2019
Harris Directory of
Mississippi
Manufacturers

Published November 2019 next update November 2020

WARNING: Purchasers and users of this directory may not use this directory to compile mailing lists, other marketing aids and other types of data, which are sold or otherwise provided to third parties. Such use is wrongful, illegal and a violation of the federal copyright laws.

CAUTION: Because of the many thousands of establishment listings contained in this directory and the possibilities of both human and mechanical error in processing this information, Mergent Inc. cannot assume liability for the correctness of the listings or information on which they are based. Hence, no information contained in this work should be relied upon in any instance where there is a possibility of any loss or damage as a consequence of any error or omission in this volume.

Publisher

Mergent Inc.
444 Madison Ave
New York, NY 10022

©Mergent Inc All Rights Reserved
2019 Mergent Business Press
ISSN 1080-2614
ISBN 978-1-64141-208-7

TABLE OF CONTENTS

Summary of Contents & Explanatory Notes 4
User's Guide to Listings 6

Geographic Section
County/City Cross-Reference Index 9
Firms Listed by Location City 11

Standard Industrial Classification (SIC) Section
SIC Alphabetical Index 203
SIC Numerical Index 205
Firms Listed by SIC 207

Alphabetic Section
Firms Listed by Firm Name 261

Product Section
Product Index 331
Firms Listed by Product Category 343

SUMMARY OF CONTENTS

Number of Companies 5,653
Number of Decision Makers 8,437
Minimum Number of Employees 1

EXPLANATORY NOTES

How to Cross-Reference in This Directory

Sequential Entry Numbers. Each establishment in the Geographic Section is numbered sequentially (G-0000). The number assigned to each establishment is referred to as its "entry number." To make cross-referencing easier, each listing in the Geographic, SIC, Alphabetic and Product Sections includes the establishment's entry number. To facilitate locating an entry in the Geographic Section, the entry numbers for the first listing on the left page and the last listing on the right page are printed at the top of the page next to the city name.

Source Suggestions Welcome

Although all known sources were used to compile this directory, it is possible that companies were inadvertently omitted. Your assistance in calling attention to such omissions would be greatly appreciated. A special form on the facing page will help you in the reporting process.

Analysis

Every effort has been made to contact all firms to verify their information. The one exception to this rule is the annual sales figure, which is considered by many companies to be confidential information. Therefore, estimated sales have been calculated by multiplying the nationwide average sales per employee for the firm's major SIC/NAICS code by the firm's number of employees. Nationwide averages for sales per employee by SIC/NAICS codes are provided by the U.S. Department of Commerce and are updated annually. All sales—sales (est)—have been estimated by this method. The exceptions are parent companies (PA), division headquarters (DH) and headquarter locations (HQ) which may include an actual corporate sales figure—sales (corporate-wide) if available.

Types of Companies

Descriptive and statistical data are included for companies in the entire state. These comprise manufacturers, machine shops, fabricators, assemblers and printers. Also identified are corporate offices in the state.

Employment Data

The employment figure shown in the Geographic Section includes male and female employees and embraces all levels of the company: administrative, clerical, sales and maintenance. This figure is for the facility listed and does not include other plants or offices. It should be recognized that these figures represent an approximate year-round average. These employment figures are broken into codes A through G and used in the Product and SIC Sections to further help you in qualifying a company. Be sure to check the footnotes on the bottom of pages for the code breakdowns.

Standard Industrial Classification (SIC)

The Standard Industrial Classification (SIC) system used in this directory was developed by the federal government for use in classifying establishments by the type of activity they are engaged in. The SIC classifications used in this directory are from the 1987 edition published by the U.S. Government's Office of Management and Budget. The SIC system separates all activities into broad industrial divisions (e.g., manufacturing, mining, retail trade). It further subdivides each division. The range of manufacturing industry classes extends from two-digit codes (major industry group) to four-digit codes (product).

For example:

Industry Breakdown	Code	Industry, Product, etc.
*Major industry group	20	Food and kindred products
Industry group	203	Canned and frozen foods
*Industry	2033	Fruits and vegetables, etc.

*Classifications used in this directory

Only two-digit and four-digit codes are used in this directory.

Arrangement

1. The **Geographic Section** contains complete in-depth corporate data. This section is sorted by cities listed in alphabetical order and companies listed alphabetically within each city. A County/City Index for referencing cities within counties precedes this section.

> IMPORTANT NOTICE: It is a violation of both federal and state law to transmit an unsolicited advertisement to a facsimile machine. Any user of this product that violates such laws may be subject to civil and criminal penalties, which may exceed $500 for each transmission of an unsolicited facsimile. Mergent Inc. provides fax numbers for lawful purposes only and expressly forbids the use of these numbers in any unlawful manner.

2. The **Standard Industrial Classification (SIC) Section** lists companies under approximately 500 four-digit SIC codes. An alphabetical and a numerical index precedes this section. A company can be listed under several codes. The codes are in numerical order with companies listed alphabetically under each code.

3. The **Alphabetic Section** lists all companies with their full physical or mailing addresses and telephone number.

4. The **Product Section** lists companies under unique Harris categories. An index preceding this section lists all product categories in alphabetical order. Companies can be listed under several categories.

USER'S GUIDE TO LISTINGS

GEOGRAPHIC SECTION

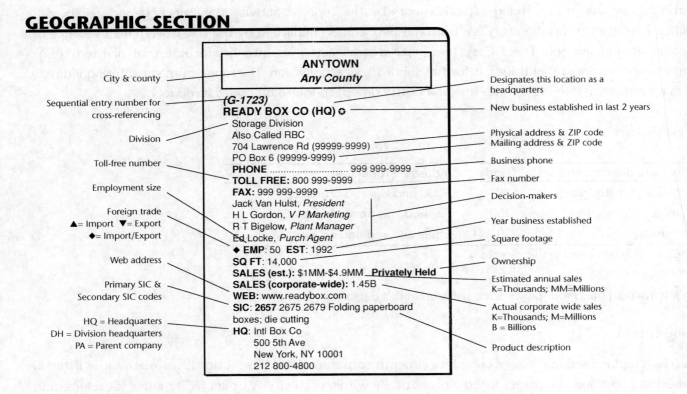

SIC SECTION

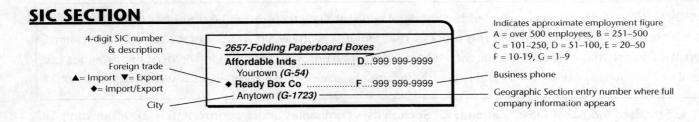

ALPHABETIC SECTION

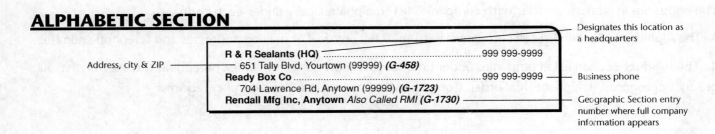

PRODUCT SECTION

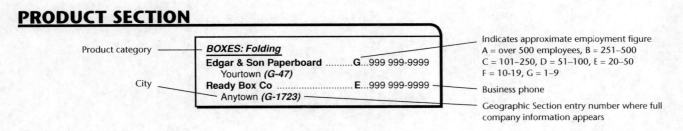

GEOGRAPHIC SECTION
Companies sorted by city in alphabetical order
In-depth company data listed

STANDARD INDUSTRIAL CLASSIFICATIONS
Alphabetical index of classifcation descriptions
Numerical index of classifcation descriptions
Companies sorted by SIC product groupings

ALPHABETIC SECTION
Company listings in alphabetical order

PRODUCT INDEX
Product categories listed in alphabetical order

PRODUCT SECTION
Companies sorted by product and manufacturing service classifications

GEOGRAPHIC

SIC

ALPHABETIC

PRDT INDEX

PRODUCT

Mississippi
County Map

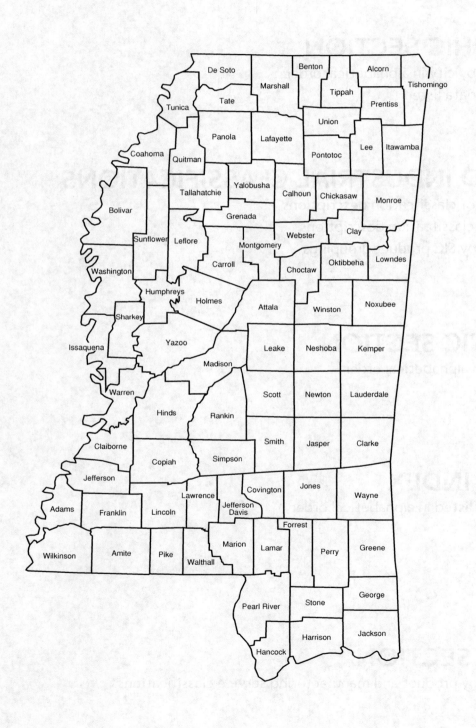

COUNTY/CITY CROSS-REFERENCE INDEX

Adams
Church Hill .... (G-754)
Natchez .... (G-3515)
Washington............. (G-5462)

Alcorn
Corinth .... (G-1056)
Glen .... (G-1506)
Rienzi .... (G-4648)

Amite
Crosby .... (G-1134)
Gloster .... (G-1509)
Liberty .... (G-2908)
Smithdale .... (G-4840)

Attala
Ethel .... (G-1282)
Kosciusko .... (G-2687)
Mc Cool .... (G-3235)
Sallis .... (G-4703)

Benton
Ashland .... (G-59)
Michigan City .... (G-3423)

Bolivar
Alligator .... (G-31)
Benoit .... (G-207)
Boyle .... (G-348)
Cleveland .... (G-785)
Mound Bayou .... (G-3509)
Rosedale .... (G-4686)
Shaw .... (G-4823)

Calhoun
Bruce .... (G-559)
Calhoun City .... (G-634)
Pittsboro .... (G-4309)
Vardaman .... (G-5324)

Carroll
Carrollton................. (G-702)
Vaiden...................... (G-5314)

Chickasaw
Houlka .... (G-2216)
Houston .... (G-2230)
Okolona .... (G-3795)
Woodland .... (G-5613)

Choctaw
Ackerman .... (G-23)
French Camp............ (G-1439)
Weir .... (G-5521)

Claiborne
Hermanville.............. (G-2121)
Pattison .... (G-4100)
Port Gibson .... (G-4400)

Clarke
Enterprise .... (G-1279)
Pachuta .... (G-4011)
Quitman .... (G-4455)
Shubuta .... (G-4827)
Stonewall .... (G-4998)

Clay
West Point .... (G-5534)

Coahoma
Clarksdale................ (G-756)

Dublin .... (G-1219)
Friars Point .... (G-1442)
Jonestown .... (G-2675)
Lyon .... (G-3041)

Copiah
Crystal Springs .... (G-1138)
Gallman .... (G-1485)
Hazlehurst .... (G-2089)
Wesson..................... (G-5523)

Covington
Collins .... (G-852)
Mount Olive .... (G-3510)
Seminary .... (G-4776)

Desoto
Hernando .... (G-2123)
Horn Lake .... (G-2196)
Lake Cormorant........ (G-2725)
Nesbit .... (G-3646)
Olive Branch .... (G-3803)
Southaven .... (G-4849)
Walls .... (G-5448)

Forrest
Brooklyn .... (G-550)
Hattiesburg .... (G-1913)
Petal .... (G-4184)

Franklin
Bude .... (G-567)
Mc Call Creek .... (G-3232)
Meadville .... (G-3274)
Roxie .... (G-4688)

George
Agricola .... (G-30)
Lucedale .... (G-2986)

Greene
Leakesville .... (G-2875)
Mc Lain .... (G-3240)
Neely .... (G-3645)
State Line .... (G-4984)

Grenada
Elliott........................ (G-1244)
Grenada .... (G-1666)

Hancock
Bay Saint Louis .... (G-133)
Bay St Louis .... (G-175)
Diamondhead .... (G-1186)
Kiln .... (G-2678)
Lakeshore................. (G-2726)
Pearlington .... (G-4160)
Stennis Space Center (G-4993)
Waveland.................. (G-5478)

Harrison
Biloxi........................ (G-214)
Diberville .... (G-1194)
Gulfport.................... (G-1714)
Long Beach .... (G-2923)
Pass Christian .... (G-4076)
Saucier .... (G-4748)

Hinds
Bolton .... (G-308)
Byram .... (G-615)

Clinton .... (G-811)
Edwards .... (G-1236)
Jackson .... (G-2312)
Raymond .... (G-4481)
Terry .... (G-5063)
Utica .... (G-5307)

Holmes
Durant....................... (G-1225)
Lexington .... (G-2897)
Pickens .... (G-4306)
West .... (G-5532)

Humphreys
Belzoni...................... (G-204)
Isola .... (G-2277)

Issaquena
Valley Park............... (G-5316)

Itawamba
Fulton .... (G-1444)
Mantachie .... (G-3197)
Nettleton .... (G-3658)
Tremont .... (G-5091)

Jackson
Escatawpa .... (G-1281)
Gautier .... (G-1488)
Hurley .... (G-2259)
Moss Point .... (G-3465)
Ocean Springs .... (G-3739)
Pascagoula .... (G-4016)
Vancleave .... (G-5317)

Jasper
Bay Springs .... (G-158)
Heidelberg .... (G-2111)
Louin........................ (G-2963)
Rose Hill .... (G-4684)
Stringer .... (G-5001)

Jefferson
Fayette .... (G-1296)
Lorman .... (G-2961)
Union Church........... (G-5305)

Jefferson Davis
Bassfield .... (G-90)
Carson...................... (G-705)
Prentiss .... (G-4415)

Jones
Ellisville................... (G-1245)
Laurel .... (G-2730)
Moselle .... (G-3455)
Ovett........................ (G-3930)
Sandersville .... (G-4725)
Soso .... (G-4846)

Kemper
De Kalb .... (G-1159)
Porterville................. (G-4410)
Preston .... (G-4426)
Scooba .... (G-4770)

Lafayette
Abbeville .... (G-1)
Oxford .... (G-3934)
Taylor .... (G-5048)
University .... (G-5306)

Lamar
Lumberton .... (G-3023)
Purvis .... (G-4432)
Sumrall .... (G-5033)

Lauderdale
Bailey .... (G-67)
Collinsville................ (G-866)
Lauderdale .... (G-2727)
Marion .... (G-3220)
Meridian................... (G-3292)
Toomsuba .... (G-5090)

Lawrence
Jayess .... (G-2674)
Monticello .... (G-3428)
Newhebron .... (G-3712)
Oak Vale .... (G-3734)
Silver Creek............. (G-4838)

Leake
Carthage................... (G-706)
Lena .... (G-2894)
Walnut Grove........... (G-5460)

Lee
Baldwyn.................... (G-70)
Belden .... (G-187)
Guntown .... (G-1896)
Mooreville .... (G-3441)
Plantersville .... (G-4310)
Saltillo .... (G-4705)
Shannon .... (G-4805)
Tupelo...................... (G-5105)
Verona .... (G-5326)

Leflore
Greenwood .... (G-1610)
Itta Bena .... (G-2279)
Minter City .... (G-3424)
Schlater .... (G-4769)

Lincoln
Bogue Chitto............ (G-301)
Brookhaven .... (G-478)
Ruth .... (G-4700)

Lowndes
Columbus .... (G-929)
Crawford .... (G-1131)
Steens .... (G-4990)

Madison
Canton .... (G-646)
Flora .... (G-1305)
Madison .... (G-3074)
Ridgeland .... (G-4545)

Marion
Columbia .... (G-877)
Foxworth................... (G-1429)
Kokomo .... (G-2686)
Sandy Hook .... (G-4727)

Marshall
Byhalia .... (G-576)
Holly Springs .... (G-2170)
Mount Pleasant .... (G-3512)

Monroe
Aberdeen .... (G-5)
Amory .... (G-32)

Becker .... (G-186)
Caledonia .... (G-627)
Hamilton .... (G-1903)
Prairie .... (G-4411)
Smithville .... (G-4843)

Montgomery
Duck Hill .... (G-1220)
Kilmichael .... (G-2677)
Winona .... (G-5595)

Neshoba
Choctaw .... (G-745)
Philadelphia .... (G-4202)
Union .... (G-5292)

Newton
Chunky .... (G-752)
Conehatta .... (G-1055)
Decatur .... (G-1170)
Hickory .... (G-2162)
Little Rock .... (G-2922)
Newton .... (G-3716)

Noxubee
Brooksville .... (G-552)
Macon .... (G-3053)
Shuqualak .... (G-4836)

Oktibbeha
Mississippi State....... (G-3425)
Starkville .... (G-4923)
Sturgis .... (G-5006)

Panola
Batesville .... (G-93)
Como .... (G-1046)
Crenshaw .... (G-1132)
Pope .... (G-4372)
Sarah .... (G-4732)
Sardis .... (G-4738)

Pearl River
Carriere .... (G-686)
Mc Neill .... (G-3241)
Nicholson .... (G-3730)
Picayune .... (G-4251)
Poplarville .... (G-4373)

Perry
Beaumont .... (G-183)
New Augusta .... (G-3710)
Richton .... (G-4526)

Pike
Fernwood .... (G-1304)
Magnolia .... (G-3188)
McComb .... (G-3242)
Osyka .... (G-3929)
Summit .... (G-5008)

Pontotoc
Ecru .... (G-1229)
Pontotoc .... (G-4319)
Randolph .... (G-4479)
Sherman .... (G-4826)
Thaxton .... (G-5078)

Prentiss
Booneville .... (G-314)
Marietta .... (G-3213)

2019 Harris Directory of
Mississippi Manufacturers

9

COUNTY/CITY CROSS-REFERENCE

Quitman
Crowder .... (G-1137)
Marks .... (G-3222)

Rankin
Brandon .... (G-353)
Florence .... (G-1314)
Flowood .... (G-1341)
Jackson .... (G-2642)
Pearl .... (G-4101)
Pelahatchie .... (G-4162)
Puckett .... (G-4429)
Richland .... (G-4496)

Scott
Forest .... (G-1409)
Lake .... (G-2722)
Morton .... (G-3446)
Pulaski .... (G-4431)
Sebastopol .... (G-4773)

Sharkey
Anguilla .... (G-58)
Delta City .... (G-1180)
Rolling Fork .... (G-4679)

Simpson
Braxton .... (G-476)
Harrisville .... (G-1911)
Magee .... (G-3174)
Mendenhall .... (G-3279)
Pinola .... (G-4308)

Smith
Mize .... (G-3426)
Raleigh .... (G-4474)
Taylorsville .... (G-5050)

Stone
Mc Henry .... (G-3239)
Perkinston .... (G-4172)
Wiggins .... (G-5568)

Sunflower
Baird .... (G-69)
Indianola .... (G-2261)
Inverness .... (G-2272)
Moorhead .... (G-3445)
Ruleville .... (G-4695)
Sunflower .... (G-5046)

Tallahatchie
Cascilla .... (G-728)
Charleston .... (G-734)
Sumner .... (G-5032)
Tutwiler .... (G-5260)
Webb .... (G-5519)

Tate
Coldwater .... (G-844)
Senatobia .... (G-4785)

Tippah
Blue Mountain .... (G-288)
Dumas .... (G-1222)
Falkner .... (G-1294)
Ripley .... (G-4651)
Tiplersville .... (G-5081)
Walnut .... (G-5452)

Tishomingo
Belmont .... (G-194)
Burnsville .... (G-572)
Dennis .... (G-1181)
Golden .... (G-1521)
Iuka .... (G-2283)

Tishomingo .... (G-5082)

Tunica
Dundee .... (G-1223)
Robinsonville .... (G-4675)
Tunica .... (G-5094)

Union
Blue Springs .... (G-294)
Etta .... (G-1284)
Myrtle .... (G-3513)
New Albany .... (G-3669)

Walthall
Tylertown .... (G-5261)

Warren
Redwood .... (G-4495)
Vicksburg .... (G-5338)

Washington
Greenville .... (G-1534)
Hollandale .... (G-2163)
Leland .... (G-2882)

Wayne
Buckatunna .... (G-564)

Waynesboro .... (G-5488)

Webster
Eupora .... (G-1285)
Maben .... (G-3044)
Mantee .... (G-3210)
Mathiston .... (G-3225)

Wilkinson
Centreville .... (G-730)
Woodville .... (G-5615)

Winston
Louisville .... (G-2964)
Noxapater .... (G-3731)

Yalobusha
Coffeeville .... (G-840)
Oakland .... (G-3737)
Tillatoba .... (G-5079)
Water Valley .... (G-5463)

Yazoo
Benton .... (G-208)
Bentonia .... (G-210)
Tinsley .... (G-5080)
Yazoo City .... (G-5620)

GEOGRAPHIC SECTION

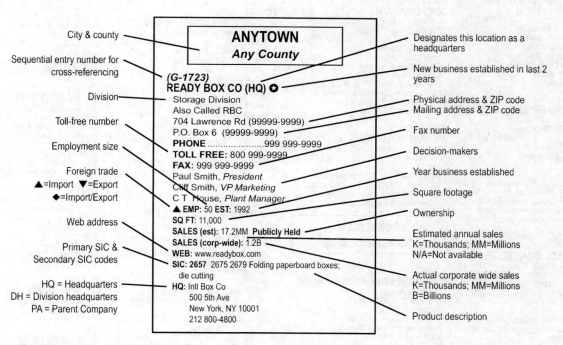

See footnotes for symbols and codes identification.
- This section is in alphabetical order by city.
- Companies are sorted alphabetically under their respective cities.
- To locate cities within a county refer to the County/City Cross Reference Index.

IMPORTANT NOTICE: It is a violation of both federal and state law to transmit an unsolicited advertisement to a facsimile machine. Any user of this product that violates such laws may be subject to civil and criminal penalties which may exceed $500 for each transmission of an unsolicited facsimile. Harris InfoSource provides fax numbers for lawful purposes only and expressly forbids the use of these numbers in any unlawful manner.

Abbeville
Lafayette County

(G-1)
ABBEVILLE MILL LLC
81 County Road 201 (38601-9623)
PHONE..................................662 238-7879
Joel Hollowell, *Owner*
EMP: 3
SALES (est): 216K Privately Held
SIC: 2491 Millwork, treated wood

(G-2)
DAVIS TOOL & DIE INC
226 County Road 235 (38601-9710)
PHONE..................................662 234-4007
Dale Davis, *President*
Durward Davis, *Admin Sec*
EMP: 12
SALES (est): 1.6MM Privately Held
SIC: 3544 Special dies & tools

(G-3)
RICHARDSON MARKETING
Also Called: Accuprint
7 County Road 2064 (38601-9692)
PHONE..................................662 234-3907
EMP: 1 **EST:** 1995
SALES (est): 61K Privately Held
SIC: 3577 Mfg Computer Peripheral Equipment

(G-4)
SMITH TOOLING
941 Highway 7 N (38601-9666)
PHONE..................................662 234-1139
Thomas Smith, *Owner*
EMP: 2 **EST:** 1996

SALES: 140K Privately Held
SIC: 3599 Machine shop, jobbing & repair

Aberdeen
Monroe County

(G-5)
3 F CHIMICA AMERICAS INC
10930 Darracott Rd (39730-9369)
P.O. Box 57 (39730-0057)
PHONE..................................662 369-2843
Leigh Guin, *Vice Pres*
▲ **EMP:** 6
SALES (est): 563.5K Privately Held
SIC: 2819 Industrial inorganic chemicals

(G-6)
ABERDEEN MACHINE WORKS INC
79 Hwy 25 S (39730)
PHONE..................................662 369-9357
Robley E Wooten, *President*
Maria Wooten, *Corp Secy*
Kelvin Wooten, *Vice Pres*
EMP: 20
SQ FT: 15,000
SALES (est): 3.3MM Privately Held
SIC: 3599 7692 3444 3443 Machine shop, jobbing & repair; custom machinery; welding repair; sheet metalwork; fabricated plate work (boiler shop)

(G-7)
ABERDEEN SCHOOL DISTRICT
115 N Long St (39730-2575)
P.O. Box 607 (39730-0607)
PHONE..................................662 369-6886
Barbara Dasser, *Branch Mgr*

EMP: 1
SALES (corp-wide): 12.5MM Privately Held
WEB: www.aberdeen.k12.ms.us
SIC: 2099 8299 Ready-to-eat meals, salads & sandwiches; arts & crafts schools
PA: Aberdeen School District
1100 W Commerce St
Aberdeen MS 39730
662 369-4682

(G-8)
ALLMOND PRINTING COMPANY INC
603 W Commerce St (39730-2405)
P.O. Box 162 (39730-0162)
PHONE..................................662 369-4848
John Allmond, *President*
EMP: 7
SQ FT: 7,860
SALES (est): 955.3K Privately Held
WEB: www.allmondprinting.com
SIC: 2752 Commercial printing, offset; lithographing on metal

(G-9)
APAC-MISSISSIPPI INC
700 S Meridian St (39730-3318)
P.O. Box 1388, Columbus (39703-1388)
PHONE..................................662 343-9300
Phil Barker, *General Mgr*
EMP: 5
SALES (corp-wide): 30.6B Privately Held
SIC: 3273 Ready-mixed concrete
HQ: Apac-Mississippi, Inc.
101 Riverview Dr
Richland MS 39218
601 376-4000

(G-10)
BIRDS NEST
121 E Commerce St (39730-2709)
PHONE..................................662 369-5757
Bea Tubb, *Owner*
EMP: 2 **EST:** 2007
SALES (est): 148.8K Privately Held
SIC: 2519 Household furniture

(G-11)
DIXIE SERVICES AND SUPPLY LLC
51741 Highway 25 S (39730-9005)
P.O. Box 144, Becker (38825-0144)
PHONE..................................662 369-0907
Sherry Case,
Charles Case,
EMP: 7
SALES (est): 521.9K Privately Held
SIC: 1389 Oil & gas wells: building, repairing & dismantling

(G-12)
DIXIE SPECIALTIES & FURN INC
525 Highway 145 N (39730-2157)
P.O. Box 177 (39730-0177)
PHONE..................................662 369-8557
EMP: 3 **EST:** 2008
SALES (est): 120K Privately Held
SIC: 3999 Mfg Misc Products

(G-13)
EVANS LOGGING
20456 Coontail Rd (39730-8590)
PHONE..................................662 369-7151
EMP: 4
SALES (est): 220K Privately Held
SIC: 2411 Logging camps & contractors

(PA)=Parent Co (HQ)=Headquarters (DH)=Div Headquarters
✪ = New Business established in last 2 years

2019 Harris Directory of Mississippi Manufacturers

Aberdeen - Monroe County (G-14)　　　　　　　　　　　　　　GEOGRAPHIC SECTION

(G-14)
IMERYS MINERALS USA INC
10033 Imc Rd (39730-8408)
PHONE.....................................662 369-6411
John Sims, *Opers-Prdtn-Mfg*
EMP: 12 **Privately Held**
SIC: **1459** Bentonite mining
HQ: Imerys Minerals Usa, Inc.
　　100 Mansell Ct E Ste 200
　　Roswell GA 30076
　　770 645-3300

(G-15)
J AND E ENTERPRISES
605 S Matubba St (39730-2927)
P.O. Box 416 (39730-0416)
PHONE.....................................662 369-7324
Robert Williams, *Owner*
Mary Jo Williams, *Partner*
EMP: 5
SQ FT: 5,400
SALES (est): 453.3K **Privately Held**
SIC: **5999** 5261 7699 5084 Engines &
parts, air-cooled; lawnmowers & tractors;
engine repair & replacement, non-auto-
motive; engines, gasoline; saws & sawing
equipment

(G-16)
LEES PRECAST CONCRETE INC
20578 Egypt Rd (39730-8545)
PHONE.....................................662 369-8935
Allen Lee, *General Mgr*
Waymon Hodge, *Project Mgr*
Lavina Koehn, *Executive*
EMP: 8
SALES (est): 1.4MM **Privately Held**
SIC: **3272** Septic tanks, concrete; concrete
products, precast

(G-17)
LEES SEPTIC INC
Also Called: Lee's Septic Tanks
20578 Egypt Rd (39730-8545)
PHONE.....................................662 369-9799
Milton Lee, *President*
Lavina Koehn, *Corp Secy*
Florence Milton, *Vice Pres*
EMP: 10
SALES (est): 740K **Privately Held**
WEB: www.leesprecast.com
SIC: **3272** 5074 5039 Septic tanks, con-
crete; plumbing fittings & supplies; septic
tanks

(G-18)
**MATTUBY CREEK MACHINE
WORKS**
21957 Highway 45 N (39730-9785)
PHONE.....................................662 369-8262
John Luker, *President*
EMP: 6
SQ FT: 5,500
SALES (est): 140K **Privately Held**
SIC: **3444** Forming machine work, sheet
metal

(G-19)
NANOCOR LLC
Also Called: Amcol International
10927 Darracott Rd (39730-9418)
P.O. Box 249 (39730-0249)
PHONE.....................................847 851-1500
Fred Nurse, *Manager*
EMP: 8 **Publicly Held**
WEB: www.nanocor.com
SIC: **2821** 3295 Plastics materials &
resins; minerals, ground or treated
HQ: Nanocor Llc
　　2870 Forbs Ave
　　Hoffman Estates IL 60192

(G-20)
**TENN TOM PALLET COMPANY
INC**
810 S Thayer Ave (39730-2818)
P.O. Box 345 (39730-0345)
PHONE.....................................662 369-9341
Chris Provias, *President*
Tony Provias, *Admin Sec*
EMP: 7 EST: 1997
SALES (est): 124.8K **Privately Held**
SIC: **2448** Pallets, wood & wood with metal

(G-21)
**WESTLAKE CHEMICAL
CORPORATION**
715 Highway 25 S (39730-3403)
P.O. Box 91 (39730-0091)
PHONE.....................................662 369-8111
Todd Toler, *Buyer*
Doug Knittig, *Manager*
EMP: 150 **Publicly Held**
WEB: www.georgiagulf.com
SIC: **2821** Polyvinyl chloride resins (PVC)
PA: Westlake Chemical Corporation
　　2801 Post Oak Blvd # 600
　　Houston TX 77056

(G-22)
WILSON SOLUTIONS LLC
10062a Homestead Rd (39730-9490)
PHONE.....................................662 319-6063
EMP: 1
SALES (est): 54.5K **Privately Held**
SIC: **3571** 7371 7389 Personal comput-
ers (microcomputers); computer software
development & applications;

Ackerman
Choctaw County

(G-23)
CHAMBERS DELIMBINATOR INC
234 Old Bellwood Rd (39735)
P.O. Box 777 (39735-0777)
PHONE.....................................662 285-2777
Eric B Chambers, *President*
Mary Chambers, *Vice Pres*
EMP: 8 EST: 1997
SQ FT: 20,000
SALES (est): 1.5MM **Privately Held**
WEB: www.chambersdelimbinator.com
SIC: **3531** Forestry related equipment

(G-24)
CHAMBERS LOGGING INC
234 Bellwood Rd (39735-8003)
P.O. Box 777 (39735-0777)
PHONE.....................................662 285-2777
Eric Chambers, *President*
EMP: 4
SALES (est): 249.1K **Privately Held**
SIC: **2411** Logging

(G-25)
**LIBERTY FUELS COMPANY
LLC**
Also Called: MISSISSIPPI LIGNITE MINING
1000 Mcintire Rd (39735-4524)
PHONE.....................................601 737-7000
Robert L Benson, *CEO*
Alfred M Rankin Jr, *Chairman*
J C Butler Jr, *Senior VP*
Michael J Gregory, *Vice Pres*
JP Sullivan Jr, *CFO*
EMP: 4
SALES: 24.7MM
SALES (corp-wide): 135.3MM **Publicly
Held**
SIC: **1221** Bituminous coal & lignite-sur-
face mining
HQ: The North American Coal Corporation
　　5340 Legacy Dr Ste 300
　　Plano TX 75024
　　972 448-5400

(G-26)
MGM INC
19440 Hwy 25 (39735)
P.O. Box 704 (39735-0704)
PHONE.....................................662 428-4646
Millan Molina, *President*
Tanya Molina, *Admin Sec*
EMP: 9
SQ FT: 1,600
SALES: 500K **Privately Held**
SIC: **3599** Machine shop, jobbing & repair

(G-27)
MISSISSIPPI FORGE (PVF) INC
400 W Main St (39735-8933)
PHONE.....................................662 285-2995
Jigar Kadakia, *Principal*
▲ EMP: 45
SQ FT: 100,000

SALES: 3MM **Privately Held**
SIC: **3494** Pipe fittings

(G-28)
MISSISSIPPI LIGNITE MINING CO
1000 Mcintire Rd (39735-4524)
PHONE.....................................662 387-5200
Robert L Benson, *President*
Alfred M Rankin Jr, *Chairman*
J C Butler Jr Sr, *Vice Pres*
Michael J Gregory, *Vice Pres*
John R Pokorny, *Controller*
EMP: 120
SALES (est): 27.8MM
SALES (corp-wide): 135.3MM **Publicly
Held**
WEB: www.mlmining.com
SIC: **1221** Bituminous coal & lignite-sur-
face mining
HQ: The North American Coal Corporation
　　5340 Legacy Dr Ste 300
　　Plano TX 75024
　　972 448-5400

(G-29)
**SOUTHEASTERN TIMBER PDTS
LLC**
240 Pca Rd (39735-5604)
P.O. Box 718 (39735-0718)
PHONE.....................................662 285-3291
William J Vandevender, *Principal*
Cindney Pallen, *CFO*
EMP: 12
SALES (est): 3MM **Privately Held**
SIC: **2421** Sawmills & planing mills, gen-
eral

Agricola
George County

(G-30)
PIERCE WELL SERVICE
5267 Highway 613 (39452-9728)
PHONE.....................................601 947-4548
Jimmy Pierce Jr, *Partner*
Michael Pierce, *Partner*
EMP: 3 EST: 1977
SALES (est): 290K **Privately Held**
SIC: **1389** Oil field services

Alligator
Bolivar County

(G-31)
**BLANK 2 BEAUTIFUL EMB
MORE LLC**
934 Allgator Rena Lara Rd (38720-9510)
PHONE.....................................662 902-6195
Karen Spinosa, *Principal*
EMP: 1
SALES (est): 42.2K **Privately Held**
SIC: **2395** Embroidery & art needlework

Amory
Monroe County

(G-32)
1529 COFFEE COMPANY
205 3rd St N (38821-3424)
PHONE.....................................662 315-6951
Danny Spreitler, *President*
EMP: 5
SQ FT: 2,100
SALES (est): 220.3K **Privately Held**
SIC: **7389** 5149 2095 Coffee service; cof-
fee & tea; coffee, green or roasted; coffee
roasting (except by wholesale grocers)

(G-33)
A STITCH IN TIME
104 Main St N (38821-3415)
PHONE.....................................662 257-0661
EMP: 1
SALES: 117K **Privately Held**
SIC: **2335** Mfg Women's/Misses' Dresses

(G-34)
A-1 FAMILY FURNITURE INC
60036 Puckett Dr (38821-9601)
PHONE.....................................662 257-6002
Patty Tomlin, *President*
Edward Tomlin, *Vice Pres*
Pamela Berryhill, *Treasurer*
EMP: 25
SALES (est): 2.7MM **Privately Held**
SIC: **2512** Upholstered household furniture

(G-35)
AMORY ADVERTISER
115 Main St S (38821-3407)
PHONE.....................................662 256-5647
Emily Tubb, *General Mgr*
Beth Bunch, *Exec Dir*
EMP: 7
SALES (est): 549.2K **Privately Held**
SIC: **7313** 2711 Newspaper advertising
representative; newspapers

(G-36)
AMORY POWDER COATING LLC
941 A S Main St Amory Ms (38821)
PHONE.....................................662 749-7081
Athena Barnett, *Vice Pres*
EMP: 8
SQ FT: 15,000
SALES (est): 532.3K **Privately Held**
SIC: **3479** Painting of metal products

(G-37)
BEASON REPAIR SHOP
108 4th Ave Nw (38821-3001)
PHONE.....................................662 256-9937
C G Beason, *Owner*
EMP: 5
SALES: 350K **Privately Held**
SIC: **3599** 7692 Machine shop, jobbing &
repair; custom machinery; welding repair

(G-38)
CHIPS AMORY INC
Also Called: Price Companies, The
100 Waterway Dr (38821-8842)
P.O. Box 609 (38821-0609)
PHONE.....................................662 256-1400
Brian Johnson, *Manager*
EMP: 11
SALES (est): 1.7MM **Privately Held**
SIC: **2421** Wood chips, produced at mill

(G-39)
COUNTRY KITCHEN OF AMORY
60395 Cotton Gin Port Rd (38821-7224)
PHONE.....................................662 257-4055
Kimberly Steele, *Principal*
EMP: 1 EST: 2011
SALES (est): 91.8K **Privately Held**
SIC: **3421** Table & food cutlery, including
butchers'

(G-40)
DAIRY KREAM
Also Called: Dairy Kream Restaurant
600 Main St N (38821-2333)
PHONE.....................................662 256-7562
Emogene Knight, *Owner*
EMP: 9
SALES: 225K **Privately Held**
SIC: **5812** 2024 5451 Ice cream stands or
dairy bars; ice cream & frozen desserts;
ice cream (packaged)

(G-41)
DOUG MCCORMICK
50020 Swan Hill Rd (38821-8608)
PHONE.....................................662 256-9506
Doug McCormick, *Owner*
EMP: 1
SALES: 150K **Privately Held**
SIC: **1442** Construction sand & gravel

(G-42)
FFM INC (PA)
1113 Hatley Rd (38821-4624)
PHONE.....................................662 256-9665
Tim Trautman, *Owner*
EMP: 27
SALES (est): 8.8MM **Privately Held**
SIC: **2511** Wood household furniture

2019 Harris Directory of
Mississippi Manufacturers

▲ = Import ▼=Export
◆ =Import/Export

GEOGRAPHIC SECTION

Baird - Sunflower County (G-69)

(G-43)
GRAVEL EQUIPMENT & SUPPLY INC
30462 Bigbee Rd (38821-8714)
P.O. Box 94 (38821-0094)
PHONE..............................662 256-2052
Judy Parrish, *President*
Norman Parrish, *Corp Secy*
EMP: 5
SQ FT: 10,000
SALES (est): 500K **Privately Held**
SIC: 3561 Pumps & pumping equipment

(G-44)
ITT ENGINEERED VALVES LLC
1110 Hatley Rd (38821-4605)
PHONE..............................662 256-7185
Dennis Jackson, *Branch Mgr*
EMP: 11
SALES (corp-wide): 2.7B **Publicly Held**
SIC: 3491 Industrial valves
HQ: Itt Engineered Valves, Llc
240 Fall St
Seneca Falls NY 13148
662 257-6982

(G-45)
ITT LLC
Also Called: ITT Engineered Valves
1110 Bankhead Ave (38821-4605)
PHONE..............................662 256-7185
Steven Loranger, *Chairman*
Richard Pate, *Safety Mgr*
Robert Honsinger, *Purch Mgr*
Tena Moreland, *Senior Buyer*
Randy Bates, *Design Engr*
EMP: 125
SALES (corp-wide): 2.7B **Publicly Held**
WEB: www.ittind.com
SIC: 3625 Control equipment, electric
HQ: Itt Llc
1133 Westchester Ave N-100
White Plains NY 10604
914 641-2000

(G-46)
JEAN PICKLE
50047 Calvary Church Rd (38821-8648)
PHONE..............................662 256-7020
Jean Pickle, *Principal*
EMP: 1
SALES (est): 51K **Privately Held**
SIC: 2035 Pickled fruits & vegetables

(G-47)
LONE STAR DEFENSE
50507 Old Highway 6 (38821-9079)
PHONE..............................662 701-5204
Jeremy Waller, *Principal*
EMP: 2
SALES (est): 92.5K **Privately Held**
SIC: 3812 Defense systems & equipment

(G-48)
MID SOUTH PUBLICATIONS INC
Also Called: Mid-South Fine Printers
111 Main St S (38821-3407)
P.O. Box 606 (38821-0606)
PHONE..............................662 256-8209
William Miles Jr, *President*
Robert Chamblee, *Corp Secy*
EMP: 7
SQ FT: 3,000
SALES (est): 900K **Privately Held**
SIC: 2752 7336 2791 2789 Commercial
printing, lithographic; commercial art &
graphic design; typesetting; bookbinding
& related work; commercial printing

(G-49)
NAUTIC STAR LLC
Also Called: Nauticstar Boats
500 Waterway Dr (38821-8207)
P.O. Box 26 (38821-0026)
PHONE..............................662 256-5636
Jay Povlin, *President*
Doug Wheeler, *COO*
Tony Watson, *Controller*
Phillip Faulkner, *Marketing Staff*
Susan Barrett, *Executive*
EMP: 120
SQ FT: 6,500

SALES: 63.7MM
SALES (corp-wide): 332.7MM **Publicly Held**
WEB: www.nauticstarboats.com
SIC: 3732 Boat building & repairing
PA: Mastercraft Boat Holdings, Inc.
100 Cherokee Cove Dr
Vonore TN 37885
423 884-2221

(G-50)
PALMER MACHINE WORKS INC
Also Called: Palmer Bodies
1106 104th St (38821-5100)
P.O. Box 359 (38821-0359)
PHONE..............................662 256-2636
Lawrence Richard Palmer Jr, *President*
Steve Gallop, *Vice Pres*
Teresa Maxey, *Shareholder*
EMP: 24
SQ FT: 35,000
SALES: 3.2MM **Privately Held**
SIC: 3715 7539 5013 Truck trailers; trailer
repair; trailer parts & accessories

(G-51)
PARISH PUMPS AND MACHINE INC
30462 Bigbee Rd (38821-8714)
P.O. Box 514 (38821-0514)
PHONE..............................662 256-2052
Norman Parish, *President*
Judy Parish, *Corp Secy*
EMP: 5
SQ FT: 5,000
SALES: 170K **Privately Held**
SIC: 3599 3561 Machine & other job shop
work; pumps & pumping equipment

(G-52)
PICKLE LARRY
60018 Country Wood Rd (38821-9185)
PHONE..............................662 256-7239
EMP: 1 EST: 2012
SALES (est): 53.1K **Privately Held**
SIC: 2035 Mfg Pickles/Sauces/Dressing

(G-53)
SANDERSON REDI-MIX INC (PA)
60068 Phllips Schlhuse Rd (38821-8697)
P.O. Box 393 (38821-0393)
PHONE..............................662 256-9301
Hobson Sanderson Jr, *President*
EMP: 20
SQ FT: 1,200
SALES (est): 1.7MM **Privately Held**
SIC: 3273 Ready-mixed concrete

(G-54)
SOUTHERN RUSTIC LOGWERKS LLC
313 Highway 278 W (38821-5112)
PHONE..............................662 315-9677
Brandi Thorne, *Mng Member*
EMP: 2 EST: 2009
SALES (est): 171K **Privately Held**
SIC: 2511 Wood household furniture

(G-55)
SOUTHERN TOOLING & MCH WORKS
Also Called: Southern Tooling and Mch Works
1421 Highway 25 S (38821-8654)
PHONE..............................662 256-7633
Ricky Camp, *President*
EMP: 3
SQ FT: 5,000
SALES (est): 302.5K **Privately Held**
SIC: 3599 Machine shop, jobbing & repair

(G-56)
STAR PRINTING CO OF AMORY INC
Also Called: Monroe County Shopper
1223 Highway 278 E (38821-5807)
P.O. Box 357 (38821-0357)
PHONE..............................662 256-8424
Robert Boozer, *President*
Jeff Boozer, *Vice Pres*
EMP: 30 EST: 1973
SQ FT: 30,000

SALES (est): 3.9MM **Privately Held**
SIC: 2759 5943 5112 5999 Commercial
printing; office forms & supplies; office
supplies; business machines & equipment; office equipment; office furniture

(G-57)
TRUE TEMPER SPORTS INC
Hgwy 25 S (38821)
PHONE..............................662 256-5605
Ray John, *Principal*
EMP: 450
SALES (corp-wide): 161.6MM **Privately Held**
WEB: www.proliteshaft.com
SIC: 3949 3312 3498 Shafts, golf club;
tubes, steel & iron; fabricated pipe & fit-
tings
HQ: True Sports, Inc.
8275 Tournament Dr # 200
Memphis TN 38125
901 746-2000

Anguilla
Sharkey County

(G-58)
CRUX INDUSTRIES
29 Nitta Yuma St (38721-9536)
PHONE..............................662 873-3317
Henry Phelps, *Owner*
EMP: 15
SALES (est): 147K **Privately Held**
SIC: 3999 5699 Manufacturing industries;
sports apparel

Ashland
Benton County

(G-59)
BETTY WRIGHT
149 Ferrell Rd (38603-6907)
PHONE..............................662 224-3000
Betty Wright, *Principal*
EMP: 4
SALES: 180K **Privately Held**
SIC: 2759 Commercial printing

(G-60)
GALLERY
5326 Pleasant Hill Rd (38603-7055)
PHONE..............................662 224-6694
Bobby Simpson, *Owner*
EMP: 1
SALES (est): 65.2K **Privately Held**
SIC: 2499 Picture & mirror frames, wood

(G-61)
INTERIOR AND EXTERIOR WD WORK
2872 Friendship Rd (38603-7832)
PHONE..............................662 587-2417
Michael Peters, *Principal*
EMP: 1
SALES (est): 83.6K **Privately Held**
SIC: 2431 Millwork

(G-62)
IRONCRAFTERS SECURITY PRODUCTS
Also Called: Iron Crafters Security Pdts
835 Iron Crafters Rd (38603-7575)
P.O. Box 277 (38603-0277)
PHONE..............................662 224-6658
Verne Kolivas, *President*
John Maclin, *Corp Secy*
John Kolivas, *Vice Pres*
▲ EMP: 20
SQ FT: 20,000
SALES (est): 3.5MM **Privately Held**
WEB: www.kolivas.com
SIC: 3442 3446 Metal doors; architectural
metalwork

(G-63)
MILPAR INC
62 Red Bud Rd (38603-6148)
P.O. Box 309 (38603-0309)
PHONE..............................662 224-0426
Delorease Lott, *President*

John A Williams, *Corp Secy*
Pat Anderson, *Controller*
EMP: 14
SQ FT: 2,500
SALES (est): 600K **Privately Held**
WEB: www.milpar.com
SIC: 3728 Aircraft parts & equipment

(G-64)
MISSISSIPPI WOOD STAKES INC
Also Called: Mws
1042 Highway 4 E (38603-7873)
PHONE..............................662 224-0975
Jim May, *President*
EMP: 1
SALES: 85K **Privately Held**
SIC: 2499 Surveyors' stakes, wood

(G-65)
SOUTHERN SINTINEL INC
Also Called: Southern Advocate
114 Church Ave (38603-7379)
P.O. Box 157 (38603-0157)
PHONE..............................662 224-6681
Tim Watson, *Manager*
EMP: 2
SALES (corp-wide): 1MM **Privately Held**
SIC: 2711 Newspapers, publishing & print-
ing
PA: Southern Sintinel Inc
1701 City Ave N
Ripley MS 38663
662 837-8111

(G-66)
TRAINUM LUMBER INC
2411 Pleasant Hill Rd (38603-7038)
PHONE..............................662 224-8346
Bobby Trainum, *President*
Sandra Trainum, *Vice Pres*
EMP: 2
SALES (est): 120K **Privately Held**
SIC: 2421 Lumber: rough, sawed or planed

Bailey
Lauderdale County

(G-67)
DAILY & SONS CONSTRUCTION INC
4580 Parker Ln (39320-8223)
P.O. Box 126 (39320-0126)
PHONE..............................601 737-5847
Chris Daily, *Owner*
EMP: 2
SALES (est): 160.8K **Privately Held**
SIC: 7389 2711 Estimating service, con-
struction; newspapers, publishing & print-
ing

(G-68)
KINARDS KOUNTRY
10059 Daniels Rd (39320-9800)
PHONE..............................601 737-8378
Gloria Kinard, *Owner*
EMP: 2
SALES: 100K **Privately Held**
SIC: 3949 Camping equipment & supplies

Baird
Sunflower County

(G-69)
TURNERS TAX SERVICE
124 Front Ave (38751-2461)
PHONE..............................662 887-2066
Franklin Turner, *Owner*
EMP: 10
SALES (est): 431.8K **Privately Held**
SIC: 3677 Filtration devices, electronic

(PA)=Parent Co (HQ)=Headquarters (DH)=Div Headquarters
✪ = New Business established in last 2 years

2019 Harris Directory of
Mississippi Manufacturers

Baldwyn — Lee County (G-70)

GEOGRAPHIC SECTION

Baldwyn
Lee County

(G-70)
ADVANCED INNOVATIVE PDTS LLC
976 Highway 45 (38824-8593)
PHONE..................................662 365-1640
EMP: 2
SALES (est): 108.7K **Privately Held**
SIC: 2392 Cushions & pillows; mattress pads

(G-71)
BALDWYN NEWS
116 W Main St (38824-1814)
P.O. Box 130 (38824-0130)
PHONE..................................662 365-3232
John Lindsey, *General Mgr*
EMP: 3 EST: 1939
SQ FT: 3,500
SALES (est): 180K **Privately Held**
SIC: 2759 5994 Newspapers: printing; news dealers & newsstands

(G-72)
BALDWYN TOOL AND DIE CO
45 County Road 6311 (38824-8531)
PHONE..................................662 365-8665
Brian Hogue, *Owner*
EMP: 2
SALES: 150K **Privately Held**
SIC: 3544 Special dies & tools

(G-73)
BALDWYN TRUCK & TRAILER REPAIR
896 Drake Dr (38824-9098)
P.O. Box 30 (38824-0030)
PHONE..................................662 365-7888
Jeffery Mathis, *Owner*
EMP: 2 EST: 2012
SALES (est): 237.5K **Privately Held**
SIC: 7699 7539 3715 Professional instrument repair services; industrial truck repair; trailer repair; semitrailers for truck tractors

(G-74)
CUSTOM ENGINEERED WHEELS INC
309 Rbert M Cggins Jr Dr (38824-6051)
P.O. Box 395 (38824-0395)
PHONE..................................662 841-0756
David Robackrewerce, *Branch Mgr*
EMP: 50 **Privately Held**
WEB: www.spartech.com
SIC: 3714 Motor vehicle wheels & parts
PA: Custom Engineered Wheels, Inc.
309 Rbert M Coggins Jr Dr
Baldwyn MS 38824

(G-75)
CUSTOM ENGINEERED WHEELS INC (PA)
309 Rbert M Coggins Jr Dr (38824-6051)
P.O. Box 395 (38824-0395)
PHONE..................................574 267-4005
Brandon Richter, *Ch of Bd*
Jason Peters, *President*
Deanna Miller, *CFO*
Michael J Mahoney,
▲ EMP: 90
SALES (est): 36.7MM **Privately Held**
SIC: 3089 3714 Injection molded finished plastic products; motor vehicle wheels & parts

(G-76)
FAB PRO WLDG & FABRICATION CO
214 Carnation St (38824-1503)
PHONE..................................662 365-5557
Cheryl King, *Principal*
EMP: 2
SALES (est): 139.9K **Privately Held**
SIC: 7692 Welding repair

(G-77)
HARRISON MOBILE WELDING
3079 Houston Palestine Rd (38824-6443)
PHONE..................................662 706-4692

Nathan Harrison, *Principal*
EMP: 1
SALES (est): 25K **Privately Held**
SIC: 7692 Welding repair

(G-78)
INNOCOR EAST LLC
976 Highway 45 (38824-8593)
PHONE..................................662 365-1640
Diane Price Baker, *Ch of Bd*
EMP: 13
SALES (corp-wide): 224.3MM **Privately Held**
SIC: 2392 Cushions & pillows; mattress pads
HQ: Innocor East, Llc
976 Highway 45
Baldwyn MS 38824
732 263-0800

(G-79)
INNOCOR EAST LLC (DH)
Also Called: Sleep Innovations
976 Highway 45 (38824-8593)
PHONE..................................732 263-0800
Carol S Eicher, *CEO*
Diane Price Baker, *Ch of Bd*
Joseph Lynch, *President*
Ray E Bailey, *Principal*
Steven Setzer, *VP Opers*
◆ EMP: 60
SQ FT: 114,000
SALES (est): 11.7MM
SALES (corp-wide): 224.3MM **Privately Held**
WEB: www.sleepinnovation.com
SIC: 2392 Cushions & pillows; mattress pads

(G-80)
INNOCOR FOAM TECH - ACP INC
1124 N 2nd St (38824-8586)
PHONE..................................662 365-5868
Eddie Googe, *Plant Mgr*
Pamela Johnson, *Human Res Dir*
Teddy Faust, *Manager*
EMP: 9
SALES (corp-wide): 224.3MM **Privately Held**
SIC: 3069 Bathmats, rubber
HQ: Innocor Foam Technologies - Acp, Inc.
200 Schulz Dr Ste 2
Red Bank NJ 07701
732 945-6222

(G-81)
KIMBERLY-CLARK CORPORATION
1337 Sheppard Cir (38824-1052)
PHONE..................................662 284-3827
EMP: 195
SALES (corp-wide): 18.4B **Publicly Held**
WEB: www.kimberly-clark.com
SIC: 2621 2676 Sanitary tissue paper; infant & baby paper products
PA: Kimberly-Clark Corporation
351 Phelps Dr
Irving TX 75038
972 281-1200

(G-82)
LIMOSS US LLC
Also Called: Linear Motion Systems
964 Highway 45 (38824-8593)
PHONE..................................662 365-2200
Damon Fisher, *Vice Pres*
Benjie Gray, *CFO*
Klaus Bellingroth,
◆ EMP: 26
SQ FT: 48,000
SALES (est): 20.5MM **Privately Held**
SIC: 3625 Actuators, industrial

(G-83)
LINDSEY MACHINE SHOP INC
655 Highway 370 (38824-6860)
PHONE..................................662 365-8189
Ralph Lindsey, *President*
EMP: 3
SALES (est): 286.3K **Privately Held**
SIC: 3599 Machine & other job shop work

(G-84)
LOCAL NATIVE CREATIVE + PRINT
111 S 2nd St (38824-2216)
PHONE..................................662 401-4767
Kayla Stone, *Principal*
EMP: 2 EST: 2017
SALES (est): 83.9K **Privately Held**
SIC: 2752 Commercial printing, lithographic

(G-85)
NORTH MISS STONE & MEM CO
684 Highway 145 S (38824-8906)
PHONE..................................662 365-2721
Mark Hamblin, *President*
Linda Hamblin, *Corp Secy*
EMP: 7
SALES: 98K **Privately Held**
SIC: 3281 Marble, building: cut & shaped; granite, cut & shaped

(G-86)
P & L EMBROIDERY
803 Highway 45 (38824-8587)
PHONE..................................662 365-9852
Paul Rowan, *Owner*
EMP: 2
SALES (est): 63K **Privately Held**
SIC: 2395 Embroidery products, except schiffli machine

(G-87)
SOUTHERN DIVERSIFIED INDS INC
Also Called: Liberty Plastics
1154 N 2nd St (38824-8586)
PHONE..................................662 365-6720
Matthew Homan, *CEO*
EMP: 75
SALES (est): 5.1MM **Privately Held**
SIC: 3083 Laminated plastics plate & sheet

(G-88)
SOUTHERN DIVERSIFIED INDS INC
1154 N 2nd St (38824-8586)
PHONE..................................662 365-8800
Daniel Zdon, *COO*
Ronda Bayer, *Vice Pres*
David Lenzen, *CFO*
Byron Wieberdink, *CFO*
▲ EMP: 1
SALES (est): 484.5K
SALES (corp-wide): 385.6MM **Privately Held**
WEB: www.libertydiversified.com
SIC: 3089 Plastic containers, except foam
PA: Liberty Diversified International, Inc.
5600 Highway 169 N
New Hope MN 55428
763 536-6600

(G-89)
WOODWORKINGS
111 E Main St (38824-1800)
PHONE..................................662 255-3421
EMP: 1 EST: 2016
SALES (est): 65.4K **Privately Held**
SIC: 2431 Millwork

Bassfield
Jefferson Davis County

(G-90)
BASS ASSOCIATES LLC
2766 Gates Rd (39421-9035)
PHONE..................................601 943-5229
Thomas Bass, *Mng Member*
EMP: 2
SALES: 500K **Privately Held**
SIC: 1382 Oil & gas exploration services

(G-91)
FASTSTOP PETROLEUM LLC
5562 N Williamsburg Rd (39421-4233)
PHONE..................................601 466-3273
Tarun Arora, *President*
EMP: 5 EST: 2015
SQ FT: 8,322

SALES (est): 1.3MM **Privately Held**
SIC: 2911 5171 5172 Petroleum refining; diesel fuels; petroleum bulk stations & terminals; diesel fuel

(G-92)
HUTCHINSON LOGGING
7585 Highway 35 (39421-9595)
P.O. Box 172 (39421-0172)
PHONE..................................601 943-5486
Dave Hutchinson, *Owner*
EMP: 2
SALES (est): 100K **Privately Held**
SIC: 2411 Logging

Batesville
Panola County

(G-93)
ACI BUILDING SYSTEMS LLC (DH)
Also Called: A C I
10125 Highway 6 W (38606-8273)
P.O. Box 1316 (38606-1316)
PHONE..................................662 563-4574
Timothy W Ritchie, *President*
James T Hansen, *CFO*
▼ EMP: 175
SQ FT: 90,000
SALES (est): 35.4MM
SALES (corp-wide): 267.5MM **Privately Held**
SIC: 3448 Prefabricated metal buildings
HQ: Associated Steel Group, Llc

Nashville TN
615 714-6234

(G-94)
ADB CANVAS ART
159 Moss Rd (38606-7701)
PHONE..................................662 934-9449
Ashley Bratcher, *Principal*
EMP: 1
SALES (est): 46.5K **Privately Held**
SIC: 2211 Canvas

(G-95)
AJINOMOTO WINDSOR INC
Also Called: AJINOMOTO WINDSOR, INC.
875 Highway 51 S (38606-2545)
PHONE..................................662 647-1594
EMP: 2 **Privately Held**
SIC: 2038 Frozen specialties
HQ: Ajinomoto Foods North America, Inc.
4200 Concours Ste 100
Ontario CA 91764

(G-96)
ART HORIZONS INC
483 Highway 6 W (38606-2561)
PHONE..................................662 561-9733
Edward E Brucker, *President*
Ruth Brucker, *Vice Pres*
Barry Brucker, *Shareholder*
May Brucker, *Shareholder*
Michael Brucker, *Shareholder*
EMP: 187
SQ FT: 300
SALES (est): 21.9MM **Privately Held**
SIC: 2499 Picture & mirror frames, wood

(G-97)
BATESVILLE RACEWAY LLC
105 Champion Dr (38606-7008)
PHONE..................................662 561-0065
Fadi Salameh, *Principal*
EMP: 6
SALES (est): 326.5K **Privately Held**
SIC: 3644 Raceways

(G-98)
BATESVILLE TOOLING & DESIGN
210 Tower Rd (38606-2724)
PHONE..................................662 563-1663
Gary Blair, *President*
Janice Blair, *Corp Secy*
EMP: 13
SQ FT: 12,500
SALES (est): 2.4MM **Privately Held**
WEB: www.btdinc.org
SIC: 3599 Machine shop, jobbing & repair

2019 Harris Directory of
Mississippi Manufacturers

▲ = Import ▼ =Export
◆ =Import/Export

GEOGRAPHIC SECTION

Batesville - Panola County (G-128)

(G-99)
BITS & PCS PRESS INC
105 Public Sq (38606-2219)
PHONE..................................662 563-8661
Brooke P Johnson, *Principal*
EMP: 2
SALES (est): 65.5K **Privately Held**
SIC: 2741 Miscellaneous publishing

(G-100)
BROCATO CONSTRUCTION INC
1847 Brewer Rd (38606-8001)
P.O. Box 627 (38606-0627)
PHONE..................................662 563-4473
Chris Brocato, *President*
Tammy Ivy, *Manager*
EMP: 6
SQ FT: 2,000
SALES: 1.8MM **Privately Held**
WEB: www.brocatoconstruction.com
SIC: 1623 3444 7692 Pipeline construction; pipe, sheet metal; welding repair

(G-101)
CARAMEL FACTORY
127 Lakewood Dr (38606-3011)
P.O. Box 1445 (38606-1445)
PHONE..................................662 563-9900
Ricky Belke, *Owner*
EMP: 2
SALES: 120K **Privately Held**
SIC: 2064 Candy & other confectionery products

(G-102)
CROWN CORK & SEAL USA INC
195 Crown Dr (38606-2711)
PHONE..................................662 563-7664
Larry Outlaw, *Manager*
EMP: 274
SALES (corp-wide): 11.1B **Publicly Held**
WEB: www.crowncork.com
SIC: 3411 3354 Metal cans; aluminum extruded products
HQ: Crown Cork & Seal Usa, Inc.
770 Township Line Rd # 100
Yardley PA 19067
215 698-5100

(G-103)
CUBE ICE CO
101 Court St (38606-2210)
P.O. Box 898 (38606-0898)
PHONE..................................662 563-8411
Dennis Lott, *President*
EMP: 2
SALES (est): 299K **Privately Held**
SIC: 2097 Manufactured ice

(G-104)
CUSTOM SIGN CO OF BATESVILLE (PA)
480 Highway 51 S (38606-2502)
P.O. Box 970 (38606-0970)
PHONE..................................662 563-7371
William Burns, *President*
Nancy C Burns, *Corp Secy*
Charlie Cook, *Vice Pres*
EMP: 50
SALES (est): 5.2MM **Privately Held**
WEB: www.customsignco.com
SIC: 1799 3993 Service station equipment installation & maintenance; gasoline pump installation; signs & advertising specialties

(G-105)
EDGE TOOLS AND DESIGNS INC
112 Compress Rd (38606-7248)
PHONE..................................662 578-0363
Barry Logue, *President*
Gene Welch, *Vice Pres*
EMP: 5
SALES (est): 593.2K **Privately Held**
SIC: 3544 Special dies & tools

(G-106)
GENERAL ELECTRIC COMPANY
1450 Highway 6 E (38606-9213)
PHONE..................................662 561-9800
Andrae Pegues, *Production*
Dwayne Tyner, *Engineer*
Kristie Sturgeon, *Manager*
EMP: 40

SALES (corp-wide): 121.6B **Publicly Held**
SIC: 3724 Aircraft engines & engine parts
PA: General Electric Company
41 Farnsworth St
Boston MA 02210
617 443-3000

(G-107)
GRANT BROTHERS MACHINE SHOP
210 Thomas St (38606-2438)
PHONE..................................662 563-2523
Ollie Grant, *Owner*
EMP: 2
SALES (est): 141.2K **Privately Held**
SIC: 3599 Machine shop, jobbing & repair

(G-108)
HELENA CHEMICAL COMPANY
3409 Farrish Gravel Rd (38606-6834)
PHONE..................................662 563-9631
EMP: 5 **Privately Held**
SIC: 5169 2899 Chemicals & allied products; chemical preparations
HQ: Helena Agri-Enterprises, Llc
255 Schilling Blvd # 300
Collierville TN 38017
901 761-0050

(G-109)
INSITUFORM TECHNOLOGIES LLC
160 Corporate Dr (38606-2716)
P.O. Box 1210 (38606-1210)
PHONE..................................662 561-1378
Charles Tramel, *Director*
EMP: 62
SALES (corp-wide): 1.3B **Publicly Held**
WEB: www.insituform.com
SIC: 2621 2295 Felts, building; tubing, textile: varnished
HQ: Insituform Technologies, Llc
17988 Edison Ave
Chesterfield MO 63005
636 530-8000

(G-110)
JASON FLY LOGGING LLC
1155 Jeff Sanders Rd (38606-9214)
PHONE..................................662 316-3499
Jason Fly, *Mng Member*
Jason F Fly,
EMP: 15
SALES (est): 7MM **Privately Held**
SIC: 2411 7389 Logging;

(G-111)
KANGAROO EXPRESS 1544
630 Highway 6 E (38606-3004)
PHONE..................................662 563-4629
Tracy Hall, *Principal*
EMP: 1
SALES (est): 77.7K **Privately Held**
SIC: 3578 Automatic teller machines (ATM)

(G-112)
KLEAN N PRESS
319 Highway 6 W (38606-2558)
PHONE..................................662 563-5515
EMP: 2
SALES (est): 45.2K **Privately Held**
SIC: 7212 3589 Garment Press/Cleaner's Agent Mfg Service Industry Machinery

(G-113)
LEHMAN-ROBERTS COMPANY
Also Called: Memphis Stone & Gravel
1775 Farrish Gravel Rd (38606-6806)
PHONE..................................662 563-2100
Joe Welch, *General Mgr*
Brenda Myers, *HR Admin*
Will Castle, *Manager*
Donald Marter, *Manager*
Patrick Nelson, *Info Tech Dir*
EMP: 15
SALES (corp-wide): 133.8MM **Privately Held**
SIC: 2951 1611 Asphalt & asphaltic paving mixtures (not from refineries); highway & street construction
PA: Lehman-Roberts Company
1111 Wilson St
Memphis TN 38106
901 774-4000

(G-114)
MASON PRINTING
344 Highway 51 N (38606-2312)
P.O. Box 657 (38606-0657)
PHONE..................................662 563-3709
Richard Mason, *Owner*
EMP: 4
SQ FT: 3,500
SALES (est): 308.3K **Privately Held**
SIC: 2752 Commercial printing, lithographic

(G-115)
NELSON MATERIALS INC
117 Vick St (38606-9360)
PHONE..................................662 563-4972
John Farrish Jr, *Vice Pres*
EMP: 60
SALES (corp-wide): 19.9MM **Privately Held**
SIC: 1442 Construction sand & gravel
PA: Nelson Materials Inc
3163 Highway 430 S
Greenwood MS

(G-116)
PANOLIAN
363 Highway 51 N (38606-2311)
P.O. Box 1616 (38606-4116)
PHONE..................................662 563-4591
John Howell, *President*
Rita M Howell, *Corp Secy*
Rupert K Howell, *Vice Pres*
EMP: 24
SALES: 950K **Privately Held**
SIC: 2711 Newspapers: publishing only, not printed on site

(G-117)
PARKER-HANNIFIN CORPORATION
Also Called: Hose Products Division
1620 Highway 6 E (38606-9376)
PHONE..................................662 563-4691
Ed Hall, *Engineer*
Jared Balistreri, *Manager*
David Peacock, *Technology*
EMP: 130
SALES (corp-wide): 14.3B **Publicly Held**
WEB: www.parker.com
SIC: 3585 3714 Air conditioning, motor vehicle; motor vehicle parts & accessories
PA: Parker-Hannifin Corporation
6035 Parkland Blvd
Cleveland OH 44124
216 896-3000

(G-118)
PEPSI-COLA METRO BTLG CO INC
Also Called: Pepsico
180 Corporate Dr (38606-2716)
PHONE..................................662 563-8622
Fax: 662 563-8056
EMP: 30
SALES (corp-wide): 62.8B **Publicly Held**
SIC: 2086 Carb Sft Drnkbtlcn
HQ: Pepsi-Cola Metropolitan Bottling Company, Inc.
1111 Westchester Ave
White Plains NY 10604
914 767-6000

(G-119)
PLASPROS INC
175 Corporate Dr (38606-2717)
PHONE..................................662 563-8635
Joel Johnson, *Prdtn Mgr*
Debbie Schneider, *Purch Agent*
Mark Doner, *Research*
Beth Neth, *Human Res Mgr*
Herbert Sanders, *Maintence Staff*
EMP: 30
SALES (corp-wide): 50.6MM **Privately Held**
WEB: www.plaspros.com
SIC: 3089 Injection molding of plastics
PA: Plaspros, Inc.
1143 Ridgeview Dr
Mchenry IL 60050
815 430-2300

(G-120)
RESOURCEMFG
101 Public Sq (38606-2219)
PHONE..................................662 563-9617
EMP: 1
SALES (est): 39.6K **Privately Held**
SIC: 3999 Manufacturing industries

(G-121)
ROBISON ADHESIVES INC
261 Murphey Ridge Rd (38606-6404)
PHONE..................................662 997-8000
Lacy Russell, *President*
EMP: 4
SALES (est): 359.7K **Privately Held**
SIC: 2891 Adhesives

(G-122)
RUSSELL TRUCKING
106 Sherwood Cv (38606-3012)
PHONE..................................662 563-2616
James Russell, *Owner*
EMP: 2
SALES (est): 150K **Privately Held**
SIC: 0115 0116 0131 3715 Corn; soybeans; cotton; cottonseed farm; truck trailers; cattle

(G-123)
SANDSTORM ENTERTAINMENT
208 Claude St (38606-5417)
PHONE..................................662 578-1357
Kerry McGhee, *Partner*
EMP: 1
SALES (est): 49.1K **Privately Held**
SIC: 3861 Sound recording & reproducing equipment, motion picture

(G-124)
SECURE SHRED LLC (PA)
36124 Highway 315 (38606-9151)
PHONE..................................662 563-5008
Wanda Charmichael, *CEO*
Cole Flint,
EMP: 5 **EST:** 2012
SQ FT: 5,000
SALES: 30K **Privately Held**
SIC: 3589 Shredders, industrial & commercial

(G-125)
SOUTHERN APPLICATION MGT
21129 Highway 6 E (38606-8562)
P.O. Box 1466 (38606-1466)
PHONE..................................662 578-4684
Mike Flatt, *President*
EMP: 8
SALES (est): 968.9K **Privately Held**
SIC: 3523 Farm machinery & equipment

(G-126)
SPECIAL TS
1883 John Branch Rd (38606-9104)
PHONE..................................662 563-5138
Philip Moore, *Owner*
EMP: 7
SQ FT: 2,400
SALES: 772K **Privately Held**
SIC: 2759 Screen printing

(G-127)
T G FERGUSON COMPANY
Also Called: Complete Computers
117 Public Sq (38606-2122)
PHONE..................................662 563-0806
Travis Ferguson Jr, *President*
Julie B Ferguson, *Treasurer*
Conor J Ferguson, *Shareholder*
Fields Ferguson, *Shareholder*
Lucas Ferguson, *Shareholder*
EMP: 8
SQ FT: 2,400
SALES (est): 1.3MM **Privately Held**
WEB: www.panola.net
SIC: 5734 5045 7371 7378 Computer & software stores; computer software; custom computer programming services; computer maintenance & repair; publishers' computer software;

(G-128)
TG MISSOURI-MISSISSIPPI
195 Corporate Dr (38606-2717)
PHONE..................................662 563-1043
EMP: 2

(PA)=Parent Co (HQ)=Headquarters (DH)=Div Headquarters
✿ = New Business established in last 2 years

2019 Harris Directory of
Mississippi Manufacturers

15

GEOGRAPHIC

Batesville - Panola County (G-129)

GEOGRAPHIC SECTION

SALES (est): 142K **Privately Held**
SIC: 3261 Vitreous plumbing fixtures

(G-129)
THERMOS LLC
355 Thermos Dr (38606-2725)
PHONE..................................800 831-9242
Gene Parker, *Managing Prtnr*
Michell Putman, *Traffic Mgr*
Mike Yeager, *Branch Mgr*
Walter Dye, *Manager*
Johnny Golden, *Manager*
EMP: 77 **Privately Held**
SIC: 3086 Padding, foamed plastic
HQ: Thermos L.L.C.
475 N Martingale Rd # 1100
Schaumburg IL 60173
847 439-7821

(G-130)
TRENS SCREEN PRINTING
348 Highway 51 N (38606-2312)
PHONE..................................662 578-9074
Trennance House, *Owner*
EMP: 2
SALES (est): 134.6K **Privately Held**
SIC: 2752 Commercial printing, lithographic

(G-131)
TUCKER MANUFACTURING CO INC
120 Crown Dr (38606-2710)
P.O. Box 1506 (38606-4006)
PHONE..................................662 563-7220
John A Tucker Sr, *President*
John A Tucker Jr, *Treasurer*
Jane W Tucker, *Admin Sec*
EMP: 35 **EST:** 1946
SQ FT: 22,500
SALES (est): 1.9MM **Privately Held**
SIC: 7699 3949 Recreational sporting equipment repair services; sporting & athletic goods; football equipment & supplies, general

(G-132)
UNIFIED BUDDIST CHURCH INC
123 Towles Rd (38606-8508)
PHONE..................................662 578-2077
Rachel Neumann, *Branch Mgr*
EMP: 1
SALES (corp-wide): 389.7K **Privately Held**
SIC: 2741 Miscellaneous publishing
PA: Unified Buddist Church, Inc.
24 S Meadow Farm Ayers Ln
Hartland Four Corner VT 05049
802 436-1103

Bay Saint Louis
Hancock County

(G-133)
AIR TECH OF WAVELAND
4111 Third St (39520-7742)
P.O. Box 142, Waveland (39576-0142)
PHONE..................................228 467-7547
Herbert Marsh, *Owner*
EMP: 1
SALES (est): 117.4K **Privately Held**
SIC: 1711 7623 1389 Warm air heating & air conditioning contractor; air conditioning repair; pumping of oil & gas wells

(G-134)
BAY PRINTING & DESIGN SHOP LLC
Also Called: Artist and Business Express
998b Highway 90 (39520-3618)
PHONE..................................228 467-5833
James H Ballard, *Partner*
EMP: 2
SALES (est): 182.8K **Privately Held**
SIC: 2752 Commercial printing, lithographic

(G-135)
BAY ST LOUIS NEWSPAPERS INC (PA)
Also Called: Sea Coast Echo
124 Court St (39520-4516)
P.O. Box 2009 (39521-2009)
PHONE..................................228 467-5474
Chark Lancaster, *President*
James D Lancaster, *President*
Geoff Belcher, *Editor*
Ellis Cuevas, *Vice Pres*
James Ponder, *Vice Pres*
EMP: 25
SQ FT: 21,000
SALES (est): 2.6MM **Privately Held**
SIC: 2711 Commercial printing & newspaper publishing combined; newspapers, publishing & printing

(G-136)
BAYOU VIEW WOODWORKS
10183 Bayou View Dr W (39520-7482)
PHONE..................................985 290-0860
Michelle Powell, *Principal*
EMP: 2
SALES (est): 93.8K **Privately Held**
SIC: 2431 Millwork

(G-137)
BIJOUBEL LLC
136 Main St (39520-4526)
PHONE..................................228 344-3393
EMP: 2
SALES (est): 131.7K **Privately Held**
SIC: 2741 Miscellaneous publishing

(G-138)
BOEING COMPANY
Bldg 4995 (39529-0001)
PHONE..................................228 688-2281
David Geiger, *Branch Mgr*
EMP: 4
SALES (corp-wide): 101.1B **Publicly Held**
SIC: 3721 Airplanes, fixed or rotary wing
PA: The Boeing Company
100 N Riverside Plz
Chicago IL 60606
312 544-2000

(G-139)
CALGON CARBON CORPORATION
13121 Webre Rd (39520-9699)
PHONE..................................228 533-7171
D M Gonsior, *Branch Mgr*
EMP: 58 **Privately Held**
WEB: www.calgoncarbon.com
SIC: 2819 Charcoal (carbon), activated
HQ: Calgon Carbon Corporation
3000 Gsk Dr
Moon Township PA 15108
412 787-6700

(G-140)
CLAY NECAISE
Also Called: Outkast Charters
1006 Washington St (39520-1522)
PHONE..................................228 233-7760
Clay Necaise, *Owner*
EMP: 4
SQ FT: 1,500
SALES (est): 146K **Privately Held**
SIC: 3949 7999 5091 Bait, artificial: fishing; tour & guide services; sporting & recreation goods

(G-141)
COAST WOOD PRODUCTS INC
Also Called: Gulf Coast Wood Tool
309 Third St (39520-4230)
PHONE..................................228 466-4302
William Adam, *President*
Margaret Adam, *Admin Sec*
EMP: 3
SALES (est): 431.9K **Privately Held**
SIC: 2434 Wood kitchen cabinets

(G-142)
DAK AMERICAS MISSISSIPPI INC (HQ)
3303 Port And Harbor Dr (39520)
PHONE..................................228 533-4000
Jorge Young, *President*
Carlos Alanis, *Vice Pres*

Javier Gonzalez, *Vice Pres*
Alejandro Gutierrez, *Vice Pres*
Jonathan McNaull, *Vice Pres*
◆ **EMP:** 41
SALES (est): 21.5MM **Privately Held**
SIC: 2821 Plastics materials & resins

(G-143)
EVERETT INDUSTRIES INC
217 Eighth St (39520-2331)
PHONE..................................228 231-1556
Joseph Everett, *President*
EMP: 7
SALES: 500K **Privately Held**
SIC: 1522 3069 3251 1771 Hotel/motel & multi-family home renovation & remodeling; flooring, rubber: tile or sheet; flooring brick, clay; flooring contractor; flooring, hardwood; parquet flooring, hardwood

(G-144)
JINDAL TUBULAR USA LLC (HQ)
13092 Sea Plane Rd (39520)
PHONE..................................228 533-7779
O P Sharma, *CEO*
Vijay Joshi, *CFO*
Sumit Agrawal, *Finance*
April Schatte, *VP Sales*
Ryan Ladner, *Manager*
▲ **EMP:** 75 **EST:** 2014
SQ FT: 6,969,600
SALES (est): 42.1MM
SALES (corp-wide): 1.3B **Privately Held**
SIC: 3317 Steel pipe & tubes
PA: Jindal Saw Limited
A1, Upsidc Industrial Area,
Mathura UP 28140
112 618-8345

(G-145)
KIRK WELDING INSPECTION SE
6021 W Grenada St (39520-8325)
PHONE..................................228 467-6586
Patsy Kirksey, *Owner*
EMP: 2
SALES (est): 96.9K **Privately Held**
SIC: 7692 Welding repair

(G-146)
LOCKHEED MARTIN CORPORATION
Stennis Space Center (39529-0001)
PHONE..................................228 688-7997
Steve Thogersen, *Manager*
EMP: 584 **Publicly Held**
WEB: www.lockheedmartin.com
SIC: 3812 Search & navigation equipment
PA: Lockheed Martin Corporation
6801 Rockledge Dr
Bethesda MD 20817

(G-147)
LOCKHEED MARTIN CORPORATION
Bldg 5100 (39529-0001)
PHONE..................................228 813-2160
Mark Hayes, *Branch Mgr*
EMP: 10 **Publicly Held**
WEB: www.lockheedmartin.com
SIC: 3812 Search & navigation equipment
PA: Lockheed Martin Corporation
6801 Rockledge Dr
Bethesda MD 20817

(G-148)
LOCKHEED MRTIN SPACE OPRATIONS
John C Stennis Cntr (39529-0001)
PHONE..................................228 688-3675
Chester Miller, *Manager*
EMP: 500 **Publicly Held**
SIC: 3721 8734 Aircraft; testing laboratories
HQ: Lockheed Martin Space Operations, Llc.
700 N Frederick Ave
Gaithersburg MD 20879
301 240-7000

(G-149)
MAC LLC
13011 Road G (39520-9671)
PHONE..................................228 533-0157
Joe Gibbons, *Manager*
Nikica Maljkovic, *Info Tech Mgr*

Nick Malkovich,
EMP: 12
SALES (est): 1MM **Privately Held**
SIC: 3482 Small arms ammunition

(G-150)
POLYCHEMIE INC (DH)
3080 Port And Harbor Dr (39520-9306)
PHONE..................................228 533-5555
Rene Pich, *CEO*
Peter W Nichols, *President*
James R Carlson, *CFO*
▲ **EMP:** 34
SALES (est): 6.1MM **Privately Held**
WEB: www.snfinc.com
SIC: 2819 Chemicals, reagent grade: refined from technical grade

(G-151)
PSL USA INC (HQ)
13092 Seaplane Rd (39520-9089)
PHONE..................................228 533-7779
Ashok Punk, *President*
EMP: 3
SALES (est): 298.7K
SALES (corp-wide): 6.8MM **Privately Held**
SIC: 3317 Steel pipe & tubes
PA: Psl Limited
Psl Towers,
Mumbai MH 40005
226 644-7777

(G-152)
PURPLE BANNANA
108 S Beach Blvd (39520-4554)
PHONE..................................228 466-2978
Robin Copeland, *Principal*
EMP: 5
SALES (est): 340.3K **Privately Held**
SIC: 2026 Yogurt

(G-153)
ROOKIE BOATS
10008 Highway 603 (39520-8604)
PHONE..................................228 466-6377
EMP: 3
SALES (est): 202.3K **Privately Held**
SIC: 3732 5551 Boat building & repairing; boat dealers

(G-154)
SABIC INNOVATIVE PLAS US LLC
13118 Webre Rd (39520-9076)
PHONE..................................228 533-7855
Wilfred Argeanton, *Engineer*
Phillip Clark, *Manager*
EMP: 20 **Privately Held**
SIC: 3083 2821 Laminated plastics plate & sheet; plastics materials & resins
HQ: Sabic Innovative Plastics Us Llc
2500 Citywest Blvd # 100
Houston TX 77042

(G-155)
SABIC INNOVATIVE PLAS US LLC
3531 Port And Harbor Dr (39520-9669)
PHONE..................................228 466-3015
Theo Van Eldik, *Plant Mgr*
Theo V Eldik, *Plant Mgr*
John Harris, *Personnel*
EMP: 200 **Privately Held**
WEB: www.sabic-ip.com
SIC: 2821 Plastics materials & resins
HQ: Sabic Innovative Plastics Us Llc
2500 Citywest Blvd # 100
Houston TX 77042

(G-156)
SOLVAY SPCLTY POLYMERS USA LLC
13233 Webre Rd (39520-9078)
PHONE..................................228 533-0238
EMP: 10
SALES (corp-wide): 379.2MM **Privately Held**
SIC: 3089 Mfg Plastic Products
HQ: Solvay Specialty Polymers Usa, L.L.C.
4500 Mcginnis Ferry Rd
Alpharetta GA 30005
770 772-8200

2019 Harris Directory of
Mississippi Manufacturers

▲ = Import ▼=Export
◆ =Import/Export

GEOGRAPHIC SECTION

Beaumont - Perry County (G-184)

(G-157)
SPORT TRIAL
5232 Highway 90 (39520-9214)
PHONE..............................228 467-1885
Kevin Desselle, *Owner*
EMP: 3
SALES (est): 240K **Privately Held**
SIC: 3799 Trailers & trailer equipment

Bay Springs
Jasper County

(G-158)
BRIAN RAND
33 Scr 185 (39422-8912)
PHONE..............................601 519-5062
Brian Rand, *Principal*
EMP: 3
SALES (est): 194.6K **Privately Held**
SIC: 3131 Rands

(G-159)
BUCKLEY NEWSPAPERS INC (PA)
Also Called: Jasper County News
Hwy 15 N (39422)
P.O. Box 449 (39422-0449)
PHONE..............................601 764-3104
Ronnie Buckley, *President*
EMP: 100
SQ FT: 3,000
SALES (est): 7.9MM **Privately Held**
WEB: www.laurelimpact.com
SIC: 2711 Newspapers: publishing only, not printed on site

(G-160)
CMC PAVING LLC
70 County Road 1717 (39422-3201)
P.O. Box 1654 (39422-1654)
PHONE..............................601 764-2787
Joe Curry, *Mng Member*
Harold McCurdy,
EMP: 4
SALES: 200K **Privately Held**
SIC: 2951 Asphalt paving mixtures & blocks

(G-161)
GEORGIA-PACIFIC LLC
71 Georgia Pacific Rd (39422)
P.O. Box 570 (39422-0570)
PHONE..............................601 764-4806
Jeff Johnson, *Manager*
EMP: 75
SALES (corp-wide): 40.9B **Privately Held**
WEB: www.gp.com
SIC: 0811 2426 2421 Timber tracts; hardwood dimension & flooring mills; sawmills & planing mills, general
HQ: Georgia-Pacific Llc
133 Peachtree St Nw
Atlanta GA 30303
404 652-4000

(G-162)
HOL-MAC CORPORATION (PA)
2730 Highway 15 (39422-7430)
P.O. Box 349 (39422-0349)
PHONE..............................601 764-4121
Jamie V Holder, *President*
Charles B Holder, *Chairman*
Jeffrey D Holder, *Corp Secy*
Joyce Holder, *Treasurer*
Paul Hill, *Admin Sec*
◆ **EMP:** 129
SQ FT: 4,000
SALES (est): 89.5MM **Privately Held**
WEB: www.e-pac-mac.com
SIC: 3593 3523 3531 3559 Fluid power cylinders, hydraulic or pneumatic; farm machinery & equipment; construction machinery; automotive related machinery

(G-163)
HOL-MAC CORPORATION
160 Commerce Dr (39422-5221)
PHONE..............................601 764-4121
C B Holder, *Principal*
EMP: 77

SALES (corp-wide): 89.5MM **Privately Held**
SIC: 3593 Fluid power cylinders, hydraulic or pneumatic
PA: Hol-Mac Corporation
2730 Highway 15
Bay Springs MS 39422
601 764-4121

(G-164)
HOL-MAC CORPORATION
Hwy 15 N (39422)
P.O. Box 349 (39422-0349)
PHONE..............................601 764-4121
Jamie Holder, *President*
EMP: 77
SALES (corp-wide): 89.5MM **Privately Held**
WEB: www.e-pac-mac.com
SIC: 3593 Fluid power cylinders, hydraulic or pneumatic
PA: Hol-Mac Corporation
2730 Highway 15
Bay Springs MS 39422
601 764-4121

(G-165)
IMPACT PRINTING & DESIGN
3362 Highway 15 N (39422)
P.O. Box 449 (39422-0449)
PHONE..............................601 764-9461
Ronnie Buckley, *Owner*
EMP: 2
SALES (est): 121.4K **Privately Held**
SIC: 2752 Commercial printing, offset

(G-166)
JAMIE VALENTINE LOGGING LLC
736 County Road 1725 (39422-9841)
PHONE..............................601 764-7271
Tony Valentine, *General Mgr*
Jamie Valentine, *Mng Member*
EMP: 5 **EST:** 2012
SALES: 180K **Privately Held**
SIC: 2411 Saw logs

(G-167)
K & T POULTRY SALES & SVC INC
573 Windham Ln (39422-8504)
PHONE..............................601 764-3918
Terry Windham, *President*
Karen Dayvolt, *Treasurer*
Tommy Wildom, *Admin Sec*
EMP: 18
SQ FT: 13,500
SALES (est): 1.4MM **Privately Held**
SIC: 1731 2452 5083 Electrical work; chicken coops, prefabricated, wood; poultry equipment

(G-168)
MCNEIL CABINET AND MILLWORK
29 County Rd 5121 (39422)
P.O. Box 386 (39422-0386)
PHONE..............................601 764-2100
Phillip Mc Neil, *President*
Diane Mc Neil, *Corp Secy*
Gabe McNeil, *Vice Pres*
EMP: 30
SQ FT: 15,000
SALES: 2.5MM **Privately Held**
SIC: 5712 2431 Cabinet work, custom; millwork

(G-169)
PECO FOODS INC
Hwy 15 N (39422)
P.O. Box 1320 (39422-1320)
PHONE..............................601 764-4964
George Hickman, *President*
EMP: 600
SALES (corp-wide): 1B **Privately Held**
WEB: www.pecofoods.com
SIC: 2015 Chicken slaughtering & processing
PA: Peco Foods, Inc.
1101 Greensboro Ave
Tuscaloosa AL 35401
205 345-4711

(G-170)
PECO FOODS INC
95 Commerce Dr (39422-5143)
P.O. Box 1905 (39422-1905)
PHONE..............................601 764-4392
Danny Hickman, *CEO*
Mark Hickman, *President*
Roddy Sanders, *Corp Secy*
Jerome Hickman, *Vice Pres*
EMP: 650
SQ FT: 120,000
SALES (est): 23.3MM
SALES (corp-wide): 1B **Privately Held**
WEB: www.pecofoods.com
SIC: 0254 0251 2015 2048 Chicken hatchery; broiling chickens, raising of; frying chickens, raising of; roasting chickens, raising of; poultry, processed; livestock feeds; poultry feeds
PA: Peco Foods, Inc.
1101 Greensboro Ave
Tuscaloosa AL 35401
205 345-4711

(G-171)
PETROCI USA INC
Also Called: Bay Springs Fields
460 County Road 2339 (39422-9398)
PHONE..............................601 764-2222
Joey McLeod, *Manager*
EMP: 2 **Privately Held**
SIC: 1311 Crude petroleum production
HQ: Petroci Usa, Inc
5100 Westheimer Rd # 420
Houston TX
713 993-9663

(G-172)
RESTORA-LIFE MINERALS INC
2140 Scr 97 (39422-8704)
PHONE..............................601 789-5545
Larry Strite, *President*
Leroy Strite, *Vice Pres*
James Landis, *Admin Sec*
EMP: 6
SALES (est): 550K **Privately Held**
SIC: 2819 3255 Ammonium compounds, except fertilizers; clay refractories

(G-173)
STRONG BROS LOGGING INC
100 County Road 182a2 (39422-9567)
PHONE..............................601 764-9191
James Strong, *President*
Mary Thomas, *Treasurer*
EMP: 7
SALES (est): 675.4K **Privately Held**
SIC: 2411 Logging

(G-174)
THOMAS E WINDHAM PUMPING
22 Hendry Rd (39422-9765)
P.O. Box 342 (39422-0342)
PHONE..............................601 764-3965
Thomas E Windham, *Owner*
Vergina A Windham, *Admin Sec*
EMP: 1
SALES (est): 91.6K **Privately Held**
SIC: 1389 Pumping of oil & gas wells

Bay St Louis
Hancock County

(G-175)
ARMORLOCK INDUSTRIES LLC
9028 Ladner St (39520-8606)
P.O. Box 4620, Bay Saint Louis (39521-4620)
PHONE..............................228 466-2990
Nicholas Savko, *Manager*
EMP: 2 **EST:** 2013
SALES (est): 160.4K **Privately Held**
SIC: 3999 Manufacturing industries

(G-176)
BETTA BOATS LLC
201 N 2nd St Ste 100 (39520-4535)
P.O. Box 2592 (39521-2592)
PHONE..............................228 363-2529
Mark Isaacs, *CEO*
EMP: 2
SALES (est): 120.6K **Privately Held**
SIC: 3732 Boat building & repairing

(G-177)
COUNTY OF HANCOCK
Also Called: Veterans Service Officer
854 Highway 90 Ste A (39520-2739)
PHONE..............................228 467-2100
Tim Bourgeors, *Principal*
EMP: 1 **Privately Held**
WEB: www.co.hancock.ms.us
SIC: 2321 9111 Men's & boys' furnishings; county supervisors' & executives' offices
PA: County Of Hancock
854 Highway 90 Ste A
Bay Saint Louis MS 39520
228 467-0172

(G-178)
DAK AMERICAS LLC
3303 Port And Harbor Dr (39520)
PHONE..............................228 533-4480
Hector Camberos, *CEO*
EMP: 226 **Privately Held**
SIC: 2821 Polyethylene resins
HQ: Dak Americas Llc
7621 Little Ave Ste 500
Charlotte NC 28226
704 940-7500

(G-179)
JM DIGITAL CORPORATION
Also Called: J M Digital Printing
10704 Highway 603 (39520-8781)
PHONE..............................601 659-0599
Fax: 228 467-9906
EMP: 5
SQ FT: 3,000
SALES: 550K **Privately Held**
SIC: 2759 Commercial Printing

(G-180)
PSL-NORTH AMERICA LLC
13092 Sea Plane Road Bay (39520)
PHONE..............................228 533-7779
John Heinemann, *CFO*
Brian J Vaill,
▲ **EMP:** 350
SALES (est): 99.4MM
SALES (corp-wide): 6.8MM **Privately Held**
SIC: 3312 Pipes & tubes
PA: Psl Limited
Psl Towers,
Mumbai MH 40005
226 644-7777

(G-181)
RIDGID MACHINING
6307 W Benton St (39520-8590)
PHONE..............................228 383-3525
Patrick Resch, *Principal*
EMP: 2 **EST:** 2017
SALES (est): 81.4K **Privately Held**
SIC: 3599 Machine & other job shop work

(G-182)
SOUTH COAST ELECTRIC LLC
Also Called: SCE
13061 Road D (39520-9676)
P.O. Box 100, Pearlington (39572-0100)
PHONE..............................228 533-0002
Ralph Lindfors, *Vice Pres*
EMP: 13 **EST:** 2016
SQ FT: 11,704
SALES (est): 921.7K **Privately Held**
SIC: 3613 3625 Switchgear & switchboard apparatus; relays & industrial controls

Beaumont
Perry County

(G-183)
601 CUSTOM WOODWORKS
204 Arlington Rd (39423-2690)
PHONE..............................601 588-0117
Norman Hinton, *Principal*
EMP: 1
SALES (est): 54.1K **Privately Held**
SIC: 2431 Millwork

(G-184)
DAVIS WLDG & FABRICATION LLC
16 Muscio Rd (39423-2076)
PHONE..............................601 258-0334

(PA)=Parent Co (HQ)=Headquarters (DH)=Div Headquarters
✪ = New Business established in last 2 years

2019 Harris Directory of
Mississippi Manufacturers

17

GEOGRAPHIC SECTION

Daniel Davis,
Carrie C Davis,
Daniel M Davis,
EMP: 5
SALES (est): 192K **Privately Held**
SIC: 7692 Welding repair

(G-185)
HOOD INDUSTRIES INC
226 Delta Pine Rd (39423-2715)
PHONE..................................601 784-3414
Jay Goree, *Credit Staff*
Jim Benefield, *Manager*
EMP: 245
SALES (corp-wide): 332.7MM **Privately Held**
WEB: www.hoodindustries.com
SIC: 2436 2435 2411 Plywood, softwood; hardwood veneer & plywood; logging
PA: Hood Industries, Inc.
15 Professional Pkwy # 8
Hattiesburg MS 39402
601 264-2962

Becker
Monroe County

(G-186)
NAUM MYATT & SONS
Hwy 25 S 52242 (38825)
P.O. Box 297, Amory (38821-0297)
PHONE..................................662 256-8104
Naum Myatt, *Partner*
Richard Donald Myatt, *Partner*
Ricky Lee Myatt, *Partner*
EMP: 4
SALES (est): 410K **Privately Held**
SIC: 3089 Reinforcing mesh, plastic

Belden
Lee County

(G-187)
BSK RESOURCES LLC
1251 Chesterville Rd (38826-9395)
PHONE..................................662 842-4716
Bryan Kelley, *Principal*
EMP: 9
SALES (est): 2.8MM **Privately Held**
SIC: 5084 3535 Elevators; conveyors & conveying equipment

(G-188)
FOREST PHARMACEUTICALS INC
3464 Mccullough Blvd (38826-9429)
PHONE..................................662 841-2321
Joe Johnson, *Principal*
EMP: 3 **Privately Held**
SIC: 2834 Pharmaceutical preparations
HQ: Forest Pharmaceuticals, Inc.
400 Interpace Pkwy Ste A1
Parsippany NJ 07054
862 261-7000

(G-189)
H & H METAL FABRICATION INC
3066 Faulkner Rd (38826-9649)
PHONE..................................662 489-4626
Michael H Huey, *President*
EMP: 2 **EST:** 2001
SALES (est): 337.8K **Privately Held**
SIC: 3449 3499 Miscellaneous metalwork; fabricated metal products

(G-190)
LFI WIND DOWN INC
Also Called: Lane Furniture
3350 Mccullough Blvd (38826-9428)
P.O. Box 360 (38826-0360)
PHONE..................................662 566-7211
Joe Johnson, *Manager*
EMP: 550
SALES (corp-wide): 258.3MM **Privately Held**
WEB: www.lanefurniture.com
SIC: 2512 Recliners: upholstered on wood frames
HQ: Lfi Wind Down, Inc.
5380 Highway 145 S
Tupelo MS 38801

(G-191)
OISEYS INTERNATIONAL INC
3325 White Dr Ste F (38826-9416)
PHONE..................................662 255-1545
Zhiyong Yuan, *CEO*
▲ **EMP:** 5
SQ FT: 25,280
SALES (est): 226.9K **Privately Held**
SIC: 2511 Rockers, except upholstered: wood

(G-192)
TRI STAR INDUSTRIAL
3269 White Dr (38826-9416)
PHONE..................................662 680-4331
Robert Beaman, *Principal*
EMP: 3
SALES (est): 292.6K **Privately Held**
SIC: 3691 Storage batteries

(G-193)
UNITED FURNITURE INDS INC
Also Called: Lane Furniture
3301 Adams Farm Rd (38826-7040)
PHONE..................................662 841-2321
Eric Huggins, *Manager*
EMP: 250
SALES (corp-wide): 353.3MM **Privately Held**
SIC: 2512 Recliners: upholstered on wood frames; couches, sofas & davenports: upholstered on wood frames
PA: United Furniture Industries, Inc.
5380 Highway 145 S
Tupelo MS 38801
662 447-4000

Belmont
Tishomingo County

(G-194)
BAYMONT WHOLESALE INC
16 Industrial Rd (38827-9103)
PHONE..................................662 424-2134
Mike Stockton, *President*
EMP: 6
SALES (est): 738.5K **Privately Held**
SIC: 2541 Wood partitions & fixtures

(G-195)
BELMONT TSHMNGO JRNL INCJURNAL
Also Called: Kema Printing
430 2nd St (38827-7700)
P.O. Box 70 (38827-0070)
PHONE..................................662 454-7196
Fax: 662 454-0055
EMP: 5
SALES (est): 409.8K **Privately Held**
SIC: 2711 Newspapers-Publishing/Printing

(G-196)
BIG STAR OF BELMONT INC
10 Fillmore St (38827-9104)
P.O. Box 719 (38827-0719)
PHONE..................................662 454-3300
Sammy Hale, *Principal*
EMP: 1
SALES (est): 125.9K **Privately Held**
SIC: 2043 Cereal breakfast foods

(G-197)
COMFORT REVOLUTION LLC
9 Industrial Rd (38827-9102)
PHONE..................................662 454-7526
Brian Bryant, *Principal*
EMP: 16
SALES (corp-wide): 2.7B **Publicly Held**
SIC: 3674 Magnetic bubble memory device
HQ: Comfort Revolution, Llc
442 Highway 35 Fl 1
Eatontown NJ 07724
732 272-9111

(G-198)
ETD INC
14 Airpark (38827)
P.O. Box 156 (38827-0156)
PHONE..................................662 454-9349
EMP: 4
SALES (est): 260K **Privately Held**
SIC: 3312 Blast Furnace-Steel Works

(G-199)
L L WOOD
10 Industrial Rd (38827-9103)
PHONE..................................662 454-0506
EMP: 2 **EST:** 2010
SALES (est): 100K **Privately Held**
SIC: 2491 Wood Preserving

(G-200)
MID-SOUTH DRAPERY INC
92 Yarber St (38827-9111)
P.O. Box 1150 (38827-1150)
PHONE..................................662 454-3855
Andrea McDonald, *President*
Shane McDonald, *Vice Pres*
◆ **EMP:** 30
SQ FT: 10,000
SALES (est): 3.6MM **Privately Held**
SIC: 2392 2391 5023 2395 Bedspreads & bed sets: made from purchased materials; draperies, plastic & textile: from purchased materials; draperies; pleating & stitching

(G-201)
POOLES STONE & MASONRY CONTRS
Also Called: Charles Pole Sons Stone Contrs
671 County Road 993 (38827-9715)
PHONE..................................662 438-6643
Charles Poole, *Owner*
EMP: 1
SALES (est): 86.9K **Privately Held**
SIC: 1521 3241 Single-family home remodeling, additions & repairs; masonry cement

(G-202)
SUN-AIR PRODUCTS INCORPORATED
18 Sun Air Dr (38827-9725)
P.O. Box 649 (38827-0649)
PHONE..................................662 454-9577
Donald D Hall, *President*
Joseph C Hall, *Corp Secy*
Joseph Hall, *Director*
EMP: 47 **EST:** 1978
SQ FT: 39,000
SALES (est): 9MM **Privately Held**
WEB: www.sunairproducts.com
SIC: 3499 Automobile seat frames, metal

(G-203)
WOOD INDUSTRIES INC
21 Front St (38827-7765)
P.O. Box 720 (38827-0720)
PHONE..................................662 454-0005
Jeff Wood, *President*
Chris Carter, *Natl Sales Mgr*
▲ **EMP:** 32
SALES (est): 8.6MM **Privately Held**
SIC: 3563 Air & gas compressors

Belzoni
Humphreys County

(G-204)
BANNER PRINTING CO INC
Also Called: Belzoni Banner The
115 E Jackson St (39038-3641)
P.O. Box 610 (39038-0610)
PHONE..................................662 247-3373
Julian Toney III, *President*
Teresa Toney, *Treasurer*
EMP: 2
SQ FT: 2,000
SALES (est): 200K **Privately Held**
SIC: 2711 2759 Job printing & newspaper publishing combined; letterpress printing

(G-205)
FRESHWATER FARMS PRODUCTS LLC
4554 State Highway 12 E (39038-4931)
P.O. Box 850 (39038-0850)
PHONE..................................662 247-4205
Dean Kiker, *General Mgr*
Harrel Potter,
EMP: 132
SQ FT: 44,000

SALES (est): 20.4MM **Privately Held**
WEB: www.freshwatercatfish.com
SIC: 2092 Fish, fresh: prepared

(G-206)
STRAUGHTER CABINETS
107 Van Buren St (39038-4050)
PHONE..................................662 247-2728
Rufus Straughter, *Owner*
EMP: 1
SALES (est): 82K **Privately Held**
SIC: 2434 Wood kitchen cabinets

Benoit
Bolivar County

(G-207)
UNITED BURIAL VAULT CO & CEMTR
205 W Preston St (38725)
P.O. Box 357 (38725-0357)
PHONE..................................662 347-9319
Robert Davis, *CEO*
EMP: 10
SALES (est): 500K **Privately Held**
SIC: 3272 7359 Burial vaults, concrete or precast terrazzo; tent & tarpaulin rental

Benton
Yazoo County

(G-208)
DIXONS HUNTING LODGE
15284 Highway 433 S (39039-8277)
PHONE..................................662 571-1908
James Dixon Jr, *Owner*
EMP: 2
SALES (est): 295.5K **Privately Held**
SIC: 3949 Sporting & athletic goods

(G-209)
M & T LOGGING
3738 Nod Rd (39039-8317)
PHONE..................................662 673-1621
Mike Kilpatrick, *Partner*
Talmadge Kilpatrick, *Partner*
EMP: 9
SALES (est): 883.7K **Privately Held**
SIC: 2411 Logging camps & contractors

Bentonia
Yazoo County

(G-210)
FOSTER MACHINE & REPAIR SVC
2023 Hilderbrand Rd (39040-8252)
PHONE..................................662 755-2656
Hillary Foster, *Owner*
EMP: 3
SALES (est): 140K **Privately Held**
SIC: 3449 Miscellaneous metalwork

(G-211)
HILDERBRAND CABINET DOORS LLC
4433 Mechanicsburg Rd (39040-8152)
PHONE..................................662 755-8626
Bradley Hilderbrand, *Principal*
EMP: 4 **EST:** 2008
SALES (est): 260.1K **Privately Held**
SIC: 2434 Wood kitchen cabinets

(G-212)
MMJ LOGGING INC
2828 Phoenix Rd (39040-8358)
PHONE..................................662 755-1163
EMP: 2 **EST:** 2017
SALES (est): 89.8K **Privately Held**
SIC: 2411 Logging

(G-213)
W S RED HANCOCK INC (PA)
Also Called: Hancock, W S Construction Co
115 Pritchard Ave (39040-8904)
P.O. Box 207 (39040-0207)
PHONE..................................662 755-0011

2019 Harris Directory of
Mississippi Manufacturers

▲ = Import ▼=Export
◆ =Import/Export

GEOGRAPHIC SECTION

Biloxi - Harrison County (G-244)

Roger Hancock, *President*
John Lewis, *Corp Secy*
EMP: 14
SQ FT: 20,000
SALES (est): 64MM **Privately Held**
SIC: 1629 1389 4212 Earthmoving contractor; construction, repair & dismantling services; local trucking, without storage

Biloxi
Harrison County

(G-214)
3D LASER SCANNING LLC
2436 Martin Rd (39531-2108)
PHONE...................................228 860-5952
Archibald April,
EMP: 2
SALES (est): 186.6K **Privately Held**
SIC: 1389 3577 3829 8713 Testing, measuring, surveying & analysis services; optical scanning devices; alidades, surveying; sextans, surveying; surveying services

(G-215)
A & A TRAILER SALES LLC
15824 Lemoyne Blvd (39532-5119)
PHONE...................................228 234-3420
Tina Andrews, *Office Mgr*
Zach Andrews,
EMP: 2
SQ FT: 120
SALES: 1.7MM **Privately Held**
SIC: 3715 7519 Truck trailers; utility trailer rental

(G-216)
ADVANCED CASTER TECH LLC
188 Main St (39530-3808)
P.O. Box 1471 (39533-1471)
PHONE...................................228 432-1384
Jody M Webster,
Melanie A Webster,
EMP: 2
SALES (est): 300K **Privately Held**
SIC: 3569 Baling machines, for scrap metal, paper or similar material

(G-217)
ADVANCED MARINE INC
337 Howard Ave (39530-4511)
PHONE...................................228 374-6747
William Allen Taylor, *President*
Lynn McGuire, *Admin Sec*
EMP: 9
SQ FT: 3,000
SALES (est): 810K **Privately Held**
SIC: 5999 3625 Electronic parts & equipment; control equipment, electric

(G-218)
ALLEN SHEETMETAL INC
14417 Cullen St (39532-8902)
PHONE...................................228 875-5336
EMP: 2
SALES (est): 350K **Privately Held**
SIC: 3444 Sheetmetal Fabrication Custom Sheetmetal Work

(G-219)
APPLIANCE TECH AUTHORIZED SVC
19701 Seymour Rd (39533)
PHONE...................................228 392-0789
Norbert Lloyd, *President*
EMP: 5
SALES (est): 413.6K **Privately Held**
SIC: 3357 Appliance fixture wire, nonferrous

(G-220)
BILOXI TENT AND AWNING CO INC
318 Howard Ave (39530-4510)
P.O. Box 329 (39533-0329)
PHONE...................................228 436-6161
Keith Parker, *President*
EMP: 4
SQ FT: 2,800

SALES (est): 230K **Privately Held**
SIC: 2394 Tents: made from purchased materials; awnings, fabric: made from purchased materials

(G-221)
BLOMS CREATIVE SIGNS INC
427 Caillavet St (39530-2049)
PHONE...................................228 374-2566
Douglas W Blom, *President*
Sylvia Blom, *Treasurer*
EMP: 2
SQ FT: 2,000
SALES: 120K **Privately Held**
SIC: 7389 3993 Lettering service; sign painting & lettering shop; signs & advertising specialties

(G-222)
BLUE CHIP SIGNS INC
13109 Shriners Blvd (39532-8747)
PHONE...................................228 918-9511
Laura Stockert, *Owner*
EMP: 1
SALES (est): 58.6K **Privately Held**
SIC: 3993 Signs & advertising specialties

(G-223)
BOOKS PLUS LLC
235 Reynoir St (39530-3003)
PHONE...................................228 209-5021
Marithis Dupre,
Andre Dupre,
EMP: 2
SALES (est): 52.5K **Privately Held**
SIC: 2731 Book publishing

(G-224)
CAMPBELL NEWSPAPERS LLC
996 Howard Ave (39530-3700)
PHONE...................................423 754-0312
Thomas Campbell,
EMP: 5 **EST:** 2017
SALES (est): 155.9K **Privately Held**
SIC: 2711 Newspapers

(G-225)
CASTLE ENCLOSURES LLC
1636 N Popps Ferry Rd M3 (39532-2217)
PHONE...................................228 238-6216
Keralyn Barnes, *Partner*
Mario Barnes, *Partner*
EMP: 1
SQ FT: 1,672
SALES (est): 63.7K **Privately Held**
SIC: 3272 Concrete products

(G-226)
CATERPILLAR DEV CTR INC
890 Vee St (39532-4204)
PHONE...................................228 385-3900
Savannh Fountain, *Director*
EMP: 2
SALES (est): 96.7K **Privately Held**
SIC: 3531 Construction machinery

(G-227)
CHARIOT WHEELCHAIR AND RPR
1636 Popps Ferry Rd (39532-2217)
PHONE...................................228 967-7991
EMP: 2
SALES (est): 86.6K **Privately Held**
SIC: 3842 Wheelchairs

(G-228)
CITY OF BILOXI
Also Called: Biloxi Fire Department
170 Porter Ave (39530-3753)
PHONE...................................228 435-6217
David Roberts, *Chief*
Mark Dronet, *Chief*
Walter Rode, *Manager*
John Miller, *Director*
EMP: 180 **Privately Held**
SIC: 5046 2759 9224 Commercial equipment; commercial printing; fire department, volunteer
PA: City Of Biloxi
140 Lameuse St
Biloxi MS 39530
228 435-6252

(G-229)
CKS PRODUCTIONS INC
Also Called: Pps Plus Software
946 Tommy Munro Dr (39532-2130)
P.O. Box 8906 (39535-8906)
PHONE...................................888 897-9136
John Shinn, *President*
EMP: 25
SALES (est): 2.3MM
SALES (corp-wide): 117.5MM **Privately Held**
WEB: www.ppsplusu.com
SIC: 7372 Business oriented computer software
HQ: Kinnser Software, Inc.
2500 Bee Caves Rd 2-300
Austin TX 78746
512 879-3135

(G-230)
CLIFFORD A CROSBY
Also Called: Crosby Surveying
716 Live Oak Dr (39532-4322)
PHONE...................................228 234-1649
Clifford Crosby, *Owner*
EMP: 1
SALES (est): 88.9K **Privately Held**
SIC: 1389 7389 Testing, measuring, surveying & analysis services;

(G-231)
CLYDE E BURTON
Also Called: Rebel Boat Works & Shipyard
161 5th St (39530-4647)
PHONE...................................228 432-0117
Clyde Burton, *Owner*
EMP: 1
SQ FT: 480
SALES (est): 133.4K **Privately Held**
SIC: 3732 Boat building & repairing

(G-232)
COASTAL SOLAR AND SEC FILMS
Also Called: Coastal S &S
620 Bay Haven Cv (39532-4331)
PHONE...................................228 369-3933
Mary Paul,
EMP: 2
SALES (est): 162.3K **Privately Held**
SIC: 3089 Plastics products

(G-233)
CONSOLIDATED PIPE SUPPLY
9337 W Oaklawn Rd (39532-8171)
PHONE...................................228 396-8818
EMP: 5
SALES (est): 195.5K **Privately Held**
SIC: 3479 Varnishing of metal products

(G-234)
CREATIONS BY STEPHANIE
152 Claiborne St (39530-4071)
P.O. Box 554 (39533-0554)
PHONE...................................228 697-2899
Stephanie Gray, *Owner*
EMP: 2
SALES (est): 91.4K **Privately Held**
SIC: 7372 Publishers' computer software

(G-235)
CUSTOM PACK INC
211 Caillavet St (39530-3031)
P.O. Box 893 (39533-0893)
PHONE...................................228 435-3632
Brent Gutierrez, *President*
Clay Gutierrez, *Corp Secy*
EMP: 10
SQ FT: 24,000
SALES (est): 1.3MM **Privately Held**
SIC: 2092 5146 Shrimp, fresh: prepared; seafoods
PA: Global Seafood Technologies, Inc.
211 Caillavet St
Biloxi MS 39530

(G-236)
DESTINY APPAREL LLC
1636 N Popps Ferry Rd # 110 (39532-2276)
PHONE...................................228 383-2665
Edwin Mallard,
EMP: 1 **EST:** 2013

SALES (est): 78.3K **Privately Held**
SIC: 2326 2329 2759 2389 Work uniforms; service apparel (baker, barber, lab, etc.), washable: men's; football uniforms: men's, youths' & boys'; letterpress & screen printing; burial garments;

(G-237)
DLA DOCUMENT SERVICES
708 Fisher St 102 (39534-2504)
PHONE...................................228 377-2612
Steve Watson, *Director*
EMP: 5 **Publicly Held**
SIC: 2752 9711 Commercial printing, lithographic; national security;
HQ: Dla Document Services
5450 Carlisle Pike Bldg 9
Mechanicsburg PA 17050
717 605-2362

(G-238)
DOCTORS SPECIALTY PHARMACY LLC
1720-A Med Pk Dr Ste 160 (39532)
P.O. Box 1412, Ocean Springs (39566-1412)
PHONE...................................228 806-1384
Gai Truong, *President*
EMP: 1
SQ FT: 2,650
SALES (est): 126.6K **Privately Held**
SIC: 2834 5122 5912 Pharmaceutical preparations; drugs, proprietaries & sundries; pharmaceuticals; druggists' sundries; drug stores

(G-239)
DUNAWAY SIGNS INC
12224 Parkers Creek Rd (39532-8100)
PHONE...................................228 392-5421
John C Dunaway Sr, *President*
Ginger Dunaway, *Vice Pres*
John Dunaway Jr, *Treasurer*
Tina Leuenberger, *Admin Sec*
EMP: 6 **EST:** 1982
SQ FT: 2,000
SALES (est): 931K **Privately Held**
WEB: www.dunawaysigns.com
SIC: 3993 Signs, not made in custom sign painting shops

(G-240)
DYNAMIC SIGNS AND MORE
1739 Pass Rd (39531-3338)
PHONE...................................228 235-5660
EMP: 2
SALES (est): 72.6K **Privately Held**
SIC: 3993 Signs & advertising specialties

(G-241)
EDCO WELDING
12416 John Lee Rd (39532-9646)
PHONE...................................228 392-5600
David Taylor, *Owner*
EMP: 1
SALES: 125K **Privately Held**
SIC: 7692 1799 3444 Welding repair; welding on site; sheet metalwork

(G-242)
FEATHERS FINS & FUR TAXIDERMY
10048 Leno Rd (39532-9675)
PHONE...................................228 860-3106
EMP: 1
SALES (est): 52.6K **Privately Held**
SIC: 3999 Mfg Misc Products

(G-243)
G HENNIG JR WELDING SHOP
213 Hoxie St (39530-4534)
PHONE...................................228 374-7836
August Hennig, *Principal*
EMP: 1
SALES (est): 51.1K **Privately Held**
SIC: 7692 Welding repair

(G-244)
GLENN WEISE
Also Called: Weise Communications
16350 Sweet Carolyn Rd (39532-7683)
PHONE...................................228 435-4455
Glen Weise, *Owner*
Glenn Weise, *Owner*
EMP: 3

(PA)=Parent Co (HQ)=Headquarters (DH)=Div Headquarters
✪ = New Business established in last 2 years

2019 Harris Directory of
Mississippi Manufacturers

19

Biloxi - Harrison County (G-245)

GEOGRAPHIC SECTION

SALES (est): 140K Privately Held
SIC: 4813 5063 3448 Data telephone communications; burglar alarm systems; prefabricated metal buildings

(G-245)
GLOBAL SEAFOOD TECH INC (PA)
211 Caillavet St (39530-3031)
P.O. Box 893 (39533-0893)
PHONE..................................228 435-3632
Brent Gutierrez, *CEO*
EMP: 50
SQ FT: 50,000
SALES (est): 9.7MM Privately Held
SIC: 2092 0273 5199 Shrimp, fresh: prepared; animal aquaculture; bait, fishing

(G-246)
GOLLOTT ICEHOUSE & OIL DOCK ✪
642 Bayview Ave (39530-2307)
PHONE..................................228 280-8033
Richard Gollott, *President*
EMP: 2 **EST:** 2018
SALES (est): 62.3K Privately Held
SIC: 2092 Fresh or frozen packaged fish

(G-247)
GOODNEWS GULF COAST
336 Rodenberg Ave (39531-3444)
PHONE..................................228 435-2456
Ray Butler, *Principal*
EMP: 3 **EST:** 2008
SALES (est): 176.1K Privately Held
SIC: 2711 Newspapers, publishing & printing

(G-248)
GTP PUBLISHING GROUP
2422 Regency Dr (39532-3024)
PHONE..................................228 348-2646
EMP: 2 **EST:** 2008
SALES (est): 110.5K Privately Held
SIC: 2741 Miscellaneous publishing

(G-249)
GULF PRIDE ENTERPRISES INC (PA)
391 Bayview Ave (39530-2502)
P.O. Box 355 (39533-0355)
PHONE..................................228 432-2488
Wally Gollott, *President*
Ann Gary, *Corp Secy*
EMP: 15
SQ FT: 16,000
SALES (est): 4.9MM Privately Held
SIC: 5146 2092 Seafoods; shrimp, fresh: prepared

(G-250)
H & L MILLWORKS INC
16001 Mcclellan Rd (39532-8529)
PHONE..................................228 392-9913
Harry Lamey Sr, *President*
EMP: 8
SQ FT: 3,600
SALES (est): 500K Privately Held
SIC: 2431 2541 5211 5046 Millwork; showcases, except refrigerated: wood; office fixtures, wood; millwork & lumber; store fixtures & display equipment; cabinet & finish carpentry

(G-251)
HIGH COUNTRY WOODWORKING
9245 Nancy Dr (39532-3774)
PHONE..................................228 396-2921
EMP: 1
SALES (est): 54.1K Privately Held
SIC: 2431 Millwork

(G-252)
HILTON NATIONAL CORPORATION
Also Called: Balloon On Wheels
2118 Lauren Dr (39532-3305)
PHONE..................................228 385-9800
Hilton Glass, *President*
Rebecca Glass, *Admin Sec*
EMP: 2 **EST:** 1993
SQ FT: 10,000

SALES (est): 240K Privately Held
WEB: www.balloononwheels.com
SIC: 2679 5947 Gift wrap & novelties, paper; gift, novelty & souvenir shop

(G-253)
IT COULD HAPPEN EMBROIDERY
265 Querens Ave (39530-2938)
PHONE..................................228 374-7674
Cathy Jasinski, *Partner*
Rose Marie Kolich, *Partner*
EMP: 4
SQ FT: 900
SALES (est): 160K Privately Held
WEB: www.itcouldhappenemb.com
SIC: 2395 Embroidery & art needlework

(G-254)
JAGG LLC
Also Called: UPS Store, The
296 Beauvoir Rd (39531-4051)
PHONE..................................228 388-1794
Jay Gannett, *Owner*
Gary Bishop, *Manager*
Allen Sands, *Manager*
EMP: 2
SQ FT: 1,600
SALES (est): 201K Privately Held
SIC: 7389 7221 5113 2759 Mailbox rental & related service; passport photographer; industrial & personal service paper; commercial printing

(G-255)
JS WOODWORKING
6820 Southwind Dr (39532-5705)
PHONE..................................228 257-6846
James Sachleben, *Mfg Staff*
EMP: 1
SALES (est): 114.3K Privately Held
SIC: 2431 Millwork

(G-256)
KENNEDY ENGINE COMPANY INC
Also Called: John Deere Authorized Dealer
980 Motsie Rd (39532-2202)
PHONE..................................228 392-2200
Thomas M Kennedy Jr, *President*
David Sean Kennedy, *Vice Pres*
Tim Kennedy, *Vice Pres*
Thomas Kennedy, *Treasurer*
Robbie Robertson, *Manager*
▼ **EMP:** 16 **EST:** 1953
SQ FT: 66,000
SALES (est): 9.9MM Privately Held
WEB: www.marineriii.com
SIC: 5084 5063 3519 Engines & parts, diesel; generators; parts & accessories, internal combustion engines

(G-257)
KNIGHT-ABBEY COML PRTRS INC
315 Caillavet St (39530-2044)
P.O. Box 1288 (39533-1288)
PHONE..................................228 702-3231
Tonya F Spiers, *President*
Ralph E Carter, *Treasurer*
Eva Sandt, *Cust Svc Dir*
John McCollins, *Manager*
EMP: 53
SQ FT: 13,000
SALES (est): 14.6MM Privately Held
SIC: 2752 Commercial printing, offset

(G-258)
L T INDUSTRIES INC
11240 Shorecrest Rd (39532-8128)
PHONE..................................228 392-1172
EMP: 2 **EST:** 2010
SALES (est): 73K Privately Held
SIC: 3999 Mfg Misc Products

(G-259)
LAURIN ENTERPRISES LLC
Also Called: Glass Etching Art
2530 Wilson Rd (39531-4737)
PHONE..................................228 207-5580
EMP: 1
SALES (est): 69.2K Privately Held
SIC: 3231 7389 Ornamental glass: cut, engraved or otherwise decorated;

(G-260)
LENOIR TECHNOLOGY LLC
8220 W Oaklawn Rd (39532-7710)
PHONE..................................769 926-5300
EMP: 3
SALES (est): 169.4K Privately Held
SIC: 3674 Semiconductors & related devices

(G-261)
LESSO FREEZING COMPANY INC
598 Bayview Ave (39530-2328)
P.O. Box 1428 (39533-1428)
PHONE..................................228 374-7200
R A Lesso Jr, *President*
Nancy Lesso, *Treasurer*
EMP: 5
SALES (est): 208.6K Privately Held
SIC: 2092 Seafoods, frozen: prepared

(G-262)
LIGHTHOUSE MARBLE WORKS INC
8212 Woolmarket Rd (39532-8148)
P.O. Box 467 (39533-0467)
PHONE..................................228 392-3038
Fred Schwan, *President*
EMP: 22
SQ FT: 32,000
SALES (est): 2.4MM Privately Held
WEB: www.lighthousemarble.com
SIC: 3281 Bathroom fixtures, cut stone

(G-263)
LIQUOR LOCKER INC
920 Cedar Lake Rd Ste O (39532-2107)
PHONE..................................228 396-8557
Andria Broach, *President*
Carolyn Handler, *Vice Pres*
David Broach, *Treasurer*
EMP: 4
SALES (est): 456.1K Privately Held
SIC: 5921 2087 Hard liquor; cocktail mixes, nonalcoholic

(G-264)
MAGNETIC ARROW LLC
Also Called: Mad House
158 Bilmarsan Dr (39531-5318)
PHONE..................................601 653-2932
Curt Simpson, *Software Dev*
Ryan Reinike, *Creative Dir*
Charles Simpson,
EMP: 2
SALES (est): 81.3K Privately Held
SIC: 2741 7311 7335 7336 Miscellaneous publishing; advertising consultant; commercial photography; commercial art & graphic design; custom computer programming services;

(G-265)
MARILYN TURNER
Also Called: Wreaths Charms and More
15628 Anderson Dr (39532-2812)
PHONE..................................228 271-2551
Marilyn Turner, *Owner*
EMP: 1
SALES (est): 56.4K Privately Held
SIC: 3999 5193 Wreaths, artificial; artificial flowers

(G-266)
MARY TIO
Also Called: Mary's Specialty Crafts
13042 Marvin St (39532-8276)
PHONE..................................228 392-0706
Mary Tio, *Owner*
EMP: 1
SALES (est): 10K Privately Held
SIC: 2499 Decorative wood & woodwork

(G-267)
MCM COMMUNICATIONS LLC
Also Called: Biloxio Newspaper
819 Jackson St (39530-4235)
P.O. Box 1209 (39533-1209)
PHONE..................................228 435-0720
Gary Michiels, *Partner*
Lisa Michiels, *Partner*
EMP: 15
SALES (est): 543.6K Privately Held
SIC: 2711 Newspapers, publishing & printing

(G-268)
METALWORX LLC
4179 Oakridge Pl (39532-9071)
PHONE..................................228 806-9112
EMP: 3 **EST:** 2012
SALES (est): 199.4K Privately Held
SIC: 3541 Vertical turning & boring machines (metalworking)

(G-269)
OCEAN SPRINGS SEAFOOD MKT INC
555 Bayview Ave (39530-2418)
PHONE..................................228 875-0104
Earl H Fayard Jr, *President*
Ruby Fayard, *Vice Pres*
Brenda Thensted, *Admin Sec*
EMP: 6
SQ FT: 2,000
SALES (est): 823.4K Privately Held
SIC: 2092 5421 Seafoods, fresh: prepared; seafoods, frozen: prepared; seafood markets

(G-270)
OMNI INSTRUMENTS
769 Whitney Dr (39532-3108)
PHONE..................................228 388-9211
Chris D Deaton, *Owner*
Bruce E Dennings, *Incorporator*
EMP: 1
SALES (est): 76K Privately Held
WEB: www.omniinstruments.com
SIC: 3823 Industrial instrmnts msrmnt display/control process variable

(G-271)
P D Q PRINTING INC
16313 Lemoyne Blvd (39532-5000)
PHONE..................................228 392-4888
Christine H Baker, *President*
EMP: 3
SALES (est): 200K Privately Held
WEB: www.pdqprinting.com
SIC: 2752 Commercial printing, offset

(G-272)
PCP P COAST
1120 Beach Blvd (39530-3631)
PHONE..................................228 202-7872
Azad Kabir, *Principal*
EMP: 2 **EST:** 2016
SALES (est): 57.8K Privately Held
SIC: 2731 Book publishing

(G-273)
PLATINUM PUBLISHING INC
630 Bay Cove Dr Unit 102 (39532-5558)
P.O. Box 6251, Diberville (39540-6251)
PHONE..................................228 219-1020
Katherine Buchanan, *Principal*
EMP: 2
SALES (est): 59.8K Privately Held
SIC: 2741 Miscellaneous publishing

(G-274)
R A LESSO SEAFOOD INC
598 Bayview Ave (39530-2328)
P.O. Box 1428 (39533-1428)
PHONE..................................228 374-7200
Rudy A Lesso Jr, *President*
R A Lesso Jr, *President*
Nancy Lesso, *Corp Secy*
Jude McDonnell, *Treasurer*
EMP: 50
SALES (est): 7.5MM Privately Held
SIC: 2092 Seafoods, fresh: prepared

(G-275)
RAINBOW SIGNS
12487 Shortcut Rd (39532-8137)
PHONE..................................228 354-8008
EMP: 2
SALES (est): 72.6K Privately Held
SIC: 3993 Signs & advertising specialties

(G-276)
REGIONAL STUCCO LLC
7301 Mccann Rd (39532-2933)
PHONE..................................228 323-0290
Jeff Johnson, *Principal*
EMP: 1 **EST:** 2010
SALES (est): 95.1K Privately Held
SIC: 3299 Stucco

2019 Harris Directory of
Mississippi Manufacturers

▲ = Import ▼=Export
◆ =Import/Export

GEOGRAPHIC SECTION

Bogue Chitto - Lincoln County (G-306)

(G-277)
RSILEDS LLC
169 Balmoral Ave (39531-4740)
PHONE..................................228 697-5967
Jeremy Palermo,
Paul Kotsakos,
EMP: 4
SALES (est): 500K **Privately Held**
SIC: 3674 7389 Light emitting diodes;

(G-278)
SENIORS BLUEBOOK
15217 Shadow Creek Dr (39532-8097)
PHONE..................................228 396-4602
Thad Anderson, *Partner*
EMP: 1 EST: 2001
SALES (est): 101.4K **Privately Held**
SIC: 2731 Books: publishing & printing

(G-279)
SHAUGHNESSY & CO INC
Also Called: Shaughnessy Clark D Prtg Co
234 Caillavet St (39530-3010)
P.O. Box 151 (39533-0151)
PHONE..................................228 436-4060
Clark Shaughnessy Jr, *President*
EMP: 2
SQ FT: 3,700
SALES: 270K **Privately Held**
SIC: 2752 2789 2791 2759 Commercial
printing, lithographic; binding only: books,
pamphlets, magazines, etc.; typesetting;
commercial printing

(G-280)
**SOPHISTICATED FABRICATIONS
LLC**
15553 Village Cir (39532-9456)
PHONE..................................228 424-8346
Jarred Jiminez, *Principal*
EMP: 1
SALES (est): 39.2K **Privately Held**
SIC: 3999 Manufacturing industries

(G-281)
**SPIRIT LIFTERS SCENTED
CANDLES**
248 Debuys Rd Apt 148 (39531-3512)
PHONE..................................210 802-0149
Memory Gause, *President*
EMP: 1 EST: 2015
SALES (est): 45.7K **Privately Held**
SIC: 3999 Candles

(G-282)
TAYLOR ENTERPRISES
2574 Hampton Ln (39531-2714)
PHONE..................................228 385-1245
Forest Taylor, *Owner*
EMP: 2
SALES (est): 135.4K **Privately Held**
SIC: 3949 Sporting & athletic goods

(G-283)
TIMBER CREEK ESTATES
6271 Pocono Way (39532-5407)
PHONE..................................228 392-0858
EMP: 6
SALES (est): 534.4K **Privately Held**
SIC: 2411 Timber, cut at logging camp

(G-284)
TNT INVESTMENTS LLC
Also Called: Sideus Technologies
176 Wisteria Ln (39530-4544)
P.O. Box 1425 (39533-1425)
PHONE..................................228 860-8207
Travis Teague, *CEO*
Dwayne Tauzin,
EMP: 2
SALES (est): 85.9K **Privately Held**
SIC: 3571 5149 Personal computers (mi-
crocomputers); spices & seasonings

(G-285)
TROPICAL WORLD INTL LLC
309 Goose Pointe Blvd (39531-6401)
PHONE..................................228 229-8413
Jacqueline Brown,
EMP: 5

SALES (est): 219.4K **Privately Held**
SIC: 6531 1422 3271 1794 Selling agent,
real estate; crushed & broken limestone;
blocks, concrete: landscape or retaining
wall; excavation & grading, building construction; commercial & office building,
new construction

(G-286)
YOUNG ELECTRIC SIGN CO
12487 Shortcut Rd (39532-8137)
PHONE..................................228 354-8008
Steve Lee, *Principal*
EMP: 3
SALES (est): 151.1K **Privately Held**
WEB: www.yesco.com
SIC: 3993 Signs & advertising specialties

(G-287)
**YOUNG ELECTRIC SIGN
COMPANY**
Also Called: Yesco
12487 Shortcut Rd (39532-8137)
PHONE..................................228 354-8008
Danny Fields, *Project Mgr*
Lonnie Trautman, *Manager*
EMP: 32
SALES (corp-wide): 331.2MM **Privately
Held**
SIC: 3993 Signs & advertising specialties
PA: Young Electric Sign Company Inc
2401 S Foothill Dr
Salt Lake City UT 84109
801 464-4600

Blue Mountain
Tippah County

(G-288)
**BLUE MOUNTAIN FURNITURE
LLC**
Hwy 15 N (38610)
P.O. Box 53 (38610-0053)
PHONE..................................662 685-4871
Greg Yates, *Mng Member*
EMP: 10
SQ FT: 11,000
SALES (est): 990K **Privately Held**
WEB: www.bluemtnwood.com
SIC: 2512 Living room furniture: uphol-
stered on wood frames

(G-289)
**BLUE MOUNTAIN REFINING
COMPANY**
31 County Road 827 (38610-9081)
PHONE..................................662 685-4386
Steve Marshall, *President*
Daniel Jaffee, *President*
James V Farrow, *Treasurer*
Becky Reaves, *Accountant*
Mike Gannon, *Admin Sec*
EMP: 70
SQ FT: 150,000
SALES (est): 18.8MM
SALES (corp-wide): 266MM **Publicly
Held**
WEB: www.oildri.com
SIC: 3295 Cat box litter
PA: Oil-Dri Corporation Of America
410 N Michigan Ave Fl 4
Chicago IL 60611
312 321-1515

(G-290)
BOBS WELDING & REPAIR
175 Hwy 15 N (38610)
PHONE..................................662 685-4217
Bobby Medland, *Owner*
EMP: 2
SALES (est): 106.4K **Privately Held**
SIC: 7692 Welding repair

(G-291)
HOFFMAN LENSES INC
105 College St (38610-9204)
PHONE..................................662 815-2803
Kent Bain, *Principal*
Roxann Dowdy, *Manager*
Janet Rock, *Manager*
Sarah Riesberg, *Asst Mgr*
Tikima Ward,
EMP: 3

SALES (est): 153.5K **Privately Held**
SIC: 3851 Ophthalmic goods

(G-292)
PROFILE PRODUCTS LLC
7250 Highway 15 (38610-9519)
PHONE..................................662 685-4741
Dwight A Schipke, *Plant Mgr*
Dwight A Schipke, *Plant Mgr*
Dwight A Schipke, *Opers-Prdtn-Mfg*
EMP: 42
SALES (corp-wide): 92MM **Privately
Held**
WEB: www.conwedfibers.com
SIC: 2611 3295 2842 3259 Pulp manu-
factured from waste or recycled paper;
minerals, ground or treated; specialty
cleaning, polishes & sanitation goods;
clay sewer & drainage pipe & tile
HQ: Profile Products Llc
750 W Lake Cook Rd # 440
Buffalo Grove IL 60089
847 215-1144

(G-293)
TIMOTHY D JETER
4740 Highway 15 (38610-9753)
PHONE..................................662 266-0968
Ashlea Jeter, *Principal*
EMP: 1
SALES (est): 39.6K **Privately Held**
SIC: 3999 Candles

Blue Springs
Union County

(G-294)
BLUE SPRINGS METALS LLC
1036 Corolla Ln (38828-8606)
PHONE..................................662 539-2700
Kirk J Lewis, *Principal*
Micheal Lamb, *Accountant*
Joe Lewis, *Sales Mgr*
Khiry Karriem, *Sales Staff*
Lakedra Washington, *Sales Staff*
EMP: 35
SQ FT: 10,000
SALES (est): 10MM **Privately Held**
SIC: 3315 Steel wire & related products

(G-295)
DIVERSITY VUTEQ LLC
1200 Magnolia Way (38828-6000)
PHONE..................................662 587-9633
EMP: 6
SALES (est): 650K **Privately Held**
SIC: 3089 Plastics products

(G-296)
GREEN METALS INC
1034 Corolla Ln (38828-8606)
PHONE..................................662 534-5447
Samuel Henry, *Branch Mgr*
EMP: 5 **Privately Held**
SIC: 3339 Primary nonferrous metals
HQ: Green Metals, Inc.
706 Triport Rd
Georgetown KY 40324
502 867-7253

(G-297)
GREENWOOD MACHINE SHOP
150 County Road 275 (38828-9067)
PHONE..................................662 316-4107
Deborah Greenwood, *Principal*
EMP: 2
SALES (est): 119.4K **Privately Held**
SIC: 3599 Machine shop, jobbing & repair

(G-298)
PINION PROD
1746 County Road 278 (38828-9234)
PHONE..................................662 891-0930
Leanna Hollis, *Principal*
EMP: 2 EST: 2013
SALES (est): 97.1K **Privately Held**
SIC: 2741 Miscellaneous publishing

(G-299)
**QUALITY PIPE & FABRICATION
LLC**
1243 Highway 9 N (38828)
PHONE..................................662 321-8542

Paul Green,
EMP: 2
SALES (est): 138.7K **Privately Held**
SIC: 3441 3498 Fabricated structural
metal; fabricated pipe & fittings

(G-300)
TOYOTA MOTOR MFG MISS INC
1200 Magnolia Way (38828-6000)
PHONE..................................662 317-3000
Masafumi Hamaguchi, *President*
Stephanie Jetson, *General Mgr*
Misao Fukuda, *Principal*
Sean Suggs, *Vice Pres*
Mark Hildenbrand, *Purch Mgr*
◆ EMP: 100
SALES (est): 44.7MM **Privately Held**
WEB: www.ttc-usa.com
SIC: 5511 3711 Automobiles, new & used;
automobile assembly, including specialty
automobiles
HQ: Toyota Motor Engineering & Manufac-
turing North America, Inc.
25 Atlantic Ave
Erlanger KY 41018

Bogue Chitto
Lincoln County

(G-301)
CORTEZ BYRD CHIPS INC
149 Auburn Dr Sw (39629-4158)
P.O. Box 547, Brookhaven (39602-0547)
PHONE..................................601 835-0333
Cortez Byrd, *President*
Tonya Stewart, *Vice Pres*
Barbara Byrd, *Treasurer*
Terry L Byrd, *Admin Sec*
EMP: 26
SQ FT: 3,000
SALES (est): 4.2MM **Privately Held**
SIC: 2499 Clip boards, wood

(G-302)
ELLIS WILLIAMS LOGGING
2622 Rlling Meadows Ln Se (39629-3202)
PHONE..................................601 734-3918
Robert Williams, *Owner*
EMP: 4
SALES (est): 256.4K **Privately Held**
SIC: 2411 Logging camps & contractors

(G-303)
LARRY SASSER LOGGING LP
Also Called: Sasser Logging Larry
913 Bogue Chitto Rd Sw (39629-9545)
PHONE..................................601 734-6002
Larry Sasser, *Partner*
EMP: 10
SALES (est): 829.5K **Privately Held**
SIC: 2411 Logging camps & contractors

(G-304)
REUBEN ALLRED
Also Called: Allred Backhoe & Gravel Co
1730 Huckleberry Trl Sw (39629-9466)
PHONE..................................601 734-2801
EMP: 2
SALES (est): 130K **Privately Held**
SIC: 3531 Backhoe Service

(G-305)
T A NETTERVILLE LOGGING INC
2910 Shannon Dr Sw (39629-5216)
PHONE..................................601 888-0054
Thomas A Netterville, *President*
Lisa T Netterville, *Admin Sec*
EMP: 12
SALES (est): 1.2MM **Privately Held**
SIC: 2411 Logging

(G-306)
TIMOTHY R OGLESBY
109 Doolittle Ln Sw (39629-8227)
PHONE..................................601 835-0673
Timothy R Oglesby, *Principal*
EMP: 2
SALES (est): 106.4K **Privately Held**
SIC: 0751 1389 0831 0214 Cattle serv-
ices; oil consultants; tree seeds gathering;
goat farm

(PA)=Parent Co (HQ)=Headquarters (DH)=Div Headquarters
✪ = New Business established in last 2 years

2019 Harris Directory of
Mississippi Manufacturers

Bogue Chitto - Lincoln County (G-307) GEOGRAPHIC SECTION

(G-307)
WALLACE WELDING LLC
1033 Montgomery Rd Sw (39629-9456)
PHONE..................................601 734-6542
Chesney Wallace, *Principal*
EMP: 1
SALES (est): 50.6K **Privately Held**
SIC: 7692 Welding repair

Bolton
Hinds County

(G-308)
DEFOREST WOOD PRESERVING CO
1400 Industrial Dr (39041-3215)
P.O. Box 357 (39041-0357)
PHONE..................................601 866-4655
Frank Deforest James III, *President*
Jewel James, *Vice Pres*
EMP: 8
SQ FT: 1,728
SALES: 7MM **Privately Held**
SIC: 2491 5031 Wood preserving; lumber, plywood & millwork

(G-309)
E & S LOGGING LLC
6277 N Chapel Hill Rd (39041-9362)
PHONE..................................601 866-7270
EMP: 2 EST: 2011
SALES (est): 163.2K **Privately Held**
SIC: 2411 Logging

(G-310)
JIMS WOODWORKS LLC
14800 Highway 22 (39041-9187)
PHONE..................................601 862-1025
Bert McLaurin, *Administration*
EMP: 1
SALES (est): 65.4K **Privately Held**
SIC: 2431 Millwork

(G-311)
KC FABRICATION AND WELDING LLC
3505 Martin Rd (39041-9226)
PHONE..................................504 427-8711
Karry Degruise, *Administration*
EMP: 1
SALES (est): 34.5K **Privately Held**
SIC: 7692 Welding repair

(G-312)
METRO MECHANICAL INC (PA)
1385 Industrial Dr (39041-3229)
P.O. Box 368 (39041-0368)
PHONE..................................601 866-9050
Frank White, *President*
Bryan Phillips, *Vice Pres*
Bryan White, *Project Mgr*
Hale Gonzales, *Opers Mgr*
Richard White, *CFO*
EMP: 100
SQ FT: 14,000
SALES (est): 22.4MM **Privately Held**
WEB: www.metroball.net
SIC: 1711 3312 Warm air heating & air conditioning contractor; ventilation & duct work contractor; plate, sheet & strip, except coated products

(G-313)
PHOENIX OPERATING INC
400 W Madison St (39041-3232)
P.O. Box 481 (39041-0481)
PHONE..................................601 866-2223
Gus Sanders, *President*
EMP: 3
SALES (est): 341.4K **Privately Held**
SIC: 1311 Crude petroleum production

Booneville
Prentiss County

(G-314)
ACCO BRANDS USA LLC
Also Called: G B C Office Products Grp
300 Quartet Ave (38829-1011)
P.O. Box 840 (38829-0840)
PHONE..................................800 541-0094
Dennis L Chandler, *Manager*
Mary Lynn Mosciano, *Info Tech Mgr*
EMP: 1
SALES (corp-wide): 1.9B **Publicly Held**
WEB: www.gbc.com
SIC: 3089 2761 3496 2675 Injection molding of plastics; manifold business forms; clips & fasteners, made from purchased wire; letters, cardboard, die-cut: from purchased materials
HQ: Acco Brands Usa Llc
4 Corporate Dr
Lake Zurich IL 60047
800 222-6462

(G-315)
ACCO BRANDS USA LLC
101 Bolton Dr Bldg 18 (38829-1409)
P.O. Box 842166, Boston MA (02284-2166)
PHONE..................................662 720-1300
EMP: 98
SALES (corp-wide): 1.9B **Publicly Held**
WEB: www.accobrands.com
SIC: 2782 3083 Looseleaf binders & devices; laminated plastic sheets
HQ: Acco Brands Usa Llc
4 Corporate Dr
Lake Zurich IL 60047
800 222-6462

(G-316)
AINZ PUBLISHING COMPANY
5 County Road 1053 (38829-7726)
PHONE..................................662 728-6131
Kathy Martin, *Principal*
EMP: 1
SALES (est): 42.4K **Privately Held**
SIC: 2741 Miscellaneous publishing

(G-317)
AMERICAN LOG HANDLERS LLC
619 Highway 30 E (38829-8012)
PHONE..................................601 927-6692
EMP: 15
SALES: 10MM **Privately Held**
SIC: 2411 Logging

(G-318)
ANDY JACKSON
6 County Road 5041 (38829-8485)
PHONE..................................662 416-2614
Andy Jackson, *Principal*
EMP: 3
SALES (est): 251K **Privately Held**
SIC: 2411 Logging

(G-319)
ASPAULJOY
404 Adams St (38829-2733)
PHONE..................................662 397-3661
Susan Gould, *Principal*
EMP: 2
SALES (est): 50.2K **Privately Held**
SIC: 2499 Wood products

(G-320)
BO ENTERPRISES INC (PA)
Also Called: Sports Zone
601 E Parker Dr (38829-5519)
P.O. Box 355 (38829-0355)
PHONE..................................662 720-1211
James C Bowens, *President*
Jessica Bowens, *Vice Pres*
EMP: 16
SQ FT: 27,500
SALES (est): 7.9MM **Privately Held**
SIC: 2389 Men's miscellaneous accessories

(G-321)
BOONEVILLE INDUSTRIAL COATINGS
100 W Veterans Dr (38829-1346)
PHONE..................................662 720-1147
George Via, *Principal*
EMP: 2
SALES (est): 139.8K **Privately Held**
SIC: 3479 Metal coating & allied service

(G-322)
BROWN LINE PRINTING INC
401 W College St (38829-3336)
P.O. Box 845 (38829-0845)
PHONE..................................662 728-9881
Tony Brown, *President*
Nora Brown, *Corp Secy*
EMP: 14
SQ FT: 20,000
SALES: 870K **Privately Held**
SIC: 2759 5199 Commercial printing; advertising specialties

(G-323)
C & W FRAMES INC
340 Highway 30 E (38829-7899)
PHONE..................................662 728-2120
Terry Cole, *President*
Linda Cole, *Co-Owner*
EMP: 16
SALES (est): 3.1MM **Privately Held**
WEB: www.cwframes.com
SIC: 2426 Frames for upholstered furniture, wood

(G-324)
CATERPILLAR INC
100 Caterpillar Dr (38829-7771)
P.O. Box 1080 (38829-7180)
PHONE..................................662 720-2400
Steve Barnett, *Engineer*
Jackie Nix, *Engineer*
Ed Maithison, *Manager*
Quincy Crabb, *Planning*
EMP: 250
SALES (corp-wide): 54.7B **Publicly Held**
WEB: www.cat.com
SIC: 3531 Construction machinery
PA: Caterpillar Inc.
510 Lake Cook Rd Ste 100
Deerfield IL 60015
224 551-4000

(G-325)
COMMUNITY BROADCASTING
1100 S Second St (38829-5408)
P.O. Box 356 (38829-0356)
PHONE..................................731 441-6962
Larry Melton, *President*
EMP: 7
SALES: 225K **Privately Held**
SIC: 4832 7372 Radio broadcasting stations; application computer software

(G-326)
DAVIS & SON LLC
Hwy 4 W (38829)
PHONE..................................662 728-8396
Ricky Davis, *Manager*
EMP: 2
SALES (est): 13.1K **Privately Held**
SIC: 2426 Frames for upholstered furniture, wood

(G-327)
DOWNS CORPORATION
Also Called: Downs' Printing & Graphic
201 Pecan Ave (38829-4613)
PHONE..................................662 728-3237
James J Downs, *President*
EMP: 4
SQ FT: 980
SALES: 100K **Privately Held**
SIC: 2759 Letterpress printing

(G-328)
EATON ELECTRIC MOTOR REPAIR
205 N 1st St (38829-2735)
PHONE..................................662 728-6187
Harold Eaton, *Owner*
EMP: 1
SQ FT: 1,200
SALES (est): 80K **Privately Held**
SIC: 7694 Electric motor repair

(G-329)
HOMELAND INC
200 Park Pl (38829-1410)
PHONE..................................662 728-7799
EMP: 2
SALES (est): 140K **Privately Held**
SIC: 2721 Periodicals

(G-330)
HOUSTON SIGN DESIGN
102 Summer Ln (38829-2612)
PHONE..................................662 728-2327
Tina Houston, *Principal*
EMP: 2
SALES (est): 132.8K **Privately Held**
SIC: 3993 Signs & advertising specialties

(G-331)
HUDDLESTON FARM SERVICE INC
Also Called: Huddleston, James Farms
424 County Road 3371 (38829-7078)
PHONE..................................662 728-5288
James A Huddleston, *President*
Shirley Huddleston, *Admin Sec*
EMP: 3
SQ FT: 4,000
SALES (est): 277.2K **Privately Held**
SIC: 5191 0116 0115 0111 Farm supplies; soybeans; corn; wheat; fertilizers, mixing only

(G-332)
JERRY HARRIS LOGGING INC
159 County Road 3151 (38829-8853)
PHONE..................................662 728-7331
Jerry Harris, *President*
EMP: 6
SALES (est): 563.1K **Privately Held**
SIC: 2411 Logging camps & contractors

(G-333)
MARATHON CHEESE CORPORATION
Also Called: Marathon Cheese of Mississippi
500 E Parker Dr (38829-5516)
PHONE..................................662 728-6242
Lisa Trace, *Plant Mgr*
Rick Underwood, *Safety Mgr*
Janie Jackson, *Finance*
Cindy Baten, *Manager*
Tina Stricklen, *Data Proc Staff*
EMP: 80
SQ FT: 80,000
SALES (corp-wide): 516.4MM **Privately Held**
WEB: www.mcheese.com
SIC: 2022 Cheese, natural & processed
PA: Marathon Cheese Corporation
304 East St
Marathon WI 54448
715 443-2211

(G-334)
MARTIN INCORPORATED
100 Caterpillar Dr (38829-7771)
PHONE..................................662 720-2445
Jim Lewis, *Manager*
EMP: 1
SALES (corp-wide): 160.8MM **Privately Held**
WEB: www.martinsupply.com
SIC: 3546 Drills & drilling tools
PA: Martin Incorporated
125 N Court St
Florence AL 35630
800 828-8116

(G-335)
MASTERBILT
Also Called: Master Bilt
213 W College St (38829-3411)
PHONE..................................662 728-3227
Craig Brown, *President*
George Loveless, *Corp Secy*
EMP: 3 EST: 1980
SALES (est): 315.9K **Privately Held**
SIC: 3442 1742 Storm doors or windows, metal; insulation, buildings

(G-336)
MID-SOUTH TRUSS CO INC
109 Magnolia Dr (38829-4405)
P.O. Box 314 (38829-0314)
PHONE..................................662 728-0016

2019 Harris Directory of
Mississippi Manufacturers

▲ = Import ▼=Export
◆ =Import/Export

GEOGRAPHIC SECTION

Brandon - Rankin County (G-367)

Toll Free:............................888   -
Kenny Claunch, *President*
Robert Dodson, *Vice Pres*
EMP: 4
SALES (est): 710.2K **Privately Held**
SIC: 2439 Trusses, wooden roof

(G-337)
NCV TESTING SERVICE
404 Pinehill Rd (38829-7904)
PHONE............................662 728-3965
EMP: 2 **EST:** 1998
SALES (est): 140K **Privately Held**
SIC: 3625 Mfg Relays/Industrial Controls

(G-338)
NORTH AMERICAN PIPE CORP
Also Called: Westlake Group
401 Industrial Park Rd (38829-1434)
PHONE............................662 728-2111
Lee Burton, *Manager*
EMP: 87 **Publicly Held**
SIC: 3354 3084 Aluminum pipe & tube;
plastics pipe
HQ: North American Pipe Corporation
2801 Post Oak Blvd # 600
Houston TX 77056

(G-339)
NORTH MISSISSIPPI TIMBER BRK
410 W College St (38829-3337)
PHONE............................662 728-7328
Robert Davis, *Owner*
EMP: 3
SALES (est): 310.6K **Privately Held**
SIC: 5099 2411 Timber products, rough;
logging camps & contractors

(G-340)
PARKER-HANNIFIN MOBILE CLIMATE
200 Quartet Ave (38829-1009)
PHONE............................662 728-3141
Donald Washkewicz, *CEO*
EMP: 1
SALES (est): 87.4K **Privately Held**
SIC: 3334 Primary aluminum

(G-341)
PAXTON MEDIA GROUP LLC
Also Called: Banner Independent
208 N Main St (38829-3317)
P.O. Box 10 (38829-0010)
PHONE............................662 728-6214
Reese Terry, *Branch Mgr*
EMP: 5
SALES (corp-wide): 234MM **Privately Held**
WEB: www.jonesborosun.com
SIC: 2711 Newspapers, publishing & printing
PA: Paxton Media Group, Llc
100 Television Ln
Paducah KY 42003
270 575-8630

(G-342)
PIERCE FOAM AND SUPPLY INC
103 Superior Dr (38829-5520)
P.O. Box 694 (38829-0694)
PHONE............................662 728-8070
Calvin W Pierce, *President*
Norma Ruth Floyd, *Treasurer*
EMP: 25
SQ FT: 35,000
SALES (est): 5.8MM **Privately Held**
SIC: 3086 Insulation or cushioning material, foamed plastic

(G-343)
PRINT BROKERS INC
219 Cedar Ridge Dr (38829-4617)
P.O. Box 1141 (38829-7241)
PHONE............................662 231-2556
Ann Ryan, *President*
EMP: 2
SALES (est): 83.9K **Privately Held**
SIC: 2752 Commercial printing, lithographic

(G-344)
PRO LOGGING INC
619 Highway 30 E (38829-8012)
PHONE............................662 720-9457

Russell M Stites, *President*
Amy Stites, *Corp Secy*
Mike Fisher, *Program Dir*
EMP: 27
SALES (est): 4.9MM **Privately Held**
SIC: 2411 Logging camps & contractors

(G-345)
SOUTH CENTRAL POLYMERS INC
Also Called: Scp
535 Highway 145 N (38829-9752)
P.O. Box 264 (38829-0264)
PHONE............................662 728-9506
Harry G Hanna, *President*
Bud Hanna, *Principal*
Daryl Finley, *Info Tech Mgr*
Kelly Hinton, *Admin Sec*
Mike Ford, *Maintence Staff*
▲ **EMP:** 55
SQ FT: 8,000
SALES (est): 14.2MM **Privately Held**
WEB: www.scpplastics.com
SIC: 3089 5162 Injection molding of plastics; plastics materials & basic shapes

(G-346)
TONY PHARR LOGGING
591b Highway 4 E (38829-8039)
PHONE............................662 728-9426
EMP: 3
SALES (est): 197.7K **Privately Held**
SIC: 2411 Logging

(G-347)
WOODRFFS PRTBLE WLDG FBRCATION
94 County Road 5131 (38829-9085)
PHONE............................662 728-3326
EMP: 2
SALES (est): 32K **Privately Held**
SIC: 7692 1791 3444 Welding Repair
Structural Steel Erection Mfg Sheet Metalwork

Boyle
Bolivar County

(G-348)
BOYLE TOOL & DIE INC
Also Called: Needle Specialty
600 Highway 446 (38730-9673)
P.O. Box 608 (38730-0608)
PHONE............................662 846-0640
Mark Meyers, *President*
Demetra Meyers, *Treasurer*
EMP: 3
SALES (est): 240K **Privately Held**
SIC: 3544 Special dies & tools

(G-349)
DELTA POSITIONS INC
631 Gaines Hwy (38730-9508)
P.O. Box 446, Cleveland (38732-0446)
PHONE............................662 719-1194
Terry Luna, *President*
Paula Luna, *Manager*
EMP: 3
SQ FT: 4,000
SALES: 700K **Privately Held**
WEB: www.deltapositions.com
SIC: 3699 Laser systems & equipment

(G-350)
M & W PUBLISHING CO LLC
93 Oakridge Rd (38730-9616)
PHONE............................662 843-1358
Margaret Hinson Tullos, *Mng Member*
EMP: 4
SALES: 2MM **Privately Held**
SIC: 2731 7389 Books: publishing only;

(G-351)
NEEDLE SPECIALTY PRODUCTS CORP
600 Highway 446 (38730-9673)
P.O. Box 608 (38730-0608)
PHONE............................662 843-8913
Vickie M Griffith, *President*
Jeffrey A Myers Sr, *Vice Pres*
EMP: 120
SQ FT: 36,800

SALES (est): 19.2MM **Privately Held**
WEB: www.needlespecialty.com
SIC: 3841 Needles, suture

(G-352)
SPAIN INCORPORATED
470 Gaines Hwy (38730-9505)
PHONE............................662 843-1301
Fred W Spain Jr, *President*
Undine B Spain, *Corp Secy*
Joy M Spain, *Vice Pres*
EMP: 6
SQ FT: 2,250
SALES (est): 460K **Privately Held**
SIC: 2531 Chairs, portable folding

Brandon
Rankin County

(G-353)
AAA HEATING & COOLING
201 Lotus Dr (39047-6246)
PHONE............................601 214-7212
Howard Branch, *Owner*
EMP: 2
SALES (est): 130K **Privately Held**
SIC: 3585 Parts for heating, cooling & refrigerating equipment

(G-354)
ACADIAN CUSTOM WOODWORKS
242 Mallard Dr (39047-7383)
PHONE............................601 572-4774
Bobby Lirette, *Principal*
EMP: 1
SALES (est): 54.1K **Privately Held**
SIC: 2431 Millwork

(G-355)
ACME BRICK COMPANY
6159 Highway 25 (39047-9303)
PHONE............................601 714-2966
EMP: 8
SALES (corp-wide): 225.3B **Publicly Held**
SIC: 3251 Brick & structural clay tile
HQ: Acme Brick Company
3024 Acme Brick Plz
Fort Worth TX 76109

(G-356)
ACTION PRSUIT GAMES OF BRANDON
44 Napoleon Cir (39047-7931)
PHONE............................601 825-1052
Barton Bankton, *President*
EMP: 2
SALES (est): 198.4K **Privately Held**
SIC: 3944 Games, toys & children's vehicles

(G-357)
ACTION SUCCESS PRESS
55 Woodgate Dr (39042-2285)
PHONE............................601 824-7775
Darryl Wheat, *Principal*
EMP: 4
SALES (est): 168K **Privately Held**
SIC: 2741 Miscellaneous publishing

(G-358)
ADVANCED TREATMENT TECH LLC
141 Peninsula Dr (39047-8282)
PHONE............................601 506-3798
Nathaniel Husman,
EMP: 1 **EST:** 2013
SALES (est): 98.8K **Privately Held**
SIC: 3589 Sewage & water treatment equipment

(G-359)
AE ENTERPRISES
312 Water Oak Rd (39047-7406)
PHONE............................601 573-5954
Alvin Edney, *Owner*
EMP: 3
SALES (est): 155.6K **Privately Held**
SIC: 2395 Embroidery & art needlework

(G-360)
ALATHEIA PROSTHETIC REHA
Also Called: Alatheia Prsthtic Rehab Centre
504 Grants Ferry Rd (39047-9049)
P.O. Box 10611, Greensboro NC (27404-0611)
PHONE............................601 919-2113
Emil Dovan, *Mng Member*
EMP: 16
SQ FT: 3,000
SALES: 1MM **Privately Held**
WEB: www.alatheia.com
SIC: 3842 8361 Prosthetic appliances; rehabilitation center, residential: health care incidental

(G-361)
ALIG LLC
Also Called: Mg Pisgah
118 Shirley Ln (39047-6603)
P.O. Box 248 (39043-0248)
PHONE............................601 829-9020
Paul Fortenberry, *Manager*
EMP: 13
SALES (corp-wide): 125.9MM **Privately Held**
WEB: www.mgindustries.com
SIC: 5169 2813 Carbon dioxide; industrial gases
HQ: Alig Llc
2700 Post Oak Blvd
Houston TX 77056
212 626-4936

(G-362)
AMARIES BATH HAPPIES & BODY
415 Turtle Ln (39047-5078)
PHONE............................601 714-1887
Amber Earles, *Principal*
EMP: 2 **EST:** 2011
SALES (est): 141.3K **Privately Held**
SIC: 3999 Soap dispensers

(G-363)
APLIMAGES INC
220 Avalon Cir Ste D (39047-7670)
PHONE............................601 992-1556
EMP: 2
SALES (est): 143.7K **Privately Held**
SIC: 3444 Sheet metalwork

(G-364)
APPLICATED IMAGES INC
220 Avalon Cir Ste D (39047-7670)
PHONE............................601 992-1556
Jacob Scott, *President*
EMP: 5 **EST:** 2008
SALES (est): 750K **Privately Held**
SIC: 3353 1791 Aluminum sheet, plate & foil; exterior wall system installation

(G-365)
ARCHITECTURAL CONCEPTS
103 Snyder Dr (39042-2819)
PHONE............................850 471-7081
Pauline Carroll, *President*
EMP: 3
SALES (est): 257K **Privately Held**
SIC: 3299 5032 5082 Ornamental & architectural plaster work; stucco; construction & mining machinery

(G-366)
ATWOOD AUTO & MARINE
117 Pine Acre Pl (39042-9706)
PHONE............................601 624-7012
Justin Atwood, *Principal*
EMP: 2
SALES (est): 65.4K **Privately Held**
SIC: 2499 Wood products

(G-367)
AUTOMTION DSIGNS SOLUTIONS INC
Also Called: AD&s
1070 Lake Village Cir D (39047-6762)
PHONE............................601 992-4121
Carolyn Rains, *President*
Doyle Rains Jr, *Vice Pres*
Melanie Toudouze, *Admin Sec*
EMP: 5
SQ FT: 1,000

(PA)=Parent Co (HQ)=Headquarters (DH)=Div Headquarters
✪ = New Business established in last 2 years

2019 Harris Directory of
Mississippi Manufacturers

Brandon - Rankin County (G-368)

GEOGRAPHIC SECTION

SALES (est): 603.5K **Privately Held**
WEB: www.fingerpro.net
SIC: **3999** Fingerprint equipment

(G-368)
B&Z SALES INC
144 Old Highway 80 (39042-3013)
P.O. Box 1958 (39043-1958)
PHONE..............................601 825-1900
Mike Ainsworth, *President*
EMP: 4
SALES (est): 753.1K **Privately Held**
WEB: www.bzsales.com
SIC: **3531** Construction machinery

(G-369)
BASF-CHEMICAL CO
809 Windlass Cv (39047-7035)
PHONE..............................478 951-9985
Nathaniel Reynolds, *Manager*
EMP: 2
SALES (est): 80.7K **Privately Held**
SIC: **2899** Chemical preparations

(G-370)
BAXTERS PRSSURE WSHG
6502 Grants Ferry Rd (39042-9333)
PHONE..............................601 825-2990
Addison Baxter, *Owner*
EMP: 1
SALES (est): 65.2K **Privately Held**
SIC: **2842** Specialty cleaning preparations

(G-371)
BIO PLUMBER OF MISSISSIPPI
210 Southampton Pl (39042-7675)
PHONE..............................601 825-5190
John Ash, *Owner*
EMP: 4
SALES (est): 317.9K **Privately Held**
SIC: **2836** Biological products, except diagnostic

(G-372)
BOX OFFICE 7 STUDIOS
27 Huntsman Cv (39042-2211)
PHONE..............................662 633-2451
Timothy Mays, *Owner*
EMP: 1
SALES: 25K **Privately Held**
SIC: **7812** 7372 7389 Video tape production; application computer software;

(G-373)
BRANDON BOC MS
159 Andrew Chapel Rd (39042-9027)
PHONE..............................601 825-1422
Heath Ahmphill, *Owner*
EMP: 2
SALES (est): 140K **Privately Held**
SIC: **2813** Industrial gases

(G-374)
BROWN BOTTLING GROUP INC
1651 Marquette Rd (39042-3271)
PHONE..............................601 824-3022
William A Brown, *Branch Mgr*
EMP: 23
SALES (corp-wide): 149.7MM **Privately Held**
SIC: **7382** 2086 Protective devices, security; bottled & canned soft drinks
PA: Brown Bottling Group, Inc.
    591 Highland Colony Pkwy
    Ridgeland MS 39157
    601 607-3011

(G-375)
CARR PLUMBING SUPPLY INC
140 Old Highway 80 Ste H (39042-3058)
PHONE..............................601 824-9711
Fred Fletcher, *Branch Mgr*
EMP: 4
SALES (corp-wide): 12.8MM **Privately Held**
SIC: **5074** 3432 Plumbing fittings & supplies; plumbing fixture fittings & trim
PA: Carr Plumbing Supply, Inc.
    2611 S Gallatin St
    Jackson MS 39204
    601 352-3999

(G-376)
CCORE ENERGY HOLDING CO LLC (PA)
2015 High Pointe Dr (39042)
P.O. Box 9287, Jackson (39286-9287)
PHONE..............................601 824-7900
James S Nippes,
EMP: 3
SALES (est): 167.7K **Privately Held**
SIC: **1381** 6719 Drilling oil & gas wells; investment holding companies, except banks

(G-377)
CCORE ENERGY/MARINER LLC
2015 High Pointe Dr (39042-3169)
PHONE..............................601 824-7900
James S Nippes,
Marsh Nippes,
EMP: 2
SALES (est): 130K **Privately Held**
SIC: **1389** Oil field services

(G-378)
CHADS LLC
120 Park Ln (39047-6120)
P.O. Box 4184 (39047-4184)
PHONE..............................601 919-3113
Dawn Ellerman, *Owner*
EMP: 3 EST: 2008
SALES (est): 266.7K **Privately Held**
SIC: **3535** Conveyors & conveying equipment

(G-379)
CHARLOTTES EMB & SCREEN PRTG
774 Trickhambridge Rd (39042-9305)
PHONE..............................601 824-1080
Jacklynn Williams, *Owner*
EMP: 2
SALES: 170K **Privately Held**
SIC: **2759** 2396 Screen printing; automotive & apparel trimmings

(G-380)
CHUCK PATRICK
Also Called: Gis Consulting
120 Dogwood Trl (39047-8600)
PHONE..............................601 278-7193
Chuck Patrick, *Owner*
EMP: 1
SALES: 25K **Privately Held**
SIC: **7372** Prepackaged software

(G-381)
CLAYFUL IMPRESSIONS
316 Woodlands Green Pl (39047-6371)
P.O. Box 5296 (39047-5296)
PHONE..............................601 918-0221
EMP: 2
SALES (est): 122.1K **Privately Held**
SIC: **2759** Commercial printing

(G-382)
COURTYARD MFG JEWELERS
210 Woodgate Dr S Ste B (39042-2415)
PHONE..............................601 825-6162
Louise Pipitone, *Owner*
EMP: 2
SALES: 150K **Privately Held**
SIC: **3911** 5944 7631 7231 Jewelry, precious metal; jewelry stores; jewelry repair services; hairdressers

(G-383)
CRECHLES THREE GENERATIONS LLC
1370 W Government St (39042-3049)
PHONE..............................601 213-8162
Phillip Crechale,
EMP: 1
SALES (est): 60.4K **Privately Held**
SIC: **2035** Pickles, sauces & salad dressings

(G-384)
CURBELL PLASTICS INC
Nationwide Plastics
112 Brooks Dr (39042-8679)
PHONE..............................888 477-8173
Mike Brown, *Manager*
EMP: 60

SALES (corp-wide): 216.5MM **Privately Held**
WEB: www.nationwideplastics.net
SIC: **5162** 3559 Plastics products; automotive related machinery
HQ: Curbell Plastics, Inc.
    7 Cobham Dr
    Orchard Park NY 14127

(G-385)
DAVION LLC
200 Jetport Rd Ste B (39047-7609)
PHONE..............................601 724-5013
Carl Davis, *Mng Member*
Joseph Davis,
EMP: 3
SQ FT: 9,000
SALES: 81K **Privately Held**
SIC: **1389** 3728 Oil consultants; target drones

(G-386)
DEEP SOUTH PHYSICS PLLC
111 Napoleon Dr (39047-8465)
PHONE..............................601 613-8076
George Harrison,
EMP: 3
SALES: 220K **Privately Held**
SIC: **3844** 0781 X-ray apparatus & tubes; horticultural counseling services

(G-387)
DELTA INDUSTRIES INC
Also Called: Jackson Ready Mix
501 E Mark Dr (39042-3811)
P.O. Box 1292, Jackson (39215-1292)
PHONE..............................601 825-7531
Donald Baker, *Manager*
EMP: 12
SALES (corp-wide): 100.3MM **Privately Held**
WEB: www.delta-ind.com
SIC: **3273** Ready-mixed concrete
PA: Delta Industries, Inc.
    100 W Woodrow Wilson Ave
    Jackson MS 39213
    601 354-3801

(G-388)
DENBURY RESOURCES INC
235 Three Prong Rd (39047-8812)
PHONE..............................601 829-0398
EMP: 7
SALES (corp-wide): 1.4B **Publicly Held**
SIC: **1311** Crude petroleum & natural gas
PA: Denbury Resources Inc.
    5320 Legacy Dr
    Plano TX 75024
    972 673-2000

(G-389)
DIXIE PRECISION RIFLES LLC
Also Called: Dpr Outdoors
100 Brooks Dr Ste B (39042-8679)
PHONE..............................601 706-9100
Alton Britt, *Partner*
EMP: 4
SALES (est): 401.9K **Privately Held**
SIC: **3484** 5941 7699 Rifles or rifle parts, 30 mm. & below; firearms; gunsmith shop

(G-390)
DOGWOOD PRESS
1022 Wakefield Pl (39047-7666)
PHONE..............................601 919-3656
Joe Lee, *Principal*
EMP: 2
SALES (est): 119.9K **Privately Held**
SIC: **2741** Miscellaneous publishing

(G-391)
DONALD E MCCAIN
33 Huntsman Cir (39042-2261)
PHONE..............................601 824-1275
Donald McCain, *Chairman*
EMP: 2
SALES (est): 79.9K **Privately Held**
SIC: **3585** Refrigeration & heating equipment

(G-392)
DVANI INNOVATION INC
123 Formosa Dr (39047-7912)
PHONE..............................601 992-5069
Krishnan Balasubramaniam, *Principal*
EMP: 2 EST: 2016

SALES (est): 88.3K **Privately Held**
SIC: **3669** Communications equipment

(G-393)
ELEMENTS COSMETICS LLC
211 Ashton Way (39047-4509)
PHONE..............................601 383-6352
Sylvia McGowan,
EMP: 1
SALES (est): 47.2K **Privately Held**
SIC: **2844** Toilet preparations

(G-394)
ELITE WOOD CARE
500 Creekstone Dr (39047-5050)
PHONE..............................601 622-2278
Lance Crockett, *Principal*
EMP: 3
SALES (est): 191.2K **Privately Held**
SIC: **2491** Wood preserving

(G-395)
ESPIRITU CUSTOM CUES
6162 Highway 18 (39042-9773)
PHONE..............................601 825-7077
Russ Espiritu, *Owner*
EMP: 2
SQ FT: 3,000
SALES (est): 162.7K **Privately Held**
WEB: www.espiritucues.com
SIC: **3949** Billiard & pool equipment & supplies, general

(G-396)
EZ MEDICAL WRAPS LLC
104 Red Oak Trl (39047-8632)
PHONE..............................321 961-0201
Nancy Vee,
Kaye Anderson,
EMP: 2
SALES (est): 126.6K **Privately Held**
SIC: **3841** Surgical & medical instruments

(G-397)
FORTENBERRY BUILDERS SUPPLY
1733 Highway 471 (39047-8301)
PHONE..............................601 825-3370
Kirby Fortenberry, *President*
Bessie Fortenberry, *Vice Pres*
Tina Greer, *Admin Sec*
EMP: 5
SQ FT: 4,000
SALES (est): 510K **Privately Held**
SIC: **2431** 5251 5211 Trim, wood; builders' hardware; lumber & other building materials

(G-398)
GILMORE BROS BUILDING SUPPLY
800 Depot Dr (39042-2908)
PHONE..............................601 825-6292
James Scott Gilmore, *President*
Jason Spencer Gilmore, *Vice Pres*
EMP: 3
SALES (est): 383.7K **Privately Held**
SIC: **3272** 5031 Building materials, except block or brick: concrete; building materials, exterior; building materials, interior

(G-399)
GLOBAL SCREEN PRINTING LLC
1301 Old Fannin Rd (39047-8734)
P.O. Box 4069 (39047-4069)
PHONE..............................601 919-2345
Gerald K Webb,
Ashley Bieliauskas,
Balys Bieliauskas,
▲ EMP: 3
SALES (est): 200K **Privately Held**
WEB: www.globalembroidery.net
SIC: **2759** 2396 7336 2261 Screen printing; screen printing on fabric articles; commercial art & graphic design; screen printing of cotton broadwoven fabrics

(G-400)
GOLD COAST COMMODITIES INC (PA)
817 Old Highway 471 (39042-2907)
P.O. Box 3 (39043-0003)
PHONE..............................601 825-2508
Tom Douglas, *President*

24

2019 Harris Directory of
Mississippi Manufacturers

▲ = Import ▼=Export
◆ =Import/Export

GEOGRAPHIC SECTION

Brandon - Rankin County (G-435)

Robert Douglas, *Vice Pres*
Chip Fisher, *Finance Spvr*
EMP: 28
SQ FT: 10,000
SALES: 7.5MM **Privately Held**
WEB: www.goldcoastcommodities.com
SIC: 2075 Soybean oil mills

(G-401)
GRAY DANIELS AUTO FAMILY
Also Called: Gray Daniels Toyota
104 Gray Daniels Blvd (39042-5512)
PHONE.................................601 948-0576
John Collins, *Sales Staff*
Steve Silberio, *Manager*
Bennie Gray, *Director*
EMP: 8 **EST:** 2007
SALES (est): 1.4MM **Privately Held**
SIC: 3944 Automobiles & trucks, toy

(G-402)
H FLEMING CONTRACTOR
525 Westwind Dr (39042-8306)
PHONE.................................601 824-0902
EMP: 2 **EST:** 1995
SALES: 250K **Privately Held**
SIC: 3645 3646 Mfg Residential Lighting Fixtures Mfg Commercial Lighting Fixtures

(G-403)
HARBOUR ENERGY INC
133 Westlake Dr (39047-9019)
PHONE.................................601 992-2277
Jim Bryan, *President*
EMP: 1
SALES (est): 110K **Privately Held**
SIC: 1389 8731 Oil consultants; natural resource research

(G-404)
HARRIS SIGNS
1496 Old Lake Rd (39042-8807)
PHONE.................................601 624-4658
Claude Harris, *Principal*
EMP: 1 **EST:** 2011
SALES (est): 66.2K **Privately Held**
SIC: 3993 Signs & advertising specialties

(G-405)
HIGHLANDS INDUSTRIES INC
132 Virginia Valley Dr (39047-4504)
PHONE.................................601 454-3901
Radim Kizek, *Partner*
EMP: 2
SALES (est): 170.6K **Privately Held**
SIC: 3999 Manufacturing industries

(G-406)
HOLLAND GRADING SERVICE
1284 Star Rd (39042-8444)
PHONE.................................601 825-2364
Francis Holland, *Owner*
EMP: 1
SALES (est): 123K **Privately Held**
WEB: www.hollandlandscape.com
SIC: 3531 Graders, road (construction machinery)

(G-407)
J & L SALES
201 Greenfield Pl (39047-9007)
PHONE.................................601 992-2495
John V Wright, *Owner*
EMP: 2
SALES (est): 121K **Privately Held**
SIC: 3699 Electrical equipment & supplies

(G-408)
J A C INDUSTRIAL TL & SUP LLC
1089 Highway 471 (39042-8746)
P.O. Box 4213 (39047-4213)
PHONE.................................601 591-1321
Josh Cochran, *Owner*
David Merrill, *Mng Member*
EMP: 7
SALES (est): 1.5MM **Privately Held**
SIC: 3545 Cutting tools for machine tools; counterbores, metalworking

(G-409)
J M I INC
100 Builders Square Dr (39047-4620)
P.O. Box 320294, Jackson (39232-0294)
PHONE.................................601 936-6800
Russell W Johnsen, *President*

Jesse McRight, *Vice Pres*
Carolyn McRight, *Treasurer*
Joanne Johnsen, *Admin Sec*
EMP: 5
SQ FT: 5,000
SALES: 1.2MM **Privately Held**
SIC: 2434 Wood kitchen cabinets

(G-410)
JARA L MILLER
Also Called: Wtf Lure Company
112 Timbercrest Ln (39047-6032)
PHONE.................................601 421-6876
Jara L Miller, *Owner*
EMP: 2
SALES (est): 101.5K **Privately Held**
SIC: 3949 Lures, fishing: artificial

(G-411)
LAMOCO INC
103 Millcreek Cors (39047-9011)
PHONE.................................601 919-3777
Fax: 601 919-3999
EMP: 6
SALES (est): 318K **Privately Held**
SIC: 1382 Oil/Gas Exploration Services

(G-412)
LEFLORE TECHNOLOGIES LLC
167 Northwind Dr (39047-8681)
PHONE.................................601 572-1491
Gene Bidwell,
EMP: 1
SALES (est): 70.5K **Privately Held**
SIC: 2834 8731 Solutions, pharmaceutical; biotechnical research, commercial

(G-413)
LENDERS SOFTWARE INCORPORATED
359 Audubon Cir (39047-7783)
P.O. Box 418, Collinsville (39325-0418)
PHONE.................................601 919-6362
Halden A Totten, *Exec Dir*
EMP: 1
SALES (est): 72.7K **Privately Held**
SIC: 7372 Prepackaged software

(G-414)
LINDE NORTH AMERICA INC
118 Shirley Ln (39047-6603)
PHONE.................................601 829-9020
Paul Fortenberry, *Manager*
EMP: 10
SALES (corp-wide): 1.4B **Privately Held**
SIC: 2813 Industrial gases
HQ: Messer North America, Inc.
200 Somerset Corporate Bl
Bridgewater NJ 08807
908 464-8100

(G-415)
LOVE YOUR LIGHT CANDLE COMPANY ✪
502 Kirsten Way (39047-8784)
PHONE.................................769 572-1733
Charleen Roth, *Principal*
EMP: 1 **EST:** 2018
SALES (est): 39.6K **Privately Held**
SIC: 3999 Candles

(G-416)
LUMS WELDING & MACHINE
2907 Highway 80 (39042-9086)
P.O. Box 652 (39043-0652)
PHONE.................................601 825-1116
Dennis Lum, *Owner*
EMP: 2
SALES (est): 117.4K **Privately Held**
SIC: 7692 Welding repair

(G-417)
MAGNOLIA BITES LLC
1252 W Government St (39042-3040)
P.O. Box 821 (39043-0821)
PHONE.................................601 709-9577
Ashley N Powell,
EMP: 1
SALES (est): 39.6K **Privately Held**
SIC: 3999 Manufacturing industries

(G-418)
MARTIN AND SONS LLC
250 Oil Well Rd (39042)
P.O. Box 99, Puckett (39151-0099)
PHONE.................................601 825-4012
Woody Martin, *Mng Member*
EMP: 25
SQ FT: 620
SALES (est): 2.8MM **Privately Held**
SIC: 2491 2449 2448 2426 Vehicle lumber, treated wood; wood containers; wood pallets & skids; hardwood dimension & flooring mills

(G-419)
MARY GIVENS
Also Called: Cee & Gee Designs
555 N Lake Dr (39042-2853)
PHONE.................................601 325-5599
Mary Givens, *Owner*
Courtney G Frisby, *Co-Owner*
EMP: 3
SALES (est): 190K **Privately Held**
SIC: 3911 5948 7389 Jewelry, precious metal; luggage & leather goods stores;

(G-420)
MCCRORY LOGGING LLC
1407 Ashley Rd (39042-7442)
PHONE.................................601 613-1702
Michael D McCrory, *President*
EMP: 2
SALES (est): 81.7K **Privately Held**
SIC: 2411 Logging

(G-421)
MCGEE MACHINE
115 Deletha Ln (39042-8984)
PHONE.................................601 825-7387
Billy McGee, *Owner*
Annelle McGee, *Admin Sec*
EMP: 1
SALES (est): 46K **Privately Held**
SIC: 3599 Machine shop, jobbing & repair

(G-422)
MCLELLAN WOODWORKS
309 Lake Harbor Rd (39047-9542)
PHONE.................................336 425-8425
EMP: 1
SALES (est): 54.1K **Privately Held**
SIC: 2431 Mfg Millwork

(G-423)
MEDIATOR LURES INC
401 Woodlands Cir (39047-8098)
PHONE.................................601 992-1577
C Baxter Kruger, *Principal*
EMP: 2
SALES (est): 143.5K **Privately Held**
SIC: 3949 Lures, fishing: artificial

(G-424)
MESSER LLC
159 Andrew Chapel Rd (39042-9027)
PHONE.................................601 825-1422
Jerry Knoll, *Manager*
Brian Blackwell, *Manager*
EMP: 28
SALES (corp-wide): 1.4B **Privately Held**
SIC: 2813 Carbon dioxide
HQ: Messer Llc
200 Somerset Corporate
Bridgewater NJ 08807
908 464-8100

(G-425)
MONOGRAM EXPRESS
131 Gateway Dr Ste A (39042-3097)
PHONE.................................601 825-1248
Stephanie Ball, *Owner*
EMP: 8 **EST:** 1999
SALES (est): 1.1MM **Privately Held**
WEB: www.monogramexpress.com
SIC: 2759 5699 5943 5949 Screen printing; customized clothing & apparel; stationery stores; sewing & needlework

(G-426)
MONOGRAM MILLS
318 Harbor Ln (39047-9533)
PHONE.................................601 749-1064
John H Mills Jr Mills, *Principal*
EMP: 1
SALES (est): 50.8K **Privately Held**
SIC: 2395 Embroidery & art needlework

(G-427)
MS YEARBOOKS LLC
Also Called: Balfour Yearbooks
1126 Pointe Cv (39042-2875)
PHONE.................................601 540-6132
Karen Loden, *Owner*
EMP: 2 **EST:** 2007
SALES (est): 75.6K **Privately Held**
SIC: 2741 Yearbooks: publishing & printing

(G-428)
NAIL LOGGING LLC
108 Blackbridge Dr (39042-2005)
PHONE.................................601 825-3375
Patricia McMahon, *Principal*
EMP: 2 **EST:** 2012
SALES (est): 140.5K **Privately Held**
SIC: 2411 Logging

(G-429)
NITAS QUILTS
3096 Highway 80 (39042-9088)
PHONE.................................601 825-2060
Mildred Stone, *Principal*
EMP: 2
SALES (est): 85K **Privately Held**
SIC: 2392 Comforters & quilts: made from purchased materials

(G-430)
OIL WELL LOGGING COMPANY INC (PA)
Also Called: Owlco
3970 Highway 43 N (39047-9517)
PHONE.................................601 477-8315
Harvey Koehne, *President*
Nettie Clark, *President*
EMP: 4 **EST:** 1983
SALES (est): 1.2MM **Privately Held**
SIC: 1389 Detection & analysis service, gas; well logging

(G-431)
PEN/RON COMPANY INC
226 Woodlake Dr (39047-6003)
P.O. Box 320373, Jackson (39232-0372)
PHONE.................................601 519-5096
Tonuia Mullins, *President*
EMP: 5 **EST:** 2012
SALES: 100K **Privately Held**
SIC: 1611 5261 1442 5211 Gravel or dirt road construction; top soil; construction sand & gravel; sand & gravel

(G-432)
PEPSI BOTTLING GROUP
Also Called: Pepsico
1651 Marquette Rd (39042-3271)
PHONE.................................601 982-4160
Jerry Staines, *Manager*
EMP: 4
SALES (est): 165.9K **Privately Held**
SIC: 2086 Carbonated soft drinks, bottled & canned

(G-433)
PERFORMANCE DRILLING CO LLC
115 E Business Park (39042-6605)
PHONE.................................601 969-6796
David Farmers, *Mng Member*
EMP: 80
SQ FT: 40,000
SALES (est): 5.7MM **Privately Held**
SIC: 1381 Directional drilling oil & gas wells

(G-434)
PEVEY PUBLISHING LLC
Also Called: Ms Sports Magazine
405 Knights Cv W (39047-4444)
PHONE.................................601 503-7205
Gregory J Pevey,
EMP: 3
SALES (est): 203.7K **Privately Held**
SIC: 2731 7389 Book clubs: publishing & printing;

(G-435)
POLLCHAPS LLC
453 Holifield Cir (39042-9376)
PHONE.................................601 706-4928
Todd Pollard, *Principal*
EMP: 2

(PA)=Parent Co (HQ)=Headquarters (DH)=Div Headquarters
✪ = New Business established in last 2 years

2019 Harris Directory of
Mississippi Manufacturers

Brandon - Rankin County (G-436)

GEOGRAPHIC SECTION

SALES (est): 214.8K **Privately Held**
SIC: 2759 Screen printing

(G-436)
POLLCHAPS CUSTOM SCREEN PRTG
100 Brooks Dr (39042-8679)
PHONE.....................769 218-0824
Todd Pollard, *Owner*
EMP: 2 EST: 2011
SALES (est): 173.5K **Privately Held**
SIC: 2752 Commercial printing, lithographic

(G-437)
PRAXAIR INC
214 Carbonic Dr (39042-7799)
PHONE.....................601 825-8214
Ron Cleary, *Chairman*
EMP: 10 **Privately Held**
SIC: 2813 Carbon dioxide
HQ: Praxair, Inc.
10 Riverview Dr
Danbury CT 06810
203 837-2000

(G-438)
PRECISION RIFLE ORDNANCE LLC
1024 Highway 471 Ste B (39042)
PHONE.....................601 825-0697
EMP: 1 EST: 2016
SALES (est): 46.6K **Privately Held**
SIC: 3482 3484 Mfg Small Arms Ammunition Mfg Small Arms

(G-439)
PREVOST WOODWORKING
318 Fairview Dr (39047-7083)
PHONE.....................615 836-9383
Stephen Prevost, *Principal*
EMP: 1
SALES (est): 54.1K **Privately Held**
SIC: 2431 Millwork

(G-440)
PRS
113 Bridlewood Dr (39047-8302)
PHONE.....................601 941-5104
Valerie Collins, *Principal*
EMP: 1
SALES (est): 41.3K **Privately Held**
SIC: 2741 Miscellaneous publishing

(G-441)
PTC INC
185 Bridlewood Dr (39047-8491)
PHONE.....................601 919-2688
George Lasseigne, *Principal*
EMP: 1
SALES (corp-wide): 1.2B **Publicly Held**
WEB: www.ptc.com
SIC: 7372 Application computer software
PA: Ptc Inc.
121 Seaport Blvd
Boston MA 02210
781 370-5000

(G-442)
QUAIL RIDGE PRESS INC
101 Brooks Dr (39042-8628)
P.O. Box 123 (39043-0123)
PHONE.....................601 825-2063
Gwen Mc Kee, *President*
Barbara Mosley, *Corp Secy*
Barney McKee, *Vice Pres*
Lacy Ward, *Sales Dir*
Corey Dunaway, *Sales Mgr*
▲ EMP: 7
SQ FT: 32,000
SALES (est): 900K **Privately Held**
WEB: www.quailridge.com
SIC: 2731 Books: publishing only

(G-443)
RAK-MASTER LLC
125 Vineyard Blvd (39047-7105)
PHONE.....................601 906-1039
Curtis A Clearman,
EMP: 4
SALES (est): 420.2K **Privately Held**
SIC: 3537 Trucks, tractors, loaders, carriers & similar equipment

(G-444)
RCN CORPORATION
Also Called: Rankin County News
207 E Government St (39042-3151)
PHONE.....................601 825-8333
Marcus Bowers, *President*
EMP: 15 EST: 1848
SQ FT: 6,528
SALES: 800K **Privately Held**
SIC: 2711 Newspapers: publishing only, not printed on site

(G-445)
REGION 8 MENTAL HEALTH RETRDAT
Also Called: Rankin County Industries
600 Marquette Rd (39042-3037)
P.O. Box 88 (39043-0088)
PHONE.....................601 591-5553
Bill Blair, *Plant Mgr*
David Mullins, *Manager*
EMP: 55
SALES (corp-wide): 12.6MM **Privately Held**
SIC: 8399 2657 3429 3999 Health systems agency; folding paperboard boxes; manufactured hardware (general); barber & beauty shop equipment; automobile recovery service; sheltered workshop
PA: Region 8 Mental Health Services
613 Marquette Rd
Brandon MS 39042
601 825-8800

(G-446)
ROCK ON INDUSTRIES LLC
116 Sunline Dr (39042-1915)
PHONE.....................601 825-4857
Roger Harrison, *Principal*
EMP: 1 EST: 2013
SALES (est): 67K **Privately Held**
SIC: 3999 Manufacturing industries

(G-447)
ROCK OR NOT LLC
Also Called: Irrock or Not
702 Pecan Ct (39042-6012)
PHONE.....................662 719-9120
Jacqueline D Boyd,
EMP: 1
SALES (est): 37.5K **Privately Held**
SIC: 2741

(G-448)
ROWELL PUBLISHING
124 Peninsula Dr (39047-8280)
PHONE.....................601 981-0933
EMP: 3 EST: 2003
SALES (est): 130K **Privately Held**
SIC: 2721 Periodicals-Publishing/Printing

(G-449)
SAFILO
2643 Highway 80 (39042-9097)
PHONE.....................601 212-4136
Tom Alexander, *Agent*
EMP: 3
SALES: 150K **Privately Held**
SIC: 3827 Optical instruments & lenses

(G-450)
SANDHILL GROUP LLC (PA)
3295 Highway 80 (39042-7774)
P.O. Box 1598 (39043-1598)
PHONE.....................601 591-4030
Linda Kinard, *Office Mgr*
Jeffrey Fry, *Mng Member*
EMP: 29
SQ FT: 6,200
SALES (est): 7.5MM **Privately Held**
SIC: 2813 Carbon dioxide

(G-451)
SERVICEKNIGHT
201 N College St Ste 201 # 201 (39042-4438)
PHONE.....................601 906-2810
Lee Ryals, *Owner*
EMP: 1
SALES (est): 46.5K **Privately Held**
SIC: 2273 Carpets & rugs

(G-452)
SIGN AND SING
151 Taylor Way (39047-7572)
PHONE.....................601 954-9172
Brandie Little, *Principal*
EMP: 1
SALES (est): 46K **Privately Held**
SIC: 3993 Signs & advertising specialties

(G-453)
SIGN CRAFTERS
316 Bay Park Dr (39047-6114)
PHONE.....................769 216-3936
Aubrey Hursh, *Owner*
Oberari Harsh, *Owner*
EMP: 1
SALES (est): 14.7K **Privately Held**
SIC: 3993 Signs & advertising specialties

(G-454)
SIPP SPINNERS AND LURES LLC
858 Willow Grande Cir (39047-8347)
PHONE.....................601 620-6445
Chance Ivy, *Principal*
EMP: 1
SALES (est): 49.3K **Privately Held**
SIC: 3949 Sporting & athletic goods

(G-455)
SISTRUNK SHEET METAL
121 Pole Bridge Dr (39042-9235)
PHONE.....................601 825-5999
Rayford Sistrunk, *Owner*
EMP: 2
SALES (est): 110K **Privately Held**
SIC: 3444 Sheet metalwork

(G-456)
SMYDA WOODWORKING INC
154 Indian Mound Rdg (39042-7572)
PHONE.....................601 591-0247
Bryan E Smyda, *President*
Laurel A Smyda, *Vice Pres*
EMP: 2
SALES (est): 311.3K **Privately Held**
SIC: 2431 Millwork

(G-457)
SOUTHEASTERN CONSTRUCTORS INC
1148 Shiloh Rd (39042-9671)
P.O. Box 1747 (39043-1747)
PHONE.....................601 825-9791
Joel Price, *President*
Virginia Price, *Corp Secy*
James S Daniels, *Vice Pres*
EMP: 30 EST: 1976
SQ FT: 15,000
SALES (est): 4.3MM **Privately Held**
SIC: 2541 2542 2521 2434 Cabinets, lockers & shelving; partitions & fixtures, except wood; wood office furniture; wood kitchen cabinets

(G-458)
SOUTHERN CANVAS
130 Belle Oak Dr (39042-8253)
PHONE.....................601 951-6266
Ashley Tullos, *Principal*
EMP: 1
SALES (est): 46.5K **Privately Held**
SIC: 2211 Canvas

(G-459)
SOUTHERN FABRICATORS LLC
980 Burnham Rd (39042-8794)
PHONE.....................601 824-8855
William Perry,
EMP: 17
SALES (est): 1.1MM **Privately Held**
SIC: 7692 Automotive welding

(G-460)
SOUTHERN FLOW
307a E Government St (39042-3238)
PHONE.....................601 591-1526
EMP: 2
SALES (est): 81.9K **Privately Held**
SIC: 1382 Oil And Gas Exploration Services

(G-461)
SOUTHERN TOUCH SOAP WORKS INC
115 Tiffany Dr (39042-8897)
PHONE.....................601 825-2676
Susan Fitts Davis, *President*
EMP: 1
SALES (est): 78.8K **Privately Held**
SIC: 2841 Soap: granulated, liquid, cake, flaked or chip

(G-462)
SPARKS WELDING SERVICE
5658 Highway 18 (39042-7881)
PHONE.....................601 519-9573
Darrin Sparks, *Principal*
EMP: 1
SALES (est): 44.2K **Privately Held**
SIC: 7692 Welding repair

(G-463)
SS DRILLING LLC
207 Pecan Blvd (39042-8371)
PHONE.....................740 207-5673
Sam Litteral, *Owner*
Sarah Litteral, *Principal*
EMP: 5 EST: 2015
SALES: 40K **Privately Held**
SIC: 1321 Fractionating natural gas liquids

(G-464)
SUN-PINE CORPORATION LTD (PA)
331 W Jasper St (39042-3034)
P.O. Box 287 (39043-0287)
PHONE.....................601 825-2463
Kenneth Courtney, *President*
Hilda Joy Courtney, *Corp Secy*
EMP: 65
SQ FT: 75,000
SALES (est): 25MM **Privately Held**
SIC: 2842 Cleaning or polishing preparations; disinfectants, household or industrial plant

(G-465)
SUPERIOR PALLET COMPANY
106 Creekwood Dr (39047)
PHONE.....................601 941-6254
Roger Dale Latham, *President*
Michele Latham, *Vice Pres*
EMP: 8
SQ FT: 20,000
SALES (est): 570K **Privately Held**
SIC: 2448 Pallets, wood & wood with metal

(G-466)
T & S MACHINE SHOP INC
1396 Highway 471 (39042-7532)
PHONE.....................601 825-8627
George Tullos, *CEO*
Michael Tullos, *President*
Kathy Tullos, *Corp Secy*
Ruby Tullos, *Vice Pres*
Ken Dollar, *Purch Agent*
EMP: 20
SQ FT: 12,500
SALES (est): 4MM **Privately Held**
WEB: www.tandsmachine.com
SIC: 3842 3812 Implants, surgical; acceleration indicators & systems components, aerospace

(G-467)
T & S PRECISION MFG INC
1396 Highway 471 (39042-7532)
PHONE.....................601 825-0878
Justin D Tullos, *Exec Dir*
EMP: 3
SALES (est): 194.1K **Privately Held**
SIC: 3999 Manufacturing industries

(G-468)
THELEG5813 PHOTOS & PRINTS
109 Quail Field Run (39042-8976)
PHONE.....................601 927-1360
Timothy Legler, *Principal*
EMP: 2
SALES (est): 83.9K **Privately Held**
SIC: 2752 Commercial printing, lithographic

GEOGRAPHIC SECTION

Brookhaven - Lincoln County (G-499)

(G-469)
TRIPLE E DOOR & HARDWARE INC
560 Turtle Ln (39047-5087)
PHONE..................................601 940-7371
Anthony Huffman, *President*
EMP: 3 EST: 2010
SALES (est): 297.8K **Privately Held**
SIC: 5072 2431 Hardware; exterior & ornamental woodwork & trim

(G-470)
VANS DEER PROCESSING INC
Also Called: Van's Deer Procesiing Sptg Gds
777 Hwy 4689 (39042)
PHONE..................................601 825-9087
Van Lorin Allen, *President*
Herman E Moore Jr, *Vice Pres*
EMP: 20
SQ FT: 8,150
SALES: 10MM **Privately Held**
SIC: 3556 Meat processing machinery

(G-471)
WALKER WELDING AND FABRICATION
1005 Prince Dr (39042-8363)
PHONE..................................601 503-0340
Allyson Walker, *Principal*
EMP: 1
SALES (est): 25K **Privately Held**
SIC: 7692 Welding repair

(G-472)
WAYNE HMPHRYS/PLYGRAPH EXMINER
101 Ferry Dr (39047-9215)
PHONE..................................601 825-8640
Wayne Humphreys, *Principal*
EMP: 3
SALES (est): 147K **Privately Held**
SIC: 2711 Newspapers, publishing & printing

(G-473)
WEBBS CSTM WDWRK & FINSHG LLC
6621 Brock Cir (39042-2051)
PHONE..................................601 824-2851
EMP: 1
SALES (est): 54.1K **Privately Held**
SIC: 2431 Mfg Millwork

(G-474)
WEEKLY LEADER
207 E Government St (39042-3151)
P.O. Box 107 (39043-0107)
PHONE..................................601 825-5133
Marcus Bowers, *Principal*
EMP: 3
SALES (est): 142.1K **Privately Held**
SIC: 2711 Newspapers

(G-475)
WESTMINSTER SOFTWARE
315 Westminster Ct (39047-7301)
PHONE..................................601 214-5028
Mike Sharpe, *President*
EMP: 2
SALES (est): 87.1K **Privately Held**
SIC: 2741 Miscellaneous publishing

Braxton
Simpson County

(G-476)
CAMPBELL CREEK PUBLISHING LLC
187 Conerly Rd (39044-9630)
PHONE..................................601 824-5932
Martha Douglass, *Principal*
EMP: 2
SALES (est): 115.2K **Privately Held**
SIC: 2741 Miscellaneous publishing

(G-477)
DONALD SPEIGHTS JR
Also Called: Speights W Repair
181 Speights Rd (39044-9333)
P.O. Box 179, Star (39167-0179)
PHONE..................................601 940-3847

Donald Speights Jr, *Owner*
EMP: 1
SALES (est): 79.4K **Privately Held**
SIC: 7692 7389 Welding repair;

Brookhaven
Lincoln County

(G-478)
ACY LOGGING
919 Smith Lake Rd Ne (39601-3574)
P.O. Box 3178 (39603-7178)
PHONE..................................601 833-5426
Johnnie M Acy, *President*
Sherry Adams, *Admin Sec*
EMP: 6
SALES (est): 538.6K **Privately Held**
SIC: 2411 Logging camps & contractors

(G-479)
AIR PRODUCTS AND CHEMICALS INC
1080 Fender Trl Ne (39601-8096)
PHONE..................................601 823-9850
EMP: 2
SALES (corp-wide): 8.9B **Publicly Held**
SIC: 2813 5047 Industrial gases; medical & hospital equipment
PA: Air Products And Chemicals, Inc.
7201 Hamilton Blvd
Allentown PA 18195
610 481-4911

(G-480)
APTIV SERVICES US LLC
Delphi Pckard Eea - Brookhaven
925 Industrial Park Rd Ne (39601-8951)
PHONE..................................601 835-1983
Ken Farlan, *Branch Mgr*
EMP: 425
SALES (corp-wide): 16.6B **Privately Held**
SIC: 3714 Motor vehicle parts & accessories
HQ: Aptiv Services Us, Llc
5725 Innovation Dr
Troy MI 48098

(G-481)
B & O MACHINE & WLDG CO INC
Also Called: Imagine Iron Works
1380 Highway 51 Ne (39601-2004)
P.O. Box 533 (39602-0533)
PHONE..................................601 833-3000
James W Minter Jr, *President*
EMP: 17
SQ FT: 25,000
SALES: 2MM **Privately Held**
SIC: 3599 1799 7389 7629 Machine shop, jobbing & repair; welding on site; crane & aerial lift service; electrical repair shops; fabricated structural metal; metal household furniture

(G-482)
BETTY MONTGOMERY
Also Called: Montgomery Electric Co
1074 Union St (39601-2373)
PHONE..................................601 833-1461
Betty Montgomery, *Owner*
James C Montgomery Jr, *General Mgr*
Gayle Onesi, *Manager*
EMP: 8 EST: 1946
SQ FT: 7,000
SALES (est): 1MM **Privately Held**
SIC: 5063 7694 Electrical supplies; electric motor repair

(G-483)
BOBBYS INDUS & OILFLD REPR
1104 Crooked Ln Ne (39601-8005)
P.O. Box 387 (39602-0387)
PHONE..................................601 833-3050
Mike McGowen, *President*
Keith McGowen, *Vice Pres*
EMP: 3
SQ FT: 1,200
SALES (est): 302K **Privately Held**
SIC: 1389 Oil field services

(G-484)
BULLOCKS GRAVEL SERVICE INC
997 Noah Trl Nw (39601-8672)
PHONE..................................601 833-7034
Jerry Bullock, *President*
EMP: 1 EST: 2001
SALES (est): 105.2K **Privately Held**
SIC: 1442 Construction sand & gravel

(G-485)
BUNYARD CABINETRY
353 Quitman Ln Nw (39601-9416)
PHONE..................................601 757-8765
Jonathan Bunyard, *Owner*
EMP: 1 EST: 2013
SALES: 50K **Privately Held**
SIC: 2434 2517 Wood kitchen cabinets; wood television & radio cabinets

(G-486)
CASES BODY & PAINT
1351 Highway 84 W (39601-8255)
PHONE..................................601 833-3153
Steve Case, *Principal*
EMP: 2
SALES (est): 137.1K **Privately Held**
SIC: 1389 Oil & gas field services

(G-487)
CAVINS CORPORATION
1224 Lofton Trl Nw (39601-8392)
P.O. Box 411 (39602-0411)
PHONE..................................601 833-2268
Bill Dickerson, *Branch Mgr*
EMP: 1
SALES (corp-wide): 0 **Privately Held**
SIC: 1389 Oil field services
PA: The Cavins Corporation
1800 Bering Dr Ste 825
Houston TX 77057
713 523-9214

(G-488)
COLUMBUS LUMBER COMPANY LLC
810 Wl Behan Rd (39601-3100)
P.O. Box 536 (39602-0536)
PHONE..................................601 833-1990
Bernard Ebbers, *CEO*
Jeff Grierson, *President*
Doug Boykin, *Vice Pres*
▼ EMP: 110
SALES (est): 13.1MM **Privately Held**
WEB: www.columbuslumber.com
SIC: 2421 2491 Sawmills & planing mills, general; structural lumber & timber, treated wood

(G-489)
DELTA INDUSTRIES INC
Also Called: Brookhaven Ready Mix
1324 Highway 51 Ne (39601-2004)
P.O. Box 1292, Jackson (39215-1292)
PHONE..................................601 833-1166
Norman Floyd, *Manager*
EMP: 7
SALES (corp-wide): 100.3MM **Privately Held**
WEB: www.delta-ind.com
SIC: 3273 Ready-mixed concrete
PA: Delta Industries, Inc.
100 W Woodrow Wilson Ave
Jackson MS 39213
601 354-3801

(G-490)
DENBURY RESOURCES INC
1151 California Rd Nw (39601-9284)
PHONE..................................601 835-0185
Chad Lofton, *Branch Mgr*
EMP: 2
SALES (corp-wide): 1.4B **Publicly Held**
SIC: 1382 Oil & gas exploration services
PA: Denbury Resources Inc.
5320 Legacy Dr
Plano TX 75024
972 673-2000

(G-491)
DENBURY RESOURCES INC
332 Rogers Ln Ne (39601-4788)
PHONE..................................601 823-4000
EMP: 10

SALES (corp-wide): 1.4B **Publicly Held**
SIC: 1382 Oil & gas exploration services
PA: Denbury Resources Inc.
5320 Legacy Dr
Plano TX 75024
972 673-2000

(G-492)
DIXIE PUMP & MACHINE WORKS
984 Highway 84 E (39601-8779)
PHONE..................................601 823-0510
EMP: 10
SALES (est): 1.3MM **Privately Held**
SIC: 3599 Mfg Industrial Machinery

(G-493)
DUNAWAYS LOGGING INC
222 S Church St (39601-3232)
PHONE..................................601 695-1232
Bailey Dunaway, *President*
Abby Dunaway, *Corp Secy*
Bailey Daniel Dunaway Jr, *Vice Pres*
EMP: 11
SALES (est): 870K **Privately Held**
SIC: 2411 Logging camps & contractors

(G-494)
GARY L THORNTON TRK
903 Highway 84 W (39601-1991)
PHONE..................................601 835-4192
EMP: 3
SALES (est): 235.2K **Privately Held**
SIC: 2411 Logging

(G-495)
GATLIN CORPORATION
58 Highway 84 E (39601-8445)
P.O. Box 1156 (39602-1156)
PHONE..................................601 833-9475
Fax: 601 833-6580
EMP: 40
SALES (est): 12.3MM **Privately Held**
SIC: 3999 Mfg Misc Products

(G-496)
GORDON REDD LUMBER COMPANY
1026 Industrial Pk Rd Ne (39601)
P.O. Box 654 (39602-0654)
PHONE..................................601 833-2311
Gordon Redd, *President*
EMP: 20 EST: 1968
SQ FT: 1,000
SALES (est): 2.9MM **Privately Held**
SIC: 2491 2421 Wood preserving; sawmills & planing mills, general

(G-497)
GREAT SOUTHERN LOG HOMES INC
111 Pritchard St (39601-7005)
PHONE..................................601 833-0700
Allen Smith, *President*
Susan E Smith, *Corp Secy*
EMP: 3
SQ FT: 1,500
SALES: 500K **Privately Held**
SIC: 2452 2499 2431 Log cabins, prefabricated, wood; handles, poles, dowels & stakes: wood; panel work, wood

(G-498)
GREAT SOUTHERN WOOD PRSV INC
111 Boyce St (39601-2104)
PHONE..................................601 823-4865
EMP: 1
SALES (corp-wide): 392.6MM **Privately Held**
SIC: 2491 Wood preserving
PA: Great Southern Wood Preserving, Incorporated
1100 Us Highway 431 S
Abbeville AL 36310
334 585-2291

(G-499)
HARPER TIMBER INC
20 E Lincoln Rd Ne (39601-8857)
PHONE..................................601 833-2121
David Dunaway, *President*
Chris Dunaway, *Vice Pres*
EMP: 25 EST: 1995

(PA)=Parent Co (HQ)=Headquarters (DH)=Div Headquarters
✿ = New Business established in last 2 years

2019 Harris Directory of
Mississippi Manufacturers

27

Brookhaven - Lincoln County (G-500)

GEOGRAPHIC SECTION

SALES (est): 2.7MM **Privately Held**
SIC: 3537 4213 4212 2411 Trucks: freight, baggage, etc.: industrial, except mining; trucking, except local; local trucking, without storage; logging

(G-500)
HOBIES SPORTS AND OUTDOORS
844 Brookway Blvd (39601-2642)
PHONE..................................601 833-9700
EMP: 2
SALES (est): 73.2K **Privately Held**
SIC: 2759 Screen printing

(G-501)
HYDRADYNE LLC
Also Called: Seal Group At Hydradyne
58 Highway 84 E (39601-8445)
PHONE..................................601 833-9475
John McConnell, *Branch Mgr*
EMP: 504
SALES (corp-wide): 371.3MM **Privately Held**
SIC: 3053 5085 Gaskets & sealing devices; pistons & valves
HQ: Hydradyne, Llc
15050 Faa Blvd
Fort Worth TX 76155
817 391-1547

(G-502)
J & P SMITH LOGGING INC
1308 Jckson Liberty Dr Nw (39601-8372)
PHONE..................................601 833-4286
Jimmy Smith, *President*
Charlotte Smith, *Corp Secy*
EMP: 10
SALES (est): 1.1MM **Privately Held**
SIC: 2411 Pulpwood contractors engaged in cutting

(G-503)
J AND S KEENE LLC
1645 Bethel Rd Se (39601-8750)
P.O. Box 459 (39602-0459)
PHONE..................................601 833-8874
James Keene, *President*
EMP: 2 **EST:** 2001
SALES (est): 90.3K **Privately Held**
SIC: 2491 Structural lumber & timber, treated wood

(G-504)
JAMES W ELLIOT JR
306 S Jackson St (39601-3302)
P.O. Box 774 (39602-0774)
PHONE..................................601 833-6201
James W Elliot Jr, *Owner*
EMP: 2
SQ FT: 1,200
SALES (est): 167.7K **Privately Held**
SIC: 1311 Crude petroleum & natural gas

(G-505)
JOHNSONS FENCING
1654 Caleb Dr Se (39601-7400)
PHONE..................................601 833-3263
Lan Johnson, *Managing Prtnr*
Lon Johnson, *Managing Prtnr*
Jordan Johnson, *Partner*
EMP: 6
SALES (est): 919.6K **Privately Held**
SIC: 3496 Fencing, made from purchased wire; shelving, made from purchased wire

(G-506)
LAGWENBRE DESIGNER CORPORATION
212 Railroad St (39601-2847)
PHONE..................................469 230-8534
Gwendolyn Sue Smith, *Exec Dir*
EMP: 1
SALES (est): 64.2K **Privately Held**
SIC: 3999 Wheelchair lifts

(G-507)
LAIRD TIMBER INC
308 Jackson Liberty Dr Sw (39601-8284)
PHONE..................................601 833-4293
EMP: 2
SALES (est): 246.9K **Privately Held**
SIC: 2411 Logging

(G-508)
LANCE SMITH LOGGING INC
1562 Zetus Rd Nw (39601-8385)
PHONE..................................601 833-4855
Lance Smith, *President*
EMP: 8 **EST:** 1998
SALES (est): 886.2K **Privately Held**
SIC: 2411 Logging

(G-509)
LEA LOGGING
1305 Sams Rd Nw (39601-4470)
PHONE..................................601 833-8983
Jeff Lea, *Owner*
EMP: 6
SALES: 350K **Privately Held**
SIC: 2411 Logging camps & contractors

(G-510)
LEE SMALL ENGINES INC
607 Country Club Rd Ne (39601-8076)
PHONE..................................601 833-5431
Julian Lee, *President*
Debbie Lee, *Vice Pres*
EMP: 2
SQ FT: 3,200
SALES (est): 210K **Privately Held**
SIC: 1389 7699 5261 Construction, repair & dismantling services; lawn mower repair shop; nurseries & garden centers

(G-511)
LEONARD PRINTING COMPANY
625 W Congress St (39601-2759)
P.O. Box 304 (39602-0304)
PHONE..................................601 833-3912
Nancy Huber, *Owner*
EMP: 2
SQ FT: 3,500
SALES (est): 252.1K **Privately Held**
SIC: 2752 Commercial printing, offset

(G-512)
LINCOLN LUMBER CO INC
410 County Farm Ln Ne (39601-3540)
P.O. Box 453 (39602-0453)
PHONE..................................601 833-4484
Terry Byrd, *President*
Cortez Byrd, *Vice Pres*
EMP: 70
SQ FT: 2,000
SALES (est): 17.2MM **Privately Held**
SIC: 5031 2421 2411 Lumber: rough, dressed & finished; sawmills & planing mills, general; logging

(G-513)
M & M MILLING INC
1056 Fender Trl Ne (39601-8096)
PHONE..................................601 823-4630
Patricia Morel, *Exec Dir*
EMP: 1
SALES (corp-wide): 11MM **Privately Held**
SIC: 3541 Milling machines
PA: M & M Milling, Inc.
33 Globe Ave
Texarkana AR 71854
870 772-3906

(G-514)
M&M LOGGING
2460 Constable Trl Nw (39601-8520)
PHONE..................................601 754-2796
Golmon Matt, *Administration*
EMP: 5
SALES (est): 311.2K **Privately Held**
SIC: 2411 Logging

(G-515)
MAPP OILFIELD SERVICES INC
941 Highway 550 Nw (39601-8548)
P.O. Box 3777 (39603-7777)
PHONE..................................601 835-2013
Stacey E Saucier, *President*
Kathy S McGehee, *Admin Sec*
EMP: 35
SALES (est): 3.1MM **Privately Held**
SIC: 1389 Oil field services

(G-516)
MAST MANAGEMENT LLC
36 Shore Dr Ne (39601-8756)
PHONE..................................601 833-8073
EMP: 1
SALES (est): 41K **Privately Held**
SIC: 3911 Jewelry, precious metal

(G-517)
MIKE SMITH LOGGING INC
1575 Friendship Ln Nw (39601-9106)
PHONE..................................601 833-2043
Mike Smith, *Principal*
EMP: 2 **EST:** 2016
SALES (est): 130.9K **Privately Held**
SIC: 2411 Logging

(G-518)
MISSISSIPPI MUDDY PRINTS LLC
1439 Pops Ln Nw (39601-9107)
PHONE..................................601 757-2990
EMP: 2
SALES (est): 83.9K **Privately Held**
SIC: 2752 Commercial printing, lithographic

(G-519)
MMC MATERIALS INC
Also Called: Mississippi Materials Co
1286 Monticello St Ne (39601-3555)
PHONE..................................601 833-4900
Rico Cain, *District Mgr*
John Crane, *Area Mgr*
EMP: 8
SALES (corp-wide): 306.5MM **Privately Held**
WEB: www.mmcmaterials.com
SIC: 3273 Ready-mixed concrete
HQ: Mmc Materials, Inc.
1052 Highland Colony Pkwy # 201
Ridgeland MS 39157
601 898-4000

(G-520)
NATIONS WELDING SERVICE INC
1127 S First St Ne (39601-8759)
PHONE..................................601 833-4949
Billy Nations, *President*
Gayle Nations, *Vice Pres*
EMP: 3
SALES (est): 349.7K **Privately Held**
SIC: 1799 7692 Welding on site; welding repair

(G-521)
OMS SHOP
Also Called: Organizational Maint Sp 5
182 Highway 84 E (39601-9209)
PHONE..................................601 835-1239
Richard King, *General Mgr*
EMP: 20
SALES (est): 1.4MM **Privately Held**
WEB: www.omsshop.com
SIC: 3731 7699 Military ships, building & repairing; welding equipment repair

(G-522)
PEPPERS MACHINE & WLDG CO INC
23 Auburn Rd Sw (39601)
P.O. Box 3038 (39603-7038)
PHONE..................................601 833-3038
Jamie Pepper, *President*
Lisa Crosby, *Corp Secy*
Terry Pepper, *Vice Pres*
EMP: 20 **EST:** 1978
SQ FT: 10,000
SALES (est): 3.1MM **Privately Held**
SIC: 1799 3559 7692 3444 Hydraulic equipment, installation & service; automotive maintenance equipment; welding repair; sheet metalwork; fabricated structural metal

(G-523)
PHILLIPS BARK PROC CO INC (PA)
428 County Farm Ln Ne (39601)
P.O. Box 1395 (39602-1395)
PHONE..................................601 605-1071
David Phillips, *President*
William C Phillips, *Vice Pres*
Phillips Jeff, *Manager*
Bill Phillips, *Manager*
EMP: 8 **EST:** 1975
SQ FT: 16,000
SALES: 7.5MM **Privately Held**
SIC: 2421 Sawmills & planing mills, general

(G-524)
POWER TORQUE SERVICES LLC
1344 Highway 84 E (39601-8859)
PHONE..................................601 835-2600
Clayton Theriot, *Branch Mgr*
EMP: 1
SALES (corp-wide): 3.6MM **Privately Held**
SIC: 1389 Oil field services
PA: Power Torque Services, L.L.C.
2133 Denley Rd
Gray LA 70359
985 223-2102

(G-525)
QUALITY METAL ROOFING LLC
3810 Bouie Mill Rd Nw (39601-8580)
P.O. Box 3968 (39603-7968)
PHONE..................................601 669-4336
Leah Henderson, *Purch Mgr*
Mathew Livings,
EMP: 4
SALES (est): 172.6K **Privately Held**
SIC: 3444 Sheet metalwork

(G-526)
REX LUMBER BROOKHAVEN LLC
810 Wl Behan Rd (39601-3100)
P.O. Box 536 (39602-0536)
PHONE..................................601 833-1990
Randy Cummings, *Manager*
EMP: 1
SALES (est): 469.4K
SALES (corp-wide): 31.5MM **Privately Held**
SIC: 2421 Lumber stacking or sticking
PA: Rex Lumber, Llc
5381 Cliff St
Graceville FL 32440
850 263-4457

(G-527)
ROBERT L LEGGETT
3525 Anderson Trl (39601)
PHONE..................................601 833-7313
Robert L Leggett, *Principal*
EMP: 6
SALES (est): 520K **Privately Held**
SIC: 2411 Logging

(G-528)
SAID MELINDA
Also Called: Melindas Fabrics and Interiors
129 W Cherokee St (39601-3310)
PHONE..................................601 990-4022
Melinda Said, *Owner*
EMP: 5
SALES (est): 428.9K **Privately Held**
SIC: 2211 2299 Draperies & drapery fabrics, cotton; slip cover fabrics, cotton; upholstery fabrics, cotton; sheers & other thin lightweight fabrics: cotton; linen fabrics

(G-529)
SAMUEL MOSES INC
112 W Highland Dr (39601-3502)
PHONE..................................601 669-0756
Samuel L Moses, *President*
EMP: 1
SALES (est): 61.6K **Privately Held**
SIC: 2051 7389 Bread, all types (white, wheat, rye, etc): fresh or frozen;

(G-530)
SELECT SIGNS MORE
664 Industrial Park Rd Ne (39601-2059)
PHONE..................................601 823-0717
Shery Purvis, *Owner*
EMP: 2
SALES: 85K **Privately Held**
SIC: 3993 Signs, not made in custom sign painting shops

(G-531)
SIGNS BY SHAFFIER
732 Zetus Rd Nw (39601-9482)
PHONE..................................601 833-8600
EMP: 1
SALES (est): 83.3K **Privately Held**
SIC: 3993 Mfg Signs Advertising Specialties

GEOGRAPHIC SECTION

Bruce - Calhoun County (G-562)

(G-532)
SMITH MOBILE WELDING LLC
718 Watts Ln Nw (39601-9449)
PHONE.................................601 695-4640
Keith L Smith, *Principal*
EMP: 1
SALES (est): 83.2K **Privately Held**
SIC: 7692 Welding repair

(G-533)
SMITH TIMBER INC
1511 Friendship Ln Nw (39601-9106)
PHONE.................................601 833-3968
Probie Lee Smith, *President*
Wanda Smith, *Admin Sec*
EMP: 3
SALES (est): 359.5K **Privately Held**
SIC: 2411 Logging camps & contractors

(G-534)
SMITHS MACHINE & WLDG CO INC
1423 Union Street Ext Ne (39601-4485)
P.O. Box 470 (39602-0470)
PHONE.................................601 833-8787
Michael K Smith, *President*
Shelby Smith, *President*
Patricia S Smith, *Corp Secy*
Chad S Smith, *Vice Pres*
Chad Smith, *Vice Pres*
EMP: 46
SQ FT: 43,000
SALES (est): 10.5MM **Privately Held**
SIC: 1541 3599 7692 Industrial buildings
& warehouses; machine shop, jobbing &
repair; welding repair

(G-535)
SOLEN INC
1706 Highway 84 E (39601-9576)
PHONE.................................601 833-0403
Marty Stephens, *President*
EMP: 23
SQ FT: 5,000
SALES: 2.4MM **Privately Held**
WEB: www.soleninc.com
SIC: 2899 Water treating compounds

(G-536)
SOUTHERN ELECTRIC WORKS INC (PA)
1557 Highway 51 Ne (39601-9091)
P.O. Box 586 (39602-0586)
PHONE.................................601 833-8323
▼ EMP: 13 EST: 1982
SQ FT: 30,000
SALES (est): 3.9MM **Privately Held**
SIC: 7694 5063 Electric motor repair; mo-
tors, electric

(G-537)
SOUTHERN GRAPHICS INC
400 Brookhaven St (39601-3651)
PHONE.................................601 833-7448
Shanna Callender, *President*
EMP: 1
SALES (est): 90K **Privately Held**
SIC: 2759 Screen printing

(G-538)
SOUTHWEST PUBLISHERS INC
Also Called: Daily Leader
128 N Railroad Ave (39601-3043)
P.O. Box 551 (39602-0551)
PHONE.................................601 833-6961
William Jacobs, *President*
Tom Goetz, *Editor*
Amy A Jacobs, *Corp Secy*
Rachel Eide, *Sales Executive*
Kristi Carney, *Marketing Staff*
EMP: 46 EST: 1883
SQ FT: 16,875
SALES (est): 3.5MM **Privately Held**
WEB: www.dailyleader.com
SIC: 2711 2752 Newspapers, publishing &
printing; commercial printing, lithographic

(G-539)
STILL BLESSED PRINTS
402 Eitel Pl (39601-2404)
PHONE.................................601 810-8285
Alvin Giddens Jr, *Principal*
EMP: 2

SALES (est): 158.6K **Privately Held**
SIC: 2752 Commercial printing, lithographic

(G-540)
STUART CHAFFIN
Also Called: Blackdog Welding
1086 Fender Trl Ne (39601)
PHONE.................................601 807-1547
Stuart Chaffin, *Principal*
EMP: 2
SALES (est): 8.7K **Privately Held**
SIC: 3999 Manufacturing industries

(G-541)
SUPERIOR WLDG FABRICATION INC
800 Magee Dr Apt 211 (39601-2609)
PHONE.................................601 823-5999
John Brister, *Principal*
EMP: 5
SALES (est): 453.2K **Privately Held**
SIC: 7692 Welding repair

(G-542)
T TOMMYS
811 Highway 51 N (39601-2079)
PHONE.................................601 833-8620
Thomas E Smith, *Owner*
EMP: 2
SALES (est): 250K **Privately Held**
SIC: 2759 2396 Screen printing; automo-
tive & apparel trimmings

(G-543)
TEES BY TARAN
300 Ash St (39601-2804)
PHONE.................................601 549-8384
Ariel Armstrong, *Principal*
EMP: 3
SALES (est): 167.6K **Privately Held**
SIC: 2759 Screen printing

(G-544)
TENCARVA MACHINERY COMPANY LLC
984 Highway 84 E (39601-8779)
PHONE.................................601 823-0510
Collins Allen, *Manager*
EMP: 10
SALES (corp-wide): 29.3MM **Privately Held**
SIC: 3599 Pump governors, for gas ma-
chines
HQ: Tencarva Machinery Company, Llc
1115 Pleasant Ridge Rd
Greensboro NC 27409
336 665-1435

(G-545)
W W W ELECTRIC COMPANY INC
523 Byrd St (39601-3758)
P.O. Box 1373 (39602-1373)
PHONE.................................601 833-6666
Ronald E Watson, *President*
Thomas Lyndon Walker, *President*
Vince Walker, *President*
EMP: 12 EST: 1951
SQ FT: 18,000
SALES (est): 1.2MM **Privately Held**
SIC: 7694 Electric motor repair

(G-546)
WATTS TIMBER COMPANY INC
1124 Wroten Ln Nw (39601-8387)
PHONE.................................601 754-0138
Steve Watts, *President*
Pam Watts, *Principal*
EMP: 13 EST: 1990
SALES (est): 715K **Privately Held**
SIC: 2411 Logging camps & contractors

(G-547)
WELL-DRESSED MAN
128 W Cherokee St (39601-3311)
PHONE.................................601 213-8311
Kensy Hoff, *Partner*
Greg Hoff, *Partner*
EMP: 3
SALES (est): 89.2K **Privately Held**
SIC: 2329 Knickers, dress (separate):
men's & boys'

(G-548)
WILLIAMS LOGGING COMPANY INC
835 Howard Rd Ne (39601-2240)
PHONE.................................601 835-2771
Andrew Williams, *President*
Rosie Williams, *Vice Pres*
EMP: 2
SALES (est): 17.7K **Privately Held**
SIC: 2411 Logging camps & contractors

(G-549)
WOOD PRESERVING INC
966 Sawmill Ln Ne (39601)
PHONE.................................601 833-8822
Gordon Redd, *Principal*
EMP: 3
SALES (est): 151.3K **Privately Held**
SIC: 2491 Wood preserving

Brooklyn
Forrest County

(G-550)
J M ARCHITECTURAL IRON WO
244 Benndale Rd (39425-9513)
PHONE.................................228 234-1747
EMP: 2
SALES (est): 112.5K **Privately Held**
SIC: 3446 Architectural metalwork

(G-551)
LAMB WOODWORKING
128 Rockhill Brklyn Rd # 54 (39425-9074)
PHONE.................................601 545-3052
EMP: 1 EST: 2010
SALES (est): 67K **Privately Held**
SIC: 2431 Mfg Millwork

Brooksville
Noxubee County

(G-552)
AGRILIANCE LLC
4408 Ms Highway 388 (39739-9129)
PHONE.................................662 738-4940
Grant Gardner, *Branch Mgr*
EMP: 15
SALES (corp-wide): 278.9MM **Privately Held**
WEB: www.agriliance.com
SIC: 2879 Agricultural chemicals
PA: Agriliance Llc
5500 Cenex Dr
Inver Grove Heights MN 55077
651 481-2031

(G-553)
GIEXCO LLC
2238 Hopewell Rd (39739)
PHONE.................................662 352-1128
Jody Giesbrecht,
EMP: 2
SALES: 175K **Privately Held**
SIC: 1389 Construction, repair & disman-
tling services

(G-554)
GRASSY RIDGE GAZEBOS
3850 Hopewell Rd (39739-5107)
PHONE.................................662 738-6556
Philip Knepp, *Partner*
EMP: 7
SALES (est): 626.3K **Privately Held**
SIC: 2511 Wood household furniture

(G-555)
HANCOCK EQUIPMENT & OIL CO LLC
18700 Us Hwy 45 S (39739)
PHONE.................................662 726-4556
Fax: 662 726-5341
EMP: 3
SQ FT: 25,000
SALES: 100K **Privately Held**
SIC: 5251 5084 5085 5172 Ret Hard-
ware Whol Industrial Equip Whol Indus-
trial Supplies Whol Petroleum Products
Whol Chemicals/Products

(G-556)
OLE COUNTRY BAKERY
Hwy 45 (39739)
PHONE.................................662 738-5795
Geneva Nightengale, *Owner*
EMP: 18 EST: 1981
SALES (est): 600K **Privately Held**
SIC: 2051 5461 Bread, all types (white,
wheat, rye, etc): fresh or frozen; cakes,
bakery: except frozen; pies, bakery: ex-
cept frozen; rolls, sweet: except frozen;
bakeries

(G-557)
PECO FOODS INC
Also Called: Peco Foods of Brooksville
559 W Main (39739)
P.O. Box 269 (39739-0269)
PHONE.................................662 738-5771
Kirt Rushing, *Manager*
Sandra Alvarez, *Personnel Assit*
EMP: 225
SALES (corp-wide): 1B **Privately Held**
WEB: www.pecofoods.com
SIC: 2015 0751 Poultry slaughtering &
processing; poultry services
PA: Peco Foods, Inc.
1101 Greensboro Ave
Tuscaloosa AL 35401
205 345-4711

(G-558)
VALLEY FARMS
Also Called: Valley Gravel Co
13462 Ms Highway 388 (39739-9167)
PHONE.................................662 738-5861
Sara C Geoghegan, *Partner*
Robert Cunningham, *Manager*
EMP: 25 EST: 1919
SALES (est): 760K **Privately Held**
SIC: 0191 1442 General farms, primarily
crop; gravel mining

Bruce
Calhoun County

(G-559)
ANTONIO TARRELL LLC
116 S Murphree Ave (38915-9709)
PHONE.................................662 983-2486
Antonio Thornton, *CEO*
EMP: 1
SQ FT: 600
SALES (est): 53.4K **Privately Held**
SIC: 7231 3999 5087 Beauty shops;
comb mountings; beauty salon & barber
shop equipment & supplies

(G-560)
CALHOUN COUNTY JOURNAL
207 N Newburger Ave (38915-9430)
P.O. Box 278 (38915-0278)
PHONE.................................662 983-2570
Joel McNeece, *Owner*
EMP: 4 EST: 1953
SALES: 300K **Privately Held**
SIC: 2711 Newspapers: publishing only,
not printed on site

(G-561)
MOJO UPRISIN INC
104 S Tyson Rd (38915-7300)
PHONE.................................662 983-8892
Teresa C Winter, *President*
EMP: 1 EST: 2011
SALES (est): 203.8K **Privately Held**
SIC: 2254 Shirts & t-shirts (underwear),
knit

(G-562)
WEYERHAEUSER COMPANY
Southern Division
106 Railroad St (38915)
PHONE.................................662 983-7311
James Dirks, *Maint Spvr*
Gerald Cooper, *Manager*
Jerry Goforth, *Manager*
EMP: 250
SALES (corp-wide): 7.4B **Publicly Held**
SIC: 2421 2426 Lumber: rough, sawed or
planed; hardwood dimension & flooring
mills

(PA)=Parent Co (HQ)=Headquarters (DH)=Div Headquarters
✿ = New Business established in last 2 years

2019 Harris Directory of
Mississippi Manufacturers

29

Bruce - Calhoun County (G-563)

GEOGRAPHIC SECTION

PA: Weyerhaeuser Company
220 Occidental Ave S
Seattle WA 98104
206 539-3000

(G-563)
WOODSON FLYING SERVICE INC
County Rd 219 Off Hwy 32 (38915)
P.O. Box 71 (38915-0071)
PHONE.................................662 983-4274
Jack Woodson, *President*
John Henry Barnes, *Corp Secy*
Annette Woodson, *Vice Pres*
EMP: 7
SQ FT: 6,400
SALES: 2.4MM **Privately Held**
SIC: 2875 5191 5531 0721 Fertilizers, mixing only; chemicals, agricultural; seeds: field, garden & flower; automotive parts; crop dusting services

Buckatunna
Wayne County

(G-564)
MASHBURNS WELDING
312 Sandbed Chicora Rd (39322-9662)
PHONE.................................601 648-2886
EMP: 1
SALES: 44K **Privately Held**
SIC: 1799 7692 3599 Trade Contractor Welding Repair Mfg Industrial Machinery

(G-565)
SMITH BROTHERS FOREST PRODUCTS
110 Carrson Rd (39322-9558)
PHONE.................................601 648-2892
Waurice K Smith, *President*
Patricia G Smith, *Corp Secy*
Rickie Smith, *Vice Pres*
EMP: 25
SALES (est): 3.8MM **Privately Held**
SIC: 2421 Sawmills & planing mills, general

(G-566)
TJ SCARBROUGH INC
2265 Hghtway 45 S Bcktnna (39322)
P.O. Box 30 (39322-0030)
PHONE.................................601 648-9987
Tj Scarbrough, *Exec Dir*
EMP: 10 EST: 2008
SALES (est): 1.4MM **Privately Held**
SIC: 1389 Oil field services

Bude
Franklin County

(G-567)
AMERICAN RAILCAR INDS INC
Also Called: Shippers Carline
S Gerard St (39630)
PHONE.................................601 384-5841
John Ward, *Branch Mgr*
EMP: 100
SALES (corp-wide): 476.8MM **Privately Held**
WEB: www.americanrailcar.com
SIC: 3743 Railroad equipment
HQ: American Railcar Industries, Inc.
100 Clark St
Saint Charles MO 63301

(G-568)
CAP CO
2325 Highway 184 E (39630-7101)
PHONE.................................601 384-3939
James E Jones, *Owner*
EMP: 4
SQ FT: 1,200
SALES: 300K **Privately Held**
WEB: www.thecapcom.com
SIC: 5699 2759 7513 T-shirts, custom printed; caps & gowns (academic vestments); commercial printing; truck rental & leasing, no drivers

(G-569)
FRANKLIN READY MIX INC
61 Wilson Ln Se (39630-5002)
PHONE.................................601 384-5445
Barry Tyson, *President*
Susan Tyson, *Vice Pres*
EMP: 6
SQ FT: 1,000
SALES (est): 580K **Privately Held**
SIC: 3273 Ready-mixed concrete

(G-570)
FRANKLIN TIMBER COMPANY
316 Railroad Ave (39630)
P.O. Box 566, Brookhaven (39602-0566)
PHONE.................................601 384-5826
EMP: 65
SQ FT: 3,000
SALES (est): 7.4MM **Privately Held**
SIC: 2421 Lumber: rough, sawed or planed; kiln drying of lumber

(G-571)
M & B LOGGING INC
140 River Rd (39630)
P.O. Box 698, Meadville (39653-0698)
PHONE.................................601 384-6611
Joseph McCormick, *Vice Pres*
EMP: 8
SALES (est): 790.9K **Privately Held**
SIC: 2411 Logging camps & contractors

Burnsville
Tishomingo County

(G-572)
MISSISSIPPI SILICON LLC
80 County Road 210 (38833-9529)
P.O. Box 316 (38833-0316)
PHONE.................................662 696-2600
Ricardo Vicintin, *Chairman*
Edward Boardwine, *COO*
John F Lalley, *VP Finance*
▲ EMP: 130 EST: 2010
SQ FT: 165,000
SALES: 100MM **Privately Held**
SIC: 3339 Silicon, pure

(G-573)
RLH TRUCKING INC
30 County Road 1461 (38833-9523)
PHONE.................................662 462-5079
Randy L Hickox, *President*
Lee Hickox, *Vice Pres*
EMP: 5
SQ FT: 20,000
SALES (est): 450K **Privately Held**
SIC: 2421 Sawmills & planing mills, general

(G-574)
TOLTEC COMPANY
364 Highway 72 (38833-9104)
P.O. Box T (38833-0325)
PHONE.................................662 427-9515
William Gregory, *President*
Tom Gregory, *Vice Pres*
▲ EMP: 15 EST: 1975
SQ FT: 49,000
SALES (est): 2.6MM **Privately Held**
WEB: www.toltecltg.com
SIC: 3646 3645 Commercial indusl & institutional electric lighting fixtures; residential lighting fixtures

(G-575)
VANLEIGH RV INC
26 Indl Access Rd (38833)
P.O. Box 445 (38833-0445)
PHONE.................................662 612-4040
Van Tiffin Jr, *President*
EMP: 12
SQ FT: 120,000
SALES: 10MM **Privately Held**
SIC: 3792 Travel trailers & campers

Byhalia
Marshall County

(G-576)
A-Z LIGHTNING PROTECTION LLC
120 Landen Cir (38611-6206)
P.O. Box 430, Collierville TN (38027-0430)
PHONE.................................662 890-7041
Eric Allred, *Superintendent*
Gerald Hutcherson, *Mng Member*
Ann Hutcherson,
Lee Hutcherson,
EMP: 6
SQ FT: 2,500
SALES (est): 854.6K **Privately Held**
SIC: 3643 Lightning protection equipment

(G-577)
ASICS AMERICA CORPORATION
549 Wingo Rd (38611-6510)
PHONE.................................662 895-6800
EMP: 16 **Privately Held**
SIC: 3149 2329 Athletic shoes, except rubber or plastic; men's & boys' sportswear & athletic clothing; men's & boys' athletic uniforms
HQ: Asics America Corporation
80 Technology Dr
Irvine CA 92618
949 453-8888

(G-578)
BEAVER BUILT CHEROKEE MFG LLC
1 Gem Blvd (38611-2307)
PHONE.................................901 258-2679
Ronnie Beaver, *Mng Member*
▼ EMP: 12
SQ FT: 40,000
SALES: 875K **Privately Held**
SIC: 3354 Aluminum extruded products

(G-579)
BILLS WELDING
181 Ponderosa Dr (38611-9167)
PHONE.................................901 216-6762
Bill Moore, *Principal*
EMP: 2
SALES (est): 88.9K **Privately Held**
SIC: 3446 Architectural metalwork

(G-580)
BILLS WELDING
181 Ponderosa Dr (38611-9167)
PHONE.................................901 216-6762
EMP: 1 EST: 2011
SALES (est): 47K **Privately Held**
SIC: 7692 Welding Repair

(G-581)
BOOK PUBLISHER LLC
132 Baicey Place Rd (38611-7870)
PHONE.................................662 838-2633
Clista Ash, *Principal*
EMP: 1
SALES (est): 37.5K **Privately Held**
SIC: 2741 Miscellaneous publishing

(G-582)
CARRIER CORPORATION
Also Called: Exel
491 Wingo Rd (38611-6512)
PHONE.................................662 890-3706
Dean Poelman, *Branch Mgr*
EMP: 115
SALES (corp-wide): 66.5B **Publicly Held**
WEB: www.carrier.com
SIC: 3585 Air conditioning equipment, complete; heating equipment, complete; room coolers, portable; heat pumps, electric
HQ: Carrier Corporation
13995 Pasteur Blvd
Palm Beach Gardens FL 33418
800 379-6484

(G-583)
CLEVELAND JOHN
Also Called: Gilliam, Susan
279 Jamie Dr (38611-7894)
PHONE.................................901 359-2737

John Cleveland, *Principal*
EMP: 2
SALES (est): 69.3K **Privately Held**
SIC: 2711 Newspapers, publishing & printing

(G-584)
ECLIPSE SCREEN PRINTS
14215 Harrison Dr (38611-7331)
PHONE.................................901 626-9029
Jill Sides, *Principal*
EMP: 2 EST: 2016
SALES (est): 83.9K **Privately Held**
SIC: 2752 Commercial printing, lithographic

(G-585)
FINE FIBERS
39 Oak Grove Dr (38611-7843)
PHONE.................................901 590-9481
Carole Woodgate, *Principal*
EMP: 1
SALES (est): 46.5K **Privately Held**
SIC: 2281 Yarn spinning mills

(G-586)
GRIFFIN INC
6562 Highway 178 (38611-9442)
PHONE.................................662 838-2128
Greg McKay, *President*
Tassie Cartwright, *Safety Mgr*
Steve Blount, *Purch Mgr*
Teresa Hubbard, *Controller*
Bill Hurst, *Sales Mgr*
▼ EMP: 70
SQ FT: 3,200
SALES (est): 22.7MM **Privately Held**
WEB: www.griffinarmor.com
SIC: 3713 3499 3711 3442 Truck bodies (motor vehicles); fire- or burglary-resistive products; doors, safe & vault: metal; motor vehicles & car bodies; metal doors, sash & trim

(G-587)
L D SHEET METAL
584 Dogwood Ranch Cir (38611-8911)
PHONE.................................662 838-6267
Linda Carpenter, *Owner*
EMP: 2
SALES (est): 228.5K **Privately Held**
SIC: 3444 Sheet metalwork

(G-588)
LAMONTS FOOD PRODUCTS INC
4212 Highway 309 S (38611-8674)
P.O. Box 8 (38611-0008)
PHONE.................................662 838-3431
Lamont Burns, *President*
EMP: 1
SALES: 150K **Privately Held**
SIC: 3556 Food products machinery

(G-589)
LOCKHEED MARTIN CORPORATION
2834 Allyson Gene Cv (38611-7359)
PHONE.................................901 795-5943
EMP: 2
SALES (corp-wide): 47.1B **Publicly Held**
SIC: 3721 Mfg Aircraft
PA: Lockheed Martin Corporation
6801 Rockledge Dr
Bethesda MD 20817
301 897-6000

(G-590)
MCCORMICK & COMPANY INC
1550 Ms 302 (38611)
PHONE.................................662 274-1732
EMP: 3
SALES (corp-wide): 5.4B **Publicly Held**
SIC: 2099 Spices, including grinding
PA: Mccormick & Company Incorporated
24 Schilling Rd Ste 1
Hunt Valley MD 21031
410 771-7301

(G-591)
MEMPHIS PALLET SERVICES LLC
236 Moore Crossing (38611-6955)
P.O. Box 838 (38611-0838)
PHONE.................................901 334-6306

2019 Harris Directory of
Mississippi Manufacturers

30

▲ = Import ▼=Export
◆ =Import/Export

GEOGRAPHIC SECTION

Byram - Hinds County (G-624)

Stanley B Page, *Principal*
EMP: 3
SALES (est): 137.5K **Privately Held**
SIC: 2448 Pallets, wood & wood with metal

(G-592)
NIAGARA BOTTLING LLC
168 E Wingo Rd (38611-7086)
PHONE.....................................215 703-0838
EMP: 5
SALES (est): 412K **Privately Held**
SIC: 2086 Bottled & canned soft drinks

(G-593)
NORTON EQUIPMENT COMPANY
60 Amy Ln (38611-6136)
P.O. Box 350 (38611-0350)
PHONE.....................................662 838-7900
J W Norton, *President*
Kathy Norton, *Corp Secy*
EMP: 10
SQ FT: 7,000
SALES (est): 1.2MM **Privately Held**
SIC: 5084 3559 Compressors, except air conditioning; recycling machinery

(G-594)
ONYX XTERIORS LLC
885 Bennett Cir (38611-6162)
PHONE.....................................901 281-2887
Jessica Lyle,
EMP: 6
SQ FT: 1,800
SALES: 225K **Privately Held**
SIC: 3334 Primary aluminum

(G-595)
ONYX XTERIRORS
885 Bennett Cir (38611-6162)
PHONE.....................................901 281-2887
William Lyle, *Principal*
EMP: 2
SALES (est): 181.4K **Privately Held**
SIC: 3444 Sheet metalwork

(G-596)
PENNINGTON WLDG SP CRANE RENTL
1041 Highway 309 N (38611-8063)
PHONE.....................................662 838-2015
Rufus Pennington, *Owner*
EMP: 3
SQ FT: 10,000
SALES (est): 160K **Privately Held**
SIC: 7692 7353 Welding repair; cranes & aerial lift equipment, rental or leasing

(G-597)
PRECISION CULTURED MARBLE
100 Lowry Dr (38611-9738)
PHONE.....................................662 838-5112
EMP: 6 EST: 2010
SALES (est): 284K **Privately Held**
SIC: 3281 Cut stone & stone products

(G-598)
PRECISION METALWORKS INC
64 Chase St (38611-7363)
PHONE.....................................662 838-4605
Asa Adkins, *President*
EMP: 9
SQ FT: 7,500
SALES: 500K **Privately Held**
SIC: 3541 Machine tools, metal cutting type

(G-599)
REBECCA MCCALLUM
14265 Harrison Dr (38611-7331)
PHONE.....................................662 501-0709
Rebecca McCallum, *Principal*
EMP: 1 EST: 2016
SALES (est): 28.2K **Privately Held**
SIC: 8748 1442 Business consulting; construction sand & gravel

(G-600)
ROXUL USA INC (HQ)
Also Called: Rockwool International
4594 Cayce Rd (38611-7550)
PHONE.....................................662 851-4755
Trent Ogilvie, *President*
Gordon Brown, *Principal*
Ken Cammarato, *Principal*
◆ EMP: 191 EST: 2004

SQ FT: 900,000
SALES (est): 35.2MM
SALES (corp-wide): 3B **Privately Held**
SIC: 3296 Insulation: rock wool, slag & silica minerals
PA: Rockwool International A/S
    Hovedgaden 584
    Hedehusene 2640
    465 603-00

(G-601)
SAMPLE LAB
3 Union Valley Rd (38611-8786)
PHONE.....................................662 564-2498
EMP: 2
SALES (est): 157.6K **Privately Held**
SIC: 2844 Mfg Beauty Products

(G-602)
SARDIS READY MIX LLC
306 E Stonewall Rd (38611-9341)
PHONE.....................................662 512-2170
EMP: 4
SALES (est): 359.3K **Privately Held**
SIC: 3273 Ready-mixed concrete

(G-603)
SISTERS SCENTS
13191 Fairview Rd (38611-9311)
PHONE.....................................901 283-9867
EMP: 2 EST: 2013
SALES (est): 118K **Privately Held**
SIC: 2844 Toilet preparations

(G-604)
SMITH TRANSPORTATION EQP INC
Also Called: Smithtrans
9045 Highway 178 (38611-8469)
P.O. Box 332 (38611-0332)
PHONE.....................................662 838-4486
Danny G Smith, *President*
Kathy Smith, *Admin Sec*
▼ EMP: 42
SQ FT: 25,500
SALES (est): 10.2MM **Privately Held**
SIC: 3537 Aircraft loading hoists; lift trucks, industrial: fork, platform, straddle, etc.

(G-605)
SOUTHERN CABINETS
7879 Highway 178 (38611-8464)
PHONE.....................................901 461-6161
EMP: 1
SALES (est): 53.7K **Privately Held**
SIC: 2434 Wood kitchen cabinets

(G-606)
SOUTHERN DESIGN FINDS
631 Desoto Rd (38611-7610)
PHONE.....................................662 893-4303
Maria Seales, *Owner*
EMP: 1
SALES (est): 71K **Privately Held**
SIC: 3999 5131 Candles; bridal supplies

(G-607)
STONE ASSOCIATES INC
Also Called: Barden-Stone Manufacturing
89 Edwards Rd (38611-6806)
PHONE.....................................662 838-4671
Billy Barden, *Manager*
EMP: 3 EST: 1997
SALES (est): 370K **Privately Held**
SIC: 5032 3281 Building stone; cut stone & stone products

(G-608)
TEMPUTECH INC
7869 Highway 178 (38611-8464)
PHONE.....................................662 838-3698
Tom Herrera, *President*
EMP: 14
SALES (est): 950K **Privately Held**
SIC: 3679 Electronic circuits

(G-609)
TLGLLC/MAGNOLIA MONOGRAMMING
11560 Byhalia Rd (38611-7204)
PHONE.....................................662 838-2000
EMP: 1 EST: 2014
SALES (est): 35.3K **Privately Held**
SIC: 2395 Embroidery & art needlework

(G-610)
TRI STATE READY MIX
2734 Highway 309 N (38611-8939)
PHONE.....................................662 893-3496
John Schumacher, *President*
EMP: 3
SALES (est): 193.1K **Privately Held**
SIC: 3273 Ready-mixed concrete

(G-611)
VAN S LEATHER CRAFTS
1909 Bubba Taylor Rd (38611-9175)
PHONE.....................................662 838-6269
Van Beasley Jr, *Owner*
EMP: 1
SALES: 15K **Privately Held**
SIC: 3172 Personal leather goods

(G-612)
WILLIAMS COMPANIES INC
772 Wingo Rd (38611-8108)
P.O. Box 522, Collierville TN (38027-0522)
PHONE.....................................662 895-7202
Mike Elverett, *Manager*
EMP: 3
SALES (corp-wide): 8.6B **Publicly Held**
WEB: www.williams.com
SIC: 1389 Pumping of oil & gas wells
PA: The Williams Companies Inc
    1 Williams Ctr
    Tulsa OK 74172
    918 573-2000

(G-613)
WIRE DISPLAY FABRICATION INC
33 Ms Sarah (38611-7796)
PHONE.....................................662 838-9650
David Stallings, *President*
Cheryl Stallings, *Admin Sec*
▲ EMP: 6
SQ FT: 15,000
SALES (est): 1.2MM **Privately Held**
SIC: 2653 Display items, corrugated: made from purchased materials

(G-614)
WOODS FARM SUPPLY INC
3248 Highway 309 S (38611-9218)
P.O. Box 366 (38611-0366)
PHONE.....................................662 838-6754
Patrick Woods, *President*
Patrick F Woods, *President*
EMP: 20
SQ FT: 55,000
SALES (est): 4.8MM **Privately Held**
SIC: 2875 5191 Fertilizers, mixing only; farm supplies; fertilizer & fertilizer materials

---

Byram
Hinds County

(G-615)
ALL AMERICAN CHECK CASHING INC
5795 Terry Rd Ste 311 (39272-9281)
PHONE.....................................601 373-6115
Randy Kirby, *Manager*
EMP: 7
SALES (corp-wide): 55.5MM **Privately Held**
SIC: 3716 Motor homes
PA: All American Check Cashing, Inc.
    505 Cobblestone Ct Ste B
    Madison MS 39110
    601 605-1678

(G-616)
ALLIED CRAWFORD JACKSON INC
212 Apache Dr (39272-9151)
PHONE.....................................769 230-2220
Bill Caldwell, *President*
April Brent, *Credit Mgr*
EMP: 35
SALES (est): 1.8MM **Privately Held**
SIC: 4119 7515 5051 3317 Automobile rental, with driver; passenger car leasing; structural shapes, iron or steel; steel pipe & tubes

(G-617)
ARIDE TAXI CAB AND TRNSP LLC
6644 Gary Rd Ste B (39272-9400)
P.O. Box 720303 (39272-0303)
PHONE.....................................601 620-4282
Alvin Brown, *Owner*
EMP: 1
SALES (est): 27.6K **Privately Held**
SIC: 7349 1799 2851 Building & office cleaning services; cleaning new buildings after construction; cleaning building exteriors; removers & cleaners

(G-618)
BARTAG CORPORATION
12550 Springridge Rd (39170-8100)
PHONE.....................................769 233-0925
Frank K Stevens, *CEO*
EMP: 1
SALES: 100K **Privately Held**
SIC: 7372 Prepackaged software

(G-619)
CHEF RAYS FAMOUS LLC
5207 Forest Hill Rd (39272-5717)
PHONE.....................................601 559-8096
Johnny Rayford, *Mng Member*
Robin Roby, *Exec Dir*
Eugene Carney,
EMP: 3 EST: 2014
SQ FT: 1,200
SALES (est): 176.8K **Privately Held**
SIC: 2099 5149 Food preparations; specialty food items

(G-620)
CLASSAIL MODELS INTERNATIONAL
117 Brampton Cv (39272-9248)
PHONE.....................................601 373-4833
EMP: 3
SALES (est): 207.4K **Privately Held**
SIC: 3732 Boatbuilding/Repairing

(G-621)
DURO-LAST INC
6200 I 55 S (39272-9100)
PHONE.....................................601 371-1973
Lee Cobb, *Manager*
EMP: 75
SALES (corp-wide): 207.6MM **Privately Held**
WEB: www.duro-last.com
SIC: 2952 Roofing materials
PA: Duro-Last, Inc.
    525 E Morley Dr
    Saginaw MI 48601
    800 248-0280

(G-622)
MICROTECH INDUSTRIES INC
2980 Davis Rd Ste A (39170-8714)
PHONE.....................................601 373-0177
Minnie Omoregie, *Principal*
EMP: 3
SALES (est): 265.4K **Privately Held**
SIC: 3999 Manufacturing industries

(G-623)
NATURES SOCIETY MAJESTIC ARTS
5038 Kay Brook Dr (39272-9653)
PHONE.....................................601 376-0447
Larry Thompson, *Principal*
EMP: 2 EST: 2008
SALES (est): 90.4K **Privately Held**
SIC: 3944 7389 8699 Craft & hobby kits & sets; ; charitable organization

(G-624)
SUPERIOR ASPHALT INC
5990 I 55 S (39272-9786)
P.O. Box 720099 (39272-0099)
PHONE.....................................601 376-3000
William G Yates III, *President*
Bobby Bullock, *Vice Pres*
Brandon Dunn, *CFO*
EMP: 125
SQ FT: 3,500

(PA)=Parent Co (HQ)=Headquarters (DH)=Div Headquarters
✿ = New Business established in last 2 years

2019 Harris Directory of
Mississippi Manufacturers

31

GEOGRAPHIC SECTION

Byram - Hinds County (G-625)

SALES: 87.1MM
SALES (corp-wide): 1.5B **Privately Held**
WEB: www.superasphalt.com
SIC: **1611** 2951 Surfacing & paving; asphalt paving mixtures & blocks; asphalt & asphaltic paving mixtures (not from refineries); paving mixtures
HQ: W. G. Yates & Sons Construction Company
1 Gully Ave
Philadelphia MS 39350
601 656-5411

(G-625)
UNIFIED BRANDS INC
Also Called: Groen
1055 Mendell Davis Dr (39272-9788)
PHONE..................................601 372-3903
Patrick Felts, *Business Mgr*
Melanie Roland, *Materials Mgr*
Mark Upton, *Opers Staff*
Scott Yohn, *Buyer*
Rick Seiss, *Engineer*
▲ EMP: 700
SALES (est): 90.5MM
SALES (corp-wide): 6.9B **Publicly Held**
SIC: **3089** Kitchenware, plastic
PA: Dover Corporation
3005 Highland Pkwy # 200
Downers Grove IL 60515
630 541-1540

(G-626)
WARREN CORPORATION UNI
121 Southpointe Dr Ste E (39272-5581)
PHONE..................................888 913-7708
Rodrick Warren, *President*
EMP: 2
SALES (est): 62.3K **Privately Held**
SIC: **2087** 2099 Syrups, drink; syrups

Caledonia
Monroe County

(G-627)
COLUMBUS ENGINE & CRANK SHAFT
700 Cal Kolola Rd (39740-9569)
PHONE..................................662 356-0068
Tim Welch, *President*
Tim Welsh, *President*
EMP: 7
SQ FT: 8,000
SALES (est): 450K **Privately Held**
SIC: **3599** 7538 Machine shop, jobbing & repair; engine rebuilding: automotive

(G-628)
DATAWARE LLC
19 Buck Egger Rd (39740-9529)
PHONE..................................662 356-4978
Thomas Morris,
EMP: 1
SALES (est): 72.4K **Privately Held**
SIC: **7372** Home entertainment computer software

(G-629)
Q P P INC
Also Called: Quality Production Products
738 Main St (39740-7604)
P.O. Box 40 (39740-0040)
PHONE..................................662 356-4848
E L Diermann, *President*
J D Diermann, *Corp Secy*
EMP: 3
SQ FT: 10,000
SALES (est): 544.5K **Privately Held**
SIC: **5084** 1389 3533 7353 Oil well machinery, equipment & supplies; oil field services; oil & gas field machinery; oil equipment rental services

(G-630)
SIGN GYPSIES GOLDEN TRIANGLE
1742 Seed Tick Rd (39740-8506)
PHONE..................................662 368-3662
Kristin Hudson, *Principal*
EMP: 1
SALES (est): 46K **Privately Held**
SIC: **3993** Signs & advertising specialties

(G-631)
SOUTHEAST MISS SCHL PDTS INC
Also Called: Southeast Miss Schl Pdts Co
151 Gin Site Rd Ste B (39740-6624)
PHONE..................................662 855-5048
Gina Pitts, *CEO*
David Pitts, *Vice Pres*
EMP: 3
SQ FT: 500
SALES: 691.7K **Privately Held**
SIC: **5021** 3949 2531 3446 Lockers; track & field athletic equipment; school furniture; flagpoles, metal

(G-632)
THOMAS LESLIE COLEMAN
Also Called: Coleman Lumber
40098 Pinebrook Cir (39740-9623)
PHONE..................................662 369-6000
Thomas Leslie Coleman, *Owner*
EMP: 8
SALES (est): 997.9K **Privately Held**
SIC: **2421** 5211 2426 Sawmills & planing mills, general; lumber products; hardwood dimension & flooring mills

(G-633)
VETERANS MONUMENT COMPANY LLC
194 Quail Rdg (39740-8622)
P.O. Box 562, Columbus (39703-0562)
PHONE..................................662 549-1422
Rodney W Glover,
EMP: 1
SALES (est): 97.7K **Privately Held**
SIC: **3281** Cut stone & stone products

Calhoun City
Calhoun County

(G-634)
A B B INC
Also Called: Med Lift
310 S Madison (38916)
P.O. Box 1221 (38916-1221)
PHONE..................................662 628-8196
A D Blount, *President*
Linda J Blount, *Vice Pres*
Alison Nichols, *Vice Pres*
David Crocker, *VP Mfg*
Ron Pollan, *Manager*
EMP: 19
SALES (est): 2.9MM **Privately Held**
SIC: **3999** 2599 Wheelchair lifts; hospital beds

(G-635)
CALHOUN PARTS INC
Hwy 8 (38916)
P.O. Box 1284 (38916-1284)
PHONE..................................662 628-6621
David Laughlin, *President*
Laura Laughlin, *Corp Secy*
Carl Laughlin, *Vice Pres*
EMP: 7 EST: 1966
SQ FT: 2,250
SALES: 850K **Privately Held**
WEB: www.calhounparts.com
SIC: **5013** 3599 5531 Automotive supplies & parts; machine shop, jobbing & repair; automotive parts

(G-636)
CAVINESS WOODWORKING COMPANY
200 N Aycock Ave (38916)
P.O. Box 710 (38916-0710)
PHONE..................................662 628-5195
James Donald Caviness, *President*
Michael Caviness, *Vice Pres*
Patricia Lee, *Treasurer*
Angela Goodson, *Admin Sec*
EMP: 75 EST: 1948
SQ FT: 175,000
SALES (est): 10.6MM **Privately Held**
WEB: www.cavinesspaddles.com
SIC: **2499** 3089 Oars & paddles, wood; injection molding of plastics

(G-637)
CUSTOM METAL FABRICATION INC
213 E Gore Ave (38916-7265)
P.O. Box 680 (38916-0680)
PHONE..................................662 628-8657
Jim Ramsey, *President*
EMP: 3
SALES (est): 480.2K **Privately Held**
SIC: **3441** Fabricated structural metal

(G-638)
DIAS LLC
Also Called: Kidz World Furniture
413 Highway 8 W (38916-7020)
P.O. Box 1250 (38916-1250)
PHONE..................................662 628-1580
Aaron Blount, *Vice Pres*
Justin Nichols, *Vice Pres*
Alison Blount Nichols,
Dwight Griffin,
▼ EMP: 50
SQ FT: 125,000
SALES: 7.5MM **Privately Held**
SIC: **2511** Children's wood furniture

(G-639)
LANGSTON LOGGING INC
675 Earnest Rd (38916-7186)
PHONE..................................662 542-8704
Sidney Langston, *Principal*
EMP: 6 EST: 2011
SALES (est): 627.3K **Privately Held**
SIC: **2411** Logging

(G-640)
LOVORN LOGGING INC
164 Dentontown Rd (38916-7168)
PHONE..................................662 637-2617
Charles Lovorn, *President*
Brenda F Lovorn, *Corp Secy*
EMP: 2
SALES (est): 407K **Privately Held**
SIC: **2411** Logging camps & contractors

(G-641)
MMC MATERIALS INC
Also Called: Vulcan Materials Company
Hgwy 8 Us (38916)
P.O. Box 703 (38916-0703)
PHONE..................................662 628-6667
Benny Rogers, *Manager*
Jay W Parker, *Manager*
EMP: 4
SALES (corp-wide): 306.5MM **Privately Held**
WEB: www.mmcmaterials.com
SIC: **3273** Ready-mixed concrete
HQ: Mmc Materials, Inc.
1052 Highland Colony Pkwy # 201
Ridgeland MS 39157
601 898-4000

(G-642)
NORTH MS TIMBER HARVESTER
502 Beadle St (38916)
PHONE..................................662 927-0013
Jeff Robertson, *Owner*
EMP: 2
SALES (est): 113.9K **Privately Held**
SIC: **2411** Timber, cut at logging camp

(G-643)
PARKER LOGGING INC
273 Highway 9 S (38916-9613)
PHONE..................................662 412-2435
Ed Parker, *President*
Melissa Parker, *Vice Pres*
EMP: 6
SALES (est): 434K **Privately Held**
SIC: **2411** Logging

(G-644)
SLATE SPRINGS GLOVE COMPANY
148 Vance St (38916-7151)
P.O. Box 267, Noxapater (39346-0267)
PHONE..................................662 637-2222
Michael Conniff, *President*
Travis Malone, *Vice Pres*
Anthony J Conniff, *Admin Sec*
EMP: 5
SQ FT: 20,000

SALES (est): 910.4K **Privately Held**
SIC: **2381** Gloves, work: woven or knit, made from purchased materials

(G-645)
VARSITY PRO INC
307 N Boland St (38916)
P.O. Box 582 (38916-0582)
PHONE..................................662 628-4172
Tony Hardin, *President*
EMP: 3 EST: 2010
SALES (est): 309.1K **Privately Held**
SIC: **2329** 2331 2519 Men's & boys' sportswear & athletic clothing; women's & misses' blouses & shirts; household furniture, except wood or metal: upholstered

---

Canton
Madison County

(G-646)
AMERICAN HOWA KENTUCKY INC
Also Called: Ahk Mississippi
151 Nissan Dr Ste J (39046-8433)
PHONE..................................601 506-0591
EMP: 8 **Privately Held**
SIC: **3714** Acceleration equipment, motor vehicle
HQ: American Howa Kentucky, Inc.
445 Jody Richards Dr
Bowling Green KY 42101
270 563-4400

(G-647)
ATCO INDUSTRIES
151 Nissan Pkwy (39046-7039)
PHONE..................................601 407-6329
EMP: 1
SALES (est): 56.1K **Privately Held**
SIC: **3999** Manufacturing industries

(G-648)
BEAR CREEK APPAREL PROMOTIONS
116 Clover Ln (39046-8842)
PHONE..................................601 259-8508
Andria White, *Managing Prtnr*
Cherie White, *Partner*
EMP: 2
SALES (est): 198.2K **Privately Held**
SIC: **2759** 7336 7319 7389 Screen printing; commercial art & graphic design; distribution of advertising material or sample services; embroidering of advertising on shirts, etc.

(G-649)
BOB LADD & ASSOCIATES INC
162a Feather Ln Ste A (39046-8510)
PHONE..................................601 859-7250
Steve Kennedy, *Branch Mgr*
EMP: 6
SALES (corp-wide): 11.4MM **Privately Held**
SIC: **3524** Lawn & garden mowers & accessories
PA: Bob Ladd & Associates, Inc.
6881 Appling Farms Pkwy
Memphis TN 38133
901 324-8801

(G-650)
BRIDGES CUSTOM CABINETS & TRIM
205 Village Cir (39046-8866)
PHONE..................................601 954-5085
David Bridges, *Principal*
EMP: 1
SALES (est): 53.7K **Privately Held**
SIC: **2434** Wood kitchen cabinets

(G-651)
BUCKRDGE SPCLTY WODS MILL WRKS
3232 S Liberty St (39046-5010)
PHONE..................................601 667-3791
Stephen Reams, *Principal*
EMP: 7
SALES (est): 505.7K **Privately Held**
SIC: **2431** Millwork

2019 Harris Directory of
Mississippi Manufacturers

▲ = Import ▼ =Export
◆ =Import/Export

GEOGRAPHIC SECTION

Canton - Madison County (G-680)

(G-652)
CANTON CONCRETE
Also Called: Lexington Concrete
153 Yandell Ave (39046-3839)
PHONE..............................601 859-4547
Watts Irving, *Owner*
EMP: 45
SALES (est): 3.8MM **Privately Held**
SIC: 3273 Ready-mixed concrete

(G-653)
CANTON HIGH PRESS BOX
529 Mace St (39046-3319)
PHONE..............................601 859-4315
Nicole Nichols, *Manager*
EMP: 1
SALES (est): 61.9K **Privately Held**
SIC: 2741 Miscellaneous publishing

(G-654)
CASTLE HILL DESIGN
205 Hill Rd (39046-9712)
PHONE..............................601 918-8234
Fabian Hill, *Owner*
EMP: 3
SALES (est): 121.3K **Privately Held**
SIC: 7389 1541 1542 1629 Design services; industrial buildings, new construction; commercial & office building, new construction; tennis court construction; excavation & grading, building construction; panels for prefabricated metal buildings

(G-655)
CRAFT EXPLORATION COMPANY LLC
325 Lakeshire Pkwy (39046-5344)
P.O. Box 2430, Madison (39130-2430)
PHONE..............................601 859-0077
Steven H Craft, *President*
EMP: 1 EST: 1967
SQ FT: 1,000
SALES: 2.7MM **Privately Held**
SIC: 1311 1382 Crude petroleum production; oil & gas exploration services

(G-656)
CRAFT OPERATING COMPANY IX LLC
325 Lakeshire Pkwy (39046-5344)
P.O. Box 2430, Madison (39130-2430)
PHONE..............................601 427-9009
E C Waytt, *Director*
EMP: 3 EST: 2010
SALES (est): 355.6K **Privately Held**
SIC: 1382 Oil & gas exploration services

(G-657)
ELECTRO NATIONAL CORPORATION
Also Called: Enc
511 Matthews Dr (39046-3251)
PHONE..............................601 859-5511
Spencer Nash, *CEO*
◆ **EMP:** 35
SQ FT: 40,000
SALES (est): 5.2MM
SALES (corp-wide): 890.5K **Privately Held**
WEB: www.electronational.com
SIC: 3672 3679 3498 3357 Printed circuit boards; electronic switches; tube fabricating (contract bending & shaping); nonferrous wiredrawing & insulating; industrial electrical relays & switches
HQ: Delta Enterprises
819 Main St Ste A
Greenville MS 38701
662 335-5291

(G-658)
FAURECIA INTERIOR SYSTEMS INC
252 Yandell Ave (39046-3840)
PHONE..............................601 855-2163
Darren Tate, *Regional Mgr*
EMP: 185
SALES (corp-wide): 38.2MM **Privately Held**
SIC: 3714 Motor vehicle parts & accessories

HQ: Faurecia Interior Systems, Inc.
2500 Executive Hills Dr
Auburn Hills MI 48326
248 724-5100

(G-659)
GRADY SHADY MUSIC INC
2352 Highway 16 E (39046-8817)
PHONE..............................601 278-3087
Grady Champion, *Owner*
EMP: 2
SALES (est): 85.9K **Privately Held**
WEB: www.gradychampion.com
SIC: 2731 Book music: publishing only, not printed on site

(G-660)
HARRIS FRM HVEN SPCLTYMILLWORK
657 John Day Rd (39046-9698)
PHONE..............................601 953-2964
Jerry M Harris, *Owner*
EMP: 2
SALES: 120K **Privately Held**
SIC: 2431 Millwork

(G-661)
HARTLEY EQUIPMENT COMPANY INC
109 Aulenbrock Dr (39046-7036)
PHONE..............................601 499-0944
Cameron L Hartley, *President*
Michael Lloyd Hartley, *Treasurer*
Joanne W Hartley, *Admin Sec*
EMP: 1
SALES (est): 54.1K **Privately Held**
SIC: 3546 Power-driven handtools

(G-662)
ITS VINYL YALL LLC
102 Aulenbrock Dr (39046-7038)
PHONE..............................601 533-8885
Austin Patrick Lasource, *Manager*
EMP: 2
SALES (est): 206.5K **Privately Held**
SIC: 3993 Signs & advertising specialties

(G-663)
JAMES K SMITH LOGGING
464 Covington Dr (39046-3822)
P.O. Box 1461 (39046-1461)
PHONE..............................601 859-1628
James Smith, *Owner*
EMP: 10
SALES (est): 361K **Privately Held**
SIC: 0811 2611 5211 Timber tracts; pulp mills; lumber products

(G-664)
JENNIFER L JOHNSON LPN
993 Dry Creek Rd (39046-8686)
PHONE..............................601 573-7582
Jennifer L Johnson Lpn, *Owner*
EMP: 2
SALES (est): 81.7K **Privately Held**
SIC: 2411 Logging

(G-665)
KTSU AMERICA LLC
279 Soldier Colony Rd (39046-8666)
PHONE..............................601 506-8148
Chris Robinson, *Marketing Mgr*
Jianliang Zou,
Mingjun Huang,
Michael Robinson,
▲ **EMP:** 12
SALES (est): 2.9MM **Privately Held**
SIC: 3531 3568 Scrapers, graders, rollers & similar equipment; drives, chains & sprockets

(G-666)
LAFARGE NORTH AMERICA INC
139 Tyler Dr (39046-5048)
PHONE..............................601 859-4488
Mark Hardy, *Branch Mgr*
EMP: 29
SALES (corp-wide): 27.6B **Privately Held**
SIC: 3241 Cement, hydraulic
HQ: Lafarge North America Inc.
8700 W Bryn Mawr Ave
Chicago IL 60631
773 372-1000

(G-667)
LARKEN LABORATORIES INC
276 Nissan Pkwy Bldg A (39046-7006)
PHONE..............................601 855-7678
Scott Allen, *President*
Clark Levi, *Vice Pres*
EMP: 7
SALES: 3.5MM **Privately Held**
SIC: 2834 Pharmaceutical preparations

(G-668)
LEXINGTON CONCRETE & BLOCK CO
153 Yandell Ave (39046-3839)
PHONE..............................601 859-4547
Watt Ervin, *Branch Mgr*
EMP: 19
SALES (corp-wide): 3.3MM **Privately Held**
SIC: 3273 1771 Ready-mixed concrete; concrete work
PA: Lexington Concrete & Block Co Inc
304a Yazoo St
Lexington MS

(G-669)
MARTIN MARIETTA MATERIALS INC
Also Called: Canton Rail Yard
139 Tyler Dr (39046-5048)
P.O. Box 266 (39046-0266)
PHONE..............................601 859-4488
Mark Hardy, *Manager*
EMP: 3 **Publicly Held**
WEB: www.martinmarietta.com
SIC: 1423 Crushed & broken granite
PA: Martin Marietta Materials Inc
2710 Wycliff Rd
Raleigh NC 27607

(G-670)
MCMASTER CUSTOM WOODWORKS LLC
106 Ashby Park (39046-8591)
PHONE..............................601 408-2252
Jason McMaster, *Principal*
EMP: 2
SALES (est): 85.2K **Privately Held**
SIC: 2431 Millwork

(G-671)
MIKES WOODWORKING
727 Miggins Rd (39046-9350)
PHONE..............................601 966-1868
Mike Elrod, *Principal*
EMP: 2
SALES (est): 140.6K **Privately Held**
SIC: 2431 Millwork

(G-672)
MUSEE LLC
123 Watford Park Way Dr (39046-9752)
PHONE..............................769 300-0485
Adam Pierce, *Owner*
EMP: 8
SALES (est): 1.4MM **Privately Held**
SIC: 2844 Toilet preparations

(G-673)
NISSAN NORTH AMERICA INC
Also Called: Canton Vehicle Assembly Plant
300 Nissan Dr (39046-8562)
P.O. Box 1606 (39046-1606)
PHONE..............................601 855-6000
Erik Fields, *Vice Pres*
Kenneth Carby, *Facilities Mgr*
Omar Walker, *Production*
Brian Adams, *Engineer*
Kelvin Doss, *Engineer*
EMP: 6400 **Privately Held**
WEB: www.nissan-na.com
SIC: 5511 3711 Automobiles, new & used; motor vehicles & car bodies; trucks, pickup, assembly of
HQ: Nissan North America Inc
1 Nissan Way
Franklin TN 37067
615 725-1000

(G-674)
OAKLOCK LLC
276 Nissan Pkwy Bldg A500 (39046-7006)
PHONE..............................601 855-7678
Rob Lewis, *Partner*
Clark Levi, *Principal*

Scott Allen, *COO*
Kay Ciarletta, *Manager*
EMP: 6
SALES (est): 827K **Privately Held**
SIC: 2834 5122 Pharmaceutical preparations; pharmaceuticals

(G-675)
PECO FOODS INC
Also Called: Peco Foods of Mississippi
1039 W Fulton St (39046-5331)
P.O. Box 419 (39046-0419)
PHONE..............................601 859-6161
Tony Pierc, *Manager*
EMP: 600
SALES (corp-wide): 1B **Privately Held**
WEB: www.pecofoods.com
SIC: 2015 Poultry slaughtering & processing
PA: Peco Foods, Inc.
1101 Greensboro Ave
Tuscaloosa AL 35401
205 345-4711

(G-676)
PECO FOODS INC
200 Feather Ln (39046-9793)
P.O. Box 419 (39046-0419)
PHONE..............................601 855-0925
Denny Hickman, *President*
Greg Walker, *Manager*
Jenna Smith, *Supervisor*
Kerry Roemer, *Director*
Tabitha Kuria, *Clerk*
EMP: 150
SALES (corp-wide): 1B **Privately Held**
SIC: 2015 Chicken, processed: cooked
HQ: Peco Foods Inc.
247 2nd Ave Se
Gordo AL 35466
205 364-7121

(G-677)
SIRCLE LABORATORIES LLC
276 Nissan Pkwy (39046-7006)
PHONE..............................601 897-4474
Dorothy Crim, *Principal*
EMP: 4
SALES (est): 441.1K **Privately Held**
SIC: 2834 Pharmaceutical preparations

(G-678)
SKYLAR LABORATORIES LLC
276 Nissan Pkwy Bldg A (39046-7006)
PHONE..............................601 855-7678
Scott Allen, *President*
EMP: 4 EST: 2015
SQ FT: 2,000
SALES (est): 176.8K **Privately Held**
SIC: 2834 Tablets, pharmaceutical; emulsions, pharmaceutical; solutions, pharmaceutical

(G-679)
SMITH BOYS TIMBER INC
464 Covington Dr (39046-3822)
P.O. Box 467 (39046-0467)
PHONE..............................601 859-1628
James K Smith Jr, *President*
EMP: 6
SQ FT: 1,800
SALES: 700K **Privately Held**
SIC: 2411 Logging

(G-680)
SUN-PINE CORPORATION LTD
340 Barfield St (39046-3846)
P.O. Box 287, Brandon (39043-0287)
PHONE..............................601 825-2463
Jimmy Marbury, *Manager*
Barry Sievers, *Manager*
Anthony Powers, *Info Tech Dir*
EMP: 50
SALES (corp-wide): 25MM **Privately Held**
SIC: 2842 Cleaning or polishing preparations; disinfectants, household or industrial plant
PA: Sun-Pine Corporation, Ltd.
331 W Jasper St
Brandon MS 39042
601 825-2463

GEOGRAPHIC

(PA)=Parent Co (HQ)=Headquarters (DH)=Div Headquarters
✿ = New Business established in last 2 years

2019 Harris Directory of
Mississippi Manufacturers

33

Canton - Madison County (G-681)

GEOGRAPHIC SECTION

(G-681)
TOPRE AMERICA CORPORATION
151 Nissan Way (39046)
PHONE..................................601 927-6723
Hideo Shimizu, *President*
EMP: 2
SALES (est): 95.9K **Privately Held**
SIC: **3714** Motor vehicle parts & accessories

(G-682)
VALEO NORTH AMERICA INC
Also Called: Valeo Front End Module
300 Nissan Dr (39046-8562)
PHONE..................................931 446-9128
EMP: 3
SALES (corp-wide): 177.9K **Privately Held**
SIC: **3714** Motor vehicle parts & accessories
HQ: Valeo North America, Inc.
150 Stephenson Hwy
Troy MI 48083

(G-683)
VERTEX AEROSPACE
133 Penn Rd (39046-9611)
PHONE..................................601 622-8940
EMP: 2
SALES (est): 146.2K **Privately Held**
SIC: **3721** Aircraft

(G-684)
WHITE RHINO FABRICATION LLC
494 Lincoln St (39046-3237)
P.O. Box 2762, Madison (39130-2762)
PHONE..................................601 397-1118
Christopher Brown,
EMP: 3
SQ FT: 5,000
SALES (est): 176.4K **Privately Held**
SIC: **3444** Sheet metalwork

(G-685)
WIREDLESS NETWORK INC
127 W Peace St Fl 2 (39046-4535)
P.O. Box 1313, Clinton (39060-1313)
PHONE..................................601 665-5307
Walt Runkis, *President*
EMP: 10
SALES: 100K **Privately Held**
SIC: **3577** Computer peripheral equipment

Carriere
Pearl River County

(G-686)
59 SIGNS LLC
426 Lakeside Dr (39426-7204)
PHONE..................................601 798-3682
James Foil, *Owner*
EMP: 1
SALES (est): 63K **Privately Held**
SIC: **3993** Electric signs

(G-687)
ARCHH LLC
103 Quail Ct (39426-9065)
PHONE..................................601 590-3519
Trenton Bond,
EMP: 1
SALES (est): 102.4K **Privately Held**
SIC: **1389** Construction, repair & dismantling services

(G-688)
BLUE BAYOU BOAT LIFTS INC
47 Paradise Ln (39426-7778)
PHONE..................................601 798-0659
Andrew M White, *Principal*
Andrew White, *Principal*
EMP: 3
SALES (est): 477.8K **Privately Held**
SIC: **3536** Boat lifts

(G-689)
CALICO JACKS LLC
19 Autumn Ln (39426-7070)
PHONE..................................504 355-9639
Sidney Martin III, *Mng Member*

EMP: 1
SALES: 100K **Privately Held**
SIC: **4212** 2086 7389 Local trucking, without storage; carbonated beverages, nonalcoholic: bottled & canned;

(G-690)
CBR PERFORMANCE
1544 Hnlyfield Mcneill Rd (39426-8411)
PHONE..................................601 337-2928
James C Bounds, *Owner*
EMP: 1
SALES (est): 127K **Privately Held**
SIC: **3444** Sheet metalwork

(G-691)
DESIGN TECH INC
919 Rock Ranch Rd (39426-7415)
PHONE..................................601 798-5844
EMP: 2
SALES: 120K **Privately Held**
SIC: **3827** Mfg Optical Instruments & Lenses

(G-692)
FORTENBERRYS SLAUGHTER HOUSE
5739 Highway 43 N (39426-2629)
PHONE..................................601 798-2156
Rick Fortenberry, *President*
EMP: 5
SALES (est): 1.2MM **Privately Held**
SIC: **5147** 2013 2011 Meats, fresh; sausages & other prepared meats; meat packing plants

(G-693)
H&M METAL EXPRESS LLC
Also Called: Adens Patt
6981 Highway 11 (39426-7648)
PHONE..................................601 798-4600
Delan Hale, *Mng Member*
Anthony Morace,
EMP: 6
SALES (est): 1.2MM **Privately Held**
SIC: **3411** Metal cans

(G-694)
LUMPKIN REPAIR SERVICE LLC
16 R N Lumpkin Ln (39426-7552)
PHONE..................................601 798-2027
Chris Lumpkin, *Mng Member*
Melinda Lumpkin, *Mng Member*
EMP: 6
SALES (est): 194.9K **Privately Held**
SIC: **7692** 7699 1799 Welding repair; industrial machinery & equipment repair; exterior cleaning, including sandblasting

(G-695)
M & M MACHINE LLC
205 Lumpkin Rd (39426-7321)
PHONE..................................601 749-4325
Frances L Miller,
EMP: 2
SALES (est): 123K **Privately Held**
SIC: **3999** Manufacturing industries

(G-696)
M&M MACHINE SHOP INC
21 Native Dancer (39426-8261)
PHONE..................................504 442-0797
Marvin Alberado, *President*
Joan Alberado, *Treasurer*
EMP: 3 EST: 1990
SALES (est): 84K **Privately Held**
SIC: **3599** Machine shop, jobbing & repair

(G-697)
MAGNOLIA CABINET WORKS
88 Paradise Ln (39426-8568)
PHONE..................................601 916-6538
Brian Bullen, *Owner*
EMP: 1
SALES (est): 80K **Privately Held**
SIC: **2434** Wood kitchen cabinets

(G-698)
MILLER ENTERPRISES
Also Called: Miller Blasting & Coating
40 Pine Hill Dr (39426-7544)
PHONE..................................601 798-3004
Neville Miller, *Owner*
Gail Miller, *Admin Sec*
EMP: 10

SQ FT: 168,000
SALES: 185K **Privately Held**
SIC: **3281** 5999 Monuments, cut stone (not finishing or lettering only); tombstones

(G-699)
PRINT ZONE
15 W Union Rd (39426-8392)
PHONE..................................601 799-3113
EMP: 2 EST: 2007
SALES (est): 213.7K **Privately Held**
SIC: **2752** Commercial printing, lithographic

(G-700)
RANDY A ELDER
Also Called: 12 Stone Consulting
155 Burgetown Rd (39426-7576)
PHONE..................................504 301-7962
Randy Elder, *Owner*
EMP: 2
SALES (est): 113K **Privately Held**
SIC: **1081** Exploration, metal mining

(G-701)
SOUTHERN TECHNICAL AQUATIC RES
Also Called: Starr
67 Hayes Rd (39426-8467)
P.O. Box 483 (39426-0483)
PHONE..................................601 590-6248
Don Mieger, *President*
Jerone Thomas, *Vice Pres*
EMP: 5
SALES (est): 212.3K **Privately Held**
SIC: **8999** 8331 8099 3429 Lecturing services; search & rescue service; job training & vocational rehabilitation services; medical rescue squad; marine hardware; firefighting apparatus & related equipment; industrial supplies

---

Carrollton
Carroll County

(G-702)
PIONEER PUBLISHING CO
20193 Highway 82 (38917)
P.O. Box 408 (38917-0408)
PHONE..................................662 237-6010
EMP: 2
SALES (est): 107.5K **Privately Held**
SIC: **2731** Books-Publishing/Printing

(G-703)
STANLEY D STOKES JR
Also Called: S & S Custom Cabinets & Trims
6796 County Road 100 (38917-7104)
P.O. Box 411 (38917-0411)
PHONE..................................662 237-6600
Stanley Stokes Jr, *Owner*
EMP: 5
SALES (est): 390.7K **Privately Held**
SIC: **2449** 2448 1751 Rectangular boxes & crates, wood; skids, wood; cabinet & finish carpentry; cabinet building & installation; finish & trim carpentry

(G-704)
WALKER ENTERPRISES
1584 County Road 121 (38917-6802)
PHONE..................................662 237-0240
EMP: 2
SALES (est): 123.3K **Privately Held**
SIC: **5531** 5999 7694 Ret Auto/Home Supplies Ret Misc Merchandise Armature Rewinding

---

Carson
Jefferson Davis County

(G-705)
STUART TIMBER INC
510 Martin Bass Rd (39427-6137)
PHONE..................................601 943-8184
Anthony Stuart, *Principal*
EMP: 2
SALES (est): 254.6K **Privately Held**
SIC: **2411** Logging

Carthage
Leake County

(G-706)
APPLIED GEO TECHNOLOGIES INC
1600 N Pearl St (39051-8701)
PHONE..................................601 267-5681
EMP: 99
SALES (est): 6.2MM
SALES (corp-wide): 17.7MM **Privately Held**
SIC: **3679** Wiring Harness Manufacturing
PA: Applied Geo Technologies, Inc.
404 Industrial Rd
Choctaw MS 39350
601 656-7350

(G-707)
BETTER BUILT PORTABLE INC
2078 Highway 16 E (39051-8901)
PHONE..................................601 267-4607
EMP: 2
SALES (est): 117.1K **Privately Held**
SIC: **3448** Mfg Prefabricated Metal Buildings

(G-708)
CARTERS MACHINE WORKS
304 Highway 16 W (39051-4424)
PHONE..................................601 507-5480
Joseph Carter, *Owner*
EMP: 1
SALES (est): 39.6K **Privately Held**
SIC: **3999** Manufacturing industries

(G-709)
CARTHAGINIAN INC
122 W Franklin St (39051-3754)
PHONE..................................601 267-4501
John H Keith, *President*
EMP: 10
SQ FT: 3,500
SALES (est): 841.4K **Privately Held**
WEB: www.thecarthaginian.com
SIC: **2711** 5943 Newspapers: publishing only, not printed on site; job printing & newspaper publishing combined; office forms & supplies

(G-710)
CENTRAL MEDICAL EQUIPMENT
807 Highway 35 S (39051-5803)
PHONE..................................661 843-6161
EMP: 2 EST: 1987
SALES (est): 145.1K **Privately Held**
SIC: **3841** Mfg Surgical/Medical Instruments

(G-711)
CENTRAL MISS MANUFACTING HSING
Also Called: Parent Co Champion HM Bldrs Co
908 Highway 16 E (39051-4218)
PHONE..................................601 267-8353
Joe Sanders II, *President*
Christine Pickering, *Director*
EMP: 5 EST: 1972
SQ FT: 1,000
SALES: 800K **Privately Held**
SIC: **2451** Mobile homes

(G-712)
CENTRAL SNACKS INC
Also Called: Dixon Central
1700 N Pearl St (39051-8635)
PHONE..................................601 267-3112
Norris Carson, *President*
Dorothy Carson, *Corp Secy*
Randy Carson, *Vice Pres*
EMP: 18
SQ FT: 14,000
SALES (est): 2.7MM **Privately Held**
WEB: www.dixoncentral.com
SIC: **2096** Pork rinds

(G-713)
CHARLES R SMITH LOGGING CO
6381 Highway 488 (39051-9573)
PHONE..................................601 267-9800

34

2019 Harris Directory of
Mississippi Manufacturers

▲ = Import ▼=Export
◆ =Import/Export

GEOGRAPHIC SECTION

Charleston - Tallahatchie County (G-743)

Charles Smith, *Principal*
EMP: 3
SALES (est): 175.3K **Privately Held**
SIC: 2411 Logging camps & contractors

(G-714)
DANNY PAT MARTIN
4568 Ebenezer Rd (39051-9279)
PHONE...................................601 267-3342
Danny Pat Martin, *Owner*
EMP: 3
SALES (est): 271.9K **Privately Held**
SIC: 2411 Logging

(G-715)
DWAIN MC NAIR SIGNS & SCREEN
4093 Highway 35 N (39051-8620)
PHONE...................................601 267-9967
Shane J McNair, *Owner*
Dwain McNair, *Owner*
EMP: 1
SALES (est): 75K **Privately Held**
SIC: 3993 Signs & advertising specialties

(G-716)
H & H CHIEF SALES INC
1309 Highway 35 N (39051-3018)
P.O. Box 456 (39051-0456)
PHONE...................................601 267-9643
Janette Sullivan, *President*
Stanley Sullivan, *Vice Pres*
EMP: 24
SQ FT: 27,000
SALES (est): 4.3MM **Privately Held**
WEB: www.hhchiefsales.com
SIC: 5521 5012 3523 Trucks, tractors & trailers: used; truck bodies; fertilizing, spraying, dusting & irrigation machinery

(G-717)
ION CHEMICAL COMPANY
247 Highway 487 W (39051-6131)
PHONE...................................601 781-0604
Zachary Faulkner, *Principal*
EMP: 3
SALES (est): 73.4K **Privately Held**
SIC: 7389 2899 2869 5961 ; chemical preparations; industrial organic chemicals; catalog & mail-order houses

(G-718)
JOHN W MCDOUGALL CO INC
151 Industrial Dr (39051-3000)
PHONE...................................601 298-0079
John McDougall Sr, *Branch Mgr*
EMP: 1
SALES (corp-wide): 43.4MM **Privately Held**
SIC: 3444 Sheet metal specialties, not stamped
PA: John W Mcdougall Co., Inc.
3731 Amy Lynn Dr
Nashville TN 37218
615 321-3900

(G-719)
MISSISSPPI BAND CHCTAW INDIANS
Also Called: Choctaw Enterprises
1600 N Pearl St (39051-8701)
PHONE...................................601 267-5279
Lemar Horne, *Branch Mgr*
EMP: 50 **Privately Held**
SIC: 3714 Automotive wiring harness sets
PA: The Mississippi Band Of Choctaw Indians
101 Industrial Rd
Choctaw MS 39350
601 656-5251

(G-720)
MMC MATERIALS INC
1201 Highway 16 E (39051-8900)
PHONE...................................601 267-8278
Tommy Warren, *Manager*
EMP: 2
SALES (corp-wide): 306.5MM **Privately Held**
WEB: www.mmcmaterials.com
SIC: 3273 Ready-mixed concrete
HQ: Mmc Materials, Inc.
1052 Highland Colony Pkwy # 201
Ridgeland MS 39157
601 898-4000

(G-721)
PEARL RIVER FOODS LLC
1012 Progress Dr (39051-4604)
PHONE...................................678 343-3265
Todd Reese,
EMP: 6 EST: 2016
SALES (est): 333.2K **Privately Held**
SIC: 3556 Poultry processing machinery

(G-722)
RYKAN INDUSTRIES
895 Greenwood Chapel Rd (39051-8392)
PHONE...................................601 900-2055
EMP: 1
SALES (est): 41.2K **Privately Held**
SIC: 3999 Manufacturing industries

(G-723)
SAMMY EVANS POULTRY
110 Cliff Roten Rd (39051)
PHONE...................................601 267-0521
Sammy Evans, *Owner*
EMP: 3 EST: 1996
SALES (est): 177.3K **Privately Held**
SIC: 2015 Bologna, poultry

(G-724)
TONY ADAMS LOGGING
7830 Ebenezer Rd (39051-7728)
PHONE...................................601 267-5174
Tony Adams, *Owner*
EMP: 2
SALES (est): 124.9K **Privately Held**
SIC: 2411 Logging camps & contractors

(G-725)
TROPHY PETROLEUM CORPORATION
2042 Red Dog Rd (39051-9342)
PHONE...................................601 298-0200
Wayne Upchurch, *President*
EMP: 2
SALES (est): 193.8K **Privately Held**
SIC: 1382 Oil & gas exploration services

(G-726)
TYSON FOODS INC
3865 Highway 35 N (39051-8613)
PHONE...................................601 298-5300
Nikki McMillan, *Manager*
Charlotte Brown, *Director*
EMP: 50
SALES (corp-wide): 40B **Publicly Held**
SIC: 2015 Poultry slaughtering & processing
PA: Tyson Foods, Inc.
2200 W Don Tyson Pkwy
Springdale AR 72762
479 290-4000

(G-727)
WENDALL HARRELL (PA)
Also Called: Carthage Ice Company Div
589 Highway 488 (39051-5811)
PHONE...................................601 267-3094
Wendall Harrell, *Owner*
EMP: 5
SQ FT: 10,500
SALES (est): 713.4K **Privately Held**
SIC: 2097 Manufactured ice

Cascilla
Tallahatchie County

(G-728)
HOOP LOGGING LLC
1011 Whitten Rd (38920-9432)
PHONE...................................662 230-7553
Mike Hoop, *Principal*
EMP: 3
SALES (est): 154.8K **Privately Held**
SIC: 2411 Logging

(G-729)
SOUTHLAND SUPPLIES
2167 Pressgrove Rd (38920-9509)
PHONE...................................662 647-2452
Don B Pressgrove, *Partner*
Mary Pressgrove, *Partner*
EMP: 2
SALES (est): 210.9K **Privately Held**
SIC: 2499 2782 Rulers & rules, wood; blankbooks & looseleaf binders

Centreville
Wilkinson County

(G-730)
EDDIE FRANKLIN
Also Called: Midway Tree Removal Co
3321 N Ms Highway 24 & 33 (39631-4304)
PHONE...................................601 225-4183
Eddie Franklin, *Owner*
EMP: 1 EST: 1999
SALES: 37K **Privately Held**
SIC: 0783 2411 Removal services, bush & tree; logging

(G-731)
J&M LOGGING INC
1665 Macedonia Rd (39631-3639)
PHONE...................................601 645-5813
Angie Darden, *Principal*
EMP: 6
SALES (est): 386.9K **Privately Held**
SIC: 2411 Logging camps & contractors

(G-732)
KRH TRANSPORT LLC
1689 Dr Anderson Rd (39631)
PHONE...................................769 244-1392
Raynauta Howard, *Principal*
EMP: 1
SALES (est): 61.9K **Privately Held**
SIC: 2542 Locker boxes, postal service: except wood

(G-733)
TIMBERLAND MANAGEMENT SERVICES (PA)
2592 Hwy 24 (39631)
P.O. Box 819 (39631-0819)
PHONE...................................601 645-6440
Michael Daughdrill, *President*
EMP: 4
SQ FT: 2,800
SALES (est): 419K **Privately Held**
SIC: 2411 0851 0811 Logging; forestry services; timber tracts

Charleston
Tallahatchie County

(G-734)
CHARLESTON PRINTING
134 S Church St (38921-2201)
P.O. Box 97 (38921-0097)
PHONE...................................662 647-2291
Lewis L Doubleday, *Owner*
EMP: 3
SALES (est): 381.7K **Privately Held**
SIC: 2752 Commercial printing, offset

(G-735)
COTTENS WELDING SHOP
1024 S Creek Rd (38921-9109)
PHONE...................................662 647-2503
James Cotten, *Owner*
EMP: 1 EST: 1965
SALES (est): 62K **Privately Held**
SIC: 7692 Welding repair

(G-736)
EDDIE REYNOLDS LOGGING
900 E Main St (38921-2508)
PHONE...................................662 647-2667
Eddie Reynolds, *Owner*
EMP: 10
SALES (est): 73.9K **Privately Held**
SIC: 2411 Poles, posts & pilings: untreated wood

(G-737)
EMMERICH NEWSPAPERS INC
Also Called: Sun Sentinel
16 S Court Sq (38921-2335)
P.O. Box 250 (38921-0250)
PHONE...................................662 647-8462
Clay McFerrin, *Manager*
EMP: 3

SALES (corp-wide): 23.8MM **Privately Held**
SIC: 2711 Newspapers, publishing & printing
PA: Emmerich Newspapers, Incorporated
246 Briarwood Dr Ste 101
Jackson MS

(G-738)
GPP CHARLESTON INDUSTRIES LLC
122 Albert Buckley Dr (38921-5400)
P.O. Box 3248, Huntsville AL (35810-0248)
PHONE...................................800 647-2384
Aubrey Smith, *Finance Dir*
EMP: 25 EST: 2015
SALES: 1.6MM **Privately Held**
SIC: 3993 1611 Electric signs; neon signs; letters for signs, metal; highway signs & guardrails

(G-739)
JAMES NEWTON
11922 Highway 35 (38921-4437)
PHONE...................................662 647-8968
James Newton, *Principal*
EMP: 1
SALES (est): 54.1K **Privately Held**
SIC: 2431 Millwork

(G-740)
KENGRO CORPORATION
6605 Ms Highway 32 (38921-9347)
P.O. Box 432 (38921-0432)
PHONE...................................662 647-2456
Gabriela Brasher, *President*
Bryan Douglas, *Director*
▲ EMP: 13
SQ FT: 25,500
SALES (est): 1.4MM **Privately Held**
WEB: www.kengro.com
SIC: 0723 3295 2842 2823 Crop preparation services for market; minerals, ground or treated; specialty cleaning, polishes & sanitation goods; cellulosic man-made fibers

(G-741)
KIRKLAND BOATS INC
1068 Factory Dr (38921-6620)
PHONE...................................662 647-0017
Tony Kirkland, *President*
Cathy Kirkland, *Treasurer*
EMP: 25
SQ FT: 81,000
SALES (est): 2.6MM **Privately Held**
WEB: www.kirklandboats.com
SIC: 3732 Boats, fiberglass: building & repairing

(G-742)
SHELBY GROUP INTERNATIONAL INC
Also Called: Shelby Manufacturing
Hwy 32 E (38921)
P.O. Box 1030, Collierville TN (38027-1030)
PHONE...................................901 795-5810
Don Carpenter, *Branch Mgr*
EMP: 79
SALES (corp-wide): 192.8MM **Privately Held**
SIC: 3151 Leather gloves & mittens
PA: Shelby Group International, Inc.
1255 W Schilling Blvd
Collierville TN 38017
901 795-5810

(G-743)
SOUTHERN DISCOUNT DRUGS OF CHA (PA)
Also Called: Diabetic Shoppe
1068 Factory Dr (38921-6620)
PHONE...................................662 647-5172
Robert L Salmon, *President*
Peyton S Boone, *Vice Pres*
Leslie S Heafner, *Vice Pres*
Sharon Salmon, *Admin Sec*
EMP: 7
SQ FT: 2,000
SALES (est): 4.8MM **Privately Held**
WEB: www.diabetic-shoppe.com
SIC: 5912 3021 5661 Drug stores; rubber & plastics footwear; custom & orthopedic shoes

---

(PA)=Parent Co (HQ)=Headquarters (DH)=Div Headquarters
✿ = New Business established in last 2 years

2019 Harris Directory of
Mississippi Manufacturers

35

Charleston - Tallahatchie County (G-744)   GEOGRAPHIC SECTION

(G-744)
TALLAHATCHIE HARDWOODS INC
336 N Market St (38921-1535)
P.O. Box 70 (38921-0070)
PHONE..................................662 647-5427
Gerald Wheatley, *President*
Gerald Wheatley Jr, *Vice Pres*
EMP: 33 EST: 1972
SQ FT: 750
SALES (est): 5.1MM **Privately Held**
SIC: 2421 2426 Lumber: rough, sawed or planed; hardwood dimension & flooring mills

Choctaw
Neshoba County

(G-745)
FIRST AMERCN PRTG DIRECT MAIL (HQ)
404 Industrial Rd Bfs1 (39350-4256)
PHONE..................................601 656-3636
Joshua Breedlove, *CEO*
Jon Murphy, *President*
Luke Schulze, *CFO*
EMP: 45
SQ FT: 72,000
SALES (est): 7.9MM **Privately Held**
WEB: www.fapdm.com
SIC: 2759 Commercial printing
PA: The Mississippi Band Of Choctaw Indians
101 Industrial Rd
Choctaw MS 39350
601 656-5251

(G-746)
MISSISSPPI BAND CHCTAW INDIANS
Also Called: Chahta Enterprises
390 Industrial Rd (39350-4259)
P.O. Box 6386 (39350-6386)
PHONE..................................601 656-7350
Ray Thomas, *President*
Brenda Barfield, *Opers Staff*
Lester Dalmer, *Branch Mgr*
Kathy Barnett, *Officer*
EMP: 1 **Privately Held**
SIC: 3651 3672 7218 7211 Household audio equipment; printed circuit boards; industrial launderers; power laundries, family & commercial
PA: The Mississippi Band Of Choctaw Indians
101 Industrial Rd
Choctaw MS 39350
601 656-5251

(G-747)
MISSISSPPI BAND CHCTAW INDIANS
Also Called: Choctaw Gaming Commission
385 Willis Rd (39350-8815)
P.O. Box 6045 (39350-6045)
PHONE..................................601 656-6038
Eddie Gibson, *Director*
EMP: 35 **Privately Held**
SIC: 3679 3651 3575 6794 Harness assemblies for electronic use: wire or cable; speaker systems; computer terminals, monitors & components; patent owners & lessors
PA: The Mississippi Band Of Choctaw Indians
101 Industrial Rd
Choctaw MS 39350
601 656-5251

(G-748)
MS BAND OF CHOCTAW INDIANS DB
Also Called: First American Printing
404 Industrial Rd (39350-4256)
PHONE..................................601 656-3636
Fax: 228 875-8198
EMP: 14 EST: 2010
SALES (est): 1.9MM **Privately Held**
SIC: 2752 Lithographic Commercial Printing

(G-749)
PEARL RIVER GRAPHICS & PRTG
404 Industrial Rd (39350-4256)
PHONE..................................601 656-3636
EMP: 2
SALES (est): 118K **Privately Held**
SIC: 2759 Screen printing

(G-750)
QUAD INC
300 Choctaw Town Ctr (39350)
P.O. Box 6342 (39350-6342)
PHONE..................................601 656-2376
EMP: 4 EST: 2012
SALES (est): 377.1K **Privately Held**
SIC: 3083 Mfg Laminated Plastic Plate/Sheet

(G-751)
REAL-TIME LABORATORIES LLC
375 Industrial Rd Ste 3 (39350-4258)
PHONE..................................601 389-2212
Bob Whiters, *Principal*
EMP: 5
SALES (corp-wide): 961MM **Privately Held**
SIC: 3823 Industrial instrmnts msrmnt display/control process variable
HQ: Real-Time Laboratories, Llc
990 S Rogers Cir Ste 5
Boca Raton FL 33487
561 988-8826

Chunky
Newton County

(G-752)
MORGAN GREG ASPHALT AND CNSTR
4273 Chunky Duffee Rd (39323-9567)
PHONE..................................601 479-3095
Greg Morgan, *Owner*
EMP: 3
SALES (est): 412.7K **Privately Held**
SIC: 2951 Asphalt paving mixtures & blocks

(G-753)
OLMSTEAD TIMBER
1031 Lisonbee Rd (39323-9655)
PHONE..................................601 655-8769
Bryan Olmstead, *Principal*
EMP: 2
SALES (est): 160.7K **Privately Held**
SIC: 2421 Lumber: rough, sawed or planed

Church Hill
Adams County

(G-754)
JAMES RACHAL
Also Called: Jr & Son Enterprises
6 Kings Ln (39120-2172)
PHONE..................................601 442-1460
James Rachal, *Owner*
EMP: 3
SALES (est): 219.2K **Privately Held**
SIC: 3531 Bulldozers (construction machinery)

(G-755)
VINES OPERATING COMPANY INC
308 Greenfield Rd (39120-7933)
PHONE..................................601 442-8034
Roy Vines, *President*
EMP: 1
SALES (est): 102K **Privately Held**
SIC: 1389 Servicing oil & gas wells

Clarksdale
Coahoma County

(G-756)
ADRIENNE BATLA CUPCAKES
131 Chancellorsville Ln (38614-2101)
PHONE..................................260 348-5364
Murtaza Batla, *Principal*
EMP: 4 EST: 2013
SALES (est): 198.8K **Privately Held**
SIC: 2051 Bread, cake & related products

(G-757)
ATKINS OFFICE SUPPLY INC
111 Highway 322 (38614-4620)
PHONE..................................662 627-2476
John T Atkins, *President*
Ann Atkins, *Corp Secy*
Randy Atkins, *Vice Pres*
EMP: 5 EST: 1974
SQ FT: 7,200
SALES: 662K **Privately Held**
SIC: 5943 5112 2752 5999 Office forms & supplies; office supplies; commercial printing, lithographic; business machines & equipment; office equipment

(G-758)
BAG CONNECTION LLC
Also Called: Southeastern Bulk Bag
408 6th St (38614-5207)
PHONE..................................662 624-6570
Carey Gammill, *Manager*
EMP: 12
SALES (corp-wide): 3.8MM **Privately Held**
SIC: 2673 3081 Garment bags (plastic film): made from purchased materials; unsupported plastics film & sheet
PA: Bag Connection Llc
1013 Tamarac Dr
Carpentersville IL 60110
847 428-6059

(G-759)
BEAUTY MART
860 S State St (38614-4804)
PHONE..................................662 624-6738
Kalil Iaisha, *Principal*
EMP: 3
SALES (est): 136.6K **Privately Held**
SIC: 7231 5999 5087 3999 Beauty shops; toiletries, cosmetics & perfumes; beauty salon & barber shop equipment & supplies; barber & beauty shop equipment

(G-760)
CAROL VINCENT & ASSOCIATES
313 Issaquena Ave (38614-4318)
PHONE..................................662 624-8406
Carol Benson, *CEO*
Gary Benson, *CFO*
EMP: 4
SQ FT: 2,945
SALES (est): 160K **Privately Held**
WEB: www.carolvincent.com
SIC: 2741 Miscellaneous publishing

(G-761)
CIRCLE S IRRIGATION INC
420 Rain St (38614-6938)
PHONE..................................662 627-7246
David Holt, *President*
▲ EMP: 13 EST: 1939
SQ FT: 7,500
SALES (est): 6.8MM **Privately Held**
WEB: www.circle-s.net
SIC: 5083 1711 5072 5085 Irrigation equipment; farm equipment parts & supplies; irrigation sprinkler system installation; nuts (hardware); bolts; filters, industrial; trailers & wagons, farm; pipe laying construction

(G-762)
CLINT WILLIAMS COMPANY
Also Called: Golden Peanut
675 Sunbelt Dr (38614-9038)
PHONE..................................662 627-3243
Clint Williams, *Principal*
EMP: 6

SALES (est): 740.2K **Privately Held**
SIC: 2076 Vegetable oil mills

(G-763)
COOPER TIRE & RUBBER COMPANY
2205 Mrtin Luther King Dr (38614-5509)
P.O. Box 130 (38614-0130)
PHONE..................................662 624-4366
Morris Favi, *Branch Mgr*
Kenny Valentine, *Administration*
EMP: 50
SALES (corp-wide): 2.8B **Publicly Held**
WEB: www.coopertire.com
SIC: 3011 Tires & inner tubes
PA: Cooper Tire & Rubber Company Inc
701 Lima Ave
Findlay OH 45840
419 423-1321

(G-764)
CROSSROADS FURNITURE INC
819 Desoto Ave (38614-6928)
PHONE..................................662 627-2114
Fred B Wells Jr, *President*
EMP: 8
SALES (est): 520K **Privately Held**
SIC: 2511 Wood household furniture

(G-765)
CROSSROADS PICKS LLC
13633 New Africa Rd (38614-8872)
PHONE..................................662 902-1026
Charles Cesare, *Mng Member*
Carie Cesare, *Admin Sec*
EMP: 2
SALES (est): 95.1K **Privately Held**
SIC: 3931 2221 7389 Guitars & parts, electric & nonelectric; glass & fiberglass broadwoven fabrics;

(G-766)
DELTA PRESS PUBLISHING CO INC
Also Called: Clarksdale Press Register
128 E 2nd St (38614-4206)
PHONE..................................662 627-2201
Wyatt Emmerich, *President*
Michael Banks, *Publisher*
Tracey Hankins, *Prdtn Dir*
Sandy Hite, *Office Mgr*
EMP: 13
SQ FT: 28,000
SALES (est): 885.8K
SALES (corp-wide): 23.8MM **Privately Held**
SIC: 2711 Newspapers: publishing only, not printed on site
PA: Emmerich Newspapers, Incorporated
246 Briarwood Dr Ste 101
Jackson MS

(G-767)
DRUMHELLER PACKAGING INC
350 Anderson Blvd (38614-4702)
PHONE..................................662 627-2207
David V Drumheller Jr, *President*
▲ EMP: 50
SALES (est): 16.2MM **Privately Held**
SIC: 2621 Bag paper

(G-768)
INFORMA BUSINESS MEDIA INC
14920 Us Hwy 61 (38614)
PHONE..................................662 624-8503
Greg Frey, *Manager*
EMP: 20
SALES (corp-wide): 3B **Privately Held**
SIC: 2741 Newsletter publishing
HQ: Informa Business Media, Inc.
605 3rd Ave
New York NY 10158
212 204-4200

(G-769)
INFORMA MEDIA INC
14920 Us Hwy 61 (38614)
PHONE..................................662 624-8503
Paul Hollis, *Editor*
Todd Fitchette, *Sales Staff*
Glenn Luedke, *Adv Dir*
EMP: 6
SALES (corp-wide): 3B **Privately Held**
SIC: 2741 Miscellaneous publishing

2019 Harris Directory of
Mississippi Manufacturers

▲ = Import ▼=Export
◆ =Import/Export

GEOGRAPHIC SECTION

Cleveland - Bolivar County (G-799)

HQ: Informa Media, Inc.
605 3rd Ave Fl 22
New York NY 10158
212 204-4200

(G-770)
KBH CORPORATION
395 Anderson Blvd (38614-4701)
P.O. Box 670 (38614-0670)
PHONE....................................662 624-5471
Buddy Bass Sr, *President*
M H Bass, *President*
Matthew H Bass, *Director*
▲ **EMP:** 150 **EST:** 1951
SQ FT: 20,000
SALES (est): 44.9MM **Privately Held**
WEB: www.kbhequipment.com
SIC: 3523 Fertilizing machinery, farm

(G-771)
KIMS PROCESSING PLANT INC
227 Leflore Ave (38614-4425)
PHONE....................................662 627-2389
EMP: 15
SQ FT: 12,000
SALES (est): 870K **Privately Held**
SIC: 2038 2096 Mfg Specialty Foods

(G-772)
LEATHER LANYARDS
9835 New Africa Rd (38614-9138)
PHONE....................................662 902-5294
EMP: 2
SALES (est): 111.8K **Privately Held**
SIC: 3199 Leather goods

(G-773)
LEMON TREE CANDLES
47 Delta Ave Apt 211 (38614-2746)
PHONE....................................662 621-4312
Pamela Bullard, *Principal*
EMP: 1
SALES (est): 42.5K **Privately Held**
SIC: 3999 Candles

(G-774)
METSO MINERALS INDUSTRIES INC
Also Called: Stephens-Adamson Division
Hwy 49 S (38614)
PHONE....................................662 627-5292
EMP: 100
SALES (corp-wide): 2.7B **Privately Held**
SIC: 3535 Mfg Conveyors/Equipment
HQ: Metso Minerals Industries Inc
20965 Crossroads Cir
Waukesha WI 53186
262 798-3994

(G-775)
MICHAELS MACHINE SHOP INC
5935 New Africa Rd (38614-9117)
PHONE....................................662 624-2376
Michael Edmonson, *President*
Karen Edmondson, *Vice Pres*
EMP: 7
SQ FT: 5,000
SALES (est): 200K **Privately Held**
SIC: 7699 7692 3599 Industrial machinery & equipment repair; welding repair; machine shop, jobbing & repair

(G-776)
MMC MATERIALS INC
1309 Highway 49 S (38614-6900)
P.O. Box 403 (38614-0403)
PHONE....................................662 624-9000
Danny Rogers, *President*
EMP: 4
SALES (corp-wide): 306.5MM **Privately Held**
WEB: www.mmcmaterials.com
SIC: 3273 Ready-mixed concrete
HQ: Mmc Materials, Inc.
1052 Highland Colony Pkwy # 201
Ridgeland MS 39157
601 898-4000

(G-777)
MOLDED ACSTCAL PDTS EASTON INC
Also Called: M A P
600 Highway 322 (38614-4719)
PHONE....................................662 627-7811
Scott Carroway, *Branch Mgr*

EMP: 40 **Privately Held**
WEB: www.mapeaston.com
SIC: 3296 Fiberglass insulation
PA: Molded Acoustical Products Of Easton, Inc.
3 Danforth Dr
Easton PA 18045

(G-778)
PO BOY WELDING INC
1012 E 2nd St (38614-4510)
P.O. Box 37 (38614-0037)
PHONE....................................662 624-3696
Sylvester Thorton, *President*
EMP: 3
SALES (est): 339.4K **Privately Held**
SIC: 5084 7692 Welding machinery & equipment; welding repair

(G-779)
RENCHERS THIS & THAT
Also Called: R & R Crafts
1768 Sycamore St (38614-6624)
PHONE....................................662 624-9825
Varner Rencher, *Owner*
EMP: 1
SALES (est): 44.8K **Privately Held**
SIC: 3914 Trophies, plated (all metals)

(G-780)
RODGERS SALES COMPANY
418 Jefferson Ave (38614-6310)
PHONE....................................662 902-1664
EMP: 1 **EST:** 2015
SALES (est): 69.6K **Privately Held**
SIC: 3523 Farm machinery & equipment

(G-781)
ROOSEVELT WALLACE
Also Called: Wallace Art & Sign Service
913 Desoto Ave (38614-6930)
PHONE....................................662 627-7513
Roosevelt Wallace, *Owner*
EMP: 2
SQ FT: 3,500
SALES: 95K **Privately Held**
SIC: 2759 3993 Screen printing; signs & advertising specialties

(G-782)
SAF T CART INC
Also Called: National Metal Products
1322 Industrial Park Dr (38614-4621)
P.O. Box 1869 (38614-7869)
PHONE....................................662 624-6492
James Walker Sr, *President*
Helen Walker, *Vice Pres*
Scott Carraway, *Purchasing*
Courtney Hays, *Engineer*
Andy Parks, *Sales Staff*
EMP: 50 **EST:** 1996
SALES (est): 12.8MM **Privately Held**
WEB: www.saftcart.com
SIC: 3589 3548 3537 3496 Janitors' carts; welding apparatus; industrial trucks & tractors; miscellaneous fabricated wire products; fabricated structural metal

(G-783)
STANDARD INDUSTRIAL CORP
1410 Industrial Park Dr (38614-4600)
PHONE....................................662 624-2436
Terry Hays, *Ch of Bd*
Steven Hays, *President*
Vance Hays, *Vice Pres*
John Hays, *Purch Mgr*
Virginia Hays, *Admin Sec*
▲ **EMP:** 60
SQ FT: 100,000
SALES (est): 9.6MM **Privately Held**
WEB: www.standard-industrial.com
SIC: 3542 Brakes, metal forming

(G-784)
TRIPLE J OF MISSISSIPPI INC
520 Sunbelt Dr (38614-9096)
PHONE....................................662 624-4630
Jerry Burchfield, *President*
Pat Burchfield, *Vice Pres*
EMP: 6
SQ FT: 15,000
SALES (est): 490K **Privately Held**
SIC: 3537 Trucks, tractors, loaders, carriers & similar equipment

---

Cleveland
Bolivar County

(G-785)
5TH AVENUE SOFTWARE LLC
600 S Fifth Ave (38732-3137)
PHONE....................................662 843-1200
Barbara Pettway, *Mng Member*
EMP: 1 **EST:** 2007
SALES (est): 76.1K **Privately Held**
SIC: 7372 Business oriented computer software

(G-786)
BAXTER HEALTHCARE CORPORATION
911 N Davis Ave (38732-2106)
PHONE....................................662 843-9421
Mark Jackson, *Plant Mgr*
Patricia Duvall, *Buyer*
Mike Howell, *Engineer*
Chris Orr, *Engineer*
Aaron Tan, *Engineer*
EMP: 20
SALES (corp-wide): 11.1B **Publicly Held**
SIC: 2834 Pharmaceutical preparations
HQ: Baxter Healthcare Corporation
1 Baxter Pkwy
Deerfield IL 60015
224 948-2000

(G-787)
BOLIVAR CNTY DEPT HUMN RSURCES
212 N Pearman Ave (38732-2634)
PHONE....................................662 843-8311
EMP: 6
SALES (est): 329.4K **Privately Held**
SIC: 2711 Newspapers, publishing & printing

(G-788)
BOLIVAR NEWSPAPER INC
Also Called: Bolivar Commercial
821 N Chrisman Ave (38732-2110)
P.O. Box 1050 (38732-1050)
PHONE....................................662 843-4241
C Lee Walls, *Ch of Bd*
Norman C Van Liew, *President*
James D Lancaster, *Admin Sec*
EMP: 25 **EST:** 1940
SQ FT: 11,200
SALES (est): 1.6MM **Privately Held**
WEB: www.bolivarcom.com
SIC: 2711 Job printing & newspaper publishing combined; commercial printing & newspaper publishing combined

(G-789)
CLARK BEVERAGE GROUP INC
Also Called: Coca-Cola
908 N Sharpe Ave (38732-2118)
PHONE....................................662 843-3241
EMP: 3
SALES (corp-wide): 167MM **Privately Held**
SIC: 2086 Carb Sft Drnkbtlcn
HQ: Clark Beverage Group, Inc.
110 Miley Dr
Starkville MS 39759
662 338-3400

(G-790)
COOPWOOD COMMUNICATIONS INC
150 N Sharpe Ave (38732-2748)
PHONE....................................662 843-2700
Scott Coopwood, *Principal*
EMP: 12
SALES (corp-wide): 6MM **Privately Held**
SIC: 2711 Newspapers
PA: Coopwood Communications, Inc.
125 S Court St
Cleveland MS 38732
662 843-3432

(G-791)
FAURECIA AUTO SEATING LLC
907 Delta Council Dr (38732-3435)
PHONE....................................248 288-1000
Jon Makamson, *Manager*
EMP: 300

SALES (corp-wide): 38.2MM **Privately Held**
WEB: www.cleveland.faurecia.com
SIC: 2531 Seats, automobile
HQ: Faurecia Automotive Seating, Llc
2800 High Meadow Cir
Auburn Hills MI 48326
248 288-1000

(G-792)
FLATLANDERS SCREEN PRINTING
1321 W Highway 8 (38732-2267)
PHONE....................................662 846-0725
Edward Gong, *President*
Penny Gong, *Corp Secy*
Marc Brinkley, *Vice Pres*
EMP: 5
SQ FT: 5,000
SALES: 500K **Privately Held**
SIC: 2759 Screen printing

(G-793)
FLEMING TRUE VALUE LBR
224 N Sharpe Ave (38732-2100)
PHONE....................................662 843-2763
EMP: 1
SALES (est): 54.1K **Privately Held**
SIC: 2431 Millwork

(G-794)
HALO SOUTHERN PUBLISHING LLC
618 Frederick Dr (38732-2006)
PHONE....................................662 299-2999
Lori Morris, *Principal*
EMP: 1
SALES (est): 37.5K **Privately Held**
SIC: 2741 Miscellaneous publishing

(G-795)
HAYNES ENTERPRISES INC
1401 S Davis Ave (38732-4316)
P.O. Box 899 (38732-0899)
PHONE....................................662 843-4411
Terry L Haynes, *President*
EMP: 2
SQ FT: 15,000
SALES: 450K **Privately Held**
SIC: 5084 5085 5087 3599 Materials handling machinery; processing & packaging equipment; industrial supplies; janitors' supplies; machine shop, jobbing & repair

(G-796)
HILLS WELDING & CRANE RENTAL
172 N Blivar Cnty Line Rd (38732-9480)
P.O. Box 235 (38732-0235)
PHONE....................................662 846-6789
Otis L Hill Jr, *Owner*
EMP: 1 **EST:** 1973
SALES (est): 160.1K **Privately Held**
SIC: 7692 7359 Welding repair; garage facility & tool rental

(G-797)
JOHN SIGN & CO INC
4139 Highway 8 (38732-8502)
PHONE....................................662 843-3548
John Yarbrough, *President*
EMP: 1
SALES (est): 148.9K **Privately Held**
SIC: 3993 Signs & advertising specialties

(G-798)
L T CORPORATION (PA)
Also Called: Quality Steel
2914 Hwy 61 S (38732)
P.O. Box 249 (38732-0249)
PHONE....................................662 843-4046
James I Tims, *Ch of Bd*
James Tims, *Executive*
EMP: 23
SQ FT: 72,000
SALES (est): 121.2MM **Privately Held**
SIC: 3443 6141 6311 Tanks for tank trucks, metal plate; consumer finance companies; life insurance

(G-799)
METHODIST AND PROSTHETICS
804 1st St (38732-2310)
PHONE....................................662 846-6555

(PA)=Parent Co (HQ)=Headquarters (DH)=Div Headquarters
✿ = New Business established in last 2 years

2019 Harris Directory of
Mississippi Manufacturers

37

Cleveland - Bolivar County (G-800)

GEOGRAPHIC SECTION

Darby Shook, *Branch Mgr*
EMP: 2
SALES (est): 122.2K **Privately Held**
SIC: 3842 Prosthetic appliances

(G-800)
MOORES WELDING & FABRICATION
198 Old Ruleville Rd (38732-9588)
PHONE.................................662 402-5503
Ernie Moore, *Principal*
EMP: 1
SALES (est): 44.6K **Privately Held**
SIC: 7692 Welding repair

(G-801)
MURPHYS WELDING LLC
3074 Highway 8 (38732-8784)
PHONE.................................662 719-3879
James A Murphy, *Manager*
EMP: 1
SALES (est): 36.6K **Privately Held**
SIC: 7692 Welding repair

(G-802)
NEHI BOTTLING CO OF CLEVELAND
310 N Sharpe Ave (38732-2340)
P.O. Box 247 (38732-0247)
PHONE.................................662 843-3431
Homer L Sledge Jr, *President*
Homer L Sledge III, *Vice Pres*
Joyce Sledge, *Admin Sec*
EMP: 18 EST: 1927
SQ FT: 18,000
SALES: 3.2MM **Privately Held**
SIC: 2086 Soft drinks: packaged in cans, bottles, etc.

(G-803)
PHARMEDIUM SERVICES LLC
913 N Davis Ave (38732-2106)
PHONE.................................662 846-5969
Timothy Rinks, *Branch Mgr*
Steven Stewart, *Maintence Staff*
EMP: 28
SALES (corp-wide): 167.9B **Publicly Held**
SIC: 2834 5912 Pharmaceutical preparations; drug stores
HQ: Pharmedium Services, Llc
150 N Field Dr Ste 350
Lake Forest IL 60045
800 523-7749

(G-804)
QUALITY STEEL CORPORATION (HQ)
Also Called: Q S C
2914 Hwy 61 (38732)
PHONE.................................662 771-4243
James I Tims, *CEO*
Clark Love, *Regional Mgr*
Brent Rogers, *Regional Mgr*
Virgil Mullins, *Vice Pres*
Dale Priemer, *Transptn Dir*
EMP: 80
SQ FT: 68,000
SALES: 120.8MM
SALES (corp-wide): 121.2MM **Privately Held**
WEB: www.propanetank.com
SIC: 3443 Tanks for tank trucks, metal plate
PA: L T Corporation
2914 Hwy 61 S
Cleveland MS 38732
662 843-4046

(G-805)
RIVERS GIST GAINSPOLETTI
38 Tiser Dr (38732-5518)
PHONE.................................662 902-5415
Rivers Gist Gainspoletti, *Principal*
EMP: 1
SALES (est): 67.8K **Privately Held**
SIC: 3952 Paints, except gold & bronze: artists'

(G-806)
ROBINSONS RETAIL INC
Also Called: Heidi's
110 N Sharpe Ave (38732-2748)
PHONE.................................662 843-3950
Heather Robinson, *President*

Brian Robinson, *Vice Pres*
EMP: 10
SQ FT: 11,000
SALES (est): 643.2K **Privately Held**
SIC: 2395 5947 Embroidery & art needlework; gift, novelty & souvenir shop

(G-807)
ROYAL CROWN BOTTLING
310 N Sharpe Ave (38732-2340)
P.O. Box 247 (38732-0247)
PHONE.................................662 843-3431
Homer Sledge III, *President*
Samir Patel, *Info Tech Mgr*
EMP: 20
SALES (est): 636.3K **Privately Held**
SIC: 2086 5149 Soft drinks: packaged in cans, bottles, etc.; soft drinks

(G-808)
SANDERS SEED (PA)
518 N Sharpe Ave (38732-2365)
PHONE.................................800 844-5533
EMP: 7
SALES (est): 7.6MM **Privately Held**
SIC: 5191 3523 Fertilizers & agricultural chemicals; sprayers & spraying machines, agricultural

(G-809)
STRYDER & ASSOCIATES LLC
Also Called: Stryder Associates
141b Walker Rd (38732-9412)
P.O. Box 25 (38732-0025)
PHONE.................................662 579-8703
Brenda Wince, *Owner*
Jalee Wince, *Managing Prtnr*
Joseph Sampson, *Prdtn Mgr*
EMP: 2
SALES: 800K **Privately Held**
SIC: 0116 5136 0762 4221 Soybeans; men's & boys' hats, scarves & gloves; farm management services; farm product warehousing & storage; fabric dress & work gloves

(G-810)
WATER WATER LLC
25 Gaston Dr (38732-9568)
PHONE.................................662 721-7098
Thomas Christopher,
EMP: 1 EST: 2014
SALES (est): 76.3K **Privately Held**
SIC: 3589 Water treatment equipment, industrial

Clinton
Hinds County

(G-811)
A TO B SIGN COMPANY
1450b E Northside Dr (39056-3552)
PHONE.................................601 924-6323
Paul Gore, *Owner*
EMP: 4
SALES (est): 50K **Privately Held**
SIC: 3993 Signs & advertising specialties

(G-812)
ARMSTRONG REMODELING
107 Lovett Dr (39056-3045)
PHONE.................................601 720-2097
Anthony Bingham, *Principal*
EMP: 10
SALES (est): 722.8K **Privately Held**
SIC: 2381 Fabric dress & work gloves

(G-813)
ARROW PRINTERS INC
447 Highway 80 E (39056-4719)
PHONE.................................601 924-1192
Penn Majors, *President*
Mary Majors, *Treasurer*
Stephaniee Briggs, *Office Mgr*
Adam Majors, *Executive*
EMP: 15
SQ FT: 3,000
SALES (est): 1.5MM **Privately Held**
WEB: www.arrowprinters.com
SIC: 2752 Commercial printing, offset

(G-814)
BLACK RVER TIMBER WILDLIFE LLC
160 Bellewood Dr (39056-4611)
PHONE.................................601 906-4099
Jenna Triplett, *Office Admin*
EMP: 2
SALES (est): 172.4K **Privately Held**
SIC: 2411 Timber, cut at logging camp

(G-815)
BRENDA RUTH DESIGNS LLC
306b Avondale Dr (39056-3461)
PHONE.................................601 708-4227
Brenda R Middleton,
Ruth A Osborn,
EMP: 2
SALES (est): 177.3K **Privately Held**
SIC: 3552 5947 5961 Embroidery machines; gifts & novelties;

(G-816)
BRYAN E PRESSON & ASSOC INC
Also Called: Mid State Welding & Mch Works
900 Industrial Park Dr (39056-3208)
P.O. Box 200 (39060-0200)
PHONE.................................601 925-0053
Bryan Presson, *President*
Tim P Presson, *Purch Mgr*
Tim Presson, *Manager*
EMP: 10
SQ FT: 6,000
SALES: 800K **Privately Held**
WEB: www.midstatewelding.com
SIC: 3441 Fabricated structural metal

(G-817)
BUILDERS MARBLE INC
108 Pinehaven Cv (39056-3123)
PHONE.................................601 922-5420
Phil Chisolm, *President*
Donna Hardy, *Treasurer*
Jan Chisolm, *Admin Sec*
EMP: 35
SALES: 1MM **Privately Held**
SIC: 3089 5032 3088 Synthetic resin finished products; brick, stone & related material; building stone; plastics plumbing fixtures

(G-818)
CAROL BAIRD
Also Called: Dolls By Carol
1008 Old Vicksburg Rd (39056-3812)
P.O. Box 276 (39060-0276)
PHONE.................................601 924-5409
Carol Baird, *Owner*
EMP: 1
SALES (est): 58.7K **Privately Held**
WEB: www.carolbaird.com
SIC: 3942 Dolls, except stuffed toy animals

(G-819)
CUSTOM PROSTHETIC & ORTHOTIC
801 E Northside Dr Ste D (39056-3663)
PHONE.................................601 708-4196
EMP: 2
SALES (est): 15.6K **Privately Held**
SIC: 3842 Mfg Surgical Appliances/Supplies

(G-820)
DANIELS LAWN AND LANSCAPE LLC
210 Dawson St (39056-3304)
PHONE.................................601 965-6982
Andrew Daniels, *Owner*
EMP: 3 EST: 2017
SALES: 15K **Privately Held**
SIC: 0782 0783 3271 Lawn & garden services; planting, pruning & trimming services; removal services, bush & tree; blocks, concrete: landscape or retaining wall

(G-821)
DATA SYSTEMS MANAGEMENT INC (PA)
1505 Clinton Business Par (39056-4443)
P.O. Box 1348, Columbus (39703-1348)
PHONE.................................601 925-6270
Glen Davis, *President*

Allan Smith, *Vice Pres*
Tracy Reynolds, *IT/INT Sup*
Brent Potter, *Prgrmr*
EMP: 18
SQ FT: 6,500
SALES: 2MM **Privately Held**
WEB: www.datasysmgt.com
SIC: 7371 7372 5734 Custom computer programming services; prepackaged software; computer software & accessories

(G-822)
DEWMAR INTERNATIONAL BMC INC (PA)
132 E Northside Dr Ste C (39056-3415)
PHONE.................................877 747-5326
Marco Moran, *President*
JD Houston, *Vice Pres*
EMP: 1
SQ FT: 4,500
SALES (est): 384.1K **Publicly Held**
SIC: 8741 7389 2086 Management services; telemarketing services; bottled & canned soft drinks

(G-823)
GOFF STEEL RECTING
285 Wells Rd (39056-9609)
PHONE.................................601 922-6014
EMP: 5
SALES (est): 427.9K **Privately Held**
SIC: 3449 Mfg Misc Structural Metalwork

(G-824)
GULF STATES CANNERS INC
1006 Indl Pk Dr (39056)
PHONE.................................601 924-0511
Albert C Clark, *President*
Hardy P Graham, *Vice Pres*
H L Williams Jr, *Vice Pres*
Randy Lee, *VP Opers*
Alysha Knight, *Purch Mgr*
EMP: 75
SQ FT: 300,000
SALES (est): 35.2MM **Privately Held**
WEB: www.gscanners.com
SIC: 2086 Carbonated beverages, nonalcoholic: bottled & canned

(G-825)
INDEPENDENT METAL CRAFT LLC
1016 Industrial Park Dr (39056-3210)
PHONE.................................601 488-4789
Davis Warren, *President*
Scott Warren, *Vice Pres*
EMP: 9
SALES (est): 1.5MM **Privately Held**
SIC: 3446 Balconies, metal

(G-826)
IRON INNOVATIONS INC
1101 Clinton Indus Pk Rd (39056-3227)
P.O. Box 2340 (39060-2340)
PHONE.................................601 924-0640
Kate Colson, *President*
Scott M Colson, *Vice Pres*
Tom Lott, *Manager*
EMP: 14
SQ FT: 11,025
SALES (est): 2.3MM **Privately Held**
WEB: www.ironinnovationsinc.com
SIC: 3446 Fences or posts, ornamental iron or steel

(G-827)
JEFF BUSBY
Also Called: Busby Office Supply & Printing
526 E College St (39056-4735)
PHONE.................................601 924-7979
Jeff Busby, *Owner*
EMP: 3
SQ FT: 3,111
SALES (est): 260K **Privately Held**
WEB: www.busbyofficesupply.com
SIC: 5943 2752 Office forms & supplies; commercial printing, lithographic

(G-828)
LADONNA R WILLIAMS
Also Called: Microscope Logic
100 Kimberly Cv (39056-9719)
PHONE.................................601 405-2200
Ladonna Williams, *Owner*
EMP: 2

2019 Harris Directory of
Mississippi Manufacturers

▲ = Import ▼=Export
◆ =Import/Export

GEOGRAPHIC SECTION

Collins - Covington County (G-859)

SALES (est): 46.9K **Privately Held**
SIC: 3944 Science kits: microscopes, chemistry sets, etc.

(G-829)
LUCKY LEAF DISCOUNT TOBACCO
509 Springridge Rd Ste C (39056-5611)
PHONE..................................601 924-8818
Charles Rodgers, *Owner*
EMP: 2
SALES (est): 210K **Privately Held**
SIC: 2141 5993 Tobacco redrying; tobacco stores & stands

(G-830)
MCNEELY PLASTIC PRODUCTS INC (PA)
Also Called: Sigma Plastics Group
1111 Industrial Park Dr (39056-3208)
PHONE..................................601 926-1000
Greg McNeely, *President*
Dave Clarke, *Vice Pres*
Edgar Davis, *Vice Pres*
Shannon Watts, *Vice Pres*
Rita Payton, *CFO*
▲ EMP: 41
SQ FT: 3,000
SALES: 58.7MM **Privately Held**
SIC: 5699 5087 2821 3999 Work clothing: janitors' supplies; thermosetting materials; barber & beauty shop equipment

(G-831)
MEGA PLASTICS INC
1111 Industrial Park Dr (39056-3208)
PHONE..................................601 924-1712
Fax: 601 924-1719
EMP: 90
SQ FT: 64,000
SALES (est): 14.2MM **Privately Held**
SIC: 2671 2673 3081 Mfg Packaging Paper/Film Mfg Bags-Plastic/Coated Paper Mfg Unsupported Plastic Film/Sheet

(G-832)
OMNI BLINDS
131 Murial St (39056-4407)
PHONE..................................601 924-0326
Robert T Ledbetter, *Owner*
Robert Ledbetter, *Owner*
EMP: 2
SALES (est): 155.6K **Privately Held**
SIC: 2591 Window blinds

(G-833)
PORTABLE BORING INC
233 Saddlewood Dr (39056-2004)
PHONE..................................601 922-9333
Anthony Edwards, *CEO*
Trish Edwards, *Vice Pres*
EMP: 3
SALES: 120K **Privately Held**
SIC: 3599 Machine shop, jobbing & repair

(G-834)
PROFESSIONAL GRAPHICS INC
154 Wickstead Dr (39056-4610)
PHONE..................................601 924-9116
Kathleen Molitor, *President*
Henry Norris, *Vice Pres*
EMP: 3
SQ FT: 1,600
SALES (est): 122.9K **Privately Held**
SIC: 2752 Commercial printing, offset

(G-835)
SANI LLC
102 Woodmoor Cv (39056-4143)
PHONE..................................601 454-6047
Steven Craig Panter, *Principal*
Willie Greer, *Manager*
EMP: 1
SALES (est): 48.4K **Privately Held**
SIC: 2079 Oil, partially hydrogenated: edible

(G-836)
SURGISURE INC
113 Trace Rdg (39056-6152)
PHONE..................................601 985-8125
Joseph Boone, *President*
EMP: 1

SALES (est): 39.6K **Privately Held**
SIC: 3999 Manufacturing industries

(G-837)
TAYLOR POWER SYSTEMS INC
947 Indl Park Dr (39056)
PHONE..................................601 932-6491
Robert D Taylor, *President*
Richard J Ballard, *Vice Pres*
Pete Reynolds, *Treasurer*
▲ EMP: 1
SALES (est): 985.3K **Privately Held**
SIC: 3621 Windmills, electric generating
PA: The Taylor Group Inc
650 N Church Ave
Louisville MS 39339

(G-838)
WALTER ALLEN
112 Country Cove Dr (39056-9792)
PHONE..................................601 924-1956
Walter Allen, *Principal*
EMP: 2 EST: 2010
SALES (est): 130.8K **Privately Held**
SIC: 1382 Oil & gas exploration services

(G-839)
WOODS TRADING CO INC
Also Called: Johnson Milling Co
100 Belmont St (39056-4274)
PHONE..................................601 924-5015
J Alvin Woods, *President*
Alvin Woods Jr, *Vice Pres*
EMP: 6
SQ FT: 20,000
SALES: 1.7MM **Privately Held**
SIC: 2048 2047 Livestock feeds; dog & cat food

Coffeeville
Yalobusha County

(G-840)
ANDY MASSEY LOGGING
2268 County Road 134 (38922-2912)
PHONE..................................662 675-2647
Andy Massey, *Owner*
EMP: 2
SALES (est): 250.7K **Privately Held**
SIC: 2411 Logging camps & contractors

(G-841)
AO LIQUIDATION TRUST INC
129 Tennessee St (38922-3345)
PHONE..................................662 675-8102
EMP: 50 **Privately Held**
SIC: 2393 3949 2381 Mfg Textile Bags Mfg Sport/Athletic Goods Mfg Fabric Gloves
PA: Ao Liquidation Trust, Inc.
405 Cumberland St
Memphis TN 38112

(G-842)
C & M TREE SVC STUMP GRINDING
766 County Road 157 (38922-2514)
PHONE..................................662 675-8884
EMP: 2 EST: 2004
SALES (est): 100K **Privately Held**
SIC: 3599 Mfg Industrial Machinery

(G-843)
K & D CULTURED MARBLE INC
Also Called: K and D Marble
17425 Okahoma St (38922)
P.O. Box 484 (38922-0484)
PHONE..................................662 675-2928
Rodney Hollowell, *President*
Diane Hollowell, *Corp Secy*
EMP: 27
SQ FT: 10,000
SALES (est): 2.5MM **Privately Held**
SIC: 3281 3088 Bathroom fixtures, cut stone; table tops, marble; plastics plumbing fixtures

---

Coldwater
Tate County

(G-844)
CZEISZPERGER DISTILLER LLC
104 Cherrydale Loop (38618-3072)
PHONE..................................662 612-6160
Czeiszperger Distillers, *Principal*
EMP: 3 EST: 2016
SALES (est): 106.4K **Privately Held**
SIC: 2085 Distilled & blended liquors

(G-845)
FEDERAL HEATH SIGN COMPANY LLC
668 Harris Rd (38618-3109)
PHONE..................................662 233-2999
David Bullock, *Manager*
EMP: 2
SALES (corp-wide): 438.7MM **Privately Held**
WEB: www.zimsign.com
SIC: 3993 Electric signs
HQ: Federal Heath Sign Company, Llc
2300 St Hwy 121
Euless TX 76039

(G-846)
G5 TEES
808 Palestine Rd (38618-7332)
PHONE..................................662 403-1339
Brett Grosmann, *Principal*
EMP: 2
SALES (est): 94.4K **Privately Held**
SIC: 2759 Screen printing

(G-847)
INNOCOR FOAM TECHNOLOGIES LLC
Also Called: Aut-Coldwater
485 Industrial Dr (38618)
PHONE..................................662 622-7221
Sally McGarrity, *Manager*
EMP: 14
SALES (corp-wide): 224.3MM **Privately Held**
SIC: 3086 Plastics foam products
HQ: Innocor Foam Technologies, Llc
200 Schulz Dr Ste 2
Red Bank NJ 07701

(G-848)
JCBC CS LLC
7660 Highway 305 (38618-7944)
PHONE..................................662 560-7235
Joshua Wilbanks,
EMP: 2
SALES (est): 33.6K **Privately Held**
SIC: 7692 Welding repair

(G-849)
METAL-TECH FABRICATORS INC
9007 Highway 51 (38618-3824)
P.O. Box 430 (38618-0430)
PHONE..................................662 622-0400
Daniel Freeman, *President*
Donna J Ford, *Corp Secy*
EMP: 15
SQ FT: 14,900
SALES (est): 2.3MM **Privately Held**
WEB: www.metaltechfab.com
SIC: 3443 3535 Industrial vessels, tanks & containers; hoppers, metal plate; cyclones, industrial: metal plate; conveyors & conveying equipment

(G-850)
PAT S PINS
470 Tanksley Rd (38618-6570)
PHONE..................................662 562-8986
Pat S Pins, *Principal*
EMP: 3
SALES (est): 142.1K **Privately Held**
SIC: 1099 Metal ores

(G-851)
TEES RIVER RELICS
796 Barr Rd (38618-3367)
PHONE..................................662 501-9936
Teresa Geeslin, *Principal*
EMP: 2

SALES (est): 73.2K **Privately Held**
SIC: 2759 Screen printing

Collins
Covington County

(G-852)
B P GRAVES LOGGING CO
156 E Williamsburg Rd (39428-4838)
PHONE..................................601 765-8956
Billy P Graves, *President*
EMP: 5
SALES (est): 290.1K **Privately Held**
SIC: 2411 Logging camps & contractors

(G-853)
DISCOUNT FIREWORKS
2542 Highway 49 (39428-4551)
PHONE..................................601 765-4295
Robert Dillen, *Owner*
EMP: 1
SALES (est): 64.7K **Privately Held**
SIC: 2899 Flares, fireworks & similar preparations

(G-854)
J & L TRANSPORT LLC
499 Lake Mike Conner Rd (39428-4028)
PHONE..................................601 292-7044
Larry Flowers, *Partner*
EMP: 5 EST: 2012
SALES (est): 307K **Privately Held**
SIC: 2411 Logging

(G-855)
JONATHAN SANFORD DBA
827 Snset Williamsburg Rd (39428-6312)
PHONE..................................601 297-2754
Jonathan Sanford, *Principal*
EMP: 2
SALES (est): 83.9K **Privately Held**
SIC: 2752 Commercial printing, lithographic

(G-856)
NEW SOUTH LOGGING LLC
464 Lake Mike Conner Rd (39428-4029)
P.O. Box 2223 (39428-2223)
PHONE..................................601 517-8457
Christi M Daniels, *Mng Member*
EMP: 1 EST: 2015
SALES (est): 125.1K **Privately Held**
SIC: 2411 Logging

(G-857)
NEWS COMMERCIAL
Also Called: News-Commercial, The
104 S First St (39428-4659)
P.O. Box 1299 (39428-1299)
PHONE..................................601 765-8275
James Arrington, *Partner*
Analyn Goff, *Partner*
Jeanie Gooch, *Partner*
Jeannie Gooch, *Partner*
EMP: 10 EST: 1902
SALES (est): 322.1K **Privately Held**
SIC: 2711 Newspapers: publishing only, not printed on site

(G-858)
OMNI FUSION LLC
123 Mount Pleasant Rd (39428-6246)
PHONE..................................601 765-6941
EMP: 1 EST: 2008
SALES (est): 39.7K **Privately Held**
SIC: 7812 2711 2721 Video production; audio-visual program production; newspapers, publishing & printing; comic books: publishing & printing; magazines: publishing & printing

(G-859)
PINE BELT READY-MIX CON INC
38 Collins Indus Pk Dr (39428-3987)
PHONE..................................601 765-4813
Tony Johnson, *Manager*
EMP: 3
SALES (corp-wide): 100.3MM **Privately Held**
SIC: 3273 Ready-mixed concrete

(PA)=Parent Co (HQ)=Headquarters (DH)=Div Headquarters
✿ = New Business established in last 2 years

2019 Harris Directory of
Mississippi Manufacturers

Collins - Covington County (G-860) — GEOGRAPHIC SECTION

HQ: Pine Belt Ready-Mix Concrete, Inc.
1104 W 1st St Ste 8
Laurel MS 39440
601 425-2026

(G-860)
RTC LOGGING INC
1731 Sunset Rd (39428-3935)
P.O. Box 2349 (39428-2349)
PHONE..................................601 517-6881
EMP: 2 EST: 2014
SALES (est): 169.8K Privately Held
SIC: 2411 Logging

(G-861)
SANDERSON FARMS INC PROC DIV
1111 N Fir Ave (39428-4178)
P.O. Box 1329 (39428-1329)
PHONE..................................601 765-8211
Dan Nicovich, Manager
Debbie Herring, Supervisor
EMP: 1100
SALES (corp-wide): 3.2B Publicly Held
SIC: 2015 Poultry slaughtering & processing
HQ: Sanderson Farms, Inc. (Processing Division)
127 Flynt Rd
Laurel MS 39443
601 649-4030

(G-862)
SANDERSON FARMS INC PROD DIV
3098 Highway 49 (39428-4578)
P.O. Box 988, Laurel (39441-0988)
PHONE..................................601 765-2221
Robert Blackwell, President
Douglas J McLoud, Manager
EMP: 444
SALES (corp-wide): 3.2B Publicly Held
SIC: 2015 Poultry slaughtering & processing
HQ: Sanderson Farms, Inc. (Production Division)
127 Flynt Rd
Laurel MS 39443
601 425-2552

(G-863)
SUNSET SCREEN PRINTING
827 Snset Williamsburg Rd (39428-6312)
PHONE..................................601 297-2754
Jonathan Sanford, Principal
EMP: 2
SALES (est): 83.9K Privately Held
SIC: 2752 Commercial printing, lithographic

(G-864)
SUPERIOR MAT COMPANY INC
1731 Sunset Rd (39428-3935)
P.O. Box 2349 (39428-2349)
PHONE..................................601 765-8268
Leslie Rutland, President
Becky Rutland, Vice Pres
▲ EMP: 6
SQ FT: 3,500
SALES: 480K Privately Held
SIC: 2448 Wood pallets & skids

(G-865)
WARREN INC
707 N Fir Ave (39428-4144)
P.O. Box 1719 (39428-1719)
PHONE..................................601 765-8221
Russell Warren, President
Duncan Buchanan, Purch Agent
Jeff Sanford, Engineer
Jesse Allday, Controller
Bob Mc Donald, Finance Mgr
▲ EMP: 120
SQ FT: 125,000
SALES (est): 28.5MM Privately Held
SIC: 3523 3715 3713 5599 Sprayers & spraying machines, agricultural; spreaders, fertilizer; fertilizing, spraying, dusting & irrigation machinery; truck trailers; dump truck bodies; utility trailers

---

Collinsville
Lauderdale County

(G-866)
AUTMAN LOGGING
23 Autman Rd (39325-9623)
PHONE..................................601 986-2555
Willie Autman, Owner
EMP: 3
SALES (est): 214.8K Privately Held
SIC: 2411 Logging camps & contractors

(G-867)
DAVIDS SIGNS INC
11560 Swearington Rd (39325-8943)
PHONE..................................601 626-8934
Fax: 601 482-8975
EMP: 4
SALES (est): 220K Privately Held
SIC: 3993 Mfg Signs/Advertising Specialties

(G-868)
GENESIS TELECOMMUNICATIONS
8487 Highway 19 N (39325-9206)
PHONE..................................601 626-7353
G Tommy Espey, President
Linda Horn, Corp Secy
Mark Joyner, Vice Pres
Todd Green, Office Mgr
EMP: 4
SQ FT: 1,000
SALES (est): 364.8K Privately Held
WEB: www.genesistelecom.net
SIC: 1731 5063 3699 Safety & security specialization; access control systems specialization; fire alarm systems; security control equipment & systems

(G-869)
HEAR AGAIN
9369 Highway 19 N (39325-9219)
PHONE..................................601 626-0050
Bart Cross, Owner
EMP: 2
SALES (est): 230.8K Privately Held
SIC: 3842 Hearing aids

(G-870)
HERITAGE PRESS PBLICATIONS LLC
10231 Shallow Creek Dr (39325-9468)
PHONE..................................601 737-2086
David L Moon, Owner
EMP: 2
SALES (est): 113.1K Privately Held
SIC: 2741 Miscellaneous publishing

(G-871)
HUNTERWORKS LLC
9291 Collinsville Cir (39325-9182)
PHONE..................................601 771-0070
Todd Eldridge, Owner
EMP: 1
SALES (est): 213.1K Privately Held
WEB: www.hunterworks.com
SIC: 3714 Motor vehicle parts & accessories

(G-872)
INDUSTRIAL MACHINE MFG
11470a Ctr Hl Martin Rd (39325-9334)
PHONE..................................601 737-5017
Steve Carlisle, Manager
EMP: 3
SALES (est): 156.8K Privately Held
SIC: 3599 Machine shop, jobbing & repair

(G-873)
MATHIS TRUCKING & CNSTR LLC
12128 Kalorama Rd (39325)
PHONE..................................601 917-0237
Charlie Mathis, Principal
EMP: 1
SALES (est): 98.8K Privately Held
SIC: 1522 3715 1542 Residential construction; truck trailers; nonresidential construction

---

(G-874)
PRECISION ASP SEALCOATING LLC
12111 Maple Leaf Ln (39325-9139)
PHONE..................................601 527-6381
Candice Myatt, CEO
EMP: 4 EST: 2017
SALES (est): 143.8K Privately Held
SIC: 1771 3292 1799 1629 Blacktop (asphalt) work; patio construction, concrete; floor tile, asphalt; erection & dismantling of forms for poured concrete; railroad & railway roadbed construction;

(G-875)
SCREENING ROOM
11611 Hitt Ln (39325-9029)
PHONE..................................601 626-0327
EMP: 1
SALES (est): 53K Privately Held
SIC: 2759 Commercial Printing

(G-876)
SOUTHERN GATE TWR FABRICATORS
Also Called: Southern Fabricators
3903 Highland Park Dr (39325)
P.O. Box 626, Meridian (39302-0626)
PHONE..................................601 483-6710
Norman L Fant, President
Roger L Fant, Vice Pres
EMP: 1
SQ FT: 2,500
SALES: 1MM Privately Held
SIC: 5039 3496 Wire fence, gates & accessories; miscellaneous fabricated wire products

---

Columbia
Marion County

(G-877)
5 K CORP
1113 Highway 98 Byp Ste A (39429-3746)
P.O. Box 292 (39429-0292)
PHONE..................................601 736-5367
Kevin L Kemp, Partner
EMP: 11
SALES (est): 572.1K Privately Held
SIC: 1381 6531 Drilling oil & gas wells; real estate managers

(G-878)
ABS WELDING INC
1133 Prospres Ridge Rd (39429-8066)
PHONE..................................601 444-9889
Stevie Anderson, President
Glenda Anderson, Vice Pres
EMP: 10
SALES (est): 1.8MM Privately Held
SIC: 7692 Welding repair

(G-879)
ANNS EMBROIDERY
730 Main St (39429-2938)
P.O. Box 704 (39429-0704)
PHONE..................................601 444-0011
Elizabeth Sanders, Owner
Jeffery Sanders, Co-Owner
EMP: 3
SALES: 100K Privately Held
SIC: 2395 Embroidery products, except schiffli machine

(G-880)
ARCHROCK INC
60 Columbia Purvis Rd (39429-9107)
PHONE..................................601 444-0055
EMP: 1 Publicly Held
SIC: 1389 5084 Gas compressing (natural gas) at the fields; compressors, except air conditioning
PA: Archrock Inc.
9807 Katy Fwy Ste 100
Houston TX 77024

(G-881)
B & P SWAB SERVICE INC
197 Airport Rd (39429-9041)
P.O. Box 906 (39429-0906)
PHONE..................................601 731-6309
Tim Buckley, President

Stacey Buckley, Vice Pres
EMP: 20
SQ FT: 2,000
SALES (est): 2MM Privately Held
SIC: 1389 Swabbing wells

(G-882)
BAKER HUGHES A GE COMPANY LLC
4025 Highway 35 N (39429-8763)
PHONE..................................601 731-5004
Chris Simmons, Branch Mgr
EMP: 40
SALES (corp-wide): 121.6B Publicly Held
SIC: 1389 Construction, repair & dismantling services; oil field services
HQ: Baker Hughes, A Ge Company, Llc
17021 Aldine Westfield Rd
Houston TX 77073
713 439-8600

(G-883)
BARN LIFE TEES
611 Williamsburg Rd (39429-8888)
PHONE..................................601 740-0696
Melanie Moree, Principal
EMP: 2
SALES (est): 73.2K Privately Held
SIC: 2759 Screen printing

(G-884)
BENGAL RESOURCES AND ASSOC INC
107 Walter Payton Dr (39429-3738)
PHONE..................................404 312-4642
Steven Perry, President
EMP: 1
SALES (est): 103K Privately Held
SIC: 3821 Laser beam alignment devices

(G-885)
CHALLNGER DPWELL SERVICING INC
4 Industrial Ln (39429)
P.O. Box 1002 (39429-1002)
PHONE..................................601 736-2511
Max Story, President
Larry Sistrunk, Corp Secy
Carolyn Riley, Manager
Jerry Davis, Admin Sec
EMP: 35
SQ FT: 4,200
SALES (est): 3.4MM Privately Held
SIC: 1389 Oil field services

(G-886)
CHIP JONES MILL INC
2438 Highway 98 E (39429-8056)
PHONE..................................601 876-6943
Brett Jones, President
EMP: 15
SALES (est): 2.5MM Privately Held
SIC: 2421 Chipper mill

(G-887)
CLYDE WOODWARD JR
51 Lake Ln (39429-9128)
PHONE..................................601 736-6115
Clyde Woodward, Principal
EMP: 5
SALES (est): 368.9K Privately Held
SIC: 3822 Auto controls regulating residntl & coml environmt & applncs

(G-888)
COLUMBIA COMPUTERS INC
1574 Highway 98 E (39429-8186)
PHONE..................................601 736-2204
Jeff Sloan, President
Randi Sloan, Vice Pres
EMP: 7 EST: 1994
SALES (est): 1.2MM Privately Held
WEB: www.columbiacomputers.com
SIC: 3571 Electronic computers

(G-889)
COLUMBIA MACHINE LLC
118a S High School Ave (39429-3410)
PHONE..................................601 441-7755
Stacy E Bozeman,
EMP: 1
SALES (est): 51.7K Privately Held
SIC: 3599 Machine shop, jobbing & repair

2019 Harris Directory of
Mississippi Manufacturers

▲ = Import ▼=Export
◆ =Import/Export

GEOGRAPHIC SECTION

Columbia - Marion County (G-920)

(G-890)
COLUMBIA WELDING & CNSTR
1278 Highway 98 Byp (39429-3703)
P.O. Box 8 (39429-0008)
PHONE....................................601 736-4332
Dan Pace, *President*
Sherman Pounds, *CFO*
EMP: 15
SQ FT: 1,600
SALES (est): 1MM **Privately Held**
WEB: www.columbiawelding.com
SIC: 7692 5084 Welding repair; welding machinery & equipment

(G-891)
COPY WRITE PRINTING INC
708 1/2 Main St (39429-2938)
PHONE....................................601 736-2679
Terry Philips, *President*
EMP: 4
SQ FT: 2,500
SALES (est): 437.2K **Privately Held**
SIC: 2752 5943 Commercial printing, lithographic; office forms & supplies

(G-892)
CRISCO SWABBING SERVICE INC
5 Stanley Barnes Ln (39429-8606)
P.O. Box 169 (39429-0169)
PHONE....................................601 731-9008
David L Parker, *President*
Koby Herring, *Vice Pres*
Joyce Parker, *Vice Pres*
Sonya McRaney, *Admin Sec*
Kathy Smith, *Admin Sec*
EMP: 31
SQ FT: 361
SALES (est): 3.1MM **Privately Held**
SIC: 1389 Oil & gas wells: building, repairing & dismantling; oil field services

(G-893)
DAVIS WELDING FABRICATION LLC
26 Seaman Bullock Rd (39429-6466)
PHONE....................................662 614-2531
EMP: 1
SALES (est): 25K **Privately Held**
SIC: 7692 Welding repair

(G-894)
DEEPWELL ENERGY SERVICES LLC (PA)
4025 Highway 35 N (39429-8763)
P.O. Box 31, Waynesboro (39367-0031)
PHONE....................................800 477-2855
Douglas Blackwell, *President*
Terry Thornton, *Corp Secy*
EMP: 63 EST: 2014
SALES (est): 231.6MM **Privately Held**
SIC: 1381 Drilling oil & gas wells

(G-895)
DIXIE MAT AND HARDWOOD CO (PA)
Also Called: Yak Mat
2438 Highway 98 E (39429-8056)
PHONE....................................601 876-2427
Jonathan Jones, *President*
Jonathan Duhon, *Corp Secy*
Lisa Jones, *Corp Secy*
Bret Jones, *Vice Pres*
Jeremy Jones, *Vice Pres*
EMP: 50
SQ FT: 5,000
SALES (est): 17.7MM **Privately Held**
WEB: www.dixiemat.com
SIC: 2448 2426 Wood pallets & skids; hardwood dimension & flooring mills

(G-896)
DIXIE OILFIELD SERVICES INC
16 Robbins Loop (39429-7813)
PHONE....................................601 731-5541
Tejay Brady, *Partner*
EMP: 2
SALES (est): 146.1K **Privately Held**
SIC: 1389 Oil field services

(G-897)
DUNNS WOODWORKING LLC
489 Enon Rd (39429-8007)
PHONE....................................601 736-0633
Terry Dunn, *Principal*

EMP: 2
SQ FT: 65.4K **Privately Held**
SIC: 2431 Millwork

(G-898)
EXTERRAN
60 Columbia Purvis Rd (39429-9107)
PHONE....................................601 444-0055
Bryan Harris, *Manager*
EMP: 2
SALES (est): 154.3K **Privately Held**
SIC: 1311 Gas & hydrocarbon liquefaction from coal

(G-899)
GAS PROCESSORS INC
21 Wesley Rd (39429-9648)
P.O. Box 683 (39429-0683)
PHONE....................................601 736-1600
Greg Robbins, *President*
Vicki Pittman, *General Mgr*
David Parson, *Corp Secy*
Dennis Little, *Vice Pres*
Vicki Laird, *Bookkeeper*
EMP: 18
SALES (est): 5.2MM **Privately Held**
SIC: 1311 Crude petroleum & natural gas production

(G-900)
GEORGIA-PACIFIC LLC
3111 Highway 13 N (39429-8505)
P.O. Box 555, Taylorsville (39168-0555)
PHONE....................................601 785-4721
Rickey Bryant, *Production*
Glenn Lott, *Manager*
EMP: 125
SALES (corp-wide): 40.9B **Privately Held**
WEB: www.gp.com
SIC: 5031 2426 2421 Building materials, exterior; hardwood dimension & flooring mills; sawmills & planing mills, general
HQ: Georgia-Pacific Llc
133 Peachtree St Nw
Atlanta GA 30303
404 652-4000

(G-901)
INTREPID DRILLING LLC
320 Second St (39429-2954)
PHONE....................................601 731-1010
William E Simmons III, *Mng Member*
Bill Simmons, *Manager*
Richard Thomas, *Manager*
Vernon L Hux,
Max E Maxwell,
EMP: 7
SALES (est): 1.5MM **Privately Held**
SIC: 1382 Oil & gas exploration services

(G-902)
KENS WELDING SHOP INC
118 S High School Ave (39429-3410)
P.O. Box 588 (39429-0588)
PHONE....................................601 736-4136
Kenneth Morgan, *President*
EMP: 3
SALES (est): 230K **Privately Held**
SIC: 7692 1799 Welding repair; welding on site

(G-903)
LISA HIBLEY
1452 Highway 98 E (39429-8103)
PHONE....................................601 736-6781
Lisa Hibley, *Owner*
EMP: 11
SQ FT: 18,000
SALES (est): 250K **Privately Held**
SIC: 2099 Food preparations

(G-904)
MACHINE SHOP INC
8 Airport Rd (39429-7946)
PHONE....................................601 736-4729
Bobby Ball, *Owner*
EMP: 2
SALES (est): 199.2K **Privately Held**
SIC: 3599 Machine shop, jobbing & repair

(G-905)
MARION PUBLISHING CO INC
Also Called: Columbia Progress
318 Second St (39429-2954)
PHONE....................................601 736-2611
Wyatt Emerich, *President*

EMP: 15
SQ FT: 3,660
SALES: 800K **Privately Held**
WEB: www.columbianprogress.com
SIC: 2711 Newspapers: publishing only, not printed on site

(G-906)
MICHAEL WILLIAMSON
Also Called: Mike's Service Center
3215 Highway 13 N (39429-8507)
PHONE....................................601 736-9156
Michael Williamson, *Owner*
EMP: 1
SQ FT: 2,500
SALES: 250K **Privately Held**
SIC: 7699 3546 Lawn mower repair shop; saws & sawing equipment

(G-907)
MIKE STRINGER SIGNS
21 Airport Rd (39429-7939)
PHONE....................................601 736-8600
Mike Stringer, *Owner*
EMP: 2
SALES: 110K **Privately Held**
SIC: 3993 5999 Signs & advertising specialties; banners

(G-908)
ODAT ENERGY LLC
919 High School Ave (39429-2747)
PHONE....................................601 736-0227
Elizabeth Pierce, *Principal*
EMP: 1 EST: 2000
SALES (est): 47.8K **Privately Held**
SIC: 1389 Oil & gas field services

(G-909)
OILFIELD PARTNERS ENERGY
Also Called: Oilfield Partners Leasing
481 Highway 98 Byp (39429-8217)
PHONE....................................601 444-0220
EMP: 6
SALES (est): 518.5K **Privately Held**
SIC: 1389 Oil field services

(G-910)
PACE BROTHERS INC
1278 Highway 98 E (39429-8101)
P.O. Box 8 (39429-0008)
PHONE....................................601 736-9225
EMP: 8
SQ FT: 600
SALES: 3MM **Privately Held**
SIC: 3531 8711 Mfg Construction Machinery Engineering Services

(G-911)
PINE BELT GAS INC
47 Pine Ln (39429-9423)
PHONE....................................601 731-1144
Steven Stringer, *President*
Jason Stringer, *Vice Pres*
EMP: 7
SQ FT: 280
SALES: 1.4MM **Privately Held**
SIC: 1321 7389 Propane (natural) production;

(G-912)
PIONEER AEROSPACE CORPORATION
1 Pioneer Dr (39429-2703)
PHONE....................................601 736-4511
Chris Powell, *Site Mgr*
Patricia Johnson, *Human Res Mgr*
Mark Moody, *Property Mgr*
Christopher Powell, *Manager*
EMP: 219
SALES (corp-wide): 833.4MM **Privately Held**
WEB: www.pioneeraero.com
SIC: 2399 5088 Parachutes; aircraft equipment & supplies
HQ: Pioneer Aerospace Corporation
45 S Satellite Rd Ste 2
South Windsor CT 06074
860 528-0092

(G-913)
QUALITY STEEL & SUPPLY LLC
2171 Highway 98 E (39429-8096)
PHONE....................................601 731-1222
Kenney R Breakfield, *Mng Member*
Kenneth R Breakfield, *Mng Member*

EMP: 10
SQ FT: 6,000
SALES (est): 1MM **Privately Held**
SIC: 3493 Steel springs, except wire

(G-914)
QUALITY WLDG & FABRICATION INC
Also Called: Quality Manufacturing Group
2171 Highway 98 E (39429-8096)
PHONE....................................601 731-1222
Kenneth R Breakfield, *President*
Natasha Baughman, *Vice Pres*
Maureen R Breakfield, *Vice Pres*
Melissa Jones, *Vice Pres*
◆ **EMP:** 83
SQ FT: 30,000
SALES (est): 24MM **Privately Held**
SIC: 3441 7692 3795 Fabricated structural metal; welding repair; tanks & tank components

(G-915)
R AND B WELDING LLC
197 Sanders Rd (39429-8075)
PHONE....................................601 441-4398
Raymond Barber, *Principal*
EMP: 1
SALES (est): 57.8K **Privately Held**
SIC: 7692 Welding repair

(G-916)
R D GRAPHIX SIGN SOLUTIONS
708 Main St (39429-2938)
PHONE....................................601 736-0663
Eddie Dement, *Principal*
EMP: 1
SALES (est): 105K **Privately Held**
SIC: 3993 Signs & advertising specialties

(G-917)
RADCO FISHING & RENTAL TLS INC
86 Pierce Ln (39429-8136)
P.O. Box 2607, Laurel (39442-2607)
PHONE....................................601 736-8580
EMP: 5
SALES: 1.2MM **Privately Held**
SIC: 7359 1389 Equipment Rental/Leasing Oil/Gas Field Services

(G-918)
RELEVANT DESIGN STUDIOS LLC
907 Main St (39429-2749)
PHONE....................................601 736-0663
Troy Ingram, *President*
EMP: 1
SQ FT: 4,500
SALES (est): 109.9K **Privately Held**
SIC: 7371 8742 8748 3993 Computer software development & applications; management consulting services; business consulting; advertising artwork

(G-919)
ROGERS LUMBER CORP (PA)
8330 Old Hwy 90 (39429)
P.O. Box 48 (39429-0048)
PHONE....................................601 736-4472
Charles L Rogers, *CEO*
Charles L Rogers Jr, *President*
EMP: 40
SQ FT: 1,500
SALES (est): 6.4MM **Privately Held**
SIC: 2421 Sawmills & planing mills, general

(G-920)
ROGERS LUMBER CORP
Also Called: Rogers Lumber 2
1120 Highway 13 S (39429)
PHONE....................................601 736-4472
Charles Rogers, *Manager*
EMP: 33
SALES (corp-wide): 6.4MM **Privately Held**
SIC: 2421 5031 Sawmills & planing mills, general; lumber: rough, dressed & finished
PA: Rogers Lumber Corp
8330 Old Hwy 90
Columbia MS 39429
601 736-4472

(PA)=Parent Co (HQ)=Headquarters (DH)=Div Headquarters
✪ = New Business established in last 2 years

2019 Harris Directory of
Mississippi Manufacturers

Columbia - Marion County (G-921)　　　　　　　　　　　　　　　　　　　　GEOGRAPHIC SECTION

(G-921)
SAFRAN USA INC
1 Pioneer Dr (39429-2703)
PHONE.....................................601 736-4511
EMP: 2
SALES (corp-wide): 833.4MM **Privately Held**
SIC: 3643 Current-carrying wiring devices
HQ: Safran Usa, Inc.
　700 S Washington St # 320
　Alexandria VA 22314
　703 351-9898

(G-922)
SOUTHERN ROOST GAME CALLS
3007 Highway 13 N (39429-8641)
PHONE.....................................601 441-0748
Josh Robertson, *Principal*
EMP: 1
SALES (est): 47K **Privately Held**
SIC: 3949 Game calls

(G-923)
ST JAMES LIGHTING LLC
1491 Highway 13 N (39429-2049)
PHONE.....................................601 444-4966
Jim Ragan,
▲ EMP: 5
SALES (est): 1.1MM **Privately Held**
SIC: 3648 Lighting fixtures, except electric:
　residential

(G-924)
STRINGERS OILFIELD SERVICE
1320 Highway 13 N (39429-2018)
P.O. Box 471 (39429-0471)
PHONE.....................................601 736-4498
Johnnie C Stringer, *President*
Peggy Stringer, *Corp Secy*
EMP: 43
SQ FT: 3,500
SALES (est): 6.4MM **Privately Held**
SIC: 1389 1382 Oil field services; oil &
　gas exploration services

(G-925)
T K STANLEY INC (PA)
4025 Highway 35 N (39429-8763)
PHONE.....................................601 735-2855
Steve Farrar, *President*
Woody Farrar, *Corp Secy*
Dennis Irle, *Foreman/Supr*
Jeremy Harrison, *CFO*
Christy Smith, *Accounting Dir*
EMP: 250
SQ FT: 3,000
SALES (est): 590MM **Privately Held**
WEB: www.tkstanley.com
SIC: 1389 Oil & gas wells: building, repair-
　ing & dismantling; oil field services

(G-926)
TRIPLE S WELL SERVICE INC
1798 Highway 98 E (39429-8042)
P.O. Box 625 (39429-0625)
PHONE.....................................601 736-8804
Tim Singley, *President*
EMP: 12
SQ FT: 2,000
SALES: 3MM **Privately Held**
SIC: 1389 1382 Servicing oil & gas wells;
　oil & gas exploration services

(G-927)
TWI INC
Also Called: Columbia Diesel Castings
1256 Highway 98 E (39429-8101)
PHONE.....................................601 736-1783
Tommy Woodward, *President*
EMP: 9
SQ FT: 14,200
SALES (est): 1.4MM **Privately Held**
SIC: 3599 3519 Machine shop, jobbing &
　repair; diesel engine rebuilding

(G-928)
WILLIAMSON & SON LOGGING LLC
317 W Reservoir Rd (39429-8554)
PHONE.....................................601 736-7858
Sandra Branch, *Bd of Directors*
EMP: 3
SALES (est): 257.5K **Privately Held**
SIC: 2411 Logging

┌─────────────────────────┐
│ **Columbus**   │
│ *Lowndes County*   │
└─────────────────────────┘

(G-929)
24 HOUR NEWS LINE
516 Main St (39701-5734)
PHONE.....................................662 241-5000
Birney Imes, *Principal*
EMP: 1
SALES (est): 60.7K **Privately Held**
SIC: 2711 Newspapers

(G-930)
ABB MOTORS AND MECHANICAL INC
Also Called: Manufacturing Plant
70 Indstrial Pk Access Rd (39701)
P.O. Box 2443 (39704-2443)
PHONE.....................................662 328-9116
Gary Beatty, *Branch Mgr*
EMP: 27
SALES (corp-wide): 36.4B **Privately Held**
WEB: www.baldor.com
SIC: 3621 3594 5063 Motors, electric;
　fluid power pumps & motors; motors,
　electric
HQ: Abb Motors And Mechanical Inc.
　5711 Rs Boreham Jr St
　Fort Smith AR 72901
　479 646-4711

(G-931)
ABILITY WORKS INC
Also Called: Abilityworks of Columbus
48 Datco Ind Dr (39702-9498)
PHONE.....................................662 328-0275
Stan Wheeler, *Branch Mgr*
EMP: 2
SALES (corp-wide): 9.6MM **Privately Held**
SIC: 8331 3949 3081 2653 Job training
　& vocational rehabilitation services; sport-
　ing & athletic goods; unsupported plastics
　film & sheet; corrugated & solid fiber
　boxes; pleating & stitching
PA: Ability Works, Inc.
　1281 Highway 51
　Madison MS 39110
　601 853-5100

(G-932)
AERO-RAD TECH LLC
2305c Highway 45 N (39705-1718)
PHONE.....................................662 328-0155
Roman Sereda,
EMP: 2
SALES (est): 184.3K **Privately Held**
SIC: 3728 Aircraft parts & equipment

(G-933)
AIRBUS HELICOPTERS INC
1782 Airport Rd (39701-9663)
PHONE.....................................662 327-6226
Rick Humphries, *Opers Mgr*
Alvin Urton, *Production*
Mike Molle, *Sales Staff*
Fred Gerard, *Manager*
Earl Walker, *Director*
EMP: 25
SALES (corp-wide): 72.9B **Privately Held**
SIC: 3721 Aircraft
HQ: Airbus Helicopters, Inc.
　2701 N Forum Dr
　Grand Prairie TX 75052
　972 641-0000

(G-934)
AMERICAN SPECIALTY ALLOYS
70 Wilcut Block Rd (39701)
P.O. Box 8430 (39705-0010)
PHONE.....................................662 368-1332
Roger D Boggs, *CEO*
Mike Davis, *CFO*
George Riel, *Marketing Staff*
EMP: 20
SQ FT: 60,000
SALES (est): 3.6MM **Privately Held**
SIC: 3353 Coils, sheet aluminum

(G-935)
ANDREWS CABINET SHOP
400 William Roberts Rd (39702-8155)
PHONE.....................................662 327-1070

William Andrews, *Owner*
EMP: 1
SALES (est): 140.1K **Privately Held**
SIC: 2434 1751 Wood kitchen cabinets;
　cabinet & finish carpentry

(G-936)
APAC-MISSISSIPPI INC
462 Lake Norris Rd (39701-7803)
P.O. Box 1388 (39703-1388)
PHONE.....................................662 328-6555
Michael W Bogue, *General Mgr*
EMP: 80
SALES (corp-wide): 30.6B **Privately Held**
SIC: 1611 2951 1442 General contractor,
　highway & street construction; asphalt
　paving mixtures & blocks; construction
　sand & gravel
HQ: Apac-Mississippi, Inc.
　101 Riverview Dr
　Richland MS 39218
　601 376-4000

(G-937)
ASSOCIATED ARCHITECTURAL PDTS
1813 8th Ave S (39701-7124)
PHONE.....................................662 245-0400
Lane Long, *Controller*
Richard Ferguson, *Branch Mgr*
EMP: 14 **Privately Held**
SIC: 2434 Wood kitchen cabinets
PA: Associated Architectural Products Inc
　129 Associated Ln
　Brandon MS 39047

(G-938)
AURORA FLIGHT SCIENCES CORP
200 Aurora Way (39701-9670)
PHONE.....................................662 328-8227
Greg Stewart, *Manager*
EMP: 16
SALES (corp-wide): 101.1B **Publicly Held**
SIC: 3721 Research & development on air-
　craft by the manufacturer
HQ: Aurora Flight Sciences Corp
　9950 Wakeman Dr
　Manassas VA 20110
　703 369-3633

(G-939)
BDM INDUSTRIAL SERVICES LLC
1235 Highway 373 (39705-8228)
PHONE.....................................662 549-3055
Bbooy McCullough, *President*
Bobby D McCullough, *Principal*
EMP: 5
SALES (est): 236.1K **Privately Held**
SIC: 3471 Sand blasting of metal parts

(G-940)
BLES CAR CARE
2305c Highway 45 N (39705-1718)
PHONE.....................................770 292-0021
Sidney Williams, *Principal*
EMP: 10
SQ FT: 2,200
SALES (est): 374.7K **Privately Held**
SIC: 3714 Radiators & radiator shells &
　cores, motor vehicle

(G-941)
BORDEN DAIRY COMPANY ALA LLC
Also Called: Dairy Fresh
85 Port Access Rd (39701)
PHONE.....................................662 328-8755
Tommy Richardson, *Branch Mgr*
EMP: 12
SQ FT: 20,000 **Privately Held**
WEB: www.dairyfreshcorp.com
SIC: 2026 5143 Fluid milk; dairy products,
　except dried or canned
HQ: Borden Dairy Company Of Alabama,
　Llc
　7572 U S Highway 49
　Hattiesburg MS 39402
　251 456-3381

(G-942)
BTM SOLUTIONS
572 Yorkville Rd E (39702-9632)
PHONE.....................................662 328-2400
Tim Beckett, *President*
Helen Stuart, *Vice Pres*
Keith Mullenix, *Project Mgr*
Dow Ford, *Manager*
EMP: 14 EST: 1998
SALES (est): 487.1K **Privately Held**
WEB: www.btmsolutions.com
SIC: 7372 Business oriented computer
　software

(G-943)
BURFORD ELECTRIC SERVICE INC
154 Cooper Rd (39702-7203)
P.O. Box 2387 (39704-2387)
PHONE.....................................662 328-5679
Kenneth R Robinson, *President*
Jonathan Robinson, *COO*
Margaret B Robinson, *Vice Pres*
Todd Jordan, *Safety Mgr*
Alex Kolassa, *Engineer*
EMP: 25 EST: 1962
SQ FT: 45,000
SALES (est): 7.8MM **Privately Held**
WEB: www.burfordinc.com
SIC: 7694 5063 5999 Electric motor re-
　pair; motors, electric; motors, electric

(G-944)
C AND P PRINTING COMPANY INC
104 Gardner Blvd (39702-5278)
PHONE.....................................662 327-9742
Dewey Petigo, *President*
Patty Petigo, *Treasurer*
EMP: 4
SQ FT: 4,200
SALES (est): 486.1K **Privately Held**
SIC: 2752 Commercial printing, offset

(G-945)
C F E N
1514 Bell Ave (39701-5953)
PHONE.....................................662 327-0031
EMP: 1
SALES (est): 57K **Privately Held**
SIC: 2759 Commercial Printing

(G-946)
CHAINS LOGGING
1800 Spurlock Rd (39702-7290)
PHONE.....................................662 327-8240
Anthony Chain, *Partner*
James Chain, *Partner*
EMP: 4
SALES (est): 497.8K **Privately Held**
SIC: 2411 Logging camps & contractors

(G-947)
CHISM RACKARD ENTERPRISES LLC
Also Called: UPS
909 Alabama St (39702-5570)
PHONE.....................................662 327-5200
Fax: 662 327-5090
EMP: 2
SALES (est): 190K **Privately Held**
SIC: 8611 3993 Business Association Mfg
　Signs/Advertising Specialties

(G-948)
CHROME DEPOSIT CORPORATION
1949 Airport Rd (39701-9526)
PHONE.....................................662 798-4149
Gary Swinford, *President*
EMP: 20
SALES (corp-wide): 22.6MM **Privately Held**
SIC: 3312 Blast furnaces & steel mills
PA: Chrome Deposit Corporation
　6640 Melton Rd
　Portage IN 46368
　219 763-1571

(G-949)
COLUMBUS BRICK COMPANY
114 Brickyard Rd (39701-5200)
P.O. Box 9630 (39705-0021)
PHONE.....................................662 328-4931
Allen B Puckett, *President*

2019 Harris Directory of
Mississippi Manufacturers

▲ = Import ▼=Export
◆ =Import/Export

GEOGRAPHIC SECTION

Columbus - Lowndes County (G-977)

Ed Thebaud, *General Mgr*
Jim Powers, *Plant Mgr*
Nigel Hough, *Engineer*
Quintin Hensley, *CFO*
▲ EMP: 50 EST: 1890
SQ FT: 4,000
SALES (est): 6.7MM **Privately Held**
SIC: 3251 Brick & structural clay tile

(G-950)
COLUMBUS MARBLE WORKS INC (PA)
2415 Highway 45 N (39705-1319)
PHONE.................................662 328-1477
R L Edmonson Jr, *President*
Hunter Gholson, *Admin Sec*
▲ EMP: 45 EST: 1800
SQ FT: 145,000
SALES (est): 7.9MM **Privately Held**
SIC: 2752 3281 3469 Commercial printing, lithographic; monument or burial stone, cut & shaped; metal stampings

(G-951)
COLUMBUS MCH & WLDG WORKS INC
Also Called: Columbus Machine & Wldg Works
807 Moss St (39701-2775)
P.O. Box 2403 (39704-2403)
PHONE.................................662 328-8473
Hank Gunter, *President*
Henry H Gunter III, *President*
Jerry Reynolds, *General Mgr*
Gina Handley, *Info Tech Mgr*
Becky Gunter, *Admin Sec*
EMP: 23
SQ FT: 12,000
SALES (est): 3.3MM **Privately Held**
WEB: www.col-mnw.com
SIC: 7692 3599 3441 Welding repair; machine shop, jobbing & repair; fabricated structural metal

(G-952)
COLUMBUS ROLL SHOP
1945 Airport Rd (39701-9526)
P.O. Box 111 (39703-0111)
PHONE.................................662 798-4149
Gary Swinford, *Principal*
EMP: 36
SALES (est): 3.4MM **Privately Held**
SIC: 3471 Plating & polishing

(G-953)
COLUMBUS SCRAP MATERIAL CO (HQ)
Also Called: Columbus Recycling
973 Island Rd (39701-8785)
P.O. Box 8670 (39705-0012)
PHONE.................................662 328-8176
Greg Rader, *President*
Debbie Daffron, *Office Mgr*
Amos Schrock, *Manager*
EMP: 25 EST: 1956
SQ FT: 2,000
SALES (est): 9MM
SALES (corp-wide): 44MM **Privately Held**
SIC: 5093 4953 3341 Junk & scrap; refuse systems; secondary nonferrous metals
PA: Trivest Partners, L.P.
550 S Dixie Hwy Ste 300
Coral Gables FL 33146
305 858-2200

(G-954)
COLUMBUS SPEEDWAY
2616 Tabernacle Rd (39702-8745)
PHONE.................................662 327-3047
EMP: 1
SALES (est): 140.4K **Privately Held**
SIC: 3644 Raceways

(G-955)
COMMERCIAL DISPATCH PUBG INC
516 Main St (39701-5734)
P.O. Box 511 (39703-0511)
PHONE.................................662 328-2424
V Birney Imes Jr, *President*
EMP: 75 EST: 1920
SQ FT: 24,000

SALES (est): 4.9MM **Privately Held**
WEB: www.cdispatch.com
SIC: 2711 Commercial printing & newspaper publishing combined; newspapers, publishing & printing

(G-956)
CREATIVE DESIGNS & SPORTS
2405 Highway 45 N (39705-1319)
P.O. Box 9444 (39705-0019)
PHONE.................................662 327-5000
Ronald O Richardson, *Owner*
EMP: 4
SQ FT: 7,500
SALES: 70K **Privately Held**
SIC: 2759 5699 2395 5941 Screen printing; sports apparel; embroidery & art needlework; sporting goods & bicycle shops; graphic arts & related design

(G-957)
CUSTOM SIGNS AND BANNERS
Also Called: JM Signs
240 Thomas Cir (39705-2864)
PHONE.................................662 327-8916
Suzanne Thomas, *Partner*
John Thomas, *Partner*
EMP: 2
SALES: 90K **Privately Held**
SIC: 2678 Stationery products

(G-958)
DALE FULTON
Also Called: Fix-Itshoppe , The
100 23rd St S (39701-6002)
PHONE.................................662 327-4800
Dale Fulton, *Owner*
EMP: 7
SQ FT: 8,500
SALES (est): 75K **Privately Held**
WEB: www.thefix-itshoppe.com
SIC: 7629 7389 3699 Electronic equipment repair; swimming pool & hot tub service & maintenance; security devices

(G-959)
DATCO INTERNATIONAL INC (PA)
15 Datco Ind Dr (39702-9742)
P.O. Box 2466 (39704-2466)
PHONE.................................248 593-9142
Ingrid Wolf, *President*
Hilary Borman, *Manager*
▲ EMP: 10
SALES (est): 2.9MM **Privately Held**
SIC: 2399 Aprons, breast (harness)

(G-960)
DATCO INTERNATIONAL INC
15 Datco Ind Dr (39702-9742)
P.O. Box 2466 (39704-2466)
PHONE.................................662 327-3995
Billy Jenkins, *Manager*
EMP: 14
SALES (est): 1MM
SALES (corp-wide): 2.9MM **Privately Held**
SIC: 2399 Aprons, breast (harness)
PA: Datco International, Inc.
15 Datco Ind Dr
Columbus MS 39702
248 593-9142

(G-961)
DC LOGGING LLC
Also Called: DC Logging
2102 Golding Rd (39702-8594)
PHONE.................................662 251-4653
EMP: 3 EST: 2013
SALES (est): 98.8K **Privately Held**
SIC: 2411 Logging

(G-962)
DILLARD MACHINING SERVICE
1023 N Lehmberg Rd (39702-3215)
P.O. Box 2553 (39704-2553)
PHONE.................................662 329-4682
Jim Dillard, *Owner*
EMP: 14
SQ FT: 5,000
SALES (est): 900K **Privately Held**
SIC: 3599 5051 1799 Machine shop, jobbing & repair; metals service centers & offices; welding on site

(G-963)
DLA DOCUMENT SERVICES
469 C St Rm 1 (39710-5000)
PHONE.................................662 434-7303
Cindy Rerby, *Branch Mgr*
EMP: 2 **Publicly Held**
SIC: 2752 9711 Commercial printing, lithographic; national security;
HQ: Dla Document Services
5450 Carlisle Pike Bldg 9
Mechanicsburg PA 17050
717 605-2362

(G-964)
DOMTAR PAPER COMPANY LLC
9620 Old Macon Rd (39701)
P.O. Box 1830 (39703-1830)
PHONE.................................662 256-3526
Kent Walker, *Vice Pres*
EMP: 157
SALES (corp-wide): 301.1MM **Privately Held**
SIC: 2421 2672 2621 2611 Sawmills & planing mills, general; coated & laminated paper; paper mills; pulp mills
HQ: Domtar Paper Company, Llc
234 Kingsley Park Dr
Fort Mill SC 29715

(G-965)
EAST SYSTEMS INC
41 Fabritek Dr (39702-7067)
PHONE.................................662 244-7070
George East, *President*
Judy East, *Vice Pres*
EMP: 6
SQ FT: 14,000
SALES (est): 1MM **Privately Held**
SIC: 3599 Amusement park equipment

(G-966)
ECOLAB INC
70 Wilcutt (39705-9623)
PHONE.................................662 327-1863
EMP: 3
SALES (corp-wide): 14.6B **Publicly Held**
SIC: 2841 Soap & other detergents
PA: Ecolab Inc.
1 Ecolab Pl
Saint Paul MN 55102
800 232-6522

(G-967)
ED DANGERFIELD CONST MILLWRKS
Also Called: Ed Dangerfield Cnstr Mfg
1090 Matson Rd (39705-9134)
PHONE.................................662 328-3877
Ed Dangerfield, *Owner*
EMP: 2 EST: 1982
SALES (est): 189.1K **Privately Held**
SIC: 2521 2449 1521 Cabinets, office: wood; shipping cases & drums, wood: wirebound & plywood; general remodeling, single-family houses

(G-968)
EKO PEROXIDE LLC
4374 Nashville Ferry Rd E (39702-7479)
PHONE.................................662 240-8571
Tim Cunningham, *CEO*
Paul Francese,
Michel Grugoire,
Malcolm Williamson,
◆ EMP: 4
SALES: 200K
SALES (corp-wide): 11.3B **Privately Held**
SIC: 2819 Peroxides, hydrogen peroxide
PA: Akzo Nobel N.V.
Christian Neefestraat 2
Amsterdam
889 697-555

(G-969)
ELECTRIC MOTOR SALES & SVC INC
232 Alabama St (39702-5204)
P.O. Box 2225 (39704-2225)
PHONE.................................662 327-1606
Michael Todd Davis, *President*
Todd Davis, *General Mgr*
Geraldine Davis, *Corp Secy*
Nettie Murrah, *Sales Staff*
Charlie Studdard, *Sales Associate*
EMP: 25

SQ FT: 40,000
SALES (est): 7.1MM **Privately Held**
WEB: www.emsonline.com
SIC: 7694 5063 Electric motor repair; motors, electric

(G-970)
ELLIS WOODWORKS
724 N Lehmberg Rd (39702-4308)
P.O. Box 5093 (39704-5093)
PHONE.................................662 329-2605
Wayne Ellis, *Owner*
EMP: 6
SALES: 300K **Privately Held**
SIC: 2434 Wood kitchen cabinets

(G-971)
EXPRESS LINE
3920 Highway 45 N (39705-1724)
PHONE.................................662 328-3720
EMP: 5
SALES (est): 461.3K **Privately Held**
SIC: 3578 Automatic teller machines (ATM)

(G-972)
F S C INC
Also Called: Graham Fabrics and Supply
7395 Highway 45 N (39705-3314)
P.O. Box 8190 (39705-0008)
PHONE.................................662 434-0025
Fred Chappell, *President*
Sue Chappell, *Exec VP*
EMP: 9
SQ FT: 15,000
SALES (est): 2.4MM **Privately Held**
SIC: 5131 2391 2394 Upholstery fabrics, woven; curtains, window: made from purchased materials; liners & covers, fabric: made from purchased materials

(G-973)
FACILITIES OUTFITTERS
2387 Jess Lyons Rd (39705-8819)
PHONE.................................662 328-1977
Martha Blanton, *Owner*
EMP: 2
SALES (est): 133.4K **Privately Held**
SIC: 2531 Public building & related furniture

(G-974)
FAST DOG PRINT CO
1925 Highway 45 N (39705-1950)
PHONE.................................662 549-4450
Kelly Ervin, *Principal*
EMP: 2 EST: 2016
SALES (est): 92.3K **Privately Held**
SIC: 2752 Commercial printing, lithographic

(G-975)
FLORENCE PARKER
Also Called: Parker Construction Materials
399 Barton Ferry Rd (39705-9371)
PHONE.................................662 434-8555
Florence Parker, *Owner*
EMP: 7
SALES (est): 1.2MM **Privately Held**
WEB: www.florencekofc.org
SIC: 1442 Construction sand & gravel

(G-976)
FLOWERS BKG CO THOMASVILLE LLC
2168 Highway 69 S (39702-7361)
P.O. Box 1458, Tuscaloosa AL (35403-1458)
PHONE.................................662 245-1188
Tim Newton, *Manager*
EMP: 1
SALES (corp-wide): 3.9B **Publicly Held**
SIC: 2051 Bread, cake & related products
HQ: Flowers Baking Co Of Thomasville Llc
300 S Madison St
Thomasville GA 31792
229 226-5331

(G-977)
FUTURE TEK INC
663 S Frontage Rd (39701-8653)
PHONE.................................662 328-0900
Kim Brock, *President*
Heather Bumgarner, *Corp Secy*
Lee Trent, *Plant Supt*
Hallman John, *Sales Staff*
Eugene Kimble, *Sales Staff*

(PA)=Parent Co (HQ)=Headquarters (DH)=Div Headquarters
✿ = New Business established in last 2 years

2019 Harris Directory of
Mississippi Manufacturers

43

Columbus - Lowndes County (G-978)

GEOGRAPHIC SECTION

EMP: 9
SQ FT: 9,000
SALES (est): 1.5MM **Privately Held**
WEB: www.futuretekinc.com
SIC: 3674 Computer logic modules

(G-978)
GLENN MACHINE WORKS INC (PA)
734 Highway 45 S (39701-8618)
P.O. Box 1247 (39703-1247)
PHONE..................................662 328-4611
Toll Free:......................................888 -
Christopher L Glenn, *President*
James A Glenn, *Corp Secy*
Lisa Burchfield, *COO*
Chris Glenn, *VP Opers*
Bryan Carr, *Project Mgr*
EMP: 25 EST: 1946
SALES (est): 19MM **Privately Held**
WEB: www.glennmachineworks.com
SIC: 3599 5085 7359 Machine shop, jobbing & repair; mill supplies; equipment rental & leasing

(G-979)
GOLDEN TRIANGE READY MIX INC
4061 Highway 50 E (39702-9542)
P.O. Box 2536 (39704-2536)
PHONE..................................662 328-0153
Ronald Davis, *President*
EMP: 14
SQ FT: 700
SALES: 1MM **Privately Held**
SIC: 3273 Ready-mixed concrete

(G-980)
GOOD NEWS INDUSTRIES INC
207 Winchester Dr (39705-3244)
PHONE..................................662 327-1988
EMP: 2
SALES (est): 7.7K **Privately Held**
SIC: 3999 Manufacturing industries

(G-981)
GRASSROOTS A NATURAL CO LLC
118 5th St N (39701-4522)
PHONE..................................662 601-8808
Christopher Lick, *Principal*
EMP: 2 EST: 2013
SALES (est): 119.8K **Privately Held**
SIC: 3999 Candles

(G-982)
H & H MACHINE SHOP
1913 Washington Ave (39701-6153)
PHONE..................................662 386-0778
EMP: 2
SALES (est): 81.4K **Privately Held**
SIC: 3599 Machine shop, jobbing & repair

(G-983)
HALFTONE PRESS LLC
129 5th St N (39701-4521)
PHONE..................................662 251-5036
Lynlee Healy, *Principal*
EMP: 1
SALES (est): 37.5K **Privately Held**
SIC: 2741 Miscellaneous publishing

(G-984)
HOOP-IT-UP EMBROIDERY
486 Elm Dr (39701-8711)
PHONE..................................662 244-7212
Tim Ketterer, *Manager*
EMP: 1
SALES (est): 62.8K **Privately Held**
SIC: 2395 Embroidery & art needlework

(G-985)
HYDROGEN PEROXIDE
4374 Nashville Ferry Rd E (39702-7479)
PHONE..................................662 329-9085
EMP: 3 EST: 2013
SALES (est): 159.3K **Privately Held**
SIC: 2813 Hydrogen

(G-986)
IMES COMMUNICATIONS OF EL PASO
Also Called: Commercial Dispatch
516 Main St (39701-5734)
P.O. Box 511 (39703-0511)
PHONE..................................662 328-2424
Birney Imes III, *Principal*
EMP: 100
SQ FT: 3,000
SALES: 3.3MM **Privately Held**
WEB: www.commercialdispatch.com
SIC: 2711 Newspapers, publishing & printing

(G-987)
INDUSTRIAL FABRICATORS INC
274 Structural Ln (39702-9686)
PHONE..................................662 327-1776
Rusty House, *President*
Henry Weiss, *Vice Pres*
Philip Atkins, *Project Mgr*
Chris Johnson, *Executive*
EMP: 35 EST: 1966
SQ FT: 40,000
SALES: 10.3MM **Privately Held**
WEB: www.indfab.net
SIC: 3441 3444 3446 Building components, structural steel; sheet metalwork; architectural metalwork

(G-988)
INNOVEX INC
210 Lake Lowndes Rd (39702-8540)
PHONE..................................662 328-9537
Bob Brandon, *President*
EMP: 20
SQ FT: 50,000
SALES (est): 2.3MM **Privately Held**
SIC: 3599 2673 Machine & other job shop work; bags: plastic, laminated & coated

(G-989)
INTERNATIONAL PAPER COMPANY
4335 Carson Rd (39701)
PHONE..................................662 243-4000
EMP: 2
SALES (corp-wide): 23.3B **Publicly Held**
SIC: 2679 Adding machine rolls, paper: made from purchased material
PA: International Paper Company
6400 Poplar Ave
Memphis TN 38197
901 419-9000

(G-990)
JASON INDUSTRIES INC
Also Called: Janesville Acoustics
221 Fabritek Dr (39702-7005)
PHONE..................................662 327-0756
Mark Benedict, *Manager*
EMP: 75
SALES (corp-wide): 612.9MM **Publicly Held**
SIC: 2297 Bonded-fiber fabrics, except felt
PA: Jason Industries, Inc.
833 E Michigan St Ste 900
Milwaukee WI 53202
414 277-9300

(G-991)
JOHNSON WILEY
Also Called: B.B. Delivery Services
42 Johnson Rd (39702-7653)
PHONE..................................662 329-1495
Wiley Johnson, *Owner*
EMP: 2
SALES (est): 113K **Privately Held**
SIC: 5531 4213 2051 4215 Batteries, automotive & truck; less-than-truckload (LTL) transport; bakery, for home service delivery; package delivery, vehicular

(G-992)
JOHNSTON-TOMBIGBEE FURN MFG CO
Also Called: JTB FURNITURE
1402 Waterworks Rd (39701-2757)
P.O. Box 2128 (39704-2128)
PHONE..................................662 328-1685
J Reau Berry, *President*
Reau Berry, *President*
Duke Berry, *COO*
Kelli Caldwell Berry, *Vice Pres*

Judy P Griffith, *CFO*
EMP: 200
SQ FT: 1,000,000
SALES: 25.3MM
SALES (corp-wide): 31.8MM **Privately Held**
WEB: www.jtbfurniture.com
SIC: 2511 Wood household furniture
PA: Lounora Industries, Inc.
1402 Waterworks Rd
Columbus MS 39701
662 328-1685

(G-993)
KING B SIGNS AND WONDERS INC
677 Golding Cir (39702-8593)
PHONE..................................815 263-1546
EMP: 2 EST: 2013
SALES (est): 84K **Privately Held**
SIC: 3993 Signs & advertising specialties

(G-994)
LOUNORA INDUSTRIES INC (PA)
Also Called: Jtb Furniture
1402 Waterworks Rd (39701-2757)
P.O. Box 2128 (39704-2128)
PHONE..................................662 328-1685
J Reau Berry, *President*
Sheila Gibson, *Purch Mgr*
Judy Griffith, *CFO*
Kelli Berry, *Treasurer*
Becky Janssen, *Accounting Mgr*
▲ EMP: 36
SQ FT: 10,000
SALES (est): 31.8MM **Privately Held**
WEB: www.jtbfurniture.com
SIC: 2511 2599 Wood household furniture; hotel furniture

(G-995)
MACKAY ENTERPRISES LLC (PA)
Also Called: Kwik Kopy Printing
411 Main St Apt C (39701-4536)
PHONE..................................662 328-8469
Susan Mackay,
EMP: 8
SQ FT: 3,000
SALES (est): 1.2MM **Privately Held**
SIC: 2752 5947 5499 Commercial printing, offset; gifts & novelties; balloon shops; party favors; gourmet food stores

(G-996)
MACKAY ENTERPRISES LLC
Also Called: Party & Paper
411 Main St Apt C (39701-4536)
PHONE..................................662 328-8469
Jesse Hazelwood, *Manager*
EMP: 5
SALES (est): 203.1K
SALES (corp-wide): 1.2MM **Privately Held**
SIC: 5499 5947 2759 Gourmet food stores; gift shop; invitation & stationery printing & engraving
PA: Mackay Enterprises Llc
411 Main St Apt C
Columbus MS 39701
662 328-8469

(G-997)
MAGNOLIA BENEKE INC (PA)
1 Tuffy Ln (39701-3838)
P.O. Box 1367 (39703-1367)
PHONE..................................662 328-4000
Thomas Whitaker, *President*
Kirk Hardy, *Controller*
Gayle Booker, *Admin Sec*
▲ EMP: 21
SALES (est): 65.9MM **Privately Held**
SIC: 2499 Seats, toilet

(G-998)
MAGNOLIA BOTTLED WATER COMPANY
302 7th Ave S (39701-6771)
P.O. Box 1824 (39703-1824)
PHONE..................................662 329-9000
Richard Watkins, *President*
EMP: 5

SALES (est): 484.9K **Privately Held**
WEB: www.magnoliawaterms.com
SIC: 2086 Water, pasteurized: packaged in cans, bottles, etc.

(G-999)
MELVIN L BREWER INC
72 Pleasant Dr (39702-9207)
PHONE..................................662 328-9191
EMP: 1
SALES (est): 103.8K **Privately Held**
SIC: 2099 Pro Audio Video Sales

(G-1000)
MICROTEK MEDICAL INC (DH)
512 N Lehmberg Rd (39702-4464)
P.O. Box 2487 (39704-2487)
PHONE..................................662 327-1863
Dan R Lee, *President*
Johnny Ellis, *Facilities Mgr*
Mary Ann Whitlock, *Mktg Dir*
Mark Dillon, *Manager*
◆ EMP: 300
SQ FT: 13,000
SALES (est): 219.8MM
SALES (corp-wide): 14.6B **Publicly Held**
WEB: www.microtekmedical.com
SIC: 3841 Surgical & medical instruments
HQ: Microtek Medical Holdings, Inc.
13000 Drfeld Pkwy Ste 300
Alpharetta GA 30004
678 896-4400

(G-1001)
MID-SOUTH SIGNS INC (PA)
Also Called: Mid-South Signs & City Elc
8643 Highway 182 E (39702-8340)
PHONE..................................662 327-7807
Mark Pridmore, *President*
Scott Pridmore, *Vice Pres*
Rice Glover, *Chief Mktg Ofcr*
Stan House, *Manager*
Jeannie King, *Graphic Designe*
EMP: 13
SQ FT: 15,500
SALES (est): 5.9MM **Privately Held**
SIC: 7389 3993 Sign painting & lettering shop; electric signs

(G-1002)
MISSISSIPPI CYLINDER HEAD SVC
Also Called: Mississippi Cylinder Head Shop
202 Tuscaloosa Rd (39702-2948)
P.O. Box 2945 (39704-2945)
PHONE..................................662 328-0170
Oran P Hill, *President*
Butch Hill, *President*
Kathy Hill, *Corp Secy*
EMP: 5
SQ FT: 5,300
SALES: 771.6K **Privately Held**
SIC: 3714 7549 Cylinder heads, motor vehicle; lubrication service, automotive

(G-1003)
MISSISSIPPI FABRITEK INC
Also Called: Americna Non Wovens
221 Fabritek Dr (39702-7005)
P.O. Box 2847 (39704-2847)
PHONE..................................662 327-0745
Ron Sancher, *COO*
Bill W Daffron, *CFO*
EMP: 100
SALES (est): 8.6MM **Privately Held**
SIC: 2297 Nonwoven fabrics

(G-1004)
MISSISSIPPI PRECISION
Also Called: Pt
356 Langston Cir (39701-5504)
P.O. Box 1407 (39703-1407)
PHONE..................................662 245-1155
Eddie Houston, *General Mgr*
James R Parrish, *Mng Member*
▲ EMP: 26
SALES (est): 5.4MM **Privately Held**
SIC: 3324 Steel investment foundries

(G-1005)
MK OILFIELD SERVICE
168 Thaxton Rd (39702-7023)
PHONE..................................662 328-2510
Mitchell Thointon, *Owner*
EMP: 2

2019 Harris Directory of
Mississippi Manufacturers

44

▲ = Import ▼=Export
◆ =Import/Export

GEOGRAPHIC SECTION

Columbus - Lowndes County (G-1031)

SALES (est): 111.1K **Privately Held**
SIC: 1389 Oil field services

(G-1006)
MMC MATERIALS INC
Also Called: Mississippi Materials
462 Lake N Rd (39705)
PHONE.................................662 327-1927
David McCool, *Manager*
EMP: 8
SALES (corp-wide): 306.5MM **Privately Held**
WEB: www.mmcmaterials.com
SIC: 3273 3272 5211 Ready-mixed concrete; concrete products; masonry materials & supplies
HQ: Mmc Materials, Inc.
1052 Highland Colony Pkwy # 201
Ridgeland MS 39157
601 898-4000

(G-1007)
MONOGRAMS PLUS
110 Chapman Rd (39705-1695)
PHONE.................................662 327-3332
Paula Gable, *Owner*
EMP: 8
SALES (est): 350K **Privately Held**
SIC: 2395 5947 3479 2759 Embroidery & art needlework; gift shop; engraving jewelry silverware, or metal; invitation & stationery printing & engraving

(G-1008)
MONROE-TUFLINE MFG CO INC
2219 Tufline Ln (39705-1730)
P.O. Box 7755 (39705-0004)
PHONE.................................662 328-8347
Tim Perkins, *President*
Sid Perkins, *Vice Pres*
Pam Reed, *Purch Mgr*
Stephanie Godfrey, *Controller*
Roy Lewis, *Manager*
▲ EMP: 33
SQ FT: 55,000
SALES (est): 8.5MM **Privately Held**
WEB: www.monroetufline.com
SIC: 3523 Soil preparation machinery, except turf & grounds; harrows: disc, spring, tine, etc.; plows, agricultural: disc, moldboard, chisel, listers, etc.

(G-1009)
MOUNT VERNON MILLS INC
339 Yorkville Park Sq (39702-8907)
PHONE.................................662 328-5670
Jerry Gee, *Engineer*
James Bowden, *Branch Mgr*
EMP: 70
SALES (corp-wide): 939.5MM **Privately Held**
WEB: www.mvmills.com
SIC: 2396 Apparel findings & trimmings; bindings, bias: made from purchased materials; trimming, fabric
HQ: Mount Vernon Mills, Inc.
900 Trail Ridge Rd Ste 3
Aiken SC 29803
864 688-7100

(G-1010)
NEW PROCESS STEEL LP
Also Called: N P S
1379 Industrial Park Rd (39701-8646)
PHONE.................................662 241-6582
Robert Reighter, *Plant Mgr*
EMP: 60
SALES (corp-wide): 346.2MM **Privately Held**
SIC: 3479 3316 3353 5051 Galvanizing of iron, steel or end-formed products; sheet, steel, cold-rolled: from purchased hot-rolled; coils, sheet aluminum; metals service centers & offices; steel; sheets, galvanized or other coated; stampings, metal
PA: New Process Steel, L.P.
1322 N Post Oak Rd
Houston TX 77055
713 686-9631

(G-1011)
NOURYON PULP & PRFMCE CHEM LLC
4374 Nashville Ferry Rd E (39702-7479)
PHONE.................................662 327-0400

Atwell Daves, *Engineer*
Tim Mayo, *Engineer*
Garrett Morrison, *Engineer*
Andy Gressett, *Branch Mgr*
Kathy Scott, *Manager*
EMP: 16
SALES (corp-wide): 110.5MM **Privately Held**
SIC: 2869 Industrial organic chemicals
PA: Nouryon Pulp And Performance Chemicals Llc
1850 Parkway Pl Se # 1200
Marietta GA 30067
770 578-0858

(G-1012)
OMNOVA SOLUTIONS INC
Also Called: Gencorp Polymer Products
133 Yorkville Rd E (39702-7643)
P.O. Box 191 (39703-0191)
PHONE.................................662 327-1522
Bob Rutkowski, *Manager*
EMP: 650
SALES (corp-wide): 769.8MM **Publicly Held**
WEB: www.omnova.com
SIC: 2824 3089 3081 2851 Organic fibers, noncellulosic; plastic processing; unsupported plastics film & sheet; paints & allied products; coated fabrics, not rubberized
PA: Omnova Solutions Inc.
25435 Harvard Rd
Beachwood OH 44122
216 682-7000

(G-1013)
ONE OF A KIND ART CREATIONS
203 N Browder St (39702-5236)
PHONE.................................662 328-1283
Dianne Ruess, *Owner*
Corinne Beauregard, *Co-Owner*
Charles Ruess, *Co-Owner*
Mike Ruess, *Co-Owner*
EMP: 4
SQ FT: 1,300
SALES (est): 311.1K **Privately Held**
SIC: 2759 Screen printing

(G-1014)
PACCAR ENGINE COMPANY
1000 Paccar Dr (39701-8815)
PHONE.................................662 329-6700
Thomas K Quinn, *President*
EMP: 3
SALES (corp-wide): 23.5B **Publicly Held**
SIC: 5013 3519 Truck parts & accessories; engines, diesel & semi-diesel or dual-fuel
HQ: Paccar Engine Company
777 106th Ave Ne
Columbus MS 39701

(G-1015)
PACCAR ENGINE COMPANY (HQ)
777 106th Ave Ne (39701)
PHONE.................................425 468-7400
Thomas K Quinn, *President*
Kevin J Fay, *Principal*
Lisa Wiborg, *COO*
Treesa Bridgewater, *Opers Staff*
Tammy Chavarria, *Sls & Mktg Exec*
◆ EMP: 2
SALES (est): 2.8MM
SALES (corp-wide): 23.5B **Publicly Held**
SIC: 5013 3519 Truck parts & accessories; engines, diesel & semi-diesel or dual-fuel
PA: Paccar Inc
777 106th Ave Ne
Bellevue WA 98004
425 468-7400

(G-1016)
PRINT PROS LLC
1112 Main St Ste 3 (39701-4711)
PHONE.................................662 327-3222
Bonnie Adair, *Manager*
EMP: 2
SALES (est): 83.9K **Privately Held**
SIC: 2752 Commercial printing, lithographic

(G-1017)
PROGRAPHICS INC (PA)
1112 Main St Ste 2 (39701-4711)
P.O. Box 1004 (39703-1004)
PHONE.................................662 329-3341
Toll Free:...............................888 -
Grady R Mordecia, *President*
Grady R Mordecai, *President*
Michael R Burks, *Vice Pres*
EMP: 7
SQ FT: 15,000
SALES (est): 750K **Privately Held**
SIC: 2752 5999 Commercial printing, lithographic; architectural supplies

(G-1018)
PUCKETT ALLEN B JR & FAMILY
114 Brickyard Rd (39701-5200)
P.O. Box 9630 (39705-0021)
PHONE.................................662 328-4931
Allen B Puckett Jr, *Owner*
EMP: 1
SALES (est): 86.1K **Privately Held**
SIC: 3559 Brick making machinery

(G-1019)
QUALITY ALUM & HM IMPRV INC
1514 Gardner Blvd (39702-2802)
PHONE.................................662 329-2525
Arlen Toews, *President*
EMP: 9 EST: 2016
SALES (est): 315.8K **Privately Held**
SIC: 1799 2394 Awning installation; canvas awnings & canopies

(G-1020)
QUALITY BEVERAGE PACKING INC
82 Yorkville Park Sq (39702-7163)
PHONE.................................662 329-5976
David Earwood, *President*
James Price, *Vice Pres*
EMP: 10
SQ FT: 16,000
SALES (est): 1.6MM **Privately Held**
SIC: 2087 Syrups, drink

(G-1021)
ROBERTSON-CECO II CORPORATION
Also Called: Ceco Building Systems
2400 Highway 45 N (39705-1398)
P.O. Box 911 (39703-0911)
PHONE.................................662 243-6400
Stephen Foreman, *Project Mgr*
Mike Maloney, *Project Mgr*
Shane Whitley, *Project Mgr*
Brian Wyatt, *Project Mgr*
Bruce Clark, *Mfg Staff*
EMP: 60
SALES (corp-wide): 2B **Publicly Held**
WEB: www.robertsonceco.com
SIC: 3448 Buildings, portable: prefabricated metal
HQ: Robertson-Ceco Ii Corporation
10943 N Sam Huston Pkwy W
Houston TX 77064

(G-1022)
RON LOR WINDOW FASHIONS
130 S Mccrary Rd (39702-6320)
P.O. Box 375, Lithia Springs GA (30122-0375)
PHONE.................................662 329-1557
Ronald Whitson, *Owner*
Lorraine Whitson, *Co-Owner*
EMP: 3
SQ FT: 1,200
SALES: 150K **Privately Held**
SIC: 2391 7699 Curtains & draperies; window blind repair services

(G-1023)
SEIMENS INDUSTRY SECTOR
1961 Airport Rd (39701-9526)
PHONE.................................662 245-4573
EMP: 4
SALES (est): 366.5K **Privately Held**
SIC: 3661 Telephones & telephone apparatus

(G-1024)
SEVERCORR LLC
1409 Highway 45 S (39701-8737)
PHONE.................................662 245-4561

EMP: 2
SALES (est): 90.8K **Privately Held**
SIC: 3312 Blast furnaces & steel mills

(G-1025)
SIGN SHOP
1835 Highway 45 N (39705-2152)
PHONE.................................662 328-7933
Robert Clark, *Owner*
EMP: 3
SALES (est): 900K **Privately Held**
SIC: 2752 Commercial printing, lithographic

(G-1026)
SIGNATURE SOUND & PRINTING
Also Called: Signature Sund Media Solutions
2116 1/2 Highway 45 N (39705-1741)
PHONE.................................601 272-5662
Orlandes Abrams,
EMP: 2
SALES (est): 141.1K **Privately Held**
SIC: 7336 2741 Graphic arts & related design; posters; publishing & printing

(G-1027)
SLEEPMADECOM LLC (PA)
179 Tradewinds Dr (39705)
P.O. Box 309 (39703-0309)
PHONE.................................662 386-2222
Matthew Fowler,
Paul F Saunders,
EMP: 5
SALES (est): 2MM **Privately Held**
SIC: 2515 Sleep furniture

(G-1028)
SOUTHERN IONICS INCORPORATED
1825 Post Access Rd (39701)
P.O. Box 1217, West Point (39773-1217)
PHONE.................................662 328-0516
Sam White, *Manager*
EMP: 5
SALES (corp-wide): 98.7MM **Privately Held**
WEB: www.southernionics.com
SIC: 2819 Alums
PA: Southern Ionics Incorporated
579 Commerce St
West Point MS 39773
662 494-3055

(G-1029)
SOUTHERN LURE COMPANY INC
201a N Browder St (39702-5202)
P.O. Box 2244 (39704-2244)
PHONE.................................662 327-4548
Dan Cunningham, *President*
EMP: 11
SALES (est): 1.3MM **Privately Held**
SIC: 3949 5091 Lures, fishing: artificial; fishing equipment & supplies

(G-1030)
SQWINCHER CORPORATION
Also Called: Sqwincher Activity Drink
1409 Highway 45 S (39701-8737)
P.O. Box 8250 (39705-0032)
PHONE.................................662 328-0400
Tommy Howard, *President*
Scott Bromley, *Vice Pres*
Davis Kelly, *CFO*
▲ EMP: 63
SQ FT: 75,000
SALES (est): 33.8MM **Privately Held**
WEB: www.sqwincher.com
SIC: 5149 2087 Beverages, except coffee & tea; beverage bases, concentrates, syrups, powders & mixes

(G-1031)
STAINED GLASSWORKS INC
3067 Old West Point Rd (39701-9594)
PHONE.................................662 329-2970
Jane Crawford, *President*
Robert Crawford, *Vice Pres*
EMP: 6
SQ FT: 2,200
SALES (est): 462.6K **Privately Held**
WEB: www.stainedglassworks.org
SIC: 5231 5947 8299 3231 Glass, leaded or stained; gift, novelty & souvenir shop; arts & crafts schools; products of purchased glass; pressed & blown glass

---

(PA)=Parent Co (HQ)=Headquarters (DH)=Div Headquarters
✿ = New Business established in last 2 years

2019 Harris Directory of
Mississippi Manufacturers

45

Columbus - Lowndes County (G-1032)

GEOGRAPHIC SECTION

(G-1032)
STARK AEROSPACE INC (DH)
319 Charleigh Ford Jr Rd (39701-9064)
PHONE..................................662 798-4075
Mike McGrevey, *CEO*
Robert Foglesong, *Ch of Bd*
Tom Ronaldi, *President*
Daniel Smith, *Project Mgr*
Chuck Bigelow, *Facilities Mgr*
◆ EMP: 75 EST: 2006
SQ FT: 100,000
SALES (est): 26.4MM
SALES (corp-wide): 993.9MM Privately
Held
SIC: 3721 Aircraft
HQ: Iai North America Inc.
1700 N Moore St Ste 1210
Arlington VA 22209
703 243-2227

(G-1033)
**STEEL DYNAMICS COLUMBUS
LLC (HQ)**
1945 Airport Rd (39701-9526)
P.O. Box 1467 (39703-1467)
PHONE..................................662 245-4200
Mark D Millett, *President*
Russell B Rinn, *Exec VP*
Theresa E Wagler, *CFO*
Jonathan Reasor, *Sales Mgr*
Zach Sheridan, *Accounts Mgr*
▲ EMP: 277
SALES (est): 307.7MM Publicly Held
SIC: 3312 Blast furnaces & steel mills

(G-1034)
SUPERIOR GRANITE & QUARTZ
341 Island Rd (39701-8519)
PHONE..................................662 241-5664
Glenn Bontrager, *President*
EMP: 4
SALES (est): 380K Privately Held
WEB: www.superiorsolidsurface.com
SIC: 2541 1799 2434 Counters or counter
display cases, wood; counter top installa-
tion; wood kitchen cabinets

(G-1035)
SWEET SCENTS
104 Sherard Cir (39705-1240)
PHONE..................................662 425-9305
Cheyenne Moseley, *Principal*
EMP: 1
SALES (est): 53.3K Privately Held
SIC: 2844 Toilet preparations

(G-1036)
**T SHIRT SHOP & DESIGN FIRM
LLC**
5489 Ridge Rd (39705-8221)
PHONE..................................662 329-9911
Dona Jo Rast, *President*
EMP: 2
SQ FT: 1,500
SALES (est): 200K Privately Held
SIC: 5651 5699 2759 2395 Family cloth-
ing stores; customized clothing & apparel;
screen printing; embroidery products, ex-
cept schiffli machine

(G-1037)
TDK LOGGING INC
6011 Highway 182 E (39702-7310)
PHONE..................................662 328-6625
Edwin Obryant, *President*
EMP: 10 EST: 1993
SALES (est): 1.5MM Privately Held
SIC: 2411 Logging camps & contractors

(G-1038)
TINKS BELLS
Also Called: Lisa Ulmer
94 South Pkwy (39705-8149)
PHONE..................................662 574-2685
Lisa Ulmer, *Owner*
EMP: 1
SALES (est): 95.3K Privately Held
SIC: 3931 7389 Bells (musical instru-
ments);

(G-1039)
TRIMJOIST CORPORATION
5146 Highway 182 E (39702-8223)
PHONE..................................662 327-7950
E Barry Sanford, *President*

Charlotte D Walker, *Corp Secy*
Marty K Hawkins, *Vice Pres*
Tony Atkins, *Engineer*
Brinton Fisackerly, *Accountant*
EMP: 50 EST: 1994
SQ FT: 110,000
SALES: 8MM Privately Held
WEB: www.trimjoist.com
SIC: 2439 Trusses, except roof: laminated
lumber

(G-1040)
**TUOHYS J SPTG GODS OF
COLUMBUS**
Also Called: J Tuohy's Apparel
113 5th St S (39701-5727)
P.O. Box 1252 (39703-1252)
PHONE..................................662 328-1440
Kyle H Connor, *President*
EMP: 40 EST: 1975
SQ FT: 5,800
SALES (est): 2.7MM Privately Held
WEB: www.camoclothes.com
SIC: 2329 2369 2361 Men's & boys'
sportswear & athletic clothing; girls' &
children's outerwear; girls' & children's
dresses, blouses & shirts

(G-1041)
VALMET INC
617 Yorkville Park Sq (39702-8909)
PHONE..................................662 328-3841
Charles Farmer, *Manager*
EMP: 100
SALES (corp-wide): 3.8B Privately Held
WEB: www.metso.com
SIC: 5084 2822 Industrial machinery &
equipment; synthetic rubber
HQ: Valmet, Inc.
2425 Commerce Ave Ste 100
Duluth GA 30096
770 263-7863

(G-1042)
WALTER L PERRIGIN
1713 Ridge Rd (39705-3289)
PHONE..................................662 240-0056
Walter L Perrigin, *Principal*
EMP: 1
SALES (est): 96.7K Privately Held
SIC: 1499 Miscellaneous nonmetallic min-
erals

(G-1043)
WEYERHAEUSER
297 Richardson Rd (39702-8852)
PHONE..................................662 327-1961
EMP: 1
SALES (est): 61K Privately Held
SIC: 2621 Paper mills

(G-1044)
WEYERHAEUSER COMPANY
Weyerhaeuser Nr Company
4335 Carson Rd (39701)
P.O. Box 1830 (39703-1830)
PHONE..................................662 243-4000
Rantle Carmes, *Branch Mgr*
EMP: 35
SALES (corp-wide): 7.4B Publicly Held
SIC: 2611 Pulp mills
PA: Weyerhaeuser Company
220 Occidental Ave S
Seattle WA 98104
206 539-3000

(G-1045)
WEYERHAEUSER COMPANY
371 Manufacturers Rd (39701-5503)
P.O. Box 8660 (39705-0012)
PHONE..................................662 243-6900
Travis Stewart, *Marketing Mgr*
Greg Parchello, *Branch Mgr*
EMP: 70
SALES (corp-wide): 7.4B Publicly Held
SIC: 2421 2824 2823 Lumber: rough,
sawed or planed; organic fibers, noncellu-
losic; cellulosic manmade fibers
PA: Weyerhaeuser Company
220 Occidental Ave S
Seattle WA 98104
206 539-3000

Como
Panola County

(G-1046)
CEMEX CNSTR MTLS FLA LLC
Also Called: Trucking Division
2179 Holston Rd (38619-6285)
PHONE..................................888 263-7093
Jimmy Glover, *Manager*
EMP: 20
SQ FT: 3,000 Privately Held
WEB: www.hansonpipeandproducts.com
SIC: 3273 Ready-mixed concrete
HQ: Cemex Construction Materials Florida,
Llc
1501 Belvedere Rd
West Palm Beach FL 33406

(G-1047)
**FORTERRA PIPE & PRECAST
LLC**
2377 Holston Rd (38619-6281)
PHONE..................................662 526-0368
Jeff Bradley, *CEO*
Steven Knotts, *Branch Mgr*
EMP: 25
SALES (corp-wide): 1.4B Publicly Held
SIC: 3272 Concrete products
HQ: Forterra Pipe & Precast, Llc
511 E John Carpenter Fwy
Irving TX 75062
469 458-7973

(G-1048)
**HOOPER SALES CO
INCORPORATED**
405 Section Line Rd (38619-7836)
PHONE..................................662 526-5668
Jerry Hudson, *Owner*
EMP: 1
SALES (corp-wide): 5MM Privately Held
SIC: 5149 2086 Beverages, except coffee
& tea; bottled & canned soft drinks
PA: Hooper Sales Co., Incorporated
316 N 5th St
West Memphis AR 72301
870 732-2259

(G-1049)
**MID SOUTH STORM SHELTERS
LLC**
201 Robinson Dr (38619-2435)
PHONE..................................901 619-0064
EMP: 2
SALES (est): 156K Privately Held
SIC: 2431 Storm windows, wood

(G-1050)
MINI SYSTEMS INC
25475 Highway 51 (38619-6383)
P.O. Box 520, Sardis (38666-0520)
PHONE..................................662 487-2240
L Tracy Crutcher, *President*
Michael Saripkin, *Vice Pres*
▼ EMP: 8
SQ FT: 5,000
SALES (est): 5.2MM Privately Held
SIC: 3448 1541 Buildings, portable: pre-
fabricated metal; prefabricated building
erection, industrial

(G-1051)
SOUTH MEMPHIS FENCE CO
307 Warren St (38619-2587)
PHONE..................................662 526-5400
Warren Price, *President*
EMP: 1
SALES (est): 91.5K Privately Held
SIC: 3446 Fences or posts, ornamental
iron or steel

(G-1052)
**THOMASVLLE MTAL
FBRICATORS INC**
305 S Main St (38619-2433)
PHONE..................................662 526-9900
Richard Weeks, *Principal*
EMP: 38
SALES (est): 6.1MM Privately Held
SIC: 3441 3498 2542 Building compo-
nents, structural steel; fabricated pipe &
fittings; partitions & fixtures, except wood

PA: Thomasville Metal Fabricators Inc.
200 Prospect Dr
Lexington NC 27292

(G-1053)
TIER-RACK CORPORATION
305 S Main St (38619-2433)
PHONE..................................662 526-9900
Richard Weeks, *Branch Mgr*
EMP: 25
SALES (corp-wide): 23.3MM Privately
Held
WEB: www.tier-rack.com
SIC: 2542 Pallet racks: except wood
PA: Tier-Rack Corporation
425 Sovereign Ct
Ballwin MO 63011
800 325-7869

(G-1054)
**TRICOUNTY FARM SERVICES
SOUTH**
Also Called: Feed Manufracturing
206 Highway 51 (38619-9334)
PHONE..................................662 526-9100
Rex Adair, *President*
Deddie Adair, *Principal*
EMP: 5
SALES (est): 820K Privately Held
SIC: 2048 Prepared feeds

Conehatta
Newton County

(G-1055)
**VAPOR OILFIELD SERVICES
LLC**
3340 Mills Rd (39057-2641)
P.O. Box 37 (39057-0037)
PHONE..................................601 741-7171
Michale Yates, *Principal*
EMP: 2
SALES (est): 126.6K Privately Held
SIC: 1389 Oil field services

Corinth
Alcorn County

(G-1056)
ALCORN FABRICATING
87 County Road 547 (38834-8106)
PHONE..................................662 462-5669
Paul Parvin, *Owner*
EMP: 1
SALES: 15K Privately Held
SIC: 7692 Welding repair

(G-1057)
AQUAVEST
1808 Highway 72 E (38834-6533)
PHONE..................................662 287-0302
EMP: 3
SALES (est): 177K Privately Held
SIC: 2819 Carbides

(G-1058)
**AUTOMATIC MACHINE
PRODUCTS INC**
1702 Sawyer Rd (38834-6331)
PHONE..................................662 287-2467
Jimmy D Manahan, *President*
Linda Wilson, *Corp Secy*
James R Manahan, *Vice Pres*
EMP: 21
SQ FT: 38,000
SALES (est): 3.7MM Privately Held
SIC: 3451 Screw machine products

(G-1059)
**AYRSHIRE ELECTRONICS MISS
LLC**
1801 S Fulton Dr (38834-9254)
PHONE..................................662 287-3771
Gary Lehren, *President*
Ed Carter, *Vice Pres*
Anthony P Meger, *Vice Pres*
W Brian Porter, *CFO*
▲ EMP: 200
SQ FT: 350,000

2019 Harris Directory of
Mississippi Manufacturers

▲ = Import ▼=Export
◆ =Import/Export

GEOGRAPHIC SECTION

Corinth - Alcorn County (G-1087)

SALES (est): 81.6MM
SALES (corp-wide): 464MM **Publicly Held**
SIC: 3672 Printed circuit boards
HQ: Cdr Manufacturing, Llc
4801 Olympia Park Plz # 1400
Louisville KY 40241

(G-1060)
B & B CONCRETE CO INC
2724 S Harper Rd (38834-9274)
P.O. Box 1978 (38835-1978)
PHONE..................................662 286-6407
Mark Drady, *Manager*
EMP: 14
SALES (corp-wide): 21.1MM **Privately Held**
SIC: 3273 Ready-mixed concrete
PA: B & B Concrete Co., Inc.
130 N Industrial Rd
Tupelo MS 38801
662 842-6312

(G-1061)
BILL PHILLIPS SAND & GRAV LLC
1299 Highway 2 (38834-8506)
PHONE..................................662 284-6061
Bill Phillips Jr, *Principal*
EMP: 2
SALES (est): 72.5K **Privately Held**
SIC: 1442 Construction sand & gravel

(G-1062)
C & D JARNAGIN COMPANY INC
103 Franklin St (38834-5640)
PHONE..................................662 287-4977
David Jarnagin, *Manager*
EMP: 20
SALES (est): 889.9K
SALES (corp-wide): 1.7MM **Privately Held**
WEB: www.jarnaginco.com
SIC: 2389 Theatrical costumes
PA: C & D Jarnagin Company, Inc
103 Franklin St
Corinth MS 38834
662 287-4977

(G-1063)
C & D JARNAGIN COMPANY INC (PA)
103 Franklin St (38834-5640)
PHONE..................................662 287-4977
Carolyn Jarnagin, *President*
David Jarnagin, *Opers Mgr*
EMP: 10 EST: 1977
SQ FT: 3,500
SALES (est): 1.7MM **Privately Held**
WEB: www.jarnaginco.com
SIC: 8733 2389 Research institute; theatrical costumes

(G-1064)
CARAUSTAR INDUSTRIAL AND CON
Also Called: Corinth Tube Plant
1504 S Fulton Dr (38834-6315)
P.O. Box 2277 (38835-2277)
PHONE..................................662 287-2492
Dick Cowart, *Manager*
EMP: 40
SALES (corp-wide): 3.8B **Publicly Held**
SIC: 2655 5113 Tubes, fiber or paper: made from purchased material; paper tubes & cores
HQ: Caraustar Industrial And Consumer Products Group Inc
5000 Austell Powder Ste
Austell GA 30106
803 548-5100

(G-1065)
CATERPILLAR
1710 Sawyer Rd (38834-6331)
PHONE..................................662 286-1274
David L Calhoun, *Principal*
▲ EMP: 7 EST: 2010
SALES (est): 776K **Privately Held**
SIC: 3531 5082 Construction machinery; construction & mining machinery

(G-1066)
CATERPILLAR INC
2500 Legacy Dr (38834)
PHONE..................................662 286-5511
Brent McCartney, *Manager*
EMP: 10
SALES (corp-wide): 54.7B **Publicly Held**
SIC: 3714 Motor vehicle engines & parts
PA: Caterpillar Inc.
510 Lake Cook Rd Ste 100
Deerfield IL 60015
224 551-4000

(G-1067)
CATERPILLAR INC
500 Cardinal Dr (38834-6376)
PHONE..................................662 284-5143
EMP: 10
SALES (corp-wide): 54.7B **Publicly Held**
SIC: 3537 Industrial trucks & tractors
PA: Caterpillar Inc.
510 Lake Cook Rd Ste 100
Deerfield IL 60015
224 551-4000

(G-1068)
CATERPILLAR INC
501 Cardinal Dr (38834-6303)
PHONE..................................662 286-5511
Kathryn Balch, *Opers Mgr*
Jeremiah Keltner, *Engineer*
Christopher A Kinney, *Engineer*
Scott Tucker, *Engineer*
Michelle Clemons, *Accountant*
EMP: 750
SALES (corp-wide): 54.7B **Publicly Held**
WEB: www.cat.com
SIC: 3531 Construction machinery
PA: Caterpillar Inc.
510 Lake Cook Rd Ste 100
Deerfield IL 60015
224 551-4000

(G-1069)
CDR MANUFACTURING INC
1801 S Fulton Dr (38834-9254)
PHONE..................................662 665-3100
EMP: 2
SALES (est): 104.3K **Privately Held**
SIC: 3999 Manufacturing industries

(G-1070)
CHRISTIANS AUTOMOTIVE MACHINE
2672 S Harper Rd Ste 2327 (38834-6723)
PHONE..................................662 287-4500
Dan Christian, *Partner*
Danny Christian, *Partner*
EMP: 6
SQ FT: 20,000
SALES: 280K **Privately Held**
SIC: 7539 3519 7549 7538 Machine shop, automotive; internal combustion engines; lubrication service, automotive; engine rebuilding: automotive; automotive parts; automotive servicing equipment

(G-1071)
CM SOLUTIONS INC
2674 S Harper Rd (38834-9268)
P.O. Box 670 (38835-0670)
PHONE..................................662 287-8810
Michael G Driste, *President*
Jack O'Rear, *Vice Pres*
Tommy Robertson, *Vice Pres*
Tabitha Patterson, *Purch Mgr*
Alecia Jones, *Engineer*
▲ EMP: 15
SQ FT: 20,000
SALES (est): 5.3MM **Privately Held**
WEB: www.cm-solutions.biz
SIC: 3672 Printed circuit boards

(G-1072)
CONAWAY LOGGING INC
1101 Cardinal Dr (38834-6817)
PHONE..................................662 287-8830
Benny Conaway, *President*
EMP: 10
SALES: 700K **Privately Held**
SIC: 2411 Logging

(G-1073)
COON CREEK CUSTOM GAME CALLS
142 County Road 546 (38834-7927)
PHONE..................................662 284-6932
Dustin Turner, *Principal*
EMP: 1 EST: 2017
SALES (est): 47K **Privately Held**
SIC: 3949 Game calls

(G-1074)
COPHARMA INC
127 Pratt Dr (38834-6026)
PHONE..................................662 594-1594
Donald King, *Owner*
EMP: 3 EST: 2013
SALES (est): 212.9K **Privately Held**
SIC: 2834 Pharmaceutical preparations

(G-1075)
CORINTH ACQUISITION CORP
Also Called: United Pioneer
504 Pinecrest Rd (38834-5331)
PHONE..................................662 287-1476
Bernie Braverman, *Owner*
EMP: 3
SQ FT: 100,000
SALES (corp-wide): 22.4MM **Privately Held**
SIC: 2211 5136 Apparel & outerwear fabrics, cotton; men's & boys' clothing
PA: Corinth Acquisition Corp
2777 Summer St Ste 206
Stamford CT 06905
203 504-6260

(G-1076)
CORINTH BRICK COMPANY INC
104 Allen St (38834-6001)
PHONE..................................662 287-2442
Allan Lee, *President*
EMP: 5 EST: 1974
SQ FT: 3,000
SALES: 700K **Privately Held**
SIC: 5032 3251 2951 Concrete & cinder block; brick, except refractory; brick & structural clay tile; asphalt paving mixtures & blocks

(G-1077)
CORINTH CC-COLA BTLG WORKS INC (PA)
601 Washington St (38834-4734)
P.O. Box 239 (38835-0239)
PHONE..................................662 287-1433
Harry Lee Williams Jr, *CEO*
Mary Martin Weaver Burress, *Ch of Bd*
Kenneth W Williams, *President*
Kenneth W Williams Sr, *Principal*
Rebecca Burress Williams, *Vice Pres*
EMP: 85 EST: 1907
SQ FT: 80,000
SALES (est): 22MM **Privately Held**
SIC: 2086 Bottled & canned soft drinks

(G-1078)
CORINTH CC-COLA BTLG WORKS INC
211 Foote St (38834)
P.O. Box 239 (38835-0239)
PHONE..................................662 286-2052
Larry Stanford, *Principal*
EMP: 50
SALES (est): 2.4MM
SALES (corp-wide): 22MM **Privately Held**
SIC: 2086 4953 3341 3231 Bottled & canned soft drinks; refuse systems; secondary nonferrous metals; products of purchased glass
PA: Corinth Coca-Cola Bottling Works, Inc.
601 Washington St
Corinth MS 38834
662 287-1433

(G-1079)
CORINTHIAN INC (PA)
Also Called: Status Leather
41 Henson Rd (38834-1423)
P.O. Box 1918 (38835-1918)
PHONE..................................662 287-7835
Vick L Etheridge, *President*
Billy J Caperton, *Principal*
Holley Foster, *Purch Agent*
Sammy Durham, *Research*

Denise McGaughy, *Research*
◆ EMP: 600
SQ FT: 425,000
SALES (est): 89MM **Privately Held**
SIC: 2512 Upholstered household furniture

(G-1080)
COTTAGE GARDEN MS LLC
997 Highway 72 E (38834-6448)
PHONE..................................662 665-1918
Jennifer Timbes,
EMP: 1
SQ FT: 1,850
SALES (est): 70.9K **Privately Held**
SIC: 2841 Soap & other detergents

(G-1081)
COTTON TOPS
311 Highway 72 W (38834-5408)
PHONE..................................662 287-4737
Terry Ross,
EMP: 2
SALES (est): 161K **Privately Held**
SIC: 2759 Screen printing

(G-1082)
D DODD JOHN OD (PA)
Also Called: Dodd, John D Dr
609 N Fillmore St (38834-4826)
P.O. Box 2100 (38835-2100)
PHONE..................................662 286-5671
John D Dood Od, *Owner*
EMP: 7
SALES (est): 556.1K **Privately Held**
SIC: 8042 3851 5995 Offices & clinics of optometrists; eyeglasses, lenses & frames; eyeglasses, prescription

(G-1083)
DEVELOPMENTAL INDUSTRIES INC
915 Highway 45 (38834-7978)
PHONE..................................662 287-6626
Todd Hight, *General Mgr*
Ted Rider, *Corp Secy*
Terry Rider, *Vice Pres*
Shane Weathers, *Plant Mgr*
DOT Rider, *Project Mgr*
▲ EMP: 24
SQ FT: 30,000
SALES (est): 6.4MM **Privately Held**
WEB: www.dimetalworks.com
SIC: 3542 3544 3599 Machine tools, metal forming type; special dies, tools, jigs & fixtures; machine shop, jobbing & repair

(G-1084)
DR ERICA AESTHETIC CENTER
2000 E Shiloh Rd (38834-3724)
PHONE..................................662 284-9600
Erica L Noyes, *Principal*
EMP: 3 EST: 2007
SALES (est): 251.4K **Privately Held**
SIC: 3841 Surgical lasers

(G-1085)
FINAL TOUCH ACCESSORIES LLC
2679 S Harper Rd (38834-9269)
PHONE..................................662 594-1348
Sandra Bonds, *Mng Member*
Jack Clark,
EMP: 30
SQ FT: 35,000
SALES: 1.7MM **Privately Held**
SIC: 2499 5719 Picture & mirror frames, wood; pictures & mirrors

(G-1086)
GARYS INDUSTRIES INC
306 Lilac St (38834-5212)
PHONE..................................662 415-1777
Gary Briggs Jr, *Partner*
EMP: 2
SALES (est): 71.4K **Privately Held**
SIC: 3999 Manufacturing industries

(G-1087)
GEARTEK
1506 S Fulton Dr (38834-6315)
P.O. Box 2160 (38835-2160)
PHONE..................................662 286-2252
Okey Thornton, *President*
Diana Dunn, *Vice Pres*

(PA)=Parent Co (HQ)=Headquarters (DH)=Div Headquarters
✪ = New Business established in last 2 years

2019 Harris Directory of
Mississippi Manufacturers

47

Corinth - Alcorn County (G-1088)

GEOGRAPHIC SECTION

Jerry Miller, *Plant Mgr*
Derrick Dunn, *Sales Mgr*
Steve Thompson, *Manager*
EMP: 17
SQ FT: 15,000
SALES (est): 5.8MM **Privately Held**
WEB: www.geartek.com
SIC: 5084 7699 3594 Hydraulic systems equipment & supplies; hydraulic equipment repair; fluid power pumps & motors

(G-1088)
H & H FABRICATION INC
243 County Road 604 (38834-8482)
PHONE..................................662 286-9475
Jimmy Hopper, *President*
EMP: 12
SALES (est): 870K **Privately Held**
SIC: 7692 Welding repair

(G-1089)
HUFFCO LLC
3263 N Polk St (38834-7229)
PHONE..................................662 284-6517
William Huff, *Principal*
EMP: 2
SALES (est): 104.2K **Privately Held**
SIC: 2842 Specialty cleaning, polishes & sanitation goods

(G-1090)
HUGHES OUTDOORS & MARIN
335a County Road 218 (38834-7536)
PHONE..................................662 287-8607
Tommy Hughes, *Principal*
EMP: 2
SALES (est): 225K **Privately Held**
SIC: 3599 Industrial machinery

(G-1091)
INDEPENDENTS SERVICE COMPANY
611 Childs St (38834-4810)
PHONE..................................662 287-2431
Katherine Forsyth, *Manager*
EMP: 3
SALES (corp-wide): 7MM **Privately Held**
WEB: www.independentsservice.com
SIC: 2759 3993 Screen printing; signs & advertising specialties
PA: Independent's Service Company
2710 Market St
Hannibal MO 63401
573 221-4615

(G-1092)
INNOVATIVE CIRCUITS INC
311a S Parkway St (38834-5914)
PHONE..................................662 287-2007
Lori Ramsey, *President*
Benny Southward, *Mfg Mgr*
EMP: 19
SQ FT: 48,000
SALES (est): 6.7MM **Privately Held**
WEB: www.icimfg.com
SIC: 3699 3993 4899 Electrical equipment & supplies; barber & beauty shop equipment; data communication services

(G-1093)
INTEX PROPERTIES PERRIS VLY LP
2733 S Harper Rd (38834-9272)
PHONE..................................662 287-1455
Tien P Zee, *President*
EMP: 9
SALES (corp-wide): 171.8MM **Privately Held**
SIC: 3081 3089 Vinyl film & sheet; polyethylene film; plastic processing
HQ: Intex Properties Perris Valley, L.P.
4130 Santa Fe Ave
Long Beach CA 90810
310 549-5400

(G-1094)
KEY TRONIC CORPORATION
Also Called: Keytronic Ems
1801 S Fulton Dr (38834-9254)
PHONE..................................662 665-3410
EMP: 7
SALES (corp-wide): 464MM **Publicly Held**
SIC: 3577 Computer peripheral equipment

PA: Key Tronic Corporation
4424 N Sullivan Rd
Spokane Valley WA 99216
509 928-8000

(G-1095)
KIMBERLY-CLARK CORPORATION
3461 County Road 100 (38834-1379)
PHONE..................................662 287-8011
Bert Calvary, *Engineer*
Fulton Garces, *Engineer*
Henry Brown, *Electrical Engi*
Steve Will, *Manager*
Terry McKee, *Manager*
EMP: 450
SALES (corp-wide): 18.4B **Publicly Held**
WEB: www.kimberly-clark.com
SIC: 2621 2676 Sanitary tissue paper; infant & baby paper products
PA: Kimberly-Clark Corporation
351 Phelps Dr
Irving TX 75038
972 281-1200

(G-1096)
KING MANUFACTURING COMPANY INC (PA)
714 S Fulton Dr (38834-6307)
P.O. Box 787 (38835-0787)
PHONE..................................662 286-5504
Thomas E Robertson, *CEO*
Frank Howell, *President*
Brian Shirley, *Vice Pres*
Betty K Robertson, *Director*
Scott Medlock, *Representative*
EMP: 37
SQ FT: 100,000
SALES (est): 12.3MM **Privately Held**
SIC: 3469 3452 3553 3661 Stamping metal for the trade; bolts, nuts, rivets & washers; screws, metal; screw eyes & hooks; woodworking machinery; telephone & telegraph apparatus

(G-1097)
KING MANUFACTURING COMPANY INC
2674 S Harper Rd (38834-9268)
P.O. Box 787 (38835-0787)
PHONE..................................662 286-5504
Frank Howell, *President*
EMP: 50
SALES (corp-wide): 12.3MM **Privately Held**
SIC: 3661 Telephone & telegraph apparatus
PA: King Manufacturing Company, Inc.
714 S Fulton Dr
Corinth MS 38834
662 286-5504

(G-1098)
LONGBRANCH
104 Taylor St (38834-5649)
PHONE..................................662 284-8585
EMP: 5
SALES (est): 336.7K **Privately Held**
SIC: 3089 Plastic processing

(G-1099)
MAGNOLIA HOSIERY MILL INC
311 S Parkway St (38834-5914)
PHONE..................................662 286-2221
Dennis Bumpas, *Treasurer*
Wayne Bumpas, *Admin Sec*
EMP: 3 EST: 1954
SQ FT: 114,061
SALES (est): 250K **Privately Held**
WEB: www.magnoliahosiery.com
SIC: 2251 Women's hosiery, except socks

(G-1100)
MERLE NORMAN COSMETICS INC
1798 Highway 72 E (38834-6502)
PHONE..................................662 287-7233
Arlene Wever, *Owner*
EMP: 5
SALES (est): 195.3K **Privately Held**
SIC: 5999 2844 Cosmetics; toilet preparations

(G-1101)
METAL PRODUCTS OF CORINTH INC
County Rd 507 (38834)
P.O. Box 1235 (38835-1235)
PHONE..................................662 287-3625
Dan Perkins, *President*
Steve Perkins, *Vice Pres*
Dorothy Perkins, *Admin Sec*
EMP: 7
SQ FT: 40,000
SALES (est): 1.4MM **Privately Held**
SIC: 3599 3544 7692 Machine shop, jobbing & repair; special dies & tools; welding repair

(G-1102)
MILITARY WAREHOUSE
51 County Road 192 (38834-9387)
P.O. Box 406 (38835-0406)
PHONE..................................662 287-8234
Jim Kindred, *Owner*
EMP: 1
SALES (est): 80K **Privately Held**
SIC: 3999 Military insignia

(G-1103)
MISSISSIPPI POLYMERS INC
2733 S Harper Rd (38834-9272)
PHONE..................................662 287-1401
Jerry Waxman, *President*
Jerold Waxman, *Principal*
Jim Jones, *Director*
James Jones, *Admin Sec*
◆ **EMP:** 300
SQ FT: 330,000
SALES (est): 83.1MM **Privately Held**
WEB: www.mississippipolymers.com
SIC: 3081 Unsupported plastics film & sheet

(G-1104)
MP LOGGING
509 Pinecrest Rd (38834-5332)
PHONE..................................662 808-5411
Michael Pittman, *Principal*
EMP: 3 EST: 2009
SALES (est): 244.5K **Privately Held**
SIC: 2411 Logging

(G-1105)
NAVISTAR INC
1710 Sawyer Rd (38834-6331)
PHONE..................................662 284-8984
EMP: 66
SALES (corp-wide): 10.2B **Publicly Held**
WEB: www.internationaldelivers.com
SIC: 3711 Motor vehicles & car bodies
HQ: Navistar, Inc.
2701 Navistar Dr
Lisle IL 60532
331 332-5000

(G-1106)
NORTH MISSISSIPPI TIMBER & LOG
648 County Road 500 (38834-7969)
PHONE..................................662 603-7944
Tom Wade, *Principal*
EMP: 3 EST: 2008
SALES (est): 302.5K **Privately Held**
SIC: 2411 Logging

(G-1107)
PALMER HANDRAIL & CUSTOM MLLWK
35 County Road 324 (38834-8836)
P.O. Box 310 (38835-0310)
PHONE..................................662 287-3090
Brent Palmer, *Owner*
EMP: 6
SQ FT: 20,000
SALES (est): 737.8K **Privately Held**
SIC: 2431 2499 Woodwork, interior & ornamental; stair railings, wood; moldings, wood; unfinished & prefinished; trim, wood; decorative wood & woodwork

(G-1108)
PAXTON MEDIA GROUP LLC
Also Called: Corinthian Daily , The
1607 S Harper Rd (38834-6653)
P.O. Box 1800 (38835-1800)
PHONE..................................662 287-6111
Reece Terry, *Manager*

EMP: 46
SALES (corp-wide): 234MM **Privately Held**
WEB: www.jonesborosun.com
SIC: 2711 Newspapers, publishing & printing
PA: Paxton Media Group, Llc
100 Television Ln
Paducah KY 42003
270 575-8630

(G-1109)
PHONE BOOTH INC
809 Tate St (38834-5600)
P.O. Box 659 (38835-0659)
PHONE..................................662 286-6600
Danny Boatman, *President*
Mark Daniel, *Vice Pres*
EMP: 10
SQ FT: 2,400
SALES (est): 1.3MM **Privately Held**
SIC: 5065 5999 1731 3651 Telephone equipment; facsimile equipment; paging & signaling equipment; telephone equipment & systems; facsimile equipment; communication equipment; telephone & telephone equipment installation; video camera-audio recorders, household use

(G-1110)
PIONEER MACHINERY AND SUP INC
901 S Tate St (38834-7979)
PHONE..................................662 286-5646
Jeff Bobo, *President*
EMP: 10
SQ FT: 8,000
SALES (est): 1.8MM **Privately Held**
SIC: 3553 5084 Sawmill machines; sawmill machinery & equipment

(G-1111)
PRODUCTION MACHINE & TOOL INC
2500 Mason Saint Luke Rd (38834)
P.O. Box 1062 (38835-1062)
PHONE..................................662 287-4752
Travis Smith, *President*
Betty B Smith, *Corp Secy*
Sheryl Webb, *Vice Pres*
EMP: 9
SQ FT: 39,000
SALES (est): 690K **Privately Held**
SIC: 3599 3544 3541 3469 Machine shop, jobbing & repair; special dies & tools; jigs: inspection, gauging & checking; screw machines, automatic; stamping metal for the trade

(G-1112)
RANKIN PRINTERY
130 S Fillmore St (38834-5636)
P.O. Box 386 (38835-0386)
PHONE..................................662 287-4426
Donald W Hutchens Jr, *Principal*
EMP: 7
SQ FT: 5,000
SALES: 800K **Privately Held**
SIC: 5943 2791 2789 2752 Office forms & supplies; typesetting; bookbinding & related work; commercial printing, lithographic; job printing, gravure

(G-1113)
REBECCAS CSTM EMB & APPLIQUES
48 County Road 258 (38834-7813)
PHONE..................................662 665-1846
EMP: 1 EST: 2017
SALES (est): 35.3K **Privately Held**
SIC: 2395 Embroidery & art needlework

(G-1114)
REED S PRINTING INC
258 State Line Rd (38834-6016)
PHONE..................................662 287-0311
Jimmy R Reed, *Owner*
EMP: 4
SALES: 300K **Privately Held**
SIC: 2752 Commercial printing, lithographic

2019 Harris Directory of
Mississippi Manufacturers

▲ = Import ▼=Export
◆ =Import/Export

GEOGRAPHIC SECTION

Crystal Springs - Copiah County (G-1142)

GEOGRAPHIC

(G-1115)
REFRESHMENTS INC
101 W Linden St (38834-4653)
P.O. Box 240 (38835-0240)
PHONE..................................662 286-6051
Kenneth W Williams, *President*
Harry L Williams Jr, *Corp Secy*
Kathy McCullem, *CFO*
Bob Holmes, *Executive*
EMP: 80 **EST:** 1965
SQ FT: 12,500
SALES (est): 11.2MM **Privately Held**
WEB: www.refreshments.net
SIC: 5962 2099 Candy & snack food
vending machines; sandwich & hot food
vending machines; food preparations

(G-1116)
ROME CHENILLE & SUPPLY CO INC
1407a N Harper Rd (38834-3749)
PHONE..................................662 286-9947
Kelly Holder, *President*
EMP: 2
SQ FT: 2,500
SALES (est): 109.9K **Privately Held**
SIC: 3999 5193 2211 5714 Grasses, arti-
ficial & preserved; flowers & florists' sup-
plies; draperies & drapery fabrics, cotton;
draperies; cemetery & funeral directors'
equipment & supplies; chair covers &
pads: made from purchased materials

(G-1117)
RUSTIC INN PUBLICATIONS INC
3233 N Polk St (38834-7229)
PHONE..................................856 983-4288
Peggy A Dobbins, *Principal*
EMP: 2
SALES (est): 76.4K **Privately Held**
SIC: 2741 Miscellaneous publishing

(G-1118)
S&G GUTTER & SHEET METAL CO
206 Norman Rd (38834-5909)
P.O. Box 1413 (38835-1413)
PHONE..................................662 286-2924
Gary Austin, *Owner*
EMP: 8
SALES (est): 700K **Privately Held**
SIC: 3441 1761 3444 Fabricated struc-
tural metal; gutter & downspout contrac-
tor; sheet metalwork

(G-1119)
SMITH CABINET SHOP INC (PA)
Also Called: Corinth Manufacturing Marble
1505 S Fulton Dr (38834-6316)
P.O. Box 1426 (38835-1426)
PHONE..................................662 287-2151
Vernon Smith, *President*
Greg Moore, *Vice Pres*
Karen Smith, *Treasurer*
Tracy Smith, *Admin Sec*
EMP: 35
SQ FT: 70,000
SALES (est): 4.5MM **Privately Held**
SIC: 2493 5031 5211 2434 Marbleboard
(stone face hard board); building materi-
als, exterior; lumber & other building ma-
terials; vanities, bathroom: wood

(G-1120)
STANLEY APPRAISAL COMPANY LLC
504 N Cass St Apt 4 (38834-4968)
PHONE..................................662 287-8543
Mike Stanley, *President*
Claire W Stanley, *Admin Sec*
EMP: 1
SALES: 30K **Privately Held**
SIC: 3999 Barber & beauty shop equip-
ment

(G-1121)
SWEET TREATS AND COFFEE TOO
501 Cardinal Dr (38834-6303)
PHONE..................................662 286-5511
Tim Davis, *Principal*
EMP: 2
SALES (est): 95.5K **Privately Held**
SIC: 3531 Construction machinery

(G-1122)
TIMBER PRODUCTS CO LTD PARTNR
Also Called: Timber Products Mississippi
2701 S Harper Rd (38834-9273)
PHONE..................................662 287-3766
Tanya Haakinson, *Safety Dir*
Levon Newsom, *Branch Mgr*
EMP: 100
SALES (corp-wide): 351.4MM **Privately Held**
WEB: www.sor.teamtp.com
SIC: 2435 8021 Hardwood veneer & ply-
wood; specialized dental practitioners
PA: Timber Products Co. Limited Partner-
ship
305 S 4th St
Springfield OR 97477
541 995-0780

(G-1123)
TRI-STATE ELECTRIC CORINTH INC
1415 Sawyer Rd (38834-6369)
P.O. Box 1268 (38835-1268)
PHONE..................................662 287-2451
Jackie Robinson, *Manager*
EMP: 12
SALES (corp-wide): 29.6MM **Privately Held**
SIC: 7694 Electric motor repair
HQ: Tri-State Electric Of Corinth, Inc.
330 E Ge Patterson Ave
Memphis TN 38126
901 527-8412

(G-1124)
TRIPLE R TRAILERS INC
194 County Road 547 (38834-8109)
PHONE..................................662 728-7975
Maris Reese, *President*
EMP: 7
SQ FT: 10,750
SALES (est): 955.2K **Privately Held**
SIC: 3799 Trailers & trailer equipment

(G-1125)
UNITED PRINT SERVICES LLC
130 S Fillmore St (38834-5636)
PHONE..................................662 287-1090
Jimmy Mitchell, *Mng Member*
Donald Hutchens Jr,
Paula Hutchens,
EMP: 6
SQ FT: 4,600
SALES (est): 677.8K **Privately Held**
SIC: 2752 Commercial printing, offset

(G-1126)
USTX CONTRACT SERVICES NC INC
311a S Parkway St (38834-5914)
PHONE..................................512 894-0008
Victoria Carter, *CEO*
Jack L Carter Jr, *Director*
EMP: 45 **EST:** 2001
SALES (est): 9.3MM **Privately Held**
WEB: www.ustxcontractservices.com
SIC: 3559 1542 Electronic component
making machinery; commercial & office
buildings, renovation & repair

(G-1127)
VIRGIL WILLIAMS LLC
46 County Road 405 (38834-8218)
PHONE..................................662 287-7734
Virgil Williams, *Mng Member*
EMP: 2
SALES (est): 180K **Privately Held**
SIC: 3312 3544 Tool & die steel & alloys;
special dies, tools, jigs & fixtures

(G-1128)
WEAVER CONSOLIDATED GROUP INC (PA)
Also Called: Coca-Cola
601 Washington St (38834-4734)
P.O. Box 239 (38835-0239)
PHONE..................................662 287-1433
Harry Lee Williams Jr, *Principal*
Kenneth W Williams, *Corp Secy*
Mary Martin Weaver Burress, *Vice Pres*
EMP: 5
SQ FT: 35,000

SALES (est): 2.9MM **Privately Held**
SIC: 2086 5149 Bottled & canned soft
drinks; soft drinks

(G-1129)
WILLIAMS PRCSION MACHINING LLC (PA)
46 County Road 405 (38834-8218)
PHONE..................................662 287-7734
Joseph Chase Williams, *Mng Member*
EMP: 1
SALES: 90K **Privately Held**
SIC: 3544 7389 Special dies, tools, jigs &
fixtures;

(G-1130)
YOUNG DGHTERS PRCSION MCH WRKS
1500 Dcomsey Way Ext Extended (38834)
PHONE..................................662 286-6538
David Young, *Owner*
EMP: 2
SQ FT: 3,200
SALES: 84K **Privately Held**
SIC: 3599 Machine shop, jobbing & repair

Crawford
Lowndes County

(G-1131)
WILDLIFE DOMINION MGT LLC
1563 Penn Station Rd (39743-9555)
PHONE..................................662 272-9550
Robert Taylor, *Principal*
Kendall Ogden, *Principal*
Jack Robertson, *Principal*
EMP: 3
SALES (est): 155.4K **Privately Held**
SIC: 3496 0971 Traps, animal & fish; hunt-
ing, commercial

Crenshaw
Panola County

(G-1132)
CLAY KENTUCKY-TENNESSEE CO
250 Kt Rd (38621-5606)
PHONE..................................662 382-5262
Donnie Cook, *Manager*
Linda Dear, *Manager*
EMP: 33
SALES (corp-wide): 3MM **Privately Held**
SIC: 1459 1455 Clays (common) quarry-
ing; kaolin & ball clay
HQ: Clay Kentucky-Tennessee Company
100 Mansell Ct E Ste 300
Roswell GA 30076
770 645-3458

(G-1133)
CONTINENTAL INTERIORS INC
219 Terry Ave (38621-5448)
PHONE..................................662 382-3061
Angela Manuel, *Principal*
EMP: 3
SALES (est): 180.3K **Privately Held**
SIC: 3423 Carpenters' hand tools, except
saws: levels, chisels, etc.

Crosby
Amite County

(G-1134)
DS WELDING SERVICES
313 Airport Rd (39633-3507)
PHONE..................................601 639-4988
David Smith, *Owner*
EMP: 1
SALES (est): 55.6K **Privately Held**
SIC: 7692 Welding repair

(G-1135)
RIVER BANK LOGGING LLC
743 Otis Jackson Rd (39633-3544)
PHONE..................................601 639-4557
Patrick O Robertson Sr, *Principal*

EMP: 6
SALES (est): 528K **Privately Held**
SIC: 2411 Logging

(G-1136)
RJB ENTERPRISES
123 E Oak St (39633)
PHONE..................................601 639-4921
Gilbert C Barbo, *Partner*
George Donald, *Partner*
EMP: 20
SALES (est): 1.4MM **Privately Held**
SIC: 2421 2426 Sawmills & planing mills,
general; hardwood dimension & flooring
mills

Crowder
Quitman County

(G-1137)
OFFICE HUDDLE SMALL BUSINESS
130 Third St (38622)
PHONE..................................601 255-8650
Henry Dorris, *Mng Member*
EMP: 10
SALES (est): 334.8K **Privately Held**
SIC: 2759 Commercial printing

Crystal Springs
Copiah County

(G-1138)
27-55 FUEL PLAZA LLC
26171 Highway 27 (39059-8742)
PHONE..................................601 892-1643
Amit Kumar Budhraja, *Principal*
EMP: 2
SALES (est): 630.5K **Privately Held**
SIC: 2869 Fuels

(G-1139)
ABB INC
Also Called: ABB Crystal Springs
101 Kuhlman Dr (39059-2110)
PHONE..................................601 892-6431
William Sistrunk, *President*
EMP: 23
SALES (corp-wide): 36.4B **Privately Held**
SIC: 3612 Transformers, except electric
HQ: Abb Inc.
305 Gregson Dr
Cary NC 27511

(G-1140)
COPIAH LUMBER COMPANY
25026 Highway 51 (39059-9033)
P.O. Box 346 (39059-0346)
PHONE..................................601 892-2241
Craig Pyron, *President*
John Pyron, *Vice Pres*
EMP: 40
SQ FT: 2,700
SALES (est): 6.8MM **Privately Held**
SIC: 2421 Specialty sawmill products

(G-1141)
DELTA INDUSTRIES INC
Also Called: Jackson Ready Mix
1006 Coor Springs Cv (39059-8789)
P.O. Box 226, Jackson (39205-0226)
PHONE..................................601 948-4245
John Watkins, *Manager*
EMP: 33
SALES (corp-wide): 100.3MM **Privately Held**
WEB: www.delta-ind.com
SIC: 1442 3273 Construction sand &
gravel; ready-mixed concrete
PA: Delta Industries, Inc.
100 W Woodrow Wilson Ave
Jackson MS 39213
601 354-3801

(G-1142)
GRAHAM CUSTOM CABINETS & TRIM
111 Dampeer St (39059-2505)
PHONE..................................803 381-6829
Marcus Graham, *Principal*

(PA)=Parent Co (HQ)=Headquarters (DH)=Div Headquarters
✿ = New Business established in last 2 years

2019 Harris Directory of
Mississippi Manufacturers

49

Crystal Springs - Copiah County (G-1143)

GEOGRAPHIC SECTION

EMP: 1
SALES (est): 53.7K **Privately Held**
SIC: 2434 Wood kitchen cabinets

(G-1143)
GREEN BROTHERS GRAVEL CO INC
5179 Harmony Rd (39059-9259)
PHONE..................................601 362-3620
Andrew T Donahoe, *Branch Mgr*
EMP: 20
SALES (corp-wide): 3.6MM **Privately Held**
WEB: www.greenbrothersgravel.com
SIC: 1442 Gravel mining
PA: Green Brothers Gravel Company
517 Cobblestone Ct 1
Madison MS 39110
601 362-3620

(G-1144)
KUHLMAN ELECTRIC CORPORATION
Also Called: Power Transformer Div
101 Kuhlman Dr (39059-2110)
PHONE..................................601 892-4661
Paul Acheson, *Opers-Prdtn-Mfg*
EMP: 252
SALES (corp-wide): 36.4B **Privately Held**
WEB: www.kuhlman.com+kuhlman+electric+versailles
SIC: 3613 3677 3612 3823 Power switching equipment; electronic coils, transformers & other inductors; transformers, except electric; industrial instrmnts msrmnt display/control process variable; auto controls regulating residntl & coml environmt & applncs
HQ: Kuhlman Electric Corporation
93 Industry Dr
Versailles KY 40383

(G-1145)
L & W LOGGING INC
24706 Highway 27 (39059-9484)
PHONE..................................601 927-3588
Robert W Haley, *President*
EMP: 2
SALES (est): 243.9K **Privately Held**
SIC: 2411 Logging camps & contractors

(G-1146)
L M & R SERVICE INC
4156 Six Mile Rd (39059-9231)
PHONE..................................601 892-3034
David Rodgers, *President*
EMP: 6
SALES: 500K **Privately Held**
SIC: 3531 Construction machinery

(G-1147)
METALINE PRODUCTS INC
1002 Metaline Dr (39059-2193)
P.O. Box 71 (39059-0071)
PHONE..................................601 892-5610
Gene Klinck, *President*
Edward N Whitton, *Vice Pres*
Charles R Klinck, *Treasurer*
EMP: 17
SQ FT: 17,500
SALES (est): 3.2MM **Privately Held**
WEB: www.metalineproducts.com
SIC: 3441 3444 Fabricated structural metal; sheet metalwork

(G-1148)
METEOR INC
201 E Georgetown St (39059-2516)
P.O. Box 353 (39059-0353)
PHONE..................................601 892-2581
Henry Carney, *President*
John H Carney, *Corp Secy*
Joyce Carney, *Vice Pres*
EMP: 12
SALES (est): 996.2K **Privately Held**
SIC: 2711 2752 5943 Newspapers, publishing & printing; offset & photolithographic printing; office forms & supplies

(G-1149)
MISSCO CORPORATION OF JACKSON
Also Called: Sheldon Laboratory Systems
102 Kirk St (39059-2850)
PHONE..................................601 892-7105

Jeff Smith, *Sales Mgr*
Carl E Adkins, *Branch Mgr*
EMP: 90
SALES (corp-wide): 36.5MM **Privately Held**
WEB: www.missco.com
SIC: 2599 3821 Hospital furniture, except beds; laboratory equipment: fume hoods, distillation racks, etc.; laboratory furniture
PA: Missco Corporation Of Jackson
2001 Airport Rd N Ste 102
Flowood MS 39232
601 987-8600

(G-1150)
MOORE MACHINE & WELDING SHOP
2156 Lake Copiah Rd (39059-9481)
PHONE..................................601 892-5026
Jerry Moore, *President*
Linda Thompson, *Vice Pres*
Mary Moore, *Treasurer*
Shannon Moore, *Admin Sec*
Mary Ratliff, *Admin Sec*
EMP: 5
SALES: 300K **Privately Held**
SIC: 7692 Welding repair

(G-1151)
NAIL FIRST
324 E Railroad Ave (39059-2848)
PHONE..................................601 892-4433
Tom Huynh, *Manager*
EMP: 2
SALES (est): 173K **Privately Held**
SIC: 2844 Manicure preparations

(G-1152)
PCW (PRINT COPY WEBDESIGN LLC
111 Thrasher St (39059-2930)
PHONE..................................601 259-1945
Kenya Cummings,
EMP: 1 **EST:** 2010
SALES (est): 99.7K **Privately Held**
SIC: 2754 Commercial printing, gravure

(G-1153)
RICHARD PRICE BATTON
2133 Harmony Rd (39059-9252)
PHONE..................................601 892-5678
Richard P Batton, *Principal*
EMP: 3
SALES (est): 190.7K **Privately Held**
SIC: 1442 Construction sand & gravel

(G-1154)
RUTN CUTN DEER PROCESSING
26029 Highway 27 (39059-9710)
PHONE..................................601 892-5527
Jason May, *Owner*
EMP: 3 **EST:** 2009
SALES (est): 212.1K **Privately Held**
SIC: 2011 Meat packing plants

(G-1155)
SHELDON LABORATORY SYSTEMS INC
102 Kirk St (39059-2850)
P.O. Box 836 (39059-0836)
PHONE..................................601 892-2731
Mark A Sorgenfrei, *CEO*
Carl E Adkins, *President*
Eddie Adkins, *President*
Jenny Phillips, *COO*
Chuck Brashier, *Vice Pres*
▲ **EMP:** 100
SALES (est): 20.3MM
SALES (corp-wide): 36.5MM **Privately Held**
WEB: www.sheldonlabs.com
SIC: 3821 Chemical laboratory apparatus
PA: Missco Corporation Of Jackson
2001 Airport Rd N Ste 102
Flowood MS 39232
601 987-8600

(G-1156)
SOJOURNER TIMBER INC
2126 Sandy Yarn Rd (39059-9202)
PHONE..................................601 892-4021
Wayne Sojourner, *President*
Susie Sojourner, *Vice Pres*
EMP: 15

SALES (est): 1.7MM **Privately Held**
SIC: 2411 Logging

(G-1157)
SPARKLES & SUCH
510 Lee Ave (39059-2548)
PHONE..................................601 750-1270
Rae Barr, *Owner*
EMP: 1
SALES (est): 40K **Privately Held**
SIC: 5961 3961 Jewelry, mail order; costume jewelry

(G-1158)
TEAM SAFETY APPAREL INC
21155 Highway 51 (39059-8502)
P.O. Box 113 (39059-0113)
PHONE..................................601 892-3571
Heyward Hodges, *President*
Barbara Jones, *COO*
Barabara Jones, *Info Tech Dir*
▲ **EMP:** 45
SQ FT: 35,000
SALES (est): 7.2MM **Privately Held**
WEB: www.tsafety.com
SIC: 2326 Work pants

De Kalb
Kemper County

(G-1159)
ALPLY ARCHTCTURAL BLDG SYSTEMS
Willow Ave Hwy 16 W (39328)
PHONE..................................601 743-2623
EMP: 47
SQ FT: 49,000
SALES (est): 9.2MM **Privately Held**
SIC: 3448 Mfg Prefabricated Metal Buildings

(G-1160)
AMERICAN METALCRAFT
14062 Highway 16 W (39328-7922)
PHONE..................................769 486-5007
Peter Pelaez, *Owner*
EMP: 2
SALES (est): 120.4K **Privately Held**
SIC: 3444 Sheet metalwork

(G-1161)
ANCERSTOR LOGGING LLC
15441 Highway 39 N (39328-8239)
PHONE..................................601 701-7020
Tony Burrage, *Principal*
EMP: 2
SALES (est): 81.7K **Privately Held**
SIC: 2411 Logging

(G-1162)
CADE RUBBER CO INC
3822 Kipling Rd (39328-6211)
PHONE..................................601 743-5717
Billy Cade, *President*
Brad Bryant, *Manager*
EMP: 6
SQ FT: 3,000
SALES: 340K **Privately Held**
SIC: 3069 Hard rubber & molded rubber products

(G-1163)
E M F CORP
Also Called: Southern Circuits & Components
299 Ponderosa Ave (39328-9102)
PHONE..................................601 743-2794
Menno Lagendyk, *Plant Mgr*
R G Keeton Jr, *Manager*
EMP: 50
SALES (corp-wide): 39MM **Privately Held**
WEB: www.emfusa.com
SIC: 3679 Electronic circuits
PA: E M F Corp
505 Pokagon Trl
Angola IN 46703
260 665-9541

(G-1164)
EMILIA RESOURCES LLC
14124 Highway 16 W (39328-7921)
P.O. Box 16114, Jackson (39236-6114)
PHONE..................................601 743-9355

Amanda Harris, *Purchasing*
Angie Smith, *Purchasing*
Bryan Ricks, *Supervisor*
Renee Barach-Niles,
▲ **EMP:** 57
SQ FT: 55,000
SALES: 10MM
SALES (corp-wide): 455.5MM **Privately Held**
SIC: 2834 Pharmaceutical preparations
HQ: Emilia Cosmetics Ltd
1 Burnstein Zvi
Yeruham 80503
732 010-369

(G-1165)
HENRY E DAVIS LOGGING
Also Called: Henry Davis & Son Logging
827 Davis Rd (39328-7417)
PHONE..................................601 677-3669
Henry E Davis, *Owner*
Modene Davis, *Bookkeeper*
EMP: 3 **EST:** 1952
SALES: 200K **Privately Held**
SIC: 2411 Wooden logs

(G-1166)
LIBERTY FUELS COMPANY LLC
4707 Highway 493 (39328-7789)
PHONE..................................601 737-7000
Robert L Benson,
EMP: 64
SALES (est): 25.4MM
SALES (corp-wide): 135.3MM **Publicly Held**
SIC: 1221 Bituminous coal & lignite-surface mining
HQ: The North American Coal Corporation
5340 Legacy Dr Ste 300
Plano TX 75024
972 448-5400

(G-1167)
NOKOMIS LLC
62 Stennis Indus Pk Rd (39328-8046)
PHONE..................................601 743-2100
Davin Talbot, *Mng Member*
EMP: 2
SALES (est): 241.3K **Privately Held**
SIC: 3431 Metal sanitary ware

(G-1168)
TOONEYS TIRE CENTER
Hwy 16 W (39328)
PHONE..................................601 479-2654
Ray Salter Hill Jr, *Owner*
EMP: 1
SALES (est): 87K **Privately Held**
SIC: 3011 Tires & inner tubes

(G-1169)
TRI-COUNTY INDUSTRIES
14066 Highway 16 W (39328-7922)
PHONE..................................601 743-9931
Doris Shaw, *Prdtn Mgr*
Jeanie Kilpatrick, *Director*
EMP: 47
SALES (est): 3.2MM **Privately Held**
SIC: 3694 3672 2679 Battery charging alternators & generators; printed circuit boards; pressed fiber & molded pulp products except food products

Decatur
Newton County

(G-1170)
ADDY METAL FABRICATION
1434 Muley Rd (39327-9132)
PHONE..................................601 635-4064
Michael Addy, *Owner*
EMP: 2 **EST:** 1995
SALES (est): 223.3K **Privately Held**
SIC: 3441 Fabricated structural metal

(G-1171)
BLONZELLS CURTAIN SHOP
83 Rr 1 Box Rd 83 1st (39327)
P.O. Box 362 (39327-0362)
PHONE..................................601 635-3811
Blonzell Brown, *Owner*
EMP: 1

2019 Harris Directory of
Mississippi Manufacturers

▲ = Import ▼=Export
◆ =Import/Export

50

GEOGRAPHIC SECTION

Diberville - Harrison County (G-1201)

SALES (est): 52.9K **Privately Held**
SIC: 2391 Curtains & draperies

(G-1172)
DAVID L VANCE LOGGING CO
2514 Erin Lucern Rd (39327-9757)
PHONE..................................601 635-2105
David Lee Vance, *Owner*
EMP: 6 **EST:** 1958
SALES (est): 265.3K **Privately Held**
SIC: 2411 Logging camps & contractors

(G-1173)
HOLMES INDUSTRIES LLC
855 County Pond Rd (39327-9421)
PHONE..................................601 635-4409
Ed Holmes,
Edward Holmes,
Gayle Holmes,
EMP: 5
SQ FT: 16,000
SALES: 150K **Privately Held**
SIC: 3544 3599 3569 Special dies, tools,
jigs & fixtures; custom machinery; filters,
general line: industrial

(G-1174)
JAMES DAVID MEASELL
Also Called: Measell Logging
2950 Mount Zion Rd (39327-8820)
PHONE..................................601 635-4441
James D Measell, *Owner*
EMP: 6
SALES (est): 466.6K **Privately Held**
SIC: 2411 Logging

(G-1175)
MCKINNION WELDING & METAL FABR
16460 Hwgy 15 (39327)
PHONE..................................601 635-3983
Richard McKinnnion, *Owner*
EMP: 2
SALES (est): 118.5K **Privately Held**
SIC: 1799 3441 3444 5211 Welding on
site; fabricated structural metal; sheet
metalwork; fencing

(G-1176)
MD METALS SCRAP & SALVAGE
7974 Decatur Conehatta Rd (39327-9790)
PHONE..................................601 635-4160
Murray McElhenney, *Owner*
EMP: 4
SALES (est): 145.8K **Privately Held**
SIC: 7692 5093 Welding repair; metal
scrap & waste materials

(G-1177)
PEAVEY ELECTRONICS CORPORATION
16389 Highway 503 (39327-9209)
PHONE..................................601 483-5365
Jack Chandler, *Plt & Fclts Mgr*
EMP: 373
SALES (corp-wide): 164.7MM **Privately Held**
WEB: www.peavey.com
SIC: 3672 Circuit boards, television & radio
printed
PA: Peavey Electronics Corporation
5022 Hartley Peavey Dr
Meridian MS 39305
601 483-5365

(G-1178)
REMAN INC
110 E 9th St (39327)
P.O. Box 900 (39327-0900)
PHONE..................................601 635-4897
Don Howington, *Vice Pres*
EMP: 50
SALES (corp-wide): 8.1MM **Privately Held**
SIC: 5013 3714 Automotive supplies &
parts; motor vehicle parts & accessories
PA: Reman Inc
6586 Highway 13
Morton MS 39117
601 537-3400

(G-1179)
SMS EMBROIDERY
891 Decatur Stratton Rd (39327-9467)
PHONE..................................601 635-2347

Stewart Smith, *Manager*
EMP: 1 **EST:** 2013
SALES (est): 76.8K **Privately Held**
SIC: 2395 Embroidery & art needlework

Delta City
Sharkey County

(G-1180)
BELL ENVIRONMENTAL SVCS LLC
Also Called: Bell Demolition & Envmtl Svcs
3016 Delta City Rd (39061)
P.O. Box 133 (39061-0133)
PHONE..................................662 873-4551
Jimmy Bell,
EMP: 4
SALES (est): 330K **Privately Held**
SIC: 1795 2842 4959 Demolition, build-
ings & other structures; specialty cleaning
preparations; sanitary services

Dennis
Tishomingo County

(G-1181)
COOPER MAR & TIMBERLANDS CORP
183 County Road 1 (38838-9753)
PHONE..................................662 454-9274
Randy Schultz, *Branch Mgr*
EMP: 6
SALES (corp-wide): 511.1MM **Privately Held**
SIC: 0811 2421 Timber tracts, hardwood;
sawmills & planing mills, general
HQ: Cooper Marine & Timberlands Corpo-
ration
118 N Royal St
Mobile AL 36602
251 434-5000

(G-1182)
KIMBERLY-CLARK CORPORATION
183 County Road 1 (38838-9753)
PHONE..................................662 454-9274
Steve Mauney, *Branch Mgr*
EMP: 17
SALES (corp-wide): 18.4B **Publicly Held**
WEB: www.kimberly-clark.com
SIC: 2621 2676 Sanitary tissue paper; in-
fant & baby paper products
PA: Kimberly-Clark Corporation
351 Phelps Dr
Irving TX 75038
972 281-1200

(G-1183)
KRISTINA THORN
809 Highway 25 (38838-9433)
PHONE..................................256 460-9798
Kristina Thorn, *Principal*
EMP: 2
SALES (est): 81.7K **Privately Held**
SIC: 2411 Logging

(G-1184)
NELSONS METAL INC
10 Old Highway 25 (38838)
P.O. Box 63, Belmont (38827-0063)
PHONE..................................662 454-7500
Ken Nelson, *President*
EMP: 1
SALES (est): 164.5K **Privately Held**
SIC: 2611 1081 5093 Pulp manufactured
from waste or recycled paper; mine devel-
opment, metal; scrap & waste materials

(G-1185)
YOUNGS LEATHER & CUSTOM TEES
2499 County Road 961 (38838-9713)
PHONE..................................662 424-3847
EMP: 2 **EST:** 2014
SALES (est): 79K **Privately Held**
SIC: 2759 Screen printing

Diamondhead
Hancock County

(G-1186)
CARROLL AIRCRAFT LLC
2379 Coelho Way (39525-3109)
PHONE..................................228 255-7460
Egan Carroll, *Principal*
EMP: 2 **EST:** 2010
SALES (est): 119K **Privately Held**
SIC: 3721 Aircraft

(G-1187)
COLQUITT WOODWORKS LLC ✿
8935 Hanalei Cir (39525-3613)
PHONE..................................229 425-6087
Tate Bowen, *Principal*
EMP: 1 **EST:** 2018
SALES (est): 54.1K **Privately Held**
SIC: 2431 Millwork

(G-1188)
CUSTOM SPORTSWEAR USA INC
6610 Alakoko Ct (39525-3488)
P.O. Box 6342 (39525-6007)
PHONE..................................228 255-4795
Monica Bologna, *President*
Monica C Bologna, *Partner*
Bill Cole, *Vice Pres*
EMP: 2
SALES (est): 110.6K **Privately Held**
SIC: 2397 2759 Schiffli machine embroi-
deries; screen printing

(G-1189)
DEEP SOUTH TRAILER SALES LLC
6812 Awini St (39525-3523)
PHONE..................................228 255-2026
Jim Adams, *Owner*
EMP: 2 **EST:** 1994
SALES: 500K **Privately Held**
SIC: 3715 Truck trailers

(G-1190)
DIAMONDHEAD AEROLEASE LLC
898 Hapuna Pl (39525-3596)
PHONE..................................228 255-8491
Victor Byrd, *Branch Mgr*
Lamar Foster, *Branch Mgr*
Cheryl Jones, *Branch Mgr*
Norbert Peterson, *Branch Mgr*
Jim Clark, *Manager*
EMP: 1
SALES (est): 80.2K **Privately Held**
SIC: 3721 Aircraft

(G-1191)
DIAZ BROTHERS PRINTING
4323 Leisure Time Dr (39525-3243)
PHONE..................................601 247-0240
EMP: 2
SALES (est): 83.9K **Privately Held**
SIC: 2752 Commercial printing, litho-
graphic

(G-1192)
NVISION SOLUTIONS INC
88360 Diamondhead Dr E (39525-3643)
PHONE..................................228 242-0010
Socorro Harvey, *CEO*
Craig Harvey, *COO*
Donald Peyton, *CFO*
EMP: 68
SQ FT: 27,000
SALES: 4.2MM **Privately Held**
WEB: www.nvisionsolutions.com
SIC: 7371 8711 7389 3829 Computer
software development; marine engineer-
ing; photogrammatic mapping; geophysi-
cal or meteorological electronic
equipment; systems engineering consult-
ant, ex. computer or professional

(G-1193)
VIZAURA LLC
6514 Hanauma Ct (39525-3430)
PHONE..................................228 363-4048
Mark Lanoue, *CEO*

Jeff Meredith, *President*
EMP: 4
SALES (est): 114.7K **Privately Held**
SIC: 7371 8731 7373 2869 Computer
software systems analysis & design, custom; computer software development &
applications; computer (hardware) development; computer integrated systems design; rocket engine fuel, organic

---

Diberville
Harrison County

(G-1194)
ADVANCED FABRICATION INC
11032 Auto Mall Pkwy (39540-2410)
PHONE..................................228 392-0400
EMP: 1 **EST:** 2017
SALES (est): 25K **Privately Held**
SIC: 7692 Welding repair

(G-1195)
BACK BAY LAWNSCAPES LLC
4459 W Gay Rd (39540-3427)
PHONE..................................228 348-1299
Lowell Fountain, *Mng Member*
Bethany Fountain, *Mng Member*
EMP: 10
SALES: 700K **Privately Held**
SIC: 3271 1771 Blocks, concrete: land-
scape or retaining wall; blacktop (asphalt)
work

(G-1196)
BALIUS DANN WELDING
4401 Arceneaux Rd (39540-2398)
PHONE..................................228 354-9647
Dann Balius, *Owner*
EMP: 1
SALES (est): 316.5K **Privately Held**
SIC: 7692 Welding repair

(G-1197)
BELLES & BEAUS
10470 Diberville Blvd C (39540-2419)
PHONE..................................228 396-1771
Vickie Stroble, *Owner*
EMP: 2
SALES (est): 137.8K **Privately Held**
SIC: 2335 Bridal & formal gowns

(G-1198)
BIG D SIGNS
684 Orchard Dr (39540-5803)
PHONE..................................228 860-1075
Frank Lassere, *Owner*
EMP: 2
SALES (est): 158.3K **Privately Held**
SIC: 3993 Signs & advertising specialties

(G-1199)
BLAX SCREEN PRINTING & EMB
4511 Popps Ferry Rd (39540-2366)
PHONE..................................228 392-5022
Doug Husley, *Principal*
EMP: 2
SALES (est): 175.3K **Privately Held**
SIC: 2759 Screen printing

(G-1200)
C&C SIGNS LLC
15240 Camelot Dr (39540-9504)
PHONE..................................228 235-4839
Laral Chandler, *Principal*
EMP: 1
SALES (est): 49.2K **Privately Held**
SIC: 3993 Signs & advertising specialties

(G-1201)
COSENTINO ENTERPRISES INC
Also Called: Auntie Anne's
3615 Sangani Blvd (39540-8770)
PHONE..................................228 392-6666
Anthony Cosentino, *Manager*
EMP: 8
SALES (corp-wide): 650K **Privately Held**
SIC: 5461 2052 Pretzels; pretzels
PA: Cosentino Enterprises, Inc.
554 Meadow Wood Curv W
Mobile AL 36609
251 422-3056

(PA)=Parent Co (HQ)=Headquarters (DH)=Div Headquarters
✿ = New Business established in last 2 years

2019 Harris Directory of
Mississippi Manufacturers

51

Diberville - Harrison County (G-1202)

GEOGRAPHIC SECTION

(G-1202)
EZ CHORD LLC
633 Octave St (39540-5813)
PHONE..................................601 329-3827
Barry M Davis, *Principal*
EMP: 2
SALES (est): 94K **Privately Held**
SIC: 3931 Musical instruments

(G-1203)
FIRST HERITAGE CREDIT CORP
11516 Lamey Bridge Rd B2 (39540-2275)
PHONE..................................228 396-2620
EMP: 1 **Privately Held**
SIC: 6141 2411 Consumer finance companies; timber, cut at logging camp
PA: First Heritage Credit Corp
605 Crescent Blvd Ste 101
Ridgeland MS 39157

(G-1204)
GREATER GULF DEVELOPMENT LLC
4263 Popps Ferry Rd (39540-2363)
P.O. Box 7408 (39540-7401)
PHONE..................................228 392-6680
Joseph B Spear, *Mng Member*
Joey Spear, *Admin Asst*
Shelley Green, *Administration*
EMP: 8
SQ FT: 2,000
SALES (est): 1.9MM **Privately Held**
SIC: 1623 1081 Underground utilities contractor; metal mining exploration & development services

(G-1205)
GULF HYDRAULICS & PNEUMATICS
10420 Lamey Bridge Rd (39540-2648)
P.O. Box 6356 (39540-6356)
PHONE..................................228 392-1275
Delores Lee, *Ch of Bd*
Webster G Lee, *President*
Terri Fournier, *Vice Pres*
Jackie Weaver, *Vice Pres*
EMP: 15
SQ FT: 14,000
SALES (est): 5MM **Privately Held**
SIC: 5085 3593 7699 Pistons & valves; fluid power cylinders & actuators; hydraulic equipment repair

(G-1206)
GWENDOLYN RUCKER
Also Called: Enoch Development
1503 Arbor View Cir (39540-4869)
PHONE..................................919 337-6218
Gwendolyn Rucker, *Owner*
EMP: 3 EST: 2012
SALES (est): 174.2K **Privately Held**
SIC: 3448 Buildings, portable: prefabricated metal

(G-1207)
HINT HUNTER LLC
10253 Diberville Blvd B (39540-2539)
PHONE..................................228 273-4064
James Anthony Tadej, *Principal*
EMP: 2
SALES (est): 64.6K **Privately Held**
SIC: 3944 Puzzles

(G-1208)
MARTINI MONDAY INC
3487 Riverbend Cv (39540-8201)
PHONE..................................228 229-4872
John McCollins, *Principal*
EMP: 2
SALES (est): 83.9K **Privately Held**
SIC: 2752 Commercial printing, lithographic

(G-1209)
R FOURNIER & SONS INC
Also Called: Waterfall Brand
9391 Fournier Ave (39540-5467)
P.O. Box 732, Biloxi (39533-0732)
PHONE..................................228 392-4293
Doty A Fournier Jr, *President*
Ray Fournier, *Vice Pres*
Carolyn F Anderson, *Admin Sec*
EMP: 25

SALES (est): 4MM **Privately Held**
SIC: 5146 2092 Seafoods; fresh or frozen packaged fish

(G-1210)
REGA ENVIRONMENTAL INC
3586 Sangani Blvd Ste L (39540-9004)
PHONE..................................228 447-1024
EMP: 12
SALES (est): 389K **Privately Held**
SIC: 1389 Oil/Gas Field Services

(G-1211)
S AND S WOODWORKING LLC
10437 Lamey Bridge Rd I (39540-2709)
PHONE..................................228 257-6846
EMP: 1
SALES (est): 59.5K **Privately Held**
SIC: 2431 Millwork

(G-1212)
SCS SIGNS AND SERVICE LLC
15240 Camelot Dr (39540-9504)
PHONE..................................228 235-4839
Ashley Clayborn, *Partner*
EMP: 2 EST: 2012
SALES (est): 159.1K **Privately Held**
SIC: 3993 Signs & advertising specialties

(G-1213)
SOLUS RX LLC
4063 Ginger Dr Ste E (39540-3705)
PHONE..................................228 365-4501
Michael McCormick,
Eva Beidelman,
Jacob Chandler,
EMP: 1
SALES (est): 123.2K **Privately Held**
SIC: 2834 Druggists' preparations (pharmaceuticals)

(G-1214)
SORG PRINTING LLC
10361 Auto Mall Pkwy (39540-3750)
PHONE..................................228 392-3299
Greg Sorg, *Partner*
John Sorg, *Partner*
Gary Sorg, *Manager*
EMP: 6
SQ FT: 6,600
SALES (est): 1.1MM **Privately Held**
SIC: 2752 Commercial printing, offset

(G-1215)
SOUTHERN-ITS CORPORATION
624 Cypress Dr (39540-3710)
PHONE..................................228 273-2585
Jason Bell, *President*
EMP: 18
SALES (est): 1.3MM
SALES (corp-wide): 1.5MM **Privately Held**
SIC: 3699 Security control equipment & systems
PA: Southern Its International, Inc.
9101 W Sahara Ave Ste 105
Las Vegas NV 89117
888 415-6609

(G-1216)
TARANTOS CRAWFISH HOUSE
11185 Gorenflo Rd Ste A (39540-2711)
PHONE..................................228 392-0806
David Taranto, *Principal*
EMP: 4 EST: 2009
SALES (est): 330.4K **Privately Held**
SIC: 2092 Fresh or frozen packaged fish

(G-1217)
TELLIERS SHEETMETAL WORKS
4270d Popps Ferry Rd (39540-2391)
PHONE..................................228 392-5319
Douglas Tellier, *Owner*
EMP: 1
SQ FT: 5,000
SALES: 150K **Privately Held**
SIC: 3444 1711 1761 Sheet metalwork; heating & air conditioning contractors; sheet metalwork

(G-1218)
TROOPER PUBLICATIONS
10536 Auto Mall Pkwy C2 (39540-3742)
PHONE..................................228 392-1442

Matt McKnight, *Owner*
EMP: 1
SALES (est): 57.5K **Privately Held**
SIC: 2741 Miscellaneous publishing

Dublin
Coahoma County

(G-1219)
LUCKETT PUMP & WELL SVC INC
1420 Emerald Rd (38739)
P.O. Box 35 (38739-0035)
PHONE..................................662 624-2398
Steve Luckett, *President*
J H Luckett, *Corp Secy*
EMP: 8
SALES: 580K **Privately Held**
SIC: 1781 3561 3581 5063 Water well drilling; pumps & pumping equipment; automatic vending machines; motor controls, starters & relays: electric; signaling equipment, electrical; data loggers, industrial process type; controllers for process variables, all types

---

Duck Hill
Montgomery County

(G-1220)
DATA MEDICAL INC
242 Eskridge Rd (38925-9523)
PHONE..................................662 283-0463
John D Malone, *President*
EMP: 2
SALES (est): 194.3K **Privately Held**
SIC: 7372 Prepackaged software

(G-1221)
GLC MFG INC
789 Fishers Crossing Rd (38925-9306)
PHONE..................................662 565-2600
Lewis B Genola, *Principal*
EMP: 2
SALES (est): 141.8K **Privately Held**
SIC: 3999 Manufacturing industries

Dumas
Tippah County

(G-1222)
M R FURNITURE LLC
530 County Road 627 (38625-9704)
PHONE..................................662 882-8483
Michael K Roebuck, *Principal*
Micahel Roebuck, *Principal*
EMP: 1 EST: 2015
SALES (est): 73.2K **Privately Held**
SIC: 2426 Frames for upholstered furniture, wood

Dundee
Tunica County

(G-1223)
DELTA DUCK HUNTS INC
4101 Dundee Rd (38626-9742)
PHONE..................................662 357-5152
David Melton, *President*
EMP: 2
SALES (est): 102K **Privately Held**
SIC: 2015 Ducks, slaughtered & dressed

(G-1224)
LAKES FARM RAISED CATFISH INC
Also Called: Lake's Catfish
10280 Old Highway 61 S (38626-9621)
P.O. Box 67 (38626-0067)
PHONE..................................662 363-1847
Earl Lake, *President*
John Lake, *Corp Secy*
Jill Lake, *Vice Pres*
EMP: 8

SALES: 450K **Privately Held**
SIC: 2092 Fish, fresh: prepared

Durant
Holmes County

(G-1225)
EXQUISITE ENTERPRISE PUBG LLC
5069 Eddisville Rd (39063-2960)
PHONE..................................708 362-4583
Javell Thompson,
EMP: 1
SALES: 25K **Privately Held**
SIC: 2731 Book music: publishing only, not printed on site

(G-1226)
HAYES TRANSPORTATION LLC
150 Woodard Ln (39063-2973)
PHONE..................................662 582-5357
Bruce Hayes,
EMP: 2
SALES (est): 95.5K **Privately Held**
SIC: 3537 Trucks, tractors, loaders, carriers & similar equipment

(G-1227)
HUNTER ENGINEERING COMPANY
33814 Hunter Engineering (39063-2957)
PHONE..................................662 653-3194
Kenny Smith, *Manager*
EMP: 180
SALES (corp-wide): 400MM **Privately Held**
WEB: www.huntersupport.com
SIC: 3549 3714 3537 3444 Metalworking machinery; motor vehicle parts & accessories; industrial trucks & tractors; sheet metalwork
PA: Hunter Engineering Company Inc
11250 Hunter Dr
Bridgeton MO 63044
314 731-3020

(G-1228)
S & S WELDING & REPAIRS
4275 Wash Bailey Rd (39063-2835)
PHONE..................................662 834-1131
Arthur Saffold, *Owner*
EMP: 1 EST: 2001
SALES (est): 57K **Privately Held**
SIC: 7692 Welding repair

Ecru
Pontotoc County

(G-1229)
ANDREWS FURNITURE COMPANY INC
Also Called: Andrews Discount Furniture Str
6584 Highway 15 N (38841-9639)
P.O. Box 426 (38841-0426)
PHONE..................................662 489-1107
Larry M Andrews, *President*
EMP: 3
SALES: 30K **Privately Held**
SIC: 2511 Wood household furniture

(G-1230)
ASHLEY FURNITURE INDS INC
447 Highway 346 (38841-9772)
PHONE..................................662 489-5655
Brent Koslo, *Exec VP*
Joe Groover, *Engineer*
Igor Karam, *Manager*
Jerry Dulaney, *Info Tech Mgr*
EMP: 120
SALES (corp-wide): 4.2B **Privately Held**
WEB: www.ashleyfurniture.com
SIC: 5712 2512 Furniture stores; upholstered household furniture
PA: Ashley Furniture Industries, Inc.
1 Ashley Way
Arcadia WI 54612
608 323-3377

2019 Harris Directory of
Mississippi Manufacturers

▲ = Import ▼=Export
◆ =Import/Export

GEOGRAPHIC SECTION

Ellisville - Jones County (G-1259)

(G-1231)
FUSION FURNITURE INC
957 Ponto Count Indus Par (38841)
P.O. Box 366 (38841-0366)
PHONE....................................662 489-1296
Kenneth L Robbins, *President*
Bo Robbins, *Principal*
Alice Robbins, *Vice Pres*
Mike Hudson, *Vice Pres*
Phillip Gough, *Manager*
◆ EMP: 30
SALES (est): 6.6MM Privately Held
SIC: 2512 5021 Living room furniture: upholstered on wood frames; furniture

(G-1232)
S&S FRAMES INC
240 Stepp Dr (38841-9755)
PHONE....................................662 488-8996
Jeff Stepp, *President*
Jane Stepp, *Vice Pres*
Norman Schotz, *Treasurer*
EMP: 17 EST: 2000
SQ FT: 9,000
SALES (est): 1.3MM Privately Held
SIC: 2426 Frames for upholstered furniture, wood

(G-1233)
SPORTMAN CAMO COVERS INC
6564 Highway 15 N (38841-9639)
PHONE....................................662 489-7074
Maury Andrews, *President*
Bobby Cooper, *Vice Pres*
EMP: 10
SQ FT: 6,000
SALES (est): 983.8K Privately Held
WEB: www.sportsmancamocovers.com
SIC: 2399 Automotive covers, except seat & tire covers

(G-1234)
TIM WILDER LOGGING INC
830 Andrews Rd (38841-7249)
P.O. Box 46 (38841-0046)
PHONE....................................662 489-7632
EMP: 12
SALES (est): 784.9K Privately Held
SIC: 2411 Logging

(G-1235)
WILDER BROS SAWMILL INC
830 Andrews Rd (38841-7249)
PHONE....................................662 488-8692
Timothy Wilder, *President*
Robbie Wilder, *Vice Pres*
Anne Wilder, *Treasurer*
EMP: 18
SALES (est): 1.6MM Privately Held
SIC: 2421 Sawmills & planing mills, general

Edwards
Hinds County

(G-1236)
CAL-MAINE FOODS INC
Hwy 467 S (39066)
P.O. Box 168 (39066-0168)
PHONE....................................601 852-4970
Wil Webb, *Manager*
EMP: 100
SALES (corp-wide): 1.3B Publicly Held
WEB: www.calmainefoods.com
SIC: 0252 2015 Chicken eggs; egg processing
PA: Cal-Maine Foods, Inc.
3320 W Woodrow Wilson Ave
Jackson MS 39209
601 948-6813

(G-1237)
CAL-MAINE FOODS INC
17521 Old Hwy 80 (39066)
P.O. Box 335 (39066-0335)
PHONE....................................601 852-4413
Jimmy Kendrick, *Branch Mgr*
EMP: 9
SALES (corp-wide): 1.3B Publicly Held
WEB: www.calmainefoods.com
SIC: 0252 2015 Chicken eggs; eggs, processed: frozen

PA: Cal-Maine Foods, Inc.
3320 W Woodrow Wilson Ave
Jackson MS 39209
601 948-6813

(G-1238)
H&R CONSULTANTS LLC
Also Called: H & R
200 Jackson St (39066-9772)
PHONE....................................601 613-2288
James Holt, *President*
Arnold Rougee, *Vice Pres*
EMP: 2
SALES (est): 91.3K Privately Held
SIC: 3272 Concrete products

(G-1239)
KC&C GENERAL CONTRACTOR
3794 Good Hope Rd (39066-9795)
PHONE....................................601 668-4615
EMP: 1
SALES (est): 70K Privately Held
SIC: 3569 Mfg General Industrial Machinery

(G-1240)
KOESTLER PALLET SALES INC
12600 I 20 (39066-9083)
P.O. Box 162 (39066-0162)
PHONE....................................601 852-2926
Leo Koestler, *President*
Steve Riddick, *Plant Mgr*
EMP: 18
SQ FT: 30,000
SALES (est): 3.1MM Privately Held
SIC: 2448 Pallets, wood

(G-1241)
MID MISSISSIPPI MAINTENANCE
4850 Smith Station Rd (39066-4419)
PHONE....................................601 953-1091
Samantha Wheeler, *President*
EMP: 10
SALES (est): 250K Privately Held
SIC: 3271 4581 Blocks, concrete: landscape or retaining wall; aircraft maintenance & repair services

(G-1242)
MR FIX IT
1422 Highway 22 (39066-9790)
P.O. Box 137 (39066-0137)
PHONE....................................601 852-4705
Curtis Herring, *Owner*
EMP: 1
SALES (est): 63.6K Privately Held
SIC: 7299 7692 Handyman service; welding repair

(G-1243)
T & T LOGGING CO
1377 Askew Ln (39066-9751)
PHONE....................................601 852-4281
Thomas Richardson, *President*
EMP: 3 EST: 1982
SALES: 207K Privately Held
SIC: 2411 Logging

Elliott
Grenada County

(G-1244)
HANKINS LUMBER COMPANY INC (PA)
496 Nat G Troutt Rd (38926)
P.O. Box 1397, Grenada (38902-1397)
PHONE....................................662 226-2961
Albert B Hankins Jr, *President*
Lee J Hankins, *Vice Pres*
Jerry A Pegg, *Officer*
EMP: 15 EST: 1950
SQ FT: 7,000
SALES (est): 40.5MM Privately Held
SIC: 5031 2421 Lumber: rough, dressed & finished; lumber: rough, sawed or planed

Ellisville
Jones County

(G-1245)
ALLIED UNIVERSAL CORP
30 Neil Gunn Dr (39437-4773)
PHONE....................................601 477-2550
Donnie Redd, *Manager*
EMP: 10
SALES (corp-wide): 152.9MM Privately Held
WEB: www.allieduniversal.com
SIC: 5169 2819 Chlorine; chemicals, industrial & heavy; sodium & potassium compounds, exc. bleaches, alkalies, alum.
PA: Allied Universal Corp.
3901 Nw 115th Ave
Doral FL 33178
305 888-2623

(G-1246)
B & B OIL WELL SERVICE CO INC
1517 Highway 588 (39437-8729)
PHONE....................................601 425-3836
Robert G Barnett, *President*
EMP: 18 EST: 1959
SQ FT: 5,000
SALES: 2.8MM Privately Held
SIC: 1389 7538 5531 Oil & gas wells: building, repairing & dismantling; general automotive repair shops; general truck repair; automotive tires

(G-1247)
BUCKHAULTS SAWMILL & PALLETS
2064 Highway 29 S (39437-8262)
PHONE....................................601 477-8403
Lynn Buckhaults, *President*
Henry Barber, *Admin Sec*
▲ EMP: 30
SQ FT: 20,000
SALES (est): 4MM Privately Held
SIC: 2421 Sawmills & planing mills, general

(G-1248)
CANDLE CREATIONS BY MELINDA
90 Holly Lake Dr (39437-4223)
PHONE....................................601 477-4942
EMP: 1
SALES (est): 44.7K Privately Held
SIC: 3999 Candles

(G-1249)
CHANCELLORS WELDING
Also Called: Chancellor Welding
1524 Highway 11 S (39437-4749)
PHONE....................................601 477-3552
Jerry Chancellor, *Owner*
EMP: 2
SALES (est): 94.3K Privately Held
SIC: 7692 Welding repair

(G-1250)
CRAFTS BY FENTON
743 Moselle Oak Grove Rd (39437-6038)
PHONE....................................601 477-9164
EMP: 2
SALES (est): 90.3K Privately Held
SIC: 3944 Mfg Games/Toys

(G-1251)
EXPRO AMERICAS LLC
5349 Highway 11 N (39437-5007)
PHONE....................................281 576-5500
Branden Napier, *Opers Spvr*
Christopher Holifield, *Manager*
EMP: 26 Privately Held
SIC: 1381 Drilling oil & gas wells
HQ: Expro Americas, Llc
1311 Brdfeld Blvd Ste 400
Houston TX 77084

(G-1252)
G & G GRANITE
9 New Hope Cutt Off Rd (39437-4791)
PHONE....................................601 319-0905
Garett Culpepper, *Partner*

David Culpepper, *Partner*
EMP: 5
SQ FT: 5,000
SALES: 900K Privately Held
SIC: 3281 Curbing, granite or stone

(G-1253)
GENERAL ELECTRIC COMPANY
135 Technology Blvd (39437-8283)
PHONE....................................769 233-2828
George Ebrown, *Branch Mgr*
EMP: 10
SQ FT: 344,000
SALES (corp-wide): 121.6B Publicly Held
SIC: 3728 3724 Nacelles, aircraft; airfoils, aircraft engine
PA: General Electric Company
41 Farnsworth St
Boston MA 02210
617 443-3000

(G-1254)
GEORGE SMITH WELDING SVC LLC
55 Jarrod Rd (39437-8209)
P.O. Box 2494, Laurel (39442-2494)
PHONE....................................601 752-5288
George Earl Smith, *Principal*
EMP: 2
SALES (est): 134.7K Privately Held
SIC: 7692 Welding repair

(G-1255)
H & H WELDING LLC
5440 Highway 11 N (39437-5071)
PHONE....................................601 428-4788
Chris M Holyfield,
EMP: 13
SQ FT: 25,000
SALES (est): 2.2MM Privately Held
WEB: www.h-hwelding.net
SIC: 7692 Welding repair

(G-1256)
HALLS WELDING SERVICE
1011 N Front St (39437-2213)
PHONE....................................601 477-3925
Randy Hall, *Owner*
EMP: 3
SQ FT: 1,000
SALES (est): 300.1K Privately Held
SIC: 7692 5051 1799 Welding repair; steel; sandblasting of building exteriors

(G-1257)
HARBISON-FISCHER INC
5417 Highway 11 N (39437-5021)
PHONE....................................601 428-7919
Keith Westmoreland, *Sales Staff*
EMP: 1
SALES (corp-wide): 1.2B Publicly Held
WEB: www.hfpumps.com
SIC: 3533 3443 Oil field machinery & equipment; tanks, lined: metal plate
HQ: Harbison-Fischer, Inc.
901 N Crowley Rd
Crowley TX 76036
817 297-2211

(G-1258)
HOWARD INDUSTRIES INC
Also Called: Howard Technology Solutions
32 Howard Dr (39437-9020)
PHONE....................................601 399-5053
Eric Brown, *Vice Pres*
Morgan Garner, *Sales Staff*
Ashley Kelly, *Sales Staff*
Kasey Merchant, *Marketing Staff*
EMP: 13 EST: 2015
SALES (est): 3.2MM Privately Held
SIC: 3577 Computer peripheral equipment

(G-1259)
IMPRESSIONS INC
Also Called: Ainsworth Impressions
78 Jordan Loop (39437-5810)
PHONE....................................601 477-9608
Bobby Ainsworth, *President*
Hilda Ainsworth, *President*
EMP: 2 EST: 1978
SALES: 300K Privately Held
SIC: 2752 Commercial printing, offset

(PA)=Parent Co (HQ)=Headquarters (DH)=Div Headquarters
✪ = New Business established in last 2 years

2019 Harris Directory of
Mississippi Manufacturers

53

Ellisville - Jones County (G-1260)　　　　　　　　　　　　　　　　　　　　　**GEOGRAPHIC SECTION**

(G-1260)
JAMES R PADGETT
Also Called: Padgett Consulting
401 Sandhill Township Rd (39437-8419)
PHONE...................................601 763-3369
James R Padgett, *Owner*
EMP: 1
SALES: 110K **Privately Held**
SIC: 1389 Oil consultants

(G-1261)
K AND A INDUSTRIES LLC
325 Blackwell Loop (39437-8909)
PHONE...................................601 763-3503
Angelia Rivers, *Principal*
EMP: 1
SALES (est): 39.6K **Privately Held**
SIC: 3999 Manufacturing industries

(G-1262)
LABELS & STAMPS OF ELLISVILLE
Also Called: Labels and Stamps
850 Three Mile Stretch Rd (39437-5787)
P.O. Box 325 (39437-0325)
PHONE...................................601 763-3092
Gerald Porter, *Owner*
EMP: 4
SALES (est): 292.6K **Privately Held**
SIC: 3953 5099 Date stamps, hand: rubber or metal; rubber stamps

(G-1263)
MEMAWS CERAMICS
513 N Deason St (39437-2117)
PHONE...................................601 319-8263
Dora Thornton, *Owner*
EMP: 1
SALES (est): 52.7K **Privately Held**
SIC: 3229 Tableware, glass or glass ceramic

(G-1264)
MID-SOUTH CONTRACTORS INC
365 Kirkland Loop (39437-5666)
P.O. Box 1982, Laurel (39441-1982)
PHONE...................................601 544-2803
George Floyd, *President*
Steve Hollaway, *Manager*
EMP: 4
SALES: 400K **Privately Held**
SIC: 1389 Construction, repair & dismantling services; oil field services; servicing oil & gas wells

(G-1265)
OIL WELL LOGGING COMPANY INC
Also Called: Oil Logging
704 County Home Rd (39437-8454)
P.O. Box 416 (39437-0416)
PHONE...................................601 477-8315
Harvey W Koehne, *President*
EMP: 8
SQ FT: 3,000
SALES (est): 474K
SALES (corp-wide): 1.2MM **Privately Held**
SIC: 1389 Oil field services
PA: Oil Well Logging Company Inc
3970 Highway 43 N
Brandon MS 39047
601 477-8315

(G-1266)
PG TECHNOLOGIES LLC
135 Technology Blvd (39437-8283)
PHONE...................................317 240-2500
Derek Hileman, *Managing Dir*
EMP: 200
SALES (corp-wide): 21.7MM **Privately Held**
SIC: 3724 Air scoops, aircraft
PA: Pg Technologies, Llc
1405 Main St
Indianapolis IN 46224
317 240-2500

(G-1267)
QUALITY DRILLING FLUIDS INC
Also Called: Quality Mud Products Co
2 Neil Gunn Dr (39437-4773)
P.O. Box 128 (39437-0128)
PHONE...................................601 477-9085

Audrey S McKay, *President*
Lottie D McKay, *Vice Pres*
EMP: 14
SQ FT: 7,500
SALES (est): 1.3MM **Privately Held**
SIC: 1389 Oil field services

(G-1268)
SANDERSON FARMS INC
195 County Line Rd (39437-5712)
PHONE...................................601 426-1316
Martha Ewing, *Branch Mgr*
EMP: 1
SALES (corp-wide): 3.2B **Publicly Held**
SIC: 2015 Poultry slaughtering & processing
PA: Sanderson Farms, Inc.
127 Flynt Rd
Laurel MS 39443
601 649-4030

(G-1269)
SIGNATURE WORKS
1101 Highway 11 S (39437-4443)
PHONE...................................601 477-6187
William L Hudson, *President*
EMP: 8
SALES: 320K **Privately Held**
SIC: 3993 Signs & advertising specialties

(G-1270)
T & T WELDING INC
Also Called: T & T Welding Service
Ellisville Tuckr Crsng Rd (39437)
P.O. Box 279 (39437-0279)
PHONE...................................601 477-2884
Terry Hinton, *President*
EMP: 30
SQ FT: 20,000
SALES: 1.3MM **Privately Held**
SIC: 1799 7692 1389 3444 Welding on site; welding repair; construction, repair & dismantling services; oil field services; sheet metalwork

(G-1271)
T & T WELDING YARD INC
Also Called: T & T Communications
1462 Tuckers Crossing Rd (39437-5124)
P.O. Box 279 (39437-0279)
PHONE...................................601 477-2299
Terry Hinton, *President*
EMP: 30
SALES (est): 1.7MM **Privately Held**
SIC: 7692 7353 5082 1799 Welding repair; oil equipment rental services; oil field equipment; welding on site; oil field services

(G-1272)
TITAN SPECIALTIES
626 County Home Rd (39437-8453)
PHONE...................................601 477-3259
EMP: 2 EST: 2008
SALES (est): 110K **Privately Held**
SIC: 2892 Mfg Explosives

(G-1273)
TRANSFORMING LIVES PUBG LLC
403 Grant St (39437-3703)
PHONE...................................601 434-6583
Daniel Baker, *Principal*
EMP: 1 EST: 2015
SALES (est): 40.8K **Privately Held**
SIC: 2741 Miscellaneous publishing

(G-1274)
W L TISDALE CABINET SHOP
2741 Highway 588 (39437-8846)
PHONE...................................601 763-3552
W L Tisdale, *Owner*
EMP: 2
SALES (est): 157.8K **Privately Held**
SIC: 2434 Wood kitchen cabinets

(G-1275)
W S RED HANCOCK INC
5349 Highway 11 N (39437-5007)
PHONE...................................601 399-0605
Linda Hancock, *Branch Mgr*
EMP: 146

SALES (corp-wide): 64MM **Privately Held**
SIC: 1629 1389 4212 Earthmoving contractor; construction, repair & dismantling services; local trucking, without storage
PA: W. S. Red Hancock, Inc.
115 Pritchard Ave
Bentonia MS 39040
662 755-0011

(G-1276)
WADE SERVICES INC (PA)
30 Currie Rd (39437-5192)
P.O. Box 399 (39437-0399)
PHONE...................................601 399-1900
Allen Wade, *President*
Gaylor Wade, *Corp Secy*
Adrian Cotten, *Purch Agent*
EMP: 40
SQ FT: 32,000
SALES (est): 6.9MM **Privately Held**
WEB: www.wadeservices.com
SIC: 3715 4213 Truck trailers; heavy hauling

(G-1277)
WATKINS
Also Called: Southern Sales and Service
3165 Monroe Rd (39437-8819)
PHONE...................................601 752-2526
Al Watkins, *Owner*
Joseph Watkins, *Owner*
EMP: 6
SALES (est): 363.3K **Privately Held**
SIC: 4213 1521 1522 1542 Trucking, except local; single-family housing construction; residential construction; commercial & office building contractors; speculative builder, single-family houses; fabricated structural metal

(G-1278)
WHITESTONE CONTRACTING LLC
503 E Holly St (39437-2809)
P.O. Box 219 (39437-0219)
PHONE...................................601 800-8077
Robert M Neill Jr,
EMP: 1
SALES (est): 100K **Privately Held**
SIC: 3568 1521 Power transmission equipment; general remodeling, single-family houses

Enterprise
Clarke County

(G-1279)
DYESS LAWN & PATIO SHOP
67 County Road 374 (39330-9709)
PHONE...................................601 659-0390
Becky Dyess, *President*
Eulus Dyess, *Vice Pres*
EMP: 3
SALES (est): 308.8K **Privately Held**
SIC: 3446 Fences, gates, posts & flagpoles

(G-1280)
KELWOOD PRODUCTS INC
Highway 513 W (39330)
P.O. Box 1079, Waynesboro (39367-1079)
PHONE...................................601 659-7027
Thomas O Kelley, *President*
Jerry R Kelley, *Vice Pres*
Terry L Kelley, *Treasurer*
EMP: 50
SQ FT: 5,000
SALES (est): 5.2MM **Privately Held**
SIC: 2426 2421 Lumber, hardwood dimension; sawmills & planing mills, general

Escatawpa
Jackson County

(G-1281)
GRAHAM BROTHERS MACHINE INC
10817 Hwy 63 (39552)
P.O. Box 2006 (39552-2006)
PHONE...................................228 474-7011
Thomas Graham, *President*
Paul Graham, *Vice Pres*
EMP: 7
SQ FT: 2,400
SALES: 180K **Privately Held**
SIC: 3599 Machine shop, jobbing & repair

Ethel
Attala County

(G-1282)
LEROY DEES
9240 Attala Road 2101 (39067-6007)
PHONE...................................662 674-5356
Leroy Dees, *Owner*
EMP: 5
SALES (est): 303.1K **Privately Held**
SIC: 2411 Logging

(G-1283)
RALPH RONE
Also Called: Rone Sawmill
11670 Attala Road 5053 (39067-5621)
PHONE...................................662 674-5796
Ralph Rone, *Owner*
EMP: 2
SALES: 76K **Privately Held**
SIC: 2421 Sawmills & planing mills, general

Etta
Union County

(G-1284)
FOLLAINE PHARMACEUTICALS LLC
147 County Road 245 (38627-9519)
PHONE...................................303 808-4104
James D McChesney, *Principal*
EMP: 4 EST: 2014
SALES (est): 245.5K **Privately Held**
SIC: 2834 Drugs affecting neoplasms & endrocrine systems

Eupora
Webster County

(G-1285)
BACKWOODS TIE AND TIMBER LLC
181 Lagrange Rd (39744-8865)
P.O. Box 424 (39744-0424)
PHONE...................................662 258-3388
EMP: 14 EST: 2015
SALES (est): 2.1MM **Privately Held**
SIC: 2421 Sawmills & planing mills, general

(G-1286)
HAWKEYE GLOVE MANUFACTURING
2985 E Roane Ave (39744-2642)
PHONE...................................662 681-6278
Jim Rodenborn, *Partner*
Justin Chance, *Opers Mgr*
EMP: 81
SALES (est): 2.7MM **Privately Held**
SIC: 2381 Fabric dress & work gloves

(G-1287)
IN MOTION ORTHOTICS
224 Meadowlane St (39744-2219)
PHONE...................................662 258-8201
Joey Leon Carney, *Principal*
EMP: 3 EST: 2010

2019 Harris Directory of
Mississippi Manufacturers

54

▲ = Import ▼=Export
◆ =Import/Export

GEOGRAPHIC SECTION

Florence - Rankin County (G-1316)

SALES (est): 307.6K **Privately Held**
SIC: 3842 Orthopedic appliances

(G-1288)
KERSHENSTINES BEEF JERKY INC
550 Industrial Park Rd (39744-2619)
PHONE..............................662 258-2049
Timothy A Kershenstine, *President*
Adelaide K Alexis, *Corp Secy*
Jerel T Kershenstine, *Vice Pres*
▲ EMP: 9 EST: 1981
SQ FT: 5,000
SALES (est): 933.7K **Privately Held**
SIC: 2013 2011 Beef, dried: from purchased meat; meat packing plants

(G-1289)
MMC MATERIALS INC
100 Mississippi St (39744-2085)
PHONE..............................662 258-6096
F Woody, *Principal*
Cully Allgood, *Sales Staff*
Dave Clay, *Manager*
Scott Craft, *Manager*
Arlene King, *Assistant*
EMP: 5
SQ FT: 1,500
SALES (est): 396.9K **Privately Held**
SIC: 3273 Ready-mixed concrete

(G-1290)
PLYMOUTH TUBE COMPANY
212 Industrial Park Rd (39744-2508)
PHONE..............................662 258-2420
Ed Reid, *General Mgr*
Holly Pugsley, *Sales Staff*
Lonnie Potts, *Manager*
Verl Hayes, *Manager*
EMP: 58
SQ FT: 80,000
SALES (corp-wide): 277.4MM **Privately Held**
WEB: www.plymouth.com
SIC: 3317 3594 Steel pipe & tubes; fluid power pumps & motors
PA: Plymouth Tube Company
29w 150 Warrenville Rd
Warrenville IL 60555
630 393-3550

(G-1291)
SIGN SHOP
559 Schaefer Rd (39744-3493)
PHONE..............................662 258-7186
EMP: 2
SALES (est): 122.4K **Privately Held**
SIC: 3993 Signs & advertising specialties

(G-1292)
SMITH TIE AND TIMBER LLC
14020 Ms Highway 9 (39744-8772)
PHONE..............................662 258-7605
EMP: 40
SALES (est): 1,000K **Privately Held**
SIC: 5211 2411 Lumber And Other Building Materials, Nsk

(G-1293)
SOUTHERN BELL CLOTHING
2860 E Roane Ave (39744-2635)
PHONE..............................662 258-2955
Kim Lovorn, *Owner*
EMP: 2
SALES (est): 79K **Privately Held**
SIC: 2759 Screen printing

Falkner
Tippah County

(G-1294)
HILLS BROTHERS CNSTR & ENGRG
20831 Highway 15 (38629-9123)
P.O. Box 131 (38629-0131)
PHONE..............................662 837-7415
EMP: 35
SALES (est): 308.9K **Privately Held**
SIC: 3272 3273 Mfg Concrete Products Mfg Ready-Mixed Concrete

(G-1295)
JACKSON FISHING SPTG ACCESSORY
23391 Highway 370 (38629-9523)
P.O. Box 45 (38629-0045)
PHONE..............................662 837-9089
Penny Robenson, *President*
EMP: 6
SALES: 300K **Privately Held**
WEB: www.jackfish.net
SIC: 3949 3089 Fishing tackle, general; hunting equipment; plastic containers, except foam

Fayette
Jefferson County

(G-1296)
FAYETTE CHRONICLE
437 Main St (39069)
PHONE..............................601 786-3661
Charles Shepphard, *Owner*
EMP: 2
SALES (est): 120K **Privately Held**
SIC: 2711 Newspapers, publishing & printing

(G-1297)
FIRST CLASS INDUSTRIES LLC
797 River Rd (39069-4364)
P.O. Box 1173 (39069-1173)
PHONE..............................601 597-4787
Tramond Colenberg, *President*
EMP: 2
SALES (est): 131.5K **Privately Held**
SIC: 3999 Manufacturing industries

(G-1298)
JOE K SMITH
2214 Dennis Cross Rd (39069-5187)
PHONE..............................601 786-8632
Joe K Smith, *Principal*
EMP: 5
SALES (est): 463.2K **Privately Held**
SIC: 2411 Logging

(G-1299)
QUALITY CNSTR & ENGRG LLC
Also Called: Quality Engineering & Cnstr
248 Medgar Evers (39069)
PHONE..............................601 786-8017
Morris Washington, *Mng Member*
James Earl Jr,
Michael Henderson,
EMP: 214
SQ FT: 10,000
SALES: 1MM **Privately Held**
SIC: 8711 3825 7539 Engineering services; signal generators & averagers; electrical services

(G-1300)
RAY SMITH LOGGING INC
979 Dennis Cross Rd (39069-5190)
PHONE..............................601 786-8428
D Ray Smith Jr, *President*
EMP: 2
SALES (est): 200K **Privately Held**
SIC: 2411 Logging camps & contractors

(G-1301)
SHABAZZ PRINTING
232 Medgar Evers Blvd (39069)
PHONE..............................601 786-9788
Michael Muhammad, *Owner*
EMP: 3 EST: 1998
SQ FT: 5,000
SALES (est): 45K **Privately Held**
SIC: 2752 Commercial printing, offset

(G-1302)
SMOOTH TRANSITIONS LLC
213 Mcginty St Ste 2247 (39069)
PHONE..............................601 493-3787
Katrina Wilson-Watson,
EMP: 1
SALES: 18K **Privately Held**
SIC: 2389 Apparel & accessories

(G-1303)
WESTWARD CORPORATION
1453 Main St (39069)
PHONE..............................601 660-3857

Janelle Edwards, *Principal*
EMP: 3 EST: 2015
SALES (est): 106.9K **Privately Held**
SIC: 2099 5145 5961 0723 Food preparations; snack foods; food, mail order; tree nuts (general) hulling & shelling services; pecan hulling & shelling services

Fernwood
Pike County

(G-1304)
FABRICATED PIPE INC
1010 Frank Oaks Dr (39635)
PHONE..............................601 684-3007
Ronnie J Polito, *Branch Mgr*
EMP: 12
SALES (est): 1.9MM
SALES (corp-wide): 17.7MM **Privately Held**
SIC: 3498 Tube fabricating (contract bending & shaping)
PA: Fabricated Pipe, Inc.
15881 Airline Hwy
Baton Rouge LA 70817
225 293-9375

Flora
Madison County

(G-1305)
EURO AMERICAN PLASTICS INC
120 Saint Charles Ave (39071-9641)
P.O. Box 69 (39071-0069)
PHONE..............................601 879-0360
Yogesh Goel, *President*
A K Goel, *Exec VP*
Rashmi Goel, *Treasurer*
EMP: 15
SQ FT: 25,000
SALES (est): 3.3MM **Privately Held**
WEB: www.euroamericanplastics.com
SIC: 3089 3544 3599 Automotive parts, plastic; special dies, tools, jigs & fixtures; machine shop, jobbing & repair

(G-1306)
FOWLER CONSULTING LLC
252 Waldrop Rd (39071-9424)
PHONE..............................601 761-3696
Cliffton Fowlrt, *President*
EMP: 1 EST: 2016
SALES (est): 50K **Privately Held**
SIC: 1389 Oil & gas field services

(G-1307)
GEM PUBLICATIONS INC
Also Called: Gpi
4860 Main St (39071-9515)
P.O. Box 87 (39071-0087)
PHONE..............................601 879-3666
Candace J McNamara, *Vice Pres*
EMP: 4
SALES (est): 519.3K **Privately Held**
SIC: 2752 Commercial printing, offset

(G-1308)
GREEN MOLD DIE & FIXTURES INC
603 Pocahontas Rd (39071-9395)
P.O. Box 39 (39071-0039)
PHONE..............................601 879-8166
Jerry Green, *President*
EMP: 10
SALES (est): 1.3MM **Privately Held**
SIC: 3544 Die sets for metal stamping (presses); industrial molds; jigs & fixtures

(G-1309)
KELLYS WELDING SERVICE
449 Moore Ave (39071)
P.O. Box 677 (39071-0677)
PHONE..............................601 879-8636
Flue Kelly, *Owner*
EMP: 1
SALES (est): 41.6K **Privately Held**
SIC: 7692 Welding repair

(G-1310)
MISSISSIPPI AGRI-PRODUCTS INC
105 Clark St (39071-9399)
P.O. Box M (39071-1601)
PHONE..............................601 879-3343
Don Lane, *President*
EMP: 3
SALES (est): 160.1K
SALES (corp-wide): 357.8K **Privately Held**
SIC: 4225 2875 General warehousing & storage; fertilizers, mixing only
PA: Mississippi Agri-Products, Inc.
105 Clark St
Flora MS 39071
601 879-3343

(G-1311)
PRIMOS INC
Also Called: Primos Hunting Calls
604 First St (39071-9356)
PHONE..............................601 879-9323
Jay Tibbets, *President*
Blake Lipham, *President*
Teresa Schroeder, *Vice Pres*
Chuck Gessler, *Treasurer*
Slade Reeves, *Producer*
▲ EMP: 91
SQ FT: 50,000
SALES (est): 15.3MM
SALES (corp-wide): 2B **Publicly Held**
WEB: www.primos.com
SIC: 3949 3695 Hunting equipment; game calls; video recording tape, blank
HQ: Bushnell Holdings, Inc.
9200 Cody St
Overland Park KS 66214
913 752-3400

(G-1312)
SOUTHLAND CONTAINER INC
493 Livingston Vernon Rd (39071-9390)
P.O. Box 128 (39071-0128)
PHONE..............................601 879-8816
John Sanders Jr, *President*
Bud Horton, *Vice Pres*
Frank Horton, *Vice Pres*
EMP: 37
SQ FT: 145,000
SALES (est): 12.6MM **Privately Held**
WEB: www.southlandcontainer.com
SIC: 2653 Boxes, corrugated: made from purchased materials

(G-1313)
TRAVIS EXPLORATION INC
636 Mount Leopard Rd (39071-9532)
PHONE..............................601 879-8664
John Harvey, *President*
Dale Sykes, *Manager*
EMP: 2
SALES (est): 226.1K **Privately Held**
SIC: 1382 Oil & gas exploration services

Florence
Rankin County

(G-1314)
B B STUMP GRINDING
435 Blue Springs Cir (39073-8165)
PHONE..............................601 506-0997
EMP: 2 EST: 2008
SALES (est): 121.8K **Privately Held**
SIC: 3599 Grinding castings for the trade

(G-1315)
BENT WRENCH INDUSTRIES LLC
3383 Star Rd (39073-9118)
PHONE..............................601 934-7851
Danny Nelms, *Principal*
EMP: 1 EST: 2013
SALES (est): 75.6K **Privately Held**
SIC: 3999 Manufacturing industries

(G-1316)
CREATIVE IRON
823 Poplar Springs Rd (39073-7710)
PHONE..............................601 845-6290
Stacy Aycox, *Owner*
EMP: 1

(PA)=Parent Co (HQ)=Headquarters (DH)=Div Headquarters
✿ = New Business established in last 2 years

2019 Harris Directory of
Mississippi Manufacturers

55

Florence - Rankin County (G-1317)

SALES: 34K **Privately Held**
SIC: 7692 Welding repair

(G-1317)
CROWN SIMPLE RENOVATIONS WDWKG
150 Highway 469 N Apt G54 (39073-8943)
PHONE..................601 850-8272
EMP: 1
SALES (est): 54.1K **Privately Held**
SIC: 2431 Millwork

(G-1318)
CROWN SIMPLE RENOVATIONS WDWKG
150 Highway 469 N (39073-8941)
PHONE..................601 850-8272
EMP: 1
SALES (est): 54.1K **Privately Held**
SIC: 2431 Millwork

(G-1319)
CUSTOM-BILT PORTABLE BUILDINGS
Also Called: Custom-Bilt Portable Bldgs
2031 Highway 49 S (39073-9422)
PHONE..................601 932-2808
Michael Finnegan, *President*
EMP: 3
SQ FT: 3,000
SALES (est): 363.6K **Privately Held**
SIC: 3448 Buildings, portable: prefabricated metal

(G-1320)
DEBRA A JONES
Also Called: Barefoot Lumber
157 Mountain Creek Frm Rd (39073-8559)
P.O. Box 313 (39073-0313)
PHONE..................601 845-8946
Debra A Jones, *Owner*
EMP: 10
SQ FT: 10,000
SALES (est): 1MM **Privately Held**
SIC: 2448 Pallets, wood

(G-1321)
ELECTRIC MOTOR & EQUIPMENT
3917 Highway 49 S (39073-8050)
PHONE..................601 845-5561
Michael Wagner, *Owner*
EMP: 1
SALES (est): 65K **Privately Held**
SIC: 7694 Electric motor repair

(G-1322)
EXIDE TECHNOLOGIES
250 Ellis St (39073)
PHONE..................601 845-2236
J T Morgan, *Manager*
EMP: 8
SALES (corp-wide): 2.3B **Privately Held**
WEB: www.exideworld.com
SIC: 3691 3629 Lead acid batteries (storage batteries); battery chargers, rectifying or nonrotating
PA: Exide Technologies
13000 Deerfield Pkwy # 200
Milton GA 30004
678 566-9000

(G-1323)
EXIDE TECHNOLOGIES
407 Briarhill Rd (39073-7824)
PHONE..................601 845-2281
Roger Howell, *Branch Mgr*
EMP: 4
SALES (corp-wide): 2.3B **Privately Held**
WEB: www.exideworld.com
SIC: 3691 4953 2819 3629 Lead acid batteries (storage batteries); recycling, waste materials; industrial inorganic chemicals; battery chargers, rectifying or nonrotating
PA: Exide Technologies
13000 Deerfield Pkwy # 200
Milton GA 30004
678 566-9000

(G-1324)
FRAGRANT FLAMES
1614 Highway 469 S (39073-9025)
PHONE..................601 845-0759
Joan Conner, *Partner*

EMP: 2
SALES (est): 98.8K **Privately Held**
SIC: 3999 Candles

(G-1325)
HERRINGTON MILLWORKS
2709 W Mountain Creek Rd (39073-8545)
P.O. Box 963 (39073-0963)
PHONE..................601 845-8056
Mike Herrington, *Owner*
EMP: 5
SALES: 540K **Privately Held**
SIC: 5211 2431 Millwork & lumber; doors, wood

(G-1326)
LEES HOT SHOT SERVICE LLC
125 Johnson Rd (39073-9472)
PHONE..................601 383-1018
Lee Ervin Clerk Sr, *Principal*
EMP: 2 **EST:** 2012
SALES (est): 108.7K **Privately Held**
SIC: 1389 Hot shot service

(G-1327)
LOGO SPORTSWEAR
211 Whitetail Blvd (39073-4021)
PHONE..................601 845-5038
David Macdonald, *Owner*
EMP: 2
SALES (est): 99K **Privately Held**
SIC: 5699 2395 Sports apparel; embroidery products, except schiffli machine

(G-1328)
MCKENZIE/LEE PUBLISHING LLC
128 Cousins Dr (39073-8565)
PHONE..................769 216-8049
Vaniessa Cousin, *Principal*
EMP: 1
SALES (est): 37.5K **Privately Held**
SIC: 2741 Miscellaneous publishing

(G-1329)
MORRISON WELDING LLC
3109 Highway 49 S (39073-9403)
P.O. Box 401 (39073-0401)
PHONE..................601 845-5187
Jared Morrison, *President*
EMP: 4
SQ FT: 8,000
SALES: 475K **Privately Held**
SIC: 1799 7692 1711 Welding on site; welding repair; mechanical contractor

(G-1330)
ONEWAY SCREEN PRTG & GRAPHICS
2142 Florence Byram Rd (39073-9352)
PHONE..................601 845-7777
Margaret Hemphill, *Owner*
EMP: 1
SALES (est): 138.4K **Privately Held**
SIC: 2759 Screen printing

(G-1331)
PRODUCT SOURCE LIMITED LLC
144 Long Dr (39073-8240)
P.O. Box 180801, Richland (39218-0801)
PHONE..................769 257-4620
George Aarons, *President*
EMP: 1
SALES: 150K **Privately Held**
SIC: 2299 Textile goods

(G-1332)
S & C WELDING & MACHINE WORKS
122 Lewis Rd S (39073-7640)
PHONE..................601 845-5483
Lawrence Pierre Cook, *Partner*
EMP: 3
SALES: 250K **Privately Held**
SIC: 7692 Welding repair

(G-1333)
STEPHENS PRINTING LLC
642 Highway 469 S (39073-9064)
PHONE..................601 845-7708
Lucy L Stephens, *Mng Member*
David W Stephens,
EMP: 5
SQ FT: 1,700

SALES (est): 461K **Privately Held**
SIC: 2752 Commercial printing, offset

(G-1334)
STEVE B WHITE
130 Shenandoah Dr (39073-9712)
PHONE..................601 939-8177
EMP: 2 **EST:** 2001
SALES (est): 130K **Privately Held**
SIC: 2759 Commercial Printing

(G-1335)
VIP VINYL AND EMBROIDERY LLC
133 Mountain Creek Frm Rd (39073-8559)
PHONE..................601 624-7366
Corri Jordan, *Principal*
EMP: 1
SALES (est): 35.7K **Privately Held**
SIC: 2395 Embroidery & art needlework

(G-1336)
VOITH FABRICS FLORENCE INC
Also Called: Voith Paper Fabrics & Roll Sys
220 Price St (39073-8488)
PHONE..................601 845-2202
David Barefield, *Principal*
Christopher Turner, *Site Mgr*
Nicole Anders, *Accountant*
Ranee Nutt, *Human Resources*
Tammy Heine, *Consultant*
◆ **EMP:** 110
SQ FT: 105,000
SALES (est): 12.8MM **Privately Held**
SIC: 2231 3496 Papermakers' felts, woven: wool, mohair or similar fibers; miscellaneous fabricated wire products

(G-1337)
W E BIRDSONG ASSOCIATES INC
1435 Monterey Rd (39073-9694)
PHONE..................601 939-7448
Walter Birdsong, *President*
EMP: 6
SALES (est): 266.2K **Privately Held**
SIC: 3479 Coating of metals & formed products

(G-1338)
WASTEWATER CONTROL INC
2056 Highway 49 S (39073-9481)
P.O. Box 1176 (39073-1176)
PHONE..................601 845-5581
Thomas E Taylor Jr, *President*
Robert O Taylor, *Treasurer*
EMP: 7
SQ FT: 4,000
SALES: 210K **Privately Held**
SIC: 3589 Sewage treatment equipment

(G-1339)
WILLIAM ZAREMBA
Also Called: Zaremba Machine
2155 Cleary Rd (39073-8848)
PHONE..................601 845-7238
William Zaremba, *Owner*
EMP: 1
SALES (est): 114.8K **Privately Held**
SIC: 3545 Machine tool accessories

(G-1340)
YNA PALLETS SALES
250 Poplar St (39073-9738)
PHONE..................601 405-6545
Yoni Cruz-Diaz, *President*
EMP: 4
SALES (est): 474.5K **Privately Held**
SIC: 2448 Pallets, wood

Flowood
Rankin County

(G-1341)
ACCURATE DRUG TESTING AND BACK
105 Katherine Dr Bldg C (39232-8857)
PHONE..................601 500-7841
Sandra McClain, *Partner*
Gina McClain, *Principal*
EMP: 3

SALES (est): 183.7K **Privately Held**
SIC: 2835 Hemotology diagnostic agents

(G-1342)
ADCAMP INC
1353 Flowood Dr Ste A (39232-2702)
P.O. Box 54246, Jackson (39288-4246)
PHONE..................601 939-4493
Ralph Barnes, *President*
Clyde B Edwards Jr, *Corp Secy*
Charles W Haley, *Vice Pres*
Bradley Barnes, *Project Mgr*
Mollie Murphey, *Controller*
EMP: 58
SQ FT: 25,000
SALES (est): 12.4MM **Privately Held**
SIC: 1611 2951 Highway & street paving contractor; asphalt & asphaltic paving mixtures (not from refineries)

(G-1343)
AMERICAN NATIONAL MOLDING LLC
3670 Flowood Dr (39232-8006)
P.O. Box 320567 (39232-0567)
PHONE..................601 936-2722
Cathy Furr, *Principal*
Derrick Dabbs, *Mng Member*
Lisa Dabbs,
EMP: 85
SQ FT: 72,000
SALES: 6MM **Privately Held**
WEB: www.americannationalmolding.com
SIC: 3089 Injection molding of plastics

(G-1344)
BED BATH & BEYOND INC
760 Mackenzie Ln (39232-5008)
PHONE..................601 939-4840
Jared Shelton, *Store Mgr*
EMP: 8
SALES (corp-wide): 12B **Publicly Held**
SIC: 5719 2299 Beddings & linens; linen fabrics
PA: Bed Bath & Beyond Inc.
650 Liberty Ave
Union NJ 07083
908 688-0888

(G-1345)
BEKESON GLASS LLC
1001 Underwood Dr (39232-2712)
PHONE..................601 932-3676
Constance M Fason, *President*
Darrell Medrano, *General Mgr*
EMP: 12
SQ FT: 36,000
SALES: 2.3MM **Privately Held**
SIC: 3229 Glassware, industrial

(G-1346)
BLACK BOX CORPORATION
3010 Lakeland Cv (39232-9784)
PHONE..................601 939-9051
EMP: 2 **Privately Held**
SIC: 3577 Computer peripheral equipment
HQ: Black Box Corporation
1000 Park Dr
Lawrence PA 15055
724 746-5500

(G-1347)
BLAKE PUBLISHING INC
Also Called: Shocase of Homes
5719 Highway 25 Ste 204 (39232-7763)
PHONE..................601 992-6220
Julie Blake, *President*
EMP: 3
SALES (est): 281.7K **Privately Held**
WEB: www.blakepub.com
SIC: 2741 Miscellaneous publishing

(G-1348)
BOYANTON PRINTING INC
1018 N Flowood Dr Ste D (39232-9791)
P.O. Box 320157 (39232-0157)
PHONE..................601 939-6725
Billy Boyanton, *President*
Nelda Boyanton, *Treasurer*
EMP: 7
SALES (est): 845.7K **Privately Held**
WEB: www.boyantonprinting.com
SIC: 2752 Commercial printing, offset

2019 Harris Directory of
Mississippi Manufacturers

▲ = Import ▼=Export
◆ =Import/Export

GEOGRAPHIC SECTION

Flowood - Rankin County (G-1377)

(G-1349)
BRAXTON FOXX LLC
232 Market St (39232-3339)
PHONE..................................800 719-6811
EMP: 1
SALES (est): 36.6K Privately Held
SIC: 2731 Books-Publishing/Printing

(G-1350)
BUZINI GROUP LLC
Also Called: Buzini Sports
1016 N Flowood Dr (39232-9532)
PHONE..................................601 398-1311
Tjay Buzini,
Christopher Collins,
Chris Walker,
EMP: 23 EST: 2014
SALES (est): 1.2MM Privately Held
SIC: 2395 2759 5091 Embroidery products, except schiffli machine; screen printing; sporting & recreation goods

(G-1351)
CAMPBELL GLOBAL
1080 River Oaks Dr A220 (39232-7658)
PHONE..................................601 932-2729
EMP: 6
SALES (est): 279.1K Privately Held
SIC: 2411 Logging

(G-1352)
COPPER SCULPTURES INC
5230 Highway 25 (39232-6184)
PHONE..................................601 992-9955
William B Shook, Principal
Kathy Shook, Vice Pres
Kimberly Mistal, Sales Staff
EMP: 15
SQ FT: 15,000
SALES (est): 2.8MM Privately Held
WEB: www.coppersculptures.com
SIC: 3648 Lanterns: electric, gas, carbide, kerosene or gasoline

(G-1353)
COX MHP INC (PA)
4400 Mangum Dr Bldg D (39232-2113)
P.O. Box 5635, Brandon (39047-5635)
PHONE..................................601 936-3949
Chester Sidney Cox, President
Joseph Cox, General Mgr
Harry Roberson, General Mgr
W Robert Jones III, Principal
Nathan Henry Cox, Vice Pres
EMP: 30
SQ FT: 70,000
SALES (est): 4.4MM Privately Held
WEB: www.coxmhp.com
SIC: 3599 Machine shop, jobbing & repair

(G-1354)
DAVID HOLLINGSWORTH
3900 Lakeland Dr (39232-8852)
PHONE..................................769 233-7769
EMP: 1 EST: 2008
SALES (est): 55.4K Privately Held
SIC: 2732 Book printing

(G-1355)
ENVIRO-FLO INC
151 Custom Dr (39232-3142)
P.O. Box 321161 (39232-1161)
PHONE..................................601 939-2948
William Lee Lacey, President
Joe W Lacey II, Corp Secy
EMP: 5
SQ FT: 3,000
SALES (est): 1.5MM Privately Held
SIC: 3589 Sewage & water treatment equipment

(G-1356)
ERGON - ST JAMES INC (HQ)
2829 Lakeland Dr Ste 2000 (39232-7611)
P.O. Box 1308, Jackson (39215-1308)
PHONE..................................601 933-3000
Leslie B Lampton Sr, CEO
Kathryn W Stone, Corp Secy
EMP: 3
SQ FT: 6,000
SALES (est): 2.9MM
SALES (corp-wide): 997.6MM Privately Held
SIC: 1382 Oil & gas exploration services

PA: Ergon, Inc.
2829 Lakeland Dr Ste 2000
Flowood MS 39232
601 933-3000

(G-1357)
ERGON - WEST VIRGINIA INC
2829 Lakeland Dr Ste 2000 (39232-7611)
P.O. Box 1639, Jackson (39215-1639)
PHONE..................................601 933-3000
H Don Davis, President
Leslie B Lampton, President
Kathryn W Stone, Corp Secy
EMP: 1
SALES (est): 309.8K Privately Held
SIC: 2911 Petroleum refining

(G-1358)
ERGON CHEMICALS LLC (HQ)
2829 Lakeland Dr Ste 2000 (39232-7611)
PHONE..................................601 933-3000
Emmitte Haddox, CEO
EMP: 345
SALES (est): 68.9MM
SALES (corp-wide): 997.6MM Privately Held
SIC: 2821 Thermosetting materials; thermoplastic materials
PA: Ergon, Inc.
2829 Lakeland Dr Ste 2000
Flowood MS 39232
601 933-3000

(G-1359)
ERGON ETHANOL INC (HQ)
2829 Lakeland Dr Ste 2000 (39232-7611)
P.O. Box 1639, Jackson (39215-1639)
PHONE..................................601 933-3000
Leslie Lampton III, President
EMP: 6
SALES (est): 16.7MM
SALES (corp-wide): 997.6MM Privately Held
SIC: 2869 Industrial organic chemicals
PA: Ergon, Inc.
2829 Lakeland Dr Ste 2000
Flowood MS 39232
601 933-3000

(G-1360)
ERGON EUROPE MEA INC
2829 Lakeland Dr (39232-9798)
PHONE..................................601 933-3000
Kathryn W Stone, Corp Secy
Leslie B Lampton III, Vice Pres
EMP: 43 EST: 2007
SALES (est): 2.2MM
SALES (corp-wide): 997.6MM Privately Held
SIC: 2911 Petroleum refining
PA: Ergon, Inc.
2829 Lakeland Dr Ste 2000
Flowood MS 39232
601 933-3000

(G-1361)
ERGON INC (PA)
2829 Lakeland Dr Ste 2000 (39232-7611)
P.O. Box 1639, Jackson (39215-1639)
PHONE..................................601 933-3000
Leslie B Lampton Sr, President
Kris Patrick, President
Gary Babb, Business Mgr
Gaylon Baumbardner, Vice Pres
Baxter Burns, Vice Pres
◆ EMP: 200
SQ FT: 66,000
SALES (est): 997.6MM Privately Held
WEB: www.ergon.com
SIC: 2911 4213 4449 4613 Gases & liquefied petroleum gases; greases, lubricating; asphalt or asphaltic materials, made in refineries; liquid petroleum transport, non-local; river transportation, except on the St. Lawrence Seaway; intracoastal (freight) transportation; refined petroleum pipelines; petroleum bulk stations; petroleum terminals; petroleum products

(G-1362)
FLOWOOD RACEWAY
202 River Pines Cv (39232-2100)
PHONE..................................601 939-5048
Bubba Barham, Principal
EMP: 3 EST: 2010

SALES (est): 288.5K Privately Held
SIC: 3644 Raceways

(G-1363)
FUDGE INC
Also Called: ASAP Printing and Copying
2801 Layfair Dr (39232-9501)
PHONE..................................601 932-4748
Chris Fudge, President
EMP: 11
SALES: 1.7MM Privately Held
WEB: www.asapprinting.com
SIC: 2759 Commercial printing

(G-1364)
GLOBAL FOOD CONCEPTS INC
Also Called: P & R Foods
679 Grants Ferry Rd (39232-6843)
PHONE..................................601 940-5425
Robert Houston, President
Patricia Houston, Shareholder
◆ EMP: 120 EST: 2009
SQ FT: 125,000
SALES (est): 13.3MM Privately Held
SIC: 2033 Fruits & fruit products in cans, jars, etc.

(G-1365)
GULF SHIP LLC
645 Lakeland East Dr # 101 (39232-9099)
P.O. Box 310, Galliano LA (70354-0310)
PHONE..................................985 601-4444
EMP: 2
SALES (est): 256.2K Privately Held
SIC: 3731 Shipbuilding & repairing

(G-1366)
IPRINT INC
2001 Airport Rd N Ste 101 (39232-8846)
PHONE..................................601 932-4414
Ashley McLain, Principal
EMP: 4
SALES (est): 340K Privately Held
SIC: 2759 Letterpress printing

(G-1367)
IT SYNERGISTICS LLC
115 Tree St (39232-7661)
PHONE..................................855 866-7648
Timothy Bryant, Mng Member
EMP: 2
SALES (est): 68.6K Privately Held
SIC: 7372 Business oriented computer software

(G-1368)
J2 MANUFACTURING INC
220 Lakeland Pkwy (39232-9552)
PHONE..................................601 573-3134
EMP: 2 EST: 2016
SALES (est): 130.5K Privately Held
SIC: 3999 Manufacturing industries

(G-1369)
JABR LLC
150 Britton Cir (39232-8109)
PHONE..................................601 502-5587
Michael Gray, Principal
Joshua Harper,
EMP: 1
SALES (est): 38.7K Privately Held
SIC: 7371 7372 Computer software systems analysis & design, custom; application computer software

(G-1370)
JACKSON BUSINESS FORM COMPANY (PA)
1125 Old Brandon Rd (39232-3130)
P.O. Box 24028, Jackson (39225-4028)
PHONE..................................601 932-5200
Mickey McCardle, President
EMP: 40
SQ FT: 48,000
SALES (est): 7MM Privately Held
SIC: 2752 2761 Business forms, lithographed; manifold business forms

(G-1371)
JOURNAL INC
Also Called: Mississippi Business Journal
132 Riverview Dr Ste E (39232-8924)
PHONE..................................601 364-1000
Joe Jones, Manager
EMP: 20 Privately Held

WEB: www.dolanmedia.com
SIC: 2721 7389 Magazines: publishing & printing; trade show arrangement
HQ: Journal, Inc.
1242 S Green St
Tupelo MS 38804
662 842-2611

(G-1372)
JTWO MANUFACTURING LLC
517 Liberty Rd (39232-8028)
PHONE..................................769 243-8914
EMP: 1
SALES (est): 39.6K Privately Held
SIC: 3999 Manufacturing industries

(G-1373)
KEY THERAPEUTICS LLC
517 Liberty Rd Ste D (39232-8031)
PHONE..................................888 981-8337
EMP: 1
SQ FT: 100
SALES (est): 50.4K Privately Held
SIC: 2834 Mfg Pharmaceutical Preparations

(G-1374)
KOCH FOODS OF MISSISSIPPI LLC (HQ)
1080 River Oaks Dr A100 (39232-9779)
PHONE..................................601 732-8911
Jamie Ford, Export Mgr
Pennye Dillard, Sales Staff
Joseph Grendys, Mng Member
Nancy Martin, Manager
Sammie Smith, Manager
▼ EMP: 50 EST: 1981
SQ FT: 10,000
SALES (est): 643.7MM
SALES (corp-wide): 2.2B Privately Held
WEB: www.bcrogers.com
SIC: 2015 Chicken, processed: fresh; chicken, processed: frozen; chicken, slaughtered & dressed
PA: Koch Foods Incorporated
1300 Higgins Rd Ste 100
Park Ridge IL 60068
601 732-8911

(G-1375)
KOPIS MOBILE LLC
3010 Lakeland Cv Ste S (39232-9709)
PHONE..................................601 345-1753
Henry Jones, Mng Member
Michael Blossom, Program Mgr
Andrew Putnam, Software Engr
Richard Sween, Software Engr
Joshua Lunn,
EMP: 7
SQ FT: 2,500
SALES (est): 1.2MM Privately Held
SIC: 3699 7371 Electrical equipment & supplies; computer software development & applications

(G-1376)
LAKESIDE MOULDING & MFG CO
5300 Mississippi 25 (39232)
P.O. Box 5157, Brandon (39047-5157)
PHONE..................................601 992-5546
Herman L Shumaker, President
Herman Shumaker, President
Amanda Shumaker, Corp Secy
Tim Shumaker, Vice Pres
Tim Tillson, Opers Staff
EMP: 55
SQ FT: 20,000
SALES (est): 8.4MM Privately Held
WEB: www.lakesidemoulding.com
SIC: 2431 Doors & door parts & trim, wood; windows & window parts & trim, wood; moldings & baseboards, ornamental & trim; planing mill, millwork

(G-1377)
LIL MS SEW & SEW INC
1679 Old Fannin Rd Ste H (39232-8101)
PHONE..................................601 992-3279
Sasha Dearman, President
EMP: 2
SALES (est): 153.6K Privately Held
SIC: 2395 Embroidery & art needlework

(PA)=Parent Co (HQ)=Headquarters (DH)=Div Headquarters
✪ = New Business established in last 2 years

2019 Harris Directory of
Mississippi Manufacturers

57

Flowood - Rankin County (G-1378)

GEOGRAPHIC SECTION

(G-1378)
LION OIL CO
2829 Lkeland Dr Ste 2000 (39232)
PHONE............................601 933-3000
James Loe, *Opers Staff*
Patrick Busby, *CFO*
Alaina Malone, *Finance Mgr*
Shawn Sellers, *Administration*
EMP: 2
SALES (est): 81.9K **Privately Held**
SIC: 1311 Crude petroleum & natural gas

(G-1379)
MAGEE ENERGY LLC
3003 Lakeland Cv (39232-9504)
PHONE............................601 709-2930
J C Sarcy Daniel, *Mng Member*
M A Sheppark,
EMP: 2
SQ FT: 3,000
SALES (est): 136.6K **Privately Held**
SIC: 1382 Oil & gas exploration services

(G-1380)
MARDIS 300 LLC
213 Katherine Dr (39232-9588)
PHONE............................601 936-3911
Jason Mardis,
Kimberly Mardis,
EMP: 1
SALES (est): 48K **Privately Held**
SIC: 2211 Luggage fabrics, cotton

(G-1381)
MID-MISSISSIPPI VINYL
4331 Lakeland Dr (39232-8947)
PHONE............................601 910-6553
EMP: 2
SALES (est): 156.2K **Privately Held**
SIC: 3993 Signs & advertising specialties

(G-1382)
MTM INDUSTRIES LLC
4701 Lakeland Dr Apt 32c (39232-9786)
PHONE............................662 402-9750
Michael Mengarelli, *Administration*
EMP: 2
SALES (est): 127.1K **Privately Held**
SIC: 3999 Manufacturing industries

(G-1383)
MURPHY USA INC
5339 Highway 25 (39232-6173)
PHONE............................601 992-2041
EMP: 14 **Publicly Held**
SIC: 5541 2911 Gasoline service stations;
petroleum refining
PA: Murphy Usa Inc.
200 E Peach St
El Dorado AR 71730

(G-1384)
**NATIONAL SEATING MOBILITY
INC**
108 N Layfair Dr (39232-9782)
PHONE............................601 664-1090
Jeffrey Matukewicz, *Branch Mgr*
EMP: 2 **Privately Held**
SIC: 3842 Wheelchairs
PA: National Seating & Mobility, Inc.
320 Premier Ct S Ste 220
Franklin TN 37067

(G-1385)
NUCOR STEEL JACKSON INC
3630 Fourth St (39232-2000)
PHONE............................601 939-1623
Daniel R Dimicco, *President*
Gim Shebel, *Vice Pres*
Craig Stovall, *Controller*
▲ EMP: 265
SQ FT: 404,694
SALES (est): 99.2MM
SALES (corp-wide): 25B **Publicly Held**
WEB: www.nsjak.com
SIC: 3312 Stainless steel
PA: Nucor Corporation
1915 Rexford Rd Ste 400
Charlotte NC 28211
704 366-7000

(G-1386)
**PACKAGING MACHINERY
SYSTEMS**
188 Webb Ln (39232-8077)
PHONE............................601 992-5011
Ladd Hay, *Principal*
EMP: 4
SALES (est): 372.9K **Privately Held**
SIC: 3565 Packaging machinery

(G-1387)
**PINNACLE PRINTING AND
COPYING**
2300 Lakeland Dr (39232-9550)
PHONE............................601 944-1470
Gary Owens, *President*
EMP: 4
SQ FT: 2,000
SALES (est): 400K **Privately Held**
SIC: 2752 Commercial printing, litho-
graphic

(G-1388)
**PLANHOUSE PUBLICATIONS
INC**
660 Katherine Dr (39232-8847)
PHONE............................601 825-1187
Micah James McCullough, *Principal*
EMP: 1 **EST:** 2016
SALES (est): 46.2K **Privately Held**
SIC: 2741 Miscellaneous publishing

(G-1389)
PREMIER PUBLISHING INC
Also Called: Premier Bride of Mississippi
640 Lakeland East Dr A (39232-9778)
P.O. Box 718, Ridgeland (39158-0718)
PHONE............................601 957-1050
Lynda Jungkind, *President*
Johnny Jungkind, *Treasurer*
EMP: 4
SALES (est): 57.3K **Privately Held**
SIC: 2721 7389 Magazines: publishing
only, not printed on site; convention &
show services

(G-1390)
**RANKIN PUBLISHING COMPANY
INC**
Also Called: Rankin Record
614 Grants Ferry Rd (39232-6844)
P.O. Box 5507, Brandon (39047-5507)
PHONE............................601 992-4869
Wyatt Emmerich, *President*
EMP: 4
SALES (est): 296.7K **Privately Held**
WEB: www.rankinrecord.com
SIC: 2711 Newspapers, publishing & print-
ing

(G-1391)
RED LAKE CEDAR CO LLC
4209 Lakeland Dr Ste 279 (39232-9212)
PHONE............................877 469-5552
Stephan Herbison, *Mng Member*
EMP: 3
SALES (est): 113.6K **Privately Held**
SIC: 2499 Carved & turned wood; en-
graved wood products

(G-1392)
REDDI MEALS INC
679 Grants Ferry Rd (39232-6843)
PHONE............................601 992-1503
EMP: 12
SALES (est): 490K **Privately Held**
SIC: 2099 Mfg Food Preparations

(G-1393)
ROCKETT INC
3640 Fourth St (39232-2003)
P.O. Box 6066, Jackson (39288-6066)
PHONE............................601 939-9347
John McGregor, *President*
Richard Autrey, *Corp Secy*
Graves Linda, *Purch Agent*
Jeff Rogers, *Engineer*
Bucky Crystal, *Business Anlyst*
▲ EMP: 105
SQ FT: 140,000

SALES (est): 24MM
SALES (corp-wide): 116.7MM **Privately
Held**
WEB: www.rockettinc.com
SIC: 3443 3449 3537 Boiler shop products: boilers, smokestacks, steel tanks;
bars, concrete reinforcing: fabricated
steel; trucks, tractors, loaders, carriers &
similar equipment
PA: Jackson Iron & Metal Company, Inc.
1404 Allen St
Jackson MS
601 969-6910

(G-1394)
**SANDERSON FARMS INC
FOODS DIV**
Food Division
4418 Mangum Dr (39232-2113)
PHONE............................601 939-9790
Paul Billingsley, *Division Mgr*
Paul Billinslgy, *Manager*
EMP: 378
SQ FT: 62,000
SALES (corp-wide): 3.2B **Publicly Held**
SIC: 2038 2015 2013 Dinners, frozen &
packaged; poultry slaughtering & pro-
cessing; sausages & other prepared
meats
HQ: Sanderson Farms, Inc. (Foods Divi-
sion)
127 Flynt Rd
Laurel MS 39443
601 649-4030

(G-1395)
SERVICE PRINTERS INC
1014 N Flowood Dr (39232-9532)
P.O. Box 320249, Jackson (39232-0249)
PHONE............................601 939-4910
M H McGee, *CEO*
Kevin M McGee, *President*
Sandra Weir Mc Gee, *Corp Secy*
Jay Peoples, *Sales Staff*
Missie Parker, *Office Admin*
EMP: 48
SQ FT: 25,000
SALES (est): 6.9MM **Privately Held**
WEB: www.serviceprintersinc.com
SIC: 2759 Screen printing

(G-1396)
**SHACKS WELDING SERVICE
INC**
1260 Old Brandon Rd (39232-3131)
P.O. Box 6164, Jackson (39288-6164)
PHONE............................601 939-5491
Thomas R Shack, *President*
Clara Shack, *Corp Secy*
EMP: 2
SQ FT: 6,400
SALES: 220K **Privately Held**
SIC: 7692 Welding repair

(G-1397)
SMART SYNCH
3010 Lakeland Cv Ste S (39232-9709)
PHONE............................601 420-9959
Steven Johnson, *President*
Paul Stoufer, *Manager*
EMP: 4
SALES (est): 290K **Privately Held**
SIC: 3825 Meters: electric, pocket,
portable, panelboard, etc.

(G-1398)
SNAPSHOT PUBLISHING LLC
3900 Lakeland Dr Ste 202 (39232-8853)
P.O. Box 320925 (39232-0925)
PHONE............................601 624-8845
EMP: 7
SALES (est): 580K **Privately Held**
SIC: 2741 Miscellaneous publishing

(G-1399)
**SOUTHEASTERN FOREST
PRODU**
502 Shalom Way (39232-8107)
PHONE............................601 988-1131
Diane Riley, *Admin Sec*
EMP: 2
SALES (est): 246.2K **Privately Held**
SIC: 2439 Timbers, structural: laminated
lumber

(G-1400)
SOUTHERN FUR DESIGN
3010 Lakeland Cv Ste V (39232-9730)
PHONE............................601 936-2005
Wilbur Pepper, *Principal*
EMP: 1
SALES (est): 100K **Privately Held**
SIC: 2371 Fur goods

(G-1401)
TAW POWER SYSTEM INC
2702 Flowood Dr (39232-9056)
PHONE............................601 939-3455
EMP: 1 **EST:** 2012
SALES (est): 77.1K **Privately Held**
SIC: 7694 Electric motor repair

(G-1402)
TMS INTERNATIONAL LLC
3630 Fourth St (39232-2000)
PHONE............................601 932-8205
EMP: 3 **Privately Held**
SIC: 3312 Blast furnaces & steel mills
HQ: Tms International, Llc
12 Monongahela Ave
Glassport PA 15045
412 678-6141

(G-1403)
TRADEWINDS PUBLICATIONS
5719 Highway 25 (39232-7105)
PHONE............................601 992-3699
Cynthia Clay, *Manager*
EMP: 4
SALES (est): 230.2K **Privately Held**
SIC: 2711 Newspapers, publishing & print-
ing

(G-1404)
**TRILOGY COMMUNICATIONS
INC**
4400 Mangum Dr (39232-2113)
P.O. Box 5918, Jackson (39288-5918)
PHONE............................601 932-4461
John Kaye, *Principal*
EMP: 130
SQ FT: 3,095
SALES (corp-wide): 27.4MM **Privately
Held**
WEB: www.trilogycoax.com
SIC: 3357 Coaxial cable, nonferrous
PA: Trilogy Communications, Inc.
2910 Highway 80 E
Pearl MS 39208
601 932-4461

(G-1405)
**VALIOSO PETROLEUM
COMPANY**
504 Keywood Cir (39232-3000)
PHONE............................601 936-3601
Karl J Kaufmann, *President*
EMP: 2
SQ FT: 2,500
SALES (est): 200K **Privately Held**
SIC: 1382 Oil & gas exploration services

(G-1406)
**WALTMAN PHARMACEUTICALS
INC**
1 Lakeland Sq Ste B (39232-8826)
P.O. Box 12442, Jackson (39236-2442)
PHONE............................601 939-0833
Herchell Waltman, *President*
Joann Waltman, *Corp Secy*
Whitney Waltman Burns, *Vice Pres*
EMP: 5
SQ FT: 5,000
SALES (est): 1.2MM **Privately Held**
WEB: www.zapzyt.com
SIC: 2834 Pharmaceutical preparations

(G-1407)
WILDERWOOD LLC
129 Indian Creek Blvd (39232-8670)
PHONE............................601 955-8539
Leslie H Miley, *President*
EMP: 1
SALES (est): 41.5K **Privately Held**
SIC: 2499 Wood products

(G-1408)
ZAVATION LLC
220 Lakeland Pkwy (39232-9552)
PHONE............................601 919-1119

▲ = Import ▼ =Export
◆ =Import/Export

58

2019 Harris Directory of
Mississippi Manufacturers

GEOGRAPHIC SECTION

Foxworth - Marion County (G-1435)

Jamie Johnson, *Opers Mgr*
Kyle Johnson, *Mfg Mgr*
Ty Pulliam, *Asst Controller*
Brad Risher, *Sales Staff*
Jeffrey Johnson, *Mng Member*
EMP: 9 **EST:** 2010
SQ FT: 9,000
SALES (est): 1.7MM **Privately Held**
SIC: 3842 Implants, surgical

Forest
Scott County

(G-1409)
BATTE & HOLLINGSWORTH LUMBER
19064 Highway 80 (39074-4438)
PHONE..................................601 469-4938
Roony Hollingsworth, *President*
Connie Hollingsworth, *Principal*
EMP: 8
SALES (est): 1.5MM **Privately Held**
SIC: 2421 Lumber: rough, sawed or planed

(G-1410)
CENTRAL INDUSTRIES INC (PA)
1300 E Third St (39074)
P.O. Box 1510 (39074-0510)
PHONE..................................601 469-4421
Barney Jarreau, *President*
EMP: 6 **EST:** 1964
SQ FT: 45,000
SALES (est): 17.3MM **Privately Held**
SIC: 5191 2048 Farm supplies; meat meal
& tankage: prepared as animal feed

(G-1411)
CENTRAL INDUSTRIES INC
13666 Highway 80 (39074-7645)
P.O. Box 1510 (39074-0510)
PHONE..................................601 469-4421
Dr Reagan Sadler, *Manager*
EMP: 40
SALES (corp-wide): 17.3MM **Privately Held**
SIC: 2048 2077 Prepared feeds; animal &
marine fats & oils
PA: Central Industries, Inc.
1300 E Third St
Forest MS 39074
601 469-4421

(G-1412)
CENTRAL MISSISSIPPI GLASS CO
502 Old Morton Rd (39074-4003)
PHONE..................................601 469-5050
David Franks, *Principal*
EMP: 8
SALES (est): 350K **Privately Held**
SIC: 3231 Products of purchased glass

(G-1413)
DAVID MOREHEAD
Also Called: Morehead Painting
428 N Woodland Dr (39074-3312)
PHONE..................................601 469-2272
David Morehead, *Owner*
EMP: 1
SALES (est): 53.3K **Privately Held**
WEB: www.davemorehead.com
SIC: 1721 2621 Residential painting; in-
dustrial painting; wallpaper (hanging
paper)

(G-1414)
DIXIE PRINT
1016 E Third St (39074-4323)
P.O. Box 322 (39074-0322)
PHONE..................................601 469-3350
Fax: 601 469-5987
EMP: 3 **EST:** 1983
SALES (est): 160K **Privately Held**
SIC: 2752 5943 Offset Printing & Ret Of-
fice Supplies

(G-1415)
DOTTED SIGNS & SCREENPRINTING
7605 Highway 35 S (39074-9480)
PHONE..................................601 506-2175
Chris Ingrahm, *Owner*
EMP: 1

SALES (est): 84.8K **Privately Held**
WEB: www.ingrammotorsports.com
SIC: 3993 Signs & advertising specialties

(G-1416)
EDDIE INC
6223 Highway 21 (39074-9593)
PHONE..................................601 663-5755
Eddie Harrison, *President*
Stephanie Harrison, *Admin Sec*
EMP: 15
SQ FT: 200
SALES: 2MM **Privately Held**
SIC: 2411 Wooden logs

(G-1417)
JACK BATTE AND SONS INC
Also Called: Batte Lumber
221 Scr 35-9 (39074-5753)
PHONE..................................601 536-3976
Bennie S Batte, *President*
Virginia Batte, *Corp Secy*
Larry Batte, *Vice Pres*
EMP: 50
SQ FT: 20,000
SALES (est): 7.8MM **Privately Held**
SIC: 2421 Sawmills & planing mills, gen-
eral

(G-1418)
JOHNSON EDUCATIONAL SALES INC
Also Called: Bob Tom Johnson
1304 Melwood Dr (39074-3030)
PHONE..................................601 469-1924
Bob Tom Johnson, *President*
Ellen Johnson, *Admin Sec*
EMP: 3
SALES: 350K **Privately Held**
SIC: 8299 7819 3652 Educational serv-
ices; video tape or disk reproduction; pre-
recorded records & tapes

(G-1419)
KANES PUBLISHING COMPANY LLC
704 Wicker St (39074-3548)
PHONE..................................601 345-5153
Shekinah Denham-Taylor, *Principal*
EMP: 2
SALES (est): 59.2K **Privately Held**
SIC: 2741 Miscellaneous publishing

(G-1420)
KING LUMBER COMPANY INC
1103 W Third St (39074-3900)
P.O. Box 1479 (39074-0479)
PHONE..................................601 469-3271
Jonette Gaddis, *Principal*
EMP: 65 **EST:** 1940
SQ FT: 5,000
SALES (est): 10.5MM **Privately Held**
SIC: 2421 Sawmills & planing mills, gen-
eral

(G-1421)
KOCH FOODS OF MISSISSIPPI LLC
921 S Main St (39074-9094)
PHONE..................................601 469-2337
Joe Grendis, *President*
David Leblanc, *Plant Mgr*
Word Strength, *Plant Mgr*
EMP: 489
SALES (corp-wide): 2.2B **Privately Held**
WEB: www.bcrogers.com
SIC: 2015 Poultry, processed
HQ: Koch Foods Of Mississippi Llc
1080 River Oaks Dr A100
Flowood MS 39232
601 732-8911

(G-1422)
METARIS CORPORATION
Also Called: Metaris Hydraulics
1519 Highway 35 N (39074-5032)
P.O. Box 387 (39074-0387)
PHONE..................................601 469-1987
Michael Smith, *President*
Stephen Smith, *Prdtn Mgr*
Anna Shumeko, *Buyer*
Shazia Dhatti, *Controller*
Kevin Leary, *Manager*
◆ **EMP:** 45
SQ FT: 70,000

SALES (est): 12.5MM **Privately Held**
WEB: www.metaris.com
SIC: 3569 5084 3594 Jacks, hydraulic;
hydraulic systems equipment & supplies;
fluid power pumps & motors
PA: Hydraulex International Holdings, Inc.
48175 Gratiot Ave
Chesterfield MI 48051

(G-1423)
MMC MATERIALS INC
13522 Hwy 80 W (39074)
PHONE..................................601 469-2741
Thomas Warren, *Manager*
EMP: 19
SALES (corp-wide): 306.5MM **Privately Held**
WEB: www.mmcmaterials.com
SIC: 3273 Ready-mixed concrete
HQ: Mmc Materials, Inc.
1052 Highland Colony Pkwy # 201
Ridgeland MS 39157
601 898-4000

(G-1424)
RAYTHEON COMPANY
19859 Highway 80 (39074-9702)
PHONE..................................601 467-3730
Gregory Bourne, *Project Mgr*
Steve Coleman, *Opers Mgr*
Gwen Laird, *Mfg Staff*
Linda Hawkins, *Production*
Teresa Price, *Purch Mgr*
EMP: 400
SALES (corp-wide): 27B **Publicly Held**
SIC: 3812 3728 Sonar systems & equip-
ment; aircraft training equipment
PA: Raytheon Company
870 Winter St
Waltham MA 02451
781 522-3000

(G-1425)
SCOTT PUBLISHING INC
Also Called: Scott County Times, The
311 Smith Ave (39074-4159)
PHONE..................................601 469-2561
Ken Belend, *President*
Brian Blackley, *President*
Sidney L Salter, *President*
Cindy Harrell, *Office Mgr*
Diane Purvis, *Manager*
EMP: 5 **EST:** 1983
SQ FT: 5,400
SALES (est): 484.1K **Privately Held**
WEB: www.sctonline.net
SIC: 2711 Commercial printing & newspa-
per publishing combined

(G-1426)
TYSON FOODS INC
305 Cleveland St (39074-3200)
PHONE..................................229 995-6800
Teresa Key, *Persnl Mgr*
Ray Able, *Manager*
Charles Cox, *Manager*
Kurt Schrock, *Director*
Tracy Shannon, *Director*
EMP: 2
SALES (corp-wide): 40B **Publicly Held**
SIC: 2015 Poultry slaughtering & process-
ing
PA: Tyson Foods, Inc.
2200 W Don Tyson Pkwy
Springdale AR 72762
479 290-4000

(G-1427)
TYSON FOODS INC
1225 Jack Lee Dr (39074-3918)
PHONE..................................601 469-1712
Fredrie Gray, *Nursing Mgr*
Charles Cox, *Manager*
EMP: 30
SALES (corp-wide): 40B **Publicly Held**
SIC: 2011 Meat packing plants
PA: Tyson Foods, Inc.
2200 W Don Tyson Pkwy
Springdale AR 72762
479 290-4000

(G-1428)
UNIPRES SOUTHEAST USA INC
1001 Fountain Dr (39074-4038)
PHONE..................................601 469-0234
Masanobu Yoshizawa, *President*

Angel Huddleston, *President*
Takayoshi Tanaka, *President*
Enisuke Tsuchiya, *President*
Dwight Vowell, *Purch Mgr*
▲ **EMP:** 123
SQ FT: 260,000
SALES (est): 24.6MM **Privately Held**
SIC: 3465 Body parts, automobile:
stamped metal
PA: Unipres Corporation
1-19-20, Shin-Yokohama, Kohoku-Ku
Yokohama KNG 222-0

Foxworth
Marion County

(G-1429)
EARS JEWLERY BOX SP FASHIONS
15 1/2 Quinn Ln (39483)
PHONE..................................769 234-1771
An'haza E White, *Owner*
EMP: 9
SALES (est): 220K **Privately Held**
SIC: 2389 Apparel & accessories

(G-1430)
FOXWORTH & THOMPSON INC
Also Called: Foxworth & Thompson Lumber
2192 Highway 98 W (39483-5023)
P.O. Box 84 (39483-0084)
PHONE..................................601 736-3602
EMP: 3
SQ FT: 500
SALES (est): 190K **Privately Held**
SIC: 2421 Planer Mill

(G-1431)
HELANBAK LLC
360 Pine Grove Church Rd (39483-3267)
PHONE..................................601 736-6112
John Bernardo, *Branch Mgr*
EMP: 9
SALES (corp-wide): 2.8MM **Privately Held**
SIC: 3553 3599 3317 Bandsaws, wood-
working; machine & other job shop work;
machine shop, jobbing & repair; pipes,
seamless steel; pipes, wrought: welded,
lock joint or heavy riveted
PA: Helanbak, Llc
1481 Highway 13 N
Columbia MS

(G-1432)
HOLMES HILTON
1438 Highway 586 (39483-3356)
PHONE..................................601 736-5757
Hilton Holmes, *Owner*
EMP: 2
SALES (est): 120.4K **Privately Held**
SIC: 2499 Trophy bases, wood

(G-1433)
MARION COUNTY TIMBER INC
168 Ten Mile Creek Rd (39483-4746)
PHONE..................................601 736-0654
Henry A Stringer, *President*
EMP: 10
SALES (est): 1.3MM **Privately Held**
SIC: 2421 Sawmills & planing mills, gen-
eral

(G-1434)
MIKE LOWERY LLC
17 Silver Creek Rd (39483-3813)
PHONE..................................601 736-1096
Mike Lower, *Manager*
EMP: 2 **EST:** 2017
SALES (est): 88.6K **Privately Held**
SIC: 1381 Drilling oil & gas wells

(G-1435)
RIVER BEND LOGGING LLC
215 Carroll Loop (39483-3367)
PHONE..................................601 466-1524
Tal Thornhill, *Principal*
EMP: 2
SALES (est): 81.7K **Privately Held**
SIC: 2411 Logging

(PA)=Parent Co (HQ)=Headquarters (DH)=Div Headquarters
✪ = New Business established in last 2 years

2019 Harris Directory of
Mississippi Manufacturers

Foxworth - Marion County (G-1436)

GEOGRAPHIC SECTION

(G-1436)
TAYLOR ENERGY COMPANY LLC
Also Called: Circle Bar East
469 Circle Bar Rd (39483-3258)
PHONE..................................601 736-9997
James Coward, *Branch Mgr*
EMP: 7
SALES (corp-wide): 3MM **Privately Held**
WEB: www.taylorenergy.com
SIC: 1311 Crude petroleum production
PA: Taylor Energy Company Llc
1 Lee Cir
New Orleans LA 70130
504 581-5491

(G-1437)
TERRYS BITS MACHINE SHOP
350 Pine Grove Church Rd (39483-3267)
PHONE..................................601 736-6112
EMP: 2
SALES (est): 81.4K **Privately Held**
SIC: 3599 Machine shop, jobbing & repair

(G-1438)
WESLEY INC
Also Called: Ceramic Studio
568 Pounds Rd (39483-4132)
PHONE..................................601 731-9288
David Wesley, *President*
Vicky Wesley, *Admin Sec*
EMP: 2
SQ FT: 5,000
SALES (est): 131.3K **Privately Held**
SIC: 3299 Ceramic fiber

French Camp
Choctaw County

(G-1439)
BOX LOGGING
115 Whites Rd (39745-8762)
PHONE..................................662 547-6692
Keith Box, *Partner*
Kevin Box, *Partner*
EMP: 7 EST: 2001
SALES (est): 703K **Privately Held**
SIC: 2411 Logging camps & contractors

(G-1440)
MARCELLAS QUILT SHOP
1588 Highway 413 (39745-9523)
PHONE..................................662 262-7870
Marcella Black, *Owner*
EMP: 1
SALES (est): 43.6K **Privately Held**
SIC: 2395 Quilting & quilting supplies

(G-1441)
PARKERSON LUMBER INC
980 Ms Highway 413 (39745-8834)
PHONE..................................662 547-6019
Keith Parkerson, *President*
Betty Parkerson, *Admin Sec*
EMP: 35
SALES: 7MM **Privately Held**
SIC: 2421 Sawmills & planing mills, general

Friars Point
Coahoma County

(G-1442)
HELENA CHEMICAL COMPANY
1500 Port Rd (38631)
PHONE..................................662 383-0004
David Cirilli, *Manager*
EMP: 9 **Privately Held**
WEB: www.helenachemical.com
SIC: 5191 2819 Fertilizers & agricultural chemicals; industrial inorganic chemicals
HQ: Helena Agri-Enterprises, Llc
255 Schilling Blvd # 300
Collierville TN 38017
901 761-0050

(G-1443)
MARTIN MARIETTA MATERIALS INC
Also Called: Friars Point Yard
1500 Port Rd (38631)
PHONE..................................662 383-2070
Bob Rice, *Branch Mgr*
EMP: 2 **Publicly Held**
WEB: www.martinmarietta.com
SIC: 1423 Crushed & broken granite
PA: Martin Marietta Materials Inc
2710 Wycliff Rd
Raleigh NC 27607

Fulton
Itawamba County

(G-1444)
AGGEOS INC
603 Dulaney Wilemon Rd (38843-9623)
PHONE..................................512 751-2160
John Walters, *CEO*
EMP: 5
SALES (est): 251.9K **Privately Held**
SIC: 7372 Prepackaged software

(G-1445)
BEANE LOGGING
3856 Peppertown Rd (38843-7418)
PHONE..................................662 862-9053
David Beane, *President*
EMP: 3 EST: 2001
SALES (est): 216.7K **Privately Held**
SIC: 2411 Logging camps & contractors

(G-1446)
BENNETTS WOOD WORKS
675 Ironwood Bluff Rd (38843-7121)
PHONE..................................662 862-6124
Stanton Bennett, *Principal*
EMP: 1 EST: 2008
SALES (est): 111.4K **Privately Held**
SIC: 2431 Millwork

(G-1447)
BROWNS ICE COMPANY
1650 Country Club Rd (38843-9702)
PHONE..................................662 862-3706
Jamie Brown, *Owner*
EMP: 2
SALES (est): 170K **Privately Held**
SIC: 2097 Manufactured ice

(G-1448)
CG MONOGRAM & GIFTS
8245 Highway 25 S (38843-9512)
PHONE..................................662 401-5344
Jeriann Grammer, *Principal*
EMP: 1
SALES (est): 45.9K **Privately Held**
SIC: 2395 Embroidery & art needlework

(G-1449)
CHAMPION CUSTOM BOW STRINGS
2716 Ptton Flat Okland Rd (38843)
PHONE..................................662 652-3499
Betsy Weaver, *Owner*
EMP: 1
SALES (est): 101.7K **Privately Held**
SIC: 3949 Archery equipment, general

(G-1450)
CLARENCE SOUTH LOGGING
Also Called: South Trucking
6 South Dr (38843-8843)
PHONE..................................662 585-3724
Clarence R South, *Owner*
EMP: 7
SALES (est): 515.3K **Privately Held**
SIC: 2411 4212 Logging camps & contractors; local trucking, without storage

(G-1451)
DELTA FABRICATORS
2 Rodgers Rd (38843-6778)
PHONE..................................662 862-2998
Randy Rodgers, *Principal*
EMP: 1
SALES (est): 95.3K **Privately Held**
SIC: 3553 Cabinet makers' machinery

(G-1452)
DSP ARMORY INC
204 N Gaither St (38843-1120)
PHONE..................................662 862-4272
Ted Chatham, *President*
Stephanie Chatham, *Principal*
Stephanie Homan, *Principal*
EMP: 4 EST: 2014
SALES (est): 394.5K **Privately Held**
SIC: 3484 Small arms

(G-1453)
FUHR INTERNATIONAL LLC
Also Called: Fuhr Research Laboratories
2841 John Frankin Hwy B (38843)
PHONE..................................662 862-4903
David R Fuhr, *Mng Member*
Jackline Fuhr,
EMP: 19 EST: 1980
SQ FT: 30,000
SALES (est): 2.1MM **Privately Held**
SIC: 2851 Paints & allied products

(G-1454)
GI ARMORY LLC
2841 John Rankin Hwy (38843-8965)
PHONE..................................662 372-3389
Will B Parker,
EMP: 3 EST: 2014
SALES: 1MM **Privately Held**
SIC: 3484 Guns (firearms) or gun parts, 30 mm. & below

(G-1455)
HOMAN FOREST PRODUCTS INC
Also Called: Homan Industries
105 Homan Rd (38843)
P.O. Box 39 (38843-0039)
PHONE..................................662 862-2145
Larry E Homan, *President*
Jason Scroggins, *Principal*
Johnny McReynolds, *Vice Pres*
Laura Homan, *Treasurer*
EMP: 25
SALES (est): 4.1MM **Privately Held**
SIC: 2421 Lumber: rough, sawed or planed

(G-1456)
HOMAN INDUSTRIES INC
1 Homan Rd (38843)
PHONE..................................662 862-2125
Larry Homan, *CEO*
Harold Reaves, *COO*
EMP: 79 EST: 2001
SQ FT: 20,000
SALES (est): 2.3MM **Privately Held**
SIC: 2421 Sawmills & planing mills, general

(G-1457)
HOMANS WOOD PRODUCTS
101 Homan Rd (38843)
P.O. Box 39 (38843-0039)
PHONE..................................662 862-2145
Larry E Homan, *President*
Tom Iseminger, *Vice Pres*
Laura Homan, *Treasurer*
Jason Scroggins, *Controller*
EMP: 27
SQ FT: 15,000
SALES (est): 3.6MM **Privately Held**
SIC: 2421 2426 Specialty sawmill products; dimension, hardwood

(G-1458)
ITAWAMBA CLASSIC LURES
35 Burch Timbers Rd (38843-9381)
PHONE..................................601 720-8810
John Collins, *Principal*
EMP: 2 EST: 2014
SALES (est): 108K **Privately Held**
SIC: 3949 Lures, fishing: artificial

(G-1459)
ITAWAMBA IND WORK ACTIVITIES C
Also Called: Itawamba Adult Training Center
1212 S Adams St (38843-2308)
PHONE..................................662 862-3392
Tammy Prude, *Director*
EMP: 40

SALES (est): 368.8K **Privately Held**
WEB: www.itawambachristianchurch.org
SIC: 8331 3999 Vocational rehabilitation agency; manufacturing industries

(G-1460)
JOURNAL INC
Also Called: Armory Advertisor
106 W Main St (38843-1146)
P.O. Box 519, Amory (38821-0519)
PHONE..................................662 862-3141
Charlotte Wolfe, *President*
Tami Jones, *Publisher*
EMP: 1 **Privately Held**
SIC: 2711 Newspapers, publishing & printing
HQ: Journal, Inc.
1242 S Green St
Tupelo MS 38804
662 842-2611

(G-1461)
KELWOOD PRODUCTS
401 Vo Tech Rd (38843-8553)
PHONE..................................662 862-9494
Jan Heering, *Principal*
EMP: 2
SALES (est): 145K **Privately Held**
SIC: 2411 Timber, cut at logging camp

(G-1462)
MAX HOME LLC
101 Max Pl (38843-6611)
PHONE..................................662 862-9966
Bruno Policicchio, *COO*
Ronald L Chapman, *Plant Mgr*
Angie Stovall, *VP Human Res*
Marcie Zello, *Human Res Dir*
Larry Stevens, *Accounts Exec*
▲ EMP: 400
SQ FT: 100,000
SALES (est): 79.5MM **Privately Held**
WEB: www.maxhome.net
SIC: 2512 Upholstered household furniture

(G-1463)
MOORE INDUSTRIES
4276 Dorsey Evergreen Rd (38843-6952)
PHONE..................................662 862-3993
Jerry Moore, *Principal*
EMP: 2
SALES (est): 115.4K **Privately Held**
SIC: 3999 Manufacturing industries

(G-1464)
MUELLER CASTINGS CO
404 Muller Rd (38843)
PHONE..................................662 862-7200
John P Fonzo, *President*
▲ EMP: 6
SALES (est): 564.8K **Privately Held**
SIC: 3498 Tube fabricating (contract bending & shaping)

(G-1465)
MUELLER COPPER FITTINGS CO
1033 Spring Street Ext (38843-8462)
PHONE..................................662 862-2181
Lee Nyman, *Principal*
EMP: 50
SQ FT: 70,000
SALES (est): 7.6MM
SALES (corp-wide): 2.5B **Publicly Held**
WEB: www.muellerbrass.com
SIC: 3463 3366 3494 Plumbing fixture forgings, nonferrous; copper foundries; valves & pipe fittings
HQ: Mueller Brass Co.
8285 Tournament Dr # 150
Memphis TN 38125
901 753-3200

(G-1466)
MUELLER COPPER TUBE CO INC
Also Called: Mueller Industries
404 Mueller Brass Rd (38843-8594)
PHONE..................................662 862-1700
Gregory Christopher, *President*
Bruce Clements, *General Mgr*
Karl J Bambas, *Vice Pres*
Kent A McKee, *CFO*
Gary C Wilkerson, *Admin Sec*
▲ EMP: 400
SQ FT: 365,000

GEOGRAPHIC SECTION

Gautier - Jackson County (G-1497)

SALES: 5MM
SALES (corp-wide): 2.5B **Publicly Held**
WEB: www.muellerbrass.com
SIC: 3351 Copper & copper alloy pipe & tube
HQ: Mueller Brass Co.
8285 Tournament Dr # 150
Memphis TN 38125
901 753-3200

(G-1467)
MUELLER COPPER TUBE PDTS INC
400 Mueller Rd (38843)
P.O. Box 849 (38843-0849)
PHONE...................................662 862-2181
Mike Baum, *Branch Mgr*
EMP: 15
SALES (corp-wide): 2.5B **Publicly Held**
SIC: 3351 Tubing, copper & copper alloy
HQ: Mueller Copper Tube Products, Inc.
8285 Tournament Dr # 150
Memphis TN 38125
901 753-3200

(G-1468)
MUELLER INDUSTRIES INC
400 Mueller Rd (38843)
PHONE...................................662 862-2181
EMP: 64
SALES (corp-wide): 2.5B **Publicly Held**
SIC: 3351 Copper & copper alloy sheet, strip, plate & products
PA: Mueller Industries, Inc.
150 Schilling Blvd # 100
Collierville TN 38017
901 753-3200

(G-1469)
MUELLER INDUSTRIES INC
Also Called: Mueller Packaging
409 Mueller Brass Rd (38843-8595)
PHONE...................................662 862-7425
Brat Wynn, *Manager*
EMP: 64
SALES (corp-wide): 2.5B **Publicly Held**
SIC: 3351 Copper & copper alloy sheet, strip, plate & products
PA: Mueller Industries, Inc.
150 Schilling Blvd # 100
Collierville TN 38017
901 753-3200

(G-1470)
NOLAN BROTHERS
Also Called: Bennett Bros Shop
2602 Highway 25 S (38843-9184)
PHONE...................................662 862-3055
Nolan Bennett, *President*
Dirk Bennettt, *Vice Pres*
EMP: 17
SALES (est): 2.3MM **Privately Held**
SIC: 2411 0851 Logging camps & contractors; forestry services

(G-1471)
OREARS GARAGE AND WRECK
3235 Ryan Salem Rd (38843-9627)
PHONE...................................662 585-3244
Kevin O'Rear, *Partner*
Dexter O'Rear, *Partner*
EMP: 4
SALES: 200K **Privately Held**
SIC: 3711 Wreckers (tow truck), assembly of

(G-1472)
PACTIV LLC
Also Called: Graham Lumber Division
21500 Old Highway 25 N (38843-9606)
PHONE...................................662 585-3151
Matt Beasley, *Principal*
EMP: 30
SALES (corp-wide): 1MM **Privately Held**
WEB: www.pactiv.com
SIC: 2656 Sanitary food containers
HQ: Pactiv Llc
1900 W Field Ct
Lake Forest IL 60045
847 482-2000

(G-1473)
REGGIE WADDLE LOGGING CO
812 W Main St (38843-1027)
PHONE...................................662 862-3106
Reggie Waddle, *Principal*

EMP: 2
SALES (est): 25.6K **Privately Held**
SIC: 2411 Logging camps & contractors

(G-1474)
SONIC OF FULTON
1620 S Adams St (38843-9096)
PHONE...................................662 862-3000
Ernie Jacobson, *Manager*
EMP: 1
SALES (est): 59.6K **Privately Held**
SIC: 3421 Table & food cutlery, including butchers'

(G-1475)
SONNY MOORE
13510 John Rankin Hwy (38843-9659)
PHONE...................................662 585-4009
Sonny Moore, *Principal*
EMP: 3
SALES (est): 184.7K **Privately Held**
SIC: 2411 Logging

(G-1476)
SOUTHERN CHARM CSTM CBNTRY LLC
261 Wilson Rd N (38843-9383)
PHONE...................................662 862-5058
Kevin L Westmoreland, *Principal*
EMP: 1 EST: 2012
SALES (est): 104.9K **Privately Held**
SIC: 2434 Wood kitchen cabinets

(G-1477)
SPIRAL FAB INC
606 S Spring St (38843-1712)
PHONE...................................662 862-7999
Thomas Kline, *President*
EMP: 8 EST: 2001
SALES (est): 1.2MM **Privately Held**
SIC: 2679 Pipes & fittings, fiber: made from purchased material

(G-1478)
SWATPRINT SCREEN PRINTING
107 N Gaither St (38843-1117)
PHONE...................................662 862-3004
EMP: 2
SALES (est): 95K **Privately Held**
SIC: 2752 Lithographic Commercial Printing

(G-1479)
THOMAS LOGGING COMPANY INC
420 E Main St (38843-2002)
PHONE...................................662 862-7342
Ronnie Thomas, *President*
EMP: 4
SALES (est): 497.7K **Privately Held**
SIC: 2411 Logging camps & contractors

(G-1480)
TOMBIGBEE LUMBER CO MS LLC
315 Vo Tech Rd (38843)
PHONE...................................662 862-7417
Gerald Washington, *Principal*
Jane Washington, *Principal*
EMP: 8
SALES (est): 318.7K **Privately Held**
SIC: 2421 Lumber: rough, sawed or planed

(G-1481)
TOMBIGBEE LUMBER COMPANY INC
315 Vo Tech Rd (38843)
P.O. Box 906 (38843-0906)
PHONE...................................662 862-7417
Clinton E Taylor, *President*
EMP: 34
SQ FT: 2,000
SALES: 43K **Privately Held**
SIC: 2421 2426 Sawmills & planing mills, general; hardwood dimension & flooring mills

(G-1482)
TRACE MOUNTAIN LLC
111 Martin Rd (38843-7690)
P.O. Box 367 (38843-0367)
PHONE...................................662 862-2345
Bryan Wilson, *Mng Member*
EMP: 4
SQ FT: 1,800

SALES (est): 277.3K **Privately Held**
SIC: 2879 Trace elements (agricultural chemicals)

(G-1483)
TRI-STATE LUMBER COMPANY INC
Also Called: Tri State Lumber Co Main
105 Homan Dr Off Hwy 25 S (38843)
P.O. Box 39 (38843-0039)
PHONE...................................662 862-2125
Larry E Homan, *President*
Laura K Homan, *Corp Secy*
Tim Weston, *Vice Pres*
▲ EMP: 60
SQ FT: 10,000
SALES (est): 10.9MM **Privately Held**
SIC: 2491 2421 Wood preserving; kiln drying of lumber

(G-1484)
VICTOR UMFRESS GAR WLDG SP INC
404 S Spring St (38843-1708)
P.O. Box 248 (38843-0248)
PHONE...................................662 862-4213
Victor Umfress, *President*
EMP: 1
SALES (est): 88.2K **Privately Held**
SIC: 7538 7692 7539 General automotive repair shops; welding repair; brake services

---

Gallman
Copiah County

(G-1485)
MOORE FABRICATION AND MCHY
19171 Hwy 51 S (39077)
P.O. Box 127 (39077-0127)
PHONE...................................601 892-5017
Shannon L Moore, *Partner*
Jerry Moore, *Partner*
EMP: 12
SQ FT: 1,000
SALES (est): 2.3MM **Privately Held**
SIC: 3441 Fabricated structural metal

(G-1486)
UNIVERSAL LIGHTING TECH INC
19120 Hwy 51 (39077)
P.O. Box 128 (39077-0128)
PHONE...................................601 892-9828
Al Tracey, *Manager*
EMP: 270 **Privately Held**
WEB: www.universalballast.com
SIC: 3315 3357 Wire & fabricated wire products; nonferrous wiredrawing & insulating
HQ: Universal Lighting Technologies, Inc.
51 Century Blvd Ste 230
Nashville TN 37214
615 316-5100

(G-1487)
WESTLAKE COMPOUNDS LLC
20043 Us Hwy 51 S (39077)
PHONE...................................601 892-5612
Andrew Lafontaine, *Branch Mgr*
EMP: 40 **Publicly Held**
SIC: 2821 Plastics materials & resins
HQ: Westlake Compounds Llc
2801 Post Oak Blvd
Houston TX 77056
713 585-2900

Gautier
Jackson County

(G-1488)
BAE SYSTEMS TECH SOL SRVC INC
330 Highway 90 (39553-5705)
PHONE...................................703 847-5820
Mike Santobianco, *Manager*
EMP: 27
SALES (corp-wide): 21.6B **Privately Held**
SIC: 3812 Search & navigation equipment

HQ: Bae Systems Technology Solutions & Services Inc.
520 Gaither Rd
Rockville MD 20850
703 847-5820

(G-1489)
BOAT MAN
1105 Highway 90 (39553-5411)
PHONE...................................228 218-3080
EMP: 1 EST: 2016
SALES (est): 26K **Privately Held**
SIC: 7699 3732 Luggage repair shop; non-motorized boat, building & repairing

(G-1490)
BUNNY BREAD INC
5600 Gautier Vancleave Rd (39553-3716)
PHONE...................................228 868-0120
Trista Keener, *Owner*
EMP: 2
SALES (est): 142.2K **Privately Held**
SIC: 2051 Bakery: wholesale or wholesale/retail combined

(G-1491)
CLOUD 12 PUBLISHING
1502 Skyline Dr (39553-7626)
PHONE...................................228 990-0434
Christine Purvis, *Principal*
EMP: 1
SALES (est): 37.5K **Privately Held**
SIC: 2741 Miscellaneous publishing

(G-1492)
FORMAL AFFAIR
4343 Gautier Vancleave Rd (39553-4800)
PHONE...................................228 497-7500
Mary Thibodeaux, *Partner*
Carroll Fritz, *Partner*
Patricia Houghton, *Partner*
EMP: 3
SALES: 240K **Privately Held**
SIC: 5699 5611 5943 7221 Formal wear; suits, men's; stationery stores; photographer, still or video; bridal shops; invitation & stationery printing & engraving

(G-1493)
GAUTIER MAYHAW CO
2603 Guillotteville Rd (39553-6517)
P.O. Box 125 (39553-0125)
PHONE...................................228 497-6896
Teri Gautier, *Partner*
EMP: 2
SQ FT: 900
SALES (est): 130.9K **Privately Held**
SIC: 2033 Jellies, edible, including imitation: in cans, jars, etc.

(G-1494)
INGALLS SHIPBUILDING INC
1109 Saint Ann St (39553-4000)
PHONE...................................228 935-2887
Mark Losset, *Principal*
EMP: 2
SALES (est): 86K **Privately Held**
SIC: 3731 Shipbuilding & repairing

(G-1495)
K M INDUSTRIES
721 Highway 90 (39553-5609)
PHONE...................................228 497-7040
EMP: 1
SALES (est): 51.6K **Privately Held**
SIC: 3999 Manufacturing industries

(G-1496)
LEGACY VULCAN LLC
Also Called: Gautier Yard
2499 Old Spanish Trl (39553-6038)
PHONE...................................228 522-6011
Ricky Austin, *Manager*
EMP: 5 **Publicly Held**
WEB: www.vulcanmaterials.com
SIC: 1442 Construction sand & gravel
HQ: Legacy Vulcan, Llc
1200 Urban Center Dr
Vestavia AL 35242
205 298-3000

(G-1497)
LOKRING GULF COAST LLC
7519 Martin Bluff Rd (39553-2352)
PHONE...................................228 497-0091
Andrew B Voda,

(PA)=Parent Co (HQ)=Headquarters (DH)=Div Headquarters
✪ = New Business established in last 2 years

2019 Harris Directory of
Mississippi Manufacturers

GEOGRAPHIC

Gautier - Jackson County (G-1498)

GEOGRAPHIC SECTION

Andrew Voda,
EMP: 2
SALES (est): 450K **Privately Held**
SIC: 3498 Pipe fittings, fabricated from purchased pipe

(G-1498)
MAINLAND SAILS INC
Also Called: Mainland Canvas
3803 Old Spanish Trl (39553-5820)
PHONE..............................228 374-7245
EMP: 6
SALES (est): 270K **Privately Held**
SIC: 2394 5091 Mfg Canvas/Related Products Whol Sporting/Recreational Goods

(G-1499)
MALLETTE BROTHERS CNSTR CO
Also Called: Mallette Brothers Cnstr Co
3708 Highway 90 (39553-5010)
PHONE..............................228 497-2523
Glynn A Mallette, *President*
Ada Barnes, *Vice Pres*
Blake L Mallette, *Vice Pres*
EMP: 41 **EST:** 1969
SQ FT: 10,000
SALES (est): 9.3MM **Privately Held**
SIC: 1611 2951 General contractor, highway & street construction; asphalt & asphaltic paving mixtures (not from refineries)

(G-1500)
OCEAN SPRINGS SIGN & GRAPHICS
Also Called: Southern Signs
1408 Highway 90 3gautier (39553-5456)
PHONE..............................228 213-7933
Matthew R Parker, *Principal*
Matthew Parker, *Vice Pres*
EMP: 2 **EST:** 2016
SALES (est): 87.5K **Privately Held**
SIC: 3993 Signs & advertising specialties

(G-1501)
PALLET EXCHANGE NETWORK
3809 Old Spanish Trl (39553-5820)
PHONE..............................251 709-7021
Ed Forness, *President*
EMP: 3
SALES (est): 142.3K **Privately Held**
SIC: 2448 Pallets, wood & wood with metal

(G-1502)
QUEENS PRINTING LLC
2009 Dartmouth Dr (39553-6653)
PHONE..............................228 234-5693
Atibba Johnson, *Principal*
EMP: 2
SALES (est): 83.9K **Privately Held**
SIC: 2752 Commercial printing, lithographic

(G-1503)
SAILMAKERS SUPPLY
3803 Old Spanish Trl (39553-5820)
PHONE..............................228 522-3232
Jean Sheldon, *Principal*
EMP: 2
SALES (est): 145.9K **Privately Held**
SIC: 2394 Sails: made from purchased materials

(G-1504)
SINGIN RIVER MENTAL HEALTH
Also Called: Georco Ind
3407 Shamrock Ct (39553-5337)
PHONE..............................228 497-0690
Carla Brookes, *Director*
EMP: 25
SALES (est): 2.3MM **Privately Held**
SIC: 3732 8331 3999 Tenders (small motor craft), building & repairing; job training & vocational rehabilitation services; manufacturing industries

(G-1505)
VANGUARD SOLUTIONS INC
1616 Bayou Vista St (39553-5404)
PHONE..............................407 230-2887
David A Vindich, *President*
EMP: 2

SALES (est): 175.5K **Privately Held**
SIC: 3699 Electrical equipment & supplies

Glen
Alcorn County

(G-1506)
DONOVAN P CAIN
145 County Road 944 (38846-9533)
PHONE..............................662 279-2124
Donovan Cain, *Principal*
EMP: 1
SALES (est): 54.1K **Privately Held**
SIC: 2431 Millwork

(G-1507)
KINGSFORD MANUFACTURING CO
2387 Highway 72 E (38846-9557)
PHONE..............................510 271-6581
Jon Balousek, *President*
G C Roeth, *Vice Pres*
C R Conradi, *Treasurer*
EMP: 2
SALES (est): 354.4K
SALES (corp-wide): 6.2B **Publicly Held**
SIC: 2861 Charcoal, except activated
PA: The Clorox Company
      1221 Broadway Ste 1300
      Oakland CA 94612
      510 271-7000

(G-1508)
REGIONAL SITES INC
6 County Road 251 (38846-9778)
PHONE..............................662 643-4595
Alan Ethridge, *CFO*
EMP: 3
SALES (est): 100K **Privately Held**
SIC: 2721 Periodicals

Gloster
Amite County

(G-1509)
AMITE BIOENERGY LLC
1763 Gp Rd No 2 (39638)
PHONE..............................770 743-4300
James Dix,
Janet Arsenault,
▲ **EMP:** 5
SQ FT: 2,000
SALES (est): 2MM
SALES (corp-wide): 36.7MM **Privately Held**
SIC: 2836 Biological products, except diagnostic
PA: Drax Biomass Inc.
      5 Concourse Pkwy Ste 3100
      Atlanta GA 30328
      770 743-4300

(G-1510)
AMITE COUNTY POLES & PILING
400 E Sterling Rd (39638)
P.O. Box 280 (39638-0280)
PHONE..............................601 225-4870
Don Alford, *President*
EMP: 6
SQ FT: 2,000
SALES (est): 668.3K **Privately Held**
SIC: 2491 Poles, posts & pilings: treated wood

(G-1511)
BATEMAN AIRCONDITIONING
Also Called: Bateman Airconditioning Rfrgn
6045 Hancock Rd (39638-6134)
PHONE..............................601 225-4442
Robert L Bateman, *Owner*
EMP: 1
SALES (est): 174.8K **Privately Held**
SIC: 3822 Refrigeration/air-conditioning defrost controls

(G-1512)
CHIPS GLOSTER INC
600 E Carney Dr (39638)
P.O. Box 309 (39638-0309)
PHONE..............................601 225-4405
John P Price, *President*
Dick Carmical, *CFO*
EMP: 12
SQ FT: 500
SALES (est): 1.5MM
SALES (corp-wide): 101.5MM **Privately Held**
SIC: 2421 Chipper mill
PA: The Price Companies Inc
      218 Midway Rte
      Monticello AR 71655
      870 367-9751

(G-1513)
CST TIMBER COMPANY
3451a Ms Hwy 24 (39638)
PHONE..............................601 225-7887
Alen Preist, *President*
Renee Priest, *Vice Pres*
Harry L Priest, *Incorporator*
EMP: 12
SQ FT: 1,400
SALES (est): 1.8MM **Privately Held**
SIC: 2439 Timbers, structural: laminated lumber

(G-1514)
FOSSIL CREEK CANDLE CO LLC
6058 Cobb Rd (39638-6026)
PHONE..............................601 730-3130
Wendy Thibodeaux, *Principal*
EMP: 1
SALES (est): 45.1K **Privately Held**
SIC: 3999 Candles

(G-1515)
GEORGIA-PACIFIC LLC
221 Frank Schuh Dr (39638-6172)
PHONE..............................601 225-4211
EMP: 7
SALES (corp-wide): 42.9B **Privately Held**
SIC: 2435 2436 Mfg Hardwood Veneer/Plywood Mfg Softwood Veneer/Plywood
HQ: Georgia-Pacific Llc
      133 Peachtree St Nw
      Atlanta GA 30303
      404 652-4000

(G-1516)
LONGLEAF ENTERPRISES LTD
155 S First St (39638)
P.O. Box 368 (39638-0368)
PHONE..............................601 225-4481
Fred A Anderson III, *Partner*
David D Anderson, *Partner*
Chris Anderson, *Treasurer*
Robert Seal, *Manager*
EMP: 12
SALES (est): 520.2K **Privately Held**
SIC: 0811 1382 Tree farm; oil & gas exploration services

(G-1517)
S L NETTERVILLE LOGGING INC
2487 Netterville Rd (39638-3541)
PHONE..............................601 639-4915
Spurdon L Netterville, *President*
EMP: 9
SALES (est): 969.2K **Privately Held**
SIC: 2411 Logging camps & contractors

(G-1518)
STERLING CUSTOM CABINETS LLC
1131 Bennie Cassels Rd (39638-3690)
PHONE..............................601 996-1906
Joseph Sterling, *President*
EMP: 2
SALES (est): 139.8K **Privately Held**
SIC: 2434 Wood kitchen cabinets

(G-1519)
T L G LOGGING INC
1881 Busy Corner Rd (39638-6313)
PHONE..............................601 225-9743
EMP: 2
SALES (est): 179K **Privately Held**
SIC: 2411 Logging

(G-1520)
TIM ROLLINS LOGGING
5785 New Hope Rd (39638-6118)
PHONE..............................601 225-4972
Tim Rollins, *Owner*
EMP: 5
SALES (est): 377K **Privately Held**
SIC: 2411 Logging camps & contractors

Golden
Tishomingo County

(G-1521)
BAYMONT INC
Also Called: Baymont Inn & Suites
30 Red Bay Rd (38847-7783)
P.O. Box 18 (38847-0018)
PHONE..............................662 454-7993
Mike Stockton, *President*
Barney Wilson, *CFO*
▲ **EMP:** 65
SQ FT: 106,000
SALES (est): 7.2MM
SALES (corp-wide): 2.2B **Publicly Held**
WEB: www.baymontbath.com
SIC: 7011 5033 3272 5091 Inns; fiberglass building materials; bathtubs, concrete; hot tubs; tile & clay products
PA: Patrick Industries, Inc.
      107 W Franklin St
      Elkhart IN 46516
      574 294-7511

(G-1522)
BOCO LOGGING LLC
24791 Highway 23 N (38847-7252)
PHONE..............................256 810-4777
Karen Boyd, *Principal*
EMP: 3 **EST:** 2012
SALES (est): 222.2K **Privately Held**
SIC: 2411 Logging

(G-1523)
C & W CUSTOM DESIGN TRAILERS
Also Called: C & W Trailers
230 Industrial Park (38847-9147)
PHONE..............................662 585-3146
Wayne Cleveland, *President*
Deborah Joyce Cleveland, *Vice Pres*
Sheila Frank, *Treasurer*
Shannon Graham, *Admin Sec*
EMP: 38
SQ FT: 12,000
SALES (est): 6.5MM **Privately Held**
SIC: 3715 Truck trailers

(G-1524)
CHARLES HORN LOGGING & TRCKG
107 Horn Dr (38847-9730)
PHONE..............................662 585-3111
Charles Horn, *President*
EMP: 10
SALES: 800K **Privately Held**
SIC: 2411 Timber, cut at logging camp

(G-1525)
GOLDEN MANUFACTURING CO INC (PA)
125 Highway 366 (38847-9702)
P.O. Box 390 (38847-0390)
PHONE..............................662 454-3428
James Fennell, *President*
William H Thorn, *Corp Secy*
EMP: 400
SQ FT: 60,000
SALES (est): 79MM **Privately Held**
SIC: 2311 2325 2321 2326 Military uniforms, men's & youths': purchased materials; trousers, dress (separate): men's, youths' & boys'; uniform shirts: made from purchased materials; jackets, overall & work

(G-1526)
HAROLD A SPARKS SEPTIC TANKS
52 County Road 8 (38847-9713)
P.O. Box 305, Belmont (38827-0305)
PHONE..............................662 454-7244
Harold Sparks, *President*

2019 Harris Directory of
Mississippi Manufacturers

▲ = Import ▼=Export
◆ =Import/Export

GEOGRAPHIC SECTION

Greenville - Washington County (G-1556)

Harold A Sparks, *President*
EMP: 4
SALES (est): 481.9K **Privately Held**
SIC: 3272 1711 Septic tanks, concrete;
septic system construction

(G-1527)
J T HORN LOGGING INC
34165 Highway 25 N (38847-9743)
PHONE.................................662 585-3417
Joel T Horn, *President*
EMP: 8
SALES (est): 1MM **Privately Held**
SIC: 2411 Logging camps & contractors

(G-1528)
JOHNSOND RV
289 Petty Rd (38847-9529)
PHONE.................................662 676-8716
Rodney Johnson, *Owner*
EMP: 2 EST: 2010
SALES (est): 217.4K **Privately Held**
SIC: 3799 Recreational vehicles

(G-1529)
LOGISTICAL SERVICES INTL INC
3649 Alice Hall Rd (38847-8465)
PHONE.................................662 676-2823
▲ EMP: 6
SQ FT: 1,500
SALES (est): 794.6K **Privately Held**
SIC: 3842 Mfg Surgical Appliances/Supplies

(G-1530)
SOUTHERN FORESTRY INC
167 Main St (38847-7721)
PHONE.................................662 416-3883
Tim Mahan, *President*
EMP: 13
SALES (est): 1.1MM **Privately Held**
SIC: 2411 Logging

(G-1531)
SUMMERFORD ENTERPRISES INC
4494 Tucker Rd (38847-8922)
PHONE.................................662 585-3584
Ricky C Summerford, *President*
Cairo Summerford, *Vice Pres*
EMP: 8
SALES (est): 307.1K **Privately Held**
SIC: 0851 2411 Timber cruising services;
logging

(G-1532)
WALKER MISSIONARY BAPTIST PARS
5 Antioch Church Rd (38847-9032)
PHONE.................................662 585-3309
David Holcomb, *Pastor*
EMP: 2 EST: 2007
SALES (est): 128.6K **Privately Held**
SIC: 3842 Walkers

(G-1533)
WOODS TRAILERS & REPAIR LLC
Also Called: Wood's Trailers
1 Industrial Park (38847-9102)
PHONE.................................662 585-3606
Donny Woods, *Mng Member*
EMP: 2
SALES: 70K **Privately Held**
SIC: 7692 7534 7539 5561 Welding repair; tire repair shop; trailer repair; recreational vehicle parts & accessories

---

Greenville
Washington County

(G-1534)
1 A LIFESAFER INC
760 S Raceway Rd (38703-8237)
PHONE.................................800 634-3077
EMP: 1
SALES (corp-wide): 4.3MM **Privately Held**
SIC: 3829 Measuring & controlling devices

PA: 1 A Lifesafer, Inc.
4290 Glendale Milford Rd
Blue Ash OH 45242
513 651-9560

(G-1535)
AI EVAC EMS INC
Also Called: Air Evac Lifeteam
1609 Hospital St (38703-3222)
PHONE.................................662 335-3034
Lee Williams, *President*
Lee Williamsm, *President*
EMP: 8
SALES (est): 529.4K **Privately Held**
SIC: 3721 Helicopters

(G-1536)
APAC-MISSISSIPPI INC
2559 Harbor Front Rd (38701-9599)
P.O. Box 5336 (38704-5336)
PHONE.................................662 378-8481
Dennis Rodgers, *Branch Mgr*
Dennis Rogers, *Manager*
EMP: 45
SALES (corp-wide): 30.6B **Privately Held**
SIC: 2951 1611 1771 Asphalt & asphaltic
paving mixtures (not from refineries);
highway & street construction; concrete
work
HQ: Apac-Mississippi, Inc.
101 Riverview Dr
Richland MS 39218
601 376-4000

(G-1537)
CHARLIE CHEMICAL AND SUPPLY
154 Stokes King Rd (38701-8504)
P.O. Box 4557 (38704-4557)
PHONE.................................662 332-9262
Robert Cooper, *President*
Connie Burfurd, *Corp Secy*
EMP: 3
SALES: 150K **Privately Held**
SIC: 2842 2841 Cleaning or polishing
preparations; soap & other detergents

(G-1538)
CHUCKS WELDING & MECH LLC
3650 Nita Ln (38701-9612)
PHONE.................................662 347-9941
William E Ramsey, *Principal*
EMP: 1
SALES (est): 48.4K **Privately Held**
SIC: 7692 Welding repair

(G-1539)
COLON CABINETS AND TRIM
2476 Hummingbird Dr (38701-8117)
PHONE.................................662 347-8608
EMP: 2
SALES (est): 142.4K **Privately Held**
SIC: 2434 Wood kitchen cabinets

(G-1540)
CONTECH ENGNERED SOLUTIONS LLC
2590 Old Leland Rd (38703-2806)
PHONE.................................601 894-2041
MO Heshmati, *Ch of Bd*
Barry Ainsworth, *Executive*
EMP: 2 **Privately Held**
SIC: 3084 3317 3441 3443 Plastics pipe;
steel pipe & tubes; fabricated structural
metal; fabricated plate work (boiler shop);
culverts, sheet metal
HQ: Contech Engineered Solutions Llc
9025 Centre Pointe Dr # 400
West Chester OH 45069
513 645-7000

(G-1541)
CONTECH ENGNERED SOLUTIONS LLC
2590 Old Leland Rd (38703-2806)
P.O. Box 1337 (38702-1337)
PHONE.................................662 332-2625
EMP: 15
SALES (corp-wide): 588.3MM **Privately Held**
SIC: 3443 3444 Mfg Fabricated Plate
Work Mfg Sheet Metalwork

PA: Contech Engineered Solutions Llc
9025 Ctr Pinte Dr Ste 400
West Chester OH 45069
513 645-7000

(G-1542)
CORRERO WOODWORKS
2267 Highway 1 N (38703-9472)
PHONE.................................662 334-9837
EMP: 2
SALES (est): 184.7K **Privately Held**
SIC: 2431 Mfg Millwork

(G-1543)
CWS GRAIN SYSTEMS INC
3746 Highway 1 S (38701-7216)
PHONE.................................662 332-5822
James Coslet, *President*
Terry Coslet, *Corp Secy*
Jason Coslet, *Vice Pres*
EMP: 20
SQ FT: 3,350
SALES (est): 2.3MM **Privately Held**
WEB: www.cws.net
SIC: 4221 7692 1791 Grain elevator, storage only; welding repair; structural steel
erection

(G-1544)
DARRELLS CUSTOM CABINETS
2221 Flannagan Rd (38701-8626)
PHONE.................................662 822-3936
Darrell L Koehn, *Principal*
EMP: 1
SALES (est): 91.1K **Privately Held**
SIC: 2434 Wood kitchen cabinets

(G-1545)
DELTA ENTERPRISES (HQ)
819 Main St Ste A (38701-4101)
P.O. Box 588 (38702-0588)
PHONE.................................662 335-5291
Spencer Nash, *CEO*
Josephine Taylor, *Asst Sec*
EMP: 2 EST: 1970
SQ FT: 12,000
SALES: 20MM
SALES (corp-wide): 890.5K **Privately Held**
SIC: 2431 3829 Staircases & stairs, wood;
measuring & controlling devices
PA: Delta Foundation Inc
819 Main St Ste A
Greenville MS 38701
662 335-5291

(G-1546)
DELTA FABRICATION LLC
1091b Little Theater Rd (38703-8242)
P.O. Box 4475 (38704-4475)
PHONE.................................662 335-2500
Tom Carter,
Bobby Brown,
EMP: 26
SALES (est): 5.4MM **Privately Held**
SIC: 3441 Fabricated structural metal

(G-1547)
DELTA FOUNDATION INC (PA)
819 Main St Ste A (38701-4101)
P.O. Box 588 (38702-0588)
PHONE.................................662 335-5291
Spencer Nash, *CEO*
EMP: 136 EST: 1969
SALES: 890.5K **Privately Held**
WEB: www.deltafoundation.com
SIC: 6163 3679 Mortgage brokers arranging for loans, using money of others; electronic switches

(G-1548)
DELTA NET & TWINE CO INC
3148 Highway 1 S (38701-7204)
PHONE.................................662 332-0841
Terry Turner, *President*
Marty Turner, *Vice Pres*
EMP: 10
SQ FT: 23,000
SALES (est): 980K **Privately Held**
WEB: www.deltanetandtwine.com
SIC: 2399 Fishing nets

(G-1549)
DELTA SIGN SHOP
1729 Highway 82 E (38703-6021)
PHONE.................................662 334-9878

Marty Childs, *Owner*
EMP: 5
SALES (est): 250K **Privately Held**
SIC: 3993 Signs & advertising specialties

(G-1550)
DELTA SIGNS AND DESIGNS LLC
2094 Highway 1 S (38701-7806)
PHONE.................................662 822-0830
Marcus Hawkins, *President*
EMP: 1
SQ FT: 1,900
SALES (est): 53.2K **Privately Held**
SIC: 3993 7299 7334 Electric signs; letters for signs, metal; signs, not made in
custom sign painting shops; portrait copying; photocopying & duplicating services

(G-1551)
DELTA-DEMOCRAT PUBG CO INC
Also Called: Delta Democrat Times
988 N Broadway St (38701-2349)
P.O. Box 1618 (38702-1618)
PHONE.................................662 335-1155
Jim Rosse, *President*
Jon Alverson, *Publisher*
David Healy, *Editor*
Heather Holland, *Business Mgr*
Eric Thomason, *Vice Pres*
EMP: 68
SQ FT: 10,000
SALES (est): 3.9MM **Privately Held**
WEB: www.ddtonline.com
SIC: 2711 2752 Newspapers, publishing &
printing; commercial printing, lithographic

(G-1552)
EASTERN GROUP LLC
2232 Highway 1 N (38703-9471)
PHONE.................................662 332-1890
Eric W Schuster, *Principal*
EMP: 2
SALES (est): 125.8K **Privately Held**
SIC: 1382 Oil & gas exploration services

(G-1553)
ELVIS AND COMPANY LLC
186 Primrose St (38701-7540)
PHONE.................................662 616-9248
Jerry L Elvis, *Mng Member*
EMP: 1
SALES (est): 157.7K **Privately Held**
SIC: 3699 Electric sound equipment

(G-1554)
ENGINE REBUILDERS CO INC
327 Highway 1 S (38701-4306)
PHONE.................................662 332-2695
George B Baroni Jr, *President*
Fred Neal Jr, *Vice Pres*
EMP: 12 EST: 1970
SQ FT: 13,000
SALES (est): 900K **Privately Held**
SIC: 3599 5013 Machine shop, jobbing &
repair; automotive supplies & parts

(G-1555)
GREENVILLE METAL WORKS INC
Also Called: Greenville Steel Sales
1254 Highway 1 N (38703-2236)
P.O. Box 4484 (38704-4484)
PHONE.................................662 335-8510
Tom Norris, *President*
Robert T Norris, *President*
Cecil A Carder, *Vice Pres*
EMP: 50
SQ FT: 14,000
SALES (est): 10.3MM **Privately Held**
SIC: 3548 1711 2296 Welding apparatus;
mechanical contractor; steel tire cords &
tire cord fabrics

(G-1556)
HALEY CLUTCH & COUPLING CO INC
1820 Highway 1 N (38703)
PHONE.................................662 332-8716
Daryl Haley, *President*
Debra Parker, *Corp Secy*
EMP: 35

(PA)=Parent Co (HQ)=Headquarters (DH)=Div Headquarters
✿ = New Business established in last 2 years

2019 Harris Directory of
Mississippi Manufacturers

63

GEOGRAPHIC

Greenville - Washington County (G-1557)　　　　　　　　　**GEOGRAPHIC SECTION**

SALES (est): 2.8MM
SALES (corp-wide): 5.8MM **Privately Held**
WEB: www.haleyinc.com
SIC: 3566 Gears, power transmission, except automotive
PA: Marine Gears, Inc.
1690 Highway 1 N
Greenville MS 38703
662 332-8716

(G-1557)
HANGER PRSTHETCS & ORTHO INC
2331 Highway 1 S (38701-8337)
PHONE..................................662 335-6828
Sam Liang, *President*
David Street, *Manager*
EMP: 4
SALES (corp-wide): 1B **Publicly Held**
SIC: 5047 3842 5999 Artificial limbs; orthopedic equipment & supplies; prosthetic appliances; orthopedic appliances; orthopedic & prosthesis applications
HQ: Hanger Prosthetics & Orthotics, Inc.
10910 Domain Dr Ste 300
Austin TX 78758
512 777-3800

(G-1558)
J & H TURBO SERVICE INC
3401 Highway 82 E (38703-8204)
PHONE..................................662 378-8715
Anthony Harper, *Manager*
EMP: 1
SALES (est): 86.6K **Privately Held**
SIC: 3519 Diesel, semi-diesel or duel-fuel engines, including marine

(G-1559)
JOE TONOS JEWELER INC
1640 Highway 1 S (38701-7108)
PHONE..................................662 335-1160
Robby Tonos, *President*
Chris Tonos, *Vice Pres*
EMP: 4 EST: 1953
SQ FT: 2,000
SALES (est): 380K **Privately Held**
SIC: 5944 7631 3911 Jewelry, precious stones & precious metals; watches; jewelry repair services; watch repair; jewelry, precious metal

(G-1560)
JOHNSON EDUCATION FIRM LLC
280 Bermuda Dr (38701-7557)
PHONE..................................662 347-9150
Authur Johnson,
EMP: 1
SALES (est): 32.5K **Privately Held**
SIC: 8299 8222 8221 3949 Educational services; community college; colleges universities & professional schools; team sports equipment

(G-1561)
KENAN TRANSPORTATION
1010 N Broadway St (38701-2004)
PHONE..................................662 332-4223
Will Mays, *President*
EMP: 2
SALES (est): 92.8K **Privately Held**
SIC: 1389 2833 Oil field services; vegetable oils, medicinal grade: refined or concentrated

(G-1562)
KENNETHS EXCAVATION DEMO
1028 Highway 1 N (38703-2204)
PHONE..................................662 379-6771
EMP: 3
SALES (est): 115.5K **Privately Held**
SIC: 1442 Construction sand & gravel

(G-1563)
L & L TOOL & MACHINE CO LLC
1225 Highway 1 N (38703-2200)
PHONE..................................662 335-1181
Casey Lindsay, *Principal*
EMP: 4
SALES (est): 414.2K **Privately Held**
SIC: 3469 Machine parts, stamped or pressed metal

(G-1564)
LOVELAND PRODUCTS INC
Also Called: Platte Chemical Co
911 Platte Rd (38703-5501)
P.O. Box 5156 (38704-5156)
PHONE..................................662 335-3394
Melanie Patterson, *Safety Mgr*
Labarron McMillian, *Manager*
EMP: 106
SALES (corp-wide): 8.8B **Privately Held**
SIC: 2879 Pesticides, agricultural or household
HQ: Loveland Products, Inc.
3005 Rocky Mountain Ave
Loveland CO 80538
970 685-3300

(G-1565)
LOVELAND PRODUCTS INC
917 Platte Rd (38703-5501)
P.O. Box 5156 (38704-5156)
PHONE..................................662 335-3394
David Hoppell, *Manager*
EMP: 40
SALES (corp-wide): 8.8B **Privately Held**
SIC: 2879 Agricultural chemicals
HQ: Loveland Products, Inc.
3005 Rocky Mountain Ave
Loveland CO 80538
970 685-3300

(G-1566)
LUVEL DAIRY PRODUCTS INC
3305 Highway 82 E (38703-8245)
PHONE..................................662 334-6372
Joseph White, *Manager*
EMP: 3
SALES (corp-wide): 1.7B **Privately Held**
SIC: 2026 2024 Fluid milk; ice cream & ice milk
HQ: Luvel Dairy Products, Inc.
926 Veterans Memorial Dr
Kosciusko MS 39090
662 289-2511

(G-1567)
MANNING SIGNS INC
Also Called: Manning Signs & Designs
881 S Raceway Rd (38703-8240)
P.O. Box 4583 (38704-4583)
PHONE..................................662 332-4496
Dale Manning, *Owner*
Amy H Manning, *Co-Owner*
EMP: 2
SQ FT: 2,500
SALES (est): 180.4K **Privately Held**
SIC: 3993 Neon signs

(G-1568)
MARINE GEARS INC (PA)
Also Called: Haley Marine Gears
1690 Highway 1 N (38703-1943)
P.O. Box 689 (38702-0689)
PHONE..................................662 332-8716
Neal Haley, *President*
Neal R Haley, *President*
Darryl Haley, *Vice Pres*
Chris Robertson, *Design Engr*
Debra Parker, *Treasurer*
▼ EMP: 29
SQ FT: 2,475
SALES (est): 5.8MM **Privately Held**
WEB: www.haleyinc.com
SIC: 3566 7699 3568 Gears, power transmission, except automotive; nautical repair services; clutches, except vehicular

(G-1569)
MARS FOOD US LLC
Also Called: Uncle Ben's
1098 N Broadway St (38701-2004)
PHONE..................................662 335-8000
Quincy Truep, *Vice Pres*
EMP: 200
SALES (corp-wide): 34.2B **Privately Held**
WEB: www.kalkan.com
SIC: 2044 Rice milling
HQ: Mars Food Us, Llc
2001 E Cashdan St Ste 201
Rancho Dominguez CA 90220
310 933-0670

(G-1570)
MASTERFOODS USA
1098 N Broadway St (38701-2004)
PHONE..................................662 335-8000

Robert Gamgort, *Principal*
EMP: 3
SALES (est): 239.8K **Privately Held**
SIC: 2044 Rice milling

(G-1571)
MAYVILLE ENGINEERING CO INC
Also Called: Mec
1281 Pickett St (38703-2454)
PHONE..................................662 335-2325
Shirley Sides, *Human Resources*
EMP: 124
SALES (corp-wide): 354.5MM **Publicly Held**
SIC: 3469 Stamping metal for the trade
PA: Mayville Engineering Co Inc
715 South St
Mayville WI 53050
920 387-4500

(G-1572)
MERLE E SULLIVAN
Also Called: Sullivan Industrial/Farm Maint
1405 E Ollie Cir (38703-7204)
PHONE..................................662 347-4494
Merle E Sullivan, *Owner*
EMP: 1
SALES (est): 35K **Privately Held**
SIC: 3569 7692 1629 5083 General industrial machinery; welding repair; heavy construction; farm equipment parts & supplies

(G-1573)
MID SOUTH ELECTRIC MOTOR SVC
3021 Highway 82 W (38701)
PHONE..................................662 332-3512
George Strickland, *President*
Susan Strickland, *Vice Pres*
EMP: 3 EST: 1971
SQ FT: 900
SALES: 250K **Privately Held**
SIC: 7694 5063 Electric motor repair; motors, electric

(G-1574)
MIGHTY MISS BREWING CO LLC
525 Washington Ave Ste B (38701-3619)
PHONE..................................662 379-6477
Jon Alverson,
EMP: 3
SQ FT: 3,000
SALES: 250K **Privately Held**
SIC: 2082 Beer (alcoholic beverage)

(G-1575)
MISSISSIPPI MARINE CORPORATION (PA)
2219 Harbor Front Rd (38701-9561)
P.O. Box 539 (38702-0539)
PHONE..................................662 332-5457
Jeff Nightingale, *President*
Melinda P Nichols, *Corp Secy*
Anita Luke, *Vice Pres*
Melinda Nichols, *Treasurer*
Barry Alderman, *Info Tech Mgr*
EMP: 150 EST: 1972
SALES (est): 21.4MM **Privately Held**
WEB: www.msmarine.net
SIC: 3731 Commercial passenger ships, building & repairing

(G-1576)
MISSISSIPPI MARINE CORPORATION
2281 Harbor Front Rd (38701-9561)
P.O. Box 539 (38702-0539)
PHONE..................................662 335-1175
Tommy McKinnon, *Manager*
EMP: 135
SALES (corp-wide): 21.4MM **Privately Held**
WEB: www.msmarine.net
SIC: 3731 3732 Shipbuilding & repairing; boat building & repairing
PA: Mississippi Marine Corporation
2219 Harbor Front Rd
Greenville MS 38701
662 332-5457

(G-1577)
MMC MATERIALS INC
1117 S Raceway Rd (38703-8246)
P.O. Box 5186 (38704-5186)
PHONE..................................662 332-5407
Glen Craft, *Manager*
EMP: 31
SQ FT: 1,400
SALES (corp-wide): 306.5MM **Privately Held**
WEB: www.mmcmaterials.com
SIC: 3273 5211 Ready-mixed concrete; cement
HQ: Mmc Materials, Inc.
1052 Highland Colony Pkwy # 201
Ridgeland MS 39157
601 898-4000

(G-1578)
MMC MATERIALS INC
313 Martin Luther King Dr (38703-9122)
P.O. Box 5186 (38704-5186)
PHONE..................................662 887-4031
James Head, *Manager*
EMP: 2
SALES (corp-wide): 306.5MM **Privately Held**
WEB: www.mmcmaterials.com
SIC: 3273 Ready-mixed concrete
HQ: Mmc Materials, Inc.
1052 Highland Colony Pkwy # 201
Ridgeland MS 39157
601 898-4000

(G-1579)
MOSLEY MFG & MCH WORKS
1516 S Theobald St (38701-5522)
P.O. Box 4922 (38704-4922)
PHONE..................................662 332-7140
E Doyle Mosley, *President*
Linda Patton Mosley, *Vice Pres*
Debra K Mosley, *Treasurer*
EMP: 8 EST: 1974
SQ FT: 7,000
SALES (est): 1.3MM **Privately Held**
SIC: 3599 Machine shop, jobbing & repair

(G-1580)
NICHOLS PROPELLER COMPANY
Also Called: Nichols Steel
640 Straughter St (38701-6126)
P.O. Box 1177 (38702-1177)
PHONE..................................662 378-2000
Joseph D Nichols, *President*
Naoma Nichols, *Vice Pres*
Mark Nichols, *Treasurer*
EMP: 38
SQ FT: 6,250
SALES (est): 11.1MM **Privately Held**
SIC: 3366 3732 Propellers; boat building & repairing

(G-1581)
NICHOLS STL SLS & FABRICATION
630 S Theobald St (38701-5155)
PHONE..................................662 378-2723
Guy Nelson, *Owner*
EMP: 1
SALES (est): 94K **Privately Held**
WEB: www.nicholspropeller.com
SIC: 3449 Bars, concrete reinforcing: fabricated steel

(G-1582)
NORMAN ACCOUNTING SERVICES
1207 Daniels St (38701-6214)
PHONE..................................662 347-4475
Takesha Norman, *Owner*
EMP: 1
SALES: 15K **Privately Held**
SIC: 6211 2782 Tax certificate dealers; account books

(G-1583)
NOYES PRINTING & RBR STAMP CO
Also Called: Greenville Printing Co
821 Highway 82 E (38701-5411)
PHONE..................................662 332-5256
Thomas Noyes, *Owner*
Ronnie Washington, *Supervisor*
EMP: 4 EST: 1947

2019 Harris Directory of
Mississippi Manufacturers

▲ = Import ▼=Export
◆ =Import/Export

GEOGRAPHIC SECTION

Greenwood - Leflore County (G-1614)

SQ FT: 2,400
SALES: 250K **Privately Held**
SIC: 2752 3953 5999 Commercial printing, offset; marking devices; rubber stamps

(G-1584)
NUFARM AMERICAS INC
1927 N Theobald St (38703-2207)
PHONE...............................708 375-9010
EMP: 2 **Privately Held**
SIC: 2869 2879 Industrial organic chemicals; agricultural chemicals
HQ: Nufarm Americas Inc.
11901 S Austin Ave
Alsip IL 60803
708 377-1330

(G-1585)
OFFICE DEPOT INC
1662 Mrtin L King Jr Blvd (38701)
PHONE...............................662 378-2995
Bradley Harger, *Office Mgr*
EMP: 35
SALES (corp-wide): 11B **Publicly Held**
WEB: www.officedepot.com
SIC: 5943 5999 5734 2759 Stationery stores; typewriters & business machines; computer & software stores; personal computers; stationery: printing
PA: Office Depot, Inc.
6600 N Military Trl
Boca Raton FL 33496
561 438-4800

(G-1586)
OUTBACK EXPRESS MISSISSIPPI
5 Orchard Pl (38701-8079)
PHONE...............................662 378-8000
Jane Oliver, *Principal*
EMP: 4
SALES (est): 228.2K **Privately Held**
SIC: 2741 Miscellaneous publishing

(G-1587)
P & S WELDING & MANUFACTURING
Also Called: P&S Welding
630 Twist St (38701-2345)
PHONE...............................662 334-9881
Stanley Saulter, *President*
EMP: 3
SQ FT: 2,000
SALES (est): 150K **Privately Held**
SIC: 7692 3599 Welding repair; machine & other job shop work

(G-1588)
PAW PRINT VISUALS LLC
910 W Lynne Cir (38703-6617)
PHONE...............................662 332-2359
Michael Morehead, *Principal*
EMP: 2
SALES (est): 83.9K **Privately Held**
SIC: 2752 Commercial printing, lithographic

(G-1589)
PAXTON EMBROIDERY
112 Bayou Rd (38701-7701)
PHONE...............................662 335-2160
EMP: 1
SALES (est): 62.7K **Privately Held**
SIC: 2395 Pleating/Stitching Services

(G-1590)
PHAE I BOBS
512 Highway 1 N (38701-3159)
PHONE...............................662 332-3505
Ora Juitt, *Manager*
EMP: 6 EST: 2008
SALES (est): 160.9K **Privately Held**
SIC: 4924 1321 Natural gas distribution; natural gas liquids

(G-1591)
PRESTO-TAP LLC
3101 Little Theater Rd (38703-8223)
P.O. Box 5095 (38704-5095)
PHONE...............................662 332-8559
Anna Fratesi, *Plant Mgr*
Paul Courson, *Sls & Mktg Exec*
H L Jim Dawkins Jr,
Robert F Vornborck,

EMP: 3
SQ FT: 9,000
SALES (est): 320K **Privately Held**
WEB: www.presto-tap.com
SIC: 3829 Liquid leak detection equipment

(G-1592)
PRODUCERS RICE MILL INC
105 Martin Luther King Dr (38703-9771)
P.O. Box 1317 (38702-1317)
PHONE...............................662 334-6266
EMP: 60
SALES (corp-wide): 420.2MM **Privately Held**
SIC: 2044 Milled rice
PA: Producers Rice Mill, Inc.
518 E Harrison St
Stuttgart AR 72160
870 673-4444

(G-1593)
RACEWAY EXPRESS SHELL
3195 Highway 82 E (38703-8233)
PHONE...............................662 335-5434
Donna Sims, *Principal*
EMP: 5
SALES (est): 348.3K **Privately Held**
SIC: 5541 3644 Filling stations, gasoline; raceways

(G-1594)
RAINBOW STITCHINGS
1047 Sisson Dr (38703-2120)
PHONE...............................662 378-5335
Iris McGee, *Owner*
EMP: 1
SALES (est): 54.7K **Privately Held**
SIC: 2395 Embroidery & art needlework

(G-1595)
REHABILITATION SVCS MISS DEPT
Also Called: Ability Works
385 W Reed Rd (38701-6967)
PHONE...............................662 335-3359
Don Walker, *Manager*
EMP: 40 **Privately Held**
SIC: 8249 9411 8331 3678 Vocational schools; administration of educational programs; ; job training & vocational rehabilitation services; electronic connectors; wood pallets & skids
HQ: Mississippi Department Of Rehabilitation Services
1281 Highway 51
Madison MS 39110

(G-1596)
SANDERS HOME HEALTH INC
Also Called: Sanders Uniform
1570 Highway 1 S (38701-7142)
PHONE...............................662 335-2326
David Hough, *CEO*
Wynn Sanders, *President*
EMP: 5
SALES (est): 300K **Privately Held**
SIC: 2326 Medical & hospital uniforms, men's

(G-1597)
SCHUDCO LTD
335 Wilmont Rd (38701-8553)
PHONE...............................662 332-8678
Bill Schultz, *President*
EMP: 2
SALES (est): 390.4K **Privately Held**
SIC: 1381 Drilling water intake wells

(G-1598)
SHOFFNER MOTOR CO INC
105 Creekmore Rd (38701-8014)
PHONE...............................662 378-2909
James Shoffner, *President*
EMP: 2
SALES (est): 162.8K **Privately Held**
SIC: 3711 Motor vehicles & car bodies

(G-1599)
SINCERE TRADING INC
1535 Sunridge Cv (38701-6932)
P.O. Box 4666 (38704-4666)
PHONE...............................662 702-3822
EMP: 3
SQ FT: 3,000

SALES (est): 313K **Privately Held**
SIC: 2337 5137 Mfg Women's/Misses' Suits/Coats Whol Women's/Child's Clothing

(G-1600)
SOUTHERN BAND SAW CO INC
Also Called: Southern Bandsaw Company
1309 Thornton St (38703-2463)
P.O. Box 4915 (38704-4915)
PHONE...............................662 332-4008
EMP: 13 EST: 1982
SQ FT: 18,000
SALES (est): 1.6MM **Privately Held**
SIC: 3425 Mfg Saw Blades/Handsaws

(G-1601)
SOUTHERN FASTENER CO MISS
Also Called: Southern Fasteners
368 Air Field Rd At Arprt (38703)
P.O. Box 906, Wheaton IL (60187-0906)
PHONE...............................662 335-2157
Christine Roche, *President*
William J Roche Jr, *Vice Pres*
Eric Jackson, *Branch Mgr*
Michael G Roche, *Admin Sec*
EMP: 148 EST: 1973
SQ FT: 75,000
SALES (est): 17.3MM **Privately Held**
SIC: 3452 Bolts, metal; screws, metal

(G-1602)
THE TOUCH
143 Bayou Rd (38701-7764)
PHONE...............................662 378-4188
Kay Newsom, *Owner*
EMP: 1
SALES: 40K **Privately Held**
SIC: 5621 2754 Women's clothing stores; stationery & invitation printing, gravure

(G-1603)
THORNTON REPAIR SHOP
248 Highway 1 S (38701-4303)
P.O. Box 5006 (38704-5006)
PHONE...............................662 332-6853
Wilma Smith, *Owner*
William Lee, *Owner*
EMP: 4
SALES (est): 235.8K **Privately Held**
WEB: www.thornton.be
SIC: 7538 7539 7692 Diesel engine repair: automotive; radiator repair shop, automotive; automotive welding

(G-1604)
THROW STRIKES BASEBALL ACADEMY
410 Solomon St (38703-3925)
PHONE...............................662 931-4948
Harold Myles, *Principal*
EMP: 2
SALES (est): 158.6K **Privately Held**
SIC: 3949 7991 Baseball equipment & supplies, general; physical fitness facilities

(G-1605)
TIM BENNETT
Also Called: B & B Sign Company
3033 Highway 1 S (38701-7203)
PHONE...............................662 332-0020
Tim Bennett, *Owner*
EMP: 2
SALES (est): 110K **Privately Held**
SIC: 3993 Signs & advertising specialties

(G-1606)
UPPER KUTZ LLC
Also Called: Upper Kutz Barbr Style College
813 S Martin Luther (38701)
PHONE...............................662 807-8707
James Preston Jr, *Mng Member*
Labella Preston,
EMP: 2 EST: 2015
SALES (est): 133.4K **Privately Held**
SIC: 3131 Footwear cut stock

(G-1607)
VANCE NIMROD
Also Called: New South Products
323 Central St (38701-4054)
PHONE...............................662 334-3713
Vance Nimrod, *Owner*
▲ **EMP:** 2
SQ FT: 2,500

SALES (est): 74K **Privately Held**
SIC: 2879 Insecticides & pesticides

(G-1608)
WASHINGTON COUNTY WIDE SHOP
3114 County Shop Rd (38703-3445)
PHONE...............................662 334-4322
Wayne Whorton, *Superintendent*
Gerald Jordan, *Director*
EMP: 70
SALES (est): 4.6MM **Privately Held**
SIC: 3531 Road construction & maintenance machinery

(G-1609)
WATSON PERCY
Also Called: Air Care Service
634 Hibiscus St (38701-5450)
PHONE...............................662 931-6490
Percy Watson, *Owner*
EMP: 1
SALES (est): 75.1K **Privately Held**
SIC: 3632 3585 5075 1761 Refrigerators, mechanical & absorption: household; refrigeration & heating equipment; air conditioning & ventilation equipment & supplies; roofing, siding & sheet metal work

---

Greenwood
Leflore County

(G-1610)
AG SPRAY EQUIPMENT INC
2900 Baldwin Rd (38930-5049)
PHONE...............................662 453-4524
Buster Norris, *President*
EMP: 8
SALES (corp-wide): 151.6MM **Privately Held**
SIC: 5046 3523 Commercial equipment; fertilizing, spraying, dusting & irrigation machinery
HQ: Ag. Spray Equipment, Inc.
3303 Pembroke Rd
Hopkinsville KY 42240
270 886-0296

(G-1611)
AINSWORTH SIGNS
406 Lamar St (38930-4531)
PHONE...............................662 453-1904
Cale Ainsworth, *Owner*
EMP: 3
SALES (est): 151.8K **Privately Held**
SIC: 3993 Signs, not made in custom sign painting shops

(G-1612)
ALFORDS DECORATING CENTER
233 County Road 231 (38930-9328)
PHONE...............................662 455-3552
Bobby Alford, *Owner*
Karon Alford, *Co-Owner*
EMP: 4
SALES (est): 349K **Privately Held**
WEB: www.moldingnet.com
SIC: 5713 5211 5714 5231 Carpets; floor tile; vinyl floor covering; flooring, wood; draperies; paint; wallpaper; trim, wood; carpet & upholstery cleaning

(G-1613)
AROUND CLOCK RECOVERY
1735 County Road 320 (38930-7040)
PHONE...............................662 455-1008
John S Mims, *Principal*
EMP: 4
SALES (est): 380K **Privately Held**
SIC: 3531 Automobile wrecker hoists

(G-1614)
BARRENTINE TRAILER MFG CO INC
271 County Road 133 (38930)
PHONE...............................662 237-9650
Jarrod Barrentine, *President*
EMP: 5
SALES (est): 840.3K **Privately Held**
SIC: 3799 Trailers & trailer equipment

(PA)=Parent Co (HQ)=Headquarters (DH)=Div Headquarters
✪ = New Business established in last 2 years

2019 Harris Directory of
Mississippi Manufacturers

65

Greenwood - Leflore County (G-1615)

GEOGRAPHIC SECTION

(G-1615)
BLUE RIDGE BEEF PLANT INC
222 Howard St (38930-4334)
PHONE..................864 338-5544
Brian Waldrop, *Principal*
Gary Waldrop, *Principal*
Steven Waldrop, *Principal*
David P Webb, *Principal*
EMP: 2
SALES (est): 62.3K Privately Held
SIC: 2077 Animal & marine fats & oils

(G-1616)
BREWER SCREEN PRINTING
1709 Grenada Blvd (38930-4714)
PHONE..................662 453-2255
Alton Brewer, *Partner*
Barry Brewer, *Partner*
EMP: 2
SALES (est): 254.2K Privately Held
SIC: 2759 Screen printing

(G-1617)
C3 DESIGN INC (PA)
1706 Cypress Ave (38930-7421)
P.O. Box 1973 (38935-1973)
PHONE..................662 392-5021
Brian Waldrop, *President*
EMP: 12
SALES (est): 1.9MM Privately Held
SIC: 5211 2452 Modular homes; modular homes, prefabricated, wood

(G-1618)
COMMONWEALTH PUBLISHING INC
Also Called: Greenwood Commonwealth
329 Highway 82 W (38930-6538)
P.O. Box 8050 (38935-8050)
PHONE..................662 453-5312
Wyatt Emmerich, *President*
J Wyatt Emmerich, *Treasurer*
Charles Dunagin, *Admin Sec*
EMP: 214
SQ FT: 12,000
SALES (est): 12.6MM
SALES (corp-wide): 23.8MM Privately Held
WEB: www.gwcommonwealth.com
SIC: 2711 2752 Newspapers, publishing & printing; commercial printing, lithographic
PA: Emmerich Newspapers, Incorporated
    246 Briarwood Dr Ste 101
    Jackson MS

(G-1619)
DELTA FARM & AUTO LLC
1607 Highway 82 W (38930-2724)
PHONE..................662 453-8340
Anthony Gammill,
EMP: 9
SALES (est): 1.6MM Privately Held
SIC: 3524 5013 5083 Lawn & garden mowers & accessories; automotive supplies; agricultural machinery & equipment

(G-1620)
DH WOODWORKS
826 County Road 185 (38930-7710)
PHONE..................662 299-5486
EMP: 1
SALES (est): 54.1K Privately Held
SIC: 2431 Millwork

(G-1621)
ECS- ELEC CNSTR SPCIALISTS INC
Also Called: Murphree Enterprises
101 Enterprise Dr (38930)
P.O. Box 1997 (38935-1997)
PHONE..................662 453-0588
Leo Murphree Jr, *President*
Christine Murphree, *Vice Pres*
EMP: 5
SQ FT: 6,250
SALES: 500K Privately Held
SIC: 1731 3648 7699 General electrical contractor; lighting contractor; airport lighting fixtures: runway approach, taxi or ramp; searchlights; industrial equipment services

(G-1622)
EXPRESS BIODIESEL LLC ☉
2015 River Road Ext (38930-4957)
P.O. Box 189, Sidon (38954-0189)
PHONE..................662 453-4312
John Coleman, *Mng Member*
Michael Coleman,
EMP: 20 EST: 2018
SALES (est): 879.6K Privately Held
SIC: 2911 Diesel fuels

(G-1623)
GALLEY KITCHEN BATH
Also Called: Favara Kitchen and Bath
320 W Park Ave Ste B (38930-2902)
PHONE..................662 455-6535
John Favara, *President*
Lisa Favara, *Vice Pres*
EMP: 5
SQ FT: 7,000
SALES (est): 609.2K Privately Held
WEB: www.favara.com
SIC: 2541 Counter & sink tops

(G-1624)
GALVIAN GROUP LLC
Also Called: None
1202 Cotton St (38930-5479)
PHONE..................662 374-1027
Jeremy Fox, *President*
EMP: 1
SALES (est): 93.7K Privately Held
SIC: 4731 4213 3559 4491 Freight transportation arrangement; heavy machinery transport; less-than-truckload (LTL) transport; semiconductor manufacturing machinery; marine cargo handling; petroleum brokers

(G-1625)
GARY BEALL ENTERPRISES LLC
15109 County Road 626 (38930-6809)
PHONE..................662 453-6100
Julian Beall, *President*
Lawson Gary, *COO*
Tommy Gary, *Officer*
EMP: 32
SALES (est): 4.2MM Privately Held
SIC: 2261 Finishing plants, cotton

(G-1626)
GECAS ASSET MGT SVCS INC
Also Called: GE Capital Aviation Services
600 Airport Rd (38930-7708)
PHONE..................662 455-1826
Jeremy Gladney, *Manager*
EMP: 4
SALES (corp-wide): 121.6B Publicly Held
SIC: 7389 7629 3728 5088 Purchasing service; aircraft electrical equipment repair; aircraft parts & equipment; aircraft engines & engine parts; aircraft & heavy equipment repair services
HQ: Gecas Asset Management Services, Inc.
    3860 E Holmes Rd Ste 108
    Memphis TN 38118
    901 362-8600

(G-1627)
HANGER PRSTHETCS & ORTHO INC
1603 Strong Ave (38930-4037)
PHONE..................662 451-7495
David Street, *Branch Mgr*
EMP: 5
SALES (corp-wide): 1B Publicly Held
SIC: 3842 Orthopedic appliances
HQ: Hanger Prosthetics & Orthotics, Inc.
    10910 Domain Dr Ste 300
    Austin TX 78758
    512 777-3800

(G-1628)
ILLUSIONS NEON & ACCESSORIES
Also Called: Illusionsneon.com
783 County Road 231 (38930-9330)
PHONE..................662 299-6366
Shanon Storms, *Principal*
EMP: 6
SALES (est): 110K Privately Held
SIC: 3993 Neon signs

(G-1629)
J J FERGUSON PRESTRESS-
4510 Highway 82 E (38930-9404)
PHONE..................662 453-5451
Jesse J Ferguson, *President*
EMP: 25
SALES (est): 2.3MM Privately Held
SIC: 3272 Concrete products, precast

(G-1630)
J J FERGUSON SAND & GRAV INC (PA)
Also Called: Hot Mix Asphalt
4510 Highway 82 E (38930-9404)
PHONE..................662 453-5451
Jerry Steen Jr, *President*
EMP: 135
SALES (est): 41.4MM Privately Held
SIC: 1622 1611 1442 3273 Bridge construction; general contractor, highway & street construction; concrete construction: roads, highways, sidewalks, etc.; common sand mining; gravel mining; ready-mixed concrete; asphalt & asphaltic paving mixtures (not from refineries)

(G-1631)
JAMES L BREWER
Also Called: Brewer Vegetable Farm
17000 Highway 7 N (38930-2635)
PHONE..................662 299-7247
James Brewer, *Owner*
EMP: 1
SALES (est): 54.6K Privately Held
SIC: 3421 7389 Table & food cutlery, including butchers';

(G-1632)
JONES SIGNS LLC
2810 Highway 82 E (38930-9706)
PHONE..................662 453-2432
Johnny M Jones,
Eddie M Jones,
EMP: 9
SQ FT: 25,000
SALES: 1MM Privately Held
SIC: 3993 Electric signs

(G-1633)
LAWRENCE PRINTING COMPANY
400 Stribling Ave (38930-2750)
P.O. Box 886 (38935-0886)
PHONE..................662 453-6301
Ellett Lawrence II, *Ch of Bd*
George Ellis Jr, *President*
Alan Ellis, *Marketing Staff*
Jeanne S Carroll, *Admin Sec*
Tabatha Sanford, *Admin Sec*
EMP: 52
SQ FT: 62,000
SALES: 3.4MM Privately Held
WEB: www.laprico.com
SIC: 2752 5943 5112 Business forms, lithographed; commercial printing, offset; office forms & supplies; stationery & office supplies

(G-1634)
LINDA F WILSON
2710 George White Cir (38930-7223)
PHONE..................662 299-9656
Linda Wilson, *Principal*
EMP: 2
SALES (est): 140.4K Privately Held
SIC: 2752 Commercial printing, lithographic

(G-1635)
LINING & COATING SOLUTIONS LLC
2606 Baldwin Rd (38930-4963)
PHONE..................662 453-6860
David Upchurch, *Principal*
EMP: 2
SALES (est): 99.8K Privately Held
SIC: 2952 Asphalt felts & coatings

(G-1636)
LOTT ENTERPRISES INC (PA)
Also Called: Pure Air Filter
204 Eastman St (38930-7000)
P.O. Box 9519 (38930-8719)
PHONE..................662 453-0034
Timmy Lott III, *President*

T W Lott Jr, *President*
James Lott, *General Mgr*
James H Lott, *COO*
Ashley Scott, *Accountant*
EMP: 150 EST: 1978
SALES (est): 30.9MM Privately Held
WEB: www.pureairco.com
SIC: 3564 Filters, air: furnaces, air conditioning equipment, etc.

(G-1637)
M AND S SALES INC
3107 Highway 82 E (38930-9751)
P.O. Box 368 (38935-0368)
PHONE..................662 453-6111
L C Ellis, *President*
Mike Ellis, *Vice Pres*
Bea Ellis, *Admin Sec*
EMP: 4
SALES (est): 340K Privately Held
SIC: 5084 3792 5531 5599 Trailers, industrial; truck campers (slide-in); truck equipment & parts; utility trailers

(G-1638)
M G K SEINING LLC
1401 Robert E Lee Dr (38930-2458)
PHONE..................662 453-8370
Larry Kelly, *Owner*
EMP: 4
SALES (est): 322.8K Privately Held
SIC: 2077 Fish oil

(G-1639)
METAL MANAGEMENT INC
405 8th St (38930-4595)
PHONE..................662 455-2540
Peggy Jeffords, *Manager*
EMP: 8 Privately Held
WEB: www.mtlm.com
SIC: 4953 3341 Recycling, waste materials; secondary nonferrous metals
HQ: Metal Management, Inc.
    200 W Madison St Ste 3600
    Chicago IL 60606
    312 645-0700

(G-1640)
MILWAUKEE ELECTRIC TOOL CORP
1003 Sycamore Ave (38930-7108)
PHONE..................662 451-5545
Josh Hardesty, *Mfg Staff*
David Creel, *Manager*
Brandon Hoover, *Administration*
Mike Young, *Maintence Staff*
EMP: 450 Privately Held
WEB: www.mil-electric-tool.com
SIC: 3546 3425 Power-driven handtools; saw blades for hand or power saws
HQ: Milwaukee Electric Tool Corporation
    13135 W Lisbon Rd
    Brookfield WI 53005
    800 729-3878

(G-1641)
MJJ INC
Also Called: New Dixie Fasteners
1910 Highway 82 W Ste G (38930-2705)
PHONE..................662 455-0126
Thomas Matthews, *Manager*
EMP: 2
SALES (corp-wide): 2MM Privately Held
SIC: 3965 5072 5251 Fasteners; brads; hardware
PA: Mjj, Inc.
    1210 Highway 1 N
    Greenville MS 38703
    662 335-6121

(G-1642)
MMC MATERIALS INC
108 Highlandale Rd (38930-7562)
PHONE..................662 453-9722
Rickie Suggs, *Branch Mgr*
EMP: 4
SALES (corp-wide): 306.5MM Privately Held
WEB: www.mmcmaterials.com
SIC: 3273 Ready-mixed concrete
HQ: Mmc Materials, Inc.
    1052 Highland Colony Pkwy # 201
    Ridgeland MS 39157
    601 898-4000

2019 Harris Directory of
Mississippi Manufacturers

▲ = Import ▼ =Export
◆ =Import/Export

GEOGRAPHIC SECTION

Grenada - Grenada County (G-1669)

GEOGRAPHIC

(G-1643)
NORRIS BOOKBINDING CO INC
107 N Stone Ave (38930-5749)
P.O. Box 305 (38935-0305)
PHONE..................................662 453-7424
Charles R Sproles, *President*
John W Sproles, *Vice Pres*
▲ EMP: 12
SALES: 500K **Privately Held**
WEB: www.norrisbookbinding.com
SIC: 2789 Binding only: books, pamphlets, magazines, etc.

(G-1644)
OUTLAW SPORTING GOODS LLC
717 Highway 82 W (38930-5027)
PHONE..................................662 459-9054
Brian Waldrop, *Principal*
EMP: 1
SALES (est): 185.1K **Privately Held**
SIC: 3949 Sporting & athletic goods

(G-1645)
PERNELLS REPAIRS INC
402 Highway 7 N (38930-4852)
PHONE..................................662 453-9702
Prentiss Pernell, *President*
Geneva Pernell, *Corp Secy*
EMP: 5
SQ FT: 5,000
SALES (est): 666.8K **Privately Held**
SIC: 3599 7699 Machine shop, jobbing & repair; industrial equipment services; agricultural equipment repair services

(G-1646)
PINNACLE AGRICULTURE DIST INC
Also Called: Sanders
62901 Highway 82 W (38930-5072)
P.O. Box 10118 (38930-0118)
PHONE..................................662 453-7010
Buzz Handwerker, *Manager*
EMP: 7
SALES (corp-wide): 1.1B **Privately Held**
SIC: 3999 Seeds, coated or treated, from purchased seeds
HQ: Pinnacle Agriculture Distribution, Inc.
1880 Fall River Dr Ste 100
Loveland CO 80538
970 800-4300

(G-1647)
PRINT SHOP
1400 Sycamore Ave (38930-5063)
P.O. Box 422 (38935-0422)
PHONE..................................662 453-8497
Dean Ainsworth, *Partner*
Cindy Hays, *Partner*
Thomas D Ainsworth, *Principal*
EMP: 4
SQ FT: 6,000
SALES (est): 340K **Privately Held**
SIC: 2752 Commercial printing, lithographic

(G-1648)
ROBERTSON FABRICATION INC
5905 Highway 49 S (38930-7543)
P.O. Box 1091 (38935-1091)
PHONE..................................662 453-1551
Richard Robertson, *President*
Janice Goodwin, *Treasurer*
EMP: 12
SALES: 690K **Privately Held**
SIC: 3499 Friction material, made from powdered metal

(G-1649)
ROG LLC
110 Main St (38930-4461)
P.O. Box 10088 (38930-1088)
PHONE..................................662 455-1364
Billy Dunn,
EMP: 6
SALES (est): 855K **Privately Held**
SIC: 3949 3151 Gloves, sport & athletic: boxing, handball, etc.; protective sporting equipment; gloves, leather: work; mittens, leather

(G-1650)
S & N AIROFLO INC
1011 Sycamore Ave (38930-5070)
PHONE..................................662 455-2804
Buster Norris, *President*
D J Norris, *President*
Donna Norris, *Vice Pres*
▼ EMP: 13 EST: 1991
SALES (est): 4.1MM **Privately Held**
WEB: www.airoflo.com
SIC: 3565 Bottling & canning machinery

(G-1651)
SHCPI GREENWOOD SITE
616 Main St (38930-5524)
PHONE..................................662 453-1445
Jackie Lewis, *Owner*
EMP: 2
SALES (est): 79.3K **Privately Held**
SIC: 2099 Emulsifiers, food

(G-1652)
SMOCKING BIRD CLOTHING LLC
1705 Highway 82 W (38930-2709)
PHONE..................................662 453-6432
Sallie Covington, *Principal*
EMP: 1
SALES (est): 43.1K **Privately Held**
SIC: 3942 Clothing, doll

(G-1653)
SUPREME ELECTRONICS CORP
Also Called: Hickok Inc-Supreme Elec Div
1714 Carrollton Ave (38930-5818)
PHONE..................................662 453-6212
Robert L Bauman, *Ch of Bd*
William Bruner, *President*
Michael Miller, *Admin Sec*
▲ EMP: 16 EST: 1926
SQ FT: 60,000
SALES (est): 3.7MM
SALES (corp-wide): 66.3MM **Publicly Held**
WEB: www.hickok-inc.com
SIC: 3825 Instruments to measure electricity
PA: Crawford United Corporation
10514 Dupont Ave
Cleveland OH 44108
216 541-8060

(G-1654)
UPHILL CONSTRUCTION LLC
402 Ione St (38930-3714)
PHONE..................................662 299-9654
Evangularnette Richards, *Partner*
EMP: 2 EST: 2015
SALES (est): 77.2K **Privately Held**
SIC: 1442 Construction sand & gravel

(G-1655)
VERA S RAY
Also Called: R & S Welding
4355 King Cir (38930-9506)
PHONE..................................662 453-1615
Vera S Ray, *Principal*
EMP: 1
SALES: 5K **Privately Held**
SIC: 7692 Welding repair

(G-1656)
VIKING CAPITAL VENTURES INC (PA)
Also Called: Viking Culinary Arts Center
111 W Front St (38930-4442)
PHONE..................................662 455-1200
Fred Carl Jr, *President*
Dave Becker, *Director*
David Webb, *Director*
Brian Waldrop, *Admin Sec*
EMP: 12 EST: 1998
SQ FT: 10,000
SALES (est): 25.3MM **Privately Held**
SIC: 2511 5064 2434 Wood household furniture; electrical appliances, major; vanities, bathroom: wood

(G-1657)
VIKING RANGE LLC
Also Called: Viking Specialty Products
5601 Viking Rd (38930-5548)
PHONE..................................770 932-7282
Baan Cunningham, *Manager*
Dale Russell, *Executive*

EMP: 85
SALES (corp-wide): 2.7B **Publicly Held**
WEB: www.vikingrange.com
SIC: 3631 3564 3444 Household cooking equipment; blowers & fans; sheet metalwork
HQ: Viking Range, Llc
111 W Front St
Greenwood MS 38930
662 455-1200

(G-1658)
VIKING RANGE LLC
5601 Viking Rd (38930-5548)
PHONE..................................662 455-7522
Fred Carl Jr, *President*
EMP: 55
SALES (corp-wide): 2.7B **Publicly Held**
WEB: www.vikingrange.com
SIC: 3631 Gas ranges, domestic; electric ranges, domestic; convection ovens, including portable: household
HQ: Viking Range, Llc
111 W Front St
Greenwood MS 38930
662 455-1200

(G-1659)
VIKING RANGE LLC
Also Called: Viking Manufacturing
5601 County Rd 525 (38930)
PHONE..................................662 455-1214
Ron Ushery, *Manager*
Brent Noah, *Director*
EMP: 675
SALES (corp-wide): 2.7B **Publicly Held**
WEB: www.vikingrange.com
SIC: 3631 3632 Gas ranges, domestic; household refrigerators & freezers
HQ: Viking Range, Llc
111 W Front St
Greenwood MS 38930
662 455-1200

(G-1660)
VIKING RANGE LLC
5601 Viking Rd (38930-5548)
PHONE..................................662 455-7521
George Demartino, *President*
EMP: 3
SALES (corp-wide): 2.7B **Publicly Held**
SIC: 3631 Household cooking equipment
HQ: Viking Range, Llc
111 W Front St
Greenwood MS 38930
662 455-1200

(G-1661)
VIKING RANGE LLC
5801 Viking Rd (38930-5546)
PHONE..................................662 455-1200
EMP: 2
SALES (corp-wide): 2.7B **Publicly Held**
SIC: 3631 Household cooking equipment
HQ: Viking Range, Llc
111 W Front St
Greenwood MS 38930
662 455-1200

(G-1662)
VIKING RANGE LLC (HQ)
111 W Front St (38930-4442)
PHONE..................................662 455-1200
Art Valentine, *President*
Clinton Wisniewski, *Regional Mgr*
Michael Beranis, *Vice Pres*
Ricky Couch, *Parts Mgr*
Rhonda Wetzbarger, *Purchasing*
◆ EMP: 450
SQ FT: 25,000
SALES (est): 248.6MM
SALES (corp-wide): 2.7B **Publicly Held**
WEB: www.vikingrange.com
SIC: 3631 5064 Household cooking equipment; dishwashers; garbage disposals; microwave ovens, non-commercial; refrigerators & freezers
PA: The Middleby Corporation
1400 Toastmaster Dr
Elgin IL 60120
847 741-3300

(G-1663)
VIKING RANGE LLC
5601 Viking Rd (38930-5548)
PHONE..................................662 455-7522

Brian Waldop, *Manager*
EMP: 297
SALES (corp-wide): 2.7B **Publicly Held**
SIC: 3631 Household cooking equipment
HQ: Viking Range, Llc
111 W Front St
Greenwood MS 38930
662 455-1200

(G-1664)
W F FERGUSON
Also Called: W F Ferguson Sand & Gravel
501 Montgomery St (38930-2817)
PHONE..................................601 453-1093
W F Ferguson, *Principal*
EMP: 2
SALES (est): 91.5K **Privately Held**
SIC: 1442 Construction sand & gravel

(G-1665)
WINERY AT WILLIAMS LANDING LLC
500 Howard St (38930-4340)
PHONE..................................662 219-0596
Lonnie Bailey, *Principal*
EMP: 2 EST: 2013
SALES (est): 111K **Privately Held**
SIC: 2084 Wines

Grenada
Grenada County

(G-1666)
ADVANCED DISTRIBUTOR PDTS LLC (HQ)
Also Called: ADP
1995 Air Industrial Pk Rd (38901-9561)
PHONE..................................662 229-3000
Tom Overs, *CEO*
David E Dorsett, *Principal*
▲ EMP: 585
SQ FT: 600,000
SALES (est): 203.5MM
SALES (corp-wide): 3.8B **Publicly Held**
SIC: 3585 Heating & air conditioning combination units
PA: Lennox International Inc.
2140 Lake Park Blvd
Richardson TX 75080
972 497-5000

(G-1667)
ALL STAR FOREST PRODUCTS INC
2498 Pryor St (38901-7914)
PHONE..................................662 294-8898
Bruce Brannan, *Branch Mgr*
EMP: 1 **Privately Held**
SIC: 5031 2448 Lumber, plywood & millwork; wood pallets & skids
PA: All Star Forest Products, Incorporated
5757 N Mcraven Rd
Jackson MS 39209

(G-1668)
BAIN MANUFACTURING CO INC
2 S Main St (38901-2620)
PHONE..................................662 226-7921
Larry Franklin, *President*
Rosemary Bain Franklin, *Treasurer*
EMP: 10 EST: 1969
SQ FT: 8,400
SALES: 791.5K **Privately Held**
WEB: www.bainsoftplastics.com
SIC: 3949 Lures, fishing: artificial

(G-1669)
BETTER SIGNS INC
11704 Highway 51 N (38901-9449)
P.O. Box 655 (38902-0655)
PHONE..................................662 227-1235
Ginger Wolfe, *President*
Freddie Wolfe, *Corp Secy*
EMP: 3
SALES (est): 447.1K **Privately Held**
WEB: www.bettersigns.com
SIC: 5046 5099 1799 7389 Signs, electrical; signs, except electric; sign installation & maintenance; awning installation; sign painting & lettering shop; awnings; signs & advertising specialties

---

(PA)=Parent Co (HQ)=Headquarters (DH)=Div Headquarters
✿ = New Business established in last 2 years

2019 Harris Directory of
Mississippi Manufacturers

67

Grenada - Grenada County (G-1670)

GEOGRAPHIC SECTION

(G-1670)
BROWNS ELECTRICAL REPAIR
317 Poplar St (38901-3023)
PHONE......................................662 226-8192
Richard Brown, *Owner*
EMP: 1
SALES (est): 65K **Privately Held**
SIC: 1711 7623 7694 Warm air heating & air conditioning contractor; air conditioning repair; electric motor repair

(G-1671)
CARROLL RAY AUTO & TRUCK SALES
23025 Highway 8 E (38901-8437)
PHONE......................................662 226-1200
Amy Denley, *Owner*
Ray Carroll, *Owner*
EMP: 3
SQ FT: 5,000
SALES (est): 308.7K **Privately Held**
SIC: 3715 5521 Truck trailers; automobiles, used cars only; pickups & vans, used

(G-1672)
COOK SALES INC
Also Called: Cook Portable Warehouses
1291 Air Industrial Pk Rd (38901-9499)
PHONE......................................662 229-9787
Shelton Cowart, *Manager*
EMP: 35
SALES (corp-wide): 19.2MM **Privately Held**
WEB: www.cookstuff.com
SIC: 2452 Prefabricated wood buildings
PA: Cook Sales, Inc.
3455 Old Highway 51 N
Cobden IL 62920
618 893-2114

(G-1673)
CRYOVAC INC
1621 Air Industrial Pk Rd (38901-9513)
PHONE......................................662 226-8804
Dave Kinard, *Branch Mgr*
EMP: 82
SALES (corp-wide): 4.7B **Publicly Held**
WEB: www.cryovac.com
SIC: 3086 2621 Packaging & shipping materials, foamed plastic; paper mills
HQ: Cryovac, Llc
2415 Cascade Pointe Blvd
Charlotte NC 28208
980 430-7000

(G-1674)
CUSTOM PRINTING
Also Called: Buzini Sports
1011 Lakeview Dr (38901-4308)
PHONE......................................662 227-9511
Chris Collins, *Owner*
EMP: 2
SALES (est): 338.2K **Privately Held**
SIC: 2752 Commercial printing, lithographic

(G-1675)
ELITE CONST AND DESIGN
1745 Jackson Ave (38901-4712)
PHONE......................................662 307-2494
EMP: 1
SALES (est): 30.7K **Privately Held**
SIC: 7389 1389 1521 1541 Design services; construction, repair & dismantling services; patio & deck construction & repair; steel building construction

(G-1676)
ENERGYZMART LLC
376 Kershaw St (38901-3307)
PHONE......................................650 630-1232
Mandala C Jones,
EMP: 2
SALES (est): 288K **Privately Held**
SIC: 2611 Pulp manufactured from waste or recycled paper

(G-1677)
FLY TIMBER CO INC (PA)
2178 Highway 7 N (38901-8662)
PHONE......................................662 226-2276
Ricky Fly, *President*
Dorothy Fly, *Corp Secy*
EMP: 15

SQ FT: 2,600
SALES (est): 2.6MM **Privately Held**
SIC: 2421 Sawmills & planing mills, general

(G-1678)
FRONTIER CONTRACTING LLC
254 Paper Mill Rd (38901-4448)
PHONE......................................662 809-1949
Heather Staten,
EMP: 5
SQ FT: 1,500
SALES (est): 196.6K **Privately Held**
SIC: 3496 1799 8744 Miscellaneous fabricated wire products; fence construction; facilities support services

(G-1679)
GRENADA ELECTRIC COMPANY INC
1055 Lakeview Dr (38901-4308)
P.O. Box 40 (38902-0040)
PHONE......................................662 226-5801
Ted R Artman, *President*
Pearl Artman, *Corp Secy*
EMP: 3
SQ FT: 1,800
SALES (est): 250K **Privately Held**
WEB: www.grenlec.com
SIC: 7694 Electric motor repair

(G-1680)
GRENADA FASTENERS INC
1518 Murff Dr (38901-9391)
P.O. Box 638, Elliott (38926-0638)
PHONE......................................662 227-1000
Glenn Dehart, *Enginr/R&D Mgr*
EMP: 5
SQ FT: 6,500
SALES (corp-wide): 5MM **Privately Held**
SIC: 3452 3965 Screws, metal; fasteners
HQ: Grenada Fasteners, Inc.
12898 Pennridge Dr
Bridgeton MO 63044
314 567-8585

(G-1681)
GRENADA NEWSPAPER INC
Also Called: Daily Sentinel Star
50 Corporate Row (38901-2823)
PHONE......................................662 226-4321
Joseph Lee III, *President*
Brenda Lee, *Vice Pres*
Chandra Burl, *Receptionist*
EMP: 29 **EST:** 1854
SQ FT: 14,100
SALES (est): 1.9MM **Privately Held**
SIC: 2711 Commercial printing & newspaper publishing combined; newspapers, publishing & printing

(G-1682)
GRENADA SALES MANAGEMENT INC
635 Highway 332 (38901-8056)
PHONE......................................662 226-1161
Howard Ice, *Ch of Bd*
Paul Bishop, *President*
Jeff Boger, *CFO*
Phil Caron, *Director*
Rodney Delong, *Director*
EMP: 175
SALES (est): 22.6MM **Privately Held**
SIC: 3469 Appliance parts, porcelain enameled

(G-1683)
HARRELLS METAL WORKS INC
1798 Highway 332 (38901-8823)
PHONE......................................662 226-0982
Howard R Harrell, *Principal*
Hunter Harrell, *Vice Pres*
Schyzell W Harrell, *Vice Pres*
EMP: 30
SQ FT: 42,000
SALES (est): 5.1MM **Privately Held**
SIC: 7692 3441 Welding repair; fabricated structural metal

(G-1684)
HARRISON LOGGING INC
29820 Highway 8 E (38901-9126)
PHONE......................................662 226-7908
EMP: 15
SALES (est): 1.4MM **Privately Held**
SIC: 2411 Logging

(G-1685)
HODGE PODGE SCREEN PRTG INC
Also Called: Sweet Thing Apparel
333 Sunset Loop (38901-4519)
PHONE......................................662 226-1636
EMP: 10
SQ FT: 13,000
SALES: 1.5MM **Privately Held**
SIC: 5947 2759 Commercial Printing Ret Gifts/Novelties

(G-1686)
ICE INDUSTRIES INC
200 American Way (38901)
PHONE......................................419 842-3612
Howard Ice, *Branch Mgr*
EMP: 20
SALES (corp-wide): 100MM **Privately Held**
SIC: 3469 Stamping metal for the trade
PA: Ice Industries, Inc.
3810 Herr Rd
Sylvania OH 43560
419 842-3600

(G-1687)
ICE INDUSTRIES INC
Also Called: Ice Industries Grenada
635 Highway 332 (38901-8056)
PHONE......................................662 226-1161
Howard Ice, *Chairman*
EMP: 9
SALES (corp-wide): 100MM **Privately Held**
SIC: 3469 Metal stampings
PA: Ice Industries, Inc.
3810 Herr Rd
Sylvania OH 43560
419 842-3600

(G-1688)
J J MONOGRAM EMBROIDERY
119 1st St (38901-2615)
PHONE......................................662 226-0304
Jeanette Langfall, *Owner*
EMP: 1
SALES: 20K **Privately Held**
SIC: 2395 Embroidery & art needlework

(G-1689)
KING HEATING & AC
5597 Sweethome Rd (38901-6833)
PHONE......................................662 227-1159
EMP: 2
SALES: 55K **Privately Held**
SIC: 3444 1711 Mfg Sheet Metalwork Plumbing/Heating/Air Cond Contractor

(G-1690)
KR STEEL & INDUSTRIAL SUPPLY
1505 South St (38901-2837)
P.O. Box 460 (38902-0460)
PHONE......................................662 294-8888
Keith Geiger, *President*
Robby Staten, *Vice Pres*
EMP: 2
SALES (est): 207.9K **Privately Held**
SIC: 3291 Abrasive metal & steel products

(G-1691)
LE CLAIR INDUSTRIES INC (PA)
2604 Sunset Dr (38901-2845)
P.O. Box 279 (38902-0279)
PHONE......................................662 226-8075
Tim Le Clair, *President*
EMP: 40
SQ FT: 42,000
SALES (est): 23.3MM **Privately Held**
SIC: 3086 Insulation or cushioning material, foamed plastic

(G-1692)
MODINE GRENADA LLC
Also Called: Aluminum Products
823a Air Industrial Pk Rd (38901-9676)
PHONE......................................662 229-2000
Norma Morgan, *Supervisor*
EMP: 1525
SALES (corp-wide): 2.2B **Publicly Held**
SIC: 3621 3585 Coils, for electric motors or generators; refrigeration equipment, complete

---

HQ: Modine Grenada Llc
3984 Highway 51 S
Grenada MS 38901
662 226-3421

(G-1693)
MODINE GRENADA LLC (HQ)
3984 Highway 51 S (38901-9318)
P.O. Box 948 (38902-0948)
PHONE......................................662 226-3421
Hannu Wahlroos, *Ch of Bd*
Thomas A Burke, *President*
John Peter Leesi, *Chairman*
Dennis Appel, *Vice Pres*
Mike Vandenbark, *Opers Staff*
▲ **EMP:** 2800
SQ FT: 650,000
SALES (est): 820.8MM
SALES (corp-wide): 2.2B **Publicly Held**
WEB: www.heatcraftheattransfer.com
SIC: 3621 3585 Coils, for electric motors or generators; refrigeration equipment, complete
PA: Modine Manufacturing Company Inc
1500 Dekoven Ave
Racine WI 53403
262 636-1200

(G-1694)
MODINE GRENADA LLC
Also Called: Commercial Coils
1000 Heat Craft Dr (38901-8843)
P.O. Box 1457 (38902-1457)
PHONE......................................662 229-4000
Michael Franklin, *Engineer*
Chris Wagner, *Manager*
EMP: 300
SALES (corp-wide): 2.2B **Publicly Held**
WEB: www.heatcraftheattransfer.com
SIC: 3585 3498 3433 Refrigeration & heating equipment; fabricated pipe & fittings; heating equipment, except electric
HQ: Modine Grenada Llc
3984 Highway 51 S
Grenada MS 38901
662 226-3421

(G-1695)
MODINE MANUFACTURING COMPANY
3984 Highway 51 S (38901-9318)
PHONE......................................662 229-2200
EMP: 5
SALES (corp-wide): 2.2B **Publicly Held**
SIC: 3443 Heat exchangers, condensers & components
PA: Modine Manufacturing Company Inc
1500 Dekoven Ave
Racine WI 53403
262 636-1200

(G-1696)
MURPHY CABINET COMPANY
2594 Pryor St (38901-7908)
PHONE......................................662 417-9717
EMP: 1
SALES (est): 187.1K **Privately Held**
SIC: 2434 Wood kitchen cabinets

(G-1697)
NOVIPAX LLC
1621 Air Industrial Pk Rd (38901-9513)
PHONE......................................662 226-8804
David Kinard, *Principal*
EMP: 64
SALES (corp-wide): 3.1B **Privately Held**
SIC: 2673 Plastic & pliofilm bags
HQ: Novipax Llc
2215 York Rd Ste 504
Oak Brook IL 60523
630 686-2735

(G-1698)
PEACOCKS SIGNS & DESIGNS
16394 Highway 8 W (38901-8099)
PHONE......................................662 226-9206
Walter Peacock, *Owner*
EMP: 1
SALES (est): 78.5K **Privately Held**
SIC: 3993 Signs, not made in custom sign painting shops

2019 Harris Directory of
Mississippi Manufacturers

▲ = Import ▼=Export
◆ =Import/Export

GEOGRAPHIC SECTION

Gulfport - Harrison County (G-1729)

(G-1699)
PERMA R PRODUCTS INC
2604 Sunset Dr (38901-2845)
P.O. Box 279 (38902-0279)
PHONE..................................662 226-8075
Tim Leclair, *CEO*
Tim Le Clair, *CEO*
Armond F Le Clair, *President*
Rick Wilbourn, *Vice Pres*
Greg Elliott, *Manager*
▲ EMP: 145
SQ FT: 43,000
SALES (est): 22.8MM
SALES (corp-wide): 23.3MM **Privately Held**
SIC: 2821 3086 *Plastics materials & resins; insulation or cushioning material, foamed plastic
PA: Le Clair Industries Inc
2604 Sunset Dr
Grenada MS 38901
662 226-8075

(G-1700)
PROVINE MACHINE WORKS
719 Air Industrial Pk Rd (38901-9518)
PHONE..................................662 226-1512
John E Provine, *Owner*
EMP: 3 EST: 1978
SQ FT: 6,200
SALES (est): 297.4K **Privately Held**
SIC: 3599 Machine shop, jobbing & repair

(G-1701)
RESOLUTE FP US INC
Also Called: Newsprint Division
1000 Paper Mill Rd (38901-4440)
P.O. Box 849 (38902-0849)
PHONE..................................662 227-7900
Steven Trew, *Superintendent*
Pat Hogg, *Opers Mgr*
Sylvain Bilodeau, *QA Dir*
Paul Ingraham, *Project Engr*
Thom Hazlett, *Electrical Engi*
EMP: 225
SALES (corp-wide): 3.7B **Privately Held**
WEB: www.bowater.com
SIC: 2621 Newsprint paper
HQ: Resolute Fp Us Inc.
5300 Cureton Ferry Rd
Catawba SC 29704
803 981-8000

(G-1702)
RESOLUTE FT US INC
1000 Paper Mill Rd (38901-4440)
P.O. Box 849 (38902-0849)
PHONE..................................662 227-7948
Richard Garneau, *CEO*
Bradley P Martin, *Ch of Bd*
Sue Keer, *General Mgr*
Robert Wise, *General Mgr*
Jacques P Vachon, *Senior VP*
EMP: 24
SALES (est): 10.5MM **Privately Held**
SIC: 2621 Paper mills

(G-1703)
SOUTHERN BELLE
2310 Sunset Dr (38901-2827)
PHONE..................................662 637-2264
Gary Worsham, *Principal*
EMP: 2
SALES (est): 108.8K **Privately Held**
SIC: 2759 Screen printing

(G-1704)
SOUTHERN MACHINING LLC
23074 Highway 8 E (38901-8597)
PHONE..................................662 229-0026
Joey Trussell, *Principal*
EMP: 3
SALES (est): 350K **Privately Held**
SIC: 3599 Machine shop, jobbing & repair

(G-1705)
SUBURBAN PLASTICS CO
1000 Enterprise Dr (38901-9509)
PHONE..................................662 227-1911
Floyd Fox, *Manager*
Cheri Baxter, *Admin Sec*
EMP: 100

SALES (est): 11.8MM
SALES (corp-wide): 93.4MM **Privately Held**
WEB: www.suburbanplastics.com
SIC: 3089 3544 Injection molding of plastics; special dies, tools, jigs & fixtures
PA: Suburban Plastics Co.
340 Renner Dr
Elgin IL 60123
847 741-4900

(G-1706)
SUNDAY BEST
10 South St (38901-2503)
PHONE..................................662 226-2214
Sunday Best, *Principal*
EMP: 2
SALES (est): 157.5K **Privately Held**
SIC: 3589 Servicing machines, except dry cleaning, laundry: coin-oper.

(G-1707)
TECH SMART LLC
570 Sunset Dr Ste C (38901-4627)
PHONE..................................662 417-8780
Eric Armstrong, *Principal*
EMP: 1 EST: 2013
SALES (est): 152.7K **Privately Held**
SIC: 3577 7378 1731 3695 Computer peripheral equipment; computer maintenance & repair; computer installation; computer software tape & disks: blank, rigid & floppy

(G-1708)
THOMAS WOOD PRESERVING INC
1964 Murff Dr (38901-8504)
PHONE..................................662 226-2350
Brent Thomas, *President*
Wesley Thomas, *Vice Pres*
EMP: 50
SQ FT: 1,900
SALES (est): 8.3MM **Privately Held**
SIC: 2491 Wood preserving

(G-1709)
TOWNES CONSTRUCTION CO INC
Also Called: Townes Ready Mix
16398 Highway 8 W (38901-8099)
PHONE..................................662 226-4894
Armistead Townes III, *President*
Lena Townes, *Corp Secy*
EMP: 18
SQ FT: 5,000
SALES: 1.5MM **Privately Held**
SIC: 1629 1794 3273 4212 Dredging contractor; excavation work; ready-mixed concrete; dump truck haulage

(G-1710)
TRAINING CONSULTANTS INC
1820 Country Club Rd (38901-4824)
PHONE..................................662 226-6637
Ryan Williams, *President*
Deborah A Rouse, *President*
EMP: 5
SALES (est): 1.1MM **Privately Held**
SIC: 3699 5999 Electronic training devices; training materials, electronic

(G-1711)
TRULITE GL ALUM SOLUTIONS LLC
501 E Govan St (38901-4324)
PHONE..................................662 226-5551
Wayne Smith, *General Mgr*
Dennis Lovell, *Plant Engr*
Leign Smith, *Branch Mgr*
Stacy Harris, *Manager*
EMP: 20 **Privately Held**
SIC: 5231 3544 Glass; forms (molds), for foundry & plastics working machinery
PA: Trulite Glass & Aluminum Solutions, Llc
403 Westpark Ct Ste 201
Peachtree City GA 30269

(G-1712)
WELL MADE GOODS LLC
81 S Church St (38901-2610)
PHONE..................................917 853-3598
Debrah Bailey, *Principal*
EMP: 1 EST: 2014

SALES (est): 112.8K **Privately Held**
SIC: 3942 Dolls & stuffed toys

(G-1713)
ZIPRINT INC
1346 Sunset Dr (38901-4000)
PHONE..................................662 226-6864
Tammy Evans, *President*
Bob Evens, *Owner*
EMP: 2
SALES (est): 286.5K **Privately Held**
SIC: 2752 Commercial printing, offset

Gulfport
Harrison County

(G-1714)
1 A LIFESAFER INC
15237 Russell Blvd (39503-4339)
PHONE..................................800 634-3077
EMP: 1
SALES (corp-wide): 4.3MM **Privately Held**
SIC: 3829 Measuring & controlling devices
PA: 1 A Lifesafer, Inc.
4290 Glendale Milford Rd
Blue Ash OH 45242
513 651-9560

(G-1715)
ACCURATE EDGE
21051 Coastal Pkwy (39503-9522)
PHONE..................................228 832-2920
Lloyd Townsend, *Owner*
Tom E Eichling, *General Mgr*
EMP: 7
SALES (est): 1.1MM **Privately Held**
SIC: 3541 Vertical turning & boring machines (metalworking)

(G-1716)
AGMYNS
102 Ruby Dr (39503-3234)
PHONE..................................228 831-0342
Eric Walker, *Owner*
EMP: 3
SALES (est): 117.1K **Privately Held**
SIC: 1389 Construction, repair & dismantling services

(G-1717)
ALDEN R STOCKERT
Also Called: Blue Chip Signs
11291 Pine Dr (39503-3940)
PHONE..................................228 731-2747
Alden R Stockert, *Owner*
EMP: 5 EST: 2016
SALES: 200K **Privately Held**
SIC: 3993 Signs & advertising specialties

(G-1718)
ALL AMERICAN STUCCO
14136 Cable Bridge Rd (39503-8650)
PHONE..................................228 669-0915
EMP: 1
SALES (est): 60.2K **Privately Held**
SIC: 3299 Stucco

(G-1719)
ALL SIGNS INC
558 Courthouse Rd (39507-2505)
P.O. Box 6265 (39506-6265)
PHONE..................................228 897-9100
Michael G Hage, *President*
EMP: 5
SQ FT: 3,500
SALES (est): 576.8K **Privately Held**
SIC: 3993 5999 Signs, not made in custom sign painting shops; decals

(G-1720)
ALL STAR FOREST PRODUCTS INC
400 Magazine Cir (39507-2859)
P.O. Box 7142 (39506-7142)
PHONE..................................228 896-4117
Charles Barnes, *Branch Mgr*
EMP: 2 **Privately Held**
SIC: 5031 2448 Lumber, plywood & millwork; wood pallets & skids
PA: All Star Forest Products, Incorporated
5757 N Mcraven Rd
Jackson MS 39209

(G-1721)
ALLEN BEVERAGES INCORPORATED
Also Called: Pepsi Cola Btlg Co Gulfport
13300 Dedeaux Rd (39503-4518)
P.O. Box 2037 (39505-2037)
PHONE..................................228 831-4343
Eustace A Allen II, *President*
Margaret Moyse, *Corp Secy*
Christie Batson, *Vice Pres*
H Grey Walker, *CFO*
EMP: 80
SQ FT: 40,000
SALES: 22.5MM **Privately Held**
WEB: www.abevinc.com
SIC: 2086 Carbonated soft drinks, bottled & canned

(G-1722)
ALLEYKAT CERAMICS LLC
2694 Broadwater Dr (39507-2839)
PHONE..................................228 224-7775
Mary Martin, *Partner*
EMP: 2
SALES (est): 155.3K **Privately Held**
SIC: 3269 Pottery products

(G-1723)
ALLISTONS
14494 Collins Blvd (39503-9132)
PHONE..................................228 832-8683
Edwin T Alliston, *Owner*
EMP: 3 EST: 1969
SQ FT: 5,000
SALES (est): 215K **Privately Held**
SIC: 2396 5999 Screen printing on fabric articles; trophies & plaques

(G-1724)
AMANDAS PUZZLES
2200 19th Ave (39501-4745)
PHONE..................................228 314-3930
EMP: 1
SALES (est): 41K **Privately Held**
SIC: 3944 Puzzles

(G-1725)
ANDREWS WOODSHOP LLC
1728 21st St (39501-4701)
PHONE..................................228 216-5563
Andrew Williams, *Principal*
EMP: 1
SALES (est): 45.6K **Privately Held**
SIC: 2499 Wood products

(G-1726)
ANI PHARMACEUTICALS INC
3600 25th Ave (39501-6922)
PHONE..................................228 863-1702
Edwin Gomez, *Branch Mgr*
EMP: 81 **Publicly Held**
SIC: 2834 Pharmaceutical preparations
PA: Ani Pharmaceuticals, Inc.
210 W Main St
Baudette MN 56623

(G-1727)
ANNA GRACE TEES LLC
402 Caribe Pl N (39507-4128)
PHONE..................................228 861-2661
Anna Grace, *Principal*
EMP: 2 EST: 2016
SALES (est): 123.7K **Privately Held**
SIC: 2759 Screen printing

(G-1728)
APM LLC
13220 N Cypress Dr (39503-7658)
PHONE..................................907 279-0204
Michael E Brown,
EMP: 6
SALES (corp-wide): 4.9MM **Privately Held**
WEB: www.apmglobal.com
SIC: 3321 5032 Sewer pipe, cast iron; sewer pipe, clay
PA: Apm, Llc
1570 N Batavia St
Orange CA 92867
714 455-0070

(G-1729)
APPLE DAPPLE
12261 Highway 49 Ste 15 (39503-2976)
PHONE..................................228 539-3100

(PA)=Parent Co (HQ)=Headquarters (DH)=Div Headquarters
✪ = New Business established in last 2 years

2019 Harris Directory of
Mississippi Manufacturers

69

Gulfport - Harrison County (G-1730)　　　　　　　　　**GEOGRAPHIC SECTION**

EMP: 2
SALES (est): 85.9K **Privately Held**
SIC: 3571 Mfg Electronic Computers

(G-1730)
AWARDS UNLIMITED
1618 25th Ave (39501-2827)
PHONE..................................228 863-1814
Freda Kelly, *Owner*
EMP: 3
SQ FT: 2,400
SALES (est): 100K **Privately Held**
SIC: 5999 7389 3479 Trophies & plaques;
engraving service; engraving jewelry sil-
verware, or metal

(G-1731)
AXSOM WOODWORKS
15215 Northrup Cuevas Rd (39503-8281)
PHONE..................................334 422-9766
EMP: 1
SALES (est): 54.1K **Privately Held**
SIC: 2431 Millwork

(G-1732)
B-LINE FABRICATION CO LTD
13465 Oneal Rd (39503-5516)
PHONE..................................228 832-3286
Rayburn Broadus Jr, *President*
Linda J Broadus, *Corp Secy*
Jeremy Broadus, *Vice Pres*
Rayburn M Broadus Jr, *Vice Pres*
EMP: 20
SQ FT: 14,000
SALES (est): 6MM **Privately Held**
SIC: 3441 Fabricated structural metal

(G-1733)
BALLY TECHNOLOGIES INC
10441 Corporate Dr (39503-4634)
PHONE..................................228 396-3480
Fax: 228 396-3485
EMP: 110
SALES (corp-wide): 1.7B **Publicly Held**
SIC: 3999 Whol Durable Goods
HQ: Bally Technologies, Inc.
6601 Bermuda Rd
Las Vegas NV 89118
770 420-2388

(G-1734)
BALLY TECHNOLOGIES INC
320 Courthouse Rd (39507-1859)
PHONE..................................228 897-9059
Mark Reid, *Supervisor*
EMP: 3
SALES (corp-wide): 3.3B **Publicly Held**
WEB: www.shufflemaster.com
SIC: 7999 3999 Card rooms; coin-oper-
ated amusement machines
HQ: Bally Technologies, Inc.
6650 El Camino Rd
Las Vegas NV 89118
702 897-2284

(G-1735)
BAY ICE COMPANY INC
1413 30th Ave (39501-2737)
PHONE..................................228 863-0981
Coileen D Renaudin, *President*
EMP: 15
SQ FT: 7,500
SALES (est): 2.1MM **Privately Held**
SIC: 2097 5999 Manufactured ice; ice

(G-1736)
BAYOU CONCRETE LLC
14312 Creosote Rd (39503-4297)
P.O. Box 3868 (39505-3868)
PHONE..................................228 868-1264
Russell Simmons, *Sales Staff*
Judd Beech, *Branch Mgr*
Bobby Dowdy, *Regional*
EMP: 70
SALES (corp-wide): 306.5MM **Privately Held**
SIC: 3273 Ready-mixed concrete
HQ: Bayou Concrete Llc
1052 Highland Colony Pkwy
Ridgeland MS 39157
601 898-4000

(G-1737)
BEACH BLVD MAG
205 Debuys Rd (39507-2838)
PHONE..................................228 896-2499

Wendy Powell, *Manager*
EMP: 1
SALES (est): 39.9K **Privately Held**
SIC: 2711 Newspapers

(G-1738)
BENVENUTTI ELCTRCL APPRTS & RP
Also Called: B.E.A.R.
9515 N Wildflower Ct (39503-8389)
PHONE..................................228 831-0445
Mary Ann Benvenutti, *President*
David M Benvenutti, *Corp Secy*
EMP: 8
SQ FT: 6,000
SALES (est): 1.4MM **Privately Held**
SIC: 3599 Machine & other job shop work

(G-1739)
BIMBO BAKERIES USA INC
901 Pass Rd (39501-6449)
PHONE..................................228 863-4302
Wayne Poke, *Branch Mgr*
EMP: 221 **Privately Held**
SIC: 2051 Bread, cake & related products
HQ: Bimbo Bakeries Usa, Inc
255 Business Center Dr # 200
Horsham PA 19044
215 347-5500

(G-1740)
BLACKLIDGE EMULSIONS INC (PA)
12251 Bernard Pkwy # 200 (39503-5086)
PHONE..................................228 863-3878
Brittany Blacklidge, *President*
Ronald Blacklidge Sr, *Chairman*
K Brooke Shoultz, *Admin Sec*
▼ EMP: 20
SQ FT: 3,000
SALES (est): 37.9MM **Privately Held**
WEB: www.blacklidgeemulsions.com
SIC: 2951 5032 Road materials, bitumi-
nous (not from refineries); paving materi-
als

(G-1741)
BLACKLIDGE EMULSIONS INC
10220 Three Rivers Rd (39503-3515)
PHONE..................................228 864-3719
Ronald Blacklidge, *Principal*
EMP: 2 EST: 2007
SALES (est): 130K **Privately Held**
SIC: 2951 2911 Asphalt paving mixtures &
blocks; asphalt or asphaltic materials,
made in refineries

(G-1742)
BLUE LINE INDUSTRIES LLC (PA)
15235 Oneal Rd Apt 14p (39503-3473)
PHONE..................................901 335-2987
Timothy Fugate, *Mng Member*
EMP: 4
SALES (est): 1MM **Privately Held**
SIC: 3999 Manufacturing industries

(G-1743)
BLUE LOTUS CREATIONS LLC
4116 Central St (39501-1528)
PHONE..................................770 714-9408
Natalie Bonner,
EMP: 2
SALES: 425K **Privately Held**
SIC: 3999

(G-1744)
BRIAN SMITH
Also Called: Brians Marine
24049 Rose Blvd (39503-7021)
PHONE..................................601 259-9745
Brian Smith, *Owner*
EMP: 2
SQ FT: 2,500
SALES (est): 197.5K **Privately Held**
SIC: 5551 5091 7699 3732 Marine sup-
plies & equipment; boat accessories &
parts; boat repair; boat building & repair-
ing; motorboats, inboard or outboard;
building & repairing; towboats, building &
repairing

(G-1745)
BRIMMER-TURAN FNDRY & MCH LLC
10021 Lorraine Rd (39503-6001)
PHONE..................................228 896-9669
Charles E Brimmer,
EMP: 9
SQ FT: 16,000
SALES: 750K **Privately Held**
SIC: 3366 3365 Castings (except die):
bronze; aluminum foundries

(G-1746)
BUZZARD REBAR FABRICATORS INC
14411 Highway 49 (39503-8424)
PHONE..................................228 832-8024
Billy R Moore, *President*
Mae B Moore, *Corp Secy*
Steven Johnson, *Manager*
EMP: 10
SQ FT: 1,000
SALES (est): 1.8MM **Privately Held**
SIC: 3449 Joists, fabricated bar; bars, con-
crete reinforcing: fabricated steel

(G-1747)
CABINETSOURCE INC
1956 E Pass Rd Ste E (39507-3768)
P.O. Box 8834, Biloxi (39535-8834)
PHONE..................................228 385-8880
Karen Lorona, *President*
EMP: 2
SALES (est): 239.8K **Privately Held**
SIC: 2434 Wood kitchen cabinets

(G-1748)
CANVAS & COCKTAILS LLC
500d Courthouse Rd (39507-2503)
PHONE..................................228 861-8444
Linda Ishee, *Mng Member*
Linda L Ishee, *Mng Member*
EMP: 3 EST: 2011
SALES (est): 158.3K **Privately Held**
SIC: 2211 5231 Canvas; paint

(G-1749)
CERBIDE INC
14115 Seaway Rd (39503-4689)
PHONE..................................228 871-7123
Jim Houlden, *President*
Xiaoying Song, *Chairman*
Bo Song, *Admin Sec*
EMP: 12
SALES (est): 161.8K **Privately Held**
SIC: 3541 Machine tools, metal cutting
type

(G-1750)
CHANNEL CHEMICAL CORPORATION
14373 Seaway Rd (39503-4637)
P.O. Box 2216 (39505-2216)
PHONE..................................228 864-6199
Brian Reid, *President*
Tim Reid, *Vice Pres*
Timothy Reid, *Vice Pres*
Kathleen Talley, *Vice Pres*
Jonathon Howell, *Director*
EMP: 20
SQ FT: 2,500
SALES (est): 2.2MM **Privately Held**
WEB: www.channelchemical.com
SIC: 2819 Industrial inorganic chemicals

(G-1751)
CHARGED UP GRILL LLC
13741 Shelby Ct (39503-5593)
PHONE..................................228 224-4461
Keithon Burnette,
EMP: 1 EST: 2017 **Privately Held**
SIC: 2099 Food preparations

(G-1752)
CHIPPEWA ENTERPRISES LLC
11451 Canal Rd (39503-7702)
PHONE..................................228 832-0032
EMP: 3
SALES (est): 230K **Privately Held**
SIC: 2431 Mfg Millwork

(G-1753)
CLAYS PRINT SHOP INC
1513 24th Ave (39501-2070)
PHONE..................................228 868-8244

Susan Clay, *President*
Guy Clay Jr, *Vice Pres*
EMP: 5
SALES: 1MM **Privately Held**
WEB: www.claysprintshop.com
SIC: 2752 7334 Commercial printing, off-
set; photocopying & duplicating services

(G-1754)
COAST COCA COLA BOTTLING CO
Also Called: Coca-Cola
3701 25th Ave (39501-6929)
PHONE..................................228 864-1122
Clifton Milner Jr, *President*
Tommy Bivings, *Warehouse Mgr*
Heather Courville, *Hum Res Coord*
Larry Cobb, *Sales Staff*
Blaine Depue, *Office Mgr*
EMP: 97
SQ FT: 175,000
SALES (est): 9.1MM **Privately Held**
SIC: 2086 Bottled & canned soft drinks

(G-1755)
COAST CONCRETE COMPANY INC
14270 Creosote Rd (39503-4298)
PHONE..................................228 863-1364
Wallace C Fore, *President*
EMP: 30
SALES (est): 826.7K
SALES (corp-wide): 8.2MM **Privately Held**
SIC: 3273 Ready-mixed concrete
PA: W. C. Fore Trucking, Inc.
14270 Creosote Rd
Gulfport MS 39503
228 863-1314

(G-1756)
COAST MOTOR NEWS
16195 Landon Rd (39503-4121)
PHONE..................................228 868-1772
Sandra P Erhard, *Principal*
EMP: 5
SALES (est): 268.8K **Privately Held**
SIC: 2711 Newspapers, publishing & print-
ing

(G-1757)
COAST PRINTING COMPANY
1623 25th Ave (39501-2834)
P.O. Box 1948 (39502-1948)
PHONE..................................228 863-1018
Jerry Maddux, *Owner*
Cindy Maddux, *Co-Owner*
EMP: 3 EST: 1958
SQ FT: 2,400
SALES (est): 125K **Privately Held**
SIC: 2752 Commercial printing, offset

(G-1758)
COAST TEES LLC
12125 Edington Pl (39503-2862)
PHONE..................................228 234-1636
Dustin Williams, *Principal*
EMP: 2
SALES (est): 128.1K **Privately Held**
SIC: 2759 Screen printing

(G-1759)
COASTAL MARINE EQUIPMENT INC
20995 Coastal Pkwy (39503-9517)
PHONE..................................228 832-7655
Mark Scairono, *President*
Scott Chauvan, *Vice Pres*
Todd Dungan, *Vice Pres*
Mark McClammy, *Project Mgr*
Jonathan Slade, *Engineer*
◆ EMP: 64
SQ FT: 11,000
SALES (est): 14.3MM **Privately Held**
WEB: www.coastalmarineequipment.com
SIC: 3731 Shipbuilding & repairing

(G-1760)
COASTAL MARINE SALES LLC
4417 Tennessee Ave (39501-7407)
PHONE..................................228 731-3955
James W Donahoo,
EMP: 1

2019 Harris Directory of
Mississippi Manufacturers

70

▲ = Import ▼=Export
◆ =Import/Export

GEOGRAPHIC SECTION

Gulfport - Harrison County (G-1792)

SALES (est): 105.2K **Privately Held**
SIC: 3732 Houseboats, building & repairing

(G-1761)
COCA-COLA BOTTLING CO UNTD INC
3701 25th Ave (39501-6929)
P.O. Box E (39502-0140)
PHONE..................................228 864-1122
Anthony Taravella, *Division Mgr*
Butch Scarborough, *Plant Mgr*
Chris Higgins, *Opers Staff*
James Honstetter, *Opers Staff*
Scott Oneal, *Opers Staff*
EMP: 5
SALES (corp-wide): 2.4B **Privately Held**
SIC: 2086 5149 Bottled & canned soft drinks; groceries & related products
PA: Coca-Cola Bottling Company United, Inc.
4600 E Lake Blvd
Birmingham AL 35217
205 841-2653

(G-1762)
COLLINS FILTER CO INC
10185 Southpark Dr (39503-6007)
PHONE..................................228 896-0582
Boyce Collins, *President*
▼ EMP: 11
SQ FT: 16,000
SALES (est): 1.2MM **Privately Held**
SIC: 3564 1711 Filters, air: furnaces, air conditioning equipment, etc.; warm air heating & air conditioning contractor

(G-1763)
COMMERCIAL MLLWK SPCIALIST INC
Also Called: CMS
1518 B 28th St (39501)
PHONE..................................228 868-3888
Trey Pennell, *President*
Drew Roan, *Project Mgr*
Rene Pennell, *Treasurer*
EMP: 25 EST: 1999
SQ FT: 12,000
SALES (est): 6.7MM **Privately Held**
SIC: 2435 Hardwood plywood, prefinished

(G-1764)
COMPETITIVE PRINTING
2400 24th St (39501-4664)
PHONE..................................228 863-4001
Larry Loveless, *Owner*
EMP: 6
SQ FT: 3,000
SALES (est): 200K **Privately Held**
WEB: www.bidsplus.com
SIC: 2752 Commercial printing, lithographic

(G-1765)
CORE SOLUTIONS LLC
651b 35th St (39501-7102)
PHONE..................................228 216-6848
Allen Harrell,
Zach Thompson,
EMP: 2
SALES (est): 274.7K **Privately Held**
SIC: 7699 7692 Garage door repair; automotive welding

(G-1766)
CROOKED LETTER PUBLISHING LLC
14055 Seaway Rd 200 (39503-4610)
PHONE..................................228 334-4575
EMP: 1
SALES (est): 40.6K **Privately Held**
SIC: 2741 Miscellaneous publishing

(G-1767)
CYRUS RESOURCES LLC
13508 John Clark Rd (39503-4892)
PHONE..................................228 669-6955
Bruce Wooten, *Mng Member*
EMP: 3
SALES (est): 87.9K **Privately Held**
SIC: 1389 Cementing oil & gas well casings

(G-1768)
DAVIS CUSTOM FABRICATION LLC
10415 7th Ave (39503-3685)
PHONE..................................228 832-7456
William B Davis, *President*
EMP: 2
SALES (est): 101.1K **Privately Held**
SIC: 3446 Architectural metalwork

(G-1769)
DEEP BLUE PRESS LLC
7 Old Oak Ln (39503-6225)
PHONE..................................228 604-4643
Frank J Wilem Jr, *Principal*
EMP: 1
SALES (est): 83.7K **Privately Held**
SIC: 2741 Miscellaneous publishing

(G-1770)
DELTA INDUSTRIES INC
Also Called: Gulf States Ready Mix
10121 Southpark Dr (39503-6007)
PHONE..................................228 896-7400
Jim Goudie, *Manager*
EMP: 50
SALES (corp-wide): 100.3MM **Privately Held**
WEB: www.delta-ind.com
SIC: 3273 Ready-mixed concrete
PA: Delta Industries, Inc.
100 W Woodrow Wilson Ave
Jackson MS 39213
601 354-3801

(G-1771)
DERN MECHANIX
13081 Canal Rd (39503-2200)
PHONE..................................228 832-3933
Gary Dern, *Principal*
EMP: 4 EST: 2009
SALES (est): 271.1K **Privately Held**
SIC: 3423 Mechanics' hand tools

(G-1772)
DESIGN PRECAST & PIPE INC (PA)
15215 Dedeaux Rd (39503-3161)
P.O. Box 2401 (39505-2401)
PHONE..................................228 831-5833
Marilyn Sellars, *President*
Pat H Fore III, *President*
Chris Fore, *Vice Pres*
Trisha Wiles, *Treasurer*
Travis Dickey, *Sales Dir*
EMP: 20
SQ FT: 1,200
SALES (est): 6.2MM **Privately Held**
WEB: www.designprecast.com
SIC: 3272 Concrete products used to facilitate drainage

(G-1773)
DOGWOOD CERAMIC SUPPLY INC
12590 Dedeaux Rd (39503-5863)
PHONE..................................228 831-4848
Francis Drollinger, *President*
EMP: 5
SQ FT: 13,000
SALES: 840K **Privately Held**
WEB: www.dogwoodceramics.com
SIC: 5945 5092 3559 Ceramics supplies; arts & crafts equipment & supplies; kilns

(G-1774)
DOUBLE C CUSTOM WELDING & FABG
3 Bandywood Ct (39503-3050)
PHONE..................................228 383-1243
Charles Pruitt, *Owner*
EMP: 1
SALES (est): 45K **Privately Held**
SIC: 7692 Welding repair

(G-1775)
DRONE ASSIST INCORPORATED
11989 Music St (39503-4455)
PHONE..................................228 265-0174
William Harwell, *Principal*
EMP: 2
SALES (est): 92.9K **Privately Held**
SIC: 3721 Motorized aircraft

(G-1776)
EDUCATE & CELEBRATE LLC
311 Cowan Rd (39507-2019)
PHONE..................................228 547-0811
Macey Young,
EMP: 2
SALES (est): 220K **Privately Held**
SIC: 2621 7389 Stationery, envelope & tablet papers;

(G-1777)
EK EMBROIDERY LLC
2219 Pass Rd Ste A (39501-4906)
PHONE..................................228 868-8469
Michael J Pornoverts,
EMP: 1
SALES (est): 53.5K **Privately Held**
SIC: 2311 Men's & boys' suits & coats

(G-1778)
EMBROIDERY NU SUN
2000 E Pass Rd (39507-3721)
PHONE..................................228 731-3781
Nina Kempton, *Manager*
EMP: 1
SALES (est): 73.5K **Privately Held**
SIC: 2395 Embroidery & art needlework

(G-1779)
ENERCEPT INC
11574 Bluff Ln (39503-6100)
PHONE..................................228 323-1666
EMP: 1 EST: 2006
SALES (est): 130K **Privately Held**
SIC: 2452 Mfg Prefabricated Wood Buildings

(G-1780)
EXCEL BY FOUR LLC
13609 Lawton Ln (39503-6503)
P.O. Box 7529, Diberville (39540-7481)
PHONE..................................228 355-8203
Leslie Jones,
EMP: 5 EST: 2015
SALES (est): 41.4K **Privately Held**
SIC: 8299 3949 8322 8748 Educational services; tutoring school; Indian clubs; disaster service; educational consultant

(G-1781)
FALLEN LEAF SERVICES LLC
2512 25th Ave Ste 4a (39501-4814)
PHONE..................................228 731-0919
Patricia Valestro,
EMP: 1 EST: 2014
SALES (est): 49.1K **Privately Held**
SIC: 8744 4213 4212 2813 Facilities support services; contract haulers; garbage collection & transport, no disposal; industrial gases; dry ice, carbon dioxide (solid)

(G-1782)
FAMCO COMPANY INC
15098 Government St (39503-2837)
P.O. Box 2936 (39505-2936)
PHONE..................................228 831-4649
EMP: 12
SALES (est): 1MM **Privately Held**
SIC: 3272 Mfg Concrete Products

(G-1783)
FAYARD MILLWORKS
3320 14th St (39501-2617)
PHONE..................................228 265-7787
Gerald Fayard, *Partner*
Linda Peterson, *Partner*
EMP: 3
SQ FT: 3,300
SALES (est): 274.4K **Privately Held**
SIC: 5211 2431 Door & window products; doors & door parts & trim, wood

(G-1784)
FED SERVICE HUB LLC
1914 24th Ave (39501-2975)
PHONE..................................228 547-3498
Andrew Schatzle,
EMP: 2
SALES (est): 56.5K **Privately Held**
SIC: 7372 5065 Application computer software; business oriented computer software; modems, computer

(G-1785)
FENNELL SAM SHEET METAL MFG C
3200 B Ave (39507-2424)
PHONE..................................228 864-1488
Sam Fennel, *Owner*
EMP: 1
SALES (est): 170.2K **Privately Held**
SIC: 3444 Sheet metal specialties, not stamped

(G-1786)
FIELD COATINGS LLC
2160 E Pass Rd (39507-3801)
PHONE..................................228 896-3535
EMP: 3
SQ FT: 8,000
SALES: 350K **Privately Held**
SIC: 3479 Coating/Engraving Service

(G-1787)
FIRST AMERCN PRTG DIRECT MAIL
1605 23rd Ave (39501-2960)
PHONE..................................228 867-9808
Jack Wilkerson, *Branch Mgr*
EMP: 4 **Privately Held**
WEB: www.fapdm.com
SIC: 2759 7331 2752 Commercial printing; direct mail advertising services; commercial printing, offset
HQ: First American Printing And Direct Mail
404 Industrial Rd Bfs1
Choctaw MS 39350

(G-1788)
FLOWERS BKG CO NEW ORLEANS LLC
14373 Creosote Rd (39503-4295)
PHONE..................................228 868-0120
Martin Cantesse, *Manager*
EMP: 3
SALES (corp-wide): 3.9B **Publicly Held**
SIC: 2051 Bakery: wholesale or wholesale/retail combined
HQ: Flowers Baking Co. Of New Orleans, Llc
5646 Lewis Rd
New Orleans LA 70126
504 241-1206

(G-1789)
FRIEDE GOLDMAN DELAWARE INC
13085 Seaway Rd (39503-4607)
PHONE..................................228 896-0029
John Corlew, *Partner*
EMP: 2 EST: 2001
SALES (est): 179.4K **Privately Held**
SIC: 8712 8711 3533 Architectural services; marine engineering; drill rigs

(G-1790)
GATEWAY AMERICA LLC
4300 Air Cargo Rd (39501-6161)
PHONE..................................228 331-1473
Frank Benso, *President*
Ryan Hollingsworth, *Vice Pres*
Frank Besno, *Administration*
EMP: 4
SQ FT: 46,000
SALES (est): 353.9K **Privately Held**
SIC: 2099 Food preparations

(G-1791)
GCP LABORATORIES INC
3600 25th Ave (39501-6922)
PHONE..................................228 863-1702
Elliot J Schindler, *President*
Roger Froit, *Manager*
Ken Fallin, *Director*
▲ EMP: 52
SALES (est): 8.8MM **Privately Held**
SIC: 2834 Pharmaceutical preparations

(G-1792)
GEMLIGHT PUBLISHING LLC
45 Hardy Court Shopg Ctr (39507-2501)
PHONE..................................601 509-1002
EMP: 1
SALES (est): 37.5K **Privately Held**
SIC: 2741 Miscellaneous publishing

(PA)=Parent Co (HQ)=Headquarters (DH)=Div Headquarters
✿ = New Business established in last 2 years

2019 Harris Directory of
Mississippi Manufacturers

71

Gulfport - Harrison County (G-1793)

GEOGRAPHIC SECTION

(G-1793)
GOLDIN METALS INCORPORATED (PA)
14231 Seaway Rd Ste 7000 (39503-4677)
PHONE.....................................228 575-7737
Alan Goldin, *President*
Martin Goldin, *Corp Secy*
Jason Goldin, *Exec VP*
Scott Goldin, *Exec VP*
Steven L Goldin, *Vice Pres*
▼ EMP: 60
SALES (est): 18.3MM **Privately Held**
WEB: www.goldinmetals.com
SIC: 3444 3448 Sheet metalwork; metal roofing & roof drainage equipment; siding, sheet metal; panels for prefabricated metal buildings

(G-1794)
GOLDIN METALS INCORPORATED
Also Called: Goldin Building Systems
12440 Seaway Rd Ste 1 (39503-6030)
P.O. Box 2909 (39505-2909)
PHONE.....................................228 575-7737
Bill Compher, *Manager*
EMP: 15
SALES (corp-wide): 18.3MM **Privately Held**
SIC: 3448 3444 Prefabricated metal buildings; sheet metalwork
PA: Goldin Metals Incorporated
14231 Seaway Rd Ste 7000
Gulfport MS 39503
228 575-7737

(G-1795)
GRASSLAWN PUBLISHING LLC
1007 Wilson Dr (39507-2740)
PHONE.....................................228 896-5532
Anthony Kalberg, *Principal*
EMP: 1
SALES (est): 37.5K **Privately Held**
SIC: 2741 Miscellaneous publishing

(G-1796)
GREAT SOUTHERN CLUB INC (PA)
2510 14th St Ste 1480 (39501-1911)
PHONE.....................................228 868-8619
Bubba Lang, *President*
EMP: 18
SALES (est): 813.1K **Privately Held**
WEB: www.greatsouthernclub.com
SIC: 7299 2531 Buyers' club; assembly hall furniture

(G-1797)
GULF COAST CABINETS & MILL
2815 22nd Ave (39501-6010)
PHONE.....................................228 206-7792
EMP: 1
SALES (est): 54.1K **Privately Held**
SIC: 2431 Millwork

(G-1798)
GULF COAST LIMB & BRACE INC
3506 Washington Ave Ste D (39507-3102)
PHONE.....................................228 864-4512
Carl Seguin, *President*
EMP: 4
SQ FT: 1,500
SALES: 600K **Privately Held**
SIC: 3842 5999 Limbs, artificial; artificial limbs

(G-1799)
GULF COAST SHIPYARD GROUP INC
13085 Seaway Rd (39503-4607)
PHONE.....................................228 276-1000
Steve Stall, *Branch Mgr*
EMP: 200 **Privately Held**
SIC: 3799 Boat trailers
PA: Gulf Coast Shipyard Group, Inc.
13085 Seaway Rd
Gulfport MS 39503

(G-1800)
GULF COAST SHIPYARD GROUP INC (PA)
13085 Seaway Rd (39503-4607)
PHONE.....................................228 276-1051

John Dane III, *President*
Marvin Serna, *COO*
Mitchell Skrmetta, *CFO*
▲ EMP: 87
SQ FT: 500,000
SALES: 165MM **Privately Held**
SIC: 3731 Shipbuilding & repairing

(G-1801)
GULF PUBLISHING COMPANY INC (HQ)
Also Called: Sun Herald
205 Debuys Rd (39507-2838)
PHONE.....................................228 896-2100
Ricky Mathews, *President*
Scott Saucier, *Safety Mgr*
Justin Batiste, *Receiver*
Michael Hunter, *Receiver*
Kevin Martinez, *Manager*
EMP: 233
SQ FT: 90,000
SALES (est): 45.7MM
SALES (corp-wide): 807.2MM **Publicly Held**
WEB: www.sunherald.com
SIC: 2711 2752 Commercial printing & newspaper publishing combined; commercial printing, lithographic
PA: The Mcclatchy Company
2100 Q St
Sacramento CA 95816
916 321-1844

(G-1802)
GULF SHIP LLC
12351 Glascock Dr (39503-4646)
PHONE.....................................228 897-9189
Gary Chouest, *Mng Member*
Damon Chouest, *Mng Member*
Dino Chouest, *Mng Member*
▲ EMP: 400
SALES (est): 66.3MM
SALES (corp-wide): 339.7MM **Privately Held**
WEB: www.chouest.com
SIC: 3731 Military ships, building & repairing
PA: Offshore Service Vessels, L.L.C.
16201 E Main St
Cut Off LA 70345
985 601-4444

(G-1803)
HANGER INC
9034 Carl Legett Rd Ste B (39503-6234)
PHONE.....................................228 604-0818
Leslie Patton, *Branch Mgr*
EMP: 36
SALES (corp-wide): 1B **Publicly Held**
SIC: 3842 Prosthetic appliances
PA: Hanger, Inc.
10910 Domain Dr Ste 300
Austin TX 78758
512 777-3800

(G-1804)
HANGER PRSTHETCS & ORTHO INC
1302 44th Ave (39501-2552)
PHONE.....................................228 822-0109
EMP: 2
SALES (corp-wide): 1B **Publicly Held**
SIC: 3842 5999 5047 Mfg Surgical Appliances/Supplies Ret Misc Merchandise Whol Medical/Hospital Equipment
HQ: Hanger Prosthetics & Orthotics, Inc.
10910 Domain Dr Ste 300
Austin TX 78758
512 777-3800

(G-1805)
HARTSON-KENNEDY CABINET TOP CO
10115 Lorraine Rd (39503-6006)
PHONE.....................................228 896-1548
Edmond Knight, *Plant Mgr*
Michael Kennedy, *Sales/Mktg Mgr*
EMP: 100
SALES (corp-wide): 99.2MM **Privately Held**
SIC: 2599 1799 2541 Cabinets, factory; counter top installation; wood partitions & fixtures

PA: Hartson-Kennedy Cabinet Top Co Inc
522 W 22nd St
Marion IN 46953
765 668-8144

(G-1806)
HERITAGE CUSTOM CABINETS LLC
22247 Tootle Rd (39503-8899)
PHONE.....................................228 323-8389
EMP: 1
SALES (est): 106.9K **Privately Held**
SIC: 2434 Wood kitchen cabinets

(G-1807)
HIGHSIDE CHEMICALS INC
11114 Reichold Rd (39503-6009)
PHONE.....................................228 896-9220
Sarah Post, *President*
Don Ashby, *Vice Pres*
Lisa Gravener, *Office Mgr*
EMP: 5
SQ FT: 11,000
SALES: 540K **Privately Held**
WEB: www.highsidechem.com
SIC: 2899 Chemical preparations

(G-1808)
HONEYWELL INTERNATIONAL INC
2012 15th St Service Bldg (39501)
PHONE.....................................228 575-3706
Jerry Byrd, *Principal*
EMP: 68
SALES (corp-wide): 41.8B **Publicly Held**
SIC: 3724 Aircraft engines & engine parts
PA: Honeywell International Inc.
300 S Tryon St
Charlotte NC 28202
973 455-2000

(G-1809)
HOOPLA MONOGRAMMING & GIFTS ○
76 48th St (39507-4029)
PHONE.....................................228 860-4774
EMP: 1 EST: 2018
SALES (est): 38.7K **Privately Held**
SIC: 2395 Embroidery & art needlework

(G-1810)
HUEY P STOCKSTILL LLC
10130 Goldin Ln (39503-6061)
PHONE.....................................228 868-8678
Jimmy Lampton, *Manager*
EMP: 15
SALES (corp-wide): 53.3MM **Privately Held**
SIC: 2951 1711 1771 Asphalt paving mixtures & blocks; fire sprinkler system installation; driveway, parking lot & blacktop contractors
PA: Huey P. Stockstill, Llc
130 Huey Stockstill Rd
Picayune MS 39466
601 798-2981

(G-1811)
I CARE OPTICAL INC
2526 16th Ave (39501-3154)
PHONE.....................................228 864-4397
David Saxton, *Manager*
EMP: 2
SALES (corp-wide): 2.9MM **Privately Held**
SIC: 3851 5099 5049 Ophthalmic goods; safety equipment & supplies; optical goods
PA: I Care Optical, Inc.
4506 Pine Lake Dr
Terry MS 39170
601 352-3576

(G-1812)
J J HILL BRACE & LIMB CO INC
1619 Broad Ave (39501-3604)
P.O. Box 1988 (39502-1988)
PHONE.....................................228 863-0381
Lawrence A Hill, *President*
Christopher Hill, *Vice Pres*
Amber Beatty, *Treasurer*
Dawn Albert, *Admin Sec*
EMP: 6 EST: 1954
SQ FT: 4,000

SALES: 500K **Privately Held**
SIC: 3842 Orthopedic appliances; prosthetic appliances

(G-1813)
JACKPOT MAGAZINE
12268 Intraplex Pkwy (39503-4642)
PHONE.....................................228 385-7707
Michael Sunderman, *Manager*
EMP: 5
SALES (est): 405.5K **Privately Held**
WEB: www.jackpotmagazine.com
SIC: 2721 Magazines: publishing & printing

(G-1814)
JOYCE TILLMAN
Also Called: Beauticontrol Cosmetic
230 Woodbine Dr (39507-1926)
PHONE.....................................228 896-4927
Joyce Tillman, *Owner*
EMP: 1
SALES (est): 84.4K **Privately Held**
SIC: 2844 7299 7231 Cosmetic preparations; personal appearance services; facial salons

(G-1815)
KD WELDING SERVICES LLC
3008 8th Ave (39501-6415)
PHONE.....................................228 863-2773
Karen Dement,
Daniel Blanchard,
Karen L Dement,
EMP: 4
SALES (est): 411.1K **Privately Held**
SIC: 7692 Welding repair

(G-1816)
KEITH HUBER CORPORATION
14220 Highway 49 (39503-8500)
P.O. Box 3368 (39505-3368)
PHONE.....................................228 832-0992
Jeffrey D Holder, *President*
Jamie V Holder, *COO*
◆ EMP: 54
SQ FT: 101,000
SALES: 20MM
SALES (corp-wide): 89.5MM **Privately Held**
WEB: www.keithhuber.com
SIC: 5084 3443 Industrial machinery & equipment; tanks for tank trucks, metal plate
PA: Hol-Mac Corporation
2730 Highway 15
Bay Springs MS 39422
601 764-4121

(G-1817)
KENNEDY MARINE INC
10220 Three Rivers Rd (39503-3515)
PHONE.....................................228 214-4392
Timothy Kennedy Sr, *CEO*
EMP: 4
SALES (est): 746.2K **Privately Held**
SIC: 3519 Diesel, semi-diesel or duel-fuel engines, including marine

(G-1818)
KITCHEN ELEGANCE LLC
39 29th St Ste H (39507)
PHONE.....................................228 248-0074
James Cox, *Mng Member*
EMP: 7
SALES (est): 600K **Privately Held**
SIC: 2434 3639 Wood kitchen cabinets; major kitchen appliances, except refrigerators & stoves

(G-1819)
KNOT JUST KITCHENS
360 Courthouse Rd Ste A (39507-1857)
PHONE.....................................228 896-0584
Jacque Childs, *Principal*
EMP: 3
SALES (est): 299.9K **Privately Held**
SIC: 3639 Major kitchen appliances, except refrigerators & stoves

(G-1820)
LAND SHAPERS INC
14270 Creosote Rd (39503-4298)
PHONE.....................................228 864-3624
Robert Parker, *President*
EMP: 3

2019 Harris Directory of
Mississippi Manufacturers

72

▲ = Import ▼ =Export
◆ =Import/Export

GEOGRAPHIC SECTION

Gulfport - Harrison County (G-1851)

SALES (est): 347K **Privately Held**
SIC: 2951 Asphalt paving mixtures & blocks

(G-1821)
LIFETIME PORTABLE BUILDING LLC
15042 Whisperwood Dr (39503-8739)
PHONE..................................228 860-7715
Donald Sessum Jr,
Gina Sessum,
EMP: 2
SQ FT: 6,200
SALES (est): 280K **Privately Held**
WEB: www.lifetimeportable.com
SIC: 2451 Mobile buildings: for commercial use

(G-1822)
LIGHTHOUSE FOR THE BLIND
424 34th St (39507-2900)
PHONE..................................228 867-1565
William Price, *Branch Mgr*
EMP: 1
SALES (corp-wide): 8.7MM **Privately Held**
SIC: 3991 Brooms & brushes
PA: The Lighthouse For The Blind In New Orleans Incorporated
123 State St
New Orleans LA 70118
504 899-4501

(G-1823)
LOCKHEED MARTIN CORPORATION
4402 Hewes Ave (39507-4304)
PHONE..................................228 864-7910
Angelo Garcia, *Branch Mgr*
EMP: 10 **Publicly Held**
WEB: www.lockheedmartin.com
SIC: 3812 Search & navigation equipment
PA: Lockheed Martin Corporation
6801 Rockledge Dr
Bethesda MD 20817

(G-1824)
MAGNOLIA PRINTING CO
1829 25th Ave (39501-2832)
PHONE..................................228 864-4401
William Holden, *Owner*
Sallie Holden, *Corp Secy*
EMP: 4
SQ FT: 4,500
SALES: 550K **Privately Held**
WEB: www.magnoliaprinting.com
SIC: 2752 Commercial printing, offset

(G-1825)
MAXIMUM AUTO PARTS & SUPPLY
14473 Creosote Rd (39503-4270)
PHONE..................................228 863-1100
Tommy Petersen, *President*
Karen Petersen, *Corp Secy*
Kevin Tringle, *Vice Pres*
EMP: 12
SQ FT: 5,200
SALES (est): 2.3MM **Privately Held**
SIC: 5531 5013 5231 3492 Automotive parts; motor vehicle supplies & new parts; paint; hose & tube fittings & assemblies, hydraulic/pneumatic

(G-1826)
MAYBELLE MFG CO INC
51 52nd St (39507-4520)
PHONE..................................228 863-4398
EMP: 1 EST: 2010
SALES (est): 47K **Privately Held**
SIC: 3999 Mfg Misc Products

(G-1827)
MCLENDON HOLDINGS LLC
2409 14th St (39501-2020)
PHONE..................................858 255-9038
Erich N Nichols, *Principal*
EMP: 1
SALES (est): 49.1K **Privately Held**
SIC: 3172 Wallets

(G-1828)
MERIDIAN BRICK LLC
Also Called: Boral Bricks Studio
1526 29th Ave (39501-2843)
PHONE..................................228 863-5451
Nuzio Caranno, *Sales/Mktg Mgr*
Gabe Necaise, *Manager*
EMP: 8
SALES (corp-wide): 441MM **Privately Held**
WEB: www.boralbricks.com
SIC: 5211 3251 3255 Brick; brick & structural clay tile; clay refractories
PA: Meridian Brick Llc
6455 Shiloh Rd D
Alpharetta GA 30005
770 645-4500

(G-1829)
METAL TECH INC (PA)
10151 Lorraine Rd (39503-6006)
P.O. Box 2327 (39505-2327)
PHONE..................................228 604-4604
Mike Funk, *President*
Jeffrey J Mattina, *Vice Pres*
EMP: 38
SQ FT: 44,000
SALES: 5.4MM **Privately Held**
WEB: www.themetaltech.com
SIC: 3441 Fabricated structural metal

(G-1830)
METRO CONCRETE
10200 Logan Cline Rd (39503-4632)
PHONE..................................228 284-1660
Brandy Shackelford, *Vice Pres*
EMP: 2
SALES (est): 146.2K **Privately Held**
SIC: 5211 5032 3273 Cement; concrete & cinder building products; ready-mixed concrete

(G-1831)
MILITARY FIREARMS PARTS
308 Tandy Dr (39503-2917)
PHONE..................................228 596-1271
James Jackson, *Owner*
EMP: 5
SALES: 45K **Privately Held**
SIC: 3484 Small arms

(G-1832)
MISSISSIPPI GULF COAST
141 Debuys Rd (39507-1612)
PHONE..................................228 896-3055
Lorriane Krohn, *Director*
EMP: 5
SALES (est): 310K **Privately Held**
SIC: 2759 Directories (except telephone): printing

(G-1833)
MMC MATERIALS INC
Also Called: Gulf Concrete
14312 Creosote Rd (39503-4297)
P.O. Box 3868 (39505-3868)
PHONE..................................251 408-0740
Dale Ladner, *General Mgr*
Julie Bradley, *Sales Mgr*
EMP: 65
SALES (corp-wide): 306.5MM **Privately Held**
WEB: www.mmcmaterials.com
SIC: 3273 Ready-mixed concrete
HQ: Mmc Materials, Inc.
1052 Highland Colony Pkwy # 201
Ridgeland MS 39157
601 898-4000

(G-1834)
MODELTRUCKIN
Also Called: Modeltruckin.com.
16078 Lizana School Rd (39503-8241)
PHONE..................................228 365-4124
EMP: 2 EST: 2010
SALES (est): 188.4K **Privately Held**
SIC: 5199 2759 2752 Posters & decals; poster & decal printing & engraving; decals, lithographed

(G-1835)
MONEY TREE LOGGING LLC
10406 Three Rivers Rd # 13 (39503-4492)
PHONE..................................740 891-1713
EMP: 2 EST: 2017

SALES (est): 81.7K **Privately Held**
SIC: 2411 Logging

(G-1836)
NECAISE LOCK SUPPLY INC
2811 23rd Ave (39501-6017)
PHONE..................................228 864-9799
Donald E Necaise, *Vice Pres*
Haley Necaise, *Treasurer*
Jason Necaise, *Admin Sec*
EMP: 6
SQ FT: 4,000
SALES (est): 1.3MM **Privately Held**
WEB: www.necaiselock.com
SIC: 5099 3442 5251 5072 Locks & lock sets; metal doors, sash & trim; door locks & lock sets; padlocks; security devices, locks

(G-1837)
NEWELL SAND & GRAVEL
11007 Wolf River Rd (39503-8119)
P.O. Box 2036 (39505-2036)
PHONE..................................228 832-1215
Terry Newell, *Owner*
EMP: 2
SALES (est): 150K **Privately Held**
SIC: 1442 Construction sand & gravel

(G-1838)
NORMAN VR INC
21 Hardy Court Shopg Ctr (39507-2501)
PHONE..................................601 352-4819
Vanessa Buckles, *President*
Gregory L Buckles, *Vice Pres*
EMP: 3
SALES (est): 131.7K **Privately Held**
SIC: 2591 2391 Window blinds; curtains & draperies

(G-1839)
NORTH WIND FABRICATION INC
12520 Glascock Cir (39503-4638)
PHONE..................................228 896-0230
Kurtis Windham, *Branch Mgr*
EMP: 1
SALES (corp-wide): 1.2MM **Privately Held**
SIC: 3423 Ironworkers' hand tools
PA: North Wind Fabrication Inc.
17095 Carlton Cuevas Rd
Gulfport MS 39503
228 896-0260

(G-1840)
OCE CORPORATE PRINTING DIV
9480 Three Rivers Rd (39503-4248)
PHONE..................................228 863-0458
Alan Balcourt, *Manager*
EMP: 2 EST: 2010
SALES (est): 148.6K **Privately Held**
SIC: 2752 Commercial printing, lithographic

(G-1841)
OUTBACK STUCCO & COATINGS LLC (PA)
45 Hardy Court Shopg Ctr (39507-2501)
PHONE..................................228 224-2824
David Jeffs, *Owner*
EMP: 1 EST: 2010
SALES (est): 188.1K **Privately Held**
SIC: 3299 Stucco

(G-1842)
P-AMERICAS LLC
Also Called: Pepsico
13300 Dedeaux Rd (39503-4518)
P.O. Box 2037 (39505-2037)
PHONE..................................228 831-4343
Drew Allen, *President*
EMP: 66
SALES (corp-wide): 64.6B **Publicly Held**
SIC: 2086 Carbonated soft drinks, bottled & canned
HQ: P-Americas Llc
1 Pepsi Way
Somers NY 10589
336 896-5740

(G-1843)
PARKER DRE INDUSTRIES ✪
12063 Carnegie Ave (39503-9529)
PHONE..................................228 383-5967
EMP: 1 EST: 2019

SALES (est): 42.8K **Privately Held**
SIC: 3999 Manufacturing industries

(G-1844)
PARTITIONS GULFPORT CORP
2604 24th Ave C (39501-4938)
PHONE..................................228 822-9908
Wayne S May, *President*
EMP: 2
SQ FT: 4,500
SALES: 800K **Privately Held**
WEB: www.partitionsofgulfport.com
SIC: 3442 Metal doors

(G-1845)
PARTS AND SUPPLY INC
14492 Dedeaux Rd (39503-3200)
PHONE..................................228 832-6272
Troy A Barbay, *President*
Jill Barbay, *Vice Pres*
EMP: 9
SALES: 950K **Privately Held**
SIC: 3714 Motor vehicle parts & accessories

(G-1846)
PARTY CITY
15224 Crossroads Pkwy (39503-3564)
PHONE..................................228 539-4476
Randy Perry, *Manager*
EMP: 18
SALES (est): 673.3K **Privately Held**
SIC: 5947 7299 2759 Gifts & novelties; costume rental; invitation & stationery printing & engraving

(G-1847)
PAV & BROME WTCHMKERS JEWELERS
1912 25th Ave (39501-4514)
P.O. Box 1738 (39502-1738)
PHONE..................................228 863-3699
John Pav, *President*
Melton Broome, *Corp Secy*
Gail Pav, *Manager*
EMP: 9
SQ FT: 4,500
SALES: 3.3MM **Privately Held**
SIC: 3911 5944 7631 Jewelry, precious metal; jewelry, precious stones & precious metals; jewelry repair services

(G-1848)
PETERMANS CABINETS
15362 Russell Rd (39503-8740)
PHONE..................................228 832-0353
Gary Peterman, *Owner*
EMP: 2 EST: 2003
SALES (est): 120K **Privately Held**
SIC: 2434 Wood kitchen cabinets

(G-1849)
PLASTICS PLUS INC
15132 Dedeaux Rd (39503-3120)
PHONE..................................228 832-4634
Ramy Ramazani, *Partner*
Charles Bouque, *Partner*
EMP: 6
SALES (est): 742.1K **Privately Held**
SIC: 3089 1799 3993 Injection molding of plastics; welding on site; signs & advertising specialties

(G-1850)
POWERLINE TAGS INC
23476 Ashleigh Dr (39503-7801)
PHONE..................................228 760-3072
Kortnie Fithian, *Principal*
Scott Brown, *Vice Pres*
Russ Carothers, *Executive*
April Lollar, *Executive*
Bruce Marie, *Executive*
EMP: 2 EST: 2010
SALES (est): 154.9K **Privately Held**
SIC: 3548 Electric welding equipment

(G-1851)
PRECIOUS CREATIVE CATERPILLARS
330 Kimberly Dr (39503-2904)
PHONE..................................228 424-3500
Saradine Celissaint, *Principal*
EMP: 1
SALES (est): 60K **Privately Held**
SIC: 3531 Construction machinery

(PA)=Parent Co (HQ)=Headquarters (DH)=Div Headquarters
✪ = New Business established in last 2 years

2019 Harris Directory of
Mississippi Manufacturers

73

GEOGRAPHIC

Gulfport - Harrison County (G-1852)　　　　　　　GEOGRAPHIC SECTION

(G-1852)
PRESTIGE CNSTR & LAND SVCS LLC
18505 Robinson Rd (39503-7763)
PHONE....................................228 861-1292
Justin Griffing, *Principal*
EMP: 1
SALES (est): 82.7K **Privately Held**
SIC: **1521** 3531 1799 1442 Single-family housing construction; finishers & spreaders (construction equipment); graders, road (construction machinery); construction site cleanup; construction sand & gravel

(G-1853)
PRESTO PRINTING INC
9471 Three Rivers Rd B (39503-4230)
P.O. Box 2095 (39505-2095)
PHONE....................................228 678-9085
EMP: 3 EST: 2011
SALES (est): 170K **Privately Held**
SIC: 2752 Lithographic Commercial Printing

(G-1854)
PRINT SHED
12100 Highway 49 Ste 906 (39503-3178)
PHONE....................................228 206-0077
Michelle Jones, *Principal*
EMP: 6 EST: 2010
SALES (est): 591.3K **Privately Held**
SIC: 2752 Commercial printing, lithographic

(G-1855)
PROSTHETIC SOLUTIONS INC
12311 Ashley Dr Ste B (39503-2950)
PHONE....................................228 220-4917
James C Patton, *Branch Mgr*
EMP: 11
SALES (corp-wide): 768.3K **Privately Held**
SIC: 3842 Prosthetic appliances
PA: Prosthetic Solutions Inc
　　4000 Bienville St
　　New Orleans LA 70119
　　504 500-1349

(G-1856)
PURE AIR FILTER
2518 Cypress Ave (39501-5354)
PHONE....................................228 867-0888
Sharon Cuevas, *Owner*
EMP: 3
SALES: 50K **Privately Held**
SIC: 3564 Blowers & fans

(G-1857)
PVH CORP
Also Called: Van Heusen
10410 Factory Shop Blvd # 410 (39503-4237)
P.O. Box 6966, Bridgewater NJ (08807-0966)
PHONE....................................228 863-0017
EMP: 6
SALES (corp-wide): 8.2B **Publicly Held**
SIC: 2321 2331 Mfg Men's/Boy's Furnishings Mfg Women's/Misses' Blouses
PA: Pvh Corp.
　　200 Madison Ave Bsmt 1
　　New York NY 10016
　　212 381-3500

(G-1858)
QUARTER INC
4300 Air Cargo Rd (39501-6161)
PHONE....................................228 701-0361
EMP: 4
SALES (est): 285.5K **Privately Held**
SIC: 3131 Quarters

(G-1859)
RED CREEK GRAPHICS LLC
Also Called: Signs First
1829 25th Ave (39501-2832)
PHONE....................................228 864-3349
Darlene Bond, *Mng Member*
Jeff Paulk, *Manager*
Kent Pearson, *Director*
Benford Bond,
EMP: 4

SALES (est): 365.3K Privately Held
WEB: www.redcreekdesign.com
SIC: 3993 Signs & advertising specialties

(G-1860)
RED STAR DIGITAL PUBLISHING
14494 Williamsburg Dr (39503-3420)
PHONE....................................228 223-7638
EMP: 1
SALES (est): 37.5K **Privately Held**
SIC: 2741 Miscellaneous publishing

(G-1861)
REEBOK INTERNATIONAL LTD
10360 Factory Shop Blvd # 360 (39503-4245)
PHONE....................................228 822-9222
Ashley Bealler, *Branch Mgr*
EMP: 14
SALES (corp-wide): 25B **Privately Held**
SIC: **5999** 2329 2339 Alarm & safety equipment stores; men's & boys' sportswear & athletic clothing; women's & misses' athletic clothing & sportswear
HQ: Reebok International Ltd.
　　25 Drydock Ste 110
　　Boston MA 02210
　　781 401-5000

(G-1862)
RFM ENTERPRISES LLC
Also Called: Ole River Fabrics
1204 E Pass Rd (39507-3403)
PHONE....................................228 896-9498
Lawanda Montana, *Mng Member*
EMP: 2
SALES: 111K **Privately Held**
SIC: 5949 2211 Fabric stores piece goods; broadwoven fabric mills, cotton

(G-1863)
RJB ENTERPRISE INC
Also Called: Slip Protector, The
11520 Briarstone Pl (39503-6170)
PHONE....................................202 830-3508
Jeanine Boyle, *Ch of Bd*
Ralph Bankston, *Principal*
EMP: 50
SALES (est): 721.6K **Privately Held**
SIC: 7349 2842 Building maintenance, except repairs; janitorial service, contract basis; ammonia, household

(G-1864)
RUN-N-TRI COMPANY LLC
9138 Carl Legett Rd D (39503-6262)
PHONE....................................228 604-2227
Kevin Goveia,
EMP: 4 EST: 2010
SALES (est): 674.3K **Privately Held**
SIC: 3021 3131 Shoes, rubber or rubber soled fabric uppers; footwear cut stock; sole parts for shoes

(G-1865)
RUNWAY LIQUIDATION LLC
Also Called: Bcbg
11240 Highway 49 (39503-4151)
PHONE....................................816 671-7922
EMP: 2
SALES (corp-wide): 576.5MM **Privately Held**
SIC: 2335 Women's, juniors' & misses' dresses
HQ: Runway Liquidation, Llc
　　2761 Fruitland Ave
　　Vernon CA 90058
　　323 589-2224

(G-1866)
S H WHOLESALE SIGN CO
17500 Racetrack Rd (39503-8081)
PHONE....................................228 865-4352
EMP: 1
SALES (est): 46K **Privately Held**
SIC: 3993 Signs & advertising specialties

(G-1867)
SEEMANN COMPOSITES LLC (PA)
12481 Glascock Dr (39503-4639)
P.O. Box 3449 (39505-3449)
PHONE....................................228 314-8000
William H Seemann III, *President*
William H Seemann IV, *Vice Pres*
EMP: 90

SQ FT: 43,000
SALES (est): 20.6MM **Privately Held**
WEB: www.seemanncomposites.com
SIC: 3089 Composition stone, plastic

(G-1868)
SIGN MINISTRIES
2068b Appleway Ct (39501-5051)
PHONE....................................678 507-9912
James Decker, *Principal*
EMP: 2
SALES (est): 74.9K **Privately Held**
SIC: 3993 Signs & advertising specialties

(G-1869)
SIGN PLEX
560 Magnolia St (39507-4104)
PHONE....................................228 896-5999
EMP: 2
SALES (est): 92K **Privately Held**
SIC: 3993 5999 Mfg Signs/Advertising Specialties Ret Misc Merchandise

(G-1870)
SIGNS PLUS
15132 Dedeaux Rd (39503-3120)
PHONE....................................228 832-4634
Charles Bourque, *Owner*
EMP: 2
SALES (est): 55.7K **Privately Held**
SIC: 3993 Signs & advertising specialties

(G-1871)
SIGNS PLUS INC
11325 Dye Rd (39503-3287)
PHONE....................................228 832-4634
EMP: 2
SALES (est): 55.7K **Privately Held**
SIC: 3993 Signs & advertising specialties

(G-1872)
SLIDE RULE LLC
139 Bayou Cir (39507-4623)
PHONE....................................228 863-8583
Kaleel Salloum, *Principal*
EMP: 2
SALES (est): 138.2K **Privately Held**
SIC: 3829 Slide rules

(G-1873)
SNAP-IT-WREATHS
12458 Crestwood Dr (39503-2748)
PHONE....................................228 596-0387
Katherine Hamiter, *Principal*
EMP: 1
SALES (est): 39.6K **Privately Held**
SIC: 3999 Wreaths, artificial

(G-1874)
SON LIGHT CANDLES AND MORE LLC
16037 Crestview Dr (39503-2689)
PHONE....................................228 263-1661
Amelia A McGuire, *Administration*
EMP: 1
SALES (est): 39K **Privately Held**
SIC: 3999 Candles

(G-1875)
SOPERMA USA INC
Also Called: Soprema
12251 Seaway Rd (39503-6072)
PHONE....................................228 701-1900
Chad Baron, *Plant Mgr*
▲ EMP: 6
SALES (est): 1.3MM **Privately Held**
SIC: 2952 Roofing materials

(G-1876)
SOUTHERN STTCH CANVAS UPHL LLC
14335 Creosote Rd (39503-4206)
PHONE....................................228 234-2515
Steven Pollard,
Jamie Boozer,
EMP: 1
SALES (est): 112.8K **Privately Held**
SIC: 2393 2394 7532 Duffle bags, canvas: made from purchased materials; canvas boat seats; convertible tops, canvas or boat: from purchased materials; shades, canvas: made from purchased materials; tops (canvas or plastic), installation or repair: automotive

(G-1877)
SPECIALTY HOSE FABRICATION INC
13309 Three Rivers Rd (39503-6902)
PHONE....................................228 831-1919
James A Jones, *President*
Janet Boykin, *Manager*
EMP: 4
SQ FT: 2,000
SALES (est): 740K **Privately Held**
SIC: 5085 3492 Hose, belting & packing; rubber goods, mechanical; hose & tube fittings & assemblies, hydraulic/pneumatic

(G-1878)
SPECIALTY MACHINE WORKS INC
11573 Three Rivers Rd (39503-3353)
P.O. Box 3959 (39505-3959)
PHONE....................................228 832-7123
H Ricky Bishop Jr, *President*
John Bishop, *Vice Pres*
Harry Bishop Sr, *Admin Sec*
▲ EMP: 38
SQ FT: 14,000
SALES (est): 8.1MM **Privately Held**
SIC: 3599 Machine shop, jobbing & repair

(G-1879)
STAIR DEPOT OF MS
9465 Creosote Rd Bldg 30 (39503-4296)
PHONE....................................334 467-5584
Neal Higgins, *President*
EMP: 2
SALES (est): 91.3K **Privately Held**
SIC: 3272 Building materials, except block or brick: concrete

(G-1880)
STANLEY MCCAFFREY SIGNS
15254 Dedeaux Rd (39503-3161)
PHONE....................................228 832-0885
EMP: 2
SALES (est): 72.6K
SALES (corp-wide): 600K **Privately Held**
SIC: 3993 Mfg Signs/Advertising Specialties
PA: Stanley Mccaffrey Signs
　　231 Bradford Dr
　　Richland MS 39218
　　228 832-0885

(G-1881)
STORSOFT TECHNOLOGY CORP
1910 31st Ave (39501-4424)
PHONE....................................954 436-9292
Jonathan Evans, *Vice Pres*
EMP: 1
SQ FT: 2,000
SALES (corp-wide): 1MM **Privately Held**
SIC: 8243 3571 3577 8748 Software training, computer; electronic computers; input/output equipment, computer; systems engineering consultant, ex. computer or professional; custom computer programming services
PA: Storsoft Technology Corp
　　1910 31st Ave
　　Gulfport MS 39501
　　954 436-9292

(G-1882)
TABER EXTRUSIONS LLC
Also Called: Tabler Metals Gulfport
1900 34th St (39501-6125)
PHONE....................................228 863-2852
Mike Keenan, *General Mgr*
EMP: 50
SALES (corp-wide): 1B **Privately Held**
WEB: www.taberextrusions.com
SIC: 3354 3444 Aluminum extruded products; sheet metalwork
HQ: Taber Extrusions, Llc
　　915 S Elmira Ave
　　Russellville AR 72802
　　479 968-1021

(G-1883)
THUGRELATEDPUBLISHING
2613 W Stevens Cir (39503-3749)
PHONE....................................228 326-2476
Brenda Williams, *Principal*
EMP: 2

2019 Harris Directory of
Mississippi Manufacturers

74

▲ = Import ▼ =Export
◆ =Import/Export

GEOGRAPHIC SECTION

Harrisville - Simpson County (G-1912)

SALES (est): 98.5K **Privately Held**
SIC: 2741 Miscellaneous publishing

(G-1884)
TONYS KING OF STEAKS INC
Also Called: Tony Nelson'
11 Pass Rd (39507-3202)
PHONE.................................228 214-9668
James A Nelson, *President*
Courtney M Fuller, *Principal*
EMP: 4 EST: 2011
SALES (est): 155K **Privately Held**
SIC: 2013 Spreads, sandwich: meat from
purchased meat

(G-1885)
TRANE US INC
14231 Seaway Rd Ste E9 (39503-4627)
PHONE.................................228 863-4445
Lawrence Miskl, *Branch Mgr*
EMP: 2 **Privately Held**
SIC: 3585 Refrigeration & heating equipment
HQ: Trane U.S. Inc.
3600 Pammel Creek Rd
La Crosse WI 54601
608 787-2000

(G-1886)
TRAVIS CONSTRUCTION CO LLC
11258 Bayou Bernard Rd (39503-7896)
PHONE.................................228 539-4849
Donald Givens, *Owner*
EMP: 13 EST: 2013
SALES (est): 1.4MM **Privately Held**
SIC: 3272 7389 Culvert pipe, concrete;

(G-1887)
TREATED MATERIALS CO INC
13334 Seaway Rd (39503-4630)
P.O. Box 2848 (39505-2848)
PHONE.................................228 896-5056
William A Randall Jr, *President*
Jackson Randall, *Plant Mgr*
Amber Scholtz, *Human Res Mgr*
Gretchen Baber, *Asst Mgr*
EMP: 15 EST: 1953
SQ FT: 3,000
SALES (est): 2.2MM **Privately Held**
WEB: www.treatedmaterials.com
SIC: 2491 Posts, treated wood; poles &
pole crossarms, treated wood

(G-1888)
UNDER ARMOUR INC
10110 Factory Shop Blvd (39503-4223)
PHONE.................................228 864-2791
Robbie Smith, *Manager*
EMP: 2
SALES (corp-wide): 5.1B **Publicly Held**
SIC: 2329 Men's & boys' sportswear & athletic clothing
PA: Under Armour, Inc.
1020 Hull St Ste 300
Baltimore MD 21230
410 454-6428

(G-1889)
UNITED ASSOC JOURNEYMEN & 5
1237 Pass Rd (39501-6234)
PHONE.................................228 863-1853
William S Wilson, *Director*
EMP: 7
SALES (est): 586.3K **Privately Held**
SIC: 3494 Pipe fittings

(G-1890)
UNITED STATES MARINE INC
Also Called: U S M I
10011 Lorraine Rd (39503-6001)
PHONE.................................228 679-1005
Barry Dreyfus, *CEO*
Bryant Bernhard, *President*
John Dane III, *Chairman*
Fernando Mejia, *Vice Pres*
Bernadette Huston, *Purchasing*
▲ EMP: 200
SQ FT: 80,000
SALES (est): 54.7MM **Privately Held**
WEB: www.usmi.com
SIC: 3732 Boat building & repairing

(G-1891)
VENEVAA JOS LLC
13230 Meadowland Ct (39503-5249)
PHONE.................................850 501-4040
Tami Boundy, *Principal*
EMP: 3
SALES (est): 168.4K **Privately Held**
SIC: 2211 5651 Apparel & outerwear fabrics, cotton; unisex clothing stores

(G-1892)
WARES AIR FILTER SERVICE
22061 E Bradis Rd (39503-7811)
PHONE.................................228 832-8918
Fred Ware, *Owner*
EMP: 1
SALES (est): 90.6K **Privately Held**
SIC: 3564 Filters, air: furnaces, air conditioning equipment, etc.

(G-1893)
WESTERGARD BOAT WORKS INC
10220 Three Rivers Rd (39503-3515)
PHONE.................................228 214-4455
Susan Courson, *Principal*
EMP: 3
SALES (est): 225.3K **Privately Held**
SIC: 3732 Boat building & repairing

(G-1894)
WOLF INDUSTRIES INC
1418 31st Ave (39501-2746)
PHONE.................................228 864-9096
EMP: 1
SALES (est): 51.6K **Privately Held**
SIC: 3999 Manufacturing industries

(G-1895)
WORTHEN BROS COASTAL LAWN
11970 Summerhaven Cir (39503-7533)
PHONE.................................228 261-4785
Jimmie Worthen, *Principal*
EMP: 4
SALES (est): 165.9K **Privately Held**
SIC: 3524 Lawn & garden equipment

Guntown
Lee County

(G-1896)
AIA COUNTERTOPS
145 H M Richards Way (38849-4002)
PHONE.................................574 457-2003
EMP: 3
SALES (est): 177.5K **Privately Held**
SIC: 3281 Cut stone & stone products

(G-1897)
APAC-MISSISSIPPI INC
331 Messner St (38849-9146)
P.O. Box 1644, Tupelo (38802-1644)
PHONE.................................662 348-2214
Mike Bogue, *Manager*
EMP: 42
SALES (corp-wide): 30.6B **Privately Held**
SIC: 1611 2951 Highway & street paving
contractor; asphalt paving mixtures &
blocks
HQ: Apac-Mississippi, Inc.
101 Riverview Dr
Richland MS 39218
601 376-4000

(G-1898)
AUTO PARTS MFG MISS INC
100 Tab Way (38849-8001)
PHONE.................................662 365-3082
Masaaki Fujii, *President*
Kiyoshi Tsuchiya, *Corp Secy*
Akitsugu Ishiguro, *Director*
▲ EMP: 330
SALES (est): 92.9MM **Privately Held**
WEB: www.mail.toyota-body.co.jp
SIC: 3089 3465 Automotive parts, plastic;
automotive stampings
HQ: Toyota Auto Body Co.,Ltd.
100, Kanayama, Ichiriyamacho
Kariya AIC 448-0

(G-1899)
HM RICHARDS INC
120 H M Richards Way (38849-4001)
P.O. Box 373, Baldwyn (38824-0373)
PHONE.................................662 365-9485
William A Quirk, *CEO*
Jeffrey Seaman, *Chairman*
Joe Tarrant, *Vice Pres*
Joey Torrent, *Vice Pres*
Thomas Wells, *VP Mfg*
◆ EMP: 838
SQ FT: 800,000
SALES: 143.1MM **Privately Held**
SIC: 2512 Living room furniture: upholstered on wood frames

(G-1900)
NORBORD MISSISSIPPI INC
1194 Highway 145 (38849-7919)
P.O. Box 390 (38849-0390)
PHONE.................................662 348-2800
John C Tremayne, *President*
Bruce Grebe, *Senior VP*
Jim Black, *Vice Pres*
Jeff Johnson, *Vice Pres*
Robin Lampard, *Director*
EMP: 125
SQ FT: 360,000
SALES (est): 24.5MM
SALES (corp-wide): 2.4B **Privately Held**
SIC: 2493 Strandboard, oriented
HQ: Norbord Industries Inc
1 Toronto St Unit 600
Toronto ON M5C 2
416 365-0705

(G-1901)
NORBORD MISSISSIPPI LLC
1194 Highway 145 (38849-7919)
PHONE.................................662 348-2800
EMP: 3
SALES (est): 109.9K **Privately Held**
SIC: 2493 Strandboard, oriented

(G-1902)
POTTERY BY HELENE
797 County Rd 5051 (38849)
PHONE.................................662 728-0988
Helene Fielder, *President*
EMP: 1 EST: 1998
SALES (est): 90.8K **Privately Held**
SIC: 3269 Stoneware pottery products

Hamilton
Monroe County

(G-1903)
BAP SERVICES INC
40227 Grubb Springs Rd (39746-9732)
P.O. Box 338 (39746-0338)
PHONE.................................662 343-5216
EMP: 1
SALES (est): 79.1K **Privately Held**
SIC: 1389 Oil & gas field services

(G-1904)
COMPUTER GRAPHICS BY CONNIE
40200 Holloway Rd (39746-9685)
PHONE.................................662 343-8399
Connie Richardson, *Owner*
EMP: 2
SALES (est): 149.1K **Privately Held**
SIC: 3993 Signs, not made in custom sign
painting shops

(G-1905)
CONFEDERATE EXPRESS LLC
40028 Hamilton Rd (39746-9679)
PHONE.................................662 315-6625
EMP: 2
SALES (est): 128.9K **Privately Held**
SIC: 7372 Prepackaged software

(G-1906)
PRAXAIR INC
40433 Old Highway 45 S (39746-9759)
P.O. Box 35 (39746-0035)
PHONE.................................662 343-8336
Andrew Graham, *Manager*
EMP: 3 **Privately Held**
SIC: 2813 Industrial gases

HQ: Praxair, Inc.
10 Riverview Dr
Danbury CT 06810
203 837-2000

(G-1907)
THOMPSON SERVICES INC
40284 Grubb Springs Rd (39746-8748)
P.O. Box 154 (39746-0154)
PHONE.................................662 369-9102
Donald Thompson, *President*
Mary Thompson, *Corp Secy*
EMP: 15
SALES (est): 1MM **Privately Held**
SIC: 1389 Swabbing wells; servicing oil &
gas wells

(G-1908)
THOMPSONS WELDING SERVICES INC (PA)
40005 Church Rd (39746-8780)
P.O. Box 308 (39746-0308)
PHONE.................................662 343-8955
Ken Thompson, *President*
Barry Thompson, *CFO*
Brent Thompson, *Finance Mgr*
EMP: 95
SQ FT: 3,200
SALES (est): 12.7MM **Privately Held**
SIC: 3443 7692 Industrial vessels, tanks &
containers; process vessels, industrial:
metal plate; tanks, standard or custom
fabricated: metal plate; heat exchangers,
condensers & components; welding repair

(G-1909)
TRONOX INCORPORATED
40034 Tronox Rd (39746-6604)
P.O. Box 180 (39746-0180)
PHONE.................................662 343-8311
Chuck Tubb, *Branch Mgr*
EMP: 100 **Privately Held**
WEB: www.tieandtimber.com
SIC: 3356 2816 Titanium & titanium alloy:
rolling, drawing or extruding; iron oxide
pigments (ochers, siennas, umbers)
HQ: Tronox Incorporated
1 Stamford Plz
Stamford CT 06901
203 705-3800

(G-1910)
TVI INC
40537 Old Highway 45 S (39746-8777)
PHONE.................................662 343-5117
EMP: 1
SALES (corp-wide): 5.3MM **Privately Held**
SIC: 3592 Valves
PA: Tvi, Inc.
3497 Stanton Rd
Memphis TN 38108
901 388-1550

Harrisville
Simpson County

(G-1911)
DIXIE DIES INC
3261 Hopewell Rd (39082-4102)
PHONE.................................601 845-6029
Tommy Brown, *President*
EMP: 3
SALES (est): 423.6K **Privately Held**
SIC: 3544 Special dies & tools

(G-1912)
SNELLS CONCRETE TANKS
180 Joe Dear Rd (39082-4001)
PHONE.................................601 845-1881
Bobby Joe Snell, *Owner*
Janice Snell, *Co-Owner*
EMP: 2
SALES (est): 182.1K **Privately Held**
SIC: 3272 1711 Septic tanks, concrete;
septic system construction

GEOGRAPHIC

Hattiesburg - Forrest County (G-1913)

GEOGRAPHIC SECTION

Hattiesburg
Forrest County

(G-1913)
1 A LIFESAFER INC
7166 U S Highway 49 (39402-9374)
PHONE..................................800 634-3077
EMP: 1
SALES (corp-wide): 4.3MM Privately Held
SIC: 3829 Measuring & controlling devices
PA: 1 A Lifesafer, Inc.
4290 Glendale Milford Rd
Blue Ash OH 45242
513 651-9560

(G-1914)
365 EXPLOSIVE ATHC PERFORMLLC
11 Longwood Place Dr (39402-4401)
PHONE..................................601 365-2318
Reginald Wilson, Principal
EMP: 2
SALES (est): 74.4K Privately Held
SIC: 2892 Explosives

(G-1915)
ADVANCED HEARING AND BALANCE
5128 Old Highway 11 Ste 8 (39402-6234)
PHONE..................................601 450-0280
Kyle McLain, Principal
EMP: 2
SALES (est): 104.6K Privately Held
SIC: 5999 7629 3842 5047 Hearing aids; hearing aid repair; hearing aids; hearing aids; hearing testing service

(G-1916)
ADVANTAGE MEDICAL AND PHRM LLC
Also Called: Pine Belt Medical Equipment
6375 U S Highway 98 # 50 (39402-7410)
PHONE..................................601 268-1422
Courtney Davis,
EMP: 3 EST: 2007
SALES (est): 185.5K Privately Held
SIC: 3842 Wheelchairs

(G-1917)
ADVANTAGE TAX & PRINTING SVC
2407 W 4th St (39401-4713)
PHONE..................................601 544-0602
Letessa Russell, Principal
EMP: 1 EST: 2010
SALES (est): 34.1K Privately Held
SIC: 7291 2759 Tax return preparation services; commercial printing

(G-1918)
AEROTEC LTD
Also Called: Aerotec Systems
5255 Old Highway 11 (39402)
PHONE..................................713 598-9410
Richard Kellogg, President
EMP: 7
SALES (est): 950K Privately Held
SIC: 3399 Primary metal products

(G-1919)
AIRDESIGNS
4407 U S Highway 49 (39401-9425)
PHONE..................................601 584-1000
EMP: 1
SALES (est): 66K Privately Held
SIC: 3993 Mfg Signs/Advertising Specialties

(G-1920)
ALLENS TROPHIES INC
Also Called: Allen's Crown's
220 Mobile St (39401-3404)
PHONE..................................601 582-7702
Arthur C Allen, President
Helen L Allen, Corp Secy
EMP: 25
SQ FT: 84,000
SALES: 2MM Privately Held
WEB: www.acrowns.com
SIC: 5094 3499 3993 3961 Coins, medals & trophies; novelties & giftware, including trophies; signs & advertising specialties; costume jewelry; hats, caps & millinery

(G-1921)
AMERICAN CONCRETE PRODUCTS INC
257 Wl Runnels Indus Dr (39401-8551)
PHONE..................................601 583-2274
Dennis Pierce, President
EMP: 26
SALES (est): 5.8MM Privately Held
SIC: 3271 5251 Blocks, concrete or cinder: standard; builders' hardware

(G-1922)
AMERICAN PRINTING BLUE PR
6186 U S Highway 49 (39401-5905)
PHONE..................................601 544-7714
Mary Hubbard, Owner
EMP: 4
SALES (est): 316.3K Privately Held
SIC: 2752 Commercial printing, lithographic

(G-1923)
ANCHOR WORKS
452 Cole Rd (39402-7918)
PHONE..................................601 264-8700
Bill Sanford, Owner
▲ EMP: 1
SALES (est): 66.3K Privately Held
SIC: 3499 Fabricated metal products

(G-1924)
ANGIES CROCHETING CORNER
127 S Pine Dr (39401-8634)
PHONE..................................228 617-9342
Angelia Snowden, Principal
EMP: 2 EST: 2017
SALES (est): 73.6K Privately Held
SIC: 2399 Hand woven & crocheted products

(G-1925)
BAD MOON CUSTOMS
610 W Pine St (39401-3834)
P.O. Box 15487 (39404-5487)
PHONE..................................601 520-7248
Paul Dunbar, Owner
EMP: 1
SALES (est): 54.3K Privately Held
SIC: 3499 Fabricated metal products

(G-1926)
BEATY STREET PUBLISHING
16 Leaf Ln (39402-9549)
PHONE..................................954 513-9441
EMP: 1
SALES (est): 57K Privately Held
SIC: 2741 Misc Publishing

(G-1927)
BENNY EVANS
Also Called: Blue Streak
307 Beverly Ln (39402-2015)
PHONE..................................601 264-8903
Benny Evans, Owner
EMP: 5
SALES (est): 411.7K Privately Held
SIC: 2819 Industrial inorganic chemicals

(G-1928)
BERRY GLOBAL INC
72 Wl Runnels Indus Dr (39401-8529)
PHONE..................................601 584-4800
Robert Kolakowski, Branch Mgr
EMP: 106 Publicly Held
SIC: 3089 3081 Bottle caps, molded plastic; unsupported plastics film & sheet
HQ: Berry Global, Inc.
101 Oakley St
Evansville IN 47710
812 424-2904

(G-1929)
BERRY GLOBAL INC
72 W L Runnels Indus Park (39401)
PHONE..................................601 584-4778
EMP: 2 Publicly Held

SIC: 3089 3081 Bottle caps, molded plastic; unsupported plastics film & sheet
HQ: Berry Global, Inc.
101 Oakley St
Evansville IN 47710
812 424-2904

(G-1930)
BERRY SIGNS & STRIPES
2125 Glendale Ave (39401-1020)
PHONE..................................601 544-5600
Wayne Berry, Owner
EMP: 3
SALES (est): 150.8K Privately Held
SIC: 3993 5999 Signs, not made in custom sign painting shops; banners

(G-1931)
BIMBO BAKERIES USA INC
Also Called: Smith S Bakery
5680 U S Highway 49 (39401-7701)
PHONE..................................601 545-3782
Warren Stafford, Branch Mgr
EMP: 10
SQ FT: 8,500 Privately Held
SIC: 2051 5461 Bakery: wholesale or wholesale/retail combined; bakeries
HQ: Bimbo Bakeries Usa, Inc
255 Business Center Dr # 200
Horsham PA 19044
215 347-5500

(G-1932)
BIO SOIL ENHANCERS INC
1161 James St (39401-4016)
PHONE..................................601 582-4000
Sabrina Baio, Controller
Nolan W Wade, Director
▲ EMP: 4
SALES (est): 718.4K Privately Held
SIC: 2879 Soil conditioners

(G-1933)
BIO-SOLUTIONS FRANCHISE CORP
1161 James St (39401-4016)
PHONE..................................601 582-4000
Len Amato, CFO
EMP: 2
SALES (est): 161.6K Privately Held
SIC: 3822 Auto controls regulating residntl & coml environmt & applncs

(G-1934)
BLACK PANTHER NEWSPAPER
209 Old Airport Rd (39401-7835)
PHONE..................................877 388-6247
Abdullah Elamin, Principal
EMP: 3
SALES (est): 83.8K Privately Held
SIC: 2711 Newspapers

(G-1935)
BLENDCO INC
Also Called: Ezy Time Foods
8 J M Tatum Industrial Dr (39401-8341)
PHONE..................................888 253-6326
Charles McCaffrey Jr, President
Chris Hatten, CFO
Katie McCaffrey, Admin Sec
EMP: 30
SQ FT: 24,500
SALES (est): 8.5MM Privately Held
SIC: 2099 Food preparations

(G-1936)
BORDEN DAIRY COMPANY ALA LLC (DH)
7572 U S Highway 49 (39402-9104)
PHONE..................................251 456-3381
Thad Riley, Prdtn Mgr
M D Brooks,
EMP: 25 EST: 1950
SQ FT: 2,000
SALES (est): 115.1MM Privately Held
WEB: www.dairyfreshcorp.com
SIC: 2026 Fluid milk
HQ: National Dairy, Llc
8750 N Cntl Expy Ste 400
Dallas TX 75231
214 459-1100

(G-1937)
BORDEN DAIRY COMPANY ALA LLC
7572 U S Highway 49 (39402-9104)
P.O. Box 16209 (39404-6209)
PHONE..................................601 268-2583
Brian McClernon, Controller
EMP: 100 Privately Held
WEB: www.dairyfreshcorp.com
SIC: 5143 2026 2099 2037 Milk & cream, fluid; fluid milk; food preparations; frozen fruits & vegetables
HQ: Borden Dairy Company Of Alabama, Llc
7572 U S Highway 49
Hattiesburg MS 39402
251 456-3381

(G-1938)
BOURNE BROTHERS PRTG CO INC
5276 Old Highway 42 (39401-1205)
PHONE..................................601 582-1808
Donnie Bourne, President
Jennifer Miley, Executive
Penny Ross, Graphic Designe
EMP: 12
SALES (est): 1.8MM Privately Held
SIC: 2752 2791 2789 Commercial printing, offset; typesetting; bookbinding & related work

(G-1939)
BPREX CLOSURES LLC
Also Called: Manufacturing Facility
72 Wl Runnels Indus Dr (39401-8529)
PHONE..................................601 584-4758
EMP: 92 Publicly Held
SIC: 3089 Bottle caps, molded plastic
HQ: Bprex Closures, Llc
101 Oakley St
Evansville IN 47710
812 424-2904

(G-1940)
CAREYS FENCING
49 Sandy Ln (39402-9240)
PHONE..................................601 434-6510
Arvelle Carey, Owner
EMP: 1
SALES (est): 55K Privately Held
SIC: 2499 Wood products

(G-1941)
CCBCC OPERATIONS LLC
Also Called: Coca-Cola
201 Coca Cola Ave (39402-1368)
P.O. Box 2368, Laurel (39442-2368)
PHONE..................................601 428-0464
John Bounds, Sales Staff
Willie Meador, Manager
EMP: 31
SALES (corp-wide): 4.6B Publicly Held
SIC: 2086 Bottled & canned soft drinks
HQ: Ccbcc Operations, Llc
4100 Coca Cola Plz
Charlotte NC 28211
704 364-8728

(G-1942)
CELEBRATIONS ETC
102 Lundy Ln (39401-6601)
PHONE..................................601 268-0390
Wanda Henderson, Owner
EMP: 4
SALES (est): 350.3K Privately Held
SIC: 2754 Stationery & invitation printing, gravure

(G-1943)
CH CUSTOM DESIGNS & PRINTS LLC
518 Sullivan Kilrain Rd (39402-8000)
PHONE..................................601 408-5068
Caleb Hinton, Mng Member
EMP: 1
SALES (est): 45K Privately Held
SIC: 2396 Screen printing on fabric articles

(G-1944)
CITIZEN HEALTH FOUNDATION
6641 Hwy 98 Ste 200 (39402)
PHONE..................................601 463-2436
Brennen Hodge, President
EMP: 7

2019 Harris Directory of
Mississippi Manufacturers

▲ = Import ▼=Export
◆ =Import/Export

GEOGRAPHIC SECTION

Hattiesburg - Forrest County (G-1973)

SALES: 100K **Privately Held**
SIC: 7372 Prepackaged software

(G-1945)
CL DEWS SONS FNDRY MCHY INC
1599 Edwards St (39401-5520)
P.O. Box 1647 (39403-1647)
PHONE....................................601 582-4427
Tommy Dews, *President*
Jody Norris, *General Mgr*
Lee Norris, *General Mgr*
Sandra B Norris, *Corp Secy*
George Boone, *Vice Pres*
EMP: 85 EST: 1939
SQ FT: 5,000
SALES (est): 27MM **Privately Held**
WEB: www.dewsfoundry.com
SIC: 3369 3441 Nonferrous foundries; fabricated structural metal

(G-1946)
CLOSE QUARTER COMBAT LLC
144 Augustine Dr (39402-7837)
PHONE....................................601 325-5610
Joseph Green, *Manager*
EMP: 1
SALES (est): 53.7K **Privately Held**
SIC: 3131 Quarters

(G-1947)
CM MANUFACTURING INC
95 WI Runnels Indstrl 6 (39401-8553)
PHONE....................................601 545-7515
EMP: 100
SALES (corp-wide): 93.7MM **Privately Held**
SIC: 3674 Manufacturer Of Semiconductors/Related Devices
HQ: Cm Manufacturing, Inc.
6321 San Ignacio Ave
San Jose CA 95119
408 284-7200

(G-1948)
COCA-COLA BOTTLING CO UNTD INC
201 Coca Cola Ave (39402-1368)
P.O. Box 17197 (39404-7197)
PHONE....................................601 264-8600
Brad Brian, *Branch Mgr*
EMP: 4
SALES (corp-wide): 2.4B **Privately Held**
SIC: 2086 Bottled & canned soft drinks
PA: Coca-Cola Bottling Company United, Inc.
4600 E Lake Blvd
Birmingham AL 35217
205 841-2653

(G-1949)
COLUMBIA BLOCK & BRICK CO INC
6686 U S Highway 98 (39402-7936)
PHONE....................................601 450-3791
Erad Pittman, *Branch Mgr*
EMP: 1
SALES (corp-wide): 3.9MM **Privately Held**
SIC: 3271 5211 Concrete block & brick; concrete & cinder block
PA: Columbia Block And Brick Company, Incorporated
401 Rustique Brick Dr
Columbia MS
601 736-3791

(G-1950)
CONSOLDTED CONVERTING SVCS INC
Also Called: Ccsi
5372 Old Highway 42 (39401-1340)
PHONE....................................601 545-1699
Lloyd E Rhian Jr, *President*
Curt Robinson, *Treasurer*
EMP: 20
SQ FT: 15,600
SALES (est): 5.4MM **Privately Held**
SIC: 2677 Envelopes

(G-1951)
COPY CATS PRINTING INC
905 Hardy St Ste 102 (39401-4163)
PHONE....................................601 582-3019
Jan Lacy, *President*

Terry Lacy, *Vice Pres*
EMP: 13
SQ FT: 52,000
SALES (est): 1.7MM **Privately Held**
WEB: www.copycats-printing.com
SIC: 2752 2796 2791 2789 Commercial printing, offset; platemaking services; typesetting; bookbinding & related work

(G-1952)
CROSBY WOOD PRESERVING CO INC
Also Called: Interpine Lumber Co
3702 Hardy St Ste 2 (39402-1579)
PHONE....................................601 264-5249
Stewart Gammill III, *President*
Lynn Gammill, *Corp Secy*
EMP: 4
SQ FT: 600
SALES (est): 412.3K **Privately Held**
SIC: 2421 5211 Silo stock, wood: sawed; planing mill products & lumber

(G-1953)
CSA LOGISTICS LLC
54 Pirate Dr (39402-9557)
PHONE....................................601 264-2455
Michael Dodds, *President*
Catherine Dodds, *Vice Pres*
EMP: 3
SQ FT: 2,000
SALES (est): 429.1K **Privately Held**
SIC: 3799 5085 All terrain vehicles (ATV); industrial supplies

(G-1954)
CUSTOM CREATIONS
11 Huckleberry Dr (39402-9746)
PHONE....................................601 450-7600
Lacey Branch, *Owner*
EMP: 6
SALES (est): 504.3K **Privately Held**
SIC: 2759 Screen printing

(G-1955)
CUSTOM ROUGH CUT LUMBER
146 Lott Town Rd (39402-9113)
PHONE....................................601 270-9518
Belinda Murphy, *Principal*
EMP: 2
SALES (est): 86.7K **Privately Held**
SIC: 2421 Sawmills & planing mills, general

(G-1956)
CUSTOMIZED STAINED GLASS
131 J C Bryant Rd (39401-8447)
PHONE....................................601 583-4720
Nancy Powe, *Owner*
EMP: 1
SALES (est): 49.8K **Privately Held**
SIC: 3229 Art, decorative & novelty glassware

(G-1957)
DIAMOND LAND & TIMBER LLC
51 Cambrooke (39402-7763)
PHONE....................................601 310-3395
Chad Diamond,
EMP: 5 EST: 2012
SALES (est): 395.1K **Privately Held**
SIC: 2411 Timber, cut at logging camp

(G-1958)
DR PEPPER/SEVEN UP INC
1000 W 63rd St (39401-6367)
PHONE....................................601 545-7511
Willie Irvy, *Branch Mgr*
EMP: 150 **Publicly Held**
SIC: 2086 Soft drinks: packaged in cans, bottles, etc.
HQ: Dr Pepper/Seven Up, Inc.
5301 Legacy Dr Fl 1
Plano TX 75024
972 673-7000

(G-1959)
EASY REACH SUPPLY LLC
32 Raspberry Ln (39402-9343)
PHONE....................................601 582-7866
Kenneth L Rakusin, *Mng Member*
R Benson Ford, *Mng Member*
EMP: 30
SQ FT: 66,000

SALES (est): 45.1K
SALES (corp-wide): 15.1MM **Privately Held**
SIC: 3991 3089 Brooms & brushes; casting of plastic
PA: Gordon Brush Mfg. Co., Inc.
3737 Capitol Ave
City Of Industry CA 90601
323 724-7777

(G-1960)
ELITE SCREEN PRINTING (PA)
107 N 40th Ave (39401-6606)
P.O. Box 17077 (39404-7077)
PHONE....................................601 450-1261
Jeremy Carothers, *Principal*
EMP: 11
SALES (est): 1.2MM **Privately Held**
SIC: 2752 Commercial printing, lithographic

(G-1961)
ELL HOLDINGS
147 Millpond Dr (39401-5559)
PHONE....................................601 325-3317
Erica Loftin, *Principal*
EMP: 5
SALES (est): 192.2K **Privately Held**
SIC: 4213 4212 2421 7389 Contract haulers; heavy machinery transport, local; hazardous waste transport; steel hauling, local; lumber: rough, sawed or planed;

(G-1962)
EMERGENT PRTCTIVE PDTS USA INC
46 Shelby Thames Dr (39402-3702)
PHONE....................................517 489-5172
Robert Kramer, *Principal*
Patrick Saam, *Principal*
EMP: 11
SQ FT: 750
SALES (est): 1MM
SALES (corp-wide): 782.4MM **Publicly Held**
SIC: 3841 Surgical & medical instruments
PA: Emergent Biosolutions Inc.
400 Professional Dr # 400
Gaithersburg MD 20879
240 631-3200

(G-1963)
ENSLIN AND SON PACKING COMPANY
2500 Glendale Ave (39401-1027)
PHONE....................................601 582-9300
August F Enslin Jr, *President*
Augustus Enslin III, *Vice Pres*
Georgie Foster, *Treasurer*
Christa Enslin, *Admin Sec*
EMP: 30
SQ FT: 10,000
SALES (est): 3.8MM **Privately Held**
WEB: www.enslin.com
SIC: 2013 2048 2011 Sausages from purchased meat; slaughtering of nonfood animals; meat packing plants

(G-1964)
ETS SIGNS INC (PA)
Also Called: Signs First
4400 Hardy St Ste A1 (39401-1309)
PHONE....................................601 268-7275
Brian Saffle, *President*
EMP: 8
SALES (est): 946.3K **Privately Held**
SIC: 3993 5999 Electric signs; banners

(G-1965)
EUGENE FLANDERS
1041 Poplar Rd (39401-8627)
PHONE....................................601 544-0345
Eugene Flanders, *Principal*
EMP: 1
SALES (est): 51K **Privately Held**
SIC: 2499 Rulers & yardsticks, wood

(G-1966)
EXCEL INJECTION MOLDING INC
977 Sullivan Dr (39401-7953)
PHONE....................................601 544-6133
John M Robinson, *President*
Jennifer M Robinson, *Corp Secy*
Randy J White, *Production*

EMP: 50
SQ FT: 45,000
SALES: 9.2MM **Privately Held**
WEB: www.excelinjection.com
SIC: 3089 Injection molding of plastics

(G-1967)
F-S PRESTRESS LLC (PA)
25 Peps Point Rd (39401)
P.O. Box 15969 (39404-5969)
PHONE....................................601 268-2006
Charlie Sutherland, *Mng Member*
Lee Sims,
EMP: 100 EST: 1957
SQ FT: 80,000
SALES (est): 15.8MM **Privately Held**
WEB: www.fsprestress.com
SIC: 3272 Prestressed concrete products; concrete products, precast

(G-1968)
FAST SIGNS
Also Called: Fastsigns
2902 Hardy St Ste 60 (39401-7031)
PHONE....................................601 602-5413
Jacquelyn Wallace, *President*
EMP: 1
SALES (est): 49.9K **Privately Held**
SIC: 3993 Signs & advertising specialties

(G-1969)
FEDEX OFFICE & PRINT SVCS INC
4600 Hardy St Ste 30 (39402-1349)
PHONE....................................601 264-6434
EMP: 11
SALES (corp-wide): 69.6B **Publicly Held**
WEB: www.kinkos.com
SIC: 7334 2796 2791 2789 Photocopying & duplicating services; platemaking services; typesetting; bookbinding & related work
HQ: Fedex Office And Print Services, Inc.
7900 Legacy Dr
Plano TX 75024
800 463-3339

(G-1970)
FIREPLACE WHOLESALE
Also Called: Trucks Unlimited
1505 N Main St (39401-1912)
PHONE....................................601 545-9876
James D Creel, *Partner*
Terry Creel, *Partner*
EMP: 8
SQ FT: 5,000
SALES (est): 1MM **Privately Held**
SIC: 3713 5074 5719 5083 Specialty motor vehicle bodies; fireplaces, prefabricated; stoves, wood burning; fireplaces & wood burning stoves; farm equipment parts & supplies; farm equipment & supplies; brick, stone & related material

(G-1971)
FLOWERS BKG CO BATON ROUGE LLC
Also Called: Flowers Bakery
5075 Old Highway 42 (39401-2874)
PHONE....................................601 583-2693
Fran Freeland, *Branch Mgr*
EMP: 1
SALES (corp-wide): 3.9B **Publicly Held**
SIC: 2051 Bread, cake & related products
HQ: Flowers Baking Co. Of Baton Rouge, Llc.
1504 Florida Blvd
Baton Rouge LA 70802
225 381-9699

(G-1972)
FOLEY TILE & MARBLE
2042 Old Highway 24 (39402-8782)
PHONE....................................601 271-8415
William Foley, *President*
EMP: 3
SALES (est): 193.1K **Privately Held**
SIC: 3281 1743 Marble, building: cut & shaped; tile installation, ceramic

(G-1973)
GAIL MCINNIS
Also Called: McInnis, Gail Productions
115 Lake Estates Dr (39402-9688)
PHONE....................................601 261-5077
Gail McInnis, *Owner*

(PA)=Parent Co (HQ)=Headquarters (DH)=Div Headquarters
✿ = New Business established in last 2 years

2019 Harris Directory of
Mississippi Manufacturers

77

GEOGRAPHIC

Hattiesburg - Forrest County (G-1974)

GEOGRAPHIC SECTION

EMP: 1 **EST:** 1999
SALES (est): 61.8K **Privately Held**
SIC: 2389 Theatrical costumes

(G-1974)
GARYS SMALL ENGINE
Also Called: Gary's Small Engine Repair
1400 1/2 E Hardy St (39401-2416)
PHONE...................................601 545-7355
Gary E Walters, *Owner*
Helen Walters, *Co-Owner*
EMP: 3
SQ FT: 3,000
SALES (est): 120K **Privately Held**
SIC: 7699 5261 3546 Engine repair & replacement, non-automotive; lawnmowers & tractors; saws & sawing equipment

(G-1975)
GOLDEN SOURCE INVENTORS LLC
710 Hillendale Dr (39402-2620)
PHONE...................................601 325-4064
Justin Clark, *Owner*
EMP: 1
SALES (est): 66.9K **Privately Held**
SIC: 2841 7389 Soap & other detergents;

(G-1976)
GRAYCO SYSTEMS & CONSULTING
201 Campbell Loop (39401-3016)
P.O. Box 17824 (39404-7824)
PHONE...................................601 583-0430
John Gray, *President*
EMP: 9
SALES (est): 778K **Privately Held**
WEB: www.graycosystems.com
SIC: 7371 7372 Computer software systems analysis & design, custom; business oriented computer software

(G-1977)
GROUP PEPPER SNAPPLE DR
117 Shadow Ridge Rd (39402-8653)
PHONE...................................601 602-3695
EMP: 3
SALES (est): 199.9K **Privately Held**
SIC: 2086 Mfg Bottled/Canned Soft Drinks

(G-1978)
GULF COAST PROTECTIVE COATING
17 Power Ln (39402-8563)
PHONE...................................601 261-9862
Ed Ryan, *Principal*
EMP: 2 **EST:** 2007
SALES (est): 162.7K **Privately Held**
SIC: 3479 Metal coating & allied service

(G-1979)
H O HUGHES
2807 Mamie St (39401-7224)
PHONE...................................601 261-3302
H Hughes, *President*
EMP: 2 **EST:** 2017
SALES (est): 81.9K **Privately Held**
SIC: 1311 Crude petroleum & natural gas

(G-1980)
HALL S CUSTOMIZED PRINTING
405 Lakewood Loop (39402-9698)
PHONE...................................601 261-2440
EMP: 2 **EST:** 2010
SALES (est): 99K **Privately Held**
SIC: 2752 Lithographic Commercial Printing

(G-1981)
HAMPTON INDUSTRIES LLC
102 Bellair Dr (39402-1913)
PHONE...................................601 441-7604
Willie Hampton, *Principal*
EMP: 1 **EST:** 2017
SALES (est): 47.3K **Privately Held**
SIC: 3999 Manufacturing industries

(G-1982)
HANGER PRSTHETCS & ORTHO INC
1104 S 28th Ave (39402-2609)
PHONE...................................601 268-5520
Charles Jakab, *Manager*
EMP: 6

SALES (corp-wide): 1B **Publicly Held**
SIC: 3842 Surgical appliances & supplies
HQ: Hanger Prosthetics & Orthotics, Inc.
10910 Domain Dr Ste 300
Austin TX 78758
512 777-3800

(G-1983)
HAT SHACK INC
1000 Turtle Creek Dr # 600 (39402-1147)
PHONE...................................601 264-1017
Mark Monroe, *Owner*
Stacy Unions, *Owner*
EMP: 3
SALES (est): 155.3K **Privately Held**
SIC: 2353 Hats & caps

(G-1984)
HATTIESBURG AMERICAN
4200 Mamie St Ste 200 (39402-1729)
PHONE...................................601 582-4321
S Haik, *Principal*
Lici Beveridge, *Editor*
Brian Broom, *Editor*
Deborah Tarwater, *Manager*
Michael Fleming, *Bd of Directors*
EMP: 8
SALES (est): 421K **Privately Held**
SIC: 2711 Newspapers, publishing & printing

(G-1985)
HATTIESBURG AMERICAN PUBG CO
4200 Mamie St Ste 200 (39402-1729)
PHONE...................................601 582-4321
Gary Watson, *President*
EMP: 150
SQ FT: 50,000
SALES (est): 22.3MM
SALES (corp-wide): 2.9B **Publicly Held**
WEB: www.hattiesburgamerican.com
SIC: 2711 Newspapers, publishing & printing
PA: Gannett Co., Inc.
7950 Jones Branch Dr
Mc Lean VA 22102
703 854-6000

(G-1986)
HATTIESBURG HYDRAULICS SLS SVC
6967 U S Highway 49 (39402-9162)
PHONE...................................601 264-6606
Mack Harrison, *President*
Kenny Harrison, *President*
Glenn Harrison, *Treasurer*
EMP: 8
SQ FT: 3,500
SALES (est): 1.1MM **Privately Held**
SIC: 5084 7699 3492 Hydraulic systems equipment & supplies; hydraulic equipment repair; hose & tube fittings & assemblies, hydraulic/pneumatic

(G-1987)
HATTIESBURG MOTORS LLC
2860 Oak Grove Rd (39402-8925)
PHONE...................................601 818-2255
EMP: 2
SALES (est): 210K **Privately Held**
SIC: 3694 Mfg Engine Electrical Equipment

(G-1988)
HATTIESBURG PAPER COMPANY LLC
1 Wl Runnels Indus Dr (39401-8320)
PHONE...................................601 545-3400
Marc Keefer, *Manager*
EMP: 162
SALES (corp-wide): 40.9B **Privately Held**
WEB: www.hattiesburg.org
SIC: 2679 Paper products, converted
HQ: Hattiesburg Paper Company, Llc
1085 Parkview Rd
Green Bay WI 54304
920 498-5100

(G-1989)
HENNS NEST INC
5317 Old Highway 11 19b (39402-6225)
PHONE...................................601 268-3577
Gradine Turnage, *President*
EMP: 2

SALES (est): 144K **Privately Held**
SIC: 2339 Maternity clothing

(G-1990)
HIRO TELEMEDICINE SYSTEMS LLC
171 Cambrooke (39402-7771)
PHONE........................312 835-1859
Italo Subbarao, *President*
Guy P Cooper,
EMP: 2
SALES (est): 32.9K **Privately Held**
SIC: 8322 3728 Telephone counseling service; target drones

(G-1991)
HOOD COMPANIES INC (PA)
623 N Main St Ste 100 (39401-3464)
P.O. Box 682 (39403-0682)
PHONE...................................601 582-1545
Warren Hood, *President*
Larry D Davis, *CFO*
John A Burnam, *Admin Sec*
◆ **EMP:** 80
SALES (est): 1B **Privately Held**
SIC: 3086 2952 6719 Insulation or cushioning material, foamed plastic; roofing materials; investment holding companies, except banks

(G-1992)
HOOD CONTAINER CORPORATION (HQ)
623 N Main St Ste 100 (39401-3464)
PHONE...................................601 582-1545
Warren A Hood Jr, *President*
Van Strahan, *Opers Mgr*
Jason Stringer, *Prdtn Mgr*
Jay St Pierre, *Safety Mgr*
Marsha Noland, *Purch Mgr*
EMP: 127
SALES (est): 135MM **Privately Held**
SIC: 2673 Bags: plastic, laminated & coated

(G-1993)
HOOD FLEXIBLE PACKAGING CORP (PA)
623 N Main St Ste 200 (39401-3464)
P.O. Box 818, Tyler TX (75710-0818)
PHONE...................................903 593-1793
Robert Morris, *President*
Gulam Harji, *Principal*
John Johnson, *Vice Pres*
R J More, *VP Human Res*
◆ **EMP:** 83
SQ FT: 200,000
SALES (est): 33MM **Privately Held**
SIC: 2673 2671 3089 Plastic bags: made from purchased materials; packaging paper & plastics film, coated & laminated; blow molded finished plastic products

(G-1994)
HOOD INDUSTRIES INC (PA)
Also Called: McEwen Lumber Co
15 Professional Pkwy # 8 (39402-2647)
PHONE...................................601 264-2962
Donald Grimm, *President*
Chris Norris, *Managing Dir*
John Hammack, *Vice Pres*
John Johnson, *Vice Pres*
Richard Mills, *Vice Pres*
◆ **EMP:** 70 **EST:** 1983
SQ FT: 18,000
SALES (est): 332.7MM **Privately Held**
WEB: www.hoodindustries.com
SIC: 2436 2421 5031 Panels, softwood plywood; resawing lumber into smaller dimensions; kiln drying of lumber; lumber, plywood & millwork; paneling, wood

(G-1995)
HOOD INDUSTRIES INC
Hood Distribution
15 Professional Pkwy # 8 (39402-2647)
PHONE...................................601 264-2962
Darrin Martin, *Partner*
Jay Gallaway, *Branch Mgr*
EMP: 1
SALES (corp-wide): 332.7MM **Privately Held**
SIC: 2411 5031 Wooden bolts, hewn; building materials, exterior

PA: Hood Industries, Inc.
15 Professional Pkwy # 8
Hattiesburg MS 39402
601 264-2962

(G-1996)
HPC LLC
1 Wl Runnels Indus Dr (39401-8320)
PHONE...................................601 545-3400
Greg Santaga, *CEO*
EMP: 2
SALES (est): 190.6K **Privately Held**
SIC: 2679 Paper products, converted

(G-1997)
HYBRID PLASTICS INCORPORATED
55 Wl Runnels Indus Dr (39401-8320)
PHONE...................................601 544-3466
Carl Hagstrom, *Vice Pres*
Joseph Schwab, *CTO*
Joseph D Lichtenhan, *Director*
Micheal J Carr, *Admin Sec*
EMP: 30
SQ FT: 35,000
SALES (est): 7.9MM **Privately Held**
SIC: 2821 2869 2819 Acrylic resins; industrial organic chemicals; charcoal (carbon), activated

(G-1998)
IDOM ENTERPRISING INC
Also Called: Idom Fabrication
508 Lakeshore Dr (39401-1048)
PHONE...................................601 583-4852
Ricky Idom, *President*
Rickey Idom, *President*
EMP: 1
SQ FT: 6,240
SALES: 130K **Privately Held**
SIC: 3448 Buildings, portable: prefabricated metal

(G-1999)
INCAPITALMGCOM LLC
5891 Hwy 49 60 Unit 205 (39402)
PHONE...................................601 268-0103
Ibrahim Mustafaa,
EMP: 1
SALES (est): 73.3K **Privately Held**
SIC: 7378 3571 5734 3575 Computer & data processing equipment repair/maintenance; electronic computers; modems, monitors, terminals & disk drives: computers; computer terminals; data processing service

(G-2000)
J M H GRAPHICS
223 S 40th Ave (39402-1604)
PHONE...................................601 261-2500
Jason Spiers, *Owner*
Melissa Spiers, *Co-Owner*
Katherine Viator, *Graphic Designe*
EMP: 6
SALES (est): 395.6K **Privately Held**
SIC: 2759 Screen printing

(G-2001)
JE PAINTING AND RENOVATIONS
275 Sandy Run Rd (39402-8951)
PHONE...................................601 470-2047
EMP: 2 **EST:** 2015
SALES (est): 87.2K **Privately Held**
SIC: 5198 2851 Paints, varnishes & supplies; wood fillers or sealers

(G-2002)
JOHNSON CONTROLS INC
77 Academy Dr (39401-7959)
PHONE...................................601 544-8911
Greg Thrash, *Manager*
EMP: 200 **Privately Held**
SIC: 2531 Seats, automobile
HQ: Johnson Controls, Inc.
5757 N Green Bay Ave
Milwaukee WI 53209
414 524-1200

(G-2003)
JONES COMPANIES AVI MGT INC
16 Office Park Dr Ste 6 (39402-6021)
PHONE...................................844 500-2438

2019 Harris Directory of
Mississippi Manufacturers

▲ = Import ▼=Export
◆ =Import/Export

GEOGRAPHIC SECTION

Hattiesburg - Forrest County (G-2032)

Jonathan Jones, *President*
Mark McCain, *CFO*
EMP: 2
SALES (est): 841.4K **Privately Held**
SIC: 5211 2869 Lumber & other building materials; fuels

(G-2004)
JPM OF MISSISSIPPI INC
Also Called: J P M
116 Wl Runnels Indus Dr (39401-8359)
P.O. Box 16449 (39404-6449)
PHONE..................................601 544-9950
William E Taber III, *Principal*
Robert M Dearman, *Vice Pres*
Dee Stuart, *Purch Mgr*
Derek Dearman, *QC Mgr*
William Taber Jr, *Shareholder*
EMP: 62
SQ FT: 28,000
SALES (est): 11.3MM **Privately Held**
WEB: www.jpm-ms.com
SIC: 3562 3463 3599 Ball & roller bearings; nonferrous forgings; machine shop, jobbing & repair

(G-2005)
KDL SOLUTIONS LLC
48 Frye Rd (39401-8850)
P.O. Box 15009 (39404-5009)
PHONE..................................601 434-0508
Les Goff,
Dean Bertram,
Kim Wright,
EMP: 5
SQ FT: 500
SALES (est): 589.2K **Privately Held**
SIC: 2899 Chemical preparations

(G-2006)
KEMP ENTERPRISES
54 Saint Charles Ave (39402-8219)
PHONE..................................662 574-0253
Brandy Nicole Kemp, *Owner*
EMP: 1
SALES (est): 100K **Privately Held**
SIC: 3621 Motors & generators

(G-2007)
KIMBERLY-CLARK CORPORATION
W L Runnels Dr (39401)
PHONE..................................601 545-3400
Steve Swiggum, *Manager*
EMP: 194
SALES (corp-wide): 18.4B **Publicly Held**
WEB: www.kimberly-clark.com
SIC: 2621 2676 Sanitary tissue paper; infant & baby paper products
PA: Kimberly-Clark Corporation
351 Phelps Dr
Irving TX 75038
972 281-1200

(G-2008)
KITCHEN TABLE
3720 Hardy St Ste 3 (39402-1596)
P.O. Box 15306 (39404-5306)
PHONE..................................601 261-3836
Kennard Mc Kay, *Principal*
EMP: 10
SALES (est): 1MM **Privately Held**
SIC: 2434 Wood kitchen cabinets

(G-2009)
KOHLER CO
182 J M Tatum Indus Dr (39401-7944)
PHONE..................................601 582-3555
Jerry Stone, *Manager*
EMP: 290
SALES (corp-wide): 7.8B **Privately Held**
SIC: 3519 Internal combustion engines
PA: Kohler Co.
444 Highland Dr
Kohler WI 53044
920 457-4441

(G-2010)
KOHLER CO
Also Called: Kohler Engine
95 W L Runnels Indus Dr (39401)
PHONE..................................601 544-2553
EMP: 3
SALES (corp-wide): 7.8B **Privately Held**
SIC: 3431 Plumbing fixtures: enameled iron cast iron or pressed metal

PA: Kohler Co.
444 Highland Dr
Kohler WI 53044
920 457-4441

(G-2011)
KOLINSKY CORP
Also Called: Nick's Ice House
2106 Hardy St (39401-5962)
PHONE..................................601 544-5987
Nick Kolinsky, *President*
Carolyn Kolinsky, *Vice Pres*
EMP: 2
SQ FT: 4,000
SALES (est): 222.2K **Privately Held**
WEB: www.nicksicehouse.com
SIC: 2097 5813 Manufactured ice; bar (drinking places)

(G-2012)
L & G MARBLE INC
2617 Lincoln Rd (39402-3132)
PHONE..................................601 268-0225
EMP: 3
SALES: 250K **Privately Held**
SIC: 3281 5713 Mfg Cut Stone/Products Ret Floor Covering

(G-2013)
LAD2 LLC
5211 Old Highway 42 (39401-1269)
PHONE..................................601 584-9026
Larry Harrington,
EMP: 2
SALES: 950K **Privately Held**
SIC: 3663 Radio & TV communications equipment

(G-2014)
LAMAR COUNTY NEWS INC
Also Called: Harrisburg Publishing
103 N 40th Ave (39401-6606)
P.O. Box 1110 (39403-1110)
PHONE..................................601 268-2331
Sonya James, *Principal*
Matt Guthrie, *Principal*
Yvette Barncastle, *Office Mgr*
EMP: 5
SALES (est): 396.4K **Privately Held**
SIC: 7313 2711 Newspaper advertising representative; newspapers

(G-2015)
LANCASTER MACHINE & WELDING
1 Lindsay Carter Rd (39401)
PHONE..................................601 582-1400
William Lancaster, *Owner*
EMP: 2
SALES (est): 81K **Privately Held**
SIC: 7692 Welding repair

(G-2016)
LASER MANIA INC
905 Hardy St Ste 223 (39401-4163)
PHONE..................................601 543-0072
Patrick Rothwell, *President*
John Craft, *Senior VP*
EMP: 9 **EST:** 1996
SQ FT: 10,000
SALES (est): 743.2K **Privately Held**
WEB: www.lasermania.com
SIC: 5941 3944 7993 Specialty sport supplies; games, toys & children's vehicles; amusement arcade

(G-2017)
LIONS PRIDE
23 Delma Dr (39401-9750)
PHONE..................................601 818-1308
Lauro S De Leon Jr, *Owner*
EMP: 2
SALES (est): 144K **Privately Held**
SIC: 3724 Aircraft engines & engine parts

(G-2018)
MAGNOLIA GREEN INDUSTRIES INC
420 S 35th Ave (39402-1711)
PHONE..................................601 466-3853
EMP: 3
SALES (est): 149.3K **Privately Held**
SIC: 3999 Manufacturing industries

(G-2019)
MAGNOLIA SEWING CENTER
6380 U S Highway 98 (39402-8532)
PHONE..................................601 261-9006
Susan Baskin, *Owner*
EMP: 2
SALES (est): 211.9K **Privately Held**
SIC: 3552 5722 Embroidery machines; sewing machines

(G-2020)
MALONE DESIGN & CONTG LLC
Also Called: Young's Trucking
104 Fox Run Dr (39402-1032)
P.O. Box 16064 (39404-6064)
PHONE..................................601 807-1279
Derrick Young,
EMP: 3
SALES (est): 263.6K **Privately Held**
SIC: 4731 1442 Freight transportation arrangement; construction sand & gravel

(G-2021)
MARSHALL DURBIN FOOD CORP
Also Called: Marshall Durbin Poultry
1301 James St (39401-4570)
P.O. Box 991 (39403-0991)
PHONE..................................601 544-3141
Chuck Handcock, *Manager*
EMP: 758
SALES (corp-wide): 404.3MM **Privately Held**
SIC: 2015 Poultry, processed
HQ: Marshall Durbin Food Corporation
2830 Commerce Blvd
Irondale AL 35210
205 841-7315

(G-2022)
MERIDIAN BRICK LLC
Also Called: Boral Bricks Studio
221 Thornhill Dr (39401-6625)
PHONE..................................601 296-0445
Jim Stewart, *Branch Mgr*
EMP: 6
SALES (corp-wide): 441MM **Privately Held**
WEB: www.boralbricks.com
SIC: 5211 3251 Brick; brick & structural clay tile
PA: Meridian Brick Llc
6455 Shiloh Rd D
Alpharetta GA 30005
770 645-4500

(G-2023)
MICHAEL A DENT
Also Called: Madness Productions
109 Claiborne Ave (39401-5339)
PHONE..................................601 543-0157
Michael Dent, *Owner*
EMP: 1
SALES (est): 48.1K **Privately Held**
SIC: 7819 9661 2741 6221 Sound (effects & music production), motion picture; space research & technology; music book & sheet music publishing; music books: publishing & printing; commodity contracts brokers, dealers

(G-2024)
MISS POLKA DOT LOLLIPOP
931 Southeast Cir (39402-2122)
PHONE..................................601 325-1779
Kristi L Henderson, *Principal*
EMP: 2
SALES (est): 62.3K **Privately Held**
SIC: 2064 Lollipops & other hard candy

(G-2025)
MISSISSIPPI COCA COLA BTLG CO
Also Called: Coca-Cola
110 Wl Runnels Indus Dr (39401-8359)
PHONE..................................601 584-6644
Bill McDonald, *Manager*
EMP: 12
SALES (corp-wide): 31.8B **Publicly Held**
SIC: 2086 Bottled & canned soft drinks
HQ: Mississippi Coca Cola Bottling Co, Inc
191 Devereaux Dr
Natchez MS

(G-2026)
MISSISSIPPI EMBROIDERY CO
Also Called: Meco
670 Weathersby Rd Ste 120 (39402-8870)
PHONE..................................601 264-3255
Gary Parker, *Owner*
EMP: 3
SALES (est): 395.7K **Privately Held**
SIC: 2395 Embroidery products, except schiffli machine; embroidery & art needlework

(G-2027)
MISSISSIPPI TANK AND MFG CO (PA)
Also Called: Mississippi Tank Company
3000 W 7th St (39401-5617)
P.O. Box 1391 (39403-1391)
PHONE..................................601 264-1800
Robert O Tatum, *Ch of Bd*
Charles Daniel Miller, *President*
Joe F Tatum Jr, *Corp Secy*
Joseph Michael Pitts, *Vice Pres*
Kim Stringer, *Purch Mgr*
▼ **EMP:** 165
SQ FT: 115,880
SALES (est): 33.4MM **Privately Held**
WEB: www.mstank.com
SIC: 3443 Tanks, standard or custom fabricated: metal plate; process vessels, industrial: metal plate; tanks for tank trucks, metal plate

(G-2028)
MMC MATERIALS INC
1920 Byron St (39402-3253)
P.O. Box 16474 (39404-6474)
PHONE..................................601 268-9599
Eddie Middleton, *Manager*
EMP: 16
SALES (corp-wide): 306.5MM **Privately Held**
WEB: www.mmcmaterials.com
SIC: 3273 Ready-mixed concrete
HQ: Mmc Materials, Inc.
1052 Highland Colony Pkwy # 201
Ridgeland MS 39157
601 898-4000

(G-2029)
MMC MATERIALS INC
22 Liberty Pl (39402-8613)
P.O. Box 16474 (39404-6474)
PHONE..................................601 268-3005
Butch Bailess, *Manager*
EMP: 3
SALES (corp-wide): 306.5MM **Privately Held**
SIC: 3273 Ready-mixed concrete
HQ: Mmc Materials, Inc.
1052 Highland Colony Pkwy # 201
Ridgeland MS 39157
601 898-4000

(G-2030)
MOHAWK STEEL COMPANY
50 Hegwood Rd (39402-9428)
PHONE..................................601 467-6959
EMP: 1 **EST:** 2016
SALES (est): 46.5K **Privately Held**
SIC: 2273 Mfg Carpets/Rugs

(G-2031)
MONOGRAM HUT
43 Turtle Creek Dr (39402-1183)
PHONE..................................601 268-9028
Dodie Robertson, *Owner*
EMP: 6
SALES (est): 447.1K **Privately Held**
SIC: 2395 7389 Embroidery products, except schiffli machine; embroidering of advertising on shirts, etc.

(G-2032)
MONOGRAMS BY RAHAIM
209 S 22nd Ave (39401-6008)
PHONE..................................601 310-0152
EMP: 1 **EST:** 2015
SALES (est): 37.8K **Privately Held**
SIC: 2395 Embroidery & art needlework

(PA)=Parent Co (HQ)=Headquarters (DH)=Div Headquarters
✪ = New Business established in last 2 years

2019 Harris Directory of
Mississippi Manufacturers

79

GEOGRAPHIC

Hattiesburg - Forrest County (G-2033)

GEOGRAPHIC SECTION

(G-2033)
MR APPLIANCE OF HATTIESBURG
5071 Old Highway 42 (39401-2874)
PHONE.....................................601 869-0434
EMP: 1
SALES (est): 56K **Privately Held**
SIC: 3639 Household appliances

(G-2034)
MR STITCH IT
2210 Alice Dr (39402-3121)
PHONE.....................................601 543-8681
EMP: 1
SALES (est): 50.8K **Privately Held**
SIC: 2395 Embroidery & art needlework

(G-2035)
MUNN ENTERPRISES INC
7712 U S Highway 49 (39402-2854)
PHONE.....................................601 264-7446
Everette C Munn, *President*
Glynda F Munn, *Corp Secy*
Harold Munn, *Vice Pres*
Howard C Munn, *Vice Pres*
Tonya Davis, *Project Mgr*
EMP: 60
SQ FT: 34,000
SALES (est): 12.1MM **Privately Held**
WEB: www.munnenterprises.com
SIC: 1799 3993 Sign installation & mainte-
nance; electric signs

(G-2036)
NEWKS EXPRESS CAFE OF H
4700 Hardy St Ste Y (39402-1300)
PHONE.....................................601 602-0189
Brent Davidson, *Manager*
EMP: 4
SALES (est): 328.4K **Privately Held**
SIC: 2741 Miscellaneous publishing

(G-2037)
NEWSON CHENORA
Also Called: Casden's Body Boutique
5056 Old Highway 42 I3 (39401-2833)
PHONE.....................................601 596-3899
Chenora Newson, *Owner*
EMP: 1
SALES: 2K **Privately Held**
SIC: 2672 2844 7389 Soap impregnated
papers & paper washcloths; toilet prepara-

(G-2038)
OWENS-BROCKWAY GLASS CONT INC
72 Wl Runnels Indus Dr (39401-8529)
PHONE.....................................601 584-4800
Robert Colacowski, *Manager*
EMP: 16
SALES (corp-wide): 6.8B **Publicly Held**
SIC: 3221 Glass containers
HQ: Owens-Brockway Glass Container Inc.
1 Michael Owens Way
Perrysburg OH 43551
567 336-8449

(G-2039)
PANAMA PUMP COMPANY
620 Meadow Lane Dr (39401-3301)
P.O. Box 15626 (39404-5626)
PHONE.....................................601 544-4251
John Freeman, *President*
EMP: 3 EST: 1933
SQ FT: 4,000
SALES: 300K **Privately Held**
WEB: www.panamapump.com
SIC: 3489 3561 Flame throwers (ord-
nance); pumps & pumping equipment

(G-2040)
PATHWAY CANDLES
45 Cherokee Rd (39402-9632)
PHONE.....................................601 297-0484
Tanya Pickering, *Principal*
EMP: 1
SALES (est): 39.6K **Privately Held**
SIC: 3999 Candles

(G-2041)
PATRICK ENTERPRISES INC
Also Called: Maxwell's Monograms
100 Pinewood Dr (39402-1452)
PHONE.....................................601 268-1115

EMP: 2 EST: 1995
SALES: 100K **Privately Held**
SIC: 2395 8711 8999 Embroidery Serv-
ices & Consulting Engineer & Geological
Consultant

(G-2042)
PINE BELT INDUSTRIES
41 Bonhomie Rd (39401-8648)
PHONE.....................................601 450-0431
Nick Hartley, *Principal*
EMP: 2
SALES (est): 117.2K **Privately Held**
SIC: 3999 Manufacturing industries

(G-2043)
PINE BELT READY MIX
2098 Glendale Ave (39401-1017)
PHONE.....................................601 544-7069
John Duff, *Manager*
EMP: 2
SALES (est): 91.3K **Privately Held**
SIC: 3273 Ready-mixed concrete

(G-2044)
PINE CREEK LLC
42 Pine Bark Cv (39401-5657)
PHONE.....................................601 255-5036
EMP: 2
SALES (est): 91.8K **Privately Held**
SIC: 1442 Construction sand & gravel

(G-2045)
PLAN HOUSE PRINTING
1 Churchill St (39402-1622)
PHONE.....................................601 336-6378
Randy Anderson, *Owner*
EMP: 1
SALES (corp-wide): 463.8K **Privately Held**
SIC: 7336 2759 Graphic arts & related de-
sign; commercial printing
PA: Plan House Printing
607 W Main St Ste A
Tupelo MS 38804
662 407-0193

(G-2046)
POWE TIMBER COMPANY (PA)
Also Called: American Wood Division
114 S 10th Ave (39401-4257)
P.O. Box 1532 (39403-1532)
PHONE.....................................601 545-7600
William Powe Jr, *President*
Joan King, *Manager*
EMP: 2
SQ FT: 2,000
SALES (est): 2.8MM **Privately Held**
WEB: www.american-woodcraft.com
SIC: 5031 2491 Lumber, plywood & mill-
work; wood products, creosoted

(G-2047)
PRECISION FAB REFURBISHING ◑
3806 U S Highway 49 (39401-8921)
PHONE.....................................601 543-7752
EMP: 1 EST: 2019
SALES (est): 25K **Privately Held**
SIC: 7692 Welding repair

(G-2048)
RAINEY MILL WORKS LLC
Also Called: Bill Rainey Millwork
1909 Country Club Rd (39401-7802)
PHONE.....................................601 583-1310
Bill Rainey, *President*
Steven Fagan, *Manager*
EMP: 15
SQ FT: 18,000
SALES: 1.2MM **Privately Held**
SIC: 2434 Wood kitchen cabinets

(G-2049)
REAVES PURE WATER LLC
2320 Eddy St (39402-2708)
PHONE.....................................601 606-6789
Jason Reaves, *Principal*
EMP: 1
SALES (est): 55.3K **Privately Held**
SIC: 2086 Pasteurized & mineral waters,
bottled & canned

(G-2050)
RESINALL MISSISSIPPI INC
102 Dixie Pine Rd (39401-4026)
PHONE.....................................252 585-1445
John M Godina Sr, *President*
Elaine L Godina, *President*
Lee T Godina, *Vice Pres*
William Gustitus, *Plant Mgr*
Linda Bryant, *Sales Staff*
▲ EMP: 110
SQ FT: 4,000
SALES (est): 23.7MM
SALES (corp-wide): 997.6MM **Privately Held**
WEB: www.resinall.com
SIC: 2821 Plastics materials & resins
HQ: Resinall Corp.
3065 High Ridge Rd
Stamford CT 06903
203 329-7100

(G-2051)
RICHARD H BOWERS
Also Called: Staco Manufacturing Co
5243 Old Highway 11 (39402-8859)
PHONE.....................................601 264-0100
Richard H Bowers, *Owner*
EMP: 7
SALES: 400K **Privately Held**
SIC: 3441 Fabricated structural metal

(G-2052)
RIVER ROAD SAND & GRAVEL LLC
406 Hemphill St (39401-3809)
PHONE.....................................601 582-9662
EMP: 6 EST: 2011
SALES (est): 566.1K **Privately Held**
SIC: 1442 Construction Sand/Gravel

(G-2053)
ROBERT R STEWART
Also Called: Pallet Depot
1701 James St (39401-8307)
PHONE.....................................601 408-0494
Robert R Stewart, *Owner*
EMP: 1
SALES (est): 140.9K **Privately Held**
SIC: 2448 Wood pallets & skids

(G-2054)
ROSEBERRY WELDING LLC
71 Walker Rd (39401-8631)
PHONE.....................................601 408-1843
Thomas Roseberry, *Principal*
EMP: 1 EST: 2015
SALES (est): 30.3K **Privately Held**
SIC: 7692 Welding repair

(G-2055)
SARAH CASE-PRICE
604 Adeline St Ste B (39401-3929)
PHONE.....................................601 818-4377
EMP: 1
SALES (est): 54.5K **Privately Held**
SIC: 3523 Farm machinery & equipment

(G-2056)
SCHOOLSTATUS LLC
6222 U S Highway 98 Fl 2 (39402-8531)
P.O. Box 18938 (39404-8938)
PHONE.....................................601 620-0613
Nick Peterman, *Vice Pres*
Terry Larabee, *Sales Staff*
Aaron Shirley, *IT/INT Sup*
Aubrey Davis,
EMP: 3
SALES (est): 281K **Privately Held**
SIC: 7372 7389 Educational computer
software;

(G-2057)
SOUTHEASTERN CONCRETE CO INC (PA)
105 Industrial Blvd (39401-2849)
P.O. Box 16748 (39404-6748)
PHONE.....................................601 544-7000
Ray A Sims, *President*
Janet Blanton, *Corp Secy*
O L Sims II, *Vice Pres*
EMP: 36
SQ FT: 1,000
SALES (est): 7.8MM **Privately Held**
WEB: www.landacontracting.com
SIC: 3273 Ready-mixed concrete

(G-2058)
SOUTHEASTERN CONCRETE CO INC
2611 Lakeview Rd (39401-1230)
P.O. Box 16748 (39404-6748)
PHONE.....................................601 545-7811
Joe Davis, *Vice Pres*
EMP: 30
SALES (corp-wide): 7.8MM **Privately Held**
WEB: www.landacontracting.com
SIC: 3531 3273 Concrete plants; ready-
mixed concrete
PA: Southeastern Concrete Company, Inc.
105 Industrial Blvd
Hattiesburg MS 39401
601 544-7000

(G-2059)
SOUTHEASTERN CONCRETE CO INC
105 Industrial Blvd (39401-2849)
P.O. Box 16748 (39404-6748)
PHONE.....................................601 544-7000
Doug Lambeth, *Branch Mgr*
EMP: 25
SALES (corp-wide): 7.8MM **Privately Held**
WEB: www.landacontracting.com
SIC: 3531 Concrete plants
PA: Southeastern Concrete Company, Inc.
105 Industrial Blvd
Hattiesburg MS 39401
601 544-7000

(G-2060)
SOUTHERN DIVERSIFIED PRODUCTS
2712 Hardy St (39401-7049)
PHONE.....................................601 271-2588
EMP: 2
SALES (est): 106K **Privately Held**
SIC: 3559 Special Industry Machinery,
Nec, Nsk

(G-2061)
SOUTHERN KERNELS
560 Weathersby Rd (39402-1164)
PHONE.....................................601 336-9080
Taj Stuart, *Owner*
EMP: 7
SALES (est): 455.8K **Privately Held**
SIC: 2064 Popcorn balls or other treated
popcorn products

(G-2062)
SOUTHERN OIL COMPANY
501 N Main St (39401-3572)
PHONE.....................................601 582-5455
Mitchell Morris, *Owner*
EMP: 3
SALES (est): 495.3K **Privately Held**
SIC: 2911 Petroleum refining

(G-2063)
SOUTHERN PROHIBITION BREWING
2056 Oak Grove Rd (39402-1475)
PHONE.....................................601 467-1057
Whitney Miracle, *Principal*
EMP: 11
SALES (est): 481.9K **Privately Held**
SIC: 2082 Beer (alcoholic beverage)

(G-2064)
SOUTHERN SYSTEMS & SERVICE CO
171 W Hills Dr (39402-1087)
P.O. Box 16212 (39404-6212)
PHONE.....................................601 264-4713
David Kean, *President*
Alice Kean, *Treasurer*
EMP: 5 EST: 1969
SQ FT: 4,500
SALES: 400K **Privately Held**
SIC: 2789 2752 Bookbinding & related
work; commercial printing, offset

(G-2065)
SOUTHERN WD PRSV HTTESBURG INC
627 Hood Rd (39401)
P.O. Box 630 (39403-0630)
PHONE.....................................601 544-1140

2019 Harris Directory of
Mississippi Manufacturers

▲ = Import ▼=Export
◆ =Import/Export

80

GEOGRAPHIC SECTION

Hazlehurst - Copiah County (G-2092)

Mark Shows, *President*
Charles Childress, *Asst Director*
EMP: 17
SQ FT: 5,000
SALES (est): 2.4MM **Privately Held**
SIC: 2491 Poles & pole crossarms, treated wood; structural lumber & timber, treated wood; posts, treated wood

(G-2066)
SQUELCHFIRE INC
46 Shelby Thames Dr (39402-3702)
PHONE..................................601 434-2048
Robert Yeats Lochhead, *President*
EMP: 2
SALES (est): 74.4K **Privately Held**
SIC: 2899 Chemical preparations

(G-2067)
STACO DECORATIVE IRON
Also Called: Bywers, Richard
5243 Old Highway 11 (39402-8859)
PHONE..................................601 264-0064
Richard Bywers, *Owner*
EMP: 2 EST: 1997
SALES (est): 146.6K **Privately Held**
SIC: 3993 Signs & advertising specialties

(G-2068)
STANDARD GRAVEL CO INC
2094 Glendale Ave (39401-1017)
PHONE..................................601 584-6436
John Green, *Branch Mgr*
EMP: 2
SALES (corp-wide): 12.9MM **Privately Held**
SIC: 1442 Construction sand & gravel
PA: Standard Gravel Co. Inc.
20258 Highway 16
Franklinton LA 70438
985 839-3442

(G-2069)
STANDARD OFFICE SUP PRTG INC
Also Called: Of/USA
400 W Pine St (39401-3830)
P.O. Box 950 (39403-0950)
PHONE..................................601 544-5361
Mike Herrin, *President*
Michael Herrin, *President*
Martha T Herrin, *Corp Secy*
Charles Downing, *Vice Pres*
EMP: 20
SQ FT: 31,000
SALES (est): 2.9MM **Privately Held**
SIC: 2754 5943 5712 2759 Rotary photogravure printing; color printing, gravure; office forms & supplies; furniture stores; commercial printing; commercial printing, lithographic

(G-2070)
SUNBEAM PRODUCTS INC
95 WI Runnels Industrial (39401-8023)
P.O. Box 860, Freeport IL (61032-0860)
PHONE..................................601 296-5000
Deidre Robinson, *Senior Mgr*
EMP: 48
SALES (corp-wide): 8.6B **Publicly Held**
SIC: 3631 3634 Barbecues, grills & braziers (outdoor cooking); electric housewares & fans
HQ: Sunbeam Products, Inc.
2381 Nw Executive Ctr Dr
Boca Raton FL 33431
561 912-4100

(G-2071)
SUNBEAM PRODUCTS INC
95 WI Runnels Industrial (39401-8023)
PHONE..................................601 296-5000
EMP: 610
SALES (corp-wide): 8.6B **Publicly Held**
SIC: 3631 2511 Manufacturing And Distribution Center For Household Division
HQ: Sunbeam Products, Inc.
2381 Nw Executive Ctr Dr
Boca Raton FL 33431
561 912-4100

(G-2072)
TATUM DEVELOPMENT CORP (PA)
3000 W 7th St (39401-5617)
P.O. Box 388 (39403-0388)
PHONE..................................601 544-6043
Robert O Tatum, *President*
Frederick E Tatum, *Corp Secy*
John M Tatum Jr, *Vice Pres*
Joseph F Tatum Jr, *Vice Pres*
Frederick Tatum, *Human Res Mgr*
EMP: 6
SQ FT: 7,500
SALES (est): 725.2MM **Privately Held**
SIC: 5141 5084 4924 3443 Groceries, general line; welding machinery & equipment; natural gas distribution; vessels, process or storage (from boiler shops): metal plate

(G-2073)
THOMAS JEWELRY
5057 Lincoln Road Ext (39402-8068)
PHONE..................................601 264-8780
Richard R Thomas, *Owner*
EMP: 1
SALES (est): 71.3K **Privately Held**
WEB: www.st-thomas.com
SIC: 5944 3911 Jewelry, precious stones & precious metals; jewelry, precious metal

(G-2074)
THOMAS WELDING AND FABRICATING
71 Walker Rd (39401-8631)
PHONE..................................601 408-1843
Thomas Roseberry, *Principal*
EMP: 1
SALES (est): 25K **Privately Held**
SIC: 7692 Welding repair

(G-2075)
TUCKER MACHINE SERVICES
507 Peps Point Rd (39401-9701)
PHONE..................................601 582-4280
Dale Tucker, *Owner*
EMP: 2
SALES (est): 100K **Privately Held**
SIC: 3599 7692 7699 5084 Machine shop, jobbing & repair; welding repair; hydraulic equipment repair; hydraulic systems equipment & supplies; hose & tube fittings & assemblies, hydraulic/pneumatic; welding on site

(G-2076)
TUFF-WALL INC
5266 Old Highway 11 (39402-7817)
PHONE..................................601 264-8649
R Hankins, *President*
EMP: 3
SALES (est): 174.3K **Privately Held**
SIC: 2851 Paints & allied products

(G-2077)
UNITED FENCE COMPANY
255 Mcleod St (39401-3816)
PHONE..................................601 582-0406
Kevin Fant, *Manager*
EMP: 1
SALES (corp-wide): 1MM **Privately Held**
WEB: www.unitedfencehattiesburg.com
SIC: 1799 3699 Swimming pool construction; security devices
PA: United Fence Company
3903 Highland Park Dr
Meridian MS 39307
601 482-3224

(G-2078)
UNIVERSITY OF SOUTHERN MISS
Also Called: Usm Science & Technology
118 College Dr (39406-0002)
P.O. Box 5046 (39406-0001)
PHONE..................................601 266-5390
Connie Morgan, *Manager*
EMP: 25
SALES (corp-wide): 189.7MM **Privately Held**
WEB: www.usm.edu
SIC: 3821 8221 Physics laboratory apparatus; university

PA: The University Of Southern Mississippi
118 College Dr
Hattiesburg MS 39406
601 266-1000

(G-2079)
USA YEAST COMPANY LLC
457 J M Tatum Indus Dr (39401-7820)
PHONE..................................601 545-2690
Gary Edwards, *CEO*
EMP: 33
SALES (est): 688.4K
SALES (corp-wide): 34.5MM **Privately Held**
WEB: www.usayeast.com
SIC: 2051 Yeast goods, sweet: except frozen
HQ: Lallemand Inc
1620 Rue Prefontaine
Montreal QC H1W 2
514 522-2131

(G-2080)
VENDWORKS LLC (HQ)
Also Called: Coca-Cola
201 Coca Cola Ave (39402-1368)
P.O. Box 17197 (39404-7197)
PHONE..................................601 268-1906
Brad Martin,
EMP: 34
SALES (est): 6.5MM
SALES (corp-wide): 2.4B **Privately Held**
SIC: 2086 Bottled & canned soft drinks
PA: Coca-Cola Bottling Company United, Inc.
4600 E Lake Blvd
Birmingham AL 35217
205 841-2653

(G-2081)
W T LEGGETT INC
Also Called: Speedy Printing & Signs
1002 Hardy St (39401-4164)
PHONE..................................601 544-2704
William T Leggett, *President*
Bill Leggett, *Administration*
EMP: 5 EST: 1973
SALES (est): 520K **Privately Held**
SIC: 2752 5943 Commercial printing, offset; office forms & supplies

(G-2082)
WESTPOINT HOME LLC
1005 Oakleigh Dr (39402-3027)
PHONE..................................601 466-6738
Mark Castracane, *Branch Mgr*
EMP: 1
SALES (corp-wide): 11.7B **Publicly Held**
SIC: 2211 Broadwoven fabric mills, cotton
HQ: Westpoint Home Llc
777 3rd Ave Fl 7
New York NY 10017
212 930-2000

(G-2083)
WILLIAM CAREY UNIVERSITY
Also Called: Newspaper Production
498 Tuscan Ave (39401-5461)
PHONE..................................601 318-6115
Merryl Cooper, *Principal*
EMP: 2
SALES (corp-wide): 69MM **Privately Held**
WEB: www.wmcarey.edu
SIC: 2711 8221 Newspapers, publishing & printing; university
PA: William Carey University
710 William Carey Pkwy
Hattiesburg MS 39401
601 318-6051

(G-2084)
WILLIE B SIMS JR CPA PLLC
908 Broadway Dr (39401-7500)
PHONE..................................601 545-3930
Dorothy Parker, *Accountant*
Willie B Sims Jr,
EMP: 3
SALES (est): 311.4K **Privately Held**
WEB: www.williesimscpa.com
SIC: 5087 2899 8721 7291 Cleaning & maintenance equipment & supplies; chemical supplies for foundries; accounting, auditing & bookkeeping; tax return preparation services

(G-2085)
WIS-PAK OF HATTIESBURG LLC
2 WI Runnels Indus Dr (39401-8529)
PHONE..................................601 544-7200
Jeff Priegnitz, *QC Mgr*
EMP: 14
SALES (est): 2.2MM **Privately Held**
SIC: 2086 Carbonated soft drinks, bottled & canned

(G-2086)
WNC SATCOM GROUP LLC (PA)
208 W Pine St Ste 100 (39401-3865)
PHONE..................................601 544-0311
Ken Brown, *Mng Member*
Rachel Brown,
EMP: 3
SALES (est): 1MM **Privately Held**
SIC: 3679 Antennas, satellite: household use

(G-2087)
YORK INTERNATIONAL CORPORATION
77 Academy Dr (39401-7959)
PHONE..................................601 544-8911
Brad Martin, *Branch Mgr*
EMP: 94 **Privately Held**
SIC: 3585 Refrigeration & heating equipment
HQ: York International Corporation
631 S Richland Ave
York PA 17403
717 771-7890

(G-2088)
ZEON CHEMICALS L P
1301 W 7th St (39401-2800)
PHONE..................................601 583-5527
Guinn Andrews, *Controller*
Ron Tarlton, *Manager*
EMP: 66 **Privately Held**
WEB: www.zeonchemicals.com
SIC: 2822 Synthetic rubber
HQ: Zeon Chemicals L.P.
4111 Bells Ln
Louisville KY 40211
502 775-7700

Hazlehurst
Copiah County

(G-2089)
AXIALL CORPORATION
20043 Highway 51 (39083-9497)
PHONE..................................601 892-5612
Glenn Wooten, *Manager*
EMP: 101
SQ FT: 60,000 **Publicly Held**
WEB: www.georgiagulf.com
SIC: 2812 2821 Alkalies & chlorine; plastics materials & resins
HQ: Axiall Corporation
1000 Abernathy Rd # 1200
Atlanta GA 30328
304 455-2200

(G-2090)
BLAYLOCKS WILD GAME PROCESSING
2142 E Whitworth St (39083-9277)
PHONE..................................601 894-0087
Michael Brent, *Owner*
EMP: 2
SALES (est): 130K **Privately Held**
SIC: 3556 Meat processing machinery

(G-2091)
CIRCLE A LLC
8161 Highway 472 (39083-9672)
PHONE..................................601 832-3698
Archie C Ashley Jr, *Mng Member*
Katherine Ashley, *Admin Sec*
EMP: 8
SALES: 1MM **Privately Held**
SIC: 2411 7389 Logging;

(G-2092)
COMMUNITY CONSTRUCTION CO LLC
1045 Hzlhurst Indus Pk Dr (39083)
PHONE..................................601 894-5239

(PA)=Parent Co (HQ)=Headquarters (DH)=Div Headquarters
✪ = New Business established in last 2 years

2019 Harris Directory of
Mississippi Manufacturers

81

Hazlehurst - Copiah County (G-2093)

GEOGRAPHIC SECTION

Hugh A Louviere Jr,
James E Stewart Jr,
EMP: 43 **EST:** 2007
SALES (est): 12.2MM **Privately Held**
SIC: 1389 Construction, repair & dismantling services

(G-2093)
COPIAH COUNTY COURIER INC
103 S Ragsdale Ave (39083-3037)
P.O. Box 351 (39083-0351)
PHONE..................................601 894-3141
James Lambert, *President*
John Carney, *Vice Pres*
EMP: 10
SALES (est): 577.4K **Privately Held**
SIC: 2711 Newspapers: publishing only, not printed on site

(G-2094)
DG FOODS LLC
1095 Industrial Dr (39083-8869)
PHONE..................................601 892-0333
Brian Jernigan, *CFO*
Jennifer Reeves, *Cust Mgr*
Gregory W O'Quinn,
EMP: 500
SALES: 58.7MM **Privately Held**
SIC: 2015 Poultry slaughtering & processing

(G-2095)
FAB- TEK CENTRAL MISS INC
19171 Highway 51 (39083-4400)
P.O. Box 127, Gallman (39077-0127)
PHONE..................................601 892-5017
Shannon Moore, *CEO*
EMP: 39
SALES (est): 2.2MM **Privately Held**
SIC: 3441 Fabricated structural metal

(G-2096)
FRANK BRADFORD WOMACK
Also Called: Magnolia Polishing Service
4032 Wilderness Rd (39083-9073)
PHONE..................................601 955-1841
Frank Bradford Womack, *Owner*
EMP: 2
SALES (est): 76.7K **Privately Held**
SIC: 2842 Polishing preparations & related products

(G-2097)
GRANGER MP AC & HTG
6032 Highway 472 (39083-9663)
PHONE..................................601 894-3774
Pat Granger, *President*
EMP: 1
SALES (est): 104.8K **Privately Held**
SIC: 3444 1711 Sheet metalwork; heating & air conditioning contractors

(G-2098)
JONES LIMBER
31050 Highway 28 (39083-9505)
PHONE..................................601 894-3839
Jones Limber, *President*
EMP: 2
SALES (est): 141.3K **Privately Held**
SIC: 2676 Towels, napkins & tissue paper products

(G-2099)
L C INDUSTRIES INC
Also Called: Signature Works Division
1 Signature Dr (39083-9195)
PHONE..................................601 894-1771
Bill Hudson, *CEO*
Michael Davis, *QC Mgr*
Marlene Cockrell, *Manager*
EMP: 300
SALES (corp-wide): 83.3MM **Privately Held**
SIC: 3089 3991 2392 2679 Tableware, plastic; brooms; brushes, household or industrial; mops, floor & dust; plates, pressed & molded pulp: from purchased material; gift wrap & novelties, paper; plastics bottles; shapes, extruded aluminum
PA: L C Industries Inc.
4500 Emperor Blvd
Durham NC 27703
919 596-8277

(G-2100)
MCNEELY PLASTIC PRODUCTS INC
Also Called: McNeely Plastics
1022 Advance Ln (39083-8629)
PHONE..................................601 926-1000
Shannon Watts, *Manager*
EMP: 15
SALES (corp-wide): 58.7MM **Privately Held**
SIC: 2673 Bags: plastic, laminated & coated
PA: Mcneely Plastic Products, Inc.
1111 Industrial Park Dr
Clinton MS 39056
601 926-1000

(G-2101)
N C ENTERPRISES INC
1006 Shady Oaks Ln (39083-8961)
PHONE..................................601 953-6977
Lee Nottingham, *President*
EMP: 3
SALES (est): 152.1K **Privately Held**
SIC: 3429 Manufactured hardware (general)

(G-2102)
NATIONAL TEXTILE AND AP INC (PA)
1018 Industrial Dr (39083-8800)
PHONE..................................601 892-4356
Frederic Lepoutre, *President*
Jennifer King, *Marketing Mgr*
▲ **EMP:** 31
SALES: 9MM **Privately Held**
WEB: www.comfortscrubs.com
SIC: 2326 Men's & boys' work clothing

(G-2103)
SANDERSON FARMS INC
Processing Division
Hwy 28 E (39083)
P.O. Box 765 (39083-0765)
PHONE..................................601 894-3721
Larry Lampkin, *Division Mgr*
David Brown, *Plant Mgr*
Tracey King, *Chief Acct*
Ken Bodman, *Manager*
EMP: 475
SALES (corp-wide): 3.2B **Publicly Held**
WEB: www.sandersonfarms.com
SIC: 2015 Poultry, slaughtered & dressed
PA: Sanderson Farms, Inc.
127 Flynt Rd
Laurel MS 39443
601 649-4030

(G-2104)
SANDERSON FARMS INC PROD DIV
19148 Highway 51 (39083-9428)
P.O. Box 506 (39083-0506)
PHONE..................................601 892-1145
Christopher B Batte, *Manager*
EMP: 120
SALES (corp-wide): 3.2B **Publicly Held**
SIC: 0251 2048 0254 Broiler, fryer & roaster chickens; prepared feeds; poultry hatcheries
HQ: Sanderson Farms, Inc. (Production Division)
127 Flynt Rd
Laurel MS 39443
601 425-2552

(G-2105)
SHAMROCK FARM
10120 Old Port Gibson Rd (39083-9012)
PHONE..................................601 277-3053
Peter McKinley, *Owner*
EMP: 5
SALES (est): 229.2K **Privately Held**
SIC: 2015 Chicken slaughtering & processing

(G-2106)
SIGNATURE WORKS INC
1 Signature Dr (39083-9195)
PHONE..................................601 894-1771
Thomas F Darnell, *Ch of Bd*
Paul A Harvey, *President*
Paul Harvey, *President*
A R Williams, *CFO*
Brand Henley, *Treasurer*

EMP: 400
SQ FT: 450,000
SALES: 26.2MM **Privately Held**
SIC: 3089 3991 2392 2679 Tableware, plastic; brooms; brushes, household or industrial; mops, floor & dust; plates, pressed & molded pulp: from purchased material; gift wrap & novelties, paper; plastics bottles; shapes, extruded aluminum

(G-2107)
SWEET SOUTH EMBROIDERY
3179 Smyrna Rd (39083-9052)
PHONE..................................601 277-3371
EMP: 1
SALES (est): 31.2K **Privately Held**
SIC: 2395 Embroidery & art needlework

(G-2108)
TANNERS ENTERPRISE LLC
4073 Tower Rd (39083-8985)
PHONE..................................601 894-5219
Damon Tanner, *Principal*
Kawana Tanner,
Kawana Stewart,
EMP: 2
SALES: 35K **Privately Held**
SIC: 0781 2759 Landscape services; screen printing

(G-2109)
WEST FARMS INC
8012 Carter Hill Rd (39083-9723)
PHONE..................................601 277-3579
James H West, *President*
Walter West, *President*
EMP: 3
SALES (est): 200.4K **Privately Held**
SIC: 0131 0811 0115 0212 Cotton; timber tracts; corn; beef cattle except feedlots; balers; farm: hay, straw, cotton, etc.

(G-2110)
WESTLAKE CHEMICAL CORPORATION
20043 Highway 51 (39083-9497)
PHONE..................................601 892-5612
Andrew La Fontaine, *Branch Mgr*
EMP: 2 **Publicly Held**
SIC: 2821 Polyethylene resins
PA: Westlake Chemical Corporation
2801 Post Oak Blvd # 600
Houston TX 77056

Heidelberg
Jasper County

(G-2111)
A & B PUMP & SUPPLY INC
710 Hwy 528 W (39439)
P.O. Box T (39439-1019)
PHONE..................................601 787-3741
Daniel W Boothe Jr, *President*
Douglas Boothe, *Vice Pres*
Angela Boothe, *Treasurer*
EMP: 8
SQ FT: 3,750
SALES (est): 2.3MM **Privately Held**
SIC: 5084 1311 5082 1389 Oil well machinery, equipment & supplies; crude petroleum production; oil field equipment; oil field services

(G-2112)
BOGUE HOMA LOGGING
40 Bill Windham Rd (39439-3111)
PHONE..................................601 426-3662
Harriett Windham, *Owner*
EMP: 5
SALES (est): 280K **Privately Held**
SIC: 2411 Logging

(G-2113)
CHRIS G GATLIN
162 County Road 377 (39439-4967)
PHONE..................................601 498-6281
Chris Gatlin, *Administration*
EMP: 2 **EST:** 2016
SALES (est): 97.5K **Privately Held**
SIC: 2411 Logging

(G-2114)
CLARKCO SERVICES INC
3313 County Road 230 (39439-3821)
P.O. Box 341 (39439-0341)
PHONE..................................601 787-3447
Thomas Lowery, *President*
Larry Rochelle, *Corp Secy*
EMP: 95
SQ FT: 2,500
SALES: 6MM **Privately Held**
SIC: 1389 Oil field services

(G-2115)
DENBURY ONSHORE LLC
175 County Road 359 (39439-3544)
P.O. Box 1003 (39439-1003)
PHONE..................................601 787-3111
Mike Hickson, *Manager*
EMP: 50
SALES (corp-wide): 1.4B **Publicly Held**
WEB: www.denbury.com
SIC: 1382 Oil & gas exploration services
HQ: Denbury Onshore, Llc
5320 Legacy Dr
Plano TX 75024
972 673-2000

(G-2116)
DONALD GATLIN LOGGING LLC
77 Arley Williams Rd (39439-3217)
PHONE..................................601 425-4320
Donald Gatlin, *Owner*
EMP: 4
SALES: 350K **Privately Held**
SIC: 2411 Logging camps & contractors

(G-2117)
HUNT REFINING COMPANY
Also Called: Hunt Southland Refining Co
177 Haney Rd (39439-3021)
PHONE..................................601 426-1821
EMP: 20
SALES (corp-wide): 8.9B **Privately Held**
SIC: 2911 Petroleum Refinery
HQ: Hunt Refining Company
2200 Jack Warner Pkwy
Tuscaloosa AL 35401
205 391-3300

(G-2118)
JOHNSTONS SAND & GRAVEL INC
65 County Road 115 (39439-3466)
PHONE..................................601 787-4326
Paula Frances Johnston, *President*
Donna Byrd, *Treasurer*
EMP: 25
SQ FT: 8,000
SALES: 3.5MM **Privately Held**
SIC: 1442 Gravel mining

(G-2119)
TELLUS OPERATING GROUP LLC
3368 County Road 8 (39439-3776)
PHONE..................................601 787-3014
EMP: 23 **Privately Held**
SIC: 4925 1311 Gas production and/or distribution; crude petroleum & natural gas production
PA: Tellus Operating Group, Llc
602 Crescent Pl Ste 100
Ridgeland MS 39157

(G-2120)
V A SAULS INC
Highway 528 E (39439)
P.O. Box 299 (39439-0299)
PHONE..................................601 787-4321
Gary W Sauls, *President*
Adam Sauls, *Corp Secy*
Joe Boyd, *Vice Pres*
EMP: 60
SQ FT: 3,200
SALES (est): 5.9MM **Privately Held**
SIC: 1389 Servicing oil & gas wells

Hermanville
Claiborne County

82

2019 Harris Directory of
Mississippi Manufacturers

▲ = Import ▼=Export
◆ =Import/Export

GEOGRAPHIC SECTION

Hernando - Desoto County (G-2150)

(G-2121)
HAZLEHURST LUMBER COMPANY INC
1027 Old Port Gibson Rd (39086-9601)
PHONE..............................601 535-7779
G J Adams, *President*
Starke Albritton, *Treasurer*
Kay Adams, *Admin Sec*
EMP: 100
SQ FT: 3,500
SALES (est): 12.5MM **Privately Held**
SIC: 2421 Lumber: rough, sawed or planed

(G-2122)
NSLC SOUTHERN INC
11167 Pttson Hrmnville Rd (39086-9615)
P.O. Box 70 (39086-0070)
PHONE..............................601 535-2205
Robert Carpenter, *Manager*
EMP: 75
SALES (corp-wide): 12.5MM **Privately Held**
WEB: www.southernlumber.net
SIC: 2421 5031 Lumber: rough, sawed or planed; lumber: rough, dressed & finished
PA: Nslc Southern, Inc.
214 Draperton Dr
Ridgeland MS 39157
601 605-0575

Hernando
Desoto County

(G-2123)
B & B PRESSURE WSHG & LDSCPG
7197 Railroad Sta (38632-8015)
PHONE..............................662 910-9105
Broin Lofton, *Owner*
EMP: 2
SQ FT: 2,500
SALES (est): 170.1K **Privately Held**
SIC: 3452 0781 Washers; landscape services

(G-2124)
CBL ARCHITECTURAL FIBERGLASS
Also Called: Cbl Architectual Fiberglass
100 E Valley St (38632-1928)
PHONE..............................662 429-2277
C Burgess Ledbetter, *President*
Joanne Ledbetter, *Treasurer*
James Garrison, *Admin Sec*
EMP: 13
SALES (est): 830K **Privately Held**
SIC: 3229 3443 Glass fiber products; fabricated plate work (boiler shop)

(G-2125)
COLES TOOL WORKS INC
Also Called: C T W
3414 Highway 51 S (38632-8692)
P.O. Box 548 (38632-0548)
PHONE..............................662 429-5191
Mark King, *CEO*
EMP: 110
SQ FT: 40,000
SALES (est): 9.9MM
SALES (corp-wide): 1.7B **Privately Held**
WEB: www.ctw-inc.com
SIC: 3841 Surgical & medical instruments
HQ: Tegra Medical, Llc
9 Forge Pkwy
Franklin MA 02038

(G-2126)
CONNECTION LABORATORIES INC
1068 Thousand Oaks Dr (38632-7742)
PHONE..............................662 429-1097
EMP: 5
SQ FT: 3,200
SALES (est): 310K **Privately Held**
SIC: 3679 Mfg Communication Equipment Parts

(G-2127)
COTHRAN MACHINE SHOP
1891 Slocum Rd (38632-8784)
PHONE..............................662 449-5983
EMP: 3
SALES (est): 220K **Privately Held**
SIC: 3599 Machine Shop

(G-2128)
D D BERRYHILL SIGNS
516 Whitfield Dr (38632-7426)
PHONE..............................662 298-3325
EMP: 1 EST: 2017
SALES (est): 50.6K **Privately Held**
SIC: 3993 Signs & advertising specialties

(G-2129)
DKH DISTRIBUTING INC
385 Green T Rd W (38632-4503)
PHONE..............................901 734-4528
Dale Hare, *President*
EMP: 5
SALES (est): 439K **Privately Held**
SIC: 3412 2096 Metal barrels, drums & pails; potato chips & similar snacks

(G-2130)
E C WELDING & FABRICATING
3320 Byhalia Rd (38632-9756)
PHONE..............................662 429-1624
Earl Caldwell, *Owner*
EMP: 1
SALES (est): 70K **Privately Held**
SIC: 7692 Welding repair

(G-2131)
FOUR STAR TRUCKING COMPANY LLC
2337 Getwell Rd S (38632-9423)
PHONE..............................662 429-5397
Nathaniel Warren Jr, *Principal*
EMP: 2
SALES (est): 292.7K **Privately Held**
SIC: 3537 Trucks, tractors, loaders, carriers & similar equipment

(G-2132)
GEORGE B READY
175 E Commerce St (38632-2343)
P.O. Box 127 (38632-0127)
PHONE..............................662 429-7088
George B Ready, *Owner*
EMP: 2
SALES (est): 158.1K **Privately Held**
SIC: 8111 3273 General practice attorney, lawyer; ready-mixed concrete

(G-2133)
HANGING BY A THREAD LLC
7401 Love Rd (38632-7302)
PHONE..............................662 449-5198
Kerry L Scott,
Taylor Buntin,
EMP: 1
SALES (est): 90K **Privately Held**
SIC: 2395 Art goods for embroidering, stamped: purchased materials

(G-2134)
HAWKS FEED MILL
7005 Holly Springs Rd (38632-9358)
PHONE..............................662 564-2920
H H Hawks, *Owner*
EMP: 3 EST: 1992
SALES (est): 96.6K **Privately Held**
SIC: 2048 5999 Livestock feeds; feed & farm supply

(G-2135)
HYDRASEP INC
Also Called: Gnesys
400 Vaiden Dr (38632-2311)
PHONE..............................662 429-4088
Preston Grace Jr, *CEO*
Larry Mathews, *President*
Naji Nassif, *Vice Pres*
EMP: 3
SALES (est): 404.3K **Privately Held**
WEB: www.hydrasep.com
SIC: 3823 On-stream gas/liquid analysis instruments, industrial

(G-2136)
KINGS WOODWORKS
1239 Cross Creek Dr E (38632-1152)
PHONE..............................662 403-0871
EMP: 1 EST: 2017
SALES (est): 57.6K **Privately Held**
SIC: 2431 Millwork

(G-2137)
KOL KRAFT MANUFACTURING CO
6514 Hwy 51 S (38632)
P.O. Box 423 (38632-0423)
PHONE..............................662 429-7561
Donald Breshears, *President*
Nyla Breshears, *Corp Secy*
EMP: 6
SQ FT: 20,000
SALES: 200K **Privately Held**
SIC: 3632 Household refrigerators & freezers

(G-2138)
LEHMAN-ROBERTS COMPANY
Also Called: Memphis Stone & Gravel
6158 Highway 51 S (38632)
P.O. Box 1603, Memphis TN (38101-1603)
PHONE..............................662 429-5237
Stan Wright, *Manager*
EMP: 10
SALES (corp-wide): 133.8MM **Privately Held**
SIC: 1611 1442 2951 Highway & street paving contractor; construction sand mining; asphalt paving mixtures & blocks
PA: Lehman-Roberts Company
1111 Wilson St
Memphis TN 38106
901 774-4000

(G-2139)
LIGHTNING MACHINE WORKS
2440 Wanda Faye Dr (38632-6701)
PHONE..............................662 449-1801
Bill Ford, *Park Mgr*
EMP: 3 EST: 1999
SALES (est): 264.4K **Privately Held**
SIC: 3599 Machine shop, jobbing & repair

(G-2140)
LINCO SAFETY SIGNS
1780 Robertson Place Dr (38632-2254)
PHONE..............................662 469-9569
EMP: 1
SALES (est): 46K **Privately Held**
SIC: 3993 Signs & advertising specialties

(G-2141)
MAGNOLIA ACCOUNTING SERVICES
3781 Mccracken Rd (38632-8860)
PHONE..............................662 429-5852
Betty Floyd, *Owner*
EMP: 3
SALES: 150K **Privately Held**
SIC: 7372 8748 Business oriented computer software; business consulting

(G-2142)
MI-DA MAPS
2868 Wren St (38632-2334)
P.O. Box 703 (38632-0703)
PHONE..............................662 429-0022
Shirley T Mc Lendon, *Owner*
EMP: 4 EST: 1994
SALES: 60K **Privately Held**
SIC: 2741 Maps: publishing & printing

(G-2143)
NATIONAL TANK INC
400 Vaiden Dr (38632-2311)
PHONE..............................662 429-5469
Preston Grace III, *President*
Larry Matthews, *Vice Pres*
John R Grace, *Admin Sec*
EMP: 10 EST: 1930
SQ FT: 2,500
SALES (est): 1.6MM **Privately Held**
WEB: www.nationaltank.com
SIC: 3443 3714 Tanks, lined: metal plate; tanks for tank trucks, metal plate; motor vehicle parts & accessories

(G-2144)
NITEO PRODUCTS LLC
720 Vaiden Dr (38632-2427)
PHONE..............................662 429-0405
Alissa Kranz, *Controller*
Robert Sheldon, *Branch Mgr*
EMP: 65
SALES (corp-wide): 180.7MM **Privately Held**
SIC: 2899 Chemical preparations
HQ: Niteo Products, Llc
5949 Sherry Ln Ste 540
Dallas TX 75225
214 245-5000

(G-2145)
NITEO PRODUCTS LLC
Also Called: Valvoline
2925 Mccracken Rd (38632-2430)
PHONE..............................662 429-8292
Robert Shelton, *Branch Mgr*
EMP: 65
SALES (corp-wide): 180.7MM **Privately Held**
SIC: 2899 Chemical preparations
HQ: Niteo Products, Llc
5949 Sherry Ln Ste 540
Dallas TX 75225
214 245-5000

(G-2146)
NORTH AMERICAN ELECTRIC INC (PA)
350 Vaiden Dr (38632-2328)
P.O. Box 130 (38632-0130)
PHONE..............................662 429-8049
David Hackman, *President*
John Eldred, *Warehouse Mgr*
Gillian Cunningham, *Treasurer*
Lashon McNeil, *Accountant*
Austin Peters, *Sales Staff*
▲ EMP: 50
SQ FT: 65,000
SALES (est): 28.6MM **Privately Held**
WEB: www.northamericanelectric.net
SIC: 5063 3621 Panelboards; motors & generators

(G-2147)
OWL CITY INDUSTRIES LLC
1227 W Oak Grove Rd (38632-7336)
P.O. Box 876 (38632-0876)
PHONE..............................901 268-6871
William Myers, *Principal*
EMP: 2
SALES (est): 109.4K **Privately Held**
SIC: 3999 Manufacturing industries

(G-2148)
PPG INDUSTRIES INC
Also Called: PPG 4483
417 E Commerce St (38632-2348)
PHONE..............................662 449-4947
EMP: 24
SALES (corp-wide): 15.3B **Publicly Held**
WEB: www.ppg.com
SIC: 2851 Paints & allied products
PA: Ppg Industries, Inc.
1 Ppg Pl
Pittsburgh PA 15272
412 434-3131

(G-2149)
PROFORMA SOUTHPRINT
857 Amanda Cv (38632-1333)
PHONE..............................901 734-2290
Bruce Orpet, *Principal*
EMP: 2
SALES (est): 231.1K **Privately Held**
SIC: 2752 Commercial printing, lithographic

(G-2150)
PUCCI PETIQUE INC
2400 Highway 51 S Ste 1 (38632-1704)
PHONE..............................662 429-3202
Tammy Croft, *Principal*
EMP: 8 EST: 2010
SALES (est): 621.2K **Privately Held**
SIC: 3999 Pet supplies

(PA)=Parent Co (HQ)=Headquarters (DH)=Div Headquarters
✪ = New Business established in last 2 years

2019 Harris Directory of
Mississippi Manufacturers

83

Hernando - Desoto County (G-2151)

GEOGRAPHIC SECTION

(G-2151)
QUALITY CABINET COMPANY INC
1662 Highway 51 S (38632-1145)
PHONE..................................662 429-1411
Jim Holt, *President*
EMP: 25
SQ FT: 19,000
SALES (est): 2.5MM **Privately Held**
SIC: 2511 2521 Kitchen & dining room furniture; cabinets, office: wood

(G-2152)
RCL COMPONENTS INC
3155 Industrail Dr (38632)
PHONE..................................662 449-0401
David Ward, *General Mgr*
EMP: 35
SALES (est): 5.7MM
SALES (corp-wide): 23.5MM **Privately Held**
WEB: www.rclcomp.com
SIC: 5084 3537 7699 Hydraulic systems equipment & supplies; industrial trucks & tractors; hydraulic equipment repair
PA: Rcl Components, Inc.
135 E Thompson St
Bogart GA 30622
770 725-0893

(G-2153)
S & S STRIPING
2340 Oak Woods Dr E (38632-6679)
P.O. Box 34697, Memphis TN (38184-0697)
PHONE..................................662 449-4498
Martha M Stacks, *Partner*
Charles B Steffey, *Partner*
EMP: 2 EST: 1969
SQ FT: 800
SALES (est): 136.8K **Privately Held**
SIC: 1721 3272 Pavement marking contractor; concrete products, precast

(G-2154)
SEW LUCKY EMBROIDERY
3022 N Wren St (38632-2556)
PHONE..................................662 550-5533
Cassie McLean, *Owner*
EMP: 3
SALES: 50K **Privately Held**
SIC: 2395 Embroidery & art needlework

(G-2155)
SPIRAL SYSTEMS INC
1700 Highway 51 S (38632-1143)
PHONE..................................901 521-8373
EMP: 2
SALES (est): 94.5K **Privately Held**
SIC: 3444 Sheet metalwork

(G-2156)
SPORTS OF ALL SORTS INC
345 E Commerce St (38632-2305)
PHONE..................................662 429-1162
Linda Carter, *President*
Danny Carter, *Vice Pres*
EMP: 3
SALES: 200K **Privately Held**
SIC: 3949 Sporting & athletic goods

(G-2157)
SXP SCHULZ XTRUDED PRODUCTS LP
2785 Mccracken Rd (38632-2429)
PHONE..................................662 429-0818
EMP: 92 **Privately Held**
SIC: 3312 Pipes, iron & steel
PA: Sxp Schulz Xtruded Products Lp
1001 Schulz Blvd
Robinsonville MS 38664

(G-2158)
TASTE MAKER FOODS LLC
495 Vaiden Dr (38632-2325)
PHONE..................................901 274-4407
Justin Reed, *Vice Pres*
William Tomlinson, *Vice Pres*
Rj Reed, *Mng Member*
John Freeman, *Manager*
EMP: 32
SALES: 10MM **Privately Held**
SIC: 2099 2045 Seasonings: dry mixes; doughnut mixes, prepared: from purchased flour

PA: Reed Food Technology, Inc.
3151 Greenfield Rd
Pearl MS 39208

(G-2159)
TEGRA MEDICAL (MS) LLC
3414 Highway 51 S (38632-8692)
PHONE..................................662 429-5191
Robert Pietrafesa, *CEO*
Josh Lee, *General Mgr*
Allie Dickey, *Buyer*
Knox Purnell, *Manager*
Betty Coleman, *Senior Mgr*
EMP: 21
SALES (est): 4.1MM
SALES (corp-wide): 1.7B **Privately Held**
SIC: 3841 Surgical & medical instruments
PA: Sfs Group Ag
Rosenbergsaustrasse 8
Heerbrugg SG 9435
717 275-151

(G-2160)
VELOCITY INC
530 Vaiden Dr (38632-2340)
PHONE..................................662 449-4026
Mark Kemper, *President*
Chris Warren, *Engineer*
Terry Harris, *Manager*
EMP: 50
SQ FT: 45,000
SALES (est): 6MM **Privately Held**
WEB: www.velocityid.com
SIC: 3993 Signs & advertising specialties

(G-2161)
WERTH SERVICING LLC
1404 Big Ben N (38632-6912)
P.O. Box 918 (38632-0918)
PHONE..................................662 449-4410
Christopher Werth,
EMP: 1
SALES: 250K **Privately Held**
SIC: 1389 Roustabout service

Hickory
Newton County

(G-2162)
J & S ENTERPRISES LLC
Also Called: Walker Printing Company
8318 Hwy 503 N (39332)
PHONE..................................601 646-3636
Johnny Walker, *Mng Member*
EMP: 6
SQ FT: 6,500
SALES: 275K **Privately Held**
SIC: 3953 Textile marking stamps, hand: rubber or metal

Hollandale
Washington County

(G-2163)
CONTINUE CARE HLTH MODEM LINE
207 East Ave N (38748-3711)
PHONE..................................662 827-7107
Robert Warrington, *Principal*
EMP: 3 EST: 2010
SALES (est): 147.1K **Privately Held**
SIC: 3661 Modems

(G-2164)
DELTA DRY LLC
204 Magnolia St (38748-3234)
PHONE..................................203 515-1528
Drew Pallotto,
Boyd Eifing,
EMP: 6
SALES (est): 267.4K **Privately Held**
SIC: 2842 Sweeping compounds, oil or water absorbent, clay or sawdust

(G-2165)
DELTA MACHINERY INC
Also Called: Geddie Machine & Repair
223 Bailey Dr (38748-3241)
P.O. Box 245 (38748-0245)
PHONE..................................662 827-2572

Ricky Grubb, *President*
EMP: 10
SALES (est): 1.7MM **Privately Held**
WEB: www.deltaportercable.com
SIC: 3441 Fabricated structural metal

(G-2166)
MONSANTO COMPANY
407 W Goldstein St (38748-3884)
P.O. Box 457 (38748-0457)
PHONE..................................662 827-7212
Kenneth Avery, *Vice Pres*
Nate Lidge, *Human Resources*
EMP: 167
SALES (corp-wide): 45.3B **Privately Held**
SIC: 2879 Agricultural chemicals
HQ: Monsanto Company
800 N Lindbergh Blvd
Saint Louis MO 63167
314 694-1000

(G-2167)
NATURES BROOM INC
204 Magnolia St (38748-3234)
PHONE..................................662 931-5844
Boyd Eifling, *President*
EMP: 5
SQ FT: 1,500
SALES: 500K **Privately Held**
WEB: www.naturalherbsktwins.com
SIC: 2842 Sweeping compounds, oil or water absorbent, clay or sawdust

(G-2168)
SUDS N SQUARES
516 East Ave N (38748-3718)
PHONE..................................662 827-9991
Sidney Christian, *Owner*
EMP: 3 EST: 2007
SALES (est): 213K **Privately Held**
SIC: 3999 Cigarette & cigar products & accessories

(G-2169)
WICKER MACHINE CO
1400 East Ave N (38748-3228)
P.O. Box 338 (38748-0338)
PHONE..................................662 827-5434
Allen W Wicker Sr, *President*
Robert Wicker, *Corp Secy*
Terry Wicker, *Vice Pres*
Sherri Ballinger, *Purchasing*
EMP: 14 EST: 1946
SQ FT: 7,600
SALES (est): 4.2MM **Privately Held**
WEB: www.wickermachinecompany.com
SIC: 3531 3523 Forestry related equipment; farm machinery & equipment

---

Holly Springs
Marshall County

(G-2170)
ALL IN ONE SIGNS & PRINTING
114 Craft St (38635-2910)
PHONE..................................662 216-0737
Melanie Wilbanks, *Owner*
EMP: 1
SALES (est): 33.9K **Privately Held**
SIC: 3993 Signs & advertising specialties

(G-2171)
AMERICAN PACIFIC INC (PA)
Also Called: American Pacific Paneling
520 Salem Ave (38635-2448)
PHONE..................................662 252-1862
Scott Beggs, *President*
Cliff Harding, *Vice Pres*
Frank Schmidt, *Vice Pres*
James Hamby, *Opers Staff*
Kerry Snyder, *Sales Mgr*
▲ EMP: 75
SQ FT: 220,000
SALES (est): 20.5MM **Privately Held**
WEB: www.americanpac.com
SIC: 2436 2493 Panels, softwood plywood; particleboard, plastic laminated; hardboard, tempered; fiberboard, other vegetable pulp

(G-2172)
BOWMAN CABINET COMPANY
456 Chulahoma Rd (38635-8325)
PHONE..................................662 564-2711
James Bowman, *Owner*
EMP: 3
SALES (est): 163.3K **Privately Held**
SIC: 2434 Wood kitchen cabinets

(G-2173)
CITE ARMORED INC
540 S Industrial Park Rd (38635-3400)
P.O. Box 5152 (38634-5152)
PHONE..................................662 551-1066
Teresa Hubbard, *President*
Kenneth Russell, *Senior VP*
Ken Russell, *Vice Pres*
Robert Lyon, *Engineer*
Joey Buchanan, *VP Sales*
EMP: 35
SQ FT: 7,500
SALES (est): 7.8MM **Privately Held**
SIC: 3711 Cars, armored, assembly of

(G-2174)
CMC READYMIX INC
516 Highway 4 W (38635-9321)
PHONE..................................662 252-6479
Harold Murphy, *President*
Donna Malone, *Bookkeeper*
EMP: 17
SALES: 1.5MM **Privately Held**
SIC: 3273 Ready-mixed concrete

(G-2175)
CONTRACT FABRICATORS INC (PA)
Also Called: C F I
105 Rolfing Rd (38635-1414)
P.O. Box 758 (38635-0758)
PHONE..................................662 252-6330
Boyce Delashmit, *President*
Mike Clarkson, *Vice Pres*
Dustin Smith, *Project Mgr*
Ray Gandy, *Purch Mgr*
Terry Byrd, *Purchasing*
◆ EMP: 110
SQ FT: 28,000
SALES (est): 33.6MM **Privately Held**
WEB: www.contractfab.com
SIC: 3443 Industrial vessels, tanks & containers; heat exchangers, condensers & components

(G-2176)
FREED PEOPLES PRESS LLC
145 S Center St (38635-3040)
P.O. Box 38, Potts Camp (38659-0038)
PHONE..................................313 717-7819
Alisea McLeod, *Principal*
EMP: 1
SALES (est): 38.8K **Privately Held**
SIC: 2741 Miscellaneous publishing

(G-2177)
HOLLY TOOL & DIE INC
805 Hwy 7 N (38635)
PHONE..................................662 252-1144
Jim Gilliam, *President*
Mary Beth Gilliam, *Corp Secy*
EMP: 6
SQ FT: 4,800
SALES: 400K **Privately Held**
SIC: 3312 Tool & die steel

(G-2178)
JEWELL AIRCRAFTING INC
Also Called: Wings Aircraft Leasing
Hwy 78 W Marshall Airport (38635)
PHONE..................................662 252-6377
John Edward Jewell, *President*
Linda F Jewell, *Corp Secy*
Charlotte Saunders, *Vice Pres*
EMP: 6
SQ FT: 9,000
SALES: 348.9K
SALES (corp-wide): 828.1K **Privately Held**
SIC: 3724 Aircraft engines & engine parts
PA: Jewell Aircraft Inc
171 A Q Greer Rd
Holly Springs MS 38635
662 252-6377

2019 Harris Directory of
Mississippi Manufacturers

84

▲ = Import ▼=Export
◆ =Import/Export

GEOGRAPHIC SECTION

Horn Lake - Desoto County (G-2207)

(G-2179)
KAYCAN INC
820 Highway 7 N (38635-1347)
PHONE..................................662 252-9991
Etienne Cambon, *Principal*
Bob Kanpik, *Branch Mgr*
EMP: 2
SALES (est): 201K **Privately Held**
SIC: 2611 Pulp mills

(G-2180)
KP BUILDING PRODUCTS INC
820 Highway 7 N (38635-1347)
PHONE..................................662 252-9991
Jay Gilletz, *Manager*
EMP: 100
SALES (corp-wide): 537.7MM **Privately Held**
SIC: 3089 5033 Siding, plastic; roofing, siding & insulation
HQ: Kp Building Products, Inc
402 Boyer Cir
Williston VT 05495
866 850-4447

(G-2181)
LAURA JANE COMPANY LLC
163 E Van Dorn Ave (38635-3025)
PHONE..................................662 629-0550
Anthony Clanton, *Principal*
EMP: 2 EST: 2016
SQ FT: 3,000
SALES (est): 52.8K **Privately Held**
SIC: 3999 5719 7389 Candles; lighting, lamps & accessories; interior design services

(G-2182)
LUND COATING TECHNOLOGIES INC
Also Called: Lund Engineered Products
400 S Industrial Park Rd (38635-3430)
PHONE..................................662 252-2340
John R Schwanbeck, *President*
James Baird, *General Mgr*
Mitch Fogle, *General Mgr*
Stephen M Coty, *Vice Pres*
Earl Hill, *Finance Mgr*
▲ EMP: 30
SQ FT: 70,000
SALES (est): 6.4MM **Privately Held**
SIC: 3524 Plows (garden tractor equipment)

(G-2183)
LUNDTEK INC
400 S Industrial Park Rd (38635-3430)
PHONE..................................662 252-2340
Stephen Cote, *President*
James Baird, *Sales Staff*
Andi Staggs, *Office Mgr*
Russell Blaski, *Manager*
EMP: 41
SQ FT: 90,000
SALES (est): 3MM **Privately Held**
SIC: 3398 Metal heat treating

(G-2184)
MAUREY MANUFACTURING CORP (PA)
410 S Industrial Park Rd (38635-3400)
PHONE..................................662 252-6583
Joseph W Maurey, *President*
Monty Wyatt, *District Mgr*
Charles Lloyd, *Exec VP*
Taylor Maurey, *Engineer*
Fitch Brenda, *Accounting Mgr*
▲ EMP: 50 EST: 1915
SQ FT: 140,000
SALES (est): 12.8MM **Privately Held**
WEB: www.maurey.com
SIC: 3568 Power transmission equipment

(G-2185)
MONOGRAM MAGICK
1280 S Red Banks Rd (38635-8355)
PHONE..................................662 544-1392
Emily Barrett, *Principal*
EMP: 1
SALES (est): 38.1K **Privately Held**
SIC: 2395 Embroidery & art needlework

(G-2186)
OLIVERS IRON WORKS
272 Rolfing Rd (38635-1404)
PHONE..................................662 252-3858
James Oliver, *Owner*
EMP: 3
SALES (est): 124K **Privately Held**
SIC: 1799 3446 3443 3442 Iron work, structural

(G-2187)
PARKER-HANNIFIN CORPORATION
Also Called: Racor Div
805 West St (38635-1412)
PHONE..................................662 252-2656
Bill Chisholm, *Manager*
EMP: 127
SALES (corp-wide): 14.3B **Publicly Held**
SIC: 3569 Filters, general line: industrial
PA: Parker-Hannifin Corporation
6035 Parkland Blvd
Cleveland OH 44124
216 896-3000

(G-2188)
PIGEON ROOST NEWS
157 S Center St (38635-3040)
PHONE..................................662 838-4844
Barry Barleson, *Manager*
EMP: 3
SALES (est): 159.5K **Privately Held**
SIC: 2711 7313 Newspapers; newspaper advertising representative

(G-2189)
READY DEFENSE LLC
481 Bonds Dr (38635-1727)
PHONE..................................662 544-3478
Kerry Reid, *Principal*
EMP: 2
SALES (est): 92.5K **Privately Held**
SIC: 3812 Defense systems & equipment

(G-2190)
ROURA ACQUISITION INC
Also Called: Roura Material Handling
100 S Industrial Park Rd (38635-7411)
PHONE..................................662 252-1421
Joy Krain, *Branch Mgr*
EMP: 20
SALES (corp-wide): 4.9MM **Privately Held**
SIC: 3444 Hoppers, sheet metal
PA: Roura Acquisition, Inc.
35355 Forton Ct
Clinton Township MI 48035
586 790-6100

(G-2191)
SOUTH CENTER PRINTING
157 S Center St (38635-3040)
P.O. Box 265 (38635-0265)
PHONE..................................662 252-2793
Lincoln Martin, *Owner*
EMP: 2 EST: 1979
SQ FT: 800
SALES (est): 212.7K **Privately Held**
SIC: 2752 Commercial printing, offset

(G-2192)
SOUTH REPORTER INC
157 S Center St (38635-3040)
P.O. Box 278 (38635-0278)
PHONE..................................662 252-4261
Barry Burleson, *Publisher*
EMP: 16
SQ FT: 4,000
SALES: 700K **Privately Held**
WEB: www.southreporter.com
SIC: 2711 Newspapers: publishing only, not printed on site; newspapers, publishing & printing

(G-2193)
SULLIVAN METALS INC
260 S Industrial Park Rd (38635-3427)
PHONE..................................662 252-5050
Edward F Sullivan, *President*
Mary Ann Sullivan, *Vice Pres*
EMP: 9
SQ FT: 10,000
SALES (est): 1.3MM **Privately Held**
SIC: 3369 Lead, zinc & white metal

(G-2194)
TEES SNOW WHITE
1403 W Woodward Ave (38635-9219)
PHONE..................................662 420-2687
Nakisha Snow, *Principal*
EMP: 3
SALES (est): 132.3K **Privately Held**
SIC: 2759 Screen printing

(G-2195)
THOMAS LP GAS INC
115 W Van Dorn Ave (38635-2901)
P.O. Box 5068 (38634-5068)
PHONE..................................662 252-5388
Kevin Thomas, *President*
Barry Thomas, *Vice Pres*
EMP: 15
SQ FT: 1,000
SALES (est): 3.8MM **Privately Held**
SIC: 5984 3634 Liquefied petroleum gas, delivered to customers' premises; heating units, electric (radiant heat): baseboard or wall

---

Horn Lake
Desoto County

(G-2196)
ELECTRIC WORKS
1721 Dancy Blvd B (38637-1908)
PHONE..................................662 342-5505
Michael Otto, *Owner*
EMP: 3
SALES (est): 254.9K **Privately Held**
SIC: 7694 Electric motor repair

(G-2197)
EMERGNCY EQP PROFESSIONALS INC
6441 Highway 51 N (38637-2414)
P.O. Box 1739, Southaven (38671-0018)
PHONE..................................662 280-4729
Jeff Kuntz, *President*
Neil Clark, *Vice Pres*
Brian Lee, *Vice Pres*
Troy Thompson, *Cust Mgr*
Marc Flanagan, *Sales Staff*
EMP: 15
SALES (est): 4.3MM **Privately Held**
SIC: 3699 Security devices

(G-2198)
EQUIPMENT MAINTENANCE CO
3780 Hilltop Dr (38637-1031)
P.O. Box 69 (38637-0069)
PHONE..................................662 393-9178
David Chadwick, *Owner*
EMP: 1
SALES (est): 107.6K **Privately Held**
SIC: 7549 7692 7699 Trailer maintenance; welding repair; industrial equipment services

(G-2199)
FIRST CLASS FIRE PRTECTION LLC
1978 Hobbs Cv (38637-1476)
P.O. Box 891, Hernando (38632-0891)
PHONE..................................901 350-0499
Bill Morrison, *Mng Member*
Jason Robertson,
EMP: 7
SALES: 1.5MM **Privately Held**
SIC: 1711 5087 3491 Fire sprinkler system installation; sprinkler systems; fire hydrant valves

(G-2200)
GRACE COMPANY OF MS INC
Also Called: Cwi
2204 Cole Rd (38637-2300)
PHONE..................................662 393-2443
William C Jones, *President*
Glenda Hardage, *Vice Pres*
EMP: 19
SQ FT: 26,500
SALES (est): 359.1K **Privately Held**
SIC: 2521 2541 Wood office furniture; store & office display cases & fixtures

(G-2201)
GROUND SUPPORT SPECIALIST LLC
Also Called: Gss
6228 Hurt Rd (38637-2306)
PHONE..................................662 342-1412
Donna Thompson, *General Mgr*
Mike Bond, *Mfg Staff*
Bill Holt, *Purch Mgr*
Kevin Kelly, *Sales Dir*
Fred Yates, *Mng Member*
EMP: 30
SALES: 9MM **Privately Held**
WEB: www.gssonline.com
SIC: 3537 7699 3728 Aircraft loading hoists; tractor repair; deicing equipment, aircraft

(G-2202)
HAVARD PRINTING CO
7431 Meadowbrook Dr (38637-9180)
PHONE..................................662 781-2613
Steven D Havard, *Owner*
EMP: 2
SALES: 30K **Privately Held**
SIC: 2752 Commercial printing, lithographic

(G-2203)
JT SHANNON LUMBER CO INC (PA)
Also Called: Shamrock Plank Flooring
2200 Cole Rd (38637-1440)
P.O. Box 16929, Memphis TN (38186-0929)
PHONE..................................662 393-3765
Jack T Shannon Jr, *CEO*
Frank Bugos, *Maint Spvr*
Lisa Kiddy, *Credit Mgr*
Staci Howery, *VP Sales*
Lisa Durbin, *Sales Mgr*
◆ EMP: 20
SQ FT: 7,000
SALES (est): 109.8MM **Privately Held**
WEB: www.jtshannon.com
SIC: 5031 3559 2421 Lumber: rough, dressed & finished; kilns, lumber; planing mills

(G-2204)
LA ILUCION
1075 Goodman Rd W (38637-1440)
PHONE..................................662 536-0046
Antoinette Vallario, *Principal*
EMP: 4
SALES (est): 79K **Privately Held**
SIC: 5461 2051 Bakeries; bread, cake & related products

(G-2205)
LAWRENCE A WITHERSPOON
Also Called: Service Connection
5784 Caroline Dr (38637-9059)
P.O. Box 10 (38637-0010)
PHONE..................................662 404-5859
Lawrence Witherspoon, *Owner*
EMP: 2
SALES (est): 115.6K **Privately Held**
SIC: 3537 7389 Industrial trucks & tractors;

(G-2206)
MAGNIFICENT PRINTS LLC
1760 Thomas St (38637-3325)
PHONE..................................662 469-5689
Roshanda Daniel, *Principal*
EMP: 2
SALES (est): 83.9K **Privately Held**
SIC: 2752 Commercial printing, lithographic

(G-2207)
MINUTEMAN PRESS INTERNATIONAL
1065 Goodman Rd W (38637-1440)
PHONE..................................662 349-6675
Ruggie Cooper, *President*
EMP: 1
SQ FT: 1,200
SALES (est): 191.9K **Privately Held**
SIC: 2752 Commercial printing, lithographic

(PA)=Parent Co (HQ)=Headquarters (DH)=Div Headquarters
✪ = New Business established in last 2 years

2019 Harris Directory of
Mississippi Manufacturers

Horn Lake - Desoto County (G-2208)

GEOGRAPHIC SECTION

(G-2208)
MMC MATERIALS INC
1955 Nail Rd W (38637-3346)
P.O. Box 673 (38637-0673)
PHONE..................................662 393-7676
Jim Wolfe, *Branch Mgr*
Scott Crast, *Manager*
EMP: 65
SALES (corp-wide): 306.5MM **Privately Held**
WEB: www.mmcmaterials.com
SIC: 3273 5211 Ready-mixed concrete; masonry materials & supplies
HQ: Mmc Materials, Inc.
1052 Highland Colony Pkwy # 201
Ridgeland MS 39157
601 898-4000

(G-2209)
NY BEAUTY
3039 Goodman Rd W (38637-1105)
PHONE..................................662 280-2573
Danny An, *Owner*
EMP: 2 EST: 2008
SALES (est): 118.3K **Privately Held**
SIC: 5087 3999 Beauty parlor equipment & supplies; barber & beauty shop equipment

(G-2210)
SHAMROCK WOOD INDUSTRIES INC
Also Called: Shamrock Plank Flooring
2200 Cole Rd (38637-2300)
P.O. Box 16929, Memphis TN (38186-0929)
PHONE..................................662 393-2125
Jack T Shannon Jr, *President*
Jeff Christian, *Manager*
EMP: 215
SQ FT: 45,000
SALES (est): 28.6MM
SALES (corp-wide): 109.8MM **Privately Held**
WEB: www.jtshannon.com
SIC: 2541 2426 Cabinets, except refrigerated: show, display, etc.: wood; furniture stock & parts, hardwood
PA: J.T. Shannon Lumber Company, Inc.
2200 Cole Rd
Horn Lake MS 38637
662 393-3765

(G-2211)
SO NUTS AND CONFECTIONS LLC
6001 Highway 51 N Ste 3 (38637-2439)
PHONE..................................901 398-9650
Terrea Fleming, *Mng Member*
EMP: 3 **Privately Held**
SIC: 5947 2053 5461 5141 Gifts & novelties; frozen bakery products, except bread; bakeries; groceries, general line; packaged frozen goods; confectionery

(G-2212)
SPEARMAN ORNAMENTAL IRONWORKS
4234 Highgate Dr (38637-5110)
PHONE..................................901 301-7061
EMP: 4 EST: 2005
SALES (est): 250K **Privately Held**
SIC: 3462 Mfg Iron/Steel Forgings

(G-2213)
SUGAR -N- SPICE CONFECTIONS
Also Called: Sugar -N- Spice Delights
3645 Pembrook Dr (38637-2615)
PHONE..................................901 210-6181
Robert Stickles, *Co-Owner*
Mary Stickles, *Co-Owner*
EMP: 1
SALES (est): 20.7K **Privately Held**
SIC: 7999 2064 2051 7389 Cake or pastry decorating instruction; fruit, chocolate covered (except dates); cakes, pies & pastries;

(G-2214)
UPCHURCH INDUSTRIAL LLC
6923 Pasadena Dr (38637-1454)
PHONE..................................662 453-6680
Jamie Rainey, *Project Mgr*
David Upchurch, *Mng Member*

Vincent Matlock,
EMP: 60
SALES: 6MM **Privately Held**
SIC: 3498 Fabricated pipe & fittings

(G-2215)
WILLIAM M STEWART
6815 Pinehurst Rd (38637-1825)
PHONE..................................662 393-7950
William M Stewart, *Owner*
EMP: 2
SALES (est): 117.3K **Privately Held**
SIC: 3571 Electronic computers

Houlka
Chickasaw County

(G-2216)
AFFORDABLE FURN MFG CO INC
6496 Redland Sarepta Rd (38850-9516)
PHONE..................................662 568-7981
Jim Sneed, *CEO*
Terry Austin, *Principal*
James C Sneed, *Principal*
Charles Boxx, *Vice Pres*
Ron Teeter, *Vice Pres*
◆ EMP: 255
SALES (est): 37.7MM **Privately Held**
SIC: 2511 Wood household furniture

(G-2217)
ARK-ELL SPRINGS INC
Also Called: Fashion
101 Industrial Dr (38850-0400)
P.O. Box 308 (38850-0308)
PHONE..................................662 568-3393
William C Stewart Jr, *President*
Stewart McKell, *Corp Secy*
Bob O'Dell Jr, *Vice Pres*
EMP: 150 EST: 1970
SQ FT: 134,000
SALES (est): 8.2MM **Privately Held**
SIC: 2515 5021 Chair & couch springs, assembled; bedsprings, assembled; beds

(G-2218)
BIGBEE INDUSTRIES
119 Industrial Dr (38850-0400)
PHONE..................................662 568-7740
Venkata Chinni, *Principal*
EMP: 2
SALES (est): 81.4K **Privately Held**
SIC: 3599 Machine & other job shop work

(G-2219)
BO LOGGING INC
192 County Road 153 (38850-9424)
PHONE..................................662 983-4225
Joe Tallent, *President*
Norma Tallent, *Vice Pres*
EMP: 2
SALES (est): 120K **Privately Held**
SIC: 2411 Logging camps & contractors

(G-2220)
CHAPTER 3 INC (PA)
958 Washington Rd (38850-9506)
PHONE..................................662 568-7830
Jennifer Schock, *CEO*
David Schock, *COO*
EMP: 70 EST: 2016
SQ FT: 175,000
SALES (est): 7.2MM **Privately Held**
SIC: 2512 Juvenile furniture: upholstered on wood frames

(G-2221)
COLLUMS FURNITURE INC
120 East St (38850-8638)
PHONE..................................662 568-7912
Ken Collums, *President*
Jimmy Collums, *Vice Pres*
◆ EMP: 65
SALES (est): 7.6MM **Privately Held**
SIC: 2512 Living room furniture: upholstered on wood frames

(G-2222)
FIBRIX LLC
101 Industrial Dr (38850-0400)
P.O. Box 308 (38850-0308)
PHONE..................................662 568-3393

Bob O'Dell, *Principal*
EMP: 4
SALES (corp-wide): 74MM **Privately Held**
WEB: www.lpfiber.com
SIC: 2515 3495 3429 Box springs, assembled; wire springs; manufactured hardware (general)
HQ: Fibrix, Llc
1820 Evans St Ne
Conover NC 28613

(G-2223)
GANN BROTHERS INC
1667 County Road 413 (38850-8709)
PHONE..................................662 568-2980
Brian Gann, *President*
Bart Gann, *Vice Pres*
EMP: 4
SALES: 800K **Privately Held**
WEB: www.gannbrothers.com
SIC: 2448 Pallets, wood

(G-2224)
LAKE ROAD FURNITURE MFG CO
2739 Highway 15 N (38850)
P.O. Box 355 (38850-0355)
PHONE..................................662 568-3329
Jimmy L Bailey, *President*
Renee Collums, *Corp Secy*
Joe Williams, *Vice Pres*
EMP: 20
SQ FT: 7,200
SALES (est): 1.7MM **Privately Held**
SIC: 2512 Living room furniture: upholstered on wood frames

(G-2225)
MASTER FIBERS INC
1 Recon Dr (38850)
P.O. Box 668, Houston (38851-0668)
PHONE..................................662 568-3455
Curtis L Clayton, *President*
James Wiygul III, *President*
EMP: 3
SQ FT: 5,000
SALES (est): 49.8K **Privately Held**
SIC: 2297 Nonwoven fabrics

(G-2226)
MILLER TIMBER LLC
865 County Road 413 (38850-9660)
PHONE..................................662 501-6150
Roger Miller,
Nellie Miller,
EMP: 7
SALES: 2MM **Privately Held**
SIC: 2411 7389 Logging;

(G-2227)
R & R LUMBER INC
2466 Highway 15 N (38850-9390)
PHONE..................................662 568-7937
Rachel Reeves, *Manager*
Randy Reeves, *Post Master*
EMP: 20
SALES (est): 3.6MM **Privately Held**
SIC: 2426 Hardwood dimension & flooring mills

(G-2228)
SOUTHERN FIBERS INC
923 Highway 32 E (38850-9016)
P.O. Box 668, Houston (38851-0668)
PHONE..................................662 568-3456
Curtis Clayton, *President*
Guy Matthew Clayton, *Vice Pres*
Jessie Carl Moore, *Admin Sec*
EMP: 2
SALES (est): 637.4K **Privately Held**
SIC: 2299 Batting, wadding, padding & fillings

(G-2229)
STEVE HAMBLIN FRAMES INC
780 County Road 408 (38850-9673)
PHONE..................................662 568-7299
Stephen Hamblin, *President*
EMP: 1
SALES (est): 187.5K **Privately Held**
SIC: 2426 Frames for upholstered furniture, wood

Houston
Chickasaw County

(G-2230)
AKERS MINERALS LLC
2476 Highway 8 E (38851-9316)
PHONE..................................207 615-7591
N B C Chestnut, *Principal*
EMP: 2
SALES (est): 92.8K **Privately Held**
SIC: 1381 Drilling oil & gas wells

(G-2231)
B & B MFG & SPECIALTY CO INC
219 County Road 94 (38851-9358)
PHONE..................................662 456-4313
William Klauser, *President*
EMP: 4
SALES (est): 302.5K **Privately Held**
SIC: 3599 3799 Custom machinery; trailers & trailer equipment

(G-2232)
B&B TRAILERS & MFG CO
219 County Road 94 (38851-9358)
PHONE..................................662 456-4313
William Klauser, *Owner*
EMP: 2
SALES (est): 66.9K **Privately Held**
SIC: 3999 Manufacturing industries

(G-2233)
CHICKASAW FARM SERVICES INC
627 Church St (38851-2002)
P.O. Box 328 (38851-0328)
PHONE..................................662 456-2008
Richard Ware, *President*
Frank Ware, *Vice Pres*
Melissa Ware, *Treasurer*
Carolyn Ware, *Admin Sec*
EMP: 10
SALES (est): 1.1MM **Privately Held**
SIC: 2048 Prepared feeds

(G-2234)
CHICKASAW WOOD PRODUCTS INC
1478 County Road 405 (38851-7216)
PHONE..................................662 456-5357
Leslie S Alford, *President*
EMP: 15
SALES (est): 4.7MM **Privately Held**
SIC: 2441 2426 Boxes, wood; furniture stock & parts, hardwood

(G-2235)
CLASSIC FURNITURE MFG
1231 County Road 515 N (38851-9033)
PHONE..................................662 456-5900
Dean Daniel, *Owner*
EMP: 20
SALES (est): 1.4MM **Privately Held**
SIC: 2511 2512 Wood household furniture; upholstered household furniture

(G-2236)
DIXIELAND FURNITURE MFG CO INC
Also Called: D M A
233 County Road 94 (38851-9358)
PHONE..................................662 456-5378
Dean Holder, *President*
EMP: 50
SALES (est): 6.7MM **Privately Held**
WEB: www.timber-ridge-school.org
SIC: 2512 Upholstered household furniture

(G-2237)
E E BAIRD MACHINE SHOP INC
221 N Jefferson St (38851-2221)
PHONE..................................662 456-2348
Bobby Baird, *President*
Doug Baird, *Vice Pres*
EMP: 3
SALES (est): 210K **Privately Held**
SIC: 3599 Machine shop, jobbing & repair

(G-2238)
E E BAIRD SHOP INC
221 N Jefferson St (38851-2221)
PHONE..................................662 456-3467

2019 Harris Directory of
Mississippi Manufacturers

▲ = Import ▼=Export
◆ =Import/Export

86

GEOGRAPHIC SECTION

Indianola - Sunflower County (G-2265)

Bobby E Baird, *President*
Bonnie Baird, *Corp Secy*
EMP: 2 **EST:** 1945
SQ FT: 6,500
SALES (est): 373.2K **Privately Held**
SIC: 7692 3599 Welding repair; machine shop, jobbing & repair

(G-2239)
EDDIE WIGGS
Also Called: Quality Engraving and Signs
1318 County Road 416 (38851-7667)
PHONE...................................662 456-7080
Eddie Wiggs, *Owner*
EMP: 1
SALES (est): 67.3K **Privately Held**
SIC: 3993 3479 7389 Name plates: except engraved, etched, etc.: metal; etching & engraving; engraving service

(G-2240)
FRANKLIN CORPORATION (PA)
600 Franklin Dr (38851-8724)
P.O. Box 569 (38851-0569)
PHONE...................................662 456-5771
Hassell H Franklin, *Ch of Bd*
Mark Franklin, *President*
Lanny Glover, *General Mgr*
Daniel Holley, *Vice Pres*
Bart Munlin, *Technical Mgr*
◆ **EMP:** 1000
SQ FT: 1,000,000
SALES (est): 238.4MM **Privately Held**
WEB: www.franklincorp.com
SIC: 2512 Recliners: upholstered on wood frames; couches, sofas & davenports: upholstered on wood frames; living room furniture: upholstered on wood frames

(G-2241)
FRANKLIN CORPORATION
600 Franklin Dr (38851-8724)
P.O. Box 569 (38851-0569)
PHONE...................................662 456-4286
Bobby Willhite, *Manager*
EMP: 300
SALES (corp-wide): 238.4MM **Privately Held**
WEB: www.franklincorp.com
SIC: 2512 Upholstered household furniture
PA: Franklin Corporation
600 Franklin Dr
Houston MS 38851
662 456-5771

(G-2242)
FRANKLIN DEVELOPMENT CO LLC
602 Franklin Dr (38851)
PHONE...................................662 456-5771
Jeffrey Cox, *CFO*
EMP: 2
SALES (est): 212.1K **Privately Held**
SIC: 2512 Upholstered household furniture

(G-2243)
GRIND
111 N Jackson St (38851-2212)
PHONE...................................662 567-5211
EMP: 2
SALES (est): 158.1K **Privately Held**
SIC: 3599 Grinding castings for the trade

(G-2244)
HARRELL WELDING SERVICE LLC
1654 Highway 8 W (38851-8655)
PHONE...................................662 456-2444
David Harrell, *Mng Member*
EMP: 1
SALES (est): 120.2K **Privately Held**
SIC: 7692 Welding repair

(G-2245)
HOUSTON NEWSPAPERS INC (HQ)
Also Called: Monitor-Herald, The
225 E Madison St (38851-2320)
PHONE...................................662 456-3771
Lisa Boyles, *President*
Gary Andrews, *General Mgr*
EMP: 12 **EST:** 1945

SALES (est): 915.3K
SALES (corp-wide): 95.3MM **Privately Held**
SIC: 2711 Commercial printing & newspaper publishing combined
PA: Boone Newspapers, Inc.
1060 Fairfax Park Ste B
Tuscaloosa AL 35406
205 330-4100

(G-2246)
INTERNATIONAL PAPER COMPANY
511 3rd St (38851-1106)
P.O. Box 431 (38851-0431)
PHONE...................................662 456-4251
Bob Bamer, *General Mgr*
Scott Doss, *Engineer*
Johnnie Hopper, *Human Res Mgr*
Bob Bammer, *Manager*
Rick Campbell, *Manager*
EMP: 150
SALES (corp-wide): 23.3B **Publicly Held**
WEB: www.internationalpaper.com
SIC: 2621 Paper mills
PA: International Paper Company
6400 Poplar Ave
Memphis TN 38197
901 419-9000

(G-2247)
J&H PRINTING INC
219 N Jackson St (38851-2214)
PHONE...................................662 456-3654
Fax: 662 456-3655
EMP: 4
SALES (est): 250K **Privately Held**
SIC: 2752 Lithographic Commercial Printing

(G-2248)
JOURNAL PUBLISHING HOUSTON
225 E Madison St (38851-2320)
PHONE...................................662 456-3771
William Crews, *Principal*
EMP: 2
SALES (est): 98.4K **Privately Held**
SIC: 2711 Newspapers, publishing & printing

(G-2249)
LEGGETT & PLATT INCORPORATED
Also Called: Leggett & Platt 1704
600 3rd Ave (38851-1337)
P.O. Box 408 (38851-0408)
PHONE...................................662 456-3053
Pat Easley, *Transptn Dir*
David Nelson, *Plant Mgr*
EMP: 92
SQ FT: 550,000
SALES (corp-wide): 4.2B **Publicly Held**
SIC: 2515 Mattresses, innerspring or box spring
PA: Leggett & Platt, Incorporated
1 Leggett Rd
Carthage MO 64836
417 358-8131

(G-2250)
LONGLEAF FOREST PRODUCTS LLC
1538 Ms 15 (38851)
P.O. Box 307 (38851-0307)
PHONE...................................662 456-4444
Joey Ferguson, *President*
EMP: 1
SALES (est): 233.2K **Privately Held**
SIC: 2431 2499 Woodwork, interior & ornamental; decorative wood & woodwork

(G-2251)
MOSS WOODTURNING INC
1560 County Road 405 (38851-9759)
PHONE...................................662 456-5043
Greg Moss, *President*
Carol Moss, *Corp Secy*
EMP: 9
SALES: 490K **Privately Held**
SIC: 2426 Turnings, furniture: wood

(G-2252)
OAK WOOD MILLS INC
130 County Road 27 (38851-9796)
PHONE...................................662 542-9158
James Kilgore, *President*
EMP: 5
SALES: 250K **Privately Held**
SIC: 2426 Frames for upholstered furniture, wood

(G-2253)
OLIGARCH INC
202 County Road 162 (38851-9737)
PHONE...................................844 321-0016
Devonta Jenkins, *President*
EMP: 2 **EST:** 2015
SALES (est): 223.3K **Privately Held**
SIC: 5044 5045 3524 5122 Office equipment; computers, peripherals & software; lawn & garden equipment; toiletries; surgical instruments & apparatus; stationery & office supplies

(G-2254)
STEELPRO LLC
120 Wright Rd (38851-2000)
P.O. Box 698 (38851-0698)
PHONE...................................662 456-3004
Jeremy Harrell, *Mng Member*
EMP: 22
SQ FT: 1,200
SALES: 2.5MM **Privately Held**
SIC: 3441 Fabricated structural metal

(G-2255)
TERRA INDUSTRIES INC
606 Franklin Dr (38851-8724)
PHONE...................................662 456-3076
Barry Shankle, *Manager*
EMP: 22
SALES (corp-wide): 4.4B **Publicly Held**
WEB: www.terraindustries.com
SIC: 2875 5191 Fertilizers, mixing only; farm supplies; fertilizer & fertilizer materials; feed
HQ: Terra Industries Inc.
600 4th St Fl 8
Sioux City IA 51101
712 943-5501

(G-2256)
TRACE INDUSTRIES INC
500 2nd Ave (38851-1334)
PHONE...................................662 456-4261
Louis Rowland, *President*
John Rowland, *Corp Secy*
Paul Uhiren, *Vice Pres*
▲ **EMP:** 50 **EST:** 1970
SQ FT: 40,000
SALES (est): 7.1MM **Privately Held**
SIC: 2299 2297 2221 Felts & felt products; nonwoven fabrics; broadwoven fabric mills, manmade

(G-2257)
U S PLASTICS INC
242 Industrial Dr (38851-7230)
P.O. Box 152 (38851-0152)
PHONE...................................662 456-5551
Wallace Norman Jr, *President*
John C Norman, *Vice Pres*
EMP: 35 **EST:** 1969
SQ FT: 20,000
SALES (est): 6.6MM **Privately Held**
WEB: www.usplastics.net
SIC: 3083 Laminated plastics plate & sheet

(G-2258)
WARE MILLING INC
150 A F L Dr (38851-8722)
P.O. Box 386 (38851-0386)
PHONE...................................662 456-9032
Richard Ware, *President*
EMP: 10
SALES (est): 1.7MM **Privately Held**
SIC: 2048 Livestock feeds

Hurley
Jackson County

(G-2259)
CHESSER PUBLISHING LLC
7064 Joe Rubino Rd (39555)
PHONE...................................228 588-1111
EMP: 2 **EST:** 2009
SALES (est): 89K **Privately Held**
SIC: 2741 Misc Publishing

(G-2260)
HURLEY FARM & FEED
7000 Hwy 614 (39555)
P.O. Box 601 (39555-0601)
PHONE...................................228 588-9156
Dean Tanner, *Owner*
EMP: 3
SQ FT: 2,400
SALES: 790K **Privately Held**
SIC: 5191 3546 Farm supplies; saws & sawing equipment

Indianola
Sunflower County

(G-2261)
B & H HILL FARM LLC
631 W Gresham St (38751-2049)
PHONE...................................662 207-7197
Barbara Hill,
EMP: 3
SALES (est): 91.3K **Privately Held**
SIC: 2075 Lecithin, soybean

(G-2262)
BAADER NORTH AMERICA CORP
505 Hwy 82 Ste A (38751)
PHONE...................................662 887-5841
Larry Downes, *Manager*
EMP: 3
SALES (corp-wide): 64.9MM **Privately Held**
SIC: 3556 Smokers, food processing equipment
HQ: Baader North America Corporation
2955 Fairfax Trfy
Kansas City KS 66115
913 621-3366

(G-2263)
DOLLYS STAINED GLASS
309 Highway 82 E Ste 29a (38751-2236)
PHONE...................................662 887-3624
EMP: 1 **EST:** 1997
SALES (est): 97K **Privately Held**
SIC: 5231 3229 Ret Stained Glass

(G-2264)
ENTERPRISE-TOCSIN
114 Main St (38751-2844)
P.O. Box 650 (38751-0650)
PHONE...................................662 887-2222
Wayne Parhan, *President*
EMP: 6 **EST:** 1980
SQ FT: 1,680
SALES (est): 404.7K **Privately Held**
SIC: 2711 Newspapers, publishing & printing

(G-2265)
INDI-BEL INC
Also Called: Delta Western
1842 Highway 82 W (38751-2084)
P.O. Box 878 (38751-0878)
PHONE...................................662 887-1226
Lester W Myers, *President*
A Turner Arant, *Corp Secy*
Kathy F Anderson, *Vice Pres*
Donna Trippe, *Vice Pres*
Liane Myers, *Human Resources*
EMP: 65 **EST:** 1978
SQ FT: 24,000
SALES (est): 15.7MM **Privately Held**
SIC: 2048 Fish food

(PA)=Parent Co (HQ)=Headquarters (DH)=Div Headquarters
✿ = New Business established in last 2 years

2019 Harris Directory of
Mississippi Manufacturers

87

Indianola - Sunflower County (G-2266)

GEOGRAPHIC SECTION

(G-2266)
INDIANOLA ELECTRIC CO INC
352 Hwy 49 N (38751)
P.O. Box 1655 (38751-1655)
PHONE..................662 887-3292
Chris McClain, *President*
Vanessa Harris, *Vice Pres*
EMP: 12 **EST:** 1981
SALES: 1.5MM **Privately Held**
SIC: 7694 1731 Armature rewinding shops; electrical work

(G-2267)
INDIANOLA PECAN HOUSE INC (PA)
1013 Highway 82 E (38751-2327)
P.O. Box 367 (38751-0367)
PHONE..................662 887-5420
Wheeler Timbs III, *President*
Ann Timbs, *Corp Secy*
Wheeler Timbs Jr, *Vice Pres*
EMP: 28 **EST:** 1974
SQ FT: 5,000
SALES (est): 10.6MM **Privately Held**
WEB: www.pecanhouse.com
SIC: 2068 Nuts: dried, dehydrated, salted or roasted

(G-2268)
JENNINGS & JENNINGS INC
1273 Highway 82 E (38751-2310)
P.O. Box 368 (38751-0368)
PHONE..................662 887-1870
William Jennings, *President*
Paula Jennings, *Vice Pres*
EMP: 1
SALES: 700K
SALES (corp-wide): 750K **Privately Held**
SIC: 7692 Welding repair
PA: Jennings Welding & Machine Works, Inc
1273 Highway 82 E
Indianola MS 38751
662 887-1870

(G-2269)
JENNINGS WELDING & MCH WORKS (PA)
1273 Highway 82 E (38751-2310)
P.O. Box 368 (38751-0368)
PHONE..................662 887-1870
William M Jennings Jr, *President*
Paula Jennings, *Corp Secy*
EMP: 8
SALES: 750K **Privately Held**
SIC: 3599 7692 Machine shop, jobbing & repair; welding repair

(G-2270)
SLATERS JIGS INC
Also Called: Slaters Quality Outdoor Pdts
185 Beaverdam Rd (38751-2654)
PHONE..................662 887-3548
James Edward Slater, *President*
Kay J Slater, *Admin Sec*
▲ **EMP:** 7 **EST:** 1971
SQ FT: 10,900
SALES (est): 811.5K **Privately Held**
WEB: www.slatersjigs.com
SIC: 3949 5941 Fishing tackle, general; hunting equipment

(G-2271)
US OIL RECOVERY LLC
1136 Highway 49 S (38751-2401)
PHONE..................662 884-1050
EMP: 3
SALES (est): 169.1K **Privately Held**
SIC: 1311 Crude Petroleum/Natural Gas Production

Inverness
Sunflower County

(G-2272)
ALABAMA CATFISH INC
Also Called: Harvest Select Catfish
83 Goldkist Ln (38753)
PHONE..................662 265-5377
Clint Dees, *Manager*
EMP: 16 **Privately Held**
SIC: 2092 Fresh or frozen packaged fish

PA: Alabama Catfish, Inc
1260 Washington St Hwy 80
Uniontown AL 36786

(G-2273)
BELL EQUIPMENT LLC
800 Moore St (38753)
P.O. Box 223 (38753-0223)
PHONE..................662 265-5841
Marion Towery, *President*
Todd Barbee, *Manager*
EMP: 24
SALES (est): 2.7MM **Privately Held**
SIC: 3523 Cabs, tractors & agricultural machinery

(G-2274)
BELL INC
Hwy 49 W (38753)
P.O. Box 223 (38753-0223)
PHONE..................662 265-5841
Marion Towery, *President*
Lawrence Long, *Shareholder*
Scott Poindexter, *Shareholder*
James Roberston Jr, *Shareholder*
Bruce Brumfield, *Admin Sec*
EMP: 28 **EST:** 1958
SQ FT: 18,100
SALES: 3.3MM **Privately Held**
WEB: www.bellinc.net
SIC: 3523 3531 Trailers & wagons, farm; harrows: disc, spring, tine, etc.; sprayers & spraying machines, agricultural; fertilizing machinery, farm; construction machinery

(G-2275)
MOSSY ISLAND LAND & FOREST LLC
657 Woodburn Rd (38753)
PHONE..................662 207-6245
Lewis Poindexter,
EMP: 6 **EST:** 2014
SALES (est): 274.1K **Privately Held**
SIC: 2411 Driving & booming timber

(G-2276)
PINNACLE AGRICULTURE DIST INC
1009 First St (38753-9703)
P.O. Box 264 (38753-0264)
PHONE..................662 265-5828
Bill Kennedy, *Branch Mgr*
EMP: 7
SALES (corp-wide): 1.1B **Privately Held**
SIC: 5191 5999 5261 2879 Insecticides; herbicides; fertilizer & fertilizer materials; seeds: field, garden & flower; insecticides; garden supplies & tools; fertilizer; nursery stock, seeds & bulbs; agricultural chemicals; fertilizers, mixing only
HQ: Pinnacle Agriculture Distribution, Inc.
1880 Fall Rver Dr Ste 100
Loveland CO 80538
970 800-4300

Isola
Humphreys County

(G-2277)
CONSOLDTED CTFISH CMPANIES LLC (PA)
Also Called: Country Select Catfish
299 South St (38754-9405)
P.O. Box 271 (38754-0271)
PHONE..................662 962-3101
Frank Davis, *Vice Pres*
Jack Perkins, *Vice Pres*
David Gray, *CFO*
David Allen, *Sales Staff*
Kim Cox, *Marketing Staff*
▲ **EMP:** 350
SQ FT: 140,000
SALES (est): 133.5MM **Privately Held**
SIC: 2092 Fish, fresh: prepared

(G-2278)
CONSOLDTED CTFISH PRDUCERS LLC
Also Called: Country Select Catfish
299 South St (38754-9405)
P.O. Box 271 (38754-0271)
PHONE..................662 962-3101
Richard D Stevens,
Lee Henry, *Maintence Staff*
David Gray,
EMP: 400
SALES (est): 62MM **Privately Held**
SIC: 2092 Fresh or frozen packaged fish
PA: Consolidated Catfish Companies, Llc
299 South St
Isola MS 38754

Itta Bena
Leflore County

(G-2279)
BELLS IRON WORKS
321 Mitchell St (38941-2110)
PHONE..................662 254-7413
William Bell, *Owner*
EMP: 1 **EST:** 1995
SALES (est): 102.7K **Privately Held**
SIC: 3634 Irons, electric: household

(G-2280)
HEARTLAND CATFISH COMPANY INC
55001 Highway 82 W (38941-9613)
PHONE..................662 254-7100
Danny Walker, *CEO*
William Tackett, *President*
Joseph A Walker, *President*
Johnny Jarrell, *Regional Mgr*
Brian L Crawford, *Corp Secy*
EMP: 415
SQ FT: 135,000
SALES (est): 86.1MM **Privately Held**
WEB: www.heartlandcatfish.com
SIC: 2092 Fresh or frozen packaged fish

(G-2281)
ITTA BENA PLANTATION III
33725 County Road 507 (38941-2384)
PHONE..................662 254-7274
Mark Kimmel, *Partner*
EMP: 8
SALES (est): 682.1K **Privately Held**
SIC: 3151 Mittens, leather

(G-2282)
MOBILE COMMUNICATIONS LLC
801 County Road 138 (38941-2309)
PHONE..................662 570-4858
Bobby Norwood,
EMP: 4
SALES (est): 516.5K **Privately Held**
SIC: 2741

Iuka
Tishomingo County

(G-2283)
AMC SIGNS & LIGHTING LLC
2304 Highway 25 (38852-6352)
PHONE..................901 831-7393
Brian Moore, *Principal*
EMP: 1
SALES (est): 46K **Privately Held**
SIC: 3993 Signs & advertising specialties

(G-2284)
ATK SPACE SYSTEMS INC
Also Called: Atk Aerospace Structures Div
751 County Road 989 Fl 1 (38852-6514)
P.O. Box 990 (38852-0990)
PHONE..................662 423-7700
Ann Davidson, *Principal*
EMP: 50 **Publicly Held**
WEB: www.psi-pci.com
SIC: 3769 3728 Guided missile & space vehicle parts & auxiliary equipment; aircraft parts & equipment

HQ: Atk Space Systems Inc.
6033 Bandini Blvd
Commerce CA 90040
323 722-0222

(G-2285)
BERRY INC
134 County Road 244 (38852-6940)
PHONE..................662 423-1984
Lance Berry, *President*
EMP: 1
SALES (est): 76.4K **Privately Held**
SIC: 7692 Welding repair

(G-2286)
CASTERS DEN
123 E Front St (38852-2324)
PHONE..................662 593-3214
EMP: 3
SALES (est): 164.5K **Privately Held**
SIC: 3562 Casters

(G-2287)
CONTRACT FABRICATORS INC
27 County Road 480 (38852-6940)
PHONE..................662 424-0061
Dustin Smith, *Principal*
Christa Smith, *General Counsel*
EMP: 23
SALES (corp-wide): 33.6MM **Privately Held**
SIC: 3312 Blast furnaces & steel mills
PA: Contract Fabricators, Inc.
105 Rolfing Rd
Holly Springs MS 38635
662 252-6330

(G-2288)
CUTSHALL D L & SONS LOGGING CO
79 County Road 299 (38852-6613)
PHONE..................662 423-6965
Douglas Lee Cutshall, *President*
Irene Cutshall, *Vice Pres*
EMP: 7 **EST:** 1971
SALES (est): 791.3K **Privately Held**
SIC: 2411 4213 Pulpwood contractors engaged in cutting; heavy hauling

(G-2289)
DAVIS WELDING LLC
537 County Road 956 (38852-8032)
PHONE..................662 423-2911
William Davis, *Principal*
EMP: 1
SALES (est): 44K **Privately Held**
SIC: 7692 Welding repair

(G-2290)
ENCORE PRODUCTS
119 S Fulton St (38852-2328)
PHONE..................662 423-3484
Charles Emmons, *Owner*
EMP: 1
SALES (est): 99.5K **Privately Held**
SIC: 2759 Screen printing

(G-2291)
ENLOW & SON INC
Also Called: Allstar
2243 Highway 25 (38852-6349)
PHONE..................662 423-9073
Donathan Enlow, *President*
EMP: 3
SALES: 150K **Privately Held**
SIC: 2421 Sawmills & planing mills, general

(G-2292)
H & H SMALL ENGINE REPAIR
1109 Battleground Dr (38852-1022)
PHONE..................662 423-2741
Rick Higginbottom, *Owner*
EMP: 2
SQ FT: 1,000
SALES: 250K **Privately Held**
SIC: 5999 7699 3546 Engine & motor equipment & supplies; lawn mower repair shop; saws & sawing equipment

(G-2293)
HAGO AUTOMOTIVE CORP
11 County Road 481 (38852-6800)
PHONE..................662 593-0491
Joerg Goeppert, *President*

2019 Harris Directory of
Mississippi Manufacturers

88

▲ = Import ▼=Export
◆ =Import/Export

GEOGRAPHIC SECTION

Jackson - Hinds County (G-2320)

EMP: 18
SALES (est): 1.1MM
SALES (corp-wide): 355.8K **Privately Held**
SIC: 1799 3465 Welding on site; automotive stampings
HQ: Feinwerktechnik Hago Gmbh
Unter Greut 4
Kussaberg 79790
774 160-030

(G-2294)
IUKA CONCRETE PRODUCTS LLC
1679 Constitution Dr (38852-7002)
PHONE..................................662 423-6238
Kelly Milligan, *Plant Mgr*
Hollie Milligan, *Mng Member*
Cory R Lancaster,
EMP: 3
SALES (est): 128.1K **Privately Held**
SIC: 3273 Ready-mixed concrete

(G-2295)
JC JOURDAN LUMBER CO INC
418 Cunty Rd 995 Arprt Rd (38852)
P.O. Box 300 (38852-0300)
PHONE..................................662 423-5238
David O Jourdan III, *Corp Secy*
EMP: 16
SQ FT: 13,350
SALES: 1.6MM **Privately Held**
SIC: 2421 5031 2448 2631 Planing mills; lumber: rough, dressed & finished; pallets, wood; container, packaging & boxboard

(G-2296)
JERRY S TROLLING MOTOR REPAIR
586 County Road 989 (38852-8561)
PHONE..................................256 431-6564
EMP: 2
SALES (est): 87.9K **Privately Held**
SIC: 3732 Non-motorized boat, building & repairing

(G-2297)
KX TECHNOLOGIES LLC
36 Wild Rose Dr (38852-7603)
PHONE..................................662 601-4140
Michael Baker, *Manager*
EMP: 50
SALES (corp-wide): 225.3B **Publicly Held**
SIC: 3589 Water purification equipment, household type
HQ: Kx Technologies Llc
55 Railroad Ave
West Haven CT 06516

(G-2298)
LARRYS EQUIPMENT INC
205 County Road 176 (38852-6734)
PHONE..................................662 423-0077
Larry Knoepflein, *President*
Emily Knoepflein, *Treasurer*
EMP: 4
SQ FT: 6,000
SALES: 500K **Privately Held**
SIC: 5087 5082 7692 Service establishment equipment; construction & mining machinery; welding repair

(G-2299)
MAX HOME LLC
1509 Paul Edmondson Dr (38852-1211)
PHONE..................................662 424-0005
Jimmy Gearren, *General Mgr*
Jim Garron, *Principal*
EMP: 2
SALES (est): 146.7K **Privately Held**
SIC: 2599 Furniture & fixtures

(G-2300)
MILLIGAN READY MIX INC
1679 Constitution Dr (38852-7002)
PHONE..................................662 423-6238
Kirk K Milligan Sr, *President*
Holly Milligan, *Admin Secy*
EMP: 14 **EST:** 1959
SQ FT: 1,700
SALES: 2MM **Privately Held**
SIC: 3273 Ready-mixed concrete

(G-2301)
MOBLEY AUTO SERVICE
821 County Road 172 (38852-7126)
PHONE..................................662 423-3516
Kenneth Mobley, *Owner*
Angela Mobley, *Co-Owner*
EMP: 1
SALES: 25K **Privately Held**
SIC: 7694 Electric motor repair

(G-2302)
MONOTECH OF MISSISSIPPI
27 County Road 342 (38852-8448)
PHONE..................................662 862-2978
Andy Easton, *Branch Mgr*
EMP: 5
SALES (corp-wide): 244.7MM **Privately Held**
SIC: 7692 Welding repair
HQ: Monotech Of Mississippi
27 County Road 342
Iuka MS 38852
662 423-2033

(G-2303)
MONOTECH OF MISSISSIPPI (DH)
27 County Road 342 (38852-8448)
PHONE..................................662 423-2033
Roger Schwab, *Ch of Bd*
Andrew Easton, *President*
Dennis Stirm, *Vice Pres*
Roy Stokes, *Vice Pres*
EMP: 180
SQ FT: 112,000
SALES (est): 20.9MM
SALES (corp-wide): 244.7MM **Privately Held**
SIC: 3569 Filters
HQ: Psp Industries, Inc.
9885 Doerr Ln
Schertz TX 78154
210 651-9595

(G-2304)
PACKAGING DYNAMICS CORPORATION
1309 Paul Edmondson Dr (38852-1210)
PHONE..................................662 424-4000
Brandon Cox, *QC Mgr*
Keith Wooley, *Branch Mgr*
EMP: 48
SALES (corp-wide): 2.9B **Privately Held**
SIC: 2621 2672 3353 Specialty papers; coated & laminated paper; foil, aluminum
HQ: Packaging Dynamics Corporation
3900 W 43rd St
Chicago IL 60632
773 254-8000

(G-2305)
PROP STRAIGHTENERS INC
2080 Paul Edmondson Dr (38852-1213)
PHONE..................................662 423-9588
Hoyt Peden, *President*
Kerry Peden, *Vice Pres*
EMP: 2
SALES (est): 194K **Privately Held**
SIC: 3732 Motorboats, inboard or outboard: building & repairing

(G-2306)
PSP INDUSTRIES INC
27 County Road 342 (38852-8448)
PHONE..................................662 423-2033
Wes Howell, *Owner*
EMP: 4
SALES (corp-wide): 244.7MM **Privately Held**
SIC: 3533 Oil & gas field machinery
HQ: Psp Industries, Inc.
9885 Doerr Ln
Schertz TX 78154
210 651-9595

(G-2307)
RIPLEY INDUSTRIES INC
Filter Division
1409 Paul Edmondson Dr (38852-1200)
PHONE..................................662 423-6733
Fax: 662 423-1874
EMP: 40

SALES (corp-wide): 8MM **Privately Held**
SIC: 3569 3496 5085 Mfg General Industrial Machinery Mfg Misc Fabricated Wire Products Whol Industrial Supplies
PA: Ripley Industries, Inc.
575 N Maple St
Adamsville TN 38310
731 632-3328

(G-2308)
SAMUEL SON & CO (USA) INC (HQ)
Also Called: Samuel Roll Form Group
26 County Road 351 (38852-7481)
PHONE..................................662 424-1460
Mark C Samuel, *President*
Rick Balaz, *Principal*
Gary C Pang, *Vice Pres*
John Megson, *Credit Mgr*
▼ EMP: 47
SQ FT: 1,000
SALES (est): 16.5MM
SALES (corp-wide): 1.8B **Privately Held**
WEB: www.rollformgroup.com
SIC: 3324 Steel investment foundries
PA: Samuel, Son & Co., Limited
2360 Dixie Rd
Mississauga ON L4Y 1
905 279-5460

(G-2309)
TIMBERLINE LOGGING INC
355 County Road 982 (38852-8266)
P.O. Box 78, Burnsville (38833-0078)
PHONE..................................662 423-3948
Brian Hickox, *President*
EMP: 14 **EST:** 2001
SALES (est): 1.9MM **Privately Held**
SIC: 2411 Driving & booming timber

(G-2310)
TISHOMINGO COUNTY NEWS INC
Also Called: Vidette-Belmont News
120 W Front St (38852-2325)
P.O. Box 70 (38852-0070)
PHONE..................................662 423-2211
John H Biggs, *President*
EMP: 10 **EST:** 1969
SQ FT: 2,250
SALES (est): 562.9K **Privately Held**
SIC: 2711 Newspapers: publishing only, not printed on site

(G-2311)
WATER-WAY INC
751 County Road 989 # 1010 (38852-6514)
P.O. Box 418 (38852-0418)
PHONE..................................662 423-0081
Bob Tiffin, *President*
Jim Shillito, *General Mgr*
Ken Hardwick, *CFO*
Tommy Hardwick, *Admin Sec*
EMP: 45
SQ FT: 126,500
SALES (est): 17MM **Privately Held**
SIC: 3088 Shower stalls, fiberglass & plastic

Jackson
Hinds County

(G-2312)
1 A LIFESAFER INC
852 Foley St (39202-3404)
PHONE..................................800 634-3077
EMP: 1
SALES (corp-wide): 4.3MM **Privately Held**
SIC: 3829 Measuring & controlling devices
PA: 1 A Lifesafer, Inc.
4290 Glendale Milford Rd
Blue Ash OH 45242
513 651-9560

(G-2313)
10 BELOW LLC
1335 Ellis Ave (39204-2235)
PHONE..................................769 243-8705
EMP: 2

SALES (corp-wide): 5.4MM **Privately Held**
SIC: 2299 Jute & flax textile products
PA: 10 Below Llc
2500 Crestwood Blvd
Irondale AL 35210
205 703-0910

(G-2314)
A PLUS SIGNS INC
4147 Northview Plz Ste B (39206-5259)
PHONE..................................601 355-9595
Dale Howie, *President*
EMP: 8
SQ FT: 7,500
SALES (est): 1.1MM **Privately Held**
WEB: www.aplusigns.com
SIC: 3993 Signs & advertising specialties

(G-2315)
A PLUS TORNADO SHELTERS O
3710 I 55 N (39211-6323)
PHONE..................................601 879-0005
Shelters Tornado, *Principal*
EMP: 4
SALES (est): 489.7K **Privately Held**
SIC: 3442 Screen & storm doors & windows

(G-2316)
A SQUARE INNOVATIVE SEC LLC
1230 Raymond Rd (39204-4583)
PHONE..................................601 937-0318
EMP: 4
SALES (est): 401.4K **Privately Held**
SIC: 3699 5065 7382 Security control equipment & systems; security control equipment & systems; protective devices, security

(G-2317)
A2Z PRINTING INC
2125 Tv Rd (39204-4025)
PHONE..................................601 487-1100
Keith Eady, *General Mgr*
Allen Taheri, *Principal*
Lisa Brown, *Project Mgr*
Cindy Minton, *Sales Mgr*
Cindy Mincon, *Sales Staff*
EMP: 18
SQ FT: 83,000
SALES (est): 2.1MM **Privately Held**
SIC: 2752 Commercial printing, offset

(G-2318)
ADAMS PRSTHTICS ORTHDNTICS LLC
931 Highway 80 W 173b (39204-3912)
PHONE..................................601 665-4000
Charleen Mitchell,
EMP: 8
SALES (est): 619.7K **Privately Held**
SIC: 3842 Prosthetic appliances

(G-2319)
ADDRESS AMERICA INC
5454 I 55 N (39211-4028)
PHONE..................................888 991-3322
David Ashley, *President*
Joshua Ashley, *Vice Pres*
Lynn Floyd, *Admin Sec*
Cherry Ashley, *Asst Sec*
▲ EMP: 7
SQ FT: 1,500
SALES: 1MM **Privately Held**
WEB: www.addressamerica.com
SIC: 3993 Signs & advertising specialties

(G-2320)
ADVANCED DRAINAGE SYSTEMS INC
205 Apache Dr (39272-9709)
PHONE..................................601 371-0678
Glen Carol, *Manager*
EMP: 76
SQ FT: 40,363
SALES (corp-wide): 1.3B **Publicly Held**
WEB: www.ads-pipe.com
SIC: 3084 Plastics pipe
PA: Advanced Drainage Systems, Inc.
4640 Trueman Blvd
Hilliard OH 43026
614 658-0050

(PA)=Parent Co (HQ)=Headquarters (DH)=Div Headquarters
✿ = New Business established in last 2 years

2019 Harris Directory of
Mississippi Manufacturers

89

Jackson - Hinds County (G-2321)

GEOGRAPHIC SECTION

(G-2321)
ALL SEASONS EVENTS
8117 Highway 18 W (39209-9219)
PHONE..................................601 405-1417
Robbie Covington, *Owner*
EMP: 6
SALES (est): 770.1K Privately Held
SIC: 2899 Fireworks

(G-2322)
ALL STAR FOREST PRODUCTS INC (PA)
5757 N Mcraven Rd (39209-5604)
P.O. Box 7538 (39284-7538)
PHONE..................................601 664-0700
William T Price, *President*
EMP: 9
SQ FT: 50,000
SALES (est): 6.5MM Privately Held
SIC: 5031 2448 Lumber, plywood & mill-work; wood pallets & skids

(G-2323)
ALL THAT GLITTERS EP INC
5968 Waverly Dr (39206-2506)
PHONE..................................601 981-1947
Tegan Smith-Cowan, *Principal*
EMP: 2
SALES (est): 69.9K Privately Held
SIC: 3471 Plating & polishing

(G-2324)
ALPHA PRINTING INC
2125 Tv Rd (39204-4025)
PHONE..................................601 371-2611
Robert E Smith, *President*
EMP: 7
SQ FT: 4,000
SALES (est): 1MM Privately Held
WEB: www.alphaprint.biz
SIC: 2752 2791 2789 Commercial printing, offset; typesetting; bookbinding & related work

(G-2325)
ALUMINUM RECYCLING OF MISS (PA)
Also Called: Can Man The
1819 Valley St (39204-2440)
PHONE..................................601 355-5777
John W Bussey Jr, *President*
Martin Fox, *Treasurer*
EMP: 30
SQ FT: 6,000
SALES (est): 8.5MM Privately Held
SIC: 5093 4953 3341 Metal scrap & waste materials; refuse systems; secondary nonferrous metals

(G-2326)
AMERICAN PAYMENT SYSTEMS
4329 N State St (39206-5261)
PHONE..................................601 368-7382
EMP: 2 EST: 2010
SALES (est): 100.4K Privately Held
SIC: 3629 Electronic generation equipment

(G-2327)
AMERICAN PAYMENT SYSTEMS
4110 Medgar Evers Blvd (39213-5207)
PHONE..................................601 713-3761
EMP: 2
SALES (est): 103.5K Privately Held
SIC: 3629 Electronic generation equipment

(G-2328)
AMERIMAC CHEMICAL CO (PA)
750 Boling St Ste J (39209-2652)
P.O. Box 1386 (39215-1386)
PHONE..................................601 918-8321
Dr Roland Powell Sr, *President*
Addie Powell, *Treasurer*
Sondra Powell, *Admin Sec*
EMP: 6
SQ FT: 1,100
SALES (est): 2.4MM Privately Held
SIC: 5169 2812 3452 Industrial chemicals; chlorine, compressed or liquefied; bolts, nuts, rivets & washers

(G-2329)
AMERIMAC MACHINING CORPORATION
750 Boling St Ste J (39209-2652)
PHONE..................................601 940-7919

Steven D Powell, *President*
EMP: 5
SQ FT: 3,500
SALES: 300K Privately Held
SIC: 3441 3599 1799 7692 Fabricated structural metal; machine shop, jobbing & repair; welding on site; welding repair; special dies, tools, jigs & fixtures

(G-2330)
AMERIMAC SYNERGY VETERANS LLC
931 Highway 80 W (39204-3912)
PHONE..................................601 326-3400
David Powell,
EMP: 2
SQ FT: 1,800
SALES (est): 86.3K Privately Held
SIC: 2879 Agricultural chemicals

(G-2331)
AMERSON CLEOPHUS JR
1603 Fairwood Dr (39213-7930)
PHONE..................................601 362-3629
Amerson Cleophus, *Owner*
Jacqueline G Jones, *Accountant*
EMP: 1
SALES (est): 66.4K Privately Held
SIC: 2591 Drapery hardware & blinds & shades

(G-2332)
APEX PRODUCTS INC (PA)
435 Cedars Of Lebanon Rd (39206-3606)
PHONE..................................601 992-5900
Terry Caves, *President*
Jean Caves, *Admin Sec*
EMP: 4 EST: 1960
SQ FT: 30,000
SALES (est): 2.2MM Privately Held
WEB: www.apexproducts.com
SIC: 3281 Marble, building: cut & shaped

(G-2333)
ARMSTRONG FLOORING INC
1085 Highway 80 W (39204-3919)
PHONE..................................601 354-1515
Dawit Teklai, *Plant Mgr*
EMP: 185
SALES (corp-wide): 728.2MM Publicly Held
WEB: www.armstrong.com
SIC: 5713 3996 3253 Floor covering stores; hard surface floor coverings; ceramic wall & floor tile
PA: Armstrong Flooring, Inc.
2500 Columbia Ave
Lancaster PA 17603
717 672-9611

(G-2334)
ASSOCIATED GEN CONTRS OF MISS (PA)
Also Called: AGC
2093 Lakeland Dr (39216-5010)
P.O. Box 12367 (39236-2367)
PHONE..................................601 981-1144
Hank Torjusen, *President*
Christy Simpson, *Accounts Mgr*
Marilyn Leiker, *Mktg Dir*
Perry L Nations, *Director*
Carl Dowden, *Director*
EMP: 7
SQ FT: 1,800
SALES: 843.5K Privately Held
WEB: www.msagc.com
SIC: 8611 2721 Contractors' association; periodicals

(G-2335)
BASF CORPORATION
600 E Mc Dowell Rd (39204)
P.O. Box 8337 (39284-8337)
PHONE..................................601 948-3966
Myron D Petruch, *Branch Mgr*
EMP: 145
SALES (corp-wide): 71.7B Privately Held
SIC: 2869 Industrial organic chemicals
HQ: Basf Corporation
100 Park Ave
Florham Park NJ 07932
973 245-6000

(G-2336)
BELGIQUE INC
752 Euclid Ave (39202-1105)
PHONE..................................601 368-1975
Fred R Ezelle, *President*
▲ EMP: 2
SALES (est): 166.9K Privately Held
SIC: 2273 Carpets & rugs

(G-2337)
BICKES INC
Also Called: Jackson Wilbert Burial Vlt Co
820 Larson St (39202-3416)
P.O. Box 569 (39205-0569)
PHONE..................................601 353-7083
Darwin May, *Manager*
EMP: 20
SALES (corp-wide): 8.5MM Privately Held
SIC: 3272 Burial vaults, concrete or precast terrazzo
PA: Bickes, Inc.
919 W Eldorado St
Decatur IL 62522
217 423-5839

(G-2338)
BISCO INDUSTRIES INC
4429 E Ridge Dr (39211-6114)
PHONE..................................601 991-3308
Don Wagner, *President*
EMP: 3
SALES (corp-wide): 193.2MM Publicly Held
SIC: 3999 Atomizers, toiletry
HQ: Bisco Industries, Inc.
1500 Lakeview Loop
Anaheim CA 92807
714 876-2400

(G-2339)
BMW PROSTHETICS ORTHOTICS LLC
1221 N West St (39202-2018)
PHONE..................................601 414-0032
Ned Mack, *Partner*
Nelson Wilson,
EMP: 50 EST: 2000
SQ FT: 3,200
SALES: 3.2MM Privately Held
SIC: 3842 Prosthetic appliances

(G-2340)
BOTTLE TREE BEVERAGE CO LLC
422 S Farish St (39201-5102)
P.O. Box 4917 (39296-4917)
PHONE..................................601 667-3038
Richard Patrick, *Mng Member*
Oustin Evans,
EMP: 10
SQ FT: 6,500
SALES (est): 366K Privately Held
SIC: 5169 2869 Alcohols; alcohols, non-beverage

(G-2341)
BOULDIN ESSENTIALS LLC
356 Sheppard Rd (39206-4037)
PHONE..................................769 216-7146
Katelyn Bouldin,
EMP: 1
SALES (est): 39.6K Privately Held
SIC: 3999 Hair & hair-based products

(G-2342)
BRAZOS BEND OIL AND GAS LLC
1837 Crane Ridge Dr (39216-4902)
PHONE..................................601 982-3444
EMP: 2 EST: 2017
SALES (est): 76.5K Privately Held
SIC: 1389 Oil & gas field services

(G-2343)
BREW BARR LLC
1485 Livingston Ln (39213-8004)
PHONE..................................601 218-7708
Mitchell Barrett, *Principal*
EMP: 1 EST: 2011
SALES (est): 60.8K Privately Held
SIC: 2741 Miscellaneous publishing

(G-2344)
BROWN BOTTLING GROUP INC
Also Called: Pepsico
2550 Medgar Evers Blvd (39213-7556)
PHONE..................................601 982-4160
Jason Sanderson, *CFO*
Jerry Stain, *Branch Mgr*
EMP: 170
SALES (corp-wide): 149.7MM Privately Held
SIC: 2086 5149 Soft drinks: packaged in cans, bottles, etc.; groceries & related products
PA: Brown Bottling Group, Inc.
591 Highland Colony Pkwy
Ridgeland MS 39157
601 607-3011

(G-2345)
BROWN BOTTLING GROUP INC
Also Called: Pepsico
535 Ford Ave (39209-2740)
PHONE..................................601 352-0366
Jim Wilson, *Manager*
EMP: 25
SALES (corp-wide): 149.7MM Privately Held
SIC: 3581 Automatic vending machines
PA: Brown Bottling Group, Inc.
591 Highland Colony Pkwy
Ridgeland MS 39157
601 607-3011

(G-2346)
BRUXOIL INC
1717 Bellewood Rd (39211-5702)
P.O. Box 16929 (39236-6929)
PHONE..................................601 981-5722
David K Brooks, *President*
Ray Helfrich, *Vice Pres*
Dorothy Jaubert, *Admin Sec*
EMP: 4
SALES (est): 314.9K Privately Held
SIC: 1311 Crude petroleum production; natural gas production

(G-2347)
BRYANTS MACHINE SHOP INC
5734 Highway 80 W (39209-3511)
P.O. Box 1239, Clinton (39060-1239)
PHONE..................................601 922-1937
Lavern G Bryant, *President*
EMP: 4
SQ FT: 500
SALES (est): 320K Privately Held
SIC: 3599 Machine shop, jobbing & repair

(G-2348)
BUDGET SIGNS INC
2358 Highway 80 W (39204-2312)
PHONE..................................601 354-4977
John Christopher Ray, *President*
Candace Ray, *Corp Secy*
Stephen Douglas, *Vice Pres*
EMP: 12
SQ FT: 3,200
SALES (est): 1.3MM Privately Held
SIC: 3993 Electric signs

(G-2349)
BURNS FENCE & WOODWORKS LLC
4233 E Ridge Dr (39211-6108)
PHONE..................................601 506-5226
EMP: 1
SALES (est): 54.1K Privately Held
SIC: 2431 Millwork

(G-2350)
BUSINESS & OFF KONNEXTIONS LLC
850 Foley St (39202-3404)
PHONE..................................601 965-5101
Patricia Reese,
Loretta Reese,
EMP: 1
SALES (est): 294.4K Privately Held
SIC: 2531 Public building & related furniture

(G-2351)
BUSINESS SYSTEMS INC
405 Briarwood Dr Ste 102b (39206-3029)
PHONE..................................601 957-1500
Graham Browne, *President*

2019 Harris Directory of
Mississippi Manufacturers

▲ = Import ▼=Export
◆ =Import/Export

90

GEOGRAPHIC SECTION

Jackson - Hinds County (G-2381)

Patricia Browne, *Corp Secy*
EMP: 6 **EST:** 1978
SQ FT: 1,200
SALES (est): 691.6K **Privately Held**
WEB: www.businesssystems.net
SIC: 5734 7372 7378 Computer peripheral equipment; prepackaged software; computer peripheral equipment repair & maintenance

(G-2352)
CABINET SPECIALISTS INC
1354 Winterview Dr (39211-3234)
PHONE..................................601 992-3929
Patricia C Jones, *President*
Charles A Jones, *Vice Pres*
EMP: 7
SALES: 120K **Privately Held**
SIC: 2434 Wood kitchen cabinets

(G-2353)
CARDINAL HEALTH 414 LLC
350 W Woodrow Wilson Ave (39213-7681)
PHONE..................................601 982-7345
Sharon Holmes, *Director*
EMP: 9
SALES (corp-wide): 145.5B **Publicly Held**
SIC: 2835 2834 Radioactive diagnostic substances; pharmaceutical preparations
HQ: Cardinal Health 414, Llc
7000 Cardinal Pl
Dublin OH 43017
614 757-5000

(G-2354)
CAREYS CONSTRUCTION CO INC
5247 Greenway Drive Ext A (39204-3204)
P.O. Box 7664 (39284-7664)
PHONE..................................601 922-7388
Carey Alexander, *President*
Inez Alexander, *Treasurer*
EMP: 20
SQ FT: 6,000
SALES (est): 3.7MM **Privately Held**
SIC: 1791 3441 Structural steel erection; fabricated structural metal

(G-2355)
CAT HEAD DISTILLERY LLC
644 Church Rd Ste 1 (39296)
P.O. Box 4917 (39296-4917)
PHONE..................................601 954-8207
Austin Evans, *Principal*
Taylor Leatherwood, *Manager*
EMP: 7
SALES (est): 530.8K **Privately Held**
SIC: 2085 Distilled & blended liquors

(G-2356)
CECO CORP
Also Called: Ceco Developement
145 Brae Burn Dr (39211-2503)
PHONE..................................601 362-4737
Cecil F Heidelberg III, *President*
Randy Peets, *Personnel*
Steve Edwards, *Sales Mgr*
EMP: 2
SQ FT: 1,000
SALES (est): 209.3K **Privately Held**
SIC: 1382 Oil & gas exploration services

(G-2357)
CENTRAL DELTA CMNTY DEV CORP
1023 Voorhees Ave (39209)
PHONE..................................601 215-0367
Ronnie Walker, *Principal*
EMP: 1
SALES (est): 60K **Privately Held**
SIC: 7699 8011 3577 Hospital equipment repair services; medical centers; computer peripheral equipment

(G-2358)
CHEMICAL PRODUCTS & SYSTEMS
124 W South St (39201-6144)
P.O. Box 3816 (39207-3816)
PHONE..................................601 354-1919
Timothy Turner, *President*
John Turner Jr, *Managing Prtnr*
EMP: 3
SQ FT: 4,500

SALES: 500K **Privately Held**
SIC: 5087 5169 2841 Janitors' supplies; detergents & soaps, except specialty cleaning; dishwashing compounds

(G-2359)
CHEP (USA) INC
750 Boling St (39209-2652)
P.O. Box 1157 (39215-1157)
PHONE..................................601 352-6500
David Rings, *Manager*
EMP: 32 **Privately Held**
WEB: www.ifcosystems.com
SIC: 2448 Pallets, wood
HQ: Chep (U.S.A.) Inc.
5897 Windward Pkwy
Alpharetta GA 30005
770 668-8100

(G-2360)
CINTAS CORPORATION NO 2
5530 Industrial Rd (39209-4553)
PHONE..................................601 923-8664
Jason Skrmetti, *General Mgr*
EMP: 90
SALES (corp-wide): 6.8B **Publicly Held**
WEB: www.cintas-corp.com
SIC: 3589 Shredders, industrial & commercial
HQ: Cintas Corporation No. 2
6800 Cintas Blvd
Mason OH 45040

(G-2361)
COLE TEMPRA HELMET & VEST LLC
707 Barwood Ct (39212-2001)
PHONE..................................601 317-3842
David Cole,
EMP: 1
SALES (est): 57.2K **Privately Held**
SIC: 2389 Apparel & accessories

(G-2362)
COMET STREET INC
5170 Galaxie Dr (39206-4308)
P.O. Box 13609 (39236-3609)
PHONE..................................601 981-4151
H G Voelkel Jr, *Treasurer*
Jackie Blackwell, *Director*
Matthew L Holleman III, *Director*
EMP: 10
SALES (est): 1.1MM **Privately Held**
SIC: 3559 Petroleum refinery equipment

(G-2363)
CONCEPTUAL DESIGNS INC
4205 W Northside Dr (39209-2519)
PHONE..................................601 923-9922
William G Dunigan, *President*
Ashley Seutze, *Vice Pres*
EMP: 13
SQ FT: 4,800
SALES (est): 2MM **Privately Held**
SIC: 2541 Counter & sink tops; table or counter tops, plastic laminated

(G-2364)
CONFLUX SOFTWARE LLC
338 Wildwood Blvd (39212-9612)
PHONE..................................601 940-0182
Stephen Handley,
EMP: 1
SALES: 20K **Privately Held**
SIC: 7372 Prepackaged software

(G-2365)
CONNECT TECHNOLOGY LLC
Also Called: Connect Software Development
18 Northtown Dr Ste C (39211-3016)
PHONE..................................601 914-1713
John Welch, *President*
Tony Bailey,
EMP: 7
SQ FT: 500
SALES: 500K **Privately Held**
SIC: 7371 7372 Computer software development; application computer software; business oriented computer software

(G-2366)
CONSUMER PRODUCTS AMERICA LLC
119 W Mayes St (39213-6212)
P.O. Box 11278 (39283-1278)
PHONE..................................601 613-8583
Earl Washington,
EMP: 4
SALES: 112K **Privately Held**
SIC: 2386 Hats & caps, leather

(G-2367)
CONTROL SYSTEMS INC
909 Quinn St (39202-2740)
P.O. Box 4852 (39296-4852)
PHONE..................................601 355-8594
John Wilkes, *President*
Bobby J Gill, *Vice Pres*
EMP: 25
SQ FT: 7,000
SALES: 8.6MM **Privately Held**
WEB: www.controlsinc.com
SIC: 3625 Control equipment, electric

(G-2368)
COOPERATION JACKSON LLC
939 W Capitol St (39203-2632)
PHONE..................................601 355-7224
Iya'falola Omobola, *Director*
Dana Gonzalez,
EMP: 10 **EST:** 2014
SALES (est): 371.4K **Privately Held**
SIC: 1521 3531 5211 Single-family housing construction; rakes, land clearing: mechanical; insulation & energy conservation products

(G-2369)
COOPERS INTL SCREEN SUPPLY LLC
1404 Whiting Rd (39209-5821)
P.O. Box 452 (39205-0452)
PHONE..................................601 353-2488
Elijah Cooper,
EMP: 1 **EST:** 1974
SQ FT: 5,000
SALES (est): 180.8K **Privately Held**
SIC: 2752 2759 2789 2796 Commercial printing, offset; letterpress printing; binding only: books, pamphlets, magazines, etc.; engraving on copper, steel, wood or rubber: printing plates; writing supplies; office forms & supplies

(G-2370)
CORCORAN LEGAL GROUP
13 Northtown Dr Ste 100 (39211-3047)
P.O. Box 2091, Ridgeland (39158-2091)
PHONE..................................601 906-8227
Sean Corcoran, *CEO*
EMP: 2
SQ FT: 1,000
SALES (est): 72.6K **Privately Held**
SIC: 7372 Business oriented computer software

(G-2371)
COUNTRY SQUIRE
1855 Lakeland Dr Ste B10 (39216-4917)
PHONE..................................601 362-2233
Kim Owen, *Owner*
EMP: 2
SALES (est): 100K **Privately Held**
SIC: 2131 Smoking tobacco; snuff

(G-2372)
CUSTOM ACCOUNTING SOLUTIONS
23 Moss Forest Cir (39211-2906)
PHONE..................................601 957-7500
EMP: 1
SALES: 250K **Privately Held**
SIC: 7372 Prepackaged Software Services

(G-2373)
CYTEC SOFTWARE SYSTEMS INC (PA)
736 S President St (39201-5623)
PHONE..................................601 362-1612
Oscar De Leon, *CEO*
Jeffrey Futterman, *President*
EMP: 12
SQ FT: 12,000

SALES (est): 2.7MM **Privately Held**
WEB: www.cytecsys.com
SIC: 3571 7378 Mainframe computers; computer & data processing equipment repair/maintenance

(G-2374)
D GRAPHICS ADVERTISING
1770 Waycona Dr (39204-3527)
PHONE..................................601 373-4667
Dominic Azogini, *CEO*
EMP: 2
SALES: 100K **Privately Held**
SIC: 2759 Screen printing

(G-2375)
DAN W BUTLER SIGNS
825 College St (39202)
PHONE..................................601 948-5059
Dan W Butler, *Owner*
EMP: 2
SALES (est): 163.5K **Privately Held**
SIC: 3993 5999 Signs, not made in custom sign painting shops; banners

(G-2376)
DARLING INGREDIENTS INC
Also Called: Darling International
1299 Prisock Rd (39272-9326)
PHONE..................................601 372-5212
Wess Laughlin, *Accounts Mgr*
EMP: 7
SALES (corp-wide): 3.3B **Publicly Held**
SIC: 2077 Animal & marine fats & oils
PA: Darling Ingredients Inc.
5601 N Macarthur Blvd
Irving TX 75038
972 717-0300

(G-2377)
DAVID K BROOKS
1717 Bellewood Rd (39211-5702)
P.O. Box 16929 (39236-6929)
PHONE..................................601 981-5722
David K Brooks, *Owner*
EMP: 4 **EST:** 1935
SQ FT: 1,200
SALES (est): 262.2K **Privately Held**
SIC: 1311 Crude petroleum & natural gas

(G-2378)
DEEP S SUSPENSION & ACC INC
303 Wilmington St (39204-5018)
PHONE..................................601 371-7373
Rusty Clark, *President*
EMP: 4
SQ FT: 12,000
SALES (est): 613.6K **Privately Held**
WEB: www.deepsouthspring.com
SIC: 3493 Automobile springs

(G-2379)
DEES WELDING SERVICE LLC
107 Stokes Robertson Rd (39212-5262)
PHONE..................................601 372-9361
Cecil Ray Dees,
EMP: 3
SQ FT: 4,000
SALES (est): 286K **Privately Held**
SIC: 7692 Welding repair

(G-2380)
DELTA INDUSTRIES INC (PA)
Also Called: South Central Ready Mix
100 W Woodrow Wilson Ave (39213-7643)
P.O. Box 1292 (39215-1292)
PHONE..................................601 354-3801
Dave Robison, *CEO*
Leland Speed, *Ch of Bd*
Phil Hickerneol, *President*
Mark Dement, *Area Mgr*
Tom Evans, *Exec VP*
EMP: 80
SQ FT: 9,000
SALES (est): 100.3MM **Privately Held**
WEB: www.delta-ind.com
SIC: 3273 Ready-mixed concrete

(G-2381)
DELTA INDUSTRIES INC
Also Called: Jackson Ready-Mix
100 W Woodrow Wilson Ave (39213-7643)
P.O. Box 1292 (39215-1292)
PHONE..................................601 354-3801
Dave Robison, *CEO*

(PA)=Parent Co (HQ)=Headquarters (DH)=Div Headquarters
✿ = New Business established in last 2 years

2019 Harris Directory of
Mississippi Manufacturers

91

Jackson - Hinds County (G-2382)　　GEOGRAPHIC SECTION

Leland Speed, *Ch of Bd*
Thomas Slough, *Vice Ch Bd*
Pete Hayes, *CFO*
W D Mounger, *Director*
EMP: 200
SALES (est): 7.6MM
SALES (corp-wide): 100.3MM **Privately Held**
WEB: www.delta-ind.com
SIC: 1611 1771 3273 3271 Concrete construction: roads, highways, sidewalks, etc.; concrete work; ready-mixed concrete; concrete block & brick
PA: Delta Industries, Inc.
100 W Woodrow Wilson Ave
Jackson MS 39213
601 354-3801

(G-2382)
DELTA ROYALTY COMPANY INC
4450 Old Canton Rd # 203 (39211-5988)
PHONE..................................601 982-0970
William D Mounger, *President*
EMP: 2
SQ FT: 1,000
SALES (est): 210.9K **Privately Held**
SIC: 1389 6211 Oil & gas wells: building, repairing & dismantling; mineral royalties dealers

(G-2383)
DIANNE GORE
Also Called: Executive Leaders of Tomorrow
248 Ridgewood Rd (39211)
PHONE..................................510 697-2569
Dianne Gore, *Owner*
EMP: 6
SALES (est): 91.9K **Privately Held**
SIC: 7819 Services allied to motion pictures; bookbinding & related work

(G-2384)
DIOMEDIA INDUSTRIES LLC
5256 Clair St (39206-4204)
PHONE..................................601 882-7724
Lamonte Pierce,
EMP: 4
SALES (est): 108K **Privately Held**
SIC: 5999 2844 Water purification equipment; lotions, shaving

(G-2385)
DIVINE CREATIONS
3537 Jackye Ln (39213-5112)
PHONE..................................601 500-2764
Katrina D Magee, *Owner*
EMP: 1
SALES: 15K **Privately Held**
SIC: 2392 Household furnishings

(G-2386)
DKC INDUSTRIES LLC
460 Briarwood Dr Ste 400 (39206-3062)
PHONE..................................800 308-5187
Darius Calvert, *Principal*
EMP: 2
SALES (est): 50K **Privately Held**
SIC: 3999 Manufacturing industries

(G-2387)
DLS TAX CONSULTANTS
1408 Deer Park St (39203-2833)
PHONE..................................601 473-6623
Deanna Shinall,
EMP: 2
SALES: 50K **Privately Held**
SIC: 7291 8721 3953 Tax return preparation services; accounting services, except auditing; seal presses, notary & hand

(G-2388)
DORIC BURIAL VAULT CO
8961 Highway 49 N (39209-9711)
P.O. Box 1377, Clinton (39060-1377)
PHONE..................................601 366-8390
Robert D Martin, *President*
EMP: 12
SQ FT: 12,000
SALES: 1.1MM **Privately Held**
SIC: 3281 Burial vaults, stone

(G-2389)
DOUBLE G COATINGS COMPANY LP
1096 Mendell Davis Dr (39272-9109)
PHONE..................................601 371-3460

Sam Moore, *Ltd Ptnr*
William Shoto, *Vice Pres*
Keith Mangum, *Plant Engr*
Becky Agostinelli, *Manager*
Jeff Roth, *Admin Asst*
EMP: 78
SQ FT: 205,000
SALES (est): 14.8MM **Privately Held**
WEB: www.dgcsteel.com
SIC: 3479 Aluminum coating of metal products; coating or wrapping steel pipe

(G-2390)
DOWNHOME PUBLICATIONS INC
Also Called: Mississippi Magazine
5 Lakeland Cir Ste 4 (39216-5006)
P.O. Box 16445 (39236-6445)
PHONE..................................601 982-8418
Richard B Roper, *President*
EMP: 10 EST: 1981
SQ FT: 2,200
SALES: 97.6K **Privately Held**
WEB: www.mismag.com
SIC: 2721 Magazines: publishing only, not printed on site

(G-2391)
DR JAMES
2004 Camellia Ln (39204-5318)
PHONE..................................601 238-7821
EMP: 1
SALES (est): 69.6K **Privately Held**
SIC: 3714 Mfg Motor Vehicle Parts/Accessories

(G-2392)
DURFOLD CORPORATION
102 Upton Dr (39209-2525)
P.O. Box 9613 (39286-9613)
PHONE..................................601 922-4144
Jim Warren, *CEO*
Wendy Colson, *President*
Jeff Gilbert, *Plant Mgr*
Dawn Warren, *CFO*
Matt Treece, *Sales Dir*
▲ **EMP:** 27
SQ FT: 22,900
SALES (est): 4.6MM **Privately Held**
WEB: www.durfold.com
SIC: 2531 Chairs, table & arm

(G-2393)
DYNASTICS SCREEN PRINTING
410 W Pascagoula St (39203-3523)
PHONE..................................601 353-1956
Richard Shaw, *Owner*
EMP: 3
SALES: 228K **Privately Held**
SIC: 2759 Screen printing

(G-2394)
EAGLE PIPE AND SUPPLY LLC
450 Industrial Dr (39209-2741)
PHONE..................................601 487-7473
Nick Patterson, *Mng Member*
EMP: 3 EST: 2014
SALES (est): 314.7K **Privately Held**
SIC: 3312 Pipes & tubes

(G-2395)
EASLEY & EASLEY MILLWORKS INC
3850 I 55 S (39212-5101)
P.O. Box 720280 (39272-0280)
PHONE..................................601 372-8881
William E Easley, *CEO*
Johnnie M Easley, *Corp Secy*
EMP: 15
SQ FT: 22,875
SALES (est): 1.2MM **Privately Held**
SIC: 2434 2431 Wood kitchen cabinets; window frames, wood; doors, wood

(G-2396)
EATON AEROSPACE LLC
5353 Highland Dr (39206-3449)
P.O. Box 10177 (39286-0177)
PHONE..................................601 981-2811
Rick Busch, *General Mgr*
George Landfair, *Maint Spvr*
Jason Nail, *Senior Buyer*
Jeff Anthony, *Engineer*
Chris Berryman, *Engineer*
EMP: 30 **Privately Held**

SIC: 3812 3561 3594 3724 Acceleration indicators & systems components, aerospace; pumps & pumping equipment; fluid power pumps & motors; aircraft engines & engine parts
HQ: Eaton Aerospace Llc
1000 Eaton Blvd
Cleveland OH 44122
216 523-5000

(G-2397)
EATON AEROSPACE LLC
Also Called: Eaton Aerospace Jackson
5353 Highland Dr (39206-3449)
PHONE..................................601 987-3273
Kirk McDaniel, *Branch Mgr*
EMP: 1 **Privately Held**
SIC: 3724 Aircraft engines & engine parts
HQ: Eaton Aerospace Llc
1000 Eaton Blvd
Cleveland OH 44122
216 523-5000

(G-2398)
ELIMS ART CNCPTS & DCRTV DSGN
350 W Woodrow Wilson Ave (39213-7681)
PHONE..................................601 540-4810
Harold Hart, *Owner*
EMP: 4
SALES (est): 304.2K **Privately Held**
SIC: 3499 Picture frames, metal

(G-2399)
ELLIS CUSTOM WOODWORK LLC
1621 W Mcdowell Rd (39204-4351)
PHONE..................................601 983-8464
EMP: 1
SALES: 120K **Privately Held**
SIC: 2431 Mfg Millwork

(G-2400)
EMERALD WATER LLC
3920 Restbrook Pl (39211-6746)
PHONE..................................601 981-2430
A Katsaboulas, *Owner*
EMP: 1
SALES (est): 51.6K **Privately Held**
SIC: 3732 Boat building & repairing

(G-2401)
ENGELHARD
600 E Mcdowell Rd (39204-5992)
PHONE..................................601 948-3966
Randy Turk, *CEO*
EMP: 2
SALES (est): 229.5K **Privately Held**
SIC: 2819 Industrial inorganic chemicals

(G-2402)
ENTERGY NUCLEAR FUELS COMPANY
1340 Echelon Pkwy (39213-8202)
PHONE..................................601 368-5750
Barrett E Green, *President*
Timothy Mitchell, *Principal*
Jeffrey S Forbes, *Exec VP*
Wanda C Curry, *Vice Pres*
Eddie D Peebles, *Vice Pres*
EMP: 10
SALES (est): 3.5MM **Publicly Held**
SIC: 2819 Nuclear fuels, uranium slug (radioactive)
PA: Entergy Corporation
639 Loyola Ave Ste 300
New Orleans LA 70113

(G-2403)
ERICKSON OIL
3969 Dogwood Dr (39211-6704)
PHONE..................................601 362-7401
J Erickson, *Principal*
EMP: 2
SALES (est): 168.4K **Privately Held**
SIC: 1382 Oil & gas exploration services

(G-2404)
EVANS REFRIGERATION
Also Called: Precast Concrete
5477 Old Byram Rd (39272-9712)
PHONE..................................601 372-3482
Otho Evans, *Owner*
EMP: 7
SQ FT: 2,400

SALES: 656.2K **Privately Held**
SIC: 3272 Concrete products, precast

(G-2405)
EVERY WORD PRESS LLC
1125 Saint Ann St (39202-2147)
PHONE..................................601 209-1379
Charles Rubisoff, *Principal*
EMP: 1 EST: 2012
SALES (est): 79.1K **Privately Held**
SIC: 2741 Miscellaneous publishing

(G-2406)
FASHIONS INCORPORATED JACKSON
Also Called: Fashion Screenprint
721 Harris St Ste A (39202-3460)
P.O. Box 604 (39205-0604)
PHONE..................................601 948-1119
Thomas M Elzen, *President*
Richard Jones, *Partner*
Thomas M Elzen Jr, *Vice Pres*
Les Kershner, *Sales Mgr*
EMP: 8 EST: 1954
SQ FT: 16,000
SALES (est): 2.4MM **Privately Held**
SIC: 5136 2396 2395 Work clothing, men's & boys'; screen printing on fabric articles; embroidery & art needlework

(G-2407)
FEDEX OFFICE & PRINT SVCS INC
6392 Ridgewood Court Dr (39211-1841)
PHONE..................................601 957-3311
EMP: 20
SALES (corp-wide): 69.6B **Publicly Held**
WEB: www.kinkos.com
SIC: 7334 2791 2789 Photocopying & duplicating services; typesetting; bookbinding & related work
HQ: Fedex Office And Print Services, Inc.
7900 Legacy Dr
Plano TX 75024
800 463-3339

(G-2408)
FISHER CONSTRUCTION COMPANY
460 Briarwood Dr Ste 110 (39206-3053)
PHONE..................................769 257-9969
Jacqueline Andrews, *CEO*
EMP: 20
SALES (est): 406.3K **Privately Held**
SIC: 1389 Construction, repair & dismantling services

(G-2409)
FLANNIGAN ELECTRIC COMPANY
1820 S West St (39201-6431)
P.O. Box 8657 (39284-8657)
PHONE..................................601 354-2756
Steve Flannigan, *President*
Michael Flannigan, *Corp Secy*
EMP: 25
SQ FT: 17,600
SALES (est): 12.6MM **Privately Held**
WEB: www.flanniganelectric.com
SIC: 5063 5084 5072 7694 Motor controls, starters & relays: electric; switchgear; pumps & pumping equipment; power tools & accessories; electric motor repair

(G-2410)
FORTERRA PIPE & PRECAST LLC
2840 W Northside Dr (39213-4654)
PHONE..................................601 982-1100
Jim Ledlow, *Vice Pres*
EMP: 25
SALES (corp-wide): 1.4B **Publicly Held**
SIC: 3272 Precast terrazo or concrete products
HQ: Forterra Pipe & Precast, Llc
511 E John Carpenter Fwy
Irving TX 75062
469 458-7973

2019 Harris Directory of
Mississippi Manufacturers

▲ = Import ▼=Export
◆ =Import/Export

GEOGRAPHIC SECTION

Jackson - Hinds County (G-2439)

(G-2411)
FORTSON INDUSTRIAL SUPPLY CO
2384 Highway 80 W (39204-2312)
PHONE...................................601 948-2053
Robert Fortson, *Owner*
EMP: 5
SALES: 1,000K **Privately Held**
SIC: 3677 Electronic coils, transformers & other inductors

(G-2412)
FRANKLIN ELECTROFLUID CO INC
Also Called: Ahc Fluid Power
1 Dutchman Row (39209-2737)
PHONE...................................601 969-7022
Barry Hunter, *Manager*
EMP: 8
SALES (corp-wide): 23.6MM **Privately Held**
WEB: www.frankelectro.com
SIC: 5084 3594 Hydraulic systems equipment & supplies; fluid power pumps & motors
PA: Franklin Electrofluid Co Inc
3854 Watman Ave
Memphis TN 38118
901 362-7504

(G-2413)
FRANKLIN PRINTERS INC
Also Called: Franklin's Printing
330 Commerce Park Dr (39213-7098)
PHONE...................................601 982-9383
Ralph Sowell Jr, *President*
Dick Warmack, *Vice Pres*
EMP: 12
SQ FT: 8,300
SALES (est): 1.5MM **Privately Held**
SIC: 2752 2759 Commercial printing, lithographic; thermography; embossing on paper

(G-2414)
FRENCH AWNING & SCREEN CO INC
4514 S Mcraven Rd (39204-2031)
PHONE...................................601 922-1132
James French, *CEO*
Judy French, *Admin Sec*
EMP: 8
SQ FT: 4,800
SALES: 700K **Privately Held**
SIC: 2211 3442 Canvas & other heavy coarse fabrics: cotton; screen & storm doors & windows

(G-2415)
FRESH PRESS CREATIVE LLC
532 Patton Ave (39216-3232)
PHONE...................................601 376-9449
EMP: 2
SALES (est): 115K **Privately Held**
SIC: 2741 Miscellaneous publishing

(G-2416)
FRIERSON BUILDING SUPPLY CO
4525 Lynch Street Ext (39209-5828)
PHONE...................................601 922-1321
Pete H Frierson, *President*
Eugene Box, *Exec VP*
John M Salter, *Vice Pres*
Virginia Salter, *Treasurer*
Lucretia T Frierson, *Admin Sec*
EMP: 175
SQ FT: 25,000
SALES: 30MM **Privately Held**
SIC: 3442 2439 2435 2431 Metal doors, sash & trim; structural wood members; hardwood veneer & plywood; millwork; millwork & lumber

(G-2417)
FUEL TIME 5
1133 Raymond Rd (39204-4509)
PHONE...................................601 372-1115
Paul Singh, *Owner*
EMP: 4
SALES (est): 417.4K **Privately Held**
SIC: 2869 Fuels

(G-2418)
G M HORNE COMMERCIAL & INDUS
135 Bounds St (39206-4121)
PHONE...................................601 981-1600
EMP: 1
SALES: 750K **Privately Held**
SIC: 3999 Manufacturing industries

(G-2419)
GALAXIE CORPORATION (PA)
5170 Galaxie Dr (39206-4308)
P.O. Box 12485 (39236-2485)
PHONE...................................601 366-8413
Matthew L Holleman III, *President*
Dan M Swain Jr, *Treasurer*
▲ EMP: 4
SALES (est): 35.7MM **Privately Held**
SIC: 2911 6141 Asphalt or asphaltic materials, made in refineries; oils, fuel; jet fuels; naphtha; licensed loan companies, small

(G-2420)
GALEXIE GLISTER
2906 N State St Ste B8 (39216-4233)
PHONE...................................601 667-0004
EMP: 2
SALES (est): 74.4K **Privately Held**
SIC: 2844 Toilet preparations

(G-2421)
GANNETT CO INC
Also Called: The Clarion Ledger
201 S Congress St (39201-4202)
P.O. Box 40 (39205-0040)
PHONE...................................601 961-7000
Larry Whitaker, *President*
Percy Perry, *District Mgr*
Tammy Ramsdell, *Producer*
Robertson Hames, *Executive*
EMP: 330
SALES (corp-wide): 2.9B **Publicly Held**
WEB: www.gannett.com
SIC: 2711 2752 Newspapers: publishing only, not printed on site; commercial printing, lithographic
PA: Gannett Co., Inc.
7950 Jones Branch Dr
Mc Lean VA 22102
703 854-6000

(G-2422)
GARRETT ROWLAND G
Also Called: G&G Enterprises
134 Richardson Dr (39209-2517)
P.O. Box 31662 (39286-1662)
PHONE...................................601 954-9841
Rowland Garrett, *Owner*
EMP: 2
SALES (est): 97.4K **Privately Held**
SIC: 2842 5087 3589 Specialty cleaning preparations; rug, upholstery, or dry cleaning detergents or spotters; carpet & rug cleaning equipment & supplies, commercial; commercial cleaning equipment

(G-2423)
GATOR GRAFIX INC
5630 Terry Rd (39272-9200)
PHONE...................................601 376-9004
Eugene W Krevz Jr, *President*
Jason Mc Ilwain, *Admin Sec*
EMP: 3
SALES: 200K **Privately Held**
SIC: 2759 2396 5699 Screen printing; screen printing on fabric articles; T-shirts, custom printed

(G-2424)
GEO SEIS PROCESSING INC
305 W Lorenz Blvd (39213-7034)
P.O. Box 822, Brandon (39043-0822)
PHONE...................................601 936-0334
Nancy Booth, *President*
Phillip Steven Ahlberg, *Corp Secy*
Kendrick H Jordan, *Vice Pres*
EMP: 2
SALES (est): 200K **Privately Held**
SIC: 1382 Oil & gas exploration services

(G-2425)
GHA ENTERPRISES INCORPORATED
822 Winthrop Cir (39206-2325)
PHONE...................................601 812-7739
George Armstrong, *CEO*
EMP: 2
SALES (est): 108.9K **Privately Held**
SIC: 2833 2879 8732 Vitamins, natural or synthetic: bulk, uncompounded; agricultural chemicals; research services, except laboratory

(G-2426)
GODSWAY ENTERPRISES INC
Also Called: Gwe
1030 Cedar Hill Dr (39206-6117)
P.O. Box 124, Clinton (39060-0124)
PHONE...................................601 517-2847
Michele Morton, *Principal*
EMP: 2 EST: 2016
SALES (est): 106.3K **Privately Held**
SIC: 3423 Garden & farm tools, including shovels

(G-2427)
GOLD TEETH CUSTOMS
1335 Ellis Ave Ste 18 (39204-2203)
PHONE...................................601 955-4653
EMP: 2
SALES (est): 86.6K **Privately Held**
SIC: 3843 Dental metal

(G-2428)
GRADY MORROW
Also Called: Morrow Affrdbl Hmes Apartments
200 Rebel Woods Dr Apt M2 (39212-3006)
PHONE...................................769 230-6226
Grady Morrow, *Owner*
Tameka Stuckey, *Superintendent*
EMP: 9
SALES (est): 277.6K **Privately Held**
SIC: 3531 Hammer mills (rock & ore crushing machines), portable

(G-2429)
GRADY MORROW
Also Called: Each Life Teach Life
532 Spryfield Rd (39212-4645)
PHONE...................................769 823-1422
Grady Morrow, *Owner*
Tameka Stuckey, *Project Mgr*
EMP: 8
SALES (est): 253K **Privately Held**
SIC: 3357 3572 Communication wire; computer disk & drum drives & components

(G-2430)
GRAND SECURITY DOOR COMPANY
140 Glenstone Cir (39212-4503)
PHONE...................................601 573-1618
Wendy Hilliard, *Principal*
EMP: 2
SALES (est): 141.5K **Privately Held**
SIC: 3446 Stairs, fire escapes, balconies, railings & ladders

(G-2431)
GREAT SOUTHERN INDUSTRIES INC (PA)
1320 Boling St (39209-2622)
P.O. Box 5325 (39296-5325)
PHONE...................................601 948-5700
C W Ellis, *President*
Sam Clark, *General Mgr*
Joe W Russell Jr, *Corp Secy*
C W Ellis Jr, *Vice Pres*
Nikki Shue, *Human Res Mgr*
▲ EMP: 90 EST: 1959
SQ FT: 189,000
SALES (est): 18.6MM **Privately Held**
WEB: www.greatsouthernindustries.com
SIC: 2653 5051 Boxes, corrugated: made from purchased materials; pads, corrugated: made from purchased materials; wire

(G-2432)
GRIFFIN GRFFIN EXPLORATION LLC
1904 Lakeland Dr Ste F (39216-5038)
PHONE...................................601 713-1146
William K Griffin III, *Mng Member*

Anna Griffin,
EMP: 5
SQ FT: 2,581
SALES (est): 1MM **Privately Held**
SIC: 1381 1382 Directional drilling oil & gas wells; oil & gas exploration services

(G-2433)
GRIFFIN INDUSTRIES LLC
1299 Prisock Rd (39272-9326)
PHONE...................................601 372-5212
Malloy Annison, *General Mgr*
Malloy Anson, *Manager*
EMP: 200
SALES (corp-wide): 3.3B **Publicly Held**
WEB: www.griffinind.com
SIC: 2077 Tallow rendering, inedible
HQ: Griffin Industries Llc
4221 Alexandria Pike
Cold Spring KY 41076
859 781-2010

(G-2434)
GROVES SHEET METAL CO INC
1369 College Hill Rd (39209)
P.O. Box 5503, Pearl (39288-5503)
PHONE...................................601 922-6464
Andy Gunn, *President*
Jamie Gunn, *Vice Pres*
Jarrett Gunn, *Treasurer*
EMP: 6
SQ FT: 7,000
SALES: 600K **Privately Held**
SIC: 3444 Sheet metal specialties, not stamped

(G-2435)
GUIDES PUBLISHING INC (PA)
Also Called: Corporate Housing Experts
228 Avalon Cir (39201)
P.O. Box 98207 (39298-8207)
PHONE...................................601 981-7368
Mike Rowell, *CEO*
EMP: 7 EST: 1997
SALES (est): 621.7K **Privately Held**
SIC: 2741 Directories: publishing & printing

(G-2436)
H AND R RACEWAY LLC
5785 Highway 18 W (39209-9604)
PHONE...................................601 373-2490
Harpreet Sood, *President*
EMP: 7 EST: 2015
SALES (est): 156.5K **Privately Held**
SIC: 3644 Raceways

(G-2437)
HARRISON MANUFACTURING LLC
126 W Mayes St (39213-6211)
P.O. Box 4901 (39296-4901)
PHONE...................................601 519-0558
Matt Harrison, *Mfg Dir*
Scott Harrison,
EMP: 20
SQ FT: 24,500
SALES (est): 3.9MM **Privately Held**
WEB: www.harrisonmfg.net
SIC: 3089 Injection molding of plastics

(G-2438)
HENRY LYELL
760 Arlington St (39202-1616)
PHONE...................................601 355-1080
Henry M Lyell, *Manager*
EMP: 2 EST: 2012
SALES (est): 93.9K **Privately Held**
SIC: 1389 Oil & gas field services

(G-2439)
HERITAGE YARNS
5875 Baxter Dr (39211-3317)
PHONE...................................601 956-1478
Margaret H Pittman, *Owner*
Don Pitman, *Principal*
Dale Poore, *Supervisor*
EMP: 2 EST: 1994
SALES (est): 75K **Privately Held**
WEB: www.heritageyarns.com
SIC: 2281 2299 5137 5949 Needle & handicraft yarns, spun; silk yarn, spun; weaving yarn, spun; yarns, specialty & novelty; scarves, women's & children's; weaving goods & supplies

---

(PA)=Parent Co (HQ)=Headquarters (DH)=Div Headquarters
✿ = New Business established in last 2 years

2019 Harris Directory of
Mississippi Manufacturers

93

Jackson - Hinds County (G-2440)

GEOGRAPHIC SECTION

(G-2440)
HIGH EDGE INC
5420 J R Lynch St Ext (39209)
PHONE....................................601 326-2025
EMP: 15
SQ FT: 1,500
SALES (est): 860K Privately Held
SIC: 5963 3679 5063 4841 Direct Retail Sales Mfg Elec Components Whol Electrical Equip Cable/Pay Tv Services

(G-2441)
HILLSHIRE BRANDS COMPANY
Also Called: Sara Lee Coffee & Tea
4201 Space Center Dr (39209-2643)
PHONE....................................601 948-4632
EMP: 7
SQ FT: 6,000
SALES (corp-wide): 40B Publicly Held
SIC: 2013 Mfg Prepared Meats
HQ: The Hillshire Brands Company
400 S Jefferson St Fl 1
Chicago IL 60607
312 614-6000

(G-2442)
HOSHIZAKI OF JACKSON
1215 High St (39202-3514)
P.O. Box 12407 (39236-2407)
PHONE....................................601 969-4200
EMP: 2
SALES (est): 188.2K Privately Held
SIC: 3822 Ice maker controls

(G-2443)
HOWARD E STOVER
1650 Lelia Dr Ste 102 (39216-4864)
PHONE....................................601 984-3702
EMP: 4
SALES (est): 280K Privately Held
SIC: 1311 Crude Petroleum/Natural Gas Production

(G-2444)
HRD SAFETY
14 Northtown Dr Ste 206 (39211-3018)
P.O. Box 13333 (39236-3333)
PHONE....................................601 213-6358
EMP: 2
SALES: 950K Privately Held
SIC: 2381 Mfg Fabric Gloves

(G-2445)
HUNTER ENGINEERING COMPANY
2125 Tv Rd (39204-4025)
PHONE....................................769 524-4949
Todd Fykes, Principal
EMP: 2
SALES (corp-wide): 400MM Privately Held
SIC: 3578 Change making machines
PA: Hunter Engineering Company Inc
11250 Hunter Dr
Bridgeton MO 63044
314 731-3020

(G-2446)
INLAND ENERGY COMPANY INC
Also Called: Miller Oil Properties
974 E Fortification St (39202-2423)
PHONE....................................601 969-1160
David Miller, President
David W Miller, Exec VP
Bryant G Miller, Vice Pres
EMP: 3
SQ FT: 2,500
SALES: 100K Privately Held
SIC: 1389 6211 1311 Oil consultants; mineral royalties dealers; crude petroleum production; natural gas production

(G-2447)
INNOVATIVE WIRELESS LLC
Also Called: Acalvin Chapman Jr.
1230 Raymond Rd (39204-4583)
PHONE....................................601 594-1201
EMP: 1
SQ FT: 1,250

SALES (est): 108.7K Privately Held
SIC: 3651 7622 1623 3661 Audio electronic systems; radio repair & installation; transmitting tower (telecommunication) construction; fiber optics communications equipment; amplifiers, RF power & IF; radios, two-way, citizens' band, weather, short-wave, etc.

(G-2448)
INTERNATIONAL GRANITE LLC
1728 Plantation Blvd (39211-2212)
PHONE....................................601 213-8287
Brian Thilders,
▲ EMP: 1
SALES (est): 400K Privately Held
SIC: 3281 Granite, cut & shaped

(G-2449)
IRONWORKS INC
300 W South St (39203-3606)
PHONE....................................601 352-3722
Pat Pigott,
Christi Gray, Admin Sec
EMP: 2
SALES (est): 204.2K Privately Held
SIC: 3446 Architectural metalwork

(G-2450)
J & R OPTICAL CO INC (PA)
Also Called: Odom's Dispensing Optician
1461 Canton Mart Rd Ste A (39211-5413)
P.O. Box 18482, Natchez (39122-8482)
PHONE....................................601 977-0272
Joseph C Odom, President
Richard Odom, Vice Pres
Rebecca O Francis, Treasurer
EMP: 4
SQ FT: 1,500
SALES (est): 2.8MM Privately Held
SIC: 5995 3851 Opticians; eyeglasses, prescription; contact lenses; eyes, glass & plastic

(G-2451)
JACKSON ADVOCATE INC
100 W Hamilton St (39202-3237)
P.O. Box 3708 (39207-3708)
PHONE....................................601 948-4122
Alice Tisdale, President
EMP: 8 EST: 1938
SQ FT: 10,000
SALES (est): 608.5K Privately Held
SIC: 2711 Commercial printing & newspaper publishing combined; newspapers, publishing & printing

(G-2452)
JACKSON ASPHALT & CONCRETE
2944 Woodbine St (39212-2845)
PHONE....................................601 371-8707
Mohammad Talee, Owner
EMP: 4 EST: 2001
SALES (est): 359.8K Privately Held
WEB: www.jacksonasphalt.com
SIC: 2951 Asphalt paving mixtures & blocks

(G-2453)
JACKSON BRACE CO
Also Called: Jackson Brace & Limb
1320 N State St (39202-2003)
PHONE....................................601 353-2477
Wesley Wilson, President
Rebecca W Dickerson, Vice Pres
Barri Delese Gordon, Treasurer
EMP: 13 EST: 1946
SQ FT: 2,400
SALES (est): 1.4MM Privately Held
SIC: 5047 3842 Orthopedic equipment & supplies; limbs, artificial

(G-2454)
JACKSON EXCAVATING & LSG CO
Also Called: Baker Engineering
1059 Deviney Dr (39282)
P.O. Box 6717 (39282-6717)
PHONE....................................601 371-7935
Jim Baker, President
W C Deviney Jr, President
EMP: 203

SALES (est): 27.6MM
SALES (corp-wide): 107.4MM Privately Held
SIC: 3629 Electronic generation equipment
PA: Deviney Construction Company Inc
1059 Deviney Dr
Raymond MS 39154
601 372-3121

(G-2455)
JACKSON FREE PRESS INC
125 S Congress St # 1324 (39201-3300)
P.O. Box 100 (39205-0100)
PHONE....................................601 362-6121
John Dongieux, Principal
Donna Ladd, Chief
Melanie Collins, Bookkeeper
Myron Cathey, Accounts Exec
Stephen Barnette, Adv Dir
EMP: 12
SALES (est): 712.1K Privately Held
SIC: 2711 Newspapers, publishing & printing

(G-2456)
JACKSON PLATING CO
228 W Lorenz Blvd (39213-7058)
P.O. Box 4667 (39296-4667)
PHONE....................................601 362-4623
Walter E Lydick Jr, President
Vince Barr, General Mgr
EMP: 24 EST: 1945
SQ FT: 25,000
SALES (est): 3.1MM Privately Held
SIC: 3471 Plating of metals or formed products; electroplating of metals or formed products

(G-2457)
JACKSON PRECAST INC
3325 Lawson St (39213-5741)
PHONE....................................601 321-8787
James Tolson, President
EMP: 20
SALES (est): 3.8MM Privately Held
WEB: www.jpi.ms
SIC: 3271 Architectural concrete: block, split, fluted, screen, etc.

(G-2458)
JANLYNN CRAFTS
5062 Sunnyvale Dr (39211-4843)
PHONE....................................601 956-1832
Lynn Ross, Owner
EMP: 1
SALES (est): 77.7K Privately Held
WEB: www.janlynncrafts.com
SIC: 3944 Craft & hobby kits & sets

(G-2459)
JASPER & ASSOC
3365 Medgar Evers Blvd (39213-6844)
PHONE....................................601 321-0811
Jasper Brenan, Principal
EMP: 1
SALES (est): 117.8K Privately Held
SIC: 2335 Wedding gowns & dresses

(G-2460)
JONES LDSCP & CONTRS SVC LLC
3172 Bilgray Dr (39212-4246)
P.O. Box 2126 (39225-2126)
PHONE....................................601 780-2042
Donald Jones, Mng Member
EMP: 1
SALES (est): 35.1K Privately Held
SIC: 0782 1389 7389 Landscape contractors; construction, repair & dismantling services;

(G-2461)
JURA-SEARCH INC
Also Called: Baria, Lawrence R
111 E Capitol St Ste 500 (39201-2122)
P.O. Box 320426, Flowood (39232-0426)
PHONE....................................601 932-0002
Lawrence R Baria, President
Carolyn Morrison, Bookkeeper
EMP: 2
SALES (est): 210K Privately Held
SIC: 1382 Oil & gas exploration services

(G-2462)
KENNEDY HALL
Also Called: Hall Metal Craft
732 Woodacre Rd (39206-2326)
PHONE....................................601 366-7301
Kennedy Hall, Owner
Toni Hall, Partner
EMP: 3
SALES (est): 210K Privately Held
WEB: www.kennedysailor.com
SIC: 2514 Metal household furniture

(G-2463)
KEREX LLC (HQ)
1421 N State St Ste 505 (39202-1652)
PHONE....................................210 494-5596
Robert Allen Smith, Director
Dr Arturo Martinez,
Mary Montalbo,
EMP: 4
SQ FT: 1,500
SALES: 750K
SALES (corp-wide): 4MM Privately Held
SIC: 3841 5999 5047 Surgical & medical instruments; medical apparatus & supplies; medical equipment & supplies
PA: Keraplast Technologies, Llc
19210 Huebner Rd Ste 103
San Antonio TX 78258
210 494-5596

(G-2464)
KIDS EXPRESS
665 Claiborne Ave (39209-6239)
P.O. Box 10992 (39289-0992)
PHONE....................................601 352-3882
EMP: 2
SALES (est): 121K Privately Held
SIC: 2741 Misc Publishing

(G-2465)
KINGDOM LIFE PRINTING
199 Raymond Rd (39204-2860)
PHONE....................................601 398-4606
EMP: 2
SALES (est): 83.9K Privately Held
SIC: 2752 Commercial printing, lithographic

(G-2466)
LA BRIOCHE LLC
2906 N State St (39216-4233)
PHONE....................................601 988-2299
Cristina Lazzari, Mng Member
EMP: 10
SALES (est): 978.1K Privately Held
SIC: 2051 Cakes, bakery: except frozen

(G-2467)
LEGACY VULCAN LLC
Also Called: Mississippi Materials
100 Commerce Park Dr (39213-6613)
PHONE....................................601 631-8833
Mark Hardy, Branch Mgr
EMP: 3 Publicly Held
WEB: www.vulcanmaterials.com
SIC: 1442 Construction sand & gravel
HQ: Legacy Vulcan, Llc
1200 Urban Center Dr
Vestavia AL 35242
205 298-3000

(G-2468)
LEGENDARY LAWN SERVICES INC
Also Called: 1967
510 George St Ste 230 (39202-3027)
PHONE....................................601 307-6381
Regina Thomas, President
EMP: 2 EST: 2017
SALES (est): 73.4K Privately Held
SIC: 3423 Hooks: bush, grass, baling, husking, etc.

(G-2469)
LIFESTORY PUBLISHING
5328 Runnymede Rd (39211-4635)
PHONE....................................601 594-0018
EMP: 2
SALES (est): 78.8K Privately Held
SIC: 2741 Miscellaneous publishing

2019 Harris Directory of
Mississippi Manufacturers

94

▲ = Import ▼=Export
◆ =Import/Export

GEOGRAPHIC SECTION

Jackson - Hinds County (G-2500)

(G-2470)
LLC GLASS HOUSE
14 Northtown Dr (39211-3018)
PHONE...................................769 251-1299
EMP: 1
SALES (est): 52.6K **Privately Held**
SIC: 3999 7231 7299 Hair & hair-based products; unisex hair salons; hair weaving or replacement

(G-2471)
LOFTON CORPORATION
6512 Dogwood View Pkwy (39213-7844)
PHONE...................................769 243-8427
EMP: 2 EST: 2015
SALES (est): 115.6K **Privately Held**
SIC: 3441 Fabricated structural metal

(G-2472)
LOW PRO PUBLISHING
133 Brenda Dr (39212-3802)
PHONE...................................601 372-1875
EMP: 1 EST: 2010
SALES (est): 54K **Privately Held**
SIC: 2741 Misc Publishing

(G-2473)
LUCKY TOWN BREWING COMPANY LLC
1710 N Mill St (39202-1536)
P.O. Box 1154 (39215-1154)
PHONE...................................601 790-0142
Lucas Simmons,
EMP: 19
SALES (est): 2.6MM **Privately Held**
SIC: 2082 5813 Beer (alcoholic beverage); bars & lounges

(G-2474)
M S RUBBER COMPANY (PA)
715 E Mcdowell Rd (39204-5908)
PHONE...................................601 948-2575
Sandra H Lewis, *President*
Susan Foster, *General Mgr*
Ella Ruth Hebert, *Chairman*
Rhonda H Fleming, *Vice Pres*
Mike Smith, *Buyer*
EMP: 17
SQ FT: 25,000
SALES (est): 7MM **Privately Held**
WEB: www.msrubber.com
SIC: 5085 3053 5162 3089 Rubber goods, mechanical; gaskets; hose, belting & packing; gaskets, all materials; plastics sheets & rods; plastics basic shapes; stock shapes, plastic

(G-2475)
MABRYS
1531 Plantation Blvd (39211-2812)
PHONE...................................601 956-7238
Walter Mabry, *Owner*
EMP: 1
SALES (est): 54.6K **Privately Held**
SIC: 3944 Craft & hobby kits & sets

(G-2476)
MADE PRINTING & DESIGNIN
5562 Queen Elizabeth Ln (39209-2135)
PHONE...................................601 572-6967
Dwanese Thomas, *Principal*
EMP: 2 EST: 2016
SALES (est): 92.3K **Privately Held**
SIC: 2752 Commercial printing, lithographic

(G-2477)
MAGNOLIA LABEL CO INC (PA)
7380 I 55 S (39272-9169)
P.O. Box 720418 (39272-0418)
PHONE...................................601 878-0951
Wallace A Fields, *President*
Gloria Fields, *Corp Secy*
EMP: 20 EST: 1971
SQ FT: 6,000
SALES (est): 2.3MM **Privately Held**
WEB: www.magnoliapest.com
SIC: 2759 Commercial printing

(G-2478)
MAGNOLIA PRINTING AND SIGNS
2252 Maddox Rd (39209-9601)
PHONE...................................601 922-5076
Melanie Morrow, *Principal*

EMP: 2
SALES (est): 85.5K **Privately Held**
SIC: 2752 Commercial printing, lithographic

(G-2479)
MAGNOLIA SCREENS LLC
176 N Sunset Ter (39212-4836)
PHONE...................................601 942-3049
Steve Honeycutt,
EMP: 1
SALES: 75K **Privately Held**
SIC: 2431 Door screens, metal covered wood; door screens, wood frame

(G-2480)
MAGNOLIA SUPPLY GROUP LLC
Also Called: Magnolia Group
315 Decelle St Jackson (39216)
PHONE...................................601 454-1368
Steven Houston, *Partner*
Tiffany Dockins,
EMP: 1
SALES (est): 93.3K **Privately Held**
SIC: 1795 3271 5047 5074 Wrecking & demolition work; blocks, concrete: landscape or retaining wall; medical equipment & supplies; heating equipment & panels, solar; towels, napkins & tissue paper products; cleaning & maintenance equipment & supplies

(G-2481)
MAJOR LEAGUE PROMOTIONS
1410 Highway 80 W (39204-2503)
PHONE...................................601 672-4798
Deborah Waguespack, *Owner*
EMP: 5
SALES (est): 104.7K **Privately Held**
SIC: 7389 5199 7319 3993 ; badges; display advertising service; signs & advertising specialties

(G-2482)
MAJOR LEAGUE PROMOTIONS LLC
1410 Highway 80 W (39204-2503)
PHONE...................................601 672-4798
Deborah Waguespack,
EMP: 5
SALES (est): 104.7K **Privately Held**
SIC: 7389 5199 7319 3993 ; badges; display advertising service; signs & advertising specialties

(G-2483)
MARSHALL DURBIN FOOD CORP
Also Called: Marshall Durbin Lab Div
650 Ford Ave (39209-2756)
PHONE...................................601 969-1248
Cassandra McCollum, *Manager*
EMP: 10
SQ FT: 2,100
SALES (corp-wide): 404.3MM **Privately Held**
SIC: 2015 Poultry slaughtering & processing
HQ: Marshall Durbin Food Corporation
2830 Commerce Blvd
Irondale AL 35210
205 841-7315

(G-2484)
MCGOWAN WORKING PARTNERS INC (PA)
1837 Crane Ridge Dr (39216-4902)
P.O. Box 55809 (39296-5809)
PHONE...................................601 982-3444
David B Russell, *President*
James A Phyfer Jr, *Vice Pres*
Sean McGowan, *Engineer*
Mart Lamar, *Senior Engr*
Debbie Chapman, *Treasurer*
EMP: 25
SQ FT: 6,000
SALES (est): 85.8MM **Privately Held**
SIC: 1311 Crude petroleum production

(G-2485)
MCMILLAN STAMP & SIGN CO INC
145 Millsaps Ave (39202-1410)
PHONE...................................601 353-4688
Thomas E Mc Daniel, *President*

Thomas B Mc Daniel, *President*
Tommy McDaniel, *General Mgr*
Faye B McDaniel, *Principal*
Garret McDaniel, *Vice Pres*
EMP: 6
SQ FT: 4,000
SALES: 700K **Privately Held**
SIC: 3953 3993 Marking devices; signs & advertising specialties

(G-2486)
MEDIA SOLUTIONS
460 Briarwood Dr Ste 400 (39206-3062)
PHONE...................................601 351-9303
George Burgess, *Owner*
EMP: 2
SALES (est): 61.8K **Privately Held**
SIC: 2752 Commercial printing, lithographic

(G-2487)
MEL VOLD SALES CO
120 Carpenter Dr (39212-9632)
P.O. Box 1475, Clinton (39060-1475)
PHONE...................................601 371-4911
Donald Melvold, *Owner*
Donald Mel Vold, *Owner*
EMP: 3
SALES (est): 140K **Privately Held**
SIC: 7372 5084 Prepackaged software; materials handling machinery

(G-2488)
METALLIC WELDING
4400 New Post Rd (39212-3612)
PHONE...................................769 798-6498
Preston Evans, *Principal*
EMP: 1
SALES (est): 42.6K **Privately Held**
SIC: 7692 Welding repair

(G-2489)
METRO CHRISTIAN LIVING
622 Duling Ave Ste 220 (39216-4000)
PHONE...................................601 790-9076
Marilyn Smith, *Principal*
EMP: 4
SALES (est): 23.3K **Privately Held**
SIC: 2721 Periodicals: publishing only

(G-2490)
MID STATE ARTIFICIAL LIMB INC (PA)
4455 Medgar Evers Blvd (39213-5202)
P.O. Box 31092 (39286-1092)
PHONE...................................601 981-2229
Troy Luster, *President*
EMP: 11
SALES (est): 881.6K **Privately Held**
SIC: 3842 Limbs, artificial

(G-2491)
MIDSOUTH ELEVATOR LLC
5810 N Commerce Plz (39206-2936)
PHONE...................................601 353-8283
Henry N Dick III,
EMP: 5
SALES (est): 902K **Privately Held**
SIC: 3534 Elevators & equipment

(G-2492)
MILLER BRYANT G OIL GAS PRPTS
1837 Peachtree St (39202-1132)
PHONE...................................601 360-2850
Bryant Miller, *Principal*
EMP: 2
SALES (est): 284K **Privately Held**
SIC: 3569 Gas producers, generators & other gas related equipment

(G-2493)
MILLER LAND PROFESSIONALS LLC
974 E Fortification St (39202-2423)
PHONE...................................601 969-1160
David Miller, *Manager*
Elizabeth Miller, *Executive*
David W Miller,
EMP: 2
SALES (est): 170K **Privately Held**
SIC: 1382 Oil & gas exploration services

(G-2494)
MILTONS AUTOMOTIVE HEAD SERVI
4539 Highway 80 W (39209-4806)
PHONE...................................601 922-8131
Milton Williams, *Owner*
EMP: 2
SALES (est): 211.7K **Privately Held**
SIC: 3599 Machine shop, jobbing & repair

(G-2495)
MILWAUKEE ELECTRIC TOOL CORP
4355 Milwaukee St (39209-2635)
PHONE...................................601 969-3033
Kenneth Allison, *General Mgr*
Charles Beeland, *Safety Mgr*
Steven Slater, *Engineer*
Tania Torres, *Engineer*
Harry Peterson, *Branch Mgr*
EMP: 400 **Privately Held**
WEB: www.mil-electric-tool.com
SIC: 3546 Power-driven handtools
HQ: Milwaukee Electric Tool Corporation
13135 W Lisbon Rd
Brookfield WI 53005
800 729-3878

(G-2496)
MISCCELLANEOUS ITEMS LLC
Also Called: Jesse L Star Sheets
6295 Old Canton Rd (39211-2908)
PHONE...................................601 918-0255
Jessee Star,
EMP: 1
SALES (est): 83K **Privately Held**
SIC: 3263 Tableware, household & commercial: semivitreous

(G-2497)
MISSCO CORPORATION OF JACKSON
4365 Michael Avalon St (39209-2633)
P.O. Box 1059 (39215-1059)
PHONE...................................601 352-7272
David Jeffreys, *Branch Mgr*
EMP: 10
SALES (corp-wide): 36.5MM **Privately Held**
WEB: www.missco.com
SIC: 5021 2531 2599 3821 School desks; school furniture; hospital furniture, except beds; laboratory equipment: fume hoods, distillation racks, etc.; laboratory furniture
PA: Missco Corporation Of Jackson
2001 Airport Rd N Ste 102
Flowood MS 39232
601 987-8600

(G-2498)
MISSISSIPPI COLD DRIP COFFEE
126 Keener Ave (39202-1007)
P.O. Box 55906 (39296-5906)
PHONE...................................601 624-5708
Michael Horn,
Raymond E Horn,
EMP: 3
SALES (est): 132.3K **Privately Held**
SIC: 2095 2099 Roasted coffee; tea blending

(G-2499)
MISSISSIPPI CATHOLIC
237 E Amite St (39201-2405)
P.O. Box 2130 (39225-2130)
PHONE...................................601 969-3581
Janna Avlon, *Exec Dir*
Joseph Latino, *Administration*
EMP: 5
SALES: 300K **Privately Held**
WEB: www.mississippicatholic.com
SIC: 2711 Newspapers: publishing only, not printed on site

(G-2500)
MISSISSIPPI IRON WORKS INC
750 S Gallatin St Ste 608 (39204-2909)
PHONE...................................601 355-0188
Tanya Crawley, *Branch Mgr*
EMP: 1 **Privately Held**
SIC: 3446 Stairs, fire escapes, balconies, railings & ladders

---

(PA)=Parent Co (HQ)=Headquarters (DH)=Div Headquarters
✪ = New Business established in last 2 years

2019 Harris Directory of
Mississippi Manufacturers

95

Jackson - Hinds County (G-2501)

GEOGRAPHIC SECTION

PA: Mississippi Iron Works, Inc.
980 S State St
Jackson MS 39201

(G-2501)
MISSISSIPPI IRON WORKS INC (PA)
980 S State St (39201-5910)
PHONE..............................601 355-0188
Carry Crawley, *President*
EMP: 7
SQ FT: 28,000
SALES (est): 1.9MM **Privately Held**
SIC: 3446 Stairs, fire escapes, balconies, railings & ladders

(G-2502)
MISSISSIPPI PHOTO & BLUPRT CO
721 Harris St Ste C (39202-3460)
PHONE..............................601 948-1119
Richard Eley, *President*
David Hawkins, *Corp Secy*
EMP: 4
SQ FT: 4,300
SALES: 325K **Privately Held**
SIC: 7334 2759 7336 5999 Photocopying & duplicating services; screen printing; graphic arts & related design; art & architectural supplies

(G-2503)
MISSISSIPPI PRISON INDS CORP (PA)
Also Called: Mpic
663 N State St (39202-3304)
PHONE..............................601 969-5760
John Miller, *CEO*
EMP: 15
SALES: 3.1MM **Privately Held**
WEB: www.mpic.net
SIC: 8331 3449 2211 2326 Vocational training agency; miscellaneous metalwork; sheets, bedding & table cloths: cotton; work uniforms; removers & cleaners

(G-2504)
MISSISSIPPI PRISON INDUSTRIES
2929 I 55 S (39212-4958)
PHONE..............................601 346-4966
EMP: 2 EST: 2009
SALES (est): 125.8K **Privately Held**
SIC: 3999 Manufacturing industries

(G-2505)
MISSISSIPPI PUPPETRY GUILD
1927 Springridge Dr (39211-3344)
P.O. Box 12123 (39236-2123)
PHONE..............................601 977-9840
Hilda Faye Hill, *President*
Patricia L Freshney, *Principal*
Clarence Hamilton, *Principal*
John Landress, *Principal*
Peter Zapletal, *Corp Secy*
EMP: 2
SALES (est): 45.9K **Privately Held**
SIC: 7929 3999 Entertainment service; puppets & marionettes

(G-2506)
MISSISSIPPI STATE PHRM ASSN
Also Called: MISSISSIPPI PHARMACISTS ASSOCI
341 Edgewood Terrace Dr (39206-6217)
PHONE..............................601 981-0416
Sam E Dalton, *Exec Dir*
Brinda Bland, *Deputy Dir*
EMP: 2
SQ FT: 3,456
SALES (est): 420.8K **Privately Held**
WEB: www.mspharm.org
SIC: 8621 2721 Medical field-related associations; periodicals

(G-2507)
MISSISSSSPPI BSKTBALL ATHLTICS
2240 Westbrook Rd (39211-4900)
PHONE..............................601 957-7373
Jefferey Lewis, *General Mgr*
Robert Holloway, *Manager*
EMP: 5

SALES (est): 274.6K **Privately Held**
WEB: www.mbahoops.net
SIC: 3949 Gymnasium equipment

(G-2508)
MMC MATERIALS INC
815 W Fortification St (39203-1702)
P.O. Box 307 (39205-0307)
PHONE..............................601 973-2093
Eddie Middleton, *Vice Pres*
Ben Tharp, *Sales Mgr*
Stanley Mangum, *Branch Mgr*
Kenny Washington, *Manager*
EMP: 100
SALES (corp-wide): 306.5MM **Privately Held**
WEB: www.mmcmaterials.com
SIC: 3273 3272 Ready-mixed concrete; concrete products
HQ: Mmc Materials, Inc.
1052 Highland Colony Pkwy # 201
Ridgeland MS 39157
601 898-4000

(G-2509)
MOLPUS TIMBERLANDS MANAGEMENT
858 North St (39202-3019)
PHONE..............................601 969-7093
EMP: 2
SALES (est): 63.8K **Privately Held**
SIC: 8741 2411 Business management; timber, cut at logging camp

(G-2510)
MONOGRAM MAGIC
1481 Canton Mart Rd Ste D (39211-5412)
PHONE..............................601 956-7117
Stacy Stovall, *Owner*
EMP: 2 EST: 1999
SALES (est): 130K **Privately Held**
SIC: 2759 Commercial printing

(G-2511)
MR FORMS PRINTING COMPANY INC
5403 Robinson Road Ext (39204-4138)
PHONE..............................601 371-2567
Russell Prisock, *President*
EMP: 3
SALES: 500K **Privately Held**
SIC: 2621 5112 Stationery, envelope & tablet papers; stationery & office supplies

(G-2512)
MRC GLOBAL (US) INC
4155 Industrial Dr (39209-2746)
PHONE..............................601 965-5275
EMP: 11 **Publicly Held**
SIC: 1311 Crude petroleum & natural gas
HQ: Mrc Global (Us) Inc.
1301 Mckinney St Ste 2300
Houston TX 77010
877 294-7574

(G-2513)
MRS GS COMPUTER SERVICES
4731 Raymond Rd (39212-3662)
P.O. Box 8271 (39284-8271)
PHONE..............................601 376-0810
Joyce Grayer, *Owner*
EMP: 1
SALES (est): 47K **Privately Held**
SIC: 2711 Job printing & newspaper publishing combined

(G-2514)
MULTIMEDIA GRAPHICS INC (PA)
Also Called: Signs First
4950 I 55 N (39211-5414)
PHONE..............................601 981-5001
Matt Jordan, *President*
EMP: 10
SQ FT: 2,000
SALES (est): 1.6MM **Privately Held**
WEB: www.signsfirstjackson.com
SIC: 3993 2399 Signs & advertising specialties; banners, made from fabric

(G-2515)
NANDYS CANDY & ICE FACTORY
1220 E Northside Dr # 380 (39211-5503)
PHONE..............................601 362-9553

Nancy King, *President*
EMP: 6
SQ FT: 2,800
SALES (est): 226.2K **Privately Held**
WEB: www.nandyscandy.com
SIC: 5441 2064 2066 Candy; candy & other confectionery products; chocolate & cocoa products

(G-2516)
NCI GROUP INC
Also Called: Metal Coaters
951 Prisock Rd (39272-9320)
PHONE..............................601 373-0374
Norman Chambers, *President*
Edwin Hastings, *QC Mgr*
Mimi Siracusa, *Treasurer*
Joseph Turjanica, *Accounts Mgr*
Tim Gray, *Marketing Staff*
EMP: 100
SALES (est): 15.9MM
SALES (corp-wide): 2B **Publicly Held**
SIC: 3355 Aluminum rolling & drawing
HQ: Nci Group, Inc.
10943 N Sam Huston Pkwy W
Houston TX 77064
281 897-7788

(G-2517)
NCI GROUP INC
Also Called: Insulated Panel Sytems
201 Apache Dr (39272-9709)
PHONE..............................601 373-3222
Fax: 601 372-8675
▲ **EMP:** 2
SALES (est): 769.5K
SALES (corp-wide): 1.6B **Publicly Held**
SIC: 3448 Mfg Prefabricated Metal Buildings
HQ: Nci Group, Inc.
10943 N Sam Huston Pkwy W
Houston TX 77064
281 897-7500

(G-2518)
NEAL CLEMENT OIL & GAS
1650 Lelia Dr Ste 101 (39216-4864)
PHONE..............................601 982-5667
EMP: 2
SALES (est): 81.9K **Privately Held**
SIC: 1311 Crude Petroleum And Natural Gas, Nsk

(G-2519)
NEILL OIL LLC
1700 Lelia Dr Ste 107 (39216-4887)
P.O. Box 1717, Brandon (39043-1717)
PHONE..............................601 984-9000
John C Neill MD, *Principal*
EMP: 3
SALES (est): 187.2K **Privately Held**
SIC: 1382 Oil & gas exploration services

(G-2520)
NEON MARKETING
188 E Capitol St Ste 800 (39201-2126)
PHONE..............................601 960-4555
EMP: 3
SALES (est): 123.2K **Privately Held**
SIC: 2813 Neon

(G-2521)
NICK STRCKLNDS QUICK PRINT INC (PA)
Also Called: Alliance Business Services
125 E South St (39201-5106)
PHONE..............................601 898-1717
Nick J Strickland, *President*
Heather Dodson, *CPA*
Cyllene Medlin, *Accounts Mgr*
Annie Bennett, *Manager*
Tony Perkins, *Manager*
EMP: 25
SQ FT: 6,000
SALES (est): 3.6MM **Privately Held**
WEB: www.alliancebusinessservices.net
SIC: 2752 2791 2789 Commercial printing, offset; typesetting; bookbinding & related work

(G-2522)
NORTHSIDE PARTNERS
Also Called: Muscle Shoals Sound Studio
3023 W Northside Dr (39213-4563)
PHONE..............................601 982-4522
Thomas J Couch, *Partner*

Stewart Madison, *Partner*
Gerald B Stephenson, *Partner*
EMP: 2
SALES (est): 238K **Privately Held**
SIC: 3652 Pre-recorded records & tapes

(G-2523)
NORTHTOWNE PRINTERS INC
Also Called: Kowalski's Printplex
2088 Dunbarton Dr (39216-5003)
PHONE..............................601 713-3200
Steve Kowalski, *President*
Kathy Kowalski, *Vice Pres*
Zachary Kowalski, *Treasurer*
EMP: 4 EST: 1976
SQ FT: 6,000
SALES: 650K **Privately Held**
SIC: 2752 Commercial printing, offset

(G-2524)
NOVELTY MACHINE WORKS INC
3120 Highway 80 W (39204-2226)
P.O. Box 8194 (39284-8194)
PHONE..............................601 948-2075
John Robinson, *President*
James Hollingsworth, *President*
John A Robinson, *Vice Pres*
EMP: 13
SQ FT: 24,000
SALES (est): 1.6MM **Privately Held**
SIC: 3599 7692 7537 3545 Machine shop, jobbing & repair; welding repair; automotive transmission repair shops; machine tool accessories

(G-2525)
NOVIA CMMNICATIONS/ NOVIA PUBG
125 S Congress St # 1338 (39201-3301)
PHONE..............................601 985-9502
Ben Minnifield, *President*
Angelique Minnifield, *Director*
EMP: 3 EST: 1997
SALES (est): 240K **Privately Held**
SIC: 2721 Comic books: publishing only, not printed on site

(G-2526)
NUMEDRX PHARMACY SOLUTIONS LLC
2 Old River Pl Ste J (39202-3435)
PHONE..............................601 973-5501
Bennie K Bostick, *Mng Member*
EMP: 9
SALES (est): 790K **Privately Held**
SIC: 2834 Pharmaceutical preparations

(G-2527)
OBSERVA-DOME LABORATORIES INC
371 Commerce Park Dr (39213-7055)
PHONE..............................601 982-3333
William R Clark, *President*
EMP: 7 EST: 1965
SQ FT: 10,000
SALES: 731K **Privately Held**
SIC: 3444 Sheet metalwork

(G-2528)
OLD BLUE PUBLISHING LLC
5406 Hialeah Dr (39211-4619)
PHONE..............................601 957-2530
Ernest L Bowen, *Principal*
EMP: 2 EST: 2010
SALES (est): 7.6K **Privately Held**
SIC: 2741 Miscellaneous publishing

(G-2529)
OLD HOUSE DEPOT LLC
639 Monroe St (39202-3423)
PHONE..............................601 592-6200
James Kopernak, *Mng Member*
EMP: 4
SALES: 450K **Privately Held**
SIC: 8712 2511 Architectural services; camp furniture: wood

(G-2530)
ORACLE AMERICA INC
Also Called: Storagetek
5723 Highway 18 W (39209-9604)
PHONE..............................601 352-6113
Larry Manuel, *Principal*
EMP: 3

2019 Harris Directory of
Mississippi Manufacturers

▲ = Import ▼=Export
◆ =Import/Export

GEOGRAPHIC SECTION

Jackson - Hinds County (G-2559)

SALES (corp-wide): 39.5B **Publicly Held**
SIC: 7372 Prepackaged software
HQ: Oracle America, Inc.
500 Oracle Pkwy
Redwood City CA 94065
650 506-7000

(G-2531)
OSBORN
4643 Medgar Evers Blvd (39213-5206)
PHONE..................................601 366-9902
Carl Brooks, *Branch Mgr*
EMP: 10
SALES (corp-wide): 612.9MM **Publicly Held**
WEB: www.schaffnermfg.com
SIC: 3291 Abrasive products
HQ: Osborn
21 Herron Ave
Pittsburgh PA 15202
412 761-9902

(G-2532)
OVATION WOMENS WELLNESS LLC
501 Marshall St (39202-1651)
PHONE..................................601 326-6401
Robert L Harris MD, *Principal*
EMP: 4
SALES (est): 242K **Privately Held**
SIC: 3842 Gynecological supplies & appliances

(G-2533)
PAINE INDUSTRIES
5000 Ridgewood Rd # 1311 (39211-5465)
PHONE..................................601 336-2069
EMP: 2 EST: 2017
SALES (est): 77K **Privately Held**
SIC: 3999 Manufacturing industries

(G-2534)
PARENTS AND KIDS MAGAZINE
817 E River Pl (39202-3403)
PHONE..................................601 366-0901
Gretchen Cook, *Principal*
Courtney Ray, *Accounts Exec*
Carrie Partridge, *Manager*
EMP: 9
SALES (est): 919.2K **Privately Held**
SIC: 2721 Magazines: publishing only, not printed on site

(G-2535)
PARTRIDGE PRODUCTION LLC
4273 I 55 N (39206-6111)
PHONE..................................601 987-4911
Richard Partridge, *Principal*
EMP: 3
SALES (est): 257.2K **Privately Held**
SIC: 1311 Crude petroleum production

(G-2536)
PATYCAKE KIDS LLC
258 Brae Burn Dr (39211-2504)
PHONE..................................601 506-7117
Shannon J Blank, *Principal*
EMP: 4
SALES (est): 218.5K **Privately Held**
SIC: 2051 Cakes, bakery: except frozen

(G-2537)
PAYMENT ALLIANCE PROC CORP
200 Briarwood West Dr (39206-3078)
PHONE..................................601 956-1222
Jeff Winkler, *Sales Staff*
John J Leehy III, *Branch Mgr*
EMP: 9
SALES (corp-wide): 52.2MM **Privately Held**
SIC: 3578 Automatic teller machines (ATM)
HQ: Payment Alliance Processing Corporation
2101 High Wickham Pl # 101
Louisville KY 40245

(G-2538)
PECANIER OIL & GAS LLC
1837 Crane Ridge Dr (39216-4902)
PHONE..................................601 982-3444
Linda Reed, *Mng Member*
David Russell,
EMP: 1

SALES (est): 158.7K **Privately Held**
SIC: 1389 Oil field services

(G-2539)
PICKENS HARDWOODS INC
127 Richardson Dr (39209-2515)
P.O. Box 1127, Clinton (39060-1127)
PHONE..................................601 924-1199
Fred Pickens, *President*
Sharon Pickens, *Vice Pres*
EMP: 2
SALES (est): 160K **Privately Held**
SIC: 5712 5211 2499 1751 Customized furniture & cabinets; lumber products; decorative wood & woodwork; carpentry work

(G-2540)
PITNEY BOWES INC
175 E Capitol St Ste 300 (39201-2110)
P.O. Box 811 (39205-0811)
PHONE..................................601 969-2900
Lindsey Glasgow, *Branch Mgr*
EMP: 3
SALES (corp-wide): 3.5B **Publicly Held**
SIC: 3579 7359 Postage meters; business machine & electronic equipment rental services
PA: Pitney Bowes Inc.
3001 Summer St Ste 3
Stamford CT 06905
203 356-5000

(G-2541)
POP-A-CART LLC
405 Briarwood Dr Ste 103a (39206-3029)
PHONE..................................931 292-2150
James Thomas, *CEO*
Elaine Gipson,
EMP: 2
SALES (est): 120K **Privately Held**
SIC: 3993 7389 Displays & cutouts, window & lobby;

(G-2542)
PORTABLE BORING & MCH WORKS
5556 Cahill Dr (39209)
PHONE..................................601 922-9333
David Edwards, *President*
Patricia D Edwards, *Vice Pres*
EMP: 2
SQ FT: 2,400
SALES (est): 50K **Privately Held**
SIC: 3599 Machine shop, jobbing & repair

(G-2543)
PORTSTONE MANUFACTURING CORP
114 Riley Dr (39209-2576)
P.O. Box 10266 (39289-0266)
PHONE..................................601 922-0902
Billy Debby Campbell, *President*
EMP: 9
SALES (est): 820K **Privately Held**
WEB: www.portstone.com
SIC: 3996 Hard surface floor coverings

(G-2544)
PRAIRIE FARMS DAIRY INC
427 Dory St (39201-6302)
PHONE..................................601 969-1307
Gary Hollis, *Manager*
EMP: 13
SALES (corp-wide): 1.7B **Privately Held**
SIC: 2026 2024 Fluid milk; ice cream & ice milk
PA: Prairie Farms Dairy, Inc.
3744 Staunton Rd
Edwardsville IL 62025
618 659-5700

(G-2545)
PRATT (MISSISSIPPI BOX) INC
Also Called: Pratt Industries
2031 Nw Progress Pkwy (39213-8310)
PHONE..................................601 366-3435
Brian McPheely, *CEO*
Anthony Pratt, *Ch of Bd*
Matt Melzer, *General Mgr*
David Wiser, *CFO*
EMP: 40
SQ FT: 65,000
SALES (est): 10.4MM
SALES (corp-wide): 2.5B **Privately Held**
SIC: 2653 Corrugated & solid fiber boxes

HQ: Jet Corr, Inc
1800 Sarasot Bus Pkwy Ne B
Conyers GA 30013
770 929-1300

(G-2546)
PRATT CORRUGATED HOLDINGS INC
2031 Nw Progress Pkwy (39213-8310)
PHONE..................................601 366-3435
EMP: 72 **Privately Held**
SIC: 2653 Corrugated & solid fiber boxes
PA: Pratt Corrugated Holdings, Inc.
1800 Sarasot Bus Pkwy Ne C
Conyers GA 30013

(G-2547)
PRECISION HEAT TREATING CORP
218 Yerger St (39203-2639)
P.O. Box 12396 (39236-2396)
PHONE..................................601 355-4208
Alfred T Bogen Jr, *Ch of Bd*
Alfred T Bogen III, *President*
Hilda Bogen, *Corp Secy*
Frank Percer, *Vice Pres*
▲ EMP: 12
SQ FT: 19,000
SALES (est): 800K **Privately Held**
SIC: 3398 Metal heat treating; brazing (hardening) of metal; tempering of metal

(G-2548)
PRECISION PACKAGING INC
2805 Meter Rd (39204-5917)
PHONE..................................601 352-2016
David G Meyer, *Vice Pres*
Carl Davidson, *Opers-Prdtn-Mfg*
EMP: 25
SALES (corp-wide): 30.6B **Privately Held**
SIC: 3272 Dry mixture concrete
HQ: Precision Packaging, Inc.
8900 Indian Creek Pkwy # 200
Shawnee Mission KS 66210
913 345-2030

(G-2549)
PRECOAT METALS INC
1095 Mendell Davis Dr (39272-9110)
PHONE..................................601 372-0325
Mike Flier, *Manager*
Brian McDonald, *Manager*
Duane Drew, *Executive*
EMP: 4
SALES (corp-wide): 2.4B **Publicly Held**
WEB: www.precoatmetals.com
SIC: 3724 3479 Aircraft engines & engine parts; coating of metals & formed products
HQ: Precoat Metals Corp.
1310 Papin St Ste 300
Saint Louis MO 63103
314 436-7010

(G-2550)
PRESTO MANUFACTURING COMPANY
109 Presto Ln (39206-2916)
PHONE..................................601 366-3481
Mike Joslyn, *Principal*
EMP: 3
SALES (est): 220.4K
SALES (corp-wide): 323.3MM **Publicly Held**
SIC: 3634 Electric housewares & fans
PA: National Presto Industries, Inc.
3925 N Hastings Way
Eau Claire WI 54703
715 839-2121

(G-2551)
PROCESS ENGINEERING CO INC
Also Called: Peco
4639 Medgar Evers Blvd (39213-5206)
P.O. Box 11189 (39283-1189)
PHONE..................................601 981-4931
Kieta Goolsby, *President*
Raymond Goolsby, *Vice Pres*
Betsy Bryant, *Human Res Mgr*
Dean Motella, *Marketing Staff*
Bessie Osgood, *Office Mgr*
EMP: 32 EST: 1935
SQ FT: 65,000

SALES (est): 9.2MM **Privately Held**
WEB: www.pecojacksonms.com
SIC: 3471 Electroplating of metals or formed products; anodizing (plating) of metals or formed products

(G-2552)
PRODUCT SERVICES COMPANY
Also Called: Gator International
266 Upton Dr (39209-2527)
P.O. Box 2337, Clinton (39060-2337)
PHONE..................................866 886-3093
Ted Dickerson, *President*
J Partick Dickerson, *Corp Secy*
▼ EMP: 37
SQ FT: 8,000
SALES (est): 4.3MM **Privately Held**
WEB: www.oilgator.com
SIC: 2843 Surface active agents

(G-2553)
PROTEES USA LLC
2650 Livingston Rd Ste A (39213-6904)
PHONE..................................601 317-3649
Linus Morgan, *Principal*
EMP: 1
SALES (est): 79.8K **Privately Held**
SIC: 2759 Screen printing

(G-2554)
PURPLE LABEL CANDLES
1127 Gentry St (39213-6624)
PHONE..................................601 955-2217
Jillian Harmon, *Principal*
EMP: 1
SALES (est): 39.6K **Privately Held**
SIC: 3999 Candles

(G-2555)
QUALITY PRINTING INC
Also Called: Mahaffey's Quality Printing
355 W Pearl St (39203-3002)
P.O. Box 23999 (39225-3999)
PHONE..................................601 353-9663
Robert A Mahaffey, *President*
Elizabeth Mahaffey, *Corp Secy*
Kevin Mahaffey, *Vice Pres*
Tim Mahaffey, *Vice Pres*
Robin Browning, *Accounts Mgr*
EMP: 38 EST: 1951
SQ FT: 15,000
SALES (est): 5.6MM **Privately Held**
SIC: 2759 2752 Flexographic printing; color lithography

(G-2556)
R & M PAINT DESIGNS
5839 N Commerce Plz Ste A (39206-2962)
PHONE..................................601 503-3631
Randy Morris, *Owner*
EMP: 1
SALES (est): 32K **Privately Held**
SIC: 2842 Automobile polish

(G-2557)
RANDELL MFG INC
1055 Mendell Davis Dr (39272-9788)
PHONE..................................601 372-3903
Randell Murphy, *Principal*
EMP: 8
SALES (est): 1.1MM **Privately Held**
SIC: 3999 Manufacturing industries

(G-2558)
RANKIN LEDGER
201 S Congress St (39201-4202)
PHONE..................................601 360-4600
Leslie Hurst, *President*
Jody Hook, *Opers Dir*
EMP: 5
SALES (est): 206.4K **Privately Held**
SIC: 2711 Newspapers, publishing & printing

(G-2559)
RAPAD DRILLING & WELL SERVICES (PA)
217 W Capitol St Ste 201 (39201-2004)
PHONE..................................601 649-0760
W Randy James, *President*
Bruce Hightower, *General Mgr*
Rick Calhoun, *Vice Pres*
Deborah Whatley, *Human Res Mgr*
James Rigney, *Manager*
EMP: 4
SQ FT: 30,000

(PA)=Parent Co (HQ)=Headquarters (DH)=Div Headquarters
✿ = New Business established in last 2 years

2019 Harris Directory of
Mississippi Manufacturers

97

Jackson - Hinds County (G-2560) GEOGRAPHIC SECTION

SALES (est): 1.3MM **Privately Held**
WEB: www.rapad-oil.com
SIC: **1389** Oil field services; roustabout
service

(G-2560)
RATLIFF FABRICATING COMPANY
100 Clay St (39213-2701)
PHONE....................................601 362-8942
Spencer Harrell, *President*
Sandra Harrell, *Vice Pres*
EMP: 10
SQ FT: 6,200
SALES (est): 1.6MM **Privately Held**
WEB: www.ratliffironworks.com
SIC: **3599** 3444 3443 3441 Machine
shop, jobbing & repair; sheet metalwork;
fabricated plate work (boiler shop); fabricated structural metal

(G-2561)
RED PENGUIN JACKSON ICE CREAM
Also Called: Good Deal Used Parts
1524 Highway 80 W (39204-2505)
PHONE....................................601 519-9901
Fernando Barone, *Owner*
Fernado Barone, *Owner*
EMP: 2 EST: 1998
SQ FT: 3,169
SALES (est): 128K **Privately Held**
SIC: **2024** Ice cream & frozen desserts

(G-2562)
REDDY ICE CORPORATION
607 S Jefferson St (39201-5620)
PHONE....................................601 948-0900
Bobby Newman, *Manager*
EMP: 22
SALES (corp-wide): 1.6B **Privately Held**
SIC: **2097** Manufactured ice
HQ: Reddy Ice Corporation
5720 Lyndon B Johnson Fwy # 200
Dallas TX 75240
214 526-6740

(G-2563)
REDI-STRIP OF JACKSON INC
Also Called: Metal Finishing Services
750 Boling St Ste C (39209-2652)
PHONE....................................601 355-3317
EMP: 10
SQ FT: 10,000
SALES (est): 1.4MM **Privately Held**
SIC: **3599** Metal Cleaning Job Shop

(G-2564)
RICHARD B BRANDON
5945 N State St (39213-9726)
PHONE....................................601 238-2383
Richard Brandon, *Owner*
EMP: 1
SALES (est): 54K **Privately Held**
SIC: **3429** 7389 Door locks, bolts &
checks;

(G-2565)
RIG MANAGERS INC
1907 Dunbarton Dr Ste A (39216-5027)
PHONE....................................601 362-5121
J Mark Hardee, *President*
EMP: 8 EST: 1997
SQ FT: 2,000
SALES (est): 643K **Privately Held**
SIC: **1389** Oil consultants

(G-2566)
RJ YOUNG
2030 Nw Progress Pkwy (39213-8302)
PHONE....................................601 948-2222
Doug Montgomery, *Executive*
EMP: 2
SALES (est): 85.9K **Privately Held**
SIC: **3579** Office machines

(G-2567)
RLT PUBLISHING LLC
3712 Thomas Jefferson Rd (39213-3025)
PHONE....................................404 956-8344
Sherry Tate, *Principal*
EMP: 1
SALES (est): 37.5K **Privately Held**
SIC: **2741** Miscellaneous publishing

(G-2568)
ROADSAFE TRAFFIC SYSTEMS INC
1416 Barnett Dr (39209-6620)
PHONE....................................601 922-5009
Charlie Bishop, *Branch Mgr*
EMP: 4 **Privately Held**
SIC: **3531** Construction machinery
PA: Roadsafe Traffic Systems, Inc.
8750 W Bryn Mawr Ave
Chicago IL 60631

(G-2569)
ROSSON EXLOPARTION COMPANY
Also Called: Bert J Rosson
4021 N State St (39206-5755)
PHONE....................................601 969-2022
Bert J Rosson, *President*
EMP: 2
SALES: 500K **Privately Held**
SIC: **1389** Oil field services

(G-2570)
ROSSON EXPLORATION COMPANY
814 N President St (39202-2560)
PHONE....................................601 969-2022
Bert J Rosson, *President*
EMP: 3 EST: 2001
SALES (est): 169.9K **Privately Held**
SIC: **1311** Crude petroleum & natural gas

(G-2571)
S & R METALS INC
2705 Lena St (39213-6913)
P.O. Box 10058 (39286-0058)
PHONE....................................601 982-1171
Scott P Tatum, *President*
Patrick F Tatum, *Vice Pres*
EMP: 16
SQ FT: 12,500
SALES (est): 2.3MM **Privately Held**
SIC: **3599** Machine shop, jobbing & repair

(G-2572)
SANDERS SONS DVRSFD WLDG ENTPS
1820 Valley St (39204-2439)
PHONE....................................601 969-3119
Joe L Sanders, *Owner*
EMP: 6
SQ FT: 5,502
SALES (est): 320K **Privately Held**
SIC: **7692** Welding repair

(G-2573)
SATCHEL LLC (PA)
121 N State St (39201-2811)
PHONE....................................901 515-8163
Frank York IV, *Principal*
EMP: 4 EST: 2017
SALES (est): 570.3K **Privately Held**
SIC: **3161** Satchels

(G-2574)
SCANLON-TAYLOR MILLWORK CO
2913 N West St (39216-3848)
P.O. Box 5029 (39296-5029)
PHONE....................................601 362-5333
Frances S Fraley, *President*
EMP: 60 EST: 1933
SQ FT: 70,000
SALES (est): 6.6MM **Privately Held**
SIC: **2431** Millwork

(G-2575)
SCENTED CREATIONS
1441 Canton Mart Rd Ste 6 (39211-5457)
PHONE....................................601 362-5926
EMP: 2
SALES (est): 129.2K **Privately Held**
SIC: **5199** 3999 Candles; manufacturing
industries

(G-2576)
SCHOLASTIC PRODUCTS AND AWARDS
Also Called: Balfour L G Co
1766 Lelia Dr (39216-4819)
PHONE....................................601 362-6990
James Nix Jr, *President*
Jimmy Nix, *Site Mgr*

▲ EMP: 10
SALES (est): 973.1K **Privately Held**
SIC: **2741** 5963 Yearbooks: publishing &
printing; jewelry sales, house-to-house

(G-2577)
SERAPHIM SOLAR USA MFG INC
3111 Lawson St (39213-5755)
PHONE....................................601 509-1265
EMP: 50
SALES (corp-wide): 2.4MM **Privately
Held**
SIC: **3674** Solar cells
PA: Seraphim Solar Usa Manufacturing,
Inc.
2150 Town Square Pl # 200
Sugar Land TX 77479
601 509-1265

(G-2578)
SHELBY LOGGING LLC
5521 Will O Run Cir (39212-3617)
PHONE....................................601 609-7796
EMP: 4
SALES (est): 255K **Privately Held**
SIC: **2411** Logging camps & contractors

(G-2579)
SHELTER FROM RAIN
2311 Breckinridge Rd (39204-5210)
P.O. Box 625 (39205-0625)
PHONE....................................601 454-7602
Brenda McConnell, *President*
Shelly Wiams, *Vice Pres*
EMP: 3
SALES (est): 137.1K **Privately Held**
SIC: **2032** Canned specialties

(G-2580)
SHORELINE POOL MFR INC
3774 I 55 S (39212-5170)
PHONE....................................601 372-0577
Larry Draughn, *Ch of Bd*
Shane Draughn, *President*
Tommy Draughn, *Vice Pres*
EMP: 7
SQ FT: 4,209
SALES (est): 1.1MM **Privately Held**
WEB: www.polymerconceptsinc.com
SIC: **3949** Swimming pools, except plastic

(G-2581)
SILLE BIOFUELS LLC
5513 Will O Run Dr (39212-3621)
PHONE....................................601 400-2227
Erick Ellis, *Mng Member*
EMP: 1
SALES (est): 55.4K **Privately Held**
SIC: **2899** 4226 Chemical preparations;
petroleum & chemical bulk stations & terminals for hire

(G-2582)
SIMPLE STONE SOLUTIONS
5760 Gallant Dr (39206-2934)
PHONE....................................601 206-5566
Edward Harrison, *Owner*
Terri Regan, *Co-Owner*
EMP: 5
SALES (est): 447.2K **Privately Held**
SIC: **5032** 3281 Granite building stone;
curbing, granite or stone

(G-2583)
SIR SPEEDY PRINTING CENTER
2701 N State St (39216-4304)
PHONE....................................601 981-3045
James Washington, *President*
Tina Murray,
EMP: 7
SQ FT: 4,000
SALES: 1.4MM **Privately Held**
SIC: **2752** Commercial printing, lithographic

(G-2584)
SNEAKER ADDICT CLOTHING
6468 Homewood Cir (39213-7813)
PHONE....................................601 212-3205
EMP: 1
SALES (est): 65.8K **Privately Held**
SIC: **3942** Clothing, doll

(G-2585)
SOCRATES GARRETT ENTPS INC
Also Called: Mississippi Link News
2659 Livingston Rd (39213-6926)
P.O. Box 11307 (39283-1307)
PHONE....................................601 896-0084
Leland Garrett, *President*
EMP: 10
SQ FT: 15,000
SALES (est): 4.2MM **Privately Held**
WEB: www.mississippilink.com
SIC: **5169** 2721 1611 1795 Chemicals &
allied products; magazines: publishing
only, not printed on site; gravel or dirt
road construction; wrecking & demolition
work; underground utilities contractor;

(G-2586)
SOMEFA LLC
2521 Harriotte Ave (39209-7408)
PHONE....................................601 506-1808
Christopher Russell,
EMP: 1
SALES (est): 68.1K **Privately Held**
SIC: **3571** Electronic computers

(G-2587)
SONNYBOYS GARMENT PRINTING LLC
3545 Rainey Rd (39212-4510)
PHONE....................................601 415-2250
Dana Williams, *Principal*
Gloria Benedict, *Principal*
EMP: 2
SALES (est): 164K **Privately Held**
SIC: **2752** Commercial printing, lithographic

(G-2588)
SOURCE
3645 Metro Dr (39209-7503)
PHONE....................................601 949-7878
Abdul Elabed, *Owner*
EMP: 9
SALES (est): 1MM **Privately Held**
SIC: **3827** Light sources, standard

(G-2589)
SOUTHERN CARBURETOR
5587 Robinson Road Ext (39204-4142)
PHONE....................................601 400-3716
EMP: 2
SALES (est): 85.9K **Privately Held**
SIC: **3592** Carburetors

(G-2590)
SOUTHERN HOSE & HYDRAULICS
4958 Highway 80 W (39209-4705)
P.O. Box 7595 (39284-7595)
PHONE....................................601 922-9990
Milam Cotten, *President*
EMP: 13
SQ FT: 15,000
SALES: 4MM **Privately Held**
SIC: **3569** Assembly machines, non-metalworking

(G-2591)
SOUTHERN RUBBER STAMP INC
121 Eltonwoods East Dr (39212-5394)
PHONE....................................601 373-6590
Vicky Chapman, *President*
EMP: 3 EST: 1970
SQ FT: 2,600
SALES (est): 260K **Privately Held**
SIC: **3953** Embossing seals & hand
stamps

(G-2592)
SOUTHLAND OIL COMPANY (HQ)
5170 Galaxie Dr (39206-4308)
P.O. Box 13609 (39236-3609)
PHONE....................................601 981-4151
James R Satcher, *President*
David Carroll, *Vice Pres*
Chris Contakos, *Vice Pres*
H G Buddy Voelkel, *CFO*
Michele Jarrell, *Treasurer*
EMP: 16
SQ FT: 11,500

2019 Harris Directory of
Mississippi Manufacturers

▲ = Import ▼=Export
◆ =Import/Export

98

GEOGRAPHIC SECTION

Jackson - Hinds County (G-2619)

SALES (est): 8.5MM
SALES (corp-wide): 35.7MM **Privately Held**
SIC: 2911 5172 Asphalt or asphaltic materials, made in refineries; oils, fuel; jet fuels; naphtha; diesel fuel; gasoline
PA: Galaxie Corporation
5170 Galaxie Dr
Jackson MS 39206
601 366-8413

(G-2593)
SPECTACLES INC
Also Called: Patton Family Optometry
120 District Blvd D109 (39211-6304)
PHONE....................................601 398-4662
Rebecca C Patton, *Exec Dir*
EMP: 10 EST: 2012
SALES (est): 1.3MM **Privately Held**
SIC: 3851 8042 Spectacles; offices & clinics of optometrists

(G-2594)
SPENCER READY-MIX JACKSON INC
9161 Highway 49 N (39209-2590)
PHONE....................................601 981-6080
Tim Spencer, *President*
EMP: 25 EST: 1989
SALES (est): 3.5MM **Privately Held**
SIC: 3273 Ready-mixed concrete

(G-2595)
SPINE STABILITY SURGICAL LLC
Also Called: S2s
2510 Lakeland Ter Ste 400 (39216-4717)
P.O. Box 1137, Ridgeland (39158-1137)
PHONE....................................800 991-3723
Larry Sudbeck, *Manager*
EMP: 6
SALES (est): 359.9K **Privately Held**
SIC: 3842 3841 Surgical appliances & supplies; surgical & medical instruments; biopsy instruments & equipment; ophthalmic instruments & apparatus; medical instruments & equipment, blood & bone work

(G-2596)
SQM NORTH AMERICA CORPORATION
Also Called: Chilean Nitrate
1325 Boling St (39209-2623)
PHONE....................................601 969-4710
Phillip Variola, *Manager*
EMP: 8
SALES (corp-wide): 242.1K **Privately Held**
WEB: www.sqmna.com
SIC: 2873 Fertilizers: natural (organic), except compost
HQ: Sqm North America Corporation
2727 Paces Ferry Rd Se 2-1425
Atlanta GA 30339
770 916-9400

(G-2597)
STAMM ADVERTISING CO INC
120 Upton Dr (39209-2525)
PHONE....................................601 922-3400
Herald Miller, *President*
EMP: 8
SQ FT: 6,025
SALES (corp-wide): 650K **Privately Held**
SIC: 2759 7311 Screen printing; advertising agencies
PA: Stamm Advertising Co Inc
3400 Drummond St
Vicksburg MS 39180
601 636-7749

(G-2598)
STORMCOM LLC
1230 Raymond Rd (39204-4583)
PHONE....................................601 918-5401
Ronnie Thompson, *Principal*
Jan Mangana, *Director*
Jasmine Thomas, *Assistant*
EMP: 1

SALES (est): 37.8K **Privately Held**
SIC: 7371 7372 7379 8742 Computer software development; utility computer software; ; management engineering; management information systems consultant

(G-2599)
SUNBELT MANUFACTURING COMPANY
5752 Gallant Dr (39206-2934)
P.O. Box 13806 (39236-3806)
PHONE....................................601 977-5292
Charles Molpus, *President*
Barry Molpus, *Vice Pres*
Ronnie Molpus, *Vice Pres*
Cynthia Molpus, *Treasurer*
EMP: 6
SQ FT: 3,750
SALES: 600K **Privately Held**
SIC: 3599 Machine shop, jobbing & repair

(G-2600)
SUNLAND PUBLISHING CO INC
Also Called: Northside Sun
246 Briarwood Dr Ste 101 (39206-3027)
PHONE....................................601 957-1122
Jimmye Sweat, *Editor*
John Wyatt, *Chairman*
Holly Dean, *Adv Dir*
Jennifer Stribling, *Adv Dir*
Wanda McCain, *Graphic Designe*
EMP: 15
SQ FT: 3,400
SALES (est): 997.7K **Privately Held**
WEB: www.northsidesun.com
SIC: 2711 Newspapers: publishing only, not printed on site

(G-2601)
SWELL O PHONIC
Also Called: Studio Chane
2906 N St St Ste 103 (39216)
PHONE....................................601 981-3547
Ronnie Chane, *Principal*
EMP: 3
SALES (est): 205.2K **Privately Held**
SIC: 5199 2389 3949 Advertising specialties; apparel for handicapped; skateboards

(G-2602)
SYNERGY PROSTHETICS CENTER
2 Old River Pl Ste D (39202-3435)
PHONE....................................601 832-4975
EMP: 2
SALES (est): 112.8K **Privately Held**
SIC: 3842 Prosthetic appliances

(G-2603)
T ENTERPRISES INC
Also Called: A 2 Z Printing
2125 Tv Rd (39204-4025)
PHONE....................................601 487-1100
Ehsan Taheri, *President*
Allen Taheri, *Owner*
Hootan Tabari, *Vice Pres*
EMP: 18
SQ FT: 4,800
SALES (est): 7.2MM **Privately Held**
SIC: 5111 7374 2752 Printing & writing paper; data processing service; commercial printing, lithographic

(G-2604)
TAYLOR RENE
Also Called: Rentay's LLC
521 N Canton Club Cir (39211-3441)
PHONE....................................601 977-8928
Rene C Taylor,
EMP: 1
SALES (est): 46.6K **Privately Held**
SIC: 3469 Household cooking & kitchen utensils, metal

(G-2605)
TAYLOR SCREEN PRINTING
700 S State St (39201-5613)
PHONE....................................601 352-9779
Greg Taylor, *Owner*
EMP: 2
SALES (est): 187.8K **Privately Held**
SIC: 2759 Screen printing

(G-2606)
THOMAS LARRY HEARN
Also Called: Belt Warehouse
1631 Westhaven Blvd (39209-5728)
PHONE....................................601 922-2700
Thomas Larry Hearn, *Owner*
EMP: 1
SQ FT: 2,500
SALES (est): 135.6K **Privately Held**
SIC: 2387 Apparel belts

(G-2607)
TIKAL PRINTS LLC
844 Lawrence Rd (39206-4922)
PHONE....................................601 954-0972
EMP: 2
SALES (est): 83.9K **Privately Held**
SIC: 2752 Commercial printing, lithographic

(G-2608)
TIPPO TIMBER COMPANY LLP
2436 Massena Dr (39211-4922)
PHONE....................................601 981-3303
Jobie T Melton Jr, *Partner*
EMP: 2 EST: 2001
SALES (est): 95.1K **Privately Held**
SIC: 2411 Timber, cut at logging camp

(G-2609)
TORCHD LLC
3325 Northview Dr (39216-3110)
PHONE....................................601 717-2044
EMP: 1
SALES (est): 39.6K **Privately Held**
SIC: 3999 Candles

(G-2610)
TRIAD OF MISSISSIPPI LLC
1685 Gregory Dr (39272-9455)
PHONE....................................601 373-7619
Chad Tyler, *Principal*
EMP: 1 EST: 1998
SALES (est): 60K **Privately Held**
SIC: 2731 Pamphlets: publishing & printing

(G-2611)
TRIANGLE RECYCLING SERVICES
Tri-Miss Services
416 W Woodrow Wilson Ave (39213-7524)
PHONE....................................601 352-5027
Ben Lilley, *Principal*
EMP: 19 **Privately Held**
SIC: 5051 4953 3341 Metals service centers & offices; refuse systems; secondary nonferrous metals
PA: Triangle Recycling Services Inc
6989 Us Highway 78 E
Anniston AL 36207

(G-2612)
TRODAT MARKING PRODUCTS INC (DH)
8339 Highway 18 W (39209-9658)
PHONE....................................601 500-5971
Poul De Martini, *President*
▲ EMP: 6
SALES: 5.7MM
SALES (corp-wide): 355.8K **Privately Held**
SIC: 5112 3953 Marking devices; marking devices
HQ: Trodat Gmbh
Linzer StraBe 156
Wels 4600
724 223-90

(G-2613)
TRONICSALES
1829 Meadowbrook Rd (39211-6526)
PHONE....................................769 218-0432
David Mims, *Owner*
EMP: 4
SALES (est): 156.6K **Privately Held**
WEB: www.getapc.net
SIC: 3577 7378 7389 Computer peripheral equipment; computer maintenance & repair;

(G-2614)
TUPELO DAILY JOURNAL NEWS BUR
Also Called: Northeast Miss Daily Jurnl
200 N Congress St Ste 400 (39201-1902)
PHONE....................................601 364-1000
Billy Truws, *Owner*
Bobby Harrison, *Chairman*
EMP: 1
SALES (est): 41.7K **Privately Held**
SIC: 2711 2721 Newspapers: publishing only, not printed on site; trade journals: publishing only, not printed on site

(G-2615)
UNIFIED BRANDS INC
Also Called: Groen
1055 Mendell Davis Dr (39272-9788)
PHONE....................................888 994-7636
Bill Scott, *Manager*
EMP: 10
SALES (corp-wide): 6.9B **Publicly Held**
SIC: 3533 Oil field machinery & equipment
HQ: Unified Brands, Inc.
2016 Gees Mill Rd Ne
Conyers GA 30013
601 372-3903

(G-2616)
UNIQUE SERVICES LLC
4955 N State St Ste A (39206-4047)
PHONE....................................601 326-9912
Roshell Baldwin, *Manager*
EMP: 3
SQ FT: 950
SALES (est): 116.7K **Privately Held**
SIC: 3499 6141 8742 Novelties & giftware, including trophies; personal credit institutions; new business start-up consultant

(G-2617)
UNITED GILSONITE LABORATORIES
3908 Beasley Rd (39213-3601)
PHONE....................................601 362-8619
Israel West, *Plant Mgr*
EMP: 20
SALES (corp-wide): 56.2MM **Privately Held**
WEB: www.ugl.com
SIC: 2851 2891 2861 2842 Varnishes; wood stains; paints & paint additives; adhesives & sealants; gum & wood chemicals; specialty cleaning, polishes & sanitation goods
PA: United Gilsonite Laboratories, Inc.
1396 Jefferson Ave
Dunmore PA 18509
570 344-1202

(G-2618)
UNITED PLASTIC MOLDERS INC
Also Called: Fish Group Company
105 E Rankin St (39201-6122)
PHONE....................................601 353-3193
W C Hoge Jr, *President*
EMP: 33 EST: 1978
SQ FT: 25,000
SALES: 3.9MM **Privately Held**
SIC: 3089 3552 Injection molding of plastics; dyeing, drying & finishing machinery & equipment

(G-2619)
UNIVERSITY PRESS MISSISSIPPI (HQ)
3825 Ridgewood Rd Unit 5 (39211-6460)
PHONE....................................601 432-6205
Craig Gill, *Director*
▲ EMP: 21
SALES: 1.9MM
SALES (corp-wide): 2.5B **Privately Held**
WEB: www.upress.state.ms.us
SIC: 2731 Book publishing
PA: Board Of Trustees Of State Institutions Of Higher Learning
3825 Ridgewood Rd
Jackson MS 39211
601 432-6198

(PA)=Parent Co (HQ)=Headquarters (DH)=Div Headquarters
✿ = New Business established in last 2 years

2019 Harris Directory of
Mississippi Manufacturers

99

Jackson - Hinds County (G-2620)
GEOGRAPHIC SECTION

(G-2620)
VAN PETROLEUM INC (PA)
Also Called: Southern Timber Venture
1300 Meadowbrook Rd # 202
(39211-6376)
P.O. Box 5327 (39296-5327)
PHONE..................................601 982-8728
William J Van Devender, *President*
Sidney P Allen, *Vice Pres*
EMP: 6 **EST:** 1981
SQ FT: 1,200
SALES (est): 869.5K **Privately Held**
SIC: 1382 Oil & gas exploration services

(G-2621)
VIBRANT SCREEN PRINTING
934 S Gallatin St (39204-3016)
P.O. Box 1192 (39215-1192)
PHONE..................................601 291-1296
Jonathan Gatlin, *Principal*
EMP: 2
SALES (est): 102.3K **Privately Held**
SIC: 2752 Commercial printing, lithographic

(G-2622)
VIZIONZ UNLIMITED LLC
Also Called: Hc2
5261 Greenway Drive Ext (39204-3212)
P.O. Box 7255 (39282-7255)
PHONE..................................601 272-5040
Putalamus White,
EMP: 2
SALES (est): 162.6K **Privately Held**
SIC: 8742 2752 2759 3993 Marketing consulting services; promotional printing, lithographic; commercial printing; promotional printing; signs & advertising specialties; commercial art & graphic design

(G-2623)
WALKER AUTO REPAIR SERVICE
624 N Mill St (39202-2905)
PHONE..................................601 969-5353
Cleophus Walker, *Owner*
EMP: 1 **EST:** 2007
SALES (est): 79.2K **Privately Held**
SIC: 7699 7694 7538 Engine repair & replacement, non-automotive; rebuilding motors, except automotive; engine repair

(G-2624)
WALLER BROS INC
524 E Pascagoula St (39201-4309)
PHONE..................................601 352-6556
Ed Waller, *President*
Donald D Waller, *Corp Secy*
Donald Waller, *Treasurer*
EMP: 4
SQ FT: 1,900
SALES (est): 388.6K **Privately Held**
WEB: www.wallerbros.com
SIC: 1382 1311 Oil & gas exploration services; crude petroleum production

(G-2625)
WASTE PLACEMENT INC
Also Called: Blueberry Hill Landfill
4164 Crestview Pl (39211-6404)
PHONE..................................601 362-5343
Joe Anglin, *President*
EMP: 4 **EST:** 1984
SALES: 50K **Privately Held**
SIC: 1241 Coal mining services

(G-2626)
WATKINS MAYOLA
Also Called: Pazzazz
900 Scr120 # 120 (39212)
PHONE..................................601 826-8310
Mayola Watkins, *Owner*
EMP: 5
SALES (est): 150K **Privately Held**
SIC: 3161 Clothing & apparel carrying cases

(G-2627)
WATKINS JR H VAUGHN
125 S Congress St # 1820 (39201-3301)
PHONE..................................601 898-9347
H Vaughn Watkins, *Manager*
EMP: 2
SALES (est): 81.9K **Privately Held**
SIC: 1382 Oil & gas exploration services

(G-2628)
WENDALL HARRELL
Also Called: Jackson Ice Co
607 S Jefferson St (39201-5620)
PHONE..................................601 353-3539
Wendall Harrell, *Branch Mgr*
EMP: 5
SALES (est): 502.6K
SALES (corp-wide): 713.4K **Privately Held**
SIC: 2097 Manufactured ice
PA: Wendall Harrell
589 Highway 488
Carthage MS 39051
601 267-3094

(G-2629)
WEST EXPRESS
3727 N West St (39216-3031)
PHONE..................................601 321-8088
Mohammed Thwayh, *Principal*
EMP: 3
SALES (est): 260.4K **Privately Held**
SIC: 2741 Miscellaneous publishing

(G-2630)
WHITE BROTHERS INC
Also Called: Hal & Mals Restaurant & Brewry
200 Commerce St Ofc (39201-4421)
PHONE..................................601 948-0888
Malcolm White, *President*
Harold White Jr, *Vice Pres*
Charles Abraham, *Manager*
Erin Pearson, *Asst Mgr*
EMP: 40
SQ FT: 36,000
SALES: 1.3MM **Privately Held**
WEB: www.halandmals.com
SIC: 5812 5813 2082 Restaurant, family: independent; bar (drinking places); malt beverages

(G-2631)
WHITEHOUSE INDUSTRIES
728 Windward Rd (39206-2316)
PHONE..................................601 981-5866
EMP: 2 **EST:** 2015
SALES (est): 99.1K **Privately Held**
SIC: 3999 Manufacturing industries

(G-2632)
WILBERT BURIAL VAULT COMPANY
820 Larson St (39202-3416)
P.O. Box 13307 (39236-3307)
PHONE..................................601 353-7084
Robert Martin, *Principal*
EMP: 3
SALES (est): 223.6K **Privately Held**
SIC: 3272 Burial vaults, concrete or precast terrazzo

(G-2633)
WILBERT FUNERAL SERVICES INC ◆
820 Larson St (39202-3416)
PHONE..................................800 323-7188
W Stellmach, *Mktg Dir*
EMP: 2 **EST:** 2018
SALES (est): 95.8K **Privately Held**
SIC: 3272 Burial vaults, concrete or precast terrazzo

(G-2634)
WILLOWOOD DVELOPMENTAL CTR INC (PA)
1635 Boling St (39213-4418)
PHONE..................................601 366-0123
Curtis Alford, *Exec Dir*
EMP: 80
SQ FT: 45,000
SALES: 4.9MM **Privately Held**
SIC: 8211 8331 7331 4783 School for physically handicapped; vocational rehabilitation agency; direct mail advertising services; packing & crating; motor vehicle parts & accessories

(G-2635)
WITHERS OIL & GAS LLC
1837 Crane Ridge Dr (39216-4902)
P.O. Box 55809 (39296-5809)
PHONE..................................601 982-3444
David Russell,
David B Russell,

EMP: 21
SALES (est): 1.1MM **Privately Held**
SIC: 3731 Drilling & production platforms, floating (oil & gas)

(G-2636)
WOLF RIVER PRESS
815 Reaves St (39204-5444)
PHONE..................................601 372-2679
Kathy R Pitts, *Owner*
EMP: 2
SALES (est): 87.3K **Privately Held**
WEB: www.wolfriverpictures.com
SIC: 8748 2721 Publishing consultant; magazines: publishing only, not printed on site

(G-2637)
WOLVERTON ENTERPRISES INC
Also Called: Micro Printing & Blueprint
225 E Pearl St (39201-3202)
PHONE..................................601 355-9543
Lorese Wolverton, *President*
Gerald Wolverton, *Exec VP*
Lorie Wolverton, *Office Mgr*
Tim Wolverton, *Manager*
James T Wolverton, *Shareholder*
EMP: 10 **EST:** 1990
SQ FT: 1,200
SALES (est): 1.3MM **Privately Held**
SIC: 7334 2752 2789 Photocopying & duplicating services; commercial printing, offset; bookbinding & related work

(G-2638)
WOMACK WILLOW
Also Called: Classic Printing
418 N Farish St (39202-3209)
P.O. Box 68696 (39286-8696)
PHONE..................................601 969-4120
Willow Womack, *Owner*
EMP: 2
SALES (est): 120K **Privately Held**
WEB: www.classic-printing.net
SIC: 2759 2791 2789 2752 Commercial printing; typesetting; bookbinding & related work; commercial printing, lithographic

(G-2639)
YANK THREADS LLC
611 Patton Ave (39216-3234)
PHONE..................................601 201-3934
Forrest Dear,
EMP: 1
SALES (est): 42.5K **Privately Held**
SIC: 2389 2759 Men's miscellaneous accessories; commercial printing

(G-2640)
ZERO DEAD MILES LLC
1245 Breckinridge Rd (39204-4577)
PHONE..................................769 208-8082
Maestro McLin, *Principal*
EMP: 2
SALES (est): 95.5K **Privately Held**
SIC: 3537 Containers (metal), air cargo

(G-2641)
ZYAA INC
2729 Bailey Ave (39213-6909)
PHONE..................................601 321-9502
Cassandra Malone, *President*
EMP: 1
SALES (est): 230.6K **Privately Held**
SIC: 5112 2396 5047 Manifold business forms; linings, apparel: made from purchased materials; beds, hospital

---

Jackson
Rankin County

(G-2642)
BOEING COMPANY
141 Military Dr Bldg 104 (39232-8851)
PHONE..................................601 936-8540
Eric King, *Manager*
Miles Webb, *IT Specialist*
EMP: 831
SALES (corp-wide): 101.1B **Publicly Held**
SIC: 3728 Aircraft parts & equipment

PA: The Boeing Company
100 N Riverside Plz
Chicago IL 60606
312 544-2000

(G-2643)
CONSTRUCTION METALS CO INC
2110 Highway 80 E Ste C (39208-3377)
P.O. Box 18, Brandon (39043-0018)
PHONE..................................601 939-2566
Don Ramsey, *President*
EMP: 1
SALES (est): 452.6K **Privately Held**
SIC: 5051 3441 Steel; fabricated structural metal

(G-2644)
DEVELOPING RESOURCES FOR EDUCA
310 Airport Rd S (39208-6649)
PHONE..................................601 933-9199
Kimberly Massey, *Principal*
EMP: 1
SALES: 1.5MM **Privately Held**
SIC: 2741 Miscellaneous publishing

(G-2645)
ERGON INC
Also Called: Paragon Technical Services
390 Carrier Blvd (39218-9400)
P.O. Box 1639 (39215-1639)
PHONE..................................601 932-8365
Paula Heard-Welch, *Office Mgr*
Scott Watson, *Branch Mgr*
EMP: 13
SQ FT: 7,200
SALES (corp-wide): 997.6MM **Privately Held**
WEB: www.ergon.com
SIC: 2911 4213 Gasoline; greases, lubricating; asphalt or asphaltic materials, made in refineries; liquid petroleum transport, non-local
PA: Ergon, Inc.
2829 Lakeland Dr Ste 2000
Flowood MS 39232
601 933-3000

(G-2646)
FRANK VILLINES
Also Called: RC Cola Bottling Co
401 Industrial Park Dr (39218-9549)
PHONE..................................601 939-5454
Walter Green, *Manager*
EMP: 2 **Privately Held**
SIC: 2086 Soft drinks: packaged in cans, bottles, etc.
PA: Frank Villines
810 Goblin Dr
Harrison AR 72601

(G-2647)
HANGER PROSTHETIC ORTHOPEDICS
Also Called: Hanger Prosthetics & Orthotics
15 River Bend Pl Ste B (39232-9524)
PHONE..................................601 939-2100
Jerrell Ballard, *Div Sub Head*
David Street, *Mktg Dir*
EMP: 7
SQ FT: 5,000
SALES (est): 675K **Privately Held**
SIC: 3842 5999 Prosthetic appliances; artificial limbs

(G-2648)
HANGER PRSTHETCS & ORTHO INC
Also Called: Hanger Clnic
15 River Bend Pl Ste B (39232-9524)
PHONE..................................601 939-2100
David Street, *Branch Mgr*
EMP: 4
SALES (corp-wide): 1B **Publicly Held**
SIC: 3842 Surgical appliances & supplies
HQ: Hanger Prosthetics & Orthotics, Inc.
10910 Domain Dr Ste 300
Austin TX 78758
512 777-3800

GEOGRAPHIC SECTION

Jonestown - Coahoma County (G-2676)

(G-2649)
INDUSTRIAL STEEL RULE DIE CORP
203 Priester Dr (39208-3305)
PHONE..................................601 932-5555
W E Baker Jr, *Principal*
EMP: 2
SALES (est): 123.4K **Privately Held**
SIC: 3544 Special dies & tools

(G-2650)
INTERNATIONAL PAPER COMPANY
211 Carrier Blvd (39218-4422)
PHONE..................................601 932-1422
Jermaine McClenty, *Purchasing*
Richard Cox, *Branch Mgr*
EMP: 130
SQ FT: 188,312
SALES (corp-wide): 23.3B **Publicly Held**
WEB: www.internationalpaper.com
SIC: 2621 2653 Paper mills; corrugated & solid fiber boxes
PA: International Paper Company
6400 Poplar Ave
Memphis TN 38197
901 419-9000

(G-2651)
JACKSON POWERTRAIN INC
1332 Old Brandon Rd (39232-3133)
PHONE..................................601 932-3159
John Middleton, *President*
Wrenn Rideout, *Vice Pres*
EMP: 8
SQ FT: 5,200
SALES (est): 1.1MM **Privately Held**
WEB: www.jacksonpowertrain.com
SIC: 3714 Crankshaft assemblies, motor vehicle

(G-2652)
JOHNS MANVILLE CORPORATION
286 Carrier Blvd (39218-9452)
PHONE..................................601 936-9841
Wayne Ishee, *Purch Mgr*
Jill Havard, *QC Mgr*
Mike Clark, *Manager*
EMP: 100
SALES (corp-wide): 225.3B **Publicly Held**
WEB: www.jm.com
SIC: 3296 Fiberglass insulation
HQ: Johns Manville Corporation
717 17th St Ste 800
Denver CO 80202
303 978-2000

(G-2653)
LEGENDARY LIGHTING LLC
1016 N Flowood Dr (39232-9532)
P.O. Box 321404, Flowood (39232-1404)
PHONE..................................601 932-0707
EMP: 22
SALES (est): 3MM **Privately Held**
WEB: www.legendarylighting.com
SIC: 3648 5063 Lanterns: electric, gas, carbide, kerosene or gasoline; electrical apparatus & equipment

(G-2654)
LOTT ENTERPRISES INC
Also Called: Pure Air Filter
1016c N Flowood Dr (39232-9532)
PHONE..................................601 932-4698
Reggie Methvin, *Branch Mgr*
EMP: 8
SALES (corp-wide): 30.9MM **Privately Held**
WEB: www.pureairco.com
SIC: 5699 3564 6515 Uniforms & work clothing; filters, air: furnaces, air conditioning equipment, etc.; mobile home site operators
PA: Lott Enterprises, Inc.
204 Eastman St
Greenwood MS 38930
662 453-0034

(G-2655)
MARUICHI LEAVITT PIPE TUBE LLC
211 Industrial Dr (39218-9548)
PHONE..................................800 532-8488
EMP: 3 **Privately Held**
SIC: 3317 Seamless pipes & tubes
HQ: Maruichi Leavitt Pipe & Tube, Llc
1717 W 115th St
Chicago IL 60643

(G-2656)
MCMILLON PALLET
540 Pemberton Dr (39208-5322)
PHONE..................................601 932-2299
EMP: 4
SALES (est): 190K **Privately Held**
SIC: 2448 Mfg Wood Pallets/Skids

(G-2657)
MIDCO SUPPLY CO INC
1420 Old Brandon Rd (39232-3221)
PHONE..................................601 932-7311
EMP: 3
SALES (est): 301.9K **Privately Held**
SIC: 3317 Mfg Steel Pipe/Tubes

(G-2658)
MUELLER PRESS COMPANY INC
631 Lakeland East Dr (39232-8815)
PHONE..................................901 753-3200
Lee R Nyman, *President*
EMP: 1
SALES (est): 52.4K
SALES (corp-wide): 2.5B **Publicly Held**
SIC: 2741 Miscellaneous publishing
HQ: Mueller Brass Co.
8285 Tournament Dr # 150
Memphis TN 38125
901 753-3200

(G-2659)
NUCOR CORPORATION
General Recycling Missisipi
2050 Flowood Dr (39232-2009)
PHONE..................................601 936-6292
Don Lemar, *Manager*
Don Le Mar, *Manager*
EMP: 30
SALES (corp-wide): 25B **Publicly Held**
WEB: www.nucor.com
SIC: 3325 3341 Steel foundries; secondary nonferrous metals
PA: Nucor Corporation
1915 Rexford Rd Ste 400
Charlotte NC 28211
704 366-7000

(G-2660)
ONEWAY INC
Also Called: Oneway Screen Printing
190 Parkison Dr (39218-4441)
P.O. Box 180149 (39218-0149)
PHONE..................................601 664-0007
Margaret Hemphill, *President*
Pam Dear, *General Mgr*
EMP: 6 EST: 1996
SALES (est): 831.9K **Privately Held**
WEB: www.onewaypromo.com
SIC: 2759 3993 5199 Screen printing; promotional printing; advertising novelties; gifts & novelties; badges; calendars

(G-2661)
PASSONS SPECIALIZED SERVICES
130 Interstate Dr (39218-9427)
P.O. Box 180056 (39218-0056)
PHONE..................................601 939-3722
Paul Passons, *President*
Stacy Adcock, *Vice Pres*
Erma Jean Passons, *Admin Sec*
EMP: 5 EST: 1981
SQ FT: 17,500
SALES (est): 901.3K **Privately Held**
SIC: 7699 3496 Printing trades machinery & equipment repair; woven wire products

(G-2662)
PEARL RUBBER STAMP & SIGN INC
Also Called: Thine Mark
228 N Pearson Rd (39208-4428)
P.O. Box 97383, Pearl (39288-7383)
PHONE..................................601 932-6699
Dale Harris, *President*
Lucy Harris, *Corp Secy*
Dwayne Harris, *Vice Pres*
EMP: 10
SQ FT: 8,000

SALES: 494.8K **Privately Held**
WEB: www.pearlstampandsign.com
SIC: 3069 7389 3993 Molded rubber products; sign painting & lettering shop; signs & advertising specialties

(G-2663)
PIERCE BODY WORKS
203 Belaire Dr (39208-3704)
PHONE..................................601 939-1768
Jeff Pierce, *Owner*
EMP: 2
SALES (est): 107.1K **Privately Held**
SIC: 3479 Painting of metal products

(G-2664)
RAYS MOBILE WELDING
1320 Old Highway 49 S (39218-9666)
PHONE..................................601 966-0848
Alex Ray, *Principal*
EMP: 1 EST: 2010
SALES (est): 39.3K **Privately Held**
SIC: 7692 Welding repair

(G-2665)
REBEL BUTCHER SUPPLY CO INC
106 Flowood Dr (39232-3205)
P.O. Box 54100 (39288-4100)
PHONE..................................601 939-2214
Michael Bush, *President*
Virginia Bush, *Corp Secy*
Kenneth Bush, *Vice Pres*
Jay Michael Bush, *Director*
EMP: 7
SQ FT: 18,000
SALES (est): 2.3MM **Privately Held**
WEB: www.rebelbutcher.com
SIC: 5084 2099 Food industry machinery; seasonings: dry mixes

(G-2666)
S & W WELDING & MACHINE WORKS
131 Walker Cir (39218-9245)
P.O. Box 180009 (39218-0009)
PHONE..................................601 939-8516
George Walker, *President*
Jerry Walker, *Corp Secy*
Bobby Walker, *Vice Pres*
EMP: 5
SQ FT: 3,000
SALES (est): 351.5K **Privately Held**
SIC: 7539 7692 Machine shop, automotive; welding repair

(G-2667)
SOUTHERN MARKETING GROUP
199 Interstate Dr Ste F (39218-9458)
PHONE..................................601 664-3880
Al Rathheim, *Branch Mgr*
EMP: 2
SALES (corp-wide): 1.2MM **Privately Held**
SIC: 3491 Industrial valves
PA: Al Rathheim
3764 Burdan Cv
Memphis TN 38118
901 547-0042

(G-2668)
STEEL SERVICE CORPORATION
2260 Flowood Dr (39232-9086)
P.O. Box 321425 (39232-1425)
PHONE..................................601 939-9222
Lawrence A Cox, *President*
Stewart C Heard, *Vice Pres*
Ray Carone, *Project Mgr*
Roger Ferril, *VP Mktg*
Joe Squyres, *Marketing Staff*
EMP: 150
SQ FT: 300,000
SALES (est): 74.9MM **Privately Held**
WEB: www.steelservicecorp.com
SIC: 3441 1791 3496 3443 Fabricated structural metal; structural steel erection; miscellaneous fabricated wire products; fabricated plate work (boiler shop)

(G-2669)
STEWARTS SCREEN PRINTING
413 Roberts St (39208-4635)
PHONE..................................601 932-8310
Sandra Hodges, *President*

EMP: 1
SALES (est): 51.9K **Privately Held**
SIC: 5699 2759 Miscellaneous apparel & accessories; screen printing

(G-2670)
TAYLOR MACHINE WORKS INC ✪
461 Highway 49 S (39218-9410)
PHONE..................................303 289-2201
Kathy Coward, *Office Mgr*
EMP: 2 EST: 2018
SALES (est): 81.4K **Privately Held**
SIC: 3599 Industrial machinery

(G-2671)
TAYLOR MADE LABELS INC
201 Industrial Dr (39218-9548)
PHONE..................................601 936-0050
Taylor Lyle, *President*
Beth Archer, *Human Res Mgr*
EMP: 4
SQ FT: 3,200
SALES (est): 509.1K **Privately Held**
WEB: www.ineedlabels.com
SIC: 2759 Labels & seals: printing

(G-2672)
ULMER MACHINE COMPANY INC
130 Aztec Dr (39218-9796)
PHONE..................................601 939-5812
James H Ulmer III, *President*
Todd Ulmer, *Vice Pres*
EMP: 10
SQ FT: 7,500
SALES: 1.9MM **Privately Held**
WEB: www.ulmcoinc.com
SIC: 3599 Machine shop, jobbing & repair; custom machinery

(G-2673)
VICTOR P SMITH OIL PRODUCERS
2 Country Pl (39208-6662)
PHONE..................................601 932-2223
Victor P Smith, *Owner*
EMP: 8
SALES (est): 660.8K **Privately Held**
SIC: 1311 Crude petroleum & natural gas

Jayess
Lawrence County

(G-2674)
MCCLOUD LOGGING INC
220 Jessie Wallace Rd (39641-9206)
PHONE..................................601 835-3217
Lance McCloud, *President*
Lowery Cpas, *Incorporator*
EMP: 1
SALES (est): 180.1K **Privately Held**
SIC: 2411 Logging camps & contractors

Jonestown
Coahoma County

(G-2675)
COTTONSEED CO-OP CORPORATION
100 Mill St (38639)
P.O. Box 9 (38639-0009)
PHONE..................................662 358-4481
Cliff Hitton, *Ch of Bd*
Jim Scott Middleton Jr, *President*
John B Laney Jr, *Treasurer*
EMP: 33 EST: 2015
SALES: 15.6MM **Privately Held**
SIC: 2079 4221 Cottonseed oil, refined: not made in cottonseed oil mills; cotton compresses & warehouses

(G-2676)
DELTA OIL MILL (PA)
100 Mill St (38639)
PHONE..................................662 358-4809
J S Middleton Jr, *President*
Scott Middleton, *General Mgr*
John B Laney Jr, *Corp Secy*
EMP: 49 EST: 1942
SQ FT: 2,000

(PA)=Parent Co (HQ)=Headquarters (DH)=Div Headquarters
✪ = New Business established in last 2 years

2019 Harris Directory of
Mississippi Manufacturers

101

GEOGRAPHIC SECTION

Kilmichael - Montgomery County (G-2677)

SALES (est): 8.7MM **Privately Held**
WEB: www.deltaoilmill.com
SIC: 2074 Cottonseed oil mills

Kilmichael
Montgomery County

(G-2677)
LOGGINS WOODWORK
237 Loggins Rd (39747-9304)
PHONE................................662 283-5882
EMP: 2
SALES (est): 25K **Privately Held**
SIC: 2499 Mfg Wood Products

Kiln
Hancock County

(G-2678)
**BLACK DIAMOND
CONSTRUCTION LLC**
17132 Bobinger Rd (39556-8444)
P.O. Box 128 (39556-0128)
PHONE................................228 342-2742
Chris Zimmerman,
Emmett Zimmerman,
EMP: 2
SALES (est): 105.1K **Privately Held**
SIC: 3537 Trucks: freight, baggage, etc.:
industrial, except mining

(G-2679)
GICLEE FINE ARTS
Also Called: Art and Photography Printing
15195 Ponotoc Dr (39556-8172)
PHONE................................228 586-2693
Judith Redshaw, *Owner*
EMP: 1
SALES: 25K **Privately Held**
SIC: 8412 2621 2741 Art gallery; printing
paper; art copy: publishing & printing

(G-2680)
**HOT STICKS MANUFACTURING
CO**
14198 Rd D Stnnis Indsl (39556)
P.O. Box 356, Waveland (39576-0356)
PHONE................................228 467-0762
Kevin Pokallus, *President*
▼ EMP: 10
SQ FT: 12,000
SALES (est): 1.2MM **Privately Held**
WEB: www.hotsticksdrumsticks.com
SIC: 3931 Drums, parts & accessories
(musical instruments)

(G-2681)
JL BROWNE INC
6182 Shawnee St (39556-8149)
P.O. Box 265 (39556-0265)
PHONE................................228 216-1137
James L Browne, *President*
Rebecca Browne, *General Mgr*
EMP: 2
SALES (est): 150K **Privately Held**
SIC: 3543 Industrial patterns

(G-2682)
KOENIG-STIMENS INC
Also Called: K S I
14258 Fred And Al Key Rd (39556-8053)
P.O. Box 360 (39556-0360)
PHONE................................228 467-3888
Edwin P Koenig, *President*
Paul Koenig, *President*
EMP: 29
SQ FT: 15,000
SALES (est): 5.4MM **Privately Held**
WEB: www.koenigstainless.com
SIC: 3444 Sheet metalwork

(G-2683)
MALLEY INC
1332 Rocky Hl Dedeaux Rd (39556-6008)
PHONE................................228 255-7467
EMP: 2
SALES (est): 100K **Privately Held**
SIC: 7692 Welding repair

(G-2684)
SELEX INC
7095 Roscoe Turner Rd (39556-8049)
PHONE................................228 467-2000
Terry Iraca, *Manager*
EMP: 3 EST: 2010
SALES (est): 211.6K **Privately Held**
SIC: 3812 Aircraft/aerospace flight instru-
ments & guidance systems

(G-2685)
**TYONEK SVCS OVERHAUL-
FACILITY**
7095 Roscoe Turner Rd (39556-8049)
PHONE................................256 258-6200
Paul Stein, *President*
Heather Hudson,
EMP: 2
SQ FT: 68,840
SALES (est): 91.4K
SALES (corp-wide): 161.3MM **Privately
Held**
SIC: 3812 Aircraft/aerospace flight instru-
ments & guidance systems
HQ: Tyonek Services Group, Inc.
1689 C St Ste 219
Anchorage AK 99501
907 272-0707

Kokomo
Marion County

(G-2686)
ANTHONY LOGGING INC
127 Rowley Rd (39643-4887)
PHONE................................601 731-2975
David Mitchell Anthony, *President*
Gayle Michael Anthony, *Admin Sec*
EMP: 2
SALES (est): 470K **Privately Held**
SIC: 2411 Logging camps & contractors

Kosciusko
Attala County

(G-2687)
ALAN DICKERSON INC
Also Called: Wamble Machine Shop
310 Knox Rd (39090-3463)
P.O. Box 886 (39090-0886)
PHONE................................662 289-1451
Glyn Alan Dickerson Jr, *President*
Joan Kelly Dickerson, *Treasurer*
EMP: 7 EST: 1932
SQ FT: 21,000
SALES (est): 600K **Privately Held**
WEB: www.alandickerson.com
SIC: 3599 3441 Machine shop, jobbing &
repair; fabricated structural metal

(G-2688)
**ATTALA STEEL INDUSTRIES
LLC (PA)**
2475 Attala Rd 2202 (39090)
P.O. Box 849 (39090-0849)
PHONE................................662 289-1980
Billy Atwood, *Mng Member*
▲ EMP: 5
SALES (est): 39.9MM **Privately Held**
SIC: 3339 Silver refining (primary)

(G-2689)
AZZ INC
2235 Attala Road 2202 (39090-6954)
PHONE................................662 290-1500
EMP: 2 EST: 2017
SALES (est): 111.1K **Privately Held**
SIC: 3699 Electrical equipment & supplies

(G-2690)
BARDO & CO
2007 Attala Road 1990 (39090-4492)
P.O. Box 1654 (39090-1654)
PHONE................................601 397-1167
Dale Bardo, *Owner*
EMP: 4
SALES (est): 240K **Privately Held**
SIC: 3589 7389 High pressure cleaning
equipment;

(G-2691)
COMPANION VANS INC (PA)
711 E Jefferson St (39090-3845)
P.O. Box 148 (39090-0148)
PHONE................................662 289-7711
Clifton D Bailey, *President*
Frank C Bailey, *Vice Pres*
EMP: 15
SQ FT: 30,000
SALES (est): 1.4MM **Privately Held**
SIC: 7532 3716 3711 Van conversion;
customizing services, non-factory basis;
motor homes; motor vehicles & car bod-
ies

(G-2692)
**DAVIDSON MARBLE & GRAN
WORKS (PA)**
318 Highway 12 E (39090-3421)
PHONE................................662 289-1337
Brian Griffin, *Owner*
EMP: 3
SALES (est): 442.6K **Privately Held**
SIC: 5999 3281 Monuments, finished to
custom order; cut stone & stone products

(G-2693)
**EYESORE YRD CLEANUP &
BUSHOGNG**
5131 Attala Road 3024 (39090-4972)
PHONE................................205 391-8232
Clint Allen, *President*
EMP: 2
SALES (est): 135.2K **Privately Held**
SIC: 3531 Backhoes

(G-2694)
GIBSON AND PICKLE INC
17757 Williamsville Rd (39090-9268)
P.O. Box 805 (39090-0805)
PHONE................................662 289-2400
Deborah Pickle, *Principal*
EMP: 2 EST: 2010
SALES (est): 96.7K **Privately Held**
SIC: 2035 Pickled fruits & vegetables

(G-2695)
**INTERSTATE INDUSTRIES MISS
LLC**
Kosciusko Attala Indl Par (39090)
PHONE................................662 289-3877
Sandra Landrum,
EMP: 125
SQ FT: 150,000
SALES (est): 15.6MM **Privately Held**
WEB: www.interstatellc.com
SIC: 3694 Harness wiring sets, internal
combustion engines

(G-2696)
JAKEN INDUSTRIES
404 Knox Rd (39090-3460)
PHONE................................662 289-7510
EMP: 2
SALES (est): 83.2K **Privately Held**
SIC: 3544 Mfg Dies/Tools/Jigs/Fixtures

(G-2697)
JOHNNY PARKS
Also Called: Premier Building Salvage
2079 Attala Road 3241 (39090-6643)
PHONE................................662 289-5844
EMP: 2
SALES: 115K **Privately Held**
SIC: 5211 3448 Ret Lumber/Building Ma-
terialsmfg Prefabricated Metal Buildings

(G-2698)
**LUVEL DAIRY PRODUCTS INC
(HQ)**
926 Veterans Memorial Dr (39090-3856)
P.O. Box 1229 (39090-1229)
PHONE................................662 289-2511
James Briscoe, *President*
Charles Terry, *Corp Secy*
Richard Briscoe, *Vice Pres*
Jack Briscoe, *Director*
EMP: 110
SQ FT: 45,000
SALES (est): 47.2MM
SALES (corp-wide): 1.7B **Privately Held**
SIC: 2026 2024 Fluid milk; ice cream & ice
milk

PA: Prairie Farms Dairy, Inc.
3744 Staunton Rd
Edwardsville IL 62025
618 659-5700

(G-2699)
**MALIBU LIGHTING
CORPORATION**
801 E Jefferson St (39090-3867)
PHONE................................662 290-1200
▲ EMP: 5
SALES (est): 627.6K **Privately Held**
SIC: 3612 Mfg Transformers

(G-2700)
**MASSEY CLOTHING COMPANY
LLC**
Also Called: Massey Kristy
104 N Jackson St (39090-3730)
PHONE................................662 792-4046
EMP: 2
SALES (est): 167.3K **Privately Held**
SIC: 5621 2329 Ret Women's Clothing
Mfg Men's/Boy's Clothing

(G-2701)
**MILK & HONEY PRTG PRESS
LLC**
305a N Natchez St (39090-3331)
P.O. Box 541 (39090-0541)
PHONE................................662 739-4949
EMP: 1
SALES (est): 40.5K **Privately Held**
SIC: 2741 Miscellaneous publishing

(G-2702)
**MISSISSIPPI MARBLE &
GRANITE**
Also Called: Monument Shop
406 E Adams St (39090-3706)
PHONE................................662 289-4111
Benard Nowell, *President*
EMP: 4
SALES (corp-wide): 7.7MM **Privately
Held**
SIC: 3281 Monument or burial stone, cut &
shaped
PA: Mississippi Marble & Granite Inc
600 N Court Ave Ste D
Louisville MS 39339
662 773-5051

(G-2703)
MITCHELLS WELDING LLC
2974 Attala Road 3024 (39090-5000)
PHONE................................601 554-6402
EMP: 5
SALES (est): 209.5K **Privately Held**
SIC: 1799 7692 Special Trade Contrac-
tors, Nec, Nsk

(G-2704)
**MOORES LOGGING &
TRUCKING**
6480 Highway 43 S (39090-9459)
PHONE................................662 289-5872
Anthony Moore, *Partner*
Brenda Moore, *Partner*
EMP: 2
SALES (est): 160K **Privately Held**
SIC: 2411 4213 Logging camps & contrac-
tors; contract haulers

(G-2705)
NAIL LOGGING
2032 Attala Road 3225 (39090)
PHONE................................601 953-0071
Benton Nail, *Owner*
EMP: 1
SALES (est): 62.6K **Privately Held**
SIC: 2411 Logging

(G-2706)
**NATIONAL COUNCIL OF NEGRO
WOME**
519 Hillview Dr (39090-3127)
PHONE................................952 361-6037
EMP: 1
SALES (est): 46.5K **Privately Held**
SIC: 2281 Yarn spinning mills

2019 Harris Directory of
Mississippi Manufacturers

▲ = Import ▼=Export
◆ =Import/Export

GEOGRAPHIC SECTION

Laurel - Jones County (G-2735)

(G-2707)
NICKERSON LOGGING
715 N Natchez St (39090-3361)
PHONE...................................662 289-9779
Albert Nickerson, *Owner*
EMP: 2
SALES (est): 102.8K **Privately Held**
SIC: 2411 Logging camps & contractors

(G-2708)
P ADAM MIDDLETON
101 Ridgewood Cir (39090-3265)
PHONE...................................662 289-7076
Susan Ellis, *Principal*
EMP:
SALES (est): 117K **Privately Held**
SIC: 3843 Enamels, dentists'

(G-2709)
PEARSON ENTERPRISES
11922 Highway 43 S (39090-4714)
PHONE...................................662 289-7625
Jerry Pearson, *Owner*
Justin Pearson, *Co-Owner*
EMP: 5
SALES: 250K **Privately Held**
SIC: 1741 1721 3271 Unit paver installa-
tion; pavement marking contractor; paving
blocks, concrete

(G-2710)
PQR INC
Also Called: Bluff Springs Paper
123 Pilsudski St (39090-3365)
P.O. Box 1139 (39090-1139)
PHONE...................................662 289-7613
Andrew Frank, *President*
Amanda Gentry, *Treasurer*
Mark Suggett, *Human Res Mgr*
EMP: 150
SQ FT: 5,000
SALES (est): 33.1MM **Privately Held**
WEB: www.bluffspringspaper.com
SIC: 2675 2679 Folders, filing, die-cut:
made from purchased materials; paper
products, converted

(G-2711)
**RIVES AND REYNOLDS LBR CO
INC**
Hwy 12 E (39090)
P.O. Box 310 (39090-0310)
PHONE...................................662 289-3823
Brant Quinn, *Manager*
EMP: 21
SALES (corp-wide): 18.4MM **Privately
Held**
SIC: 5031 2426 2421 Lumber: rough,
dressed & finished; hardwood dimension
& flooring mills; sawmills & planing mills,
general
PA: Rives And Reynolds Lumber Company,
Inc.
Hwy 15 N
Louisville MS 39339
662 773-5157

(G-2712)
SOUTHERN TEES PLUS
110 Aponaug Rd (39090-3506)
PHONE...................................601 896-7468
EMP: 2 EST: 2014
SALES (est): 89.2K **Privately Held**
SIC: 2759 Screen printing

(G-2713)
**SPOT CASH TIRE AND
APPLIANCE (PA)**
140 Highway 12 W (39090-3206)
PHONE...................................662 289-2611
Kenneth B Fowler III, *President*
Sandra Fowler, *Vice Pres*
EMP: 7
SQ FT: 7,500
SALES (est): 1.1MM **Privately Held**
SIC: 5531 7534 3639 Automotive tires;
tire repair shop; major kitchen appliances,
except refrigerators & stoves

(G-2714)
STACY ROBINSON
3077 Attala Road 1154 (39090-6522)
PHONE...................................662 289-4640
Stacy Robinson, *Principal*
EMP: 1

SALES (est): 80.8K **Privately Held**
SIC: 2741 Miscellaneous publishing

(G-2715)
STAR HERALD
207 N Madison St (39090-3626)
PHONE...................................662 289-2251
Stan Beall, *Editor*
Shelley Darwin, *Bookkeeper*
Daphne Dabbs, *Manager*
Jennifer McCaskill, *Graphic Designe*
EMP: 6 EST: 2014
SALES (est): 218.3K **Privately Held**
SIC: 2711 Newspapers, publishing & print-
ing

(G-2716)
TAVARES SIGNS
12038 Highway 12 W (39090-3651)
PHONE...................................662 289-5366
Art Tavares, *Owner*
EMP: 3
SALES (est): 242.3K **Privately Held**
SIC: 3993 Neon signs

(G-2717)
TECHNO-CATCH LLC
2087 Attala Road 5257 (39090-5133)
P.O. Box 1138 (39090-1138)
PHONE...................................662 289-1631
Hollis C Cheek, *Mng Member*
▲ EMP: 2
SQ FT: 20,000
SALES (est): 2.5MM **Privately Held**
SIC: 3523 Barn, silo, poultry, dairy & live-
stock machinery

(G-2718)
**TOWNSNDS AUTO REPR
WRICKER SVC**
Also Called: Townsend Wrecker & Auto Re-
pair
806 Highway 12 W (39090-9127)
P.O. Box 1642 (39090-1642)
PHONE...................................662 289-6845
EMP: 1 EST: 1967
SQ FT: 1,000
SALES (est): 69K **Privately Held**
SIC: 7549 3599 Machine Shop & Wreck-
ing Service

(G-2719)
**TRINITY HIGHWAY PRODUCTS
LLC**
2235 Attala Road 2202 (39090-6954)
PHONE...................................662 290-1500
Roger Bingham, *Branch Mgr*
EMP: 6
SALES (corp-wide): 2.5B **Publicly Held**
SIC: 3743 Freight cars & equipment
HQ: Trinity Highway Products, Llc.
2525 N Stemmons Fwy
Dallas TX 75207

(G-2720)
**WELL LOGGING SOLUTIONS
LLC**
1011 Hickory Ridge Dr (39090-4209)
PHONE...................................601 416-9241
James Thomas, *Manager*
EMP: 2
SALES (est): 65.5K **Privately Held**
SIC: 1389 Well logging

(G-2721)
YOUNG WELDING SUPPLY INC
723 Veterans Memorial Dr (39090-3854)
PHONE...................................662 792-4061
EMP: 1
SALES (corp-wide): 2.5MM **Privately
Held**
SIC: 7692 Welding repair
PA: Young Welding Supply Inc
101 E 1st St
Sheffield AL 35660
256 383-5429

Lake
Scott County

(G-2722)
GIBBS & SONS INC
1197 Old 80 Rd (39092-9253)
PHONE...................................601 775-3467
Jimmie Dale Gibbs, *President*
EMP: 1
SALES (est): 78.6K **Privately Held**
SIC: 7692 Welding repair

(G-2723)
LAKE MESSENGER
24642 Highway 80 (39092)
PHONE...................................601 775-3857
Frank Edmondson, *Owner*
EMP: 3
SALES: 80K **Privately Held**
SIC: 2711 Newspapers: publishing only,
not printed on site

(G-2724)
RANDY JUDGE LOGGING INC
122 Little Warrior Rd (39092-9644)
PHONE...................................601 775-3027
Terry R Judge, *President*
Amy Judge, *Corp Secy*
EMP: 13
SALES (est): 1.5MM **Privately Held**
SIC: 2411 Logging

Lake Cormorant
Desoto County

(G-2725)
LEGACY VULCAN LLC
15581 Graves Rd (38641)
PHONE...................................662 357-7675
EMP: 2 **Publicly Held**
SIC: 1442 Construction sand & gravel
HQ: Legacy Vulcan, Llc
1200 Urban Center Dr
Vestavia AL 35242
205 298-3000

Lakeshore
Hancock County

(G-2726)
**GULF SHORES SEA PRODUCTS
INC**
5122 Ship Yard Rd (39558)
P.O. Box 509 (39558-0509)
PHONE...................................228 323-6370
EMP: 3 EST: 2004
SALES: 250K **Privately Held**
SIC: 2499 Mfg Wood Products

Lauderdale
Lauderdale County

(G-2727)
FAITH INDUSTRIES LLC
3667 N Lake Dr (39335-9433)
P.O. Box 49 (39335-0049)
PHONE...................................662 618-0839
Judy Kimberly, *Principal*
EMP: 1
SALES (est): 42.8K **Privately Held**
SIC: 3999 Manufacturing industries

(G-2728)
RALPH MORGAN LOGGING INC
3714 Lauderdale Rd (39335-9632)
PHONE...................................601 679-5291
EMP: 30 EST: 1947
SALES (est): 3.3MM **Privately Held**
SIC: 2411 0212 Logging Beef Cattle-Ex-
cept Feedlot

(G-2729)
WOODIES WOODWORKS
3840 York Rd (39335-9599)
PHONE...................................478 973-8851

Woodie Stubbs, *Principal*
EMP: 1
SALES (est): 54.1K **Privately Held**
SIC: 2431 Millwork

Laurel
Jones County

(G-2730)
A B S WOODWORKS
258 Flynt Rd (39443-9059)
PHONE...................................601 425-3306
Allen Blankenship, *Owner*
EMP: 3
SALES (est): 267.9K **Privately Held**
SIC: 2431 Millwork

(G-2731)
**APPLIED INDUS TECH - DIXIE
INC**
Also Called: Applied Industrial Tech 0670
556 S 16th Ave (39440-4210)
PHONE...................................601 649-4312
Edgar Bartran, *Principal*
EMP: 5
SALES (corp-wide): 3.4B **Publicly Held**
SIC: 5085 5063 3492 Bearings; motors,
electric; hose & tube fittings & assem-
blies, hydraulic/pneumatic
HQ: Applied Industrial Technologies - Dixie,
Inc.
1 Applied Plz
Cleveland OH 44115
216 426-4000

(G-2732)
ASHLEY PRINTING CO
527 Hines Rd (39443-5707)
PHONE...................................601 729-8950
Robert Ashley, *Partner*
Mary A Ashley, *Partner*
EMP: 6
SALES (est): 494.1K **Privately Held**
SIC: 2759 Commercial printing

(G-2733)
**BAKER HGHES OLFLD
OPRTIONS LLC**
2628 Ellisville Blvd (39440-6006)
P.O. Box 1769 (39441-1769)
PHONE...................................601 649-4400
Don Bilbo, *Branch Mgr*
EMP: 16
SALES (corp-wide): 121.6B **Publicly
Held**
WEB: www.bot.bhi-net.com
SIC: 1389 Oil field services
HQ: Baker Hughes Oilfield Operations Llc
17021 Aldine Westfield Rd
Houston TX 77073
713 879-1000

(G-2734)
**BAKER HGHES OLFLD
OPRTIONS LLC**
270 Victory Rd (39443-2614)
PHONE...................................601 649-2704
Russell Brooks, *Manager*
EMP: 3
SALES (corp-wide): 121.6B **Publicly
Held**
WEB: www.bot.bhi-net.com
SIC: 1389 5084 Oil field services; pumps
& pumping equipment
HQ: Baker Hughes Oilfield Operations Llc
17021 Aldine Westfield Rd
Houston TX 77073
713 879-1000

(G-2735)
**BAKER HUGHES A GE
COMPANY LLC**
111 Avenue C (39440-5942)
PHONE...................................601 649-7400
EMP: 2
SALES (corp-wide): 121.6B **Publicly
Held**
SIC: 1389 Oil field services
HQ: Baker Hughes, A Ge Company, Llc
17021 Aldine Westfield Rd
Houston TX 77073
713 439-8600

(PA)=Parent Co (HQ)=Headquarters (DH)=Div Headquarters
✿ = New Business established in last 2 years

2019 Harris Directory of
Mississippi Manufacturers

103

Laurel - Jones County (G-2736)

GEOGRAPHIC SECTION

(G-2736)
BAKER HUGHES A GE COMPANY LLC
3705 Industrial Blvd (39440-5840)
PHONE..................601 649-1955
EMP: 2
SALES (corp-wide): 121.6B **Publicly Held**
SIC: 1389 Oil field services
HQ: Baker Hughes, A Ge Company, Llc
17021 Aldine Westfield Rd
Houston TX 77073
713 439-8600

(G-2737)
BAKER HUGHES A GE COMPANY LLC
2628 Ellisville Blvd (39440-6006)
PHONE..................601 649-4400
Todd Davis, *Engineer*
Jeremy Sokovich, *Accounts Mgr*
Don Bilbo, *Branch Mgr*
EMP: 15
SALES (corp-wide): 121.6B **Publicly Held**
WEB: www.bakerhughes.com
SIC: 1389 Oil field services
HQ: Baker Hughes, A Ge Company, Llc
17021 Aldine Westfield Rd
Houston TX 77073
713 439-8600

(G-2738)
BAKER HUGHES A GE COMPANY LLC
Also Called: B J Coiltech
2850 Industrial Blvd (39440-5900)
P.O. Box 24 (39441-0024)
PHONE..................601 425-1599
David Welborn, *Manager*
EMP: 18
SALES (corp-wide): 121.6B **Publicly Held**
WEB: www.bjservices.com
SIC: 1389 Oil field services
HQ: Baker Hughes, A Ge Company, Llc
17021 Aldine Westfield Rd
Houston TX 77073
713 439-8600

(G-2739)
BAKER PETROLITE LLC
3705 Industrial Blvd (39440-5840)
PHONE..................601 649-1955
Steve Martin, *Division Mgr*
David Speed, *Mfg Staff*
Jerry Fenton, *Branch Mgr*
EMP: 15
SALES (corp-wide): 121.6B **Publicly Held**
WEB: www.bakerpetrolite.com
SIC: 1389 5169 5084 Oil field services; chemicals & allied products; cleaning equipment, high pressure, sand or steam
HQ: Baker Petrolite Llc
12645 W Airport Blvd
Sugar Land TX 77478
281 276-5400

(G-2740)
BILLYS WELDING SERVICE INC
281 Freedom Rd (39443-7020)
PHONE..................601 649-1432
Billy Ray Hinton, *Principal*
EMP: 1
SALES (est): 59K **Privately Held**
SIC: 7692 Welding repair

(G-2741)
BOOMERANG SERVICES LLC
4398 Sharon Rd (39443-8026)
PHONE..................601 649-6474
EMP: 1
SALES (est): 63.2K **Privately Held**
SIC: 3949 Mfg Sporting/Athletic Goods

(G-2742)
BRADY ELECTRIC INC
510 Ellisville Blvd (39440-5049)
PHONE..................601 649-7862
Ricky Brady, *President*
Jerene Homes, *Vice Pres*
Cindy Sumter, *Admin Sec*
EMP: 14
SQ FT: 2,400
SALES: 2.5MM **Privately Held**
SIC: 7694 1731 Electric motor repair; electrical work

(G-2743)
BRANDON PETROLEUM PROPERTIES
544 Central Ave (39440-3955)
P.O. Box 2766 (39442-2766)
PHONE..................601 649-2261
Alexander Lindsey, *Partner*
John L Lindsey, *Partner*
Lex Lindsey, *Mng Member*
EMP: 4 EST: 1956
SALES (est): 314.2K **Privately Held**
WEB: www.brandonpetro.com
SIC: 1382 Oil & gas exploration services

(G-2744)
BRYAN INDUSTRIAL CO INC
822 Lake Como Rd (39443-8673)
PHONE..................601 649-8786
Paul Bryan, *President*
Keith Bryan, *President*
EMP: 15
SQ FT: 75,000
SALES (est): 2MM **Privately Held**
SIC: 2448 2441 Pallets, wood; nailed wood boxes & shook

(G-2745)
BURROUGHS BUS SALES INC
3626 Industrial Blvd (39440-5839)
PHONE..................601 649-3062
Robert Burroughs, *President*
EMP: 2
SALES (est): 226.7K **Privately Held**
SIC: 3711 Bus & other large specialty vehicle assembly

(G-2746)
C B R MACHINIST INC
11 County Barn Rd (39443-7507)
P.O. Box 1900 (39441-1900)
PHONE..................601 426-2326
Rayford Graham, *President*
Eva Graham, *Corp Secy*
EMP: 9
SALES (est): 750K **Privately Held**
SIC: 3599 7692 Machine shop, jobbing & repair; welding repair

(G-2747)
CAMERON INTERNATIONAL CORP
1020 Hillcrest Dr (39440-4728)
P.O. Box 3039 (39442-3039)
PHONE..................601 649-8900
Richard Brown, *Manager*
EMP: 6 **Publicly Held**
SIC: 1389 5082 Oil field services; oil field equipment
HQ: Cameron International Corporation
4646 W Sam Houston Pkwy N
Houston TX 77041

(G-2748)
CAMERON INTERNATIONAL CORP
16 Donald Dr (39440-4724)
P.O. Box 2594 (39442-2594)
PHONE..................601 425-2377
Ronnie Williams, *Manager*
EMP: 3 **Publicly Held**
SIC: 1389 Oil field services
HQ: Cameron International Corporation
4646 W Sam Houston Pkwy N
Houston TX 77041

(G-2749)
CAVINS CORPORATION
19 Nemo Clark Dr (39443-8847)
PHONE..................601 428-0670
Ezell Dickerson, *Owner*
EMP: 1
SALES (corp-wide): 0 **Privately Held**
SIC: 5084 1389 Oil well machinery, equipment & supplies; oil field services
PA: The Cavins Corporation
1800 Bering Dr Ste 825
Houston TX 77057
713 523-9214

(G-2750)
CENTERPINT ENRGY RSOURCES CORP
Centerpoint Energy-Entex
26 Mason St (39440-4438)
PHONE..................601 425-1461
Charlie William, *Sales/Mktg Mgr*
EMP: 23
SALES (corp-wide): 10.5B **Publicly Held**
WEB: www.reliantresources.com
SIC: 4924 1311 Natural gas distribution; crude petroleum & natural gas
HQ: Centerpoint Energy Resources Corp.
1111 Louisiana St
Houston TX 77002
713 207-1111

(G-2751)
CG WELDING SERVICES LLC
540 Norton Rd (39443-6979)
PHONE..................601 426-3922
Charles B Griffith, *Principal*
EMP: 1
SALES (est): 40.6K **Privately Held**
SIC: 7692 Welding repair

(G-2752)
CHANCELLOR INC
505 Avenue C (39440-5938)
PHONE..................601 518-0412
EMP: 10
SALES (corp-wide): 35MM **Privately Held**
SIC: 2869 Hydraulic fluids, synthetic base
PA: Chancellor, Inc.
1228 W 5th St
Laurel MS 39440
601 518-6455

(G-2753)
CHANCELLORS BUSINESS SUP INC (PA)
Also Called: Quality Office Supply
1325 W 5th St (39440-3809)
P.O. Box 224 (39441-0224)
PHONE..................601 426-6396
Sam Chancellor, *President*
Reba Chancellor, *Corp Secy*
Bill Chancellor, *Vice Pres*
David Chancellor, *Vice Pres*
EMP: 11 EST: 1967
SQ FT: 2,000
SALES (est): 1.3MM **Privately Held**
SIC: 5943 2711 Office forms & supplies; newspapers

(G-2754)
CHRONICLE
130 Leontyne Price Blvd B (39440-4428)
PHONE..................601 651-2000
Wyatt Emmerich, *Exec Dir*
EMP: 7 EST: 2012
SALES (est): 346.3K **Privately Held**
SIC: 2711 Newspapers

(G-2755)
CLINE LTD
366 Lower Myrick Rd (39443-6460)
PHONE..................601 649-6274
Lee Cline, *Owner*
EMP: 2
SALES (est): 176.5K **Privately Held**
SIC: 1311 Crude petroleum & natural gas

(G-2756)
COMMERCIAL CONSTRUCTION CO INC
1939 N Mississippi Ave (39440-2468)
P.O. Box 2794 (39442-2794)
PHONE..................601 649-5300
Charles V Landrum Sr, *President*
EMP: 70 EST: 1974
SQ FT: 18,800
SALES (est): 10.9MM **Privately Held**
WEB: www.ccctank.com
SIC: 3443 Tanks, standard or custom fabricated: metal plate

(G-2757)
CONSOLIDATED INC
1195 Trace Rd (39443-8433)
P.O. Box 424 (39441-0424)
PHONE..................601 425-2196
Sony Nail, *President*
▲ EMP: 10

SALES: 1MM **Privately Held**
SIC: 2511 2426 Wood household furniture; furniture stock & parts, hardwood

(G-2758)
DANNY BYRD LLC
1416 Sndrsville Sharon Rd (39443-8466)
PHONE..................601 649-2524
Danny M Byrd, *CEO*
EMP: 50
SQ FT: 28,500
SALES (est): 11.3MM **Privately Held**
WEB: www.dannybyrdinc.com
SIC: 1799 7353 1389 Rigging & scaffolding; oil field equipment, rental or leasing; construction, repair & dismantling services

(G-2759)
DAVIS & COOKE CUSTOM CABINETRY
203 S Magnolia St (39440-4433)
PHONE..................601 580-0181
Charles Davis, *Principal*
EMP: 1
SALES (est): 53.7K **Privately Held**
SIC: 2434 Wood kitchen cabinets

(G-2760)
DECIBEL AUDIO
2514 Highway 15 N (39440-1827)
PHONE..................601 649-1144
Shan Budley, *Owner*
EMP: 2
SALES (est): 188.7K **Privately Held**
SIC: 3651 Audio electronic systems

(G-2761)
DIXIE OILFIELD SUPPLY LLC
20 Crumbly Dr (39443-9344)
P.O. Box 2711 (39442-2711)
PHONE..................601 408-6027
John M Dubose III, *Mng Member*
EMP: 2 EST: 2015
SQ FT: 1,000
SALES: 127K **Privately Held**
SIC: 1389 Oil field services

(G-2762)
DNOW LP
Also Called: Distributionnow
2930 Industrial Blvd (39440-5914)
PHONE..................601 649-8671
Atley Lidlow, *Manager*
EMP: 9
SALES (corp-wide): 3.1B **Publicly Held**
WEB: www.natoil.com
SIC: 5084 7699 5082 1389 Oil well machinery, equipment & supplies; industrial equipment services; oil field equipment; oil field services
HQ: Dnow L.P.
7402 N Eldridge Pkwy
Houston TX 77041
281 823-4700

(G-2763)
DONALD L MCKINNON
548 Highway 533 (39443-8906)
PHONE..................601 319-3311
Donald L McKinnon, *Owner*
EMP: 1
SALES: 25K **Privately Held**
SIC: 1389 Oil consultants

(G-2764)
DUBOSE ELECTRIC
3963 Sharon Rd (39443-8412)
PHONE..................601 425-5116
Robin Dubose, *Principal*
EMP: 3
SALES (est): 163.2K **Privately Held**
SIC: 7694 1731 Coil winding service; electrical work

(G-2765)
E & D SERVICES INC
2300 Hwy 11 N (39440)
PHONE..................601 649-9044
Lavon Evans Jr, *President*
EMP: 50
SQ FT: 14,000
SALES (est): 3.8MM **Privately Held**
SIC: 1381 Drilling oil & gas wells

2019 Harris Directory of
Mississippi Manufacturers

▲ = Import ▼=Export
◆ =Import/Export

104

GEOGRAPHIC SECTION

Laurel - Jones County (G-2795)

(G-2766)
EASTERN FISHING & RENTAL TL CO
2406 Moose Dr (39440-3728)
P.O. Box 292 (39441-0292)
PHONE..................601 649-1454
Nick Welch, *President*
Darren Welch, *Controller*
EMP: 69
SQ FT: 2,300
SALES (est): 12.5MM **Privately Held**
SIC: 1389 Oil field services

(G-2767)
ESSMUELLER COMPANY
Also Called: Essmueller Home Offices
334 Ave A Airbase (39440)
PHONE..................601 649-2400
William L Mc Lean, *Ch of Bd*
Patricia E Mc Lean, *Principal*
Donald R Merten, *Exec VP*
Matthew McLean, *Vice Pres*
Dale Harris, *CFO*
▼ **EMP:** 100
SQ FT: 175,000
SALES (est): 45.8MM **Privately Held**
WEB: www.essmueller.com
SIC: 3535 Bulk handling conveyor systems

(G-2768)
FRETWELL (NOT INCORPORATED)
Also Called: Fretwell's
3031 Ellisville Blvd (39440-6022)
P.O. Box 385 (39441-0385)
PHONE..................601 649-0003
Windell F Fretwell, *Owner*
Windell Fretwell, *Owner*
EMP: 3
SQ FT: 5,000
SALES (est): 312K **Privately Held**
SIC: 5082 3599 Oil field equipment; machine & other job shop work

(G-2769)
GE OIL & GAS PRESSURE CTRL LP
Also Called: ERC Wellheads
20 Service Blvd (39440-6014)
PHONE..................601 425-1436
Ryan Thrash, *Manager*
EMP: 7
SALES (corp-wide): 121.6B **Publicly Held**
WEB: www.woodgroup.com
SIC: 7699 1389 Welding equipment repair; oil field services
HQ: Ge Oil & Gas Pressure Control Lp
4424 W Sam Houston Pkwy N # 100
Houston TX 77041
281 398-8901

(G-2770)
GIN CREEK PUBLISHING
318 N Magnolia St (39440-3932)
PHONE..................601 649-9388
Jim Cegielski, *Principal*
EMP: 8
SALES: 300K **Privately Held**
SIC: 2711 Newspapers

(G-2771)
GLAD INDUSTRIES
1001 S 4th Ave (39440-5110)
PHONE..................601 422-0261
EMP: 1 **EST:** 2006
SALES (est): 49K **Privately Held**
SIC: 3999 Mfg Misc Products

(G-2772)
GLOBAL VESSEL TANK ✪
1939 N Mississippi Ave (39440-2468)
PHONE..................601 649-5300
EMP: 2 **EST:** 2019
SALES (est): 95.5K **Privately Held**
SIC: 3533 Oil & gas field machinery

(G-2773)
GULF STATES FABRICATION INC
5311 Highway 15 N (39443-8255)
PHONE..................601 426-9006
Steven A Gavin, *President*
Brenda Gavin, *Vice Pres*
EMP: 11
SQ FT: 18,000

SALES (est): 2.4MM **Privately Held**
SIC: 3441 5947 Fabricated structural metal; artcraft & carvings

(G-2774)
GULF STATES FORMING SYSTEMS
528 Avenue B (39440-5929)
P.O. Box 1348 (39441-1348)
PHONE..................601 428-1582
Joe M McCann, *President*
Pamela G McCann, *Vice Pres*
EMP: 15
SALES: 1.5MM **Privately Held**
SIC: 3272 Concrete stuctural support & building material

(G-2775)
HAROLD KNIGHT SEW MCHS & APPLS (PA)
Also Called: Harold Sewing Center & Trctrs
721 S Magnolia St (39440-4423)
PHONE..................601 425-2220
Harold W Knight, *President*
William Harold Knight Jr, *President*
EMP: 2 **EST:** 1948
SQ FT: 1,200
SALES: 1MM **Privately Held**
SIC: 3523 5999 5719 Planting machines, agricultural; farm tractors; bedding (sheets, blankets, spreads & pillows)

(G-2776)
HEADRICK SIGNS & GRAPHICS INC
1 Freedom Sq (39440-3367)
PHONE..................601 649-1977
Richard Headrick, *President*
Terry Busbea, *Vice Pres*
Buddy McCardle, *CFO*
◆ **EMP:** 60
SQ FT: 50,000
SALES (est): 9.5MM **Privately Held**
SIC: 3993 Electric signs

(G-2777)
HEAVY DUTY INDUSTRIES INC
841 Masonite Dr (39440-5126)
PHONE..................601 425-1011
John Hanna, *President*
Mack Strickland, *Treasurer*
EMP: 3
SQ FT: 3,600
SALES: 200K **Privately Held**
SIC: 3469 Metal stampings

(G-2778)
HOLCOMB HANDIMAN SVCS CSTM WOO
1137 W 20th St (39440-2107)
PHONE..................601 394-4284
EMP: 1
SALES (est): 54.1K **Privately Held**
SIC: 2431 Millwork

(G-2779)
HOWARD INDUSTRIES INC
Also Called: Howard Computers
580 Eastview Dr (39443-5332)
P.O. Box 1590 (39441-1590)
PHONE..................601 422-0033
Billy Howrd Sr, *President*
Kyle Mc Coy, *Exec VP*
David Ditirro, *Vice Pres*
Roger May, *Vice Pres*
Derral Ward, *Vice Pres*
EMP: 500
SALES (corp-wide): 19.3MM **Privately Held**
WEB: www.howard-ind.com
SIC: 4213 5063 3612 3646 Contract haulers; electrical apparatus & equipment; transformers, except electric; commercial indusl & institutional electric lighting fixtures
PA: Howard Industries, Inc.
36 Howard Dr
Ellisville MS 39437
601 425-3151

(G-2780)
HOWARD INDUSTRIES INC
3225 Pendorff Rd (39440-5820)
P.O. Box 1588 (39441-1588)
PHONE..................601 425-3151

Donald Saget, *Vice Pres*
Renee Jones, *Purchasing*
Michelle Howard, *Treasurer*
Tina Adams, *Accounting Mgr*
Lonnie J Hodnett, *VP Sales*
EMP: 1
SALES (corp-wide): 19.3MM **Privately Held**
SIC: 4213 3612 Contract haulers; power transformers, electric; ballasts for lighting fixtures; power & distribution transformers
PA: Howard Industries, Inc.
36 Howard Dr
Ellisville MS 39437
601 425-3151

(G-2781)
HOWARD TECHNOLOGY SOLUTIONS
580 Eastview Dr (39443-5332)
PHONE..................601 428-2200
Jennifer McLelland, *Sales Staff*
Andy Finnegan, *IT/INT Sup*
EMP: 3
SALES (est): 94.5K **Privately Held**
SIC: 3571 Electronic computers

(G-2782)
HOWSE IMPLEMENT COMPANY INC
Also Called: Agrimotive Division
2013 Highway 184 (39443-8302)
P.O. Box 365 (39441-0365)
PHONE..................601 428-0841
Benjamin T Howse, *President*
Ben Howse, *President*
Barry D Howse, *Treasurer*
▲ **EMP:** 120 **EST:** 1964
SQ FT: 268,811
SALES (est): 31.5MM **Privately Held**
SIC: 3523 Grounds mowing equipment

(G-2783)
HUNTIN CAMP LLC
2110 Sandy Ln (39443-9087)
PHONE..................601 649-6334
Mike Wages,
Bob Sullivan,
EMP: 2
SALES (est): 402K **Privately Held**
SIC: 3949 Sporting & athletic goods

(G-2784)
ISHEE PRODUCE
1654 Highway 184 (39443-9549)
PHONE..................601 651-6643
Floyd Ishee, *Owner*
EMP: 4
SALES (est): 142.5K **Privately Held**
SIC: 2037 Frozen fruits & vegetables

(G-2785)
J R POUNDS INC
805 W 5th St (39440-3430)
P.O. Box 991 (39441-0991)
PHONE..................601 649-1743
J Ray Pounds Sr, *President*
James R Pounds Jr, *President*
EMP: 5
SQ FT: 1,400
SALES (est): 772.1K **Privately Held**
SIC: 1311 Crude petroleum & natural gas production

(G-2786)
JAKES WOODWORK LLC
817 W 7th St (39440-3458)
PHONE..................601 651-6278
Jacob Moore, *Principal*
EMP: 1
SALES (est): 80.8K **Privately Held**
SIC: 2434 2511 Wood kitchen cabinets; wood household furniture

(G-2787)
JEREMY RAY WELDING SERVICE LLC
34 Kennon Ave (39443-6423)
PHONE..................601 433-4905
EMP: 1
SALES (est): 56.7K **Privately Held**
SIC: 7692 Welding repair

(G-2788)
JOHNNIE WRIGHT RADIATOR & WLDG
315 E 15th St (39440-3000)
P.O. Box 174 (39441-0174)
PHONE..................601 428-5013
Mike Wilkerson, *President*
Penny Wilkerson, *Vice Pres*
EMP: 4
SQ FT: 6,300
SALES (est): 233.9K **Privately Held**
SIC: 7539 7692 Radiator repair shop, automotive; automotive welding

(G-2789)
K&D WRIGHT LOGGING
28 E Brushy Rd (39443-0781)
PHONE..................601 729-5675
Kevin Wright, *Principal*
EMP: 6
SALES (est): 603.4K **Privately Held**
SIC: 2411 Logging camps & contractors

(G-2790)
KSJ INDUSTRIES
4630 Sharon Rd (39443-8084)
PHONE..................601 493-3991
Karla Jordan, *Principal*
EMP: 1
SALES (est): 52.6K **Privately Held**
SIC: 3999 Manufacturing industries

(G-2791)
LACKNOTHING ENTERPRISES LLC
19 Sunset Rd (39440-3741)
PHONE..................601 498-1000
Adam Lack,
EMP: 2
SALES (est): 62.5K **Privately Held**
SIC: 3999 Manufacturing industries

(G-2792)
LADNER LOGGING LLC ✪
1727 Highway 184 (39443-9585)
PHONE..................601 422-7822
EMP: 2 **EST:** 2018
SALES (est): 81.7K **Privately Held**
SIC: 2411 Logging

(G-2793)
LAUREL MACHINE AND FOUNDRY CO
Also Called: Lmf
810 Front St (39440-3548)
P.O. Box 1049 (39441-1049)
PHONE..................601 428-0541
Patrick Mulloy, *CEO*
Trent A Mulloy, *President*
Chuck Bridges, *CFO*
Norman Hinton, *Information Mgr*
Ray Robinson, *Admin Sec*
EMP: 140
SQ FT: 400,000
SALES (est): 35.9MM **Privately Held**
WEB: www.lmfco.com
SIC: 3599 3441 5051 3443 Machine shop, jobbing & repair; fabricated structural metal; metals service centers & offices; fabricated plate work (boiler shop); mill supplies; gray & ductile iron foundries

(G-2794)
LEE & LEE SERVICES INC
542 Lake Como Rd (39443-0962)
PHONE..................601 425-1060
Hilton Lee, *President*
Lola Lee, *Vice Pres*
EMP: 11
SQ FT: 800
SALES (est): 1MM **Privately Held**
SIC: 1389 Oil field services

(G-2795)
LEECO WELDING SERVICE
67 Victory Rd (39443-9567)
PHONE..................601 428-7896
EMP: 1
SALES (est): 48K **Privately Held**
SIC: 7692 Welding Repair

(PA)=Parent Co (HQ)=Headquarters (DH)=Div Headquarters
✪ = New Business established in last 2 years

2019 Harris Directory of
Mississippi Manufacturers

105

Laurel - Jones County (G-2796)

GEOGRAPHIC SECTION

(G-2796)
LIVINGSTON LOG & TIMBER CO INC
64 Jess Livingston Rd (39443-6417)
PHONE..................601 425-2095
Billy W Livingston, *President*
Scott Livingston, *Vice Pres*
EMP: 5
SALES (est): 325.1K **Privately Held**
SIC: 2411 7389 Logging; personal service agents, brokers & bureaus

(G-2797)
MASCO WIRELINE SERVICE INC
337 Avenue A (39440-5836)
PHONE..................601 428-7966
Nola Adams, *President*
Cindy Mercer, *Corp Secy*
Keith Mercer, *Vice Pres*
EMP: 33
SQ FT: 1,500
SALES (est): 3.8MM **Privately Held**
SIC: 1389 Gas field services; oil field services

(G-2798)
MASONITE CORPORATION
1001 S 4th Ave (39440-5110)
PHONE..................601 422-2200
Jim Rabe, *Vice Pres*
Vera Ross, *Production*
Linda Shivers, *Buyer*
Rick Woodfield, *Cust Mgr*
Frederick J Lynch, *Branch Mgr*
EMP: 96
SALES (corp-wide): 2.1B **Publicly Held**
SIC: 2431 Doors, wood
HQ: Masonite Corporation
201 N Franklin St Ste 300
Tampa FL 33602
813 877-2726

(G-2799)
MERCER WELDING SERVICE
636 Poole Creek Rd (39443-6224)
P.O. Box 2923 (39442-2923)
PHONE..................601 649-4269
Thomas Mercer, *Owner*
EMP: 1
SALES (est): 70K **Privately Held**
WEB: www.mercervufarms.com
SIC: 1799 7692 Welding on site; welding repair

(G-2800)
MERIDIAN BRICK LLC
Boral Bricks Studio
1 Brickyard Dr (39440-2416)
PHONE..................601 428-4364
Jim Stewart, *Manager*
EMP: 12
SALES (corp-wide): 441MM **Privately Held**
WEB: www.boralbricks.com
SIC: 5211 3251 Brick; brick & structural clay tile
PA: Meridian Brick Llc
6455 Shiloh Rd D
Alpharetta GA 30005
770 645-4500

(G-2801)
METAL BUILDING SYSTEMS LLC
2 Twin Oaks Pl (39440-9004)
P.O. Box 63 (39441-0063)
PHONE..................601 649-9949
Gregory D Rustin, *Principal*
Joan Byrd,
EMP: 15 EST: 1998
SQ FT: 30,000
SALES (est): 3MM **Privately Held**
SIC: 3441 Fabricated structural metal

(G-2802)
MICKEYS TROPHY & SIGN SHOP
444 Front St (39440-3902)
P.O. Box 171 (39441-0171)
PHONE..................601 649-1263
Mickey Arledge, *Owner*
EMP: 5
SQ FT: 5,000
SALES (est): 489.5K **Privately Held**
WEB: www.mickeys.net
SIC: 5999 3993 Trophies & plaques; signs & advertising specialties

(G-2803)
MID-SOUTH INDUSTRIES INC
Also Called: Thermo-Kool
723 E 21st St (39440-2457)
P.O. Box 989 (39441-0989)
PHONE..................601 649-4600
M Randolph McLaughlin, *President*
Teri Brewer, *Vice Pres*
Lee Thames, *Vice Pres*
Carl Stevenson, *Plant Supt*
Paul Moss, *Accounting Mgr*
▼ EMP: 154
SQ FT: 122,000
SALES (est): 40MM **Privately Held**
WEB: www.thermokool.com
SIC: 3585 Lockers, refrigerated

(G-2804)
MISSISSIPPI BAPTIST PAPER
4228 Highway 15 N (39440-1026)
P.O. Box 8181 (39441-8181)
PHONE..................601 426-3293
Don Brown, *Principal*
EMP: 1
SALES (est): 75K **Privately Held**
WEB: www.msbaptist.org
SIC: 2721 Periodicals

(G-2805)
MONCLA COMPANIES
1250 1/2 Hillcrest Dr (39440-4734)
PHONE..................601 428-4322
Buck Moncla, *Sales Staff*
Johnny Cook, *Branch Mgr*
Jeff Casey, *Manager*
EMP: 45 EST: 2015
SALES (est): 887.7K **Privately Held**
SIC: 1389 Oil field services

(G-2806)
MONOGRAM STITCH LLC
688 Sharon Moss Rd (39443-8454)
PHONE..................601 649-1582
Kimberly Johnson, *Principal*
EMP: 1
SALES (est): 65.1K **Privately Held**
SIC: 2395 Embroidery & art needlework

(G-2807)
MORGAN BROTHERS MILLWORK INC (PA)
Bruce Ave Ste 1 (39440)
P.O. Box 4343 (39441-4343)
PHONE..................601 649-9188
Steve Morgan, *President*
Mark Morgan, *Corp Secy*
Alan Morgan, *Vice Pres*
Dale Caves, *Human Res Mgr*
Linda Phillips, *Receptionist*
EMP: 180
SQ FT: 100,000
SALES (est): 28.3MM **Privately Held**
SIC: 2431 Doors, wood

(G-2808)
MORRIS WELDING SERVICE
183 Lebanon Rd (39443-2937)
PHONE..................601 729-2737
John David Morris, *Owner*
EMP: 2
SALES (est): 110K **Privately Held**
SIC: 7692 Welding repair

(G-2809)
MULTI-CHEM GROUP LLC
1643 Highway 184 (39443-9272)
PHONE..................601 425-1131
EMP: 19 **Publicly Held**
SIC: 1389 Oil/Gas Field Services
HQ: Multi-Chem Group, Llc
424 S Chadbourne St
San Angelo TX 77032

(G-2810)
N-R-G CHEMICAL COMPANY
2933 Industrial Blvd (39440-5953)
P.O. Box 777, Raleigh (39153-0777)
PHONE..................601 519-5363
Fd Grant, *Owner*
EMP: 2
SALES (est): 92K **Privately Held**
SIC: 1479 Fertilizer mineral mining

(G-2811)
NEEDLE WORKS
1115 W 6th St (39440-3815)
PHONE..................601 425-4692
Owen Ousley, *Owner*
EMP: 2
SALES (est): 101.3K **Privately Held**
SIC: 2395 Embroidery & art needlework; embroidery products, except schiffli machine

(G-2812)
NOVI CREATIONS LLC
3815 Baldwin Dr (39440-1306)
PHONE..................601 335-1902
Shauna Stockstill,
EMP: 2
SALES (est): 62.5K **Privately Held**
SIC: 3999 Manufacturing industries

(G-2813)
OILFIELD SERVICE & SUP CO INC
Also Called: Oil Field Service & Supply Co
1991 Highway 184 (39443-9692)
P.O. Box 454 (39441-0454)
PHONE..................601 649-4461
Robert Stone Sr, *President*
Robert Stone Jr, *Admin Sec*
EMP: 30
SQ FT: 7,200
SALES (est): 2.5MM **Privately Held**
SIC: 1389 5082 Oil field services; oil field equipment

(G-2814)
OLD GES INC
Also Called: Greene's Energy Services
1250 1 A Half Hllcrest Dr Hillcrest (39440)
PHONE..................601 649-4920
Fax: 601 649-4911
EMP: 6
SALES (corp-wide): 544.3MM **Privately Held**
SIC: 1389 Oil/Gas Field Services
PA: Old Ges, Inc.
11757 Katy Fwy Ste 700
Houston TX 70503
281 598-6830

(G-2815)
OPEN AIR M R I OF LAUREL
227 S 13th Ave (39440-4225)
PHONE..................601 428-5026
Bob Jicks, *President*
EMP: 5
SALES (est): 445.4K **Privately Held**
SIC: 3841 Diagnostic apparatus, medical

(G-2816)
PANTHER PRINTING LLC
58 Robert Walters Rd (39443-7360)
PHONE..................601 425-4414
Richard Oneal, *Owner*
EMP: 2 EST: 2013
SALES (est): 183.4K **Privately Held**
SIC: 2752 Commercial printing, lithographic

(G-2817)
PAWN INVESTMENTS INC
9 Heritage Trl (39440-1066)
PHONE..................601 649-4059
Neil Scrimpshire, *Owner*
EMP: 1
SALES (est): 94.6K **Privately Held**
SIC: 3533 Derricks, oil or gas field

(G-2818)
PAYNE PORTABLE BUILDING INC
342 Maxey Rd (39443-8520)
PHONE..................601 426-9484
Fonda Payne, *President*
EMP: 1
SQ FT: 720
SALES (est): 264.6K **Privately Held**
SIC: 3448 2452 Buildings, portable: prefabricated metal; prefabricated wood buildings

(G-2819)
PINE BELT READY MIX CONCRETE
1104 W 1st St Ste 8 (39440-4357)
P.O. Box 3032 (39442-3032)
PHONE..................601 425-2559
Ronald Crocker, *Manager*
EMP: 15
SALES (corp-wide): 100.3MM **Privately Held**
SIC: 3272 3273 Concrete products; ready-mixed concrete
HQ: Pine Belt Ready-Mix Concrete, Inc.
1104 W 1st St Ste 8
Laurel MS 39440
601 425-2026

(G-2820)
PINE BELT READY-MIX CON INC (HQ)
Also Called: Delta Industries
1104 W 1st St Ste 8 (39440-4357)
P.O. Box 3032 (39442-3032)
PHONE..................601 425-2026
Dave Robison, *President*
Paul Duff, *Vice Pres*
Pete Hayes, *Admin Sec*
EMP: 3 EST: 1971
SQ FT: 1,300
SALES (est): 4MM
SALES (corp-wide): 100.3MM **Privately Held**
SIC: 3273 Ready-mixed concrete
PA: Delta Industries, Inc.
100 W Woodrow Wilson Ave
Jackson MS 39213
601 354-3801

(G-2821)
PIONEER WELL SERVICE
1475 Highway 84 E (39443-9298)
PHONE..................601 399-1648
Laura White, *Principal*
Tony White, *Office Mgr*
EMP: 40
SALES (est): 1.2MM **Privately Held**
SIC: 1389 Oil field services

(G-2822)
PIPE ORGAN SPECIALTIES INC
3104 N 5th Ave (39440-1714)
P.O. Box 8201 (39441-8201)
PHONE..................601 649-5581
Nell Smith, *Corp Secy*
Troy Scott, *Vice Pres*
Henry Madison Lindsey III, *Director*
EMP: 5
SQ FT: 1,000
SALES: 600K **Privately Held**
SIC: 7699 3931 Organ tuning & repair; organ parts & materials

(G-2823)
PISTOL RIDGE PARTNERS LLC
2300 Hwy 11 N (39440)
PHONE..................601 649-7639
S Lavon Evans Jr,
EMP: 2
SALES (est): 81.9K **Privately Held**
SIC: 1382 Oil & gas exploration services

(G-2824)
PITTS SWABBING SERVICE INC
2777 Highway 84 E (39443-8321)
P.O. Box 554 (39441-0554)
PHONE..................601 422-0111
Billy J Pitts Sr, *President*
Billy J Pitts Jr, *Vice Pres*
Belinda Harrison, *Admin Sec*
EMP: 25
SQ FT: 2,400
SALES (est): 2.9MM **Privately Held**
SIC: 1389 Oil field services

(G-2825)
PREMIUM OILFIELD SERVICES
19 Service Blvd (39440-6014)
PHONE..................601 425-5211
Kevin Letbetter, *Opers Mgr*
Jerry Cosby, *Branch Mgr*
Randall Welch, *Supervisor*
EMP: 2
SALES (est): 141.3K **Privately Held**
SIC: 1389 Oil field services

2019 Harris Directory of
Mississippi Manufacturers

▲ = Import ▼=Export
◆ =Import/Export

106

GEOGRAPHIC SECTION

Laurel - Jones County (G-2853)

(G-2826)
PRESSURE CONTROL
1643 Highway 184 (39443-9272)
PHONE..................................601 342-8051
Pat Schumaker, *Owner*
EMP: 5
SALES (est): 260.3K **Privately Held**
SIC: 3533 Oil field machinery & equipment

(G-2827)
PRINT PRESS
5229 Highway 84 W (39443-8588)
P.O. Box 2085 (39442-2085)
PHONE..................................601 342-2645
Chris Karnes, *Owner*
EMP: 1
SALES (est): 71.4K **Privately Held**
SIC: 2741 Miscellaneous publishing

(G-2828)
PRINT SHOP INC
1108 Trace Rd (39443-8700)
PHONE..................................601 428-4602
Bobbie Rawls, *President*
Danny Simmons, *Vice Pres*
EMP: 4
SQ FT: 1,800
SALES (est): 452.7K **Privately Held**
SIC: 2752 Commercial printing, offset

(G-2829)
PRYOR PACKERS INC
382 Trace Rd (39443-9412)
P.O. Box 2754 (39442-2754)
PHONE..................................601 649-4535
Barry Pryor, *President*
Karen Gatlin, *Office Mgr*
EMP: 10
SQ FT: 2,700
SALES (est): 4.6MM **Privately Held**
WEB: www.pryorpackers.com
SIC: 5082 1389 Oil field equipment; oil
field services

(G-2830)
QUALITY WELDING
3270 Ellisville Blvd (39440-6018)
PHONE..................................601 428-4724
Chris Sumrall, *Owner*
EMP: 5
SQ FT: 5,000
SALES (est): 343.5K **Privately Held**
SIC: 3599 7692 7699 Machine shop, job-
bing & repair; welding repair; hydraulic
equipment repair

(G-2831)
R & W HYDRAULICS INC
3039 Ellisville Blvd (39440-6013)
PHONE..................................601 649-0565
Freddie Welch, *President*
Charlie Robine, *Vice Pres*
Charlotte Robine, *Treasurer*
Barbara Welch, *Admin Sec*
EMP: 7
SQ FT: 6,000
SALES (est): 665.5K **Privately Held**
SIC: 7692 Welding repair

(G-2832)
R&R WELDING LLC
18 E L Loper Rd (39443-9690)
PHONE..................................601 335-2470
Anthony Rayner, *Principal*
EMP: 2
SALES (est): 108.3K **Privately Held**
SIC: 7692 Welding repair

(G-2833)
**RAINBOW RENTL FISHING TLS
INC**
12 Donald Dr (39440-4724)
P.O. Box 6533 (39441-6533)
PHONE..................................601 425-3309
Roy M Wyrick, *President*
Su R Wyrick, *Vice Pres*
EMP: 10
SQ FT: 600
SALES (est): 1.1MM **Privately Held**
WEB: www.rainbowrental.com
SIC: 7353 1389 Oil field equipment, rental
or leasing; fishing for tools, oil & gas field

(G-2834)
RALPH CRAVEN LLC
Also Called: Jimco Pumps
526 E 21st St (39440-2461)
P.O. Box 6255 (39441-6255)
PHONE..................................601 425-0294
Wanda Craven, *Office Mgr*
Ralph Craven, *Mng Member*
EMP: 8
SALES: 3MM **Privately Held**
SIC: 1389 Oil field services

(G-2835)
**RAPAD DRILLING & WELL
SERVICES**
1309 Hillcrest Dr (39440-4737)
P.O. Box 4240 (39441-4240)
PHONE..................................601 649-0760
Donald Wilson, *Manager*
EMP: 1
SALES (corp-wide): 1.3MM **Privately
Held**
WEB: www.rapad-oil.com
SIC: 1389 Oil field services
PA: Rapad Drilling & Well Services Inc
217 W Capitol St Ste 201
Jackson MS 39201
601 649-0760

(G-2836)
RICHARD PLASTICS CO
1024 Hillcrest Dr (39440-4728)
PHONE..................................601 426-2810
David Buck, *President*
▲ EMP: 15
SQ FT: 21,250
SALES (est): 3MM **Privately Held**
SIC: 3089 Injection molded finished plastic
products; injection molding of plastics

(G-2837)
**RIVER RADS DRECTIONAL
DRLG LLC (PA)**
3616 Industrial Blvd (39440-5839)
P.O. Box 286, Soso (39480-0286)
PHONE..................................601 778-7179
David M Murray, *Mng Member*
Bobby Busby, *Mng Member*
EMP: 2
SALES (est): 1MM **Privately Held**
SIC: 1381 Directional drilling oil & gas
wells

(G-2838)
**ROBINE & WELCH MACHINE &
TL CO**
3037 Ellisville Blvd (39440-6013)
P.O. Box 252 (39441-0252)
PHONE..................................601 428-1545
Freddie G Welch, *President*
Charles Robine Jr, *President*
Freddie Welch, *Treasurer*
Barbara Welch, *Admin Sec*
EMP: 30 EST: 1980
SQ FT: 10,000
SALES (est): 7.5MM **Privately Held**
SIC: 3533 3546 Oil & gas field machinery;
power-driven handtools

(G-2839)
ROGER WELCH
Also Called: Roger's Inspection Service
4457 Indian Springs Rd (39443-9174)
PHONE..................................601 649-3767
Roger Welch, *Owner*
EMP: 1
SALES (est): 72K **Privately Held**
SIC: 1389 Pipe testing, oil field service

(G-2840)
ROY S RIDES INC
94 Highway 28 W (39443-4944)
PHONE..................................601 425-3700
Vickie Harrington, *President*
EMP: 2
SALES (est): 276.5K **Privately Held**
SIC: 3711 Cars, armored, assembly of

(G-2841)
**S LAVON EVANS JR OPER CO
INC**
2300 Hwy 11 N (39440)
P.O. Box 2336 (39442-2336)
PHONE..................................601 649-7639
S Lavon Evans Jr, *President*

Pam Evans, *Corp Secy*
EMP: 12
SALES (est): 1.4MM **Privately Held**
SIC: 1311 Crude petroleum & natural gas
production

(G-2842)
SANDERSON FARMS INC (PA)
127 Flynt Rd (39443-9062)
P.O. Box 988 (39441-0988)
PHONE..................................601 649-4030
Joe F Sanderson Jr, *Ch of Bd*
Lampkin Butts, *President*
Heath Parker, *Division Mgr*
Carrie Carter, *Plant Mgr*
Mickey Kelly, *Prdtn Mgr*
◆ EMP: 125
SALES: 3.2B **Publicly Held**
WEB: www.sandersonfarms.com
SIC: 2015 0251 Chicken, slaughtered &
dressed; chicken, processed: fresh;
chicken, processed: frozen; broiling chick-
ens, raising of

(G-2843)
**SANDERSON FARMS INC
FOODS DIV (HQ)**
127 Flynt Rd (39443-9062)
P.O. Box 988 (39441-0988)
PHONE..................................601 649-4030
Joe Frank Sanderson Jr, *President*
D Michael Cockrell, *CFO*
Timothy Rigney, *Controller*
James A Grimes, *Admin Sec*
▼ EMP: 4
SQ FT: 25,000
SALES (est): 153.3MM
SALES (corp-wide): 3.2B **Publicly Held**
SIC: 2038 2092 Dinners, frozen & pack-
aged; ethnic foods, frozen; seafoods,
frozen: prepared
PA: Sanderson Farms, Inc.
127 Flynt Rd
Laurel MS 39443
601 649-4030

(G-2844)
**SANDERSON FARMS INC PROC
DIV (HQ)**
127 Flynt Rd (39443-9062)
P.O. Box 988 (39441-0988)
PHONE..................................601 649-4030
Joe F Sanderson Jr, *President*
Lampkin Butts, *President*
D Michael Cockrell, *CFO*
Mike Cockrell, *Treasurer*
Beverly Wade Hogan, *Director*
▼ EMP: 125
SQ FT: 25,000
SALES (est): 614MM
SALES (corp-wide): 3.2B **Publicly Held**
SIC: 2015 Chicken, slaughtered &
dressed; chicken, processed: fresh;
chicken, processed: frozen
PA: Sanderson Farms, Inc.
127 Flynt Rd
Laurel MS 39443
601 649-4030

(G-2845)
**SANDERSON FARMS INC PROC
DIV**
2535 Sanderson Dr (39440-4741)
P.O. Box 988 (39441-0988)
PHONE..................................601 428-5261
Gary Clayton, *Sales Mgr*
Chris McBride, *Manager*
EMP: 675
SALES (corp-wide): 3.2B **Publicly Held**
SIC: 2015 Chicken slaughtering & process-
ing
HQ: Sanderson Farms, Inc. (Processing Di-
vision)
127 Flynt Rd
Laurel MS 39443
601 649-4030

(G-2846)
**SCHLUMBERGER
TECHNOLOGY CORP**
Also Called: Schlumberger Wireline & Tstg
3750 Industrial Blvd (39440-5973)
PHONE..................................601 649-3200
Tim Morrison, *Branch Mgr*
EMP: 15 **Publicly Held**

SIC: 1389 Oil field services
HQ: Schlumberger Technology Corp
100 Gillingham Ln
Sugar Land TX 77478
281 285-8500

(G-2847)
**SECORP INDUS & SAFETY SUPS
INC**
294 Victory Rd (39443-9533)
PHONE..................................601 422-0203
Fax: 601 422-0162
EMP: 13
SALES (corp-wide): 7.1MM **Privately
Held**
SIC: 8748 1389 Business Consulting
Services Oil/Gas Field Services
PA: Secorp Industrial & Safety Supplies,
Inc.
2101 Jefferson St
Lafayette LA 70501
337 237-3471

(G-2848)
SHIRTZ STUFF
180 Johnny Watkins Rd (39443-9041)
PHONE..................................601 729-2472
Janet Smith, *Owner*
Randall Smith, *Co-Owner*
EMP: 4
SALES: 60K **Privately Held**
SIC: 3552 Silk screens for textile industry

(G-2849)
SHOULDER CORDS UNLIMITED
1008 Strngthfrd Plsnt Grv (39443-7398)
PHONE..................................601 425-2195
Deloris P Stegall, *Principal*
EMP: 2 EST: 2008
SALES (est): 186K **Privately Held**
SIC: 2241 Cords, fabric

(G-2850)
SIMS METAL INC
87 Crepe Myrtle Ln (39443-7865)
PHONE..................................601 649-2555
Jack Sims, *President*
EMP: 7
SALES (est): 780.3K **Privately Held**
SIC: 3444 Sheet metalwork

(G-2851)
**SOUTHEASTERN OILFIELD
PDTS LLC**
Also Called: M & D Sales
1250 Ellisville Blvd (39440-5420)
PHONE..................................601 428-0603
Mike Ishee, *Owner*
EMP: 4
SALES (est): 200K **Privately Held**
SIC: 1389 Oil consultants

(G-2852)
**SOUTHERN IMAGES PRINTING
INC**
121 N 15th Ave (39440-4119)
PHONE..................................601 649-3501
Bill Reddoch, *President*
Janice Reddoch, *Admin Sec*
EMP: 5
SALES: 300K **Privately Held**
WEB: www.southernimagesprinting.com
SIC: 2791 Hand composition typesetting;
typesetting, computer controlled

(G-2853)
**SOUTHERN METALS CO MISS
INC**
144 Don Curt Rd (39440-5423)
P.O. Box 782 (39441-0782)
PHONE..................................601 649-7475
Jack L Moran, *President*
Judy Moran, *Corp Secy*
Michael Moran, *Vice Pres*
EMP: 30
SALES (est): 4.2MM **Privately Held**
SIC: 3599 3429 3469 3444 Machine
shop, jobbing & repair; manufactured
hardware (general); metal stampings;
sheet metalwork; fabricated plate work
(boiler shop); aluminum sheet, plate & foil

(PA)=Parent Co (HQ)=Headquarters (DH)=Div Headquarters
✪ = New Business established in last 2 years

2019 Harris Directory of
Mississippi Manufacturers

107

GEOGRAPHIC SECTION

Laurel - Jones County (G-2854)

(G-2854)
SOUTHERN PETROLEUM LABS INC
1961 Bush Dairy Rd (39443-9066)
P.O. Box 3079 (39442-3079)
PHONE.................................601 428-0842
Randy McCullum, *Branch Mgr*
EMP: 6
SALES (corp-wide): 165.4MM **Privately Held**
WEB: www.spl-inc.com
SIC: 1389 Oil field services
PA: Southern Petroleum Laboratories, Inc.
8850 Interchange Dr
Houston TX 77054
713 660-0901

(G-2855)
SPRINGER TRCKG & CAR CRUSHING
1500 Highway 84 E (39443-9289)
PHONE.................................601 649-4238
Darrell Springer, *Owner*
EMP: 15
SQ FT: 5,700
SALES (est): 836.4K **Privately Held**
SIC: 4212 4213 1542 7389 Local truck-
ing, without storage; heavy hauling; com-
mercial & office building contractors;
salvaging of damaged merchandise, serv-
ice only; construction, repair & disman-
tling services

(G-2856)
T JS WELDING
244 Victory Rd (39443-9569)
PHONE.................................601 498-1409
T Estilette, *Owner*
EMP: 1
SALES (est): 39.5K **Privately Held**
SIC: 7692 Welding repair

(G-2857)
TAYLOR CONSTRUCTION CO INC
Also Called: Taylor Redi-Mix Co
28 Taylors Cir (39443-9515)
PHONE.................................601 426-2987
Larry Taylor, *President*
Pat Taylor, *Corp Secy*
Kyle Taylor, *Vice Pres*
Melanie Beard, *Office Mgr*
EMP: 68
SQ FT: 525
SALES: 13.3MM **Privately Held**
SIC: 1389 Oil field services; gas field serv-
ices

(G-2858)
THORNTON & SONS CABINET SHOP
2065 Highway 184 (39443-8302)
PHONE.................................601 425-2172
Paul Thornton, *Partner*
Mark Thornton, *General Mgr*
Michael Thorton, *Office Mgr*
EMP: 3
SALES (est): 430.7K **Privately Held**
SIC: 2434 Wood kitchen cabinets

(G-2859)
TRICO INDUSTRIES INC
1317 Hillcrest Dr (39440-4737)
PHONE.................................601 649-4467
Charlotte Mosley, *Principal*
EMP: 2
SALES (est): 255.1K **Privately Held**
SIC: 3533 Oil & gas field machinery

(G-2860)
U S WEATHERFORD L P
1315 Hillcrest Dr (39440-4737)
PHONE.................................601 428-1551
Bobo White, *Manager*
EMP: 8 **Privately Held**
WEB: www.gaslift.com
SIC: 1389 Oil field services
HQ: U S Weatherford L P
179 Weatherford Dr
Schriever LA 70395
985 493-6100

(G-2861)
VARCO LP
721 E 22nd St (39440)
P.O. Box 6518 (39441-6518)
PHONE.................................601 428-1555
Butch Red, *Branch Mgr*
EMP: 10
SALES (corp-wide): 8.4B **Publicly Held**
WEB: www.tuboscope.com
SIC: 1389 Testing, measuring, surveying &
analysis services
HQ: Varco, L.P.
2835 Holmes Rd
Houston TX 77051
713 799-5272

(G-2862)
VENTURE OIL & GAS INC
207 S 13th Ave (39440-4225)
PHONE.................................601 428-3653
Jay Fenton, *President*
Jarvis Hensley, *Vice Pres*
Tony Stuart, *Director*
EMP: 12
SQ FT: 4,000
SALES (est): 3.3MM **Privately Held**
SIC: 1382 Oil & gas exploration services

(G-2863)
VULCAN MATERIALS COMPANY
606 Avenue C (39440-5971)
PHONE.................................601 425-3509
Brett Vanbermeeben, *General Mgr*
Brett Vandermeeden, *Branch Mgr*
EMP: 2 **Publicly Held**
SIC: 5211 3295 Masonry materials & sup-
plies; slag, crushed or ground
PA: Vulcan Materials Company
1200 Urban Center Dr
Vestavia AL 35242

(G-2864)
WADE SERVICES INC
500 Eastview Dr (39443-5332)
P.O. Box 399, Ellisville (39437-0399)
PHONE.................................601 399-1900
Allen Wade, *President*
EMP: 2 **Privately Held**
SIC: 4213 3715 Heavy hauling; truck trail-
ers
PA: Wade Services, Inc.
30 Currie Rd
Ellisville MS 39437

(G-2865)
WALKER MACHINE
1104 Susie B Ruffin Ave (39440-3066)
P.O. Box 4308 (39441-4308)
PHONE.................................601 425-4635
Chuck Walker, *Owner*
EMP: 4
SQ FT: 3,500
SALES: 180K **Privately Held**
SIC: 7699 3599 Industrial machinery &
equipment repair; machine shop, jobbing
& repair

(G-2866)
WALKER MEMORIAL CO INC
1220 Ellisville Blvd (39440-5420)
P.O. Box 2006 (39442-2006)
PHONE.................................601 428-5337
Fred Stringfellow, *President*
EMP: 7 EST: 1950
SQ FT: 2,800
SALES: 850K **Privately Held**
SIC: 3281 Monuments, cut stone (not fin-
ishing or lettering only)

(G-2867)
WALTERS MACHINE WORKS INC
1507 Highway 84 E (39443-9595)
P.O. Box 1944 (39441-1944)
PHONE.................................601 426-6092
Roger Walters, *President*
EMP: 5
SQ FT: 8,000
SALES: 500K **Privately Held**
SIC: 3599 7692 Machine shop, jobbing &
repair; welding repair

(G-2868)
WARRIOR ENERGY SERVICES CORP
339 Avenue A (39440-5836)
P.O. Box 4396, Odessa TX (79760-4396)
PHONE.................................601 425-9684
Roy Boney, *Manager*
EMP: 15 **Publicly Held**
SIC: 1389 Oil field services
HQ: Warrior Energy Services Corporation
5801 Highway 90 E
Broussard LA 70518
337 243-3488

(G-2869)
WAYNE FARMS LLC
525 N Mississippi Ave (39440-4088)
P.O. Box 328 (39441-0328)
PHONE.................................601 425-4721
Glen Caves, *Branch Mgr*
Terry McGowen, *Manager*
Steven Oneal, *Manager*
Laura Echenique, *Maintence Staff*
EMP: 102
SALES (corp-wide): 2.6B **Privately Held**
SIC: 2015 Poultry slaughtering & process-
ing
HQ: Wayne Farms Llc
4110 Continental Dr
Oakwood GA 30566

(G-2870)
WAYNE FARMS LLC
Also Called: General Offices & Proc Plant
525 Wayne Dr (39440)
PHONE.................................601 399-7000
EMP: 102
SALES (corp-wide): 2.6B **Privately Held**
SIC: 2015 Poultry slaughtering & process-
ing
HQ: Wayne Farms Llc
4110 Continental Dr
Oakwood GA 30566

(G-2871)
WEATHERFORD ARTIFICIA
2932 Industrial Blvd (39440-5914)
P.O. Box 285 (39441-0285)
PHONE.................................601 649-4467
Dwight Powers, *Manager*
EMP: 6 **Privately Held**
WEB: www.johnsonscreens.com
SIC: 1389 Oil field services
HQ: Weatherford Artificial Lift Systems, Llc
2000 Saint James Pl
Houston TX 77056
713 836-4000

(G-2872)
WELBORN DEVICES LLC
1596 Sndrsville Sharon Rd (39443-5418)
PHONE.................................601 428-5912
Larry Welborn,
EMP: 6
SALES: 400K **Privately Held**
SIC: 3523 3556 Farm machinery & equip-
ment; food products machinery

(G-2873)
WEST JONES PRESS BOX
254 Springhill Rd (39443-7874)
PHONE.................................601 729-2216
Wayde Clark, *Principal*
EMP: 1
SALES (est): 54.9K **Privately Held**
SIC: 2741 Miscellaneous publishing

(G-2874)
WILLIAMS TRANSPORTATION CO LLC
46 Don Curt Rd (39440-5430)
P.O. Box 131, Stringer (39481-0131)
PHONE.................................601 428-2214
Scott A Williams,
EMP: 70
SALES (est): 12.5MM **Privately Held**
SIC: 4789 1389 1623 Cargo loading &
unloading services; gas field services;
pipeline construction
PA: Scott Williams Companies
46 Don Curt Rd
Laurel MS

Leakesville
Greene County

(G-2875)
ADVANTAGE TAX & PRINTING INC
314a Main St (39451-6504)
PHONE.................................601 394-2898
Letessa Russell, *Owner*
EMP: 2
SALES (est): 158.9K **Privately Held**
SIC: 2752 Commercial printing, litho-
graphic

(G-2876)
BLOCK & CHIP IRON WORKS INC
21912 Highway 63 (39451-5798)
P.O. Box 758 (39451-0758)
PHONE.................................601 394-2964
Elvie Robertson, *President*
Lynn Robertson, *Vice Pres*
EMP: 5
SALES (est): 66.5K **Privately Held**
SIC: 7692 3599 1799 Welding repair; ma-
chine shop, jobbing & repair; welding on
site

(G-2877)
INSPECTION PLUS LLC
1806 Texas St (39451-2883)
PHONE.................................601 525-6744
Jeremy Mizell,
EMP: 1 EST: 2016
SALES (est): 55.2K **Privately Held**
SIC: 2899 Fluxes: brazing, soldering, gal-
vanizing & welding

(G-2878)
PAUL BOLLING
Also Called: B & B Contractors
6400 Old 24 (39451)
PHONE.................................601 466-3398
Paul Bolling, *Owner*
EMP: 10
SALES (est): 657.7K **Privately Held**
SIC: 1442 Construction sand & gravel

(G-2879)
TNC LOGGING LLC ✪
1741 Mcdonald Rd (39451-4745)
PHONE.................................601 394-9760
EMP: 2 EST: 2019
SALES (est): 81.7K **Privately Held**
SIC: 2411 Logging

(G-2880)
TURNER GROUP LLC
Also Called: Greene County Herald
431 Main St (39451-6502)
PHONE.................................601 394-5070
John F Turner, *Mng Member*
Rusell Turner, *Administration*
EMP: 5
SALES (est): 356.1K **Privately Held**
SIC: 2711 2752 Newspapers: publishing
only, not printed on site; commercial print-
ing, offset

(G-2881)
ULYSSES COOLEY
506 Steer Holw (39451-5216)
PHONE.................................601 394-5485
Ulysses Cooley, *Principal*
EMP: 6 EST: 2010
SALES (est): 388.4K **Privately Held**
SIC: 2411 Logging

Leland
Washington County

(G-2882)
BAYER COTTON SEED INTL
117 Kennedy Flat Rd (38756-9577)
PHONE.................................662 686-9235
Emil Lansu, *President*
Franz Evesheim, *President*
Mike Gilbert, *Vice Pres*
Dale Shelley, *Treasurer*
Heather Benjamin, *Admin Sec*

2019 Harris Directory of
Mississippi Manufacturers

▲ = Import ▼=Export
◆ =Import/Export

GEOGRAPHIC SECTION

Liberty - Amite County (G-2910)

EMP: 7
SALES: 650K
SALES (corp-wide): 71.7B **Privately Held**
SIC: 2834 Pharmaceutical preparations
HQ: Bayer Cropscience Lp
2 Tw Alexander Dr
Durham NC 27709
919 549-2000

(G-2883)
BAYER CROPSCIENCE LP
206 Kennedy Flat Rd (38756-9327)
P.O. Box 167, Stoneville (38776-0167)
PHONE....................................662 686-2334
Charles Graham, *Branch Mgr*
EMP: 78
SALES (corp-wide): 71.7B **Privately Held**
SIC: 2879 Fungicides, herbicides
HQ: Bayer Cropscience Lp
2 Tw Alexander Dr
Durham NC 27709
919 549-2000

(G-2884)
BAYER CROPSCIENCE LP
Also Called: Field Technology Station
206 Kennedy Flat Rd (38756-9327)
PHONE....................................662 686-9323
Charles Graham, *Manager*
EMP: 6
SALES (corp-wide): 71.7B **Privately Held**
SIC: 2879 Insecticides, agricultural or
household
HQ: Bayer Cropscience Lp
2 Tw Alexander Dr
Durham NC 27709
919 549-2000

(G-2885)
BAYER CROPSCIENCE LP
Also Called: Cotton Breeding Research Stn
117 Kennedy Flat Rd (38756-9577)
PHONE....................................662 686-9235
Joe Johnson, *Manager*
EMP: 10
SALES (corp-wide): 71.7B **Privately Held**
SIC: 2879 Agricultural chemicals
HQ: Bayer Cropscience Lp
2 Tw Alexander Dr
Durham NC 27709
919 549-2000

(G-2886)
CONNIE S KITCHEN
112 Mimosa Dr (38756-3014)
PHONE....................................662 686-2255
Connie Coehn, *Owner*
EMP: 10
SQ FT: 4,800
SALES (est): 705.5K **Privately Held**
SIC: 2052 Bakery products, dry

(G-2887)
EARLS MACHINING CENTER INC
264 Saint Christopher Rd (38756-9530)
PHONE....................................662 820-7565
James Earl Vance Jr, *President*
EMP: 4
SQ FT: 2,500
SALES (est): 150K **Privately Held**
SIC: 3599 Machine shop, jobbing & repair

(G-2888)
KNU LLC (PA)
Also Called: La-Z-Boy Contract Furniture
1300 N Broad St (38756-2511)
P.O. Box 9, Ferdinand IN (47532-0009)
PHONE....................................812 367-1761
Glenn A Lange, *President*
Richard N Franey, *Vice Pres*
Steven M Wahl, *Treasurer*
Samantha Gray, *Mktg Coord*
Patrick L Miller, *General Counsel*
▲ EMP: 69
SALES: 27.8MM **Privately Held**
SIC: 2599 Hospital furniture, except beds

(G-2889)
LINAS INTERIORS INC
109 E 3rd St (38756-2705)
PHONE....................................662 332-7226
Patty Gibbs, *President*
▲ EMP: 2

SALES (est): 296.5K **Privately Held**
WEB: www.linasinteriors.com
SIC: 5199 5714 2391 5712 Gifts & novelties; draperies; draperies, plastic & textile:
from purchased materials; furniture
stores; wallpaper

(G-2890)
MAREL USA INC
438 Burdett Rd (38756-9774)
PHONE....................................662 686-2269
Russ McPherson, *Principal*
Michael Lanier, *Engineer*
Robert Beauregard, *Sales Staff*
Michael McMann, *Sales Staff*
Don Stone, *Sales Staff*
EMP: 1
SALES (est): 95K **Privately Held**
SIC: 3556 Food products machinery

(G-2891)
NIGHTENGALE CABINETS
60 Kuhn Rd (38756-9532)
PHONE....................................662 686-9004
Randall Nightengale, *Owner*
EMP: 6
SQ FT: 3,500
SALES: 300K **Privately Held**
SIC: 2434 Wood kitchen cabinets

(G-2892)
SABBATINI & SONS INCORPORATION
410 N Broad St (38756-2795)
PHONE....................................662 686-7713
Paul Sabbatini, *President*
Bobbi Sabbatini, *Partner*
EMP: 3
SALES: 50K **Privately Held**
SIC: 7538 7699 7692 General automotive
repair shops; tractor repair; automotive
welding

(G-2893)
WORLD CLASS ATHLTCSURFACES INC
817 N Broad St (38756-2546)
P.O. Box 152 (38756-0152)
PHONE....................................662 686-9997
Radford E Dubois III, *President*
Mike Fulgham, *Vice Pres*
Margaret Dubois, *Treasurer*
EMP: 15
SQ FT: 35,000
SALES (est): 4.1MM **Privately Held**
WEB: www.worldclasspaints.com
SIC: 2851 Coating, air curing

Lena
Leake County

(G-2894)
AMERICAN APPAREL INC
52 Pleasant Hill Rd (39094-9152)
P.O. Box 1330, Carthage (39051-1330)
PHONE....................................601 654-9211
William W Corhern, *President*
EMP: 4
SQ FT: 35,000
SALES (est): 553.4K **Privately Held**
SIC: 2253 Shirts (outerwear), knit

(G-2895)
GREAT AMERICAN PUBLISHERS
171 Lone Pine Church Rd (39094-9350)
PHONE....................................601 854-5956
Sheila Simmons, *Owner*
EMP: 4
SALES (est): 415.9K **Privately Held**
SIC: 2741 Miscellaneous publishing

(G-2896)
REAL MEAL PUBLISHING LLC
7657 Highway 13 N (39094-9781)
PHONE....................................601 697-7199
Jojuan Johnson,
EMP: 1
SALES (est): 45.7K **Privately Held**
SIC: 2741 Miscellaneous publishing

Lexington
Holmes County

(G-2897)
BALDWIN SAND & GRAVEL
1422 Coxburg Rd (39095-5940)
PHONE....................................662 834-6167
Richard Smith, *Manager*
EMP: 3
SALES (est): 196.1K **Privately Held**
SIC: 1442 Construction sand & gravel

(G-2898)
CHENOA COFFEE COMPANY
212 Court Sq (39095-3628)
PHONE....................................662 834-3917
Chuck Lovorn, *CEO*
Nancy Barrett, *President*
EMP: 5
SALES (est): 139.9K **Privately Held**
SIC: 2095 2099 Roasted coffee; tea
blending

(G-2899)
CLAUDE W CARNATHAN
Also Called: CWC Computers & Cstm Databases
652 Boulevard Ext (39095-3411)
PHONE....................................662 834-3855
EMP: 1
SALES: 160K **Privately Held**
SIC: 3577 5734 Mfg Computer Peripheral
Equipment Ret Computers/Software

(G-2900)
DESIGN PRINT & ADVERTISE BY PJ
260 Mason Rd (39095-7108)
PHONE....................................662 299-1148
Pamela Gaines, *Principal*
EMP: 2
SALES (est): 156.5K **Privately Held**
SIC: 2752 Commercial printing, lithographic

(G-2901)
EAST HOLMES PUBLISHING ENTPS
Also Called: Holmes County Herald
308 Court Sq (39095-3636)
P.O. Box 60 (39095-0060)
PHONE....................................662 834-1151
Allen Bruce Hill, *President*
Mary C Hill, *Treasurer*
EMP: 3
SQ FT: 1,200
SALES (est): 450.9K **Privately Held**
WEB: www.holmescountyherald.com
SIC: 2711 5943 Newspapers, publishing &
printing; office forms & supplies

(G-2902)
EMERALD TRANSFORMER
491 Bowling Green Rd (39095-5183)
PHONE....................................800 346-6164
EMP: 4
SALES (est): 416.8K **Privately Held**
SIC: 3612 Power transformers, electric;
voltage regulators, transmission & distribution

(G-2903)
HAMMETT GRAVEL CO INC (PA)
72 Hammett Dr (39095-7341)
P.O. Box 209 (39095-0209)
PHONE....................................662 834-1867
Harold P Hammett III, *President*
Heyward C Green, *Vice Pres*
John Green, *Treasurer*
Tim Deason, *Admin Sec*
EMP: 6 EST: 1941
SQ FT: 16,100
SALES (est): 8.5MM **Privately Held**
SIC: 1442 1611 Sand mining; gravel mining; general contractor, highway & street
construction

(G-2904)
LEXINGTON CONCRETE & BLOCK CO
Also Called: Cancon Concrete
304a Yazoo St (39095-3623)
PHONE....................................662 834-3892
H Watt Ervin, *Branch Mgr*
EMP: 6
SALES (corp-wide): 3.3MM **Privately Held**
SIC: 3273 3271 Ready-mixed concrete;
concrete block & brick
PA: Lexington Concrete & Block Co Inc
304a Yazoo St
Lexington MS

(G-2905)
SUPERIOR UNIFORM GROUP INC
Also Called: Mississippi Uniform Industries
Hwy 12 Bowling Green Rd (39095)
PHONE....................................662 834-4485
Thomas E Cox Jr, *Manager*
EMP: 4
SALES (corp-wide): 346.3MM **Publicly Held**
WEB: www.superiorsurgicalmfg.com
SIC: 2326 2393 Medical & hospital uniforms, men's; textile bags
PA: Superior Group Of Companies, Inc.
10055 Seminole Blvd
Seminole FL 33772
727 397-9611

(G-2906)
TRANSFRMER GSKETS CMPNENTS LLC
Also Called: T G C
491 Bowling Green Rd (39095-5183)
P.O. Box 158, Pelahatchie (39145-0158)
PHONE....................................601 854-6624
Justin Sarrett, *President*
Marlo Sarrett, *Vice Pres*
EMP: 6
SALES (est): 1.8MM **Privately Held**
SIC: 3443 Boiler shop products: boilers,
smokestacks, steel tanks

(G-2907)
WILLIE MORGAN
159 Mallory Rd (39095-6556)
PHONE....................................662 834-4366
Willie Morgan, *Principal*
EMP: 1
SALES (est): 49.8K **Privately Held**
SIC: 7692 Welding repair

Liberty
Amite County

(G-2908)
ADAM STERLING LOGGING LLC
4730 Graves Chapel Rd (39645-5335)
PHONE....................................601 657-1091
Adam Sterling, *Mng Member*
EMP: 12
SALES (est): 1.1MM **Privately Held**
SIC: 2411 Logging camps & contractors

(G-2909)
AIR CRUISERS COMPANY LLC
269 Main St (39645)
P.O. Box 515 (39645-0515)
PHONE....................................601 657-8043
Chris Campbell, *Principal*
EMP: 170
SALES (corp-wide): 833.4MM **Privately Held**
WEB: www.aircruisers.com
SIC: 3069 Air-supported rubber structures
HQ: Air Cruisers Company, Llc
1747 State Route 34
Wall Township NJ 07727
732 681-3527

(G-2910)
BLAYLOCKS CEMENT MANUFACTURING
4608 Austin Ln (39645-6142)
PHONE....................................225 627-1006
Winston Blaylock, *Owner*
EMP: 4

(PA)=Parent Co (HQ)=Headquarters (DH)=Div Headquarters
✪ = New Business established in last 2 years

2019 Harris Directory of
Mississippi Manufacturers

Liberty - Amite County (G-2911)
GEOGRAPHIC SECTION

SALES (est): 365.1K **Privately Held**
SIC: 5211 3272 Masonry materials & supplies; concrete products

(G-2911)
C E WELCH TIMBER CO INC
409 Roberts Rd (39645-5119)
PHONE...................................601 657-4577
EMP: 6
SALES (est): 350K **Privately Held**
SIC: 2411 Logging Contractor

(G-2912)
F W GRAVES & SON INC
Also Called: Graves, F W & Son Logging Co
3930 Graves Rd (39645-5123)
PHONE...................................601 657-8750
Leslie W Graves, *President*
I Leslie Ward Graves II, *Vice Pres*
Debra T Graves, *Treasurer*
EMP: 4
SALES (est): 341.5K **Privately Held**
SIC: 2411 Logging camps & contractors

(G-2913)
KDH TRUCKING LLC
5800 Good Hope Ln (39645-5182)
PHONE...................................601 730-2052
Lakendred Hughes, *Principal*
EMP: 3
SALES (est): 133.9K **Privately Held**
SIC: 4212 1389 3743 4731 Local trucking, without storage; hot shot service; freight cars & equipment; transportation agents & brokers

(G-2914)
LARRY D BRABHAM
4662 E Fork Rd (39645-7212)
PHONE...................................601 551-4777
Larry D Brabham, *Principal*
EMP: 3
SALES (est): 272.9K **Privately Held**
SIC: 2411 Logging

(G-2915)
LIBERTY OILFIELD SERVICES & RE
4018 Meadville Rd (39645-5065)
PHONE...................................601 398-8511
EMP: 1
SALES (est): 108.8K **Privately Held**
SIC: 1389 Oil field services

(G-2916)
RONALD D STERLING
3471 King Rd (39645-5143)
PHONE...................................601 225-7772
Ronald Sterling, *Principal*
EMP: 1
SALES (est): 153.1K **Privately Held**
SIC: 2411 Logging

(G-2917)
SOUTHERN LOGGING INC
5411 Ms Highway 567 (39645-5280)
PHONE...................................601 657-4449
Worth A Smith III, *President*
T F Badon, *Principal*
Wayne McGraw, *Principal*
Randell J Smith, *Vice Pres*
Meghan A Phenald, *Admin Sec*
EMP: 12 EST: 1980
SALES (est): 500K **Privately Held**
SIC: 2411 Logging camps & contractors

(G-2918)
TW LOGGING LLC
3333b Highway 48 (39645-8280)
PHONE...................................601 657-8838
Terry Woodside, *Administration*
EMP: 4
SALES (est): 108.7K **Privately Held**
SIC: 2411 Logging camps & contractors

(G-2919)
U S METAL WORKS INC
438 Industrial Dr (39645)
PHONE...................................601 657-4676
Robert Nipper, *Manager*
EMP: 30

SALES (est): 7.1MM
SALES (corp-wide): 12.1MM **Privately Held**
WEB: www.usmetalworks.com
SIC: 3564 3537 Blowers & fans; industrial trucks & tractors
PA: U. S. Metal Works, Inc.
36370 Industrial Way
Sandy OR 97055
503 668-8036

(G-2920)
WINDSHIELD REPAIR SYSTEMS
3028 Highway 569 S (39645-8120)
PHONE...................................601 657-8303
Benny Stevens, *Owner*
EMP: 1
SALES (est): 53K **Privately Held**
SIC: 3231 5231 Windshields, glass: made from purchased glass; glass

(G-2921)
ZODIAC AEROSPACE
269 Main St (39645)
PHONE...................................601 657-8719
Ed Dundis, *Manager*
Rick Angley, *Manager*
EMP: 2
SALES (est): 201K **Privately Held**
SIC: 3728 Aircraft parts & equipment

Little Rock
Newton County

(G-2922)
CIRCLE G HAULING LLC
1410 Goforth Rd (39337-9218)
PHONE...................................662 436-7028
Erika Gordon,
EMP: 5 EST: 2017
SALES (est): 188K **Privately Held**
SIC: 2411 Logging

Long Beach
Harrison County

(G-2923)
BACKYARD ESCAPES
8468 County Farm Rd (39560-9087)
PHONE...................................228 868-3938
Tanya Sprinkler, *Owner*
EMP: 2
SALES (est): 181.8K **Privately Held**
SIC: 2369 Bathing suits & swimwear: girls', children's & infants'

(G-2924)
BAY MOTOR WINDING INC
125 N Ocean Wave Ave (39560-5017)
P.O. Box 411 (39560-0411)
PHONE...................................228 863-0666
Edward M Benvenutti, *President*
Patrick T Benvenutti, *Vice Pres*
Mary Kay Wicks, *Admin Sec*
EMP: 17
SQ FT: 12,000
SALES: 3.5MM **Privately Held**
WEB: www.baymotorwinding.com
SIC: 7694 Electric motor repair

(G-2925)
BAY TECHNICAL ASSOCIATES INC
Also Called: Baytech
5239 A Ave (39560-9703)
PHONE...................................228 563-7334
Jane R Storey, *President*
Nancy Ramsey, *Corp Secy*
Charles A Ramsey, *Vice Pres*
Charles R Ramsey, *Vice Pres*
Alex North, *Opers Mgr*
▲ EMP: 100
SQ FT: 31,000
SALES (est): 23.5MM **Privately Held**
WEB: www.baytechdcd.com
SIC: 3577 Computer peripheral equipment

(G-2926)
BBQ WORLD MAGAZINE
650 E Railroad St (39560-4934)
PHONE...................................228 363-2716
Terry Welch, *Owner*
EMP: 12
SALES: 200K **Privately Held**
SIC: 2721 Magazines: publishing only, not printed on site

(G-2927)
BEADED OWLS
200 Jeff Davis Ave Ste 10 (39560-6183)
PHONE...................................228 284-2712
Catherine Thomas, *Owner*
EMP: 3
SALES (est): 164.1K **Privately Held**
SIC: 5944 3999 Jewelry, precious stones & precious metals; beads, unassembled

(G-2928)
BEARHAWK TAILWHEELS LLC
205 Kuyrkendall Pl (39560-3307)
PHONE...................................228 424-5096
Michelle Newton, *Administration*
Eric Newton,
EMP: 2 EST: 2011
SALES: 30K **Privately Held**
SIC: 3728 Wheels, aircraft

(G-2929)
BELL GRAVEL CO INC
7290 Red Creek Rd (39560-8804)
PHONE...................................228 452-2872
David Bell, *President*
Billy Bell, *Vice Pres*
EMP: 2
SQ FT: 400
SALES: 135K **Privately Held**
SIC: 1442 Construction sand & gravel

(G-2930)
CAJUN PLANTERS LLC
205 S Burke Ave (39560-6151)
PHONE...................................770 363-5638
Forrest Garriga,
EMP: 4 EST: 2017
SALES (est): 125.1K **Privately Held**
SIC: 3999 Manufacturing industries

(G-2931)
CHRISMAN MANUFACTURING INC
7399 Beatline Rd (39560-9109)
PHONE...................................228 864-6293
Mark Chrisman, *President*
Lori Chrisman, *Vice Pres*
Norris Danny, *Plant Mgr*
Calena Roberts, *Parts Mgr*
Tom Glaze, *Engineer*
▲ EMP: 50
SQ FT: 26,000
SALES (est): 15.2MM **Privately Held**
WEB: www.navigatorforklift.com
SIC: 3537 5084 Forklift trucks; lift trucks, industrial: fork, platform, straddle, etc.; lift trucks & parts

(G-2932)
CHUCK RYAN CARS INC
Also Called: Mississippi Sound & Recording
18012 Pineville Rd (39560-4535)
PHONE...................................228 864-9706
Thomas Ryan Jr, *President*
EMP: 8 EST: 1975
SALES (est): 1MM **Privately Held**
WEB: www.chuckryancars.com
SIC: 3711 5012 7389 Cars, electric, assembly of; automobiles & other motor vehicles; recording studio, noncommercial records

(G-2933)
CL CABINETS LLC
109 N Ocean Wave Ave (39560-5017)
PHONE...................................228 860-9678
EMP: 1
SALES (est): 53.7K **Privately Held**
SIC: 2434 Wood kitchen cabinets

(G-2934)
COASTAL TIRE WHOLESALERS LLC
19079 Pineville Rd (39560-4542)
PHONE...................................810 257-9977

Jason Walker, *Principal*
EMP: 2
SALES (est): 88.9K **Privately Held**
SIC: 3089 Plastics products

(G-2935)
DAVIS WELDING
20391 Jones Mill Rd (39560-8938)
PHONE...................................228 257-5231
Steven Deboard, *Principal*
EMP: 1
SALES (est): 28.1K **Privately Held**
SIC: 7692 Welding repair

(G-2936)
EXCITING LIGHTING
1102 E Railroad St (39560-5052)
PHONE...................................228 864-2995
EMP: 10
SALES (est): 70.6K **Privately Held**
SIC: 3647 Manufacture Fiber-Optic Lighting

(G-2937)
FASTWAY FUELS 3 LLC
9069 County Farm Rd (39560-9112)
P.O. Box 6458, Diamondhead (39525-6440)
PHONE...................................228 452-7009
Ricky Stegall, *Principal*
EMP: 5
SALES (est): 432.6K **Privately Held**
SIC: 2869 5411 Fuels; convenience stores, independent

(G-2938)
GULF CONCRETE TECHNOLOGY LLC
4739 W Oreck Rd (39560-3702)
PHONE...................................228 575-3500
Edgar Figueroa,
◆ EMP: 4
SALES (est): 604.4K **Privately Held**
SIC: 2821 Polystyrene resins

(G-2939)
GULFPORT HARBOR FUEL
720 S Cleveland Ave (39560-6271)
PHONE...................................228 248-3474
Justin M Roland, *Principal*
EMP: 4
SALES (est): 231.6K **Privately Held**
SIC: 2869 Fuels

(G-2940)
HIGH TECH INC
21120 Johnson Rd (39560-3721)
PHONE...................................228 868-6632
Brian S Spychalski, *President*
Stephen E Spychalski, *Treasurer*
Elizabeth A Spychalski, *Admin Sec*
EMP: 22
SQ FT: 10,000
SALES (est): 4.4MM **Privately Held**
SIC: 3699 Electrical equipment & supplies

(G-2941)
KEWL KITES
200 Jeff Davis Ave Ste 4 (39560-6183)
PHONE...................................228 206-0322
Chris Barker, *Owner*
EMP: 6
SALES (est): 78.8K **Privately Held**
SIC: 3944 5947 Kites; gift shop

(G-2942)
LA ROSA GLASS INC
Also Called: La Rosa Glass & Hardware
6303 Beatline Rd (39560-2105)
PHONE...................................228 864-0751
Frank La Rosa, *President*
Debbie La Rosa, *Corp Secy*
Jeri La Rosa, *Vice Pres*
EMP: 8
SQ FT: 3,000
SALES (est): 730K **Privately Held**
SIC: 3442 1793 5039 5231 Storm doors or windows, metal; glass & glazing work; exterior flat glass: plate or window; interior flat glass: plate or window; paint; hardware

---

2019 Harris Directory of
Mississippi Manufacturers

▲ = Import ▼=Export
◆ =Import/Export

110

GEOGRAPHIC SECTION

Louisville - Winston County (G-2974)

(G-2943)
LEGACY VULCAN LLC
Also Called: Long Beach Yard
4010 Espy Ave (39560)
PHONE...................................228 452-3000
Johnny Williams, *Manager*
EMP: 1 **Publicly Held**
WEB: www.vulcanmaterials.com
SIC: 3273 Ready-mixed concrete
HQ: Legacy Vulcan, Llc
1200 Urban Center Dr
Vestavia AL 35242
205 298-3000

(G-2944)
LEISURE HOME PRODUCTS INC
7085 Turner Rd (39560-9043)
PHONE...................................228 860-7727
Richard Armstrong, *President*
EMP: 2 EST: 2007
SALES (est): 264.7K **Privately Held**
SIC: 3999 Hot tubs

(G-2945)
MOULTON TILE & MARBLE INC
5125 Gates Ave (39560-2415)
PHONE...................................228 863-7587
EMP: 4
SQ FT: 5,000
SALES (est): 381.1K **Privately Held**
SIC: 3281 1743 Mfg Cut Stone/Products
Tile/Marble Contractor

(G-2946)
NATIONAL STONE IMPORTS INC
1314 E Old Pass Rd 2 (39560-5041)
PHONE...................................228 323-7239
Andrew Vega, *President*
Thomas Alterburg, *Corp Secy*
▲ EMP: 4
SQ FT: 20,000
SALES (est): 461.2K **Privately Held**
WEB: www.nationalstoneimports.com
SIC: 3272 Stone, cast concrete

(G-2947)
ONSWOLL GRAFIX LLC
107 Twin Cedar Dr (39560-5320)
PHONE...................................228 596-8409
Clifford Lowe, *Manager*
EMP: 1
SALES (est): 55K **Privately Held**
SIC: 2759 Letterpress & screen printing

(G-2948)
PASSPORT AMERICA CORPORATION (PA)
21263 Tucker Rd (39560-9041)
PHONE...................................228 452-9972
Ray Fernandez, *President*
Dresden Simmons, *Admin Sec*
EMP: 14
SALES (est): 2.3MM **Privately Held**
WEB: www.campsave50percent.com
SIC: 3792 Travel trailers & campers

(G-2949)
PHILUMINA LLC
122 Carroll Ave (39560-5809)
PHONE...................................228 363-4048
Mark Lanoue, *Branch Mgr*
EMP: 4
SALES (corp-wide): 134.8K **Privately Held**
SIC: 3826 Spectrometers
PA: Philumina, Llc
45 Hardy Court Ctr 355
Gulfport MS

(G-2950)
RICHARD ARMSTRONG
Also Called: Armstrong Spa & Hot Tubs
7085 Turner Rd (39560-9043)
PHONE...................................228 822-2238
Richard Armstrong, *Owner*
EMP: 1
SALES (est): 122.9K **Privately Held**
SIC: 3999 5091 Hot tubs; hot tubs

(G-2951)
ROBCO INC
113 E Second St (39560-6145)
P.O. Box 104 (39560-0104)
PHONE...................................769 218-6457
Russell Brashear, *President*
EMP: 1
SALES: 75K **Privately Held**
SIC: 3663 Radio & TV communications
equipment

(G-2952)
ROBERTS WELDING LLC
19451 28th St (39560-9056)
PHONE...................................228 697-4816
Robert Thomas,
EMP: 1
SALES (est): 71.3K **Privately Held**
SIC: 7692 Welding repair

(G-2953)
SMITH & ASSOCIATES INC
207 Mcguire Dr (39560-3312)
PHONE...................................228 864-2786
EMP: 1
SALES (est): 130K **Privately Held**
SIC: 2421 5031 Sawmill/Planing Mill Whol
Lumber/Plywood/Millwork

(G-2954)
SPORTZ ZONE LLC
100 Jeff Davis Ave (39560-6180)
PHONE...................................228 284-1654
EMP: 1 EST: 2012
SALES (est): 88.2K **Privately Held**
SIC: 3949 Sporting & athletic goods

(G-2955)
STITCHING AND STUFF LLC
4401 Beatline Rd Apt 3d (39560-4124)
P.O. Box 1171 (39560-1171)
PHONE...................................228 365-4735
Megin Murphy, *Principal*
EMP: 1
SALES (est): 62.7K **Privately Held**
SIC: 2395 Embroidery & art needlework

(G-2956)
TACKLE TECHNOLOGIES LLC
5244 A Ave (39560-9705)
PHONE...................................228 206-1449
Jacob Steinle, *VP Business*
Keith Fulton,
EMP: 5
SALES (est): 2.7MM **Privately Held**
SIC: 2842 4959 8744 Sweeping compounds, oil or water absorbent, clay or
sawdust; oil spill cleanup;

(G-2957)
TRITON AUTOMATIC TELLER MCHS
522 E Railroad St (39560-4933)
PHONE...................................228 575-3292
Don Dover, *Project Mgr*
EMP: 1
SALES (est): 54.5K **Privately Held**
SIC: 3578 Calculating & accounting equipment

(G-2958)
TRITON SYSTEMS DELAWARE LLC (PA)
Also Called: Atm Gurus
21405 B St (39560-3141)
PHONE...................................228 575-3100
Daryl Cornell, *CEO*
Donald Lett, *CFO*
Stephanie Siaris, *Senior Mgr*
▲ EMP: 125 EST: 1979
SQ FT: 90,000
SALES (est): 18.4MM **Privately Held**
SIC: 7629 3578 Electrical repair shops;
automatic teller machines (ATM)

(G-2959)
TWISTED CANVAS
6190 Beatline Rd Ste 2 (39560-2551)
PHONE...................................228 596-9332
EMP: 1
SALES (est): 46.5K **Privately Held**
SIC: 2211 Canvas

(G-2960)
WOODEN ARTS LLC
Also Called: Wooden Arts Workshop
22332 Freddie Frank Rd (39560-9728)
PHONE...................................228 452-9943
Peter McCarthy, *Mng Member*
EMP: 1

SALES (est): 94K **Privately Held**
SIC: 2431 Millwork

Lorman
Jefferson County

(G-2961)
JONES LOGGING CO INC
1045 Allen Jones Rd (39096-9761)
PHONE...................................601 877-3814
EMP: 3
SALES (est): 150K **Privately Held**
SIC: 2411 Logging

(G-2962)
SHARONES INNOVATIVE PRTG LLC
5009 Alcorn Rd 552 W (39096-9743)
PHONE...................................601 877-3727
Jerry Howard,..*Principal*
EMP: 2
SALES (est): 83.9K **Privately Held**
SIC: 2752 Commercial printing, lithographic

Louin
Jasper County

(G-2963)
R & J BROWN LOGGING & TRUCKING
639 County Road 13 (39338-4623)
PHONE...................................601 739-3338
Ronnie Brown, *Principal*
Joseph Brown, *Vice Pres*
EMP: 4
SALES (est): 400K **Privately Held**
SIC: 2411 5031 Logging camps & contractors; lumber: rough, dressed & finished

Louisville
Winston County

(G-2964)
BAKER READY MIX & CNSTR LLC
11000 Highway 15 S (39339-3497)
PHONE...................................662 773-8054
Billy D Baker,
EMP: 22 EST: 1976
SALES (est): 3.5MM **Privately Held**
SIC: 3273 Ready-mixed concrete

(G-2965)
D & T MOTORS INC (PA)
Also Called: D & T Services
55 N Columbus Ave (39339-2600)
P.O. Box 268 (39339-0268)
PHONE...................................662 773-5021
Jerry L Donald, *President*
Jeanette Donald, *Corp Secy*
EMP: 8
SQ FT: 40,000
SALES (est): 1.8MM **Privately Held**
SIC: 5999 5531 5013 3531 Electronic
parts & equipment; automotive parts; automotive supplies & parts; logging equipment

(G-2966)
D & T MOTORS INC
Also Called: D & T Services
53 Mill St (39339-2627)
PHONE...................................662 773-9041
Meredith Matthews, *Manager*
EMP: 2
SALES (corp-wide): 1.8MM **Privately Held**
SIC: 3599 Machine & other job shop work
PA: D & T Motors Inc
55 N Columbus Ave
Louisville MS 39339
662 773-5021

(G-2967)
DELBERT T DICKERSON
Also Called: Dale Dickerson Logging
534 White Rd (39339-5162)
PHONE...................................662 773-4747
Delbert Dickerson, *Owner*
EMP: 8
SALES (est): 622.1K **Privately Held**
SIC: 2411 Logging

(G-2968)
GEORGE PACIFIC
1487 S Church Ave (39339-3474)
PHONE...................................662 779-1300
Teresa Ming, *Clerk*
EMP: 2
SALES (est): 78.4K **Privately Held**
SIC: 2821 Plastics materials & resins

(G-2969)
GEORGIA-PACIFIC LLC
300 Giffen Industrial Dr (39339)
PHONE...................................662 773-9454
Willy B Moore, *Manager*
EMP: 6
SALES (corp-wide): 40.9B **Privately Held**
WEB: www.gp.com
SIC: 2621 Paper mills
HQ: Georgia-Pacific Llc
133 Peachtree St Nw
Atlanta GA 30303
404 652-4000

(G-2970)
GRAYSON BLU LLC
5695 Old Robinson Rd (39339-7440)
PHONE...................................662 779-1291
Melaine Sylvester,
EMP: 43
SQ FT: 10,000
SALES (est): 6.6MM **Privately Held**
SIC: 3312 Stainless steel

(G-2971)
HARDWIRE INC
926 S Church Ave (39339-3443)
P.O. Box 1183, Ackerman (39735-1183)
PHONE...................................662 285-2312
David Forster, *President*
EMP: 18
SQ FT: 5,000
SALES (est): 5.9MM **Privately Held**
SIC: 3679 Harness assemblies for electronic use: wire or cable

(G-2972)
HOBBY CONST CO
4985 Shiloh Rd (39339-8465)
PHONE...................................662 803-1599
Lonnie Hobby, *Principal*
EMP: 2
SALES (est): 217.2K **Privately Held**
SIC: 2431 Millwork

(G-2973)
LOUISVILLE BRICK COMPANY
750 N Church Ave (39339-9704)
PHONE...................................800 530-7102
John D Mitchell, *President*
EMP: 40 EST: 1926
SQ FT: 2,000
SALES (est): 3.7MM **Privately Held**
WEB: www.louisvillebrick.com
SIC: 3251 Brick clay: common face,
glazed, vitrified or hollow

(G-2974)
LOUISVILLE PUBLISHING INC
Also Called: Winston County Journal
233 N Court Ave (39339-2648)
P.O. Box 469 (39339-0469)
PHONE...................................662 773-6241
Susan Adcock, *Manager*
Joseph McCain, *Director*
EMP: 20 EST: 1892
SQ FT: 20,000
SALES: 900K **Privately Held**
WEB: www.winstoncountyjournal.com
SIC: 2711 7261 Newspapers: publishing
only, not printed on site; funeral service &
crematories

GEOGRAPHIC

(PA)=Parent Co (HQ)=Headquarters (DH)=Div Headquarters
✿ = New Business established in last 2 years

2019 Harris Directory of
Mississippi Manufacturers

111

Louisville - Winston County (G-2975) | GEOGRAPHIC SECTION

(G-2975)
MMC MATERIALS INC
Also Called: Mississippi Materials Co
306 S Spring Ave (39339-2928)
PHONE...................................662 773-5656
EMP: 6
SALES (corp-wide): 288.2MM Privately Held
SIC: 3273 Mfg Ready-Mixed Concrete
HQ: Mmc Materials, Inc.
1052 Highland Colony Pkwy # 201
Ridgeland MS 39157
601 898-4000

(G-2976)
POLO CUSTOM PRODUCTS INC
15730 W Main St (39339-9497)
PHONE...................................662 779-2009
Randolph Lyons, QC Mgr
David Mills, Branch Mgr
EMP: 140
SALES (corp-wide): 68MM Privately Held
WEB: www.mcind.com
SIC: 3069 2393 Medical & laboratory rubber sundries & related products; bags & containers, except sleeping bags: textile
PA: Polo Custom Products, Inc.
3601 Sw 29th St Ste 250
Topeka KS 66614
888 828-9702

(G-2977)
PRISOCK BROTHERS LOGGING INC
8270 Bluff Lake Rd (39339-9334)
PHONE...................................662 773-8443
Deborah Prisock, Vice Pres
Deborah L Prisock, Vice Pres
EMP: 2
SALES (est): 288.6K Privately Held
SIC: 2411 Logging camps & contractors

(G-2978)
QUINTON HILL LOGGING
4825 Bond Rd (39339-9446)
PHONE...................................662 773-6864
Quinton Hill, Owner
EMP: 12
SALES: 200K Privately Held
SIC: 2411 Logging camps & contractors

(G-2979)
RIVES AND REYNOLDS LBR CO INC (PA)
Hwy 15 N (39339)
P.O. Box 490 (39339-0490)
PHONE...................................662 773-5157
Terry E Reynolds, President
Ann Reynolds, Corp Secy
William Bruce Reynolds, Vice Pres
EMP: 55 EST: 1972
SQ FT: 8,000
SALES (est): 18.4MM Privately Held
SIC: 2421 Planing mills

(G-2980)
RONNIES AUTO SALES
Also Called: Eubanks Records Service
601 S Church Ave (39339)
PHONE...................................662 773-9327
Ronnie Eubanks, Owner
EMP: 2
SALES (est): 268.6K Privately Held
SIC: 3711 Wreckers (tow truck), assembly of

(G-2981)
ROSEBURG FOREST PRODUCTS CO
Also Called: Eupora Cut-To-Size
122 Armstrong St (39339-9201)
PHONE...................................662 773-9868
EMP: 32
SALES (corp-wide): 625.9MM Privately Held
SIC: 2431 2493 2421 Mfg Millwork Mfg Reconstituted Wood Products Sawmill/Planing Mill
HQ: Roseburg Forest Products Co
10599 Old Hwy 99 S
Dillard OR 97477
541 679-3311

(G-2982)
SANTAS & SUCH
2090 Evergreen Rd (39339-9387)
PHONE...................................662 773-2711
Frankie Matthews, Owner
EMP: 2
SALES (est): 71K Privately Held
SIC: 3269 Figures: pottery, china, earthenware & stoneware

(G-2983)
SWAIN PRINTING & SIGNS
15185 Highway 397 (39339-5150)
PHONE...................................662 773-7584
Eva Sullivan, Owner
EMP: 2 EST: 1973
SQ FT: 1,000
SALES: 180K Privately Held
SIC: 2759 2791 2789 2752 Screen printing; typesetting; bookbinding & related work; commercial printing, lithographic

(G-2984)
TAYLOR DEFENSE PRODUCTS LLC
3690 N Church Ave (39339-2070)
PHONE...................................662 773-3421
Richard P Ballard, Principal
EMP: 1
SALES (est): 72.6K Privately Held
SIC: 3812 Defense systems & equipment

(G-2985)
TAYLOR ENVIRONMENTAL PRODUCTS
3690 N Church Ave (39339-2070)
PHONE...................................662 773-8056
Lex Taylor, President
Joe Boykin, MIS Staff
EMP: 7
SALES (est): 1.1MM Privately Held
SIC: 3826 3443 Environmental testing equipment; fabricated plate work (boiler shop)
PA: The Taylor Group Inc
650 N Church Ave
Louisville MS 39339

Lucedale
George County

(G-2986)
AMERICAN TANK & VESSEL INC
274 Evanston Rd (39452-6432)
P.O. Box 118 (39452-0118)
PHONE...................................601 947-7210
Joe Watts, Traffic Mgr
Kelvin McLeod, Engineer
David Perkins, Engineer
Christine Fairley, Human Res Dir
James Davidson, Manager
EMP: 150
SALES (corp-wide): 68MM Privately Held
WEB: www.at-v.com
SIC: 3443 7699 Tanks, lined: metal plate; tank repair & cleaning services
PA: American Tank & Vessel, Inc.
1005 Government St
Mobile AL 36604
251 432-8265

(G-2987)
CASTON CREAT & COATINGS LLC
24001 Robert E Lee Rd (39452-9048)
PHONE...................................228 588-0055
Sonia Caston, Principal
EMP: 2
SALES (est): 92.7K Privately Held
SIC: 3479 Metal coating & allied service

(G-2988)
COASTAL PRTECTIVE COATINGS LLC
1260 Plum Bulff Dr (39452)
PHONE...................................214 882-8036
Enoch Capps,
EMP: 1 EST: 2017
SALES (est): 48.8K Privately Held
SIC: 3479 Metal coating & allied service

(G-2989)
COMPLETE WELDING SOLUTIONS
103 Jodie Baxter Rd (39452-4809)
P.O. Box 765 (39452-0765)
PHONE...................................601 791-5370
Michelle Shepherd, CEO
Walter Shepherd, President
Robert Langley,
EMP: 2
SALES (est): 150.3K Privately Held
SIC: 1541 1623 3443 3731 Paper/pulp mill construction; steel building construction; prefabricated building erection, industrial; oil & gas pipeline construction; boilers: industrial, power, or marine; lighters, marine: building & repairing

(G-2990)
COOL BABY WATER LLC
124 Easy St (39452-3757)
PHONE...................................850 748-0921
Gina Fairley Harries, Principal
Margeaux Fairley Domangue,
Meagan Fairley Kinnard,
EMP: 1
SALES (est): 39.5K Privately Held
SIC: 2086 5149 7389 Water, pasteurized: packaged in cans, bottles, etc.; mineral or spring water bottling

(G-2991)
COUNTRY FARMS QUAIL
4284 Dickerson Sawmill Rd (39452-2781)
PHONE...................................601 947-4263
Ann Davis, Owner
EMP: 9
SALES (est): 765.3K Privately Held
SIC: 2015 Poultry slaughtering & processing

(G-2992)
CRYSTAL CROWN INC
183 Webb Davis Rd (39452-3645)
PHONE...................................601 947-8074
Ernest A Snelgrove Jr, President
Crystal Williams, Principal
EMP: 8
SALES (est): 1MM Privately Held
WEB: www.crystalcrown.com
SIC: 3961 Costume jewelry

(G-2993)
DESIGNS OF TIMES INC
11289 Old 63 S (39452-6649)
PHONE...................................601 791-5299
Jason Scott, Principal
EMP: 1
SALES: 250K Privately Held
SIC: 3993 Signs & advertising specialties

(G-2994)
EMERSONS
Also Called: Emerson's Sports
26102 Highway 613 (39452-9695)
PHONE...................................228 588-3952
Pat Naramore, Owner
EMP: 4 EST: 1989
SQ FT: 2,500
SALES (est): 220K Privately Held
SIC: 5941 2759 Sporting goods & bicycle shops; commercial printing

(G-2995)
EUBANKS AND EUBANKS INC
1179 Evanston Rd (39452-6244)
PHONE...................................601 947-2509
Steve Eubanks, President
Tyler Eubanks, Vice Pres
EMP: 7
SQ FT: 2,500
SALES (est): 1.3MM Privately Held
SIC: 2411 Poles, posts & pilings: untreated wood

(G-2996)
FRYFOGLE MANUFACTURING INC
Also Called: FMI Trailers
106 Holmes Dr (39452-8712)
P.O. Box 1388 (39452-1388)
PHONE...................................601 947-8088
Gordon Fryfogle, President
EMP: 10

SALES (est): 374.7K Privately Held
SIC: 3715 5531 7539 Truck trailer chassis; truck equipment & parts; trailer repair

(G-2997)
GEORGE COUNTY TIMES
5133 Main St (39452-6523)
P.O. Box 238 (39452-0238)
PHONE...................................601 947-2967
Og Sellers, Owner
Joann Hardson, Officer
EMP: 7
SALES (est): 305K Privately Held
SIC: 2711 Commercial printing & newspaper publishing combined; newspapers, publishing & printing

(G-2998)
H AND H FABRICATIONS
Also Called: H & H Fabricators
833 Seldom Rest Rd (39452-6182)
PHONE...................................601 508-7558
Norman Ricky Havard, Owner
EMP: 4
SALES: 80K Privately Held
SIC: 3599 Machine shop, jobbing & repair

(G-2999)
HARPER INDUSTRIES INC
Also Called: Lucedale Sportswear Co
52 Virginia St Ste A (39452-6588)
PHONE...................................601 947-2746
Kathy McLaud, Branch Mgr
EMP: 2
SALES (corp-wide): 7.5MM Privately Held
WEB: www.harperindustries.com
SIC: 2253 5136 T-shirts & tops, knit; shirts, men's & boys'
PA: Harper Industries, Inc
29 Hillcrest Rd
Berkeley CA 94705
601 947-2746

(G-3000)
HAVARD MFG INC
1235 Henry Cochran Rd (39452-9408)
PHONE...................................601 766-9170
Jennifer Havard, President
Shane Havard, Vice Pres
EMP: 8
SALES (est): 1.4MM Privately Held
SIC: 3535 Conveyors & conveying equipment

(G-3001)
HAVARDS CONSTRUCTION LLC
5219 Main St (39452-6513)
PHONE...................................601 766-9841
Charles E Havard,
Melissa G Havard,
EMP: 3
SQ FT: 10,500
SALES (est): 294.7K Privately Held
SIC: 1799 3441 Welding on site; ship sections, prefabricated metal

(G-3002)
HUDSON OUTDOOR SIGN LLC
170 N Lake Rd (39452-3457)
PHONE...................................601 947-4608
Hudson Henderson, Principal
EMP: 1
SALES (est): 47.5K Privately Held
SIC: 3993 Signs & advertising specialties

(G-3003)
HUDSON SALVAGE INC
12101 Old 63 S (39452-6619)
PHONE...................................601 947-0092
Martha Willburn, Manager
EMP: 3
SALES (est): 185.1K Privately Held
SIC: 3643 Outlets, electric: convenience

(G-3004)
JIFFY MART
110 Airport Rd (39452-4724)
PHONE...................................601 947-6589
Eddie Dueitt, Owner
EMP: 2 EST: 2015
SALES (est): 148K Privately Held
SIC: 1382 5411 Oil & gas exploration services; convenience stores

---

2019 Harris Directory of
Mississippi Manufacturers

112

▲ = Import ▼=Export
◆ =Import/Export

GEOGRAPHIC SECTION

Lumberton - Lamar County (G-3037)

(G-3005)
JMS MANUFACTURING INC
Also Called: JMS Energy Services
3247 Highway 63 S Bldg 8 (39452-7202)
PHONE....................................601 514-0660
Christopher Johnson, *President*
Monty Johnson, *General Mgr*
EMP: 2
SQ FT: 6,400
SALES (est): 73.4K **Privately Held**
SIC: 3484 3482 3544 7373 Guns
(firearms) or gun parts, 30 mm. & below;
small arms ammunition; industrial molds;
computer-aided design (CAD) systems
service; computer software systems
analysis & design, custom

(G-3006)
JOES CUSTOM CABINETS
134 Alford Howard Rd (39452-5426)
PHONE....................................601 508-8284
Patrick Hewitt, *Owner*
EMP: 2
SALES (est): 150.2K **Privately Held**
SIC: 2434 Wood kitchen cabinets

(G-3007)
LAKEVIEW METAL WORKS
155 Lakeview Dr (39452-3588)
PHONE....................................601 947-8019
Don Lowery, *President*
Larry Lowery, *Vice Pres*
Larry R Lowery, *Vice Pres*
EMP: 3
SALES (est): 335.8K **Privately Held**
SIC: 3448 Buildings, portable: prefabri-
cated metal

(G-3008)
LEGACY VULCAN LLC
201 County Industrial Rd (39452-5784)
PHONE....................................601 947-9717
EMP: 2 **Publicly Held**
SIC: 1442 Construction sand & gravel
HQ: Legacy Vulcan, Llc
1200 Urban Center Dr
Vestavia AL 35242
205 298-3000

(G-3009)
**LUCEDALE READY MIX
CONCRETE CO**
139 Evanston Rd (39452-6219)
P.O. Box 828 (39452-0828)
PHONE....................................601 947-4741
Edward R Evans Sr, *President*
Mary Evelyn Evans, *Corp Secy*
Edward R Evans Jr, *Vice Pres*
EMP: 6
SQ FT: 3,000
SALES (est): 460K **Privately Held**
SIC: 3273 Ready-mixed concrete

(G-3010)
MAGNOLIA TRAILERS INC
144 Airport Cafe Cir (39452-4732)
P.O. Box 1146 (39452-1146)
PHONE....................................601 947-7990
Connie Langley, *President*
Robert Langley, *Vice Pres*
▼ EMP: 25
SQ FT: 15,000
SALES (est): 7.2MM **Privately Held**
WEB: www.magnoliatrailers.com
SIC: 3715 7539 Trailer bodies; trailer re-
pair

(G-3011)
MERR EXPRESS LLC
278 Gyther Fairley Rd (39452-2221)
PHONE....................................601 327-1554
Maurice Reed,
Ruby Reed,
EMP: 2
SALES (est): 100K **Privately Held**
SIC: 3537 Trucks: freight, baggage, etc.:
industrial, except mining

(G-3012)
PROSIGNS INC
17252 Highway 26 W (39452-3809)
PHONE....................................601 791-5299
EMP: 1
SALES (est): 48.6K **Privately Held**
SIC: 3993 Signs & advertising specialties

(G-3013)
PURVIS MACHINE
Also Called: Purvis Machine New Hope
147 New Hope Church Rd (39452-9590)
PHONE....................................601 947-6617
Earl Purvis, *Partner*
Connie Purvis, *Partner*
EMP: 3
SALES (est): 323K **Privately Held**
SIC: 3599 7692 Machine shop, jobbing &
repair; welding repair

(G-3014)
QUALIFIED FABRICATION INC
174 Nancy Ln (39452-4401)
PHONE....................................601 508-4389
Sanford Howell, *Principal*
EMP: 14 EST: 2009
SALES (est): 2MM **Privately Held**
SIC: 3999 Manufacturing industries

(G-3015)
RAYMOND YOUNG PRINTING
7188 Highway 198 E (39452-7850)
PHONE....................................601 947-8999
Raymond Young, *Owner*
EMP: 6
SALES (est): 453.1K **Privately Held**
SIC: 2752 Lithographing on metal

(G-3016)
RIVER ROAD WELDING INC
1313 Vernal River Rd (39452-5935)
PHONE....................................601 947-2511
Franklin D Hinton, *President*
EMP: 2
SALES (est): 268.7K **Privately Held**
SIC: 3499 Fire- or burglary-resistive prod-
ucts

(G-3017)
SOUTHEAST SUPPLY HEADER
1154 Pete Miles Rd (39452-5656)
PHONE....................................601 947-9842
EMP: 2
SALES (est): 124.3K **Privately Held**
SIC: 3542 Headers

(G-3018)
SPIDER BLUE PRESS LLC
116 Milton Murrah Rd (39452-3716)
PHONE....................................601 770-0846
Jeremy Defatta, *Principal*
EMP: 2
SALES (est): 45.4K **Privately Held**
SIC: 2741 Miscellaneous publishing

(G-3019)
STRINGER GUN WORKS LLC
18117 Highway 98 (39452-8509)
PHONE....................................601 947-6796
Wynn Stringer,
Wynn Stringar,
EMP: 1
SALES (est): 56K **Privately Held**
SIC: 3484 Guns (firearms) or gun parts, 30
mm. & below

(G-3020)
TRI-STATE POLE & PILING INC
103 Tri State Rd (39452-6221)
P.O. Box 166 (39452-0166)
PHONE....................................601 947-4285
Jack Harlan, *President*
Mary Jane Harlan, *Corp Secy*
EMP: 13
SQ FT: 3,300
SALES (est): 5MM **Privately Held**
SIC: 2491 Pilings, treated wood; poles &
pole crossarms, treated wood; piles, foun-
dation & marine construction: treated
wood

(G-3021)
WILLIE LYNN HUNT
Also Called: Lynn Hunt Trucking
161 Hunt Rd (39452-3967)
PHONE....................................601 945-2237
Willie Lynn Hunt, *Owner*
EMP: 7
SALES (est): 620.7K **Privately Held**
SIC: 2411 Logging

(G-3022)
X TREME RACING
109 Mcmahan Dr (39452-9721)
PHONE....................................601 947-9686
Sam McClure, *Owner*
EMP: 2
SALES (est): 218.7K **Privately Held**
SIC: 3599 Machine shop, jobbing & repair

Lumberton
Lamar County

(G-3023)
ADVANCED FABRICATION INC
644 Hickory Grove Rd (39455-9637)
P.O. Box 402 (39455-0402)
PHONE....................................601 796-7977
Anthony Fetterolf, *President*
Gail Fetterolf, *President*
EMP: 3
SALES (est): 323.1K **Privately Held**
SIC: 1761 3444 3441 1799 Sheet metal-
work; sheet metalwork; fabricated struc-
tural metal; welding on site

(G-3024)
**BURGE TIMBER CONTRACTORS
INC**
142 Lower Airport Rd (39455-9148)
PHONE....................................601 796-3471
Larry Burge, *President*
Edna Burge, *Admin Sec*
EMP: 11
SALES: 1MM **Privately Held**
SIC: 2411 4213 Logging; contract haulers

(G-3025)
CLEAR ENTERPRISE
1298 Gumpond Beall Rd (39455-5219)
PHONE....................................601 796-2429
Mark Korczak, *Owner*
EMP: 3
SALES (est): 308.4K **Privately Held**
SIC: 3599 7692 3339 Machine shop, job-
bing & repair; welding repair; babbitt
metal (primary)

(G-3026)
**COMMERCIAL METALS
COMPANY**
18 Lavelle Ladner Rd (39455-5401)
PHONE....................................601 796-5474
Brant Smith, *Manager*
EMP: 12
SALES (corp-wide): 4.6B **Publicly Held**
SIC: 3312 Blast furnaces & steel mills
PA: Commercial Metals Company
6565 N Mcarthr Blvd # 800
Irving TX 75039
214 689-4300

(G-3027)
**CUSTOM PRECAST PRODUCTS
INC**
68 Industrial Parkway Rd (39455-2314)
PHONE....................................601 796-8531
Fax: 601 796-8539
EMP: 35
SQ FT: 1,600
SALES (est): 3.8MM **Privately Held**
SIC: 3272 Mfg Concrete Products

(G-3028)
DEVON ENERGY CORPORATION
4 Gulf Camp Cir (39455-8204)
PHONE....................................601 796-4243
Dale Wood, *Principal*
EMP: 8
SALES (corp-wide): 10.7B **Publicly Held**
WEB: www.dvn.com
SIC: 1311 Natural gas production
PA: Devon Energy Corporation
333 W Sheridan Ave
Oklahoma City OK 73102
405 235-3611

(G-3029)
**FRESH DISTRIBUTING
COMPANY LLC**
515j Magnolia Rd (39455-9413)
PHONE....................................228 297-7655
Mike Wilson,

EMP: 3
SALES: 509.3K **Privately Held**
SIC: 2051 Bakery: wholesale or whole-
sale/retail combined

(G-3030)
HUNT REFINING COMPANY
7539 U S Highway 11 (39455)
PHONE....................................601 796-2331
Bill McPhillips, *Opers Staff*
EMP: 30
SALES (corp-wide): 5.3B **Privately Held**
SIC: 2911 Petroleum refining
HQ: Hunt Refining Company
2200 Jack Warner Pkwy # 400
Tuscaloosa AL 35401
205 391-3300

(G-3031)
**INTEGRITY VNYL SDING DECKS
LLC**
104 Flagstaff St (39455-9461)
PHONE....................................601 723-1257
Tammy Miller,
EMP: 2
SALES (est): 74.4K **Privately Held**
SIC: 2821 Vinyl resins

(G-3032)
J & K SERVICES LLC
Also Called: Clear Enterprises
1290 Gumpond Beall Rd (39455-5219)
PHONE....................................601 310-7728
John Korczak, *Mng Member*
EMP: 3
SQ FT: 2,000
SALES (est): 89.5K **Privately Held**
SIC: 1389 Lease tanks, oil field: erecting,
cleaning & repairing

(G-3033)
**JASONS CUSTOM LOGGING
LLC**
26 Victory Ln (39455-9281)
PHONE....................................601 270-6818
Jason Miley,
EMP: 4
SALES (est): 275.4K **Privately Held**
SIC: 2411 Logging

(G-3034)
JUSTIN ALAN RANKIN
145 Carroll Rd (39455-9238)
PHONE....................................601 297-4365
Justin Alan Rankin, *Administration*
EMP: 2
SALES (est): 103K **Privately Held**
SIC: 2411 Logging

(G-3035)
KNR FARM SUPPLIES INC
863 Magnolia Rd (39455-9474)
PHONE....................................228 574-8397
EMP: 3
SALES: 250K **Privately Held**
SIC: 3523 Mfg Farm Machinery/Equipment

(G-3036)
MYLES SMITH
Also Called: Jr Smith Assemble Plant
100 W Main Ave (39455-2526)
PHONE....................................228 323-5052
Myles Smith, *Owner*
EMP: 10
SALES (est): 400K **Privately Held**
SIC: 3711 Automobile assembly, including
specialty automobiles

(G-3037)
**PINE BELT ENERGY SERVICES
LLC**
6466 Highway 13 (39455-9300)
PHONE....................................601 796-3299
Freddy Entrekin, *Superintendent*
Frederick Allen Entrekin,
Mary Pat Entrekin,
EMP: 130
SALES: 25MM **Privately Held**
SIC: 1389 Oil & gas wells: building, repair-
ing & dismantling; construction, repair &
dismantling services

(PA)=Parent Co (HQ)=Headquarters (DH)=Div Headquarters
✿ = New Business established in last 2 years

2019 Harris Directory of
Mississippi Manufacturers

Lumberton - Lamar County (G-3038)
GEOGRAPHIC SECTION

(G-3038)
SOUTHLAND OIL COMPANY
7539 U S Highway 11 (39455-7619)
P.O. Box 241 (39455-0241)
PHONE..................................601 796-2331
David Johnson, *Managing Dir*
Rick Kohnke, *Div Sub Head*
EMP: 25
SALES (corp-wide): 35.7MM **Privately Held**
SIC: 2911 2951 Petroleum refining; asphalt paving mixtures & blocks
HQ: Southland Oil Company
5170 Galaxie Dr
Jackson MS 39206
601 981-4151

(G-3039)
TEXAS PETROLEUM INVESTMENT CO
1497 Clear Creek Ch Rd (39455-8725)
PHONE..................................601 796-4921
Cliff Rice, *Controller*
EMP: 6
SALES (corp-wide): 1.4B **Privately Held**
SIC: 1311 Crude petroleum production
PA: Texas Petroleum Investment Company Inc
5850 San Felipe St # 250
Houston TX 77057
713 789-9225

(G-3040)
WALT MACHINE INC
891 Otho Davis Rd (39455-5672)
PHONE..................................601 796-8269
Tommy Caughey Jr, *President*
EMP: 4
SQ FT: 2,240
SALES: 200K **Privately Held**
SIC: 3599 Machine shop, jobbing & repair

Lyon
Coahoma County

(G-3041)
BIG CREEK GIN COMPANY INC
4150 Highway 6 (38645-9425)
PHONE..................................662 624-5233
John B Laney Jr, *President*
EMP: 30
SALES (est): 526.5K **Privately Held**
SIC: 0724 3559 Cotton ginning; cotton ginning machinery

(G-3042)
CONVEYOR TECH
1350 Old Highway 61 (38645-9553)
PHONE..................................901 831-4760
Harold Jackson, *Owner*
Katy Jackson, *Co-Owner*
EMP: 10
SALES: 1.5MM **Privately Held**
SIC: 3535 Conveyors & conveying equipment

(G-3043)
OWENS CUSTOM MARBLE
18680 Highway 61 N (38645-9768)
P.O. Box 291 (38645-0291)
PHONE..................................662 627-7256
Ray Owens, *Owner*
EMP: 4
SALES: 160K **Privately Held**
SIC: 2493 Marbleboard (stone face hard board)

Maben
Webster County

(G-3044)
DAVID KIRKMAN
2433 Us Highway 82 (39750-8855)
PHONE..................................662 418-5048
David Kirkman, *Principal*
EMP: 3
SALES (est): 283.8K **Privately Held**
SIC: 2411 Logging

(G-3045)
FLORA LOGGING LLC
270 Cordell Rd (39750-6874)
PHONE..................................662 552-5408
Jason Flora,
Jeremy Flora,
EMP: 4
SALES (est): 538.4K **Privately Held**
SIC: 2411 Logging camps & contractors

(G-3046)
HUDSPETH WOOD PRODUCTS INC
3800 Webster St (39750-8638)
P.O. Box 270, Mantee (39751-0270)
PHONE..................................662 263-5902
Jim Hudspeth, *President*
Keith Hudspeth, *Manager*
▲ EMP: 10
SQ FT: 10,000
SALES (est): 660K **Privately Held**
SIC: 2448 2441 Pallets, wood; nailed wood boxes & shook

(G-3047)
MARK TAYLOR LOGGING
Also Called: Taylor, Mark Logging
12990 Sturgis Maben Rd (39750-8873)
PHONE..................................662 418-0812
Mark Taylor, *Owner*
EMP: 3
SALES (est): 181.5K **Privately Held**
SIC: 2411 Logging camps & contractors

(G-3048)
MKS CROCHET
618 Ms Highway 50 E (39750-6836)
PHONE..................................662 769-4982
Melinda Hardin, *Principal*
EMP: 1
SALES (est): 40.9K **Privately Held**
SIC: 2399 Hand woven & crocheted products

(G-3049)
RONNIE KOLB
Also Called: Dewberry Sawmill
Douglastown Rd (39750)
P.O. Box 281 (39750-0281)
PHONE..................................662 263-5252
Ronnie Kolb, *Owner*
EMP: 8 EST: 1956
SQ FT: 600
SALES (est): 937.2K **Privately Held**
SIC: 2421 Sawmills & planing mills, general

(G-3050)
SHANNON FULGHAM LOGGING INC
1694 County Line Rd (39750)
PHONE..................................662 418-4449
Shannon Fulgham, *Exec Dir*
EMP: 3
SALES (est): 358.4K **Privately Held**
SIC: 2411 Logging camps & contractors

(G-3051)
SPRINGER DRY GOODS
Hwy 15 N (39750)
P.O. Box 189 (39750-0189)
PHONE..................................662 263-8144
J O Springer, *Owner*
EMP: 10
SQ FT: 300,000
SALES (est): 550K **Privately Held**
SIC: 5699 5399 5712 2519 Work clothing; country general stores; furniture stores; household furniture, except wood or metal: upholstered

(G-3052)
TOMBSTONE GAME CALLS
3622 N County Line Rd (39750-9626)
PHONE..................................662 769-6364
Chadd Garnett, *Principal*
EMP: 2
SALES (est): 134.7K **Privately Held**
SIC: 3949 Game calls

Macon
Noxubee County

(G-3053)
506 PRINTING
2837 Jefferson St (39341-2271)
P.O. Box 293 (39341-0293)
PHONE..................................662 361-4411
EMP: 2
SALES (est): 83.9K **Privately Held**
SIC: 2752 Lithographic Commercial Printing

(G-3054)
AERWAY MANUFACTURING CO
1721 Deerbrook Rd (39341-9423)
PHONE..................................662 726-4246
Roland Schmidt, *Partner*
Robert Schmidt, *Partner*
EMP: 6
SALES (est): 76.4K **Privately Held**
SIC: 3523 Farm machinery & equipment

(G-3055)
BARGE FOREST PRODUCTS CO
Also Called: Barge Timberland Manageme
Forest Lake Rd (39341)
PHONE..................................662 726-4426
Travis Lindsey, *Manager*
EMP: 5
SALES (corp-wide): 10.1MM **Privately Held**
SIC: 2421 5031 Lumber: rough, sawed or planed; lumber: rough, dressed & finished
PA: Barge Forest Products Co
900 Buggs Ferry Rd
Macon MS
662 726-5841

(G-3056)
D&J TWINE CO
1907 Paulette Rd (39341-8628)
PHONE..................................662 726-2594
Judy Card, *Owner*
EMP: 1
SALES (est): 81K **Privately Held**
SIC: 3552 Rope & cordage machines

(G-3057)
DANIEL PETRE
Also Called: Prairie Welding & Supply
19 Deerbrook Rd (39341-9614)
PHONE..................................662 726-2462
Daniel Petre, *Owner*
EMP: 3
SALES (est): 400K **Privately Held**
SIC: 7692 1799 3444 Welding repair; welding on site; sheet metalwork

(G-3058)
DAVID M EAVES
Also Called: Eaves Brothers Logging
5765 Yellow Creek Rd (39341-9306)
PHONE..................................662 773-7056
EMP: 3
SALES (est): 130K **Privately Held**
SIC: 2411 Logging

(G-3059)
EAST MISSISSIPPI POLE COMPANY
15029 Us Highway 45 (39341-4512)
P.O. Box 108 (39341-0108)
PHONE..................................662 726-2932
William Brent Gray, *President*
Jane Thomasson, *Corp Secy*
Patricia Thomasson, *Vice Pres*
EMP: 20
SQ FT: 120,000
SALES (est): 2.9MM
SALES (corp-wide): 15.3MM **Privately Held**
SIC: 2411 Peeler logs
PA: Thomasson Company
1007 Saint Francis Dr
Philadelphia MS 39350
601 656-6000

(G-3060)
EXQUISITE READS PUBLICATIONS
242 Prairie St (39341-2493)
PHONE..................................662 400-0743
EMP: 2
SALES (est): 47.6K **Privately Held**
SIC: 2741 Music book & sheet music publishing

(G-3061)
FIANNA SYSTEMS LLC
Also Called: Latitude Armory
2974 Jefferson St (39341-2273)
PHONE..................................662 726-5200
Michael Sennett, *Mng Member*
Ralph Sennett,
EMP: 3
SALES (est): 305.3K **Privately Held**
SIC: 3483 3484 Ammunition, except for small arms; small arms

(G-3062)
FOREST PENICK PRODUCTS INC
5734 Ms Highway 145 (39341-2777)
P.O. Box 479 (39341-0479)
PHONE..................................662 726-5224
Eugene B Penick Jr, *Admin Sec*
EMP: 25
SQ FT: 2,500
SALES (est): 5.7MM **Privately Held**
SIC: 2873 2491 Nitrogenous fertilizers; wood preserving

(G-3063)
GUYS LOGGING
40461 Ms Highway 14 W (39341-7663)
PHONE..................................662 726-9301
Brad Guy, *Owner*
EMP: 2
SALES (est): 143.8K **Privately Held**
SIC: 2411 7389 Logging camps & contractors; timber, cut at logging camp;

(G-3064)
MACON BEACON
Also Called: Macon Beacon, The
2904 Jefferson St (39341-2273)
PHONE..................................662 726-4747
Scott Boyd, *Owner*
EMP: 5 EST: 1849
SQ FT: 7,200
SALES: 300K **Privately Held**
SIC: 2711 2752 7383 Newspapers, publishing & printing; lithographing on metal; news reporting services for newspapers & periodicals

(G-3065)
MACON READY-MIX CONCRETE CO
46712 Ms Highway 14 E (39341-2587)
PHONE..................................662 726-4733
Galen Schrock, *President*
Jeanie Schrock, *Admin Sec*
EMP: 14 EST: 1961
SQ FT: 500
SALES (est): 1.5MM **Privately Held**
SIC: 3273 5211 3272 Ready-mixed concrete; concrete & cinder block; concrete products

(G-3066)
MACON TREATING COMPANY
15029 Us Highway 45 (39341-4512)
PHONE..................................662 726-2767
William Brent Gray, *President*
Patricia Thomasson, *Vice Pres*
Helen Thomasson, *Treasurer*
Jane Thomas, *Admin Sec*
EMP: 2
SALES: 794K
SALES (corp-wide): 15.3MM **Privately Held**
SIC: 2491 Poles & pole crossarms, treated wood
PA: Thomasson Company
1007 Saint Francis Dr
Philadelphia MS 39350
601 656-6000

2019 Harris Directory of
Mississippi Manufacturers

▲ = Import ▼=Export
◆ =Import/Export

114

GEOGRAPHIC SECTION

Madison - Madison County (G-3098)

(G-3067)
MISSISSIPPI WELDING AND MCHS
40737 Ms Highway 14 W (39341-7665)
PHONE..................................662 726-5593
Larry Robins, *Owner*
EMP: 5
SQ FT: 2,500
SALES (est): 460K **Privately Held**
SIC: 7692 Welding repair

(G-3068)
MURRAYS DEER PROCESSING
227 Murray Hill Rd (39341-8204)
PHONE..................................601 720-2769
Leroy Murray, *Principal*
EMP: 3
SALES (est): 166.7K **Privately Held**
SIC: 2011 Meat packing plants

(G-3069)
NOXUBEE COUNTY PRODUCERS INC
Also Called: Superior Fish Products
11751 Highway 45 (39341-2250)
P.O. Box 700 (39341-0700)
PHONE..................................662 726-2502
Norman Koehn, *CEO*
Melissa Unruh, *Engineer*
Richard Johnson, *Treasurer*
Kenneth Johnson, *Admin Sec*
EMP: 118
SQ FT: 32,000
SALES (est): 19MM **Privately Held**
SIC: 2092 Fish, fresh: prepared; fish, frozen: prepared

(G-3070)
PALLET MACHINERY SVC
6285 Pearl St (39341-2259)
PHONE..................................662 726-5101
EMP: 2
SALES (est): 81.4K **Privately Held**
SIC: 3599 Industrial Machinery, Nec, Nsk

(G-3071)
PROBUILT LLC
47121 Ms Highway 14 E (39341-2679)
PHONE..................................662 312-2159
Daniel Yoder, *Principal*
EMP: 8
SALES (est): 1.1MM **Privately Held**
SIC: 3448 Prefabricated metal buildings

(G-3072)
PURINA ANIMAL NUTRITION LLC
600 Pearl St (39341)
PHONE..................................662 726-4262
Todd Kennedy, *Manager*
EMP: 35
SALES (corp-wide): 8.4B **Privately Held**
WEB: www.landolakesidd.com
SIC: 2048 Prepared feeds
HQ: Purina Animal Nutrition Llc
100 Danforth Dr
Gray Summit MO 63039

(G-3073)
TRAILBOSS TRAILERS INC
15722 Us Highway 45 (39341-4508)
PHONE..................................800 345-2452
Michael R Banks, *Exec Dir*
EMP: 28
SALES (corp-wide): 13.3MM **Privately Held**
SIC: 3799 Trailers & trailer equipment
PA: Trailboss Trailers, Inc
15722 Us Highway 45
Macon MS 39341
662 726-5666

Madison
Madison County

(G-3074)
3V SOLUTIONS LLC
1888 Main St Ste C296 (39110-6337)
P.O. Box 18639, Atlanta GA (31126-0639)
PHONE..................................601 720-4999
Mark Dendinger, *Mng Member*
EMP: 2 EST: 2010

SALES (est): 244.8K **Privately Held**
SIC: 7372 Business oriented computer software

(G-3075)
ACME PRINTING COMPANY INC
1112 Windrose Cir (39110-7753)
PHONE..................................601 856-7766
Mike Waggener, *President*
Steve Waggener, *Vice Pres*
EMP: 10 EST: 1961
SQ FT: 10,000
SALES (est): 1.4MM **Privately Held**
WEB: www.acmeprinting.net
SIC: 2752 Commercial printing, offset

(G-3076)
AIR VENT
110 Lake Village Dr (39110-6520)
PHONE..................................601 790-9397
EMP: 2
SALES (est): 106.7K **Privately Held**
SIC: 3444 Mfg Sheet Metalwork

(G-3077)
ALARM COMPANY INC
Also Called: B & S Alarm Service
338 Distribution Dr (39110-9066)
P.O. Box 13633, Jackson (39236-3633)
PHONE..................................601 898-3105
Tony Collums, *President*
Christina Collums, *Office Mgr*
EMP: 12
SQ FT: 2,000
SALES: 1.2MM **Privately Held**
WEB: www.thugproof.com
SIC: 3669 5946 Burglar alarm apparatus, electric; fire alarm apparatus, electric; camera & photographic supply stores

(G-3078)
AMERICAN PACKAGING COMPANY INC
Also Called: American Printing & Converting
158 American Way (39110-7968)
PHONE..................................601 856-0986
John W Campbell Jr, *President*
Janice V Campbell, *Vice Pres*
James Marcus Campbell, *Admin Sec*
EMP: 10
SQ FT: 5,000
SALES (est): 2.4MM **Privately Held**
SIC: 2673 Plastic bags: made from purchased materials

(G-3079)
AUTOFLOW LLC
Also Called: 8209
1294 Mannsdale Rd (39110-9730)
P.O. Box 1550 (39130-1550)
PHONE..................................601 853-1021
Paul Watson, *President*
Vanessa Watson, *Vice Pres*
EMP: 3
SALES (est): 157.9K **Privately Held**
SIC: 3523 Farm machinery & equipment

(G-3080)
AXIALL LLC
210 Industrial Dr N (39110-9481)
PHONE..................................601 856-8993
◆ EMP: 25
SALES (est): 8.9MM **Publicly Held**
SIC: 2821 Plastics materials & resins
HQ: Axiall Corporation
1000 Abernathy Rd # 1200
Atlanta GA 30328
304 455-2200

(G-3081)
AXIALL CORPORATION
Also Called: Westlake Compound
210 Industrial Dr N (39110-9481)
PHONE..................................601 206-3200
Mike Meccardeo, *Manager*
EMP: 70 **Publicly Held**
WEB: www.georgiagulf.com
SIC: 2812 2821 Alkalies & chlorine; vinyl resins
HQ: Axiall Corporation
1000 Abernathy Rd # 1200
Atlanta GA 30328
304 455-2200

(G-3082)
BACALLAO SILVA GRAN & TILE LLC
110 Lexington Dr (39110-6951)
PHONE..................................769 798-8816
Reed B Ingramc,
EMP: 2
SALES (est): 62.6K **Privately Held**
SIC: 3281 Granite, cut & shaped

(G-3083)
BANGERS AND MASH TEES LLC
1888 Main St Ste C-292 (39110-6337)
PHONE..................................801 803-8970
Lindsay Mitchell, *Manager*
EMP: 2
SALES (est): 131.5K **Privately Held**
SIC: 2759 Screen printing

(G-3084)
BEMIS COMPANY INC
25 Woodgreen Pl (39110-9531)
PHONE..................................402 734-6262
Nathan Creen, *Plt & Fclts Mgr*
EMP: 300
SQ FT: 80,000
SALES (corp-wide): 256.8K **Privately Held**
WEB: www.bemis.com
SIC: 2671 2674 Paper coated or laminated for packaging; plastic film, coated or laminated for packaging; paper bags: made from purchased materials; shipping bags or sacks, including multiwall & heavy duty
HQ: Bemis Company, Inc.
2301 Industrial Dr
Neenah WI 54956
920 727-4100

(G-3085)
BEN SESSUMS
Also Called: Ben's Printing & Graphics
624 Live Oak Dr (39110-9509)
PHONE..................................601 856-3401
Ben Sessums, *Owner*
EMP: 1
SALES (est): 105.8K **Privately Held**
SIC: 2752 7336 Commercial printing, lithographic; commercial art & graphic design

(G-3086)
BEVERLY ROBINSON DECOR
357 Kiowa Dr (39110-8814)
PHONE..................................601 201-1520
Beverly Robinson, *Principal*
EMP: 2
SALES (est): 108.3K **Privately Held**
SIC: 2391 Curtains & draperies

(G-3087)
CANNON BOAT LIFTS LLC
99 Ingleside Rd (39110-8510)
PHONE..................................601 540-8691
Caleb Cannon, *Principal*
EMP: 2
SALES (est): 95.5K **Privately Held**
SIC: 3536 Boat lifts

(G-3088)
CANOPY BREEZES LLC
401 Pebble Creek Dr (39110-9191)
PHONE..................................972 207-2045
Frank Arnold, *CEO*
Jeffrey Snuggs, *CFO*
Don Foote,
Blane Taylor,
EMP: 5 EST: 2011
SALES (est): 296.7K **Privately Held**
SIC: 3089 3634 Injection molding of plastics; kits, plastic; personal electrical appliances

(G-3089)
CORREY ELDER
Also Called: Entrepreneur
104 Mulberry Way (39110-9122)
P.O. Box 872 (39130-0872)
PHONE..................................769 257-3240
Correy Elder, *Owner*
EMP: 1
SALES (est): 45.6K **Privately Held**
SIC: 3953 6798 1531 Marking devices; real estate investment trusts; operative builders

(G-3090)
COX HARDWARE LLC
Also Called: Southern Door & Hardware
47 Deer Haven Dr (39110-8055)
PHONE..................................713 923-9458
Perry N Cox, *Mng Member*
EMP: 26
SQ FT: 55,000
SALES: 8MM **Privately Held**
SIC: 5031 3442 Doors; window & door frames

(G-3091)
CYPRESS PHARMACEUTICAL INC
135 Industrial Dr N (39110-9290)
PHONE..................................800 856-4393
EMP: 8
SALES (est): 750.3K **Privately Held**
SIC: 2834 Pharmaceutical preparations

(G-3092)
DARRELL CRUM LLC
Also Called: Labelsrx
136 Saint Charles Pl (39110-8879)
PHONE..................................806 224-7337
Darrell L Crum, *Principal*
EMP: 3
SALES (est): 147.6K **Privately Held**
SIC: 2672 Adhesive papers, labels or tapes: from purchased material

(G-3093)
DBC CORPORATION
Also Called: De Beukelaer Cookie Company
228 Industrial Dr N (39110-9481)
P.O. Box 456 (39130-0456)
PHONE..................................601 856-7454
Peter De Beukelaer, *President*
Mirelle De Beukelaer, *Corp Secy*
Herwig Debeukelaer, *Plant Mgr*
▲ EMP: 86
SQ FT: 100,000
SALES (est): 22.3MM **Privately Held**
WEB: www.pirouline.com
SIC: 2052 Cookies; sugar wafers

(G-3094)
DEBEUKELAER CORPORATION
228 Industrial Dr N (39110-9481)
P.O. Box 1697 (39130-1697)
PHONE..................................601 856-7454
◆ EMP: 17
SALES (est): 3.6MM **Privately Held**
SIC: 3421 Table & food cutlery, including butchers'

(G-3095)
DEBRA THIGPEN
Also Called: Garden Interiors
538 Lake Pointe Ln (39110-8752)
PHONE..................................601 856-0019
EMP: 1
SALES (est): 52K **Privately Held**
SIC: 3999 Floral Designer

(G-3096)
DIGNITY GARMENTS LLC
520 Silverstone Dr (39110-7647)
PHONE..................................601 941-4636
Douglas Eric Parsell, *Principal*
Ruonan Wu, *Manager*
EMP: 3
SALES (est): 170.5K **Privately Held**
SIC: 2389 Hospital gowns

(G-3097)
EMERGENT TECHNOLOGIES LLC
299 Woodland Brook Dr (39110-7379)
PHONE..................................601 497-8239
Ryan Bohling, *Principal*
Edward Ellington, *Principal*
EMP: 2
SALES (est): 104.1K **Privately Held**
SIC: 3721 8713 Motorized aircraft;

(G-3098)
FAURECIA MDSON AUTO SATING INC
272 Old Jackson Rd (39110-4718)
PHONE..................................601 407-2200
Collin Malcolm, *President*
▲ EMP: 250

(PA)=Parent Co (HQ)=Headquarters (DH)=Div Headquarters
✿ = New Business established in last 2 years

2019 Harris Directory of
Mississippi Manufacturers

115

Madison - Madison County (G-3099)

GEOGRAPHIC SECTION

SALES (est): 62.6MM
SALES (corp-wide): 38.2MM **Privately Held**
SIC: 3499 Automobile seat frames, metal
HQ: Faurecia Usa Holdings, Inc.
2800 High Meadow Cir
Auburn Hills MI 48326
248 724-5100

(G-3099)
FISHER LUDLOW
211 Industrial Dr N (39110-9783)
PHONE...................................601 853-9996
Andra Johnson, *Manager*
EMP: 2
SALES (est): 88.9K **Privately Held**
SIC: 3446 Architectural metalwork

(G-3100)
FISKE INTERNATIONAL GROUP CORP
268 Hawthorne Dr (39110-9334)
PHONE...................................601 622-5767
Babatunde Abioye, *President*
EMP: 3
SALES (est): 461.2K **Privately Held**
SIC: 5172 2097 5075 7389 Petroleum products; manufactured ice; warm air heating & air conditioning;

(G-3101)
FROM OUR HOUSE TO YOURS
214 Heritage Dr (39110-8676)
PHONE...................................601 956-1818
Kimi Fancher, *Owner*
EMP: 3
SALES (est): 332.8K **Privately Held**
SIC: 2511 Wood household furniture

(G-3102)
GARRETT & SON INC
130 American Way (39110-8246)
PHONE...................................601 853-7865
Robert E Garrett, *President*
Dorris B Garrett, *Vice Pres*
Jason Peacock, *Treasurer*
Mark Garrett, *Admin Sec*
EMP: 35
SALES (est): 8.4MM **Privately Held**
WEB: www.garrettandson.net
SIC: 5063 7629 3612 Transformers, electric; electrical equipment repair, high voltage; transformers, except electric

(G-3103)
GATOR ARCHERY & OUTDOORS LLC
464 Church Rd (39110-6940)
PHONE...................................601 940-3570
Elizabeth Greer,
EMP: 3 EST: 2017
SQ FT: 1,400
SALES (est): 88.4K **Privately Held**
SIC: 3949 Bows, archery

(G-3104)
GERRER INDUSTRIAL LLC
1888 Main St Ste C186 (39110-6337)
PHONE...................................601 506-2709
EMP: 1
SALES: 50K **Privately Held**
SIC: 3429 Mfg Hardware

(G-3105)
HEDERMAN BROTHERS LLC
247 Industrial Dr N (39110-9783)
PHONE...................................601 853-7300
Doug Hederman, *CEO*
Bert Jackson, *President*
Rick Smith, *Exec VP*
Jim McBrayer, *CFO*
Bob Curtis, *Administration*
EMP: 83
SQ FT: 73,000
SALES: 490.6K **Privately Held**
SIC: 2752 Commercial printing, offset

(G-3106)
HOOD PACKAGING CORPORATION
Also Called: Hood Flexible Packaging
25 Woodgreen Pl (39110-9531)
PHONE...................................770 981-5400
EMP: 95

SALES (corp-wide): 622.5MM **Privately Held**
SIC: 2674 2673 Mfg Bags-Uncoated Paper Mfg Bags-Plastic/Coated Paper
HQ: Hood Packaging Corporation
25 Woodgreen Pl
Madison MS 39110
601 853-7260

(G-3107)
HOOD PACKAGING CORPORATION (HQ)
25 Woodgreen Pl (39110-9531)
PHONE...................................601 853-7260
Robert Morris, *President*
John Johnson, *Vice Pres*
Warren A Hood Jr, *Treasurer*
Nick Arato, *Finance Mgr*
John Burnam, *Admin Sec*
▲ EMP: 25
SQ FT: 11,000
SALES (est): 353.5MM **Privately Held**
WEB: www.hoodpkg.com
SIC: 2674 Bags: uncoated paper & multiwall

(G-3108)
HOSPITALITY SIGN COMPANY
123 Munich Dr (39110-9082)
PHONE...................................601 898-8393
Hank McMahan, *Principal*
EMP: 1
SALES (est): 72K **Privately Held**
SIC: 3993 Signs & advertising specialties

(G-3109)
INFO SERVICES INC
125 Solleftea Dr (39110-7258)
P.O. Box 936 (39130-0936)
PHONE...................................601 898-7858
Tommy Ladner, *President*
Anthony Tharpe, *Vice Pres*
Lori Ladner, *Treasurer*
EMP: 10 EST: 1984
SALES: 500K **Privately Held**
WEB: www.infosvcsinc.com
SIC: 7372 8721 Application computer software; billing & bookkeeping service

(G-3110)
INGRAM ROMAN INC
386 Green Oak Ln (39110-7516)
PHONE...................................601 954-8367
Roman Ingram, *President*
EMP: 9
SALES: 800K **Privately Held**
SIC: 2899 Patching plaster, household

(G-3111)
INTEGRITY FIRE EXTINGUISH
120 E Hill Dr (39110-8961)
PHONE...................................601 953-1927
EMP: 2
SALES (est): 91.4K **Privately Held**
SIC: 3999 Fire extinguishers, portable

(G-3112)
J S IUPES
101 Village Blvd Ste D (39110-8439)
P.O. Box 2736 (39130-2736)
PHONE...................................601 856-7776
Joe Iupe Jr, *Owner*
EMP: 6
SALES (est): 548.7K **Privately Held**
SIC: 5699 2759 Customized clothing & apparel; screen printing

(G-3113)
J&I&R RACEWAY LLC
106 Fairfax Ct (39110-7381)
PHONE...................................601 622-8458
EMP: 2
SALES (est): 88.3K **Privately Held**
SIC: 3644 Raceways

(G-3114)
K&A CUSTOMIZE PRINTING LLC
427 Autumn Oak Dr (39110-9149)
PHONE...................................225 326-9054
Kathleen McPherson, *Principal*
EMP: 1
SALES (est): 107.2K **Privately Held**
SIC: 2752 Commercial printing, lithographic

(G-3115)
KELSEY BAILEY CONSULTING LLC
107 Kenzie Dr (39110-7081)
PHONE...................................601 622-8319
Kelsey Bailey, *Owner*
Tisha Bailey, *Principal*
EMP: 2
SALES (est): 115.6K **Privately Held**
SIC: 3829 8742 8748 8711 Plotting instruments, drafting & map reading; industrial & labor consulting services; systems analysis & engineering consulting services; industrial engineers

(G-3116)
KSQUARED INC
Also Called: Reservoir Stationers
106 Lone Wolf Dr (39110-7028)
PHONE...................................601 956-2951
EMP: 10
SQ FT: 4,000
SALES (est): 1.2MM **Privately Held**
WEB: www.rsiop.com
SIC: 5943 2752 Office forms & supplies; commercial printing, lithographic

(G-3117)
L3 TECHNOLOGIES INC
Also Called: L3 Technologies Systems
555 Industrial Dr S (39110-9072)
PHONE...................................601 856-2274
Cassandra Bradley, *Purch Mgr*
S Gordon Walsh, *Branch Mgr*
Joe Bryant, *Manager*
Susan Rigby, *Manager*
Roy Chaisson, *Info Tech Mgr*
EMP: 25
SALES (corp-wide): 6.8B **Publicly Held**
SIC: 3663 3669 3679 3812 Telemetering equipment, electronic; receiver-transmitter units (transceiver); amplifiers, RF power & IF; sirens, electric: vehicle, marine, industrial & air raid; intercommunication systems, electric; microwave components; aircraft control systems, electronic; guided missile & space vehicle parts & auxiliary equipment
HQ: L3 Technologies, Inc.
600 3rd Ave Fl 34
New York NY 10016
212 697-1111

(G-3118)
LAG CONSTRUCTORS
700 Woods Rd (39110-9328)
PHONE...................................601 720-0404
EMP: 2
SALES (est): 140K **Privately Held**
SIC: 1442 Construction sand & gravel

(G-3119)
LANDING
Also Called: Tailored South
111 Colony Crossing Way (39110-7778)
PHONE...................................601 707-7505
Whitney Giordano, *Principal*
EMP: 6
SALES (est): 527.1K **Privately Held**
SIC: 2331 2337 2361 T-shirts & tops, women's: made from purchased materials; jackets & vests, except fur & leather: women's; blouses: girls', children's & infants'

(G-3120)
LOST SOCK LLC
104 Golden Pond Dr (39110-8323)
PHONE...................................601 946-1155
David Parks,
EMP: 4
SALES (est): 239.4K **Privately Held**
SIC: 2252 Socks

(G-3121)
LULUS SWEET SHOP LLC
102 Dees Drive Madison (39110)
PHONE...................................601 790-1951
Paris McDougal,
EMP: 1
SALES (est): 99.1K **Privately Held**
SIC: 2051 Cakes, bakery: except frozen

(G-3122)
M & M MONOGRAMS
2019 Silver Ln (39110-8984)
PHONE...................................601 856-7459
Merry P Farris, *Owner*
EMP: 1
SALES: 40K **Privately Held**
SIC: 2395 Embroidery & art needlework

(G-3123)
M-TEK INC
Also Called: M-Tek Mississippi
435 Church Rd (39110-9051)
PHONE...................................601 407-5000
Glenn Lowe, *Plant Mgr*
Calvin Whitehead, *Engineer*
Shunji Yokoyama, *Branch Mgr*
EMP: 542 **Privately Held**
WEB: www.m-tek.com
SIC: 3089 Automotive parts, plastic
HQ: Kasai North America, Inc.
1225 Garrison Dr
Murfreesboro TN 37129
615 546-6040

(G-3124)
MADISON COUNTY HERALD
794 Highway 51 Ste B (39110-9662)
PHONE...................................601 853-2899
Fax: 601 853-8720
EMP: 5
SALES (est): 310.1K **Privately Held**
SIC: 2711 5994 7313 Newspapers-Publishing/Printing Ret News Dealer/Newsstand Advertising Representative

(G-3125)
MADISON HOUSE INC ✪
160 Weisenberger Rd (39110-7993)
PHONE...................................601 898-8090
EMP: 2 EST: 2019
SALES (est): 72.9K **Privately Held**
SIC: 2519 Household furniture

(G-3126)
MAJESTIC METALS INC (PA)
192 American Way (39110-7968)
P.O. Box 12266, Jackson (39236-2266)
PHONE...................................601 856-3600
C A Hall III, *President*
Steffen Hancock, *Sales Staff*
Johnny Reid, *Sales Executive*
Jill Becnel, *Manager*
EMP: 20 EST: 1967
SALES (est): 6.4MM **Privately Held**
WEB: www.majesticmetals.com
SIC: 3448 5039 3446 3444 Buildings, portable: prefabricated metal; prefabricated buildings; architectural metalwork; sheet metalwork; fabricated structural metal; asphalt felts & coatings

(G-3127)
MATHESON TRI-GAS INC
218 Weisenberger Rd (39110-9723)
PHONE...................................601 856-3000
Wayne Dooley, *Branch Mgr*
EMP: 12 **Privately Held**
WEB: www.airliquide.com
SIC: 5084 2813 Welding machinery & equipment; safety equipment; nitrogen
HQ: Matheson Tri-Gas, Inc.
150 Allen Rd Ste 302
Basking Ridge NJ 07920
908 991-9200

(G-3128)
MEDI-VATION LLC
115 Homestead Dr (39110-7087)
PHONE...................................800 643-2134
Kevin G Johnson, *President*
EMP: 3
SALES (est): 324K **Privately Held**
SIC: 3842 Sutures, absorbable & non-absorbable

(G-3129)
MILIEU OUTDOOR IMAGE SOLUTIONS
990 Highway 51 2905 (39110-8409)
PHONE...................................601 259-8570
Bryce Davis, *Principal*
EMP: 2 EST: 2010
SQ FT: 4,600

2019 Harris Directory of
Mississippi Manufacturers

116

▲ = Import ▼=Export
◆ =Import/Export

GEOGRAPHIC SECTION

Madison - Madison County (G-3162)

SALES (est): 53.3K **Privately Held**
SIC: **0781** 3271 0782 Landscape services; blocks, concrete: landscape or retaining wall; landscape contractors

(G-3130)
MIN SHENG HEALTHCARE LLC
232 Tifton Dr (39110-6939)
PHONE.............................601 212-6189
Ruisheng Liu,
EMP: 2
SALES (est): 130K **Privately Held**
SIC: 8742 3845 Hospital & health services consultant; electromedical equipment

(G-3131)
MOLLYGRAMS
11 Twelve Oaks Dr (39110-9377)
PHONE.............................601 856-5598
EMP: 1
SALES (est): 39.3K **Privately Held**
SIC: 2395 Pleating/Stitching Services

(G-3132)
MONOGRAM MAGIC
3011 Tidewater Cir (39110-8980)
PHONE.............................601 624-6917
Monogram Magic Warren, *Principal*
EMP: 1
SALES (est): 47K **Privately Held**
SIC: 2395 Embroidery & art needlework

(G-3133)
NICK CLARK PRINTING AND SIGNS
965 Highway 51 Ste 4 (39110-8922)
PHONE.............................601 607-7722
Nick Clark, *Owner*
EMP: 6
SALES (est): 396.6K **Privately Held**
SIC: 2759 Commercial printing

(G-3134)
NUCOR GRATING
211 Industrial Dr N (39110-9783)
PHONE.............................601 853-9996
EMP: 9
SALES (est): 1.6MM **Privately Held**
SIC: 3827 Optical instruments & lenses

(G-3135)
OOLITE INVESTMENTS INC
160 Autumn Woods Dr (39110-8601)
PHONE.............................601 853-0408
Lynn Harmount, *President*
James Harmount, *Director*
EMP: 2
SALES (est): 500K **Privately Held**
SIC: 1382 Oil & gas exploration services

(G-3136)
PACKAGING RESEARCH AND DESIGN
107 Bristol Ct (39110-9435)
P.O. Box 149, Brandon (39043-0149)
PHONE.............................800 833-9364
William Beck, *President*
EMP: 5
SALES (est): 1MM **Privately Held**
WEB: www.packagingresearch.com
SIC: 3069 Linings, vulcanizable rubber

(G-3137)
PARKER-HANNIFIN CORPORATION
Also Called: Fluid Control Division
147 W Hoy Rd (39110-9357)
PHONE.............................601 856-4123
Joey Ray, *Accounts Mgr*
Larry Ryba, *Branch Mgr*
Ronnie Shields, *Data Proc Dir*
EMP: 160
SQ FT: 69,116
SALES (corp-wide): 14.3B **Publicly Held**
WEB: www.parker.com
SIC: 3491 3494 3492 Solenoid valves; valves & pipe fittings; fluid power valves & hose fittings
PA: Parker-Hannifin Corporation
6035 Parkland Blvd
Cleveland OH 44124
216 896-3000

(G-3138)
PHOSPHATE HOLDINGS INC
100 Webster Cir Ste 4 (39110-7366)
P.O. Box 848, Pascagoula (39568-0848)
PHONE.............................601 898-9004
James L Sherbert, *CEO*
Rex M Deloach, *Ch of Bd*
Ed McCraw, *COO*
James G Perkins, *Vice Pres*
W Thomas Jagodinski, *Director*
EMP: 315
SALES (est): 39.7MM **Privately Held**
WEB: www.missphosphate.com
SIC: 2874 Phosphatic fertilizers

(G-3139)
PINK PEPPERMINT PAPER LLC
404 Saint Ives Dr (39110-6944)
PHONE.............................601 898-9232
Eleanor Touchet, *Principal*
EMP: 4
SALES (est): 202.7K **Privately Held**
SIC: 2754 Invitations: gravure printing

(G-3140)
PIRANHA BUSINESS CARDS LLC
Also Called: BCT
106 Lone Wolf Dr (39110-7028)
P.O. Box 16628, Jackson (39236-6628)
PHONE.............................800 281-1916
Christopher McCoy,
Wanda McCoy,
EMP: 11
SQ FT: 6,000
SALES: 130K **Privately Held**
SIC: 2752 Commercial printing, lithographic

(G-3141)
POLYCON INTERNATIONAL LLC
350 Industrial Dr S (39110-8284)
P.O. Box 4567, Jackson (39296-4567)
PHONE.............................601 898-1024
Bradley Wilson, *Exec VP*
Jack H Wilson, *Mng Member*
John Howard,
▼ EMP: 19 EST: 1995
SQ FT: 22,000
SALES (est): 3.8MM **Privately Held**
SIC: 2951 2952 Concrete, asphaltic (not from refineries); asphalt felts & coatings

(G-3142)
PREMIER SHOOTING SOLUTIONS LLC
557 Silverstone Dr (39110-7646)
PHONE.............................601 297-5778
James Duncan,
EMP: 1
SALES (est): 52.6K **Privately Held**
SIC: 3489 Artillery or artillery parts, over 30 mm.

(G-3143)
RESERVOIR SIGNS LLC
323 Trace Harbor Rd (39110-8767)
PHONE.............................601 898-1111
Tyler Johnson, *Principal*
EMP: 2 EST: 2010
SALES (est): 205.9K **Privately Held**
SIC: 3993 Signs & advertising specialties

(G-3144)
ROADSTER DREAM PUBLISHING LLC
809 Steels Pt (39110-7294)
PHONE.............................601 853-4443
Andrew Thomas, *Principal*
EMP: 2
SALES (est): 59.2K **Privately Held**
SIC: 2741 Miscellaneous publishing

(G-3145)
SCHUYLER C JONES
Also Called: Vetguard Solutions
115 Coventry Cv (39110-8481)
PHONE.............................601 540-5841
Schuyler C Jones, *Owner*
EMP: 1
SALES (est): 51.6K **Privately Held**
SIC: 3069 Medical & laboratory rubber sundries & related products

(G-3146)
SIGNATURE ACCENTS
297 Ingleside Dr (39110-9528)
PHONE.............................601 853-9020
Rebecca Henley, *Owner*
EMP: 1
SALES (est): 47.4K **Privately Held**
SIC: 2395 Embroidery & art needlework

(G-3147)
SKIN SAKE LLC
2187 Highway 51 (39110-7491)
P.O. Box 948 (39130-0948)
PHONE.............................870 853-5544
Jeff Foote,
▲ EMP: 6
SALES (est): 1MM **Privately Held**
WEB: www.skinsake.com
SIC: 2834 Dermatologicals

(G-3148)
SOLOMON ENERGY LLC
132 Adderley Blvd (39110-9487)
PHONE.............................601 607-3070
EMP: 2
SALES (est): 170K **Privately Held**
SIC: 1382 Oil/Gas Exploration Services

(G-3149)
SOUTHEASTERN SIGN COMPANY INC
120 Lone Wolf Dr (39110-7028)
PHONE.............................601 391-0023
Robert W Buchanan, *President*
Paula Nutt, *Sales Staff*
Cindy Stitchley, *Office Mgr*
EMP: 4 EST: 2009
SALES: 84K **Privately Held**
SIC: 3993 Signs & advertising specialties

(G-3150)
SOUTHERN PRINT COMPANY
130 Langdon Dr (39110-7076)
PHONE.............................601 898-8796
Chad Collins Biggs, *Owner*
EMP: 2
SALES (est): 360.4K **Privately Held**
SIC: 2752 Commercial printing, lithographic

(G-3151)
SOUTHLAND LOG HOMES
421 Business Park Dr (39110-9498)
PHONE.............................601 605-4900
EMP: 2 EST: 2003
SALES (est): 160K **Privately Held**
SIC: 2452 Mfg Prefabricated Wood Buildings

(G-3152)
STA-PUT-HOOK LLC
204 Belle Pointe (39110-8286)
PHONE.............................601 622-7313
Tom Root, *Owner*
Thomas M Root,
EMP: 2
SALES (est): 116.6K **Privately Held**
SIC: 3965 Fasteners, buttons, needles & pins

(G-3153)
STEEL TECHNOLOGIES LLC
576 Church Rd (39110-8023)
PHONE.............................601 855-7242
Hamid Muhammad, *Manager*
EMP: 40
SQ FT: 134,860 **Privately Held**
SIC: 3316 3325 Cold finishing of steel shapes; steel foundries
HQ: Steel Technologies Llc
700 N Hurstbourne Pkwy # 400
Louisville KY 40222
502 245-2110

(G-3154)
SURFACETECHS
188 Woods Crossing Blvd (39110-7092)
PHONE.............................601 605-1900
Andy Wiley, *Manager*
EMP: 1 EST: 2008
SALES (est): 156.1K **Privately Held**
SIC: 3398 Shot peening (treating steel to reduce fatigue)

(G-3155)
SWEET SENSATIONS-JACKSON
534 Brookstone Dr (39110-8881)
PHONE.............................601 790-7553
Jacqueline Coleman, *Principal*
EMP: 4
SALES (est): 227.8K **Privately Held**
SIC: 2051 Cakes, bakery: except frozen

(G-3156)
SYSTEMS ELECTRO COATING LLC
253 Old Jackson Rd (39110-9485)
PHONE.............................601 407-2340
William M Cooley, *Mng Member*
Joshua E Ashaka,
Toni D Cooley,
Delbert Hosemann Jr,
James Mike McGuffie,
EMP: 60
SQ FT: 105,000
SALES: 106.7MM **Privately Held**
SIC: 3479 Coating of metals & formed products

(G-3157)
TAYLOR INDUSTRIES LLC
308 Distribution Dr (39110-9066)
P.O. Box 280 (39130-0280)
PHONE.............................601 856-8439
Lucy Taylor, *Mng Member*
John Taylor, *Manager*
EMP: 6
SALES (est): 1.1MM **Privately Held**
SIC: 2899 5169 Chemical preparations; specialty cleaning & sanitation preparations; industrial chemicals

(G-3158)
TENAX TM LLC
124 One Madison Plz # 2100 (39110-2021)
PHONE.............................601 352-1107
Terry Ryan, *CEO*
Gregory Holloway, *Principal*
Jl Holloway, *Chairman*
Timothy Cantrell, *CFO*
EMP: 16
SQ FT: 12,000
SALES (est): 288.3K **Privately Held**
SIC: 3699 7359 4581 8711 Electrical equipment & supplies; aircraft rental; aircraft maintenance & repair services; engineering services; air cargo carriers, nonscheduled

(G-3159)
TIMBER CREEK CANDLES
436 Longwood Trl (39110-9631)
PHONE.............................601 818-6400
Renee Strait, *Owner*
EMP: 2
SALES (est): 121.3K **Privately Held**
SIC: 3999 Candles

(G-3160)
TOWER AUTOMOTIVE OPERATIONS
440 Church Rd (39110-8022)
PHONE.............................601 499-3300
Paul Meisel, *Manager*
Katrina Moten, *Supervisor*
EMP: 169 **Publicly Held**
SIC: 3465 Automotive stampings
HQ: Tower Automotive Operations Usa Ii, Llc
17672 N Laurel Park Dr 400e
Livonia MI 48152

(G-3161)
TREMAC RESTEEL INC
2064 Main St (39110-8353)
P.O. Box 1422 (39130-1422)
PHONE.............................601 853-3123
Phyllis Trevathan, *President*
Angela McThil, *Vice Pres*
EMP: 28
SALES (est): 2.7MM **Privately Held**
SIC: 3462 1799 Iron & steel forgings; rigging & scaffolding

(G-3162)
TWISTER LLC
36 Jennifer Ct (39110-9542)
PHONE.............................601 371-7276
Suzanne Belk, *Mng Member*

(PA)=Parent Co (HQ)=Headquarters (DH)=Div Headquarters
✿ = New Business established in last 2 years

2019 Harris Directory of
Mississippi Manufacturers

117

Madison - Madison County (G-3163)

GEOGRAPHIC SECTION

Kay Black,
EMP: 4
SALES (est): 173.8K **Privately Held**
SIC: 2731 8999 7389 Book publishing;
writing for publication;

(G-3163)
UNIK INK CSTM SCREEN PRTG INC
555 Hoy Rd (39110-8769)
PHONE..................................601 259-1004
Justin Vaughn, *Owner*
EMP: 2
SALES (est): 149K **Privately Held**
SIC: 2752 Commercial printing, lithographic

(G-3164)
USWEBWORX LLC
455 Brookstone Dr (39110-8837)
PHONE..................................601 813-8927
Clay Thornton, *Mng Member*
EMP: 1 **EST:** 2011
SALES: 50K **Privately Held**
SIC: 2741 8742 ; marketing consulting services

(G-3165)
VERTEX AEROSPACE LLC
555 Industrial Dr S (39110-9072)
PHONE..................................601 856-2274
EMP: 3500
SALES (corp-wide): 665.3MM **Privately Held**
WEB: www.l-3vertex.com
SIC: 3721 Aircraft
HQ: Vertex Aerospace Llc
555 Industrial Dr S
Madison MS 39110
800 774-4927

(G-3166)
VITAL CARE OF CENTRAL MS
159 Fountains Blvd (39110-6344)
PHONE..................................601 859-8200
Wade Philipps, *Principal*
Meredith Hegi, *Pharmacist*
EMP: 5
SALES (est): 369.8K **Privately Held**
SIC: 3845 Ultrasonic medical equipment, except cleaning

(G-3167)
WARHORSE INDUSTRIES LLC
100 Darrowsby Pl (39110-7434)
PHONE..................................601 856-2990
Charles Maris, *Manager*
EMP: 2
SALES (est): 83.1K **Privately Held**
SIC: 3999 Manufacturing industries

(G-3168)
WESTLAKE COMPOUNDS LLC
210 Industrial Dr N (39110-9481)
PHONE..................................601 206-3200
Albert Chao,
EMP: 1 **Publicly Held**
SIC: 2821 Plastics materials & resins
HQ: Westlake Compounds Llc
2801 Post Oak Blvd
Houston TX 77056
713 585-2900

(G-3169)
WHERE WE PRINT SHIRTS LLC
108 Kenbridge Ln (39110-8369)
PHONE..................................601 348-5754
Derrick Smith, *Principal*
EMP: 2
SALES (est): 83.9K **Privately Held**
SIC: 2752 Commercial printing, lithographic

(G-3170)
WHITE SHIRT NETWORKS LLC
Also Called: Loud Technology
742 Magnolia St (39110-8903)
P.O. Box 473 (39130-0473)
PHONE..................................601 292-7900
Donna Mathews, *Mng Member*
EMP: 5
SALES (est): 264.2K **Privately Held**
SIC: 7372 7382 Application computer software; security systems services

(G-3171)
WIDUPS WOODWORKS LLC
128 Rockwood Dr (39110-8838)
PHONE..................................601 966-0593
Kevin Widup, *Principal*
EMP: 2
SALES (est): 95.7K **Privately Held**
SIC: 2431 Millwork

(G-3172)
WONDER WOODS INC
376 Distribution Dr (39110-8745)
P.O. Box 1394 (39130-1394)
PHONE..................................601 853-1956
Jim Druey, *President*
EMP: 7
SQ FT: 8,000
SALES (est): 730K **Privately Held**
WEB: www.wonderwoodsinc.com
SIC: 5941 3949 Playground equipment; sporting & athletic goods

(G-3173)
YALLS PRODUCTS
644 Church Rd (39110-7061)
PHONE..................................601 391-3698
EMP: 1 **EST:** 2017
SALES (est): 39.6K **Privately Held**
SIC: 3999 Combs, except hard rubber

Magee
Simpson County

(G-3174)
CITY OF MAGEE
Also Called: Magee Police Department
124 1st St Ne (39111-3513)
PHONE..................................601 849-2366
Randy Crawford, *Chief*
Casey Bowen, *Officer*
EMP: 25 **Privately Held**
WEB: www.cityofmagee.com
SIC: 9221 7363 3711 ; medical help service; fire department vehicles (motor vehicles); assembly of
PA: City Of Magee
123 Main Ave N
Magee MS 39111
601 849-3344

(G-3175)
COUNTRY PRINTER INC
207 Main Ave N (39111-3535)
P.O. Box 765 (39111-0765)
PHONE..................................601 849-3637
Robert L Vinson, *President*
EMP: 3
SQ FT: 500
SALES (est): 383.8K **Privately Held**
SIC: 2752 2759 Commercial printing, offset; letterpress printing

(G-3176)
DELTA INDUSTRIES INC
Also Called: Simpson County Ready Mix
801 Industrial Park Dr Se (39111-4398)
P.O. Box 157 (39111-0157)
PHONE..................................601 849-2661
Robert Sullivan, *Manager*
EMP: 9
SALES (corp-wide): 100.3MM **Privately Held**
WEB: www.delta-ind.com
SIC: 3273 Ready-mixed concrete
PA: Delta Industries, Inc.
100 W Woodrow Wilson Ave
Jackson MS 39213
601 354-3801

(G-3177)
HARLAN SERVICES LLC
301 5th Ave Se (39111-3734)
PHONE..................................601 513-5318
Lance Harlan, *CEO*
Bert Usry, *Senior VP*
EMP: 8
SALES: 950K **Privately Held**
WEB: www.harlanservices.com
SIC: 3571 5734 7373 7389 Personal computers (microcomputers); computer & software stores; computer integrated systems design; ; fiber optic cable installation

(G-3178)
K & D FUEL INJECTION SERVICE
108 Ray Dr (39111-8707)
PHONE..................................601 849-9113
Kent Luckey, *Owner*
EMP: 5 **EST:** 2001
SALES (est): 436.9K **Privately Held**
SIC: 7539 2869 Fuel system repair, motor vehicle; fuels

(G-3179)
MURPHYS MACHINE & WELDING LLC
260 Simpson Highway 149 (39111-8868)
PHONE..................................601 849-2771
David Murphy,
EMP: 5
SQ FT: 2,500
SALES (est): 75K **Privately Held**
SIC: 3599 7692 Machine shop, jobbing & repair; welding repair

(G-3180)
POLKS MEAT PRODUCTS INC
1801 Simpson Highway 49 (39111-5391)
P.O. Box 1190 (39111-1190)
PHONE..................................601 849-9997
Julie Breazeale, *President*
Jan B Polk, *Corp Secy*
Michael Hand, *COO*
Veronica White, *Production*
Lenny Chisholm, *Engineer*
EMP: 105
SALES (est): 19.1MM **Privately Held**
WEB: www.polksmeat.com
SIC: 2011 Meat packing plants

(G-3181)
REALPURE BEVERAGE GROUP LLC
130 Coby Dr (39111-4391)
PHONE..................................601 849-9910
John E Solomon,
David Cox,
EMP: 10
SALES (est): 707.9K **Privately Held**
SIC: 2037 Fruit juices

(G-3182)
REALPURE BOTTLING INC
130 Coby Dr (39111-4391)
PHONE..................................601 849-9910
Kane Richmond, *President*
Keith Richmond, *Treasurer*
Karl Richmond, *Director*
EMP: 13 **EST:** 2016
SALES: 567.6K
SALES (corp-wide): 39.8MM **Privately Held**
SIC: 2086 Pasteurized & mineral waters, bottled & canned
PA: Silver Springs Bottled Water Co Inc
2445 Nw 42nd St
Ocala FL 34475
352 368-6806

(G-3183)
ROBERT W STUBBS
Also Called: Robert W Stubbs Logging
275 George Turner Rd (39111-5748)
PHONE..................................601 849-9857
EMP: 6
SALES (est): 270K **Privately Held**
SIC: 2411 Logging

(G-3184)
ROGERS AUTOMATIC SCREW MACHINE
412 Raleigh Dr Ne (39111-3244)
PHONE..................................601 849-2431
Fax: 601 849-2424
EMP: 1
SALES (est): 110K **Privately Held**
SIC: 3599 3451 Mfg Industrial Machinery Mfg Screw Machine Products

(G-3185)
SIMPSON PUBLISHING CO INC
Also Called: Simpson County News
206 Main Ave N (39111-3536)
P.O. Box 338 (39111-0338)
PHONE..................................601 849-3434
Wyatt Emmerich, *President*
EMP: 20

SQ FT: 2,000
SALES (est): 970K **Privately Held**
SIC: 2711 5943 Job printing & newspaper publishing combined; office forms & supplies

(G-3186)
SOUTHEASTERN E & P SVCS INC
148 Clovis Jones Rd (39111-5132)
P.O. Box 682 (39111-0682)
PHONE..................................601 849-9218
William S Carlton, *President*
EMP: 9 **EST:** 2008
SALES (est): 1.4MM **Privately Held**
SIC: 1623 1389 Oil & gas pipeline construction; building oil & gas well foundations on site; grading oil & gas well foundations; servicing oil & gas wells

(G-3187)
TYSON FOODS INC
855 Industrial Park Dr Se (39111-4398)
PHONE..................................601 849-3351
Cindy Sullivan, *Purch Mgr*
Mack Walker, *Director*
EMP: 130
SALES (corp-wide): 40B **Publicly Held**
SIC: 2015 Poultry slaughtering & processing
PA: Tyson Foods, Inc.
2200 W Don Tyson Pkwy
Springdale AR 72762
479 290-4000

Magnolia
Pike County

(G-3188)
AGRI-AFC LLC
310 E Railroad Ave N (39652-2639)
PHONE..................................601 783-6080
Gene Jay, *Branch Mgr*
EMP: 26
SALES (corp-wide): 384.6MM **Privately Held**
SIC: 5191 5261 2899 2875 Fertilizers & agricultural chemicals; nurseries & garden centers; chemical preparations; fertilizers, mixing only; crop preparation services for market
PA: Agri-Afc, Llc
121 Somerville Rd Ne
Decatur AL 35601
256 560-2848

(G-3189)
ANDERSON REPAIR SHOP
1015 Highway 48 E (39652-8994)
PHONE..................................601 783-2654
James D Anderson, *Owner*
Jimmy D Anderson, *Owner*
EMP: 1
SALES (est): 66.7K **Privately Held**
SIC: 7538 7692 Diesel engine repair: automotive; welding repair

(G-3190)
DELTA INDUSTRIES INC
Also Called: Pike County Ready-Mix Concrete
1012 Highway 48 E Lot 1 (39652-9117)
PHONE..................................601 783-6030
Rudolph Joseph, *Manager*
EMP: 12
SALES (corp-wide): 100.3MM **Privately Held**
WEB: www.delta-ind.com
SIC: 3273 Ready-mixed concrete
PA: Delta Industries, Inc.
100 W Woodrow Wilson Ave
Jackson MS 39213
601 354-3801

(G-3191)
INTERNATIONAL PAPER COMPANY
350 Prescott Dr (39652-2146)
PHONE..................................601 783-5011
EMP: 12
SALES (corp-wide): 23.3B **Publicly Held**
SIC: 2621 Paper mills

2019 Harris Directory of
Mississippi Manufacturers

118

▲ = Import ▼=Export
◆ =Import/Export

GEOGRAPHIC SECTION

Marion - Lauderdale County (G-3221)

PA: International Paper Company
6400 Poplar Ave
Memphis TN 38197
901 419-9000

(G-3192)
LOMBARDO INDUSTRIES LLC
3481 Smiley Honea Rd (39652-9425)
PHONE...................................601 783-3643
Steve Lombardo, *Principal*
EMP: 1 **EST:** 2016
SALES (est): 42.8K **Privately Held**
SIC: 3999 Manufacturing industries

(G-3193)
MAC FINANCIAL MGMT LLC
1006 Highway 48 E (39652-9117)
PHONE...................................844 622-6468
Brandon McDaniel, *Principal*
EMP: 1
SQ FT: 2,351
SALES (est): 76.1K **Privately Held**
SIC: 8742 5734 7372 7299 Financial
consultant; software, business & non-
game; business oriented computer soft-
ware; tax refund discounting

(G-3194)
MANOLIA GAZETTE
280 Magnolia St (39652-2828)
P.O. Box 152 (39652-0152)
PHONE...................................601 783-2441
Lucius Lampton, *President*
EMP: 3
SALES (est): 187.2K **Privately Held**
SIC: 2711 Newspapers, publishing & print-
ing; newspapers: publishing only, not
printed on site

(G-3195)
TRINITY STEEL FABRICATORS
INC
5005 Highway 568 W (39652-2971)
PHONE...................................601 783-6625
Derrick Graves, *President*
Dane Graves, *Vice Pres*
EMP: 9
SQ FT: 15,000
SALES: 1.4MM **Privately Held**
SIC: 3441 Fabricated structural metal

(G-3196)
WHITE LOGGING
7759 Highway 568 W (39652-9372)
PHONE...................................601 783-2738
Willie White, *Owner*
EMP: 2
SALES (est): 80K **Privately Held**
SIC: 2411 Logging camps & contractors

Mantachie
Itawamba County

(G-3197)
500 DEGREEZ ENTRMT LLC NOT
LLC
250 Ivie Ln Apt 1 (38855-9717)
PHONE...................................678 948-8710
Edward Patterson, *Principal*
EMP: 1 **EST:** 2015
SALES (est): 40K **Privately Held**
SIC: 2741 Miscellaneous publishing

(G-3198)
BEN MEARS TAXIDERMISTS &
SUPS
223 Lake Rd (38855-8290)
P.O. Box 131 (38855-0131)
PHONE...................................662 282-4594
Joe Mears Jr, *Owner*
Melinda Mears, *Owner*
EMP: 3 **EST:** 1991
SALES (est): 198.9K **Privately Held**
SIC: 3824 Taximeters

(G-3199)
INDUSTRIAL TIMBER LLC
415 Devaughn Rd (38855-7019)
PHONE...................................662 282-4000
EMP: 60

SALES (corp-wide): 72MM **Privately**
Held
SIC: 2493 5031 Reconstituted wood prod-
ucts; lumber, plywood & millwork
PA: Industrial Timber, Llc
6441 Hendry Rd
Charlotte NC 28269
704 919-1215

(G-3200)
IRVIN MACHINE SPECIALTY CO
1430 Bankhead Rd Sw (38855-8707)
PHONE...................................662 862-3781
EMP: 2
SALES: 50K **Privately Held**
SIC: 3599 Machine shop, jobbing & repair

(G-3201)
MAGNOLIA CABINET & MLLWK
INC
3031 Highway 371 (38855)
PHONE...................................662 282-7683
Dan W Moore Jr, *President*
EMP: 2
SALES (est): 209.1K **Privately Held**
SIC: 2434 Wood kitchen cabinets

(G-3202)
NICHOLS MOLD SHOP
1453 Centerville Rd (38855-8457)
PHONE...................................662 282-7560
Joel Nichols, *Principal*
EMP: 2
SALES (est): 215K **Privately Held**
SIC: 3544 Industrial molds

(G-3203)
PRO TOOL INC
3320 Highway 371 N (38855-7146)
P.O. Box 99 (38855-0099)
PHONE...................................662 282-4419
David Pearce, *President*
EMP: 4
SALES (est): 744.1K **Privately Held**
SIC: 3544 Die sets for metal stamping
(presses)

(G-3204)
ROBERT SMITH CUSTOM
CABINETS
869 Shiloh Rd (38855-8718)
PHONE...................................662 282-5007
Rebecca Smith, *President*
Robert Smith, *Vice Pres*
EMP: 19
SQ FT: 20,000
SALES (est): 1.6MM **Privately Held**
SIC: 2434 Wood kitchen cabinets

(G-3205)
SOUTHEASTERN SAMPLE
COMPANY
2710 Highway 371 N (38855-9111)
P.O. Box 339 (38855-0339)
PHONE...................................662 282-4063
Brian Sugg, *President*
Amanda Sugg, *Vice Pres*
EMP: 15
SALES (est): 1.6MM **Privately Held**
SIC: 2392 Household furnishings

(G-3206)
SYSTEMS AUTO INTERIORS LLC
1 Tb Way (38855-6000)
PHONE...................................662 862-1360
Naomi Munger, *Mng Member*
EMP: 70
SALES (est): 7.5MM **Privately Held**
SIC: 2396 Automotive & apparel trimmings

(G-3207)
TECHFORM MANUFACTURING
LLC
100 Industrial Park Rd (38855-9310)
P.O. Box 250 (38855-0250)
PHONE...................................662 282-7771
Stanley Dewayne Thornton, *Manager*
EMP: 2 **EST:** 2017
SALES (est): 139.2K **Privately Held**
SIC: 3999 Manufacturing industries

(G-3208)
TOMBIGBEE TOOLING INC
100 W E Hodges Indl Pk Rd (38855)
P.O. Box 280 (38855-0280)
PHONE...................................662 282-4273
Dewayne Thornton, *President*
Deborah Carol Thornton, *Admin Sec*
EMP: 25
SALES (est): 4.4MM **Privately Held**
WEB: www.tombigbeetooling.com
SIC: 3544 Special dies, tools, jigs & fix-
tures

(G-3209)
TOYOTA BOSHOKU MISSISSIPPI
LLC
1 Tb Way (38855-6000)
PHONE...................................662 862-3322
Kiyoshi Furuta, *Mng Member*
▲ **EMP:** 21
SALES (est): 4.4MM **Privately Held**
SIC: 2531 Seats, automobile

Mantee
Webster County

(G-3210)
CECIL D JOHNSON
Also Called: Johnson Timber Co
12546 Ms Highway 15 (39751-5552)
PHONE...................................662 456-5846
Cecil D Johnson, *Owner*
Peggy Johnson, *Owner*
EMP: 10
SALES (est): 522.8K **Privately Held**
SIC: 2411 Logging camps & contractors

(G-3211)
CRIMM LOGGING LLC
11646 Ms Highway 15 (39751-5548)
PHONE...................................662 552-8511
Justin Crimm, *Principal*
EMP: 2
SALES (est): 81.7K **Privately Held**
SIC: 2411 Logging

(G-3212)
S & F LOGGING INC
597 Eddie Lee Rd (39751-5575)
PHONE...................................662 552-4701
William F Sanford, *President*
Barrett Lance Sanford, *Vice Pres*
EMP: 10
SALES (est): 16.3K **Privately Held**
SIC: 2411 Logging

Marietta
Prentiss County

(G-3213)
DAVIDS SATELLITE
31 Griggs Rd (38856-6184)
PHONE...................................662 416-4697
David Badeau, *Principal*
EMP: 2 **EST:** 1993
SALES (est): 112K **Privately Held**
SIC: 3663 Satellites, communications

(G-3214)
GOLDEN MANUFACTURING CO
INC
450 Highway 371 (38856)
PHONE...................................662 728-8200
James Fennell, *Owner*
EMP: 20
SALES (corp-wide): 79MM **Privately**
Held
SIC: 5699 2325 2311 Work clothing;
men's & boys' trousers & slacks; men's &
boys' suits & coats
PA: Golden Manufacturing Co., Inc.
125 Highway 366
Golden MS 38847
662 454-3428

(G-3215)
GOLDEN MANUFACTURING CO
INC
450 Highway 371 (38856)
PHONE...................................662 728-1300

Dennis Colin, *Manager*
EMP: 15
SALES (corp-wide): 79MM **Privately**
Held
SIC: 2389 Men's miscellaneous acces-
sories
PA: Golden Manufacturing Co., Inc.
125 Highway 366
Golden MS 38847
662 454-3428

(G-3216)
HODGES WOOD PRODUCTS
INC
289 Highway 371 (38856-6250)
P.O. Box 69 (38856-0069)
PHONE...................................662 728-3716
Frances Hodges, *President*
James W Hodges, *Treasurer*
EMP: 20
SQ FT: 21,000
SALES (est): 1.2MM **Privately Held**
WEB: www.hodgeswood.com
SIC: 2426 Furniture stock & parts, hard-
wood

(G-3217)
MARIETTA WOOD SUPPLY INC
349 Highway 371 (38856-6204)
P.O. Box 225 (38856-0225)
PHONE...................................662 728-9874
Craig Pharr, *President*
Felicia Pharr, *Corp Secy*
EMP: 25
SALES (est): 4.2MM **Privately Held**
SIC: 2421 2426 Lumber: rough, sawed or
planed; hardwood dimension & flooring
mills

(G-3218)
STEVENS MACHINE & TOOL
INC
291 Highway 371 (38856-6250)
P.O. Box 25 (38856-0025)
PHONE...................................662 728-6005
Marshall Stevens, *President*
Mark Stevens, *Vice Pres*
EMP: 9
SQ FT: 6,000
SALES (est): 1.3MM **Privately Held**
SIC: 3544 Special dies & tools

(G-3219)
W & W SPECIAL COMPONENTS
INC
10040 Highway 371 (38856-5852)
PHONE...................................662 365-5648
Mike Wilburn, *President*
Phil Wilburn, *Vice Pres*
EMP: 50
SQ FT: 31,000
SALES (est): 3.5MM **Privately Held**
SIC: 2675 3086 Cardboard cut-outs, pan-
els & foundations: die-cut; packaging &
shipping materials, foamed plastic

Marion
Lauderdale County

(G-3220)
ALOHA PRINTING CO
6429 Confederate Dr (39342-9497)
PHONE...................................601 483-6677
EMP: 1
SALES (est): 61.9K **Privately Held**
SIC: 2752 Lithographic Commercial Print-
ing

(G-3221)
CANVASBEAUTY BEAUTY
6103 Dale Dr (39342-8209)
PHONE...................................601 282-5430
EMP: 2
SALES (est): 124.5K **Privately Held**
SIC: 2211 Canvas

(PA)=Parent Co (HQ)=Headquarters (DH)=Div Headquarters
✿ = New Business established in last 2 years

2019 Harris Directory of
Mississippi Manufacturers

Marks
Quitman County

(G-3222)
QUITMAN COUNTY DEMOCRAT
330 Locust St (38646-1229)
P.O. Box 328 (38646-0328)
PHONE..................................662 326-2181
Carol Knight, *Owner*
Bill Knight, *Co-Owner*
EMP: 3
SALES (est): 216.1K **Privately Held**
SIC: 2752 7313 2711 Commercial print-
ing, lithographic; newspaper advertising
representative; newspapers

(G-3223)
REBEL QUICK CASH
225 Martin Luther King Dr (38646-1102)
PHONE..................................662 326-9228
Larry Bailey, *Owner*
EMP: 1 **EST:** 2007
SALES (est): 59.3K **Privately Held**
SIC: 2782 Checkbooks

(G-3224)
RIVERSIDE AG SUPPLY LLC
109 Hwy 6 E (38646)
PHONE..................................662 444-0600
Jack Butler Jr,
EMP: 4 **EST:** 2017
SALES (est): 56.1K **Privately Held**
SIC: 7699 7692 Miscellaneous automotive
repair services; automotive welding

Mathiston
Webster County

(G-3225)
1 A LIFESAFER INC
17769 U S Highway 82 (39752-4531)
PHONE..................................800 634-3077
EMP: 1
SALES (corp-wide): 4.3MM **Privately
Held**
SIC: 3829 Measuring & controlling devices
PA: 1 A Lifesafer, Inc.
4290 Glendale Milford Rd
Blue Ash OH 45242
513 651-9560

(G-3226)
**BK EDWARDS FABRICATION &
WLDG**
Cumberland Rd (39752)
PHONE..................................662 263-4320
Bruce Edwards, *President*
Tammy Edwards, *Corp Secy*
EMP: 4
SALES (est): 301.1K **Privately Held**
SIC: 7692 Welding repair

(G-3227)
**BROWN WOOD PRESERVING
CO INC**
266 Crossroads Church Rd (39752-6800)
PHONE..................................662 263-8272
Mark Dean, *Manager*
EMP: 8
SALES (corp-wide): 13.8MM **Privately
Held**
WEB: www.brownwoodpoles.com
SIC: 2491 Wood preserving
PA: Brown Wood Preserving Company, Inc.
6201 Camp Ground Rd
Louisville KY 40216
800 537-1765

(G-3228)
**CRIMM BROS LOG LTD LBLTY
CO**
49 Crimm Rd (39752-5651)
PHONE..................................662 552-0122
Randy E Crimm, *Principal*
EMP: 2
SALES (est): 81.7K **Privately Held**
SIC: 2411 Logging

(G-3229)
**EVERGREEN AG ENVMTL &
TURF LLC**
18385 U S Highway 82 (39752-4445)
PHONE..................................662 263-4419
Michael D Maddox,
EMP: 10
SALES (est): 1.2MM **Privately Held**
SIC: 3523 Farm machinery & equipment

(G-3230)
S AND M LOGGING LLC ☉
200 Fulton St (39752-9416)
PHONE..................................662 263-6711
Spencer Carden, *Managing Prtnr*
EMP: 2 **EST:** 2018
SALES (est): 81.7K **Privately Held**
SIC: 2411 Timber, cut at logging camp

(G-3231)
SLY INC
4526 Reed Rd (39752-7754)
P.O. Box 210 (39752-0210)
PHONE..................................662 263-8234
Billy E Wynne, *Branch Mgr*
EMP: 1
SQ FT: 20,000
SALES (corp-wide): 5MM **Privately Held**
WEB: www.slyinc.com
SIC: 3564 3567 5075 Dust or fume col-
lecting equipment, industrial; industrial
furnaces & ovens; dust collecting equip-
ment
PA: Sly, Inc.
8300 Dow Cir Ste 600
Strongsville OH 44136
440 891-3200

Mc Call Creek
Franklin County

(G-3232)
CHARLES LANCE GRIFFIN
Also Called: Griffin Lodging
9144 Bogue Chitto Rd Se (39647-8085)
PHONE..................................601 734-2683
Charles Lance Griffin, *Owner*
EMP: 9
SALES: 3MM **Privately Held**
SIC: 2411 5031 Logging; lumber, plywood
& millwork

(G-3233)
DIXIE LOGGING INC
3770 Veto Rd Ne (39647-5208)
PHONE..................................601 532-6583
Ronnie Priest, *President*
Kim Priest, *Admin Sec*
EMP: 10
SALES (est): 963.9K **Privately Held**
SIC: 2411 Logging camps & contractors

(G-3234)
J W PRIEST & SONS LOGGING
Off Hwy 84 (39647)
PHONE..................................601 532-6237
L Ray Priest, *Owner*
John W Priest, *Owner*
EMP: 6
SALES (est): 385.8K **Privately Held**
SIC: 2411 Logging camps & contractors

Mc Cool
Attala County

(G-3235)
D J S EMBROIDERY LLC
3248 Highway 407 (39108-4457)
P.O. Box 10 (39108-0010)
PHONE..................................662 547-9000
Diane Keen, *Owner*
EMP: 1
SALES (est): 52.2K **Privately Held**
SIC: 5949 2395 Sewing, needlework &
piece goods; embroidery & art needle-
work

(G-3236)
LARRY WHEELESS LOGGING
2232 Highway 407 (39108-4393)
P.O. Box 3 (39108-0003)
PHONE..................................662 547-6863
Larry R Wheeless, *President*
EMP: 2
SALES (est): 196.6K **Privately Held**
SIC: 2411 Logging

(G-3237)
SIMPSON BROTHERS INC
4796 Attala Rd (39108)
PHONE..................................678 451-4259
Roger Simpson, *President*
Joe Simpson, *Admin Sec*
EMP: 9 **EST:** 1997
SALES (est): 1.3MM **Privately Held**
SIC: 2411 7389 Logging;

(G-3238)
WHEEL POLISHING PROS INC
31234 Highway 12 (39108-8953)
PHONE..................................601 259-9379
Morris Massey, *Manager*
EMP: 3
SALES (est): 172.4K **Privately Held**
SIC: 3471 Polishing, metals or formed
products

Mc Henry
Stone County

(G-3239)
**WEDGEWORTH WELDING AND
FAB**
558 W Mchenry Rd (39561)
PHONE..................................228 326-0937
EMP: 1
SALES (est): 37.2K **Privately Held**
SIC: 7692 Welding Repair

Mc Lain
Greene County

(G-3240)
LEON SCHOMMER SAWMILL
Little Creek Rd (39456)
PHONE..................................601 753-2687
EMP: 1
SALES: 80K **Privately Held**
SIC: 2421 Sawmill

Mc Neill
Pearl River County

(G-3241)
M & M INDUSTRIES INC
15 Sones Chapel Rd (39457)
P.O. Box 241 (39457-0241)
PHONE..................................601 799-2615
Joey McClinton, *President*
Kimberly Necaise, *Vice Pres*
Nan C McClinton, *Treasurer*
EMP: 40
SALES (est): 3MM **Privately Held**
SIC: 2311 Men's & boys' suits & coats

McComb
Pike County

(G-3242)
1 A LIFESAFER INC
1046 Highway 98 And 51 (39648-8710)
PHONE..................................800 634-3077
EMP: 1
SALES (corp-wide): 4.3MM **Privately
Held**
SIC: 3829 Measuring & controlling devices
PA: 1 A Lifesafer, Inc.
4290 Glendale Milford Rd
Blue Ash OH 45242
513 651-9560

(G-3243)
ABACUS PUBLISHING CO
1060 Addo Barnes Rd (39648)
PHONE..................................601 684-0001
Clark Hale, *Owner*
EMP: 6
SALES: 260K **Privately Held**
WEB: www.abacuspublishing.com
SIC: 2741 Miscellaneous publishing

(G-3244)
BULLOCKS WASHTERIA
Also Called: Your Dollar and More
130 Saint Augustine Ave (39648-3140)
PHONE..................................601 684-2332
Theodore Bullock, *Owner*
EMP: 1
SQ FT: 1,500
SALES (est): 82K **Privately Held**
SIC: 3582 Washing machines, laundry;
commercial, incl. coin-operated

(G-3245)
CABLE ONE INC
230 5th Ave (39648-4128)
PHONE..................................601 833-7991
Amanda Everett, *Manager*
EMP: 1
SALES (corp-wide): 1B **Publicly Held**
SIC: 7389 7372 4841 4813 Telephone
services; prepackaged software; cable &
other pay television services; telephone
communication, except radio
PA: Cable One, Inc.
210 E Earll Dr
Phoenix AZ 85012
602 364-6000

(G-3246)
**COCA-COLA BOTTLING CO
UNTD INC**
310 W Presley Blvd (39648-5526)
P.O. Box 568 (39649-0568)
PHONE..................................601 684-8223
James Brumfield, *Sales/Mktg Mgr*
EMP: 60
SALES (corp-wide): 2.4B **Privately Held**
SIC: 2086 Bottled & canned soft drinks;
soft drinks: packaged in cans, bottles, etc.
PA: Coca-Cola Bottling Company United,
Inc.
4600 E Lake Blvd
Birmingham AL 35217
205 841-2653

(G-3247)
CROFT LLC (PA)
107 Oliver Emmerich Dr (39648-6317)
P.O. Box 826 (39649-0826)
PHONE..................................601 684-6121
Gerald M Abdalla, *President*
John Reeves, *Business Mgr*
Steve Lewis, *VP Opers*
Steve Magee, *Chief Mktg Ofcr*
Victor C Donati,
▼ **EMP:** 25 **EST:** 1920
SQ FT: 30,000
SALES (est): 43.4MM **Privately Held**
SIC: 2431 3334 Windows, wood; primary
aluminum

(G-3248)
DAVE STRONG CIRCUIT JUDGE
119 N Broadway St (39648-3901)
PHONE..................................601 684-3400
David Strong, *Executive*
EMP: 2 **EST:** 2007
SALES (est): 131.2K **Privately Held**
SIC: 3699 Electrical equipment & supplies

(G-3249)
**EIGHTY-FIVE 15 CANDLE CO
LLC**
1328 Parklane Rd Apt 402 (39648-4930)
P.O. Box 1453 (39649-1453)
PHONE..................................601 324-3064
Carolyn Junius, *Principal*
EMP: 1 **EST:** 2017
SALES (est): 39.6K **Privately Held**
SIC: 3999 Candles

▲ = Import ▼=Export
◆ =Import/Export

GEOGRAPHIC SECTION

Mendenhall - Simpson County (G-3281)

(G-3250)
FLOWERS BKG CO THOMASVILLE LLC
605 Avenue C (39648-4213)
PHONE..................................601 684-5481
Ed Coker, *Manager*
EMP: 13
SALES (corp-wide): 3.9B **Publicly Held**
SIC: 2051 Bread, cake & related products
HQ: Flowers Baking Co Of Thomasville Llc
300 S Madison St
Thomasville GA 31792
229 226-5331

(G-3251)
GATOR SIGN & IMAGE CONCEPTS
1027 Karey Andrews Rd (39648-9446)
PHONE..................................601 684-8686
Daryl Redditt, *Owner*
Steven Powels, *Owner*
Denise Allen, *Project Mgr*
Chris McEwen, *Project Mgr*
Matt Hamilton, *Opers Mgr*
EMP: 3
SQ FT: 2,000
SALES: 200K **Privately Held**
WEB: www.gatorsigncompany.com
SIC: 3993 7311 Signs & advertising specialties; advertising consultant

(G-3252)
HILGERSON PRINTING
400 Delaware Ave Ste A (39648-4021)
P.O. Box 1109 (39649-1109)
PHONE..................................601 684-6978
Harold Hilgerson, *Owner*
EMP: 3
SQ FT: 800
SALES (est): 224.5K **Privately Held**
SIC: 2759 2752 Commercial printing; commercial printing, lithographic

(G-3253)
INTELLABUY INC
312 N James Ave (39648-2918)
PHONE..................................601 249-0508
Charles Paulk, *President*
Dana Persons, *Director*
EMP: 4 EST: 1999
SQ FT: 1,000
SALES: 460K **Privately Held**
SIC: 3089 8748 Plates, plastic; business consulting

(G-3254)
J O EMMERICH & ASSOC INC
Also Called: Enterprise-Journal
112 Oliver Emmerich Dr (39648-6330)
P.O. Box 2009 (39649-2009)
PHONE..................................601 684-2421
John Wyatt Emmerich, *President*
EMP: 40
SQ FT: 18,000
SALES (est): 2.7MM **Privately Held**
WEB: www.enterprisejournal.com
SIC: 2711 Commercial printing & newspaper publishing combined; newspapers, publishing & printing

(G-3255)
K B M S
1703 Delaware Ave (39648-3611)
PHONE..................................601 684-0510
Jennifer Zorek, *Manager*
EMP: 2
SALES (est): 100.3K **Privately Held**
SIC: 2836 Vaccines & other immunizing products

(G-3256)
KDH KUSTOMS LLC
1028 Highway 98 E (39648-9451)
PHONE..................................601 730-2052
Yolanda L Hughes,
EMP: 1
SQ FT: 6,500
SALES (est): 93.7K **Privately Held**
SIC: 2231 3111 7641 Upholstery fabrics, wool; upholstery leather; upholstery work; reupholstery

(G-3257)
L&E LOGISTICS LLC
411 Aston Ave (39648-3809)
PHONE..................................877 884-8889
Erica Brown,
EMP: 1
SALES: 90K **Privately Held**
SIC: 3537 Trucks, tractors, loaders, carriers & similar equipment

(G-3258)
MC COMB WELDING & MCH WORKS
110 E Presley Blvd (39648-5908)
P.O. Box 989 (39649-0989)
PHONE..................................601 684-1921
Louise D Smith, *President*
Tercy Smith, *Chairman*
EMP: 8
SQ FT: 12,000
SALES: 200K **Privately Held**
SIC: 7692 3523 Welding repair; trailers & wagons, farm; cattle feeding, handling & watering equipment

(G-3259)
MCCOMB PRINTING INC
210 S Broadway St (39648-4144)
P.O. Box 805 (39649-0805)
PHONE..................................601 684-9841
Forrest L Adair, *President*
Judy Adair, *Corp Secy*
EMP: 10
SALES (est): 1.7MM **Privately Held**
WEB: www.mccombprinting.com
SIC: 2752 Commercial printing, offset

(G-3260)
MMC MATERIALS INC
906 S Locust St (39648-4848)
PHONE..................................601 684-7373
Bruce McGuire, *Manager*
EMP: 23
SALES (corp-wide): 306.5MM **Privately Held**
SIC: 3273 Ready-mixed concrete
HQ: Mmc Materials, Inc.
1052 Highland Colony Pkwy # 201
Ridgeland MS 39157
601 898-4000

(G-3261)
MODERN MILL INC
1140 Frank Oaks Rd (39648)
PHONE..................................601 869-5050
EMP: 2
SALES (est): 62.3K **Privately Held**
SIC: 2044 Rice milling

(G-3262)
OTIS LOGGING INC
116 Price St (39648-3739)
PHONE..................................601 249-0963
Wayne Hutchison, *President*
EMP: 3 EST: 2010
SALES (est): 339.2K **Privately Held**
SIC: 2411 Logging

(G-3263)
P-AMERICAS LLC
Also Called: Pepsico
1096 Highway 98 E (39648-9451)
P.O. Box 728 (39649-0728)
PHONE..................................601 684-2281
Ricky Ivey, *Manager*
EMP: 40
SALES (corp-wide): 64.6B **Publicly Held**
SIC: 2086 5149 Carbonated soft drinks, bottled & canned; groceries & related products
HQ: P-Americas Llc
1 Pepsi Way
Somers NY 10589
336 896-5740

(G-3264)
SAF-T COMPLIANCE INTL LLC
1312c Harrison Ave (39648-2830)
P.O. Box 108 (39649-0108)
PHONE..................................601 684-9495
David Coon, *Owner*
EMP: 6

SALES (est): 322.1K **Privately Held**
SIC: 1381 3589 3999 Service well drilling; asbestos removal equipment; atomizers, toiletry

(G-3265)
SEAGO ENTERPRISES INC
Also Called: Seago Lumber
614 W Presley Blvd (39648-5306)
P.O. Box 607 (39649-0607)
PHONE..................................601 684-3000
D G Seago, *President*
Eda Vita Seago, *Treasurer*
Eda Vita, *Treasurer*
EMP: 55
SQ FT: 6,000
SALES (est): 49.7K **Privately Held**
SIC: 2421 8742 5172 Lumber: rough, sawed or planed; financial consultant; petroleum products

(G-3266)
SHARP CYPRESS INC
3194 Highway 98 E (39648-9459)
PHONE..................................601 249-2936
Glenn Sharp, *President*
EMP: 4
SALES (est): 262.8K **Privately Held**
SIC: 2741 Miscellaneous publishing

(G-3267)
SOKHOM TO
Also Called: Donut Palace
912 Delaware Ave (39648-3826)
PHONE..................................601 684-3300
Sokhom To, *Owner*
EMP: 3
SALES (est): 195.2K **Privately Held**
SIC: 2051 Doughnuts, except frozen

(G-3268)
SPIC-N-SPAN CREW LLC
1019 Little Rock Ln (39648-8119)
PHONE..................................601 248-2090
Diane Martin, *Owner*
EMP: 2
SALES (est): 110.2K **Privately Held**
SIC: 2842 Cleaning or polishing preparations

(G-3269)
STEWART SIGN & SCREEN GRAPHICS
2107 Highway 48 W (39648-7532)
PHONE..................................601 783-5377
Jim Stewart, *Owner*
EMP: 2
SALES (est): 194.5K **Privately Held**
SIC: 3086 Plastics foam products

(G-3270)
TC ENGRAVING & GIFTS
1722 Veterans Blvd (39648-2038)
PHONE..................................601 684-6834
Carol Hardin, *Principal*
EMP: 2
SALES (est): 96.3K **Privately Held**
SIC: 3479 Etching & engraving

(G-3271)
TRAVIS WELDING SERVICES
905 S Magnolia St (39648-4821)
PHONE..................................601 684-9578
Lynn Travis, *Owner*
EMP: 2
SQ FT: 5,000
SALES (est): 86K **Privately Held**
SIC: 7692 Welding repair

(G-3272)
VENDWORKS LLC
Also Called: Coca-Cola
301 Oakdale Ave (39648-5942)
P.O. Box 17197, Hattiesburg (39404-7197)
PHONE..................................601 684-2085
Richard Mabile, *Branch Mgr*
EMP: 8
SALES (corp-wide): 2.4B **Privately Held**
SIC: 2086 Bottled & canned soft drinks
HQ: Vendworks, Llc
201 Coca Cola Ave
Hattiesburg MS 39402
601 268-1906

(G-3273)
W A MATHIS TIMBER CO
Also Called: Mathis, W A Logging Co
210 E Georgia Ave (39648-3331)
PHONE..................................601 684-7839
EMP: 6
SQ FT: 400
SALES (est): 638.1K **Privately Held**
SIC: 2411 Logging Pulpwood Center

Meadville
Franklin County

(G-3274)
DIER LOGGING INC
331 Cotten Rd Se (39653-7332)
PHONE..................................601 384-5963
Thomas R Dier, *President*
EMP: 6
SALES (est): 606.1K **Privately Held**
SIC: 2411 Logging camps & contractors

(G-3275)
INCITEFUL ANALYTICS CORP
915 Dillard Ln Se (39653-7300)
PHONE..................................601 870-4004
Rhonda Petty, *President*
EMP: 2
SALES: 50K **Privately Held**
SIC: 3826 Analytical instruments

(G-3276)
JULIUS WHITTINGTON
1889 Round Top Hill Rd Se (39653-8038)
PHONE..................................601 532-6519
Julius Whittington, *Principal*
EMP: 3
SALES (est): 386.7K **Privately Held**
SIC: 1382 Oil & gas exploration services

(G-3277)
LISAS CANDLES
652 Low Wtr Bridge Rd Se (39653-8096)
PHONE..................................601 384-7406
Clifton Cannon, *Principal*
EMP: 1
SALES (est): 39.6K **Privately Held**
SIC: 3999 Candles

(G-3278)
WARDS CUSTOM SCREEN PRIN
3055 Highway 84 W (39653-8495)
PHONE..................................601 384-4635
Shawn Ward, *Owner*
EMP: 3
SALES (est): 284.8K **Privately Held**
SIC: 2752 Commercial printing, lithographic

Mendenhall
Simpson County

(G-3279)
BRANDI BONNER
Also Called: B&G Dirt Work
114 Dane Ln (39114-6244)
PHONE..................................601 906-7224
Brandi Bonner, *Owner*
EMP: 2 EST: 2016
SALES (est): 115.1K **Privately Held**
SIC: 3531 Construction machinery

(G-3280)
CLAY STEWART INDUSTRIES LLC
122 Don Stewart Dr (39114-8981)
PHONE..................................601 946-2332
Joseph Stewart, *Principal*
EMP: 2
SALES (est): 97.1K **Privately Held**
SIC: 3999 Manufacturing industries

(G-3281)
HOWARD INDUSTRIES INC
Howard Technology Solutions
2778 Simpson Highway 49 (39114-5421)
PHONE..................................601 847-5278
Jerry Williams, *Branch Mgr*
EMP: 1

(PA)=Parent Co (HQ)=Headquarters (DH)=Div Headquarters
✪ = New Business established in last 2 years

2019 Harris Directory of
Mississippi Manufacturers

121

Mendenhall - Simpson County (G-3282)

GEOGRAPHIC SECTION

SALES (corp-wide): 19.3MM **Privately Held**
WEB: www.howard-ind.com
SIC: 3612 4213 Power transformers, electric; contract haulers
PA: Howard Industries, Inc.
36 Howard Dr
Ellisville MS 39437
601 425-3151

(G-3282)
JOHN J ISHEE
201 Wilson Welch Rd (39114-4832)
PHONE..................................601 847-2723
John J Ishee, *Owner*
EMP: 2
SALES (est): 122K **Privately Held**
SIC: 3484 Guns (firearms) or gun parts, 30 mm. & below

(G-3283)
MAR-CAL INC
951 Cato Rd (39114-4450)
PHONE..................................601 825-7520
Kenneth Martin, *President*
Rupert Martin, *President*
EMP: 8
SALES: 1.5MM **Privately Held**
WEB: www.mar-cal.com
SIC: 2411 Logging camps & contractors; pulpwood contractors engaged in cutting

(G-3284)
MCCOY FARMS & GRAVEL
1215 Main St S (39114-6070)
PHONE..................................601 847-5962
Lee McCoy, *Principal*
EMP: 2
SALES (est): 66K **Privately Held**
SIC: 1442 Construction sand & gravel

(G-3285)
MISSISSIPPI DIESEL PRODUCTS
1562 Simpson Highway 149 (39114-3633)
PHONE..................................601 847-2500
David Mitchell, *Owner*
EMP: 22
SALES (est): 3.2MM **Privately Held**
SIC: 3714 5084 Fuel systems & parts, motor vehicle; fuel injection systems

(G-3286)
NORTH SIMPSON GRAVEL CO
376 Old Gravel 49 (39114-5406)
PHONE..................................601 847-9500
Randy Beckham, *Principal*
EMP: 1 EST: 2011
SALES (est): 100.4K **Privately Held**
SIC: 1442 Gravel mining

(G-3287)
ROBBYS SMALL ENGINE & SAW REPR
3661 Simpson Hwy 493 (39114)
PHONE..................................601 847-0323
Robby Wester, *Owner*
Karen Wester, *Co-Owner*
EMP: 2
SQ FT: 2,800
SALES (est): 199.8K **Privately Held**
SIC: 5261 5251 7699 5084 Lawnmowers & tractors; tools, power; engine repair & replacement, non-automotive; lawn mower repair shop; engines, gasoline; saws & sawing equipment

(G-3288)
SIGN HERE
507 N West St (39114-3348)
PHONE..................................601 847-3537
Glen Floyd, *Principal*
EMP: 1
SALES (est): 77.7K **Privately Held**
SIC: 3993 Signs & advertising specialties

(G-3289)
SIMPSON COUNTY NEWS
120 W Court Ave (39114-3526)
PHONE..................................601 847-2525
Patt Brown, *General Mgr*
EMP: 1
SALES (est): 124.3K **Privately Held**
SIC: 2711 Job printing & newspaper publishing combined

(G-3290)
SMALLBERRY MFG CO
125 Rosebud Trl (39114-5132)
PHONE..................................601 847-3692
Linda Morgan, *Principal*
EMP: 2
SALES (est): 73K **Privately Held**
SIC: 3999 Manufacturing industries

(G-3291)
Z A CONSTRUCTION LLC
834 Cato Rd (39114-4451)
PHONE..................................601 259-5276
Zach Ainsworth,
EMP: 10
SALES (est): 1.3MM **Privately Held**
SIC: 8748 3537 Business consulting; industrial trucks & tractors

---

Meridian
Lauderdale County

(G-3292)
1 A LIFESAFER INC
2600 N Hills St (39305-2639)
PHONE..................................800 634-3077
EMP: 1
SALES (corp-wide): 4.3MM **Privately Held**
SIC: 3829 Measuring & controlling devices
PA: 1 A Lifesafer, Inc.
4290 Glendale Milford Rd
Blue Ash OH 45242
513 651-9560

(G-3293)
A AND Y UNIFORM SHOP
1720 N Frontage Rd (39301-6154)
PHONE..................................601 553-1377
Talat Hussein, *Partner*
EMP: 1 EST: 2008
SALES (est): 117K **Privately Held**
SIC: 2326 Work uniforms

(G-3294)
ACCUSTEER LLC
901 Dst (39301)
P.O. Box 1265 (39302-1265)
PHONE..................................601 483-0225
Ann Alexander,
John Forde, *Assoc Prof*
EMP: 1
SALES (est): 105K **Privately Held**
SIC: 3559 Automotive related machinery

(G-3295)
ALEXANDER FABRICATING CO INC
686 Murphy Rd (39301-8948)
PHONE..................................601 485-5414
EMP: 4 EST: 1973
SALES (est): 50K **Privately Held**
SIC: 3429 3448 Manufactured hardware (general); prefabricated metal buildings

(G-3296)
ALGIX LLC
5168 Water Tower Rd (39301-8850)
PHONE..................................877 972-5449
Ashton Zeller, *Research*
Ralph Reed, *CFO*
Barbara Zeller, *Marketing Staff*
Michael Van Drunen,
Michael V Drunen,
◆ **EMP:** 4 EST: 2011
SALES (est): 847.8K **Privately Held**
SIC: 2836 Biological products, except diagnostic

(G-3297)
AMERICRETE INC (HQ)
Also Called: Americrete Ready Mix Inc
220 65th Ave (39307-7018)
P.O. Box 4391 (39304-4391)
PHONE..................................601 485-6507
David Robison, *President*
EMP: 16
SQ FT: 1,000
SALES (est): 32.1MM
SALES (corp-wide): 100.3MM **Privately Held**
SIC: 3273 Ready-mixed concrete

PA: Delta Industries, Inc.
100 W Woodrow Wilson Ave
Jackson MS 39213
601 354-3801

(G-3298)
ANCESTOR LOGGING
1719 Highway 19 N Apt 30 (39307-5344)
PHONE..................................925 895-2306
Michael Larkin, *Principal*
EMP: 2
SALES (est): 81.7K **Privately Held**
SIC: 2411 Logging

(G-3299)
APAC-MISSISSIPPI INC
4412 Interchange Rd (39307-7203)
P.O. Box 748 (39302-0748)
PHONE..................................601 693-5025
Jimmy Ivy, *Branch Mgr*
EMP: 45
SALES (corp-wide): 30.6B **Privately Held**
SIC: 1622 2951 1771 1611 Bridge, tunnel & elevated highway; asphalt paving mixtures & blocks; concrete work; highway & street construction
HQ: Apac-Mississippi, Inc.
101 Riverview Dr
Richland MS 39218
601 376-4000

(G-3300)
ATLAS ROOFING CORPORATION (HQ)
802 Highway 19 N Ste 190 (39307-5815)
PHONE..................................601 484-8900
Warren A Hood Jr, *Ch of Bd*
Kenneth Farrish, *President*
James W Hood, *Vice Pres*
Jeff Hedden, *Production*
Sheri Paul, *Purch Agent*
◆ **EMP:** 27 EST: 1982
SQ FT: 5,000
SALES (est): 565.5MM **Privately Held**
WEB: www.atlasroofing.com
SIC: 3086 2952 Insulation or cushioning material, foamed plastic; roofing materials

(G-3301)
ATLAS ROOFING CORPORATION
Also Called: Research and Development
2564 Valley Rd (39307-9401)
PHONE..................................601 481-1474
Andy McLaughin, *Director*
EMP: 10 **Privately Held**
WEB: www.atlasroofing.com
SIC: 3086 Insulation or cushioning material, foamed plastic
HQ: Atlas Roofing Corporation
802 Highway 19 N Ste 190
Meridian MS 39307
601 484-8900

(G-3302)
ATLAS ROOFING CORPORATION
2322 Valley Rd (39307-9531)
PHONE..................................601 483-7111
Roger Reeves, *VP Opers*
Anthony Steele, *Opers Staff*
Joe Ogg, *Purch Mgr*
Tammy Sessums, *Credit Staff*
Philip Bush, *Manager*
EMP: 50 **Privately Held**
WEB: www.atlasroofing.com
SIC: 3086 2952 Insulation or cushioning material, foamed plastic; asphalt felts & coatings
HQ: Atlas Roofing Corporation
802 Highway 19 N Ste 190
Meridian MS 39307
601 484-8900

(G-3303)
AUTO TRIM DESIGN OF MERIDIAN
3115 5th Ave (39305-4891)
P.O. Box 3832 (39303-3832)
PHONE..................................601 482-8037
David A Winford, *President*
EMP: 4
SALES (est): 470.2K **Privately Held**
SIC: 3993 Signs & advertising specialties

(G-3304)
AVERY PRODUCTS CORPORATION
4100 Highway 45 N (39301-1203)
PHONE..................................601 483-0611
Bill Cofield, *Branch Mgr*
EMP: 250
SALES (corp-wide): 3.9B **Privately Held**
WEB: www.avery.com
SIC: 2678 2782 Notebooks: made from purchased paper; blankbooks & looseleaf binders
HQ: Avery Products Corporation
50 Pointe Dr
Brea CA 92821
714 675-8500

(G-3305)
B-N/ASSOCIATES
4913 55th Pl (39305-2404)
PHONE..................................601 482-3939
Nancy Snowden, *Owner*
EMP: 4
SALES (est): 186.1K **Privately Held**
SIC: 3999 Identification tags, except paper

(G-3306)
BILLY PURVIS DISTRIBUTING LLC
5394 Vmvlle Cuseyville Rd (39301)
PHONE..................................601 480-3147
William Purvis Jr,
EMP: 1 EST: 2017
SALES: 270K **Privately Held**
SIC: 2096 Potato chips & similar snacks

(G-3307)
BIMBO BAKERIES USA INC
624 Natures Way (39305-6901)
PHONE..................................601 479-8887
EMP: 24 **Privately Held**
SIC: 2051 Bakery: wholesale or wholesale/retail combined
HQ: Bimbo Bakeries Usa, Inc
255 Business Center Dr # 200
Horsham PA 19044
215 347-5500

(G-3308)
BIMBO BAKERIES USA INC
3400 Saint Paul St (39301-6417)
PHONE..................................601 693-4871
EMP: 24
SALES (corp-wide): 13.7B **Privately Held**
SIC: 2051 Mfg Bread/Related Products
HQ: Bimbo Bakeries Usa, Inc
255 Business Center Dr # 200
Horsham PA 19044
215 347-5500

(G-3309)
BIMBO BAKERIES USA INC
3400 Saint Paul St (39301-6417)
P.O. Box 1071 (39302-1071)
PHONE..................................601 693-4871
Marshall S Maddox, *Principal*
EMP: 120 **Privately Held**
SIC: 2051 Bread, all types (white, wheat, rye, etc): fresh or frozen
HQ: Bimbo Bakeries Usa, Inc
255 Business Center Dr # 200
Horsham PA 19044
215 347-5500

(G-3310)
BLUE SOUTH PUBLISHING CORP
2320 8th St (39301-5049)
P.O. Box 3663 (39303-3663)
PHONE..................................601 604-2963
Marianne Todd, *President*
EMP: 4
SALES: 450K **Privately Held**
SIC: 2721 Magazines: publishing & printing

(G-3311)
BO ENTERPRISES INC
Also Called: Sports Zone 2
1380 Bonita Lakes Cir (39301-6976)
PHONE..................................601 483-5571
EMP: 3
SALES (corp-wide): 8.1MM **Privately Held**
SIC: 2389 Manufacture Apparel

2019 Harris Directory of
Mississippi Manufacturers

▲ = Import ▼=Export
◆ =Import/Export

GEOGRAPHIC SECTION

Meridian - Lauderdale County (G-3341)

PA: Bo Enterprises, Inc.
601 E Parker Dr
Booneville MS 38829
662 720-1211

(G-3312)
BOLT COMPANY LLC
5321 1st St (39307-6662)
PHONE.................................601 696-9191
Roger Henderson,
EMP: 5
SALES (est): 693.3K Privately Held
SIC: 3965 Fasteners

(G-3313)
BUDGET PRINTING COMPANY
721 Front Street Ext # 720 (39301-4586)
PHONE.................................601 693-6003
Joe M Young, Partner
W R Patterson, Partner
EMP: 4
SQ FT: 1,500
SALES (est): 347K Privately Held
SIC: 2752 Commercial printing, offset

(G-3314)
BURTONI FINE ART INC
Also Called: Custom Frame & Gift
4900 Poplar Sprng Dr Ste 8 (39305)
PHONE.................................601 581-1557
John Wesley Burton, President
Ron Burton, Vice Pres
EMP: 5
SQ FT: 3,500
SALES: 310K Privately Held
SIC: 2499 5947 Picture & mirror frames, wood; gift, novelty & souvenir shop

(G-3315)
CARAUSTAR INDUSTRIES INC
1242 Montgomery Dr (39301-7963)
PHONE.................................601 703-0550
Ken Dezarn, Branch Mgr
EMP: 1
SALES (corp-wide): 3.8B Publicly Held
SIC: 2655 Tubes, fiber or paper: made from purchased material
HQ: Caraustar Industries, Inc.
5000 Austell Powder Sprin
Austell GA 30106
770 948-3101

(G-3316)
CATONTECH MGT SYSTEMS LLC
4825 37th Ave (39305-2549)
P.O. Box 3759 (39303-3759)
PHONE.................................601 207-1047
Joel Caton, Mng Member
EMP: 1
SALES (est): 47K Privately Held
SIC: 7372 Publishers' computer software

(G-3317)
CENTER FOR PREGNANCY CHOICES
4927 Poplar Springs Dr (39305-1618)
P.O. Box 3301 (39303-3301)
PHONE.................................601 482-1230
Karen Sims, Director
EMP: 2
SALES: 50.7K Privately Held
SIC: 3999 Education aids, devices & supplies

(G-3318)
CERTAINTEED GYPSUM INC
2710 Highway 11 S (39307-9580)
PHONE.................................601 693-0254
Terry Stoddard, Manager
EMP: 180
SALES (corp-wide): 215.9MM Privately Held
WEB: www.bpb-na.com
SIC: 5033 3275 3296 2493 Insulation materials; building board, gypsum; acoustical board & tile, mineral wool; fiberboard, other vegetable pulp; roofing materials
HQ: Certainteed Gypsum, Inc.
20 Moores Rd
Malvern PA 19355

(G-3319)
CHARLES ON CALL MOLD REMOVAL
806 Highway 19 N Ste 299 (39307-5875)
PHONE.................................662 352-8009
EMP: 2 EST: 2010
SALES (est): 100K Privately Held
SIC: 3544 Mfg Dies/Tools/Jigs/Fixtures

(G-3320)
CI METAL FABRICATION LLC
6205 Saint Louis St (39307-9575)
PHONE.................................601 483-6281
Walter O Hatfield, President
EMP: 25
SALES (est): 4.4MM Privately Held
SIC: 3441 Fabricated structural metal
PA: Mhs Legacy Group, Inc.
1054 Central Indus Dr
Saint Louis MO 63110

(G-3321)
CLEARSPAN COMPONENTS INC
6110 Old Highway 80 W (39307-6113)
P.O. Box 4195 (39304-4195)
PHONE.................................601 483-3941
Daniel Holland, President
James McRae, Director
EMP: 140 EST: 1960
SQ FT: 150,000
SALES (est): 21.9MM Privately Held
WEB: www.clearspaninc.com
SIC: 2431 2439 2426 Panel work, wood; trusses, wooden roof; timbers, structural: laminated lumber; flooring, hardwood

(G-3322)
COMPLETE CNC MACHINE REPAIR
2440 N Hills St Ste 105 (39305-2653)
PHONE.................................601 604-2063
Eldon Richardson, Owner
EMP: 1
SALES (est): 69K Privately Held
WEB: www.completecncmachinerepair.com
SIC: 3599 Machine shop, jobbing & repair

(G-3323)
COOK EYE CENTER
2024 15th St Ste 5d (39301-4130)
PHONE.................................601 553-2100
Brenda Thornhill, Principal
EMP: 3
SALES (est): 357.2K Privately Held
SIC: 3851 Eyeglasses, lenses & frames

(G-3324)
CRAIG WILKES DESIGN
2910 Highland Ave (39307-4453)
PHONE.................................917 664-7255
Gerald Wilkes, Principal
EMP: 1
SALES (est): 38.8K Privately Held
SIC: 3999 Manufacturing industries

(G-3325)
CUSTODIS MGT SYSTEMS LLC
4905b Poplar Springs Dr (39305-1618)
PHONE.................................601 207-1047
Joel Caton, Principal
EMP: 2
SALES (est): 88.3K Privately Held
SIC: 7372 Prepackaged software

(G-3326)
D&H CONSTRUCTION CABINETRY INC
8589 A C Brown Rd (39305-9273)
PHONE.................................601 737-2010
Donald R Massey, President
Donald Massey, Owner
C M Hewey, Vice Pres
Beth Dorman, Treasurer
Leneal P Massey, Admin Sec
EMP: 7
SALES (est): 1.2MM Privately Held
SIC: 2434 1521 Wood kitchen cabinets; new construction, single-family houses

(G-3327)
DEA MISSISSIPPI INC
Also Called: Pioneer
5184 Pioneer Rd (39301-8833)
P.O. Box 490, Marion (39342-0490)
PHONE.................................800 821-2302
Doron Arad, President
Efrat Arad, Admin Sec
▲ EMP: 150
SQ FT: 100,000
SALES (est): 49.1MM Privately Held
WEB: www.pioneerautoinc.com
SIC: 5013 3714 Automotive supplies & parts; motor vehicle parts & accessories

(G-3328)
DEARLENS INC
Also Called: Dearman Optical
910 23rd Ave Ste A (39301-5017)
PHONE.................................601 693-1841
Rocky Dearman, President
Jennifer Boyd, Office Mgr
EMP: 8
SQ FT: 2,500
SALES (est): 1MM Privately Held
SIC: 3851 Lens grinding, except prescription: ophthalmic; lens coating, ophthalmic

(G-3329)
DEMENT PRINTING COMPANY
2002 6th St (39301-5135)
PHONE.................................601 693-2721
John Dement, President
Judy Dement, Treasurer
EMP: 6
SALES (est): 1.5MM Privately Held
SIC: 2759 2752 5943 2789 Commercial printing; lithographing on metal; office forms & supplies; binding only: books, pamphlets, magazines, etc.; typesetting

(G-3330)
DUB STREET FASHION CENTER LLC
3316 20th St (39301-2832)
PHONE.................................601 483-0036
Freddie Miller, Mng Member
EMP: 2 EST: 2014
SALES: 280K Privately Held
SIC: 5651 2759 2284 Unisex clothing stores; screen printing; embroidery thread

(G-3331)
DUBLIN STEEL CORPORATION INC
7730 Highway 45 N (39305-8506)
PHONE.................................601 482-2102
David McKelvey, President
Shannon Danylieko, General Mgr
EMP: 5
SALES (est): 472.5K Privately Held
SIC: 3441 Fabricated structural metal

(G-3332)
DUFFELL METAL AWNING CO
Also Called: Duffell Awning Co
3903 Highland Park Dr (39307-5596)
P.O. Box 4834 (39304-4834)
PHONE.................................601 483-2181
William Vince Barber, Owner
EMP: 1 EST: 1948
SQ FT: 1,600
SALES (est): 88.5K Privately Held
SIC: 2394 3444 1731 Canvas awnings & canopies; awnings, sheet metal; safety & security specialization

(G-3333)
DUFOUR BATTERY ONE SOURCE LLC
2618 N Frontage Rd (39301-6546)
PHONE.................................601 693-1500
Genia Dufour,
Reginald Dufour,
EMP: 8
SALES (est): 929.7K Privately Held
SIC: 5531 3679 Batteries, automotive & truck; commutators, electronic

(G-3334)
ELEMENTS ESTATE SALES
6144 13th Ave (39305-1227)
PHONE.................................601 482-4099
EMP: 2

SALES (est): 74.4K Privately Held
SIC: 2819 Mfg Industrial Inorganic Chemicals

(G-3335)
EXPRESS LANE INC
500 Highway 19 N (39307-6347)
PHONE.................................601 483-8872
Adam Obed, CEO
EMP: 6
SALES (corp-wide): 2.4B Publicly Held
SIC: 2741 Miscellaneous publishing
HQ: Express Lane, Inc.
645 Hamilton St Ste 500
Allentown PA

(G-3336)
EYECATCHER SIGNS
2920 8th St (39301-4846)
PHONE.................................601 604-2595
Jim Brashier, Owner
EMP: 1
SALES (est): 46K Privately Held
SIC: 3993 Signs & advertising specialties

(G-3337)
FAIRBANKS SCALES INC
239 69th Ave (39307-5671)
PHONE.................................601 482-2073
Fax: 601 485-2733
EMP: 40
SALES (corp-wide): 197MM Privately Held
SIC: 3829 Mfg Measuring/Controlling Devices
HQ: Fairbanks Scales Inc.
821 Locust St
Kansas City MO 64106
816 471-0231

(G-3338)
FILTER SERVICE INC
10158 County Road 430 (39301-7619)
PHONE.................................601 644-9840
Larry Key, Manager
EMP: 5
SALES (est): 523.4K Privately Held
SIC: 3569 Filters

(G-3339)
FILTER SERVICE MISSISSIPPI LLC
2371 Freedom Baptst Ch Rd (39301-7310)
P.O. Box 300, Marion (39342-0300)
PHONE.................................601 693-4614
Thomas G Bradshaw, CEO
Ladonna Bradshaw, President
EMP: 5
SALES (est): 380K Privately Held
SIC: 3564 5999 Filters, air: furnaces, air conditioning equipment, etc.; plumbing & heating supplies

(G-3340)
GIPSON STEEL INC
Also Called: G S
2770 Sellers Dr (39301-1736)
P.O. Box 5225 (39302-5225)
PHONE.................................601 482-5131
Scott Gipson, CEO
Keith Gipson, President
Ernest M Gipson, Principal
Mark Gipson, Vice Pres
Michelle Hollan, CFO
EMP: 75 EST: 1976
SQ FT: 80,000
SALES (est): 25.1MM Privately Held
WEB: www.gipsonsteel.com
SIC: 3441 Bridge sections, prefabricated highway

(G-3341)
GLENN MACHINE WORKS INC
2120 31st Ave S (39307-8517)
PHONE.................................601 482-5554
Sonny Glenn, Branch Mgr
EMP: 3
SALES (corp-wide): 17.7MM Privately Held
SIC: 3599 Machine shop, jobbing & repair
PA: Glenn Machine Works, Inc.
734 Highway 45 S
Columbus MS 39701
662 328-4611

(PA)=Parent Co (HQ)=Headquarters (DH)=Div Headquarters
✪ = New Business established in last 2 years

2019 Harris Directory of
Mississippi Manufacturers

123

Meridian - Lauderdale County (G-3342) GEOGRAPHIC SECTION

(G-3342)
GOODMAN LOGGING LLC
10253 County Road 420 (39301-9201)
PHONE...............................601 644-3443
Robert E Goodman,
Lynese Goodman,
EMP: 7 EST: 2001
SALES (est): 782.7K **Privately Held**
SIC: 2411 Logging camps & contractors

(G-3343)
GULLEY S WELDING SERVICE
2510 B St (39301-5935)
PHONE...............................601 938-6336
Rodney Gulley, *Owner*
EMP: 4
SALES (est): 523K **Privately Held**
SIC: 3441 Fabricated structural metal

(G-3344)
GULLEYS WLDG STL ERECTORS INC
5107 1st St (39307-6629)
P.O. Box 1660 (39302-1660)
PHONE...............................601 482-3767
Rodney Gulley, *President*
EMP: 35
SALES (est): 3.7MM **Privately Held**
SIC: 7692 Welding repair

(G-3345)
HANGER PRSTHETCS & ORTHO INC
Also Called: Hanger Clinic
1903 23rd Ave (39301-3108)
PHONE...............................601 693-1002
Sam Liang, *President*
Kyle Temple, *Branch Mgr*
EMP: 4
SALES (corp-wide): 1B **Publicly Held**
SIC: 3842 Prosthetic appliances
HQ: Hanger Prosthetics & Orthotics, Inc.
10910 Domain Dr Ste 300
Austin TX 78758
512 777-3800

(G-3346)
HASTYS MULCH & STONE LLC
5321 Arundel Rd (39307-7269)
P.O. Box 383, Toomsuba (39364-0383)
PHONE...............................601 485-2120
EMP: 3
SALES (est): 220K **Privately Held**
SIC: 1741 2499 Masonry/Stone Contractor Mfg Wood Products

(G-3347)
ICE PLANT INC
202 Highway 19 N (39307-6600)
P.O. Box 4057 (39304-4057)
PHONE...............................601 485-9111
Phillip Maples, *President*
Sean Odom, *General Mgr*
EMP: 10
SQ FT: 5,000
SALES (est): 1.5MM **Privately Held**
WEB: www.iceplant.net
SIC: 2097 Ice cubes

(G-3348)
IDEAL SOFTWARE SYSTEMS INC
3839 Old Highway 45 N (39301-1518)
P.O. Box 3065 (39303-3065)
PHONE...............................601 693-1673
David Goldman, *President*
Amy Goldman, *Corp Secy*
Jason Southwell, *Vice Pres*
Alvin Brown, *Engineer*
Bridgett Hare, *CFO*
EMP: 55
SQ FT: 13,000
SALES (est): 8.6MM **Privately Held**
WEB: www.idealss.com
SIC: 7372 Prepackaged software

(G-3349)
IDENTITIES GRAPHIC SOLUTIONS
3115 5th Ave (39305-4891)
PHONE...............................601 917-9983
David Winford, *Principal*
EMP: 1
SALES (est): 46K **Privately Held**
SIC: 3993 Signs & advertising specialties

(G-3350)
IMMUNOTEK BIO CENTERS LLC
416 18th Ave (39301-5216)
PHONE...............................601 462-5145
Darryl King, *Manager*
EMP: 34
SALES (corp-wide): 27MM **Privately Held**
SIC: 2836 Blood derivatives
PA: Immunotek Bio Centers, L.L.C.
3900 N Causeway Blvd # 1200
Metairie LA 70002
337 500-1175

(G-3351)
INDIANOLA PECAN HOUSE INC
1410 Bonita Lakes Cir (39301-6975)
PHONE...............................601 693-1998
Fax: 601 693-1995
EMP: 5 EST: 1999
SALES (est): 330K **Privately Held**
SIC: 2068 Mfg Salted/Roasted Nuts/Seeds

(G-3352)
INDUSTRIAL ELC MTR WORKS INC
1551 Redman Rd (39305-8428)
P.O. Box 638, Marion (39342-0638)
PHONE...............................601 679-5500
Thomas E Mc Daniel, *Ch of Bd*
Thomas E McDaniel, *Ch of Bd*
Thomas A McDaniel, *President*
Kathy M Temple, *Corp Secy*
Stephen McDaniel, *Vice Pres*
▲ EMP: 38
SQ FT: 100,000
SALES (est): 26.2MM **Privately Held**
WEB: www.industrialelectricmotor.net
SIC: 5063 7694 Motors, electric; electric motor repair

(G-3353)
INNOVATIVE FABRICATIONS LLC
1110 B St (39301-5413)
PHONE...............................601 485-1400
Julie Lynch, *CEO*
Zane Royal,
EMP: 3
SQ FT: 6,000
SALES (est): 295.9K **Privately Held**
SIC: 3449 3715 3799 3713 Miscellaneous metalwork; truck trailers; trailers & trailer equipment; beverage truck bodies; truck beds

(G-3354)
JONES & YOUNG LOGGING LLC
8998 Chapel Rd (39305-9678)
P.O. Box 3702 (39303-3702)
PHONE...............................601 681-6801
Bruce Young, *Mng Member*
EMP: 8
SALES (est): 2MM **Privately Held**
SIC: 2411 Logging camps & contractors

(G-3355)
JOSEPH L BROWN PRINTING CO
Also Called: Brown Printing Co
204 20th Ave (39301-5107)
PHONE...............................601 693-6184
Benji D Brown, *President*
Choxie D Brown, *Corp Secy*
EMP: 7 EST: 1973
SQ FT: 5,000
SALES (est): 1.4MM **Privately Held**
SIC: 2752 Lithographing on metal

(G-3356)
LAUDERDALE COUNTY FARM SUP INC
203 49th Ave S (39307-7227)
P.O. Box 4256 (39304-4256)
PHONE...............................601 483-3363
Steve Windsted, *President*
Duane Maust, *Vice Pres*
Ron James, *Treasurer*
EMP: 29
SQ FT: 5,600
SALES (est): 10.4MM **Privately Held**
SIC: 5191 2048 5651 Feed; feed concentrates; family clothing stores

(G-3357)
LAUNDRY DEPOT LLC
613 Crosscreek Private St (39301)
PHONE...............................601 527-2774
La Fondra D Porter Kenney,
An'dria D Kenney,
James A Kenney III,
Jamesia L Kenney,
EMP: 12
SQ FT: 5,500
SALES: 375K **Privately Held**
SIC: 3582 Washing machines, laundry: commercial, incl. coin-operated

(G-3358)
LEGACY VULCAN LLC
2785 Sellers Dr (39301)
PHONE...............................601 553-2902
EMP: 2 **Publicly Held**
SIC: 1442 Construction sand & gravel
HQ: Legacy Vulcan, Llc
1200 Urban Center Dr
Vestavia AL 35242
205 298-3000

(G-3359)
LEGACY VULCAN LLC
Also Called: Meridian Yard
5226 Arundel Rd (39307-7213)
PHONE...............................601 482-7007
Greg Wolverton, *Manager*
EMP: 11 **Publicly Held**
WEB: www.vulcanmaterials.com
SIC: 1442 Construction sand & gravel
HQ: Legacy Vulcan, Llc
1200 Urban Center Dr
Vestavia AL 35242
205 298-3000

(G-3360)
LIGHTING INVESTMENT GROUP INC (PA)
Also Called: Specialty Lamps
6325 Specior St (39307-9586)
PHONE...............................601 482-3983
Julie Hagan-Bailey, *President*
David Bailey, *Vice Pres*
EMP: 2
SALES (est): 950K **Privately Held**
SIC: 3648 Lighting equipment

(G-3361)
LUKE PRINTING CO INC
2959 Alpine Way (39301-6664)
PHONE...............................601 693-1144
EMP: 6
SQ FT: 5,400
SALES: 400K **Privately Held**
SIC: 2752 Commercial printing, offset

(G-3362)
LUVEL DAIRY PRODUCTS INC
2659 Sellers Dr (39301-1752)
PHONE...............................601 693-0038
Russel Reed, *Manager*
EMP: 6
SALES (corp-wide): 1.7B **Privately Held**
SIC: 2026 2024 Fluid milk; ice cream & ice milk
HQ: Luvel Dairy Products, Inc.
926 Veterans Memorial Dr
Kosciusko MS 39090
662 289-2511

(G-3363)
MAGNOLIA STEEL CO INC
17 17th Ave S (39301-5401)
P.O. Box 5007 (39302-5007)
PHONE...............................601 693-4301
Christopher D Crowe, *President*
Kathryn C Coleman, *Vice Pres*
Debbie S Gibson, *Admin Sec*
EMP: 108 EST: 1950
SALES: 27.7MM **Privately Held**
WEB: www.magnoliasteel.com
SIC: 3441 Building components, structural steel

(G-3364)
MARTIN LOGGING INC (PA)
336 County Road 432 (39301-9250)
PHONE...............................601 644-3374
Robert Martin, *President*
Darron J Martin, *Vice Pres*
Sarah Martin, *Treasurer*

Robin Martin, *Admin Sec*
EMP: 12
SALES (est): 1.4MM **Privately Held**
SIC: 2411 Logging camps & contractors

(G-3365)
MCDEVITT ENTERPRISES LLC
3125 5th Ave (39305-4891)
PHONE...............................601 453-2290
Beverly McDevitt, *CEO*
Ronald McDevitt, *COO*
EMP: 5
SALES: 150K **Privately Held**
SIC: 1522 1629 1422 1771 Residential construction; rock removal; crushed & broken limestone; parking lot construction; janitorial service, contract basis

(G-3366)
MEDICAL ARTS SURGICAL GROUP
2111 14th St (39301-4095)
PHONE...............................601 693-3834
Frank H Tucker Jr, *Owner*
Karen Todd, *Med Doctor*
Stephen Tartt, *Surgeon*
EMP: 16
SQ FT: 3,000
SALES (est): 2.2MM **Privately Held**
WEB: www.medicalartssg.com
SIC: 3841 Surgical & medical instruments

(G-3367)
MERIDIAN COCA-COLA BOTTLING CO (PA)
2016 Highway 45 N (39301-2705)
P.O. Box 5207 (39302-5207)
PHONE...............................601 483-5272
Hardy P Graham Jr, *Ch of Bd*
Richard D James, *Corp Secy*
EMP: 170 EST: 1902
SQ FT: 100,000
SALES (est): 31.3MM **Privately Held**
SIC: 2086 Bottled & canned soft drinks

(G-3368)
MERIDIAN MATTRESS FACTORY INC
Also Called: Bemco Bedding
200 Rubush Ave (39301-5743)
P.O. Box 5127 (39302-5127)
PHONE...............................601 693-3875
Thomas L Crudup, *President*
William C Crudup, *Admin Sec*
▲ EMP: 10 EST: 1928
SQ FT: 40,000
SALES (est): 1.9MM **Privately Held**
WEB: www.mermat.com
SIC: 5712 2515 Mattresses; mattresses & bedsprings

(G-3369)
MERIDIAN WOODWORKING
2405 State Blvd (39307-5033)
PHONE...............................601 604-6147
Curtis Trussell, *Principal*
EMP: 2
SALES (est): 139.5K **Privately Held**
SIC: 2431 Millwork

(G-3370)
MET-TECH CORP
3405 Industrial Dr (39307-9585)
PHONE...............................601 693-0061
George McLean, *CEO*
Tommy E Dulaney, *President*
James Dean Jr, *Exec VP*
Tom Larkins, *Vice Pres*
Donna Reed, *Treasurer*
EMP: 8
SQ FT: 32,000
SALES (est): 845.6K
SALES (corp-wide): 54.3MM **Privately Held**
SIC: 8711 3599 3549 Designing: ship, boat, machine & product; pump governors, for gas machines; metalworking machinery
HQ: Structural Steel Services, Inc.
6215 Saint Louis St
Meridian MS 39307
601 482-1668

2019 Harris Directory of
Mississippi Manufacturers

▲ = Import ▼=Export
◆ =Import/Export

124

GEOGRAPHIC SECTION

Meridian - Lauderdale County (G-3399)

(G-3371)
MGC TERMINAL LLC
101 65th Ave (39307-7017)
P.O. Box 292 (39302-0292)
PHONE...................................601 482-5012
Phillip M Maples, *Principal*
EMP: 2
SALES (est): 150K **Privately Held**
SIC: 1321 Liquefied petroleum gases (natural) production

(G-3372)
MISSISSIPPI BEVERAGE CO INC
2620 A St (39301-5755)
PHONE...................................601 693-3853
EMP: 25
SQ FT: 15,000
SALES (est): 2MM **Privately Held**
SIC: 3221 Water bottles, glass

(G-3373)
MISSISSPPI INDS FOR THE BLIND
6603 Laurel Dr (39307-5674)
PHONE...................................601 693-5525
Danny Cooper, *Vice Pres*
Ronny Salter, *Director*
EMP: 35
SQ FT: 15,000
SALES (corp-wide): 21MM **Privately Held**
WEB: www.msblind.org
SIC: 7363 8331 3469 Help supply services; job training & vocational rehabilitation services; metal stampings
PA: Mississippi Industries For The Blind
2501 N West St
Jackson MS 39216
601 984-3200

(G-3374)
MITCHELL SIGNS INC
3200 Highway 45 N (39301-1505)
PHONE...................................601 553-1557
Melanie M Mitchell, *President*
Timothy D Hogan, *President*
John Mitchell Jr, *Vice Pres*
Stephanie Nowell, *Project Mgr*
Randy Robinson, *Project Mgr*
◆ **EMP:** 53
SQ FT: 10,000
SALES (est): 7.7MM **Privately Held**
SIC: 3993 3552 Electric signs; silk screens for textile industry

(G-3375)
MMC MATERIALS INC
5226 Arundel Rd (39307-7213)
PHONE...................................601 482-7007
Elton Cook, *President*
James Toler, *Manager*
Greg Wolverton, *Director*
EMP: 34
SALES (corp-wide): 306.5MM **Privately Held**
WEB: www.mmcmaterials.com
SIC: 3273 Ready-mixed concrete
HQ: Mmc Materials, Inc.
1052 Highland Colony Pkwy # 201
Ridgeland MS 39157
601 898-4000

(G-3376)
NATIONAL SCRUBWEAR INC
Also Called: M Prints
3200 Highway 45 N (39301-1505)
PHONE...................................601 483-0796
John Mitchell, *President*
Manny Mitchell, *President*
Jon Hamm, *Sales Staff*
EMP: 12
SALES (est): 1.5MM **Privately Held**
SIC: 2759 3993 Screen printing; signs & advertising specialties

(G-3377)
NEWSPAPER HOLDING INC
Also Called: Meridian Star, The
812814 22nd Ave (39301)
P.O. Box 1591 (39302-1591)
PHONE...................................601 693-1551
Cristal Dupre, *Branch Mgr*
EMP: 70 **Privately Held**
WEB: www.clintonnc.com

SIC: 2711 2752 Newspapers: publishing only, not printed on site; commercial printing, lithographic
HQ: Newspaper Holding, Inc.
425 Locust St
Johnstown PA 15901
814 532-5102

(G-3378)
OPEL CORP
Also Called: John's Welding Service
1414 Rubush Ave (39301-6615)
PHONE...................................601 693-0771
John Opel, *President*
Bonnie Opel, *Vice Pres*
EMP: 3
SQ FT: 3,200
SALES: 0 **Privately Held**
SIC: 7692 Welding repair

(G-3379)
ORRIN F FUELLING
573 Purvis Rd (39301-8620)
PHONE...................................601 485-2598
Orrin F Fuelling, *Owner*
EMP: 1
SALES (est): 55K **Privately Held**
SIC: 2869 Fuels

(G-3380)
PARTRIDGE ORNAMENTAL IRON INC
4816 Arundel Rd (39307-9541)
P.O. Box 3564 (39303-3564)
PHONE...................................601 693-4021
Terry Plummer, *President*
EMP: 25 **EST:** 1957
SALES (est): 2.4MM **Privately Held**
SIC: 1791 1799 3496 Iron work, structural; ornamental metal work; miscellaneous fabricated wire products

(G-3381)
PEAVEY ELECTRONICS CORPORATION (PA)
5022 Hartley Peavey Dr (39305-8733)
P.O. Box 1150 (39302-1150)
PHONE...................................601 483-5365
Hartley D Peavey, *Ch of Bd*
Mary Peavey, *President*
Courtland Gray, *COO*
Ed Heath, *Design Engr*
Bill Ford, *Natl Sales Mgr*
◆ **EMP:** 277
SQ FT: 1,500,000
SALES (est): 164.7MM **Privately Held**
WEB: www.peavey.com
SIC: 3931 Musical instruments

(G-3382)
PEAVEY ELECTRONICS CORPORATION
4500 8th Ave (39305)
PHONE...................................601 483-5365
Tony Roberson, *Principal*
EMP: 6
SALES (corp-wide): 164.7MM **Privately Held**
WEB: www.peavey.com
SIC: 3651 Audio electronic systems
PA: Peavey Electronics Corporation
5022 Hartley Peavey Dr
Meridian MS 39305
601 483-5365

(G-3383)
PEAVEY ELECTRONICS CORPORATION
710 A St (39301-4517)
PHONE...................................601 486-1760
Hartley Peavey, *Branch Mgr*
EMP: 5
SALES (corp-wide): 164.7MM **Privately Held**
SIC: 3651 Audio electronic systems
PA: Peavey Electronics Corporation
5022 Hartley Peavey Dr
Meridian MS 39305
601 483-5365

(G-3384)
PEAVEY ELECTRONICS CORPORATION
412 Highway 11 And 80 (39301-2778)
PHONE...................................601 486-1878

Hartley D Peavey, *Ch of Bd*
EMP: 6
SALES (corp-wide): 164.7MM **Privately Held**
SIC: 3931 Musical instruments
PA: Peavey Electronics Corporation
5022 Hartley Peavey Dr
Meridian MS 39305
601 483-5365

(G-3385)
PEAVEY ELECTRONICS CORPORATION
Also Called: Crest Audio
4886 Peavey Dr (39301-8026)
PHONE...................................601 486-1127
Lee Peavey, *Branch Mgr*
EMP: 9
SALES (corp-wide): 164.7MM **Privately Held**
WEB: www.peavey.com
SIC: 3651 Audio electronic systems
PA: Peavey Electronics Corporation
5022 Hartley Peavey Dr
Meridian MS 39305
601 483-5365

(G-3386)
PEAVEY ELECTRONICS CORPORATION
711 A St (39301-5422)
PHONE...................................601 483-5365
Hartley Peavey, *Manager*
EMP: 14
SALES (corp-wide): 164.7MM **Privately Held**
WEB: www.peavey.com
SIC: 3651 Audio electronic systems
PA: Peavey Electronics Corporation
5022 Hartley Peavey Dr
Meridian MS 39305
601 483-5365

(G-3387)
PELLER ELECTRIC MOTOR SRVS
2125 Grand Ave (39301-6652)
P.O. Box 5755 (39302-5755)
PHONE...................................601 693-4621
Burley Linton, *President*
EMP: 4
SQ FT: 2,400
SALES (est): 344.7K **Privately Held**
SIC: 7694 5999 Electric motor repair; motors, electric

(G-3388)
PERFECT PROMOTIONS LLC
504b Highway 19 N Ste B (39307-6347)
PHONE...................................601 482-7710
EMP: 11
SALES (est): 1MM **Privately Held**
SIC: 2395 Pleating/Stitching Services

(G-3389)
QUALITY TRIM & UPHOLSTERY
3313 State Blvd (39307-4374)
PHONE...................................601 483-0077
Fax: 601 483-4582
EMP: 3
SALES: 170K **Privately Held**
SIC: 2512 7532 Mfg Upholstered Household Furniture Auto Body Repair/Painting

(G-3390)
QUICK PRINTS
2318 12th St (39301-3933)
PHONE...................................601 485-3278
Margaret Remy, *Owner*
John Remy, *Owner*
EMP: 3
SQ FT: 3,000
SALES: 110K **Privately Held**
SIC: 2752 Commercial printing, offset

(G-3391)
RIEDESIGNS EMBROIDERY
7869 County Road 350 (39301-9643)
PHONE...................................601 262-5130
EMP: 1
SALES (est): 37.3K **Privately Held**
SIC: 2395 Embroidery & art needlework

(G-3392)
ROBCHEM LLC
Also Called: Robchem Paints and Coatings
981 Highway 19 S (39301-8229)
P.O. Box 1429 (39302-1429)
PHONE...................................601 485-5502
Nan F Robinson, *President*
Thomas Robinson, *President*
EMP: 4
SQ FT: 20,000
SALES (est): 569.4K **Privately Held**
WEB: www.robchem.com
SIC: 2851 Paints & allied products

(G-3393)
RUNWAY LIQUIDATION LLC
Also Called: Bcbg
2024 15th St (39301-4104)
PHONE...................................406 388-1988
EMP: 2
SALES (corp-wide): 576.5MM **Privately Held**
SIC: 2335 Women's, juniors' & misses' dresses
HQ: Runway Liquidation, Llc
2761 Fruitland Ave
Vernon CA 90058
323 589-2224

(G-3394)
SAUNDERS MFG CO INC
6604 Highway 80 W (39307-6107)
PHONE...................................601 693-3482
Theron White, *Manager*
EMP: 12
SALES (corp-wide): 13.5MM **Privately Held**
WEB: www.saunders-usa.com
SIC: 8741 3354 2493 Administrative management; aluminum extruded products; reconstituted wood products
PA: Saunders Mfg. Co., Inc.
65 Nickerson Hill Rd
Readfield ME 04355
207 685-9860

(G-3395)
SIGN DOCTOR LLC
422 N Point Dr (39305-8722)
PHONE...................................601 286-3387
Roger Fortenberry,
EMP: 2 **EST:** 2011
SALES (est): 208.6K **Privately Held**
SIC: 3993 Signs & advertising specialties

(G-3396)
SIGN PRO WHOLESALE LLC
345 Hawkins Crossing Dr (39301-9571)
PHONE...................................601 453-3082
Mark Brittain Covington, *Principal*
EMP: 11
SALES (est): 1.4MM **Privately Held**
SIC: 3993 Signs & advertising specialties

(G-3397)
SIGNS PLUS
9218 Whippoorwill Rd (39307-9266)
PHONE...................................601 482-4217
Toni Lewis, *Partner*
Jeff Lee, *Partner*
EMP: 4
SALES (est): 489.9K **Privately Held**
SIC: 3993 Electric signs

(G-3398)
SLAY STEEL INC
6215 5th St (39307-6169)
P.O. Box 4009 (39304-4009)
PHONE...................................601 483-3911
Ronnie Slay, *President*
Greg Slay, *Vice Pres*
Phillip Slay, *Treasurer*
Todd Nosco, *Sales Mgr*
Ginger Delaney, *Office Mgr*
EMP: 65
SQ FT: 34,000
SALES (est): 65.1MM **Privately Held**
SIC: 5051 3441 Steel; fabricated structural metal

(G-3399)
SOLAPLAST LLC
Also Called: Algix
5168 Water Tower Rd (39301-8850)
PHONE...................................877 972-5449
Mike Van Drunen, *Principal*

(PA)=Parent Co (HQ)=Headquarters (DH)=Div Headquarters
✪ = New Business established in last 2 years

2019 Harris Directory of
Mississippi Manufacturers

125

Meridian - Lauderdale County (G-3400)

GEOGRAPHIC SECTION

EMP: 5
SALES (est): 505.8K **Privately Held**
SIC: 2821 Plastics materials & resins

(G-3400)
SOUTH TXAS LGHTHOUSE FOR BLIND
Also Called: 1 Store Solution
224 Allen Rd (39309-0001)
PHONE..............................601 679-3180
Lisa Easterwood, *Branch Mgr*
EMP: 2 **EST:** 2007
SALES (est): 213.1K **Privately Held**
SIC: 2782 5112 5021 Ledger, inventory & account books; looseleaf binders; office & public building furniture

(G-3401)
SOUTHERN CAST PRODUCTS INC
1010 Wile Rd (39301-8894)
P.O. Box 3644 (39303-3644)
PHONE..............................601 482-8518
Frederick A Wile, *President*
Sarah Wile, *Corp Secy*
EMP: 160
SQ FT: 62,000
SALES (est): 41.1MM **Privately Held**
WEB: www.southerncastproducts.com
SIC: 3325 Alloy steel castings, except investment

(G-3402)
SOUTHERN CRAFTSMEN INC
1193 Bonita Lakes Cir (39301-6967)
PHONE..............................601 484-5757
EMP: 7
SALES (corp-wide): 5.2MM **Privately Held**
SIC: 2511 Wood household furniture
PA: Southern Craftsmen, Inc.
2301 Highway 39 N
Meridian MS 39301
601 483-4717

(G-3403)
SOUTHERN SCRAP MERIDIAN LLC
Also Called: Columbus Recycling Corporation
75 Highway 19 N (39307-7217)
P.O. Box 1636 (39302-1636)
PHONE..............................601 693-5323
Greg Rader,
EMP: 25
SQ FT: 14,000
SALES (est): 3.5MM **Privately Held**
SIC: 5093 3341 3312 Ferrous metal scrap & waste; nonferrous metals scrap; secondary nonferrous metals; blast furnaces & steel mills

(G-3404)
SPECIALTY ROLL PRODUCTS INC
601 25th Ave (39301-4918)
P.O. Box 5374 (39302-5374)
PHONE..............................601 693-1771
Larry Love, *President*
Lisa N Love, *Corp Secy*
Brad Huff, *Vice Pres*
Gordon Parker, *Sales Staff*
◆ **EMP:** 35
SQ FT: 100,000
SALES (est): 12.6MM **Privately Held**
WEB: www.specialtyroll.com
SIC: 2679 Paper products, converted

(G-3405)
SPECTECH SERVICE & SIGNS LLC
202 Highway 19 N (39307-6600)
PHONE..............................601 482-0816
Phillip Maples, *President*
EMP: 15
SALES (est): 1.1MM **Privately Held**
WEB: www.maplesgas.com
SIC: 3993 Signs, not made in custom sign painting shops

(G-3406)
SPEEDS WELDING WORKS
2653 Russell Mt Gilead Rd (39301-8165)
PHONE..............................601 917-2571
Charles F Speed, *Owner*
EMP: 1

SALES (est): 95.1K **Privately Held**
SIC: 7692 Welding repair

(G-3407)
STRUCTURAL STEEL HOLDING INC
1601 60th Pl S (39307)
PHONE..............................601 485-1503
Tommy Dulaney, *Branch Mgr*
EMP: 15
SALES (corp-wide): 54.3MM **Privately Held**
WEB: www.structuralsteeldetailing.com
SIC: 3441 Building components, structural steel
PA: Structural Steel Holding, Inc.
6210 Saint Louis St
Meridian MS 39307
601 483-5381

(G-3408)
STRUCTURAL STEEL HOLDING INC (PA)
6210 Saint Louis St (39307-7209)
P.O. Box 2929 (39302-2929)
PHONE..............................601 483-5381
Tommy E Dulaney, *President*
Donna Reid, *Corp Secy*
James T Dean Jr, *Exec VP*
Robert Cardwell, *Purch Mgr*
John Height, *Data Proc Exec*
EMP: 125
SQ FT: 600,000
SALES (est): 54.3MM **Privately Held**
WEB: www.sssvc-inc.com
SIC: 3441 3443 4213 Fabricated structural metal; fabricated plate work (boiler shop); trucking, except local

(G-3409)
STRUCTURAL STEEL SERVICES INC (HQ)
Also Called: S S S
6215 Saint Louis St (39307-9575)
P.O. Box 2929 (39302-2929)
PHONE..............................601 482-1668
Tommy Dulaney, *President*
Donna Reid, *Corp Secy*
James Dean Jr, *Exec VP*
Tony Dean, *Vice Pres*
Harold Reed, *Plant Mgr*
EMP: 225
SQ FT: 550,000
SALES (est): 51.6MM
SALES (corp-wide): 54.3MM **Privately Held**
SIC: 3441 Building components, structural steel
PA: Structural Steel Holding, Inc.
6210 Saint Louis St
Meridian MS 39307
601 483-5381

(G-3410)
STRUCTURAL STEEL SERVICES INC
533 65th Ave (39307-5644)
PHONE..............................601 485-2619
Ted Devalcourt, *Manager*
EMP: 24
SALES (corp-wide): 54.3MM **Privately Held**
SIC: 3441 3443 Building components, structural steel; fabricated plate work (boiler shop)
HQ: Structural Steel Services, Inc.
6215 Saint Louis St
Meridian MS 39307
601 482-1668

(G-3411)
TAYLOR & SONS INC
2622 N Frontage Rd (39301-6546)
PHONE..............................601 483-0714
Priestly Taylor, *President*
Janice Taylor, *Corp Secy*
▲ **EMP:** 6
SQ FT: 7,600
SALES: 1.5MM **Privately Held**
SIC: 5999 5261 5571 3599 Feed & farm supply; nurseries & garden centers; lawn & garden equipment; motorcycle dealers; all-terrain vehicles; motorcycles; all terrain vehicle parts and accessories; machine shop, jobbing & repair

(G-3412)
TEIKURO CORPORATION
4847 Peavey Dr (39301-8856)
PHONE..............................601 482-0432
Jim Purdue, *Superintendent*
EMP: 8 **Privately Held**
SIC: 3471 Plating of metals or formed products
HQ: Teikuro Corporation
101 Clay St
San Francisco CA 94111
415 273-2650

(G-3413)
TEN BELOW LLC
1814 N Frontage Rd (39301-6155)
PHONE..............................601 453-2041
EMP: 2
SALES (est): 73.4K **Privately Held**
SIC: 2299 Jute & flax textile products

(G-3414)
TIMBER RESOURCES INC
8998 Chapel Rd (39305-9678)
P.O. Box 3396 (39303-3396)
PHONE..............................601 681-6801
Bruce Young, *President*
Laura Young, *Vice Pres*
EMP: 1
SALES: 5MM **Privately Held**
SIC: 2411 Logging

(G-3415)
TOWER AUTOMOTIVE OPERATIONS
6305 Saint Louis St (39307-9577)
PHONE..............................601 678-4000
Christina Shepard, *Production*
Darnell Montgomery, *Manager*
EMP: 110 **Publicly Held**
SIC: 3465 Automotive stampings
HQ: Tower Automotive Operations Usa Ii, Llc
17672 N Laurel Park Dr 400e
Livonia MI 48152

(G-3416)
WATCO CO INC
Also Called: Watco Mobile Services
400 18th Ave S (39301-6057)
PHONE..............................601 553-1332
EMP: 3 **EST:** 2004
SALES (est): 260K **Privately Held**
SIC: 3743 Mfg Railroad Equipment

(G-3417)
WATKINS TRIM SHOP INC
Also Called: Upholstry
2503 8th St (39301-4946)
PHONE..............................601 485-5512
Tim Watkins, *Owner*
EMP: 3
SALES: 50K **Privately Held**
SIC: 2759 2752 Commercial printing; commercial printing, lithographic

(G-3418)
WATSON TJ PROPERTY LLC
Also Called: Big T'S Moving
2440 N Hills St 105 Mrdian (39305)
PHONE..............................601 527-3587
Tommy Watson,
EMP: 1
SALES (est): 73.3K **Privately Held**
SIC: 4212 3537 7363 4731 Moving services; trucks: freight, baggage, etc.: industrial, except mining; truck driver services; freight transportation arrangement

(G-3419)
WEBSTER - PORTALLOY CHAINS INC (HQ)
Also Called: Portland Chain
3800 2nd St (39301-6219)
P.O. Box 640172, Cincinnati OH (45264-0001)
PHONE..............................419 447-8232
Fred Spurck, *President*
Andrew Felter, *Vice Pres*
Chris English, *Treasurer*
▲ **EMP:** 150 **EST:** 1971
SQ FT: 8,000

SALES (est): 12.3MM
SALES (corp-wide): 55MM **Privately Held**
SIC: 3496 Chain, welded
PA: Webster Industries, Inc.
325 Hall St
Tiffin OH 44883
419 447-8232

(G-3420)
WEBSTER INDUSTRY INC
3800 2nd St (39301-6219)
PHONE..............................601 482-0183
Dan Jackson, *Principal*
EMP: 2
SALES (est): 257.9K **Privately Held**
SIC: 3535 Conveyors & conveying equipment

(G-3421)
WILSON WELDING
3211 Bolen Long Creek Rd (39301-8428)
PHONE..............................601 483-3696
Sylmon Wilson, *Owner*
Dorothy Wilson, *Co-Owner*
EMP: 3
SALES: 260K **Privately Held**
SIC: 7692 Welding repair

(G-3422)
YOUNG E F JR MANUFACTURING CO
425 26th Ave (39301-5722)
PHONE..............................601 483-8864
Charles L Young Sr, *President*
Eugene F Young III, *Corp Secy*
Abdul Lala, *Vice Pres*
Charles L Young Jr, *Vice Pres*
EMP: 46 **EST:** 1931
SQ FT: 35,000
SALES (est): 7.2MM **Privately Held**
WEB: www.efyoungjr.com
SIC: 2844 Cosmetic preparations

Michigan City
Benton County

(G-3423)
MID-SOUTH ORNAMENTAL CONCRETE
6488 Highway 72 (38647-8839)
PHONE..............................662 224-3170
Edward Carpenter, *President*
EMP: 15
SQ FT: 12,000
SALES (est): 2.6MM **Privately Held**
SIC: 3272 Concrete products, precast

Minter City
Leflore County

(G-3424)
LEAS REPAIR
27538 County Road 550 (38944-2708)
PHONE..............................662 658-4462
Robert Lea, *Owner*
EMP: 2
SALES (est): 110K **Privately Held**
SIC: 7699 3537 Farm machinery repair; aircraft loading hoists

---

Mississippi State
Oktibbeha County

(G-3425)
MISSISSIPPI STATE UNIVERSITY
Also Called: MSU Electrical Computer Design
Hardy Rd (39762)
P.O. Box 9571 (39762-9571)
PHONE..............................662 325-3149
Dr Malcolm Potera, *President*
EMP: 9
SALES (corp-wide): 489.2MM **Privately Held**
WEB: www.msstate.edu
SIC: 3571 8221 Electronic computers; university

2019 Harris Directory of
Mississippi Manufacturers

▲ = Import ▼=Export
◆ =Import/Export

GEOGRAPHIC SECTION

Morton - Scott County (G-3454)

PA: Mississippi State University
245 Barr Ave Mcrthur Hl Mcarthur Hall
Mississippi State MS 39762
662 325-2302

Mize
Smith County

(G-3426)
FREEMAN MILLING LLC
112 Eucalyptus St (39116-5758)
PHONE..................................601 733-5444
Jared Freeman, *Principal*
EMP: 10 **EST:** 2010
SALES (est): 1.6MM **Privately Held**
SIC: 3541 Milling machines

(G-3427)
JWB CONSTRUCTION LLC
4141 Scr 83 Mize (39116)
P.O. Box 303, Taylorsville (39168-0303)
PHONE..................................601 439-7190
Joseph Blakeney,
EMP: 10
SALES (est): 1.2MM **Privately Held**
SIC: 1389 1629 1799 1521 Grading oil &
gas well foundations; land clearing con-
tractor; building site preparation; single-
family housing construction

Monticello
Lawrence County

(G-3428)
ATLAS-SSI INC
622 E Mcpherson Dr (39654-3709)
P.O. Box 1969 (39654-1969)
PHONE..................................601 587-4511
Larry Crowell Sr, *President*
Jeri Newsom, *Corp Secy*
William F Wall, *Vice Pres*
William Wall, *Buyer*
Anthony Everett, *Sales Staff*
◆ **EMP:** 70 **EST:** 1998
SALES (est): 12.6MM **Privately Held**
WEB: www.atlasmanufacturing.net
SIC: 5084 3291 Industrial machinery &
equipment; abrasive metal & steel prod-
ucts

(G-3429)
CARNEY PUBLICATIONS LLC
1655 Carmel New Hope Rd (39654-9631)
P.O. Box 1663, Madison (39130-1663)
PHONE..................................601 427-5694
Jennifer Carney,
EMP: 1 **EST:** 2011
SALES (est): 72K **Privately Held**
SIC: 2741 Miscellaneous publishing

(G-3430)
CKC LOGGING INC
182 Brother In Law Ln (39654-9679)
PHONE..................................601 754-1344
Charles Carr, *President*
Hope Carr, *Vice Pres*
EMP: 6
SALES (est): 669.2K **Privately Held**
SIC: 2411 Fuel wood harvesting

(G-3431)
GEO SPECIALTY CHEMICAL INC
107 Cytec Rd (39654)
PHONE..................................601 587-7481
Stanley Stephens, *General Mgr*
EMP: 3
SALES (est): 381.6K **Privately Held**
SIC: 2819 Aluminum sulfate

(G-3432)
GEORGIA-PACIFIC LLC
604 Na Sandifer Hwy (39654-7601)
PHONE..................................601 587-7570
Fred Sheffield, *Purchasing*
David Oliver, *Train & Dev Mgr*
Jimmy Johnson, *Manager*
Hugh Lewing, *Director*
EMP: 9
SALES (corp-wide): 40.9B **Privately Held**
SIC: 2621 Paper mills

HQ: Georgia-Pacific Llc
133 Peachtree St Nw
Atlanta GA 30303
404 652-4000

(G-3433)
GEORGIA-PACIFIC LLC
1477 Highway 84 (39654)
PHONE..................................601 587-7711
Walt Schimmel, *Branch Mgr*
EMP: 9
SALES (corp-wide): 40.9B **Privately Held**
WEB: www.gp.com
SIC: 2431 Millwork
HQ: Georgia-Pacific Llc
133 Peachtree St Nw
Atlanta GA 30303
404 652-4000

(G-3434)
JOHN READY DAMOND
547 Old Highway 27 N (39654-8411)
PHONE..................................601 587-4381
John Ready, *Principal*
EMP: 1
SALES (est): 110K **Privately Held**
SIC: 3273 Ready-mixed concrete

(G-3435)
LAWRENCE COUNTY PRESS INC
296 F E Sellers Hwy (39654-9555)
P.O. Box 549 (39654-0549)
PHONE..................................601 587-2781
John Henry Carney Jr, *President*
John Carney, *CIO*
EMP: 8 **EST:** 1888
SQ FT: 2,250
SALES (est): 647.7K **Privately Held**
WEB: www.governmax.com
SIC: 2711 5943 Commercial printing &
newspaper publishing combined; office
forms & supplies

(G-3436)
MEDICAL CLINIC
Also Called: Medical Clinic, The
713 Watts St (39654-9313)
P.O. Box 518 (39654-0518)
PHONE..................................601 587-7795
Brantley B Pace MD, *Owner*
EMP: 4
SQ FT: 2,800
SALES (est): 520.1K **Privately Held**
SIC: 8011 1382 General & family practice,
physician/surgeon; oil & gas exploration
services

(G-3437)
NO HOPE LOGGING INC
453 Carmel New Hope Rd (39654-9659)
PHONE..................................601 587-5515
EMP: 2
SALES (est): 180K **Privately Held**
SIC: 2411 Logging

(G-3438)
NO HOPE TRUCKING INC
388 Renfroe Rd (39654-9093)
PHONE..................................601 320-1919
Michael H Sistrunk, *Principal*
EMP: 7
SALES (est): 664.1K **Privately Held**
SIC: 2411 Logging

(G-3439)
PEARL RIVER LOGGING LLC
465 Na Sandifer Hwy (39654-7692)
P.O. Box 789 (39654-0789)
PHONE..................................601 587-2516
Eric Brown, *Partner*
EMP: 4
SALES (est): 636.1K **Privately Held**
SIC: 2411 Logging

(G-3440)
USACCESS LLC
Also Called: Enviro-Mats, LLC
1005 W Broad St (39654-7726)
PHONE..................................601 806-5034
Gregory Pomerleau,
Kevin Pomerleau,
EMP: 22
SALES (est): 1.5MM **Privately Held**
SIC: 2273 Carpets & rugs

Mooreville
Lee County

(G-3441)
BURCHWOOD INC
155 Road 1445 (38857-8008)
P.O. Box 479 (38857-0479)
PHONE..................................662 841-2609
Brad Stanford, *President*
Cindy Stanford, *Admin Sec*
EMP: 18
SQ FT: 23,000
SALES (est): 2.2MM **Privately Held**
WEB: www.burchwood.com
SIC: 2431 Moldings & baseboards, orna-
mental & trim

(G-3442)
CANTRELL HOT RODS LLC
166 Road 1492 (38857-7440)
PHONE..................................662 213-7184
Stephen Cantrell, *Principal*
EMP: 2
SALES (est): 119.9K **Privately Held**
SIC: 3714 Motor vehicle parts & acces-
sories

(G-3443)
PRINT SHOP OF TUPELO
144 Hillview Dr (38857-7716)
PHONE..................................662 841-0004
Jeff Senter, *Owner*
EMP: 1
SQ FT: 1,400
SALES (est): 270K **Privately Held**
SIC: 2759 Screen printing

(G-3444)
WICKS N MORE INC
Also Called: Wicks N More Wholesale
558 Highway 371 (38857-7310)
PHONE..................................662 205-4025
Cynthia Albanese, *CEO*
Becky Neal, *President*
Beckey Neal, *Vice Pres*
▲ **EMP:** 20
SALES (est): 205.7K **Privately Held**
SIC: 3999 Candles

Moorhead
Sunflower County

(G-3445)
FISHBELT FEEDS INC
33 Moorhead Itta Bena Rd (38761)
P.O. Box 609 (38761-0609)
PHONE..................................662 246-5065
Joe Oglesby Jr, *President*
Bob Harris, *General Mgr*
Ed Pentecost, *Corp Secy*
Jimmy D Carter, *Vice Pres*
Alvin Simpson, *Plant Mgr*
EMP: 46
SQ FT: 24,000
SALES: 58MM **Privately Held**
SIC: 2048 5191 Fish food; animal feeds

Morton
Scott County

(G-3446)
COX MHP INC
2348 Highway 80 (39117-7936)
PHONE..................................601 732-6600
John Smith, *Principal*
Mike Davis, *Marketing Staff*
EMP: 1 **Privately Held**
WEB: www.coxmhp.com
SIC: 3599 Machine shop, jobbing & repair
PA: Cox Mhp, Inc.
4400 Mangum Dr Bldg D
Flowood MS 39232

(G-3447)
HONDUMEX GLOBAL LLC
38 W Second Ave (39117-3400)
PHONE..................................601 732-6505
Ruiz Luz, *Bd of Directors*

EMP: 1
SALES (est): 172.4K **Privately Held**
SIC: 3421 Table & food cutlery, including
butchers'

(G-3448)
KDEB MANUFACTURING LLC
2246 Highway 80 (39117-9036)
PHONE..................................601 750-9659
Albert Bozeman White, *Mng Member*
EMP: 1
SALES (est): 60K **Privately Held**
SIC: 3531 3496 3955 Pavers; mats &
matting; print cartridges for laser & other
computer printers

(G-3449)
KOCH FOODS OF MISSISSIPPI LLC
278 Herring Rd (39117)
PHONE..................................601 732-3026
Richard Morrison, *Manager*
EMP: 50
SALES (corp-wide): 2.2B **Privately Held**
SIC: 2015 Chicken, processed: fresh;
chicken, processed: frozen; chicken,
slaughtered & dressed
HQ: Koch Foods Of Mississippi Llc
1080 River Oaks Dr A100
Flowood MS 39232
601 732-8911

(G-3450)
MISSISSIPPI POULTRY
4013 Highway 80 (39117-3350)
PHONE..................................601 732-8670
Liang WEI Bin, *Principal*
EMP: 2
SALES (est): 190.2K **Privately Held**
SIC: 5046 2011 Commercial cooking &
food service equipment; meat packing
plants

(G-3451)
MORTON INDUSTRY
3986 Highway 80 (39117-3304)
PHONE..................................601 732-6486
Lisa Till, *Manager*
EMP: 2
SALES (est): 222.5K **Privately Held**
SIC: 3999 Manufacturing industries

(G-3452)
NEXTEER AUTOMOTIVE CORPORATION
6586 Highway 13 (39117-5352)
PHONE..................................601 537-3099
Christine Felix, *Branch Mgr*
EMP: 409 **Privately Held**
SIC: 3714 Motor vehicle parts & acces-
sories
HQ: Nexteer Automotive Corporation
1272 Doris Rd
Auburn Hills MI 48326

(G-3453)
PARKER TRUCKING AND HLG LLC
339 Scr 150 (39117-5182)
PHONE..................................601 537-3670
Ricky Parker,
EMP: 5 **EST:** 1989
SALES: 300K **Privately Held**
SIC: 2411 Logging

(G-3454)
REMAN INC (PA)
6586 Highway 13 (39117-5352)
PHONE..................................601 537-3400
James Alexander, *President*
Henry Burns, *Corp Secy*
EMP: 30
SQ FT: 21,000
SALES (est): 8.1MM **Privately Held**
SIC: 3714 Steering mechanisms, motor ve-
hicle

(PA)=Parent Co (HQ)=Headquarters (DH)=Div Headquarters
✿ = New Business established in last 2 years

2019 Harris Directory of
Mississippi Manufacturers

127

GEOGRAPHIC SECTION

Moselle - Jones County (G-3455)

Moselle
Jones County

(G-3455)
BURR CREEK SCREEN PRINTING
179 Stewart Dr (39459-9599)
PHONE.................................601 297-2853
Michelle Bell, *Principal*
EMP: 2
SALES (est): 111.6K **Privately Held**
SIC: 2752 Commercial printing, lithographic

(G-3456)
COMPOSITE FBRICATION GROUP LLC
26 Dean Anderson Rd (39459-9777)
PHONE.................................601 549-1789
Judith Riddle, *Mng Member*
Grant Riddle,
▼ EMP: 2
SALES: 1MM **Privately Held**
SIC: 3441 7389 Fabricated structural metal;

(G-3457)
DIXIE WELDING SERVICE INC
608 R V Lindley Rd (39459-9416)
PHONE.................................601 268-6949
Barney L Poole, *Principal*
EMP: 1
SALES (est): 54K **Privately Held**
SIC: 7692 Welding repair

(G-3458)
M & M CHASSIS SHOP LLC
442 Old Progress Rd (39459-9726)
PHONE.................................601 310-6078
Brian Mooney,
Marla Mooney,
EMP: 3
SALES (est): 66.9K **Privately Held**
SIC: 7692 7389 Automotive welding;

(G-3459)
RIVER RADS DRECTIONAL DRLG LLC
3078 Highway 11 (39459)
PHONE.................................601 778-7179
David M Murray, *Principal*
EMP: 23
SALES (corp-wide): 1MM **Privately Held**
SIC: 1381 Directional drilling oil & gas wells
PA: River & Roads Directional Drilling Llc
3616 Industrial Blvd
Laurel MS 39440
601 778-7179

(G-3460)
SOUTHERN HENS INC
327 Moselle Seminary Rd (39459-8935)
P.O. Box 8000 (39459-8000)
PHONE.................................601 582-2262
Ken Primm, *President*
Bob Kenney, *President*
John Comino, *General Mgr*
Mark Kaminsky, *Treasurer*
Randy Sanford, *Sales Executive*
EMP: 600
SQ FT: 152,000
SALES (est): 153.2MM **Privately Held**
SIC: 3556 Meat processing machinery

(G-3461)
SUPERIOR MFG GROUP INC
Also Called: No Trax
133 Superior Dr (39459-8913)
PHONE.................................601 544-8119
Jim Wood, *Principal*
▼ EMP: 3
SALES (corp-wide): 1.7B **Privately Held**
SIC: 3083 Plastic finished products, laminated
HQ: Superior Manufacturing Group, Inc.
5655 W 73rd St
Bedford Park IL 60638
708 458-4600

(G-3462)
SUPERIOR MFG GROUP INC
133 Superior Dr (39459-8913)
PHONE.................................601 544-8119
Kyle Miller, *Branch Mgr*
EMP: 80
SALES (corp-wide): 1.7B **Privately Held**
WEB: www.notrax.com
SIC: 3069 2273 Mats or matting, rubber; carpets & rugs
HQ: Superior Manufacturing Group, Inc.
5655 W 73rd St
Bedford Park IL 60638
708 458-4600

(G-3463)
SWEETWATER STUDIOS INC
318 Cook Rd (39459-9682)
PHONE.................................601 584-8035
John Whitt, *President*
Kimberly Whitt, *Vice Pres*
EMP: 2 EST: 1979
SALES (est): 175.7K **Privately Held**
SIC: 3231 Stained glass: made from purchased glass

(G-3464)
WILLIAM KILGORE
702 Sanford Rd (39459-9580)
PHONE.................................601 582-3702
EMP: 1
SALES (est): 70K **Privately Held**
SIC: 2521 Mfg Wood Office Furniture

Moss Point
Jackson County

(G-3465)
ACCU-FAB AND CONSTRUCTION INC
5313 Mirror Lake Rd (39562-7034)
PHONE.................................228 475-0082
Paul A Bosarge, *President*
Janet M Bosargee, *Treasurer*
EMP: 40
SQ FT: 40,000
SALES: 6.5MM **Privately Held**
SIC: 3441 1629 Building components, structural steel; industrial plant construction

(G-3466)
AZZ INCORPORATED
Also Called: Automatic Processing Co
4212 Dutch Bayou Rd (39563-9537)
P.O. Box 8580 (39562-0009)
PHONE.................................228 475-0342
Phillip Vance, *Project Mgr*
Rick Pribanic, *Manager*
EMP: 12
SALES (corp-wide): 927MM **Publicly Held**
WEB: www.aztecgalvanizing.com
SIC: 3699 3547 3479 Electrical equipment & supplies; galvanizing lines (rolling mill equipment); painting, coating & hot dipping
PA: Azz Inc.
3100 W 7th St Ste 500
Fort Worth TX 76107
817 810-0095

(G-3467)
B AND P CSTOME META L FBRCTION
14036 Highway 613 (39562-9145)
PHONE.................................228 474-0097
EMP: 2
SALES (est): 63.9K **Privately Held**
SIC: 3999 Manufacturing industries

(G-3468)
BAKERS AUTO MACHINE & RAD SP
Also Called: Bakers Automotive Machine Shop
4512 Main St (39563-3938)
PHONE.................................228 474-1222
Tim Baker, *President*
EMP: 4
SQ FT: 3,000

SALES (est): 400K **Privately Held**
SIC: 7538 7692 Engine repair; welding repair

(G-3469)
BELZONA MISSISSIPPI INC
9720 Highway 63 Ste A (39562-8867)
PHONE.................................228 475-1110
Maurice Nulta, *President*
EMP: 1
SALES (est): 162K **Privately Held**
SIC: 2851 Epoxy coatings

(G-3470)
BOO ENTERPRISES LLC
4016 Rosa Ln (39563-9616)
PHONE.................................228 475-8929
Darryl Nettles, *Principal*
EMP: 2
SALES (est): 67K **Privately Held**
SIC: 2331 T-shirts & tops, women's: made from purchased materials

(G-3471)
BP AMERICA PRODUCTION COMPANY
6800 Stennis Blvd (39562-7609)
P.O. Box 5, Grand Chenier LA (70643-0005)
PHONE.................................228 762-3996
Joseph Zurovec, *Safety Mgr*
Steven Richardson, *Manager*
EMP: 26
SALES (corp-wide): 298.7B **Privately Held**
WEB: www.firstchurchtulsa.org
SIC: 1311 4613 Crude petroleum production; refined petroleum pipelines
HQ: Bp America Production Company
501 Westlake Park Blvd
Houston TX 77079
281 366-2000

(G-3472)
BP CORPORATION NORTH AMER INC
Also Called: BP Pascagoula Gas Proc Plant
6800 Stennis Blvd (39562-7609)
PHONE.................................228 712-3500
Stephen Richardson, *Engineer*
Richard Rose, *Manager*
EMP: 30
SALES (corp-wide): 298.7B **Privately Held**
WEB: www.bpamoco.com
SIC: 1311 Natural gas production
HQ: Bp Corporation North America Inc.
501 Westlake Park Blvd
Houston TX 77079
281 366-2000

(G-3473)
CENTERPOINT ENERGY INC
17717 Highway 63 (39562-8509)
PHONE.................................228 588-2977
EMP: 10
SALES (corp-wide): 7.4B **Publicly Held**
SIC: 4924 1382 Natural Gas Distribution Oil/Gas Exploration Services
PA: Centerpoint Energy, Inc.
1111 Louisiana St Ste 264
Houston TX 77002
713 207-1111

(G-3474)
CITY SPORTS CENTER
Also Called: Can't Miss Embroidery
3631 Main St (39563-5154)
PHONE.................................228 474-2033
Charlotte Carpenter, *President*
Ralph Carpenter, *Corp Secy*
EMP: 8 EST: 1969
SQ FT: 10,500
SALES (est): 744.3K **Privately Held**
SIC: 2395 Embroidery products, except schiffli machine

(G-3475)
COMPUTER WORKS LLC
4006 Kreole Ave B (39563-5831)
PHONE.................................228 696-8889
Jeffery Richmond,
EMP: 2

SALES (est): 100K **Privately Held**
SIC: 7372 7378 Operating systems computer software; computer maintenance & repair

(G-3476)
DELTA INDUSTRIES INC
8207 Old Stage Rd (39562-9753)
PHONE.................................228 475-2419
Jim Goudie, *Branch Mgr*
EMP: 2
SALES (corp-wide): 100.3MM **Privately Held**
SIC: 5211 3273 Cement; ready-mixed concrete
PA: Delta Industries, Inc.
100 W Woodrow Wilson Ave
Jackson MS 39213
601 354-3801

(G-3477)
FAST FLOW PUMPS
9700 Highway 63 (39562-8867)
PHONE.................................228 475-2468
Steve Pemderton, *Owner*
Jordan Dupree, *Prdtn Mgr*
Eric Perez, *Sales Engr*
Mike Earle, *Mktg Dir*
Andrew Eaton, *Manager*
▼ EMP: 9
SALES (est): 1.2MM **Privately Held**
SIC: 3561 Pumps & pumping equipment

(G-3478)
G&K FABRICATION & TRAILER REPR
Also Called: G&B Trailers
11205 Lily Orchard Rd (39562-7490)
P.O. Box 1307, Escatawpa (39552-1307)
PHONE.................................228 249-6336
EMP: 1
SALES: 29.2K **Privately Held**
SIC: 7692 Steel Welding And Fabrication

(G-3479)
HJ NORRIS LLC (PA)
9720b Highway 63 (39562-8867)
PHONE.................................228 217-6704
Rosemary Walker, *Mng Member*
Huey Walker,
Justin Walker,
EMP: 9
SQ FT: 3,000
SALES: 2.5MM **Privately Held**
SIC: 1711 1623 1099 Plumbing contractors; oil & gas pipeline construction; aluminum & beryllium ores mining

(G-3480)
HORIZON SHIPBUILDING INC
Also Called: Metal Shark
17629 Highway 613 (39562-6106)
PHONE.................................251 824-1660
Travis R Short Sr, *President*
Mickey Cook, *Vice Pres*
Ron Gunter, *Vice Pres*
Shirl Manche, *Warehouse Mgr*
▲ EMP: 244
SALES (est): 61.1MM
SALES (corp-wide): 153.3MM **Privately Held**
WEB: www.horizonshipbuilding.com
SIC: 3731 Shipbuilding & repairing
PA: Gravois Aluminum Boats, Llc
6814 E Admiral Doyle Dr
Jeanerette LA 70544
337 364-0777

(G-3481)
INTERNTNAL WLDG FBRICATION INC
11401 Highway 63 (39562-7478)
P.O. Box 193, Hurley (39555-0193)
PHONE.................................228 474-9353
Beth Ray, *President*
Keith Ray, *Vice Pres*
EMP: 50
SQ FT: 11,000
SALES: 14MM **Privately Held**
SIC: 3441 Fabricated structural metal

2019 Harris Directory of
Mississippi Manufacturers

128

▲ = Import ▼ =Export
◆ =Import/Export

GEOGRAPHIC SECTION

Mount Olive - Covington County (G-3511)

(G-3482)
J L MCCOOL CONTRACTORS INC
11700 Highway 613 (39562-7991)
P.O. Box 1765, Pascagoula (39568-1765)
PHONE..................................228 769-9771
Richard D McCool, *President*
EMP: 15
SQ FT: 250
SALES (est): 1.2MM **Privately Held**
SIC: 1721 3669 1799 Pavement marking contractor; transportation signaling devices; sign installation & maintenance

(G-3483)
LEGACY VULCAN LLC
5500 Hwy 613 (39563)
PHONE..................................228 474-1414
Don Fender, *Manager*
EMP: 1 **Publicly Held**
WEB: www.vulcanmaterials.com
SIC: 3273 Ready-mixed concrete
HQ: Legacy Vulcan, Llc
1200 Urban Center Dr
Vestavia AL 35242
205 298-3000

(G-3484)
LYNN HOLLIS REBEL CABINETS
7109 E Central Park Dr (39562-9444)
PHONE..................................228 588-2572
EMP: 1
SALES (est): 53.7K **Privately Held**
SIC: 2434 Wood kitchen cabinets

(G-3485)
MATCO INDUSTRIES LLC
10950 Highway 614 (39562-6336)
PHONE..................................228 218-9813
Matthew Byrd, *President*
EMP: 1
SALES (est): 45.5K **Privately Held**
SIC: 3999 Manufacturing industries

(G-3486)
MITCHELL BUCKHALTER
Also Called: Precision Automotive Machine
2908 Jr Davis Rd (39562-7129)
PHONE..................................228 588-2040
Mitchell Buckhalter, *Owner*
Susanne Buckhalter, *Vice Pres*
EMP: 3
SALES: 146K **Privately Held**
SIC: 3599 Machine shop, jobbing & repair

(G-3487)
MITCHELLS MACHINE SHOP
19002 Highway 63 (39562-8494)
PHONE..................................228 588-2040
Mitchell Buckhalter, *Principal*
EMP: 2
SALES (est): 140K **Privately Held**
SIC: 3599 Machine shop, jobbing & repair

(G-3488)
MOSS POINT EXPRESS
4130 Main St (39563-4177)
PHONE..................................228 475-4370
Meim Thai, *Principal*
EMP: 2
SALES (est): 113.6K **Privately Held**
SIC: 2741 Miscellaneous publishing

(G-3489)
NEW HORIZON INC
9749 Donchester Cir (39562-8063)
PHONE..................................228 474-9918
EMP: 2
SALES: 30K **Privately Held**
SIC: 3751 Mfg Motorcycles/Bicycles

(G-3490)
NORTHROP GRUMMAN SYSTEMS CORP
Northrop Grmman Arpace Systems
8319 Avtech Pkwy (39563-9399)
PHONE..................................228 474-3700
Anthony Hatcher, *Sales Mgr*
Berry Elliot, *Manager*
EMP: 99 **Publicly Held**
SIC: 3812 3761 3721 Search & navigation equipment; guided missiles & space vehicles; aircraft

HQ: Northrop Grumman Systems Corporation
2980 Fairview Park Dr
Falls Church VA 22042
703 280-2900

(G-3491)
NSC TECHNOLOGIES LLC
4519 Jefferson Ave Ste A (39563-5211)
PHONE..................................251 338-0725
Belinda Hinton, *Branch Mgr*
EMP: 10
SALES (corp-wide): 14.9MM **Privately Held**
SIC: 7361 3731 Employment agencies; shipbuilding & repairing
PA: Nsc Technologies, Llc
500 Crawford St Ste 401
Portsmouth VA 23704
866 672-2677

(G-3492)
OMEGA PROTEIN CORPORATION
5735 Elder Ferry Rd (39563-9501)
PHONE..................................228 475-1252
Tom Reichardt, *General Mgr*
Wanda Davis, *Purchasing*
Marty Triplett, *QC Mgr*
Jeff Blaylock, *Manager*
EMP: 200
SALES (corp-wide): 268.6MM **Privately Held**
WEB: www.omegaproteininc.com
SIC: 2077 2092 2074 Fish meal, except as animal feed; fish oil; fresh or frozen packaged fish; cottonseed oil mills
HQ: Omega Protein Corporation
610 Menhaden Rd
Reedville VA 22539
804 453-6262

(G-3493)
OMEGA SHIPYARD INC
5659 Elder Ferry Rd (39563-9533)
PHONE..................................228 475-9052
Michael Wilson, *President*
EMP: 30
SALES (est): 4.1MM **Privately Held**
SIC: 3731 Shipbuilding & repairing

(G-3494)
PERSONAL TOUCH STONE
6321 Gavin Hamilton Rd (39562-9322)
P.O. Box 893, Hurley (39555-0893)
PHONE..................................228 219-3359
Dalton Gregory Morrison, *Owner*
EMP: 6
SALES: 200K **Privately Held**
SIC: 3281 Granite, cut & shaped

(G-3495)
PRECISION PRODUCTS INC
6500 Shortcut Rd (39563-6477)
PHONE..................................228 475-7400
Kenneth Steiner, *President*
Debbie Steiner, *Treasurer*
EMP: 18
SQ FT: 16,000
SALES: 3.2MM **Privately Held**
SIC: 3599 3441 Machine shop, jobbing & repair; fabricated structural metal

(G-3496)
PROGRESSIVE ATMS
10000 Saracennia Rd (39562-7813)
PHONE..................................228 475-7234
EMP: 1
SALES (est): 76K **Privately Held**
SIC: 3578 Mfg Calculating Equipment

(G-3497)
ROMAR OFFSHORE WLDG SVCS LLC
6524 Shortcut Rd (39563-6477)
P.O. Box 5539 (39563-1539)
PHONE..................................228 475-4220
Marcus Hennis, *Engineer*
Mark R Fletcher, *Mng Member*
Rodney Ellis,
EMP: 6
SALES (est): 1.4MM **Privately Held**
SIC: 7692 Welding repair

(G-3498)
SIMPLE SOLUTIONS
7004 Bentwood Dr (39562-6317)
PHONE..................................228 588-9509
Barry Langley, *Principal*
EMP: 2
SALES (est): 205.6K **Privately Held**
WEB: www.ssolutionsonline.com
SIC: 7372 7378 Prepackaged software; computer maintenance & repair

(G-3499)
SOUTHERN CABINET & WOODWORK
Also Called: South Coast Architectural
6312 Shortcut Rd (39563-6471)
P.O. Box 5308 (39563-1308)
PHONE..................................228 475-0912
Brian Harmon, *President*
Pat Lambert, *Corp Secy*
EMP: 25
SQ FT: 23,000
SALES (est): 3.2MM **Privately Held**
SIC: 2434 2431 1751 Wood kitchen cabinets; millwork; cabinet & finish carpentry

(G-3500)
STRINGER RANDAL
Also Called: Rls Transport and Welding Svc
7402 Frank Griffin Rd (39563)
PHONE..................................228 623-0037
Randal Stringer, *Owner*
EMP: 1
SALES (est): 44.4K **Privately Held**
SIC: 7549 7692 Towing, mobile homes; welding repair

(G-3501)
TAMPA SIGN CO
5625 Grierson St (39563-4623)
PHONE..................................228 474-1945
Mel Hatampa, *Owner*
EMP: 3
SQ FT: 1,500
SALES (est): 140.4K **Privately Held**
SIC: 3993 Signs & advertising specialties

(G-3502)
TINDALL CORPORATION
11450 Saracennia Rd (39562-6786)
PHONE..................................228 246-0798
Jeff Woodruff, *Manager*
EMP: 130
SALES (corp-wide): 374.9MM **Privately Held**
WEB: www.tindallcorp.com
SIC: 3272 Concrete products, precast
PA: Tindall Corporation
3076 N Blackstock Rd
Spartanburg SC 29301
864 576-3230

(G-3503)
TURNER FLY RODS LLC
Also Called: Turner Bamboo Fly Rods
8005 Pecan Ridge Dr (39562-6101)
PHONE..................................228 623-6475
Gary Turner, *Co-Owner*
EMP: 2
SALES (est): 98.7K **Privately Held**
SIC: 3949 Rods & rod parts, fishing

(G-3504)
VT HALTER MARINE INC
5801 Elder Ferry Rd (39563-9613)
P.O. Box 1328, Pascagoula (39568-1328)
PHONE..................................228 475-1211
Fax: 228 474-5707
EMP: 150 **Privately Held**
SIC: 3731 3732 Shipbuilding/Repairing Boatbuilding/Repairing
HQ: Vt Halter Marine, Inc.
900 Bayou Casotte Pkwy
Pascagoula MS 39581
228 696-6888

(G-3505)
VT HALTER MARINE INC
Also Called: Moss Point Marine
7801 Trinity Dr (39562-6458)
PHONE..................................228 712-2278
Ralph Havard, *Principal*
EMP: 175

SALES (corp-wide): 4.8B **Privately Held**
SIC: 3731 3732 Shipbuilding & repairing; boat building & repairing
HQ: Vt Halter Marine, Inc.
900 Bayou Casotte Pkwy
Pascagoula MS 39581
228 696-6888

(G-3506)
WESCO GAS & WELDING SUPPLY INC
3830 Highway 63 (39563-6455)
P.O. Box 10456, Mobile AL (36610-0456)
PHONE..................................228 475-1955
Brett Williams, *Branch Mgr*
EMP: 6
SALES (corp-wide): 38.1MM **Privately Held**
WEB: www.wescoweld.com
SIC: 5084 5085 2813 Welding machinery & equipment; welding supplies; acetylene
PA: Wesco Gas & Welding Supply, Inc.
940 N Dr M L King Jr Dr Martin L
Prichard AL 36610
251 457-8681

(G-3507)
WILLIAMS JP MCH & FABRICATION
Also Called: Williams J P Mch & Fabrication
7206 Grierson St (39563-4916)
PHONE..................................228 474-1099
Josh Williams, *President*
EMP: 8
SALES (est): 1MM **Privately Held**
SIC: 3599 Machine shop, jobbing & repair

(G-3508)
WILLIAMS MACHINE WORKS INC (PA)
5624 Main St (39563-2252)
P.O. Box 8640 (39562-0010)
PHONE..................................228 475-7651
David C Hicks, *President*
EMP: 17
SQ FT: 10,000
SALES (est): 1.3MM **Privately Held**
SIC: 3599 3441 Machine shop, jobbing & repair; fabricated structural metal

---

Mound Bayou
Bolivar County

(G-3509)
DELTA MUNICIPAL ENERGY INC
Also Called: Delta Municipal Energy Group
404 Holt St (38762-9759)
PHONE..................................800 217-1519
Darryl Johnson Sr, *Ch of Bd*
Ellsworth James, *Principal*
Larry Haywood Sr, *Treasurer*
EMP: 20
SALES (est): 746.9K **Privately Held**
SIC: 3612 Transformers, except electric

Mount Olive
Covington County

(G-3510)
C5 TRUCKING LLC
183 J D Herrington Rd (39119-5321)
PHONE..................................601 797-9335
Truitt D Crawford, *Principal*
EMP: 1
SALES (est): 63.6K **Privately Held**
SIC: 4212 3131 0191 Local trucking, without storage; quarters; general farms, primarily crop

(G-3511)
T S CAR PORTS
Also Called: T/S Car Ports
5091 Highway 49 (39119-6089)
PHONE..................................601 797-9600
Detrich Thompson, *Owner*
Rebecca Thompson, *Owner*
EMP: 2
SQ FT: 9,900

Mount Pleasant - Marshall County (G-3512)

GEOGRAPHIC SECTION

SALES (est): 232.2K **Privately Held**
SIC: 7299 2531 Porter service; picnic tables or benches, park

---

Mount Pleasant
Marshall County

(G-3512)
PALLET SOURCE INC (PA)
228 Mount Pleasant Rd (38649)
P.O. Box 36 (38649-0036)
PHONE................................662 851-3118
William D Schaefer, *President*
Ronda Mitchell, *General Mgr*
Brandon Mitchell, *Vice Pres*
John S Pflaumer, *Vice Pres*
EMP: 31
SQ FT: 30,000
SALES (est): 5.4MM **Privately Held**
WEB: www.palletsourceinc.com
SIC: 2448 Pallets, wood

Myrtle
Union County

(G-3513)
PROSHOP INC
Also Called: Pro Shop The
200 Dogwood Cir (38650-9209)
P.O. Box 529, Calhoun City (38916-0529)
PHONE................................662 333-7511
Jarvis Umphers, *President*
Joyce Umphers, *Admin Sec*
EMP: 6
SALES (est): 550K **Privately Held**
SIC: 3648 3812 3199 5961 Lighting equipment; search & detection systems & instruments; dog furnishings: collars, leashes, muzzles, etc.: leather; catalog & mail-order houses; sporting & athletic goods

(G-3514)
TURNER JIMMY BACKHOE DOZER SVC
1875 County Road 478 (38650-9665)
PHONE................................662 988-2701
Jimmy Turner, *Owner*
EMP: 2
SALES (est): 251.2K **Privately Held**
SIC: 1623 3599 Sewer line construction; machine shop, jobbing & repair

---

Natchez
Adams County

(G-3515)
1 A LIFESAFER INC
747 Highway 61 N (39120-8411)
PHONE................................800 634-3077
EMP: 1
SALES (corp-wide): 4.3MM **Privately Held**
SIC: 3829 Measuring & controlling devices
PA: 1 A Lifesafer, Inc.
4290 Glendale Milford Rd
Blue Ash OH 45242
513 651-9560

(G-3516)
AAA PORTABLE BUILDINGS LLC
658 Highway 61 N (39120-9102)
PHONE................................601 445-4034
Brandon Atkins,
EMP: 1 EST: 1974
SALES (est): 167.6K **Privately Held**
SIC: 3448 Buildings, portable: prefabricated metal

(G-3517)
ALDRIDGE OPERATING CO LLC
151 Providence Rd (39120-9364)
P.O. Box 629 (39121-0629)
PHONE................................601 446-5585
Courtney G Aldridge,
EMP: 2
SALES (est): 797.2K **Privately Held**
SIC: 1382 Oil & gas exploration services

(G-3518)
ALLEN PETROLEUM SERVICE INC
Also Called: Allen Operating Company
521 Main St Ste M1 (39120-3369)
P.O. Box 1364 (39121-1364)
PHONE................................601 442-3662
Woodrow W Allen, *President*
EMP: 2
SALES (est): 200K **Privately Held**
SIC: 1382 Oil & gas exploration services

(G-3519)
ALPINE WELL SERVICE INC
144 Providence Rd (39120-8121)
PHONE................................601 442-0021
Stanley Parks, *President*
Debra Parks, *President*
Deborah Parks, *Corp Secy*
EMP: 9
SALES (est): 660K **Privately Held**
SIC: 1389 Oil field services

(G-3520)
ANDERSON OIL COMPANY INC
679 Highway 61 N (39120-8442)
P.O. Box 2216 (39121-2216)
PHONE................................601 442-2960
Jack Cox, *President*
Patsy Cox, *Corp Secy*
EMP: 3
SQ FT: 2,100
SALES (est): 420K **Privately Held**
SIC: 1311 Crude petroleum production; natural gas production

(G-3521)
AUTOMOTIVE MACHINE COMPANY
30 Saint Catherine St (39120-3612)
P.O. Box 772 (39121-0772)
PHONE................................601 442-0422
Curtis Wilson, *President*
EMP: 6
SQ FT: 4,900
SALES (est): 742.2K **Privately Held**
SIC: 3599 Machine shop, jobbing & repair

(G-3522)
BAKER PETROLITE
Also Called: Baker Hughes
17 Marion E Syfarth Sr Rd (39120-4429)
PHONE................................601 442-2401
Gary Jones, *Manager*
EMP: 4
SALES (corp-wide): 121.6B **Publicly Held**
SIC: 2819 Industrial inorganic chemicals
HQ: Baker Petrolite
2121 W Mary St
Garden City KS 67846

(G-3523)
BANKINGFORMSCOM INC
322a Highland Blvd (39120-4611)
P.O. Box 17728 (39122-7728)
PHONE................................601 445-2245
Mark Smitherman, *President*
Dixie Smitherman, *Vice Pres*
EMP: 5
SQ FT: 4,000
SALES (est): 550K **Privately Held**
WEB: www.smithermanprinting.com
SIC: 2752 Commercial printing, offset

(G-3524)
BAYOU OIL FILL SUPPLY LLC
242 Highway 61 S (39120-5219)
PHONE................................601 446-6284
John Hardie, *Principal*
EMP: 2
SALES (est): 114.1K **Privately Held**
SIC: 1389 Oil field services

(G-3525)
BE JOYFUL SIGNS
305 S Wall St (39120-3429)
PHONE................................601 540-6602
Shannon Jex, *Principal*
EMP: 1
SALES (est): 46K **Privately Held**
SIC: 3993 Signs & advertising specialties

(G-3526)
BEACH HARVEY & SON LOGGING
398 Greenfield Rd (39120-7933)
PHONE................................601 446-5771
Harvey Beach Jr, *President*
Linda Beach, *Corp Secy*
EMP: 15
SQ FT: 5,000
SALES: 1MM **Privately Held**
SIC: 2411 Logging camps & contractors

(G-3527)
BELLE EXPLORATION INC
280 Highland Blvd (39120-4609)
P.O. Box 952 (39121-0952)
PHONE................................601 442-6648
Alton Ogden Jr, *President*
Jeff Burkhalter, *Vice Pres*
EMP: 1
SQ FT: 5,000
SALES (est): 200.2K
SALES (corp-wide): 2MM **Privately Held**
SIC: 1382 Oil & gas exploration services
PA: Belle Oil, Inc.
280 Highland Blvd
Natchez MS 39120
601 442-6648

(G-3528)
BELLE OIL INC (PA)
280 Highland Blvd (39120-4609)
P.O. Box 952 (39121-0952)
PHONE................................601 442-6648
Alton Ogden Jr, *President*
EMP: 7
SQ FT: 5,000
SALES: 2MM **Privately Held**
SIC: 1311 Crude petroleum production

(G-3529)
BERYL JONES
Also Called: Bonnie's Babies & Ladies
102 Catalpa Dr (39120-5209)
PHONE................................601 442-4597
Beryl Jones, *Owner*
EMP: 1 EST: 1998
SALES (est): 47.5K **Privately Held**
SIC: 3942 Dolls & stuffed toys

(G-3530)
BIG JOE OIL CO INC
251 Highway 61 S (39120-5218)
P.O. Box 1087 (39121-1087)
PHONE................................601 442-5481
Noland E Biglane, *President*
Dorothy Biglane, *Corp Secy*
Joe F Fortunato, *Vice Pres*
EMP: 3
SQ FT: 3,500
SALES (est): 270K **Privately Held**
SIC: 1382 1311 Oil & gas exploration services; crude petroleum production

(G-3531)
BIG JOE OPERATING CO INC
Hwy 61 S (39120)
P.O. Box 1087 (39121-1087)
PHONE................................601 442-5481
Joe Fortunato, *President*
EMP: 2
SQ FT: 3,500
SALES (est): 232.8K **Privately Held**
SIC: 1311 Crude petroleum production

(G-3532)
BIGLANE OPERATING CO
75 Melrose St (39120)
P.O. Box 966 (39121-0966)
PHONE................................601 442-2783
James M Biglane, *President*
Nancy Biglane, *Vice Pres*
EMP: 3 EST: 1962
SALES (est): 399.2K **Privately Held**
SIC: 1311 Crude petroleum production

(G-3533)
BLUFF CITY POST NEWSPAPER
719 Franklin St (39120-3313)
P.O. Box 681 (39121-0681)
PHONE................................601 446-5218
William H Terrell, *Owner*
Danielle Terrell, *Co-Owner*
Flora Terrell, *Co-Owner*
EMP: 4

SALES (est): 177.4K **Privately Held**
SIC: 2711 Newspapers

(G-3534)
BLUFFS & BAYOU MAGAZINE
423 Main St Ste 7 (39120-3463)
PHONE................................601 442-6847
Cheryl Morace, *Owner*
EMP: 1
SALES (est): 82K **Privately Held**
SIC: 2721 Magazines: publishing & printing

(G-3535)
BOB BERTOLET
517 S Canal St (39120-3481)
P.O. Box 2090 (39121-2090)
PHONE................................601 442-0424
Bob Bertolet, *Owner*
EMP: 3
SQ FT: 1,500
SALES (est): 243.4K **Privately Held**
SIC: 1382 Oil & gas exploration services

(G-3536)
BOOKPRO PUBLISHING COMPANY
705 Washington St (39120-3544)
PHONE................................769 208-6806
Dan M Gibson, *Principal*
EMP: 1
SALES (est): 44.3K **Privately Held**
SIC: 2741 Miscellaneous publishing

(G-3537)
BOONE NEWSPAPERS (PA)
Also Called: Natchez Democrat
503 N Canal St (39120-2902)
P.O. Box 1447 (39121-1447)
PHONE................................601 442-9101
James B Boone, *Ch of Bd*
Todd Carpenter, *President*
EMP: 50
SQ FT: 12,000
SALES (est): 2.9MM **Privately Held**
WEB: www.shopnatchez.com
SIC: 2711 2791 2752 Newspapers, publishing & printing; typesetting; commercial printing, lithographic

(G-3538)
BRADFORD ENTERPRISES
3 James Brown Ave (39120-8706)
PHONE................................601 442-2339
Luther Bradford, *Owner*
EMP: 4
SALES (est): 137.8K **Privately Held**
SIC: 3823 4213 Data loggers, industrial process type; heavy hauling

(G-3539)
BROWN BOTTLING GROUP INC
Also Called: Pepsico
265 Liberty Rd (39120)
PHONE................................601 442-5805
Ricky Ivey, *Manager*
EMP: 1
SALES (corp-wide): 149.7MM **Privately Held**
SIC: 2086 5499 5046 Bottled & canned soft drinks; carbonated soft drinks, bottled & canned; beverage stores; soda fountain fixtures, except refrigerated
PA: Brown Bottling Group, Inc.
591 Highland Colony Pkwy
Ridgeland MS 39157
601 607-3011

(G-3540)
BROWNING OIL TOOLS INC
Also Called: Scarborough Oilfield Supply Co
6 Ridgeway Rd (39120-5253)
PHONE................................601 442-1800
James C Browning, *President*
Fred Rogers, *Corp Secy*
Frank Grantham, *Vice Pres*
Doug Fisher, *Sales Mgr*
Billy Smith, *Office Mgr*
EMP: 35
SQ FT: 24,500
SALES (est): 9.6MM **Privately Held**
SIC: 5084 3561 3533 Pumps & pumping equipment; pumps, oil well & field; oil & gas field machinery

---

2019 Harris Directory of
Mississippi Manufacturers

130

▲ = Import ▼=Export
◆ =Import/Export

GEOGRAPHIC SECTION

Natchez - Adams County (G-3570)

(G-3541)
BYRNE FURN CO & SAWMILL SVCS
Also Called: Byrne Sawmill Services
18 Old Devereaux St (39120-3636)
P.O. Box 1302 (39121-1302)
PHONE.................................601 442-7363
Joseph Byrne, *President*
Donald Byrne, *Vice Pres*
EMP: 7
SQ FT: 4,800
SALES: 800K **Privately Held**
WEB: www.byrnefurniture.com
SIC: 2421 Sawmills & planing mills, general

(G-3542)
CALLON OFFSHORE PRODUCTION
200 N Canal St (39120-3212)
P.O. Box 1287 (39121-1287)
PHONE.................................601 442-1601
Tom Schwager, *Vice Pres*
EMP: 65 EST: 1983
SALES (est): 3.6MM
SALES (corp-wide): 587.6MM **Publicly Held**
WEB: www.callon.com
SIC: 1311 1382 Crude petroleum production; natural gas production; oil & gas exploration services
PA: Callon Petroleum Company
2000 W Sam Houston Pkwy S
Houston TX 77042
281 589-5200

(G-3543)
CAND M PUPWOOD
100 Redd Loop Rd (39120-2139)
PHONE.................................601 445-9200
Jake Morris, *Owner*
EMP: 1 EST: 2009
SALES (est): 71.8K **Privately Held**
SIC: 2621 Pressed pulp products

(G-3544)
CARPENTER NEWSMEDIA LLC
503 N Canal St (39120-2902)
P.O. Box 1447 (39121-1447)
PHONE.................................601 445-3618
Todd H Carpenter, *Manager*
Todd Carpenter, *Manager*
EMP: 1 EST: 2016
SALES (est): 47.5K **Privately Held**
SIC: 2711 Commercial printing & newspaper publishing combined

(G-3545)
CENTRAL MACHINE SHOP
639 Highway 61 S (39120-8685)
PHONE.................................601 446-8732
Robert Smith, *Owner*
EMP: 1
SALES (est): 96.6K **Privately Held**
SIC: 3599 Machine shop, jobbing & repair

(G-3546)
CHOPS WRECKER & WELDING SVC
283 Lower Woodville Rd (39120-4467)
P.O. Box 18004 (39122-8004)
PHONE.................................601 442-0092
Michael Wheeler, *Owner*
EMP: 1
SALES (est): 72K **Privately Held**
SIC: 7692 7549 Welding repair; towing service, automotive

(G-3547)
COASTAL PETROLEUM SERVICES INC
138 Col John Pitchford Pa (39120-5291)
P.O. Box 17733 (39122-7733)
PHONE.................................601 446-5888
Fax: 601 446-5996
EMP: 20
SQ FT: 1,800
SALES (est): 2.1MM **Privately Held**
SIC: 1381 4212 Drilling Oil And Gas Wells, Nsk

(G-3548)
COCA-COLA REFRESHMENTS USA INC
191 Devereaux Dr (39120-3754)
PHONE.................................601 442-1641
EMP: 7
SALES (corp-wide): 31.8B **Publicly Held**
SIC: 2086 Bottled & canned soft drinks
HQ: Coca-Cola Refreshments Usa, Inc.
2500 Windy Ridge Pkwy Se
Atlanta GA 30339
770 989-3000

(G-3549)
CONSOLIDATED GULF SERVICES LLC
1117 Main St (39120-3643)
P.O. Box 822 (39121-0822)
PHONE.................................601 446-5992
Michael Rinehart, *Manager*
EMP: 3
SALES (est): 98.5K **Privately Held**
SIC: 1389 Construction, repair & dismantling services; excavating slush pits & cellars; lease tanks, oil field: erecting, cleaning & repairing

(G-3550)
COOK LAWN & TRACTOR LLC
Also Called: Kubota Authorized Dealer
114 Northgate Rd (39120-9161)
PHONE.................................601 445-0718
William S Cook Jr, *Mng Member*
EMP: 6
SALES (est): 1.1MM **Privately Held**
SIC: 3524 5083 Lawn & garden equipment; farm & garden machinery

(G-3551)
COTTONPORT HARDWOODS LLC
209 State St (39120-3470)
PHONE.................................601 442-9888
A V Davis, *Administration*
EMP: 2
SALES (est): 60.7K **Privately Held**
SIC: 2499 Wood products

(G-3552)
CRTNEY G ALDRIDGE PTRO GLOGIST
Also Called: Aldridge Operating Co.
316 Main St (39120-3462)
P.O. Box 629 (39121-0629)
PHONE.................................601 446-5585
Courtney G Aldridge,
EMP: 2
SALES (est): 148.1K **Privately Held**
SIC: 1382 Oil & gas exploration services

(G-3553)
DARRELLS SCREEN PRINTING
175 Highway 61 S Ste 8 (39120-5285)
PHONE.................................601 653-6924
Darrell Hash, *Principal*
EMP: 6
SALES (est): 502.7K **Privately Held**
SIC: 2759 Commercial printing

(G-3554)
DELTA BIOFUELS INC
151 L E Barry Rd (39120-6201)
PHONE.................................601 442-5330
Clint Vegas, *President*
EMP: 14
SQ FT: 28,690
SALES (est): 2.1MM **Privately Held**
WEB: www.deltabiofuels.com
SIC: 2869 Fuels

(G-3555)
DELTA-ENERGY GROUP LLC
Also Called: Delta Energy Group
61 Carthage Point Rd (39120-4442)
PHONE.................................601 348-4610
Richard Lee, *CEO*
EMP: 1
SALES (est): 311.5K **Privately Held**
SIC: 2895 Carbon black

(G-3556)
DOZER INC
14 Minor St (39120-3035)
P.O. Box 2031 (39121-2031)
PHONE.................................601 442-1671
William T Jones Jr, *President*
William Jones, *General Mgr*
Kathy Jones, *Corp Secy*
Kathy F Jones, *Manager*
EMP: 15
SQ FT: 6,000
SALES (est): 1.5MM **Privately Held**
WEB: www.dozer.com
SIC: 1389 Construction, repair & dismantling services

(G-3557)
DUTCH ANN FOODS INC
716 Liberty Rd (39120-7914)
P.O. Box 2031 (39121-2031)
PHONE.................................601 445-4496
William T Jones Jr, *President*
EMP: 28
SQ FT: 6,000
SALES: 1.5MM **Privately Held**
SIC: 2038 2053 Frozen specialties; frozen bakery products, except bread

(G-3558)
EL TORO PRODUCTION CO INC
66 Springfield Rd (39120-8783)
PHONE.................................601 442-4159
Phillip W Vasser, *President*
Page Blackwell, *Corp Secy*
Jimmie Vasser, *Vice Pres*
EMP: 3
SQ FT: 1,000
SALES (est): 399.4K **Privately Held**
SIC: 1311 Crude petroleum production

(G-3559)
ELEVANCE NATCHEZ INC
151 L E Barry Rd (39120-6201)
PHONE.................................601 442-5330
K'Lynne Johnson, *President*
Kara Lawrence, *Corp Secy*
Mel Luetkens, *Vice Pres*
David Kelsey, *CFO*
EMP: 14 EST: 2011
SALES (est): 2.9MM **Privately Held**
SIC: 2869 Industrial organic chemicals
PA: Elevance Renewable Sciences, Inc.
2501 Davey Rd
Woodridge IL 60517

(G-3560)
ENERGY DRILLING COMPANY
413 Liberty Rd (39120-4313)
P.O. Box 905 (39121-0905)
PHONE.................................601 446-5259
John Dale IV, *President*
Pat Burns Jr, *Vice Pres*
David Cothren, *CFO*
Mike Jagneaux, *Manager*
EMP: 200
SQ FT: 5,000
SALES (est): 27.6MM **Privately Held**
WEB: www.energydrilling.com
SIC: 1381 Directional drilling oil & gas wells

(G-3561)
FREEMAN REASON LOGGING
45 Brenham Ave (39120-3022)
PHONE.................................601 446-5938
Freeman Reason, *Owner*
EMP: 1
SALES (est): 46.7K **Privately Held**
SIC: 2411 Logging camps & contractors

(G-3562)
G MARK LAFRANCIS
9 Janice Cir (39120-4340)
PHONE.................................601 442-0980
G Mark Lafrancis, *Principal*
EMP: 2
SALES (est): 111K **Privately Held**
SIC: 2741 Miscellaneous publishing

(G-3563)
GEORGE NOSSER JR
Also Called: Old River Peddler
103 Lwer Wdville Rd Ste 4 (39120)
P.O. Box 18142 (39122-8142)
PHONE.................................601 446-7998
George Nosser Jr, *Owner*

EMP: 2
SALES (est): 200K **Privately Held**
WEB: www.oldriverpeddler.com
SIC: 5192 2711 Newspapers; newspapers

(G-3564)
GREAT RIVER INDUSTRIES LLC (PA)
21 Moran Rd (39120-4074)
PHONE.................................601 442-7568
Kenny Lawson, *President*
Aaron Shermer, *Vice Pres*
Devin Evans, *Safety Mgr*
Kevin Sullivan, *Opers Staff*
Pat Powers, *Director*
▲ EMP: 5
SALES (est): 24.3MM **Privately Held**
SIC: 3449 Bars, concrete reinforcing: fabricated steel

(G-3565)
HALL MANUFACTURING LLC
Also Called: H&M Syrup
92 Mullins Rd (39120-8469)
PHONE.................................601 445-6640
Rodney D Hall, *Vice Pres*
Dale Hall,
EMP: 2
SALES (est): 98.2K **Privately Held**
SIC: 2099 Syrups

(G-3566)
HANGER PRSTHETCS & ORTHO INC
304 Highland Blvd Ste C (39120-4624)
PHONE.................................601 442-7742
David Street, *Manager*
EMP: 3
SALES (corp-wide): 1B **Publicly Held**
SIC: 5999 3842 Orthopedic & prosthesis applications; prosthetic appliances
HQ: Hanger Prosthetics & Orthotics, Inc.
10910 Domain Dr Ste 300
Austin TX 78758
512 777-3800

(G-3567)
HARBISON-FISCHER INC
24 Feltus St (39120-4243)
PHONE.................................601 442-7961
Fred Slover, *Manager*
EMP: 1
SALES (corp-wide): 1.2B **Publicly Held**
WEB: www.hfpumps.com
SIC: 3561 7699 5084 Pumps & pumping equipment; pumps & pumping equipment repair; pumps & pumping equipment
HQ: Harbison-Fischer, Inc.
901 N Crowley Rd
Crowley TX 76036
817 297-2211

(G-3568)
HEAVENLY CONFECTIONS
1106 First St (39120-2732)
PHONE.................................601 660-1986
Kira Byrd, *Principal*
EMP: 1
SALES (est): 67.9K **Privately Held**
SIC: 2053 7389 Cakes, bakery: frozen;

(G-3569)
J M JONES LUMBER COMPANY INC
1 Jones Sawmill Rd (39120-1000)
P.O. Box 1368 (39121-1368)
PHONE.................................601 442-7471
H Lee Jones Jr, *President*
Howard Jones III, *Treasurer*
Lee Jones, *Sales Staff*
▼ EMP: 120
SQ FT: 6,250
SALES (est): 15.8MM **Privately Held**
SIC: 2421 Lumber: rough, sawed or planed; kiln drying of lumber

(G-3570)
JACK BLACK OIL COMPANY INC
305 Creek Bend Rd (39120-5011)
P.O. Box 214, Sibley (39165-0214)
PHONE.................................601 442-2620
Kevin L Wilson, *President*
Becky Wilson, *Vice Pres*
Brena Willis, *Admin Sec*
EMP: 2

(PA)=Parent Co (HQ)=Headquarters (DH)=Div Headquarters
✪ = New Business established in last 2 years

2019 Harris Directory of
Mississippi Manufacturers

131

Natchez - Adams County (G-3571)

GEOGRAPHIC SECTION

SALES (est): 1MM **Privately Held**
SIC: **1381** 1389 Drilling oil & gas wells; oil & gas wells: building, repairing & dismantling

(G-3571)
JAMES BIGLANE
Also Called: D A Biglane Oil Co
75 Melrose Mntebello Pkwy (39120-4747)
P.O. Box 966 (39121-0966)
PHONE..................................601 442-2783
James Biglane, *Owner*
EMP: 2 EST: 1961
SQ FT: 10,000
SALES (est): 245.2K **Privately Held**
SIC: **1311** 0191 Crude petroleum production; natural gas production; general farms, primarily crop

(G-3572)
JOE FORTUNATO OIL PRODCR RES
111 Woodhaven Dr (39120-5256)
PHONE..................................601 442-6397
EMP: 2
SALES (est): 104.4K **Privately Held**
SIC: **1311** Crude petroleum & natural gas production

(G-3573)
JONES LUMBER CO INC
3 Dave Levite Rd (39120-3184)
PHONE..................................601 445-8206
Billy Joe Pritchett, *Manager*
EMP: 65
SALES (corp-wide): 54.3MM **Privately Held**
SIC: **2421** Planing mills
HQ: Jones Lumber Co., Inc.
16 Office Park Dr Ste 6
Hattiesburg MS 39402

(G-3574)
K C S LUMBER CO INC
3 Dave Levite Rd (39120-3184)
P.O. Box 1619, Hot Springs AR (71902-1619)
PHONE..................................601 446-8525
Marie Wilson, *Corp Secy*
EMP: 4
SQ FT: 32,500
SALES (est): 310K **Privately Held**
SIC: **2421** Lumber: rough, sawed or planed; kiln drying of lumber

(G-3575)
K F G PETROLEUM CORPORATION
118 Lwer Wdvlle Rd Unit 2 (39120)
PHONE..................................601 446-5219
Stephen Guido, *President*
Robert Kadene, *Vice Pres*
James Gilbert, *Admin Sec*
EMP: 4
SQ FT: 800
SALES (est): 380K **Privately Held**
WEB: www.kfgresources.com
SIC: **1382** Oil & gas exploration services

(G-3576)
KFG RESOURCES LTD
118 Lwer Wdvlle Rd Unit 2 (39120)
PHONE..................................601 446-5219
Stephen Guido, *President*
EMP: 2
SALES (est): 2.6MM **Privately Held**
SIC: **1382** Oil & gas exploration services

(G-3577)
KREWE OF NATCHEZ INDN YTH LDRS
14 Fatherland Rd (39120-4734)
PHONE..................................601 392-1709
Robert McNeely, *President*
Lekeshia Jones, *Consultant*
EMP: 35 EST: 2014
SALES (est): 2.2MM **Privately Held**
SIC: **3949** Indian clubs

(G-3578)
LAZARUS ARTS
Also Called: Lazarus Green Arts
55 Sgt Prentiss Dr # 103 (39120-4791)
PHONE..................................601 445-4576
Mike Lazarus, *Owner*

Kim Lazarus, *Co-Owner*
EMP: 2
SQ FT: 1,000
SALES (est): 168.4K **Privately Held**
SIC: **2759** Screen printing

(G-3579)
LEVAN INDUSTRIES
1200 Highway 61 S (39120-8617)
PHONE..................................601 446-7390
Fax: 601 446-7390
EMP: 2 EST: 2010
SALES (est): 67K **Privately Held**
SIC: **3999** Mfg Misc Products

(G-3580)
LOUISIANA WELL SERVICE CO INC
Also Called: Bell Exploration
280 Highland Blvd (39120-4609)
P.O. Box 952 (39121-0952)
PHONE..................................601 442-6648
Alton Ogden Jr, *President*
Jeff Burkhalter, *Treasurer*
EMP: 6
SALES (est): 494.3K
SALES (corp-wide): 2MM **Privately Held**
SIC: **1382** 1389 Geophysical exploration, oil & gas field; oil field services
PA: Belle Oil, Inc.
280 Highland Blvd
Natchez MS 39120
601 442-6648

(G-3581)
M&M BOOK PUBLISHING CO
9 Janice Cir (39120-4340)
PHONE..................................601 442-0980
Galen M Lafrancis, *Principal*
EMP: 1 EST: 2017
SALES (est): 40.4K **Privately Held**
SIC: **2741** Miscellaneous publishing

(G-3582)
MAGNOLIA FRAC SAND
100 State St (39120-3469)
PHONE..................................601 446-6023
Marc Godfrey, *Owner*
EMP: 6
SALES (est): 189K **Privately Held**
SIC: **1442** Construction sand & gravel

(G-3583)
MAGNOLIA MARIEE LLC
200 Main St (39120-3460)
PHONE..................................601 446-6400
Sarah W Williams, *Mng Member*
Jennifer Smith,
EMP: 2 EST: 2016
SALES (est): 90K **Privately Held**
SIC: **2335** Wedding gowns & dresses

(G-3584)
MARK WILLIAMS WELDING LLC
726 Liberty Rd (39120-7914)
PHONE..................................601 431-5324
Mark Williams,
EMP: 1
SALES (est): 30K **Privately Held**
SIC: **7692** Welding repair

(G-3585)
MCGEE WELDING LLC
106 E Franklin St (39120-3661)
PHONE..................................769 355-2339
Lawanda Green, *Principal*
EMP: 1
SALES (est): 25K **Privately Held**
SIC: **7692** Welding repair

(G-3586)
MEASON OPERATING CO
188 Highway 61 S (39120-5279)
PHONE..................................601 442-3668
J Robert Meason Jr, *President*
EMP: 15
SQ FT: 2,000
SALES (est): 1.7MM **Privately Held**
SIC: **1311** Crude petroleum production

(G-3587)
MID SOUTH SIGN COUNCIL
214 S Pearl St (39120-3421)
PHONE..................................601 446-6688
Casey Hughes, *Owner*

EMP: 1
SALES (est): 61.4K **Privately Held**
SIC: **3993** Signs & advertising specialties

(G-3588)
MISS LOU GUIDE
503 N Canal St (39120-2902)
PHONE..................................601 442-9101
EMP: 2
SALES (est): 79.6K **Privately Held**
SIC: **2711** Newspapers, publishing & printing

(G-3589)
MISS-LOU STEEL SUPPLY INC
186 N Palestine Rd (39120-9089)
P.O. Box 217, Washington (39190-0217)
PHONE..................................601 442-0846
John D Scruggs, *President*
Doug Scruggs, *Corp Secy*
EMP: 6
SQ FT: 20,900
SALES (est): 2.2MM **Privately Held**
SIC: **5051** 3316 Steel; cold finishing of steel shapes

(G-3590)
MMC MATERIALS INC
30 Feltus St (39120-4243)
PHONE..................................601 445-5641
Alonzo Evans, *Manager*
EMP: 10
SALES (corp-wide): 306.5MM **Privately Held**
WEB: www.mmcmaterials.com
SIC: **3273** Ready-mixed concrete
HQ: Mmc Materials, Inc.
1052 Highland Colony Pkwy # 201
Ridgeland MS 39157
601 898-4000

(G-3591)
MOBILE DIAGNOSTICS INC
133 Jefferson Davis Blvd (39120-5103)
PHONE..................................601 445-9895
Randall Tillman, *President*
EMP: 9
SALES (est): 910K **Privately Held**
SIC: **3841** Diagnostic apparatus, medical

(G-3592)
MODEM GUEST
201 N Pearl St (39120-3240)
PHONE..................................601 442-5202
EMP: 3
SALES (est): 192.4K **Privately Held**
SIC: **3661** Mfg Telephone/Telegraph Apparatus

(G-3593)
MURRAY PRINTING
154 E Franklin St (39120-3610)
PHONE..................................601 446-6558
Sid Murray, *Owner*
EMP: 2
SQ FT: 1,500
SALES: 150K **Privately Held**
SIC: **2752** Commercial printing, offset

(G-3594)
NATCHEZ EXPLORATION LLC
416 Main St (39120-3464)
PHONE..................................601 442-7400
John McCullough,
EMP: 2
SALES (est): 110K **Privately Held**
SIC: **1382** Oil & gas exploration services

(G-3595)
NATCHEZ NEWSPAPERS INC
503 N Canal St (39120-2902)
P.O. Box 2590, Selma AL (36702-2590)
PHONE..................................601 442-9101
Todd H Carpenter, *President*
Oseph C Davis Jr, *Corp Secy*
James B Boone Jr, *Director*
EMP: 5
SALES (est): 286.6K **Privately Held**
SIC: **2711** Newspapers

(G-3596)
NATCHEZ PRINTING CO
520 Main St (39120-3324)
P.O. Box 1165 (39121-1165)
PHONE..................................601 442-3693
Nancy Kimbrell, *President*

T Scott Kimbrell, *Corp Secy*
Jane S Kimbrell, *Vice Pres*
David Alford, *Mfg Staff*
EMP: 3
SQ FT: 4,000
SALES (est): 240K **Privately Held**
WEB: www.kimbrells.net
SIC: **2752** 2759 2789 Commercial printing, offset; letterpress printing; bookbinding & related work

(G-3597)
NATCHEZ SMOKEHOUSE & COLD STOR
1144 Liberty Rd (39120-9512)
PHONE..................................601 442-6116
Marvin Hammack, *President*
EMP: 2
SALES (est): 74K **Privately Held**
SIC: **2011** 5812 Meat packing plants; eating places

(G-3598)
NAVIDAD PETROLEUM LLC
109 Southampton Rd (39120-5254)
PHONE..................................601 442-9812
Wayne Potter, *Principal*
EMP: 2
SALES (est): 81.9K **Privately Held**
SIC: **1381** Drilling oil & gas wells

(G-3599)
NEW DAVID OIL COMPANY INC
231 Highway 61 S (39120-5218)
PHONE..................................601 442-1607
David A New Sr, *Ch of Bd*
David A New Jr, *President*
Beverly Massey, *Corp Secy*
Suzanne New, *Vice Pres*
EMP: 10
SQ FT: 10,000
SALES (est): 892.2K **Privately Held**
SIC: **1311** Crude petroleum production

(G-3600)
NICHOLES CTURE FASHION BTQ LLC
105 Brooklyn Dr (39120-2715)
PHONE..................................601 493-6469
Gwendolyn Harris,
EMP: 1
SALES (est): 49.1K **Privately Held**
SIC: **3161** Clothing & apparel carrying cases

(G-3601)
NMHG FINANCIAL SERVICES
Also Called: Hyster Capital
1258 Highway 61 S (39120-8617)
PHONE..................................601 304-0112
EMP: 1
SALES (est): 108K **Privately Held**
SIC: **3537** Mfg Industrial Trucks/Tractors

(G-3602)
OIL TOOLS & SUPPLIES INC
519 Liberty Rd (39120-7903)
P.O. Box 1021 (39121-1021)
PHONE..................................601 446-7229
Betty Blanay, *President*
EMP: 5
SALES (est): 565.1K **Privately Held**
SIC: **1389** Cleaning wells

(G-3603)
ON THE RIVER LLC
216 Linton Ave (39120-2316)
PHONE..................................601 442-7103
Ed Godfrey, *Owner*
EMP: 2
SALES (est): 179.3K **Privately Held**
SIC: **1382** 6531 Oil & gas exploration services; real estate managers

(G-3604)
OTTOS CUSTOM TRAILERS
581 Old Highway 84 No 3 (39120-8479)
PHONE..................................601 446-6469
EMP: 1
SALES (est): 93K **Privately Held**
SIC: **5599** 3714 Ret Misc Vehicles

2019 Harris Directory of
Mississippi Manufacturers

▲ = Import ▼=Export
◆ =Import/Export

GEOGRAPHIC SECTION

Natchez - Adams County (G-3635)

(G-3605)
PAR-CO DRILLING INC
144 Providence Rd (39120-8121)
P.O. Box 873 (39121-0873)
PHONE..................................601 442-6421
Stanley Parks, *President*
Deborah Parks, *Treasurer*
EMP: 2
SQ FT: 2,000
SALES (est): 267.3K **Privately Held**
SIC: 1382 Oil & gas exploration services

(G-3606)
PARADISE & ASSOCIATES INC
296 Highland Blvd (39120-4609)
P.O. Box 18939 (39122-8939)
PHONE..................................601 445-9710
David E Paradise, *President*
Robert Hill, *Opers Staff*
EMP: 9
SALES (est): 580K **Privately Held**
WEB: www.paradisefoods.net
SIC: 6531 1382 Real estate brokers & agents; geological exploration, oil & gas field

(G-3607)
PHOENIX ENERGY INC MISSISSIPPI
118 Lower Woodville Rd (39120-4448)
P.O. Box 668 (39121-0668)
PHONE..................................601 445-3200
Joseph J Ring III, *President*
William H McDonald, *Vice Pres*
EMP: 15
SQ FT: 900
SALES (est): 2.2MM **Privately Held**
SIC: 1382 Oil & gas exploration services

(G-3608)
PLEDGER PETROLEUM INC
606 Washington St (39120-3527)
PHONE..................................601 442-9871
Harris Butler, *President*
Tim Chesteen, *Vice Pres*
EMP: 2 **EST:** 1990
SALES (est): 190K **Privately Held**
SIC: 1382 Geological exploration, oil & gas field

(G-3609)
R W DELANEY CONSTRUCTION CO (PA)
155 River Terminal Rd (39120-9608)
PHONE..................................601 442-0352
Randy Irvin, *Partner*
Jimmy R Delaney, *Partner*
Clayton Delaney, *General Mgr*
EMP: 64 **EST:** 1962
SQ FT: 1,200
SALES (est): 53.9MM **Privately Held**
SIC: 1389 1542 Oil field services; nonresidential construction

(G-3610)
RADZEWICZ EXPLRATION DRLG CORP
Also Called: Redco
655 Highway 61 S (39120-8686)
PHONE..................................601 445-8659
Maurine Radzewicz, *President*
Ethel Radzewicz, *Treasurer*
EMP: 12
SALES (est): 1.4MM **Privately Held**
SIC: 1389 1382 Servicing oil & gas wells; oil & gas exploration services

(G-3611)
RC LONESTAR INC
60 Le Barry Rd (39120)
P.O. Box 961 (39121-0961)
PHONE..................................601 442-8651
David Nepereny, *Branch Mgr*
EMP: 9
SALES (corp-wide): 367.6MM **Privately Held**
SIC: 3241 Portland cement
HQ: Rc Lonestar Inc.
100 Brodhead Rd Ste 230
Bethlehem PA 18017

(G-3612)
REEDS REYNOLDS
33 Vaughn Dr (39120-2019)
PHONE..................................601 445-8206

Terry Reynolds, *President*
Bruce Reynolds, *Vice Pres*
EMP: 50
SQ FT: 1,440
SALES (est): 4.1MM **Privately Held**
SIC: 2421 2426 Specialty sawmill products; hardwood dimension & flooring mills

(G-3613)
RHINO GRAPHICS
20 Fourth St (39120-3673)
P.O. Box 688 (39121-0688)
PHONE..................................601 445-8777
Lorra Maxwell, *President*
George B Maxwell, *Vice Pres*
EMP: 9
SQ FT: 6,000
SALES: 500K **Privately Held**
WEB: www.maxwellprinting.net
SIC: 2752 5734 Commercial printing, offset; modems, monitors, terminals & disk drives: computers

(G-3614)
RIVER CEMENT CO
60 L E Barry Rd (39121)
P.O. Box 961 (39121-0961)
PHONE..................................601 442-4881
Jack Norman, *Principal*
EMP: 2
SALES (est): 131.6K **Privately Held**
SIC: 3241 Portland cement

(G-3615)
ROCK SHOP LLC
241 John R Junkin Dr (39120-3821)
PHONE..................................601 446-7625
Marshall Gibson, *Mng Member*
EMP: 6
SALES (est): 495.6K **Privately Held**
SIC: 3281 Granite, cut & shaped; table tops, marble; limestone, cut & shaped; blackboards, slate

(G-3616)
SCHLUMBERGER TECHNOLOGY CORP
Also Called: Schlumberger Well Services
9 Covington Rd (39120-2773)
PHONE..................................601 442-7481
William Gardner, *Branch Mgr*
EMP: 11 **Publicly Held**
SIC: 1389 Oil field services
HQ: Schlumberger Technology Corp
100 Gillingham Ln
Sugar Land TX 77478
281 285-8500

(G-3617)
SCOTT O GALBREATH JR
Also Called: Old South Winery
65 S Concord Ave (39120-6806)
PHONE..................................601 445-9924
Dr Scott O Galbreath Jr, *Owner*
EMP: 3
SALES (est): 160.9K **Privately Held**
WEB: www.newu.net
SIC: 0742 2084 Animal hospital services, pets & other animal specialties; wines

(G-3618)
SEW SWEET
4 Jason Ct (39120-8862)
PHONE..................................601 431-2304
Nicole Brown, *Owner*
EMP: 1
SALES (est): 48.1K **Privately Held**
SIC: 3999 2395 Artificial flower arrangements; decorative & novelty stitching, for the trade

(G-3619)
SHAMROCK DRILLING INC
118 Lwer Wdvlle Rd Unit 2 (39120)
PHONE..................................601 442-0785
G Stephen Guido, *President*
Bradley Pickens, *General Mgr*
Robert A Kadane, *Treasurer*
James F Gilbert, *Admin Sec*
EMP: 15 **EST:** 1981
SQ FT: 1,500
SALES (est): 2.2MM **Privately Held**
SIC: 1382 Oil & gas exploration services

(G-3620)
SIGN GRAPHICS
166 E Franklin St (39120-3610)
PHONE..................................601 445-0463
Nancy Laird, *Owner*
EMP: 4
SALES: 180K **Privately Held**
SIC: 3993 Signs & advertising specialties

(G-3621)
SMITH PRINTING & OFF SUP INC (PA)
294 1/2 Sgt Prentiss Dr (39120-4142)
PHONE..................................601 442-2441
Charles Smith, *President*
Donald Smith, *Vice Pres*
Greg Smith, *Vice Pres*
EMP: 9
SQ FT: 3,000
SALES (est): 1.2MM **Privately Held**
SIC: 5943 2759 2791 2789 Office forms & supplies; commercial printing; typesetting; bookbinding & related work; commercial printing, lithographic

(G-3622)
SOUTH CARLTON OPERATING CO LLC
11179 St (39120)
P.O. Box 822 (39121-0822)
PHONE..................................601 446-5992
EMP: 8
SALES (est): 1.7MM **Privately Held**
SIC: 1382 Oil & gas exploration services

(G-3623)
SOUTH CENTRAL GROUP INC
Also Called: Creative Marine Products
1124 Lower Woodville Rd (39120-8132)
P.O. Box 2120 (39121-2120)
PHONE..................................601 445-5101
Andrew L Peabody, *President*
Debbie Foster, *Corp Secy*
Richard Durkin, *Vice Pres*
EMP: 3 **EST:** 1971
SQ FT: 1,700
SALES: 200K **Privately Held**
SIC: 3462 1311 Anchors, forged; crude petroleum production; natural gas production

(G-3624)
SOUTHERN SIGNS INC
406 Liberty Rd (39120-4314)
PHONE..................................601 445-5564
Glenn Wisner, *President*
Mandy Wisner, *Vice Pres*
EMP: 5 **EST:** 1963
SQ FT: 6,600
SALES (est): 625.3K **Privately Held**
SIC: 3993 1799 7629 Electric signs; neon signs; signs, not made in custom sign painting shops; sign installation & maintenance; electronic equipment repair

(G-3625)
ST CATHERINE READY MIX INC (PA)
319 Lower Woodville Rd (39120-5367)
P.O. Box 1443 (39121-1443)
PHONE..................................601 445-8891
Dick Junkin, *President*
Johnny Junkin, *Vice Pres*
Patricia S Junkin, *Admin Sec*
EMP: 15
SALES: 1MM **Privately Held**
SIC: 3273 Ready-mixed concrete

(G-3626)
SWD ACIDIZING INC
429 Lower Woodville Rd (39120)
PHONE..................................601 442-7172
Ken Janette, *President*
EMP: 3
SQ FT: 3,000
SALES: 495K **Privately Held**
SIC: 1389 Acidizing wells; impounding & storing salt water, oil & gas field; servicing oil & gas wells

(G-3627)
SYNERGY SERVICE AND SUPPLY LLC
1106 Highway 61 S (39120-8658)
PHONE..................................601 597-9902

Jack Ryan, *Branch Mgr*
EMP: 1
SALES (corp-wide): 1.2MM **Privately Held**
SIC: 1389 Construction, repair & dismantling services
PA: Synergy Service And Supply Llc
294 Highland Blvd
Natchez MS 39120
601 492-4000

(G-3628)
SYNERGY SERVICE AND SUPPLY LLC (PA)
294 Highland Blvd (39120-4609)
P.O. Box 3008 (39121-3008)
PHONE..................................601 492-4000
Jack Morgan Ryan, *Mng Member*
EMP: 10
SALES (est): 1.2MM **Privately Held**
SIC: 1389 Construction, repair & dismantling services

(G-3629)
T O KIMBRELL LLC
118 Lower Woodville Rd (39120-4448)
PHONE..................................601 446-6099
Thomas O Kimbrell,
EMP: 2 **EST:** 2013
SALES (est): 129.3K **Privately Held**
SIC: 1382 Oil & gas exploration services

(G-3630)
TIMBERLAND PRODUCTS INC
310 Auburn Ave (39120-3939)
PHONE..................................601 442-8102
Kenan S Gwin, *President*
Rebecca S Gwin, *Admin Sec*
EMP: 6
SALES: 1.5MM **Privately Held**
SIC: 2411 Logging

(G-3631)
TMC EXPLORATION INC
116 Lower Woodville Rd (39120-4472)
P.O. Box 2162 (39121-2162)
PHONE..................................601 807-1124
Michael J Fields, *President*
Charles P Fields, *Vice Pres*
EMP: 2 **EST:** 1994
SALES (est): 277.1K **Privately Held**
SIC: 1081 Exploration, metal mining

(G-3632)
TWO-J RANCH INC
25 Hawthorne Pl (39120-4431)
P.O. Box 991 (39121-0991)
PHONE..................................601 445-8540
Bettye Jenkins, *President*
Carla Jenkins, *Vice Pres*
EMP: 8
SALES (est): 1MM **Privately Held**
SIC: 1422 Limestones, ground

(G-3633)
VON DREHLE CORPORATION
30 Majorca Rd (39120-4075)
PHONE..................................601 445-0100
Kevin Avera, *Regional Mgr*
Joe Paynecratz, *Branch Mgr*
EMP: 48
SALES (corp-wide): 177.2MM **Privately Held**
SIC: 2621 Towels, tissues & napkins: paper & stock
PA: Von Drehle Corporation
612 3rd Ave Ne Ste 200
Hickory NC 28601
828 322-1805

(G-3634)
VONCO OF MISSISSIPPI INC
188 Highway 61 S (39120-5279)
PHONE..................................601 446-7274
Todd Bertolet, *President*
Susan Hewitt, *Corp Secy*
EMP: 2
SQ FT: 1,800
SALES (est): 290.2K **Privately Held**
SIC: 1381 Drilling oil & gas wells

(G-3635)
W E BLAIN & SONS INC
Also Called: Blain Sand & Gravel
693 Highway 61 N (39120-8442)
PHONE..................................601 442-3032

(PA)=Parent Co (HQ)=Headquarters (DH)=Div Headquarters

✪ = New Business established in last 2 years

2019 Harris Directory of
Mississippi Manufacturers

133

Natchez - Adams County (G-3636)　　　　　　　　**GEOGRAPHIC SECTION**

Nick Blain, *Superintendent*
Michael Blain, *Manager*
Margaret Steele, *Associate*
EMP: 50
SALES (corp-wide): 66.9MM **Privately Held**
WEB: www.blain-co.com
SIC: 1611 2951 1442 General contractor, highway & street construction; asphalt paving mixtures & blocks; construction sand & gravel
PA: W. E. Blain & Sons, Inc.
　　98 Pearce Rd
　　Mount Olive MS 39119
　　601 797-9777

(G-3636)
W T DRILLING CO INC
231 Highway 61 S (39120-5218)
PHONE......................601 442-1607
Leo Joseph Jr, *President*
Nannette New, *Corp Secy*
Wayne Johnson, *Vice Pres*
EMP: 77
SQ FT: 1,200
SALES (est): 11.4MM **Privately Held**
SIC: 1381 Directional drilling oil & gas wells

(G-3637)
WALSWORTH LOGGING
530 Tate Rd (39120)
PHONE......................601 442-5406
Kenneth R Walswworth, *Principal*
EMP: 3
SALES (est): 183.1K **Privately Held**
SIC: 2411 Logging camps & contractors

(G-3638)
WAYNE A POTTER
417 Main St (39120-3463)
PHONE......................601 446-6090
Wayne Potter, *Principal*
EMP: 2
SALES (est): 176.5K **Privately Held**
SIC: 6211 1311 Oil royalties dealers; crude petroleum & natural gas

(G-3639)
WELCO INC
114 Foster Mound Rd (39120-8492)
PHONE......................601 445-9851
EMP: 2
SALES (est): 150K **Privately Held**
SIC: 1389 Oil/Gas Field Services

(G-3640)
WHITTINGTON CONSTRUCTION CO
706 Orleans St (39120-3529)
PHONE......................601 442-8096
Alan Whittington, *Owner*
EMP: 1
SALES (est): 120K **Privately Held**
SIC: 1521 1542 2434 New construction, single-family houses; commercial & office building, new construction; wood kitchen cabinets

(G-3641)
WILCOX ENERGY COMPANY
304 Franklin St (39120-3262)
P.O. Box 3021 (39121-3021)
PHONE......................601 442-5191
Fred Callon, *President*
Mike Hopkins, *Vice Pres*
EMP: 6
SQ FT: 3,000
SALES (est): 1.3MM **Privately Held**
SIC: 1311 8742 Crude petroleum production; management consulting services

(G-3642)
WILLIAM BARNES
Also Called: Scotts Welding
198 Devereaux Dr (39120-3750)
PHONE......................601 446-6122
William Barnes, *Owner*
Jennifer Mullins, *Admin Sec*
EMP: 8 EST: 1977
SQ FT: 1,500
SALES: 700K **Privately Held**
SIC: 7692 Welding repair

(G-3643)
WILSON FABRICATION INC
252 Lower Woodville Rd (39120-4001)
PHONE......................601 445-8119
EMP: 5
SQ FT: 3,000
SALES: 75K **Privately Held**
WEB: www.fishcooker.net
SIC: 3949 Shooting equipment & supplies, general

(G-3644)
WNTZ TV
26 Col John Ptchford Pkwy (39120-5379)
PHONE......................601 442-4800
EMP: 1
SALES (est): 92K **Privately Held**
SIC: 3663 Mfg Radio/Tv Communication Equipment

Neely
Greene County

(G-3645)
NORMAN K HILLMAN
Also Called: Kent Hillman Logging
4022 Forrest Breland Rd (39461-2557)
PHONE......................601 525-3735
Norman Kent Hillman, *Owner*
EMP: 6
SQ FT: 800
SALES (est): 636.1K **Privately Held**
SIC: 2411 Logging

Nesbit
Desoto County

(G-3646)
AD LINES INC
3902 Windermere Rd S (38651-8306)
PHONE......................662 893-6400
Lindor Signoss, *President*
Annetta B Tice, *Vice Pres*
Jackie Tice, *Vice Pres*
EMP: 2
SQ FT: 600
SALES: 200K **Privately Held**
SIC: 7311 3993 Advertising agencies; signs, not made in custom sign painting shops

(G-3647)
ALLENS CANE SHOP
2038 Getwell Rd (38651-9194)
P.O. Box 525 (38651-0525)
PHONE......................662 429-2016
Anna Allen, *Owner*
EMP: 1
SALES (est): 77.1K **Privately Held**
SIC: 2519 Cane chairs

(G-3648)
AMS SERVICES LLC
960 Old Highway 51 N (38651-7700)
P.O. Box 156, Mendenhall (39114-0156)
PHONE......................662 449-2672
Jeffrey McLaughlin, *Manager*
Jim Eichenberger,
Andy Broadhead,
Micah C Usry,
EMP: 6
SALES (est): 418.1K **Privately Held**
SIC: 1629 3713 Railroad & subway construction; automobile wrecker truck bodies

(G-3649)
D & D SIGNS AND LABELS
1418 Dogwood Hollow Dr (38651-8314)
PHONE......................662 449-4956
Debbie Campbell, *Owner*
EMP: 3
SALES (est): 188.5K **Privately Held**
SIC: 3993 Signs & advertising specialties

(G-3650)
DIRECT AG SOURCE
2720 Itasca Dr (38651-9745)
PHONE......................901 246-1487
EMP: 2

SALES (est): 157.7K **Privately Held**
SIC: 2879 Agricultural chemicals

(G-3651)
FORCE BEEKEEPING LLC
2651 S Hunter Rd (38651-6203)
PHONE......................662 429-7586
James Forbush, *Bd of Directors*
EMP: 2
SALES (est): 76.8K **Privately Held**
SIC: 3999 Beekeepers' supplies

(G-3652)
GARYS GRAPHICS
1117 Broady Rd (38651-9164)
PHONE......................662 429-2924
Gary K Loyd, *Owner*
EMP: 1
SALES: 20K **Privately Held**
SIC: 3993 Signs, not made in custom sign painting shops

(G-3653)
HERNANDO REDI MIX INC
190 Motor Scooter Dr (38651-9219)
P.O. Box 97 (38651-0097)
PHONE......................662 429-7571
Robert Davis, *President*
EMP: 12
SALES (est): 1.9MM **Privately Held**
SIC: 3273 Ready-mixed concrete

(G-3654)
MORGAN BILLINGSLEY LIGHTING
1636 Star Landing Rd (38651-9386)
PHONE......................662 429-3685
EMP: 2
SALES (est): 156.1K **Privately Held**
SIC: 3648 Mfg Lighting Equipment

(G-3655)
OMEGA SYSTEM SPECIALISTS LLC
2671 White Oak Dr (38651-9056)
PHONE......................901 334-6742
James Hall,
EMP: 1
SALES: 150K **Privately Held**
SIC: 1796 3625 4841 1751 Installing building equipment; relays, for electronic use; closed circuit television services; carpentry work; garage door, installation or erection

(G-3656)
RAYMOND MUCILLO JR
Also Called: Universal Scale & Conveyor
400 Getwell Rd (38651-9171)
PHONE......................662 429-8976
Raymond Muccillo Jr, *Owner*
EMP: 3
SQ FT: 1,800
SALES: 240K **Privately Held**
SIC: 3535 3596 Conveyors & conveying equipment; scales & balances, except laboratory

(G-3657)
SPIRAL SYSTEMS INC (PA)
860 Old Highway 51 N (38651-9591)
P.O. Box 513 (38651-0513)
PHONE......................662 429-0373
Dan Snell, *President*
Sandra Snell, *Admin Sec*
EMP: 15
SALES (est): 2.4MM **Privately Held**
WEB: www.spiralsystems.com
SIC: 3444 1711 Pipe, sheet metal; heating & air conditioning contractors

---

Nettleton
Itawamba County

(G-3658)
COLD MIX INC (PA)
32807 Highway 45 N (38858-9336)
P.O. Box 333 (38858-0333)
PHONE......................662 256-4529
Joyce Blasingame, *President*
William Walton, *President*
Jane M Davis, *Vice Pres*
Elizabeth Lea Hudson, *Treasurer*

Glenda Garver, *Admin Sec*
EMP: 8
SQ FT: 1,050
SALES: 1.3MM **Privately Held**
WEB: www.coldmix.net
SIC: 2951 1611 5032 Asphalt & asphaltic paving mixtures (not from refineries); highway & street paving contractor; paving materials

(G-3659)
D & C LOGGING INC
3480 Van Buren Rd (38858-8180)
PHONE......................662 862-9316
Donald Bennett, *President*
EMP: 7
SALES (est): 911.3K **Privately Held**
SIC: 2411 Logging camps & contractors

(G-3660)
HOMESTRETCH INC
146 Furniture Dr (38858-6124)
P.O. Box 379 (38858-0379)
PHONE......................662 963-2494
William Holliman, *President*
Gentry Long, *Vice Pres*
Jan Coggin, *Office Mgr*
◆ **EMP:** 10 EST: 2013
SALES (est): 246.1K **Privately Held**
SIC: 2512 Upholstered household furniture

(G-3661)
HOMESTRETCH HOLDINGS LLC
146 Furniture Dr (38858-6124)
P.O. Box 379 (38858-0379)
PHONE......................662 963-2494
William Holliman, *President*
▲ **EMP:** 300
SQ FT: 15,000
SALES (est): 39.1MM **Privately Held**
SIC: 2512 Upholstered household furniture

(G-3662)
MOCKINGBIRD MONOGRAMS ✪
170 Young Ave (38858-6010)
PHONE......................662 315-6213
Emily Payne, *Principal*
EMP: 1 EST: 2018
SALES (est): 42.1K **Privately Held**
SIC: 2395 Embroidery & art needlework

(G-3663)
NATIONAL CUSTOM CRAFT INC
30081 Highway 6 (38858-9514)
PHONE......................662 963-7373
Jerald D Sullivan, *President*
Donna Gillentine, *Admin Sec*
EMP: 5
SQ FT: 5,000
SALES (est): 720.6K **Privately Held**
WEB: www.nationalcustomcraft.com
SIC: 3442 Storm doors or windows, metal; shutters, door or window; metal; louvers, shutters, jalousies & similar items

(G-3664)
NATURAL OZONE SOLUTIONS LLC
684a Road 1463 (38858-9401)
PHONE......................662 963-2157
Jeff Knowles,
EMP: 2
SALES: 60K **Privately Held**
SIC: 3564 Air cleaning systems

(G-3665)
NATURAL WOOD SOLUTIONS LLC
276 Pennington Lake Rd (38858-8171)
P.O. Box 130, Mooreville (38857-0130)
PHONE......................662 871-1625
Shane Kitchens, *CEO*
Jeffrey Broadfoot, *President*
Brian Lindsey, *Opers Mgr*
EMP: 3
SALES (est): 8MM **Privately Held**
SIC: 2491 Bridges, treated wood; railroad cross bridges & switch ties, treated wood; railroad cross-ties, treated wood

(G-3666)
OUTBACK INDUSTRIES LLC
30093 Old Highway 6 (38858-8154)
PHONE......................662 591-5100
Mike Harris,

2019 Harris Directory of
Mississippi Manufacturers

▲ = Import ▼=Export
◆ =Import/Export

134

GEOGRAPHIC SECTION

New Albany - Union County (G-3693)

EMP: 14
SALES (est): 2.1MM **Privately Held**
SIC: 7699 3548 Industrial equipment services; welding apparatus

(G-3667)
SHUMPERT MEDIA
30081 Seymore Rd (38858-6801)
PHONE....................................662 678-3742
Helen Wilson, *Principal*
EMP: 2
SALES (est): 144.5K **Privately Held**
SIC: 2721 Magazines: publishing & printing

(G-3668)
TIM BLAKE
Also Called: Double E Farms
30225 Johnson Mill Rd (38858-8340)
PHONE....................................662 256-8218
EMP: 7 **EST:** 1994
SALES (est): 600K **Privately Held**
SIC: 1382 Oil/Gas Exploration Services

New Albany
Union County

(G-3669)
2A ARMAMENTS LLC
107 W Bankhead St (38652-3314)
PHONE....................................662 538-8118
Joshua Hardy, *Principal*
EMP: 3
SALES (est): 89.6K **Privately Held**
SIC: 5091 5941 3484 3482 Firearms, sporting; firearms; guns (firearms) or gun parts, 30 mm. & below; small arms ammunition; shot, steel (ammunition)

(G-3670)
ABBY MANUFACTURING CO INC
1100 Denmill Rd (38652-5328)
PHONE....................................662 223-5339
Terry Abby, *Manager*
EMP: 20
SALES (corp-wide): 17.7MM **Privately Held**
SIC: 3441 Fabricated structural metal
PA: Abby Manufacturing, Llc
501 Pulliam Rd
Walnut MS 38683
662 223-5339

(G-3671)
ALBANY FIBER SALES INC
120 Snyder St (38652-3411)
P.O. Box 235, Belden (38826-0235)
PHONE....................................662 401-2342
Kevin Brown, *President*
Sunni Brown, *Admin Sec*
▲ **EMP:** 6 **EST:** 2006
SQ FT: 10,000
SALES (est): 3.4MM **Privately Held**
SIC: 3429 Furniture builders' & other household hardware

(G-3672)
ALBANY INDUSTRIES LLC (HQ)
504 N Glenfield Rd (38652-2214)
PHONE....................................662 534-9800
Richie McClarty, *President*
Bentley Jones, *Marketing Staff*
Phillip Jamieson, *Admin Sec*
Tuck Karen, *Graphic Designe*
Chama McKnight, *Services*
◆ **EMP:** 350
SQ FT: 831,000
SALES (est): 137.7MM
SALES (corp-wide): 241.1MM **Privately Held**
WEB: www.albanyindustries.com
SIC: 2512 Couches, sofas & davenports: upholstered on wood frames
PA: Standard Furniture Manufacturing Company, Llc
801 S Us Highway 31
Bay Minette AL 36507
251 937-6741

(G-3673)
B & B CONCRETE CO INC
1220 W Bankhead St (38652-2102)
P.O. Box 580 (38652-0580)
PHONE....................................662 534-2626
Larry Scott, *Manager*
EMP: 10
SALES (corp-wide): 21.1MM **Privately Held**
SIC: 3273 Ready-mixed concrete
PA: B & B Concrete Co., Inc.
130 N Industrial Rd
Tupelo MS 38801
662 842-6312

(G-3674)
B K INDUSTRIES INC
908 State Highway 15 N (38652-9507)
P.O. Box 59 (38652-0059)
PHONE....................................864 963-3471
EMP: 18
SALES (corp-wide): 791.5MM **Publicly Held**
SIC: 2099 Food preparations
HQ: B K Industries, Inc.
2812 Grandview Dr
Simpsonville SC 29680
864 963-3471

(G-3675)
BLUFF CITY SERVICE COMPANY
213 W Bankhead St (38652-3316)
PHONE....................................662 534-2500
Larry Roberts, *Manager*
EMP: 4
SALES (corp-wide): 616.5K **Privately Held**
SIC: 2819 5087 Chemicals, high purity: refined from technical grade; janitors' supplies
PA: Bluff City Service Company Inc
4187 Lamar Ave
Memphis TN
901 363-5000

(G-3676)
BURGESS KUSTOM CABINETRY
1344 State Highway 30 E (38652-9615)
PHONE....................................662 316-4294
Barry Burgess, *Principal*
EMP: 2
SALES (est): 206.1K **Privately Held**
SIC: 2434 Wood kitchen cabinets

(G-3677)
COZZYTYMZZ CANDLES LLC
1119 Bratton Rd Apt 1112 (38652-9330)
PHONE....................................662 471-1607
Terry Cosey, *Principal*
EMP: 2 **EST:** 2016
SALES (est): 48K **Privately Held**
SIC: 3999 Candles

(G-3678)
CUSTOM CAMS INC
1143 County Road 50 (38652-8943)
PHONE....................................662 534-4881
Tommy Kirk, *President*
Kennell Kirk, *Vice Pres*
EMP: 2
SQ FT: 2,500
SALES (est): 220.1K **Privately Held**
SIC: 3714 Camshafts, motor vehicle

(G-3679)
CUSTOM NONWOVEN INC
1015 Munsford Dr (38652-2124)
PHONE....................................662 539-6103
J M Kim, *President*
Kevin Lee, *Corp Secy*
▲ **EMP:** 14
SQ FT: 5,000
SALES (est): 5.2MM **Privately Held**
WEB: www.custom-nonwoven.com
SIC: 2823 Cellulosic manmade fibers

(G-3680)
DAVIS WOOD PRODUCTS OF MISS
102 Industrial Dr (38652-3002)
PHONE....................................662 534-2211
Al Wallace, *President*
Dennis Davis, *Corp Secy*
J Donald Davis Sr, *Director*
EMP: 196

SQ FT: 20,000
SALES (est): 11.6MM
SALES (corp-wide): 35.4MM **Privately Held**
WEB: www.daviswoodproducts.com
SIC: 2435 Hardwood veneer & plywood
PA: Davis Wood Products, Inc.
1 Davis St
Hudson NC
828 728-8444

(G-3681)
DIVERSITY-VUTEQ LLC
2300 Munsford Dr (38652-7415)
PHONE....................................662 534-9250
Christopher Spence, *President*
Lawrence Crawford, *Mng Member*
Hiseo Nagahiro, *Mng Member*
▼ **EMP:** 750
SQ FT: 196,000
SALES (est): 173.4MM **Privately Held**
SIC: 3089 Automotive parts, plastic

(G-3682)
HMC METAL FORMING INC
Also Called: AMC
1100 Denmill Rd (38652-5328)
PHONE....................................662 538-5447
David McMillen, *President*
John Cobb, *General Mgr*
Donn Owen, *Engineer*
Tony Robbins, *Sales Mgr*
EMP: 32
SQ FT: 43,000
SALES: 950K **Privately Held**
SIC: 3354 Aluminum extruded products

(G-3683)
JNS BIOFUEL LLC
823 State Highway 15 N (38652-9556)
PHONE....................................662 538-1005
Stevan Bolin, *President*
EMP: 10 **EST:** 2011
SALES (est): 1.1MM **Privately Held**
SIC: 2869 Fuels

(G-3684)
LEATHER WORKS INC
1107 Denmill Rd (38652-5327)
PHONE....................................662 538-4455
Dale Manning, *President*
▲ **EMP:** 3
SQ FT: 20,000
SALES: 800K **Privately Held**
WEB: www.leatherrepair.com
SIC: 3111 Upholstery leather

(G-3685)
METAL IMPACT SOUTH LLC (HQ)
795 Sam T Barkley Dr (38652-9537)
PHONE....................................662 538-6500
Kevin Prunsky, *Manager*
John Newell, *Manager*
EMP: 28
SQ FT: 250,000
SALES (est): 24.2MM
SALES (corp-wide): 84.5MM **Privately Held**
SIC: 3354 Aluminum extruded products
PA: Thunderbird Llc
1501 Oakton St
Elk Grove Village IL 60007
847 718-9300

(G-3686)
METAL MANAGEMENT INC
844 State Highway 15 N (38652-9504)
PHONE....................................662 844-6441
Ben Morris, *Branch Mgr*
EMP: 17 **Privately Held**
WEB: www.mtlm.com
SIC: 5093 3341 Ferrous metal scrap & waste; secondary nonferrous metals
HQ: Metal Management, Inc.
200 W Madison St Ste 3600
Chicago IL 60606
312 645-0700

(G-3687)
NA FOOD DASH LLC
720 W Bankhead St (38652-2801)
PHONE....................................662 266-0738
Robert Scott Hancock,
EMP: 2 **EST:** 2017
SALES (est): 56.5K **Privately Held**
SIC: 7372 Prepackaged software

(G-3688)
NEW ALBANY PUBLISHING COMPANY
Also Called: New Albany Gazette, The
713 Carter Ave (38652-3310)
P.O. Box 300 (38652-0300)
PHONE....................................662 534-6321
Larry R Coffey, *President*
Max Heath, *Vice Pres*
Randall G Mast, *Vice Pres*
Lawrence Paden, *Vice Pres*
Brian Roy, *Manager*
EMP: 14
SQ FT: 10,000
SALES (est): 796.4K **Privately Held**
WEB: www.leaderunion.com
SIC: 2711 Commercial printing & newspaper publishing combined
HQ: Journal, Inc.
1242 S Green St
Tupelo MS 38804
662 842-2611

(G-3689)
NEW ALBANY SIGN CO
919 Sam T Barkley Dr (38652-9506)
PHONE....................................662 538-5599
Jerry Burke, *Owner*
EMP: 1
SALES (est): 101.3K **Privately Held**
SIC: 3993 Signs & advertising specialties

(G-3690)
NEWPORT HOME FURNISHINGS LLC
1201 W Bankhead St (38652-2104)
PHONE....................................662 534-3030
Wayne Stewart, *Mng Member*
▲ **EMP:** 75
SALES: 15MM **Privately Held**
SIC: 2512 Upholstered household furniture

(G-3691)
PIPER METAL FORMING CORP
Also Called: Piper Impact
795 Sam T Barkley Dr (38652-9537)
PHONE....................................508 363-3937
Cyral Narishkin, *President*
EMP: 220
SQ FT: 500,000
SALES (est): 32MM
SALES (corp-wide): 81.9MM **Privately Held**
SIC: 3354 3351 3356 3312 Shapes, extruded aluminum; extruded shapes, copper & copper alloy; magnesium & magnesium alloy: rolling, drawing or extruding; primary finished or semifinished shapes
PA: Essex Industries, Inc.
7700 Gravois Rd
Saint Louis MO 63123
314 644-3000

(G-3692)
PUGH TACKLE CO INC
1111 St Hwy 348 (38652-9144)
PHONE....................................662 534-7393
Melba Pugh, *President*
Joseph T Pugh, *Treasurer*
EMP: 6
SALES (est): 624.5K **Privately Held**
SIC: 3949 5941 Fishing tackle, general; bait & tackle

(G-3693)
RUNWAY LIQUIDATION LLC
Also Called: Bcbg
109 State Highway 15 S (38652-5206)
PHONE....................................406 259-1280
EMP: 2
SALES (corp-wide): 576.5MM **Privately Held**
SIC: 2335 Women's, juniors' & misses' dresses
HQ: Runway Liquidation, Llc
2761 Fruitland Ave
Vernon CA 90058
323 589-2224

(PA)=Parent Co (HQ)=Headquarters (DH)=Div Headquarters
✿ = New Business established in last 2 years

2019 Harris Directory of
Mississippi Manufacturers

New Albany - Union County (G-3694)

GEOGRAPHIC SECTION

(G-3694)
RUTLEDGE PUBLISHING CO INC
100 Main St W (38652-3323)
P.O. Box 29 (38652-0029)
PHONE....................662 534-2116
William O Rutledge, *President*
Ken Owen, *Vice Pres*
EMP: 6 EST: 1936
SQ FT: 9,000
SALES (est): 933.7K **Privately Held**
WEB: www.houseofsharks.com
SIC: 2752 2759 5112 2791 Commercial printing, offset; letterpress printing; business forms; typesetting

(G-3695)
S & A INDUSTRIES CORPORATION
303 Futorian Way (38652-2305)
PHONE....................330 733-6040
Greg Anderson, *Branch Mgr*
EMP: 40 **Privately Held**
SIC: 3086 Plastics foam products
HQ: S & A Industries Corporation
571 Kennedy Rd Ste R
Akron OH 44305

(G-3696)
S & A INDUSTRIES CORPORATION
2300 Munsford Dr (38652-7415)
PHONE....................330 733-6040
Earl Evans, *Controller*
Greg Anderson, *Branch Mgr*
Dillon Rockwell, *Manager*
EMP: 6 **Privately Held**
SIC: 3086 Plastics foam products
HQ: S & A Industries Corporation
571 Kennedy Rd Ste R
Akron OH 44305

(G-3697)
SCREENCO INC
Also Called: Screen-Co
214 Carter Ave (38652-3321)
PHONE....................662 534-8750
Jimmy Garrett, *President*
EMP: 3
SQ FT: 4,000
SALES (est): 104.5K **Privately Held**
SIC: 2759 Screen printing

(G-3698)
SOUTHERN TRADITIONS
120 W Bankhead St (38652-3313)
PHONE....................662 534-0410
Darlene Williams, *Owner*
Bobby Williams, *Co-Owner*
EMP: 8
SQ FT: 2,500
SALES: 500K **Privately Held**
SIC: 5947 5632 3911 Gift shop; costume jewelry; jewelry, precious metal

(G-3699)
STANDEX INTERNATIONAL CORP
Also Called: Standex Food Service Group
908 Highway 15 N (38652-9507)
PHONE....................662 534-9061
Cassandra Crane, *Purch Agent*
Simon Pearman, *Credit Staff*
John Minahan, *Branch Mgr*
EMP: 12
SALES (corp-wide): 791.5MM **Publicly Held**
SIC: 3556 Smokers, food processing equipment
PA: Standex International Corporation
11 Keewaydin Dr Ste 300
Salem NH 03079
603 893-9701

(G-3700)
STANDEX INTERNATIONAL CORP
Also Called: Master-Bilt Products
908 State Highway 15 N (38652-9507)
PHONE....................662 534-9061
David Parks, *Branch Mgr*
EMP: 350

SALES (corp-wide): 791.5MM **Publicly Held**
SIC: 3585 3993 3556 2542 Refrigeration equipment, complete; signs & advertising specialties; food products machinery; partitions & fixtures, except wood
PA: Standex International Corporation
11 Keewaydin Dr Ste 300
Salem NH 03079
603 893-9701

(G-3701)
STANDEX INTERNATIONAL CORP
Also Called: Masterbilt
Hwy 15 Bldg 2900 (38652)
P.O. Box 59 (38652-0059)
PHONE....................662 534-9061
Duane Burger, *Branch Mgr*
EMP: 150
SALES (corp-wide): 791.5MM **Publicly Held**
SIC: 3632 Household refrigerators & freezers
PA: Standex International Corporation
11 Keewaydin Dr Ste 300
Salem NH 03079
603 893-9701

(G-3702)
STRYKE RYTE LURES
1026 County Road 358 (38652-9783)
PHONE....................217 370-9461
EMP: 2
SALES (est): 120.9K **Privately Held**
SIC: 3949 Lures, fishing: artificial

(G-3703)
TSA EMBROIDERY LLC
1186 State Highway 348 (38652-9143)
PHONE....................662 538-1007
Rick L Murry, *Principal*
EMP: 2 EST: 2015
SALES (est): 118.5K **Privately Held**
SIC: 2395 Embroidery & art needlework

(G-3704)
TUPELO ADVERTISER INC
Also Called: Advertiser, The
713 Carter Ave (38652-3310)
PHONE....................601 534-6635
Jim Gray, *Manager*
EMP: 25
SALES (est): 1.1MM **Privately Held**
SIC: 2711 Newspapers, publishing & printing

(G-3705)
ULTRA COMFORT FOAM COMPANY
431 Garfield St (38652-5012)
P.O. Box 522 (38652-0522)
PHONE....................662 539-6004
David Smith, *President*
EMP: 12
SALES (est): 2.9MM **Privately Held**
SIC: 3086 Padding, foamed plastic

(G-3706)
UNITED SERVICE EQUIPMENT CO
908 State Highway 15 N (38652-9507)
PHONE....................662 534-9061
Paul Roberts, *Owner*
EMP: 5
SALES (est): 534.4K
SALES (corp-wide): 791.5MM **Publicly Held**
SIC: 3585 Refrigeration & heating equipment
PA: Standex International Corporation
11 Keewaydin Dr Ste 300
Salem NH 03079
603 893-9701

(G-3707)
VIP CINEMA LLC (PA)
Also Called: VIP Cinema Seating
101 Industrial Dr (38652-3016)
P.O. Box 1689 (38652-1689)
PHONE....................662 841-5866
Lakedra Crum, *Project Mgr*
Terry Johnson, *Engineer*
Steve Simons, *Mng Member*
Lisa Crockett, *Office Admin*

Edward O Powell,
EMP: 74
SQ FT: 40,000
SALES (est): 24MM **Privately Held**
SIC: 2531 Stadium seating

(G-3708)
WORTHINGTON CYLINDER CORP
795 Sam Barkley Dr (38652)
PHONE....................662 538-6500
Chuck Bauman, *Vice Pres*
EMP: 191
SALES (corp-wide): 3.7B **Publicly Held**
SIC: 3443 Cylinders, pressure: metal plate
HQ: Worthington Cylinder Corporation
200 W Old Wlson Bridge Rd
Worthington OH 43085
614 840-3210

(G-3709)
WORTHINGTON CYLINDERS MISS LLC
Also Called: Worthington Industries
795 Sam T Barkley Dr (38652-9537)
PHONE....................614 840-3802
John P McConnell, *CEO*
Sonja Huffman, *Manager*
EMP: 22
SALES (est): 5.9MM
SALES (corp-wide): 3.7B **Publicly Held**
SIC: 3316 Cold finishing of steel shapes
PA: Worthington Industries, Inc.
200 W Old Wlson Bridge Rd
Worthington OH 43085
614 438-3210

New Augusta
Perry County

(G-3710)
CONWAY INVESTMENTS INC
Also Called: Conway Pole & Piling Company
Hwy 98 (39462)
P.O. Box 162 (39462-0162)
PHONE....................601 964-3215
Kenneth Conway, *President*
Jessie M Conway, *Principal*
EMP: 8
SQ FT: 400
SALES (est): 971.6K **Privately Held**
SIC: 2411 Poles, wood: untreated; piling, wood: untreated

(G-3711)
LEAF RIVER CELLULOSE LLC
157 Buck Creek Rd (39462-6070)
P.O. Box 329 (39462-0329)
PHONE....................601 964-8411
Richard King, *Mng Member*
Anja Dubose, *Info Tech Mgr*
Brad Hoefler, *Info Tech Mgr*
Arlis Hicks, *Lab Dir*
▼ EMP: 300
SQ FT: 40,500
SALES (est): 125.8MM
SALES (corp-wide): 40.9B **Privately Held**
WEB: www.gpcellulose.com
SIC: 2676 Diapers, paper (disposable): made from purchased paper
HQ: Gp Cellulose, Llc
133 Peachtree St Ne # 1
Atlanta GA 30303
404 652-6630

Newhebron
Lawrence County

(G-3712)
GULF PINE ENERGY LP (PA)
8970 Highway 13 (39140-5635)
PHONE....................587 287-5400
Ian Atkinson, *Partner*
EMP: 32
SALES (est): 2.1MM **Privately Held**
SIC: 1389 Oil field services

(G-3713)
JANE LITTLE INC
Also Called: Buddys Jeans
306b Franklin St (39140-5484)
P.O. Box 90 (39140-0090)
PHONE....................601 694-2767
Jane Little, *President*
Michael Little, *Treasurer*
EMP: 3
SQ FT: 50,000
SALES (est): 787.5K **Privately Held**
WEB: www.buddysjeans.com
SIC: 2211 Jean fabrics

(G-3714)
S CIRCLE INC
187 Rodeo Rd (39140-5629)
P.O. Box 529 (39140-0529)
PHONE....................601 792-4104
Jill Steverson, *President*
Lonnie Steverson, *Vice Pres*
Tonya Huffman, *Admin Sec*
EMP: 80
SQ FT: 28,000
SALES (est): 10MM **Privately Held**
WEB: www.circlesinc.com
SIC: 1799 1771 1721 3471 Exterior cleaning, including sandblasting; foundation & footing contractor; commercial painting; plating & polishing; exhibit construction by industrial contractors

(G-3715)
TRINITY RIVER ENERGY OPER LLC
8970 Highway 13 (39140-5635)
PHONE....................601 792-9686
EMP: 3 **Publicly Held**
SIC: 1382 Oil/Gas Exploration Services
HQ: Trinity River Energy Operating, Llc
15021 Katy Fwy Ste 200
Houston TX 77094
817 872-7800

Newton
Newton County

(G-3716)
AT XTREE
259 Northside Dr (39345-9597)
PHONE....................601 683-6494
EMP: 1 EST: 2007
SALES (est): 64K **Privately Held**
SIC: 3578 Mfg Calculating Equipment

(G-3717)
BIEWER SAWMILL-NEWTON LLC
331 Coliseum Dr (39345-9004)
PHONE....................601 357-6001
EMP: 17
SALES (est): 3.1MM
SALES (corp-wide): 4.2MM **Privately Held**
SIC: 2491 Wood preserving
PA: Biewer Sawmill-Newton, Llc
812 S Riverside Ave
Saint Clair MI 48079
810 329-4789

(G-3718)
C & L LOGGING INC
99 Horne Rd (39345-9221)
PHONE....................601 683-6349
EMP: 2
SALES: 50K **Privately Held**
SIC: 2411 Logging camps & contractors

(G-3719)
DELTA DIRECTIONAL DRILLING LLC
9027 Eastside Drive Ext (39345-8056)
P.O. Box 219 (39345-0219)
PHONE....................601 683-0879
Billy Cleveland, *Mng Member*
Brian Dawson, *Administration*
EMP: 155
SQ FT: 5,000
SALES (est): 154.4K
SALES (corp-wide): 1.2B **Privately Held**
SIC: 1389 Mud service, oil field drilling

2019 Harris Directory of
Mississippi Manufacturers

▲ = Import ▼=Export
◆ =Import/Export

GEOGRAPHIC SECTION

Ocean Springs - Jackson County (G-3749)

PA: Strike, Llc
1800 Hughes Landing Blvd # 500
The Woodlands TX 77380
713 389-2400

(G-3720)
ESCO GROUP LLC
9098 Eastside Drive Ext (39345-8715)
PHONE..................................601 683-3192
Alan Sims, *Buyer*
Body Cooper, *Branch Mgr*
Chris Rule, *Director*
EMP: 250
SALES (corp-wide): 3.1B **Privately Held**
SIC: 3535 Conveyors & conveying equipment
HQ: Esco Group Llc
2141 Nw 25th Ave
Portland OR 97210
503 228-2141

(G-3721)
HEARZ YER SIGN
702 Decatur St (39345-2322)
PHONE..................................601 683-3636
James Nance, *Owner*
EMP: 1
SALES: 250K **Privately Held**
SIC: 3993 Signs & advertising specialties

(G-3722)
LA-Z-BOY INC
133 Scanlan St (39345-2329)
PHONE..................................601 683-3354
Charles Knabusch, *General Mgr*
Earl Bryan, *Principal*
Kevin Davis, *Manager*
Randy Barrett, *Executive*
▲ **EMP:** 3 **EST:** 1960
SALES: 391.4K **Privately Held**
SIC: 2512 Chairs: upholstered on wood frames; couches, sofas & davenports: upholstered on wood frames

(G-3723)
LA-Z-BOY INCORPORATED
33 Scanlan St (39345-2348)
PHONE..................................601 683-3354
Don Mather, *Manager*
EMP: 600
SALES (corp-wide): 1.7B **Publicly Held**
SIC: 2512 Upholstered household furniture
PA: La-Z-Boy Incorporated
1 Lazboy Dr
Monroe MI 48162
734 242-1444

(G-3724)
LMG DIVERSIFIED LLC
110 Russell St (39345-2866)
P.O. Box 811 (39345-0811)
PHONE..................................601 635-5955
Ryan Weaver, *Principal*
EMP: 2
SALES (est): 236.9K **Privately Held**
SIC: 8741 0782 3271 Business management; mowing services, lawn; blocks, concrete: landscape or retaining wall

(G-3725)
NELSONS PRINTING INC
Also Called: Nelson Printing
308 N Main St (39345-2336)
PHONE..................................601 683-6651
Terry Nelson, *President*
Tawana Clark, *Partner*
EMP: 4
SQ FT: 2,000
SALES: 150K **Privately Held**
SIC: 2752 Commercial printing, offset

(G-3726)
NEWTON APPEAL
128 S Main St (39345-2657)
PHONE..................................601 683-7810
Jack Tannehill, *Owner*
EMP: 2 **EST:** 2009
SALES (est): 143.7K **Privately Held**
SIC: 2754 Stationery & invitation printing, gravure

(G-3727)
NEWTON DISCOUNT TOBACCO
300 Northside Dr (39345-2378)
PHONE..................................601 683-6555
David Brashier, *Owner*

EMP: 4
SALES (est): 253.6K **Privately Held**
SIC: 5194 2111 Cigarettes; cigarettes

(G-3728)
SPECIALTEES ETC
108 Doolittle St (39345-2645)
PHONE..................................601 683-2552
Judy Beckly, *Owner*
EMP: 1
SALES (est): 54K **Privately Held**
SIC: 2759 Screen printing

(G-3729)
SPOONFUDGE SHOPPE LLC (PA)
113 S Main St (39345-2656)
PHONE..................................601 685-2000
Tarah Boykin, *Principal*
Aleisa Johnson,
EMP: 2
SALES (est): 871.9K **Privately Held**
SIC: 2064 Fruits: candied, crystallized, or glazed

Nicholson
Pearl River County

(G-3730)
CHEMTRADE CHEMICALS US LLC
187 J J Holcomb Rd (39463)
P.O. Box 890 (39463-0890)
PHONE..................................601 799-2380
Lloyd Lineske, *Manager*
EMP: 7
SALES (corp-wide): 1.2B **Privately Held**
SIC: 2819 Aluminum sulfate
HQ: Chemtrade Chemicals Us Llc
90 E Halsey Rd
Parsippany NJ 07054

Noxapater
Winston County

(G-3731)
CHOCTAW GLOVE & SAFETY CO INC (PA)
10 Laura St (39346)
P.O. Box 411 (39346-0411)
PHONE..................................662 724-4178
Kenny Tubby, *President*
Steve Weeks, *Vice Pres*
▲ **EMP:** 62
SQ FT: 10,000
SALES (est): 42MM **Privately Held**
SIC: 3151 3842 2259 5084 Leather gloves & mittens; gloves, safety; gloves & mittens, knit; safety equipment

(G-3732)
LARRY WELLS
Also Called: Wells Wood Products
817 Highway 490 (39346-3225)
P.O. Box 261 (39346-0261)
PHONE..................................662 724-4355
Larry Wells, *Owner*
EMP: 13
SALES (est): 1.1MM **Privately Held**
WEB: www.noxapatertel.net
SIC: 2531 Church furniture

(G-3733)
LOBELL SALES LLC
2258 Oak Grove Rd (39346)
P.O. Box 307 (39346-0307)
PHONE..................................662 724-2940
Jeffrey Hugh Terry,
Gerald A Lobell,
EMP: 6
SALES (est): 7.2MM **Privately Held**
SIC: 3585 Refrigeration & heating equipment

Oak Vale
Lawrence County

(G-3734)
FRANK J MILLER
96 Highway 43 (39656-8009)
PHONE..................................601 792-8795
Frank Miller, *Principal*
EMP: 3
SALES (est): 173.2K **Privately Held**
SIC: 3678 Electronic connectors

(G-3735)
LEMONWOOD LLC
455 Park Fortenberry Rd (39656-8096)
PHONE..................................601 792-5748
Byron Harrell, *Principal*
EMP: 1
SALES (est): 41.5K **Privately Held**
SIC: 2499 Wood products

(G-3736)
TAYLOR MCKINLEY
337 Park Fortenberry Rd (39656-8094)
PHONE..................................601 792-2739
Taylor McKinley, *Owner*
EMP: 11
SALES (est): 748K **Privately Held**
SIC: 2411 Logging

Oakland
Yalobusha County

(G-3737)
AJINOMOTO FOODS NORTH AMER INC
10646 Highway 51 (38948-2314)
P.O. Box 179 (38948-0179)
PHONE..................................662 623-7400
Tom Eckenrode, *Controller*
Kevin Lake, *Branch Mgr*
EMP: 54 **Privately Held**
SIC: 2038 Frozen specialties
HQ: Ajinomoto Foods North America, Inc.
4200 Concours Ste 100
Ontario CA 91764

(G-3738)
OAKLAND YLBSHA NATURAL GAS DST
286 Holly St (38948-2899)
PHONE..................................662 623-5005
James Swerengen, *Chairman*
EMP: 5
SALES (est): 179.2K **Privately Held**
SIC: 4924 1321 Natural gas distribution; natural gas liquids

Ocean Springs
Jackson County

(G-3739)
ADVANCED PHARMACEUTICALS LLC
998 N Halstead Rd Ste A (39564-3109)
PHONE..................................228 215-1911
Erin W Hollis,
EMP: 4
SALES (est): 283.5K **Privately Held**
SIC: 2834 Pharmaceutical preparations

(G-3740)
ALVIX LABORATORIES LLC
6601 Sunplex Dr (39564-8691)
PHONE..................................601 714-1677
Scott Allen, *Mng Member*
Clark Levi,
Jeffrey Rollins,
EMP: 22
SALES (est): 852.5K **Privately Held**
SIC: 2834 2899 Pharmaceutical preparations; chemical preparations

(G-3741)
AMERICAN PRINTING COPY CENTER
Also Called: Quick Printer
3064b Bienville Blvd (39564-4354)
PHONE..................................228 875-1398
Frank Acevedo, *President*
EMP: 4
SQ FT: 4,000
SALES (est): 331K **Privately Held**
SIC: 2759 2752 Commercial printing; commercial printing, offset

(G-3742)
B & D PLASTICS MISSISSIPPI INC
5500 Allen Rd (39565-8671)
PHONE..................................228 875-5865
Thomas L Reeves Jr, *President*
Trina H Reeves, *Admin Sec*
Kim Bray, *Administration*
EMP: 14
SQ FT: 20,000
SALES: 1.4MM **Privately Held**
SIC: 2821 Plastics materials & resins

(G-3743)
BEST DRESSED BUNNIES
13400 Mount Pleasant Rd (39565-8865)
PHONE..................................228 826-4619
Diane Robinson, *Owner*
EMP: 1
SALES (est): 49.4K **Privately Held**
SIC: 3942 Dolls & stuffed toys

(G-3744)
BUY A BARRICADE LLC
707 Russell Ave Apt A (39564-4751)
PHONE..................................228 355-0146
Heather Eason, *Principal*
EMP: 2
SALES (est): 109.7K **Privately Held**
SIC: 3499 Barricades, metal

(G-3745)
CABOOSE CONES
1009 Pesoto Ave (39566)
P.O. Box 121 (39566-0121)
PHONE..................................228 860-4030
John Tue, *Owner*
EMP: 4 **EST:** 2010
SALES (est): 248.6K **Privately Held**
SIC: 2024 Ice cream & frozen desserts

(G-3746)
CARLISS PHARMACEUTICALS
1306 Bienville Blvd (39564-2914)
PHONE..................................228 875-2748
EMP: 3
SALES (est): 179.3K **Privately Held**
SIC: 2834 Mfg Pharmaceutical Preparations

(G-3747)
CARROLLS WELDING SERVICE
7509 Highway 90 E (39564-7402)
PHONE..................................228 875-3800
Alice Carroll, *Owner*
EMP: 3
SQ FT: 2,500
SALES (est): 130K **Privately Held**
SIC: 7692 1799 Welding repair; welding on site

(G-3748)
CCBCC OPERATIONS LLC
Also Called: Coca-Cola
7900 Highway 57 (39565-8211)
PHONE..................................228 875-5426
Fax: 228 872-4347
EMP: 65
SALES (corp-wide): 1.7B **Publicly Held**
SIC: 2086 Carb Sft Drnkbtlcn
HQ: Ccbcc Operations, Llc
4100 Coca Cola Plz
Charlotte NC 28211
704 364-8728

(G-3749)
COAST OBSERVER
7604 Clamshell Ave (39564-7694)
PHONE..................................228 875-0090
EMP: 2

(PA)=Parent Co (HQ)=Headquarters (DH)=Div Headquarters

✪ = New Business established in last 2 years

2019 Harris Directory of
Mississippi Manufacturers

137

Ocean Springs - Jackson County (G-3750)
GEOGRAPHIC SECTION

SALES (est): 150K **Privately Held**
SIC: **6531** 6519 2711 Real Estate Agent/Manager Real Property Lessor Newspapers-Publishing/Printing

(G-3750)
COMPUTER CONSULTANT
3604 Portree Pl (39564-3438)
PHONE.................................228 818-4486
Richard Huffman, *Chairman*
EMP: 2
SALES (est): 85.9K **Privately Held**
SIC: **3571** Electronic computers

(G-3751)
DAHLS AUTOMOTIVE PARTS INC
2904a Bienville Blvd (39564-4303)
PHONE.................................228 875-8154
Freddie J Dahl III, *President*
Joey Dahl, *Principal*
EMP: 3
SQ FT: 4,000
SALES (est): 440.7K **Privately Held**
SIC: **5531** 5013 3492 Automotive parts; automotive supplies & parts; hose & tube fittings & assemblies, hydraulic/pneumatic

(G-3752)
DIMENSIONS WOOD WORKS
8504 Clamshell Ave (39564-9498)
PHONE.................................228 254-6623
J D Cutrer, *Principal*
EMP: 1
SALES (est): 54.1K **Privately Held**
SIC: **2431** Millwork

(G-3753)
DUNGANS OUTDOOR SOLUTIONS CO
5100 Midway St (39564-9277)
PHONE.................................228 382-7156
Racheal Dungan, *President*
EMP: 3 EST: 2016
SALES (est): 61.4K **Privately Held**
SIC: **7349** 7699 2499 1799 Cleaning service, industrial or commercial; brick cleaning; fencing, docks & other outdoor wood structural products; cleaning building exteriors

(G-3754)
DZT PHOTOGRAPHY AND EVENT PRTG ✪
9105 Margurite Dr (39564-7687)
PHONE.................................228 334-5253
EMP: 1 EST: 2018
SALES (est): 20.7K **Privately Held**
SIC: **7221** 2752 Photographer, still or video; commercial printing, lithographic

(G-3755)
EMBROIDME
9321 Live Oak Ave (39564-8530)
PHONE.................................228 284-1689
EMP: 1
SALES (est): 48.8K **Privately Held**
SIC: **2395** Pleating And Stitching, Nsk

(G-3756)
FAB PRODUCTS
1312 Iberville Dr (39564-2926)
PHONE.................................228 324-4133
Michael B McDermott, *Principal*
▲ EMP: 3
SALES (est): 316.8K **Privately Held**
SIC: **3559** Sewing machines & attachments, industrial

(G-3757)
FERSON LLC
Also Called: Ferson Technologies
5801 Gulf Tech Dr (39564-8225)
PHONE.................................228 875-8146
Louis Peters, *CEO*
William Wilburn, *Vice Pres*
Debra Jones, *QC Mgr*
Bill Wilburn, *Controller*
Connie Spence, *Technology*
▲ EMP: 16
SQ FT: 10,000
SALES (est): 3MM **Privately Held**
WEB: www.ferson.com
SIC: **3827** 5049 Optical instruments & apparatus; optical goods

(G-3758)
FORTUS PHARMA LLC
996 N Halstead Rd Ste C (39564-3107)
PHONE.................................662 420-3094
EMP: 2 EST: 2017
SALES (est): 101.6K **Privately Held**
SIC: **2834** Analgesics

(G-3759)
GREAT AMERICAN GRANOLA CO LLC
10 Sauvolle Ct (39564-1052)
PHONE.................................228 369-0902
James Sutton, *Principal*
EMP: 1
SALES (est): 41.8K **Privately Held**
SIC: **2043** Granola & muesli, except bars & clusters

(G-3760)
GUICE WOODWORKS
122 Halstead Rd (39564-5317)
PHONE.................................323 384-1826
Wade Guice, *Principal*
EMP: 2
SALES (est): 85.2K **Privately Held**
SIC: **2431** Millwork

(G-3761)
HANGER PRSTHETCS & ORTHO INC
7350 Ms 57 I (39565)
PHONE.................................228 875-8354
EMP: 2
SALES (corp-wide): 1B **Publicly Held**
SIC: **3842** Surgical appliances & supplies
HQ: Hanger Prosthetics & Orthotics, Inc.
10910 Domain Dr Ste 300
Austin TX 78758
512 777-3800

(G-3762)
HARVEST TRENDS INC
6336 Point Porteaux Rd (39564-2546)
P.O. Box 201 (39566-0201)
PHONE.................................716 514-6788
Jackie Parker, *CEO*
Colleen Cutler, *Director*
EMP: 9
SALES (est): 240K **Privately Held**
SIC: **3695** Computer software tape & disks: blank, rigid & floppy

(G-3763)
HEY THERE APP LLC
9405 Meadowlark Ave (39564-9149)
PHONE.................................228 238-0344
EMP: 1
SALES (est): 50K **Privately Held**
SIC: **7372** Prepackaged Software Services

(G-3764)
HONEY BAKED
Also Called: Heavenly Ham
1533 Bienville Blvd (39564-3082)
PHONE.................................228 875-5828
Teresa Young, *President*
Todd Deruce, *President*
EMP: 4
SALES (est): 360K **Privately Held**
SIC: **5421** 2013 Meat markets, including freezer provisioners; ham, boiled: from purchased meat

(G-3765)
HYDROLEVEL
505 Jackson Ave (39564-4619)
PHONE.................................228 875-1821
EMP: 2
SQ FT: 1,000
SALES (est): 110K **Privately Held**
SIC: **3823** Mfg Process Control Instruments

(G-3766)
IMAGES GALORE SIGNS LLC
3002 Bienville Blvd Ste A (39564-4328)
PHONE.................................228 818-5449
Jennifer Delage,
EMP: 1
SQ FT: 2,500
SALES (est): 132.7K **Privately Held**
SIC: **3993** Signs & advertising specialties

(G-3767)
IN THE BLACK SOFTWARE LLC
202 Woodland Cir (39564-4124)
PHONE.................................228 697-2120
Tim Anderson, *Principal*
EMP: 2
SALES (est): 84K **Privately Held**
SIC: **7372** Prepackaged software

(G-3768)
INKY PRINTING LLC
12621 Hanover Dr (39564-2711)
PHONE.................................504 858-6461
Dodie Bertolino, *Principal*
EMP: 2
SALES (est): 92.3K **Privately Held**
SIC: **2752** Commercial printing, lithographic

(G-3769)
LE FLEUR DE LUIS
6650 Rose Farm Rd (39564-2117)
PHONE.................................228 875-6628
John Tomsik, *Principal*
EMP: 2 EST: 2010
SALES (est): 135.1K **Privately Held**
SIC: **2335** Wedding gowns & dresses

(G-3770)
LEVINS LABS LLC
801 Washington Ave Ste H (39564-4637)
PHONE.................................228 334-2411
Eva Beidelman, *Officer*
EMP: 4
SALES (est): 179.4K **Privately Held**
SIC: **2834** Druggists' preparations (pharmaceuticals)

(G-3771)
LINTON SYSTEMS
6608 Sunscope Dr (39564-8608)
PHONE.................................228 872-7300
Martin Simoni, *Manager*
EMP: 1
SALES (est): 76.5K **Privately Held**
SIC: **3812** Navigational systems & instruments

(G-3772)
MISSISSIPPI MUD WORKS POTTERY
2011 Kensington St (39564-3907)
PHONE.................................228 875-8773
James Francis, *Principal*
EMP: 2
SALES (est): 78K **Privately Held**
SIC: **5719** 3269 Pottery; pottery products

(G-3773)
NORTHROP GRUMMAN SYSTEMS CORP
6608 Sunscope Dr (39564-8608)
PHONE.................................228 872-7300
Roland Reynolds, *General Mgr*
Jerry Storey, *Mfg Staff*
Michael Ebl, *Engineer*
Steven Reiling, *Engineer*
Stacy Sibley, *Engineer*
EMP: 52 **Publicly Held**
WEB: www.sperry.ngc.com
SIC: **3812** 8711 Navigational systems & instruments; engineering services
HQ: Northrop Grumman Systems Corporation
2980 Fairview Park Dr
Falls Church VA 22042
703 280-2900

(G-3774)
OCEAN SPRINGS GAZETTE
3064 Bienville Blvd (39564-4354)
PHONE.................................228 875-1241
EMP: 3
SALES (est): 126.8K **Privately Held**
SIC: **2711** Newspapers

(G-3775)
PHARMACEUTICAL TRADE SVCS INC
Also Called: Durbin USA
5820 Gulf Tech Dr (39564-8212)
P.O. Box 561, Gautier (39553-0561)
PHONE.................................228 244-1530
Leslie Morgan, *Principal*
EMP: 19

SQ FT: 5,400
SALES (est): 8.1MM **Privately Held**
WEB: www.ptsinc-usa.com
SIC: **5122** 2834 Pharmaceuticals; pharmaceutical preparations

(G-3776)
PLAY COAST
1403 Churchill Dr (39564-3303)
PHONE.................................228 369-4582
Arturo Barajas, *President*
EMP: 2 EST: 2017
SALES (est): 67K **Privately Held**
SIC: **2711** Newspapers

(G-3777)
PLR LABS LLC
996 N Halstead Rd (39564-3107)
PHONE.................................228 327-0939
Samuel Levi,
EMP: 4
SALES (est): 156.7K **Privately Held**
SIC: **2834** Analgesics

(G-3778)
PRIMARY PHARMACEUTICALS
1019 Government St Ste E (39564-3862)
PHONE.................................228 872-1167
Darrell Ritchey, *President*
Debra Ritchey, *Administration*
EMP: 7
SALES (est): 701.9K **Privately Held**
SIC: **2834** Pharmaceutical preparations

(G-3779)
PUBLIC ART PROJECT OCEAN
1924 Kensington St (39564-3906)
P.O. Box 552 (39566-0552)
PHONE.................................228 872-0846
Herb Moore, *Ch of Bd*
EMP: 1
SALES (est): 62K **Privately Held**
SIC: **3299** Architectural sculptures: gypsum, clay, papier mache, etc.

(G-3780)
R F EDERER CO INC
4000 Bienville Blvd (39564-5953)
P.O. Box 874 (39566-0874)
PHONE.................................228 875-9345
Mark Ederer, *President*
Maryann Ederer, *Corp Secy*
Laura Bolton, *Vice Pres*
Laura E Bolton, *Vice Pres*
George Booth, *Vice Pres*
▲ EMP: 24 EST: 1969
SQ FT: 35,000
SALES (est): 4.9MM **Privately Held**
WEB: www.rfederer.com
SIC: **2298** Fishing lines, nets, seines: made in cordage or twine mills

(G-3781)
RECON CONCEALMENT FURN EQP LLC
7421 Joe Fountain Rd (39564-9626)
PHONE.................................228 238-9149
EMP: 3
SALES (est): 137K **Privately Held**
SIC: **2599** Furniture & fixtures

(G-3782)
RICHARDS HOME SERVICES
9009 Seahorse Ave (39564-9607)
PHONE.................................228 324-3482
EMP: 1
SALES (est): 56K **Privately Held**
SIC: **1751** 3443 Carpentry Contractor Mfg Fabricated Plate Work

(G-3783)
SERENDIPITEE
918 Washington Ave (39564-4640)
PHONE.................................228 872-4766
EMP: 2
SALES (est): 116.9K **Privately Held**
SIC: **2395** Pleating And Stitching, Nsk

(G-3784)
SHEARWATER POTTERY LTD
102 Shearwater Dr (39564-4829)
P.O. Box 737 (39566-0737)
PHONE.................................228 875-7320
James Anderson, *President*
Beth Ashley, *Business Mgr*

2019 Harris Directory of
Mississippi Manufacturers

▲ = Import ▼=Export
◆ =Import/Export

GEOGRAPHIC SECTION

Olive Branch - Desoto County (G-3812)

Annette Ashley, *Vice Pres*
EMP: 13
SALES (est): 1.3MM **Privately Held**
SIC: 3269 Pottery household articles, except kitchen articles

(G-3785)
SHED SAUCERY LLC
Also Called: Shed Bbq, The
2 Choctaw Trl (39564-8694)
PHONE.............................228 875-7373
S Craig Orrison, *Mng Member*
Kurt Koegler,
Brooke Lewis,
Brent Orrison,
Linda Orrison,
▼ **EMP:** 3
SALES (est): 1.2MM **Privately Held**
SIC: 2035 5149 Pickles, sauces & salad dressings; natural & organic foods

(G-3786)
SJ ELLINGTON INC
5604 Belle Vale Dr (39565-8679)
PHONE.............................228 369-0089
EMP: 2
SALES (est): 140K **Privately Held**
SIC: 1389 Oil consultants

(G-3787)
SMART SNACKS LLC
8724 Live Oak Ave (39564-9235)
PHONE.............................228 239-6507
EMP: 2
SALES (est): 50K **Privately Held**
SIC: 3581 Automatic vending machines

(G-3788)
SOAP & STUFF LLC
611 Pine Hills Rd (39564-5520)
PHONE.............................228 875-1721
EMP: 3
SALES (est): 110K **Privately Held**
SIC: 2841 Mfg Soap/Other Detergents

(G-3789)
SOUTH COAST PADDLING COMPANY (PA)
614 Magnolia Ave (39564-4823)
PHONE.............................228 818-9442
Robert Wiygul, *Principal*
EMP: 8
SALES (est): 882.7K **Privately Held**
SIC: 2499 Oars & paddles, wood

(G-3790)
SUPERIOR OPTICAL LABS INC (PA)
6525 Sunplex Dr (39564-8704)
P.O. Box 1290 (39566-1290)
PHONE.............................228 875-3796
Harold Walker, *President*
Jonathon Jacobs, *Vice Pres*
Robert Colucci, *Treasurer*
Melinda Baker, *Human Res Mgr*
Amber Janes, *Admin Asst*
EMP: 37
SQ FT: 7,000
SALES (est): 14.6MM **Privately Held**
WEB: www.superioroptical.com
SIC: 5049 3851 Optical goods; frames, lenses & parts, eyeglass & spectacle

(G-3791)
TATO-NUT DONUT SHOP
1114 Government St (39564-3818)
PHONE.............................228 872-2076
David Mohler, *Owner*
EMP: 10
SQ FT: 1,100
SALES (est): 327.2K **Privately Held**
SIC: 5461 2051 Doughnuts; doughnuts, except frozen

(G-3792)
TRIPLE SHOTS
1415 Bienville Blvd (39564-2915)
PHONE.............................228 872-2696
David Buchanan, *Owner*
EMP: 3
SALES (est): 216K **Privately Held**
SIC: 3354 Bars, extruded, aluminum

(G-3793)
VAPE AND BAKE LLC
Also Called: High Roads
6716 Washington Ave Ste C (39564-2129)
PHONE.............................228 447-1566
Jerry Brown, *Mng Member*
EMP: 1
SQ FT: 3,000
SALES (est): 45.2K **Privately Held**
SIC: 7389 3229 Balloons, novelty & toy; ; novelty glassware

(G-3794)
WELLCHECK INC
4013 Bienville Blvd (39564-5806)
PHONE.............................228 872-3633
William Rogers, *President*
EMP: 11
SQ FT: 6,000
SALES (est): 600K **Privately Held**
WEB: www.wellcheck.net
SIC: 3599 Machine shop, jobbing & repair

Okolona
Chickasaw County

(G-3795)
CHICKASAW CONTAINER COMPANY
219 S Carter St (38860-8308)
P.O. Box 49 (38860-0049)
PHONE.............................662 447-3339
Bud Davis, *President*
Davis Travis, *President*
John Sutherland, *Division Mgr*
Barry Gladney, *Vice Pres*
Bobby Easter, *Opers Staff*
EMP: 70 EST: 1981
SQ FT: 110,000
SALES (est): 16.7MM **Privately Held**
WEB: www.chickasawboxes.com
SIC: 2653 Boxes, corrugated: made from purchased materials

(G-3796)
OKOLONA MESSENGER INC
249 W Main St (38860-1498)
PHONE.............................662 447-5501
Murry Blankenship, *President*
Sue Blankenship, *Treasurer*
EMP: 2 EST: 1966
SALES: 44K **Privately Held**
SIC: 2711 Job printing & newspaper publishing combined

(G-3797)
SEMINOLE FURNITURE LLC
Also Called: Seminole Furniture Mfg
269 S Carter St (38860-1905)
P.O. Box 620 (38860-0620)
PHONE.............................662 447-5222
Ricky Stroupe, *Principal*
Mark Dauler, *Principal*
Adam Paxton, *Principal*
EMP: 100 EST: 2011
SALES (est): 8.9MM **Privately Held**
SIC: 2512 Upholstered household furniture

(G-3798)
SEMINOLE FURNITURE MFG INC
269 S Carter St (38860-1905)
P.O. Box 620 (38860-0620)
PHONE.............................662 447-5222
Bobby D Beard, *President*
Bobby Beard, *President*
Thomas A Beard, *Admin Sec*
◆ **EMP:** 100
SQ FT: 130,000
SALES (est): 13.4MM **Privately Held**
SIC: 2512 3999 Chairs: upholstered on wood frames; juvenile furniture: upholstered on wood frames; atomizers, toiletry

(G-3799)
SOUTHERN CABINETS & MILLWORK
106 N Gatlin St (38860-1403)
P.O. Box 587 (38860-0587)
PHONE.............................662 447-3885
George Carter, *President*
Hoyet Pitts, *Corp Secy*

EMP: 8
SALES (est): 971K **Privately Held**
SIC: 2431 2541 Millwork; wood partitions & fixtures

(G-3800)
UNITED FURNITURE INDS CA INC
431 Highway 41 N (38860-9792)
PHONE.............................800 458-7212
Larry George, *President*
Hayley S Hildreth, *Sales Staff*
Douglas A Hanby, *Exec Dir*
EMP: 3
SALES (est): 188.7K
SALES (corp-wide): 353.3MM **Privately Held**
SIC: 2512 Living room furniture: upholstered on wood frames
PA: United Furniture Industries, Inc.
5380 Highway 145 S
Tupelo MS 38801
662 447-4000

(G-3801)
UNITED FURNITURE INDS INC
431 Highway 41 N (38860-9792)
PHONE.............................662 447-4000
Larry George, *CEO*
EMP: 64
SALES (corp-wide): 353.3MM **Privately Held**
SIC: 2512 Living room furniture: upholstered on wood frames
PA: United Furniture Industries, Inc.
5380 Highway 145 S
Tupelo MS 38801
662 447-4000

(G-3802)
UNITED FURNITURE INDS NC LLC
431 Highway 41 N (38860-9792)
PHONE.............................662 447-5504
Larry George, *President*
▼ **EMP:** 79
SALES (est): 8.7MM
SALES (corp-wide): 353.3MM **Privately Held**
WEB: www.unitedfurnitureindustries.com
SIC: 2512 Living room furniture: upholstered on wood frames
PA: United Furniture Industries, Inc.
5380 Highway 145 S
Tupelo MS 38801
662 447-4000

Olive Branch
Desoto County

(G-3803)
901 SAFETY LLC
7328 Wind Dr (38654-5564)
PHONE.............................901 493-3841
Kelly McQuage, *Owner*
EMP: 2
SALES (est): 86.6K **Privately Held**
SIC: 3842 5047 3851 Personal safety equipment; linemen's safety belts; industrial safety devices: first aid kits & masks; goggles: sun, safety, industrial, underwater, etc.

(G-3804)
ACCRABOND CORPORATION
8848 Hacks Cross Rd (38654-3827)
P.O. Box 17945, Memphis TN (38187-0945)
PHONE.............................662 895-4480
Michael Reddoch Sr, *President*
Melissa Dula Reddoch, *Corp Secy*
▲ **EMP:** 11 EST: 1972
SQ FT: 12,000
SALES (est): 3.6MM **Privately Held**
WEB: www.accrabond.com
SIC: 2891 Adhesives; epoxy adhesives; sealants

(G-3805)
ADP HEARING INC
6915 Crumpler Blvd Ste E (38654-1967)
PHONE.............................662 874-6279
Brian K Harvey, *President*

EMP: 1
SALES (est): 60.5K **Privately Held**
SIC: 3842 Hearing aids

(G-3806)
ADVANCED DIGITAL FIRE & SEC
9818 Southern Gum Way (38654-6743)
PHONE.............................901 240-8030
James Wooldridge, *Owner*
EMP: 4
SALES (est): 292.2K **Privately Held**
SIC: 3699 Security control equipment & systems

(G-3807)
AERIAL TRUCK EQUIPMENT CO INC
8270 New Craft Rd (38654-8876)
P.O. Box 716 (38654-0716)
PHONE.............................662 895-0993
Richard L Easley, *President*
EMP: 8
SQ FT: 11,200
SALES (est): 2.2MM **Privately Held**
WEB: www.aerialtruck.com
SIC: 5012 5013 5531 7532 Truck bodies; truck parts & accessories; truck equipment & parts; van conversion; contractors' materials; truck bodies & parts

(G-3808)
AFCO INDUSTRIES INC
Also Called: Afco Millwork
11000 Green Valley Dr (38654-3820)
PHONE.............................662 895-8686
Todd Harnett, *Branch Mgr*
EMP: 150
SQ FT: 18,000
SALES (corp-wide): 84.9MM **Privately Held**
WEB: www.afco-ind.com
SIC: 3442 3081 3354 Metal doors, sash & trim; unsupported plastics film & sheet; aluminum extruded products
PA: Afco Industries, Inc.
3400 Roy Ave
Alexandria LA 71302
318 448-1651

(G-3809)
AIR + MAK INDUSTRIES INC
11154 Wildwood Dr (38654-3838)
PHONE.............................662 893-3444
Manickam Gounder, *President*
Athapa Manickam, *President*
Sundaram P S, *Vice Pres*
Vance Robertson, *Treasurer*
Saravanan Manickam, *Exec Dir*
▲ **EMP:** 12 EST: 1997
SQ FT: 38,650
SALES (est): 3.3MM **Privately Held**
WEB: www.airmak.com
SIC: 3523 3728 3721 Turf & grounds equipment; military aircraft equipment & armament; aircraft

(G-3810)
AMERICAN CONTAINER INC
8530 W Sandidge Rd (38654-3410)
P.O. Box 743 (38654-0743)
PHONE.............................662 890-0325
Steve Harris, *President*
Scott Appell, *General Mgr*
EMP: 50
SQ FT: 150,000
SALES (est): 10.5MM **Privately Held**
WEB: www.americancontainer1.com
SIC: 2653 5199 Boxes, corrugated: made from purchased materials; packaging materials

(G-3811)
AMERICAN ENERGY SOLUTIONS LLC
6155 Autumn Oaks Dr (38654-6611)
PHONE.............................757 846-3261
Isaac Belton, *Mng Member*
EMP: 1
SALES (est): 24K **Privately Held**
SIC: 4911 3621 ; windmills, electric generating

(G-3812)
AMERICAN PLASTIC TOYS INC
11200 Wildwood Dr (38654-3838)
PHONE.............................662 895-4055

(PA)=Parent Co (HQ)=Headquarters (DH)=Div Headquarters
✿ = New Business established in last 2 years

2019 Harris Directory of
Mississippi Manufacturers

139

Olive Branch - Desoto County (G-3813)

GEOGRAPHIC SECTION

Don Debourge, *Opers-Prdtn-Mfg*
EMP: 110
SALES (est): 13.7MM
SALES (corp-wide): 48.5MM **Privately Held**
WEB: www.aptoys.net
SIC: 3944 Craft & hobby kits & sets
PA: American Plastic Toys, Inc.
  799 Ladd Rd
  Walled Lake MI 48390
  248 624-4881

(G-3813)
AMERICAN STAMPING CORPORATION
15451 Goodman Rd Ste A (38654-7604)
P.O. Box 547 (38654-0547)
PHONE.................................662 895-5300
Barry Carter, *President*
EMP: 3
SQ FT: 2,000
SALES (est): 365.9K **Privately Held**
SIC: 3544 Special dies & tools

(G-3814)
AN AMC LLC
Also Called: An American Made Coffee Co
14150 Knightsbridge Ln (38654-8484)
PHONE.................................662 292-6973
Sherry Cash,
Rohn Cash,
EMP: 1
SALES (est): 116.3K **Privately Held**
SIC: 2095 Roasted coffee

(G-3815)
ANGELS TRUCK SERVICE LLC
11153 Highway 178 (38654-8415)
P.O. Box 1458 (38654-0925)
PHONE.................................662 890-0417
Joseph Paul Gibson,
Clare Gibson,
Joseph Gibson,
EMP: 12
SQ FT: 2,000
SALES (est): 2MM **Privately Held**
SIC: 7538 7539 7549 7692 General truck repair; wheel alignment, automotive; road service, automotive; welding repair

(G-3816)
AROMICA COFFEE LLC
8079 Caitlin Dr (38654-6718)
PHONE.................................901 848-1687
Jeffery Hunter,
EMP: 1
SALES (est): 52.6K **Privately Held**
SIC: 2095 Roasted coffee

(G-3817)
AUTOLIV ASP INC
Also Called: Autoliv Combined Warehouse-Aoa
8989 Hacks Cross Rd # 3 (38654-3802)
PHONE.................................801 620-8018
Jay Ward, *Business Mgr*
EMP: 7
SALES (corp-wide): 8.6B **Publicly Held**
SIC: 3714 Sanders, motor vehicle safety
HQ: Autoliv Asp, Inc.
  1000 W 3300 S
  Ogden UT 84401
  248 475-9000

(G-3818)
BARNES SAWMILL WOODWORKS
9480 Miranda Dr (38654-7431)
PHONE.................................901 605-7104
Jeff and Alisha Barnes, *Principal*
EMP: 1 **EST:** 2017
SALES (est): 54.1K **Privately Held**
SIC: 2431 Millwork

(G-3819)
BILLS ORGANTIC GRDNNG & LEAF
7204 Highway 178 (38654-8592)
PHONE.................................901 315-8888
Bill Abresch, *Owner*
EMP: 1
SALES: 3.5K **Privately Held**
SIC: 2295 Coated fabrics, not rubberized

(G-3820)
BLUE LIGHTNING ENTERPRISE LLC
4045 Davall Dr (38654-7083)
P.O. Box 1533 (38654-0935)
PHONE.................................901 626-8587
John Wagner,
EMP: 2
SALES (est): 157.2K **Privately Held**
SIC: 1311 Crude petroleum production

(G-3821)
BSC SALES LLC
8363 Industrial Dr (38654-1918)
PHONE.................................662 890-1079
Johnny D Lucas,
EMP: 2
SALES (est): 414.5K **Privately Held**
SIC: 3561 Pumps & pumping equipment

(G-3822)
CHARLESTON MANUFACTURING LLC
10500 Highway 178 (38654-8186)
PHONE.................................901 853-3070
Edward J Odom, *Mng Member*
EMP: 1
SALES (est): 54.6K **Privately Held**
SIC: 3993 Signs & advertising specialties

(G-3823)
CLASSIC WINDOW DESIGN
4495 Miranda Dr (38654-8866)
PHONE.................................662 893-5892
Barbara East, *Owner*
EMP: 2
SALES (est): 130.8K **Privately Held**
SIC: 2391 1791 Curtains & draperies; structural steel erection

(G-3824)
COMMERCIAL DRAPERY SVCS LLC
8450 W Sandidge Rd (38654-3412)
P.O. Box 624 (38654-0624)
PHONE.................................662 893-1510
EMP: 28
SALES (est): 2.3MM **Privately Held**
SIC: 2211 Mfg Bedspreads & Draperies

(G-3825)
COMPETITION CAMS INC
8649 Hacks Cross Rd (38654-3841)
PHONE.................................662 224-8972
EMP: 2
SALES (corp-wide): 40.3MM **Privately Held**
SIC: 3714 Motor vehicle parts & accessories
PA: Competition Cams, Inc.
  3406 Democrat Rd
  Memphis TN 38118
  901 795-2400

(G-3826)
COMPETITION CAMS INC
8649 Hacks Cross Rd (38654-3841)
PHONE.................................662 890-9825
Ronald L Coleman, *Branch Mgr*
EMP: 1
SALES (corp-wide): 40.3MM **Privately Held**
SIC: 3714 Motor vehicle parts & accessories
PA: Competition Cams, Inc.
  3406 Democrat Rd
  Memphis TN 38118
  901 795-2400

(G-3827)
COMPRESSED AIR TECH INC
7187 Old Craft Cv (38654-1160)
PHONE.................................662 890-9782
Allen Cox, *Branch Mgr*
EMP: 7
SALES (est): 663.7K **Privately Held**
SIC: 3563 Air & gas compressors
PA: Compressed Air Technologies, Inc.
  1758 Highway 49 S
  Florence MS 39073

(G-3828)
CONTROL PRODUCTS INC
11222 Green Valley Dr (38654-3824)
PHONE.................................662 890-7920

Stuart Ransom, *President*
Frank Greganti, *Prdtn Mgr*
Brenda Looney, *Admin Sec*
EMP: 9
SQ FT: 30,000
SALES (est): 1.9MM **Privately Held**
WEB: www.controlproducts.us
SIC: 3625 Motor controls, electric; control equipment, electric

(G-3829)
COTTON PATCH FRAMERY
9086 Pigeon Roost Rd # 106 (38654-1692)
PHONE.................................662 895-6605
Joyce Lyon, *Owner*
Edward Lyon, *Co-Owner*
EMP: 2
SALES: 20K **Privately Held**
SIC: 5999 2499 Picture frames, ready made; picture frame molding, finished

(G-3830)
COVIDIEN LP
Also Called: Medical Supplies
6750 Legacy Dr 101 (38654-5219)
PHONE.................................815 744-3766
Erick Smrt, *Branch Mgr*
EMP: 200 **Privately Held**
WEB: www.tycohealthcare.com
SIC: 3291 5047 Abrasive products; medical & hospital equipment
HQ: Covidien Lp
  15 Hampshire St
  Mansfield MA 02048
  508 261-8000

(G-3831)
CRANE CAMS INC
8649 Hacks Cross Rd (38654-3841)
P.O. Box 12057, Daytona Beach FL (32120-2057)
PHONE.................................386 310-4875
Sean Holly, *Mng Member*
▲ **EMP:** 20
SALES (est): 4.5MM **Privately Held**
SIC: 3559 3714 Automotive maintenance equipment; motor vehicle parts & accessories

(G-3832)
D & G ENTERPRISES
Also Called: Scentsational Scents
4400 Bonner Dr (38654-8149)
PHONE.................................662 895-4471
Greg King, *Partner*
Debra King, *Co-Owner*
EMP: 2
SALES (est): 92K **Privately Held**
SIC: 3999 Potpourri

(G-3833)
DESOTO CONCRETE PRODUCTS INC
220 Highway 305 N (38654-9054)
P.O. Box 336 (38654-0336)
PHONE.................................662 890-1688
Lauren Harry, *Vice Pres*
EMP: 9
SQ FT: 200
SALES (est): 1.4MM **Privately Held**
SIC: 3272 Tanks, concrete

(G-3834)
DESOTO DIGITAL SERVICES LLC
7840 Allen Ridge Ln (38654-9782)
PHONE.................................662 336-2233
Tawanna Jones,
EMP: 1
SALES: 20K **Privately Held**
SIC: 3993 Signs & advertising specialties

(G-3835)
DESOTO FUR TRAPPERS LLC
5816 Brice Cv S (38654-3533)
PHONE.................................662 874-5605
Bradley K Witt, *Principal*
EMP: 2
SALES (est): 154.5K **Privately Held**
SIC: 3999 Furs

(G-3836)
DIGITAL KANVAS LLC
9930 Goodman Rd (38654-1720)
PHONE.................................901 896-9690

Robert Richard Cadwallder, *Principal*
EMP: 2
SALES (est): 126.1K **Privately Held**
SIC: 2759 Screen printing

(G-3837)
DRIVEN RACING OIL LLC
8649 Hacks Cross Rd (38654-3841)
PHONE.................................866 611-1820
Scott Diehl, *Sales Mgr*
Lake C Speed Jr, *Mng Member*
▼ **EMP:** 5
SALES: 5MM **Privately Held**
SIC: 2843 Oils & greases

(G-3838)
ELLIS STEEL COMPANY INC
10290 Old Hwy 78 (38654)
P.O. Box 642 (38654-0642)
PHONE.................................662 893-5955
Shawn Howell, *Manager*
EMP: 7
SALES (corp-wide): 19.5MM **Privately Held**
SIC: 3441 3449 Fabricated structural metal; miscellaneous metalwork
PA: Ellis Steel Company, Inc.
  642 Highway 45 N Altn
  West Point MS 39773
  662 494-5955

(G-3839)
ENGLANDER SLEEP PRODUCTS LLC
Also Called: Englander South Central
8300 Industrial Dr (38654-1917)
P.O. Box 88 (38654-0088)
PHONE.................................800 370-8700
Ronald Clevenger, *CEO*
Mark Savel,
EMP: 125
SALES (est): 6.1MM **Privately Held**
SIC: 2515 Mattresses & foundations

(G-3840)
EVERCOMPOUNDS LLC
7046 Stateline Rd (38654-5709)
PHONE.................................309 256-1166
Mateo Mosconi, *Mng Member*
Shaun Miller, *Mng Member*
EMP: 9
SQ FT: 280,000
SALES (est): 287.1K
SALES (corp-wide): 3MM **Privately Held**
SIC: 3069 Reclaimed rubber & specialty rubber compounds
PA: Cm Group, Llc
  1291 Galleria Dr Ste 200
  Henderson NV 89014
  702 739-9090

(G-3841)
GANSMAN SHEET METAL CONTRS
8251 Industrial Dr (38654-1914)
PHONE.................................662 890-6215
Larry Gansman, *President*
EMP: 1 **EST:** 1960
SALES (est): 230.3K **Privately Held**
SIC: 3444 Sheet metalwork

(G-3842)
GE WIND ENERGY LLC
9124 Polk Ln (38654-7809)
PHONE.................................662 892-2900
Mary Keenum, *President*
EMP: 127
SALES (corp-wide): 121.6B **Publicly Held**
SIC: 3511 Turbines & turbine generator sets
HQ: Ge Wind Energy, Llc
  13000 Jameson Rd
  Tehachapi CA 93561

(G-3843)
HAMILTON BEACH BRANDS INC
11624 S Distribution Cv (38654-7380)
PHONE.................................662 890-9869
Ken Gieszler, *Director*
EMP: 13

2019 Harris Directory of
Mississippi Manufacturers

140

▲ = Import ▼=Export
◆ =Import/Export

GEOGRAPHIC SECTION

Olive Branch - Desoto County (G-3871)

SALES (corp-wide): 743.1MM **Publicly Held**
WEB: www.hamiltonbeach.com
SIC: **4225** 3634 5064 General warehousing & storage; electric housewares & fans; electrical appliances, television & radio
HQ: Hamilton Beach Brands, Inc.
4421 Waterfront Dr
Glen Allen VA 23060
804 273-9777

(G-3844)
HARRIS CUSTOM INK LLC
6810 Crumpler Blvd # 203 (38654-1933)
PHONE.................................662 338-4242
Riqell Wallace,
EMP: 33
SQ FT: 11,000
SALES: 330K **Privately Held**
SIC: **2329** 2262 2261 2211 Athletic (warmup, sweat & jogging) suits: men's & boys'; screen printing: manmade fiber & silk broadwoven fabrics; screen printing of cotton broadwoven fabrics; print cloths, cotton; letterpress & screen printing; screen printing; men's & boys' clothing

(G-3845)
HART & COOLEY INC
8601 Hacks Cross Rd (38654-3841)
PHONE.................................662 890-8000
Jim Scott, *Manager*
EMP: 250 **Privately Held**
SIC: **3446** Registers (air), metal; grillwork, ornamental metal
HQ: Hart & Cooley, Inc.
5030 Corp Exch Blvd Se
Grand Rapids MI 49512
616 656-8200

(G-3846)
HEALTHY GROWTH NTRTN PROGRAM
4725 Deer Run Rd (38654-5626)
PHONE.................................901 493-7991
Claudia Thomas, *President*
EMP: 1
SALES: 10K **Privately Held**
SIC: **2099** Food preparations

(G-3847)
HELMITIN INC
11110 Airport Rd (38654-4004)
PHONE.................................662 895-4565
Steven Edward, *President*
Adrian Holzscherer, *Vice Pres*
Darren Kaine, *Vice Pres*
Mike Walsh, *Accounting Mgr*
Will Riske, *Manager*
▲ EMP: 19 EST: 1978
SQ FT: 36,000
SALES (est): 5.8MM **Privately Held**
WEB: www.helmitinadhesives.com
SIC: **2891** Adhesives, paste; glue
HQ: Itochu International Inc.
1251 Avenue Of The Americ
New York NY 10020
212 818-8000

(G-3848)
HILLSHIRE BRANDS COMPANY
8110 Camp Creek Rd # 125 (38654-1614)
PHONE.................................662 890-6069
EMP: 322
SALES (corp-wide): 40B **Publicly Held**
SIC: **2013** Sausages & other prepared meats
HQ: The Hillshire Brands Company
400 S Jefferson St Fl 1
Chicago IL 60607
312 614-6000

(G-3849)
HUNTER TRADING COMPANY LLC
7282 Maygan Dr (38654-1027)
PHONE.................................866 521-5012
EMP: 3
SALES (est): 388.2K **Privately Held**
SIC: **2329** Mfg Men's/Boy's Clothing

(G-3850)
ICON OUTDOORS LLC (PA)
Also Called: Drake Waterfowl
7282 Maygan Dr (38654-1027)
PHONE.................................662 895-3651
Bobby L Windham Jr, *Mng Member*
Michael Wood,
▲ EMP: 9
SALES (est): 2.3MM **Privately Held**
SIC: **3949** 2329 Hunting equipment; hunting coats & vests, men's

(G-3851)
INCOME ONLINE RESIDUAL
4199 Robinson Crossing (38654-6789)
PHONE.................................662 420-7636
Wade Tarence, *Principal*
EMP: 3 EST: 2011
SALES (est): 264.1K **Privately Held**
SIC: **2911** Residues

(G-3852)
INTERNATIONAL PAPER COMPANY
8301 Hacks Cross Rd (38654-4087)
PHONE.................................662 893-3100
Roger Stafford, *COO*
EMP: 12
SALES (corp-wide): 23.3B **Publicly Held**
SIC: **2621** Paper mills
PA: International Paper Company
6400 Poplar Ave
Memphis TN 38197
901 419-9000

(G-3853)
J & A MECHANICAL INC
10600 Ridge Wood Dr (38654-3917)
PHONE.................................662 890-4565
Ed Nenon, *Owner*
EMP: 1 EST: 1999
SALES (est): 91.9K **Privately Held**
WEB: www.coolofftexas.com
SIC: **1711** 3498 3444 Mechanical contractor; fabricated pipe & fittings; sheet metalwork

(G-3854)
J STRICKLAND AND CO
Also Called: J Strickland Products
10420 Desoto Rd (38654-5301)
P.O. Box 1637 (38654-0955)
PHONE.................................662 890-2306
Linda L Clifton, *President*
Marcus Mobley, *COO*
James E McKelroy, *Vice Pres*
Donna Paine, *Vice Pres*
Tom Dearing, *Opers Mgr*
◆ EMP: 70 EST: 1936
SQ FT: 300,000
SALES (est): 22.5MM **Privately Held**
WEB: www.jstrickland.net
SIC: **2844** Shampoos, rinses, conditioners: hair

(G-3855)
JENKINS GRAPHICS INC
7083 Commerce Dr (38654-2115)
PHONE.................................662 890-2851
Joseph E Jenkins Jr, *President*
Barbara A Jenkins, *Corp Secy*
Wayne Jenkins, *Vice Pres*
EMP: 7
SQ FT: 2,000
SALES: 425K **Privately Held**
WEB: www.jenkinsgraphics.com
SIC: **2752** 2791 2789 2759 Commercial printing, offset; typesetting; bookbinding & related work; commercial printing

(G-3856)
JIMS TOOL & DIE INC
Also Called: Jtd Manufacturing Solutions
12605 Whispering Pines Dr (38654-6034)
PHONE.................................662 895-3287
Jim Cole, *President*
EMP: 17
SQ FT: 31,000
SALES: 1.7MM **Privately Held**
SIC: **3544** 3599 Special dies & tools; custom machinery

(G-3857)
JOHN D MURLEY
Also Called: Integrity Systems
8417 Industrial Dr (38654-1923)
PHONE.................................662 890-3920
John D Murley, *Owner*
Jeremy Wray, *Mfg Mgr*
EMP: 13
SALES (est): 1.6MM **Privately Held**
SIC: **3599** Machine shop, jobbing & repair

(G-3858)
KAYO TECHNOLOGIES
4702 Center Hill Rd (38654-8218)
PHONE.................................662 893-7569
Kevin Odom, *Owner*
EMP: 2
SALES: 350K **Privately Held**
SIC: **3599** Machine shop, jobbing & repair

(G-3859)
KAZ USA
7159 Polk Ln (38654-8983)
PHONE.................................800 477-0457
EMP: 6
SALES (est): 1.3MM **Privately Held**
SIC: **3585** Refrigeration & heating equipment

(G-3860)
KIK CUSTOM PRODUCTS INC
11170 Green Valley Dr (38654-3822)
PHONE.................................901 947-5400
Roger Bos, *Branch Mgr*
EMP: 300
SALES (corp-wide): 3.2MM **Privately Held**
SIC: **2844** 5122 2841 Toilet preparations; cosmetics, perfumes & hair products; soap & other detergents
HQ: Kik Custom Products, Inc.
1 W Hegeler Ln
Danville IL 61832

(G-3861)
KOGLER EQUIPMENT SERVICE INC
8155 Industrial Dr (38654-1912)
PHONE.................................901 521-9742
James Kogler, *President*
Shelia Kogler, *Admin Sec*
EMP: 30 EST: 1980
SALES (est): 2.9MM **Privately Held**
SIC: **7539** 7692 7538 Trailer repair; automotive welding; general automotive repair shops

(G-3862)
L & W PRINT FINISHERS LLC
7472b Highway 178 (38654-8596)
PHONE.................................662 890-0505
Brad Lindley,
Ray Wilson,
EMP: 2
SQ FT: 1,400
SALES: 300K **Privately Held**
SIC: **3559** Recycling machinery

(G-3863)
L AND J GLOBAL MARKETING LLC
8544 Caroma St Unit 77 (38654-2806)
PHONE.................................662 420-9480
Jack Turner, *Principal*
Lilly Turner,
EMP: 2
SALES (est): 56.5K **Privately Held**
SIC: **7372** Educational computer software

(G-3864)
LANDAU UNIFORMS INCORPORATED
Chefwear
8410 W Sandidge Rd (38654-3412)
PHONE.................................662 895-7200
Jason Bowen, *Regional Mgr*
Stephen Brown, *Vice Pres*
Tim Shelton, *Vice Pres*
Alex Fairly, *Inv Control Mgr*
Frank Gubera, *Credit Mgr*
EMP: 45

SALES (corp-wide): 104.7MM **Privately Held**
SIC: **2326** 2339 5136 5137 Service apparel (baker, barber, lab, etc.), washable: men's; service apparel, washable: women's; uniforms, men's & boys'; uniforms, women's & children's; uniforms; work clothing; industrial launderers
PA: Landau Uniforms, Incorporated
1004 Madison Ave
Memphis TN 38104
662 895-7200

(G-3865)
LINING & COATING SOLUTIONS LLC
7122 Highway 178 (38654-8589)
P.O. Box 298 (38654-0298)
PHONE.................................662 893-0984
David Upchurch, *Mng Member*
EMP: 17 EST: 2015
SALES: 3MM **Privately Held**
SIC: **4619** 2851 Coal pipeline operation; epoxy coatings

(G-3866)
LOGITECH INC
8640 Nail Rd Ste 100 (38654-9031)
PHONE.................................510 713-5429
EMP: 7
SALES (corp-wide): 2.2B **Privately Held**
SIC: **3577** Computer peripheral equipment
HQ: Logitech Inc.
7700 Gateway Blvd
Newark CA 94560
510 795-8500

(G-3867)
LUCITE INTERNATIONAL
10500 High Point Rd (38654-3912)
PHONE.................................662 893-5450
Rex Kerby, *Maintence Staff*
EMP: 2
SALES (est): 77.4K **Privately Held**
SIC: **3081** Unsupported plastics film & sheet

(G-3868)
LUNATI LLC
Also Called: Lunati CAM Shafts
8649 Hacks Cross Rd (38654-3841)
PHONE.................................662 892-1518
Jason Kruter, *Principal*
Brian Yon, *Buyer*
Pam Barber, *Purchasing*
Mark Scott, *Purchasing*
Gemma Ryan, *Accounting Mgr*
▲ EMP: 25
SALES (est): 5.4MM **Privately Held**
SIC: **3592** 3545 3356 Carburetors, pistons, rings, valves; machine tool accessories; nonferrous rolling & drawing

(G-3869)
MANUFACTURING -
12380 Kirk Rd (38654-8633)
PHONE.................................408 514-6512
EMP: 1
SALES (est): 39.6K **Privately Held**
SIC: **3999** Manufacturing industries

(G-3870)
MARIETTA AMERICAN INC
11170 Green Valley Dr (38654-3822)
PHONE.................................662 892-6959
James E Woods, *President*
▲ EMP: 225
SALES (est): 35.7K
SALES (corp-wide): 256.4MM **Privately Held**
SIC: **2841** 5169 Soap: granulated, liquid, cake, flaked or chip; detergents
HQ: Marietta Corporation
37 Huntington St
Cortland NY 13045
607 753-6746

(G-3871)
MARIETTA CORPORATION
11170 Green Valley Dr (38654-3822)
PHONE.................................662 893-4233
Steve Odum, *Branch Mgr*
EMP: 250

(PA)=Parent Co (HQ)=Headquarters (DH)=Div Headquarters
✿ = New Business established in last 2 years

2019 Harris Directory of
Mississippi Manufacturers

141

GEOGRAPHIC SECTION

Olive Branch - Desoto County (G-3872)

SALES (corp-wide): 284.9MM **Privately Held**
SIC: 2841 Soap: granulated, liquid, cake, flaked or chip
HQ: Marietta Corporation
37 Huntington St
Cortland NY 13045
607 753-6746

(G-3872)
MEDICAL MCHNING SPECIALSTS LLC
7221 Old Craft Cv (38654-1147)
P.O. Box 2016 (38654-2209)
PHONE..................................662 890-7006
Tim May,
EMP: 40
SALES (est): 1.6MM **Privately Held**
SIC: 3599 Machine shop, jobbing & repair

(G-3873)
MEDTRONIC INC
6047 Choctaw Trl (38654-3106)
PHONE..................................662 895-2016
EMP: 204 **Privately Held**
SIC: 3841 Surgical & medical instruments
HQ: Medtronic, Inc.
710 Medtronic Pkwy
Minneapolis MN 55432
763 514-4000

(G-3874)
MID SOUTH CAST STONE
10258 Highway 178 (38654-3304)
PHONE..................................662 890-7669
Mid Cast, Principal
EMP: 3 EST: 2011
SALES (est): 321.1K **Privately Held**
SIC: 3272 Concrete products

(G-3875)
MID-SOUTH FOAM & ASSEMBLY INC
125 Downing St Ste 8 (38654-7689)
P.O. Box 23 (38654-0023)
PHONE..................................662 895-3334
Jim Cosby, President
Ramah Cosby, Corp Secy
EMP: 10
SALES (est): 490.2K **Privately Held**
SIC: 3086 7336 Packaging & shipping materials, foamed plastic; package design

(G-3876)
MIDLAND COLOR CORP
8489 Summit Cv (38654-4019)
PHONE..................................662 895-4100
Amy Ellison, Controller
Jeff Eleizesmes, Manager
EMP: 6 EST: 2015
SALES (est): 779.1K **Privately Held**
SIC: 2653 Corrugated & solid fiber boxes

(G-3877)
MIDSOUTH CORPORATE HOUSING
1973 Planters Rd (38654-9141)
PHONE..................................901 239-4514
EMP: 2
SALES (est): 149.8K **Privately Held**
SIC: 3953 Embossing seals, corporate & official

(G-3878)
MIDSOUTH MEDIA GROUP
6920 Oak Forest Dr (38654-1332)
PHONE..................................662 890-3359
Kristi Rowan, President
EMP: 11
SALES (est): 1.4MM **Privately Held**
WEB: www.midsouthmediagroup.com
SIC: 2721 5812 Magazines: publishing only, not printed on site; eating places

(G-3879)
MILWAUKEE ELECTRIC TOOL CORP
Also Called: Milwaukee Tool
12385 Crossroads Rd (38654-8972)
PHONE..................................662 895-4560
Darrin Thurmond, Engineer
Steve Nelson, Manager
Calvin Jones, Network Mgr
EMP: 200 **Privately Held**
WEB: www.mil-electric-tool.com

SIC: 3546 3425 5072 Power-driven hand-tools; saw blades for hand or power saws; hardware
HQ: Milwaukee Electric Tool Corporation
13135 W Lisbon Rd
Brookfield WI 53005
800 729-3878

(G-3880)
MONKEY BUSINESS UNLIMIT
5730 Malone Rd (38654-9606)
PHONE..................................662 895-1912
EMP: 2 EST: 2004
SALES (est): 64K **Privately Held**
SIC: 2395 Pleating/Stitching Services

(G-3881)
MY FANTASY HAIR INC
1980 Ingram Cv (38654-7339)
PHONE..................................925 289-4247
Ashley Stanga, President
EMP: 2
SALES (est): 23.6K **Privately Held**
SIC: 7231 5131 3999 2844 Hairdressers; hair accessories; hair & hair-based products; hair preparations, including shampoos; shampoos, rinses, conditioners: hair; cosmetics, perfumes & hair products

(G-3882)
MY SONGS OF LIFE
6322 Chickasaw Dr Ste 2 (38654-3102)
PHONE..................................901 303-8687
June Ann Santonastasi, Partner
EMP: 1
SALES (est): 47.9K **Privately Held**
SIC: 7389 2731 Lecture bureau; ; books: publishing only

(G-3883)
NATIONAL DIAMOND CORP (PA)
8101 Longwood Dr (38654-1643)
PHONE..................................662 895-9633
Milton Cox, President
James E Slade, Exec VP
EMP: 5
SQ FT: 1,100
SALES (est): 867.1K **Privately Held**
SIC: 5094 3915 Diamonds (gems); diamond cutting & polishing

(G-3884)
NATIONAL FILTER MEDIA CORP
8895 Deerfield Dr (38654-3888)
PHONE..................................662 895-4660
Tom Harrison, Branch Mgr
EMP: 100
SALES (corp-wide): 922.9MM **Privately Held**
WEB: www.nfm-filter.com
SIC: 3569 Filters, general line: industrial
HQ: The National Filter Media Corporation
691 N 400 W
Salt Lake City UT 84103
801 363-6736

(G-3885)
NATIONAL PUMP CO LLC
11176 Green Valley Dr (38654-3822)
PHONE..................................662 895-1110
Stan Dodson,
◆ EMP: 32
SALES (est): 5.6MM **Privately Held**
WEB: www.nationalpumpcompany.com
SIC: 3561 Pumps & pumping equipment

(G-3886)
NATIONAL PUMP COMPANY
11176 Green Valley Dr (38654-3822)
PHONE..................................662 895-1110
Steve Anglin, Branch Mgr
EMP: 1
SALES (corp-wide): 414.3MM **Publicly Held**
WEB: www.rainbird.com
SIC: 3432 Plumbing fixture fittings & trim
HQ: National Pump Company
7706 N 71st Ave
Glendale AZ 85303

(G-3887)
NATIONAL SIGN TENNESSEE CORP
6400 Davidson Rd (38654-7153)
PHONE..................................901 210-8023
Mona L Simmons, President

EMP: 1
SALES (est): 65.8K **Privately Held**
SIC: 3993 Signs & advertising specialties

(G-3888)
NCE GROUP INC
8405 National Dr (38654)
PHONE..................................662 890-8778
Shili Fan, Manager
EMP: 1
SALES (corp-wide): 302.9K **Privately Held**
SIC: 3999 Barber & beauty shop equipment
PA: Nce Group Inc.
9970 Irvine Center Dr
Irvine CA 92618
949 585-9008

(G-3889)
ONE GROWER PUBLISHING
6515 Goodman Rd Ste 4 (38654-7336)
PHONE..................................901 767-4020
Mike Lamensdorf, Partner
Lia Guthrie, Partner
Kathy Killingsworth, Prdtn Mgr
EMP: 4
SALES (est): 249.6K **Privately Held**
SIC: 2741 Miscellaneous publishing

(G-3890)
ONEIDA FARMS PARTNERSHIP
8679 Saddlecreek Dr (38654-5866)
P.O. Box 424, Nesbit (38651-0424)
PHONE..................................901 652-4182
Lan Burns, Partner
EMP: 3
SALES: 75K **Privately Held**
SIC: 3523 Driers (farm): grain, hay & seed

(G-3891)
ORBIS RPM LLC
10800 Marina Dr (38654-3716)
PHONE..................................662 890-7646
John McKinley, Manager
EMP: 10
SALES (corp-wide): 1.6B **Privately Held**
WEB: www.cartonplast.com
SIC: 3081 Unsupported plastics film & sheet
HQ: Orbis Rpm, Llc
1055 Corporate Center Dr
Oconomowoc WI 53066
262 560-5000

(G-3892)
OVERNIGHT PRINTING SERVICE
6335 Autumn Oaks Dr (38654-9342)
PHONE..................................662 895-9262
Jukoby Fentress, Owner
EMP: 1
SALES (est): 77K **Privately Held**
SIC: 2752 Commercial printing, offset

(G-3893)
PACKAGING CORPORATION AMERICA
Also Called: PCA/Olive Branch 341
8489 Summit Cv (38654-4019)
PHONE..................................662 895-4100
Eric Underwood, Principal
Lavada Turner, Manager
EMP: 39
SALES (corp-wide): 7B **Publicly Held**
WEB: www.packagingcorp.com
SIC: 2653 Boxes, corrugated: made from purchased materials
PA: Packaging Corporation Of America
1 N Field Ct
Lake Forest IL 60045
847 482-3000

(G-3894)
PARKER-HANNIFIN CORPORATION
Also Called: Chelsea Products
8225 Hacks Cross Rd (38654-4007)
PHONE..................................662 895-1011
James Blalock, Engineer
Mark Bordwell, Project Engr
Tamara Gilder, HR Admin
Artie Young, Branch Mgr
Nancy Crooks, Manager
EMP: 120
SQ FT: 75,000

SALES (corp-wide): 14.3B **Publicly Held**
WEB: www.parker.com
SIC: 3714 3713 Motor vehicle parts & accessories; truck & bus bodies
PA: Parker-Hannifin Corporation
6035 Parkland Blvd
Cleveland OH 44124
216 896-3000

(G-3895)
PICKETT EQUIPMENT CO INC
8464 Summit Cv (38654-4019)
PHONE..................................662 890-9095
William B Everett Jr, President
Mary Everett, Vice Pres
EMP: 7
SQ FT: 16,000
SALES (est): 2.8MM **Privately Held**
SIC: 5084 3594 Pumps & pumping equipment; fluid power pumps & motors

(G-3896)
PILLOWS PLUS
6645 Blue Bird Ln (38654-9626)
PHONE..................................662 890-3699
Sandra Bass, Owner
EMP: 1
SALES: 20K **Privately Held**
SIC: 2392 Cushions & pillows

(G-3897)
PLANTRONICS INC
7769 Pleasant Hill Rd (38654-8085)
PHONE..................................662 893-7221
Rosanne Thomas, Manager
EMP: 1
SALES (corp-wide): 1.6B **Publicly Held**
WEB: www.plantronics.com
SIC: 3661 Telephone & telegraph apparatus
PA: Plantronics, Inc.
345 Encinal St
Santa Cruz CA 95060
831 426-5858

(G-3898)
PLASKOLITE SOUTH LLC
10500 High Point Rd (38654-3912)
PHONE..................................662 895-7007
Mitchell P Grindley, President
EMP: 120
SALES (est): 3.7MM
SALES (corp-wide): 267.7MM **Privately Held**
SIC: 2821 Plastics materials & resins
PA: Plaskolite, Llc
400 W Nationwide Blvd # 400
Columbus OH 43215
614 294-3281

(G-3899)
PRECISION ELECTRIC & LTG SVC
6229 Highway 305 N Ste G (38654-3083)
PHONE..................................662 893-3200
Larry Hawkins, Principal
EMP: 4
SALES (est): 242.3K **Privately Held**
SIC: 5063 3699 Lighting fixtures; electrical equipment & supplies

(G-3900)
PREMIER AIR PRODUCTS LLC
5230 Hacks Cross Rd (38654-8158)
PHONE..................................662 890-9233
Lauren Conde, General Mgr
EMP: 7
SALES (est): 1.5MM **Privately Held**
SIC: 2813 Industrial gases

(G-3901)
PRESS 4 U
10340 Palmer Cv (38654-3332)
PHONE..................................901 361-0256
Jordan Hodge, Principal
EMP: 1
SALES (est): 37.5K **Privately Held**
SIC: 2741 Miscellaneous publishing

(G-3902)
PRO-STONE LLC
8855 Cypress Woods Ln (38654-3805)
PHONE..................................334 281-0048
EMP: 11
SALES (est): 1.6MM **Privately Held**
SIC: 2434 Mfg Wood Kitchen Cabinets

2019 Harris Directory of
Mississippi Manufacturers

▲ = Import ▼=Export
◆ =Import/Export

142

GEOGRAPHIC SECTION

Oxford - Lafayette County (G-3935)

(G-3903)
PROTANK LLC (PA)
8971 Yahweh Rd (38654-7754)
P.O. Box 490, Belmont (38827-0490)
PHONE..................................662 895-4337
Donald Thomas Plumpton, *President*
Brendon E Plumpton, *Vice Pres*
Brenadene Kathleen Plumpton, *Treasurer*
Fran Shaw, *Admin Asst*
EMP: 8 EST: 2000
SQ FT: 8,000
SALES (est): 2.1MM **Privately Held**
WEB: www.protankms.com
SIC: 3089 Plastic & fiberglass tanks; septic
tanks, plastic

(G-3904)
**REVOLUTION PRINTING &
GRAPHICS**
8610 Highway 178 (38654-1202)
PHONE..................................662 932-8176
EMP: 2
SALES (est): 28.3K **Privately Held**
SIC: 7336 2759 Graphic arts & related de-
sign; commercial printing

(G-3905)
RONALD E CHRISTOPHER III
7377 Grove Park Rd (38654-1388)
PHONE..................................901 301-5922
Ronald Christopher III, *Owner*
EMP: 7 EST: 2016
SALES (est): 331.4K **Privately Held**
SIC: 3569 7389 Assembly machines, non-
metalworking;

(G-3906)
SANDERS INDUSTRIES INC
8158 Industrial Dr (38654-1911)
P.O. Box 1575, Mineral Wells (38654-0945)
PHONE..................................662 895-1337
EMP: 2
SALES (est): 82.7K **Privately Held**
SIC: 3999 Mfg Misc Products

(G-3907)
**SENTIMENTS BY SHELE -
WHMSICAL**
4257 Forest Hill Rd S (38654-6161)
PHONE..................................662 812-3506
EMP: 1 EST: 2017
SALES (est): 54.1K **Privately Held**
SIC: 2431 Millwork

(G-3908)
SERIGRAPHICS
7275 Lamb Rd (38654-7739)
PHONE..................................662 895-3553
Carolyn Mc Donald, *Partner*
Joey Knecht, *Partner*
EMP: 2
SQ FT: 10,000
SALES: 400K **Privately Held**
WEB: www.serigraphics.com
SIC: 2759 Screen printing

(G-3909)
SIGNS BY SCHACK
9093 Deerfield Cv (38654-5720)
PHONE..................................662 890-3683
Rick Shackleford, *Owner*
EMP: 2
SALES (est): 220.1K **Privately Held**
SIC: 3993 Signs & advertising specialties

(G-3910)
SIMS BARK CO INC
5060 Hacks Xrd (38654)
PHONE..................................662 895-6501
Doug Nelson, *General Mgr*
EMP: 15
SALES (corp-wide): 13.4MM **Privately
Held**
SIC: 2421 Sawmills & planing mills, gen-
eral
PA: Sims Bark Co., Inc.
1765 Spring Valley Rd
Tuscumbia AL 35674
256 381-8323

(G-3911)
SMITH CHEMICAL COMPANY
9821 Bethel Rd (38654-9288)
PHONE..................................901 849-4074
EMP: 2 EST: 2010

SALES (est): 130K **Privately Held**
SIC: 3312 Blast Furnace-Steel Works

(G-3912)
SMITHS MEDICAL ASD INC
9124 Polk Ln Ste 101 (38654-7809)
PHONE..................................662 895-8000
Glenn Boylan, *President*
EMP: 11
SALES (corp-wide): 4.1B **Privately Held**
SIC: 3841 Surgical & medical instruments
HQ: Smiths Medical Asd, Inc.
6000 Nathan Ln N Ste 100
Plymouth MN 55442
763 383-3000

(G-3913)
STEINER PLASTICS INC
8805 Cypress Woods Ln (38654-3805)
PHONE..................................662 895-7350
John R Steiner, *President*
EMP: 5
SQ FT: 10,000
SALES (est): 1MM **Privately Held**
SIC: 3089 Injection molded finished plastic
products

(G-3914)
STONE PERFECTION
8822 Cypress Woods Ln (38654-3806)
PHONE..................................662 895-4442
Dawn Burdick, *Principal*
EMP: 2
SALES (est): 256.9K **Privately Held**
SIC: 2541 Counter & sink tops

(G-3915)
**TAYLOR COML FOODSERVICE
INC**
11042 Wildwood Dr (38654-3834)
PHONE..................................662 895-4455
Roger Brown, *Manager*
EMP: 130
SALES (corp-wide): 2.7B **Publicly Held**
WEB: www.ccr.carrier.com
SIC: 3585 5078 5064 Air conditioning
equipment, complete; commercial refrig-
eration equipment; refrigerators & freez-
ers
HQ: Taylor Commercial Foodservice Inc.
750 N Blackhawk Blvd
Rockton IL 61072
815 624-8333

(G-3916)
**TELEFLEX MEDICAL
INCORPORATED**
11245 N Distribution Cv (38654-7840)
PHONE..................................662 892-9100
Ernest Waaser, *President*
Kevin Gordon, *Vice Pres*
Jeffrey Jacobs, *Treasurer*
◆ EMP: 71
SALES (est): 24.2MM **Privately Held**
SIC: 3841 Surgical & medical instruments

(G-3917)
THIBIDEAU ENTERPRISES LLC
9461 Taylor Cv (38654-6588)
PHONE..................................662 471-3168
Terrence Thibideau, *Principal*
EMP: 1
SALES (est): 37.5K **Privately Held**
SIC: 2741 Miscellaneous publishing

(G-3918)
TIN ROOF MERCANTILE
9808 Sequoia Ln (38654-3200)
PHONE..................................901 596-6803
EMP: 3
SALES (est): 214.2K **Privately Held**
SIC: 3356 Tin

(G-3919)
**TRINER SCALE AND MFG CO
INC (PA)**
8411 Hacks Cross Rd (38654-4010)
PHONE..................................800 238-0152
Arthur Wendt, *President*
Ray Wendt, *Vice Pres*
Matthew Wendt, *CTO*
Cecelia Wendt, *Admin Sec*
▲ EMP: 13
SALES (est): 2.2MM **Privately Held**
SIC: 3596 Industrial scales; mail scales

(G-3920)
**VERTEX MANUFACTURING
CORP**
8341 Industrial Dr (38654-1918)
P.O. Box 949 (38654-0910)
PHONE..................................662 895-6263
David B Dorris, *President*
EMP: 8
SQ FT: 10,500
SALES (est): 1.7MM **Privately Held**
SIC: 3511 Hydraulic turbine generator set
units, complete

(G-3921)
VIEW INC
12380 Kirk Rd (38654-8633)
PHONE..................................662 892-3415
Joe Crouson, *Branch Mgr*
EMP: 75 **Privately Held**
SIC: 3211 Window glass, clear & colored
PA: View, Inc.
195 S Milpitas Blvd
Milpitas CA 95035

(G-3922)
**WALLACE EXPRESS FREIGHT
INC**
9305 Stateline Rd Apt 32a (38654-3770)
PHONE..................................662 890-3080
Emmanuel Wallace, *CEO*
Riqell Buckley Wallace, *President*
Mollie Johnson, *Treasurer*
EMP: 15 EST: 2015
SALES (est): 823.5K **Privately Held**
SIC: 3537 6411 6399 Trucks: freight, bag-
gage, etc.: industrial, except mining; in-
surance agents; warranty insurance,
product; except automobile

(G-3923)
WATERSPRINGS MEDIA HOUSE
10719 Oak Cir N (38654-4814)
PHONE..................................662 812-1568
Athena Smith, *Principal*
EMP: 2 EST: 2015
SALES (est): 55.3K **Privately Held**
SIC: 8742 2731 Marketing consulting
services; book publishing

(G-3924)
**WEBBS WELDING & REPAIR
LLC**
14414 Hedge Row Cv (38654-8706)
PHONE..................................901 487-2400
EMP: 1
SALES: 10K **Privately Held**
SIC: 7692 Welding repair

(G-3925)
WESTROCK CP LLC
10333 High Point Rd (38654-3911)
PHONE..................................662 895-1627
Loren Allman, *Manager*
EMP: 50
SQ FT: 50,000
SALES (corp-wide): 16.2B **Publicly Held**
SIC: 2653 Boxes, corrugated: made from
purchased materials
HQ: Westrock Cp, Llc
1000 Abernathy Rd
Atlanta GA 30328

(G-3926)
WHITING WOODCRAFT LLC
8823 Deerfield Dr (38654-3815)
PHONE..................................662 895-1688
Clarence Whiting Jr, *Owner*
EMP: 6
SQ FT: 5,000
SALES (est): 596K **Privately Held**
WEB: www.whitingwoodcraft.com
SIC: 2431 Millwork

(G-3927)
WILLIAMS SONOMA
7755 Polk Ln (38654-8313)
PHONE..................................901 795-2625
EMP: 14
SALES (est): 834.4K **Privately Held**
SIC: 3269 Cookware: stoneware, coarse
earthenware & pottery

(G-3928)
WOOD WORK SOLUTIONS
155 Downing St (38654-7691)
PHONE..................................662 890-8954
EMP: 2
SALES (est): 140.7K **Privately Held**
SIC: 2431 Mfg Millwork

Osyka
Pike County

(G-3929)
SASSONES TIMBER LLC
566 E Railroad Ave (39657)
P.O. Box 215 (39657-0215)
PHONE..................................601 542-5558
Anthony O Sassone, *President*
Chris Sassone, *Vice Pres*
EMP: 40
SQ FT: 500
SALES (est): 5.1MM **Privately Held**
SIC: 2411 5099 Logging; pulpwood

Ovett
Jones County

(G-3930)
**ADAMS WELDING &
FABRICATION**
136 Widow Landrum Rd (39464-3812)
PHONE..................................601 319-1865
Narvel E Adams, *Principal*
EMP: 2
SALES (est): 221.2K **Privately Held**
SIC: 7692 Welding repair

(G-3931)
FRANKS SAWMILL INC
1780 Ovett Petal Rd (39464-3459)
PHONE..................................601 344-7437
Frank A Hamby, *President*
EMP: 5 EST: 1993
SALES (est): 664.6K **Privately Held**
SIC: 2421 Lumber: rough, sawed or planed

(G-3932)
RISING SON WELDING LLC
269 Will Young Rd (39464-3836)
PHONE..................................601 344-0077
Charles East, *Owner*
EMP: 1 EST: 2010
SALES (est): 62.4K **Privately Held**
SIC: 7692 Welding repair

(G-3933)
**SUMRALL WELDING SERVICE
LLC**
157 George Boutwell Rd (39464-3762)
PHONE..................................601 498-1075
EMP: 2
SALES (est): 57K **Privately Held**
SIC: 7692 Welding repair

Oxford
Lafayette County

(G-3934)
**3 MEN MOVING & STORAGE
LLC**
419 Jackson Ave W (38655)
P.O. Box 1035 (38655-1035)
PHONE..................................662 238-7774
Pat Patterson,
EMP: 3
SALES (est): 270K **Privately Held**
SIC: 5941 2759 Sporting goods & bicycle
shops; screen printing

(G-3935)
ARBOR THERAPEUTICS LLC
851b Highway 30 E (38655-5819)
PHONE..................................303 808-4104
James D McChesney, *Director*
EMP: 5
SALES (est): 290K **Privately Held**
SIC: 2834 Pharmaceutical preparations

(PA)=Parent Co (HQ)=Headquarters (DH)=Div Headquarters
✪ = New Business established in last 2 years

2019 Harris Directory of
Mississippi Manufacturers

143

Oxford - Lafayette County (G-3936)

GEOGRAPHIC SECTION

(G-3936)
ARTISTIC TEES
1453 S Lamar Blvd (38655-4740)
PHONE..................................662 234-5051
Tatum Mike, *CEO*
EMP: 2
SALES (est): 165.4K **Privately Held**
SIC: 2759 Screen printing

(G-3937)
B & B CONCRETE CO INC
Oxford Div
2304 University Ave (38655-8905)
P.O. Box 825 (38655-0825)
PHONE..................................662 234-7088
Bean Blick, *Opers-Prdtn-Mfg*
EMP: 14
SALES (corp-wide): 21.1MM **Privately Held**
SIC: 3273 Ready-mixed concrete
PA: B & B Concrete Co., Inc.
130 N Industrial Rd
Tupelo MS 38801
662 842-6312

(G-3938)
BALL SIGN CO
Highway 334 Ste 36a (38655)
PHONE..................................662 236-2338
Coolidge Ball, *Owner*
EMP: 1
SALES (est): 84K **Privately Held**
WEB: www.ballsign.com
SIC: 3993 Signs & advertising specialties

(G-3939)
BECKHAM WELDING LLC
73 County Road 420 (38655-8257)
PHONE..................................662 832-0071
Steve Beckham, *Principal*
EMP: 1
SALES (est): 25K **Privately Held**
SIC: 7692 Welding repair

(G-3940)
BILL BRISCOE
Also Called: Briscoe Woodworks
71 County Road 327 (38655-5919)
PHONE..................................662 234-5669
Bill Briscoe, *Owner*
EMP: 1
SALES (est): 93K **Privately Held**
SIC: 1751 2511 Cabinet building & installation; wood household furniture

(G-3941)
BLAUER MANUFACTURING CO INC
Also Called: Suzuki of Western Mass
156 County Rd (38655)
P.O. Box 1438 (38655-1438)
PHONE..................................662 281-0097
Michael Blauer, *Principal*
EMP: 100
SALES (corp-wide): 63.4MM **Privately Held**
WEB: www.blauer.com
SIC: 2311 2326 Policemen's uniforms: made from purchased materials; work uniforms
PA: Blauer Manufacturing Co, Inc.
20 Aberdeen St
Boston MA 02215
800 225-6715

(G-3942)
BLAUER MANUFACTURING CO INC
Also Called: S W M Company
10 Lafayette Park Dr (38655)
P.O. Box 1438 (38655-1438)
PHONE..................................662 281-0097
Kerry Martin, *Branch Mgr*
EMP: 100
SALES (corp-wide): 63.4MM **Privately Held**
WEB: www.blauer.com
SIC: 2311 2321 2326 Policemen's uniforms: made from purchased materials; men's & boys' furnishings; work uniforms
PA: Blauer Manufacturing Co, Inc.
20 Aberdeen St
Boston MA 02215
800 225-6715

(G-3943)
BLUE NOTE MANAGEMENT LLC
Also Called: SERVPRO Oxfrd/Btsvll/Clrksdale
1197 Highway 6 W (38655-8565)
PHONE..................................662 281-1881
Steven Jones,
Tara Jones,
EMP: 10
SQ FT: 13,000
SALES: 1.5MM **Privately Held**
SIC: 1623 7389 1446 7699 Water, sewer & utility lines; fire protection service other than forestry or public; molding sand mining; cleaning services

(G-3944)
CALLAHANS QUICK PRINT INC
191 Highway 6 E (38655-9298)
PHONE..................................662 234-8060
Robert L Callahan, *Partner*
EMP: 8
SQ FT: 4,000
SALES (est): 1.3MM **Privately Held**
WEB: www.callahansquickprint.com
SIC: 2752 Commercial printing, offset

(G-3945)
CATAWOMPER PRESS LLC
206 Northpointe Blvd (38655-7724)
PHONE..................................662 832-3897
Kath Hood, *Principal*
EMP: 1
SALES (est): 67.6K **Privately Held**
SIC: 2741 Miscellaneous publishing

(G-3946)
CLAY CANVAS
113 County Road 401 (38655-9581)
PHONE..................................662 236-9798
Cheryl Davis, *Partner*
Duke Hussey, *Partner*
EMP: 3 **EST:** 2002
SALES (est): 170K **Privately Held**
SIC: 3269 Pottery cooking & kitchen articles

(G-3947)
COLEMAN BUILDERS INC
14 County Road 466 (38655-6309)
PHONE..................................662 234-0376
Gary Coleman, *President*
Debbie Coleman, *Vice Pres*
EMP: 3
SALES (est): 410K **Privately Held**
WEB: www.colemanbuilders.com
SIC: 1521 1531 2541 New construction, single-family houses; speculative builder, single-family houses; cabinets, except refrigerated: show, display, etc.: wood

(G-3948)
CONSTRUCTION WASTE MANAGEMENT
17 County Road 4018 (38655)
P.O. Box 399 (38655-0399)
PHONE..................................662 513-7999
Lee Martuis, *Owner*
EMP: 2
SALES (est): 235.1K **Privately Held**
SIC: 3443 Dumpsters, garbage

(G-3949)
COTTONS CAFE LLC
Also Called: Cotton's Cafe Dog Treat Bakery
850 Insight Park Ave (38655)
PHONE..................................662 380-1463
Janet McCarty, *Mng Member*
EMP: 1
SALES (est): 122K **Privately Held**
SIC: 5812 2047 Cafe; dog food

(G-3950)
DEALS XPRESS LUBE
2211 University Ave (38655-3526)
PHONE..................................662 281-4417
Tony Deal, *Owner*
EMP: 6
SALES (est): 462.2K **Privately Held**
SIC: 2741 Miscellaneous publishing

(G-3951)
DOCUMART OF MID-SOUTH LLC
1105 Jackson Ave W (38655-2509)
PHONE..................................662 281-1474
Diane Wade, *Branch Mgr*

EMP: 1
SALES (corp-wide): 2.7MM **Privately Held**
SIC: 3953 Marking devices
PA: Documart Of The Mid-South Llc
2085 E Winchester Blvd # 101
Collierville TN 38017
901 854-8405

(G-3952)
DOGMAN INDUSTRIES LLC
419 County Road 321 (38655-8911)
PHONE..................................662 832-3644
William Schaffer, *Principal*
EMP: 1 **EST:** 2017
SALES (est): 57.6K **Privately Held**
SIC: 3999 Manufacturing industries

(G-3953)
EAGLE EYE PERSONAL DEFENSE
23 County Road 277 (38655-8739)
PHONE..................................662 816-2310
Nora Webb, *Principal*
EMP: 3
SALES (est): 173.7K **Privately Held**
SIC: 3812 Defense systems & equipment

(G-3954)
END2END PUBLIC SAFETY LLC
Also Called: Arms
2627 West Oxford Loop F (38655-5442)
PHONE..................................662 513-0999
Michael Bryant, *Mng Member*
EMP: 1
SALES (corp-wide): 2.1MM **Privately Held**
WEB: www.arms.com
SIC: 7372 Prepackaged software
PA: End2end Public Safety, Llc
351 State St
Mobile AL 36603
800 776-6783

(G-3955)
FIELDERS WELDING AND ORNA IR
Also Called: Fielders Welding & Orna Ir
43 County Road 3056 (38655-9320)
PHONE..................................662 234-4256
Steve Fielder, *Owner*
EMP: 5
SQ FT: 1,500
SALES (est): 190K **Privately Held**
WEB: www.fielderswelding.com
SIC: 7692 3444 Welding repair; sheet metalwork

(G-3956)
FITMATE SOCIAL INC
108 Mulberry Ln (38655-6093)
PHONE..................................206 849-2447
Luke McKey, *CEO*
EMP: 2
SALES (est): 62.1K **Privately Held**
SIC: 7372 7389 Application computer software;

(G-3957)
HUBBARD PUBLISHING LLC
76 County Road 1061 (38655-5956)
PHONE..................................662 638-3821
James Hubbard, *Principal*
EMP: 1
SALES (est): 37.5K **Privately Held**
SIC: 2741 Miscellaneous publishing

(G-3958)
HUNTERS HOLLOW INC
658 Highway 6 W (38655-9074)
PHONE..................................662 234-5945
Donald A Guest, *President*
Star Guest, *Corp Secy*
Ishmael L Guest, *Vice Pres*
EMP: 10
SQ FT: 12,000
SALES (est): 1.2MM **Privately Held**
WEB: www.huntershollow.com
SIC: 5941 5999 7699 3479 Archery supplies; hunting equipment; fishing equipment; trophies & plaques; gun services; engraving jewelry silverware, or metal

(G-3959)
INK SPOT INC
Also Called: Cat Daddy's
304 S Lamar Blvd (38655-4012)
PHONE..................................662 236-2639
Chris Riddell, *President*
EMP: 6 **Privately Held**
SIC: 2759 Screen printing
PA: Ink Spot Inc
1301 N Lamar Blvd
Oxford MS 38655

(G-3960)
INK SPOT INC (PA)
1301 N Lamar Blvd (38655-2846)
PHONE..................................662 236-1985
Chris Riddell, *President*
Eric Boling, *Corp Secy*
EMP: 11
SALES (est): 1MM **Privately Held**
SIC: 5699 2759 T-shirts, custom printed; screen printing

(G-3961)
INVITATION OXFORD MAGAZINE
908 N Lamar Blvd (38655-2851)
P.O. Box 776 (38655-0776)
PHONE..................................662 701-8365
EMP: 12
SALES (est): 563.2K **Privately Held**
SIC: 2721 Periodicals-Publishing/Printing

(G-3962)
IRON AND STEEL DESIGN WORKS
606 Kates Cv (38655-8487)
PHONE..................................662 380-5662
EMP: 3
SQ FT: 2,500
SALES: 750K **Privately Held**
SIC: 3446 3631 Mfg Architectural Metalwork Mfg Household Cooking Equipment

(G-3963)
JC GRAPHICS LLC
1415 University Ave (38655-4031)
PHONE..................................662 832-9291
Michael N Lott, *Principal*
Nathan Lott, *Software Dev*
Michael Lott,
EMP: 30
SALES (est): 2.6MM **Privately Held**
SIC: 2759 Screen printing

(G-3964)
JJS WOODSHED
714 Long Meadow Dr (38655-9792)
PHONE..................................662 380-5034
James Craig Garvin, *President*
EMP: 2
SALES (est): 151.9K **Privately Held**
SIC: 2431 Millwork

(G-3965)
LIGHTNING BLOOM PRESS LLC
303 River Run Rd (38655-6909)
PHONE..................................662 638-3611
Deslin Chapman, *Principal*
EMP: 1
SALES (est): 37.5K **Privately Held**
SIC: 2741 Miscellaneous publishing

(G-3966)
LOCAL VOICE LLC
1503 White Oak Ln (38655-2311)
PHONE..................................662 232-8900
Paige Smith, *Principal*
EMP: 4
SALES (est): 163.4K **Privately Held**
SIC: 2711 Newspapers, publishing & printing

(G-3967)
LONG-DELAYED PUBLISHING LLC ✪
1802 Jackson Ave W # 175 (38655-4260)
PHONE..................................662 202-6229
Richard Swinney,
EMP: 1 **EST:** 2018
SALES (est): 39.8K **Privately Held**
SIC: 2741 Miscellaneous publishing

2019 Harris Directory of
Mississippi Manufacturers

▲ = Import ▼=Export
◆ =Import/Export

GEOGRAPHIC SECTION

Oxford - Lafayette County (G-4000)

(G-3968)
MAA GLOBAL SUPPLY LTD
9 Industrial Park Dr # 103 (38655-9332)
PHONE......................................662 816-4802
Nathan Yow, *President*
EMP: 11
SALES: 950K **Privately Held**
WEB: www.mississippiautoarms.com
SIC: 3484 5099 Small arms; machine guns

(G-3969)
MALIUS PRESS LLC
200 Tanner Dr (38655-8176)
PHONE......................................662 281-0955
Gregg Davidson, *Bd of Directors*
EMP: 1
SALES (est): 48.7K **Privately Held**
SIC: 2741 Miscellaneous publishing

(G-3970)
MARTIN CADERWOOD
Also Called: Caen Engineering
905 Bonnie Blue Dr (38655-6199)
P.O. Box 2005 (38655-8005)
PHONE......................................714 456-0800
Martin Caderwood, *Owner*
EMP: 2
SALES: 750K **Privately Held**
SIC: 3572 Computer storage devices

(G-3971)
MARY MARGARET ANDREWS
Also Called: Cookbook Marketplace
130 Leighton Rd (38655-2010)
PHONE......................................901 233-5463
Mary Margaret Andrews, *Owner*
EMP: 1
SALES (est): 41.5K **Privately Held**
WEB: www.frpbooks.com
SIC: 2741 Miscellaneous publishing

(G-3972)
MAX WHITE LOGGING INC
194 County Road 461 (38655-8750)
PHONE......................................662 560-3460
Max White, *President*
Max L White, *Owner*
EMP: 6
SALES (est): 490K **Privately Held**
SIC: 2411 Logging

(G-3973)
MCGREGOR INDSTL STEEL FABRCATN
658 Highway 7 S (38655-9552)
PHONE......................................662 236-7006
Bill McGregor, *President*
Tanya Thweatt, *Corp Secy*
EMP: 25
SQ FT: 25,000
SALES (est): 4.7MM **Privately Held**
WEB: www.mcgregorsteel.com
SIC: 3599 1799 Machine & other job shop work; welding on site

(G-3974)
MCKEWENS OXFORD
1110 Van Buren Ave (38655-3912)
PHONE......................................662 234-7003
EMP: 4
SALES (est): 323.3K **Privately Held**
SIC: 3421 Table & food cutlery, including butchers'

(G-3975)
NAUTILUS PUBLISHING COMPANY
426 S Lamar Blvd Ste 16 (38655-4055)
PHONE......................................662 513-0159
Deborah Hodges Bell, *President*
Carroll Chiles, *Publisher*
Neil White, *Vice Pres*
EMP: 5
SQ FT: 2,100
SALES (est): 684.3K **Privately Held**
SIC: 2721 2711 2731 Magazines: publishing only, not printed on site; newspapers: publishing only, not printed on site; book publishing

(G-3976)
NO TIME 2 COOK LLC
6 County Road 1014 (38655-8445)
P.O. Box 2880 (38655-2898)
PHONE......................................662 236-9456
Karen Kurr,
EMP: 7
SALES (est): 965.7K **Privately Held**
SIC: 2099 Emulsifiers, food

(G-3977)
NORTH MISS CONVEYOR CO INC
125 C R 370 Hwy 7 S (38655)
P.O. Box 1375 (38655-1375)
PHONE......................................662 236-1000
Darrick Vanderford, *President*
Darrell Vanderford, *Vice Pres*
David Vanderford, *Vice Pres*
Gary Carroll, *Purch Agent*
John Vanderford, *Shareholder*
EMP: 40
SQ FT: 30,000
SALES (est): 12.9MM **Privately Held**
WEB: www.nmconveyor.com
SIC: 3535 Conveyors & conveying equipment

(G-3978)
NORTH MISS ENTP INITIATIVE INC
Also Called: NMEI
9 Industrial Park Dr # 104 (38655-9332)
PHONE......................................662 281-0720
Justin Robison, *Principal*
Holly Kelly, *Exec Dir*
EMP: 1
SALES: 358.2K **Privately Held**
SIC: 3821 7389 Incubators, laboratory; office facilities & secretarial service rental

(G-3979)
OLIN CORPORATION
33 County Road 166 (38655-9721)
PHONE......................................662 281-7900
Alan Martens, *Branch Mgr*
EMP: 136
SALES (corp-wide): 6.9B **Publicly Held**
PA: Olin Corporation
190 Carondelet Plz # 1530
Saint Louis MO 63105
314 480-1400

(G-3980)
OLIN CORPORATION
411 County Road 101 (38655-8441)
PHONE......................................662 234-4056
Elaine Clark, *Manager*
EMP: 136
SALES (corp-wide): 6.9B **Publicly Held**
WEB: www.olin.com
SIC: 2812 Chlorine, compressed or liquefied
PA: Olin Corporation
190 Carondelet Plz # 1530
Saint Louis MO 63105
314 480-1400

(G-3981)
OLIN CORPORATION
Also Called: Winchester Ammunition
411 County Road 101 (38655-8441)
PHONE......................................662 513-2002
Steve Goldschmidt, *Vice Pres*
EMP: 8
SALES (corp-wide): 6.9B **Publicly Held**
SIC: 3482 Small arms ammunition
PA: Olin Corporation
190 Carondelet Plz # 1530
Saint Louis MO 63105
314 480-1400

(G-3982)
ORCHARD OXFORD
295 Highway 7 N (38655-9718)
PHONE......................................662 259-0094
EMP: 2
SALES (est): 34.7K **Privately Held**
SIC: 8699 7372 Charitable organization; application computer software

(G-3983)
ORMAN CABINET CO LLC
114 Cypress Cir (38655-9031)
P.O. Box 2515 (38655-5700)
PHONE......................................662 837-6352
Jonathan Orman, *Principal*
EMP: 2 EST: 2009
SALES (est): 164.9K **Privately Held**
SIC: 2434 Wood kitchen cabinets

(G-3984)
OXFORD ALARM CMMUNICATIONS INC
Also Called: Oxford Alarm Company
179 Highway 6 E (38655-9298)
PHONE......................................662 234-0505
William Vick, *President*
EMP: 6
SALES: 1MM **Privately Held**
WEB: www.oxfordalarm.com
SIC: 1731 3699 Telephone & telephone equipment installation; security devices

(G-3985)
OXFORD CANDLE COMPANY LLC
2 County Road 148 (38655-9698)
PHONE......................................662 816-7429
Anna Brown, *Principal*
EMP: 1
SALES (est): 43.6K **Privately Held**
SIC: 3999 Candles

(G-3986)
OXFORD EAGLE INC
4 Private Road 2050 (38655-8887)
P.O. Box 866 (38655-0866)
PHONE......................................662 234-2222
Jesse P Phillips, *President*
Jonathan Scott, *Editor*
Rita Vasilyev, *Treasurer*
Delia Childers, *Adv Dir*
Anne Smith, *Marketing Staff*
EMP: 25 EST: 1867
SQ FT: 8,000
SALES (est): 1.8MM **Privately Held**
WEB: www.oxfordeagle.com
SIC: 2711 2721 2741 Newspapers: publishing only, not printed on site; periodicals; miscellaneous publishing

(G-3987)
OXFORD LABORATORIES
213 Timber Ln (38655-5851)
PHONE......................................662 801-9764
Paige Hamann, *CEO*
Mark Hamann, *Mng Member*
EMP: 2
SALES (est): 111.9K **Privately Held**
SIC: 2844 Toilet preparations

(G-3988)
OXFORD METAL WORKS LLC
27 County Road 316 (38655-9557)
PHONE......................................662 801-7969
EMP: 2
SALES (est): 180K **Privately Held**
SIC: 3441 Structural Metal Fabrication

(G-3989)
OXFORD PRINTWEAR LLC
1722 University Ave (38655-4110)
PHONE......................................662 234-5051
Mike Tatum, *Owner*
James T Fergensun,
EMP: 13
SALES (est): 1.3MM **Privately Held**
SIC: 2759 Screen printing

(G-3990)
OXFORD SAND-CONCRETE PLANT
693 Highway 30 E (38655-8891)
PHONE......................................662 281-0355
J B Purvis, *Principal*
EMP: 2
SALES (est): 159.3K **Privately Held**
SIC: 3273 Ready-mixed concrete

(G-3991)
OXFORD SCRUBS
1151 Frontage Rd (38655-5103)
PHONE......................................662 513-0341
Lisa Gay, *Manager*
EMP: 3

SALES (est): 261.6K **Privately Held**
SIC: 3842 Clothing, fire resistant & protective

(G-3992)
P PRESS
1903 University Ave (38655-4144)
PHONE......................................662 638-3571
EMP: 1
SALES (est): 63K **Privately Held**
SIC: 2741 Miscellaneous publishing

(G-3993)
PIG NEON
711 N Lamar Blvd (38655-3242)
PHONE......................................662 638-3257
EMP: 3 EST: 2015
SALES (est): 135.6K **Privately Held**
SIC: 2813 Neon

(G-3994)
PINPLANFIX21 LLC
307 Park Dr (38655-2818)
PHONE......................................662 380-1961
Natasha Bankhead,
EMP: 1
SALES (est): 34.5K **Privately Held**
SIC: 7372 Application computer software

(G-3995)
PMQ INC
Also Called: Green Advertising
612 Mclarty Rd (38655-4500)
PHONE......................................662 234-5481
Steven Green, *President*
Linda Green, *Vice Pres*
Anna Zemek, *Accounts Exec*
EMP: 15
SALES (est): 910K **Privately Held**
WEB: www.pmq.com
SIC: 2721 Periodicals

(G-3996)
PMQ INC
605 Edison St (38655-2901)
PHONE......................................662 234-5481
Steve Green, *President*
Linda Green, *Vice Pres*
EMP: 15
SALES (est): 1.6MM **Privately Held**
SIC: 8742 2741 Marketing consulting services; miscellaneous publishing

(G-3997)
QUALITY COATINGS OXFORD
521 College Hill Rd (38655-2027)
PHONE......................................662 234-2944
Robert Northern, *Principal*
EMP: 2
SALES (est): 101.9K **Privately Held**
SIC: 3479 Metal coating & allied service

(G-3998)
RAVEN HAPPY HOUR LLC
1739 University Ave 132 (38655-4109)
PHONE......................................662 607-6604
Mandy Roth, *Mng Member*
EMP: 3 EST: 2016
SALES (est): 220.3K **Privately Held**
SIC: 2731 Book publishing

(G-3999)
RAYBURN PUBLISHING LLC
1503 White Oak Ln Ste A (38655-2311)
PHONE......................................662 232-8900
Paige Smith, *Principal*
EMP: 2
SALES (est): 95.4K **Privately Held**
SIC: 2741 Miscellaneous publishing

(G-4000)
ROSEBURG FOREST PRODUCTS CO
Oxford Melamine
26 County Road 122 (38655-8457)
PHONE......................................662 236-8080
Mike Reardon, *Opers Staff*
EMP: 300
SALES (corp-wide): 949.4MM **Privately Held**
WEB: www.rfpco.com
SIC: 2493 5031 Particleboard, plastic laminated; plywood

(PA)=Parent Co (HQ)=Headquarters (DH)=Div Headquarters

✿ = New Business established in last 2 years

2019 Harris Directory of
Mississippi Manufacturers

145

Oxford - Lafayette County (G-4001)

GEOGRAPHIC SECTION

HQ: Roseburg Forest Products Co
3660 Gateway St Ste A
Springfield OR 97477
541 679-3311

(G-4001)
RUBY PRESS LLC
207 Birch Tree Loop (38655-6911)
PHONE....................................662 832-2255
Margaret Goodwyn Bankston, *Principal*
EMP: 1
SALES (est): 45.4K **Privately Held**
SIC: 2741 Miscellaneous publishing

(G-4002)
SINHATECH
3607 Lyles Dr (38655-5708)
PHONE....................................662 234-6248
Sumon Sinha, *Owner*
EMP: 4
SALES (est): 103K **Privately Held**
WEB: www.sinhatech.com
SIC: 3728 8999 3714 3721 Aircraft parts
& equipment; scientific consulting; motor
vehicle parts & accessories; aircraft; plas-
tic processing

(G-4003)
SMW MANUFACTURING
36 County Road 166 (38655-8493)
PHONE....................................517 596-3300
Kevin McCarty, *Partner*
EMP: 3
SALES (est): 48K **Privately Held**
SIC: 3999 Manufacturing industries

(G-4004)
**SOUTHERN BELLE TRESSES
LLC ⊙**
426 Saddle Creek Dr (38655-5306)
P.O. Box 3058 (38655-3025)
PHONE....................................470 645-1777
Ladonna Cooperwood,
EMP: 1 EST: 2019
SALES (est): 39.6K **Privately Held**
SIC: 3999 Hair & hair-based products

(G-4005)
SPECTRUM III LIMITED
Also Called: Joel Little Construction
108 Sivley St (38655-3122)
PHONE....................................662 234-2461
Joel C Little, *President*
EMP: 1
SALES (est): 100K **Privately Held**
SIC: 1442 Construction sand & gravel

(G-4006)
SPIRIT ENTERPRISES
Also Called: Ole Miss Spirit, The
1296 N Lamar Blvd (38655-2812)
PHONE....................................662 236-2667
Charles Rounsaville, *Owner*
EMP: 4
SALES (est): 355.9K **Privately Held**
SIC: 2711 Newspapers

(G-4007)
TJX COMPANIES INC
Also Called: T.J. Maxx
500 Merchants Dr (38655-0038)
PHONE....................................662 236-2856
EMP: 3
SALES (corp-wide): 38.9B **Publicly Held**
SIC: 7699 7694 7538 5311 Lawn mower
repair shop; armature rewinding shops;
engine repair; department stores
PA: The Tjx Companies Inc
770 Cochituate Rd Ste 1
Framingham MA 01701
508 390-1000

(G-4008)
TROPHY SHOP
1533 University Ave (38655-4033)
PHONE....................................662 236-3726
David Pryor, *Owner*
EMP: 4
SQ FT: 3,500
SALES: 125K **Privately Held**
SIC: 5999 3479 Trophies & plaques; en-
graving jewelry silverware, or metal

(G-4009)
**WILLOW ANSTHESIA
SOLUTIONS LLC**
2704 West Oxford Loop (38655-5723)
PHONE....................................662 550-4299
Paul Carpenter, *CEO*
David McCullen, *President*
Camille Mitchell, *COO*
EMP: 4
SALES (est): 126.9K **Privately Held**
SIC: 3841 8099 Anesthesia apparatus;
blood related health services

(G-4010)
WILSONART LLC
98 County Road 122 (38655-8457)
PHONE....................................828 785-2796
EMP: 2
SALES (corp-wide): 14.7B **Publicly Held**
SIC: 3431 Sinks: enameled iron, cast iron
or pressed metal
HQ: Wilsonart Llc
2501 Wilsonart Dr
Temple TX 76504
254 207-7000

Pachuta
Clarke County

(G-4011)
CHARLES JORDAN
Also Called: Jordan Logging
49 County Road 226 (39347-5058)
PHONE....................................601 727-4753
Charles Jordan, *Owner*
EMP: 1
SALES (est): 94.3K **Privately Held**
SIC: 2411 Logging camps & contractors

(G-4012)
COOK TIMBER CO INC
20 Lake Eddins 1638 (39347)
PHONE....................................601 727-4782
Richard Cook, *President*
EMP: 6
SALES (est): 555K **Privately Held**
SIC: 2411 Logging camps & contractors

(G-4013)
**DIVERSIFIED PETROLEUM INC
(PA)**
Also Called: Reclamation Resources
741 County Road 313 (39347-9619)
PHONE....................................601 727-4926
Steve Mc Kenna Sr, *President*
Christopher Mc Kenna, *Principal*
Mark Mc Kenna, *Vice Pres*
Steve Mc Kenna Jr, *Vice Pres*
Cetty Carolyn Mc Kenna, *Treasurer*
EMP: 4
SALES (est): 2.1MM **Privately Held**
SIC: 5172 2899 Crude oil; fuel tank or en-
gine cleaning chemicals

(G-4014)
ODOM INDUSTRIES INC
100 Chestnut St (39347)
PHONE....................................601 776-2035
Jimmie Spencer, *Manager*
EMP: 33
SALES (corp-wide): 9.6MM **Privately
Held**
WEB: www.odomind.com
SIC: 2819 2879 2899 Industrial inorganic
chemicals; agricultural chemicals; chemi-
cal preparations
PA: Odom Industries, Inc.
800 Odom Industrial Rd
Waynesboro MS 39367
601 735-0088

(G-4015)
PURPOSE DESIGNS LLC
131 County Road 289 (39347-9633)
PHONE....................................601 480-2197
Victoria Johnson, *CEO*
EMP: 1
SALES (est): 43.8K **Privately Held**
SIC: 2741 7336 ; graphic arts & related
design

Pascagoula
Jackson County

(G-4016)
1 A LIFESAFER INC
1340 Denny Ave (39567-3023)
PHONE....................................800 634-3077
EMP: 1
SALES (corp-wide): 4.3MM **Privately
Held**
SIC: 3829 Measuring & controlling devices
PA: 1 A Lifesafer, Inc.
4290 Glendale Milford Rd
Blue Ash OH 45242
513 651-9560

(G-4017)
**ACCU-FAB MANUFACTURING
LLC**
1804 Roswell St (39581-2442)
PHONE....................................228 769-2532
Jackie Grimes, *Principal*
EMP: 1 EST: 2010
SALES (est): 93.1K **Privately Held**
SIC: 3999 Manufacturing industries

(G-4018)
ACTION PRINTING CENTER INC
3315 Market St (39567-3228)
PHONE....................................228 769-2676
Bob Nusko Jr, *President*
Denise Nusko, *Admin Sec*
EMP: 12 EST: 1975
SQ FT: 3,000
SALES (est): 1.9MM **Privately Held**
WEB: www.actionprintingcenter.com
SIC: 2752 Lithographing on metal; com-
mercial printing, offset

(G-4019)
**AMERICAN PLANT SERVICES
INC**
5705 Telephone Rd (39567-1128)
PHONE....................................228 762-1397
Pan Dessawoods, *Manager*
EMP: 51
SALES (est): 5.5MM
SALES (corp-wide): 8.9MM **Privately
Held**
SIC: 3312 Blast furnaces & steel mills
PA: American Plant Services Inc
6242 N Paramount Blvd
Long Beach CA 90805
562 630-1773

(G-4020)
**B-GONE STUMP GRINDING
SERVICE**
3407 Chicago Ave (39581-4255)
PHONE....................................228 762-2196
Johnny Horton, *Principal*
EMP: 1
SALES (est): 102.2K **Privately Held**
SIC: 3599 Grinding castings for the trade

(G-4021)
**BATH IRON WORKS
CORPORATION**
1000 Access Rd (39567-4485)
PHONE....................................228 935-3872
Peter Card,
EMP: 2
SALES (corp-wide): 36.1B **Publicly Held**
WEB: www.gdbiw.com
SIC: 3441 Fabricated structural metal for
ships
HQ: Bath Iron Works Corporation
700 Washington St Stop 1
Bath ME 04530
207 443-3311

(G-4022)
BAYOU CONCRETE LLC
5509 Industrial Rd (39581-5116)
PHONE....................................228 762-8911
Mike Pepper, *Manager*
EMP: 10
SALES (corp-wide): 306.5MM **Privately
Held**
WEB: www.gulfconcretellc.com
SIC: 3273 Ready-mixed concrete

HQ: Bayou Concrete Llc
1052 Highland Colony Pkwy
Ridgeland MS 39157
601 898-4000

(G-4023)
BOSARGE BOATS INC
5301 Ladner Ave (39581-2573)
PHONE....................................228 762-0888
Steven Bosarge, *President*
Sandra Bosarge, *Corp Secy*
EMP: 9
SQ FT: 2,000
SALES (est): 605.7K **Privately Held**
SIC: 0912 3799 Finfish; boat trailers

(G-4024)
**C E RUSSELL FRAMING
COMPONENTS**
715 Morgan Ave (39567-2116)
PHONE....................................228 762-9267
Calvin Russell, *Owner*
EMP: 1
SALES (est): 300K **Privately Held**
SIC: 2431 Window frames, wood

(G-4025)
CHEVRON CORPORATION
250 Industrial Rd (39581-3201)
P.O. Box 7002 (39568-7002)
PHONE....................................228 938-4600
John Watson, *CEO*
Christina King, *Safety Mgr*
Rick Grubb, *Engineer*
Guy Davis, *Design Engr*
Ed Rogers, *Electrical Engi*
▲ EMP: 120
SALES (est): 32.9MM **Privately Held**
SIC: 5541 5172 3533 Filling stations;
gasoline; petroleum products; oil & gas
drilling rigs & equipment

(G-4026)
**CHEVRON PHILLIPS CHEM CO
LLC**
250 Industrial Rd (39581-3201)
P.O. Box 7002 (39568-7002)
PHONE....................................228 938-4600
Roland Kell, *General Mgr*
Joe Robison, *Maintence Staff*
EMP: 1600
SALES (corp-wide): 8B **Privately Held**
WEB: www.chevrontexaco.com
SIC: 2911 Petroleum refining
PA: Chevron Phillips Chemical Company
Llc
10001 Six Pines Dr
The Woodlands TX 77380
832 813-4100

(G-4027)
**COASTAL FIRE AND SAFETY
LLC**
2706 Lynwood St (39567-5278)
PHONE....................................228 327-0563
James Roe,
Timothy S Andrews,
EMP: 3 EST: 2015
SALES (est): 192.9K **Privately Held**
SIC: 3999 Manufacturing industries

(G-4028)
**CONSOLIDATED PIPE & SUP CO
INC**
4220 Industrial Rd (39581-5221)
PHONE....................................228 769-1920
Allen Hudson, *Sales/Mktg Mgr*
EMP: 14
SALES (corp-wide): 518.1MM **Privately
Held**
WEB: www.consolidatedpipe.com
SIC: 5051 3494 3312 Pipe & tubing,
steel; valves & pipe fittings; blast furnaces
& steel mills
PA: Consolidated Pipe & Supply Company,
Inc.
1205 Hilltop Pkwy
Birmingham AL 35204
205 323-7261

(G-4029)
CUPITSIGNSCOM LLC
1914 Denny Ave (39567-3400)
PHONE....................................228 712-2322
Thomas Golson,

2019 Harris Directory of
Mississippi Manufacturers

▲ = Import ▼=Export
◆ =Import/Export

146

GEOGRAPHIC SECTION

Pascagoula - Jackson County (G-4054)

Jessie McNeese, *Graphic Designe*
EMP: 4
SALES (est): 320K **Privately Held**
SIC: 3993 Signs & advertising specialties

(G-4030)
E I DU PONT DE NEMOURS & CO
1001 Industrial Rd (39581-3237)
PHONE....................228 762-0870
EMP: 378
SALES (corp-wide): 7.5B **Publicly Held**
SIC: 2879 Agricultural chemicals
HQ: E. I. Du Pont De Nemours And Company
974 Centre Rd Bldg 735
Wilmington DE 19805
302 485-3000

(G-4031)
FIRST CHEMICAL CORPORATION
1001 Industrial Rd (39581-3237)
PHONE....................228 762-0870
Karen Crossman, *President*
Phillip N Perry, *Treasurer*
James L McArthur, *Admin Sec*
◆ **EMP:** 77
SQ FT: 20,000
SALES (est): 1.4MM
SALES (corp-wide): 6.6B **Publicly Held**
SIC: 2865 Aniline, nitrobenzene; nitroaniline
HQ: The Chemours Company Fc Llc
1007 Market St
Wilmington DE 19898
302 773-1000

(G-4032)
FIRST HERITAGE CREDIT CORP
3529 Denny Ave (39581-5416)
PHONE....................228 762-7000
EMP: 1 **Privately Held**
SIC: 6141 2411 Consumer finance companies; timber, cut at logging camp
PA: First Heritage Credit Corp
605 Crescent Blvd Ste 101
Ridgeland MS 39157

(G-4033)
GIBSON ELECTRIC MOTOR SVC INC
5505 Veterans St (39581-5600)
P.O. Box 1589 (39568-1589)
PHONE....................228 762-4923
Wiley Gibson, *President*
Belinda Green, *President*
Sandra Gibson, *Corp Secy*
F P Martin, *Vice Pres*
Belinda Reeves, *Vice Pres*
EMP: 8
SQ FT: 22,000
SALES (est): 2.7MM **Privately Held**
SIC: 5063 5084 7694 8734 Motors, electric; generators; meters, consumption registering; electric motor repair; rebuilding motors, except automotive; calibration & certification

(G-4034)
GOODGAMES INC
5402 Industrial Rd (39581-5109)
P.O. Box 1663 (39568-1663)
PHONE....................228 769-1827
Cheryl Wells, *President*
Robert Goodgame, *Vice Pres*
Imogene Goodgame, *Treasurer*
EMP: 10
SQ FT: 4,000
SALES (est): 1.8MM **Privately Held**
WEB: www.goodgames.com
SIC: 2752 2759 Commercial printing, offset; letterpress printing

(G-4035)
GULF COAST MARINE SUPPLY CO
3703 Industrial Rd (39581-5232)
P.O. Box 1117, Mobile AL (36633-1117)
PHONE....................228 762-9282
Brigette Nicholson, *Sales Staff*
Jim Cotten, *Manager*
EMP: 14

SALES (corp-wide): 52.6MM **Privately Held**
WEB: www.gulfcoastmarine.com
SIC: 3596 Industrial scales
PA: Gulf Coast Marine Supply Company
501 Stimrad Rd
Mobile AL 36610
251 452-8066

(G-4036)
HAYGOODS INDUSTRIAL ENGRAVERS
2114 Chicot St (39581-2815)
PHONE....................228 769-7488
Steve Haygood, *President*
Mana Haygood, *Corp Secy*
Jim Haygood, *Vice Pres*
EMP: 4
SQ FT: 6,500
SALES: 460K **Privately Held**
SIC: 5074 5078 2396 Plumbing fittings & supplies; refrigeration equipment & supplies; automotive & apparel trimmings

(G-4037)
HUNTINGTON INGALLS INC
Also Called: Ingalls Shipbuilding
1000 Access Rd (39567-4485)
P.O. Box 149 (39568-0149)
PHONE....................228 935-1122
Brian Cuccias, *President*
Judy Applegate, *General Mgr*
Rick Spaulding, *Vice Pres*
Roberto Griffin, *Engineer*
EMP: 9558 **Publicly Held**
WEB: www.avondale.com
SIC: 3731 Combat vessels, building & repairing
HQ: Huntington Ingalls Incorporated
4101 Washington Ave
Newport News VA 23607
757 380-2000

(G-4038)
HUNTINGTON INGALLS INDUSTRIES
1000 Access Rd (39567-4485)
PHONE....................228 935-1122
Philip Teek, *President*
Eric Crooker, *Vice Pres*
Wendell Scarborough, *Design Engr Mgr*
Gaylene McHale, *Engineer*
James L Sanford, *Treasurer*
EMP: 12
SALES (est): 121.6MM **Publicly Held**
WEB: www.sperry.ngc.com
SIC: 3731 Combat vessels, building & repairing
HQ: Huntington Ingalls Incorporated
4101 Washington Ave
Newport News VA 23607
757 380-2000

(G-4039)
INDUSTRIAL & CRANE SVCS INC
Also Called: I C S
2301 Petit Bois St (39581-3109)
PHONE....................601 914-4491
Robert T Williams, *President*
Ashley Williams, *Corp Secy*
Charlie McVea, *COO*
Brice Walters, *Opers Staff*
Ryan Purvis, *Chief Engr*
▲ **EMP:** 35
SQ FT: 5,000
SALES (est): 14.7MM **Privately Held**
WEB: www.industrialcraneservices.com
SIC: 3441 7389 1796 7699 Fabricated structural metal; crane & aerial lift service; machinery installation; industrial machinery & equipment repair

(G-4040)
INGALLS SHIPBUILDING INC
1000 Access Rd (39567-4485)
P.O. Box 149 (39568-0149)
PHONE....................877 871-2058
Brian Cuccias, *President*
Dave Belanger, *Vice Pres*
Mike Duthu, *Vice Pres*
Thomas Stiehle, *Vice Pres*
Joe Stockert, *Plant Mgr*
▲ **EMP:** 1
SALES (est): 204.4K **Publicly Held**
SIC: 3731 Shipbuilding & repairing

PA: Huntington Ingalls Industries, Inc.
4101 Washington Ave
Newport News VA 23607

(G-4041)
JAMESTOWN METAL MARINE SLS INC
4502 Chicot St (39581-4704)
PHONE....................228 762-3156
Pat Sutherland, *Purch Agent*
John Hacard, *Branch Mgr*
EMP: 97
SALES (corp-wide): 25.6MM **Privately Held**
SIC: 1751 3731 Ship joinery; shipbuilding & repairing
PA: Jamestown Metal Marine Sales, Inc.
4710 Nw Boca Raton Blvd
Boca Raton FL 33431
561 994-3900

(G-4042)
JP WILLIAMS MACHINE & FABRICAT
7206 Grierson St (39563-4916)
P.O. Box 1529 (39568-1529)
PHONE....................228 474-1099
J Williams, *Principal*
Josh Williams, *Principal*
EMP: 2
SALES (est): 200K **Privately Held**
SIC: 3552 Fabric forming machinery & equipment

(G-4043)
JUST FOR YOU EMBROIDERY
1915 Ingalls Ave (39567-5765)
PHONE....................228 769-8388
Katherine R Ruckdeschel, *Owner*
EMP: 1
SALES (est): 89.1K **Privately Held**
SIC: 5949 2395 Sewing & needlework; embroidery products, except schiffli machine

(G-4044)
KATHYS FRAME WORKS INC
2300 Ingalls Ave (39567-5858)
PHONE....................228 769-7672
Kevin Skelton, *President*
EMP: 3
SQ FT: 2,000
SALES: 190K **Privately Held**
SIC: 2499 5999 Picture & mirror frames, wood; picture frames, ready made

(G-4045)
KNIGHTS MAR & INDUS SVCS INC
3421 Industrial Rd (39581-5213)
PHONE....................228 769-5550
Brian Knight, *President*
David Knight, *COO*
David E Knight, *Vice Pres*
Jim Patano, *Vice Pres*
Kaley Knight, *Project Engr*
EMP: 242
SQ FT: 33,500
SALES (est): 40.8MM **Privately Held**
WEB: www.knightsmarine.com
SIC: 3441 3732 7361 Fabricated structural metal; boat building & repairing; labor contractors (employment agency)

(G-4046)
LEWIS YAGER MELBALEEN J
Also Called: Lewis Printing Service
501 Krebs Ave (39567-3123)
PHONE....................228 762-3152
Melbaleen J Lewis-Yager, *Owner*
EMP: 3
SQ FT: 4,000
SALES: 500K **Privately Held**
SIC: 2752 7334 2791 2789 Commercial printing, offset; blueprinting service; typesetting; bookbinding & related work

(G-4047)
M M FLECHAS SHIPYARD CO INC
4514 Flechas St (39567-1604)
PHONE....................228 762-3628
Miguel M Flechas III, *President*
Karen Johnson, *Corp Secy*
EMP: 7

SQ FT: 20,000
SALES (est): 854.9K **Privately Held**
SIC: 3732 Motorboats, inboard or outboard: building & repairing; fishing boats: lobster, crab, oyster, etc.: small

(G-4048)
MAELSTROM SQUARE LLC
4112 Victor St (39567-3448)
PHONE....................470 378-9064
Julius Wells, *President*
Carlos Wells, *Vice Pres*
EMP: 2
SALES (est): 71.7K **Privately Held**
SIC: 3911 5094 5399 5621 Rosaries or other small religious articles, precious metal; jewelry & precious stones; warehouse club stores; teenage apparel;

(G-4049)
MAIN STREET PASCAGOULA
Also Called: PASCAGOULA MAIN STREET
303 Delmas Ave Cottagea (39567-4106)
PHONE....................228 219-1114
Michele Coats, *Ch of Bd*
Joe Stout, *Vice Pres*
Herman Smith, *Treasurer*
Dj Garrison, *Bookkeeper*
Rebecca Davis, *Director*
EMP: 1
SALES (est): 84.5K **Privately Held**
SIC: 3369 Nonferrous foundries

(G-4050)
MARINE FLOORING LLC
2827 Andrew Ave (39567-1801)
PHONE....................832 472-0661
EMP: 2
SALES (est): 86K **Privately Held**
SIC: 3731 Shipbuilding & repairing

(G-4051)
MARITIME DEFENSE STRATEGY LLC
Also Called: Ephesians Security
1405 General Lee St (39567-6413)
PHONE....................352 302-1442
Joseph Powell,
Mark Perry,
EMP: 2
SALES (est): 85.1K **Privately Held**
SIC: 3812 Defense systems & equipment

(G-4052)
MAYMAR MARINE SUPPLY INC
Also Called: Mike P Mavromihalis
4929 Denny Ave (39581-5521)
P.O. Box 351 (39568-0351)
PHONE....................228 762-2241
George Mavromihalis, *President*
Gary L Roberts, *Principal*
George Halis, *Vice Pres*
Mike Mavromihalis, *Director*
▲ **EMP:** 7
SALES (est): 1.5MM **Privately Held**
WEB: www.maymarmarine.com
SIC: 3531 Marine related equipment

(G-4053)
MDH MARINE ART
1015 Kell Ave (39567-2211)
PHONE....................228 769-1692
Robert Hardy, *Owner*
EMP: 1
SALES (est): 54.5K **Privately Held**
SIC: 3519 Internal combustion engines

(G-4054)
N ROLLS-RYCE AMER HOLDINGS INC
1000 W River Rd (39568)
P.O. Box 1528 (39568-1528)
PHONE....................228 762-0728
Peter Lapp, *Branch Mgr*
▲ **EMP:** 4
SALES (corp-wide): 20.2B **Privately Held**
SIC: 3599 Propellers, ship & boat: machined
HQ: Rolls-Royce North America Holdings Inc.
1875 Explorer St Ste 200
Reston VA 20190
703 834-1700

(PA)=Parent Co (HQ)=Headquarters (DH)=Div Headquarters
✿ = New Business established in last 2 years

2019 Harris Directory of
Mississippi Manufacturers

147

Pascagoula - Jackson County (G-4055)

GEOGRAPHIC SECTION

(G-4055)
NAVAL ENGINEERING WORKS INC
3614 Frederic St (39567-3136)
PHONE..................................228 769-1080
Bobby Ray Green, *President*
Carolyn A Green, *Corp Secy*
▼ EMP: 9
SALES (est): 1.1MM **Privately Held**
SIC: 3731 8711 Shipbuilding & repairing; designing: ship, boat, machine & product

(G-4056)
NGSS INGALLS OPERATIONS
1000 Jerry St Pes Hwy Pe S (39568)
P.O. Box 149 (39568-0149)
PHONE..................................228 935-5731
EMP: 4 EST: 2008
SALES (est): 240K **Privately Held**
SIC: 3731 Shipbuilding/Repairing

(G-4057)
NORTHROP GRUMMAN CORP ◆
510 Krebs Ave (39567-3124)
PHONE..................................434 845-9181
EMP: 2 EST: 2019
SALES (est): 86K **Privately Held**
SIC: 3721 Aircraft

(G-4058)
PAK UNIFORM & EMB SHOPPE LLC
4002 Alandale St (39581-4608)
PHONE..................................228 365-6695
Tommie Kelly, *CEO*
Patricia Kelly,
EMP: 3 EST: 2014
SALES (est): 163.5K **Privately Held**
SIC: 2329 2326 Men's & boys' athletic uniforms; football uniforms: men's, youths' & boys'; basketball uniforms: men's, youths' & boys'; work apparel, except uniforms; medical & hospital uniforms, men's

(G-4059)
PANDLE INC
2401 Petit Bois St (39581-3103)
P.O. Box 2039 (39569-2039)
PHONE..................................228 762-3300
Walter Randle, *President*
EMP: 25
SALES (est): 5.6MM **Privately Held**
SIC: 2951 Asphalt & asphaltic paving mixtures (not from refineries)

(G-4060)
PASCAGOULA REFINERY
250 Industrial Rd (39581-3201)
PHONE..................................228 938-4563
Warren Bosarge, *Principal*
▲ EMP: 6
SALES (est): 874.4K **Privately Held**
SIC: 3559 Petroleum refinery equipment

(G-4061)
PAVCO INDUSTRIES INC (PA)
4703 Pascagoula St (39567-1711)
P.O. Box 612 (39568-0612)
PHONE..................................228 762-3959
David Boland, *President*
Linda Grimes, *CFO*
Shelley Tanner, *Sales Staff*
Mary Boland, *Admin Sec*
EMP: 81 EST: 1947
SQ FT: 190,000
SALES (est): 8.8MM **Privately Held**
WEB: www.pavcoind.com
SIC: 2435 2752 6552 Panels, hardwood plywood; commercial printing, offset; subdividers & developers

(G-4062)
PEMCO-NAVAL ENGRG WORKS INC
3614 Frederic St (39567-3136)
PHONE..................................228 769-1080
Bobby R Green, *CEO*
Jason E Broadus, *President*
Jason Broadus, *General Mgr*
Jessica Broadus, *Treasurer*
Pam Perkins, *Manager*
▲ EMP: 42 EST: 1971
SQ FT: 94,000

SALES (est): 9MM **Privately Held**
WEB: www.pemco-inc.com
SIC: 3441 Fabricated structural metal

(G-4063)
RAINBOW SPRING WATER INC
3310 Old Mobile Ave (39581-3740)
PHONE..................................228 769-6262
Camille C Sykes, *President*
John O Sykes, *Corp Secy*
EMP: 16
SQ FT: 4,400
SALES: 1.5MM **Privately Held**
SIC: 5499 2899 Water: distilled mineral or spring; chemical preparations

(G-4064)
ROLLS-ROYCE MARINE NORTH AMER
Rolls-Royce Naval Marine
3719 Industrial Rd (39581-5232)
P.O. Box 1528 (39568-1528)
PHONE..................................228 762-0728
Don Roussinos, *President*
Derek Jenkins, *General Mgr*
William T Powers, *CFO*
Scott Sibley, *Sales Mgr*
James Travis, *Sales Mgr*
EMP: 59
SALES (corp-wide): 20.2B **Privately Held**
SIC: 3599 3429 3366 5091 Propellers, ship & boat: machined; manufactured hardware (general); copper foundries; boat accessories & parts; marine crafts & supplies
HQ: Rolls-Royce Marine North America Inc
110 Norfolk St
Walpole MA 02081
508 668-9610

(G-4065)
RUBBER & SPECIALTIES INC
2802 Andrew Ave (39567-1802)
PHONE..................................228 762-6103
Glen Culpepper, *Manager*
EMP: 5
SQ FT: 7,600
SALES (corp-wide): 31.9MM **Privately Held**
SIC: 5085 3492 Rubber goods, mechanical; hose & tube fittings & assemblies, hydraulic/pneumatic
PA: Rubber & Specialties, Inc.
5011 Commerce Park Cir
Pensacola FL 32505
850 478-9778

(G-4066)
S W KREBS WOODWORKING CO LLC
2009 Resca De La Palma St (39567-5675)
P.O. Box 773 (39568-0773)
PHONE..................................228 762-1064
Stephen W Krebs Jr,
EMP: 4
SQ FT: 18,000
SALES: 200K **Privately Held**
SIC: 2541 Cabinets, lockers & shelving

(G-4067)
SELF SERVE MARINE INC
4514 Flechas St (39567-1604)
PHONE..................................228 762-3628
Miguel M Flechas III, *President*
EMP: 3
SALES (est): 187.2K **Privately Held**
SIC: 3799 Boat trailers

(G-4068)
ST ENGINEER HALTER MARINE AND
601 Bayou Casotte Pkwy (39581-9600)
PHONE..................................228 762-0010
Nian Hua Lim, *President*
Tom Vecchiolla, *Principal*
Jeffrey Gehrmann, *Vice Pres*
Meng Twang Lim, *Director*
Sing Chan Ng, *Director*
EMP: 90
SALES: 1.2MM
SALES (corp-wide): 4.8B **Privately Held**
SIC: 1389 Construction, repair & dismantling services

HQ: St Engineering North America, Inc.
99 Canal Center Plz # 220
Alexandria VA 22314
703 739-2610

(G-4069)
STEVE HARRIS
Also Called: Harris Sheet Metal
1902 Chicot St (39581-2813)
PHONE..................................228 769-8350
Steve Harris, *Owner*
EMP: 3
SALES: 125K **Privately Held**
SIC: 3444 Sheet metalwork

(G-4070)
STITCHES BY LEE LLC
903 Tucker Ave (39567-4358)
P.O. Box 1431 (39568-1431)
PHONE..................................228 769-7460
Beverly Lee, *Mng Member*
EMP: 3
SQ FT: 900
SALES (est): 213.8K **Privately Held**
SIC: 5699 2395 Uniforms; embroidery & art needlework

(G-4071)
TRI-COAST INDUSTRIES INC
1007 Del Norte Cir (39581-2021)
PHONE..................................228 369-9924
EMP: 2
SALES (est): 98.6K **Privately Held**
SIC: 3999 Mfg Misc Products

(G-4072)
VISION TECHNOLOGIES MARINE INC
Also Called: VT Marine
601 Bayou Casotte Pkwy (39581-9600)
P.O. Box 1308 (39568-1308)
PHONE..................................228 762-0010
Lim Lim Nian Hua, *President*
Pawan Agrawal, *Vice Pres*
Lee Stokes, *Vice Pres*
EMP: 50
SALES: 10MM
SALES (corp-wide): 4.8B **Privately Held**
SIC: 3731 Shipbuilding & repairing
HQ: Vt Systems
99 Canal Center Plz # 220
Alexandria VA 22314
703 739-2610

(G-4073)
VT HALTER MARINE INC (DH)
900 Bayou Casotte Pkwy (39581-9602)
P.O. Box 1328 (39568-1328)
PHONE..................................228 696-6888
William E Skinner, *CEO*
D Margaret Gambrell, *Principal*
Paul J Albert, *COO*
Rear Admiral John, *Exec VP*
Robert A Socha, *Senior VP*
▲ EMP: 143
SQ FT: 33,600
SALES (est): 445.5MM
SALES (corp-wide): 4.8B **Privately Held**
SIC: 3731 Shipbuilding & repairing
HQ: St Engineering North America, Inc.
99 Canal Center Plz # 220
Alexandria VA 22314
703 739-2610

(G-4074)
WILLIAMS MACHINE WORKS INC
5309 Industrial Rd (39581-5110)
PHONE..................................228 712-2667
David Hicks, *Branch Mgr*
EMP: 3
SALES (corp-wide): 1.3MM **Privately Held**
SIC: 3599 Machine shop, jobbing & repair
PA: Williams Machine Works Inc
5624 Main St
Moss Point MS 39563
228 475-7651

(G-4075)
WORLD MARINE MISSISSIPPI LLC
601 Bayou Casotte Pkwy (39581-9600)
P.O. Box 2007, Mobile AL (36652-2007)
PHONE..................................228 762-0010

Richard Marler, *President*
Ronald Schnoor, *Senior VP*
Christopher Cunningham, *CFO*
EMP: 200
SALES (est): 8.2MM **Privately Held**
SIC: 3731 Shipbuilding & repairing
HQ: World Marine, Llc
601 S Royal St
Mobile AL 36603
251 338-7400

┌─────────────────────────┐
│ **Pass Christian**   │
│ *Harrison County*   │
└─────────────────────────┘

(G-4076)
A STEP ABOVE MARINE CONTRS LLC
224 W North St (39571-3711)
PHONE..................................228 452-5122
Don Coulon,
EMP: 2
SALES (est): 264.5K **Privately Held**
SIC: 3732 Boat building & repairing

(G-4077)
BARBARA OMEALLIE
29002 Sixteen Section Rd (39571-9300)
P.O. Box 5 (39571-0005)
PHONE..................................228 255-7573
Barbara O'Meallie, *Owner*
EMP: 1
SALES (est): 91K **Privately Held**
SIC: 5199 2752 Advertising specialties; commercial printing, lithographic

(G-4078)
CHEMOURS COMPANY FC LLC
Also Called: De Lisle Plant
7685 Kiln Delisle Rd (39571-9423)
P.O. Box 430 (39571-0430)
PHONE..................................228 255-2100
Steve Phillips, *Project Mgr*
Aldo Morell, *Manager*
Eduardo Ramos, *Manager*
EMP: 50
SALES (corp-wide): 6.6B **Publicly Held**
WEB: www.dupont.com
SIC: 2819 2816 Industrial inorganic chemicals; inorganic pigments
HQ: The Chemours Company Fc Llc
1007 Market St
Wilmington DE 19898
302 773-1000

(G-4079)
CHRISTIAN PASS SOAP
Also Called: PC Soap
330 W North St (39571-3834)
PHONE..................................228 222-4303
Paula Winsey, *General Mgr*
EMP: 5
SALES (est): 980.5K **Privately Held**
SIC: 2844 5999 Toilet preparations; toiletries, cosmetics & perfumes

(G-4080)
COLLINS WOODWORKS
6328 Menge Ave (39571-8877)
PHONE..................................228 452-2627
Harry Collins, *Owner*
EMP: 1
SALES (est): 85.6K **Privately Held**
SIC: 2599 Furniture & fixtures

(G-4081)
DIXIE SIGNS LLC
9329 Edwin Ladner Rd (39571-8319)
PHONE..................................228 255-5548
Glen Lidner,
Monica Lidner,
EMP: 2
SALES (est): 171.2K **Privately Held**
SIC: 3993 Signs & advertising specialties

(G-4082)
E VEGELY SIGNS
28453 Sixteen Section Rd (39571-9343)
PHONE..................................228 255-7543
Edward Vegely, *Owner*
EMP: 1
SALES (est): 76.8K **Privately Held**
SIC: 3993 Signs & advertising specialties

2019 Harris Directory of
Mississippi Manufacturers

▲ = Import ▼=Export
◆ =Import/Export

GEOGRAPHIC SECTION

Pearl - Rankin County (G-4114)

(G-4083)
FINNESSE FABRICATIONS & STEEL
11661 Katie Dr (39571-5422)
PHONE....................................228 216-2102
Jeremie Ramond, *Principal*
EMP: 1
SALES (est): 39.6K Privately Held
SIC: 3999 Manufacturing industries

(G-4084)
GOLD COAST MANUFACTURING INC
220 Mcdonald Dr (39571-3923)
PHONE....................................228 261-6290
Walter Dees, *President*
EMP: 1
SALES (est): 62.3K Privately Held
SIC: 3999 Atomizers, toiletry

(G-4085)
GOODINGS FINE WOODWORKING
23220 Enchanted Ave (39571-8998)
PHONE....................................228 255-9037
John Gooding, *Owner*
EMP: 1 EST: 1994
SALES (est): 88.1K Privately Held
SIC: 3553 Cabinet makers' machinery

(G-4086)
GULF COAST PRE-STRESS INC (PA)
494 N Market St (39571-2712)
P.O. Box 825 (39571-0419)
PHONE....................................228 452-7270
Michael Spruill, *President*
Ben Spruill, *Project Mgr*
Dusty Carver, *Purch Mgr*
Andrew Levens, *Chief Engr*
Peter Wareing, *Treasurer*
▲ EMP: 130
SALES (est): 21.9MM Privately Held
WEB: www.gcprestress.com
SIC: 3272 Prestressed concrete products

(G-4087)
HI TECH CONCRETE INC
327 Courtenay Ave (39571-4109)
P.O. Box 251 (39571-0251)
PHONE....................................228 452-2125
EMP: 1
SALES (est): 110K Privately Held
SIC: 3273 Mfg Ready-Mixed Concrete

(G-4088)
HONEYLAND INC
25439 Elmer Ladner Rd (39571-8948)
P.O. Box 807, Earle AR (72331-0800)
PHONE....................................870 635-1160
Lloyd Shynes, *President*
Lloyd S Hynes, *President*
EMP: 1
SALES: 200K Privately Held
SIC: 2099 Honey, strained & bottled

(G-4089)
IMAGING INFORMATICS LLC
Also Called: Imaging Infomatics
529 E Second St (39571-4530)
P.O. Box 4005, Bay St Louis (39521-4005)
PHONE....................................228 332-0674
Katherine Breath, *Principal*
EMP: 2
SALES (est): 87.9K Privately Held
SIC: 7372 5045 8748 Prepackaged software; computers, peripherals & software; business consulting

(G-4090)
INLINE BARRICADES MET PDTS INC
7114 Kiln Delisle Rd (39571-9218)
P.O. Box 6219, Diamondhead (39525-6003)
PHONE....................................800 229-4790
Joseph C Gallagher, *President*
Jeannine Gallagher, *Admin Sec*
EMP: 3
SQ FT: 5,000
SALES (est): 406.2K Privately Held
WEB: www.inlinebarricades.com
SIC: 3499 Barricades, metal

(G-4091)
MATHESON TRI-GAS INC
7635 Kiln Delisle Rd (39571-9423)
PHONE....................................228 255-6661
James Wartin, *Branch Mgr*
EMP: 10 Privately Held
WEB: www.matheson-trigas.com
SIC: 2813 3443 Oxygen, compressed or liquefied; nitrogen; argon; acetylene; fabricated plate work (boiler shop)
HQ: Matheson Tri-Gas, Inc.
150 Allen Rd Ste 302
Basking Ridge NJ 07920
908 991-9200

(G-4092)
PANGAEA EXPLORATION INC
104 Vista Dr (39571-3519)
PHONE....................................228 452-7544
EMP: 1 EST: 1997
SALES (est): 130K Privately Held
SIC: 1382 Oil/Gas Exploration Services

(G-4093)
PATCO SALES INC
100 Birch Dr (39571-2300)
PHONE....................................228 207-4171
Patricia Meyer, *President*
EMP: 3
SALES (est): 139.8K Privately Held
SIC: 3731 Commercial cargo ships, building & repairing

(G-4094)
PROTEC STEEL INDUSTRIES LLC
24101 Spyders Dr (39571-9414)
PHONE....................................228 364-4240
Andrew Marshall, *Mng Member*
EMP: 3
SALES (est): 270.6K Privately Held
SIC: 3999 Atomizers, toiletry

(G-4095)
SOUTHERN PRTG & SILK SCREENING
230 Davis Ave (39571-4506)
PHONE....................................228 452-7309
Connie Jenkins, *President*
Homer Jenkins, *Vice Pres*
EMP: 15
SQ FT: 5,000
SALES (est): 1.5MM Privately Held
SIC: 2253 2752 7299 5621 T-shirts & tops, knit; commercial printing, lithographic; calendars, lithographed; stitching services; ready-to-wear apparel, women's; shirts, men's & boys'

(G-4096)
SOUTHERN SIGNS
13117 C Necaise Rd (39571-9566)
PHONE....................................228 255-4122
Travis Necaise, *Owner*
Donna Necaise, *Co-Owner*
EMP: 3
SALES (est): 194.5K Privately Held
SIC: 3993 1799 Signs & advertising specialties; sign installation & maintenance

(G-4097)
TOMMY L HENDERSON
Also Called: Tlh Consturction
607 W North St (39571-2607)
PHONE....................................228 452-4484
Tommy L Henderson, *Owner*
Penny Henderson, *Co-Owner*
EMP: 4 EST: 1998
SALES: 275K Privately Held
SIC: 1521 1542 2426 Single-family housing construction; commercial & office building, new construction; furniture dimension stock, hardwood

(G-4098)
WRESTLING USA MAGAZINE INC
590 Royal Oak Dr Apt 18 (39571-2539)
PHONE....................................406 360-9421
Lanny Bryant, *President*
Ann Bryant, *Vice Pres*
EMP: 4
SALES: 100K Privately Held
SIC: 2721 Magazines: publishing & printing

(G-4099)
WRESTLING USA MAGAZINE INC
590 Royal Oak Dr Apt 18 (39571-2539)
PHONE....................................406 549-4448
EMP: 4
SALES: 569K Privately Held
SIC: 2721 Magazine Publishing

Pattison
Claiborne County

(G-4100)
DEBBIE F SHELTON
7126 Mcbride Rd (39144-6111)
PHONE....................................601 535-7162
Debbie F Shelton, *Owner*
EMP: 1
SALES: 275K Privately Held
SIC: 2015 Poultry slaughtering & processing

Pearl
Rankin County

(G-4101)
4M ENTERPRISES LLC
Also Called: Line-X of Jackson
5219 Highway 80 E (39208-9302)
PHONE....................................601 664-0030
EMP: 5
SALES (est): 711.4K Privately Held
SIC: 2821 Plastics materials & resins

(G-4102)
A-SQUARED PRINTING LLC
211 Eldorado Cir (39208-9397)
PHONE....................................601 497-0280
Anna Nicole Montgomery, *Principal*
EMP: 2
SALES (est): 83.9K Privately Held
SIC: 2752 Commercial printing, lithographic

(G-4103)
AD ART SIGN
Also Called: Ad Art Signs Promotions
424 N Bierdeman Rd (39208-4616)
P.O. Box 5537 (39288-5537)
PHONE....................................601 939-8000
Jerome Taylor, *Owner*
EMP: 1
SQ FT: 3,000
SALES (est): 120.3K Privately Held
SIC: 3993 Signs & advertising specialties

(G-4104)
ADVANCE TOOL AND DIE INC
2750 Old Brandon Rd (39208-4701)
P.O. Box 5465 (39288-5465)
PHONE....................................601 939-1291
Riley Dewain Miller, *President*
Dewain Scott Miller, *Vice Pres*
Webbie Miller, *Admin Sec*
EMP: 6
SQ FT: 13,800
SALES (est): 400K Privately Held
SIC: 3312 3469 Tool & die steel; metal stampings

(G-4105)
AUTO-CHLOR SYSTEM OF MID S LLC
193 Country Place Pkwy (39208-6676)
PHONE....................................601 420-0331
Clyde McDaniel, *Branch Mgr*
EMP: 8
SALES (corp-wide): 61.9MM Privately Held
SIC: 3589 Dishwashing machines, commercial
HQ: Auto-Chlor System Of The Mid South, Llc
746 Poplar Ave
Memphis TN 38105

(G-4106)
B FICKLIN INVESTMENTS LLC
184 Beechwood Cir (39208-5070)
PHONE....................................601 454-2724

Brandon Ficklin,
EMP: 1
SALES (est): 82.4K Privately Held
SIC: 2085 Vodka (alcoholic beverage)

(G-4107)
BIG RIVER CLASSICS INC
198 Van Doren Ct (39208-3822)
PHONE....................................601 856-6607
Bobby Clark, *Principal*
EMP: 1
SALES (est): 67.5K Privately Held
SIC: 2389 Apparel & accessories

(G-4108)
CAPITAL CITY METAL WORKS INC
817 Airport Rd S (39208)
PHONE....................................601 939-7467
Brent Quarles, *President*
Kimberly Quarles, *Corp Secy*
EMP: 2
SQ FT: 10,000
SALES: 600K Privately Held
SIC: 3444 1711 Sheet metal specialties, not stamped; ventilation & duct work contractor

(G-4109)
CAPITOL CITY LABEL INC
46 Valley Dr (39208-6782)
P.O. Box 734, Brandon (39043-0734)
PHONE....................................601 420-2375
Jimmy Briggs, *President*
EMP: 9
SALES: 5MM Privately Held
SIC: 2679 Tags & labels, paper

(G-4110)
CLAYTON HOMES INC
2318 Highway 80 E (39208-3323)
PHONE....................................601 939-0461
Clayton Stutts, *Branch Mgr*
EMP: 4
SALES (corp-wide): 225.3B Publicly Held
SIC: 2451 Mobile homes
HQ: Clayton Homes, Inc.
5000 Clayton Rd
Maryville TN 37804
865 380-3000

(G-4111)
COMFORT DESIGNS INC
1732 Old Whitfield Rd (39208-9135)
PHONE....................................601 932-7555
Gregory E Taylor, *President*
Chris D Taylor, *Corp Secy*
EMP: 19
SALES (est): 3.7MM Privately Held
SIC: 3634 5074 Electric household fans, heaters & humidifiers; heating equipment (hydronic)

(G-4112)
CORRUGATED SERVICES AMERICA
1440 Sweetwater Dr (39208-6418)
PHONE....................................601 209-6297
EMP: 3
SALES (est): 197.8K Privately Held
SIC: 2653 Corrugated & solid fiber boxes

(G-4113)
CR CUSTOM WOODWORKS
304 Creek Ct (39208-4159)
PHONE....................................601 624-2310
Chris Renaldo, *Principal*
EMP: 1
SALES (est): 54.1K Privately Held
SIC: 2431 Millwork

(G-4114)
DESTINIS CREATIONS AND EXQUIS
523 Fox Run Trl Apt H8 (39208-5707)
PHONE....................................601 317-3764
Da'vina Fairley-Horne,
EMP: 1
SALES (est): 25K Privately Held
SIC: 7692 5947 7299 Automotive welding; gift, novelty & souvenir shop; miscellaneous personal service

---

(PA)=Parent Co (HQ)=Headquarters (DH)=Div Headquarters
✿ = New Business established in last 2 years

2019 Harris Directory of
Mississippi Manufacturers

149

Pearl - Rankin County (G-4115)   GEOGRAPHIC SECTION

(G-4115)
DURACO INC
2000 Old Whitfield Rd (39208-9170)
P.O. Box 6127, Jackson (39288-6127)
PHONE..................................601 932-2100
Mark Hefty, *President*
Greg Longcore, *Treasurer*
Nat Alford, *VP Sales*
J Scott Timmer, *Admin Sec*
EMP: 25
SQ FT: 4,500
SALES (est): 5.3MM **Privately Held**
SIC: 3531 Drags, road (construction & road maintenance equipment)

(G-4116)
EXIDE TECHNOLOGIES
154 Concourse Dr (39208-6747)
PHONE..................................601 936-7788
Dana Ellis, *Coordinator*
EMP: 10
SALES (corp-wide): 2.3B **Privately Held**
WEB: www.exideworld.com
SIC: 3691 4953 2819 3629 Storage batteries; refuse systems; industrial inorganic chemicals; battery chargers, rectifying or nonrotating
PA: Exide Technologies
13000 Deerfield Pkwy # 200
Milton GA 30004
678 566-9000

(G-4117)
FIRST COASTAL EXTERIORS LLC
203 Priester Dr (39208-3305)
PHONE..................................769 251-1894
Richard Miller, *Branch Mgr*
EMP: 1
SALES (corp-wide): 2.4MM **Privately Held**
SIC: 5039 2952 Doors, sliding; siding materials
PA: First Coastal Exteriors, Llc
3349a Halls Mill Rd
Mobile AL 36606
251 725-1118

(G-4118)
FLAMBEAUX CANDLE COMPANY
3064 Highway 80 E (39208-3420)
PHONE..................................769 251-0142
EMP: 1
SALES (est): 75.6K **Privately Held**
SIC: 3999 Candles

(G-4119)
FLOWERS BKG CO BATON ROUGE LLC
4635 Highway 80 E (39208-4226)
PHONE..................................601 932-7843
Merlyn Walton, *Manager*
EMP: 1
SALES (corp-wide): 3.9B **Publicly Held**
SIC: 2051 Bread, cake & related products
HQ: Flowers Baking Co. Of Baton Rouge, Llc.
1504 Florida Blvd
Baton Rouge LA 70802
225 381-9699

(G-4120)
FOWLER BUICK-GMC INC (PA)
5801 Highway 80 E (39208-8932)
P.O. Box 106, Brandon (39043-0106)
PHONE..................................601 360-0200
James E Fowler Sr, *Ch of Bd*
Larry Cruise, *President*
Frances Fowler, *Corp Secy*
Jim Wright, *CFO*
Joy Cruise, *Data Proc Exec*
EMP: 45
SQ FT: 150,000
SALES (est): 22.1MM **Privately Held**
WEB: www.fowlerusedcars.com
SIC: 5511 5521 7515 7513 Automobiles, new & used; used car dealers; passenger car leasing; truck rental & leasing, no drivers; automobiles & other motor vehicles; motor vehicle parts & accessories

(G-4121)
FROM OUR CUP TO YOURS
729 Woodrun Dr (39208-7913)
PHONE..................................601 214-7689
Tamara Jackson,
Timothy Jackson,
EMP: 2 **EST:** 2012
SALES (est): 95.3K **Privately Held**
SIC: 5149 2095 5963 Coffee & tea; instant coffee; food service, mobile, except coffee-cart

(G-4122)
GEORGIA-PACIFIC LLC
555 Gulf Line Rd (39208-3402)
PHONE..................................601 939-7797
Bruce Keith, *Manager*
EMP: 12
SQ FT: 4,523
SALES (corp-wide): 40.9B **Privately Held**
WEB: www.gp.com
SIC: 2431 2621 2631 2421 Millwork; paper mills; paperboard mills; sawmills & planing mills, general; pulp mills; gypsum products
HQ: Georgia-Pacific Llc
133 Peachtree St Nw
Atlanta GA 30303
404 652-4000

(G-4123)
GILCORP
Also Called: Duraco Industries, Inc.
2000 Old Whitfield Rd (39208-9170)
P.O. Box 6127 (39288-6127)
PHONE..................................601 932-2100
Robert Gilchrist, *CEO*
Nat Alford, *Vice Pres*
EMP: 58
SALES (est): 1.5MM
SALES (corp-wide): 204.2MM **Privately Held**
SIC: 3743 Railroad equipment
HQ: Cimline, Inc.
2601 Niagara Ln N
Minneapolis MN 55447
763 557-1982

(G-4124)
GT SCREEN PRTG & PROMOTIONS
5909 Old Brandon Rd Ste 4 (39208-9015)
PHONE..................................601 759-9858
Patricia Peppers, *Principal*
EMP: 2
SQ FT: 1,250
SALES (est): 242.5K **Privately Held**
SIC: 2759 Commercial printing

(G-4125)
HAGEN CORPORATION
Also Called: AAA Printing & Graphics
108 Jetport Dr (39208-6746)
P.O. Box 5477 (39288-5477)
PHONE..................................601 932-3138
Bob Brooker, *President*
Robert Hagen, *President*
Donna Hagen, *Vice Pres*
Michael Schwarz, *Vice Pres*
Mickey Ray, *Admin Sec*
EMP: 8
SQ FT: 10,000
SALES (est): 1.4MM **Privately Held**
SIC: 2752 2789 2759 Commercial printing, offset; bookbinding & related work; commercial printing

(G-4126)
HELMERICH & PAYNE INTL DRLG CO
Also Called: Southern Division
102 Ware St (39208-9470)
P.O. Box 6173 (39288-6173)
PHONE..................................601 939-1589
Scott Strack, *Opers Mgr*
Tom Freeny, *Branch Mgr*
EMP: 18
SALES (corp-wide): 1.8B **Publicly Held**
SIC: 1381 Directional drilling oil & gas wells
HQ: Helmerich & Payne International Drilling Co Inc
1437 S Boulder Ave # 1400
Tulsa OK 74119
918 742-5531

(G-4127)
INDUSTRIAL STEEL CORPORATION (PA)
821 Highway 475 S (39208-6635)
P.O. Box 98108, Jackson (39298-8108)
PHONE..................................601 932-5555
Robert Donald, *President*
▲ **EMP:** 9
SQ FT: 27,400
SALES (est): 1.7MM **Privately Held**
WEB: www.indsteel.com
SIC: 3312 Blast furnaces & steel mills

(G-4128)
LEC INC
110 Excell Dr (39208-6752)
P.O. Box 127, Brandon (39043-0127)
PHONE..................................601 939-8535
Harold A Hogue, *President*
Justin Hogue, *Vice Pres*
Brady Sims, *Engineer*
Joe Mixon, *Treasurer*
Melissa Weaver, *Controller*
EMP: 28
SQ FT: 12,000
SALES: 5.9MM **Privately Held**
WEB: www.lecinc.com
SIC: 8711 3625 3823 Engineering services; electric controls & control accessories, industrial; industrial instrmnts msrmnt display/control process variable

(G-4129)
LEONARD METAL FABRICATORS INC
5012 Highway 80 E (39208-4224)
PHONE..................................601 936-4994
Mariel Leonard, *President*
Mike Mann, *Plant Mgr*
Vic Boggs, *Representative*
EMP: 24
SQ FT: 48,000
SALES (est): 5.6MM **Privately Held**
WEB: www.leonardmetal.com
SIC: 3556 3444 Food products machinery; sheet metalwork

(G-4130)
MASON OVERSTREET WLDG MCH WORK
720 M And O Dr (39208-3335)
P.O. Box 5791 (39288-5791)
PHONE..................................601 932-1794
John Mason, *President*
John Overstreet, *Vice Pres*
EMP: 35 **EST:** 1975
SQ FT: 17,800
SALES (est): 5.2MM **Privately Held**
SIC: 3599 7692 7629 Machine shop, jobbing & repair; welding repair; electrical repair shops

(G-4131)
METAL BUILDERS SUPPLY INC
632 N Bierdeman Rd (39208-3303)
PHONE..................................601 932-0202
Carolyn Castens, *President*
R W Castens, *Vice Pres*
EMP: 8
SALES (est): 980K **Privately Held**
WEB: www.metalbuilderssupply.com
SIC: 3448 Buildings, portable: prefabricated metal

(G-4132)
MILLENNIUM OUTDOORS LLC
Also Called: Millennium Treestands
201 Fairmont Plz (39208-3414)
PHONE..................................601 932-5832
Robert Willard, *COO*
Edwin Welsh, *CFO*
EMP: 12
SQ FT: 30,000
SALES (est): 2.4MM **Privately Held**
SIC: 5091 2421 Fishing equipment & supplies; outdoor wood structural products

(G-4133)
MSU VETERINARY DIAGNOSTICS LAB
Also Called: Missippi Vtrnary RES Diagnstc
3137 Highway 468 W (39208-9007)
P.O. Box 97813 (39288-7813)
PHONE..................................601 420-4700
Susan Sloop, *Manager*

Lanny Pace, *Director*
Floyd Wilson, *Professor*
EMP: 40
SALES (est): 4.7MM **Privately Held**
WEB: www.cvm.msstate.edu
SIC: 2835 0742 Veterinary diagnostic substances; animal hospital services, pets & other animal specialties

(G-4134)
NICK STRCKLNDS QUICK PRINT INC
3086 Highway 80 E (39208-3435)
PHONE..................................601 939-2781
EMP: 2
SALES (corp-wide): 3.6MM **Privately Held**
SIC: 2752 Lithographic Commercial Printing
PA: Nick Strickland's Quick Print, Inc.
125 E South St
Jackson MS 39201
601 898-1717

(G-4135)
OFFICE CHAIRS MISSISSIPPI LLC
Also Called: K Contract
3209 Greenfield Rd (39208-8101)
PHONE..................................601 842-1004
James Patterson, *President*
EMP: 1 **EST:** 2012
SALES: 182K **Privately Held**
SIC: 2521 2522 Wood office furniture; office furniture, except wood

(G-4136)
PACKAGING CORPORATION AMERICA
Also Called: PCA/Pearl 340
100 Willie Dr (39208-3400)
P.O. Box 6283, Jackson (39288-6283)
PHONE..................................601 939-5111
Donnie Crabtree, *Sales Mgr*
Daine Bowmen, *Manager*
EMP: 101
SALES (corp-wide): 7B **Publicly Held**
SIC: 2653 Boxes, corrugated: made from purchased materials; boxes, solid fiber: made from purchased materials
PA: Packaging Corporation Of America
1 N Field Ct
Lake Forest IL 60045
847 482-3000

(G-4137)
PEARL RIVER DOOR COMPANY
878 N Bierdeman Rd (39208-3337)
PHONE..................................601 573-2572
Jon Carter, *President*
EMP: 1
SALES (est): 174.7K **Privately Held**
SIC: 2431 Millwork

(G-4138)
PPG INDUSTRIES INC
2106 Highway 80 E (39208-3329)
PHONE..................................601 932-0898
Sammy Ditta, *Manager*
EMP: 11
SALES (corp-wide): 15.3B **Publicly Held**
WEB: www.ppg.com
SIC: 2851 Paints & allied products
PA: Ppg Industries, Inc.
1 Ppg Pl
Pittsburgh PA 15272
412 434-3131

(G-4139)
PRECISION SPINE INC
5177 Old Brandon Rd (39208-9025)
PHONE..................................601 420-4244
EMP: 1
SALES (corp-wide): 1.9MM **Privately Held**
SIC: 3841 Anesthesia apparatus
PA: Precision Spine, Inc.
5 Sylvan Way Ste 2
Parsippany NJ 07054
601 420-4244

2019 Harris Directory of
Mississippi Manufacturers

▲ = Import ▼=Export
◆ =Import/Export

150

GEOGRAPHIC SECTION

Pelahatchie - Rankin County (G-4167)

(G-4140)
REED FOOD TECHNOLOGY INC (PA)
3151 Greenfield Rd (39208-8808)
PHONE....................................601 939-4001
Justin Reed, *Principal*
Peggy Smith, *Vice Pres*
Cory Jackson, *Prdtn Mgr*
Bob Gross, *VP Sales*
Merrilee Hall, *Manager*
▲ EMP: 35
SQ FT: 35,000
SALES (est): 10.4MM **Privately Held**
SIC: 2041 2035 Bread & bread-type roll mixes; dressings, salad: raw & cooked (except dry mixes)

(G-4141)
S & H STEEL CORP
2110 Highway 80 E Ste D (39208-3378)
P.O. Box 54081, Jackson (39288-4081)
PHONE....................................601 932-0250
David S Harris, *President*
EMP: 18
SQ FT: 12,000
SALES (est): 4.5MM **Privately Held**
WEB: www.sandhsteel.com
SIC: 3312 3444 3441 Blast furnaces & steel mills; sheet metalwork; fabricated structural metal

(G-4142)
SARUB INC
Also Called: Signs First
5020 Highway 80 E Ste A (39208-4224)
PHONE....................................601 936-4490
Linda Buras, *President*
Jeffery Buras, *Vice Pres*
EMP: 4
SQ FT: 15,000
SALES: 200K **Privately Held**
SIC: 3993 Signs, not made in custom sign painting shops

(G-4143)
SEAL MASTER MISSISSIPPI
1124 Weems St (39208-6256)
PHONE....................................601 936-0080
Huey Smith, *Principal*
EMP: 1 EST: 2011
SALES (est): 91K **Privately Held**
SIC: 2951 Asphalt paving mixtures & blocks

(G-4144)
SHILPAM CORP
Also Called: AlphaGraphics
115 Metroplex Blvd (39208-9204)
PHONE....................................601 933-9550
Ramesh Gajjar, *Director*
EMP: 15
SALES (est): 2.3MM **Privately Held**
SIC: 2752 Commercial printing, lithographic

(G-4145)
SIGNMARK INC
Also Called: Victor Dale Harris, Exec Dir
228 N Pearson Rd (39208-4428)
P.O. Box 97383 (39288-7383)
PHONE....................................601 932-6699
Victor Dale Harris, *Exec Dir*
EMP: 5
SALES (est): 493.2K **Privately Held**
SIC: 3993 Signs & advertising specialties

(G-4146)
SKILLEM ENTREPRISES INC
Also Called: All Bright Sign and Neon
5020 Highway 80 E Ste D (39208-4224)
PHONE....................................601 936-4461
Frank J Buras, *Principal*
EMP: 3
SQ FT: 15,000
SALES (est): 447.3K **Privately Held**
SIC: 3993 Signs, not made in custom sign painting shops

(G-4147)
SOUTHERN PHARMACEUTICAL CORP
5905 Old Brandon Rd # 10 (39208-9021)
PHONE....................................601 939-2525
Doug E Martin, *Vice Pres*
EMP: 1 **Privately Held**

SIC: 8082 2834 Home health care services; pharmaceutical preparations
PA: Southern Pharmaceutical Corporation
165 Rosecrest Dr
Columbus MS 39701

(G-4148)
SPINAL USA INC (PA)
Also Called: Precision Spine
2050 Executive Dr (39208-4282)
PHONE....................................601 420-4244
James Pastena, *CEO*
Rich Dickerson, *President*
Christopher A Denicola, *COO*
Joe Deluca, *Vice Pres*
Herb Epstein, *Vice Pres*
EMP: 60
SQ FT: 9,450
SALES (est): 34MM **Privately Held**
WEB: www.spinalusa.com
SIC: 3841 Surgical & medical instruments

(G-4149)
STEEL SPECIALTIES MISS INC
111 Midco Rd (39208-5506)
P.O. Box 54128 (39288-4128)
PHONE....................................601 939-2690
Richard Harding, *CEO*
Linda Bradshaw, *President*
Lee Harding, *Vice Pres*
▼ EMP: 17
SQ FT: 46,000
SALES (est): 3.5MM **Privately Held**
SIC: 3441 Expansion joints (structural shapes), iron or steel

(G-4150)
STEVENS SHEET METAL & IR WORKS
420 Childre Rd (39208-5508)
P.O. Box 6176, Jackson (39288-6176)
PHONE....................................601 939-6943
Charles M Stevens Jr, *President*
Jayne Stevens, *Corp Secy*
Charles M Stevens III, *Vice Pres*
Joan Lovett, *Manager*
EMP: 20 EST: 1945
SQ FT: 20,000
SALES (est): 3.7MM **Privately Held**
SIC: 3441 Fabricated structural metal

(G-4151)
THERMOPROBE INC
112a Jetport Dr (39208-6746)
P.O. Box 532, Ocean Springs (39566-0532)
PHONE....................................601 939-1831
Luke Bartkiewicz, *President*
Mc Goff Bartkiewicz, *Corp Secy*
EMP: 10
SALES (est): 2MM **Privately Held**
WEB: www.thermoprobe.net
SIC: 3829 Measuring & controlling devices

(G-4152)
TOKINS INC
127 Tokins Dr (39208-9140)
P.O. Box 6287 (39288-6287)
PHONE....................................601 939-1093
John T Larkins, *President*
Peggy Larkins, *Owner*
EMP: 5
SQ FT: 8,000
SALES (est): 450K **Privately Held**
SIC: 3599 3544 3443 Machine shop, jobbing & repair; special dies, tools, jigs & fixtures; fabricated plate work (boiler shop)

(G-4153)
TRI COUNTY SHEET METAL & WLDG
1001 S Pearson Rd (39208-6268)
P.O. Box 97364 (39288-7364)
PHONE....................................601 939-0803
David Rigby, *Owner*
EMP: 2
SALES (est): 103.8K **Privately Held**
SIC: 7692 1761 3535 Welding repair; sheet metalwork; conveyors & conveying equipment

(G-4154)
TRILOGY COMMUNICATIONS INC (PA)
2910 Highway 80 E (39208-3495)
PHONE....................................601 932-4461
Sidney Shinn Lee, *CEO*
Grace Lee, *President*
William T Lea, *Vice Pres*
Gary Cohen, *Treasurer*
Grace Pao-Chu Lee, *Admin Sec*
▲ EMP: 100
SQ FT: 265,000
SALES (est): 27.4MM **Privately Held**
WEB: www.trilogycoax.com
SIC: 3355 3357 Aluminum wire & cable; coaxial cable, nonferrous; communication wire

(G-4155)
TYSON FOODS INC
110 Metroplex Blvd Ste F (39208-9210)
PHONE....................................601 664-9102
Mike Warren, *Branch Mgr*
EMP: 6
SALES (corp-wide): 40B **Publicly Held**
SIC: 2011 Meat packing plants
PA: Tyson Foods, Inc.
2200 W Don Tyson Pkwy
Springdale AR 72762
479 290-4000

(G-4156)
VAPOR EXPRESS LLC
3553 Dale Cir (39208-5417)
PHONE....................................601 559-8004
Teresa Wheat,
EMP: 2
SALES (est): 235.7K **Privately Held**
SIC: 3634 Vaporizers, electric: household

(G-4157)
WALLS DRAPERY & BEDSPREAD MFG
Also Called: Walls Drapery & Bedspreads
422 Roberts St (39208-4634)
P.O. Box 5495 (39288-5495)
PHONE....................................601 939-6014
John Walls, *Owner*
Lillian Walls, *Principal*
EMP: 6
SALES (est): 220K **Privately Held**
SIC: 2211 Draperies & drapery fabrics, cotton; bedspreads, cotton

(G-4158)
WATTHOUR ENGINEERING CO INC
333 Cross Park Dr (39208-8905)
PHONE....................................601 933-0900
Charles S Weimer, *President*
Sue S Weimer, *Vice Pres*
▲ EMP: 32
SQ FT: 6,000
SALES (est): 7.3MM **Privately Held**
WEB: www.watthour.com
SIC: 3825 7371 Electrical energy measuring equipment; test equipment for electronic & electric measurement; computer software development & applications

(G-4159)
WYNNES CUSTOM COATINGS
2560 Highway 80 E (39208-3327)
PHONE....................................601 664-3474
Don A Wynne, *Principal*
EMP: 2
SALES (est): 121.5K **Privately Held**
SIC: 3479 Metal coating & allied service

Pearlington
Hancock County

(G-4160)
HONEY ISLAND SOFTWARE INC
16048 Oahu Rd (39572-7507)
PHONE....................................985 265-4192
Christine M Combel, *Director*
EMP: 2
SALES (est): 119.5K **Privately Held**
SIC: 7372 Prepackaged software

(G-4161)
PRETTY VIXEN DEFENSE LLC
6136 11th Ave (39572-7694)
PHONE....................................228 304-2173
Stevie Bello, *Principal*
EMP: 3
SALES (est): 226.5K **Privately Held**
SIC: 3812 Defense systems & equipment

Pelahatchie
Rankin County

(G-4162)
COLOR-BOX LLC
Also Called: Georgia-Pacific
108 Industrial Dr (39145-2915)
PHONE....................................601 854-6020
Mike Farley, *Branch Mgr*
EMP: 107
SALES (corp-wide): 40.9B **Privately Held**
WEB: www.gp.com
SIC: 2653 Boxes, corrugated: made from purchased materials
HQ: Color-Box Llc
623 S G St
Richmond IN 47374
765 966-7588

(G-4163)
DENBURY RESOURCES INC
1919 Holly Bush Rd (39145-2847)
PHONE....................................972 673-2787
Purvis Don, *Principal*
EMP: 2
SALES (est): 186K **Privately Held**
SIC: 1389 Oil field services

(G-4164)
FALVEY LOGGING
160 Gardenia Dr (39145-3308)
PHONE....................................601 546-2922
EMP: 2
SALES (est): 160K **Privately Held**
SIC: 2411 Logging

(G-4165)
MISSISSIPPI BAKING CO LLC
Also Called: Central Mississippi Baking
4311 Highway 80 (39145-2918)
PHONE....................................601 854-5000
Tom McLemore, *General Mgr*
Tom Shuler, *Vice Pres*
Steve Warren, *Manager*
EMP: 90 **Privately Held**
SIC: 2051 Rolls, bread type: fresh or frozen; buns, bread type: fresh or frozen
PA: Mississippi Baking Co. L.L.C.
600 Phil Gramm Blvd
Bryan TX 77807

(G-4166)
MULTICRAFT ENTERPRISES INC
201 Old Highway 80 (39145-3003)
PHONE....................................601 854-5516
A Mallinson, *President*
H Post, *Vice Pres*
G Love, *Treasurer*
EMP: 2
SALES (est): 175.2K **Privately Held**
SIC: 3714 Motor vehicle parts & accessories

(G-4167)
MULTICRAFT INTL LTD PARTNR
Also Called: Trillium Specialty Parts
301 N Brooks Ave (39145-2973)
PHONE....................................601 854-5516
Jesse Havard, *QC Mgr*
Chris Schooler, *Research*
Tommy Nichols, *Program Mgr*
EMP: 1
SALES (corp-wide): 29.4MM **Privately Held**
SIC: 3694 3625 3089 3465 Automotive electrical equipment; solenoid switches (industrial controls); injection molded finished plastic products; automotive stampings; electronic resistors

---

(PA)=Parent Co (HQ)=Headquarters (DH)=Div Headquarters
✿ = New Business established in last 2 years

2019 Harris Directory of
Mississippi Manufacturers

151

Pelahatchie - Rankin County (G-4168)   **GEOGRAPHIC SECTION**

PA: Multicraft International Limited Partnership
4341 Highway 80
Pelahatchie MS 39145
601 854-1200

(G-4168)
MULTICRAFT INTL LTD PARTNR (PA)
4341 Highway 80 (39145-2918)
P.O. Box 180 (39145-0180)
PHONE..................................601 854-1200
Andrew Mallinson, *General Ptnr*
Caleb Crosby, *Technician*
▲ EMP: 6
SQ FT: 150,000
SALES (est): 29.4MM **Privately Held**
WEB: www.multicraft.com
SIC: 3699 3711 Electrical equipment & supplies; automobile assembly, including specialty automobiles

(G-4169)
MULTICRAFT INTL LTD PARTNR
Also Called: Trillium International
4341 Highway 80 (39145-2918)
P.O. Box 180 (39145-0180)
PHONE..................................601 854-1200
Vernon Lowery, *Branch Mgr*
EMP: 100
SALES (corp-wide): 29.4MM **Privately Held**
SIC: 3679 Harness assemblies for electronic use: wire or cable
PA: Multicraft International Limited Partnership
4341 Highway 80
Pelahatchie MS 39145
601 854-1200

(G-4170)
MULTICRAFT INTL LTD PARTNR
Also Called: Trilloma Industries
4341 Highway 80 (39145-2918)
P.O. Box 180 (39145-0180)
PHONE..................................601 854-1200
Vernon Weathersby, *Principal*
EMP: 25
SALES (corp-wide): 29.4MM **Privately Held**
SIC: 3699 3711 Electrical equipment & supplies; motor vehicles & car bodies
PA: Multicraft International Limited Partnership
4341 Highway 80
Pelahatchie MS 39145
601 854-1200

(G-4171)
PERFORMANCE DRILLING COMPANY
4326 Highway 80 (39145-3533)
P.O. Box 1748, Brandon (39043-1748)
PHONE..................................601 854-5661
EMP: 9
SALES (est): 800K **Privately Held**
SIC: 1381 Oil/Gas Well Drilling

Perkinston
Stone County

(G-4172)
ACME FABRICATION LLC
190 Wire Rd W (39573-5702)
PHONE..................................228 669-0004
David Gunter,
EMP: 9 EST: 2012
SALES (est): 1.3MM **Privately Held**
SIC: 3441 7389 Fabricated structural metal;

(G-4173)
BAYOU INOVATIONS
38 South Park Dr (39573-3025)
PHONE..................................601 928-4143
William Purvis, *President*
EMP: 3
SALES (est): 110.9K **Privately Held**
SIC: 2851 Paints: oil or alkyd vehicle or water thinned

(G-4174)
BERRY ENTERPRISES OF MISS
1035 Wire Rd W (39573-5721)
P.O. Box 483 (39573-0009)
PHONE..................................601 928-4006
Kevin Berry, *President*
EMP: 4
SQ FT: 1,500
SALES (est): 748K **Privately Held**
SIC: 3441 7389 Fabricated structural metal; drafting service, except temporary help

(G-4175)
FAST TRACK PLANNERS LLC
82 Roy Oneal Rd (39573-3352)
PHONE..................................601 528-0558
Stephanie Whitfield,
EMP: 1
SALES (est): 51.7K **Privately Held**
SIC: 2741 7389 Miscellaneous publishing;

(G-4176)
GULF COAST FILTERS INC
45 South Park Dr (39573-3063)
P.O. Box 2787, Gulfport (39505-2787)
PHONE..................................601 528-5762
Jerry Sims, *President*
▲ EMP: 6
SQ FT: 5,000
SALES (est): 400K **Privately Held**
SIC: 3569 5085 Filters, general line: industrial; industrial supplies

(G-4177)
JOSH GUS GARCIA
6040 Jordan Rd (39573-3657)
PHONE..................................228 255-7157
Josh G Garcia, *Principal*
EMP: 1
SALES (est): 45K **Privately Held**
SIC: 2395 Embroidery & art needlework

(G-4178)
KINGS JUDAH PUBLISHING CO LLC
269 Sweet Beulah Rd (39573-5739)
PHONE..................................228 342-3648
Sharon Mack, *Manager*
EMP: 1 EST: 2017
SALES (est): 37.5K **Privately Held**
SIC: 2741 Miscellaneous publishing

(G-4179)
ONEAL POWER CORPORATION
17 Lawson Oneal Rd (39573-5161)
PHONE..................................228 323-1059
Darel O'Neal, *Principal*
EMP: 2
SALES (est): 96.3K **Privately Held**
SIC: 2411 Logging

(G-4180)
SCOTT STRICKLAND SONS INC
32 Lawson Oneal Rd (39573-5144)
PHONE..................................601 928-2321
Scott Strickland, *President*
EMP: 7 EST: 1998
SALES (est): 611.4K **Privately Held**
SIC: 2411 Timber, cut at logging camp

(G-4181)
SOUTHERN EXTERIORS FENCE CO
31023 Crane Creek Rd (39573-3920)
PHONE..................................228 586-2110
Rance Necaise, *President*
Jessica Necaise, *Corp Secy*
Gwen Smith, *Vice Pres*
EMP: 5
SALES (est): 421.4K **Privately Held**
SIC: 1799 3089 3312 3315 Fence construction; fences, gates & accessories: plastic; fence posts, iron & steel; fence gates posts & fittings: steel; wire fence, gates & accessories

(G-4182)
TRIPLE M LURES LLC
13 Summit View Dr (39573-4092)
PHONE..................................601 919-5515
Ryan D Brown, *Mng Member*
EMP: 1
SALES (est): 62.6K **Privately Held**
SIC: 3949 Lures, fishing: artificial

(G-4183)
WILSONS WELDING SERVICE INC (PA)
5229 Jordan Rd (39573-3893)
PHONE..................................228 255-4825
Terry Wilson, *President*
Melissa Wilson, *Corp Secy*
Verble Wilson, *Vice Pres*
EMP: 12
SQ FT: 5,500
SALES (est): 2.1MM **Privately Held**
SIC: 7692 Welding repair

Petal
Forrest County

(G-4184)
ASH MILLWORKS INC
65 Springfield Rd (39465-9839)
PHONE..................................601 544-3962
A S Herring, *President*
EMP: 30
SQ FT: 9,000
SALES (est): 5.2MM **Privately Held**
SIC: 2431 5031 5211 1751 Millwork; millwork; millwork & lumber; cabinet & finish carpentry; wood kitchen cabinets

(G-4185)
FLATHAUS FINE FOODS LLC
209 W Second Ave (39465-2403)
PHONE..................................601 582-9629
Heather Flathau, *President*
Jeff Flathau, *Vice Pres*
▼ EMP: 14
SQ FT: 10,000
SALES (est): 1MM **Privately Held**
WEB: www.flathausfinefoods.com
SIC: 2052 Cookies

(G-4186)
GLENN MCH WORKS CRANE RIGGING
1505 Highway 11 (39465-7980)
PHONE..................................601 544-1275
Brent Stockstill, *Manager*
EMP: 2
SALES (est): 166.1K **Privately Held**
SIC: 3532 Mining machinery

(G-4187)
HUB CITY BRUSH INC
106 Mc Aulay Dr (39465-4008)
P.O. Box 503 (39465-0503)
PHONE..................................601 584-7314
Robert Cedotal, *President*
Cecil J Cedotal, *Vice Pres*
Wayne L Cedotal, *Treasurer*
▲ EMP: 12
SQ FT: 60,000
SALES (est): 1.1MM **Privately Held**
SIC: 3991 Brushes, household or industrial

(G-4188)
JONATHAN BIGBIE
Also Called: Big B Granite
1409 Highway 42 (39465-9855)
PHONE..................................601 498-9890
Jonathan Bigbie, *Owner*
EMP: 3
SALES (est): 60K **Privately Held**
SIC: 5032 3281 Granite building stone; cut stone & stone products

(G-4189)
K & B MISSISSIPPI CORPORATION
100 Highway 42 (39465-2881)
PHONE..................................601 545-2056
EMP: 10
SALES (est): 100.8K
SALES (corp-wide): 21.5B **Publicly Held**
SIC: 2836 Mfg Biological Products
PA: Rite Aid Corporation
30 Hunter Ln
Camp Hill PA 17011
717 761-2633

(G-4190)
LARS JORDAN
296 Kelly Rose Ln (39465-4041)
PHONE..................................601 544-2424

Lars Jordan, *Owner*
EMP: 1
SALES (est): 64.2K **Privately Held**
SIC: 7692 Welding repair

(G-4191)
LEGACY VULCAN LLC
Also Called: Hattiesburg Yard
157 Chevis Lee Rd (39465-4218)
P.O. Box 385016, Birmingham AL (35238-5016)
PHONE..................................601 544-3523
Mike Graham, *Manager*
EMP: 4 **Publicly Held**
WEB: www.vulcanmaterials.com
SIC: 3272 Concrete products
HQ: Legacy Vulcan, Llc
1200 Urban Center Dr
Vestavia AL 35242
205 298-3000

(G-4192)
LONDON WAR ROOM
41 Beverly Hills Loop (39465-9345)
PHONE..................................601 584-8533
EMP: 2
SALES (est): 89.5K **Privately Held**
SIC: 3999 Mfg Misc Products

(G-4193)
MMC MATERIALS INC
157 Chevis Lee Rd (39465-4218)
PHONE..................................601 582-8493
EMP: 2
SALES (corp-wide): 306.5MM **Privately Held**
SIC: 3273 Ready-mixed concrete
HQ: Mmc Materials, Inc.
1052 Highland Colony Pkwy # 201
Ridgeland MS 39157
601 898-4000

(G-4194)
MULTIFORMS
20 Lee St (39465-8124)
PHONE..................................601 545-2312
Ernie Martin, *Owner*
Scott Cordman, *Co-Owner*
EMP: 4
SALES (est): 215.7K **Privately Held**
SIC: 2741 Technical papers: publishing & printing

(G-4195)
PIAVE BROOM & MOP INC
106 Mc Aulay Dr (39465-4008)
P.O. Box 503 (39465-0503)
PHONE..................................601 584-7314
Robert Cedotal, *President*
Cecil J Cedotal, *Vice Pres*
Brant Lee Cedotal, *Treasurer*
Wayne L Cedotal, *Admin Sec*
EMP: 18
SQ FT: 18,360
SALES (est): 1.2MM **Privately Held**
SIC: 2392 3991 Mops, floor & dust; brooms

(G-4196)
PIERCE CNSTR & MAINT CO INC
1505 Highway 11 (39465-7980)
P.O. Box 485 (39465-0485)
PHONE..................................601 544-1321
Willie D Pierce, *President*
Edith Pierce, *Corp Secy*
Werner Pierce, *Vice Pres*
Mark Breland, *Manager*
EMP: 85
SQ FT: 31,000
SALES: 28.1MM **Privately Held**
SIC: 3553 Woodworking machinery

(G-4197)
TRI RESOURCES INC
Also Called: Dynegy
18 Chappell Hill Rd (39465-3019)
P.O. Box 587 (39465-0587)
PHONE..................................601 583-8711
EMP: 6
SALES (corp-wide): 8.6B **Publicly Held**
SIC: 1389 Oil/Gas Field Services
HQ: Tri Resources Inc.
1000 Louisiana St # 4300
Houston TX 77002
713 584-1000

2019 Harris Directory of
Mississippi Manufacturers

▲ = Import ▼=Export
◆ =Import/Export

GEOGRAPHIC SECTION

Philadelphia - Neshoba County (G-4229)

(G-4198)
TRI-STATE ENVIRONMENTAL LLC
4901 Highway 29 (39465-7840)
P.O. Box 403 (39465-0403)
PHONE..................................888 554-9792
Judy Carter, *Mng Member*
EMP: 20
SALES (corp-wide): 8MM **Privately Held**
SIC: 1389 Oil field services
PA: Tri-State Environmental, Llc
141 Thompson Rd
Houma LA 70363
888 554-9792

(G-4199)
VELOCITY CNSLTING SPCALIST LLC
46 Edgeware (39465-9021)
PHONE..................................229 726-6047
Jamison Roberts, *Mng Member*
EMP: 1 **EST:** 2011
SALES (est): 84.2K **Privately Held**
SIC: 2834 7389 Pharmaceutical preparations;

(G-4200)
WREATH HAVEN
102 Little John Dr (39465-8824)
PHONE..................................205 393-3015
EMP: 1 **EST:** 2017
SALES (est): 52.6K **Privately Held**
SIC: 3999 Wreaths, artificial

(G-4201)
YONCE & COMANS PRODUCTS LLC
9128 Old River Rd (39465-9230)
PHONE..................................601 270-7712
Angela C Yonce,
EMP: 1 **EST:** 2016
SALES (est): 108.4K **Privately Held**
SIC: 2841 2844 Soap & other detergents; perfumes & colognes; lotions, shaving

---

Philadelphia
Neshoba County

(G-4202)
AIRBRUSH & SIGNS BY DEBBY
15821 Highway 21 S (39350-7750)
PHONE..................................601 656-6953
Debby Lundy, *Owner*
EMP: 1
SALES (est): 67.5K **Privately Held**
SIC: 3993 5699 Signs, not made in custom sign painting shops; T-shirts, custom printed

(G-4203)
AMERICAN TARP & AWNING CO
11500 Highway 482 Lot 3 (39350-8059)
P.O. Box 457 (39350-0457)
PHONE..................................601 656-5177
Manuel Goforth, *President*
Geraldine Goforth, *Vice Pres*
EMP: 7
SQ FT: 25,000
SALES (est): 450K **Privately Held**
WEB: www.mississippi.net
SIC: 2394 Tarpaulins, fabric: made from purchased materials

(G-4204)
AMERICRETE READY MIX INC
10350 Road 383 (39350-4034)
PHONE..................................601 656-5590
Danny Napp, *Manager*
EMP: 3
SALES (corp-wide): 100.3MM **Privately Held**
SIC: 3273 Ready-mixed concrete
HQ: Americrete, Inc.
220 65th Ave
Meridian MS 39307

(G-4205)
ANTHONY SYRUP COMPANY
11191 Highway 21 N (39350-6745)
PHONE..................................601 656-7052
Faye Anthony, *Owner*
EMP: 1 **EST:** 1931
SQ FT: 3,456
SALES (est): 133.7K **Privately Held**
SIC: 2087 Flavoring extracts & syrups

(G-4206)
B & S FARMS
10391 Road 525 (39350-7318)
PHONE..................................601 656-5157
Bunkie Smith, *Partner*
EMP: 2
SALES (est): 192.2K **Privately Held**
SIC: 2015 Poultry slaughtering & processing

(G-4207)
BENNY MCDANIEL
Also Called: Benny McDaniel Logging
1869 Peoples Rd (39350-2596)
P.O. Box 123, Walnut Grove (39189-0123)
PHONE..................................601 253-0564
Benny McDaniel, *Owner*
EMP: 4
SALES (est): 523.4K **Privately Held**
WEB: www.bennymcdaniel.com
SIC: 2411 Logging

(G-4208)
BOSWELL MEAT PROCESSING
10481 Road 836 (39350-4817)
PHONE..................................601 656-6015
Keith Boswell, *Owner*
EMP: 2
SALES (est): 66.6K **Privately Held**
SIC: 2011 Meat packing plants

(G-4209)
BROWN WOOD PRESERVING CO INC
433 E Beacon St (39350-2952)
PHONE..................................601 656-2607
EMP: 8
SALES (corp-wide): 13.2MM **Privately Held**
SIC: 2491 Wood preserving
PA: Brown Wood Preserving Company, Inc.
6201 Camp Ground Rd
Louisville KY 40216
502 448-2337

(G-4210)
CENTRAL MISSISSIPPI WOOD INC
449 Ryles Rd S (39350-1913)
PHONE..................................662 724-2447
EMP: 5
SQ FT: 500
SALES: 114K **Privately Held**
SIC: 2421 Sawmill

(G-4211)
CLARENCE SANSING JR
Also Called: Williamson, James Co
324 Williamson Ave (39350-2063)
PHONE..................................601 656-4771
Clarence Sansing Jr, *Owner*
EMP: 4
SALES (est): 400K **Privately Held**
SIC: 1711 3444 Ventilation & duct work contractor; sheet metalwork

(G-4212)
COSCO AUTHORIZED XEROX DEALER ✪
423 Center Ave N (39350-2919)
PHONE..................................601 568-5006
EMP: 2 **EST:** 2018
SALES (est): 85.9K **Privately Held**
SIC: 3577 Computer peripheral equipment

(G-4213)
D D RUSHING
17960 Road 339 (39350-7131)
PHONE..................................601 656-8842
Dwight D Rushing, *Owner*
EMP: 2
SALES (est): 261.8K **Privately Held**
SIC: 2273 7389 Carpets, hand & machine made;

(G-4214)
DAVID DREW SULLIVAN
10050 Eastmore Ln (39350-3536)
PHONE..................................601 656-3556
EMP: 3

(G-4215)
GARAN INCORPORATED
Also Called: Garan Manufacturing
1015 Holland Ave (39350-2161)
P.O. Box 629 (39350-0629)
PHONE..................................601 656-1501
Judy Witt, *Branch Mgr*
EMP: 30
SALES (corp-wide): 225.3B **Publicly Held**
WEB: www.garanimals.com
SIC: 4225 2331 2321 General warehousing; T-shirts & tops, women's: made from purchased materials; shirts, women's & juniors': made from purchased materials; men's & boys' furnishings; sport shirts, men's & boys': from purchased materials
HQ: Garan, Incorporated
200 Madison Ave Fl 4
New York NY 10016
212 563-1292

(G-4216)
HANSON ATHLETIC INC
Also Called: Athletic Action
170 Canal Pl (39350-8908)
PHONE..................................601 389-0403
EMP: 6 **EST:** 1980
SQ FT: 1,500
SALES (est): 527.4K **Privately Held**
SIC: 3949 Mfg Sporting/Athletic Goods

(G-4217)
HARDY MANUFACTURING CO INC
12345 Road 505 (39350-3366)
PHONE..................................601 656-5866
Jerome Hardy, *Ch of Bd*
Frank L Moore, *President*
Janet H Moore, *Corp Secy*
B R Smith, *Vice Pres*
Willard Posey, *Sales Staff*
▲ **EMP:** 39
SQ FT: 5,000
SALES (est): 5.5MM **Privately Held**
WEB: www.hardyheater.com
SIC: 3433 Heating equipment, except electric

(G-4218)
JC WELDING LLC
106 Pinecrest Dr (39350-3334)
PHONE..................................601 575-1307
Joshua Coghlan, *Principal*
EMP: 1
SALES (est): 25K **Privately Held**
SIC: 7692 Welding repair

(G-4219)
JEFF SHEPHERD LOGGING INC
17221 Highway 19 S (39350-4599)
PHONE..................................601 416-1832
Jeff Shepherd, *President*
Tammy Shepherd, *Admin Sec*
EMP: 10
SALES (est): 1.5MM **Privately Held**
SIC: 2411 Logging camps & contractors

(G-4220)
JEFF WINSTEAD LOGGING
16931 Highway 19 S (39350-4593)
PHONE..................................601 656-1448
Jeff Winstead, *Owner*
EMP: 10
SALES: 100K **Privately Held**
SIC: 2411 Logging camps & contractors

(G-4221)
KUSTOM MACHINE AND SHEET METAL
10091 Road 375 (39350-9303)
PHONE..................................601 469-1062
James V Jones, *President*
Larry Crimm, *Vice Pres*
EMP: 14
SALES (est): 2.2MM **Privately Held**
SIC: 3312 1799 Tool & die steel & alloys; welding on site

(G-4222)
LAMONT WELLS LLC
Also Called: Wells Lamont Div
299a W Beacon St (39350-3151)
PHONE..................................601 656-2772
Carl Powe, *Manager*
EMP: 64
SALES (corp-wide): 225.3B **Publicly Held**
SIC: 2381 Gloves, woven or knit: made from purchased materials; mittens, woven or knit: made from purchased materials
HQ: Wells Lamont Llc
5215 Old Orchard Rd # 725
Skokie IL 60077

(G-4223)
LARRY WINSTEAD
Also Called: L and S Logging
1028 Highway 427 (39350)
PHONE..................................601 656-6438
Larry Winstead, *Managing Prtnr*
Samantha Winstead, *Partner*
EMP: 10
SALES (est): 78.7K **Privately Held**
SIC: 2411 Logging

(G-4224)
MARK A WHITNEY
Also Called: Whitney Engineering
429 E Beacon St (39350-2952)
PHONE..................................601 575-4952
Mark Whitney, *Owner*
EMP: 1
SALES (est): 36.2K **Privately Held**
SIC: 8711 1389 Civil engineering; professional engineer; testing, measuring, surveying & analysis services

(G-4225)
MCDANIEL TRUCKING
12140 Highway 16 E (39350-4359)
PHONE..................................601 656-1028
EMP: 1
SALES (est): 61.4K **Privately Held**
SIC: 4213 2411 Trucking, except local; logging

(G-4226)
MISSISSIPPI IMAGING
439 Center Ave N (39350-2918)
P.O. Box 117 (39350-0117)
PHONE..................................601 656-6759
EMP: 5 **EST:** 2008
SALES (est): 639.4K **Privately Held**
SIC: 2835 Mfg Diagnostic Substances

(G-4227)
NESHOBA COUNTY GIN ASSN AAL
264 Railroad Ave (39350-3458)
P.O. Box 326 (39350-0326)
PHONE..................................601 656-3463
Dwight Mulholland, *COO*
Jasper Commer, *Vice Pres*
EMP: 14
SQ FT: 2,500
SALES (est): 5.5MM **Privately Held**
SIC: 5999 2875 Feed & farm supply; fertilizers, mixing only

(G-4228)
NESHOBA DEMOCRAT PUBLISHING CO
439 E Beacon St (39350-2950)
P.O. Box 30 (39350-0030)
PHONE..................................601 656-4000
James E Prince III, *President*
Summer Hines, *General Mgr*
Thomas Rayburn, *Editor*
EMP: 18
SQ FT: 6,000
SALES: 652.1K **Privately Held**
WEB: www.neshobademocrat.com
SIC: 2711 Newspapers: publishing only, not printed on site

(G-4229)
NHC DISTRIBUTORS INC
Also Called: Crosstec
212 Lewis Ave S (39350-2844)
PHONE..................................601 656-7911
Willie Vaughn, *President*
Shirley Vaughn, *Corp Secy*
▲ **EMP:** 25

(PA)=Parent Co (HQ)=Headquarters (DH)=Div Headquarters
✪ = New Business established in last 2 years

2019 Harris Directory of
Mississippi Manufacturers

153

Philadelphia - Neshoba County (G-4230)

GEOGRAPHIC SECTION

SQ FT: 20,000
SALES (est): 17.6MM **Privately Held**
WEB: www.crosstec.com
SIC: 5051 5084 2298 5172 Rope, wire (not insulated); chainsaws; wire rope centers; petroleum products; miscellaneous fabricated wire products

(G-4230)
PEARL RIVER EXXON
Hwy 16 W (39350)
PHONE..........................601 650-9393
Ken Banks, *General Mgr*
EMP: 11
SALES (est): 1.1MM **Privately Held**
WEB: www.pearlriverresort.com
SIC: 3578 Automatic teller machines (ATM)

(G-4231)
PECO FOODS INC
999 Herman Alford Mem Hwy (39350)
P.O. Box 646 (39350-0646)
PHONE..........................601 656-1865
Duane Weens, *President*
EMP: 125
SALES (corp-wide): 1B **Privately Held**
WEB: www.pecofoods.com
SIC: 0254 0251 2015 2048 Chicken hatchery; broiling chickens, raising of; frying chickens, raising of; roasting chickens, raising of; poultry, processed; livestock feeds; poultry feeds
PA: Peco Foods, Inc.
1101 Greensboro Ave
Tuscaloosa AL 35401
205 345-4711

(G-4232)
PERFORMANCE LOGGING LLC
10050 Eastmore Ln (39350-3536)
PHONE..........................601 656-3556
EMP: 2
SALES (est): 160K **Privately Held**
SIC: 2411 Logging

(G-4233)
PHOTOWIRE SOLAR PRODUCERS
10530 Road 747 (39350-5943)
PHONE..........................228 627-0088
Dolonte A Riley, *Principal*
EMP: 3
SALES (est): 220K **Privately Held**
SIC: 3612 Transformers, except electric

(G-4234)
QUARTERMASTER SECURITY PR
10371 Road 391 (39350-8941)
PHONE..........................601 656-9882
Norman Adcock, *Owner*
EMP: 1
SALES (est): 92.2K **Privately Held**
SIC: 3699 Security devices

(G-4235)
RICHARDSON MOLDING LLC
931 Herman Alford Mem Hwy (39350-8701)
PHONE..........................601 656-7921
Sam Holden, *COO*
George Smith, *Plant Mgr*
George Brice, *Opers Mgr*
Mike Mynk, *QC Mgr*
Keith Toll, *Sales Staff*
EMP: 6
SALES (corp-wide): 106.7MM **Privately Held**
SIC: 3089 Injection molding of plastics
HQ: Richardson Molding Incorporated
2405 Norcross Dr
Columbus IN 47201
812 342-0139

(G-4236)
SMOKERS EXPRESS
804 Holland Ave (39350-2114)
PHONE..........................601 483-5789
Billy Spears, *Owner*
EMP: 3
SALES (est): 181.3K **Privately Held**
SIC: 3911 Cigar & cigarette accessories

(G-4237)
STITCHED IN TIME
12631 Road 759 (39350-6930)
PHONE..........................601 562-6715
Autumn Fulton, *Principal*
EMP: 1 EST: 2016
SALES (est): 51.9K **Privately Held**
SIC: 2395 Embroidery & art needlework

(G-4238)
STRIBLING PRINTING
409 Center Ave N (39350-2920)
PHONE..........................601 656-4194
Teresa Pace, *Owner*
EMP: 4
SQ FT: 1,200
SALES (est): 340K **Privately Held**
SIC: 2752 2759 Offset & photolithographic printing; business form & card printing, lithographic; invitation & stationery printing & engraving

(G-4239)
SUDDEN SERVICE INC
Taylor Precision Industries
103 Industrial Park Rd (39350-8973)
P.O. Box 1234 (39350-1234)
PHONE..........................601 650-9600
Donald Hardin, *Plant Mgr*
Doris Wheeler, *Manager*
Bobby Kennedy, *Supervisor*
EMP: 40 **Privately Held**
WEB: www.taylorenviro.com
SIC: 3451 Screw machine products
HQ: Sudden Service Inc
3637 N Church Ave
Louisville MS 39339

(G-4240)
TAYLOR MACHINE
103 Industrial Park Rd (39350-8973)
PHONE..........................601 650-9600
EMP: 2
SALES (est): 81.4K **Privately Held**
SIC: 3599 Industrial machinery

(G-4241)
THOMAS DAVIS GAMBLIN
Also Called: Thomas Gamblin Logging
12220 Marty Stuart Dr (39350-8947)
PHONE..........................601 656-2759
Thomas Gamblin, *Owner*
EMP: 13
SALES (est): 1.1MM **Privately Held**
SIC: 2411 Logging

(G-4242)
THOMASSON COMPANY (PA)
1007 Saint Francis Dr (39350-2029)
P.O. Box 490 (39350-0490)
PHONE..........................601 656-6000
Patricia Thomasson, *CEO*
William Brent Gray, *President*
Randy Deweese, *Vice Pres*
Patricia Stokes, *Vice Pres*
Jane Thomas, *CFO*
◆ EMP: 25
SQ FT: 8,000
SALES (est): 15.3MM **Privately Held**
WEB: www.thomassonlumber.com
SIC: 5099 5031 2421 Wood & wood by-products; lumber: rough, dressed & finished; lumber: rough, sawed or planed

(G-4243)
TIM BRELAND LOGGING INC
10580 Road 537 (39350-5811)
PHONE..........................601 656-0382
Tim Breland, *President*
Sandy Breland, *Admin Sec*
EMP: 15
SQ FT: 1,000
SALES (est): 500K **Privately Held**
SIC: 2411 Logging camps & contractors

(G-4244)
TIMBER HARVESTERS INC
27 Tommy Dr (39350-2003)
PHONE..........................601 416-2078
Timothy S Allen, *President*
EMP: 6
SALES (est): 518.4K **Privately Held**
SIC: 2411 Logging

(G-4245)
TRIPLE G LOGGING
11700 Road 397 (39350-3960)
PHONE..........................601 416-8733
EMP: 9 EST: 2008
SALES (est): 766.6K **Privately Held**
SIC: 2411 Logging camps & contractors

(G-4246)
TRIPLE J TIE AND TIMBER LLC
12920 Road 832 (39350-6860)
PHONE..........................601 663-4275
EMP: 2
SALES (est): 55.3K **Privately Held**
SIC: 5093 2421 Metal scrap & waste materials; sawmills & planing mills, general

(G-4247)
TRIPLE L LOGGING
11761 Road 539 (39350-4508)
PHONE..........................601 656-9313
Lori Long, *Partner*
Ricky Long, *Partner*
EMP: 13
SALES (est): 1.1MM **Privately Held**
SIC: 2411 Logging camps & contractors

(G-4248)
W G YATES & SONS CNSTR CO (HQ)
1 Gully Ave (39350)
P.O. Box 456 (39350-0456)
PHONE..........................601 656-5411
William G Yates III, *President*
David Fulmer, *Superintendent*
Thompson James, *Superintendent*
Greg Sims, *Superintendent*
Chester Nadolski, *Vice Pres*
EMP: 1919 EST: 1964
SQ FT: 50,000
SALES: 1.2B
SALES (corp-wide): 1.5B **Privately Held**
WEB: www.wgyates.com
SIC: 1542 1541 2339 1611 Commercial & office building, new construction; industrial buildings, new construction; jeans: women's, misses' & juniors'; resurfacing contractor; home centers; general electrical contractor
PA: The Yates Companies Inc
1 Gully Ave
Philadelphia MS 39350
601 656-5411

(G-4249)
WEYERHAEUSER COMPANY
1016 Weyerhaeuser Rd (39350-6505)
PHONE..........................601 650-7200
Stan Webb, *Opers-Prdtn-Mfg*
EMP: 210
SALES (corp-wide): 7.4B **Publicly Held**
SIC: 2421 Lumber: rough, sawed or planed; chipper mill
PA: Weyerhaeuser Company
220 Occidental Ave S
Seattle WA 98104
206 539-3000

(G-4250)
WILSON BRANCH PUBLISHING LLC
31 Terri Dr (39350-9769)
PHONE..........................601 656-2718
EMP: 1
SALES (est): 54.3K **Privately Held**
SIC: 2741 Misc Publishing

Picayune
Pearl River County

(G-4251)
AMERICAN MIDSTREAM LLC
148 Runway Rd (39466-8120)
PHONE..........................601 798-9145
EMP: 2 EST: 2017
SALES (est): 81.9K **Privately Held**
SIC: 1311 Crude petroleum & natural gas

(G-4252)
ATLAS MACHINE & MFG LLC
1928 Palestine Rd (39466-3606)
PHONE..........................601 799-2616

EMP: 5
SALES (est): 410K **Privately Held**
SIC: 3599 Mfg Industrial Machinery

(G-4253)
AVALON MARBLE LLC (PA)
424 Memorial Blvd (39466-5544)
PHONE..........................601 798-3378
Joseph Lafaye III,
EMP: 10
SQ FT: 5,000
SALES: 300K **Privately Held**
WEB: www.avalonmarble.com
SIC: 1411 3281 1799 Marble, dimension-quarrying; marble, building: cut & shaped; counter top installation

(G-4254)
AVON ENGNERED FABRICATIONS LLC
Also Called: Avon Engnered Fabrications Inc
113 Street A (39466-5467)
PHONE..........................601 889-9050
Jamie Rogers, *Opers Mgr*
Richard Heath,
▲ EMP: 80
SQ FT: 80,000
SALES: 18.9MM
SALES (corp-wide): 4.5MM **Privately Held**
WEB: www.avon-rubber.com
SIC: 3443 3069 Industrial vessels, tanks & containers; air-supported rubber structures
HQ: Performance Inflatables Co., Llc
7975 E Mcclain Dr Ste 201
Scottsdale AZ 85260
602 315-2391

(G-4255)
AWESOME SIGHT AND SOUND
Also Called: Jim Ballenger
170 Cypress Pt (39466-9272)
P.O. Box 1777 (39466-1777)
PHONE..........................601 215-8846
Jim Ballenger, *Owner*
EMP: 2
SALES: 80K **Privately Held**
SIC: 3699 1731 4813 Security devices; sound equipment specialization;

(G-4256)
BEAVERS ENTERPRISES
85 Woodridge Ln (39466-8834)
PHONE..........................601 569-1557
Dan Beavers, *Owner*
EMP: 1
SALES (est): 74.9K **Privately Held**
SIC: 3559 Special industry machinery

(G-4257)
BREAKTIME VENDING INC
Also Called: Usedvending.com
2001 Cooper Rd (39466-2205)
P.O. Box 321, Carriere (39426-0321)
PHONE..........................601 749-8424
Eric Normand, *President*
EMP: 6
SQ FT: 6,000
SALES (est): 892.2K **Privately Held**
WEB: www.newvending.com
SIC: 5962 2721 Food vending machines; periodicals

(G-4258)
C WELLS TRUCKING LLC
15464 Lott Mccarty Rd (39466-8903)
PHONE..........................601 273-0972
EMP: 1
SALES (est): 54.6K **Privately Held**
SIC: 3732 Boat building & repairing

(G-4259)
CAPT MIKES STUMP GRINDING AND
165 Will Thompson Rd (39466-6616)
PHONE..........................985 892-9162
Pamela Slemmer, *Principal*
EMP: 1
SALES (est): 98.2K **Privately Held**
SIC: 3599 Grinding castings for the trade

2019 Harris Directory of
Mississippi Manufacturers

▲ = Import ▼=Export
◆ =Import/Export

GEOGRAPHIC SECTION

Picayune - Pearl River County (G-4290)

(G-4260)
COASTAL CHARTING CONSULTANTS
215 Boley Dr (39466-2525)
PHONE..............................601 590-0540
Jesse H Costolo III, *Owner*
EMP: 1
SALES (est): 52K **Privately Held**
SIC: 3812 Search & navigation equipment

(G-4261)
COASTAL METAL WORKS LLC
1821 Palestine Rd (39466-3603)
P.O. Box 10069, New Orleans LA (70181-0069)
PHONE..............................601 749-2611
Carl F Ducote,
Brenda B Ducote,
Martha Flick,
Robert C Flick,
EMP: 12
SQ FT: 13,200
SALES: 4.5MM **Privately Held**
SIC: 3441 Fabricated structural metal

(G-4262)
CPP LLC
1900 Rocha St (39466)
PHONE..............................601 749-7140
Preston Carpenter,
EMP: 8
SALES (est): 1MM **Privately Held**
SIC: 2491 Wood preserving

(G-4263)
CREATIVE IRON WORKS MS LLC
23050 Felix Rd N (39466-9524)
PHONE..............................985 960-2386
James Payne, *Principal*
EMP: 1
SALES (est): 55.3K **Privately Held**
SIC: 3462 Iron & steel forgings

(G-4264)
CREATIVE VENTURES LLC
49 Werner Rd Bldg A (39466-9500)
PHONE..............................601 798-7758
Sheila Fletcher,
Randy Fletcher,
EMP: 2
SQ FT: 1,086
SALES (est): 146K **Privately Held**
WEB: www.creativeventures.biz
SIC: 7336 3993 Graphic arts & related design; signs & advertising specialties

(G-4265)
EAGLE FIRE WORKS CO INC
24 Hodge Dr5 (39466)
P.O. Box 10, Nicholson (39463-0010)
PHONE..............................601 798-9291
Carl A Hodge, *President*
Eileen M Hodge, *Vice Pres*
Holly D Hodge, *Vice Pres*
▲ EMP: 2
SALES (est): 200K **Privately Held**
SIC: 2899 5999 Fireworks; fireworks

(G-4266)
FIRST HERITAGE CREDIT CORP
1 Sycamore Rd Ste E (39466-2666)
PHONE..............................601 799-1972
Scott Duffy, *CEO*
EMP: 1 **Privately Held**
SIC: 6141 2411 Consumer finance companies; timber, cut at logging camp
PA: First Heritage Credit Corp
605 Crescent Blvd Ste 101
Ridgeland MS 39157

(G-4267)
GLOBAL FABRICATION II LLC
1934 Palestine Rd (39466-3606)
PHONE..............................601 749-2209
Stuart Pender, *Sales Staff*
Ed Pender,
▲ EMP: 40
SQ FT: 50,000
SALES (est): 10.1MM **Privately Held**
WEB: www.globalfabrication.com
SIC: 3441 Fabricated structural metal

(G-4268)
GULF COAST FABRICATION INC
616 E Canal St (39466-4516)
PHONE..............................601 347-8403
Nanette Hardin, *President*
Frederick Hardin, *Vice Pres*
EMP: 2 EST: 2013
SQ FT: 10,000
SALES (est): 144.5K **Privately Held**
SIC: 3599 Machine & other job shop work

(G-4269)
GULF CONCRETE CO INC
106 S Beech St (39466-4206)
PHONE..............................601 798-3181
Berton Swook, *President*
Anna Lou Wilkes, *Principal*
EMP: 12 EST: 1963
SQ FT: 1,700
SALES (est): 1.1MM **Privately Held**
SIC: 3273 5032 Ready-mixed concrete; brick, except refractory

(G-4270)
H S I READY MIX
130 Huey Stockstill Rd (39466-8361)
PHONE..............................601 798-1665
David Stockstill, *Owner*
▲ EMP: 1
SALES (est): 130.8K **Privately Held**
SIC: 3273 Ready-mixed concrete

(G-4271)
HERITAGE PLASTICS INC (PA)
1002 Hunt St (39466-5200)
PHONE..............................404 425-1905
Carl F Allen, *Ch of Bd*
Paul Lewis, *President*
Justin Jones, *Vice Pres*
Tommy Chisolm, *Opers Mgr*
Lynn Smith, *Buyer*
◆ EMP: 115
SQ FT: 106,000
SALES (est): 49.8MM **Privately Held**
WEB: www.heritage-plastics.com
SIC: 2821 Plastics materials & resins

(G-4272)
HUEY P STOCKSTILL LLC (PA)
Also Called: Hsi Ready Mix
130 Huey Stockstill Rd (39466-8361)
P.O. Box 758 (39466-0758)
PHONE..............................601 798-2981
Huey Stockstill Jr, *CEO*
Huey P Stockstill Jr, *CEO*
Huey P Stockstill Sr, *President*
Richard W Stockstill, *Vice Pres*
Ricky Stockstill, *Vice Pres*
EMP: 180
SQ FT: 4,000
SALES (est): 53.3MM **Privately Held**
WEB: www.hueystockstill.com
SIC: 1611 3272 Highway & street paving contractor; building materials, except block or brick: concrete

(G-4273)
HUEY P STOCKSTILL LLC
130 Huey Stockstill Rd (39466-8361)
P.O. Box 758 (39466-0758)
PHONE..............................601 798-2981
Huey Stockstill Jr,
EMP: 150 EST: 2015
SQ FT: 3,000
SALES (est): 2.4MM **Privately Held**
SIC: 1442 1611 1622 3273 Construction sand & gravel; highway & street construction; bridge, tunnel & elevated highway; highway construction, elevated; ready-mixed concrete

(G-4274)
HUTCHINSON ISLAND MINING CORP
216 Dan Stewart Rd (39466-8339)
PHONE..............................601 799-4070
Richard W Stockstill, *President*
David Stockstill, *Corp Secy*
Susan McDonald, *Vice Pres*
Huey P Stockstill Jr, *Vice Pres*
EMP: 10
SQ FT: 320
SALES (est): 920K **Privately Held**
SIC: 1442 Sand mining; gravel & pebble mining

(G-4275)
LAGNIAPPE BOOKS LLC
313 Telly Rd (39466-5552)
PHONE..............................769 242-8104
EMP: 1
SALES (est): 36.1K **Privately Held**
SIC: 2731 Books: publishing only

(G-4276)
M & M PRINTING LLC
29 Alex Pl (39466-9697)
PHONE..............................601 798-4316
Debra Sharff,
EMP: 6
SALES: 15K **Privately Held**
SIC: 2752 Commercial printing, offset

(G-4277)
M & M PRINTING CO
29 Alex Pl (39466-9697)
PHONE..............................601 798-4316
Deborah Sharff, *Mng Member*
EMP: 2
SALES: 100K **Privately Held**
SIC: 2752 2791 Commercial printing, lithographic; typesetting

(G-4278)
MILITARY DEFENSE SYSTEMS INC
1817 Palestine Rd (39466-3603)
PHONE..............................850 449-1910
Ada Wolfe, *President*
EMP: 6
SALES (est): 620.8K **Privately Held**
SIC: 3053 3429 Gaskets, packing & sealing devices; manufactured hardware (general)

(G-4279)
MILLION DOLLAR MAKEUP LLC
145 Arbor Gate Cir Apt H (39466-6006)
PHONE..............................318 331-5363
Taylor McMillion,
EMP: 1
SALES (est): 47.2K **Privately Held**
SIC: 2844 7231 Cosmetic preparations; cosmetologist

(G-4280)
MISSISSIPPI AEROSPACE CORP
501 S Main St (39466-4419)
PHONE..............................601 749-5659
Amy Jo Formby, *CEO*
Ira Ned Formby Jr, *COO*
Ashley Mitchell, *Treasurer*
Becky Highnote, *Office Mgr*
EMP: 10
SQ FT: 5,100
SALES (est): 1.8MM **Privately Held**
SIC: 8711 3721 3812 3441 Aviation &/or aeronautical engineering; aircraft; search & navigation equipment; fabricated structural metal

(G-4281)
NEWSPAPER HOLDING INC
Also Called: Picayune Item
17 Richardson Ozona Rd (39466-7865)
P.O. Box 580 (39466-0580)
PHONE..............................601 798-4766
Linda Gilmore, *Manager*
EMP: 24
SQ FT: 7,000 **Privately Held**
WEB: www.clintonnc.com
SIC: 2711 Newspapers, publishing & printing
HQ: Newspaper Holding, Inc.
425 Locust St
Johnstown PA 15901
814 532-5102

(G-4282)
OUTDOOR DIMENSIONS INC
62 Hidden Hills Dr E (39466-6800)
PHONE..............................601 749-9981
Charles Rogers, *Owner*
Tawny Simmons, *Project Mgr*
Richelle Jensen, *Sales Staff*
Kimberly Sanchez, *Receptionist*
EMP: 1
SALES (est): 70.8K **Privately Held**
SIC: 3993 Signs & advertising specialties

(G-4283)
PARR PROSTHETICS
1125 Highway 43 N Ste F (39466-2173)
PHONE..............................601 749-7254
Larry Loughlin, *Owner*
EMP: 5
SALES (est): 270K **Privately Held**
SIC: 3842 Prosthetic appliances

(G-4284)
PAULS PASTRY PRODUCTION LLC
1 Sycamore Rd Ste A (39466-2666)
PHONE..............................601 798-7457
Laci Brunson,
EMP: 13
SALES (est): 320.1K **Privately Held**
SIC: 5461 2051 2052 Bakeries; bread, cake & related products; cookies & crackers

(G-4285)
PAULS PASTRY SHOP
1 Sycamore Rd Ste A (39466-2666)
PHONE..............................601 798-7457
Sherri Thigpen, *Owner*
Laci Brunson, *Purch Dir*
EMP: 25
SQ FT: 5,500
SALES (est): 826.6K **Privately Held**
SIC: 5461 2052 2051 Cakes; cookies & crackers; bread, cake & related products

(G-4286)
PICAYUNE MONUMENT & GRAN WORKS
Also Called: Mid State Coatings
411 Memorial Blvd (39466-5545)
P.O. Box 774 (39466-0774)
PHONE..............................601 798-7926
Foy R Williams, *Owner*
EMP: 2
SALES (est): 211.8K **Privately Held**
SIC: 3272 1721 5999 Monuments & grave markers, except terrazo; painting & paper hanging; monuments, finished to custom order

(G-4287)
POWER DYNAMICS INNOVATIONS LLC
1301 Mlk Blvd (39466-5426)
PHONE..............................601 229-0960
Carl Liberty, *President*
Charles La Biche, *Vice Pres*
Kenneth Hesler, *Opers Mgr*
Larry Metting, *VP Engrg*
Kenneth Mitchell, *Project Engr*
▲ EMP: 50 EST: 1999
SQ FT: 60,000
SALES (est): 17.7MM **Privately Held**
WEB: www.pdi-entech.com
SIC: 3569 8711 Jacks, hydraulic; industrial engineers

(G-4288)
PURVIS JEWELRY CANDLES
505 S Main St (39466-4419)
PHONE..............................601 270-9687
EMP: 1
SALES (est): 39.6K **Privately Held**
SIC: 3999 Candles

(G-4289)
QUALITY MACHINE & WLDG OF MISS
64 Mars Island Rd (39466-9057)
PHONE..............................601 798-8568
Kennon Peterson, *President*
Ernest Odom, *Vice Pres*
EMP: 32
SQ FT: 1,400
SALES (est): 3MM **Privately Held**
SIC: 3599 7692 Machine shop, jobbing & repair; welding repair

(G-4290)
QUIKRETE COMPANIES LLC
178 Huey Stockstill Rd (39466-8361)
PHONE..............................601 798-6021
Kelli Bennett, *Branch Mgr*
EMP: 39 **Privately Held**
SIC: 3272 Concrete products

(PA)=Parent Co (HQ)=Headquarters (DH)=Div Headquarters
✿ = New Business established in last 2 years

2019 Harris Directory of
Mississippi Manufacturers

155

Picayune - Pearl River County (G-4291) — GEOGRAPHIC SECTION

HQ: The Quikrete Companies Llc
5 Concourse Pkwy Ste 1900
Atlanta GA 30328
404 634-9100

(G-4291)
RHEOGISTICS LLC
100 Polymer Dr (39466-5441)
PHONE..........................601 749-8845
Henry Renken, *Mng Member*
Jean R Pedersen,
Tom Pedersen,
▲ EMP: 24
SQ FT: 42,000
SALES (est): 12.8MM **Privately Held**
WEB: www.rheogistics.com
SIC: 2822 Ethylene-propylene rubbers, EPDM polymers

(G-4292)
RIVER ROCK AND SAND CO
79 Emmett Meitzler Rd (39466-7956)
P.O. Box 1538 (39466-1538)
PHONE..........................601 798-4292
William Gilmore, *Owner*
EMP: 2
SALES (est): 194.7K **Privately Held**
SIC: 1442 Construction sand & gravel

(G-4293)
SEA ROBIN FORGE
1423 Third Ave (39466-2415)
PHONE..........................601 798-0060
Charles H Robinson, *Principal*
EMP: 2
SALES (est): 103.5K **Privately Held**
SIC: 3199 Aprons: welders', blacksmiths', etc.: leather

(G-4294)
SHABBY CHIC S ETC
505 S Main St (39466-4419)
PHONE..........................601 799-2800
Rosemary Ladner, *Owner*
EMP: 2
SALES (est): 223K **Privately Held**
SIC: 3643 Outlets, electric: convenience

(G-4295)
SHALE ENERGY SUPPORT LLC
Also Called: Shale Support
105 Street A (39466-5467)
PHONE..........................601 798-7821
Jeff Bartlan, *President*
EMP: 70
SALES (est): 1.9MM **Privately Held**
SIC: 1442 Sand mining

(G-4296)
SOUTHERN PROSTHETIC CARE LLC
4201 Highway 11 N Ste D (39466-2014)
PHONE..........................769 242-2555
William Kenny,
EMP: 1
SALES (est): 93.7K **Privately Held**
SIC: 3842 Prosthetic appliances

(G-4297)
ST TAMMANY BOX COMPANY
205 Street A (39466-5468)
PHONE..........................601 799-0775
Tina Dubroc, *President*
Scott Dubroc, *Exec VP*
EMP: 35
SQ FT: 3,000,000
SALES (est): 10.5MM **Privately Held**
SIC: 2653 Boxes, corrugated: made from purchased materials

(G-4298)
STOCKSTILL BROS INVSTMENTS LLC
Also Called: Metro Concrete
130 Huey Stockstill Rd (39466-8361)
PHONE..........................601 798-2981
David Stockstill,
EMP: 40
SALES (est): 3.2MM **Privately Held**
SIC: 1611 3273 Concrete construction: roads, highways, sidewalks, etc.; ready-mixed concrete

(G-4299)
STONE TREATED MATERIALS
403 Davis St (39466-4313)
PHONE..........................601 798-4422
Doug Seal, *Principal*
EMP: 2
SALES (est): 65.4K **Privately Held**
SIC: 2491 Wood preserving

(G-4300)
TEXAS PACKAGING
711 Neal Rd (39466-3019)
PHONE..........................214 912-5833
Gerry Wilson, *Owner*
EMP: 1
SALES: 125K **Privately Held**
SIC: 2653 Corrugated & solid fiber boxes

(G-4301)
TINY PRINTS 3D IMAGING LLC
118 E Canal St (39466-4506)
P.O. Box 765 (39466-0765)
PHONE..........................866 846-9733
EMP: 2
SALES (est): 109.4K **Privately Held**
SIC: 2752 Lithographic Commercial Printing

(G-4302)
WAY MANUFACTURE INC
204 Street A (39466-5458)
PHONE..........................601 749-0362
Wayne R Wiggins, *President*
EMP: 20
SALES (est): 3.5MM **Privately Held**
SIC: 2842 2899 2841 Specialty cleaning preparations; chemical preparations; soap & other detergents
PA: The Way Inc
204 Street A
Picayune MS
601 798-5757

(G-4303)
WHEELER ENTERPRISES INC
Also Called: X Press Copy Centre
1620 Highway 11 N Ste B (39466-2070)
PHONE..........................601 799-1440
Bob Wheeler, *President*
Mary Wheeler, *Treasurer*
EMP: 3 EST: 1992
SQ FT: 1,400
SALES (est): 130K **Privately Held**
SIC: 2759 Commercial printing

(G-4304)
WILLIES WOODWORKS
12471 Old Kiln Rd (39466-9387)
PHONE..........................601 916-3574
EMP: 1 EST: 2016
SALES (est): 54.1K **Privately Held**
SIC: 2431 Mfg Millwork

(G-4305)
WRJW 1320 AM
Also Called: Swap Shop Newspaper
2438 Highway 43 S (39466)
P.O. Box 907 (39466-0907)
PHONE..........................601 798-4835
John Pigott, *President*
Delores Wood, *Manager*
EMP: 15
SALES (est): 857.7K **Privately Held**
SIC: 4832 2711 Radio broadcasting stations; newspapers

Pickens
Holmes County

(G-4306)
CRUISE STREET PRESS LLC
277 Rocky Hill Rd (39146-9415)
PHONE..........................601 720-4848
Douglas Cruise, *Principal*
EMP: 1
SALES (est): 37.5K **Privately Held**
SIC: 2741 Miscellaneous publishing

(G-4307)
TWIN RIVERS PAPER COMPANY LLC
Also Called: Burrows Southern Division
196 Burrows Dr (39146)
P.O. Box 98 (39146-0098)
PHONE..........................662 468-2183
Don Durrell, *Manager*
EMP: 39 **Privately Held**
WEB: www.burrowspaper.com
SIC: 2621 2676 Tissue paper; sanitary paper products
PA: Twin Rivers Paper Company Llc
82 Bridge Ave
Madawaska ME 04756

Pinola
Simpson County

(G-4308)
ECO RECOVERY MACHINE LLC
1118 Highway 472 (39149-3014)
PHONE..........................713 829-1083
EMP: 2 EST: 2012
SQ FT: 250
SALES: 51MM **Privately Held**
SIC: 3599 Oil filters, internal combustion engine, except automotive

Pittsboro
Calhoun County

(G-4309)
OLDTOWN TRUSS
239 County Road 102 (38951-9703)
PHONE..........................662 412-2500
Terry Davis, *Partner*
Benny Bryant, *Partner*
John Wooten, *Partner*
EMP: 4
SQ FT: 7,500
SALES (est): 800K **Privately Held**
SIC: 2439 Trusses, except roof: laminated lumber; trusses, wooden roof

Plantersville
Lee County

(G-4310)
KEDRON FURNITURE MFG INC
Also Called: Kedron Surplus & Sales
3867 Highway 6 (38862-3917)
PHONE..........................662 963-3366
Billy Joe Finney, *President*
Betty Finney, *Treasurer*
EMP: 3
SQ FT: 13,800
SALES (est): 224K **Privately Held**
SIC: 2512 2392 Living room furniture: upholstered on wood frames; household furnishings

(G-4311)
NATIONAL MATTRESS LLC
224 Poplar St (38862-7306)
P.O. Box 485 (38862-0485)
PHONE..........................662 205-4891
Debby Harmon, *Owner*
EMP: 9
SQ FT: 40,000
SALES (est): 800K **Privately Held**
SIC: 2515 5021 Mattresses & bedsprings; furniture

(G-4312)
NORTHEAST METAL PROCESSORS
551 Central St (38862)
PHONE..........................662 844-2164
Walter D Fleishhacker, *President*
Larry Bert, *Vice Pres*
Regina Todd, *Finance*
EMP: 22 EST: 1974
SQ FT: 10,000
SALES (est): 4.3MM **Privately Held**
SIC: 3341 5093 Secondary nonferrous metals; ferrous metal scrap & waste

(G-4313)
PETTIGREW CABINETS INC
3449 Highway 6 (38862-7622)
PHONE..........................662 844-1368
Jeff Pettigrew, *President*
Brenda Pettigrew, *Corp Secy*
Fred Pettigrew, *Vice Pres*
EMP: 23
SQ FT: 32,000
SALES (est): 4.1MM **Privately Held**
WEB: www.pettigrewcabinets.com
SIC: 5712 5722 5211 2517 Cabinet work, custom; kitchens, complete (sinks, cabinets, etc.); bathroom fixtures, equipment & supplies; counter tops; wood television & radio cabinets; wood kitchen cabinets

(G-4314)
RAUSCHS WELDING & REPAIR
County Rd 736 Ste 136 (38862)
P.O. Box 325 (38862-0325)
PHONE..........................662 841-0499
Alvin Rausch, *Manager*
EMP: 1
SALES (est): 64.7K **Privately Held**
SIC: 7692 Welding repair

(G-4315)
SLEEPER KRAFT LLC
131 Cedar St (38862-9778)
P.O. Box 7176, Tupelo (38802-7176)
PHONE..........................662 620-9797
Larry Jackson,
Michele Jackson,
▼ EMP: 32
SQ FT: 70,000
SALES: 5MM **Privately Held**
SIC: 2515 Mattresses, innerspring or box spring

(G-4316)
SUPERIOR BEDDING PRODUCTS OF M
Also Called: Royal Products
224 Poplar St (38862-7306)
P.O. Box 130 (38862-0130)
PHONE..........................662 841-1632
▲ EMP: 31
SALES (est): 1.8MM **Privately Held**
SIC: 2515 Mfg Mattresses/Bedsprings

(G-4317)
SUPERIOR MANUFACTURED FIBERS (PA)
117 Cedar St (38862-9778)
PHONE..........................662 844-8255
James Matthews Sr, *President*
James Matthews Jr, *Vice Pres*
EMP: 5
SQ FT: 50,000
SALES (est): 884K **Privately Held**
SIC: 2824 Polyester fibers

(G-4318)
W & W PALLETS LLC
106 Woodgreen Rd (38862-9709)
P.O. Box 313, Nettleton (38858-0313)
PHONE..........................662 706-0050
Michael Woolven, *Principal*
EMP: 4
SALES (est): 170K **Privately Held**
SIC: 2448 Pallets, wood & wood with metal

Pontotoc
Pontotoc County

(G-4319)
ACTION INDUSTRIES
338 Stafford Blvd (38863-1106)
P.O. Box 1627, Tupelo (38802-1627)
PHONE..........................662 566-3173
Fax: 662 566-7418
EMP: 8 EST: 2005
SALES (est): 560K **Privately Held**
SIC: 3999 Mfg Misc Products

(G-4320)
ALBANY INDUSTRIES INC
388 Highway 15 S (38863-3713)
P.O. Box 1258 (38863-1259)
PHONE..........................662 488-8281
EMP: 4

2019 Harris Directory of Mississippi Manufacturers

▲ = Import ▼=Export
◆ =Import/Export

GEOGRAPHIC SECTION

Pontotoc - Pontotoc County (G-4349)

SALES (corp-wide): 241.1MM **Privately Held**
SIC: 2512 Upholstered household furniture
HQ: Albany Industries, Llc
504 N Glenfield Rd
New Albany MS 38652

(G-4321)
B & B CONCRETE CO INC
291 W 8th St (38863-3606)
P.O. Box 1178 (38863-1199)
PHONE..................................662 489-2233
Henry Brevard, *President*
Stony Sappington, *Manager*
EMP: 9
SALES (corp-wide): 21.1MM **Privately Held**
SIC: 3273 Ready-mixed concrete
PA: B & B Concrete Co., Inc.
130 N Industrial Rd
Tupelo MS 38801
662 842-6312

(G-4322)
BEHOLD WASHINGTON LLC
Also Called: Washington Furniture Sales
206 Magee Dr (38863-1114)
P.O. Box 540 (38863-0540)
PHONE..................................662 489-6117
Carlyle Smith Harris Jr, *CEO*
Gerald Washington, *Managing Dir*
Bo Rusell, *CFO*
Janet Washington, *Manager*
◆ EMP: 438
SQ FT: 9,000
SALES (est): 79MM **Privately Held**
SIC: 2511 Wood household furniture

(G-4323)
BRAZIL FURNITURE INC
110 Maggie Dr (38863-8668)
P.O. Box 1397 (38863-1440)
PHONE..................................662 489-2063
Mike Brazil, *President*
Mac Reeder, *Vice Pres*
EMP: 40
SQ FT: 35,000
SALES (est): 3.6MM **Privately Held**
SIC: 2512 Recliners: upholstered on wood
frames; rockers: upholstered on wood
frames

(G-4324)
C & CS MACHINE SHOP INC
420 E Oxford St (38863-2316)
PHONE..................................662 489-3376
Mark Clemons, *President*
EMP: 12 EST: 1993
SQ FT: 10,000
SALES (est): 891K **Privately Held**
SIC: 3599 Machine shop, jobbing & repair

(G-4325)
CARNES FRAMES INC (PA)
263 Brookwood Dr (38863-1332)
P.O. Box 720 (38863-0720)
PHONE..................................662 489-1984
Howard Carnes, *President*
Julie M Shelly Carnes, *Vice Pres*
EMP: 35 EST: 1988
SQ FT: 21,000
SALES (est): 17MM **Privately Held**
SIC: 2426 Frames for upholstered furniture, wood

(G-4326)
COUNTRY KIDS PUBLISHING LLC
729 Maffett Rd (38863-8057)
PHONE..................................662 509-0427
Beverly Gunter, *Principal*
EMP: 1
SALES (est): 70.5K **Privately Held**
SIC: 2741 Miscellaneous publishing

(G-4327)
CUSHIONS TO GO LLC
370 Henry Southern Dr (38863-8988)
PHONE..................................662 488-0350
Albert G Delgadillo, *Principal*
Roger Bland, *Manager*
H Guy Lipscomb Sr, *Manager*
Larry Witcher, *Manager*
EMP: 1
SALES (est): 124.8K **Privately Held**
SIC: 2392 Mattress pads

(G-4328)
DAVIS ENTERPRISES INC
Also Called: Davis Cardboard
715 Q T Todd Dr (38863-6233)
P.O. Box 47, Ecru (38841-0047)
PHONE..................................662 488-9972
Tracy Davis, *President*
Kay Davis, *Vice Pres*
EMP: 5
SQ FT: 1,600
SALES (est): 640K **Privately Held**
SIC: 5113 2675 Cardboard & products;
die-cut paper & board

(G-4329)
DELTA FURNITURE MFG LLC
292 Industrial Dr (38863-1324)
PHONE..................................662 489-2128
Terry Wages, *President*
Wesley Walls, *Principal*
Jeff Hamilton, *CFO*
Corey Wages, *CFO*
EMP: 52
SQ FT: 73,000
SALES (est): 10MM **Privately Held**
SIC: 2511 Wood household furniture

(G-4330)
EATON CUSTOM SEATING LLC
Also Called: E C S
263 Coffee St (38863-2612)
P.O. Box 1449 (38863-1499)
PHONE..................................662 489-4242
Craig Clawson, *Chairman*
Caleb Mills, *Purchasing*
Keith Sanders, *CFO*
EMP: 100
SQ FT: 200,000
SALES (est): 6.7MM **Privately Held**
SIC: 3646 Commercial indusl & institutional electric lighting fixtures

(G-4331)
FIBRIX LLC
Also Called: Cumulus Fibres - Pontotoc
226 Prestige Dr (38863-1121)
PHONE..................................662 489-7908
Mark Buskirk, *Manager*
EMP: 30
SALES (corp-wide): 74MM **Privately Held**
WEB: www.lpfiber.com
SIC: 2284 2824 2823 2297 Thread from
manmade fibers; organic fibers, noncellulosic; cellulosic manmade fibers; nonwoven fabrics
HQ: Fibrix, Llc
1820 Evans St Ne
Conover NC 28613

(G-4332)
HICKORY SPRINGS MFG CO
397 Stafford Blvd (38863)
PHONE..................................662 489-6684
Steve Pannell, *Manager*
EMP: 33
SALES (corp-wide): 898MM **Privately Held**
WEB: www.hickorysprings.com
SIC: 3086 Insulation or cushioning material, foamed plastic
PA: Hickory Springs Manufacturing Company
235 2nd Ave Nw
Hickory NC 28601
828 328-2201

(G-4333)
HYPERCO
260 Industrial Dr (38863-1338)
PHONE..................................662 488-4567
EMP: 2 EST: 2017
SALES (est): 141.8K **Privately Held**
SIC: 3714 Motor vehicle parts & accessories

(G-4334)
IDEAL FOAM LLC
300 Stafford Blvd (38863-1106)
P.O. Box 563 (38863-0563)
PHONE..................................662 489-2264
Todd Bushkirk,
▲ EMP: 60
SQ FT: 1,500
SALES (est): 19.2MM **Privately Held**
SIC: 3086 Plastics foam products

(G-4335)
ILLINOIS TOOL WORKS INC
ITW Paslode
364 Stafford Blvd (38863-1119)
PHONE..................................662 489-4151
Don Wilson, *Manager*
EMP: 150
SALES (corp-wide): 14.7B **Publicly Held**
SIC: 3965 3452 3315 Fasteners, buttons,
needles & pins; bolts, nuts, rivets & washers; steel wire & related products
PA: Illinois Tool Works Inc.
155 Harlem Ave
Glenview IL 60025
847 724-7500

(G-4336)
IMAGE SCREEN PRINTING INC
2111 Highway 15 N (38863-9607)
PHONE..................................662 489-5668
Denita Sneed, *President*
Harold Sneed, *Vice Pres*
Tammy Hannon, *Sales Staff*
EMP: 22
SQ FT: 6,000
SALES (est): 2.3MM **Privately Held**
WEB: www.imagescreenprinting.com
SIC: 2759 Screen printing

(G-4337)
INNER SANCTUARY INC
137 Oak Dr (38863-1527)
PHONE..................................662 489-6772
EMP: 3 EST: 2000
SALES (est): 140K **Privately Held**
SIC: 2731 8661 Books-Publishing/Printing
Religious Organization

(G-4338)
J & W FURNITURE FRAMES INC
435 Warren Ln (38863-8641)
PHONE..................................662 489-1991
Jeff Warren, *President*
Jimmie Warren, *Corp Secy*
EMP: 25
SQ FT: 6,000
SALES (est): 3.9MM **Privately Held**
SIC: 2426 Frames for upholstered furniture, wood

(G-4339)
JOHN ALBERT WARE
Also Called: Jj & W Trucking
28 Ben Hardin Rd (38863-7031)
PHONE..................................662 489-7824
John Albert Ware, *Owner*
EMP: 2
SALES (est): 140K **Privately Held**
SIC: 4212 2411 Local trucking, without
storage; logging

(G-4340)
K & L FURNITURE FRAMES INC
1080 Pontotoc Cnty Ind Pk (38863)
P.O. Box 970 (38863-0970)
PHONE..................................662 489-5355
Shirley Willard, *President*
Linda Willard, *Treasurer*
EMP: 48
SQ FT: 27,500
SALES (est): 7.5MM **Privately Held**
SIC: 2426 Furniture stock & parts, hardwood

(G-4341)
LANE FURNITURE INDUSTRIES INC
Industrial Pk Stafford Dr (38863)
PHONE..................................662 489-3815
EMP: 700
SALES (corp-wide): 1B **Privately Held**
SIC: 2512 Mfg Upholstered Household
Furniture
HQ: Lane Furniture Industries, Inc.
5380 Highway 145 S
Tupelo MS 38801
662 566-7211

(G-4342)
MAGNOLIA FURNITURE LLC
4333 Highway 9 S (38863-9322)
PHONE..................................662 489-9337
Delma Lathel Ward,
EMP: 5

SALES (est): 1.1MM **Privately Held**
WEB: www.magnoliafurniture.com
SIC: 3069 5031 2426 2515 Foam rubber;
lumber: rough, dressed & finished; plywood; frames for upholstered furniture,
wood; mattresses & foundations; excavation work; general farms, primarily crop

(G-4343)
MARTIN CARDBOARD COMPANY INC
103 Cruse Dr (38863)
P.O. Box 812 (38863-0812)
PHONE..................................662 489-5416
Tim Martin, *President*
James R Martin, *Vice Pres*
EMP: 8
SALES (est): 1.5MM **Privately Held**
SIC: 2675 Panels, cardboard, die-cut:
made from purchased materials

(G-4344)
MATTHEW WARREN INC
Also Called: Pontotoc Spring
260 Industrial Dr (38863-1338)
PHONE..................................662 489-7846
Allen Roye, *General Mgr*
EMP: 100
SALES (corp-wide): 185.9MM **Privately Held**
SIC: 3493 3495 Steel springs, except
wire; wire springs
HQ: Matthew Warren, Inc.
9501 Tech Blvd Ste 401
Rosemont IL 60018
847 349-5760

(G-4345)
MATTHEW WARREN INC
Also Called: Hyperco
260 Industrial Dr (38863-1338)
PHONE..................................574 753-6622
McClain Kipp, *Branch Mgr*
EMP: 4
SALES (corp-wide): 185.9MM **Privately Held**
SIC: 3493 Coiled flat springs; cold formed
springs; helical springs, hot wound: railroad equipment etc.; hot wound springs,
except wire
HQ: Matthew Warren, Inc.
9501 Tech Blvd Ste 401
Rosemont IL 60018
847 349-5760

(G-4346)
MISS EATON INC
Also Called: Eaton Seating
263 Coffee St (38863-2612)
P.O. Box 1449 (38863-1499)
PHONE..................................662 489-4242
Bill Cotter, *President*
Ed Bartee, *Corp Secy*
Todd Torrence, *Manager*
Craig S Clawson, *Director*
▲ EMP: 97
SQ FT: 120,000
SALES (est): 12.2MM **Privately Held**
SIC: 2512 Chairs: upholstered on wood
frames

(G-4347)
MITCHELL GROUP
204 Brookwood Dr (38863-1302)
PHONE..................................662 488-0025
▲ EMP: 5
SALES (est): 524.7K **Privately Held**
SIC: 2231 5131 Upholstery fabrics, wool;
upholstery fabrics, woven

(G-4348)
MOORES FEED STORE INC
157 Highway 15 S (38863-3103)
PHONE..................................662 488-0024
EMP: 2
SALES (est): 62.3K **Privately Held**
SIC: 2048 Feeds from meat & from meat &
vegetable meals

(G-4349)
MOORES II INC
Also Called: Moore's Feed Store & Mill
439 Highway 9 S (38863-2406)
PHONE..................................662 488-0024
EMP: 20

(PA)=Parent Co (HQ)=Headquarters (DH)=Div Headquarters
✪ = New Business established in last 2 years

2019 Harris Directory of
Mississippi Manufacturers

157

Pontotoc - Pontotoc County (G-4350)

GEOGRAPHIC SECTION

SALES (corp-wide): 11.3MM **Privately Held**
SIC: 2048 Prepared feeds
PA: Moore's Ii, Inc
  3261 Highway 15 N
  Pontotoc MS 38863
  662 489-1411

(G-4350)
MOORES JOHN
3261 Highway 15 N (38863-8512)
PHONE..................................662 488-2980
John Moores, *Principal*
EMP: 2
SALES (est): 111.8K **Privately Held**
SIC: 5999 3429 Feed & farm supply; manufactured hardware (general)

(G-4351)
MW INDUSTRIES
260 Industrial Dr (38863-1338)
PHONE..................................662 488-4551
Barry Ehrensaft, *Sales Staff*
EMP: 3
SALES (est): 262.4K **Privately Held**
SIC: 3999 Manufacturing industries

(G-4352)
OLIVES & APPLES LLC ◒
624 E Ridge Hts (38863-1217)
PHONE..................................662 419-0224
EMP: 2 **EST:** 2018
SALES (est): 85.9K **Privately Held**
SIC: 3571 Mfg Electronic Computers

(G-4353)
PASLODE CORPORATION
364 Stafford Blvd (38863-1119)
PHONE..................................662 489-4151
David B Speer, *President*
Robert V McGrath, *Vice Pres*
Valery Vanstaan, *Engineer*
Michael J Robinson, *Treasurer*
Stewart S Hudnut, *Admin Sec*
EMP: 8
SALES (est): 1.6MM **Privately Held**
SIC: 3423 Hand & edge tools

(G-4354)
PONTOTOC DIE CUTTING LLC
363 Stafford Blvd (38863-1112)
P.O. Box 594 (38863-0594)
PHONE..................................662 489-5874
Ken Pruett,
Tami Lorick,
EMP: 10
SQ FT: 4,200
SALES (est): 700K **Privately Held**
SIC: 2631 2675 Paperboard mills; die-cut paper & board

(G-4355)
PONTOTOC MACHINE WORKS INC
312 Highway 15 S (38863)
P.O. Box 587 (38863-0587)
PHONE..................................662 489-8944
James W Todd, *President*
Ted McVay, *President*
Elise Todd, *Owner*
Louise Todd, *Vice Pres*
EMP: 6
SQ FT: 10,000
SALES: 1MM **Privately Held**
SIC: 3599 Custom machinery

(G-4356)
PONTOTOC PROGRESS INC
Also Called: Northeast Miss Cmnty Newsppr
13 E Jefferson St (38863-2807)
P.O. Box 210 (38863-0210)
PHONE..................................662 489-3511
Paul Sims, *General Mgr*
EMP: 8 **EST:** 1928
SQ FT: 6,000
SALES (est): 612.4K **Privately Held**
WEB: www.tupeloelvisfestival.com
SIC: 2711 Job printing & newspaper publishing combined
HQ: Journal, Inc.
  1242 S Green St
  Tupelo MS 38804
  662 842-2611

(G-4357)
PREMIERE PLASTICS INC
109 Ford St (38863-2309)
P.O. Box 359 (38863-0359)
PHONE..................................662 489-2007
John Metcalf, *President*
Johnny Metcalf, *Manager*
Janice Metcalf, *Admin Sec*
EMP: 20
SQ FT: 70,000
SALES (est): 3.7MM **Privately Held**
SIC: 3088 Tubs (bath, shower & laundry), plastic

(G-4358)
PREMIERE PRINTING
269 W Reynolds St (38863-1925)
P.O. Box 572 (38863-0572)
PHONE..................................662 488-9591
Michael Bailey, *Owner*
EMP: 5
SALES: 285K **Privately Held**
SIC: 2752 Commercial printing, offset

(G-4359)
PRINTSHOP PLUS INC
461 Barry Spur (38863-6350)
PHONE..................................662 231-4790
Barry Jaggers, *President*
EMP: 1
SALES: 150K **Privately Held**
SIC: 2759 Commercial printing

(G-4360)
RESURFACING CONCEPTS INC
5024 New Hope Rd (38863-9511)
P.O. Box 1012 (38863-1012)
PHONE..................................662 489-6867
Don Dye Jr, *President*
EMP: 2
SALES (est): 211.4K **Privately Held**
SIC: 1799 3471 3312 3479 Welding on site; sand blasting of metal parts; pipes, iron & steel; painting of metal products

(G-4361)
S & S MANUFACTURERS INC
Also Called: Stacy Furniture
1998 Campground Rd (38863-7068)
PHONE..................................662 489-2223
Dale Stacy, *President*
Mike Stacy, *Vice Pres*
Helen Stacy, *Director*
Helen I Stacy, *Admin Sec*
Sara Saxon,
EMP: 35
SALES (est): 5MM **Privately Held**
SIC: 2512 Living room furniture: upholstered on wood frames

(G-4362)
SMOKEHOUSE MEATS
426 Highway 41 (38863-9778)
PHONE..................................662 489-5764
Steve McMinn, *Owner*
EMP: 6
SALES (est): 374.1K **Privately Held**
WEB: www.smokehousemeats.com
SIC: 2011 Meat packing plants

(G-4363)
SOUTHERN MOTION INC
298 Henry Southern Dr (38863)
P.O. Box 1064 (38863-1064)
PHONE..................................662 488-9301
Larry Todd, *Vice Pres*
Tonya Jackson,
EMP: 121 **Privately Held**
SIC: 2512 Upholstered household furniture
PA: Southern Motion, Inc.
  298 Henry Southern Dr
  Pontotoc MS 38863

(G-4364)
TRACEWAY ENGINEERING AND MFG
Also Called: Traceway Tooling
344 Presidents Dr (38863-2322)
P.O. Box 548 (38863-0548)
PHONE..................................662 489-1314
Bart Hardee, *President*
Linda Hardee, *Corp Secy*
EMP: 10
SQ FT: 22,000

SALES (est): 1MM **Privately Held**
SIC: 3544 3599 Special dies & tools; custom machinery

(G-4365)
TRU-CUT INC
Also Called: Tru-Cut Frames
89 Possum Trot Rd (38863-6210)
PHONE..................................662 489-1879
Willie Frank Stark, *President*
Willie Stark, *Partner*
EMP: 30
SQ FT: 20,000
SALES (est): 4MM **Privately Held**
SIC: 2511 Wood household furniture

(G-4366)
UNION SPRING & MFG CORP
Also Called: Pontotoc Springs
260 Industrial Dr (38863-1338)
PHONE..................................662 489-7846
Allan Roye, *Manager*
EMP: 80
SALES (corp-wide): 22.7MM **Privately Held**
WEB: www.pontotocspring.com
SIC: 3493 3542 Automobile springs; machine tools, metal forming type
PA: Union Spring & Manufacturing Corporation
  4268 N Pike Ste 1
  Monroeville PA 15146
  412 843-5900

(G-4367)
UNITED STATES WORLDWIDE INC
7118 Highway 41 (38863-8862)
PHONE..................................662 488-1840
Robert Foster, *President*
EMP: 3
SALES (corp-wide): 3MM **Privately Held**
WEB: www.univ.cc
SIC: 2511 Children's wood furniture
PA: United States Worldwide, Inc.
  237 Burgess Rd Ste C
  Greensboro NC 27409
  336 664-5920

(G-4368)
VOLUPTUOUS E-JUICE LLC
1085 Wise Bend Rd (38863-8551)
PHONE..................................662 297-8353
Bryan Robbins, *Principal*
EMP: 1
SQ FT: 312
SALES (est): 113.3K **Privately Held**
SIC: 2111 5194 5993 Cigarettes; tobacco & tobacco products; tobacco stores & stands

(G-4369)
WDTM INC
Also Called: Tupelo Manufacturing
3185 Highway 9 S (38863-9319)
PHONE..................................662 842-6161
Kevin Mills, *President*
EMP: 85 **EST:** 1921
SQ FT: 100,000
SALES (est): 12.6MM **Privately Held**
WEB: www.tupelomfg.com
SIC: 2531 Public building & related furniture

(G-4370)
WILDER FITNESS SYSTEMS
215 E Oxford St (38863-2212)
PHONE..................................662 489-8365
Jimmy Wilder, *Owner*
EMP: 2
SALES (est): 209K **Privately Held**
WEB: www.wilderfitness.com
SIC: 3949 Exercise equipment

(G-4371)
WILDERS WELDING SHOP
Also Called: Wilder Architecheral Designs
321 W Oxford St (38863-1203)
PHONE..................................662 489-2772
Johnny Wilder, *Owner*
EMP: 2
SQ FT: 3,200
SALES (est): 202.8K **Privately Held**
SIC: 7692 7539 Welding repair; radiator repair shop, automotive

---

Pope
Panola County

(G-4372)
PITCOCKS MEAT PROCESSING INC
483 Liberty Hill Rd (38658-2860)
PHONE..................................662 563-9627
Tony Capwill, *President*
EMP: 3
SALES (est): 260K **Privately Held**
SIC: 5421 2011 7299 Meat markets, including freezer provisioners; meat packing plants; butcher service, processing only

---

Poplarville
Pearl River County

(G-4373)
ALTHEES JELLIES & JAMS LLC
110 Long Leaf Ln (39470-4200)
PHONE..................................601 795-4118
Althea Tavai, *Principal*
EMP: 2
SALES (est): 104.3K **Privately Held**
SIC: 2033 Canned fruits & specialties

(G-4374)
ANUSAYA FRESH USA LLC
576 Slade Woodward Rd (39470-7154)
PHONE..................................601 795-2008
EMP: 6 **EST:** 2015
SALES (est): 220.5K **Privately Held**
SIC: 0171 0179 2037 5431 Berry Crop Farm Fruit/Nut Farm Mfg Frozen Fruits/Vegtbl Ret Fruits/Vegetables

(G-4375)
BERGERON MACHINE & MARINE
107 Indian Spgs (39470-3688)
PHONE..................................504 416-6461
Todd Bergeros, *Owner*
EMP: 3
SALES (est): 247.5K **Privately Held**
SIC: 7692 Welding repair

(G-4376)
BEST EQUIPMENT TECH INC
100 Industrial Dr (39470)
P.O. Box 429 (39470-0429)
PHONE..................................601 795-2208
David Miller, *President*
Gary Silva, *Corp Secy*
James Cicardo, *Vice Pres*
William Wetta II, *Vice Pres*
▼ **EMP:** 40
SQ FT: 36,200
SALES (est): 4.3MM **Privately Held**
WEB: www.uetmixers.com
SIC: 3531 Dredging machinery
PA: Dsc Dredge, Llc
  156 Airport Rd
  Reserve LA 70084

(G-4377)
BIG JOHNS WELDING LLC
78 C J Harrell Rd (39470-4126)
PHONE..................................570 660-1972
John Penton, *Principal*
EMP: 1
SALES (est): 74K **Privately Held**
SIC: 7692 Welding repair

(G-4378)
BOTR PRESS LLC
676b Dpont Hrts Chapel Rd (39470-4028)
PHONE..................................708 431-9668
Mary E Magee, *Principal*
EMP: 1
SALES (est): 35.9K **Privately Held**
SIC: 2741 Miscellaneous publishing

(G-4379)
C & C MACHINE INCORPORATED
2940 Highway 53 (39470-4127)
PHONE..................................601 795-6377
David Crovetto, *President*

2019 Harris Directory of
Mississippi Manufacturers

▲ = Import ▼=Export
◆ =Import/Export

158

GEOGRAPHIC SECTION

Porterville - Kemper County (G-4410)

Debbie Crovetto, *Treasurer*
EMP: 7
SQ FT: 1,800
SALES: 1.4MM **Privately Held**
SIC: 3599 Machine shop, jobbing & repair

(G-4380)
CUEVAS MACHINE CO INC
Also Called: C M C
5548 Highway 53 (39470-8467)
PHONE..................................228 255-1384
Paul Cuevas, *President*
Linda Smith, *Corp Secy*
Todd Smith, *Vice Pres*
Vince Allen, *Opers Staff*
EMP: 53
SQ FT: 10,000
SALES (est): 9.5MM **Privately Held**
WEB: www.cuevasmachine.com
SIC: 3599 7692 Machine shop, jobbing & repair; welding repair

(G-4381)
E FAIRLEY UNLIMITED SVC LLC
28 Bob Simpson Rd (39470-7416)
PHONE..................................601 795-6933
Emilia Fairley, *Mng Member*
EMP: 3
SALES: 350K **Privately Held**
SIC: 2411 Logging

(G-4382)
FOH GROUP INC
100 Highway 11 N (39470-2217)
PHONE..................................601 795-6470
David Hannaford, *Division Pres*
EMP: 105
SALES (corp-wide): 86.5MM **Privately Held**
SIC: 2341 2384 Pajamas & bedjackets: women's & children's; nightgowns & negligees: women's & children's; women's & children's undergarments; robes & dressing gowns
PA: Foh Group Inc.
6255 W Sunset Blvd # 2212
Los Angeles CA 90028
323 466-5151

(G-4383)
IRONHORSE ENVIRONMENTAL LLC
9989 Highway 43 N (39470-8801)
PHONE..................................504 952-2516
Lacey Latkovic, *CEO*
EMP: 1
SALES (est): 21K **Privately Held**
SIC: 0851 4212 2411 Forestry services; local trucking, without storage; logging

(G-4384)
JERRY D SMITH
Also Called: J.D. Smith Contracting
281 Cowart Holiday Rd (39470-6423)
PHONE..................................601 795-8760
Jerry D Smith, *Owner*
EMP: 6
SALES (est): 423.1K **Privately Held**
SIC: 3999 Straw goods

(G-4385)
NEWSPAPER HOLDING INC
Also Called: Poplarville Democrat
418 S Main St (39470-2826)
PHONE..................................601 795-2247
Butch Weir, *Principal*
EMP: 2 **Privately Held**
WEB: www.clintonnc.com
SIC: 7313 2711 Newspaper advertising representative; newspapers
HQ: Newspaper Holding, Inc.
425 Locust St
Johnstown PA 15901
814 532-5102

(G-4386)
OPEN WINDOWS LLC
203 Frank Smith Rd (39470-6274)
PHONE..................................601 798-5757
EMP: 2
SALES (est): 88.9K **Privately Held**
SIC: 3442 Metal doors, sash & trim

(G-4387)
P DELTA INC
306 Highway 26 E (39470-3304)
PHONE..................................601 403-8100
John Tims Red, *President*
Wayne Dupre, *Prdtn Mgr*
Jennifer Clayton, *Executive*
EMP: 25
SALES: 5.8MM **Privately Held**
SIC: 3533 Oil field machinery & equipment

(G-4388)
PEARL RIVER TIMBER LLC
80 P M Hall Rd (39470)
PHONE..................................985 516-7951
Earl Scott, *President*
EMP: 1 **EST:** 2012
SALES (est): 55.6K **Privately Held**
SIC: 2491 Structural lumber & timber, treated wood

(G-4389)
QUANTUM SCIENTIFIC IMAGING INC
12 Coteau Dr (39470-9030)
PHONE..................................601 795-8824
Neal L Barry, *President*
Kevin Nelson, *Vice Pres*
EMP: 11
SALES (est): 1.6MM **Privately Held**
SIC: 3861 Cameras & related equipment

(G-4390)
RESTEEL EXPRESS INC
9 Saw Rd (39470-3804)
P.O. Box 547 (39470-0547)
PHONE..................................601 795-6110
Curt P Stasny, *President*
Amanda Lee, *Office Admin*
EMP: 11
SQ FT: 3,000
SALES (est): 2.3MM **Privately Held**
SIC: 3449 Bars, concrete reinforcing: fabricated steel

(G-4391)
RFC-EMBROIDERY
401 Highway 26 E (39470-3556)
PHONE..................................601 463-0491
EMP: 1 **EST:** 2017
SALES (est): 36.4K **Privately Held**
SIC: 2395 Embroidery & art needlework

(G-4392)
ROBICHEAUXS SPECIALTY CANDY
2103 Fords Creek Rd (39470-9218)
PHONE..................................601 795-6833
Laura Robicheaux, *President*
Francis J Robicheaux, *Corp Secy*
EMP: 12
SALES (est): 532.4K **Privately Held**
SIC: 2064 2066 Candy & other confectionery products; chocolate & cocoa products

(G-4393)
SHEAR VIEW MULCHING LLC
35 Magnolia Ln (39470-7409)
PHONE..................................985 637-8402
Casamir James Acosta, *Mng Member*
Casamere Acosta, *Manager*
Ryan Ross, *Manager*
EMP: 2
SALES: 350K **Privately Held**
SIC: 1629 1799 1442 0783 Land preparation construction; building site preparation; construction sand & gravel; ornamental shrub & tree services

(G-4394)
SMITH GRAVEL AND TRUCKING LLC
5564 Highway 53 (39470-8467)
PHONE..................................228 518-0766
Heidi Smith,
EMP: 2
SALES (est): 318.8K **Privately Held**
SIC: 1442 Construction sand & gravel

(G-4395)
STEVENS PACKING
52 Foots Stevens Rd (39470-3520)
PHONE..................................601 795-6999
Kathy Stevens, *Owner*

EMP: 4
SALES (est): 120K **Privately Held**
SIC: 2011 Meat packing plants

(G-4396)
STOCKSTILL LAND DEV LLC
20 Joyce Dr (39470-9601)
PHONE..................................601 273-2409
Joshua Stockstill,
EMP: 3
SALES: 180K **Privately Held**
SIC: 1629 4212 1794 3531 Heavy construction; local trucking, without storage; excavation work; construction machinery

(G-4397)
STOUT WOODWORKS INC
59 Castleberry Dr (39470-7230)
PHONE..................................601 795-0727
Hubert Ladner, *Principal*
EMP: 2
SALES (est): 136.4K **Privately Held**
SIC: 2431 Millwork

(G-4398)
T & J MACHINE
689 Progress Rd (39470-3615)
PHONE..................................601 795-0853
Thomas E Hudnell, *Owner*
Jane Hudnell, *Co-Owner*
EMP: 4
SALES: 80K **Privately Held**
SIC: 3449 Miscellaneous metalwork

(G-4399)
WHEAT CONSTRUCTION INC
8124 Highway 43 N (39470-8739)
PHONE..................................601 772-9074
Richard Wheat, *President*
EMP: 3 **EST:** 1972
SALES: 430K **Privately Held**
SIC: 1459 Clays (common) quarrying

Port Gibson
Claiborne County

(G-4400)
CHARLES DONALD PULPWOOD INC (PA)
Also Called: Charles Donald Timber
1024 Noble Rd (39150-5630)
P.O. Box 398 (39150-0398)
PHONE..................................601 437-4012
Charles Donald Jr, *President*
David Donald, *Vice Pres*
George Donald, *Vice Pres*
Mary Donald, *Treasurer*
EMP: 23
SQ FT: 750
SALES (est): 4.5MM **Privately Held**
WEB: www.charlesdonaldtimber.com
SIC: 2411 Pulpwood contractors engaged in cutting

(G-4401)
CLAIRBORNE PUBLISHING CO
Also Called: Port Gibson Reville News
708 Market St (39150-2332)
PHONE..................................601 437-5103
Emma Crisler, *President*
EMP: 4
SQ FT: 2,100
SALES (est): 335K **Privately Held**
SIC: 2711 Newspapers, publishing & printing

(G-4402)
J W B LOGGING CO LLC
403 Pecan St (39150-2229)
P.O. Box 923 (39150-0923)
PHONE..................................601 437-8743
Joe Barnes, *Mng Member*
EMP: 3 **EST:** 2011
SALES (est): 214.4K **Privately Held**
SIC: 2411 Logging

(G-4403)
MMC MATERIALS INC
1083 Highway 18 (39150-4201)
PHONE..................................601 437-4321
Chris Cacio, *Manager*
EMP: 2

SALES (corp-wide): 306.5MM **Privately Held**
WEB: www.mmcmaterials.com
SIC: 3273 Ready-mixed concrete
HQ: Mmc Materials, Inc.
1052 Highland Colony Pkwy # 201
Ridgeland MS 39157
601 898-4000

(G-4404)
NICKS ONE STOP PORT GBSON LLC
2154 Highway 61 N (39150-4264)
PHONE..................................601 437-3380
Valerie Beesley, *Partner*
EMP: 2
SALES (est): 175.9K **Privately Held**
SIC: 1321 Natural gas liquids

(G-4405)
PROLON LLC
305 Industrial Ave (39150-2868)
P.O. Box 568 (39150-0568)
PHONE..................................601 437-4211
Robert E Mc Afee,
Stephen E Dowling,
Greg L Wertz,
EMP: 55
SQ FT: 120,000
SALES (est): 7.5MM **Privately Held**
SIC: 3089 Plastic kitchenware, tableware & houseware

(G-4406)
R2PG INC
Also Called: Reid II Port Gibson
507 Market St (39150-2041)
PHONE..................................601 747-0522
Kendrick E Reid II, *Principal*
EMP: 10
SQ FT: 10,000
SALES: 40K **Privately Held**
SIC: 2392 2299 Tablecloths & table settings; hand woven fabrics

(G-4407)
SHENISE PRODUCTIONS INC
30 Pinehurst St (39150-2850)
PHONE..................................601 437-3665
Courtney S Bailey, *President*
EMP: 2
SALES (est): 80.6K **Privately Held**
SIC: 2759 Commercial printing

(G-4408)
V & B INTERNATIONAL INC
810 Market St (39150-2334)
PHONE..................................601 437-8279
Valory G Beesley, *President*
Jane Puckett, *Corp Secy*
Cindi Beesley, *Vice Pres*
EMP: 25
SQ FT: 2,500
SALES: 2.3MM **Privately Held**
WEB: www.vbinternational.com
SIC: 5031 2426 Lumber: rough, dressed & finished; hardwood dimension & flooring mills

(G-4409)
WALKER PARRIS
Also Called: Walker Construction
1017 Riley Thomas Cir (39150-3131)
P.O. Box 274 (39150-0274)
PHONE..................................601 953-3023
Parris Walker, *Owner*
EMP: 5
SALES (est): 137.7K **Privately Held**
SIC: 1799 1389 1522 Construction site cleanup; construction, repair & dismantling services; remodeling, multi-family dwellings

---

Porterville
Kemper County

(G-4410)
NARKEETA FOREST SERVICES INC
4016 Highway 498 E (39352-6831)
PHONE..................................601 692-4777
Russ Calvert, *President*
EMP: 10

(PA)=Parent Co (HQ)=Headquarters (DH)=Div Headquarters
✪ = New Business established in last 2 years

2019 Harris Directory of
Mississippi Manufacturers

159

GEOGRAPHIC SECTION

Prairie - Monroe County (G-4411)

SALES (est): 1.3MM **Privately Held**
SIC: 2411 Logging

Prairie
Monroe County

(G-4411)
AXIALL CORPORATION
10068 Summit Dr (39756-9200)
PHONE....................................662 369-9586
Mark Reeds, *Branch Mgr*
EMP: 23 **Publicly Held**
WEB: www.georgiagulf.com
SIC: 2812 2821 Alkalies & chlorine;
polyvinyl chloride resins (PVC)
HQ: Axiall Corporation
1000 Abernathy Rd # 1200
Atlanta GA 30328
304 455-2200

(G-4412)
C W EMBROIDERY INC
10032 Lenoir Loop (39756-9758)
PHONE....................................662 231-9206
EMP: 1
SALES (est): 37.3K **Privately Held**
SIC: 2395 Pleating & stitching

(G-4413)
**SOUTHERN LAND
EXPLORATION INC**
20671 Old Magnolia Hwy (39756-9732)
PHONE....................................662 369-7390
EMP: 2 EST: 2008
SALES (est): 110K **Privately Held**
SIC: 1382 Oil/Gas Exploration Services

(G-4414)
STEVE SCHROCK
Also Called: Prairie Mills Feed & Farm Sup
10111 Prairie Mills Rd (39756-9743)
PHONE....................................662 369-6062
Steve Schrock, *Owner*
EMP: 2
SQ FT: 3,780
SALES: 600K **Privately Held**
SIC: 2048 5999 5191 Prepared feeds;
farm equipment & supplies; animal feeds

Prentiss
Jefferson Davis County

(G-4415)
CURTIS WILSON LOGGING
83 Sam Graham Rd (39474-3038)
PHONE....................................601 943-6808
EMP: 2
SALES (est): 81.7K **Privately Held**
SIC: 2411 Logging

(G-4416)
DELTA INDUSTRIES INC
Also Called: South Central Ready Mix
1780 John Street Ext (39474-4845)
P.O. Box 698 (39474-0698)
PHONE....................................601 792-4286
Wayne Dailey, *Manager*
EMP: 7
SALES (corp-wide): 100.3MM **Privately
Held**
WEB: www.delta-ind.com
SIC: 3273 Ready-mixed concrete
PA: Delta Industries, Inc.
100 W Woodrow Wilson Ave
Jackson MS 39213
601 354-3801

(G-4417)
FOLEY PRODUCTS COMPANY
1650 John Street Ext (39474-4847)
PHONE....................................601 792-3202
Doug Doty, *Branch Mgr*
EMP: 25
SALES (corp-wide): 192.8MM **Privately
Held**
SIC: 3272 Concrete products
HQ: The Foley Products Company
1030 1st Ave
Columbus GA 31901
706 563-7882

(G-4418)
**FORTERRA PIPE & PRECAST
LLC**
1650 John Street Ext (39474-4847)
PHONE....................................601 268-2081
Robert Burgess, *Manager*
EMP: 35
SALES (corp-wide): 1.4B **Publicly Held**
SIC: 3272 Precast terrazo or concrete
products
HQ: Forterra Pipe & Precast, Llc
511 E John Carpenter Fwy
Irving TX 75062
469 458-7973

(G-4419)
**FORTERRA PIPE & PRECAST
LLC**
1650 John Street Ext (39474-4847)
PHONE....................................601 792-3202
EMP: 3
SALES (est): 275.8K **Privately Held**
SIC: 3272 Precast terrazo or concrete
products

(G-4420)
GOLDEN PINE RACEWAY LLC
103 Golden Pine Rd (39474-4175)
PHONE....................................601 506-8669
EMP: 3 EST: 2011
SALES (est): 259K **Privately Held**
SIC: 3644 Mfg Nonconductive Wiring De-
vices

(G-4421)
HALLS WOODWORKING
265 Williamson Mill Rd (39474-4342)
PHONE....................................601 792-5955
Grover Thall, *Principal*
EMP: 4 EST: 2011
SALES (est): 308.5K **Privately Held**
SIC: 2431 Millwork

(G-4422)
**NORWOOD MEDICAL SUPPLY
LLC**
2218 Columbia Ave (39474-5406)
PHONE....................................601 792-2224
Von Norwood, *Mng Member*
EMP: 3
SALES: 1.5MM **Privately Held**
SIC: 5047 3841 5999 Medical equipment
& supplies; medical instruments & equip-
ment, blood & bone work; medical appa-
ratus & supplies

(G-4423)
PRENTISS PUBLISHERS INC
Also Called: Prentiss Headlight
1020 Third St (39474-6002)
PHONE....................................601 792-4221
Bill Jacobs, *President*
Patsy Speights, *Principal*
EMP: 7
SQ FT: 1,200
SALES: 140K **Privately Held**
WEB: www.prentissheadlight.com
SIC: 2711 Newspapers: publishing only,
not printed on site

(G-4424)
PRINTERS INC
2233 Columbia Ave (39474)
P.O. Box 1077 (39474-1077)
PHONE....................................601 792-8493
Robert L Jones, *Owner*
EMP: 2
SQ FT: 4,000
SALES (est): 288.6K **Privately Held**
SIC: 2752 2791 Commercial printing, off-
set; typesetting, computer controlled

(G-4425)
WHITE JERLEEN
Also Called: Joelprinting
5641 Highway 84 (39474-4457)
PHONE....................................601 941-6886
Jerleen White, *Owner*
EMP: 1
SALES (est): 29.2K **Privately Held**
SIC: 2731 2741 Pamphlets: publishing &
printing; business service newsletters:
publishing & printing

Preston
Kemper County

(G-4426)
ADVANCED DYNAMICS INC
4048 Kellis Store Rd (39354-8737)
PHONE....................................601 677-3423
Ron Poole, *Director*
Charles Lin, *Intl Dir*
EMP: 3
SALES (est): 230K **Privately Held**
WEB: www.advanceddynamics.com
SIC: 3721 5191 5199 5052 Helicopters;
fertilizer & fertilizer materials; art goods &
supplies; coal & other minerals & ores

(G-4427)
GRADY 1&2
249 Grady Rd (39354-9263)
PHONE....................................601 677-3390
Linda Grady, *Owner*
EMP: 2
SALES (est): 95K **Privately Held**
SIC: 2449 Chicken coops (crates), wood:
wirebound

(G-4428)
**SULLIVANS CUSTOM
PROCESSING**
610 Sullivan Rd (39354-9500)
PHONE....................................662 773-2839
Jean Sullivan, *Owner*
Doyle Sullivan, *Owner*
EMP: 4
SALES (est): 190K **Privately Held**
SIC: 2011 Meat packing plants

Puckett
Rankin County

(G-4429)
R- SQUARED ALUMINIUM LLC
2650 Hwy 18 (39151)
P.O. Box 306 (39151-0306)
PHONE....................................601 825-1171
Naveen Bhojraj, *General Mgr*
Ramesh Mehra,
▲ EMP: 130
SALES: 17MM **Privately Held**
SIC: 3714 Manifolds, motor vehicle

(G-4430)
R-SQUARED PUCKETT INC
2650 Hwy 18 (39151)
PHONE....................................601 825-1171
Ramesh Mehra, *President*
Naveen Bhojray, *Vice Pres*
Cathy Nokes, *Treasurer*
Tynti Parikh, *Admin Sec*
▲ EMP: 40
SQ FT: 5,000
SALES (est): 12.8MM
SALES (corp-wide): 1.4B **Privately Held**
SIC: 3714 Motor vehicle parts & acces-
sories
PA: Sanhua Holding Group Co., Ltd.
Xialiquan Village, Qixing St., Xinchang
County
Shaoxing 31250

Pulaski
Scott County

(G-4431)
**HARRISON BROTHERS
INCORPORATED**
3243 Scr 558 (39152-9532)
PHONE....................................601 536-2069
Charles R Harrison, *President*
Willy Harrison, *Vice Pres*
EMP: 9
SALES (est): 1MM **Privately Held**
SIC: 2411 Logging camps & contractors

Purvis
Lamar County

(G-4432)
ALVIN SCHILLING WDWKG LLC
241 Bayberry Loop (39475-3455)
PHONE....................................601 268-1070
Alvin Schilling, *Principal*
EMP: 2 EST: 2012
SALES (est): 145.7K **Privately Held**
SIC: 2431 Millwork

(G-4433)
ARROWMAKER
1065 Lee Rd (39475-3531)
PHONE....................................601 264-4748
John Fletcher Beaver, *Partner*
EMP: 2
SALES (est): 98.1K **Privately Held**
SIC: 3949 Arrows, archery

(G-4434)
B & L INTERNATIONAL INC
1189 Carter Cir (39475-3337)
PHONE....................................601 261-5127
William Kester, *President*
EMP: 2
SALES: 219.7K **Privately Held**
SIC: 3546 5088 Power-driven handtools;
aircraft & parts

(G-4435)
CARLMAC INDUSTRIES INC
Hwy 589 & Interstate 59 I 59 (39475)
P.O. Box 508 (39475-0508)
PHONE....................................601 794-5000
Carl McMurphy, *President*
Carol McMurphy, *Corp Secy*
EMP: 8
SQ FT: 50,000
SALES (est): 1.4MM **Privately Held**
SIC: 2493 Hardboard, tempered; particle-
board products

(G-4436)
**DOVES MACHINE & WELDING
SVC**
39 Deep South Ln (39475-4546)
P.O. Box 657 (39475-0657)
PHONE....................................601 794-8112
Joel Dove, *President*
Deidra Dove, *Treasurer*
EMP: 5
SQ FT: 7,800
SALES: 200K **Privately Held**
SIC: 3599 7692 Machine shop, jobbing &
repair; welding repair

(G-4437)
**EVERGREEN LUMBER & TRUSS
INC (HQ)**
84 Central Industrial Row (39475-5832)
PHONE....................................601 794-8404
T H Buce III, *President*
Mike Mosley, *General Mgr*
Tom Oldweiler, *Corp Secy*
EMP: 42 EST: 2005
SQ FT: 80,000
SALES (est): 10.8MM
SALES (corp-wide): 13.2MM **Privately
Held**
SIC: 2439 Structural wood members
PA: Gst Holdings Inc
222 Rochester Rd
Mobile AL 36608
251 344-4206

(G-4438)
FRED WINDHAM SIGNS
34 Stonefield Dr (39475-3047)
PHONE....................................601 794-1445
EMP: 2
SALES (est): 155.1K **Privately Held**
SIC: 3993 Mfg Signs/Advertising Special-
ties

(G-4439)
GRUMPY MAN LLC
31 Yellow Bird Rd (39475-6014)
P.O. Box 1767 (39475-1767)
PHONE....................................601 606-8683
Nathan Sanford,

2019 Harris Directory of
Mississippi Manufacturers

▲ = Import ▼=Export
◆ =Import/Export

160

GEOGRAPHIC SECTION

Quitman - Clarke County (G-4470)

EMP: 4 EST: 2013
SQ FT: 400
SALES (est): 127.7K **Privately Held**
SIC: 2035 Pickles, sauces & salad dressings

(G-4440)
J & K ENTERPRISE INC
184 Central Indus Row (39475-4199)
PHONE......................................601 794-6005
Kent Stuart, *President*
Jimmy Stuart, *Vice Pres*
Becky Stuart, *Treasurer*
Stephanie Stuart, *Admin Sec*
EMP: 18
SQ FT: 4,000
SALES: 1.8MM **Privately Held**
SIC: 2411 Logging camps & contractors

(G-4441)
JAMES E MATTISON JR
Also Called: J'S Modular Installations
28 Aldon Rd (39475-3099)
PHONE......................................601 543-7313
James E Mattison Jr, *Owner*
EMP: 4
SALES: 25K **Privately Held**
SIC: 2531 Public building & related furniture

(G-4442)
JJ MERCHANT
S Mill Creek Rd (39475)
PHONE......................................601 596-4430
Jeff Clearman, *Owner*
James Durham, *Owner*
EMP: 2
SALES (est): 95.5K **Privately Held**
SIC: 3531 Subgraders (construction equipment)

(G-4443)
KINARD BURGE & SONS INC
24 Kinard Burge Rd (39475)
P.O. Box 23 (39475-0023)
PHONE......................................601 794-6829
Kinard Burge, *President*
Jean Burge, *Admin Sec*
EMP: 12
SALES (est): 1MM **Privately Held**
SIC: 2411 Logging camps & contractors

(G-4444)
LAMAR CONCRETE INC
5697 Us Highway 11 (39475-3104)
P.O. Box 616 (39475-0616)
PHONE......................................601 794-0049
Danny Anderson, *President*
Marie Anderson, *Corp Secy*
EMP: 18
SALES (est): 2MM **Privately Held**
SIC: 3273 Ready-mixed concrete

(G-4445)
LORESCO INC
875 Old Richburg Rd (39475-3137)
PHONE......................................601 544-7490
Tom Lewis, *President*
Joe F Tatum Jr, *Treasurer*
Mary Tatum, *Admin Sec*
▼ EMP: 1
SALES (est): 312K **Privately Held**
WEB: www.loresco.com
SIC: 2999 Coke

(G-4446)
MALT INDUSTRIES INC
43 Mangum Ln (39475-4550)
P.O. Box 287 (39475-0287)
PHONE......................................601 794-4200
Max Dyar Jr, *President*
Todd Little, *Vice Pres*
▲ EMP: 20 EST: 1998
SQ FT: 60,000
SALES (est): 4.3MM **Privately Held**
WEB: www.maltindustries.com
SIC: 2326 Men's & boys' work clothing

(G-4447)
PORTABULL FUEL SERVICE LLC
343 Highway 589 (39475-3035)
PHONE......................................601 549-5655
Jonathan Duhon, *Mng Member*
EMP: 4

SALES (est): 392.6K **Privately Held**
SIC: 2869 Fuels

(G-4448)
PURVIS FOREST PRODUCTS INC
630 Highway 589 (39475-4101)
P.O. Box 1300 (39475-1300)
PHONE......................................601 794-8593
John Wendell Hudson, *President*
Tonia Hudson, *Treasurer*
▼ EMP: 25
SQ FT: 5,000
SALES (est): 15.8MM **Privately Held**
SIC: 5031 2493 Lumber: rough, dressed & finished; reconstituted wood products

(G-4449)
PURVIS JEWELRY CANDLES LLC
176 Shelby Speights Dr # 9 (39475-4554)
P.O. Box 1414, Walker LA (70785-1414)
PHONE......................................601 794-8977
Destry Lott, *Administration*
EMP: 2
SALES (est): 144.9K **Privately Held**
SIC: 3999 Candles

(G-4450)
PURVIS JEWERLY RLC LLC
176 Shelby Speights Dr # 9 (39475-4554)
PHONE......................................601 329-9002
Aaron Lott, *Manager*
EMP: 1 EST: 2015
SALES (est): 71.4K **Privately Held**
SIC: 3339 Primary nonferrous metals

(G-4451)
RAIN CII CARBON LLC
863 Old Richburg Rd (39475-3137)
P.O. Box 349 (39475-0349)
PHONE......................................601 794-2753
Mickey Harrison, *Manager*
EMP: 8 **Privately Held**
WEB: www.ciicarbon.com
SIC: 2999 3312 Coke, calcined petroleum: made from purchased materials; blast furnaces & steel mills
HQ: Rain Cii Carbon Llc
2627 Chestnut Ridge Dr # 200
Kingwood TX 77339
281 318-2400

(G-4452)
SMITHS SPEED SHOP
Also Called: Smith Speed Shop
1185 Rckhill To Brklyn Rd (39475-4394)
PHONE......................................601 794-2855
Michael Smith, *Owner*
EMP: 1 EST: 1993
SALES (est): 52K **Privately Held**
SIC: 7699 3484 Gun services; guns (firearms) or gun parts, 30 mm. & below

(G-4453)
SOUPBONE INDUSTRIES LLC
10 Melody Ln (39475-3587)
PHONE......................................601 520-1317
Robert Ross, *Principal*
EMP: 1
SALES (est): 62.8K **Privately Held**
SIC: 3999 Manufacturing industries

(G-4454)
YATES INDUSTRIAL SERVICES LLC
131 Calvin Purvis Rd (39475-5368)
PHONE......................................601 467-6232
Billy Yates, *Mng Member*
Denise Yates, *Manager*
EMP: 7
SALES (est): 1.4MM **Privately Held**
SIC: 1629 3441 7692 Industrial plant construction; fabricated structural metal; welding repair

---

Quitman
Clarke County

(G-4455)
ADVANTAGE TAX AND PRINT
109 W Church St (39355-2134)
PHONE......................................601 557-5055
David Stevens, *Principal*
EMP: 2
SALES (est): 73.2K **Privately Held**
SIC: 2759 Commercial printing

(G-4456)
AMERICAN MIDSTREAM LLC
103 E Franklin St (39355-2319)
PHONE......................................601 776-6721
Sandra Flower, *Branch Mgr*
EMP: 3
SALES (corp-wide): 805.3MM **Privately Held**
SIC: 1311 Crude petroleum & natural gas
HQ: American Midstream, Llc
2103 Citywest Blvd # 800
Houston TX 77042
713 815-3900

(G-4457)
BAZOR LUMBER COMPANY LLC
300 N Archusa Ave (39355-2419)
P.O. Box 9 (39355-0009)
PHONE......................................601 776-2181
EMP: 37 EST: 2002
SALES (est): 3.8MM **Privately Held**
SIC: 2421 Sawmill/Plaining Mill

(G-4458)
BDM IT SERVICES (US) INC
142 County Road 159 (39355-9447)
PHONE......................................601 274-0347
Patricia Jefcoat, *President*
EMP: 4 EST: 2012
SALES (est): 222.9K
SALES (corp-wide): 4.7MM **Privately Held**
SIC: 7371 7372 Computer software development & applications; business oriented computer software
PA: Bdm It Solutions Inc
306 Ontario Ave
Saskatoon SK S7K 2
306 933-3000

(G-4459)
CENTRAL RESOURCES INC
1667 Apache Loop (39355)
PHONE......................................601 776-3281
EMP: 2
SALES (est): 140K **Privately Held**
SIC: 1311 Crude Petroleum/Natural Gas Production

(G-4460)
CLARKE COUNTY TRIBUNE INC
Also Called: Clark Publishing
101 Main St (39355-2119)
P.O. Box 900 (39355-0900)
PHONE......................................601 776-3726
Wyatt Emmrich, *President*
Glen Cochran, *Financial Exec*
Scott Evans, *Associate*
EMP: 3
SALES (est): 255.8K **Privately Held**
SIC: 2711 Newspapers, publishing & printing

(G-4461)
DART CONT CO MISS LTD LBLTY CO
197 Harris Ave (39355-2107)
PHONE......................................601 776-3555
Robert C Dart, *CEO*
EMP: 140
SALES (est): 4.3MM **Privately Held**
SIC: 3086 Cups & plates, foamed plastic

(G-4462)
DYEHOUSE INC
601 Harris Ave (39355)
PHONE......................................601 776-2189
Paul Brown, *President*
Charlotte Brown, *Vice Pres*
EMP: 5
SQ FT: 8,750

SALES (est): 534.8K **Privately Held**
SIC: 2261 Dyeing cotton broadwoven fabrics

(G-4463)
EDWARD C MATHIS LOGGING
206 County Road 450 (39355-9119)
PHONE......................................601 776-2379
Edward C Mathis, *Owner*
EMP: 1
SALES (est): 67K **Privately Held**
SIC: 2411 Logging

(G-4464)
FC MEYER PACKAGING LLC
101 Ascher St (39355-2147)
PHONE......................................601 776-2117
Nazira Wightman, *Branch Mgr*
Shirley Giles, *Clerk*
EMP: 16
SALES (corp-wide): 100.3MM **Privately Held**
SIC: 2657 Folding paperboard boxes
HQ: Meyer Fc Packaging Llc
108 Main St Ste 3
Norwalk CT 06851
203 847-8500

(G-4465)
FLEMING BOOK BINDING COMPANY
180 Harris Ave (39355-2103)
PHONE......................................601 776-3761
Charles E Fleming, *Owner*
EMP: 5
SQ FT: 3,200
SALES (est): 362.2K **Privately Held**
WEB: www.flemingbookbinding.com
SIC: 2789 Binding only: books, pamphlets, magazines, etc.

(G-4466)
J & B ATHLETICS
100 Main St (39355-2120)
PHONE......................................601 776-7557
Jeff Lewis, *Partner*
EMP: 3
SALES (est): 240K **Privately Held**
SIC: 3842 Hearing aids

(G-4467)
MIKE CULBRETH WOODYARD
19 Donald Woodyard Ln (39355)
P.O. Box 802 (39355-0802)
PHONE......................................601 776-2422
Mike Culbreth, *Owner*
EMP: 1
SALES (est): 100K **Privately Held**
SIC: 2611 Pulp mills

(G-4468)
QUITMAN SPORTING GOODS & PAWN
113 Sanders Ave (39355-2131)
PHONE......................................601 776-3212
Joe Walters, *Owner*
Norma Walters, *Co-Owner*
EMP: 3
SALES (est): 120K **Privately Held**
SIC: 3949 5944 5932 Sporting & athletic goods; jewelry stores; pawnshop

(G-4469)
QUITMAN TANK SOLUTIONS LLC
502 S Archusa Ave (39355-2330)
P.O. Box 90 (39355-0090)
PHONE......................................601 776-3800
Jason Smith, *Partner*
John Smith, *Mng Member*
EMP: 25 EST: 2011
SALES (est): 5.1MM **Privately Held**
SIC: 3443 Tanks, standard or custom fabricated: metal plate

(G-4470)
RONNY P MOORE
Also Called: R&M Harvesting
543 Moorewood Ln (39355-7816)
PHONE......................................601 934-0113
Ronny P Moore, *Owner*
EMP: 1
SALES (est): 600K **Privately Held**
SIC: 2411 Timber, cut at logging camp

(PA)=Parent Co (HQ)=Headquarters (DH)=Div Headquarters
✪ = New Business established in last 2 years

2019 Harris Directory of
Mississippi Manufacturers

161

Quitman - Clarke County (G-4471) | **GEOGRAPHIC SECTION**

(G-4471)
RUFUS M CHANCELLOR
276 County Road 658 (39355-8909)
PHONE..............................601 776-5557
Rufus M Chancellor, *Principal*
EMP: 2
SALES (est): 120.8K **Privately Held**
SIC: **1389** Oil field services

(G-4472)
X L JOHNSON & SONS INC
9110 County Road 511 (39355-8324)
PHONE..............................601 776-3685
Jack Johnson, *President*
Charlotte Johnson, *Vice Pres*
EMP: 4
SALES (est): 375.6K **Privately Held**
SIC: **2411** Logging

(G-4473)
YELLOW DOG PRINTING CO LLC
1065 County Road 430 (39355-9567)
PHONE..............................601 776-6853
Josh Miller, *Principal*
EMP: 2
SALES (est): 150.7K **Privately Held**
SIC: **2752** Commercial printing, lithographic

Raleigh
Smith County

(G-4474)
BOON DOCKS DEER PROCESSING
6308 Highway 501 (39153-5241)
PHONE..............................601 789-5843
Natasha Nelson, *Principal*
EMP: 3
SALES (est): 219.1K **Privately Held**
SIC: **2011** Meat packing plants

(G-4475)
DONALD W MASON
Also Called: Masons Millworks
1348 Scr 540-2 (39153)
PHONE..............................601 269-3782
Donald W Mason, *Owner*
EMP: 1
SALES (est): 120.7K **Privately Held**
SIC: **1522** 1542 2431 Residential construction; nonresidential construction; millwork

(G-4476)
ROBERT BRAY LOGGING
101 Scr 516 (39153-6394)
PHONE..............................601 269-3437
EMP: 2
SALES (est): 130K **Privately Held**
SIC: **2411** Logging

(G-4477)
STICKMAN LOGGING LLC
3367 Scr 540-2 (39153-6328)
PHONE..............................601 782-4597
Ricky Baldwin,
EMP: 4
SALES (est): 250K **Privately Held**
SIC: **2411** Logging camps & contractors

(G-4478)
TALLY STUDENT SERVICE LLC
Also Called: Tally Trophies & Awards
214 Mimosa Dr (39153-9700)
PHONE..............................601 782-9606
Joe Tally, *Mng Member*
Ken Tally,
Phil Tally,
EMP: 5
SALES (est): 356.8K **Privately Held**
SIC: **2499** Trophy bases, wood

Randolph
Pontotoc County

(G-4479)
AUSTIN LOGGING LLC
15 Robbs Rd (38864-9795)
PHONE..............................662 296-6566
Cody Austin, *Mng Member*
EMP: 9 EST: 2016
SALES (est): 330.3K **Privately Held**
SIC: **2411** Timber, cut at logging camp

(G-4480)
ROBINSON WOODWORKS ◆
2986 Topsy Rd (38864-9159)
PHONE..............................662 419-1864
EMP: 1 EST: 2018
SALES (est): 54.1K **Privately Held**
SIC: **2431** Millwork

Raymond
Hinds County

(G-4481)
5D NATURAL FARM LLC
2629 Neil Collins Rd (39154-5002)
PHONE..............................601 906-8763
Virgil Dennis, *CEO*
EMP: 4
SALES (est): 132.1K **Privately Held**
SIC: **0191** 0182 2035 0161 General farms, primarily crop; tomatoes grown under cover; cucumbers, pickles & pickle salting; squash farm

(G-4482)
AIRWORKS ENTERPRISES INC
5080 Springridge Rd (39154-9479)
PHONE..............................601 372-8304
Robert Cheesman, *President*
Hank E Cooper, *Vice Pres*
EMP: 3 EST: 1990
SQ FT: 1,500
SALES: 200K **Privately Held**
SIC: **3721** Blimps

(G-4483)
APPLIED SAFETY COATINGS INC
232 Wakeland Dr (39154-7621)
PHONE..............................601 940-3004
Terry Tynes, *Principal*
EMP: 2
SALES (est): 138.5K **Privately Held**
SIC: **3479** Coating of metals & formed products

(G-4484)
ARMADILLO SERVICE INC ALABAMA
126 Oak Ridge Ln (39154-9525)
PHONE..............................601 857-0440
EMP: 14 EST: 1990
SALES: 3MM **Privately Held**
SIC: **1389** 1381 Oil Field Svc & Drilling Contractor

(G-4485)
CENTRAL MISS RES & EXT CTR
1320 Seven Springs Dr (39154-2202)
PHONE..............................601 857-2284
Frank Withers, *Manager*
EMP: 6 EST: 2008
SALES (est): 637.7K **Privately Held**
SIC: **3081** Unsupported plastics film & sheet

(G-4486)
CHUCK JENNINGS
Also Called: About Time PC and Electronics
1783 Pine Hill Dr (39154-8887)
P.O. Box 1290 (39154-1290)
PHONE..............................601 668-5704
Chuck Jennings, *Owner*
Amy Blaylock-Jennigs, *Corp Secy*
EMP: 2
SQ FT: 1,200

SALES (est): 130K **Privately Held**
WEB: www.abouttimepc.com
SIC: **5734** 3645 3535 1731 Computer & software stores; residential lighting fixtures; conveyors & conveying equipment; access control systems specialization

(G-4487)
DWIGHTS CUSTOM DEER PROCESSING
10237 Highway 18 (39154-9669)
PHONE..............................601 857-2324
Dwight Traxler, *Principal*
EMP: 3
SALES (est): 201.4K **Privately Held**
SIC: **2011** Meat packing plants

(G-4488)
FLOWERS BKG CO LYNCHBURG LLC
9483 Highway 18 (39154-8908)
PHONE..............................601 502-1305
Willie Brown, *Principal*
EMP: 2
SALES (corp-wide): 3.9B **Publicly Held**
SIC: **2051** Bread, cake & related products
HQ: Flowers Baking Co. Of Lynchburg, Llc
1905 Hollins Mill Rd
Lynchburg VA 24503
434 528-0441

(G-4489)
HUNTER ENGINEERING COMPANY
2489 Raymond Clinton Rd (39154)
P.O. Box 819 (39154-0819)
PHONE..............................601 857-8883
Bill O'Connor, *Manager*
EMP: 175
SALES (corp-wide): 400MM **Privately Held**
WEB: www.huntersupport.com
SIC: **3559** 3672 Wheel balancing equipment, automotive; automotive maintenance equipment; printed circuit boards
PA: Hunter Engineering Company Inc
11250 Hunter Dr
Bridgeton MO 63044
314 731-3020

(G-4490)
INKY BS CUSTOM TEES LLC
Also Called: Inky B Tees
4292 Bill Downing Rd (39154-9251)
PHONE..............................601 988-8558
Brandy Renfroe, *Mng Member*
EMP: 4 EST: 2015
SALES (est): 252.1K **Privately Held**
SIC: **2759** Screen printing

(G-4491)
MCLAN ELECTRONICS INC
7770 Jackson Raymond Rd (39154-8342)
PHONE..............................601 373-2392
Ray McCall, *President*
Danny McCall, *President*
EMP: 4
SQ FT: 3,000
SALES (est): 340K **Privately Held**
WEB: www.mclan.com
SIC: **3699** 5065 Electrical equipment & supplies; electronic parts & equipment

(G-4492)
NOVARTIS CORPORATION
303 Foxton Cv (39154-8861)
PHONE..............................601 373-6148
Michael Crain, *Manager*
EMP: 1
SALES (corp-wide): 51.9B **Privately Held**
WEB: www.novartis.com
SIC: **2834** Pharmaceutical preparations
HQ: Novartis Corporation
1 S Ridgedale Ave
East Hanover NJ 07936
212 307-1122

(G-4493)
STRINGER WOODWORKS
6795 Springridge Rd (39154-9015)
PHONE..............................601 372-5725
EMP: 2
SALES: 67K **Privately Held**
SIC: **2499** Mfr Wood Kitchen Items

(G-4494)
VICTORY MOTOR COMPANY
9373 Highway 18 (39154-8907)
PHONE..............................601 573-1441
EMP: 2
SALES (est): 116.1K **Privately Held**
SIC: **3711** Motor vehicles & car bodies

Redwood
Warren County

(G-4495)
INTERNATIONAL PAPER COMPANY
Highway 3 N (39156)
PHONE..............................601 638-3665
John Grover, *Manager*
Amos Nixon, *Receptionist*
EMP: 365
SALES (corp-wide): 23.3B **Publicly Held**
WEB: www.internationalpaper.com
SIC: **2621** 2631 Paper mills; paperboard mills
PA: International Paper Company
6400 Poplar Ave
Memphis TN 38197
901 419-9000

Richland
Rankin County

(G-4496)
A QUARTER CAN INC
855 Richland East Dr (39218-9572)
P.O. Box 180444 (39218-0444)
PHONE..............................601 936-9915
Mayoung McClendon, *Owner*
EMP: 1
SALES (est): 66.7K **Privately Held**
SIC: **3131** Quarters

(G-4497)
AD VISUALS INC
587 Old Highway 49 S (39218-8409)
P.O. Box 180007 (39218-0007)
PHONE..............................601 932-3060
Donnie Chapman, *President*
Clara Chapman, *Treasurer*
EMP: 4
SQ FT: 9,000
SALES (est): 300K **Privately Held**
SIC: **2759** Screen printing

(G-4498)
ADA NEWSON
Also Called: Ada S Sweetz and Treats
321 Washington Ave (39218-9582)
PHONE..............................601 810-6614
Ada Newson, *Owner*
EMP: 1
SALES (est): 36.9K **Privately Held**
SIC: **2064** 2096 2087 7389 Nuts, candy covered; lollipops & other hard candy; chewing candy, not chewing gum; popcorn, already popped (except candy covered); colorings, bakers';

(G-4499)
ADEMCO INC
Also Called: ADI Global Distribution
197 Interstate Dr (39218-4427)
PHONE..............................601 936-4842
EMP: 5
SALES (corp-wide): 4.8B **Publicly Held**
SIC: **5063** 3669 3822 Electrical apparatus & equipment; emergency alarms; auto controls regulating residntl & coml environmt & applncs
HQ: Ademco Inc.
1985 Douglas Dr N
Golden Valley MN 55422
800 468-1502

(G-4500)
AMERICAN BOTTLING COMPANY
401 Industrial Park Dr (39218-9549)
PHONE..............................601 939-5454
Quinton Northrup, *Branch Mgr*
EMP: 70 **Publicly Held**

2019 Harris Directory of
Mississippi Manufacturers

▲ = Import ▼=Export
◆ =Import/Export

GEOGRAPHIC SECTION

Richland - Rankin County (G-4525)

SIC: **2086** Soft drinks: packaged in cans, bottles, etc.
HQ: The American Bottling Company
5301 Legacy Dr
Plano TX 75024

(G-4501)
APAC-MISSISSIPPI INC
101 Riverview Dr (39218-4401)
P.O. Box 24508, Jackson (39225-4508)
PHONE......................................601 376-4000
John May, *Area Mgr*
Dwayne Boyd, *Manager*
EMP: 100
SALES (corp-wide): 30.6B **Privately Held**
SIC: **1611** 1771 3531 2951 Highway & street paving contractor; concrete construction: roads, highways, sidewalks, etc.; airport runway construction; parking lot construction; asphalt plant, including gravel-mix type; asphalt paving mixtures & blocks
HQ: Apac-Mississippi, Inc.
101 Riverview Dr
Richland MS 39218
601 376-4000

(G-4502)
APAC-MISSISSIPPI INC (DH)
101 Riverview Dr (39218-4401)
P.O. Box 24508, Jackson (39225-4508)
PHONE......................................601 376-4000
Dwayne H Boyd, *President*
Jimmy Ivy, *Area Mgr*
Wilma G Foreman, *Corp Secy*
Michael W Bogue, *Vice Pres*
Ladell N Estes, *Vice Pres*
EMP: 6
SQ FT: 10,000
SALES (est): 142.2MM
SALES (corp-wide): 30.6B **Privately Held**
SIC: **1611** 1771 3531 5032 Highway & street paving contractor; concrete construction: roads, highways, sidewalks, etc.; airport runway construction; parking lot construction; asphalt plant, including gravel-mix type; sand, construction; gravel; asphalt paving mixtures & blocks

(G-4503)
ARROW MATERIAL SERVICES LLC
187 Transload Dr (39218-4447)
PHONE......................................601 939-3113
Alan Dorman, *Branch Mgr*
EMP: 1 **Privately Held**
SIC: **3537** Loading docks: portable, adjustable & hydraulic
PA: Modern Materials Services, Llc
2605 Nicholson Rd # 5200
Sewickley PA 15143

(G-4504)
AZTEC INDUSTRIES INC
125 Aztec Dr (39218-4408)
P.O. Box 180067, Jackson (39218-0067)
PHONE......................................601 939-8522
L C Martin, *Principal*
Dana Perry, *Principal*
EMP: 18
SQ FT: 15,000
SALES (est): 2MM
SALES (corp-wide): 927MM **Publicly Held**
WEB: www.gulfcoastgalv.com
SIC: **3479** Hot dip coating of metals or formed products
PA: Azz Inc.
3100 W 7th St Ste 500
Fort Worth TX 76107
817 810-0095

(G-4505)
AZZ INC
120 Aztec Dr (39218-9796)
P.O. Box 180067 (39218-0067)
PHONE......................................601 939-9191
Ken Outt, *Project Mgr*
Aaron Tupman, *Project Mgr*
Derrick Henderson, *Safety Mgr*
Ron Poitra, *Site Mgr*
Mike Kobb, *Purch Mgr*
EMP: 37
SALES (corp-wide): 927MM **Publicly Held**
SIC: **3699** Electrical equipment & supplies

PA: Azz Inc.
3100 W 7th St Ste 500
Fort Worth TX 76107
817 810-0095

(G-4506)
BEAVER INDUSTRIES INC
583 Old Highway 49 S (39218-8409)
P.O. Box 180458 (39218-0458)
PHONE......................................601 664-6610
Thomas P McDonnell III, *Exec Dir*
EMP: 5
SALES (est): 566.2K **Privately Held**
SIC: **3999** Manufacturing industries

(G-4507)
BONDS COMPANY INC
Also Called: Bonds Paving
101 Riverview Dr (39218-4401)
P.O. Box 24508, Jackson (39225-4508)
PHONE......................................601 376-4000
EMP: 25
SALES (corp-wide): 6.8MM **Privately Held**
WEB: www.bondscompany.com
SIC: **3531** 1611 Asphalt plant, including gravel-mix type; surfacing & paving
PA: Bonds Company, Inc.
201 County Road 227
Iuka MS 38852
662 427-9581

(G-4508)
BUREL PHARMACEUTICALS INC
199 Interstate Dr Ste N (39218-9433)
PHONE......................................601 720-0111
Jay Edwards, *President*
EMP: 2 EST: 2007
SQ FT: 1,900
SALES: 968.3K **Privately Held**
SIC: **2834** Pharmaceutical preparations

(G-4509)
CALVERT COMPANY INC
120 Aztec Dr (39218-9796)
P.O. Box 180358 (39218-0358)
PHONE......................................601 939-9191
David Dingus, *CEO*
Dr H Kirk Downey, *Ch of Bd*
Tom Ferguson, *President*
Dana Perry, *Corp Secy*
Steve Powell, *IT/INT Sup*
▼ EMP: 83
SQ FT: 50,000
SALES: 35MM
SALES (corp-wide): 927MM **Publicly Held**
WEB: www.calvertbus.com
SIC: **3613** Bus bar structures; switchgear & switchgear accessories
PA: Azz Inc.
3100 W 7th St Ste 500
Fort Worth TX 76107
817 810-0095

(G-4510)
CONKLIN METAL INDUSTRIES INC
2900 Benton H Green Blvd (39218-4437)
PHONE......................................601 933-0402
Robert A Thompson, *Branch Mgr*
EMP: 17
SALES (corp-wide): 51.9MM **Privately Held**
SIC: **3444** Sheet metalwork
PA: Conklin Metal Industries, Inc.
684 Antone St Nw Ste 100
Atlanta GA 30318
404 688-4510

(G-4511)
DALLAS PRINTING INC
315 Carrier Blvd (39218-4420)
P.O. Box 902, Jackson (39205-0902)
PHONE......................................601 968-9354
Harvey Dallas, *CEO*
Bryan Dallas, *President*
Brenda Dallas, *CFO*
EMP: 25
SALES: 1MM **Privately Held**
WEB: www.harveydallasprinting.com
SIC: **2759** 2752 7331 Business forms: printing; commercial printing, lithographic; direct mail advertising services

(G-4512)
DEEPWELL ENERGY SERVICES LLC
134 Riverview Dr (39218-4400)
PHONE......................................601 735-1393
EMP: 28
SALES (corp-wide): 231.6MM **Privately Held**
SIC: **1381** Drilling oil & gas wells
PA: Deepwell Energy Services, Llc
4025 Highway 35 N
Columbia MS 39429
800 477-2855

(G-4513)
DESICCARE INC
211 Industrial Dr (39218-9548)
P.O. Box 180359, Jackson (39218-0359)
PHONE......................................601 932-0405
Ted Mc Intyre, *Purch Mgr*
Ted Tedintyre, *VP Engrg*
Marc Laporte, *Financial Exec*
Ted McIntrye, *Branch Mgr*
Marcus Dukes, *Director*
EMP: 25 **Privately Held**
WEB: www.desiccare.com
SIC: **3295** 2842 2819 Desiccants, clay: activated; specialty cleaning, polishes & sanitation goods; industrial inorganic chemicals
PA: Desiccare, Inc.
3930 W Windmill Ln # 100
Las Vegas NV 89139

(G-4514)
ERGON CONSTRUCTION GROUP INC
Also Called: ISO Panels, Inc.
630 Industrial Dr (39218-9730)
P.O. Box 180639 (39218-0639)
PHONE......................................601 939-3909
Robert H Lampton, *President*
Leslie Lampton, *President*
Kathryn W Stone, *Corp Secy*
Jimmy Langdon, *Vice Pres*
Roger Bynum, *Sales Staff*
EMP: 25
SQ FT: 22,000
SALES: 7MM
SALES (corp-wide): 997.6MM **Privately Held**
WEB: www.isopanels.com
SIC: **2911** Petroleum refining
PA: Ergon, Inc.
2829 Lakeland Dr Ste 2000
Flowood MS 39232
601 933-3000

(G-4515)
FIRST HERITAGE CREDIT CORP
129 Center St Ste C (39218-4800)
PHONE......................................601 939-9309
Tammy McCue, *Principal*
EMP: 1 **Privately Held**
SIC: **6141** 2411 Consumer finance companies; timber, cut at logging camp
PA: First Heritage Credit Corp
605 Crescent Blvd Ste 101
Ridgeland MS 39157

(G-4516)
FOREMOST DAIRIES
425 Highway 49 S (39218-9410)
PHONE......................................601 936-9606
Bryan Morris, *Manager*
EMP: 2 EST: 2008
SALES (est): 122K **Privately Held**
SIC: **2026** Fluid milk

(G-4517)
FUEL CENTER
1167 Highway 49 S (39218-4409)
PHONE......................................601 664-1861
EMP: 3
SALES (est): 180.7K **Privately Held**
SIC: **2869** Mfg Industrial Organic Chemicals

(G-4518)
GRD DISTRIBUTORS LLC
307 Walker Cir Bldg O (39218-8411)
P.O. Box 1, Star (39167-0001)
PHONE......................................601 382-8802
Jim Deweese,
EMP: 4 EST: 2010

(G-4519)
SQ FT: 8,000
SALES (est): 441.8K **Privately Held**
SIC: **2086** 5149 Iced tea & fruit drinks, bottled & canned; water, pasteurized: packaged in cans, bottles, etc.; mineral or spring water bottling; water, distilled

HABE-ISE USA INC
160 Interstate Dr (39218-9427)
PHONE......................................769 235-6650
Aaron Broussard, *Principal*
EMP: 11
SALES (est): 2.8MM **Privately Held**
SIC: **3714** Motor vehicle parts & accessories

(G-4520)
INTELATOOL SOLUTIONS LLC
309a Monterey Rd (39218-9403)
PHONE......................................601 594-8451
EMP: 5
SALES (est): 611K **Privately Held**
SIC: **7379** 7372 Computer related consulting services; prepackaged software

(G-4521)
MACS SMALL ENGINE SERVICE
Also Called: Mechanical Therapy
160 Scarbrough St (39218-9770)
PHONE......................................601 932-8076
Mac Scarbrough, *Owner*
EMP: 10
SALES (est): 70.3K **Privately Held**
SIC: **7699** 2431 Engine repair & replacement, non-automotive; millwork

(G-4522)
MINTON FLOORCOVERING LLC
522 Quinn Dr (39218-9220)
PHONE......................................601 540-3764
Rusty Minton, *Mng Member*
EMP: 2
SALES: 800K **Privately Held**
SIC: **3069** Rubber floor coverings, mats & wallcoverings

(G-4523)
RANKIN PLASTICS LLC
307 Walker Cir Bldg L (39218-8411)
P.O. Box 1844, Brandon (39043-1844)
PHONE......................................601 919-7883
Leslie Hambrick, *President*
William Beck, *Corp Secy*
Damon Hawk, *Vice Pres*
EMP: 3
SALES (est): 246.2K **Privately Held**
SIC: **2673** Bags: plastic, laminated & coated; plastic bags: made from purchased materials

(G-4524)
SIEMENS INDUSTRY INC
44 Old Highway 49 S (39218-4318)
P.O. Box 6289, Pearl (39288-6289)
PHONE......................................601 939-0550
EMP: 5
SALES (corp-wide): 95B **Privately Held**
SIC: **3822** Air conditioning & refrigeration controls
HQ: Siemens Industry, Inc.
1000 Deerfield Pkwy
Buffalo Grove IL 60089
847 215-1000

(G-4525)
STANLEY MCCAFFREY SIGNS (PA)
Also Called: McCaffrey Supply Co
231 Bradford Dr (39218-9676)
PHONE......................................228 832-0885
Stanley McCaffrey Jr, *President*
Debbie McCaffrey, *Corp Secy*
EMP: 7
SQ FT: 6,000
SALES: 600K **Privately Held**
SIC: **5734** 5046 3089 Computer & software stores; neon signs; display equipment, except refrigerated; scales, except laboratory; plastic processing

---

(PA)=Parent Co (HQ)=Headquarters (DH)=Div Headquarters

✪ = New Business established in last 2 years

2019 Harris Directory of
Mississippi Manufacturers

163

GEOGRAPHIC SECTION

Richton - Perry County (G-4526)

Richton
Perry County

(G-4526)
AL-TOM FOREST PRODUCTS INC
335 Al Tom Rd (39476-7866)
P.O. Box 595, Waynesboro (39367-0595)
PHONE..............................601 989-2631
Thomas O Kelley Jr, *President*
Jerry Kelly, *Vice Pres*
Bessie Kelly, *Treasurer*
Terry Kelley, *Admin Sec*
EMP: 47
SQ FT: 5,000
SALES (est): 6.8MM
SALES (corp-wide): 89.5MM **Privately Held**
SIC: 2426 2421 Lumber, hardwood dimension; sawmills & planing mills, general
PA: Kelley Brothers Contractors, Inc.
401 County Farm Rd
Waynesboro MS 39367
601 735-2541

(G-4527)
BURNIE DYKES LOGGING CO INC
67 Jim Easterling Rd (39476-8916)
PHONE..............................601 788-6211
Burnie Dykes, *President*
Lynn Dykes, *Director*
Don Bishop, *Admin Sec*
EMP: 7
SALES (est): 1.3MM **Privately Held**
SIC: 2411 Logging

(G-4528)
CANDLES BY VALORIE
3251 W Salem Rd (39476-7705)
PHONE..............................601 394-3153
Valorie Riles, *Principal*
EMP: 1
SALES (est): 39.6K **Privately Held**
SIC: 3999 Candles

(G-4529)
DEEP S MCH WRKS HYDRAULICS LLC
44430 Highway 63 N (39476-8046)
PHONE..............................601 989-2977
Scott Elmore, *Mng Member*
EMP: 2 EST: 2006
SALES (est): 351.7K **Privately Held**
SIC: 7539 7699 3599 Machine shop, automotive; hydraulic equipment repair; machine shop, jobbing & repair

(G-4530)
ELMORE MACHINE SHOP INC
2898 Lovewell Rd (39476-7989)
PHONE..............................601 989-2508
Ottice Neval Elmore, *Owner*
Thelma Elmore, *Vice Pres*
EMP: 8
SQ FT: 4,200
SALES (est): 580K **Privately Held**
SIC: 3599 Machine shop, jobbing & repair

(G-4531)
G&K SERVICES LLC
411 Oak St (39476)
P.O. Box 587 (39476-0587)
PHONE..............................601 788-6375
Danny Thompson, *Manager*
EMP: 30
SALES (corp-wide): 6.8B **Publicly Held**
WEB: www.gkservices.com
SIC: 7218 2326 Industrial uniform supply; men's & boys' work clothing
HQ: G&K Services, Llc
6800 Cintas Blvd
Mason OH 45040
952 912-5500

(G-4532)
GLENDON HENDERSON LOG & TRCKG
4797 Lovewell Rd (39476-7858)
P.O. Box 1092 (39476-1092)
PHONE..............................601 989-2638
J Henderson, *Principal*

EMP: 10
SALES (est): 1.1MM **Privately Held**
SIC: 2411 Logging camps & contractors

(G-4533)
GRACE WELDING FABRICATION LLC
11 Willis Edwards Dr (39476-8600)
PHONE..............................601 788-2478
Christopher L Cooper, *Principal*
EMP: 1
SALES (est): 43.8K **Privately Held**
SIC: 7692 Welding repair

(G-4534)
H DELANE TUCKER LOGGING INC
Camp Eight Rd Rr 51 # 8 (39476)
P.O. Box 655 (39476-0655)
PHONE..............................601 788-6320
Homer D Tucker, *President*
Kathy Tucker, *Admin Sec*
EMP: 4
SALES: 1MM **Privately Held**
SIC: 2411 Logging camps & contractors

(G-4535)
INTERNATIONAL LASER SUPS LLC
602 Cherry St (39476-9656)
P.O. Box 1090 (39476-1090)
PHONE..............................601 788-6475
Bruce Walley, *General Mgr*
Herbert Walley, *Mng Member*
Ollie Walley,
Sonya Walley,
EMP: 4
SQ FT: 1,600
SALES (est): 29.2K **Privately Held**
SIC: 3577 Computer peripheral equipment

(G-4536)
J D SMITH DRILLING COMPANY
Also Called: Seismic Drilling Contractor
5797 Union Rd (39476-7830)
PHONE..............................601 989-2475
John D Smith, *President*
Sundra Smith, *Treasurer*
EMP: 2
SALES (est): 810K **Privately Held**
SIC: 3829 Seismographs

(G-4537)
JEROLD HENDERSON LOGGING INC
5207 Lovewell Rd (39476-7855)
PHONE..............................601 989-2399
Jerold Henderson, *President*
Ruby Henderson, *Admin Sec*
EMP: 10
SALES (est): 1.2MM **Privately Held**
SIC: 2411 Logging

(G-4538)
JOHNNY W MILLS TIMBER COMPANY
4839 Lovewell Rd (39476-7919)
PHONE..............................601 989-2398
Johnny W Mills, *President*
EMP: 2 EST: 2001
SALES (est): 244.1K **Privately Held**
SIC: 2411 Logging camps & contractors

(G-4539)
MANNING DRILLING COMPANY INC
1335 Mount Zion Rd (39476-2623)
PHONE..............................601 989-2805
Freddie Matt Manning, *President*
Debora Manning, *Vice Pres*
EMP: 4
SALES (est): 462.2K **Privately Held**
SIC: 1382 Oil & gas exploration services

(G-4540)
MAYO LOGGING
90 Will Best Rd (39476-8201)
PHONE..............................601 270-4426
EMP: 2
SALES (est): 81.7K **Privately Held**
SIC: 2411 Logging

(G-4541)
NOWELL STEPS INCORPORATED
438 Hickory Grove Ch Rd (39476-8806)
PHONE..............................601 964-8455
Roy Nowell, *President*
Joyce Nowell, *Vice Pres*
EMP: 6
SALES (est): 330K **Privately Held**
SIC: 2514 Breakfast sets, household: metal

(G-4542)
POWE TIMBER COMPANY
Also Called: American Wood
1356 Highway 15 (39476-8918)
P.O. Box 1617 (39476-1617)
PHONE..............................601 788-6564
Larry Polk, *Manager*
EMP: 7
SALES (corp-wide): 2.8MM **Privately Held**
WEB: www.american-woodcraft.com
SIC: 2491 Railroad cross-ties, treated wood
PA: Powe Timber Company
114 S 10th Ave
Hattiesburg MS 39401
601 545-7600

(G-4543)
RICHTON DISPATCH INC
110 Walnut St (39476)
PHONE..............................601 788-6031
Larry Wilson, *President*
Dean D Wilson, *Vice Pres*
EMP: 3
SQ FT: 1,200
SALES (est): 321.4K **Privately Held**
SIC: 2752 Newspapers, lithographed only; commercial printing, offset

(G-4544)
STINSON & SON LOGGING
Also Called: Loggers Depot
Rr 1 Box 88 (39476)
PHONE..............................601 989-2311
Bobby Stinson, *Owner*
Bobbie Stinson, *Owner*
EMP: 6
SALES (est): 243.7K **Privately Held**
SIC: 2411 5541 Logging camps & contractors; truck stops

Ridgeland
Madison County

(G-4545)
ADWARE
310b Hawthorne Cir (39157-2510)
PHONE..............................601 898-9194
Tom Vinson, *Owner*
EMP: 2
SALES (est): 230.5K **Privately Held**
SIC: 2752 Commercial printing, lithographic

(G-4546)
AIRLOCK INSULATION LLC
121 E State St Ste A (39157-4516)
PHONE..............................601 526-4141
EMP: 10
SALES (est): 1.2MM **Privately Held**
SIC: 3443 Airlocks

(G-4547)
ALEX CAROL LIMITED
834 Wilson Dr Ste C (39157-4510)
PHONE..............................601 956-0536
Alex Carro, *Principal*
EMP: 2 EST: 2007
SALES (est): 163.2K **Privately Held**
SIC: 5137 2342 2341 2331 Women's & children's clothing; bras, girdles & allied garments; women's & children's underwear; women's & misses' blouses & shirts

(G-4548)
AMEITECH/SOUTH
210 Industrial Dr (39157-2704)
PHONE..............................601 853-0830
Joe Leach, *Owner*
EMP: 3

SQ FT: 10,000
SALES (est): 190K **Privately Held**
WEB: www.woodworkingtools.net
SIC: 2431 5084 Millwork; industrial machinery & equipment

(G-4549)
AMERICAN STITCHING LLC
119 Deer Cir (39157-5020)
PHONE..............................601 919-7882
Paul Ray Bunch Jr, *Principal*
EMP: 2
SALES (est): 81K **Privately Held**
SIC: 2395 Embroidery & art needlework

(G-4550)
APPLIED SOFTWARE SYSTEM LLC
177 Green Glades (39157-8661)
PHONE..............................601 605-0877
Chris Crawford, *Principal*
EMP: 2 EST: 2011
SALES (est): 44.2K **Privately Held**
SIC: 7372 Prepackaged software

(G-4551)
ASCEND SURGICAL SALES LLC
574 Highland Colony Pkwy 320l (39157-6073)
PHONE..............................601 351-9866
Jeff Jones, *Branch Mgr*
EMP: 3
SALES (corp-wide): 382.2K **Privately Held**
SIC: 3842 Implants, surgical
PA: Ascend Surgical Sales, Llc
5510 Pine Lane Dr
Jackson MS 39211
601 573-1890

(G-4552)
BATTCO INC
Also Called: Interstate All Battery Center
243 Highway 51 (39157-4423)
PHONE..............................601 898-1200
Kevin Erwin, *President*
Debra Erwin, *Vice Pres*
EMP: 8 EST: 2001
SALES (est): 678.5K **Privately Held**
SIC: 5531 3691 3692 5063 Batteries, automotive & truck; alkaline cell storage batteries; primary batteries, dry & wet; batteries; storage batteries, industrial

(G-4553)
BAYOU CONCRETE LLC (HQ)
1052 Highland Colony Pkwy (39157-8764)
P.O. Box 2569, Madison (39130-2569)
PHONE..............................601 898-4000
Mike Pepper, *President*
Danny Rodgers, *Chairman*
Walter Verneuille, *Sales Mgr*
EMP: 1
SALES (est): 32MM
SALES (corp-wide): 306.5MM **Privately Held**
WEB: www.gulfconcretellc.com
SIC: 3273 Ready-mixed concrete
PA: Dunn Investment Company
3900 Messer Airport Hwy
Birmingham AL 35222
205 592-3866

(G-4554)
BECKS CONFECTION
Also Called: Food Manufacturing
270 Highpoint Dr (39157-6019)
P.O. Box 531 (39158-0531)
PHONE..............................601 927-3137
Annie Beck, *Owner*
EMP: 3 EST: 2013
SQ FT: 4,000
SALES: 50K **Privately Held**
SIC: 2099 Baking powder & soda, yeast & other leavening agents

(G-4555)
BEYONDTRUST CORPORATION
Also Called: Bomgar
578 Highland Colony Pkwy (39157-8779)
PHONE..............................601 519-0213
Daniel Derosa, *Vice Pres*
Joe Durante, *Vice Pres*
Jeff Newlin, *Vice Pres*
Davy Durham, *Engineer*
Adam Lien, *Engineer*

2019 Harris Directory of
Mississippi Manufacturers

▲ = Import ▼=Export
◆ =Import/Export

GEOGRAPHIC SECTION

Ridgeland - Madison County (G-4587)

EMP: 50
SALES (corp-wide): 66.4MM **Privately Held**
SIC: 7372 Business oriented computer software
PA: Beyondtrust Corporation
11695 Johns Creek Pkwy
Duluth GA 30097
770 407-1800

(G-4556)
BIG BUCK SPORTS
242 Highway 51 (39157-4422)
P.O. Box 908, Columbia (39429-0908)
PHONE..........................601 605-2661
Louis Swarts, *Principal*
EMP: 1
SALES (est): 57K **Privately Held**
SIC: 7699 5941 5661 2759 Gunsmith shop; archery supplies; shoe stores; screen printing

(G-4557)
BLACKSTONE INVESTMENTS LLC
603 Northpark Dr Ste 300 (39157-5232)
PHONE..........................601 978-1763
Todd Bertolet, *Owner*
EMP: 2
SALES (est): 227.1K **Privately Held**
SIC: 1382 Oil & gas exploration services

(G-4558)
BOYD EDUCTL SOLUTIONS TECH LLC
241 Pine Knoll Dr (39157-1364)
PHONE..........................601 951-2305
Alfred Boyd,
EMP: 1
SALES (est): 32.7K **Privately Held**
SIC: 7372 Educational computer software

(G-4559)
BUSINESS COMMUNICATIONS INC (PA)
Also Called: BCI
442 Highland Colony Pkwy (39157-8727)
PHONE..........................601 898-1890
Tony Bailey, *CEO*
Greg Latour, *President*
Niki Papazoglakis, *General Mgr*
Craig Henley, *Business Mgr*
Sheila Pike, *Purch Mgr*
EMP: 35
SQ FT: 30,000
SALES (est): 34.6MM **Privately Held**
WEB: www.buscominc.com
SIC: 7378 1731 7372 Computer mainte-nance & repair; fiber optic cable installa-tion; telephone & telephone equipment installation; operating systems computer software

(G-4560)
CARNECERIA VALDEZ
6530 Old Canton Rd (39157-1313)
PHONE..........................601 899-6992
Adalberto Valdez, *Principal*
EMP: 1
SALES (est): 121.3K **Privately Held**
SIC: 3421 Table & food cutlery, including butchers'

(G-4561)
CEDOTAL INC
Also Called: Tech Assurance
330 Ne Madison Dr (39157-2021)
P.O. Box 726 (39158-0726)
PHONE..........................601 605-2660
Jonathan Cedotal, *President*
Shelle Cedotal, *Vice Pres*
EMP: 5
SALES: 750K **Privately Held**
SIC: 3555 Type cases, printers'

(G-4562)
CELGENE CORP
100 Brighton Ln (39157-8774)
PHONE..........................908 673-9000
EMP: 3
SALES (est): 157K **Privately Held**
SIC: 2834 Pharmaceutical preparations

(G-4563)
CIVIL PRECAST CORPORATION
854 Wilson Dr Ste B (39157-4521)
PHONE..........................601 853-1870
Anthony J Bertas, *President*
EMP: 5
SALES (est): 400K **Privately Held**
SIC: 3272 Precast terrazo or concrete products

(G-4564)
COAST INK WHOLESALE CLUB
1200 E County Line Rd # 186 (39157-1941)
PHONE..........................601 948-4849
Cartez Pollard, *Owner*
Anthony Joe, *Principal*
EMP: 2
SALES (est): 129.6K **Privately Held**
SIC: 2395 Embroidery & art needlework

(G-4565)
COOKIE PLACE INC
1200 E County Line Rd # 111 (39157-1904)
PHONE..........................601 957-2891
Mary Carrier, *Manager*
EMP: 8 **Privately Held**
WEB: www.thecookieplace.com
SIC: 5461 2052 Cookies; cookies
PA: The Cookie Place Inc
2140 11th Ave S Ste 305
Birmingham AL 35205

(G-4566)
CORPORATE HOUSING
761 Rice Rd (39157-1085)
PHONE..........................601 853-8982
EMP: 1 EST: 2011
SALES (est): 40K **Privately Held**
SIC: 2392 Mfg Household Furnishings

(G-4567)
CROSBYS CREEK OIL & GAS LLC
Also Called: Hughes Eastern
605 Northpark Dr Ste A (39157-5211)
PHONE..........................601 898-0051
Emil Pawlik,
EMP: 6
SQ FT: 2,700
SALES (est): 621.1K **Privately Held**
SIC: 1311 Crude petroleum & natural gas

(G-4568)
CRYSTAL SPRINGS APPAREL LLC (PA)
216 Bellewether Pass (39157-8762)
PHONE..........................601 856-8831
Donna Nigro, *Mng Member*
EMP: 50
SQ FT: 17,500
SALES (est): 2.9MM **Privately Held**
SIC: 2331 2321 8741 Women's & misses' blouses & shirts; men's & boys' sports & polo shirts; management services

(G-4569)
CUFF TOUGHENER
327 Arlington Cir (39157-2576)
PHONE..........................601 209-1609
Doug Parsell, *President*
EMP: 2
SALES (est): 167.5K **Privately Held**
SIC: 3841 Surgical instruments & appara-tus

(G-4570)
DAVES MOBILE CAR WASH
102 Hawks Nest Blf (39157-2874)
PHONE..........................601 940-6855
EMP: 4 EST: 2011
SALES (est): 339.4K **Privately Held**
SIC: 2842 Automobile polish

(G-4571)
DAVIS SPECIALTY CHEMICALS INC
220 Davis Dr (39157-2230)
P.O. Box 1080 (39158-1080)
PHONE..........................601 856-5774
John D Davis III, *President*
EMP: 4
SQ FT: 8,000

SALES (est): 741.6K **Privately Held**
SIC: 5087 2842 Janitors' supplies; indus-trial plant disinfectants or deodorants

(G-4572)
DAVISCOMMS (S) PTE LTD
Also Called: Daviscomms USA
120 Travis Rodgers Ln (39157-5032)
PHONE..........................601 416-5043
EMP: 3
SALES (est): 198.7K **Privately Held**
SIC: 3674 Semiconductors & related de-vices

(G-4573)
DENOVO LABS LLC
202 W Jackson St (39157-2310)
PHONE..........................615 587-3099
John Brewer,
EMP: 1
SALES (est): 47.2K **Privately Held**
SIC: 2834 Pharmaceutical preparations

(G-4574)
DRAGON BREATH PRESS LLC
212 Salem Sq (39157-2818)
PHONE..........................601 607-7007
Janet Taylor-Perry, *Principal*
EMP: 1
SALES (est): 40.7K **Privately Held**
SIC: 2741 Miscellaneous publishing

(G-4575)
DURANGO OPERATING LLC
419 Northpark Dr A (39157-5109)
PHONE..........................601 420-2525
John D Herlihy,
EMP: 16
SALES (est): 1.6MM **Privately Held**
SIC: 1382 Oil & gas exploration services

(G-4576)
EFMA CONTRACTING LLC
107 Pine Knoll Dr Apt 8 (39157-1317)
PHONE..........................901 292-7221
EMP: 13
SALES (est): 1MM **Privately Held**
SIC: 2952 1751 1742 1752 Asphalt Felts And Coatings

(G-4577)
ENVIRONMENTAL TECH OF AMER
403 Towne Center Blvd # 404 (39157-4887)
P.O. Box 1230 (39158-1230)
PHONE..........................601 607-3151
Bob Mailly, *Branch Mgr*
EMP: 9
SALES (corp-wide): 2.9MM **Privately Held**
SIC: 7372 Prepackaged software
PA: Environmental Technology Of America Inc
403 D Townctr Blvd 3&
Ridgeland MS 39157
601 939-3313

(G-4578)
ESOFTWARE SOLUTIONS INC
Also Called: Ecash Software Systems
403 Legacy Park (39157-4316)
P.O. Box 1968 (39158-1968)
PHONE..........................601 919-2275
Scott Putnam, *CEO*
Jennifer Tabb, *Vice Pres*
Bradley Tompkins, *Vice Pres*
Lisa Freeze, *CFO*
Tony Huffman, *Treasurer*
EMP: 25
SQ FT: 5,000
SALES: 3MM **Privately Held**
SIC: 7372 Prepackaged software

(G-4579)
EXPRESS PRINTING
614 Highway 51 (39157-2571)
PHONE..........................601 856-5458
EMP: 2
SALES (est): 120.5K **Privately Held**
SIC: 2759 Commercial Printing

(G-4580)
FILING AND STORAGE MISS LLC
751 Avignon Dr Ste G (39157-5161)
PHONE..........................601 397-6452
Kevin McKay,
Lisa Williams McKay,
EMP: 2
SQ FT: 400
SALES (est): 360.2K **Privately Held**
WEB: www.filingandstorageofms.com
SIC: 2599 7699 3499 Stools with casters (not household or office), metal; photo-copy machine repair; furniture parts, metal

(G-4581)
FINAL TOUCH PRODUCTIONS
609 Bryceland Blvd (39157-1206)
PHONE..........................601 750-3940
Marques Walker, *Partner*
EMP: 2
SALES (est): 158.7K **Privately Held**
SIC: 2752 Commercial printing, litho-graphic

(G-4582)
FISHYRHYTHMS PUBLISHING LLC
287 Longwood Cv (39157-3562)
PHONE..........................601 573-6771
B L Buddy Fish, *Principal*
EMP: 2 EST: 2011
SALES (est): 109.5K **Privately Held**
SIC: 2741 Miscellaneous publishing

(G-4583)
FLAMBEAUX COCKTAIL CANDLE LLC
580 S Pear Orchard Rd # 1503 (39157-4200)
PHONE..........................601 826-1642
Wonda Taylor, *Mng Member*
EMP: 1
SQ FT: 500
SALES: 10K **Privately Held**
SIC: 3999 7389 Candles;

(G-4584)
FLETCHER COX
6817 Cole Rd (39157-6005)
P.O. Box 188, Tougaloo (39174-0188)
PHONE..........................601 956-2610
Flectcher Cox, *Principal*
EMP: 1
SALES (est): 68K **Privately Held**
SIC: 2531 Public building & related furni-ture

(G-4585)
FOSSIL FUEL
150 Sunnycrest Dr (39157-2566)
PHONE..........................601 790-7955
EMP: 3
SALES (est): 176.2K **Privately Held**
SIC: 2869 Fuels

(G-4586)
GASMAX FLTRATION SOLUTIONS LLC
368 Highland Colony Pkwy (39157-6036)
PHONE..........................601 790-1225
William Nicholas, *Principal*
EMP: 2
SALES (est): 151.9K **Privately Held**
SIC: 3569 1321 1389 Gas producers, generators & other gas related equip-ment; natural gas liquids; processing service, gas

(G-4587)
GENTEX PHARMA LLC
Also Called: Gentexpharma
121 Marketridge Dr Ste C (39157-6027)
P.O. Box 1724, Madison (39130-1724)
PHONE..........................601 990-9497
Ford Mundy, *President*
Heath Wray, *Director*
EMP: 2
SALES (est): 200K **Privately Held**
SIC: 2834 Pills, pharmaceutical

(PA)=Parent Co (HQ)=Headquarters (DH)=Div Headquarters
✿ = New Business established in last 2 years

2019 Harris Directory of
Mississippi Manufacturers

165

Ridgeland - Madison County (G-4588) GEOGRAPHIC SECTION

(G-4588)
GULF STATES GOLF CARS
Also Called: Gulf States Yamaha
235 Highway 51 (39157-4423)
PHONE..................................601 853-1510
Stuart Conway, *General Mgr*
EMP: 6
SALES (est): 821.7K **Privately Held**
SIC: 3949 Sporting & athletic goods

(G-4589)
HEMLINE
140 Township Ave Ste 102 (39157-2094)
PHONE..................................601 898-3456
EMP: 1
SALES (est): 51.2K **Privately Held**
SIC: 2253 Dresses & skirts

(G-4590)
HUGHES EASTERN CORPORATION (PA)
605 Northpark Dr Ste A (39157-5211)
PHONE..................................601 957-1778
Emil Pawlik, *President*
Jim Stephens, *Vice Pres*
EMP: 6
SQ FT: 2,600
SALES (est): 2.3MM **Privately Held**
WEB: www.hugheseastern.com
SIC: 1311 Crude petroleum production

(G-4591)
HUNT PROCESS CORP-SOUTHERN
138 N Wheatley St (39157-2339)
P.O. Box 688 (39158-0688)
PHONE..................................601 856-8811
Richard W Largent, *Ch of Bd*
James Watts, *President*
Margie C Largent, *Treasurer*
Gina Lee Rutherford, *Office Mgr*
EMP: 7 EST: 1952
SQ FT: 16,000
SALES (est): 1.4MM **Privately Held**
WEB: www.huntprocess.com
SIC: 2891 2899 Epoxy adhesives; concrete curing & hardening compounds

(G-4592)
ID GROUP INC (PA)
280 Trace Colony Park Dr (39157-8810)
PHONE..................................601 982-2651
Sam King, *President*
Nora T King, *Vice Pres*
EMP: 6
SQ FT: 4,300
SALES (est): 3.8MM **Privately Held**
WEB: www.idgroupinfo.com
SIC: 3999 Identification tags, except paper

(G-4593)
INTEGRITY HOT SHOT SVCS LLC
317 Pear Orchard Cir (39157-4116)
PHONE..................................601 850-8881
Brad Warrinton,
Bradley W Warrington, *Administration*
EMP: 2
SALES (est): 1.2MM **Privately Held**
SIC: 1389 Hot shot service

(G-4594)
INTERSTATE INDUSTRIES MISS LL
353 Hillview Dr (39157-8607)
PHONE..................................601 856-5941
EMP: 2 EST: 2001
SALES (est): 120.7K **Privately Held**
SIC: 3999 Manufacturing industries

(G-4595)
KLAAS-ROBBINS PAVEMENT MAINT
2362 W County Line Rd (39157-5077)
PHONE..................................601 362-4091
Trena Klaas, *Partner*
EMP: 3
SALES: 500K **Privately Held**
SIC: 2951 Asphalt & asphaltic paving mixtures (not from refineries)

(G-4596)
LA JOLIE ENTERPRISES LLC
340 Arbor Dr Apt 1317 (39157-4825)
PHONE..................................601 909-8840
Rena Smith, *Owner*
EMP: 2
SQ FT: 300
SALES (est): 48.1K **Privately Held**
SIC: 7389 7231 5122 3999 Personal service agents, brokers & bureaus; cosmetology & personal hygiene salons; cosmetics; eyelashes, artificial

(G-4597)
LC IND SIGNATURE WORKS DIV
920 E County Line Rd (39157-1932)
PHONE..................................601 206-9564
Timothy Hurst, *Manager*
EMP: 1
SALES (est): 104.3K **Privately Held**
SIC: 2621 Paper mills

(G-4598)
LIBERTY SOUTHERN PARTNERS LP
Also Called: Liberty Southern Energy
611 S Pear Orchard Rd (39158-6000)
P.O. Box 3342 (39158-3342)
PHONE..................................214 450-8838
EMP: 1
SALES (est): 110K **Privately Held**
SIC: 1382 Oil And Gas Exploration Services

(G-4599)
M S I/POZZI
829 Wilson Dr Ste C (39157-4507)
PHONE..................................601 957-0085
Philip Richards, *Manager*
Philip Richards -Dist, *Manager*
EMP: 5 EST: 2001
SALES (est): 494.7K **Privately Held**
SIC: 2431 Windows, wood

(G-4600)
MADISON COUNTY PUBLISHING INC
Also Called: Madison County Journal
293 Commerce Park Dr (39157-2233)
P.O. Box 219 (39158-0219)
PHONE..................................601 853-4222
James E Prince III, *President*
EMP: 7
SALES (est): 519.3K **Privately Held**
SIC: 2711 Newspapers, publishing & printing

(G-4601)
MAGNOLIA THERAPEUTICS LLC
605 Crescent Blvd Ste 200 (39157-8659)
PHONE..................................662 281-0502
Kevin M Patterson,
EMP: 2
SALES (est): 74.4K **Privately Held**
SIC: 2834 Pharmaceutical preparations

(G-4602)
MAGNOLIA TOOL & MFG CO (PA)
111 E State St (39157)
PHONE..................................601 856-4333
Dallas Mc Crory, *President*
Deborah Mc Crory, *Vice Pres*
EMP: 6
SQ FT: 10,000
SALES (est): 1.6MM **Privately Held**
SIC: 3469 3544 Stamping metal for the trade; die sets for metal stamping (presses)

(G-4603)
MAGNOLIA TOOL & MFG CO
110-111 E State St (39157)
P.O. Box 426 (39158-0426)
PHONE..................................601 856-4333
Dallas McCrory, *Manager*
EMP: 5
SALES (est): 375.3K
SALES (corp-wide): 1.6MM **Privately Held**
SIC: 3469 Stamping metal for the trade
PA: Magnolia Tool & Manufacturing Co Inc
111 E State St
Ridgeland MS 39157
601 856-4333

(G-4604)
MEDICAL GRADE INNOVATIONS LLC
605 Northpark Dr Ste C (39157-5211)
PHONE..................................601 899-9207
Allen Salvage, *CIO*
Bert Rubinsky,
Kenny Perry,
Kenneth A Primos III,
EMP: 2
SALES (est): 174.6K **Privately Held**
SIC: 2299 Towels & towelings, linen & linen-and-cotton mixtures

(G-4605)
MEDWORX COMPOUNDING LLC
500 Highway 51 Ste Q (39157-2886)
PHONE..................................601 859-5008
Rett Crowder, *Owner*
EMP: 10
SALES (est): 145.7K **Privately Held**
SIC: 8069 3841 Orthopedic hospital; surgical instruments & apparatus

(G-4606)
MISSISSIPPI RAINBOW PRINTING
217a Industrial Dr (39157-2703)
PHONE..................................601 853-9513
Edward Rouse, *President*
Lesia Rouse, *Vice Pres*
EMP: 4
SALES: 190K **Privately Held**
SIC: 2752 Commercial printing, offset

(G-4607)
MISSISSIPPI VALLEY PUBLISHING
Also Called: Stockman Grass Farmer
234 W School St (39157-2707)
P.O. Box 2300 (39158-2300)
PHONE..................................601 853-1861
Glenda Dandofort, *President*
H Allan Nation, *President*
Allan Nation, *Publisher*
EMP: 14
SALES (est): 1.2MM **Privately Held**
SIC: 2721 Magazines: publishing only, not printed on site

(G-4608)
MMC MATERIALS INC (HQ)
1052 Highland Colony Pkwy # 201 (39157-8764)
P.O. Box 2569, Madison (39130-2569)
PHONE..................................601 898-4000
James Overstreet Jr, *President*
Rodney Grogan, *President*
Brian McDonald, *General Mgr*
Johnny Sides, *Area Mgr*
Butch Bailess, *Vice Pres*
EMP: 15 EST: 1927
SQ FT: 7,872
SALES (est): 101.3MM
SALES (corp-wide): 306.5MM **Privately Held**
WEB: www.mmcmaterials.com
SIC: 3273 Ready-mixed concrete
PA: Dunn Investment Company
3900 Messer Airport Hwy
Birmingham AL 35222
205 592-3866

(G-4609)
MOCO INC
603 Northpark Dr Ste 100 (39157-5232)
PHONE..................................601 957-3550
Michael L Blackwell, *President*
Don Noblitt, *Corp Secy*
EMP: 2 EST: 1982
SQ FT: 3,000
SALES (est): 299.4K **Privately Held**
SIC: 1311 Crude petroleum production; natural gas production

(G-4610)
MOON-HNS-TIGRETT OPERATING INC
599 Northpark Dr Ste A (39157-5111)
P.O. Box 3216 (39158-3216)
PHONE..................................601 572-8300
Scott Hines, *President*
Terry A Tigrett Jr, *President*
Todd Hines, *Admin Sec*
EMP: 6 EST: 1982

SQ FT: 4,800
SALES (est): 1.2MM **Privately Held**
SIC: 1382 Oil & gas exploration services

(G-4611)
NICK STRCKLNDS QUICK PRINT INC
Also Called: Alliance Business Services
250 Highpoint Dr (39157-6019)
PHONE..................................601 353-8672
EMP: 17
SALES (corp-wide): 2.7MM **Privately Held**
SIC: 2752 2791 2789 Lithographic commercial Printing Typesetting Services Bookbinding/Related Work
PA: Nick Strickland's Quick Print, Inc.
109 E State St
Ridgeland MS 39201
601 898-1717

(G-4612)
NICK STRCKLNDS QUICK PRINT INC
109 E State St (39157-4504)
PHONE..................................601 355-8195
Fajor Payne, *Manager*
EMP: 6
SALES (corp-wide): 3.6MM **Privately Held**
WEB: www.alliancebusinessservices.net
SIC: 2752 2791 Commercial printing, offset; typesetting
PA: Nick Strickland's Quick Print, Inc.
125 E South St
Jackson MS 39201
601 898-1717

(G-4613)
NSLC SOUTHERN INC (PA)
214 Draperton Dr (39157-3907)
P.O. Box 70, Hermanville (39086-0070)
PHONE..................................601 605-0575
Floyd Sulser Sr, *Ch of Bd*
Floyd M Sulser Jr, *Admin Sec*
EMP: 80
SQ FT: 4,700
SALES (est): 12.5MM **Privately Held**
WEB: www.southernlumber.net
SIC: 2421 Sawmills & planing mills, general

(G-4614)
OMNI TECHNOLOGIES LLC
7048 Old Canton Rd # 2008 (39157-1021)
PHONE..................................601 427-5898
Bobby Fricke, *Owner*
Rodney Neease, *Co-Owner*
EMP: 2
SALES (est): 125.3K **Privately Held**
SIC: 3571 7371 7379 Electronic computers; custom computer programming services; computer related services

(G-4615)
PATRICIA BETTS
Also Called: Mspatticakes
614 Kinsington Ct (39157-4160)
PHONE..................................601 863-9058
Patricia Betts, *Owner*
EMP: 1
SALES (est): 38.8K **Privately Held**
SIC: 2052 Cookies & crackers

(G-4616)
PEPSI SOUTH BOTTLING
591 Highland Colony Pkwy (39157-8784)
PHONE..................................601 607-3011
Willam A Brown,
Drew Allen,
Dennis Smith,
Ray Wilkins,
EMP: 50
SALES (est): 3.1MM **Privately Held**
SIC: 2086 Bottled & canned soft drinks

(G-4617)
PERFORMANCE PAPERBOARD INC
218 N Wheatley St (39157-2344)
P.O. Box 776 (39158-0776)
PHONE..................................601 856-3939
EMP: 22
SQ FT: 45,000

2019 Harris Directory of
Mississippi Manufacturers

166

▲ = Import ▼=Export
◆ =Import/Export

GEOGRAPHIC SECTION

Rienzi - Alcorn County (G-4648)

SALES (est): 4.3MM **Privately Held**
SIC: 2631 Paperboard Mill

(G-4618)
PITNEY BOWES INC
119 Marketridge Dr Ste H (39157-6028)
PHONE...................................601 206-9039
Leon Bankston, *Branch Mgr*
EMP: 35
SALES (corp-wide): 3.5B **Publicly Held**
SIC: 3579 7359 Postage meters; business
machine & electronic equipment rental
services
PA: Pitney Bowes Inc.
3001 Summer St Ste 3
Stamford CT 06905
203 356-5000

(G-4619)
PRESSURE PRO
142 Ne Madison Dr (39157-2400)
PHONE...................................601 331-7070
EMP: 2
SALES (est): 131.7K **Privately Held**
SIC: 3589 High pressure cleaning equipment

(G-4620)
PRINTING ON TIME SCREEN
230 Christopher Cv (39157-2000)
PHONE...................................601 707-7207
EMP: 2 EST: 2017
SALES (est): 83.9K **Privately Held**
SIC: 2752 Lithographic Commercial Printing

(G-4621)
PROCESS MECHANICAL EQP CO
110 Windrush Dr (39157-9782)
PHONE...................................601 291-4082
Dan Hobbs, *President*
EMP: 1
SALES (est): 500K **Privately Held**
SIC: 3498 Fabricated pipe & fittings

(G-4622)
RED SQUARE CLOTHING CO
1000 Highland Pkwy # 9004 (39157-2073)
PHONE...................................601 853-8960
Codie Harris, *Principal*
EMP: 5
SALES (est): 556.9K **Privately Held**
SIC: 2329 Men's & boys' clothing

(G-4623)
RK MANUFACTURING INC
119 Marketridge Dr Ste D (39157-6028)
PHONE...................................601 956-7774
Anne Klinglar, *Branch Mgr*
EMP: 15 **Privately Held**
SIC: 3089 Injection molding of plastics
PA: Rk Manufacturing, Inc.
810 Cooper Rd
Jackson MS

(G-4624)
ROBOT-COUPE INC USA
264 S Perkins St (39157-2719)
P.O. Box 16625, Jackson (39236-6625)
PHONE...................................601 898-8411
Jay A Williams, *President*
Cliff Reding, *Vice Pres*
Mitchell Reed, *Vice Pres*
Robert Sherrod, *Vice Pres*
Deel Frankie, *Credit Mgr*
▲ EMP: 39 EST: 1967
SQ FT: 30,000
SALES (est): 10MM **Privately Held**
WEB: www.robotcoupeusa.com
SIC: 3556 Choppers, commercial, food

(G-4625)
ROUNDTREE & ASSOCIATES INC
210 Trace Colony Park Dr (39157-8810)
PHONE...................................601 355-4530
Ronald Roundtree, *President*
Brian Roundtree, *Vice Pres*
Susan Pridgen, *Admin Sec*
EMP: 14
SQ FT: 8,000

SALES (est): 2.7MM **Privately Held**
SIC: 1311 1389 Crude petroleum production; oil & gas wells: building, repairing & dismantling

(G-4626)
ROYAL CANVAS STUDIOS
110 Pine Knoll Dr Apt 261 (39157-1343)
PHONE...................................601 419-0809
Kashundra Taylor, *Principal*
EMP: 1
SALES (est): 46.5K **Privately Held**
SIC: 2211 Canvas

(G-4627)
SC3 LLC
Also Called: Shavers' Choice
112 Overlook Pointe Dr (39157-8653)
P.O. Box 980, Madison (39130-0980)
PHONE...................................601 853-3690
Brenda Van Velkinburgh, *Mng Member*
Michael Van Velkinburgh,
Michael V Velkinburgh,
EMP: 2
SALES (est): 60K **Privately Held**
WEB: www.shaverschoice.com
SIC: 2844 Face creams or lotions

(G-4628)
SCREENCO PRINTING LLC
280 Christopher Cv Ste C (39157-2039)
PHONE...................................601 507-1986
EMP: 2
SALES (est): 129.9K **Privately Held**
SIC: 2752 Commercial printing, lithographic

(G-4629)
SIGNATURELINK INC
605 Crescent Blvd Ste 200 (39157-8659)
PHONE...................................601 898-7359
Greg Wooten, *CEO*
Greg Stamatis, *President*
James Packer, *COO*
EMP: 2
SALES (est): 177.9K **Privately Held**
SIC: 7372 Business oriented computer software

(G-4630)
SKYHAWKE TECHNOLOGIES LLC
Also Called: Skygolf
274 Commerce Park Dr (39157-2236)
P.O. Box 2960 (39158-2960)
PHONE...................................601 605-6100
Richard C Edmonson, *CEO*
Jim Meadows, *Vice Pres*
Richard Root, *Vice Pres*
Rob Spell, *Vice Pres*
Jacqui Surman, *Vice Pres*
▲ EMP: 275
SQ FT: 35,000
SALES (est): 37.2MM **Privately Held**
WEB: www.skyhawke.com
SIC: 7372 Prepackaged software

(G-4631)
SMART SOURCE
Also Called: DSI
356 Highway 51 (39157-3433)
PHONE...................................601 707-1150
Jim Combee, *President*
EMP: 6
SALES (corp-wide): 55MM **Privately Held**
SIC: 2752 2754 2759 7389 Promotional printing, lithographic; commercial printing, gravure; envelopes: gravure printing; envelopes: printing; printing broker
HQ: Smart Source Of Georgia, Llc
7270 Mcginnis Ferry Rd
Suwanee GA 30024
770 449-6300

(G-4632)
SOUTHSTERN FOAM FBRICATION LLC
141 Township Ave Ste 305 (39157-8697)
PHONE...................................601 540-8880
Hunter Travis, *President*
EMP: 2
SALES (est): 88.2K **Privately Held**
SIC: 2515 Mattresses, containing felt, foam rubber, urethane, etc.

(G-4633)
SPEED BOX LLC
375 Whippoorwill Ln (39157-9448)
PHONE...................................910 964-7947
Matthew Summers,
EMP: 6
SALES (est): 248.5K **Privately Held**
SIC: 3089 Plastic containers, except foam

(G-4634)
SPOONER PETROLEUM INC
154 Meadowlark Ln (39157-9233)
PHONE...................................601 969-1831
Ronnie Turner, *President*
EMP: 1
SALES (est): 74.9K **Privately Held**
SIC: 1382 Oil & gas exploration services

(G-4635)
STOCKMAN GRASS FARMER (PA)
Also Called: Stockman Grass Farmers
234 W School St (39157-2707)
P.O. Box 2300 (39158-2300)
PHONE...................................601 853-1861
Glinda Davenport, *Owner*
EMP: 14 EST: 1975
SALES (est): 1MM **Privately Held**
SIC: 2721 Magazines: publishing only, not printed on site

(G-4636)
SUNBELT RESOURCES INC
700 Northlake Ave V (39157-1712)
PHONE...................................601 853-8195
Bowman S Tighe Jr, *President*
EMP: 2
SALES (est): 211.8K **Privately Held**
SIC: 1389 Oil consultants

(G-4637)
TARGET DOOR AND SUPPLY INC
208 Industrial Dr (39157-2704)
PHONE...................................601 790-9006
Russell Ingram, *President*
Francis Ingram, *Vice Pres*
EMP: 6
SQ FT: 10,000
SALES: 3MM **Privately Held**
SIC: 2431 Door sashes, wood

(G-4638)
TELLUS OPERATING GROUP LLC (PA)
602 Crescent Pl Ste 100 (39157-8676)
PHONE...................................601 898-7444
Tom Payton, *COO*
Darrell Bracey, *Foreman/Supr*
Tom Wofford, *Finance Mgr*
Phyllis Slawson, *Accountant*
Ken Rushing, *Comptroller*
EMP: 3
SQ FT: 4,500
SALES (est): 60.8MM **Privately Held**
WEB: www.tellusoperating.com
SIC: 1311 Crude petroleum production

(G-4639)
TELPICO LLC
602 Crescent Pl Ste 100 (39157-8676)
PHONE...................................601 898-7444
Richard H Mills Jr, *Mng Member*
EMP: 3 EST: 2003
SALES (est): 466.5K **Privately Held**
SIC: 1382 Oil & gas exploration services

(G-4640)
TENRGYS LLC (PA)
602 Crescent Pl Ste 100 (39157-8676)
PHONE...................................601 898-7444
EMP: 3
SALES (est): 851.3K **Privately Held**
SIC: 1382 Oil & gas exploration services

(G-4641)
TICO INVESTMENTS LLC
Also Called: Pura Vida
131 Canterbury Pl (39157-8732)
PHONE...................................601 559-8161
Danny Bolanos,
EMP: 1 EST: 2015
SALES: 100K **Privately Held**
SIC: 5149 2099 Groceries & related products; food preparations

(G-4642)
TOUBA HAIR BRAIDING MS
1910 E County Line Rd (39157-1921)
PHONE...................................769 524-4641
Ndey Diop, *Principal*
EMP: 2
SALES (est): 132.8K **Privately Held**
SIC: 3999 Hair, dressing of, for the trade

(G-4643)
TRIANGLE FASTENER CORPORATION
854 Centre St (39157-4501)
PHONE...................................601 956-1824
Steve Harper, *Manager*
EMP: 4
SALES (corp-wide): 66.6MM **Privately Held**
SIC: 3965 Fasteners
PA: Triangle Fastener Corporation
1925 Preble Ave
Pittsburgh PA 15233
412 321-5000

(G-4644)
VENABLE GLASS SERVICES LLC (PA)
660 Highway 51 (39157-2127)
PHONE...................................601 605-4443
Roger Venable, *Owner*
Dustin Venable, *Manager*
EMP: 18
SALES (est): 1.9MM **Privately Held**
SIC: 3231 Products of purchased glass

(G-4645)
VINEYARD
801 S Wheatley St Ste E (39157-5196)
PHONE...................................769 251-1322
EMP: 2
SALES (est): 84.3K **Privately Held**
SIC: 2084 Wines

(G-4646)
VT CONSOLIDATED INC (DH)
Also Called: Venture Technologies
860 Centre St (39157-4501)
PHONE...................................601 956-5440
Gerard R Gibert, *CEO*
Win Farnsworth, *President*
Joseph Rucker, *COO*
John Bergeron, *Exec VP*
Mark Frye, *Exec VP*
EMP: 6
SALES (est): 171.6MM
SALES (corp-wide): 79.4MM **Privately Held**
SIC: 7372 Business oriented computer software

(G-4647)
XSPIRE PHARMA LLC
121 Marketridge Dr Ste B (39157-6027)
PHONE...................................870 243-1687
Ford J Mundy,
EMP: 3
SALES (est): 250K **Privately Held**
SIC: 2834 Pharmaceutical preparations

Rienzi
Alcorn County

(G-4648)
C & W EMBROIDERY INC
386 Highway 356 (38865-9706)
P.O. Box 133 (38865-0133)
PHONE...................................662 462-8526
Elizabeth Carnell, *President*
Roye Carnell, *President*
Stephanie L Denley, *Vice Pres*
Edward Parsons, *Info Tech Mgr*
EMP: 40 EST: 1991
SQ FT: 13,500
SALES (est): 3.4MM **Privately Held**
SIC: 2395 Embroidery products, except schiffli machine; embroidery & art needlework

---

(PA)=Parent Co (HQ)=Headquarters (DH)=Div Headquarters
✪ = New Business established in last 2 years

2019 Harris Directory of
Mississippi Manufacturers

167

Rienzi - Alcorn County (G-4649) · GEOGRAPHIC SECTION

(G-4649)
ELIZABETH NEWCOMB
Also Called: A Port In The Storm
458 County Road 550 (38865-9419)
P.O. Box 1498, Booneville (38829-6498)
PHONE................................662 596-1536
Elizabeth Newcomb, *Principal*
Nona Mayhall, *Principal*
John Newcomb, *Principal*
Guy Staggs, *Principal*
EMP: 7
SALES (est): 224.2K **Privately Held**
SIC: 2833 8011 8049 2741 Medicinals &
botanicals; physicians' office, including
specialists; Christian Science practitioner;
miscellaneous publishing; custom sawmill

(G-4650)
LLOYD COX JR
60 County Road 449 (38865-9791)
PHONE................................662 462-5226
Lloyd Cox, *Principal*
EMP: 2
SALES (est): 81.7K **Privately Held**
SIC: 2411 Logging

Ripley
Tippah County

(G-4651)
ALACO OF MISSISSIPPI INC
Also Called: Alaco Sale
151 County Rd 565 (38663)
P.O. Box 284 (38663-0284)
PHONE................................662 837-4041
Sheila Singleton, *President*
Al E Singleton Jr, *General Mgr*
EMP: 25
SALES (est): 3.8MM **Privately Held**
SIC: 3086 Insulation or cushioning mate-
rial, foamed plastic

(G-4652)
ASHLEY FURNITURE INDS INC
15900 Highway 15 N (38663-9208)
PHONE................................662 837-7146
EMP: 200
SALES (corp-wide): 5.2B **Privately Held**
SIC: 2512 2515 Mfg Upholstered House-
hold Furniture Mfg Mattresses/Bedsprings
PA: Ashley Furniture Industries, Inc.
1 Ashley Way
Arcadia WI 54612
608 323-3377

(G-4653)
B & B CONCRETE CO INC
Hwy 15 S (38663)
P.O. Box 596 (38663-0596)
PHONE................................662 837-3221
Perry Ward, *Branch Mgr*
EMP: 8
SALES (corp-wide): 21.1MM **Privately
Held**
SIC: 3273 Ready-mixed concrete
PA: B & B Concrete Co., Inc.
130 N Industrial Rd
Tupelo MS 38801
662 842-6312

(G-4654)
**BILTRITE RIPLEY OPERATIONS
LLC**
Also Called: Warco
16310 Highway 15 N (38663-9213)
PHONE................................662 837-9231
Larry Babcock,
▲ EMP: 1
SALES (est): 11.2MM
SALES (corp-wide): 73.4MM **Privately
Held**
SIC: 3069 3131 3053 2273 Heels, boot
or shoe: rubber, composition or fiber;
soles, boot or shoe: rubber, composition
or fiber; footwear cut stock; gaskets,
packing & sealing devices; carpets & rugs
PA: West American Rubber Company Llc
1337 W Braden Ct
Orange CA 92868
714 532-3355

(G-4655)
CECA LLC
171 County Road 562 (38663-8404)
PHONE................................662 993-8880
Thomas Kreher, *Mng Member*
EMP: 29
SQ FT: 38,000
SALES: 10.2MM **Privately Held**
WEB: www.ceca.org
SIC: 3316 3462 Bars, steel, cold finished,
from purchased hot-rolled; iron & steel
forgings

(G-4656)
ECOWATER SYSTEMS LLC
17471 Highway 15 N (38663-9225)
PHONE................................662 837-9349
Anne Rushing, *Branch Mgr*
EMP: 120
SALES (corp-wide): 225.3B **Publicly
Held**
WEB: www.ecowater.com
SIC: 3589 Water filters & softeners, house-
hold type; sewage & water treatment
equipment; water treatment equipment,
industrial
HQ: Ecowater Systems Llc
1890 Woodlane Dr
Saint Paul MN 55125
651 739-5330

(G-4657)
ELITE ELASTOMERS INC
200 County Rd 565 (38663)
P.O. Box 496 (38663-0496)
PHONE................................662 512-1770
Steve Glidewell, *President*
Jimmy Miller, *Vice Pres*
EMP: 30
SALES: 10MM **Privately Held**
WEB: www.eliteelastomers.com
SIC: 2824 Elastomeric fibers

(G-4658)
**FAIRVIEW PORTABLE
BUILDINGS**
10590 Highway 15 S (38663-2923)
PHONE................................662 837-8709
Keith Thurmond, *President*
Jerry Windham, *Vice Pres*
EMP: 8
SALES (est): 719.6K **Privately Held**
SIC: 3448 Buildings, portable: prefabri-
cated metal
PA: First Monday Trade Day
10590 Highway 15 S
Ripley MS 38663

(G-4659)
FIRST MONDAY TRADE DAY (PA)
Also Called: Fairview Portable Buildings
10590 Highway 15 S (38663-2923)
PHONE................................662 837-4051
Wayne Windham, *President*
Jerry Windham, *Vice Pres*
Cheryl Thurmond, *Admin Sec*
EMP: 9
SALES: 1MM **Privately Held**
SIC: 7389 3448 Flea market; buildings,
portable: prefabricated metal

(G-4660)
G & S AUTO PARTS INC
410 City Ave S (38663-2515)
PHONE................................662 837-9292
Paula Mc Bride, *President*
Barbara Graddy, *Vice Pres*
Mary Smith, *Treasurer*
EMP: 2
SQ FT: 4,800
SALES (est): 408.9K **Privately Held**
SIC: 5013 5531 3599 Automotive sup-
plies & parts; automotive parts; machine
shop, jobbing & repair

(G-4661)
INDUSTRIAL TIMBER LLC
781 County Road 549 (38663-8476)
PHONE................................662 837-3213
Mitch Lambert, *Branch Mgr*
Mike Rook,
EMP: 90
SALES (corp-wide): 72MM **Privately
Held**
SIC: 2493 5031 Reconstituted wood prod-
ucts; lumber, plywood & millwork

PA: Industrial Timber, Llc
6441 Hendry Rd
Charlotte NC 28269
704 919-1215

(G-4662)
JEFFREY ROBERSON
Also Called: Stakes Unlimited
107 Carter Ln (38663-1126)
PHONE................................662 587-1991
EMP: 3 EST: 1992
SQ FT: 2,400
SALES (est): 191.8K **Privately Held**
SIC: 2421 Lumber stacking or sticking

(G-4663)
LIT INDUSTRIES INC
12051 Highway 4 E (38663-9335)
PHONE................................662 993-8088
Thomas Walter, *Manager*
EMP: 2 EST: 2014
SALES (est): 137.4K **Privately Held**
SIC: 3999 Manufacturing industries

(G-4664)
**MISEMER PHARMACEUTICAL
INC**
203 N Main St (38663-2027)
PHONE................................732 762-6577
Arun Kapoor, *President*
EMP: 3
SALES (est): 12.1K **Privately Held**
SIC: 2834 Pharmaceutical preparations

(G-4665)
NORTH MISSISSIPPI TOOL INC
158 Bails Rd (38663-1265)
PHONE................................662 720-9530
George N Thomas, *President*
Ricky Bolen, *Corp Secy*
Jeff White, *Vice Pres*
EMP: 10
SALES (est): 1.3MM **Privately Held**
SIC: 3599 Machine shop, jobbing & repair

(G-4666)
**OIL-DRI PRODUCTION
COMPANY**
1800 City Ave N (38663-1111)
P.O. Box 476 (38663-0476)
PHONE................................662 837-9263
Daniel S Jaffee, *President*
Diego Mejia, *Plant Supt*
Amanda Liles, *Safety Mgr*
Bobby Brannan, *Manager*
Bradley Knight, *Manager*
▲ EMP: 75 EST: 1962
SQ FT: 201,000
SALES (est): 24.9MM
SALES (corp-wide): 266MM **Publicly
Held**
WEB: www.oildri.com
SIC: 2842 3295 Specialty cleaning, pol-
ishes & sanitation goods; clay, ground or
otherwise treated
PA: Oil-Dri Corporation Of America
410 N Michigan Ave Fl 4
Chicago IL 60611
312 321-1515

(G-4667)
ORALIA MEJIA
903 N Main St (38663-1422)
PHONE................................662 512-1906
Oralia Mejia, *Principal*
EMP: 2
SALES (est): 145.7K **Privately Held**
SIC: 3999 Barber & beauty shop equip-
ment

(G-4668)
PRO SIGNS
550 County Road 538 (38663-8864)
PHONE................................662 587-6036
Brandon Jones, *Principal*
EMP: 1 EST: 2017
SALES (est): 46K **Privately Held**
SIC: 3993 Signs & advertising specialties

(G-4669)
**QUALITY GLASS AND
ALUMINUM**
Also Called: Quality Glass Inc-Ripley Miss
1725 City Ave N (38663-1100)
P.O. Box 504 (38663-0504)
PHONE................................662 837-3615
Greg Ward, *President*
David Ward, *Vice Pres*
EMP: 4 EST: 1982
SQ FT: 3,500
SALES (est): 548.2K **Privately Held**
SIC: 3442 5211 5999 5231 Storm doors
or windows, metal; siding; awnings; glass

(G-4670)
ROLISON & SONS LOGGING INC
Also Called: Rolison Logging
101 Walker Dr (38663-1028)
PHONE................................662 837-9066
Gary Rolison Sr, *President*
EMP: 11
SALES (est): 1.2MM **Privately Held**
SIC: 2411 Logging

(G-4671)
ROLISON TIMBER LOGGING ○
1116 City Ave N (38663-1415)
PHONE................................662 993-8115
EMP: 2 EST: 2018
SALES (est): 81.7K **Privately Held**
SIC: 2411 Logging

(G-4672)
SOUTHERN SINTINEL INC (PA)
Also Called: Southern Sentinel
1701 City Ave N (38663-1124)
P.O. Box 558 (38663-0558)
PHONE................................662 837-8111
Albert Thompson, *President*
Brian Roy, *Publisher*
Barbara Steverson, *Vice Pres*
EMP: 15
SQ FT: 5,000
SALES (est): 1MM **Privately Held**
SIC: 2711 Newspapers: publishing only,
not printed on site

(G-4673)
**STERLNG-KNGHT
PHRMCUTICALS LLC**
106 E Mulberry St (38663-1736)
PHONE................................662 661-3232
Arun Kapoor, *President*
EMP: 1
SQ FT: 4,000
SALES (est): 67.1K **Privately Held**
SIC: 2834 Pharmaceutical preparations

(G-4674)
**VICEROY PHARMACEUTICALS
INC**
106 E Mulberry St (38663-1736)
PHONE................................732 762-6577
Arun Kapoor, *President*
EMP: 1
SALES (est): 47.2K **Privately Held**
SIC: 2834 Pharmaceutical preparations

Robinsonville
Tunica County

(G-4675)
GREENTECH AUTOMOTIVE INC
1 Greentech Dr (38664-6002)
PHONE................................662 996-1118
Charles Xiaolin Wang, *CEO*
Paul Ritchie, *Vice Pres*
Gary Yi Tang, *Vice Pres*
Didier Verriest, *Vice Pres*
Michael McCarthy, *Admin Sec*
▲ EMP: 92
SQ FT: 125,000
SALES: 17.1MM
SALES (corp-wide): 18.5MM **Privately
Held**
SIC: 3711 Automobile assembly, including
specialty automobiles
HQ: Greentech Automotive Corp.
21355 Ridgetop Cir # 250
Sterling VA 20166
703 666-9001

2019 Harris Directory of
Mississippi Manufacturers

▲ = Import ▼=Export
◆ =Import/Export

GEOGRAPHIC SECTION

Ruth - Lincoln County (G-4701)

(G-4676)
POWERTRAIN N FEUER AMER INC
2130 Csino Ctr Dr Extnded (38664-9603)
PHONE.....................................662 373-0050
James Howell, *Controller*
Marco Illig, *Director*
▲ EMP: 90
SQ FT: 200,000
SALES (est): 11.3MM
SALES (corp-wide): 149.5MM **Privately Held**
SIC: 3599 3714 Crankshafts & camshafts, machining; crankshaft assemblies, motor vehicle
PA: Feuer Powertrain Gmbh & Co.Kg
Rothenburgstr. 27
Nordhausen 99734
363 147-00

(G-4677)
RICHARD MELOS
Also Called: Melos Manufacturing
11562 Old Highway 61 N (38664-9199)
PHONE.....................................434 401-9496
Richard Melos, *Owner*
EMP: 2
SALES (est): 146K **Privately Held**
SIC: 3694 7389 Engine electrical equipment;

(G-4678)
SXP SCHULZ XTRUDED PRODUCTS LP (PA)
1001 Schulz Blvd (38664-7016)
P.O. Box 2178, Tunica (38676-2178)
PHONE.....................................662 373-4114
Rainer Floeth, *CEO*
Dave Calhoun, *General Mgr*
Heike Ballik, *COO*
Bobbie Hood, *Production*
Melissa Mire, *Production*
▲ EMP: 108
SQ FT: 1,000
SALES (est): 48.9MM **Privately Held**
SIC: 3312 Pipes, iron & steel

Rolling Fork
Sharkey County

(G-4679)
AUTOMATED TECH & ASSEMBLY LLC
316 Maple St (39159-5056)
PHONE.....................................662 213-9352
Curtis Johnson,
Edward Bronston,
Teresa Graham,
EMP: 5
SALES (est): 162.6K **Privately Held**
SIC: 4226 3714 7389 Special warehousing & storage; motor vehicle body components & frame;

(G-4680)
DEER CREEK PUBLISHING COMPANY
Also Called: Deer Creek Pilot
145 N First St (39159-2749)
P.O. Box 398 (39159-0398)
PHONE.....................................662 873-4354
H Ray Mosby, *Owner*
EMP: 2
SALES (est): 153.1K **Privately Held**
SIC: 2711 Commercial printing & newspaper publishing combined; newspapers, publishing & printing

(G-4681)
JESSICA WILLIAMS
1519 Bear Lake Rd (39159-4911)
PHONE.....................................601 738-0090
Jessica Williams, *Owner*
EMP: 1
SALES (est): 35.3K **Privately Held**
SIC: 2741 5111 Guides: publishing only, not printed on site; patterns, paper: publishing only, not printed on site; writing paper

(G-4682)
SERVICE LUMBER COMPANY INC
20558 Highway 61 (39159-5014)
P.O. Box 457 (39159-0457)
PHONE.....................................662 873-4334
Thad C Virden, *President*
Dora R Alexander, *Vice Pres*
EMP: 17
SQ FT: 15,000
SALES: 3.1MM
SALES (corp-wide): 2.9MM **Privately Held**
SIC: 5211 5031 3273 Planing mill products & lumber; lumber, plywood & millwork; ready-mixed concrete
PA: Service Lumber Holding Corp.
20558 Highway 61
Rolling Fork MS 39159
662 873-4334

(G-4683)
SERVICE LUMBER HOLDING CORP (PA)
20558 Highway 61 (39159-5014)
P.O. Box 457 (39159-0457)
PHONE.....................................662 873-4334
Thad C Virden, *President*
Nancy Virden, *Admin Sec*
EMP: 4
SALES: 2.9MM **Privately Held**
SIC: 5211 5031 3273 Lumber & other building materials; lumber, plywood & millwork; ready-mixed concrete

---

Rose Hill
Jasper County

(G-4684)
CHATHAM ENTERPRISES INC
Hwy 18 W (39356)
P.O. Box 81 (39356-0081)
PHONE.....................................601 727-4951
Charles Chatham, *President*
EMP: 25
SQ FT: 9,600
SALES (est): 4.7MM **Privately Held**
SIC: 3448 Prefabricated metal buildings

(G-4685)
T AND S DEER PROCESSING
4419 County Road 31 (39356-5423)
PHONE.....................................601 727-3725
Suzanne Magill, *Owner*
EMP: 6
SALES (est): 160K **Privately Held**
SIC: 2011 Meat packing plants

Rosedale
Bolivar County

(G-4686)
AXEL AMERICAS LLC
Also Called: Jesco Resources
150 Russell Crutcher Rd S (38769-5503)
P.O. Box 308 (38769-0308)
PHONE.....................................662 759-6808
Gayle Dill, *Branch Mgr*
EMP: 18
SALES (corp-wide): 352.2K **Privately Held**
WEB: www.jescolube.com
SIC: 2992 Brake fluid (hydraulic): made from purchased materials
HQ: Axel Americas, Llc
1440 Erie St
Kansas City MO 64116
816 471-4590

(G-4687)
CIVES CORPORATION
Also Called: Mid-South Division
219 Port Terminal Rd S (38769-5500)
P.O. Box 609 (38769-0609)
PHONE.....................................662 759-6265
William R Reed Jr, *Manager*
Jim Maloney, *Manager*
EMP: 150

SALES (corp-wide): 651.3MM **Privately Held**
WEB: www.cives.com
SIC: 3441 Fabricated structural metal
PA: Cives Corporation
3700 Mansell Rd Ste 500
Alpharetta GA 30022
770 993-4424

Roxie
Franklin County

(G-4688)
ABC SCRITY FBRCTION SLTION LLC
9920 Highway 84 W (39661-4532)
PHONE.....................................601 828-9010
Joseph Carbery, *Principal*
EMP: 1 EST: 2016
SALES (est): 42.2K **Privately Held**
SIC: 3999 Manufacturing industries

(G-4689)
FISHBOWL INTERNATIONAL INC
3218 Bdford Tillman Rd Nw (39661)
PHONE.....................................601 384-0219
Cassandra Vaughn, *Exec Dir*
EMP: 2 EST: 2015
SALES (est): 91.8K **Privately Held**
SIC: 2741 Miscellaneous publishing

(G-4690)
K & J LOGGING INC
10569 Highway 33 S (39661-4062)
PHONE.....................................601 639-4607
Darcy Kermit Shell, *President*
EMP: 4
SALES (est): 441.4K **Privately Held**
SIC: 2411 Logging camps & contractors

(G-4691)
LARRY D WALLACE
782 Martin Bonds Rd Nw (39661-7158)
PHONE.....................................601 384-4409
Larry Wallace, *Principal*
EMP: 1
SALES (est): 72K **Privately Held**
SIC: 7692 7389 Welding repair;

(G-4692)
MCDANIEL LOGGING CO INC
6603 Highway 33 S (39661-4043)
PHONE.....................................601 322-7701
Dennis McDaniel, *President*
EMP: 5
SALES (est): 703.7K **Privately Held**
SIC: 2411 Logging camps & contractors

(G-4693)
RARE STUDIOS PUBLISHING
194 Davis Hill Rd Nw (39661-7177)
PHONE.....................................770 316-0683
Antoine Manning, *Manager*
EMP: 1 EST: 2017
SALES (est): 41.3K **Privately Held**
SIC: 2741 Miscellaneous publishing

(G-4694)
SMITH BROTHERS LOGGING INC
5769 Highway 33 S (39661-4057)
PHONE.....................................601 322-7362
Alfred Smith, *President*
Ellis Smith, *Exec Dir*
EMP: 14
SALES (est): 1.9MM **Privately Held**
SIC: 2411 Logging camps & contractors

Ruleville
Sunflower County

(G-4695)
BAGIT SYSTEM INC
301 W Sunflower St (38771-3823)
P.O. Box 307 (38771-0307)
PHONE.....................................662 756-2600
Henry Pani, *Manager*
EMP: 28

SALES (corp-wide): 5.6MM **Privately Held**
WEB: www.bagitsystem.com
SIC: 2673 Plastic bags: made from purchased materials; trash bags (plastic film): made from purchased materials
PA: Bagit System, Inc.
459 Sw 9th St
Dundee OR 97115
503 538-8180

(G-4696)
CHAMPION CHEMICAL COMPANY LLC
802 N Oak Ave (38771-3215)
PHONE.....................................601 720-8908
William Jeffrey Champion,
EMP: 2
SALES (est): 106K **Privately Held**
SIC: 3559 Chemical machinery & equipment

(G-4697)
OVERSTREET WELDING LLC
309 Sylvia St (38771-4117)
PHONE.....................................662 719-1269
William Overstreet, *Principal*
EMP: 1
SALES (est): 28.4K **Privately Held**
SIC: 7692 Welding repair

(G-4698)
PRECISION/DELTA CORPORATION
205 W Floyce St (38771-3402)
P.O. Box 128 (38771-0128)
PHONE.....................................662 756-2810
Joe Tranum Jr, *President*
Judy Tranum, *Corp Secy*
Patricia Lott, *Vice Pres*
EMP: 16
SQ FT: 12,000
SALES (est): 5.8MM **Privately Held**
WEB: www.precisiondelta.com
SIC: 3482 Small arms ammunition

(G-4699)
RULEVILLE MANUFACTURING CO INC
902 N Oak Ave (38771-3217)
P.O. Box 397 (38771-0397)
PHONE.....................................662 756-4363
Steve Hardman, *General Mgr*
EMP: 80
SALES (corp-wide): 17.7MM **Privately Held**
WEB: www.spiewak.com
SIC: 2329 2326 Men's & boys' sportswear & athletic clothing; men's & boys' work clothing
PA: Ruleville Manufacturing Company, Incorporated
469 Fashion Ave Fl 10
New York NY

Ruth
Lincoln County

(G-4700)
DENBURY ONSHORE LLC
4047 Shell Oil Rd (39662-9545)
PHONE.....................................601 276-2147
Gareth Roberts, *Branch Mgr*
EMP: 48
SALES (corp-wide): 1.4B **Publicly Held**
WEB: www.denbury.com
SIC: 3731 1382 Drilling & production platforms, floating (oil & gas); oil & gas exploration services
HQ: Denbury Onshore, Llc
5320 Legacy Dr
Plano TX 75024
972 673-2000

(G-4701)
GREER ENVIRONMENTAL SERVICES
3955 Primitive Dr Se (39662-9732)
PHONE.....................................601 734-2883
Robin S Greer, *President*
Wayne Greer, *Vice Pres*
EMP: 3

(PA)=Parent Co (HQ)=Headquarters (DH)=Div Headquarters
✪ = New Business established in last 2 years

2019 Harris Directory of
Mississippi Manufacturers

169

Ruth - Lincoln County (G-4702)

GEOGRAPHIC SECTION

SQ FT: 3,000
SALES (est): 311.9K **Privately Held**
WEB: www.ebac2000.com
SIC: 8748 3564 Environmental consultant; dust or fume collecting equipment, industrial

(G-4702)
ISAIAH ARD TIMBER INC
3622 Junction Ln Se (39662-9749)
PHONE..................................601 833-9359
EMP: 20
SALES (est): 1.8MM **Privately Held**
SIC: 2411 Logging

Sallis
Attala County

(G-4703)
OXFORD FALLS
9465 Highway 14 (39160-5132)
P.O. Box 2424, Starkville (39760-2424)
PHONE..................................662 323-9696
Kathy Mosier, *Owner*
EMP: 2
SALES: 125K **Privately Held**
SIC: 2035 2099 Pickles, sauces & salad dressings; food preparations

(G-4704)
RAYMOND GRANGER
2309 Attala Road 4237 (39160-5587)
PHONE..................................662 289-2502
Raymond Granger, *Principal*
EMP: 3
SALES (est): 246.1K **Privately Held**
SIC: 2411 Logging

Saltillo
Lee County

(G-4705)
1810 VAPORS
174 County Road 1810 (38866-9336)
PHONE..................................662 523-7924
Terrin Snipes, *Co-Owner*
EMP: 2
SALES (est): 88.3K **Privately Held**
SIC: 3634 Vaporizers, electric: household

(G-4706)
B & B CONCRETE CO INC
Hwy 45 N (38866)
P.O. Box 407, Tupelo (38802-0407)
PHONE..................................662 869-1927
David Brevard, *President*
EMP: 25
SALES (corp-wide): 21.1MM **Privately Held**
SIC: 3273 Ready-mixed concrete
PA: B & B Concrete Co., Inc.
130 N Industrial Rd
Tupelo MS 38801
662 842-6312

(G-4707)
BAUHAUS FURNITURE GROUP LLC
1 Bauhaus Dr (38866-6974)
PHONE..................................662 869-2664
James Al Wiygul, *CEO*
Britt Allred, *President*
Louis M Riccio Jr, *Vice Pres*
Blair Taylor, *CFO*
Otis S Sawyer, *Director*
◆ **EMP:** 500
SQ FT: 155,000
SALES (est): 86.9MM **Privately Held**
WEB: www.bauhaususa.com
SIC: 2512 Upholstered household furniture

(G-4708)
BOXCAR FLOORING COMPANY LLC
2673 Highway 145 (38866-9771)
PHONE..................................662 871-1417
Brian Martin,
Chuck Hopkins,
Will Troxler,
EMP: 2

SALES (est): 106.2K **Privately Held**
SIC: 1771 2273 Flooring contractor; carpets & rugs

(G-4709)
BROCK OUTDOORS
1026 County Road 821 (38866-8800)
PHONE..................................662 255-1121
Sandra Brock, *Owner*
EMP: 6
SALES: 55K **Privately Held**
SIC: 3949 7381 Game calls; guard services

(G-4710)
C & S MARBLE CO
918 Dixie Creek Rd (38866-9306)
PHONE..................................662 844-6873
Billy W Scruggs, *Owner*
EMP: 3
SQ FT: 5,000
SALES (est): 159.7K **Privately Held**
SIC: 3281 5211 Marble, building: cut & shaped; counter tops

(G-4711)
ELLIS CERTIFIED WELDING
676 Pulltight Rd (38866)
PHONE..................................662 869-2295
Mike Alis, *Owner*
EMP: 1
SALES (est): 445.5K **Privately Held**
SIC: 7692 Welding repair

(G-4712)
INDUSTRIAL CLEANING SVCS LLC
101 County Road 461 (38866-6824)
P.O. Box 597 (38866-0597)
PHONE..................................662 397-6735
Richard Finley,
Jack Quartaro Jr,
EMP: 14
SALES (est): 1.2MM **Privately Held**
SIC: 2842 7389 Specialty cleaning preparations;

(G-4713)
INDUSTRIAL TIMBER LLC
200 Mccomb Ave (38866)
PHONE..................................662 346-4488
Ralph Riggs, *Branch Mgr*
EMP: 22
SALES (corp-wide): 72MM **Privately Held**
SIC: 2493 5031 Reconstituted wood products; lumber, plywood & millwork
PA: Industrial Timber, Llc
6441 Hendry Rd
Charlotte NC 28269
704 919-1215

(G-4714)
JACKSON WELDING LLC
234 County Road 1806 (38866-9323)
PHONE..................................662 680-4325
EMP: 8
SALES (est): 88.7K **Privately Held**
SIC: 7692 Welding repair

(G-4715)
KING MFG
341 County Road 521 (38866-9576)
PHONE..................................662 869-2069
Tami King,
EMP: 3 **EST:** 2015
SALES (est): 293.2K **Privately Held**
SIC: 3999 Atomizers, toiletry

(G-4716)
KS TOBACCO & BREW
2546 Highway 145 (38866-6981)
PHONE..................................662 869-0086
Nadia Piatt, *CEO*
Wayne Piatt, *Vice Pres*
EMP: 2
SALES: 700K **Privately Held**
SIC: 2111 Cigarettes

(G-4717)
LEGGETT & PLATT INCORPORATED
Also Called: Omega Motion
241 Jamie Whitten Blvd (38866-8701)
PHONE..................................662 869-1060

Rick Lake, *President*
Jason Bryant, *Opers Staff*
Billie J Stewart, *Officer*
EMP: 300
SALES (corp-wide): 4.2B **Publicly Held**
SIC: 2515 Mattresses & bedsprings
PA: Leggett & Platt, Incorporated
1 Leggett Rd
Carthage MO 64836
417 358-8131

(G-4718)
MSI INC
688 Pulltight Rd (38866-6922)
P.O. Box 1031 (38866-1031)
PHONE..................................662 401-9781
Jimmy Glover, *President*
EMP: 4
SALES (est): 502.2K **Privately Held**
SIC: 3599 Machine & other job shop work

(G-4719)
PRECISION BLADES INC
120 Bauhaus Dr (38866-9104)
P.O. Box 1408 (38866-1408)
PHONE..................................662 869-1034
Michael Davis, *President*
Hugh Davis, *Vice Pres*
◆ **EMP:** 15
SQ FT: 15,000
SALES (est): 2.9MM **Privately Held**
WEB: www.precisionblades.net
SIC: 3425 Saw blades & handsaws

(G-4720)
SALTILLO GUNTOWN GAZETTE
2686 Highway 145 (38866-6941)
P.O. Box 647 (38866-0647)
PHONE..................................662 869-8380
Sam Grisham, *Owner*
EMP: 2
SALES (est): 101.3K **Privately Held**
SIC: 2711 Newspapers, publishing & printing

(G-4721)
SYNTRON MATERIAL HANDLING LLC (HQ)
2730 Highway 145 (38866-6814)
PHONE..................................662 869-5711
Andy Blanchard, *President*
Don Mann, *General Mgr*
Dean Mitchell, *Dean*
Rob Drew, *Vice Pres*
Ronnie Dunaway, *Maint Spvr*
◆ **EMP:** 153
SALES (est): 101.4MM
SALES (corp-wide): 633.7MM **Publicly Held**
SIC: 3532 Mining machinery
PA: Kadant Inc.
1 Technology Park Dr # 210
Westford MA 01886
978 776-2000

(G-4722)
SYNTRON MTL HDLG GROUP LLC
2730 Highway 145 (38866-6814)
PHONE..................................662 869-5711
Jonathan W Painter, *President*
EMP: 250
SALES (est): 7.8MM
SALES (corp-wide): 633.7MM **Publicly Held**
SIC: 3532 Mining machinery
PA: Kadant Inc.
1 Technology Park Dr # 210
Westford MA 01886
978 776-2000

(G-4723)
WESTROCK CP LLC
Smurfit-Stone Container
324 Turner Indus Pk Rd (38866-8700)
PHONE..................................662 869-5771
Steve White, *General Mgr*
EMP: 196
SALES (corp-wide): 16.2B **Publicly Held**
WEB: www.sto.com
SIC: 2653 Boxes, corrugated: made from purchased materials
HQ: Westrock Cp, Llc
1000 Abernathy Rd
Atlanta GA 30328

(G-4724)
WICKS N CANDLE COMPANY
703 Pulltight Rd (38866-9179)
PHONE..................................662 891-4237
Jim Troxler, *Principal*
EMP: 1
SALES (est): 39.6K **Privately Held**
SIC: 3999 Candles

Sandersville
Jones County

(G-4725)
HALLIBURTON ENERGY SERVICES
Also Called: Halliburton Service Division
1384 Sndrsville Sharon Rd (39477)
P.O. Box 622 (39477-0622)
PHONE..................................601 649-9290
Fax: 601 649-3077
EMP: 70 **Publicly Held**
SIC: 1389 Oil/Gas Field Services
HQ: Halliburton Energy Services, Inc.
10200 Bellaire Blvd
Houston TX 77032
713 839-3950

(G-4726)
WCS OIL & GAS CORPORATION
Also Called: Eagle Oil & Gas
141 Hale Rd (39477)
PHONE..................................601 787-4565
Danny Riley, *Manager*
EMP: 1
SALES (est): 94K
SALES (corp-wide): 4.5MM **Privately Held**
SIC: 1311 Crude petroleum production
PA: Wcs Oil & Gas Corporation
4807 W Lovers Ln
Dallas TX 75209
214 357-9116

Sandy Hook
Marion County

(G-4727)
DIXIE MAT LLC
216 Herring Rd (39478-9680)
PHONE..................................601 876-2427
Jonathan Duhon, *Finance*
Sam Herring, *Sales Associate*
Jason Dunn, *Mng Member*
Adam Wilson, *Manager*
John Morris, *Supervisor*
EMP: 12
SALES (est): 925.3K **Privately Held**
SIC: 2273 Carpets & rugs

(G-4728)
FORBES MEAT PROCESSORS
Hurricane Creek Rd (39478)
PHONE..................................601 736-6992
Frank Forbes, *Owner*
EMP: 4
SALES: 300K **Privately Held**
SIC: 2011 Meat packing plants

(G-4729)
FORTENBERRYS MEAT PROCESSING
39 Enoch Hines Rd (39478-9631)
PHONE..................................601 876-2291
John Fortenberry, *Owner*
EMP: 2
SALES (est): 65K **Privately Held**
SIC: 2011 Meat packing plants

(G-4730)
JONES READY MIX LLC
216 Herring Rd (39478-9680)
P.O. Box 636, Foxworth (39483-0636)
PHONE..................................601 222-1919
Jeremy Jones,
EMP: 7
SALES: 989K **Privately Held**
SIC: 3273 Ready-mixed concrete

2019 Harris Directory of
Mississippi Manufacturers

▲ = Import ▼=Export
◆ =Import/Export

170

GEOGRAPHIC SECTION

Saucier - Harrison County (G-4762)

(G-4731)
SANDY HOOK MACHINE SHOP INC
283 Highway 48 E (39478-9449)
P.O. Box 38 (39478-0038)
PHONE..................................601 736-4041
Wayne Herring, *President*
EMP: 14
SQ FT: 160,000
SALES: 2MM **Privately Held**
SIC: 3599 1799 Machine shop, jobbing & repair; welding on site

Sarah
Panola County

(G-4732)
BARBERS TIMBER & LOGGING
14224 Brownsferry Rd (38665-3009)
PHONE..................................662 382-7649
Randell Barber, *Owner*
EMP: 9
SALES (est): 428.7K **Privately Held**
SIC: 2411 7359 Logging camps & contractors; industrial truck rental

(G-4733)
CUSTOM ARCHITECTURAL MILLWORK
2016 Egypt Creek Rd (38665-4174)
PHONE..................................662 562-7011
John Lake, *President*
EMP: 2
SALES (est): 150K **Privately Held**
SIC: 2431 Millwork

(G-4734)
GOAT RANCHER
731 Sandy Branch Rd (38665-3013)
PHONE..................................662 562-9529
Terry Hankins, *Owner*
Yvonne Zweede, *Author*
EMP: 2 **EST:** 1996
SALES (est): 124.5K **Privately Held**
WEB: www.goatrancher.com
SIC: 2721 Magazines: publishing only, not printed on site

(G-4735)
PINK STAR INDUSTRIES
1386 Rader Creek Rd (38665-3184)
PHONE..................................702 546-9883
EMP: 2
SALES (est): 109.2K **Privately Held**
SIC: 3999 Manufacturing industries

(G-4736)
STRAYHORN TRUCKING & CNSTR LLC
1250 Matthews Rd (38665-3515)
PHONE..................................662 560-6516
Tracy Matthews,
EMP: 4
SALES (est): 881.6K **Privately Held**
SIC: 1442 Construction sand & gravel

(G-4737)
WHITNEY WHITEHEAD
127 Ashley Way (38665)
PHONE..................................662 380-0614
EMP: 1
SALES (est): 35K **Privately Held**
SIC: 2099 7389 Ready-to-eat meals, salads & sandwiches;

Sardis
Panola County

(G-4738)
DELTA PETROLEUM SERVICE INC
651 E Lee St (38666-1200)
PHONE..................................662 487-1701
Mustafa Zayed, *President*
EMP: 3
SALES (est): 99.1K **Privately Held**
SIC: 1381 Drilling oil & gas wells

(G-4739)
FLETCHER PRINTING & OFFICE SUP
105 S Pocahontas St (38666-1624)
PHONE..................................662 487-3200
Chrisler Fletcher, *Owner*
EMP: 1 **EST:** 1855
SQ FT: 6,000
SALES: 50K **Privately Held**
SIC: 5943 2752 Office forms & supplies; commercial printing, offset

(G-4740)
HONNOLL SAND & GRAVEL LLC
3013 Viney Creek Rd (38666-1537)
PHONE..................................662 487-3854
David Honnoll, *Manager*
EMP: 2
SALES (est): 72.6K **Privately Held**
SIC: 1442 Construction sand & gravel

(G-4741)
INCA PRESSWOOD-PALLETS LTD
2333 S Frontage Rd (38666-2132)
P.O. Box 129 (38666-0129)
PHONE..................................662 487-1016
EMP: 1
SALES (corp-wide): 5.6MM **Privately Held**
SIC: 2448 Wood pallets & skids
PA: Inca Presswood-Pallets, Ltd.
3005 Progress St
Dover OH 44622
330 343-3361

(G-4742)
INCA PRESSWOOD-PALLETS LTD
2333 S Frontage Sardis In (38666)
P.O. Box 129 (38666-0129)
PHONE..................................662 487-1016
Dale Hart, *Branch Mgr*
EMP: 25
SALES (corp-wide): 5.6MM **Privately Held**
SIC: 5031 2448 Pallets, wood; wood pallets & skids
PA: Inca Presswood-Pallets, Ltd.
3005 Progress St
Dover OH 44622
330 343-3361

(G-4743)
PLEASANT GROVE SOAPS
9360 Highway 315 (38666-2574)
PHONE..................................662 487-3050
Deborah Robinson, *Owner*
EMP: 1
SALES (est): 80.7K **Privately Held**
WEB: www.pleasantgrovesoaps.com
SIC: 2841 Soap: granulated, liquid, cake, flaked or chip

(G-4744)
SECURE SHRED LLC
5850 Barnacre Rd (38666-5270)
PHONE..................................662 563-5008
Wanda Charmichael,
EMP: 2
SALES (corp-wide): 30K **Privately Held**
SIC: 3589 Shredders, industrial & commercial
PA: Secure Shred Llc
36124 Highway 315
Batesville MS 38606
662 563-5008

(G-4745)
SWEETEES
101 Sycamore St (38666-2016)
PHONE..................................662 404-1966
Chelsea Anderson, *Principal*
EMP: 3
SALES (est): 112.1K **Privately Held**
SIC: 2759 Screen printing

(G-4746)
UNITED COMB & NOVELTY CORP
Also Called: United Plastics
1052 Industrial Park Rd (38666-2138)
PHONE..................................662 487-9248
Phil Waldrup, *Principal*
EMP: 14
SALES (corp-wide): 33.4MM **Privately Held**
SIC: 3089 Molding primary plastic
PA: United Comb & Novelty Corp
33 Patriots Cir
Leominster MA 01453
978 537-2096

(G-4747)
UNITED SOLUTIONS INC
100 Rainwater St (38666-1128)
PHONE..................................662 487-0068
◆ **EMP:** 11
SALES (est): 1.9MM **Privately Held**
SIC: 2673 Food storage & trash bags (plastic)

Saucier
Harrison County

(G-4748)
A & W MARBLE INC
19290 Frontier Rd (39574-8506)
PHONE..................................228 832-5037
Stanley C Whitfield, *President*
EMP: 3
SALES: 250K **Privately Held**
SIC: 5032 3281 Marble building stone; marble, building: cut & shaped

(G-4749)
AT HOME EMBROIDERY
19461 Dixie Rd (39574-9499)
PHONE..................................228 365-4034
EMP: 1
SALES (est): 31.2K **Privately Held**
SIC: 2395 Embroidery & art needlework

(G-4750)
COX WORKS
19202 Frontier Rd (39574-8506)
PHONE..................................228 236-8402
Elaine Cox, *Principal*
EMP: 1
SALES (est): 54.1K **Privately Held**
SIC: 2431 Millwork

(G-4751)
CWG WELDING
19487 Wallace Way (39574-5403)
PHONE..................................228 539-4121
EMP: 1 **EST:** 2010
SALES (est): 55K **Privately Held**
SIC: 7692 Welding Repair

(G-4752)
DELTA INDUSTRIES INC
17478 Nobles Rd (39574-6077)
PHONE..................................228 539-9333
Jerry Gable, *Branch Mgr*
EMP: 2
SALES (corp-wide): 100.3MM **Privately Held**
SIC: 3273 Ready-mixed concrete
PA: Delta Industries, Inc.
100 W Woodrow Wilson Ave
Jackson MS 39213
601 354-3801

(G-4753)
DISON ELECTRICAL SOLUTIONS LLC
18311 Shaw Rd (39574-9566)
PHONE..................................228 234-7767
William Dison, *President*
EMP: 5
SALES (est): 228.6K **Privately Held**
SIC: 3679 Harness assemblies for electronic use: wire or cable

(G-4754)
HICKORY CREEK INC
21595 Yankee Town Rd (39574-8238)
PHONE..................................228 832-2649
Jerry Goff, *President*
Annette Goff, *Treasurer*
Sherwood Goff, *Admin Sec*
EMP: 3
SALES (est): 240K **Privately Held**
SIC: 3949 5941 Archery equipment, general; archery supplies

(G-4755)
HILLBILLY WINES LLC
21310 Yankee Town Rd (39574-9136)
PHONE..................................228 234-4411
Brenda Lee Simoneaux, *President*
EMP: 1
SALES (est): 46.6K **Privately Held**
SIC: 2084 Wines

(G-4756)
ILLUSTRATIVE INK LLC
1844 Blaylock Rd (39574)
PHONE..................................228 354-9559
Diana Punzo,
EMP: 6
SQ FT: 2,650
SALES (est): 331.1K **Privately Held**
SIC: 2741 Posters: publishing & printing

(G-4757)
LARKOWSKI INC
Also Called: Mike's Heating & AC
19486 Borzik Rd (39574-9699)
PHONE..................................601 928-9501
Michael Larkowski, *President*
Diana B Larkowski, *Shareholder*
EMP: 5
SALES (est): 512.1K **Privately Held**
SIC: 1711 3444 Warm air heating & air conditioning contractor; sheet metalwork

(G-4758)
MARINE SERVICE SOLUTIONS
17042 E Adams Rd Lot 4 (39574-8175)
PHONE..................................601 658-0772
Jeffrey Compton, *Owner*
EMP: 2 **EST:** 2016
SQ FT: 1,200
SALES (est): 86K **Privately Held**
SIC: 3731 Shipbuilding & repairing

(G-4759)
MCMURTRYS AUTOMOTIVE MCH SVC
19076 Pete Hickman Rd (39574-9462)
PHONE..................................228 832-8335
David McMurtry, *President*
Bonnie McMurtry, *Treasurer*
EMP: 3
SALES (est): 300K **Privately Held**
WEB: www.mcmurtrys.com
SIC: 3599 7549 5531 Machine shop, jobbing & repair; lubrication service, automotive; speed shops, including race car supplies

(G-4760)
PALMER TOOL LLC
Also Called: Palmer Companies, The
24125 Hwy 49 S (39574)
P.O. Box 340 (39574-0340)
PHONE..................................228 832-0805
Eddie Haynes, *General Mgr*
EMP: 20
SALES (corp-wide): 27.1MM **Privately Held**
WEB: www.palmertool.com
SIC: 3599 3444 Machine shop, jobbing & repair; sheet metalwork
PA: Palmer Tool, Llc
3385 Highway 70 E
Camden TN 38320
731 584-2265

(G-4761)
PRECISION IRON WORKS
23213 Road 508 (39574-8577)
PHONE..................................228 341-0736
Marlin Ladner, *Owner*
EMP: 1
SALES (est): 41.1K **Privately Held**
SIC: 7692 Welding repair

(G-4762)
RUFROGGY MONOGRAMS
18205 Prairie Dr (39574-4409)
PHONE..................................228 547-7060
EMP: 1
SALES (est): 43.9K **Privately Held**
SIC: 2395 Embroidery & art needlework

(PA)=Parent Co (HQ)=Headquarters (DH)=Div Headquarters
✿ = New Business established in last 2 years

2019 Harris Directory of
Mississippi Manufacturers

Saucier - Harrison County (G-4763)
GEOGRAPHIC SECTION

(G-4763)
SEAMLESS ONE SEAMLES GUTTERS
23044 N Carr Bridge Rd (39574-9338)
P.O. Box 6236, Diberville (39540-6236)
PHONE..................228 832-0516
Todd Fayaral, *Owner*
EMP: 2 EST: 2001
SALES (est): 184K **Privately Held**
SIC: 1761 3448 Gutter & downspout contractor; screen enclosures

(G-4764)
SHAW SIGNS LLC
21797 Ridgeview Dr (39574-6066)
PHONE..................228 224-4971
Algernon Shaw, *Principal*
EMP: 2
SALES (est): 157.3K **Privately Held**
SIC: 3993 Signs & advertising specialties

(G-4765)
SIGN SOLUTIONS OF SAUCIER
13056 Teague Rd (39574-8337)
PHONE..................228 265-4325
EMP: 2
SALES (est): 140K **Privately Held**
SIC: 3993 Mfg Signs/Advertising Specialties

(G-4766)
SOUTHERN SEWAGE SYSTEMS
23018 Highway 49 (39574-9158)
PHONE..................228 832-7400
Joe Nahlik, *Owner*
EMP: 3
SALES (est): 190K **Privately Held**
SIC: 3272 1623 5999 3589 Tanks, concrete; water & sewer line construction; plumbing & heating supplies; sewage treatment equipment; septic system construction

(G-4767)
TOP OF LINE WOODWORK
17477 Robinwood Dr (39574-9590)
PHONE..................228 669-3363
EMP: 2
SALES (est): 154.6K **Privately Held**
SIC: 2431 Millwork

(G-4768)
WEEMS INDUSTRIES LLC
20053 Yaupon Dr (39574-8266)
PHONE..................228 382-4423
Sherman Weems, *Principal*
EMP: 1
SALES (est): 44.5K **Privately Held**
SIC: 3999 Manufacturing industries

Schlater
Leflore County

(G-4769)
BROOKS FARMS INC
28052 County Road 559 (38952-3010)
PHONE..................662 299-8780
Greg Carr, *President*
EMP: 3
SALES: 15K **Privately Held**
SIC: 3523 Driers (farm): grain, hay & seed

Scooba
Kemper County

(G-4770)
ELECTRIC MILLS WOOD PRSV LLC
13539 Highway 45 (39358-7611)
P.O. Box 1496, Tacoma WA (98401-1496)
PHONE..................662 476-8000
Corry Mc Farland, *Mng Member*
EMP: 2
SALES (est): 165.2K **Privately Held**
SIC: 2491 Wood preserving

(G-4771)
MCFARLAND CASCADE HOLDINGS INC
13539 Highway 45 (39358-7611)
PHONE..................662 476-8000
Kay Ratcliff, *Manager*
EMP: 30
SALES (corp-wide): 1.6B **Privately Held**
SIC: 2491 2411 Wood products, creosoted; logging
HQ: Mcfarland Cascade Holdings, Inc.
1640 E Marc St
Tacoma WA 98421
253 572-3033

(G-4772)
REED LOGGING INC
231 Reed Rd (39358-7562)
PHONE..................662 793-4951
Mike Reed, *President*
Jean Reed, *Admin Sec*
EMP: 6
SALES (est): 826.7K **Privately Held**
SIC: 2411 4212 Logging; local trucking, without storage

Sebastopol
Scott County

(G-4773)
5M ENTERPRISES LLC
193 North St (39359-6600)
PHONE..................601 416-0210
Sara Marshall,
EMP: 4
SALES (est): 206.7K **Privately Held**
SIC: 3669 1795 Railroad signaling devices, electric; demolition, buildings & other structures

(G-4774)
MAXIM HOLDING COMPANY INC (PA)
Also Called: Maxim Manufacturing
16741 Highway 21 S (39359)
P.O. Box 110 (39359-0110)
PHONE..................601 625-7471
Albert G Easom Jr, *President*
Sarah Easom, *Corp Secy*
Albert G Easom III, *Vice Pres*
◆ EMP: 50
SQ FT: 100,000
SALES (est): 8.2MM **Privately Held**
WEB: www.maximmfg.com
SIC: 3524 Rototillers (garden machinery)

(G-4775)
PECO FOODS INC
Hwy 21 (39359)
P.O. Box 319 (39359-0319)
PHONE..................601 625-7819
Keith Tollett, *Manager*
EMP: 500
SALES (corp-wide): 1B **Privately Held**
SIC: 2015 Poultry slaughtering & processing
HQ: Peco Foods Inc.
247 2nd Ave Se
Gordo AL 35466
205 364-7121

Seminary
Covington County

(G-4776)
DEEP SOUTH FIRE TRUCKS INC (PA)
2342 Hwy 49 N (39479)
P.O. Box 293 (39479-0293)
PHONE..................601 722-4166
Charles R Barber, *President*
Richard Ellis, *President*
Christopher M Taormina, *Corp Secy*
EMP: 56
SALES (est): 10MM **Privately Held**
SIC: 3711 Fire department vehicles (motor vehicles), assembly of

(G-4777)
EAKES NURSERY MATERIALS INC
249 Bethel Church Rd (39479-9392)
PHONE..................601 722-4797
Pamela Eakes, *President*
William Eakes, *Vice Pres*
EMP: 9
SALES (est): 1.4MM **Privately Held**
SIC: 5193 2875 5191 Nursery stock; fertilizers, mixing only; greenhouse equipment & supplies

(G-4778)
ELLIS DOZER LLC
253 Earl Brashier Rd (39479-4024)
PHONE..................601 752-2207
Johnny Kirkley, *Manager*
EMP: 4
SALES (est): 454.6K **Privately Held**
SIC: 1794 1442 Excavation work; construction sand & gravel

(G-4779)
ELLIS WELDING
59 Rogers Rd (39479-9270)
PHONE..................601 752-2207
Susan B Ellis, *Principal*
EMP: 1
SALES (est): 84.5K **Privately Held**
SIC: 7692 Welding repair

(G-4780)
FAYE NELDRA RAND SPEARS
51 Wood Bridge Ln (39479-4194)
PHONE..................601 722-0104
EMP: 3
SALES (est): 201.9K **Privately Held**
SIC: 3131 Mfg Footwear Cut Stock

(G-4781)
G&L LOGGING LLC
49 Tom Leggett Rd (39479-9234)
PHONE..................601 722-9781
Lane Crosby, *President*
EMP: 2
SALES (est): 117K **Privately Held**
SIC: 2411 Logging

(G-4782)
KA POTTERY
Also Called: Ka Pottery Studio
506 Shirley Sanford Rd (39479-8916)
PHONE..................601 722-4948
Troy Cartee, *Manager*
EMP: 2
SALES (est): 113.7K **Privately Held**
SIC: 3269 5719 Stoneware pottery products; pottery

(G-4783)
MACKIES SLIP INC
492 Shirley Sanford Rd (39479-8910)
PHONE..................601 722-4395
Heber Newton, *President*
EMP: 5
SQ FT: 4,000
SALES (est): 651.7K **Privately Held**
SIC: 3299 Ceramic fiber

(G-4784)
TIMOTHY TRIGG
Also Called: Custom BLT Gooseneck Trailers
1335 Highway 49 (39479-4482)
PHONE..................601 722-9581
Timothy Trigg, *Owner*
EMP: 1
SALES (est): 92.5K **Privately Held**
SIC: 3715 Truck trailers

Senatobia
Tate County

(G-4785)
ABB INC
1555 Scott St (38668-2863)
PHONE..................662 562-0700
EMP: 19
SALES (corp-wide): 36.4B **Privately Held**
SIC: 3612 Transformers, except electric
HQ: Abb Inc.
305 Gregson Dr
Cary NC 27511

(G-4786)
AEI LLC
Also Called: Aluminum Extrusion Industries
140 Matthews Dr (38668-2303)
P.O. Box 886 (38668-0886)
PHONE..................662 562-6663
Floyd F Markling, *Vice Pres*
Amanda Hancock, *Manager*
EMP: 100
SALES (est): 2.3MM
SALES (corp-wide): 229MM **Privately Held**
SIC: 3354 Aluminum extruded products
PA: Larson Manufacturing Company Of South Dakota, Inc.
2333 Eastbrook Dr
Brookings SD 57006
605 692-6115

(G-4787)
BADDOUR MEMORIAL CENTER INC
3297 Highway 51 S (38668-2926)
P.O. Box 97 (38668-0097)
PHONE..................662 562-0100
Parke Pepper, *CEO*
Jerry Harmon, *CFO*
EMP: 315 EST: 1978
SQ FT: 80,540
SALES: 7.3MM **Privately Held**
WEB: www.baddour.org
SIC: 8361 2875 0181 5261 Home for the mentally retarded; potting soil, mixed; plants, foliage & shrubberies; flowers: grown under cover (e.g. greenhouse production); nurseries & garden centers; furniture finishing; packaging & labeling services; job training & vocational rehabilitation services

(G-4788)
CARLISLE CONSTRUCTION MTLS LLC
1201 Scott St (38668-2820)
PHONE..................662 560-6474
Jerry Ingle, *Manager*
EMP: 80
SALES (corp-wide): 4.4B **Publicly Held**
WEB: www.premiumroofs.com
SIC: 3086 Plastics foam products
HQ: Carlisle Construction Materials, Llc
1285 Ritner Hwy
Carlisle PA 17013

(G-4789)
CARLISLE SYNTEC
1201 Scott St (38668-2820)
PHONE..................662 301-4509
Joe Gregory, *President*
Burke Nichols, *Plant Mgr*
EMP: 9
SALES (est): 1MM **Privately Held**
SIC: 3083 Laminated plastics plate & sheet

(G-4790)
CHROMCRAFT CORPORATION
Also Called: Chromcraft Furniture
1 Quality Ln (38668-2333)
PHONE..................662 562-8203
Matthew Prochaska, *President*
Samuel Kidston, *Chairman*
Michael Hanna, *Senior VP*
▲ EMP: 180 EST: 1965
SQ FT: 560,000
SALES (est): 34.4MM
SALES (corp-wide): 70.7MM **Privately Held**
SIC: 2522 2514 Office chairs, benches & stools, except wood; metal kitchen & dining room furniture
HQ: Chromcraft Revington, Inc.
140 Bradford Dr Ste A
West Berlin NJ 08091

(G-4791)
D M YOUNT GRAVEL
780 Woolfolk Rd (38668-4017)
P.O. Box 661 (38668-0661)
PHONE..................662 292-1040
Tee Dandridge, *Mng Member*
EMP: 3 EST: 2008
SALES: 307K **Privately Held**
SIC: 1442 Construction sand & gravel

2019 Harris Directory of Mississippi Manufacturers

▲ = Import ▼ =Export
◆ =Import/Export

GEOGRAPHIC SECTION

Shannon - Lee County (G-4821)

(G-4792)
DEMOCRAT
Also Called: Democrat , The
219 E Main St (38668-2123)
PHONE...............................662 562-4414
Joe Lee III, *President*
Brenda Lee, *CFO*
EMP: 11
SQ FT: 5,000
SALES (est): 827.1K **Privately Held**
WEB: www.thedemocrat.com
SIC: 2711 Newspapers: publishing only,
not printed on site

(G-4793)
KEITH MURPHREE
Also Called: Sandy Ridge Sweet Potato Farm
620 Sides Bottom Rd (38668-7301)
P.O. Box 1278 (38668-1278)
PHONE...............................662 292-7644
Keith Murphree, *Owner*
Keith Murphre, *Owner*
Anna Murphree, *Business Mgr*
EMP: 2
SALES: 1.3MM **Privately Held**
SIC: 0191 2037 General farms, primarily
crop; vegetables, quick frozen & cold
pack, excl. potato products

(G-4794)
LSC COMMUNICATIONS US LLC
121 Matthews Dr (38668-2304)
PHONE...............................601 562-5252
EMP: 5
SALES (corp-wide): 3.8B **Publicly Held**
SIC: 2732 Book printing
HQ: Lsc Communications Us, Llc
191 N Wacker Dr Ste 1400
Chicago IL 60606
844 572-5720

(G-4795)
MAINLINE PRINTING
1893 Merryhill Ranch Rd (38668-6393)
PHONE...............................662 301-8298
EMP: 2
SALES (est): 127.2K **Privately Held**
SIC: 2759 Commercial printing

(G-4796)
MIMS TIMBER LLC
Also Called: TMI
934 Yellowdog Rd (38668-7040)
PHONE...............................662 301-5022
Sonia Mims, *Co-Owner*
Todd E Mims, *Mng Member*
EMP: 6
SALES: 600K **Privately Held**
SIC: 2411 Timber, cut at logging camp

(G-4797)
PAT SCREEN PRINTING
214 E Main St (38668-2140)
PHONE...............................662 301-8176
Patrick Alexander, *Owner*
EMP: 2
SALES (est): 77.9K **Privately Held**
SIC: 2759 Commercial printing

(G-4798)
PK USA INC
150 Industrial Dr (38668-2822)
PHONE...............................662 301-4800
Terrance Holmes, *President*
Eddie Washington, *Plant Mgr*
EMP: 21 EST: 2010
SALES (est): 3.6MM **Privately Held**
SIC: 3469 Metal stampings

(G-4799)
PRIME MANUFACTURING SVCS LLC
622 Highway 305 N (38668-6920)
PHONE...............................901 463-5844
Kim Hartzog, *Manager*
Clay Hartzog Jr,
EMP: 38
SALES: 2MM **Privately Held**
SIC: 3999 Barber & beauty shop equipment

(G-4800)
ROBERT E MONK
30 Gwen Rd (38668-6356)
PHONE...............................662 562-8729

Robert Monk, *President*
EMP: 2
SALES (est): 87K **Privately Held**
SIC: 3489 3423 Guns or gun parts, over
30 mm.; soldering guns or tools, hand:
electric

(G-4801)
ROSSVILLE ALUMINUM CASTINGS
211 Gwen Rd (38668-6361)
PHONE...............................662 301-1147
EMP: 15
SQ FT: 1,250
SALES: 800K **Privately Held**
SIC: 3363 3369 3365 Mfg Aluminum Die-
Castings Nonferrous Metal Foundry Alu-
minum Foundry

(G-4802)
RR DONNELLEY & SONS COMPANY
Also Called: R R Donnelley
121 Matthews Dr (38668-2304)
P.O. Box 568 (38668-0568)
PHONE...............................662 562-5252
Richard Utley, *Director*
EMP: 395
SALES (corp-wide): 6.8B **Publicly Held**
WEB: www.rrdonnelley.com
SIC: 2721 2796 2791 2789 Trade jour-
nals: publishing only, not printed on site;
platemaking services; typesetting; book-
binding & related work; book printing
PA: R. R. Donnelley & Sons Company
35 W Wacker Dr
Chicago IL 60601
312 326-8000

(G-4803)
SYCPOWERSPORTS
468 Christian College Rd (38668-3604)
PHONE...............................662 301-1563
Thomas Syc, *Executive*
EMP: 2
SALES (est): 117.9K **Privately Held**
SIC: 3484 Small arms

(G-4804)
TEEZERS
111 S Front St (38668-2600)
P.O. Box 473 (38668-0473)
PHONE...............................662 560-5099
Jeff Jones, *Owner*
EMP: 1
SALES (est): 54K **Privately Held**
WEB: www.teezersprintwear.com
SIC: 2759 Screen printing

Shannon
Lee County

(G-4805)
ADLAM FILMS LLC
62 County Road 520 (38868-9243)
PHONE...............................662 823-1345
Terry Goggans, *CFO*
John Bryce,
EMP: 50
SQ FT: 7,000
SALES: 25MM **Privately Held**
SIC: 3081 Plastic film & sheet
PA: Adaw Llc
62 County Road 520
Shannon MS 38868

(G-4806)
AW MANUFACTURING INC
111 South St (38868-9075)
PHONE...............................662 767-2800
Phil Collam, *General Mgr*
EMP: 145
SALES (corp-wide): 20.5MM **Privately Held**
SIC: 2512 Chairs: upholstered on wood
frames; couches, sofas & davenports: up-
holstered on wood frames
PA: Aw Manufacturing, Inc
111 South St
Shannon MS 38868
662 767-2800

(G-4807)
GRAMMER INC
231 Laney Rd (38868-9354)
PHONE...............................662 566-1660
◆ EMP: 7 EST: 2014
SALES (est): 430.6K **Privately Held**
SIC: 2531 3711 Mfg Public Building Furni-
ture Mfg Motor Vehicle/Car Bodies

(G-4808)
GRAMMER INC (DH)
231 Laney Rd (38868-9354)
PHONE...............................864 672-0702
Thomas Schleuchardt, *President*
Ed Nelson, *Principal*
Joel Snead, *Controller*
Milton Cardoso, *Admin Sec*
▲ EMP: 80
SQ FT: 65,000
SALES (est): 50.9MM
SALES (corp-wide): 3MM **Privately Held**
SIC: 5013 2396 Motor vehicle supplies &
new parts; automotive trimmings, fabric
HQ: Grammer Ag
Georg-Grammer-Str. 2
Amberg 92224
962 166-0

(G-4809)
HER HEART SHOP
240 County Road 501 (38868-9067)
PHONE...............................662 523-9568
Markisa Bailey,
EMP: 1
SALES (est): 46.5K **Privately Held**
SIC: 2759 Letterpress & screen printing

(G-4810)
HUNTER DOUGLAS INC
Also Called: Hunter Douglas Window Fash-
ions
222 Laney Rd (38868-8746)
P.O. Box 89, Tupelo (38802-0089)
PHONE...............................662 690-8190
Mike Robinson, *Mfg Staff*
Whitney Williams, *Controller*
EMP: 173 **Privately Held**
SIC: 2591 3444 5084 3469 Window
blinds; window shades; venetian blinds;
sheet metalwork; industrial machinery &
equipment; metal stampings
HQ: Hunter Douglas Inc.
2550 W Midway Blvd
Broomfield CO 80020
845 664-7000

(G-4811)
JOHNSON FOAM SALES INC
6312 Hwy 145 S (38868)
PHONE...............................662 767-9007
Greg Johnson, *President*
Nicole Campbell, *Admin Sec*
EMP: 20 EST: 1999
SQ FT: 40,000
SALES (est): 4.6MM **Privately Held**
SIC: 3069 Foam rubber

(G-4812)
KELLY DIRT & GRAVEL LLC
718 County Road 300 (38868-9790)
P.O. Box 575 (38868-0575)
PHONE...............................662 231-0249
John Kelly, *Principal*
EMP: 3
SALES (est): 79.9K **Privately Held**
SIC: 1442 Construction sand & gravel

(G-4813)
LAUDERDALE-HAMILTON INC
Hwy 45 S Alt (38868)
PHONE...............................662 767-3928
Dave Hamilton, *President*
Margaret Hamilton, *Vice Pres*
EMP: 18 EST: 1980
SQ FT: 13,750
SALES (est): 3.3MM **Privately Held**
SIC: 3599 Custom machinery

(G-4814)
MARTINREA ATMTV-STRUCTURES USA
Also Called: Martinrea Tupelo Division
323 C D F Blvd (38868-8767)
PHONE...............................662 566-1023
Brian Duivesteyn, *General Mgr*

Rita Cunningham, *Buyer*
Lora Clark, *Executive*
EMP: 2
SALES (corp-wide): 2.7B **Privately Held**
WEB: www.reedcitytool.com
SIC: 3714 Motor vehicle parts & acces-
sories
HQ: Martinrea Automotive-Structures (Usa),
Inc
2800 Livernois Rd Ste 450
Troy MI 48083

(G-4815)
MAX PRIVATE LABEL INC
103 Green Dr (38868-9001)
PHONE...............................773 362-2601
Akhtar Ali, *President*
Babatunde Oduniyi, *Vice Pres*
▲ EMP: 14
SQ FT: 70,000
SALES (est): 2.6MM **Privately Held**
SIC: 2844 Shampoos, rinses, conditioners:
hair

(G-4816)
MEGA TECH SOUTH LLC
5525 Highway 145 (38868-9351)
PHONE...............................662 538-3366
Ken Metts, *Principal*
EMP: 2
SALES (est): 124.2K **Privately Held**
SIC: 7372 Business oriented computer
software

(G-4817)
OKIN AMERICA INC
291 Cdf Blvd (38868)
PHONE...............................662 566-1000
Greg Bowen, *Branch Mgr*
EMP: 100
SALES (corp-wide): 738.4MM **Privately Held**
SIC: 3479 Aluminum coating of metal prod-
ucts
HQ: Okin America, Inc.
7330 Executive Way
Frederick MD 21704

(G-4818)
S & S FRAME SALES LLC
155 Old Highway 45 (38868-9304)
P.O. Box 693 (38868-0693)
PHONE...............................662 397-3725
James B Sisk,
EMP: 6 EST: 2010
SALES (est): 540K **Privately Held**
SIC: 2511 Bed frames, except water bed
frames: wood

(G-4819)
TOM LAUDERDALE PAPER SVCS INC
127 Bynum Ave (38868-8618)
P.O. Box 35 (38868-0035)
PHONE...............................662 767-9744
James B Lauderdale, *President*
Tommy Lauderdale, *Corp Secy*
EMP: 12
SQ FT: 30,000
SALES: 1MM **Privately Held**
SIC: 2493 2675 Fiberboard, other veg-
etable pulp; die-cut paper & board

(G-4820)
TRADER PRINTING
Also Called: Northeast Mississippi Trader
215 Broad St (38868-9301)
P.O. Box 405, Amory (38821-0405)
PHONE...............................662 767-9411
Angel Fawer, *Owner*
Angel Fower, *Owner*
EMP: 2
SALES (est): 180.7K **Privately Held**
SIC: 2752 Commercial printing, litho-
graphic

(G-4821)
WEST GROUP HOLDING COMPANY LLC
251 County Road 631 (38868-9221)
PHONE...............................662 871-2344
Joshua West, *Principal*
James Homan, *Principal*
Nicholas Weaver, *Principal*
EMP: 3

(PA)=Parent Co (HQ)=Headquarters (DH)=Div Headquarters
✿ = New Business established in last 2 years

2019 Harris Directory of
Mississippi Manufacturers

Shannon - Lee County (G-4822)　　　　　　　　　　**GEOGRAPHIC SECTION**

SALES (est): 93.1K **Privately Held**
SIC: **2099** 2325 7389 4783 Box lunches, for sale off premises; men's & boys' jeans & dungarees; sewing contractor; packing goods for shipping; general warehousing & storage; mattresses, containing felt, foam rubber, urethane, etc.

(G-4822)
WEY VALVE INC
175 Bryan Blvd (38868-9502)
P.O. Box 387, Nettleton (38858-0387)
PHONE.............................662 963-2020
Don Trott, *President*
Sharron Cresap, *Vice Pres*
Joey Umfress, *Purchasing*
Tim Martin, *Engineer*
Ryan Ericksen, *Sales Staff*
▲ EMP: 19
SQ FT: 16,000
SALES (est): 4MM
SALES (corp-wide): 16.9MM **Privately Held**
WEB: www.weyvalve.com
SIC: **3491** Industrial valves
PA: Sistag Ag
　Alte Kantonsstrasse 7
　Eschenbach 6274
　414 499-944

Shaw
Bolivar County

(G-4823)
GLENDA BROCK WOODS MUSIC LLC
364 Highway 442 (38773-9612)
PHONE.............................662 588-8343
Leroy Woods, *Principal*
EMP: 1
SALES (est): 41.5K **Privately Held**
SIC: **2499** Wood products

(G-4824)
GUNNS TRANSPORT SERVICES LLC
408 Jackson St (38773)
PHONE.............................662 402-3586
Jemarcus Gunns,
EMP: 2
SALES (est): 95.5K **Privately Held**
SIC: **3537** Trucks, tractors, loaders, carriers & similar equipment

(G-4825)
SHORT LINE MANUFACTURING CO
36 Choctaw Gin Rd (38773-9558)
PHONE.............................662 754-6858
Dennis G Short, *President*
Sammye M Short, *Vice Pres*
▲ EMP: 4
SQ FT: 5,400
SALES (est): 320K **Privately Held**
SIC: **3523** Planting, haying, harvesting & processing machinery

Sherman
Pontotoc County

(G-4826)
BEST FOAM INC
481 3rd Ave (38869)
P.O. Box 288 (38869-0288)
PHONE.............................662 840-6700
Tommy Thompson, *President*
William Hodges, *Vice Pres*
Margaret Thompson, *Vice Pres*
EMP: 25
SQ FT: 35,000
SALES: 800K **Privately Held**
SIC: **3069** Foam rubber

Shubuta
Clarke County

(G-4827)
C & F SWABBING INC
458 Shubuta Eucutta Rd (39360-9632)
PHONE.............................601 687-1171
EMP: 2
SALES (est): 86.7K **Privately Held**
SIC: **1389** Bailing, cleaning, swabbing & treating of wells

(G-4828)
CAREY F STANLEY
Also Called: Stanley Logging
739 Waynesboro Shubuta Rd (39360-9625)
PHONE.............................601 687-5247
EMP: 13
SALES (est): 540K **Privately Held**
SIC: **2411** Logging

(G-4829)
CIRCLE LANE CONTRACTORS LLC
263 Hall St (39360)
P.O. Box 540 (39360-0540)
PHONE.............................601 776-0129
EMP: 13
SQ FT: 2,000
SALES (est): 1.1MM **Privately Held**
SIC: **2411** 4212 Logging Local Trucking Operator

(G-4830)
DENBURY RESOURCES INC
50 Woodrow Reynolds Rd (39360)
PHONE.............................601 687-0089
Brian Dew, *Branch Mgr*
EMP: 7
SALES (corp-wide): 1.4B **Publicly Held**
SIC: **1382** Oil & gas exploration services
PA: Denbury Resources Inc.
　5320 Legacy Dr
　Plano TX 75024
　972 673-2000

(G-4831)
MISSISSIPPI LAMINATORS INC
1151 County Road 210 (39360-8432)
PHONE.............................601 687-1621
Elizabeth Henderson, *President*
Mary Douglas, *Vice Pres*
EMP: 40
SQ FT: 48,000
SALES (est): 5.6MM **Privately Held**
SIC: **2439** Timbers, structural: laminated lumber; trusses, wooden roof

(G-4832)
ODOM INDUSTRIES
26593 Highway 45 (39360-8412)
PHONE.............................601 687-6325
EMP: 1
SALES (est): 39.6K **Privately Held**
SIC: **3999** Manufacturing industries

(G-4833)
ROBIN JONES LOGGING CO
665 W Eucutta St (39360)
P.O. Box 362 (39360-0362)
PHONE.............................601 687-5837
Robin Jones, *Owner*
EMP: 7
SALES (est): 541.5K **Privately Held**
SIC: **2411** Logging camps & contractors

(G-4834)
W L S INC (PA)
851 County Road 253 (39360-9188)
P.O. Box 28, Quitman (39355-0028)
PHONE.............................601 687-1761
Harriet H Waltman, *President*
Michael Sullivan, *Assistant VP*
Gerald Waltman Jr, *Vice Pres*
Theresa Hamrick, *Admin Sec*
EMP: 6
SALES (est): 1.4MM **Privately Held**
SIC: **1389** Oil field services

(G-4835)
W L S INC
Also Called: Well Lease Service
8207 County Road 630 (39360-9399)
P.O. Box 28, Quitman (39355-0028)
PHONE.............................601 687-1761
Gerald Waltman, *General Mgr*
EMP: 12
SALES (corp-wide): 1.4MM **Privately Held**
SIC: **1389** Oil field services
PA: W L S Inc
　851 County Road 253
　Shubuta MS 39360
　601 687-1761

Shuqualak
Noxubee County

(G-4836)
PINECREST WOODWORKS
414 Randy Coleman Rd (39361-8806)
PHONE.............................601 677-3015
EMP: 1
SALES (est): 41.5K **Privately Held**
SIC: **2499** Rulers & yardsticks, wood

(G-4837)
SHUQUALAK LUMBER COMPANY INC
86 College St (39361-8914)
P.O. Box 25 (39361-0025)
PHONE.............................662 425-5339
EMP: 100
SALES (corp-wide): 21.3MM **Privately Held**
WEB: www.shuqualak.com
SIC: **2421** Lumber: rough, sawed or planed
PA: Shuqualak Lumber Company, Inc.
　402 Oak St
　Shuqualak MS 39361
　662 793-4528

Silver Creek
Lawrence County

(G-4838)
GHE MACHINE SHOP
430 Garrett Rd (39663-2210)
PHONE.............................601 886-0304
Christopher C Grantham, *Principal*
EMP: 2 EST: 2011
SALES (est): 159.8K **Privately Held**
SIC: **3599** Machine shop, jobbing & repair

(G-4839)
RAC N SPURS GAME CALLS
578 Crooked Creek Rd (39663-4409)
PHONE.............................601 455-9484
EMP: 1
SALES (est): 76.8K **Privately Held**
SIC: **3949** Game calls

Smithdale
Amite County

(G-4840)
ADAMS LOGGING INC
6587 Adams Rd (39664-7007)
PHONE.............................601 567-2988
Warren Adams, *President*
Margaret Adams, *Treasurer*
EMP: 9
SALES (est): 1.1MM **Privately Held**
SIC: **2411** Logging camps & contractors

(G-4841)
CASES CNTRPINT HNTING CLB INC
2295 Sw Bogue Chitto Rd (39664-7429)
PHONE.............................601 734-2373
Billy Joe Case, *Manager*
EMP: 1
SALES (est): 54.5K **Privately Held**
SIC: **3523** Farm machinery & equipment

(G-4842)
PHILLIP SPRING LOGGING IN
319 Evans Rd Se (39664-3796)
PHONE.............................601 567-2138
Pamela W Spring, *Vice Pres*
EMP: 6 EST: 2001
SALES (est): 675.3K **Privately Held**
SIC: **2411** Logging camps & contractors

Smithville
Monroe County

(G-4843)
BEHOLD HOME INC
60012 Industrial St (38870-7770)
PHONE.............................662 651-4510
Lyle Harris, *CEO*
Larry Todd, *COO*
Bo Russell, *CFO*
▲ EMP: 43 EST: 2014
SALES (est): 5.2MM **Privately Held**
SIC: **2512** Chairs: upholstered on wood frames

(G-4844)
KHLOES CLOSET AND MONOGRAMS
60014 Parkview Dr (38870-7743)
PHONE.............................662 315-9425
Kelli Steadman, *Principal*
EMP: 1 EST: 2015
SALES (est): 45.5K **Privately Held**
SIC: **2395** Embroidery & art needlework

(G-4845)
TOWNHOUSE HOME FURNISHINGS LLC (PA)
60012 Industrial St D (38870-7770)
P.O. Box 360 (38870-0360)
PHONE.............................662 651-5442
Kevin Trautman, *Mng Member*
Jermey Lafayette,
◆ EMP: 120
SALES (est): 11.7MM **Privately Held**
SIC: **2231** Upholstery fabrics, wool

Soso
Jones County

(G-4846)
DENBURY RESOURCES INC
80 County Road 7 (39480-5548)
PHONE.............................601 729-2266
Sandy Sandusky, *Branch Mgr*
EMP: 2
SALES (corp-wide): 1.4B **Publicly Held**
SIC: **1382** Oil & gas exploration services
PA: Denbury Resources Inc.
　5320 Legacy Dr
　Plano TX 75024
　972 673-2000

(G-4847)
PINE BELT TRUSS COMPANY INC
246 Northridge Rd (39480-5185)
P.O. Box 9 (39480-0009)
PHONE.............................601 729-4298
Pete Ward, *President*
Sherrah Ward, *Vice Pres*
Angela Bynum, *Admin Sec*
EMP: 8
SQ FT: 3,200
SALES (est): 1.1MM **Privately Held**
SIC: **2439** Trusses, wooden roof

(G-4848)
SUPERIOR MULCH INC
1701 Sw Macedo Blvd (39480)
PHONE.............................772 878-5220
Tony Gilvimazzl, *Manager*
EMP: 1
SALES (corp-wide): 842.9K **Privately Held**
SIC: **3523** Turf & grounds equipment
PA: Superior Mulch Inc.
　7457 Park Lane Rd
　Lake Worth FL 33449
　561 439-2898

2019 Harris Directory of
Mississippi Manufacturers

▲ = Import ▼=Export
◆ =Import/Export

GEOGRAPHIC SECTION

Southaven - Desoto County (G-4879)

Southaven
Desoto County

(G-4849)
1 A LIFESAFER INC
1262 Main St (38671-1430)
PHONE...................................800 634-3077
EMP: 1
SALES (corp-wide): 4.3MM **Privately Held**
SIC: 3829 Measuring & controlling devices
PA: 1 A Lifesafer, Inc.
4290 Glendale Milford Rd
Blue Ash OH 45242
513 651-9560

(G-4850)
A K SANDERS MFG INC
2116 Pryne Dr (38672-9612)
PHONE...................................901 647-1830
Albert Kirk Sanders Sr, *President*
Victoria Sanders, *Director*
EMP: 8
SALES (est): 832.4K **Privately Held**
SIC: 3444 3599 Forming machine work, sheet metal; machine & other job shop work

(G-4851)
ABB INSTALLATION PRODUCTS INC
8735 Hamilton Rd (38671-3103)
P.O. Box 100 (38671-0100)
PHONE...................................662 342-1545
Anthony Moore, *Buyer*
Michael O'Neil, *Engineer*
Patrick George, *Manager*
Scott Carpenter, *Info Tech Dir*
Krish Eastlick, *Administration*
EMP: 300
SQ FT: 250,000
SALES (corp-wide): 36.4B **Privately Held**
WEB: www.tnb.com
SIC: 3699 3643 3471 Electrical equipment & supplies; current-carrying wiring devices; plating & polishing
HQ: Abb Installation Products Inc.
860 Ridge Lake Blvd
Memphis TN 38120
901 252-5000

(G-4852)
ADVENTURE LEADERSHIP CONS LLC
606 Scarlet Oak St # 301 (38671-6337)
PHONE...................................662 915-6736
Joshua Norris, *Executive*
EMP: 2
SALES (est): 85.9K **Privately Held**
SIC: 3577 Computer peripheral equipment

(G-4853)
AMERIONE SECURITY
8361 Pinnacle Dr (38672-6590)
PHONE...................................901 502-2295
Jeremy K Coker, *Owner*
EMP: 4
SALES: 70K **Privately Held**
SIC: 3669 Burglar alarm apparatus, electric

(G-4854)
BELOVED POTTERY
1555 Stonehedge Dr (38671-8811)
PHONE...................................662 349-4430
Paula Stephenson, *Owner*
EMP: 1
SALES: 50K **Privately Held**
SIC: 3269 7389 Art & ornamental ware, pottery;

(G-4855)
BF KAUFMAN INC
9020 Highway 51 N Ste 1 (38671-1231)
PHONE...................................662 253-8093
Brian Kaufman, *President*
EMP: 2
SALES (est): 128.7K **Privately Held**
SIC: 3011 Tires & inner tubes

(G-4856)
BRADFORD ENTERPRISES LLC
7426 Overlook Dr (38671-5841)
P.O. Box 1223 (38671-0112)
PHONE...................................901 652-1491
Leighton Bradford,
EMP: 4
SALES (est): 201.4K **Privately Held**
SIC: 3812 Aircraft/aerospace flight instruments & guidance systems

(G-4857)
CATER 2U EMBROIDERY
1654 Main St (38671-1237)
PHONE...................................662 253-8713
Michael Chaffen, *Manager*
EMP: 1
SALES (est): 58.8K **Privately Held**
SIC: 2395 Embroidery products, except schiffli machine; embroidery & art needlework

(G-4858)
CENTRAL FABRICATION INC
401 Suthcrest Cir Ste 102 (38671)
PHONE...................................662 349-7122
Ronald Snell, *Branch Mgr*
EMP: 8
SALES (corp-wide): 4.6MM **Privately Held**
SIC: 3842 Orthopedic appliances
PA: Central Fabrication, Inc.
1665 Shelby Oaks Dr N # 105
Memphis TN 38134
901 725-0060

(G-4859)
CLARK BEVERAGE GROUP INC
Also Called: Coca-Cola
5645 Pepper Chase Dr (38671-9634)
PHONE...................................662 280-8540
Jeff Brasher, *Branch Mgr*
EMP: 32
SALES (corp-wide): 167MM **Privately Held**
SIC: 2086 Bottled & canned soft drinks
HQ: Clark Beverage Group, Inc.
110 Miley Dr
Starkville MS 39759
662 338-3400

(G-4860)
COLLEGE STATION SPT STORES INC
6519 Towne Center Xing (38671-8100)
PHONE...................................662 349-8988
Adam York, *Manager*
EMP: 9
SALES (corp-wide): 3.4MM **Privately Held**
SIC: 3949 Sporting & athletic goods
PA: The College Station Sports Stores Inc
4674 Merchants Park Cir
Collierville TN 38017
901 854-0225

(G-4861)
COMPOSING ROOM INC
8098 Chesterfield Dr (38671-3809)
PHONE...................................662 393-6652
Debra Cupps, *President*
Roscoe Langford, *Corp Secy*
EMP: 2
SQ FT: 1,690
SALES: 180K **Privately Held**
SIC: 2791 Typesetting

(G-4862)
CON AIR
711 Venture Dr (38672-8133)
P.O. Box 904 (38671-0010)
PHONE...................................662 280-6499
Doug Ray, *Plant Mgr*
◆ EMP: 7
SALES (est): 1.7MM **Privately Held**
SIC: 3634 Hair dryers, electric

(G-4863)
CONAIR CORPORATION
711 Venture Dr (38672-8133)
P.O. Box 904 (38671-0010)
PHONE...................................662 280-6499
Doug Ray, *Branch Mgr*
EMP: 22

SALES (corp-wide): 2B **Privately Held**
WEB: www.conair.com
SIC: 3634 Electric housewares & fans
PA: Conair Corporation
1 Cummings Point Rd
Stamford CT 06902
203 351-9000

(G-4864)
COOPER LIGHTING LLC
100 Airport Industrial Dr (38671-5848)
PHONE...................................662 342-3100
Raymond Hollins, *Branch Mgr*
EMP: 12 **Privately Held**
WEB: www.corelite.com
SIC: 3648 Lighting equipment
HQ: Cooper Lighting, Llc
1121 Highway 74 S
Peachtree City GA 30269
770 486-4800

(G-4865)
COUNTER CONNECTIONS INC
2085 First Coml Dr S (38671)
PHONE...................................662 342-5111
John P Jacobs, *President*
Kathy G Jacobs, *Treasurer*
EMP: 5
SALES: 650K **Privately Held**
SIC: 2541 Table or counter tops, plastic laminated

(G-4866)
CTA PRODUCTS GROUP LLC
1899 Kings Castle Dr (38671-8805)
PHONE...................................662 536-1446
Barbara Murray,
EMP: 1
SALES (est): 155.4K **Privately Held**
SIC: 5169 2833 2869 2899 Chemicals & allied products; medicinals & botanicals; industrial organic chemicals; chemical preparations

(G-4867)
DESOTO SLEEP DIAGNOSTICS
7600 Airways Blvd Ste G (38671-5138)
PHONE...................................662 349-9802
Brian Redden, *Principal*
EMP: 2
SALES (est): 180.9K **Privately Held**
SIC: 3841 Diagnostic apparatus, medical

(G-4868)
DIMS GROUP
4091 Davis Rd (38671-9620)
PHONE...................................302 562-2697
Della Miller, *Vice Pres*
EMP: 2
SALES (est): 72.6K **Privately Held**
SIC: 3993 Electric signs; signs, not made in custom sign painting shops

(G-4869)
DIPSTIX LUBE
3255 Goodman Rd E (38672-6449)
PHONE...................................662 349-2810
Jeff Corton, *General Mgr*
EMP: 4
SALES (est): 187.6K **Privately Held**
SIC: 1389 Oil field services

(G-4870)
EAGLE SPECIALTY PRODUCTS INC
8530 Aaron Ln (38671-1002)
P.O. Box 1079 (38671-0011)
PHONE...................................662 796-7373
James A Dorris, *President*
Robert Dorris, *Purchasing*
Dore Dorris, *Treasurer*
EMP: 21
SQ FT: 3,200
SALES (est): 3.8MM **Privately Held**
SIC: 3462 5531 3312 Automotive & internal combustion engine forgings; speed shops, including race car supplies; blast furnaces & steel mills

(G-4871)
ELECTRIC CONTRACTORS
8945 Hamilton Rd (38671-2504)
PHONE...................................662 470-3102
EMP: 2

SALES (est): 93.7K **Privately Held**
SIC: 5082 3699 General construction machinery & equipment; electrical equipment & supplies

(G-4872)
EXEL LOGISTICS XEROX
228 Access Dr Ste 105 (38671-5887)
PHONE...................................662 393-7122
EMP: 6
SALES (est): 24.4K **Privately Held**
SIC: 3861 Photographic equipment & supplies

(G-4873)
FISKARS BRANDS INC
330 Stateline Rd E (38671-1722)
PHONE...................................662 393-3236
Jane Scott, *President*
EMP: 250
SALES (corp-wide): 1.2B **Privately Held**
SIC: 3423 5049 Garden & farm tools, including shovels; school supplies
HQ: Fiskars Brands, Inc.
7800 Discovery Dr
Middleton WI 53562
608 259-1649

(G-4874)
GENIE INDUSTRIES
8800 Rostin Rd (38671-1022)
PHONE...................................662 393-1800
Genie Henson, *Principal*
EMP: 3 EST: 2010
SALES (est): 279.7K **Privately Held**
SIC: 3999 Manufacturing industries

(G-4875)
GLASSBRIDGE ENTERPRISES INC
8680 Swinnea Rd (38671-2807)
PHONE...................................662 280-6268
EMP: 8 **Publicly Held**
SIC: 3572 3695 Computer storage devices; computer tape drives & components; disk drives, computer; magnetic storage devices, computer; magnetic disks & drums
PA: Glassbridge Enterprises, Inc.
1099 Helmo Ave N Ste 250
Oakdale MN 55128

(G-4876)
HATCHETT PERFECTION PRINTS LLC
1155 Dorshire Dr (38671-6262)
PHONE...................................662 260-6244
EMP: 2
SALES (est): 83.9K **Privately Held**
SIC: 2752 Commercial printing, lithographic

(G-4877)
HOFFINGER INDUSTRIES
6928 Cobblestone Blvd # 200 (38672-8301)
PHONE...................................662 890-7930
Martin I Hoffinger, *Principal*
EMP: 2
SALES (est): 215.2K **Privately Held**
SIC: 3544 Special dies, tools, jigs & fixtures

(G-4878)
HUMAN TECHNOLOGY INC
Also Called: Hi-Tech Prosthetics Orthotics
1880 Goodman Rd E (38671-9552)
PHONE...................................662 349-4909
Ramesh Dubey, *Principal*
EMP: 2
SALES (est): 77.1K **Privately Held**
SIC: 5961 3842 Television, home shopping; surgical appliances & supplies

(G-4879)
ITT LLC
Also Called: I T T
8890 Commerce Dr (38671-7358)
PHONE...................................662 393-0275
Lonny Birkelbach, *Manager*
EMP: 20
SALES (corp-wide): 2.7B **Publicly Held**
WEB: www.ittind.com
SIC: 3625 Control equipment, electric

(PA)=Parent Co (HQ)=Headquarters (DH)=Div Headquarters
✪ = New Business established in last 2 years

2019 Harris Directory of
Mississippi Manufacturers

175

GEOGRAPHIC

Southhaven - Desoto County (G-4880)

GEOGRAPHIC SECTION

HQ: Itt Llc
1133 Westchester Ave N-100
White Plains NY 10604
914 641-2000

(G-4880)
J N S MARBLE & GRANITE LLC
8950 Highway 51 N (38671-2004)
PHONE....................................662 280-2272
Elzie Lynn Ellis,
EMP: 10
SALES (est): 109.4K Privately Held
SIC: 2541 Counter & sink tops

(G-4881)
J&J SCREEN PRINTING
Also Called: J & J Screen Printing
1810 Veterans Dr (38671-2006)
PHONE....................................662 342-6131
Kim Jones, Owner
EMP: 5
SALES: 400K Privately Held
SIC: 2752 2759 Commercial printing, litho-
graphic; screen printing

(G-4882)
JACKSON PUBLISHING
7661 Forstoria Cv (38672-6470)
PHONE....................................662 349-2866
Jeffery Jackson, Principal
EMP: 2
SALES (est): 100.5K Privately Held
SIC: 2741 Miscellaneous publishing

(G-4883)
JERRY HAILEY
Also Called: Jerry's Mobile Repair Service
6605 Tchulahoma Rd (38671-9207)
PHONE....................................662 349-2582
Jerry Hailey, Owner
EMP: 2
SALES: 55K Privately Held
SIC: 7538 7699 7692 General automotive
repair shops; industrial equipment serv-
ices; welding repair

(G-4884)
JOHNSON MACHINE NORTH MISS
3636 Stateline Rd W (38671-1023)
PHONE....................................662 393-3567
John Johnson, Owner
EMP: 2
SQ FT: 2,600
SALES: 50K Privately Held
SIC: 3599 Machine shop, jobbing & repair

(G-4885)
KRAZY KAT MONOGRAMS
9095 Millbranch Rd (38671-1421)
PHONE....................................901 832-1339
EMP: 1
SALES (est): 40.3K Privately Held
SIC: 2395 Embroidery & art needlework

(G-4886)
M P JOHNSON PUBLISHING LLC ✪
1246 Mcgowan Dr (38671-8420)
PHONE....................................662 270-5544
Michael Johnson, Principal
EMP: 1 EST: 2019
SALES (est): 37.5K Privately Held
SIC: 2741 Miscellaneous publishing

(G-4887)
M2 CORP
8362 Lake Shore Dr W (38671-4220)
PHONE....................................662 342-2173
David Rayburn, President
EMP: 2
SALES (est): 410K Privately Held
SIC: 2421 Railroad ties, sawed

(G-4888)
MAM MACHINE & MFG LLC
8490 Tulane Rd (38671-1024)
PHONE....................................901 216-1960
Donald McCommon,
David McCommon,
EMP: 5
SQ FT: 2,000
SALES (est): 401K Privately Held
SIC: 3599 Machine shop, jobbing & repair

(G-4889)
MEMPHIS OBSTETRICS & GYNECOLOG
7900 Airways Blvd Bldg C6 (38671-4115)
PHONE....................................662 349-5554
George Worthom, President
EMP: 8
SALES (est): 1.1MM Privately Held
WEB: www.memphisobgynpc.com
SIC: 3842 Gynecological supplies & appli-
ances

(G-4890)
NEBCO INC
7065 Airways Blvd Ste 111 (38671-5874)
PHONE....................................662 349-1400
Jimmy Neblett, Branch Mgr
EMP: 1 Privately Held
SIC: 2759 Business forms: printing
PA: Nebco Inc

Clinton MS

(G-4891)
NIDEC MOTOR CORPORATION
Also Called: Emerson Motor Company
710 Venture Dr Ste 100 (38672-8164)
PHONE....................................662 393-6910
EMP: 415 Privately Held
SIC: 3621 Motors, electric
HQ: Nidec Motor Corporation
8050 West Florissant Ave
Saint Louis MO 63136

(G-4892)
PINK APPLE
1686 Main St (38671-1240)
PHONE....................................901 412-3926
EMP: 2
SALES (est): 91.2K Privately Held
SIC: 3571 Mfg Electronic Computers

(G-4893)
PROSPERITY7 HELPING HANDS LLC
1046 Church Rd W # 106234
(38671-7139)
PHONE....................................800 597-6599
Sharon Mitchell, Vice Pres
Ernest Hall,
EMP: 3
SQ FT: 5,900
SALES (est): 296.1K Privately Held
SIC: 3953 7389 Seal presses, notary &
hand; paralegal service

(G-4894)
RA MAXX LLC
Also Called: Signs First
3380 Goodman Rd E (38672-6433)
PHONE....................................662 342-6212
Hobbs Milton D Jr, Director
EMP: 2
SALES (est): 260.2K Privately Held
SIC: 3993 Signs & advertising specialties

(G-4895)
RAY BROOKS ENTERPRISES
8068 Buckingham Dr (38671-3908)
PHONE....................................662 342-0555
Ray Brooks, Owner
Betty Brooks, Partner
EMP: 2 EST: 1982
SALES: 150K Privately Held
SIC: 3555 Printing trades machinery

(G-4896)
RECORD IMAGING SYSTEMS
963 Town And Country Dr (38671-1514)
P.O. Box 2017 (38671-0024)
PHONE....................................662 280-1286
Paul Mauller, Owner
EMP: 1
SALES (est): 49.1K Privately Held
SIC: 3861 Photographic equipment & sup-
plies

(G-4897)
RPM PIPING AND SUPPLY LLC
1615 Epping Forest Dr (38671-8873)
PHONE....................................901 633-6083
Morgan Simpson,
EMP: 2
SALES (est): 85.6K Privately Held
SIC: 3494 Pipe fittings

(G-4898)
SANDYS AUTO PARTS & MACHINE SP
1759 Veterans Dr (38671-2013)
PHONE....................................662 342-1900
Sandy Tolson, Partner
Doris Tolson, Partner
EMP: 4 EST: 1978
SALES: 350K Privately Held
SIC: 3599 5531 7694 3621 Machine
shop, jobbing & repair; automotive parts;
armature rewinding shops; motors & gen-
erators

(G-4899)
SAUL JAY ENTERPRISES INC
Also Called: Eye/Ear Optical
3044 Goodman Rd E (38672-8760)
PHONE....................................662 349-1660
Carol Karesh, President
Saul Karesh, President
Dr Michael Cook, Owner
EMP: 11
SQ FT: 4,000
SALES: 1MM Privately Held
SIC: 5995 3851 8042 Contact lenses,
prescription; eyeglasses, prescription;
glasses, sun or glare; offices & clinics of
optometrists

(G-4900)
SIGN GYPSIES DF NORTH MS
4764 Thornbury Cv (38672-9588)
PHONE....................................901 484-7357
EMP: 2
SALES (est): 54.3K Privately Held
SIC: 3993 Signs & advertising specialties

(G-4901)
SIGNS & STUFF
910 Goodman Rd E Apt C (38671-8891)
PHONE....................................662 393-9314
Sherry Jones, Owner
EMP: 1
SALES (est): 102.5K Privately Held
SIC: 3993 Signs, not made in custom sign
painting shops

(G-4902)
SIGNS & STUFF INC
3674 Goodman Rd S Ste 1 (38672)
PHONE....................................662 895-4505
Cherie Jones, President
Rodney Jones, Vice Pres
EMP: 6
SALES (est): 711.7K Privately Held
WEB: www.signsandstuff.biz
SIC: 3993 Signs, not made in custom sign
painting shops

(G-4903)
SMITH SR WILLIAM SHAYNE
Also Called: American Dream Handyman Svc
2807 Oliver Cv (38672-9106)
PHONE....................................901 832-1998
William Smith, Owner
EMP: 7
SALES (est): 547.2K Privately Held
SIC: 3599 Machine shop, jobbing & repair

(G-4904)
SMITHS MOBILE WELDING
828 Parham Cir (38671-8973)
PHONE....................................901 626-1616
Blake Smith, Principal
EMP: 1 EST: 2017
SALES (est): 38.7K Privately Held
SIC: 7692 Welding repair

(G-4905)
SOUTHAVEN RACEWAY
580 Stateline Rd W (38671-1604)
P.O. Box 1450 (38671-0015)
PHONE....................................662 393-9945
Fadi Salameh, Principal
EMP: 6
SALES (est): 577.6K Privately Held
SIC: 3644 Raceways

(G-4906)
SOUTHERN BLLE SWEET DSIGNS LLC
Also Called: Candy Bouquet 6625
917 Cloverleaf Dr (38671-9789)
P.O. Box 740 (38671-0008)
PHONE....................................901 598-7938
Jane Shenks,
Rosa Alford,
Rebecca White,
EMP: 3
SALES: 5K Privately Held
SIC: 2064 Candy & other confectionery
products

(G-4907)
SOUTHWARK METAL MFG CO
8680 Stanton Rd (38671-1000)
PHONE....................................662 342-7805
Peter Schroder, Branch Mgr
EMP: 125
SALES (corp-wide): 119.5MM Privately
Held
SIC: 3444 Ducts, sheet metal
PA: Southwark Metal Manufacturing Com-
pany
2800 Red Lion Rd
Philadelphia PA 19154
215 735-3401

(G-4908)
STAYBRITE SIGNS
819 Autumn Woods Cv (38671-4918)
PHONE....................................901 490-0431
Steve Lee, Principal
EMP: 1
SALES (est): 46K Privately Held
SIC: 3993 Signs & advertising specialties

(G-4909)
STYLECRAFT HOME COLLECTION INC
Also Called: Stylecraft Home Collections
8474 Market Place Dr # 104 (38671-5881)
PHONE....................................662 429-5279
Jimmy D Webster Jr, President
Ron Armstrong, Exec VP
Andy Estes, Vice Pres
James C Poffenberger III, Vice Pres
Ed Swanson, Opers Staff
◆ EMP: 225
SQ FT: 250,000
SALES (est): 57.7MM Privately Held
SIC: 3645 3641 Electric lamps; table
lamps

(G-4910)
SUPERIOR BLINDS AND SHUTTERS
3664 New Pointe Dr S (38672-6384)
PHONE....................................901 270-8061
Charles Ledbetter, Principal
EMP: 1
SALES (est): 57.3K Privately Held
SIC: 2591 Window blinds

(G-4911)
T AND W MAINTENANCE LLC
902 Acorn Cv (38671-4926)
PHONE....................................901 848-2511
Wesley Benedict,
EMP: 2
SALES (est): 40.6K Privately Held
SIC: 7692 Welding repair

(G-4912)
T R GENERAL WELDING
5790 Landau Dr (38671-8943)
PHONE....................................901 481-0425
EMP: 1
SALES (est): 51.4K Privately Held
SIC: 7692 Welding repair

(G-4913)
TEREX CORPORATION
Terex Construction Americas
8800 Rostin Rd (38671-1099)
PHONE....................................662 393-1800
Rob Roche, Counsel
Dean Hays, Prdtn Mgr
Ed Cox, Materials Mgr
Richard Leisen, Materials Mgr
Kevin Hamer, Safety Mgr
EMP: 200

2019 Harris Directory of
Mississippi Manufacturers

▲ = Import ▼=Export
◆ =Import/Export

GEOGRAPHIC SECTION

Starkville - Oktibbeha County (G-4943)

SALES (corp-wide): 5.1B **Publicly Held**
WEB: www.terex.com
SIC: **3531** Construction machinery
PA: Terex Corporation
200 Nyala Farms Rd Ste 2
Westport CT 06880
203 222-7170

(G-4914)
TERUMO MEDICAL CORPORATION
8655 Commerce Dr Ste 105 (38671-7382)
PHONE..............................662 280-2643
Sandi Hartka, *Manager*
EMP: 13 **Privately Held**
SIC: **3841** Surgical & medical instruments
HQ: Terumo Medical Corporation
265 Davidson Ave Ste 320
Somerset NJ 08873

(G-4915)
TOMLINSON MACHINE & TOOL LLC
2989 Stateline Rd W (38671-1043)
PHONE..............................662 342-5043
Brandy Tomlinson,
Brian Tomlinson,
EMP: 2
SALES (est): 288K **Privately Held**
SIC: **3599** Machine shop, jobbing & repair

(G-4916)
TRI-STATE ATHLETIC GROUP
Also Called: Tri-State Ballers
2893 Broadway Dr (38672-6518)
PHONE..............................901 395-6359
Danny Trezvant, *Director*
Samantha Trezvant, *Administration*
EMP: 2
SALES (est): 89.7K **Privately Held**
SIC: **3949** Sporting & athletic goods

(G-4917)
TRITON STONE HOLDINGS LLC
2363 Stateline Rd W (38671-1103)
PHONE..............................662 280-8041
EMP: 73
SALES (corp-wide): 44.2MM **Privately Held**
SIC: **3281** 5032 1752 3253 Granite, cut & shaped; brick, stone & related material; floor laying & floor work; ceramic wall & floor tile
PA: Triton Stone Holdings, Llc
800 Nw 65th St
Fort Lauderdale FL 33309
219 669-4890

(G-4918)
UNDER ARMOUR INC
5205 Airways Blvd Ste 700 (38671-6539)
PHONE..............................662 298-5269
EMP: 2
SALES (corp-wide): 5.1B **Publicly Held**
SIC: **2329** Men's & boys' sportswear & athletic clothing
PA: Under Armour, Inc.
1020 Hull St Ste 300
Baltimore MD 21230
410 454-6428

(G-4919)
VERTIV CORPORATION
710 Venture Dr Ste 200 (38672-8165)
PHONE..............................662 313-0813
Floyd Gaston, *Branch Mgr*
EMP: 10
SALES (corp-wide): 3.1B **Privately Held**
WEB: www.liebert.com
SIC: **3613** Switchgear & switchboard apparatus
HQ: Vertiv Corporation
1050 Dearborn Dr
Columbus OH 43085
614 888-0246

(G-4920)
XOOMA WORLDWIDE
2258 Linda Shore Dr (38672-8386)
PHONE..............................662 548-5361
EMP: 2
SALES (est): 91.8K **Privately Held**
SIC: **2023** 5169 Mfg Dry/Evaporated Dairy Products Whol Chemicals/Products

(G-4921)
XYLEM WATER SOLUTIONS USA
1085 Sttline Rd E Ste 107 (38671)
PHONE..............................662 393-0275
▲ EMP: 15
SALES (est): 3.5MM **Privately Held**
SIC: **3561** Pumps & pumping equipment

(G-4922)
YUM YUMS GOURMET POPCORN LLC
9049 Highway 51 N (38671-1230)
PHONE..............................662 470-6047
Samuel McClenton, *Mng Member*
EMP: 7
SQ FT: 1,250
SALES: 212.9K **Privately Held**
SIC: **5145** 5441 2064 Popcorn & supplies; popcorn, including caramel corn; popcorn balls or other treated popcorn products

---

Starkville
Oktibbeha County

(G-4923)
ADVANCED GNSLNGER ARMAMENT LLC
Also Called: AGA
313 Critz St (39759-2259)
PHONE..............................775 343-5633
Benjamin Tower, *Principal*
EMP: 1
SALES (est): 45K **Privately Held**
SIC: **3949** 7389 Targets, archery & rifle shooting;

(G-4924)
ALLEY KATS GLASS
1628 Highway 389 (39759-8465)
PHONE..............................662 324-3002
Katherine Davis, *Owner*
EMP: 1
SQ FT: 1,500
SALES: 24K **Privately Held**
SIC: **5231** 8999 3479 Glass, leaded or stained; stained glass art; etching & engraving

(G-4925)
ASSURED REVENUE CORPORATION
Also Called: Doorswap
325 1/2 Highway 12 W (39759-3632)
PHONE..............................662 323-5350
William Ford, *President*
Claire Sewell, *Manager*
EMP: 3
SQ FT: 2,000
SALES (est): 199.1K **Privately Held**
SIC: **7372** Business oriented computer software

(G-4926)
BARNETTS SMALL ENGINES
54 Old Highway 12 (39759-5656)
PHONE..............................662 323-8993
Charles Barnett, *Owner*
EMP: 2
SALES (est): 200K **Privately Held**
SIC: **5999** 5261 5084 3546 Engines & parts, air-cooled; lawnmowers & tractors; engines, gasoline; saws & sawing equipment

(G-4927)
BATTLEBELLS LLC (PA)
307 1/2 Scales St Lot 2 (39759-3165)
PHONE..............................662 312-5901
John Howell, *Mng Member*
Stephen Caples,
EMP: 2
SALES: 26.7K **Privately Held**
SIC: **3499** 7389 Novelties & giftware, including trophies;

(G-4928)
BELLES
Also Called: Belles Nail Bar
500 Russell St Ste 35 (39759-5405)
PHONE..............................662 617-8171
Aaron Weiss, *Owner*

EMP: 9
SALES (est): 722K **Privately Held**
SIC: **2844** Manicure preparations

(G-4929)
BOARDTOWN TRADING POST
307 Hillside Dr (39759-2630)
PHONE..............................662 324-7296
EMP: 1
SALES: 150K **Privately Held**
SIC: **7384** 3479 5932 5999 Photofinishing Laboratory Coating/Engraving Service Ret Used Merchandise Ret Misc Merchandise

(G-4930)
BOOK MART CORPORATION
318 E Lee Blvd (39759-5343)
PHONE..............................662 323-2844
EMP: 43
SALES (corp-wide): 8.5MM **Privately Held**
SIC: **2741** Miscellaneous publishing
PA: Book Mart Corporation
120 E Main St
Starkville MS 39759
662 323-2844

(G-4931)
C C CLARK INC (PA)
501 Academy Rd (39759-4047)
P.O. Box 966 (39760-0966)
PHONE..............................662 323-4317
Albert C Clark, *President*
Larry Parker, *Partner*
Albert C Clark, *Vice Pres*
Albert Clark, *Vice Pres*
Harold N Clark, *Vice Pres*
EMP: 30 EST: 1932
SQ FT: 2,500
SALES: 167MM **Privately Held**
SIC: **5149** 2086 Groceries & related products; bottled & canned soft drinks

(G-4932)
CANDLELORE INC
101 E Pointe Dr (39759-3696)
PHONE..............................662 312-1060
EMP: 1
SALES (est): 39.6K **Privately Held**
SIC: **3999** Candles

(G-4933)
CEMCO INC
Also Called: Top Brass Tackle
909a Lynn Ln (39759-4408)
P.O. Box 209 (39760-0209)
PHONE..............................662 323-1559
Arthur G Cosby III, *President*
Eric Cosby, *Treasurer*
EMP: 20
SQ FT: 22,500
SALES (est): 3.3MM **Privately Held**
WEB: www.cemcotubecutting.com
SIC: **3498** 3451 3949 Tube fabricating (contract bending & shaping); screw machine products; fishing tackle, general

(G-4934)
CLARK BEVERAGE GROUP INC (HQ)
Also Called: Coca-Cola
110 Miley Dr (39759-7728)
P.O. Box 968 (39760-0968)
PHONE..............................662 338-3400
Robert H Clark, *President*
Robert Clark, *President*
Albert C Clark, *Vice Pres*
Dallas Clark, *Vice Pres*
Morgan E Clark, *Admin Sec*
▲ EMP: 52 EST: 1905
SQ FT: 80,000
SALES (est): 74.9MM
SALES (corp-wide): 167MM **Privately Held**
SIC: **5149** 5181 2086 Soft drinks; beer & ale; bottled & canned soft drinks
PA: C. C. Clark, Inc.
501 Academy Rd
Starkville MS 39759
662 323-4317

(G-4935)
COASTAL WATERS LLC
220 Brook Ave (39759-4343)
PHONE..............................662 769-2944

Dean O'Neal, *Mng Member*
EMP: 8
SALES (est): 602.9K **Privately Held**
SIC: **2389** Apparel & accessories

(G-4936)
CREEKSIDE ENVMTL PDTS LLC
1 Southern Cross Way (39759)
PHONE..............................662 617-5553
Todd Mlsna,
EMP: 1
SALES (est): 47.2K **Privately Held**
SIC: **2875** 7389 Compost;

(G-4937)
CURAHE LLC
1305 Nottingham Rd (39759-4023)
PHONE..............................662 325-2176
Raymond S Winton, *Exec Dir*
EMP: 3
SALES (est): 159.5K **Privately Held**
SIC: **3845** Electromedical equipment

(G-4938)
DAVID BREAZEALE LOGGING LLC
6478 Us Highway 82 (39759-3044)
PHONE..............................662 323-9991
David Breazeale, *Principal*
EMP: 10
SALES (est): 1.7MM **Privately Held**
SIC: **2411** Logging camps & contractors

(G-4939)
DELTA INDUSTRIES INC
311 Industrial Park Rd (39759-3993)
PHONE..............................662 323-7224
EMP: 1
SALES (corp-wide): 100.3MM **Privately Held**
SIC: **5211** 3273 Cement; ready-mixed concrete
PA: Delta Industries, Inc.
100 W Woodrow Wilson Ave
Jackson MS 39213
601 354-3801

(G-4940)
DESIREPATH MISSISSIPPI LLC
Also Called: Aspen Bay Candles
1010 Lynn Ln (39759-3963)
P.O. Box 1446 (39760-1446)
PHONE..............................662 324-2231
Tom Reed, *President*
Timothy D Hernly,
Mark Radzik,
Brian Sauers,
▲ EMP: 50
SQ FT: 40,000
SALES (est): 8MM
SALES (corp-wide): 3.8MM **Privately Held**
SIC: **3999** Candles
PA: Spring Thymes Holdings, Llc
629 9th St Se
Minneapolis MN 55414
612 338-4471

(G-4941)
DITTOS PRINT & COPY SHOP
602 Highway 12 E (39759-3826)
PHONE..............................662 324-3838
Brittney Holdr, *Owner*
EMP: 60
SALES (est): 2.8MM **Privately Held**
SIC: **2752** Commercial printing, lithographic

(G-4942)
DIXON-DRONE
162 Park Cir Apt D (39759-4407)
PHONE..............................662 545-9303
EMP: 2
SALES (est): 86K **Privately Held**
SIC: **3721** Mfg Aircraft

(G-4943)
DOGPOUND PRINTING LLC
319 E Dr Martn L Kng Dr Martin Luther Kin (39759)
PHONE..............................662 323-7425
Rick Welch, *Principal*
EMP: 2
SALES (est): 168.8K **Privately Held**
SIC: **2752** Commercial printing, lithographic

(PA)=Parent Co (HQ)=Headquarters (DH)=Div Headquarters
✿ = New Business established in last 2 years

2019 Harris Directory of
Mississippi Manufacturers

177

Starkville - Oktibbeha County (G-4944)

GEOGRAPHIC SECTION

(G-4944)
FLEXSTEEL INDUSTRIES INC
Commercial Seating Division
212 Industrial Park Rd (39759-3990)
P.O. Box 825 (39760-0825)
PHONE...................................662 323-5481
Chad Stowell, *Plant Mgr*
Gary McMinn, *Project Engr*
Pat Salmon, *Sales/Mktg Mgr*
Roy Pollard, *Human Res Mgr*
Albert Frazier, *Manager*
EMP: 328
SQ FT: 235,000
SALES (corp-wide): 489.1MM **Publicly Held**
WEB: www.flexsteel.com
SIC: 2512 2531 2522 2521 Upholstered household furniture; public building & related furniture; office furniture, except wood; wood office furniture
PA: Flexsteel Industries, Inc.
385 Bell St
Dubuque IA 52001
563 556-7730

(G-4945)
GARAN MANUFACTURING CORP
Highway 12 W (39759)
P.O. Box 100 (39760-0100)
PHONE...................................662 323-4731
Phillip Rush, *Branch Mgr*
EMP: 120
SALES (corp-wide): 225.3B **Publicly Held**
WEB: www.garanimals.com
SIC: 2361 2369 2331 2339 T-shirts & tops: girls', children's & infants'; slacks: girls' & children's; T-shirts & tops, women's: made from purchased materials; shirts, women's & juniors': made from purchased materials; jeans: women's, misses' & juniors'; men's & boys' furnishings; sport shirts, men's & boys': from purchased materials
HQ: Garan Manufacturing Corp.
200 Madison Ave Fl 4
New York NY 10016

(G-4946)
GENTRY SIGNS
9 Lynn Ln (39759-3989)
P.O. Box 494 (39760-0494)
PHONE...................................662 323-3652
Hillman M Gentry, *Owner*
EMP: 1
SALES (est): 99.5K **Privately Held**
SIC: 3993 Signs & advertising specialties

(G-4947)
HANGER PRSTHETCS & ORTHO INC
100 Brandon Rd Ste D (39759-2571)
PHONE...................................662 323-3349
Terry Goin, *Manager*
EMP: 1
SALES (corp-wide): 1B **Publicly Held**
SIC: 5999 3842 Orthopedic & prosthesis applications; prosthetic appliances
HQ: Hanger Prosthetics & Orthotics, Inc.
10910 Domain Dr Ste 300
Austin TX 78758
512 777-3800

(G-4948)
HEWLETT INDUSTRIES INC (PA)
407 Industrial Park Rd (39759-3943)
P.O. Box 170 (39760-0170)
PHONE...................................662 773-4626
Richard Hewlett, *President*
▲ EMP: 56
SALES (est): 3.8MM **Privately Held**
SIC: 3089 Pallets, plastic

(G-4949)
HIGH YIELD AG SOLUTIONS LLC
Also Called: Hyas
123 Jefferson St (39759-2919)
PHONE...................................662 546-4463
EMP: 2
SALES (est): 166.4K **Privately Held**
SIC: 3825 Network analyzers

(G-4950)
HORIZON PUBLICATIONS INC
Also Called: Starkville Daily News
304 E Lampkin St (39759-2910)
P.O. Box 1068 (39760-1068)
PHONE...................................662 323-1642
Mona Howell, *Business Mgr*
EMP: 25
SALES (corp-wide): 71.5MM **Privately Held**
WEB: www.malvern-online.com
SIC: 2711 Newspapers, publishing & printing
PA: Horizon Publications, Inc.
1120 N Carbon St Ste 100
Marion IL 62959
618 993-1711

(G-4951)
II-VI INCORPORATED
60 Technology Blvd (39759-1301)
PHONE...................................662 615-5040
EMP: 8
SALES (corp-wide): 1.3B **Publicly Held**
SIC: 3827 Optical instruments & lenses
PA: Ii-Vi Incorporated
375 Saxonburg Blvd
Saxonburg PA 16056
724 352-4455

(G-4952)
JC MANUFACTURING LLC
3111 Old Highway 12 (39759-7637)
PHONE...................................662 338-9004
John W Campbell, *Mng Member*
EMP: 6
SQ FT: 3,000
SALES: 5MM **Privately Held**
SIC: 2431 3442 Doors, wood; metal doors

(G-4953)
JOANNA FREELY
781 Rachel Turner Rd (39759-6826)
PHONE...................................662 272-8679
Joanna Freely, *Owner*
Michael Freely, *Co-Owner*
EMP: 2 EST: 1998
SALES (est): 85K **Privately Held**
SIC: 2399 Horse harnesses & riding crops, etc.: non-leather

(G-4954)
KIRBY BLDG SYSTEMS MISS LLC
101 Airport Rd (39759-9682)
P.O. Box 1128 (39760-1128)
PHONE...................................662 323-8021
Denny Cole, *Engineer*
Irving Pylate, *Engineer*
Matthew McKenzie, *Design Engr*
Kimberly Norman, *Credit Staff*
Bill Holloway, *Regl Sales Mgr*
EMP: 198
SALES: 39MM
SALES (corp-wide): 25B **Publicly Held**
SIC: 3448 Prefabricated metal buildings
PA: Nucor Corporation
1915 Rexford Rd Ste 400
Charlotte NC 28211
704 366-7000

(G-4955)
LANDMARK SPATIAL SOLUTIONS LLC
4635 County Lake Rd (39759-8193)
PHONE...................................662 769-5344
Johnny Thompson, *Mng Member*
EMP: 3
SQ FT: 200
SALES: 1.3MM **Privately Held**
SIC: 5734 3728 5961 3699 Computer & software stores; target drones; computer equipment & electronics, mail order; laser systems & equipment

(G-4956)
LEOPOLD INDS INTRGLAETICAL LLC
211 Hickory Dr (39759-6926)
PHONE...................................662 324-0536
Bruce D Leopold, *Principal*
EMP: 1
SALES (est): 56.3K **Privately Held**
SIC: 3999 Manufacturing industries

(G-4957)
MATHIS PLOW INC
Also Called: Fesco
1281 Old Hwy 82 E (39759)
PHONE...................................662 323-5600
◆ EMP: 10
SQ FT: 12,000
SALES: 700K **Privately Held**
WEB: www.mathisplow.com
SIC: 3531 Forestry related equipment

(G-4958)
MFJ ENTERPRISES INC (PA)
Also Called: Ameritron
300 Industrial Park Rd (39759-3992)
P.O. Box 494, Mississippi State (39762-0494)
PHONE...................................662 323-5869
Martin Fun Gwon Jue, *President*
Betty Lou Quong Jue, *Corp Secy*
Steven Pan, *Vice Pres*
Sushing Pan, *Vice Pres*
Betty L Jue, *Treasurer*
◆ EMP: 100
SQ FT: 21,000
SALES (est): 21.2MM **Privately Held**
WEB: www.mfjenterprises.com
SIC: 5731 3651 Radio, television & electronic stores; household video equipment

(G-4959)
MFJ ENTERPRISES INC
Also Called: Hy Gain
308 Industrial Park Rd (39759-3992)
P.O. Box 494, Mississippi State (39762-0494)
PHONE...................................662 323-9538
Martin Jue, *President*
EMP: 50
SALES (corp-wide): 21.2MM **Privately Held**
WEB: www.mfjenterprises.com
SIC: 3663 5065 Antennas, transmitting & communications; radio & television equipment & parts
PA: Mfj Enterprises, Inc.
300 Industrial Park Rd
Starkville MS 39759
662 323-5869

(G-4960)
MISSISSIPPI STATE UNIVERSITY
Also Called: Diagnostic Instrmntn & Anlys L
205 Research Blvd (39759-7704)
PHONE...................................662 325-2510
John Plodinec, *Director*
Charles Waggoner, *Deputy Dir*
Leslie Bauman, *Professor*
Leanne Long, *Assistant*
Jeremy Lasalle, *Associate*
EMP: 70
SALES (corp-wide): 489.2MM **Privately Held**
WEB: www.msstate.edu
SIC: 3829 8221 Measuring & controlling devices; university
PA: Mississippi State University
245 Barr Ave Mcrthur Hl Mcarthur Hall
Mississippi State MS 39762
662 325-2302

(G-4961)
MMC MATERIALS INC
217 Industrial Park Rd (39759-3991)
P.O. Box 1347 (39760-1347)
PHONE...................................662 323-0644
Rock McBride, *Manager*
EMP: 14
SALES (corp-wide): 306.5MM **Privately Held**
WEB: www.mmcmaterials.com
SIC: 3273 Ready-mixed concrete
HQ: Mmc Materials, Inc.
1052 Highland Colony Pkwy # 201
Ridgeland MS 39157
601 898-4000

(G-4962)
MSTATE TECHNOLOGIES LLC
2608 Pinoak Dr (39759-3546)
P.O. Box 2039 (39760-2039)
PHONE...................................662 418-0110
EMP: 1

(G-4963)
SALES (est): 94.8K **Privately Held**
SIC: 3949 3663 Mfg Sporting/Athletic Goods Mfg Radio/Tv Communication Equipment

NCI GROUP INC
Also Called: Nci Drafting Division
530 Vine St (39759-3271)
PHONE...................................662 324-1845
Danny Henson, *Branch Mgr*
Donny Hanson, *Manager*
EMP: 75
SALES (corp-wide): 2B **Publicly Held**
SIC: 3448 Buildings, portable: prefabricated metal
HQ: Nci Group, Inc.
10943 N Sam Huston Pkwy W
Houston TX 77064
281 897-7788

(G-4964)
NEW PATIENTS NUMBER
407 University Dr (39759-2915)
PHONE...................................662 323-2803
EMP: 2
SALES (est): 120K **Privately Held**
SIC: 3843 Mfg Dental Equipment/Supplies

(G-4965)
P & B ENTERPRISES INC
200 Morrill Rd (39759-5390)
PHONE...................................662 323-8565
Richard Patton, *President*
Albert George Benette Jr, *Vice Pres*
EMP: 3
SALES (est): 279K **Privately Held**
SIC: 3519 Internal combustion engines

(G-4966)
PAUL YEATMAN
Also Called: Paul's Welding
254 Longview Rd (39759-4917)
PHONE...................................662 323-7140
Paul Yeatman, *Owner*
EMP: 3
SALES (est): 130.4K **Privately Held**
SIC: 7692 Welding repair

(G-4967)
REEVES CABINETS
112 Miley Dr (39759-7728)
PHONE...................................662 323-3633
Dwight Reeves, *President*
EMP: 1
SALES (est): 110.2K **Privately Held**
SIC: 2434 Wood kitchen cabinets

(G-4968)
RICE EQUIPMENT CO LLC
5893 Ms Highway 182 (39759-2386)
PHONE...................................662 323-5502
Tim Rice, *President*
EMP: 1
SQ FT: 7,500
SALES: 250K **Privately Held**
SIC: 7692 Welding repair

(G-4969)
RONDA K GENTRY
Also Called: Rkr Woodworking
2225 Old Highway 12 (39759-7498)
PHONE...................................662 418-9844
Ronda Gentry, *Owner*
EMP: 1
SALES (est): 60K **Privately Held**
SIC: 2441 7389 Boxes, wood;

(G-4970)
SEVLO SOLUTIONS LLC
Also Called: Computer Systems
39a Sadye Weir St (39759-2475)
PHONE...................................662 312-9507
Henry Antonio Sudduth, *Mng Member*
EMP: 1
SALES (est): 57.9K **Privately Held**
SIC: 7819 3089 7335 Services allied to motion pictures; identification cards, plastic; aerial photography, except mapmaking

(G-4971)
SISTERS OF CREATIONS
102 Green Hill Dr (39759-2269)
PHONE...................................662 615-3978
Turnesia Fason, *Owner*

2019 Harris Directory of
Mississippi Manufacturers

178

▲ = Import ▼=Export
◆ =Import/Export

GEOGRAPHIC SECTION

Stonewall - Clarke County (G-5000)

EMP: 3
SALES: 200K **Privately Held**
SIC: 3999 Manufacturing industries

(G-4972)
SONOCO PRODUCTS COMPANY
1025 Lynn Ln (39759-3905)
PHONE..................................662 615-6204
David Hughs, *Branch Mgr*
EMP: 57
SALES (corp-wide): 5.3B **Publicly Held**
SIC: 2631 Paperboard mills
PA: Sonoco Products Company
1 N 2nd St
Hartsville SC 29550
843 383-7000

(G-4973)
SOUTHERN SCENTS BY CARLA LLC
41 Augusta Dr (39759-6066)
PHONE..................................662 312-5610
Carla Cummings, *Principal*
EMP: 2 EST: 2014
SALES (est): 140.7K **Privately Held**
SIC: 2844 Toilet preparations

(G-4974)
SOUTHWIRE COMPANY LLC
103 Airport Rd (39759-9682)
P.O. Box 967 (39760-0967)
PHONE..................................662 324-6600
Kathy Brown, *Principal*
Ross Alldread, *Buyer*
Blakelee Morgan, *Engineer*
Heath Street, *Engineer*
Mike Pankey, *Manager*
EMP: 40
SALES (corp-wide): 2.2B **Privately Held**
WEB: www.southwire.com
SIC: 3355 3357 3315 Aluminum wire &
cable; nonferrous wiredrawing & insulat-
ing; steel wire & related products
PA: Southwire Company, Llc
1 Southwire Dr
Carrollton GA 30119
770 832-4242

(G-4975)
STANDARD DYNAMICS LLC
822 Taylor St (39760-4401)
P.O. Box 1582 (39760-1582)
PHONE..................................228 383-2070
Cory Krivanec, *Mng Member*
EMP: 5
SALES (est): 239.7K **Privately Held**
SIC: 3829 Measuring & controlling devices

(G-4976)
STOCKMANS SUPPLY LLC
13545 Ms Highway 12 W (39759-6062)
P.O. Box 921 (39760-0921)
PHONE..................................601 750-2726
Clint Eaves, *President*
EMP: 13
SALES (est): 564.4K **Privately Held**
SIC: 0742 2834 Veterinarian, animal spe-
cialties; veterinary pharmaceutical prepa-
rations

(G-4977)
TECH WIRE
4588 Rock Hill Rd (39759-7504)
PHONE..................................773 669-7583
EMP: 26 EST: 2005
SALES (est): 2.3MM **Privately Held**
SIC: 3312 Nonclassifiable Establishments

(G-4978)
UNIVERSITY SCREEN PRINT INC
Also Called: Logo Specialties
414 Highway 12 E (39759-3822)
PHONE..................................662 324-8277
John M Hendricks, *President*
Marc Anthony, *Vice Pres*
Holley Gardner, *Sales Dir*
Wilson Gardner, *Manager*
EMP: 11
SQ FT: 2,400
SALES (est): 1.3MM **Privately Held**
SIC: 3993 2261 Signs & advertising spe-
cialties; screen printing of cotton broad-
woven fabrics

(G-4979)
WATERMARK PRINTERS LLC
1085 Stark Rd (39759-3682)
PHONE..................................662 323-8750
Jimmy Covin, *Executive Asst*
EMP: 2
SALES (est): 214.7K **Privately Held**
SIC: 2759 Commercial printing

(G-4980)
WEAVEXX LLC
401 Mississippi 12 W (39759)
P.O. Box 1067 (39760-1067)
PHONE..................................662 323-4064
Keith Rising, *Systems Mgr*
EMP: 200
SALES (corp-wide): 6.9B **Privately Held**
WEB: www.weavexx.com
SIC: 2221 5199 2299 Specialty broadwo-
ven fabrics, including twisted weaves; felt;
felts & felt products
HQ: Weavexx, Llc
14101 Capital Blvd
Youngsville NC 27596

(G-4981)
WELDING WORKS LLC
307 Industrial Park Rd (39759-3993)
PHONE..................................662 323-8684
Justin Lindley, *Mng Member*
Katie Lindley,
EMP: 6 EST: 2014
SQ FT: 300
SALES: 500K **Privately Held**
SIC: 7692 Welding repair

(G-4982)
WHITNEY
96 Lummus Dr (39759-1500)
PHONE..................................662 268-8379
EMP: 2
SALES (est): 112K **Privately Held**
SIC: 3724 Aircraft engines & engine parts

(G-4983)
XERIUM TECHNOLOGIES INC
401 Highway 12 W (39759-3602)
PHONE..................................662 323-4064
EMP: 8
SALES (corp-wide): 6.9B **Privately Held**
SIC: 3069 Medical & laboratory rubber
sundries & related products
HQ: Andritz Fabrics And Rolls Inc.
14101 Capital Blvd
Youngsville NC 27596
919 526-1400

State Line
Greene County

(G-4984)
CLAUDE GUY
5 Gandy St (39362-6027)
P.O. Box 263 (39362-0263)
PHONE..................................601 848-7859
Claude Guy, *Principal*
EMP: 2
SALES (est): 81.7K **Privately Held**
SIC: 2411 Logging

(G-4985)
D & D OILFIELD CONSULTANTS INC
57 Gaines Hinton Rd (39362-9475)
PHONE..................................601 648-2282
Bobby Hudson, *Principal*
EMP: 2
SALES (est): 81.9K **Privately Held**
SIC: 1311 Crude petroleum & natural gas

(G-4986)
DUCKWRTH DRLG COMPLETION L L C
504 Miller Wicks Rd (39362-8459)
PHONE..................................601 848-6486
N Eugene Duckworth Jr, *Owner*
EMP: 2
SALES (est): 144.8K **Privately Held**
SIC: 1389 Construction, repair & disman-
tling services

(G-4987)
KENNETH SMITH
Also Called: Triple S Logging
283 Woulard Bend River Rd (39362-9411)
PHONE..................................601 848-7956
Eric Smith, *Principal*
EMP: 3
SALES (est): 232.6K **Privately Held**
SIC: 2411 Logging

(G-4988)
RICHARD FICK
15438 Old Avera Rd (39362-7106)
PHONE..................................601 848-7420
Richard Fick, *Owner*
EMP: 1
SALES (est): 53.5K **Privately Held**
SIC: 1751 3531 Carpentry work; back-
hoes, tractors, cranes, plows & similar
equipment

(G-4989)
WALLEY TRUCKING
19645 Mrtn Luther King Dr (39362-8803)
PHONE..................................601 848-7576
Stance Walley, *Owner*
EMP: 2
SALES (est): 120K **Privately Held**
SIC: 2411 Logging

Steens
Lowndes County

(G-4990)
BOWEN TITUS
Also Called: Bowen Backhoe Service
462 Dickerson Rd (39766-9570)
PHONE..................................662 327-3084
William Bowen, *Owner*
EMP: 1 EST: 1970
SALES (est): 80.1K **Privately Held**
SIC: 3531 Construction machinery

(G-4991)
MINI MTRS UNLIMITED SLS & SVC
2186 Sanders Mill Rd (39766-9613)
PHONE..................................662 356-4900
Charles Bush, *Owner*
EMP: 2
SALES (est): 134.2K **Privately Held**
SIC: 7699 3599 5084 Lawn mower repair
shop; boiler tube cleaners; engines, gaso-
line

(G-4992)
WHITE SEPTIC BACKHOE LLC
69 Mohave Ln (39766-9544)
PHONE..................................662 251-8989
EMP: 2
SALES (est): 83K **Privately Held**
SIC: 3531 Backhoes

Stennis Space Center
Hancock County

(G-4993)
AEROJET ROCKETDYNE INC
9101 Lnard Kmble Rd Rrm07
(39529-0001)
PHONE..................................228 813-1511
Michael McDaniel, *Branch Mgr*
EMP: 148
SALES (corp-wide): 1.9B **Publicly Held**
SIC: 3724 Air scoops, aircraft
HQ: Aerojet Rocketdyne, Inc.
2001 Aerojet Rd
Rancho Cordova CA 95742
916 355-4000

(G-4994)
DQSI LLC
John C Stennis Space Cent (39529-0001)
PHONE..................................228 688-3796
Kenny Enclade, *Branch Mgr*
EMP: 2
SALES (corp-wide): 4MM **Privately Held**
SIC: 7372 Prepackaged software

PA: Dqsi, Llc
19218 N 5th St
Covington LA 70433
985 871-7472

(G-4995)
JKS INTERNATIONAL LLC
Msaap Bldg 9353 (39529-0001)
PHONE..................................228 689-8999
EMP: 10
SALES (est): 143.3K **Privately Held**
SIC: 3089 Mfg Plastic Products

(G-4996)
PERSPECTA ENGINEERING INC
1103 Balch Blvd Ste 218 (39529-0001)
PHONE..................................571 313-6000
John Curtis, *CEO*
Brad Perniciaro, *Software Engr*
EMP: 3
SQ FT: 10,000
SALES (corp-wide): 12.1B **Publicly Held**
SIC: 8733 3812 7372 8711 Economic re-
search, noncommercial; defense systems
& equipment; radio magnetic instrumenta-
tion; application computer software; pro-
fessional engineer
HQ: Perspecta Engineering Inc.
15050 Conference Ctr Dr
Chantilly VA 20151
571 313-6000

(G-4997)
ROLLS-ROYCE NORTH AMERICA INC
5002 Test Site H1 (39529-0001)
PHONE..................................228 688-1003
EMP: 8
SALES (corp-wide): 20.2B **Privately Held**
SIC: 3825 Internal combustion engine ana-
lyzers, to test electronics
HQ: Rolls-Royce North America Inc.
1875 Explorer St Ste 200
Reston VA 20190
703 834-1700

Stonewall
Clarke County

(G-4998)
PINE BELT PROCESSING INC
1122 Erwin Rd (39363-9784)
P.O. Box 557, Taylorsville (39168-0557)
PHONE..................................601 785-4476
Donald C Saxon, *President*
Roger D Lack, *Vice Pres*
▲ EMP: 25
SALES (est): 1.9MM **Privately Held**
SIC: 2311 Military uniforms, men's &
youths': purchased materials

(G-4999)
S&S SIGNS
117 Harper Ln (39363-9714)
PHONE..................................601 659-7783
Scotty Allen, *Principal*
EMP: 2 EST: 2008
SALES (est): 134.2K **Privately Held**
SIC: 3993 Signs, not made in custom sign
painting shops

(G-5000)
WARMKRAFT INC
1122 Erwin Rd (39363-9784)
P.O. Box 549 (39363-0549)
PHONE..................................601 659-3317
Ron Lack, *General Mgr*
EMP: 49
SALES (corp-wide): 25.2MM **Privately
Held**
SIC: 3634 Electric housewares & fans
PA: Warmkraft, Inc
113 Fellowship Rd
Taylorsville MS 39168
601 785-4476

(PA)=Parent Co (HQ)=Headquarters (DH)=Div Headquarters
✿ = New Business established in last 2 years

2019 Harris Directory of
Mississippi Manufacturers

179

GEOGRAPHIC SECTION

Stringer - Jasper County (G-5001)

Stringer
Jasper County

(G-5001)
HICKS HOT SHOT SERVICES LLC
593 County Road 79 (39481-4553)
PHONE..................601 498-7482
EMP: 2 **EST:** 2017
SALES (est): 65.5K **Privately Held**
SIC: 1389 Hot shot service

(G-5002)
HOLLOWAYS WELDING SERVICE LLC
468 County Road 7 (39481-4607)
PHONE..................601 729-4403
James Hollowaly, *Principal*
James A Holloway, *Principal*
EMP: 1 **EST:** 2013
SALES (est): 53.1K **Privately Held**
SIC: 7692 Welding repair

(G-5003)
JASPER COOPERATIVE
34 County Road 17 (39481-4466)
PHONE..................601 428-4968
Bobby Sykes, *President*
Forrest R Sims, *President*
JC Duckworth, *General Mgr*
EMP: 8 **EST:** 1946
SQ FT: 24,000
SALES (est): 2.5MM **Privately Held**
SIC: 5191 2048 Farm supplies; prepared feeds

(G-5004)
SOUTHERN INDUSTRIAL TECH LLC
25 County Road 17 (39481-4468)
P.O. Box 7 (39481-0007)
PHONE..................601 426-3866
Billy Van Sumrall, *Mng Member*
Connie Sumrall, *Admin Sec*
Reggie Sumrall,
EMP: 16
SALES (est): 2.6MM **Privately Held**
SIC: 3441 Fabricated structural metal

(G-5005)
TRICOUNTY READY MIX INC
1241 Highway 15 (39481-4541)
P.O. Box 148 (39481-0148)
PHONE..................601 649-2887
Howard King, *Principal*
EMP: 10
SALES (est): 1.3MM **Privately Held**
SIC: 3273 Ready-mixed concrete

Sturgis
Oktibbeha County

(G-5006)
CARPENTERS CABINETS
3881 Highway 12 W (39769-9744)
P.O. Box 112 (39769-0112)
PHONE..................662 465-6453
Earl Carpenter, *Owner*
EMP: 1
SALES (est): 150.3K **Privately Held**
SIC: 2434 Wood kitchen cabinets

(G-5007)
MAT STURGIS CO INC
4062 Strgis Louisville Rd (39769)
PHONE..................662 465-8879
George Bowman, *CEO*
EMP: 30
SALES (est): 4.1MM **Privately Held**
SIC: 2273 Mats & matting

Summit
Pike County

(G-5008)
CLEAR CREEK CABINETRY INC
1014 Clear Creek Ln (39666-7903)
PHONE..................601 684-7130
James M Hewitt, *President*
EMP: 9
SALES (est): 204.9K **Privately Held**
SIC: 2434 Wood kitchen cabinets

(G-5009)
CORNWELL WELL SERVICE INC
1004 Magee Rd (39666-7012)
P.O. Box 647 (39666-0647)
PHONE..................601 684-4951
Cathy Davis, *President*
Martin Van Cornwell Jr, *Vice Pres*
EMP: 20 **EST:** 1951
SQ FT: 1,500
SALES (est): 1.4MM **Privately Held**
SIC: 1389 Oil field services

(G-5010)
DANNY BERRY
Also Called: Southwest Ready Mix Concrete
1178 Old Brookhaven Rd (39666-8164)
P.O. Box 1285 (39666-1285)
PHONE..................601 276-6200
Balinda Gilmone Vandan, *Owner*
EMP: 6
SALES (est): 618.1K **Privately Held**
WEB: www.dannyberry.com
SIC: 3273 Ready-mixed concrete

(G-5011)
DENBURY RESOURCES INC
7969 Robert Jones Rd (39666-7036)
PHONE..................601 276-2677
Tom Cole, *Branch Mgr*
EMP: 18
SALES (corp-wide): 1.4B **Publicly Held**
SIC: 1382 Oil & gas exploration services
PA: Denbury Resources Inc.
5320 Legacy Dr
Plano TX 75024
972 673-2000

(G-5012)
DIXIE PACKAGING INC
1183 Dixie Springs Rd (39666-9117)
P.O. Box 788 (39666-0788)
PHONE..................601 276-9317
Barry Hart, *President*
Jamie Hart, *Vice Pres*
June Hart, *Vice Pres*
Jerry Robison, *Vice Pres*
Ricky Welch, *Vice Pres*
EMP: 25
SQ FT: 20,000
SALES (est): 6.7MM **Privately Held**
SIC: 2673 3081 Plastic bags: made from purchased materials; unsupported plastics film & sheet

(G-5013)
EIGHTEEN-SEVENTEEN PRTG LLC
2142 Willis Cotton Rd (39666-7078)
PHONE..................601 300-0506
Lora Vance, *Principal*
EMP: 2
SALES (est): 170.6K **Privately Held**
SIC: 2752 Commercial printing, lithographic

(G-5014)
EMPIRE SERVICES INC
6451 County Line Rd (39666-7043)
PHONE..................601 276-2500
Leighton Davis, *President*
EMP: 150
SQ FT: 3,500
SALES: 30MM **Privately Held**
SIC: 3317 Steel pipe & tubes

(G-5015)
HOLIFIELD ENGINEERING INC
1062 Golf Ln (39666-8907)
PHONE..................601 276-3391
Robert W Holifield, *President*
EMP: 1

SQ FT: 2,400
SALES (est): 204.6K **Privately Held**
WEB: www.holifieldengineering.com
SIC: 3449 Bars, concrete reinforcing: fabricated steel

(G-5016)
HOLMES STATIONARY AND GIFTS
Also Called: Moores Living and Storage
1136 Highway 51 N (39666-9127)
P.O. Box 729 (39666-0729)
PHONE..................601 276-2700
Susan Gibbes, *Owner*
EMP: 7
SALES (est): 376.7K **Privately Held**
SIC: 5947 2791 2759 2752 Gift shop; typesetting; commercial printing; commercial printing, lithographic

(G-5017)
LYLE MACHINERY CO
298 Lawrence St (39666-8190)
PHONE..................601 276-3528
EMP: 1 **Privately Held**
SIC: 5084 5082 3599 Whol Industrial Equipment Whol Construction/Mining Equipment Mfg Industrial Machinery
PA: Lyle Machinery Co.
650 Highway 49 S
Jackson MS 39218

(G-5018)
NEWPARK DRILLING FLUIDS LLC
1024 Highpoint Rd (39666-8066)
PHONE..................281 362-6800
Daniela Quast, *Asst Treas*
EMP: 10
SQ FT: 40,000
SALES (corp-wide): 946.5MM **Publicly Held**
SIC: 1389 Oil field services
HQ: Newpark Drilling Fluids Llc
21920 Merchants Way
Katy TX 77449
281 754-8600

(G-5019)
PRECISION WELDING
3069 Johnston Chapel Rd (39666-8214)
PHONE..................601 730-0224
Mike Dickerson, *President*
Donna Dickerson, *Owner*
EMP: 1
SALES: 50K **Privately Held**
SIC: 7692 Welding repair

(G-5020)
REID ELECTRIC MOTOR SERVICES
1008 Office Park Ct (39666-7188)
PHONE..................601 684-6040
Sharon Lambert, *Owner*
EMP: 2
SALES (est): 171.5K **Privately Held**
SIC: 7694 Electric motor repair

(G-5021)
SANDERSON FARMS INC PROC DIV
4039 River Rdg Rd (39666)
P.O. Box 867, McComb (39649-0867)
PHONE..................601 684-9375
Ray Tucker, *Purch Dir*
Cecil Jackson, *Manager*
Steven McFarland, *Manager*
EMP: 2029
SALES (corp-wide): 3.2B **Publicly Held**
SIC: 2015 2011 Chicken slaughtering & processing; meat packing plants
HQ: Sanderson Farms, Inc. (Processing Division)
127 Flynt Rd
Laurel MS 39443
601 649-4030

(G-5022)
SOUTHWEST MISSISSIPPI ROBOTICS
1062 Golf Ln (39666-8907)
PHONE..................601 276-4276
Robert Holifield, *Principal*
EMP: 2

SALES (est): 81.4K **Privately Held**
SIC: 3599 Industrial machinery

(G-5023)
SUMMIT CABINET CO LLC
2060 Moak Rd (39666-9297)
PHONE..................601 684-1639
EMP: 2
SALES: 100K **Privately Held**
SIC: 2434 Wood kitchen cabinets

(G-5024)
SUMMIT PLASTICS INC
107 S Laurel St (39666-9349)
PHONE..................601 276-7500
Michael Monteferrante, *President*
Frank Clepper, *Principal*
Mike Stephens, *Vice Pres*
Greg Unruh, *Treasurer*
Kent Wilson, *Treasurer*
▲ **EMP:** 45
SALES (est): 10.6MM
SALES (corp-wide): 192.4MM **Privately Held**
WEB: www.envisionus.com
SIC: 3081 Polyethylene film
PA: Envision, Inc.
2301 S Water St
Wichita KS 67213
316 267-2244

(G-5025)
SWEET TEE SCREEN PRINTING
803 Robb St (39666-8247)
PHONE..................601 757-3435
EMP: 2
SALES (est): 89.2K **Privately Held**
SIC: 2759 Commercial printing

(G-5026)
THORNHILL WELDING
5228 Wilson Rd (39666-9290)
PHONE..................601 248-6472
H Thornhill, *Principal*
EMP: 1
SALES (est): 38.2K **Privately Held**
SIC: 7692 Welding repair

(G-5027)
TRINITY THREE LLC
1009 Meadville St (39666-9485)
PHONE..................601 249-8851
Anthony C Dillon Sr, *Manager*
EMP: 1
SALES (est): 57.8K **Privately Held**
SIC: 4212 1799 2411 Local trucking, without storage; special trade contractors; logging

(G-5028)
W L BYRD LUMBER CO INC (PA)
2145 Highway 98 W (39666-7210)
P.O. Box 150, Fernwood (39635-0150)
PHONE..................601 783-5711
Jerry Byrd, *President*
James Byrd, *Treasurer*
Kevin Byrd, *Director*
Larue Byrd, *Director*
Keith Byrd, *Admin Sec*
EMP: 48
SQ FT: 1,200
SALES (est): 5.5MM **Privately Held**
SIC: 2421 Lumber: rough, sawed or planed

(G-5029)
W L BYRD LUMBER CO INC
2145 Highway 98 W (39666-7210)
PHONE..................601 567-2314
Jerry Byrd, *Branch Mgr*
EMP: 22
SALES (corp-wide): 5.5MM **Privately Held**
SIC: 2421 2411 Sawmills & planing mills, general; logging
PA: W L Byrd Lumber Co Inc
2145 Highway 98 W
Summit MS 39666
601 783-5711

(G-5030)
WALLACE LUMBER COMPANY
6521 County Line Rd (39666-7044)
PHONE..................601 276-2834
Mark Wallace, *President*
Melinda Wallace, *Corp Secy*
Wendell Forest, *Sales Executive*

2019 Harris Directory of
Mississippi Manufacturers

▲ = Import ▼ =Export
◆ =Import/Export

180

GEOGRAPHIC SECTION

Taylorsville - Smith County (G-5058)

Wendell Forrest, *Sales Executive*
Leslie Johnson, *Manager*
EMP: 50
SALES (est): 10.1MM **Privately Held**
WEB: www.empiremat.com
SIC: 2421 Lumber: rough, sawed or planed

(G-5031)
WREN PEST CONTROL
1160 Robb Street Ext E (39666-9721)
P.O. Box 143, McComb (39649-0143)
PHONE..................................601 276-6117
Glenn Wren, *Owner*
EMP: 2
SALES (est): 93K **Privately Held**
SIC: 3993 7342 Signs & advertising specialties; pest control services

Sumner
Tallahatchie County

(G-5032)
SMITH MACHINE & IRON INC
2479 Hwy 49 E (38957)
PHONE..................................662 375-8551
Brian Smith, *President*
Yvonne J Smith, *Treasurer*
EMP: 3 EST: 1967
SQ FT: 600
SALES (est): 120K **Privately Held**
SIC: 3599 Machine shop, jobbing & repair

Sumrall
Lamar County

(G-5033)
AJS WELDING REPAIR
601 Nobles Rd (39482-3821)
PHONE..................................601 264-2571
EMP: 1
SALES (est): 44.6K **Privately Held**
SIC: 7692 Welding Repair

(G-5034)
BEC FIRE AND SAFETY LLC
94a Gussy Nobles Rd (39482-3897)
PHONE..................................601 498-9108
Diana B Ishee,
Kevin Ishee,
EMP: 2
SALES (est): 184.2K **Privately Held**
SIC: 2899 7389 Chemical preparations;

(G-5035)
BILAL 100 ALL NATURAL SPRING
26 Regan Rd (39482-3611)
PHONE..................................601 323-2237
EMP: 1
SALES (est): 67.1K **Privately Held**
SIC: 2899 Distilled water

(G-5036)
FAMILY MEAT PROCESSING
142 N Black Creek Rd (39482-3909)
PHONE..................................601 264-2344
Sarad Mohamed, *Owner*
EMP: 2
SALES: 75K **Privately Held**
SIC: 2011 7299 5421 Meat packing plants; butcher service, processing only; meat markets, including freezer provisioners

(G-5037)
KERMIT BROOME SONS WD CHIPPING
113 W Black Creek Rd (39482-3839)
PHONE..................................601 264-8470
Kermit Broome, *President*
Michael Broome, *Vice Pres*
Linda Broome, *Admin Sec*
EMP: 38
SQ FT: 4,500
SALES (est): 7MM **Privately Held**
SIC: 2421 Wood chips, produced at mill

(G-5038)
MAILBOX RANCH
84 Sonny Carter Dr (39482-9729)
PHONE..................................601 758-4767
Martha Carter, *Principal*
EMP: 2
SALES (est): 262.3K **Privately Held**
WEB: www.themailboxranch.com
SIC: 2542 7389 Mail racks & lock boxes; postal service: except wood; mailbox rental & related service

(G-5039)
MCMAHAN BULLDOG ENTERPRISES
Also Called: Bulldog Brackets
203 Canty Rayborn Rd (39482-4733)
PHONE..................................601 606-5711
Victor McMahan, *Owner*
EMP: 2
SALES (est): 162.5K **Privately Held**
SIC: 3441 Fabricated structural metal

(G-5040)
PARTHENON ENVELOPE COMPANY LLC
10 Veterans Memorial Dr (39482-5602)
P.O. Box 347 (39482-0347)
PHONE..................................601 758-4788
Trey Rhian,
Louis Rhian,
EMP: 22
SALES (est): 2.4MM **Privately Held**
WEB: www.parthenonenvelope.com
SIC: 2677 Envelopes

(G-5041)
PLUM TROPHY SALES
4882 Highway 589 (39482-3950)
P.O. Box 673 (39482-0673)
PHONE..................................601 758-4834
Judy Pfalum, *General Ptnr*
EMP: 3
SALES (est): 175K **Privately Held**
SIC: 5999 7389 3231 Trophies & plaques; engraving service; decorated glassware: chipped, engraved, etched, etc.

(G-5042)
POWER PLUS INC
923 Highway 42 (39482-4342)
PHONE..................................601 264-1950
Billy Montgomery, *President*
David Montgomery, *President*
Betty Montgomery, *Corp Secy*
Brian Montgomery, *Treasurer*
EMP: 16
SALES (est): 2.2MM **Privately Held**
WEB: www.outdoorpowersales.com
SIC: 5261 7699 5084 3546 Lawnmowers & tractors; lawn mower repair shop; engines, gasoline; saws & sawing equipment; outdoor wood structural products

(G-5043)
ROCKY BR DIRECTIONAL DRLG LLC
196 Bob Graham Rd (39482-3500)
PHONE..................................601 758-3340
EMP: 2
SALES (est): 224.9K **Privately Held**
SIC: 1381 Oil/Gas Well Drilling

(G-5044)
SHIRLEY MCARTHUR NOBLES
956 Wpa Rd (39482-4068)
PHONE..................................601 310-0890
EMP: 1
SALES (est): 54.1K **Privately Held**
SIC: 2431 Millwork

(G-5045)
SPECIALTY SERVICES GROUP LLC
71 Fillingane Rd (39482-5019)
PHONE..................................601 543-9474
Russell R Griffith,
Milton G Richards,
EMP: 3
SALES: 83K **Privately Held**
SIC: 2911 Oils, fuel

Sunflower
Sunflower County

(G-5046)
DELTA PROTEIN INTL INC
200 Itta Bena Rd (38778-9637)
PHONE..................................662 279-8728
Christopher Gorski, *Principal*
Peter Noble, *Vice Pres*
Jason Gorski, *Mfg Staff*
Josh Nelson, *QC Mgr*
▲ **EMP:** 12
SQ FT: 660,000
SALES (est): 2.5MM **Privately Held**
SIC: 2899 Chemical preparations

(G-5047)
PROTEIN PRODUCTS INC
1042 Highway 3 (38778-9795)
PHONE..................................662 569-3396
Dallas Gay, *President*
Lacy Lary, *Enginr/R&D Mgr*
EMP: 42
SALES (corp-wide): 6.7MM **Privately Held**
SIC: 2077 2048 Fish meal, except as animal feed; prepared feeds
PA: Protein Products, Inc.
454 Green St Ne
Gainesville GA 30501
770 536-3922

Taylor
Lafayette County

(G-5048)
FONDREN AND SONS LLC
County Rd 343 Apt 249 (38673)
P.O. Box 31 (38673-0031)
PHONE..................................662 816-8640
EMP: 6
SQ FT: 5,000
SALES: 150K **Privately Held**
SIC: 3585 Parts for heating, cooling & refrigerating equipment

(G-5049)
LIVE AND LAFF LLC
Also Called: Mardis Honey
518 County Road 303 (38673-4556)
PHONE..................................662 816-5144
Karen Lafferty,
Michael Lafferty,
EMP: 2
SALES (est): 34.7K **Privately Held**
SIC: 0279 2099 Apiary (bee & honey farm); honey, strained & bottled

Taylorsville
Smith County

(G-5050)
AUTOMATIC PLATING INC
204 Fellowship Rd (39168-4475)
P.O. Box 239 (39168-0239)
PHONE..................................601 785-6923
EMP: 12
SQ FT: 20,000
SALES (est): 1.2MM **Privately Held**
SIC: 3471 Plating/Polishing Service

(G-5051)
BORGWARNER INC
Also Called: Borg Warner
214 Fellowship Rd (39168-4475)
PHONE..................................601 785-9504
Tim Stevens, *Branch Mgr*
EMP: 2
SALES (corp-wide): 10.5B **Publicly Held**
SIC: 3714 Motor vehicle parts & accessories
PA: Borgwarner Inc.
3850 Hamlin Rd
Auburn Hills MI 48326
248 754-9200

(G-5052)
BRYANT MEATS INC
Also Called: Bryant's Meat Processing
104 Fellowship Rd (39168-5501)
P.O. Box 321 (39168-0321)
PHONE..................................601 785-6507
Robert Hunt, *President*
Kay Hunt, *Corp Secy*
▲ **EMP:** 22
SQ FT: 20,000
SALES (est): 3.2MM **Privately Held**
SIC: 2013 Sausages & other prepared meats

(G-5053)
DELCO REMY AMERICA
214 Fellowship Rd (39168-4475)
PHONE..................................601 785-6690
John Gladney, *Principal*
EMP: 2
SALES (est): 167.5K **Privately Held**
SIC: 3694 Engine electrical equipment

(G-5054)
JAN SIGNS INC
1215 Highway 28 (39168-5647)
P.O. Box 304 (39168-0304)
PHONE..................................601 785-9800
Jan Heisey, *President*
EMP: 3
SALES (est): 100K **Privately Held**
SIC: 3993 Signs & advertising specialties

(G-5055)
KOCH INDUSTRIES INC
Hwy 28 W (39168)
P.O. Box 556 (39168-0556)
PHONE..................................601 785-6523
Harward Stevens, *Manager*
EMP: 14
SALES (corp-wide): 40.9B **Privately Held**
WEB: www.kochind.com
SIC: 2869 Formaldehyde (formalin)
PA: Koch Industries, Inc.
4111 E 37th St N
Wichita KS 67220
316 828-5500

(G-5056)
PAUL GARNER MOTORS LLC
417 Hwy 28 E (39168)
P.O. Box 247 (39168-0247)
PHONE..................................601 785-4924
Paul Garner, *Mng Member*
EMP: 4
SALES (est): 849.4K **Privately Held**
SIC: 5521 5511 3524 Automobiles, used cars only; trucks, tractors & trailers: new & used; lawn & garden equipment

(G-5057)
REMY REMAN LLC (DH)
214 Fellowship Rd (39168-4475)
PHONE..................................601 785-9504
John M Mayfield,
David Harbert,
Tim Hill,
David Stoll,
▲ **EMP:** 29
SALES (est): 45.5MM
SALES (corp-wide): 10.5B **Publicly Held**
SIC: 3714 Motor vehicle electrical equipment
HQ: Reman Holdings, Llc
600 Corporation Dr
Pendleton IN 46064
800 372-5131

(G-5058)
ROSEBURG FOREST PRODUCTS CO
Taylorsville Particleboard
10599 Old Hwy 99 S (39168)
PHONE..................................601 785-4734
Dean Leist, *Controller*
Chuck Tasma, *Branch Mgr*
EMP: 450
SALES (corp-wide): 949.4MM **Privately Held**
WEB: www.rfpco.com
SIC: 2493 Particleboard products
HQ: Roseburg Forest Products Co
3660 Gateway St Ste A
Springfield OR 97477
541 679-3311

(PA)=Parent Co (HQ)=Headquarters (DH)=Div Headquarters
✪ = New Business established in last 2 years

2019 Harris Directory of
Mississippi Manufacturers

181

Taylorsville - Smith County (G-5059)　　　　　　　　**GEOGRAPHIC SECTION**

(G-5059)
SOUTHERN STATES BEE SUPPLY LLC
109 Back St (39168-9502)
PHONE..................................601 513-5151
John Mosby, *Mng Member*
EMP: 1
SALES (est): 76.2K **Privately Held**
SIC: 3999 Beekeepers' supplies

(G-5060)
THE POST
124 Main St (39168)
P.O. Box 100 (39168-0100)
PHONE..................................601 785-4333
Harold Bynum, *Owner*
Ann Bynum, *Co-Owner*
EMP: 3
SALES (est): 159.7K **Privately Held**
SIC: 2711 Newspapers

(G-5061)
VIBRA SHINE INC
Also Called: Vibrashine
113 Fellowship Rd (39168-5500)
P.O. Box 557 (39168-0557)
PHONE..................................601 785-9854
EMP: 5
SALES (est): 209K **Privately Held**
SIC: 3471 Mfg Vibratory Polishing Machines

(G-5062)
WARMKRAFT INC (PA)
113 Fellowship Rd (39168-5500)
P.O. Box 557 (39168-0557)
PHONE..................................601 785-4476
Don Saxon, *President*
Roger Lack, *Vice Pres*
▼ EMP: 180
SQ FT: 104,000
SALES (est): 25.2MM **Privately Held**
SIC: 3634 7389 Heating units, electric (radiant heat): baseboard or wall; textile & apparel services

Terry
Hinds County

(G-5063)
AIR COND HTG & S/M SOLUTIONS
144 Pinedale Rd (39170-9646)
PHONE..................................601 720-5085
Jeff Johns, *Owner*
EMP: 2
SALES (est): 139.2K **Privately Held**
SIC: 3585 Air conditioning equipment, complete

(G-5064)
CARNET TECHNOLOGY
6097 Oakley Palestine Rd (39170-8834)
PHONE..................................601 857-8641
Carnet Wayne O'Neal, *Owner*
EMP: 1
SALES: 30K **Privately Held**
SIC: 3829 Measuring & controlling devices

(G-5065)
DOUBLETAP INDUSTRIES
104 Country Oaks Dr (39170-9799)
PHONE..................................601 506-3218
Steven Roberts, *Principal*
EMP: 2 EST: 2011
SALES (est): 91.5K **Privately Held**
SIC: 3999 Manufacturing industries

(G-5066)
ELIZABETH CLAYTON
201 Springwood Dr (39170-9716)
PHONE..................................601 371-1172
Betty Derrick Clayton, *Owner*
EMP: 1
SALES (est): 25.2K **Privately Held**
SIC: 8999 7389 2731 Author; ; book publishing

(G-5067)
EMBROIDERY DESIGN LLC
14893 Midway Rd (39170-8317)
PHONE..................................601 878-2606

Susan Coulson, *Mng Member*
EMP: 3
SALES: 125K **Privately Held**
SIC: 2395 Embroidery products, except schiffli machine

(G-5068)
GARRETT WELDING & IRON
4388 Pine Lake Dr (39170-8740)
PHONE..................................601 372-3889
L Garrett, *Owner*
Joann Garrett, *Co-Owner*
EMP: 1
SALES (est): 88K **Privately Held**
SIC: 3312 Fence posts, iron & steel

(G-5069)
I CARE OPTICAL INC
160 Mctyere Ave (39170)
PHONE..................................601 372-3801
Sandra Leach, *Vice Pres*
EMP: 17
SALES (corp-wide): 2.9MM **Privately Held**
SIC: 3851 Ophthalmic goods
PA: I Care Optical, Inc.
　4506 Pine Lake Dr
　Terry MS 39170
　601 352-3576

(G-5070)
I CARE OPTICAL INC (PA)
4506 Pine Lake Dr (39170-9760)
PHONE..................................601 352-3576
Sandra Leach, *President*
Mike Leach Sr, *President*
Kimberly Baughan, *Corp Secy*
Mike Leach Jr, *Vice Pres*
EMP: 22
SQ FT: 7,500
SALES (est): 2.9MM **Privately Held**
SIC: 3851 Eyeglasses, lenses & frames

(G-5071)
JORDON CONSTRUCTION LLC
309 Pleasant Lakes Cv (39170-8229)
PHONE..................................601 502-6019
EMP: 1
SALES (est): 63.6K **Privately Held**
SIC: 4212 1442 Dump truck haulage; construction sand & gravel; gravel & pebble mining

(G-5072)
MAURICE HINTON
Also Called: Beaux Bijoux
5057 Myers Rd (39170-9429)
PHONE..................................601 857-5168
Maurice Hinton, *Owner*
EMP: 1 EST: 1998
SALES (est): 97.6K **Privately Held**
SIC: 3999 3961 Beads, unassembled; jewelry apparel, non-precious metals

(G-5073)
MIRACLEWORKS PRESS
19405 Midway Rd (39170-8744)
PHONE..................................601 878-6686
Jo-Ann Lawrence, *Principal*
EMP: 1
SALES (est): 45.2K **Privately Held**
SIC: 2741 Miscellaneous publishing

(G-5074)
OLD RIVER LURE COMPANY LLC
1965 George Rd (39170-9432)
PHONE..................................601 259-4323
Joseph Rader,
Steven Davis,
EMP: 4
SALES (est): 40K **Privately Held**
SIC: 3949 Lures, fishing: artificial

(G-5075)
PRINTING ALLEY LTD
349 Springhill Dr (39170-7100)
PHONE..................................601 371-1243
EMP: 2
SALES (est): 158.8K **Privately Held**
SIC: 2752 Commercial printing, lithographic

(G-5076)
RAYS WELDING
101 Garrett Rd (39170-9522)
PHONE..................................601 741-1114
Raymond May, *Principal*
EMP: 1
SALES (est): 25K **Privately Held**
SIC: 7692 Welding repair

(G-5077)
SOUTHERN LAND SOLUTIONS LLC
1203 Crisler Rd (39170-9027)
PHONE..................................601 622-8581
Tyler Gregory, *Principal*
EMP: 2
SALES (est): 33.8K **Privately Held**
SIC: 0783 1799 3531 1629 Tree trimming services for public utility lines; building site preparation; rakes, land clearing: mechanical; land clearing contractor

Thaxton
Pontotoc County

(G-5078)
IRON EFFECTS
14668 Highway 6 (38871-8216)
PHONE..................................662 871-5565
EMP: 2 EST: 2007
SALES (est): 143.8K **Privately Held**
SIC: 3446 Ornamental metalwork

Tillatoba
Yalobusha County

(G-5079)
ANDERSON & SON LOGGING LLC
462 County Road 117 (38961-2765)
PHONE..................................662 688-1211
Brent Anderson, *Principal*
EMP: 2
SALES (est): 81.7K **Privately Held**
SIC: 2411 Logging

Tinsley
Yazoo County

(G-5080)
REAL YELLOW PAGES
7144 Tinsley Rd (39173)
PHONE..................................662 746-4958
EMP: 1 EST: 2007
SALES (est): 65K **Privately Held**
SIC: 2741 Misc Publishing

Tiplersville
Tippah County

(G-5081)
MILLS LOGGING
1221 County Road 249 (38674-9412)
PHONE..................................662 665-2718
James Hollis, *Manager*
EMP: 3
SALES (est): 175.5K **Privately Held**
SIC: 2411 Logging

Tishomingo
Tishomingo County

(G-5082)
BRIAN SCOTT MOORE
370 Highway 364 (38873-9724)
PHONE..................................901 831-7393
Brian Moore, *Principal*
EMP: 1
SALES (est): 46K **Privately Held**
SIC: 3993 Signs & advertising specialties

(G-5083)
BUCHANAN CUSTOM CABINETS
215 County Road 55 (38873-9712)
PHONE..................................662 438-7435
Robert Buchanan Jr, *Owner*
EMP: 3 EST: 1979
SALES (est): 214.8K **Privately Held**
SIC: 2434 Wood kitchen cabinets

(G-5084)
CUSTOM PALLETT LLC
421 Highway 365 (38873-9341)
PHONE..................................662 423-8127
Johnny Prince, *Mng Member*
EMP: 5 EST: 2012
SALES: 200K **Privately Held**
SIC: 2448 7389 Pallets, wood;

(G-5085)
DOMES INTERNATIONAL INC (PA)
5 Murphy St (38873-8427)
PHONE..................................662 438-7186
Dicky Sparks, *President*
Dean Deaton, *Corp Secy*
David Deaton, *Vice Pres*
EMP: 25
SQ FT: 3,200
SALES: 10MM **Privately Held**
WEB: www.domesintl.com
SIC: 1521 1542 3448 Prefabricated single-family house erection; commercial & office building, new construction; prefabricated metal buildings

(G-5086)
MAIN STREET CYCLE INC
1295 Main St (38873-9410)
PHONE..................................662 438-6407
James Crane, *President*
EMP: 9
SQ FT: 80,000
SALES: 1.2MM **Privately Held**
SIC: 3799 5571 5091 All terrain vehicles (ATV); motorcycle parts & accessories; bicycles

(G-5087)
TISHOMINGO ACQUISITION LLC
1425 Highway 25 (38873-9770)
PHONE..................................662 438-7800
Robert Fines, *President*
Monty Jeter, *Plant Mgr*
EMP: 200
SALES (est): 24.7MM
SALES (corp-wide): 1B **Publicly Held**
WEB: www.oxbodies.com
SIC: 3714 Motor vehicle parts & accessories
HQ: Ox Bodies, Inc.
　719 Columbus St E
　Fayette AL 35555
　205 932-5720

(G-5088)
TRUCK BODIES & EQP INTL INC
182 County Road 123 (38873-8737)
PHONE..................................662 438-7800
Bob Fines, *Branch Mgr*
EMP: 7
SALES (corp-wide): 1B **Publicly Held**
SIC: 3713 Truck & bus bodies
HQ: Truck Bodies & Equipment International, Inc.
　5336 Stadium Trace Pkwy
　Hoover AL 35244

(G-5089)
TRUCK BODIES & EQP INTL INC
Also Called: Tbei
1425 Highway 25 (38873-9770)
PHONE..................................800 255-4345
Bob Fines, *CEO*
Kurt Meyer, *CFO*
EMP: 9
SALES (est): 416.4K **Privately Held**
SIC: 3715 3999 Truck trailers; atomizers, toiletry

Toomsuba
Lauderdale County

2019 Harris Directory of
Mississippi Manufacturers

▲ = Import ▼=Export
◆ =Import/Export

GEOGRAPHIC SECTION

Tupelo - Lee County (G-5117)

(G-5090)
BUNYARDS GARAGE
194 Will Garrett Rd (39364-9762)
P.O. Box 17 (39364-0017)
PHONE..................................601 632-4892
Artis Bunyard, *Owner*
EMP: 2 **EST:** 1972
SALES (est): 139.7K **Privately Held**
SIC: 3714 Rebuilding engines & transmissions, factory basis

Tremont
Itawamba County

(G-5091)
ATLAS MANUFACTURING CO INC
51 Dow Dr (38876-8425)
PHONE..................................662 652-3900
Darrell C Harp Jr, *President*
Susan Harp, *Admin Sec*
▲ **EMP:** 23
SQ FT: 5,000
SALES (est): 5.2MM **Privately Held**
SIC: 3523 Trailers & wagons, farm

(G-5092)
BIGBEE METAL MANUFACTURING CO
10310 Highway 178 E (38876-8942)
P.O. Box 147 (38876-0147)
PHONE..................................662 652-3372
Darrell Harp, *President*
Ruth Harp, *Corp Secy*
Boyd Grimes, *Vice Pres*
▲ **EMP:** 50 **EST:** 1974
SQ FT: 5,000
SALES (est): 7.2MM **Privately Held**
SIC: 3523 Farm machinery & equipment

(G-5093)
MARTIN MARIETTA MATERIALS INC
Also Called: R & S Sand & Gravel
2050 Cotton Gin Rd (38876-8652)
P.O. Box 289, Vance AL (35490-0003)
PHONE..................................662 652-3836
Dennis Tharab, *Manager*
EMP: 1 **Publicly Held**
WEB: www.martinmarietta.com
SIC: 5211 1423 Sand & gravel; crushed & broken granite
PA: Martin Marietta Materials Inc
2710 Wycliff Rd
Raleigh NC 27607

Tunica
Tunica County

(G-5094)
A & J PLANTING COMPANY
Also Called: 52 Mp Farms
1318 Edwards Ave (38676-9374)
P.O. Box 2128 (38676-2128)
PHONE..................................662 363-0039
William Allen, *President*
Hellen Nash, *Admin Sec*
EMP: 8
SQ FT: 3,000
SALES (est): 680K **Privately Held**
SIC: 2044 0131 0161 Bran, rice; cottonseed farm; pea & bean farms

(G-5095)
ABBOTT INDUSTRIES INC
211 S Airport Blvd (38676-6003)
PHONE..................................662 357-7360
EMP: 1
SALES (corp-wide): 10.9MM **Privately Held**
SIC: 3724 Aircraft engines & engine parts

PA: Abbott Industries, Inc.
12801 Highway 75
Okmulgee OK 74447
918 756-8320

(G-5096)
DELTA AGRICULTURAL MGT INC
Also Called: Daniels Farms
21698 Highway 3 (38676-9264)
PHONE..................................865 210-4605
Kyle Adkins, *Principal*
James Daniels, *Principal*
EMP: 2 **EST:** 2014
SALES (est): 180.2K **Privately Held**
SIC: 8611 0191 2875 7389 Growers' associations; general farms, primarily crop; fertilizers, mixing only;

(G-5097)
DELTA OIL MILL
1723 Main St (38676-9391)
P.O. Box 29, Jonestown (38639-0029)
PHONE..................................662 363-1121
Scot Midleton, *Manager*
EMP: 3
SALES (corp-wide): 8.7MM **Privately Held**
WEB: www.deltaoilmill.com
SIC: 2074 Cottonseed oil, cake or meal
PA: Delta Oil Mill
100 Mill St
Jonestown MS 38639
662 358-4809

(G-5098)
DREXEL CHEMICAL COMPANY
1099 Drexel Rd (38676-9163)
P.O. Box 1096 (38676-1096)
PHONE..................................662 363-1791
Peggy Riley, *Purch Mgr*
William Carlew, *Manager*
EMP: 50
SALES (corp-wide): 104.6MM **Privately Held**
SIC: 2879 Agricultural chemicals
PA: Drexel Chemical Company
1700 Channel Ave
Memphis TN 38106
901 774-4370

(G-5099)
DUNNS JEWELRY
1225 Main St (38676)
PHONE..................................662 363-1501
B H Papasan, *Owner*
Ann Papasan, *Co-Owner*
EMP: 2
SALES: 120K **Privately Held**
SIC: 5944 7631 3911 Jewelry, precious stones & precious metals; watches; jewelry repair services; watch repair; rings, finger: precious metal

(G-5100)
FAMILY FEEDING DEV PROGRAM
1126 Flagg St (38676-9356)
PHONE..................................662 357-8917
Felecia Burks, *President*
EMP: 2
SALES (est): 62.3K **Privately Held**
SIC: 2099 Food preparations

(G-5101)
MAGNOLIA PROCESSING INC
Also Called: Pride of The Pond
5255 Highway 4 (38676-6136)
P.O. Box 609 (38676-0609)
PHONE..................................662 363-3600
William Gidden, *President*
Paul Battle Jr, *Vice Pres*
Sterling W Owen III, *Treasurer*
EMP: 150
SQ FT: 11,000
SALES (est): 20MM **Privately Held**
SIC: 2092 Fish, fresh: prepared

(G-5102)
RELIABLE 2 SCREEN PRINTING
1558 Woolfolk Rd (38676-9265)
PHONE..................................662 910-8272
Major Taylor Jr, *Principal*
EMP: 2
SALES (est): 83.9K **Privately Held**
SIC: 2752 Commercial printing, lithographic

(G-5103)
TUNICA PUBLISHING CO INC
Also Called: Tunica Times
986 Magnolia St (38676-9742)
P.O. Box 308 (38676-0308)
PHONE..................................662 363-1511
Brooks Taylor, *President*
Mary Cox, *Publisher*
EMP: 4
SALES (est): 324.8K **Privately Held**
WEB: www.tunicatimes.com
SIC: 2711 Commercial printing & newspaper publishing combined; newspapers, publishing & printing

(G-5104)
VITAL SIGNS UNBOUND
1286 Houston Ln (38676-9139)
PHONE..................................662 363-6940
David Doernbach, *Owner*
EMP: 2 **EST:** 2010
SALES (est): 176.6K **Privately Held**
SIC: 3993 Signs & advertising specialties

Tupelo
Lee County

(G-5105)
1 A LIFESAFER INC
1345 Palmetto Rd (38801-9088)
PHONE..................................800 634-3077
EMP: 1
SALES (corp-wide): 4.3MM **Privately Held**
SIC: 3829 Measuring & controlling devices
PA: 1 A Lifesafer, Inc.
4290 Glendale Milford Rd
Blue Ash OH 45242
513 651-9560

(G-5106)
ABILITY PROSTHETICS LLC
223 E Franklin St (38804-4007)
PHONE..................................662 842-3220
John P Smith, *Principal*
EMP: 1
SALES (est): 106K **Privately Held**
SIC: 3842 Orthopedic appliances

(G-5107)
ABILITY WORKS INC
Also Called: Abilityworks of Tupelo
613 Pegram Dr (38801-6321)
P.O. Box 1543 (38802-1543)
PHONE..................................662 842-2144
Greg Hughes, *Branch Mgr*
EMP: 40
SALES (corp-wide): 9.6MM **Privately Held**
SIC: 8331 3088 2653 2631 Job training & vocational rehabilitation services; plastics plumbing fixtures; corrugated & solid fiber boxes; paperboard mills
PA: Ability Works, Inc.
1281 Highway 51
Madison MS 39110
601 853-5100

(G-5108)
ADVANCED SCREENING SOLUTIIONS
2005 W Main St (38801-3214)
PHONE..................................662 205-4139
EMP: 2
SALES (est): 120K **Privately Held**
SIC: 2899 Mfg Chemical Preparations

(G-5109)
AMERICAN BOTTLING COMPANY
2945 Mattox St (38801-8759)
PHONE..................................662 844-7047
EMP: 70
SALES (corp-wide): 6B **Publicly Held**
SIC: 2086 Mfg Bottled/Canned Soft Drinks
HQ: The American Bottling Company
5301 Legacy Dr
Plano TX 75024
972 673-7000

(G-5110)
ASHLEY FURNITURE INDS INC
108 Lipford Ave (38801-9121)
PHONE..................................608 323-3377
James Evanson, *Manager*
EMP: 1
SALES (corp-wide): 4.2B **Privately Held**
SIC: 5712 2512 Furniture stores; upholstered household furniture
PA: Ashley Furniture Industries, Inc.
1 Ashley Way
Arcadia WI 54612
608 323-3377

(G-5111)
B & B CONCRETE CO INC
Also Called: Senter's Transit Mix
401 Elizabeth St (38804)
P.O. Box 106 (38802-0106)
PHONE..................................662 842-7305
Jimmy Westbrook, *Branch Mgr*
EMP: 20
SALES (corp-wide): 6MM **Privately Held**
WEB: www.concreteindustries.com
SIC: 3273 Ready-mixed concrete
PA: B & B Concrete Co Inc
Brewer Rd
Verona MS 38879
662 842-6312

(G-5112)
BARBER PRINTING INC
Also Called: Barber Planning
811a Varsity Dr (38801-4615)
PHONE..................................662 841-1584
Bill Morgan, *President*
EMP: 11
SQ FT: 11,000
SALES: 1MM **Privately Held**
SIC: 2759 2732 2761 Letterpress printing; pamphlets: printing only, not published on site; computer forms, manifold or continuous

(G-5113)
BARRYS FINE WDWKG & CRAFTS LLC
150 Limousine Dr (38804-6105)
PHONE..................................662 808-2268
Barry Cox, *Principal*
EMP: 1
SALES (est): 57.8K **Privately Held**
SIC: 2431 Millwork

(G-5114)
BASSCO FOAM INC
108 Air Park Rd (38801-7012)
P.O. Box 2731 (38803-2731)
PHONE..................................662 842-4321
Robert C Bass, *President*
Charlotte Bass, *Corp Secy*
EMP: 20
SQ FT: 47,500
SALES (est): 3.8MM **Privately Held**
WEB: www.basscofoam.com
SIC: 3086 Plastics foam products

(G-5115)
BEST FIBER INC
1644a S Eason Blvd (38804-5990)
PHONE..................................662 840-1118
Billy Hodges, *President*
John Hodges, *Corp Secy*
Randy Roper, *Vice Pres*
EMP: 27
SQ FT: 30,000
SALES (est): 5.5MM **Privately Held**
SIC: 2824 Polyester fibers

(G-5116)
C&C MCHINE FABRICATION MGT LLC ✪
Also Called: C & C Machine Shop
2383 S Green St (38801-6562)
PHONE..................................662 269-2534
Mark Clemons,
EMP: 2 **EST:** 2018
SALES (est): 89.6K **Privately Held**
SIC: 3599 Machine shop, jobbing & repair

(G-5117)
CAPRI LIGHTING
776 S Green St (38804-5510)
PHONE..................................662 842-7212
Omega Capri, *Vice Pres*

(PA)=Parent Co (HQ)=Headquarters (DH)=Div Headquarters
✪ = New Business established in last 2 years

2019 Harris Directory of
Mississippi Manufacturers

183

Tupelo - Lee County (G-5118)

GEOGRAPHIC SECTION

EMP: 2
SALES (est): 210.8K **Privately Held**
SIC: 3641 Electric lamps

(G-5118)
CARDINAL HEALTH 414 LLC
1930 International Dr (38804-5807)
PHONE...................662 680-8644
Beven Callicott, *Manager*
EMP: 7
SALES (corp-wide): 145.5B **Publicly Held**
WEB: www.syncor.com
SIC: 2835 2834 In vitro & in vivo diagnostic substances; pharmaceutical preparations
HQ: Cardinal Health 414, Llc
7000 Cardinal Pl
Dublin OH 43017
614 757-5000

(G-5119)
CARTERS INC
3822 Market Center Dr (38804-0923)
PHONE...................662 844-2667
EMP: 2
SALES (corp-wide): 3.4B **Publicly Held**
SIC: 2361 5641 Girls' & children's dresses, blouses & shirts; children's wear
PA: Carter's, Inc.
3438 Peachtree Rd Ne # 1800
Atlanta GA 30326
678 791-1000

(G-5120)
CIRCLE J MEAT MANUFACTURING
104 Marquette Cir (38801-2462)
PHONE...................662 790-3448
Matt Hitt, *Principal*
EMP: 1
SALES (est): 47.9K **Privately Held**
SIC: 3999 Manufacturing industries

(G-5121)
CONFORTAIRE INC
2133 S Veterans Mem Blvd (38804-5828)
PHONE...................662 842-2966
Jane Aggers, *President*
EMP: 74
SQ FT: 80,000
SALES (est): 6MM **Privately Held**
WEB: www.confortaire.net
SIC: 3086 Padding, foamed plastic

(G-5122)
CORINTH CC-COLA BTLG WORKS INC
1 Hadley St (38801)
P.O. Box 1068 (38802-1068)
PHONE...................662 842-1753
Buddy Long, *Safety Mgr*
Kathy Lewis, *Human Res Mgr*
Chris Porterfield, *Human Res Mgr*
EMP: 55
SALES (est): 6.5MM
SALES (corp-wide): 22MM **Privately Held**
SIC: 2086 5149 Bottled & canned soft drinks; groceries & related products
PA: Corinth Coca-Cola Bottling Works, Inc.
601 Washington St
Corinth MS 38834
662 287-1433

(G-5123)
CREATIVE CAKES & SUPPLIES INC
1422 E Main St (38804-2956)
PHONE...................662 844-3080
Rose McCoy, *President*
EMP: 8
SQ FT: 2,000
SALES (est): 876K **Privately Held**
SIC: 2051 5999 7999 Cakes, bakery: except frozen; cake decorating supplies; cake or pastry decorating instruction

(G-5124)
CULP INC
Also Called: Culp of Mississippi
2307 W Main St Ste C (38801-3105)
PHONE...................662 844-7144
Tanya Scott, *Manager*
EMP: 15

SALES (corp-wide): 296.6MM **Publicly Held**
WEB: www.culpinc.com
SIC: 2211 5131 Upholstery fabrics, cotton; piece goods & notions
PA: Culp, Inc.
1823 Eastchester Dr
High Point NC 27265
336 889-5161

(G-5125)
CUSTOM SIGN CO OF BATESVILLE
1219 Nelle St (38801-3415)
PHONE...................662 844-6333
EMP: 1
SALES (corp-wide): 5.3MM **Privately Held**
SIC: 3993 Mfg Signs/Advertising Specialties
PA: Custom Sign Co Of Batesville, Inc
480 Highway 51 S
Batesville MS 38606
662 563-7371

(G-5126)
DEALERSHIP SERVICES LLC
Also Called: Linex Tupelo
851 Mitchell Road Ext (38801-6579)
P.O. Box 826 (38802-0826)
PHONE...................662 269-3897
EMP: 7 EST: 2015
SALES: 350K **Privately Held**
SIC: 5531 2821 Ret Auto/Home Supplies

(G-5127)
DUNCAN SIGNS INC
3900 Westgate Dr (38801-9478)
P.O. Box 344 (38802-0344)
PHONE...................662 842-0226
Lee Duncan, *President*
EMP: 4
SQ FT: 3,600
SALES: 550K **Privately Held**
WEB: www.duncansign.com
SIC: 3993 Electric signs

(G-5128)
ECONO SIGNS
707 Daybrite Dr (38801-4913)
PHONE...................662 844-1554
Lorie Carson, *Owner*
Josh Smith, *Marketing Mgr*
EMP: 4
SQ FT: 1,250
SALES (est): 161K **Privately Held**
SIC: 3993 Signs & advertising specialties

(G-5129)
EDDIE MARTIN GOLF CARS INC
502 Air Park Rd (38801-7020)
PHONE...................662 620-7242
Eddie Martin, *Principal*
▼ **EMP:** 3
SALES (est): 247.8K **Privately Held**
SIC: 3799 5521 Golf carts, powered; automobiles, used cars only

(G-5130)
ENTEK INC
4126 Westside Dr (38801-7007)
P.O. Box 3128 (38803-3128)
PHONE...................662 841-5134
Carl Ganaway, *President*
EMP: 4
SQ FT: 5,000
SALES: 420K **Privately Held**
SIC: 3599 Machine shop, jobbing & repair

(G-5131)
FASTWRAPZCOM LLC
502 Crossover Rd (38801-4946)
P.O. Box 1344 (38802-1344)
PHONE...................662 213-8771
Patricia R Hych, *Partner*
EMP: 2
SALES (est): 182.9K **Privately Held**
SIC: 3993 Signs & advertising specialties

(G-5132)
FIBRIX LLC
Also Called: Cumulus Fibres - Verona
2119 Dalton St (38801-6471)
PHONE...................662 844-3803
EMP: 20
SQ FT: 20,000

SALES (corp-wide): 74MM **Privately Held**
SIC: 2297 2823 2299 Mfg Nonwoven Fabrics Mfg Cellulosic Manmade Fibers Mfg Textile Goods
HQ: Fibrix, Llc
1820 Evans St Ne
Conover NC 28613

(G-5133)
FIBRIX LLC
Also Called: Tupelo Fibers
2119 Dalton St (38801-6471)
PHONE...................662 844-5595
Tommy Wood, *Manager*
EMP: 52
SALES (corp-wide): 74MM **Privately Held**
WEB: www.lpfiber.com
SIC: 2297 2273 2393 Nonwoven fabrics; carpets & rugs; cushions, except spring & carpet: purchased materials
HQ: Fibrix, Llc
1820 Evans St Ne
Conover NC 28613

(G-5134)
FLOWERS BKG CO TUSCALOOSA LLC
Also Called: Flowers Bakery Thrift Store
1078 Cliff Gookin Blvd (38801-6458)
PHONE...................662 842-8613
Chuck Weaver, *Manager*
EMP: 17
SALES (corp-wide): 3.9B **Publicly Held**
SIC: 2051 Bread, cake & related products
HQ: Flowers Baking Co Of Tuscaloosa, Llc
546 15th St
Tuscaloosa AL 35401
205 752-5586

(G-5135)
FOAMCRAFT INC
281 Highway 178 W (38804-6907)
P.O. Box 2901 (38803-2901)
PHONE...................662 844-6399
Robert Wiles, *Principal*
EMP: 21
SALES (corp-wide): 7.6MM **Privately Held**
WEB: www.foamcraftinc.com
SIC: 2392 Pillows, bed: made from purchased materials
PA: Foamcraft, Inc.
115 Old Runway Rd
Tupelo MS 38801
662 844-6399

(G-5136)
FOAMCRAFT INC (PA)
115 Old Runway Rd (38801-7033)
P.O. Box 2901 (38803-2901)
PHONE...................662 844-6399
Jim Hensley, *President*
Phoebe Hensley, *Corp Secy*
EMP: 40
SQ FT: 75,000
SALES (est): 7.6MM **Privately Held**
WEB: www.foamcraftinc.com
SIC: 3086 Insulation or cushioning material, foamed plastic

(G-5137)
FORKLIFT LLC (PA)
912 George Ave (38801-2426)
PHONE...................813 527-4093
David Leathers, *Principal*
EMP: 3
SALES (est): 432.9K **Privately Held**
SIC: 3537 Forklift trucks

(G-5138)
FORKLIFT LLC
1103 W Jackson St (38804-2515)
PHONE...................662 255-2581
David Leathers, *Branch Mgr*
EMP: 2
SALES (corp-wide): 432.9K **Privately Held**
SIC: 3537 Forklift trucks
PA: Forklift, Llc
912 George Ave
Tupelo MS 38801
813 527-4093

(G-5139)
GARNER MILLWORK INC
Also Called: Garner Millwork & Cabinet
177 Road 1758 (38804-7143)
PHONE...................662 844-7007
Percy Garner, *President*
Dwayne Garner, *Vice Pres*
EMP: 10
SQ FT: 5,040
SALES: 1MM **Privately Held**
SIC: 2431 2434 Millwork; wood kitchen cabinets; vanities, bathroom: wood

(G-5140)
GENERAL PACKAGING SPECIALTIES
3255 Westover Park (38803)
P.O. Box 3244 (38803-3244)
PHONE...................662 844-7882
EMP: 13 EST: 1975
SALES: 1.5MM **Privately Held**
SIC: 2653 2671 Mfg Corrugated/Solid Fiber Boxes Mfg Packaging Paper/Film

(G-5141)
GENERAL SHALE BRICK INC
2027 Mccullough Blvd (38801-7109)
P.O. Box 7065 (38802-7065)
PHONE...................662 840-8221
EMP: 10
SALES (corp-wide): 3.5B **Privately Held**
SIC: 3271 5211 Mfg Concrete Block/Brick Ret Lumber/Building Materials
HQ: General Shale Brick, Inc.
3015 Bristol Hwy
Johnson City TN 37601
423 282-4661

(G-5142)
GENERATOR POWER SYSTEMS LLC
411 N Joann St (38801-3134)
P.O. Box 3912 (38803-3912)
PHONE...................662 231-0092
Clay McDonald,
EMP: 1
SALES: 20K **Privately Held**
SIC: 3621 Motors & generators

(G-5143)
GIBSON CORRUGATED LLC
1920 E Main St (38804-2937)
P.O. Box 380 (38802-0380)
PHONE...................662 842-1862
Waymon Gibson,
Charles Dale Gibson,
Terry Gibson,
EMP: 93
SQ FT: 330,000
SALES (est): 30.1MM **Privately Held**
WEB: www.gibsoncorrugated.com
SIC: 2653 Boxes, corrugated: made from purchased materials

(G-5144)
GODS INSPIRATION FOR THE SOUL
913 Clayton Ave Apt 1 (38804-1933)
PHONE...................662 374-7785
Tiara Brown, *President*
EMP: 1
SALES (est): 33.3K **Privately Held**
SIC: 2731 Pamphlets: publishing & printing

(G-5145)
GOLDEN NEEDLE
4139 W Main St (38801-8129)
PHONE...................662 842-0515
Brenda West, *Partner*
Linda Burton, *Partner*
EMP: 2
SALES (est): 189.8K **Privately Held**
SIC: 2395 Embroidery products, except schiffli machine

(G-5146)
GPAL LLC
302 N Highland Dr (38801-3426)
P.O. Box 4325 (38803-4325)
PHONE...................662 422-9351
George Smith, *Manager*
EMP: 1
SALES (est): 63K **Privately Held**
SIC: 2761 Manifold business forms

2019 Harris Directory of
Mississippi Manufacturers

▲ = Import ▼=Export
◆ =Import/Export

GEOGRAPHIC SECTION

Tupelo - Lee County (G-5173)

(G-5147)
GRECIAN OIL IMPORTERS LLC
850 N Gloster St (38804-1926)
PHONE..................................662 372-4933
Demetrios L Pappas,
Sam Calloway,
EMP: 3
SALES (est): 91.3K **Privately Held**
SIC: 2079 Olive oil

(G-5148)
GUTH LIGHTING
938 S Green St (38804-5514)
PHONE..................................800 234-1890
Robert Catone, *Mng Member*
▲ EMP: 2 EST: 2012
SALES (est): 150K **Privately Held**
SIC: 3648 Lighting equipment

(G-5149)
HANCOCK ADVG SPECIALITIES
4008 W Main St Ste 4 (38801-0407)
PHONE..................................662 842-1820
Sandra Hancock, *Owner*
EMP: 2
SALES (est): 82K **Privately Held**
SIC: 3993 Signs & advertising specialties

(G-5150)
HANGER PRSTHETCS & ORTHO INC
502 Council Cir (38801-4940)
PHONE..................................662 844-6734
Terry Goings, *Manager*
EMP: 6
SALES (corp-wide): 1B **Publicly Held**
SIC: 3842 5999 Limbs, artificial; artificial limbs
HQ: Hanger Prosthetics & Orthotics, Inc.
10910 Domain Dr Ste 300
Austin TX 78758
512 777-3800

(G-5151)
HARDEN ENTERPRISES INC
Also Called: Sprint Print of Tupelo
114 N Spring St (38804-3922)
PHONE..................................662 841-9292
Rubye Del Hardin, *President*
Rubye Del Harden, *Personnel Exec*
EMP: 5
SALES (corp-wide): 1.2MM **Privately Held**
SIC: 2752 Commercial printing, offset
PA: Harden Enterprises, Inc.
114 N Spring St
Tupelo MS 38804
662 841-9292

(G-5152)
HARDEN ENTERPRISES INC (PA)
Also Called: Sprint Print
114 N Spring St (38804-3922)
PHONE..................................662 841-9292
Peggy Browne, *Office Mgr*
Teresa Floyd, *Software Dev*
Rubye Del Hardin, *Post Master*
EMP: 18
SALES (est): 1.2MM **Privately Held**
SIC: 2752 2791 2789 Commercial printing, lithographic; typesetting; bookbinding & related work

(G-5153)
HARRIS JA INC
Also Called: Doricvaults North Mississipi
107 Old Runway Rd (38801-7033)
P.O. Box 2273 (38803-2273)
PHONE..................................662 205-4370
John Harris, *President*
Amy Harris, *Vice Pres*
EMP: 7
SALES: 1MM **Privately Held**
SIC: 3272 Grave markers, concrete

(G-5154)
HAWKEYE INDUSTRIES INC
1126 N Eason Blvd (38804-7522)
P.O. Box 1277 (38802-1277)
PHONE..................................662 842-3333
J Bryan Hawkins, *President*
EMP: 34
SQ FT: 59,000

SALES (est): 11.4MM **Privately Held**
WEB: www.hawkeye.ws
SIC: 3441 3444 Fabricated structural metal; sheet metalwork; forming machine work, sheet metal; sheet metal specialties, not stamped

(G-5155)
HESTERS CERTIFIED WELDING
1060 Road 261 (38801-8135)
PHONE..................................662 566-7305
Greg Hester, *Owner*
EMP: 1
SALES (est): 54K **Privately Held**
SIC: 7692 1791 7699 Welding repair; structural steel erection; tank repair

(G-5156)
HOERNER BOXES INC
100 Old Runway Rd (38801-7032)
P.O. Box 2382 (38803-2382)
PHONE..................................662 842-2491
Van Jackson, *President*
EMP: 45
SQ FT: 100,000
SALES (est): 12.5MM **Privately Held**
SIC: 2653 Boxes, corrugated: made from purchased materials

(G-5157)
HOME DECOR COMPANY
Also Called: Stanley Home Decor
1141 Ryder St (38804-5815)
PHONE..................................662 844-7191
Richard Daendurand, *CEO*
Jeff Tartamella, *President*
James Bennett, *CFO*
◆ EMP: 250
SALES (est): 22.2MM **Privately Held**
WEB: www.homedecorcompany.com
SIC: 3231 Mirrored glass

(G-5158)
HOOPSNAKE PRESS -
1249 N Coley Rd (38801-8167)
PHONE..................................662 260-5133
EMP: 1
SALES (est): 37.5K **Privately Held**
SIC: 2741 Miscellaneous publishing

(G-5159)
HYDRO HOSE CORP
1731 Mccullough Blvd (38801-7102)
P.O. Box 737 (38802-0737)
PHONE..................................662 842-2761
Merrill Johnston, *President*
Ellen Johnston, *Corp Secy*
Greg Harris, *Sales Mgr*
Cindy Harris, *Manager*
▲ EMP: 13
SQ FT: 34,000
SALES: 2.5MM **Privately Held**
WEB: www.hydrohose.com
SIC: 5085 3052 Hose, belting & packing; garden hose, rubber; garden hose, plastic

(G-5160)
HYDROSTATIC TRANSM SVC LLC
404 Air Park Rd (38801-7015)
PHONE..................................662 680-8899
EMP: 3
SALES (est): 192K **Privately Held**
SIC: 3594 Hydrostatic drives (transmissions)

(G-5161)
INDEPENDENT FURN SUP CO INC
3609 W Jackson St (38801-7060)
P.O. Box 2186 (38803-2186)
PHONE..................................662 844-8411
James E Wiygul III, *President*
Michael R Thomas, *Corp Secy*
Linda Poe, *Executive*
▲ EMP: 285
SQ FT: 150,000
SALES (est): 62.5MM **Privately Held**
SIC: 3086 Packaging & shipping materials, foamed plastic

(G-5162)
INNOCOR FOAM TECH - ACP INC
1665 S Veterans Blvd (38804-5825)
P.O. Box 1767 (38802-1767)
PHONE..................................662 842-0123
Chris Lacorata, *CEO*
Steve Lindsey, *Manager*
EMP: 9
SALES (corp-wide): 224.3MM **Privately Held**
SIC: 3086 Plastics foam products
HQ: Innocor Foam Technologies - Acp, Inc.
200 Schulz Dr Ste 2
Red Bank NJ 07701
732 945-6222

(G-5163)
JJI LIGHTING GROUP INC
Also Called: Guth Lighting Systems
938 S Green St (38804-5514)
PHONE..................................662 842-7212
Walter Coleman, *Branch Mgr*
EMP: 7
SALES (corp-wide): 20.8B **Privately Held**
WEB: www.alkco.com
SIC: 3646 3648 Commercial indusl & institutional electric lighting fixtures; lighting equipment
HQ: Jji Lighting Group, Inc.
11500 Melrose Ave
Franklin Park IL 60131
847 451-0700

(G-5164)
JOURNAL INC (HQ)
Also Called: Northeast Miss Daily Jurnl
1242 S Green St (38804-6301)
P.O. Box 909 (38802-0909)
PHONE..................................662 842-2611
Henry Foster Jr, *CEO*
William L Crews, *Ch of Bd*
Quincy Ward, *President*
Lisa Bryant, *General Mgr*
Rod Guajardo, *Editor*
EMP: 150 EST: 1924
SQ FT: 26,400
SALES (est): 13.6MM **Privately Held**
SIC: 2711 6512 Newspapers, publishing & printing; insurance building operation

(G-5165)
K & K SYSTEMS INC
687 Palmetto Rd (38801-7662)
P.O. Box 1065, Verona (38879-1065)
PHONE..................................662 566-2025
Troy G Keith, *President*
Timothy Keith, *Vice Pres*
Jerry McCool, *Plant Mgr*
Barbara R Keith, *Treasurer*
Mark Faust, *Sales Staff*
▲ EMP: 88
SQ FT: 44,000
SALES (est): 7.9MM **Privately Held**
SIC: 1611 3993 Highway signs & guardrails; signs & advertising specialties

(G-5166)
K D M CUSTOM COATINGS LLC
1989 Royal Maid Dr (38804-5812)
P.O. Box 445, Belden (38826-0445)
PHONE..................................662 842-9725
EMP: 12
SQ FT: 5,000
SALES (est): 605K **Privately Held**
SIC: 3479 Coating of metals with plastic or resins

(G-5167)
KRUEGER INTERNATIONAL INC
K I
2112 S Green St (38804-6507)
PHONE..................................662 842-3124
Bob Easley, *Purch Mgr*
Becky Malone, *Buyer*
Duane Fishel, *Branch Mgr*
Amy Barrett, *Technician*
Travis Drewery, *Technician*
EMP: 621
SQ FT: 282,000

SALES (corp-wide): 649.9MM **Privately Held**
WEB: www.ki.com
SIC: 2514 2531 3821 2522 Metal household furniture; public building & related furniture; laboratory apparatus & furniture; office furniture, except wood; wood office furniture; wood household furniture
PA: Krueger International, Inc.
1330 Bellevue St
Green Bay WI 54302
920 468-8100

(G-5168)
KRUEGER INTERNATIONAL INC
2112 S Green St (38804-6507)
PHONE..................................662 840-7368
Stevens Anna, *Sales Staff*
Duane Fischel, *Manager*
EMP: 100
SALES (corp-wide): 649.9MM **Privately Held**
WEB: www.ki.com
SIC: 2514 Metal household furniture
PA: Krueger International, Inc.
1330 Bellevue St
Green Bay WI 54302
920 468-8100

(G-5169)
L & J PRODUCTS & SALES INC (PA)
281 Highway 178 W (38804-6907)
P.O. Box 189, Sherman (38869-0189)
PHONE..................................662 841-0710
Ken Lockhart, *President*
Larry Jackson, *Vice Pres*
EMP: 27
SQ FT: 40,000
SALES (est): 13.5MM **Privately Held**
SIC: 2821 Polyurethane resins

(G-5170)
L C INDUSTRIES INC
Also Called: Lc Industries
1151 S Veterans Blvd (38804-5809)
PHONE..................................662 841-1640
Laura BR, *Manager*
Larue Peters, *Manager*
EMP: 40
SQ FT: 40,000
SALES (corp-wide): 83.3MM **Privately Held**
SIC: 2621 8331 2675 2392 Facial tissue stock; job training & vocational rehabilitation services; die-cut paper & board; household furnishings
PA: L C Industries Inc.
4500 Emperor Blvd
Durham NC 27703
919 596-8277

(G-5171)
LARRY JOE GIBSON
503a State Park Rd (38804-7304)
PHONE..................................662 844-9113
Joey Gibson, *Principal*
EMP: 2
SALES (est): 213K **Privately Held**
SIC: 2655 Tubes, for chemical or electrical uses: paper or fiber

(G-5172)
LAVASTONE INDUSTRIES MID SOUTH
Also Called: Lavastone Inds Fireplace Sp
4115 W Main St (38801-8129)
PHONE..................................662 844-5178
H Steve Hester, *President*
Martha Hester, *Corp Secy*
EMP: 5
SQ FT: 7,200
SALES: 1MM **Privately Held**
WEB: www.hillcountrystone.net
SIC: 3281 5719 Marble, building: cut & shaped; fireplaces & wood burning stoves; fireplace equipment & accessories

(G-5173)
LEE COUNTY COURIER INC
303 W Main St (38804-3919)
PHONE..................................662 840-8819
Jim Clark, *President*
Larry Hancock, *Treasurer*
Linda Clark, *Admin Sec*

(PA)=Parent Co (HQ)=Headquarters (DH)=Div Headquarters
✪ = New Business established in last 2 years

2019 Harris Directory of
Mississippi Manufacturers

185

Tupelo - Lee County (G-5174)

GEOGRAPHIC SECTION

EMP: 8
SQ FT: 1,200
SALES (est): 493.7K **Privately Held**
WEB: www.leecountycourier.com
SIC: 2711 Newspapers, publishing & printing

(G-5174)
LEGEND PUBLISHING
499 Gloster Creek Vlg B (38801-4600)
P.O. Box 1388 (38802-1388)
PHONE..................................662 844-2602
Westley Wells, *Owner*
EMP: 2
SALES (est): 125K **Privately Held**
SIC: 2721 Magazines: publishing only, not printed on site

(G-5175)
LEGGETT & PLATT INCORPORATED
Super Sagless
1961 S Green St (38804-6514)
PHONE..................................662 842-5704
EMP: 7
SALES (corp-wide): 4.2B **Publicly Held**
SIC: 2515 2514 3495 2392 Box springs, assembled; frames for box springs or bedsprings: metal; wire springs; mattress pads; fixtures: display, office or store: except wood; aluminum die-castings
PA: Leggett & Platt, Incorporated
1 Leggett Rd
Carthage MO 64836
417 358-8131

(G-5176)
LEGGETT & PLATT INCORPORATED
Also Called: Super Sagless
2071 S Green St (38804-6512)
P.O. Box 1027, Carthage MO (64836-5027)
PHONE..................................662 842-5704
EMP: 37
SALES (corp-wide): 4.2B **Publicly Held**
SIC: 2515 Box springs, assembled; mattresses, innerspring or box spring; chair & couch springs, assembled; bedsprings, assembled
PA: Leggett & Platt, Incorporated
1 Leggett Rd
Carthage MO 64836
417 358-8131

(G-5177)
LEGGETT & PLATT INCORPORATED
Also Called: Leggett & Platt 4201
2071 S Green St (38804-6512)
PHONE..................................662 842-5704
Dan Newman, *Manager*
EMP: 92
SALES (corp-wide): 4.2B **Publicly Held**
WEB: www.leggett.com
SIC: 2515 Mattresses, innerspring or box spring
PA: Leggett & Platt, Incorporated
1 Leggett Rd
Carthage MO 64836
417 358-8131

(G-5178)
LEGGETT & PLATT INCORPORATED
Also Called: Tupelo Sleeper 0341
115 N Industrial Rd (38801-3434)
PHONE..................................662 842-5237
Traci Carlack, *Purch Agent*
Robby Scruggs, *Engineer*
Ben Galijour, *Branch Mgr*
EMP: 28
SALES (corp-wide): 4.2B **Publicly Held**
WEB: www.leggett.com
SIC: 2514 2515 2512 Frames for box springs or bedsprings: metal; mattresses & bedsprings; upholstered household furniture
PA: Leggett & Platt, Incorporated
1 Leggett Rd
Carthage MO 64836
417 358-8131

(G-5179)
LEGGETT PLATT COMPONENTS INC (HQ)
Also Called: Cameo Fibers
115 N Industrial Rd (38801-3434)
P.O. Box 310, Conover NC (28613-0310)
PHONE..................................662 844-4224
Karl Glassman, *CEO*
▲ EMP: 10 EST: 1982
SALES (est): 6.4MM
SALES (corp-wide): 4.2B **Publicly Held**
WEB: www.lpfiber.com
SIC: 2299 2823 Batting, wadding, padding & fillings; cellulosic manmade fibers
PA: Leggett & Platt, Incorporated
1 Leggett Rd
Carthage MO 64836
417 358-8131

(G-5180)
LOS PORTRILLOS
831 S Gloster St (38801-4933)
PHONE..................................662 844-7350
Juana Cubillo, *Principal*
EMP: 5
SALES (est): 475.6K **Privately Held**
SIC: 2032 Mexican foods: packaged in cans, jars, etc.

(G-5181)
LUCKY DOG MONOGRAMS LLC
124 Herdtown Dr (38804-9106)
PHONE..................................662 321-7903
Stephanie Rial, *Principal*
EMP: 1
SALES (est): 48.7K **Privately Held**
SIC: 2395 Embroidery & art needlework

(G-5182)
LUCKY STAR INDUSTRIES INC (PA)
1016 N Gloster St (38804-1202)
P.O. Box 1010 (38802-1010)
PHONE..................................662 840-4465
Larry E Gibens, *President*
Leighton Gibens, *CFO*
EMP: 12 EST: 1953
SALES (est): 9MM **Privately Held**
WEB: www.advantagefurniture.com
SIC: 2512 Living room furniture: upholstered on wood frames

(G-5183)
MANTACHIE PRINTING & MKTG LLC
372 Road 1438 (38804-7595)
PHONE..................................662 282-7625
Robert Rieves, *Owner*
EMP: 2
SALES: 125K **Privately Held**
SIC: 2759 Commercial printing

(G-5184)
MCCULLAR LONG & MCCULLOUGH INC
Also Called: M L M
108 S Spring St (38804-4820)
P.O. Box 717 (38802-0717)
PHONE..................................662 842-4165
James C Long, *President*
Joe Yarber, *Vice Pres*
Sharon Long, *Admin Sec*
EMP: 3
SQ FT: 4,800
SALES (est): 583K **Privately Held**
WEB: www.mlmclothiers.com
SIC: 5611 3131 Men's & boys' clothing stores; boot & shoe accessories

(G-5185)
MDN LASER ENGRAVING INC
1223 Nelle St (38801-3415)
PHONE..................................662 397-5799
Michael Neely, *Principal*
EMP: 3
SALES (est): 168.2K **Privately Held**
SIC: 2796 Platemaking services

(G-5186)
MERIDIAN BRICK LLC
1735 Mccullough Blvd (38801-7102)
PHONE..................................662 840-8884
Bill Zieren, *Manager*
EMP: 5

SALES (corp-wide): 441MM **Privately Held**
WEB: www.boralbricks.com
SIC: 5211 3251 Brick; brick & structural clay tile
PA: Meridian Brick Llc
6455 Shiloh Rd D
Alpharetta GA 30005
770 645-4500

(G-5187)
MICROWAVE SERVICE CO (PA)
1359 Beech Springs Rd (38801)
PHONE..................................662 842-7620
Frank K Spain, *Owner*
EMP: 3 EST: 1959
SQ FT: 4,500
SALES (est): 450.1K **Privately Held**
WEB: www.microwaveservice.com
SIC: 3663 Microwave communication equipment; studio equipment, radio & television broadcasting

(G-5188)
MISSISSIPI FURNITURE COMPONENT
Also Called: M F C A
118 Road 752 (38801-9319)
PHONE..................................662 566-8855
Kenny Hankins, *President*
Tina Wilburn, *Vice Pres*
▲ EMP: 7
SALES (est): 872.3K **Privately Held**
WEB: www.countryroadfurniture.com
SIC: 2521 Benches, office: wood

(G-5189)
MOAK BOTTLING CO INC
510 S Spring St (38804)
PHONE..................................662 844-0012
John Surrette, *Manager*
EMP: 5
SALES (corp-wide): 1.1MM **Privately Held**
SIC: 2086 Bottled & canned soft drinks
PA: Moak Bottling Co Inc
5345 Hickory Hill Rd
Memphis TN 38141
901 369-0483

(G-5190)
MOUNT VERNON FOAM SALES
575 Mount Vernon Rd (38804-7162)
PHONE..................................662 844-3107
Terry Robbins, *Owner*
EMP: 12
SALES: 390K **Privately Held**
SIC: 3069 Foam rubber

(G-5191)
MTD PRODUCTS INC
5484 Hwy 145 S (38804)
PHONE..................................662 566-2332
Jerilynn Billingsley, *Controller*
Tab Cherry, *Branch Mgr*
EMP: 700
SALES (corp-wide): 2.3B **Privately Held**
WEB: www.mtdproducts.com
SIC: 3524 Lawn & garden equipment
HQ: Mtd Products Inc
5965 Grafton Rd
Valley City OH 44280
330 225-2600

(G-5192)
NICHOLS SAW SERVICE
1236 Nelle St (38801-3490)
PHONE..................................662 842-2129
Leo Davis, *President*
Kelly Barlow, *Vice Pres*
EMP: 10
SQ FT: 14,000
SALES: 1.8MM **Privately Held**
SIC: 7699 3546 Knife, saw & tool sharpening & repair; power-driven handtools

(G-5193)
NIGHTWIND INDUSTRIES
2839 S Eason Blvd (38804-5985)
PHONE..................................662 690-9709
EMP: 2 EST: 2007
SALES (est): 76K **Privately Held**
SIC: 3999 Mfg Misc Products

(G-5194)
NORTHEAST MISS DAILY JURNL
1242 S Green St (38802-6301)
P.O. Box 909 (38802-0909)
PHONE..................................662 842-2622
EMP: 4
SALES (est): 192.6K **Privately Held**
WEB: www.djournal.com
SIC: 2711 Newspapers, publishing & printing

(G-5195)
NOVARTIS CORPORATION
1203 Queensgate Dr (38801-5624)
PHONE..................................662 844-2271
EMP: 1
SALES (corp-wide): 56.6B **Privately Held**
SIC: 2834 Mfg Pharmaceutical Preparations
HQ: Novartis Corporation
608 5th Ave Fl 10
New York NY 07936
212 307-1122

(G-5196)
OUTDOORS ADVANTAGE
1171 Country Wood Cv (38801-8937)
PHONE..................................662 257-9601
Misty Gann, *Manager*
EMP: 2 EST: 2010
SALES (est): 182.4K **Privately Held**
SIC: 3949 Sporting & athletic goods

(G-5197)
P P I INC
Also Called: Printing and Promotional Items
5280 Cliff Gookin Blvd (38801-7091)
PHONE..................................662 680-4332
Toll Free:..................................888 -
Jesse L Mc Neece, *President*
Donna H Mc Neece, *Vice Pres*
Kim Harper, *Sales Staff*
Patsy Thompson, *Consultant*
EMP: 10
SQ FT: 7,800
SALES (est): 1.6MM **Privately Held**
WEB: www.ppims.net
SIC: 2752 7389 Promotional printing, lithographic; printing broker

(G-5198)
P-AMERICAS LLC
Also Called: Pepsico
620 E President Ave (38801-5522)
PHONE..................................662 841-8750
Bobby Bryant, *Manager*
EMP: 123
SALES (corp-wide): 64.6B **Publicly Held**
SIC: 2086 Carbonated soft drinks, bottled & canned
HQ: P-Americas Llc
1 Pepsi Way
Somers NY 10589
336 896-5740

(G-5199)
PAT THE CAT PRINTS
1404 Pinecrest Dr (38804-1230)
PHONE..................................662 397-1038
Louis Armour, *Owner*
EMP: 2
SALES: 100K **Privately Held**
SIC: 2752 Commercial printing, lithographic

(G-5200)
PATTERSON & COMPANY INC
Also Called: Electric and Machine Svcs
3893 Cliff Gookin Blvd (38801-7170)
P.O. Box 2243 (38803-2243)
PHONE..................................662 842-2807
Sam G Patterson, *President*
Billy Haygood, *Corp Secy*
Hardin Patterson, *Vice Pres*
Lauren Patterson, *Vice Pres*
EMP: 25
SQ FT: 20,000
SALES (est): 1.6MM **Privately Held**
WEB: www.electricandmachine.com
SIC: 7692 3599 5063 7694 Welding repair; machine shop, jobbing & repair; motors, electric; electric motor repair

---

2019 Harris Directory of
Mississippi Manufacturers

▲ = Import ▼=Export
◆ =Import/Export

186

GEOGRAPHIC SECTION

Tupelo - Lee County (G-5229)

(G-5201)
PAXTON SALES INC
Also Called: Vogue Home Furnishings
1020 N Gloster St Ste 116 (38804-1202)
PHONE......................................662 841-1929
Adam Paxton, *President*
Lisa Crouch, *Vice Pres*
Rebecca Nicholson, *VP Sales*
◆ EMP: 25
SQ FT: 1,500
SALES: 34MM **Privately Held**
SIC: 2519 Household furniture, except wood or metal: upholstered

(G-5202)
PEPSI BEVERAGES COMPANY
Also Called: Pepsi America
620 E President Ave (38801-5522)
PHONE......................................662 841-8750
Jeff Coley, *Manager*
EMP: 40
SALES (corp-wide): 64.6B **Publicly Held**
SIC: 2086 4212 Carbonated soft drinks, bottled & canned; delivery service, vehicular
HQ: Pepsi Beverages Company
110 S Byhalia Rd
Collierville TN 38017
901 853-5736

(G-5203)
PHILLIPS COMPANY INC
372 Road 1438 (38804-7595)
PHONE......................................662 844-3898
Joe Phillips, *CEO*
EMP: 1
SALES (est): 162.8K **Privately Held**
SIC: 2759 Labels & seals: printing

(G-5204)
PIERCE CABINETS INC
2259 Graham Dr (38801-6797)
PHONE......................................662 840-6795
Berry Pierce, *President*
EMP: 22
SQ FT: 10,000
SALES (est): 2.6MM **Privately Held**
SIC: 1751 5722 2541 2434 Cabinet building & installation; household appliance stores; wood partitions & fixtures; wood kitchen cabinets

(G-5205)
PITTS COMPANIES CABINETS MLLWK (PA)
1644 Cliff Gookin Blvd (38801)
PHONE......................................662 844-2772
Hoyt Pitts, *President*
EMP: 2 EST: 1973
SQ FT: 10,000
SALES (est): 915.3K **Privately Held**
SIC: 2431 5712 Millwork; cabinet work, custom

(G-5206)
PLAN HOUSE PRINTING (PA)
607 W Main St Ste A (38804-3732)
PHONE......................................662 407-0193
Phillip Eaves, *Principal*
EMP: 3 EST: 2008
SALES (est): 463.8K **Privately Held**
SIC: 2759 Commercial printing

(G-5207)
PRECISION MCH MET FBRCTION INC
502 Crossover Rd (38801-4946)
P.O. Box 7006 (38802-7006)
PHONE......................................662 844-4606
Charles L Michael, *President*
EMP: 40
SQ FT: 102,000
SALES (est): 8.2MM
SALES (corp-wide): 8.3MM **Privately Held**
SIC: 3444 3599 Sheet metalwork; custom machinery
PA: Transport Trailer Service, Inc.
502 Crossover Rd
Tupelo MS 38801
662 844-4606

(G-5208)
PRIME HOSPITALITY GROUP LLC
95 Old Runway Rd (38801-0369)
PHONE......................................662 269-2892
Tom Gilmer, *Administration*
EMP: 30
SALES (corp-wide): 11.4MM **Privately Held**
SIC: 2599 5021 Hotel furniture; restaurant furniture
PA: Prime Hospitality Group, Llc
2000 Remke Ave
Lawrenceburg TN 38464
931 762-5611

(G-5209)
PRO DESIGNS INC
1835 Nelle St Ste A (38801-3339)
PHONE......................................662 841-1867
W E Dickerson Jr, *President*
James Bryan, *Admin Sec*
EMP: 5
SQ FT: 5,280
SALES (est): 599.1K **Privately Held**
SIC: 2759 Screen printing

(G-5210)
QUALITY FIBERS INC
858 Mitchell Road Ext (38801-6578)
PHONE......................................662 620-7775
Randy Roper, *President*
EMP: 4
SQ FT: 6,000
SALES (est): 860.2K **Privately Held**
WEB: www.qualityfibers.com
SIC: 2824 Polyester fibers

(G-5211)
QUEENS REWARD MEADERY LLC
1719 Mccullough Blvd (38801-7102)
P.O. Box 444, Belden (38826-0444)
PHONE......................................662 823-6323
Jeri Carter,
EMP: 8
SALES: 125K **Privately Held**
SIC: 2084 Wines

(G-5212)
R & B SPECIALTY PRINTING LLC
398 E Main St Ste 119 (38804-4037)
PHONE......................................662 260-2145
Shirley Hendrix, *Owner*
EMP: 1
SALES (est): 116.5K **Privately Held**
SIC: 2752 Commercial printing, lithographic

(G-5213)
R K METALS LLC
703 Westmoreland Dr (38801-6521)
P.O. Box 3455 (38803-3455)
PHONE......................................662 840-6060
Mark Lovil,
EMP: 6
SALES (est): 606.5K **Privately Held**
SIC: 3471 Plating & polishing

(G-5214)
RC COLA COMPANY
2945 Mattox St (38801-8759)
PHONE......................................662 844-7947
Logan Young, *President*
EMP: 12
SALES (est): 568.6K **Privately Held**
SIC: 2086 5149 Soft drinks: packaged in cans, bottles, etc.; beverages, except coffee & tea

(G-5215)
READY MIX DISPATCH
130 N Industrial Rd (38801-3423)
PHONE......................................662 842-6313
David Dredard, *Principal*
EMP: 3
SALES (est): 197K **Privately Held**
SIC: 3273 Ready-mixed concrete

(G-5216)
REED MANUFACTURING COMPANY INC (PA)
1321 S Veterans Mem Blvd (38804-5813)
P.O. Box 650 (38802-0650)
PHONE......................................662 842-4472

Edward R Nelson, *President*
Dave Lendon, *Exec VP*
Jack Reed, *Vice Pres*
John Gaines, *Purch Agent*
Kenneth J Krason, *Treasurer*
◆ EMP: 45
SQ FT: 155,000
SALES (est): 14.9MM **Privately Held**
WEB: www.reedflex.com
SIC: 2326 2325 Work uniforms; shorts (outerwear): men's, youths' & boys'; jeans: men's, youths' & boys'

(G-5217)
RENIN US LLC
1141 Ryder St (38804-5815)
PHONE......................................662 844-7191
Kevin Campbell, *President*
Aziz Hirji, *CFO*
▲ EMP: 30
SQ FT: 240,000
SALES (est): 6.3MM
SALES (corp-wide): 947.5MM **Publicly Held**
SIC: 3231 Mirrored glass
HQ: Renin Holdings Llc
401 E Las Olas Blvd Fl 8
Fort Lauderdale FL 33301
954 940-4000

(G-5218)
RITE-KEM INC
703 Westmoreland Dr (38801-6521)
P.O. Box 3454 (38803-3454)
PHONE......................................662 840-6060
Mark Lovil, *President*
Alisha Bryant, *Vice Pres*
Olha Lovil, *Admin Sec*
EMP: 11
SQ FT: 30,000
SALES (est): 5MM **Privately Held**
WEB: www.ritekem.com
SIC: 5087 2841 Janitors' supplies; soap & other detergents

(G-5219)
RUSKEN PACKAGING INC
1720 S Green St (38801)
P.O. Box 7173 (38802-7173)
PHONE......................................662 680-5060
Christopher Lindsey, *Branch Mgr*
EMP: 8
SALES (corp-wide): 160.3MM **Privately Held**
SIC: 5199 2652 Packaging materials; filing boxes, paperboard: made from purchased materials
PA: Rusken Packaging, Inc.
64 Walnut St Nw
Cullman AL 35055
256 734-0092

(G-5220)
SCRUBS ELITE LLC (PA)
Also Called: Uniforms Unlimited of Tupelo
917 S Gloster St (38801-6311)
PHONE......................................662 842-4011
Charles Vinson,
Rita Kay Vinson,
EMP: 4
SALES (est): 524.1K **Privately Held**
SIC: 2211 Scrub cloths

(G-5221)
SIGNATURE BEDDING LLC
515 Crump Rd (38801-9367)
PHONE......................................663 523-8477
EMP: 5
SALES (est): 350K **Privately Held**
SIC: 2515 Mfg Mattresses/Bedsprings

(G-5222)
SIGNIFY NORTH AMERICA CORP
Also Called: Philips Lighting Company
938 S Green St (38804-5514)
PHONE......................................662 842-7212
Jim O'Hargan, *Principal*
EMP: 650
SALES (corp-wide): 7.2B **Privately Held**
WEB: www.lightguard.com
SIC: 3646 Commercial indusl & institutional electric lighting fixtures
HQ: Signify North America Corporation
200 Franklin Square Dr
Somerset NJ 08873
732 563-3000

(G-5223)
SIGNIFY NORTH AMERICA CORP
Also Called: Philips Day-Brite
938 S Green St (38804-5514)
PHONE......................................662 842-7212
Rick Spencer, *Branch Mgr*
EMP: 132
SALES (corp-wide): 7.2B **Privately Held**
SIC: 3646 Commercial indusl & institutional electric lighting fixtures
HQ: Signify North America Corporation
200 Franklin Square Dr
Somerset NJ 08873
732 563-3000

(G-5224)
SMITH MOBILE HOME COMPANY
2703 S Gloster St (38801-6905)
PHONE......................................662 566-7998
Willie P Smith, *Owner*
EMP: 2
SALES (est): 182K **Privately Held**
SIC: 2451 Mobile homes

(G-5225)
SONOCO PRTECTIVE SOLUTIONS INC
2612 President Ave (38801)
PHONE......................................662 842-1043
Arnold Chatman, *Manager*
EMP: 20
SALES (corp-wide): 5.3B **Publicly Held**
WEB: www.tuscarora.com
SIC: 3086 2821 Packaging & shipping materials, foamed plastic; plastics materials & resins
HQ: Sonoco Protective Solutions, Inc.
1 N 2nd St
Hartsville SC 29550
843 383-7000

(G-5226)
SOUTHERN COMPONENTS INC
Also Called: Fibre Craft
114 Old Runway Rd (38801-7032)
PHONE......................................662 844-7884
Robert Dexter, *Owner*
Steve Johnson, *Vice Pres*
Theresa Childress, *Admin Sec*
▲ EMP: 55
SQ FT: 122,000
SALES (est): 9.9MM **Privately Held**
WEB: www.fibrecraft.net
SIC: 2823 Cellulosic manmade fibers

(G-5227)
SOUTHERN PHARMACEUTICAL CORP
444 E President Ave (38801-5500)
PHONE......................................662 844-5858
Marinda Bandre, *President*
EMP: 1 **Privately Held**
SIC: 8082 2834 Home health care services; pharmaceutical preparations
PA: Southern Pharmaceutical Corporation
165 Rosecrest Dr
Columbus MS 39701

(G-5228)
SOUTHERN SPEED
2028 Mccullough Blvd (38801-7108)
PHONE......................................662 842-3799
John Johnson, *Owner*
EMP: 2
SALES (est): 193.9K **Privately Held**
SIC: 2396 Automotive & apparel trimmings

(G-5229)
SPARKO INC (PA)
Also Called: Golf First
868 Mississippi Dr (38804-0942)
P.O. Box 100, Belmont (38827-0100)
PHONE......................................662 690-5800
Hollis Sparks, *President*
Edward Tucker, *Vice Pres*
Mark McCrory, *Manager*
EMP: 5 EST: 1964
SQ FT: 105,000
SALES (est): 754K **Privately Held**
SIC: 8741 7389 3949 Management services; purchasing service; golf equipment

---

(PA)=Parent Co (HQ)=Headquarters (DH)=Div Headquarters
✪ = New Business established in last 2 years

2019 Harris Directory of
Mississippi Manufacturers

187

Tupelo - Lee County (G-5230)　　　　　　　　　　　　　　　　　　　　　**GEOGRAPHIC SECTION**

(G-5230)
SPARKS PRINTING & GRAPHICS
529 Road 1460 (38804-8233)
PHONE..................................662 842-4481
William F Sparks, *Owner*
EMP: 5 **EST:** 1957
SQ FT: 2,700
SALES (est): 388.7K **Privately Held**
WEB: www.sparkprintsolutions.com
SIC: 2752 Commercial printing, offset

(G-5231)
STANLEY BLACK & DECKER INC
1141 Ryder St (38804-5815)
PHONE..................................662 844-7191
D H Eckenrode, *Branch Mgr*
EMP: 40
SQ FT: 120,000
SALES (corp-wide): 13.9B **Publicly Held**
WEB: www.stanleyworks.com
SIC: 2542 Cabinets: show, display or storage: except wood
PA: Stanley Black & Decker, Inc.
　　1000 Stanley Dr
　　New Britain CT 06053
　　860 225-5111

(G-5232)
SUMMIT TRUCK GROUP MISS LLC
1007 International Dr (38804-5814)
P.O. Box 529 (38802-0529)
PHONE..................................662 842-3401
Glynn Franklin, *General Mgr*
David McGinnis, *Supervisor*
EMP: 9
SALES (est): 291.7K **Privately Held**
SIC: 7694 Motor repair services

(G-5233)
SUNSHINE MILLS INC
2103 S Gloster St (38801)
P.O. Box 1483 (38802-1483)
PHONE..................................662 842-6714
Phillip Bates, *General Mgr*
EMP: 100
SQ FT: 65,000
SALES (corp-wide): 355MM **Privately Held**
WEB: www.sportsmanspride.net
SIC: 2047 2048 Dog food; cat food; fish food
PA: Sunshine Mills, Inc.
　　500 6th St Sw
　　Red Bay AL 35582
　　256 356-9541

(G-5234)
SUNSHINE MILLS INC
Also Called: American Pet Food
2103 S Gloster St (38801)
P.O. Box 1483 (38802-1483)
PHONE..................................662 842-6175
Phillip Bates, *Manager*
Brad Stubblefield, *Director*
EMP: 100
SALES (corp-wide): 355MM **Privately Held**
WEB: www.sportsmanspride.net
SIC: 5149 2048 Pet foods; prepared feeds
PA: Sunshine Mills, Inc.
　　500 6th St Sw
　　Red Bay AL 35582
　　256 356-9541

(G-5235)
SWIRLZ
109 N Spring St (38804-3921)
PHONE..................................662 791-7822
Casey H Ferguson Jr, *Principal*
Jessica Clayton, *Manager*
EMP: 4
SALES (est): 331.2K **Privately Held**
SIC: 2754 Stationery & invitation printing, gravure

(G-5236)
T & L SPECIALTY COMPANY INC
300 Air Park Rd (38801-7016)
P.O. Box 2144 (38803-2144)
PHONE..................................662 842-8143
Cecil Overton, *CEO*
Tim Overton, *President*

Kim Overton, *Admin Sec*
Lisa A Robinson, *Admin Sec*
▲ **EMP:** 34 **EST:** 1982
SQ FT: 60,000
SALES (est): 8.8MM **Privately Held**
WEB: www.tlspecialty.com
SIC: 2899 2841 1799 Chemical preparations; soap & other detergents; paint & wallpaper stripping

(G-5237)
T & T INC
Also Called: T & T Plating
2348 S Green St (38801-6569)
PHONE..................................662 840-7500
Tom Towner, *President*
EMP: 8
SQ FT: 9,000
SALES (est): 470K **Privately Held**
SIC: 3471 Plating of metals or formed products; chromium plating of metals or formed products

(G-5238)
TAPCO INC
1813 Mccullough Blvd (38801-7176)
P.O. Box 1427 (38802-1427)
PHONE..................................662 841-1635
J Willford Roberts, *President*
Betty Roberts, *Treasurer*
◆ **EMP:** 30
SQ FT: 50,000
SALES (est): 5.9MM **Privately Held**
SIC: 3442 5031 Screen & storm doors & windows; storm doors or windows, metal; screens, window, metal; doors & windows

(G-5239)
TECUMSEH PRODUCTS COMPANY
158 Plant Rd (38804-4939)
PHONE..................................662 407-0428
EMP: 225
SALES (corp-wide): 876.5MM **Privately Held**
SIC: 3585 Parts for heating, cooling & refrigerating equipment
HQ: Tecumseh Products Company Llc
　　5683 Hines Dr
　　Ann Arbor MI 48108
　　734 585-9500

(G-5240)
TOYOTA TSUSHO AMERICA INC
203 Service Dr (38804-4034)
PHONE..................................662 620-8890
Shuhei Yamashita, *Manager*
EMP: 2 **Privately Held**
WEB: www.taiamerica.com
SIC: 2796 3462 3463 Steel line engraving for the printing trade; automotive forgings, ferrous: crankshaft, engine, axle, etc.; automotive forgings, nonferrous
HQ: Toyota Tsusho America, Inc.
　　805 3rd Ave Fl 17
　　New York NY 10022
　　212 355-3600

(G-5241)
TRANSPORT TRAILER SERVICE INC (PA)
502 Crossover Rd (38801-4946)
P.O. Box 7006 (38802-7006)
PHONE..................................662 844-4606
Gabe Boykin, *Partner*
David McKinney, *General Mgr*
C Larry Michael, *Principal*
Peggy Rhinehart, *Corp Secy*
EMP: 69
SQ FT: 102,000
SALES (est): 8.3MM **Privately Held**
SIC: 7539 5012 3599 Trailer repair; trailers for trucks, new & used; trailers for passenger vehicles; custom machinery

(G-5242)
TRI-STATE TRUCK CENTER INC
3025 International Dr (38801-7133)
P.O. Box 7008 (38802-7008)
PHONE..................................662 844-6000
Al Stephens, *Branch Mgr*
EMP: 27

SALES (corp-wide): 163.8MM **Privately Held**
WEB: www.tristatemack.com
SIC: 7538 5012 3713 General truck repair; truck tractors; truck bodies & parts
PA: Tri-State Truck Center, Inc.
　　494 E Eh Crump Blvd
　　Memphis TN 38126
　　901 947-5000

(G-5243)
TUPELO CONCRETE PRODUCTS INC
120 N Industrial Rd (38801-3423)
PHONE..................................662 842-7811
John Sisson, *President*
Jeff Stout, *Plant Mgr*
Tommy Bigham, *Sales Staff*
EMP: 19 **EST:** 1945
SQ FT: 5,000
SALES (est): 4.2MM **Privately Held**
WEB: www.div2-4.com
SIC: 3271 5032 5211 Blocks, concrete or cinder: standard; brick, except refractory; brick

(G-5244)
TUPELO CUPCAKES INC
3978 N Gloster St Ste C (38804-0913)
PHONE..................................205 269-4130
Colby Lee Dodd, *Principal*
EMP: 4
SALES (est): 111.5K **Privately Held**
SIC: 2051 Bread, cake & related products

(G-5245)
TUPELO ELVIS PRESLEY FAN CLUB
114 Lake Crest Cir (38801-8631)
PHONE..................................662 610-5301
V Armstrong, *Principal*
EMP: 1
SALES (est): 56K **Privately Held**
SIC: 3635 Household vacuum cleaners

(G-5246)
TUPELO ENGRAVING & RBR STAMP
605 W Main St Ste 15 (38804-3728)
PHONE..................................662 842-0574
Gail Collins, *President*
Tom Collins, *Vice Pres*
EMP: 2
SQ FT: 4,000
SALES (est): 213.1K **Privately Held**
SIC: 5999 3479 3993 Rubber stamps; name plates: engraved, etched, etc.; signs & advertising specialties

(G-5247)
TUPELO SCREEN PRINTING LLC
408 W Franklin St (38804-3822)
P.O. Box 4334 (38803-4334)
PHONE..................................662 523-0092
Russell Stafford, *Owner*
EMP: 3
SALES (est): 205.7K **Privately Held**
SIC: 2752 Commercial printing, lithographic

(G-5248)
UNION DIRECTORIES
818 Shell St (38801-6419)
PHONE..................................662 620-6366
Jamie Hunter, *Owner*
EMP: 12
SALES (est): 1.1MM **Privately Held**
SIC: 2721 Periodicals: publishing only

(G-5249)
V E BRACKETT & CO INC
1203 Maxwell St (38801-2528)
PHONE..................................662 840-5656
EMP: 3
SALES (est): 210.6K **Privately Held**
SIC: 3568 Mfg Power Transmission Equipment

(G-5250)
VEGASIGNS LLC
932 William St (38801-6720)
PHONE..................................662 871-7337
Jintana Richardson, *Principal*
EMP: 2 **EST:** 2012

SALES (est): 185.8K **Privately Held**
SIC: 3993 Signs & advertising specialties

(G-5251)
VICTORY LOGISTICS LLC
4110 Westside Dr Ste C (38801-7007)
PHONE..................................662 620-2829
Daniel H Purnell, *President*
EMP: 1
SALES (est): 54K **Privately Held**
SIC: 3151 Leather gloves & mittens

(G-5252)
WAG CORPORATION
5522 W Main St (38801-8036)
PHONE..................................662 844-8478
John William Denton, *President*
Jim Denton, *Treasurer*
EMP: 6
SQ FT: 12,000
SALES (est): 680K **Privately Held**
WEB: www.wagcorp.com
SIC: 3585 Refrigeration & heating equipment

(G-5253)
WEAVER CONSOLIDATED GROUP INC
Also Called: Coca-Cola
1 Hadley St (38804)
P.O. Box 1068 (38802-1068)
PHONE..................................662 842-1753
Willian H Long, *Branch Mgr*
EMP: 50
SALES (corp-wide): 2.9MM **Privately Held**
SIC: 2086 5149 Bottled & canned soft drinks; soft drinks
PA: The Weaver Consolidated Group Inc
　　601 Washington St
　　Corinth MS 38834
　　662 287-1433

(G-5254)
WELDING RESEARCH & FABRICATN
201 Milford St Apt 59 (38801-4655)
PHONE..................................870 551-5650
Hong Zhao,
EMP: 1
SALES (est): 33.5K **Privately Held**
SIC: 7692 Welding repair

(G-5255)
WELDING SERVICES
680a Road 1460 (38804-8232)
PHONE..................................662 321-2472
William Lewis, *Principal*
EMP: 1
SALES (est): 33.8K **Privately Held**
SIC: 7692 Welding repair

(G-5256)
WEST BACKHOE INC
132 Gum Tree Run (38801-8809)
PHONE..................................662 566-7828
Belinda West, *Principal*
EMP: 2
SALES (est): 137.8K **Privately Held**
SIC: 3531 Backhoes

(G-5257)
WESTROCK CP LLC
1590 S Green St (38802)
PHONE..................................662 842-4940
Steve White, *General Mgr*
Troy Beck, *Plant Mgr*
Peggy Smith, *Purch Agent*
EMP: 45
SALES (corp-wide): 16.2B **Publicly Held**
WEB: www.smurfit-stone.com
SIC: 2653 2657 Boxes, corrugated: made from purchased materials; folding paperboard boxes
HQ: Westrock Cp, Llc
　　1000 Abernathy Rd
　　Atlanta GA 30328

(G-5258)
WET PAINT LLC
4344 Mall Dr (38804-0907)
PHONE..................................662 269-2412
Tracy Clark, *Mng Member*
EMP: 7

GEOGRAPHIC SECTION

Union - Neshoba County (G-5292)

SALES: 95K **Privately Held**
SIC: 3269 3952 Art & ornamental ware, pottery; paints for china painting

(G-5259)
WILLCOXON ENTERPRISES INC
Also Called: Signs First of North Miss
510 S Gloster St (38801-5528)
PHONE..................................662 840-2300
E H Willcoxon, *President*
EMP: 3
SALES (est): 341.4K **Privately Held**
SIC: 3993 Signs & advertising specialties

Tutwiler
Tallahatchie County

(G-5260)
TROY CUSTOM CABINETS LLC
3246 Us Highway 49 E (38963)
PHONE..................................662 902-5559
EMP: 2 **EST:** 2009
SALES (est): 110K **Privately Held**
SIC: 2434 Mfg Wood Kitchen Cabinets

Tylertown
Walthall County

(G-5261)
9R SCREEN PRINTING
9 Percy Pittman Rd (39667-7720)
PHONE..................................601 303-0520
EMP: 2
SALES (est): 128.7K **Privately Held**
SIC: 2752 Commercial printing, lithographic

(G-5262)
AMERICAN PRINTING AND CONVERTI
210 Beulah Ave (39667-2304)
PHONE..................................601 222-0555
Julius Bacot, *Vice Pres*
EMP: 2
SALES (est): 231.6K **Privately Held**
SIC: 2752 Commercial printing, offset

(G-5263)
BATES VAULT & SERVICES LLC
136 Claude Smith Rd (39667-5826)
P.O. Box 306 (39667-0306)
PHONE..................................601 303-0508
Oliver Bates, *Principal*
EMP: 3 **EST:** 2007
SALES (est): 200.4K **Privately Held**
SIC: 3272 Burial vaults, concrete or precast terrazzo

(G-5264)
BRADLEY REID INC
263 Highway 27 S (39667-5502)
PHONE..................................601 810-6655
Bradley Reid, *President*
EMP: 11
SALES (est): 1.2MM **Privately Held**
SIC: 2411 Logging

(G-5265)
BRIGADE MANUFACTURING INC
101 Ostrover Dr (39667-6241)
PHONE..................................601 827-5062
Alton Spurlock, *President*
EMP: 70
SALES: 950K **Privately Held**
SIC: 2311 Men's & boys' suits & coats

(G-5266)
BROCK BIT CO INC
43 Walt Brock Rd (39667-5424)
PHONE..................................601 876-4237
Norman Brock, *President*
EMP: 3
SQ FT: 2,000
SALES: 800K **Privately Held**
SIC: 3533 Bits, oil & gas field tools: rock

(G-5267)
COASTAL TIE & TIMBER CO INC
34 Pallets Rd (39667-6001)
P.O. Box 539 (39667-0539)
PHONE..................................601 876-2688
Steve Jones, *President*
EMP: 48
SQ FT: 3,500
SALES (est): 7.6MM **Privately Held**
SIC: 2448 Pallets, wood

(G-5268)
COASTAL TRANSPORTATION LLC
34 Pallets Rd (39667-6001)
PHONE..................................601 876-2688
EMP: 3
SALES (est): 119.9K **Privately Held**
SIC: 2448 Wood pallets & skids

(G-5269)
COTTON CAPITOL LLC
100 Ostrover Dr (39667-6226)
PHONE..................................601 498-4770
Mason Pearce, *President*
Tiffany Langlinais, *Vice Pres*
EMP: 55
SQ FT: 40,000
SALES (est): 1.5MM **Privately Held**
SIC: 2211 Apparel & outerwear fabrics, cotton

(G-5270)
FOIL J BRANTON
Also Called: Foil, J Branton Office
810 N Railroad Ave (39667-2743)
PHONE..................................601 876-9678
J Branton Foil, *Owner*
Alicia K Foil, *Incorporator*
EMP: 2
SALES: 300K **Privately Held**
SIC: 1382 Oil & gas exploration services

(G-5271)
HARD ROCK SAND & GRAVEL
787 Highway 27 S (39667-5599)
PHONE..................................601 876-2929
James Denman, *Principal*
James J Denman, *Principal*
EMP: 6 **EST:** 2008
SALES (est): 380K **Privately Held**
SIC: 1442 Construction sand & gravel

(G-5272)
HAWAS INC
Also Called: Mg Custom Metal Works
225 Hobgood Rd (39667-5044)
PHONE..................................601 876-0806
Michael Hobgood, *President*
Carol Hobgood, *Vice Pres*
EMP: 2
SQ FT: 3,500
SALES (est): 200K **Privately Held**
SIC: 3599 Machine shop, jobbing & repair

(G-5273)
JAMES H KEMP
5 Jackson Rd (39667-6018)
P.O. Box 522 (39667-0522)
PHONE..................................601 876-2331
Mary Ann Kemp, *Principal*
EMP: 1
SALES (est): 39.6K **Privately Held**
SIC: 3999 Candles

(G-5274)
JEROME RUSHING WELDING
51 Highway 48 W (39667-6169)
PHONE..................................601 303-0139
Jerome Rushing, *Owner*
EMP: 2
SALES (est): 72.7K **Privately Held**
SIC: 7692 Welding repair

(G-5275)
JONES WOOD PRODUCTS INC
34 Pallets Rd (39667-6001)
PHONE..................................601 876-2688
Everett Jones, *President*
EMP: 1
SALES (est): 75.3K **Privately Held**
SIC: 2421 4226 Lumber: rough, sawed or planed; lumber terminal (storage for hire)

(G-5276)
KUT TOOLS INC
110 Beulah Ave (39667-2302)
PHONE..................................601 876-4467
Brent Boyd, *President*
Jason Boyd, *Vice Pres*
Josh Boyd, *Manager*
EMP: 5
SQ FT: 3,500
SALES: 500K **Privately Held**
SIC: 3421 Cutlery

(G-5277)
MAIN STREET EMBROIDERY
715 Beulah Ave (39667-2709)
PHONE..................................601 876-0003
EMP: 1
SALES (est): 33.7K **Privately Held**
SIC: 2395 Embroidery & art needlework

(G-5278)
PALLETS INC
34 Pallets Rd (39667-6001)
P.O. Box 441 (39667-0441)
PHONE..................................601 876-2688
Everett K Jones, *President*
Pamela Jones, *Vice Pres*
EMP: 15
SQ FT: 2,000
SALES: 3.5MM **Privately Held**
SIC: 2448 Pallets, wood

(G-5279)
PARK AVENUE PRINTING
305 Beulah Ave (39667-2701)
PHONE..................................601 876-9095
Rebecca Smith, *Owner*
EMP: 2
SALES: 50K **Privately Held**
SIC: 2752 7336 5699 2759 Commercial printing, offset; commercial art & graphic design; shirts, custom made; screen printing

(G-5280)
PEZANT LOGGING LLC
169 New River Rd (39667-6236)
PHONE..................................601 303-3025
EMP: 2 **EST:** 2017
SALES (est): 81.7K **Privately Held**
SIC: 2411 Logging

(G-5281)
RAM PETROLEUM LLC
84 A C Dillon Rd 1 (39667-5524)
PHONE..................................601 876-0807
Gary Wray,
EMP: 8
SALES (est): 449.8K **Privately Held**
SIC: 1382 Oil & gas exploration services

(G-5282)
RAND S WELDING
44 Rand Rd (39667-6630)
PHONE..................................601 876-3736
Kenneth Rand, *Owner*
Thersea Rand, *Co-Owner*
EMP: 2
SQ FT: 2,100
SALES (est): 96K **Privately Held**
SIC: 7692 Welding repair

(G-5283)
REID & DEESE LLC
263 Highway 27 S (39667-5502)
PHONE..................................601 248-3143
Bradley Reid, *Manager*
Robert Deese,
EMP: 4
SALES (est): 261.2K **Privately Held**
SIC: 2411 Logging

(G-5284)
ROGERS MACHINE
298 Rushingtown Rd (39667-7835)
PHONE..................................601 876-4476
EMP: 3
SALES (est): 40K **Privately Held**
SIC: 3532 Machine/Equipment Parts Manufacturer

(G-5285)
SOUTHERN FIBERGLASS INC
194 Cemetery Rd (39667-5986)
PHONE..................................601 876-2111

Joe Penn Jr, *Principal*
EMP: 15
SALES (est): 970K **Privately Held**
WEB: www.southernfiberglasshoods.com
SIC: 3714 Hoods, motor vehicle

(G-5286)
STRINGER INDUSTRIES INC (PA)
11 Highway 48 E (39667-7146)
P.O. Box 450 (39667-0450)
PHONE..................................601 876-3376
Tony P Stringer, *President*
Charlene P Stringer, *Corp Secy*
Trent S Stringer, *Vice Pres*
Trent Stringer, *Vice Pres*
Jeff Fortenberry, *Plant Mgr*
EMP: 50
SQ FT: 30,000
SALES (est): 11.7MM **Privately Held**
WEB: www.stringerind.com
SIC: 3553 Sawmill machines; planing mill machinery

(G-5287)
SUMRALL WELDING
980 Highway 48 E (39667-7115)
PHONE..................................601 876-4653
Dana Sumrall, *Owner*
Bridget Burris, *Analyst*
EMP: 1
SALES (est): 96.4K **Privately Held**
SIC: 7692 Welding repair

(G-5288)
TULLAHOMA INDUSTRIES LLC
101 Ostrover Dr (39667-6241)
PHONE..................................601 222-2255
EMP: 5
SALES (corp-wide): 122MM **Privately Held**
SIC: 2311 Mfg Men's/Boy's Suits/Coats
PA: Tullahoma Industries, Llc
    401 Nw Atlantic St
    Tullahoma TN 37388
    931 455-1314

(G-5289)
TYLERTOWN TIMES
727 Beulah Ave (39667-2709)
PHONE..................................601 876-5111
Carolyn Dillon, *Owner*
EMP: 15
SQ FT: 1,800
SALES (est): 1MM **Privately Held**
SIC: 2711 5943 5699 Job printing & newspaper publishing combined; newspapers: publishing only, not printed on site; writing supplies; T-shirts, custom printed

(G-5290)
TYLERTOWN WEAR PARTS INC
25 Industrial Park Rd (39667-6009)
PHONE..................................601 876-4659
Joan Cantrell, *President*
EMP: 22 **EST:** 1975
SQ FT: 12,000
SALES (est): 3.8MM **Privately Held**
WEB: www.tylertownwearparts.com
SIC: 3469 Machine parts, stamped or pressed metal

(G-5291)
WINDMILL PALLET WORKS INC (PA)
70 Old Settlement Rd (39667-4977)
PHONE..................................601 876-4498
EMP: 13
SALES (est): 1.5MM **Privately Held**
SIC: 2448 5031 Mfg & Whls Pallets

Union
Neshoba County

(G-5292)
APPEAL PUBLISHING CO INC
102 Main St (39365-2520)
P.O. Box 287 (39365-0287)
PHONE..................................601 774-9433
Luke Horton, *President*
Amy Thompson, *General Mgr*
EMP: 5 **EST:** 1967
SQ FT: 7,000

(PA)=Parent Co (HQ)=Headquarters (DH)=Div Headquarters
✪ = New Business established in last 2 years

2019 Harris Directory of
Mississippi Manufacturers

189

Union - Neshoba County (G-5293)　　　　　　　　　　**GEOGRAPHIC SECTION**

SALES (est): 392.6K **Privately Held**
SIC: 2711 Job printing & newspaper publishing combined

(G-5293)
B R SMITH ENTERPRISES INC
11840 Road 505 (39365-7324)
PHONE..................................601 656-0846
BR Smith, *President*
B R Smith, *President*
Bobby E Smith, *Vice Pres*
Bobby R Smith, *Vice Pres*
EMP: 18
SALES: 2MM **Privately Held**
SIC: 3433 7692 Stoves, wood & coal burning; welding repair

(G-5294)
BRAD WARREN LOG & TRCKG LLC
11281 Road 270 (39365-7003)
PHONE..................................601 416-8113
Brad Warren, *Mng Member*
EMP: 5
SALES (est): 765.5K **Privately Held**
SIC: 2411 Logging camps & contractors

(G-5295)
BUNTYN SAWMILL
44 Buntyn Rd (39365-9677)
PHONE..................................601 774-8128
James Buntyn, *Owner*
EMP: 8
SALES (est): 580K **Privately Held**
SIC: 2421 Sawmills & planing mills, general

(G-5296)
CHOCTAW GLOVE & SAFETY CO INC
100 Kate Thomas Dr (39365)
P.O. Box 405 (39365-0405)
PHONE..................................601 774-5555
Larry Pearson, *Manager*
EMP: 9 **Privately Held**
SIC: 2512 5699 5085 Upholstered household furniture; work clothing; industrial supplies
PA: Choctaw Glove & Safety Company, Inc.
10 Laura St
Noxapater MS 39346

(G-5297)
GREG WINSTEAD LOGGING INC
259 Tullus Rd (39365-9422)
PHONE..................................601 774-9565
Greg Winstead, *President*
EMP: 10
SALES (est): 1.1MM **Privately Held**
SIC: 2411 Logging

(G-5298)
HOWELLS WELDING & FABRICATING
12320 Highway 492 E (39365-9521)
PHONE..................................601 663-6098
Amber Howell, *Principal*
EMP: 1 EST: 2017
SALES (est): 25K **Privately Held**
SIC: 7692 Welding repair

(G-5299)
IRON HORSE LOGGING LLC
711 Rufus Gill Rd (39365-8716)
PHONE..................................601 416-5966
William Beckham, *Principal*
EMP: 2
SALES (est): 81.7K **Privately Held**
SIC: 2411 Logging

(G-5300)
LOCALNET
108 Ware St (39365-2439)
PHONE..................................601 774-9338
EMP: 2 EST: 2007
SALES (est): 96K **Privately Held**
SIC: 4813 7372 Telephone Communications Prepackaged Software Services

(G-5301)
MC LOGGING LLC
10480 Road 313 (39365-9512)
PHONE..................................601 678-6681
EMP: 2

SALES (est): 81.7K **Privately Held**
SIC: 2411 Logging

(G-5302)
MMC MATERIALS INC
Also Called: Mississippi Materials Company
105 Compress Rd (39365-2003)
PHONE..................................601 774-0443
Randy Crapse, *Manager*
EMP: 2
SALES (corp-wide): 306.5MM **Privately Held**
WEB: www.mmcmaterials.com
SIC: 3273 5211 Ready-mixed concrete; masonry materials & supplies
HQ: Mmc Materials, Inc.
1052 Highland Colony Pkwy # 201
Ridgeland MS 39157
601 898-4000

(G-5303)
TRI-C WOOD PRODUCTS INC (PA)
610 S Decatur St (39365-2634)
P.O. Box 189 (39365-0189)
PHONE..................................601 774-8295
Harold Cleveland, *President*
Bobby Cleveland, *Corp Secy*
Ricky Cleveland, *Vice Pres*
EMP: 29
SQ FT: 75,000
SALES: 1.5MM **Privately Held**
SIC: 2431 Floor baseboards, wood

(G-5304)
TYSON FOODS INC
13001 Road 2219 (39365-9585)
PHONE..................................601 774-7551
Jeff McNeece, *Manager*
Shawn Gamber, *Supervisor*
Wayne Culliver, *Executive*
Carolyn Jones, *Administration*
EMP: 150
SALES (corp-wide): 40B **Publicly Held**
SIC: 0254 2048 Chicken hatchery; prepared feeds
PA: Tyson Foods, Inc.
2200 W Don Tyson Pkwy
Springdale AR 72762
479 290-4000

Union Church
Jefferson County

(G-5305)
BUIE LOGGIN
4566 Nw Homochitto Rd (39668-7116)
PHONE..................................601 532-7186
Elmer Buie, *Owner*
John D Buie, *Co-Owner*
Ruby Buie, *Co-Owner*
EMP: 4
SALES (est): 198.8K **Privately Held**
SIC: 2411 Logging

University
Lafayette County

(G-5306)
UNIVERSITY OF MISSISSIPPI
Also Called: Living Blues Magazine
301 Hill HI (38677)
PHONE..................................662 915-5742
Mickey McLaurin, *Manager*
Charlie Ball, *Director*
Joe Swingle, *Art Dir*
Yvonne Cockrell, *Clerk*
EMP: 5
SALES (corp-wide): 2.5B **Privately Held**
WEB: www.olemiss.edu
SIC: 2721 8221 Periodicals; university
PA: University Of Mississippi
113 Falkner
University MS 38677
662 915-6538

Utica
Hinds County

(G-5307)
CLEMENTINE FRAZIER
Also Called: Neeto's Bargains
1970 Lebanon Pinegrove Rd (39175-8810)
PHONE..................................601 572-7698
Clemetine Frazier, *Owner*
EMP: 2
SALES (est): 25K **Privately Held**
SIC: 2395 Embroidery & art needlework

(G-5308)
H & G SAWMILL LLC
3213 Chapman Rd (39175-9726)
PHONE..................................601 885-2179
EMP: 2
SALES (est): 97K **Privately Held**
SIC: 2421 Sawmill/Planing Mill

(G-5309)
KITCHENS BROTHERS MFG CO
4854 Reed Town Rd (39175)
PHONE..................................601 885-6001
D Greg Kitchens, *President*
◆ EMP: 250 EST: 1946
SQ FT: 160,000
SALES (est): 31.5MM **Privately Held**
SIC: 2421 Furniture dimension stock, softwood

(G-5310)
PICKETT PRODUCTIONS
1923 Breeden Rd (39175-4001)
P.O. Box 337, Raymond (39154-0337)
PHONE..................................601 885-2720
Steven W Pickett, *Partner*
Fred Pickett, *Partner*
EMP: 2
SALES (est): 140K **Privately Held**
SIC: 3993 Signs & advertising specialties

(G-5311)
PRINTING PLACE
4038 Old Port Gibson Rd (39175-9694)
PHONE..................................601 885-8327
Kathleen Mc Griggs, *Owner*
EMP: 2
SALES (est): 130K **Privately Held**
SIC: 2752 Commercial printing, offset

(G-5312)
SHEARS FABRICATION & WLDG LLC
1045 Chapel Hill Rd (39175-8908)
PHONE..................................601 946-3268
Nichlas Shears,
EMP: 1 EST: 2017
SALES (est): 54.9K **Privately Held**
SIC: 3441 7692 Fabricated structural metal; welding repair

(G-5313)
TAYLOR S FLYING SERVICE INC
1460 Charlie Brown Rd (39175-9418)
PHONE..................................601 885-9959
Tommy Taylor, *Principal*
EMP: 1
SALES (est): 97.7K **Privately Held**
SIC: 2411 Logging camps & contractors

Vaiden
Carroll County

(G-5314)
KRESEC ENTERPRISES CORP
502 Mulberry St Rear Bldg (39176-9648)
P.O. Box 466, Olive Branch (38654-0466)
PHONE..................................601 292-7015
Simon Woody, *President*
EMP: 3
SQ FT: 800
SALES (est): 170K **Privately Held**
SIC: 3613 Panel & distribution boards & other related apparatus

(G-5315)
VAIDEN TIMBER CO
300 Hwy 51 (39176)
P.O. Box 97 (39176-0097)
PHONE..................................662 464-7740
Charles Dismuke, *Owner*
EMP: 5
SQ FT: 2,200
SALES: 2MM **Privately Held**
SIC: 2411 Pulpwood contractors engaged in cutting

Valley Park
Issaquena County

(G-5316)
DANNY R JANSEN
4411 Highway 61 N (39177-9700)
P.O. Box 206 (39177-0206)
PHONE..................................601 636-1070
Danny Jansen, *Owner*
Danny R Jansen, *Owner*
EMP: 1
SALES: 40K **Privately Held**
SIC: 2851 Removers & cleaners

Vancleave
Jackson County

(G-5317)
B & D PLASTICS LLC
5500 Allen Rd (39565-8671)
PHONE..................................228 875-5865
EMP: 17
SALES (est): 2.9MM **Privately Held**
SIC: 3083 Laminated plastics plate & sheet

(G-5318)
B&M MAINTENANCE LLC
10393 Cherokee Rose Rd (39565-9085)
PHONE..................................228 273-5821
Matthew Ivey,
EMP: 1
SALES (est): 61K **Privately Held**
SIC: 2431 1711 7389 Millwork; plumbing, heating, air-conditioning contractors;

(G-5319)
GLENN MACHINE WORKS INC
Also Called: Crane Rentals
8100 Highway 57 (39565-8237)
PHONE..................................228 875-1877
Toll Free:...............................877 -
Tim Stockstill, *Manager*
EMP: 30
SALES (corp-wide): 19MM **Privately Held**
WEB: www.glennmachineworks.com
SIC: 3599 5085 7359 7353 Machine shop, jobbing & repair; mill supplies; equipment rental & leasing; heavy construction equipment rental; crane & aerial lift service
PA: Glenn Machine Works, Inc.
734 Highway 45 S
Columbus MS 39701
662 328-4611

(G-5320)
SEB MINING
8400 Jim Ramsay Rd (39565-6479)
PHONE..................................228 826-4466
Elaine Bright, *Owner*
EMP: 2
SALES (est): 274K **Privately Held**
SIC: 3648 Miners' lamps

(G-5321)
SIGN LANGUAGE
17300 Popcorn Ave (39565-6340)
PHONE..................................228 990-3609
EMP: 1
SALES (est): 46K **Privately Held**
SIC: 3993 Signs & advertising specialties

(G-5322)
SWAMP DONKEY LLC ✪
14508 Low Point Rd (39565-8503)
PHONE..................................228 369-4927
Tad Fairley, *Principal*

GEOGRAPHIC SECTION

Vicksburg - Warren County (G-5348)

EMP: 5 **EST:** 2019
SALES (est): 202.2K **Privately Held**
SIC: 3799 All terrain vehicles (ATV)

(G-5323)
VANCLEAVE PORTABLE BUILDINGS
Also Called: Vancleave Bait and Tackle
12214 Highway 57 (39565-8272)
PHONE 228 826-5151
John Mizelle, *Owner*
EMP: 2 **EST:** 2013
SALES (est): 206.2K **Privately Held**
SIC: 3448 5941 Buildings, portable: prefabricated metal; bait & tackle

---

Vardaman
Calhoun County

(G-5324)
FOSTER & THOMAS MANUFACTURING
1088 County Road 102 (38878-9228)
PHONE 662 682-9094
Grady Foster, *Principal*
EMP: 1
SALES (est): 58K **Privately Held**
SIC: 3999 Manufacturing industries

(G-5325)
P & R ALUMINUM
Also Called: Vardaman Hardware
202 Main St (38878)
P.O. Box 198 (38878-0198)
PHONE 662 682-7939
Fax: 662 682-7939
EMP: 2
SALES (est): 120K **Privately Held**
SIC: 3442 5251 1751 Mfg Metal Doors/Sash/Trim Ret Hardware Carpentry Contractor

---

Verona
Lee County

(G-5326)
AIRFLOAT SYSTEMS INC
110 Second St (38879)
P.O. Box 1476 (38879-1476)
PHONE 662 566-0158
Bryan White, *President*
Sally White, *Vice Pres*
Chad West, *Webmaster*
EMP: 9
SQ FT: 22,000
SALES (est): 1.7MM **Privately Held**
WEB: www.airfloatsys.com
SIC: 2653 Boxes, corrugated: made from purchased materials

(G-5327)
B & B CONCRETE CO INC (PA)
Also Called: Senter's Transit Mix
Brewer Rd (38879)
P.O. Box 407, Tupelo (38802-0407)
PHONE 662 842-6312
Henry C Brevard, *President*
Beth Brevard, *Corp Secy*
David E Brevard, *Vice Pres*
Chris Sokol, *Engineer*
EMP: 35
SQ FT: 5,000
SALES (est): 6MM **Privately Held**
WEB: www.concreteindustries.com
SIC: 3273 6519 Ready-mixed concrete; real property lessors

(G-5328)
CAPITAL BEDDING INC
5262 S Raymond St (38879)
P.O. Box 2460 (38879-2460)
PHONE 662 566-1144
Douglas West, *President*
Crystal McGregory, *Purchasing*
Bud Allbritton Jr, *Technology*
◆ **EMP:** 100 **EST:** 1969
SQ FT: 120,000

SALES (est): 17.5MM **Privately Held**
WEB: www.capital-bedding.com
SIC: 2515 Mattresses, containing felt, foam rubber, urethane, etc.; box springs, assembled

(G-5329)
CARPENTER CO
184 Lipford Rd (38879)
P.O. Box 1070, Tupelo (38802-1070)
PHONE 662 566-2392
Al Servati, *Manager*
EMP: 500
SALES (corp-wide): 1.8B **Privately Held**
WEB: www.carpenter.com
SIC: 3086 2821 2297 Insulation or cushioning material, foamed plastic; plastics materials & resins; nonwoven fabrics
PA: Carpenter Co.
5016 Monument Ave
Richmond VA 23230
804 359-0800

(G-5330)
ELITE COMFORT SOLUTIONS LLC
Also Called: Verona Foam
234 Cdf Blvd Lee Indus Pa Lee Industrial Park (38879)
P.O. Box 517 (38879-0517)
PHONE 662 566-2322
Robert Kieffer, *Manager*
Bob Kieffer, *Manager*
EMP: 47
SALES (corp-wide): 4.2B **Publicly Held**
WEB: www.hickorysprings.com
SIC: 3069 2821 2515 2392 Foam rubber; plastics materials & resins; mattresses & bedsprings; household furnishings
HQ: Elite Comfort Solutions Llc
24 Herring Rd
Newnan GA 30265
828 267-7813

(G-5331)
FXI INC
Also Called: Foamex
154 Lipford Rd (38879)
P.O. Box 1063 (38879-1063)
PHONE 662 566-2382
Mark Dailey, *Branch Mgr*
EMP: 174 **Privately Held**
SIC: 3086 2821 Carpet & rug cushions, foamed plastic; plastics materials & resins
HQ: Fxi, Inc.
1400 N Providence Rd # 2000
Media PA 19063

(G-5332)
GREEN SAVE INC
162 Greystone Dr (38879)
P.O. Box 508, Plantersville (38862-0508)
PHONE 662 566-0717
Les Ellis, *President*
EMP: 2
SALES (est): 186K **Privately Held**
SIC: 3949 5091 5941 Golf equipment; golf equipment; golf goods & equipment

(G-5333)
HSM SOLUTIONS
234 Cdf Blvd Lee City (38879)
P.O. Box 459 (38879-0459)
PHONE 352 622-7583
EMP: 3
SALES (est): 97.9K **Privately Held**
SIC: 5719 3469 Bedding (sheets, blankets, spreads & pillows); furniture components, porcelain enameled

(G-5334)
LABEL EXPRESS INC
100 Quality Ln (38879)
P.O. Box 489 (38879-0489)
PHONE 662 566-7075
Jim Barber, *President*
Kenny Simmons, *Vice Pres*
EMP: 18 **EST:** 1996
SQ FT: 43,000
SALES: 3MM **Privately Held**
WEB: www.labelexpress.net
SIC: 2759 2891 Labels & seals: printing; adhesives & sealants

(G-5335)
STYLE-LINE FURN INC
116 Godfrey Rd (38879)
P.O. Box 2450 (38879-2450)
PHONE 662 566-1113
Margie Anderson, *President*
Mark Anderson, *Vice Pres*
▼ **EMP:** 135
SQ FT: 355,500
SALES (est): 19.2MM **Privately Held**
SIC: 2512 Living room furniture: upholstered on wood frames

(G-5336)
TECUMSEH PRODUCTS COMPANY
5424 Hwy 145 S (38879)
P.O. Box 527, Tupelo (38802-0527)
PHONE 662 566-2231
Joel Kulovitz, *Branch Mgr*
EMP: 1
SALES (corp-wide): 876.5MM **Privately Held**
WEB: www.tecumseh.com
SIC: 3585 3563 Compressors for refrigeration & air conditioning equipment; air & gas compressors
HQ: Tecumseh Products Company Llc
5683 Hines Dr
Ann Arbor MI 48108
734 585-9500

(G-5337)
WEST BODY SHOP & SALVAGE INC
1383 W Palmetto Rd (38879)
PHONE 662 566-2161
Tim West, *President*
Joe West, *Vice Pres*
EMP: 6 **EST:** 1974
SALES: 210K **Privately Held**
SIC: 7532 7692 Body shop, automotive; automotive welding

Vicksburg
Warren County

(G-5338)
ADVANCED DRAINAGE SYSTEMS INC
5695 Highway 61 S (39180-9537)
PHONE 601 629-9040
John Tomlinson, *Branch Mgr*
EMP: 2
SALES (corp-wide): 1.3B **Publicly Held**
SIC: 3084 Plastics pipe
PA: Advanced Drainage Systems, Inc.
4640 Trueman Blvd
Hilliard OH 43026
614 658-0050

(G-5339)
ANDERSON-TULLY COMPANY
Also Called: Veneer Division
1735 N Washington St (39183-7696)
PHONE 601 629-3283
Richard Wilkerson, *Manager*
EMP: 286 **Privately Held**
WEB: www.andersontully.com
SIC: 2421 5031 2435 2426 Sawmills & planing mills, general; veneer; hardwood veneer & plywood; hardwood dimension & flooring mills
HQ: Anderson-Tully Company
565 Industrial Dr
Vicksburg MS 39183
601 636-3876

(G-5340)
ANDERSON-TULLY COMPANY
Also Called: Anderson Tully Co
565 Industrial Dr (39183-8689)
P.O. Box 38 (39181-0038)
PHONE 601 636-3876
Tony Parks, *President*
EMP: 286 **Privately Held**
WEB: www.andersontully.com
SIC: 2421 5031 2426 Box lumber; lumber, plywood & millwork; hardwood dimension & flooring mills

HQ: Anderson-Tully Company
565 Industrial Dr
Vicksburg MS 39183
601 636-3876

(G-5341)
APAC-MISSISSIPPI INC
4441 Rifle Range Rd (39180-5911)
PHONE 601 634-6600
Andy Atkins, *Manager*
EMP: 29
SALES (corp-wide): 30.6B **Privately Held**
SIC: 1611 2951 Highway & street paving contractor; asphalt paving mixtures & blocks
HQ: Apac-Mississippi, Inc.
101 Riverview Dr
Richland MS 39218
601 376-4000

(G-5342)
ARC-UP WELDING INC
76 Business Park Dr (39180-8323)
PHONE 601 638-1202
Sidney A Meacham Sr, *President*
Gail C Meacham, *Treasurer*
EMP: 7
SQ FT: 2,500
SALES (est): 426.6K **Privately Held**
SIC: 7692 Welding repair

(G-5343)
B AND L MEAT PROCESSING
73 Standard Hill Rd (39183-4030)
PHONE 601 218-0918
Daniel Boler, *Principal*
EMP: 3
SALES (est): 161.2K **Privately Held**
SIC: 2011 Meat packing plants

(G-5344)
BG3 DELTA LLC
Also Called: Delta Discount Wine & Spirits
415 Tiffintown Rd (39183-7490)
PHONE 601 636-9828
William Kitchens, *Owner*
EMP: 3
SALES (est): 188.7K **Privately Held**
SIC: 5921 7999 5411 3519 Wine; lottery tickets, sale of; grocery stores; gasoline engines

(G-5345)
BIG RIVER SHIPBUILDERS INC (PA)
404 Port Terminal Cir (39183-1175)
PHONE 601 636-9161
J O Smith III, *President*
Hugh Smith Jr, *General Mgr*
Teresia White, *Corp Secy*
Patrick Smith, *Vice Pres*
EMP: 34
SQ FT: 20,000
SALES: 8.7MM **Privately Held**
SIC: 3731 3531 3441 Shipbuilding & repairing; marine related equipment; fabricated structural metal

(G-5346)
BIG RIVER SHIPBUILDERS INC
1063 Haining Rd (39183-9005)
PHONE 601 802-9994
Kerry Southern, *Branch Mgr*
EMP: 8
SALES (corp-wide): 8.7MM **Privately Held**
SIC: 3531 Marine related equipment
PA: Big River Shipbuilders, Inc.
404 Port Terminal Cir
Vicksburg MS 39183
601 636-9161

(G-5347)
BOBS WOODWORKING LLC
2211 Tiffintown Rd (39183-1530)
PHONE 601 661-8093
Robert Breland, *Principal*
EMP: 1
SALES (est): 41.5K **Privately Held**
SIC: 2499 Wood products

(G-5348)
BRM LLC
Also Called: Billy's Original Foods
121 Thalweg Dr (39183-7390)
PHONE 601 501-1444

Vicksburg - Warren County (G-5349)　　　　　　　　　　　　　　　**GEOGRAPHIC SECTION**

William Lieberman, *Managing Prtnr*
Manivanh Chanprasith,
Rita P Cook,
Robin Lieberman,
EMP: 9
SQ FT: 5,000
SALES (est): 296K **Privately Held**
SIC: 2038 5812 Dinners, frozen & packaged; Italian restaurant

(G-5349)
BUTTON UP CANDLES
6023 Castle Rd (39180-9313)
PHONE..................................317 522-8060
Kylie Hager, *Principal*
EMP: 1
SALES (est): 39.6K **Privately Held**
SIC: 3999 Candles

(G-5350)
CAM2 INTERNATIONAL LLC
685 Haining Rd (39183-9069)
PHONE..................................601 661-5382
Jack Baker, *Branch Mgr*
EMP: 45
SALES (corp-wide): 43MM **Privately Held**
SIC: 1389 Gas field services
PA: Cam2 International, L.L.C.
685 Haining Rd
Vicksburg MS 39183
800 338-2262

(G-5351)
CAM2 INTERNATIONAL LLC (PA)
685 Haining Rd (39183-9069)
PHONE..................................800 338-2262
Jack Baker, *CEO*
Walter Tyson, *President*
Stephen Kelley, *CFO*
Edgar Ray Smith III,
EMP: 3
SALES (est): 43MM **Privately Held**
SIC: 1389 Gas field services

(G-5352)
CAM2 INTERNATIONAL LLC
685 Haining Rd (39183-9069)
PHONE..................................601 661-5382
Jack Baker, *Vice Pres*
EMP: 10
SALES (corp-wide): 43MM **Privately Held**
SIC: 3714 Hydraulic fluid power pumps for auto steering mechanism
PA: Cam2 International, L.L.C.
685 Haining Rd
Vicksburg MS 39183
800 338-2262

(G-5353)
CAMERON RIG SOLUTIONS INC
500 Letourneau Rd (39180-1203)
PHONE..................................601 629-3300
EMP: 2
SALES (est): 86.6K **Privately Held**
SIC: 3441 Fabricated structural metal

(G-5354)
CARSONS CONSTRUCTION LLC
1127 Openwood St (39183-2533)
PHONE..................................601 301-0841
Malcolm Carson, *Owner*
Clifton Jeffery, *Co-Owner*
EMP: 30 **EST:** 2015
SALES (est): 914.9K **Privately Held**
SIC: 3423 3272 Carpenters' hand tools, except saws: levels, chisels, etc.; wall base, precast terrazzo

(G-5355)
CARUTHERS AC & HTG LLC
3300 Washington St (39180-5058)
PHONE..................................601 636-9433
Georgia Caruthers, *Treasurer*
Thomas Caruthers IV,
EMP: 6
SALES: 950K **Privately Held**
SIC: 3585 Refrigeration & heating equipment

(G-5356)
CLEAR SIGHT WINDSHIELD REPAIR
1712 Sky Farm Ave (39183-2306)
PHONE..................................601 638-2892
EMP: 1
SALES (est): 87K **Privately Held**
SIC: 3231 Windshields, glass: made from purchased glass

(G-5357)
COOPER LIGHTING LLC
5035 Highway 61 S (39180-9538)
PHONE..................................601 638-1522
Dustin Pittman, *Engineer*
Lucian Greco, *Manager*
EMP: 500 **Privately Held**
WEB: www.corelite.com
SIC: 3645 3648 3646 Residential lighting fixtures; lighting equipment; commercial indusl & institutional electric lighting fixtures
HQ: Cooper Lighting, Llc
1121 Highway 74 S
Peachtree City GA 30269
770 486-4800

(G-5358)
CREATIVE HANDS PRINTING SVCS
3895 Highway 80 (39180-7804)
PHONE..................................601 631-1262
Constance Lenoir, *Principal*
EMP: 4
SALES (est): 202.7K **Privately Held**
SIC: 2752 Commercial printing, lithographic

(G-5359)
CREATIVE MACHINING INC
508 Goodrum Rd (39180-8924)
PHONE..................................601 630-5536
Clay Lahatte, *President*
Steve Lahatte, *Vice Pres*
EMP: 2
SALES: 75K **Privately Held**
WEB: www.creative-machining.com
SIC: 3599 Machine shop, jobbing & repair

(G-5360)
DELLA WEST PUBLISHING LLC
743 Lakeside Dr (39180-8596)
PHONE..................................601 618-8429
Trina Girard, *President*
EMP: 1
SALES (est): 39.4K **Privately Held**
SIC: 2741 Miscellaneous publishing

(G-5361)
DELTA INDUSTRIES INC
1730 Highway 80 (39180-0936)
PHONE..................................601 634-6001
Terry Merideth, *Principal*
EMP: 11
SALES (corp-wide): 100.3MM **Privately Held**
WEB: www.delta-ind.com
SIC: 3273 Ready-mixed concrete
PA: Delta Industries, Inc.
100 W Woodrow Wilson Ave
Jackson MS 39213
601 354-3801

(G-5362)
DOTTLEYS SPICE MART INC
5626 Highway 61 S (39180-7281)
PHONE..................................601 629-6100
William Dottley, *President*
Teresa Dottley, *Director*
Cathy Blagg, *Admin Sec*
EMP: 1
SALES (est): 17.2K **Privately Held**
SIC: 2099 Seasonings & spices

(G-5363)
EAP LLC
102 Danawood Ln (39180-9146)
PHONE..................................601 636-1621
EMP: 5
SALES (est): 270K **Privately Held**
SIC: 3648 Mfg Lighting Equipment

(G-5364)
EASTERS CUSTOM WOODWORKS LLC
110 King Arthurs Rdg (39180-9767)
PHONE..................................740 502-2039
John Easter,
EMP: 1
SALES (est): 39.6K **Privately Held**
SIC: 3999 Manufacturing industries

(G-5365)
ELECTRO MECH SOLUTIONS EMS INC
5589 Highway 61 S (39180-9654)
PHONE..................................601 631-0138
Christina R Davidson, *President*
Brad Davidson, *Principal*
Chandler Jackson, *Human Res Mgr*
EMP: 2
SALES (est): 565.9K **Privately Held**
SIC: 3556 3541 1799 5084 Food products machinery; lathes, metal cutting & polishing; welding on site; welding machinery & equipment

(G-5366)
EMMA ROBERTS
Also Called: E & J Distributors
4908 Gibson Rd (39180-6306)
PHONE..................................601 638-3062
Emma Roberts, *Owner*
EMP: 2
SALES (est): 204.7K **Privately Held**
SIC: 3577 1799 Computer peripheral equipment; cleaning building exteriors

(G-5367)
ERGON INC
Also Called: Specialty Process Fabricators
2353 Haining Rd (39183-9056)
PHONE..................................601 636-6888
Don May, *Branch Mgr*
Larry Jones, *Manager*
EMP: 50
SALES (corp-wide): 997.6MM **Privately Held**
WEB: www.ergon.com
SIC: 4213 2911 Trucking, except local; petroleum refining
PA: Ergon, Inc.
2829 Lakeland Dr Ste 2000
Flowood MS 39232
601 933-3000

(G-5368)
ERGON BIOFUELS LLC
1833 Haining Rd (39183-9036)
P.O. Box 1639, Jackson (39215-1639)
PHONE..................................601 636-1976
Joe Branch, *Asst Mgr*
Don Davis,
EMP: 25
SALES (est): 16.7MM
SALES (corp-wide): 997.6MM **Privately Held**
SIC: 2869 2879 Industrial organic chemicals; agricultural chemicals
HQ: Ergon Ethanol, Inc.
2829 Lakeland Dr Ste 2000
Flowood MS 39232

(G-5369)
ERGON MARINE & INDUSTRIAL SUP
100 Lee St (39180-5070)
PHONE..................................601 636-6552
Danny Kessler, *Manager*
EMP: 1
SALES (corp-wide): 1.1MM **Privately Held**
SIC: 2911 4213 Gasoline; greases, lubricating; asphalt or asphaltic materials, made in refineries; liquid petroleum transport, non-local
PA: Ergon Marine & Industrial Supply Inc
2829 Lakeland Dr Ste 2000
Flowood MS

(G-5370)
ERGON REFINING INC
2611 Haining Rd (39183-9056)
P.O. Box 309 (39181-0309)
PHONE..................................601 638-4960
Jeff Cochran, *Engineer*
Kim Deller, *Manager*

Debbie Beach, *Manager*
Steve Elwart, *Manager*
Larry Jones, *Manager*
EMP: 114
SALES (corp-wide): 997.6MM **Privately Held**
SIC: 2911 Oils, lubricating
HQ: Ergon Refining, Inc.
2829 Lakeland Dr
Flowood MS 39232
601 933-3000

(G-5371)
FIELDER MFG
2358 Redbone Rd (39180-8947)
PHONE..................................601 630-9295
Mike Fielder, *Owner*
EMP: 1
SALES: 100K **Privately Held**
SIC: 7692 Welding repair

(G-5372)
FIRST HERITAGE CREDIT CORP
2480 S Frontage Rd (39180-5251)
PHONE..................................601 636-6060
EMP: 1 **Privately Held**
SIC: 6141 2411 Consumer finance companies; timber, cut at logging camp
PA: First Heritage Credit Corp
605 Crescent Blvd Ste 101
Ridgeland MS 39157

(G-5373)
FIVE STARS LIGHTING CO LTD
95 Waring Rd (39183-9071)
PHONE..................................610 533-6522
John Tselepis, *Principal*
▲ **EMP:** 2
SALES (est): 237.6K **Privately Held**
SIC: 3645 3646 Residential lighting fixtures; commercial indusl & institutional electric lighting fixtures

(G-5374)
GLEN JONES & ASSOCIATES INC
107 Cherrybark Ln (39180-1820)
PHONE..................................601 634-0877
Glen Jones, *Owner*
EMP: 2
SALES (est): 128.8K **Privately Held**
SIC: 2392 Household furnishings

(G-5375)
GULF STATES SILVER
810 Fort Hill Dr (39183-2046)
PHONE..................................601 415-4365
Gordon Longmire, *Principal*
EMP: 4 **EST:** 2010
SALES (est): 363.8K **Privately Held**
SIC: 3559 Silver recovery equipment

(G-5376)
HANCOR INC
5695 Highway 61 S (39180-9537)
PHONE..................................601 629-9040
Allen Rush, *Manager*
EMP: 22
SALES (corp-wide): 1.3B **Publicly Held**
SIC: 3084 3088 3089 Plastics pipe; plastics plumbing fixtures; septic tanks, plastic; engraving of plastic
HQ: Hancor, Inc.
4640 Trueman Blvd
Hilliard OH 43026
614 658-0050

(G-5377)
HANGER PRSTHETCS & ORTHO INC
1111 N Frontage Rd (39180-5102)
PHONE..................................601 883-3341
EMP: 7
SALES (corp-wide): 1B **Publicly Held**
SIC: 3842 Surgical appliances & supplies
HQ: Hanger Prosthetics & Orthotics, Inc.
10910 Domain Dr Ste 300
Austin TX 78758
512 777-3800

192

2019 Harris Directory of
Mississippi Manufacturers

▲ = Import ▼=Export
◆ =Import/Export

GEOGRAPHIC SECTION

Vicksburg - Warren County (G-5409)

(G-5378)
HELPING HAND FAMILY PHARMACY
Also Called: Helping Hands Pharmacy
1670 Highway 61 N (39183-3411)
PHONE....................................601 631-6837
Michael Jones, *Owner*
EMP: 3
SALES (est): 453.5K **Privately Held**
SIC: 2834 Medicines, capsuled or ampuled

(G-5379)
HUNT REFINING COMPANY
2600 Dorsey St (39180-4661)
PHONE....................................843 236-5098
EMP: 2
SALES (corp-wide): 5.3B **Privately Held**
SIC: 2911 Petroleum refining
HQ: Hunt Refining Company
     2200 Jack Warner Pkwy # 400
     Tuscaloosa AL 35401
     205 391-3300

(G-5380)
HYDESOFT COMPUTING LLC
110 Roseland Dr (39180-5540)
PHONE....................................601 629-8607
David Hyde,
EMP: 1
SALES: 80K **Privately Held**
SIC: 7372 Application computer software

(G-5381)
J & K RESTAURANTS INC (PA)
Also Called: Billys Original Food
121 Thalweg Dr (39183-7390)
PHONE....................................601 501-1444
Billy Lieberman, *CEO*
EMP: 8 EST: 2001
SQ FT: 5,000
SALES: 555K **Privately Held**
SIC: 2038 Dinners, frozen & packaged;
lunches, frozen & packaged

(G-5382)
JH DIRT & GRAVEL LLC
114 Blackwell Dr (39180-8518)
PHONE....................................601 831-3990
EMP: 2
SALES (est): 66K **Privately Held**
SIC: 1442 Construction sand & gravel

(G-5383)
JOHNNY MCCOOL LOGGING
315 Silver Creek Dr (39180-9251)
PHONE....................................601 636-3824
Johnny E McCool, *President*
Judy McCool, *Vice Pres*
EMP: 50 EST: 1973
SQ FT: 29,000
SALES: 7MM **Privately Held**
SIC: 2411 Logging camps & contractors

(G-5384)
KAR KLEEN
1955 Highway 80 (39180-0938)
PHONE....................................601 638-8816
Jack Hill Sr, *Owner*
Sandy Hill, *Office Mgr*
EMP: 3
SALES (est): 200K **Privately Held**
SIC: 3599 7538 7539 7542 Machine
shop, jobbing & repair; engine rebuilding;
automotive; machine shop, automotive;
washing & polishing, automotive; engines
& transportation equipment

(G-5385)
KENNITH HUMPHREY - PAINTINGS &
1407 Parkway Dr (39180-4730)
PHONE....................................601 218-2786
EMP: 2
SALES (est): 83.9K **Privately Held**
SIC: 2752 Commercial printing, lithographic

(G-5386)
KEPLER BOYS WEAR LLC
3301 Washington St (39180-5057)
PHONE....................................601 738-1664
Deborah Reul,
Douglas Reul, *Associate*
EMP: 3 EST: 2016
SQ FT: 1,500

SALES (est): 137.1K **Privately Held**
SIC: 2311 Suits, men's & boys': made from
purchased materials

(G-5387)
L AND H INVESTMENT INC
1880 S Frontage Rd (39180-5259)
PHONE....................................601 636-4642
Hayes Latham, *President*
EMP: 6
SALES (est): 304.6K **Privately Held**
SIC: 2273 Carpets & rugs

(G-5388)
LACLEDE CHAIN MFG CO LLC
101 W Ceres Blvd (39183-8026)
PHONE....................................601 802-0134
EMP: 1
SALES (corp-wide): 39.6MM **Privately Held**
SIC: 3315 Chain link fencing
PA: Laclede Chain Manufacturing Company, Llc
     1549 Fenpark Dr
     Fenton MO 63026
     636 680-2320

(G-5389)
LIPSTICK AND LABELS LLC
1208 Washington St (39183-2962)
PHONE....................................601 501-4029
Jasmine Wheatley, *Principal*
EMP: 2
SALES (est): 74.4K **Privately Held**
SIC: 2844 Lipsticks

(G-5390)
LYNN WELDING SHOP LLC
Also Called: Lynns Custom Boats
7355 Highway 61 S (39180-8321)
PHONE....................................601 638-7235
James E Lynn Sr,
Teresa Lynn,
EMP: 3
SALES: 100K **Privately Held**
SIC: 3732 7692 Boat building & repairing;
welding repair

(G-5391)
LYNNS WELDING SHOP LLC
7355 Highway 61 S (39180-8321)
PHONE....................................601 415-0012
Danny Lynn, *Partner*
EMP: 3 EST: 2016
SALES (est): 142.6K **Privately Held**
SIC: 3731 Lighters, marine: building & repairing

(G-5392)
MAGNOLIA MOBILITY LLC
Also Called: Magnolia Group The
3101 Washington St (39180-4968)
PHONE....................................601 400-7292
Steven A Houston, *Owner*
EMP: 3
SALES (est): 220K **Privately Held**
SIC: 5047 0851 0711 2879 Medical &
hospital equipment; forestry services; soil
preparation services; agricultural chemicals; lawn & garden services

(G-5393)
MAGNOLIA MTAL PLASTIC PDTS INC
Also Called: Magnoliascreencomp
101 County Ln (39183-3487)
P.O. Box 822049 (39182-2049)
PHONE....................................601 638-6912
Tony Malik, *President*
Fred Malik Jr, *President*
Laurie Malik, *Treasurer*
▼ EMP: 40
SALES (est): 9MM **Privately Held**
WEB: www.magnoliametal.com
SIC: 3355 3089 Aluminum rolling & drawing; injection molding of plastics

(G-5394)
MCHAN CABINETS
3250 Tiffintown Rd (39183-1524)
PHONE....................................601 636-8821
EMP: 2
SALES (est): 208.4K **Privately Held**
SIC: 2434 Wood kitchen cabinets

(G-5395)
MISSISSIPPI CENTER FOR FREEDOM
1601f N Frontage Rd (39180-5149)
P.O. Box 821668 (39182-1668)
PHONE....................................601 638-0962
EMP: 1
SALES (est): 54.5K **Privately Held**
SIC: 3523 Farm machinery & equipment

(G-5396)
MISSISSIPPI LIME COMPANY
Also Called: Falco Lime
1543 Haining Rd (39183-9036)
PHONE....................................601 636-0932
Eustas Conway, *Branch Mgr*
EMP: 25
SALES (corp-wide): 324.1MM **Privately Held**
WEB: www.mississippilime.com
SIC: 3274 Lime
HQ: Mississippi Lime Company
     3870 S Lindbergh Blvd # 200
     Saint Louis MO 63127
     314 543-6300

(G-5397)
MISSISSIPPI SAND SOLUTIONS LL
255 C J Fisher Dr (39180-7460)
PHONE....................................870 291-8802
EMP: 3
SALES (est): 229.6K **Privately Held**
SIC: 1442 Construction sand & gravel

(G-5398)
MISSISSIPPI TANTEC LEATHER INC
101 Tantec Way (39183-8796)
PHONE....................................601 429-6081
Thomas Schneider, *CEO*
Uwe Hutzler, *President*
Mariano Fleita, *Vice Pres*
Jens Kaufhold, *Vice Pres*
Lisa Ainsworth, *Accounting Mgr*
▲ EMP: 1
SALES (est): 383.1K **Privately Held**
SIC: 3172 Personal leather goods

(G-5399)
MMC MATERIALS INC
4450 Rifle Range Rd (39180-5912)
PHONE....................................601 634-8787
Stanley Mangum, *Manager*
EMP: 56
SALES (corp-wide): 306.5MM **Privately Held**
WEB: www.mmcmaterials.com
SIC: 3273 1442 Ready-mixed concrete;
construction sand & gravel
HQ: Mmc Materials, Inc.
     1052 Highland Colony Pkwy # 201
     Ridgeland MS 39157
     601 898-4000

(G-5400)
MOBILE ONE LUBE EXPRESS PLUS
3420 Halls Ferry Rd (39180-5504)
PHONE....................................601 631-8000
Charles Pendleton, *Owner*
EMP: 7
SALES (est): 441.8K **Privately Held**
SIC: 2741 Miscellaneous publishing

(G-5401)
MONOGRAM CREATIONS
1890 S Frontage Rd Ste 3 (39180-5633)
PHONE....................................601 415-4970
Becky Chennault, *Principal*
EMP: 1
SALES (est): 62.6K **Privately Held**
SIC: 2395 Embroidery products, except
schiffli machine

(G-5402)
OMEGA-TEC LLC
Also Called: Isplacement Loop Antenna
1025 Jackson St (39183-2521)
PHONE....................................601 750-8082
Barrie McArthur,
Bill Bolick,
Matt Holmes,
EMP: 8

SALES (est): 841.4K **Privately Held**
SIC: 7373 3663 1731 8748 Computer integrated systems design; antennas, transmitting & communications; safety &
security specialization; systems analysis
or design

(G-5403)
ONE SOURCE SYSTEMS LLC
120 Holt Collier Dr Ste C (39183-4408)
PHONE....................................601 636-6888
Mike Ford, *Owner*
EMP: 32
SALES (corp-wide): 11.3MM **Privately Held**
SIC: 3823 Industrial process measurement
equipment
PA: One Source Systems, L.L.C.
     18359 Petroleum Dr
     Baton Rouge LA 70809
     225 752-0267

(G-5404)
PELTZ MEDICAL LLC
3211 Wisconsin Ave Ste A (39180-5635)
PHONE....................................601 831-3135
Jeffrey Peltz, *Partner*
EMP: 2 EST: 2014
SALES (est): 110K **Privately Held**
SIC: 3841 Surgical instruments & apparatus

(G-5405)
PETRO-HUNT LLC
4940 Freetown Rd (39183-7838)
PHONE....................................601 636-3448
EMP: 19
SALES (corp-wide): 5B **Privately Held**
SIC: 1311 Crude Petroleum/Natural Gas
Production
HQ: Petro-Hunt, L.L.C.
     2101 Cedar Springs Rd # 600
     Dallas TX 75201
     214 880-8400

(G-5406)
PITTSBURGH STONE & PLASTER
715 China St (39183-2923)
PHONE....................................601 631-0006
John Tuminello, *CEO*
EMP: 1
SALES (est): 96.6K **Privately Held**
SIC: 1743 3253 5211 Tile installation, ceramic; ceramic wall & floor tile; masonry
materials & supplies; tile, ceramic

(G-5407)
POLYVULC USA INC
695 Industrial Dr (39183-8653)
PHONE....................................601 638-8040
Fred Farrell, *Ch of Bd*
Larry L Lambiotte, *President*
J Fred Farrell, *Vice Pres*
Dean Andrews Jr, *Bd of Directors*
Eustace Conway, *Admin Sec*
EMP: 50
SQ FT: 125,000
SALES (est): 10.5MM **Privately Held**
WEB: www.polyvulcusa.com
SIC: 3069 3089 3585 Reclaimed rubber
(reworked by manufacturing processes);
plastic processing; refrigeration & heating
equipment

(G-5408)
PRINT SHOP
3510 Manor Dr (39180-5693)
P.O. Box 820638 (39182-0638)
PHONE....................................601 638-0962
William Cotton, *Owner*
EMP: 2
SALES (est): 249K **Privately Held**
SIC: 2752 Commercial printing, lithographic

(G-5409)
QUARTER REST CLASSICS
2170 N Washington St (39183-5093)
PHONE....................................601 638-4207
EMP: 1 EST: 2014
SALES (est): 63.6K **Privately Held**
SIC: 3131 Quarters

(PA)=Parent Co (HQ)=Headquarters (DH)=Div Headquarters
✿ = New Business established in last 2 years

2019 Harris Directory of
Mississippi Manufacturers

193

GEOGRAPHIC

Vicksburg - Warren County (G-5410)
GEOGRAPHIC SECTION

(G-5410)
RICKYS WELDING AND MACHINE SP
1721 Levee St (39180-3511)
PHONE..................................601 638-8238
Ricky Lowery, *President*
Debra Lowery, *Corp Secy*
Otis Lowery, *Vice Pres*
EMP: 8
SQ FT: 12,000
SALES (est): 1.4MM **Privately Held**
SIC: **1791** 7699 3444 3443 Iron work, structural; industrial machinery & equipment repair; sheet metalwork; fabricated plate work (boiler shop); fabricated structural metal; aluminum sheet, plate & foil

(G-5411)
RIVER CITY PALLET CO
30 Sherard Dr (39180-9671)
PHONE..................................601 415-0386
EMP: 4
SALES (est): 363.5K **Privately Held**
SIC: **2448** Pallets, wood & wood with metal

(G-5412)
RIVER ROAD JEAN COMPANY
2250 Eagle Lake Shore Rd (39183-7382)
PHONE..................................601 279-6571
Steve Koppman, *President*
EMP: 2
SALES (est): 154.6K **Privately Held**
WEB: www.riverroadjeancompany.com
SIC: **2325** Jeans: men's, youths' & boys'

(G-5413)
ROES RIMS AND ACCESSORIES
2840 Clay St (39183-3133)
PHONE..................................601 619-4489
Roosevelt Harris, *Owner*
EMP: 1
SALES: 70K **Privately Held**
SIC: **5014** 5531 3312 Tires & tubes; automotive accessories; wheels

(G-5414)
ROGER FILLEBAUM
Also Called: Creative Signs
7935 Warriors Trl (39180-7771)
PHONE..................................601 638-5473
Roger Fillebaum, *Owner*
EMP: 1
SALES (est): 101.2K **Privately Held**
SIC: **3993** Signs, not made in custom sign painting shops

(G-5415)
SERI
1000 Rubber Way (39180-8322)
PHONE..................................601 638-3355
Wes Johnson, *Owner*
EMP: 5
SALES (est): 681.6K **Privately Held**
SIC: **3069** Molded rubber products

(G-5416)
SHAWN KURTZ
Also Called: Kurtz Custom Cabinets
344 Stenson Rd (39180-7789)
PHONE..................................601 415-9540
Shawn Kurtz, *Principal*
EMP: 1
SALES (est): 106.4K **Privately Held**
SIC: **2434** Wood kitchen cabinets

(G-5417)
SHELBY DEAN DISTRIBUTING
800 Newitt Vick Dr (39183-8749)
PHONE..................................601 529-7936
Shelby Dean, *Owner*
EMP: 1
SALES (est): 53K **Privately Held**
SIC: **3423** Hand & edge tools

(G-5418)
SHELL PIPE LINE CORPORATION
20 Freetown Rd (39183-8600)
PHONE..................................601 638-1921
EMP: 4
SALES (corp-wide): 388.3B **Privately Held**
SIC: **2911** Gasoline

HQ: Shell Pipe Line Corporation
2 Shell Plz Ste 1160
Houston TX 77002
713 241-6161

(G-5419)
SKYHAWK LLC
1661 N Frontage Rd (39180-5149)
PHONE..................................601 619-6805
EMP: 2
SALES (est): 206.4K **Privately Held**
SIC: **3663** Radio And Tv Communications Equipment,Nsk

(G-5420)
SOUTH FORK LOGGING LLC
6624 Warriors Trl (39180-0842)
PHONE..................................601 218-4524
Audrey Christmas, *Principal*
EMP: 2
SALES (est): 81.7K **Privately Held**
SIC: **2411** Logging

(G-5421)
SOUTHLAND OIL COMPANY
2600 Dorsey St (39180-4661)
P.O. Box 663 (39181-0663)
PHONE..................................601 634-1361
Carl Brock, *Manager*
EMP: 6
SALES (corp-wide): 35.7MM **Privately Held**
SIC: **2911** Petroleum refining
HQ: Southland Oil Company
5170 Galaxie Dr
Jackson MS 39206
601 981-4151

(G-5422)
SPLIT ENDS
3412 Pemberton Square Blv (39180-5541)
PHONE..................................601 619-0088
Bonny East, *Owner*
EMP: 2
SALES (est): 77K **Privately Held**
SIC: **3999** Barber & beauty shop equipment

(G-5423)
STAMM ADVERTISING CO INC (PA)
3400 Drummond St (39180-5006)
PHONE..................................601 636-7749
John C Stamm, *President*
Laurin Stamm, *Corp Secy*
John C Stamm Jr, *Vice Pres*
EMP: 1
SALES: 650K **Privately Held**
SIC: **2759** Screen printing

(G-5424)
STEELSUMMIT HOLDINGS INC
Also Called: Vicksmetal Company
901 Haining Rd (39183-9000)
PHONE..................................601 638-1819
Takahiro Saito, *President*
Tracy Warren, *Admin Asst*
EMP: 13
SALES (est): 3.9MM **Privately Held**
SIC: **3699** Electrical equipment & supplies

(G-5425)
SUPREME INTERNATIONAL LLC
Also Called: Duck Head Apparel
4000 S Frontage Rd # 101 (39180-4462)
PHONE..................................601 638-2403
Ramona Goff, *Manager*
EMP: 5
SALES (corp-wide): 874.8MM **Privately Held**
WEB: www.supreme.com
SIC: **2325** Men's & boys' trousers & slacks
HQ: Supreme International, Llc
3000 Nw 107th Ave
Doral FL 33172
305 592-2830

(G-5426)
T-N-T PRINTING
1211 Grammar St (39180-3603)
PHONE..................................601 630-9553
Perri Johnson, *Principal*
EMP: 2
SALES (est): 139.1K **Privately Held**
SIC: **2752** Commercial printing, lithographic

(G-5427)
TAYLOR BROTHERS CNSTR CO
213 Greenbriar Dr (39180-6210)
PHONE..................................601 636-1749
Reginal Taylor, *Owner*
EMP: 7
SALES (est): 168K **Privately Held**
SIC: **1522** 1623 1771 1751 Residential construction; sewer line construction; concrete work; carpentry work; welding repair; grading

(G-5428)
TERMINAL
639 Industrial Dr (39183-8653)
PHONE..................................601 636-7781
EMP: 2
SALES (est): 91.3K **Privately Held**
SIC: **3273** Ready-mixed concrete

(G-5429)
TRANSFRAC LOGISTICS LLC
1350 Fonsylvania Rd (39180-6916)
P.O. Box 525, Pea Ridge AR (72751-0525)
PHONE..................................479 659-8186
James Marble, *CEO*
Tom Waggoner, *Agent*
EMP: 1
SQ FT: 200
SALES (est): 45.1K **Privately Held**
SIC: **1389** Haulage, oil field

(G-5430)
TYLER PRINTING AND CMPT SVC
225 Sea Island Dr (39183-7958)
PHONE..................................601 279-6105
Ronnie Tyler, *Principal*
EMP: 1
SALES (est): 69.3K **Privately Held**
SIC: **2752** Commercial printing, lithographic

(G-5431)
TYSON FOODS INC
1785 Interplex Cir (39183-7433)
PHONE..................................601 631-3600
Aretha Carmichael, *Finance*
Shannon Hendry, *Branch Mgr*
Sharon Robinson, *Director*
EMP: 750
SQ FT: 2,797
SALES (corp-wide): 40B **Publicly Held**
SIC: **2015** Poultry sausage, luncheon meats & other poultry products
PA: Tyson Foods, Inc.
2200 W Don Tyson Pkwy
Springdale AR 72762
479 290-4000

(G-5432)
UNION CORRUGATING COMPANY
Also Called: Vicksburg Metal Products
1463 Interplex Cir (39183-7434)
PHONE..................................601 661-0577
Dwight Berry, *Manager*
EMP: 6
SALES (corp-wide): 36.2MM **Privately Held**
WEB: www.unioncorrugating.com
SIC: **3444** 3441 2952 3446 Roof deck, sheet metal; siding, sheet metal; fabricated structural metal; asphalt felts & coatings; architectural metalwork
PA: Union Corrugating Company
701 S King St
Fayetteville NC 28301
910 483-0479

(G-5433)
VAMPCO INC
Also Called: Vicksburg Alum & Met Pdts Co
247 Armory Rd (39183-7475)
P.O. Box 822049 (39182-2049)
PHONE..................................601 638-5133
Tony Malik, *CEO*
Marguerite Malik, *CEO*
Fred A Malik Sr, *President*
Fred A Malik Jr, *Controller*
EMP: 5
SQ FT: 18,000

SALES (est): 799.9K **Privately Held**
WEB: www.vampco.com
SIC: **3442** Screens, window, metal; screen doors, metal; sash, door or window: metal

(G-5434)
VBG WOODWORKS LLC
766 Rollingwood Dr (39183-6932)
PHONE..................................601 634-0313
Thad Pratt, *Owner*
EMP: 1
SALES (est): 82.4K **Privately Held**
SIC: **2431** Millwork

(G-5435)
VICKSBURG ENTERPRISE MFG LLC
Also Called: Vicksburg Engineering & Mfg
4 Chelsea Ln (39180-9173)
P.O. Box 820040 (39182-0040)
PHONE..................................601 631-0304
Ronnie Runnels, *Manager*
EMP: 5
SALES (corp-wide): 1.5MM **Privately Held**
SIC: **3644** 3643 Noncurrent-carrying wiring services; current-carrying wiring devices
PA: Vicksburg Enterprise Manufacturing, Llc
1514 Walnut St
Vicksburg MS 39180
601 631-0304

(G-5436)
VICKSBURG ENTERPRISE MFG LLC (PA)
Also Called: Vicksburg Engineering & Mfg
1514 Walnut St (39180-3536)
P.O. Box 820040 (39182-0040)
PHONE..................................601 631-0304
Marco Bubani, *Network Enginr*
Ronnie G Runnels,
EMP: 5
SQ FT: 4,500
SALES (est): 1.5MM **Privately Held**
SIC: **3644** 3643 Noncurrent-carrying wiring services; current-carrying wiring devices

(G-5437)
VICKSBURG NEWSMEDIA LLC
Also Called: Vicksburg Posts, The
1601 N Frontage Rd Ste F (39180-5149)
P.O. Box 821668 (39182-1668)
PHONE..................................601 636-4545
Timothy Reeves,
EMP: 1
SALES (est): 197.2K **Privately Held**
SIC: **2752** 3993 2711 Commercial printing, offset; signs & advertising specialties; newspapers

(G-5438)
VICKSBURG PRINTING AND PUBG CO (PA)
Also Called: Vicksburg Post
1601 N Frontage Rd (39180-5149)
P.O. Box 821668 (39182-1668)
PHONE..................................601 636-4545
Louis P Cashman III, *President*
Jan Griffey, *Editor*
Rob Sigler, *Editor*
Barbara Cashman, *Vice Pres*
Shandale Goodman, *Controller*
EMP: 86 EST: 1883
SQ FT: 14,000
SALES (est): 5.8MM **Privately Held**
WEB: www.vicksburgpost.com
SIC: **2711** Commercial printing & newspaper publishing combined

(G-5439)
VICKSBURG PRINTING AND PUBG CO
Also Called: Speediprint
1601c N Frontage Rd Ste C (39180-5149)
P.O. Box 821668 (39182-1668)
PHONE..................................601 638-2900
David Willis, *Manager*
EMP: 5
SALES (corp-wide): 5.8MM **Privately Held**
WEB: www.vicksburgpost.com
SIC: **2759** Commercial printing

2019 Harris Directory of
Mississippi Manufacturers

▲ = Import ▼=Export
◆ =Import/Export

GEOGRAPHIC SECTION

Water Valley - Yalobusha County (G-5467)

PA: Vicksburg Printing And Publishing
Company
1601 N Frontage Rd
Vicksburg MS 39180
601 636-4545

(G-5440)
VICKSBURG PRINTING AND PUBG CO
Also Called: Signs First
1601b N Frontage Rd (39180-5149)
P.O. Box 821668 (39182-1668)
PHONE..................................601 631-0400
Sammy Ross, *Office Mgr*
EMP: 3
SALES (corp-wide): 5.8MM Privately Held
WEB: www.vicksburgpost.com
SIC: 5199 3993 Advertising specialties; signs & advertising specialties
PA: Vicksburg Printing And Publishing Company
1601 N Frontage Rd
Vicksburg MS 39180
601 636-4545

(G-5441)
VICKSBURG READY MIX CONCRETE
1730 Highway 80 (39180-0936)
PHONE..................................601 634-6001
Warren Brown, *Manager*
EMP: 9
SALES (est): 787.1K Privately Held
SIC: 3273 Ready-mixed concrete

(G-5442)
VICKSMETAL CORPORATION
Also Called: Steelsummit Mississippi
155 Industrial Dr (39183-9072)
PHONE..................................601 636-1314
Gene Kuoda, *President*
EMP: 20
SQ FT: 53,000
SALES (est): 30.7K Privately Held
SIC: 3312 Blast furnaces & steel mills
HQ: Sumitomo Corporation Of Americas
300 Madison Ave Frnt 3
New York NY 10017
212 207-0700

(G-5443)
VMI MARINE INC
4477 Highway 61 S (39180-1346)
P.O. Box 821406 (39182-1406)
PHONE..................................601 636-8700
Henry H Smith Jr, *President*
▲ EMP: 55
SQ FT: 40,000
SALES (est): 13.9MM Privately Held
SIC: 5084 1389 Drilling bits; drilling equipment, excluding bits; oil well machinery, equipment & supplies; construction, repair & dismantling services

(G-5444)
WHO IS SED PUBLISHING LLC
5015 Rllngwood Esttes Dr (39180-6334)
PHONE..................................601 634-8939
Sederick Williams, *Principal*
EMP: 2
SALES (est): 59.2K Privately Held
SIC: 2741 Miscellaneous publishing

(G-5445)
WHOLESALE ELECTRIC SUPPLY
520 Depot St (39180-3504)
PHONE..................................601 501-6928
EMP: 1
SALES (est): 37.7K Privately Held
SIC: 5099 5063 3699 Durable goods; electrical apparatus & equipment; electrical equipment & supplies

(G-5446)
WILLIAM R GATEWOOD
Also Called: Gatewood Farms
1431 Wisteria Dr (39180-4756)
PHONE..................................601 636-0107
William R Gatewood, *Owner*
EMP: 7
SALES (est): 350K Privately Held
SIC: 2015 Chicken slaughtering & processing

(G-5447)
WILLIAM STEPHENS
Also Called: Magnolia Molds
3995 Highway 80 (39180-7742)
PHONE..................................601 634-0498
William Stephens, *Owner*
EMP: 1
SQ FT: 4,600
SALES (est): 99.4K Privately Held
WEB: www.magnoliamolds.net
SIC: 3269 Pottery cooking & kitchen articles

Walls
Desoto County

(G-5448)
BRENTWOOD ORIGINALS INC
9759 Church Rd (38680-8409)
PHONE..................................662 781-5301
Ryan Meinhardt, *VP Sales*
Jack Domer, *Branch Mgr*
EMP: 250
SALES (corp-wide): 145.3MM Privately Held
SIC: 2393 Canvas bags
PA: Brentwood Originals, Inc.
20639 S Fordyce Ave
Carson CA 90810
310 637-6804

(G-5449)
DELTA PALLETS AND CRATES I
6590 Hickory Crest Dr (38680-8920)
PHONE..................................662 781-1633
Judith Durham, *Principal*
EMP: 4
SALES (est): 279.7K Privately Held
SIC: 2448 Pallets, wood & wood with metal

(G-5450)
NATIONAL BANK BUILDERS & EQP
6081 Highway 161 (38680-9793)
PHONE..................................662 781-0702
Fax: 662 781-1368
EMP: 18
SQ FT: 80,000
SALES (est): 3.1MM Privately Held
SIC: 1542 3441 8742 8711 Modular Bank Building Construction Mfg Building Components Consultants & Engineers

(G-5451)
SATIN LOCS LLC
6930 Black Oak Dr (38680-9276)
PHONE..................................901 282-6823
EMP: 1
SALES (est): 53.4K Privately Held
SIC: 2221 Satins

Walnut
Tippah County

(G-5452)
ABBY MANUFACTURING LLC (PA)
Also Called: AMC
501 Pulliam Rd (38683-8925)
P.O. Box 7120, Tupelo (38802-7120)
PHONE..................................662 223-5339
Linda Abby, *President*
Terry L Abby, *Vice Pres*
Stacie Roberson, *Office Mgr*
EMP: 63
SQ FT: 10,300
SALES (est): 17.7MM Privately Held
SIC: 3441 Fabricated structural metal

(G-5453)
ABBY MANUFACTURING CO INC
Also Called: Ripley Precision Tool & Die
501 Pulliam Rd (38683-8925)
PHONE..................................662 223-5339
Terry Abby, *President*
Joe Spencer, *General Mgr*
Linda Abby, *Vice Pres*
Andy Hall, *Opers Staff*
Lindsey Davis, *Accountant*
EMP: 3

SQ FT: 10,000
SALES (est): 322.1K Privately Held
SIC: 3599 Machine shop, jobbing & repair

(G-5454)
ALUMA-FORM INC
141 Pulliam Rd (38683)
PHONE..................................662 677-6000
Tim Harper, *Manager*
EMP: 80
SALES (corp-wide): 50.7MM Privately Held
SIC: 3629 3354 Electronic generation equipment; bars, extruded, aluminum
PA: Aluma-Form, Inc.
3625 Old Getwell Rd
Memphis TN 38118
901 362-0100

(G-5455)
B S MONOGRAMMING
260 Frederick Dr (38683-9607)
PHONE..................................662 750-0505
Bethany Young, *Principal*
EMP: 1
SALES (est): 44K Privately Held
SIC: 2395 Embroidery & art needlework

(G-5456)
CV SUNGLASSES LLC
21418 Highway 72 (38683-7109)
P.O. Box 568 (38683-0568)
PHONE..................................662 212-0993
Jerry Brown, *Mng Member*
EMP: 1
SQ FT: 1,500
SALES (est): 50K Privately Held
SIC: 3851 Glasses, sun or glare

(G-5457)
KEITH CONAWAY LOGGING LLC
23 County Road 607 (38683-8320)
PHONE..................................662 415-5646
Keith Conaway, *Principal*
EMP: 2
SALES (est): 81.7K Privately Held
SIC: 2411 Logging

(G-5458)
THYSSENKRUPP ELEVATOR CORP
50 Mitchell Ave (38683-6001)
P.O. Box 300 (38683-0300)
PHONE..................................662 223-4025
Chris Horn, *Branch Mgr*
EMP: 165
SQ FT: 65,000
SALES (corp-wide): 39.8B Privately Held
WEB: www.tyssenkrupp.com
SIC: 3534 3625 3577 Elevators & equipment; relays & industrial controls; computer peripheral equipment
HQ: Thyssenkrupp Elevator Corporation
11605 Haynes Bridge Rd # 650
Alpharetta GA 30009
678 319-3240

(G-5459)
WOOLY BOOGER GAME CALLS
520 County Road 308 (38683-9157)
PHONE..................................662 587-3763
John Chapman, *Owner*
EMP: 1
SALES (est): 69.1K Privately Held
SIC: 3949 Game calls

Walnut Grove
Leake County

(G-5460)
JIMMY JONES & SONS SAWMILL
4546 Gunter Rd (39189-6398)
PHONE..................................601 253-2533
Jimmy Jones, *Owner*
EMP: 9
SQ FT: 3,000
SALES (est): 460K Privately Held
SIC: 2421 2411 Sawmills & planing mills, general; logging camps & contractors

(G-5461)
MISSISSIPPI QUARTERHORSE ASSN
2653 Clyde B Rd (39189-6213)
PHONE..................................601 692-5128
Tom McBeath, *Principal*
EMP: 1 EST: 2017
SALES (est): 74.2K Privately Held
SIC: 3131 Quarters

Washington
Adams County

(G-5462)
ST CATHERINE GRAVEL CO INC
879 Hwy 61 N (39190)
PHONE..................................601 442-1674
Dick Junkin, *President*
Johnny Junkin, *Vice Pres*
EMP: 6
SQ FT: 1,500
SALES (est): 445.9K Privately Held
SIC: 1442 Gravel mining

Water Valley
Yalobusha County

(G-5463)
BORGWARNER INC
600 Highway 32 (38965-6431)
PHONE..................................662 473-3100
Davy Doss, *Engineer*
Kent Tobin, *Branch Mgr*
Kathy Elliott, *Manager*
Tommy Edwards, *Prgrmr*
Bud McCluskey, *Director*
EMP: 39
SALES (corp-wide): 10.5B Publicly Held
SIC: 3714 Motor vehicle parts & accessories
PA: Borgwarner Inc.
3850 Hamlin Rd
Auburn Hills MI 48326
248 754-9200

(G-5464)
BORGWRNER EMSSIONS SYSTEMS LLC
600 Highway 32 (38965-6431)
P.O. Box 727 (38965-0727)
PHONE..................................662 473-3100
Ray Robertson, *Plant Mgr*
EMP: 700
SALES (corp-wide): 10.5B Publicly Held
SIC: 3592 3714 Carburetors; fuel systems & parts, motor vehicle
HQ: Borgwarner Emissions Systems Llc
3800 Automation Ave # 200
Auburn Hills MI 48326
248 754-9600

(G-5465)
CIC INTERNATIONAL LLC
Also Called: Crews International Cons
178 Askew St (38965-3913)
PHONE..................................662 473-4724
EMP: 2 EST: 2003
SALES (est): 130K Privately Held
SIC: 2211 Cotton Broadwoven Fabric Mill

(G-5466)
DAVID BUFORD
Also Called: Ethel Benson Quilt Collection
576 County Road 121 (38965-5955)
PHONE..................................662 714-3031
David Buford, *Owner*
EMP: 1
SALES (est): 46.5K Privately Held
SIC: 2221 Comforters & quilts, manmade fiber & silk

(G-5467)
DELTA GRIND STONE GROUND PDTS
111 Industrial Park Rd (38965-4681)
PHONE..................................662 816-1254
Julia Tatum, *Owner*
EMP: 1

(PA)=Parent Co (HQ)=Headquarters (DH)=Div Headquarters
✪ = New Business established in last 2 years

2019 Harris Directory of
Mississippi Manufacturers

195

GEOGRAPHIC SECTION

Water Valley - Yalobusha County (G-5468)

SALES (est): 43.5K **Privately Held**
SIC: 2041 Corn grits & flakes, for brewers' use

(G-5468)
GMN GROUP LLC (PA)
Also Called: Valley Thing'y
1112 County Road 103 (38965-5220)
PHONE..................................662 473-3094
Jason Bailey, *Mng Member*
Jerry Bailey,
EMP: 2
SALES: 20K **Privately Held**
SIC: 0191 0252 0254 2531 General farms, primarily crop; chicken eggs; chicken hatchery; picnic tables or benches, park; general merchandise, mail order;

(G-5469)
GW MINISTRIES
148 County Road 294 (38965-4794)
PHONE..................................662 832-9756
Gregory Wilson, *Director*
EMP: 1 EST: 2016
SALES (est): 67.8K **Privately Held**
SIC: 3669 7389 Transportation signaling devices;

(G-5470)
H&S SIGN COMPANY
234 County Road 550 (38965-3482)
PHONE..................................662 473-9300
Joseph Spence, *Owner*
EMP: 1
SALES: 20K **Privately Held**
SIC: 3993 Signs, not made in custom sign painting shops

(G-5471)
MAHANS CONCRETE SEPTIC TANKS
26 County Road 375 (38965-3751)
PHONE..................................662 234-3767
Larry Mahan, *Owner*
EMP: 1
SALES (est): 62.4K **Privately Held**
SIC: 3272 Concrete products

(G-5472)
MID SOUTH COMMUNICATIONS INC
50 County Road 122 (38965-5900)
PHONE..................................662 832-0538
Robert Craig Swanner, *Partner*
EMP: 5
SALES (corp-wide): 1.3B **Privately Held**
WEB: www.memphisbusinessjournal.com
SIC: 3663 Radio & TV communications equipment
HQ: Mid South Communications Inc
651 Oakleaf Office Ln
Memphis TN 38117
901 523-1000

(G-5473)
MORRIS READY MIX INC
133 Gore Cir (38965-3316)
PHONE..................................662 473-2505
Ricky Morris, *President*
Donny Morris, *Vice Pres*
EMP: 3
SALES (est): 355K **Privately Held**
SIC: 3273 Ready-mixed concrete

(G-5474)
SATISFACTION WELDING
49 County Road 484 (38965-2884)
PHONE..................................662 473-1518
EMP: 1
SALES (est): 42.5K **Privately Held**
SIC: 7692 Welding repair

(G-5475)
VALLEY PUBLISHING INC
Also Called: North Mississippi Herald
416 N Main St (38965-2506)
P.O. Box 648 (38965-0648)
PHONE..................................662 473-1473
David Howell, *President*
EMP: 5
SALES: 200K **Privately Held**
SIC: 7313 2711 Newspaper advertising representative; newspapers; newspapers: publishing only, not printed on site

(G-5476)
VALLEY TOOL INC (PA)
Also Called: VT
101 Industrial Park Rd (38965-4681)
P.O. Box 663 (38965-0663)
PHONE..................................662 473-3066
Cayce Washington, *President*
Michelle Washington, *Vice Pres*
Lee Jackson, *Mfg Mgr*
Les Gilley, *Production*
Jacob Edwards, *Office Mgr*
EMP: 25 EST: 1997
SQ FT: 7,500
SALES: 5.2MM **Privately Held**
WEB: www.valleytoolinc.com
SIC: 3599 Machine shop, jobbing & repair

(G-5477)
WATER VALLEY POULTRY INC
507 Lafayette St (38965-1636)
PHONE..................................662 473-0016
John Craig, *President*
Mona Nicholas, *President*
Marco Barahmand, *Engineer*
Philip Tallant, *Manager*
Woody Johnson, *Executive*
EMP: 20
SALES (est): 3.8MM **Privately Held**
SIC: 2015 Poultry slaughtering & processing

Waveland
Hancock County

(G-5478)
C & D CABINETS LLC
2225 Kiln Waveland Rd (39576-2039)
PHONE..................................228 466-4644
Neely Whites, *Accountant*
Chris Harmon, *Mng Member*
EMP: 14
SQ FT: 3,000
SALES (est): 575.7K **Privately Held**
SIC: 2434 Wood kitchen cabinets

(G-5479)
CYNTHIA BOWEN
Also Called: Bowens and Company
302 Sandy St (39576-3934)
PHONE..................................228 463-7131
Cynithia Bowen, *Owner*
EMP: 2 EST: 2000
SALES (est): 82K **Privately Held**
SIC: 2426 8999 Carvings, furniture: wood; artist

(G-5480)
DIAMONDHEAD ADVERTISER
723 Faith St (39576-2610)
PHONE..................................228 263-4377
Christie Clark, *Owner*
EMP: 1 EST: 2007
SALES (est): 79.5K **Privately Held**
SIC: 2741 7313 Telephone & other directory publishing; magazine advertising representative

(G-5481)
GET STITCHED
545 Highway 90 (39576-2405)
PHONE..................................228 231-1162
Anna La Fontaine, *President*
EMP: 1
SALES (est): 58.3K **Privately Held**
SIC: 2395 Pleating & stitching

(G-5482)
LIGHTNING QUICK SIGNS
208 Highway 90 (39576-2621)
PHONE..................................228 467-1718
Gary Knoblock, *Owner*
EMP: 4
SQ FT: 2,000
SALES (est): 343K **Privately Held**
WEB: www.gohigherky.org
SIC: 3993 5999 Signs, not made in custom sign painting shops; decals

(G-5483)
MOMBO GRAPHIXS
541 Highway 90 (39576-2405)
PHONE..................................228 466-2551
Scott Blackwell, *Owner*

EMP: 2
SALES (est): 223.8K **Privately Held**
SIC: 2759 Screen printing

(G-5484)
SHERWIN-WILLIAMS COMPANY
214 Highway 90 (39576-2621)
PHONE..................................228 467-3938
Volme Swanier, *Principal*
EMP: 3
SALES (corp-wide): 17.5B **Publicly Held**
WEB: www.sherwin.com
SIC: 5231 2851 Paint & painting supplies; paints & paint additives
PA: The Sherwin-Williams Company
101 W Prospect Ave # 1020
Cleveland OH 44115
216 566-2000

(G-5485)
SPEEDY PRINTING
304 Highway 90 Ste D (39576-2653)
PHONE..................................228 466-5766
Bruce Darby, *Owner*
EMP: 1
SALES: 47K **Privately Held**
SIC: 2752 Commercial printing, offset

(G-5486)
VERTECHS DESIGN SOLUTIONS LLC
Also Called: Cust-Alum Marine
712 Spruce St (39576-3006)
PHONE..................................228 671-1442
Byron Farver, *Mng Member*
EMP: 3
SALES (est): 80K **Privately Held**
SIC: 3441 7692 Boat & barge sections, prefabricated metal; welding repair

(G-5487)
WAVELAND CANDLE COMPANY LLC
1815 Nicholson Ave (39576-3347)
PHONE..................................228 220-4716
EMP: 1
SALES (est): 39.6K **Privately Held**
SIC: 3999 Candles

Waynesboro
Wayne County

(G-5488)
ADVANTAGE TAX & PRINTING
308 Mississippi Dr (39367-2810)
PHONE..................................601 735-2023
Letessa Russell, *President*
EMP: 6
SALES (est): 713.7K **Privately Held**
SIC: 2752 Commercial printing, lithographic

(G-5489)
ALAMISS INC
91 Airport Rd (39367-9581)
P.O. Box 250, State Line (39362-0250)
PHONE..................................601 671-0840
Mark Dailey, *Manager*
EMP: 1
SALES (corp-wide): 14.3MM **Privately Held**
SIC: 5082 2411 Logging equipment & supplies; logging
PA: Alamiss, Inc.
467 Old Saint Peter St
State Line MS 39362
601 394-7470

(G-5490)
AMERICAN MIDSTREAM ✪
595 Ceamon Pittman Rd (39367-7336)
PHONE..................................601 671-8800
EMP: 2 EST: 2019
SALES (est): 81.9K **Privately Held**
SIC: 1311 Crude petroleum & natural gas

(G-5491)
ATWOOD MCH WLDG & HYDRAULICS
640 Industrial Park Rd (39367-3038)
P.O. Box 51 (39367-0051)
PHONE..................................601 735-0398

Kenneth Atwood, *Owner*
EMP: 10
SALES (est): 460K **Privately Held**
SIC: 3599 7692 7699 Machine shop, jobbing & repair; welding repair; hydraulic equipment repair

(G-5492)
BAZOR PULPWOOD COMPANY INC
165 Big Creek Rd (39367-9549)
PHONE..................................601 735-4017
Colon Fred Bazor, *President*
Betsy Bazor, *Corp Secy*
Brantley Bazor, *Director*
EMP: 12
SALES (est): 1.1MM **Privately Held**
SIC: 2411 4212 Logging camps & contractors; lumber & timber trucking

(G-5493)
BTC LOGGING CO
Also Called: M.J. Bunch and Sons Logging
26 Bobby Bunch Dr (39367-9504)
PHONE..................................601 735-3259
Bobby Bunch, *Owner*
EMP: 5
SALES (est): 418.6K **Privately Held**
SIC: 2411 Logging camps & contractors

(G-5494)
BYNUM PRINTING
220 Azalea Dr (39367-7713)
PHONE..................................601 735-5269
Glen Bynum, *Partner*
Silva Bynum, *Partner*
EMP: 6
SQ FT: 3,000
SALES: 190K **Privately Held**
SIC: 2752 Commercial printing, offset

(G-5495)
CANVAS CREATIONS & EATERY
93 E Robinson Junction Rd (39367-9426)
PHONE..................................404 514-3399
Marilyn Smith, *Principal*
EMP: 1
SALES (est): 46.5K **Privately Held**
SIC: 2211 Canvas

(G-5496)
CRAGER WELDING
1480 Coyt Rd (39367-9612)
PHONE..................................601 687-0019
Alton Crager, *Owner*
EMP: 1
SALES (est): 68.6K **Privately Held**
SIC: 7692 Welding repair

(G-5497)
ENBRIDGE PROCESSING LLC
595 Ceamon Pittman Rd (39367-7336)
PHONE..................................601 671-8800
Dan C Tutcher, *Principal*
EMP: 3
SALES (est): 267.4K **Privately Held**
SIC: 1311 Crude petroleum & natural gas production

(G-5498)
FIRST HERITAGE CREDIT CORP
903 Robinson St (39367-2455)
PHONE..................................601 735-4543
EMP: 1 **Privately Held**
SIC: 6141 2411 Consumer finance companies; timber, cut at logging camp
PA: First Heritage Credit Corp
605 Crescent Blvd Ste 101
Ridgeland MS 39157

(G-5499)
GUSOIL INC
705 Azalea Dr Ste A (39367-2722)
P.O. Box 865 (39367-0865)
PHONE..................................601 735-2731
Rayford B Gustafson Jr, *Owner*
EMP: 1
SQ FT: 2,000
SALES: 500K **Privately Held**
SIC: 1311 Crude petroleum production; natural gas production

2019 Harris Directory of
Mississippi Manufacturers

▲ = Import ▼=Export
◆ =Import/Export

GEOGRAPHIC SECTION

Wesson - Copiah County (G-5529)

(G-5500)
HOOD INDUSTRIES INC
915 Industrial Park Rd (39367-3008)
P.O. Box 569 (39367-0569)
PHONE..................................601 735-5038
Ben Crim, *Research*
Don Crim, *Manager*
EMP: 100
SALES (corp-wide): 332.7MM **Privately Held**
WEB: www.hoodindustries.com
SIC: 2435 2426 Hardwood veneer & plywood; hardwood dimension & flooring mills
PA: Hood Industries, Inc.
15 Professional Pkwy # 8
Hattiesburg MS 39402
601 264-2962

(G-5501)
KELLEY BROTHERS CONTRS INC (PA)
401 County Farm Rd (39367-8772)
P.O. Box 1079 (39367-1079)
PHONE..................................601 735-2541
Jerry Kelley, *President*
Thomas O Kelley Jr, *Vice Pres*
Bessie Kelley, *Treasurer*
Terry L Kelley, *Admin Sec*
EMP: 100 EST: 1955
SQ FT: 2,000
SALES (est): 89.5MM **Privately Held**
SIC: 1389 1382 1381 Oil field services; oil & gas exploration services; drilling oil & gas wells

(G-5502)
KEYES MACHINE SHOP LLC
93 Dub Beasley Rd (39367-8011)
PHONE..................................601 671-8646
James Keyes, *Principal*
EMP: 2
SALES (est): 131.2K **Privately Held**
SIC: 3599 Machine shop, jobbing & repair

(G-5503)
LADY BUGS AND LILY PADS
801a Mississippi Dr (39367-2437)
PHONE..................................601 735-0071
EMP: 2 EST: 2008
SALES (est): 88K **Privately Held**
SIC: 3663 Mfg Radio/Tv Communication Equipment

(G-5504)
LOGAN OIL FIELD SERVICES
379 Eucutta Rd (39367)
PHONE..................................601 787-4407
Butch Logan, *Managing Prtnr*
Johnny Logan, *Partner*
EMP: 2
SALES (est): 168.3K **Privately Held**
SIC: 1389 Oil field services

(G-5505)
MAR-JAC POULTRY MS LLC (PA)
261 Marshall Durbin Dr (39367)
PHONE..................................601 735-3132
Dwayne Rawson, *General Mgr*
EMP: 1000
SALES (est): 134.8MM **Privately Held**
SIC: 2048 Prepared feeds

(G-5506)
MC CONSULTING LLC
950 Dyess Bridge Rd (39367-8941)
PHONE..................................601 735-2000
Michael Clanton, *President*
Pamela Clanton, *Treasurer*
EMP: 2
SALES (est): 145.9K **Privately Held**
SIC: 1381 7389 Redrilling oil & gas wells;

(G-5507)
MCILWAINS ELECTRICAL SUPPLY (PA)
808 Fagan Ave (39367-2723)
PHONE..................................601 735-1145
Shelia D McIlwain, *Owner*
EMP: 7 EST: 1978
SQ FT: 4,000

SALES (est): 1MM **Privately Held**
SIC: 5063 7694 5999 Electrical supplies; electric motor repair; cake decorating supplies

(G-5508)
ODOM INDUSTRIES INC (PA)
800 Odom Industrial Rd (39367-3026)
P.O. Box 866 (39367-0866)
PHONE..................................601 735-0088
Richard D James, *President*
Jessica West, *General Mgr*
Debra McMichael, *Corp Secy*
William Richard Odom, *Vice Pres*
Richard James, *Opers Mgr*
▲ EMP: 175
SQ FT: 200,000
SALES: 9.6MM **Privately Held**
WEB: www.odomind.com
SIC: 2819 2879 Industrial inorganic chemicals; agricultural chemicals

(G-5509)
PALMER VENEER INC
216 Mozingo Richey Rd (39367-8403)
PHONE..................................601 735-9717
EMP: 15 EST: 1978
SALES (est): 1.5MM **Privately Held**
SIC: 2436 Mfg Softwood Veneer/Plywood

(G-5510)
QUALITY PLYWOOD COMPANY INC (PA)
160 Marshall Durbin Dr (39367-3013)
P.O. Box 187 (39367-0187)
PHONE..................................601 735-3106
Virgil Palmer, *CEO*
Reggie Palmer, *President*
Rebecca Walker, *Purch Mgr*
Matthew Thompson, *Engineer*
Kristi Wright, *CFO*
◆ EMP: 74
SQ FT: 50,000
SALES: 8MM **Privately Held**
WEB: www.qualityplywood.com
SIC: 2435 Hardwood veneer & plywood

(G-5511)
RAY DAVIS LOGGING INC
Also Called: Ray's Trucking
377 Matherville Poplar (39367)
PHONE..................................601 687-1392
EMP: 5
SALES (est): 280K **Privately Held**
SIC: 2411 Logging

(G-5512)
RICHARD E JOHNSON (PA)
Also Called: Church's Chicken
148 Russell Dr (39367-4409)
P.O. Box 111 (39367-0111)
PHONE..................................601 735-4737
Richard E Johnson, *President*
William G Johnson, *Vice Pres*
EMP: 7
SQ FT: 10,000
SALES (est): 733.5K **Privately Held**
SIC: 5812 1389 5084 5172 Chicken restaurant; oil field services; drilling equipment, excluding bits; gasoline; diesel fuel

(G-5513)
SCOTCH PLYWOOD COMPANY MISS
110 Industrial Park Rd (39367)
P.O. Box 959 (39367-0959)
PHONE..................................601 735-2881
Buddy Douglas, *Manager*
EMP: 70
SALES (est): 10.1MM
SALES (corp-wide): 47.7MM **Privately Held**
SIC: 2436 2435 Veneer stock, softwood; hardwood veneer & plywood
PA: Scotch Plywood Company Of Mississippi
101 Main St
Fulton AL 36446
334 636-2731

(G-5514)
SIGN SHOP
1204 Mississippi Dr (39367-2418)
PHONE..................................601 735-1383
Timothy Johnson, *Owner*
EMP: 1

SALES (est): 53.1K **Privately Held**
SIC: 3993 7532 5049 Signs, not made in custom sign painting shops; paint shop, automotive; religious supplies

(G-5515)
SOUTHEAST READY MIX INC
3594 Highway 145 S (39367-7745)
PHONE..................................601 735-4823
Greg Kelley, *President*
EMP: 15
SALES (est): 2MM **Privately Held**
SIC: 3273 Ready-mixed concrete

(G-5516)
SUNBEAM PRODUCTS INC
224 Russell Dr (39367-7739)
P.O. Box 469 (39367-0469)
PHONE..................................601 671-2200
Charles Murin, *QC Mgr*
Steve Ulery, *Manager*
EMP: 80
SALES (corp-wide): 8.6B **Publicly Held**
WEB: www.healthometer.com
SIC: 3634 Blankets, electric
HQ: Sunbeam Products, Inc.
2381 Nw Executive Ctr Dr
Boca Raton FL 33431
561 912-4100

(G-5517)
T K STANLEY INC
6739 Highway 184 (39367-9201)
PHONE..................................601 735-2855
Steve Farrar, *Owner*
EMP: 28
SALES (corp-wide): 590MM **Privately Held**
WEB: www.tkstanley.com
SIC: 1389 Haulage, oil field
PA: T. K. Stanley, Inc.
4025 Highway 35 N
Columbia MS 39429
601 735-2855

(G-5518)
TEDDY DOGGETT LOGGING INC
1631 Pleasant Grove Chapp (39367-8902)
PHONE..................................601 687-5233
Teddy E Doggett, *President*
EMP: 3
SALES (est): 284.4K **Privately Held**
SIC: 2411 Logging camps & contractors

Webb
Tallahatchie County

(G-5519)
FLAUTT FARMS
1529 Swan Lake Rd (38966)
PHONE..................................662 375-2116
Mike Flautt, *Partner*
EMP: 10
SALES (est): 950K **Privately Held**
SIC: 3523 Driers (farm): grain, hay & seed

(G-5520)
WEBB MACHINE AND SUPPLY INC
303 Hwy 49 E (38966)
P.O. Box 187 (38966-0187)
PHONE..................................662 375-8309
Fred M Goss, *President*
EMP: 10
SQ FT: 15,625
SALES (est): 1.3MM **Privately Held**
SIC: 5531 7692 Automotive parts; welding repair

Weir
Choctaw County

(G-5521)
RANDY CUMMINGS
516 Erwin Rd (39772-8801)
PHONE..................................662 547-2008
Randy Cummings, *Owner*
Larry Cummings, *Co-Owner*
EMP: 7

SALES (est): 460K **Privately Held**
WEB: www.randycummingsonline.com
SIC: 2411 Logging

(G-5522)
TRIPLE J TIE AND TIMBER LLC
609 Stewart Weir Rd (39772-8882)
PHONE..................................662 547-6600
Betty Parkerson, *Principal*
EMP: 2
SALES (est): 229.8K **Privately Held**
SIC: 2411 Timber, cut at logging camp

Wesson
Copiah County

(G-5523)
ACTION DRILLING COMPANY INC
2933 Old Church Dr Nw (39191-9686)
P.O. Box 909, Crystal Springs (39059-0909)
PHONE..................................601 892-5105
Wayne Jackson, *President*
John Harris Jr, *Vice Pres*
Theresa Harris, *Admin Sec*
EMP: 3
SALES (est): 416.9K **Privately Held**
SIC: 1382 Oil & gas exploration services

(G-5524)
BOLING CONSTRUCTION INC
2779 Bahalia Rd Ne (39191-9422)
PHONE..................................601 833-0122
Jerry B Boling Sr, *President*
Dorothea J Boling, *Vice Pres*
EMP: 5
SALES (est): 511.3K **Privately Held**
SIC: 2951 Asphalt paving mixtures & blocks

(G-5525)
CADE & CADE LOGGING INC
2782 Jckson Liberty Dr Nw (39191-9533)
PHONE..................................601 833-2557
Chad Cade, *President*
Celeste Cade, *Admin Sec*
EMP: 4 EST: 1992
SALES (est): 194K **Privately Held**
SIC: 2411 Logging

(G-5526)
DEAN WEEKS REPAIR & WELDING
3146 Jckson Liberty Dr Nw (39191-9609)
PHONE..................................601 833-2669
Dean Weeks, *Owner*
EMP: 5
SALES (est): 396.7K **Privately Held**
SIC: 7538 7692 Truck engine repair, except industrial; welding repair

(G-5527)
DWAYNE TIMBER COMPANY
1466 Mission Hill Rd Ne (39191-6083)
PHONE..................................601 695-6177
Dwayne Pendleton, *Officer*
EMP: 9
SALES (est): 649.5K **Privately Held**
SIC: 7389 2411 ; logging camps & contractors

(G-5528)
MAXWELL SAWMILL LLC
9071 Highway 51 (39191-9188)
PHONE..................................601 894-3194
Patrick A Maxwell, *Principal*
EMP: 2
SALES (est): 90K **Privately Held**
WEB: www.maxhuff.com
SIC: 2421 Sawmills & planing mills, general

(G-5529)
S & S TIMBER
2411 Highway 550 Nw (39191-6029)
PHONE..................................601 833-8844
Darrell O Smith, *Owner*
Diana Smith, *Owner*
EMP: 12 EST: 1984
SALES: 1MM **Privately Held**
SIC: 3823 Data loggers, industrial process type

(PA)=Parent Co (HQ)=Headquarters (DH)=Div Headquarters
♣ = New Business established in last 2 years

2019 Harris Directory of
Mississippi Manufacturers

197

GEOGRAPHIC SECTION

Wesson - Copiah County (G-5530)

(G-5530)
THOMPSON DOZER & GRAVEL
Also Called: Thompson Backhoe Service
1633 Furrs Mill Dr Ne (39191-9455)
PHONE..................................601 835-2406
Anthony D Thompson, *Owner*
Virginia C Thompson, *Nurse*
EMP: 2
SALES: 140K **Privately Held**
SIC: 3531 Dozers, tractor mounted: material moving

(G-5531)
U S SAFETY SERVICES INC
1878 Pleasant Ridge Rd Nw (39191-5003)
P.O. Box 44, Brookhaven (39602-0044)
PHONE..................................601 833-3627
EMP: 7
SQ FT: 1,350
SALES (est): 710K **Privately Held**
SIC: 1389 1629 Oil field services; earthmoving contractor

West
Holmes County

(G-5532)
CHAMBERS AIR AND HEAT
401 County Line Rd (39192-8349)
P.O. Box 5 (39192-0005)
PHONE..................................662 967-2002
David Danburs, *Owner*
EMP: 1 **EST:** 2009
SALES (est): 86.3K **Privately Held**
SIC: 1711 3263 5999 Warm air heating & air conditioning contractor; commercial tableware or kitchen articles, fine earthenware; alarm signal systems

(G-5533)
FISHERS SAWMILL
8074 Emory Rd (39192-8227)
PHONE..................................662 967-2502
EMP: 2
SALES (est): 130K **Privately Held**
SIC: 2421 Sawmill/Planing Mill

West Point
Clay County

(G-5534)
ADVANTAGE CABINET DOORS
715 Airport Rd (39773)
PHONE..................................662 494-9700
Mike Henson, *Owner*
Haley Mitchell, *Sales Staff*
EMP: 4
SALES (est): 437.3K **Privately Held**
WEB: www.advantagecabinetdoors.com
SIC: 2434 Wood kitchen cabinets

(G-5535)
APAC-MISSISSIPPI INC
753 Mayhew St (39773-2753)
P.O. Box 1388, Columbus (39703-1388)
PHONE..................................662 494-5772
Ashley Sansing, *Sales Associate*
Scott Glusenkamp, *Manager*
EMP: 7
SALES (corp-wide): 30.6B **Privately Held**
SIC: 3273 Ready-mixed concrete
HQ: Apac-Mississippi, Inc.
101 Riverview Dr
Richland MS 39218
601 376-4000

(G-5536)
ARKY WELDING & HANDY MAN
119 J T Britt Rd (39773-9623)
PHONE..................................662 494-4233
Elva Beal, *Owner*
EMP: 1
SALES (est): 41K **Privately Held**
SIC: 7692 Welding repair

(G-5537)
BABCOCK & WILCOX COMPANY
900 Bnw Dr (39773)
PHONE..................................662 494-1323
John Yash, *Regional Mgr*

Jay Mordecai, *Project Mgr*
Robby Pierce, *Mfg Staff*
Davis Slone, *Manager*
Donald Whitman Jr, *Manager*
EMP: 190
SALES (corp-wide): 1B **Publicly Held**
SIC: 3433 3498 3444 3443 Heating equipment, except electric; fabricated pipe & fittings; sheet metalwork; fabricated plate work (boiler shop)
HQ: The Babcock & Wilcox Company
20 S Van Buren Ave
Barberton OH 44203
330 753-4511

(G-5538)
BLUE DEER CANDLES LLP
184 Court St (39773-7990)
PHONE..................................662 275-2016
Leslie Earnest, *Principal*
EMP: 1
SALES (est): 48K **Privately Held**
SIC: 3999 Candles

(G-5539)
CANADA BREAD
1340 N Eshman Ave (39773)
PHONE..................................662 494-1607
EMP: 2
SALES (est): 62.3K **Privately Held**
SIC: 2051 Bakery: wholesale or wholesale/retail combined

(G-5540)
CCCL PALLET LLC
372 Court St (39773-2954)
PHONE..................................662 494-0141
Willie Key, *Principal*
EMP: 3
SALES (est): 157.4K **Privately Held**
SIC: 2448 Pallets, wood & wood with metal

(G-5541)
CONVICTION GAME CALLS
582 Windy Ridge Rd (39773-4134)
PHONE..................................662 295-9972
Corey Ellis, *Principal*
EMP: 1
SALES (est): 47K **Privately Held**
SIC: 3949 Game calls

(G-5542)
ELLIS STEEL COMPANY INC (PA)
642 Highway 45 N Altn (39773-2340)
P.O. Box 816 (39773-0816)
PHONE..................................662 494-5955
Frank Hopper, *President*
Marvin Blanks, *Corp Secy*
Gene Childress, *Vice Pres*
W G Yates Jr, *Vice Pres*
Stephanie Vanven Vranden, *Manager*
EMP: 80
SALES (est): 19.5MM **Privately Held**
SIC: 3441 Fabricated structural metal

(G-5543)
GENERAL MACHINE WORKS INC
112 N Forest St (39773)
PHONE..................................662 494-5155
John Wooten, *President*
Kathy Wooten, *Treasurer*
EMP: 3
SQ FT: 15,000
SALES: 100K **Privately Held**
SIC: 3599 Machine shop, jobbing & repair

(G-5544)
GRAPHIC ARTS PRODUCTIONS INC
1223 N Eshman Ave (39773-7581)
P.O. Box 1116 (39773-1116)
PHONE..................................662 494-2549
Ed C Rice, *President*
Linda Rice, *Bookkeeper*
EMP: 5
SALES: 225K **Privately Held**
SIC: 2396 2759 Screen printing on fabric articles; screen printing

(G-5545)
GRIFFIN ARMOR
901 E Half Mile St (39773-2208)
P.O. Box 1054 (39773-1054)
PHONE..................................662 494-3421
Ron Munroe, *Owner*
EMP: 5
SALES (est): 542K **Privately Held**
SIC: 3471 Plating of metals or formed products

(G-5546)
HORIZON PUBLICATIONS INC
Also Called: Daily Times Leader
26463 E Main St (39773-7995)
P.O. Box 1176 (39773-1176)
PHONE..................................662 494-1422
William Carroll, *Branch Mgr*
EMP: 7
SALES (corp-wide): 71.5MM **Privately Held**
WEB: www.malvern-online.com
SIC: 2711 Newspapers
PA: Horizon Publications, Inc.
1120 N Carbon St Ste 100
Marion IL 62959
618 993-1711

(G-5547)
JIMS AUTO PARTS INC
130 Highway 45 N (39773)
P.O. Box 130
PHONE..................................662 494-4541
J C Write, *President*
EMP: 5
SALES (corp-wide): 5.4MM **Privately Held**
SIC: 5531 3599 Speed shops, including race car supplies; machine shop, jobbing & repair
PA: Jim's Auto Parts Inc
2844 E Roane Ave
Eupora MS 39744
662 258-3191

(G-5548)
JUBILATIONS INC
Also Called: Jubilations Cheesecake
950 Highway 45 S (39773)
PHONE..................................662 328-9210
Tamara Craddock, *President*
George Purnell, *Vice Pres*
Neda Powell, *Executive*
James Craddock, *Admin Sec*
EMP: 10
SQ FT: 4,500
SALES (est): 1.3MM **Privately Held**
WEB: www.jubilations.com
SIC: 2053 5461 Cakes, bakery: frozen; cakes

(G-5549)
LEGGETT & PLATT INCORPORATED
Blazon Tube Company
61 Mapleview Rd (39773-3967)
PHONE..................................417 358-8131
EMP: 10
SALES (corp-wide): 3.7B **Publicly Held**
SIC: 3317 Mfg Steel Pipe/Tubes
PA: Leggett & Platt, Incorporated
1 Leggett Rd
Carthage MO 64836
417 358-8131

(G-5550)
LIBERATIONS PUBLISHING LLC
29680 Highway 50 E (39773-5589)
PHONE..................................662 605-0382
Nicole Deanes Mangum, *President*
Stanley Mangum Jr, *President*
EMP: 1
SQ FT: 2,400
SALES: 10K **Privately Held**
SIC: 2731 Book publishing

(G-5551)
LIMECO INC
14611 Highway 47 (39773-4863)
PHONE..................................662 456-4226
Mike W Juckes, *President*
EMP: 6
SQ FT: 50,000
SALES (est): 470K **Privately Held**
SIC: 3274 Lime

(G-5552)
MISCELLANEOUS STEEL SUPPLY LLC
210 E Morrow St 50w (39773-2407)
P.O. Box 330 (39773-0330)
PHONE..................................662 494-0090
Don Childress,
Ken Bill,
EMP: 9
SQ FT: 5,000
SALES (est): 1.4MM **Privately Held**
SIC: 3449 Bars, concrete reinforcing: fabricated steel

(G-5553)
MOSSY OAK 3D FLUID GRPHICS LLC
Also Called: 3d Graphics
1251 Hwy 45 Alt S (39773)
P.O. Box 757 (39773-0757)
PHONE..................................662 494-9092
Toxey Haas, *CEO*
Bill Sugg, *President*
Fox Haas, *Corp Secy*
Ronnie Strickland, *Senior VP*
EMP: 4
SALES (est): 455.9K **Privately Held**
SIC: 2211 Camouflage nets

(G-5554)
MOSSYOAK WILDLIFE CONSERVATORY
Also Called: Biologic
26420 E Main St (39773-7995)
P.O. Box 757 (39773-0757)
PHONE..................................662 495-9292
Toxey Haas, *Owner*
EMP: 5
SQ FT: 30,000
SALES (est): 949.1K
SALES (corp-wide): 60.8MM **Privately Held**
WEB: www.mossyoak.com
SIC: 2321 Men's & boys' furnishings
PA: Haas Outdoors, Inc.
26420 E Main St
West Point MS 39773
662 494-8859

(G-5555)
MS PUBLISHING GROUP LLC
25140 Highway 50 W (39773-0411)
PHONE..................................662 323-8800
Michal Salyer, *Principal*
EMP: 3 **EST:** 2016
SALES (est): 55K **Privately Held**
SIC: 2741 Miscellaneous publishing

(G-5556)
ORMANS WELDING & FAB INC
640 Curtis Orman Rd (39773-5041)
PHONE..................................662 494-9471
David L Orman, *President*
Debbie Lofton, *Corp Secy*
EMP: 16
SQ FT: 12,600
SALES (est): 2.1MM **Privately Held**
SIC: 1799 3599 7692 3549 Welding on site; machine shop, jobbing & repair; welding repair; metalworking machinery

(G-5557)
PC ACE COMPUTER SERVICE
228 Mccord St (39773-3279)
PHONE..................................662 494-1925
Kenneth Andrews, *Principal*
EMP: 2
SALES (est): 85.9K **Privately Held**
SIC: 3571 Electronic computers

(G-5558)
PRAIRIE ADVENTURE LLC
126 Bus Blankenship Rd (39773-5003)
PHONE..................................662 295-8807
David Estes,
EMP: 4
SALES (est): 187K **Privately Held**
WEB: www.prairieadventure.com
SIC: 3732 Hydrofoil boats

(G-5559)
PRAIRIE WILDLIFE
3990 Old Vinton Rd (39773-4271)
PHONE..................................662 494-1235
Harry Pasisis, *Principal*

2019 Harris Directory of
Mississippi Manufacturers

▲ = Import ▼=Export
◆ =Import/Export

198

GEOGRAPHIC SECTION

Wiggins - Stone County (G-5589)

Bennie Atkinson, *Manager*
EMP: 6
SALES (est): 413.8K **Privately Held**
SIC: 3421 Table & food cutlery, including butchers'

(G-5560)
PRESTAGE FARMS INC
1550 W Church Hill Rd (39773-9077)
P.O. Box 1425 (39773-1425)
PHONE.................................662 494-0813
Terry Emerson, *Manager*
EMP: 210
SALES (corp-wide): 373.8MM **Privately Held**
WEB: www.prestagefarms.com
SIC: 0213 2011 Hogs; meat packing plants
PA: Prestage Farms, Inc.
4651 Taylors Bridge Hwy
Clinton NC 28328
910 596-5700

(G-5561)
RODGER HOLDEMAN S SIGNS
155 Northwood Forest Rd (39773-9088)
PHONE.................................662 436-0911
EMP: 2
SALES (est): 136.3K **Privately Held**
SIC: 3993 Signs & advertising specialties

(G-5562)
SIGNS & MORE
Also Called: Sign Design Plus
1050 Northwood Forest Rd (39773-9002)
PHONE.................................662 494-9451
Rodger Holdeman, *Owner*
Mark Koehn, *Owner*
EMP: 1
SALES (est): 77K **Privately Held**
SIC: 3993 Signs & advertising specialties

(G-5563)
SOUTHERN IONICS INCORPORATED (PA)
579 Commerce St (39773-7543)
P.O. Box 1217 (39773-1217)
PHONE.................................662 494-3055
Milton O Sundbeck Jr, *President*
Randy Weimer, *Vice Pres*
Steven D Mitchener, *CFO*
Mary Ann Briggs, *Accountant*
▲ **EMP:** 50
SALES (est): 98.7MM **Privately Held**
WEB: www.southernionics.com
SIC: 2819 Alums

(G-5564)
SOUTHERN IONICS INCORPORATED
506 W Broad St (39773)
P.O. Box 1217 (39773-1217)
PHONE.................................662 495-2583
Jerry Blackwell, *Manager*
EMP: 30
SALES (corp-wide): 98.7MM **Privately Held**
WEB: www. southernionics.com
SIC: 2819 Alums
PA: Southern Ionics Incorporated
579 Commerce St
West Point MS 39773
662 494-3055

(G-5565)
ULTRA DRYING TECHNOLOGY
Also Called: Udt
2867 Oak Ridge Rd (39773-8517)
PHONE.................................662 494-5025
EMP: 3
SALES (est): 750K **Privately Held**
SIC: 3564 Mfg Drying Machines

(G-5566)
YOKOHAMA TIRE MANUFACTU
1 Yokohama Blvd (39773-6009)
PHONE.................................800 423-4544
EMP: 5 **Privately Held**
SIC: 3011 Tire & inner tube materials & related products
HQ: Yokohama Tire Manufacturing Virginia, Llc
1500 Indiana St
Salem VA 24153
540 389-5426

(G-5567)
YOKOHAMA TIRE MFG MISS LLC
1 Yokohama Blvd (39773-6009)
PHONE.................................800 423-4544
Naoki Takeda, *Vice Pres*
Jeremy Brown, *Engineer*
Tadaharu Yamamoto,
Thomas Masuguchi, *Admin Sec*
EMP: 3
SQ FT: 30,000
SALES (est): 1.6MM **Privately Held**
SIC: 3011 Tire & inner tube materials & related products
HQ: Yokohama Tire Corporation
1 Macarthur Pl Ste 800
Santa Ana CA 92707
714 870-3800

Wiggins
Stone County

(G-5568)
A & D TIMBER COMPANY INC
465 Thelma Andrews Rd (39577-8170)
P.O. Box 550 (39577-0550)
PHONE.................................601 528-9357
Michael Alexander, *President*
Barbara S Alexander, *Corp Secy*
Timothy M Alexander, *Vice Pres*
EMP: 17
SALES (est): 3.5MM **Privately Held**
SIC: 2411 7389 4212 Logging camps & contractors; ; lumber & timber trucking

(G-5569)
ALL-TECH METAL WORKS INC
99 Fairley Bridge Rd (39577-8505)
PHONE.................................228 396-3800
Michael Strayham, *President*
EMP: 2
SALES (est): 100K **Privately Held**
SIC: 7692 Welding repair

(G-5570)
ANDERSON ENTERPRISES LLC
1825 Highway 49 (39577-8190)
P.O. Box 525, Perkinston (39573-0010)
PHONE.................................601 928-0030
Mickey Anderson, *President*
EMP: 9
SALES (est): 1.2MM **Privately Held**
SIC: 3448 Prefabricated metal buildings

(G-5571)
BALDWIN POLE MISSISSIPPI LLC
1633 First St S (39577-3338)
PHONE.................................601 928-5475
Thomas McMillan Jr, *Principal*
EMP: 1
SALES (est): 211.1K **Privately Held**
SIC: 2491 Poles, posts & pilings: treated wood

(G-5572)
BBS PRINTING
33 Lacy Evans Rd (39577-9128)
PHONE.................................601 606-6980
Cassandra Buckley, *Principal*
EMP: 2
SALES (est): 141.1K **Privately Held**
SIC: 2752 Commercial printing, lithographic

(G-5573)
BRENT HICKMAN LOGGING LLC
47 Stillmore Rd (39577-5504)
PHONE.................................601 928-8840
Brent A Hickman, *Principal*
EMP: 3
SALES (est): 458.5K **Privately Held**
SIC: 2411 Logging camps & contractors

(G-5574)
BRITTANY H DAVIS
365a E Bond Rd (39577-8429)
PHONE.................................251 348-8858
Brittany Davis, *Principal*
EMP: 2
SALES (est): 98.8K **Privately Held**
SIC: 2411 Logging

(G-5575)
BUMPER TO BUMPER
338 Magnolia Dr N (39577-3232)
PHONE.................................601 928-5603
Manny Brooks, *Manager*
EMP: 2
SALES (est): 95.5K **Privately Held**
SIC: 3537 Industrial trucks & tractors

(G-5576)
CARPENTERS POLE & PILING CO
1513 Magnolia Dr N (39577-8010)
P.O. Box 758 (39577-0758)
PHONE.................................601 928-7400
Ben Carpenter II, *President*
Ben Carpenter III, *Vice Pres*
Preston Carpenter, *Vice Pres*
Janice Carpenter, *Treasurer*
Donna Pearson, *Sales Staff*
EMP: 42
SQ FT: 1,200
SALES (est): 11.1MM **Privately Held**
SIC: 2491 Poles & pole crossarms, treated wood; pilings, treated wood

(G-5577)
CLARK HARVISON
435 Marshall Taylor Rd (39577-8640)
PHONE.................................601 928-7929
Clark D Harvison, *Principal*
EMP: 2
SALES (est): 100K **Privately Held**
SIC: 2411 Logging

(G-5578)
D & R INDUSTRIAL SERVICES LLC
738 Hickman St (39577-8125)
P.O. Box 1436 (39577-1322)
PHONE.................................601 716-3140
Shermon Davis,
Jose Ramos,
EMP: 15 **EST:** 2014
SALES (est): 1.3MM **Privately Held**
SIC: 1796 3441 Installing building equipment; fabricated structural metal

(G-5579)
DERKSEN PORTABLE BUILDINGS
329 First St N (39577-3346)
PHONE.................................601 528-5778
Donovan S Nelson, *Principal*
EMP: 2 **EST:** 2010
SALES (est): 252.1K **Privately Held**
SIC: 3448 Buildings, portable: prefabricated metal

(G-5580)
DESOTO TREATED MATERIALS INC
Also Called: Utility Poles & Piling
941 Magnolia Dr S (39577-2707)
P.O. Box 460 (39577-0460)
PHONE.................................601 928-3921
Wynn Alexander, *President*
EMP: 35
SALES (est): 5.6MM **Privately Held**
WEB: www.dtmpoleandpile.com
SIC: 2491 Wood preserving

(G-5581)
DUNN PAPER INC
1321 Magnolia Dr S (39577-8160)
PHONE.................................800 253-1889
Brent Earnshaw, *President*
EMP: 105
SALES (corp-wide): 139.6MM **Privately Held**
SIC: 2671 Packaging paper & plastics film, coated & laminated
HQ: Dunn Paper, Inc.
218 Riverview St
Port Huron MI 48060
810 984-5521

(G-5582)
F & F TIMBER INC
939 Pine Ave E (39577-2967)
PHONE.................................601 528-0023
Arlin Fore, *President*
EMP: 10

SALES (est): 862.9K **Privately Held**
SIC: 2411 4212 Logging; local trucking, without storage

(G-5583)
G A PEARSON LOGGING INC
Also Called: GA Pearson Logging
71 Timber Ridge Rd (39577-9610)
PHONE.................................601 928-2105
George A Pearson, *President*
Connie Pearson, *Corp Secy*
EMP: 7
SALES: 673K **Privately Held**
SIC: 2411 Logging camps & contractors

(G-5584)
HOOD INDUSTRIES INC
1945 First St S (39577-2227)
PHONE.................................601 928-3737
Larry Stephens, *Manager*
EMP: 380
SALES (corp-wide): 332.7MM **Privately Held**
WEB: www.hoodindustries.com
SIC: 2435 2436 2411 Hardwood veneer & plywood; softwood veneer & plywood; logging
PA: Hood Industries, Inc.
15 Professional Pkwy # 8
Hattiesburg MS 39402
601 264-2962

(G-5585)
KKAM SERVICES LLC
620 Frontage Dr W (39577-8131)
PHONE.................................903 707-0110
EMP: 2
SALES (est): 139K **Privately Held**
SIC: 1389 Oil/Gas Field Services

(G-5586)
MMC MATERIALS INC
607 Stapp St (39577-2852)
PHONE.................................601 928-4941
Steve Covington, *Branch Mgr*
EMP: 5
SALES (corp-wide): 306.5MM **Privately Held**
WEB: www.mmcmaterials.com
SIC: 3273 Ready-mixed concrete
HQ: Mmc Materials, Inc.
1052 Highland Colony Pkwy # 201
Ridgeland MS 39157
601 898-4000

(G-5587)
PETERS BROTHERS LOGGING
60 Lacy Evans Rd (39577-9127)
PHONE.................................601 928-3591
Jesse Peter, *Partner*
Edio Peter, *Partner*
EMP: 2
SALES (est): 144.9K **Privately Held**
SIC: 2411 Logging camps & contractors

(G-5588)
POLE MILL OPTIMIZER LLC
2175 Hwy 49 S (39577)
P.O. Box 508 (39577-0508)
PHONE.................................601 928-8860
Lenfield Ritchey Oneal,
EMP: 2
SALES (est): 150.1K **Privately Held**
SIC: 2411 Pole cutting contractors

(G-5589)
STONE COUNTY ENTERPRISES INC
143 First St S (39577-2733)
P.O. Box 157 (39577-0157)
PHONE.................................601 928-4802
Ellis Cuevas, *President*
Heather Freret, *Vice Pres*
EMP: 4
SALES (est): 353.6K
SALES (corp-wide): 2.6MM **Privately Held**
WEB: www.stonecountyenterprise.com
SIC: 2711 Newspapers, publishing & printing
PA: Bay St. Louis Newspapers, Inc.
124 Court St
Bay Saint Louis MS 39520
228 467-5474

(PA)=Parent Co (HQ)=Headquarters (DH)=Div Headquarters
✪ = New Business established in last 2 years

2019 Harris Directory of
Mississippi Manufacturers

199

Wiggins - Stone County (G-5590)

GEOGRAPHIC SECTION

(G-5590)
STONE PRINTING INC
2919 Highway 26 (39577-9585)
PHONE..................................601 928-7050
Dale Davis, *President*
Mary Alice Davis, *Director*
EMP: 3
SALES: 225K **Privately Held**
SIC: 2752 Commercial printing, offset

(G-5591)
TINKERBELLE INDUSTRIES INC
230 Clear Creek Rd (39577-8621)
PHONE..................................601 928-3520
Samuel Bond, *Principal*
EMP: 1 EST: 2017
SALES (est): 39.6K **Privately Held**
SIC: 3999 Manufacturing industries

(G-5592)
TOOL TEK LLC
365 Highway 13 (39577-8812)
PHONE..................................937 399-4333
Michael Whitney, *Mng Member*
Jay K Jordan, *Principal*
EMP: 2
SALES (est): 126.5K **Privately Held**
SIC: 3544 Die sets for metal stamping (presses)

(G-5593)
VISION CENTER PA
Also Called: Gregory D Loose Od
1113 Central Ave E (39577-9605)
PHONE..................................601 928-3914
Gregory D Loose, *Owner*
EMP: 3
SALES (est): 370.6K **Privately Held**
SIC: 3851 Contact lenses

(G-5594)
WORD ALIVE
727 Central Ave W (39577-2522)
PHONE..................................601 307-3639
EMP: 2
SALES (est): 107.9K **Privately Held**
SIC: 2741 Miscellaneous publishing

Winona
Montgomery County

(G-5595)
BUBBA BOND LOGGING LLC
1503 Highway 51 (38967-9720)
PHONE..................................662 417-5242
James C Bond, *Mng Member*
EMP: 3
SALES (est): 255.2K **Privately Held**
SIC: 2411 Logging

(G-5596)
CADE ENTERPRISES 2
107 Pine Dr (38967-2009)
PHONE..................................662 283-3678
William Cade Jr, *Owner*
EMP: 1 EST: 1995
SALES (est): 158.3K **Privately Held**
SIC: 2411 Logging

(G-5597)
DIXIE WELDING
337 Sawyer Rd (38967-9527)
PHONE..................................662 417-0938
EMP: 1
SALES (est): 28.1K **Privately Held**
SIC: 7692 Welding repair

(G-5598)
FIRST HERITAGE CREDIT CORP
408 N Applegate St (38967-1827)
PHONE..................................662 283-4696
EMP: 1 **Privately Held**
SIC: 6141 2411 Personal credit institutions; timber, cut at logging camp
PA: First Heritage Credit Corp
605 Crescent Blvd Ste 101
Ridgeland MS 39157

(G-5599)
HEATH AVIATION
219 Airport Dr (38967-9605)
PHONE..................................662 283-9833
David Heath, *Owner*
EMP: 6
SALES (est): 911.9K **Privately Held**
WEB: www.heathaviation.com
SIC: 7363 3829 Pilot service, aviation; measuring & controlling devices

(G-5600)
HELENA AGRI-ENTERPRISES LLC
1199 Highway 51 (38967-9711)
PHONE..................................662 283-3990
EMP: 9 **Privately Held**
SIC: 5191 2819 Chemicals, agricultural; chemicals, high purity: refined from technical grade
HQ: Helena Agri-Enterprises, Llc
255 Schilling Blvd # 300
Collierville TN 38017
901 761-0050

(G-5601)
HH SERVICES
708 S Applegate St (38967-3001)
PHONE..................................662 283-1131
Barry Hardin, *Principal*
EMP: 1
SALES (est): 85.6K **Privately Held**
SIC: 2711 Newspapers, publishing & printing

(G-5602)
INHEALTH MEDICAL
107 N Front St (38967-2219)
PHONE..................................662 283-5750
Keith Wire, *Owner*
EMP: 3
SALES (est): 236.5K **Privately Held**
SIC: 2599 Hospital beds

(G-5603)
LUCY LUS MONOGRAMMING LLC
202 Summit St (38967-2235)
PHONE..................................662 417-9552
Christy Oliver, *Principal*
EMP: 1
SALES (est): 39.8K **Privately Held**
SIC: 2395 Embroidery & art needlework

(G-5604)
MONTGOMERY PUBLISHING CO INC
Also Called: Winona Times, The
401 Summit St Rm 108 (38967-2240)
PHONE..................................662 283-1131
White Emerich, *President*
Pat Brown, *Vice Pres*
Dan Strack, *Vice Pres*
EMP: 10
SALES (est): 760.1K **Privately Held**
SIC: 2711 Commercial printing & newspaper publishing combined

(G-5605)
PARKER BROTHERS 2 INC
4 Old Highway 51 N (38967-9742)
PHONE..................................662 283-2224
EMP: 1
SALES (est): 41K **Privately Held**
SIC: 3944 Games, toys & children's vehicles

(G-5606)
SCREW CONVEYOR CORPORATION
781 Church St (38967-2813)
PHONE..................................662 283-3142
Mark Middleton, *Branch Mgr*
EMP: 120
SALES (corp-wide): 31.2MM **Privately Held**
SIC: 3535 3715 3537 3532 Conveyors & conveying equipment; truck trailers; industrial trucks & tractors; mining machinery
PA: Screw Conveyor Corporation
700 Hoffman St
Hammond IN 46327
219 931-1450

(G-5607)
SEW SOUTHERN MONOGRAMS
1394 Highway 51 (38967-9122)
PHONE..................................662 229-6564
EMP: 1
SALES (est): 37.3K **Privately Held**
SIC: 2395 Embroidery & art needlework

(G-5608)
TIMBERWOOD LOGGING LLC
1238 Highway 51 (38967-9709)
PHONE..................................662 633-7744
Alicia Alvarado, *Principal*
EMP: 2 EST: 2016
SALES (est): 89.8K **Privately Held**
SIC: 2411 Logging

(G-5609)
TRI B TIMBER & LOGGING LLC
646 Sawyer Rd (38967-9601)
PHONE..................................662 283-4824
Larry Blaylock, *Owner*
EMP: 2
SALES (est): 207.4K **Privately Held**
SIC: 2411 Logging camps & contractors

(G-5610)
WELCH PRINTING
705 Fairground St (38967-1603)
PHONE..................................662 283-3692
Wayne Welch, *Owner*
Gloria Welch, *Owner*
EMP: 2
SALES: 93K **Privately Held**
SIC: 2752 Commercial printing, offset

(G-5611)
WINONA HARDWOOD INC
164 Sawyer Rd (38967)
PHONE..................................662 283-3050
Ricky Kilgore, *President*
Jeremy Kilgore, *Vice Pres*
EMP: 9
SQ FT: 1,500
SALES (est): 1.3MM **Privately Held**
SIC: 2421 Sawmills & planing mills, general

(G-5612)
WORLD EVANGELISM
600 Devine St (38967-1607)
P.O. Box 72 (38967-0072)
PHONE..................................662 283-1192
J C Choate, *Owner*
▲ EMP: 5
SALES (est): 424.2K **Privately Held**
SIC: 2731 Books: publishing only

Woodland
Chickasaw County

(G-5613)
J & J WELDING
1783 Highway 15 S (39776-9723)
PHONE..................................662 456-6065
Jeremy Chandler, *Principal*
EMP: 1 EST: 2013
SALES (est): 72.1K **Privately Held**
SIC: 7692 Welding repair

(G-5614)
R AND R FURNITURE INC
112 County Road 66 (39776-9700)
PHONE..................................662 456-5888
Rodney Oswalt, *President*
EMP: 40
SQ FT: 5,000
SALES (est): 3.5MM **Privately Held**
WEB: www.randrfurniture.com
SIC: 2512 Recliners: upholstered on wood frames; rockers: upholstered on wood frames

---

Woodville
Wilkinson County

(G-5615)
ALICIA VAUGHN
Also Called: Candy Lady AV
613 Main St (39669)
PHONE..................................601 888-7830
Alicia Vaughn, *Owner*
EMP: 1
SALES: 15K **Privately Held**
SIC: 2064 Candy & other confectionery products

(G-5616)
DMI PIPE FABRICATION LLC
1495 Us Highway 61 S (39669-3562)
PHONE..................................225 272-1420
Julie Folse,
EMP: 12 EST: 2010
SALES: 1MM **Privately Held**
SIC: 3498 Fabricated pipe & fittings

(G-5617)
DOOLEY BROTHERS READY MIX INC
2622 Woodville Jackson Ln (39669)
P.O. Box 961 (39669-0961)
PHONE..................................601 888-3530
Ricky Dooley, *President*
Herbert Dooley, *Vice Pres*
EMP: 3
SALES (est): 352.7K **Privately Held**
SIC: 3273 Ready-mixed concrete

(G-5618)
FRED NETTERVILLE LUMBER CO
3975 Buffalo Rd (39669-3659)
P.O. Box 857 (39669-0857)
PHONE..................................601 888-4343
Charles T Netterville, *President*
Tommie J Netterville, *Vice Pres*
Jerry Beauchamp, *CFO*
Matthew Netterville, *Treasurer*
Scott Wesberry, *Sales Mgr*
EMP: 120
SQ FT: 5,000
SALES (est): 24.5MM **Privately Held**
WEB: www.netcolbr.com
SIC: 2421 Lumber: rough, sawed or planed; planing mills

(G-5619)
WILKINSON COUNTY MUSEUM
Also Called: Woodville Civic Club
203 Boston Row (39669-5501)
P.O. Box 1055 (39669-1055)
PHONE..................................601 888-7151
David Smith, *Director*
Ernesto Coldeira, *Director*
EMP: 5
SALES: 18K **Privately Held**
SIC: 8412 2731 Museum; books: publishing only

Yazoo City
Yazoo County

(G-5620)
AA CALIBRATION SERVICES LLC
111 Roosevelt Hudson Dr (39194-8831)
PHONE..................................662 716-0202
Dorothy White, *COO*
Larry White,
White Dorothy,
EMP: 11
SALES (est): 278.5K **Privately Held**
WEB: www.aacalibrationservices.com
SIC: 7629 3825 8734 Electrical measuring instrument repair & calibration; standards & calibration equipment for electrical measuring; calibration & certification

(G-5621)
AMCO MANUFACTURING COMPANY LLC
800 S Industrial Pkwy (39194)
P.O. Box 1107 (39194-1107)
PHONE..................................662 746-4464
Drew Coker, *Sales Staff*
Michael Atwood, *Marketing Mgr*
Bernard Whalen, *Mng Member*
EMP: 27
SQ FT: 85,000
SALES (est): 1MM **Privately Held**
SIC: 3523 Soil preparation machinery, except turf & grounds

(G-5622)
AMERICAN T SHIRT PRINTING CO
251 Freeman Ln (39194-9287)
PHONE..................................662 590-3272

2019 Harris Directory of
Mississippi Manufacturers

▲ = Import ▼=Export
◆ =Import/Export

200

GEOGRAPHIC SECTION

Yazoo City - Yazoo County (G-5650)

Carol White, *Owner*
EMP: 2
SALES (est): 75.2K **Privately Held**
SIC: 2759 Screen printing

(G-5623)
APAC-MISSISSIPPI INC
22431 Hwy 3 (39194)
PHONE...................................662 746-7983
Andy Atkins, *Branch Mgr*
EMP: 5
SALES (corp-wide): 30.6B **Privately Held**
SIC: 5032 2951 Brick, stone & related material; asphalt paving mixtures & blocks
HQ: Apac-Mississippi, Inc.
101 Riverview Dr
Richland MS 39218
601 376-4000

(G-5624)
BRENT AUBRY
927 Prentiss Ave (39194-2832)
PHONE...................................662 746-7600
Aubry Brent, *Principal*
EMP: 1
SALES (est): 59.7K **Privately Held**
SIC: 2711 Newspapers, publishing & printing

(G-5625)
CF INDUSTRIES INC
4608 Highway 49 E (39194-2318)
P.O. Box 1348 (39194-1348)
PHONE...................................662 746-4131
Steve Moore, *Plant Mgr*
Hui Wang, *Project Engr*
EMP: 214
SALES (corp-wide): 4.4B **Publicly Held**
WEB: www.terraindustries.com
SIC: 2873 2874 Anhydrous ammonia; urea; phosphoric acid; superphosphates, ammoniated or not ammoniated; diammonium phosphate; calcium meta-phosphate
HQ: Cf Industries, Inc.
4 Parkway North Blvd # 400
Deerfield IL 60015
847 405-2400

(G-5626)
CF INDUSTRIES NITROGEN LLC
4612 Highway 49 E (39194-2318)
P.O. Box 1348 (39194-1348)
PHONE...................................662 751-2616
EMP: 28
SALES (corp-wide): 4.4B **Publicly Held**
SIC: 2873 2874 Nitrogenous fertilizers; phosphatic fertilizers
HQ: Cf Industries Nitrogen, Llc
4 Parkway North Blvd # 400
Deerfield IL 60015
847 405-2400

(G-5627)
CG&P MANUFACTURING INC
800 S Industrial Pkwy (39194)
PHONE...................................662 746-4464
Jody Carr, *President*
David Shylko, *Managing Dir*
Kasia Arent, *Prdtn Mgr*
▲ **EMP:** 27
SALES (est): 6.3MM **Privately Held**
WEB: www.amcomanufacturing.com
SIC: 3523 Farm machinery & equipment

(G-5628)
CJW HUNTING LLC
213 S Main St (39194-4009)
P.O. Box 567 (39194-0567)
PHONE...................................662 746-1863
James Wayne Morrison, *President*
EMP: 2
SALES (est): 88.5K **Privately Held**
SIC: 3949 Hunting equipment

(G-5629)
CRABTREE MANUFACTURING INC
970 S Industrial Pkwy (39194-9489)
PHONE...................................662 746-3041
Jim Crabtree, *CEO*
EMP: 13
SQ FT: 43,000
SALES (est): 2.1MM **Privately Held**
SIC: 3599 3531 Machine shop, jobbing & repair; backhoes, tractors, cranes, plows & similar equipment

(G-5630)
DELTA AUTO PARTS INC
Also Called: Ace Hardware
647 Haley Barbour Pkwy (39194-4750)
P.O. Box 15 (39194-0015)
PHONE...................................662 746-1143
Sean King, *President*
Peggy King, *Vice Pres*
EMP: 13 **EST:** 1967
SQ FT: 15,000
SALES (est): 2.5MM **Privately Held**
SIC: 5261 5531 5251 3429 Lawn & garden equipment; automotive parts; hardware; aircraft & marine hardware, inc. pulleys & similar items

(G-5631)
DELTA INDUSTRIES INC
Also Called: Yazoo Ready Mix Concrete
1011 S Industrial Pkwy (39194-9488)
PHONE...................................662 746-6646
Mark Dement, *Manager*
EMP: 3
SALES (corp-wide): 100.3MM **Privately Held**
WEB: www.delta-ind.com
SIC: 3273 Ready-mixed concrete
PA: Delta Industries, Inc.
100 W Woodrow Wilson Ave
Jackson MS 39213
601 354-3801

(G-5632)
DELTA LOGGING & COMPANY INC
700 S Industrial Pkwy (39194-9403)
P.O. Box 1542 (39194-1542)
PHONE...................................662 746-2066
C Pat Ramsay, *President*
Paula Pyles, *Corp Secy*
EMP: 25
SQ FT: 20,000
SALES: 2.5MM **Privately Held**
SIC: 2411 Logging camps & contractors

(G-5633)
EMBROIDERY PLUS
1563 Jerry Clower Blvd (39194-2718)
PHONE...................................662 590-7102
Judy Griffin, *Principal*
EMP: 1
SALES (est): 46.9K **Privately Held**
SIC: 2395 Embroidery products, except schiffli machine

(G-5634)
EVH PROPERTIES LLC
700 Edgar Rd (39194-9698)
PHONE...................................662 571-1980
Angela Edgar, *President*
Angela H Edgar, *Owner*
Emily Vick,
EMP: 1
SALES (est): 60.1K **Privately Held**
SIC: 2211 Luggage fabrics, cotton

(G-5635)
HELENA AGRI-ENTERPRISES LLC
1205 Rialto Rd (39194)
P.O. Box 72 (39194-0072)
PHONE...................................662 746-7466
Ward Bloodworgh, *Manager*
EMP: 15 **Privately Held**
WEB: www.helenachemical.com
SIC: 2875 5191 Fertilizers, mixing only; farm supplies
HQ: Helena Agri-Enterprises, Llc
255 Schilling Blvd # 300
Collierville TN 38017
901 761-0050

(G-5636)
INTERNATIONAL PAPER COMPANY
270 S Industrial Pkwy (39194-9319)
PHONE...................................800 207-4003
Mark Brown, *Manager*
EMP: 1
SALES (corp-wide): 23.3B **Publicly Held**
WEB: www.internationalpaper.com
SIC: 2621 Paper mills

PA: International Paper Company
6400 Poplar Ave
Memphis TN 38197
901 419-9000

(G-5637)
J & J BAGGING LLC
1312 Rialto Rd (39194-9111)
PHONE...................................662 746-5155
Joseph A Mohamed III,
James A Davis,
EMP: 23
SALES (est): 9.7MM **Privately Held**
SIC: 2048 5191 Prepared feeds; fertilizers & agricultural chemicals

(G-5638)
LAVELLE CRABTREE WELDING
401 S Industrial Pkwy (39194-9320)
PHONE...................................662 746-7177
D Lavelle, *Owner*
EMP: 3
SALES (est): 100K **Privately Held**
SIC: 7692 Welding repair

(G-5639)
MELAMINE CHEMICALS INC
Hwy 49 (39194)
P.O. Box 1348 (39194-1348)
PHONE...................................662 746-4131
Carl Wallace, *Manager*
▲ **EMP:** 4
SALES (est): 250.8K
SALES (corp-wide): 4.4B **Publicly Held**
WEB: www.misschem.com
SIC: 2873 Nitrogenous fertilizers
HQ: Terra Mississippi Nitrogen, Inc.
4612 Highway 49 E
Yazoo City MS 39194
662 746-4131

(G-5640)
MISSISSIPPI CHEESE STRAW FCTRY
741 E Eighth St (39194-3309)
PHONE...................................662 746-7171
Hunter Yerger, *President*
Robert Yerger, *Vice Pres*
Mary M Yerger, *Shareholder*
EMP: 15
SQ FT: 10,000
SALES (est): 2.1MM **Privately Held**
SIC: 2022 Natural cheese

(G-5641)
MISSISSIPPI DELTA ENERGY AGCY
210 S Mound St (39194-4043)
P.O. Box 660 (39194-0660)
PHONE...................................662 746-3741
William N Nelson, *Ch of Bd*
Melville Tillis, *Ch of Bd*
Jimmy Wever, *Treasurer*
Marvin Carraway, *Admin Sec*
EMP: 4 **EST:** 2001
SALES (est): 300K **Privately Held**
SIC: 3648 Reflectors for lighting equipment: metal

(G-5642)
MONOGRAM EXPRESSIONS
3779 Old Dover Rd (39194-9550)
PHONE...................................662 571-0582
Bonnie Durden, *Principal*
EMP: 1
SALES (est): 45.4K **Privately Held**
SIC: 2395 Embroidery & art needlework

(G-5643)
MOTOR PARTS CO OF YAZOO CITY
Also Called: NAPA Auto Parts
322 S Washington St (39194-4462)
P.O. Box 169 (39194-0169)
PHONE...................................662 746-1462
Ben P Estes, *President*
EMP: 7
SQ FT: 8,100
SALES (est): 1.3MM **Privately Held**
SIC: 5531 5251 5261 3599 Automobile & truck equipment & parts; chainsaws; lawnmowers & tractors; machine shop, jobbing & repair

(G-5644)
NITROUS OXIDE CORP
1226 Rialto Rd (39194-9485)
P.O. Box 1085 (39194-1085)
PHONE...................................662 746-7607
Roger Millay, *Principal*
Dell Walton, *Manager*
▲ **EMP:** 5 **EST:** 2010
SALES (est): 803.3K **Privately Held**
SIC: 2813 Nitrous oxide

(G-5645)
PARTY TIME ICE INC
677 E Sunflower Dr (39194-2726)
PHONE...................................662 746-8899
Kevin Helton, *President*
Kenneth Helton, *Corp Secy*
Charlotte Helton, *Vice Pres*
EMP: 10
SALES: 1MM **Privately Held**
SIC: 5199 5999 2097 Ice, manufactured or natural; ice; manufactured ice

(G-5646)
SIMMONS FRM RAISED CATFISH INC (PA)
Also Called: Simmons Farms
2628 Erickson Rd (39194-9457)
PHONE...................................662 746-5687
Harry D Simmons Jr, *President*
Mark Henderson, *Sales Mgr*
Katy Prosser, *Mktg Dir*
EMP: 41
SQ FT: 3,000
SALES (est): 23.3MM **Privately Held**
SIC: 2092 Fish, frozen: prepared; fish, fresh: prepared

(G-5647)
T & G PALLET INC
1138 Rialto Rd (39194)
PHONE...................................662 746-4499
EMP: 15 **EST:** 2000
SQ FT: 24,000
SALES (est): 970K **Privately Held**
SIC: 2448 Mfg Wood Pallets/Skids

(G-5648)
TERRA HOUSTON AMMONIA INC
Hwy 49 (39194)
PHONE...................................662 746-4131
Coley Bailey, *CEO*
EMP: 45
SALES (est): 7.2MM
SALES (corp-wide): 4.4B **Publicly Held**
WEB: www.misschem.com
SIC: 2873 Nitrogenous fertilizers
HQ: Terra Mississippi Nitrogen, Inc.
4612 Highway 49 E
Yazoo City MS 39194
662 746-4131

(G-5649)
TERRA MISSISSIPPI NITROGEN INC (DH)
4612 Highway 49 E (39194-2318)
P.O. Box 388 (39194-0388)
PHONE...................................662 746-4131
W Mark Rosenbury, *Vice Pres*
Francis G Meyer, *Treasurer*
Mark A Kalafut, *Admin Sec*
▲ **EMP:** 459
SQ FT: 65,000
SALES (est): 103.7MM
SALES (corp-wide): 4.4B **Publicly Held**
WEB: www.misschem.com
SIC: 2873 2874 1474 Nitrogenous fertilizers; phosphatic fertilizers; potash mining
HQ: Terra Industries Inc.
600 4th St Fl 8
Sioux City IA 51101
712 943-5501

(G-5650)
THREE CRAFTY WOMEN
519 Webster St (39194-3757)
PHONE...................................662 746-6844
Sheila Boston, *Owner*
EMP: 1
SALES (est): 37K **Privately Held**
SIC: 2395 Embroidery products, except schiffli machine

(PA)=Parent Co (HQ)=Headquarters (DH)=Div Headquarters
✿ = New Business established in last 2 years

2019 Harris Directory of
Mississippi Manufacturers

201

Yazoo City - Yazoo County (G-5651)

GEOGRAPHIC SECTION

(G-5651)
TIM ROARK
494 Eola Dr (39194-8241)
PHONE..................................662 746-8871
Tim Roark, *Principal*
EMP: 2
SALES (est): 157.9K **Privately Held**
SIC: 3479 Painting, coating & hot dipping

(G-5652)
WILLIAMSON GIN REPAIR
1200 Rialto Rd (39194-9485)
PHONE..................................662 571-6084
Clay Williamson, *Owner*
EMP: 2
SALES (est): 81K **Privately Held**
SIC: 7699 3559 Farm machinery repair;
cotton ginning machinery

(G-5653)
YAZOO NEWSPAPER CO INC
Also Called: Yazoo Herald, The
1035 Grand Ave (39194-2946)
P.O. Box 720 (39194-0720)
PHONE..................................662 746-4911
Wyatt Emmerich Jr, *President*
EMP: 11
SALES (est): 786.2K **Privately Held**
SIC: 2711 7313 Commercial printing &
newspaper publishing combined; newspa-
per advertising representative

SIC INDEX

Standard Industrial Classification Alphabetical Index

SIC NO	PRODUCT

A

3291 Abrasive Prdts
2891 Adhesives & Sealants
3563 Air & Gas Compressors
3585 Air Conditioning & Heating Eqpt
3721 Aircraft
3724 Aircraft Engines & Engine Parts
3728 Aircraft Parts & Eqpt, NEC
2812 Alkalies & Chlorine
3363 Aluminum Die Castings
3354 Aluminum Extruded Prdts
3365 Aluminum Foundries
3355 Aluminum Rolling & Drawing, NEC
3353 Aluminum Sheet, Plate & Foil
3483 Ammunition, Large
3826 Analytical Instruments
2077 Animal, Marine Fats & Oils
2389 Apparel & Accessories, NEC
2387 Apparel Belts
3446 Architectural & Ornamental Metal Work
7694 Armature Rewinding Shops
3292 Asbestos products
2952 Asphalt Felts & Coatings
3822 Automatic Temperature Controls
3581 Automatic Vending Machines
3465 Automotive Stampings
2396 Automotive Trimmings, Apparel Findings, Related Prdts

B

2673 Bags: Plastics, Laminated & Coated
2674 Bags: Uncoated Paper & Multiwall
3562 Ball & Roller Bearings
2836 Biological Prdts, Exc Diagnostic Substances
1221 Bituminous Coal & Lignite: Surface Mining
2782 Blankbooks & Looseleaf Binders
3312 Blast Furnaces, Coke Ovens, Steel & Rolling Mills
3564 Blowers & Fans
3732 Boat Building & Repairing
3452 Bolts, Nuts, Screws, Rivets & Washers
2732 Book Printing, Not Publishing
2789 Bookbinding
2731 Books: Publishing & Printing
3131 Boot & Shoe Cut Stock & Findings
2342 Brassieres, Girdles & Garments
2051 Bread, Bakery Prdts Exc Cookies & Crackers
3251 Brick & Structural Clay Tile
3991 Brooms & Brushes

C

3578 Calculating & Accounting Eqpt
2064 Candy & Confectionery Prdts
2033 Canned Fruits, Vegetables & Preserves
2032 Canned Specialties
2394 Canvas Prdts
2895 Carbon Black
3955 Carbon Paper & Inked Ribbons
3592 Carburetors, Pistons, Rings & Valves
2273 Carpets & Rugs
2823 Cellulosic Man-Made Fibers
3241 Cement, Hydraulic
3253 Ceramic Tile
2043 Cereal Breakfast Foods
2022 Cheese
1479 Chemical & Fertilizer Mining
2899 Chemical Preparations, NEC
2361 Children's & Infants' Dresses & Blouses
3261 China Plumbing Fixtures & Fittings
2066 Chocolate & Cocoa Prdts
2111 Cigarettes
3255 Clay Refractories
1459 Clay, Ceramic & Refractory Minerals, NEC
1241 Coal Mining Svcs
3479 Coating & Engraving, NEC
2095 Coffee
3316 Cold Rolled Steel Sheet, Strip & Bars
3582 Commercial Laundry, Dry Clean & Pressing Mchs
2759 Commercial Printing
2754 Commercial Printing: Gravure
2752 Commercial Printing: Lithographic
3646 Commercial, Indl & Institutional Lighting Fixtures
3669 Communications Eqpt, NEC
3577 Computer Peripheral Eqpt, NEC
3572 Computer Storage Devices

3575 Computer Terminals
3271 Concrete Block & Brick
3272 Concrete Prdts
3531 Construction Machinery & Eqpt
1442 Construction Sand & Gravel
2679 Converted Paper Prdts, NEC
3535 Conveyors & Eqpt
2052 Cookies & Crackers
3366 Copper Foundries
2298 Cordage & Twine
2653 Corrugated & Solid Fiber Boxes
3961 Costume Jewelry & Novelties
2261 Cotton Fabric Finishers
2211 Cotton, Woven Fabric
2074 Cottonseed Oil Mills
1311 Crude Petroleum & Natural Gas
1423 Crushed & Broken Granite
1422 Crushed & Broken Limestone
3643 Current-Carrying Wiring Devices
2391 Curtains & Draperies
3281 Cut Stone Prdts
3421 Cutlery
2865 Cyclic-Crudes, Intermediates, Dyes & Org Pigments

D

3843 Dental Eqpt & Splys
2835 Diagnostic Substances
2675 Die-Cut Paper & Board
3544 Dies, Tools, Jigs, Fixtures & Indl Molds
1411 Dimension Stone
2047 Dog & Cat Food
3942 Dolls & Stuffed Toys
2591 Drapery Hardware, Window Blinds & Shades
2381 Dress & Work Gloves
1381 Drilling Oil & Gas Wells

E

3263 Earthenware, Whiteware, Table & Kitchen Articles
3634 Electric Household Appliances
3641 Electric Lamps
3694 Electrical Eqpt For Internal Combustion Engines
3629 Electrical Indl Apparatus, NEC
3699 Electrical Machinery, Eqpt & Splys, NEC
3845 Electromedical & Electrotherapeutic Apparatus
3677 Electronic Coils & Transformers
3679 Electronic Components, NEC
3571 Electronic Computers
3678 Electronic Connectors
3676 Electronic Resistors
3471 Electroplating, Plating, Polishing, Anodizing & Coloring
3534 Elevators & Moving Stairways
3431 Enameled Iron & Metal Sanitary Ware
2677 Envelopes
2892 Explosives

F

2241 Fabric Mills, Cotton, Wool, Silk & Man-Made
3499 Fabricated Metal Prdts, NEC
3498 Fabricated Pipe & Pipe Fittings
3443 Fabricated Plate Work
3069 Fabricated Rubber Prdts, NEC
3441 Fabricated Structural Steel
2399 Fabricated Textile Prdts, NEC
2295 Fabrics Coated Not Rubberized
2297 Fabrics, Nonwoven
3523 Farm Machinery & Eqpt
3965 Fasteners, Buttons, Needles & Pins
2875 Fertilizers, Mixing Only
2655 Fiber Cans, Tubes & Drums
2092 Fish & Seafoods, Fresh & Frozen
3211 Flat Glass
2087 Flavoring Extracts & Syrups
2045 Flour, Blended & Prepared
2041 Flour, Grain Milling
3824 Fluid Meters & Counters
3593 Fluid Power Cylinders & Actuators
3594 Fluid Power Pumps & Motors
3492 Fluid Power Valves & Hose Fittings
2657 Folding Paperboard Boxes
3556 Food Prdts Machinery
2099 Food Preparations, NEC
3149 Footwear, NEC
2053 Frozen Bakery Prdts
2037 Frozen Fruits, Juices & Vegetables

2038 Frozen Specialties
2371 Fur Goods
2599 Furniture & Fixtures, NEC

G

3944 Games, Toys & Children's Vehicles
3524 Garden, Lawn Tractors & Eqpt
3053 Gaskets, Packing & Sealing Devices
2369 Girls' & Infants' Outerwear, NEC
3221 Glass Containers
3231 Glass Prdts Made Of Purchased Glass
3321 Gray Iron Foundries
3769 Guided Missile/Space Vehicle Parts & Eqpt, NEC
3761 Guided Missiles & Space Vehicles
2861 Gum & Wood Chemicals
3275 Gypsum Prdts

H

3423 Hand & Edge Tools
3425 Hand Saws & Saw Blades
3429 Hardware, NEC
2426 Hardwood Dimension & Flooring Mills
2435 Hardwood Veneer & Plywood
2353 Hats, Caps & Millinery
3433 Heating Eqpt
3536 Hoists, Cranes & Monorails
2252 Hosiery, Except Women's
2251 Hosiery, Women's Full & Knee Length
2392 House furnishings: Textile
3639 Household Appliances, NEC
3651 Household Audio & Video Eqpt
3631 Household Cooking Eqpt
2519 Household Furniture, NEC
3632 Household Refrigerators & Freezers
3635 Household Vacuum Cleaners

I

2097 Ice
2024 Ice Cream
2819 Indl Inorganic Chemicals, NEC
3823 Indl Instruments For Meas, Display & Control
3569 Indl Machinery & Eqpt, NEC
3567 Indl Process Furnaces & Ovens
3537 Indl Trucks, Tractors, Trailers & Stackers
2813 Industrial Gases
2869 Industrial Organic Chemicals, NEC
3543 Industrial Patterns
1446 Industrial Sand
3491 Industrial Valves
2816 Inorganic Pigments
3825 Instrs For Measuring & Testing Electricity
3519 Internal Combustion Engines, NEC
3462 Iron & Steel Forgings

J

3915 Jewelers Findings & Lapidary Work
3911 Jewelry: Precious Metal

K

1455 Kaolin & Ball Clay
2253 Knit Outerwear Mills
2254 Knit Underwear Mills
2259 Knitting Mills, NEC

L

3821 Laboratory Apparatus & Furniture
3952 Lead Pencils, Crayons & Artist's Mtrls
2386 Leather & Sheep Lined Clothing
3151 Leather Gloves & Mittens
3199 Leather Goods, NEC
3111 Leather Tanning & Finishing
3648 Lighting Eqpt, NEC
3274 Lime
3996 Linoleum & Hard Surface Floor Coverings, NEC
2085 Liquors, Distilled, Rectified & Blended
2411 Logging
2992 Lubricating Oils & Greases
3161 Luggage

M

3545 Machine Tool Access
3541 Machine Tools: Cutting
3542 Machine Tools: Forming
3599 Machinery & Eqpt, Indl & Commercial, NEC
2082 Malt Beverages

SIC

2019 Harris Directory of
Mississippi Manufactures

203

SIC INDEX

SIC NO	PRODUCT
2761	Manifold Business Forms
3999	Manufacturing Industries, NEC
3953	Marking Devices
2515	Mattresses & Bedsprings
3829	Measuring & Controlling Devices, NEC
2011	Meat Packing Plants
3568	Mechanical Power Transmission Eqpt, NEC
2833	Medicinal Chemicals & Botanical Prdts
2329	Men's & Boys' Clothing, NEC
2325	Men's & Boys' Separate Trousers & Casual Slacks
2321	Men's & Boys' Shirts
2311	Men's & Boys' Suits, Coats & Overcoats
2326	Men's & Boys' Work Clothing
3412	Metal Barrels, Drums, Kegs & Pails
3411	Metal Cans
3442	Metal Doors, Sash, Frames, Molding & Trim
3398	Metal Heat Treating
2514	Metal Household Furniture
1081	Metal Mining Svcs
1099	Metal Ores, NEC
3469	Metal Stampings, NEC
3549	Metalworking Machinery, NEC
2026	Milk
2023	Milk, Condensed & Evaporated
2431	Millwork
3296	Mineral Wool
3295	Minerals & Earths: Ground Or Treated
3532	Mining Machinery & Eqpt
3496	Misc Fabricated Wire Prdts
2741	Misc Publishing
3449	Misc Structural Metal Work
1499	Miscellaneous Nonmetallic Mining
2451	Mobile Homes
3716	Motor Homes
3714	Motor Vehicle Parts & Access
3711	Motor Vehicles & Car Bodies
3751	Motorcycles, Bicycles & Parts
3621	Motors & Generators
3931	Musical Instruments

N

SIC NO	PRODUCT
1321	Natural Gas Liquids
2711	Newspapers: Publishing & Printing
2873	Nitrogenous Fertilizers
3644	Noncurrent-Carrying Wiring Devices
3463	Nonferrous Forgings
3369	Nonferrous Foundries: Castings, NEC
3357	Nonferrous Wire Drawing
3299	Nonmetallic Mineral Prdts, NEC

O

SIC NO	PRODUCT
2522	Office Furniture, Except Wood
3579	Office Machines, NEC
1382	Oil & Gas Field Exploration Svcs
1389	Oil & Gas Field Svcs, NEC
3533	Oil Field Machinery & Eqpt
3851	Ophthalmic Goods
3827	Optical Instruments
3489	Ordnance & Access, NEC
3842	Orthopedic, Prosthetic & Surgical Appliances/Splys

P

SIC NO	PRODUCT
3565	Packaging Machinery
2851	Paints, Varnishes, Lacquers, Enamels
2671	Paper Coating & Laminating for Packaging
2672	Paper Coating & Laminating, Exc for Packaging
2621	Paper Mills
2631	Paperboard Mills
2542	Partitions & Fixtures, Except Wood
2951	Paving Mixtures & Blocks
2844	Perfumes, Cosmetics & Toilet Preparations
2721	Periodicals: Publishing & Printing
3172	Personal Leather Goods
2879	Pesticides & Agricultural Chemicals, NEC
2911	Petroleum Refining
2834	Pharmaceuticals

SIC NO	PRODUCT
3652	Phonograph Records & Magnetic Tape
2874	Phosphatic Fertilizers
3861	Photographic Eqpt & Splys
2035	Pickled Fruits, Vegetables, Sauces & Dressings
3085	Plastic Bottles
3086	Plastic Foam Prdts
3083	Plastic Laminated Plate & Sheet
3084	Plastic Pipe
3088	Plastic Plumbing Fixtures
3089	Plastic Prdts
3081	Plastic Unsupported Sheet & Film
2821	Plastics, Mtrls & Nonvulcanizable Elastomers
2796	Platemaking & Related Svcs
2395	Pleating & Stitching For The Trade
3432	Plumbing Fixture Fittings & Trim, Brass
1474	Potash, Soda & Borate Minerals
2096	Potato Chips & Similar Prdts
3269	Pottery Prdts, NEC
2015	Poultry Slaughtering, Dressing & Processing
3546	Power Hand Tools
3612	Power, Distribution & Specialty Transformers
3448	Prefabricated Metal Buildings & Cmpnts
2452	Prefabricated Wood Buildings & Cmpnts
7372	Prepackaged Software
2048	Prepared Feeds For Animals & Fowls
3229	Pressed & Blown Glassware, NEC
3692	Primary Batteries: Dry & Wet
3399	Primary Metal Prdts, NEC
3339	Primary Nonferrous Metals, NEC
3334	Primary Production Of Aluminum
3672	Printed Circuit Boards
3555	Printing Trades Machinery & Eqpt
2999	Products Of Petroleum & Coal, NEC
2531	Public Building & Related Furniture
2611	Pulp Mills
3561	Pumps & Pumping Eqpt

R

SIC NO	PRODUCT
3663	Radio & T V Communications, Systs & Eqpt, Broadcast/Studio
3743	Railroad Eqpt
3273	Ready-Mixed Concrete
2493	Reconstituted Wood Prdts
3695	Recording Media
3625	Relays & Indl Controls
3645	Residential Lighting Fixtures
2044	Rice Milling
2384	Robes & Dressing Gowns
3547	Rolling Mill Machinery & Eqpt
3351	Rolling, Drawing & Extruding Of Copper
3356	Rolling, Drawing-Extruding Of Nonferrous Metals
3021	Rubber & Plastic Footwear
3052	Rubber & Plastic Hose & Belting

S

SIC NO	PRODUCT
2068	Salted & Roasted Nuts & Seeds
2656	Sanitary Food Containers
2676	Sanitary Paper Prdts
2013	Sausages & Meat Prdts
2421	Saw & Planing Mills
3596	Scales & Balances, Exc Laboratory
2397	Schiffli Machine Embroideries
3451	Screw Machine Prdts
3812	Search, Detection, Navigation & Guidance Systs & Instrs
3341	Secondary Smelting & Refining Of Nonferrous Metals
3674	Semiconductors
3589	Service Ind Machines, NEC
2652	Set-Up Paperboard Boxes
3444	Sheet Metal Work
3731	Shipbuilding & Repairing
2079	Shortening, Oils & Margarine
3993	Signs & Advertising Displays
2262	Silk & Man-Made Fabric Finishers
2221	Silk & Man-Made Fiber
3914	Silverware, Plated & Stainless Steel Ware
3484	Small Arms

SIC NO	PRODUCT
3482	Small Arms Ammunition
2841	Soap & Detergents
2086	Soft Drinks
2436	Softwood Veneer & Plywood
2075	Soybean Oil Mills
2842	Spec Cleaning, Polishing & Sanitation Preparations
3559	Special Ind Machinery, NEC
3566	Speed Changers, Drives & Gears
3949	Sporting & Athletic Goods, NEC
2678	Stationery Prdts
3511	Steam, Gas & Hydraulic Turbines & Engines
3325	Steel Foundries, NEC
3324	Steel Investment Foundries
3317	Steel Pipe & Tubes
3493	Steel Springs, Except Wire
3315	Steel Wire Drawing & Nails & Spikes
3691	Storage Batteries
3259	Structural Clay Prdts, NEC
2439	Structural Wood Members, NEC
2843	Surface Active & Finishing Agents, Sulfonated Oils
3841	Surgical & Medical Instrs & Apparatus
3613	Switchgear & Switchboard Apparatus
2824	Synthetic Organic Fibers, Exc Cellulosic
2822	Synthetic Rubber (Vulcanizable Elastomers)

T

SIC NO	PRODUCT
3795	Tanks & Tank Components
3661	Telephone & Telegraph Apparatus
2393	Textile Bags
2299	Textile Goods, NEC
3552	Textile Machinery
2284	Thread Mills
2296	Tire Cord & Fabric
3011	Tires & Inner Tubes
2141	Tobacco Stemming & Redrying
2131	Tobacco, Chewing & Snuff
3799	Transportation Eqpt, NEC
3792	Travel Trailers & Campers
3713	Truck & Bus Bodies
3715	Truck Trailers
2791	Typesetting

V

SIC NO	PRODUCT
3494	Valves & Pipe Fittings, NEC
2076	Vegetable Oil Mills
3647	Vehicular Lighting Eqpt

W

SIC NO	PRODUCT
3548	Welding Apparatus
7692	Welding Repair
2084	Wine & Brandy
3495	Wire Springs
2331	Women's & Misses' Blouses
2335	Women's & Misses' Dresses
2339	Women's & Misses' Outerwear, NEC
2337	Women's & Misses' Suits, Coats & Skirts
2341	Women's, Misses' & Children's Underwear & Nightwear
2441	Wood Boxes
2449	Wood Containers, NEC
2511	Wood Household Furniture
2512	Wood Household Furniture, Upholstered
2434	Wood Kitchen Cabinets
2521	Wood Office Furniture
2448	Wood Pallets & Skids
2499	Wood Prdts, NEC
2491	Wood Preserving
2517	Wood T V, Radio, Phono & Sewing Cabinets
2541	Wood, Office & Store Fixtures
3553	Woodworking Machinery
2231	Wool, Woven Fabric

X

SIC NO	PRODUCT
3844	X-ray Apparatus & Tubes

Y

SIC NO	PRODUCT
2281	Yarn Spinning Mills

SIC INDEX

Standard Industrial Classification Numerical Index

SIC NO	PRODUCT

10 metal mining
1081 Metal Mining Svcs
1099 Metal Ores, NEC

12 coal mining
1221 Bituminous Coal & Lignite: Surface Mining
1241 Coal Mining Svcs

13 oil and gas extraction
1311 Crude Petroleum & Natural Gas
1321 Natural Gas Liquids
1381 Drilling Oil & Gas Wells
1382 Oil & Gas Field Exploration Svcs
1389 Oil & Gas Field Svcs, NEC

14 mining and quarrying of nonmetallic minerals, except fuels
1411 Dimension Stone
1422 Crushed & Broken Limestone
1423 Crushed & Broken Granite
1442 Construction Sand & Gravel
1446 Industrial Sand
1455 Kaolin & Ball Clay
1459 Clay, Ceramic & Refractory Minerals, NEC
1474 Potash, Soda & Borate Minerals
1479 Chemical & Fertilizer Mining
1499 Miscellaneous Nonmetallic Mining

20 food and kindred products
2011 Meat Packing Plants
2013 Sausages & Meat Prdts
2015 Poultry Slaughtering, Dressing & Processing
2022 Cheese
2023 Milk, Condensed & Evaporated
2024 Ice Cream
2026 Milk
2032 Canned Specialties
2033 Canned Fruits, Vegetables & Preserves
2035 Pickled Fruits, Vegetables, Sauces & Dressings
2037 Frozen Fruits, Juices & Vegetables
2038 Frozen Specialties
2041 Flour, Grain Milling
2043 Cereal Breakfast Foods
2044 Rice Milling
2045 Flour, Blended & Prepared
2047 Dog & Cat Food
2048 Prepared Feeds For Animals & Fowls
2051 Bread, Bakery Prdts Exc Cookies & Crackers
2052 Cookies & Crackers
2053 Frozen Bakery Prdts
2064 Candy & Confectionery Prdts
2066 Chocolate & Cocoa Prdts
2068 Salted & Roasted Nuts & Seeds
2074 Cottonseed Oil Mills
2075 Soybean Oil Mills
2076 Vegetable Oil Mills
2077 Animal, Marine Fats & Oils
2079 Shortening, Oils & Margarine
2082 Malt Beverages
2084 Wine & Brandy
2085 Liquors, Distilled, Rectified & Blended
2086 Soft Drinks
2087 Flavoring Extracts & Syrups
2092 Fish & Seafoods, Fresh & Frozen
2095 Coffee
2096 Potato Chips & Similar Prdts
2097 Ice
2099 Food Preparations, NEC

21 tobacco products
2111 Cigarettes
2131 Tobacco, Chewing & Snuff
2141 Tobacco Stemming & Redrying

22 textile mill products
2211 Cotton, Woven Fabric
2221 Silk & Man-Made Fiber
2231 Wool, Woven Fabric
2241 Fabric Mills, Cotton, Wool, Silk & Man-Made
2251 Hosiery, Women's Full & Knee Length
2252 Hosiery, Except Women's
2253 Knit Outerwear Mills
2254 Knit Underwear Mills
2259 Knitting Mills, NEC

2261 Cotton Fabric Finishers
2262 Silk & Man-Made Fabric Finishers
2273 Carpets & Rugs
2281 Yarn Spinning Mills
2284 Thread Mills
2295 Fabrics Coated Not Rubberized
2296 Tire Cord & Fabric
2297 Fabrics, Nonwoven
2298 Cordage & Twine
2299 Textile Goods, NEC

23 apparel and other finished products made from fabrics and similar material
2311 Men's & Boys' Suits, Coats & Overcoats
2321 Men's & Boys' Shirts
2325 Men's & Boys' Separate Trousers & Casual Slacks
2326 Men's & Boys' Work Clothing
2329 Men's & Boys' Clothing, NEC
2331 Women's & Misses' Blouses
2335 Women's & Misses' Dresses
2337 Women's & Misses' Suits, Coats & Skirts
2339 Women's & Misses' Outerwear, NEC
2341 Women's, Misses' & Children's Underwear & Nightwear
2342 Brassieres, Girdles & Garments
2353 Hats, Caps & Millinery
2361 Children's & Infants' Dresses & Blouses
2369 Girls' & Infants' Outerwear, NEC
2371 Fur Goods
2381 Dress & Work Gloves
2384 Robes & Dressing Gowns
2386 Leather & Sheep Lined Clothing
2387 Apparel Belts
2389 Apparel & Accessories, NEC
2391 Curtains & Draperies
2392 House furnishings: Textile
2393 Textile Bags
2394 Canvas Prdts
2395 Pleating & Stitching For The Trade
2396 Automotive Trimmings, Apparel Findings, Related Prdts
2397 Schiffli Machine Embroideries
2399 Fabricated Textile Prdts, NEC

24 lumber and wood products, except furniture
2411 Logging
2421 Saw & Planing Mills
2426 Hardwood Dimension & Flooring Mills
2431 Millwork
2434 Wood Kitchen Cabinets
2435 Hardwood Veneer & Plywood
2436 Softwood Veneer & Plywood
2439 Structural Wood Members, NEC
2441 Wood Boxes
2448 Wood Pallets & Skids
2449 Wood Containers, NEC
2451 Mobile Homes
2452 Prefabricated Wood Buildings & Cmpnts
2491 Wood Preserving
2493 Reconstituted Wood Prdts
2499 Wood Prdts, NEC

25 furniture and fixtures
2511 Wood Household Furniture
2512 Wood Household Furniture, Upholstered
2514 Metal Household Furniture
2515 Mattresses & Bedsprings
2517 Wood T V, Radio, Phono & Sewing Cabinets
2519 Household Furniture, NEC
2521 Wood Office Furniture
2522 Office Furniture, Except Wood
2531 Public Building & Related Furniture
2541 Wood, Office & Store Fixtures
2542 Partitions & Fixtures, Except Wood
2591 Drapery Hardware, Window Blinds & Shades
2599 Furniture & Fixtures, NEC

26 paper and allied products
2611 Pulp Mills
2621 Paper Mills
2631 Paperboard Mills
2652 Set-Up Paperboard Boxes
2653 Corrugated & Solid Fiber Boxes
2655 Fiber Cans, Tubes & Drums
2656 Sanitary Food Containers

2657 Folding Paperboard Boxes
2671 Paper Coating & Laminating for Packaging
2672 Paper Coating & Laminating, Exc for Packaging
2673 Bags: Plastics, Laminated & Coated
2674 Bags: Uncoated Paper & Multiwall
2675 Die-Cut Paper & Board
2676 Sanitary Paper Prdts
2677 Envelopes
2678 Stationery Prdts
2679 Converted Paper Prdts, NEC

27 printing, publishing, and allied industries
2711 Newspapers: Publishing & Printing
2721 Periodicals: Publishing & Printing
2731 Books: Publishing & Printing
2732 Book Printing, Not Publishing
2741 Misc Publishing
2752 Commercial Printing: Lithographic
2754 Commercial Printing: Gravure
2759 Commercial Printing
2761 Manifold Business Forms
2782 Blankbooks & Looseleaf Binders
2789 Bookbinding
2791 Typesetting
2796 Platemaking & Related Svcs

28 chemicals and allied products
2812 Alkalies & Chlorine
2813 Industrial Gases
2816 Inorganic Pigments
2819 Indl Inorganic Chemicals, NEC
2821 Plastics, Mtrls & Nonvulcanizable Elastomers
2822 Synthetic Rubber (Vulcanizable Elastomers)
2823 Cellulosic Man-Made Fibers
2824 Synthetic Organic Fibers, Exc Cellulosic
2833 Medicinal Chemicals & Botanical Prdts
2834 Pharmaceuticals
2835 Diagnostic Substances
2836 Biological Prdts, Exc Diagnostic Substances
2841 Soap & Detergents
2842 Spec Cleaning, Polishing & Sanitation Preparations
2843 Surface Active & Finishing Agents, Sulfonated Oils
2844 Perfumes, Cosmetics & Toilet Preparations
2851 Paints, Varnishes, Lacquers, Enamels
2861 Gum & Wood Chemicals
2865 Cyclic-Crudes, Intermediates, Dyes & Org Pigments
2869 Industrial Organic Chemicals, NEC
2873 Nitrogenous Fertilizers
2874 Phosphatic Fertilizers
2875 Fertilizers, Mixing Only
2879 Pesticides & Agricultural Chemicals, NEC
2891 Adhesives & Sealants
2892 Explosives
2895 Carbon Black
2899 Chemical Preparations, NEC

29 petroleum refining and related industries
2911 Petroleum Refining
2951 Paving Mixtures & Blocks
2952 Asphalt Felts & Coatings
2992 Lubricating Oils & Greases
2999 Products Of Petroleum & Coal, NEC

30 rubber and miscellaneous plastics products
3011 Tires & Inner Tubes
3021 Rubber & Plastic Footwear
3052 Rubber & Plastic Hose & Belting
3053 Gaskets, Packing & Sealing Devices
3069 Fabricated Rubber Prdts, NEC
3081 Plastic Unsupported Sheet & Film
3083 Plastic Laminated Plate & Sheet
3084 Plastic Pipe
3085 Plastic Bottles
3086 Plastic Foam Prdts
3088 Plastic Plumbing Fixtures
3089 Plastic Prdts

31 leather and leather products
3111 Leather Tanning & Finishing
3131 Boot & Shoe Cut Stock & Findings
3149 Footwear, NEC
3151 Leather Gloves & Mittens
3161 Luggage
3172 Personal Leather Goods

S
I
C

2019 Harris Directory of
Mississippi Manufacturers

SIC INDEX

SIC NO	PRODUCT

3199 Leather Goods, NEC

32 stone, clay, glass, and concrete products

3211 Flat Glass
3221 Glass Containers
3229 Pressed & Blown Glassware, NEC
3231 Glass Prdts Made Of Purchased Glass
3241 Cement, Hydraulic
3251 Brick & Structural Clay Tile
3253 Ceramic Tile
3255 Clay Refractories
3259 Structural Clay Prdts, NEC
3261 China Plumbing Fixtures & Fittings
3263 Earthenware, Whiteware, Table & Kitchen Articles
3269 Pottery Prdts, NEC
3271 Concrete Block & Brick
3272 Concrete Prdts
3273 Ready-Mixed Concrete
3274 Lime
3275 Gypsum Prdts
3281 Cut Stone Prdts
3291 Abrasive Prdts
3292 Asbestos products
3295 Minerals & Earths: Ground Or Treated
3296 Mineral Wool
3299 Nonmetallic Mineral Prdts, NEC

33 primary metal industries

3312 Blast Furnaces, Coke Ovens, Steel & Rolling Mills
3315 Steel Wire Drawing & Nails & Spikes
3316 Cold Rolled Steel Sheet, Strip & Bars
3317 Steel Pipe & Tubes
3321 Gray Iron Foundries
3324 Steel Investment Foundries
3325 Steel Foundries, NEC
3334 Primary Production Of Aluminum
3339 Primary Nonferrous Metals, NEC
3341 Secondary Smelting & Refining Of Nonferrous Metals
3351 Rolling, Drawing & Extruding Of Copper
3353 Aluminum Sheet, Plate & Foil
3354 Aluminum Extruded Prdts
3355 Aluminum Rolling & Drawing, NEC
3356 Rolling, Drawing-Extruding Of Nonferrous Metals
3357 Nonferrous Wire Drawing
3363 Aluminum Die Castings
3365 Aluminum Foundries
3366 Copper Foundries
3369 Nonferrous Foundries: Castings, NEC
3398 Metal Heat Treating
3399 Primary Metal Prdts, NEC

34 fabricated metal products, except machinery and transportation equipment

3411 Metal Cans
3412 Metal Barrels, Drums, Kegs & Pails
3421 Cutlery
3423 Hand & Edge Tools
3425 Hand Saws & Saw Blades
3429 Hardware, NEC
3431 Enameled Iron & Metal Sanitary Ware
3432 Plumbing Fixture Fittings & Trim, Brass
3433 Heating Eqpt
3441 Fabricated Structural Steel
3442 Metal Doors, Sash, Frames, Molding & Trim
3443 Fabricated Plate Work
3444 Sheet Metal Work
3446 Architectural & Ornamental Metal Work
3448 Prefabricated Metal Buildings & Cmpnts
3449 Misc Structural Metal Work
3451 Screw Machine Prdts
3452 Bolts, Nuts, Screws, Rivets & Washers
3462 Iron & Steel Forgings
3463 Nonferrous Forgings
3465 Automotive Stampings
3469 Metal Stampings, NEC
3471 Electroplating, Plating, Polishing, Anodizing & Coloring
3479 Coating & Engraving, NEC
3482 Small Arms Ammunition
3483 Ammunition, Large
3484 Small Arms
3489 Ordnance & Access, NEC

3491 Industrial Valves
3492 Fluid Power Valves & Hose Fittings
3493 Steel Springs, Except Wire
3494 Valves & Pipe Fittings, NEC
3495 Wire Springs
3496 Misc Fabricated Wire Prdts
3498 Fabricated Pipe & Pipe Fittings
3499 Fabricated Metal Prdts, NEC

35 industrial and commercial machinery and computer equipment

3511 Steam, Gas & Hydraulic Turbines & Engines
3519 Internal Combustion Engines, NEC
3523 Farm Machinery & Eqpt
3524 Garden, Lawn Tractors & Eqpt
3531 Construction Machinery & Eqpt
3532 Mining Machinery & Eqpt
3533 Oil Field Machinery & Eqpt
3534 Elevators & Moving Stairways
3535 Conveyors & Eqpt
3536 Hoists, Cranes & Monorails
3537 Indl Trucks, Tractors, Trailers & Stackers
3541 Machine Tools: Cutting
3542 Machine Tools: Forming
3543 Industrial Patterns
3544 Dies, Tools, Jigs, Fixtures & Indl Molds
3545 Machine Tool Access
3546 Power Hand Tools
3547 Rolling Mill Machinery & Eqpt
3548 Welding Apparatus
3549 Metalworking Machinery, NEC
3552 Textile Machinery
3553 Woodworking Machinery
3555 Printing Trades Machinery & Eqpt
3556 Food Prdts Machinery
3559 Special Ind Machinery, NEC
3561 Pumps & Pumping Eqpt
3562 Ball & Roller Bearings
3563 Air & Gas Compressors
3564 Blowers & Fans
3565 Packaging Machinery
3566 Speed Changers, Drives & Gears
3567 Indl Process Furnaces & Ovens
3568 Mechanical Power Transmission Eqpt, NEC
3569 Indl Machinery & Eqpt, NEC
3571 Electronic Computers
3572 Computer Storage Devices
3575 Computer Terminals
3577 Computer Peripheral Eqpt, NEC
3578 Calculating & Accounting Eqpt
3579 Office Machines, NEC
3581 Automatic Vending Machines
3582 Commercial Laundry, Dry Clean & Pressing Mchs
3585 Air Conditioning & Heating Eqpt
3589 Service Ind Machines, NEC
3592 Carburetors, Pistons, Rings & Valves
3593 Fluid Power Cylinders & Actuators
3594 Fluid Power Pumps & Motors
3596 Scales & Balances, Exc Laboratory
3599 Machinery & Eqpt, Indl & Commercial, NEC

36 electronic and other electrical equipment and components, except computer

3612 Power, Distribution & Specialty Transformers
3613 Switchgear & Switchboard Apparatus
3621 Motors & Generators
3625 Relays & Indl Controls
3629 Electrical Indl Apparatus, NEC
3631 Household Cooking Eqpt
3632 Household Refrigerators & Freezers
3634 Electric Household Appliances
3635 Household Vacuum Cleaners
3639 Household Appliances, NEC
3641 Electric Lamps
3643 Current-Carrying Wiring Devices
3644 Noncurrent-Carrying Wiring Devices
3645 Residential Lighting Fixtures
3646 Commercial, Indl & Institutional Lighting Fixtures
3647 Vehicular Lighting Eqpt
3648 Lighting Eqpt, NEC

3651 Household Audio & Video Eqpt
3652 Phonograph Records & Magnetic Tape
3661 Telephone & Telegraph Apparatus
3663 Radio & T V Communications, Systs & Eqpt, Broadcast/Studio
3669 Communications Eqpt, NEC
3672 Printed Circuit Boards
3674 Semiconductors
3676 Electronic Resistors
3677 Electronic Coils & Transformers
3678 Electronic Connectors
3679 Electronic Components, NEC
3691 Storage Batteries
3692 Primary Batteries: Dry & Wet
3694 Electrical Eqpt For Internal Combustion Engines
3695 Recording Media
3699 Electrical Machinery, Eqpt & Splys, NEC

37 transportation equipment

3711 Motor Vehicles & Car Bodies
3713 Truck & Bus Bodies
3714 Motor Vehicle Parts & Access
3715 Truck Trailers
3716 Motor Homes
3721 Aircraft
3724 Aircraft Engines & Engine Parts
3728 Aircraft Parts & Eqpt, NEC
3731 Shipbuilding & Repairing
3732 Boat Building & Repairing
3743 Railroad Eqpt
3751 Motorcycles, Bicycles & Parts
3761 Guided Missiles & Space Vehicles
3769 Guided Missile/Space Vehicle Parts & Eqpt, NEC
3792 Travel Trailers & Campers
3795 Tanks & Tank Components
3799 Transportation Eqpt, NEC

38 measuring, analyzing and controlling instruments; photographic, medical an

3812 Search, Detection, Navigation & Guidance Systs & Instrs
3821 Laboratory Apparatus & Furniture
3822 Automatic Temperature Controls
3823 Indl Instruments For Meas, Display & Control
3824 Fluid Meters & Counters
3825 Instrs For Measuring & Testing Electricity
3826 Analytical Instruments
3827 Optical Instruments
3829 Measuring & Controlling Devices, NEC
3841 Surgical & Medical Instrs & Apparatus
3842 Orthopedic, Prosthetic & Surgical Appliances/Splys
3843 Dental Eqpt & Splys
3844 X-ray Apparatus & Tubes
3845 Electromedical & Electrotherapeutic Apparatus
3851 Ophthalmic Goods
3861 Photographic Eqpt & Splys

39 miscellaneous manufacturing industries

3911 Jewelry: Precious Metal
3914 Silverware, Plated & Stainless Steel Ware
3915 Jewelers Findings & Lapidary Work
3931 Musical Instruments
3942 Dolls & Stuffed Toys
3944 Games, Toys & Children's Vehicles
3949 Sporting & Athletic Goods, NEC
3952 Lead Pencils, Crayons & Artist's Mtrls
3953 Marking Devices
3955 Carbon Paper & Inked Ribbons
3961 Costume Jewelry & Novelties
3965 Fasteners, Buttons, Needles & Pins
3991 Brooms & Brushes
3993 Signs & Advertising Displays
3996 Linoleum & Hard Surface Floor Coverings, NEC
3999 Manufacturing Industries, NEC

73 business services

7372 Prepackaged Software

76 miscellaneous repair services

7692 Welding Repair
7694 Armature Rewinding Shops

SIC SECTION

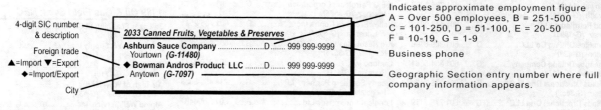

See footnotes for symbols and codes identification.

- The SIC codes in this section are from the latest Standard Industrial Classification manual published by the U.S. Government's Office of Management and Budget. For more information regarding SICs, see the Explanatory Notes.
- Companies may be listed under multiple classifications.

10 METAL MINING

1081 Metal Mining Svcs

Greater Gulf Development LLC ....G....... 228 392-6680
  Diberville *(G-1204)*
Nelsons Metal Inc.............................G....... 662 454-7500
  Dennis *(G-1184)*
Randy A Elder....................................G....... 504 301-7962
  Carriere *(G-700)*
TMC Exploration Inc ....G....... 601 807-1124
  Natchez *(G-3631)*

1099 Metal Ores, NEC

Hj Norris LLC......................................G....... 228 217-6704
  Moss Point *(G-3479)*
Pat S Pins ....G....... 662 562-8986
  Coldwater *(G-850)*

12 COAL MINING

1221 Bituminous Coal & Lignite: Surface Mining

Liberty Fuels Company LLC ....G....... 601 737-7000
  Ackerman *(G-25)*
Liberty Fuels Company LLC ....D....... 601 737-7000
  De Kalb *(G-1166)*
Mississippi Lignite Mining Co ....C....... 662 387-5200
  Ackerman *(G-28)*

1241 Coal Mining Svcs

Waste Placement Inc ....G....... 601 362-5343
  Jackson *(G-2625)*

13 OIL AND GAS EXTRACTION

1311 Crude Petroleum & Natural Gas

A & B Pump & Supply Inc ....G....... 601 787-3741
  Heidelberg *(G-2111)*
American Midstream ....G....... 601 671-8800
  Waynesboro *(G-5490)*
American Midstream LLC ....G....... 601 776-6721
  Quitman *(G-4456)*
American Midstream LLC ....G....... 601 798-9145
  Picayune *(G-4251)*
Anderson Oil Company Inc...............G....... 601 442-2960
  Natchez *(G-3520)*
Belle Oil Inc ....G....... 601 442-6648
  Natchez *(G-3528)*
Big Joe Oil Co Inc ....G....... 601 442-5481
  Natchez *(G-3530)*
Big Joe Operating Co Inc ....G....... 601 442-5481
  Natchez *(G-3531)*
Biglane Operating Co ....G....... 601 442-2783
  Natchez *(G-3532)*
Blue Lightning Enterprise LLC ....G....... 901 626-8587
  Olive Branch *(G-3820)*
BP America Production Company ....E....... 228 762-3996
  Moss Point *(G-3471)*
BP Corporation North Amer Inc ....E....... 228 712-3500
  Moss Point *(G-3472)*
Bruxoil Inc ....G....... 601 981-5722
  Jackson *(G-2346)*
Callon Offshore Production ....D....... 601 442-1601
  Natchez *(G-3542)*
Centerpint Enrgy Rsources Corp ......E....... 601 425-1461
  Laurel *(G-2750)*

Central Resources Inc ....G....... 601 776-3281
  Quitman *(G-4459)*
Cline Ltd ....G....... 601 649-6274
  Laurel *(G-2755)*
Craft Exploration Company LLC ......G....... 601 859-0077
  Canton *(G-655)*
Crosbys Creek Oil & Gas LLC ....G....... 601 898-0051
  Ridgeland *(G-4567)*
D & D Oilfield Consultants Inc ....G....... 601 648-2282
  State Line *(G-4985)*
David K Brooks ....G....... 601 981-5722
  Jackson *(G-2377)*
Denbury Resources Inc ....G....... 601 829-0398
  Brandon *(G-388)*
Devon Energy Corporation ....G....... 601 796-4243
  Lumberton *(G-3028)*
El Toro Production Co Inc ....G....... 601 442-4159
  Natchez *(G-3558)*
Enbridge Processing LLC ....G....... 601 671-8800
  Waynesboro *(G-5497)*
Exterran ....G....... 601 444-0055
  Columbia *(G-898)*
Gas Processors Inc ....F....... 601 736-1600
  Columbia *(G-899)*
Gusoil Inc ....G....... 601 735-2731
  Waynesboro *(G-5499)*
H O Hughes ....G....... 601 261-3302
  Hattiesburg *(G-1979)*
Howard E Stover ....G....... 601 984-3702
  Jackson *(G-2443)*
Hughes Eastern Corporation ....G....... 601 957-1778
  Ridgeland *(G-4590)*
Inland Energy Company Inc..............G....... 601 969-1160
  Jackson *(G-2446)*
J R Pounds Inc ....G....... 601 649-1743
  Laurel *(G-2785)*
James Biglane ....G....... 601 442-2783
  Natchez *(G-3571)*
James W Elliot Jr ....G....... 601 833-6201
  Brookhaven *(G-504)*
Joe Fortunato Oil Prodcr RES ....G....... 601 442-6397
  Natchez *(G-3572)*
Lion Oil Co ....G....... 601 933-3000
  Flowood *(G-1378)*
McGowan Working Partners Inc ....E....... 601 982-3444
  Jackson *(G-2484)*
Meason Operating Co ....F....... 601 442-3668
  Natchez *(G-3586)*
Moco Inc ....G....... 601 957-3550
  Ridgeland *(G-4609)*
MRC Global (us) Inc ....F....... 601 965-5275
  Jackson *(G-2512)*
Neal Clement Oil & Gas ....G....... 601 982-5667
  Jackson *(G-2518)*
New David Oil Company Inc ....F....... 601 442-1607
  Natchez *(G-3599)*
Partridge Production LLC ....G....... 601 987-4911
  Jackson *(G-2535)*
Petro-Hunt LLC ....G....... 601 636-3448
  Vicksburg *(G-5405)*
Petroci Usa Inc ....G....... 601 764-2222
  Bay Springs *(G-171)*
Phoenix Operating Inc ....G....... 601 866-2223
  Bolton *(G-313)*
Rosson Exploration Company ....G....... 601 969-2022
  Jackson *(G-2475)*
Roundtree & Associates Inc ....F....... 601 355-4530
  Ridgeland *(G-4625)*
S Lavon Evans Jr Oper Co Inc ....F....... 601 649-7639
  Laurel *(G-2841)*

South Central Group Inc ....G....... 601 445-5101
  Natchez *(G-3623)*
Taylor Energy Company LLC ....G....... 601 736-9997
  Foxworth *(G-1436)*
Tellus Operating Group LLC ....E....... 601 787-3014
  Heidelberg *(G-2119)*
Tellus Operating Group LLC ....G....... 601 898-7444
  Ridgeland *(G-4638)*
Texas Petroleum Investment Co ....G....... 601 796-4921
  Lumberton *(G-3039)*
US Oil Recovery LLC ....G....... 662 884-1050
  Indianola *(G-2271)*
Victor P Smith Oil Producers ....G....... 601 932-2223
  Jackson *(G-2673)*
Waller Bros Inc ....G....... 601 352-6556
  Jackson *(G-2624)*
Wayne A Potter ....G....... 601 446-6090
  Natchez *(G-3638)*
Wcs Oil & Gas Corporation ....G....... 601 787-4565
  Sandersville *(G-4726)*
Wilcox Energy Company ....G....... 601 442-5191
  Natchez *(G-3641)*

1321 Natural Gas Liquids

Gasmax Fltration Solutions LLC ....G....... 601 790-1225
  Ridgeland *(G-4586)*
Mgc Terminal LLC ....G....... 601 482-5012
  Meridian *(G-3371)*
Nicks One Stop Port Gbson LLC ....G....... 601 437-3380
  Port Gibson *(G-4404)*
Oakland Ylbsha Natural Gas Dst ....G....... 662 623-5005
  Oakland *(G-3738)*
Phae I Bobs ....G....... 662 332-3505
  Greenville *(G-1590)*
Pine Belt Gas Inc ....G....... 601 731-1144
  Columbia *(G-911)*
Ss Drilling LLC ....G....... 740 207-5673
  Brandon *(G-463)*

1381 Drilling Oil & Gas Wells

5 K Corp ....F....... 601 736-5367
  Columbia *(G-877)*
Akers Minerals LLC ....G....... 207 615-7591
  Houston *(G-2230)*
Armadillo Service Inc Alabama ....F....... 601 857-0440
  Raymond *(G-4484)*
Ccore Energy Holding Co LLC ....G....... 601 824-7900
  Brandon *(G-376)*
Coastal Petroleum Services Inc ....E....... 601 446-5888
  Natchez *(G-3547)*
Deepwell Energy Services LLC ....D....... 800 477-2855
  Columbia *(G-894)*
Deepwell Energy Services LLC ....E....... 601 735-1393
  Richland *(G-4512)*
Delta Petroleum Service Inc ....G....... 662 487-1701
  Sardis *(G-4738)*
E & D Services Inc ....E....... 601 649-9044
  Laurel *(G-2765)*
Energy Drilling Company ....C....... 601 446-5259
  Natchez *(G-3560)*
Expro Americas LLC ....E....... 281 576-5500
  Ellisville *(G-1251)*
Griffin Grffin Exploration LLC ....G....... 601 713-1146
  Jackson *(G-2432)*
Helmerich & Payne Intl Drlg Co ....F....... 601 939-1589
  Pearl *(G-4126)*
Jack Black Oil Company Inc ....G....... 601 442-2620
  Natchez *(G-3570)*
Kelley Brothers Contrs Inc ....D....... 601 735-2541
  Waynesboro *(G-5501)*

Employee Codes: A=Over 500 employees, B=251-500
C=101-250, D=51-100, E=20-50, F=10-19, G=1-9

2019 Harris Directory of Mississippi Manufacturers

13 OIL AND GAS EXTRACTION

SIC SECTION

Mc Consulting LLC ....G..... 601 735-2000
Waynesboro *(G-5506)*

Mike Lowery LLC ....G..... 601 736-1096
Foxworth *(G-1434)*

Navidad Petroleum LLC ....G..... 601 442-9812
Natchez *(G-3598)*

Performance Drilling Co LLC ....D..... 601 969-6796
Brandon *(G-433)*

Performance Drilling Company ....G..... 601 854-5661
Pelahatchie *(G-4171)*

River Rads Drectional Drlg LLC ...E..... 601 778-7179
Moselle *(G-3459)*

River Rads Drectional Drlg LLC ...G..... 601 778-7179
Laurel *(G-2837)*

Rocky BR Directional Drlg LLC ....G..... 601 758-3340
Sumrall *(G-5043)*

Saf-T Compliance Intl LLC ....G..... 601 684-9495
McComb *(G-3264)*

Schudco Ltd ....G..... 662 332-8678
Greenville *(G-1597)*

Vonco of Mississippi Inc ....G..... 601 446-7274
Natchez *(G-3634)*

W T Drilling Co Inc ....D..... 601 442-1607
Natchez *(G-3636)*

1382 Oil & Gas Field Exploration Svcs

Action Drilling Company Inc ....G..... 601 892-5105
Wesson *(G-5523)*

Aldridge Operating Co LLC ....G..... 601 446-5585
Natchez *(G-3517)*

Allen Petroleum Service Inc ....G..... 601 442-3562
Natchez *(G-3518)*

Bass Associates LLC ....G..... 601 943-5229
Bassfield *(G-90)*

Belle Exploration Inc ....G..... 601 442-6648
Natchez *(G-3527)*

Big Joe Oil Co Inc ....G..... 601 442-5481
Natchez *(G-3530)*

Blackstone Investments LLC ....G..... 601 978-1763
Ridgeland *(G-4557)*

Bob Bertolet ....G..... 601 442-0424
Natchez *(G-3535)*

Brandon Petroleum Properties .....G..... 601 649-2261
Laurel *(G-2743)*

Callon Offshore Production ....D..... 601 442-1601
Natchez *(G-3542)*

Ceco Corp ....G..... 601 362-4737
Jackson *(G-2356)*

Centerpoint Energy Inc ....F..... 228 588-2977
Moss Point *(G-3473)*

Craft Exploration Company LLC ....G..... 601 859-0077
Canton *(G-655)*

Craft Operating Company Ix LLC ...G..... 601 427-9009
Canton *(G-656)*

Crtney G Aldridge Ptro Glogist .....G..... 601 446-5585
Natchez *(G-3552)*

Denbury Onshore LLC ....E..... 601 787-3111
Heidelberg *(G-2115)*

Denbury Onshore LLC ....E..... 601 276-2147
Ruth *(G-4700)*

Denbury Resources Inc ....G..... 601 729-2266
Soso *(G-4846)*

Denbury Resources Inc ....G..... 601 687-0089
Shubuta *(G-4830)*

Denbury Resources Inc ....G..... 601 835-0185
Brookhaven *(G-490)*

Denbury Resources Inc ....F..... 601 276-2677
Summit *(G-5011)*

Denbury Resources Inc ....F..... 601 823-4000
Brookhaven *(G-491)*

Durango Operating LLC ....F..... 601 420-2525
Ridgeland *(G-4575)*

Eastern Group LLC ....G..... 662 332-1890
Greenville *(G-1552)*

Ergon - St James Inc ....G..... 601 933-3000
Flowood *(G-1356)*

Erickson Oil ....G..... 601 362-7401
Jackson *(G-2403)*

Foil J Branton ....G..... 601 876-9678
Tylertown *(G-5270)*

Geo Seis Processing Inc ....G..... 601 936-0334
Jackson *(G-2424)*

Griffin Grffin Exploration LLC ....G..... 601 713-1146
Jackson *(G-2432)*

Intrepid Drilling LLC ....G..... 601 731-1010
Columbia *(G-901)*

Jiffy Mart ....G..... 601 947-6589
Lucedale *(G-3004)*

Julius Whittington ....G..... 601 532-6519
Meadville *(G-3276)*

Jura-Search Inc ....G..... 601 932-0002
Jackson *(G-2461)*

K F G Petroleum Corporation ....G..... 601 446-5219
Natchez *(G-3575)*

Kelley Brothers Contrs Inc ....D..... 601 735-2541
Waynesboro *(G-5501)*

Kfg Resources Ltd ....G..... 601 446-5219
Natchez *(G-3576)*

Lamoco Inc ....G..... 601 919-3777
Brandon *(G-411)*

Liberty Southern Partners LP ....G..... 214 450-8838
Ridgeland *(G-4598)*

Longleaf Enterprises Ltd ....F..... 601 225-4481
Gloster *(G-1516)*

Louisiana Well Service Co Inc ....G..... 601 442-6648
Natchez *(G-3580)*

Magee Energy LLC ....G..... 601 709-2930
Flowood *(G-1379)*

Manning Drilling Company Inc ......G..... 601 989-2805
Richton *(G-4539)*

Medical Clinic ....G..... 601 587-7795
Monticello *(G-3436)*

Miller Land Professionals LLC ....G..... 601 969-1160
Jackson *(G-2493)*

Moon-Hns-Tigrett Operating Inc ...G..... 601 572-8300
Ridgeland *(G-4610)*

Natchez Exploration LLC ....G..... 601 442-7400
Natchez *(G-3594)*

Neill Oil LLC ....G..... 601 984-9000
Jackson *(G-2519)*

On The River LLC ....G..... 601 442-7103
Natchez *(G-3603)*

Oolite Investments Inc ....G..... 601 853-0408
Madison *(G-3135)*

Pangaea Exploration Inc ....G..... 228 452-7544
Pass Christian *(G-4092)*

Par-Co Drilling Inc ....G..... 601 442-6421
Natchez *(G-3605)*

Paradise & Associates Inc ....G..... 601 445-9710
Natchez *(G-3606)*

Phoenix Energy Inc Mississippi .....F..... 601 445-3200
Natchez *(G-3607)*

Pistol Ridge Partners LLC ....G..... 601 649-7639
Laurel *(G-2823)*

Pledger Petroleum Inc ....G..... 601 442-9871
Natchez *(G-3608)*

Radzewicz Explration Drlg Corp ....F..... 601 445-8659
Natchez *(G-3610)*

Ram Petroleum LLC ....G..... 601 876-0807
Tylertown *(G-5281)*

Shamrock Drilling Inc ....F..... 601 442-0785
Natchez *(G-3619)*

Solomon Energy LLC ....G..... 601 607-3070
Madison *(G-3148)*

South Carlton Operating Co LLC ...G..... 601 446-5992
Natchez *(G-3622)*

Southern Flow ....G..... 601 591-1526
Brandon *(G-460)*

Southern Land Exploration Inc .....G..... 662 369-7390
Prairie *(G-4413)*

Spooner Petroleum Inc ....G..... 601 969-1831
Ridgeland *(G-4634)*

Stringers Oilfield Service ....E..... 601 736-4498
Columbia *(G-924)*

T O Kimbrell LLC ....G..... 601 446-6099
Natchez *(G-3629)*

Telpico LLC ....G..... 601 898-7444
Ridgeland *(G-4639)*

Tenrgys LLC ....G..... 601 898-7444
Ridgeland *(G-4640)*

Tim Blake ....G..... 662 256-8218
Nettleton *(G-3668)*

Travis Exploration Inc ....G..... 601 879-8664
Flora *(G-1313)*

Trinity River Energy Oper LLC ....G..... 601 792-9686
Newhebron *(G-3715)*

Triple S Well Service Inc ....F..... 601 736-8804
Columbia *(G-926)*

Trophy Petroleum Corporation .....G..... 601 298-0200
Carthage *(G-725)*

Valioso Petroleum Company ....G..... 601 936-3601
Flowood *(G-1405)*

Van Petroleum Inc ....G..... 601 982-8728
Jackson *(G-2620)*

Venture Oil & Gas Inc ....F..... 601 428-3653
Laurel *(G-2862)*

Waller Bros Inc ....G..... 601 352-6556
Jackson *(G-2624)*

Walter Allen ....G..... 601 924-1956
Clinton *(G-838)*

Watkins Jr H Vaughn ....G..... 601 898-9347
Jackson *(G-2627)*

1389 Oil & Gas Field Svcs, NEC

3d Laser Scanning LLC ....G..... 228 860-5952
Biloxi *(G-214)*

A & B Pump & Supply Inc ....G..... 601 787-3741
Heidelberg *(G-2111)*

Agmyns ....G..... 228 831-0342
Gulfport *(G-1716)*

Air Tech of Waveland ....G..... 228 467-7547
Bay Saint Louis *(G-133)*

Alpine Well Service Inc ....G..... 601 442-0021
Natchez *(G-3519)*

Archh LLC ....G..... 601 590-3519
Carriere *(G-687)*

Archrock Inc ....G..... 601 444-0055
Columbia *(G-880)*

Armadillo Service Inc Alabama .....F..... 601 857-0440
Raymond *(G-4484)*

B & B Oil Well Service Co Inc ....F..... 601 425-3836
Ellisville *(G-1246)*

B & P Swab Service Inc ....E..... 601 731-6309
Columbia *(G-881)*

Baker Hghes Olfld Oprtions LLC ....F..... 601 649-4400
Laurel *(G-2733)*

Baker Hghes Olfld Oprtions LLC ....G..... 601 649-2704
Laurel *(G-2734)*

Baker Hughes A GE Company LLC ..E..... 601 731-5004
Columbia *(G-882)*

Baker Hughes A GE Company LLC ..G..... 601 649-7400
Laurel *(G-2735)*

Baker Hughes A GE Company LLC ..G..... 601 649-1955
Laurel *(G-2736)*

Baker Hughes A GE Company LLC ..F..... 601 649-4400
Laurel *(G-2737)*

Baker Hughes A GE Company LLC ..G..... 601 425-1599
Laurel *(G-2738)*

Baker Petrolite LLC ....F..... 601 649-1955
Laurel *(G-2739)*

Bap Services Inc ....G..... 662 343-5216
Hamilton *(G-1903)*

Bayou Oil Fill Supply LLC ....G..... 601 446-6284
Natchez *(G-3524)*

Bobbys Indus & Oilfield Repr ....G..... 601 833-3050
Brookhaven *(G-483)*

Brazos Bend Oil and Gas LLC ....G..... 601 982-3444
Jackson *(G-2342)*

C & F Swabbing Inc ....G..... 601 687-1171
Shubuta *(G-4827)*

Cam2 International LLC ....E..... 601 661-5382
Vicksburg *(G-5350)*

Cam2 International LLC ....G..... 800 338-2262
Vicksburg *(G-5351)*

Cameron International Corp ....G..... 601 649-8900
Laurel *(G-2747)*

Cameron International Corp ....G..... 601 425-2377
Laurel *(G-2748)*

Cases Body & Paint ....G..... 601 833-3153
Brookhaven *(G-486)*

Cavins Corporation ....G..... 601 833-2268
Brookhaven *(G-487)*

Cavins Corporation ....G..... 601 428-0670
Laurel *(G-2749)*

Ccore Energy/Mariner LLC ....G..... 601 824-7900
Brandon *(G-377)*

Challnger Dpwell Servicing Inc ......E..... 601 736-2511
Columbia *(G-885)*

Clarkco Services Inc ....D..... 601 787-3447
Heidelberg *(G-2114)*

Clifford A Crosby ....G..... 228 234-1649
Biloxi *(G-230)*

Community Construction Co LLC ....E..... 601 894-5239
Hazlehurst *(G-2092)*

Consolidated Gulf Services LLC .....S..... 601 446-5992
Natchez *(G-3549)*

Cornwell Well Service Inc ....E..... 601 684-4951
Summit *(G-5009)*

Crisco Swabbing Service Inc ....E..... 601 731-9008
Columbia *(G-892)*

Cyrus Resources LLC ....G..... 228 669-6955
Gulfport *(G-1767)*

Danny Byrd LLC ....E..... 601 649-2524
Laurel *(G-2758)*

DAvion LLC ....G..... 601 724-5013
Brandon *(G-385)*

Delta Directional Drilling LLC ....C..... 601 683-0879
Newton *(G-3719)*

Delta Royalty Company Inc ....G..... 601 982-0970
Jackson *(G-2382)*

2019 Harris Directory of
Mississippi Manufacturers

208

SIC SECTION

14 MINING AND QUARRYING OF NONMETALLIC MINERALS, EXCEPT FUELS

Denbury Resources Inc ....G 972 673-2787
Pelahatchie *(G-4163)*

Dipstix Lube ....G 662 349-2810
Southaven *(G-4869)*

Dixie Oilfield Services Inc ....G 601 731-5541
Columbia *(G-896)*

Dixie Oilfield Supply LLC ....G 601 408-6027
Laurel *(G-2761)*

Dixie Services and Supply LLC .....G 662 369-0907
Aberdeen *(G-11)*

Dnow LP ....G 601 649-8671
Laurel *(G-2762)*

Donald L McKinnon ....G 601 319-3311
Laurel *(G-2763)*

Dozer Inc ....F 601 442-1671
Natchez *(G-3556)*

Duckwrth Drlg Completion L L C ...G 601 848-6486
State Line *(G-4986)*

Eastern Fishing & Rental Tl Co .....D 601 649-1454
Laurel *(G-2766)*

Elite Const and Design ....G 662 307-2494
Grenada *(G-1675)*

Fisher Construction Company ....E 769 257-9969
Jackson *(G-2408)*

Fowler Consulting LLC ....G 601 761-3696
Flora *(G-1306)*

Gasmax Fltration Solutions LLC .....G 601 790-1225
Ridgeland *(G-4586)*

GE Oil & Gas Pressure Ctrl LP ......G 601 425-1436
Laurel *(G-2769)*

Giexco LLC ....G 662 352-1128
Brooksville *(G-553)*

Gulf Pine Energy LP ....E 587 287-5400
Newhebron *(G-3712)*

Halliburton Energy Services ....D 601 649-9290
Sandersville *(G-4725)*

Harbour Energy Inc ....G 601 992-2277
Brandon *(G-403)*

Henry Lyell ....G 601 355-1080
Jackson *(G-2438)*

Hicks Hot Shot Services LLC ....G 601 498-7482
Stringer *(G-5001)*

Inland Energy Company Inc ....G 601 969-1160
Jackson *(G-2446)*

Integrity Hot Shot Svcs LLC ....G 601 850-8881
Ridgeland *(G-4593)*

J & K Services LLC ....G 601 310-7728
Lumberton *(G-3032)*

Jack Black Oil Company Inc ....G 601 442-2620
Natchez *(G-3570)*

James R Padgett ....G 601 763-3369
Ellisville *(G-1260)*

Jones Ldscp & Contrs Svc LLC .....G 601 780-2042
Jackson *(G-2460)*

Jwb Construction LLC ....F 601 439-7190
Mize *(G-3427)*

Kdh Trucking LLC ....G 601 730-2052
Liberty *(G-2913)*

Kelley Brothers Contrs Inc ....D 601 735-2541
Waynesboro *(G-5501)*

Kenan Transportation ....G 662 332-4223
Greenville *(G-1561)*

Kkam Services LLC ....G 903 707-0110
Wiggins *(G-5585)*

Lee & Lee Services Inc ....F 601 425-1060
Laurel *(G-2794)*

Lee Small Engines Inc ....G 601 833-5431
Brookhaven *(G-510)*

Lees Hot Shot Service LLC ....G 601 383-1018
Florence *(G-1326)*

Liberty Oilfield Services & RE ....G 601 398-8511
Liberty *(G-2915)*

Logan Oil Field Services ....G 601 787-4407
Waynesboro *(G-5504)*

Louisiana Well Service Co Inc ....G 601 442-6648
Natchez *(G-3580)*

Mapp Oilfield Services Inc ....E 601 835-2013
Brookhaven *(G-515)*

Mark A Whitney ....G 601 575-4952
Philadelphia *(G-4224)*

Masco Wireline Service Inc ....E 601 428-7966
Laurel *(G-2797)*

Mid-South Contractors Inc ....G 601 544-2803
Ellisville *(G-1264)*

Mk Oilfield Service ....G 662 328-2510
Columbus *(G-1005)*

Moncla Companies ....E 601 428-4322
Laurel *(G-2805)*

Multi-Chem Group LLC ....F 601 425-1131
Laurel *(G-2809)*

Newpark Drilling Fluids LLC ....F 281 362-6800
Summit *(G-5018)*

Odat Energy LLC ....G 601 736-0227
Columbia *(G-908)*

Oil Tools & Supplies Inc ....G 601 446-7229
Natchez *(G-3602)*

Oil Well Logging Company Inc ....G 601 477-8315
Brandon *(G-430)*

Oil Well Logging Company Inc ....G 601 477-8315
Ellisville *(G-1265)*

Oilfield Partners Energy ....G 601 444-0220
Columbia *(G-909)*

Oilfield Service & Sup Co Inc ....E 601 649-4461
Laurel *(G-2813)*

Old Ges Inc ....G 601 649-4920
Laurel *(G-2814)*

Pecanier Oil & Gas LLC ....G 601 982-3444
Jackson *(G-2538)*

Pierce Well Service ....G 601 947-4548
Agricola *(G-30)*

Pine Belt Energy Services LLC ......C 601 796-3299
Lumberton *(G-3037)*

Pioneer Well Service ....E 601 399-1648
Laurel *(G-2821)*

Pitts Swabbing Service Inc ....E 601 422-0111
Laurel *(G-2824)*

Power Torque Services LLC ....G 601 835-2600
Brookhaven *(G-524)*

Premium Oilfield Services ....G 601 425-5211
Laurel *(G-2825)*

Pryor Packers Inc ....F 601 649-4535
Laurel *(G-2829)*

Q P P Inc ....G 662 356-4848
Caledonia *(G-629)*

Quality Drilling Fluids Inc ....F 601 477-9085
Ellisville *(G-1267)*

R W Delaney Construction Co ....D 601 442-0352
Natchez *(G-3609)*

Radco Fishing & Rental Tls Inc ......G 601 736-8580
Columbia *(G-917)*

Radzewicz Explration Drlg Corp .....F 601 445-8659
Natchez *(G-3610)*

Rainbow Rentl Fishing Tls Inc ....F 601 425-3309
Laurel *(G-2833)*

Ralph Craven LLC ....G 601 425-0294
Laurel *(G-2834)*

Rapad Drilling & Well Services ....G 601 649-0760
Jackson *(G-2559)*

Rapad Drilling & Well Services ....G 601 649-0760
Laurel *(G-2835)*

Rega Environmental Inc ....F 228 447-1024
Diberville *(G-1210)*

Richard E Johnson ....G 601 735-4737
Waynesboro *(G-5512)*

Rig Managers Inc ....G 601 362-5121
Jackson *(G-2565)*

Roger Welch ....G 601 649-3767
Laurel *(G-2839)*

Rosson Exlopartion Company ....G 601 969-2022
Jackson *(G-2569)*

Roundtree & Associates Inc ....F 601 355-4530
Ridgeland *(G-4625)*

Rufus M Chancellor ....G 601 776-5557
Quitman *(G-4471)*

Schlumberger Technology Corp ......F 601 649-3200
Laurel *(G-2846)*

Schlumberger Technology Corp ......F 601 442-7481
Natchez *(G-3616)*

Secorp Indus & Safety Sups Inc .....F 601 422-0203
Laurel *(G-2847)*

SJ Ellington Inc ....G 228 369-0089
Ocean Springs *(G-3786)*

Southeastern E & P Svcs Inc ....G 601 849-9218
Magee *(G-3186)*

Southeastern Oilfield Pdts LLC ......G 601 428-0603
Laurel *(G-2851)*

Southern Petroleum Labs Inc ....G 601 428-0842
Laurel *(G-2854)*

Springer Trckg & Car Crushing ......F 601 649-4238
Laurel *(G-2855)*

St Engineer Halter Marine and ....D 228 762-0010
Pascagoula *(G-4068)*

Stringers Oilfield Service ....E 601 736-4498
Columbia *(G-924)*

Sunbelt Resources Inc ....G 601 853-8195
Ridgeland *(G-4636)*

Swd Acidizing Inc ....G 601 442-7172
Natchez *(G-3626)*

Synergy Service and Supply LLC ....G 601 597-9902
Natchez *(G-3627)*

Synergy Service and Supply LLC ....F 601 492-4000
Natchez *(G-3628)*

T & T Welding Inc ....E 601 477-2884
Ellisville *(G-1270)*

T & T Welding Yard Inc ....E 601 477-2299
Ellisville *(G-1271)*

T K Stanley Inc ....C 601 735-2855
Columbia *(G-925)*

T K Stanley Inc ....E 601 735-2855
Waynesboro *(G-5517)*

Taylor Construction Co Inc ....D 601 426-2987
Laurel *(G-2857)*

Thomas E Windham Pumping ....G 601 764-3965
Bay Springs *(G-174)*

Thompson Services Inc ....F 662 369-9102
Hamilton *(G-1907)*

Timothy R Oglesby ....G 601 835-0673
Bogue Chitto *(G-306)*

Tj Scarbrough Inc ....F 601 648-9987
Buckatunna *(G-566)*

Transfrac Logistics LLC ....G 479 659-8186
Vicksburg *(G-5429)*

Tri Resources Inc ....G 601 583-8711
Petal *(G-4197)*

Tri-State Environmental LLC ....E 888 554-9792
Petal *(G-4198)*

Triple S Well Service Inc ....F 601 736-8804
Columbia *(G-926)*

U S Safety Services Inc ....G 601 833-3627
Wesson *(G-5531)*

U S Weatherford L P ....G 601 428-1551
Laurel *(G-2860)*

V A Sauls Inc ....D 601 787-4321
Heidelberg *(G-2120)*

Vapor Oilfield Services LLC ....G 601 741-7171
Conehatta *(G-1055)*

Varco LP ....F 601 428-1555
Laurel *(G-2861)*

Vines Operating Company Inc ....G 601 442-8034
Church Hill *(G-755)*

▲ Vmi Marine Inc ....D 601 636-8700
Vicksburg *(G-5443)*

W L S Inc ....G 601 687-1761
Shubuta *(G-4834)*

W L S Inc ....F 601 687-1761
Shubuta *(G-4835)*

W S Red Hancock Inc ....F 662 755-0011
Bentonia *(G-213)*

W S Red Hancock Inc ....C 601 399-0605
Ellisville *(G-1275)*

Walker Parris ....G 601 953-3023
Port Gibson *(G-4409)*

Warrior Energy Services Corp ....F 601 425-9684
Laurel *(G-2868)*

Weatherford Artificia ....G 601 649-4467
Laurel *(G-2871)*

Welco Inc ....G 601 445-9851
Natchez *(G-3639)*

Well Logging Solutions LLC ....G 601 416-9241
Kosciusko *(G-2720)*

Werth Servicing LLC ....G 662 449-4410
Hernando *(G-2161)*

Williams Companies Inc ....G 662 895-7202
Byhalia *(G-612)*

Williams Transportation Co LLC .....D 601 428-2214
Laurel *(G-2874)*

14 MINING AND QUARRYING OF NONMETALLIC MINERALS, EXCEPT FUELS

1411 Dimension Stone

Avalon Marble LLC ....F 601 798-3378
Picayune *(G-4253)*

1422 Crushed & Broken Limestone

McDevitt Enterprises LLC ....G 601 453-2290
Meridian *(G-3365)*

Tropical World Intl LLC ....G 228 229-8413
Biloxi *(G-285)*

Two-J Ranch Inc ....G 601 445-8540
Natchez *(G-3632)*

1423 Crushed & Broken Granite

Martin Marietta Materials Inc ....G 662 383-2070
Friars Point *(G-1443)*

Martin Marietta Materials Inc ....G 601 859-4488
Canton *(G-669)*

Employee Codes: A=Over 500 employees, B=251-500
C=101-250, D=51-100, E=20-50, F=10-19, G=1-9

14 MINING AND QUARRYING OF NONMETALLIC MINERALS, EXCEPT FUELS

Martin Marietta Materials Inc................G....... 662 652-3836
Tremont *(G-5093)*

1442 Construction Sand & Gravel

Apac-Mississippi Inc.........................D....... 662 328-6555
Columbus *(G-936)*
Baldwin Sand & Gravel........................G....... 662 834-6167
Lexington *(G-2897)*
Bell Gravel Co Inc..............................G....... 228 452-2872
Long Beach *(G-2929)*
Bill Phillips Sand & Grav LLC...............G....... 662 284-6061
Corinth *(G-1061)*
Bullocks Gravel Service Inc.................G....... 601 833-7034
Brookhaven *(G-484)*
D M Yount Gravel..............................G....... 662 292-1040
Senatobia *(G-4791)*
Delta Industries Inc..........................E....... 601 948-4245
Crystal Springs *(G-1141)*
Doug McCormick..............................G....... 662 256-9506
Amory *(G-41)*
Ellis Dozer LLC..................................G....... 601 752-2207
Seminary *(G-4778)*
Florence Parker................................G....... 662 434-8555
Columbus *(G-975)*
Green Brothers Gravel Co Inc..............E....... 601 362-3620
Crystal Springs *(G-1143)*
Hammett Gravel Co Inc......................G....... 662 834-1867
Lexington *(G-2903)*
Hard Rock Sand & Gravel...................G....... 601 876-2929
Tylertown *(G-5271)*
Honnoll Sand & Gravel LLC................G....... 662 487-3854
Sardis *(G-4740)*
Huey P Stockstill LLC.......................C....... 601 798-2981
Picayune *(G-4273)*
Hutchinson Island Mining Corp...........F....... 601 799-4070
Picayune *(G-4274)*
J J Ferguson Sand & Grav Inc...........C....... 662 453-5451
Greenwood *(G-1630)*
Jh Dirt & Gravel Llc...........................G....... 601 831-3990
Vicksburg *(G-5382)*
Johnstons Sand & Gravel Inc.............E....... 601 787-4326
Heidelberg *(G-2118)*
Jordon Construction LLC...................G....... 601 502-6019
Terry *(G-5071)*
Kelly Dirt & Gravel LLC......................G....... 662 231-0249
Shannon *(G-4812)*
Kenneths Excavation Demo................G....... 662 379-6771
Greenville *(G-1562)*
Lag Constructors..............................G....... 601 720-0404
Madison *(G-3118)*
Legacy Vulcan LLC............................G....... 662 357-7675
Lake Cormorant *(G-2725)*
Legacy Vulcan LLC............................G....... 601 947-9717
Lucedale *(G-3008)*
Legacy Vulcan LLC............................G....... 601 553-2902
Meridian *(G-3358)*
Legacy Vulcan LLC............................G....... 228 522-6011
Gautier *(G-1496)*
Legacy Vulcan LLC............................F....... 601 482-7007
Meridian *(G-3359)*
Legacy Vulcan LLC............................G....... 601 631-8833
Jackson *(G-2467)*
Lehman-Roberts Company..................F....... 662 429-5237
Hernando *(G-2138)*
Magnolia Frac Sand..........................G....... 601 446-6023
Natchez *(G-3582)*
Malone Design & Contg LLC...............G....... 601 807-1279
Hattiesburg *(G-2020)*
McCoy Farms & Gravel......................G....... 601 847-5962
Mendenhall *(G-3284)*
Mississippi Sand Solutions LL.........G....... 870 291-8802
Vicksburg *(G-5397)*
MMC Materials Inc............................D....... 601 634-8787
Vicksburg *(G-5399)*
Nelson Materials Inc.........................D....... 662 563-4972
Batesville *(G-115)*
Newell Sand & Gravel........................G....... 228 832-1215
Gulfport *(G-1837)*
North Simpson Gravel Co...................G....... 601 847-9500
Mendenhall *(G-3286)*
Paul Bolling......................................F....... 601 466-3398
Leakesville *(G-2878)*
Pen/Ron Company Inc........................G....... 601 519-5096
Brandon *(G-431)*
Pine Creek LLC..................................G....... 601 255-5036
Hattiesburg *(G-2044)*
Prestige Cnstr & Land Svcs LLC.........G....... 228 861-1292
Gulfport *(G-1852)*
Rebecca McCallum............................G....... 662 501-0709
Byhalia *(G-599)*

Richard Price Batton.........................G....... 601 892-5678
Crystal Springs *(G-1153)*
River Road Sand & Gravel LLC............G....... 601 582-9662
Hattiesburg *(G-2052)*
River Rock and Sand Co.....................G....... 601 798-4292
Picayune *(G-4292)*
Shale Energy Support LLC.................D....... 601 798-7821
Picayune *(G-4295)*
Shear View Mulching LLC...................G....... 985 637-8402
Poplarville *(G-4393)*
Smith Gravel and Trucking LLC..........G....... 228 518-0766
Poplarville *(G-4394)*
Spectrum III Limited.........................G....... 662 234-2461
Oxford *(G-4005)*
St Catherine Gravel Co Inc................G....... 601 442-1674
Washington *(G-5462)*
Standard Gravel Co Inc......................G....... 601 584-6436
Hattiesburg *(G-2068)*
Strayhorn Trucking & Cnstr LLC.........G....... 662 560-6516
Sarah *(G-4736)*
Uphill Construction LLC.....................G....... 662 299-9654
Greenwood *(G-1654)*
Valley Farms.....................................E....... 662 738-5861
Brooksville *(G-558)*
W E Blain & Sons Inc.........................E....... 601 442-3032
Natchez *(G-3635)*
W F Ferguson....................................G....... 601 453-1093
Greenwood *(G-1664)*

1446 Industrial Sand

Blue Note Management LLC................F....... 662 281-1881
Oxford *(G-3943)*

1455 Kaolin & Ball Clay

Clay Kentucky-Tennessee Co..............E....... 662 382-5262
Crenshaw *(G-1132)*

1459 Clay, Ceramic & Refractory Minerals, NEC

Clay Kentucky-Tennessee Co..............E....... 662 382-5262
Crenshaw *(G-1132)*
Imerys Minerals Usa Inc.....................F....... 662 369-6411
Aberdeen *(G-14)*
Wheat Construction Inc.....................G....... 601 772-9074
Poplarville *(G-4399)*

1474 Potash, Soda & Borate Minerals

▲ **Terra Mississippi Nitrogen Inc**..........B....... 662 746-4131
Yazoo City *(G-5649)*

1479 Chemical & Fertilizer Mining

N-R-G Chemical Company...................G....... 601 519-5363
Laurel *(G-2810)*

1499 Miscellaneous Nonmetallic Mining

Walter L Perrigin..............................G....... 662 240-0056
Columbus *(G-1042)*

20 FOOD AND KINDRED PRODUCTS

2011 Meat Packing Plants

B and L Meat Processing...................G....... 601 218-0918
Vicksburg *(G-5343)*
Boon Docks Deer Processing...............G....... 601 789-5843
Raleigh *(G-4474)*
Boswell Meat Processing...................G....... 601 656-6015
Philadelphia *(G-4208)*
Dwights Custom Deer Processing.......G....... 601 857-2324
Raymond *(G-4487)*
Enslin and Son Packing Company........E....... 601 582-9300
Hattiesburg *(G-1963)*
Family Meat Processing.....................G....... 601 264-2344
Sumrall *(G-5036)*
Forbes Meat Processors....................G....... 601 736-6992
Sandy Hook *(G-4728)*
Fortenberrys Meat Processing............G....... 601 876-2291
Sandy Hook *(G-4729)*
Fortenberrys Slaughter House............G....... 601 798-2156
Carriere *(G-692)*
▲ **Kershenstines Beef Jerky Inc**...........G....... 662 258-2049
Eupora *(G-1288)*
Mississippi Poultry...........................G....... 601 732-8670
Morton *(G-3450)*
Murrays Deer Processing....................G....... 601 720-2769
Macon *(G-3068)*
Natchez Smokehouse & Cold Stor......G....... 601 442-6116
Natchez *(G-3597)*

Pitcocks Meat Processing Inc.............G....... 662 563-9627
Pope *(G-4372)*
Polks Meat Products Inc....................C....... 601 849-9997
Magee *(G-3180)*
Prestage Farms Inc............................C....... 662 494-0813
West Point *(G-5560)*
Rutn Cutn Deer Processing.................G....... 601 892-5527
Crystal Springs *(G-1154)*
Sanderson Farms Inc Proc Div............A....... 601 684-9375
Summit *(G-5021)*
Smokehouse Meats...........................G....... 662 489-5764
Pontotoc *(G-4362)*
Stevens Packing................................G....... 601 795-6999
Poplarville *(G-4395)*
Sullivans Custom Processing.............G....... 662 773-2839
Preston *(G-4428)*
T and S Deer Processing....................G....... 601 727-3725
Rose Hill *(G-4685)*
Tyson Foods Inc................................G....... 601 664-9102
Pearl *(G-4155)*
Tyson Foods Inc................................E....... 601 469-1712
Forest *(G-1427)*

2013 Sausages & Meat Prdts

▲ **Bryant Meats Inc**..............................E....... 601 785-6507
Taylorsville *(G-5052)*
Enslin and Son Packing Company........E....... 601 582-9300
Hattiesburg *(G-1963)*
Fortenberrys Slaughter House............G....... 601 798-2156
Carriere *(G-692)*
Hillshire Brands Company...................B....... 662 890-6069
Olive Branch *(G-3848)*
Hillshire Brands Company...................G....... 601 948-4632
Jackson *(G-2441)*
Honey Baked.....................................G....... 228 875-5828
Ocean Springs *(G-3764)*
▲ **Kershenstines Beef Jerky Inc**...........G....... 662 258-2049
Eupora *(G-1288)*
Sanderson Farms Inc Foods Div..........B....... 601 939-9790
Flowood *(G-1394)*
Tonys King of Steaks Inc...................G....... 228 214-9668
Gulfport *(G-1884)*

2015 Poultry Slaughtering, Dressing & Processing

B & S Farms......................................G....... 601 656-5157
Philadelphia *(G-4206)*
Cal-Maine Foods Inc.........................D....... 601 852-4970
Edwards *(G-1236)*
Cal-Maine Foods Inc.........................G....... 601 852-4413
Edwards *(G-1237)*
Country Farms Quail..........................G....... 601 947-4263
Lucedale *(G-2991)*
Debbie F Shelton..............................G....... 601 535-7162
Pattison *(G-4100)*
Delta Duck Hunts Inc.........................G....... 662 357-5152
Dundee *(G-1223)*
Dg Foods LLC....................................B....... 601 892-0333
Hazlehurst *(G-2094)*
▼ **Koch Foods of Mississippi LLC**.........E....... 601 732-8911
Flowood *(G-1374)*
Koch Foods of Mississippi LLC...........B....... 601 469-2337
Forest *(G-1421)*
Koch Foods of Mississippi LLC...........E....... 601 732-3026
Morton *(G-3449)*
Marshall Durbin Food Corp.................F....... 601 969-1248
Jackson *(G-2483)*
Marshall Durbin Food Corp.................A....... 601 544-3141
Hattiesburg *(G-2021)*
Peco Foods Inc..................................A....... 601 859-6161
Canton *(G-675)*
Peco Foods Inc..................................A....... 601 764-4964
Bay Springs *(G-169)*
Peco Foods Inc..................................C....... 662 738-5771
Brooksville *(G-557)*
Peco Foods Inc..................................C....... 601 656-1865
Philadelphia *(G-4231)*
Peco Foods Inc..................................A....... 601 764-4392
Bay Springs *(G-170)*
Peco Foods Inc..................................C....... 601 855-0925
Canton *(G-676)*
Peco Foods Inc..................................B....... 601 625-7819
Sebastopol *(G-4775)*
Sammy Evans Poultry.........................G....... 601 267-0521
Carthage *(G-723)*
◆ **Sanderson Farms Inc**.......................C....... 601 649-4030
Laurel *(G-2842)*
Sanderson Farms Inc.........................G....... 601 426-1316
Ellisville *(G-1268)*

SIC SECTION

20 FOOD AND KINDRED PRODUCTS

Sanderson Farms Inc ....B 601 894-3721
Hazlehurst (G-2103)
Sanderson Farms Inc Foods Div ....B 601 939-9790
Flowood (G-1394)
Sanderson Farms Inc Proc Div ....A 601 765-8211
Collins (G-861)
▼ Sanderson Farms Inc Proc Div ....C 601 649-4030
Laurel (G-2844)
Sanderson Farms Inc Proc Div ....A 601 428-5261
Laurel (G-2845)
Sanderson Farms Inc Proc Div ....A 601 684-9375
Summit (G-5021)
Sanderson Farms Inc Prod Div ....B 601 765-2221
Collins (G-862)
Shamrock Farm ....G 601 277-3053
Hazlehurst (G-2105)
Tyson Foods Inc ....E 601 298-5300
Carthage (G-726)
Tyson Foods Inc ....G 229 995-6800
Forest (G-1426)
Tyson Foods Inc ....C 601 849-3351
Magee (G-3187)
Tyson Foods Inc ....A 601 631-3600
Vicksburg (G-5431)
Water Valley Poultry Inc ....E 662 473-0016
Water Valley (G-5477)
Wayne Farms LLC ....C 601 425-4721
Laurel (G-2869)
Wayne Farms LLC ....C 601 399-7000
Laurel (G-2870)
William R Gatewood ....G 601 636-0107
Vicksburg (G-5446)

2022 Cheese

Marathon Cheese Corporation ....D 662 728-6242
Booneville (G-333)
Mississippi Cheese Straw Fctry ....F 662 746-7171
Yazoo City (G-5640)

2023 Milk, Condensed & Evaporated

Xooma Worldwide ....G 662 548-5361
Southaven (G-4920)

2024 Ice Cream

Caboose Cones ....G 228 860-4030
Ocean Springs (G-3745)
Dairy Kream ....G 662 256-7562
Amory (G-40)
Luvel Dairy Products Inc ....C 662 289-2511
Kosciusko (G-2698)
Luvel Dairy Products Inc ....G 601 693-0038
Meridian (G-3362)
Luvel Dairy Products Inc ....G 662 334-6372
Greenville (G-1566)
Prairie Farms Dairy Inc ....F 601 969-1307
Jackson (G-2544)
Red Penguin Jackson Ice Cream ....G 601 519-9901
Jackson (G-2561)

2026 Milk

Borden Dairy Company Ala LLC ....E 251 456-3381
Hattiesburg (G-1936)
Borden Dairy Company Ala LLC ....F 662 328-8755
Columbus (G-941)
Borden Dairy Company Ala LLC ....D 601 268-2583
Hattiesburg (G-1937)
Foremost Dairies ....G 601 936-9606
Richland (G-4516)
Luvel Dairy Products Inc ....C 662 289-2511
Kosciusko (G-2698)
Luvel Dairy Products Inc ....G 601 693-0038
Meridian (G-3362)
Luvel Dairy Products Inc ....G 662 334-6372
Greenville (G-1566)
Prairie Farms Dairy Inc ....F 601 969-1307
Jackson (G-2544)
Purple Bannana ....G 228 466-2978
Bay Saint Louis (G-152)

2032 Canned Specialties

Los Portrillos ....G 662 844-7350
Tupelo (G-5180)
Shelter From Rain ....G 601 454-7602
Jackson (G-2579)

2033 Canned Fruits, Vegetables & Preserves

Althees Jellies & Jams LLC ....G 601 795-4118
Poplarville (G-4373)

Gautier Mayhaw Co ....G 228 497-6896
Gautier (G-1493)
◆ Global Food Concepts Inc ....C 601 940-5425
Flowood (G-1364)

2035 Pickled Fruits, Vegetables, Sauces & Dressings

5d Natural Farm LLc ....G 601 906-8763
Raymond (G-4481)
Crechles Three Generations LLC ....G 601 213-8162
Brandon (G-383)
Gibson and Pickle Inc ....G 662 289-2400
Kosciusko (G-2694)
Grumpy Man LLC ....G 601 606-8683
Purvis (G-4439)
Jean Pickle ....G 662 256-7020
Amory (G-46)
Oxford Falls ....G 662 323-9696
Sallis (G-4703)
Pickle Larry ....G 662 256-7239
Amory (G-52)
▲ Reed Food Technology Inc ....E 601 939-4001
Pearl (G-4140)
▼ Shed Saucery LLC ....G 228 875-7373
Ocean Springs (G-3785)

2037 Frozen Fruits, Juices & Vegetables

Anusaya Fresh USA LLC ....G 601 795-2008
Poplarville (G-4374)
Borden Dairy Company Ala LLC ....D 601 268-2583
Hattiesburg (G-1937)
Ishee Produce ....G 601 651-6643
Laurel (G-2784)
Keith Murphree ....G 662 292-7644
Senatobia (G-4793)
Realpure Beverage Group LLC ....F 601 849-9910
Magee (G-3181)

2038 Frozen Specialties

Ajinomoto Foods North Amer Inc ....D 662 623-7400
Oakland (G-3737)
Ajinomoto Windsor Inc ....G 662 647-1594
Batesville (G-95)
Brm LLC ....G 601 501-1444
Vicksburg (G-5348)
Dutch Ann Foods Inc ....E 601 445-4496
Natchez (G-3557)
J & K Restaurants Inc ....G 601 501-1444
Vicksburg (G-5381)
Kims Processing Plant Inc ....F 662 627-2389
Clarksdale (G-771)
▼ Sanderson Farms Inc Foods Div ....G 601 649-4030
Laurel (G-2843)
Sanderson Farms Inc Foods Div ....B 601 939-9790
Flowood (G-1394)

2041 Flour, Grain Milling

Delta Grind Stone Ground Pdts ....G 662 816-1254
Water Valley (G-5467)
▲ Reed Food Technology Inc ....E 601 939-4001
Pearl (G-4140)

2043 Cereal Breakfast Foods

Big Star of Belmont Inc ....G 662 454-3300
Belmont (G-196)
Great American Granola Co LLC ....G 228 369-0902
Ocean Springs (G-3759)

2044 Rice Milling

A & J Planting Company ....G 662 363-0039
Tunica (G-5094)
Mars Food Us LLC ....G 662 335-8000
Greenville (G-1569)
Masterfoods USA ....G 662 335-8000
Greenville (G-1570)
Modern Mill Inc ....G 601 869-5050
McComb (G-3261)
Producers Rice Mill Inc ....D 662 334-6266
Greenville (G-1592)

2045 Flour, Blended & Prepared

Taste Maker Foods LLC ....E 901 274-4407
Hernando (G-2158)

2047 Dog & Cat Food

Cottons Cafe LLC ....G 662 380-1463
Oxford (G-3949)

Sunshine Mills Inc ....D 662 842-6714
Tupelo (G-5233)
Woods Trading Co Inc ....G 601 924-5015
Clinton (G-839)

2048 Prepared Feeds For Animals & Fowls

Central Industries Inc ....E 601 469-4421
Forest (G-1411)
Central Industries Inc ....G 601 469-4421
Forest (G-1410)
Chickasaw Farm Services Inc ....F 662 456-2008
Houston (G-2233)
Enslin and Son Packing Company ....E 601 582-9300
Hattiesburg (G-1963)
Fishbelt Feeds Inc ....E 662 246-5065
Moorhead (G-3445)
Hawks Feed Mill ....G 662 564-2920
Hernando (G-2134)
Indi-Bel Inc ....D 662 887-1226
Indianola (G-2265)
J & J Bagging LLC ....E 662 746-5155
Yazoo City (G-5637)
Jasper Cooperative ....G 601 428-4968
Stringer (G-5003)
Lauderdale County Farm Sup Inc ....E 601 483-3363
Meridian (G-3356)
Mar-Jac Poultry Ms LLC ....A 601 735-3132
Waynesboro (G-5505)
Moores Feed Store Inc ....G 662 488-0024
Pontotoc (G-4348)
Moores II Inc ....E 662 488-0024
Pontotoc (G-4349)
Peco Foods Inc ....C 601 656-1865
Philadelphia (G-4231)
Peco Foods Inc ....A 601 764-4392
Bay Springs (G-170)
Protein Products Inc ....E 662 569-3396
Sunflower (G-5047)
Purina Animal Nutrition LLC ....E 662 726-4262
Macon (G-3072)
Sanderson Farms Inc Prod Div ....C 601 892-1145
Hazlehurst (G-2104)
Steve Schrock ....G 662 369-6062
Prairie (G-4414)
Sunshine Mills Inc ....D 662 842-6714
Tupelo (G-5233)
Sunshine Mills Inc ....D 662 842-6175
Tupelo (G-5234)
Tricounty Farm Services South ....G 662 526-9100
Como (G-1054)
Tyson Foods Inc ....C 601 774-7551
Union (G-5304)
Ware Milling Inc ....F 662 456-9032
Houston (G-2258)
Woods Trading Co Inc ....G 601 924-5015
Clinton (G-839)

2051 Bread, Bakery Prdts Exc Cookies & Crackers

Adrienne Batla Cupcakes ....G 260 348-5364
Clarksdale (G-756)
Bimbo Bakeries Usa Inc ....F 601 545-3782
Hattiesburg (G-1931)
Bimbo Bakeries Usa Inc ....C 228 863-4302
Gulfport (G-1739)
Bimbo Bakeries Usa Inc ....E 601 479-8887
Meridian (G-3307)
Bimbo Bakeries Usa Inc ....G 601 693-4871
Meridian (G-3308)
Bimbo Bakeries Usa Inc ....C 601 693-4871
Meridian (G-3309)
Bunny Bread Inc ....G 228 868-0120
Gautier (G-1490)
Canada Bread ....G 662 494-1607
West Point (G-5539)
Creative Cakes & Supplies Inc ....G 662 844-3080
Tupelo (G-5123)
Flowers Bkg Co Baton Rouge LLC ....G 601 932-7843
Pearl (G-4119)
Flowers Bkg Co Baton Rouge LLC ....G 601 583-2693
Hattiesburg (G-1971)
Flowers Bkg Co Lynchburg LLC ....G 601 502-1305
Raymond (G-4488)
Flowers Bkg Co New Orleans LLC ....G 228 868-0120
Gulfport (G-1788)
Flowers Bkg Co Thomasville LLC ....G 662 245-1188
Columbus (G-976)
Flowers Bkg Co Thomasville LLC ....F 601 684-5481
McComb (G-3250)

Employee Codes: A=Over 500 employees, B=251-500
C=101-250, D=51-100, E=20-50, F=10-19, G=1-9

2019 Harris Directory of
Mississippi Manufacturers

20 FOOD AND KINDRED PRODUCTS

SIC SECTION

Flowers Bkg Co Tuscaloosa LLC ....F 662 842-8613
Tupelo (G-5134)
Fresh Distributing Company LLC.........G..... 228 297-7655
Lumberton (G-3029)
Johnson Wiley.....................................G..... 662 329-1495
Columbus (G-991)
La Brioche LLC ....F 601 988-2299
Jackson (G-2466)
La Ilucion ....G..... 662 536-0046
Horn Lake (G-2204)
Lulus Sweet Shop LLC ....G..... 601 790-1951
Madison (G-3121)
Mississippi Baking Co LLC ....D..... 601 854-5000
Pelahatchie (G-4165)
Ole Country Bakery ....F 662 738-5795
Brooksville (G-556)
Patycake Kids LLC ....G..... 601 506-7117
Jackson (G-2536)
Pauls Pastry Production LLC ....F 601 798-7457
Picayune (G-4284)
Pauls Pastry Shop ....E 601 798-7457
Picayune (G-4285)
Samuel Moses Inc ....G..... 601 669-0756
Brookhaven (G-529)
Sokhom To..G..... 601 684-3300
McComb (G-3267)
Sugar -N- Spice Confections ....G..... 901 210-6181
Horn Lake (G-2213)
Sweet Sensations-Jackson ....G..... 601 790-7553
Madison (G-3155)
Tato-Nut Donut Shop ....F 228 872-2076
Ocean Springs (G-3791)
Tupelo Cupcakes Inc ....G..... 205 269-4130
Tupelo (G-5244)
USA Yeast Company LLC......................E 601 545-2690
Hattiesburg (G-2079)

2052 Cookies & Crackers

Connie S Kitchen ....F 662 686-2255
Leland (G-2886)
Cookie Place Inc ....G..... 601 957-2891
Ridgeland (G-4565)
Cosentino Enterprises Inc ....G..... 228 392-6666
Diberville (G-1201)
▲ DBC Corporation...............................D..... 601 856-7454
Madison (G-3093)
▼ Flathaus Fine Foods LLC ....F 601 582-9629
Petal (G-4185)
Patricia Betts ....G..... 601 863-9058
Ridgeland (G-4615)
Pauls Pastry Production LLC ....F 601 798-7457
Picayune (G-4284)
Pauls Pastry Shop ....E 601 798-7457
Picayune (G-4285)

2053 Frozen Bakery Prdts

Dutch Ann Foods Inc ....E 601 445-4496
Natchez (G-3557)
Heavenly Confections ....G..... 601 660-1986
Natchez (G-3568)
Jubilations Inc ....F 662 328-9210
West Point (G-5548)
So Nuts and Confections LLC ....G..... 901 398-9650
Horn Lake (G-2211)

2064 Candy & Confectionery Prdts

Ada Newson ....G..... 601 810-6614
Richland (G-4498)
Alicia Vaughn ....G..... 601 888-7830
Woodville (G-5615)
Caramel Factory ....G..... 662 563-9900
Batesville (G-101)
Miss Polka DOT Lollipop ....G..... 601 325-1779
Hattiesburg (G-2024)
Nandys Candy & Ice Factory ....G..... 601 362-9553
Jackson (G-2515)
Robicheauxs Specialty Candy ....F 601 795-6833
Poplarville (G-4392)
Southern Blle Sweet Dsigns LLC ....G..... 901 598-7938
Southaven (G-4906)
Southern Kernels ....G..... 601 336-9080
Hattiesburg (G-2061)
Spoonfudge Shoppe LLC ....G..... 601 685-2000
Newton (G-3729)
Sugar -N- Spice Confections ....G..... 901 210-6181
Horn Lake (G-2213)
Yum Yums Gourmet Popcorn LLC ....G..... 662 470-6047
Southaven (G-4922)

2066 Chocolate & Cocoa Prdts

Nandys Candy & Ice Factory ....G..... 601 362-9553
Jackson (G-2515)
Robicheauxs Specialty Candy ....F 601 795-6833
Poplarville (G-4392)

2068 Salted & Roasted Nuts & Seeds

Indianola Pecan House Inc ....E 662 887-5420
Indianola (G-2267)
Indianola Pecan House Inc ....G..... 601 693-1998
Meridian (G-3351)

2074 Cottonseed Oil Mills

Delta Oil Mill ....E 662 358-4809
Jonestown (G-2676)
Delta Oil Mill ....G..... 662 363-1121
Tunica (G-5097)
Omega Protein Corporation ....C 228 475-1252
Moss Point (G-3492)

2075 Soybean Oil Mills

B & H Hill Farm LLC ....G..... 662 207-7197
Indianola (G-2261)
Gold Coast Commodities Inc.................E 601 825-2508
Brandon (G-400)

2076 Vegetable Oil Mills

Clint Williams Company ....G..... 662 627-3243
Clarksdale (G-762)

2077 Animal, Marine Fats & Oils

Blue Ridge Beef Plant Inc ....G..... 864 338-5544
Greenwood (G-1615)
Central Industries Inc ....E 601 469-4421
Forest (G-1411)
Darling Ingredients Inc ....G..... 601 372-5212
Jackson (G-2376)
Griffin Industries LLC ....G..... 601 372-5212
Jackson (G-2433)
M G K Seining LLC ....G..... 662 453-8370
Greenwood (G-1638)
Omega Protein Corporation ....C 228 475-1252
Moss Point (G-3492)
Protein Products Inc.............................E 662 569-3396
Sunflower (G-5047)

2079 Shortening, Oils & Margarine

Cottonseed Co-Op Corporation.............E 662 358-4481
Jonestown (G-2675)
Grecian Oil Importers LLC ....G..... 662 372-4933
Tupelo (G-5147)
Sani LLC ....G..... 601 454-6047
Clinton (G-835)

2082 Malt Beverages

Lucky Town Brewing Company LLC.....F 601 790-0142
Jackson (G-2473)
Mighty Miss Brewing Co LLC ....G..... 662 379-6477
Greenville (G-1574)
Southern Prohibition Brewing ....F 601 467-1057
Hattiesburg (G-2063)
White Brothers Inc ....E 601 948-0888
Jackson (G-2630)

2084 Wine & Brandy

Hillbilly Wines LLC...............................G..... 228 234-4411
Saucier (G-4755)
Queens Reward Meadery LLC ....G..... 662 823-6323
Tupelo (G-5211)
Scott O Galbreath Jr.............................G..... 601 445-9924
Natchez (G-3617)
Vineyard ....G..... 769 251-1322
Ridgeland (G-4645)
Winery At Williams Landing LLC ....G..... 662 219-0596
Greenwood (G-1665)

2085 Liquors, Distilled, Rectified & Blended

B Ficklin Investments LLC ....G..... 601 454-2724
Pearl (G-4106)
Cat Head Distillery LLC ....G..... 601 954-8207
Jackson (G-2355)
Czeiszperger Distiller LLC ....G..... 662 612-6160
Coldwater (G-844)

2086 Soft Drinks

Allen Beverages Incorporated ....D..... 228 831-4343
Gulfport (G-1721)
American Bottling Company...................D..... 601 939-5454
Richland (G-4500)
American Bottling Company...................D..... 662 844-7047
Tupelo (G-5109)
Brown Bottling Group Inc ....C 601 982-4160
Jackson (G-2344)
Brown Bottling Group Inc ....D..... 601 442-5805
Natchez (G-3539)
Brown Bottling Group Inc ....E 601 824-3022
Brandon (G-374)
C C Clark Inc ....E 662 323-4317
Starkville (G-4931)
Calico Jacks Llc ....G..... 504 355-9639
Carriere (G-689)
Ccbcc Operations LLC ....D..... 228 875-5426
Ocean Springs (G-3748)
Ccbcc Operations LLC ....E 601 428-0464
Hattiesburg (G-1941)
Clark Beverage Group Inc ....E 662 280-8540
Southaven (G-4859)
Clark Beverage Group Inc ....G..... 662 843-3241
Cleveland (G-789)
▲ Clark Beverage Group Inc ....D..... 662 338-3400
Starkville (G-4934)
Coast Coca Cola Bottling Co ....D..... 228 864-1122
Gulfport (G-1754)
Coca-Cola Bottling Co Untd Inc ....G..... 228 864-1122
Gulfport (G-1761)
Coca-Cola Bottling Co Untd Inc ....D..... 601 684-8223
McComb (G-3246)
Coca-Cola Bottling Co Untd Inc ....G..... 601 264-8600
Hattiesburg (G-1948)
Coca-Cola Refreshments USA Inc ....G..... 601 442-1641
Natchez (G-3548)
Cool Baby Water LLC ....G..... 850 748-0921
Lucedale (G-2990)
Corinth Cc-Cola Btlg Works Inc ....D..... 662 287-1433
Corinth (G-1077)
Corinth Cc-Cola Btlg Works Inc ....E 662 286-2052
Corinth (G-1078)
Corinth Cc-Cola Btlg Works Inc ....D..... 662 842-1753
Tupelo (G-5122)
Dewmar International Bmc Inc ....G..... 877 747-5326
Clinton (G-822)
Dr Pepper/Seven Up Inc ....G..... 601 545-7511
Hattiesburg (G-1958)
Frank Villines ....G..... 601 939-5454
Jackson (G-2646)
Grd Distributors LLC ....G..... 601 382-8802
Richland (G-4518)
Group Pepper Snapple Dr ....G..... 601 602-3695
Hattiesburg (G-1977)
Gulf States Canners Inc ....D..... 601 924-0511
Clinton (G-824)
Hooper Sales Co Incorporated ....G..... 662 526-5668
Como (G-1048)
Magnolia Bottled Water Company.........G..... 662 329-9000
Columbus (G-998)
Meridian Coca-Cola Bottling Co ....C 601 483-5272
Meridian (G-3367)
Mississippi Coca Cola Btlg Co ....F 601 584-6644
Hattiesburg (G-2025)
Moak Bottling Co Inc ....G..... 662 844-0012
Tupelo (G-5189)
Nehi Bottling Co of Cleveland ....F 662 843-3431
Cleveland (G-802)
Niagara Bottling LLC ....G..... 215 703-0838
Byhalia (G-592)
P-Americas LLC ....D..... 228 831-4343
Gulfport (G-1842)
P-Americas LLC ....E 601 684-2281
McComb (G-3263)
P-Americas LLC ....C 662 841-8750
Tupelo (G-5198)
Pepsi Beverages Company ....G..... 662 841-8750
Tupelo (G-5202)
Pepsi Bottling Group ....G..... 601 982-4160
Brandon (G-432)
Pepsi South Bottling.............................E 601 607-3011
Ridgeland (G-4616)
Pepsi-Cola Metro Btlg Co Inc................E 662 563-8622
Batesville (G-118)
RC Cola Company ....F 662 844-7947
Tupelo (G-5214)
Realpure Bottling Inc ....F 601 849-9910
Magee (G-3182)

212

2019 Harris Directory of
Mississippi Manufacturers

SIC SECTION

22 TEXTILE MILL PRODUCTS

Reaves Pure Water LLC ....G..... 601 606-6789
  Hattiesburg *(G-2049)*
Royal Crown Bottling ....E....... 662 843-3431
  Cleveland *(G-807)*
Vendworks LLC ....E....... 601 268-1906
  Hattiesburg *(G-2080)*
Vendworks LLC ....G....... 601 684-2085
  McComb *(G-3272)*
Weaver Consolidated Group Inc ....G....... 662 287-1433
  Corinth *(G-1128)*
Weaver Consolidated Group Inc ....E....... 662 842-1753
  Tupelo *(G-5253)*
Wis-Pak of Hattiesburg LLC ....F....... 601 544-7200
  Hattiesburg *(G-2085)*

2087 Flavoring Extracts & Syrups

Ada Newson ....G....... 601 810-6614
  Richland *(G-4498)*
Anthony Syrup Company ....G....... 601 656-7052
  Philadelphia *(G-4205)*
Liquor Locker Inc ....G....... 228 396-8557
  Biloxi *(G-263)*
Quality Beverage Packing Inc ....F....... 662 329-5976
  Columbus *(G-1020)*
▲ Sqwincher Corporation ....D....... 662 328-0400
  Columbus *(G-1030)*
Warren Corporation UNI ....G....... 888 913-7708
  Byram *(G-626)*

2092 Fish & Seafoods, Fresh & Frozen

Alabama Catfish Inc ....F....... 662 265-5377
  Inverness *(G-2272)*
▲ Consoldted Ctfish Cmpanies LLC ....B....... 662 962-3101
  Isola *(G-2277)*
Consoldted Ctfish Prducers LLC ......B....... 662 962-3101
  Isola *(G-2278)*
Custom Pack Inc ....F....... 228 435-3632
  Biloxi *(G-235)*
Freshwater Farms Products LLC ......C....... 662 247-4205
  Belzoni *(G-205)*
Global Seafood Tech Inc ....E....... 228 435-3632
  Biloxi *(G-245)*
Gollott Icehouse & Oil Dock ....G....... 228 280-8033
  Biloxi *(G-246)*
Gulf Pride Enterprises Inc ....F....... 228 432-2488
  Biloxi *(G-249)*
Heartland Catfish Company Inc ....B....... 662 254-7100
  Itta Bena *(G-2280)*
Lakes Farm Raised Catfish Inc ....G....... 662 363-1847
  Dundee *(G-1224)*
Lesso Freezing Company Inc ....G....... 228 374-7200
  Biloxi *(G-261)*
Magnolia Processing Inc ....C....... 662 363-3600
  Tunica *(G-5101)*
Noxubee County Producers Inc ....G....... 662 726-2502
  Macon *(G-3069)*
Ocean Springs Seafood Mkt Inc ....G....... 228 875-0104
  Biloxi *(G-269)*
Omega Protein Corporation ....C....... 228 475-1252
  Moss Point *(G-3492)*
R A Lesso Seafood Inc ....E....... 228 374-7200
  Biloxi *(G-274)*
R Fournier & Sons Inc ....E....... 228 392-4293
  Diberville *(G-1209)*
▼ Sanderson Farms Inc Foods Div ......G....... 601 649-4030
  Laurel *(G-2843)*
Simmons Frm Raised Catfish Inc ....E....... 662 746-5687
  Yazoo City *(G-5646)*
Tarantos Crawfish House ....G....... 228 392-0806
  Diberville *(G-1216)*

2095 Coffee

1529 Coffee Company ....G....... 662 315-6951
  Amory *(G-32)*
An AMC LLC ....G....... 662 292-6973
  Olive Branch *(G-3814)*
Aromica Coffee LLC ....G....... 901 848-1687
  Olive Branch *(G-3816)*
Chenoa Coffee Company ....G....... 662 834-3917
  Lexington *(G-2898)*
From Our Cup To Yours ....G....... 601 214-7689
  Pearl *(G-4121)*
Mississippi Cold Drip Coffee ....G....... 601 624-5708
  Jackson *(G-2498)*

2096 Potato Chips & Similar Prdts

Ada Newson ....G....... 601 810-6614
  Richland *(G-4498)*

Billy Purvis Distributing LLC ....G....... 601 480-3147
  Meridian *(G-3306)*
Central Snacks Inc ....F....... 601 267-3112
  Carthage *(G-712)*
Dkh Distributing Inc.......................G....... 901 734-4528
  Hernando *(G-2129)*
Kims Processing Plant Inc ....F....... 662 627-2389
  Clarksdale *(G-771)*

2097 Ice

Bay Ice Company Inc ....F....... 228 863-0981
  Gulfport *(G-1735)*
Browns Ice Company ....G....... 662 862-3706
  Fulton *(G-1447)*
Cube Ice Co ....G....... 662 563-8411
  Batesville *(G-103)*
Fiske International Group Corp ....G....... 601 622-5767
  Madison *(G-3100)*
Ice Plant Inc ....F....... 601 485-9111
  Meridian *(G-3347)*
Kolinsky Corp.................................G....... 601 544-5987
  Hattiesburg *(G-2011)*
Party Time Ice Inc ....G....... 662 746-8899
  Yazoo City *(G-5645)*
Reddy Ice Corporation ....E....... 601 948-0900
  Jackson *(G-2562)*
Wendall Harrell ....G....... 601 267-3094
  Carthage *(G-727)*
Wendall Harrell ....G....... 601 353-3539
  Jackson *(G-2628)*

2099 Food Preparations, NEC

Aberdeen School District.................G....... 662 369-6886
  Aberdeen *(G-7)*
B K Industries Inc ....F....... 864 963-3471
  New Albany *(G-3674)*
Becks Confection ....G....... 601 927-3137
  Ridgeland *(G-4554)*
Blendco Inc....................................E....... 888 253-6326
  Hattiesburg *(G-1935)*
Borden Dairy Company Ala LLC ....D....... 601 268-2583
  Hattiesburg *(G-1937)*
Charged Up Grill LLC ....G....... 228 224-4461
  Gulfport *(G-1751)*
Chef Rays Famous LLC....................G....... 601 559-8096
  Byram *(G-619)*
Chenoa Coffee Company ....G....... 662 834-3917
  Lexington *(G-2898)*
Dottleys Spice Mart Inc ....G....... 601 629-6100
  Vicksburg *(G-5362)*
Family Feeding Dev Program ....G....... 662 357-8917
  Tunica *(G-5100)*
Gateway America LLC ....G....... 228 331-1473
  Gulfport *(G-1790)*
Hall Manufacturing LLC ....G....... 601 445-6640
  Natchez *(G-3565)*
Healthy Growth Ntrtn Program ....G....... 901 493-7991
  Olive Branch *(G-3846)*
Honeyland Inc ....G....... 870 635-1160
  Pass Christian *(G-4088)*
Lisa Hibley ....F....... 601 736-6781
  Columbia *(G-903)*
Live and Laff LLC ....G....... 662 816-5144
  Taylor *(G-5049)*
McCormick & Company Inc ....G....... 662 274-1732
  Byhalia *(G-590)*
Melvin L Brewer Inc ....G....... 662 328-9191
  Columbus *(G-999)*
Mississippi Cold Drip Coffee ....G....... 601 624-5708
  Jackson *(G-2498)*
No Time 2 Cook LLC ....G....... 662 236-9456
  Oxford *(G-3976)*
Oxford Falls ....G....... 662 323-9696
  Sallis *(G-4703)*
Rebel Butcher Supply Co Inc ....G....... 601 939-2214
  Jackson *(G-2665)*
Reddi Meals Inc ....F....... 601 992-1503
  Flowood *(G-1392)*
Refreshments Inc ....D....... 662 286-6051
  Corinth *(G-1115)*
Shcpi Greenwood Site ....G....... 662 453-1445
  Greenwood *(G-1651)*
Taste Maker Foods LLC ....G....... 901 274-4407
  Hernando *(G-2158)*
Tico Investments LLC ....G....... 601 559-8161
  Ridgeland *(G-4641)*
Warren Corporation UNI ....G....... 888 913-7708
  Byram *(G-626)*
West Group Holding Company LLC ......G....... 662 871-2344
  Shannon *(G-4821)*

Westward Corporation ....G....... 601 660-3857
  Fayette *(G-1303)*
Whitney Whitehead ....G....... 662 380-0614
  Sarah *(G-4737)*

21 TOBACCO PRODUCTS

2111 Cigarettes

KS Tobacco & Brew ....G....... 662 869-0086
  Saltillo *(G-4716)*
Newton Discount Tobacco ....G....... 601 683-6555
  Newton *(G-3727)*
Voluptuous E-Juice LLC....................G....... 662 297-8353
  Pontotoc *(G-4368)*

2131 Tobacco, Chewing & Snuff

Country Squire ....G....... 601 362-2233
  Jackson *(G-2371)*

2141 Tobacco Stemming & Redrying

Lucky Leaf Discount Tobacco ....G....... 601 924-8818
  Clinton *(G-829)*

22 TEXTILE MILL PRODUCTS

2211 Cotton, Woven Fabric

ADB Canvas Art ....G....... 662 934-9449
  Batesville *(G-94)*
Canvas & Cocktails LLC ....G....... 228 861-8444
  Gulfport *(G-1748)*
Canvas Creations & Eatery ....G....... 404 514-3399
  Waynesboro *(G-5495)*
Canvasbeauty Beauty ....G....... 601 282-5430
  Marion *(G-3221)*
CIC International LLC ....G....... 662 473-4724
  Water Valley *(G-5465)*
Commercial Drapery Svcs LLC ....E....... 662 893-1510
  Olive Branch *(G-3824)*
Corinth Acquisition Corp ....G....... 662 287-1476
  Corinth *(G-1075)*
Cotton Capitol LLC ....D....... 601 498-4770
  Tylertown *(G-5269)*
Culp Inc ....F....... 662 844-7144
  Tupelo *(G-5124)*
Evh Properties LLC ....G....... 662 571-1980
  Yazoo City *(G-5634)*
French Awning & Screen Co Inc ....G....... 601 922-1132
  Jackson *(G-2414)*
Harris Custom Ink LLC ....E....... 662 338-4242
  Olive Branch *(G-3844)*
Jane Little Inc ....G....... 601 694-2767
  Newhebron *(G-3713)*
Mardis 300 LLC ....G....... 601 936-3911
  Flowood *(G-1380)*
Mississippi Prison Inds Corp............F....... 601 969-5760
  Jackson *(G-2503)*
Mossy Oak 3d Fluid Grphics LLC........G....... 662 494-9092
  West Point *(G-5553)*
Rfm Enterprises LLC ....G....... 228 896-9498
  Gulfport *(G-1862)*
Rome Chenille & Supply Co Inc ....G....... 662 286-9947
  Corinth *(G-1116)*
Royal Canvas Studios ....G....... 601 419-0809
  Ridgeland *(G-4626)*
Said Melinda ....G....... 601 990-4022
  Brookhaven *(G-528)*
Scrubs Elite LLC ....G....... 662 842-4011
  Tupelo *(G-5220)*
Southern Canvas ....G....... 601 951-6266
  Brandon *(G-458)*
Twisted Canvas ....G....... 228 596-9332
  Long Beach *(G-2959)*
Venevaa Jos LLC ....G....... 850 501-4040
  Gulfport *(G-1891)*
Walls Drapery & Bedspread Mfg ....G....... 601 939-6014
  Pearl *(G-4157)*
Westpoint Home LLC ....G....... 601 466-6738
  Hattiesburg *(G-2082)*

2221 Silk & Man-Made Fiber

Crossroads Picks LLC ....G....... 662 902-1026
  Clarksdale *(G-765)*
David Buford ....G....... 662 714-3031
  Water Valley *(G-5466)*
Satin Locs LLC ....G....... 901 282-6823
  Walls *(G-5451)*
▲ Trace Industries Inc ....E....... 662 456-4261
  Houston *(G-2256)*

Employee Codes: A=Over 500 employees, B=251-500
C=101-250, D=51-100, E=20-50, F=10-19, G=1-9

2019 Harris Directory of
Mississippi Manufacturers

213

22 TEXTILE MILL PRODUCTS

Weavexx LLC ....C...... 662 323-4064
Starkville (G-4980)

2231 Wool, Woven Fabric

Kdh Kustoms LLC ....G...... 601 730-2052
McComb (G-3256)
▲ Mitchell Group ....G...... 662 488-0025
Pontotoc (G-4347)
◆ Townhouse Home Furnishings LLC .C...... 662 651-5442
Smithville (G-4845)
◆ Voith Fabrics Florence Inc ....C...... 601 845-2202
Florence (G-1336)

2241 Fabric Mills, Cotton, Wool, Silk & Man-Made

Shoulder Cords Unlimited ....G...... 601 425-2195
Laurel (G-2849)

2251 Hosiery, Women's Full & Knee Length

Magnolia Hosiery Mill Inc ....G...... 662 286-2221
Corinth (G-1099)

2252 Hosiery, Except Women's

Lost Sock LLC ....G...... 601 946-1155
Madison (G-3120)

2253 Knit Outerwear Mills

American Apparel Inc ....G...... 601 654-9211
Lena (G-2894)
Harper Industries Inc ....G...... 601 947-2746
Lucedale (G-2999)
Hemline ....G...... 601 898-3456
Ridgeland (G-4589)
Southern Prtg & Silk Screening ....F...... 228 452-7309
Pass Christian (G-4095)

2254 Knit Underwear Mills

Mojo Uprisin Inc ....G...... 662 983-8892
Bruce (G-561)

2259 Knitting Mills, NEC

▲ Choctaw Glove & Safety Co Inc ....D...... 662 724-4178
Noxapater (G-3731)

2261 Cotton Fabric Finishers

Dyehouse Inc ....G...... 601 776-2189
Quitman (G-4462)
Gary Beall Enterprises LLC ....E...... 662 453-6100
Greenwood (G-1625)
▲ Global Screen Printing LLC ....G...... 601 919-2345
Brandon (G-399)
Harris Custom Ink LLC ....E...... 662 338-4242
Olive Branch (G-3844)
University Screen Print Inc ....F...... 662 324-8277
Starkville (G-4978)

2262 Silk & Man-Made Fabric Finishers

Harris Custom Ink LLC ....E...... 662 338-4242
Olive Branch (G-3844)

2273 Carpets & Rugs

▲ Belgique Inc ....G...... 601 368-1975
Jackson (G-2336)
▲ Biltrite Ripley Operations LLC ....G...... 662 837-9231
Ripley (G-4654)
Boxcar Flooring Company LLC ....G...... 662 871-1417
Saltillo (G-4708)
D D Rushing ....G...... 601 656-8842
Philadelphia (G-4213)
Dixie Mat LLC ....F...... 601 876-2427
Sandy Hook (G-4727)
Fibrix LLC ....D...... 662 844-5595
Tupelo (G-5133)
L and H Investment Inc ....G...... 601 636-4642
Vicksburg (G-5387)
Mat Sturgis Co Inc ....E...... 662 465-8879
Sturgis (G-5007)
Mohawk Steel Company ....G...... 601 467-6959
Hattiesburg (G-2030)
Serviceknight ....G...... 601 906-2810
Brandon (G-451)
Superior Mfg Group Inc ....D...... 601 544-8119
Moselle (G-3462)
Usaccess LLC ....E...... 601 806-5034
Monticello (G-3440)

2281 Yarn Spinning Mills

Fine Fibers ....G...... 901 590-9481
Byhalia (G-585)
Heritage Yarns ....G...... 601 956-1478
Jackson (G-2439)
National Council of Negro Wome ....G...... 952 361-6037
Kosciusko (G-2706)

2284 Thread Mills

Dub Street Fashion Center LLC ....G...... 601 483-0036
Meridian (G-3330)
Fibrix LLC ....E...... 662 489-7908
Pontotoc (G-4331)

2295 Fabrics Coated Not Rubberized

Bills Organtic Grdnng & Leaf ....G...... 901 315-8888
Olive Branch (G-3819)
Insituform Technologies LLC ....D...... 662 561-1378
Batesville (G-109)
Omnova Solutions Inc ....A...... 662 327-1522
Columbus (G-1012)

2296 Tire Cord & Fabric

Greenville Metal Works Inc ....E...... 662 335-8510
Greenville (G-1555)

2297 Fabrics, Nonwoven

Carpenter Co ....B...... 662 566-2392
Verona (G-5329)
Fibrix LLC ....E...... 662 844-3803
Tupelo (G-5132)
Fibrix LLC ....D...... 662 844-5595
Tupelo (G-5133)
Fibrix LLC ....E...... 662 489-7908
Pontotoc (G-4331)
Jason Industries Inc ....D...... 662 327-0756
Columbus (G-990)
Master Fibers Inc ....G...... 662 568-3455
Houlka (G-2225)
Mississippi Fabritek Inc ....D...... 662 327-0745
Columbus (G-1003)
▲ Trace Industries Inc ....G...... 662 456-4261
Houston (G-2256)

2298 Cordage & Twine

▲ Nhc Distributors Inc ....E...... 601 656-7911
Philadelphia (G-4229)
▲ R F Ederer Co Inc ....E...... 228 875-9345
Ocean Springs (G-3780)

2299 Textile Goods, NEC

10 Below LLC ....G...... 769 243-8705
Jackson (G-2313)
Bed Bath & Beyond Inc ....G...... 601 939-4840
Flowood (G-1344)
Fibrix LLC ....E...... 662 844-3803
Tupelo (G-5132)
Heritage Yarns ....G...... 601 956-1478
Jackson (G-2439)
▲ Leggett Platt Components Inc ....F...... 662 844-4224
Tupelo (G-5179)
Medical Grade Innovations LLC ....G...... 601 899-9207
Ridgeland (G-4604)
Product Source Limited LLC ....G...... 769 257-4620
Florence (G-1331)
R2pg Inc ....F...... 601 747-0522
Port Gibson (G-4406)
Said Melinda ....G...... 601 990-4022
Brookhaven (G-528)
Southern Fibers Inc ....G...... 662 568-3456
Houlka (G-2228)
Ten Below LLC ....G...... 601 453-2041
Meridian (G-3413)
▲ Trace Industries Inc ....E...... 662 456-4261
Houston (G-2256)
Weavexx LLC ....C...... 662 323-4064
Starkville (G-4980)

23 APPAREL AND OTHER FINISHED PRODUCTS MADE FROM FABRICS AND SIMILAR MATERIAL

2311 Men's & Boys' Suits, Coats & Overcoats

Blauer Manufacturing Co Inc ....D...... 662 281-0097
Oxford (G-3941)

Blauer Manufacturing Co Inc ....D...... 662 281-0097
Oxford (G-3942)
Brigade Manufacturing Inc ....D...... 601 827-5062
Tylertown (G-5265)
Ek Embroidery LLC ....G...... 228 868-8469
Gulfport (G-1777)
Golden Manufacturing Co Inc ....B...... 662 454-3428
Golden (G-1525)
Golden Manufacturing Co Inc ....G...... 662 728-8200
Marietta (G-3214)
Kepler Boys Wear LLC ....G...... 601 738-1664
Vicksburg (G-5386)
M & M Industries Inc ....E...... 601 799-2615
Mc Neill (G-3241)
▲ Pine Belt Processing Inc ....E...... 601 785-4476
Stonewall (G-4998)
Tullahoma Industries LLC ....G...... 601 222-2255
Tylertown (G-5288)

2321 Men's & Boys' Shirts

Blauer Manufacturing Co Inc ....D...... 662 281-0097
Oxford (G-3942)
County of Hancock ....G...... 228 467-2100
Bay St Louis (G-177)
Crystal Springs Apparel LLC ....E...... 601 856-8831
Ridgeland (G-4568)
Garan Incorporated ....E...... 601 656-1501
Philadelphia (G-4215)
Garan Manufacturing Corp ....C...... 662 323-4731
Starkville (G-4945)
Golden Manufacturing Co Inc ....B...... 662 454-3428
Golden (G-1525)
Mossyoak Wildlife Conservatory ....G...... 662 495-9292
West Point (G-5554)
Pvh Corp ....G...... 228 863-0017
Gulfport (G-1857)

2325 Men's & Boys' Separate Trousers & Casual Slacks

Golden Manufacturing Co Inc ....B...... 662 454-3428
Golden (G-1525)
Golden Manufacturing Co Inc ....E...... 662 728-8200
Marietta (G-3214)
◆ Reed Manufacturing Company Inc ...E...... 662 842-4472
Tupelo (G-5216)
River Road Jean Company ....G...... 601 279-6571
Vicksburg (G-5412)
Supreme International LLC ....G...... 601 638-2403
Vicksburg (G-5425)
West Group Holding Company LLC ......G...... 662 871-2344
Shannon (G-4821)

2326 Men's & Boys' Work Clothing

A and Y Uniform Shop ....G...... 601 553-1377
Meridian (G-3293)
Blauer Manufacturing Co Inc ....D...... 662 281-0097
Oxford (G-3941)
Blauer Manufacturing Co Inc ....D...... 662 281-0097
Oxford (G-3942)
Destiny Apparel LLC ....G...... 228 383-2665
Biloxi (G-236)
G&K Services LLC ....E...... 601 788-6375
Richton (G-4531)
Golden Manufacturing Co Inc ....B...... 662 454-3428
Golden (G-1525)
Landau Uniforms Incorporated ....E...... 662 895-7200
Olive Branch (G-3864)
▲ Malt Industries Inc ....E...... 601 794-4200
Purvis (G-4446)
Mississippi Prison Inds Corp ....F...... 601 969-5760
Jackson (G-2503)
▲ National Textile and AP Inc ....E...... 601 892-4356
Hazlehurst (G-2102)
Pak Uniform & EMB Shoppe LLC ....G...... 228 365-6695
Pascagoula (G-4058)
◆ Reed Manufacturing Company Inc ...E...... 662 842-4472
Tupelo (G-5216)
Ruleville Manufacturing Co Inc ....D...... 662 756-4363
Ruleville (G-4699)
Sanders Home Health Inc ....G...... 662 335-2326
Greenville (G-1596)
Superior Uniform Group Inc ....G...... 662 834-4485
Lexington (G-2905)
▲ Team Safety Apparel Inc ....E...... 601 892-3571
Crystal Springs (G-1158)

2329 Men's & Boys' Clothing, NEC

Asics America Corporation ....F...... 662 895-6800
Byhalia (G-577)

SIC SECTION
23 APPAREL AND OTHER FINISHED PRODUCTS MADE FROM FABRICS AND SIMILAR MATERIAL

Destiny Apparel LLC ....G...... 228 383-2665
Biloxi (G-236)
Harris Custom Ink LLC ....E...... 662 338-4242
Olive Branch (G-3844)
Hunter Trading Company LLC ....G...... 866 521-5012
Olive Branch (G-3849)
▲ Icon Outdoors LLC ....G...... 662 895-3651
Olive Branch (G-3850)
Massey Clothing Company LLC ....G...... 662 792-4046
Kosciusko (G-2700)
Pak Uniform & EMB Shoppe LLC ....G...... 228 365-6695
Pascagoula (G-4058)
Red Square Clothing Co ....G...... 601 853-8960
Ridgeland (G-4622)
Reebok International Ltd ....F...... 228 822-9222
Gulfport (G-1861)
Ruleville Manufacturing Co Inc ....D...... 662 756-4363
Ruleville (G-4699)
Tuohys J Sptg Gods of Columbus ....E...... 662 328-1440
Columbus (G-1040)
Under Armour Inc ....G...... 228 864-2791
Gulfport (G-1888)
Under Armour Inc ....G...... 662 298-5269
Southaven (G-4918)
Varsity Pro Inc ....G...... 662 628-4172
Calhoun City (G-645)
Well-Dressed Man ....G...... 601 213-8311
Brookhaven (G-547)

2331 Women's & Misses' Blouses

Alex Carol Limited ....G...... 601 956-0536
Ridgeland (G-4547)
Boo Enterprises LLC ....G...... 228 475-8929
Moss Point (G-3470)
Crystal Springs Apparel LLC ....E...... 601 856-8831
Ridgeland (G-4568)
Garan Incorporated ....E...... 601 656-1501
Philadelphia (G-4215)
Garan Manufacturing Corp ....C...... 662 323-4731
Starkville (G-4945)
Landing ....G...... 601 707-5505
Madison (G-3119)
Pvh Corp ....G...... 228 863-0017
Gulfport (G-1857)
Varsity Pro Inc ....G...... 662 628-4172
Calhoun City (G-645)

2335 Women's & Misses' Dresses

A Stitch In Time ....G...... 662 257-0661
Amory (G-33)
Belles & Beaus ....G...... 228 396-1771
Diberville (G-1197)
Jasper & Assoc ....G...... 601 321-0811
Jackson (G-2459)
Le Fleur De Luis ....G...... 228 875-6628
Ocean Springs (G-3769)
Magnolia Mariee LLC ....G...... 601 446-6400
Natchez (G-3583)
Runway Liquidation LLC ....G...... 406 388-1988
Meridian (G-3393)
Runway Liquidation LLC ....G...... 406 259-1280
New Albany (G-3693)
Runway Liquidation LLC ....G...... 816 671-7922
Gulfport (G-1865)

2337 Women's & Misses' Suits, Coats & Skirts

Landing ....G...... 601 707-5505
Madison (G-3119)
Sincere Trading Inc ....G...... 662 702-3822
Greenville (G-1599)

2339 Women's & Misses' Outerwear, NEC

Garan Manufacturing Corp ....C...... 662 323-4731
Starkville (G-4945)
Henns Nest Inc ....G...... 601 268-3577
Hattiesburg (G-1989)
Landau Uniforms Incorporated ....E...... 662 895-7200
Olive Branch (G-3864)
Reebok International Ltd ....F...... 228 822-9222
Gulfport (G-1861)
W G Yates & Sons Cnstr Co ....A...... 601 656-5411
Philadelphia (G-4248)

2341 Women's, Misses' & Children's Underwear & Nightwear

Alex Carol Limited ....G...... 601 956-0536
Ridgeland (G-4547)

Foh Group Inc ....C...... 601 795-6470
Poplarville (G-4382)

2342 Brassieres, Girdles & Garments

Alex Carol Limited ....G...... 601 956-0536
Ridgeland (G-4547)

2353 Hats, Caps & Millinery

Allens Trophies Inc ....E...... 601 582-7702
Hattiesburg (G-1920)
Hat Shack Inc ....G...... 601 264-1017
Hattiesburg (G-1983)

2361 Children's & Infants' Dresses & Blouses

Carters Inc ....G...... 662 844-2667
Tupelo (G-5119)
Garan Manufacturing Corp ....C...... 662 323-4731
Starkville (G-4945)
Landing ....G...... 601 707-5505
Madison (G-3119)
Tuohys J Sptg Gods of Columbus ....E...... 662 328-1440
Columbus (G-1040)

2369 Girls' & Infants' Outerwear, NEC

Backyard Escapes ....G...... 228 868-3938
Long Beach (G-2923)
Garan Manufacturing Corp ....C...... 662 323-4731
Starkville (G-4945)
Tuohys J Sptg Gods of Columbus ....E...... 662 328-1440
Columbus (G-1040)

2371 Fur Goods

Southern Fur Design ....G...... 601 936-2005
Flowood (G-1400)

2381 Dress & Work Gloves

Ao Liquidation Trust Inc ....E...... 662 675-8102
Coffeeville (G-841)
Armstrong Remodeling ....F...... 601 720-2097
Clinton (G-812)
Hawkeye Glove Manufacturing ....D...... 662 681-6278
Eupora (G-1286)
Hrd Safety ....G...... 601 213-6358
Jackson (G-2444)
Lamont Wells LLC ....D...... 601 656-2772
Philadelphia (G-4222)
Slate Springs Glove Company ....G...... 662 637-2222
Calhoun City (G-644)
Stryder & Associates LLC ....G...... 662 579-8703
Cleveland (G-809)

2384 Robes & Dressing Gowns

Foh Group Inc ....C...... 601 795-6470
Poplarville (G-4382)

2386 Leather & Sheep Lined Clothing

Consumer Products America LLC ....G...... 601 613-8583
Jackson (G-2366)

2387 Apparel Belts

Thomas Larry Hearn ....G...... 601 922-2700
Jackson (G-2606)

2389 Apparel & Accessories, NEC

Big River Classics Inc ....G...... 601 856-6607
Pearl (G-4107)
Bo Enterprises Inc ....F...... 662 720-1211
Booneville (G-320)
Bo Enterprises Inc ....G...... 601 483-5571
Meridian (G-3311)
C & D Jarnagin Company Inc ....E...... 662 287-4977
Corinth (G-1062)
C & D Jarnagin Company Inc ....F...... 662 287-4977
Corinth (G-1063)
Coastal Waters LLC ....C...... 662 769-2944
Starkville (G-4935)
Cole Tempra Helmet & Vest LLC ....G...... 601 317-3842
Jackson (G-2361)
Destiny Apparel LLC ....G...... 228 383-2665
Biloxi (G-236)
Dignity Garments LLC ....G...... 601 941-4636
Madison (G-3096)
Ears Jewlery Box Sp Fashions ....G...... 769 234-1771
Foxworth (G-1429)
Gail McInnis ....G...... 601 261-5077
Hattiesburg (G-1973)

Golden Manufacturing Co Inc ....F...... 662 728-1300
Marietta (G-3215)
Smooth Transitions LLC ....G...... 601 493-3787
Fayette (G-1302)
Swell O Phonic ....G...... 601 981-3547
Jackson (G-2601)
Yank Threads LLC ....G...... 601 201-3934
Jackson (G-2639)

2391 Curtains & Draperies

Beverly Robinson Decor ....G...... 601 201-1520
Madison (G-3086)
Blonzells Curtain Shop ....G...... 601 635-3811
Decatur (G-1171)
Classic Window Design ....G...... 662 893-5892
Olive Branch (G-3823)
F S C Inc ....G...... 662 434-0025
Columbus (G-972)
▲ Linas Interiors Inc ....G...... 662 332-7226
Leland (G-2889)
◆ Mid-South Drapery Inc ....E...... 662 454-3855
Belmont (G-200)
Norman Vr Inc ....G...... 601 352-4819
Gulfport (G-1838)
Ron Lor Window Fashions ....G...... 662 329-1557
Columbus (G-1022)

2392 House furnishings: Textile

Advanced Innovative Pdts LLC ....G...... 662 365-1640
Baldwyn (G-70)
Corporate Housing ....G...... 601 853-8982
Ridgeland (G-4566)
Cushions To Go LLC ....G...... 662 488-0350
Pontotoc (G-4327)
Divine Creations ....G...... 601 500-2764
Jackson (G-2385)
Elite Comfort Solutions LLC ....E...... 662 566-2322
Verona (G-5330)
Foamcraft Inc ....E...... 662 844-6399
Tupelo (G-5135)
Glen Jones & Associates Inc ....G...... 601 634-0877
Vicksburg (G-5374)
Innocor East LLC ....F...... 662 365-1640
Baldwyn (G-78)
◆ Innocor East LLC ....D...... 732 263-0800
Baldwyn (G-79)
Kedron Furniture Mfg Inc ....G...... 662 963-3366
Plantersville (G-4310)
L C Industries Inc ....B...... 601 894-1771
Hazlehurst (G-2099)
L C Industries Inc ....G...... 662 841-1640
Tupelo (G-5170)
Leggett & Platt Incorporated ....G...... 662 842-5704
Tupelo (G-5175)
◆ Mid-South Drapery Inc ....E...... 662 454-3855
Belmont (G-200)
Nitas Quilts ....G...... 601 825-2060
Brandon (G-429)
Piave Broom & Mop Inc ....F...... 601 584-7314
Petal (G-4195)
Pillows Plus ....G...... 662 890-3699
Olive Branch (G-3896)
R2pg Inc ....F...... 601 747-0522
Port Gibson (G-4406)
Rome Chenille & Supply Co Inc ....G...... 662 286-9947
Corinth (G-1116)
Signature Works Inc ....B...... 601 894-1771
Hazlehurst (G-2106)
Southeastern Sample Company ....F...... 662 282-4063
Mantachie (G-3205)

2393 Textile Bags

Ao Liquidation Trust Inc ....E...... 662 675-8102
Coffeeville (G-841)
Brentwood Originals Inc ....C...... 662 781-5301
Walls (G-5448)
Fibrix LLC ....D...... 662 844-5595
Tupelo (G-5133)
Polo Custom Products Inc ....C...... 662 779-2009
Louisville (G-2976)
Southern Sttch Canvas Uphl LLC ....G...... 228 234-2515
Gulfport (G-1876)
Superior Uniform Group Inc ....G...... 662 834-4485
Lexington (G-2905)

2394 Canvas Prdts

American Tarp & Awning Co ....G...... 601 656-5177
Philadelphia (G-4203)

Employee Codes: A=Over 500 employees, B=251-500
C=101-250, D=51-100, E=20-50, F=10-19, G=1-9

2019 Harris Directory of
Mississippi Manufacturers

215

23 APPAREL AND OTHER FINISHED PRODUCTS MADE FROM FABRICS AND SIMILAR MATERIAL

Biloxi Tent and Awning Co Inc .... G 228 436-6161
Biloxi (G-220)
Duffell Metal Awning Co .... G 601 483-2181
Meridian (G-3332)
F S C Inc .... G 662 434-0025
Columbus (G-972)
Mainland Sails Inc .... G 228 374-7245
Gautier (G-1498)
Quality Alum & HM Imprv Inc .... G 662 329-2525
Columbus (G-1019)
Sailmakers Supply .... G 228 522-3232
Gautier (G-1503)
Southern Sttch Canvas Uphl LLC .... G 228 234-2515
Gulfport (G-1876)

2395 Pleating & Stitching For The Trade

Ability Works Inc .... G 662 328-0275
Columbus (G-931)
Ae Enterprises .... G 601 573-5954
Brandon (G-359)
American Stitching LLC .... G 601 919-7882
Ridgeland (G-4549)
Anns Embroidery .... G 601 444-0011
Columbia (G-879)
At Home Embroidery .... G 228 365-4034
Saucier (G-4749)
B S Monogramming .... G 662 750-0505
Walnut (G-5455)
Blank 2 Beautiful EMB More LLC .... G 662 902-6195
Alligator (G-31)
Buzini Group LLC .... E 601 398-1311
Flowood (G-1350)
C & W Embroidery Inc .... E 662 462-8526
Rienzi (G-4648)
C W Embroidery Inc .... G 662 231-9206
Prairie (G-4412)
Cater 2u Embroidery .... G 662 253-8713
Southaven (G-4857)
Cg Monogram & Gifts .... G 662 401-5344
Fulton (G-1448)
City Sports Center .... G 228 474-2033
Moss Point (G-3474)
Clementine Frazier .... G 601 572-7698
Utica (G-5307)
Coast Ink Wholesale Club .... G 601 948-4849
Ridgeland (G-4564)
Creative Designs & Sports .... G 662 327-5000
Columbus (G-956)
D J S Embroidery LLC .... G 662 547-9000
Mc Cool (G-3235)
Embroidery Design LLC .... G 601 878-2606
Terry (G-5067)
Embroidery Nu Sun .... G 228 731-3781
Gulfport (G-1778)
Embroidery Plus .... G 662 590-7102
Yazoo City (G-5633)
Embroidme .... G 228 284-1689
Ocean Springs (G-3755)
Fashions Incorporated Jackson .... G 601 948-1119
Jackson (G-2406)
Get Stitched .... G 228 231-1162
Waveland (G-5481)
Golden Needle .... G 662 842-0515
Tupelo (G-5145)
Hanging By A Thread LLC .... G 662 449-5198
Hernando (G-2133)
Hoop-It-Up Embroidery .... G 662 244-7212
Columbus (G-984)
Hoopla Monogramming & Gifts .... G 228 860-4774
Gulfport (G-1809)
It Could Happen Embroidery .... G 228 374-7674
Biloxi (G-253)
J J Monogram Embroidery .... G 662 226-0304
Grenada (G-1688)
Josh Gus Garcia .... G 228 255-7157
Perkinston (G-4177)
Just For You Embroidery .... G 228 769-8388
Pascagoula (G-4043)
Khloes Closet and Monograms .... G 662 315-9425
Smithville (G-4844)
Krazy Kat Monograms .... G 901 832-1339
Southaven (G-4885)
Lil Ms Sew & Sew Inc .... G 601 992-3279
Flowood (G-1377)
Logo Sportswear .... G 601 845-5038
Florence (G-1327)
Lucky Dog Monograms LLC .... G 662 321-7903
Tupelo (G-5181)
Lucy Lus Monogramming LLC .... G 662 417-9552
Winona (G-5603)

M & M Monograms .... G 601 856-7459
Madison (G-3122)
Main Street Embroidery .... G 601 876-0003
Tylertown (G-5277)
Marcellas Quilt Shop .... G 662 262-7870
French Camp (G-1440)
◆ Mid-South Drapery Inc .... E 662 454-3855
Belmont (G-200)
Mississippi Embroidery Co .... G 601 264-3255
Hattiesburg (G-2026)
Mockingbird Monograms .... G 662 315-6213
Nettleton (G-3662)
Mollygrams .... G 601 856-5598
Madison (G-3131)
Monkey Business Unlimit .... G 662 895-1912
Olive Branch (G-3880)
Monogram Creations .... G 601 415-4970
Vicksburg (G-5401)
Monogram Expressions .... G 662 571-0582
Yazoo City (G-5642)
Monogram Hut .... G 601 268-9028
Hattiesburg (G-2031)
Monogram Magic .... G 601 624-6917
Madison (G-3132)
Monogram Magick .... G 662 544-1392
Holly Springs (G-2185)
Monogram Mills .... G 601 749-1064
Brandon (G-426)
Monogram Stitch LLC .... G 601 649-1582
Laurel (G-2806)
Monograms By Rahaim .... G 601 310-0152
Hattiesburg (G-2032)
Monograms Plus .... G 662 327-3332
Columbus (G-1007)
Mr Stitch It .... G 601 543-8681
Hattiesburg (G-2034)
Needle Works .... G 601 425-4692
Laurel (G-2811)
P & L Embroidery .... G 662 365-9852
Baldwyn (G-86)
Patrick Enterprises Inc .... G 601 268-1115
Hattiesburg (G-2041)
Paxton Embroidery .... G 662 335-2160
Greenville (G-1589)
Perfect Promotions LLC .... F 601 482-7710
Meridian (G-3388)
Rainbow Stitchings .... G 662 378-5335
Greenville (G-1594)
Rebeccas Cstm EMB & Appliques .... G 662 665-1846
Corinth (G-1113)
Rfc-Embroidery .... G 601 463-0491
Poplarville (G-4391)
Riedesigns Embroidery .... G 601 262-5130
Meridian (G-3391)
Robinsons Retail Inc .... F 662 843-3950
Cleveland (G-806)
Rufroggy Monograms .... G 228 547-7060
Saucier (G-4762)
Serendipitee .... G 228 872-4766
Ocean Springs (G-3783)
Sew Lucky Embroidery .... G 662 550-5533
Hernando (G-2154)
Sew Southern Monograms .... G 662 229-6564
Winona (G-5607)
Sew Sweet .... G 601 431-2304
Natchez (G-3618)
Signature Accents .... G 601 853-9020
Madison (G-3146)
SMS Embroidery .... G 601 635-2347
Decatur (G-1179)
Stitched In Time .... G 601 562-6715
Philadelphia (G-4237)
Stitches By Lee LLC .... G 228 769-7460
Pascagoula (G-4070)
Stitching and Stuff LLC .... G 228 365-4735
Long Beach (G-2955)
Sweet South Embroidery .... G 601 277-3371
Hazlehurst (G-2107)
T Shirt Shop & Design Firm LLC .... G 662 329-9911
Columbus (G-1036)
Three Crafty Women .... G 662 746-6844
Yazoo City (G-5650)
Tlgllc/Magnolia Monogramming .... G 662 838-2000
Byhalia (G-609)
TSA Embroidery LLC .... G 662 538-1007
New Albany (G-3703)
VIP Vinyl and Embroidery LLC .... G 601 624-7366
Florence (G-1335)

2396 Automotive Trimmings, Apparel Findings, Related Prdts

Allistons .... G 228 832-8683
Gulfport (G-1723)
Ch Custom Designs & Prints LLC .... G 601 408-5068
Hattiesburg (G-1943)
Charlottes EMB & Screen Prtg .... G 601 824-1080
Brandon (G-379)
Fashions Incorporated Jackson .... G 601 948-1119
Jackson (G-2406)
Gator Grafix Inc .... G 601 376-9004
Jackson (G-2423)
▲ Global Screen Printing LLC .... G 601 919-2345
Brandon (G-399)
▲ Grammer Inc .... D 864 672-0702
Shannon (G-4808)
Graphic Arts Productions Inc .... G 662 494-2549
West Point (G-5544)
Haygoods Industrial Engravers .... G 228 769-7488
Pascagoula (G-4036)
Mount Vernon Mills Inc .... D 662 328-5670
Columbus (G-1009)
Southern Speed .... G 662 842-3799
Tupelo (G-5228)
Systems Auto Interiors LLC .... D 662 862-1360
Mantachie (G-3206)
T Tommys .... G 601 833-8620
Brookhaven (G-542)
Zyaa Inc .... G 601 321-9502
Jackson (G-2641)

2397 Schiffli Machine Embroideries

Custom Sportswear USA Inc .... G 228 255-4795
Diamondhead (G-1188)

2399 Fabricated Textile Prdts, NEC

Angies Crocheting Corner .... G 228 617-9342
Hattiesburg (G-1924)
▲ Datco International Inc .... F 248 593-9142
Columbus (G-959)
Datco International Inc .... F 662 327-3995
Columbus (G-960)
Delta Net & Twine Co Inc .... F 662 332-0841
Greenville (G-1548)
Joanna Freely .... G 662 272-8679
Starkville (G-4953)
Mks Crochet .... G 662 769-4982
Maben (G-3048)
Multimedia Graphics Inc .... G 601 981-5001
Jackson (G-2514)
Pioneer Aerospace Corporation .... C 601 736-4511
Columbia (G-912)
Sportman Camo Covers Inc .... F 662 489-7074
Ecru (G-1233)

24 LUMBER AND WOOD PRODUCTS, EXCEPT FURNITURE

2411 Logging

A & D Timber Company Inc .... F 601 528-9357
Wiggins (G-5568)
Acy Logging .... G 601 833-5426
Brookhaven (G-478)
Adam Sterling Logging LLC .... F 601 657-1091
Liberty (G-2908)
Adams Logging Inc .... G 601 567-2988
Smithdale (G-4840)
Alamiss Inc .... G 601 671-0840
Waynesboro (G-5489)
American Log Handlers LLC .... F 601 927-6692
Booneville (G-317)
Ancerstor Logging LLC .... G 601 701-7020
De Kalb (G-1161)
Ancestor Logging .... G 925 895-2306
Meridian (G-3298)
Anderson & Son Logging LLC .... G 662 688-1211
Tillatoba (G-5079)
Andy Jackson .... G 662 416-2614
Booneville (G-318)
Andy Massey Logging .... G 662 675-2647
Coffeeville (G-840)
Anthony Logging Inc .... G 601 731-2975
Kokomo (G-2686)
Austin Logging LLC .... G 662 296-6566
Randolph (G-4479)
Autman Logging .... G 601 986-2555
Collinsville (G-866)

SIC SECTION

24 LUMBER AND WOOD PRODUCTS, EXCEPT FURNITURE

B P Graves Logging Co ....G...... 601 765-8956
Collins *(G-852)*

Barbers Timber & Logging ....G.... 662 382-7649
Sarah *(G-4732)*

Bazor Pulpwood Company Inc ....F...... 601 735-4017
Waynesboro *(G-5492)*

Beach Harvey & Son Logging ....F...... 601 446-5771
Natchez *(G-3526)*

Beane Logging ....G..... 662 862-9053
Fulton *(G-1445)*

Benny McDaniel ....G..... 601 253-0564
Philadelphia *(G-4207)*

Black Rver Timber Wildlife LLC ....G...... 601 906-4099
Clinton *(G-814)*

Bo Logging Inc ....G..... 662 983-4225
Houlka *(G-2219)*

Boco Logging LLC ....G..... 256 810-4777
Golden *(G-1522)*

Bogue Homa Logging ....G..... 601 426-3662
Heidelberg *(G-2112)*

Box Logging ....G..... 662 547-6692
French Camp *(G-1439)*

Brad Warren Log & Trckg LLC ....G...... 601 416-8113
Union *(G-5294)*

Bradley Reid Inc ....F...... 601 810-6655
Tylertown *(G-5264)*

Brent Hickman Logging LLC ....G...... 601 928-8840
Wiggins *(G-5573)*

Brittany H Davis ....G..... 251 348-8858
Wiggins *(G-5574)*

Btc Logging Co ....G..... 601 735-3259
Waynesboro *(G-5493)*

Bubba Bond Logging LLC ....G..... 662 417-5242
Winona *(G-5595)*

Buie Loggin ....G..... 601 532-7186
Union Church *(G-5305)*

Burge Timber Contractors Inc ....F...... 601 796-3471
Lumberton *(G-3024)*

Burnie Dykes Logging Co Inc ....G...... 601 788-6211
Richton *(G-4527)*

C & L Logging Inc ....G..... 601 683-6349
Newton *(G-3718)*

C E Welch Timber Co Inc ....G..... 601 657-4577
Liberty *(G-2911)*

Cade & Cade Logging Inc ....G..... 601 833-2557
Wesson *(G-5525)*

Cade Enterprises 2 ....G..... 662 283-3678
Winona *(G-5596)*

Campbell Global ....G..... 601 932-2729
Flowood *(G-1351)*

Carey F Stanley ....F...... 601 687-5247
Shubuta *(G-4828)*

Cecil D Johnson ....F...... 662 456-5846
Mantee *(G-3210)*

Chains Logging ....G..... 662 327-8240
Columbus *(G-946)*

Chambers Logging Inc ....G..... 662 285-2777
Ackerman *(G-24)*

Charles Donald Pulpwood Inc ....E...... 601 437-4012
Port Gibson *(G-4400)*

Charles Horn Logging & Trckg ....F...... 662 585-3111
Golden *(G-1524)*

Charles Jordan ....G..... 601 727-4753
Pachuta *(G-4011)*

Charles Lance Griffin ....G..... 601 734-2683
Mc Call Creek *(G-3232)*

Charles R Smith Logging Co ....G...... 601 267-9800
Carthage *(G-713)*

Chris G Gatlin ....G..... 601 498-6281
Heidelberg *(G-2113)*

Circle A LLC ....G..... 601 832-3698
Hazlehurst *(G-2091)*

Circle G Hauling LLC ....G..... 662 436-7028
Little Rock *(G-2922)*

Circle Lane Contractors LLC ....F...... 601 776-0129
Shubuta *(G-4829)*

Ckc Logging Inc ....G..... 601 754-1344
Monticello *(G-3430)*

Clarence South Logging ....G..... 662 585-3724
Fulton *(G-1450)*

Clark Harvison ....G..... 601 928-7929
Wiggins *(G-5577)*

Claude Guy ....G..... 601 848-7859
State Line *(G-4984)*

Conaway Logging Inc ....F...... 662 287-8830
Corinth *(G-1072)*

Conway Investments Inc ....G..... 601 964-3215
New Augusta *(G-3710)*

Cook Timber Co Inc ....G..... 601 727-4782
Pachuta *(G-4012)*

Crimm Bros Log Ltd Lblty Co ....G...... 662 552-0122
Mathiston *(G-3228)*

Crimm Logging LLC ....G..... 662 552-8511
Mantee *(G-3211)*

Curtis Wilson Logging ....G..... 601 943-6808
Prentiss *(G-4415)*

Cutshall D L & Sons Logging Co ....G...... 662 423-6965
Iuka *(G-2288)*

D & C Logging Inc ....G..... 662 862-9316
Nettleton *(G-3659)*

Danny Pat Martin ....G..... 601 267-3342
Carthage *(G-714)*

David Breazeale Logging LLC ....F...... 662 323-9991
Starkville *(G-4938)*

David Drew Sullivan ....G..... 601 656-3556
Philadelphia *(G-4214)*

David Kirkman ....G..... 662 418-5048
Maben *(G-3044)*

David L Vance Logging Co ....G..... 601 635-2105
Decatur *(G-1172)*

David M Eaves ....G..... 662 773-7056
Macon *(G-3058)*

DC Logging LLC ....G..... 662 251-4653
Columbus *(G-961)*

Delbert T Dickerson ....G..... 662 773-4747
Louisville *(G-2967)*

Delta Logging & Company Inc ....E...... 662 746-2066
Yazoo City *(G-5632)*

Diamond Land & Timber LLC ....G...... 601 310-3395
Hattiesburg *(G-1957)*

Dier Logging Inc ....G..... 601 384-5963
Meadville *(G-3274)*

Dixie Logging Inc ....F...... 601 532-6583
Mc Call Creek *(G-3233)*

Donald Gatlin Logging LLC ....G..... 601 425-4320
Heidelberg *(G-2116)*

Dunaways Logging Inc ....F...... 601 695-1232
Brookhaven *(G-493)*

Dwayne Timber Company ....G..... 601 695-6177
Wesson *(G-5527)*

E & S Logging LLC ....G..... 601 866-7270
Bolton *(G-309)*

E Fairley Unlimited Svc LLC ....G...... 601 795-6933
Poplarville *(G-4381)*

East Mississippi Pole Company ....E...... 662 726-2932
Macon *(G-3059)*

Eddie Inc ....F...... 601 663-5755
Forest *(G-1416)*

Eddie Franklin ....G..... 601 225-4183
Centreville *(G-730)*

Eddie Reynolds Logging ....G..... 662 647-2667
Charleston *(G-736)*

Edward C Mathis Logging ....G..... 601 776-2379
Quitman *(G-4463)*

Ellis Williams Logging ....G..... 601 734-3918
Bogue Chitto *(G-303)*

Eubanks and Eubanks Inc ....G..... 601 947-2509
Lucedale *(G-2995)*

Evans Logging ....G..... 662 369-7151
Aberdeen *(G-13)*

F & F Timber Inc ....F...... 601 528-0023
Wiggins *(G-5582)*

F W Graves & Son Inc ....G..... 601 657-8750
Liberty *(G-2912)*

Falvey Logging ....G..... 601 546-2922
Pelahatchie *(G-4164)*

First Heritage Credit Corp ....G..... 228 762-7000
Pascagoula *(G-4032)*

First Heritage Credit Corp ....G..... 228 396-2620
Diberville *(G-1203)*

First Heritage Credit Corp ....G..... 601 636-6060
Vicksburg *(G-5372)*

First Heritage Credit Corp ....G..... 601 735-4543
Waynesboro *(G-5498)*

First Heritage Credit Corp ....G..... 601 799-1972
Picayune *(G-4266)*

First Heritage Credit Corp ....G..... 662 283-4696
Winona *(G-5598)*

First Heritage Credit Corp ....G..... 601 939-9309
Richland *(G-4515)*

Flora Logging LLC ....G..... 662 552-5408
Maben *(G-3045)*

Freeman Reason Logging ....G..... 601 446-5938
Natchez *(G-3561)*

G A Pearson Logging Inc ....G..... 601 928-2105
Wiggins *(G-5583)*

G&L Logging LLC ....G..... 601 722-9781
Seminary *(G-4781)*

Gary L Thornton Trk ....G..... 601 835-4192
Brookhaven *(G-494)*

Glendon Henderson Log & Trckg ....F...... 601 989-2638
Richton *(G-4532)*

Goodman Logging LLC ....G..... 601 644-3443
Meridian *(G-3342)*

Greg Winstead Logging Inc ....F...... 601 774-9565
Union *(G-5297)*

Guys Logging ....G..... 662 726-9301
Macon *(G-3063)*

H Delane Tucker Logging Inc ....G...... 601 788-6320
Richton *(G-4534)*

Harper Timber Inc ....E...... 601 833-2121
Brookhaven *(G-499)*

Harrison Brothers Incorporated ....G...... 601 536-2069
Pulaski *(G-4431)*

Harrison Logging Inc ....F...... 662 226-7908
Grenada *(G-1684)*

Henry E Davis Logging ....G..... 601 677-3669
De Kalb *(G-1165)*

Hood Industries Inc ....G..... 601 264-2962
Hattiesburg *(G-1995)*

Hood Industries Inc ....B...... 601 928-3737
Wiggins *(G-5584)*

Hood Industries Inc ....C...... 601 784-3414
Beaumont *(G-185)*

Hoop Logging LLC ....G..... 662 230-7553
Cascilla *(G-728)*

Hutchinson Logging ....G..... 601 943-5486
Bassfield *(G-92)*

Iron Horse Logging LLC ....G..... 601 416-5966
Union *(G-5299)*

Ironhorse Environmental LLC ....G...... 504 952-2516
Poplarville *(G-4383)*

Isaiah Ard Timber Inc ....E...... 601 833-9359
Ruth *(G-4702)*

J & K Enterprise Inc ....F...... 601 794-6005
Purvis *(G-4440)*

J & L Transport LLC ....G..... 601 292-7044
Collins *(G-854)*

J & P Smith Logging Inc ....F...... 601 833-4286
Brookhaven *(G-502)*

J T Horn Logging Inc ....G..... 662 585-3417
Golden *(G-1527)*

J W B Logging Co LLC ....G..... 601 437-8743
Port Gibson *(G-4402)*

J W Priest & Sons Logging ....G..... 601 532-6237
Mc Call Creek *(G-3234)*

J&M Logging Inc ....G..... 601 645-5813
Centreville *(G-731)*

James David Measell ....G..... 601 635-4441
Decatur *(G-1174)*

Jamie Valentine Logging LLC ....G...... 601 764-7271
Bay Springs *(G-166)*

Jason Fly Logging LLC ....F...... 662 316-3499
Batesville *(G-110)*

Jasons Custom Logging LLC ....G...... 601 270-6818
Lumberton *(G-3033)*

Jeff Shepherd Logging Inc ....F...... 601 416-1832
Philadelphia *(G-4219)*

Jeff Winstead Logging ....F...... 601 656-1448
Philadelphia *(G-4220)*

Jennifer L Johnson Lpn ....G..... 601 573-7582
Canton *(G-664)*

Jerold Henderson Logging Inc ....F...... 601 989-2399
Richton *(G-4537)*

Jerry Harris Logging Inc ....G..... 662 728-7331
Booneville *(G-332)*

Jimmy Jones & Sons Sawmill ....G...... 601 253-2533
Walnut Grove *(G-5460)*

Joe K Smith ....G..... 601 786-8632
Fayette *(G-1298)*

John Albert Ware ....G..... 662 489-7824
Pontotoc *(G-4339)*

Johnny McCool Logging ....E...... 601 636-3824
Vicksburg *(G-5383)*

Johnny W Mills Timber Company ....G...... 601 989-2398
Richton *(G-4538)*

Jones & Young Logging LLC ....G...... 601 681-6801
Meridian *(G-3354)*

Jones Logging Co Inc ....G..... 601 877-3814
Lorman *(G-2961)*

Justin Alan Rankin ....G..... 601 297-4365
Lumberton *(G-3034)*

K & J Logging Inc ....G..... 601 639-4607
Roxie *(G-4690)*

K&D Wright Logging ....G..... 601 729-5675
Laurel *(G-2789)*

Keith Conaway Logging LLC ....G...... 662 415-5646
Walnut *(G-5457)*

Kelwood Products ....G..... 662 862-9494
Fulton *(G-1461)*

Employee Codes: A=Over 500 employees, B=251-500
C=101-250, D=51-100, E=20-50, F=10-19, G=1-9

2019 Harris Directory of
Mississippi Manufacturers

217

24 LUMBER AND WOOD PRODUCTS, EXCEPT FURNITURE

Kenneth Smith ....G.....601 848-7956
State Line (G-4987)

Kinard Burge & Sons Inc ....F.....601 794-6829
Purvis (G-4443)

Kristina Thorn ....G.....256 460-9798
Dennis (G-1183)

L & W Logging Inc ....G.....601 927-3588
Crystal Springs (G-1145)

Ladner Logging LLC ....G.....601 422-7822
Laurel (G-2792)

Laird Timber Inc ....G.....601 833-4293
Brookhaven (G-507)

Lance Smith Logging Inc ....G.....601 833-4855
Brookhaven (G-508)

Langston Logging Inc ....G.....662 542-8704
Calhoun City (G-639)

Larry D Brabham ....G.....601 551-4777
Liberty (G-2914)

Larry Sasser Logging LP ....F.....601 734-6002
Bogue Chitto (G-303)

Larry Wheeless Logging ....G.....662 547-6863
Mc Cool (G-3236)

Larry Winstead ....F.....601 656-6438
Philadelphia (G-4223)

Lea Logging................................G.....601 833-8983
Brookhaven (G-509)

Leroy Dees ....G.....662 674-5356
Ethel (G-1282)

Lincoln Lumber Co Inc ....D.....601 833-4484
Brookhaven (G-512)

Livingston Log & Timber Co Inc......G.....601 425-2095
Laurel (G-2796)

Lloyd Cox Jr ....G.....662 462-5226
Rienzi (G-4650)

Lovorn Logging Inc ....G.....662 637-2617
Calhoun City (G-640)

M & B Logging Inc ....G.....601 384-6611
Bude (G-571)

M & T Logging ....G.....662 673-1621
Benton (G-209)

M&M Logging ....G.....601 754-2796
Brookhaven (G-514)

Mar-Cal Inc ....G.....601 825-7520
Mendenhall (G-3283)

Mark Taylor Logging ....G.....662 418-0812
Maben (G-3047)

Martin Logging Inc ....F.....601 644-3374
Meridian (G-3364)

Max White Logging Inc ....G.....662 560-3460
Oxford (G-3972)

Mayo Logging ....G.....601 270-4426
Richton (G-4540)

Mc Logging LLC ....G.....601 678-6681
Union (G-5301)

McCloud Logging Inc ....G.....601 835-3217
Jayess (G-2674)

McCrory Logging LLC ....G.....601 613-1702
Brandon (G-420)

McDaniel Logging Co Inc ....G.....601 322-7701
Roxie (G-4692)

McDaniel Trucking ....G.....601 656-1028
Philadelphia (G-4225)

McFarland Cascade Holdings Inc........E.....662 476-8000
Scooba (G-4771)

Mike Smith Logging Inc.................G.....601 833-2043
Brookhaven (G-517)

Miller Timber LLC.......................G.....662 501-6150
Houlka (G-2226)

Mills Logging ....G.....662 665-2718
Tiplersville (G-5081)

Mims Timber LLC ....G.....662 301-5022
Senatobia (G-4796)

Mmj Logging Inc ....G.....662 755-1163
Bentonia (G-212)

Molpus Timberlands Management ......G.....601 969-7093
Jackson (G-2509)

Money Tree Logging LLC ....G.....740 891-1713
Gulfport (G-1835)

Moores Logging & Trucking ....G.....662 289-5872
Kosciusko (G-2704)

Mossy Island Land & Forest LLC ......G.....662 207-6245
Inverness (G-2275)

Mp Logging ....G.....662 808-5411
Corinth (G-1104)

Nail Logging ....G.....601 953-0071
Kosciusko (G-2705)

Nail Logging LLC ....G.....601 825-3375
Brandon (G-428)

Narkeeta Forest Services Inc..........F.....601 692-4777
Porterville (G-4410)

New South Logging LLC ....G.....601 517-8457
Collins (G-856)

Nickerson Logging ....G.....662 289-9779
Kosciusko (G-2707)

No Hope Logging Inc ....G.....601 587-5515
Monticello (G-3437)

No Hope Trucking Inc ....G.....601 320-1919
Monticello (G-3438)

Nolan Brothers ....F.....662 862-3055
Fulton (G-1470)

Norman K Hillman ....G.....601 525-3735
Neely (G-3645)

North Mississippi Timber & Log ......G.....662 603-7944
Corinth (G-1106)

North Mississippi Timber Brk ....G.....662 728-7328
Booneville (G-339)

North Ms Timber Harvester ....G.....662 927-0013
Calhoun City (G-642)

ONeal Power Corporation ....G.....228 323-1059
Perkinston (G-4179)

Otis Logging Inc.........................G.....601 249-0963
McComb (G-3262)

Parker Logging Inc ....G.....662 412-2435
Calhoun City (G-643)

Parker Trucking and Hlg LLC..........G.....601 537-3670
Morton (G-3453)

Pearl River Logging LLC ....G.....601 587-2516
Monticello (G-3439)

Performance Logging LLC ....G.....601 656-3556
Philadelphia (G-4232)

Peters Brothers Logging ....G.....601 928-3591
Wiggins (G-5587)

Pezant Logging LLC ....G.....601 303-3025
Tylertown (G-5280)

Phillip Spring Logging In ....G.....601 567-2138
Smithdale (G-4842)

Pole Mill Optimizer LLC ....G.....601 928-8860
Wiggins (G-5588)

Prisock Brothers Logging Inc ....G.....662 773-8443
Louisville (G-2977)

Pro Logging Inc..........................E.....662 720-9457
Booneville (G-344)

Quinton Hill Logging ....G.....662 773-6864
Louisville (G-2978)

R & J Brown Logging & Trucking ......G.....601 739-3338
Louin (G-2963)

Ralph Morgan Logging Inc ....E.....601 679-5291
Lauderdale (G-2728)

Randy Cummings ....G.....662 547-2008
Weir (G-5521)

Randy Judge Logging Inc ....F.....601 775-3027
Lake (G-2724)

Ray Davis Logging Inc ....G.....601 687-1392
Waynesboro (G-5511)

Ray Smith Logging Inc ....G.....601 786-8428
Fayette (G-1300)

Raymond Granger ....G.....662 289-2502
Sallis (G-4704)

Reed Logging Inc ....G.....601 793-4951
Scooba (G-4772)

Reggie Waddle Logging Co ....G.....662 862-3106
Fulton (G-1473)

Reid & Deese Llc ....G.....601 248-3143
Tylertown (G-5283)

River Bank Logging LLC ....G.....601 639-4557
Crosby (G-1135)

River Bend Logging LLC ....G.....601 466-1524
Foxworth (G-1435)

Robert Bray Logging ....G.....601 269-3437
Raleigh (G-4476)

Robert L Leggett ....G.....601 833-7313
Brookhaven (G-527)

Robert W Stubbs ....G.....601 849-9857
Magee (G-3183)

Robin Jones Logging Co ....G.....601 687-5837
Shubuta (G-4833)

Rolison & Sons Logging Inc ....F.....662 837-9066
Ripley (G-4670)

Rolison Timber Logging ....G.....662 993-8115
Ripley (G-4671)

Ronald D Sterling ....G.....601 225-7772
Liberty (G-2916)

Ronny P Moore ....G.....601 934-0113
Quitman (G-4470)

RTC Logging Inc ....G.....601 517-6881
Collins (G-860)

S & F Logging Inc ....F.....662 552-4701
Mantee (G-3212)

S and M Logging LLC ....G.....662 263-6711
Mathiston (G-3230)

S L Netterville Logging Inc ....G.....601 639-4915
Gloster (G-1517)

Sassones Timber LLC ....E.....601 542-5558
Osyka (G-3929)

Scott Strickland Sons Inc ....G.....601 928-2321
Perkinston (G-4180)

Shannon Fulgham Logging Inc ....G.....662 418-4449
Maben (G-3050)

Shelby Logging LLC ....G.....601 609-7796
Jackson (G-2578)

Simpson Brothers Inc ....G.....678 451-4259
Mc Cool (G-3237)

Smith Boys Timber Inc ....G.....601 859-1628
Canton (G-679)

Smith Brothers Logging Inc ....F.....601 322-7362
Roxie (G-4694)

Smith Tie and Timber LLC ....E.....662 258-7605
Eupora (G-1292)

Smith Timber Inc ....G.....601 833-3968
Brookhaven (G-533)

Sojourner Timber Inc ....F.....601 892-4021
Crystal Springs (G-1156)

Sonny Moore ....G.....662 585-4009
Fulton (G-1475)

South Fork Logging LLC ....G.....601 218-4524
Vicksburg (G-5420)

Southern Forestry Inc ....F.....662 416-3883
Golden (G-1530)

Southern Logging Inc ....F.....601 657-4449
Liberty (G-2917)

Stickman Logging LLC ....G.....601 782-4597
Raleigh (G-4477)

Stinson & Son Logging ....G.....601 989-2311
Richton (G-4544)

Strong Bros Logging Inc ....G.....601 764-9191
Bay Springs (G-173)

Stuart Timber Inc ....G.....601 943-8184
Carson (G-705)

Summerford Enterprises Inc ....G.....662 585-3584
Golden (G-1531)

T & T Logging Co ....G.....601 852-4281
Edwards (G-1243)

T A Netterville Logging Inc ....F.....601 888-0054
Bogue Chitto (G-305)

T L G Logging Inc ....G.....601 225-9743
Gloster (G-1519)

Taylor McKinley ....F.....601 792-2739
Oak Vale (G-3736)

Taylor S Flying Service Inc ....G.....601 885-9959
Utica (G-5313)

Tdk Logging Inc ....F.....662 328-6625
Columbus (G-1037)

Teddy Doggett Logging Inc.............G.....601 687-5233
Waynesboro (G-5518)

Thomas Davis Gamblin ....F.....601 656-2759
Philadelphia (G-4241)

Thomas Logging Company Inc ....G.....662 862-7342
Fulton (G-1479)

Tim Breland Logging Inc ....G.....601 656-0382
Philadelphia (G-4243)

Tim Rollins Logging ....G.....601 225-4972
Gloster (G-1520)

Tim Wilder Logging Inc ....F.....662 489-7632
Ecru (G-1234)

Timber Creek Estates ....G.....228 392-0858
Biloxi (G-283)

Timber Harvesters Inc ....G.....601 416-2078
Philadelphia (G-4244)

Timber Resources Inc ....G.....601 681-6801
Meridian (G-3414)

Timberland Management Services ......G.....601 645-6440
Centreville (G-733)

Timberland Products Inc ....G.....601 442-8102
Natchez (G-3630)

Timberline Logging Inc ....F.....662 423-3948
Iuka (G-2309)

Timberwood Logging LLC ....G.....662 633-7744
Winona (G-5608)

Tippo Timber Company LLP ....G.....601 981-3303
Jackson (G-2608)

Tnc Logging Llc ....G.....601 394-9760
Leakesville (G-2879)

Tony Adams Logging ....G.....601 267-5174
Carthage (G-724)

Tony Pharr Logging ....G.....662 728-9426
Booneville (G-346)

Tri B Timber & Logging LLC ....G.....662 283-4824
Winona (G-5609)

Trinity Three LLC ....G.....601 249-8851
Summit (G-5027)

SIC SECTION

24 LUMBER AND WOOD PRODUCTS, EXCEPT FURNITURE

Triple G Logging ....G...... 601 416-8733
Philadelphia *(G-4245)*

Triple J Tie and Timber LLC ....G...... 662 547-6600
Weir *(G-5522)*

Triple L Logging ....F...... 601 656-9313
Philadelphia *(G-4247)*

TW Logging LLC ....G...... 601 657-8838
Liberty *(G-2918)*

Ulysses Cooley ....G...... 601 394-5485
Leakesville *(G-2881)*

Vaiden Timber Co ....G...... 662 464-7740
Vaiden *(G-5315)*

W A Mathis Timber Co ....G...... 601 684-7839
McComb *(G-3273)*

W L Byrd Lumber Co Inc ....E...... 601 567-2314
Summit *(G-5029)*

Walley Trucking ....G...... 601 848-7576
State Line *(G-4989)*

Walsworth Logging ....G...... 601 442-5406
Natchez *(G-3637)*

Watts Timber Company Inc ....F...... 601 754-0138
Brookhaven *(G-546)*

White Logging ....G...... 601 783-2738
Magnolia *(G-3196)*

Williams Logging Company Inc ....G...... 601 835-2771
Brookhaven *(G-548)*

Williamson & Son Logging LLC ....G...... 601 736-7858
Columbia *(G-928)*

Willie Lynn Hunt ....G...... 601 945-2237
Lucedale *(G-3021)*

X L Johnson & Sons Inc ....G...... 601 776-3685
Quitman *(G-4472)*

2421 Saw & Planing Mills

Al-Tom Forest Products Inc ....E...... 601 989-2631
Richton *(G-4526)*

Anderson-Tully Company ....B...... 601 629-3283
Vicksburg *(G-5339)*

Anderson-Tully Company ....B...... 601 636-3876
Vicksburg *(G-5340)*

Backwoods Tie and Timber LLC ....F...... 662 258-3388
Eupora *(G-1285)*

Barge Forest Products Co ....G...... 662 726-4426
Macon *(G-3055)*

Batte & Hollingsworth Lumber ....G...... 601 469-4938
Forest *(G-1409)*

Bazor Lumber Company LLC ....E...... 601 776-2181
Quitman *(G-4457)*

▲ Buckhaults Sawmill & Pallets ....E...... 601 477-8403
Ellisville *(G-1247)*

Buntyn Sawmill ....G...... 601 774-8128
Union *(G-5295)*

Byrne Furn Co & Sawmill Svcs ....G...... 601 442-7363
Natchez *(G-3541)*

Central Mississippi Wood Inc ....G...... 662 724-2447
Philadelphia *(G-4210)*

Chip Jones Mill Inc ....F...... 601 876-6943
Columbia *(G-886)*

Chips Amory Inc ....F...... 662 256-1400
Amory *(G-38)*

Chips Gloster Inc ....F...... 601 225-4405
Gloster *(G-1512)*

▼ Columbus Lumber Company LLC ....C...... 601 833-1990
Brookhaven *(G-488)*

Cooper Mar & Timberlands Corp ....G...... 662 454-9274
Dennis *(G-1181)*

Copiah Lumber Company ....E...... 601 892-2241
Crystal Springs *(G-1140)*

Crosby Wood Preserving Co Inc ....G...... 601 264-5249
Hattiesburg *(G-1952)*

Custom Rough Cut Lumber ....G...... 601 270-9518
Hattiesburg *(G-1955)*

Domtar Paper Company LLC ....C...... 662 256-3526
Columbus *(G-964)*

Elizabeth Newcomb ....G...... 662 596-1536
Rienzi *(G-4649)*

Ell Holdings ....G...... 601 325-3317
Hattiesburg *(G-1961)*

Enlow & Son Inc ....G...... 662 423-9073
Iuka *(G-2291)*

Fishers Sawmill ....G...... 662 967-2502
West *(G-5533)*

Fly Timber Co Inc ....F...... 662 226-2276
Grenada *(G-1677)*

Foxworth & Thompson Inc ....G...... 601 736-3602
Foxworth *(G-1430)*

Franklin Timber Company ....D...... 601 384-5826
Bude *(G-570)*

Franks Sawmill Inc ....G...... 601 344-7437
Ovett *(G-3931)*

Fred Netterville Lumber Co ....C...... 601 888-4343
Woodville *(G-5618)*

Georgia-Pacific LLC ....D...... 601 764-4806
Bay Springs *(G-161)*

Georgia-Pacific LLC ....C...... 601 785-4721
Columbia *(G-900)*

Georgia-Pacific LLC ....F...... 601 939-7797
Pearl *(G-4122)*

Gordon Redd Lumber Company ....E...... 601 833-2311
Brookhaven *(G-496)*

H & G Sawmill LLC ....G...... 601 885-2179
Utica *(G-5308)*

Hankins Lumber Company Inc ....F...... 662 226-2961
Elliott *(G-1244)*

Hazlehurst Lumber Company Inc ....D...... 601 535-7779
Hermanville *(G-2121)*

Homan Forest Products Inc ....G...... 662 862-2145
Fulton *(G-1455)*

Homan Industries Inc ....D...... 662 862-2125
Fulton *(G-1456)*

Homans Wood Products ....E...... 662 862-2145
Fulton *(G-1457)*

◆ Hood Industries Inc ....E...... 601 264-2962
Hattiesburg *(G-1994)*

▼ J M Jones Lumber Company Inc ....C...... 601 442-7471
Natchez *(G-3569)*

Jack Batte and Sons Inc ....E...... 601 536-3976
Forest *(G-1417)*

JC Jourdan Lumber Co Inc ....F...... 662 423-5238
Iuka *(G-2295)*

Jeffrey Roberson ....G...... 662 587-1991
Ripley *(G-4662)*

Jimmy Jones & Sons Sawmill ....G...... 601 253-2533
Walnut Grove *(G-5460)*

Jones Lumber Co Inc ....G...... 601 445-8206
Natchez *(G-3573)*

Jones Wood Products Inc ....G...... 601 876-2688
Tylertown *(G-5275)*

◆ JT Shannon Lumber Co Inc ....E...... 662 393-3765
Horn Lake *(G-2203)*

K C S Lumber Co Inc ....G...... 601 446-8525
Natchez *(G-3574)*

Kelwood Products Inc ....G...... 601 659-7027
Enterprise *(G-1280)*

Kermit Broome Sons WD Chipping ....E...... 601 264-8470
Sumrall *(G-5037)*

King Lumber Company Inc ....D...... 601 469-3271
Forest *(G-1420)*

◆ Kitchens Brothers Mfg Co ....E...... 601 885-6001
Utica *(G-5309)*

Leon Schommer Sawmill ....G...... 601 753-2687
Mc Lain *(G-3240)*

Lincoln Lumber Co Inc ....D...... 601 833-4484
Brookhaven *(G-512)*

M2 Corp ....G...... 662 342-2173
Southaven *(G-4887)*

Marietta Wood Supply Inc ....E...... 662 728-9874
Marietta *(G-3217)*

Marion County Timber Inc ....E...... 601 736-0654
Foxworth *(G-1433)*

Maxwell Sawmill LLC ....G...... 601 894-3194
Wesson *(G-5528)*

Millennium Outdoors LLC ....E...... 601 932-5832
Pearl *(G-4132)*

Nslc Southern Inc ....D...... 601 535-2205
Hermanville *(G-2122)*

Nslc Southern Inc ....E...... 601 605-0575
Ridgeland *(G-4613)*

Olmstead Timber ....G...... 601 655-8769
Chunky *(G-753)*

Parkerson Lumber Inc ....E...... 662 547-6019
French Camp *(G-1441)*

Phillips Bark Proc Co Inc ....G...... 601 605-1071
Brookhaven *(G-523)*

Power Plus Inc ....F...... 601 264-1950
Sumrall *(G-5042)*

Ralph Rone ....G...... 662 674-5796
Ethel *(G-1283)*

Reeds Reynolds ....E...... 601 445-8206
Natchez *(G-3612)*

Rex Lumber Brookhaven Llc ....G...... 601 833-1990
Brookhaven *(G-526)*

Rives and Reynolds Lbr Co Inc ....D...... 662 773-5157
Louisville *(G-2979)*

Rives and Reynolds Lbr Co Inc ....E...... 662 289-3823
Kosciusko *(G-2711)*

Rjb Enterprises ....E...... 601 639-4921
Crosby *(G-1136)*

RLH Trucking Inc ....G...... 662 462-5079
Burnsville *(G-573)*

Rogers Lumber Corp ....E...... 601 736-4472
Columbia *(G-919)*

Rogers Lumber Corp ....E...... 601 736-4472
Columbia *(G-920)*

Ronnie Kolb ....G...... 662 263-5252
Maben *(G-3049)*

Roseburg Forest Products Co ....E...... 662 773-9868
Louisville *(G-2981)*

Seago Enterprises Inc ....D...... 601 684-3000
McComb *(G-3265)*

Shuqualak Lumber Company Inc ....D...... 662 425-5339
Shuqualak *(G-4837)*

Sims Bark Co Inc ....F...... 662 895-6501
Olive Branch *(G-3910)*

Smith & Associates Inc ....G...... 228 864-2786
Long Beach *(G-2953)*

Smith Brothers Forest Products ....E...... 601 648-2892
Buckatunna *(G-565)*

Southeastern Timber Pdts LLC ....F...... 662 285-3291
Ackerman *(G-29)*

Tallahatchie Hardwoods Inc ....E...... 662 647-5427
Charleston *(G-744)*

Thomas Leslie Coleman ....G...... 662 369-6000
Caledonia *(G-632)*

◆ Thomasson Company ....E...... 601 656-6000
Philadelphia *(G-4242)*

Tombigbee Lumber Co Ms LLC ....G...... 662 862-7417
Fulton *(G-1480)*

Tombigbee Lumber Company Inc ....E...... 662 862-7417
Fulton *(G-1481)*

Trainum Lumber Inc ....G...... 662 224-8346
Ashland *(G-66)*

▲ Tri-State Lumber Company Inc ....D...... 662 862-2125
Fulton *(G-1483)*

Triple J Tie and Timber LLC ....G...... 601 663-4275
Philadelphia *(G-4246)*

W L Byrd Lumber Co Inc ....E...... 601 783-5711
Summit *(G-5028)*

W L Byrd Lumber Co Inc ....E...... 601 567-2314
Summit *(G-5029)*

Wallace Lumber Company ....E...... 601 276-2834
Summit *(G-5030)*

Weyerhaeuser Company ....C...... 601 650-7200
Philadelphia *(G-4249)*

Weyerhaeuser Company ....C...... 662 983-7311
Bruce *(G-562)*

Weyerhaeuser Company ....D...... 662 243-6900
Columbus *(G-1045)*

Wilder Bros Sawmill Inc ....E...... 662 488-8692
Ecru *(G-1235)*

Winona Hardwood Inc ....G...... 662 283-3050
Winona *(G-5611)*

2426 Hardwood Dimension & Flooring Mills

Al-Tom Forest Products Inc ....E...... 601 989-2631
Richton *(G-4526)*

Anderson-Tully Company ....B...... 601 636-3876
Vicksburg *(G-5340)*

Anderson-Tully Company ....B...... 601 629-3283
Vicksburg *(G-5339)*

C & W Frames Inc ....F...... 662 728-2120
Booneville *(G-323)*

Carnes Frames Inc ....E...... 662 489-1984
Pontotoc *(G-4325)*

Chickasaw Wood Products Inc ....F...... 662 456-5357
Houston *(G-2234)*

Clearspan Components Inc ....C...... 601 483-3941
Meridian *(G-3321)*

▲ Consolidated Inc ....F...... 601 425-2196
Laurel *(G-2757)*

Cynthia Bowen ....G...... 228 463-7131
Waveland *(G-5479)*

Davis & Son LLC ....G...... 662 728-8396
Booneville *(G-326)*

Dixie Mat and Hardwood Co ....E...... 601 876-2427
Columbia *(G-895)*

Everett Industries Inc ....G...... 228 231-1556
Bay Saint Louis *(G-143)*

Georgia-Pacific LLC ....D...... 601 764-4806
Bay Springs *(G-161)*

Georgia-Pacific LLC ....C...... 601 785-4721
Columbia *(G-900)*

Hodges Wood Products Inc ....E...... 662 728-3716
Marietta *(G-3216)*

Homans Wood Products ....E...... 662 862-2145
Fulton *(G-1457)*

Hood Industries Inc ....D...... 601 735-5038
Waynesboro *(G-5500)*

J & W Furniture Frames Inc ....E...... 662 489-1991
Pontotoc *(G-4338)*

Employee Codes: A=Over 500 employees, B=251-500
C=101-250, D=51-100, E=20-50, F=10-19, G=1-9

24 LUMBER AND WOOD PRODUCTS, EXCEPT FURNITURE

SIC SECTION

K & L Furniture Frames Inc ....E 662 489-5355
Pontotoc *(G-4340)*

Kelwood Products Inc ....E 601 659-7027
Enterprise *(G-1280)*

M R Furniture LLC ....G 662 882-8483
Dumas *(G-1222)*

Magnolia Furniture LLC ....G 662 489-9337
Pontotoc *(G-4342)*

Marietta Wood Supply Inc ....G 662 728-9874
Marietta *(G-3217)*

Martin and Sons LLC ....E 601 825-4012
Brandon *(G-418)*

Moss Woodturning Inc ....G 662 456-5043
Houston *(G-2251)*

Oak Wood Mills Inc ....G 662 542-9158
Houston *(G-2252)*

R & R Lumber Inc ....G 662 568-7937
Houlka *(G-2227)*

Reeds Reynolds ....E 601 445-8206
Natchez *(G-3612)*

Rives and Reynolds Lbr Co Inc ....E 662 289-3823
Kosciusko *(G-2711)*

Rjb Enterprises ....E 601 639-4921
Crosby *(G-1136)*

S&S Frames Inc ....F 662 488-8996
Ecru *(G-1232)*

Shamrock Wood Industries Inc ....C 662 393-2125
Horn Lake *(G-2210)*

Steve Hamblin Frames Inc ....G 662 568-7299
Houlka *(G-2229)*

Tallahatchie Hardwoods Inc ....E 662 647-5427
Charleston *(G-744)*

Thomas Leslie Coleman ....G 662 369-6000
Caledonia *(G-632)*

Tombigbee Lumber Company Inc ....E 662 862-7417
Fulton *(G-1481)*

Tommy L Henderson ....G 228 452-4484
Pass Christian *(G-4097)*

V & B International Inc ....E 601 437-8279
Port Gibson *(G-4408)*

Weyerhaeuser Company ....C 662 983-7311
Bruce *(G-562)*

2431 Millwork

601 Custom Woodworks ....G 601 588-0117
Beaumont *(G-183)*

A B S Woodworks ....G 601 425-3306
Laurel *(G-2730)*

Acadian Custom Woodworks ....G 601 572-4774
Brandon *(G-354)*

Alfords Decorating Center ....G 662 455-3552
Greenwood *(G-1612)*

Alvin Schilling Wdwkg LLC ....G 601 268-1070
Purvis *(G-4432)*

Ameitech/South ....G 601 853-0830
Ridgeland *(G-4548)*

Ash Millworks Inc ....E 601 544-3962
Petal *(G-4184)*

Axsom Woodworks ....G 334 422-9766
Gulfport *(G-1731)*

B&M Maintenance LLC ....G 228 273-5821
Vancleave *(G-5318)*

Barnes Sawmill Woodworks ....G 901 605-7104
Olive Branch *(G-3818)*

Barrys Fine Wdwkg & Crafts LLC ....G 662 808-2268
Tupelo *(G-5113)*

Bayou View Woodworks ....G 985 290-0860
Bay Saint Louis *(G-136)*

Bennetts Wood Works ....G 662 862-6124
Fulton *(G-1446)*

Buckrdge Spclty Wods Mill Wrks ....G 601 667-3791
Canton *(G-651)*

Burchwood Inc ....F 662 841-2609
Mooreville *(G-3441)*

Burns Fence & Woodworks LLC ....G 601 506-5226
Jackson *(G-2349)*

C E Russell Framing Components ....G 228 762-9267
Pascagoula *(G-4024)*

Chippewa Enterprises LLC ....G 228 832-0032
Gulfport *(G-1752)*

Clearspan Components Inc ....C 601 483-3941
Meridian *(G-3321)*

Colquitt Woodworks LLC ....G 229 425-6087
Diamondhead *(G-1187)*

Correro Woodworks ....G 662 334-9837
Greenville *(G-1542)*

Cox Works ....G 228 236-8402
Saucier *(G-4750)*

Cr Custom Woodworks ....G 601 624-2310
Pearl *(G-4113)*

▼ Croft LLC ....E 601 684-6121
McComb *(G-3247)*

Crown Simple Renovations Wdwkg ......G 601 850-8272
Florence *(G-1317)*

Crown Simple Renovations Wdwkg ......G 601 850-8272
Florence *(G-1318)*

Custom Architectural Millwork ....G 662 562-7011
Sarah *(G-4733)*

Delta Enterprises ....G 662 335-5291
Greenville *(G-1545)*

DH Woodworks ....G 662 299-5486
Greenwood *(G-1620)*

Dimensions Wood Works ....G 228 254-6623
Ocean Springs *(G-3752)*

Donald W Mason ....G 601 269-3782
Raleigh *(G-4475)*

Donovan P Cain ....G 662 279-2124
Glen *(G-1506)*

Dunns Woodworking LLC ....G 601 736-0633
Columbia *(G-897)*

Easley & Easley Millworks Inc ....F 601 372-8881
Jackson *(G-2395)*

Ellis Custom Woodwork LLC ....G 601 983-8464
Jackson *(G-2399)*

Fayard Millworks ....G 228 265-7787
Gulfport *(G-1783)*

Fleming True Value Lbr ....G 662 843-2763
Cleveland *(G-793)*

Fortenberry Builders Supply ....G 601 825-3370
Brandon *(G-397)*

Frierson Building Supply Co ....C 601 922-1321
Jackson *(G-2456)*

Garner Millwork Inc ....F 662 844-7007
Tupelo *(G-5139)*

Georgia-Pacific LLC ....F 601 939-7797
Pearl *(G-4122)*

Georgia-Pacific LLC ....G 601 587-7711
Monticello *(G-3433)*

Great Southern Log Homes Inc ....G 601 833-0700
Brookhaven *(G-497)*

Guice Woodworks ....G 323 384-1826
Ocean Springs *(G-3760)*

Gulf Coast Cabinets & Mill ....G 228 206-7792
Gulfport *(G-1797)*

H & L Millworks Inc ....G 228 392-9913
Biloxi *(G-250)*

Halls Woodworking ....G 601 792-5955
Prentiss *(G-4421)*

Harris Frm Hven Spcltymillwork ....G 601 953-2964
Canton *(G-660)*

Herrington Millworks ....G 601 845-8056
Florence *(G-1325)*

High Country Woodworking ....G 228 396-2921
Biloxi *(G-251)*

Hobby Const Co ....G 662 803-1599
Louisville *(G-2972)*

Holcomb Handiman Svcs Cstm Woo ....G 601 394-4284
Laurel *(G-2778)*

Interior and Exterior WD Work ....G 662 587-2417
Ashland *(G-61)*

James Newton ....G 662 647-8968
Charleston *(G-739)*

JC Manufacturing LLC ....G 662 338-9004
Starkville *(G-4952)*

Jims Woodworks LLC ....G 601 862-1025
Bolton *(G-310)*

Jjs Woodshed ....G 662 380-5034
Oxford *(G-3964)*

Js Woodworking ....G 228 257-6846
Biloxi *(G-255)*

Kings Woodworks ....G 662 403-0871
Hernando *(G-2136)*

Lakeside Moulding & Mfg Co ....D 601 992-5546
Flowood *(G-1376)*

Lamb Woodworking ....G 601 545-3052
Brooklyn *(G-551)*

Longleaf Forest Products LLC ....G 662 456-4444
Houston *(G-2250)*

M S I/Pozzi ....G 601 957-0085
Ridgeland *(G-4599)*

Macs Small Engine Service ....F 601 932-8076
Richland *(G-4521)*

Magnolia Screens LLC ....G 601 942-3049
Jackson *(G-2479)*

Masonite Corporation ....D 601 422-2200
Laurel *(G-2798)*

McLellan Woodworks ....G 336 425-8425
Brandon *(G-422)*

McMaster Custom Woodworks LLC ......G 601 408-2252
Canton *(G-670)*

McNeil Cabinet and Millwork ....E 601 764-2100
Bay Springs *(G-168)*

Meridian Woodworking ....G 601 604-6147
Meridian *(G-3369)*

Mid South Storm Shelters LLC ....G 901 619-0064
Como *(G-1049)*

Mikes Woodworking ....G 601 966-1868
Canton *(G-671)*

Morgan Brothers Millwork Inc ....C 601 649-9188
Laurel *(G-2807)*

Palmer Handrail & Custom Mllwk ....G 662 287-3090
Corinth *(G-1107)*

Pearl River Door Company ....G 601 573-2572
Pearl *(G-4137)*

Pitts Companies Cabinets Mllwk ....G 662 844-2772
Tupelo *(G-5205)*

Prevost Woodworking ....G 615 836-9383
Brandon *(G-439)*

Robinson Woodworks ....G 662 419-1864
Randolph *(G-4480)*

Roseburg Forest Products Co ....E 662 773-9868
Louisville *(G-2981)*

S and S Woodworking LLC ....G 228 257-6846
Diberville *(G-1211)*

Scanlon-Taylor Millwork Co ....D 601 362-5333
Jackson *(G-2574)*

Sentiments By Shele - Whmsical ....G 662 812-3506
Olive Branch *(G-3907)*

Shirley McArthur Nobles ....G 601 310-0890
Sumrall *(G-5044)*

Smyda Woodworking Inc ....G 601 591-0247
Brandon *(G-456)*

Southern Cabinet & Woodwork ....E 228 475-0912
Moss Point *(G-3499)*

Southern Cabinets & Millwork ....G 662 447-3885
Okolona *(G-3799)*

Stout Woodworks Inc ....G 601 795-0727
Poplarville *(G-4397)*

Target Door and Supply Inc ....G 601 790-9006
Ridgeland *(G-4637)*

Top of Line Woodwork ....G 228 669-3363
Saucier *(G-4767)*

Tri-C Wood Products Inc ....E 601 774-8295
Union *(G-5303)*

Triple E Door & Hardware Inc ....G 601 940-7371
Brandon *(G-469)*

Vbg Woodworks LLC ....G 601 634-0313
Vicksburg *(G-5434)*

Webbs Cstm Wdwrk & Fnshg LLC ....G 601 824-2851
Brandon *(G-473)*

Whiting Woodcraft LLC ....G 662 895-1688
Olive Branch *(G-3926)*

Widups Woodworks LLC ....G 601 966-0593
Madison *(G-3171)*

Willies Woodworks ....G 601 916-3574
Picayune *(G-4304)*

Wood Work Solutions ....G 662 890-8954
Olive Branch *(G-3928)*

Wooden Arts LLC ....G 228 452-9943
Long Beach *(G-2960)*

Woodies Woodworks ....G 478 973-8851
Lauderdale *(G-2729)*

Woodworkings ....G 662 255-3421
Baldwyn *(G-89)*

2434 Wood Kitchen Cabinets

Advantage Cabinet Doors ....G 662 494-9700
West Point *(G-5534)*

Andrews Cabinet Shop ....G 662 327-1070
Columbus *(G-935)*

Ash Millworks Inc ....E 601 544-3962
Petal *(G-4184)*

Associated Architectural Pdts ....F 662 245-0400
Columbus *(G-937)*

Bowman Cabinet Company ....G 662 564-2711
Holly Springs *(G-2172)*

Bridges Custom Cabinets & Trim ....G 601 954-5085
Canton *(G-650)*

Buchanan Custom Cabinets ....G 662 438-7435
Tishomingo *(G-5083)*

Bunyard Cabinetry ....G 601 757-8765
Brookhaven *(G-485)*

Burgess Kustom Cabinetry ....G 662 316-4294
New Albany *(G-3676)*

C & D Cabinets LLC ....F 228 466-4644
Waveland *(G-5478)*

Cabinet Specialists Inc ....G 601 992-3929
Jackson *(G-2352)*

Cabinetsource Inc ....G 228 385-8880
Gulfport *(G-1747)*

2019 Harris Directory of
Mississippi Manufacturers

SIC SECTION

24 LUMBER AND WOOD PRODUCTS, EXCEPT FURNITURE

Carpenters Cabinets ....G...... 662 465-6453
Sturgis (G-5006)

CL Cabinets LLC ....G...... 228 860-9678
Long Beach (G-2933)

Clear Creek Cabinetry Inc ....G...... 601 684-7130
Summit (G-5008)

Coast Wood Products Inc ....G...... 228 466-4302
Bay Saint Louis (G-141)

Colon Cabinets and Trim ....G...... 662 347-8608
Greenville (G-1539)

D&H Construction Cabinetry Inc ....G...... 601 737-2010
Meridian (G-3326)

Darrells Custom Cabinets ....G...... 662 822-3936
Greenville (G-1544)

Davis & Cooke Custom Cabinetry ....G...... 601 580-0181
Laurel (G-2759)

Easley & Easley Millworks Inc ....F....... 601 372-8881
Jackson (G-2395)

Ellis Woodworks ....G...... 662 329-2605
Columbus (G-970)

Garner Millwork Inc ....F....... 662 844-7007
Tupelo (G-5139)

Graham Custom Cabinets & Trim ....G...... 803 381-6829
Crystal Springs (G-1142)

Heritage Custom Cabinets LLC ....G...... 228 323-8389
Gulfport (G-1806)

Hilderbrand Cabinet Doors LLC ....G...... 662 755-8626
Bentonia (G-211)

J M I Inc ....G...... 601 936-6800
Brandon (G-409)

Jakes Woodwork LLC ....G...... 601 651-6278
Laurel (G-2786)

Joes Custom Cabinets ....G...... 601 508-8284
Lucedale (G-3006)

Kitchen Elegance LLC ....G...... 228 248-0074
Gulfport (G-1818)

Kitchen Table ....F....... 601 261-3836
Hattiesburg (G-2008)

Lynn Hollis Rebel Cabinets ....G...... 228 588-2572
Moss Point (G-3484)

Magnolia Cabinet & Mllwk Inc ....G...... 662 282-7683
Mantachie (G-3201)

Magnolia Cabinet Works ....G...... 601 916-6538
Carriere (G-697)

McHan Cabinets ....G...... 601 636-8821
Vicksburg (G-5394)

Murphy Cabinet Company ....G...... 662 417-9717
Grenada (G-1696)

Nightengale Cabinets ....G...... 662 686-9004
Leland (G-2891)

Orman Cabinet Co LLC ....G...... 662 837-6352
Oxford (G-3983)

Petermans Cabinets ....G...... 228 832-0353
Gulfport (G-1848)

Pettigrew Cabinets Inc ....E....... 662 844-1368
Plantersville (G-4313)

Pierce Cabinets Inc ....E....... 662 840-6795
Tupelo (G-5204)

Pro-Stone LLC ....F....... 334 281-0048
Olive Branch (G-3902)

Rainey Mill Works LLC ....F....... 601 583-1310
Hattiesburg (G-2048)

Reeves Cabinets ....G...... 662 323-3633
Starkville (G-4967)

Robert Smith Custom Cabinets ....F....... 662 282-5007
Mantachie (G-3204)

Shawn Kurtz ....G...... 601 415-9540
Vicksburg (G-5416)

Smith Cabinet Shop Inc ....E....... 662 287-2151
Corinth (G-1119)

Southeastern Constructors Inc ....E....... 601 825-9791
Brandon (G-457)

Southern Cabinet & Woodwork ....E....... 228 475-0912
Moss Point (G-3499)

Southern Cabinets ....G...... 901 461-6161
Byhalia (G-605)

Southern Charm Cstm Cbntry LLC ....G...... 662 862-5058
Fulton (G-1476)

Sterling Custom Cabinets LLC ....G...... 601 996-1906
Gloster (G-1518)

Straughter Cabinets ....G...... 662 247-2728
Belzoni (G-206)

Summit Cabinet Co LLC ....G...... 601 684-1639
Summit (G-5023)

Superior Granite & Quartz ....G...... 662 241-5664
Columbus (G-1034)

Thornton & Sons Cabinet Shop ....G...... 601 425-2172
Laurel (G-2858)

Troy Custom Cabinets LLC ....G...... 662 902-5559
Tutwiler (G-5260)

Viking Capital Ventures Inc ....F....... 662 455-1200
Greenwood (G-1656)

W L Tisdale Cabinet Shop ....G...... 601 763-3552
Ellisville (G-1274)

Whittington Construction Co ....G...... 601 442-8096
Natchez (G-3640)

2435 Hardwood Veneer & Plywood

Anderson-Tully Company ....B...... 601 629-3283
Vicksburg (G-5339)

Commercial Mllwk Spcialist Inc ....E...... 228 868-3888
Gulfport (G-1763)

Davis Wood Products of Miss ....C...... 662 534-2211
New Albany (G-3680)

Frierson Building Supply Co ....C...... 601 922-1321
Jackson (G-2416)

Georgia-Pacific LLC ....G...... 601 225-4211
Gloster (G-1515)

Hood Industries Inc ....B...... 601 928-3737
Wiggins (G-5584)

Hood Industries Inc ....D...... 601 735-5038
Waynesboro (G-5500)

Hood Industries Inc ....C...... 601 784-3414
Beaumont (G-185)

Pavco Industries Inc ....D...... 228 762-3959
Pascagoula (G-4061)

◆ Quality Plywood Company Inc ....D...... 601 735-3106
Waynesboro (G-5510)

Scotch Plywood Company Miss ....D...... 601 735-2881
Waynesboro (G-5513)

Timber Products Co Ltd Partnr ....D...... 662 287-3766
Corinth (G-1122)

2436 Softwood Veneer & Plywood

▲ American Pacific Inc ....D...... 662 252-1862
Holly Springs (G-2171)

Georgia-Pacific LLC ....G...... 601 225-4211
Gloster (G-1515)

◆ Hood Industries Inc ....D...... 601 264-2962
Hattiesburg (G-1994)

Hood Industries Inc ....C...... 601 784-3414
Beaumont (G-185)

Hood Industries Inc ....B...... 601 928-3737
Wiggins (G-5584)

Palmer Veneer Inc ....F....... 601 735-9717
Waynesboro (G-5509)

Scotch Plywood Company Miss ....D...... 601 735-2881
Waynesboro (G-5513)

2439 Structural Wood Members, NEC

Clearspan Components Inc ....C...... 601 483-3941
Meridian (G-3321)

CST Timber Company ....F....... 601 225-7887
Gloster (G-1513)

Evergreen Lumber & Truss Inc ....E...... 601 794-8404
Purvis (G-4437)

Frierson Building Supply Co ....C...... 601 922-1321
Jackson (G-2416)

Mid-South Truss Co Inc ....G...... 662 728-0016
Booneville (G-336)

Mississippi Laminators Inc ....E...... 601 687-1621
Shubuta (G-4831)

Oldtown Truss ....G...... 662 412-2500
Pittsboro (G-4309)

Pine Belt Truss Company Inc ....G...... 601 729-4298
Soso (G-4847)

Southeastern Forest Produ ....G...... 601 988-1131
Flowood (G-1399)

Trimjoist Corporation ....E...... 662 327-7950
Columbus (G-1039)

2441 Wood Boxes

Bryan Industrial Co Inc ....F....... 601 649-8786
Laurel (G-2744)

Chickasaw Wood Products Inc ....F....... 662 456-5357
Houston (G-2234)

▲ Hudspeth Wood Products Inc ....F....... 662 263-5902
Maben (G-3046)

Ronda K Gentry ....G...... 662 418-9844
Starkville (G-4969)

2448 Wood Pallets & Skids

All Star Forest Products Inc ....G...... 228 896-4117
Gulfport (G-1720)

All Star Forest Products Inc ....G...... 662 294-8898
Grenada (G-1667)

All Star Forest Products Inc ....G...... 601 664-0700
Jackson (G-2322)

Bryan Industrial Co Inc ....F....... 601 649-8786
Laurel (G-2744)

Cccl Pallet LLC ....G...... 662 494-0141
West Point (G-5540)

Chep (usa) Inc ....E...... 601 352-6500
Jackson (G-2359)

Coastal Tie & Timber Co Inc ....E...... 601 876-2688
Tylertown (G-5267)

Coastal Transportation LLC ....G...... 601 876-2688
Tylertown (G-5268)

Custom Pallett LLC ....G...... 662 423-8127
Tishomingo (G-5084)

Debra A Jones ....F....... 601 845-8946
Florence (G-1320)

Delta Pallets and Crates I ....G...... 662 781-1633
Walls (G-5449)

Dixie Mat and Hardwood Co ....E...... 601 876-2427
Columbia (G-895)

Gann Brothers Inc ....G...... 662 568-2980
Houlka (G-2223)

▲ Hudspeth Wood Products Inc ....F....... 662 263-5902
Maben (G-3046)

Inca Presswood-Pallets Ltd ....G...... 662 487-1016
Sardis (G-4741)

Inca Presswood-Pallets Ltd ....E...... 662 487-1016
Sardis (G-4742)

JC Jourdan Lumber Co Inc ....F....... 662 423-5238
Iuka (G-2295)

Koestler Pallet Sales Inc ....F....... 601 852-2926
Edwards (G-1240)

Martin and Sons LLC ....E...... 601 825-4012
Brandon (G-418)

McMillon Pallet ....G...... 601 932-2299
Jackson (G-2656)

Memphis Pallet Services LLC ....G...... 901 334-6306
Byhalia (G-591)

Pallet Exchange Network ....G...... 251 709-7021
Gautier (G-1501)

Pallet Source Inc ....E...... 662 851-3118
Mount Pleasant (G-3512)

Pallets Inc ....F....... 601 876-2688
Tylertown (G-5278)

Rehabilitation Svcs Miss Dept ....E...... 662 335-3359
Greenville (G-1595)

River City Pallet Co ....G...... 601 415-0386
Vicksburg (G-5411)

Robert R Stewart ....G...... 601 408-0494
Hattiesburg (G-2053)

Stanley D Stokes Jr ....G...... 662 237-6600
Carrollton (G-703)

▲ Superior Mat Company Inc ....G...... 601 765-8268
Collins (G-864)

Superior Pallet Company ....G...... 601 941-6254
Brandon (G-465)

T & G Pallet Inc ....F....... 662 746-4499
Yazoo City (G-5647)

Tenn Tom Pallet Company Inc ....G...... 662 369-9341
Aberdeen (G-20)

W & W Pallets LLC ....G...... 662 706-0050
Plantersville (G-4318)

Windmill Pallet Works Inc ....F....... 601 876-4498
Tylertown (G-5291)

Yna Pallets Sales ....G...... 601 405-6545
Florence (G-1340)

2449 Wood Containers, NEC

Ed Dangerfield Const Millwrks ....G...... 662 328-3877
Columbus (G-967)

Grady 1&2 ....G...... 601 677-3390
Preston (G-4427)

Martin and Sons LLC ....E...... 601 825-4012
Brandon (G-418)

Stanley D Stokes Jr ....G...... 662 237-6600
Carrollton (G-703)

2451 Mobile Homes

Central Miss Manufacturing Hsing ....G...... 601 267-8353
Carthage (G-711)

Clayton Homes Inc ....G...... 601 939-0461
Pearl (G-4110)

Lifetime Portable Building LLC ....G...... 228 860-7715
Gulfport (G-1821)

Smith Mobile Home Company ....G...... 662 566-7998
Tupelo (G-5224)

2452 Prefabricated Wood Buildings & Cmpnts

C3 Design Inc ....F....... 662 392-5021
Greenwood (G-1617)

Employee Codes: A=Over 500 employees, B=251-500
C=101-250, D=51-100, E=20-50, F=10-19, G=1-9

2019 Harris Directory of
Mississippi Manufacturers

24 LUMBER AND WOOD PRODUCTS, EXCEPT FURNITURE

SIC SECTION

Cook Sales Inc ....E 662 229-9787
Grenada **(G-1672)**
Enercept Inc ....G 228 323-1666
Gulfport **(G-1779)**
Great Southern Log Homes Inc ....G 601 833-0700
Brookhaven **(G-497)**
K & T Poultry Sales & Svc Inc ....F 601 764-3918
Bay Springs **(G-167)**
Payne Portable Building Inc ....G 601 426-9484
Laurel **(G-2818)**
Southland Log Homes ....G 601 605-4900
Madison **(G-3151)**

2491 Wood Preserving

Abbeville Mill LLC ....G 662 238-7879
Abbeville **(G-1)**
Amite County Poles & Piling ....G 601 225-4870
Gloster **(G-1510)**
Baldwin Pole Mississippi LLC ....G 601 928-5475
Wiggins **(G-5571)**
Biewer Sawmill-Newton LLC ....F 601 357-6001
Newton **(G-3717)**
Brown Wood Preserving Co Inc ....G 601 656-2607
Philadelphia **(G-4209)**
Brown Wood Preserving Co Inc ....G 662 263-8272
Mathiston **(G-3227)**
Carpenters Pole & Piling Co ....E 601 928-7400
Wiggins **(G-5576)**
▼ Columbus Lumber Company LLC ...C 601 833-1990
Brookhaven **(G-488)**
Cpp LLC ....G 601 749-7140
Picayune **(G-4262)**
Deforest Wood Preserving Co ....G 601 866-4655
Bolton **(G-308)**
Desoto Treated Materials Inc ....E 601 928-3921
Wiggins **(G-5580)**
Electric Mills Wood Prsv LLC ....G 662 476-8000
Scooba **(G-4770)**
Elite Wood Care ....G 601 622-2278
Brandon **(G-394)**
Forest Penick Products Inc ....E 662 726-5224
Macon **(G-3062)**
Gordon Redd Lumber Company ....E 601 833-2311
Brookhaven **(G-496)**
Great Southern Wood Prsv Inc ....G 601 823-4865
Brookhaven **(G-498)**
J and S Keene LLC ....G 601 833-8874
Brookhaven **(G-503)**
L L Wood ....G 662 454-0506
Belmont **(G-199)**
Macon Treating Company ....G 662 726-2767
Macon **(G-3066)**
Martin and Sons LLC ....E 601 825-4012
Brandon **(G-418)**
McFarland Cascade Holdings Inc ....E 662 476-8000
Scooba **(G-4771)**
Natural Wood Solutions LLC ....G 662 871-1625
Nettleton **(G-3665)**
Pearl River Timber Llc ....G 985 516-7951
Poplarville **(G-4388)**
Powe Timber Company ....G 601 788-6564
Richton **(G-4542)**
Powe Timber Company ....G 601 545-7600
Hattiesburg **(G-2046)**
Southern WD Prsv Httesburg Inc ....F 601 544-1140
Hattiesburg **(G-2065)**
Stone Treated Materials................G 601 798-4422
Picayune **(G-4299)**
Thomas Wood Preserving Inc ....E 662 226-2350
Grenada **(G-1708)**
Treated Materials Co Inc ....F 228 896-5056
Gulfport **(G-1887)**
▲ Tri-State Lumber Company Inc ....D 662 862-2125
Fulton **(G-1483)**
Tri-State Pole & Piling Inc ....F 601 947-4285
Lucedale **(G-3020)**
Wood Preserving Inc ....G 601 833-8822
Brookhaven **(G-549)**

2493 Reconstituted Wood Prdts

▲ American Pacific Inc ....D 662 252-1862
Holly Springs **(G-2171)**
Carlmac Industries Inc ....G 601 794-5000
Purvis **(G-4435)**
Certainteed Gypsum Inc ....C 601 693-0254
Meridian **(G-3318)**
Industrial Timber LLC ....E 662 346-4488
Saltillo **(G-4713)**
Industrial Timber LLC ....D 662 282-4000
Mantachie **(G-3199)**

Industrial Timber LLC ....D 662 837-3213
Ripley **(G-4661)**
Norbord Mississippi Inc ....C 662 348-2800
Guntown **(G-1900)**
Norbord Mississippi LLC ....G 662 348-2800
Guntown **(G-1901)**
Owens Custom Marble ....G 662 627-7256
Lyon **(G-3043)**
▼ Purvis Forest Products Inc ....E 601 794-8593
Purvis **(G-4448)**
Roseburg Forest Products Co ....B 601 785-4734
Taylorsville **(G-5058)**
Roseburg Forest Products Co ....B 662 236-8080
Oxford **(G-4000)**
Roseburg Forest Products Co ....E 662 773-9868
Louisville **(G-2981)**
Saunders Mfg Co Inc ....F 601 693-3482
Meridian **(G-3394)**
Smith Cabinet Shop Inc ....G 662 287-2151
Corinth **(G-1119)**
Tom Lauderdale Paper Svcs Inc ....F 662 767-9744
Shannon **(G-4819)**

2499 Wood Prdts, NEC

Andrews Woodshop LLC ....G 228 216-5563
Gulfport **(G-1725)**
Art Horizons Inc ....C 662 561-9733
Batesville **(G-96)**
ASpauljoy ....G 662 397-3661
Booneville **(G-319)**
Atwood Auto & Marine ....G 601 624-7012
Brandon **(G-366)**
Bobs Woodworking LLC ....G 601 661-8093
Vicksburg **(G-5347)**
Burtoni Fine Art Inc ....G 601 581-1557
Meridian **(G-3314)**
Careys Fencing ....G 601 434-6510
Hattiesburg **(G-1940)**
Caviness Woodworking Company ....D 662 628-5195
Calhoun City **(G-636)**
Cortez Byrd Chips Inc ....E 601 835-0333
Bogue Chitto **(G-301)**
Cotton Patch Framery ....G 662 895-6605
Olive Branch **(G-3829)**
Cottonport Hardwoods LLC ....G 601 442-9888
Natchez **(G-3551)**
Dungans Outdoor Solutions Co ....G 228 382-7156
Ocean Springs **(G-3753)**
Eugene Flanders ....G 601 544-0345
Hattiesburg **(G-1965)**
Final Touch Accessories LLC ....E 662 594-1348
Corinth **(G-1085)**
Gallery ....G 662 224-6694
Ashland **(G-60)**
Glenda Brock Woods Music LLC ....G 662 588-8343
Shaw **(G-4823)**
Great Southern Log Homes Inc ....G 601 833-0700
Brookhaven **(G-497)**
Gulf Shores Sea Products Inc ....G 228 323-6370
Lakeshore **(G-2726)**
Hastys Mulch & Stone LLC ....G 601 485-2120
Meridian **(G-3346)**
Holmes Hilton ....G 601 736-5757
Foxworth **(G-1432)**
Kathys Frame Works Inc ....G 228 769-7672
Pascagoula **(G-4044)**
Lemonwood LLC ....G 601 792-5748
Oak Vale **(G-3735)**
Loggins Woodwork ....G 662 283-5882
Kilmichael **(G-2677)**
Longleaf Forest Products LLC ....G 662 456-4444
Houston **(G-2250)**
▲ Magnolia Beneke Inc ....E 662 328-4000
Columbus **(G-997)**
Mary Tio ....G 228 392-0706
Biloxi **(G-266)**
Mississippi Wood Stakes Inc ....G 662 224-0975
Ashland **(G-64)**
Palmer Handrail & Custom Mllwk.........G 662 287-3090
Corinth **(G-1107)**
Pickens Hardwoods Inc ....G 601 924-1199
Jackson **(G-2539)**
Pinecrest Woodworks ....G 601 677-3015
Shuqualak **(G-4836)**
Red Lake Cedar Co LLC ....G 877 469-5552
Flowood **(G-1391)**
South Coast Paddling Company ....G 228 818-9442
Ocean Springs **(G-3789)**
Southland Supplies ....G 662 647-2452
Cascilla **(G-729)**

Stringer Woodworks ....G 601 372-5725
Raymond **(G-4493)**
Tally Student Service LLC ....G 601 782-9606
Raleigh **(G-4478)**
Wilderwood LLC ....G 601 955-8539
Flowood **(G-1407)**

25 FURNITURE AND FIXTURES

2511 Wood Household Furniture

◆ Affordable Furn Mfg Co Inc ....B 662 568-7981
Houlka **(G-2216)**
Andrews Furniture Company Inc ....G 662 489-1107
Ecru **(G-1229)**
◆ Behold Washington LLC ....B 662 489-6117
Pontotoc **(G-4322)**
Bill Briscoe ....G 662 234-5669
Oxford **(G-3940)**
Classic Furniture Mfg ....E 662 456-5900
Houston **(G-2235)**
▲ Consolidated Inc ....F 601 425-2196
Laurel **(G-2757)**
Crossroads Furniture Inc ....G 662 627-2114
Clarksdale **(G-764)**
Delta Furniture Mfg LLC ....D 662 489-2128
Pontotoc **(G-4329)**
▼ DIAS LLC ....E 662 628-1580
Calhoun City **(G-638)**
Ffm Inc ....E 662 256-9665
Amory **(G-42)**
From Our House To Yours ....G 601 956-1818
Madison **(G-3101)**
Grassy Ridge Gazebos ....G 662 738-6556
Brooksville **(G-554)**
Jakes Woodwork LLC ....G 601 651-6278
Laurel **(G-2786)**
Johnston-Tombigbee Furn Mfg Co ....C 662 328-1685
Columbus **(G-992)**
Krueger International Inc ....A 662 842-3124
Tupelo **(G-5167)**
▲ Lounora Industries Inc ....E 662 328-1685
Columbus **(G-994)**
▲ Oiseys International Inc ....G 662 255-1545
Belden **(G-191)**
Old House Depot LLC ....G 601 592-6200
Jackson **(G-2529)**
Quality Cabinet Company Inc ....E 662 429-1411
Hernando **(G-2151)**
S & S Frame Sales LLC ....G 662 397-3725
Shannon **(G-4818)**
Southern Craftsmen Inc ....G 601 484-5757
Meridian **(G-3402)**
Southern Rustic Logwerks LLC ....G 662 315-9677
Amory **(G-54)**
Sunbeam Products Inc ....A 601 296-5000
Hattiesburg **(G-2071)**
Tru-Cut Inc ....E 662 489-1879
Pontotoc **(G-4365)**
United States Worldwide Inc ....G 662 488-1840
Pontotoc **(G-4367)**
Viking Capital Ventures Inc ....F 662 455-1200
Greenwood **(G-1656)**

2512 Wood Household Furniture, Upholstered

A-1 Family Furniture Inc ....E 662 257-6002
Amory **(G-34)**
Albany Industries Inc ....G 662 488-8281
Pontotoc **(G-4320)**
◆ Albany Industries LLC ....B 662 534-9800
New Albany **(G-3672)**
Ashley Furniture Inds Inc ....C 662 837-7146
Ripley **(G-4652)**
Ashley Furniture Inds Inc ....G 608 323-3377
Tupelo **(G-5110)**
Ashley Furniture Inds Inc ....C 662 489-5655
Ecru **(G-1230)**
Aw Manufacturing Inc ....C 662 767-2800
Shannon **(G-4806)**
◆ Bauhaus Furniture Group LLC........B 662 869-2664
Saltillo **(G-4707)**
▲ Behold Home Inc ....E 662 651-4510
Smithville **(G-4843)**
Blue Mountain Furniture LLC ....F 662 685-4871
Blue Mountain **(G-288)**
Brazil Furniture Inc ....E 662 489-2063
Pontotoc **(G-4323)**
Chapter 3 Inc ....D 662 568-7830
Houlka **(G-2220)**

222

2019 Harris Directory of
Mississippi Manufacturers

SIC SECTION

25 FURNITURE AND FIXTURES

Choctaw Glove & Safety Co Inc............G....... 601 774-5555
Union (G-5296)

Classic Furniture Mfg ....E....... 662 456-5900
Houston (G-2235)

◆ Collums Furniture Inc ....D....... 662 568-7912
Houlka (G-2221)

◆ Corinthian Inc ....A....... 662 287-7835
Corinth (G-1079)

Dixieland Furniture Mfg Co Inc............E....... 662 456-5378
Houston (G-2236)

Flexsteel Industries Inc ....B....... 662 323-5481
Starkville (G-4944)

◆ Franklin Corporation ....A....... 662 456-5771
Houston (G-2240)

Franklin Corporation ....B....... 662 456-4286
Houston (G-2241)

Franklin Development Co LLC ....G....... 662 456-5771
Houston (G-2242)

◆ Fusion Furniture Inc ....E....... 662 489-1296
Ecru (G-1231)

◆ HM Richards Inc ....A....... 662 365-9485
Guntown (G-1899)

◆ Homestretch Inc ....F....... 662 963-2494
Nettleton (G-3660)

▲ Homestretch Holdings LLC ....B....... 662 963-2494
Nettleton (G-3661)

Kedron Furniture Mfg Inc ....G....... 662 963-3366
Plantersville (G-4310)

▲ La-Z-Boy Inc ....G....... 601 683-3354
Newton (G-3722)

La-Z-Boy Incorporated ....A....... 601 683-3354
Newton (G-3723)

Lake Road Furniture Mfg Co ....E....... 662 568-3329
Houlka (G-2224)

Lane Furniture Industries Inc ....A....... 662 489-3815
Pontotoc (G-4341)

Leggett & Platt Incorporated................E....... 662 842-5237
Tupelo (G-5178)

LFI Wind Down Inc ....A....... 662 566-7211
Belden (G-190)

Lucky Star Industries Inc ....F....... 662 840-4465
Tupelo (G-5182)

▲ Max Home LLC ....B....... 662 862-9966
Fulton (G-1462)

▲ Miss Eaton Inc ....D....... 662 489-4242
Pontotoc (G-4346)

▲ Newport Home Furnishings LLC .....D....... 662 534-3030
New Albany (G-3690)

Quality Trim & Upholstery ....G....... 601 483-0077
Meridian (G-3389)

R and R Furniture Inc ....E....... 662 456-5888
Woodland (G-5614)

S & S Manufacturers Inc ....E....... 662 489-2223
Pontotoc (G-4361)

Seminole Furniture LLC ....D....... 662 447-5222
Okolona (G-3797)

◆ Seminole Furniture Mfg Inc ....D....... 662 447-5222
Okolona (G-3798)

Southern Motion Inc ....C....... 662 488-9301
Pontotoc (G-4363)

▼ Style-Line Furn Inc ....C....... 662 566-1113
Verona (G-5335)

United Furniture Inds CA Inc ....G....... 800 458-7212
Okolona (G-3800)

United Furniture Inds Inc ....D....... 662 447-4000
Okolona (G-3801)

United Furniture Inds Inc ....C....... 662 841-2321
Belden (G-193)

▼ United Furniture Inds NC LLC ....D....... 662 447-5504
Okolona (G-3802)

2514 Metal Household Furniture

B & O Machine & Wldg Co Inc ....F....... 601 833-3000
Brookhaven (G-481)

▲ Chromcraft Corporation ....C....... 662 562-8203
Senatobia (G-4790)

Kennedy Hall ....G....... 601 366-7301
Jackson (G-2462)

Krueger International Inc ....A....... 662 842-3124
Tupelo (G-5167)

Krueger International Inc ....D....... 662 840-7368
Tupelo (G-5168)

Leggett & Platt Incorporated................G....... 662 842-5704
Tupelo (G-5175)

Leggett & Platt Incorporated................E....... 662 842-5237
Tupelo (G-5178)

Nowell Steps Incorporated ....G....... 601 964-8455
Richton (G-4541)

2515 Mattresses & Bedsprings

Ark-Ell Springs Inc ....C....... 662 568-3393
Houlka (G-2217)

Ashley Furniture Inds Inc ....C....... 662 837-7146
Ripley (G-4652)

◆ Capital Bedding Inc ....D....... 662 566-1144
Verona (G-5328)

Elite Comfort Solutions LLC ....E....... 662 566-2322
Verona (G-5330)

Englander Sleep Products LLC ....C....... 800 370-8700
Olive Branch (G-3839)

Fibrix LLC ....G....... 662 568-3393
Houlka (G-2222)

Leggett & Platt Incorporated................D....... 662 456-3053
Houston (G-2249)

Leggett & Platt Incorporated................G....... 662 842-5704
Tupelo (G-5175)

Leggett & Platt Incorporated................E....... 662 842-5704
Tupelo (G-5176)

Leggett & Platt Incorporated................D....... 662 842-5704
Tupelo (G-5177)

Leggett & Platt Incorporated................B....... 662 869-1060
Saltillo (G-4717)

Leggett & Platt Incorporated................E....... 662 842-5237
Tupelo (G-5178)

Magnolia Furniture LLC ....G....... 662 489-9337
Pontotoc (G-4342)

▲ Meridian Mattress Factory Inc ....F....... 601 693-3875
Meridian (G-3368)

National Mattress LLC ....G....... 662 205-4891
Plantersville (G-4311)

Signature Bedding LLC ....G....... 663 523-8477
Tupelo (G-5221)

▼ Sleeper Kraft LLC ....G....... 662 620-9797
Plantersville (G-4315)

Sleepmadecom LLC ....G....... 662 386-2222
Columbus (G-1027)

Southstern Foam Fbrication LLC ....G....... 601 540-8880
Ridgeland (G-4632)

▲ Superior Bedding Products of M ....E....... 662 841-1632
Plantersville (G-4316)

West Group Holding Company LLC ......G....... 662 871-2344
Shannon (G-4821)

2517 Wood T V, Radio, Phono & Sewing Cabinets

Bunyard Cabinetry ....G....... 601 757-8765
Brookhaven (G-485)

Pettigrew Cabinets Inc ....E....... 662 844-1368
Plantersville (G-4313)

2519 Household Furniture, NEC

Allens Cane Shop ....G....... 662 429-2016
Nesbit (G-3647)

Birds Nest ....G....... 662 369-5757
Aberdeen (G-10)

Madison House Inc ....G....... 601 898-8090
Madison (G-3125)

◆ Paxton Sales Inc ....E....... 662 841-1929
Tupelo (G-5201)

Springer Dry Goods ....F....... 662 263-8144
Maben (G-3051)

Varsity Pro Inc ....G....... 662 628-4172
Calhoun City (G-645)

2521 Wood Office Furniture

Ed Dangerfield Const Millwrks ....G....... 662 328-3877
Columbus (G-967)

Flexsteel Industries Inc ....B....... 662 323-5481
Starkville (G-4944)

Grace Company of Ms Inc ....F....... 662 393-2443
Horn Lake (G-2200)

Krueger International Inc ....A....... 662 842-3124
Tupelo (G-5167)

▲ Mississipi Furniture Component ....G....... 662 566-8855
Tupelo (G-5188)

Office Chairs Mississippi LLC ....G....... 601 842-1004
Pearl (G-4135)

Quality Cabinet Company Inc ....E....... 662 429-1411
Hernando (G-2151)

Southeastern Constructors Inc ....E....... 601 825-9791
Brandon (G-457)

William Kilgore ....G....... 601 582-3702
Moselle (G-3464)

2522 Office Furniture, Except Wood

▲ Chromcraft Corporation ....C....... 662 562-8203
Senatobia (G-4790)

Flexsteel Industries Inc ....B....... 662 323-5481
Starkville (G-4944)

Krueger International Inc ....A....... 662 842-3124
Tupelo (G-5167)

Office Chairs Mississippi LLC ....G....... 601 842-1004
Pearl (G-4135)

2531 Public Building & Related Furniture

Business & Off Konnextions LLC ....G....... 601 965-5101
Jackson (G-2350)

▲ Durfold Corporation ....E....... 601 922-4144
Jackson (G-2392)

Facilities Outfitters ....G....... 662 328-1977
Columbus (G-973)

Faurecia Auto Seating LLC ....B....... 248 288-1000
Cleveland (G-791)

Fletcher Cox ....G....... 601 956-2610
Ridgeland (G-4584)

Flexsteel Industries Inc ....B....... 662 323-5481
Starkville (G-4944)

Gmn Group LLC ....G....... 662 473-3094
Water Valley (G-5468)

◆ Grammer Inc ....G....... 662 566-1660
Shannon (G-4807)

Great Southern Club Inc ....F....... 228 868-8619
Gulfport (G-1796)

James E Mattison Jr ....G....... 601 543-7313
Purvis (G-4441)

Johnson Controls Inc ....C....... 601 544-8911
Hattiesburg (G-2002)

Krueger International Inc ....A....... 662 842-3124
Tupelo (G-5167)

Larry Wells ....F....... 662 724-4355
Noxapater (G-3732)

Missco Corporation of Jackson ....F....... 601 352-7272
Jackson (G-2497)

Southeast Miss Schl Pdts Inc ....G....... 662 855-5048
Caledonia (G-631)

Spain Incorporated ....G....... 662 843-1301
Boyle (G-352)

T S Car Ports ....G....... 601 797-9600
Mount Olive (G-3511)

▲ Toyota Boshoku Mississippi LLC ......E....... 662 862-3322
Mantachie (G-3209)

VIP Cinema LLC ....D....... 662 841-5866
New Albany (G-3707)

Wdtm Inc ....D....... 662 842-6161
Pontotoc (G-4369)

2541 Wood, Office & Store Fixtures

Baymont Wholesale Inc ....G....... 662 424-2134
Belmont (G-194)

Coleman Builders Inc ....G....... 662 234-0376
Oxford (G-3947)

Conceptual Designs Inc ....F....... 601 923-9922
Jackson (G-2363)

Counter Connections Inc ....G....... 662 342-5111
Southaven (G-4865)

Galley Kitchen Bath ....G....... 662 455-6535
Greenwood (G-1623)

Grace Company of Ms Inc ....F....... 662 393-2443
Horn Lake (G-2200)

H & L Millworks Inc ....G....... 228 392-9913
Biloxi (G-250)

Hartson-Kennedy Cabinet Top Co........D....... 228 896-1548
Gulfport (G-1805)

J N S Marble & Granite LLC ....F....... 662 280-2272
Southaven (G-4880)

Pierce Cabinets Inc ....E....... 662 840-6795
Tupelo (G-5204)

S W Krebs Woodworking Co LLC ....G....... 228 762-1064
Pascagoula (G-4066)

Shamrock Wood Industries Inc ....C....... 662 393-2125
Horn Lake (G-2210)

Southeastern Constructors Inc ....E....... 601 825-9791
Brandon (G-457)

Southern Cabinets & Millwork ....G....... 662 447-3885
Okolona (G-3799)

Stone Perfection ....G....... 662 895-4442
Olive Branch (G-3914)

Superior Granite & Quartz ....G....... 662 241-5664
Columbus (G-1034)

2542 Partitions & Fixtures, Except Wood

Krh Transport LLC ....G....... 769 244-1392
Centreville (G-732)

Leggett & Platt Incorporated................G....... 662 842-5704
Tupelo (G-5175)

Mailbox Ranch ....G....... 601 758-4767
Sumrall (G-5038)

25 FURNITURE AND FIXTURES

Southeastern Constructors Inc ....E 601 825-9791
Brandon *(G-457)*
Standex International Corp ....B 662 534-9061
New Albany *(G-3700)*
Stanley Black & Decker Inc ....E 662 844-7191
Tupelo *(G-5231)*
Thomasvlle Mtal Fbricators Inc ....E 662 526-9900
Como *(G-1052)*
Tier-Rack Corporation ....E 662 526-9900
Como *(G-1053)*

2591 Drapery Hardware, Window Blinds & Shades

Amerson Cleophus Jr ....G 601 362-3629
Jackson *(G-2331)*
Hunter Douglas Inc ....C 662 690-8190
Shannon *(G-4810)*
Norman Vr Inc ....G 601 352-4819
Gulfport *(G-1838)*
Omni Blinds ....G 601 924-0326
Clinton *(G-832)*
Superior Blinds and Shutters ....G 901 270-8061
Southaven *(G-4910)*

2599 Furniture & Fixtures, NEC

A B B Inc ....F 662 628-8196
Calhoun City *(G-634)*
Collins Woodworks ....G 228 452-2627
Pass Christian *(G-4080)*
Filing and Storage Miss LLC ....G 601 397-6452
Ridgeland *(G-4580)*
Hartson-Kennedy Cabinet Top Co ....D 228 896-1548
Gulfport *(G-1805)*
Inhealth Medical ....G 662 283-5750
Winona *(G-5602)*
▲ **Knu LLC** ....D 812 367-1761
Leland *(G-2888)*
▲ **Lounora Industries Inc** ....E 662 328-1685
Columbus *(G-994)*
Max Home LLC ....G 662 424-0005
Iuka *(G-2299)*
Missco Corporation of Jackson ....D 601 892-7105
Crystal Springs *(G-1149)*
Missco Corporation of Jackson ....F 601 352-7272
Jackson *(G-2497)*
Prime Hospitality Group LLC ....E 662 269-2892
Tupelo *(G-5208)*
Recon Concealment Furn Eqp LLC ....G 228 238-9149
Ocean Springs *(G-3781)*

26 PAPER AND ALLIED PRODUCTS

2611 Pulp Mills

Domtar Paper Company LLC ....C 662 256-3526
Columbus *(G-964)*
Energyzmart LLC ....G 650 630-1232
Grenada *(G-1676)*
Georgia-Pacific LLC ....F 601 939-7797
Pearl *(G-4122)*
James K Smith Logging ....F 601 859-1628
Canton *(G-663)*
Kaycan Inc ....G 662 252-9991
Holly Springs *(G-2179)*
Mike Culbreth Woodyard ....G 601 776-2422
Quitman *(G-4467)*
Nelsons Metal Inc ....G 662 454-7500
Dennis *(G-1184)*
Profile Products LLC ....E 662 685-4741
Blue Mountain *(G-292)*
Weyerhaeuser Company ....E 662 243-4000
Columbus *(G-1044)*

2621 Paper Mills

Cand M Pupwood ....G 601 445-9200
Natchez *(G-3543)*
Cryovac Inc ....D 662 226-8804
Grenada *(G-1673)*
David Morehead ....G 601 469-2272
Forest *(G-1413)*
Domtar Paper Company LLC ....C 662 256-3526
Columbus *(G-964)*
▲ **Drumheller Packaging Inc** ....E 662 627-2207
Clarksdale *(G-767)*
Educate & Celebrate LLC ....G 228 547-0811
Gulfport *(G-1776)*
Georgia-Pacific LLC ....G 662 773-9454
Louisville *(G-2969)*
Georgia-Pacific LLC ....G 601 587-7570
Monticello *(G-3432)*

Georgia-Pacific LLC ....F 601 939-7797
Pearl *(G-4122)*
Giclee Fine Arts ....G 228 586-2693
Kiln *(G-2679)*
Insituform Technologies LLC ....D 662 561-1378
Batesville *(G-109)*
International Paper Company ....B 601 638-3665
Redwood *(G-4495)*
International Paper Company ....C 601 932-1422
Jackson *(G-2650)*
International Paper Company ....F 601 783-5011
Magnolia *(G-3191)*
International Paper Company ....F 662 893-3100
Olive Branch *(G-3852)*
International Paper Company ....C 662 456-4251
Houston *(G-2246)*
International Paper Company ....G 800 207-4003
Yazoo City *(G-5636)*
Kimberly-Clark Corporation ....C 601 545-3400
Hattiesburg *(G-2007)*
Kimberly-Clark Corporation ....B 662 287-8011
Corinth *(G-1095)*
Kimberly-Clark Corporation ....E 662 454-9274
Dennis *(G-1182)*
Kimberly-Clark Corporation ....G 662 284-3827
Baldwyn *(G-81)*
L C Industries Inc ....E 662 841-1640
Tupelo *(G-5170)*
Lc Ind Signature Works Div ....G 601 206-9564
Ridgeland *(G-4597)*
Mr Forms Printing Company Inc ....G 601 371-2567
Jackson *(G-2511)*
Packaging Dynamics Corporation ....E 662 424-4000
Iuka *(G-2304)*
Resolute FP US Inc ....E 662 227-7900
Grenada *(G-1701)*
Resolute Ft US Inc ....E 662 227-7948
Grenada *(G-1702)*
Twin Rivers Paper Company LLC ....E 662 468-2183
Pickens *(G-4307)*
Von Drehle Corporation ....E 601 445-0100
Natchez *(G-3633)*
Weyerhaeuser ....G 662 327-1961
Columbus *(G-1043)*

2631 Paperboard Mills

Ability Works Inc ....E 662 842-2144
Tupelo *(G-5107)*
Georgia-Pacific LLC ....F 601 939-7797
Pearl *(G-4122)*
International Paper Company ....B 601 638-3665
Redwood *(G-4495)*
JC Jourdan Lumber Co Inc ....F 662 423-5238
Iuka *(G-2295)*
Performance Paperboard Inc ....G 601 856-3939
Ridgeland *(G-4617)*
Pontotoc Die Cutting LLC ....F 662 489-5874
Pontotoc *(G-4354)*
Sonoco Products Company ....D 662 615-6204
Starkville *(G-4972)*

2652 Set-Up Paperboard Boxes

Rusken Packaging Inc ....E 662 680-5060
Tupelo *(G-5219)*

2653 Corrugated & Solid Fiber Boxes

Ability Works Inc ....E 662 842-2144
Tupelo *(G-5107)*
Ability Works Inc ....G 662 328-0275
Columbus *(G-931)*
Airfloat Systems Inc ....G 662 566-0158
Verona *(G-5326)*
American Container Inc ....E 662 890-0325
Olive Branch *(G-3810)*
Chickasaw Container Company ....D 662 447-3339
Okolona *(G-3795)*
Color-Box LLC ....C 601 854-6020
Pelahatchie *(G-4162)*
Corrugated Services America ....G 601 209-6297
Pearl *(G-5012)*
General Packaging Specialties ....F 662 844-7882
Tupelo *(G-5140)*
Gibson Corrugated LLC ....D 662 842-1862
Tupelo *(G-5143)*
▲ **Great Southern Industries Inc** ....D 601 948-5700
Jackson *(G-2431)*
Hoerner Boxes Inc ....E 662 842-2491
Tupelo *(G-5156)*
International Paper Company ....C 601 932-1422
Jackson *(G-2650)*

Midland Color Corp ....G 662 895-4100
Olive Branch *(G-3876)*
Packaging Corporation America ....C 601 939-5111
Pearl *(G-4136)*
Packaging Corporation America ....E 662 895-4100
Olive Branch *(G-3893)*
Pratt (mississippi Box) Inc ....E 601 366-3435
Jackson *(G-2545)*
Pratt Corrugated Holdings Inc ....D 601 366-3435
Jackson *(G-2546)*
Southland Container Inc ....E 601 879-8816
Flora *(G-1312)*
St Tammany Box Company ....E 601 799-0775
Picayune *(G-4297)*
Texas Packaging ....G 214 912-5833
Picayune *(G-4300)*
Westrock Cp LLC ....E 662 842-4940
Tupelo *(G-5257)*
Westrock Cp LLC ....G 662 895-1627
Olive Branch *(G-3925)*
Westrock Cp LLC ....C 662 869-5771
Saltillo *(G-4723)*
▲ **Wire Display Fabrication Inc** ....G 662 838-9650
Byhalia *(G-613)*

2655 Fiber Cans, Tubes & Drums

Caraustar Industrial and Con ....E 662 287-2492
Corinth *(G-1064)*
Caraustar Industries Inc ....G 601 703-0550
Meridian *(G-3315)*
Larry Joe Gibson ....G 662 844-9113
Tupelo *(G-5171)*

2656 Sanitary Food Containers

Pactiv LLC ....E 662 585-3151
Fulton *(G-1472)*

2657 Folding Paperboard Boxes

Fc Meyer Packaging LLC ....F 601 776-2117
Quitman *(G-4464)*
Region 8 Mental Health Retrdat ....D 601 591-5553
Brandon *(G-445)*
Westrock Cp LLC ....E 662 842-4940
Tupelo *(G-5257)*

2671 Paper Coating & Laminating for Packaging

Bemis Company Inc ....B 402 734-6262
Madison *(G-3084)*
Dunn Paper Inc ....C 800 253-1889
Wiggins *(G-5581)*
General Packaging Specialties ....F 662 844-7882
Tupelo *(G-5140)*
◆ **Hood Flexible Packaging Corp** ....D 903 593-1793
Hattiesburg *(G-1993)*
Mega Plastics Inc ....D 601 924-1712
Clinton *(G-831)*

2672 Paper Coating & Laminating, Exc for Packaging

Darrell Crum LLC ....G 806 224-7337
Madison *(G-3092)*
Domtar Paper Company LLC ....C 662 256-3526
Columbus *(G-964)*
Newson Chenora ....G 601 596-3899
Hattiesburg *(G-2037)*
Packaging Dynamics Corporation ....E 662 424-4000
Iuka *(G-2304)*

2673 Bags: Plastics, Laminated & Coated

American Packaging Company Inc ....F 601 856-0986
Madison *(G-3078)*
Bag Connection LLC ....F 662 624-6570
Clarksdale *(G-758)*
Bagit System Inc ....E 662 756-2600
Ruleville *(G-4695)*
Dixie Packaging Inc ....E 601 276-9317
Summit *(G-5012)*
Hood Container Corporation ....C 601 582-1545
Hattiesburg *(G-1992)*
◆ **Hood Flexible Packaging Corp** ....D 903 593-1793
Hattiesburg *(G-1993)*
Hood Packaging Corporation ....D 770 981-5400
Madison *(G-3106)*
Innovex Inc ....E 662 328-9537
Columbus *(G-988)*
McNeely Plastic Products Inc ....F 601 926-1000
Hazlehurst *(G-2100)*

2019 Harris Directory of
Mississippi Manufacturers

SIC SECTION

27 PRINTING, PUBLISHING, AND ALLIED INDUSTRIES

Mega Plastics Inc ....D...... 601 924-1712
Clinton (G-831)

Novipax LLC ....D...... 662 226-8804
Grenada (G-1697)

Rankin Plastics LLC ....G...... 601 919-7883
Richland (G-4523)

◆ United Solutions Inc ....F...... 662 487-0068
Sardis (G-4747)

2674 Bags: Uncoated Paper & Multiwall

Bemis Company Inc ....B...... 402 734-6262
Madison (G-3084)

Hood Packaging Corporation ....D...... 770 981-5400
Madison (G-3106)

▲ Hood Packaging Corporation ....E...... 601 853-7260
Madison (G-3107)

2675 Die-Cut Paper & Board

Acco Brands USA LLC ....G...... 800 541-0094
Booneville (G-314)

Davis Enterprises Inc ....G...... 662 488-9972
Pontotoc (G-4328)

L C Industries Inc ....E...... 662 841-1640
Tupelo (G-5170)

Martin Cardboard Company Inc ....G...... 662 489-5416
Pontotoc (G-4343)

Pontotoc Die Cutting LLC ....F...... 662 489-5874
Pontotoc (G-4354)

Pqr Inc ....C...... 662 289-7613
Kosciusko (G-2710)

Tom Lauderdale Paper Svcs Inc ....F...... 662 767-9744
Shannon (G-4819)

W & W Special Components Inc ....E...... 662 365-5648
Marietta (G-3219)

2676 Sanitary Paper Prdts

Jones Limber ....G...... 601 894-3839
Hazlehurst (G-2098)

Kimberly-Clark Corporation ....C...... 601 545-3400
Hattiesburg (G-2007)

Kimberly-Clark Corporation ....B...... 662 287-8011
Corinth (G-1095)

Kimberly-Clark Corporation ....F...... 662 454-9274
Dennis (G-1182)

Kimberly-Clark Corporation ....C...... 662 284-3827
Baldwyn (G-81)

▼ Leaf River Cellulose LLC ....B...... 601 964-8411
New Augusta (G-3711)

Magnolia Supply Group LLC ....G...... 601 454-1368
Jackson (G-2480)

Twin Rivers Paper Company LLC ....E...... 662 468-2183
Pickens (G-4307)

2677 Envelopes

Consoldted Converting Svcs Inc ....E...... 601 545-1699
Hattiesburg (G-1950)

Parthenon Envelope Company LLC ......E...... 601 758-4788
Sumrall (G-5040)

2678 Stationery Prdts

Avery Products Corporation ....C...... 601 483-0611
Meridian (G-3304)

Custom Signs and Banners ....G...... 662 327-8916
Columbus (G-957)

2679 Converted Paper Prdts, NEC

Capitol City Label Inc ....G...... 601 420-2375
Pearl (G-4109)

Hattiesburg Paper Company LLC ....C...... 601 545-3400
Hattiesburg (G-1988)

Hilton National Corporation ....G...... 228 385-9800
Biloxi (G-252)

Hpc LLC ....G...... 601 545-3400
Hattiesburg (G-1996)

International Paper Company ....G...... 662 243-4000
Columbus (G-989)

L C Industries Inc ....B...... 601 894-1771
Hazlehurst (G-2099)

Pqr Inc ....C...... 662 289-7613
Kosciusko (G-2710)

Signature Works Inc ....B...... 601 894-1771
Hazlehurst (G-2106)

◆ Specialty Roll Products Inc ....E...... 601 693-1771
Meridian (G-3404)

Spiral Fab Inc ....G...... 662 862-7999
Fulton (G-1477)

Tri-County Industries ....E...... 601 743-9931
De Kalb (G-1169)

27 PRINTING, PUBLISHING, AND ALLIED INDUSTRIES

2711 Newspapers: Publishing & Printing

24 Hour News Line ....G...... 662 241-5000
Columbus (G-929)

Amory Advertiser ....G...... 662 256-5647
Amory (G-35)

Appeal Publishing Co Inc ....G...... 601 774-9433
Union (G-5292)

Banner Printing Co Inc ....G...... 662 247-3373
Belzoni (G-204)

Bay St Louis Newspapers Inc ....E...... 228 467-5474
Bay Saint Louis (G-135)

Beach Blvd Mag ....G...... 228 896-2499
Gulfport (G-1737)

Belmont Tshmngo Jrnl Incjurnal ....G...... 662 454-7196
Belmont (G-195)

Black Panther Newspaper ....G...... 877 388-6247
Hattiesburg (G-1934)

Bluff City Post Newspaper ....G...... 601 446-5218
Natchez (G-3533)

Bolivar Cnty Dept Humn Rsurces ....G...... 662 843-8311
Cleveland (G-787)

Bolivar Newspaper Inc ....G...... 662 843-4241
Cleveland (G-788)

Boone Newspapers ....E...... 601 442-9101
Natchez (G-3537)

Brent Aubry ....G...... 662 746-7600
Yazoo City (G-5624)

Buckley Newspapers Inc ....D...... 601 764-3104
Bay Springs (G-159)

Calhoun County Journal ....G...... 662 983-2570
Bruce (G-560)

Campbell Newspapers LLC ....G...... 423 754-0312
Biloxi (G-224)

Carpenter Newsmedia LLC ....G...... 601 445-3618
Natchez (G-3544)

Carthaginian Inc ....F...... 601 267-4501
Carthage (G-709)

Chancellors Business Sup Inc ....F...... 601 426-6396
Laurel (G-2753)

Chronicle ....G...... 601 651-2000
Laurel (G-2754)

Clairborne Publishing Co ....G...... 601 437-5103
Port Gibson (G-4401)

Clarke County Tribune Inc ....G...... 601 776-3726
Quitman (G-4460)

Cleveland John ....G...... 901 359-2737
Byhalia (G-583)

Coast Motor News ....G...... 228 868-1772
Gulfport (G-1756)

Coast Observer ....G...... 228 875-0090
Ocean Springs (G-3749)

Commercial Dispatch Pubg Inc ....D...... 662 328-2424
Columbus (G-955)

Commonwealth Publishing Inc ....C...... 662 453-5312
Greenwood (G-1618)

Coopwood Communications Inc ....F...... 662 843-2700
Cleveland (G-790)

Copiah County Courier Inc ....F...... 601 894-3141
Hazlehurst (G-2093)

Daily & Sons Construction Inc ....G...... 601 737-5847
Bailey (G-67)

Deer Creek Publishing Company ....G...... 662 873-4354
Rolling Fork (G-4680)

Delta Press Publishing Co Inc ....F...... 662 627-2201
Clarksdale (G-766)

Delta-Democrat Pubg Co Inc ....D...... 662 335-1155
Greenville (G-1551)

Democrat ....G...... 662 562-4414
Senatobia (G-4792)

East Holmes Publishing Entps ....G...... 662 834-1151
Lexington (G-2901)

Emmerich Newspapers Inc ....G...... 662 647-8462
Charleston (G-737)

Enterprise-Tocsin ....G...... 662 887-2222
Indianola (G-2264)

Fayette Chronicle ....G...... 601 786-3661
Fayette (G-1296)

Gannett Co Inc ....G...... 601 961-7000
Jackson (G-2421)

George County Times ....G...... 601 947-2967
Lucedale (G-2997)

George Nosser Jr ....G...... 601 446-7998
Natchez (G-3563)

Gin Creek Publishing ....G...... 601 649-9388
Laurel (G-2770)

Goodnews Gulf Coast ....G...... 228 435-2456
Biloxi (G-247)

Grenada Newspaper Inc ....E...... 662 226-4321
Grenada (G-1681)

Gulf Publishing Company Inc ....C...... 228 896-2100
Gulfport (G-1801)

Hattiesburg American ....G...... 601 582-4321
Hattiesburg (G-1984)

Hattiesburg American Pubg Co ....C...... 601 582-4321
Hattiesburg (G-1985)

Hh Services ....G...... 662 283-1131
Winona (G-5601)

Horizon Publications Inc ....G...... 662 494-1422
West Point (G-5546)

Horizon Publications Inc ....E...... 662 323-1642
Starkville (G-4950)

Houston Newspapers Inc ....F...... 662 456-3771
Houston (G-2245)

Imes Communications of El Paso ....D...... 662 328-2424
Columbus (G-986)

J O Emmerich & Assoc Inc ....E...... 601 684-2421
McComb (G-3254)

Jackson Advocate Inc ....G...... 601 948-4122
Jackson (G-2451)

Jackson Free Press Inc ....F...... 601 362-6121
Jackson (G-2455)

Journal Inc ....C...... 662 842-2611
Tupelo (G-5164)

Journal Inc ....G...... 662 862-3141
Fulton (G-1460)

Journal Publishing Houston ....G...... 662 456-3771
Houston (G-2248)

Lake Messenger ....G...... 601 775-3857
Lake (G-2723)

Lamar County News Inc ....G...... 601 268-2331
Hattiesburg (G-2014)

Lawrence County Press Inc ....G...... 601 587-2781
Monticello (G-3435)

Lee County Courier Inc ....G...... 662 840-8819
Tupelo (G-5173)

Local Voice LLC ....G...... 662 232-8900
Oxford (G-3966)

Louisville Publishing Inc ....E...... 662 773-6241
Louisville (G-2974)

Macon Beacon ....G...... 662 726-4747
Macon (G-3064)

Madison County Herald ....G...... 601 853-2899
Madison (G-3124)

Madison County Publishing Inc ....G...... 601 853-4222
Ridgeland (G-4600)

Manolia Gazette ....G...... 601 783-2441
Magnolia (G-3194)

Marion Publishing Co Inc ....F...... 601 736-2611
Columbia (G-905)

McM Communications LLC ....F...... 228 435-0720
Biloxi (G-267)

Meteor Inc ....F...... 601 892-2581
Crystal Springs (G-1148)

Miss Lou Guide ....G...... 601 442-9101
Natchez (G-3588)

Mississippi Catholic ....G...... 601 969-3581
Jackson (G-2499)

Montgomery Publishing Co Inc ....G...... 662 283-1131
Winona (G-5604)

Mrs GS Computer Services ....G...... 601 376-0810
Jackson (G-2513)

Natchez Newspapers Inc ....G...... 601 442-9101
Natchez (G-3595)

Nautilus Publishing Company ....G...... 662 513-0159
Oxford (G-3975)

Neshoba Democrat Publishing Co ....F...... 601 656-4000
Philadelphia (G-4228)

New Albany Publishing Company ....F...... 662 534-6321
New Albany (G-3688)

News Commercial ....F...... 601 765-8275
Collins (G-857)

Newspaper Holding Inc ....E...... 601 798-4766
Picayune (G-4281)

Newspaper Holding Inc ....D...... 601 693-1551
Meridian (G-3377)

Newspaper Holding Inc ....G...... 601 795-2247
Poplarville (G-4385)

Northeast Miss Daily Jurnl ....G...... 662 842-2622
Tupelo (G-5194)

Ocean Springs Gazette ....G...... 228 875-1241
Ocean Springs (G-3774)

Okolona Messenger Inc ....G...... 662 447-5501
Okolona (G-3796)

Omni Fusion LLC ....G...... 601 765-6941
Collins (G-858)

SIC

Employee Codes: A=Over 500 employees, B=251-500
C=101-250, D=51-100, E=20-50, F=10-19, G=1-9

2019 Harris Directory of
Mississippi Manufacturers

225

27 PRINTING, PUBLISHING, AND ALLIED INDUSTRIES

SIC SECTION

Oxford Eagle Inc ....E....... 662 234-2222
Oxford *(G-3986)*

Panolian ....E....... 662 563-4591
Batesville *(G-116)*

Paxton Media Group LLC ....E....... 662 287-6111
Corinth *(G-1108)*

Paxton Media Group LLC ....G....... 662 728-6214
Booneville *(G-341)*

Pigeon Roost News ....G....... 662 838-4844
Holly Springs *(G-2188)*

Play Coast ....G....... 228 369-4582
Ocean Springs *(G-3776)*

Pontotoc Progress Inc ....G....... 662 489-3511
Pontotoc *(G-4356)*

Prentiss Publishers Inc ....G....... 601 792-4221
Prentiss *(G-4423)*

Quitman County Democrat ....G....... 662 326-2181
Marks *(G-3222)*

Rankin Ledger ....G....... 601 360-4600
Jackson *(G-2558)*

Rankin Publishing Company Inc ....G....... 601 992-4869
Flowood *(G-1390)*

Rcn Corporation ....F....... 601 825-8333
Brandon *(G-444)*

Saltillo Guntown Gazette ....G....... 662 869-8380
Saltillo *(G-4720)*

Scott Publishing Inc ....G....... 601 469-2561
Forest *(G-1425)*

Simpson County News ....G....... 601 847-2525
Mendenhall *(G-3289)*

Simpson Publishing Co Inc ....E....... 601 849-3434
Magee *(G-3185)*

South Reporter Inc ....F....... 662 252-4261
Holly Springs *(G-2192)*

Southern Sintinel Inc ....F....... 662 837-8111
Ripley *(G-4672)*

Southern Sintinel Inc ....G....... 662 224-6681
Ashland *(G-65)*

Southwest Publishers Inc ....G....... 601 833-6961
Brookhaven *(G-538)*

Spirit Enterprises ....G....... 662 236-2667
Oxford *(G-4006)*

Star Herald ....G....... 662 289-2251
Kosciusko *(G-2715)*

Stone County Enterprises Inc ....G....... 601 928-4802
Wiggins *(G-5589)*

Sunland Publishing Co Inc ....F....... 601 957-1122
Jackson *(G-2600)*

The Post ....G....... 601 785-4333
Taylorsville *(G-5060)*

Tishomingo County News Inc ....F....... 662 423-2211
Iuka *(G-2310)*

Tradewinds Publications ....G....... 601 992-3699
Flowood *(G-1403)*

Tunica Publishing Co Inc ....G....... 662 363-1511
Tunica *(G-5103)*

Tupelo Advertiser Inc ....E....... 601 534-6635
New Albany *(G-3704)*

Tupelo Daily Journal News Bur ....G....... 601 364-1000
Jackson *(G-2614)*

Turner Group LLC ....G....... 601 394-5070
Leakesville *(G-2880)*

Tylertown Times ....F....... 601 876-5111
Tylertown *(G-5289)*

Valley Publishing Inc ....G....... 662 473-1473
Water Valley *(G-5475)*

Vicksburg Newsmedia LLC ....G....... 601 636-4545
Vicksburg *(G-5437)*

Vicksburg Printing and Pubg Co ....D....... 601 636-4545
Vicksburg *(G-5438)*

Wayne Hmphrys/Plygraph Exminer ....G....... 601 825-8640
Brandon *(G-472)*

Weekly Leader ....G....... 601 825-5133
Brandon *(G-474)*

William Carey University ....G....... 601 318-6115
Hattiesburg *(G-2083)*

Wrjw 1320 AM ....F....... 601 798-4835
Picayune *(G-4305)*

Yazoo Newspaper Co Inc ....F....... 662 746-4911
Yazoo City *(G-5653)*

2721 Periodicals: Publishing & Printing

Associated Gen Contrs of Miss ....G....... 601 981-1144
Jackson *(G-2334)*

Bbq World Magazine ....F....... 228 363-2716
Long Beach *(G-2926)*

Blue South Publishing Corp ....G....... 601 604-2963
Meridian *(G-3310)*

Bluffs & Bayou Magazine ....G....... 601 442-6847
Natchez *(G-3534)*

Breaktime Vending Inc ....G....... 601 749-8424
Picayune *(G-4257)*

Downhome Publications Inc ....F....... 601 982-8418
Jackson *(G-2390)*

Goat Rancher ....G....... 662 562-9529
Sarah *(G-4734)*

Homeland Inc ....G....... 662 728-7799
Booneville *(G-329)*

Invitation Oxford Magazine ....F....... 662 701-8365
Oxford *(G-3961)*

Jackpot Magazine ....G....... 228 385-7707
Gulfport *(G-1813)*

Journal Inc ....G....... 601 364-1000
Flowood *(G-1371)*

Legend Publishing ....G....... 662 844-2602
Tupelo *(G-5174)*

Metro Christian Living ....G....... 601 790-9076
Jackson *(G-2489)*

Midsouth Media Group ....F....... 662 890-3359
Olive Branch *(G-3878)*

Mississippi Baptist Paper ....G....... 601 426-3293
Laurel *(G-2804)*

Mississippi State Phrm Assn ....G....... 601 981-0416
Jackson *(G-2506)*

Mississippi Valley Publishing ....F....... 601 853-1861
Ridgeland *(G-4607)*

Nautilus Publishing Company ....G....... 662 513-0159
Oxford *(G-3975)*

Novia Cmmnications/ Novia Pubg ....G....... 601 985-9502
Jackson *(G-2525)*

Omni Fusion LLC ....G....... 601 765-6941
Collins *(G-858)*

Oxford Eagle Inc ....E....... 662 234-2222
Oxford *(G-3986)*

Parents and Kids Magazine ....G....... 601 366-0901
Jackson *(G-2534)*

Pmq Inc ....F....... 662 234-5481
Oxford *(G-3995)*

Premier Publishing Inc ....G....... 601 957-1050
Flowood *(G-1389)*

Regional Sites Inc ....G....... 662 643-4595
Glen *(G-1508)*

Rowell Publishing ....G....... 601 981-0933
Brandon *(G-448)*

RR Donnelley & Sons Company ....B....... 662 562-5252
Senatobia *(G-4802)*

Shumpert Media ....G....... 662 678-3742
Nettleton *(G-3667)*

Socrates Garrett Entps Inc ....F....... 601 896-0084
Jackson *(G-2585)*

Stockman Grass Farmer ....F....... 601 853-1861
Ridgeland *(G-4635)*

Tupelo Daily Journal News Bur ....G....... 601 364-1000
Jackson *(G-2614)*

Union Directories ....F....... 662 620-6366
Tupelo *(G-5248)*

University of Mississippi ....G....... 662 915-5742
University *(G-5306)*

Wolf River Press ....G....... 601 372-2679
Jackson *(G-2636)*

Wrestling USA Magazine Inc ....G....... 406 360-9421
Pass Christian *(G-4098)*

Wrestling USA Magazine Inc ....G....... 406 549-4448
Pass Christian *(G-4099)*

2731 Books: Publishing & Printing

Books Plus LLC ....G....... 228 209-5021
Biloxi *(G-223)*

Braxton Foxx LLC ....G....... 800 719-6811
Flowood *(G-1349)*

Elizabeth Clayton ....G....... 601 371-1172
Terry *(G-5066)*

Exquisite Enterprise Pubg LLC ....G....... 708 362-4583
Durant *(G-1225)*

Gods Inspiration For The Soul ....G....... 662 374-7785
Tupelo *(G-5144)*

Grady Shady Music Inc ....G....... 601 278-3087
Canton *(G-659)*

Inner Sanctuary Inc ....G....... 662 489-6772
Pontotoc *(G-4337)*

Lagniappe Books LLC ....G....... 769 242-8104
Picayune *(G-4275)*

Liberations Publishing LLC ....G....... 662 605-0382
West Point *(G-5550)*

M & W Publishing Co LLC ....G....... 662 843-1358
Boyle *(G-350)*

My Songs of Life ....G....... 901 303-8687
Olive Branch *(G-3882)*

Nautilus Publishing Company ....G....... 662 513-0159
Oxford *(G-3975)*

Pcp P Coast ....G....... 228 202-7872
Biloxi *(G-272)*

Pevey Publishing LLC ....G....... 601 503-7205
Brandon *(G-434)*

Pioneer Publishing Co ....G....... 662 237-6010
Carrollton *(G-702)*

▲ Quail Ridge Press Inc ....G....... 601 825-2063
Brandon *(G-442)*

Raven Happy Hour LLC ....G....... 662 607-6604
Oxford *(G-3998)*

Seniors Bluebook ....G....... 228 396-4602
Biloxi *(G-278)*

Triad of Mississippi LLC ....G....... 601 373-7619
Jackson *(G-2610)*

Twister LLC ....G....... 601 371-7276
Madison *(G-3162)*

▲ University Press Mississippi ....E....... 601 432-6205
Jackson *(G-2619)*

Watersprings Media House ....G....... 662 812-1568
Olive Branch *(G-3923)*

White Jerleen ....G....... 601 941-6886
Prentiss *(G-4425)*

Wilkinson County Museum ....G....... 601 888-7151
Woodville *(G-5619)*

▲ World Evangelism ....G....... 662 283-1192
Winona *(G-5612)*

2732 Book Printing, Not Publishing

Barber Printing Inc ....F....... 662 841-1584
Tupelo *(G-5112)*

David Hollingsworth ....G....... 769 233-7769
Flowood *(G-1354)*

Lsc Communications Us LLC ....G....... 601 562-5252
Senatobia *(G-4794)*

RR Donnelley & Sons Company ....B....... 662 562-5252
Senatobia *(G-4802)*

2741 Misc Publishing

500 Degreez Entrmt LLC Not LLC ....G....... 678 948-8710
Mantachie *(G-3197)*

Abacus Publishing Co ....G....... 601 684-0001
McComb *(G-3243)*

Action Success Press ....G....... 601 824-7775
Brandon *(G-357)*

Ainz Publishing Company ....G....... 662 728-6131
Booneville *(G-316)*

Beaty Street Publishing ....G....... 954 513-9441
Hattiesburg *(G-1926)*

Bijoubel LLC ....G....... 228 344-3393
Bay Saint Louis *(G-137)*

Bits & PCs Press Inc ....G....... 662 563-8661
Batesville *(G-99)*

Blake Publishing Inc ....G....... 601 992-6220
Flowood *(G-1347)*

Book Mart Corporation ....E....... 662 323-2844
Starkville *(G-4930)*

Book Publisher LLC ....G....... 662 838-2633
Byhalia *(G-581)*

Bookpro Publishing Company ....G....... 769 208-6806
Natchez *(G-3536)*

Botr Press LLC ....G....... 708 431-9668
Poplarville *(G-4378)*

Brew Barr LLC ....G....... 601 218-7708
Jackson *(G-2343)*

Campbell Creek Publishing LLC ....G....... 601 824-5932
Braxton *(G-476)*

Canton High Press Box ....G....... 601 859-4315
Canton *(G-653)*

Carney Publications LLC ....G....... 601 427-5694
Monticello *(G-3429)*

Carol Vincent & Associates ....G....... 662 624-8406
Clarksdale *(G-760)*

Catawomper Press LLC ....G....... 662 832-3897
Oxford *(G-3945)*

Chesser Publishing LLC ....G....... 228 588-1111
Hurley *(G-2259)*

Cloud 12 Publishing ....G....... 228 990-0434
Gautier *(G-1491)*

Country Kids Publishing LLC ....G....... 662 509-0427
Pontotoc *(G-4326)*

Crooked Letter Publishing LLC ....G....... 228 334-4575
Gulfport *(G-1766)*

Cruise Street Press LLC ....G....... 601 720-4848
Pickens *(G-4306)*

Deals Xpress Lube ....G....... 662 281-4417
Oxford *(G-3950)*

Deep Blue Press LLC ....G....... 228 604-4643
Gulfport *(G-1769)*

Della West Publishing LLC ....G....... 601 618-8429
Vicksburg *(G-5360)*

SIC SECTION
27 PRINTING, PUBLISHING, AND ALLIED INDUSTRIES

Developing Resources For Educa..........G....... 601 933-9199
Jackson *(G-2644)*
Diamondhead Advertiser ....G....... 228 263-4377
Waveland *(G-5480)*
Dogwood Press..........G....... 601 919-3656
Brandon *(G-390)*
Dragon Breath Press LLC ....G....... 601 607-7007
Ridgeland *(G-4574)*
Elizabeth Newcomb ....G....... 662 596-1536
Rienzi *(G-4649)*
Every Word Press LLC ....G....... 601 209-1379
Jackson *(G-2405)*
Express Lane Inc ....G....... 601 483-8872
Meridian *(G-3335)*
Exquisite Reads Publications ....G....... 662 400-0743
Macon *(G-3060)*
Fast Track Planners LLC ....G....... 601 528-0558
Perkinston *(G-4175)*
Fishbowl International Inc ....G....... 601 384-0219
Roxie *(G-4689)*
Fishyrhythms Publishing LLC ....G....... 601 573-6771
Ridgeland *(G-4582)*
Freed Peoples Press LLC ....G....... 313 717-7819
Holly Springs *(G-2176)*
Fresh Press Creative LLC ....G....... 601 376-9449
Jackson *(G-2415)*
G Mark Lafrancis ....G....... 601 442-0980
Natchez *(G-3562)*
Gemlight Publishing LLC ....G....... 601 509-1002
Gulfport *(G-1792)*
Giclee Fine Arts..........G....... 228 586-2693
Kiln *(G-2679)*
Grasslawn Publishing LLC ....G....... 228 896-5532
Gulfport *(G-1795)*
Great American Publishers ....G....... 601 854-5956
Lena *(G-2895)*
Gtp Publishing Group ....G....... 228 348-2646
Biloxi *(G-248)*
Guides Publishing Inc ....G....... 601 981-7368
Jackson *(G-2435)*
Halftone Press LLC ....G....... 662 251-5036
Columbus *(G-983)*
Halo Southern Publishing LLC ....G....... 662 299-2999
Cleveland *(G-794)*
Heritage Press Pblications LLC..........G....... 601 737-2086
Collinsville *(G-870)*
Hoopsnake Press -..........G....... 662 260-5133
Tupelo *(G-5158)*
Hubbard Publishing LLC ....G....... 662 638-3821
Oxford *(G-3957)*
Illustrative Ink LLC ....G....... 228 354-9559
Saucier *(G-4756)*
Informa Business Media Inc ....E....... 662 624-8503
Clarksdale *(G-768)*
Informa Media Inc ....G....... 662 624-8503
Clarksdale *(G-769)*
Jackson Publishing ....G....... 662 349-2866
Southaven *(G-4882)*
Jessica Williams ....G....... 601 738-0090
Rolling Fork *(G-4681)*
Kanes Publishing Company LLC ....G....... 601 345-5153
Forest *(G-1419)*
Kids Express ....G....... 601 352-3882
Jackson *(G-2464)*
Kings Judah Publishing Co LLC ....G....... 228 342-3648
Perkinston *(G-4178)*
Lifestory Publishing ....G....... 601 594-0018
Jackson *(G-2469)*
Lightning Bloom Press LLC ....G....... 662 638-3611
Oxford *(G-3965)*
Long-Delayed Publishing LLC ....G....... 662 202-6229
Oxford *(G-3967)*
Low Pro Publishing ....G....... 601 372-1875
Jackson *(G-2472)*
M P Johnson Publishing LLC ....G....... 662 270-5544
Southaven *(G-4886)*
M&M Book Publishing Co ....G....... 601 442-0980
Natchez *(G-3581)*
Magnetic Arrow LLC ....G....... 601 653-2932
Biloxi *(G-264)*
Malius Press LLC ....G....... 662 281-0955
Oxford *(G-3969)*
Mary Margaret Andrews ....G....... 901 233-5463
Oxford *(G-3971)*
McKenzie/Lee Publishing LLC..........G....... 769 216-8049
Florence *(G-1328)*
MI-Da Maps ....G....... 662 429-0022
Hernando *(G-2142)*
Michael A Dent ....G....... 601 543-0157
Hattiesburg *(G-2023)*

Milk & Honey Prtg Press LLC ....G....... 662 739-4949
Kosciusko *(G-2701)*
Miracleworks Press ....G....... 601 878-6686
Terry *(G-5073)*
Mobile Communications LLC ....G....... 662 570-4858
Itta Bena *(G-2282)*
Mobile One Lube Express Plus ....G....... 601 631-8000
Vicksburg *(G-5400)*
Moss Point Express ....G....... 228 475-4370
Moss Point *(G-3488)*
Ms Publishing Group LLC ....G....... 662 323-8800
West Point *(G-5555)*
Ms Yearbooks LLC ....G....... 601 540-6132
Brandon *(G-427)*
Mueller Press Company Inc ....G....... 901 753-3200
Jackson *(G-2658)*
Multiforms..........G....... 601 545-2312
Petal *(G-4194)*
Newks Express Cafe of H ....G....... 601 602-0189
Hattiesburg *(G-2036)*
Old Blue Publishing LLC ....G....... 601 957-2530
Jackson *(G-2528)*
One Grower Publishing ....G....... 901 767-4020
Olive Branch *(G-3889)*
Outback Express Mississippi ....G....... 662 378-8000
Greenville *(G-1586)*
Oxford Eagle Inc ....E....... 662 234-2222
Oxford *(G-3986)*
P Press ....G....... 662 638-3571
Oxford *(G-3992)*
Pinion Prod ....G....... 662 891-0930
Blue Springs *(G-298)*
Planhouse Publications Inc ....G....... 601 825-1187
Flowood *(G-1388)*
Platinum Publishing Inc ....G....... 228 219-1020
Biloxi *(G-273)*
Pmq Inc ....F....... 662 234-5481
Oxford *(G-3996)*
Press 4 U ....G....... 901 361-0256
Olive Branch *(G-3901)*
Print Press ....G....... 601 342-2645
Laurel *(G-2827)*
Prs ....G....... 601 941-5104
Brandon *(G-440)*
Purpose Designs LLC ....G....... 601 480-2197
Pachuta *(G-4015)*
Rare Studios Publishing ....G....... 770 316-0683
Roxie *(G-4693)*
Rayburn Publishing LLC ....G....... 662 232-8900
Oxford *(G-3999)*
Real Meal Publishing LLC ....G....... 601 697-7199
Lena *(G-2896)*
Real Yellow Pages ....G....... 662 746-4958
Tinsley *(G-5080)*
Red Star Digital Publishing ....G....... 228 223-7638
Gulfport *(G-1860)*
Rlt Publishing LLC ....G....... 404 956-8344
Jackson *(G-2567)*
Roadster Dream Publishing LLC ....G....... 601 853-4443
Madison *(G-3144)*
Rock or Not LLC..........G....... 662 719-9120
Brandon *(G-447)*
Ruby Press LLC ....G....... 662 832-2255
Oxford *(G-4001)*
Rustic Inn Publications Inc ....G....... 856 983-4288
Corinth *(G-1117)*
▲ Scholastic Products and Awards ....F....... 601 362-6990
Jackson *(G-2576)*
Sharp Cypress Inc ....G....... 601 249-2936
McComb *(G-3266)*
Signature Sound & Printing ....G....... 601 272-5662
Columbus *(G-1026)*
Snapshot Publishing LLC ....G....... 601 624-8845
Flowood *(G-1398)*
Spider Blue Press LLC ....G....... 601 770-0846
Lucedale *(G-3018)*
Stacy Robinson ....G....... 662 289-4640
Kosciusko *(G-2714)*
Thibideau Enterprises LLC ....G....... 662 471-3168
Olive Branch *(G-3917)*
Thugrelatedpublishing ....G....... 228 326-2476
Gulfport *(G-1883)*
Transforming Lives Pubg LLC ....G....... 601 434-6583
Ellisville *(G-1273)*
Trooper Publications ....G....... 228 392-1442
Diberville *(G-1218)*
Unified Buddist Church Inc ....G....... 662 578-2077
Batesville *(G-132)*
Uswebworx LLC ....G....... 601 813-8927
Madison *(G-3164)*

West Express ....G....... 601 321-8088
Jackson *(G-2629)*
West Jones Press Box ....G....... 601 729-2216
Laurel *(G-2873)*
Westminster Software ....G....... 601 214-5028
Brandon *(G-475)*
White Jerleen ....G....... 601 941-6886
Prentiss *(G-4425)*
Who Is Sed Publishing LLC ....G....... 601 634-8939
Vicksburg *(G-5444)*
Wilson Branch Publishing LLC ....G....... 601 656-2718
Philadelphia *(G-4250)*
Word Alive ....G....... 601 307-3639
Wiggins *(G-5594)*

2752 Commercial Printing: Lithographic

506 Printing ....G....... 662 361-4411
Macon *(G-3053)*
9r Screen Printing ....G....... 601 303-0520
Tylertown *(G-5261)*
A-Squared Printing LLC ....G....... 601 497-0280
Pearl *(G-4102)*
A2z Printing Inc ....F....... 601 487-1100
Jackson *(G-2317)*
Acme Printing Company Inc ....F....... 601 856-7766
Madison *(G-3075)*
Action Printing Center Inc ....F....... 228 769-2676
Pascagoula *(G-4018)*
Advantage Tax & Printing ....G....... 601 735-2023
Waynesboro *(G-5488)*
Advantage Tax & Printing Inc ....G....... 601 394-2898
Leakesville *(G-2875)*
Adware ....G....... 601 898-9194
Ridgeland *(G-4545)*
Allmond Printing Company Inc ....G....... 662 369-4848
Aberdeen *(G-8)*
Aloha Printing Co. ....G....... 601 483-6677
Marion *(G-3220)*
Alpha Printing Inc ....G....... 601 371-2611
Jackson *(G-2324)*
American Printing and Converti ....G....... 601 222-0555
Tylertown *(G-5262)*
American Printing Blue PR ....G....... 601 544-7714
Hattiesburg *(G-1922)*
American Printing Copy Center ....G....... 228 875-1398
Ocean Springs *(G-3741)*
Arrow Printers Inc ....F....... 601 924-1192
Clinton *(G-813)*
Atkins Office Supply Inc ....G....... 662 627-2476
Clarksdale *(G-757)*
Bankingformscom Inc ....G....... 601 445-2245
Natchez *(G-3523)*
Barbara OMeallie ....G....... 228 255-7573
Pass Christian *(G-4077)*
Bay Printing & Design Shop LLC ....G....... 228 467-5833
Bay Saint Louis *(G-134)*
Bbs Printing ....G....... 601 606-6980
Wiggins *(G-5572)*
Ben Sessums ....G....... 601 856-3401
Madison *(G-3085)*
Boone Newspapers ....E....... 601 442-9101
Natchez *(G-3537)*
Bourne Brothers Prtg Co Inc ....F....... 601 582-1808
Hattiesburg *(G-1938)*
Boyanton Printing Inc. ....G....... 601 939-6725
Flowood *(G-1348)*
Budget Printing Company ....G....... 601 693-6003
Meridian *(G-3313)*
Burr Creek Screen Printing ....G....... 601 297-2853
Moselle *(G-3455)*
Bynum Printing ....G....... 601 735-5269
Waynesboro *(G-5494)*
C and P Printing Company Inc ....G....... 662 327-9742
Columbus *(G-944)*
Callahans Quick Print Inc. ....G....... 662 234-8060
Oxford *(G-3944)*
Charleston Printing ....G....... 662 647-2291
Charleston *(G-734)*
Clays Print Shop Inc ....G....... 228 868-8244
Gulfport *(G-1753)*
Coast Printing Company ....G....... 228 863-1018
Gulfport *(G-1757)*
▲ Columbus Marble Works Inc ....E....... 662 328-1477
Columbus *(G-950)*
Commonwealth Publishing Inc..........C....... 662 453-5312
Greenwood *(G-1618)*
Competitive Printing ....G....... 228 863-4001
Gulfport *(G-1764)*
Coopers Intl Screen Supply LLC ....G....... 601 353-2488
Jackson *(G-2369)*

Employee Codes: A=Over 500 employees, B=251-500
C=101-250, D=51-100, E=20-50, F=10-19, G=1-9

2019 Harris Directory of
Mississippi Manufacturers

227

27 PRINTING, PUBLISHING, AND ALLIED INDUSTRIES

SIC SECTION

Copy Cats Printing Inc ....F 601 582-3019
Hattiesburg *(G-1951)*
Copy Write Printing Inc ....G 601 736-2679
Columbia *(G-891)*
Country Printer Inc ....G 601 849-3637
Magee *(G-3175)*
Creative Hands Printing Svcs ....G 601 631-1262
Vicksburg *(G-5358)*
Custom Printing ....G 662 227-9511
Grenada *(G-1674)*
Dallas Printing Inc ....E 601 968-9354
Richland *(G-4511)*
Delta-Democrat Pubg Co Inc ......D 662 335-1155
Greenville *(G-1551)*
Dement Printing Company ....G 601 693-2721
Meridian *(G-3329)*
Design Print & Advertise By Pj ....G 662 299-1148
Lexington *(G-2900)*
Diaz Brothers Printing ....G 601 247-0240
Diamondhead *(G-1191)*
Dittos Print & Copy Shop ....D 662 324-3838
Starkville *(G-4941)*
Dixie Print ....G 601 469-3350
Forest *(G-1414)*
Dla Document Services ....G 662 434-7303
Columbus *(G-963)*
Dla Document Services ....G 228 377-2612
Biloxi *(G-237)*
Dogpound Printing LLC ....G 662 323-7425
Starkville *(G-4943)*
Dzt Photography and Event Prtg ...G 228 334-5253
Ocean Springs *(G-3754)*
Eclipse Screen Prints ....G 901 626-9029
Byhalia *(G-584)*
Eighteen-Seventeen Prtg LLC .....G 601 300-0506
Summit *(G-5013)*
Elite Screen Printing ....F 601 450-1261
Hattiesburg *(G-1960)*
Fast Dog Print Co ....G 662 549-4450
Columbus *(G-974)*
Final Touch Productions ....G 601 750-3940
Ridgeland *(G-4581)*
First Amercn Prtg Direct Mail ......G 228 867-9808
Gulfport *(G-1787)*
Fletcher Printing & Office Sup ......G 662 487-3200
Sardis *(G-4739)*
Franklin Printers Inc ....F 601 982-9383
Jackson *(G-2413)*
Gannett Co Inc ....B 601 961-7000
Jackson *(G-2421)*
Gem Publications Inc ....G 601 879-3666
Flora *(G-1307)*
Goodgames Inc ....F 228 769-1827
Pascagoula *(G-4034)*
Gulf Publishing Company Inc ......C 228 896-2100
Gulfport *(G-1801)*
Hagen Corporation ....G 601 932-3138
Pearl *(G-4125)*
Hall S Customized Printing ....G 601 261-2440
Hattiesburg *(G-1980)*
Harden Enterprises Inc ....G 662 841-9292
Tupelo *(G-5151)*
Harden Enterprises Inc ....F 662 841-9292
Tupelo *(G-5152)*
Hatchett Perfection Prints LLC .....G 662 260-6244
Southaven *(G-4876)*
Havard Printing Co ....G 662 781-2613
Horn Lake *(G-2202)*
Hederman Brothers LLC ....D 601 853-7300
Madison *(G-3105)*
Hilgerson Printing ....G 601 684-6978
McComb *(G-3252)*
Holmes Stationary and Gifts ......G 601 276-2700
Summit *(G-5016)*
Impact Printing & Design ....G 601 764-9461
Bay Springs *(G-165)*
Impressions Inc ....G 601 477-9608
Ellisville *(G-1259)*
Inky Printing LLC ....G 504 858-6461
Ocean Springs *(G-3768)*
J&H Printing Inc ....G 662 456-3654
Houston *(G-2247)*
J&J Screen Printing ....G 662 342-6131
Southaven *(G-4881)*
Jackson Business Form Company ...E 601 932-5200
Flowood *(G-1370)*
Jeff Busby ....G 601 924-7979
Clinton *(G-827)*
Jenkins Graphics Inc ....G 662 890-2851
Olive Branch *(G-3855)*

Jonathan Sanford DBA ....G 601 297-2754
Collins *(G-855)*
Joseph L Brown Printing Co ....G 601 693-6184
Meridian *(G-3355)*
K&A Customize Printing LLC ....G 225 326-9054
Madison *(G-3114)*
Kennith Humphrey - Paintings & ...G 601 218-2786
Vicksburg *(G-5385)*
Kingdom Life Printing ....G 601 398-4606
Jackson *(G-2465)*
Knight-Abbey Coml Prtrs Inc ......D 228 702-3231
Biloxi *(G-257)*
Ksquared Inc ....F 601 956-2951
Madison *(G-3116)*
Lawrence Printing Company ....D 662 453-6301
Greenwood *(G-1633)*
Leonard Printing Company ....G 601 833-3912
Brookhaven *(G-511)*
Lewis Yager Melbaleen J ....G 228 762-3152
Pascagoula *(G-4046)*
Linda F Wilson ....G 662 299-9656
Greenwood *(G-1634)*
Local Native Creative + Print ......G 662 401-4767
Baldwyn *(G-84)*
Luke Printing Co Inc ....G 601 693-1144
Meridian *(G-3361)*
M & M Printing LLC ....G 601 798-4316
Picayune *(G-4276)*
M & M Printing Co ....G 601 798-4316
Picayune *(G-4277)*
Mackay Enterprises LLC ....G 662 328-8469
Columbus *(G-995)*
Macon Beacon ....G 662 726-4747
Macon *(G-3064)*
MADE Printing & Designin ....G 601 572-6967
Jackson *(G-2476)*
Magnificent Prints LLC ....G 662 469-5689
Horn Lake *(G-2206)*
Magnolia Printing and Signs ......G 601 922-5076
Jackson *(G-2478)*
Magnolia Printing Co ....G 228 864-4401
Gulfport *(G-1824)*
Martini Monday Inc ....G 228 229-4872
Diberville *(G-1208)*
Mason Printing ....G 662 563-3709
Batesville *(G-114)*
McComb Printing Inc ....F 601 684-9841
McComb *(G-3259)*
Media Solutions ....G 601 351-9303
Jackson *(G-2486)*
Meteor Inc ....F 601 892-2581
Crystal Springs *(G-1148)*
Mid South Publications Inc ....G 662 256-8209
Amory *(G-48)*
Minuteman Press International ......G 662 349-6675
Horn Lake *(G-2207)*
Mississippi Muddy Prints LLC ......G 601 757-2990
Brookhaven *(G-518)*
Mississippi Rainbow Printing ......G 601 853-9513
Ridgeland *(G-4606)*
Modeltruckin ....G 228 365-4124
Gulfport *(G-1834)*
Ms Band of Choctaw Indians Db ...F 601 656-3636
Choctaw *(G-748)*
Murray Printing ....G 601 446-6558
Natchez *(G-3593)*
Natchez Printing Co ....G 601 442-3693
Natchez *(G-3596)*
Nelsons Printing Inc ....G 601 683-6651
Newton *(G-3725)*
Newspaper Holding Inc ....D 601 693-1551
Meridian *(G-3377)*
Nick Strcklnds Quick Print Inc ......F 601 353-8672
Ridgeland *(G-4611)*
Nick Strcklnds Quick Print Inc ......E 601 898-1717
Jackson *(G-2521)*
Nick Strcklnds Quick Print Inc ......G 601 939-2781
Pearl *(G-4134)*
Nick Strcklnds Quick Print Inc ......G 601 355-8195
Ridgeland *(G-4612)*
Northtowne Printers Inc ....G 601 713-3200
Jackson *(G-2523)*
Noyes Printing & Rbr Stamp Co ...G 662 332-5256
Greenville *(G-1583)*
Oce Corporate Printing Div ....G 228 863-0458
Gulfport *(G-1840)*
Overnight Printing Service ....G 662 895-9262
Olive Branch *(G-3892)*
P D Q Printing Inc ....G 228 392-4888
Biloxi *(G-271)*

P P I Inc ....F 662 680-4332
Tupelo *(G-5197)*
Panther Printing LLC ....G 601 425-4414
Laurel *(G-2816)*
Park Avenue Printing ....G 601 876-9095
Tylertown *(G-5279)*
Pat The Cat Prints ....G 662 397-1038
Tupelo *(G-5199)*
Pavco Industries Inc ....D 228 762-3959
Pascagoula *(G-4061)*
Paw Print Visuals LLC ....G 662 332-2359
Greenville *(G-1588)*
Pinnacle Printing and Copying ....G 601 944-1470
Flowood *(G-1387)*
Piranha Business Cards LLC ......F 800 281-1916
Madison *(G-3140)*
Pollchaps Custom Screen Prtg ....G 769 218-0824
Brandon *(G-436)*
Premiere Printing ....G 662 488-9591
Pontotoc *(G-4358)*
Presto Printing Inc ....G 228 678-9085
Gulfport *(G-1853)*
Print Brokers Inc ....G 662 231-2556
Booneville *(G-343)*
Print Pros LLC ....G 662 327-3222
Columbus *(G-1016)*
Print Shed ....G 228 206-0077
Gulfport *(G-1854)*
Print Shop ....G 662 453-8497
Greenwood *(G-1647)*
Print Shop ....G 601 638-0962
Vicksburg *(G-5408)*
Print Shop Inc ....G 601 428-4602
Laurel *(G-2828)*
Print Zone ....G 601 799-3113
Carriere *(G-699)*
Printers Inc ....G 601 792-8493
Prentiss *(G-4424)*
Printing Alley Ltd ....G 601 371-1243
Terry *(G-5075)*
Printing On Time Screen ....G 601 707-7207
Ridgeland *(G-4620)*
Printing Place ....G 601 885-8327
Utica *(G-5311)*
Professional Graphics Inc ....G 601 924-9116
Clinton *(G-834)*
Proforma Southprint ....G 901 734-2290
Hernando *(G-2149)*
Prographics Inc ....G 662 329-3341
Columbus *(G-1017)*
Quality Printing Inc ....E 601 353-9663
Jackson *(G-2555)*
Queens Printing LLC ....G 228 234-5693
Gautier *(G-1502)*
Quick Prints ....G 601 485-3278
Meridian *(G-3390)*
Quitman County Democrat ....G 662 326-2181
Marks *(G-3222)*
R & B Specialty Printing LLC ....G 662 260-2145
Tupelo *(G-5212)*
Rankin Printery ....G 662 287-4426
Corinth *(G-1112)*
Raymond Young Printing ....G 601 947-8999
Lucedale *(G-3015)*
Reed S Printing Inc ....G 662 287-0311
Corinth *(G-1114)*
Reliable 2 Screen Printing ....G 662 910-8272
Tunica *(G-5102)*
Rhino Graphics ....G 601 445-8777
Natchez *(G-3613)*
Richton Dispatch Inc ....G 601 788-6031
Richton *(G-4543)*
Rutledge Publishing Co Inc ....G 662 534-2116
New Albany *(G-3694)*
Screenco Printing LLC ....G 601 507-1986
Ridgeland *(G-4628)*
Shabazz Printing ....G 601 786-9788
Fayette *(G-1301)*
Sharones Innovative Prtg LLC ......G 601 877-3727
Lorman *(G-2962)*
Shaughnessy & Co Inc ....G 228 436-4060
Biloxi *(G-279)*
Shilpam Corp ....F 601 933-9550
Pearl *(G-4144)*
Sign Shop ....G 662 328-7933
Columbus *(G-1025)*
Sir Speedy Printing Center ....G 601 981-3045
Jackson *(G-2583)*
Smart Source ....G 601 707-1150
Ridgeland *(G-4631)*

228

2019 Harris Directory of
Mississippi Manufacturers

SIC SECTION
27 PRINTING, PUBLISHING, AND ALLIED INDUSTRIES

Smith Printing & Off Sup Inc....G....601 442-2441
Natchez *(G-3621)*
Sonnyboys Garment Printing LLC....G....601 415-2250
Jackson *(G-2587)*
Sorg Printing LLC....G....228 392-3299
Diberville *(G-1214)*
South Center Printing....G....662 252-2793
Holly Springs *(G-2191)*
Southern Print Company....G....601 898-8796
Madison *(G-3150)*
Southern Prtg & Silk Screening....F....228 452-7309
Pass Christian *(G-4095)*
Southern Systems & Service Co....G....601 264-4713
Hattiesburg *(G-2064)*
Southwest Publishers Inc....E....601 833-6961
Brookhaven *(G-538)*
Sparks Printing & Graphics....G....662 842-4481
Tupelo *(G-5230)*
Speedy Printing....G....228 466-5766
Waveland *(G-5485)*
Standard Office Sup Prtg Inc....E....601 544-5361
Hattiesburg *(G-2069)*
Stephens Printing LLC....G....601 845-7708
Florence *(G-1333)*
Still Blessed Prints....G....601 810-8285
Brookhaven *(G-539)*
Stone Printing Inc....G....601 928-7050
Wiggins *(G-5590)*
Stribling Printing....G....601 656-4194
Philadelphia *(G-4238)*
Sunset Screen Printing....G....601 297-2754
Collins *(G-863)*
Swain Printing & Signs....G....662 773-7584
Louisville *(G-2983)*
Swatprint Screen Printing....G....662 862-3004
Fulton *(G-1478)*
T Enterprises Inc....F....601 487-1100
Jackson *(G-2603)*
T-N-T Printing....G....601 630-9553
Vicksburg *(G-5426)*
Theleg5813 Photos & Prints....G....601 927-1360
Brandon *(G-468)*
Tikal Prints LLC....G....601 954-0972
Jackson *(G-2607)*
Tiny Prints 3d Imaging LLC....G....866 846-9733
Picayune *(G-4301)*
Trader Printing....G....662 767-9411
Shannon *(G-4820)*
Trens Screen Printing....G....662 578-9074
Batesville *(G-130)*
Tupelo Screen Printing LLC....G....662 523-0092
Tupelo *(G-5247)*
Turner Group LLC....G....601 394-5070
Leakesville *(G-2880)*
Tyler Printing and Cmpt Svc....G....601 279-6105
Vicksburg *(G-5430)*
Unik Ink Cstm Screen Prtg Inc....G....601 259-1004
Madison *(G-3163)*
United Print Services LLC....G....662 287-1090
Corinth *(G-1125)*
Vibrant Screen Printing....G....601 291-1296
Jackson *(G-2621)*
Vicksburg Newsmedia LLC....G....601 636-4545
Vicksburg *(G-5437)*
Vizionz Unlimited LLC....G....601 272-5040
Jackson *(G-2622)*
W T Leggett Inc....G....601 544-2704
Hattiesburg *(G-2081)*
Wards Custom Screen Prin....G....601 384-4635
Meadville *(G-3278)*
Watkins Trim Shop Inc....G....601 485-5512
Meridian *(G-3417)*
Welch Printing....G....662 283-3692
Winona *(G-5610)*
Where We Print Shirts LLC....G....601 348-5754
Madison *(G-3169)*
Wolverton Enterprises Inc....F....601 355-9543
Jackson *(G-2637)*
Womack Willow....G....601 969-4120
Jackson *(G-2638)*
Yellow Dog Printing Co LLC....G....601 776-6853
Quitman *(G-4473)*
Ziprint Inc....G....662 226-6864
Grenada *(G-1713)*

2754 Commercial Printing: Gravure

Celebrations Etc....G....601 268-0390
Hattiesburg *(G-1942)*
Newton Appeal....G....601 683-7810
Newton *(G-3726)*
Pcw (print Copy Webdesign LLC....G....601 259-1945
Crystal Springs *(G-1152)*
Pink Peppermint Paper LLC....G....601 898-9232
Madison *(G-3139)*
Rankin Printery....G....662 287-4426
Corinth *(G-1112)*
Smart Source....G....601 707-1150
Ridgeland *(G-4631)*
Standard Office Sup Prtg Inc....E....601 544-5361
Hattiesburg *(G-2069)*
Swirlz....G....662 791-7822
Tupelo *(G-5235)*
The Touch....G....662 378-4188
Greenville *(G-1602)*

2759 Commercial Printing

3 Men Moving & Storage LLC....G....662 238-7774
Oxford *(G-3934)*
Ad Visuals Inc....G....601 932-3060
Richland *(G-4497)*
Advantage Tax & Printing Svc....G....601 544-0602
Hattiesburg *(G-1917)*
Advantage Tax and Print....G....601 557-5055
Quitman *(G-4455)*
American Printing Copy Center....G....228 875-1398
Ocean Springs *(G-3741)*
American T Shirt Printing Co....G....662 590-3272
Yazoo City *(G-5622)*
Anna Grace Tees LLC....G....228 861-2661
Gulfport *(G-1727)*
Artistic Tees....G....662 234-5051
Oxford *(G-3936)*
Ashley Printing Co....G....601 729-8950
Laurel *(G-2732)*
Baldwyn News....G....662 365-3232
Baldwyn *(G-71)*
Bangers and Mash Tees LLC....G....801 803-8970
Madison *(G-3083)*
Banner Printing Co Inc....G....662 247-3373
Belzoni *(G-204)*
Barber Printing Inc....F....662 841-1584
Tupelo *(G-5112)*
Barn Life Tees....G....601 740-0696
Columbia *(G-883)*
Bear Creek Apparel Promotions....G....601 259-8508
Canton *(G-648)*
Betty Wright....G....662 224-3000
Ashland *(G-59)*
Big Buck Sports....G....601 605-2661
Ridgeland *(G-4556)*
Blax Screen Printing & EMB....G....228 392-5022
Diberville *(G-1199)*
Brewer Screen Printing....G....662 453-2255
Greenwood *(G-1616)*
Brown Line Printing Inc....F....662 728-9881
Booneville *(G-322)*
Buzini Group LLC....E....601 398-1311
Flowood *(G-1350)*
C F E N....G....662 327-0031
Columbus *(G-945)*
Cap Co....G....601 384-3939
Bude *(G-568)*
Charlottes EMB & Screen Prtg....G....601 824-1080
Brandon *(G-379)*
City of Biloxi....C....228 435-6217
Biloxi *(G-228)*
Clayful Impressions....G....601 918-0221
Brandon *(G-381)*
Coast Tees LLC....G....228 234-1636
Gulfport *(G-1758)*
Coopers Intl Screen Supply LLC....G....601 353-2488
Jackson *(G-2369)*
Cotton Tops....G....662 287-4737
Corinth *(G-1081)*
Country Printer Inc....G....601 849-3637
Magee *(G-3175)*
Creative Designs & Sports....G....662 327-5000
Columbus *(G-956)*
Custom Creations....G....601 450-7600
Hattiesburg *(G-1954)*
Custom Sportswear USA Inc....G....228 255-4795
Diamondhead *(G-1188)*
D Graphics Advertising....G....601 373-4667
Jackson *(G-2374)*
Dallas Printing Inc....E....601 968-9354
Richland *(G-4511)*
Darrells Screen Printing....G....601 653-6924
Natchez *(G-3553)*
Dement Printing Company....G....601 693-2721
Meridian *(G-3329)*
Destiny Apparel LLC....G....228 383-2665
Biloxi *(G-236)*
Digital Kanvas LLC....G....901 896-9690
Olive Branch *(G-3836)*
Downs Corporation....G....662 728-3237
Booneville *(G-327)*
Dub Street Fashion Center LLC....G....601 483-0036
Meridian *(G-3330)*
Dynastics Screen Printing....G....601 353-1956
Jackson *(G-2393)*
Emersons....G....228 588-3952
Lucedale *(G-2994)*
Encore Products....G....662 423-3484
Iuka *(G-2290)*
Express Printing....G....601 856-5458
Ridgeland *(G-4579)*
First Amercn Prtg Direct Mail....G....228 867-9808
Gulfport *(G-1787)*
First Amercn Prtg Direct Mail....E....601 656-3636
Choctaw *(G-745)*
Flatlanders Screen Printing....G....662 846-0725
Cleveland *(G-792)*
Formal Affair....G....228 497-7500
Gautier *(G-1492)*
Franklin Printers Inc....F....601 982-9383
Jackson *(G-2413)*
Fudge Inc....F....601 932-4748
Flowood *(G-1363)*
G5 Tees....G....662 403-1339
Coldwater *(G-846)*
Gator Grafix Inc....G....601 376-9004
Jackson *(G-2423)*
▲ Global Screen Printing LLC....G....601 919-2345
Brandon *(G-399)*
Goodgames Inc....F....228 769-1827
Pascagoula *(G-4034)*
Graphic Arts Productions Inc....G....662 494-2549
West Point *(G-5544)*
Gt Screen Prtg & Promotions....G....601 759-9858
Pearl *(G-4124)*
Hagen Corporation....G....601 932-3138
Pearl *(G-4125)*
Harris Custom Ink LLC....E....662 338-4242
Olive Branch *(G-3844)*
Her Heart Shop....G....662 523-9568
Shannon *(G-4809)*
Hilgerson Printing....G....601 684-6978
McComb *(G-3252)*
Hobies Sports and Outdoors....G....601 833-9700
Brookhaven *(G-500)*
Hodge Podge Screen Prtg Inc....F....662 226-1636
Grenada *(G-1685)*
Holmes Stationary and Gifts....G....601 276-2700
Summit *(G-5016)*
Image Screen Printing Inc....E....662 489-5668
Pontotoc *(G-4336)*
Independents Service Company....G....662 287-2431
Corinth *(G-1091)*
Ink Spot Inc....G....662 236-2639
Oxford *(G-3959)*
Ink Spot Inc....F....662 236-1985
Oxford *(G-3960)*
Inky BS Custom Tees LLC....G....601 988-8558
Raymond *(G-4490)*
Iprint Inc....G....601 932-4414
Flowood *(G-1366)*
J M H Graphics....G....601 261-2500
Hattiesburg *(G-2000)*
J S Iupes....G....601 856-7776
Madison *(G-3112)*
J&J Screen Printing....G....662 342-6131
Southaven *(G-4881)*
Jagg LLC....G....228 388-1794
Biloxi *(G-254)*
JC Graphics LLC....E....662 832-9291
Oxford *(G-3963)*
Jenkins Graphics Inc....G....662 890-2851
Olive Branch *(G-3855)*
JM Digital Corporation....G....601 659-0599
Bay St Louis *(G-179)*
Label Express Inc....F....662 566-7075
Verona *(G-5334)*
Lazarus Arts....G....601 445-4576
Natchez *(G-3578)*
Mackay Enterprises LLC....G....662 328-8469
Columbus *(G-996)*
Magnolia Label Co Inc....E....601 878-0951
Jackson *(G-2477)*
Mainline Printing....G....662 301-8298
Senatobia *(G-4795)*

S I C

Employee Codes: A=Over 500 employees, B=251-500
C=101-250, D=51-100, E=20-50, F=10-19, G=1-9
2019 Harris Directory of
Mississippi Manufacturers
229

27 PRINTING, PUBLISHING, AND ALLIED INDUSTRIES

SIC SECTION

Mantachie Printing & Mktg LLC .... G 662 282-7625
Tupelo (G-5183)
Mid South Publications Inc .... G 662 256-8209
Amory (G-48)
Mississippi Gulf Coast .... G 228 896-3055
Gulfport (G-1832)
Mississippi Photo & Bluprt Co .... G 601 948-1119
Jackson (G-2502)
Modeltruckin .... G 228 365-4124
Gulfport (G-1834)
Mombo Graphixs .... G 228 466-2551
Waveland (G-5483)
Monogram Express .... G 601 825-1248
Brandon (G-425)
Monogram Magic .... G 601 956-7117
Jackson (G-2510)
Monograms Plus .... G 662 327-3332
Columbus (G-1007)
Natchez Printing Co .... G 601 442-3693
Natchez (G-3596)
National Scrubwear Inc .... F 601 483-0796
Meridian (G-3376)
Nebco Inc .... G 662 349-1400
Southaven (G-4890)
Nick Clark Printing and Signs .... G 601 607-7722
Madison (G-3133)
Office Depot Inc .... E 662 378-2995
Greenville (G-1585)
Office Huddle Small Business .... F 601 255-8650
Crowder (G-1137)
One of A Kind Art Creations .... G 662 328-1283
Columbus (G-1013)
Oneway Inc .... G 601 664-0007
Jackson (G-2660)
Oneway Screen Prtg & Graphics .... G 601 845-7777
Florence (G-1330)
Onswoll Grafix LLC .... G 228 596-8409
Long Beach (G-2947)
Oxford Printwear LLC .... F 662 234-5051
Oxford (G-3989)
Park Avenue Printing .... G 601 876-9095
Tylertown (G-5279)
Party City .... F 228 539-4476
Gulfport (G-1846)
Pat Screen Printing .... G 662 301-8176
Senatobia (G-4797)
Pearl River Graphics & Prtg .... G 601 656-3636
Choctaw (G-749)
Phillips Company Inc .... G 662 844-3898
Tupelo (G-5203)
Plan House Printing .... G 662 407-0193
Tupelo (G-5206)
Plan House Printing .... G 601 336-6378
Hattiesburg (G-2045)
Pollchaps LLC .... G 601 706-4928
Brandon (G-435)
Print Shop of Tupelo .... G 662 841-0004
Mooreville (G-3443)
Printshop Plus Inc .... G 662 231-4790
Pontotoc (G-4359)
Pro Designs Inc .... G 662 841-1867
Tupelo (G-5209)
Protees USA LLC .... G 601 317-3649
Jackson (G-2553)
Quality Printing Inc .... E 601 353-9663
Jackson (G-2555)
Revolution Printing & Graphics .... G 662 932-8176
Olive Branch (G-3904)
Roosevelt Wallace .... G 662 627-7513
Clarksdale (G-781)
Rutledge Publishing Co Inc .... G 662 534-2116
New Albany (G-3694)
Screenco Inc .... G 662 534-8750
New Albany (G-3697)
Screening Room .... G 601 626-0327
Collinsville (G-875)
Serigraphics .... G 662 895-3553
Olive Branch (G-3908)
Service Printers Inc .... E 601 939-4910
Flowood (G-1395)
Shaughnessy & Co Inc .... G 228 436-4060
Biloxi (G-279)
Shenise Productions Inc .... G 601 437-3665
Port Gibson (G-4407)
Smart Source .... G 601 707-1150
Ridgeland (G-4631)
Smith Printing & Off Sup Inc .... G 601 442-2441
Natchez (G-3621)
Southern Bell Clothing .... G 662 258-2955
Eupora (G-1293)

Southern Belle .... G 662 637-2264
Grenada (G-1703)
Southern Graphics Inc .... G 601 833-7448
Brookhaven (G-537)
Southern Tees Plus .... G 601 896-7468
Kosciusko (G-2712)
Special TS .... G 662 563-5138
Batesville (G-126)
Specialtees Etc .... G 601 683-2552
Newton (G-3728)
Stamm Advertising Co Inc .... G 601 636-7749
Vicksburg (G-5423)
Stamm Advertising Co Inc .... G 601 922-3400
Jackson (G-2597)
Standard Office Sup Prtg Inc .... E 601 544-5361
Hattiesburg (G-2069)
Star Printing Co of Amory Inc .... E 662 256-8424
Amory (G-56)
Steve B White .... G 601 939-8177
Florence (G-1334)
Stewarts Screen Printing .... G 601 932-8310
Jackson (G-2669)
Stribling Printing .... G 601 656-4194
Philadelphia (G-4238)
Swain Printing & Signs .... G 662 773-7584
Louisville (G-2983)
Sweet Tee Screen Printing .... G 601 757-3435
Summit (G-5025)
Sweetees .... G 662 404-1966
Sardis (G-4745)
T Shirt Shop & Design Firm LLC .... G 662 329-9911
Columbus (G-1036)
T Tommys .... G 601 833-8620
Brookhaven (G-542)
Tanners Enterprise LLC .... G 601 894-5219
Hazlehurst (G-2108)
Taylor Made Labels Inc .... G 601 936-0050
Jackson (G-2671)
Taylor Screen Printing .... G 601 352-9779
Jackson (G-2605)
Tees By Taran .... G 601 549-8384
Brookhaven (G-543)
Tees River Relics .... G 662 501-9936
Coldwater (G-851)
Tees Snow White .... G 662 420-2687
Holly Springs (G-2194)
Teezers .... G 662 560-5099
Senatobia (G-4804)
Vicksburg Printing and Pubg Co .... G 601 638-2900
Vicksburg (G-5439)
Vizionz Unlimited LLC .... G 601 272-5040
Jackson (G-2622)
Watermark Printers LLC .... G 662 323-8750
Starkville (G-4979)
Watkins Trim Shop Inc .... G 601 485-5512
Meridian (G-3417)
Wheeler Enterprises Inc .... G 601 799-1440
Picayune (G-4303)
Womack Willow .... G 601 969-4120
Jackson (G-2638)
Yank Threads LLC .... G 601 201-3934
Jackson (G-2639)
Youngs Leather & Custom Tees .... G 662 424-3847
Dennis (G-1185)

2761 Manifold Business Forms

Acco Brands USA LLC .... G 800 541-0094
Booneville (G-314)
Barber Printing Inc .... F 662 841-1584
Tupelo (G-5112)
Gpal LLC .... G 662 422-9351
Tupelo (G-5146)
Jackson Business Form Company .... E 601 932-5200
Flowood (G-1370)

2782 Blankbooks & Looseleaf Binders

Acco Brands USA LLC .... D 662 720-1300
Booneville (G-315)
Avery Products Corporation .... C 601 483-0611
Meridian (G-3304)
Norman Accounting Services .... G 662 347-4475
Greenville (G-1582)
Rebel Quick Cash .... G 662 326-9228
Marks (G-3223)
South Txas Lghthouse For Blind .... G 601 679-3180
Meridian (G-3400)
Southland Supplies .... G 662 647-2452
Cascilla (G-729)

2789 Bookbinding

Alpha Printing Inc .... G 601 371-2611
Jackson (G-2324)
Bourne Brothers Prtg Co Inc .... F 601 582-1808
Hattiesburg (G-1938)
Coopers Intl Screen Supply LLC .... G 601 353-2488
Jackson (G-2369)
Copy Cats Printing Inc .... F 601 582-3019
Hattiesburg (G-1951)
Dement Printing Company .... G 601 693-2721
Meridian (G-3329)
Dianne Gore .... G 510 697-2569
Jackson (G-2383)
Fedex Office & Print Svcs Inc .... E 601 957-3311
Jackson (G-2407)
Fedex Office & Print Svcs Inc .... F 601 264-6434
Hattiesburg (G-1969)
Fleming Book Binding Company .... G 601 776-3761
Quitman (G-4465)
Hagen Corporation .... G 601 932-3138
Pearl (G-4125)
Harden Enterprises Inc .... F 662 841-9292
Tupelo (G-5152)
Jenkins Graphics Inc .... G 662 890-2851
Olive Branch (G-3855)
Lewis Yager Melbaleen J .... G 228 762-3152
Pascagoula (G-4046)
Mid South Publications Inc .... G 662 256-8209
Amory (G-48)
Natchez Printing Co .... G 601 442-3693
Natchez (G-3596)
Nick StrckInds Quick Print Inc .... F 601 353-8672
Ridgeland (G-4611)
Nick StrckInds Quick Print Inc .... E 601 898-1717
Jackson (G-2521)
▲ Norris Bookbinding Co Inc .... F 662 453-7424
Greenwood (G-1643)
Rankin Printery .... G 662 287-4426
Corinth (G-1112)
RR Donnelley & Sons Company .... B 662 562-5252
Senatobia (G-4802)
Shaughnessy & Co Inc .... G 228 436-4060
Biloxi (G-279)
Smith Printing & Off Sup Inc .... G 601 442-2441
Natchez (G-3621)
Southern Systems & Service Co .... G 601 264-4713
Hattiesburg (G-2064)
Swain Printing & Signs .... G 662 773-7584
Louisville (G-2983)
Wolverton Enterprises Inc .... F 601 355-9543
Jackson (G-2637)
Womack Willow .... G 601 969-4120
Jackson (G-2638)

2791 Typesetting

Alpha Printing Inc .... G 601 371-2611
Jackson (G-2324)
Boone Newspapers .... E 601 442-9101
Natchez (G-3537)
Bourne Brothers Prtg Co Inc .... F 601 582-1808
Hattiesburg (G-1938)
Composing Room Inc .... G 662 393-6652
Southaven (G-4861)
Copy Cats Printing Inc .... F 601 582-3019
Hattiesburg (G-1951)
Dement Printing Company .... G 601 693-2721
Meridian (G-3329)
Fedex Office & Print Svcs Inc .... E 601 957-3311
Jackson (G-2407)
Fedex Office & Print Svcs Inc .... F 601 264-6434
Hattiesburg (G-1969)
Harden Enterprises Inc .... F 662 841-9292
Tupelo (G-5152)
Holmes Stationary and Gifts .... G 601 276-2700
Summit (G-5016)
Jenkins Graphics Inc .... G 662 890-2851
Olive Branch (G-3855)
Lewis Yager Melbaleen J .... G 228 762-3152
Pascagoula (G-4046)
M & M Printing Co .... G 601 798-4316
Picayune (G-4277)
Mid South Publications Inc .... G 662 256-8209
Amory (G-48)
Nick StrckInds Quick Print Inc .... F 601 353-8672
Ridgeland (G-4611)
Nick StrckInds Quick Print Inc .... E 601 898-1717
Jackson (G-2521)
Nick StrckInds Quick Print Inc .... G 601 355-8195
Ridgeland (G-4612)

230

2019 Harris Directory of
Mississippi Manufacturers

SIC SECTION

28 CHEMICALS AND ALLIED PRODUCTS

Printers Inc ....G....... 601 792-8493
Prentiss (G-4424)
Rankin Printery ....G....... 662 287-4426
Corinth (G-1112)
RR Donnelley & Sons Company..........B....... 662 562-5252
Senatobia (G-4802)
Rutledge Publishing Co Inc ....G....... 662 534-2116
New Albany (G-3694)
Shaughnessy & Co Inc ....G....... 228 436-4060
Biloxi (G-279)
Smith Printing & Off Sup Inc ....G....... 601 442-2441
Natchez (G-3621)
Southern Images Printing Inc ....G....... 601 649-3501
Laurel (G-2852)
Swain Printing & Signs ....G....... 662 773-7584
Louisville (G-2983)
Womack Willow ....G....... 601 969-4120
Jackson (G-2638)

2796 Platemaking & Related Svcs

Coopers Intl Screen Supply LLC ....G....... 601 353-2488
Jackson (G-2369)
Copy Cats Printing Inc ....F....... 601 582-3019
Hattiesburg (G-1951)
Fedex Office & Print Svcs Inc ....F....... 601 264-6434
Hattiesburg (G-1969)
MDN Laser Engraving Inc ....G....... 662 397-5799
Tupelo (G-5185)
RR Donnelley & Sons Company..........B....... 662 562-5252
Senatobia (G-4802)
Toyota Tsusho America Inc................G....... 662 620-8890
Tupelo (G-5240)

28 CHEMICALS AND ALLIED PRODUCTS

2812 Alkalies & Chlorine

Amerimac Chemical Co ....G....... 601 918-8321
Jackson (G-2328)
Axiall Corporation ....C....... 601 892-5612
Hazlehurst (G-2089)
Axiall Corporation ....D....... 601 206-3200
Madison (G-3081)
Axiall Corporation ....E....... 662 369-9586
Prairie (G-4411)
Olin Corporation ....C....... 662 281-7900
Oxford (G-3979)
Olin Corporation ....C....... 662 234-4056
Oxford (G-3980)

2813 Industrial Gases

Air Products and Chemicals Inc ....G....... 601 823-9850
Brookhaven (G-479)
Alig LLC ....F....... 601 829-9020
Brandon (G-361)
Brandon Boc Ms ....G....... 601 825-1422
Brandon (G-373)
Fallen Leaf Services LLC ....G....... 228 731-0919
Gulfport (G-1781)
Hydrogen Peroxide ....G....... 662 329-9085
Columbus (G-985)
Linde North America Inc ....F....... 601 829-9020
Brandon (G-414)
Matheson Tri-Gas Inc ....F....... 228 255-6661
Pass Christian (G-4091)
Matheson Tri-Gas Inc ....F....... 601 856-3000
Madison (G-3127)
Messer LLC ....E....... 601 825-1422
Brandon (G-424)
Neon Marketing ....G....... 601 960-4555
Jackson (G-2520)
▲ Nitrous Oxide Corp ....G....... 662 746-7607
Yazoo City (G-5644)
Pig Neon ....G....... 662 638-3257
Oxford (G-3993)
Praxair Inc ....G....... 662 343-8336
Hamilton (G-1906)
Praxair Inc ....F....... 601 825-8214
Brandon (G-437)
Premier Air Products LLC ....G....... 662 890-9233
Olive Branch (G-3900)
Sandhill Group LLC ....E....... 601 591-4030
Brandon (G-450)
Wesco Gas & Welding Supply Inc ....G....... 228 475-1955
Moss Point (G-3506)

2816 Inorganic Pigments

Chemours Company Fc LLC...............E....... 228 255-2100
Pass Christian (G-4078)
Tronox Incorporated ....D....... 662 343-8311
Hamilton (G-1909)

2819 Indl Inorganic Chemicals, NEC

▲ 3 F Chimica Americas Inc..............G....... 662 369-2843
Aberdeen (G-5)
Allied Universal Corp........................F....... 601 477-2550
Ellisville (G-1245)
Aquavest ....G....... 662 287-0302
Corinth (G-1057)
Baker Petrolite.................................G....... 601 442-2401
Natchez (G-3522)
Benny Evans ....G....... 601 264-8903
Hattiesburg (G-1927)
Bluff City Service Company ....G....... 662 534-2500
New Albany (G-3675)
Calgon Carbon Corporation...............D....... 228 533-7171
Bay Saint Louis (G-139)
Channel Chemical Corporation ....E....... 228 864-6199
Gulfport (G-1750)
Chemours Company Fc LLC...............E....... 228 255-2100
Pass Christian (G-4078)
Chemtrade Chemicals US LLC ....G....... 601 799-2380
Nicholson (G-3730)
Desiccare Inc ....E....... 601 932-0405
Richland (G-4513)
◆ Eko Peroxide LLC ....G....... 662 240-8571
Columbus (G-968)
Elements Estate Sales ....G....... 601 482-4099
Meridian (G-3334)
Engelhard ....G....... 601 948-3966
Jackson (G-2401)
Entergy Nuclear Fuels Company.........F....... 601 368-5750
Jackson (G-2402)
Exide Technologies ....G....... 601 936-7788
Pearl (G-4116)
Exide Technologies ....G....... 601 845-2281
Florence (G-1323)
Geo Specialty Chemical Inc ....G....... 601 587-7481
Monticello (G-3431)
Helena Agri-Enterprises LLC ....G....... 662 283-3990
Winona (G-5600)
Helena Chemical Company ....G....... 662 383-0004
Friars Point (G-1442)
Hybrid Plastics Incorporated ....E....... 601 544-3466
Hattiesburg (G-1997)
▲ Odom Industries Inc ....C....... 601 735-0088
Waynesboro (G-5508)
Odom Industries Inc ....E....... 601 776-2035
Pachuta (G-4014)
▲ Polychemie Inc............................E....... 228 533-5555
Bay Saint Louis (G-150)
Restora-Life Minerals Inc ....G....... 601 789-5545
Bay Springs (G-172)
▲ Southern Ionics Incorporated.........E....... 662 494-3055
West Point (G-5563)
Southern Ionics Incorporated.............E....... 662 495-2583
West Point (G-5564)
Southern Ionics Incorporated.............E....... 662 328-0516
Columbus (G-1028)

2821 Plastics, Mtrls & Nonvulcanizable Elastomers

4m Enterprises LLC ....G....... 601 664-0030
Pearl (G-4101)
◆ Axiall LLC....................................E....... 601 856-8993
Madison (G-3080)
Axiall Corporation ....C....... 601 892-5612
Hazlehurst (G-2089)
Axiall Corporation ....D....... 601 206-3200
Madison (G-3081)
Axiall Corporation ....E....... 662 369-9586
Prairie (G-4411)
B & D Plastics Mississippi Inc............F....... 228 875-5865
Ocean Springs (G-3742)
Carpenter Co ....B....... 662 566-2392
Verona (G-5329)
Dak Americas LLC ....C....... 228 533-4480
Bay St Louis (G-178)
◆ Dak Americas Mississippi Inc ....E....... 228 533-4000
Bay Saint Louis (G-142)
Dealership Services LLC....................G....... 662 269-3897
Tupelo (G-5126)
Elite Comfort Solutions LLC ....E....... 662 566-2322
Verona (G-5330)

28 CHEMICALS AND ALLIED PRODUCTS

Ergon Chemicals LLC.......................B....... 601 933-3000
Flowood (G-1358)
Fxi Inc ....C....... 662 566-2382
Verona (G-5331)
George Pacific ....G....... 662 779-1300
Louisville (G-2968)
◆ Gulf Concrete Technology LLC.........G....... 228 575-3500
Long Beach (G-2938)
◆ Heritage Plastics Inc ....C....... 404 425-1905
Picayune (G-4271)
Hybrid Plastics Incorporated ....E....... 601 544-3466
Hattiesburg (G-1997)
Integrity Vnyl Sding Decks LLC...........G....... 601 723-1257
Lumberton (G-3031)
L & J Products & Sales Inc ....E....... 662 841-0710
Tupelo (G-5169)
▲ McNeely Plastic Products Inc.........E....... 601 926-1000
Clinton (G-830)
Nanocor LLC ....G....... 847 851-1500
Aberdeen (G-19)
▲ Perma R Products Inc....................C....... 662 226-8075
Grenada (G-1699)
Plaskolite South LLC ....C....... 662 895-7007
Olive Branch (G-3898)
▲ Resinall Mississippi Inc.................C....... 252 585-1445
Hattiesburg (G-2050)
Sabic Innovative Plas US LLC ....C....... 228 466-3015
Bay Saint Louis (G-155)
Sabic Innovative Plas US LLC ....E....... 228 533-7855
Bay Saint Louis (G-154)
Solaplast LLC ....G....... 877 972-5449
Meridian (G-3399)
Sonoco Prtective Solutions Inc ....E....... 662 842-1043
Tupelo (G-5225)
Westlake Chemical Corporation..........G....... 601 892-5612
Hazlehurst (G-2110)
Westlake Chemical Corporation..........C....... 662 369-8111
Aberdeen (G-21)
Westlake Compounds LLC ....G....... 601 206-3200
Madison (G-3168)
Westlake Compounds LLC ....G....... 601 892-5612
Gallman (G-1487)

2822 Synthetic Rubber (Vulcanizable Elastomers)

▲ Rheogistics LLC............................E....... 601 749-8845
Picayune (G-4291)
Valmet Inc ....D....... 662 328-3841
Columbus (G-1041)
Zeon Chemicals L P ....D....... 601 583-5527
Hattiesburg (G-2088)

2823 Cellulosic Man-Made Fibers

▲ Custom Nonwoven Inc ....F....... 662 539-6103
New Albany (G-3679)
Fibrix LLC ....E....... 662 844-3803
Tupelo (G-5132)
Fibrix LLC ....E....... 662 489-7908
Pontotoc (G-4331)
▲ Kengro Corporation.......................F....... 662 647-2456
Charleston (G-740)
▲ Leggett Platt Components Inc.........F....... 662 844-4224
Tupelo (G-5179)
▲ Southern Components Inc ....D....... 662 844-7884
Tupelo (G-5226)
Weyerhaeuser Company ....D....... 662 243-6900
Columbus (G-1045)

2824 Synthetic Organic Fibers, Exc Cellulosic

Best Fiber Inc ....E....... 662 840-1118
Tupelo (G-5115)
Elite Elastomers Inc ....E....... 662 512-1770
Ripley (G-4657)
Fibrix LLC ....E....... 662 489-7908
Pontotoc (G-4331)
Omnova Solutions Inc ....A....... 662 327-1522
Columbus (G-1012)
Quality Fibers Inc.............................G....... 662 620-7775
Tupelo (G-5210)
Superior Manufactured Fibers............G....... 662 844-8255
Plantersville (G-4317)
Weyerhaeuser Company ....D....... 662 243-6900
Columbus (G-1045)

2833 Medicinal Chemicals & Botanical Prdts

CTA Products Group LLC...................G....... 662 536-1446
Southaven (G-4866)

S
I
C

Employee Codes: A=Over 500 employees, B=251-500
C=101-250, D=51-100, E=20-50, F=10-19, G=1-9

2019 Harris Directory of
Mississippi Manufacturers

231

28 CHEMICALS AND ALLIED PRODUCTS

SIC SECTION

Elizabeth Newcomb ....G 662 596-1536
Rienzi *(G-4649)*

Gha Enterprises Incorporated ....G 601 812-7739
Jackson *(G-2425)*

Kenan Transportation ....G 662 332-4223
Greenville *(G-1561)*

2834 Pharmaceuticals

Advanced Pharmaceuticals LLC ....G 228 215-1911
Ocean Springs *(G-3739)*

Alvix Laboratories LLC ....E 601 714-1677
Ocean Springs *(G-3740)*

Ani Pharmaceuticals Inc ....D 228 863-1702
Gulfport *(G-1726)*

Arbor Therapeutics LLC ....G 303 808-4104
Oxford *(G-3935)*

Baxter Healthcare Corporation ....E 662 843-9421
Cleveland *(G-786)*

Bayer Cotton Seed Intl ....G 662 686-9235
Leland *(G-2882)*

Burel Pharmaceuticals Inc ....G 601 720-0111
Richland *(G-4508)*

Cardinal Health 414 LLC ....G 601 982-7345
Jackson *(G-2353)*

Cardinal Health 414 LLC ....G 662 680-8644
Tupelo *(G-5118)*

Carliss Pharmaceuticals ....G 228 875-2748
Ocean Springs *(G-3746)*

Celgene Corp ....G 908 673-9000
Ridgeland *(G-4562)*

Copharma Inc ....G 662 594-1594
Corinth *(G-1074)*

Cypress Pharmaceutical Inc ....G 800 856-4393
Madison *(G-3091)*

Denovo Labs LLC ....G 615 587-3099
Ridgeland *(G-4573)*

Doctors Specialty Pharmacy LLC ....G 228 806-1384
Biloxi *(G-238)*

▲ Emilia Resources LLC ....D 601 743-9355
De Kalb *(G-1164)*

Follaine Pharmaceuticals LLC ....G 303 808-4104
Etta *(G-1284)*

Forest Pharmaceuticals Inc ....G 662 841-2321
Belden *(G-188)*

Fortus Pharma LLC ....G 662 420-3094
Ocean Springs *(G-3758)*

▲ Gcp Laboratories Inc ....D 228 863-1702
Gulfport *(G-1791)*

Gentex Pharma LLC ....G 601 990-9497
Ridgeland *(G-4587)*

Helping Hand Family Pharmacy ....G 601 631-6837
Vicksburg *(G-5378)*

Key Therapeutics LLC ....G 888 981-8337
Flowood *(G-1373)*

Larken Laboratories Inc ....G 601 855-7678
Canton *(G-667)*

Leflore Technologies LLC ....G 601 572-1491
Brandon *(G-412)*

Levins Labs LLC ....G 228 334-2411
Ocean Springs *(G-3770)*

Magnolia Therapeutics LLC ....G 662 281-0502
Ridgeland *(G-4601)*

Misemer Pharmaceutical Inc ....G 732 762-6577
Ripley *(G-4664)*

Novartis Corporation ....G 601 373-6148
Raymond *(G-4492)*

Novartis Corporation ....G 662 844-2271
Tupelo *(G-5195)*

Numedrx Pharmacy Solutions LLC ....G 601 973-5501
Jackson *(G-2526)*

Oaklock LLC ....G 601 855-7678
Canton *(G-674)*

Pharmaceutical Trade Svcs Inc ....F 228 244-1530
Ocean Springs *(G-3775)*

Pharmedium Services LLC ....E 662 846-5969
Cleveland *(G-803)*

Plr Labs LLC ....G 228 327-0939
Ocean Springs *(G-3777)*

Primary Pharmaceuticals ....G 228 872-1167
Ocean Springs *(G-3778)*

Sircle Laboratories LLC ....G 601 897-4474
Canton *(G-677)*

▲ Skin Sake LLC ....G 870 853-5544
Madison *(G-3147)*

Skylar Laboratories LLC ....G 601 855-7678
Canton *(G-678)*

Solus Rx LLC ....G 228 365-4501
Diberville *(G-1213)*

Southern Pharmaceutical Corp ....G 601 939-2525
Pearl *(G-4147)*

Southern Pharmaceutical Corp ....G 662 844-5858
Tupelo *(G-5227)*

Sterling-Knght Phrmcuticals LLC ....G 662 661-3232
Ripley *(G-4673)*

Stockmans Supply LLC ....F 601 750-2726
Starkville *(G-4976)*

Velocity Cnslting Spcalist LLC ....G 229 726-6047
Petal *(G-4199)*

Viceroy Pharmaceuticals Inc ....G 732 762-6577
Ripley *(G-4674)*

Waltman Pharmaceuticals Inc ....G 601 939-0833
Flowood *(G-1406)*

Xspire Pharma LLC ....G 870 243-1687
Ridgeland *(G-4647)*

2835 Diagnostic Substances

Accurate Drug Testing and Back ....G 601 500-7841
Flowood *(G-1341)*

Cardinal Health 414 LLC ....G 601 982-7345
Jackson *(G-2353)*

Cardinal Health 414 LLC ....G 662 680-8644
Tupelo *(G-5118)*

Mississippi Imaging ....G 601 656-6759
Philadelphia *(G-4226)*

MSU Veterinary Diagnostics Lab ....E 601 420-4700
Pearl *(G-4133)*

2836 Biological Prdts, Exc Diagnostic Substances

◆ Algix LLC ....G 877 972-5449
Meridian *(G-3296)*

▲ Amite Bioenergy LLC ....G 770 743-4300
Gloster *(G-1509)*

Bio Plumber of Mississippi ....G 601 825-5190
Brandon *(G-371)*

Immunotek Bio Centers LLC ....E 601 462-5145
Meridian *(G-3350)*

K & B Mississippi Corporation ....F 601 545-2056
Petal *(G-4189)*

K B Ms ....G 601 684-0510
McComb *(G-3255)*

2841 Soap & Detergents

Charlie Chemical and Supply ....G 662 332-9262
Greenville *(G-1537)*

Chemical Products & Systems ....G 601 354-1919
Jackson *(G-2358)*

Cottage Garden Ms LLC ....G 662 665-1918
Corinth *(G-1080)*

Ecolab Inc ....G 662 327-1863
Columbus *(G-966)*

Golden Source Inventors LLC ....G 601 325-4064
Hattiesburg *(G-1975)*

Kik Custom Products Inc ....B 901 947-5400
Olive Branch *(G-3860)*

▲ Marietta American Inc ....C 662 892-6959
Olive Branch *(G-3870)*

Marietta Corporation ....G 662 893-4233
Olive Branch *(G-3871)*

Pleasant Grove Soaps ....G 662 487-3050
Sardis *(G-4743)*

Rite-Kem LLC ....F 662 840-6060
Tupelo *(G-5218)*

Soap & Stuff LLC ....G 228 875-1721
Ocean Springs *(G-3788)*

Southern Touch Soap Works Inc ....G 601 825-2676
Brandon *(G-461)*

▲ T & L Specialty Company Inc ....E 662 842-8143
Tupelo *(G-5236)*

Way Manufacture Inc ....E 601 749-0362
Picayune *(G-4302)*

Yonce & Comans Products LLC ....G 601 270-7712
Petal *(G-4201)*

2842 Spec Cleaning, Polishing & Sanitation Preparations

Baxters Prssure Wshg ....G 601 825-2990
Brandon *(G-370)*

Bell Environmental Svcs LLC ....G 662 873-4551
Delta City *(G-1180)*

Charlie Chemical and Supply ....G 662 332-9262
Greenville *(G-1537)*

Daves Mobile Car Wash ....G 601 940-6855
Ridgeland *(G-4570)*

Davis Specialty Chemicals Inc ....G 601 856-5774
Ridgeland *(G-4571)*

Delta Dry LLC ....G 203 515-1528
Hollandale *(G-2164)*

Desiccare Inc ....E 601 932-0405
Richland *(G-4513)*

Frank Bradford Womack ....G 601 955-1841
Hazlehurst *(G-2096)*

Garrett Rowland G ....G 601 954-9841
Jackson *(G-2422)*

Huffco LLC ....G 662 284-6517
Corinth *(G-1089)*

Industrial Cleaning Svcs LLC ....F 662 397-6735
Saltillo *(G-4712)*

▲ Kengro Corporation ....F 662 647-2456
Charleston *(G-740)*

Natures Broom Inc ....G 662 931-5844
Hollandale *(G-2167)*

▲ Oil-Dri Production Company ....D 662 837-9263
Ripley *(G-4666)*

Profile Products LLC ....E 662 685-4741
Blue Mountain *(G-292)*

R & M Paint Designs ....G 601 503-3631
Jackson *(G-2556)*

Rjb Enterprise Inc ....E 202 830-3508
Gulfport *(G-1863)*

Spic-N-Span Crew LLC ....G 601 248-2090
McComb *(G-3268)*

Sun-Pine Corporation Ltd ....E 601 825-2463
Canton *(G-680)*

Sun-Pine Corporation Ltd ....D 601 825-2463
Brandon *(G-464)*

Tackle Technologies LLC ....G 228 206-1449
Long Beach *(G-2956)*

United Gilsonite Laboratories ....E 601 362-8619
Jackson *(G-2617)*

Way Manufacture Inc ....E 601 749-0362
Picayune *(G-4302)*

2843 Surface Active & Finishing Agents, Sulfonated Oils

▼ Driven Racing Oil LLC ....G 866 611-1820
Olive Branch *(G-3837)*

▼ Product Services Company ....E 866 886-3093
Jackson *(G-2552)*

2844 Perfumes, Cosmetics & Toilet Preparations

Belles ....G 662 617-8171
Starkville *(G-4928)*

Christian Pass Soap ....G 228 222-4303
Pass Christian *(G-4079)*

Diomedia Industries LLC ....G 601 882-7724
Jackson *(G-2384)*

Elements Cosmetics LLC ....G 601 383-6352
Brandon *(G-393)*

Galexie Glister ....G 601 667-0004
Jackson *(G-2420)*

◆ J Strickland and Co ....D 662 890-2306
Olive Branch *(G-3854)*

Joyce Tillman ....G 228 896-4927
Gulfport *(G-1814)*

Kik Custom Products Inc ....B 901 947-5400
Olive Branch *(G-3860)*

Lipstick and Labels LLC ....G 601 501-4029
Vicksburg *(G-5389)*

▲ Max Private Label Inc ....F 773 362-2601
Shannon *(G-4815)*

Merle Norman Cosmetics Inc ....G 662 287-7233
Corinth *(G-1100)*

Million Dollar Makeup LLC ....G 318 331-5363
Picayune *(G-4279)*

Musee LLC ....G 769 300-0485
Canton *(G-672)*

My Fantasy Hair Inc ....G 925 289-4247
Olive Branch *(G-3881)*

Nail First ....G 601 892-4433
Crystal Springs *(G-1151)*

Newson Chenora ....G 601 596-3899
Hattiesburg *(G-2037)*

Oxford Laboratories ....G 662 801-9764
Oxford *(G-3987)*

Sample Lab ....G 662 564-2498
Byhalia *(G-601)*

Sc3 LLC ....G 601 853-3690
Ridgeland *(G-4627)*

Sisters Scents ....G 901 283-9867
Byhalia *(G-603)*

Southern Scents By Carla LLC ....G 662 312-5610
Starkville *(G-4973)*

Sweet Scents ....G 662 425-9305
Columbus *(G-1035)*

*2019 Harris Directory of
Mississippi Manufacturers*

SIC SECTION

28 CHEMICALS AND ALLIED PRODUCTS

Yonce & Comans Products LLC ....G..... 601 270-7712
Petal (G-4201)
Young E F Jr Manufacturing Co ....E..... 601 483-8864
Meridian (G-3422)

2851 Paints, Varnishes, Lacquers, Enamels

Aride Taxi Cab and Trnsp LLC ....G..... 601 620-4282
Byram (G-617)
Bayou Inovations ....G..... 601 928-4143
Perkinston (G-4173)
Belzona Mississippi Inc ....G..... 228 475-1110
Moss Point (G-3469)
Danny R Jansen ....G..... 601 636-1070
Valley Park (G-5316)
Fuhr International LLC ....F..... 662 862-4903
Fulton (G-1453)
Je Painting and Renovations ....G..... 601 470-2047
Hattiesburg (G-2001)
Lining & Coating Solutions LLC ....F..... 662 893-0984
Olive Branch (G-3865)
Mississippi Prison Inds Corp ....F..... 601 969-5760
Jackson (G-2503)
Omnova Solutions Inc ....A..... 662 327-1522
Columbus (G-1012)
PPG Industries Inc ....F..... 601 932-0898
Pearl (G-4138)
PPG Industries Inc ....E..... 662 449-4947
Hernando (G-2148)
Robchem LLC ....G..... 601 485-5502
Meridian (G-3392)
Sherwin-Williams Company ....G..... 228 467-3938
Waveland (G-5484)
Tuff-Wall Inc ....G..... 601 264-8649
Hattiesburg (G-2076)
United Gilsonite Laboratories ....E..... 601 362-8619
Jackson (G-2617)
World Class Athltcsurfaces Inc ....F..... 662 686-9997
Leland (G-2893)

2861 Gum & Wood Chemicals

Kingsford Manufacturing Co ....G..... 510 271-6581
Glen (G-1507)
United Gilsonite Laboratories ....E..... 601 362-8619
Jackson (G-2617)

2865 Cyclic-Crudes, Intermediates, Dyes & Org Pigments

◆ First Chemical Corporation ....D..... 228 762-0870
Pascagoula (G-4031)

2869 Industrial Organic Chemicals, NEC

27-55 Fuel Plaza LLC ....G..... 601 892-1643
Crystal Springs (G-1138)
BASF Corporation ....C..... 601 948-3966
Jackson (G-2335)
Bottle Tree Beverage Co LLC ....F..... 601 667-3038
Jackson (G-2340)
Chancellor Inc ....F..... 601 518-0412
Laurel (G-2752)
CTA Products Group LLC ....G..... 662 536-1446
Southaven (G-4866)
Delta Biofuels Inc ....F..... 601 442-5330
Natchez (G-3554)
Elevance Natchez Inc ....F..... 601 442-5330
Natchez (G-3559)
Ergon Biofuels LLC ....E..... 601 636-1976
Vicksburg (G-5368)
Ergon Ethanol Inc ....G..... 601 933-3000
Flowood (G-1359)
Fastway Fuels 3 LLC ....G..... 228 452-7009
Long Beach (G-2937)
Fossil Fuel ....G..... 601 790-7955
Ridgeland (G-4585)
Fuel Center ....G..... 601 664-1861
Richland (G-4517)
Fuel Time 5 ....G..... 601 372-1115
Jackson (G-2417)
Gulfport Harbor Fuel ....G..... 228 248-3474
Long Beach (G-2939)
Hybrid Plastics Incorporated ....E..... 601 544-3466
Hattiesburg (G-1997)
Ion Chemical Company ....G..... 601 781-0604
Carthage (G-717)
Jns Biofuel LLC ....F..... 662 538-1005
New Albany (G-3683)
Jones Companies AVI MGT Inc ....G..... 844 500-2438
Hattiesburg (G-2003)
K & D Fuel Injection Service ....G..... 601 849-9113
Magee (G-3178)

Koch Industries Inc ....F..... 601 785-6523
Taylorsville (G-5055)
Nouryon Pulp & Prfmce Chem LLC ....F..... 662 327-0400
Columbus (G-1011)
Nufarm Americas Inc ....G..... 708 375-9010
Greenville (G-1584)
Orrin F Fuelling ....G..... 601 485-2598
Meridian (G-3379)
Portabull Fuel Service LLC ....G..... 601 549-5655
Purvis (G-4447)
Vizaura LLC ....G..... 228 363-4048
Diamondhead (G-1193)

2873 Nitrogenous Fertilizers

CF Industries Inc ....C..... 662 746-4131
Yazoo City (G-5625)
CF Industries Nitrogen LLC ....E..... 662 751-2616
Yazoo City (G-5626)
Forest Penick Products Inc ....E..... 662 726-5224
Macon (G-3062)
▲ Melamine Chemicals Inc ....E..... 662 746-4131
Yazoo City (G-5639)
Sqm North America Corporation ....G..... 601 969-4710
Jackson (G-2596)
Terra Houston Ammonia Inc ....E..... 662 746-4131
Yazoo City (G-5648)
▲ Terra Mississippi Nitrogen Inc ....B..... 662 746-4131
Yazoo City (G-5649)

2874 Phosphatic Fertilizers

CF Industries Inc ....C..... 662 746-4131
Yazoo City (G-5625)
CF Industries Nitrogen LLC ....E..... 662 751-2616
Yazoo City (G-5626)
Phosphate Holdings Inc ....B..... 601 898-9004
Madison (G-3138)
▲ Terra Mississippi Nitrogen Inc ....B..... 662 746-4131
Yazoo City (G-5649)

2875 Fertilizers, Mixing Only

Agri-Afc LLC ....E..... 601 783-6080
Magnolia (G-3188)
Baddour Memorial Center Inc ....B..... 662 562-0100
Senatobia (G-4787)
Creekside Envmtl Pdts LLC ....G..... 662 617-5553
Starkville (G-4936)
Delta Agricultural MGT Inc ....G..... 865 210-4605
Tunica (G-5096)
Eakes Nursery Materials Inc ....G..... 601 722-4797
Seminary (G-4777)
Helena Agri-Enterprises LLC ....F..... 662 746-7466
Yazoo City (G-5635)
Huddleston Farm Service Inc ....G..... 662 728-5288
Booneville (G-331)
Mississippi Agri-Products Inc ....G..... 601 879-3343
Flora (G-1310)
Neshoba County Gin Assn AAL ....F..... 601 656-3463
Philadelphia (G-4227)
Pinnacle Agriculture Dist Inc ....G..... 662 265-5828
Inverness (G-2276)
Terra Industries Inc ....E..... 662 456-3076
Houston (G-2255)
Woods Farm Supply Inc ....E..... 662 838-6754
Byhalia (G-614)
Woodson Flying Service Inc ....G..... 662 983-4274
Bruce (G-563)

2879 Pesticides & Agricultural Chemicals, NEC

Agriliance LLC ....F..... 662 738-4940
Brooksville (G-552)
Amerimac Synergy Veterans LLC ....G..... 601 326-3400
Jackson (G-2330)
Bayer Cropscience LP ....D..... 662 686-2334
Leland (G-2883)
Bayer Cropscience LP ....G..... 662 686-9323
Leland (G-2884)
Bayer Cropscience LP ....F..... 662 686-9235
Leland (G-2885)
▲ Bio Soil Enhancers Inc ....G..... 601 582-4000
Hattiesburg (G-1932)
Direct AG Source ....G..... 901 246-1487
Nesbit (G-3650)
Drexel Chemical Company ....E..... 662 363-1791
Tunica (G-5098)
E I Du Pont De Nemours & Co ....B..... 228 762-0870
Pascagoula (G-4030)
Ergon Biofuels LLC ....E..... 601 636-1976
Vicksburg (G-5368)

Gha Enterprises Incorporated ....G..... 601 812-7739
Jackson (G-2425)
Loveland Products Inc ....C..... 662 335-3394
Greenville (G-1564)
Loveland Products Inc ....E..... 662 335-3394
Greenville (G-1565)
Magnolia Mobility LLC ....G..... 601 400-7292
Vicksburg (G-5392)
Monsanto Company ....C..... 662 827-7212
Hollandale (G-2166)
Nufarm Americas Inc ....G..... 708 375-9010
Greenville (G-1584)
▲ Odom Industries Inc ....G..... 601 735-0088
Waynesboro (G-5508)
Odom Industries Inc ....E..... 601 776-2035
Pachuta (G-4014)
Pinnacle Agriculture Dist Inc ....G..... 662 265-5828
Inverness (G-2276)
Trace Mountain LLC ....G..... 662 862-2345
Fulton (G-1482)
▲ Vance Nimrod ....G..... 662 334-3713
Greenville (G-1607)

2891 Adhesives & Sealants

▲ Accrabond Corporation ....F..... 662 895-4480
Olive Branch (G-3804)
▲ Helmitin Inc ....F..... 662 895-4565
Olive Branch (G-3847)
Hunt Process Corp-Southern ....G..... 601 856-8811
Ridgeland (G-4591)
Label Express Inc ....F..... 662 566-7075
Verona (G-5334)
Robison Adhesives Inc ....G..... 662 997-8000
Batesville (G-121)
United Gilsonite Laboratories ....E..... 601 362-8619
Jackson (G-2617)

2892 Explosives

365 Explosive Athc Performllc ....G..... 601 365-2318
Hattiesburg (G-1914)
Titan Specialties ....G..... 601 477-3259
Ellisville (G-1272)

2895 Carbon Black

Delta-Energy Group LLC ....G..... 601 348-4610
Natchez (G-3555)

2899 Chemical Preparations, NEC

Advanced Screening Solutiions ....G..... 662 205-4139
Tupelo (G-5108)
Agri-Afc LLC ....E..... 601 783-6080
Magnolia (G-3188)
All Seasons Events ....G..... 601 405-1417
Jackson (G-2321)
Alvix Laboratories LLC ....E..... 601 714-1677
Ocean Springs (G-3740)
Basf-Chemical Co ....G..... 478 951-9985
Brandon (G-369)
BEC Fire and Safety LLC ....G..... 601 498-9108
Sumrall (G-5034)
Bilal 100 All Natural Spring ....G..... 601 323-2237
Sumrall (G-5035)
CTA Products Group LLC ....G..... 662 536-1446
Southaven (G-4866)
▲ Delta Protein Intl Inc ....F..... 662 279-8728
Sunflower (G-5046)
Discount Fireworks ....G..... 601 765-4295
Collins (G-853)
Diversified Petroleum Inc ....G..... 601 727-4926
Pachuta (G-4013)
▲ Eagle Fire Works Co Inc ....G..... 601 798-9291
Picayune (G-4265)
Helena Chemical Company ....G..... 662 563-9631
Batesville (G-108)
Highside Chemicals Inc ....G..... 228 896-9220
Gulfport (G-1807)
Hunt Process Corp-Southern ....G..... 601 856-8811
Ridgeland (G-4591)
Ingram Roman Inc ....G..... 601 954-8367
Madison (G-3110)
Inspection Plus LLC ....G..... 601 525-6744
Leakesville (G-2877)
Ion Chemical Company ....G..... 601 781-0604
Carthage (G-717)
Kdl Solutions LLC ....G..... 601 434-0508
Hattiesburg (G-2005)
Niteo Products LLC ....D..... 662 429-0405
Hernando (G-2144)

Employee Codes: A=Over 500 employees, B=251-500
C=101-250, D=51-100, E=20-50, F=10-19, G=1-9

2019 Harris Directory of
Mississippi Manufacturers

233

28 CHEMICALS AND ALLIED PRODUCTS

SIC SECTION

Niteo Products LLC ....D 662 429-8292
Hernando *(G-2145)*

Odom Industries Inc ....E 601 776-2035
Pachuta *(G-4014)*

Rainbow Spring Water Inc ....F 228 769-6262
Pascagoula *(G-4063)*

Sille Biofuels LLC ....G 601 400-2227
Jackson *(G-2581)*

Solen Inc ....E 601 833-0403
Brookhaven *(G-535)*

Squelchfire Inc ....G 601 434-2048
Hattiesburg *(G-2066)*

▲ T & L Specialty Company Inc ...E 662 842-8143
Tupelo *(G-5236)*

Taylor Industries LLC ....G 601 856-8439
Madison *(G-3157)*

Way Manufacture Inc ....E 601 749-0362
Picayune *(G-4302)*

Willie B Sims Jr CPA Pllc ....G 601 545-3930
Hattiesburg *(G-2084)*

29 PETROLEUM REFINING AND RELATED INDUSTRIES

2911 Petroleum Refining

Blacklidge Emulsions Inc.............G 228 864-3719
Gulfport *(G-1741)*

Chevron Phillips Chem Co LLC.....A 228 938-4600
Pascagoula *(G-4026)*

Ergon Inc ....E 601 636-6888
Vicksburg *(G-5367)*

Ergon - West Virginia Inc ....G 601 933-3000
Flowood *(G-1357)*

Ergon Construction Group Inc .....E 601 939-3909
Richland *(G-4514)*

Ergon Europe Mea Inc ....E 601 933-3000
Flowood *(G-1360)*

Ergon Inc ....F 601 932-8365
Jackson *(G-2645)*

◆ Ergon Inc ....C 601 933-3000
Flowood *(G-1361)*

Ergon Marine & Industrial Sup ....G 601 636-6552
Vicksburg *(G-5369)*

Ergon Refining Inc ....C 601 638-4960
Vicksburg *(G-5370)*

Express Biodiesel LLC ....E 662 453-4312
Greenwood *(G-1622)*

Faststop Petroleum LLC ....G 601 466-3273
Bassfield *(G-91)*

▲ Galaxie Corporation ....G 601 366-8413
Jackson *(G-2419)*

Hunt Refining Company ....G 843 236-5098
Vicksburg *(G-5379)*

Hunt Refining Company ....E 601 426-1821
Heidelberg *(G-2117)*

Hunt Refining Company ....E 601 796-2331
Lumberton *(G-3030)*

Income Online Residual ....G 662 420-7636
Olive Branch *(G-3851)*

Murphy USA Inc ....F 601 992-2041
Flowood *(G-1383)*

Shell Pipe Line Corporation.........G 601 638-1921
Vicksburg *(G-5418)*

Southern Oil Company ....G 601 582-5455
Hattiesburg *(G-2062)*

Southland Oil Company ....E 601 796-2331
Lumberton *(G-3038)*

Southland Oil Company ....F 601 981-4151
Jackson *(G-2592)*

Southland Oil Company ....G 601 634-1361
Vicksburg *(G-5421)*

Specialty Services Group LLC......G 601 543-9474
Sumrall *(G-5045)*

2951 Paving Mixtures & Blocks

Adcamp Inc ....D 601 939-4493
Flowood *(G-1342)*

Apac-Mississippi Inc ....E 662 378-8481
Greenville *(G-1536)*

Apac-Mississippi Inc ....D 662 328-6555
Columbus *(G-936)*

Apac-Mississippi Inc ....E 601 693-5025
Meridian *(G-3299)*

Apac-Mississippi Inc ....E 662 348-2214
Guntown *(G-1897)*

Apac-Mississippi Inc ....E 601 634-6600
Vicksburg *(G-5341)*

Apac-Mississippi Inc ....G 662 746-7983
Yazoo City *(G-5623)*

Apac-Mississippi Inc ....D 601 376-4000
Richland *(G-4501)*

Apac-Mississippi Inc ....E 601 376-4000
Richland *(G-4502)*

▼ Blacklidge Emulsions Inc..........E 228 863-3878
Gulfport *(G-1740)*

Blacklidge Emulsions Inc.............G 228 864-3719
Gulfport *(G-1741)*

Boling Construction Inc ....G 601 833-0122
Wesson *(G-5524)*

CMC Paving LLC ....G 601 764-2787
Bay Springs *(G-160)*

Cold Mix Inc ....G 662 256-4529
Nettleton *(G-3658)*

Corinth Brick Company Inc...........G 662 287-2442
Corinth *(G-1076)*

Huey P Stockstill LLC ....F 228 868-8678
Gulfport *(G-1810)*

J J Ferguson Sand & Grav Inc ......C 662 453-5451
Greenwood *(G-1630)*

Jackson Asphalt & Concrete ....G 601 371-8707
Jackson *(G-2452)*

Klaas-Robbins Pavement Maint ....G 601 362-4091
Ridgeland *(G-4595)*

Land Shapers Inc ....G 228 864-3624
Gulfport *(G-1820)*

Lehman-Roberts Company ....F 662 563-2100
Batesville *(G-113)*

Lehman-Roberts Company ....F 662 429-5237
Hernando *(G-2138)*

Mallette Brothers Cnstr Co ....E 228 497-2523
Gautier *(G-1499)*

Morgan Greg Asphalt and Cnstr....G 601 479-3095
Chunky *(G-752)*

Pandle Inc ....E 228 762-3300
Pascagoula *(G-4059)*

▼ Polycon International LLC...........F 601 898-1024
Madison *(G-3141)*

Seal Master Mississippi...............G 601 936-0080
Pearl *(G-4143)*

Southland Oil Company ....E 601 796-2331
Lumberton *(G-3038)*

Superior Asphalt Inc ....C 601 376-3000
Byram *(G-624)*

W E Blain & Sons Inc ....E 601 442-3032
Natchez *(G-3635)*

2952 Asphalt Felts & Coatings

◆ Atlas Roofing Corporation ....E 601 484-8900
Meridian *(G-3300)*

Atlas Roofing Corporation ....E 601 483-7111
Meridian *(G-3302)*

Certainteed Gypsum Inc...............C 601 693-0254
Meridian *(G-3318)*

Duro-Last Inc ....D 601 371-1973
Byram *(G-621)*

Efma Contracting LLC ....F 901 292-7221
Ridgeland *(G-4576)*

First Coastal Exteriors LLC..........G 769 251-1894
Pearl *(G-4117)*

◆ Hood Companies Inc ....D 601 582-1545
Hattiesburg *(G-1991)*

Lining & Coating Solutions LLC ....G 662 453-6860
Greenwood *(G-1635)*

Majestic Metals Inc ....E 601 856-3600
Madison *(G-3126)*

▼ Polycon International LLC ....F 601 898-1024
Madison *(G-3141)*

▲ Soperma USA Inc ....G 228 701-1900
Gulfport *(G-1875)*

Union Corrugating Company ....G 601 661-0577
Vicksburg *(G-5432)*

2992 Lubricating Oils & Greases

Axel Americas LLC ....F 662 759-6808
Rosedale *(G-4686)*

2999 Products Of Petroleum & Coal, NEC

▼ Loresco Inc ....G 601 544-7490
Purvis *(G-4445)*

Rain Cii Carbon LLC ....G 601 794-2753
Purvis *(G-4451)*

30 RUBBER AND MISCELLANEOUS PLASTICS PRODUCTS

3011 Tires & Inner Tubes

BF Kaufman Inc..........................G 662 253-8093
Southaven *(G-4855)*

Cooper Tire & Rubber Company ....E 662 624-4366
Clarksdale *(G-763)*

Tooneys Tire Center ....G 601 479-2654
De Kalb *(G-1168)*

Yokohama Tire Manufactu ....G 800 423-4544
West Point *(G-5566)*

Yokohama Tire Mfg Miss LLC ....G 800 423-4544
West Point *(G-5567)*

3021 Rubber & Plastic Footwear

Run-N-Tri Company Llc ....G 228 604-2227
Gulfport *(G-1864)*

Southern Discount Drugs of Cha ...G 662 647-5172
Charleston *(G-743)*

3052 Rubber & Plastic Hose & Belting

▲ Hydro Hose Corp ....F 662 842-2761
Tupelo *(G-5159)*

3053 Gaskets, Packing & Sealing Devices

▲ Biltrite Ripley Operations LLC ...G 662 837-9231
Ripley *(G-4654)*

Hydradyne LLC ....A 601 833-9475
Brookhaven *(G-501)*

M S Rubber Company ....F 601 948-2575
Jackson *(G-2474)*

Military Defense Systems Inc ....G 850 449-1910
Picayune *(G-4278)*

3069 Fabricated Rubber Prdts, NEC

Air Cruisers Company LLC ....C 601 657-8043
Liberty *(G-2909)*

▲ Avon Engnered Fabrications LLC ...D 601 889-9050
Picayune *(G-4254)*

Best Foam Inc ....E 662 840-6700
Sherman *(G-4826)*

▲ Biltrite Ripley Operations LLC ...G 662 837-9231
Ripley *(G-4654)*

Cade Rubber Co Inc ....G 601 743-5717
De Kalb *(G-1162)*

Elite Comfort Solutions LLC ....E 662 566-2322
Verona *(G-5330)*

Evercompounds LLC....................G 309 256-1166
Olive Branch *(G-3840)*

Everett Industries Inc ....G 228 231-1556
Bay Saint Louis *(G-143)*

Innocor Foam Tech - Acp Inc ....G 662 365-5868
Baldwyn *(G-80)*

Johnson Foam Sales Inc ....E 662 767-9007
Shannon *(G-4811)*

Magnolia Furniture LLC ....G 662 489-9337
Pontotoc *(G-4342)*

Minton Floorcovering LLC ....G 601 540-3764
Richland *(G-4522)*

Mount Vernon Foam Sales ....F 662 844-3107
Tupelo *(G-5190)*

Packaging Research and Design ...G 800 833-9364
Madison *(G-3136)*

Pearl Rubber Stamp & Sign Inc ....F 601 932-6699
Jackson *(G-2662)*

Polo Custom Products Inc ....C 662 779-2009
Louisville *(G-2976)*

Polyvulc Usa Inc ....E 601 638-8040
Vicksburg *(G-5407)*

Schuyler C Jones ....G 601 540-5841
Madison *(G-3145)*

Seri ....G 601 638-3355
Vicksburg *(G-5415)*

Superior Mfg Group Inc ....D 601 544-8119
Moselle *(G-3462)*

Xerium Technologies Inc ....G 662 323-4064
Starkville *(G-4983)*

3081 Plastic Unsupported Sheet & Film

Ability Works Inc ....G 662 328-0275
Columbus *(G-931)*

Adlam Films LLC ....E 662 823-1345
Shannon *(G-4805)*

Afco Industries Inc ....C 662 895-8686
Olive Branch *(G-3808)*

2019 Harris Directory of
Mississippi Manufacturers

SIC SECTION

31 LEATHER AND LEATHER PRODUCTS

Bag Connection LLC ....F 662 624-6570
Clarksdale (G-758)
Berry Global Inc ....C 601 584-4800
Hattiesburg (G-1928)
Berry Global Inc ....G 601 584-4778
Hattiesburg (G-1929)
Central Miss RES & EXT Ctr ....G 601 857-2284
Raymond (G-4485)
Dixie Packaging Inc ....E 601 276-9317
Summit (G-5012)
Intex Properties Perris Vly LP ....G 662 287-1455
Corinth (G-1093)
Lucite International ....G 662 893-5450
Olive Branch (G-3867)
Mega Plastics Inc ....D 601 924-1712
Clinton (G-831)
◆ Mississippi Polymers Inc ....B 662 287-1401
Corinth (G-1103)
Omnova Solutions Inc ....A 662 327-1522
Columbus (G-1012)
Orbis Rpm LLC ....F 662 890-7646
Olive Branch (G-3891)
▲ Summit Plastics Inc ....E 601 276-7500
Summit (G-5024)

3083 Plastic Laminated Plate & Sheet

Acco Brands USA LLC ....D 662 720-1300
Booneville (G-315)
B & D Plastics LLC ....F 228 875-5865
Vancleave (G-5317)
Carlisle Syntec ....G 662 301-4509
Senatobia (G-4789)
Quad Inc ....G 601 656-2376
Choctaw (G-750)
Sabic Innovative Plas US LLC ....E 228 533-7855
Bay Saint Louis (G-154)
Southern Diversified Inds Inc ....D 662 365-6720
Baldwyn (G-87)
▼ Superior Mfg Group Inc ....G 601 544-8119
Moselle (G-3461)
U S Plastics Inc ....E 662 456-5551
Houston (G-2257)

3084 Plastic Pipe

Advanced Drainage Systems Inc .....G 601 629-9040
Vicksburg (G-5338)
Advanced Drainage Systems Inc .....D 601 371-0678
Jackson (G-2320)
Contech Engnered Solutions LLC ....G 601 894-2041
Greenville (G-1540)
Hancor Inc ....E 601 629-9040
Vicksburg (G-5376)
North American Pipe Corp ....D 662 728-2111
Booneville (G-338)

3085 Plastic Bottles

L C Industries Inc ....B 601 894-1771
Hazlehurst (G-2099)
Signature Works Inc ....B 601 894-1771
Hazlehurst (G-2106)

3086 Plastic Foam Prdts

Alaco of Mississippi Inc ....E 662 837-4041
Ripley (G-4651)
◆ Atlas Roofing Corporation ....E 601 484-8900
Meridian (G-3300)
Atlas Roofing Corporation ....F 601 481-1474
Meridian (G-3301)
Atlas Roofing Corporation ....E 601 483-7111
Meridian (G-3302)
Bassco Foam Inc ....E 662 842-4321
Tupelo (G-5114)
Carlisle Construction Mtls LLC ......D 662 560-6474
Senatobia (G-4788)
Carpenter Co ....B 662 566-2392
Verona (G-5329)
Confortaire Inc ....D 662 842-2966
Tupelo (G-5121)
Cryovac Inc ....D 662 226-8804
Grenada (G-1673)
Dart Cont Co Miss Ltd Lblty Co ......C 601 776-3555
Quitman (G-4461)
Foamcraft Inc ....E 662 844-6399
Tupelo (G-5136)
Fxi Inc ....C 662 566-2382
Verona (G-5331)
Hickory Springs Mfg Co ....E 662 489-6684
Pontotoc (G-4332)

◆ Hood Companies Inc ....D 601 582-1545
Hattiesburg (G-1991)
▲ Ideal Foam LLC ....D 662 489-2264
Pontotoc (G-4334)
▲ Independent Furn Sup Co Inc .....B 662 844-8411
Tupelo (G-5161)
Innocor Foam Tech - Acp Inc ....D 662 842-0123
Tupelo (G-5162)
Innocor Foam Technologies LLC .....F 662 622-7221
Coldwater (G-847)
Le Clair Industries Inc ....E 662 226-8075
Grenada (G-1691)
Mid-South Foam & Assembly Inc .....F 662 895-3334
Olive Branch (G-3875)
▲ Perma R Products Inc ....C 662 226-8075
Grenada (G-1699)
Pierce Foam and Supply Inc ....E 662 728-8070
Booneville (G-342)
S & A Industries Corporation ....G 330 733-6040
New Albany (G-3695)
S & A Industries Corporation ....G 330 733-6040
New Albany (G-3696)
Sonoco Prtective Solutions Inc ......E 662 842-1043
Tupelo (G-5225)
Stewart Sign & Screen Graphics .....G 601 783-5377
McComb (G-3269)
Thermos LLC ....D 800 831-9242
Batesville (G-129)
Ultra Comfort Foam Company ....G 662 539-6004
New Albany (G-3705)
W & W Special Components Inc ......E 662 365-5648
Marietta (G-3219)

3088 Plastic Plumbing Fixtures

Ability Works Inc ....E 662 842-2144
Tupelo (G-5107)
Builders Marble Inc ....E 601 922-5420
Clinton (G-817)
Hancor Inc ....E 601 629-9040
Vicksburg (G-5376)
K & D Cultured Marble Inc ....E 662 675-2928
Coffeeville (G-843)
Premiere Plastics Inc ....E 662 489-2007
Pontotoc (G-4357)
Water-Way Inc ....E 662 423-0081
Iuka (G-2311)

3089 Plastic Prdts

Acco Brands USA LLC ....G 800 541-0094
Booneville (G-314)
American National Molding LLC ....D 601 936-2722
Flowood (G-1343)
▲ Auto Parts Mfg Miss Inc ....B 662 365-3082
Guntown (G-1898)
Berry Global Inc ....C 601 584-4800
Hattiesburg (G-1928)
Berry Global Inc ....G 601 584-4778
Hattiesburg (G-1929)
Bprex Closures LLC ....D 601 584-4758
Hattiesburg (G-1939)
Builders Marble Inc ....E 601 922-5420
Clinton (G-817)
Canopy Breezes LLC ....G 972 207-2045
Madison (G-3088)
Caviness Woodworking Company ....D 662 628-5195
Calhoun City (G-636)
Coastal Solar and SEC Films ....G 228 369-3933
Biloxi (G-232)
Coastal Tire Wholesalers LLC ....G 810 257-9977
Long Beach (G-2934)
▲ Custom Engineered Wheels Inc ...D 574 267-4005
Baldwyn (G-75)
Diversity Vuteq LLC ....G 662 587-9633
Blue Springs (G-295)
▼ Diversity-Vuteq LLC ....A 662 534-9250
New Albany (G-3681)
Easy Reach Supply LLC ....E 601 582-7866
Hattiesburg (G-1959)
Euro American Plastics Inc ....F 601 879-0360
Flora (G-1305)
Excel Injection Molding Inc ....E 601 544-6133
Hattiesburg (G-1966)
Hancor Inc ....E 601 629-9040
Vicksburg (G-5376)
Harrison Manufacturing LLC ....E 601 519-0558
Jackson (G-2437)
▲ Hewlett Industries Inc ....D 662 773-4626
Starkville (G-4948)
◆ Hood Flexible Packaging Corp .....D 903 593-1793
Hattiesburg (G-1993)

Intellabuy Inc ....G 601 249-0508
McComb (G-3253)
Intex Properties Perris Vly LP ....G 662 287-1455
Corinth (G-1093)
Jackson Fishing Sptg Accessory .....G 662 837-9089
Falkner (G-1295)
JKS International LLC ....F 228 689-8999
Stennis Space Center (G-4995)
Kp Building Products Inc ....D 662 252-9991
Holly Springs (G-2180)
L C Industries Inc ....B 601 894-1771
Hazlehurst (G-2099)
Longbranch ....G 662 284-8585
Corinth (G-1098)
M S Rubber Company ....F 601 948-2575
Jackson (G-2474)
M-Tek Inc ....A 601 407-5000
Madison (G-3123)
▼ Magnolia Mtal Plastic Pdts Inc ....E 601 638-6912
Vicksburg (G-5393)
Multicraft Intl Ltd Partnr ....G 601 854-5516
Pelahatchie (G-4167)
Naum Myatt & Sons ....G 662 256-8104
Becker (G-186)
Omnova Solutions Inc ....A 662 327-1522
Columbus (G-1012)
Plaspros Inc ....E 662 563-8635
Batesville (G-119)
Plastics Plus Inc ....G 228 832-4634
Gulfport (G-1849)
Polyvulc Usa Inc ....E 601 638-8004
Vicksburg (G-5407)
Prolon LLC ....D 601 437-4211
Port Gibson (G-4405)
Protank LLC ....G 662 895-4337
Olive Branch (G-3903)
▲ Richard Plastics Co ....F 601 426-2810
Laurel (G-2836)
Richardson Molding LLC ....G 601 656-7921
Philadelphia (G-4235)
Rk Manufacturing Inc ....F 601 956-7774
Ridgeland (G-4623)
Seemann Composites LLC ....D 228 314-8000
Gulfport (G-1867)
Sevlo Solutions LLC ....G 662 312-9507
Starkville (G-4970)
Signature Works Inc ....B 601 894-1771
Hazlehurst (G-2106)
Sinhatech ....G 662 234-6248
Oxford (G-4002)
Solvay Spclty Polymers USA LLC ....F 228 533-0238
Bay Saint Louis (G-156)
▲ South Central Polymers Inc ....D 662 728-9506
Booneville (G-345)
▲ Southern Diversified Inds Inc ......G 662 365-8800
Baldwyn (G-88)
Southern Exteriors Fence Co ....G 228 586-2110
Perkinston (G-4181)
Speed Box LLC ....G 910 964-7947
Ridgeland (G-4633)
Stanley McCaffrey Signs ....G 228 832-0885
Richland (G-4525)
Steiner Plastics Inc ....G 662 895-7350
Olive Branch (G-3913)
Suburban Plastics Co ....D 662 227-1911
Grenada (G-1705)
▲ Unified Brands Inc ....A 601 372-3903
Byram (G-625)
United Comb & Novelty Corp ....F 662 487-9248
Sardis (G-4746)
United Plastic Molders Inc ....E 601 353-3193
Jackson (G-2618)

31 LEATHER AND LEATHER PRODUCTS

3111 Leather Tanning & Finishing

Kdh Kustoms LLC ....G 601 730-2052
McComb (G-3256)
▲ Leather Works Inc ....G 662 538-4455
New Albany (G-3684)

3131 Boot & Shoe Cut Stock & Findings

A Quarter Can Inc ....G 601 936-9915
Richland (G-4496)
▲ Biltrite Ripley Operations LLC .....G 662 837-9231
Ripley (G-4654)
Brian Rand ....G 601 519-5062
Bay Springs (G-158)

Employee Codes: A=Over 500 employees, B=251-500
C=101-250, D=51-100, E=20-50, F=10-19, G=1-9

2019 Harris Directory of
Mississippi Manufacturers

235

31 LEATHER AND LEATHER PRODUCTS

C5 Trucking LLC ....G...... 601 797-9335
Mount Olive *(G-3510)*
Close Quarter Combat LLC ....G...... 601 325-5610
Hattiesburg *(G-1946)*
Faye Neldra Rand Spears ....G...... 601 722-0104
Seminary *(G-4780)*
McCullar Long & Mccullough Inc ....G...... 662 842-4165
Tupelo *(G-5184)*
Mississippi Quarterhorse Assn ....G...... 601 692-5128
Walnut Grove *(G-5461)*
Quarter Inc ....G...... 228 701-0361
Gulfport *(G-1858)*
Quarter Rest Classics ....G...... 601 638-4207
Vicksburg *(G-5409)*
Run-N-Tri Company Llc ....G...... 228 604-2227
Gulfport *(G-1864)*
Upper Kutz LLC ....G...... 662 807-8707
Greenville *(G-1606)*

3149 Footwear, NEC

Asics America Corporation ....F...... 662 895-6800
Byhalia *(G-577)*

3151 Leather Gloves & Mittens

▲ **Choctaw Glove & Safety Co Inc** ....D...... 662 724-4178
Noxapater *(G-3731)*
Itta Bena Plantation III ....G...... 662 254-7274
Itta Bena *(G-2281)*
Rog LLC ....G...... 662 455-1364
Greenwood *(G-1649)*
Shelby Group International Inc ....D...... 901 795-5810
Charleston *(G-742)*
Victory Logistics LLC ....G...... 662 620-2829
Tupelo *(G-5251)*

3161 Luggage

Nicholes Cture Fashion Btq LLC ....G...... 601 493-6469
Natchez *(G-3600)*
Satchel LLC ....G...... 901 515-8163
Jackson *(G-2573)*
Watkins Mayola ....G...... 601 826-8310
Jackson *(G-2626)*

3172 Personal Leather Goods

McLendon Holdings LLC ....G...... 858 255-9038
Gulfport *(G-1827)*
▲ **Mississippi Tantec Leather Inc** ....G...... 601 429-6081
Vicksburg *(G-5398)*
Van S Leather Crafts ....G...... 662 838-6269
Byhalia *(G-611)*

3199 Leather Goods, NEC

Leather Lanyards ....G...... 662 902-5294
Clarksdale *(G-772)*
Proshop Inc ....G...... 662 333-7511
Myrtle *(G-3513)*
Sea Robin Forge ....G...... 601 798-0060
Picayune *(G-4293)*

32 STONE, CLAY, GLASS, AND CONCRETE PRODUCTS

3211 Flat Glass

View Inc ....D...... 662 892-3415
Olive Branch *(G-3921)*

3221 Glass Containers

Mississippi Beverage Co Inc ....E...... 601 693-3853
Meridian *(G-3372)*
Owens-Brockway Glass Cont Inc ....F...... 601 584-4800
Hattiesburg *(G-2038)*

3229 Pressed & Blown Glassware, NEC

Bekeson Glass LLC ....F...... 601 932-3676
Flowood *(G-1345)*
Cbl Architectural Fiberglass ....F...... 662 429-2277
Hernando *(G-2124)*
Customized Stained Glass ....G...... 601 583-4720
Hattiesburg *(G-1956)*
Dollys Stained Glass ....G...... 662 887-3624
Indianola *(G-2263)*
Memaws Ceramics ....G...... 601 319-8263
Ellisville *(G-1263)*
Stained Glassworks Inc ....G...... 662 329-2970
Columbus *(G-1031)*
Vape and Bake LLC ....G...... 228 447-1566
Ocean Springs *(G-3793)*

3231 Glass Prdts Made Of Purchased Glass

Central Mississippi Glass Co ....G...... 601 469-5050
Forest *(G-1412)*
Clear Sight Windshield Repair ....G...... 601 638-2892
Vicksburg *(G-5356)*
Corinth Cc-Cola Btlg Works Inc ....E...... 662 286-2052
Corinth *(G-1078)*
◆ **Home Decor Company** ....C...... 662 844-7191
Tupelo *(G-5157)*
Laurin Enterprises LLC ....G...... 228 207-5580
Biloxi *(G-259)*
Plum Trophy Sales ....G...... 601 758-4834
Sumrall *(G-5041)*
▲ **Renin US LLC** ....E...... 662 844-7191
Tupelo *(G-5217)*
Stained Glassworks Inc ....G...... 662 329-2970
Columbus *(G-1031)*
Sweetwater Studios Inc ....G...... 601 584-8035
Moselle *(G-3463)*
Venable Glass Services LLC ....F...... 601 605-4443
Ridgeland *(G-4644)*
Windshield Repair Systems ....G...... 601 657-8303
Liberty *(G-2920)*

3241 Cement, Hydraulic

Lafarge North America Inc ....E...... 601 859-4488
Canton *(G-666)*
Pooles Stone & Masonry Contrs ....G...... 662 438-6643
Belmont *(G-201)*
RC Lonestar Inc ....G...... 601 442-8651
Natchez *(G-3611)*
River Cement Co ....G...... 601 442-4881
Natchez *(G-3614)*

3251 Brick & Structural Clay Tile

Acme Brick Company ....G...... 601 714-2966
Brandon *(G-355)*
▲ **Columbus Brick Company** ....E...... 662 328-4931
Columbus *(G-949)*
Corinth Brick Company Inc ....G...... 662 287-2442
Corinth *(G-1076)*
Everett Industries Inc ....G...... 228 231-1556
Bay Saint Louis *(G-143)*
Louisville Brick Company ....E...... 800 530-7102
Louisville *(G-2973)*
Meridian Brick LLC ....G...... 228 863-5451
Gulfport *(G-1828)*
Meridian Brick LLC ....G...... 601 296-0445
Hattiesburg *(G-2022)*
Meridian Brick LLC ....F...... 601 428-4364
Laurel *(G-2800)*
Meridian Brick LLC ....G...... 662 840-8884
Tupelo *(G-5186)*

3253 Ceramic Tile

Armstrong Flooring Inc ....C...... 601 354-1515
Jackson *(G-2333)*
Pitsburgh Stone & Plaster ....G...... 601 631-0006
Vicksburg *(G-5406)*
Triton Stone Holdings LLC ....G...... 662 280-8041
Southaven *(G-4917)*

3255 Clay Refractories

Meridian Brick LLC ....G...... 228 863-5451
Gulfport *(G-1828)*
Restora-Life Minerals Inc ....G...... 601 789-5545
Bay Springs *(G-172)*

3259 Structural Clay Prdts, NEC

Profile Products LLC ....E...... 662 685-4741
Blue Mountain *(G-292)*

3261 China Plumbing Fixtures & Fittings

Tg Missouri-Mississippi ....G...... 662 563-1043
Batesville *(G-128)*

3263 Earthenware, Whiteware, Table & Kitchen Articles

Chambers Air and Heat ....G...... 662 967-2002
West *(G-5532)*
Misccellaneous Items LLC ....G...... 601 918-0255
Jackson *(G-2496)*

3269 Pottery Prdts, NEC

Alleykat Ceramics LLC ....G...... 228 224-7775
Gulfport *(G-1722)*

Beloved Pottery ....G...... 662 349-4430
Southaven *(G-4854)*
Clay Canvas ....G...... 662 236-9798
Oxford *(G-3946)*
Ka Pottery ....G...... 601 722-4948
Seminary *(G-4782)*
Mississippi Mud Works Pottery ....G...... 228 875-8773
Ocean Springs *(G-3772)*
Pottery By Helene ....G...... 662 728-0988
Guntown *(G-1902)*
Santas & Such ....G...... 662 773-2711
Louisville *(G-2982)*
Shearwater Pottery Ltd ....F...... 228 875-7320
Ocean Springs *(G-3784)*
Wet Paint LLC ....G...... 662 269-2412
Tupelo *(G-5258)*
William Stephens ....G...... 601 634-0498
Vicksburg *(G-5447)*
Williams Sonoma ....F...... 901 795-2625
Olive Branch *(G-3927)*

3271 Concrete Block & Brick

American Concrete Products Inc ....E...... 601 583-2274
Hattiesburg *(G-1921)*
Back Bay Lawnscapes LLC ....F...... 228 348-1299
Diberville *(G-1195)*
Columbia Block & Brick Co Inc ....G...... 601 450-3791
Hattiesburg *(G-1949)*
Daniels Lawn and Lanscape LLC ....G...... 601 965-6982
Clinton *(G-820)*
Delta Industries Inc ....C...... 601 354-3801
Jackson *(G-2381)*
General Shale Brick Inc ....F...... 662 840-8221
Tupelo *(G-5141)*
Jackson Precast Inc ....E...... 601 321-8787
Jackson *(G-2457)*
Lexington Concrete & Block Co ....G...... 662 834-3892
Lexington *(G-2904)*
Lmg Diversified LLC ....G...... 601 635-5955
Newton *(G-3724)*
Magnolia Supply Group LLC ....G...... 601 454-1368
Jackson *(G-2480)*
Mid Mississippi Maintenance ....F...... 601 953-1091
Edwards *(G-1241)*
Milieu Outdoor Image Solutions ....G...... 601 259-8570
Madison *(G-3129)*
Pearson Enterprises ....G...... 662 289-7625
Kosciusko *(G-2709)*
Tropical World Intl LLC ....G...... 228 229-8413
Biloxi *(G-285)*
Tupelo Concrete Products Inc ....F...... 662 842-7811
Tupelo *(G-5243)*

3272 Concrete Prdts

Bates Vault & Services LLC ....G...... 601 303-0508
Tylertown *(G-5263)*
▲ **Baymont Inc** ....D...... 662 454-7993
Golden *(G-1521)*
Bickes Inc ....E...... 601 353-7083
Jackson *(G-2337)*
Blaylocks Cement Manufacturing ....G...... 225 627-1006
Liberty *(G-2910)*
Carsons Construction LLC ....E...... 601 301-0841
Vicksburg *(G-5354)*
Castle Enclosures LLC ....G...... 228 238-6216
Biloxi *(G-225)*
Civil Precast Corporation ....G...... 601 853-1870
Ridgeland *(G-4563)*
Custom Precast Products Inc ....E...... 601 796-8531
Lumberton *(G-3027)*
Design Precast & Pipe Inc ....E...... 228 831-5833
Gulfport *(G-1772)*
Desoto Concrete Products Inc ....G...... 662 890-1688
Olive Branch *(G-3833)*
Evans Refrigeration ....G...... 601 372-3482
Jackson *(G-2404)*
F-S Prestress LLC ....D...... 601 268-2006
Hattiesburg *(G-1967)*
Famco Company Inc ....F...... 228 831-4649
Gulfport *(G-1782)*
Foley Products Company ....E...... 601 792-3202
Prentiss *(G-4417)*
Forterra Pipe & Precast LLC ....E...... 662 526-0368
Como *(G-1047)*
Forterra Pipe & Precast LLC ....E...... 601 268-2081
Prentiss *(G-4418)*
Forterra Pipe & Precast LLC ....E...... 601 982-1100
Jackson *(G-2410)*
Forterra Pipe & Precast LLC ....G...... 601 792-3202
Prentiss *(G-4419)*

2019 Harris Directory of Mississippi Manufacturers

SIC SECTION

32 STONE, CLAY, GLASS, AND CONCRETE PRODUCTS

Gilmore Bros Building Supply ....G 601 825-6292
Brandon (G-398)

▲ Gulf Coast Pre-Stress Inc ....C 228 452-7270
Pass Christian (G-4086)

Gulf States Forming Systems ....F 601 428-1582
Laurel (G-2774)

H&R Consultants LLC ....G 601 613-2288
Edwards (G-1238)

Harold A Sparks Septic Tanks ....G 662 454-7244
Golden (G-1526)

Harris Ja Inc ....G 662 205-4370
Tupelo (G-5153)

Hills Brothers Cnstr & Engrg ....E 662 837-7415
Falkner (G-1294)

Huey P Stockstill LLC ....C 601 798-2981
Picayune (G-4272)

J J Ferguson Prestress- ....E 662 453-5451
Greenwood (G-1629)

Lees Precast Concrete Inc ....G 662 369-8935
Aberdeen (G-16)

Lees Septic Inc ....F 662 369-9799
Aberdeen (G-17)

Legacy Vulcan LLC ....G 601 544-3523
Petal (G-4191)

Macon Ready-Mix Concrete Co ....F 662 726-4733
Macon (G-3065)

Mahans Concrete Septic Tanks ....G 662 234-3767
Water Valley (G-5471)

Mid South Cast Stone ....G 662 890-7669
Olive Branch (G-3874)

Mid-South Ornamental Concrete...........F 662 224-3170
Michigan City (G-3423)

MMC Materials Inc ....G 662 327-1927
Columbus (G-1006)

MMC Materials Inc ....D 601 973-2093
Jackson (G-2508)

▲ National Stone Imports Inc ....G 228 323-7239
Long Beach (G-2946)

Picayune Monument & Gran Works .....G 601 798-7926
Picayune (G-4286)

Pine Belt Ready Mix Concrete ....F 601 425-2559
Laurel (G-2819)

Precision Packaging Inc ....E 601 352-2016
Jackson (G-2548)

Quikrete Companies LLC ....E 601 798-6021
Picayune (G-4290)

S & S Striping ....G 662 449-4498
Hernando (G-2153)

Snells Concrete Tanks ....G 601 845-1881
Harrisville (G-1912)

Southern Sewage Systems ....G 228 832-7400
Saucier (G-4766)

Stair Depot of Ms ....G 334 467-5584
Gulfport (G-1879)

Tindall Corporation ....C 228 246-0798
Moss Point (G-3502)

Travis Construction Co LLC ....F 228 539-4849
Gulfport (G-1886)

United Burial Vault Co & Cemtr ....F 662 347-9319
Benoit (G-207)

Wilbert Burial Vault Company ....G 601 353-7084
Jackson (G-2632)

Wilbert Funeral Services Inc ....G 800 323-7188
Jackson (G-2633)

3273 Ready-Mixed Concrete

Americrete Inc ....F 601 485-6507
Meridian (G-3297)

Americrete Ready Mix Inc ....G 601 656-5590
Philadelphia (G-4204)

Apac-Mississippi Inc ....G 662 494-5772
West Point (G-5535)

Apac-Mississippi Inc ....G 662 343-9300
Aberdeen (G-9)

B & B Concrete Co Inc ....F 662 286-6407
Corinth (G-1060)

B & B Concrete Co Inc ....G 662 489-2233
Pontotoc (G-4321)

B & B Concrete Co Inc ....F 662 234-7088
Oxford (G-3937)

B & B Concrete Co Inc ....G 662 837-3221
Ripley (G-4653)

B & B Concrete Co Inc ....F 662 534-2626
New Albany (G-3673)

B & B Concrete Co Inc ....E 662 869-1927
Saltillo (G-4706)

B & B Concrete Co Inc ....E 662 842-6312
Verona (G-5327)

B & B Concrete Co Inc ....E 662 842-7305
Tupelo (G-5111)

Baker Ready Mix & Cnstr LLC ....E 662 773-8054
Louisville (G-2964)

Bayou Concrete LLC ....D 228 868-1264
Gulfport (G-1736)

Bayou Concrete LLC ....G 601 898-4000
Ridgeland (G-4553)

Bayou Concrete LLC ....F 228 762-8911
Pascagoula (G-4022)

Canton Concrete ....E 601 859-4547
Canton (G-652)

Cemex Cnstr Mtls Fla LLC ....E 888 263-7093
Como (G-1046)

CMC Readymix Inc ....F 662 252-6479
Holly Springs (G-2174)

Coast Concrete Company Inc ....E 228 863-1364
Gulfport (G-1755)

Danny Berry ....G 601 276-6200
Summit (G-5010)

Delta Industries Inc ....G 601 634-6001
Vicksburg (G-5361)

Delta Industries Inc ....E 228 896-7400
Gulfport (G-1770)

Delta Industries Inc ....F 601 783-6030
Magnolia (G-3190)

Delta Industries Inc ....G 228 539-9333
Saucier (G-4752)

Delta Industries Inc ....G 601 849-2661
Magee (G-3176)

Delta Industries Inc ....D 601 354-3801
Jackson (G-2380)

Delta Industries Inc ....G 601 833-1166
Brookhaven (G-489)

Delta Industries Inc ....G 662 746-6646
Yazoo City (G-5631)

Delta Industries Inc ....F 601 825-7531
Brandon (G-387)

Delta Industries Inc ....G 228 475-2419
Moss Point (G-3476)

Delta Industries Inc ....G 662 323-7224
Starkville (G-4939)

Delta Industries Inc ....E 601 948-4245
Crystal Springs (G-1141)

Delta Industries Inc ....C 601 354-3801
Jackson (G-2381)

Delta Industries Inc ....F 601 792-4286
Prentiss (G-4416)

Dooley Brothers Ready Mix Inc ....G 601 888-3530
Woodville (G-5617)

Franklin Ready Mix Inc ....G 601 384-5445
Bude (G-569)

George B Ready ....G 662 429-7088
Hernando (G-2132)

Golden Triange Ready Mix Inc ....F 662 328-0153
Columbus (G-979)

Gulf Concrete Co Inc ....F 601 798-3181
Picayune (G-4269)

▲ H S I Ready Mix ....G 601 798-1665
Picayune (G-4270)

Hernando Redi Mix Inc ....F 662 429-7571
Nesbit (G-3653)

HI Tech Concrete Inc ....G 228 452-2125
Pass Christian (G-4087)

Hills Brothers Cnstr & Engrg ....E 662 837-7415
Falkner (G-1294)

Huey P Stockstill LLC ....C 601 798-2981
Picayune (G-4273)

Iuka Concrete Products LLC ....G 662 423-6238
Iuka (G-2294)

J J Ferguson Sand & Grav Inc ....G 662 453-5451
Greenwood (G-1630)

John Ready Damond ....G 601 587-4381
Monticello (G-3434)

Jones Ready Mix LLC ....G 601 222-1919
Sandy Hook (G-4730)

Lamar Concrete Inc ....F 601 794-0049
Purvis (G-4444)

Legacy Vulcan LLC ....G 228 452-3000
Long Beach (G-2943)

Legacy Vulcan LLC ....G 228 474-1414
Moss Point (G-3483)

Lexington Concrete & Block Co ....F 601 859-4547
Canton (G-668)

Lexington Concrete & Block Co ....G 662 834-3892
Lexington (G-2904)

Lucedale Ready Mix Concrete Co ....G 601 947-4741
Lucedale (G-3009)

Macon Ready-Mix Concrete Co ....F 662 726-4733
Macon (G-3065)

Metro Concrete ....G 228 284-1660
Gulfport (G-1830)

Milligan Ready Mix Inc ....F 662 423-6238
Iuka (G-2300)

MMC Materials Inc ....F 601 898-4000
Ridgeland (G-4608)

MMC Materials Inc ....G 601 928-4941
Wiggins (G-5586)

MMC Materials Inc ....G 601 774-0443
Union (G-5302)

MMC Materials Inc ....G 601 833-4900
Brookhaven (G-519)

MMC Materials Inc ....E 601 684-7373
McComb (G-3260)

MMC Materials Inc ....F 601 469-2741
Forest (G-1423)

MMC Materials Inc ....G 601 582-8493
Petal (G-4193)

MMC Materials Inc ....G 662 624-9000
Clarksdale (G-776)

MMC Materials Inc ....G 662 332-5407
Greenville (G-1577)

MMC Materials Inc ....E 601 482-7007
Meridian (G-3375)

MMC Materials Inc ....G 662 628-6667
Calhoun City (G-641)

MMC Materials Inc ....D 662 393-7676
Horn Lake (G-2208)

MMC Materials Inc ....D 601 634-8787
Vicksburg (G-5399)

MMC Materials Inc ....G 662 453-9722
Greenwood (G-1642)

MMC Materials Inc ....F 601 268-9599
Hattiesburg (G-2028)

MMC Materials Inc ....D 251 408-0740
Gulfport (G-1833)

MMC Materials Inc ....G 662 887-4031
Greenville (G-1578)

MMC Materials Inc ....G 601 268-3005
Hattiesburg (G-2029)

MMC Materials Inc ....G 601 267-8278
Carthage (G-720)

MMC Materials Inc ....G 601 437-4321
Port Gibson (G-4403)

MMC Materials Inc ....F 601 445-5641
Natchez (G-3590)

MMC Materials Inc ....G 662 327-1927
Columbus (G-1006)

MMC Materials Inc ....D 601 973-2093
Jackson (G-2508)

MMC Materials Inc ....G 662 773-5656
Louisville (G-2975)

MMC Materials Inc ....F 662 323-0644
Starkville (G-4961)

MMC Materials Inc ....G 662 258-6096
Eupora (G-1289)

Morris Ready Mix Inc ....G 662 473-2505
Water Valley (G-5473)

Oxford Sand-Concrete Plant ....G 662 281-0355
Oxford (G-3990)

Pine Belt Ready Mix ....G 601 544-7069
Hattiesburg (G-2043)

Pine Belt Ready Mix Concrete ....F 601 425-2559
Laurel (G-2819)

Pine Belt Ready-Mix Con Inc ....G 601 425-2026
Laurel (G-2820)

Pine Belt Ready-Mix Con Inc ....G 601 765-4813
Collins (G-859)

Ready Mix Dispatch ....G 662 842-6313
Tupelo (G-5215)

Sanderson Redi-Mix Inc ....G 662 256-9301
Amory (G-53)

Sardis Ready Mix LLC ....G 662 512-2170
Byhalia (G-602)

Service Lumber Company Inc ....F 662 873-4334
Rolling Fork (G-4682)

Service Lumber Holding Corp ....G 662 873-4334
Rolling Fork (G-4683)

Southeast Ready Mix Inc ....F 601 735-4823
Waynesboro (G-5515)

Southeastern Concrete Co Inc ....E 601 544-7000
Hattiesburg (G-2057)

Southeastern Concrete Co Inc ....E 601 545-7811
Hattiesburg (G-2058)

Spencer Ready-Mix Jackson Inc ....E 601 981-6080
Jackson (G-2594)

St Catherine Ready Mix Inc ....F 601 445-8891
Natchez (G-3625)

Stockstill Bros Invstments LLC ....E 601 798-2981
Picayune (G-4298)

Terminal ....G 601 636-7781
Vicksburg (G-5428)

Employee Codes: A=Over 500 employees, B=251-500
C=101-250, D=51-100, E=20-50, F=10-19, G=1-9

2019 Harris Directory of
Mississippi Manufacturers

237

S I C

32 STONE, CLAY, GLASS, AND CONCRETE PRODUCTS

Townes Construction Co Inc ....F 662 226-4894
Grenada *(G-1709)*

Tri State Ready Mix ....G 662 893-3496
Byhalia *(G-610)*

Tricounty Ready Mix Inc ....F 601 649-2887
Stringer *(G-5005)*

Vicksburg Ready Mix Concrete ....G 601 634-6001
Vicksburg *(G-5441)*

3274 Lime

Limeco Inc ....G 662 456-4226
West Point *(G-5551)*

Mississippi Lime Company ....E 601 636-0932
Vicksburg *(G-5396)*

3275 Gypsum Prdts

Certainteed Gypsum Inc ....C 601 693-0254
Meridian *(G-3318)*

Georgia-Pacific LLC ....F 601 939-7797
Pearl *(G-4122)*

3281 Cut Stone Prdts

A & W Marble Inc ....G 228 832-5037
Saucier *(G-4748)*

AIA Countertops ....G 574 457-2003
Guntown *(G-1896)*

Apex Products Inc ....G 601 992-5900
Jackson *(G-2332)*

Avalon Marble LLC ....F 601 798-3378
Picayune *(G-4253)*

Bacallao Silva Gran & Tile LLC..........G 769 798-8816
Madison *(G-3082)*

C & S Marble Co ....G 662 844-6873
Saltillo *(G-4710)*

▲ Columbus Marble Works Inc..........E 662 328-1477
Columbus *(G-950)*

Davidson Marble & Gran Works ....G 662 289-1337
Kosciusko *(G-2692)*

Doric Burial Vault Co ....F 601 366-8390
Jackson *(G-2388)*

Foley Tile & Marble ....G 601 271-8415
Hattiesburg *(G-1972)*

G & G Granite ....G 601 319-0905
Ellisville *(G-1252)*

▲ International Granite LLC ....G 601 213-8287
Jackson *(G-2448)*

Jonathan Bigbie ....G 601 498-9890
Petal *(G-4188)*

K & D Cultured Marble Inc ....E 662 675-2928
Coffeeville *(G-843)*

L & G Marble Inc ....G 601 268-0225
Hattiesburg *(G-2012)*

Lavastone Industries Mid South...........G 662 844-5178
Tupelo *(G-5172)*

Lighthouse Marble Works Inc ....E 228 392-3038
Biloxi *(G-262)*

Miller Enterprises ....F 601 798-3004
Carriere *(G-698)*

Mississippi Marble & Granite ....G 662 289-4111
Kosciusko *(G-2702)*

Moulton Tile & Marble Inc ....G 228 863-7587
Long Beach *(G-2945)*

North Miss Stone & Mem Co ....G 662 365-5721
Baldwyn *(G-85)*

Personal Touch Stone ....G 228 219-3359
Moss Point *(G-3494)*

Precision Cultured Marble ....G 662 838-5112
Byhalia *(G-597)*

Rock Shop LLC ....G 601 446-7625
Natchez *(G-3615)*

Simple Stone Solutions ....G 601 206-5566
Jackson *(G-2582)*

Stone Associates Inc ....G 662 838-4671
Byhalia *(G-607)*

Triton Stone Holdings LLC................D 662 280-8041
Southaven *(G-4917)*

Veterans Monument Company LLC .....G 662 549-1422
Caledonia *(G-633)*

Walker Memorial Co Inc ....G 601 428-5337
Laurel *(G-2866)*

3291 Abrasive Prdts

◆ Atlas-Ssi Inc ....D 601 587-4511
Monticello *(G-3428)*

Covidien LP ....C 815 744-3766
Olive Branch *(G-3830)*

Kr Steel & Industrial Supply.............G 662 294-8888
Grenada *(G-1690)*

Osborn ....F 601 366-9902
Jackson *(G-2531)*

3292 Asbestos products

Precision Asp Sealcoating LLC..........G 601 527-6381
Collinsville *(G-874)*

3295 Minerals & Earths: Ground Or Treated

Blue Mountain Refining Company ....D 662 685-4386
Blue Mountain *(G-289)*

Desiccare Inc ....G 601 932-0405
Richland *(G-4513)*

▲ Kengro Corporation ....F 662 647-2456
Charleston *(G-740)*

Nanocor LLC ....G 847 851-1500
Aberdeen *(G-19)*

▲ Oil-Dri Production Company............D 662 837-9263
Ripley *(G-4666)*

Profile Products LLC ....E 662 685-4741
Blue Mountain *(G-292)*

Vulcan Materials Company ....G 601 425-3509
Laurel *(G-2863)*

3296 Mineral Wool

Certainteed Gypsum Inc ....C 601 693-0254
Meridian *(G-3318)*

Johns Manville Corporation ....D 601 936-9841
Jackson *(G-2652)*

Molded Acstcal Pdts Easton Inc ....E 662 627-7811
Clarksdale *(G-777)*

◆ Roxul USA Inc ....C 662 851-4755
Byhalia *(G-600)*

3299 Nonmetallic Mineral Prdts, NEC

All American Stucco ....G 228 669-0915
Gulfport *(G-1718)*

Architectural Concepts ....G 850 471-7081
Brandon *(G-365)*

Mackies Slip Inc ....G 601 722-4395
Seminary *(G-4783)*

Outback Stucco & Coatings LLC.........G 228 224-2824
Gulfport *(G-1841)*

Public Art Project Ocean ....G 228 872-0846
Ocean Springs *(G-3779)*

Regional Stucco LLC ....G 228 323-0290
Biloxi *(G-276)*

Wesley Inc ....G 601 731-9288
Foxworth *(G-1438)*

33 PRIMARY METAL INDUSTRIES

3312 Blast Furnaces, Coke Ovens, Steel & Rolling Mills

Advance Tool and Die Inc ....G 601 939-1291
Pearl *(G-4104)*

American Plant Services Inc ....D 228 762-1397
Pascagoula *(G-4019)*

Chrome Deposit Corporation ....E 662 798-4149
Columbus *(G-948)*

Commercial Metals Company ....F 601 796-5474
Lumberton *(G-3026)*

Consolidated Pipe & Sup Co Inc ....F 228 769-1920
Pascagoula *(G-4028)*

Contract Fabricators Inc ....E 662 424-0061
Iuka *(G-2287)*

Eagle Pipe and Supply LLC ....G 601 487-7473
Jackson *(G-2394)*

Eagle Specialty Products Inc ....E 662 796-7373
Southaven *(G-4870)*

Etd Inc ....G 662 454-9349
Belmont *(G-198)*

Garrett Welding & Iron ....G 601 372-3889
Terry *(G-5068)*

Grayson Blu LLC ....E 662 779-1291
Louisville *(G-2970)*

Holly Tool & Die Inc ....G 662 252-1144
Holly Springs *(G-2177)*

▲ Industrial Steel Corporation............G 601 932-5555
Pearl *(G-4127)*

Kustom Machine and Sheet Metal ....F 601 469-1062
Philadelphia *(G-4221)*

Metro Mechanical Inc......................D 601 866-9050
Bolton *(G-312)*

▲ Nucor Steel Jackson Inc ....B 601 939-1623
Flowood *(G-1385)*

Piper Metal Forming Corp ....C 508 363-3937
New Albany *(G-3691)*

▲ PSL-North America LLC ....B 228 533-7779
Bay St Louis *(G-180)*

Rain Cii Carbon LLC ....G 601 794-2753
Purvis *(G-4451)*

Resurfacing Concepts Inc ....G 662 489-6867
Pontotoc *(G-4360)*

Roes Rims and Accessories ....G 601 619-4489
Vicksburg *(G-5413)*

S & H Steel Corp ....F 601 932-0250
Pearl *(G-4141)*

Severcorr LLC ....G 662 245-4561
Columbus *(G-1024)*

Smith Chemical Company ....G 901 849-4074
Olive Branch *(G-3911)*

Southern Exteriors Fence Co ....G 228 586-2110
Perkinston *(G-4181)*

Southern Scrap Meridian LLC ....E 601 693-5323
Meridian *(G-3403)*

▲ Steel Dynamics Columbus LLC........B 662 245-4200
Columbus *(G-1033)*

Sxp Schulz Xtruded Products LP ....D 662 429-0818
Hernando *(G-2157)*

▲ Sxp Schulz Xtruded Products LP .....C 662 373-4114
Robinsonville *(G-4678)*

Tech Wire ....E 773 669-7583
Starkville *(G-4977)*

Tms International LLC ....G 601 932-8205
Flowood *(G-1402)*

True Temper Sports Inc ....B 662 256-5605
Amory *(G-57)*

Vicksmetal Corporation ....E 601 636-1314
Vicksburg *(G-5442)*

Virgil Williams LLC ....G 662 287-7734
Corinth *(G-1127)*

3315 Steel Wire Drawing & Nails & Spikes

Blue Springs Metals LLC ....E 662 539-2700
Blue Springs *(G-294)*

Illinois Tool Works Inc ....C 662 489-4151
Pontotoc *(G-4335)*

Laclede Chain Mfg Co LLC ....G 601 802-0134
Vicksburg *(G-5388)*

Southern Exteriors Fence Co ....G 228 586-2110
Perkinston *(G-4181)*

Southwire Company LLC ....E 662 324-6600
Starkville *(G-4974)*

Universal Lighting Tech Inc ....B 601 892-9828
Gallman *(G-1486)*

3316 Cold Rolled Steel Sheet, Strip & Bars

Ceca LLC ....E 662 993-8880
Ripley *(G-4655)*

Miss-Lou Steel Supply Inc ....G 601 442-0846
Natchez *(G-3589)*

New Process Steel LP ....D 662 241-6582
Columbus *(G-1010)*

Steel Technologies LLC ....E 601 855-7242
Madison *(G-3153)*

Worthington Cylinders Miss LLC ....E 614 840-3802
New Albany *(G-3709)*

3317 Steel Pipe & Tubes

Allied Crawford Jackson Inc..............E 769 230-2220
Byram *(G-616)*

Contech Engnered Solutions LLC.........G 601 894-2041
Greenville *(G-1540)*

Empire Services Inc ....C 601 276-2500
Summit *(G-5014)*

Helanbak LLC ....G 601 736-6112
Foxworth *(G-1431)*

▲ Jindal Tubular USA LLC ....D 228 533-7779
Bay Saint Louis *(G-144)*

Leggett & Platt Incorporated ....F 417 358-8131
West Point *(G-5549)*

Maruichi Leavitt Pipe Tube LLC..........G 800 532-8488
Jackson *(G-2655)*

Midco Supply Co Inc ....G 601 932-7311
Jackson *(G-2657)*

Plymouth Tube Company ....D 662 258-2420
Eupora *(G-1290)*

PSL USA Inc ....G 228 533-7779
Bay Saint Louis *(G-151)*

3321 Gray Iron Foundries

Apm LLC ....G 907 279-0204
Gulfport *(G-1728)*

Laurel Machine and Foundry Co ....C 601 428-0541
Laurel *(G-2793)*

2019 Harris Directory of
Mississippi Manufacturers

238

SIC SECTION

34 FABRICATED METAL PRODUCTS, EXCEPT MACHINERY AND TRANSPORTATION EQUIPMENT

3324 Steel Investment Foundries

▲ Mississippi Precision ....E 662 245-1155
Columbus (G-1004)
▼ Samuel Son & Co (usa) Inc ....E 662 424-1460
Iuka (G-2308)

3325 Steel Foundries, NEC

Nucor Corporation ....E 601 936-6292
Jackson (G-2659)
Southern Cast Products Inc ....C 601 482-8518
Meridian (G-3401)
Steel Technologies LLC ....E 601 855-7242
Madison (G-3153)

3334 Primary Production Of Aluminum

▼ Croft LLC ....E 601 684-6121
McComb (G-3247)
Onyx Xteriors LLC ....G 901 281-2887
Byhalia (G-594)
Parker-Hannifin Mobile Climate ....G 662 728-3141
Booneville (G-340)

3339 Primary Nonferrous Metals, NEC

▲ Attala Steel Industries LLC ....G 662 289-1980
Kosciusko (G-2688)
Clear Enterprise ....G 601 796-2429
Lumberton (G-3025)
Green Metals Inc ....G 662 534-5447
Blue Springs (G-296)
▲ Mississippi Silicon LLC ....C 662 696-2600
Burnsville (G-572)
Purvis Jewerly Rlc LLC ....G 601 329-9002
Purvis (G-4450)

3341 Secondary Smelting & Refining Of Non-ferrous Metals

Aluminum Recycling of Miss ....E 601 355-5777
Jackson (G-2325)
Columbus Scrap Material Co ....E 662 328-8176
Columbus (G-953)
Corinth Cc-Cola Btlg Works Inc ....E 662 286-2052
Corinth (G-1078)
Metal Management Inc ....G 662 455-2540
Greenwood (G-1639)
Metal Management Inc ....F 662 844-6441
New Albany (G-3686)
Northeast Metal Processors ....E 662 844-2164
Plantersville (G-4312)
Nucor Corporation ....E 601 936-6292
Jackson (G-2659)
Southern Scrap Meridian LLC ....E 601 693-5323
Meridian (G-3403)
Triangle Recycling Services ....F 601 352-5027
Jackson (G-2611)

3351 Rolling, Drawing & Extruding Of Copper

▲ Mueller Copper Tube Co Inc ....B 662 862-1700
Fulton (G-1466)
Mueller Copper Tube Pdts Inc ....F 662 862-2181
Fulton (G-1467)
Mueller Industries Inc ....D 662 862-2181
Fulton (G-1468)
Mueller Industries Inc ....D 662 862-7425
Fulton (G-1469)
Piper Metal Forming Corp ....C 508 363-3937
New Albany (G-3691)

3353 Aluminum Sheet, Plate & Foil

American Specialty Alloys ....E 662 368-1332
Columbus (G-934)
Applicated Images Inc ....G 601 992-1556
Brandon (G-364)
New Process Steel LP ....D 662 241-6582
Columbus (G-1010)
Packaging Dynamics Corporation ......E 662 424-4000
Iuka (G-2304)
Rickys Welding and Machine Sp ....G 601 638-8238
Vicksburg (G-5410)
Southern Metals Co Miss Inc ....E 601 649-7475
Laurel (G-2853)

3354 Aluminum Extruded Prdts

Aei LLC ....D 662 562-6663
Senatobia (G-4786)
Afco Industries Inc ....C 662 895-8686
Olive Branch (G-3808)

Aluma-Form Inc ....D 662 677-6000
Walnut (G-5454)
▼ Beaver Built Cherokee Mfg LLC .....F 901 258-2679
Byhalia (G-578)
Crown Cork & Seal Usa Inc ....B 662 563-7664
Batesville (G-102)
HMC Metal Forming Inc ....E 662 538-5447
New Albany (G-3682)
L C Industries Inc ....B 601 894-1771
Hazlehurst (G-2099)
Metal Impact South LLC ....E 662 538-6500
New Albany (G-3685)
North American Pipe Corp ....E 662 728-2111
Booneville (G-338)
Piper Metal Forming Corp ....C 508 363-3937
New Albany (G-3691)
Saunders Mfg Co Inc ....F 601 693-3482
Meridian (G-3394)
Signature Works Inc ....E 601 894-1771
Hazlehurst (G-2106)
Taber Extrusions LLC ....E 228 863-2852
Gulfport (G-1882)
Triple Shots ....G 228 872-2696
Ocean Springs (G-3792)

3355 Aluminum Rolling & Drawing, NEC

▼ Magnolia Mtal Plastic Pdts Inc ......E 601 638-6912
Vicksburg (G-5393)
Nci Group Inc ....D 601 373-0374
Jackson (G-2516)
Southwire Company LLC ....E 662 324-6600
Starkville (G-4974)
▲ Trilogy Communications Inc ....D 601 932-4461
Pearl (G-4154)

3356 Rolling, Drawing-Extruding Of Nonferrous Metals

▲ Lunati LLC ....E 662 892-1518
Olive Branch (G-3868)
Piper Metal Forming Corp ....C 508 363-3937
New Albany (G-3691)
Tin Roof Mercantile ....G 901 596-6803
Olive Branch (G-3918)
Tronox Incorporated ....D 662 343-8311
Hamilton (G-1909)

3357 Nonferrous Wire Drawing

Appliance Tech Authorized Svc ....G 228 392-0789
Biloxi (G-219)
◆ Electro National Corporation ....E 601 859-5511
Canton (G-657)
Grady Morrow ....G 769 823-1422
Jackson (G-2429)
Southwire Company LLC ....E 662 324-6600
Starkville (G-4974)
Trilogy Communications Inc ....C 601 932-4461
Flowood (G-1404)
▲ Trilogy Communications Inc ....D 601 932-4461
Pearl (G-4154)
Universal Lighting Tech Inc ....B 601 892-9828
Gallman (G-1486)

3363 Aluminum Die Castings

Leggett & Platt Incorporated ....G 662 842-5704
Tupelo (G-5175)
Rossville Aluminum Castings ....F 662 301-1147
Senatobia (G-4801)

3365 Aluminum Foundries

Brimmer-Turan Fndry & Mch LLC ......G 228 896-9669
Gulfport (G-1745)
Rossville Aluminum Castings ....F 662 301-1147
Senatobia (G-4801)

3366 Copper Foundries

Brimmer-Turan Fndry & Mch LLC ......G 228 896-9669
Gulfport (G-1745)
Mueller Copper Fittings Co ....E 662 862-2181
Fulton (G-1465)
Nichols Propeller Company ....E 662 378-2000
Greenville (G-1580)
Rolls-Royce Marine North Amer ....D 228 762-0728
Pascagoula (G-4064)

3369 Nonferrous Foundries: Castings, NEC

CL Dews Sons Fndry McHy Inc ....D 601 582-4427
Hattiesburg (G-1945)

Main Street Pascagoula ....G 228 219-1114
Pascagoula (G-4049)
Rossville Aluminum Castings ....F 662 301-1147
Senatobia (G-4801)
Sullivan Metals Inc ....G 662 252-5050
Holly Springs (G-2193)

3398 Metal Heat Treating

Lundtek Inc ....E 662 252-2340
Holly Springs (G-2183)
▲ Precision Heat Treating Corp ....F 601 355-4208
Jackson (G-2547)
Surfacetechs ....G 601 605-1900
Madison (G-3154)

3399 Primary Metal Prdts, NEC

Aerotec Ltd ....G 713 598-9410
Hattiesburg (G-1918)

34 FABRICATED METAL PRODUCTS, EXCEPT MACHINERY AND TRANSPORTATION EQUIPMENT

3411 Metal Cans

Crown Cork & Seal Usa Inc ....B 662 563-7664
Batesville (G-102)
H&M Metal Express LLC ....G 601 798-4600
Carriere (G-693)

3412 Metal Barrels, Drums, Kegs & Pails

Dkh Distributing Inc ....G 901 734-4528
Hernando (G-2129)

3421 Cutlery

Carneceria Valdez ....G 601 899-6992
Ridgeland (G-4560)
Country Kitchen of Amory ....G 662 257-4055
Amory (G-39)
◆ Debeukelaer Corporation ....E 601 856-7454
Madison (G-3094)
Hondumex Global LLC ....G 601 732-6505
Morton (G-3447)
James L Brewer ....G 662 299-7247
Greenwood (G-1631)
Kut Tools Inc ....G 601 876-4467
Tylertown (G-5276)
McKewens Oxford ....G 662 234-7003
Oxford (G-3974)
Prairie Wildlife ....G 662 494-1235
West Point (G-5559)
Sonic of Fulton ....G 662 862-3000
Fulton (G-1474)

3423 Hand & Edge Tools

Carsons Construction LLC ....E 601 301-0841
Vicksburg (G-5354)
Continental Interiors Inc ....G 662 382-3061
Crenshaw (G-1133)
Dern Mechanix ....G 228 832-3933
Gulfport (G-1771)
Fiskars Brands Inc ....G 662 393-3236
Southaven (G-4873)
Godsway Enterprises Inc ....G 601 517-2847
Jackson (G-2426)
Legendary Lawn Services Inc ....G 601 307-6381
Jackson (G-2468)
North Wind Fabrication Inc ....G 228 896-0230
Gulfport (G-1839)
Paslode Corporation ....G 662 489-4151
Pontotoc (G-4353)
Robert E Monk ....G 662 562-8729
Senatobia (G-4800)
Shelby Dean Distributing ....G 601 529-7936
Vicksburg (G-5417)

3425 Hand Saws & Saw Blades

Milwaukee Electric Tool Corp ....B 662 451-5545
Greenwood (G-1640)
Milwaukee Electric Tool Corp ....C 662 895-4560
Olive Branch (G-3879)
◆ Precision Blades Inc ....F 662 869-1034
Saltillo (G-4719)
Southern Band Saw Co Inc ....F 662 332-4008
Greenville (G-1600)

Employee Codes: A=Over 500 employees, B=251-500
C=101-250, D=51-100, E=20-50, F=10-19, G=1-9

2019 Harris Directory of
Mississippi Manufacturers

239

S I C

34 FABRICATED METAL PRODUCTS, EXCEPT MACHINERY AND TRANSPORTATION EQUIPMENT

SIC SECTION

3429 Hardware, NEC

▲ Albany Fiber Sales Inc ....G...... 662 401-2342
New Albany *(G-3671)*

Alexander Fabricating Co Inc ....G...... 601 485-5414
Meridian *(G-3295)*

Delta Auto Parts Inc ....F...... 662 746-1143
Yazoo City *(G-5630)*

Fibrix LLC ....G...... 662 568-3393
Houlka *(G-2222)*

Gerrer Industrial LLC ....G...... 601 506-2709
Madison *(G-3104)*

Military Defense Systems Inc ....G...... 850 449-1910
Picayune *(G-4278)*

Moores John ....G...... 662 488-2980
Pontotoc *(G-4350)*

N C Enterprises Inc ....G...... 601 953-6977
Hazlehurst *(G-2101)*

Region 8 Mental Health Retrdat ......D...... 601 591-5553
Brandon *(G-445)*

Richard B Brandon ....G...... 601 238-2383
Jackson *(G-2564)*

Rolls-Royce Marine North Amer ....D...... 228 762-0728
Pascagoula *(G-4064)*

Southern Metals Co Miss Inc ....E...... 601 649-7475
Laurel *(G-2853)*

Southern Technical Aquatic RES ......G...... 601 590-6248
Carriere *(G-701)*

3431 Enameled Iron & Metal Sanitary Ware

Kohler Co ....G...... 601 544-2553
Hattiesburg *(G-2010)*

Nokomis LLC ....G...... 601 743-2100
De Kalb *(G-1167)*

Wilsonart LLC ....G...... 828 785-2796
Oxford *(G-4010)*

3432 Plumbing Fixture Fittings & Trim, Brass

Carr Plumbing Supply Inc ....G...... 601 824-9711
Brandon *(G-375)*

National Pump Company ....G...... 662 895-1110
Olive Branch *(G-3886)*

3433 Heating Eqpt

B R Smith Enterprises Inc ....F...... 601 656-0846
Union *(G-5293)*

Babcock & Wilcox Company ....C...... 662 494-1323
West Point *(G-5537)*

▲ Hardy Manufacturing Co Inc ....E...... 601 656-5866
Philadelphia *(G-4217)*

Modine Grenada LLC ....B...... 662 229-4000
Grenada *(G-1694)*

3441 Fabricated Structural Steel

Abby Manufacturing LLC ....D...... 662 223-5339
Walnut *(G-5452)*

Abby Manufacturing Co Inc ....E...... 662 223-5339
New Albany *(G-3670)*

Accu-Fab and Construction Inc ....E...... 228 475-0082
Moss Point *(G-3465)*

Acme Fabrication LLC ....G...... 228 669-0004
Perkinston *(G-4172)*

Addy Metal Fabrication ....G...... 601 635-4064
Decatur *(G-1170)*

Advanced Fabrication Inc ....G...... 601 796-7977
Lumberton *(G-3023)*

Alan Dickerson Inc ....G...... 662 289-1451
Kosciusko *(G-2687)*

Amerimac Machining Corporation .....G...... 601 940-7919
Jackson *(G-2329)*

B & O Machine & Wldg Co Inc ....F...... 601 833-3000
Brookhaven *(G-481)*

B-Line Fabrication Co Ltd ....E...... 228 832-3286
Gulfport *(G-1732)*

Bath Iron Works Corporation ....G...... 228 935-3872
Pascagoula *(G-4021)*

Berry Enterprises of Miss ....G...... 601 928-4006
Perkinston *(G-4174)*

Big River Shipbuilders Inc ....E...... 601 636-9161
Vicksburg *(G-5345)*

Bryan E Presson & Assoc Inc ....F...... 601 925-0053
Clinton *(G-816)*

Cameron Rig Solutions Inc ....G...... 601 629-3300
Vicksburg *(G-5353)*

Careys Construction Co Inc ....E...... 601 922-7388
Jackson *(G-2354)*

Ci Metal Fabrication LLC ....E...... 601 483-6281
Meridian *(G-3320)*

Cives Corporation ....C...... 662 759-6265
Rosedale *(G-4687)*

CL Dews Sons Fndry McHy Inc ....D...... 601 582-4427
Hattiesburg *(G-1945)*

Coastal Metal Works LLC ....F...... 601 749-2611
Picayune *(G-4261)*

Columbus Mch & Wldg Works Inc ......E...... 662 328-8473
Columbus *(G-951)*

▼ Composite Fbrication Group LLC ...G...... 601 549-1789
Moselle *(G-3456)*

Construction Metals Co Inc ....G...... 601 939-2566
Jackson *(G-2643)*

Contech Engnered Solutions LLC ......G...... 601 894-2041
Greenville *(G-1540)*

Custom Metal Fabrication Inc ....G...... 662 628-8657
Calhoun City *(G-637)*

D & R Industrial Services LLC ....F...... 601 716-3140
Wiggins *(G-5578)*

Delta Fabrication LLC ....E...... 662 335-2500
Greenville *(G-1546)*

Delta Machinery Inc ....G...... 662 827-2572
Hollandale *(G-2165)*

Dublin Steel Corporation Inc ....G...... 601 482-2102
Meridian *(G-3331)*

Ellis Steel Company Inc ....G...... 662 494-5955
West Point *(G-5542)*

Ellis Steel Company Inc ....G...... 662 893-5955
Olive Branch *(G-3838)*

Fab- Tek Central Miss Inc ....G...... 601 892-5017
Hazlehurst *(G-2095)*

Gipson Steel Inc ....G...... 601 482-5131
Meridian *(G-3340)*

▲ Global Fabrication II LLC ....E...... 601 749-2209
Picayune *(G-4267)*

Gulf States Fabrication Inc ....F...... 601 426-9006
Laurel *(G-2773)*

Gulley S Welding Service ....G...... 601 938-6336
Meridian *(G-3343)*

Harrells Metal Works Inc ....E...... 662 226-0982
Grenada *(G-1683)*

Havards Construction LLC ....G...... 601 766-9841
Lucedale *(G-3001)*

Hawkeye Industries Inc ....E...... 662 842-3333
Tupelo *(G-5154)*

▲ Industrial & Crane Svcs Inc ....E...... 601 914-4491
Pascagoula *(G-4039)*

Industrial Fabricators Inc ....G...... 662 327-1776
Columbus *(G-987)*

Interntnl Wldg Fbrication Inc ....E...... 228 474-9353
Moss Point *(G-3481)*

Knights Mar & Indus Svcs Inc ....C...... 228 769-5550
Pascagoula *(G-4045)*

Laurel Machine and Foundry Co ....C...... 601 428-0541
Laurel *(G-2793)*

Lofton Corporation ....G...... 769 243-8427
Jackson *(G-2471)*

Magnolia Steel Co Inc ....G...... 601 693-4301
Meridian *(G-3363)*

Majestic Metals Inc ....E...... 601 856-3600
Madison *(G-3126)*

McKinnion Welding & Metal Fabr ....G...... 601 635-3983
Decatur *(G-1175)*

McMahan Bulldog Enterprises ....G...... 601 606-5711
Sumrall *(G-5039)*

Metal Building Systems LLC ....F...... 601 649-9949
Laurel *(G-2801)*

Metal Tech Inc ....E...... 228 604-4604
Gulfport *(G-1829)*

Metaline Products Inc ....F...... 601 892-5610
Crystal Springs *(G-1147)*

Mississippi Aerospace Corp ....F...... 601 749-5659
Picayune *(G-4280)*

Moore Fabrication and McHy ....G...... 601 892-5017
Gallman *(G-1485)*

National Bank Builders & Eqp ....F...... 662 781-0702
Walls *(G-5450)*

Olivers Iron Works ....G...... 662 252-3858
Holly Springs *(G-2186)*

Oxford Metal Works LLC ....G...... 662 801-7969
Oxford *(G-3988)*

▲ Pemco-Naval Engrg Works Inc ....E...... 228 769-1080
Pascagoula *(G-4062)*

Peppers Machine & Wldg Co Inc ....E...... 601 833-3038
Brookhaven *(G-522)*

Precision Products Inc ....F...... 228 475-7400
Moss Point *(G-3495)*

Quality Pipe & Fabrication LLC ....G...... 662 321-8542
Blue Springs *(G-299)*

◆ Quality Wldg & Fabrication Inc ......D...... 601 731-1222
Columbia *(G-914)*

Ratliff Fabricating Company ....F...... 601 362-8942
Jackson *(G-2560)*

Richard H Bowers ....G...... 601 264-0100
Hattiesburg *(G-2051)*

Rickys Welding and Machine Sp ....G...... 601 638-8238
Vicksburg *(G-5410)*

S & H Steel Corp ....F...... 601 932-0250
Pearl *(G-4141)*

S&G Gutter & Sheet Metal Co ....G...... 662 286-2924
Corinth *(G-1118)*

Saf T Cart Inc ....E...... 662 624-6492
Clarksdale *(G-782)*

Shears Fabrication & Wldg LLC ....G...... 601 946-3268
Utica *(G-5312)*

Slay Steel Inc ....D...... 601 483-3911
Meridian *(G-3398)*

Southern Industrial Tech LLC ....F...... 601 426-3866
Stringer *(G-5004)*

Steel Service Corporation ....C...... 601 939-9222
Jackson *(G-2668)*

▼ Steel Specialties Miss Inc ....F...... 601 939-2690
Pearl *(G-4149)*

Steelpro LLC ....E...... 662 456-3004
Houston *(G-2254)*

Stevens Sheet Metal & Ir Works ......E...... 601 939-6943
Pearl *(G-4150)*

Structural Steel Holding Inc ....F...... 601 485-1503
Meridian *(G-3407)*

Structural Steel Holding Inc ....C...... 601 483-5381
Meridian *(G-3408)*

Structural Steel Services Inc ....C...... 601 482-1668
Meridian *(G-3409)*

Structural Steel Services Inc ....E...... 601 485-2619
Meridian *(G-3410)*

Thomasvlle Mtal Fbricators Inc ....E...... 662 526-9900
Como *(G-1052)*

Trinity Steel Fabricators Inc ....G...... 601 783-6625
Magnolia *(G-3195)*

Union Corrugating Company ....G...... 601 661-0577
Vicksburg *(G-5432)*

Vertechs Design Solutions LLC ....G...... 228 671-1442
Waveland *(G-5486)*

Watkins ....G...... 601 752-2526
Ellisville *(G-1277)*

Williams Machine Works Inc ....F...... 228 475-7651
Moss Point *(G-3508)*

Yates Industrial Services LLC ....G...... 601 467-6232
Purvis *(G-4454)*

3442 Metal Doors, Sash, Frames, Molding & Trim

A Plus Tornado Shelters O ....G...... 601 879-0005
Jackson *(G-2315)*

Afco Industries Inc ....C...... 662 895-8686
Olive Branch *(G-3808)*

Cox Hardware LLC ....E...... 713 923-9458
Madison *(G-3090)*

French Awning & Screen Co Inc ....G...... 601 922-1132
Jackson *(G-2414)*

Frierson Building Supply Co ....C...... 601 922-1321
Jackson *(G-2416)*

▼ Griffin Inc ....D...... 662 838-2128
Byhalia *(G-586)*

▲ Ironcrafters Security Products ....E...... 662 224-6658
Ashland *(G-62)*

JC Manufacturing LLC ....G...... 662 338-9004
Starkville *(G-4952)*

La Rosa Glass Inc ....G...... 228 864-0751
Long Beach *(G-2942)*

Masterbilt ....G...... 662 728-3227
Booneville *(G-335)*

National Custom Craft Inc ....G...... 662 963-7373
Nettleton *(G-3663)*

Necaise Lock Supply Inc ....G...... 228 864-9799
Gulfport *(G-1836)*

Olivers Iron Works ....G...... 662 252-3858
Holly Springs *(G-2186)*

Open Windows LLC ....G...... 601 798-5757
Poplarville *(G-4386)*

P & R Aluminum ....G...... 662 682-7939
Vardaman *(G-5325)*

Partitions Gulfport Corp ....G...... 228 822-9908
Gulfport *(G-1844)*

Quality Glass and Aluminum ....G...... 662 837-3615
Ripley *(G-4669)*

◆ Tapco Inc ....E...... 662 841-1635
Tupelo *(G-5238)*

Vampco Inc ....G...... 601 638-5133
Vicksburg *(G-5433)*

240

2019 Harris Directory of
Mississippi Manufacturers

SIC SECTION — 34 FABRICATED METAL PRODUCTS, EXCEPT MACHINERY AND TRANSPORTATION EQUIPMENT

3443 Fabricated Plate Work

Aberdeen Machine Works Inc ....E 662 369-9357
Aberdeen (G-6)
Airlock Insulation LLC ....F 601 526-4141
Ridgeland (G-4546)
American Tank & Vessel Inc ....C 601 947-7210
Lucedale (G-2986)
▲ Avon Engnered Fabrications LLC ....D 601 889-9050
Picayune (G-4254)
Babcock & Wilcox Company ....C 662 494-1323
West Point (G-5537)
Cbl Architectural Fiberglass ....F 662 429-2277
Hernando (G-2124)
Commercial Construction Co Inc ....D 601 649-5300
Laurel (G-2756)
Complete Welding Solutions ....G 601 791-5370
Lucedale (G-2989)
Construction Waste Management ....G 662 513-7999
Oxford (G-3948)
Contech Engnered Solutions LLC ....F 662 332-2625
Greenville (G-1541)
Contech Engnered Solutions LLC ....G 601 894-2041
Greenville (G-1540)
◆ Contract Fabricators Inc ....C 662 252-6330
Holly Springs (G-2175)
Harbison-Fischer Inc ....G 601 428-7919
Ellisville (G-1257)
◆ Keith Huber Corporation ....D 228 832-0992
Gulfport (G-1816)
L T Corporation ....E 662 843-4046
Cleveland (G-798)
Laurel Machine and Foundry Co ....C 601 428-0541
Laurel (G-2793)
Matheson Tri-Gas Inc ....F 228 255-6661
Pass Christian (G-4091)
Metal-Tech Fabricators Inc ....F 662 622-0400
Coldwater (G-849)
▼ Mississippi Tank and Mfg Co ....C 601 264-1800
Hattiesburg (G-2027)
Modine Manufacturing Company ....G 662 229-2200
Grenada (G-1695)
National Tank Inc ....F 662 429-5469
Hernando (G-2143)
Olivers Iron Works ....G 662 252-3858
Holly Springs (G-2186)
Quality Steel Corporation ....D 662 771-4243
Cleveland (G-804)
Quitman Tank Solutions LLC ....E 601 776-3800
Quitman (G-4469)
Ratliff Fabricating Company ....F 601 362-8942
Jackson (G-2560)
Richards Home Services ....G 228 324-3482
Ocean Springs (G-3782)
Rickys Welding and Machine Sp ....G 601 638-8238
Vicksburg (G-5410)
▲ Rockett Inc ....C 601 939-9347
Flowood (G-1393)
Southern Metals Co Miss Inc ....E 601 649-7475
Laurel (G-2853)
Steel Service Corporation ....G 601 939-9222
Jackson (G-2668)
Structural Steel Holding Inc ....C 601 483-5381
Meridian (G-3408)
Structural Steel Services Inc ....E 601 485-2619
Meridian (G-3410)
Tatum Development Corp ....G 601 544-6043
Hattiesburg (G-2072)
Taylor Environmental Products ....G 662 773-8056
Louisville (G-2985)
Thompsons Welding Services Inc ....D 662 343-8955
Hamilton (G-1908)
Tokins Inc ....G 601 939-1093
Pearl (G-4152)
Transfrmer Gskets Cmpnents LLC ....G 601 854-6624
Lexington (G-2906)
Worthington Cylinder Corp ....C 662 538-6500
New Albany (G-3708)

3444 Sheet Metal Work

A K Sanders Mfg Inc ....G 901 647-1830
Southaven (G-4850)
Aberdeen Machine Works Inc ....E 662 369-9357
Aberdeen (G-6)
Advanced Fabrication Inc ....G 601 796-7977
Lumberton (G-3023)
Air Vent ....G 601 790-9397
Madison (G-3076)
Allen Sheetmetal Inc ....G 228 875-5336
Biloxi (G-218)

American Metalcraft ....G 769 486-5007
De Kalb (G-1160)
Aplimages Inc ....G 601 992-1556
Brandon (G-363)
Babcock & Wilcox Company ....C 662 494-1323
West Point (G-5537)
Brocato Construction Inc ....G 662 563-4473
Batesville (G-100)
Capital City Metal Works Inc ....G 601 939-7467
Pearl (G-4108)
Cbr Performance ....G 601 337-2928
Carriere (G-690)
Clarence Sansing Jr ....G 601 656-4771
Philadelphia (G-4211)
Conklin Metal Industries Inc ....F 601 933-0402
Richland (G-4510)
Contech Engnered Solutions LLC ....F 662 332-2625
Greenville (G-1541)
Contech Engnered Solutions LLC ....G 601 894-2041
Greenville (G-1540)
Daniel Petre ....G 662 726-2462
Macon (G-3057)
Duffell Metal Awning Co ....G 601 483-2181
Meridian (G-3332)
Edco Welding ....G 228 392-5600
Biloxi (G-241)
Fennell Sam Sheet Metal Mfg C ....G 228 864-1488
Gulfport (G-1785)
Fielders Welding and Orna Ir ....G 662 234-4256
Oxford (G-3955)
Gansman Sheet Metal Contrs ....G 662 890-6215
Olive Branch (G-3841)
▼ Goldin Metals Incorporated ....D 228 575-7737
Gulfport (G-1793)
Goldin Metals Incorporated ....F 228 575-7737
Gulfport (G-1794)
Granger Mp AC & Htg ....G 601 894-3774
Hazlehurst (G-2097)
Groves Sheet Metal Co Inc ....G 601 922-6464
Jackson (G-2434)
Hawkeye Industries Inc ....E 662 842-3333
Tupelo (G-5154)
Hunter Douglas Inc ....C 662 690-8190
Shannon (G-4810)
Hunter Engineering Company ....C 662 653-3194
Durant (G-1227)
Industrial Fabricators Inc ....E 662 327-1776
Columbus (G-987)
J & A Mechanical Inc ....G 662 890-4565
Olive Branch (G-3853)
John W McDougall Co Inc ....G 601 298-0079
Carthage (G-718)
King Heating & AC ....G 662 227-1159
Grenada (G-1689)
Koenig-Stimens Inc ....E 228 467-3888
Kiln (G-2682)
L D Sheet Metal ....G 662 838-6267
Byhalia (G-587)
Larkowski Inc ....G 601 928-9501
Saucier (G-4757)
Leonard Metal Fabricators Inc ....E 601 936-4994
Pearl (G-4129)
Majestic Metals Inc ....E 601 856-3600
Madison (G-3126)
Mattuby Creek Machine Works ....G 662 369-8262
Aberdeen (G-18)
McKinnion Welding & Metal Fabr ....G 601 635-3983
Decatur (G-1175)
Metaline Products Inc ....E 601 892-5610
Crystal Springs (G-1147)
Observa-Dome Laboratories Inc ....G 601 982-3333
Jackson (G-2527)
Onyx Xterirors ....G 901 281-2887
Byhalia (G-595)
Palmer Tool LLC ....E 228 832-0805
Saucier (G-4760)
Peppers Machine & Wldg Co Inc ....E 601 833-3038
Brookhaven (G-522)
Precision Mch Met Fbrction Inc ....G 662 844-4606
Tupelo (G-5207)
Quality Metal Roofing LLC ....G 601 669-4336
Brookhaven (G-525)
Ratliff Fabricating Company ....F 601 362-8942
Jackson (G-2560)
Rickys Welding and Machine Sp ....G 601 638-8238
Vicksburg (G-5410)
Roura Acquisition Inc ....F 662 252-1421
Holly Springs (G-2190)
S & H Steel Corp ....F 601 932-0250
Pearl (G-4141)

S&G Gutter & Sheet Metal Co ....G 662 286-2924
Corinth (G-1118)
Sims Metal Inc ....G 601 649-2555
Laurel (G-2850)
Sistrunk Sheet Metal ....G 601 825-5999
Brandon (G-455)
Southern Metals Co Miss Inc ....E 601 649-7475
Laurel (G-2853)
Southwark Metal Mfg Co ....C 662 342-7805
Southaven (G-4907)
Spiral Systems Inc ....F 662 429-0373
Nesbit (G-3657)
Spiral Systems Inc ....G 901 521-8373
Hernando (G-2155)
Steve Harris ....G 228 769-8350
Pascagoula (G-4069)
T & T Welding Inc ....E 601 477-2884
Ellisville (G-1270)
Taber Extrusions LLC ....E 228 863-2852
Gulfport (G-1882)
Telliers Sheetmetal Works ....G 228 392-5319
Diberville (G-1217)
Union Corrugating Company ....G 601 661-0577
Vicksburg (G-5432)
Viking Range LLC ....D 770 932-7282
Greenwood (G-1657)
White Rhino Fabrication LLC ....G 601 397-1118
Canton (G-684)
Woodrffs Prtble Wldg Fbrcation ....G 662 728-3326
Booneville (G-347)

3446 Architectural & Ornamental Metal Work

Bills Welding ....G 901 216-6762
Byhalia (G-579)
Davis Custom Fabrication LLC ....G 228 832-7456
Gulfport (G-1768)
Dyess Lawn & Patio Shop ....G 601 659-0390
Enterprise (G-1279)
Fisher Ludlow ....G 601 853-9996
Madison (G-3099)
Grand Security Door Company ....G 601 573-1618
Jackson (G-2430)
Hart & Cooley Inc ....C 662 890-8000
Olive Branch (G-3845)
Independent Metal Craft LLC ....G 601 488-4789
Clinton (G-825)
Industrial Fabricators Inc ....E 662 327-1776
Columbus (G-987)
Iron and Steel Design Works ....G 662 380-5662
Oxford (G-3962)
Iron Effects ....G 662 871-5565
Thaxton (G-5078)
Iron Innovations Inc ....F 601 924-0640
Clinton (G-826)
▲ Ironcrafters Security Products ....E 662 224-6658
Ashland (G-62)
Ironworks Inc ....G 601 352-3722
Jackson (G-2449)
J M Architectural Iron Wo ....G 228 234-1747
Brooklyn (G-550)
Majestic Metals Inc ....E 601 856-3600
Madison (G-3126)
Mississippi Iron Works Inc ....G 601 355-0188
Jackson (G-2500)
Mississippi Iron Works Inc ....G 601 355-0188
Jackson (G-2501)
Olivers Iron Works ....G 662 252-3858
Holly Springs (G-2186)
South Memphis Fence Co ....G 662 526-5400
Como (G-1051)
Southeast Miss Schl Pdts Inc ....G 662 855-5048
Caledonia (G-631)
Union Corrugating Company ....G 601 661-0577
Vicksburg (G-5432)

3448 Prefabricated Metal Buildings & Cmpnts

AAA Portable Buildings LLC ....G 601 445-4034
Natchez (G-3516)
▼ Aci Building Systems LLC ....C 662 563-4574
Batesville (G-93)
Alexander Fabricating Co Inc ....G 601 485-5414
Meridian (G-3295)
Alply Archtctural Bldg Systems ....E 601 743-2623
De Kalb (G-1159)
Anderson Enterprises LLC ....G 601 928-0030
Wiggins (G-5570)
Better Built Portable Inc ....G 601 267-4607
Carthage (G-707)

Employee Codes: A=Over 500 employees, B=251-500
C=101-250, D=51-100, E=20-50, F=10-19, G=1-9

2019 Harris Directory of
Mississippi Manufacturers

241

34 FABRICATED METAL PRODUCTS, EXCEPT MACHINERY AND TRANSPORTATION EQUIPMENT

SIC SECTION

Castle Hill Design................................G...... 601 918-8234
Canton *(G-654)*
Chatham Enterprises Inc ....E...... 601 727-4951
Rose Hill *(G-4684)*
Custom-Bilt Portable Buildings............G...... 601 932-2808
Florence *(G-1319)*
Derksen Portable Buildings ....G...... 601 528-5778
Wiggins *(G-5579)*
Domes International Inc ....E...... 662 438-7186
Tishomingo *(G-5085)*
Fairview Portable Buildings ....G...... 662 837-8709
Ripley *(G-4658)*
First Monday Trade Day ....G...... 662 837-4051
Ripley *(G-4659)*
Glenn Weise ....G...... 228 435-4455
Biloxi *(G-244)*
Goldin Metals Incorporated ....F...... 228 575-7737
Gulfport *(G-1794)*
▼ Goldin Metals Incorporated ....D...... 228 575-7737
Gulfport *(G-1793)*
Gwendolyn Rucker ....G...... 919 337-6218
Diberville *(G-1206)*
Idom Enterprising Inc ....G...... 601 583-4852
Hattiesburg *(G-1998)*
Johnny Parks ....G...... 662 289-5844
Kosciusko *(G-2697)*
Kirby Bldg Systems Miss LLC ....C...... 662 323-8021
Starkville *(G-4954)*
Lakeview Metal Works ....G...... 601 947-8019
Lucedale *(G-3007)*
Majestic Metals Inc ....E...... 601 856-3600
Madison *(G-3126)*
Metal Builders Supply Inc ....G...... 601 932-0202
Pearl *(G-4131)*
▼ Mini Systems Inc ....G...... 662 487-2240
Como *(G-1050)*
Nci Group Inc ....D...... 662 324-1845
Starkville *(G-4963)*
▲ Nci Group Inc ....G...... 601 373-3222
Jackson *(G-2517)*
Payne Portable Building Inc ....G...... 601 426-9484
Laurel *(G-2818)*
Probuilt LLC ....G...... 662 312-2159
Macon *(G-3071)*
Robertson-Ceco II Corporation ....D...... 662 243-6400
Columbus *(G-1021)*
Seamless One Seamles Gutters ....G...... 228 832-0516
Saucier *(G-4763)*
Vancleave Portable Buildings ....G...... 228 826-5151
Vancleave *(G-5323)*

3449 Misc Structural Metal Work

Buzzard Rebar Fabricators Inc ....F...... 228 832-8024
Gulfport *(G-1746)*
Ellis Steel Company Inc ....G...... 662 893-5955
Olive Branch *(G-3838)*
Foster Machine & Repair Svc ....G...... 662 755-2656
Bentonia *(G-210)*
Goff Steel Recting ....G...... 601 922-6014
Clinton *(G-823)*
▲ Great River Industries LLC ....G...... 601 442-7568
Natchez *(G-3564)*
H & H Metal Fabrication Inc ....G...... 662 489-4626
Belden *(G-189)*
Holifield Engineering Inc ....G...... 601 276-3391
Summit *(G-5015)*
Innovative Fabrications LLC..................G...... 601 485-1400
Meridian *(G-3353)*
Miscellaneous Steel Supply LLC ....G...... 662 494-0090
West Point *(G-5552)*
Mississippi Prison Inds Corp ....F...... 601 969-5760
Jackson *(G-2503)*
Nichols Stl Sls & Fabrication ....G...... 662 378-2723
Greenville *(G-1581)*
Resteel Express Inc ....F...... 601 795-6110
Poplarville *(G-4390)*
▲ Rockett Inc..................................C...... 601 939-9347
Flowood *(G-1393)*
T & J Machine ....G...... 601 795-0853
Poplarville *(G-4398)*

3451 Screw Machine Prdts

Automatic Machine Products Inc ....E...... 662 287-2467
Corinth *(G-1058)*
Cemco Inc..E...... 662 323-1559
Starkville *(G-4933)*
Rogers Automatic Screw Machine ....G...... 601 849-2431
Magee *(G-3184)*
Sudden Service Inc ....E...... 601 650-9600
Philadelphia *(G-4239)*

3452 Bolts, Nuts, Screws, Rivets & Washers

Amerimac Chemical Co ....G...... 601 918-8321
Jackson *(G-2328)*
B & B Pressure Wshg & Ldscpg............G...... 662 910-9105
Hernando *(G-2123)*
Grenada Fasteners Inc ....G...... 662 227-1000
Grenada *(G-1680)*
Illinois Tool Works Inc ....C...... 662 489-4151
Pontotoc *(G-4335)*
King Manufacturing Company Inc ....E...... 662 286-5504
Corinth *(G-1096)*
Southern Fastener Co Miss ....C...... 662 335-2157
Greenville *(G-1601)*

3462 Iron & Steel Forgings

Ceca LLC ....E...... 662 993-8880
Ripley *(G-4655)*
Creative Iron Works Ms LLC..................G...... 985 960-2386
Picayune *(G-4263)*
Eagle Specialty Products Inc ....E...... 662 796-7373
Southaven *(G-4870)*
South Central Group Inc ....G...... 601 445-5101
Natchez *(G-3623)*
Spearman Ornamental Ironworks ....G...... 901 301-7061
Horn Lake *(G-2212)*
Toyota Tsusho America Inc ....G...... 662 620-8890
Tupelo *(G-5240)*
Tremac Resteel Inc ....E...... 601 853-3123
Madison *(G-3161)*

3463 Nonferrous Forgings

Jpm of Mississippi Inc ....D...... 601 544-9950
Hattiesburg *(G-2004)*
Mueller Copper Fittings Co ....G...... 662 862-2181
Fulton *(G-1465)*
Toyota Tsusho America Inc ....G...... 662 620-8890
Tupelo *(G-5240)*

3465 Automotive Stampings

▲ Auto Parts Mfg Miss Inc ....B...... 662 365-3082
Guntown *(G-1898)*
Hago Automotive Corp ....F...... 662 593-0491
Iuka *(G-2293)*
Multicraft Intl Ltd Partnr ....G...... 601 854-5516
Pelahatchie *(G-4167)*
Tower Automotive Operations ....C...... 601 499-3300
Madison *(G-3160)*
Tower Automotive Operations ....G...... 601 678-4000
Meridian *(G-3415)*
▲ Unipres Southeast USA Inc..............C...... 601 469-0234
Forest *(G-1428)*

3469 Metal Stampings, NEC

Advance Tool and Die Inc ....G...... 601 939-1291
Pearl *(G-4104)*
▲ Columbus Marble Works Inc ....E...... 662 328-1477
Columbus *(G-950)*
Grenada Sales Management Inc ....C...... 662 226-1161
Grenada *(G-1682)*
Heavy Duty Industries Inc ....G...... 601 425-1011
Laurel *(G-2777)*
Hsm Solutions ....G...... 352 622-7583
Verona *(G-5333)*
Hunter Douglas Inc ....C...... 662 690-8190
Shannon *(G-4810)*
Ice Industries Inc ....E...... 419 842-3612
Grenada *(G-1686)*
Ice Industries Inc ....G...... 662 226-1161
Grenada *(G-1687)*
King Manufacturing Company Inc..........E...... 662 286-5504
Corinth *(G-1096)*
L & L Tool & Machine Co LLC ....G...... 662 335-1181
Greenville *(G-1563)*
Magnolia Tool & Mfg Co ....G...... 601 856-4333
Ridgeland *(G-4602)*
Magnolia Tool & Mfg Co ....G...... 601 856-4333
Ridgeland *(G-4603)*
Mayville Engineering Co Inc ....G...... 662 335-2325
Greenville *(G-1571)*
Mississppi Inds For The Blind ....E...... 601 693-5525
Meridian *(G-3373)*
Pk USA Inc ....E...... 662 301-4800
Senatobia *(G-4798)*
Production Machine & Tool Inc ....G...... 662 287-4752
Corinth *(G-1111)*
Southern Metals Co Miss Inc ....E...... 601 649-7475
Laurel *(G-2853)*
Taylor Rene ....G...... 601 977-8928
Jackson *(G-2604)*

Tylertown Wear Parts Inc ....E...... 601 876-4659
Tylertown *(G-5290)*

3471 Electroplating, Plating, Polishing, Anodizing & Coloring

ABB Installation Products Inc ....B...... 662 342-1545
Southaven *(G-4851)*
All That Glitters Ep Inc ....G...... 601 981-1947
Jackson *(G-2323)*
Automatic Plating Inc ....F...... 601 785-6923
Taylorsville *(G-5050)*
Bdm Industrial Services LLC..................G...... 662 549-3055
Columbus *(G-939)*
Columbus Roll Shop ....E...... 662 798-4149
Columbus *(G-952)*
Griffin Armor ....G...... 662 494-3421
West Point *(G-5545)*
Jackson Plating Co ....G...... 601 362-4623
Jackson *(G-2456)*
Process Engineering Co Inc ....E...... 601 981-4931
Jackson *(G-2551)*
R K Metals LLC....................................G...... 662 840-6060
Tupelo *(G-5213)*
Resurfacing Concepts Inc ....G...... 662 489-6867
Pontotoc *(G-4360)*
S Circle Inc ....D...... 601 792-4104
Newhebron *(G-3714)*
T & T Inc ....G...... 662 840-7500
Tupelo *(G-5237)*
Teikuro Corporation..............................G...... 601 482-0432
Meridian *(G-3412)*
Vibra Shine Inc ....G...... 601 785-9854
Taylorsville *(G-5061)*
Wheel Polishing Pros Inc ....G...... 601 259-9379
Mc Cool *(G-3238)*

3479 Coating & Engraving, NEC

Alley Kats Glass ....G...... 662 324-3002
Starkville *(G-4924)*
Amory Powder Coating LLC ....G...... 662 749-7081
Amory *(G-36)*
Applied Safety Coatings Inc ....G...... 601 940-3004
Raymond *(G-4483)*
Awards Unlimited..................................G...... 228 863-1814
Gulfport *(G-1730)*
Aztec Industries Inc ....F...... 601 939-8522
Richland *(G-4504)*
Azz Incorporated..................................F...... 228 475-0342
Moss Point *(G-3466)*
Boardtown Trading Post ....G...... 662 324-7296
Starkville *(G-4929)*
Booneville Industrial Coatings ....G...... 662 720-1147
Booneville *(G-321)*
Caston Creat & Coatings LLC................G...... 228 588-0055
Lucedale *(G-2987)*
Coastal Prtective Coatings LLC ....G...... 214 882-8036
Lucedale *(G-2988)*
Consolidated Pipe Supply......................G...... 228 396-8818
Biloxi *(G-233)*
Double G Coatings Company LP............D...... 601 371-3460
Jackson *(G-2389)*
Eddie Wiggs ....G...... 662 456-7080
Houston *(G-2239)*
Field Coatings LLC ....G...... 228 896-3535
Gulfport *(G-1786)*
Gulf Coast Protective Coating ....G...... 601 261-9862
Hattiesburg *(G-1978)*
Hunters Hollow Inc ....F...... 662 234-5945
Oxford *(G-3958)*
K D M Custom Coatings LLC ....F...... 662 842-9725
Tupelo *(G-5166)*
Monograms Plus ....G...... 662 327-3332
Columbus *(G-1007)*
New Process Steel LP..........................D...... 662 241-6582
Columbus *(G-1010)*
Okin America Inc ....D...... 662 566-1000
Shannon *(G-4817)*
Pierce Body Works ....G...... 601 939-1768
Jackson *(G-2663)*
Precoat Metals Inc ....G...... 601 372-0325
Jackson *(G-2549)*
Quality Coatings Oxford........................G...... 662 234-2944
Oxford *(G-3997)*
Resurfacing Concepts Inc.....................G...... 662 489-6867
Pontotoc *(G-4360)*
Systems Electro Coating LLC................D...... 601 407-2340
Madison *(G-3156)*
Tc Engraving & Gifts............................G...... 601 684-6834
McComb *(G-3270)*

242

2019 Harris Directory of
Mississippi Manufacturers

SIC SECTION
35 INDUSTRIAL AND COMMERCIAL MACHINERY AND COMPUTER EQUIPMENT

Tim Roark ....G...... 662 746-8871
Yazoo City (G-5651)

Trophy Shop ....G...... 662 236-3726
Oxford (G-4008)

Tupelo Engraving & Rbr Stamp ....G...... 662 842-0574
Tupelo (G-5246)

W E Birdsong Associates Inc ....G...... 601 939-7448
Florence (G-1337)

Wynnes Custom Coatings ....G...... 601 664-3474
Pearl (G-4159)

3482 Small Arms Ammunition

2a Armaments LLC ....G...... 662 538-8118
New Albany (G-3669)

JMS Manufacturing Inc ....G...... 601 514-0660
Lucedale (G-3005)

Mac LLC ....F...... 228 533-0157
Bay Saint Louis (G-149)

Olin Corporation ....G...... 662 513-2002
Oxford (G-3981)

Precision Rifle Ordnance LLC ....G...... 601 825-0697
Brandon (G-438)

Precision/Delta Corporation ....F...... 662 756-2810
Ruleville (G-4698)

3483 Ammunition, Large

Fianna Systems LLC....................G...... 662 726-5200
Macon (G-3061)

3484 Small Arms

2a Armaments LLC ....G...... 662 538-8118
New Albany (G-3669)

Dixie Precision Rifles LLC ....G...... 601 706-9100
Brandon (G-389)

Dsp Armory Inc ....G...... 662 862-4272
Fulton (G-1452)

Fianna Systems LLC....................G...... 662 726-5200
Macon (G-3061)

GI Armory LLC ....G...... 662 372-3389
Fulton (G-1454)

JMS Manufacturing Inc ....G...... 601 514-0660
Lucedale (G-3005)

John J Ishee ....G...... 601 847-2723
Mendenhall (G-3282)

Maa Global Supply Ltd ....F...... 662 816-4802
Oxford (G-3968)

Military Firearms Parts ....G...... 228 596-1271
Gulfport (G-1831)

Precision Rifle Ordnance LLC ....G...... 601 825-0697
Brandon (G-438)

Smiths Speed Shop ....G...... 601 794-2855
Purvis (G-4452)

Stringer Gun Works LLC ....G...... 601 947-6796
Lucedale (G-3019)

Sycpowersports ....G...... 662 301-1563
Senatobia (G-4803)

3489 Ordnance & Access, NEC

Panama Pump Company ....G...... 601 544-4251
Hattiesburg (G-2039)

Premier Shooting Solutions LLC.......G...... 601 297-5778
Madison (G-3142)

Robert E Monk ....G...... 662 562-8729
Senatobia (G-4800)

3491 Industrial Valves

First Class Fire Prtection LLC ....G...... 901 350-0499
Horn Lake (G-2199)

ITT Engineered Valves LLC...........F...... 662 256-7185
Amory (G-44)

Parker-Hannifin Corporation...........C...... 601 856-4123
Madison (G-3137)

Southern Marketing Group ....G...... 601 664-3880
Jackson (G-2667)

▲ Wey Valve Inc ....F...... 662 963-2020
Shannon (G-4822)

3492 Fluid Power Valves & Hose Fittings

Applied Indus Tech - Dixie Inc ....G...... 601 649-4312
Laurel (G-2731)

Dahls Automotive Parts Inc ....G...... 228 875-8154
Ocean Springs (G-3751)

Hattiesburg Hydraulics Sls Svc........G...... 601 264-6606
Hattiesburg (G-1986)

Maximum Auto Parts & Supply ....F...... 228 863-1100
Gulfport (G-1825)

Parker-Hannifin Corporation...........C...... 601 856-4123
Madison (G-3137)

Rubber & Specialties Inc ....G...... 228 762-6103
Pascagoula (G-4065)

Specialty Hose Fabrication Inc........G...... 228 831-1919
Gulfport (G-1877)

Tucker Machine Services ....G...... 601 582-4280
Hattiesburg (G-2075)

3493 Steel Springs, Except Wire

Deep S Suspension & ACC Inc........G...... 601 371-7373
Jackson (G-2378)

Matthew Warren Inc ....D...... 662 489-7846
Pontotoc (G-4344)

Matthew Warren Inc ....G...... 574 753-6622
Pontotoc (G-4345)

Quality Steel & Supply LLC ....F...... 601 731-1222
Columbia (G-913)

Union Spring & Mfg Corp ....D...... 662 489-7846
Pontotoc (G-4366)

3494 Valves & Pipe Fittings, NEC

Consolidated Pipe & Sup Co Inc ......F...... 228 769-1920
Pascagoula (G-4028)

▲ Mississippi Forge (pvf) Inc ....E...... 662 285-2995
Ackerman (G-27)

Mueller Copper Fittings Co ....E...... 662 862-2181
Fulton (G-1465)

Parker-Hannifin Corporation...........C...... 601 856-4123
Madison (G-3137)

RPM Piping and Supply LLC...........G...... 901 633-6083
Southaven (G-4897)

United Assoc Journeymen & 5 ....G...... 228 863-1853
Gulfport (G-1889)

3495 Wire Springs

Fibrix LLC ....G...... 662 568-3393
Houlka (G-2222)

Leggett & Platt Incorporated..........G...... 662 842-5704
Tupelo (G-5175)

Matthew Warren Inc ....D...... 662 489-7846
Pontotoc (G-4344)

3496 Misc Fabricated Wire Prdts

Acco Brands USA LLC ....G...... 800 541-0094
Booneville (G-314)

Frontier Contracting LLC ....G...... 662 809-1949
Grenada (G-1678)

Johnsons Fencing ....G...... 601 833-3263
Brookhaven (G-505)

Kdeb Manufacturing LLC ....G...... 601 750-9659
Morton (G-3448)

▲ Nhc Distributors Inc ....E...... 601 656-7911
Philadelphia (G-4229)

Partridge Ornamental Iron Inc ....E...... 601 693-4021
Meridian (G-3380)

Passons Specialized Services.........G...... 601 939-3722
Jackson (G-2661)

Ripley Industries Inc ....E...... 662 423-6733
Iuka (G-2307)

Saf T Cart Inc ....E...... 662 624-6492
Clarksdale (G-782)

Southern Gate Twr Fabricators ......G...... 601 483-6710
Collinsville (G-876)

Steel Service Corporation ....C...... 601 939-9222
Jackson (G-2668)

◆ Voith Fabrics Florence Inc.........C...... 601 845-2202
Florence (G-1336)

▲ Webster - Portalloy Chains Inc ......G...... 419 447-8232
Meridian (G-3419)

Wildlife Dominion MGT LLC..........G...... 662 272-9550
Crawford (G-1131)

3498 Fabricated Pipe & Pipe Fittings

Babcock & Wilcox Company ....C...... 662 494-1323
West Point (G-5537)

Cemco Inc ....E...... 662 323-1559
Starkville (G-4933)

Dmi Pipe Fabrication LLC ....F...... 225 272-1420
Woodville (G-5616)

◆ Electro National Corporation........G...... 601 859-5511
Canton (G-657)

Fabricated Pipe Inc ....F...... 601 684-3007
Fernwood (G-1304)

J & A Mechanical Inc ....G...... 662 890-4565
Olive Branch (G-3853)

Lokring Gulf Coast LLC...............G...... 228 497-0091
Gautier (G-1497)

Modine Grenada LLC...................B...... 662 229-4000
Grenada (G-1694)

▲ Mueller Castings Co ....G...... 662 862-7200
Fulton (G-1464)

Process Mechanical Eqp Co ....G...... 601 291-4082
Ridgeland (G-4621)

Quality Pipe & Fabrication LLC ....G...... 662 321-8542
Blue Springs (G-299)

Thomasvlle Mtal Fbricators Inc ....E...... 662 526-9900
Como (G-1052)

True Temper Sports Inc ....B...... 662 256-5605
Amory (G-57)

Upchurch Industrial LLC ....D...... 662 453-6680
Horn Lake (G-2214)

3499 Fabricated Metal Prdts, NEC

Allens Trophies Inc ....E...... 601 582-7702
Hattiesburg (G-1920)

▲ Anchor Works ....G...... 601 264-8700
Hattiesburg (G-1923)

Bad Moon Customs ....G...... 601 520-7248
Hattiesburg (G-1925)

Battlebells LLC ....G...... 662 312-5901
Starkville (G-4927)

Buy A Barricade LLC ....G...... 228 355-0146
Ocean Springs (G-3744)

Elims Art Cncpts & Dcrtv Dsgn ....G...... 601 540-4810
Jackson (G-2398)

▲ Faurecia Mdson Auto Sating Inc ....C...... 601 407-2200
Madison (G-3098)

Filing and Storage Miss LLC..........G...... 601 397-6452
Ridgeland (G-4580)

▼ Griffin Inc ....D...... 662 838-2128
Byhalia (G-586)

H & H Metal Fabrication Inc ....G...... 662 489-4626
Belden (G-189)

Inline Barricades Met Pdts Inc.........G...... 800 229-4790
Pass Christian (G-4090)

River Road Welding Inc ....G...... 601 947-2511
Lucedale (G-3016)

Robertson Fabrication Inc ....F...... 662 453-1551
Greenwood (G-1648)

Sun-Air Products Incorporated ....E...... 662 454-9577
Belmont (G-202)

Unique Services LLC ....G...... 601 326-9912
Jackson (G-2616)

35 INDUSTRIAL AND COMMERCIAL MACHINERY AND COMPUTER EQUIPMENT

3511 Steam, Gas & Hydraulic Turbines & Engines

GE Wind Energy LLC...................C...... 662 892-2900
Olive Branch (G-3842)

Vertex Manufacturing Corp ....G...... 662 895-6263
Olive Branch (G-3920)

3519 Internal Combustion Engines, NEC

Bg3 Delta LLC ....G...... 601 636-9828
Vicksburg (G-5344)

Christians Automotive Machine ....G...... 662 287-4500
Corinth (G-1070)

J & H Turbo Service Inc ....G...... 662 378-8715
Greenville (G-1558)

▼ Kennedy Engine Company Inc ......F...... 228 392-2200
Biloxi (G-256)

Kennedy Marine Inc ....G...... 228 214-4392
Gulfport (G-1817)

Kohler Co ....B...... 601 582-3555
Hattiesburg (G-2009)

Mdh Marine Art ....G...... 228 769-1692
Pascagoula (G-4053)

P & B Enterprises Inc ....G...... 662 323-8565
Starkville (G-4965)

Paccar Engine Company ....G...... 662 329-6700
Columbus (G-1014)

◆ Paccar Engine Company ....G...... 425 468-7400
Columbus (G-1015)

TWI Inc ....G...... 601 736-1783
Columbia (G-927)

3523 Farm Machinery & Eqpt

Aerway Manufacturing Co ....G...... 662 726-4246
Macon (G-3054)

Ag Spray Equipment Inc ....G...... 662 453-4524
Greenwood (G-1610)

▲ Air + Mak Industries Inc............F...... 662 893-3444
Olive Branch (G-3809)

Employee Codes: A=Over 500 employees, B=251-500
C=101-250, D=51-100, E=20-50, F=10-19, G=1-9

2019 Harris Directory of
Mississippi Manufacturers

243

35 INDUSTRIAL AND COMMERCIAL MACHINERY AND COMPUTER EQUIPMENT

Amco Manufacturing Company LLC.....E....... 662 746-4464
Yazoo City *(G-5621)*

▲ Atlas Manufacturing Co Inc.............E....... 662 652-3900
Tremont *(G-5091)*

Autoflow LLC..G....... 601 853-1021
Madison *(G-3079)*

Bell Equipment LLC.............................E....... 662 265-5841
Inverness *(G-2273)*

Bell Inc...E....... 662 265-5841
Inverness *(G-2274)*

▲ Bigbee Metal Manufacturing Co ....E....... 662 652-3372
Tremont *(G-5092)*

Brooks Farms Inc...............................G....... 662 299-8780
Schlater *(G-4769)*

Cases Cntrpint Hnting CLB Inc ....G....... 601 734-2373
Smithdale *(G-4841)*

▲ CG&p Manufacturing Inc..................E....... 662 746-4464
Yazoo City *(G-5627)*

◆ Circle S Irrigation Inc ....F....... 662 627-7246
Clarksdale *(G-761)*

Evergreen AG Envmtl & Turf LLC ....F....... 662 263-4419
Mathiston *(G-3229)*

Flautt Farms ....F....... 662 375-2116
Webb *(G-5519)*

H & H Chief Sales Inc........................E....... 601 267-9643
Carthage *(G-716)*

Harold Knight Sew Mchs & Appls ....G....... 601 425-2220
Laurel *(G-2775)*

◆ Hol-Mac Corporation........................C....... 601 764-4121
Bay Springs *(G-162)*

▲ Howse Implement Company Inc.......C....... 601 428-0841
Laurel *(G-2782)*

▲ Kbh Corporation..............................C....... 662 624-5471
Clarksdale *(G-770)*

Knr Farm Supplies Inc.......................G....... 228 574-8397
Lumberton *(G-3035)*

Mc Comb Welding & Mch Works ....G....... 601 684-1921
McComb *(G-3258)*

Mississippi Center For Freedom ....G....... 601 638-0962
Vicksburg *(G-5395)*

▲ Monroe-Tufline Mfg Co Inc ....E....... 662 328-8347
Columbus *(G-1008)*

Oneida Farms Partnership ....G....... 901 652-4182
Olive Branch *(G-3890)*

Rodgers Sales Company.....................G....... 662 902-1664
Clarksdale *(G-780)*

Sanders Seed ....G....... 800 844-5533
Cleveland *(G-808)*

Sarah Case-Price ....G....... 601 818-4377
Hattiesburg *(G-2055)*

▲ Short Line Manufacturing Co............G....... 662 754-6858
Shaw *(G-4825)*

Southern Application MGT...................G....... 662 578-4684
Batesville *(G-125)*

Superior Mulch Inc.............................G....... 772 878-5220
Soso *(G-4848)*

▲ Techno-Catch LLC ....G....... 662 289-1631
Kosciusko *(G-2717)*

▲ Warren Inc......................................C....... 601 765-8221
Collins *(G-865)*

Welborn Devices LLC.........................G....... 601 428-5912
Laurel *(G-2872)*

West Farms Inc ....G....... 601 277-3579
Hazlehurst *(G-2109)*

Wicker Machine Co ....F....... 662 827-5434
Hollandale *(G-2169)*

3524 Garden, Lawn Tractors & Eqpt

Bob Ladd & Associates Inc.................G....... 601 859-7250
Canton *(G-649)*

Cook Lawn & Tractor LLC....................G....... 601 445-0718
Natchez *(G-3550)*

Delta Farm & Auto LLC.......................G....... 662 453-8340
Greenwood *(G-1619)*

▲ Lund Coating Technologies Inc.........E....... 662 252-2340
Holly Springs *(G-2182)*

◆ Maxim Holding Company Inc ....E....... 601 625-7471
Sebastopol *(G-4774)*

Mtd Products Inc................................A....... 662 566-2332
Tupelo *(G-5191)*

Oligarch Inc.......................................G....... 844 321-0016
Houston *(G-2253)*

Paul Garner Motors LLC......................G....... 601 785-4924
Taylorsville *(G-5056)*

Worthen Bros Coastal Lawn ....G....... 228 261-4785
Gulfport *(G-1895)*

3531 Construction Machinery & Eqpt

Apac-Mississippi Inc ....D....... 601 376-4000
Richland *(G-4501)*

Apac-Mississippi Inc ....G....... 601 376-4000
Richland *(G-4502)*

Around Clock Recovery ....G....... 662 455-1008
Greenwood *(G-1613)*

B&Z Sales Inc....................................G....... 601 825-1900
Brandon *(G-368)*

Bell Inc...E....... 662 265-5841
Inverness *(G-2274)*

▼ Best Equipment Tech Inc ....E....... 601 795-2208
Poplarville *(G-4376)*

Big River Shipbuilders Inc ....G....... 601 802-9994
Vicksburg *(G-5346)*

Big River Shipbuilders Inc ....G....... 601 636-9161
Vicksburg *(G-5345)*

Bonds Company Inc............................E....... 601 376-4000
Richland *(G-4507)*

Bowen Titus......................................G....... 662 327-3084
Steens *(G-4990)*

Brandi Bonner ....G....... 601 906-7224
Mendenhall *(G-3279)*

▲ Caterpillar ....G....... 662 286-1274
Corinth *(G-1065)*

Caterpillar Dev Ctr Inc ....G....... 228 385-3900
Biloxi *(G-226)*

Caterpillar Inc ....C....... 662 720-2400
Booneville *(G-324)*

Caterpillar Inc ....A....... 662 286-5511
Corinth *(G-1068)*

Chambers Delimbinator Inc ....C....... 662 285-2777
Ackerman *(G-23)*

Cooperation Jackson LLC ....F....... 601 355-7224
Jackson *(G-2368)*

Crabtree Manufacturing Inc ....F....... 662 746-3041
Yazoo City *(G-5629)*

D & T Motors Inc ....G....... 662 773-5021
Louisville *(G-2965)*

Duraco Inc ....E....... 601 932-2100
Pearl *(G-4115)*

Eyesore Yrd Cleanup & Bushogng ....G....... 205 391-8232
Kosciusko *(G-2693)*

Grady Morrow ....G....... 769 230-6226
Jackson *(G-2428)*

◆ Hol-Mac Corporation........................C....... 601 764-4121
Bay Springs *(G-162)*

Holland Grading Service ....G....... 601 825-2364
Brandon *(G-406)*

James Rachal ....G....... 601 442-1460
Church Hill *(G-754)*

Jj Merchant ....G....... 601 596-4430
Purvis *(G-4442)*

Kdeb Manufacturing LLC ....G....... 601 750-9659
Morton *(G-3448)*

▲ Ktsu America LLC ....F....... 601 506-8148
Canton *(G-665)*

L M & R Service Inc...........................G....... 601 892-3034
Crystal Springs *(G-1146)*

◆ Mathis Plow Inc ....F....... 662 323-5600
Starkville *(G-4957)*

▲ Maymar Marine Supply Inc ....G....... 228 762-2241
Pascagoula *(G-4052)*

Pace Brothers Inc ....G....... 601 736-9225
Columbia *(G-910)*

Precious Creative Caterpillars.............G....... 228 424-3500
Gulfport *(G-1851)*

Prestige Cnstr & Land Svcs LLC..........G....... 228 861-1292
Gulfport *(G-1852)*

Reuben Allred ....G....... 601 734-2801
Bogue Chitto *(G-304)*

Richard Fick ....G....... 601 848-7420
State Line *(G-4988)*

Roadsafe Traffic Systems Inc..............G....... 601 922-5009
Jackson *(G-2568)*

Southeastern Concrete Co Inc ....E....... 601 545-7811
Hattiesburg *(G-2058)*

Southeastern Concrete Co Inc ....E....... 601 544-7000
Hattiesburg *(G-2059)*

Southern Land Solutions LLC ....G....... 601 622-8581
Terry *(G-5077)*

Stockstill Land Dev LLC......................G....... 601 273-2409
Poplarville *(G-4396)*

Sweet Treats and Coffee Too ....G....... 662 286-5511
Corinth *(G-1121)*

Terex Corporation ....C....... 662 393-1800
Southaven *(G-4913)*

Thompson Dozer & Gravel...................G....... 601 835-2406
Wesson *(G-5530)*

Washington County Wide Shop ....D....... 662 334-4322
Greenville *(G-1608)*

West Backhoe Inc ....G....... 662 566-7828
Tupelo *(G-5256)*

White Septic Backhoe LLC ....G....... 662 251-8989
Steens *(G-4992)*

Wicker Machine Co ....F....... 662 827-5434
Hollandale *(G-2169)*

3532 Mining Machinery & Eqpt

Glenn Mch Works Crane Rigging ....G....... 601 544-1275
Petal *(G-4186)*

Rogers Machine ....G....... 601 876-4476
Tylertown *(G-5284)*

Screw Conveyor Corporation ....C....... 662 283-3142
Winona *(G-5606)*

◆ Syntron Material Handling LLC.........C....... 662 869-5711
Saltillo *(G-4721)*

Syntron Mtl Hdlg Group LLC ....C....... 662 869-5711
Saltillo *(G-4722)*

3533 Oil Field Machinery & Eqpt

Brock Bit Co Inc.................................G....... 601 876-4237
Tylertown *(G-5266)*

Browning Oil Tools Inc ....E....... 601 442-1800
Natchez *(G-3540)*

▲ Chevron Corporation........................C....... 228 938-4600
Pascagoula *(G-4025)*

Friede Goldman Delaware Inc..............G....... 228 896-0029
Gulfport *(G-1789)*

Global Vessel Tank ....G....... 601 649-5300
Laurel *(G-2772)*

Harbison-Fischer Inc ....G....... 601 428-7919
Ellisville *(G-1257)*

P Delta Inc..E....... 601 403-8100
Poplarville *(G-4387)*

Pawn Investments Inc ....G....... 601 649-4059
Laurel *(G-2817)*

Pressure Control ....G....... 601 342-8051
Laurel *(G-2826)*

Psp Industries Inc ....G....... 662 423-2033
Iuka *(G-2306)*

Q P P Inc...G....... 662 356-4848
Caledonia *(G-629)*

Robine & Welch Machine & TI Co.........E....... 601 428-1545
Laurel *(G-2838)*

Trico Industries Inc............................G....... 601 649-4467
Laurel *(G-2859)*

Unified Brands Inc ....F....... 888 994-7636
Jackson *(G-2615)*

3534 Elevators & Moving Stairways

Midsouth Elevator LLC ....G....... 601 353-8283
Jackson *(G-2491)*

Thyssenkrupp Elevator Corp................C....... 662 223-4025
Walnut *(G-5458)*

3535 Conveyors & Eqpt

BSK Resources LLC............................G....... 662 842-4716
Belden *(G-187)*

Chads LLC ....G....... 601 919-3113
Brandon *(G-378)*

Chuck Jennings ....G....... 601 668-5704
Raymond *(G-4486)*

Conveyor Tech ....F....... 901 831-4760
Lyon *(G-3042)*

Esco Group LLC ....G....... 601 683-3192
Newton *(G-3720)*

▼ Essmueller Company ....D....... 601 649-2400
Laurel *(G-2767)*

Havard Mfg Inc ....G....... 601 766-9170
Lucedale *(G-3000)*

Metal-Tech Fabricators Inc..................F....... 662 622-0400
Coldwater *(G-849)*

Metso Minerals Industries Inc..............D....... 662 627-5292
Clarksdale *(G-774)*

North Miss Conveyor Co Inc ....G....... 662 236-1000
Oxford *(G-3977)*

Raymond Mucillo Jr............................G....... 662 429-8976
Nesbit *(G-3656)*

Screw Conveyor Corporation ....C....... 662 283-3142
Winona *(G-5606)*

Tri County Sheet Metal & Wldg.............G....... 601 939-0803
Pearl *(G-4153)*

Webster Industry Inc ....G....... 601 482-0183
Meridian *(G-3420)*

3536 Hoists, Cranes & Monorails

Blue Bayou Boat Lifts Inc ....G....... 601 798-0659
Carriere *(G-688)*

Cannon Boat Lifts LLC ....G....... 601 540-8691
Madison *(G-3087)*

35 INDUSTRIAL AND COMMERCIAL MACHINERY AND COMPUTER EQUIPMENT

3537 Indl Trucks, Tractors, Trailers & Stackers

Arrow Material Services LLC ....G....... 601 939-3113
Richland (G-4503)

Black Diamond Construction LLC........G...... 228 342-2742
Kiln (G-2678)

Bumper To Bumper ....G...... 601 928-5603
Wiggins (G-5575)

Caterpillar Inc ....F...... 662 284-5143
Corinth (G-1067)

▲ Chrisman Manufacturing Inc ....E...... 228 864-6293
Long Beach (G-2931)

Forklift LLC ....G...... 813 527-4093
Tupelo (G-5137)

Forklift LLC ....G...... 662 255-2581
Tupelo (G-5138)

Four Star Trucking Company LLC........G...... 662 429-5397
Hernando (G-2131)

Ground Support Specialist LLC ....E...... 662 342-1412
Horn Lake (G-2201)

Gunns Transport Services LLC ....G...... 662 402-3586
Shaw (G-4824)

Harper Timber Inc ....E...... 601 833-2121
Brookhaven (G-499)

Hayes Transportation LLC ....G...... 662 582-5357
Durant (G-1226)

Hunter Engineering Company ....C...... 662 653-3194
Durant (G-1227)

L&E Logistics LLC ....G...... 877 884-8889
McComb (G-3257)

Lawrence A Witherspoon ....G...... 662 404-5859
Horn Lake (G-2205)

Leas Repair...G...... 662 658-4462
Minter City (G-3424)

MERR Express LLC ....G...... 601 327-1554
Lucedale (G-3011)

Nmhg Financial Services ....G...... 601 304-0112
Natchez (G-3601)

Rak-Master LLC ....G...... 601 906-1039
Brandon (G-443)

Rcl Components Inc ....E...... 662 449-0401
Hernando (G-2152)

▲ Rockett Inc ....C...... 601 939-9347
Flowood (G-1393)

Saf T Cart Inc ....E...... 662 624-6492
Clarksdale (G-782)

Screw Conveyor Corporation ....C...... 662 283-3142
Winona (G-5606)

▼ Smith Transportation Eqp Inc ....E...... 662 838-4486
Byhalia (G-604)

Triple J of Mississippi Inc ....G...... 662 624-4630
Clarksdale (G-784)

U S Metal Works Inc ....E...... 601 657-4676
Liberty (G-2919)

Wallace Express Freight Inc ....F...... 662 890-3080
Olive Branch (G-3922)

Watson Tj Property LLC ....G...... 601 527-3587
Meridian (G-3418)

Z A Construction LLC ....F...... 601 259-5276
Mendenhall (G-3291)

Zero Dead Miles LLC ....G...... 769 208-8082
Jackson (G-2640)

3541 Machine Tools: Cutting

Accurate Edge.......................................G...... 228 832-2920
Gulfport (G-1715)

Cerbide Inc ....F...... 228 871-7123
Gulfport (G-1749)

Electro Mech Solutions Ems Inc ....G...... 601 631-0138
Vicksburg (G-5365)

Freeman Milling LLC..............................F...... 601 733-5444
Mize (G-3426)

M & M Milling Inc ....G...... 601 823-4630
Brookhaven (G-513)

Metalworx LLC ....G...... 228 806-9112
Biloxi (G-268)

Precision Metalworks Inc ....G...... 662 838-4605
Byhalia (G-598)

Production Machine & Tool Inc ....G...... 662 287-4752
Corinth (G-1111)

3542 Machine Tools: Forming

▲ Developmental Industries Inc ....E...... 662 287-6626
Corinth (G-1083)

Southeast Supply Header ....G...... 601 947-9842
Lucedale (G-3017)

▲ Standard Industrial Corp ....D...... 662 624-2436
Clarksdale (G-783)

Union Spring & Mfg Corp ....D...... 662 489-7846
Pontotoc (G-4366)

3543 Industrial Patterns

JI Browne Inc ....G...... 228 216-1137
Kiln (G-2681)

3544 Dies, Tools, Jigs, Fixtures & Indl Molds

American Stamping Corporation...........G...... 662 895-5300
Olive Branch (G-3813)

Amerimac Machining Corporation ....G...... 601 940-7919
Jackson (G-2329)

Baldwyn Tool and Die Co ....G...... 662 365-8665
Baldwyn (G-72)

Boyle Tool & Die Inc ....G...... 662 846-0640
Boyle (G-348)

Charles On Call Mold Removal ....G...... 662 352-8009
Meridian (G-3319)

Davis Tool & Die Inc ....F...... 662 234-4007
Abbeville (G-2)

▲ Developmental Industries Inc ....E...... 662 287-6626
Corinth (G-1083)

Dixie Dies Inc ....G...... 601 845-6029
Harrisville (G-1911)

Edge Tools and Designs Inc ....G...... 662 578-0363
Batesville (G-105)

Euro American Plastics Inc ....F...... 601 879-0360
Flora (G-1305)

Green Mold Die & Fixtures Inc ....F...... 601 879-8166
Flora (G-1308)

Hoffinger Industries ....G...... 662 890-7930
Southaven (G-4877)

Holmes Industries LLC ....G...... 601 635-4409
Decatur (G-1173)

Industrial Steel Rule Die Corp ....G...... 601 932-5555
Jackson (G-2649)

Jaken Industries...................................G...... 662 289-7510
Kosciusko (G-2696)

Jims Tool & Die Inc ....F...... 662 895-3287
Olive Branch (G-3856)

JMS Manufacturing Inc ....G...... 601 514-0660
Lucedale (G-3005)

Magnolia Tool & Mfg Co ....G...... 601 856-4333
Ridgeland (G-4602)

Metal Products of Corinth Inc................G...... 662 287-3625
Corinth (G-1101)

Nichols Mold Shop ....G...... 662 282-7560
Mantachie (G-3202)

Pro Tool Inc ....G...... 662 282-4419
Mantachie (G-3203)

Production Machine & Tool Inc ....G...... 662 287-4752
Corinth (G-1111)

Stevens Machine & Tool Inc..................G...... 662 728-6005
Marietta (G-3218)

Suburban Plastics Co ....D...... 662 227-1911
Grenada (G-1705)

Tokins Inc ....G...... 601 939-1093
Pearl (G-4152)

Tombigbee Tooling Inc ....G...... 662 282-4273
Mantachie (G-3208)

Tool Tek LLC ....G...... 937 399-4333
Wiggins (G-5592)

Traceway Engineering and Mfg ....F...... 662 489-1314
Pontotoc (G-4364)

Trulite GL Alum Solutions LLC ....E...... 662 226-5551
Grenada (G-1711)

Virgil Williams LLC ....G...... 662 287-7734
Corinth (G-1127)

Williams Prcsion Machining LLC ....G...... 662 287-7734
Corinth (G-1129)

3545 Machine Tool Access

J A C Industrial Tl & Sup LLC ....G...... 601 591-1321
Brandon (G-408)

▲ Lunati LLC ....E...... 662 892-1518
Olive Branch (G-3868)

Novelty Machine Works Inc ....F...... 601 948-2075
Jackson (G-2524)

William Zaremba ....G...... 601 845-7238
Florence (G-1339)

3546 Power Hand Tools

B & L International Inc ....G...... 601 261-5127
Purvis (G-4434)

Barnetts Small Engines ....G...... 662 323-8993
Starkville (G-4926)

Garys Small Engine ....G...... 601 545-7355
Hattiesburg (G-1974)

H & H Small Engine Repair ....G...... 662 423-2741
Iuka (G-2292)

Hartley Equipment Company Inc ....G...... 601 499-0944
Canton (G-661)

Hurley Farm & Feed ....G...... 228 588-9156
Hurley (G-2260)

J and E Enterprises ....G...... 662 369-7324
Aberdeen (G-15)

Martin Incorporated ....G...... 662 720-2445
Booneville (G-334)

Michael Williamson ....G...... 601 736-9156
Columbia (G-906)

Milwaukee Electric Tool Corp ....B...... 601 969-3033
Jackson (G-2495)

Milwaukee Electric Tool Corp ....B...... 662 451-5545
Greenwood (G-1640)

Milwaukee Electric Tool Corp ....C...... 662 895-4560
Olive Branch (G-3879)

Nichols Saw Service ....F...... 662 842-2129
Tupelo (G-5192)

Power Plus Inc ....F...... 601 264-1950
Sumrall (G-5042)

Robbys Small Engine & Saw Repr ....G...... 601 847-0323
Mendenhall (G-3287)

Robine & Welch Machine & Tl Co...........G...... 601 428-1545
Laurel (G-2838)

3547 Rolling Mill Machinery & Eqpt

Azz Incorporated ....F...... 228 475-0342
Moss Point (G-3466)

3548 Welding Apparatus

Greenville Metal Works Inc ....E...... 662 335-8510
Greenville (G-1555)

Outback Industries LLC ....F...... 662 591-5100
Nettleton (G-3666)

Powerline Tags Inc ....G...... 228 760-3072
Gulfport (G-1850)

Saf T Cart Inc ....E...... 662 624-6492
Clarksdale (G-782)

3549 Metalworking Machinery, NEC

Hunter Engineering Company ....C...... 662 653-3194
Durant (G-1227)

Met-Tech Corp ....G...... 601 693-0061
Meridian (G-3370)

Ormans Welding & Fab Inc ....F...... 662 494-9471
West Point (G-5556)

3552 Textile Machinery

Brenda Ruth Designs LLC ....G...... 601 708-4227
Clinton (G-815)

D&J Twine Co ....G...... 662 726-2594
Macon (G-3056)

JP Williams Machine & Fabricat ....G...... 228 474-1099
Pascagoula (G-4042)

Magnolia Sewing Center ....G...... 601 261-9006
Hattiesburg (G-2019)

◆ Mitchell Signs Inc ....D...... 601 553-1557
Meridian (G-3374)

Shirtz Stuff...G...... 601 729-2472
Laurel (G-2848)

United Plastic Molders Inc ....E...... 601 353-3193
Jackson (G-2618)

3553 Woodworking Machinery

Delta Fabricators..................................G...... 662 862-2998
Fulton (G-1451)

Goodings Fine Woodworking ....G...... 228 255-9037
Pass Christian (G-4085)

Helanbak LLC ....G...... 601 736-6112
Foxworth (G-1431)

King Manufacturing Company Inc...........E...... 662 286-5504
Corinth (G-1096)

Pierce Cnstr & Maint Co Inc ....D...... 601 544-1321
Petal (G-4196)

Pioneer Machinery and Sup Inc ....F...... 662 286-5646
Corinth (G-1110)

Stringer Industries Inc ....E...... 601 876-3376
Tylertown (G-5286)

3555 Printing Trades Machinery & Eqpt

Cedotal Inc ....G...... 601 605-2660
Ridgeland (G-4561)

Ray Brooks Enterprises ....G...... 662 342-0555
Southaven (G-4895)

Employee Codes: A=Over 500 employees, B=251-500
C=101-250, D=51-100, E=20-50, F=10-19, G=1-9

35 INDUSTRIAL AND COMMERCIAL MACHINERY AND COMPUTER EQUIPMENT

3556 Food Prdts Machinery

Baader North America Corp ....G 662 887-5841
  Indianola *(G-2262)*
Blaylocks Wild Game Processing ....G 601 894-0087
  Hazlehurst *(G-2090)*
Electro Mech Solutions Ems Inc ....G 601 631-0138
  Vicksburg *(G-5365)*
Lamonts Food Products Inc ....G 662 838-3431
  Byhalia *(G-588)*
Leonard Metal Fabricators Inc ....E 601 936-4994
  Pearl *(G-4129)*
Marel USA Inc ....G 662 686-2269
  Leland *(G-2890)*
Pearl River Foods LLC ....G 678 343-3265
  Carthage *(G-721)*
▲ Robot-Coupe Inc USA ....E 601 898-8411
  Ridgeland *(G-4624)*
Southern Hens Inc ....A 601 582-2262
  Moselle *(G-3460)*
Standex International Corp ....F 662 534-9061
  New Albany *(G-3699)*
Standex International Corp ....B 662 534-9061
  New Albany *(G-3700)*
Vans Deer Processing Inc ....E 601 825-9087
  Brandon *(G-470)*
Welborn Devices LLC ....G 601 428-5912
  Laurel *(G-2872)*

3559 Special Ind Machinery, NEC

Accusteer LLC ....G 601 483-0225
  Meridian *(G-3294)*
Beavers Enterprises ....G 601 569-1557
  Picayune *(G-4256)*
Big Creek Gin Company Inc ....E 662 624-5233
  Lyon *(G-3041)*
Champion Chemical Company LLC .....G 601 720-8908
  Ruleville *(G-4696)*
Comet Street Inc ....F 601 981-4151
  Jackson *(G-2362)*
▲ Crane Cams Inc ....E 386 310-4875
  Olive Branch *(G-3831)*
Curbell Plastics Inc ....D 888 477-8173
  Brandon *(G-384)*
Dogwood Ceramic Supply Inc ....G 228 831-4848
  Gulfport *(G-1773)*
▲ Fab Products ....G 228 324-4133
  Ocean Springs *(G-3756)*
Galvian Group LLC ....G 662 374-1027
  Greenwood *(G-1624)*
Gulf States Silver ....G 601 415-4365
  Vicksburg *(G-5375)*
◆ Hol-Mac Corporation ....C 601 764-4121
  Bay Springs *(G-162)*
Hunter Engineering Company ....C 601 857-8883
  Raymond *(G-4489)*
◆ JT Shannon Lumber Co Inc ....E 662 393-3765
  Horn Lake *(G-2203)*
L & W Print Finishers LLC ....G 662 890-0505
  Olive Branch *(G-3862)*
Norton Equipment Company ....F 662 838-7900
  Byhalia *(G-593)*
▲ Pascagoula Refinery ....G 228 938-4563
  Pascagoula *(G-4060)*
Peppers Machine & Wldg Co Inc ....E 601 833-3038
  Brookhaven *(G-522)*
Puckett Allen B Jr & Family ....G 662 328-4931
  Columbus *(G-1018)*
Southern Diversified Products ....G 601 271-2588
  Hattiesburg *(G-2060)*
Ustx Contract Services NC Inc ....E 512 894-0008
  Corinth *(G-1126)*
Williamson Gin Repair ....G 662 571-6084
  Yazoo City *(G-5652)*

3561 Pumps & Pumping Eqpt

Browning Oil Tools Inc ....E 601 442-1800
  Natchez *(G-3540)*
BSC Sales LLC ....G 662 890-1079
  Olive Branch *(G-3821)*
Eaton Aerospace LLC ....E 601 981-2811
  Jackson *(G-2396)*
▼ Fast Flow Pumps ....G 228 475-2468
  Moss Point *(G-3477)*
Gravel Equipment & Supply Inc ....G 662 256-2052
  Amory *(G-43)*
Harbison-Fischer Inc ....G 601 442-7961
  Natchez *(G-3567)*
Luckett Pump & Well Svc Inc ....G 662 624-2398
  Dublin *(G-1219)*

◆ National Pump Co LLC ....E 662 895-1110
  Olive Branch *(G-3885)*
Panama Pump Company ....G 601 544-4251
  Hattiesburg *(G-2039)*
Parish Pumps and Machine Inc ....G 662 256-2052
  Amory *(G-51)*
▲ Xylem Water Solutions Usa ....F 662 393-0275
  Southaven *(G-4921)*

3562 Ball & Roller Bearings

Casters Den ....G 662 593-3214
  Iuka *(G-2286)*
Jpm of Mississippi Inc ....D 601 544-9950
  Hattiesburg *(G-2004)*

3563 Air & Gas Compressors

Compressed Air Tech Inc ....G 662 890-9782
  Olive Branch *(G-3827)*
Tecumseh Products Company ....G 662 566-2231
  Verona *(G-5336)*
▲ Wood Industries Inc ....E 662 454-0005
  Belmont *(G-203)*

3564 Blowers & Fans

▼ Collins Filter Co Inc ....F 228 896-0582
  Gulfport *(G-1762)*
Filter Service Mississippi LLC ....G 601 693-4614
  Meridian *(G-3339)*
Greer Environmental Services ....G 601 734-2883
  Ruth *(G-4701)*
Lott Enterprises Inc ....C 662 453-0034
  Greenwood *(G-1636)*
Lott Enterprises Inc ....G 601 932-4698
  Jackson *(G-2654)*
Natural Ozone Solutions LLC ....G 662 963-2157
  Nettleton *(G-3664)*
Pure Air Filter ....G 228 867-0888
  Gulfport *(G-1856)*
Sly Inc ....G 662 263-8234
  Mathiston *(G-3231)*
U S Metal Works Inc ....E 601 657-4676
  Liberty *(G-2919)*
Ultra Drying Technology ....G 662 494-5025
  West Point *(G-5565)*
Viking Range LLC ....D 770 932-7282
  Greenwood *(G-1657)*
Wares Air Filter Service ....G 228 832-8918
  Gulfport *(G-1892)*

3565 Packaging Machinery

Packaging Machinery Systems ....G 601 992-5011
  Flowood *(G-1386)*
▼ S & N Airoflo Inc ....F 662 455-2804
  Greenwood *(G-1650)*

3566 Speed Changers, Drives & Gears

Haley Clutch & Coupling Co Inc ....E 662 332-8716
  Greenville *(G-1556)*
▼ Marine Gears Inc ....G 662 332-8716
  Greenville *(G-1568)*

3567 Indl Process Furnaces & Ovens

Sly Inc ....G 662 263-8234
  Mathiston *(G-3231)*

3568 Mechanical Power Transmission Eqpt, NEC

▲ Ktsu America LLC ....F 601 506-8148
  Canton *(G-665)*
▼ Marine Gears Inc ....E 662 332-8716
  Greenville *(G-1568)*
▲ Maurey Manufacturing Corp ....E 662 252-6583
  Holly Springs *(G-2184)*
V E Brackett & Co Inc ....G 662 840-5656
  Tupelo *(G-5249)*
Whitestone Contracting LLC ....G 601 800-8077
  Ellisville *(G-1278)*

3569 Indl Machinery & Eqpt, NEC

Advanced Caster Tech LLC ....G 228 432-1384
  Biloxi *(G-216)*
Filter Service Inc ....G 601 644-9840
  Meridian *(G-3338)*
Gasmax Fltration Solutions LLC ....G 601 790-1225
  Ridgeland *(G-4586)*
▲ Gulf Coast Filters Inc ....G 601 528-5762
  Perkinston *(G-4176)*

Holmes Industries LLC ....G 601 635-4409
  Decatur *(G-1173)*
KC&c General Contractor ....G 601 668-4615
  Edwards *(G-1239)*
Merle E Sullivan ....G 662 347-4494
  Greenville *(G-1572)*
◆ Metaris Corporation ....E 601 469-1987
  Forest *(G-1422)*
Miller Bryant G Oil Gas Prpts ....G 601 360-2850
  Jackson *(G-2492)*
Monotech of Mississippi ....C 662 423-2033
  Iuka *(G-2303)*
National Filter Media Corp ....D 662 895-4660
  Olive Branch *(G-3884)*
Parker-Hannifin Corporation ....C 662 252-2656
  Holly Springs *(G-2187)*
▲ Power Dynamics Innovations LLC .....G 601 229-0960
  Picayune *(G-4287)*
Ripley Industries Inc ....E 662 423-6733
  Iuka *(G-2307)*
Ronald E Christopher III ....G 901 301-5922
  Olive Branch *(G-3905)*
Southern Hose & Hydraulics ....F 601 922-9990
  Jackson *(G-2590)*
Southern Technical Aquatic RES ....G 601 590-6248
  Carriere *(G-701)*

3571 Electronic Computers

Apple Dapple ....G 228 539-3100
  Gulfport *(G-1729)*
Columbia Computers Inc ....G 601 736-2204
  Columbia *(G-888)*
Computer Consultant ....G 228 818-4486
  Ocean Springs *(G-3750)*
Cytec Software Systems Inc ....F 601 362-1612
  Jackson *(G-2373)*
Harlan Services LLC ....G 601 513-5318
  Magee *(G-3177)*
Howard Technology Solutions ....G 601 428-2200
  Laurel *(G-2781)*
Incapitalmgcom LLC ....G 601 268-0103
  Hattiesburg *(G-1999)*
Mississippi State University ....G 662 325-3149
  Mississippi State *(G-3425)*
Olives & Apples LLC ....G 662 419-0224
  Pontotoc *(G-4352)*
Omni Technologies LLC ....G 601 427-5898
  Ridgeland *(G-4614)*
PC Ace Computer Service ....G 662 494-1925
  West Point *(G-5557)*
Pink Apple ....G 901 412-3926
  Southaven *(G-4892)*
Somefa LLC ....G 601 506-1808
  Jackson *(G-2586)*
Storsoft Technology Corp ....G 954 436-9292
  Gulfport *(G-1881)*
TNT Investments LLC ....G 228 860-8207
  Biloxi *(G-284)*
William M Stewart ....G 662 393-7950
  Horn Lake *(G-2215)*
Wilson Solutions LLC ....G 662 319-6063
  Aberdeen *(G-22)*

3572 Computer Storage Devices

Glassbridge Enterprises Inc ....G 662 280-6268
  Southaven *(G-4875)*
Grady Morrow ....G 769 823-1422
  Jackson *(G-2429)*
Martin Caderwood ....G 714 456-0800
  Oxford *(G-3970)*

3575 Computer Terminals

Incapitalmgcom LLC ....G 601 268-0103
  Hattiesburg *(G-1999)*
Mississppi Band Chctaw Indians ....E 601 656-6038
  Choctaw *(G-747)*

3577 Computer Peripheral Eqpt, NEC

3d Laser Scanning LLC ....G 228 860-5952
  Biloxi *(G-214)*
Adventure Leadership Cons LLC ....G 662 915-6736
  Southaven *(G-4852)*
▲ Bay Technical Associates Inc ....D 228 563-7334
  Long Beach *(G-2925)*
Black Box Corporation ....G 601 939-9051
  Flowood *(G-1346)*
Central Delta Cmnty Dev Corp ....G 601 215-0367
  Jackson *(G-2357)*

2019 Harris Directory of
Mississippi Manufacturers

246

SIC SECTION

35 INDUSTRIAL AND COMMERCIAL MACHINERY AND COMPUTER EQUIPMENT

Claude W Carnathan ....G....... 662 834-3855
Lexington (G-2899)
Cosco Authorized Xerox Dealer ....G....... 601 568-5006
Philadelphia (G-4212)
Emma Roberts ....G....... 601 638-3062
Vicksburg (G-5366)
Howard Industries Inc ....F....... 601 399-5053
Ellisville (G-1258)
International Laser Sups LLC ....G....... 601 788-6475
Richton (G-4535)
Key Tronic Corporation ....G....... 662 665-3410
Corinth (G-1094)
Logitech Inc ....G....... 510 713-5429
Olive Branch (G-3866)
Richardson Marketing ....G....... 662 234-3907
Abbeville (G-3)
Storsoft Technology Corp ....G....... 954 436-9292
Gulfport (G-1881)
Tech Smart LLC ....G....... 662 417-8780
Grenada (G-1707)
Thyssenkrupp Elevator Corp ....C....... 662 223-4025
Walnut (G-5458)
Tronicsales ....G....... 769 218-0432
Jackson (G-2613)
Wireless Network Inc ....F....... 601 665-5307
Canton (G-685)

3578 Calculating & Accounting Eqpt

At Xtree ....G....... 601 683-6494
Newton (G-3716)
Express Line ....G....... 662 328-3720
Columbus (G-971)
Hunter Engineering Company ....G....... 769 524-4949
Jackson (G-2445)
Kangaroo Express 1544 ....G....... 662 563-4629
Batesville (G-111)
Payment Alliance Proc Corp ....G....... 601 956-1222
Jackson (G-2537)
Pearl River Exxon ....F....... 601 650-9393
Philadelphia (G-4230)
Progressive Atms ....G....... 228 475-7234
Moss Point (G-3496)
Triton Automatic Teller Mchs ....G....... 228 575-3292
Long Beach (G-2957)
▲ Triton Systems Delaware LLC ....C....... 228 575-3100
Long Beach (G-2958)

3579 Office Machines, NEC

Pitney Bowes Inc ....G....... 601 969-2900
Jackson (G-2540)
Pitney Bowes Inc ....E....... 601 206-9039
Ridgeland (G-4618)
Rj Young ....G....... 601 948-2222
Jackson (G-2566)

3581 Automatic Vending Machines

Brown Bottling Group Inc ....E....... 601 352-0366
Jackson (G-2345)
Luckett Pump & Well Svc Inc ....G....... 662 624-2398
Dublin (G-1219)
Smart Snacks LLC ....G....... 228 239-6507
Ocean Springs (G-3787)

3582 Commercial Laundry, Dry Clean & Pressing Mchs

Bullocks Washteria ....G....... 601 684-2332
McComb (G-3244)
Laundry Depot LLC ....F....... 601 527-2774
Meridian (G-3357)

3585 Air Conditioning & Heating Eqpt

AAA Heating & Cooling ....G....... 601 214-7212
Brandon (G-353)
▲ Advanced Distributor Pdts LLC ....A....... 662 229-3000
Grenada (G-1666)
Air Cond Htg & S/M Solutions ....G....... 601 720-5085
Terry (G-5063)
Carrier Corporation ....C....... 662 890-3706
Byhalia (G-582)
Caruthers AC & Htg LLC ....G....... 601 636-9433
Vicksburg (G-5355)
Donald E McCain ....G....... 601 824-1275
Brandon (G-391)
Fondren and Sons LLC ....G....... 662 816-8640
Taylor (G-5048)
Kaz USA ....G....... 800 477-0457
Olive Branch (G-3859)
Lobell Sales LLC ....G....... 662 724-2940
Noxapater (G-3733)

▼ Mid-South Industries Inc ....C....... 601 649-4600
Laurel (G-2803)
Modine Grenada LLC ....B....... 662 229-4000
Grenada (G-1694)
Modine Grenada LLC ....A....... 662 229-2000
Grenada (G-1692)
▲ Modine Grenada LLC ....C....... 662 226-3421
Grenada (G-1693)
Parker-Hannifin Corporation ....C....... 662 563-4691
Batesville (G-117)
Polyvulc Usa Inc ....E....... 601 638-8040
Vicksburg (G-5407)
Standex International Corp ....B....... 662 534-9061
New Albany (G-3700)
Taylor Coml Foodservice Inc ....C....... 662 895-4455
Olive Branch (G-3915)
Tecumseh Products Company ....G....... 662 566-2231
Verona (G-5336)
Tecumseh Products Company ....G....... 662 407-0428
Tupelo (G-5239)
Trane US Inc ....G....... 228 863-4445
Gulfport (G-1885)
United Service Equipment Co ....G....... 662 534-9061
New Albany (G-3706)
Wag Corporation ....G....... 662 844-8478
Tupelo (G-5252)
Watson Percy ....G....... 662 931-6490
Greenville (G-1609)
York International Corporation ....D....... 601 544-8911
Hattiesburg (G-2087)

3589 Service Ind Machines, NEC

Advanced Treatment Tech LLC ....G....... 601 506-3798
Brandon (G-358)
Auto-Chlor System of Mid S LLC ....G....... 601 420-0331
Pearl (G-4105)
Bardo & Co ....G....... 601 397-1167
Kosciusko (G-2690)
Cintas Corporation No 2 ....G....... 601 923-8664
Jackson (G-2360)
Ecowater Systems LLC ....C....... 662 837-9349
Ripley (G-4656)
Enviro-Flo Inc ....G....... 601 939-2948
Flowood (G-1355)
Garrett Rowland G ....G....... 601 954-9841
Jackson (G-2422)
Hancock Equipment & Oil Co LLC ....G....... 662 726-4556
Brooksville (G-555)
Klean N Press ....G....... 662 563-5515
Batesville (G-112)
Kx Technologies LLC ....E....... 662 601-4140
Iuka (G-2297)
Pressure Pro ....G....... 601 331-7070
Ridgeland (G-4619)
Saf T Cart Inc ....E....... 662 624-6492
Clarksdale (G-782)
Saf-T Compliance Intl LLC ....G....... 601 684-9495
McComb (G-3264)
Secure Shred LLC ....G....... 662 563-5008
Batesville (G-124)
Secure Shred LLC ....G....... 662 563-5008
Sardis (G-4744)
Southern Sewage Systems ....G....... 228 832-7400
Saucier (G-4766)
Sunday Best ....G....... 662 226-2214
Grenada (G-1706)
Wastewater Control Inc ....G....... 601 845-5581
Florence (G-1338)
Water Water LLC ....G....... 662 721-7098
Cleveland (G-810)

3592 Carburetors, Pistons, Rings & Valves

Borgwrner Emssions Systems LLC ....A....... 662 473-3100
Water Valley (G-5464)
▲ Lunati LLC ....E....... 662 892-1518
Olive Branch (G-3868)
Southern Carburetor ....G....... 601 400-3716
Jackson (G-2589)
Tvi Inc ....G....... 662 343-5117
Hamilton (G-1910)

3593 Fluid Power Cylinders & Actuators

Gulf Hydraulics & Pneumatics ....F....... 228 392-1275
Diberville (G-1205)
◆ Hol-Mac Corporation ....C....... 601 764-4121
Bay Springs (G-162)
Hol-Mac Corporation ....D....... 601 764-4121
Bay Springs (G-163)
Hol-Mac Corporation ....D....... 601 764-4121
Bay Springs (G-164)

3594 Fluid Power Pumps & Motors

ABB Motors and Mechanical Inc ....E....... 662 328-9116
Columbus (G-930)
Eaton Aerospace LLC ....E....... 601 981-2811
Jackson (G-2396)
Franklin Electrofluid Co Inc ....G....... 601 969-7022
Jackson (G-2412)
Geartek ....F....... 662 286-2252
Corinth (G-1087)
Hydrostatic Transm Svc LLC ....G....... 662 680-8899
Tupelo (G-5160)
◆ Metaris Corporation ....E....... 601 469-1987
Forest (G-1422)
Pickett Equipment Co Inc ....G....... 662 890-9095
Olive Branch (G-3895)
Plymouth Tube Company ....D....... 662 258-2420
Eupora (G-1290)

3596 Scales & Balances, Exc Laboratory

Gulf Coast Marine Supply Co ....F....... 228 762-9282
Pascagoula (G-4035)
Raymond Mucillo Jr ....G....... 662 429-8976
Nesbit (G-3656)
▲ Triner Scale and Mfg Co Inc ....F....... 800 238-0152
Olive Branch (G-3919)

3599 Machinery & Eqpt, Indl & Commercial, NEC

A K Sanders Mfg Inc ....G....... 901 647-1830
Southaven (G-4850)
Abby Manufacturing Co Inc ....G....... 662 223-5339
Walnut (G-5453)
Aberdeen Machine Works Inc ....E....... 662 369-9357
Aberdeen (G-6)
Alan Dickerson Inc ....G....... 662 289-1451
Kosciusko (G-2687)
Amerimac Machining Corporation ....G....... 601 940-7919
Jackson (G-2329)
Atlas Machine & Mfg LLC ....G....... 601 799-2616
Picayune (G-4252)
Atwood Mch Wldg & Hydraulics ....F....... 601 735-0398
Waynesboro (G-5491)
Automotive Machine Company ....G....... 601 442-0422
Natchez (G-3521)
B & B Mfg & Specialty Co Inc ....G....... 662 456-4313
Houston (G-2231)
B & O Machine & Wldg Co Inc ....G....... 601 833-3000
Brookhaven (G-481)
B B Stump Grinding ....G....... 601 506-0997
Florence (G-1314)
B-Gone Stump Grinding Service ....G....... 228 762-2196
Pascagoula (G-4020)
Batesville Tooling & Design ....F....... 662 563-1663
Batesville (G-98)
Beason Repair Shop ....G....... 662 256-9937
Amory (G-37)
Benvenutti Elctrcl Apprts & Rp ....G....... 228 831-0445
Gulfport (G-1738)
Bigbee Industries ....G....... 662 568-7740
Houlka (G-2218)
Block & Chip Iron Works Inc ....G....... 601 394-2964
Leakesville (G-2876)
Bryants Machine Shop Inc ....G....... 601 922-1937
Jackson (G-2347)
C & C Machine Incorporated ....G....... 601 795-6377
Poplarville (G-4379)
C & CS Machine Shop Inc ....F....... 662 489-3376
Pontotoc (G-4324)
C & M Tree Svc Stump Grinding ....G....... 662 675-8884
Coffeeville (G-842)
C B R Machinist Inc ....G....... 601 426-2326
Laurel (G-2746)
C&C McHine Fabrication MGT LLC ....G....... 662 269-2534
Tupelo (G-5116)
Calhoun Parts Inc ....G....... 662 628-6621
Calhoun City (G-635)
Capt Mikes Stump Grinding and ....G....... 985 892-9162
Picayune (G-4259)
Central Machine Shop ....G....... 601 446-8732
Natchez (G-3545)
Clear Enterprise ....G....... 601 796-2429
Lumberton (G-3025)
Columbia Machine LLC ....G....... 601 441-7755
Columbia (G-889)
Columbus Engine & Crank Shaft ....G....... 662 356-0068
Caledonia (G-627)
Columbus Mch & Wldg Works Inc ....E....... 662 328-8473
Columbus (G-951)

SIC

Employee Codes: A=Over 500 employees, B=251-500
C=101-250, D=51-100, E=20-50, F=10-19, G=1-9

2019 Harris Directory of
Mississippi Manufacturers

247

35 INDUSTRIAL AND COMMERCIAL MACHINERY AND COMPUTER EQUIPMENT

SIC SECTION

Complete Cnc Machine Repair ....G...... 601 604-2063
Meridian *(G-3322)*

Cothran Machine Shop ....G...... 662 449-5983
Hernando *(G-2127)*

Cox Mhp Inc ....G...... 601 732-6600
Morton *(G-3446)*

Cox Mhp Inc ....E...... 601 936-3949
Flowood *(G-1353)*

Crabtree Manufacturing Inc ....F...... 662 746-3041
Yazoo City *(G-5629)*

Creative Machining Inc ....G...... 601 630-5536
Vicksburg *(G-5359)*

Cuevas Machine Co Inc ....D...... 228 255-1384
Poplarville *(G-4380)*

D & T Motors Inc ....G...... 662 773-9041
Louisville *(G-2966)*

Deep S Mch Wrks Hydraulics LLC ....G...... 601 989-2977
Richton *(G-4529)*

▲ Developmental Industries Inc ....E...... 662 287-6626
Corinth *(G-1083)*

Dillard Machining Service ....F...... 662 329-4682
Columbus *(G-962)*

Dixie Pump & Machine Works ....F...... 601 823-0510
Brookhaven *(G-492)*

Doves Machine & Welding Svc ....G...... 601 794-8112
Purvis *(G-4436)*

E E Baird Machine Shop Inc ....G...... 662 456-2348
Houston *(G-2237)*

E E Baird Shop Inc ....G...... 662 456-3467
Houston *(G-2238)*

Earls Machining Center Inc ....G...... 662 820-7565
Leland *(G-2887)*

East Systems Inc ....G...... 662 244-7070
Columbus *(G-965)*

Eco Recovery Machine LLC ....G...... 713 829-1083
Pinola *(G-4308)*

Elmore Machine Shop Inc ....G...... 601 989-2508
Richton *(G-4530)*

Engine Rebuilders Co Inc ....F...... 662 332-2695
Greenville *(G-1554)*

Entek Inc ....G...... 662 841-5134
Tupelo *(G-5130)*

Euro American Plastics Inc ....F...... 601 879-0360
Flora *(G-1305)*

Fretwell (not Incorporated) ....G...... 601 649-0003
Laurel *(G-2768)*

G & S Auto Parts Inc ....G...... 662 837-9292
Ripley *(G-4660)*

General Machine Works Inc ....G...... 662 494-5155
West Point *(G-5543)*

Ghe Machine Shop ....G...... 601 886-0304
Silver Creek *(G-4838)*

Glenn Machine Works Inc ....E...... 662 328-4611
Columbus *(G-978)*

Glenn Machine Works Inc ....E...... 228 875-1877
Vancleave *(G-5319)*

Glenn Machine Works Inc ....G...... 601 482-5554
Meridian *(G-3341)*

Graham Brothers Machine Inc ....G...... 228 474-7011
Escatawpa *(G-1281)*

Grant Brothers Machine Shop ....G...... 662 563-2523
Batesville *(G-107)*

Greenwood Machine Shop ....G...... 662 316-4107
Blue Springs *(G-297)*

Grind ....G...... 662 567-5211
Houston *(G-2243)*

Gulf Coast Fabrication Inc ....G...... 601 347-8403
Picayune *(G-4268)*

H & H Machine Shop ....G...... 662 386-0778
Columbus *(G-982)*

H and H Fabrications ....G...... 601 508-7558
Lucedale *(G-2998)*

Hawas Inc ....G...... 601 876-0806
Tylertown *(G-5272)*

Haynes Enterprises Inc ....G...... 662 843-4411
Cleveland *(G-795)*

Helanbak LLC ....G...... 601 736-6112
Foxworth *(G-1431)*

Holmes Industries LLC ....G...... 601 635-4409
Decatur *(G-1173)*

Hughes Outdoors & Marin ....E...... 662 287-8607
Corinth *(G-1090)*

Industrial Machine Mfg ....G...... 601 737-5017
Collinsville *(G-872)*

Innovex Inc ....E...... 662 328-9537
Columbus *(G-988)*

Irvin Machine Specialty Co ....G...... 662 862-3781
Mantachie *(G-3200)*

Jennings Welding & Mch Works ....G...... 662 887-1870
Indianola *(G-2269)*

Jims Auto Parts Inc ....G...... 662 494-4541
West Point *(G-5547)*

Jims Tool & Die Inc ....F...... 662 895-3287
Olive Branch *(G-3856)*

John D Murley ....F...... 662 890-3920
Olive Branch *(G-3857)*

Johnson Machine North Miss ....G...... 662 393-3567
Southaven *(G-4884)*

Jpm of Mississippi Inc ....D...... 601 544-9950
Hattiesburg *(G-2004)*

Kar Kleen ....G...... 601 638-8816
Vicksburg *(G-5384)*

Kayo Technologies ....G...... 662 893-7569
Olive Branch *(G-3858)*

Keyes Machine Shop LLC ....G...... 601 671-8646
Waynesboro *(G-5502)*

Lauderdale-Hamilton Inc ....F...... 662 767-3928
Shannon *(G-4813)*

Laurel Machine and Foundry Co ....C...... 601 428-0541
Laurel *(G-2793)*

Lightning Machine Works ....G...... 662 449-1801
Hernando *(G-2139)*

Lindsey Machine Shop Inc ....G...... 662 365-8189
Baldwyn *(G-83)*

Lyle Machinery Co ....G...... 601 276-3528
Summit *(G-5017)*

M&M Machine Shop Inc ....G...... 504 442-0797
Carriere *(G-696)*

Machine Shop Inc ....G...... 601 736-4729
Columbia *(G-904)*

Mam Machine & Mfg LLC ....G...... 901 216-1960
Southaven *(G-4888)*

Mashburns Welding ....G...... 601 648-2886
Buckatunna *(G-564)*

Mason Overstreet Wldg Mch Work ....E...... 601 932-1794
Pearl *(G-4130)*

McGee Machine ....G...... 601 825-7387
Brandon *(G-421)*

McGregor Indstl Steel Fabrcatn ....E...... 662 236-7006
Oxford *(G-3973)*

McMurtrys Automotive Mch Svc ....G...... 228 832-8335
Saucier *(G-4759)*

Medical McHning Specialsts LLC ....E...... 662 890-7006
Olive Branch *(G-3872)*

Met-Tech Corp ....G...... 601 693-0061
Meridian *(G-3370)*

Metal Products of Corinth Inc ....G...... 662 287-3625
Corinth *(G-1101)*

MGM Inc ....G...... 662 428-4646
Ackerman *(G-26)*

Michaels Machine Shop Inc ....G...... 662 624-2376
Clarksdale *(G-775)*

Miltons Automotive Head Servi ....G...... 601 922-8131
Jackson *(G-2494)*

Mini Mtrs Unlimited Sls & Svc ....G...... 662 356-4900
Steens *(G-4991)*

Mitchell Buckhalter ....G...... 228 588-2040
Moss Point *(G-3486)*

Mitchells Machine Shop ....G...... 228 588-2040
Moss Point *(G-3487)*

Mosley Mfg & Mch Works ....G...... 662 332-7140
Greenville *(G-1579)*

Motor Parts Co of Yazoo City ....G...... 662 746-1462
Yazoo City *(G-5643)*

Msi Inc ....G...... 662 401-9781
Saltillo *(G-4718)*

Murphys Machine & Welding LLC ....G...... 601 849-2771
Magee *(G-3179)*

▲ N Rolls-Ryce Amer Holdings Inc ....G...... 228 762-0728
Pascagoula *(G-4054)*

North Mississippi Tool Inc ....F...... 662 720-9530
Ripley *(G-4665)*

Novelty Machine Works Inc ....G...... 601 948-2075
Jackson *(G-2524)*

Ormans Welding & Fab Inc ....F...... 662 494-9471
West Point *(G-5556)*

P & S Welding & Manufacturing ....G...... 662 334-9881
Greenville *(G-1587)*

Pallet Machinery Svc ....G...... 662 726-5101
Macon *(G-3070)*

Palmer Tool LLC ....E...... 228 832-0805
Saucier *(G-4760)*

Parish Pumps and Machine Inc ....G...... 662 256-2052
Amory *(G-51)*

Patterson & Company Inc ....E...... 662 842-2807
Tupelo *(G-5200)*

Pernells Repairs Inc ....G...... 662 453-9702
Greenwood *(G-1645)*

Pontotoc Machine Works Inc ....G...... 662 489-8944
Pontotoc *(G-4355)*

Portable Boring & Mch Works ....G...... 601 922-9333
Jackson *(G-2542)*

Portable Boring Inc ....G...... 601 922-9333
Clinton *(G-833)*

▲ Powertrain N Feuer Amer Inc ....D...... 662 373-0050
Robinsonville *(G-4676)*

Precision Mch Met Fbrction Inc ....E...... 662 844-4606
Tupelo *(G-5207)*

Precision Products Inc ....F...... 228 475-7400
Moss Point *(G-3495)*

Production Machine & Tool Inc ....G...... 662 287-4752
Corinth *(G-1111)*

Provine Machine Works ....G...... 662 226-1512
Grenada *(G-1700)*

Purvis Machine ....G...... 601 947-6617
Lucedale *(G-3013)*

Quality Machine & Wldg of Miss ....E...... 601 798-8568
Picayune *(G-4289)*

Quality Welding ....G...... 601 428-4724
Laurel *(G-2830)*

Ratliff Fabricating Company ....F...... 601 362-8942
Jackson *(G-2560)*

Redi-Strip of Jackson Inc ....F...... 601 355-3317
Jackson *(G-2563)*

Ridgid Machining ....G...... 228 383-3525
Bay St Louis *(G-181)*

Rogers Automatic Screw Machine ....G...... 601 849-2431
Magee *(G-3184)*

Rolls-Royce Marine North Amer ....D...... 228 762-0728
Pascagoula *(G-4064)*

S & R Metals Inc ....F...... 601 982-1171
Jackson *(G-2571)*

Sandy Hook Machine Shop Inc ....F...... 601 736-4041
Sandy Hook *(G-4731)*

Sandys Auto Parts & Machine Sp ....G...... 662 342-1900
Southaven *(G-4898)*

Smith Machine & Iron Inc ....G...... 662 375-8551
Sumner *(G-5032)*

Smith Sr William Shayne ....G...... 901 832-1998
Southaven *(G-4903)*

Smith Tooling ....G...... 662 234-1139
Abbeville *(G-4)*

Smiths Machine & Wldg Co Inc ....E...... 601 833-8787
Brookhaven *(G-534)*

Southern Machining LLC ....G...... 662 229-0026
Grenada *(G-1704)*

Southern Metals Co Miss Inc ....E...... 601 649-7475
Laurel *(G-2853)*

Southern Tooling & Mch Works ....G...... 662 256-7633
Amory *(G-55)*

Southwest Mississippi Robotics ....G...... 601 276-4276
Summit *(G-5022)*

▲ Specialty Machine Works Inc ....E...... 228 832-7123
Gulfport *(G-1878)*

Sunbelt Manufacturing Company ....G...... 601 977-5292
Jackson *(G-2599)*

▲ Taylor & Sons Inc ....G...... 601 483-0714
Meridian *(G-3411)*

Taylor Machine ....G...... 601 650-9600
Philadelphia *(G-4240)*

Taylor Machine Works Inc ....G...... 303 289-2201
Jackson *(G-2670)*

Tencarva Machinery Company LLC ....F...... 601 823-0510
Brookhaven *(G-544)*

Terrys Bits Machine Shop ....G...... 601 736-6112
Foxworth *(G-1437)*

Tokins Inc ....G...... 601 939-1093
Pearl *(G-4152)*

Tomlinson Machine & Tool LLC ....G...... 662 342-5043
Southaven *(G-4915)*

Townsnds Auto Repr Wricker Svc ....G...... 662 289-6845
Kosciusko *(G-2718)*

Traceway Engineering and Mfg ....F...... 662 489-1314
Pontotoc *(G-4364)*

Transport Trailer Service Inc ....D...... 662 844-4606
Tupelo *(G-5241)*

Tucker Machine Services ....G...... 601 582-4280
Hattiesburg *(G-2075)*

Turner Jimmy Backhoe Dozer Svc ....G...... 662 988-2701
Myrtle *(G-3514)*

TWI Inc ....G...... 601 736-1783
Columbia *(G-927)*

Ulmer Machine Company Inc ....F...... 601 939-5812
Jackson *(G-2672)*

Valley Tool Inc ....E...... 662 473-3066
Water Valley *(G-5476)*

Walker Machine ....G...... 601 425-4635
Laurel *(G-2865)*

Walt Machine Inc ....G...... 601 796-8269
Lumberton *(G-3040)*

SIC SECTION
36 ELECTRONIC AND OTHER ELECTRICAL EQUIPMENT AND COMPONENTS, EXCEPT COMPUTER

Walters Machine Works Inc .... G 601 426-6092
Laurel (G-2867)
Wellcheck Inc .... F 228 872-3633
Ocean Springs (G-3794)
Williams JP Mch & Fabrication .... G 228 474-1099
Moss Point (G-3507)
Williams Machine Works Inc .... G 228 712-2667
Pascagoula (G-4074)
Williams Machine Works Inc .... F 228 475-7651
Moss Point (G-3508)
X Treme Racing .... G 601 947-9686
Lucedale (G-3022)
Young Dghters Prcsion Mch Wrks .... G 662 286-6538
Corinth (G-1130)

36 ELECTRONIC AND OTHER ELECTRICAL EQUIPMENT AND COMPONENTS, EXCEPT COMPUTER

3612 Power, Distribution & Specialty Transformers

ABB Inc .... E 601 892-6431
Crystal Springs (G-1139)
ABB Inc .... F 662 562-0700
Senatobia (G-4785)
Delta Municipal Energy Inc .... E 800 217-1519
Mound Bayou (G-3509)
Emerald Transformer .... G 800 346-6164
Lexington (G-2902)
Garrett & Son Inc .... E 601 853-7865
Madison (G-3102)
Howard Industries Inc .... G 601 847-5278
Mendenhall (G-3281)
Howard Industries Inc .... G 601 425-3151
Laurel (G-2780)
Howard Industries Inc .... B 601 422-0033
Laurel (G-2779)
Kuhlman Electric Corporation .... B 601 892-4661
Crystal Springs (G-1144)
▲ Malibu Lighting Corporation .... G 662 290-1200
Kosciusko (G-2699)
Photowire Solar Producers .... G 228 627-0088
Philadelphia (G-4233)

3613 Switchgear & Switchboard Apparatus

▼ Calvert Company Inc .... D 601 939-9191
Richland (G-4509)
Kresec Enterprises Corp .... G 601 292-7015
Vaiden (G-5314)
Kuhlman Electric Corporation .... B 601 892-4661
Crystal Springs (G-1144)
South Coast Electric LLC .... F 228 533-0002
Bay St Louis (G-182)
Vertiv Corporation .... F 662 313-0813
Southaven (G-4919)

3621 Motors & Generators

ABB Motors and Mechanical Inc .... E 662 328-9116
Columbus (G-930)
American Energy Solutions LLC .... G 757 846-3261
Olive Branch (G-3811)
Generator Power Systems LLC .... G 662 231-0092
Tupelo (G-5142)
Kemp Enterprises .... G 662 574-0253
Hattiesburg (G-2006)
Modine Grenada LLC .... A 662 229-2000
Grenada (G-1692)
▲ Modine Grenada LLC .... A 662 226-3421
Grenada (G-1693)
Nidec Motor Corporation .... B 662 393-6910
Southaven (G-4891)
▲ North American Electric Inc .... E 662 429-8049
Hernando (G-2146)
Sandys Auto Parts & Machine Sp .... G 662 342-1900
Southaven (G-4898)
▲ Taylor Power Systems Inc .... G 601 932-6491
Clinton (G-837)

3625 Relays & Indl Controls

Advanced Marine Inc .... G 228 374-6747
Biloxi (G-217)
Control Products Inc .... G 662 890-7920
Olive Branch (G-3828)
Control Systems Inc .... E 601 355-8594
Jackson (G-2367)

◆ Electro National Corporation .... E 601 859-5511
Canton (G-657)
ITT LLC .... E 601 393-0275
Southaven (G-4879)
ITT LLC .... C 662 256-7185
Amory (G-45)
Lec Inc .... G 601 939-8535
Pearl (G-4128)
◆ Limoss Us LLC .... E 662 365-2200
Baldwyn (G-82)
Multicraft Intl Ltd Partnr .... G 601 854-5516
Pelahatchie (G-4167)
Ncv Testing Service .... G 662 728-3965
Booneville (G-337)
Omega System Specialists LLC .... G 901 334-6742
Nesbit (G-3655)
South Coast Electric LLC .... F 228 533-0002
Bay St Louis (G-182)
Thyssenkrupp Elevator Corp .... C 662 223-4025
Walnut (G-5458)

3629 Electrical Indl Apparatus, NEC

Aluma-Form Inc .... D 662 677-6000
Walnut (G-5454)
American Payment Systems .... G 601 368-7382
Jackson (G-2326)
American Payment Systems .... G 601 713-3761
Jackson (G-2327)
Exide Technologies .... G 601 845-2236
Florence (G-1322)
Exide Technologies .... F 601 936-7788
Pearl (G-4116)
Exide Technologies .... G 601 845-2281
Florence (G-1323)
Jackson Excavating & Lsg Co .... G 601 371-7935
Jackson (G-2454)

3631 Household Cooking Eqpt

Iron and Steel Design Works .... G 662 380-5662
Oxford (G-3962)
Sunbeam Products Inc .... E 601 296-5000
Hattiesburg (G-2070)
Sunbeam Products Inc .... A 601 296-5000
Hattiesburg (G-2071)
Viking Range LLC .... D 770 932-7282
Greenwood (G-1657)
Viking Range LLC .... D 662 455-7522
Greenwood (G-1658)
Viking Range LLC .... A 662 455-1214
Greenwood (G-1659)
Viking Range LLC .... G 662 455-7521
Greenwood (G-1660)
Viking Range LLC .... G 662 455-1200
Greenwood (G-1661)
◆ Viking Range LLC .... B 662 455-1200
Greenwood (G-1662)
Viking Range LLC .... B 662 455-7522
Greenwood (G-1663)

3632 Household Refrigerators & Freezers

Kol Kraft Manufacturing Co .... G 662 429-7561
Hernando (G-2137)
Standex International Corp .... C 662 534-9061
New Albany (G-3701)
Viking Range LLC .... A 662 455-1214
Greenwood (G-1659)
Watson Percy .... G 662 931-6490
Greenville (G-1609)

3634 Electric Household Appliances

1810 Vapors .... G 662 523-7924
Saltillo (G-4705)
Bells Iron Works .... G 662 254-7413
Itta Bena (G-2279)
Canopy Breezes LLC .... G 972 207-2045
Madison (G-3088)
Comfort Designs Inc .... F 601 932-7555
Pearl (G-4111)
◆ Con Air .... G 662 280-6499
Southaven (G-4862)
Conair Corporation .... E 662 280-6499
Southaven (G-4863)
Hamilton Beach Brands Inc .... F 662 890-9869
Olive Branch (G-3843)
Presto Manufacturing Company .... G 601 366-3481
Jackson (G-2550)
Sunbeam Products Inc .... D 601 671-2200
Waynesboro (G-5516)

Sunbeam Products Inc .... E 601 296-5000
Hattiesburg (G-2070)
Thomas LP Gas Inc .... F 662 252-5388
Holly Springs (G-2195)
Vapor Express LLC .... G 601 559-8004
Pearl (G-4156)
Warmkraft Inc .... E 601 659-3317
Stonewall (G-5000)
▼ Warmkraft Inc .... C 601 785-4476
Taylorsville (G-5062)

3635 Household Vacuum Cleaners

Tupelo Elvis Presley Fan Club .... G 662 610-5301
Tupelo (G-5245)

3639 Household Appliances, NEC

Kitchen Elegance LLC .... G 228 248-0074
Gulfport (G-1818)
Knot Just Kitchens .... G 228 896-0584
Gulfport (G-1819)
Mr Appliance of Hattiesburg .... G 601 869-0434
Hattiesburg (G-2033)
Spot Cash Tire and Appliance .... G 662 289-2611
Kosciusko (G-2713)

3641 Electric Lamps

Capri Lighting .... G 662 842-7212
Tupelo (G-5117)
◆ Stylecraft Home Collection Inc .... C 662 429-5279
Southaven (G-4909)

3643 Current-Carrying Wiring Devices

A-Z Lightning Protection LLC .... G 662 890-7041
Byhalia (G-576)
ABB Installation Products Inc .... B 662 342-1545
Southaven (G-4851)
Hudson Salvage Inc .... G 601 947-0092
Lucedale (G-3003)
Safran Usa Inc .... G 601 736-4511
Columbia (G-921)
Shabby Chic S Etc .... G 601 799-2800
Picayune (G-4294)
Vicksburg Enterprise Mfg LLC .... G 601 631-0304
Vicksburg (G-5435)
Vicksburg Enterprise Mfg LLC .... G 601 631-0304
Vicksburg (G-5436)

3644 Noncurrent-Carrying Wiring Devices

Batesville Raceway LLC .... G 662 561-0065
Batesville (G-97)
Columbus Speedway .... G 662 327-3047
Columbus (G-954)
Flowood Raceway .... G 601 939-5048
Flowood (G-1362)
Golden Pine Raceway LLC .... G 601 506-8669
Prentiss (G-4420)
H and R Raceway LLC .... G 601 373-2490
Jackson (G-2436)
J&I&r Raceway LLC .... G 601 622-8458
Madison (G-3113)
Raceway Express Shell .... G 662 335-5434
Greenville (G-1593)
Southaven Raceway .... G 662 393-9945
Southaven (G-4905)
Vicksburg Enterprise Mfg LLC .... G 601 631-0304
Vicksburg (G-5435)
Vicksburg Enterprise Mfg LLC .... G 601 631-0304
Vicksburg (G-5436)

3645 Residential Lighting Fixtures

Chuck Jennings .... G 601 668-5704
Raymond (G-4486)
Cooper Lighting LLC .... B 601 638-1522
Vicksburg (G-5357)
▲ Five Stars Lighting Co Ltd .... G 610 533-6522
Vicksburg (G-5373)
H Fleming Contractor .... G 601 824-0902
Brandon (G-402)
◆ Stylecraft Home Collection Inc .... C 662 429-5279
Southaven (G-4909)
▲ Toltec Company .... F 662 427-9515
Burnsville (G-574)

3646 Commercial, Indl & Institutional Lighting Fixtures

Cooper Lighting LLC .... B 601 638-1522
Vicksburg (G-5357)

Employee Codes: A=Over 500 employees, B=251-500
C=101-250, D=51-100, E=20-50, F=10-19, G=1-9

2019 Harris Directory of
Mississippi Manufacturers

249

36 ELECTRONIC AND OTHER ELECTRICAL EQUIPMENT AND COMPONENTS, EXCEPT COMPUTER

SIC SECTION

Eaton Custom Seating LLC..............D...... 662 489-4242
Pontotoc *(G-4330)*
▲ Five Stars Lighting Co Ltd..............G...... 610 533-6522
Vicksburg *(G-5373)*
H Fleming Contractor.....................G...... 601 824-0902
Brandon *(G-402)*
Howard Industries Inc...................B...... 601 422-0033
Laurel *(G-2779)*
Jji Lighting Group Inc....................G...... 662 842-7212
Tupelo *(G-5163)*
Signify North America Corp..............A...... 662 842-7212
Tupelo *(G-5222)*
Signify North America Corp..............C...... 662 842-7212
Tupelo *(G-5223)*
▲ Toltec Company.......................F...... 662 427-9515
Burnsville *(G-574)*

3647 Vehicular Lighting Eqpt

Exciting Lighting........................F...... 228 864-2995
Long Beach *(G-2936)*

3648 Lighting Eqpt, NEC

Cooper Lighting LLC....................F...... 662 342-3100
Southaven *(G-4864)*
Cooper Lighting LLC....................B...... 601 638-1522
Vicksburg *(G-5357)*
Copper Sculptures Inc...................F...... 601 992-9955
Flowood *(G-1352)*
Eap LLC..................................G...... 601 636-1621
Vicksburg *(G-5363)*
Ecs- Elec Cnstr Spcialists Inc..........G...... 662 453-0588
Greenwood *(G-1621)*
▲ Guth Lighting........................G...... 800 234-1890
Tupelo *(G-5148)*
Jji Lighting Group Inc....................G...... 662 842-7212
Tupelo *(G-5163)*
Legendary Lighting LLC.................E...... 601 932-0707
Jackson *(G-2653)*
Lighting Investment Group Inc..........G...... 601 482-3983
Meridian *(G-3360)*
Mississppi Delta Energy Agcy...........G...... 662 746-3741
Yazoo City *(G-5641)*
Morgan Billingsley Lighting.............G...... 662 429-3685
Nesbit *(G-3654)*
Proshop Inc.............................G...... 662 333-7511
Myrtle *(G-3513)*
Seb Mining..............................G...... 228 826-4466
Vancleave *(G-5320)*
▲ St James Lighting LLC...............G...... 601 444-4966
Columbia *(G-923)*

3651 Household Audio & Video Eqpt

Decibel Audio...........................G...... 601 649-1144
Laurel *(G-2760)*
Innovative Wireless LLC.................G...... 601 594-1201
Jackson *(G-2447)*
◆ Mfj Enterprises Inc..................D...... 662 323-5869
Starkville *(G-4958)*
Mississppi Band Chctaw Indians.........G...... 601 656-7350
Choctaw *(G-746)*
Mississppi Band Chctaw Indians.........E...... 601 656-6038
Choctaw *(G-747)*
Peavey Electronics Corporation.........G...... 601 483-5365
Meridian *(G-3382)*
Peavey Electronics Corporation.........G...... 601 486-1760
Meridian *(G-3383)*
Peavey Electronics Corporation.........G...... 601 486-1127
Meridian *(G-3385)*
Peavey Electronics Corporation.........F...... 601 483-5365
Meridian *(G-3386)*
Phone Booth Inc.........................F...... 662 286-6600
Corinth *(G-1109)*

3652 Phonograph Records & Magnetic Tape

Johnson Educational Sales Inc..........G...... 601 469-1924
Forest *(G-1418)*
Northside Partners......................G...... 601 982-4522
Jackson *(G-2522)*

3661 Telephone & Telegraph Apparatus

Continue Care Hlth Modem Line..........G...... 662 827-7107
Hollandale *(G-2163)*
Innovative Wireless LLC.................G...... 601 594-1201
Jackson *(G-2447)*
King Manufacturing Company Inc.........E...... 662 286-5504
Corinth *(G-1097)*
King Manufacturing Company Inc.........E...... 662 286-5504
Corinth *(G-1096)*

Modem Guest.............................G...... 601 442-5202
Natchez *(G-3592)*
Plantronics Inc.........................G...... 662 893-7221
Olive Branch *(G-3897)*
Seimens Industry Sector.................G...... 662 245-4573
Columbus *(G-1023)*

3663 Radio & T V Communications, Systs & Eqpt, Broadcast/Studio

Davids Satellite.........................G...... 662 416-4697
Marietta *(G-3213)*
Innovative Wireless LLC.................G...... 601 594-1201
Jackson *(G-2447)*
L3 Technologies Inc.....................E...... 601 856-2274
Madison *(G-3117)*
Lad2 LLC................................G...... 601 584-9026
Hattiesburg *(G-2013)*
Lady Bugs and Lily Pads.................G...... 601 735-0071
Waynesboro *(G-5503)*
Mfj Enterprises Inc.....................G...... 662 323-9538
Starkville *(G-4959)*
Microwave Service Co...................G...... 662 842-7620
Tupelo *(G-5187)*
Mid South Communications Inc...........G...... 662 832-0538
Water Valley *(G-5472)*
Mstate Technologies LLC................G...... 662 418-0110
Starkville *(G-4962)*
Omega-Tec LLC..........................G...... 601 750-8082
Vicksburg *(G-5402)*
Robco Inc...............................G...... 769 218-6457
Long Beach *(G-2951)*
Skyhawk LLC............................G...... 601 619-6805
Vicksburg *(G-5419)*
Wntz TV.................................G...... 601 442-4800
Natchez *(G-3644)*

3669 Communications Eqpt, NEC

5m Enterprises LLC.....................G...... 601 416-0210
Sebastopol *(G-4773)*
Ademco Inc.............................G...... 601 936-4842
Richland *(G-4499)*
Alarm Company Inc.....................F...... 601 898-3105
Madison *(G-3077)*
Amerione Security......................G...... 901 502-2295
Southaven *(G-4853)*
Dvani Innovation Inc....................G...... 601 992-5069
Brandon *(G-392)*
Gw Ministries...........................G...... 662 832-9756
Water Valley *(G-5469)*
J L McCool Contractors Inc..............F...... 228 769-9771
Moss Point *(G-3482)*
L3 Technologies Inc.....................E...... 601 856-2274
Madison *(G-3117)*

3672 Printed Circuit Boards

▲ Ayrshire Electronics Miss LLC.........C...... 662 287-3771
Corinth *(G-1059)*
▲ CM Solutions Inc....................F...... 662 287-8810
Corinth *(G-1071)*
◆ Electro National Corporation.........E...... 601 859-5511
Canton *(G-657)*
Hunter Engineering Company............C...... 601 857-8883
Raymond *(G-4489)*
Mississppi Band Chctaw Indians.........G...... 601 656-7350
Choctaw *(G-746)*
Peavey Electronics Corporation.........B...... 601 483-5365
Decatur *(G-1177)*
Tri-County Industries...................E...... 601 743-9931
De Kalb *(G-1169)*

3674 Semiconductors

CM Manufacturing Inc...................D...... 601 545-7515
Hattiesburg *(G-1947)*
Comfort Revolution LLC.................F...... 662 454-7526
Belmont *(G-197)*
Daviscomms (s) Pte Ltd.................G...... 601 416-5043
Ridgeland *(G-4572)*
Future Tek Inc..........................G...... 662 328-0900
Columbus *(G-977)*
Lenoir Technology LLC..................G...... 769 926-5300
Biloxi *(G-260)*
Rsileds LLC.............................G...... 228 697-5967
Biloxi *(G-277)*
Seraphim Solar USA Mfg Inc.............E...... 601 509-1265
Jackson *(G-2577)*

3676 Electronic Resistors

Multicraft Intl Ltd Partnr...............G...... 601 854-5516
Pelahatchie *(G-4167)*

3677 Electronic Coils & Transformers

Fortson Industrial Supply Co............G...... 601 948-2053
Jackson *(G-2411)*
Kuhlman Electric Corporation...........B...... 601 892-4661
Crystal Springs *(G-1144)*
Turners Tax Service....................F...... 662 887-2066
Baird *(G-69)*

3678 Electronic Connectors

Frank J Miller.........................G...... 601 792-8795
Oak Vale *(G-3734)*
Rehabilitation Svcs Miss Dept...........E...... 662 335-3359
Greenville *(G-1595)*

3679 Electronic Components, NEC

Applied Geo Technologies Inc...........D...... 601 267-5681
Carthage *(G-706)*
Connection Laboratories Inc.............G...... 662 429-1097
Hernando *(G-2126)*
Delta Foundation Inc...................C...... 662 335-5291
Greenville *(G-1547)*
Dison Electrical Solutions LLC..........G...... 228 234-7767
Saucier *(G-4753)*
Dufour Battery One Source LLC..........G...... 601 693-1500
Meridian *(G-3333)*
E M F Corp.............................E...... 601 743-2794
De Kalb *(G-1163)*
◆ Electro National Corporation.........E...... 601 859-5511
Canton *(G-657)*
Hardwire Inc............................F...... 662 285-2312
Louisville *(G-2971)*
High Edge Inc...........................F...... 601 326-2025
Jackson *(G-2440)*
L3 Technologies Inc.....................E...... 601 856-2274
Madison *(G-3117)*
Mississppi Band Chctaw Indians.........E...... 601 656-6038
Choctaw *(G-747)*
Multicraft Intl Ltd Partnr...............D...... 601 854-1200
Pelahatchie *(G-4169)*
Temputech Inc..........................F...... 662 838-3698
Byhalia *(G-608)*
Wnc Satcom Group LLC.................G...... 601 544-0311
Hattiesburg *(G-2086)*

3691 Storage Batteries

Battco Inc..............................G...... 601 898-1200
Ridgeland *(G-4552)*
Exide Technologies.....................G...... 601 845-2236
Florence *(G-1322)*
Exide Technologies.....................F...... 601 936-7788
Pearl *(G-4116)*
Exide Technologies.....................G...... 601 845-2281
Florence *(G-1323)*
Tri Star Industrial.....................G...... 662 680-4331
Belden *(G-192)*

3692 Primary Batteries: Dry & Wet

Battco Inc..............................G...... 601 898-1200
Ridgeland *(G-4552)*

3694 Electrical Eqpt For Internal Combustion Engines

Delco Remy America.....................G...... 601 785-6690
Taylorsville *(G-5053)*
Hattiesburg Motors LLC.................G...... 601 818-2255
Hattiesburg *(G-1987)*
Interstate Industries Miss LLC..........C...... 662 289-3877
Kosciusko *(G-2695)*
Multicraft Intl Ltd Partnr...............G...... 601 854-5516
Pelahatchie *(G-4167)*
Richard Melos...........................G...... 434 401-9496
Robinsonville *(G-4677)*
Tri-County Industries...................E...... 601 743-9931
De Kalb *(G-1169)*

3695 Recording Media

Glassbridge Enterprises Inc.............G...... 662 280-6268
Southaven *(G-4875)*
Harvest Trends Inc......................G...... 716 514-6788
Ocean Springs *(G-3762)*
▲ Primos Inc...........................D...... 601 879-9323
Flora *(G-1311)*
Tech Smart LLC.........................G...... 662 417-8780
Grenada *(G-1707)*

2019 Harris Directory of
Mississippi Manufacturers

250

3699 Electrical Machinery, Eqpt & Splys, NEC

A Square Innovative SEC LLC ....G.... 601 937-0318
Jackson *(G-2316)*
ABB Installation Products Inc ....B.... 662 342-1545
Southaven *(G-4851)*
Advanced Digital Fire & SEC ....G.... 901 240-8030
Olive Branch *(G-3806)*
Awesome Sight and Sound ....G.... 601 215-8846
Picayune *(G-4255)*
Azz Inc ....G.... 662 290-1500
Kosciusko *(G-2689)*
Azz Inc ....E.... 601 939-9191
Richland *(G-4505)*
Azz Incorporated ....F.... 228 475-0342
Moss Point *(G-3466)*
Dale Fulton ....G.... 662 327-4800
Columbus *(G-958)*
Dave Strong Circuit Judge ....G.... 601 684-3400
McComb *(G-3248)*
Delta Positions Inc ....G.... 662 719-1194
Boyle *(G-349)*
Electric Contractors ....G.... 662 470-3102
Southaven *(G-4871)*
Elvis and Company LLC ....G.... 662 616-9248
Greenville *(G-1553)*
Emergncy Eqp Professionals Inc ....F.... 662 280-4729
Horn Lake *(G-2197)*
Genesis Telecommunications ....G.... 601 626-7353
Collinsville *(G-868)*
High Tech Inc ....E.... 228 868-6632
Long Beach *(G-2940)*
Innovative Circuits Inc ....F.... 662 287-2007
Corinth *(G-1092)*
J & L Sales ....G.... 601 992-2495
Brandon *(G-407)*
Kopis Mobile LLC ....G.... 601 345-1753
Flowood *(G-1375)*
Landmark Spatial Solutions LLC ....G.... 662 769-5344
Starkville *(G-4955)*
McLan Electronics Inc ....G.... 601 373-2392
Raymond *(G-4491)*
▲ **Multicraft Intl Ltd Partnr** ....G.... 601 854-1200
Pelahatchie *(G-4168)*
Multicraft Intl Ltd Partnr ....E.... 601 854-1200
Pelahatchie *(G-4170)*
Oxford Alarm Cmmunications Inc ....G.... 662 234-0505
Oxford *(G-3984)*
Precision Electric & Ltg Svc ....G.... 662 893-3200
Olive Branch *(G-3899)*
Quartermaster Security PR ....G.... 601 656-9882
Philadelphia *(G-4234)*
Southern-Its Corporation ....F.... 228 273-2585
Diberville *(G-1215)*
Steelsummit Holdings Inc ....F.... 601 638-1819
Vicksburg *(G-5424)*
Tenax Tm LLC ....F.... 601 352-1107
Madison *(G-3158)*
Training Consultants Inc ....G.... 662 226-6637
Grenada *(G-1710)*
United Fence Company ....G.... 601 582-0406
Hattiesburg *(G-2077)*
Vanguard Solutions Inc ....G.... 407 230-2887
Gautier *(G-1505)*
Wholesale Electric Supply ....G.... 601 501-6928
Vicksburg *(G-5445)*

37 TRANSPORTATION EQUIPMENT

3711 Motor Vehicles & Car Bodies

Burroughs Bus Sales Inc ....G.... 601 649-3062
Laurel *(G-2745)*
Chuck Ryan Cars Inc ....G.... 228 864-9706
Long Beach *(G-2932)*
Cite Armored Inc ....E.... 662 551-1066
Holly Springs *(G-2173)*
City of Magee ....E.... 601 849-2366
Magee *(G-3174)*
Companion Vans Inc ....F.... 662 289-7711
Kosciusko *(G-2691)*
Deep South Fire Trucks Inc ....D.... 601 722-4166
Seminary *(G-4776)*
◆ **Grammer Inc** ....G.... 662 566-1660
Shannon *(G-4807)*
▲ **Greentech Automotive Inc** ....D.... 662 996-1118
Robinsonville *(G-4675)*
▼ **Griffin Inc** ....D.... 662 838-2128
Byhalia *(G-586)*
▲ **Multicraft Intl Ltd Partnr** ....G.... 601 854-1200
Pelahatchie *(G-4168)*
Multicraft Intl Ltd Partnr ....E.... 601 854-1200
Pelahatchie *(G-4170)*
Myles Smith ....F.... 228 323-5052
Lumberton *(G-3036)*
Navistar Inc ....D.... 662 284-8984
Corinth *(G-1105)*
Nissan North America Inc ....A.... 601 855-6000
Canton *(G-673)*
ORears Garage and Wreck ....G.... 662 585-3244
Fulton *(G-1471)*
Ronnies Auto Sales ....G.... 662 773-9327
Louisville *(G-2980)*
Roy S Rides Inc ....G.... 601 425-3700
Laurel *(G-2840)*
Shoffner Motor Co Inc ....G.... 662 378-2909
Greenville *(G-1598)*
◆ **Toyota Motor Mfg Miss Inc** ....D.... 662 317-3000
Blue Springs *(G-300)*
Victory Motor Company ....G.... 601 573-1441
Raymond *(G-4494)*

3713 Truck & Bus Bodies

Aerial Truck Equipment Co Inc ....G.... 662 895-0993
Olive Branch *(G-3807)*
AMS Services LLC ....G.... 662 449-2672
Nesbit *(G-3648)*
Fireplace Wholesale ....G.... 601 545-9876
Hattiesburg *(G-1970)*
▼ **Griffin Inc** ....D.... 662 838-2128
Byhalia *(G-586)*
Innovative Fabrications LLC ....G.... 601 485-1400
Meridian *(G-3353)*
Parker-Hannifin Corporation ....C.... 662 895-1011
Olive Branch *(G-3894)*
Tri-State Truck Center Inc ....E.... 662 844-6000
Tupelo *(G-5242)*
Truck Bodies & Eqp Intl Inc ....G.... 662 438-7800
Tishomingo *(G-5088)*
▲ **Warren Inc** ....C.... 601 765-8221
Collins *(G-865)*

3714 Motor Vehicle Parts & Access

American Howa Kentucky Inc ....G.... 601 506-0591
Canton *(G-646)*
Aptiv Services Us LLC ....B.... 601 835-1983
Brookhaven *(G-480)*
Autoliv Asp Inc ....G.... 801 620-8018
Olive Branch *(G-3817)*
Automated Tech & Assembly LLC ....G.... 662 213-9352
Rolling Fork *(G-4679)*
Bles Car Care ....F.... 770 292-0021
Columbus *(G-940)*
Borgwarner Inc ....G.... 601 785-9504
Taylorsville *(G-5051)*
Borgwarner Inc ....E.... 662 473-3100
Water Valley *(G-5463)*
Borgwarner Emssions Systems LLC ....A.... 662 473-3100
Water Valley *(G-5464)*
Bunyards Garage ....G.... 601 632-4892
Toomsuba *(G-5090)*
Cam2 International LLC ....F.... 601 661-5382
Vicksburg *(G-5352)*
Cantrell Hot Rods LLC ....G.... 662 213-7184
Mooreville *(G-3442)*
Caterpillar Inc ....F.... 662 286-5511
Corinth *(G-1066)*
Competition Cams Inc ....G.... 662 224-8972
Olive Branch *(G-3825)*
Competition Cams Inc ....G.... 662 890-9825
Olive Branch *(G-3826)*
▲ **Crane Cams Inc** ....E.... 386 310-4875
Olive Branch *(G-3831)*
Custom Cams Inc ....G.... 662 534-4881
New Albany *(G-3678)*
Custom Engineered Wheels Inc ....E.... 662 841-0756
Baldwyn *(G-74)*
▲ **Custom Engineered Wheels Inc** ....D.... 574 267-4005
Baldwyn *(G-75)*
▲ **DEA Mississippi Inc** ....C.... 800 821-2302
Meridian *(G-3327)*
Dr James ....G.... 601 238-7821
Jackson *(G-2391)*
Faurecia Interior Systems Inc ....C.... 601 855-2163
Canton *(G-658)*
Fowler Buick-Gmc Inc ....E.... 601 360-0200
Pearl *(G-4120)*
Habe-ISE USA Inc ....F.... 769 235-6650
Richland *(G-4519)*
Hunter Engineering Company ....C.... 662 653-3194
Durant *(G-1227)*
Hunterworks LLC ....G.... 601 771-0070
Collinsville *(G-871)*
Hyperco ....G.... 662 488-4567
Pontotoc *(G-4333)*
Jackson Powertrain Inc ....G.... 601 932-3159
Jackson *(G-2651)*
Martinrea Atmtv-Structures USA ....G.... 662 566-1023
Shannon *(G-4814)*
Mississippi Cylinder Head Svc ....G.... 662 328-0170
Columbus *(G-1002)*
Mississippi Diesel Products ....E.... 601 847-2500
Mendenhall *(G-3285)*
Mississppi Band Chctaw Indians ....E.... 601 267-5279
Carthage *(G-719)*
Multicraft Enterprises Inc ....G.... 601 854-5516
Pelahatchie *(G-4166)*
National Tank Inc ....F.... 662 429-5469
Hernando *(G-2143)*
Nexteer Automotive Corporation ....B.... 601 537-3099
Morton *(G-3452)*
Ottos Custom Trailers ....G.... 601 446-6469
Natchez *(G-3604)*
Parker-Hannifin Corporation ....C.... 662 895-1011
Olive Branch *(G-3894)*
Parker-Hannifin Corporation ....C.... 662 563-4691
Batesville *(G-117)*
Parts and Supply Inc ....G.... 228 832-6272
Gulfport *(G-1845)*
▲ **Powertrain N Feuer Amer Inc** ....D.... 662 373-0050
Robinsonville *(G-4676)*
▲ **R- Squared Aluminium LLC** ....C.... 601 825-1171
Puckett *(G-4429)*
▲ **R-Squared Puckett Inc** ....E.... 601 825-1171
Puckett *(G-4430)*
Reman Inc ....E.... 601 537-3400
Morton *(G-3454)*
Reman Inc ....E.... 601 635-4897
Decatur *(G-1178)*
▲ **Remy Reman LLC** ....E.... 601 785-9504
Taylorsville *(G-5057)*
Sinhatech ....G.... 662 234-6248
Oxford *(G-4002)*
Southern Fiberglass Inc ....F.... 601 876-2111
Tylertown *(G-5285)*
Tishomingo Acquisition LLC ....C.... 662 438-7800
Tishomingo *(G-5087)*
Topre America Corporation ....G.... 601 927-6723
Canton *(G-681)*
Valeo North America Inc ....G.... 931 446-9128
Canton *(G-682)*
Willowood Dvelopmental Ctr Inc ....D.... 601 366-0123
Jackson *(G-2634)*

3715 Truck Trailers

A & A Trailer Sales LLC ....G.... 228 234-3420
Biloxi *(G-215)*
Baldwyn Truck & Trailer Repair ....G.... 662 365-7888
Baldwyn *(G-73)*
C & W Custom Design Trailers ....E.... 662 585-3146
Golden *(G-1523)*
Carroll Ray Auto & Truck Sales ....G.... 662 226-1200
Grenada *(G-1671)*
Deep South Trailer Sales LLC ....G.... 228 255-2026
Diamondhead *(G-1189)*
Fryfogle Manufacturing Inc ....F.... 601 947-8088
Lucedale *(G-2996)*
Innovative Fabrications LLC ....G.... 601 485-1400
Meridian *(G-3353)*
▼ **Magnolia Trailers Inc** ....E.... 601 947-7990
Lucedale *(G-3010)*
Mathis Trucking & Cnstr LLC ....G.... 601 917-0237
Collinsville *(G-873)*
Palmer Machine Works Inc ....E.... 662 256-2636
Amory *(G-50)*
Russell Trucking ....G.... 662 563-2616
Batesville *(G-122)*
Screw Conveyor Corporation ....C.... 662 283-3142
Winona *(G-5606)*
Timothy Trigg ....G.... 601 722-9581
Seminary *(G-4784)*
Truck Bodies & Eqp Intl Inc ....G.... 800 255-4345
Tishomingo *(G-5089)*
Wade Services Inc ....E.... 601 399-1900
Ellisville *(G-1276)*
Wade Services Inc ....G.... 601 399-1900
Laurel *(G-2864)*
▲ **Warren Inc** ....C.... 601 765-8221
Collins *(G-865)*

SIC

Employee Codes: A=Over 500 employees, B=251-500
C=101-250, D=51-100, E=20-50, F=10-19, G=1-9
2019 Harris Directory of
Mississippi Manufacturers
251

37 TRANSPORTATION EQUIPMENT

SIC SECTION

3716 Motor Homes

All American Check Cashing Inc ....G 601 373-6115
  Byram (G-615)
Companion Vans Inc ....F 662 289-7711
  Kosciusko (G-2691)

3721 Aircraft

Advanced Dynamics Inc ....G 601 677-3423
  Preston (G-4426)
Ai Evac Ems Inc ....G 662 335-3034
  Greenville (G-1535)
▲ Air + Mak Industries Inc ....F 662 893-3444
  Olive Branch (G-3809)
Airbus Helicopters Inc ....E 662 327-6226
  Columbus (G-933)
Airworks Enterprises Inc ....G 601 372-8304
  Raymond (G-4482)
Aurora Flight Sciences Corp ....F 662 328-8227
  Columbus (G-938)
Boeing Company ....G 228 688-2281
  Bay Saint Louis (G-138)
Carroll Aircraft LLC ....G 228 255-7460
  Diamondhead (G-1186)
Diamondhead Aerolease LLC ....G 228 255-8491
  Diamondhead (G-1190)
Dixon-Drone ....G 662 545-9303
  Starkville (G-4942)
Drone Assist Incorporated ....G 228 265-0174
  Gulfport (G-1775)
Emergent Technologies LLC ....G 601 497-8239
  Madison (G-3097)
Lockheed Martin Corporation ....G 901 795-5943
  Byhalia (G-589)
Lockheed Mrtin Space Oprations ....B 228 688-3675
  Bay Saint Louis (G-148)
Mississippi Aerospace Corp ....F 601 749-5659
  Picayune (G-4280)
Northrop Grumman Corp ....G 434 845-9181
  Pascagoula (G-4057)
Northrop Grumman Systems Corp ....D 228 474-3700
  Moss Point (G-3490)
Sinhatech ....G 662 234-6248
  Oxford (G-4002)
◆ Stark Aerospace Inc ....D 662 798-4075
  Columbus (G-1032)
Vertex Aerospace ....G 601 622-8940
  Canton (G-683)
Vertex Aerospace LLC ....A 601 856-2274
  Madison (G-3165)

3724 Aircraft Engines & Engine Parts

Abbott Industries Inc ....G 662 357-7360
  Tunica (G-5095)
Aerojet Rocketdyne Inc ....C 228 813-1511
  Stennis Space Center (G-4993)
Eaton Aerospace LLC ....G 601 987-3273
  Jackson (G-2397)
Eaton Aerospace LLC ....E 601 981-2811
  Jackson (G-2396)
General Electric Company ....E 662 561-9800
  Batesville (G-106)
General Electric Company ....F 769 233-2828
  Ellisville (G-1253)
Honeywell International Inc ....D 228 575-3706
  Gulfport (G-1808)
Jewell Aircrafting Inc ....G 662 252-6377
  Holly Springs (G-2178)
Lions Pride ....G 601 818-1308
  Hattiesburg (G-2017)
Pg Technologies LLC ....C 317 240-2500
  Ellisville (G-1266)
Precoat Metals Inc ....G 601 372-0325
  Jackson (G-2549)
Whitney ....G 662 268-8379
  Starkville (G-4982)

3728 Aircraft Parts & Eqpt, NEC

Aero-RAD Tech LLC ....G 662 328-0155
  Columbus (G-932)
▲ Air + Mak Industries Inc ....F 662 893-3444
  Olive Branch (G-3809)
Atk Space Systems Inc ....E 662 423-7700
  Iuka (G-2284)
Bearhawk Tailwheels LLC ....G 228 424-5096
  Long Beach (G-2928)
Boeing Company ....A 601 936-8540
  Jackson (G-2642)
DAvion LLC ....G 601 724-5013
  Brandon (G-385)

Gecas Asset MGT Svcs Inc ....G 662 455-1826
  Greenwood (G-1626)
General Electric Company ....F 769 233-2828
  Ellisville (G-1253)
Ground Support Specialist LLC ....E 662 342-1412
  Horn Lake (G-2201)
Hiro Telemedicine Systems LLC ....G 312 835-1859
  Hattiesburg (G-1990)
Landmark Spatial Solutions LLC ....G 662 769-5344
  Starkville (G-4955)
Milpar Inc ....F 662 224-0426
  Ashland (G-63)
Raytheon Company ....B 601 467-3730
  Forest (G-1424)
Sinhatech ....G 662 234-6248
  Oxford (G-4002)
Zodiac Aerospace ....G 601 657-8719
  Liberty (G-2921)

3731 Shipbuilding & Repairing

Big River Shipbuilders Inc ....E 601 636-9161
  Vicksburg (G-5345)
Brian Smith ....G 601 259-9745
  Gulfport (G-1744)
◆ Coastal Marine Equipment Inc ....D 228 832-7655
  Gulfport (G-1759)
Complete Welding Solutions ....G 601 791-5370
  Lucedale (G-2989)
Denbury Onshore LLC ....E 601 276-2147
  Ruth (G-4700)
▲ Gulf Coast Shipyard Group Inc ....D 228 276-1051
  Gulfport (G-1800)
▲ Gulf Ship LLC ....B 228 897-9189
  Gulfport (G-1802)
Gulf Ship LLC ....G 985 601-4444
  Flowood (G-1365)
▲ Horizon Shipbuilding Inc ....C 251 824-1660
  Moss Point (G-3480)
Huntington Ingalls Inc ....A 228 935-1122
  Pascagoula (G-4037)
Huntington Ingalls Industries ....F 228 935-1122
  Pascagoula (G-4038)
▲ Ingalls Shipbuilding Inc ....G 877 871-2058
  Pascagoula (G-4040)
Ingalls Shipbuilding Inc ....G 228 935-2887
  Gautier (G-1494)
Jamestown Metal Marine Sls Inc ....D 228 762-3156
  Pascagoula (G-4041)
Lynns Welding Shop LLC ....G 601 415-0012
  Vicksburg (G-5391)
Marine Flooring LLC ....G 832 472-0661
  Pascagoula (G-4050)
Marine Service Solutions ....G 601 658-0772
  Saucier (G-4758)
Mississippi Marine Corporation ....C 662 332-5457
  Greenville (G-1575)
Mississippi Marine Corporation ....C 662 335-1175
  Greenville (G-1576)
▼ Naval Engineering Works Inc ....A 228 769-1080
  Pascagoula (G-4055)
Ngss Ingalls Operations ....G 228 935-5731
  Pascagoula (G-4056)
Nsc Technologies LLC ....F 251 338-0725
  Moss Point (G-3491)
Omega Shipyard Inc ....E 228 475-9052
  Moss Point (G-3493)
Oms Shop ....E 601 835-1239
  Brookhaven (G-521)
Patco Sales Inc ....G 228 207-4171
  Pass Christian (G-4093)
Vision Technologies Marine Inc ....E 228 762-0010
  Pascagoula (G-4072)
VT Halter Marine Inc ....C 228 475-1211
  Moss Point (G-3504)
▲ VT Halter Marine Inc ....G 228 696-6888
  Pascagoula (G-4073)
VT Halter Marine Inc ....C 228 712-2278
  Moss Point (G-3505)
Withers Oil & Gas LLC ....E 601 982-3444
  Jackson (G-2635)
World Marine Mississippi LLC ....C 228 762-0010
  Pascagoula (G-4075)

3732 Boat Building & Repairing

A Step Above Marine Contrs LLC ....G 228 452-5122
  Pass Christian (G-4076)
Betta Boats LLC ....G 228 363-2529
  Bay St Louis (G-176)
Boat Man ....G 228 218-3080
  Gautier (G-1489)

Brian Smith ....G 601 259-9745
  Gulfport (G-1744)
C Wells Trucking LLC ....G 601 273-0972
  Picayune (G-4258)
Classail Models International ....G 601 373-4833
  Byram (G-620)
Clyde E Burton ....G 228 432-0117
  Biloxi (G-231)
Coastal Marine Sales LLC ....G 228 731-3955
  Gulfport (G-1760)
Emerald Water LLC ....G 601 981-2430
  Jackson (G-2400)
Jerry S Trolling Motor Repair ....G 256 431-6564
  Iuka (G-2296)
Kirkland Boats Inc ....E 662 647-0017
  Charleston (G-741)
Knights Mar & Indus Svcs Inc ....C 228 769-5550
  Pascagoula (G-4045)
Lynn Welding Shop LLC ....G 601 638-7235
  Vicksburg (G-5390)
M M Flechas Shipyard Co Inc ....G 228 762-3628
  Pascagoula (G-4047)
Mississippi Marine Corporation ....C 662 335-1175
  Greenville (G-1576)
Nautic Star LLC ....G 662 256-5636
  Amory (G-49)
Nichols Propeller Company ....E 662 378-2000
  Greenville (G-1580)
Prairie Adventure LLC ....G 662 295-8807
  West Point (G-5558)
Prop Straighteners Inc ....G 662 423-9588
  Iuka (G-2305)
Rookie Boats ....G 228 466-6377
  Bay Saint Louis (G-153)
Singin River Mental Health ....E 228 497-0690
  Gautier (G-1504)
▲ United States Marine Inc ....C 228 679-1005
  Gulfport (G-1890)
VT Halter Marine Inc ....C 228 475-1211
  Moss Point (G-3504)
VT Halter Marine Inc ....C 228 712-2278
  Moss Point (G-3505)
Westergard Boat Works Inc ....G 228 214-4455
  Gulfport (G-1893)

3743 Railroad Eqpt

American Railcar Inds Inc ....D 601 384-5841
  Bude (G-567)
Gilcorp ....D 601 932-2100
  Pearl (G-4123)
Kdh Trucking LLC ....G 601 730-2052
  Liberty (G-2913)
Trinity Highway Products Llc ....G 662 290-1500
  Kosciusko (G-2719)
Watco Co Inc ....G 601 553-1332
  Meridian (G-3416)

3751 Motorcycles, Bicycles & Parts

New Horizon Inc ....G 228 474-9918
  Moss Point (G-3489)

3761 Guided Missiles & Space Vehicles

Northrop Grumman Systems Corp ....D 228 474-3700
  Moss Point (G-3490)

3769 Guided Missile/Space Vehicle Parts & Eqpt, NEC

Atk Space Systems Inc ....E 662 423-7700
  Iuka (G-2284)
L3 Technologies Inc ....E 601 856-2274
  Madison (G-3117)

3792 Travel Trailers & Campers

M and S Sales LLC ....G 662 453-6111
  Greenwood (G-1637)
Passport America Corporation ....F 228 452-9972
  Long Beach (G-2948)
Vanleigh Rv Inc ....F 662 612-4040
  Burnsville (G-575)

3795 Tanks & Tank Components

◆ Quality Wldg & Fabrication Inc ....D 601 731-1222
  Columbia (G-914)

3799 Transportation Eqpt, NEC

B & B Mfg & Specialty Co Inc ....G 662 456-4313
  Houston (G-2231)

SIC SECTION
38 MEASURING, ANALYZING AND CONTROLLING INSTRUMENTS; PHOTOGRAPHIC, MEDICAL AN

Barrentine Trailer Mfg Co Inc .... G 662 237-9650
Greenwood *(G-1614)*

Bosarge Boats Inc .... G 228 762-0888
Pascagoula *(G-4023)*

Csa Logistics LLC .... G 601 264-2455
Hattiesburg *(G-1953)*

▼ Eddie Martin Golf Cars Inc .... G 662 620-7242
Tupelo *(G-5129)*

Gulf Coast Shipyard Group Inc .... C 228 276-1000
Gulfport *(G-1799)*

Innovative Fabrications LLC .... G 601 485-1400
Meridian *(G-3353)*

Johnsond Rv .... G 662 676-8716
Golden *(G-1528)*

Main Street Cycle Inc .... G 662 438-6407
Tishomingo *(G-5086)*

Self Serve Marine Inc .... G 228 762-3628
Pascagoula *(G-4067)*

Sport Trial .... G 228 467-1885
Bay Saint Louis *(G-157)*

Swamp Donkey LLC .... G 228 369-4927
Vancleave *(G-5322)*

Trailboss Trailers Inc .... E 800 345-2452
Macon *(G-3073)*

Triple R Trailers Inc .... G 662 728-7975
Corinth *(G-1124)*

38 MEASURING, ANALYZING AND CONTROLLING INSTRUMENTS; PHOTOGRAPHIC, MEDICAL AN

3812 Search, Detection, Navigation & Guidance Systs & Instrs

Bae Systems Tech Sol Srvc Inc .... E 703 847-5820
Gautier *(G-1488)*

Bradford Enterprises LLC .... G 901 652-1491
Southaven *(G-4856)*

Coastal Charting Consultants .... G 601 590-0540
Picayune *(G-4260)*

Eagle Eye Personal Defense .... G 662 816-2310
Oxford *(G-3953)*

Eaton Aerospace LLC .... E 601 981-2811
Jackson *(G-2396)*

L3 Technologies Inc .... E 601 856-2274
Madison *(G-3117)*

Linton Systems .... G 228 872-7300
Ocean Springs *(G-3771)*

Lockheed Martin Corporation .... F 228 864-7910
Gulfport *(G-1823)*

Lockheed Martin Corporation .... A 228 688-7997
Bay Saint Louis *(G-146)*

Lockheed Martin Corporation .... F 228 813-2160
Bay Saint Louis *(G-147)*

Lone Star Defense .... G 662 701-5204
Amory *(G-47)*

Maritime Defense Strategy LLC .... G 352 302-1442
Pascagoula *(G-4051)*

Mississippi Aerospace Corp .... F 601 749-5659
Picayune *(G-4280)*

Northrop Grumman Systems Corp .... D 228 872-7300
Ocean Springs *(G-3773)*

Northrop Grumman Systems Corp .... D 228 474-3700
Moss Point *(G-3490)*

Perspecta Engineering Inc .... G 571 313-6000
Stennis Space Center *(G-4996)*

Pretty Vixen Defense LLC .... G 228 304-2173
Pearlington *(G-4161)*

Proshop Inc .... G 662 333-7511
Myrtle *(G-3513)*

Raytheon Company .... B 601 467-3730
Forest *(G-1424)*

Ready Defense LLC .... G 662 544-3478
Holly Springs *(G-2189)*

Selex Inc .... G 228 467-2000
Kiln *(G-2684)*

T & S Machine Shop Inc .... E 601 825-8627
Brandon *(G-466)*

Taylor Defense Products LLC .... G 662 773-3421
Louisville *(G-2984)*

Tyonek Svcs Overhaul-Facility .... G 256 258-6200
Kiln *(G-2685)*

3821 Laboratory Apparatus & Furniture

Bengal Resources and Assoc Inc .... G 404 312-4642
Columbia *(G-884)*

Krueger International Inc .... A 662 842-3124
Tupelo *(G-5167)*

Missco Corporation of Jackson .... D 601 892-7105
Crystal Springs *(G-1149)*

Missco Corporation of Jackson .... F 601 352-7272
Jackson *(G-2497)*

North Miss Entp Initiative Inc .... G 662 281-0720
Oxford *(G-3978)*

▲ Sheldon Laboratory Systems Inc ..... D 601 892-2731
Crystal Springs *(G-1155)*

University of Southern Miss .... E 601 266-5390
Hattiesburg *(G-2078)*

3822 Automatic Temperature Controls

Ademco Inc .... G 601 936-4842
Richland *(G-4499)*

Bateman Airconditioning .... G 601 225-4442
Gloster *(G-1511)*

Bio-Solutions Franchise Corp .... G 601 582-4000
Hattiesburg *(G-1933)*

Clyde Woodward Jr .... G 601 736-6115
Columbia *(G-887)*

Hoshizaki of Jackson .... G 601 969-4200
Jackson *(G-2442)*

Kuhlman Electric Corporation .... B 601 892-4661
Crystal Springs *(G-1144)*

Siemens Industry Inc .... G 601 939-0550
Richland *(G-4524)*

3823 Indl Instruments For Meas, Display & Control

Bradford Enterprises .... G 601 442-2339
Natchez *(G-3538)*

Hydrasep Inc .... G 662 429-4088
Hernando *(G-2135)*

Hydrolevel .... G 228 875-1821
Ocean Springs *(G-3765)*

Kuhlman Electric Corporation .... B 601 892-4661
Crystal Springs *(G-1144)*

Lec Inc .... E 601 939-8535
Pearl *(G-4128)*

Luckett Pump & Well Svc Inc .... G 662 624-2398
Dublin *(G-1219)*

Omni Instruments .... G 228 388-9211
Biloxi *(G-270)*

One Source Systems LLC .... E 601 636-6888
Vicksburg *(G-5403)*

Real-Time Laboratories LLC .... G 601 389-2212
Choctaw *(G-751)*

S & S Timber .... F 601 833-8844
Wesson *(G-5529)*

3824 Fluid Meters & Counters

Ben Mears Taxidermists & Sups .... G 662 282-4594
Mantachie *(G-3198)*

3825 Instrs For Measuring & Testing Electricity

AA Calibration Services LLC .... F 662 716-0202
Yazoo City *(G-5620)*

High Yield AG Solutions LLC .... G 662 546-4463
Starkville *(G-4949)*

Quality Cnstr & Engrg LLC .... C 601 786-8017
Fayette *(G-1299)*

Rolls-Royce North America Inc .... G 228 688-1003
Stennis Space Center *(G-4997)*

Smart Synch .... G 601 420-9959
Flowood *(G-1397)*

▲ Supreme Electronics Corp .... F 662 453-6212
Greenwood *(G-1653)*

▲ Watthour Engineering Co Inc .... E 601 933-0900
Pearl *(G-4158)*

3826 Analytical Instruments

Inciteful Analytics Corp .... G 601 870-4004
Meadville *(G-3275)*

Philumina LLC .... G 228 363-4048
Long Beach *(G-2949)*

Taylor Environmental Products .... G 662 773-8056
Louisville *(G-2985)*

3827 Optical Instruments

Design Tech Inc .... G 601 798-5844
Carriere *(G-691)*

▲ Ferson LLC .... F 228 875-8146
Ocean Springs *(G-3757)*

Ii-VI Incorporated .... G 662 615-5040
Starkville *(G-4951)*

Nucor Grating .... G 601 853-9996
Madison *(G-3134)*

Safilo .... G 601 212-4136
Brandon *(G-449)*

Source .... G 601 949-7878
Jackson *(G-2588)*

3829 Measuring & Controlling Devices, NEC

1 A Lifesafer Inc .... G 800 634-3077
McComb *(G-3242)*

1 A Lifesafer Inc .... G 800 634-3077
Southaven *(G-4849)*

1 A Lifesafer Inc .... G 800 634-3077
Tupelo *(G-5105)*

1 A Lifesafer Inc .... G 800 634-3077
Pascagoula *(G-4016)*

1 A Lifesafer Inc .... G 800 634-3077
Gulfport *(G-1714)*

1 A Lifesafer Inc .... G 800 634-3077
Mathiston *(G-3225)*

1 A Lifesafer Inc .... G 800 634-3077
Meridian *(G-3292)*

1 A Lifesafer Inc .... G 800 634-3077
Hattiesburg *(G-1913)*

1 A Lifesafer Inc .... G 800 634-3077
Natchez *(G-3515)*

1 A Lifesafer Inc .... G 800 634-3077
Greenville *(G-1534)*

1 A Lifesafer Inc .... G 800 634-3077
Jackson *(G-2312)*

3d Laser Scanning LLC .... G 228 860-5952
Biloxi *(G-214)*

Carnet Technology .... G 601 857-8641
Terry *(G-5064)*

Delta Enterprises .... G 662 335-5291
Greenville *(G-1545)*

Fairbanks Scales Inc .... E 601 482-2073
Meridian *(G-3337)*

Heath Aviation .... G 662 283-9833
Winona *(G-5599)*

J D Smith Drilling Company .... G 601 989-2475
Richton *(G-4536)*

Kelsey Bailey Consulting LLC .... G 601 622-8319
Madison *(G-3115)*

Mississippi State University .... D 662 325-2510
Starkville *(G-4960)*

Nvision Solutions Inc .... D 228 242-0010
Diamondhead *(G-1192)*

Presto-Tap LLC .... G 662 332-8559
Greenville *(G-1591)*

Slide Rule LLC .... G 228 863-8583
Gulfport *(G-1872)*

Standard Dynamics LLC .... G 228 383-2070
Starkville *(G-4975)*

Thermoprobe Inc .... F 601 939-1831
Pearl *(G-4151)*

3841 Surgical & Medical Instrs & Apparatus

Central Medical Equipment .... G 661 843-6161
Carthage *(G-710)*

Coles Tool Works Inc .... C 662 429-5191
Hernando *(G-2125)*

Cuff Toughener .... G 601 209-1609
Ridgeland *(G-4569)*

Desoto Sleep Diagnostics .... G 662 349-9802
Southaven *(G-4867)*

Dr Erica Aesthetic Center .... G 662 284-9600
Corinth *(G-1084)*

Emergent Prtctive Pdts USA Inc .... F 517 489-5172
Hattiesburg *(G-1962)*

EZ Medical Wraps LLC .... G 321 961-0201
Brandon *(G-396)*

Kerex LLC .... G 210 494-5596
Jackson *(G-2463)*

Medical Arts Surgical Group .... F 601 693-3834
Meridian *(G-3366)*

Medtronic Inc .... C 662 895-2016
Olive Branch *(G-3873)*

Medworx Compounding LLC .... F 601 859-5008
Ridgeland *(G-4605)*

◆ Microtek Medical Inc .... B 662 327-1863
Columbus *(G-1000)*

Mobile Diagnostics Inc .... G 601 445-9895
Natchez *(G-3591)*

Needle Specialty Products Corp .... C 662 843-8913
Boyle *(G-351)*

Norwood Medical Supply LLC .... G 601 792-2224
Prentiss *(G-4422)*

Oligarch Inc .... G 844 321-0016
Houston *(G-2253)*

Open Air M R I of Laurel .... G 601 428-5026
Laurel *(G-2815)*

S I C

Employee Codes: A=Over 500 employees, B=251-500
C=101-250, D=51-100, E=20-50, F=10-19, G=1-9

2019 Harris Directory of
Mississippi Manufacturers

253

38 MEASURING, ANALYZING AND CONTROLLING INSTRUMENTS; PHOTOGRAPHIC, MEDICAL AN

SIC SECTION

Peltz Medical LLC ....G...... 601 831-3135
Vicksburg (G-5404)

Precision Spine Inc ....G...... 601 420-4244
Pearl (G-4139)

Smiths Medical Asd Inc ....F...... 662 895-8000
Olive Branch (G-3912)

Spinal Usa Inc ....D...... 601 420-4244
Pearl (G-4148)

Spine Stability Surgical LLC ....G...... 800 991-3723
Jackson (G-2595)

Tegra Medical (ms) LLC ....E...... 662 429-5191
Hernando (G-2159)

◆ Teleflex Medical Incorporated ....D...... 662 892-9100
Olive Branch (G-3916)

Terumo Medical Corporation ....F...... 662 280-2643
Southaven (G-4914)

Willow Ansthesia Solutions LLC ....G...... 662 550-4299
Oxford (G-4009)

3842 Orthopedic, Prosthetic & Surgical Appliances/Splys

901 Safety LLC ....G...... 901 493-3841
Olive Branch (G-3803)

Ability Prosthetics LLC ....G...... 662 842-3220
Tupelo (G-5106)

Adams Prsthtics Orthdntics LLC ....G...... 601 665-4000
Jackson (G-2318)

ADP Hearing Inc ....G...... 662 874-6279
Olive Branch (G-3805)

Advanced Hearing and Balance ....G...... 601 450-0280
Hattiesburg (G-1915)

Advantage Medical and Phrm LLC .....G...... 601 268-1422
Hattiesburg (G-1916)

Alatheia Prosthetic Reha ....F...... 601 919-2113
Brandon (G-360)

Ascend Surgical Sales LLC ....G...... 601 351-9866
Ridgeland (G-4551)

BMW Prosthetics Orthotics LLC ....E...... 601 414-0032
Jackson (G-2339)

Central Fabrication Inc ....G...... 662 349-7122
Southaven (G-4858)

Chariot Wheelchair and RPR ....G...... 228 967-7991
Biloxi (G-227)

▲ Choctaw Glove & Safety Co Inc ......D...... 662 724-4178
Noxapater (G-3731)

Custom Prosthetic & Orthotic ....G...... 601 708-4196
Clinton (G-819)

Gulf Coast Limb & Brace Inc ....G...... 228 864-4512
Gulfport (G-1798)

Hanger Inc ....E...... 228 604-0818
Gulfport (G-1803)

Hanger Prosthetic Orthopedics ....G...... 601 939-2100
Jackson (G-2647)

Hanger Prsthetcs & Ortho Inc ....G...... 662 451-7495
Greenwood (G-1627)

Hanger Prsthetcs & Ortho Inc ....G...... 601 268-5520
Hattiesburg (G-1982)

Hanger Prsthetcs & Ortho Inc ....G...... 601 883-3341
Vicksburg (G-5377)

Hanger Prsthetcs & Ortho Inc ....G...... 228 822-0109
Gulfport (G-1804)

Hanger Prsthetcs & Ortho Inc ....G...... 228 875-8354
Ocean Springs (G-3761)

Hanger Prsthetcs & Ortho Inc ....G...... 601 939-2100
Jackson (G-2648)

Hanger Prsthetcs & Ortho Inc ....G...... 662 844-6734
Tupelo (G-5150)

Hanger Prsthetcs & Ortho Inc ....G...... 601 693-1002
Meridian (G-3345)

Hanger Prsthetcs & Ortho Inc ....G...... 662 335-6828
Greenville (G-1557)

Hanger Prsthetcs & Ortho Inc ....G...... 601 442-7742
Natchez (G-3566)

Hanger Prsthetcs & Ortho Inc ....G...... 662 323-3349
Starkville (G-4947)

Hear Again ....G...... 601 626-0050
Collinsville (G-869)

Human Technology Inc ....G...... 662 349-4909
Southaven (G-4878)

In Motion Orthotics ....G...... 662 258-8201
Eupora (G-1287)

J & B Athletics ....G...... 601 776-7557
Quitman (G-4466)

J J Hill Brace & Limb Co Inc ....G...... 228 863-0381
Gulfport (G-1812)

Jackson Brace Co ....F...... 601 353-2477
Jackson (G-2453)

▲ Logistical Services Intl Inc ....G...... 662 676-2823
Golden (G-1529)

Medi-Vation LLC ....G...... 800 643-2134
Madison (G-3128)

Memphis Obstetrics & Gynecolog ....G...... 662 349-5554
Southaven (G-4889)

Methodist and Prosthetics ....G...... 662 846-6555
Cleveland (G-799)

Mid State Artificial Limb Inc ....F...... 601 981-2229
Jackson (G-2490)

National Seating Mobility Inc ....G...... 601 664-1090
Flowood (G-1384)

Ovation Womens Wellness LLC ....G...... 601 326-6401
Jackson (G-2532)

Oxford Scrubs ....G...... 662 513-0341
Oxford (G-3991)

Parr Prosthetics ....G...... 601 749-7254
Picayune (G-4283)

Prosthetic Solutions Inc ....F...... 228 220-4917
Gulfport (G-1855)

Southern Prosthetic Care LLC ....G...... 769 242-2555
Picayune (G-4296)

Spine Stability Surgical LLC ....G...... 800 991-3723
Jackson (G-2595)

Synergy Prosthetics Center ....G...... 601 832-4975
Jackson (G-2602)

T & S Machine Shop Inc ....E...... 601 825-8627
Brandon (G-466)

Walker Missionary Baptist Pars ....G...... 662 585-3309
Golden (G-1532)

Zavation LLC ....G...... 601 919-1119
Flowood (G-1408)

3843 Dental Eqpt & Splys

Gold Teeth Customs ....G...... 601 955-4653
Jackson (G-2427)

New Patients Number ....G...... 662 323-2803
Starkville (G-4964)

P Adam Middleton ....G...... 662 289-7076
Kosciusko (G-2708)

3844 X-ray Apparatus & Tubes

Deep South Physics Pllc ....G...... 601 613-8076
Brandon (G-386)

3845 Electromedical & Electrotherapeutic Apparatus

Curahe LLC ....G...... 662 325-2176
Starkville (G-4937)

Min Sheng Healthcare LLC ....G...... 601 212-6189
Madison (G-3130)

Vital Care of Central Ms ....G...... 601 859-8200
Madison (G-3166)

3851 Ophthalmic Goods

901 Safety LLC ....G...... 901 493-3841
Olive Branch (G-3803)

Cook Eye Center ....G...... 601 553-2100
Meridian (G-3323)

Cv Sunglasses LLC ....G...... 662 212-0993
Walnut (G-5456)

D Dodd John Od ....G...... 662 286-5671
Corinth (G-1082)

Dearlens Inc ....G...... 601 693-1841
Meridian (G-3328)

Hoffman Lenses Inc ....G...... 662 815-2803
Blue Mountain (G-291)

I Care Optical Inc ....F...... 601 372-3801
Terry (G-5069)

I Care Optical Inc ....G...... 228 864-4397
Gulfport (G-1811)

I Care Optical Inc ....E...... 601 352-3576
Terry (G-5070)

J & R Optical Co Inc ....G...... 601 977-0272
Jackson (G-2450)

Saul Jay Enterprises Inc ....F...... 662 349-1660
Southaven (G-4899)

Spectacles Inc ....F...... 601 398-4662
Jackson (G-2593)

Superior Optical Labs Inc ....E...... 228 875-3796
Ocean Springs (G-3790)

Vision Center PA ....G...... 601 928-3914
Wiggins (G-5593)

3861 Photographic Eqpt & Splys

Exel Logistics Xerox ....G...... 662 393-7122
Southaven (G-4872)

Quantum Scientific Imaging Inc ....F...... 601 795-8824
Poplarville (G-4389)

Record Imaging Systems ....G...... 662 280-1286
Southaven (G-4896)

Sandstorm Entertainment ....G...... 662 578-1357
Batesville (G-123)

39 MISCELLANEOUS MANUFACTURING INDUSTRIES

3911 Jewelry: Precious Metal

Courtyard Mfg Jewelers ....G...... 601 825-6162
Brandon (G-382)

Dunns Jewelry ....G...... 662 363-1501
Tunica (G-5099)

Joe Tonos Jeweler Inc ....G...... 662 335-1160
Greenville (G-1559)

Maelstrom Square LLC ....G...... 470 378-9064
Pascagoula (G-4048)

Mary Givens ....G...... 601 325-5599
Brandon (G-419)

Mast Management LLC ....G...... 601 833-8073
Brookhaven (G-516)

Pav & Brome Wtchmkers Jewelers ....G...... 228 863-3699
Gulfport (G-1847)

Smokers Express ....G...... 601 483-5789
Philadelphia (G-4236)

Southern Traditions ....G...... 662 534-0410
New Albany (G-3698)

Thomas Jewelry ....G...... 601 264-8780
Hattiesburg (G-2073)

3914 Silverware, Plated & Stainless Steel Ware

Renchers This & That ....G...... 662 624-9825
Clarksdale (G-779)

3915 Jewelers Findings & Lapidary Work

National Diamond Corp ....G...... 662 895-9633
Olive Branch (G-3883)

3931 Musical Instruments

Crossroads Picks LLC ....G...... 662 902-1026
Clarksdale (G-765)

EZ Chord LLC ....G...... 601 329-3827
Diberville (G-1202)

▼ Hot Sticks Manufacturing Co ....F...... 228 467-0762
Kiln (G-2680)

◆ Peavey Electronics Corporation ....B...... 601 483-5365
Meridian (G-3381)

Peavey Electronics Corporation ....G...... 601 486-1878
Meridian (G-3384)

Pipe Organ Specialties Inc ....G...... 601 649-5581
Laurel (G-2822)

Tinks Bells ....G...... 662 574-2685
Columbus (G-1038)

3942 Dolls & Stuffed Toys

Beryl Jones ....G...... 601 442-4597
Natchez (G-3529)

Best Dressed Bunnies ....G...... 228 826-4619
Ocean Springs (G-3743)

Carol Baird ....G...... 601 924-5409
Clinton (G-818)

Smocking Bird Clothing LLC ....G...... 662 453-6432
Greenwood (G-1652)

Sneaker Addict Clothing ....G...... 601 212-3205
Jackson (G-2584)

Well Made Goods LLC ....G...... 917 853-3598
Grenada (G-1712)

3944 Games, Toys & Children's Vehicles

Action Prsuit Games of Brandon ....G...... 601 825-1052
Brandon (G-356)

Amandas Puzzles ....G...... 228 314-3930
Gulfport (G-1724)

American Plastic Toys Inc ....C...... 662 895-4055
Olive Branch (G-3812)

Crafts By Fenton ....G...... 601 477-9164
Ellisville (G-1250)

Gray Daniels Auto Family ....G...... 601 948-0576
Brandon (G-401)

Hint Hunter LLC ....G...... 228 273-4064
Diberville (G-1207)

Janlynn Crafts ....G...... 601 956-1832
Jackson (G-2458)

Kewl Kites ....G...... 228 206-0322
Long Beach (G-2941)

Ladonna R Williams ....G...... 601 405-2200
Clinton (G-828)

2019 Harris Directory of
Mississippi Manufacturers

254

SIC SECTION

39 MISCELLANEOUS MANUFACTURING INDUSTRIES

Laser Mania Inc ....G...... 601 543-0072
Hattiesburg (G-2016)

Mabrys ....G...... 601 956-7238
Jackson (G-2475)

Natures Society Majestic Arts ....G...... 601 376-0447
Byram (G-623)

Parker Brothers 2 Inc ....G...... 662 283-2224
Winona (G-5605)

3949 Sporting & Athletic Goods, NEC

Ability Works Inc ....G...... 662 328-0275
Columbus (G-931)

Advanced GnsInger Armament LLC .....G...... 775 343-5633
Starkville (G-4923)

Ao Liquidation Trust Inc ....E...... 662 675-8102
Coffeeville (G-841)

Arrowmaker ....G...... 601 264-4748
Purvis (G-4433)

Bain Manufacturing Co Inc ....F...... 662 226-7921
Grenada (G-1668)

Boomerang Services LLC ....G...... 601 649-6474
Laurel (G-2741)

Brock Outdoors ....G...... 662 255-1121
Saltillo (G-4709)

Cemco Inc ....E...... 662 323-1559
Starkville (G-4933)

Champion Custom Bow Strings ....G...... 662 652-3499
Fulton (G-1449)

Cjw Hunting LLC ....G...... 662 746-1863
Yazoo City (G-5628)

Clay Necaise ....G...... 228 233-7760
Bay Saint Louis (G-140)

College Station Spt Stores Inc ....G...... 662 349-8988
Southaven (G-4860)

Conviction Game Calls ....G...... 662 295-9972
West Point (G-5541)

Coon Creek Custom Game Calls ....G...... 662 284-6932
Corinth (G-1073)

Dixons Hunting Lodge ....G...... 662 571-1908
Benton (G-208)

Espiritu Custom Cues ....G...... 601 825-7077
Brandon (G-395)

Excel By Four LLC ....G...... 228 355-8203
Gulfport (G-1780)

Gator Archery & Outdoors LLC ....G...... 601 940-3570
Madison (G-3103)

Green Save Inc ....G...... 662 566-0717
Verona (G-5332)

Gulf States Golf Cars ....G...... 601 853-1510
Ridgeland (G-4588)

Hanson Athletic Inc ....G...... 601 389-0403
Philadelphia (G-4216)

Hickory Creek Inc ....G...... 228 832-2649
Saucier (G-4754)

Huntin Camp LLC ....G...... 601 649-6334
Laurel (G-2783)

▲ Icon Outdoors LLC ....G...... 662 895-3651
Olive Branch (G-3850)

Itawamba Classic Lures ....G...... 601 720-8810
Fulton (G-1458)

Jackson Fishing Sptg Accessory ....G...... 662 837-9089
Falkner (G-1295)

Jara L Miller ....G...... 601 421-6876
Brandon (G-410)

Johnson Education Firm LLC ....G...... 662 347-9150
Greenville (G-1560)

Kinards Kountry ....G...... 601 737-8378
Bailey (G-68)

Krewe of Natchez Indn Yth Ldrs ....E...... 601 392-1709
Natchez (G-3577)

Mediator Lures Inc ....G...... 601 992-1577
Brandon (G-423)

Mississssppi Bsktball Athltics ....G...... 601 957-7373
Jackson (G-2507)

Mstate Technologies LLC ....G...... 662 418-0110
Starkville (G-4962)

Old River Lure Company LLC ....G...... 601 259-4323
Terry (G-5074)

Outdoors Advantage ....G...... 662 257-9601
Tupelo (G-5196)

Outlaw Sporting Goods LLC ....G...... 662 459-9054
Greenwood (G-1644)

▲ Primos Inc ....D...... 601 879-9323
Flora (G-1311)

Proshop Inc ....G...... 662 333-7511
Myrtle (G-3513)

Pugh Tackle Co Inc ....G...... 662 534-7393
New Albany (G-3692)

Quitman Sporting Goods & Pawn ....G...... 601 776-3212
Quitman (G-4468)

RAC N Spurs Game Calls ....G...... 601 455-9484
Silver Creek (G-4839)

Rog LLC ....G...... 662 455-1364
Greenwood (G-1649)

Shoreline Pool Mfr Inc ....G...... 601 372-0577
Jackson (G-2580)

Sipp Spinners and Lures LLC ....G...... 601 620-6445
Brandon (G-454)

▲ Slaters Jigs Inc ....G...... 662 887-3548
Indianola (G-2270)

Southeast Miss Schl Pdts Inc ....G...... 662 855-5048
Caledonia (G-631)

Southern Lure Company Inc ....F...... 662 327-4548
Columbus (G-1029)

Southern Roost Game Calls ....G...... 601 441-0748
Columbia (G-922)

Sparko Inc ....G...... 662 690-5800
Tupelo (G-5229)

Sports of All Sorts Inc ....G...... 662 429-1162
Hernando (G-2156)

Sportz Zone LLC ....G...... 228 284-1654
Long Beach (G-2954)

Stryke Ryte Lures ....G...... 217 370-9461
New Albany (G-3702)

Swell O Phonic ....G...... 601 981-3547
Jackson (G-2601)

Taylor Enterprises ....G...... 228 385-1245
Biloxi (G-282)

Throw Strikes Baseball Academy ....G...... 662 931-4948
Greenville (G-1604)

Tombstone Game Calls ....G...... 662 769-6364
Maben (G-3052)

Tri-State Athletic Group ....G...... 901 395-6359
Southaven (G-4916)

Triple M Lures LLC ....G...... 601 919-5515
Perkinston (G-4182)

True Temper Sports Inc ....B...... 662 256-5605
Amory (G-57)

Tucker Manufacturing Co Inc ....E...... 662 563-7220
Batesville (G-131)

Turner Fly Rods LLC ....G...... 228 623-6475
Moss Point (G-3503)

Wilder Fitness Systems ....G...... 662 489-8365
Pontotoc (G-4370)

Wilson Fabrication Inc ....G...... 601 445-8119
Natchez (G-3643)

Wonder Woods Inc ....G...... 601 853-1956
Madison (G-3172)

Wooly Booger Game Calls ....G...... 662 587-3763
Walnut (G-5459)

3952 Lead Pencils, Crayons & Artist's Mtrls

Rivers Gist Gainspoletti ....G...... 662 902-5415
Cleveland (G-805)

Wet Paint LLC ....G...... 662 269-2412
Tupelo (G-5258)

3953 Marking Devices

Correy Elder ....G...... 769 257-3240
Madison (G-3089)

DLS Tax Consultants ....G...... 601 473-6623
Jackson (G-2387)

Documart of Mid-South LLC ....G...... 662 281-1474
Oxford (G-3951)

J & S Enterprises LLC ....G...... 601 646-3636
Hickory (G-2162)

Labels & Stamps of Ellisville ....G...... 601 763-3092
Ellisville (G-1262)

McMillan Stamp & Sign Co Inc ....G...... 601 353-4688
Jackson (G-2485)

Midsouth Corporate Housing ....G...... 901 239-4514
Olive Branch (G-3877)

Noyes Printing & Rbr Stamp Co ....G...... 662 332-5256
Greenville (G-1583)

Prosperity7 Helping Hands LLC ....G...... 800 597-6599
Southaven (G-4893)

Southern Rubber Stamp Inc ....G...... 601 373-6590
Jackson (G-2591)

▲ Trodat Marking Products Inc ....G...... 601 500-5971
Jackson (G-2612)

3955 Carbon Paper & Inked Ribbons

Kdeb Manufacturing LLC ....G...... 601 750-9659
Morton (G-3448)

3961 Costume Jewelry & Novelties

Allens Trophies Inc ....E...... 601 582-7702
Hattiesburg (G-1920)

Crystal Crown Inc ....G...... 601 947-8074
Lucedale (G-2992)

Maurice Hinton ....G...... 601 857-5168
Terry (G-5072)

Sparkles & Such ....G...... 601 750-1270
Crystal Springs (G-1157)

3965 Fasteners, Buttons, Needles & Pins

Bolt Company LLC ....G...... 601 696-9191
Meridian (G-3312)

Grenada Fasteners Inc ....G...... 662 227-1000
Grenada (G-1680)

Illinois Tool Works Inc ....C...... 662 489-4151
Pontotoc (G-4335)

Mjj Inc ....G...... 662 455-0126
Greenwood (G-1641)

Sta-Put-Hook LLC ....G...... 601 622-7313
Madison (G-3152)

Triangle Fastener Corporation ....G...... 601 956-1824
Ridgeland (G-4643)

3991 Brooms & Brushes

Easy Reach Supply LLC ....E...... 601 582-7866
Hattiesburg (G-1959)

▲ Hub City Brush Inc ....F...... 601 584-7314
Petal (G-4187)

L C Industries Inc ....B...... 601 894-1771
Hazlehurst (G-2099)

Lighthouse For The Blind ....G...... 228 867-1565
Gulfport (G-1822)

Piave Broom & Mop Inc ....F...... 601 584-7314
Petal (G-4195)

Signature Works Inc ....B...... 601 894-1771
Hazlehurst (G-2106)

3993 Signs & Advertising Displays

59 Signs LLC ....G...... 601 798-3682
Carriere (G-686)

A Plus Signs Inc ....G...... 601 355-9595
Jackson (G-2314)

A To B Sign Company ....G...... 601 924-6323
Clinton (G-811)

Ad Art Sign ....G...... 601 939-8000
Pearl (G-4103)

Ad Lines Inc ....G...... 662 893-6400
Nesbit (G-3646)

▲ Address America Inc ....G...... 888 991-3322
Jackson (G-2319)

Ainsworth Signs ....G...... 662 453-1904
Greenwood (G-1611)

Airbrush & Signs By Debby ....G...... 601 656-6953
Philadelphia (G-4202)

Airdesigns ....G...... 601 584-1000
Hattiesburg (G-1919)

Alden R Stockert ....G...... 228 731-2747
Gulfport (G-1717)

All In One Signs & Printing ....G...... 662 216-0737
Holly Springs (G-2170)

All Signs Inc ....G...... 228 897-9100
Gulfport (G-1719)

Allens Trophies Inc ....E...... 601 582-7702
Hattiesburg (G-1920)

AMC Signs & Lighting LLC ....G...... 901 831-7393
Iuka (G-2283)

Auto Trim Design of Meridian ....G...... 601 482-8037
Meridian (G-3303)

Ball Sign Co ....G...... 662 236-2338
Oxford (G-3938)

Be Joyful Signs ....G...... 601 540-6602
Natchez (G-3525)

Berry Signs & Stripes ....G...... 601 544-5600
Hattiesburg (G-1930)

Better Signs Inc ....G...... 662 227-1235
Grenada (G-1669)

Big D Signs ....G...... 228 860-1075
Diberville (G-1198)

Bloms Creative Signs Inc ....G...... 228 374-2566
Biloxi (G-221)

Blue Chip Signs Inc ....G...... 228 918-9511
Biloxi (G-221)

Brian Scott Moore ....G...... 901 831-7393
Tishomingo (G-5082)

Budget Signs Inc ....F...... 601 354-4977
Jackson (G-2348)

C&C Signs LLC ....G...... 228 235-4839
Diberville (G-1200)

Charleston Manufacturing LLC ....G...... 901 853-3070
Olive Branch (G-3822)

Chism Rackard Enterprises LLC ....G...... 662 327-5200
Columbus (G-947)

S I C

Employee Codes: A=Over 500 employees, B=251-500
C=101-250, D=51-100, E=20-50, F=10-19, G=1-9

2019 Harris Directory of
Mississippi Manufacturers

255

39 MISCELLANEOUS MANUFACTURING INDUSTRIES SIC SECTION

Computer Graphics By Connie..............G....... 662 343-8399
Hamilton ***(G-1904)***
Creative Ventures LLC..............G....... 601 798-7758
Picayune ***(G-4264)***
Cupitsignscom LLC..............G....... 228 712-2322
Pascagoula ***(G-4029)***
Custom Sign Co of Batesville..............G....... 662 844-6333
Tupelo ***(G-5125)***
Custom Sign Co of Batesville..............E....... 662 563-7371
Batesville ***(G-104)***
D & D Signs and Labels..............G....... 662 449-4956
Nesbit ***(G-3649)***
D D Berryhill Signs..............G....... 662 298-3325
Hernando ***(G-2128)***
Dan W Butler Signs..............G....... 601 948-5059
Jackson ***(G-2375)***
Davids Signs Inc..............G....... 601 626-8934
Collinsville ***(G-867)***
Delta Sign Shop..............G....... 662 334-9878
Greenville ***(G-1549)***
Delta Signs and Designs LLC..............G....... 662 822-0830
Greenville ***(G-1550)***
Designs of Times Inc..............G....... 601 791-5299
Lucedale ***(G-2993)***
Desoto Digital Services Llc..............G....... 662 336-2233
Olive Branch ***(G-3834)***
Dims Group..............G....... 302 562-2697
Southaven ***(G-4868)***
Dixie Signs LLC..............G....... 228 255-5548
Pass Christian ***(G-4081)***
Dotted Signs & Screenprinting..............G....... 601 506-2175
Forest ***(G-1415)***
Dunaway Signs Inc..............G....... 228 392-5421
Biloxi ***(G-239)***
Duncan Signs Inc..............G....... 662 842-0226
Tupelo ***(G-5127)***
Dwain Mc Nair Signs & Screen..............G....... 601 267-9967
Carthage ***(G-715)***
Dynamic Signs and More..............G....... 228 235-5660
Biloxi ***(G-240)***
E Vegely Signs..............G....... 228 255-7543
Pass Christian ***(G-4082)***
Econo Signs..............G....... 662 844-1554
Tupelo ***(G-5128)***
Eddie Wiggs..............G....... 662 456-7080
Houston ***(G-2239)***
Ets Signs Inc..............G....... 601 268-7275
Hattiesburg ***(G-1964)***
Eyecatcher Signs..............G....... 601 604-2595
Meridian ***(G-3336)***
Fast Signs..............G....... 601 602-5413
Hattiesburg ***(G-1968)***
Fastwrapzcom LLC..............G....... 662 213-8771
Tupelo ***(G-5131)***
Federal Heath Sign Company LLC..............G....... 662 233-2999
Coldwater ***(G-845)***
Fred Windham Signs..............G....... 601 794-1445
Purvis ***(G-4438)***
Garys Graphics..............G....... 662 429-2924
Nesbit ***(G-3652)***
Gator Sign & Image Concepts..............G....... 601 684-8686
McComb ***(G-3251)***
Gentry Signs..............G....... 662 323-3652
Starkville ***(G-4946)***
Gpp Charleston Industries LLC..............E....... 800 647-2384
Charleston ***(G-738)***
H&S Sign Company..............G....... 662 473-9300
Water Valley ***(G-5470)***
Hancock Advg Specialities..............G....... 662 842-1820
Tupelo ***(G-5149)***
Harris Signs..............G....... 601 624-4658
Brandon ***(G-404)***
◆ **Headrick Signs & Graphics Inc**..............D....... 601 649-1977
Laurel ***(G-2776)***
Hearz Yer Sign..............G....... 601 683-3636
Newton ***(G-3721)***
Hospitality Sign Company..............G....... 601 898-8393
Madison ***(G-3108)***
Houston Sign Design..............G....... 662 728-2327
Booneville ***(G-330)***
Hudson Outdoor Sign LLC..............G....... 601 947-4608
Lucedale ***(G-3002)***
Identities Graphic Solutions..............G....... 601 917-9983
Meridian ***(G-3349)***
Illusions Neon & Accessories..............G....... 662 299-6366
Greenwood ***(G-1628)***
Images Galore Signs LLC..............G....... 228 818-5449
Ocean Springs ***(G-3766)***
Independents Service Company..............G....... 662 287-2431
Corinth ***(G-1091)***
Its Vinyl YAll LLC..............G....... 601 533-8885
Canton ***(G-662)***
Jan Signs Inc..............G....... 601 785-9800
Taylorsville ***(G-5054)***
John Sign & Co Inc..............G....... 662 843-3548
Cleveland ***(G-797)***
Jones Signs LLC..............G....... 662 453-2432
Greenwood ***(G-1632)***
▲ **K & K Systems Inc**..............D....... 662 566-2025
Tupelo ***(G-5165)***
King B Signs and Wonders Inc..............G....... 815 263-1546
Columbus ***(G-993)***
Lightning Quick Signs..............G....... 228 467-1718
Waveland ***(G-5482)***
Linco Safety Signs..............G....... 662 469-9569
Hernando ***(G-2140)***
Major League Promotions..............G....... 601 672-4798
Jackson ***(G-2481)***
Major League Promotions LLC..............G....... 601 672-4798
Jackson ***(G-2482)***
Manning Signs Inc..............G....... 662 332-4496
Greenville ***(G-1567)***
McMillan Stamp & Sign Co Inc..............G....... 601 353-4688
Jackson ***(G-2485)***
Mickeys Trophy & Sign Shop..............G....... 601 649-1263
Laurel ***(G-2802)***
Mid South Sign Council..............G....... 601 446-6688
Natchez ***(G-3587)***
Mid-Mississippi Vinyl..............G....... 601 910-6553
Flowood ***(G-1381)***
Mid-South Signs Inc..............F....... 662 327-7807
Columbus ***(G-1001)***
Mike Stringer Signs..............G....... 601 736-8600
Columbia ***(G-907)***
◆ **Mitchell Signs Inc**..............D....... 601 553-1557
Meridian ***(G-3374)***
Multimedia Graphics Inc..............F....... 601 981-5001
Jackson ***(G-2514)***
Munn Enterprises Inc..............D....... 601 264-7446
Hattiesburg ***(G-2035)***
National Scrubwear Inc..............F....... 601 483-0796
Meridian ***(G-3376)***
National Sign Tennessee Corp..............G....... 901 210-8023
Olive Branch ***(G-3887)***
New Albany Sign Co..............G....... 662 538-5599
New Albany ***(G-3689)***
Ocean Springs Sign & Graphics..............G....... 228 213-7933
Gautier ***(G-1500)***
Oneway Inc..............G....... 601 664-0007
Jackson ***(G-2660)***
Outdoor Dimensions Inc..............G....... 601 749-9981
Picayune ***(G-4282)***
Peacocks Signs & Designs..............G....... 662 226-9206
Grenada ***(G-1698)***
Pearl Rubber Stamp & Sign Inc..............F....... 601 932-6699
Jackson ***(G-2662)***
Pickett Productions..............G....... 601 885-2720
Utica ***(G-5310)***
Plastics Plus Inc..............G....... 228 832-4634
Gulfport ***(G-1849)***
Pop-A-Cart LLC..............G....... 931 292-2150
Jackson ***(G-2541)***
Pro Signs..............G....... 662 587-6036
Ripley ***(G-4668)***
Prosigns Inc..............G....... 601 791-5299
Lucedale ***(G-3012)***
R D Graphix Sign Solutions..............G....... 601 736-0663
Columbia ***(G-916)***
Ra Maxx LLC..............G....... 662 342-6212
Southaven ***(G-4894)***
Rainbow Signs..............G....... 228 354-8008
Biloxi ***(G-275)***
Red Creek Graphics LLC..............G....... 228 864-3349
Gulfport ***(G-1859)***
Relevant Design Studios LLC..............G....... 601 736-0663
Columbia ***(G-918)***
Reservoir Signs LLC..............G....... 601 898-1111
Madison ***(G-3143)***
Rodger Holdeman S Signs..............G....... 662 436-0911
West Point ***(G-5561)***
Roger Fillebaum..............G....... 601 638-5473
Vicksburg ***(G-5414)***
Roosevelt Wallace..............G....... 662 627-7513
Clarksdale ***(G-781)***
S H Wholesale Sign Co..............G....... 228 865-4352
Gulfport ***(G-1866)***
S&S Signs..............G....... 601 659-7783
Stonewall ***(G-4999)***
Sarub Inc..............G....... 601 936-4490
Pearl ***(G-4142)***
Scs Signs and Service LLC..............G....... 228 235-4839
Diberville ***(G-1212)***
Select Signs More..............G....... 601 823-0717
Brookhaven ***(G-530)***
Shaw Signs LLC..............G....... 228 224-4971
Saucier ***(G-4764)***
Sign and Sing..............G....... 601 954-9172
Brandon ***(G-452)***
Sign Crafters..............G....... 769 216-3936
Brandon ***(G-453)***
Sign Doctor LLC..............G....... 601 286-3387
Meridian ***(G-3395)***
Sign Graphics..............G....... 601 445-0463
Natchez ***(G-3620)***
Sign Gypsies Df North Ms..............G....... 901 484-7357
Southaven ***(G-4900)***
Sign Gypsies Golden Triangle..............G....... 662 368-3662
Caledonia ***(G-630)***
Sign Here..............G....... 601 847-3537
Mendenhall ***(G-3288)***
Sign Language..............G....... 228 990-3609
Vancleave ***(G-5321)***
Sign Ministries..............G....... 678 507-9912
Gulfport ***(G-1868)***
Sign Plex..............G....... 228 896-5999
Gulfport ***(G-1869)***
Sign Pro Wholesale LLC..............F....... 601 453-3082
Meridian ***(G-3396)***
Sign Shop..............G....... 662 258-7186
Eupora ***(G-1291)***
Sign Shop..............G....... 601 735-1383
Waynesboro ***(G-5514)***
Sign Solutions of Saucier..............G....... 228 265-4325
Saucier ***(G-4765)***
Signature Works..............G....... 601 477-6187
Ellisville ***(G-1269)***
Signmark Inc..............G....... 601 932-6699
Pearl ***(G-4145)***
Signs & More..............G....... 662 494-9451
West Point ***(G-5562)***
Signs & Stuff..............G....... 662 393-9314
Southaven ***(G-4901)***
Signs & Stuff Inc..............G....... 662 895-4505
Southaven ***(G-4902)***
Signs By Schack..............G....... 662 890-3683
Olive Branch ***(G-3909)***
Signs By Shaffier..............G....... 601 833-8600
Brookhaven ***(G-531)***
Signs Plus..............G....... 228 832-4634
Gulfport ***(G-1870)***
Signs Plus..............G....... 601 482-4217
Meridian ***(G-3397)***
Signs Plus Inc..............G....... 228 832-4634
Gulfport ***(G-1871)***
Skillem Entreprises Inc..............G....... 601 936-4461
Pearl ***(G-4146)***
Southeastern Sign Company Inc..............G....... 601 391-0023
Madison ***(G-3149)***
Southern Signs..............G....... 228 255-4122
Pass Christian ***(G-4096)***
Southern Signs Inc..............G....... 601 445-5564
Natchez ***(G-3624)***
Spectech Service & Signs LLC..............F....... 601 482-0816
Meridian ***(G-3405)***
Staco Decorative Iron..............G....... 601 264-0064
Hattiesburg ***(G-2067)***
Standex International Corp..............B....... 662 534-9061
New Albany ***(G-3700)***
Stanley McCaffrey Signs..............G....... 228 832-0885
Gulfport ***(G-1880)***
Staybrite Signs..............G....... 901 490-0431
Southaven ***(G-4908)***
Tampa Sign Co..............G....... 228 474-1945
Moss Point ***(G-3501)***
Tavares Signs..............G....... 662 289-5366
Kosciusko ***(G-2716)***
Tim Bennett..............G....... 662 332-0020
Greenville ***(G-1605)***
Tupelo Engraving & Rbr Stamp..............G....... 662 842-0574
Tupelo ***(G-5246)***
University Screen Print Inc..............F....... 662 324-8277
Starkville ***(G-4978)***
Vegasigns LLC..............G....... 662 871-7337
Tupelo ***(G-5250)***
Velocity Inc..............E....... 662 449-4026
Hernando ***(G-2160)***
Vicksburg Newsmedia LLC..............G....... 601 636-4545
Vicksburg ***(G-5437)***
Vicksburg Printing and Pubg Co..............G....... 601 631-0400
Vicksburg ***(G-5440)***

256 2019 Harris Directory of Mississippi Manufacturers

SIC SECTION

39 MISCELLANEOUS MANUFACTURING INDUSTRIES

Vital Signs Unbound ....G....... 662 363-6940
Tunica (G-5104)
Vizionz Unlimited LLC ....G....... 601 272-5040
Jackson (G-2622)
Willcoxon Enterprises Inc ....G....... 662 840-2300
Tupelo (G-5259)
Wren Pest Control ....G....... 601 276-6117
Summit (G-5031)
Young Electric Sign Co ....G....... 228 354-8008
Biloxi (G-286)
Young Electric Sign Company ....E....... 228 354-8008
Biloxi (G-287)

3996 Linoleum & Hard Surface Floor Coverings, NEC

Armstrong Flooring Inc ....C....... 601 354-1515
Jackson (G-2333)
Portstone Manufacturing Corp ....G....... 601 922-0902
Jackson (G-2543)

3999 Manufacturing Industries, NEC

A B B Inc ....F....... 662 628-8196
Calhoun City (G-634)
ABC Scrity Fbrction Sltion LLC ....G....... 601 828-9010
Roxie (G-4688)
Accu-Fab Manufacturing LLC ....G....... 228 769-2532
Pascagoula (G-4017)
Action Industries ....G....... 662 566-3173
Pontotoc (G-4319)
AMaries Bath Happies & Body ....G....... 601 714-1887
Brandon (G-362)
Antonio Tarrell LLC ....G....... 662 983-2486
Bruce (G-559)
Armorlock Industries LLC ....G....... 228 466-2990
Bay St Louis (G-175)
Atco Industries ....G....... 601 407-6329
Canton (G-647)
Automtion Dsigns Solutions Inc ....G....... 601 992-4121
Brandon (G-367)
B and P Cstome Meta L Fbrction ....G....... 228 474-0097
Moss Point (G-3467)
B&B Trailers & Mfg Co ....G....... 662 456-4313
Houston (G-2232)
B-N/Associates ....G....... 601 482-3939
Meridian (G-3305)
Bally Technologies Inc ....C....... 228 396-3480
Gulfport (G-1733)
Bally Technologies Inc ....G....... 228 897-9059
Gulfport (G-1734)
Beaded Owls ....G....... 228 284-2712
Long Beach (G-2927)
Beauty Mart ....G....... 662 624-6738
Clarksdale (G-759)
Beaver Industries Inc ....G....... 601 664-6610
Richland (G-4506)
Bent Wrench Industries LLC ....G....... 601 934-7851
Florence (G-1315)
Bisco Industries Inc ....G....... 601 991-3308
Jackson (G-2338)
Blue Deer Candles LLP ....G....... 662 275-2016
West Point (G-5538)
Blue Line Industries LLC ....G....... 901 335-2987
Gulfport (G-1742)
Blue Lotus Creations LLC ....G....... 770 714-9408
Gulfport (G-1743)
Bouldin Essentials LLC ....G....... 769 216-7146
Jackson (G-2341)
Button Up Candles ....G....... 317 522-8060
Vicksburg (G-5349)
Cajun Planters LLC ....G....... 770 363-5638
Long Beach (G-2930)
Candle Creations By Melinda ....G....... 601 477-4942
Ellisville (G-1248)
Candlelore Inc ....G....... 662 312-1060
Starkville (G-4932)
Candles By Valorie ....G....... 601 394-3153
Richton (G-4528)
Carters Machine Works ....G....... 601 507-5480
Carthage (G-708)
Cdr Manufacturing Inc ....G....... 662 665-3100
Corinth (G-1069)
Center For Pregnancy Choices ....G....... 601 482-1230
Meridian (G-3317)
Circle J Meat Manufacturing ....G....... 662 790-3448
Tupelo (G-5120)
Clay Stewart Industries LLC ....G....... 601 946-2332
Mendenhall (G-3280)
Coastal Fire and Safety LLC ....G....... 228 327-0563
Pascagoula (G-4027)

Cozzytymzz Candles LLC ....G....... 662 471-1607
New Albany (G-3677)
Craig Wilkes Design ....G....... 917 664-7255
Meridian (G-3324)
Crux Industries ....F....... 662 873-3317
Anguilla (G-58)
D & G Enterprises ....G....... 662 895-4471
Olive Branch (G-3832)
Debra Thigpen ....G....... 601 856-0019
Madison (G-3095)
▲ Desirepath Mississippi LLC ....E....... 662 324-2231
Starkville (G-4940)
Desoto Fur Trappers LLC ....G....... 662 874-5605
Olive Branch (G-3835)
Dixie Specialties & Furn Inc ....G....... 662 369-8557
Aberdeen (G-12)
Dkc Industries LLC ....G....... 800 308-5187
Jackson (G-2386)
Dogman Industries LLC ....G....... 662 832-3644
Oxford (G-3952)
Doubletap Industries ....G....... 601 506-3218
Terry (G-5065)
Easters Custom Woodworks LLC ....G....... 740 502-2039
Vicksburg (G-5364)
Eighty-Five 15 Candle Co LLC ....G....... 601 324-3064
McComb (G-3249)
Faith Industries LLC ....G....... 662 618-0839
Lauderdale (G-2727)
Feathers Fins & Fur Taxidermy ....G....... 228 860-3106
Biloxi (G-242)
Finnesse Fabrications & Steel ....G....... 228 216-2102
Pass Christian (G-4083)
First Class Industries LLC ....G....... 601 597-4787
Fayette (G-1297)
Flambeaux Candle Company ....G....... 769 251-0142
Pearl (G-4118)
Flambeaux Cocktail Candle LLC ....G....... 601 826-1642
Ridgeland (G-4583)
Force Beekeeping LLC ....G....... 662 429-7586
Nesbit (G-3651)
Fossil Creek Candle Co LLC ....G....... 601 730-3130
Gloster (G-1514)
Foster & Thomas Manufacturing ....G....... 662 682-9094
Vardaman (G-5324)
Fragrant Flames ....G....... 601 845-0759
Florence (G-1324)
G M Horne Commercial & Indus ....G....... 601 981-1600
Jackson (G-2418)
Garys Industries Inc ....G....... 662 415-1777
Corinth (G-1086)
Gatlin Corporation ....E....... 601 833-9475
Brookhaven (G-495)
Genie Industries ....G....... 662 393-1800
Southaven (G-4874)
Glad Industries ....G....... 601 422-0261
Laurel (G-2771)
GLC Mfg Inc ....G....... 662 565-2600
Duck Hill (G-1221)
Gold Coast Manufacturing Inc ....G....... 228 261-6290
Pass Christian (G-4084)
Good News Industries Inc ....G....... 662 327-1988
Columbus (G-980)
Grassroots A Natural Co LLC ....G....... 662 601-8808
Columbus (G-981)
Hampton Industries LLC ....G....... 601 441-7604
Hattiesburg (G-1981)
Highlands Industries Inc ....G....... 601 454-3901
Brandon (G-405)
ID Group Inc ....G....... 601 982-2651
Ridgeland (G-4592)
Innovative Circuits Inc ....F....... 662 287-2007
Corinth (G-1092)
Integrity Fire Extinguish ....G....... 601 953-1927
Madison (G-3111)
Interstate Industries Miss LL ....G....... 601 856-5941
Ridgeland (G-4594)
Itawamba Ind Work Activities C ....E....... 662 862-3392
Fulton (G-1459)
J2 Manufacturing Inc ....G....... 601 573-3134
Flowood (G-1368)
James H Kemp ....G....... 601 876-2331
Tylertown (G-5273)
Jerry D Smith ....G....... 601 795-8760
Poplarville (G-4384)
Jtwo Manufacturing LLC ....G....... 769 243-8914
Flowood (G-1372)
K and A Industries LLC ....G....... 601 763-3503
Ellisville (G-1261)
K M Industries ....G....... 228 497-7040
Gautier (G-1495)

King Mfg ....G....... 662 869-2069
Saltillo (G-4715)
Ksj Industries ....G....... 601 493-3991
Laurel (G-2790)
L T Industries Inc ....G....... 228 392-1172
Biloxi (G-258)
La Jolie Enterprises LLC ....G....... 601 909-8840
Ridgeland (G-4596)
Lacknothing Enterprises LLC ....G....... 601 498-1000
Laurel (G-2791)
Lagwenbre Designer Corporation ....G....... 469 230-8534
Brookhaven (G-506)
Laura Jane Company LLC ....G....... 662 629-0550
Holly Springs (G-2181)
Leisure Home Products Inc ....G....... 228 860-7727
Long Beach (G-2944)
Lemon Tree Candles ....G....... 662 621-4312
Clarksdale (G-773)
Leopold Inds Intrglaetical LLC ....G....... 662 324-0536
Starkville (G-4956)
Levan Industries ....G....... 601 446-7390
Natchez (G-3579)
Lisas Candles ....G....... 601 384-7406
Meadville (G-3277)
Lit Industries Inc ....G....... 662 993-8088
Ripley (G-4663)
LLC Glass House ....G....... 769 251-1299
Jackson (G-2470)
Lombardo Industries LLC ....G....... 601 783-3643
Magnolia (G-3192)
London War Room ....G....... 601 584-8533
Petal (G-4192)
Love Your Light Candle Company ....G....... 769 572-1733
Brandon (G-415)
M & M Machine LLC ....G....... 601 749-4325
Carriere (G-695)
Magnolia Bites LLC ....G....... 601 709-9577
Brandon (G-417)
Magnolia Green Industries Inc ....G....... 601 466-3853
Hattiesburg (G-2018)
Manufacturing - ....G....... 408 514-6512
Olive Branch (G-3869)
Marilyn Turner ....G....... 228 271-2551
Biloxi (G-265)
Matco Industries LLC ....G....... 228 218-9813
Moss Point (G-3485)
Maurice Hinton ....G....... 601 857-5168
Terry (G-5072)
Maybelle Mfg Co Inc ....G....... 228 863-4398
Gulfport (G-1826)
▲ McNeely Plastic Products Inc ....E....... 601 926-1000
Clinton (G-830)
Microtech Industries Inc ....G....... 601 373-0177
Byram (G-622)
Military Warehouse ....G....... 662 287-8234
Corinth (G-1102)
Mississippi Prison Industries ....G....... 601 346-4966
Jackson (G-2504)
Mississippi Puppetry Guild ....G....... 601 977-9840
Jackson (G-2505)
Moore Industries ....G....... 662 862-3993
Fulton (G-1463)
Morton Industry ....G....... 601 732-6486
Morton (G-3451)
Mtm Industries LLC ....G....... 662 402-9750
Flowood (G-1382)
Mw Industries ....G....... 662 488-4551
Pontotoc (G-4351)
My Fantasy Hair Inc ....G....... 925 289-4247
Olive Branch (G-3881)
Nce Group Inc ....G....... 662 890-8778
Olive Branch (G-3888)
Nightwind Industries ....G....... 662 690-9709
Tupelo (G-5193)
Novi Creations LLC ....G....... 601 335-1902
Laurel (G-2812)
NY Beauty ....G....... 662 280-2573
Horn Lake (G-2209)
Odom Industries ....G....... 601 687-6325
Shubuta (G-4832)
Oralia Mejia ....G....... 662 512-1906
Ripley (G-4667)
Owl City Industries LLC ....G....... 901 268-6871
Hernando (G-2147)
Oxford Candle Company LLC ....G....... 662 816-7429
Oxford (G-3985)
Paine Industries ....G....... 601 336-2069
Jackson (G-2533)
Parker Dre Industries ....G....... 228 383-5967
Gulfport (G-1843)

Employee Codes: A=Over 500 employees, B=251-500
C=101-250, D=51-100, E=20-50, F=10-19, G=1-9

2019 Harris Directory of
Mississippi Manufacturers

257

SIC

39 MISCELLANEOUS MANUFACTURING INDUSTRIES

Pathway Candles ....G....... 601 297-0484
Hattiesburg *(G-2040)*
Pine Belt Industries ....G....... 601 450-0431
Hattiesburg *(G-2042)*
Pink Star Industries ....G....... 702 546-9883
Sarah *(G-4735)*
Pinnacle Agriculture Dist Inc ....G....... 662 453-7010
Greenwood *(G-1646)*
Prime Manufacturing Svcs LLC ....E....... 901 463-5844
Senatobia *(G-4799)*
Protec Steel Industries LLC ....G....... 228 364-4240
Pass Christian *(G-4094)*
Pucci Petique Inc ....G....... 662 429-3202
Hernando *(G-2150)*
Purple Label Candles ....G....... 601 955-2217
Jackson *(G-2554)*
Purvis Jewelry Candles ....G....... 601 270-9687
Picayune *(G-4288)*
Purvis Jewelry Candles LLC ....G....... 601 794-8977
Purvis *(G-4449)*
Qualified Fabrication Inc ....F....... 601 508-4389
Lucedale *(G-3014)*
Randell Mfg Inc ....G....... 601 372-3903
Jackson *(G-2557)*
Region 8 Mental Health Retrdat ....D....... 601 591-5553
Brandon *(G-445)*
Resourcemfg ....G....... 662 563-9617
Batesville *(G-120)*
Richard Armstrong ....G....... 228 822-2238
Long Beach *(G-2950)*
Rock On Industries LLC ....G....... 601 825-4857
Brandon *(G-446)*
Rome Chenille & Supply Co Inc ....G....... 662 286-9947
Corinth *(G-1116)*
Rykan Industries ....G....... 601 900-2055
Carthage *(G-722)*
Saf-T Compliance Intl LLC ....G....... 601 684-9495
McComb *(G-3264)*
Sanders Industries Inc ....G....... 662 895-1337
Olive Branch *(G-3906)*
Scented Creations ....G....... 601 362-5926
Jackson *(G-2575)*
◆ **Seminole Furniture Mfg Inc** .....D....... 662 447-5222
Okolona *(G-3798)*
Sew Sweet ....G....... 601 431-2304
Natchez *(G-3618)*
Singin River Mental Health ....E....... 228 497-0690
Gautier *(G-1504)*
Sisters of Creations ....G....... 662 615-3978
Starkville *(G-4971)*
Smallberry Mfg Co ....G....... 601 847-3692
Mendenhall *(G-3290)*
Smw Manufacturing ....G....... 517 596-3300
Oxford *(G-4003)*
Snap-It-Wreaths ....G....... 228 596-0387
Gulfport *(G-1873)*
Son Light Candles and More LLC ...G....... 228 263-1661
Gulfport *(G-1874)*
Sophisticated Fabrications LLC ....G....... 228 424-8346
Biloxi *(G-280)*
Soupbone Industries LLC ....G....... 601 520-1317
Purvis *(G-4453)*
Southern Belle Tresses LLC ....G....... 470 645-1777
Oxford *(G-4004)*
Southern Design Finds ....G....... 662 893-4303
Byhalia *(G-606)*
Southern States Bee Supply LLC ...G....... 601 513-5151
Taylorsville *(G-5059)*
Spirit Lifters Scented Candles ......G....... 210 802-0149
Biloxi *(G-281)*
Split Ends ....G....... 601 619-0088
Vicksburg *(G-5422)*
Stanley Appraisal Company LLC ....G....... 662 287-8543
Corinth *(G-1120)*
Stuart Chaffin ....G....... 601 807-1547
Brookhaven *(G-540)*
Suds N Squares ....G....... 662 827-9991
Hollandale *(G-2168)*
Surgisure Inc ....G....... 601 985-8125
Clinton *(G-836)*
T & S Precision Mfg Inc ....G....... 601 825-0878
Brandon *(G-467)*
Techform Manufacturing LLC ....G....... 662 282-7771
Mantachie *(G-3207)*
Timber Creek Candles ....G....... 601 818-6400
Madison *(G-3159)*
Timothy D Jeter ....G....... 662 266-0968
Blue Mountain *(G-293)*
Tinkerbelle Industries Inc ....G....... 601 928-3520
Wiggins *(G-5591)*

Torchd LLC ....G....... 601 717-2044
Jackson *(G-2609)*
Touba Hair Braiding Ms ....G....... 769 524-4641
Ridgeland *(G-4642)*
Tri-Coast Industries Inc ....G....... 228 369-9924
Pascagoula *(G-4071)*
Truck Bodies & Eqp Intl Inc ....G....... 800 255-4345
Tishomingo *(G-5089)*
Warhorse Industries LLC ....G....... 601 856-2990
Madison *(G-3167)*
Waveland Candle Company LLC ....G....... 228 220-4716
Waveland *(G-5487)*
Weems Industries LLC ....G....... 228 382-4423
Saucier *(G-4768)*
Whitehouse Industries ....G....... 601 981-5866
Jackson *(G-2631)*
Wicks N Candle Company ....G....... 662 891-4237
Saltillo *(G-4724)*
▲ **Wicks N More Inc** ....E....... 662 205-4025
Mooreville *(G-3444)*
Wolf Industries Inc ....G....... 228 864-9096
Gulfport *(G-1894)*
Wreath Haven ....G....... 205 393-3015
Petal *(G-4200)*
Yalls Products ....G....... 601 391-3698
Madison *(G-3173)*

73 BUSINESS SERVICES

7372 Prepackaged Software

3v Solutions LLC ....G....... 601 720-4999
Madison *(G-3074)*
5th Avenue Software LLC ....G....... 662 843-1200
Cleveland *(G-785)*
Aggeos Inc ....G....... 512 751-2160
Fulton *(G-1444)*
Applied Software System LLC ......G....... 601 605-0877
Ridgeland *(G-4550)*
Assured Revenue Corporation .....G....... 662 323-5350
Starkville *(G-4925)*
Bartag Corporation ....G....... 769 233-0925
Byram *(G-618)*
Bdm It Services (us) Inc ....G....... 601 274-0347
Quitman *(G-4458)*
Beyondtrust Corporation ....E....... 601 519-0213
Ridgeland *(G-4555)*
Box Office 7 Studios ....G....... 662 633-2451
Brandon *(G-372)*
Boyd Eductl Solutions Tech LLC ....G....... 601 951-2305
Ridgeland *(G-4558)*
Btm Solutions ....F....... 662 328-2400
Columbus *(G-942)*
Business Communications Inc ......E....... 601 898-1890
Ridgeland *(G-4559)*
Business Systems Inc ....G....... 601 957-1500
Jackson *(G-2351)*
Cable One Inc ....G....... 601 833-7991
McComb *(G-3245)*
Catontech MGT Systems LLC ....G....... 601 207-1047
Meridian *(G-3316)*
Chuck Patrick ....G....... 601 278-7193
Brandon *(G-380)*
Citizen Health Foundation ....G....... 601 463-2436
Hattiesburg *(G-1944)*
Cks Productions Inc ....E....... 888 897-9136
Biloxi *(G-229)*
Community Broadcasting ....G....... 731 441-6962
Booneville *(G-325)*
Computer Works LLC ....G....... 228 696-8889
Moss Point *(G-3475)*
Confederate Express LLC ....G....... 662 315-6625
Hamilton *(G-1905)*
Conflux Software LLC ....G....... 601 940-0182
Jackson *(G-2364)*
Connect Technology LLC ....G....... 601 914-1713
Jackson *(G-2365)*
Corcoran Legal Group ....G....... 601 906-8227
Jackson *(G-2370)*
Creations By Stephanie ....G....... 228 697-2899
Biloxi *(G-234)*
Custodis MGT Systems LLC ....G....... 601 207-1047
Meridian *(G-3325)*
Custom Accounting Solutions ......G....... 601 957-7500
Jackson *(G-2372)*
Data Medical Inc ....G....... 662 283-0463
Duck Hill *(G-1220)*
Data Systems Management Inc .....F....... 601 925-6270
Clinton *(G-821)*
Dataware LLC ....G....... 662 356-4978
Caledonia *(G-628)*

Dqsi LLC ....G....... 228 688-3796
Stennis Space Center *(G-4994)*
End2end Public Safety LLC ....G....... 662 513-0999
Oxford *(G-3954)*
Environmental Tech of Amer ....G....... 601 607-3151
Ridgeland *(G-4577)*
Esoftware Solutions Inc ....E....... 601 919-2275
Ridgeland *(G-4578)*
Fed Service Hub LLC ....G....... 228 547-3498
Gulfport *(G-1784)*
Fitmate Social Inc ....G....... 206 849-2447
Oxford *(G-3956)*
Grayco Systems & Consulting ......G....... 601 583-0430
Hattiesburg *(G-1976)*
Hey There App LLC ....G....... 228 238-0344
Ocean Springs *(G-3763)*
Honey Island Software Inc ....G....... 985 265-4192
Pearlington *(G-4160)*
Hydesoft Computing LLC ....G....... 601 629-8607
Vicksburg *(G-5380)*
Ideal Software Systems Inc ....D....... 601 693-1673
Meridian *(G-3348)*
Imaging Informatics LLC ....G....... 228 332-0674
Pass Christian *(G-4089)*
In The Black Software LLC ....G....... 228 697-2120
Ocean Springs *(G-3767)*
Info Services Inc ....F....... 601 898-7858
Madison *(G-3109)*
Intelatool Solutions LLC ....G....... 601 594-8451
Richland *(G-4520)*
It Synergistics LLC ....G....... 855 866-7648
Flowood *(G-1367)*
Jabr LLC ....G....... 601 502-5587
Flowood *(G-1369)*
L and J Global Marketing LLC ....G....... 662 420-9480
Olive Branch *(G-3863)*
Lenders Software Incorporated .....G....... 601 919-6362
Brandon *(G-413)*
Localnet ....G....... 601 774-9338
Union *(G-5300)*
Mac Financial Mgmt LLC ....G....... 844 622-6468
Magnolia *(G-3193)*
Magnolia Accounting Services ......G....... 662 429-5852
Hernando *(G-2141)*
Mega Tech South LLC ....G....... 662 538-3366
Shannon *(G-4816)*
Mel Vold Sales Co ....G....... 601 371-4911
Jackson *(G-2487)*
NA Food Dash LLC ....G....... 662 266-0738
New Albany *(G-3687)*
Oracle America Inc ....G....... 601 352-6113
Jackson *(G-2530)*
Orchard Oxford ....G....... 662 259-0094
Oxford *(G-3982)*
Perspecta Engineering Inc ....G....... 571 313-6000
Stennis Space Center *(G-4996)*
Pinplanfix21 LLC ....G....... 662 380-1961
Oxford *(G-3994)*
Ptc Inc ....G....... 601 919-2688
Brandon *(G-441)*
Schoolstatus LLC ....G....... 601 620-0613
Hattiesburg *(G-2056)*
Signaturelink Inc ....G....... 601 898-7359
Ridgeland *(G-4629)*
Simple Solutions ....G....... 228 588-9509
Moss Point *(G-3498)*
▲ **Skyhawke Technologies LLC** ....B....... 601 605-6100
Ridgeland *(G-4630)*
Stormcom LLC ....G....... 601 918-5401
Jackson *(G-2598)*
T G Ferguson Company ....G....... 662 563-0806
Batesville *(G-127)*
VT Consolidated Inc ....G....... 601 956-5440
Ridgeland *(G-4646)*
White Shirt Networks LLC ....G....... 601 292-7900
Madison *(G-3170)*

76 MISCELLANEOUS REPAIR SERVICES

7692 Welding Repair

Aberdeen Machine Works Inc ....E....... 662 369-9357
Aberdeen *(G-6)*
ABS Welding Inc ....F....... 601 444-9889
Columbia *(G-878)*
Adams Welding & Fabrication ....G....... 601 319-1865
Ovett *(G-3930)*
Advanced Fabrication Inc ....G....... 228 392-0400
Diberville *(G-1194)*

258

2019 Harris Directory of
Mississippi Manufacturers

SIC SECTION
76 MISCELLANEOUS REPAIR SERVICES

Ajs Welding Repair ....G...... 601 264-2571
Sumrall (G-5033)

Alcorn Fabricating ....G...... 662 462-5669
Corinth (G-1056)

All-Tech Metal Works Inc.....................G...... 228 396-3800
Wiggins (G-5569)

Amerimac Machining Corporation ....G...... 601 940-7919
Jackson (G-2329)

Anderson Repair Shop ....G...... 601 783-2654
Magnolia (G-3189)

Angels Truck Service LLC ....F...... 662 890-0417
Olive Branch (G-3815)

ARC-Up Welding Inc ....G...... 601 638-1202
Vicksburg (G-5342)

Arky Welding & Handy Man ....G...... 662 494-4233
West Point (G-5536)

Atwood Mch Wldg & Hydraulics............F...... 601 735-0398
Waynesboro (G-5491)

B R Smith Enterprises Inc ....F...... 601 656-0846
Union (G-5293)

Bakers Auto Machine & RAD Sp ....G...... 228 474-1222
Moss Point (G-3468)

Balius Dann Welding ....G...... 228 354-9647
Diberville (G-1196)

Beason Repair Shop ....G...... 662 256-9937
Amory (G-37)

Beckham Welding LLC..........................G...... 662 832-0071
Oxford (G-3939)

Bergeron Machine & Marine ....G...... 504 416-6461
Poplarville (G-4375)

Berry Inc ....G...... 662 423-1984
Iuka (G-2285)

Big Johns Welding LLC..........................G...... 570 660-1972
Poplarville (G-4377)

Bills Welding ....G...... 901 216-6762
Byhalia (G-580)

Billys Welding Service Inc ....G...... 601 649-1432
Laurel (G-2740)

Bk Edwards Fabrication & Wldg...........G...... 662 263-4320
Mathiston (G-3226)

Block & Chip Iron Works Inc ....G...... 601 394-2964
Leakesville (G-2876)

Bobs Welding & Repair ....G...... 662 685-4217
Blue Mountain (G-290)

Brocato Construction Inc..................G...... 662 563-4473
Batesville (G-100)

C B R Machinist Inc ....G...... 601 426-2326
Laurel (G-2746)

Carrolls Welding Service....................G...... 228 875-3800
Ocean Springs (G-3747)

Cg Welding Services LLC ....G...... 601 426-3922
Laurel (G-2751)

Chancellors Welding ....G...... 601 477-3552
Ellisville (G-1249)

Chops Wrecker & Welding Svc............G...... 601 442-0092
Natchez (G-3546)

Chucks Welding & Mech LLC ....G...... 662 347-9941
Greenville (G-1538)

Clear Enterprise ....G...... 601 796-2429
Lumberton (G-3025)

Columbia Welding & Cnstr.................F...... 601 736-4332
Columbia (G-890)

Columbus Mch & Wldg Works Inc......E...... 662 328-8473
Columbus (G-951)

Core Solutions LLC ....G...... 228 216-6848
Gulfport (G-1765)

Cottens Welding Shop..........................G...... 662 647-2503
Charleston (G-735)

Crager Welding ....G...... 601 687-0019
Waynesboro (G-5496)

Creative Iron ....G...... 601 845-6290
Florence (G-1316)

Cuevas Machine Co Inc.......................D...... 228 255-1384
Poplarville (G-4380)

Cwg Welding ....G...... 228 539-4121
Saucier (G-4751)

Cws Grain Systems Inc ....E...... 662 332-5822
Greenville (G-1543)

Daniel Petre ....G...... 662 726-2462
Macon (G-3057)

Davis Welding ....G...... 228 257-5231
Long Beach (G-2935)

Davis Welding Fabrication LLC...........G...... 662 614-2531
Columbia (G-893)

Davis Welding LLC ....G...... 662 423-2911
Iuka (G-2289)

Davis Wldg & Fabrication LLC ....G...... 601 258-0334
Beaumont (G-184)

Dean Weeks Repair & Welding ....G...... 601 833-2669
Wesson (G-5526)

Dees Welding Service LLC...................G...... 601 372-9361
Jackson (G-2379)

Destinis Creations and Exquis ....G...... 601 317-3764
Pearl (G-4114)

Dixie Welding ....G...... 662 417-0938
Winona (G-5597)

Dixie Welding Service Inc ....G...... 601 268-6949
Moselle (G-3457)

Donald Speights Jr ....G...... 601 940-3847
Braxton (G-477)

Double C Custom Welding & Fabg........G...... 228 383-1243
Gulfport (G-1774)

Doves Machine & Welding Svc ....G...... 601 794-8112
Purvis (G-4436)

Ds Welding Services............................G...... 601 639-4988
Crosby (G-1134)

E C Welding & Fabricating ....G...... 662 429-1624
Hernando (G-2130)

E E Baird Shop Inc ....G...... 662 456-3467
Houston (G-2238)

Edco Welding ....G...... 228 392-5600
Biloxi (G-241)

Ellis Certified Welding ....G...... 662 869-2295
Saltillo (G-4711)

Ellis Welding ....G...... 601 752-2207
Seminary (G-4779)

Equipment Maintenance Co ....G...... 662 393-9178
Horn Lake (G-2198)

Fab Pro Wldg & Fabrication Co ....G...... 662 365-5557
Baldwyn (G-76)

Fielder Mfg..G...... 601 630-9295
Vicksburg (G-5371)

Fielders Welding and Orna Ir ....G...... 662 234-4256
Oxford (G-3955)

G Hennig Jr Welding Shop..................G...... 228 374-7836
Biloxi (G-243)

G&K Fabrication & Trailer Repr ....G...... 228 249-6336
Moss Point (G-3478)

George Smith Welding Svc LLC ....G...... 601 752-5288
Ellisville (G-1254)

Gibbs & Sons Inc ....G...... 601 775-3467
Lake (G-2722)

Grace Welding Fabrication LLC ....G...... 601 788-2478
Richton (G-4533)

Gulleys Wldg Stl Erectors Inc ....E...... 601 482-3767
Meridian (G-3344)

H & H Fabrication Inc.........................F...... 662 286-9475
Corinth (G-1088)

H & H Welding LLC ....G...... 601 428-4788
Ellisville (G-1255)

Halls Welding Service..........................G...... 601 477-3925
Ellisville (G-1256)

Harrell Welding Service LLC ....G...... 662 456-2444
Houston (G-2244)

Harrells Metal Works Inc ....E...... 662 226-0982
Grenada (G-1683)

Harrison Mobile Welding ....G...... 662 706-4692
Baldwyn (G-77)

Hesters Certified Welding ....G...... 662 566-7305
Tupelo (G-5155)

Hills Welding & Crane Rental..............G...... 662 846-6789
Cleveland (G-796)

Holloways Welding Service LLC ....G...... 601 729-4403
Stringer (G-5002)

Howells Welding & Fabricating ....G...... 601 663-6098
Union (G-5298)

J & J Welding ....G...... 662 456-6065
Woodland (G-5613)

Jackson Welding LLC...........................G...... 662 680-4325
Saltillo (G-4714)

JC Welding LLC ....G...... 601 575-1307
Philadelphia (G-4218)

Jcbc Cs LLC ....G...... 662 560-7235
Coldwater (G-848)

Jennings & Jennings Inc.....................G...... 662 887-1870
Indianola (G-2268)

Jennings Welding & Mch Works ....G...... 662 887-1870
Indianola (G-2269)

Jeremy Ray Welding Service LLC ....G...... 601 433-4905
Laurel (G-2787)

Jerome Rushing Welding ....G...... 601 303-0139
Tylertown (G-5274)

Jerry Hailey ....G...... 662 349-2582
Southaven (G-4883)

Johnnie Wright Radiator & Wldg..........G...... 601 428-5013
Laurel (G-2788)

Kc Fabrication and Welding LLC...........G...... 504 427-8711
Bolton (G-311)

Kd Welding Services LLC ....G...... 228 863-2773
Gulfport (G-1815)

Kellys Welding Service.........................G...... 601 879-8636
Flora (G-1309)

Kens Welding Shop Inc ....G...... 601 736-4136
Columbia (G-902)

Kirk Welding Inspection SE ....G...... 228 467-6586
Bay Saint Louis (G-145)

Kogler Equipment Service Inc ....E...... 901 521-9742
Olive Branch (G-3861)

Lancaster Machine & Welding ....G...... 601 582-1400
Hattiesburg (G-2015)

Larry D Wallace ....G...... 601 384-4409
Roxie (G-4691)

Larrys Equipment Inc ....G...... 662 423-0077
Iuka (G-2298)

Lars Jordan ....G...... 601 544-2424
Petal (G-4190)

Lavelle Crabtree Welding ....G...... 662 746-7177
Yazoo City (G-5638)

Leeco Welding Service ....G...... 601 428-7896
Laurel (G-2795)

Lumpkin Repair Service LLC ....G...... 601 798-2027
Carriere (G-694)

Lums Welding & Machine ....G...... 601 825-1116
Brandon (G-416)

Lynn Welding Shop LLC.......................G...... 601 638-7235
Vicksburg (G-5390)

M & M Chassis Shop LLC ....G...... 601 310-6078
Moselle (G-3458)

Malley Inc ....G...... 228 255-7467
Kiln (G-2683)

Mark Williams Welding LLC ....G...... 601 431-5324
Natchez (G-3584)

Mashburns Welding ....G...... 601 648-2886
Buckatunna (G-564)

Mason Overstreet Wldg Mch Work.......E...... 601 932-1794
Pearl (G-4130)

Mc Comb Welding & Mch Works ....G...... 601 684-1921
McComb (G-3258)

McGee Welding LLC ....G...... 769 355-2339
Natchez (G-3585)

MD Metals Scrap & Salvage ....G...... 601 635-4160
Decatur (G-1176)

Mercer Welding Service ....G...... 601 649-4269
Laurel (G-2799)

Merle E Sullivan ....G...... 662 347-4494
Greenville (G-1572)

Metal Products of Corinth Inc.............G...... 662 287-3625
Corinth (G-1101)

Metallic Welding ....G...... 769 798-6498
Jackson (G-2488)

Michaels Machine Shop Inc ....G...... 662 624-2376
Clarksdale (G-775)

Mississippi Welding and Mchs ....G...... 662 726-5593
Macon (G-3067)

Mitchells Welding LLC..........................G...... 601 554-6402
Kosciusko (G-2703)

Monotech of Mississippi ....G...... 662 862-2978
Iuka (G-2302)

Moore Machine & Welding Shop ....G...... 601 892-5026
Crystal Springs (G-1150)

Moores Welding & Fabrication ....G...... 662 402-5503
Cleveland (G-800)

Morris Welding Service ....G...... 601 729-2737
Laurel (G-2808)

Morrison Welding LLC..........................G...... 601 845-5187
Florence (G-1329)

Mr Fix It ....G...... 601 852-4705
Edwards (G-1242)

Murphys Machine & Welding LLC ....G...... 601 849-2771
Magee (G-3179)

Murphys Welding LLC ....G...... 662 719-3879
Cleveland (G-801)

Nations Welding Service Inc ....G...... 601 833-4949
Brookhaven (G-520)

Novelty Machine Works Inc ....F...... 601 948-2075
Jackson (G-2524)

Opel Corp..G...... 601 693-0771
Meridian (G-3378)

Ormans Welding & Fab Inc ....F...... 662 494-9471
West Point (G-5556)

Overstreet Welding LLC ....G...... 662 719-1269
Ruleville (G-4697)

P & S Welding & Manufacturing ....G...... 662 334-9881
Greenville (G-1587)

Patterson & Company Inc ....E...... 662 842-2807
Tupelo (G-5200)

Paul Yeatman ....G...... 662 323-7140
Starkville (G-4966)

Pennington Wldg Sp Crane Rentl.........G...... 662 838-2015
Byhalia (G-596)

Employee Codes: A=Over 500 employees, B=251-500
C=101-250, D=51-100, E=20-50, F=10-19, G=1-9

2019 Harris Directory of
Mississippi Manufacturers

259

SIC

76 MISCELLANEOUS REPAIR SERVICES

Peppers Machine & Wldg Co Inc ....E 601 833-3038
Brookhaven **(G-522)**

PO Boy Welding Inc..................................G....... 662 624-3696
Clarksdale **(G-778)**

Precision Fab Refurbishing ....G....... 601 543-7752
Hattiesburg **(G-2047)**

Precision Iron Works ....G....... 228 341-0736
Saucier **(G-4761)**

Precision Welding ....G....... 601 730-0224
Summit **(G-5019)**

Purvis Machine ....G....... 601 947-6617
Lucedale **(G-3013)**

Quality Machine & Wldg of Miss ....E 601 798-8568
Picayune **(G-4289)**

Quality Welding ....G....... 601 428-4724
Laurel **(G-2830)**

◆ Quality Wldg & Fabrication Inc ....D...... 601 731-1222
Columbia **(G-914)**

R & W Hydraulics Inc ....G....... 601 649-0565
Laurel **(G-2831)**

R and B Welding LLC ....G....... 601 441-4398
Columbia **(G-915)**

R&R Welding LLC ....G....... 601 335-2470
Laurel **(G-2832)**

Rand S Welding......................................G....... 601 876-3736
Tylertown **(G-5282)**

Rauschs Welding & Repair ....G....... 662 841-0499
Plantersville **(G-4314)**

Rays Mobile Welding ....G....... 601 966-0848
Jackson **(G-2664)**

Rays Welding ....G....... 601 741-1114
Terry **(G-5076)**

Rice Equipment Co LLC ....G....... 662 323-5502
Starkville **(G-4968)**

Rising Son Welding LLC ....G....... 601 344-0077
Ovett **(G-3932)**

Riverside AG Supply LLC ....G....... 662 444-0600
Marks **(G-3224)**

Roberts Welding LLC ....G....... 228 697-4816
Long Beach **(G-2952)**

Romar Offshore Wldg Svcs LLC ....G....... 228 475-4220
Moss Point **(G-3497)**

Roseberry Welding LLC ....G....... 601 408-1843
Hattiesburg **(G-2054)**

S & C Welding & Machine Works ....G....... 601 845-5483
Florence **(G-1332)**

S & S Welding & Repairs ....G....... 662 834-1131
Durant **(G-1228)**

S & W Welding & Machine Works ....G....... 601 939-8516
Jackson **(G-2666)**

Sabbatini & Sons Incorporation ....G....... 662 686-7713
Leland **(G-2892)**

Sanders Sons Dvrsfd Wldg Entps ....G....... 601 969-3119
Jackson **(G-2572)**

Satisfaction Welding..............................G....... 662 473-1518
Water Valley **(G-5474)**

Shacks Welding Service Inc ....G....... 601 939-5491
Flowood **(G-1396)**

Shears Fabrication & Wldg LLC ....G....... 601 946-3268
Utica **(G-5312)**

Smith Mobile Welding LLC....................G....... 601 695-4640
Brookhaven **(G-532)**

Smiths Machine & Wldg Co Inc ....E 601 833-8787
Brookhaven **(G-534)**

Smiths Mobile Welding ....G....... 901 626-1616
Southaven **(G-4904)**

Southern Fabricators LLC.....................F 601 824-8855
Brandon **(G-459)**

Sparks Welding Service ....G....... 601 519-9573
Brandon **(G-462)**

Speeds Welding Works ....G....... 601 917-2571
Meridian **(G-3406)**

Stringer Randal ....G....... 228 623-0037
Moss Point **(G-3500)**

Sumrall Welding ....G....... 601 876-4653
Tylertown **(G-5287)**

Sumrall Welding Service LLC ....G....... 601 498-1075
Ovett **(G-3933)**

Superior Wldg Fabrication Inc ....G....... 601 823-5999
Brookhaven **(G-541)**

T & T Welding Inc ....E 601 477-2884
Ellisville **(G-1270)**

T & T Welding Yard Inc ....E 601 477-2299
Ellisville **(G-1271)**

T and W Maintenance LLC ....G....... 901 848-2511
Southaven **(G-4911)**

T JS Welding ....G....... 601 498-1409
Ellisville **(G-2856)**

T R General Welding ....G....... 901 481-0425
Southaven **(G-4912)**

Taylor Brothers Cnstr Co ....G....... 601 636-1749
Vicksburg **(G-5427)**

Thomas Welding and Fabricating ....G....... 601 408-1843
Hattiesburg **(G-2074)**

Thompsons Welding Services Inc.........D....... 662 343-8955
Hamilton **(G-1908)**

Thornhill Welding...................................G....... 601 248-6472
Summit **(G-5026)**

Thornton Repair Shop ....G....... 662 332-6853
Greenville **(G-1603)**

Travis Welding Services ....G....... 601 684-9578
McComb **(G-3271)**

Tri County Sheet Metal & Wldg.............G....... 601 939-0803
Pearl **(G-4153)**

Tucker Machine Services ....G....... 601 582-4280
Hattiesburg **(G-2075)**

Vera S Ray ....G....... 662 453-1615
Greenwood **(G-1655)**

Vertechs Design Solutions LLC............G....... 228 671-1442
Waveland **(G-5486)**

Victor Umfress Gar Wldg Sp Inc...........G....... 662 862-4213
Fulton **(G-1484)**

Walker Welding and Fabrication ....G....... 601 503-0340
Brandon **(G-471)**

Wallace Welding LLC..............................G....... 601 734-6542
Bogue Chitto **(G-307)**

Walters Machine Works Inc...................G....... 601 426-6092
Laurel **(G-2867)**

Webb Machine and Supply Inc ....F 662 375-8309
Webb **(G-5520)**

Webbs Welding & Repair LLC ....G....... 901 487-2400
Olive Branch **(G-3924)**

Wedgeworth Welding and Fab...............G....... 228 326-0937
Mc Henry **(G-3239)**

Welding Research & Fabricatn ....G....... 870 551-5650
Tupelo **(G-5254)**

Welding Services ....G....... 662 321-2472
Tupelo **(G-5255)**

Welding Works LLC ....G....... 662 323-8684
Starkville **(G-4981)**

West Body Shop & Salvage Inc ....G....... 662 566-2161
Verona **(G-5337)**

Wilders Welding Shop ....G....... 662 489-2772
Pontotoc **(G-4371)**

William Barnes ....G....... 601 446-6122
Natchez **(G-3642)**

Willie Morgan ....G....... 662 834-4366
Lexington **(G-2907)**

Wilson Welding ....G....... 601 483-3696
Meridian **(G-3421)**

Wilsons Welding Service Inc ....F 228 255-4825
Perkinston **(G-4183)**

Woodrffs Prtble Wldg Fbrcation............G....... 662 728-3326
Booneville **(G-347)**

Woods Trailers & Repair LLC ....G....... 662 585-3606
Golden **(G-1533)**

Yates Industrial Services LLC...............G....... 601 467-6232
Purvis **(G-4454)**

Young Welding Supply Inc ....G....... 662 792-4061
Kosciusko **(G-2721)**

7694 Armature Rewinding Shops

Bay Motor Winding Inc ....F 228 863-0666
Long Beach **(G-2924)**

Betty Montgomery ....G....... 601 833-1461
Brookhaven **(G-482)**

Brady Electric Inc...................................F 601 649-7862
Laurel **(G-2742)**

Browns Electrical Repair........................G....... 662 226-8192
Grenada **(G-1670)**

Burford Electric Service Inc ....E 662 328-5679
Columbus **(G-943)**

Dubose Electric ....G....... 601 425-5116
Laurel **(G-2764)**

Eaton Electric Motor Repair..................G....... 662 728-6187
Booneville **(G-328)**

Electric Motor & Equipment...................G....... 601 845-5561
Florence **(G-1321)**

Electric Motor Sales & Svc Inc ....E 662 327-1606
Columbus **(G-969)**

Electric Works ....G....... 662 342-5505
Horn Lake **(G-2196)**

Flannigan Electric Company..................E 601 354-2756
Jackson **(G-2409)**

Gibson Electric Motor Svc Inc ....G....... 228 762-4923
Pascagoula **(G-4033)**

Grenada Electric Company Inc ....G....... 662 226-5801
Grenada **(G-1679)**

Indianola Electric Co Inc ....F 662 887-3292
Indianola **(G-2266)**

▲ Industrial Elc Mtr Works Inc..............E 601 679-5500
Meridian **(G-3352)**

McIlwains Electrical Supply ....G....... 601 735-1145
Waynesboro **(G-5507)**

Mid South Electric Motor Svc ....G....... 662 332-3512
Greenville **(G-1573)**

Mobley Auto Service..............................G....... 662 423-3516
Iuka **(G-2301)**

Patterson & Company Inc ....E 662 842-2807
Tupelo **(G-5200)**

Peller Electric Motor Srvs ....G....... 601 693-4621
Meridian **(G-3387)**

Reid Electric Motor Services ....G....... 601 684-6040
Summit **(G-5020)**

Sandys Auto Parts & Machine Sp ....G....... 662 342-1900
Southaven **(G-4898)**

▼ Southern Electric Works Inc ....F 601 833-8323
Brookhaven **(G-536)**

Summit Truck Group Miss LLC ....G....... 662 842-3401
Tupelo **(G-5232)**

Taw Power System Inc ....G....... 601 939-3455
Flowood **(G-1401)**

TJX Companies Inc ....G....... 662 236-2856
Oxford **(G-4007)**

Tri-State Electric Corinth Inc.................F 662 287-2451
Corinth **(G-1123)**

W W W Electric Company Inc ....F 601 833-6666
Brookhaven **(G-545)**

Walker Auto Repair Service ....G....... 601 969-5353
Jackson **(G-2623)**

Walker Enterprises ....G....... 662 237-0240
Carrollton **(G-704)**

ALPHABETIC SECTION

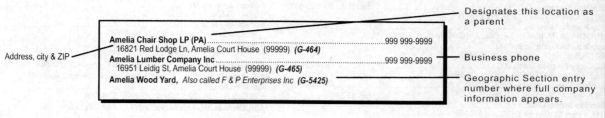

See footnotes for symbols and codes identification.
* Companies listed alphabetically.
* Complete physical or mailing address.

1 A Lifesafer Inc 800 634-3077
1046 Highway 98 And 51 McComb (39648) *(G-3242)*
1 A Lifesafer Inc 800 634-3077
1262 Main St Southaven (38671) *(G-4849)*
1 A Lifesafer Inc 800 634-3077
1345 Palmetto Rd Tupelo (38801) *(G-5105)*
1 A Lifesafer Inc 800 634-3077
1340 Denny Ave Pascagoula (39567) *(G-4016)*
1 A Lifesafer Inc 800 634-3077
15237 Russell Blvd Gulfport (39503) *(G-1714)*
1 A Lifesafer Inc 800 634-3077
17769 U S Highway 82 Mathiston (39752) *(G-3225)*
1 A Lifesafer Inc 800 634-3077
2600 N Hills St Meridian (39305) *(G-3292)*
1 A Lifesafer Inc 800 634-3077
7166 U S Highway 49 Hattiesburg (39402) *(G-1913)*
1 A Lifesafer Inc 800 634-3077
747 Highway 61 N Natchez (39120) *(G-3515)*
1 A Lifesafer Inc 800 634-3077
760 S Raceway Rd Greenville (38703) *(G-1534)*
1 A Lifesafer Inc 800 634-3077
852 Foley St Jackson (39202) *(G-2312)*
1 Store Solution, Meridian *Also called South Txas Lghthouse For Blind (G-3400)*
10 Below LLC 769 243-8705
1335 Ellis Ave Jackson (39204) *(G-2313)*
12 Stone Consulting, Carriere *Also called Randy A Elder (G-700)*
1529 Coffee Company 662 315-6951
205 3rd St N Amory (38821) *(G-32)*
1810 Vapors 662 523-7924
174 County Road 1810 Saltillo (38866) *(G-4705)*
1967, Jackson *Also called Legendary Lawn Services Inc (G-2468)*
24 Hour News Line 662 241-5000
516 Main St Columbus (39701) *(G-929)*
27-55 Fuel Plaza LLC 601 892-1643
26171 Highway 27 Crystal Springs (39059) *(G-1138)*
2a Armaments LLC 662 538-8118
107 W Bankhead St New Albany (38652) *(G-3669)*
3 F Chimica Americas Inc 662 369-2843
10930 Darracott Rd Aberdeen (39730) *(G-5)*
3 Men Moving & Storage LLC 662 238-7774
419 Jackson Ave W Oxford (38655) *(G-3934)*
365 Explosive Athc Performllc 601 365-2318
11 Longwood Place Dr Hattiesburg (39402) *(G-1914)*
3d Graphics, West Point *Also called Mossy Oak 3d Fluid Grphics LLC (G-5553)*
3d Laser Scanning LLC 228 860-5952
2436 Martin Rd Biloxi (39531) *(G-214)*
3v Solutions LLC 601 720-4999
1888 Main St Ste C296 Madison (39110) *(G-3074)*
4m Enterprises LLC 601 664-0030
5219 Highway 80 E Pearl (39208) *(G-4101)*
5 K Corp 601 736-5367
1113 Highway 98 Byp Ste A Columbia (39429) *(G-877)*
500 Degreez Entrmt LLC Not LLC 678 948-8710
250 Ivie Ln Apt 1 Mantachie (38855) *(G-3197)*
506 Printing 662 361-4411
2837 Jefferson St Macon (39341) *(G-3053)*
52 Mp Farms, Tunica *Also called A & J Planting Company (G-5094)*
59 Signs LLC 601 798-3682
426 Lakeside Dr Carriere (39426) *(G-686)*
5d Natural Farm LLc 601 906-8763
2629 Neil Collins Rd Raymond (39154) *(G-4481)*
5m Enterprises LLC 601 416-0210
193 North St Sebastopol (39359) *(G-4773)*
5th Avenue Software LLC 662 843-1200
600 S Fifth Ave Cleveland (38732) *(G-785)*
601 Custom Woodworks 601 588-0117
204 Arlington Rd Beaumont (39423) *(G-183)*
8209, Madison *Also called Autoflow LLC (G-3079)*

901 Safety LLC 901 493-3841
7328 Wind Dr Olive Branch (38654) *(G-3803)*
9r Screen Printing 601 303-0520
9 Percy Pittman Rd Tylertown (39667) *(G-5261)*
A & A Trailer Sales LLC 228 234-3420
15824 Lemoyne Blvd Biloxi (39532) *(G-215)*
A & B Pump & Supply Inc 601 787-3741
710 Hwy 528 W Heidelberg (39439) *(G-2111)*
A & D Timber Company Inc 601 528-9357
465 Thelma Andrews Rd Wiggins (39577) *(G-5568)*
A & J Planting Company 662 363-0039
1318 Edwards Ave Tunica (38676) *(G-5094)*
A & W Marble Inc 228 832-5037
19290 Frontier Rd Saucier (39574) *(G-4748)*
A 2 Z Printing, Jackson *Also called T Enterprises Inc (G-2603)*
A and Y Uniform Shop 601 553-1377
1720 N Frontage Rd Meridian (39301) *(G-3293)*
A B B Inc 662 628-8196
310 S Madison Calhoun City (38916) *(G-634)*
A B S Woodworks 601 425-3306
258 Flynt Rd Laurel (39443) *(G-2730)*
A C I, Batesville *Also called Aci Building Systems LLC (G-93)*
A K Sanders Mfg Inc 901 647-1830
2116 Pryne Dr Southaven (38672) *(G-4850)*
A Plus Signs Inc 601 355-9595
4147 Northview Plz Ste B Jackson (39206) *(G-2314)*
A Plus Tornado Shelters O 601 879-0005
3710 I 55 N Jackson (39211) *(G-2315)*
A Port In The Storm, Rienzi *Also called Elizabeth Newcomb (G-4649)*
A Quarter Can Inc 601 936-9915
855 Richland East Dr Richland (39218) *(G-4496)*
A Square Innovative SEC LLC 601 937-0318
1230 Raymond Rd Jackson (39204) *(G-2316)*
A Step Above Marine Contrs LLC 228 452-5122
224 W North St Pass Christian (39571) *(G-4076)*
A Stitch In Time 662 257-0661
104 Main St N Amory (38821) *(G-33)*
A To B Sign Company 601 924-6323
1450b E Northside Dr Clinton (39056) *(G-811)*
A-1 Family Furniture Inc 662 257-6002
60036 Puckett Dr Amory (38821) *(G-34)*
A-Squared Printing LLC 601 497-0280
211 Eldorado Cir Pearl (39208) *(G-4102)*
A-Z Lightning Protection LLC 662 890-7041
120 Landen Cir Byhalia (38611) *(G-576)*
A2z Printing Inc 601 487-1100
2125 Tv Rd Jackson (39204) *(G-2317)*
AA Calibration Services LLC 662 716-0202
111 Roosevelt Hudson Dr Yazoo City (39194) *(G-5620)*
AAA Heating & Cooling 601 214-7212
201 Lotus Dr Brandon (39047) *(G-353)*
AAA Portable Buildings LLC 601 445-4034
658 Highway 61 N Natchez (39120) *(G-3516)*
AAA Printing & Graphics, Pearl *Also called Hagen Corporation (G-4125)*
Abacus Publishing Co 601 684-0001
1060 Addo Barnes Rd McComb (39648) *(G-3243)*
ABB Crystal Springs, Crystal Springs *Also called ABB Inc (G-1139)*
ABB Inc 601 892-6431
101 Kuhlman Dr Crystal Springs (39059) *(G-1139)*
ABB Inc 662 562-0700
1555 Scott St Senatobia (38668) *(G-4785)*
ABB Installation Products Inc 662 342-1545
8735 Hamilton Rd Southaven (38671) *(G-4851)*
ABB Motors and Mechanical Inc 662 328-9116
70 Indstrial Pk Access Rd Columbus (39701) *(G-930)*
Abbeville Mill LLC 662 238-7879
81 County Road 201 Abbeville (38601) *(G-1)*

(PA)=Parent Co (HQ)=Headquarters (DH)=Div Headquarters

2019 Harris Directory of
Mississippi Manufacturers

Abbott Industries Inc

ALPHABETIC SECTION

Abbott Industries Inc..........662 357-7360
211 S Airport Blvd Tunica (38676) *(G-5095)*

Abby Manufacturing LLC (PA)..........662 223-5339
501 Pulliam Rd Walnut (38683) *(G-5452)*

Abby Manufacturing Co Inc..........662 223-5339
1100 Denmill Rd New Albany (38652) *(G-3670)*

Abby Manufacturing Co Inc..........662 223-5339
501 Pulliam Rd Walnut (38683) *(G-5453)*

ABC Scrity Fbrction Sltion LLC..........601 828-9010
9920 Highway 84 W Roxie (39661) *(G-4688)*

Aberdeen Machine Works Inc..........662 369-9357
79 Hwy 25 S Aberdeen (39730) *(G-6)*

Aberdeen School District..........662 369-6886
115 N Long St Aberdeen (39730) *(G-7)*

Ability Prosthetics LLC..........662 842-3220
223 E Franklin St Tupelo (38804) *(G-5106)*

Ability Works, Greenville Also called Rehabilitation Svcs Miss Dept *(G-1595)*

Ability Works Inc..........662 328-0275
48 Datco Ind Dr Columbus (39702) *(G-931)*

Ability Works Inc..........662 842-2144
613 Pegram Dr Tupelo (38801) *(G-5107)*

Abilityworks of Columbus, Columbus Also called Ability Works Inc *(G-931)*

Abilityworks of Tupelo, Tupelo Also called Ability Works Inc *(G-5107)*

About Time PC and Electronics, Raymond Also called Chuck Jennings *(G-4486)*

ABS Welding Inc..........601 444-9889
1133 Prospres Ridge Rd Columbia (39429) *(G-878)*

Acadian Custom Woodworks..........601 572-4774
242 Mallard Dr Brandon (39047) *(G-354)*

Acalvin Chapman Jr., Jackson Also called Innovative Wireless LLC *(G-2447)*

Acco Brands USA LLC..........800 541-0094
300 Quartet Ave Booneville (38829) *(G-314)*

Acco Brands USA LLC..........662 720-1300
101 Bolton Dr Bldg 18 Booneville (38829) *(G-315)*

Accrabond Corporation..........662 895-4480
8848 Hacks Cross Rd Olive Branch (38654) *(G-3804)*

Accu-Fab and Construction Inc..........228 475-0082
5313 Mirror Lake Rd Moss Point (39562) *(G-3465)*

Accu-Fab Manufacturing LLC..........228 769-2532
1804 Roswell St Pascagoula (39581) *(G-4017)*

Accuprint, Abbeville Also called Richardson Marketing *(G-3)*

Accurate Drug Testing and Back..........601 500-7841
105 Katherine Dr Bldg C Flowood (39232) *(G-1341)*

Accurate Edge..........228 832-2920
21051 Coastal Pkwy Gulfport (39503) *(G-1715)*

Accusteer LLC..........601 483-0225
901 Dst Meridian (39301) *(G-3294)*

Ace Hardware, Yazoo City Also called Delta Auto Parts Inc *(G-5630)*

Aci Building Systems LLC (HQ)..........662 563-4574
10125 Highway 6 W Batesville (38606) *(G-93)*

Acme Brick Company..........601 714-2966
6159 Highway 25 Brandon (39047) *(G-355)*

Acme Fabrication LLC..........228 669-0004
190 Wire Rd W Perkinston (39573) *(G-4172)*

Acme Printing Company Inc..........601 856-7766
1112 Windrose Cir Madison (39110) *(G-3075)*

Action Drilling Company Inc..........601 892-5105
2933 Old Church Dr Nw Wesson (39191) *(G-5523)*

Action Industries..........662 566-3173
338 Stafford Blvd Pontotoc (38863) *(G-4319)*

Action Printing Center Inc..........228 769-2676
3315 Market St Pascagoula (39567) *(G-4018)*

Action Prsuit Games of Brandon..........601 825-1052
44 Napoleon Dr Brandon (39047) *(G-356)*

Action Success Press..........601 824-7775
55 Woodgate Dr Brandon (39042) *(G-357)*

Acy Logging..........601 833-5426
919 Smith Lake Rd Ne Brookhaven (39601) *(G-478)*

Ad Art Sign..........601 939-8000
424 N Bierdeman Rd Pearl (39208) *(G-4103)*

Ad Art Signs Promotions, Pearl Also called Ad Art Sign *(G-4103)*

Ad Lines Inc..........662 893-6400
3902 Windermere Rd S Nesbit (38651) *(G-3646)*

Ad Visuals Inc..........601 932-3060
587 Old Highway 49 S Richland (39218) *(G-4497)*

AD&s, Brandon Also called Automtion Dsigns Solutions Inc *(G-367)*

Ada Newson..........601 810-6614
321 Washington Ave Richland (39218) *(G-4498)*

Ada S Sweetz and Treats, Richland Also called Ada Newson *(G-4498)*

Adam Sterling Logging LLC..........601 657-1091
4730 Graves Chapel Rd Liberty (39645) *(G-2908)*

Adams Logging Inc..........601 567-2988
6587 Adams Rd Smithdale (39664) *(G-4840)*

Adams Prsthtics Orthdntics LLC..........601 665-4000
931 Highway 80 W 173b Jackson (39204) *(G-2318)*

Adams Welding & Fabrication..........601 319-1865
136 Widow Landrum Rd Ovett (39464) *(G-3930)*

ADB Canvas Art..........662 934-9449
159 Moss Rd Batesville (38606) *(G-94)*

Adcamp Inc..........601 939-4493
1353 Flowood Dr Ste A Flowood (39232) *(G-1342)*

Address America Inc..........888 991-3322
5454 I 55 N Jackson (39211) *(G-2319)*

Addy Metal Fabrication..........601 635-4064
1434 Muley Rd Decatur (39327) *(G-1170)*

Ademco Inc..........601 936-4842
197 Interstate Dr Richland (39218) *(G-4499)*

Adens Patt, Carriere Also called H&M Metal Express LLC *(G-693)*

ADI Global Distribution, Richland Also called Ademco Inc *(G-4499)*

Adlam Films LLC..........662 823-1345
62 County Road 520 Shannon (38868) *(G-4805)*

ADP, Grenada Also called Advanced Distributor Pdts LLC *(G-1666)*

ADP Hearing Inc..........662 874-6279
6915 Crumpler Blvd Ste E Olive Branch (38654) *(G-3805)*

Adrienne Batla Cupcakes..........260 348-5364
131 Chancellorsville Ln Clarksdale (38614) *(G-756)*

Advance Tool and Die Inc..........601 939-1291
2750 Old Brandon Rd Pearl (39208) *(G-4104)*

Advanced Caster Tech LLC..........228 432-1384
188 Main St Biloxi (39530) *(G-216)*

Advanced Digital Fire & SEC..........901 240-8030
9818 Southern Gum Way Olive Branch (38654) *(G-3806)*

Advanced Distributor Pdts LLC (HQ)..........662 229-3000
1995 Air Industrial Pk Rd Grenada (38901) *(G-1666)*

Advanced Drainage Systems Inc..........601 629-9040
5695 Highway 61 S Vicksburg (39180) *(G-5338)*

Advanced Drainage Systems Inc..........601 371-0678
205 Apache Dr Jackson (39272) *(G-2320)*

Advanced Dynamics Inc..........601 677-3423
4048 Kellis Store Rd Preston (39354) *(G-4426)*

Advanced Fabrication Inc..........228 392-0400
11032 Auto Mall Pkwy Diberville (39540) *(G-1194)*

Advanced Fabrication Inc..........601 796-7977
644 Hickory Grove Rd Lumberton (39455) *(G-3023)*

Advanced GnsInger Armament LLC..........775 343-5633
313 Critz St Starkville (39759) *(G-4923)*

Advanced Hearing and Balance..........601 450-0280
5128 Old Highway 11 Ste 8 Hattiesburg (39402) *(G-1915)*

Advanced Innovative Pdts LLC..........662 365-1640
976 Highway 45 Baldwyn (38824) *(G-70)*

Advanced Marine Inc..........228 374-6747
337 Howard Ave Biloxi (39530) *(G-217)*

Advanced Pharmaceuticals LLC..........228 215-1911
998 N Halstead Rd Ste A Ocean Springs (39564) *(G-3739)*

Advanced Screening Solutiions..........662 205-4139
2005 W Main St Tupelo (38801) *(G-5108)*

Advanced Treatment Tech LLC..........601 506-3798
141 Peninsula Dr Brandon (39047) *(G-358)*

Advantage Cabinet Doors..........662 494-9700
715 Airport Rd West Point (39773) *(G-5534)*

Advantage Medical and Phrm LLC..........601 268-1422
6375 U S Highway 98 # 50 Hattiesburg (39402) *(G-1916)*

Advantage Tax & Printing..........601 735-2023
308 Mississippi Dr Waynesboro (39367) *(G-5488)*

Advantage Tax & Printing Inc..........601 394-2898
314a Main St Leakesville (39451) *(G-2875)*

Advantage Tax & Printing Svc..........601 544-0602
2407 W 4th St Hattiesburg (39401) *(G-1917)*

Advantage Tax and Print..........601 557-5055
109 W Church St Quitman (39355) *(G-4455)*

Adventure Leadership Cons LLC..........662 915-6736
606 Scarlet Oak St # 301 Southaven (38671) *(G-4852)*

Advertiser, The, New Albany Also called Tupelo Advertiser Inc *(G-3704)*

Adware..........601 898-9194
310b Hawthorne Cir Ridgeland (39157) *(G-4545)*

Ae Enterprises..........601 573-5954
312 Water Oak Rd Brandon (39047) *(G-359)*

Aei LLC..........662 562-6663
140 Matthews Dr Senatobia (38668) *(G-4786)*

Aerial Truck Equipment Co Inc..........662 895-0993
8270 New Craft Rd Olive Branch (38654) *(G-3807)*

Aero-RAD Tech LLC..........662 328-0155
2305c Highway 45 N Columbus (39705) *(G-932)*

Aerojet Rocketdyne Inc..........228 813-1511
9101 Lnard Kmble Rd Rrm07 Stennis Space Center (39529) *(G-4993)*

Aerotec Ltd..........713 598-9410
5255 Old Highway 11 Hattiesburg (39402) *(G-1918)*

Aerotec Systems, Hattiesburg Also called Aerotec Ltd *(G-1918)*

Aerway Manufacturing Co..........662 726-4246
1721 Deerbrook Rd Macon (39341) *(G-3054)*

Afco Industries Inc..........662 895-8686
11000 Green Valley Dr Olive Branch (38654) *(G-3808)*

Afco Millwork, Olive Branch Also called Afco Industries Inc *(G-3808)*

Affordable Furn Mfg Co Inc..........662 568-7981
6496 Redland Sarepta Rd Houlka (38850) *(G-2216)*

Ag Spray Equipment Inc..........662 453-4524
2900 Baldwin Rd Greenwood (38930) *(G-1610)*

AGA, Starkville Also called Advanced GnsInger Armament LLC *(G-4923)*

2019 Harris Directory of
Mississippi Manufacturers

(G-0000) Company's Geographic Section entry number

AGC, Jackson *Also called Associated Gen Contrs of Miss* ***(G-2334)***
Aggeos Inc 512 751-2160
603 Dulaney Wilemon Rd Fulton (38843) ***(G-1444)***
Agmyns 228 831-0342
102 Ruby Dr Gulfport (39503) ***(G-1716)***
Agri-Afc LLC 601 783-6080
310 E Railroad Ave N Magnolia (39652) ***(G-3188)***
Agriliance LLC 662 738-4940
4408 Ms Highway 388 Brooksville (39739) ***(G-552)***
Agrimotive Division, Laurel *Also called Howse Implement Company Inc* ***(G-2782)***
Ahc Fluid Power, Jackson *Also called Franklin Electrofluid Co Inc* ***(G-2412)***
Ahk Mississippi, Canton *Also called American Howa Kentucky Inc* ***(G-646)***
Ai Evac Ems Inc 662 335-3034
1609 Hospital St Greenville (38703) ***(G-1535)***
AIA Countertops 574 457-2003
145 H M Richards Way Guntown (38849) ***(G-1896)***
Ainsworth Impressions, Ellisville *Also called Impressions Inc* ***(G-1259)***
Ainsworth Signs 662 453-1904
406 Lamar St Greenwood (38930) ***(G-1611)***
Ainz Publishing Company 662 728-6131
5 County Road 1053 Booneville (38829) ***(G-316)***
Air + Mak Industries Inc 662 893-3444
11154 Wildwood Dr Olive Branch (38654) ***(G-3809)***
Air Care Service, Greenville *Also called Watson Percy* ***(G-1609)***
Air Cond Htg & S/M Solutions 601 720-5085
144 Pinedale Rd Terry (39170) ***(G-5063)***
Air Cruisers Company LLC 601 657-8043
269 Main St Liberty (39645) ***(G-2909)***
Air Evac Lifeteam, Greenville *Also called Ai Evac Ems Inc* ***(G-1535)***
Air Products and Chemicals Inc 601 823-9850
1080 Fender Trl Ne Brookhaven (39601) ***(G-479)***
Air Tech of Waveland 228 467-7547
4111 Third St Bay Saint Louis (39520) ***(G-133)***
Air Vent 601 790-9397
110 Lake Village Dr Madison (39110) ***(G-3076)***
Airbrush & Signs By Debby 601 656-6953
15821 Highway 21 S Philadelphia (39350) ***(G-4202)***
Airbus Helicopters Inc 662 327-6226
1782 Airport Rd Columbus (39701) ***(G-933)***
Airdesigns 601 584-1000
4407 U S Highway 49 Hattiesburg (39401) ***(G-1919)***
Airfloat Systems Inc 662 566-0158
110 Second St Verona (38879) ***(G-5326)***
Airlock Insulation LLC 601 526-4141
121 E State St Ste A Ridgeland (39157) ***(G-4546)***
Airworks Enterprises Inc 601 372-8304
5080 Springridge Rd Raymond (39154) ***(G-4482)***
Ajinomoto Foods North Amer Inc 662 623-7400
10646 Highway 51 Oakland (38948) ***(G-3737)***
Ajinomoto Windsor Inc 662 647-1594
875 Highway 51 S Batesville (38606) ***(G-95)***
AJINOMOTO WINDSOR, INC., Batesville *Also called Ajinomoto Windsor Inc* ***(G-95)***
Ajs Welding Repair 601 264-2571
601 Nobles Rd Sumrall (39482) ***(G-5033)***
Akers Minerals LLC 207 615-7591
2476 Highway 8 E Houston (38851) ***(G-2230)***
Al-Tom Forest Products Inc 601 989-2631
335 Al Tom Rd Richton (39476) ***(G-4526)***
Alabama Catfish Inc 662 265-5377
83 Goldkist Ln Inverness (38753) ***(G-2272)***
Alaco of Mississippi Inc 662 837-4041
151 County Rd 565 Ripley (38663) ***(G-4651)***
Alaco Sale, Ripley *Also called Alaco of Mississippi Inc* ***(G-4651)***
Alamiss Inc 601 671-0840
91 Airport Rd Waynesboro (39367) ***(G-5489)***
Alan Dickerson Inc 662 289-1451
310 Knox Rd Kosciusko (39090) ***(G-2687)***
Alarm Company Inc 601 898-3105
338 Distribution Dr Madison (39110) ***(G-3077)***
Alatheia Prosthetic Reha 601 919-2113
504 Grants Ferry Rd Brandon (39047) ***(G-360)***
Alatheia Prsthtic Rehab Centre, Brandon *Also called Alatheia Prosthetic Reha* ***(G-360)***
Albany Fiber Sales Inc 662 401-2342
120 Snyder St New Albany (38652) ***(G-3671)***
Albany Industries Inc 662 488-8281
388 Highway 15 S Pontotoc (38863) ***(G-4320)***
Albany Industries LLC (HQ) 662 534-9800
504 N Glenfield Rd New Albany (38652) ***(G-3672)***
Alcorn Fabricating 662 462-5669
87 County Road 547 Corinth (38834) ***(G-1056)***
Alden R Stockert 228 731-2747
11291 Pine Dr Gulfport (39503) ***(G-1717)***
Aldridge Operating Co LLC 601 446-5585
151 Providence Rd Natchez (39120) ***(G-3517)***
Aldridge Operating Co., Natchez *Also called Crtney G Aldridge Ptro Glogist* ***(G-3552)***
Alex Carol Limited 601 956-0536
834 Wilson Dr Ste C Ridgeland (39157) ***(G-4547)***
Alexander Fabricating Co Inc 601 485-5414
686 Murphy Rd Meridian (39301) ***(G-3295)***
Alfords Decorating Center 662 455-3552
233 County Road 231 Greenwood (38930) ***(G-1612)***
Algix, Meridian *Also called Solaplast LLC* ***(G-3399)***
Algix LLC 877 972-5449
5168 Water Tower Rd Meridian (39301) ***(G-3296)***
Alicia Vaughn 601 888-7830
613 Main St Woodville (39669) ***(G-5615)***
Alig LLC 601 829-9020
118 Shirley Ln Brandon (39047) ***(G-361)***
All American Check Cashing Inc 601 373-6115
5795 Terry Rd Ste 311 Byram (39272) ***(G-615)***
All American Stucco 228 669-0915
14136 Cable Bridge Rd Gulfport (39503) ***(G-1718)***
All Bright Sign and Neon, Pearl *Also called Skillem Entreprises Inc* ***(G-4146)***
All In One Signs & Printing 662 216-0737
114 Craft St Holly Springs (38635) ***(G-2170)***
All Seasons Events 601 405-1417
8117 Highway 18 W Jackson (39209) ***(G-2321)***
All Signs Inc 228 897-9100
558 Courthouse Rd Gulfport (39507) ***(G-1719)***
All Star Forest Products Inc 228 896-4117
400 Magazine Cir Gulfport (39507) ***(G-1720)***
All Star Forest Products Inc 662 294-8898
2498 Pryor St Grenada (38901) ***(G-1667)***
All Star Forest Products Inc (PA) 601 664-0700
5757 N Mcraven Rd Jackson (39209) ***(G-2322)***
All That Glitters Ep Inc 601 981-1947
5968 Waverly Dr Jackson (39206) ***(G-2323)***
All-Tech Metal Works Inc 228 396-3800
99 Fairley Bridge Rd Wiggins (39577) ***(G-5569)***
Allen Beverages Incorporated 228 831-4343
13300 Dedeaux Rd Gulfport (39503) ***(G-1721)***
Allen Operating Company, Natchez *Also called Allen Petroleum Service Inc* ***(G-3518)***
Allen Petroleum Service Inc 601 442-3562
521 Main St Ste M1 Natchez (39120) ***(G-3518)***
Allen Sheetmetal Inc 228 875-5336
14417 Cullen St Biloxi (39532) ***(G-218)***
Allen's Crown's, Hattiesburg *Also called Allens Trophies Inc* ***(G-1920)***
Allens Cane Shop 662 429-2016
2038 Getwell Rd Nesbit (38651) ***(G-3647)***
Allens Trophies Inc 601 582-7702
220 Mobile St Hattiesburg (39401) ***(G-1920)***
Alley Kats Glass 662 324-3002
1628 Highway 389 Starkville (39759) ***(G-4924)***
Alleykat Ceramics LLC 228 224-7775
2694 Broadwater Dr Gulfport (39507) ***(G-1722)***
Alliance Business Services, Ridgeland *Also called Nick Strcklnds Quick Print Inc* ***(G-4611)***
Alliance Business Services, Jackson *Also called Nick Strcklnds Quick Print Inc* ***(G-2521)***
Allied Crawford Jackson Inc 769 230-2220
212 Apache Dr Byram (39272) ***(G-616)***
Allied Universal Corp 601 477-2550
30 Neil Gunn Dr Ellisville (39437) ***(G-1245)***
Allistons 228 832-8683
14494 Collins Blvd Gulfport (39503) ***(G-1723)***
Allmond Printing Company Inc 662 369-4848
603 W Commerce St Aberdeen (39730) ***(G-8)***
Allred Backhoe & Gravel Co, Bogue Chitto *Also called Reuben Allred* ***(G-304)***
Allstar, Iuka *Also called Enlow & Son Inc* ***(G-2291)***
Aloha Printing Co 601 483-6677
6429 Confederate Dr Marion (39342) ***(G-3220)***
Alpha Printing Inc 601 371-2611
2125 Tv Rd Jackson (39204) ***(G-2324)***
AlphaGraphics, Pearl *Also called Shilpam Corp* ***(G-4144)***
Alpine Well Service Inc 601 442-0021
144 Providence Rd Natchez (39120) ***(G-3519)***
Alply Archtctural Bldg Systems 601 743-2623
Willow Ave Hwy 16 W De Kalb (39328) ***(G-1159)***
Althees Jellies & Jams LLC 601 795-4118
110 Long Leaf Ln Poplarville (39470) ***(G-4373)***
Aluma-Form Inc 662 677-6000
141 Pulliam Rd Walnut (38683) ***(G-5454)***
Aluminum Extrusion Industries, Senatobia *Also called Aei LLC* ***(G-4786)***
Aluminum Products, Grenada *Also called Modine Grenada LLC* ***(G-1692)***
Aluminum Recycling of Miss (PA) 601 355-5777
1819 Valley St Jackson (39204) ***(G-2325)***
Alvin Schilling Wdwkg LLC 601 268-1070
241 Bayberry Loop Purvis (39475) ***(G-4432)***
Alvix Laboratories LLC 601 714-1677
6601 Sunplex Dr Ocean Springs (39564) ***(G-3740)***
Amandas Puzzles 228 314-3930
2200 19th Ave Gulfport (39501) ***(G-1724)***
AMaries Bath Happies & Body 601 714-1887
415 Turtle Ln Brandon (39047) ***(G-362)***
AMC, Walnut *Also called Abby Manufacturing LLC* ***(G-5452)***
AMC, New Albany *Also called HMC Metal Forming Inc* ***(G-3682)***
AMC Signs & Lighting LLC 901 831-7393
2304 Highway 25 Iuka (38852) ***(G-2283)***

ALPHABETIC

(PA)=Parent Co (HQ)=Headquarters (DH)=Div Headquarters
2019 Harris Directory of Mississippi Manufacturers
263

Amco Manufacturing Company LLC

ALPHABETIC SECTION

Amco Manufacturing Company LLC 662 746-4464
800 S Industrial Pkwy Yazoo City (39194) *(G-5621)*

Amcol International, Aberdeen *Also called Nanocor LLC* *(G-19)*

Ameitech/South 601 853-0830
210 Industrial Dr Ridgeland (39157) *(G-4548)*

American Apparel Inc 601 654-9211
52 Pleasant Hill Rd Lena (39094) *(G-2894)*

American Bottling Company 601 939-5454
401 Industrial Park Dr Richland (39218) *(G-4500)*

American Bottling Company 662 844-7047
2945 Mattox St Tupelo (38801) *(G-5109)*

American Concrete Products Inc 601 583-2274
257 Wl Runnels Indus Dr Hattiesburg (39401) *(G-1921)*

American Container Inc 662 890-0325
8530 W Sandidge Rd Olive Branch (38654) *(G-3810)*

American Dream Handyman Svc, Southaven *Also called Smith Sr William Shayne* *(G-4903)*

American Energy Solutions LLC 757 846-3261
6155 Autumn Oaks Dr Olive Branch (38654) *(G-3811)*

American Howa Kentucky Inc 601 506-0591
151 Nissan Dr Ste J Canton (39046) *(G-646)*

American Log Handlers LLC 601 927-6692
619 Highway 30 E Booneville (38829) *(G-317)*

American Metalcraft 769 486-5007
14062 Highway 16 W De Kalb (39328) *(G-1160)*

American Midstream 601 671-8800
595 Ceamon Pittman Rd Waynesboro (39367) *(G-5490)*

American Midstream LLC 601 776-6721
103 E Franklin St Quitman (39355) *(G-4456)*

American Midstream LLC 601 798-9145
148 Runway Rd Picayune (39466) *(G-4251)*

American National Molding LLC 601 936-2722
3670 Flowood Dr Flowood (39232) *(G-1343)*

American Pacific Inc (PA) 662 252-1862
520 Salem Ave Holly Springs (38635) *(G-2171)*

American Pacific Paneling, Holly Springs *Also called American Pacific Inc* *(G-2171)*

American Packaging Company Inc 601 856-0986
158 American Way Madison (39110) *(G-3078)*

American Payment Systems 601 368-7382
4329 N State St Jackson (39206) *(G-2326)*

American Payment Systems 601 713-3761
4110 Medgar Evers Blvd Jackson (39213) *(G-2327)*

American Pet Food, Tupelo *Also called Sunshine Mills Inc* *(G-5234)*

American Plant Services Inc 228 762-1397
5705 Telephone Rd Pascagoula (39567) *(G-4019)*

American Plastic Toys Inc 662 895-4055
11200 Wildwood Dr Olive Branch (38654) *(G-3812)*

American Printing & Converting, Madison *Also called American Packaging Company Inc* *(G-3078)*

American Printing and Converti 601 222-0555
210 Beulah Ave Tylertown (39667) *(G-5262)*

American Printing Blue PR 601 544-7714
6186 U S Highway 49 Hattiesburg (39401) *(G-1922)*

American Printing Copy Center 228 875-1398
3064b Bienville Blvd Ocean Springs (39564) *(G-3741)*

American Railcar Inds Inc 601 384-5841
S Gerard St Bude (39630) *(G-567)*

American Specialty Alloys 662 368-1332
70 Wilcut Block Rd Columbus (39701) *(G-934)*

American Stamping Corporation 662 895-5300
15451 Goodman Rd Ste A Olive Branch (38654) *(G-3813)*

American Stitching LLC 601 919-7882
119 Deer Cir Ridgeland (39157) *(G-4549)*

American T Shirt Printing Co 662 590-3272
251 Freeman Ln Yazoo City (39194) *(G-5622)*

American Tank & Vessel Inc 601 947-7210
274 Evanston Rd Lucedale (39452) *(G-2986)*

American Tarp & Awning Co 601 656-5177
11500 Highway 482 Lot 3 Philadelphia (39350) *(G-4203)*

American Wood, Richton *Also called Powe Timber Company* *(G-4542)*

American Wood Division, Hattiesburg *Also called Powe Timber Company* *(G-2046)*

Americrete Inc (HQ) 601 485-6507
220 65th Ave Meridian (39307) *(G-3297)*

Americrete Ready Mix Inc, Meridian *Also called Americrete Inc* *(G-3297)*

Americrete Ready Mix Inc 601 656-5590
10350 Road 383 Philadelphia (39350) *(G-4204)*

Amerimac Chemical Co (PA) 601 918-8321
750 Boling St Ste J Jackson (39209) *(G-2328)*

Amerimac Machining Corporation 601 940-7919
750 Boling St Ste J Jackson (39209) *(G-2329)*

Amerimac Synergy Veterans LLC 601 326-3400
931 Highway 80 W Jackson (39204) *(G-2330)*

Amerinca Non Wovens, Columbus *Also called Mississippi Fabritek Inc* *(G-1003)*

Amerione Security 901 502-2295
8361 Pinnacle Dr Southaven (38672) *(G-4853)*

Ameritron, Starkville *Also called Mfj Enterprises Inc* *(G-4958)*

Amerson Cleophus Jr 601 362-3629
1603 Fairwood Dr Jackson (39213) *(G-2331)*

Amite Bioenergy LLC 770 743-4300
1763 Gp Rd No 2 Gloster (39638) *(G-1509)*

Amite County Poles & Piling 601 225-4870
400 E Sterling Rd Gloster (39638) *(G-1510)*

Amory Advertiser 662 256-5647
115 Main St S Amory (38821) *(G-35)*

Amory Powder Coating LLC 662 749-7081
941 A S Main St Amory Ms Amory (38821) *(G-36)*

AMS Services LLC 662 449-2672
960 Old Highway 51 N Nesbit (38651) *(G-3648)*

An AMC LLC 662 292-6973
14150 Knightsbridge Ln Olive Branch (38654) *(G-3814)*

An American Made Coffee Co, Olive Branch *Also called An AMC LLC* *(G-3814)*

Ancerstor Logging LLC 601 701-7020
15441 Highway 39 N De Kalb (39328) *(G-1161)*

Ancestor Logging 925 895-2306
1719 Highway 19 N Apt 30 Meridian (39307) *(G-3298)*

Anchor Works 601 264-8700
452 Cole Rd Hattiesburg (39402) *(G-1923)*

Anderson & Son Logging LLC 662 688-1211
462 County Road 117 Tillatoba (38961) *(G-5079)*

Anderson Enterprises LLC 601 928-0030
1825 Highway 49 Wiggins (39577) *(G-5570)*

Anderson Oil Company Inc 601 442-2960
679 Highway 61 N Natchez (39120) *(G-3520)*

Anderson Repair Shop 601 783-2654
1015 Highway 48 E Magnolia (39652) *(G-3189)*

Anderson Tully Co, Vicksburg *Also called Anderson-Tully Company* *(G-5340)*

Anderson-Tully Company 601 629-3283
1735 N Washington St Vicksburg (39183) *(G-5339)*

Anderson-Tully Company 601 636-3876
565 Industrial Dr Vicksburg (39183) *(G-5340)*

Andrews Cabinet Shop 662 327-1070
400 William Roberts Rd Columbus (39702) *(G-935)*

Andrews Discount Furniture Str, Ecru *Also called Andrews Furniture Company Inc* *(G-1229)*

Andrews Furniture Company Inc 662 489-1107
6584 Highway 15 N Ecru (38841) *(G-1229)*

Andrews Woodshop LLC 228 216-5563
1728 21st St Gulfport (39501) *(G-1725)*

Andy Jackson 662 416-2614
6 County Road 5041 Booneville (38829) *(G-318)*

Andy Massey Logging 662 675-2647
2268 County Road 134 Coffeeville (38922) *(G-840)*

Angels Truck Service LLC 662 890-0417
11153 Highway 178 Olive Branch (38654) *(G-3815)*

Angies Crocheting Corner 228 617-9342
127 S Pine Dr Hattiesburg (39401) *(G-1924)*

Ani Pharmaceuticals Inc 228 863-1702
3600 25th Ave Gulfport (39501) *(G-1726)*

Anna Grace Tees LLC 228 861-2661
402 Caribe Pl N Gulfport (39507) *(G-1727)*

Anns Embroidery 601 444-0011
730 Main St Columbia (39429) *(G-879)*

Anthony Logging Inc 601 731-2975
127 Rowley Rd Kokomo (39643) *(G-2686)*

Anthony Syrup Company 601 656-7052
11191 Highway 21 N Philadelphia (39350) *(G-4205)*

Antonio Tarrell LLC 662 983-2486
116 S Murphree Ave Bruce (38915) *(G-559)*

Anusaya Fresh USA LLC 601 795-2008
576 Slade Woodward Rd Poplarville (39470) *(G-4374)*

Ao Liquidation Trust Inc 662 675-8102
129 Tennessee St Coffeeville (38922) *(G-841)*

Apac-Mississippi Inc 662 494-5772
753 Mayhew St West Point (39773) *(G-5535)*

Apac-Mississippi Inc 601 376-4000
101 Riverview Dr Richland (39218) *(G-4501)*

Apac-Mississippi Inc 662 328-6555
462 Lake Norris Rd Columbus (39701) *(G-936)*

Apac-Mississippi Inc 662 378-8481
2559 Harbor Front Rd Greenville (38701) *(G-1536)*

Apac-Mississippi Inc (HQ) 601 376-4000
101 Riverview Dr Richland (39218) *(G-4502)*

Apac-Mississippi Inc 601 693-5025
4412 Interchange Rd Meridian (39307) *(G-3299)*

Apac-Mississippi Inc 662 348-2214
331 Messner St Guntown (38849) *(G-1897)*

Apac-Mississippi Inc 601 634-6600
4441 Rifle Range Rd Vicksburg (39180) *(G-5341)*

Apac-Mississippi Inc 662 343-9300
700 S Meridian St Aberdeen (39730) *(G-9)*

Apac-Mississippi Inc 662 746-7983
22431 Hwy 3 Yazoo City (39194) *(G-5623)*

Apex Products Inc (PA) 601 992-5900
435 Cedars Of Lebanon Rd Jackson (39206) *(G-2332)*

Aplimages Inc 601 992-1556
220 Avalon Cir Ste D Brandon (39047) *(G-363)*

Apm LLC 907 279-0204
13220 N Cypress Dr Gulfport (39503) *(G-1728)*

Appeal Publishing Co Inc 601 774-9433
102 Main St Union (39365) *(G-5292)*

2019 Harris Directory of
Mississippi Manufacturers

(G-0000) Company's Geographic Section entry number

264

ALPHABETIC SECTION

Aztec Industries Inc

Apple Dapple..228 539-3100
12261 Highway 49 Ste 15 Gulfport (39503) *(G-1729)*

Appliance Tech Authorized Svc................228 392-0789
19701 Seymour Rd Biloxi (39533) *(G-219)*

Applicated Images Inc...............................601 992-1556
220 Avalon Cir Ste D Brandon (39047) *(G-364)*

Applied Geo Technologies Inc...................601 267-5681
1600 N Pearl St Carthage (39051) *(G-706)*

Applied Indus Tech - Dixie Inc..................601 649-4312
556 S 16th Ave Laurel (39440) *(G-2731)*

Applied Industrial Tech 0670, Laurel *Also called Applied Indus Tech - Dixie Inc (G-2731)*

Applied Safety Coatings Inc.....................601 940-3004
232 Wakeland Dr Raymond (39154) *(G-4483)*

Applied Software System LLC....................601 605-0877
177 Green Glades Ridgeland (39157) *(G-4550)*

Aptiv Services Us LLC..............................601 835-1983
925 Industrial Park Rd Ne Brookhaven (39601) *(G-480)*

Aquavest...662 287-0302
1808 Highway 72 E Corinth (38834) *(G-1057)*

Arbor Therapeutics LLC............................303 808-4104
851b Highway 30 E Oxford (38655) *(G-3935)*

ARC-Up Welding Inc.................................601 638-1202
76 Business Park Dr Vicksburg (39180) *(G-5342)*

Archh LLC...601 590-3519
103 Quail Ct Carriere (39426) *(G-687)*

Architectural Concepts.............................850 471-7081
103 Snyder Dr Brandon (39042) *(G-365)*

Archrock Inc..601 444-0055
60 Columbia Purvis Rd Columbia (39429) *(G-880)*

Aride Taxi Cab and Trnsp LLC...................601 620-4282
6644 Gary Rd Ste B Byram (39272) *(G-617)*

Ark-Ell Springs Inc...................................662 568-3393
101 Industrial Dr Houlka (38850) *(G-2217)*

Arky Welding & Handy Man........................662 494-4233
119 J T Britt Rd West Point (39773) *(G-5536)*

Armadillo Service Inc Alabama..................601 857-0440
126 Oak Ridge Ln Raymond (39154) *(G-4484)*

Armorlock Industries LLC..........................228 466-2990
9028 Ladner St Bay St Louis (39520) *(G-175)*

Armory Advertisor, Fulton *Also called Journal Inc (G-1460)*

Arms, Oxford *Also called End2end Public Safety LLC (G-3954)*

Armstrong Flooring Inc.............................601 354-1515
1085 Highway 80 W Jackson (39204) *(G-2333)*

Armstrong Remodeling...............................601 720-2097
107 Lovett Dr Clinton (39056) *(G-812)*

Armstrong Spa & Hot Tubs, Long Beach *Also called Richard Armstrong (G-2950)*

Aromica Coffee LLC...................................901 848-1687
8079 Caitlin Dr Olive Branch (38654) *(G-3816)*

Around Clock Recovery..............................662 455-1008
1735 County Road 320 Greenwood (38930) *(G-1613)*

Arrow Material Services LLC.....................601 939-3113
187 Transload Dr Richland (39218) *(G-4503)*

Arrow Printers Inc.....................................601 924-1192
447 Highway 80 E Clinton (39056) *(G-813)*

Arrowmaker..601 264-4748
1065 Lee Rd Purvis (39475) *(G-4433)*

Art and Photography Printing, Kiln *Also called Giclee Fine Arts (G-2679)*

Art Horizons Inc..662 561-9733
483 Highway 6 W Batesville (38606) *(G-96)*

Artist and Business Express, Bay Saint Louis *Also called Bay Printing & Design Shop LLC (G-134)*

Artistic Tees..662 234-5051
1453 S Lamar Blvd Oxford (38655) *(G-3936)*

ASAP Printing and Copying, Flowood *Also called Fudge Inc (G-1363)*

Ascend Surgical Sales LLC.........................601 351-9866
574 Highland Colony Pkwy 320l Ridgeland (39157) *(G-4551)*

Ash Millworks Inc......................................601 544-3962
65 Springfield Rd Petal (39465) *(G-4184)*

Ashley Furniture Inds Inc...........................608 323-3377
108 Lipford Ave Tupelo (38801) *(G-5110)*

Ashley Furniture Inds Inc...........................662 489-5655
447 Highway 346 Ecru (38841) *(G-1230)*

Ashley Furniture Inds Inc...........................662 837-7146
15900 Highway 15 N Ripley (38663) *(G-4652)*

Ashley Printing Co.....................................601 729-8950
527 Hines Rd Laurel (39443) *(G-2732)*

Asics America Corporation.........................662 895-6800
549 Wingo Rd Byhalia (38611) *(G-577)*

ASpauljoy..662 397-3661
404 Adams St Booneville (38829) *(G-319)*

Aspen Bay Candles, Starkville *Also called Desirepath Mississippi LLC (G-4940)*

Associated Architectural Pdts...................662 245-0400
1813 8th Ave S Columbus (39701) *(G-937)*

Associated Gen Contrs of Miss (PA)...........601 981-1144
2093 Lakeland Dr Jackson (39216) *(G-2334)*

Assured Revenue Corporation....................662 323-5350
325 1/2 Highway 12 W Starkville (39759) *(G-4925)*

At Home Embroidery...................................228 365-4034
19461 Dixie Rd Saucier (39574) *(G-4749)*

At Xtree...601 683-6494
259 Northside Dr Newton (39345) *(G-3716)*

Atco Industries..601 407-6329
151 Nissan Pkwy Canton (39046) *(G-647)*

Athletic Action, Philadelphia *Also called Hanson Athletic Inc (G-4216)*

Atk Aerospace Structures Div, Iuka *Also called Atk Space Systems Inc (G-2284)*

Atk Space Systems Inc...............................662 423-7700
751 County Road 989 Fl 1 Iuka (38852) *(G-2284)*

Atkins Office Supply Inc............................662 627-2476
111 Highway 322 Clarksdale (38614) *(G-757)*

Atlas Machine & Mfg LLC...........................601 799-2616
1928 Palestine Rd Picayune (39466) *(G-4252)*

Atlas Manufacturing Co Inc........................662 652-3900
51 Dow Dr Tremont (38876) *(G-5091)*

Atlas Roofing Corporation (HQ).................601 484-8900
802 Highway 19 N Ste 190 Meridian (39307) *(G-3300)*

Atlas Roofing Corporation.........................601 481-1474
2564 Valley Rd Meridian (39307) *(G-3301)*

Atlas Roofing Corporation.........................601 483-7111
2322 Valley Rd Meridian (39307) *(G-3302)*

Atlas-Ssi Inc...601 587-4511
622 E Mcpherson Dr Monticello (39654) *(G-3428)*

Atm Gurus, Long Beach *Also called Triton Systems Delaware LLC (G-2958)*

Attala Steel Industries LLC (PA)...............662 289-1980
2475 Attala Rd 2202 Kosciusko (39090) *(G-2688)*

Atwood Auto & Marine................................601 624-7012
117 Pine Acre Pl Brandon (39042) *(G-366)*

Atwood Mch Wldg & Hydraulics..................601 735-0398
640 Industrial Park Rd Waynesboro (39367) *(G-5491)*

Auntie Anne's, Diberville *Also called Cosentino Enterprises Inc (G-1201)*

Aurora Flight Sciences Corp.......................662 328-8227
200 Aurora Way Columbus (39701) *(G-938)*

Austin Logging LLC....................................662 296-6566
15 Robbs Rd Randolph (38864) *(G-4479)*

Aut-Coldwater, Coldwater *Also called Innocor Foam Technologies LLC (G-847)*

Autman Logging...601 986-2555
23 Autman Rd Collinsville (39325) *(G-866)*

Auto Parts Mfg Miss Inc.............................662 365-3082
100 Tab Way Guntown (38849) *(G-1898)*

Auto Trim Design of Meridian......................601 482-8037
3115 5th Ave Meridian (39305) *(G-3303)*

Auto-Chlor System of Mid S LLC.................601 420-0331
193 Country Place Pkwy Pearl (39208) *(G-4105)*

Autoflow LLC..601 853-1021
1294 Mannsdale Rd Madison (39110) *(G-3079)*

Autoliv Asp Inc...801 620-8018
8989 Hacks Cross Rd # 3 Olive Branch (38654) *(G-3817)*

Autoliv Combined Warehouse-Aoa, Olive Branch *Also called Autoliv Asp Inc (G-3817)*

Automated Tech & Assembly LLC.................662 213-9352
316 Maple St Rolling Fork (39159) *(G-4679)*

Automatic Machine Products Inc.................662 287-2467
1702 Sawyer Rd Corinth (38834) *(G-1058)*

Automatic Plating Inc................................601 785-6923
204 Fellowship Rd Taylorsville (39168) *(G-5050)*

Automatic Processing Co, Moss Point *Also called Azz Incorporated (G-3466)*

Automotive Machine Company....................601 442-0422
30 Saint Catherine St Natchez (39120) *(G-3521)*

Automtion Dsigns Solutions Inc.................601 992-4121
1070 Lake Village Cir D Brandon (39047) *(G-367)*

Avalon Marble LLC (PA)............................601 798-3378
424 Memorial Blvd Picayune (39466) *(G-4253)*

Avery Products Corporation.......................601 483-0611
4100 Highway 45 N Meridian (39301) *(G-3304)*

Avon Engnered Fabrications Inc, Picayune *Also called Avon Engnered Fabrications LLC (G-4254)*

Avon Engnered Fabrications LLC................601 889-9050
113 Street A Picayune (39466) *(G-4254)*

Aw Manufacturing Inc...............................662 767-2800
111 South St Shannon (38868) *(G-4806)*

Awards Unlimited.......................................228 863-1814
1618 25th Ave Gulfport (39501) *(G-1730)*

Awesome Sight and Sound..........................601 215-8846
170 Cypress Pt Picayune (39466) *(G-4255)*

Axel Americas LLC....................................662 759-6808
150 Russell Crutcher Rd S Rosedale (38769) *(G-4686)*

Axiall LLC...601 856-8993
210 Industrial Dr N Madison (39110) *(G-3080)*

Axiall Corporation.....................................601 892-5612
20043 Highway 51 Hazlehurst (39083) *(G-2089)*

Axiall Corporation.....................................601 206-3200
210 Industrial Dr N Madison (39110) *(G-3081)*

Axiall Corporation.....................................662 369-9586
10068 Summit Dr Prairie (39756) *(G-4411)*

Axsom Woodworks......................................334 422-9766
15215 Northrup Cuevas Rd Gulfport (39503) *(G-1731)*

Ayrshire Electronics Miss LLC....................662 287-3771
1801 S Fulton Dr Corinth (38834) *(G-1059)*

Aztec Industries Inc.................................601 939-8522
125 Aztec Dr Richland (39218) *(G-4504)*

(PA)=Parent Co (HQ)=Headquarters (DH)=Div Headquarters

2019 Harris Directory of
Mississippi Manufacturers

ALPHABETIC

265

Azz Inc

ALPHABETIC SECTION

Azz Inc 662 290-1500
2235 Attala Road 2202 Kosciusko (39090) *(G-2689)*

Azz Inc 601 939-9191
120 Aztec Dr Richland (39218) *(G-4505)*

Azz Incorporated 228 475-0342
4212 Dutch Bayou Rd Moss Point (39563) *(G-3466)*

B & B Concrete Co Inc 662 286-6407
2724 S Harper Rd Corinth (38834) *(G-1060)*

B & B Concrete Co Inc 662 489-2233
291 W 8th St Pontotoc (38863) *(G-4321)*

B & B Concrete Co Inc 662 234-7088
2304 University Ave Oxford (38655) *(G-3937)*

B & B Concrete Co Inc 662 837-3221
Hwy 15 S Ripley (38663) *(G-4653)*

B & B Concrete Co Inc 662 534-2626
1220 W Bankhead St New Albany (38652) *(G-3673)*

B & B Concrete Co Inc 662 869-1927
Hwy 45 N Saltillo (38866) *(G-4706)*

B & B Concrete Co Inc (PA) 662 842-6312
Brewer Rd Verona (38879) *(G-5327)*

B & B Concrete Co Inc 662 842-7305
401 Elizabeth St Tupelo (38804) *(G-5111)*

B & B Contractors, Leakesville *Also called Paul Bolling (G-2878)*

B & B Mfg & Specialty Co Inc 662 456-4313
219 County Road 94 Houston (38851) *(G-2231)*

B & B Oil Well Service Co Inc 601 425-3836
1517 Highway 588 Ellisville (39437) *(G-1246)*

B & B Pressure Wshg & Ldscpg 662 910-9105
7197 Railroad Sta Hernando (38632) *(G-2123)*

B & B Sign Company, Greenville *Also called Tim Bennett (G-1605)*

B & D Plastics LLC 228 875-5865
5500 Allen Rd Vancleave (39565) *(G-5317)*

B & D Plastics Mississippi Inc 228 875-5865
5500 Allen Rd Ocean Springs (39565) *(G-3742)*

B & H Hill Farm LLC 662 207-7197
631 W Gresham St Indianola (38751) *(G-2261)*

B & L International Inc 601 261-5127
1189 Carter Cir Purvis (39475) *(G-4434)*

B & O Machine & Wldg Co Inc 601 833-3000
1380 Highway 51 Ne Brookhaven (39601) *(G-481)*

B & P Swab Service Inc 601 731-6309
197 Airport Rd Columbia (39429) *(G-881)*

B & S Alarm Service, Madison *Also called Alarm Company Inc (G-3077)*

B & S Farms 601 656-5157
10391 Road 525 Philadelphia (39350) *(G-4206)*

B and L Meat Processing 601 218-0918
73 Standard Hill Rd Vicksburg (39183) *(G-5343)*

B and P Cstome Meta L Fbrction 228 474-0097
14036 Highway 613 Moss Point (39562) *(G-3467)*

B B Stump Grinding 601 506-0997
435 Blue Springs Cir Florence (39073) *(G-1314)*

B Ficklin Investments LLC 601 454-2724
184 Beechwood Cir Pearl (39208) *(G-4106)*

B J Coiltech, Laurel *Also called Baker Hughes A GE Company LLC (G-2738)*

B K Industries Inc 864 963-3471
908 State Highway 15 N New Albany (38652) *(G-3674)*

B P Graves Logging Co 601 765-8956
156 E Williamsburg Rd Collins (39428) *(G-852)*

B R Smith Enterprises Inc 601 656-0846
11840 Road 505 Union (39365) *(G-5293)*

B S Monogramming 662 750-0505
260 Frederick Dr Walnut (38683) *(G-5455)*

B&B Trailers & Mfg Co 662 456-4313
219 County Road 94 Houston (38851) *(G-2232)*

B&G Dirt Work, Mendenhall *Also called Brandi Bonner (G-3279)*

B&M Maintenance LLC 228 273-5821
10393 Cherokee Rose Rd Vancleave (39565) *(G-5318)*

B&Z Sales Inc 601 825-1900
144 Old Highway 80 Brandon (39042) *(G-368)*

B-Gone Stump Grinding Service 228 762-2196
3407 Chicago Ave Pascagoula (39581) *(G-4020)*

B-Line Fabrication Co Ltd 228 832-3286
13465 Oneal Rd Gulfport (39503) *(G-1732)*

B-N/Associates 601 482-3939
4913 55th Pl Meridian (39305) *(G-3305)*

B.B. Delivery Services, Columbus *Also called Johnson Wiley (G-991)*

B.E.A.R., Gulfport *Also called Benvenutti Elctrcl Apprts & Rp (G-1738)*

Baader North America Corp 662 887-5841
505 Hwy 82 Ste A Indianola (38751) *(G-2262)*

Babcock & Wilcox Company 662 494-1323
900 Bnw Dr West Point (39773) *(G-5537)*

Bacallao Silva Gran & Tile LLC 769 798-8816
110 Lexington Dr Madison (39110) *(G-3082)*

Back Bay Lawnscapes LLC 228 348-1299
4459 W Gay Rd Diberville (39540) *(G-1195)*

Backwoods Tie and Timber LLC 662 258-3388
181 Lagrange Rd Eupora (39744) *(G-1285)*

Backyard Escapes 228 868-3938
8468 County Farm Rd Long Beach (39560) *(G-2923)*

Bad Moon Customs 601 520-7248
610 W Pine St Hattiesburg (39401) *(G-1925)*

Baddour Memorial Center Inc 662 562-0100
3297 Highway 51 S Senatobia (38668) *(G-4787)*

Bae Systems Tech Sol Srvc Inc 703 847-5820
330 Highway 90 Gautier (39553) *(G-1488)*

Bag Connection LLC 662 624-6570
408 6th St Clarksdale (38614) *(G-758)*

Bagit System Inc 662 756-2600
301 W Sunflower St Ruleville (38771) *(G-4695)*

Bain Manufacturing Co Inc 662 226-7921
2 S Main St Grenada (38901) *(G-1668)*

Baker Engineering, Jackson *Also called Jackson Excavating & Lsg Co (G-2454)*

Baker Hghes Olfld Oprtions LLC 601 649-4400
2628 Ellisville Blvd Laurel (39440) *(G-2733)*

Baker Hghes Olfld Oprtions LLC 601 649-2704
270 Victory Rd Laurel (39443) *(G-2734)*

Baker Hughes, Natchez *Also called Baker Petrolite (G-3522)*

Baker Hughes A GE Company LLC 601 731-5004
4025 Highway 35 N Columbia (39429) *(G-882)*

Baker Hughes A GE Company LLC 601 649-7400
111 Avenue C Laurel (39440) *(G-2735)*

Baker Hughes A GE Company LLC 601 649-1955
3705 Industrial Blvd Laurel (39440) *(G-2736)*

Baker Hughes A GE Company LLC 601 649-4400
2628 Ellisville Blvd Laurel (39440) *(G-2737)*

Baker Hughes A GE Company LLC 601 425-1599
2850 Industrial Blvd Laurel (39440) *(G-2738)*

Baker Petrolite 601 442-2401
17 Marion E Syfarth Sr Rd Natchez (39120) *(G-3522)*

Baker Petrolite 601 649-1955
3705 Industrial Blvd Laurel (39440) *(G-2739)*

Baker Ready Mix & Cnstr LLC 662 773-8054
11000 Highway 15 S Louisville (39339) *(G-2964)*

Bakers Auto Machine & RAD Sp 228 474-1222
4512 Main St Moss Point (39563) *(G-3468)*

Bakers Automotive Machine Shop, Moss Point *Also called Bakers Auto Machine & RAD Sp (G-3468)*

Baldwin Pole Mississippi LLC 601 928-5475
1633 First St S Wiggins (39577) *(G-5571)*

Baldwin Sand & Gravel 662 834-6167
1422 Coxburg Rd Lexington (39095) *(G-2897)*

Baldwyn News 662 365-3232
116 W Main St Baldwyn (38824) *(G-71)*

Baldwyn Tool and Die Co 662 365-8665
45 County Road 6311 Baldwyn (38824) *(G-72)*

Baldwyn Truck & Trailer Repair 662 365-7888
896 Drake Dr Baldwyn (38824) *(G-73)*

Balfour L G Co, Jackson *Also called Scholastic Products and Awards (G-2576)*

Balfour Yearbooks, Brandon *Also called Ms Yearbooks LLC (G-427)*

Balius Dann Welding 228 354-9647
4401 Arceneaux Rd Diberville (39540) *(G-1196)*

Ball Sign Co 662 236-2338
Highway 334 Ste 36a Oxford (38655) *(G-3938)*

Balloon On Wheels, Biloxi *Also called Hilton National Corporation (G-252)*

Bally Technologies Inc 228 396-3480
10441 Corporate Dr Gulfport (39503) *(G-1733)*

Bally Technologies Inc 228 897-9059
320 Courthouse Rd Gulfport (39507) *(G-1734)*

Bangers and Mash Tees LLC 801 803-8970
1888 Main St Ste C-292 Madison (39110) *(G-3083)*

Bankingformscom Inc 601 445-2245
322a Highland Blvd Natchez (39120) *(G-3523)*

Banner Independent, Booneville *Also called Paxton Media Group LLC (G-341)*

Banner Printing Co Inc 662 247-3373
115 E Jackson St Belzoni (39038) *(G-204)*

Bap Services Inc 662 343-5216
40227 Grubb Springs Rd Hamilton (39746) *(G-1903)*

Barbara OMeallie 228 255-7573
29002 Sixteen Section Rd Pass Christian (39571) *(G-4077)*

Barber Planning, Tupelo *Also called Barber Printing Inc (G-5112)*

Barber Printing Inc 662 841-1584
811a Varsity Dr Tupelo (38801) *(G-5112)*

Barbers Timber & Logging 662 382-7649
14224 Brownsferry Rd Sarah (38665) *(G-4732)*

Barden-Stone Manufacturing, Byhalia *Also called Stone Associates Inc (G-607)*

Bardo & Co 601 397-1167
2007 Attala Road 1990 Kosciusko (39090) *(G-2690)*

Barefoot Lumber, Florence *Also called Debra A Jones (G-1320)*

Barge Forest Products Co 662 726-4426
Forest Lake Rd Macon (39341) *(G-3055)*

Barge Timberland Manageme, Macon *Also called Barge Forest Products Co (G-3055)*

Baria, Lawrence R, Jackson *Also called Jura-Search Inc (G-2461)*

Barn Life Tees 601 740-0696
611 Williamsburg Rd Columbia (39429) *(G-883)*

Barnes Sawmill Woodworks 901 605-7104
9480 Miranda Dr Olive Branch (38654) *(G-3818)*

2019 Harris Directory of
Mississippi Manufacturers

(G-0000) Company's Geographic Section entry number

266

ALPHABETIC SECTION
Bennett Bros Shop, Fulton

Barnetts Small Engines 662 323-8993
54 Old Highway 12 Starkville (39759) ***(G-4926)***
Barrentine Trailer Mfg Co Inc 662 237-9650
271 County Road 133 Greenwood (38930) ***(G-1614)***
Barrys Fine Wdwkg & Crafts LLC 662 808-2268
150 Limousine Dr Tupelo (38804) ***(G-5113)***
Bartag Corporation 769 233-0925
12550 Springridge Rd Byram (39170) ***(G-618)***
BASF Corporation 601 948-3966
600 E Mc Dowell Rd Jackson (39204) ***(G-2335)***
Basf-Chemical Co 478 951-9985
809 Windlass Cv Brandon (39047) ***(G-369)***
Bass Associates LLC 601 943-5229
2766 Gates Rd Bassfield (39421) ***(G-90)***
Bassco Foam Inc 662 842-4321
108 Air Park Rd Tupelo (38801) ***(G-5114)***
Bateman Airconditioning 601 225-4442
6045 Hancock Rd Gloster (39638) ***(G-1511)***
Bateman Airconditioning Rfrgn, Gloster *Also called Bateman Airconditioning* ***(G-1511)***
Bates Vault & Services LLC 601 303-0508
136 Claude Smith Rd Tylertown (39667) ***(G-5263)***
Batesville Raceway LLC 662 561-0065
105 Champion Dr Batesville (38606) ***(G-97)***
Batesville Tooling & Design 662 563-1663
210 Tower Rd Batesville (38606) ***(G-98)***
Bath Iron Works Corporation 228 935-3872
1000 Access Rd Pascagoula (39567) ***(G-4021)***
Battco Inc 601 898-1200
243 Highway 51 Ridgeland (39157) ***(G-4552)***
Batte & Hollingsworth Lumber 601 469-4938
19064 Highway 80 Forest (39074) ***(G-1409)***
Batte Lumber, Forest *Also called Jack Batte and Sons Inc* ***(G-1417)***
Battlebells LLC (PA) 662 312-5901
307 1/2 Scales St Lot 2 Starkville (39759) ***(G-4927)***
Bauhaus Furniture Group LLC 662 869-2664
1 Bauhaus Dr Saltillo (38866) ***(G-4707)***
Baxter Healthcare Corporation 662 843-9421
911 N Davis Ave Cleveland (38732) ***(G-786)***
Baxters Prssure Wshg 601 825-2990
6502 Grants Ferry Rd Brandon (39042) ***(G-370)***
Bay Ice Company Inc 228 863-0981
1413 30th Ave Gulfport (39501) ***(G-1735)***
Bay Motor Winding Inc 228 863-0666
125 N Ocean Wave Ave Long Beach (39560) ***(G-2924)***
Bay Printing & Design Shop LLC 228 467-5833
998b Highway 90 Bay Saint Louis (39520) ***(G-134)***
Bay Springs Fields, Bay Springs *Also called Petroci Usa Inc* ***(G-171)***
Bay St Louis Newspapers Inc (PA) 228 467-5474
124 Court St Bay Saint Louis (39520) ***(G-135)***
Bay Technical Associates Inc 228 563-7334
5239 A Ave Long Beach (39560) ***(G-2925)***
Bayer Cotton Seed Intl 662 686-9235
117 Kennedy Flat Rd Leland (38756) ***(G-2882)***
Bayer Cropscience LP 662 686-2334
206 Kennedy Flat Rd Leland (38756) ***(G-2883)***
Bayer Cropscience LP 662 686-9323
206 Kennedy Flat Rd Leland (38756) ***(G-2884)***
Bayer Cropscience LP 662 686-9235
117 Kennedy Flat Rd Leland (38756) ***(G-2885)***
Baymont Inc 662 454-7993
30 Red Bay Rd Golden (38847) ***(G-1521)***
Baymont Inn & Suites, Golden *Also called Baymont Inc* ***(G-1521)***
Baymont Wholesale Inc 662 424-2134
16 Industrial Rd Belmont (38827) ***(G-194)***
Bayou Concrete LLC 228 868-1264
14312 Creosote Rd Gulfport (39503) ***(G-1736)***
Bayou Concrete LLC (HQ) 601 898-4000
1052 Highland Colony Pkwy Ridgeland (39157) ***(G-4553)***
Bayou Concrete LLC 228 762-8911
5509 Industrial Rd Pascagoula (39581) ***(G-4022)***
Bayou Inovations 601 928-4143
38 South Park Dr Perkinston (39573) ***(G-4173)***
Bayou Oil Fill Supply LLC 601 446-6284
242 Highway 61 S Natchez (39120) ***(G-3524)***
Bayou View Woodworks 985 290-0860
10183 Bayou View Dr W Bay Saint Louis (39520) ***(G-136)***
Baytech, Long Beach *Also called Bay Technical Associates Inc* ***(G-2925)***
Bazor Lumber Company LLC 601 776-2181
300 N Archusa Ave Quitman (39355) ***(G-4457)***
Bazor Pulpwood Company Inc 601 735-4017
165 Big Creek Rd Waynesboro (39367) ***(G-5492)***
Bbq World Magazine 228 363-2716
650 E Railroad St Long Beach (39560) ***(G-2926)***
Bbs Printing 601 606-6980
33 Lacy Evans Rd Wiggins (39577) ***(G-5572)***
Bcbg, Meridian *Also called Runway Liquidation LLC* ***(G-3393)***
Bcbg, New Albany *Also called Runway Liquidation LLC* ***(G-3693)***
Bcbg, Gulfport *Also called Runway Liquidation LLC* ***(G-1865)***
BCI, Ridgeland *Also called Business Communications Inc* ***(G-4559)***
BCT, Madison *Also called Piranha Business Cards LLC* ***(G-3140)***
Bdm Industrial Services LLC 662 549-3055
1235 Highway 373 Columbus (39705) ***(G-939)***
Bdm It Services (us) Inc 601 274-0347
142 County Road 159 Quitman (39355) ***(G-4458)***
Be Joyful Signs 601 540-6602
305 S Wall St Natchez (39120) ***(G-3525)***
Beach Blvd Mag 228 896-2499
205 Debuys Rd Gulfport (39507) ***(G-1737)***
Beach Harvey & Son Logging 601 446-5771
398 Greenfield Rd Natchez (39120) ***(G-3526)***
Beaded Owls 228 284-2712
200 Jeff Davis Ave Ste 10 Long Beach (39560) ***(G-2927)***
Beane Logging 662 862-9053
3856 Peppertown Rd Fulton (38843) ***(G-1445)***
Bear Creek Apparel Promotions 601 259-8508
116 Clover Ln Canton (39046) ***(G-648)***
Bearhawk Tailwheels LLC 228 424-5096
205 Kuyrkendall Pl Long Beach (39560) ***(G-2928)***
Beason Repair Shop 662 256-9937
108 4th Ave Nw Amory (38821) ***(G-37)***
Beaty Street Publishing 954 513-9441
16 Leaf Ln Hattiesburg (39402) ***(G-1926)***
Beauticontrol Cosmetic, Gulfport *Also called Joyce Tillman* ***(G-1814)***
Beauty Mart 662 624-6738
860 S State St Clarksdale (38614) ***(G-759)***
Beaux Bijoux, Terry *Also called Maurice Hinton* ***(G-5072)***
Beaver Built Cherokee Mfg LLC 901 258-2679
1 Gem Blvd Byhalia (38611) ***(G-578)***
Beaver Industries Inc 601 664-6610
583 Old Highway 49 S Richland (39218) ***(G-4506)***
Beavers Enterprises 601 569-1557
85 Woodridge Ln Picayune (39466) ***(G-4256)***
BEC Fire and Safety LLC 601 498-9108
94a Gussy Nobles Rd Sumrall (39482) ***(G-5034)***
Beckham Welding LLC 662 832-0071
73 County Road 420 Oxford (38655) ***(G-3939)***
Becks Confection 601 927-3137
270 Highpoint Dr Ridgeland (39157) ***(G-4554)***
Bed Bath & Beyond Inc 601 939-4840
760 Mackenzie Ln Flowood (39232) ***(G-1344)***
Behold Home Inc 662 651-4510
60012 Industrial St Smithville (38870) ***(G-4843)***
Behold Washington LLC 662 489-6117
206 Magee Dr Pontotoc (38863) ***(G-4322)***
Bekeson Glass LLC 601 932-3676
1001 Underwood Dr Flowood (39232) ***(G-1345)***
Belgique Inc 601 368-1975
752 Euclid Ave Jackson (39202) ***(G-2336)***
Bell Demolition & Envmtl Svcs, Delta City *Also called Bell Environmental Svcs LLC* ***(G-1180)***
Bell Environmental Svcs LLC 662 873-4551
3016 Delta City Rd Delta City (39061) ***(G-1180)***
Bell Equipment LLC 662 265-5841
800 Moore St Inverness (38753) ***(G-2273)***
Bell Exploration, Natchez *Also called Louisiana Well Service Co Inc* ***(G-3580)***
Bell Gravel Co Inc 228 452-2872
7290 Red Creek Rd Long Beach (39560) ***(G-2929)***
Bell Inc 662 265-5841
Hwy 49 W Inverness (38753) ***(G-2274)***
Belle Exploration Inc 601 442-6648
280 Highland Blvd Natchez (39120) ***(G-3527)***
Belle Oil Inc (PA) 601 442-6648
280 Highland Blvd Natchez (39120) ***(G-3528)***
Belles 662 617-8171
500 Russell St Ste 35 Starkville (39759) ***(G-4928)***
Belles & Beaus 228 396-1771
10470 Diberville Blvd C Diberville (39540) ***(G-1197)***
Belles Nail Bar, Starkville *Also called Belles* ***(G-4928)***
Bells Iron Works 662 254-7413
321 Mitchell St Itta Bena (38941) ***(G-2279)***
Belmont Tshmngo Jrnl Incjurnal 662 454-7196
430 2nd St Belmont (38827) ***(G-195)***
Beloved Pottery 662 349-4430
1555 Stonehedge Dr Southaven (38671) ***(G-4854)***
Belt Warehouse, Jackson *Also called Thomas Larry Hearn* ***(G-2606)***
Belzona Mississippi Inc 228 475-1110
9720 Highway 63 Ste A Moss Point (39562) ***(G-3469)***
Belzoni Banner The, Belzoni *Also called Banner Printing Co Inc* ***(G-204)***
Bemco Bedding, Meridian *Also called Meridian Mattress Factory Inc* ***(G-3368)***
Bemis Company Inc 402 734-6262
25 Woodgreen Pl Madison (39110) ***(G-3084)***
Ben Mears Taxidermists & Sups 662 282-4594
223 Lake Rd Mantachie (38855) ***(G-3198)***
Ben Sessums 601 856-3401
624 Live Oak Dr Madison (39110) ***(G-3085)***
Ben's Printing & Graphics, Madison *Also called Ben Sessums* ***(G-3085)***
Bengal Resources and Assoc Inc 404 312-4642
107 Walter Payton Dr Columbia (39429) ***(G-884)***
Bennett Bros Shop, Fulton *Also called Nolan Brothers* ***(G-1470)***

ALPHABETIC

(PA)=Parent Co (HQ)=Headquarters (DH)=Div Headquarters
2019 Harris Directory of Mississippi Manufacturers
267

Bennetts Wood Works

ALPHABETIC SECTION

Bennetts Wood Works 662 862-6124
675 Ironwood Bluff Rd Fulton (38843) *(G-1446)*

Benny Evans 601 264-8903
307 Beverly Ln Hattiesburg (39402) *(G-1927)*

Benny McDaniel 601 253-0564
1869 Peoples Rd Philadelphia (39350) *(G-4207)*

Benny McDaniel Logging, Philadelphia *Also called Benny McDaniel (G-4207)*

Bent Wrench Industries LLC 601 934-7851
3383 Star Rd Florence (39073) *(G-1315)*

Benvenutti Elctrcl Apprts & Rp 228 831-0445
9515 N Wildflower Ct Gulfport (39503) *(G-1738)*

Bergeron Machine & Marine 504 416-6461
107 Indian Spgs Poplarville (39470) *(G-4375)*

Berry Enterprises of Miss 601 928-4006
1035 Wire Rd W Perkinston (39573) *(G-4174)*

Berry Global Inc 601 584-4800
72 Wl Runnels Indus Dr Hattiesburg (39401) *(G-1928)*

Berry Global Inc 601 584-4778
72 W L Runnels Indus Park Hattiesburg (39401) *(G-1929)*

Berry Inc 662 423-1984
134 County Road 244 Iuka (38852) *(G-2285)*

Berry Signs & Stripes 601 544-5600
2125 Glendale Ave Hattiesburg (39401) *(G-1930)*

Bert J Rosson, Jackson *Also called Rosson Exlopartion Company (G-2569)*

Beryl Jones 601 442-4597
102 Catalpa Dr Natchez (39120) *(G-3529)*

Best Dressed Bunnies 228 826-4619
13400 Mount Pleasant Rd Ocean Springs (39565) *(G-3743)*

Best Equipment Tech Inc 601 795-2208
100 Industrial Dr Poplarville (39470) *(G-4376)*

Best Fiber Inc 662 840-1118
1644a S Eason Blvd Tupelo (38804) *(G-5115)*

Best Foam Inc 662 840-6700
481 3rd Ave Sherman (38869) *(G-4826)*

Betta Boats LLC 228 363-2529
201 N 2nd St Ste 100 Bay St Louis (39520) *(G-176)*

Better Built Portable Inc 601 267-4607
2078 Highway 16 E Carthage (39051) *(G-707)*

Better Signs Inc 662 227-1235
11704 Highway 51 N Grenada (38901) *(G-1669)*

Betty Montgomery 601 833-1461
1074 Union St Brookhaven (39601) *(G-482)*

Betty Wright 662 224-3000
149 Ferrell Rd Ashland (38603) *(G-59)*

Beverly Robinson Decor 601 201-1520
357 Kiowa Dr Madison (39110) *(G-3086)*

Beyondtrust Corporation 601 519-0213
578 Highland Colony Pkwy Ridgeland (39157) *(G-4555)*

BF Kaufman Inc 662 253-8093
9020 Highway 51 N Ste 1 Southaven (38671) *(G-4855)*

Bg3 Delta LLC 601 636-9828
415 Tiffintown Rd Vicksburg (39183) *(G-5344)*

Bickes Inc 601 353-7083
820 Larson St Jackson (39202) *(G-2337)*

Biewer Sawmill-Newton LLC 601 357-6001
331 Coliseum Dr Newton (39345) *(G-3717)*

Big B Granite, Petal *Also called Jonathan Bigbie (G-4188)*

Big Buck Sports 601 605-2661
242 Highway 51 Ridgeland (39157) *(G-4556)*

Big Creek Gin Company Inc 662 624-5233
4150 Highway 6 Lyon (38645) *(G-3041)*

Big D Signs 228 860-1075
684 Orchard Dr Diberville (39540) *(G-1198)*

Big Joe Oil Co Inc 601 442-5481
251 Highway 61 S Natchez (39120) *(G-3530)*

Big Joe Operating Co Inc 601 442-5481
Hwy 61 S Natchez (39120) *(G-3531)*

Big Johns Welding LLC 570 660-1972
78 C J Harrell Rd Poplarville (39470) *(G-4377)*

Big River Classics Inc 601 856-6607
198 Van Doren Ct Pearl (39208) *(G-4107)*

Big River Shipbuilders Inc (PA) 601 636-9161
404 Port Terminal Cir Vicksburg (39183) *(G-5345)*

Big River Shipbuilders Inc 601 802-9994
1063 Haining Rd Vicksburg (39183) *(G-5346)*

Big Star of Belmont Inc 662 454-3300
10 Fillmore St Belmont (38827) *(G-196)*

Big T'S Moving, Meridian *Also called Watson Tj Property LLC (G-3418)*

Bigbee Industries 662 568-7740
119 Industrial Dr Houlka (38850) *(G-2218)*

Bigbee Metal Manufacturing Co 662 652-3372
10310 Highway 178 E Tremont (38876) *(G-5092)*

Biglane Operating Co 601 442-2783
75 Melrose St Natchez (39120) *(G-3532)*

Bijoubel LLC 228 344-3393
136 Main St Bay Saint Louis (39520) *(G-137)*

Bilal 100 All Natural Spring 601 323-2237
26 Regan Rd Sumrall (39482) *(G-5035)*

Bill Briscoe 662 234-5669
71 County Road 327 Oxford (38655) *(G-3940)*

Bill Phillips Sand & Grav LLC 662 284-6061
1299 Highway 2 Corinth (38834) *(G-1061)*

Bill Rainey Millwork, Hattiesburg *Also called Rainey Mill Works LLC (G-2048)*

Bills Organic Grdnng & Leaf 901 315-8888
7204 Highway 178 Olive Branch (38654) *(G-3819)*

Bills Welding 901 216-6762
181 Ponderosa Dr Byhalia (38611) *(G-579)*

Bills Welding 901 216-6762
181 Ponderosa Dr Byhalia (38611) *(G-580)*

Billy Purvis Distributing LLC 601 480-3147
5394 Vmvlle Cuseyville Rd Meridian (39301) *(G-3306)*

Billy's Original Foods, Vicksburg *Also called Brm LLC (G-5348)*

Billys Original Food, Vicksburg *Also called J & K Restaurants Inc (G-5381)*

Billys Welding Service Inc 601 649-1432
281 Freedom Rd Laurel (39443) *(G-2740)*

Biloxi Fire Department, Biloxi *Also called City of Biloxi (G-228)*

Biloxi Tent and Awning Co Inc 228 436-6161
318 Howard Ave Biloxi (39530) *(G-220)*

Biloxio Newspaper, Biloxi *Also called McM Communications LLC (G-267)*

Biltrite Ripley Operations LLC 662 837-9231
16310 Highway 15 N Ripley (38663) *(G-4654)*

Bimbo Bakeries Usa Inc 601 545-3782
5680 U S Highway 49 Hattiesburg (39401) *(G-1931)*

Bimbo Bakeries Usa Inc 228 863-4302
901 Pass Rd Gulfport (39501) *(G-1739)*

Bimbo Bakeries Usa Inc 601 479-8887
624 Natures Way Meridian (39305) *(G-3307)*

Bimbo Bakeries Usa Inc 601 693-4871
3400 Saint Paul St Meridian (39301) *(G-3308)*

Bimbo Bakeries Usa Inc 601 693-4871
3400 Saint Paul St Meridian (39301) *(G-3309)*

Bio Plumber of Mississippi 601 825-5190
210 Southampton Pl Brandon (39042) *(G-371)*

Bio Soil Enhancers Inc 601 582-4000
1161 James St Hattiesburg (39401) *(G-1932)*

Bio-Solutions Franchise Corp 601 582-4000
1161 James St Hattiesburg (39401) *(G-1933)*

Biologic, West Point *Also called Mossyoak Wildlife Conservatory (G-5554)*

Birds Nest 662 369-5757
121 E Commerce St Aberdeen (39730) *(G-10)*

Bisco Industries Inc 601 991-3308
4429 E Ridge Dr Jackson (39211) *(G-2338)*

Bits & PCs Press Inc 662 563-8661
105 Public Sq Batesville (38606) *(G-99)*

Bk Edwards Fabrication & Wldg 662 263-4320
Cumberland Rd Mathiston (39752) *(G-3226)*

Black Box Corporation 601 939-9051
3010 Lakeland Cv Flowood (39232) *(G-1346)*

Black Diamond Construction LLC 228 342-2742
17132 Bobinger Rd Kiln (39556) *(G-2678)*

Black Panther Newspaper 877 388-6247
209 Old Airport Rd Hattiesburg (39401) *(G-1934)*

Black Rver Timber Wildlife LLC 601 906-4099
160 Bellewood Dr Clinton (39056) *(G-814)*

Blackdog Welding, Brookhaven *Also called Stuart Chaffin (G-540)*

Blacklidge Emulsions Inc (PA) 228 863-3878
12251 Bernard Pkwy # 200 Gulfport (39503) *(G-1740)*

Blacklidge Emulsions Inc 228 864-3719
10220 Three Rivers Rd Gulfport (39503) *(G-1741)*

Blackstone Investments LLC 601 978-1763
603 Northpark Dr Ste 300 Ridgeland (39157) *(G-4557)*

Blain Sand & Gravel, Natchez *Also called W E Blain & Sons Inc (G-3635)*

Blake Publishing Inc 601 992-6220
5719 Highway 25 Ste 204 Flowood (39232) *(G-1347)*

Blank 2 Beautiful EMB More LLC 662 902-6195
934 Allgator Rena Lara Rd Alligator (38720) *(G-31)*

Blauer Manufacturing Co Inc 662 281-0097
156 County Rd Oxford (38655) *(G-3941)*

Blauer Manufacturing Co Inc 662 281-0097
10 Lafayette Park Dr Oxford (38655) *(G-3942)*

Blax Screen Printing & EMB 228 392-5022
4511 Popps Ferry Rd Diberville (39540) *(G-1199)*

Blaylocks Cement Manufacturing 225 627-1006
4608 Austin Ln Liberty (39645) *(G-2910)*

Blaylocks Wild Game Processing 601 894-0087
2142 E Whitworth St Hazlehurst (39083) *(G-2090)*

Blendco Inc 888 253-6326
8 J M Tatum Industrial Dr Hattiesburg (39401) *(G-1935)*

Bles Car Care 770 292-0021
2305c Highway 45 N Columbus (39705) *(G-940)*

Block & Chip Iron Works Inc 601 394-2964
21912 Highway 63 Leakesville (39451) *(G-2876)*

Bloms Creative Signs Inc 228 374-2566
427 Caillavet St Biloxi (39530) *(G-221)*

Blonzells Curtain Shop 601 635-3811
83 Rr 1 Box Rd 83 1st Decatur (39327) *(G-1171)*

Blue Bayou Boat Lifts Inc 601 798-0659
47 Paradise Ln Carriere (39426) *(G-688)*

Blue Chip Signs, Gulfport *Also called Alden R Stockert (G-1717)*

268

2019 Harris Directory of
Mississippi Manufacturers

(G-0000) Company's Geographic Section entry number

ALPHABETIC SECTION

Blue Chip Signs Inc 228 918-9511
13109 Shriners Blvd Biloxi (39532) *(G-222)*

Blue Deer Candles LLP 662 275-2016
184 Court St West Point (39773) *(G-5538)*

Blue Lightning Enterprise LLC 901 626-8587
4045 Davall Dr Olive Branch (38654) *(G-3820)*

Blue Line Industries LLC (PA) 901 335-2987
15235 Oneal Rd Apt 14p Gulfport (39503) *(G-1742)*

Blue Lotus Creations LLC 770 714-9408
4116 Central St Gulfport (39501) *(G-1743)*

Blue Mountain Furniture LLC 662 685-4871
Hwy 15 N Blue Mountain (38610) *(G-288)*

Blue Mountain Refining Company 662 685-4386
31 County Road 827 Blue Mountain (38610) *(G-289)*

Blue Note Management LLC 662 281-1881
1197 Highway 6 W Oxford (38655) *(G-3943)*

Blue Ridge Beef Plant Inc 864 338-5544
222 Howard St Greenwood (38930) *(G-1615)*

Blue South Publishing Corp 601 604-2963
2320 8th St Meridian (39301) *(G-3310)*

Blue Springs Metals LLC 662 539-2700
1036 Corolla Ln Blue Springs (38828) *(G-294)*

Blue Streak, Hattiesburg *Also called Benny Evans (G-1927)*

Blueberry Hill Landfill, Jackson *Also called Waste Placement Inc (G-2625)*

Bluff City Post Newspaper 601 446-5218
719 Franklin St Natchez (39120) *(G-3533)*

Bluff City Service Company 662 534-2500
213 W Bankhead St New Albany (38652) *(G-3675)*

Bluff Springs Paper, Kosciusko *Also called Pqr Inc (G-2710)*

Bluffs & Bayou Magazine 601 442-6847
423 Main St Ste 7 Natchez (39120) *(G-3534)*

BMW Prosthetics Orthotics LLC 601 414-0032
1221 N West St Jackson (39202) *(G-2339)*

Bo Enterprises Inc (PA) 662 720-1211
601 E Parker Dr Booneville (38829) *(G-320)*

Bo Enterprises Inc 601 483-5571
1380 Bonita Lakes Cir Meridian (39301) *(G-3311)*

Bo Logging Inc 662 983-4225
192 County Road 153 Houlka (38850) *(G-2219)*

Boardtown Trading Post 662 324-7296
307 Hillside Dr Starkville (39759) *(G-4929)*

Boat Man 228 218-3080
1105 Highway 90 Gautier (39553) *(G-1489)*

Bob Bertolet 601 442-0424
517 S Canal St Natchez (39120) *(G-3535)*

Bob Ladd & Associates Inc 601 859-7250
162a Feather Ln Ste A Canton (39046) *(G-649)*

Bob Tom Johnson, Forest *Also called Johnson Educational Sales Inc (G-1418)*

Bobbys Indus & Oilfld Repr 601 833-3050
1104 Crooked Ln Ne Brookhaven (39601) *(G-483)*

Bobs Welding & Repair 662 685-4217
175 Hwy 15 N Blue Mountain (38610) *(G-290)*

Bobs Woodworking LLC 601 661-8093
2211 Tiffintown Rd Vicksburg (39183) *(G-5347)*

Boco Logging LLC 256 810-4777
24791 Highway 23 N Golden (38847) *(G-1522)*

Boeing Company 228 688-2281
Bldg 4995 Bay Saint Louis (39529) *(G-138)*

Boeing Company 601 936-8540
141 Military Dr Bldg 104 Jackson (39232) *(G-2642)*

Bogue Homa Logging 601 426-3662
40 Bill Windham Rd Heidelberg (39439) *(G-2112)*

Boling Construction Inc 601 833-0122
2779 Bahalia Rd Ne Wesson (39191) *(G-5524)*

Bolivar Cnty Dept Humn Rsurces 662 843-8311
212 N Pearman Ave Cleveland (38732) *(G-787)*

Bolivar Commercial, Cleveland *Also called Bolivar Newspaper Inc (G-788)*

Bolivar Newspaper Inc 662 843-4241
821 N Chrisman Ave Cleveland (38732) *(G-788)*

Bolt Company LLC 601 696-9191
5321 1st St Meridian (39307) *(G-3312)*

Bomgar, Ridgeland *Also called Beyondtrust Corporation (G-4555)*

Bonds Company Inc 601 376-4000
101 Riverview Dr Richland (39218) *(G-4507)*

Bonds Paving, Richland *Also called Bonds Company Inc (G-4507)*

Bonnie's Babies & Ladies, Natchez *Also called Beryl Jones (G-3529)*

Boo Enterprises LLC 228 475-8929
4016 Rosa Ln Moss Point (39563) *(G-3470)*

Book Mart Corporation 662 323-2844
318 E Lee Blvd Starkville (39759) *(G-4930)*

Book Publisher LLC 662 838-2633
132 Baicey Place Rd Byhalia (38611) *(G-581)*

Bookpro Publishing Company 769 208-6806
705 Washington St Natchez (39120) *(G-3536)*

Books Plus LLC 228 209-5021
235 Reynoir St Biloxi (39530) *(G-223)*

Boomerang Services LLC 601 649-6474
4398 Sharon Rd Laurel (39443) *(G-2741)*

Boon Docks Deer Processing 601 789-5843
6308 Highway 501 Raleigh (39153) *(G-4474)*

Boone Newspapers (PA) 601 442-9101
503 N Canal St Natchez (39120) *(G-3537)*

Booneville Industrial Coatings 662 720-1147
100 W Veterans Dr Booneville (38829) *(G-321)*

Boral Bricks Studio, Gulfport *Also called Meridian Brick LLC (G-1828)*

Boral Bricks Studio, Hattiesburg *Also called Meridian Brick LLC (G-2022)*

Borden Dairy Company Ala LLC (HQ) 251 456-3381
7572 U S Highway 49 Hattiesburg (39402) *(G-1936)*

Borden Dairy Company Ala LLC 601 268-2583
7572 U S Highway 49 Hattiesburg (39402) *(G-1937)*

Borden Dairy Company Ala LLC 662 328-8755
85 Port Access Rd Columbus (39701) *(G-941)*

Borg Warner, Taylorsville *Also called Borgwarner Inc (G-5051)*

Borgwarner Inc 601 785-9504
214 Fellowship Rd Taylorsville (39168) *(G-5051)*

Borgwarner Inc 662 473-3100
600 Highway 32 Water Valley (38965) *(G-5463)*

Borgwrner Emssions Systems LLC 662 473-3100
600 Highway 32 Water Valley (38965) *(G-5464)*

Bosarge Boats Inc 228 762-0888
5301 Ladner Ave Pascagoula (39581) *(G-4023)*

Boswell Meat Processing 601 656-6015
10481 Road 836 Philadelphia (39350) *(G-4208)*

Botr Press LLC 708 431-9668
676b Dpont Hrts Chapel Rd Poplarville (39470) *(G-4378)*

Bottle Tree Beverage Co LLC 601 667-3038
422 S Farish St Jackson (39201) *(G-2340)*

Bouldin Essentials LLC 769 216-7146
356 Sheppard Rd Jackson (39206) *(G-2341)*

Bourne Brothers Prtg Co Inc 601 582-1808
5276 Old Highway 42 Hattiesburg (39401) *(G-1938)*

Bowen Backhoe Service, Steens *Also called Bowen Titus (G-4990)*

Bowen Titus 662 327-3084
462 Dickerson Rd Steens (39766) *(G-4990)*

Bowens and Company, Waveland *Also called Cynthia Bowen (G-5479)*

Bowman Cabinet Company 662 564-2711
456 Chulahoma Rd Holly Springs (38635) *(G-2172)*

Box Logging 662 547-6692
115 Whites Rd French Camp (39745) *(G-1439)*

Box Office 7 Studios 662 633-2451
27 Huntsman Cv Brandon (39042) *(G-372)*

Boxcar Flooring Company LLC 662 871-1417
2673 Highway 145 Saltillo (38866) *(G-4708)*

Boyanton Printing Inc 601 939-6725
1018 N Flowood Dr Ste D Flowood (39232) *(G-1348)*

Boyd Eductl Solutions Tech LLC 601 951-2305
241 Pine Knoll Dr Ridgeland (39157) *(G-4558)*

Boyle Tool & Die Inc 662 846-0640
600 Highway 446 Boyle (38730) *(G-348)*

BP America Production Company 228 762-3996
6800 Stennis Blvd Moss Point (39562) *(G-3471)*

BP Corporation North Amer Inc 228 712-3500
6800 Stennis Blvd Moss Point (39562) *(G-3472)*

BP Pascagoula Gas Proc Plant, Moss Point *Also called BP Corporation North Amer Inc (G-3472)*

Bprex Closures LLC 601 584-4758
72 Wl Runnels Indus Dr Hattiesburg (39401) *(G-1939)*

Brad Warren Log & Trckg LLC 601 416-8113
11281 Road 270 Union (39365) *(G-5294)*

Bradford Enterprises 601 442-2339
3 James Brown Ave Natchez (39120) *(G-3538)*

Bradford Enterprises LLC 901 652-1491
7426 Overlook Dr Southaven (38671) *(G-4856)*

Bradley Reid Inc 601 810-6655
263 Highway 27 S Tylertown (39667) *(G-5264)*

Brady Electric Inc 601 649-7862
510 Ellisville Blvd Laurel (39440) *(G-2742)*

Brandi Bonner 601 906-7224
114 Dane Ln Mendenhall (39114) *(G-3279)*

Brandon Boc Ms 601 825-1422
159 Andrew Chapel Rd Brandon (39042) *(G-373)*

Brandon Petroleum Properties 601 649-2261
544 Central Ave Laurel (39440) *(G-2743)*

Braxton Foxx LLC 800 719-6811
232 Market St Flowood (39232) *(G-1349)*

Brazil Furniture Inc 662 489-2063
110 Maggie Dr Pontotoc (38863) *(G-4323)*

Brazos Bend Oil and Gas LLC 601 982-3444
1837 Crane Ridge Dr Jackson (39216) *(G-2342)*

Breaktime Vending Inc 601 749-8424
2001 Cooper Rd Picayune (39466) *(G-4257)*

Brenda Ruth Designs LLC 601 708-4227
306b Avondale Dr Clinton (39056) *(G-815)*

Brent Aubry 662 746-7600
927 Prentiss Ave Yazoo City (39194) *(G-5624)*

Brent Hickman Logging LLC 601 928-8840
47 Stillmore Rd Wiggins (39577) *(G-5573)*

(PA)=Parent Co (HQ)=Headquarters (DH)=Div Headquarters

Brentwood Originals Inc

ALPHABETIC SECTION

Brentwood Originals Inc 662 781-5301
9759 Church Rd Walls (38680) *(G-5448)*

Brew Barr LLC 601 218-7708
1485 Livingston Ln Jackson (39213) *(G-2343)*

Brewer Screen Printing 662 453-2255
1709 Grenada Blvd Greenwood (38930) *(G-1616)*

Brewer Vegetable Farm, Greenwood Also called James L Brewer *(G-1631)*

Brian Rand 601 519-5062
33 Scr 185 Bay Springs (39422) *(G-158)*

Brian Scott Moore 901 831-7393
370 Highway 364 Tishomingo (38873) *(G-5082)*

Brian Smith 601 259-9745
24049 Rose Blvd Gulfport (39503) *(G-1744)*

Brians Marine, Gulfport Also called Brian Smith *(G-1744)*

Bridges Custom Cabinets & Trim 601 954-5085
205 Village Cir Canton (39046) *(G-650)*

Brigade Manufacturing Inc 601 827-5062
101 Ostrover Dr Tylertown (39667) *(G-5265)*

Brimmer-Turan Fndry & Mch LLC 228 896-9669
10021 Lorraine Rd Gulfport (39503) *(G-1745)*

Briscoe Woodworks, Oxford Also called Bill Briscoe *(G-3940)*

Brittany H Davis 251 348-8858
365a E Bond Rd Wiggins (39577) *(G-5574)*

Brm LLC 601 501-1444
121 Thalweg Dr Vicksburg (39183) *(G-5348)*

Brocato Construction Inc 662 563-4473
1847 Brewer Rd Batesville (38606) *(G-100)*

Brock Bit Co Inc 601 876-4237
43 Walt Brock Rd Tylertown (39667) *(G-5266)*

Brock Outdoors 662 255-1121
1026 County Road 821 Saltillo (38866) *(G-4709)*

Brookhaven Ready Mix, Brookhaven Also called Delta Industries Inc *(G-489)*

Brooks Farms Inc 662 299-8780
28052 County Road 559 Schlater (38952) *(G-4769)*

Brown Bottling Group Inc 601 982-4160
2550 Medgar Evers Blvd Jackson (39213) *(G-2344)*

Brown Bottling Group Inc 601 824-3022
1651 Marquette Rd Brandon (39042) *(G-374)*

Brown Bottling Group Inc 601 352-0366
535 Ford Ave Jackson (39209) *(G-2345)*

Brown Bottling Group Inc 601 442-5805
265 Liberty Rd Natchez (39120) *(G-3539)*

Brown Line Printing Inc 662 728-9881
401 W College St Booneville (38829) *(G-322)*

Brown Printing Co, Meridian Also called Joseph L Brown Printing Co *(G-3355)*

Brown Wood Preserving Co Inc 601 656-2607
433 E Beacon St Philadelphia (39350) *(G-4209)*

Brown Wood Preserving Co Inc 662 263-8272
266 Crossroads Church Rd Mathiston (39752) *(G-3227)*

Browning Oil Tools Inc 601 442-1800
6 Ridgeway Rd Natchez (39120) *(G-3540)*

Browns Electrical Repair 662 226-8192
317 Poplar St Grenada (38901) *(G-1670)*

Browns Ice Company 662 862-3706
1650 Country Club Rd Fulton (38843) *(G-1447)*

Bruxoil Inc 601 981-5722
1717 Bellewood Rd Jackson (39211) *(G-2346)*

Bryan E Presson & Assoc Inc 601 925-0053
900 Industrial Park Dr Clinton (39056) *(G-816)*

Bryan Industrial Co Inc 601 649-8786
822 Lake Como Rd Laurel (39443) *(G-2744)*

Bryant Meats Inc 601 785-6507
104 Fellowship Rd Taylorsville (39168) *(G-5052)*

Bryant's Meat Processing, Taylorsville Also called Bryant Meats Inc *(G-5052)*

Bryants Machine Shop Inc 601 922-1937
5734 Highway 80 W Jackson (39209) *(G-2347)*

BSC Sales LLC 662 890-1079
8363 Industrial Dr Olive Branch (38654) *(G-3821)*

BSK Resources LLC 662 842-4716
1251 Chesterville Rd Belden (38826) *(G-187)*

Btc Logging Co 601 735-3259
26 Bobby Bunch Dr Waynesboro (39367) *(G-5493)*

Btm Solutions 662 328-2400
572 Yorkville Rd E Columbus (39702) *(G-942)*

Bubba Bond Logging LLC 662 417-5242
1503 Highway 51 Winona (38967) *(G-5595)*

Buchanan Custom Cabinets 662 438-7435
215 County Road 55 Tishomingo (38873) *(G-5083)*

Buckhaults Sawmill & Pallets 601 477-8403
2064 Highway 29 S Ellisville (39437) *(G-1247)*

Buckley Newspapers Inc (PA) 601 764-3104
Hwy 15 N Bay Springs (39422) *(G-159)*

Buckrdge Spclty Wods Mill Wrks 601 667-3791
3232 S Liberty St Canton (39046) *(G-651)*

Buddys Jeans, Newhebron Also called Jane Little Inc *(G-3713)*

Budget Printing Company 601 693-6003
721 Front Street Ext # 720 Meridian (39301) *(G-3313)*

Budget Signs Inc 601 354-4977
2358 Highway 80 W Jackson (39204) *(G-2348)*

Buie Loggin 601 532-7186
4566 Nw Homochitto Rd Union Church (39668) *(G-5305)*

Builders Marble Inc 601 922-5420
108 Pinehaven Cv Clinton (39056) *(G-817)*

Bulldog Brackets, Sumrall Also called McMahan Bulldog Enterprises *(G-5039)*

Bullocks Gravel Service Inc 601 833-7034
997 Noah Trl Nw Brookhaven (39601) *(G-484)*

Bullocks Washteria 601 684-2332
130 Saint Augustine Ave McComb (39648) *(G-3244)*

Bumper To Bumper 601 928-5603
338 Magnolia Dr N Wiggins (39577) *(G-5575)*

Bunny Bread Inc 228 868-0120
5600 Gautier Vancleave Rd Gautier (39553) *(G-1490)*

Buntyn Sawmill 601 774-8128
44 Buntyn Rd Union (39365) *(G-5295)*

Bunyard Cabinetry 601 757-8765
353 Quitman Ln Nw Brookhaven (39601) *(G-485)*

Bunyards Garage 601 632-4892
194 Will Garrett Rd Toomsuba (39364) *(G-5090)*

Burchwood Inc 662 841-2609
155 Road 1445 Mooreville (38857) *(G-3441)*

Burel Pharmaceuticals Inc 601 720-0111
199 Interstate Dr Ste N Richland (39218) *(G-4508)*

Burford Electric Service Inc 662 328-5679
154 Cooper Rd Columbus (39702) *(G-943)*

Burge Timber Contractors Inc 601 796-3471
142 Lower Airport Rd Lumberton (39455) *(G-3024)*

Burgess Kustom Cabinetry 662 316-4294
1344 State Highway 30 E New Albany (38652) *(G-3676)*

Burnie Dykes Logging Co Inc 601 788-6211
67 Jim Easterling Rd Richton (39476) *(G-4527)*

Burns Fence & Woodworks LLC 601 506-5226
4233 E Ridge Dr Jackson (39211) *(G-2349)*

Burr Creek Screen Printing 601 297-2853
179 Stewart Dr Moselle (39459) *(G-3455)*

Burroughs Bus Sales Inc 601 649-3062
3626 Industrial Blvd Laurel (39440) *(G-2745)*

Burrows Southern Division, Pickens Also called Twin Rivers Paper Company LLC *(G-4307)*

Burtoni Fine Art Inc 601 581-1557
4900 Pplar Sprng Dr Ste 8 Meridian (39305) *(G-3314)*

Busby Office Supply & Printing, Clinton Also called Jeff Busby *(G-827)*

Business & Off Konnextions LLC 601 965-5101
850 Foley St Jackson (39202) *(G-2350)*

Business Communications Inc (PA) 601 898-1890
442 Highland Colony Pkwy Ridgeland (39157) *(G-4559)*

Business Systems Inc 601 957-1500
405 Briarwood Dr Ste 102b Jackson (39206) *(G-2351)*

Button Up Candles 317 522-8060
6023 Castle Rd Vicksburg (39180) *(G-5349)*

Buy A Barricade LLC 228 355-0146
707 Russell Ave Apt A Ocean Springs (39564) *(G-3744)*

Buzini Group LLC 601 398-1311
1016 N Flowood Dr Flowood (39232) *(G-1350)*

Buzini Sports, Flowood Also called Buzini Group LLC *(G-1350)*

Buzini Sports, Grenada Also called Custom Printing *(G-1674)*

Buzzard Rebar Fabricators Inc 228 832-8024
14411 Highway 49 Gulfport (39503) *(G-1746)*

Bynum Printing 601 735-5269
220 Azalea Dr Waynesboro (39367) *(G-5494)*

Byrne Furn Co & Sawmill Svcs 601 442-7363
18 Old Devereaux St Natchez (39120) *(G-3541)*

Byrne Sawmill Services, Natchez Also called Byrne Furn Co & Sawmill Svcs *(G-3541)*

Bywers, Richard, Hattiesburg Also called Staco Decorative Iron *(G-2067)*

C & C Machine Incorporated 601 795-6377
2940 Highway 53 Poplarville (39470) *(G-4379)*

C & C Machine Shop, Tupelo Also called C&C McHine Fabrication MGT LLC *(G-5116)*

C & CS Machine Shop Inc 662 489-3376
420 E Oxford St Pontotoc (38863) *(G-4324)*

C & D Cabinets LLC 228 466-4644
2225 Kiln Waveland Rd Waveland (39576) *(G-5478)*

C & D Jarnagin Company Inc 662 287-4977
103 Franklin St Corinth (38834) *(G-1062)*

C & D Jarnagin Company Inc (PA) 662 287-4977
103 Franklin St Corinth (38834) *(G-1063)*

C & F Swabbing Inc 601 687-1171
458 Shubuta Eucutta Rd Shubuta (39360) *(G-4827)*

C & L Logging Inc 601 683-6349
99 Horne Rd Newton (39345) *(G-3718)*

C & M Tree Svc Stump Grinding 662 675-8884
766 County Road 157 Coffeeville (38922) *(G-842)*

C & S Marble Co 662 844-6873
918 Dixie Creek Rd Saltillo (38866) *(G-4710)*

C & W Custom Design Trailers 662 585-3146
230 Industrial Park Golden (38847) *(G-1523)*

C & W Embroidery Inc 662 462-8526
386 Highway 356 Rienzi (38865) *(G-4648)*

C & W Frames Inc 662 728-2120
340 Highway 30 E Booneville (38829) *(G-323)*

C & W Trailers, Golden Also called C & W Custom Design Trailers *(G-1523)*

2019 Harris Directory of
Mississippi Manufacturers

(G-0000) Company's Geographic Section entry number

ALPHABETIC SECTION

Carroll Ray Auto & Truck Sales

C and P Printing Company Inc 662 327-9742
104 Gardner Blvd Columbus (39702) *(G-944)*

C B R Machinist Inc 601 426-2326
11 County Barn Rd Laurel (39443) *(G-2746)*

C C Clark Inc (PA) 662 323-4317
501 Academy Rd Starkville (39759) *(G-4931)*

C E Russell Framing Components 228 762-9267
715 Morgan Ave Pascagoula (39567) *(G-4024)*

C E Welch Timber Co Inc 601 657-4577
409 Roberts Rd Liberty (39645) *(G-2911)*

C F E N 662 327-0031
1514 Bell Ave Columbus (39701) *(G-945)*

C F I, Holly Springs Also called Contract Fabricators Inc *(G-2175)*

C M C, Poplarville Also called Cuevas Machine Co Inc *(G-4380)*

C T W, Hernando Also called Coles Tool Works Inc *(G-2125)*

C W Embroidery Inc 662 231-9206
10032 Lenoir Loop Prairie (39756) *(G-4412)*

C Wells Trucking LLC 601 273-0972
15464 Lott Mccarty Rd Picayune (39466) *(G-4258)*

C&C McHine Fabrication MGT LLC 662 269-2534
2383 S Green St Tupelo (38801) *(G-5116)*

C&C Signs LLC 228 235-4839
15240 Camelot Dr Diberville (39540) *(G-1200)*

C3 Design Inc (PA) 662 392-5021
1706 Cypress Ave Greenwood (38930) *(G-1617)*

C5 Trucking LLC 601 797-9335
183 J D Herrington Rd Mount Olive (39119) *(G-3510)*

Cabinet Specialists Inc 601 992-3929
1354 Winterview Dr Jackson (39211) *(G-2352)*

Cabinetsource Inc 228 385-8880
1956 E Pass Rd Ste E Gulfport (39507) *(G-1747)*

Cable One Inc 601 833-7991
230 5th Ave McComb (39648) *(G-3245)*

Caboose Cones 228 860-4030
1009 Pesoto Ave Ocean Springs (39566) *(G-3745)*

Cade & Cade Logging Inc 601 833-2557
2782 Jckson Liberty Dr Nw Wesson (39191) *(G-5525)*

Cade Enterprises 2 .... 662 283-3678
107 Pine Dr Winona (38967) *(G-5596)*

Cade Rubber Co Inc 601 743-5717
3822 Kipling Rd De Kalb (39328) *(G-1162)*

Caen Engineering, Oxford Also called Martin Caderwood *(G-3970)*

Cajun Planters LLC 770 363-5638
205 S Burke Ave Long Beach (39560) *(G-2930)*

Cal-Maine Foods Inc 601 852-4970
Hwy 467 S Edwards (39066) *(G-1236)*

Cal-Maine Foods Inc 601 852-4413
17521 Old Hwy 80 Edwards (39066) *(G-1237)*

Calgon Carbon Corporation 228 533-7171
13121 Webre Rd Bay Saint Louis (39520) *(G-139)*

Calhoun County Journal 662 983-2570
207 N Newburger Ave Bruce (38915) *(G-560)*

Calhoun Parts Inc 662 628-6621
Hwy 8 Calhoun City (38916) *(G-635)*

Calico Jacks Llc 504 355-9639
19 Autumn Ln Carriere (39426) *(G-689)*

Callahans Quick Print Inc 662 234-8060
191 Highway 6 E Oxford (38655) *(G-3944)*

Callon Offshore Production 601 442-1601
200 N Canal St Natchez (39120) *(G-3542)*

Calvert Company Inc 601 939-9191
120 Aztec Dr Richland (39218) *(G-4509)*

Cam2 International LLC 601 661-5382
685 Haining Rd Vicksburg (39183) *(G-5350)*

Cam2 International LLC (PA) 800 338-2262
685 Haining Rd Vicksburg (39183) *(G-5351)*

Cam2 International LLC 601 661-5382
685 Haining Rd Vicksburg (39183) *(G-5352)*

Cameo Fibers, Tupelo Also called Leggett Platt Components Inc *(G-5179)*

Cameron International Corp 601 649-8900
1020 Hillcrest Dr Laurel (39440) *(G-2747)*

Cameron International Corp 601 425-2377
16 Donald Dr Laurel (39440) *(G-2748)*

Cameron Rig Solutions Inc 601 629-3300
500 Letourneau Rd Vicksburg (39180) *(G-5353)*

Campbell Creek Publishing LLC 601 824-5932
187 Conerly Rd Braxton (39044) *(G-476)*

Campbell Global 601 932-2729
1080 River Oaks Dr A220 Flowood (39232) *(G-1351)*

Campbell Newspapers LLC 423 754-0312
996 Howard Ave Biloxi (39530) *(G-224)*

Can Man The, Jackson Also called Aluminum Recycling of Miss *(G-2325)*

Can't Miss Embroidery, Moss Point Also called City Sports Center *(G-3474)*

Canada Bread 662 494-1607
1340 N Eshman Ave West Point (39773) *(G-5539)*

Cancon Concrete, Lexington Also called Lexington Concrete & Block Co *(G-2904)*

Cand M Pupwood 601 445-9200
100 Redd Loop Rd Natchez (39120) *(G-3543)*

Candle Creations By Melinda 601 477-4942
90 Holly Lake Dr Ellisville (39437) *(G-1248)*

Candlelore Inc 662 312-1060
101 E Pointe Dr Starkville (39759) *(G-4932)*

Candles By Valorie 601 394-3153
3251 W Salem Rd Richton (39476) *(G-4528)*

Candy Bouquet 6625, Southaven Also called Southern Blle Sweet Dsigns LLC *(G-4906)*

Candy Lady AV, Woodville Also called Alicia Vaughn *(G-5615)*

Cannon Boat Lifts LLC 601 540-8691
99 Ingleside Rd Madison (39110) *(G-3087)*

Canopy Breezes LLC 972 207-2045
401 Pebble Creek Dr Madison (39110) *(G-3088)*

Canton Concrete 601 859-4547
153 Yandell Ave Canton (39046) *(G-652)*

Canton High Press Box 601 859-4315
529 Mace St Canton (39046) *(G-653)*

Canton Rail Yard, Canton Also called Martin Marietta Materials Inc *(G-669)*

Canton Vehicle Assembly Plant, Canton Also called Nissan North America Inc *(G-673)*

Cantrell Hot Rods LLC 662 213-7184
166 Road 1492 Mooreville (38857) *(G-3442)*

Canvas & Cocktails LLC 228 861-8444
500d Courthouse Rd Gulfport (39507) *(G-1748)*

Canvas Creations & Eatery 404 514-3399
93 E Robinson Junction Rd Waynesboro (39367) *(G-5495)*

Canvasbeauty Beauty 601 282-5430
6103 Dale Dr Marion (39342) *(G-3221)*

Cap Co 601 384-3939
2325 Highway 184 E Bude (39630) *(G-568)*

Capital Bedding Inc 662 566-1144
5262 S Raymond St Verona (38879) *(G-5328)*

Capital City Metal Works Inc 601 939-7467
817 Airport Rd S Pearl (39208) *(G-4108)*

Capitol City Label Inc 601 420-2375
46 Valley Dr Pearl (39208) *(G-4109)*

Capri Lighting 662 842-7212
776 S Green St Tupelo (38804) *(G-5117)*

Capt Mikes Stump Grinding and 985 892-9162
165 Will Thompson Rd Picayune (39466) *(G-4259)*

Caramel Factory 662 563-9900
127 Lakewood Dr Batesville (38606) *(G-101)*

Caraustar Industrial and Con 662 287-2492
1504 S Fulton Dr Corinth (38834) *(G-1064)*

Caraustar Industries Inc 601 703-0550
1242 Montgomery Dr Meridian (39301) *(G-3315)*

Cardinal Health 414 LLC 601 982-7345
350 W Woodrow Wilson Ave Jackson (39213) *(G-2353)*

Cardinal Health 414 LLC 662 680-8644
1930 International Dr Tupelo (38804) *(G-5118)*

Carey F Stanley 601 687-5247
739 Waynesboro Shubuta Rd Shubuta (39360) *(G-4828)*

Careys Construction Co Inc 601 922-7388
5247 Greenway Drive Ext A Jackson (39204) *(G-2354)*

Careys Fencing 601 434-6510
49 Sandy Ln Hattiesburg (39402) *(G-1940)*

Carlisle Construction Mtls LLC 662 560-6474
1201 Scott St Senatobia (38668) *(G-4788)*

Carlisle Syntec 662 301-4509
1201 Scott St Senatobia (38668) *(G-4789)*

Carliss Pharmaceuticals 228 875-2748
1306 Bienville Blvd Ocean Springs (39564) *(G-3746)*

Carlmac Industries Inc 601 794-5000
Hwy 589 & Interstate 59 I 59 Purvis (39475) *(G-4435)*

Carneceria Valdez 601 899-6992
6530 Old Canton Rd Ridgeland (39157) *(G-4560)*

Carnes Frames Inc (PA) 662 489-1984
263 Brookwood Dr Pontotoc (38863) *(G-4325)*

Carnet Technology 601 857-8641
6097 Oakley Palestine Rd Terry (39170) *(G-5064)*

Carney Publications LLC 601 427-5694
1655 Carmel New Hope Rd Monticello (39654) *(G-3429)*

Carol Baird 601 924-5409
1008 Old Vicksburg Rd Clinton (39056) *(G-818)*

Carol Vincent & Associates 662 624-8406
313 Issaquena Ave Clarksdale (38614) *(G-760)*

Carpenter Co 662 566-2392
184 Lipford Rd Verona (38879) *(G-5329)*

Carpenter Newsmedia LLC 601 445-3618
503 N Canal St Natchez (39120) *(G-3544)*

Carpenters Cabinets 662 465-6453
3881 Highway 12 W Sturgis (39769) *(G-5006)*

Carpenters Pole & Piling Co 601 928-7400
1513 Magnolia Dr N Wiggins (39577) *(G-5576)*

Carr Plumbing Supply Inc 601 824-9711
140 Old Highway 80 Ste H Brandon (39042) *(G-375)*

Carrier Corporation 662 890-3706
491 Wingo Rd Byhalia (38611) *(G-582)*

Carroll Aircraft LLC 228 255-7460
2379 Coelho Way Diamondhead (39525) *(G-1186)*

Carroll Ray Auto & Truck Sales 662 226-1200
23025 Highway 8 E Grenada (38901) *(G-1671)*

A
L
P
H
A
B
E
T
I
C

(PA)=Parent Co (HQ)=Headquarters (DH)=Div Headquarters

2019 Harris Directory of
Mississippi Manufacturers

Carrolls Welding Service

Carrolls Welding Service 228 875-3800
7509 Highway 90 E Ocean Springs (39564) *(G-3747)*

Carsons Construction LLC 601 301-0841
1127 Openwood St Vicksburg (39183) *(G-5354)*

Carters Inc 662 844-2667
3822 Market Center Dr Tupelo (38804) *(G-5119)*

Carters Machine Works 601 507-5480
304 Highway 16 W Carthage (39051) *(G-708)*

Carthage Ice Company Div, Carthage *Also called Wendall Harrell (G-727)*

Carthaginian Inc 601 267-4501
122 W Franklin St Carthage (39051) *(G-709)*

Caruthers AC & Htg LLC 601 636-9433
3300 Washington St Vicksburg (39180) *(G-5355)*

Casden's Body Boutique, Hattiesburg *Also called Newson Chenora (G-2037)*

Cases Body & Paint 601 833-3153
1351 Highway 84 W Brookhaven (39601) *(G-486)*

Cases Cntrpint Hnting CLB Inc 601 734-2373
2295 Sw Bogue Chitto Rd Smithdale (39664) *(G-4841)*

Casters Den 662 593-3214
123 E Front St Iuka (38852) *(G-2286)*

Castle Enclosures LLC 228 238-6216
1636 N Popps Ferry Rd M3 Biloxi (39532) *(G-225)*

Castle Hill Design 601 918-8234
205 Hill Rd Canton (39046) *(G-654)*

Caston Creat & Coatings LLC 228 588-0055
24001 Robert E Lee Rd Lucedale (39452) *(G-2987)*

Cat Daddy's, Oxford *Also called Ink Spot Inc (G-3959)*

Cat Head Distillery LLC 601 954-8207
644 Church Rd Ste 1 Jackson (39296) *(G-2355)*

Catawomper Press LLC 662 832-3897
206 Northpointe Blvd Oxford (38655) *(G-3945)*

Cater 2u Embroidery 662 253-8713
1654 Main St Southaven (38671) *(G-4857)*

Caterpillar 662 286-1274
1710 Sawyer Rd Corinth (38834) *(G-1065)*

Caterpillar Dev Ctr Inc 228 385-3900
890 Vee St Biloxi (39532) *(G-226)*

Caterpillar Inc 662 720-2400
100 Caterpillar Dr Booneville (38829) *(G-324)*

Caterpillar Inc 662 286-5511
2500 Legacy Dr Corinth (38834) *(G-1066)*

Caterpillar Inc 662 284-5143
500 Cardinal Dr Corinth (38834) *(G-1067)*

Caterpillar Inc 662 286-5511
501 Cardinal Dr Corinth (38834) *(G-1068)*

Catontech MGT Systems LLC 601 207-1047
4825 37th Ave Meridian (39305) *(G-3316)*

Caviness Woodworking Company 662 628-5195
200 N Aycock Ave Calhoun City (38916) *(G-636)*

Cavins Corporation 601 428-0670
19 Nemo Clark Dr Laurel (39443) *(G-2749)*

Cavins Corporation 601 833-2268
1224 Lofton Trl Nw Brookhaven (39601) *(G-487)*

Cbl Architectual Fiberglass, Hernando *Also called Cbl Architectural Fiberglass (G-2124)*

Cbl Architectural Fiberglass 662 429-2277
100 E Valley St Hernando (38632) *(G-2124)*

Cbr Performance 601 337-2928
1544 Hnlyfield Mcneill Rd Carriere (39426) *(G-690)*

Ccbcc Operations LLC 228 875-5426
7900 Highway 57 Ocean Springs (39565) *(G-3748)*

Ccbcc Operations LLC 601 428-0464
201 Coca Cola Ave Hattiesburg (39402) *(G-1941)*

Cccl Pallet LLC 662 494-0141
372 Court St West Point (39773) *(G-5540)*

Ccore Energy Holding Co LLC (PA) 601 824-7900
2015 High Pointe Dr Brandon (39042) *(G-376)*

Ccore Energy/Mariner LLC 601 824-7900
2015 High Pointe Dr Brandon (39042) *(G-377)*

Ccsi, Hattiesburg *Also called Consoldted Converting Svcs Inc (G-1950)*

Cdr Manufacturing Inc 662 665-3100
1801 S Fulton Dr Corinth (38834) *(G-1069)*

Ceca LLC 662 993-8880
171 County Road 562 Ripley (38663) *(G-4655)*

Cecil D Johnson 662 456-5846
12546 Ms Highway 15 Mantee (39751) *(G-3210)*

Ceco Building Systems, Columbus *Also called Robertson-Ceco II Corporation (G-1021)*

Ceco Corp 601 362-4737
145 Brae Burn Dr Jackson (39211) *(G-2356)*

Ceco Developement, Jackson *Also called Ceco Corp (G-2356)*

Cedotal Inc 601 605-2660
330 Ne Madison Dr Ridgeland (39157) *(G-4561)*

Cee & Gee Designs, Brandon *Also called Mary Givens (G-419)*

Celebrations Etc 601 268-0390
102 Lundy Ln Hattiesburg (39401) *(G-1942)*

Celgene Corp 908 673-9000
100 Brighton Ln Ridgeland (39157) *(G-4562)*

Cemco Inc 662 323-1559
909a Lynn Ln Starkville (39759) *(G-4933)*

Cemex Cnstr Mtls Fla LLC 888 263-7093
2179 Holston Rd Como (38619) *(G-1046)*

Center For Pregnancy Choices 601 482-1230
4927 Poplar Springs Dr Meridian (39305) *(G-3317)*

Centerpint Enrgy Rsources Corp 601 425-1461
26 Mason St Laurel (39440) *(G-2750)*

Centerpoint Energy Inc 228 588-2977
17717 Highway 63 Moss Point (39562) *(G-3473)*

Central Delta Cmnty Dev Corp 601 215-0367
1023 Voorhees Ave Jackson (39209) *(G-2357)*

Central Fabrication Inc 662 349-7122
401 Suthcrest Cir Ste 102 Southaven (38671) *(G-4858)*

Central Industries Inc (PA) 601 469-4421
1300 E Third St Forest (39074) *(G-1410)*

Central Industries Inc 601 469-4421
13666 Highway 80 Forest (39074) *(G-1411)*

Central Machine Shop 601 446-8732
639 Highway 61 S Natchez (39120) *(G-3545)*

Central Medical Equipment 661 843-6161
807 Highway 35 S Carthage (39051) *(G-710)*

Central Miss Manufacting Hsing 601 267-8353
908 Highway 16 E Carthage (39051) *(G-711)*

Central Miss RES & EXT Ctr 601 857-2284
1320 Seven Springs Dr Raymond (39154) *(G-4485)*

Central Mississippi Baking, Pelahatchie *Also called Mississippi Baking Co LLC (G-4165)*

Central Mississippi Glass Co 601 469-5050
502 Old Morton Rd Forest (39074) *(G-1412)*

Central Mississippi Wood Inc 662 724-2447
449 Ryles Rd S Philadelphia (39350) *(G-4210)*

Central Resources Inc 601 776-3281
1667 Apache Loop Quitman (39355) *(G-4459)*

Central Snacks Inc 601 267-3112
1700 N Pearl St Carthage (39051) *(G-712)*

Ceramic Studio, Foxworth *Also called Wesley Inc (G-1438)*

Cerbide Inc 228 871-7123
14115 Seaway Rd Gulfport (39503) *(G-1749)*

Certainteed Gypsum Inc 601 693-0254
2710 Highway 11 S Meridian (39307) *(G-3318)*

CF Industries Inc 662 746-4131
4608 Highway 49 E Yazoo City (39194) *(G-5625)*

CF Industries Nitrogen LLC 662 751-2616
4612 Highway 49 E Yazoo City (39194) *(G-5626)*

Cg Monogram & Gifts 662 401-5344
8245 Highway 25 S Fulton (38843) *(G-1448)*

Cg Welding Services LLC 601 426-3922
540 Norton Rd Laurel (39443) *(G-2751)*

CG&p Manufacturing Inc 662 746-4464
800 S Industrial Pkwy Yazoo City (39194) *(G-5627)*

Ch Custom Designs & Prints LLC 601 408-5068
518 Sullivan Kilrain Rd Hattiesburg (39402) *(G-1943)*

Chads LLC 601 919-3113
120 Park Ln Brandon (39047) *(G-378)*

Chahta Enterprises, Choctaw *Also called Mississppi Band Chctaw Indians (G-746)*

Chains Logging 662 327-8240
1800 Spurlock Rd Columbus (39702) *(G-946)*

Challnger Dpwell Servicing Inc 601 736-2511
4 Industrial Ln Columbia (39429) *(G-885)*

Chambers Air and Heat 662 967-2002
401 County Line Rd West (39192) *(G-5532)*

Chambers Delimbinator Inc 662 285-2777
234 Old Bellwood Rd Ackerman (39735) *(G-23)*

Chambers Logging Inc 662 285-2777
234 Bellwood Rd Ackerman (39735) *(G-24)*

Champion Chemical Company LLC 601 720-8908
802 N Oak Ave Ruleville (38771) *(G-4696)*

Champion Custom Bow Strings 662 652-3499
2716 Ptton Flat Okland Rd Fulton (38843) *(G-1449)*

Chancellor Inc 601 518-0412
505 Avenue C Laurel (39440) *(G-2752)*

Chancellor Welding, Ellisville *Also called Chancellors Welding (G-1249)*

Chancellors Business Sup Inc (PA) 601 426-6396
1325 W 5th St Laurel (39440) *(G-2753)*

Chancellors Welding 601 477-3552
1524 Highway 11 S Ellisville (39437) *(G-1249)*

Channel Chemical Corporation 228 864-6199
14373 Seaway Rd Gulfport (39503) *(G-1750)*

Chapter 3 Inc (PA) 662 568-7830
958 Washington Rd Houlka (38850) *(G-2220)*

Charged Up Grill LLC 228 224-4461
13741 Shelby Ct Gulfport (39503) *(G-1751)*

Chariot Wheelchair and RPR 228 967-7991
1636 Popps Ferry Rd Biloxi (39532) *(G-227)*

Charles Donald Pulpwood Inc (PA) 601 437-4012
1024 Noble Rd Port Gibson (39150) *(G-4400)*

Charles Donald Timber, Port Gibson *Also called Charles Donald Pulpwood Inc (G-4400)*

Charles Horn Logging & Trckg 662 585-3111
107 Horn Dr Golden (38847) *(G-1524)*

Charles Jordan 601 727-4753
49 County Road 226 Pachuta (39347) *(G-4011)*

2019 Harris Directory of
Mississippi Manufacturers

(G-0000) Company's Geographic Section entry number

Charles Lance Griffin 601 734-2683
9144 Bogue Chitto Rd Se Mc Call Creek (39647) ***(G-3232)***
Charles On Call Mold Removal 662 352-8009
806 Highway 19 N Ste 299 Meridian (39307) ***(G-3319)***
Charles Pole Sons Stone Contrs, Belmont *Also called Pooles Stone & Masonry Contrs* ***(G-201)***
Charles R Smith Logging Co 601 267-9800
6381 Highway 488 Carthage (39051) ***(G-713)***
Charleston Manufacturing LLC 901 853-3070
10500 Highway 178 Olive Branch (38654) ***(G-3822)***
Charleston Printing 662 647-2291
134 S Church St Charleston (38921) ***(G-734)***
Charlie Chemical and Supply 662 332-9262
154 Stokes King Rd Greenville (38701) ***(G-1537)***
Charlottes EMB & Screen Prtg 601 824-1080
774 Trickhambridge Rd Brandon (39042) ***(G-379)***
Chatham Enterprises Inc 601 727-4951
Hwy 18 W Rose Hill (39356) ***(G-4684)***
Chef Rays Famous LLC 601 559-8096
5207 Forest Hill Rd Byram (39272) ***(G-619)***
Chelsea Products, Olive Branch *Also called Parker-Hannifin Corporation* ***(G-3894)***
Chemical Products & Systems 601 354-1919
124 W South St Jackson (39201) ***(G-2358)***
Chemours Company Fc LLC 228 255-2100
7685 Kiln Delisle Rd Pass Christian (39571) ***(G-4078)***
Chemtrade Chemicals US LLC 601 799-2380
187 J J Holcomb Rd Nicholson (39463) ***(G-3730)***
Chenoa Coffee Company 662 834-3917
212 Court Sq Lexington (39095) ***(G-2898)***
Chep (usa) Inc 601 352-6500
750 Boling St Jackson (39209) ***(G-2359)***
Chesser Publishing LLC 228 588-1111
7064 Joe Rubino Rd Hurley (39555) ***(G-2259)***
Chevron Corporation 228 938-4600
250 Industrial Rd Pascagoula (39581) ***(G-4025)***
Chevron Phillips Chem Co LLC 228 938-4600
250 Industrial Rd Pascagoula (39581) ***(G-4026)***
Chickasaw Container Company 662 447-3339
219 S Carter St Okolona (38860) ***(G-3795)***
Chickasaw Farm Services Inc 662 456-2008
627 Church St Houston (38851) ***(G-2233)***
Chickasaw Wood Products Inc 662 456-5357
1478 County Road 405 Houston (38851) ***(G-2234)***
Chilean Nitrate, Jackson *Also called Sqm North America Corporation* ***(G-2596)***
Chip Jones Mill Inc 601 876-6943
2438 Highway 98 E Columbia (39429) ***(G-886)***
Chippewa Enterprises LLC 228 832-0032
11451 Canal Rd Gulfport (39503) ***(G-1752)***
Chips Amory Inc 662 256-1400
100 Waterway Dr Amory (38821) ***(G-38)***
Chips Gloster Inc 601 225-4405
600 E Carney Dr Gloster (39638) ***(G-1512)***
Chism Rackard Enterprises LLC 662 327-5200
909 Alabama St Columbus (39702) ***(G-947)***
Choctaw Enterprises, Carthage *Also called Mississppi Band Chctaw Indians* ***(G-719)***
Choctaw Gaming Commission, Choctaw *Also called Mississppi Band Chctaw Indians* ***(G-747)***
Choctaw Glove & Safety Co Inc 601 774-5555
100 Kate Thomas Dr Union (39365) ***(G-5296)***
Choctaw Glove & Safety Co Inc (PA) 662 724-4178
10 Laura St Noxapater (39346) ***(G-3731)***
Chops Wrecker & Welding Svc 601 442-0092
283 Lower Woodville Rd Natchez (39120) ***(G-3546)***
Chris G Gatlin 601 498-6281
162 County Road 377 Heidelberg (39439) ***(G-2113)***
Chrisman Manufacturing Inc 228 864-6293
7399 Beatline Rd Long Beach (39560) ***(G-2931)***
Christian Pass Soap 228 222-4303
330 W North St Pass Christian (39571) ***(G-4079)***
Christians Automotive Machine 662 287-4500
2672 S Harper Rd Ste 2327 Corinth (38834) ***(G-1070)***
Chromcraft Corporation 662 562-8203
1 Quality Ln Senatobia (38668) ***(G-4790)***
Chromcraft Furniture, Senatobia *Also called Chromcraft Corporation* ***(G-4790)***
Chrome Deposit Corporation 662 798-4149
1949 Airport Rd Columbus (39701) ***(G-948)***
Chronicle 601 651-2000
130 Leontyne Price Blvd B Laurel (39440) ***(G-2754)***
Chuck Jennings 601 668-5704
1783 Pine Hill Dr Raymond (39154) ***(G-4486)***
Chuck Patrick 601 278-7193
120 Dogwood Trl Brandon (39047) ***(G-380)***
Chuck Ryan Cars Inc 228 864-9706
18012 Pineville Rd Long Beach (39560) ***(G-2932)***
Chucks Welding & Mech LLC 662 347-9941
3650 Nita Ln Greenville (38701) ***(G-1538)***
Church's Chicken, Waynesboro *Also called Richard E Johnson* ***(G-5512)***
Ci Metal Fabrication LLC 601 483-6281
6205 Saint Louis St Meridian (39307) ***(G-3320)***
CIC International LLC 662 473-4724
178 Askew St Water Valley (38965) ***(G-5465)***
Cintas Corporation No 2 ......601 923-8664
5530 Industrial Rd Jackson (39209) ***(G-2360)***
Circle A LLC 601 832-3698
8161 Highway 472 Hazlehurst (39083) ***(G-2091)***
Circle Bar East, Foxworth *Also called Taylor Energy Company LLC* ***(G-1436)***
Circle G Hauling LLC 662 436-7028
1410 Goforth Rd Little Rock (39337) ***(G-2922)***
Circle J Meat Manufacturing 662 790-3448
104 Marquette Cir Tupelo (38801) ***(G-5120)***
Circle Lane Contractors LLC 601 776-0129
263 Hall St Shubuta (39360) ***(G-4829)***
Circle S Irrigation Inc 662 627-7246
420 Rain St Clarksdale (38614) ***(G-761)***
Cite Armored Inc 662 551-1066
540 S Industrial Park Rd Holly Springs (38635) ***(G-2173)***
Citizen Health Foundation 601 463-2436
6641 Hwy 98 Ste 200 Hattiesburg (39402) ***(G-1944)***
City of Biloxi 228 435-6217
170 Porter Ave Biloxi (39530) ***(G-228)***
City of Magee 601 849-2366
124 1st St Ne Magee (39111) ***(G-3174)***
City Sports Center 228 474-2033
3631 Main St Moss Point (39563) ***(G-3474)***
Cives Corporation 662 759-6265
219 Port Terminal Rd S Rosedale (38769) ***(G-4687)***
Civil Precast Corporation 601 853-1870
854 Wilson Dr Ste B Ridgeland (39157) ***(G-4563)***
Cjw Hunting LLC 662 746-1863
213 S Main St Yazoo City (39194) ***(G-5628)***
Ckc Logging Inc 601 754-1344
182 Brother In Law Ln Monticello (39654) ***(G-3430)***
Cks Productions Inc 888 897-9136
946 Tommy Munro Dr Biloxi (39532) ***(G-229)***
CL Cabinets LLC 228 860-9678
109 N Ocean Wave Ave Long Beach (39560) ***(G-2933)***
CL Dews Sons Fndry McHy Inc 601 582-4427
1599 Edwards St Hattiesburg (39401) ***(G-1945)***
Clairborne Publishing Co 601 437-5103
708 Market St Port Gibson (39150) ***(G-4401)***
Clarence Sansing Jr 601 656-4771
324 Williamson Ave Philadelphia (39350) ***(G-4211)***
Clarence South Logging 662 585-3724
6 South Dr Fulton (38843) ***(G-1450)***
Clark Beverage Group Inc (HQ) 662 338-3400
110 Miley Dr Starkville (39759) ***(G-4934)***
Clark Beverage Group Inc 662 280-8540
5645 Pepper Chase Dr Southaven (38671) ***(G-4859)***
Clark Beverage Group Inc 662 843-3241
908 N Sharpe Ave Cleveland (38732) ***(G-789)***
Clark Harvison 601 928-7929
435 Marshall Taylor Rd Wiggins (39577) ***(G-5577)***
Clark Publishing, Quitman *Also called Clarke County Tribune Inc* ***(G-4460)***
Clarkco Services Inc 601 787-3447
3313 County Road 230 Heidelberg (39439) ***(G-2114)***
Clarke County Tribune Inc 601 776-3726
101 Main St Quitman (39355) ***(G-4460)***
Clarksdale Press Register, Clarksdale *Also called Delta Press Publishing Co Inc* ***(G-766)***
Classail Models International 601 373-4833
117 Brampton Cv Byram (39272) ***(G-620)***
Classic Furniture Mfg 662 456-5900
1231 County Road 515 N Houston (38851) ***(G-2235)***
Classic Printing, Jackson *Also called Womack Willow* ***(G-2638)***
Classic Window Design 662 893-5892
4495 Miranda Dr Olive Branch (38654) ***(G-3823)***
Claude Guy 601 848-7859
5 Gandy St State Line (39362) ***(G-4984)***
Claude W Carnathan 662 834-3855
652 Boulevard Ext Lexington (39095) ***(G-2899)***
Clay Canvas 662 236-9798
113 County Road 401 Oxford (38655) ***(G-3946)***
Clay Kentucky-Tennessee Co 662 382-5262
250 Kt Rd Crenshaw (38621) ***(G-1132)***
Clay Necaise 228 233-7760
1006 Washington St Bay Saint Louis (39520) ***(G-140)***
Clay Stewart Industries LLC 601 946-2332
122 Don Stewart Dr Mendenhall (39114) ***(G-3280)***
Clayful Impressions 601 918-0221
316 Woodlands Green Pl Brandon (39047) ***(G-381)***
Clays Print Shop Inc 228 868-8244
1513 24th Ave Gulfport (39501) ***(G-1753)***
Clayton Homes Inc 601 939-0461
2318 Highway 80 E Pearl (39208) ***(G-4110)***
Clear Creek Cabinetry Inc 601 684-7130
1014 Clear Creek Ln Summit (39666) ***(G-5008)***
Clear Enterprise 601 796-2429
1298 Gumpond Beall Rd Lumberton (39455) ***(G-3025)***
Clear Enterprises, Lumberton *Also called J & K Services LLC* ***(G-3032)***

ALPHABETIC

(PA)=Parent Co (HQ)=Headquarters (DH)=Div Headquarters
2019 Harris Directory of Mississippi Manufacturers
273

Clear Sight Windshield Repair — ALPHABETIC SECTION

Clear Sight Windshield Repair 601 638-2892
1712 Sky Farm Ave Vicksburg (39183) *(G-5356)*

Clearspan Components Inc 601 483-3941
6110 Old Highway 80 W Meridian (39307) *(G-3321)*

Clementine Frazier 601 572-7698
1970 Lebanon Pinegrove Rd Utica (39175) *(G-5307)*

Cleveland John 901 359-2737
279 Jamie Dr Byhalia (38611) *(G-583)*

Clifford A Crosby 228 234-1649
716 Live Oak Dr Biloxi (39532) *(G-230)*

Cline Ltd 601 649-6274
366 Lower Myrick Rd Laurel (39443) *(G-2755)*

Clint Williams Company 662 627-3243
675 Sunbelt Dr Clarksdale (38614) *(G-762)*

Close Quarter Combat LLC 601 325-5610
144 Augustine Dr Hattiesburg (39402) *(G-1946)*

Cloud 12 Publishing 228 990-0434
1502 Skyline Dr Gautier (39553) *(G-1491)*

Clyde E Burton 228 432-0117
161 5th St Biloxi (39530) *(G-231)*

Clyde Woodward Jr 601 736-6115
51 Lake Ln Columbia (39429) *(G-887)*

CM Manufacturing Inc 601 545-7515
95 Wl Runnels Indstrl 6 Hattiesburg (39401) *(G-1947)*

CM Solutions Inc 662 287-8810
2674 S Harper Rd Corinth (38834) *(G-1071)*

CMC Paving LLC 601 764-2787
70 County Road 1717 Bay Springs (39422) *(G-160)*

CMC Readymix Inc 662 252-6479
516 Highway 4 W Holly Springs (38635) *(G-2174)*

CMS, Gulfport *Also called Commercial Mllwk Spcialist Inc (G-1763)*

Coast Coca Cola Bottling Co 228 864-1122
3701 25th Ave Gulfport (39501) *(G-1754)*

Coast Concrete Company Inc 228 863-1364
14270 Creosote Rd Gulfport (39503) *(G-1755)*

Coast Ink Wholesale Club 601 948-4849
1200 E County Line Rd # 186 Ridgeland (39157) *(G-4564)*

Coast Motor News 228 868-1772
16195 Landon Rd Gulfport (39503) *(G-1756)*

Coast Observer 228 875-0090
7604 Clamshell Ave Ocean Springs (39564) *(G-3749)*

Coast Printing Company 228 863-1018
1623 25th Ave Gulfport (39501) *(G-1757)*

Coast Tees LLC 228 234-1636
12125 Edington Pl Gulfport (39503) *(G-1758)*

Coast Wood Products Inc 228 466-4302
309 Third St Bay Saint Louis (39520) *(G-141)*

Coastal Charting Consultants 601 590-0540
215 Boley Dr Picayune (39466) *(G-4260)*

Coastal Fire and Safety LLC 228 327-0563
2706 Lynwood St Pascagoula (39567) *(G-4027)*

Coastal Marine Equipment Inc 228 832-7655
20995 Coastal Pkwy Gulfport (39503) *(G-1759)*

Coastal Marine Sales LLC 228 731-3955
4417 Tennessee Ave Gulfport (39501) *(G-1760)*

Coastal Metal Works LLC 601 749-2611
1821 Palestine Rd Picayune (39466) *(G-4261)*

Coastal Petroleum Services Inc 601 446-5888
138 Col John Pitchford Pa Natchez (39120) *(G-3547)*

Coastal Prtective Coatings LLC 214 882-8036
1260 Plum Bulff Dr Lucedale (39452) *(G-2988)*

Coastal S &S, Biloxi *Also called Coastal Solar and SEC Films (G-232)*

Coastal Solar and SEC Films 228 369-3933
620 Bay Haven Cv Biloxi (39532) *(G-232)*

Coastal Tie & Timber Co Inc 601 876-2688
34 Pallets Rd Tylertown (39667) *(G-5267)*

Coastal Tire Wholesalers LLC 810 257-9977
19079 Pineville Rd Long Beach (39560) *(G-2934)*

Coastal Transportation LLC 601 876-2688
34 Pallets Rd Tylertown (39667) *(G-5268)*

Coastal Waters LLC 662 769-2944
220 Brook Ave Starkville (39759) *(G-4935)*

Coca-Cola, Starkville *Also called Clark Beverage Group Inc (G-4934)*

Coca-Cola, Gulfport *Also called Coast Coca Cola Bottling Co (G-1754)*

Coca-Cola, Hattiesburg *Also called Mississippi Coca Cola Btlg Co (G-2025)*

Coca-Cola, Corinth *Also called Weaver Consolidated Group Inc (G-1128)*

Coca-Cola, Tupelo *Also called Weaver Consolidated Group Inc (G-5253)*

Coca-Cola, Ocean Springs *Also called Ccbcc Operations LLC (G-3748)*

Coca-Cola, Hattiesburg *Also called Vendworks LLC (G-2080)*

Coca-Cola, Hattiesburg *Also called Ccbcc Operations LLC (G-1941)*

Coca-Cola, McComb *Also called Vendworks LLC (G-3272)*

Coca-Cola, Southaven *Also called Clark Beverage Group Inc (G-4859)*

Coca-Cola, Cleveland *Also called Clark Beverage Group Inc (G-789)*

Coca-Cola Bottling Co Untd Inc 228 864-1122
3701 25th Ave Gulfport (39501) *(G-1761)*

Coca-Cola Bottling Co Untd Inc 601 684-8223
310 W Presley Blvd McComb (39648) *(G-3246)*

Coca-Cola Bottling Co Untd Inc 601 264-8600
201 Coca Cola Ave Hattiesburg (39402) *(G-1948)*

Coca-Cola Refreshments USA Inc 601 442-1641
191 Devereaux Dr Natchez (39120) *(G-3548)*

Cold Mix Inc (PA) 662 256-4529
32807 Highway 45 N Nettleton (38858) *(G-3658)*

Cole Tempra Helmet & Vest LLC 601 317-3842
707 Barwood Ct Jackson (39212) *(G-2361)*

Coleman Builders Inc 662 234-0376
14 County Road 466 Oxford (38655) *(G-3947)*

Coleman Lumber, Caledonia *Also called Thomas Leslie Coleman (G-632)*

Coles Tool Works Inc 662 429-5191
3414 Highway 51 S Hernando (38632) *(G-2125)*

College Station Spt Stores Inc 662 349-8988
6519 Towne Center Xing Southaven (38671) *(G-4860)*

Collins Filter Co Inc 228 896-0582
10185 Southpark Dr Gulfport (39503) *(G-1762)*

Collins Woodworks 228 452-2627
6328 Menge Ave Pass Christian (39571) *(G-4080)*

Collums Furniture Inc 662 568-7912
120 East St Houlka (38850) *(G-2221)*

Colon Cabinets and Trim 662 347-8608
2476 Hummingbird Dr Greenville (38701) *(G-1539)*

Color-Box LLC 601 854-6020
108 Industrial Dr Pelahatchie (39145) *(G-4162)*

Colquitt Woodworks LLC 229 425-6087
8935 Hanalei Cir Diamondhead (39525) *(G-1187)*

Columbia Block & Brick Co Inc 601 450-3791
6686 U S Highway 98 Hattiesburg (39402) *(G-1949)*

Columbia Computers Inc 601 736-2204
1574 Highway 98 E Columbia (39429) *(G-888)*

Columbia Diesel Castings, Columbia *Also called TWI Inc (G-927)*

Columbia Machine LLC 601 441-7755
118a S High School Ave Columbia (39429) *(G-889)*

Columbia Progress, Columbia *Also called Marion Publishing Co Inc (G-905)*

Columbia Welding & Cnstr 601 736-4332
1278 Highway 98 Byp Columbia (39429) *(G-890)*

Columbus Brick Company 662 328-4931
114 Brickyard Rd Columbus (39701) *(G-949)*

Columbus Engine & Crank Shaft 662 356-0068
700 Cal Kolola Rd Caledonia (39740) *(G-627)*

Columbus Lumber Company LLC 601 833-1990
810 Wl Behan Rd Brookhaven (39601) *(G-488)*

Columbus Machine & Wldg Works, Columbus *Also called Columbus Mch & Wldg Works Inc (G-951)*

Columbus Marble Works Inc (PA) 662 328-1477
2415 Highway 45 N Columbus (39705) *(G-950)*

Columbus Mch & Wldg Works Inc 662 328-8473
807 Moss St Columbus (39701) *(G-951)*

Columbus Recycling, Columbus *Also called Columbus Scrap Material Co (G-953)*

Columbus Recycling Corporation, Meridian *Also called Southern Scrap Meridian LLC (G-3403)*

Columbus Roll Shop 662 798-4149
1945 Airport Rd Columbus (39701) *(G-952)*

Columbus Scrap Material Co (HQ) 662 328-8176
973 Island Rd Columbus (39701) *(G-953)*

Columbus Speedway 662 327-3047
2616 Tabernacle Rd Columbus (39702) *(G-954)*

Comet Street Inc 601 981-4151
5170 Galaxie Dr Jackson (39206) *(G-2362)*

Comfort Designs Inc 601 932-7555
1732 Old Whitfield Rd Pearl (39208) *(G-4111)*

Comfort Revolution LLC 662 454-7526
9 Industrial Rd Belmont (38827) *(G-197)*

Commercial Coils, Grenada *Also called Modine Grenada LLC (G-1694)*

Commercial Construction Co Inc 601 649-5300
1939 N Mississippi Ave Laurel (39440) *(G-2756)*

Commercial Dispatch, Columbus *Also called Imes Communications of El Paso (G-986)*

Commercial Dispatch Pubg Inc 662 328-2424
516 Main St Columbus (39701) *(G-955)*

Commercial Drapery Svcs LLC 662 893-1510
8450 W Sandidge Rd Olive Branch (38654) *(G-3824)*

Commercial Metals Company 601 796-5474
18 Lavelle Ladner Rd Lumberton (39455) *(G-3026)*

Commercial Mllwk Spcialist Inc 228 868-3888
1518 B 28th St Gulfport (39501) *(G-1763)*

Commonwealth Publishing Inc 662 453-5312
329 Highway 82 W Greenwood (38930) *(G-1618)*

Community Broadcasting 731 441-6962
1100 S Second St Booneville (38829) *(G-325)*

Community Construction Co LLC 601 894-5239
1045 Hzlhurst Indus Pk Dr Hazlehurst (39083) *(G-2092)*

Companion Vans Inc (PA) 662 289-7711
711 E Jefferson St Kosciusko (39090) *(G-2691)*

Competition Cams Inc 662 224-8972
8649 Hacks Cross Rd Olive Branch (38654) *(G-3825)*

Competition Cams Inc 662 890-9825
8649 Hacks Cross Rd Olive Branch (38654) *(G-3826)*

ALPHABETIC SECTION

Cotton Tops

Competitive Printing 228 863-4001
2400 24th St Gulfport (39501) *(G-1764)*

Complete Cnc Machine Repair 601 604-2063
2440 N Hills St Ste 105 Meridian (39305) *(G-3322)*

Complete Computers, Batesville Also called T G Ferguson Company *(G-127)*

Complete Welding Solutions 601 791-5370
103 Jodie Baxter Rd Lucedale (39452) *(G-2989)*

Composing Room Inc 662 393-6652
8098 Chesterfield Dr Southaven (38671) *(G-4861)*

Composite Fbrication Group LLC 601 549-1789
26 Dean Anderson Rd Moselle (39459) *(G-3456)*

Compressed Air Tech Inc 662 890-9782
7187 Old Craft Cv Olive Branch (38654) *(G-3827)*

Computer Consultant 228 818-4486
3604 Portree Pl Ocean Springs (39564) *(G-3750)*

Computer Graphics By Connie 662 343-8399
40200 Holloway Rd Hamilton (39746) *(G-1904)*

Computer Systems, Starkville Also called Sevlo Solutions LLC *(G-4970)*

Computer Works LLC 228 696-8889
4006 Kreole Ave B Moss Point (39563) *(G-3475)*

Con Air 662 280-6499
711 Venture Dr Southaven (38672) *(G-4862)*

Conair Corporation 662 280-6499
711 Venture Dr Southaven (38672) *(G-4863)*

Conaway Logging Inc 662 287-8830
1101 Cardinal Dr Corinth (38834) *(G-1072)*

Conceptual Designs Inc 601 923-9922
4205 W Northside Dr Jackson (39209) *(G-2363)*

Confederate Express LLC 662 315-6625
40028 Hamilton Rd Hamilton (39746) *(G-1905)*

Conflux Software LLC 601 940-0182
338 Wildwood Blvd Jackson (39212) *(G-2364)*

Confortaire Inc 662 842-2966
2133 S Veterans Mem Blvd Tupelo (38804) *(G-5121)*

Conklin Metal Industries Inc 601 933-0402
2900 Benton H Green Blvd Richland (39218) *(G-4510)*

Connect Software Development, Jackson Also called Connect Technology LLC *(G-2365)*

Connect Technology LLC 601 914-1713
18 Northtown Dr Ste C Jackson (39211) *(G-2365)*

Connection Laboratories Inc 662 429-1097
1068 Thousand Oaks Dr Hernando (38632) *(G-2126)*

Connie S Kitchen 662 686-2255
112 Mimosa Dr Leland (38756) *(G-2886)*

Consoldted Converting Svcs Inc 601 545-1699
5372 Old Highway 42 Hattiesburg (39401) *(G-1950)*

Consoldted Ctfish Cmpanies LLC (PA) 662 962-3101
299 South St Isola (38754) *(G-2277)*

Consoldted Ctfish Prducers LLC 662 962-3101
299 South St Isola (38754) *(G-2278)*

Consolidated Gulf Services LLC 601 446-5992
1117 Main St Natchez (39120) *(G-3549)*

Consolidated Inc 601 425-2196
1195 Trace Rd Laurel (39443) *(G-2757)*

Consolidated Pipe & Sup Co Inc 228 769-1920
4220 Industrial Rd Pascagoula (39581) *(G-4028)*

Consolidated Pipe Supply 228 396-8818
9337 W Oaklawn Rd Biloxi (39532) *(G-233)*

Construction Metals Co Inc 601 939-2566
2110 Highway 80 E Ste C Jackson (39208) *(G-2643)*

Construction Waste Management 662 513-7999
17 County Road 4018 Oxford (38655) *(G-3948)*

Consumer Products America LLC 601 613-8583
119 W Mayes St Jackson (39213) *(G-2366)*

Contech Engnered Solutions LLC 601 894-2041
2590 Old Leland Rd Greenville (38703) *(G-1540)*

Contech Engnered Solutions LLC 662 332-2625
2590 Old Leland Rd Greenville (38703) *(G-1541)*

Continental Interiors Inc 662 382-3061
219 Terry Ave Crenshaw (38621) *(G-1133)*

Continue Care Hlth Modem Line 662 827-7107
207 East Ave N Hollandale (38748) *(G-2163)*

Contract Fabricators Inc 662 424-0061
27 County Road 480 Iuka (38852) *(G-2287)*

Contract Fabricators Inc (PA) 662 252-6330
105 Rolfing Rd Holly Springs (38635) *(G-2175)*

Control Products Inc 662 890-7920
11222 Green Valley Dr Olive Branch (38654) *(G-3828)*

Control Systems Inc 601 355-8594
909 Quinn St Jackson (39202) *(G-2367)*

Conveyor Tech 901 831-4760
1350 Old Highway 61 Lyon (38645) *(G-3042)*

Conviction Game Calls 662 295-9972
582 Windy Ridge Rd West Point (39773) *(G-5541)*

Conway Investments Inc 601 964-3215
Hwy 98 New Augusta (39462) *(G-3710)*

Conway Pole & Piling Company, New Augusta Also called Conway Investments Inc *(G-3710)*

Cook Eye Center 601 553-2100
2024 15th St Ste 5d Meridian (39301) *(G-3323)*

Cook Lawn & Tractor LLC 601 445-0718
114 Northgate Rd Natchez (39120) *(G-3550)*

Cook Portable Warehouses, Grenada Also called Cook Sales Inc *(G-1672)*

Cook Sales Inc 662 229-9787
1291 Air Industrial Pk Rd Grenada (38901) *(G-1672)*

Cook Timber Co Inc 601 727-4782
20 Lake Eddins 1638 Pachuta (39347) *(G-4012)*

Cookbook Marketplace, Oxford Also called Mary Margaret Andrews *(G-3971)*

Cookie Place Inc 601 957-2891
1200 E County Line Rd # 111 Ridgeland (39157) *(G-4565)*

Cool Baby Water LLC 850 748-0921
124 Easy St Lucedale (39452) *(G-2990)*

Coon Creek Custom Game Calls 662 284-6932
142 County Road 546 Corinth (38834) *(G-1073)*

Cooper Lighting LLC 601 638-1522
5035 Highway 61 S Vicksburg (39180) *(G-5357)*

Cooper Lighting LLC 662 342-3100
100 Airport Industrial Dr Southaven (38671) *(G-4864)*

Cooper Mar & Timberlands Corp 662 454-9274
183 County Road 1 Dennis (38838) *(G-1181)*

Cooper Tire & Rubber Company 662 624-4366
2205 Mrtin Luther King Dr Clarksdale (38614) *(G-763)*

Cooperation Jackson LLC 601 355-7224
939 W Capitol St Jackson (39203) *(G-2368)*

Coopers Intl Screen Supply LLC 601 353-2488
1404 Whiting Rd Jackson (39209) *(G-2369)*

Coopwood Communications Inc 662 843-2700
150 N Sharpe Ave Cleveland (38732) *(G-790)*

Copharma Inc 662 594-1594
127 Pratt Dr Corinth (38834) *(G-1074)*

Copiah County Courier Inc 601 894-3141
103 S Ragsdale Ave Hazlehurst (39083) *(G-2093)*

Copiah Lumber Company 601 892-2241
25026 Highway 51 Crystal Springs (39059) *(G-1140)*

Copper Sculptures Inc 601 992-9955
5230 Highway 25 Flowood (39232) *(G-1352)*

Copy Cats Printing Inc 601 582-3019
905 Hardy St Ste 102 Hattiesburg (39401) *(G-1951)*

Copy Write Printing Inc 601 736-2679
708 1/2 Main St Columbia (39429) *(G-891)*

Corcoran Legal Group 601 906-8227
13 Northtown Dr Ste 100 Jackson (39211) *(G-2370)*

Core Solutions LLC 228 216-6848
651b 35th St Gulfport (39501) *(G-1765)*

Corinth Acquisition Corp 662 287-1476
504 Pinecrest Rd Corinth (38834) *(G-1075)*

Corinth Brick Company Inc 662 287-2442
104 Allen St Corinth (38834) *(G-1076)*

Corinth Cc-Cola Btlg Works Inc (PA) 662 287-1433
601 Washington St Corinth (38834) *(G-1077)*

Corinth Cc-Cola Btlg Works Inc 662 286-2052
211 Foote St Corinth (38834) *(G-1078)*

Corinth Cc-Cola Btlg Works Inc 662 842-1753
1 Hadley St Tupelo (38801) *(G-5122)*

Corinth Manufacturing Marble, Corinth Also called Smith Cabinet Shop Inc *(G-1119)*

Corinth Tube Plant, Corinth Also called Caraustar Industrial and Con *(G-1064)*

Corinthian Inc (PA) 662 287-7835
41 Henson Rd Corinth (38834) *(G-1079)*

Corinthian Daily , The, Corinth Also called Paxton Media Group LLC *(G-1108)*

Cornwell Well Service Inc 601 684-4951
1004 Magee Rd Summit (39666) *(G-5009)*

Corporate Housing 601 853-8982
761 Rice Rd Ridgeland (39157) *(G-4566)*

Corporate Housing Experts, Jackson Also called Guides Publishing Inc *(G-2435)*

Correro Woodworks 662 334-9837
2267 Highway 1 N Greenville (38703) *(G-1542)*

Correy Elder 769 257-3240
104 Mulberry Way Madison (39110) *(G-3089)*

Corrugated Services America 601 209-6297
1440 Sweetwater Dr Pearl (39208) *(G-4112)*

Cortez Byrd Chips Inc 601 835-0333
149 Auburn Dr Sw Bogue Chitto (39629) *(G-301)*

Cosco Authorized Xerox Dealer 601 568-5006
423 Center Ave N Philadelphia (39350) *(G-4212)*

Cosentino Enterprises Inc 228 392-6666
3615 Sangani Blvd Diberville (39540) *(G-1201)*

Cothran Machine Shop 662 449-5983
1891 Slocum Rd Hernando (38632) *(G-2127)*

Cottage Garden Ms LLC 662 665-1918
997 Highway 72 E Corinth (38834) *(G-1080)*

Cottens Welding Shop 662 647-2503
1024 S Creek Rd Charleston (38921) *(G-735)*

Cotton Breeding Research Stn, Leland Also called Bayer Cropscience LP *(G-2885)*

Cotton Capitol LLC 601 498-4770
100 Ostrover Dr Tylertown (39667) *(G-5269)*

Cotton Patch Framery 662 895-6605
9086 Pigeon Roost Rd # 106 Olive Branch (38654) *(G-3829)*

Cotton Tops 662 287-4737
311 Highway 72 W Corinth (38834) *(G-1081)*

(PA)=Parent Co (HQ)=Headquarters (DH)=Div Headquarters

2019 Harris Directory of
Mississippi Manufacturers

275

Cotton's Cafe Dog Treat Bakery, Oxford Also called Cottons Cafe LLC *(G-3949)*

Cottonport Hardwoods LLC 601 442-9888
209 State St Natchez (39120) *(G-3551)*

Cottons Cafe LLC 662 380-1463
850 Insight Park Ave Oxford (38655) *(G-3949)*

Cottonseed Co-Op Corporation 662 358-4481
100 Mill St Jonestown (38639) *(G-2675)*

Counter Connections Inc 662 342-5111
2085 First Coml Dr S Southaven (38671) *(G-4865)*

Country Farms Quail 601 947-4263
4284 Dickerson Sawmill Rd Lucedale (39452) *(G-2991)*

Country Kids Publishing LLC 662 509-0427
729 Maffett Rd Pontotoc (38863) *(G-4326)*

Country Kitchen of Amory 662 257-4055
60395 Cotton Gin Port Rd Amory (38821) *(G-39)*

Country Printer Inc 601 849-3637
207 Main Ave N Magee (39111) *(G-3175)*

Country Select Catfish, Isola Also called Consoldted Ctfish Cmpanies LLC *(G-2277)*

Country Select Catfish, Isola Also called Consoldted Ctfish Prducers LLC *(G-2278)*

Country Squire 601 362-2233
1855 Lakeland Dr Ste B10 Jackson (39216) *(G-2371)*

County of Hancock 228 467-2100
854 Highway 90 Ste A Bay St Louis (39520) *(G-177)*

Courtyard Mfg Jewelers 601 825-6162
210 Woodgate Dr S Ste B Brandon (39042) *(G-382)*

Covidien LP 815 744-3766
6750 Legacy Dr 101 Olive Branch (38654) *(G-3830)*

Cox Hardware LLC 713 923-9458
47 Deer Haven Dr Madison (39110) *(G-3090)*

Cox Mhp Inc 601 732-6600
2348 Highway 80 Morton (39117) *(G-3446)*

Cox Mhp Inc (PA) 601 936-3949
4400 Mangum Dr Bldg D Flowood (39232) *(G-1353)*

Cox Works 228 236-8402
19202 Frontier Rd Saucier (39574) *(G-4750)*

Cozzytymzz Candles LLC 662 471-1607
1119 Bratton Rd Apt 1112 New Albany (38652) *(G-3677)*

Cpp LLC 601 749-7140
1900 Rocha St Picayune (39466) *(G-4262)*

Cr Custom Woodworks 601 624-2310
304 Creek Ct Pearl (39208) *(G-4113)*

Crabtree Manufacturing Inc 662 746-3041
970 S Industrial Pkwy Yazoo City (39194) *(G-5629)*

Craft Exploration Company LLC 601 859-0077
325 Lakeshire Pkwy Canton (39046) *(G-655)*

Craft Operating Company Ix LLC 601 427-9009
325 Lakeshire Pkwy Canton (39046) *(G-656)*

Crafts By Fenton 601 477-9164
743 Moselle Oak Grove Rd Ellisville (39437) *(G-1250)*

Crager Welding 601 687-0019
1480 Coyt Rd Waynesboro (39367) *(G-5496)*

Craig Wilkes Design 917 664-7255
2910 Highland Ave Meridian (39307) *(G-3324)*

Crane Cams Inc 386 310-4875
8649 Hacks Cross Rd Olive Branch (38654) *(G-3831)*

Crane Rentals, Vancleave Also called Glenn Machine Works Inc *(G-5319)*

Creations By Stephanie 228 697-2899
152 Claiborne St Biloxi (39530) *(G-234)*

Creative Cakes & Supplies Inc 662 844-3080
1422 E Main St Tupelo (38804) *(G-5123)*

Creative Designs & Sports 662 327-5000
2405 Highway 45 N Columbus (39705) *(G-956)*

Creative Hands Printing Svcs 601 631-1262
3895 Highway 80 Vicksburg (39180) *(G-5358)*

Creative Iron 601 845-6290
823 Poplar Springs Rd Florence (39073) *(G-1316)*

Creative Iron Works Ms LLC 985 960-2386
23050 Felix Rd N Picayune (39466) *(G-4263)*

Creative Machining Inc 601 630-5536
508 Goodrum Rd Vicksburg (39180) *(G-5359)*

Creative Marine Products, Natchez Also called South Central Group Inc *(G-3623)*

Creative Signs, Vicksburg Also called Roger Fillebaum *(G-5414)*

Creative Ventures LLC 601 798-7758
49 Werner Rd Bldg A Picayune (39466) *(G-4264)*

Crechles Three Generations LLC 601 213-8162
1370 W Government St Brandon (39042) *(G-383)*

Creekside Envmtl Pdts LLC 662 617-5553
1 Southern Cross Way Starkville (39759) *(G-4936)*

Crest Audio, Meridian Also called Peavey Electronics Corporation *(G-3385)*

Crews International Cons, Water Valley Also called CIC International LLC *(G-5465)*

Crimm Bros Log Ltd Lblty Co 662 552-0122
49 Crimm Rd Mathiston (39752) *(G-3228)*

Crimm Logging LLC 662 552-8511
11646 Ms Highway 15 Mantee (39751) *(G-3211)*

Crisco Swabbing Service Inc 601 731-9008
5 Stanley Barnes Ln Columbia (39429) *(G-892)*

Croft LLC (PA) 601 684-6121
107 Oliver Emmerich Dr McComb (39648) *(G-3247)*

Crooked Letter Publishing LLC 228 334-4575
14055 Seaway Rd 200 Gulfport (39503) *(G-1766)*

Crosby Surveying, Biloxi Also called Clifford A Crosby *(G-230)*

Crosby Wood Preserving Co Inc 601 264-5249
3702 Hardy St Ste 2 Hattiesburg (39402) *(G-1952)*

Crosbys Creek Oil & Gas LLC 601 898-0051
605 Northpark Dr Ste A Ridgeland (39157) *(G-4567)*

Crossroads Furniture Inc 662 627-2114
819 Desoto Ave Clarksdale (38614) *(G-764)*

Crossroads Picks LLC 662 902-1026
13633 New Africa Rd Clarksdale (38614) *(G-765)*

Crosstec, Philadelphia Also called Nhc Distributors Inc *(G-4229)*

Crown Cork & Seal Usa Inc 662 563-7664
195 Crown Dr Batesville (38606) *(G-102)*

Crown Simple Renovations Wdwkg 601 850-8272
150 Highway 469 N Apt G54 Florence (39073) *(G-1317)*

Crown Simple Renovations Wdwkg 601 850-8272
150 Highway 469 N Florence (39073) *(G-1318)*

Crtney G Aldridge Ptro Glogist 601 446-5585
316 Main St Natchez (39120) *(G-3552)*

Cruise Street Press LLC 601 720-4848
277 Rocky Hill Rd Pickens (39146) *(G-4306)*

Crux Industries 662 873-3317
29 Nitta Yuma St Anguilla (38721) *(G-58)*

Cryovac Inc 662 226-8804
1621 Air Industrial Pk Rd Grenada (38901) *(G-1673)*

Crystal Crown Inc 601 947-8074
183 Webb Davis Rd Lucedale (39452) *(G-2992)*

Crystal Springs Apparel LLC (PA) 601 856-8831
216 Bellewether Pass Ridgeland (39157) *(G-4568)*

Csa Logistics LLC 601 264-2455
54 Pirate Dr Hattiesburg (39402) *(G-1953)*

CST Timber Company 601 225-7887
3451a Ms Hwy 24 Gloster (39638) *(G-1513)*

CTA Products Group LLC 662 536-1446
1899 Kings Castle Dr Southaven (38671) *(G-4866)*

Cube Ice Co 662 563-8411
101 Court St Batesville (38606) *(G-103)*

Cuevas Machine Co Inc 228 255-1384
5548 Highway 53 Poplarville (39470) *(G-4380)*

Cuff Toughener 601 209-1609
327 Arlington Cir Ridgeland (39157) *(G-4569)*

Culp Inc 662 844-7144
2307 W Main St Ste C Tupelo (38801) *(G-5124)*

Culp of Mississippi, Tupelo Also called Culp Inc *(G-5124)*

Cumulus Fibres - Pontotoc, Pontotoc Also called Fibrix LLC *(G-4331)*

Cumulus Fibres - Verona, Tupelo Also called Fibrix LLC *(G-5132)*

Cupitsignscom LLC 228 712-2322
1914 Denny Ave Pascagoula (39567) *(G-4029)*

Curahe LLC 662 325-2176
1305 Nottingham Rd Starkville (39759) *(G-4937)*

Curbell Plastics Inc 888 477-8173
112 Brooks Dr Brandon (39042) *(G-384)*

Curtis Wilson Logging 601 943-6808
83 Sam Graham Rd Prentiss (39474) *(G-4415)*

Cushions To Go LLC 662 488-0350
370 Henry Southern Dr Pontotoc (38863) *(G-4327)*

Cust-Alum Marine, Waveland Also called Vertechs Design Solutions LLC *(G-5486)*

Custodis MGT Systems LLC 601 207-1047
4905b Poplar Springs Dr Meridian (39305) *(G-3325)*

Custom Accounting Solutions 601 957-7500
23 Moss Forest Cir Jackson (39211) *(G-2372)*

Custom Architectural Millwork 662 562-7011
2016 Egypt Creek Rd Sarah (38665) *(G-4733)*

Custom BLT Gooseneck Trailers, Seminary Also called Timothy Trigg *(G-4784)*

Custom Cams Inc 662 534-4881
1143 County Road 50 New Albany (38652) *(G-3678)*

Custom Creations 601 450-7600
11 Huckleberry Dr Hattiesburg (39402) *(G-1954)*

Custom Engineered Wheels Inc 662 841-0756
309 Rbert M Cggins Jr Dr Baldwyn (38824) *(G-74)*

Custom Engineered Wheels Inc (PA) 574 267-4005
309 Rbert M Coggins Jr Dr Baldwyn (38824) *(G-75)*

Custom Frame & Gift, Meridian Also called Burtoni Fine Art Inc *(G-3314)*

Custom Metal Fabrication Inc 662 628-8657
213 E Gore Ave Calhoun City (38916) *(G-637)*

Custom Nonwoven Inc 662 539-6103
1015 Munsford Dr New Albany (38652) *(G-3679)*

Custom Pack Inc 228 435-3632
211 Caillavet St Biloxi (39530) *(G-235)*

Custom Pallett Inc 662 423-8127
421 Highway 365 Tishomingo (38873) *(G-5084)*

Custom Precast Products Inc 601 796-8531
68 Industrial Parkway Rd Lumberton (39455) *(G-3027)*

Custom Printing 662 227-9511
1011 Lakeview Dr Grenada (38901) *(G-1674)*

Custom Prosthetic & Orthotic 601 708-4196
801 E Northside Dr Ste D Clinton (39056) *(G-819)*

ALPHABETIC SECTION

Custom Rough Cut Lumber 601 270-9518
146 Lott Town Rd Hattiesburg (39402) *(G-1955)*

Custom Sign Co of Batesville (PA) 662 563-7371
480 Highway 51 S Batesville (38606) *(G-104)*

Custom Sign Co of Batesville 662 844-6333
1219 Nelle St Tupelo (38801) *(G-5125)*

Custom Signs and Banners 662 327-8916
240 Thomas Cir Columbus (39705) *(G-957)*

Custom Sportswear USA Inc 228 255-4795
6610 Alakoko Ct Diamondhead (39525) *(G-1188)*

Custom-Bilt Portable Bldgs, Florence *Also called Custom-Bilt Portable Buildings (G-1319)*

Custom-Bilt Portable Buildings 601 932-2808
2031 Highway 49 S Florence (39073) *(G-1319)*

Customized Stained Glass 601 583-4720
131 J C Bryant Rd Hattiesburg (39401) *(G-1956)*

Cutshall D L & Sons Logging Co 662 423-6965
79 County Road 299 Iuka (38852) *(G-2288)*

Cv Sunglasses LLC 662 212-0993
21418 Highway 72 Walnut (38683) *(G-5456)*

CWC Computers & Cstm Databases, Lexington *Also called Claude W Carnathan (G-2899)*

Cwg Welding 228 539-4121
19487 Wallace Way Saucier (39574) *(G-4751)*

Cwi, Horn Lake *Also called Grace Company of Ms Inc (G-2200)*

Cws Grain Systems Inc 662 332-5822
3746 Highway 1 S Greenville (38701) *(G-1543)*

Cynthia Bowen 228 463-7131
302 Sandy St Waveland (39576) *(G-5479)*

Cypress Pharmaceutical Inc 800 856-4393
135 Industrial Dr N Madison (39110) *(G-3091)*

Cyrus Resources LLC 228 669-6955
13508 John Clark Rd Gulfport (39503) *(G-1767)*

Cytec Software Systems Inc (PA) 601 362-1612
736 S President St Jackson (39201) *(G-2373)*

Czeiszperger Distiller LLC 662 612-6160
104 Cherrydale Loop Coldwater (38618) *(G-844)*

D & C Logging Inc 662 862-9316
3480 Van Buren Rd Nettleton (38858) *(G-3659)*

D & D Oilfield Consultants Inc 601 648-2282
57 Gaines Hinton Rd State Line (39362) *(G-4985)*

D & D Signs and Labels 662 449-4956
1418 Dogwood Hollow Dr Nesbit (38651) *(G-3649)*

D & G Enterprises 662 895-4471
4400 Bonner Dr Olive Branch (38654) *(G-3832)*

D & R Industrial Services LLC 601 716-3140
738 Hickman St Wiggins (39577) *(G-5578)*

D & T Motors Inc (PA) 662 773-5021
55 N Columbus Ave Louisville (39339) *(G-2965)*

D & T Motors Inc 662 773-9041
53 Mill St Louisville (39339) *(G-2966)*

D & T Services, Louisville *Also called D & T Motors Inc (G-2965)*

D & T Services, Louisville *Also called D & T Motors Inc (G-2966)*

D A Biglane Oil Co, Natchez *Also called James Biglane (G-3571)*

D D Berryhill Signs 662 298-3325
516 Whitfield Dr Hernando (38632) *(G-2128)*

D D Rushing 601 656-8842
17960 Road 339 Philadelphia (39350) *(G-4213)*

D Dodd John Od (PA) 662 286-5671
609 N Fillmore St Corinth (38834) *(G-1082)*

D Graphics Advertising 601 373-4667
1770 Waycona Dr Jackson (39204) *(G-2374)*

D J S Embroidery LLC 662 547-9000
3248 Highway 407 Mc Cool (39108) *(G-3235)*

D M A, Houston *Also called Dixieland Furniture Mfg Co Inc (G-2236)*

D M Yount Gravel 662 292-1040
780 Woolfolk Rd Senatobia (38668) *(G-4791)*

D&H Construction Cabinetry Inc 601 737-2010
8589 A C Brown Rd Meridian (39305) *(G-3326)*

D&J Twine Co. 662 726-2594
1907 Paulette Rd Macon (39341) *(G-3056)*

Dahls Automotive Parts Inc 228 875-8154
2904a Bienville Blvd Ocean Springs (39564) *(G-3751)*

Daily & Sons Construction Inc 601 737-5847
4580 Parker Ln Bailey (39320) *(G-67)*

Daily Leader, Brookhaven *Also called Southwest Publishers Inc (G-538)*

Daily Sentinel Star, Grenada *Also called Grenada Newspaper Inc (G-1681)*

Daily Times Leader, West Point *Also called Horizon Publications Inc (G-5546)*

Dairy Fresh, Columbus *Also called Borden Dairy Company Ala LLC (G-941)*

Dairy Kream 662 256-7562
600 Main St N Amory (38821) *(G-40)*

Dairy Kream Restaurant, Amory *Also called Dairy Kream (G-40)*

Dak Americas LLC 228 533-4480
3303 Port And Harbor Dr Bay St Louis (39520) *(G-178)*

Dak Americas Mississippi Inc (HQ) 228 533-4000
3303 Port And Harbor Dr Bay Saint Louis (39520) *(G-142)*

Dale Dickerson Logging, Louisville *Also called Delbert T Dickerson (G-2967)*

Dale Fulton 662 327-4800
100 23rd St S Columbus (39701) *(G-958)*

Dallas Printing Inc 601 968-9354
315 Carrier Blvd Richland (39218) *(G-4511)*

Dan W Butler Signs 601 948-5059
825 College St Jackson (39202) *(G-2375)*

Daniel Petre 662 726-2462
19 Deerbrook Rd Macon (39341) *(G-3057)*

Daniels Farms, Tunica *Also called Delta Agricultural MGT Inc (G-5096)*

Daniels Lawn and Lanscape LLC 601 965-6982
210 Dawson St Clinton (39056) *(G-820)*

Danny Berry 601 276-6200
1178 Old Brookhaven Rd Summit (39666) *(G-5010)*

Danny Byrd LLC 601 649-2524
1416 Sndrsville Sharon Rd Laurel (39443) *(G-2758)*

Danny Pat Martin 601 267-3342
4568 Ebenezer Rd Carthage (39051) *(G-714)*

Danny R Jansen 601 636-1070
4411 Highway 61 N Valley Park (39177) *(G-5316)*

Darling Ingredients Inc 601 372-5212
1299 Prisock Rd Jackson (39272) *(G-2376)*

Darling International, Jackson *Also called Darling Ingredients Inc (G-2376)*

Darrell Crum LLC 806 224-7337
136 Saint Charles Pl Madison (39110) *(G-3092)*

Darrells Custom Cabinets 662 822-3936
2221 Flannagan Rd Greenville (38701) *(G-1544)*

Darrells Screen Printing 601 653-6924
175 Highway 61 S Ste 8 Natchez (39120) *(G-3553)*

Dart Cont Co Miss Ltd Lblty Co 601 776-3555
197 Harris Ave Quitman (39355) *(G-4461)*

Data Medical Inc 662 283-0463
242 Eskridge Rd Duck Hill (38925) *(G-1220)*

Data Systems Management Inc (PA) 601 925-6270
1505 Clinton Business Par Clinton (39056) *(G-821)*

Dataware LLC 662 356-4978
19 Buck Egger Rd Caledonia (39740) *(G-628)*

Datco International Inc (PA) 248 593-9142
15 Datco Ind Dr Columbus (39702) *(G-959)*

Datco International Inc 662 327-3995
15 Datco Ind Dr Columbus (39702) *(G-960)*

Dave Strong Circuit Judge 601 684-3400
119 N Broadway St McComb (39648) *(G-3248)*

Daves Mobile Car Wash 601 940-6855
102 Hawks Nest Blf Ridgeland (39157) *(G-4570)*

David Breazeale Logging LLC 662 323-9991
6478 Us Highway 82 Starkville (39759) *(G-4938)*

David Buford 662 714-3031
576 County Road 121 Water Valley (38965) *(G-5466)*

David Drew Sullivan 601 656-3556
10050 Eastmore Ln Philadelphia (39350) *(G-4214)*

David Hollingsworth 769 233-7769
3900 Lakeland Dr Flowood (39232) *(G-1354)*

David K Brooks 601 981-5722
1717 Bellewood Rd Jackson (39211) *(G-2377)*

David Kirkman 662 418-5048
2433 Us Highway 82 Maben (39750) *(G-3044)*

David L Vance Logging Co 601 635-2105
2514 Erin Lucern Rd Decatur (39327) *(G-1172)*

David M Eaves 662 773-7056
5765 Yellow Creek Rd Macon (39341) *(G-3058)*

David Morehead 601 469-2272
428 N Woodland Dr Forest (39074) *(G-1413)*

Davids Satellite 662 416-4697
31 Griggs Rd Marietta (38856) *(G-3213)*

Davids Signs Inc 601 626-8934
11560 Swearington Rd Collinsville (39325) *(G-867)*

Davidson Marble & Gran Works (PA) 662 289-1337
318 Highway 12 E Kosciusko (39090) *(G-2692)*

DAvion LLC 601 724-5013
200 Jetport Rd Ste B Brandon (39047) *(G-385)*

Davis & Cooke Custom Cabinetry 601 580-0181
203 S Magnolia St Laurel (39440) *(G-2759)*

Davis & Son LLC 662 728-8396
Hwy 4 W Booneville (38829) *(G-326)*

Davis Cardboard, Pontotoc *Also called Davis Enterprises Inc (G-4328)*

Davis Custom Fabrication LLC 228 832-7456
10415 7th Ave Gulfport (39503) *(G-1768)*

Davis Enterprises Inc 662 488-9972
715 Q T Todd Dr Pontotoc (38863) *(G-4328)*

Davis Specialty Chemicals Inc 601 856-5774
220 Davis Dr Ridgeland (39157) *(G-4571)*

Davis Tool & Die Inc 662 234-4007
226 County Road 235 Abbeville (38601) *(G-2)*

Davis Welding 228 257-5231
20391 Jones Mill Rd Long Beach (39560) *(G-2935)*

Davis Welding Fabrication LLC 662 614-2531
26 Seaman Bullock Rd Columbia (39429) *(G-893)*

Davis Welding LLC 662 423-2911
537 County Road 956 Iuka (38852) *(G-2289)*

Davis Wldg & Fabrication LLC 601 258-0334
16 Muscio Rd Beaumont (39423) *(G-184)*

Davis Wood Products of Miss ALPHABETIC SECTION

Davis Wood Products of Miss 662 534-2211
102 Industrial Dr New Albany (38652) *(G-3680)*

Daviscomms (s) Pte Ltd 601 416-5043
120 Travis Rodgers Ln Ridgeland (39157) *(G-4572)*

Daviscomms USA, Ridgeland *Also called Daviscomms (s) Pte Ltd* *(G-4572)*

DBC Corporation 601 856-7454
228 Industrial Dr N Madison (39110) *(G-3093)*

DC Logging, Columbus *Also called DC Logging LLC* *(G-961)*

DC Logging LLC 662 251-4653
2102 Golding Rd Columbus (39702) *(G-961)*

De Beukelaer Cookie Company, Madison *Also called DBC Corporation* *(G-3093)*

De Lisle Plant, Pass Christian *Also called Chemours Company Fc LLC* *(G-4078)*

DEA Mississippi Inc 800 821-2302
5184 Pioneer Rd Meridian (39301) *(G-3327)*

Dealership Services LLC 662 269-3897
851 Mitchell Road Ext Tupelo (38801) *(G-5126)*

Deals Xpress Lube 662 281-4417
2211 University Ave Oxford (38655) *(G-3950)*

Dean Weeks Repair & Welding 601 833-2669
3146 Jckson Liberty Dr Nw Wesson (39191) *(G-5526)*

Dearlens Inc 601 693-1841
910 23rd Ave Ste A Meridian (39301) *(G-3328)*

Dearman Optical, Meridian *Also called Dearlens Inc* *(G-3328)*

Debbie F Shelton 601 535-7162
7126 Mcbride Rd Pattison (39144) *(G-4100)*

Debeukelaer Corporation 601 856-7454
228 Industrial Dr N Madison (39110) *(G-3094)*

Debra A Jones 601 845-8946
157 Mountain Creek Frm Rd Florence (39073) *(G-1320)*

Debra Thigpen 601 856-0019
538 Lake Pointe Ln Madison (39110) *(G-3095)*

Decibel Audio 601 649-1144
2514 Highway 15 N Laurel (39440) *(G-2760)*

Deep Blue Press LLC 228 604-4643
7 Old Oak Ln Gulfport (39503) *(G-1769)*

Deep S Mch Wrks Hydraulics LLC 601 989-2977
44430 Highway 63 N Richton (39476) *(G-4529)*

Deep S Suspension & ACC Inc 601 371-7373
303 Wilmington St Jackson (39204) *(G-2378)*

Deep South Fire Trucks Inc (PA) 601 722-4166
2342 Hwy 49 N Seminary (39479) *(G-4776)*

Deep South Physics Pllc 601 613-8076
111 Napoleon Dr Brandon (39047) *(G-386)*

Deep South Trailer Sales LLC 228 255-2026
6812 Awini St Diamondhead (39525) *(G-1189)*

Deepwell Energy Services LLC (PA) 800 477-2855
4025 Highway 35 N Columbia (39429) *(G-894)*

Deepwell Energy Services LLC 601 735-1393
134 Riverview Dr Richland (39218) *(G-4512)*

Deer Creek Pilot, Rolling Fork *Also called Deer Creek Publishing Company* *(G-4680)*

Deer Creek Publishing Company 662 873-4354
145 N First St Rolling Fork (39159) *(G-4680)*

Dees Welding Service LLC 601 372-9361
107 Stokes Robertson Rd Jackson (39212) *(G-2379)*

Deforest Wood Preserving Co 601 866-4655
1400 Industrial Dr Bolton (39041) *(G-308)*

Delbert T Dickerson 662 773-4747
534 White Rd Louisville (39339) *(G-2967)*

Delco Remy America 601 785-6690
214 Fellowship Rd Taylorsville (39168) *(G-5053)*

Della West Publishing LLC 601 618-8429
743 Lakeside Dr Vicksburg (39180) *(G-5360)*

Delta Agricultural MGT Inc 865 210-4605
21698 Highway 3 Tunica (38676) *(G-5096)*

Delta Auto Parts Inc 662 746-1143
647 Haley Barbour Pkwy Yazoo City (39194) *(G-5630)*

Delta Biofuels Inc 601 442-5330
151 L E Barry Rd Natchez (39120) *(G-3554)*

Delta Democrat Times, Greenville *Also called Delta-Democrat Pubg Co Inc* *(G-1551)*

Delta Directional Drilling LLC 601 683-0879
9027 Eastside Drive Ext Newton (39345) *(G-3719)*

Delta Discount Wine & Spirits, Vicksburg *Also called Bg3 Delta LLC* *(G-5344)*

Delta Dry LLC 203 515-1528
204 Magnolia St Hollandale (38748) *(G-2164)*

Delta Duck Hunts Inc 662 357-5152
4101 Dundee Rd Dundee (38626) *(G-1223)*

Delta Energy Group, Natchez *Also called Delta-Energy Group LLC* *(G-3555)*

Delta Enterprises (HQ) 662 335-5291
819 Main St Ste A Greenville (38701) *(G-1545)*

Delta Fabrication LLC 662 335-2500
1091b Little Theater Rd Greenville (38703) *(G-1546)*

Delta Fabricators 662 862-2998
2 Rodgers Rd Fulton (38843) *(G-1451)*

Delta Farm & Auto LLC 662 453-8340
1607 Highway 82 W Greenwood (38930) *(G-1619)*

Delta Foundation Inc (PA) 662 335-5291
819 Main St Ste A Greenville (38701) *(G-1547)*

Delta Furniture Mfg LLC 662 489-2128
292 Industrial Dr Pontotoc (38863) *(G-4329)*

Delta Grind Stone Ground Pdts 662 816-1254
111 Industrial Park Rd Water Valley (38965) *(G-5467)*

Delta Industries, Laurel *Also called Pine Belt Ready-Mix Con Inc* *(G-2820)*

Delta Industries Inc 601 634-6001
1730 Highway 80 Vicksburg (39180) *(G-5361)*

Delta Industries Inc 228 475-2419
8207 Old Stage Rd Moss Point (39562) *(G-3476)*

Delta Industries Inc 228 896-7400
10121 Southpark Dr Gulfport (39503) *(G-1770)*

Delta Industries Inc 601 783-6030
1012 Highway 48 E Lot 1 Magnolia (39652) *(G-3190)*

Delta Industries Inc 662 323-7224
311 Industrial Park Rd Starkville (39759) *(G-4939)*

Delta Industries Inc 228 539-9333
17478 Nobles Rd Saucier (39574) *(G-4752)*

Delta Industries Inc 601 849-2661
801 Industrial Park Dr Se Magee (39111) *(G-3176)*

Delta Industries Inc (PA) 601 354-3801
100 W Woodrow Wilson Ave Jackson (39213) *(G-2380)*

Delta Industries Inc 601 833-1166
1324 Highway 51 Ne Brookhaven (39601) *(G-489)*

Delta Industries Inc 601 948-4245
1006 Coor Springs Cv Crystal Springs (39059) *(G-1141)*

Delta Industries Inc 601 354-3801
100 W Woodrow Wilson Ave Jackson (39213) *(G-2381)*

Delta Industries Inc 662 746-6646
1011 S Industrial Pkwy Yazoo City (39194) *(G-5631)*

Delta Industries Inc 601 825-7531
501 E Mark Dr Brandon (39042) *(G-387)*

Delta Industries Inc 601 792-4286
1780 John Street Ext Prentiss (39474) *(G-4416)*

Delta Logging & Company Inc 662 746-2066
700 S Industrial Pkwy Yazoo City (39194) *(G-5632)*

Delta Machinery Inc 662 827-2572
223 Bailey Dr Hollandale (38748) *(G-2165)*

Delta Municipal Energy Group, Mound Bayou *Also called Delta Municipal Energy Inc (G-3509)*

Delta Municipal Energy Inc 800 217-1519
404 Holt St Mound Bayou (38762) *(G-3509)*

Delta Net & Twine Co Inc 662 332-0841
3148 Highway 1 S Greenville (38701) *(G-1548)*

Delta Oil Mill (PA) 662 358-4809
100 Mill St Jonestown (38639) *(G-2676)*

Delta Oil Mill 662 363-1121
1723 Main St Tunica (38676) *(G-5097)*

Delta Pallets and Crates I 662 781-1633
6590 Hickory Crest Dr Walls (38680) *(G-5449)*

Delta Petroleum Service Inc 662 487-1701
651 E Lee St Sardis (38666) *(G-4738)*

Delta Positions Inc 662 719-1194
631 Gaines Hwy Boyle (38730) *(G-349)*

Delta Press Publishing Co Inc 662 627-2201
128 E 2nd St Clarksdale (38614) *(G-766)*

Delta Protein Intl Inc 662 279-8728
200 Itta Bena Rd Sunflower (38778) *(G-5046)*

Delta Royalty Company Inc 601 982-0970
4450 Old Canton Rd # 203 Jackson (39211) *(G-2382)*

Delta Sign Shop 662 334-9878
1729 Highway 82 E Greenville (38703) *(G-1549)*

Delta Signs and Designs LLC 662 822-0830
2094 Highway 1 S Greenville (38701) *(G-1550)*

Delta Western, Indianola *Also called Indi-Bel Inc* *(G-2265)*

Delta-Democrat Pubg Co Inc 662 335-1155
988 N Broadway St Greenville (38701) *(G-1551)*

Delta-Energy Group LLC 601 348-4610
61 Carthage Point Rd Natchez (39120) *(G-3555)*

Dement Printing Company 601 693-2721
2002 6th St Meridian (39301) *(G-3329)*

Democrat 662 562-4414
219 E Main St Senatobia (38668) *(G-4792)*

Democrat , The, Senatobia *Also called Democrat* *(G-4792)*

Denbury Onshore LLC 601 787-3111
175 County Road 359 Heidelberg (39439) *(G-2115)*

Denbury Onshore LLC 601 276-2147
4047 Shell Oil Rd Ruth (39662) *(G-4700)*

Denbury Resources Inc 601 829-0398
235 Three Prong Rd Brandon (39047) *(G-388)*

Denbury Resources Inc 601 729-2266
80 County Road 7 Soso (39480) *(G-4846)*

Denbury Resources Inc 601 687-0089
50 Woodrow Reynolds Rd Shubuta (39360) *(G-4830)*

Denbury Resources Inc 601 835-0185
1151 California Rd Nw Brookhaven (39601) *(G-490)*

Denbury Resources Inc 972 673-2787
1919 Holly Bush Rd Pelahatchie (39145) *(G-4163)*

Denbury Resources Inc 601 276-2677
7969 Robert Jones Rd Summit (39666) *(G-5011)*

Denbury Resources Inc 601 823-4000
332 Rogers Ln Ne Brookhaven (39601) *(G-491)*

2019 Harris Directory of
Mississippi Manufacturers

(G-0000) Company's Geographic Section entry number

278

ALPHABETIC SECTION

Doorswap, Starkville

Denovo Labs LLC 615 587-3099
202 W Jackson St Ridgeland (39157) *(G-4573)*

Derksen Portable Buildings 601 528-5778
329 First St N Wiggins (39577) *(G-5579)*

Dern Mechanix 228 832-3933
13081 Canal Rd Gulfport (39503) *(G-1771)*

Desiccare Inc 601 932-0405
211 Industrial Dr Richland (39218) *(G-4513)*

Design Precast & Pipe Inc (PA) 228 831-5833
15215 Dedeaux Rd Gulfport (39503) *(G-1772)*

Design Print & Advertise By Pj 662 299-1148
260 Mason Rd Lexington (39095) *(G-2900)*

Design Tech Inc 601 798-5844
919 Rock Ranch Rd Carriere (39426) *(G-691)*

Designs of Times Inc 601 791-5299
11289 Old 63 S Lucedale (39452) *(G-2993)*

Desirepath Mississippi LLC 662 324-2231
1010 Lynn Ln Starkville (39759) *(G-4940)*

Desoto Concrete Products Inc 662 890-1688
220 Highway 305 N Olive Branch (38654) *(G-3833)*

Desoto Digital Services Llc 662 336-2233
7840 Allen Ridge Ln Olive Branch (38654) *(G-3834)*

Desoto Fur Trappers LLC 662 874-5605
5816 Brice Cv S Olive Branch (38654) *(G-3835)*

Desoto Sleep Diagnostics 662 349-9802
7600 Airways Blvd Ste G Southaven (38671) *(G-4867)*

Desoto Treated Materials Inc 601 928-3921
941 Magnolia Dr S Wiggins (39577) *(G-5580)*

Destinis Creations and Exquis 601 317-3764
523 Fox Run Trl Apt H8 Pearl (39208) *(G-4114)*

Destiny Apparel LLC 228 383-2665
1636 N Popps Ferry Rd # 110 Biloxi (39532) *(G-236)*

Developing Resources For Educa 601 933-9199
310 Airport Rd S Jackson (39208) *(G-2644)*

Developmental Industries Inc 662 287-6626
915 Highway 45 Corinth (38834) *(G-1083)*

Devon Energy Corporation 601 796-4243
4 Gulf Camp Cir Lumberton (39455) *(G-3028)*

Dewberry Sawmill, Maben Also called Ronnie Kolb *(G-3049)*

Dewmar International Bmc Inc (PA) 877 747-5326
132 E Northside Dr Ste C Clinton (39056) *(G-822)*

Dg Foods LLC 601 892-0333
1095 Industrial Dr Hazlehurst (39083) *(G-2094)*

DH Woodworks 662 299-5486
826 County Road 185 Greenwood (38930) *(G-1620)*

Diabetic Shoppe, Charleston Also called Southern Discount Drugs of Cha *(G-743)*

Diagnostic Instrmntn & Anlys L, Starkville Also called Mississippi State University *(G-4960)*

Diamond Land & Timber LLC 601 310-3395
51 Cambrooke Hattiesburg (39402) *(G-1957)*

Diamondhead Advertiser 228 263-4377
723 Faith St Waveland (39576) *(G-5480)*

Diamondhead Aerolease LLC 228 255-8491
898 Hapuna Pl Diamondhead (39525) *(G-1190)*

Dianne Gore 510 697-2569
248 Ridgewood Rd Jackson (39211) *(G-2383)*

DIAS LLC 662 628-1580
413 Highway 8 W Calhoun City (38916) *(G-638)*

Diaz Brothers Printing 601 247-0240
4323 Leisure Time Dr Diamondhead (39525) *(G-1191)*

Dier Logging Inc 601 384-5963
331 Cotten Rd Se Meadville (39653) *(G-3274)*

Digital Kanvas LLC 901 896-9690
9930 Goodman Rd Olive Branch (38654) *(G-3836)*

Dignity Garments LLC 601 941-4636
520 Silverstone Dr Madison (39110) *(G-3096)*

Dillard Machining Service 662 329-4682
1023 N Lehmberg Rd Columbus (39702) *(G-962)*

Dimensions Wood Works 228 254-6623
8504 Clamshell Ave Ocean Springs (39564) *(G-3752)*

Dims Group 302 562-2697
4091 Davis Rd Southaven (38671) *(G-4868)*

Diomedia Industries LLC 601 882-7724
5256 Clair St Jackson (39206) *(G-2384)*

Dipstix Lube 662 349-2810
3255 Goodman Rd E Southaven (38672) *(G-4869)*

Direct AG Source 901 246-1487
2720 Itasca Dr Nesbit (38651) *(G-3650)*

Discount Fireworks 601 765-4295
2542 Highway 49 Collins (39428) *(G-853)*

Dison Electrical Solutions LLC 228 234-7767
18311 Shaw Rd Saucier (39574) *(G-4753)*

Distributionnow, Laurel Also called Dnow LP *(G-2762)*

Dittos Print & Copy Shop 662 324-3838
602 Highway 12 E Starkville (39759) *(G-4941)*

Diversified Petroleum Inc (PA) 601 727-4926
741 County Road 313 Pachuta (39347) *(G-4013)*

Diversity Vuteq LLC 662 587-9633
1200 Magnolia Way Blue Springs (38828) *(G-295)*

Diversity-Vuteq LLC 662 534-9250
2300 Munsford Dr New Albany (38652) *(G-3681)*

Divine Creations 601 500-2764
3537 Jackye Ln Jackson (39213) *(G-2385)*

Dixie Dies Inc 601 845-6029
3261 Hopewell Rd Harrisville (39082) *(G-1911)*

Dixie Logging Inc 601 532-6583
3770 Veto Rd Ne Mc Call Creek (39647) *(G-3233)*

Dixie Mat LLC 601 876-2427
216 Herring Rd Sandy Hook (39478) *(G-4727)*

Dixie Mat and Hardwood Co (PA) 601 876-2427
2438 Highway 98 E Columbia (39429) *(G-895)*

Dixie Oilfield Services Inc 601 731-5541
16 Robbins Loop Columbia (39429) *(G-896)*

Dixie Oilfield Supply LLC 601 408-6027
20 Crumbly Dr Laurel (39443) *(G-2761)*

Dixie Packaging Inc 601 276-9317
1183 Dixie Springs Rd Summit (39666) *(G-5012)*

Dixie Precision Rifles LLC 601 706-9100
100 Brooks Dr Ste B Brandon (39042) *(G-389)*

Dixie Print 601 469-3350
1016 E Third St Forest (39074) *(G-1414)*

Dixie Pump & Machine Works 601 823-0510
984 Highway 84 E Brookhaven (39601) *(G-492)*

Dixie Services and Supply LLC 662 369-0907
51741 Highway 25 S Aberdeen (39730) *(G-11)*

Dixie Signs LLC 228 255-5548
9329 Edwin Ladner Rd Pass Christian (39571) *(G-4081)*

Dixie Specialties & Furn Inc 662 369-8557
525 Highway 145 N Aberdeen (39730) *(G-12)*

Dixie Welding 662 417-0938
337 Sawyer Rd Winona (38967) *(G-5597)*

Dixie Welding Service Inc 601 268-6949
608 R V Lindley Rd Moselle (39459) *(G-3457)*

Dixieland Furniture Mfg Co Inc 662 456-5378
233 County Road 94 Houston (38851) *(G-2236)*

Dixon Central, Carthage Also called Central Snacks Inc *(G-712)*

Dixon-Drone 662 545-9303
162 Park Cir Apt D Starkville (39759) *(G-4942)*

Dixons Hunting Lodge 662 571-1908
15284 Highway 433 S Benton (39039) *(G-208)*

Dkc Industries LLC 800 308-5187
460 Briarwood Dr Ste 400 Jackson (39206) *(G-2386)*

Dkh Distributing Inc 901 734-4528
385 Green T Rd W Hernando (38632) *(G-2129)*

Dla Document Services 662 434-7303
469 C St Rm 1 Columbus (39710) *(G-963)*

Dla Document Services 228 377-2612
708 Fisher St 102 Biloxi (39534) *(G-237)*

DLS Tax Consultants 601 473-6623
1408 Deer Park St Jackson (39203) *(G-2387)*

Dmi Pipe Fabrication LLC 225 272-1420
1495 Us Highway 61 S Woodville (39669) *(G-5616)*

Dnow LP 601 649-8671
2930 Industrial Blvd Laurel (39440) *(G-2762)*

Doctors Specialty Pharmacy LLC 228 806-1384
1720-A Med Pk Dr Ste 160 Biloxi (39532) *(G-238)*

Documart of Mid-South LLC 662 281-1474
1105 Jackson Ave W Oxford (38655) *(G-3951)*

Dodd, John D Dr, Corinth Also called D Dodd John Od *(G-1082)*

Dogman Industries LLC 662 832-3644
419 County Road 321 Oxford (38655) *(G-3952)*

Dogpound Printing LLC 662 323-7425
319 E Dr Martn L Kng Dr Martin Luther Kin Starkville (39759) *(G-4943)*

Dogwood Ceramic Supply Inc 228 831-4848
12590 Dedeaux Rd Gulfport (39503) *(G-1773)*

Dogwood Press 601 919-3656
1022 Wakefield Pl Brandon (39047) *(G-390)*

Dolls By Carol, Clinton Also called Carol Baird *(G-818)*

Dollys Stained Glass 662 887-3624
309 Highway 82 E Ste 29a Indianola (38751) *(G-2263)*

Domes International Inc (PA) 662 438-7186
5 Murphy St Tishomingo (38873) *(G-5085)*

Domtar Paper Company LLC 662 256-3526
9620 Old Macon Rd Columbus (39701) *(G-964)*

Donald E McCain 601 824-1275
33 Huntsman Cir Brandon (39042) *(G-391)*

Donald Gatlin Logging LLC 601 425-4320
77 Arley Williams Rd Heidelberg (39439) *(G-2116)*

Donald L McKinnon 601 319-3311
548 Highway 533 Laurel (39443) *(G-2763)*

Donald Speights Jr 601 940-3847
181 Speights Rd Braxton (39044) *(G-477)*

Donald W Mason 601 269-3782
1348 Scr 540-2 Raleigh (39153) *(G-4475)*

Donovan P Cain 662 279-2124
145 County Road 944 Glen (38846) *(G-1506)*

Donut Palace, McComb Also called Sokhom To *(G-3267)*

Dooley Brothers Ready Mix Inc 601 888-3530
2622 Woodville Jackson Ln Woodville (39669) *(G-5617)*

Doorswap, Starkville Also called Assured Revenue Corporation *(G-4925)*

ALPHABETIC

(PA)=Parent Co (HQ)=Headquarters (DH)=Div Headquarters

2019 Harris Directory of
Mississippi Manufacturers

279

Doric Burial Vault Co

Doric Burial Vault Co 601 366-8390
  8961 Highway 49 N Jackson (39209) *(G-2388)*

Doricvaults North Mississippi, Tupelo *Also called Harris Ja Inc (G-5153)*

Dotted Signs & Screenprinting 601 506-2175
  7605 Highway 35 S Forest (39074) *(G-1415)*

Dottleys Spice Mart Inc 601 629-6100
  5626 Highway 61 S Vicksburg (39180) *(G-5362)*

Double C Custom Welding & Fabg 228 383-1243
  3 Bandywood Ct Gulfport (39503) *(G-1774)*

Double E Farms, Nettleton *Also called Tim Blake (G-3668)*

Double G Coatings Company LP 601 371-3460
  1096 Mendell Davis Dr Jackson (39272) *(G-2389)*

Doubletap Industries 601 506-3218
  104 Country Oaks Dr Terry (39170) *(G-5065)*

Doug McCormick 662 256-9506
  50020 Swan Hill Rd Amory (38821) *(G-41)*

Doves Machine & Welding Svc 601 794-8112
  39 Deep South Ln Purvis (39475) *(G-4436)*

Downhome Publications Inc 601 982-8418
  5 Lakeland Cir Ste 4 Jackson (39216) *(G-2390)*

Downs Corporation 662 728-3237
  201 Pecan Ave Booneville (38829) *(G-327)*

Downs' Printing & Graphic, Booneville *Also called Downs Corporation (G-327)*

Dozer Inc 601 442-1671
  14 Minor St Natchez (39120) *(G-3556)*

Dpr Outdoors, Brandon *Also called Dixie Precision Rifles LLC (G-389)*

Dqsi LLC 228 688-3796
  John C Stennis Space Cent Stennis Space Center (39529) *(G-4994)*

Dr Erica Aesthetic Center 662 284-9600
  2000 E Shiloh Rd Corinth (38834) *(G-1084)*

Dr James 601 238-7821
  2004 Camellia Ln Jackson (39204) *(G-2391)*

Dr Pepper/Seven Up Inc 601 545-7511
  1000 W 63rd St Hattiesburg (39401) *(G-1958)*

Dragon Breath Press LLC 601 607-7007
  212 Salem Sq Ridgeland (39157) *(G-4574)*

Drake Waterfowl, Olive Branch *Also called Icon Outdoors LLC (G-3850)*

Drexel Chemical Company 662 363-1791
  1099 Drexel Rd Tunica (38676) *(G-5098)*

Driven Racing Oil LLC 866 611-1820
  8649 Hacks Cross Rd Olive Branch (38654) *(G-3837)*

Drone Assist Incorporated 228 265-0174
  11989 Music St Gulfport (39503) *(G-1775)*

Drumheller Packaging Inc 662 627-2207
  350 Anderson Blvd Clarksdale (38614) *(G-767)*

Ds Welding Services 601 639-4988
  313 Airport Rd Crosby (39633) *(G-1134)*

DSI, Ridgeland *Also called Smart Source (G-4631)*

Dsp Armory Inc 662 862-4272
  204 N Gaither St Fulton (38843) *(G-1452)*

Dub Street Fashion Center LLC 601 483-0036
  3316 20th St Meridian (39301) *(G-3330)*

Dublin Steel Corporation Inc 601 482-2102
  7730 Highway 45 N Meridian (39305) *(G-3331)*

Dubose Electric 601 425-5116
  3963 Sharon Rd Laurel (39443) *(G-2764)*

Duck Head Apparel, Vicksburg *Also called Supreme International LLC (G-5425)*

Duckwrth Drlg Completion L L C 601 848-6486
  504 Miller Wicks Rd State Line (39362) *(G-4986)*

Duffell Awning Co, Meridian *Also called Duffell Metal Awning Co (G-3332)*

Duffell Metal Awning Co 601 483-2181
  3903 Highland Park Dr Meridian (39307) *(G-3332)*

Dufour Battery One Source LLC 601 693-1500
  2618 N Frontage Rd Meridian (39301) *(G-3333)*

Dunaway Signs Inc 228 392-5421
  12224 Parkers Creek Rd Biloxi (39532) *(G-239)*

Dunaways Logging Inc 601 695-1232
  222 S Church St Brookhaven (39601) *(G-493)*

Duncan Signs Inc 662 842-0226
  3900 Westgate Dr Tupelo (38801) *(G-5127)*

Dungans Outdoor Solutions Co 228 382-7156
  5100 Midway St Ocean Springs (39564) *(G-3753)*

Dunn Paper Inc 800 253-1889
  1321 Magnolia Dr S Wiggins (39577) *(G-5581)*

Dunns Jewelry 662 363-1501
  1225 Main St Tunica (38676) *(G-5099)*

Dunns Woodworking LLC 601 736-0633
  489 Enon Rd Columbia (39429) *(G-897)*

Duraco Inc 601 932-2100
  2000 Old Whitfield Rd Pearl (39208) *(G-4115)*

Duraco Industries, Inc., Pearl *Also called Gilcorp (G-4123)*

Durango Operating LLC 601 420-2525
  419 Northpark Dr A Ridgeland (39157) *(G-4575)*

Durbin USA, Ocean Springs *Also called Pharmaceutical Trade Svcs Inc (G-3775)*

Durfold Corporation 601 922-4144
  102 Upton Dr Jackson (39209) *(G-2392)*

Duro-Last Inc 601 371-1973
  6200 I 55 S Byram (39272) *(G-621)*

Dutch Ann Foods Inc 601 445-4496
  716 Liberty Rd Natchez (39120) *(G-3557)*

Dvani Innovation Inc 601 992-5069
  123 Formosa Dr Brandon (39047) *(G-392)*

Dwain Mc Nair Signs & Screen 601 267-9967
  4093 Highway 35 N Carthage (39051) *(G-715)*

Dwayne Timber Company 601 695-6177
  1466 Mission Hill Rd Ne Wesson (39191) *(G-5527)*

Dwights Custom Deer Processing 601 857-2324
  10237 Highway 18 Raymond (39154) *(G-4487)*

Dyehouse Inc 601 776-2189
  601 Harris Ave Quitman (39355) *(G-4462)*

Dyess Lawn & Patio Shop 601 659-0390
  67 County Road 374 Enterprise (39330) *(G-1279)*

Dynamic Signs and More 228 235-5660
  1739 Pass Rd Biloxi (39531) *(G-240)*

Dynastics Screen Printing 601 353-1956
  410 W Pascagoula St Jackson (39203) *(G-2393)*

Dynegy, Petal *Also called Tri Resources Inc (G-4197)*

Dzt Photography and Event Prtg 228 334-5253
  9105 Margurite Dr Ocean Springs (39564) *(G-3754)*

E & D Services Inc 601 649-9044
  2300 Hwy 11 N Laurel (39440) *(G-2765)*

E & J Distributors, Vicksburg *Also called Emma Roberts (G-5366)*

E & S Logging LLC 601 866-7270
  6277 N Chapel Hill Rd Bolton (39041) *(G-309)*

E C S, Pontotoc *Also called Eaton Custom Seating LLC (G-4330)*

E C Welding & Fabricating 662 429-1624
  3320 Byhalia Rd Hernando (38632) *(G-2130)*

E E Baird Machine Shop Inc 662 456-2348
  221 N Jefferson St Houston (38851) *(G-2237)*

E E Baird Shop Inc 662 456-3467
  221 N Jefferson St Houston (38851) *(G-2238)*

E Fairley Unlimited Svc LLC 601 795-6933
  28 Bob Simpson Rd Poplarville (39470) *(G-4381)*

E I Du Pont De Nemours & Co 228 762-0870
  1001 Industrial Rd Pascagoula (39581) *(G-4030)*

E M F Corp 601 743-2794
  299 Ponderosa Ave De Kalb (39328) *(G-1163)*

E Vegely Signs 228 255-7543
  28453 Sixteen Section Rd Pass Christian (39571) *(G-4082)*

Each Life Teach Life, Jackson *Also called Grady Morrow (G-2429)*

Eagle Eye Personal Defense 662 816-2310
  23 County Road 277 Oxford (38655) *(G-3953)*

Eagle Fire Works Co Inc 601 798-9291
  24 Hodge Dr5 Picayune (39466) *(G-4265)*

Eagle Oil & Gas, Sandersville *Also called Wcs Oil & Gas Corporation (G-4726)*

Eagle Pipe and Supply LLC 601 487-7473
  450 Industrial Dr Jackson (39209) *(G-2394)*

Eagle Specialty Products Inc 662 796-7373
  8530 Aaron Ln Southaven (38671) *(G-4870)*

Eakes Nursery Materials Inc.....................................601 722-4797
  249 Bethel Church Rd Seminary (39479) *(G-4777)*

Eap LLC 601 636-1621
  102 Danawood Ln Vicksburg (39180) *(G-5363)*

Earls Machining Center Inc 662 820-7565
  264 Saint Christopher Rd Leland (38756) *(G-2887)*

Ears Jewelry Box Sp Fashions 769 234-1771
  15 1/2 Quinn Ln Foxworth (39483) *(G-1429)*

Easley & Easley Millworks Inc..................................601 372-8881
  3850 I 55 S Jackson (39212) *(G-2395)*

East Holmes Publishing Entps 662 834-1151
  308 Court Sq Lexington (39095) *(G-2901)*

East Mississippi Pole Company 662 726-2932
  15029 Us Highway 45 Macon (39341) *(G-3059)*

East Systems Inc 662 244-7070
  41 Fabritek Dr Columbus (39702) *(G-965)*

Eastern Fishing & Rental Tl Co 601 649-1454
  2406 Moose Dr Laurel (39440) *(G-2766)*

Eastern Group LLC..662 332-1890
  2232 Highway 1 N Greenville (38703) *(G-1552)*

Easters Custom Woodworks LLC 740 502-2039
  110 King Arthurs Rdg Vicksburg (39180) *(G-5364)*

Easy Reach Supply LLC 601 582-7866
  32 Raspberry Ln Hattiesburg (39402) *(G-1959)*

Eaton Aerospace Jackson, Jackson *Also called Eaton Aerospace LLC (G-2397)*

Eaton Aerospace Inc 601 981-2811
  5353 Highland Dr Jackson (39206) *(G-2396)*

Eaton Aerospace LLC 601 987-3273
  5353 Highland Dr Jackson (39206) *(G-2397)*

Eaton Custom Seating LLC 662 489-4242
  263 Coffee St Pontotoc (38863) *(G-4330)*

Eaton Electric Motor Repair 662 728-6187
  205 N 1st St Booneville (38829) *(G-328)*

Eaton Seating, Pontotoc *Also called Miss Eaton Inc (G-4346)*

Eaves Brothers Logging, Macon *Also called David M Eaves (G-3058)*

Ecash Software Systems, Ridgeland *Also called Esoftware Solutions Inc (G-4578)*

Eclipse Screen Prints 901 626-9029
  14215 Harrison Dr Byhalia (38611) *(G-584)*

ALPHABETIC SECTION

Ergon - St James Inc (HQ)

Eco Recovery Machine LLC 713 829-1083
1118 Highway 472 Pinola (39149) *(G-4308)*

Ecolab Inc 662 327-1863
70 Wilcutt Columbus (39705) *(G-966)*

Econo Signs 662 844-1554
707 Daybrite Dr Tupelo (38801) *(G-5128)*

Ecowater Systems LLC 662 837-9349
17471 Highway 15 N Ripley (38663) *(G-4656)*

Ecs- Elec Cnstr Spcialists Inc 662 453-0588
101 Enterprise Dr Greenwood (38930) *(G-1621)*

Ed Dangerfield Cnstr Mfg, Columbus *Also called Ed Dangerfield Const Millwrks (G-967)*

Ed Dangerfield Const Millwrks 662 328-3877
1090 Matson Rd Columbus (39705) *(G-967)*

Edco Welding 228 392-5600
12416 John Lee Rd Biloxi (39532) *(G-241)*

Eddie Inc 601 663-5755
6223 Highway 21 Forest (39074) *(G-1416)*

Eddie Franklin 601 225-4183
3321 N Ms Highway 24 & 33 Centreville (39631) *(G-730)*

Eddie Martin Golf Cars Inc 662 620-7242
502 Air Park Rd Tupelo (38801) *(G-5129)*

Eddie Reynolds Logging 662 647-2667
900 E Main St Charleston (38921) *(G-736)*

Eddie Wiggs 662 456-7080
1318 County Road 416 Houston (38851) *(G-2239)*

Edge Tools and Designs Inc 662 578-0363
112 Compress Rd Batesville (38606) *(G-105)*

Educate & Celebrate LLC 228 547-0811
311 Cowan Rd Gulfport (39507) *(G-1776)*

Edward C Mathis Logging 601 776-2379
206 County Road 450 Quitman (39355) *(G-4463)*

Efma Contracting LLC 901 292-7221
107 Pine Knoll Dr Apt 8 Ridgeland (39157) *(G-4576)*

Eighteen-Seventeen Prtg LLC 601 300-0506
2142 Willis Cotton Rd Summit (39666) *(G-5013)*

Eighty-Five 15 Candle Co LLC 601 324-3064
1328 Parklane Rd Apt 402 McComb (39648) *(G-3249)*

Ek Embroidery LLC 228 868-8469
2219 Pass Rd Ste A Gulfport (39501) *(G-1777)*

Eko Peroxide LLC 662 240-8571
4374 Nashville Ferry Rd E Columbus (39702) *(G-968)*

El Toro Production Co Inc 601 442-4159
66 Springfield Rd Natchez (39120) *(G-3558)*

Electric and Machine Svcs, Tupelo *Also called Patterson & Company Inc (G-5200)*

Electric Contractors 662 470-3102
8945 Hamilton Rd Southaven (38671) *(G-4871)*

Electric Mills Wood Prsv LLC 662 476-8000
13539 Highway 45 Scooba (39358) *(G-4770)*

Electric Motor & Equipment 601 845-5561
3917 Highway 49 S Florence (39073) *(G-1321)*

Electric Motor Sales & Svc Inc 662 327-1606
232 Alabama St Columbus (39702) *(G-969)*

Electric Works 662 342-5505
1721 Dancy Blvd B Horn Lake (38637) *(G-2196)*

Electro Mech Solutions Ems Inc 601 631-0138
5589 Highway 61 S Vicksburg (39180) *(G-5365)*

Electro National Corporation 601 859-5511
511 Matthews Dr Canton (39046) *(G-657)*

Elements Cosmetics LLC 601 383-6352
211 Ashton Way Brandon (39047) *(G-393)*

Elements Estate Sales 601 482-4099
6144 13th Ave Meridian (39305) *(G-3334)*

Elevance Natchez Inc 601 442-5330
151 L E Barry Rd Natchez (39120) *(G-3559)*

Elims Art Cncpts & Dcrtv Dsgn 601 540-4810
350 W Woodrow Wilson Ave Jackson (39213) *(G-2398)*

Elite Comfort Solutions LLC 662 566-2322
234 Cdf Blvd Lee Indus Pa Lee Industrial Park Verona (38879) *(G-5330)*

Elite Const and Design 662 307-2494
1745 Jackson Ave Grenada (38901) *(G-1675)*

Elite Elastomers Inc 662 512-1770
200 County Rd 565 Ripley (38663) *(G-4657)*

Elite Screen Printing (PA) 601 450-1261
107 N 40th Ave Hattiesburg (39401) *(G-1960)*

Elite Wood Care 601 622-2278
500 Creekstone Dr Brandon (39047) *(G-394)*

Elizabeth Clayton 601 371-1172
201 Springwood Dr Terry (39170) *(G-5066)*

Elizabeth Newcomb 662 596-1536
458 County Road 550 Rienzi (38865) *(G-4649)*

Ell Holdings 601 325-3317
147 Millpond Dr Hattiesburg (39401) *(G-1961)*

Ellis Certified Welding 662 869-2295
676 Pulltight Rd Saltillo (38866) *(G-4711)*

Ellis Custom Woodwork LLC 601 983-8464
1621 W Mcdowell Rd Jackson (39204) *(G-2399)*

Ellis Dozer LLC 601 752-2207
253 Earl Brashier Rd Seminary (39479) *(G-4778)*

Ellis Steel Company Inc (PA) 662 494-5955
642 Highway 45 N Altn West Point (39773) *(G-5542)*

Ellis Steel Company Inc 662 893-5955
10290 Old Hwy 78 Olive Branch (38654) *(G-3838)*

Ellis Welding 601 752-2207
59 Rogers Rd Seminary (39479) *(G-4779)*

Ellis Williams Logging 601 734-3918
2622 Rlling Meadows Ln Se Bogue Chitto (39629) *(G-302)*

Ellis Woodworks 662 329-2605
724 N Lehmberg Rd Columbus (39702) *(G-970)*

Elmore Machine Shop Inc 601 989-2508
2898 Lovewell Rd Richton (39476) *(G-4530)*

Elvis and Company LLC 662 616-9248
186 Primrose St Greenville (38701) *(G-1553)*

Embroidery Design LLC 601 878-2606
14893 Midway Rd Terry (39170) *(G-5067)*

Embroidery Nu Sun 228 731-3781
2000 E Pass Rd Gulfport (39507) *(G-1778)*

Embroidery Plus 662 590-7102
1563 Jerry Clower Blvd Yazoo City (39194) *(G-5633)*

Embroidme 228 284-1689
9321 Live Oak Ave Ocean Springs (39564) *(G-3755)*

Emerald Transformer 800 346-6164
491 Bowling Green Rd Lexington (39095) *(G-2902)*

Emerald Water LLC 601 981-2430
3920 Restbrook Pl Jackson (39211) *(G-2400)*

Emergent Prtctive Pdts USA Inc 517 489-5172
46 Shelby Thames Dr Hattiesburg (39402) *(G-1962)*

Emergent Technologies LLC 601 497-8239
299 Woodland Brook Dr Madison (39110) *(G-3097)*

Emergncy Eqp Professionals Inc 662 280-4729
6441 Highway 51 N Horn Lake (38637) *(G-2197)*

Emerson Motor Company, Southaven *Also called Nidec Motor Corporation (G-4891)*

Emerson's Sports, Lucedale *Also called Emersons (G-2994)*

Emersons 228 588-3952
26102 Highway 613 Lucedale (39452) *(G-2994)*

Emilia Resources LLC 601 743-9355
14124 Highway 16 W De Kalb (39328) *(G-1164)*

Emma Roberts 601 638-3062
4908 Gibson Rd Vicksburg (39180) *(G-5366)*

Emmerich Newspapers Inc 662 647-8462
16 S Court Sq Charleston (38921) *(G-737)*

Empire Services Inc 601 276-2500
6451 County Line Rd Summit (39666) *(G-5014)*

Enbridge Processing LLC 601 671-8800
595 Ceamon Pittman Rd Waynesboro (39367) *(G-5497)*

Enc, Canton *Also called Electro National Corporation (G-657)*

Encore Products 662 423-3484
119 S Fulton St Iuka (38852) *(G-2290)*

End2end Public Safety LLC 662 513-0999
2627 West Oxford Loop F Oxford (38655) *(G-3954)*

Enercept Inc 228 323-1666
11574 Bluff Ln Gulfport (39503) *(G-1779)*

Energy Drilling Company 601 446-5259
413 Liberty Rd Natchez (39120) *(G-3560)*

Energyzmart LLC 650 630-1232
376 Kershaw St Grenada (38901) *(G-1676)*

Engelhard 601 948-3966
600 E Mcdowell Rd Jackson (39204) *(G-2401)*

Engine Rebuilders Co Inc 662 332-2695
327 Highway 1 S Greenville (38701) *(G-1554)*

Englander Sleep Products LLC 800 370-8700
8300 Industrial Dr Olive Branch (38654) *(G-3839)*

Englander South Central, Olive Branch *Also called Englander Sleep Products LLC (G-3839)*

Enlow & Son Inc 662 423-9073
2243 Highway 25 Iuka (38852) *(G-2291)*

Enoch Development, Diberville *Also called Gwendolyn Rucker (G-1206)*

Enslin and Son Packing Company 601 582-9300
2500 Glendale Ave Hattiesburg (39401) *(G-1963)*

Entek Inc 662 841-5134
4126 Westside Dr Tupelo (38801) *(G-5130)*

Entergy Nuclear Fuels Company 601 368-5750
1340 Echelon Pkwy Jackson (39213) *(G-2402)*

Enterprise-Journal, McComb *Also called J O Emmerich & Assoc Inc (G-3254)*

Enterprise-Tocsin 662 887-2222
114 Main St Indianola (38751) *(G-2264)*

Entrepreneur, Madison *Also called Correy Elder (G-3089)*

Enviro-Flo Inc 601 939-2948
151 Custom Dr Flowood (39232) *(G-1355)*

Enviro-Mats, LLC, Monticello *Also called Usaccess LLC (G-3440)*

Environmental Tech of Amer 601 607-3151
403 Towne Center Blvd # 404 Ridgeland (39157) *(G-4577)*

Ephesians Security, Pascagoula *Also called Maritime Defense Strategy LLC (G-4051)*

Equipment Maintenance Co 662 393-9178
3780 Hilltop Dr Horn Lake (38637) *(G-2198)*

ERC Wellheads, Laurel *Also called GE Oil & Gas Pressure Ctrl LP (G-2769)*

Ergon Inc 601 636-6888
2353 Haining Rd Vicksburg (39183) *(G-5367)*

Ergon - St James Inc (HQ) 601 933-3000
2829 Lakeland Dr Ste 2000 Flowood (39232) *(G-1356)*

(PA)=Parent Co (HQ)=Headquarters (DH)=Div Headquarters

2019 Harris Directory of
Mississippi Manufacturers

281

A L P H A B E T I C

ALPHABETIC SECTION

Ergon - West Virginia Inc 601 933-3000
2829 Lakeland Dr Ste 2000 Flowood (39232) *(G-1357)*

Ergon Biofuels LLC 601 636-1976
1833 Haining Rd Vicksburg (39183) *(G-5368)*

Ergon Chemicals LLC (HQ) 601 933-3000
2829 Lakeland Dr Ste 2000 Flowood (39232) *(G-1358)*

Ergon Construction Group Inc 601 939-3909
630 Industrial Dr Richland (39218) *(G-4514)*

Ergon Ethanol Inc (HQ) 601 933-3000
2829 Lakeland Dr Ste 2000 Flowood (39232) *(G-1359)*

Ergon Europe Mea Inc 601 933-3000
2829 Lakeland Dr Flowood (39232) *(G-1360)*

Ergon Inc 601 932-8365
390 Carrier Blvd Jackson (39218) *(G-2645)*

Ergon Inc (PA) 601 933-3000
2829 Lakeland Dr Ste 2000 Flowood (39232) *(G-1361)*

Ergon Marine & Industrial Sup 601 636-6552
100 Lee St Vicksburg (39180) *(G-5369)*

Ergon Refining Inc 601 638-4960
2611 Haining Rd Vicksburg (39183) *(G-5370)*

Erickson Oil 601 362-7401
3969 Dogwood Dr Jackson (39211) *(G-2403)*

Esco Group LLC 601 683-3192
9098 Eastside Drive Ext Newton (39345) *(G-3720)*

Esoftware Solutions Inc 601 919-2275
403 Legacy Park Ridgeland (39157) *(G-4578)*

Espiritu Custom Cues 601 825-7077
6162 Highway 18 Brandon (39042) *(G-395)*

Essmueller Company 601 649-2400
334 Ave A Airbase Laurel (39440) *(G-2767)*

Essmueller Home Offices, Laurel *Also called Essmueller Company (G-2767)*

Etd Inc 662 454-9349
14 Airpark Belmont (38827) *(G-198)*

Ethel Benson Quilt Collection, Water Valley *Also called David Buford (G-5466)*

Ets Signs Inc (PA) 601 268-7275
4400 Hardy St Ste A1 Hattiesburg (39402) *(G-1964)*

Eubanks and Eubanks Inc 601 947-2509
1179 Evanston Rd Lucedale (39452) *(G-2995)*

Eubanks Records Service, Louisville *Also called Ronnies Auto Sales (G-2980)*

Eugene Flanders 601 544-0345
1041 Poplar Rd Hattiesburg (39401) *(G-1965)*

Eupora Cut-To-Size, Louisville *Also called Roseburg Forest Products Co (G-2981)*

Euro American Plastics Inc 601 879-0360
120 Saint Charles Ave Flora (39071) *(G-1305)*

Evans Logging 662 369-7151
20456 Coontail Rd Aberdeen (39730) *(G-13)*

Evans Refrigeration 601 372-3482
5477 Old Byram Rd Jackson (39272) *(G-2404)*

Evercompounds LLC 309 256-1166
7046 Stateline Rd Olive Branch (38654) *(G-3840)*

Everett Industries Inc 228 231-1556
217 Eighth St Bay Saint Louis (39520) *(G-143)*

Evergreen AG Envmtl & Turf LLC 662 263-4419
18385 U S Highway 82 Mathiston (39752) *(G-3229)*

Evergreen Lumber & Truss Inc (HQ) 601 794-8404
84 Central Industrial Row Purvis (39475) *(G-4437)*

Every Word Press LLC 601 209-1379
1125 Saint Ann St Jackson (39202) *(G-2405)*

Evh Properties LLC 662 571-1980
700 Edgar Rd Yazoo City (39194) *(G-5634)*

Excel By Four LLC 228 355-8203
13609 Lawton Ln Gulfport (39503) *(G-1780)*

Excel Injection Molding Inc 601 544-6133
977 Sullivan Dr Hattiesburg (39401) *(G-1966)*

Exciting Lighting 228 864-2995
1102 E Railroad St Long Beach (39560) *(G-2936)*

Executive Leaders of Tomorrow, Jackson *Also called Dianne Gore (G-2383)*

Exel, Byhalia *Also called Carrier Corporation (G-582)*

Exel Logistics Xerox 662 393-7122
228 Access Dr Ste 105 Southaven (38671) *(G-4872)*

Exide Technologies 601 845-2236
250 Ellis St Florence (39073) *(G-1322)*

Exide Technologies 601 936-7788
154 Concourse Dr Pearl (39208) *(G-4116)*

Exide Technologies 601 845-2281
407 Briarhill Rd Florence (39073) *(G-1323)*

Express Biodiesel LLC 662 453-4312
2015 River Road Ext Greenwood (38930) *(G-1622)*

Express Lane Inc 601 483-8872
500 Highway 19 N Meridian (39307) *(G-3335)*

Express Line 662 328-3720
3920 Highway 45 N Columbus (39705) *(G-971)*

Express Printing 601 856-5458
614 Highway 51 Ridgeland (39157) *(G-4579)*

Expro Americas LLC 281 576-5500
5349 Highway 11 N Ellisville (39437) *(G-1251)*

Exquisite Enterprise Pubg LLC 708 362-4583
5069 Eddisville Rd Durant (39063) *(G-1225)*

Exquisite Reads Publications 662 400-0743
242 Prairie St Macon (39341) *(G-3060)*

Exterran 601 444-0055
60 Columbia Purvis Rd Columbia (39429) *(G-898)*

Eye/Ear Optical, Southaven *Also called Saul Jay Enterprises Inc (G-4899)*

Eyecatcher Signs 601 604-2595
2920 8th St Meridian (39301) *(G-3336)*

Eyesore Yrd Cleanup & Bushogng 205 391-8232
5131 Attala Road 3024 Kosciusko (39090) *(G-2693)*

EZ Chord LLC 601 329-3827
633 Octave St Diberville (39540) *(G-1202)*

EZ Medical Wraps LLC 321 961-0201
104 Red Oak Trl Brandon (39047) *(G-396)*

Ezy Time Foods, Hattiesburg *Also called Blendco Inc (G-1935)*

F & F Timber Inc 601 528-0023
939 Pine Ave E Wiggins (39577) *(G-5582)*

F S C Inc 662 434-0025
7395 Highway 45 N Columbus (39705) *(G-972)*

F W Graves & Son Inc 601 657-8750
3930 Graves Rd Liberty (39645) *(G-2912)*

F-S Prestress LLC (PA) 601 268-2006
25 Peps Point Rd Hattiesburg (39401) *(G-1967)*

Fab Pro Wldg & Fabrication Co 662 365-5557
214 Carnation St Baldwyn (38824) *(G-76)*

Fab Products 228 324-4133
1312 Iberville Dr Ocean Springs (39564) *(G-3756)*

Fab- Tek Central Miss Inc 601 892-5017
19171 Highway 51 Hazlehurst (39083) *(G-2095)*

Fabricated Pipe Inc 601 684-3007
1010 Frank Oaks Dr Fernwood (39635) *(G-1304)*

Facilities Outfitters 662 328-1977
2387 Jess Lyons Rd Columbus (39705) *(G-973)*

Fairbanks Scales Inc 601 482-2073
239 69th Ave Meridian (39307) *(G-3337)*

Fairview Portable Buildings, Ripley *Also called First Monday Trade Day (G-4659)*

Fairview Portable Buildings 662 837-8709
10590 Highway 15 S Ripley (38663) *(G-4658)*

Faith Industries LLC 662 618-0839
3667 N Lake Dr Lauderdale (39335) *(G-2727)*

Falco Lime, Vicksburg *Also called Mississippi Lime Company (G-5396)*

Fallen Leaf Services LLC 228 731-0919
2512 25th Ave Ste 4a Gulfport (39501) *(G-1781)*

Falvey Logging 601 546-2922
160 Gardenia Dr Pelahatchie (39145) *(G-4164)*

Famco Company Inc 228 831-4649
15098 Government St Gulfport (39503) *(G-1782)*

Family Feeding Dev Program 662 357-8917
1126 Flagg St Tunica (38676) *(G-5100)*

Family Meat Processing 601 264-2344
142 N Black Creek Rd Sumrall (39482) *(G-5036)*

Fashion, Houlka *Also called Ark-Ell Springs Inc (G-2217)*

Fashion Screenprint, Jackson *Also called Fashions Incorporated Jackson (G-2406)*

Fashions Incorporated Jackson 601 948-1119
721 Harris St Ste A Jackson (39202) *(G-2406)*

Fast Dog Print Co 662 549-4450
1925 Highway 45 N Columbus (39705) *(G-974)*

Fast Flow Pumps 228 475-2468
9700 Highway 63 Moss Point (39562) *(G-3477)*

Fast Signs 601 602-5413
2902 Hardy St Ste 60 Hattiesburg (39401) *(G-1968)*

Fast Track Planners 601 528-0558
82 Roy Oneal Rd Perkinston (39573) *(G-4175)*

Fastsigns, Hattiesburg *Also called Fast Signs (G-1968)*

Faststop Petroleum LLC 601 466-3273
5562 N Williamsburg Rd Bassfield (39421) *(G-91)*

Fastway Fuels 3 LLC 228 452-7009
9069 County Farm Rd Long Beach (39560) *(G-2937)*

Fastwrapzcom LLC 662 213-8771
502 Crossover Rd Tupelo (38801) *(G-5131)*

Faurecia Auto Seating LLC 248 288-1000
907 Delta Council Dr Cleveland (38732) *(G-791)*

Faurecia Interior Systems Inc 601 855-2163
252 Yandell Ave Canton (39046) *(G-658)*

Faurecia Mdson Auto Sating Inc 601 407-2200
272 Old Jackson Rd Madison (39110) *(G-3098)*

Favara Kitchen and Bath, Greenwood *Also called Galley Kitchen Bath (G-1623)*

Fayard Millworks 228 265-7787
3320 14th St Gulfport (39501) *(G-1783)*

Faye Neldra Rand Spears 601 722-0104
51 Wood Bridge Ln Seminary (39479) *(G-4780)*

Fayette Chronicle 601 786-3661
437 Main St Fayette (39069) *(G-1296)*

Fc Meyer Packaging LLC 601 776-2117
101 Ascher St Quitman (39355) *(G-4464)*

Feathers Fins & Fur Taxidermy 228 860-3106
10048 Leno Rd Biloxi (39532) *(G-242)*

Fed Service Hub LLC 228 547-3498
1914 24th Ave Gulfport (39501) *(G-1784)*

Federal Heath Sign Company LLC 662 233-2999
668 Harris Rd Coldwater (38618) *(G-845)*

282

2019 Harris Directory of
Mississippi Manufacturers

(G-0000) Company's Geographic Section entry number

ALPHABETIC SECTION

Forest Pharmaceuticals Inc

Fedex Office & Print Svcs Inc......................601 264-6434
4600 Hardy St Ste 30 Hattiesburg (39402) *(G-1969)*
Fedex Office & Print Svcs Inc......................601 957-3311
6392 Ridgewood Court Dr Jackson (39211) *(G-2407)*
Feed Manufracturing, Como *Also called Tricounty Farm Services South (G-1054)*
Fennell Sam Sheet Metal Mfg C....................228 864-1488
3200 B Ave Gulfport (39507) *(G-1785)*
Ferson LLC..228 875-8146
5801 Gulf Tech Dr Ocean Springs (39564) *(G-3757)*
Ferson Technologies, Ocean Springs *Also called Ferson LLC (G-3757)*
Fesco, Starkville *Also called Mathis Plow Inc (G-4957)*
Ffm Inc (PA).......................................662 256-9665
1113 Hatley Rd Amory (38821) *(G-42)*
Fianna Systems LLC..................................662 726-5200
2974 Jefferson St Macon (39341) *(G-3061)*
Fibre Craft, Tupelo *Also called Southern Components Inc (G-5226)*
Fibrix LLC..662 489-7908
226 Prestige Dr Pontotoc (38863) *(G-4331)*
Fibrix LLC..662 844-3803
2119 Dalton St Tupelo (38801) *(G-5132)*
Fibrix LLC..662 568-3393
101 Industrial Dr Houlka (38850) *(G-2222)*
Fibrix LLC..662 844-5595
2119 Dalton St Tupelo (38801) *(G-5133)*
Field Coatings LLC.................................228 896-3535
2160 E Pass Rd Gulfport (39507) *(G-1786)*
Field Technology Station, Leland *Also called Bayer Cropscience LP (G-2884)*
Fielder Mfg...601 630-9295
2358 Redbone Rd Vicksburg (39180) *(G-5371)*
Fielders Welding & Orna Ir, Oxford *Also called Fielders Welding and Orna Ir (G-3955)*
Fielders Welding and Orna Ir......................662 234-4256
43 County Road 3056 Oxford (38655) *(G-3955)*
Filing and Storage Miss LLC.......................601 397-6452
751 Avignon Dr Ste G Ridgeland (39157) *(G-4580)*
Filter Service Inc.................................601 644-9840
10158 County Road 430 Meridian (39301) *(G-3338)*
Filter Service Mississippi LLC....................601 693-4614
2371 Freedom Baptst Ch Rd Meridian (39301) *(G-3339)*
Final Touch Accessories LLC.......................662 594-1348
2679 S Harper Rd Corinth (38834) *(G-1085)*
Final Touch Productions...........................601 750-3940
609 Bryceland Blvd Ridgeland (39157) *(G-4581)*
Fine Fibers..901 590-9481
39 Oak Grove Dr Byhalia (38611) *(G-585)*
Finnesse Fabrications & Steel.....................228 216-2102
11661 Katie Dr Pass Christian (39571) *(G-4083)*
Fireplace Wholesale...............................601 545-9876
1505 N Main St Hattiesburg (39401) *(G-1970)*
First Amercn Prtg Direct Mail.....................228 867-9808
1605 23rd Ave Gulfport (39501) *(G-1787)*
First Amercn Prtg Direct Mail (HQ)................601 656-3636
404 Industrial Rd Bfs1 Choctaw (39350) *(G-745)*
First American Printing, Choctaw *Also called Ms Band of Choctaw Indians Db (G-748)*
First Chemical Corporation........................228 762-0870
1001 Industrial Rd Pascagoula (39581) *(G-4031)*
First Class Fire Prtection LLC....................901 350-0499
1978 Hobbs Cv Horn Lake (38637) *(G-2199)*
First Class Industries LLC........................601 597-4787
797 River Rd Fayette (39069) *(G-1297)*
First Coastal Exteriors LLC.......................769 251-1894
203 Priester Dr Pearl (39208) *(G-4117)*
First Heritage Credit Corp........................228 762-7000
3529 Denny Ave Pascagoula (39581) *(G-4032)*
First Heritage Credit Corp........................228 396-2620
11516 Lamey Bridge Rd B2 Diberville (39540) *(G-1203)*
First Heritage Credit Corp........................601 636-6060
2480 S Frontage Rd Vicksburg (39180) *(G-5372)*
First Heritage Credit Corp........................601 735-4543
903 Robinson St Waynesboro (39367) *(G-5498)*
First Heritage Credit Corp........................601 799-1972
1 Sycamore Rd Ste E Picayune (39466) *(G-4266)*
First Heritage Credit Corp........................662 283-4696
408 N Applegate St Winona (38967) *(G-5598)*
First Heritage Credit Corp........................601 939-9309
129 Center St Ste C Richland (39218) *(G-4515)*
First Monday Trade Day (PA).......................662 837-4051
10590 Highway 15 S Ripley (38663) *(G-4659)*
Fish Group Company, Jackson *Also called United Plastic Molders Inc (G-2618)*
Fishbelt Feeds Inc.................................662 246-5065
33 Moorhead Itta Bena Rd Moorhead (38761) *(G-3445)*
Fishbowl International Inc.........................601 384-0219
3218 Bdford Tillman Rd Nw Roxie (39661) *(G-4689)*
Fisher Construction Company.......................769 257-9969
460 Briarwood Dr Ste 110 Jackson (39206) *(G-2408)*
Fisher Ludlow......................................601 853-9996
211 Industrial Dr N Madison (39110) *(G-3099)*
Fishers Sawmill....................................662 967-2502
8074 Emory Rd West (39192) *(G-5533)*

Fishyrhythms Publishing LLC.......................601 573-6771
287 Longwood Cv Ridgeland (39157) *(G-4582)*
Fiskars Brands Inc.................................662 393-3236
330 Stateline Rd E Southaven (38671) *(G-4873)*
Fiske International Group Corp.....................601 622-5767
268 Hawthorne Dr Madison (39110) *(G-3100)*
Fitmate Social Inc.................................206 849-2447
108 Mulberry Ln Oxford (38655) *(G-3956)*
Five Stars Lighting Co Ltd........................610 533-6522
95 Waring Rd Vicksburg (39183) *(G-5373)*
Fix-Itshoppe , The, Columbus *Also called Dale Fulton (G-958)*
Flambeaux Candle Company..........................769 251-0142
3064 Highway 80 E Pearl (39208) *(G-4118)*
Flambeaux Cocktail Candle LLC.....................601 826-1642
580 S Pear Orchard Rd # 1503 Ridgeland (39157) *(G-4583)*
Flannigan Electric Company........................601 354-2756
1820 S West St Jackson (39201) *(G-2409)*
Flathaus Fine Foods LLC...........................601 582-9629
209 W Second Ave Petal (39465) *(G-4185)*
Flatlanders Screen Printing.......................662 846-0725
1321 W Highway 8 Cleveland (38732) *(G-792)*
Flautt Farms.......................................662 375-2116
1529 Swan Lake Rd Webb (38966) *(G-5519)*
Fleming Book Binding Company......................601 776-3761
180 Harris Ave Quitman (39355) *(G-4465)*
Fleming True Value Lbr............................662 843-2763
224 N Sharpe Ave Cleveland (38732) *(G-793)*
Fletcher Cox.......................................601 956-2610
6817 Cole Rd Ridgeland (39157) *(G-4584)*
Fletcher Printing & Office Sup....................662 487-3200
105 S Pocahontas St Sardis (38666) *(G-4739)*
Flexsteel Industries Inc..........................662 323-5481
212 Industrial Park Rd Starkville (39759) *(G-4944)*
Flora Logging LLC..................................662 552-5408
270 Cordell Rd Maben (39750) *(G-3045)*
Florence Parker....................................662 434-8555
399 Barton Ferry Rd Columbus (39705) *(G-975)*
Flowers Bakery, Hattiesburg *Also called Flowers Bkg Co Baton Rouge LLC (G-1971)*
Flowers Bakery Thrift Store, Tupelo *Also called Flowers Bkg Co Tuscaloosa LLC (G-5134)*
Flowers Bkg Co Baton Rouge LLC....................601 932-7843
4635 Highway 80 E Pearl (39208) *(G-4119)*
Flowers Bkg Co Baton Rouge LLC....................601 583-2693
5075 Old Highway 42 Hattiesburg (39401) *(G-1971)*
Flowers Bkg Co Lynchburg LLC......................601 502-1305
9483 Highway 18 Raymond (39154) *(G-4488)*
Flowers Bkg Co New Orleans LLC....................228 868-0120
14373 Creosote Rd Gulfport (39503) *(G-1788)*
Flowers Bkg Co Thomasville LLC....................662 245-1188
2168 Highway 69 S Columbus (39702) *(G-976)*
Flowers Bkg Co Thomasville LLC....................601 684-5481
605 Avenue C McComb (39648) *(G-3250)*
Flowers Bkg Co Tuscaloosa LLC.....................662 842-8613
1078 Cliff Gookin Blvd Tupelo (38801) *(G-5134)*
Flowood Raceway....................................601 939-5048
202 River Pines Cv Flowood (39232) *(G-1362)*
Fluid Control Division, Madison *Also called Parker-Hannifin Corporation (G-3137)*
Fly Timber Co Inc (PA)............................662 226-2276
2178 Highway 7 N Grenada (38901) *(G-1677)*
FMI Trailers, Lucedale *Also called Fryfogle Manufacturing Inc (G-2996)*
Foamcraft Inc......................................662 844-6399
281 Highway 178 W Tupelo (38804) *(G-5135)*
Foamcraft Inc (PA).................................662 844-6399
115 Old Runway Rd Tupelo (38801) *(G-5136)*
Foamex, Verona *Also called Fxi Inc (G-5331)*
Foh Group Inc......................................601 795-6470
100 Highway 11 N Poplarville (39470) *(G-4382)*
Foil J Branton.....................................601 876-9678
810 N Railroad Ave Tylertown (39667) *(G-5270)*
Foil, J Branton Office, Tylertown *Also called Foil J Branton (G-5270)*
Foley Products Company............................601 792-3202
1650 John Street Ext Prentiss (39474) *(G-4417)*
Foley Tile & Marble...............................601 271-8415
2042 Old Highway 24 Hattiesburg (39402) *(G-1972)*
Follaine Pharmaceuticals LLC......................303 808-4104
147 County Road 245 Etta (38627) *(G-1284)*
Fondren and Sons LLC..............................662 816-8640
County Rd 343 Apt 249 Taylor (38673) *(G-5048)*
Food Manufacturing, Ridgeland *Also called Becks Confection (G-4554)*
Forbes Meat Processors............................601 736-6992
Hurricane Creek Rd Sandy Hook (39478) *(G-4728)*
Force Beekeeping LLC..............................662 429-7586
2651 S Hunter Rd Nesbit (38651) *(G-3651)*
Foremost Dairies..................................601 936-9606
425 Highway 49 S Richland (39218) *(G-4516)*
Forest Penick Products Inc........................662 726-5224
5734 Ms Highway 145 Macon (39341) *(G-3062)*
Forest Pharmaceuticals Inc........................662 841-2321
3464 Mccullough Blvd Belden (38826) *(G-188)*

ALPHABETIC

(PA)=Parent Co (HQ)=Headquarters (DH)=Div Headquarters

2019 Harris Directory of
Mississippi Manufacturers

283

Forklift LLC (PA)

ALPHABETIC SECTION

Forklift LLC (PA) 813 527-4093
912 George Ave Tupelo (38801) *(G-5137)*

Forklift LLC 662 255-2581
1103 W Jackson St Tupelo (38804) *(G-5138)*

Formal Affair 228 497-7500
4343 Gautier Vancleave Rd Gautier (39553) *(G-1492)*

Fortenberry Builders Supply 601 825-3370
1733 Highway 471 Brandon (39047) *(G-397)*

Fortenberrys Meat Processing 601 876-2291
39 Enoch Hines Rd Sandy Hook (39478) *(G-4729)*

Fortenberrys Slaughter House 601 798-2156
5739 Highway 43 N Carriere (39426) *(G-692)*

Forterra Pipe & Precast LLC 662 526-0368
2377 Holston Rd Como (38619) *(G-1047)*

Forterra Pipe & Precast LLC 601 268-2081
1650 John Street Ext Prentiss (39474) *(G-4418)*

Forterra Pipe & Precast LLC 601 982-1100
2840 W Northside Dr Jackson (39213) *(G-2410)*

Forterra Pipe & Precast LLC 601 792-3202
1650 John Street Ext Prentiss (39474) *(G-4419)*

Fortson Industrial Supply Co 601 948-2053
2384 Highway 80 W Jackson (39204) *(G-2411)*

Fortus Pharma LLC 662 420-3094
996 N Halstead Rd Ste C Ocean Springs (39564) *(G-3758)*

Fossil Creek Candle Co LLC 601 730-3130
6058 Cobb Rd Gloster (39638) *(G-1514)*

Fossil Fuel 601 790-7955
150 Sunnycrest Dr Ridgeland (39157) *(G-4585)*

Foster & Thomas Manufacturing 662 682-9094
1088 County Road 102 Vardaman (38878) *(G-5324)*

Foster Machine & Repair Svc 662 755-2656
2023 Hilderbrand Rd Bentonia (39040) *(G-210)*

Four Star Trucking Company LLC 662 429-5397
2337 Getwell Rd S Hernando (38632) *(G-2131)*

Fowler Buick-Gmc Inc (PA) 601 360-0200
5801 Highway 80 E Pearl (39208) *(G-4120)*

Fowler Consulting LLC 601 761-3696
252 Waldrop Rd Flora (39071) *(G-1306)*

Foxworth & Thompson Inc 601 736-3602
2192 Highway 98 W Foxworth (39483) *(G-1430)*

Foxworth & Thompson Lumber, Foxworth *Also called Foxworth & Thompson Inc* *(G-1430)*

Fragrant Flames 601 845-0759
1614 Highway 469 S Florence (39073) *(G-1324)*

Frank Bradford Womack 601 955-1841
4032 Wilderness Rd Hazlehurst (39083) *(G-2096)*

Frank J Miller 601 792-8795
96 Highway 43 Oak Vale (39656) *(G-3734)*

Frank Villines 601 939-5454
401 Industrial Park Dr Jackson (39218) *(G-2646)*

Franklin Corporation (PA) 662 456-5771
600 Franklin Dr Houston (38851) *(G-2240)*

Franklin Corporation 662 456-4286
600 Franklin Dr Houston (38851) *(G-2241)*

Franklin Development Co LLC 662 456-5771
602 Franklin Dr Houston (38851) *(G-2242)*

Franklin Electrofluid Co Inc 601 969-7022
1 Dutchman Row Jackson (39209) *(G-2412)*

Franklin Printers Inc 601 982-9383
330 Commerce Park Dr Jackson (39213) *(G-2413)*

Franklin Ready Mix Inc 601 384-5445
61 Wilson Ln Se Bude (39630) *(G-569)*

Franklin Timber Company 601 384-5826
316 Railroad Ave Bude (39630) *(G-570)*

Franklin's Printing, Jackson *Also called Franklin Printers Inc* *(G-2413)*

Franks Sawmill Inc 601 344-7437
1780 Ovett Petal Rd Ovett (39464) *(G-3931)*

Fred Netterville Lumber Co 601 888-4343
3975 Buffalo Rd Woodville (39669) *(G-5618)*

Fred Windham Signs 601 794-1445
34 Stonefield Dr Purvis (39475) *(G-4438)*

Freed Peoples Press LLC 313 717-7819
145 S Center St Holly Springs (38635) *(G-2176)*

Freeman Milling LLC 601 733-5444
112 Eucalyptus St Mize (39116) *(G-3426)*

Freeman Reason Logging 601 446-5938
45 Brenham Ave Natchez (39120) *(G-3561)*

French Awning & Screen Co Inc 601 922-1132
4514 S Mcraven Rd Jackson (39204) *(G-2414)*

Fresh Distributing Company LLC 228 297-7655
515j Magnolia Rd Lumberton (39455) *(G-3029)*

Fresh Press Creative LLC 601 376-9449
532 Patton Ave Jackson (39216) *(G-2415)*

Freshwater Farms Products LLC 662 247-4205
4554 State Highway 12 E Belzoni (39038) *(G-205)*

Fretwell (not Incorporated) 601 649-0003
3031 Ellisville Blvd Laurel (39440) *(G-2768)*

Fretwell's, Laurel *Also called Fretwell (not Incorporated)* *(G-2768)*

Friars Point Yard, Friars Point *Also called Martin Marietta Materials Inc* *(G-1443)*

Friede Goldman Delaware Inc 228 896-0029
13085 Seaway Rd Gulfport (39503) *(G-1789)*

Frierson Building Supply Co 601 922-1321
4525 Lynch Street Ext Jackson (39209) *(G-2416)*

From Our Cup To Yours 601 214-7689
729 Woodrun Dr Pearl (39208) *(G-4121)*

From Our House To Yours 601 956-1818
214 Heritage Dr Madison (39110) *(G-3101)*

Frontier Contracting LLC 662 809-1949
254 Paper Mill Rd Grenada (38901) *(G-1678)*

Fryfogle Manufacturing Inc 601 947-8088
106 Holmes Dr Lucedale (39452) *(G-2996)*

Fudge Inc 601 932-4748
2801 Layfair Dr Flowood (39232) *(G-1363)*

Fuel Center 601 664-1861
1167 Highway 49 S Richland (39218) *(G-4517)*

Fuel Time 5 ....601 372-1115
1133 Raymond Rd Jackson (39204) *(G-2417)*

Fuhr International LLC 662 862-4903
2841 John Frankin Hwy B Fulton (38843) *(G-1453)*

Fuhr Research Laboratories, Fulton *Also called Fuhr International LLC* *(G-1453)*

Fusion Furniture Inc 662 489-1296
957 Ponto Count Indus Par Ecru (38841) *(G-1231)*

Future Tek Inc 662 328-0900
663 S Frontage Rd Columbus (39701) *(G-977)*

Fxi Inc 662 566-2382
154 Lipford Rd Verona (38879) *(G-5331)*

G & G Granite 601 319-0905
9 New Hope Cutt Off Rd Ellisville (39437) *(G-1252)*

G & S Auto Parts Inc 662 837-9292
410 City Ave S Ripley (38663) *(G-4660)*

G A Pearson Logging Inc 601 928-2105
71 Timber Ridge Rd Wiggins (39577) *(G-5583)*

G B C Office Products Grp, Booneville *Also called Acco Brands USA LLC* *(G-314)*

G Hennig Jr Welding Shop 228 374-7836
213 Hoxie St Biloxi (39530) *(G-243)*

G M Horne Commercial & Indus 601 981-1600
135 Bounds St Jackson (39206) *(G-2418)*

G Mark Lafrancis 601 442-0980
9 Janice Cir Natchez (39120) *(G-3562)*

G S, Meridian *Also called Gipson Steel Inc* *(G-3340)*

G&B Trailers, Moss Point *Also called G&K Fabrication & Trailer Repr* *(G-3478)*

G&G Enterprises, Jackson *Also called Garrett Rowland G* *(G-2422)*

G&K Fabrication & Trailer Repr 228 249-6336
11205 Lily Orchard Rd Moss Point (39562) *(G-3478)*

G&K Services LLC 601 788-6375
411 Oak St Richton (39476) *(G-4531)*

G&L Logging LLC 601 722-9781
49 Tom Leggett Rd Seminary (39479) *(G-4781)*

G5 Tees 662 403-1339
808 Palestine Rd Coldwater (38618) *(G-846)*

GA Pearson Logging, Wiggins *Also called G A Pearson Logging Inc* *(G-5583)*

Gail McInnis 601 261-5077
115 Lake Estates Dr Hattiesburg (39402) *(G-1973)*

Galaxie Corporation (PA) 601 366-8413
5170 Galaxie Dr Jackson (39206) *(G-2419)*

Galexie Glister 601 667-0004
2906 N State St Ste B8 Jackson (39216) *(G-2420)*

Gallery 662 224-6694
5326 Pleasant Hill Rd Ashland (38603) *(G-60)*

Galley Kitchen Bath 662 455-6535
320 W Park Ave Ste B Greenwood (38930) *(G-1623)*

Galvian Group LLC 662 374-1027
1202 Cotton St Greenwood (38930) *(G-1624)*

Gann Brothers Inc 662 568-2980
1667 County Road 413 Houlka (38850) *(G-2223)*

Gannett Co Inc 601 961-7000
201 S Congress St Jackson (39201) *(G-2421)*

Gansman Sheet Metal Contrs 662 890-6215
8251 Industrial Dr Olive Branch (38654) *(G-3841)*

Garan Incorporated 601 656-1501
1015 Holland Ave Philadelphia (39350) *(G-4215)*

Garan Manufacturing, Philadelphia *Also called Garan Incorporated* *(G-4215)*

Garan Manufacturing Corp 662 323-4731
Highway 12 W Starkville (39759) *(G-4945)*

Garden Interiors, Madison *Also called Debra Thigpen* *(G-3095)*

Garner Millwork & Cabinet, Tupelo *Also called Garner Millwork Inc* *(G-5139)*

Garner Millwork Inc 662 844-7007
177 Road 1758 Tupelo (38804) *(G-5139)*

Garrett Rowland G 601 954-9841
134 Richardson Dr Jackson (39209) *(G-2422)*

Garrett & Son Inc 601 853-7865
130 American Way Madison (39110) *(G-3102)*

Garrett Welding & Iron 601 372-3889
4388 Pine Lake Dr Terry (39170) *(G-5068)*

Gary Beall Enterprises LLC 662 453-6100
15109 County Road 626 Greenwood (38930) *(G-1625)*

Gary L Thornton Trk 601 835-4192
903 Highway 84 W Brookhaven (39601) *(G-494)*

Gary's Small Engine Repair, Hattiesburg *Also called Garys Small Engine* *(G-1974)*

2019 Harris Directory of
Mississippi Manufacturers

(G-0000) Company's Geographic Section entry number

284

Garys Graphics 662 429-2924
1117 Broady Rd Nesbit (38651) **(G-3652)**
Garys Industries Inc 662 415-1777
306 Lilac St Corinth (38834) **(G-1086)**
Garys Small Engine 601 545-7355
1400 1/2 E Hardy St Hattiesburg (39401) **(G-1974)**
Gas Processors Inc 601 736-1600
21 Wesley Rd Columbia (39429) **(G-899)**
Gasmax Fltration Solutions LLC 601 790-1225
368 Highland Colony Pkwy Ridgeland (39157) **(G-4586)**
Gateway America LLC 228 331-1473
4300 Air Cargo Rd Gulfport (39501) **(G-1790)**
Gatewood Farms, Vicksburg *Also called William R Gatewood* **(G-5446)**
Gatlin Corporation 601 833-9475
58 Highway 84 E Brookhaven (39601) **(G-495)**
Gator Archery & Outdoors LLC 601 940-3570
464 Church Rd Madison (39110) **(G-3103)**
Gator Grafix Inc 601 376-9004
5630 Terry Rd Jackson (39272) **(G-2423)**
Gator International, Jackson *Also called Product Services Company* **(G-2552)**
Gator Sign & Image Concepts 601 684-8686
1027 Karey Andrews Rd McComb (39648) **(G-3251)**
Gautier Mayhaw Co 228 497-6896
2603 Guillotteville Rd Gautier (39553) **(G-1493)**
Gautier Yard, Gautier *Also called Legacy Vulcan LLC* **(G-1496)**
Gcp Laboratories Inc 228 863-1702
3600 25th Ave Gulfport (39501) **(G-1791)**
GE Capital Aviation Services, Greenwood *Also called Gecas Asset MGT Svcs Inc* **(G-1626)**
GE Oil & Gas Pressure Ctrl LP 601 425-1436
20 Service Blvd Laurel (39440) **(G-2769)**
GE Wind Energy LLC 662 892-2900
9124 Polk Ln Olive Branch (38654) **(G-3842)**
Geartek 662 286-2252
1506 S Fulton Dr Corinth (38834) **(G-1087)**
Gecas Asset MGT Svcs Inc 662 455-1826
600 Airport Rd Greenwood (38930) **(G-1626)**
Geddie Machine & Repair, Hollandale *Also called Delta Machinery Inc* **(G-2165)**
Gem Publications Inc 601 879-3666
4860 Main St Flora (39071) **(G-1307)**
Gemlight Publishing LLC 601 509-1002
45 Hardy Court Shopg Ctr Gulfport (39507) **(G-1792)**
Gencorp Polymer Products, Columbus *Also called Omnova Solutions Inc* **(G-1012)**
General Electric Company 769 233-2828
135 Technology Blvd Ellisville (39437) **(G-1253)**
General Electric Company 662 561-9800
1450 Highway 6 E Batesville (38606) **(G-106)**
General Machine Works Inc 662 494-5155
112 N Forest St West Point (39773) **(G-5543)**
General Offices & Proc Plant, Laurel *Also called Wayne Farms LLC* **(G-2870)**
General Packaging Specialties 662 844-7882
3255 Westover Park Tupelo (38803) **(G-5140)**
General Shale Brick Inc 662 840-8221
2027 Mccullough Blvd Tupelo (38801) **(G-5141)**
Generator Power Systems LLC 662 231-0092
411 N Joann St Tupelo (38801) **(G-5142)**
Genesis Telecommunications 601 626-7353
8487 Highway 19 N Collinsville (39325) **(G-868)**
Genie Industries 662 393-1800
8800 Rostin Rd Southaven (38671) **(G-4874)**
Gentex Pharma LLC 601 990-9497
121 Marketridge Dr Ste C Ridgeland (39157) **(G-4587)**
Gentexpharma, Ridgeland *Also called Gentex Pharma LLC* **(G-4587)**
Gentry Signs 662 323-3652
9 Lynn Ln Starkville (39759) **(G-4946)**
Geo Seis Processing Inc 601 936-0334
305 W Lorenz Blvd Jackson (39213) **(G-2424)**
Geo Specialty Chemical Inc 601 587-7481
107 Cytec Rd Monticello (39654) **(G-3431)**
Georco Ind, Gautier *Also called Singin River Mental Health* **(G-1504)**
George B Ready 662 429-7088
175 E Commerce St Hernando (38632) **(G-2132)**
George County Times 601 947-2967
5133 Main St Lucedale (39452) **(G-2997)**
George Nosser Jr 601 446-7998
103 Lwer Wdville Rd Ste 4 Natchez (39120) **(G-3563)**
George Pacific 662 779-1300
1487 S Church Ave Louisville (39339) **(G-2968)**
George Smith Welding Svc LLC 601 752-5288
55 Jarrod Rd Ellisville (39437) **(G-1254)**
Georgia-Pacific, Pelahatchie *Also called Color-Box LLC* **(G-4162)**
Georgia-Pacific LLC 601 764-4806
71 Georgia Pacific Rd Bay Springs (39422) **(G-161)**
Georgia-Pacific LLC 601 225-4211
221 Frank Schuh Dr Gloster (39638) **(G-1515)**
Georgia-Pacific LLC 662 773-9454
300 Giffen Industrial Dr Louisville (39339) **(G-2969)**
Georgia-Pacific LLC 601 939-7797
555 Gulf Line Rd Pearl (39208) **(G-4122)**
Georgia-Pacific LLC 601 785-4721
3111 Highway 13 N Columbia (39429) **(G-900)**
Georgia-Pacific LLC 601 587-7570
604 Na Sandifer Hwy Monticello (39654) **(G-3432)**
Georgia-Pacific LLC 601 587-7711
1477 Highway 84 Monticello (39654) **(G-3433)**
Gerrer Industrial LLC 601 506-2709
1888 Main St Ste C186 Madison (39110) **(G-3104)**
Get Stitched 228 231-1162
545 Highway 90 Waveland (39576) **(G-5481)**
Gha Enterprises Incorporated 601 812-7739
822 Winthrop Cir Jackson (39206) **(G-2425)**
Ghe Machine Shop 601 886-0304
430 Garrett Rd Silver Creek (39663) **(G-4838)**
Gl Armory LLC 662 372-3389
2841 John Rankin Hwy Fulton (38843) **(G-1454)**
Gibbs & Sons Inc 601 775-3467
1197 Old 80 Rd Lake (39092) **(G-2722)**
Gibson and Pickle Inc 662 289-2400
17757 Williamsville Rd Kosciusko (39090) **(G-2694)**
Gibson Corrugated LLC 662 842-1862
1920 E Main St Tupelo (38804) **(G-5143)**
Gibson Electric Motor Svc Inc 228 762-4923
5505 Veterans St Pascagoula (39581) **(G-4033)**
Giclee Fine Arts 228 586-2693
15195 Ponotoc Dr Kiln (39556) **(G-2679)**
Giexco LLC 662 352-1128
2238 Hopewell Rd Brooksville (39739) **(G-553)**
Gilcorp 601 932-2100
2000 Old Whitfield Rd Pearl (39208) **(G-4123)**
Gilliam, Susan, Byhalia *Also called Cleveland John* **(G-583)**
Gilmore Bros Building Supply 601 825-6292
800 Depot Dr Brandon (39042) **(G-398)**
Gin Creek Publishing 601 649-9388
318 N Magnolia St Laurel (39440) **(G-2770)**
Gipson Steel Inc 601 482-5131
2770 Sellers Dr Meridian (39301) **(G-3340)**
Gis Consulting, Brandon *Also called Chuck Patrick* **(G-380)**
Glad Industries 601 422-0261
1001 S 4th Ave Laurel (39440) **(G-2771)**
Glass Etching Art, Biloxi *Also called Laurin Enterprises LLC* **(G-259)**
Glassbridge Enterprises Inc 662 280-6268
8680 Swinnea Rd Southaven (38671) **(G-4875)**
GLC Mfg Inc 662 565-2600
789 Fishers Crossing Rd Duck Hill (38925) **(G-1221)**
Glen Jones & Associates Inc 601 634-0877
107 Cherrybark Ln Vicksburg (39180) **(G-5374)**
Glenda Brock Woods Music LLC 662 588-8343
364 Highway 442 Shaw (38773) **(G-4823)**
Glendon Henderson Log & Trckg 601 989-2638
4797 Lovewell Rd Richton (39476) **(G-4532)**
Glenn Machine Works Inc (PA) 662 328-4611
734 Highway 45 S Columbus (39701) **(G-978)**
Glenn Machine Works Inc 228 875-1877
8100 Highway 57 Vancleave (39565) **(G-5319)**
Glenn Machine Works Inc 601 482-5554
2120 31st Ave S Meridian (39307) **(G-3341)**
Glenn Mch Works Crane Rigging 601 544-1275
1505 Highway 11 Petal (39465) **(G-4186)**
Glenn Weise 228 435-4455
16350 Sweet Carolyn Rd Biloxi (39532) **(G-244)**
Global Fabrication II LLC 601 749-2209
1934 Palestine Rd Picayune (39466) **(G-4267)**
Global Food Concepts Inc 601 940-5425
679 Grants Ferry Rd Flowood (39232) **(G-1364)**
Global Screen Printing LLC 601 919-2345
1301 Old Fannin Rd Brandon (39047) **(G-399)**
Global Seafood Tech Inc (PA) 228 435-3632
211 Caillavet St Biloxi (39530) **(G-245)**
Global Vessel Tank 601 649-5300
1939 N Mississippi Ave Laurel (39440) **(G-2772)**
Gmn Group LLC (PA) 662 473-3094
1112 County Road 103 Water Valley (38965) **(G-5468)**
Gnesys, Hernando *Also called Hydrasep Inc* **(G-2135)**
Goat Rancher 662 562-9529
731 Sandy Branch Rd Sarah (38665) **(G-4734)**
Gods Inspiration For The Soul 662 374-7785
913 Clayton Ave Apt 1 Tupelo (38804) **(G-5144)**
Godsway Enterprises Inc 601 517-2847
1030 Cedar Hill Dr Jackson (39206) **(G-2426)**
Goff Steel Recting 601 922-6014
285 Wells Rd Clinton (39056) **(G-823)**
Gold Coast Commodities Inc (PA) 601 825-2508
817 Old Highway 471 Brandon (39042) **(G-400)**
Gold Coast Manufacturing Inc 228 261-6290
220 Mcdonald Dr Pass Christian (39571) **(G-4084)**
Gold Teeth Customs 601 955-4653
1335 Ellis Ave Ste 18 Jackson (39204) **(G-2427)**
Golden Manufacturing Co Inc (PA) 662 454-3428
125 Highway 366 Golden (38847) **(G-1525)**

ALPHABETIC

(PA)=Parent Co (HQ)=Headquarters (DH)=Div Headquarters
2019 Harris Directory of Mississippi Manufacturers
285

Golden Manufacturing Co Inc

ALPHABETIC SECTION

Golden Manufacturing Co Inc 662 728-8200
450 Highway 371 Marietta (38856) *(G-3214)*

Golden Manufacturing Co Inc 662 728-1300
450 Highway 371 Marietta (38856) *(G-3215)*

Golden Needle 662 842-0515
4139 W Main St Tupelo (38801) *(G-5145)*

Golden Peanut, Clarksdale *Also called Clint Williams Company* *(G-762)*

Golden Pine Raceway LLC 601 506-8669
103 Golden Pine Rd Prentiss (39474) *(G-4420)*

Golden Source Inventors LLC 601 325-4064
710 Hillendale Dr Hattiesburg (39402) *(G-1975)*

Golden Triange Ready Mix Inc 662 328-0153
4061 Highway 50 E Columbus (39702) *(G-979)*

Goldin Building Systems, Gulfport *Also called Goldin Metals Incorporated* *(G-1794)*

Goldin Metals Incorporated (PA) 228 575-7737
14231 Seaway Rd Ste 7000 Gulfport (39503) *(G-1793)*

Goldin Metals Incorporated 228 575-7737
12440 Seaway Rd Ste 1 Gulfport (39503) *(G-1794)*

Golf First, Tupelo *Also called Sparko Inc* *(G-5229)*

Gollott Icehouse & Oil Dock 228 280-8033
642 Bayview Ave Biloxi (39530) *(G-246)*

Good Deal Used Parts, Jackson *Also called Red Penguin Jackson Ice Cream* *(G-2561)*

Good News Industries Inc 662 327-1988
207 Winchester Dr Columbus (39705) *(G-980)*

Goodgames Inc 228 769-1827
5402 Industrial Rd Pascagoula (39581) *(G-4034)*

Goodings Fine Woodworking 228 255-9037
23220 Enchanted Ave Pass Christian (39571) *(G-4085)*

Goodman Logging LLC 601 644-3443
10253 County Road 420 Meridian (39301) *(G-3342)*

Goodnews Gulf Coast 228 435-2456
336 Rodenberg Ave Biloxi (39531) *(G-247)*

Gordon Redd Lumber Company 601 833-2311
1026 Industrial Pk Rd Ne Brookhaven (39601) *(G-496)*

Gpal LLC 662 422-9351
302 N Highland Dr Tupelo (38801) *(G-5146)*

Gpi, Flora *Also called Gem Publications Inc* *(G-1307)*

Gpp Charleston Industries LLC 800 647-2384
122 Albert Buckley Dr Charleston (38921) *(G-738)*

Grace Company of Ms Inc 662 393-2443
2204 Cole Rd Horn Lake (38637) *(G-2200)*

Grace Welding Fabrication LLC 601 788-2478
11 Willis Edwards Dr Richton (39476) *(G-4533)*

Grady 1&2 ....601 677-3390
249 Grady Rd Preston (39354) *(G-4427)*

Grady Morrow 769 230-6226
200 Rebel Woods Dr Apt M2 Jackson (39212) *(G-2428)*

Grady Morrow 769 823-1422
532 Spryfield Rd Jackson (39212) *(G-2429)*

Grady Shady Music Inc 601 278-3087
2352 Highway 16 E Canton (39046) *(G-659)*

Graham Brothers Machine Inc 228 474-7011
10817 Hwy 63 Escatawpa (39552) *(G-1281)*

Graham Custom Cabinets & Trim 803 381-6829
111 Dampeer St Crystal Springs (39059) *(G-1142)*

Graham Fabrics and Supply, Columbus *Also called F S C Inc* *(G-972)*

Graham Lumber Division, Fulton *Also called Pactiv LLC* *(G-1472)*

Grammer Inc 662 566-1660
231 Laney Rd Shannon (38868) *(G-4807)*

Grammer Inc (HQ) 864 672-0702
231 Laney Rd Shannon (38868) *(G-4808)*

Grand Security Door Company 601 573-1618
140 Glenstone Cir Jackson (39212) *(G-2430)*

Granger Mp AC & Htg 601 894-3774
6032 Highway 472 Hazlehurst (39083) *(G-2097)*

Grant Brothers Machine Shop 662 563-2523
210 Thomas St Batesville (38606) *(G-107)*

Graphic Arts Productions Inc 662 494-2549
1223 N Eshman Ave West Point (39773) *(G-5544)*

Grasslawn Publishing LLC 228 896-5532
1007 Wilson Dr Gulfport (39507) *(G-1795)*

Grassroots A Natural Co LLC 662 601-8808
118 5th St N Columbus (39701) *(G-981)*

Grassy Ridge Gazebos 662 738-6556
3850 Hopewell Rd Brooksville (39739) *(G-554)*

Gravel Equipment & Supply Inc 662 256-2052
30462 Bigbee Rd Amory (38821) *(G-43)*

Graves, F W & Son Logging Co, Liberty *Also called F W Graves & Son Inc* *(G-2912)*

Gray Daniels Auto Family 601 948-0576
104 Gray Daniels Blvd Brandon (39042) *(G-401)*

Gray Daniels Toyota, Brandon *Also called Gray Daniels Auto Family* *(G-401)*

Grayco Systems & Consulting 601 583-0430
201 Campbell Loop Hattiesburg (39401) *(G-1976)*

Grayson Blu LLC 662 779-1291
5695 Old Robinson Rd Louisville (39339) *(G-2970)*

Grd Distributors LLC 601 382-8802
307 Walker Cir Bldg O Richland (39218) *(G-4518)*

Great American Granola Co LLC 228 369-0902
10 Sauville Ct Ocean Springs (39564) *(G-3759)*

Great American Publishers 601 854-5956
171 Lone Pine Church Rd Lena (39094) *(G-2895)*

Great River Industries LLC (PA) 601 442-7568
21 Moran Rd Natchez (39120) *(G-3564)*

Great Southern Club Inc (PA) 228 868-8619
2510 14th St Ste 1480 Gulfport (39501) *(G-1796)*

Great Southern Industries Inc (PA) 601 948-5700
1320 Boling St Jackson (39209) *(G-2431)*

Great Southern Log Homes Inc 601 833-0700
111 Pritchard St Brookhaven (39601) *(G-497)*

Great Southern Wood Prsv Inc 601 823-4865
111 Boyce St Brookhaven (39601) *(G-498)*

Greater Gulf Development LLC 228 392-6680
4263 Popps Ferry Rd Diberville (39540) *(G-1204)*

Grecian Oil Importers LLC 662 372-4933
850 N Gloster St Tupelo (38804) *(G-5147)*

Green Advertising, Oxford *Also called Pmq Inc* *(G-3995)*

Green Brothers Gravel Co Inc 601 362-3620
5179 Harmony Rd Crystal Springs (39059) *(G-1143)*

Green Metals Inc 662 534-5447
1034 Corolla Ln Blue Springs (38828) *(G-296)*

Green Mold Die & Fixtures Inc 601 879-8166
603 Pocahontas Rd Flora (39071) *(G-1308)*

Green Save Inc 662 566-0717
162 Greystone Dr Verona (38879) *(G-5332)*

Greene County Herald, Leakesville *Also called Turner Group LLC* *(G-2880)*

Greene's Energy Services, Laurel *Also called Old Ges Inc* *(G-2814)*

Greentech Automotive Inc 662 996-1118
1 Greentech Dr Robinsonville (38664) *(G-4675)*

Greenville Metal Works Inc 662 335-8510
1254 Highway 1 N Greenville (38703) *(G-1555)*

Greenville Printing Co, Greenville *Also called Noyes Printing & Rbr Stamp Co* *(G-1583)*

Greenville Steel Sales, Greenville *Also called Greenville Metal Works Inc* *(G-1555)*

Greenwood Commonwealth, Greenwood *Also called Commonwealth Publishing Inc* *(G-1618)*

Greenwood Machine Shop 662 316-4107
150 County Road 275 Blue Springs (38828) *(G-297)*

Greer Environmental Services 601 734-2883
3955 Primitive Dr Se Ruth (39662) *(G-4701)*

Greg Winstead Logging Inc 601 774-9565
259 Tullus Rd Union (39365) *(G-5297)*

Gregory D Loose Od, Wiggins *Also called Vision Center PA* *(G-5593)*

Grenada Electric Company Inc 662 226-5801
1055 Lakeview Dr Grenada (38901) *(G-1679)*

Grenada Fasteners Inc 662 227-1000
1518 Murff Dr Grenada (38901) *(G-1680)*

Grenada Newspaper Inc 662 226-4321
50 Corporate Row Grenada (38901) *(G-1681)*

Grenada Sales Management Inc 662 226-1161
635 Highway 332 Grenada (38901) *(G-1682)*

Griffin Inc 662 838-2128
6562 Highway 178 Byhalia (38611) *(G-586)*

Griffin Armor 662 494-3421
901 E Half Mile St West Point (39773) *(G-5545)*

Griffin Grffin Exploration LLC 601 713-1146
1904 Lakeland Dr Ste F Jackson (39216) *(G-2432)*

Griffin Industries LLC 601 372-5212
1299 Prisock Rd Jackson (39272) *(G-2433)*

Griffin Lodging, Mc Call Creek *Also called Charles Lance Griffin* *(G-3232)*

Grind 662 567-5211
111 N Jackson St Houston (38851) *(G-2243)*

Groen, Jackson *Also called Unified Brands Inc* *(G-2615)*

Groen, Byram *Also called Unified Brands Inc* *(G-625)*

Ground Support Specialist LLC 662 342-1412
6228 Hurt Rd Horn Lake (38637) *(G-2201)*

Group Pepper Snapple Dr 601 602-3695
117 Shadow Ridge Rd Hattiesburg (39402) *(G-1977)*

Groves Sheet Metal Co Inc 601 922-6464
1369 College Hill Dr Jackson (39209) *(G-2434)*

Grumpy Man LLC 601 606-8683
31 Yellow Bird Rd Purvis (39475) *(G-4439)*

Gss, Horn Lake *Also called Ground Support Specialist LLC* *(G-2201)*

Gt Screen Prtg & Promotions 601 759-9858
5909 Old Brandon Rd Ste 4 Pearl (39208) *(G-4124)*

Gtp Publishing Group 228 348-2646
2422 Regency Dr Biloxi (39532) *(G-248)*

Guice Woodworks 323 384-1826
122 Halstead Rd Ocean Springs (39564) *(G-3760)*

Guides Publishing Inc (PA) 601 981-7368
228 Avalon Cir Jackson (39201) *(G-2435)*

Gulf Coast Cabinets & Mill 228 206-7792
2815 22nd Ave Gulfport (39501) *(G-1797)*

Gulf Coast Fabrication Inc 601 347-8403
616 E Canal St Picayune (39466) *(G-4268)*

Gulf Coast Filters Inc 601 528-5762
45 South Park Dr Perkinston (39573) *(G-4176)*

Gulf Coast Limb & Brace Inc 228 864-4512
3506 Washington Ave Ste D Gulfport (39507) *(G-1798)*

Gulf Coast Marine Supply Co 228 762-9282
3703 Industrial Rd Pascagoula (39581) *(G-4035)*

2019 Harris Directory of
Mississippi Manufacturers

(G-0000) Company's Geographic Section entry number

ALPHABETIC SECTION

Harbison-Fischer Inc

Gulf Coast Pre-Stress Inc (PA) 228 452-7270
494 N Market St Pass Christian (39571) *(G-4086)*

Gulf Coast Protective Coating 601 261-9862
17 Power Ln Hattiesburg (39402) *(G-1978)*

Gulf Coast Shipyard Group Inc 228 276-1000
13085 Seaway Rd Gulfport (39503) *(G-1799)*

Gulf Coast Shipyard Group Inc (PA) 228 276-1051
13085 Seaway Rd Gulfport (39503) *(G-1800)*

Gulf Coast Wood Tool, Bay Saint Louis Also called Coast Wood Products Inc *(G-141)*

Gulf Concrete, Gulfport Also called MMC Materials Inc *(G-1833)*

Gulf Concrete Co Inc 601 798-3181
106 S Beech St Picayune (39466) *(G-4269)*

Gulf Concrete Technology LLC 228 575-3500
4739 W Oreck Rd Long Beach (39560) *(G-2938)*

Gulf Hydraulics & Pneumatics 228 392-1275
10420 Lamey Bridge Rd Diberville (39540) *(G-1205)*

Gulf Pine Energy LP (PA) 587 287-5400
8970 Highway 13 Newhebron (39140) *(G-3712)*

Gulf Pride Enterprises Inc (PA) 228 432-2488
391 Bayview Ave Biloxi (39530) *(G-249)*

Gulf Publishing Company Inc (HQ) 228 896-2100
205 Debuys Rd Gulfport (39507) *(G-1801)*

Gulf Ship LLC 228 897-9189
12351 Glascock Dr Gulfport (39503) *(G-1802)*

Gulf Ship LLC 985 601-4444
645 Lakeland East Dr # 101 Flowood (39232) *(G-1365)*

Gulf Shores Sea Products Inc 228 323-6370
5122 Ship Yard Rd Lakeshore (39558) *(G-2726)*

Gulf States Canners Inc 601 924-0511
1006 Indl Pk Dr Clinton (39056) *(G-824)*

Gulf States Fabrication Inc 601 426-9006
5311 Highway 15 N Laurel (39443) *(G-2773)*

Gulf States Forming Systems 601 428-1582
528 Avenue B Laurel (39440) *(G-2774)*

Gulf States Golf Cars 601 853-1510
235 Highway 51 Ridgeland (39157) *(G-4588)*

Gulf States Ready Mix, Gulfport Also called Delta Industries Inc *(G-1770)*

Gulf States Silver 601 415-4365
810 Fort Hill Dr Vicksburg (39183) *(G-5375)*

Gulf States Yamaha, Ridgeland Also called Gulf States Golf Cars *(G-4588)*

Gulfport Harbor Fuel 228 248-3474
720 S Cleveland Ave Long Beach (39560) *(G-2939)*

Gulley S Welding Service 601 938-6336
2510 B St Meridian (39301) *(G-3343)*

Gulleys Wldg Stl Erectors Inc 601 482-3767
5107 1st St Meridian (39307) *(G-3344)*

Gunns Transport Services LLC 662 402-3586
408 Jackson St Shaw (38773) *(G-4824)*

Gusoil Inc 601 735-2731
705 Azalea Dr Ste A Waynesboro (39367) *(G-5499)*

Guth Lighting 800 234-1890
938 S Green St Tupelo (38804) *(G-5148)*

Guth Lighting Systems, Tupelo Also called Jji Lighting Group Inc *(G-5163)*

Guys Logging 662 726-9301
40461 Ms Highway 14 W Macon (39341) *(G-3063)*

Gw Ministries 662 832-9756
148 County Road 294 Water Valley (38965) *(G-5469)*

Gwe, Jackson Also called Godsway Enterprises Inc *(G-2426)*

Gwendolyn Rucker 919 337-6218
1503 Arbor View Cir Diberville (39540) *(G-1206)*

H & G Sawmill LLC 601 885-2179
3213 Chapman Rd Utica (39175) *(G-5308)*

H & H Chief Sales Inc 601 267-9643
1309 Highway 35 N Carthage (39051) *(G-716)*

H & H Fabrication Inc 662 286-9475
243 County Road 604 Corinth (38834) *(G-1088)*

H & H Fabricators, Lucedale Also called H and H Fabrications *(G-2998)*

H & H Machine Shop 662 386-0778
1913 Washington Ave Columbus (39701) *(G-982)*

H & H Metal Fabrication LLC 662 489-4626
3066 Faulkner Rd Belden (38826) *(G-189)*

H & H Small Engine Repair 662 423-2741
1109 Battleground Dr Iuka (38852) *(G-2292)*

H & H Welding LLC 601 428-4788
5440 Highway 11 N Ellisville (39437) *(G-1255)*

H & L Millworks Inc 228 392-9913
16001 Mcclellan Rd Biloxi (39532) *(G-250)*

H & R, Edwards Also called H&R Consultants LLC *(G-1238)*

H and H Fabrications 601 508-7558
833 Seldom Rest Rd Lucedale (39452) *(G-2998)*

H and R Raceway LLC 601 373-2490
5785 Highway 18 W Jackson (39209) *(G-2436)*

H Delane Tucker Logging Inc 601 788-6320
Camp Eight Rd Rr 51 # 8 Richton (39476) *(G-4534)*

H Fleming Contractor 601 824-0902
525 Westwind Dr Brandon (39042) *(G-402)*

H O Hughes 601 261-3302
2807 Mamie St Hattiesburg (39401) *(G-1979)*

H S I Ready Mix 601 798-1665
130 Huey Stockstill Rd Picayune (39466) *(G-4270)*

H&M Metal Express LLC 601 798-4600
6981 Highway 11 Carriere (39426) *(G-693)*

H&M Syrup, Natchez Also called Hall Manufacturing LLC *(G-3565)*

H&R Consultants LLC 601 613-2288
200 Jackson St Edwards (39066) *(G-1238)*

H&S Sign Company 662 473-9300
234 County Road 550 Water Valley (38965) *(G-5470)*

Habe-ISE USA Inc 769 235-6650
160 Interstate Dr Richland (39218) *(G-4519)*

Hagen Corporation 601 932-3138
108 Jetport Dr Pearl (39208) *(G-4125)*

Hago Automotive Corp 662 593-0491
11 County Road 481 Iuka (38852) *(G-2293)*

Hal & Mals Restaurant & Brewry, Jackson Also called White Brothers Inc *(G-2630)*

Haley Clutch & Coupling Co Inc 662 332-8716
1820 Highway 1 N Greenville (38703) *(G-1556)*

Haley Marine Gears, Greenville Also called Marine Gears Inc *(G-1568)*

Halftone Press LLC 662 251-5036
129 5th St N Columbus (39701) *(G-983)*

Hall Manufacturing LLC 601 445-6640
92 Mullins Rd Natchez (39120) *(G-3565)*

Hall Metal Craft, Jackson Also called Kennedy Hall *(G-2462)*

Hall S Customized Printing 601 261-2440
405 Lakewood Loop Hattiesburg (39402) *(G-1980)*

Halliburton Energy Services 601 649-9290
1384 Sndrsville Sharon Rd Sandersville (39477) *(G-4725)*

Halliburton Service Division, Sandersville Also called Halliburton Energy Services *(G-4725)*

Halls Welding Service 601 477-3925
1011 N Front St Ellisville (39437) *(G-1256)*

Halls Woodworking 601 792-5955
265 Williamson Mill Rd Prentiss (39474) *(G-4421)*

Halo Southern Publishing LLC 662 299-2999
618 Frederick Dr Cleveland (38732) *(G-794)*

Hamilton Beach Brands Inc 662 890-9869
11624 S Distribution Cv Olive Branch (38654) *(G-3843)*

Hammett Gravel Co Inc (PA) 662 834-1867
72 Hammett Dr Lexington (39095) *(G-2903)*

Hampton Industries LLC 601 441-7604
102 Bellair Dr Hattiesburg (39402) *(G-1981)*

Hancock Advg Specialities 662 842-1820
4008 W Main St Ste 4 Tupelo (38801) *(G-5149)*

Hancock Equipment & Oil Co LLC 662 726-4556
18700 Us Hwy 45 S Brooksville (39739) *(G-555)*

Hancock, W S Construction Co, Bentonia Also called W S Red Hancock Inc *(G-213)*

Hancor Inc 601 629-9040
5695 Highway 61 S Vicksburg (39180) *(G-5376)*

Hanger Inc 228 604-0818
9034 Carl Legett Rd Ste B Gulfport (39503) *(G-1803)*

Hanger Clinic, Meridian Also called Hanger Prsthetcs & Ortho Inc *(G-3345)*

Hanger Clnic, Jackson Also called Hanger Prsthetcs & Ortho Inc *(G-2648)*

Hanger Prosthetic Orthopedics 601 939-2100
15 River Bend Pl Ste B Jackson (39232) *(G-2647)*

Hanger Prosthetics & Orthotics, Jackson Also called Hanger Prosthetic Orthopedics *(G-2647)*

Hanger Prsthetcs & Ortho Inc 662 451-7495
1603 Strong Ave Greenwood (38930) *(G-1627)*

Hanger Prsthetcs & Ortho Inc 601 268-5520
1104 S 28th Ave Hattiesburg (39402) *(G-1982)*

Hanger Prsthetcs & Ortho Inc 601 883-3341
1111 N Frontage Rd Vicksburg (39180) *(G-5377)*

Hanger Prsthetcs & Ortho Inc 228 822-0109
1302 44th Ave Gulfport (39501) *(G-1804)*

Hanger Prsthetcs & Ortho Inc 228 875-8354
7350 Ms 57 I Ocean Springs (39565) *(G-3761)*

Hanger Prsthetcs & Ortho Inc 601 939-2100
15 River Bend Pl Ste B Jackson (39232) *(G-2648)*

Hanger Prsthetcs & Ortho Inc 662 844-6734
502 Council Cir Tupelo (38801) *(G-5150)*

Hanger Prsthetcs & Ortho Inc 601 693-1002
1903 23rd Ave Meridian (39301) *(G-3345)*

Hanger Prsthetcs & Ortho Inc 662 335-6828
2331 Highway 1 S Greenville (38701) *(G-1557)*

Hanger Prsthetcs & Ortho Inc 601 442-7742
304 Highland Blvd Ste C Natchez (39120) *(G-3566)*

Hanger Prsthetcs & Ortho Inc 662 323-3349
100 Brandon Rd Ste D Starkville (39759) *(G-4947)*

Hanging By A Thread LLC 662 449-5198
7401 Love Rd Hernando (38632) *(G-2133)*

Hankins Lumber Company Inc (PA) 662 226-2961
496 Nat G Troutt Rd Elliott (38926) *(G-1244)*

Hanson Athletic Inc 601 389-0403
170 Canal Pl Philadelphia (39350) *(G-4216)*

Harbison-Fischer Inc 601 442-7961
24 Feltus St Natchez (39120) *(G-3567)*

Harbison-Fischer Inc 601 428-7919
5417 Highway 11 N Ellisville (39437) *(G-1257)*

(PA)=Parent Co (HQ)=Headquarters (DH)=Div Headquarters

2019 Harris Directory of
Mississippi Manufacturers

287

Harbour Energy Inc

ALPHABETIC SECTION

Harbour Energy Inc 601 992-2277
133 Westlake Dr Brandon (39047) *(G-403)*

Hard Rock Sand & Gravel 601 876-2929
787 Highway 27 S Tylertown (39667) *(G-5271)*

Harden Enterprises Inc 662 841-9292
114 N Spring St Tupelo (38804) *(G-5151)*

Harden Enterprises Inc (PA) 662 841-9292
114 N Spring St Tupelo (38804) *(G-5152)*

Hardwire Inc 662 285-2312
926 S Church Ave Louisville (39339) *(G-2971)*

Hardy Manufacturing Co Inc 601 656-5866
12345 Road 505 Philadelphia (39350) *(G-4217)*

Harlan Services LLC 601 513-5318
301 5th Ave Se Magee (39111) *(G-3177)*

Harold A Sparks Septic Tanks 662 454-7244
52 County Road 8 Golden (38847) *(G-1526)*

Harold Knight Sew Mchs & Appls (PA) 601 425-2220
721 S Magnolia St Laurel (39440) *(G-2775)*

Harold Sewing Center & Trctrs, Laurel *Also called Harold Knight Sew Mchs & Appls* *(G-2775)*

Harper Industries Inc 601 947-2746
52 Virginia St Ste A Lucedale (39452) *(G-2999)*

Harper Timber Inc 601 833-2121
20 E Lincoln Rd Ne Brookhaven (39601) *(G-499)*

Harrell Welding Service LLC 662 456-2444
1654 Highway 8 W Houston (38851) *(G-2244)*

Harrells Metal Works Inc 662 226-0982
1798 Highway 332 Grenada (38901) *(G-1683)*

Harris Custom Ink LLC 662 338-4242
6810 Crumpler Blvd # 203 Olive Branch (38654) *(G-3844)*

Harris Frm Hven Spcltymillwork 601 953-2964
657 John Day Rd Canton (39046) *(G-660)*

Harris Ja Inc 662 205-4370
107 Old Runway Rd Tupelo (38801) *(G-5153)*

Harris Sheet Metal, Pascagoula *Also called Steve Harris* *(G-4069)*

Harris Signs 601 624-4658
1496 Old Lake Rd Brandon (39042) *(G-404)*

Harrisburg Publishing, Hattiesburg *Also called Lamar County News Inc* *(G-2014)*

Harrison Brothers Incorporated 601 536-2069
3243 Scr 558 Pulaski (39152) *(G-4431)*

Harrison Logging Inc 662 226-7908
29820 Highway 8 E Grenada (38901) *(G-1684)*

Harrison Manufacturing LLC 601 519-0558
126 W Mayes St Jackson (39213) *(G-2437)*

Harrison Mobile Welding 662 706-4692
3079 Houston Palestine Rd Baldwyn (38824) *(G-77)*

Hart & Cooley Inc 662 890-8000
8601 Hacks Cross Rd Olive Branch (38654) *(G-3845)*

Hartley Equipment Company Inc 601 499-0944
109 Aulenbrock Dr Canton (39046) *(G-661)*

Hartson-Kennedy Cabinet Top Co 228 896-1548
10115 Lorraine Rd Gulfport (39503) *(G-1805)*

Harvest Select Catfish, Inverness *Also called Alabama Catfish Inc* *(G-2272)*

Harvest Trends Inc 716 514-6788
6336 Point Porteaux Rd Ocean Springs (39564) *(G-3762)*

Hastys Mulch & Stone LLC 601 485-2120
5321 Arundel Rd Meridian (39307) *(G-3346)*

Hat Shack Inc 601 264-1017
1000 Turtle Creek Dr # 600 Hattiesburg (39402) *(G-1983)*

Hatchett Perfection Prints LLC 662 260-6244
1155 Dorshire Dr Southaven (38671) *(G-4876)*

Hattiesburg American 601 582-4321
4200 Mamie St Ste 200 Hattiesburg (39402) *(G-1984)*

Hattiesburg American Pubg Co 601 582-4321
4200 Mamie St Ste 200 Hattiesburg (39402) *(G-1985)*

Hattiesburg Hydraulics Sls Svc 601 264-6606
6967 U S Highway 49 Hattiesburg (39402) *(G-1986)*

Hattiesburg Motors LLC 601 818-2255
2860 Oak Grove Rd Hattiesburg (39402) *(G-1987)*

Hattiesburg Paper Company LLC 601 545-3400
1 Wl Runnels Indus Dr Hattiesburg (39401) *(G-1988)*

Hattiesburg Yard, Petal *Also called Legacy Vulcan LLC* *(G-4191)*

Havard Mfg Inc 601 766-9170
1235 Henry Cochran Rd Lucedale (39452) *(G-3000)*

Havard Printing Co 662 781-2613
7431 Meadowbrook Dr Horn Lake (38637) *(G-2202)*

Havards Construction LLC 601 766-9841
5219 Main St Lucedale (39452) *(G-3001)*

Hawas Inc 601 876-0806
225 Hobgood Rd Tylertown (39667) *(G-5272)*

Hawkeye Glove Manufacturing 662 681-6278
2985 E Roane Ave Eupora (39744) *(G-1286)*

Hawkeye Industries Inc 662 842-3333
1126 N Eason Blvd Tupelo (38804) *(G-5154)*

Hawks Feed Mill 662 564-2920
7005 Holly Springs Rd Hernando (38632) *(G-2134)*

Hayes Transportation LLC 662 582-5357
150 Woodard Ln Durant (39063) *(G-1226)*

Haygoods Industrial Engravers 228 769-7488
2114 Chicot St Pascagoula (39581) *(G-4036)*

Haynes Enterprises Inc 662 843-4411
1401 S Davis Ave Cleveland (38732) *(G-795)*

Hazlehurst Lumber Company Inc 601 535-7779
1027 Old Port Gibson Rd Hermanville (39086) *(G-2121)*

Hc2, Jackson *Also called Vizionz Unlimited LLC* *(G-2622)*

Headrick Signs & Graphics Inc 601 649-1977
1 Freedom Sq Laurel (39440) *(G-2776)*

Healthy Growth Ntrtn Program 901 493-7991
4725 Deer Run Rd Olive Branch (38654) *(G-3846)*

Hear Again 601 626-0050
9369 Highway 19 N Collinsville (39325) *(G-869)*

Heartland Catfish Company Inc 662 254-7100
55001 Highway 82 W Itta Bena (38941) *(G-2280)*

Hearz Yer Sign 601 683-3636
702 Decatur St Newton (39345) *(G-3721)*

Heath Aviation 662 283-9833
219 Airport Dr Winona (38967) *(G-5599)*

Heavenly Confections 601 660-1986
1106 First St Natchez (39120) *(G-3568)*

Heavenly Ham, Ocean Springs *Also called Honey Baked* *(G-3764)*

Heavy Duty Industries Inc 601 425-1011
841 Masonite Dr Laurel (39440) *(G-2777)*

Hederman Brothers LLC 601 853-7300
247 Industrial Dr N Madison (39110) *(G-3105)*

Heidi's, Cleveland *Also called Robinsons Retail Inc* *(G-806)*

Helanbak LLC 601 736-6112
360 Pine Grove Church Rd Foxworth (39483) *(G-1431)*

Helena Agri-Enterprises LLC 662 746-7466
1205 Rialto Rd Yazoo City (39194) *(G-5635)*

Helena Agri-Enterprises LLC 662 283-3990
1199 Highway 51 Winona (38967) *(G-5600)*

Helena Chemical Company 662 563-9631
3409 Farrish Gravel Rd Batesville (38606) *(G-108)*

Helena Chemical Company 662 383-0004
1500 Port Rd Friars Point (38631) *(G-1442)*

Helmerich & Payne Intl Drlg Co 601 939-1589
102 Ware St Pearl (39208) *(G-4126)*

Helmitin Inc 662 895-4565
11110 Airport Rd Olive Branch (38654) *(G-3847)*

Helping Hand Family Pharmacy 601 631-6837
1670 Highway 61 N Vicksburg (39183) *(G-5378)*

Helping Hands Pharmacy, Vicksburg *Also called Helping Hand Family Pharmacy* *(G-5378)*

Hemline 601 898-3456
140 Township Ave Ste 102 Ridgeland (39157) *(G-4589)*

Henns Nest Inc 601 268-3577
5317 Old Highway 11 19b Hattiesburg (39402) *(G-1989)*

Henry Davis & Son Logging, De Kalb *Also called Henry E Davis Logging* *(G-1165)*

Henry E Davis Logging 601 677-3669
827 Davis Rd De Kalb (39328) *(G-1165)*

Henry Lyell 601 355-1080
760 Arlington St Jackson (39202) *(G-2438)*

Her Heart Shop 662 523-9568
240 County Road 501 Shannon (38868) *(G-4809)*

Heritage Custom Cabinets LLC 228 323-8389
22247 Tootle Rd Gulfport (39503) *(G-1806)*

Heritage Plastics Inc (PA) 404 425-1905
1002 Hunt St Picayune (39466) *(G-4271)*

Heritage Press Pblications LLC 601 737-2086
10231 Shallow Creek Dr Collinsville (39325) *(G-870)*

Heritage Yarns 601 956-1478
5875 Baxter Dr Jackson (39211) *(G-2439)*

Hernando Redi Mix Inc 662 429-7571
190 Motor Scooter Dr Nesbit (38651) *(G-3653)*

Herrington Millworks 601 845-8056
2709 W Mountain Creek Rd Florence (39073) *(G-1325)*

Hesters Certified Welding 662 566-7305
1060 Road 261 Tupelo (38801) *(G-5155)*

Hewlett Industries Inc (PA) 662 773-4626
407 Industrial Park Rd Starkville (39759) *(G-4948)*

Hey There App LLC 228 238-0344
9405 Meadowlark Ave Ocean Springs (39564) *(G-3763)*

Hh Services 662 283-1131
708 S Applegate St Winona (38967) *(G-5601)*

HI Tech Concrete Inc 228 452-2125
327 Courtenay Ave Pass Christian (39571) *(G-4087)*

Hi-Tech Prosthetics Orthotics, Southaven *Also called Human Technology Inc* *(G-4878)*

Hickok Inc-Supreme Elec Div, Greenwood *Also called Supreme Electronics Corp* *(G-1653)*

Hickory Creek Inc 228 832-2649
21595 Yankee Town Rd Saucier (39574) *(G-4754)*

Hickory Springs Mfg Co 662 489-6684
397 Stafford Blvd Pontotoc (38863) *(G-4332)*

Hicks Hot Shot Services LLC 601 498-7482
593 County Road 79 Stringer (39481) *(G-5001)*

High Country Woodworking 228 396-2921
9245 Nancy Dr Biloxi (39532) *(G-251)*

High Edge Inc 601 326-2025
5420 J R Lynch St Ext Jackson (39209) *(G-2440)*

High Roads, Ocean Springs *Also called Vape and Bake LLC* *(G-3793)*

2019 Harris Directory of
Mississippi Manufacturers

(G-0000) Company's Geographic Section entry number

288

ALPHABETIC SECTION

Huddleston, James Farms, Booneville

High Tech Inc 228 868-6632
21120 Johnson Rd Long Beach (39560) *(G-2940)*

High Yield AG Solutions LLC 662 546-4463
123 Jefferson St Starkville (39759) *(G-4949)*

Highlands Industries Inc 601 454-3901
132 Virginia Valley Dr Brandon (39047) *(G-405)*

Highside Chemicals Inc 228 896-9220
11114 Reichold Rd Gulfport (39503) *(G-1807)*

Hilderbrand Cabinet Doors LLC 662 755-8626
4433 Mechanicsburg Rd Bentonia (39040) *(G-211)*

Hilgerson Printing 601 684-6978
400 Delaware Ave Ste A McComb (39648) *(G-3252)*

Hillbilly Wines LLC 228 234-4411
21310 Yankee Town Rd Saucier (39574) *(G-4755)*

Hills Brothers Cnstr & Engrg 662 837-7415
20831 Highway 15 Falkner (38629) *(G-1294)*

Hills Welding & Crane Rental 662 846-6789
172 N Blivar Cnty Line Rd Cleveland (38732) *(G-796)*

Hillshire Brands Company 662 890-6069
8110 Camp Creek Rd # 125 Olive Branch (38654) *(G-3848)*

Hillshire Brands Company 601 948-4632
4201 Space Center Dr Jackson (39209) *(G-2441)*

Hilton National Corporation 228 385-9800
2118 Lauren Dr Biloxi (39532) *(G-252)*

Hint Hunter LLC 228 273-4064
10253 Diberville Blvd B Diberville (39540) *(G-1207)*

Hiro Telemedicine Systems LLC 312 835-1859
171 Cambrooke Hattiesburg (39402) *(G-1990)*

Hj Norris LLC (PA) 228 217-6704
9720b Highway 63 Moss Point (39562) *(G-3479)*

HM Richards Inc 662 365-9485
120 H M Richards Way Guntown (38849) *(G-1899)*

HMC Metal Forming Inc 662 538-5447
1100 Denmill Rd New Albany (38652) *(G-3682)*

Hobby Const Co 662 803-1599
4985 Shiloh Rd Louisville (39339) *(G-2972)*

Hobies Sports and Outdoors 601 833-9700
844 Brookway Blvd Brookhaven (39601) *(G-500)*

Hodge Podge Screen Prtg Inc 662 226-1636
333 Sunset Loop Grenada (38901) *(G-1685)*

Hodges Wood Products Inc 662 728-3716
289 Highway 371 Marietta (38856) *(G-3216)*

Hoerner Boxes Inc 662 842-2491
100 Old Runway Rd Tupelo (38801) *(G-5156)*

Hoffinger Industries 662 890-7930
6928 Cobblestone Blvd # 200 Southaven (38672) *(G-4877)*

Hoffman Lenses Inc 662 815-2803
105 College St Blue Mountain (38610) *(G-291)*

Hol-Mac Corporation (PA) 601 764-4121
2730 Highway 15 Bay Springs (39422) *(G-162)*

Hol-Mac Corporation 601 764-4121
160 Commerce Dr Bay Springs (39422) *(G-163)*

Hol-Mac Corporation 601 764-4121
Hwy 15 N Bay Springs (39422) *(G-164)*

Holcomb Handiman Svcs Cstm Woo 601 394-4284
1137 W 20th St Laurel (39440) *(G-2778)*

Holifield Engineering Inc 601 276-3391
1062 Golf Ln Summit (39666) *(G-5015)*

Holland Grading Service 601 825-2364
1284 Star Rd Brandon (39042) *(G-406)*

Holloways Welding Service LLC 601 729-4403
468 County Road 7 Stringer (39481) *(G-5002)*

Holly Tool & Die Inc 662 252-1144
805 Hwy 7 N Holly Springs (38635) *(G-2177)*

Holmes County Herald, Lexington *Also called East Holmes Publishing Entps* *(G-2901)*

Holmes Hilton 601 736-5757
1438 Highway 586 Foxworth (39483) *(G-1432)*

Holmes Industries LLC 601 635-4409
855 County Pond Rd Decatur (39327) *(G-1173)*

Holmes Stationary and Gifts 601 276-2700
1136 Highway 51 N Summit (39666) *(G-5016)*

Homan Forest Products Inc 662 862-2145
105 Homan Rd Fulton (38843) *(G-1455)*

Homan Industries, Fulton *Also called Homan Forest Products Inc* *(G-1455)*

Homan Industries Inc 662 862-2125
1 Homan Rd Fulton (38843) *(G-1456)*

Homans Wood Products 662 862-2145
101 Homan Rd Fulton (38843) *(G-1457)*

Home Decor Company 662 844-7191
1141 Ryder St Tupelo (38804) *(G-5157)*

Homeland Inc 662 728-7799
200 Park Pl Booneville (38829) *(G-329)*

Homestretch Inc 662 963-2494
146 Furniture Dr Nettleton (38858) *(G-3660)*

Homestretch Holdings LLC 662 963-2494
146 Furniture Dr Nettleton (38858) *(G-3661)*

Hondumex Global LLC 601 732-6505
38 W Second Ave Morton (39117) *(G-3447)*

Honey Baked 228 875-5828
1533 Bienville Blvd Ocean Springs (39564) *(G-3764)*

Honey Island Software Inc 985 265-4192
16048 Oahu Rd Pearlington (39572) *(G-4160)*

Honeyland Inc 870 635-1160
25439 Elmer Ladner Rd Pass Christian (39571) *(G-4088)*

Honeywell International Inc 228 575-3706
2012 15th St Service Bldg Gulfport (39501) *(G-1808)*

Honnoll Sand & Gravel LLC 662 487-3854
3013 Viney Creek Rd Sardis (38666) *(G-4740)*

Hood Companies Inc (PA) 601 582-1545
623 N Main St Ste 100 Hattiesburg (39401) *(G-1991)*

Hood Container Corporation (HQ) 601 582-1545
623 N Main St Ste 100 Hattiesburg (39401) *(G-1992)*

Hood Flexible Packaging, Madison *Also called Hood Packaging Corporation* *(G-3106)*

Hood Flexible Packaging Corp (PA) 903 593-1793
623 N Main St Ste 200 Hattiesburg (39401) *(G-1993)*

Hood Industries Inc (PA) 601 264-2962
15 Professional Pkwy # 8 Hattiesburg (39402) *(G-1994)*

Hood Industries Inc 601 928-3737
1945 First St S Wiggins (39577) *(G-5584)*

Hood Industries Inc 601 735-5038
915 Industrial Park Rd Waynesboro (39367) *(G-5500)*

Hood Industries Inc 601 784-3414
226 Delta Pine Rd Beaumont (39423) *(G-185)*

Hood Industries Inc 601 264-2962
15 Professional Pkwy # 8 Hattiesburg (39402) *(G-1995)*

Hood Packaging Corporation 770 981-5400
25 Woodgreen Pl Madison (39110) *(G-3106)*

Hood Packaging Corporation (HQ) 601 853-7260
25 Woodgreen Pl Madison (39110) *(G-3107)*

Hoop Logging LLC 662 230-7553
1011 Whitten Rd Cascilla (38920) *(G-728)*

Hoop-It-Up Embroidery 662 244-7212
486 Elm Dr Columbus (39701) *(G-984)*

Hooper Sales Co Incorporated 662 526-5668
405 Section Line Rd Como (38619) *(G-1048)*

Hoopla Monogramming & Gifts 228 860-4774
76 48th St Gulfport (39507) *(G-1809)*

Hoopsnake Press - 662 260-5133
1249 N Coley Rd Tupelo (38801) *(G-5158)*

Horizon Publications Inc 662 494-1422
26463 E Main St West Point (39773) *(G-5546)*

Horizon Publications Inc 662 323-1642
304 E Lampkin St Starkville (39759) *(G-4950)*

Horizon Shipbuilding Inc 251 824-1660
17629 Highway 613 Moss Point (39562) *(G-3480)*

Hose Products Division, Batesville *Also called Parker-Hannifin Corporation* *(G-117)*

Hoshizaki of Jackson 601 969-4200
1215 High St Jackson (39202) *(G-2442)*

Hospitality Sign Company 601 898-8393
123 Munich Dr Madison (39110) *(G-3108)*

Hot Mix Asphalt, Greenwood *Also called J J Ferguson Sand & Grav Inc* *(G-1630)*

Hot Sticks Manufacturing Co 228 467-0762
14198 Rd D Stnnis Indsl Kiln (39556) *(G-2680)*

Houston Newspapers Inc (HQ) 662 456-3771
225 E Madison St Houston (38851) *(G-2245)*

Houston Sign Design 662 728-2327
102 Summer Ln Booneville (38829) *(G-330)*

Howard Computers, Laurel *Also called Howard Industries Inc* *(G-2779)*

Howard E Stover 601 984-3702
1650 Lelia Dr Ste 102 Jackson (39216) *(G-2443)*

Howard Industries Inc 601 422-0033
580 Eastview Dr Laurel (39443) *(G-2779)*

Howard Industries Inc 601 847-5278
2778 Simpson Highway 49 Mendenhall (39114) *(G-3281)*

Howard Industries Inc 601 399-5053
32 Howard Dr Ellisville (39437) *(G-1258)*

Howard Industries Inc 601 425-3151
3225 Pendorff Rd Laurel (39440) *(G-2780)*

Howard Technology Solutions, Ellisville *Also called Howard Industries Inc* *(G-1258)*

Howard Technology Solutions 601 428-2200
580 Eastview Dr Laurel (39443) *(G-2781)*

Howells Welding & Fabricating 601 663-6098
12320 Highway 492 E Union (39365) *(G-5298)*

Howse Implement Company Inc 601 428-0841
2013 Highway 184 Laurel (39443) *(G-2782)*

Hpc LLC 601 545-3400
1 Wl Runnels Indus Dr Hattiesburg (39401) *(G-1996)*

Hrd Safety 601 213-6358
14 Northtown Dr Ste 206 Jackson (39211) *(G-2444)*

Hsi Ready Mix, Picayune *Also called Huey P Stockstill LLC* *(G-4272)*

Hsm Solutions 352 622-7583
234 Cdf Blvd Lee City Verona (38879) *(G-5333)*

Hub City Brush Inc 601 584-7314
106 Mc Aulay Dr Petal (39465) *(G-4187)*

Hubbard Publishing LLC 662 638-3821
76 County Road 1061 Oxford (38655) *(G-3957)*

Huddleston Farm Service Inc 662 728-5288
424 County Road 3371 Booneville (38829) *(G-331)*

Huddleston, James Farms, Booneville *Also called Huddleston Farm Service Inc* *(G-331)*

ALPHABETIC

(PA)=Parent Co (HQ)=Headquarters (DH)=Div Headquarters

2019 Harris Directory of
Mississippi Manufacturers

289

Hudson Outdoor Sign LLC

ALPHABETIC SECTION

Hudson Outdoor Sign LLC 601 947-4608
170 N Lake Rd Lucedale (39452) *(G-3002)*

Hudson Salvage Inc 601 947-0092
12101 Old 63 S Lucedale (39452) *(G-3003)*

Hudspeth Wood Products Inc 662 263-5902
3800 Webster St Maben (39750) *(G-3046)*

Huey P Stockstill LLC (PA) 601 798-2981
130 Huey Stockstill Rd Picayune (39466) *(G-4272)*

Huey P Stockstill LLC 601 798-2981
130 Huey Stockstill Rd Picayune (39466) *(G-4273)*

Huey P Stockstill LLC 228 868-8678
10130 Goldin Ln Gulfport (39503) *(G-1810)*

Huffco LLC 662 284-6517
3263 N Polk St Corinth (38834) *(G-1089)*

Hughes Eastern, Ridgeland *Also called Crosbys Creek Oil & Gas LLC* *(G-4567)*

Hughes Eastern Corporation (PA) 601 957-1778
605 Northpark Dr Ste A Ridgeland (39157) *(G-4590)*

Hughes Outdoors & Marin 662 287-8607
335a County Road 218 Corinth (38834) *(G-1090)*

Human Technology Inc 662 349-4909
1880 Goodman Rd E Southaven (38671) *(G-4878)*

Hunt Process Corp-Southern 601 856-8811
138 N Wheatley St Ridgeland (39157) *(G-4591)*

Hunt Refining Company 843 236-5098
2600 Dorsey St Vicksburg (39180) *(G-5379)*

Hunt Refining Company 601 426-1821
177 Haney Rd Heidelberg (39439) *(G-2117)*

Hunt Refining Company 601 796-2331
7539 U S Highway 11 Lumberton (39455) *(G-3030)*

Hunt Southland Refining Co, Heidelberg *Also called Hunt Refining Company* *(G-2117)*

Hunter Douglas Inc 662 690-8190
222 Laney Rd Shannon (38868) *(G-4810)*

Hunter Douglas Window Fashions, Shannon *Also called Hunter Douglas Inc* *(G-4810)*

Hunter Engineering Company 769 524-4949
2125 Tv Rd Jackson (39204) *(G-2445)*

Hunter Engineering Company 662 653-3194
33814 Hunter Engineering Durant (39063) *(G-1227)*

Hunter Engineering Company 601 857-8883
2489 Raymond Clinton Rd Raymond (39154) *(G-4489)*

Hunter Trading Company LLC 866 521-5012
7282 Maygan Dr Olive Branch (38654) *(G-3849)*

Hunters Hollow Inc 662 234-5945
658 Highway 6 W Oxford (38655) *(G-3958)*

Hunterworks LLC 601 771-0070
9291 Collinsville Cir Collinsville (39325) *(G-871)*

Huntin Camp LLC 601 649-6334
2110 Sandy Ln Laurel (39443) *(G-2783)*

Huntington Ingalls Inc 228 935-1122
1000 Access Rd Pascagoula (39567) *(G-4037)*

Huntington Ingalls Industries 228 935-1122
1000 Access Rd Pascagoula (39567) *(G-4038)*

Hurley Farm & Feed 228 588-9156
7000 Hwy 614 Hurley (39555) *(G-2260)*

Hutchinson Island Mining Corp 601 799-4070
216 Dan Stewart Rd Picayune (39466) *(G-4274)*

Hutchinson Logging 601 943-5486
7585 Highway 35 Bassfield (39421) *(G-92)*

Hy Gain, Starkville *Also called Mfj Enterprises Inc* *(G-4959)*

Hyas, Starkville *Also called High Yield AG Solutions LLC* *(G-4949)*

Hybrid Plastics Incorporated 601 544-3466
55 Wl Runnels Indus Dr Hattiesburg (39401) *(G-1997)*

Hydesoft Computing LLC 601 629-8607
110 Roseland Dr Vicksburg (39180) *(G-5380)*

Hydradyne LLC 601 833-9475
58 Highway 84 E Brookhaven (39601) *(G-501)*

Hydrasep Inc 662 429-4088
400 Vaiden Dr Hernando (38632) *(G-2135)*

Hydro Hose Corp 662 842-2761
1731 Mccullough Blvd Tupelo (38801) *(G-5159)*

Hydrogen Peroxide 662 329-9085
4374 Nashville Ferry Rd E Columbus (39702) *(G-985)*

Hydrolevel 228 875-1821
505 Jackson Ave Ocean Springs (39564) *(G-3765)*

Hydrostatic Transm Svc LLC 662 680-8899
404 Air Park Rd Tupelo (38801) *(G-5160)*

Hyperco, Pontotoc *Also called Matthew Warren Inc* *(G-4345)*

Hyperco 662 488-4567
260 Industrial Dr Pontotoc (38863) *(G-4333)*

Hyster Capital, Natchez *Also called Nmhg Financial Services* *(G-3601)*

I C S, Pascagoula *Also called Industrial & Crane Svcs Inc* *(G-4039)*

I Care Optical Inc 601 372-3801
160 Mctyere Ave Terry (39170) *(G-5069)*

I Care Optical Inc 228 864-4397
2526 16th Ave Gulfport (39501) *(G-1811)*

I Care Optical Inc (PA) 601 352-3576
4506 Pine Lake Dr Terry (39170) *(G-5070)*

I T T, Southaven *Also called ITT LLC* *(G-4879)*

Ice Industries Inc 419 842-3612
200 American Way Grenada (38901) *(G-1686)*

Ice Industries Inc 662 226-1161
635 Highway 332 Grenada (38901) *(G-1687)*

Ice Industries Grenada, Grenada *Also called Ice Industries Inc* *(G-1687)*

Ice Plant Inc 601 485-9111
202 Highway 19 N Meridian (39307) *(G-3347)*

Icon Outdoors LLC (PA) 662 895-3651
7282 Maygan Dr Olive Branch (38654) *(G-3850)*

ID Group Inc (PA) 601 982-2651
280 Trace Colony Park Dr Ridgeland (39157) *(G-4592)*

Ideal Foam LLC 662 489-2264
300 Stafford Blvd Pontotoc (38863) *(G-4334)*

Ideal Software Systems Inc 601 693-1673
3839 Old Highway 45 N Meridian (39301) *(G-3348)*

Identities Graphic Solutions 601 917-9983
3115 5th Ave Meridian (39305) *(G-3349)*

Idom Enterprising Inc 601 583-4852
508 Lakeshore Dr Hattiesburg (39401) *(G-1998)*

Idom Fabrication, Hattiesburg *Also called Idom Enterprising Inc* *(G-1998)*

Ii-VI Incorporated 662 615-5040
60 Technology Blvd Starkville (39759) *(G-4951)*

Illinois Tool Works Inc 662 489-4151
364 Stafford Blvd Pontotoc (38863) *(G-4335)*

Illusions Neon & Accessories 662 299-6366
783 County Road 231 Greenwood (38930) *(G-1628)*

Illusionsneon.com, Greenwood *Also called Illusions Neon & Accessories* *(G-1628)*

Illustrative Ink LLC 228 354-9559
1844 Blaylock Rd Saucier (39574) *(G-4756)*

Image Screen Printing Inc 662 489-5668
2111 Highway 15 N Pontotoc (38863) *(G-4336)*

Images Galore Signs LLC 228 818-5449
3002 Bienville Blvd Ste A Ocean Springs (39564) *(G-3766)*

Imagine Iron Works, Brookhaven *Also called B & O Machine & Wldg Co Inc* *(G-481)*

Imaging Infomatics, Pass Christian *Also called Imaging Informatics LLC* *(G-4089)*

Imaging Informatics LLC 228 332-0674
529 E Second St Pass Christian (39571) *(G-4089)*

Imerys Minerals Usa Inc 662 369-6411
10033 Imc Rd Aberdeen (39730) *(G-14)*

Imes Communications of El Paso 662 328-2424
516 Main St Columbus (39701) *(G-986)*

Immunotek Bio Centers LLC 601 462-5145
416 18th Ave Meridian (39301) *(G-3350)*

Impact Printing & Design 601 764-9461
3362 Highway 15 N Bay Springs (39422) *(G-165)*

Impressions Inc 601 477-9608
78 Jordan Loop Ellisville (39437) *(G-1259)*

In Motion Orthotics 662 258-8201
224 Meadowlane St Eupora (39744) *(G-1287)*

In The Black Software LLC 228 697-2120
202 Woodland Cir Ocean Springs (39564) *(G-3767)*

Inca Presswood-Pallets Ltd 662 487-1016
2333 S Frontage Rd Sardis (38666) *(G-4741)*

Inca Presswood-Pallets Ltd 662 487-1016
2333 S Frontage Sardis In Sardis (38666) *(G-4742)*

Incapitalmgcom LLC 601 268-0103
5891 Hwy 49 60 Unit 205 Hattiesburg (39402) *(G-1999)*

Inciteful Analytics Corp 601 870-4004
915 Dillard Ln Se Meadville (39653) *(G-3275)*

Income Online Residual 662 420-7636
4199 Robinson Crossing Olive Branch (38654) *(G-3851)*

Independent Furn Sup Co Inc 662 844-8411
3609 W Jackson St Tupelo (38801) *(G-5161)*

Independent Metal Craft LLC 601 488-4789
1016 Industrial Park Dr Clinton (39056) *(G-825)*

Independents Service Company 662 287-2431
611 Childs St Corinth (38834) *(G-1091)*

Indi-Bel Inc 662 887-1226
1842 Highway 82 W Indianola (38751) *(G-2265)*

Indianola Electric Co Inc 662 887-3292
352 Hwy 49 N Indianola (38751) *(G-2266)*

Indianola Pecan House Inc (PA) 662 887-5420
1013 Highway 82 E Indianola (38751) *(G-2267)*

Indianola Pecan House Inc 601 693-1998
1410 Bonita Lakes Cir Meridian (39301) *(G-3351)*

Industrial & Crane Svcs Inc 601 914-4491
2301 Petit Bois St Pascagoula (39581) *(G-4039)*

Industrial Cleaning Svcs LLC 662 397-6735
101 County Road 461 Saltillo (38866) *(G-4712)*

Industrial Elc Mtr Works Inc 601 679-5500
1551 Redman Rd Meridian (39305) *(G-3352)*

Industrial Fabricators Inc 662 327-1776
274 Structural Ln Columbus (39702) *(G-987)*

Industrial Machine Mfg 601 737-5017
11470a Ctr Hl Martin Rd Collinsville (39325) *(G-872)*

Industrial Steel Corporation (PA) 601 932-5555
821 Highway 475 S Pearl (39208) *(G-4127)*

Industrial Steel Rule Die Corp 601 932-5555
203 Priester Dr Jackson (39208) *(G-2649)*

Industrial Timber LLC 662 346-4488
200 Mccomb Ave Saltillo (38866) *(G-4713)*

2019 Harris Directory of
Mississippi Manufacturers

(G-0000) Company's Geographic Section entry number

ALPHABETIC SECTION

J & S Enterprises LLC

Industrial Timber LLC 662 282-4000
415 Devaughn Rd Mantachie (38855) *(G-3199)*

Industrial Timber LLC 662 837-3213
781 County Road 549 Ripley (38663) *(G-4661)*

Info Services Inc 601 898-7858
125 Solleftea Dr Madison (39110) *(G-3109)*

Informa Business Media Inc 662 624-8503
14920 Us Hwy 61 Clarksdale (38614) *(G-768)*

Informa Media Inc 662 624-8503
14920 Us Hwy 61 Clarksdale (38614) *(G-769)*

Ingalls Shipbuilding, Pascagoula *Also called Huntington Ingalls Inc* *(G-4037)*

Ingalls Shipbuilding Inc 877 871-2058
1000 Access Rd Pascagoula (39567) *(G-4040)*

Ingalls Shipbuilding Inc 228 935-2887
1109 Saint Ann St Gautier (39553) *(G-1494)*

Ingram Roman Inc 601 954-8367
386 Green Oak Ln Madison (39110) *(G-3110)*

Inhealth Medical 662 283-5750
107 N Front St Winona (38967) *(G-5602)*

Ink Spot Inc 662 236-2639
304 S Lamar Blvd Oxford (38655) *(G-3959)*

Ink Spot Inc (PA) 662 236-1985
1301 N Lamar Blvd Oxford (38655) *(G-3960)*

Inky B Tees, Raymond *Also called Inky BS Custom Tees LLC* *(G-4490)*

Inky BS Custom Tees LLC 601 988-8558
4292 Bill Downing Rd Raymond (39154) *(G-4490)*

Inky Printing LLC 504 858-6461
12621 Hanover Dr Ocean Springs (39564) *(G-3768)*

Inland Energy Company Inc 601 969-1160
974 E Fortification St Jackson (39202) *(G-2446)*

Inline Barricades Met Pdts Inc 800 229-4790
7114 Kiln Delisle Rd Pass Christian (39571) *(G-4090)*

Inner Sanctuary Inc 662 489-6772
137 Oak Dr Pontotoc (38863) *(G-4337)*

Innocor East LLC 662 365-1640
976 Highway 45 Baldwyn (38824) *(G-78)*

Innocor East LLC (HQ) 732 263-0800
976 Highway 45 Baldwyn (38824) *(G-79)*

Innocor Foam Tech - Acp Inc 662 365-5868
1124 N 2nd St Baldwyn (38824) *(G-80)*

Innocor Foam Tech - Acp Inc 662 842-0123
1665 S Veterans Blvd Tupelo (38804) *(G-5162)*

Innocor Foam Technologies LLC 662 622-7221
485 Industrial Dr Coldwater (38618) *(G-847)*

Innovative Circuits Inc 662 287-2007
311a S Parkway St Corinth (38834) *(G-1092)*

Innovative Fabrications LLC 601 485-1400
1110 B St Meridian (39301) *(G-3353)*

Innovative Wireless LLC 601 594-1201
1230 Raymond Rd Jackson (39204) *(G-2447)*

Innovex Inc 662 328-9537
210 Lake Lowndes Rd Columbus (39702) *(G-988)*

Insituform Technologies LLC 662 561-1378
160 Corporate Dr Batesville (38606) *(G-109)*

Inspection Plus LLC 601 525-6744
1806 Texas St Leakesville (39451) *(G-2877)*

Insulated Panel Sytems, Jackson *Also called Nci Group Inc* *(G-2517)*

Integrity Fire Extinguish 601 953-1927
120 E Hill Dr Madison (39110) *(G-3111)*

Integrity Hot Shot Svcs LLC 601 850-8881
317 Pear Orchard Cir Ridgeland (39157) *(G-4593)*

Integrity Systems, Olive Branch *Also called John D Murley* *(G-3857)*

Integrity Vnyl Sding Decks LLC 601 723-1257
104 Flagstaff St Lumberton (39455) *(G-3031)*

Intelatool Solutions LLC 601 594-8451
309a Monterey Rd Richland (39218) *(G-4520)*

Intellabuy Inc 601 249-0508
312 N James Ave McComb (39648) *(G-3253)*

Interior and Exterior WD Work 662 587-2417
2872 Friendship Rd Ashland (38603) *(G-61)*

International Granite LLC 601 213-8287
1728 Plantation Blvd Jackson (39211) *(G-2448)*

International Laser Sups LLC 601 788-6475
602 Cherry St Richton (39476) *(G-4535)*

International Paper Company 601 638-3665
Highway 3 N Redwood (39156) *(G-4495)*

International Paper Company 601 932-1422
211 Carrier Blvd Jackson (39218) *(G-2650)*

International Paper Company 601 783-5011
350 Prescott Dr Magnolia (39652) *(G-3191)*

International Paper Company 662 893-3100
8301 Hacks Cross Rd Olive Branch (38654) *(G-3852)*

International Paper Company 662 243-4000
4335 Carson Rd Columbus (39701) *(G-989)*

International Paper Company 662 456-4251
511 3rd St Houston (38851) *(G-2246)*

International Paper Company 800 207-4003
270 S Industrial Pkwy Yazoo City (39194) *(G-5636)*

Interntnal Wldg Fbrication Inc 228 474-9353
11401 Highway 63 Moss Point (39562) *(G-3481)*

Interpine Lumber Co, Hattiesburg *Also called Crosby Wood Preserving Co Inc* *(G-1952)*

Interstate All Battery Center, Ridgeland *Also called Battco Inc* *(G-4552)*

Interstate Industries Miss LL 601 856-5941
353 Hillview Dr Ridgeland (39157) *(G-4594)*

Interstate Industries Miss LLC 662 289-3877
Kosciusko Attala Indl Par Kosciusko (39090) *(G-2695)*

Intex Properties Perris Vly LP 662 287-1455
2733 S Harper Rd Corinth (38834) *(G-1093)*

Intrepid Drilling LLC 601 731-1010
320 Second St Columbia (39429) *(G-901)*

Invitation Oxford Magazine 662 701-8365
908 N Lamar Blvd Oxford (38655) *(G-3961)*

Ion Chemical Company 601 781-0604
247 Highway 487 W Carthage (39051) *(G-717)*

Iprint Inc 601 932-4414
2001 Airport Rd N Ste 101 Flowood (39232) *(G-1366)*

Irock or Not, Brandon *Also called Rock or Not LLC* *(G-447)*

Iron and Steel Design Works 662 380-5662
606 Kates Cv Oxford (38655) *(G-3962)*

Iron Crafters Security Pdts, Ashland *Also called Ironcrafters Security Products* *(G-62)*

Iron Effects 662 871-5565
14668 Highway 6 Thaxton (38871) *(G-5078)*

Iron Horse Logging LLC 601 416-5966
711 Rufus Gill Rd Union (39365) *(G-5299)*

Iron Innovations Inc 601 924-0640
1101 Clinton Indus Pk Rd Clinton (39056) *(G-826)*

Ironcrafters Security Products 662 224-6658
835 Iron Crafters Rd Ashland (38603) *(G-62)*

Ironhorse Environmental LLC 504 952-2516
9989 Highway 43 N Poplarville (39470) *(G-4383)*

Ironworks Inc 601 352-3722
300 W South St Jackson (39203) *(G-2449)*

Irvin Machine Specialty Co 662 862-3781
1430 Bankhead Rd Sw Mantachie (38855) *(G-3200)*

Isaiah Ard Timber Inc 601 833-9359
3622 Junction Ln Se Ruth (39662) *(G-4702)*

Ishee Produce 601 651-6643
1654 Highway 184 Laurel (39443) *(G-2784)*

ISO Panels, Inc., Richland *Also called Ergon Construction Group Inc* *(G-4514)*

Isplacement Loop Antenna, Vicksburg *Also called Omega-Tec LLC* *(G-5402)*

It Could Happen Embroidery 228 374-7674
265 Querens Ave Biloxi (39530) *(G-253)*

It Synergistics LLC 855 866-7648
115 Tree St Flowood (39232) *(G-1367)*

Itawamba Adult Training Center, Fulton *Also called Itawamba Ind Work Activities C* *(G-1459)*

Itawamba Classic Lures 601 720-8810
35 Burch Timbers Rd Fulton (38843) *(G-1458)*

Itawamba Ind Work Activities C 662 862-3392
1212 S Adams St Fulton (38843) *(G-1459)*

Its Vinyl YAll LLC 601 533-8885
102 Aulenbrock Dr Canton (39046) *(G-662)*

ITT Engineered Valves, Amory *Also called ITT LLC* *(G-45)*

ITT Engineered Valves LLC 662 256-7185
1110 Hatley Rd Amory (38821) *(G-44)*

ITT LLC 662 393-0275
8890 Commerce Dr Southaven (38671) *(G-4879)*

ITT LLC 662 256-7185
1110 Bankhead Ave Amory (38821) *(G-45)*

Itta Bena Plantation III 662 254-7274
33725 County Road 507 Itta Bena (38941) *(G-2281)*

Iuka Concrete Products LLC 662 423-6238
1679 Constitution Dr Iuka (38852) *(G-2294)*

J & A Mechanical Inc 662 890-4565
10600 Ridge Wood Dr Olive Branch (38654) *(G-3853)*

J & B Athletics 601 776-7557
100 Main St Quitman (39355) *(G-4466)*

J & H Turbo Service Inc 662 378-8715
3401 Highway 82 E Greenville (38703) *(G-1558)*

J & J Bagging LLC 662 746-5155
1312 Rialto Rd Yazoo City (39194) *(G-5637)*

J & J Screen Printing, Southaven *Also called J&J Screen Printing* *(G-4881)*

J & J Welding 662 456-6065
1783 Highway 15 S Woodland (39776) *(G-5613)*

J & K Enterprise Inc 601 794-6005
184 Central Indus Row Purvis (39475) *(G-4440)*

J & K Restaurants Inc (PA) 601 501-1444
121 Thalweg Dr Vicksburg (39183) *(G-5381)*

J & K Services LLC 601 310-7728
1290 Gumpond Beall Rd Lumberton (39455) *(G-3032)*

J & L Sales 601 992-2495
201 Greenfield Pl Brandon (39047) *(G-407)*

J & L Transport LLC 601 292-7044
499 Lake Mike Conner Rd Collins (39428) *(G-854)*

J & P Smith Logging Inc 601 833-4286
1308 Jckson Liberty Dr Nw Brookhaven (39601) *(G-502)*

J & R Optical Co Inc (PA) 601 977-0272
1461 Canton Mart Rd Ste A Jackson (39211) *(G-2450)*

J & S Enterprises LLC 601 646-3636
8318 Hwy 503 N Hickory (39332) *(G-2162)*

(PA)=Parent Co (HQ)=Headquarters (DH)=Div Headquarters

2019 Harris Directory of
Mississippi Manufacturers

291

J & W Furniture Frames Inc

ALPHABETIC SECTION

J & W Furniture Frames Inc......................662 489-1991
435 Warren Ln Pontotoc (38863) *(G-4338)*

J A C Industrial Tl & Sup LLC..................601 591-1321
1089 Highway 471 Brandon (39042) *(G-408)*

J and E Enterprises..............................662 369-7324
605 S Matubba St Aberdeen (39730) *(G-15)*

J and S Keene LLC...............................601 833-8874
1645 Bethel Rd Se Brookhaven (39601) *(G-503)*

J D Smith Drilling Company....................601 989-2475
5797 Union Rd Richton (39476) *(G-4536)*

J J Ferguson Prestress-........................662 453-5451
4510 Highway 82 E Greenwood (38930) *(G-1629)*

J J Ferguson Sand & Grav Inc (PA)............662 453-5451
4510 Highway 82 E Greenwood (38930) *(G-1630)*

J J Hill Brace & Limb Co Inc..................228 863-0381
1619 Broad Ave Gulfport (39501) *(G-1812)*

J J Monogram Embroidery.......................662 226-0304
119 1st St Grenada (38901) *(G-1688)*

J L McCool Contractors Inc....................228 769-9771
11700 Highway 613 Moss Point (39562) *(G-3482)*

J M Architectural Iron Wo......................228 234-1747
244 Benndale Rd Brooklyn (39425) *(G-550)*

J M Digital Printing, Bay St Louis *Also called JM Digital Corporation (G-179)*

J M H Graphics..................................601 261-2500
223 S 40th Ave Hattiesburg (39402) *(G-2000)*

J M I Inc..601 936-6800
100 Builders Square Dr Brandon (39047) *(G-409)*

J M Jones Lumber Company Inc..................601 442-7471
1 Jones Sawmill Rd Natchez (39120) *(G-3569)*

J N S Marble & Granite LLC....................662 280-2272
8950 Highway 51 N Southaven (38671) *(G-4880)*

J O Emmerich & Assoc Inc......................601 684-2421
112 Oliver Emmerich Dr McComb (39648) *(G-3254)*

J P M, Hattiesburg *Also called Jpm of Mississippi Inc (G-2004)*

J R Pounds Inc..................................601 649-1743
805 W 5th St Laurel (39440) *(G-2785)*

J S Iupes.......................................601 856-7776
101 Village Blvd Ste D Madison (39110) *(G-3112)*

J Strickland and Co............................662 890-2306
10420 Desoto Rd Olive Branch (38654) *(G-3854)*

J Strickland Products, Olive Branch *Also called J Strickland and Co (G-3854)*

J T Horn Logging Inc...........................662 585-3417
34165 Highway 25 N Golden (38847) *(G-1527)*

J Tuohy's Apparel, Columbus *Also called Tuohys J Sptg Gods of Columbus (G-1040)*

J W B Logging Co LLC...........................601 437-8743
403 Pecan St Port Gibson (39150) *(G-4402)*

J W Priest & Sons Logging.....................601 532-6237
Off Hwy 84 Mc Call Creek (39647) *(G-3234)*

J&H Printing Inc................................662 456-3654
219 N Jackson St Houston (38851) *(G-2247)*

J&I&r Raceway LLC..............................601 622-8458
106 Fairfax Ct Madison (39110) *(G-3113)*

J&J Screen Printing............................662 342-6131
1810 Veterans Dr Southaven (38671) *(G-4881)*

J&M Logging Inc.................................601 645-5813
1665 Macedonia Rd Centreville (39631) *(G-731)*

J'S Modular Installations, Purvis *Also called James E Mattison Jr (G-4441)*

J.D. Smith Contracting, Poplarville *Also called Jerry D Smith (G-4384)*

J2 Manufacturing Inc...........................601 573-3134
220 Lakeland Pkwy Flowood (39232) *(G-1368)*

Jabr LLC..601 502-5587
150 Britton Cir Flowood (39232) *(G-1369)*

Jack Batte and Sons Inc.......................601 536-3976
221 Scr 35-9 Forest (39074) *(G-1417)*

Jack Black Oil Company Inc....................601 442-2620
305 Creek Bend Rd Natchez (39120) *(G-3570)*

Jackpot Magazine...............................228 385-7707
12268 Intraplex Pkwy Gulfport (39503) *(G-1813)*

Jackson Advocate Inc...........................601 948-4122
100 W Hamilton St Jackson (39202) *(G-2451)*

Jackson Asphalt & Concrete....................601 371-8707
2944 Woodbine St Jackson (39212) *(G-2452)*

Jackson Brace & Limb, Jackson *Also called Jackson Brace Co (G-2453)*

Jackson Brace Co................................601 353-2477
1320 N State St Jackson (39202) *(G-2453)*

Jackson Business Form Company (PA)............601 932-5200
1125 Old Brandon Rd Flowood (39232) *(G-1370)*

Jackson Excavating & Lsg Co...................601 371-7935
1059 Deviney Dr Jackson (39282) *(G-2454)*

Jackson Fishing Sptg Accessory................662 837-9089
23391 Highway 370 Falkner (38629) *(G-1295)*

Jackson Free Press Inc.........................601 362-6121
125 S Congress St # 1324 Jackson (39201) *(G-2455)*

Jackson Ice Co, Jackson *Also called Wendall Harrell (G-2628)*

Jackson Plating Co..............................601 362-4623
228 W Lorenz Blvd Jackson (39213) *(G-2456)*

Jackson Powertrain Inc.........................601 932-3159
1332 Old Brandon Rd Jackson (39232) *(G-2651)*

Jackson Precast Inc.............................601 321-8787
3325 Lawson St Jackson (39213) *(G-2457)*

Jackson Publishing..............................662 349-2866
7661 Forstoria Cv Southaven (38672) *(G-4882)*

Jackson Ready Mix, Crystal Springs *Also called Delta Industries Inc (G-1141)*

Jackson Ready Mix, Brandon *Also called Delta Industries Inc (G-387)*

Jackson Ready-Mix, Jackson *Also called Delta Industries Inc (G-2381)*

Jackson Welding LLC............................662 680-4325
234 County Road 1806 Saltillo (38866) *(G-4714)*

Jackson Wilbert Burial Vlt Co, Jackson *Also called Bickes Inc (G-2337)*

Jagg LLC..228 388-1794
296 Beauvoir Rd Biloxi (39531) *(G-254)*

Jaken Industries................................662 289-7510
404 Knox Rd Kosciusko (39090) *(G-2696)*

Jakes Woodwork LLC.............................601 651-6278
817 W 7th St Laurel (39440) *(G-2786)*

James Biglane...................................601 442-2783
75 Melrose Mntebello Pkwy Natchez (39120) *(G-3571)*

James David Measell............................601 635-4441
2950 Mount Zion Rd Decatur (39327) *(G-1174)*

James E Mattison Jr.............................601 543-7313
28 Aldon Rd Purvis (39475) *(G-4441)*

James H Kemp....................................601 876-2331
5 Jackson Rd Tylertown (39667) *(G-5273)*

James K Smith Logging..........................601 859-1628
464 Covington Dr Canton (39046) *(G-663)*

James L Brewer..................................662 299-7247
17000 Highway 7 N Greenwood (38930) *(G-1631)*

James Newton....................................662 647-8968
11922 Highway 35 Charleston (38921) *(G-739)*

James R Padgett.................................601 763-3369
401 Sandhill Township Rd Ellisville (39437) *(G-1260)*

James Rachal....................................601 442-1460
6 Kings Ln Church Hill (39120) *(G-754)*

James W Elliot Jr...............................601 833-6201
306 S Jackson St Brookhaven (39601) *(G-504)*

Jamestown Metal Marine Sls Inc................228 762-3156
4502 Chicot St Pascagoula (39581) *(G-4041)*

Jamie Valentine Logging LLC...................601 764-7271
736 County Road 1725 Bay Springs (39422) *(G-166)*

Jan Signs Inc...................................601 785-9800
1215 Highway 28 Taylorsville (39168) *(G-5054)*

Jane Little Inc.................................601 694-2767
306b Franklin St Newhebron (39140) *(G-3713)*

Janesville Acoustics, Columbus *Also called Jason Industries Inc (G-990)*

Janlynn Crafts..................................601 956-1832
5062 Sunnyvale Dr Jackson (39211) *(G-2458)*

Jara L Miller...................................601 421-6876
112 Timbercrest Ln Brandon (39047) *(G-410)*

Jason Fly Logging LLC...........................662 316-3499
1155 Jeff Sanders Rd Batesville (38606) *(G-110)*

Jason Industries Inc............................662 327-0756
221 Fabritek Dr Columbus (39702) *(G-990)*

Jasons Custom Logging LLC......................601 270-6818
26 Victory Ln Lumberton (39455) *(G-3033)*

Jasper & Assoc..................................601 321-0811
3365 Medgar Evers Blvd Jackson (39213) *(G-2459)*

Jasper Cooperative..............................601 428-4968
34 County Road 17 Stringer (39481) *(G-5003)*

Jasper County News, Bay Springs *Also called Buckley Newspapers Inc (G-159)*

JC Graphics LLC.................................662 832-9291
1415 University Ave Oxford (38655) *(G-3963)*

JC Jourdan Lumber Co Inc.......................662 423-5238
418 Cunty Rd 995 Arprt Rd Iuka (38852) *(G-2295)*

JC Manufacturing LLC...........................662 338-9004
3111 Old Highway 12 Starkville (39759) *(G-4952)*

JC Welding LLC..................................601 575-1307
106 Pinecrest Dr Philadelphia (39350) *(G-4218)*

Jcbc Cs LLC.....................................662 560-7235
7660 Highway 305 Coldwater (38618) *(G-848)*

Je Painting and Renovations...................601 470-2047
275 Sandy Run Rd Hattiesburg (39402) *(G-2001)*

Jean Pickle.....................................662 256-7020
50047 Calvary Church Rd Amory (38821) *(G-46)*

Jeff Busby......................................601 924-7979
526 E College St Clinton (39056) *(G-827)*

Jeff Shepherd Logging Inc......................601 416-1832
17221 Highway 19 S Philadelphia (39350) *(G-4219)*

Jeff Winstead Logging..........................601 656-1448
16931 Highway 19 S Philadelphia (39350) *(G-4220)*

Jeffrey Roberson................................662 587-1991
107 Carter Ln Ripley (38663) *(G-4662)*

Jenkins Graphics Inc............................662 890-2851
7083 Commerce Dr Olive Branch (38654) *(G-3855)*

Jennifer L Johnson Lpn.........................601 573-7582
993 Dry Creek Rd Canton (39046) *(G-664)*

Jennings & Jennings Inc........................662 887-1870
1273 Highway 82 E Indianola (38751) *(G-2268)*

Jennings Welding & Mch Works (PA).............662 887-1870
1273 Highway 82 E Indianola (38751) *(G-2269)*

2019 Harris Directory of
Mississippi Manufacturers

(G-0000) Company's Geographic Section entry number

292

ALPHABETIC SECTION

Just For You Embroidery

Jeremy Ray Welding Service LLC..............601 433-4905
34 Kennon Ave Laurel (39443) *(G-2787)*

Jerold Henderson Logging Inc..............601 989-2399
5207 Lovewell Rd Richton (39476) *(G-4537)*

Jerome Rushing Welding..............601 303-0139
51 Highway 48 W Tylertown (39667) *(G-5274)*

Jerry D Smith..............601 795-8760
281 Cowart Holiday Rd Poplarville (39470) *(G-4384)*

Jerry Hailey..............662 349-2582
6605 Tchulahoma Rd Southaven (38671) *(G-4883)*

Jerry Harris Logging Inc..............662 728-7331
159 County Road 3151 Booneville (38829) *(G-332)*

Jerry S Trolling Motor Repair..............256 431-6564
586 County Road 989 Iuka (38852) *(G-2296)*

Jerry's Mobile Repair Service, Southaven *Also called Jerry Hailey* *(G-4883)*

Jesco Resources, Rosedale *Also called Axel Americas LLC* *(G-4686)*

Jesse L Star Sheets, Jackson *Also called Misccellaneous Items LLC* *(G-2496)*

Jessica Williams..............601 738-0090
1519 Bear Lake Rd Rolling Fork (39159) *(G-4681)*

Jewell Aircrafting Inc..............662 252-6377
Hwy 78 W Marshall Airport Holly Springs (38635) *(G-2178)*

Jh Dirt & Gravel Llc..............601 831-3990
114 Blackwell Dr Vicksburg (39180) *(G-5382)*

Jiffy Mart..............601 947-6589
110 Airport Rd Lucedale (39452) *(G-3004)*

Jim Ballenger, Picayune *Also called Awesome Sight and Sound* *(G-4255)*

Jimco Pumps, Laurel *Also called Ralph Craven LLC* *(G-2834)*

Jimmy Jones & Sons Sawmill..............601 253-2533
4546 Gunter Rd Walnut Grove (39189) *(G-5460)*

Jims Auto Parts Inc..............662 494-4541
130 Highway 45 N West Point (39773) *(G-5547)*

Jims Tool & Die Inc..............662 895-3287
12605 Whispering Pines Dr Olive Branch (38654) *(G-3856)*

Jims Woodworks LLC..............601 862-1025
14800 Highway 22 Bolton (39041) *(G-310)*

Jindal Tubular USA LLC (HQ)..............228 533-7779
13092 Sea Plane Rd Bay Saint Louis (39520) *(G-144)*

Jj & W Trucking, Pontotoc *Also called John Albert Ware* *(G-4339)*

Jj Merchant..............601 596-4430
S Mill Creek Rd Purvis (39475) *(G-4442)*

Jji Lighting Group Inc..............662 842-7212
938 S Green St Tupelo (38804) *(G-5163)*

Jjs Woodshed..............662 380-5034
714 Long Meadow Dr Oxford (38655) *(G-3964)*

JKS International LLC..............228 689-8999
Msaap Bldg 9353 Stennis Space Center (39529) *(G-4995)*

Jl Browne Inc..............228 216-1137
6182 Shawnee St Kiln (39556) *(G-2681)*

JM Digital Corporation..............601 659-0599
10704 Highway 603 Bay St Louis (39520) *(G-179)*

JM Signs, Columbus *Also called Custom Signs and Banners* *(G-957)*

JMS Energy Services, Lucedale *Also called JMS Manufacturing Inc* *(G-3005)*

JMS Manufacturing Inc..............601 514-0660
3247 Highway 63 S Bldg 8 Lucedale (39452) *(G-3005)*

Jns Biofuel LLC..............662 538-1005
823 State Highway 15 N New Albany (38652) *(G-3683)*

Joanna Freely..............662 272-8679
781 Rachel Turner Rd Starkville (39759) *(G-4953)*

Joe Fortunato Oil Prodcr RES..............601 442-6397
111 Woodhaven Dr Natchez (39120) *(G-3572)*

Joe K Smith..............601 786-8632
2214 Dennis Cross Rd Fayette (39069) *(G-1298)*

Joe Tonos Jeweler Inc..............662 335-1160
1640 Highway 1 S Greenville (38701) *(G-1559)*

Joel Little Construction, Oxford *Also called Spectrum III Limited* *(G-4005)*

Joelprinting, Prentiss *Also called White Jerleen* *(G-4425)*

Joes Custom Cabinets..............601 508-8284
134 Alford Howard Rd Lucedale (39452) *(G-3006)*

John Albert Ware..............662 489-7824
28 Ben Hardin Rd Pontotoc (38863) *(G-4339)*

John D Murley..............662 890-3920
8417 Industrial Dr Olive Branch (38654) *(G-3857)*

John Deere Authorized Dealer, Biloxi *Also called Kennedy Engine Company Inc* *(G-256)*

John J Ishee..............601 847-2723
201 Wilson Welch Rd Mendenhall (39114) *(G-3282)*

John Ready Damond..............601 587-4381
547 Old Highway 27 N Monticello (39654) *(G-3434)*

John Sign & Co Inc..............662 843-3548
4139 Highway 8 Cleveland (38732) *(G-797)*

John W McDougall Co Inc..............601 298-0079
151 Industrial Dr Carthage (39051) *(G-718)*

John's Welding Service, Meridian *Also called Opel Corp* *(G-3378)*

Johnnie Wright Radiator & Wldg..............601 428-5013
315 E 15th St Laurel (39440) *(G-2788)*

Johnny McCool Logging..............601 636-3824
315 Silver Creek Dr Vicksburg (39180) *(G-5383)*

Johnny Parks..............662 289-5844
2079 Attala Road 3241 Kosciusko (39090) *(G-2697)*

Johnny W Mills Timber Company..............601 989-2398
4839 Lovewell Rd Richton (39476) *(G-4538)*

Johns Manville Corporation..............601 936-9841
286 Carrier Blvd Jackson (39218) *(G-2652)*

Johnson Wiley..............662 329-1495
42 Johnson Rd Columbus (39702) *(G-991)*

Johnson Controls Inc..............601 544-8911
77 Academy Dr Hattiesburg (39401) *(G-2002)*

Johnson Education Firm LLC..............662 347-9150
280 Bermuda Dr Greenville (38701) *(G-1560)*

Johnson Educational Sales Inc..............601 469-1924
1304 Melwood Dr Forest (39074) *(G-1418)*

Johnson Foam Sales Inc..............662 767-9007
6312 Hwy 145 S Shannon (38868) *(G-4811)*

Johnson Machine North Miss..............662 393-3567
3636 Stateline Rd W Southaven (38671) *(G-4884)*

Johnson Milling Co, Clinton *Also called Woods Trading Co Inc* *(G-839)*

Johnson Timber Co, Mantee *Also called Cecil D Johnson* *(G-3210)*

Johnsond Rv..............662 676-8716
289 Petty Rd Golden (38847) *(G-1528)*

Johnsons Fencing..............601 833-3263
1654 Caleb Dr Se Brookhaven (39601) *(G-505)*

Johnston-Tombigbee Furn Mfg Co..............662 328-1685
1402 Waterworks Rd Columbus (39701) *(G-992)*

Johnstons Sand & Gravel Inc..............601 787-4326
65 County Road 115 Heidelberg (39439) *(G-2118)*

Jonathan Bigbie..............601 498-9890
1409 Highway 42 Petal (39465) *(G-4188)*

Jonathan Sanford DBA..............601 297-2754
827 Snset Williamsburg Rd Collins (39428) *(G-855)*

Jones & Young Logging LLC..............601 681-6801
8998 Chapel Rd Meridian (39305) *(G-3354)*

Jones Companies AVI MGT Inc..............844 500-2438
16 Office Park Dr Ste 6 Hattiesburg (39402) *(G-2003)*

Jones Ldscp & Contrs Svc LLC..............601 780-2042
3172 Bilgray Dr Jackson (39212) *(G-2460)*

Jones Limber..............601 894-3839
31050 Highway 28 Hazlehurst (39083) *(G-2098)*

Jones Logging Co Inc..............601 877-3814
1045 Allen Jones Rd Lorman (39096) *(G-2961)*

Jones Lumber Co Inc..............601 445-8206
3 Dave Levite Rd Natchez (39120) *(G-3573)*

Jones Ready Mix LLC..............601 222-1919
216 Herring Rd Sandy Hook (39478) *(G-4730)*

Jones Signs LLC..............662 453-2432
2810 Highway 82 E Greenwood (38930) *(G-1632)*

Jones Wood Products Inc..............601 876-2688
34 Pallets Rd Tylertown (39667) *(G-5275)*

Jordan Logging, Pachuta *Also called Charles Jordan* *(G-4011)*

Jordon Construction LLC..............601 502-6019
309 Pleasant Lakes Cv Terry (39170) *(G-5071)*

Joseph L Brown Printing Co..............601 693-6184
204 20th Ave Meridian (39301) *(G-3355)*

Josh Gus Garcia..............228 255-7157
6040 Jordan Rd Perkinston (39573) *(G-4177)*

Journal Inc (HQ)..............662 842-2611
1242 S Green St Tupelo (38804) *(G-5164)*

Journal Inc..............662 862-3141
106 W Main St Fulton (38843) *(G-1460)*

Journal Inc..............601 364-1000
132 Riverview Dr Ste E Flowood (39232) *(G-1371)*

Journal Publishing Houston..............662 456-3771
225 E Madison St Houston (38851) *(G-2248)*

Joyce Tillman..............228 896-4927
230 Woodbine Dr Gulfport (39507) *(G-1814)*

JP Williams Machine & Fabricat..............228 474-1099
7206 Grierson St Pascagoula (39563) *(G-4042)*

Jpm of Mississippi Inc..............601 544-9950
116 Wi Runnels Indus Dr Hattiesburg (39401) *(G-2004)*

Jr & Son Enterprises, Church Hill *Also called James Rachal* *(G-754)*

Jr Smith Assemble Plant, Lumberton *Also called Myles Smith* *(G-3036)*

Js Woodworking..............228 257-6846
6820 Southwind Dr Biloxi (39532) *(G-255)*

JT Shannon Lumber Co Inc (PA)..............662 393-3765
2200 Cole Rd Horn Lake (38637) *(G-2203)*

JTB FURNITURE, Columbus *Also called Johnston-Tombigbee Furn Mfg Co* *(G-992)*

Jtb Furniture, Columbus *Also called Lounora Industries Inc* *(G-994)*

Jtd Manufacturing Solutions, Olive Branch *Also called Jims Tool & Die Inc* *(G-3856)*

Jtwo Manufacturing LLC..............769 243-8914
517 Liberty Rd Flowood (39232) *(G-1372)*

Jubilations Inc..............662 328-9210
950 Highway 45 S West Point (39773) *(G-5548)*

Jubilations Cheesecake, West Point *Also called Jubilations Inc* *(G-5548)*

Julius Whittington..............601 532-6519
1889 Round Top Hill Rd Se Meadville (39653) *(G-3276)*

Jura-Search Inc..............601 932-0002
111 E Capitol St Ste 500 Jackson (39201) *(G-2461)*

Just For You Embroidery..............228 769-8388
1915 Ingalls Ave Pascagoula (39567) *(G-4043)*

ALPHABETIC

(PA)=Parent Co (HQ)=Headquarters (DH)=Div Headquarters

2019 Harris Directory of
Mississippi Manufacturers

Justin Alan Rankin 601 297-4365
145 Carroll Rd Lumberton (39455) *(G-3034)*

Jwb Construction LLC 601 439-7190
4141 Scr 83 Mize Mize (39116) *(G-3427)*

K & B Mississippi Corporation 601 545-2056
100 Highway 42 Petal (39465) *(G-4189)*

K & D Cultured Marble Inc 662 675-2928
17425 Okahoma St Coffeeville (38922) *(G-843)*

K & D Fuel Injection Service 601 849-9113
108 Ray Dr Magee (39111) *(G-3178)*

K & J Logging Inc 601 639-4607
10569 Highway 33 S Roxie (39661) *(G-4690)*

K & K Systems Inc 662 566-2025
687 Palmetto Rd Tupelo (38801) *(G-5165)*

K & L Furniture Frames Inc 662 489-5355
1080 Pontotoc Cnty Ind Pk Pontotoc (38863) *(G-4340)*

K & T Poultry Sales & Svc Inc 601 764-3918
573 Windham Ln Bay Springs (39422) *(G-167)*

K and A Industries LLC 601 763-3503
325 Blackwell Loop Ellisville (39437) *(G-1261)*

K and D Marble, Coffeeville *Also called K & D Cultured Marble Inc (G-843)*

K B Ms 601 684-0510
1703 Delaware Ave McComb (39648) *(G-3255)*

K C S Lumber Co Inc 601 446-8525
3 Dave Levite Rd Natchez (39120) *(G-3574)*

K Contract, Pearl *Also called Office Chairs Mississippi LLC (G-4135)*

K D M Custom Coatings LLC 662 842-9725
1989 Royal Maid Dr Tupelo (38804) *(G-5166)*

K F G Petroleum Corporation 601 446-5219
118 Lwer Wdvlle Rd Unit 2 Natchez (39120) *(G-3575)*

K M Industries 228 497-7040
721 Highway 90 Gautier (39553) *(G-1495)*

K S I, Kiln *Also called Koenig-Stimens Inc (G-2682)*

K&A Customize Printing LLC 225 326-9054
427 Autumn Oak Dr Madison (39110) *(G-3114)*

K&D Wright Logging 601 729-5675
28 E Brushy Rd Laurel (39443) *(G-2789)*

Ka Pottery 601 722-4948
506 Shirley Sanford Rd Seminary (39479) *(G-4782)*

Ka Pottery Studio, Seminary *Also called Ka Pottery (G-4782)*

Kanes Publishing Company LLC 601 345-5153
704 Wicker St Forest (39074) *(G-1419)*

Kangaroo Express 1544 .... 662 563-4629
630 Highway 6 E Batesville (38606) *(G-111)*

Kar Kleen 601 638-8816
1955 Highway 80 Vicksburg (39180) *(G-5384)*

Kathys Frame Works Inc 228 769-7672
2300 Ingalls Ave Pascagoula (39567) *(G-4044)*

Kaycan Inc 662 252-9991
820 Highway 7 N Holly Springs (38635) *(G-2179)*

Kayo Technologies 662 893-7569
4702 Center Hill Rd Olive Branch (38654) *(G-3858)*

Kaz USA 800 477-0457
7159 Polk Ln Olive Branch (38654) *(G-3859)*

Kbh Corporation 662 624-5471
395 Anderson Blvd Clarksdale (38614) *(G-770)*

Kc Fabrication and Welding LLC 504 427-8711
3505 Martin Rd Bolton (39041) *(G-311)*

KC&c General Contractor 601 668-4615
3794 Good Hope Rd Edwards (39066) *(G-1239)*

Kd Welding Services LLC 228 863-2773
3008 8th Ave Gulfport (39501) *(G-1815)*

Kdeb Manufacturing LLC 601 750-9659
2246 Highway 80 Morton (39117) *(G-3448)*

Kdh Kustoms LLC 601 730-2052
1028 Highway 98 E McComb (39648) *(G-3256)*

Kdh Trucking LLC 601 730-2052
5800 Good Hope Ln Liberty (39645) *(G-2913)*

Kdl Solutions LLC 601 434-0508
48 Frye Rd Hattiesburg (39401) *(G-2005)*

Kedron Furniture Mfg Inc 662 963-3366
3867 Highway 6 Plantersville (38862) *(G-4310)*

Kedron Surplus & Sales, Plantersville *Also called Kedron Furniture Mfg Inc (G-4310)*

Keith Conaway Logging LLC 662 415-5646
23 County Road 607 Walnut (38683) *(G-5457)*

Keith Huber Corporation 228 832-0992
14220 Highway 49 Gulfport (39503) *(G-1816)*

Keith Murphree 662 292-7644
620 Sides Bottom Rd Senatobia (38668) *(G-4793)*

Kelley Brothers Contrs Inc (PA) 601 735-2541
401 County Farm Rd Waynesboro (39367) *(G-5501)*

Kelly Dirt & Gravel LLC 662 231-0249
718 County Road 300 Shannon (38868) *(G-4812)*

Kellys Welding Service 601 879-8636
449 Moore Ave Flora (39071) *(G-1309)*

Kelsey Bailey Consulting LLC 601 622-8319
107 Kenzie Dr Madison (39110) *(G-3115)*

Kelwood Products 662 862-9494
401 Vo Tech Rd Fulton (38843) *(G-1461)*

Kelwood Products Inc 601 659-7027
Highway 513 W Enterprise (39330) *(G-1280)*

Kema Printing, Belmont *Also called Belmont Tshmngo Jrnl Incjurnal (G-195)*

Kemp Enterprises 662 574-0253
54 Saint Charles Ave Hattiesburg (39402) *(G-2006)*

Kenan Transportation 662 332-4223
1010 N Broadway St Greenville (38701) *(G-1561)*

Kengro Corporation 662 647-2456
6605 Ms Highway 32 Charleston (38921) *(G-740)*

Kennedy Engine Company Inc 228 392-2200
980 Motsie Rd Biloxi (39532) *(G-256)*

Kennedy Hall 601 366-7301
732 Woodacre Rd Jackson (39206) *(G-2462)*

Kennedy Marine Inc 228 214-4392
10220 Three Rivers Rd Gulfport (39503) *(G-1817)*

Kenneth Smith 601 848-7956
283 Woulard Bend River Rd State Line (39362) *(G-4987)*

Kenneths Excavation Demo 662 379-6771
1028 Highway 1 N Greenville (38703) *(G-1562)*

Kennith Humphrey - Paintings & 601 218-2786
1407 Parkway Dr Vicksburg (39180) *(G-5385)*

Kens Welding Shop Inc 601 736-4136
118 S High School Ave Columbia (39429) *(G-902)*

Kent Hillman Logging, Neely *Also called Norman K Hillman (G-3645)*

Kepler Boys Wear LLC 601 738-1664
3301 Washington St Vicksburg (39180) *(G-5386)*

Kerex LLC (HQ) 210 494-5596
1421 N State St Ste 505 Jackson (39202) *(G-2463)*

Kermit Broome Sons WD Chipping 601 264-8470
113 W Black Creek Rd Sumrall (39482) *(G-5037)*

Kershenstines Beef Jerky Inc 662 258-2049
550 Industrial Park Rd Eupora (39744) *(G-1288)*

Kewl Kites 228 206-0322
200 Jeff Davis Ave Ste 4 Long Beach (39560) *(G-2941)*

Key Therapeutics LLC 888 981-8337
517 Liberty Rd Ste D Flowood (39232) *(G-1373)*

Key Tronic Corporation 662 665-3410
1801 S Fulton Dr Corinth (38834) *(G-1094)*

Keyes Machine Shop LLC 601 671-8646
93 Dub Beasley Rd Waynesboro (39367) *(G-5502)*

Keytronic Ems, Corinth *Also called Key Tronic Corporation (G-1094)*

Kfg Resources Ltd 601 446-5219
118 Lwer Wdvlle Rd Unit 2 Natchez (39120) *(G-3576)*

Khloes Closet and Monograms 662 315-9425
60014 Parkview Dr Smithville (38870) *(G-4844)*

Kids Express 601 352-3882
665 Claiborne Ave Jackson (39209) *(G-2464)*

Kidz World Furniture, Calhoun City *Also called DIAS LLC (G-638)*

Kik Custom Products Inc 901 947-5400
11170 Green Valley Dr Olive Branch (38654) *(G-3860)*

Kimberly-Clark Corporation 601 545-3400
W L Runnels Dr Hattiesburg (39401) *(G-2007)*

Kimberly-Clark Corporation 662 287-8011
3461 County Road 100 Corinth (38834) *(G-1095)*

Kimberly-Clark Corporation 662 454-9274
183 County Road 1 Dennis (38838) *(G-1182)*

Kimberly-Clark Corporation 662 284-3827
1337 Sheppard Cir Baldwyn (38824) *(G-81)*

Kims Processing Plant Inc 662 627-2389
227 Leflore Ave Clarksdale (38614) *(G-771)*

Kinard Burge & Sons Inc 601 794-6829
24 Kinard Burge Rd Purvis (39475) *(G-4443)*

Kinards Kountry 601 737-8378
10059 Daniels Rd Bailey (39320) *(G-68)*

King B Signs and Wonders Inc 815 263-1546
677 Golding Cir Columbus (39702) *(G-993)*

King Heating & AC 662 227-1159
5597 Sweethome Rd Grenada (38901) *(G-1689)*

King Lumber Company Inc 601 469-3271
1103 W Third St Forest (39074) *(G-1420)*

King Manufacturing Company Inc (PA) 662 286-5504
714 S Fulton Dr Corinth (38834) *(G-1096)*

King Manufacturing Company Inc 662 286-5504
2674 S Harper Rd Corinth (38834) *(G-1097)*

King Mfg 662 869-2069
341 County Road 521 Saltillo (38866) *(G-4715)*

Kingdom Life Printing 601 398-4606
199 Raymond Rd Jackson (39204) *(G-2465)*

Kings Judah Publishing Co LLC 228 342-3648
269 Sweet Beulah Rd Perkinston (39573) *(G-4178)*

Kings Woodworks 662 403-0871
1239 Cross Creek Dr E Hernando (38632) *(G-2136)*

Kingsford Manufacturing Co 510 271-6581
2387 Highway 72 E Glen (38846) *(G-1507)*

Kirby Bldg Systems Miss LLC 662 323-8021
101 Airport Rd Starkville (39759) *(G-4954)*

Kirk Welding Inspection SE 228 467-6586
6021 W Grenada St Bay Saint Louis (39520) *(G-145)*

Kirkland Boats Inc 662 647-0017
1068 Factory Dr Charleston (38921) *(G-741)*

ALPHABETIC SECTION

Lamb Woodworking

Kitchen Elegance LLC 228 248-0074
39 29th St Ste H Gulfport (39507) *(G-1818)*

Kitchen Table 601 261-3836
3720 Hardy St Ste 3 Hattiesburg (39402) *(G-2008)*

Kitchens Brothers Mfg Co 601 885-6001
4854 Reed Town Rd Utica (39175) *(G-5309)*

Kkam Services LLC 903 707-0110
620 Frontage Dr W Wiggins (39577) *(G-5585)*

Klaas-Robbins Pavement Maint 601 362-4091
2362 W County Line Rd Ridgeland (39157) *(G-4595)*

Klean N Press 662 563-5515
319 Highway 6 W Batesville (38606) *(G-112)*

Knight-Abbey Coml Prtrs Inc 228 702-3231
315 Caillavet St Biloxi (39530) *(G-257)*

Knights Mar & Indus Svcs Inc 228 769-5550
3421 Industrial Rd Pascagoula (39581) *(G-4045)*

Knot Just Kitchens 228 896-0584
360 Courthouse Rd Ste A Gulfport (39507) *(G-1819)*

Knr Farm Supplies Inc 228 574-8397
863 Magnolia Rd Lumberton (39455) *(G-3035)*

Knu LLC (PA) 812 367-1761
1300 N Broad St Leland (38756) *(G-2888)*

Koch Foods of Mississippi LLC (HQ) 601 732-8911
1080 River Oaks Dr A100 Flowood (39232) *(G-1374)*

Koch Foods of Mississippi LLC 601 469-2337
921 S Main St Forest (39074) *(G-1421)*

Koch Foods of Mississippi LLC 601 732-3026
278 Herring Rd Morton (39117) *(G-3449)*

Koch Industries Inc 601 785-6523
Hwy 28 W Taylorsville (39168) *(G-5055)*

Koenig-Stimens Inc 228 467-3888
14258 Fred And Al Key Rd Kiln (39556) *(G-2682)*

Koestler Pallet Sales Inc 601 852-2926
12600 I 20 Edwards (39066) *(G-1240)*

Kogler Equipment Service Inc. 901 521-9742
8155 Industrial Dr Olive Branch (38654) *(G-3861)*

Kohler Co 601 582-3555
182 J M Tatum Indus Dr Hattiesburg (39401) *(G-2009)*

Kohler Co 601 544-2553
95 W L Runnels Indus Dr Hattiesburg (39401) *(G-2010)*

Kohler Engine, Hattiesburg Also called Kohler Co *(G-2010)*

Kol Kraft Manufacturing Co 662 429-7561
6514 Hwy 51 S Hernando (38632) *(G-2137)*

Kolinsky Corp 601 544-5987
2106 Hardy St Hattiesburg (39401) *(G-2011)*

Kopis Mobile LLC 601 345-1753
3010 Lakeland Cv Ste S Flowood (39232) *(G-1375)*

Kowalski's Printplex, Jackson Also called Northtowne Printers Inc *(G-2523)*

Kp Building Products Inc 662 252-9991
820 Highway 7 N Holly Springs (38635) *(G-2180)*

Kr Steel & Industrial Supply 662 294-8888
1505 South St Grenada (38901) *(G-1690)*

Krazy Kat Monograms 901 832-1339
9095 Millbranch Rd Southaven (38671) *(G-4885)*

Kresec Enterprises Corp 601 292-7015
502 Mulberry St Rear Bldg Vaiden (39176) *(G-5314)*

Krewe of Natchez Indn Yth Ldrs 601 392-1709
14 Fatherland Rd Natchez (39120) *(G-3577)*

Krh Transport LLC 769 244-1392
1689 Dr Anderson Rd Centreville (39631) *(G-732)*

Kristina Thorn 256 460-9798
809 Highway 25 Dennis (38838) *(G-1183)*

Krueger International Inc 662 842-3124
2112 S Green St Tupelo (38804) *(G-5167)*

Krueger International Inc 662 840-7368
2112 S Green St Tupelo (38804) *(G-5168)*

KS Tobacco & Brew 662 869-0086
2546 Highway 145 Saltillo (38866) *(G-4716)*

Ksj Industries 601 493-3991
4630 Sharon Rd Laurel (39443) *(G-2790)*

Ksquared Inc 601 956-2951
106 Lone Wolf Dr Madison (39110) *(G-3116)*

Ktsu America LLC 601 506-8148
279 Soldier Colony Rd Canton (39046) *(G-665)*

Kubota Authorized Dealer, Natchez Also called Cook Lawn & Tractor LLC *(G-3550)*

Kuhlman Electric Corporation 601 892-4661
101 Kuhlman Dr Crystal Springs (39059) *(G-1144)*

Kurtz Custom Cabinets, Vicksburg Also called Shawn Kurtz *(G-5416)*

Kustom Machine and Sheet Metal 601 469-1062
10091 Road 375 Philadelphia (39350) *(G-4221)*

Kut Tools Inc 601 876-4467
110 Beulah Ave Tylertown (39667) *(G-5276)*

Kwik Kopy Printing, Columbus Also called Mackay Enterprises LLC *(G-995)*

Kx Technologies LLC 662 601-4140
36 Wild Rose Dr Iuka (38852) *(G-2297)*

L & G Marble Inc 601 268-0225
2617 Lincoln Rd Hattiesburg (39402) *(G-2012)*

L & J Products & Sales Inc (PA) 662 841-0710
281 Highway 178 W Tupelo (38804) *(G-5169)*

L & L Tool & Machine Co LLC 662 335-1181
1225 Highway 1 N Greenville (38703) *(G-1563)*

L & W Logging Inc 601 927-3588
24706 Highway 27 Crystal Springs (39059) *(G-1145)*

L & W Print Finishers LLC 662 890-0505
7472b Highway 178 Olive Branch (38654) *(G-3862)*

L and H Investment Inc 601 636-4642
1880 S Frontage Rd Vicksburg (39180) *(G-5387)*

L and J Global Marketing LLC 662 420-9480
8544 Caroma St Unit 77 Olive Branch (38654) *(G-3863)*

L and S Logging, Philadelphia Also called Larry Winstead *(G-4223)*

L C Industries Inc 662 841-1640
1151 S Veterans Blvd Tupelo (38804) *(G-5170)*

L C Industries Inc 601 894-1771
1 Signature Dr Hazlehurst (39083) *(G-2099)*

L D Sheet Metal 662 838-6267
584 Dogwood Ranch Cir Byhalia (38611) *(G-587)*

L L Wood 662 454-0506
10 Industrial Rd Belmont (38827) *(G-199)*

L M & R Service Inc 601 892-3034
4156 Six Mile Rd Crystal Springs (39059) *(G-1146)*

L T Corporation (PA) 662 843-4046
2914 Hwy 61 S Cleveland (38732) *(G-798)*

L T Industries Inc 228 392-1172
11240 Shorecrest Rd Biloxi (39532) *(G-258)*

L&E Logistics LLC 877 884-8889
411 Aston Ave McComb (39648) *(G-3257)*

L3 Technologies Inc 601 856-2274
555 Industrial Dr S Madison (39110) *(G-3117)*

L3 Technologies Systems, Madison Also called L3 Technologies Inc *(G-3117)*

La Brioche LLC 601 988-2299
2906 N State St Jackson (39216) *(G-2466)*

La Ilucion 662 536-0046
1075 Goodman Rd W Horn Lake (38637) *(G-2204)*

La Jolie Enterprises LLC 601 909-8840
340 Arbor Dr Apt 1317 Ridgeland (39157) *(G-4596)*

La Rosa Glass & Hardware, Long Beach Also called La Rosa Glass Inc *(G-2942)*

La Rosa Glass Inc 228 864-0751
6303 Beatline Rd Long Beach (39560) *(G-2942)*

La-Z-Boy Inc 601 683-3354
133 Scanlan St Newton (39345) *(G-3722)*

La-Z-Boy Contract Furniture, Leland Also called Knu LLC *(G-2888)*

La-Z-Boy Incorporated 601 683-3354
33 Scanlan St Newton (39345) *(G-3723)*

Label Express Inc 662 566-7075
100 Quality Ln Verona (38879) *(G-5334)*

Labels & Stamps of Ellisville 601 763-3092
850 Three Mile Stretch Rd Ellisville (39437) *(G-1262)*

Labels and Stamps, Ellisville Also called Labels & Stamps of Ellisville *(G-1262)*

Labelsrx, Madison Also called Darrell Crum LLC *(G-3092)*

Lacknothing Enterprises LLC 601 498-1000
19 Sunset Rd Laurel (39440) *(G-2791)*

Laclede Chain Mfg Co LLC 601 802-0134
101 W Ceres Blvd Vicksburg (39183) *(G-5388)*

Lad2 LLC 601 584-9026
5211 Old Highway 42 Hattiesburg (39401) *(G-2013)*

Ladner Logging LLC 601 422-7822
1727 Highway 184 Laurel (39443) *(G-2792)*

Ladonna R Williams 601 405-2200
100 Kimberly Cv Clinton (39056) *(G-828)*

Lady Bugs and Lily Pads 601 735-0071
801a Mississippi Dr Waynesboro (39367) *(G-5503)*

Lafarge North America Inc 601 859-4488
139 Tyler Dr Canton (39046) *(G-666)*

Lag Constructors 601 720-0404
700 Woods Rd Madison (39110) *(G-3118)*

Lagniappe Books LLC 769 242-8104
313 Telly Rd Picayune (39466) *(G-4275)*

Lagwenbre Designer Corporation 469 230-8534
212 Railroad St Brookhaven (39601) *(G-506)*

Laird Timber Inc 601 833-4293
308 Jackson Liberty Dr Sw Brookhaven (39601) *(G-507)*

Lake Messenger 601 775-3857
24642 Highway 80 Lake (39092) *(G-2723)*

Lake Road Furniture Mfg Co 662 568-3329
2739 Highway 15 N Houlka (38850) *(G-2224)*

Lake's Catfish, Dundee Also called Lakes Farm Raised Catfish Inc *(G-1224)*

Lakes Farm Raised Catfish Inc 662 363-1847
10280 Old Highway 61 S Dundee (38626) *(G-1224)*

Lakeside Moulding & Mfg Co 601 992-5546
5300 Mississippi 25 Flowood (39232) *(G-1376)*

Lakeview Metal Works 601 947-8019
155 Lakeview Dr Lucedale (39452) *(G-3007)*

Lamar Concrete Inc 601 794-0049
5697 Us Highway 11 Purvis (39475) *(G-4444)*

Lamar County News Inc 601 268-2331
103 N 40th Ave Hattiesburg (39401) *(G-2014)*

Lamb Woodworking 601 545-3052
128 Rockhill Brklyn Rd # 54 Brooklyn (39425) *(G-551)*

(PA)=Parent Co (HQ)=Headquarters (DH)=Div Headquarters

2019 Harris Directory of
Mississippi Manufacturers

Lamoco Inc

Lamoco Inc..601 919-3777
103 Millcreek Cors Brandon (39047) *(G-411)*

Lamont Wells LLC...601 656-2772
299a W Beacon St Philadelphia (39350) *(G-4222)*

Lamonts Food Products Inc.............................662 838-3431
4212 Highway 309 S Byhalia (38611) *(G-588)*

Lancaster Machine & Welding..........................601 582-1400
1 Lindsay Carter Rd Hattiesburg (39401) *(G-2015)*

Lance Smith Logging Inc................................601 833-4855
1562 Zetus Rd Nw Brookhaven (39601) *(G-508)*

Land Shapers Inc...228 864-3624
14270 Creosote Rd Gulfport (39503) *(G-1820)*

Landau Uniforms Incorporated.........................662 895-7200
8410 W Sandidge Rd Olive Branch (38654) *(G-3864)*

Landing..601 707-7505
111 Colony Crossing Way Madison (39110) *(G-3119)*

Landmark Spatial Solutions LLC........................662 769-5344
4635 County Lake Rd Starkville (39759) *(G-4955)*

Lane Furniture, Belden *Also called United Furniture Inds Inc (G-193)*

Lane Furniture, Belden *Also called LFI Wind Down Inc (G-190)*

Lane Furniture Industries Inc...........................662 489-3815
Industrial Pk Stafford Dr Pontotoc (38863) *(G-4341)*

Langston Logging Inc...................................662 542-8704
675 Earnest Rd Calhoun City (38916) *(G-639)*

Larken Laboratories Inc................................601 855-7678
276 Nissan Pkwy Bldg A Canton (39046) *(G-667)*

Larkowski Inc...601 928-9501
19486 Borzik Rd Saucier (39574) *(G-4757)*

Larry D Brabham...601 551-4777
4662 E Fork Rd Liberty (39645) *(G-2914)*

Larry D Wallace..601 384-4409
782 Martin Bonds Rd Nw Roxie (39661) *(G-4691)*

Larry Joe Gibson...662 844-9113
503a State Park Rd Tupelo (38804) *(G-5171)*

Larry Sasser Logging LP.................................601 734-6002
913 Bogue Chitto Rd Sw Bogue Chitto (39629) *(G-303)*

Larry Wells..662 724-4355
817 Highway 490 Noxapater (39346) *(G-3732)*

Larry Wheeless Logging.................................662 547-6863
2232 Highway 407 Mc Cool (39108) *(G-3236)*

Larry Winstead...601 656-6438
1028 Highway 427 Philadelphia (39350) *(G-4223)*

Larrys Equipment Inc....................................662 423-0077
205 County Road 176 Iuka (38852) *(G-2298)*

Lars Jordan...601 544-2424
296 Kelly Rose Ln Petal (39465) *(G-4190)*

Laser Mania Inc...601 543-0072
905 Hardy St Ste 223 Hattiesburg (39401) *(G-2016)*

Latitude Armory, Macon *Also called Fianna Systems LLC (G-3061)*

Lauderdale County Farm Sup Inc.......................601 483-3363
203 49th Ave S Meridian (39307) *(G-3356)*

Lauderdale-Hamilton Inc.................................662 767-3928
Hwy 45 S Alt Shannon (38868) *(G-4813)*

Laundry Depot LLC......................................601 527-2774
613 Crosscreek Private St Meridian (39301) *(G-3357)*

Laura Jane Company LLC................................662 629-0550
163 E Van Dorn Ave Holly Springs (38635) *(G-2181)*

Laurel Machine and Foundry Co.........................601 428-0541
810 Front St Laurel (39440) *(G-2793)*

Laurin Enterprises LLC...................................228 207-5580
2530 Wilson Rd Biloxi (39531) *(G-259)*

Lavastone Inds Fireplace Sp, Tupelo *Also called Lavastone Industries Mid South (G-5172)*

Lavastone Industries Mid South.........................662 844-5178
4115 W Main St Tupelo (38801) *(G-5172)*

Lavelle Crabtree Welding................................662 746-7177
401 S Industrial Pkwy Yazoo City (39194) *(G-5638)*

Lawrence A Witherspoon................................662 404-5859
5784 Caroline Dr Horn Lake (38637) *(G-2205)*

Lawrence County Press Inc..............................601 587-2781
296 F E Sellers Hwy Monticello (39654) *(G-3435)*

Lawrence Printing Company.............................662 453-6301
400 Stribling Ave Greenwood (38930) *(G-1633)*

Lazarus Arts..601 445-4576
55 Sgt Prentiss Dr # 103 Natchez (39120) *(G-3578)*

Lazarus Green Arts, Natchez *Also called Lazarus Arts (G-3578)*

Lc Ind Signature Works Div..............................601 206-9564
920 E County Line Rd Ridgeland (39157) *(G-4597)*

Lc Industries, Tupelo *Also called L C Industries Inc (G-5170)*

Le Clair Industries Inc (PA)..............................662 226-8075
2604 Sunset Dr Grenada (38901) *(G-1691)*

Le Fleur De Luis..228 875-6628
6650 Rose Farm Rd Ocean Springs (39564) *(G-3769)*

Lea Logging...601 833-8983
1305 Sams Rd Nw Brookhaven (39601) *(G-509)*

Leaf River Cellulose LLC................................601 964-8411
157 Buck Creek Rd New Augusta (39462) *(G-3711)*

Leas Repair...662 658-4462
27538 County Road 550 Minter City (38944) *(G-3424)*

Leather Lanyards...662 902-5294
9835 New Africa Rd Clarksdale (38614) *(G-772)*

Leather Works Inc.......................................662 538-4455
1107 Denmill Rd New Albany (38652) *(G-3684)*

Lec Inc..601 939-8535
110 Excell Dr Pearl (39208) *(G-4128)*

Lee & Lee Services Inc...................................601 425-1060
542 Lake Como Rd Laurel (39443) *(G-2794)*

Lee County Courier Inc...................................662 840-8819
303 W Main St Tupelo (38804) *(G-5173)*

Lee Small Engines Inc....................................601 833-5431
607 Country Club Rd Ne Brookhaven (39601) *(G-510)*

Lee's Septic Tanks, Aberdeen *Also called Lees Septic Inc (G-17)*

Leeco Welding Service...................................601 428-7896
67 Victory Rd Laurel (39443) *(G-2795)*

Lees Hot Shot Service LLC...............................601 383-1018
125 Johnson Rd Florence (39073) *(G-1326)*

Lees Precast Concrete Inc...............................662 369-8935
20578 Egypt Rd Aberdeen (39730) *(G-16)*

Lees Septic Inc...662 369-9799
20578 Egypt Rd Aberdeen (39730) *(G-17)*

Leflore Technologies LLC.................................601 572-1491
167 Northwind Dr Brandon (39047) *(G-412)*

Legacy Vulcan LLC......................................662 357-7675
15581 Graves Rd Lake Cormorant (38641) *(G-2725)*

Legacy Vulcan LLC......................................601 947-9717
201 County Industrial Rd Lucedale (39452) *(G-3008)*

Legacy Vulcan LLC......................................601 553-2902
2785 Sellers Dr Meridian (39301) *(G-3358)*

Legacy Vulcan LLC......................................228 452-3000
4010 Espy Ave Long Beach (39560) *(G-2943)*

Legacy Vulcan LLC......................................601 544-3523
157 Chevis Lee Rd Petal (39465) *(G-4191)*

Legacy Vulcan LLC......................................228 474-1414
5500 Hwy 613 Moss Point (39563) *(G-3483)*

Legacy Vulcan LLC......................................228 522-6011
2499 Old Spanish Trl Gautier (39553) *(G-1496)*

Legacy Vulcan LLC......................................601 482-7007
5226 Arundel Rd Meridian (39307) *(G-3359)*

Legacy Vulcan LLC......................................601 631-8833
100 Commerce Park Dr Jackson (39213) *(G-2467)*

Legend Publishing..662 844-2602
499 Gloster Creek Vlg B Tupelo (38801) *(G-5174)*

Legendary Lawn Services Inc............................601 307-6381
510 George St Ste 230 Jackson (39202) *(G-2468)*

Legendary Lighting LLC..................................601 932-0707
1016 N Flowood Dr Jackson (39232) *(G-2653)*

Leggett & Platt Incorporated...........................662 456-3053
600 3rd Ave Houston (38851) *(G-2249)*

Leggett & Platt Incorporated...........................662 842-5704
1961 S Green St Tupelo (38804) *(G-5175)*

Leggett & Platt Incorporated...........................662 842-5704
2071 S Green St Tupelo (38804) *(G-5176)*

Leggett & Platt Incorporated...........................662 842-5704
2071 S Green St Tupelo (38804) *(G-5177)*

Leggett & Platt Incorporated...........................662 869-1060
241 Jamie Whitten Blvd Saltillo (38866) *(G-4717)*

Leggett & Platt Incorporated...........................417 358-8131
61 Mapleview Rd West Point (39773) *(G-5549)*

Leggett & Platt 1704, Houston *Also called Leggett & Platt Incorporated (G-2249)*

Leggett & Platt 4201, Tupelo *Also called Leggett & Platt Incorporated (G-5177)*

Leggett & Platt Incorporated............................662 842-5237
115 N Industrial Rd Tupelo (38801) *(G-5178)*

Leggett Platt Components Inc (HQ).....................662 844-4224
115 N Industrial Rd Tupelo (38801) *(G-5179)*

Lehman-Roberts Company...............................662 563-2100
1775 Farrish Gravel Rd Batesville (38606) *(G-113)*

Lehman-Roberts Company...............................662 429-5237
6158 Highway 51 S Hernando (38632) *(G-2138)*

Leisure Home Products Inc..............................228 860-7727
7085 Turner Rd Long Beach (39560) *(G-2944)*

Lemon Tree Candles......................................662 621-4312
47 Delta Ave Apt 211 Clarksdale (38614) *(G-773)*

Lemonwood LLC..601 792-5748
455 Park Fortenberry Rd Oak Vale (39656) *(G-3735)*

Lenders Software Incorporated..........................601 919-6362
359 Audubon Cir Brandon (39047) *(G-413)*

Lenoir Technology LLC...................................769 926-5300
8220 W Oaklawn Rd Biloxi (39532) *(G-260)*

Leon Schommer Sawmill.................................601 753-2687
Little Creek Rd Mc Lain (39456) *(G-3240)*

Leonard Metal Fabricators Inc...........................601 936-4994
5012 Highway 80 E Pearl (39208) *(G-4129)*

Leonard Printing Company...............................601 833-3912
625 W Congress St Brookhaven (39601) *(G-511)*

Leopold Inds Intrglaetical LLC...........................662 324-0536
211 Hickory Dr Starkville (39759) *(G-4956)*

Leroy Dees..662 674-5356
9240 Attala Road 2101 Ethel (39067) *(G-1282)*

Lesso Freezing Company Inc...........................228 374-7200
598 Bayview Ave Biloxi (39530) *(G-261)*

2019 Harris Directory of
Mississippi Manufacturers

(G-0000) Company's Geographic Section entry number

ALPHABETIC SECTION

Lucedale Sportswear Co, Lucedale

Levan Industries 601 446-7390
1200 Highway 61 S Natchez (39120) *(G-3579)*

Levins Labs LLC 228 334-2411
801 Washington Ave Ste H Ocean Springs (39564) *(G-3770)*

Lewis Printing Service, Pascagoula *Also called Lewis Yager Melbaleen J (G-4046)*

Lewis Yager Melbaleen J 228 762-3152
501 Krebs Ave Pascagoula (39567) *(G-4046)*

Lexington Concrete, Canton *Also called Canton Concrete (G-652)*

Lexington Concrete & Block Co 601 859-4547
153 Yandell Ave Canton (39046) *(G-668)*

Lexington Concrete & Block Co 662 834-3892
304a Yazoo St Lexington (39095) *(G-2904)*

LFI Wind Down Inc 662 566-7211
3350 Mccullough Blvd Belden (38826) *(G-190)*

Liberations Publishing LLC 662 605-0382
29680 Highway 50 E West Point (39773) *(G-5550)*

Liberty Fuels Company LLC 601 737-7000
1000 Mcintire Rd Ackerman (39735) *(G-25)*

Liberty Fuels Company LLC 601 737-7000
4707 Highway 493 De Kalb (39328) *(G-1166)*

Liberty Oilfield Services & RE 601 398-8511
4018 Meadville Rd Liberty (39645) *(G-2915)*

Liberty Plastics, Baldwyn *Also called Southern Diversified Inds Inc (G-87)*

Liberty Southern Energy, Ridgeland *Also called Liberty Southern Partners LP (G-4598)*

Liberty Southern Partners LP 214 450-8838
611 S Pear Orchard Rd Ridgeland (39158) *(G-4598)*

Lifestory Publishing 601 594-0018
5328 Runnymede Rd Jackson (39211) *(G-2469)*

Lifetime Portable Building LLC 228 860-7715
15042 Whisperwood Dr Gulfport (39503) *(G-1821)*

Lighthouse For The Blind 228 867-1565
424 34th St Gulfport (39507) *(G-1822)*

Lighthouse Marble Works Inc 228 392-3038
8212 Woolmarket Rd Biloxi (39532) *(G-262)*

Lighting Investment Group Inc (PA) 601 482-3983
6325 Spector St Meridian (39307) *(G-3360)*

Lightning Bloom Press LLC 662 638-3611
303 River Run Rd Oxford (38655) *(G-3965)*

Lightning Machine Works 662 449-1801
2440 Wanda Faye Dr Hernando (38632) *(G-2139)*

Lightning Quick Signs 228 467-1718
208 Highway 90 Waveland (39576) *(G-5482)*

Lil Ms Sew & Sew Inc 601 992-3279
1679 Old Fannin Rd Ste H Flowood (39232) *(G-1377)*

Limeco Inc 662 456-4226
14611 Highway 47 West Point (39773) *(G-5551)*

Limoss Us LLC 662 365-2200
964 Highway 45 Baldwyn (38824) *(G-82)*

Linas Interiors Inc 662 332-7226
109 E 3rd St Leland (38756) *(G-2889)*

Linco Safety Signs 662 469-9569
1780 Robertson Place Dr Hernando (38632) *(G-2140)*

Lincoln Lumber Co Inc 601 833-4484
410 County Farm Ln Ne Brookhaven (39601) *(G-512)*

Linda F Wilson 662 299-9656
2710 George White Cir Greenwood (38930) *(G-1634)*

Linde North America Inc 601 829-9020
118 Shirley Ln Brandon (39047) *(G-414)*

Lindsey Machine Shop Inc 662 365-8189
655 Highway 370 Baldwyn (38824) *(G-83)*

Line-X of Jackson, Pearl *Also called 4m Enterprises LLC (G-4101)*

Linear Motion Systems, Baldwyn *Also called Limoss Us LLC (G-82)*

Linex Tupelo, Tupelo *Also called Dealership Services LLC (G-5126)*

Lining & Coating Solutions LLC 662 453-6860
2606 Baldwin Rd Greenwood (38930) *(G-1635)*

Lining & Coating Solutions LLC 662 893-0984
7122 Highway 178 Olive Branch (38654) *(G-3865)*

Linton Systems 228 872-7300
6608 Sunscope Dr Ocean Springs (39564) *(G-3771)*

Lion Oil Co 601 933-3000
2829 Lkeland Dr Ste 2000 Flowood (39232) *(G-1378)*

Lions Pride 601 818-1308
23 Delma Dr Hattiesburg (39401) *(G-2017)*

Lipstick and Labels LLC 601 501-4029
1208 Washington St Vicksburg (39183) *(G-5389)*

Liquor Locker Inc 228 396-8557
920 Cedar Lake Rd Ste O Biloxi (39532) *(G-263)*

Lisa Hibley 601 736-6781
1452 Highway 98 E Columbia (39429) *(G-903)*

Lisa Ulmer, Columbus *Also called Tinks Bells (G-1038)*

Lisas Candles 601 384-7406
652 Low Wtr Bridge Rd Se Meadville (39653) *(G-3277)*

Lit Industries Inc 662 993-8088
12051 Highway 4 E Ripley (38663) *(G-4663)*

Live and Laff LLC 662 816-5144
518 County Road 303 Taylor (38673) *(G-5049)*

Living Blues Magazine, University *Also called University of Mississippi (G-5306)*

Livingston Log & Timber Co Inc 601 425-2095
64 Jess Livingston Rd Laurel (39443) *(G-2796)*

LLC Glass House 769 251-1299
14 Northtown Dr Jackson (39211) *(G-2470)*

Lloyd Cox Jr 662 462-5226
60 County Road 449 Rienzi (38865) *(G-4650)*

Lmf, Laurel *Also called Laurel Machine and Foundry Co (G-2793)*

Lmg Diversified LLC 601 635-5955
110 Russell St Newton (39345) *(G-3724)*

Lobell Sales LLC 662 724-2940
2258 Oak Grove Rd Noxapater (39346) *(G-3733)*

Local Native Creative + Print 662 401-4767
111 S 2nd St Baldwyn (38824) *(G-84)*

Local Voice LLC 662 232-8900
1503 White Oak Ln Oxford (38655) *(G-3966)*

Localnet 601 774-9338
108 Ware St Union (39365) *(G-5300)*

Lockheed Martin Corporation 901 795-5943
2834 Allyson Gene Cv Byhalia (38611) *(G-589)*

Lockheed Martin Corporation 228 864-7910
4402 Hewes Ave Gulfport (39507) *(G-1823)*

Lockheed Martin Corporation 228 688-7997
Stennis Space Center Bay Saint Louis (39529) *(G-146)*

Lockheed Martin Corporation 228 813-2160
Bldg 5100 Bay Saint Louis (39529) *(G-147)*

Lockheed Mrtin Space Oprations 228 688-3675
John C Stennis Cntr Bay Saint Louis (39529) *(G-148)*

Lofton Corporation 769 243-8427
6512 Dogwood View Pkwy Jackson (39213) *(G-2471)*

Logan Oil Field Services 601 787-4407
379 Eucutta Rd Waynesboro (39367) *(G-5504)*

Loggers Depot, Richton *Also called Stinson & Son Logging (G-4544)*

Loggins Woodwork 662 283-5882
237 Loggins Rd Kilmichael (39747) *(G-2677)*

Logistical Services Intl Inc 662 676-2823
3649 Alice Hall Rd Golden (38847) *(G-1529)*

Logitech Inc 510 713-5429
8640 Nail Rd Ste 100 Olive Branch (38654) *(G-3866)*

Logo Specialties, Starkville *Also called University Screen Print Inc (G-4978)*

Logo Sportswear 601 845-5038
211 Whitetail Blvd Florence (39073) *(G-1327)*

Lokring Gulf Coast LLC 228 497-0091
7519 Martin Bluff Rd Gautier (39553) *(G-1497)*

Lombardo Industries LLC 601 783-3643
3481 Smiley Honea Rd Magnolia (39652) *(G-3192)*

London War Room 601 584-8533
41 Beverly Hills Loop Petal (39465) *(G-4192)*

Lone Star Defense 662 701-5204
50507 Old Highway 6 Amory (38821) *(G-47)*

Long Beach Yard, Long Beach *Also called Legacy Vulcan LLC (G-2943)*

Long-Delayed Publishing LLC 662 202-6229
1802 Jackson Ave W # 175 Oxford (38655) *(G-3967)*

Longbranch 662 284-8585
104 Taylor St Corinth (38834) *(G-1098)*

Longleaf Enterprises Ltd 601 225-4481
155 S First St Gloster (39638) *(G-1516)*

Longleaf Forest Products LLC 662 456-4444
1538 Ms 15 Houston (38851) *(G-2250)*

Loresco Inc 601 544-7490
875 Old Richburg Rd Purvis (39475) *(G-4445)*

Los Portrillos 662 844-7350
831 S Gloster St Tupelo (38801) *(G-5180)*

Lost Sock LLC 601 946-1155
104 Golden Pond Dr Madison (39110) *(G-3120)*

Lott Enterprises Inc (PA) 662 453-0034
204 Eastman St Greenwood (38930) *(G-1636)*

Lott Enterprises Inc 601 932-4698
1016c N Flowood Dr Jackson (39232) *(G-2654)*

Loud Technology, Madison *Also called White Shirt Networks LLC (G-3170)*

Louisiana Well Service Co Inc 601 442-6648
280 Highland Blvd Natchez (39120) *(G-3580)*

Louisville Brick Company 800 530-7102
750 N Church Ave Louisville (39339) *(G-2973)*

Louisville Publishing Inc 662 773-6241
233 N Court Ave Louisville (39339) *(G-2974)*

Lounora Industries Inc (PA) 662 328-1685
1402 Waterworks Rd Columbus (39701) *(G-994)*

Love Your Light Candle Company 769 572-1733
502 Kirsten Way Brandon (39047) *(G-415)*

Loveland Products Inc 662 335-3394
911 Platte Rd Greenville (38703) *(G-1564)*

Loveland Products Inc 662 335-3394
917 Platte Rd Greenville (38703) *(G-1565)*

Lovorn Logging Inc 662 637-2617
164 Dentontown Rd Calhoun City (38916) *(G-640)*

Low Pro Publishing 601 372-1875
133 Brenda Dr Jackson (39212) *(G-2472)*

Lsc Communications Us LLC 601 562-5252
121 Matthews Dr Senatobia (38668) *(G-4794)*

Lucedale Ready Mix Concrete Co 601 947-4741
139 Evanston Rd Lucedale (39452) *(G-3009)*

Lucedale Sportswear Co, Lucedale *Also called Harper Industries Inc (G-2999)*

(PA)=Parent Co (HQ)=Headquarters (DH)=Div Headquarters

2019 Harris Directory of
Mississippi Manufacturers

Lucite International..........662 893-5450
10500 High Point Rd Olive Branch (38654) *(G-3867)*
Luckett Pump & Well Svc Inc..........662 624-2398
1420 Emerald Rd Dublin (38739) *(G-1219)*
Lucky Dog Monograms LLC..........662 321-7903
124 Herdtown Dr Tupelo (38804) *(G-5181)*
Lucky Leaf Discount Tobacco..........601 924-8818
509 Springridge Rd Ste C Clinton (39056) *(G-829)*
Lucky Star Industries Inc (PA)..........662 840-4465
1016 N Gloster St Tupelo (38804) *(G-5182)*
Lucky Town Brewing Company LLC..........601 790-0142
1710 N Mill St Jackson (39202) *(G-2473)*
Lucy Lus Monogramming LLC..........662 417-9552
202 Summit St Winona (38967) *(G-5603)*
Luke Printing Co Inc..........601 693-1144
2959 Alpine Way Meridian (39301) *(G-3361)*
Lulus Sweet Shop LLC..........601 790-1951
102 Dees Drive Madison Madison (39110) *(G-3121)*
Lumpkin Repair Service LLC..........601 798-2027
16 R N Lumpkin Ln Carriere (39426) *(G-694)*
Lums Welding & Machine..........601 825-1116
2907 Highway 80 Brandon (39042) *(G-416)*
Lunati CAM Shafts, Olive Branch *Also called Lunati LLC (G-3868)*
Lunati LLC..........662 892-1518
8649 Hacks Cross Rd Olive Branch (38654) *(G-3868)*
Lund Coating Technologies Inc..........662 252-2340
400 S Industrial Park Rd Holly Springs (38635) *(G-2182)*
Lund Engineered Products, Holly Springs *Also called Lund Coating Technologies Inc (G-2182)*
Lundtek Inc..........662 252-2340
400 S Industrial Park Rd Holly Springs (38635) *(G-2183)*
Luvel Dairy Products Inc (HQ)..........662 289-2511
926 Veterans Memorial Dr Kosciusko (39090) *(G-2698)*
Luvel Dairy Products Inc..........601 693-0038
2659 Sellers Dr Meridian (39301) *(G-3362)*
Luvel Dairy Products Inc..........662 334-6372
3305 Highway 82 E Greenville (38703) *(G-1566)*
Lyle Machinery Co..........601 276-3528
298 Lawrence St Summit (39666) *(G-5017)*
Lynn Hollis Rebel Cabinets..........228 588-2572
7109 E Central Park Dr Moss Point (39562) *(G-3484)*
Lynn Hunt Trucking, Lucedale *Also called Willie Lynn Hunt (G-3021)*
Lynn Welding Shop LLC..........601 638-7235
7355 Highway 61 S Vicksburg (39180) *(G-5390)*
Lynns Custom Boats, Vicksburg *Also called Lynn Welding Shop LLC (G-5390)*
Lynns Welding Shop LLC..........601 415-0012
7355 Highway 61 S Vicksburg (39180) *(G-5391)*
M & B Logging Inc..........601 384-6611
140 River Rd Bude (39630) *(G-571)*
M & D Sales, Laurel *Also called Southeastern Oilfield Pdts LLC (G-2851)*
M & M Chassis Shop LLC..........601 310-6078
442 Old Progress Rd Moselle (39459) *(G-3458)*
M & M Industries Inc..........601 799-2615
15 Sones Chapel Rd Mc Neill (39457) *(G-3241)*
M & M Machine LLC..........601 749-4325
205 Lumpkin Rd Carriere (39426) *(G-695)*
M & M Milling Inc..........601 823-4630
1056 Fender Trl Ne Brookhaven (39601) *(G-513)*
M & M Monograms..........601 856-7459
2019 Silver Ln Madison (39110) *(G-3122)*
M & M Printing LLC..........601 798-4316
29 Alex Pl Picayune (39466) *(G-4276)*
M & M Printing Co..........601 798-4316
29 Alex Pl Picayune (39466) *(G-4277)*
M & T Logging..........662 673-1621
3738 Nod Rd Benton (39039) *(G-209)*
M & W Publishing Co LLC..........662 843-1358
93 Oakridge Rd Boyle (38730) *(G-350)*
M A P, Clarksdale *Also called Molded Acstcal Pdts Easton Inc (G-777)*
M and S Sales Inc..........662 453-6111
3107 Highway 82 E Greenwood (38930) *(G-1637)*
M F C A, Tupelo *Also called Mississipi Furniture Component (G-5188)*
M G K Seining LLC..........662 453-8370
1401 Robert E Lee Dr Greenwood (38930) *(G-1638)*
M L M, Tupelo *Also called McCullar Long & Mccullough Inc (G-5184)*
M M Flechas Shipyard Co Inc..........228 762-3628
4514 Flechas St Pascagoula (39567) *(G-4047)*
M P Johnson Publishing LLC..........662 270-5544
1246 Mcgowan Dr Southaven (38671) *(G-4886)*
M Prints, Meridian *Also called National Scrubwear Inc (G-3376)*
M R Furniture LLC..........662 882-8483
530 County Road 627 Dumas (38625) *(G-1222)*
M S I/Pozzi..........601 957-0085
829 Wilson Dr Ste C Ridgeland (39157) *(G-4599)*
M S Rubber Company (PA)..........601 948-2575
715 E Mcdowell Rd Jackson (39204) *(G-2474)*
M&M Book Publishing Co..........601 442-0980
9 Janice Cir Natchez (39120) *(G-3581)*
M&M Logging..........601 754-2796
2460 Constable Trl Nw Brookhaven (39601) *(G-514)*
M&M Machine Shop Inc..........504 442-0797
21 Native Dancer Carriere (39426) *(G-696)*
M-Tek Inc..........601 407-5000
435 Church Rd Madison (39110) *(G-3123)*
M-Tek Mississippi, Madison *Also called M-Tek Inc (G-3123)*
M.J. Bunch and Sons Logging, Waynesboro *Also called Btc Logging Co (G-5493)*
M2 Corp..........662 342-2173
8362 Lake Shore Dr W Southaven (38671) *(G-4887)*
Maa Global Supply Ltd..........662 816-4802
9 Industrial Park Dr # 103 Oxford (38655) *(G-3968)*
Mabrys..........601 956-7238
1531 Plantation Blvd Jackson (39211) *(G-2475)*
Mac LLC..........228 533-0157
13011 Road G Bay Saint Louis (39520) *(G-149)*
Mac Financial Mgmt LLC..........844 622-6468
1006 Highway 48 E Magnolia (39652) *(G-3193)*
Machine Shop Inc..........601 736-4729
8 Airport Rd Columbia (39429) *(G-904)*
Mackay Enterprises LLC (PA)..........662 328-8469
411 Main St Apt C Columbus (39701) *(G-995)*
Mackay Enterprises LLC..........662 328-8469
411 Main St Apt C Columbus (39701) *(G-996)*
Mackies Slip Inc..........601 722-4395
492 Shirley Sanford Rd Seminary (39479) *(G-4783)*
Macon Beacon..........662 726-4747
2904 Jefferson St Macon (39341) *(G-3064)*
Macon Beacon, The, Macon *Also called Macon Beacon (G-3064)*
Macon Ready-Mix Concrete Co..........662 726-4733
46712 Ms Highway 14 E Macon (39341) *(G-3065)*
Macon Treating Company..........662 726-2767
15029 Us Highway 45 Macon (39341) *(G-3066)*
Macs Small Engine Service..........601 932-8076
160 Scarbrough St Richland (39218) *(G-4521)*
Mad House, Biloxi *Also called Magnetic Arrow LLC (G-264)*
MADE Printing & Designin..........601 572-6967
5562 Queen Elizabeth Ln Jackson (39209) *(G-2476)*
Madison County Herald..........601 853-2899
794 Highway 51 Ste B Madison (39110) *(G-3124)*
Madison County Journal, Ridgeland *Also called Madison County Publishing Inc (G-4600)*
Madison County Publishing Inc..........601 853-4222
293 Commerce Park Dr Ridgeland (39157) *(G-4600)*
Madison House Inc..........601 898-8090
160 Weisenberger Rd Madison (39110) *(G-3125)*
Madness Productions, Hattiesburg *Also called Michael A Dent (G-2023)*
Maelstrom Square LLC..........470 378-9064
4112 Victor St Pascagoula (39567) *(G-4048)*
Magee Energy LLC..........601 709-2930
3003 Lakeland Cv Flowood (39232) *(G-1379)*
Magee Police Department, Magee *Also called City of Magee (G-3174)*
Magnetic Arrow LLC..........601 653-2932
158 Bilmarsan Dr Biloxi (39531) *(G-264)*
Magnificent Prints LLC..........662 469-5689
1760 Thomas St Horn Lake (38637) *(G-2206)*
Magnolia Accounting Services..........662 429-5852
3781 Mccracken Rd Hernando (38632) *(G-2141)*
Magnolia Beneke Inc (PA)..........662 328-4000
1 Tuffy Ln Columbus (39701) *(G-997)*
Magnolia Bites LLC..........601 709-9577
1252 W Government St Brandon (39042) *(G-417)*
Magnolia Bottled Water Company..........662 329-9000
302 7th Ave S Columbus (39701) *(G-998)*
Magnolia Cabinet & Mllwk Inc..........662 282-7683
3031 Highway 371 Mantachie (38855) *(G-3201)*
Magnolia Cabinet Works..........601 916-6538
88 Paradise Ln Carriere (39426) *(G-697)*
Magnolia Frac Sand..........601 446-6023
100 State St Natchez (39120) *(G-3582)*
Magnolia Furniture LLC..........662 489-9337
4333 Highway 9 S Pontotoc (38863) *(G-4342)*
Magnolia Green Industries Inc..........601 466-3853
420 S 35th Ave Hattiesburg (39402) *(G-2018)*
Magnolia Group, Jackson *Also called Magnolia Supply Group LLC (G-2480)*
Magnolia Group The, Vicksburg *Also called Magnolia Mobility LLC (G-5392)*
Magnolia Hosiery Mill Inc..........662 286-2221
311 S Parkway St Corinth (38834) *(G-1099)*
Magnolia Label Co Inc (PA)..........601 878-0951
7380 I 55 S Jackson (39272) *(G-2477)*
Magnolia Mariee LLC..........601 446-6400
200 Main St Natchez (39120) *(G-3583)*
Magnolia Mobility LLC..........601 400-7292
3101 Washington St Vicksburg (39180) *(G-5392)*
Magnolia Molds, Vicksburg *Also called William Stephens (G-5447)*
Magnolia Mtal Plastic Pdts Inc..........601 638-6912
101 County Ln Vicksburg (39183) *(G-5393)*
Magnolia Polishing Service, Hazlehurst *Also called Frank Bradford Womack (G-2096)*
Magnolia Printing and Signs..........601 922-5076
2252 Maddox Rd Jackson (39209) *(G-2478)*

298 2019 Harris Directory of Mississippi Manufacturers (G-0000) Company's Geographic Section entry number

ALPHABETIC SECTION

Masterfoods USA

Magnolia Printing Co..........................228 864-4401
1829 25th Ave Gulfport (39501) *(G-1824)*

Magnolia Processing Inc.......................662 363-3600
5255 Highway 4 Tunica (38676) *(G-5101)*

Magnolia Screens LLC.........................601 942-3049
176 N Sunset Ter Jackson (39212) *(G-2479)*

Magnolia Sewing Center......................601 261-9006
6380 U S Highway 98 Hattiesburg (39402) *(G-2019)*

Magnolia Steel Co Inc.........................601 693-4301
17 17th Ave S Meridian (39301) *(G-3363)*

Magnolia Supply Group LLC..................601 454-1368
315 Decelle St Jackson Jackson (39216) *(G-2480)*

Magnolia Therapeutics LLC..................662 281-0502
605 Crescent Blvd Ste 200 Ridgeland (39157) *(G-4601)*

Magnolia Tool & Mfg Co (PA).................601 856-4333
111 E State St Ridgeland (39157) *(G-4602)*

Magnolia Tool & Mfg Co.......................601 856-4333
110-111 E State St Ridgeland (39157) *(G-4603)*

Magnolia Trailers Inc..........................601 947-7990
144 Airport Cafe Cir Lucedale (39452) *(G-3010)*

Magnoliascreencomp, Vicksburg Also called Magnolia Mtal Plastic Pdts Inc *(G-5393)*

Mahaffey's Quality Printing, Jackson Also called Quality Printing Inc *(G-2555)*

Mahans Concrete Septic Tanks...............662 234-3767
26 County Road 375 Water Valley (38965) *(G-5471)*

Mailbox Ranch...................................601 758-4767
84 Sonny Carter Dr Sumrall (39482) *(G-5038)*

Main Street Cycle Inc..........................662 438-6407
1295 Main St Tishomingo (38873) *(G-5086)*

Main Street Embroidery.......................601 876-0003
715 Beulah Ave Tylertown (39667) *(G-5277)*

Main Street Pascagoula......................228 219-1114
303 Delmas Ave Cottagea Pascagoula (39567) *(G-4049)*

Mainland Canvas, Gautier Also called Mainland Sails Inc *(G-1498)*

Mainland Sails Inc.............................228 374-7245
3803 Old Spanish Trl Gautier (39553) *(G-1498)*

Mainline Printing...............................662 301-8298
1893 Merryhill Ranch Rd Senatobia (38668) *(G-4795)*

Majestic Metals Inc (PA)......................601 856-3600
192 American Way Madison (39110) *(G-3126)*

Major League Promotions....................601 672-4798
1410 Highway 80 W Jackson (39204) *(G-2481)*

Major League Promotions LLC...............601 672-4798
1410 Highway 80 W Jackson (39204) *(G-2482)*

Malibu Lighting Corporation.................662 290-1200
801 E Jefferson St Kosciusko (39090) *(G-2699)*

Malius Press LLC...............................662 281-0955
200 Tanner Dr Oxford (38655) *(G-3969)*

Mallette Brothers Cnstr Co, Gautier Also called Mallette Brothers Cnstr Co *(G-1499)*

Mallette Brothers Cnstr Co..................228 497-2523
3708 Highway 90 Gautier (39553) *(G-1499)*

Malley Inc..228 255-7467
1332 Rocky Hl Dedeaux Rd Kiln (39556) *(G-2683)*

Malone Design & Contg LLC.................601 807-1279
104 Fox Run Dr Hattiesburg (39402) *(G-2020)*

Malt Industries Inc............................601 794-4200
43 Mangum Ln Purvis (39475) *(G-4446)*

Mam Machine & Mfg LLC.....................901 216-1960
8490 Tulane Rd Southaven (38671) *(G-4888)*

Manning Drilling Company Inc...............601 989-2805
1335 Mount Zion Rd Richton (39476) *(G-4539)*

Manning Signs & Designs, Greenville Also called Manning Signs Inc *(G-1567)*

Manning Signs Inc.............................662 332-4496
881 S Raceway Rd Greenville (38703) *(G-1567)*

Manolia Gazette................................601 783-2441
280 Magnolia St Magnolia (39652) *(G-3194)*

Mantachie Printing & Mktg LLC.............662 282-7625
372 Road 1438 Tupelo (38804) *(G-5183)*

Manufacturing -.................................408 514-6512
12380 Kirk Rd Olive Branch (38654) *(G-3869)*

Manufacturing Facility, Hattiesburg Also called Bprex Closures LLC *(G-1939)*

Manufacturing Plant, Columbus Also called ABB Motors and Mechanical Inc *(G-930)*

Mapp Oilfield Services Inc...................601 835-2013
941 Highway 550 Nw Brookhaven (39601) *(G-515)*

Mar-Cal Inc......................................601 825-7520
951 Cato Rd Mendenhall (39114) *(G-3283)*

Mar-Jac Poultry Ms LLC (PA)................601 735-3132
261 Marshall Durbin Dr Waynesboro (39367) *(G-5505)*

Marathon Cheese Corporation...............662 728-6242
500 E Parker Dr Booneville (38829) *(G-333)*

Marathon Cheese of Mississippi, Booneville Also called Marathon Cheese Corporation *(G-333)*

Marcellas Quilt Shop..........................662 262-7870
1588 Highway 413 French Camp (39745) *(G-1440)*

Mardis 300 LLC.................................601 936-3911
213 Katherine Dr Flowood (39232) *(G-1380)*

Mardis Honey, Taylor Also called Live and Laff LLC *(G-5049)*

Marel USA Inc...................................662 686-2269
438 Burdett Rd Leland (38756) *(G-2890)*

Marietta American Inc.........................662 892-6959
11170 Green Valley Dr Olive Branch (38654) *(G-3870)*

Marietta Corporation..........................662 893-4233
11170 Green Valley Dr Olive Branch (38654) *(G-3871)*

Marietta Wood Supply Inc....................662 728-9874
349 Highway 371 Marietta (38856) *(G-3217)*

Marilyn Turner..................................228 271-2551
15628 Anderson Dr Biloxi (39532) *(G-265)*

Marine Flooring LLC...........................832 472-0661
2827 Andrew Ave Pascagoula (39567) *(G-4050)*

Marine Gears Inc (PA)........................662 332-8716
1690 Highway 1 N Greenville (38703) *(G-1568)*

Marine Service Solutions.....................601 658-0772
17042 E Adams Rd Lot 4 Saucier (39574) *(G-4758)*

Marion County Timber Inc....................601 736-0654
168 Ten Mile Creek Rd Foxworth (39483) *(G-1433)*

Marion Publishing Co Inc.....................601 736-2611
318 Second St Columbia (39429) *(G-905)*

Maritime Defense Strategy LLC.............352 302-1442
1405 General Lee St Pascagoula (39567) *(G-4051)*

Mark A Whitney.................................601 575-4952
429 E Beacon St Philadelphia (39350) *(G-4224)*

Mark Taylor Logging..........................662 418-0812
12990 Sturgis Maben Rd Maben (39750) *(G-3047)*

Mark Williams Welding LLC..................601 431-5324
726 Liberty Rd Natchez (39120) *(G-3584)*

Mars Food Us LLC.............................662 335-8000
1098 N Broadway St Greenville (38701) *(G-1569)*

Marshall Durbin Food Corp..................601 969-1248
650 Ford Ave Jackson (39209) *(G-2483)*

Marshall Durbin Food Corp..................601 544-3141
1301 James St Hattiesburg (39401) *(G-2021)*

Marshall Durbin Lab Div, Jackson Also called Marshall Durbin Food Corp *(G-2483)*

Marshall Durbin Poultry, Hattiesburg Also called Marshall Durbin Food Corp *(G-2021)*

Martin and Sons LLC..........................601 825-4012
250 Oil Well Rd Brandon (39042) *(G-418)*

Martin Caderwood.............................714 456-0800
905 Bonnie Blue Dr Oxford (38655) *(G-3970)*

Martin Cardboard Company Inc.............662 489-5416
103 Cruse Dr Pontotoc (38863) *(G-4343)*

Martin Incorporated...........................662 720-2445
100 Caterpillar Dr Booneville (38829) *(G-334)*

Martin Logging Inc (PA)......................601 644-3374
336 County Road 432 Meridian (39301) *(G-3364)*

Martin Marietta Materials Inc................662 383-2070
1500 Port Rd Friars Point (38631) *(G-1443)*

Martin Marietta Materials Inc................662 652-3836
2050 Cotton Gin Rd Tremont (38876) *(G-5093)*

Martin Marietta Materials Inc................601 859-4488
139 Tyler Dr Canton (39046) *(G-669)*

Martini Monday Inc............................228 229-4872
3487 Riverbend Cv Diberville (39540) *(G-1208)*

Martinrea Atmtv-Structures USA............662 566-1023
323 C D F Blvd Shannon (38868) *(G-4814)*

Martinrea Tupelo Division, Shannon Also called Martinrea Atmtv-Structures USA *(G-4814)*

Maruichi Leavitt Pipe Tube LLC.............800 532-8488
211 Industrial Dr Jackson (39218) *(G-2655)*

Mary Givens.....................................601 325-5599
555 N Lake Dr Brandon (39042) *(G-419)*

Mary Margaret Andrews......................901 233-5463
130 Leighton Rd Oxford (38655) *(G-3971)*

Mary Tio..228 392-0706
13042 Marvin St Biloxi (39532) *(G-266)*

Mary's Specialty Crafts, Biloxi Also called Mary Tio *(G-266)*

Masco Wireline Service Inc...................601 428-7966
337 Avenue A Laurel (39440) *(G-2797)*

Mashburns Welding............................601 648-2886
312 Sandbed Chicora Rd Buckatunna (39322) *(G-564)*

Mason Overstreet Wldg Mch Work.........601 932-1794
720 M And O Dr Pearl (39208) *(G-4130)*

Mason Printing..................................662 563-3709
344 Highway 51 N Batesville (38606) *(G-114)*

Masonite Corporation.........................601 422-2200
1001 S 4th Ave Laurel (39440) *(G-2798)*

Masons Millworks, Raleigh Also called Donald W Mason *(G-4475)*

Massey Clothing Company LLC..............662 792-4046
104 N Jackson St Kosciusko (39090) *(G-2700)*

Massey Kristy, Kosciusko Also called Massey Clothing Company LLC *(G-2700)*

Mast Management LLC........................601 833-8073
36 Shore Dr Ne Brookhaven (39601) *(G-516)*

Master Bilt, Booneville Also called Masterbilt *(G-335)*

Master Fibers Inc..............................662 568-3455
1 Recon Dr Houlka (38850) *(G-2225)*

Master-Bilt Products, New Albany Also called Standex International Corp *(G-3700)*

Masterbilt, New Albany Also called Standex International Corp *(G-3701)*

Masterbilt..662 728-3227
213 W College St Booneville (38829) *(G-335)*

Masterfoods USA..............................662 335-8000
1098 N Broadway St Greenville (38701) *(G-1570)*

(PA)=Parent Co (HQ)=Headquarters (DH)=Div Headquarters

2019 Harris Directory of
Mississippi Manufacturers

299

Mat Sturgis Co Inc 662 465-8879
4062 Strgis Louisville Rd Sturgis (39769) **(G-5007)**

Matco Industries LLC 228 218-9813
10950 Highway 614 Moss Point (39562) **(G-3485)**

Matheson Tri-Gas Inc 228 255-6661
7635 Kiln Delisle Rd Pass Christian (39571) **(G-4091)**

Matheson Tri-Gas Inc 601 856-3000
218 Weisenberger Rd Madison (39110) **(G-3127)**

Mathis Plow Inc 662 323-5600
1281 Old Hwy 82 E Starkville (39759) **(G-4957)**

Mathis Trucking & Cnstr LLC 601 917-0237
12128 Kalorama Rd Collinsville (39325) **(G-873)**

Mathis, W A Logging Co, McComb Also called W A Mathis Timber Co **(G-3273)**

Matthew Warren Inc 662 489-7846
260 Industrial Dr Pontotoc (38863) **(G-4344)**

Matthew Warren Inc 574 753-6622
260 Industrial Dr Pontotoc (38863) **(G-4345)**

Mattuby Creek Machine Works 662 369-8262
21957 Highway 45 N Aberdeen (39730) **(G-18)**

Maurey Manufacturing Corp (PA) 662 252-6583
410 S Industrial Park Rd Holly Springs (38635) **(G-2184)**

Maurice Hinton 601 857-5168
5057 Myers Rd Terry (39170) **(G-5072)**

Max Home LLC 662 862-9966
101 Max Pl Fulton (38843) **(G-1462)**

Max Home LLC 662 424-0005
1509 Paul Edmondson Dr Iuka (38852) **(G-2299)**

Max Private Label Inc 773 362-2601
103 Green Dr Shannon (38868) **(G-4815)**

Max White Logging Inc 662 560-3460
194 County Road 461 Oxford (38655) **(G-3972)**

Maxim Holding Company Inc (PA) 601 625-7471
16741 Highway 21 S Sebastopol (39359) **(G-4774)**

Maxim Manufacturing, Sebastopol Also called Maxim Holding Company Inc **(G-4774)**

Maximum Auto Parts & Supply 228 863-1100
14473 Creosote Rd Gulfport (39503) **(G-1825)**

Maxwell Sawmill LLC 601 894-3194
9071 Highway 51 Wesson (39191) **(G-5528)**

Maxwell's Monograms, Hattiesburg Also called Patrick Enterprises Inc **(G-2041)**

Maybelle Mfg Co Inc 228 863-4398
51 52nd St Gulfport (39507) **(G-1826)**

Maymar Marine Supply Inc 228 762-2241
4929 Denny Ave Pascagoula (39581) **(G-4052)**

Mayo Logging 601 270-4426
90 Will Best Rd Richton (39476) **(G-4540)**

Mayville Engineering Co Inc 662 335-2325
1281 Pickett St Greenville (38703) **(G-1571)**

Mc Comb Welding & Mch Works 601 684-1921
110 E Presley Blvd McComb (39648) **(G-3258)**

Mc Consulting LLC 601 735-2000
950 Dyess Bridge Rd Waynesboro (39367) **(G-5506)**

Mc Logging LLC 601 678-6681
10480 Road 313 Union (39365) **(G-5301)**

McCaffrey Supply Co, Richland Also called Stanley McCaffrey Signs **(G-4525)**

McCloud Logging Inc 601 835-3217
220 Jessie Wallace Rd Jayess (39641) **(G-2674)**

McComb Printing Inc 601 684-9841
210 S Broadway St McComb (39648) **(G-3259)**

McCormick & Company Inc 662 274-1732
1550 Ms 302 Byhalia (38611) **(G-590)**

McCoy Farms & Gravel 601 847-5962
1215 Main St S Mendenhall (39114) **(G-3284)**

McCrory Logging LLC 601 613-1702
1407 Ashley Rd Brandon (39042) **(G-420)**

McCullar Long & Mccullough Inc 662 842-4165
108 S Spring St Tupelo (38804) **(G-5184)**

McDaniel Logging Co Inc 601 322-7701
6603 Highway 33 S Roxie (39661) **(G-4692)**

McDaniel Trucking 601 656-1028
12140 Highway 16 E Philadelphia (39350) **(G-4225)**

McDevitt Enterprises LLC 601 453-2290
3125 5th Ave Meridian (39305) **(G-3365)**

McEwen Lumber Co, Hattiesburg Also called Hood Industries Inc **(G-1994)**

McFarland Cascade Holdings Inc 662 476-8000
13539 Highway 45 Scooba (39358) **(G-4771)**

McGee Machine 601 825-7387
115 Deletha Ln Brandon (39042) **(G-421)**

McGee Welding LLC 769 355-2339
106 E Franklin St Natchez (39120) **(G-3585)**

McGowan Working Partners Inc (PA) 601 982-3444
1837 Crane Ridge Dr Jackson (39216) **(G-2484)**

McGregor Indstl Steel Fabrcatn 662 236-7006
658 Highway 7 S Oxford (38655) **(G-3973)**

McHan Cabinets 601 636-8821
3250 Tiffintown Rd Vicksburg (39183) **(G-5394)**

McIlwains Electrical Supply (PA) 601 735-1145
808 Fagan Ave Waynesboro (39367) **(G-5507)**

McInnis, Gail Productions, Hattiesburg Also called Gail McInnis **(G-1973)**

McKenzie/Lee Publishing LLC 769 216-8049
128 Cousins Dr Florence (39073) **(G-1328)**

McKewens Oxford 662 234-7003
1110 Van Buren Ave Oxford (38655) **(G-3974)**

McKinnion Welding & Metal Fabr 601 635-3983
16460 Hgwy 15 Decatur (39327) **(G-1175)**

McLan Electronics Inc 601 373-2392
7770 Jackson Raymond Rd Raymond (39154) **(G-4491)**

McLellan Woodworks 336 425-8425
309 Lake Harbor Rd Brandon (39047) **(G-422)**

McLendon Holdings LLC 858 255-9038
2409 14th St Gulfport (39501) **(G-1827)**

McM Communications LLC 228 435-0720
819 Jackson St Biloxi (39530) **(G-267)**

McMahan Bulldog Enterprises 601 606-5711
203 Canty Rayborn Rd Sumrall (39482) **(G-5039)**

McMaster Custom Woodworks LLC 601 408-2252
106 Ashby Park Canton (39046) **(G-670)**

McMillan Stamp & Sign Co Inc 601 353-4688
145 Millsaps Ave Jackson (39202) **(G-2485)**

McMillon Pallet 601 932-2299
540 Pemberton Dr Jackson (39208) **(G-2656)**

McMurtrys Automotive Mch Svc 228 832-8335
19076 Pete Hickman Rd Saucier (39574) **(G-4759)**

McNeely Plastic Products Inc 601 926-1000
1022 Advance Ln Hazlehurst (39083) **(G-2100)**

McNeely Plastic Products Inc (PA) 601 926-1000
1111 Industrial Park Dr Clinton (39056) **(G-830)**

McNeely Plastics, Hazlehurst Also called McNeely Plastic Products Inc **(G-2100)**

McNeil Cabinet and Millwork 601 764-2100
29 County Rd 5121 Bay Springs (39422) **(G-168)**

MD Metals Scrap & Salvage 601 635-4160
7974 Decatur Conehatta Rd Decatur (39327) **(G-1176)**

Mdh Marine Art 228 769-1692
1015 Kell Ave Pascagoula (39567) **(G-4053)**

MDN Laser Engraving Inc 662 397-5799
1223 Nelle St Tupelo (38801) **(G-5185)**

Measell, Decatur Also called James David Measell **(G-1174)**

Meason Operating Co 601 442-3668
188 Highway 61 S Natchez (39120) **(G-3586)**

Mec, Greenville Also called Mayville Engineering Co Inc **(G-1571)**

Mechanical Therapy, Richland Also called Macs Small Engine Service **(G-4521)**

Meco, Hattiesburg Also called Mississippi Embroidery Co **(G-2026)**

Med Lift, Calhoun City Also called A B B Inc **(G-634)**

Medi-Vation LLC 800 643-2134
115 Homestead Dr Madison (39110) **(G-3128)**

Media Solutions 601 351-9303
460 Briarwood Dr Ste 400 Jackson (39206) **(G-2486)**

Mediator Lures Inc 601 992-1577
401 Woodlands Cir Brandon (39047) **(G-423)**

Medical Arts Surgical Group 601 693-3834
2111 14th St Meridian (39301) **(G-3366)**

Medical Clinic 601 587-7795
713 Watts St Monticello (39654) **(G-3436)**

Medical Clinic, The, Monticello Also called Medical Clinic **(G-3436)**

Medical Grade Innovations LLC 601 899-9207
605 Northpark Dr Ste C Ridgeland (39157) **(G-4604)**

Medical McHning Specialsts LLC 662 890-7006
7221 Old Craft Cv Olive Branch (38654) **(G-3872)**

Medical Supplies, Olive Branch Also called Covidien LP **(G-3830)**

Medtronic Inc 662 895-2016
6047 Choctaw Trl Olive Branch (38654) **(G-3873)**

Medworx Compounding LLC 601 859-5008
500 Highway 51 Ste Q Ridgeland (39157) **(G-4605)**

Mega Plastics Inc 601 924-1712
1111 Industrial Park Dr Clinton (39056) **(G-831)**

Mega Tech South LLC 662 538-3366
5525 Highway 145 Shannon (38868) **(G-4816)**

Mel Vold Sales Co 601 371-4911
120 Carpenter Dr Jackson (39212) **(G-2487)**

Melamine Chemicals Inc 662 746-4131
Hwy 49 Yazoo City (39194) **(G-5639)**

Melindas Fabrics and Interiors, Brookhaven Also called Said Melinda **(G-528)**

Melos Manufacturing, Robinsonville Also called Richard Melos **(G-4677)**

Melvin L Brewer Inc 662 328-9191
72 Pleasant Dr Columbus (39702) **(G-999)**

Memaws Ceramics 601 319-8263
513 N Deason St Ellisville (39437) **(G-1263)**

Memphis Obstetrics & Gynecolog 662 349-5554
7900 Airways Blvd Bldg C6 Southaven (38671) **(G-4889)**

Memphis Pallet Services LLC 901 334-6306
236 Moore Crossing Byhalia (38611) **(G-591)**

Memphis Stone & Gravel, Batesville Also called Lehman-Roberts Company **(G-113)**

Memphis Stone & Gravel, Hernando Also called Lehman-Roberts Company **(G-2138)**

Mercer Welding Service 601 649-4269
636 Poole Creek Rd Laurel (39443) **(G-2799)**

Meridian Brick LLC 228 863-5451
1526 29th Ave Gulfport (39501) **(G-1828)**

Meridian Brick LLC 601 296-0445
221 Thornhill Dr Hattiesburg (39401) **(G-2022)**

Meridian Brick LLC ...601 428-4364
1 Brickyard Dr Laurel (39440) ***(G-2800)***
Meridian Brick LLC ...662 840-8884
1735 Mccullough Blvd Tupelo (38801) ***(G-5186)***
Meridian Coca-Cola Bottling Co (PA) ...601 483-5272
2016 Highway 45 N Meridian (39301) ***(G-3367)***
Meridian Mattress Factory Inc ...601 693-3875
200 Rubush Ave Meridian (39301) ***(G-3368)***
Meridian Star, The, Meridian *Also called Newspaper Holding Inc **(G-3377)***
Meridian Woodworking ...601 604-6147
2405 State Blvd Meridian (39307) ***(G-3369)***
Meridian Yard, Meridian *Also called Legacy Vulcan LLC **(G-3359)***
Merle E Sullivan ...662 347-4494
1405 E Ollie Cir Greenville (38703) ***(G-1572)***
Merle Norman Cosmetics Inc ...662 287-7233
1798 Highway 72 E Corinth (38834) ***(G-1100)***
MERR Express LLC ...601 327-1554
278 Gyther Fairley Rd Lucedale (39452) ***(G-3011)***
Messer LLC ...601 825-1422
159 Andrew Chapel Rd Brandon (39042) ***(G-424)***
Met-Tech Corp ...601 693-0061
3405 Industrial Dr Meridian (39307) ***(G-3370)***
Metal Builders Supply Inc ...601 932-0202
632 N Bierdeman Rd Pearl (39208) ***(G-4131)***
Metal Building Systems LLC ...601 649-9949
2 Twin Oaks Pl Laurel (39440) ***(G-2801)***
Metal Coaters, Jackson *Also called Nci Group Inc **(G-2516)***
Metal Finishing Services, Jackson *Also called Redi-Strip of Jackson Inc **(G-2563)***
Metal Impact South LLC (HQ) ...662 538-6500
795 Sam T Barkley Dr New Albany (38652) ***(G-3685)***
Metal Management Inc ...662 455-2540
405 8th St Greenwood (38930) ***(G-1639)***
Metal Management Inc ...662 844-6441
844 State Highway 15 N New Albany (38652) ***(G-3686)***
Metal Products of Corinth Inc ...662 287-3625
County Rd 507 Corinth (38834) ***(G-1101)***
Metal Shark, Moss Point *Also called Horizon Shipbuilding Inc **(G-3480)***
Metal Tech Inc (PA) ...228 604-4604
10151 Lorraine Rd Gulfport (39503) ***(G-1829)***
Metal-Tech Fabricators Inc ...662 622-0400
9007 Highway 51 Coldwater (38618) ***(G-849)***
Metaline Products Inc ...601 892-5610
1002 Metaline Dr Crystal Springs (39059) ***(G-1147)***
Metallic Welding ...769 798-6498
4400 New Post Rd Jackson (39212) ***(G-2488)***
Metalworx LLC ...228 806-9112
4179 Oakridge Pl Biloxi (39532) ***(G-268)***
Metaris Corporation ...601 469-1987
1519 Highway 35 N Forest (39074) ***(G-1422)***
Metaris Hydraulics, Forest *Also called Metaris Corporation **(G-1422)***
Meteor Inc ...601 892-2581
201 E Georgetown St Crystal Springs (39059) ***(G-1148)***
Methodist and Prosthetics ...662 846-6555
804 1st St Cleveland (38732) ***(G-799)***
Metro Christian Living ...601 790-9076
622 Duling Ave Ste 220 Jackson (39216) ***(G-2489)***
Metro Concrete, Picayune *Also called Stockstill Bros Invstments LLC **(G-4298)***
Metro Concrete ...228 284-1660
10200 Logan Cline Rd Gulfport (39503) ***(G-1830)***
Metro Mechanical Inc (PA) ...601 866-9050
1385 Industrial Dr Bolton (39041) ***(G-312)***
Metso Minerals Industries Inc ...662 627-5292
Hwy 49 S Clarksdale (38614) ***(G-774)***
Mfj Enterprises Inc (PA) ...662 323-5869
300 Industrial Park Rd Starkville (39759) ***(G-4958)***
Mfj Enterprises Inc ...662 323-9538
308 Industrial Park Rd Starkville (39759) ***(G-4959)***
Mg Custom Metal Works, Tylertown *Also called Hawas Inc **(G-5272)***
Mg Pisgah, Brandon *Also called Alig LLC **(G-361)***
Mgc Terminal LLC ...601 482-5012
101 65th Ave Meridian (39307) ***(G-3371)***
MGM Inc ...662 428-4646
19440 Hwy 25 Ackerman (39735) ***(G-26)***
MI-Da Maps ...662 429-0022
2868 Wren St Hernando (38632) ***(G-2142)***
Michael A Dent ...601 543-0157
109 Claiborne Ave Hattiesburg (39401) ***(G-2023)***
Michael Williamson ...601 736-9156
3215 Highway 13 N Columbia (39429) ***(G-906)***
Michaels Machine Shop Inc ...662 624-2376
5935 New Africa Rd Clarksdale (38614) ***(G-775)***
Mickeys Trophy & Sign Shop ...601 649-1263
444 Front St Laurel (39440) ***(G-2802)***
Micro Printing & Blueprint, Jackson *Also called Wolverton Enterprises Inc **(G-2637)***
Microscope Logic, Clinton *Also called Ladonna R Williams **(G-828)***
Microtech Industries Inc ...601 373-0177
2980 Davis Rd Ste A Byram (39170) ***(G-622)***
Microtek Medical Inc (HQ) ...662 327-1863
512 N Lehmberg Rd Columbus (39702) ***(G-1000)***
Microwave Service Co (PA) ...662 842-7620
1359 Beech Springs Rd Tupelo (38801) ***(G-5187)***
Mid Mississippi Maintenance ...601 953-1091
4850 Smith Station Rd Edwards (39066) ***(G-1241)***
Mid South Cast Stone ...662 890-7669
10258 Highway 178 Olive Branch (38654) ***(G-3874)***
Mid South Communications Inc ...662 832-0538
50 County Road 122 Water Valley (38965) ***(G-5472)***
Mid South Electric Motor Svc ...662 332-3512
3021 Highway 82 W Greenville (38701) ***(G-1573)***
Mid South Publications Inc ...662 256-8209
111 Main St S Amory (38821) ***(G-48)***
Mid South Sign Council ...601 446-6688
214 S Pearl St Natchez (39120) ***(G-3587)***
Mid South Storm Shelters LLC ...901 619-0064
201 Robinson Dr Como (38619) ***(G-1049)***
Mid State Artificial Limb Inc (PA) ...601 981-2229
4455 Medgar Evers Blvd Jackson (39213) ***(G-2490)***
Mid State Coatings, Picayune *Also called Picayune Monument & Gran Works **(G-4286)***
Mid State Welding & Mch Works, Clinton *Also called Bryan E Presson & Assoc Inc **(G-816)***
Mid-Mississippi Vinyl ...601 910-6553
4331 Lakeland Dr Flowood (39232) ***(G-1381)***
Mid-South Contractors Inc ...601 544-2803
365 Kirkland Loop Ellisville (39437) ***(G-1264)***
Mid-South Division, Rosedale *Also called Cives Corporation **(G-4687)***
Mid-South Drapery Inc ...662 454-3855
92 Yarber St Belmont (38827) ***(G-200)***
Mid-South Fine Printers, Amory *Also called Mid South Publications Inc **(G-48)***
Mid-South Foam & Assembly Inc ...662 895-3334
125 Downing St Ste 8 Olive Branch (38654) ***(G-3875)***
Mid-South Industries Inc ...601 649-4600
723 E 21st St Laurel (39440) ***(G-2803)***
Mid-South Ornamental Concrete ...662 224-3170
6488 Highway 72 Michigan City (38647) ***(G-3423)***
Mid-South Signs & City Elc, Columbus *Also called Mid-South Signs Inc **(G-1001)***
Mid-South Signs Inc (PA) ...662 327-7807
8643 Highway 182 E Columbus (39702) ***(G-1001)***
Mid-South Truss Co Inc ...662 728-0016
109 Magnolia Dr Booneville (38829) ***(G-336)***
Midco Supply Co Inc ...601 932-7311
1420 Old Brandon Rd Jackson (39232) ***(G-2657)***
Midland Color Corp ...662 895-4100
8489 Summit Cv Olive Branch (38654) ***(G-3876)***
Midsouth Corporate Housing ...901 239-4514
1973 Planters Rd Olive Branch (38654) ***(G-3877)***
Midsouth Elevator LLC ...601 353-8283
5810 N Commerce Plz Jackson (39206) ***(G-2491)***
Midsouth Media Group ...662 890-3359
6920 Oak Forest Dr Olive Branch (38654) ***(G-3878)***
Midway Tree Removal Co, Centreville *Also called Eddie Franklin **(G-730)***
Mighty Miss Brewing Co LLC ...662 379-6477
525 Washington Ave Ste B Greenville (38701) ***(G-1574)***
Mike Culbreth Woodyard ...601 776-2422
19 Donald Woodyard Ln Quitman (39355) ***(G-4467)***
Mike Lowery LLC ...601 736-1096
17 Silver Creek Rd Foxworth (39483) ***(G-1434)***
Mike P Mavromihalis, Pascagoula *Also called Maymar Marine Supply Inc **(G-4052)***
Mike Smith Logging Inc ...601 833-2043
1575 Friendship Ln Nw Brookhaven (39601) ***(G-517)***
Mike Stringer Signs ...601 736-8600
21 Airport Rd Columbia (39429) ***(G-907)***
Mike's Heating & AC, Saucier *Also called Larkowski Inc **(G-4757)***
Mike's Service Center, Columbia *Also called Michael Williamson **(G-906)***
Mikes Woodworking ...601 966-1868
727 Miggins Rd Canton (39046) ***(G-671)***
Milieu Outdoor Image Solutions ...601 259-8570
990 Highway 51 2905 Madison (39110) ***(G-3129)***
Military Defense Systems Inc ...850 449-1910
1817 Palestine Rd Picayune (39466) ***(G-4278)***
Military Firearms Parts ...228 596-1271
308 Tandy Dr Gulfport (39503) ***(G-1831)***
Military Warehouse ...662 287-8234
51 County Road 192 Corinth (38834) ***(G-1102)***
Milk & Honey Prtg Press LLC ...662 739-4949
305a N Natchez St Kosciusko (39090) ***(G-2701)***
Millennium Outdoors LLC ...601 932-5832
201 Fairmont Plz Pearl (39208) ***(G-4132)***
Millennium Treestands, Pearl *Also called Millennium Outdoors LLC **(G-4132)***
Miller Blasting & Coating, Carriere *Also called Miller Enterprises **(G-698)***
Miller Bryant G Oil Gas Prpts ...601 360-2850
1837 Peachtree St Jackson (39202) ***(G-2492)***
Miller Enterprises ...601 798-3004
40 Pine Hill Dr Carriere (39426) ***(G-698)***
Miller Land Professionals LLC ...601 969-1160
974 E Fortification St Jackson (39202) ***(G-2493)***
Miller Oil Properties, Jackson *Also called Inland Energy Company Inc **(G-2446)***
Miller Timber LLC ...662 501-6150
865 County Road 413 Houlka (38850) ***(G-2226)***

ALPHABETIC

(PA)=Parent Co (HQ)=Headquarters (DH)=Div Headquarters
2019 Harris Directory of Mississippi Manufacturers
301

ALPHABETIC SECTION

Milligan Ready Mix Inc 662 423-6238
1679 Constitution Dr Iuka (38852) *(G-2300)*

Million Dollar Makeup LLC 318 331-5363
145 Arbor Gate Cir Apt H Picayune (39466) *(G-4279)*

Mills Logging 662 665-2718
1221 County Road 249 Tiplersville (38674) *(G-5081)*

Milpar Inc 662 224-0426
62 Red Bud Rd Ashland (38603) *(G-63)*

Miltons Automotive Head Servi 601 922-8131
4539 Highway 80 W Jackson (39209) *(G-2494)*

Milwaukee Electric Tool Corp 601 969-3033
4355 Milwaukee St Jackson (39209) *(G-2495)*

Milwaukee Electric Tool Corp 662 451-5545
1003 Sycamore Ave Greenwood (38930) *(G-1640)*

Milwaukee Electric Tool Corp 662 895-4560
12385 Crossroads Rd Olive Branch (38654) *(G-3879)*

Milwaukee Tool, Olive Branch Also called Milwaukee Electric Tool Corp *(G-3879)*

Mims Timber LLC 662 301-5022
934 Yellowdog Rd Senatobia (38668) *(G-4796)*

Min Sheng Healthcare LLC 601 212-6189
232 Tifton Dr Madison (39110) *(G-3130)*

Mini Mtrs Unlimited Sls & Svc 662 356-4900
2186 Sanders Mill Rd Steens (39766) *(G-4991)*

Mini Systems Inc 662 487-2240
25475 Highway 51 Como (38619) *(G-1050)*

Minton Floorcovering LLC 601 540-3764
522 Quinn Dr Richland (39218) *(G-4522)*

Minuteman Press International 662 349-6675
1065 Goodman Rd W Horn Lake (38637) *(G-2207)*

Miracleworks Press 601 878-6686
19405 Midway Rd Terry (39170) *(G-5073)*

Misccellaneous Items LLC 601 918-0255
6295 Old Canton Rd Jackson (39211) *(G-2496)*

Miscellaneous Steel Supply LLC 662 494-0090
210 E Morrow St 50w West Point (39773) *(G-5552)*

Misemer Pharmaceutical Inc 732 762-6577
203 N Main St Ripley (38663) *(G-4664)*

Miss Eaton Inc 662 489-4242
263 Coffee St Pontotoc (38863) *(G-4346)*

Miss Lou Guide 601 442-9101
503 N Canal St Natchez (39120) *(G-3588)*

Miss Polka DOT Lollipop 601 325-1779
931 Southeast Cir Hattiesburg (39402) *(G-2024)*

Miss-Lou Steel Supply Inc 601 442-0846
186 N Palestine Rd Natchez (39120) *(G-3589)*

Missco Corporation of Jackson 601 892-7105
102 Kirk St Crystal Springs (39059) *(G-1149)*

Missco Corporation of Jackson 601 352-7272
4365 Michael Avalon St Jackson (39209) *(G-2497)*

Missisppi Vtrnary RES Diagnstc, Pearl Also called MSU Veterinary Diagnostics Lab *(G-4133)*

Mississipi Furniture Component 662 566-8855
118 Road 752 Tupelo (38801) *(G-5188)*

Mississippi Cold Drip Coffee 601 624-5708
126 Keener Ave Jackson (39202) *(G-2498)*

Mississippi Aerospace Corp 601 749-5659
501 S Main St Picayune (39466) *(G-4280)*

Mississippi Agri-Products Inc 601 879-3343
105 Clark St Flora (39071) *(G-1310)*

Mississippi Baking Co LLC 601 854-5000
4311 Highway 80 Pelahatchie (39145) *(G-4165)*

Mississippi Baptist Paper 601 426-3293
4228 Highway 15 N Laurel (39440) *(G-2804)*

Mississippi Beverage Co Inc 601 693-3853
2620 A St Meridian (39301) *(G-3372)*

Mississippi Business Journal, Flowood Also called Journal Inc *(G-1371)*

Mississippi Catholic 601 969-3581
237 E Amite St Jackson (39201) *(G-2499)*

Mississippi Center For Freedom 601 638-0962
1601f N Frontage Rd Vicksburg (39180) *(G-5395)*

Mississippi Cheese Straw Fctry 662 746-7171
741 E Eighth St Yazoo City (39194) *(G-5640)*

Mississippi Coca Cola Btlg Co 601 584-6644
110 WI Runnels Indus Dr Hattiesburg (39401) *(G-2025)*

Mississippi Cylinder Head Shop, Columbus Also called Mississippi Cylinder Head Svc *(G-1002)*

Mississippi Cylinder Head Svc 662 328-0170
202 Tuscaloosa Rd Columbus (39702) *(G-1002)*

Mississippi Delta Energy Agcy 662 746-3741
210 S Mound St Yazoo City (39194) *(G-5641)*

Mississippi Diesel Products 601 847-2500
1562 Simpson Highway 149 Mendenhall (39114) *(G-3285)*

Mississippi Embroidery Co 601 264-3255
670 Weathersby Rd Ste 120 Hattiesburg (39402) *(G-2026)*

Mississippi Fabritek Inc 662 327-0745
221 Fabritek Dr Columbus (39702) *(G-1003)*

Mississippi Forge (pvf) Inc 662 285-2995
400 W Main St Ackerman (39735) *(G-27)*

Mississippi Gulf Coast 228 896-3055
141 Debuys Rd Gulfport (39507) *(G-1832)*

Mississippi Imaging 601 656-6759
439 Center Ave N Philadelphia (39350) *(G-4226)*

Mississippi Iron Works Inc 601 355-0188
750 S Gallatin St Ste 608 Jackson (39204) *(G-2500)*

Mississippi Iron Works Inc (PA) 601 355-0188
980 S State St Jackson (39201) *(G-2501)*

Mississippi Laminators Inc 601 687-1621
1151 County Road 210 Shubuta (39360) *(G-4831)*

MISSISSIPPI LIGNITE MINING, Ackerman Also called Liberty Fuels Company LLC *(G-25)*

Mississippi Lignite Mining Co 662 387-5200
1000 Mcintire Rd Ackerman (39735) *(G-28)*

Mississippi Lime Company 601 636-0932
1543 Haining Rd Vicksburg (39183) *(G-5396)*

Mississippi Link News, Jackson Also called Socrates Garrett Entps Inc *(G-2585)*

Mississippi Magazine, Jackson Also called Downhome Publications Inc *(G-2390)*

Mississippi Marble & Granite 662 289-4111
406 E Adams St Kosciusko (39090) *(G-2702)*

Mississippi Marine Corporation (PA) 662 332-5457
2219 Harbor Front Rd Greenville (38701) *(G-1575)*

Mississippi Marine Corporation 662 335-1175
2281 Harbor Front Rd Greenville (38701) *(G-1576)*

Mississippi Materials, Columbus Also called MMC Materials Inc *(G-1006)*

Mississippi Materials, Jackson Also called Legacy Vulcan LLC *(G-2467)*

Mississippi Materials Co, Brookhaven Also called MMC Materials Inc *(G-519)*

Mississippi Materials Co, Louisville Also called MMC Materials Inc *(G-2975)*

Mississippi Materials Company, Union Also called MMC Materials Inc *(G-5302)*

Mississippi Mud Works Pottery 228 875-8773
2011 Kensington St Ocean Springs (39564) *(G-3772)*

Mississippi Muddy Prints LLC 601 757-2990
1439 Pops Ln Nw Brookhaven (39601) *(G-518)*

MISSISSIPPI PHARMACISTS ASSOCI, Jackson Also called Mississippi State Phrm Assn *(G-2506)*

Mississippi Photo & Bluprt Co 601 948-1119
721 Harris St Ste C Jackson (39202) *(G-2502)*

Mississippi Polymers Inc 662 287-1401
2733 S Harper Rd Corinth (38834) *(G-1103)*

Mississippi Poultry 601 732-8670
4013 Highway 80 Morton (39117) *(G-3450)*

Mississippi Precision 662 245-1155
356 Langston Cir Columbus (39701) *(G-1004)*

Mississippi Prison Inds Corp (PA) 601 969-5760
663 N State St Jackson (39202) *(G-2503)*

Mississippi Prison Industries 601 346-4966
2929 I 55 S Jackson (39212) *(G-2504)*

Mississippi Puppetry Guild 601 977-9840
1927 Springridge Dr Jackson (39211) *(G-2505)*

Mississippi Quarterhorse Assn 601 692-5128
2653 Clyde B Rd Walnut Grove (39189) *(G-5461)*

Mississippi Rainbow Printing 601 853-9513
217a Industrial Dr Ridgeland (39157) *(G-4606)*

Mississippi Sand Solutions LL 870 291-8802
255 C J Fisher Dr Vicksburg (39180) *(G-5397)*

Mississippi Silicon LLC 662 696-2600
80 County Road 210 Burnsville (38833) *(G-572)*

Mississippi Sound & Recording, Long Beach Also called Chuck Ryan Cars Inc *(G-2932)*

Mississippi State Phrm Assn 601 981-0416
341 Edgewood Terrace Dr Jackson (39206) *(G-2506)*

Mississippi State University 662 325-2510
205 Research Blvd Starkville (39759) *(G-4960)*

Mississippi State University 662 325-3149
Hardy Rd Mississippi State (39762) *(G-3425)*

Mississippi Tank and Mfg Co (PA) 601 264-1800
3000 W 7th St Hattiesburg (39401) *(G-2027)*

Mississippi Tank Company, Hattiesburg Also called Mississippi Tank and Mfg Co *(G-2027)*

Mississippi Tantec Leather Inc 601 429-6081
101 Tantec Way Vicksburg (39183) *(G-5398)*

Mississippi Uniform Industries, Lexington Also called Superior Uniform Group Inc *(G-2905)*

Mississippi Valley Publishing 601 853-1861
234 W School St Ridgeland (39157) *(G-4607)*

Mississippi Welding and Mchs 662 726-5593
40737 Ms Highway 14 W Macon (39341) *(G-3067)*

Mississippi Wood Stakes Inc 662 224-0975
1042 Highway 4 E Ashland (38603) *(G-64)*

Mississppi Band Chctaw Indians 601 267-5279
1600 N Pearl St Carthage (39051) *(G-719)*

Mississppi Band Chctaw Indians 601 656-7350
390 Industrial Rd Choctaw (39350) *(G-746)*

Mississippi Band Chctaw Indians 601 656-6038
385 Willis Rd Choctaw (39350) *(G-747)*

Mississppi Inds For The Blind 601 693-5525
6603 Laurel Dr Meridian (39307) *(G-3373)*

Mississssppi Bsktball Athltics 601 957-7373
2240 Westbrook Rd Jackson (39211) *(G-2507)*

Mitchell Buckhalter 228 588-2040
2908 Jr Davis Rd Moss Point (39562) *(G-3486)*

Mitchell Group 662 488-0025
204 Brookwood Dr Pontotoc (38863) *(G-4347)*

2019 Harris Directory of
Mississippi Manufacturers

(G-0000) Company's Geographic Section entry number

302

ALPHABETIC SECTION

Morris Welding Service

Mitchell Signs Inc..601 553-1557
3200 Highway 45 N Meridian (39301) *(G-3374)*

Mitchells Machine Shop.......................................228 588-2040
19002 Highway 63 Moss Point (39562) *(G-3487)*

Mitchells Welding LLC..601 554-6402
2974 Attala Road 3024 Kosciusko (39090) *(G-2703)*

Mjj Inc..662 455-0126
1910 Highway 82 W Ste G Greenwood (38930) *(G-1641)*

Mk Oilfield Service..662 328-2510
168 Thaxton Rd Columbus (39702) *(G-1005)*

Mks Crochet...662 769-4982
618 Ms Highway 50 E Maben (39750) *(G-3048)*

MMC Materials Inc (HQ)......................................601 898-4000
1052 Highland Colony Pkwy # 201 Ridgeland (39157) *(G-4608)*

MMC Materials Inc..601 928-4941
607 Stapp St Wiggins (39577) *(G-5586)*

MMC Materials Inc..601 774-0443
105 Compress Rd Union (39365) *(G-5302)*

MMC Materials Inc..601 833-4900
1286 Monticello St Ne Brookhaven (39601) *(G-519)*

MMC Materials Inc..601 684-7373
906 S Locust St McComb (39648) *(G-3260)*

MMC Materials Inc..601 469-2741
13522 Hwy 80 W Forest (39074) *(G-1423)*

MMC Materials Inc..601 582-8493
157 Chevis Lee Rd Petal (39465) *(G-4193)*

MMC Materials Inc..662 624-9000
1309 Highway 49 S Clarksdale (38614) *(G-776)*

MMC Materials Inc..662 332-5407
1117 S Raceway Rd Greenville (38703) *(G-1577)*

MMC Materials Inc..601 482-7007
5226 Arundel Rd Meridian (39307) *(G-3375)*

MMC Materials Inc..662 628-6667
Hgwy 8 Us Calhoun City (38916) *(G-641)*

MMC Materials Inc..662 393-7676
1955 Nail Rd W Horn Lake (38637) *(G-2208)*

MMC Materials Inc..601 634-8787
4450 Rifle Range Rd Vicksburg (39180) *(G-5399)*

MMC Materials Inc..662 453-9722
108 Highlandale Rd Greenwood (38930) *(G-1642)*

MMC Materials Inc..601 268-9599
1920 Byron St Hattiesburg (39402) *(G-2028)*

MMC Materials Inc..251 408-0740
14312 Creosote Rd Gulfport (39503) *(G-1833)*

MMC Materials Inc..662 887-4031
313 Martin Luther King Dr Greenville (38703) *(G-1578)*

MMC Materials Inc..601 268-3005
22 Liberty Pl Hattiesburg (39402) *(G-2029)*

MMC Materials Inc..601 267-8278
1201 Highway 16 E Carthage (39051) *(G-720)*

MMC Materials Inc..601 437-4321
1083 Highway 18 Port Gibson (39150) *(G-4403)*

MMC Materials Inc..601 445-5641
30 Feltus St Natchez (39120) *(G-3590)*

MMC Materials Inc..662 327-1927
462 Lake N Rd Columbus (39705) *(G-1006)*

MMC Materials Inc..601 973-2093
815 W Fortification St Jackson (39203) *(G-2508)*

MMC Materials Inc..662 773-5656
306 S Spring Ave Louisville (39339) *(G-2975)*

MMC Materials Inc..662 323-0644
217 Industrial Park Rd Starkville (39759) *(G-4961)*

MMC Materials Inc..662 258-6096
100 Mississippi St Eupora (39744) *(G-1289)*

Mmj Logging Inc...662 755-1163
2828 Phoenix Rd Bentonia (39040) *(G-212)*

Moak Bottling Co Inc...662 844-0012
510 S Spring St Tupelo (38804) *(G-5189)*

Mobile Communications LLC...............................662 570-4858
801 County Road 138 Itta Bena (38941) *(G-2282)*

Mobile Diagnostics Inc..601 445-9895
133 Jefferson Davis Blvd Natchez (39120) *(G-3591)*

Mobile One Lube Express Plus............................601 631-8000
3420 Halls Ferry Rd Vicksburg (39180) *(G-5400)*

Mobley Auto Service...662 423-3516
821 County Road 172 Iuka (38852) *(G-2301)*

Mockingbird Monograms.....................................662 315-6213
170 Young Ave Nettleton (38858) *(G-3662)*

Moco Inc...601 957-3550
603 Northpark Dr Ste 100 Ridgeland (39157) *(G-4609)*

Modeltruckin..228 365-4124
16078 Lizana School Rd Gulfport (39503) *(G-1834)*

Modeltruckin.com., Gulfport Also called Modeltruckin *(G-1834)*

Modem Guest..601 442-5202
201 N Pearl St Natchez (39120) *(G-3592)*

Modern Mill Inc...601 869-5050
1140 Frank Oaks Rd McComb (39648) *(G-3261)*

Modine Grenada LLC...662 229-2000
823a Air Industrial Pk Rd Grenada (38901) *(G-1692)*

Modine Grenada LLC (HQ)...................................662 226-3421
3984 Highway 51 S Grenada (38901) *(G-1693)*

Modine Grenada LLC...662 229-4000
1000 Heat Craft Dr Grenada (38901) *(G-1694)*

Modine Manufacturing Company.........................662 229-2200
3984 Highway 51 S Grenada (38901) *(G-1695)*

Mohawk Steel Company......................................601 467-6959
50 Hegwood Rd Hattiesburg (39402) *(G-2030)*

Mojo Uprisin Inc...662 983-8892
104 S Tyson Rd Bruce (38915) *(G-561)*

Molded Acstcal Pdts Easton Inc..........................662 627-7811
600 Highway 322 Clarksdale (38614) *(G-777)*

Mollygrams..601 856-5598
11 Twelve Oaks Dr Madison (39110) *(G-3131)*

Molpus Timberlands Management........................601 969-7093
858 North St Jackson (39202) *(G-2509)*

Mombo Graphixs..228 466-2551
541 Highway 90 Waveland (39576) *(G-5483)*

Moncla Companies...601 428-4322
1250 1/2 Hillcrest Dr Laurel (39440) *(G-2805)*

Money Tree Logging LLC.....................................740 891-1713
10406 Three Rivers Rd # 13 Gulfport (39503) *(G-1835)*

Monitor-Herald, The, Houston Also called Houston Newspapers Inc *(G-2245)*

Monkey Business Unlimit.....................................662 895-1912
5730 Malone Rd Olive Branch (38654) *(G-3880)*

Monogram Creations..601 415-4970
1890 S Frontage Rd Ste 3 Vicksburg (39180) *(G-5401)*

Monogram Express...601 825-1248
131 Gateway Dr Ste A Brandon (39042) *(G-425)*

Monogram Expressions.......................................662 571-0582
3779 Old Dover Rd Yazoo City (39194) *(G-5642)*

Monogram Hut..601 268-9028
43 Turtle Creek Dr Hattiesburg (39402) *(G-2031)*

Monogram Magic..601 956-7117
1481 Canton Mart Rd Ste D Jackson (39211) *(G-2510)*

Monogram Magic..601 624-6917
3011 Tidewater Cir Madison (39110) *(G-3132)*

Monogram Magick..662 544-1392
1280 S Red Banks Rd Holly Springs (38635) *(G-2185)*

Monogram Mills...601 749-1064
318 Harbor Ln Brandon (39047) *(G-426)*

Monogram Stitch LLC..601 649-1582
688 Sharon Moss Rd Laurel (39443) *(G-2806)*

Monograms By Rahaim.......................................601 310-0152
209 S 22nd Ave Hattiesburg (39401) *(G-2032)*

Monograms Plus..662 327-3332
110 Chapman Rd Columbus (39705) *(G-1007)*

Monotech of Mississippi......................................662 862-2978
27 County Road 342 Iuka (38852) *(G-2302)*

Monotech of Mississippi (HQ).............................662 423-2033
27 County Road 342 Iuka (38852) *(G-2303)*

Monroe County Shopper, Amory Also called Star Printing Co of Amory Inc *(G-56)*

Monroe-Tufline Mfg Co Inc..................................662 328-8347
2219 Tufline Ln Columbus (39705) *(G-1008)*

Monsanto Company..662 827-7212
407 W Goldstein St Hollandale (38748) *(G-2166)*

Montgomery Electric Co, Brookhaven Also called Betty Montgomery *(G-482)*

Montgomery Publishing Co Inc.............................662 283-1131
401 Summit St Rm 108 Winona (38967) *(G-5604)*

Monument Shop, Kosciusko Also called Mississippi Marble & Granite *(G-2702)*

Moon-Hns-Tigrett Operating Inc...........................601 572-8300
599 Northpark Dr Ste A Ridgeland (39157) *(G-4610)*

Moore Fabrication and McHy...............................601 892-5017
19171 Hwy 51 S Gallman (39077) *(G-1485)*

Moore Industries..662 862-3993
4276 Dorsey Evergreen Rd Fulton (38843) *(G-1463)*

Moore Machine & Welding Shop..........................601 892-5026
2156 Lake Copiah Rd Crystal Springs (39059) *(G-1150)*

Moore's Feed Store & Mill, Pontotoc Also called Moores II Inc *(G-4349)*

Moores Feed Store Inc..662 488-0024
157 Highway 15 S Pontotoc (38863) *(G-4348)*

Moores II Inc..662 488-0024
439 Highway 9 S Pontotoc (38863) *(G-4349)*

Moores John..662 488-2980
3261 Highway 15 N Pontotoc (38863) *(G-4350)*

Moores Living and Storage, Summit Also called Holmes Stationary and Gifts *(G-5016)*

Moores Logging & Trucking.................................662 289-5872
6480 Highway 43 S Kosciusko (39090) *(G-2704)*

Moores Welding & Fabrication.............................662 402-5503
198 Old Ruleville Rd Cleveland (38732) *(G-800)*

Morehead Painting, Forest Also called David Morehead *(G-1413)*

Morgan Billingsley Lighting.................................662 429-3685
1636 Star Landing Rd Nesbit (38651) *(G-3654)*

Morgan Brothers Millwork Inc (PA).......................601 649-9188
Bruce Ave Ste 1 Laurel (39440) *(G-2807)*

Morgan Greg Asphalt and Cnstr...........................601 479-3095
4273 Chunky Duffee Rd Chunky (39323) *(G-752)*

Morris Ready Mix Inc..662 473-2505
133 Gore Cir Water Valley (38965) *(G-5473)*

Morris Welding Service.......................................601 729-2737
183 Lebanon Rd Laurel (39443) *(G-2808)*

(PA)=Parent Co (HQ)=Headquarters (DH)=Div Headquarters

2019 Harris Directory of
Mississippi Manufacturers

303

ALPHABETIC

Morrison Welding LLC | ALPHABETIC SECTION

Morrison Welding LLC 601 845-5187
3109 Highway 49 S Florence (39073) *(G-1329)*

Morrow Affrdbl Hmes Apartments, Jackson *Also called Grady Morrow* *(G-2428)*

Morton Industry 601 732-6486
3986 Highway 80 Morton (39117) *(G-3451)*

Mosley Mfg & Mch Works 662 332-7140
1516 S Theobald St Greenville (38701) *(G-1579)*

Moss Point Express 228 475-4370
4130 Main St Moss Point (39563) *(G-3488)*

Moss Point Marine, Moss Point *Also called VT Halter Marine Inc* *(G-3505)*

Moss Woodturning Inc 662 456-5043
1560 County Road 405 Houston (38851) *(G-2251)*

Mossy Island Land & Forest LLC 662 207-6245
657 Woodburn Rd Inverness (38753) *(G-2275)*

Mossy Oak 3d Fluid Grphics LLC 662 494-9092
1251 Hwy 45 Alt S West Point (39773) *(G-5553)*

Mossyoak Wildlife Conservatory 662 495-9292
26420 E Main St West Point (39773) *(G-5554)*

Motor Parts Co of Yazoo City 662 746-1462
322 S Washington St Yazoo City (39194) *(G-5643)*

Moulton Tile & Marble Inc 228 863-7587
5125 Gates Ave Long Beach (39560) *(G-2945)*

Mount Vernon Foam Sales 662 844-3107
575 Mount Vernon Rd Tupelo (38804) *(G-5190)*

Mount Vernon Mills Inc 662 328-5670
339 Yorkville Park Sq Columbus (39702) *(G-1009)*

Mp Logging 662 808-5411
509 Pinecrest Rd Corinth (38834) *(G-1104)*

Mpic, Jackson *Also called Mississippi Prison Inds Corp* *(G-2503)*

Mr Appliance of Hattiesburg 601 869-0434
5071 Old Highway 42 Hattiesburg (39401) *(G-2033)*

Mr Fix It 601 852-4705
1422 Highway 22 Edwards (39066) *(G-1242)*

Mr Forms Printing Company Inc 601 371-2567
5403 Robinson Road Ext Jackson (39204) *(G-2511)*

Mr Stitch It 601 543-8681
2210 Alice Dr Hattiesburg (39402) *(G-2034)*

MRC Global (us) Inc 601 965-5275
4155 Industrial Dr Jackson (39209) *(G-2512)*

Mrs GS Computer Services 601 376-0810
4731 Raymond Rd Jackson (39212) *(G-2513)*

Ms Band of Choctaw Indians Db 601 656-3636
404 Industrial Rd Choctaw (39350) *(G-748)*

Ms Publishing Group LLC 662 323-8800
25140 Highway 50 W West Point (39773) *(G-5555)*

Ms Sports Magazine, Brandon *Also called Pevey Publishing LLC* *(G-434)*

Ms Yearbooks LLC 601 540-6132
1126 Pointe Cv Brandon (39042) *(G-427)*

Msi Inc 662 401-9781
688 Pulltight Rd Saltillo (38866) *(G-4718)*

Mspatticakes, Ridgeland *Also called Patricia Betts* *(G-4615)*

Mstate Technologies LLC 662 418-0110
2608 Pinoak Dr Starkville (39759) *(G-4962)*

MSU Electrical Computer Design, Mississippi State *Also called Mississippi State University* *(G-3425)*

MSU Veterinary Diagnostics Lab 601 420-4700
3137 Highway 468 W Pearl (39208) *(G-4133)*

Mtd Products Inc 662 566-2332
5484 Hwy 145 S Tupelo (38804) *(G-5191)*

Mtm Industries LLC 662 402-9750
4701 Lakeland Dr Apt 32c Flowood (39232) *(G-1382)*

Mueller Castings Co 662 862-7200
404 Muller Rd Fulton (38843) *(G-1464)*

Mueller Copper Fittings Co 662 862-2181
1033 Spring Street Ext Fulton (38843) *(G-1465)*

Mueller Copper Tube Co Inc 662 862-1700
404 Mueller Brass Rd Fulton (38843) *(G-1466)*

Mueller Copper Tube Pdts Inc 662 862-2181
400 Mueller Rd Fulton (38843) *(G-1467)*

Mueller Industries, Fulton *Also called Mueller Copper Tube Co Inc* *(G-1466)*

Mueller Industries Inc 662 862-2181
400 Mueller Rd Fulton (38843) *(G-1468)*

Mueller Industries Inc 662 862-7425
409 Mueller Brass Rd Fulton (38843) *(G-1469)*

Mueller Packaging, Fulton *Also called Mueller Industries Inc* *(G-1469)*

Mueller Press Company Inc 901 753-3200
631 Lakeland East Dr Jackson (39232) *(G-2658)*

Multi-Chem Group LLC 601 425-1131
1643 Highway 184 Laurel (39443) *(G-2809)*

Multicraft Enterprises Inc 601 854-5516
201 Old Highway 80 Pelahatchie (39145) *(G-4166)*

Multicraft Intl Ltd Partnr 601 854-5516
301 N Brooks Ave Pelahatchie (39145) *(G-4167)*

Multicraft Intl Ltd Partnr (PA) 601 854-1200
4341 Highway 80 Pelahatchie (39145) *(G-4168)*

Multicraft Intl Ltd Partnr 601 854-1200
4341 Highway 80 Pelahatchie (39145) *(G-4169)*

Multicraft Intl Ltd Partnr 601 854-1200
4341 Highway 80 Pelahatchie (39145) *(G-4170)*

Multiforms 601 545-2312
20 Lee St Petal (39465) *(G-4194)*

Multimedia Graphics Inc (PA) 601 981-5001
4950 I 55 N Jackson (39211) *(G-2514)*

Munn Enterprises Inc 601 264-7446
7712 U S Highway 49 Hattiesburg (39402) *(G-2035)*

Murphree Enterprises, Greenwood *Also called Ecs- Elec Cnstr Spcialists Inc* *(G-1621)*

Murphy Cabinet Company 662 417-9717
2594 Pryor St Grenada (38901) *(G-1696)*

Murphy USA Inc 601 992-2041
5339 Highway 25 Flowood (39232) *(G-1383)*

Murphys Machine & Welding LLC 601 849-2771
260 Simpson Highway 149 Magee (39111) *(G-3179)*

Murphys Welding LLC 662 719-3879
3074 Highway 8 Cleveland (38732) *(G-801)*

Murray Printing 601 446-6558
154 E Franklin St Natchez (39120) *(G-3593)*

Murrays Deer Processing 601 720-2769
227 Murray Hill Rd Macon (39341) *(G-3068)*

Muscle Shoals Sound Studio, Jackson *Also called Northside Partners* *(G-2522)*

Musee LLC 769 300-0485
123 Watford Park Way Dr Canton (39046) *(G-672)*

Mw Industries 662 488-4551
260 Industrial Dr Pontotoc (38863) *(G-4351)*

Mws, Ashland *Also called Mississippi Wood Stakes Inc* *(G-64)*

My Fantasy Hair Inc 925 289-4247
1980 Ingram Cv Olive Branch (38654) *(G-3881)*

My Songs of Life 901 303-8687
6322 Chickasaw Dr Ste 2 Olive Branch (38654) *(G-3882)*

Myles Smith 228 323-5052
100 W Main Ave Lumberton (39455) *(G-3036)*

N C Enterprises Inc 601 953-6977
1006 Shady Oaks Ln Hazlehurst (39083) *(G-2101)*

N P S, Columbus *Also called New Process Steel LP* *(G-1010)*

N Rolls-Ryce Amer Holdings Inc 228 762-0728
1000 W River Rd Pascagoula (39568) *(G-4054)*

N-R-G Chemical Company 601 519-5363
2933 Industrial Blvd Laurel (39440) *(G-2810)*

NA Food Dash LLC 662 266-0738
720 W Bankhead St New Albany (38652) *(G-3687)*

Nail First 601 892-4433
324 E Railroad Ave Crystal Springs (39059) *(G-1151)*

Nail Logging 601 953-0071
2032 Attala Road 3225 Kosciusko (39090) *(G-2705)*

Nail Logging LLC 601 825-3375
108 Blackbridge Dr Brandon (39042) *(G-428)*

Nandys Candy & Ice Factory 601 362-9553
1220 E Northside Dr # 380 Jackson (39211) *(G-2515)*

Nanocor LLC 847 851-1500
10927 Darracott Rd Aberdeen (39730) *(G-19)*

NAPA Auto Parts, Yazoo City *Also called Motor Parts Co of Yazoo City* *(G-5643)*

Narkeeta Forest Services Inc 601 692-4777
4016 Highway 498 E Porterville (39352) *(G-4410)*

Natchez Democrat, Natchez *Also called Boone Newspapers* *(G-3537)*

Natchez Exploration LLC 601 442-7400
416 Main St Natchez (39120) *(G-3594)*

Natchez Newspapers Inc 601 442-9101
503 N Canal St Natchez (39120) *(G-3595)*

Natchez Printing Co 601 442-3693
520 Main St Natchez (39120) *(G-3596)*

Natchez Smokehouse & Cold Stor 601 442-6116
1144 Liberty Rd Natchez (39120) *(G-3597)*

National Bank Builders & Eqp 662 781-0702
6081 Highway 161 Walls (38680) *(G-5450)*

National Council of Negro Wome 952 361-6037
519 Hillview Dr Kosciusko (39090) *(G-2706)*

National Custom Craft Inc 662 963-7373
30081 Highway 6 Nettleton (38858) *(G-3663)*

National Diamond Corp (PA) 662 895-9633
8101 Longwood Dr Olive Branch (38654) *(G-3883)*

National Filter Media Corp 662 895-4660
8895 Deerfield Dr Olive Branch (38654) *(G-3884)*

National Mattress LLC 662 205-4891
224 Poplar St Plantersville (38862) *(G-4311)*

National Metal Products, Clarksdale *Also called Saf T Cart Inc* *(G-782)*

National Pump Co LLC 662 895-1110
11176 Green Valley Dr Olive Branch (38654) *(G-3885)*

National Pump Company 662 895-1110
11176 Green Valley Dr Olive Branch (38654) *(G-3886)*

National Scrubwear Inc 601 483-0796
3200 Highway 45 N Meridian (39301) *(G-3376)*

National Seating Mobility Inc 601 664-1090
108 N Layfair Dr Flowood (39232) *(G-1384)*

National Sign Tennessee Corp 901 210-8023
6400 Davidson Rd Olive Branch (38654) *(G-3887)*

National Stone Imports Inc 228 323-7239
1314 E Old Pass Rd 2 Long Beach (39560) *(G-2946)*

National Tank Inc 662 429-5469
400 Vaiden Dr Hernando (38632) *(G-2143)*

2019 Harris Directory of
Mississippi Manufacturers

(G-0000) Company's Geographic Section entry number

304

ALPHABETIC SECTION

National Textile and AP Inc (PA).................................601 892-4356
1018 Industrial Dr Hazlehurst (39083) *(G-2102)*

Nations Welding Service Inc.................................601 833-4949
1127 S First St Ne Brookhaven (39601) *(G-520)*

Natural Ozone Solutions LLC.................................662 963-2157
684a Road 1463 Nettleton (38858) *(G-3664)*

Natural Wood Solutions LLC.................................662 871-1625
276 Pennington Lake Rd Nettleton (38858) *(G-3665)*

Natures Broom Inc.................................662 931-5844
204 Magnolia St Hollandale (38748) *(G-2167)*

Natures Society Majestic Arts.................................601 376-0447
5038 Kay Brook Dr Byram (39272) *(G-623)*

Naum Myatt & Sons.................................662 256-8104
Hwy 25 S 52242 Becker (38825) *(G-186)*

Nautic Star LLC.................................662 256-5636
500 Waterway Dr Amory (38821) *(G-49)*

Nauticstar Boats, Amory *Also called Nautic Star LLC (G-49)*

Nautilus Publishing Company.................................662 513-0159
426 S Lamar Blvd Ste 16 Oxford (38655) *(G-3975)*

Naval Engineering Works Inc.................................228 769-1080
3614 Frederic St Pascagoula (39567) *(G-4055)*

Navidad Petroleum LLC.................................601 442-9812
109 Southampton Rd Natchez (39120) *(G-3598)*

Navistar Inc.................................662 284-8984
1710 Sawyer Rd Corinth (38834) *(G-1105)*

Nce Group Inc.................................662 890-8778
8405 National Dr Olive Branch (38654) *(G-3888)*

Nci Drafting Division, Starkville *Also called Nci Group Inc (G-4963)*

Nci Group Inc.................................601 373-0374
951 Prisock Rd Jackson (39272) *(G-2516)*

Nci Group Inc.................................662 324-1845
530 Vine St Starkville (39759) *(G-4963)*

Nci Group Inc.................................601 373-3222
201 Apache Dr Jackson (39272) *(G-2517)*

Ncv Testing Service.................................662 728-3965
404 Pinehill Rd Booneville (38829) *(G-337)*

Neal Clement Oil & Gas.................................601 982-5667
1650 Lelia Dr Ste 101 Jackson (39216) *(G-2518)*

Nebco Inc.................................662 349-1400
7065 Airways Blvd Ste 111 Southaven (38671) *(G-4890)*

Necaise Lock Supply Inc.................................228 864-9799
2811 23rd Ave Gulfport (39501) *(G-1836)*

Needle Specialty, Boyle *Also called Boyle Tool & Die Inc (G-348)*

Needle Specialty Products Corp.................................662 843-8913
600 Highway 446 Boyle (38730) *(G-351)*

Needle Works.................................601 425-4692
1115 W 6th St Laurel (39440) *(G-2811)*

Neeto's Bargains, Utica *Also called Clementine Frazier (G-5307)*

Nehi Bottling Co of Cleveland.................................662 843-3431
310 N Sharpe Ave Cleveland (38732) *(G-802)*

Neill Oil LLC.................................601 984-9000
1700 Lelia Dr Ste 107 Jackson (39216) *(G-2519)*

Nelson Materials Inc.................................662 563-4972
117 Vick St Batesville (38606) *(G-115)*

Nelson Printing, Newton *Also called Nelsons Printing Inc (G-3725)*

Nelsons Metal Inc.................................662 454-7500
10 Old Highway 25 Dennis (38838) *(G-1184)*

Nelsons Printing Inc.................................601 683-6651
308 N Main St Newton (39345) *(G-3725)*

Neon Marketing.................................601 960-4555
188 E Capitol St Ste 800 Jackson (39201) *(G-2520)*

Neshoba County Gin Assn AAL.................................601 656-3463
264 Railroad Ave Philadelphia (39350) *(G-4227)*

Neshoba Democrat Publishing Co.................................601 656-4000
439 E Beacon St Philadelphia (39350) *(G-4228)*

New David Oil Company Inc.................................601 442-1607
231 Highway 61 S Natchez (39120) *(G-3599)*

New Albany Gazette, The, New Albany *Also called New Albany Publishing Company (G-3688)*

New Albany Publishing Company.................................662 534-6321
713 Carter Ave New Albany (38652) *(G-3688)*

New Albany Sign Co.................................662 538-5599
919 Sam T Barkley Dr New Albany (38652) *(G-3689)*

New Dixie Fasteners, Greenwood *Also called Mjj Inc (G-1641)*

New Horizon Inc.................................228 474-9918
9749 Donchester Cir Moss Point (39562) *(G-3489)*

New Patients Number.................................662 323-2803
407 University Dr Starkville (39759) *(G-4964)*

New Process Steel LP.................................662 241-6582
1379 Industrial Park Rd Columbus (39701) *(G-1010)*

New South Logging LLC.................................601 517-8457
464 Lake Mike Conner Rd Collins (39428) *(G-856)*

New South Products, Greenville *Also called Vance Nimrod (G-1607)*

Newell Sand & Gravel.................................228 832-1215
11007 Wolf River Rd Gulfport (39503) *(G-1837)*

Newks Express Cafe of H.................................601 602-0189
4700 Hardy St Ste Y Hattiesburg (39402) *(G-2036)*

Newpark Drilling Fluids LLC.................................281 362-6800
1024 Highpoint Rd Summit (39666) *(G-5018)*

Newport Home Furnishings LLC.................................662 534-3030
1201 W Bankhead St New Albany (38652) *(G-3690)*

News Commercial.................................601 765-8275
104 S First St Collins (39428) *(G-857)*

News-Commercial, The, Collins *Also called News Commercial (G-857)*

Newson Chenora.................................601 596-3899
5056 Old Highway 42 l3 Hattiesburg (39401) *(G-2037)*

Newspaper Holding Inc.................................601 798-4766
17 Richardson Ozona Rd Picayune (39466) *(G-4281)*

Newspaper Holding Inc.................................601 693-1551
812814 22nd Ave Meridian (39301) *(G-3377)*

Newspaper Holding Inc.................................601 795-2247
418 S Main St Poplarville (39470) *(G-4385)*

Newspaper Production, Hattiesburg *Also called William Carey University (G-2083)*

Newsprint Division, Grenada *Also called Resolute FP US Inc (G-1701)*

Newton Appeal.................................601 683-7810
128 S Main St Newton (39345) *(G-3726)*

Newton Discount Tobacco.................................601 683-6555
300 Northside Dr Newton (39345) *(G-3727)*

Nexteer Automotive Corporation.................................601 537-3099
6586 Highway 13 Morton (39117) *(G-3452)*

Ngss Ingalls Operations.................................228 935-5731
1000 Jerry St Pes Hwy Pe S Pascagoula (39568) *(G-4056)*

Nhc Distributors Inc.................................601 656-7911
212 Lewis Ave S Philadelphia (39350) *(G-4229)*

Niagara Bottling LLC.................................215 703-0838
168 E Wingo Rd Byhalia (38611) *(G-592)*

Nicholes Cture Fashion Btq LLC.................................601 493-6469
105 Brooklyn Dr Natchez (39120) *(G-3600)*

Nichols Mold Shop.................................662 282-7560
1453 Centerville Rd Mantachie (38855) *(G-3202)*

Nichols Propeller Company.................................662 378-2000
640 Straughter St Greenville (38701) *(G-1580)*

Nichols Saw Service.................................662 842-2129
1236 Nelle St Tupelo (38801) *(G-5192)*

Nichols Steel, Greenville *Also called Nichols Propeller Company (G-1580)*

Nichols Stl Sls & Fabrication.................................662 378-2723
630 S Theobald St Greenville (38701) *(G-1581)*

Nick Clark Printing and Signs.................................601 607-7722
965 Highway 51 Ste 4 Madison (39110) *(G-3133)*

Nick Strcklnds Quick Print Inc.................................601 353-8672
250 Highpoint Dr Ridgeland (39157) *(G-4611)*

Nick Strcklnds Quick Print Inc (PA).................................601 898-1717
125 E South St Jackson (39201) *(G-2521)*

Nick Strcklnds Quick Print Inc.................................601 939-2781
3086 Highway 80 E Pearl (39208) *(G-4134)*

Nick Strcklnds Quick Print Inc.................................601 355-8195
109 E State St Ridgeland (39157) *(G-4612)*

Nick's Ice House, Hattiesburg *Also called Kolinsky Corp (G-2011)*

Nickerson Logging.................................662 289-9779
715 N Natchez St Kosciusko (39090) *(G-2707)*

Nicks One Stop Port Gbson LLC.................................601 437-3380
2154 Highway 61 N Port Gibson (39150) *(G-4404)*

Nidec Motor Corporation.................................662 393-6910
710 Venture Dr Ste 100 Southaven (38672) *(G-4891)*

Nightengale Cabinets.................................662 686-9004
60 Kuhn Rd Leland (38756) *(G-2891)*

Nightwind Industries.................................662 690-9709
2839 S Eason Blvd Tupelo (38804) *(G-5193)*

Nissan North America Inc.................................601 855-6000
300 Nissan Dr Canton (39046) *(G-673)*

Nitas Quilts.................................601 825-2060
3096 Highway 80 Brandon (39042) *(G-429)*

Niteo Products LLC.................................662 429-0405
720 Vaiden Dr Hernando (38632) *(G-2144)*

Niteo Products LLC.................................662 429-8292
2925 Mccracken Rd Hernando (38632) *(G-2145)*

Nitrous Oxide Corp.................................662 746-7607
1226 Rialto Rd Yazoo City (39194) *(G-5644)*

NMEI, Oxford *Also called North Miss Entp Initiative Inc (G-3978)*

Nmhg Financial Services.................................601 304-0112
1258 Highway 61 S Natchez (39120) *(G-3601)*

No Hope Logging Inc.................................601 587-5515
453 Carmel New Hope Rd Monticello (39654) *(G-3437)*

No Hope Trucking Inc.................................601 320-1919
388 Renfroe Rd Monticello (39654) *(G-3438)*

No Time 2 Cook LLC.................................662 236-9456
6 County Road 1014 Oxford (38655) *(G-3976)*

No Trax, Moselle *Also called Superior Mfg Group Inc (G-3461)*

Nokomis LLC.................................601 743-2100
62 Stennis Indus Pk Rd De Kalb (39328) *(G-1167)*

Nolan Brothers.................................662 862-3055
2602 Highway 25 S Fulton (38843) *(G-1470)*

None, Greenwood *Also called Galvian Group LLC (G-1624)*

Norbord Mississippi Inc.................................662 348-2800
1194 Highway 145 Guntown (38849) *(G-1900)*

Norbord Mississippi LLC.................................662 348-2800
1194 Highway 145 Guntown (38849) *(G-1901)*

(PA)=Parent Co (HQ)=Headquarters (DH)=Div Headquarters

Norman Accounting Services

Norman Accounting Services......................662 347-4475
1207 Daniels St Greenville (38701) *(G-1582)*

Norman K Hillman......................601 525-3735
4022 Forrest Breland Rd Neely (39461) *(G-3645)*

Norman Vr Inc......................601 352-4819
21 Hardy Court Shopg Ctr Gulfport (39507) *(G-1838)*

Norris Bookbinding Co Inc......................662 453-7424
107 N Stone Ave Greenwood (38930) *(G-1643)*

North American Electric Inc (PA)......................662 429-8049
350 Vaiden Dr Hernando (38632) *(G-2146)*

North American Pipe Corp......................662 728-2111
401 Industrial Park Rd Booneville (38829) *(G-338)*

North Miss Conveyor Co Inc......................662 236-1000
125 C R 370 Hwy 7 S Oxford (38655) *(G-3977)*

North Miss Entp Initiative Inc......................662 281-0720
9 Industrial Park Dr # 104 Oxford (38655) *(G-3978)*

North Miss Stone & Mem Co......................662 365-2721
684 Highway 145 S Baldwyn (38824) *(G-85)*

North Mississippi Herald, Water Valley *Also called Valley Publishing Inc (G-5475)*

North Mississippi Timber & Log......................662 603-7944
648 County Road 500 Corinth (38834) *(G-1106)*

North Mississippi Timber Brk......................662 728-7328
410 W College St Booneville (38829) *(G-339)*

North Mississippi Tool Inc......................662 720-9530
158 Bails Rd Ripley (38663) *(G-4665)*

North Ms Timber Harvester......................662 927-0013
502 Beadle St Calhoun City (38916) *(G-642)*

North Simpson Gravel Co......................601 847-9500
376 Old Gravel 49 Mendenhall (39114) *(G-3286)*

North Wind Fabrication Inc......................228 896-0230
12520 Glascock Cir Gulfport (39503) *(G-1839)*

Northeast Metal Processors......................662 844-2164
551 Central St Plantersville (38862) *(G-4312)*

Northeast Miss Cmnty Newsppr, Pontotoc *Also called Pontotoc Progress Inc (G-4356)*

Northeast Miss Daily Jurnl, Tupelo *Also called Journal Inc (G-5164)*

Northeast Miss Daily Jurnl, Jackson *Also called Tupelo Daily Journal News Bur (G-2614)*

Northeast Miss Daily Jurnl......................662 842-2622
1242 S Green St Tupelo (38804) *(G-5194)*

Northeast Mississippi Trader, Shannon *Also called Trader Printing (G-4820)*

Northrop Grumman Corp......................434 845-9181
510 Krebs Ave Pascagoula (39567) *(G-4057)*

Northrop Grumman Systems Corp......................228 872-7300
6608 Sunscope Dr Ocean Springs (39564) *(G-3773)*

Northrop Grumman Systems Corp......................228 474-3700
8319 Avtech Pkwy Moss Point (39563) *(G-3490)*

Northside Partners......................601 982-4522
3023 W Northside Dr Jackson (39213) *(G-2522)*

Northside Sun, Jackson *Also called Sunland Publishing Co Inc (G-2600)*

Northtowne Printers Inc......................601 713-3200
2088 Dunbarton Dr Jackson (39216) *(G-2523)*

Norton Equipment Company......................662 838-7900
60 Amy Ln Byhalia (38611) *(G-593)*

Norwood Medical Supply LLC......................601 792-2224
2218 Columbia Ave Prentiss (39474) *(G-4422)*

Nouryon Pulp & Prfmce Chem LLC......................662 327-0400
4374 Nashville Ferry Rd E Columbus (39702) *(G-1011)*

Novartis Corporation......................601 373-6148
303 Foxton Cv Raymond (39154) *(G-4492)*

Novartis Corporation......................662 844-2271
1203 Queensgate Dr Tupelo (38801) *(G-5195)*

Novelty Machine Works Inc......................601 948-2075
3120 Highway 80 W Jackson (39204) *(G-2524)*

Novi Creations LLC......................601 335-1902
3815 Baldwin Dr Laurel (39440) *(G-2812)*

Novia Cmmnications/ Novia Pubg......................601 985-9502
125 S Congress St # 1338 Jackson (39201) *(G-2525)*

Novipax LLC......................662 226-8804
1621 Air Industrial Pk Rd Grenada (38901) *(G-1697)*

Nowell Steps Incorporated......................601 964-8455
438 Hickory Grove Ch Rd Richton (39476) *(G-4541)*

Noxubee County Producers Inc......................662 726-2502
11751 Highway 45 Macon (39341) *(G-3069)*

Noyes Printing & Rbr Stamp Co......................662 332-5256
821 Highway 82 E Greenville (38701) *(G-1583)*

Nsc Technologies LLC......................251 338-0725
4519 Jefferson Ave Ste A Moss Point (39563) *(G-3491)*

Nslc Southern Inc......................601 535-2205
11167 Pttson Hrmnville Rd Hermanville (39086) *(G-2122)*

Nslc Southern Inc (PA)......................601 605-0575
214 Draperton Dr Ridgeland (39157) *(G-4613)*

Nucor Corporation......................601 936-6292
2050 Flowood Dr Jackson (39232) *(G-2659)*

Nucor Grating......................601 853-9996
211 Industrial Dr N Madison (39110) *(G-3134)*

Nucor Steel Jackson Inc......................601 939-1623
3630 Fourth St Flowood (39232) *(G-1385)*

Nufarm Americas Inc......................708 375-9010
1927 N Theobald St Greenville (38703) *(G-1584)*

Numedrx Pharmacy Solutions LLC......................601 973-5501
2 Old River Pl Ste J Jackson (39202) *(G-2526)*

ALPHABETIC SECTION

Nvision Solutions Inc......................228 242-0010
88360 Diamondhead Dr E Diamondhead (39525) *(G-1192)*

NY Beauty......................662 280-2573
3039 Goodman Rd W Horn Lake (38637) *(G-2209)*

Oak Wood Mills Inc......................662 542-9158
130 County Road 27 Houston (38851) *(G-2252)*

Oakland Ylbsha Natural Gas Dst......................662 623-5005
286 Holly St Oakland (38948) *(G-3738)*

Oaklock LLC......................601 855-7678
276 Nissan Pkwy Bldg A500 Canton (39046) *(G-674)*

Observa-Dome Laboratories Inc......................601 982-3333
371 Commerce Park Dr Jackson (39213) *(G-2527)*

Oce Corporate Printing Div......................228 863-0458
9480 Three Rivers Rd Gulfport (39503) *(G-1840)*

Ocean Springs Gazette......................228 875-1241
3064 Bienville Blvd Ocean Springs (39564) *(G-3774)*

Ocean Springs Seafood Mkt Inc......................228 875-0104
555 Bayview Ave Biloxi (39530) *(G-269)*

Ocean Springs Sign & Graphics......................228 213-7933
1408 Highway 90 3gautier Gautier (39553) *(G-1500)*

Odat Energy LLC......................601 736-0227
919 High School Ave Columbia (39429) *(G-908)*

Odom Industries......................601 687-6325
26593 Highway 45 Shubuta (39360) *(G-4832)*

Odom Industries Inc (PA)......................601 735-0088
800 Odom Industrial Rd Waynesboro (39367) *(G-5508)*

Odom Industries Inc......................601 776-2035
100 Chestnut St Pachuta (39347) *(G-4014)*

Odom's Dispensing Optician, Jackson *Also called J & R Optical Co Inc (G-2450)*

Of/USA, Hattiesburg *Also called Standard Office Sup Prtg Inc (G-2069)*

Office Chairs Mississippi LLC......................601 842-1004
3209 Greenfield Rd Pearl (39208) *(G-4135)*

Office Depot Inc......................662 378-2995
1662 Mrtin L King Jr Blvd Greenville (38701) *(G-1585)*

Office Huddle Small Business......................601 255-8650
130 Third St Crowder (38622) *(G-1137)*

Oil Field Service & Supply Co, Laurel *Also called Oilfield Service & Sup Co Inc (G-2813)*

Oil Logging, Ellisville *Also called Oil Well Logging Company Inc (G-1265)*

Oil Tools & Supplies Inc......................601 446-7229
519 Liberty Rd Natchez (39120) *(G-3602)*

Oil Well Logging Company Inc (PA)......................601 477-8315
3970 Highway 43 N Brandon (39047) *(G-430)*

Oil Well Logging Company Inc.......................601 477-8315
704 County Home Rd Ellisville (39437) *(G-1265)*

Oil-Dri Production Company......................662 837-9263
1800 City Ave N Ripley (38663) *(G-4666)*

Oilfield Partners Energy......................601 444-0220
481 Highway 98 Byp Columbia (39429) *(G-909)*

Oilfield Partners Leasing, Columbia *Also called Oilfield Partners Energy (G-909)*

Oilfield Service & Sup Co Inc......................601 649-4461
1991 Highway 184 Laurel (39443) *(G-2813)*

Oiseys International Inc......................662 255-1545
3325 White Dr Ste F Belden (38826) *(G-191)*

Okin America Inc......................662 566-1000
291 Cdf Blvd Shannon (38868) *(G-4817)*

Okolona Messenger Inc......................662 447-5501
249 W Main St Okolona (38860) *(G-3796)*

Old Blue Publishing LLC......................601 957-2530
5406 Hialeah Dr Jackson (39211) *(G-2528)*

Old Ges Inc......................601 649-4920
1250 1 A Half Hllcrest Dr Hillcrest Laurel (39440) *(G-2814)*

Old House Depot Inc......................601 592-6200
639 Monroe St Jackson (39202) *(G-2529)*

Old River Lure Company LLC......................601 259-4323
1965 George Rd Terry (39170) *(G-5074)*

Old River Peddler, Natchez *Also called George Nosser Jr (G-3563)*

Old South Winery, Natchez *Also called Scott O Galbreath Jr (G-3617)*

Oldtown Truss......................662 412-2500
239 County Road 102 Pittsboro (38951) *(G-4309)*

Ole Country Bakery......................662 738-5795
Hwy 45 Brooksville (39739) *(G-556)*

Ole Miss Spirit, The, Oxford *Also called Spirit Enterprises (G-4006)*

Ole River Fabrics, Gulfport *Also called Rfm Enterprises LLC (G-1862)*

Oligarch Inc......................844 321-0016
202 County Road 162 Houston (38851) *(G-2253)*

Olin Corporation......................662 281-7900
33 County Road 166 Oxford (38655) *(G-3979)*

Olin Corporation......................662 234-4056
411 County Road 101 Oxford (38655) *(G-3980)*

Olin Corporation......................662 513-2002
411 County Road 101 Oxford (38655) *(G-3981)*

Olivers Iron Works......................662 252-3858
272 Rolfing Rd Holly Springs (38635) *(G-2186)*

Olives & Apples LLC......................662 419-0224
624 E Ridge Hts Pontotoc (38863) *(G-4352)*

Olmstead Timber......................601 655-8769
1031 Lisonbee Rd Chunky (39323) *(G-753)*

Omega Motion, Saltillo *Also called Leggett & Platt Incorporated (G-4717)*

306

2019 Harris Directory of
Mississippi Manufacturers

(G-0000) Company's Geographic Section entry number

ALPHABETIC SECTION

Palmer Bodies, Amory

Omega Protein Corporation 228 475-1252
5735 Elder Ferry Rd Moss Point (39563) *(G-3492)*

Omega Shipyard Inc 228 475-9052
5659 Elder Ferry Rd Moss Point (39563) *(G-3493)*

Omega System Specialists LLC 901 334-6742
2671 White Oak Dr Nesbit (38651) *(G-3655)*

Omega-Tec LLC 601 750-8082
1025 Jackson St Vicksburg (39183) *(G-5402)*

Omni Blinds 601 924-0326
131 Murial St Clinton (39056) *(G-832)*

Omni Fusion LLC 601 765-6941
123 Mount Pleasant Rd Collins (39428) *(G-858)*

Omni Instruments 228 388-9211
769 Whitney Dr Biloxi (39532) *(G-270)*

Omni Technologies LLC 601 427-5898
7048 Old Canton Rd # 2008 Ridgeland (39157) *(G-4614)*

Omnova Solutions Inc 662 327-1522
133 Yorkville Rd E Columbus (39702) *(G-1012)*

Oms Shop 601 835-1239
182 Highway 84 E Brookhaven (39601) *(G-521)*

On The River LLC 601 442-7103
216 Linton Ave Natchez (39120) *(G-3603)*

One Grower Publishing 901 767-4020
6515 Goodman Rd Ste 4 Olive Branch (38654) *(G-3889)*

One of A Kind Art Creations 662 328-1283
203 N Browder St Columbus (39702) *(G-1013)*

One Source Systems LLC 601 636-6888
120 Holt Collier Dr Ste C Vicksburg (39183) *(G-5403)*

ONeal Power Corporation 228 323-1059
17 Lawson Oneal Rd Perkinston (39573) *(G-4179)*

Oneida Farms Partnership 901 652-4182
8679 Saddlecreek Dr Olive Branch (38654) *(G-3890)*

Oneway Inc 601 664-0007
190 Parkison Dr Jackson (39218) *(G-2660)*

Oneway Screen Printing, Jackson Also called Oneway Inc *(G-2660)*

Oneway Screen Prtg & Graphics 601 845-7777
2142 Florence Byram Rd Florence (39073) *(G-1330)*

Onswoll Grafix LLC 228 596-8409
107 Twin Cedar Dr Long Beach (39560) *(G-2947)*

Onyx Xteriors LLC 901 281-2887
885 Bennett Cir Byhalia (38611) *(G-594)*

Onyx Xterirors 901 281-2887
885 Bennett Cir Byhalia (38611) *(G-595)*

Oolite Investments Inc 601 853-0408
160 Autumn Woods Dr Madison (39110) *(G-3135)*

Opel Corp 601 693-0771
1414 Rubush Ave Meridian (39301) *(G-3378)*

Open Air M R I of Laurel 601 428-5026
227 S 13th Ave Laurel (39440) *(G-2815)*

Open Windows LLC 601 798-5757
203 Frank Smith Rd Poplarville (39470) *(G-4386)*

Oracle America Inc 601 352-6113
5723 Highway 18 W Jackson (39209) *(G-2530)*

Oralia Mejia 662 512-1906
903 N Main St Ripley (38663) *(G-4667)*

Orbis Rpm LLC 662 890-7646
10800 Marina Dr Olive Branch (38654) *(G-3891)*

Orchard Oxford 662 259-0094
295 Highway 7 N Oxford (38655) *(G-3982)*

ORears Garage and Wreck 662 585-3244
3235 Ryan Salem Rd Fulton (38843) *(G-1471)*

Organizational Maint Sp 5, Brookhaven Also called Oms Shop *(G-521)*

Orman Cabinet Co LLC 662 837-6352
114 Cypress Cir Oxford (38655) *(G-3983)*

Ormans Welding & Fab Inc 662 494-9471
640 Curtis Orman Rd West Point (39773) *(G-5556)*

Orrin F Fuelling 601 485-2598
573 Purvis Rd Meridian (39301) *(G-3379)*

Osborn 601 366-9902
4643 Medgar Evers Blvd Jackson (39213) *(G-2531)*

Otis Logging Inc 601 249-0963
116 Price St McComb (39648) *(G-3262)*

Ottos Custom Trailers 601 446-6469
581 Old Highway 84 No 3 Natchez (39120) *(G-3604)*

Outback Express Mississippi 901 378-8000
5 Orchard Pl Greenville (38701) *(G-1586)*

Outback Industries LLC 662 591-5100
30093 Old Highway 6 Nettleton (38858) *(G-3666)*

Outback Stucco & Coatings LLC (PA) 228 224-2824
45 Hardy Court Shopg Ctr Gulfport (39507) *(G-1841)*

Outdoor Dimensions Inc 601 749-9981
62 Hidden Hills Dr E Picayune (39466) *(G-4282)*

Outdoors Advantage 662 257-9601
1171 Country Wood Cv Tupelo (38801) *(G-5196)*

Outkast Charters, Bay Saint Louis Also called Clay Necaise *(G-140)*

Outlaw Sporting Goods LLC 662 459-9054
717 Highway 82 W Greenwood (38930) *(G-1644)*

Ovation Womens Wellness LLC 601 326-6401
501 Marshall St Jackson (39202) *(G-2532)*

Overnight Printing Service 662 895-9262
6335 Autumn Oaks Dr Olive Branch (38654) *(G-3892)*

Overstreet Welding LLC 662 719-1269
309 Sylvia St Ruleville (38771) *(G-4697)*

Owens Custom Marble 662 627-7256
18680 Highway 61 N Lyon (38645) *(G-3043)*

Owens-Brockway Glass Cont Inc 601 584-4800
72 Wl Runnels Indus Dr Hattiesburg (39401) *(G-2038)*

Owl City Industries LLC 901 268-6871
1227 W Oak Grove Rd Hernando (38632) *(G-2147)*

Owlco, Brandon Also called Oil Well Logging Company Inc *(G-430)*

Oxford Alarm Cmmunications Inc 662 234-0505
179 Highway 6 E Oxford (38655) *(G-3984)*

Oxford Alarm Company, Oxford Also called Oxford Alarm Cmmunications Inc *(G-3984)*

Oxford Candle Company LLC 662 816-7429
2 County Road 148 Oxford (38655) *(G-3985)*

Oxford Eagle Inc 662 234-2222
4 Private Road 2050 Oxford (38655) *(G-3986)*

Oxford Falls 662 323-9696
9465 Highway 14 Sallis (39160) *(G-4703)*

Oxford Laboratories 662 801-9764
213 Timber Ln Oxford (38655) *(G-3987)*

Oxford Metal Works LLC 662 801-7969
27 County Road 316 Oxford (38655) *(G-3988)*

Oxford Printwear LLC 662 234-5051
1722 University Ave Oxford (38655) *(G-3989)*

Oxford Sand-Concrete Plant 662 281-0355
693 Highway 30 E Oxford (38655) *(G-3990)*

Oxford Scrubs 662 513-0341
1151 Frontage Rd Oxford (38655) *(G-3991)*

P & B Enterprises Inc 662 323-8565
200 Morrill Rd Starkville (39759) *(G-4965)*

P & L Embroidery 662 365-9852
803 Highway 45 Baldwyn (38824) *(G-86)*

P & R Aluminum 662 682-7939
202 Main St Vardaman (38878) *(G-5325)*

P & R Foods, Flowood Also called Global Food Concepts Inc *(G-1364)*

P & S Welding & Manufacturing 662 334-9881
630 Twist St Greenville (38701) *(G-1587)*

P Adam Middleton 662 289-7076
101 Ridgewood Cir Kosciusko (39090) *(G-2708)*

P D Q Printing Inc 228 392-4888
16313 Lemoyne Blvd Biloxi (39532) *(G-271)*

P Delta Inc 601 403-8100
306 Highway 26 E Poplarville (39470) *(G-4387)*

P P I Inc 662 680-4332
5280 Cliff Gookin Blvd Tupelo (38801) *(G-5197)*

P Press 662 638-3571
1903 University Ave Oxford (38655) *(G-3992)*

P&S Welding, Greenville Also called P & S Welding & Manufacturing *(G-1587)*

P-Americas LLC 228 831-4343
13300 Dedeaux Rd Gulfport (39503) *(G-1842)*

P-Americas LLC 601 684-2281
1096 Highway 98 E McComb (39648) *(G-3263)*

P-Americas LLC 662 841-8750
620 E President Ave Tupelo (38801) *(G-5198)*

Paccar Engine Company 662 329-6700
1000 Paccar Dr Columbus (39701) *(G-1014)*

Paccar Engine Company (HQ) 425 468-7400
777 106th Ave Ne Columbus (39701) *(G-1015)*

Pace Brothers Inc 601 736-9225
1278 Highway 98 E Columbia (39429) *(G-910)*

Packaging Corporation America 601 939-5111
100 Willie Dr Pearl (39208) *(G-4136)*

Packaging Corporation America 662 895-4100
8489 Summit Cv Olive Branch (38654) *(G-3893)*

Packaging Dynamics Corporation 662 424-4000
1309 Paul Edmondson Dr Iuka (38852) *(G-2304)*

Packaging Machinery Systems 601 992-5011
188 Webb Ln Flowood (39232) *(G-1386)*

Packaging Research and Design 800 833-9364
107 Bristol Ct Madison (39110) *(G-3136)*

Pactiv LLC 662 585-3151
21500 Old Highway 25 N Fulton (38843) *(G-1472)*

Padgett Consulting, Ellisville Also called James R Padgett *(G-1260)*

Paine Industries 601 336-2069
5000 Ridgewood Rd # 1311 Jackson (39211) *(G-2533)*

Pak Uniform & EMB Shoppe LLC 228 365-6695
4002 Alandale St Pascagoula (39581) *(G-4058)*

Pallet Depot, Hattiesburg Also called Robert R Stewart *(G-2053)*

Pallet Exchange Network 251 709-7021
3809 Old Spanish Trl Gautier (39553) *(G-1501)*

Pallet Machinery Svc 662 726-5101
6285 Pearl St Macon (39341) *(G-3070)*

Pallet Source Inc (PA) 662 851-3118
228 Mount Pleasant Rd Mount Pleasant (38649) *(G-3512)*

Pallets Inc 601 876-2688
34 Pallets Rd Tylertown (39667) *(G-5278)*

Palmer Bodies, Amory Also called Palmer Machine Works Inc *(G-50)*

(PA)=Parent Co (HQ)=Headquarters (DH)=Div Headquarters

2019 Harris Directory of
Mississippi Manufacturers

307

Palmer Companies, The, Saucier

Palmer Companies, The, Saucier Also called Palmer Tool LLC *(G-4760)*

Palmer Handrail & Custom Mllwk 662 287-3090
35 County Road 324 Corinth (38834) *(G-1107)*

Palmer Machine Works Inc 662 256-2636
1106 104th St Amory (38821) *(G-50)*

Palmer Tool LLC 228 832-0805
24125 Hwy 49 S Saucier (39574) *(G-4760)*

Palmer Veneer Inc 601 735-9717
216 Mozingo Richey Rd Waynesboro (39367) *(G-5509)*

Panama Pump Company 601 544-4251
620 Meadow Lane Dr Hattiesburg (39401) *(G-2039)*

Pandle Inc 228 762-3300
2401 Petit Bois St Pascagoula (39581) *(G-4059)*

Pangaea Exploration Inc 228 452-7544
104 Vista Dr Pass Christian (39571) *(G-4092)*

Panolian 662 563-4591
363 Highway 51 N Batesville (38606) *(G-116)*

Panther Printing LLC 601 425-4414
58 Robert Walters Rd Laurel (39443) *(G-2816)*

Par-Co Drilling Inc 601 442-6421
144 Providence Rd Natchez (39120) *(G-3605)*

Paradise & Associates Inc 601 445-9710
296 Highland Blvd Natchez (39120) *(G-3606)*

Paragon Technical Services, Jackson Also called Ergon Inc *(G-2645)*

Parent Co Champion HM Bldrs Co, Carthage Also called Central Miss Manufacturing Hsing *(G-711)*

Parents and Kids Magazine 601 366-0901
817 E River Pl Jackson (39202) *(G-2534)*

Parish Pumps and Machine Inc 662 256-2052
30462 Bigbee Rd Amory (38821) *(G-51)*

Park Avenue Printing 601 876-9095
305 Beulah Ave Tylertown (39667) *(G-5279)*

Parker Brothers 2 Inc 662 283-2224
4 Old Highway 51 N Winona (38967) *(G-5605)*

Parker Construction Materials, Columbus Also called Florence Parker *(G-975)*

Parker Dre Industries 228 383-5967
12063 Carnegie Ave Gulfport (39503) *(G-1843)*

Parker Logging Inc 662 412-2435
273 Highway 9 S Calhoun City (38916) *(G-643)*

Parker Trucking and Hlg LLC 601 537-3670
339 Scr 150 Morton (39117) *(G-3453)*

Parker-Hannifin Corporation 601 856-4123
147 W Hoy Rd Madison (39110) *(G-3137)*

Parker-Hannifin Corporation 662 563-4691
1620 Highway 6 E Batesville (38606) *(G-117)*

Parker-Hannifin Corporation 662 895-1011
8225 Hacks Cross Rd Olive Branch (38654) *(G-3894)*

Parker-Hannifin Corporation 662 252-2656
805 West St Holly Springs (38635) *(G-2187)*

Parker-Hannifin Mobile Climate 662 728-3141
200 Quartet Ave Booneville (38829) *(G-340)*

Parkerson Lumber Inc 662 547-6019
980 Ms Highway 413 French Camp (39745) *(G-1441)*

Parr Prosthetics 601 749-7254
1125 Highway 43 N Ste F Picayune (39466) *(G-4283)*

Parthenon Envelope Company LLC 601 758-4788
10 Veterans Memorial Dr Sumrall (39482) *(G-5040)*

Partitions Gulfport Corp 228 822-9908
2604 24th Ave C Gulfport (39501) *(G-1844)*

Partridge Ornamental Iron Inc 601 693-4021
4816 Arundel Rd Meridian (39307) *(G-3380)*

Partridge Production LLC 601 987-4911
4273 I 55 N Jackson (39206) *(G-2535)*

Parts and Supply Inc 228 832-6272
14492 Dedeaux Rd Gulfport (39503) *(G-1845)*

Party & Paper, Columbus Also called Mackay Enterprises LLC *(G-996)*

Party City 228 539-4476
15224 Crossroads Pkwy Gulfport (39503) *(G-1846)*

Party Time Ice Inc 662 746-8899
677 E Sunflower Dr Yazoo City (39194) *(G-5645)*

PASCAGOULA MAIN STREET, Pascagoula Also called Main Street Pascagoula *(G-4049)*

Pascagoula Refinery 228 938-4563
250 Industrial Rd Pascagoula (39581) *(G-4060)*

Paslode Corporation 662 489-4151
364 Stafford Blvd Pontotoc (38863) *(G-4353)*

Passons Specialized Services 601 939-3722
130 Interstate Dr Jackson (39218) *(G-2661)*

Passport America Corporation (PA) 228 452-9972
21263 Tucker Rd Long Beach (39560) *(G-2948)*

Pat S Pins 662 562-8986
470 Tanksley Rd Coldwater (38618) *(G-850)*

Pat Screen Printing 662 301-8176
214 E Main St Senatobia (38668) *(G-4797)*

Pat The Cat Prints 662 397-1038
1404 Pinecrest Dr Tupelo (38804) *(G-5199)*

Patco Sales Inc 228 207-4171
100 Birch Dr Pass Christian (39571) *(G-4093)*

Pathway Candles 601 297-0484
45 Cherokee Rd Hattiesburg (39402) *(G-2040)*

Patricia Betts 601 863-9058
614 Kinsington Ct Ridgeland (39157) *(G-4615)*

Patrick Enterprises Inc 601 268-1115
100 Pinewood Dr Hattiesburg (39402) *(G-2041)*

Patterson & Company Inc 662 842-2807
3893 Cliff Gookin Blvd Tupelo (38801) *(G-5200)*

Patton Family Optometry, Jackson Also called Spectacles Inc *(G-2593)*

Patycake Kids LLC 601 506-7117
258 Brae Burn Dr Jackson (39211) *(G-2536)*

Paul Bolling 601 466-3398
6400 Old 24 Leakesville (39451) *(G-2878)*

Paul Garner Motors LLC 601 785-4924
417 Hwy 28 E Taylorsville (39168) *(G-5056)*

Paul Yeatman 662 323-7140
254 Longview Rd Starkville (39759) *(G-4966)*

Paul's Welding, Starkville Also called Paul Yeatman *(G-4966)*

Pauls Pastry Production LLC 601 798-7457
1 Sycamore Rd Ste A Picayune (39466) *(G-4284)*

Pauls Pastry Shop 601 798-7457
1 Sycamore Rd Ste A Picayune (39466) *(G-4285)*

Pav & Brome Wtchmkrs Jewelers 228 863-3699
1912 25th Ave Gulfport (39501) *(G-1847)*

Pavco Industries Inc (PA) 228 762-3959
4703 Pascagoula St Pascagoula (39567) *(G-4061)*

Paw Print Visuals LLC 662 332-2359
910 W Lynne Cir Greenville (38703) *(G-1588)*

Pawn Investments Inc 601 649-4059
9 Heritage Trl Laurel (39440) *(G-2817)*

Paxton Embroidery 662 335-2160
112 Bayou Rd Greenville (38701) *(G-1589)*

Paxton Media Group LLC 662 287-6111
1607 S Harper Rd Corinth (38834) *(G-1108)*

Paxton Media Group LLC 662 728-6214
208 N Main St Booneville (38829) *(G-341)*

Paxton Sales Inc 662 841-1929
1020 N Gloster St Ste 116 Tupelo (38804) *(G-5201)*

Payment Alliance Proc Corp 601 956-1222
200 Briarwood West Dr Jackson (39206) *(G-2537)*

Payne Portable Building Inc 601 426-9484
342 Maxey Rd Laurel (39443) *(G-2818)*

Pazzazz, Jackson Also called Watkins Mayola *(G-2626)*

PC Ace Computer Service 662 494-1925
228 Mccord St West Point (39773) *(G-5557)*

PC Soap, Pass Christian Also called Christian Pass Soap *(G-4079)*

PCA/Olive Branch 341, Olive Branch Also called Packaging Corporation America *(G-3893)*

PCA/Pearl 340, Pearl Also called Packaging Corporation America *(G-4136)*

Pcp P Coast 228 202-7872
1120 Beach Blvd Biloxi (39530) *(G-272)*

Pcw (print Copy Webdesign LLC 601 259-1945
111 Thrasher St Crystal Springs (39059) *(G-1152)*

Peacocks Signs & Designs 662 226-9206
16394 Highway 8 W Grenada (38901) *(G-1698)*

Pearl River Door Company 601 573-2572
878 N Bierdeman Rd Pearl (39208) *(G-4137)*

Pearl River Exxon 601 650-9393
Hwy 16 W Philadelphia (39350) *(G-4230)*

Pearl River Foods LLC 678 343-3265
1012 Progress Dr Carthage (39051) *(G-721)*

Pearl River Graphics & Prtg 601 656-3636
404 Industrial Rd Choctaw (39350) *(G-749)*

Pearl River Logging Inc 601 587-2516
465 Na Sandifer Hwy Monticello (39654) *(G-3439)*

Pearl River Timber Llc 985 516-7951
80 P M Hall Rd Poplarville (39470) *(G-4388)*

Pearl Rubber Stamp & Sign Inc 601 932-6699
228 N Pearson Rd Jackson (39208) *(G-2662)*

Pearson Enterprises 662 289-7625
11922 Highway 43 S Kosciusko (39090) *(G-2709)*

Peavey Electronics Corporation (PA) 601 483-5365
5022 Hartley Peavey Dr Meridian (39305) *(G-3381)*

Peavey Electronics Corporation 601 483-5365
4500 8th Ave Meridian (39305) *(G-3382)*

Peavey Electronics Corporation 601 486-1760
710 A St Meridian (39301) *(G-3383)*

Peavey Electronics Corporation 601 486-1878
412 Highway 11 And 80 Meridian (39301) *(G-3384)*

Peavey Electronics Corporation 601 486-1127
4886 Peavey Dr Meridian (39301) *(G-3385)*

Peavey Electronics Corporation 601 483-5365
16389 Highway 503 Decatur (39327) *(G-1177)*

Peavey Electronics Corporation 601 483-5365
711 A St Meridian (39301) *(G-3386)*

Pecanier Oil & Gas LLC 601 982-3444
1837 Crane Ridge Dr Jackson (39216) *(G-2538)*

Peco, Jackson Also called Process Engineering Co Inc *(G-2551)*

Peco Foods Inc 601 859-6161
1039 W Fulton St Canton (39046) *(G-675)*

Peco Foods Inc 601 656-1865
999 Herman Alford Mem Hwy Philadelphia (39350) *(G-4231)*

308

2019 Harris Directory of
Mississippi Manufacturers

(G-0000) Company's Geographic Section entry number

ALPHABETIC SECTION

Pioneer Machinery and Sup Inc

Peco Foods Inc 601 764-4964
  Hwy 15 N Bay Springs (39422) *(G-169)*

Peco Foods Inc 601 764-4392
  95 Commerce Dr Bay Springs (39422) *(G-170)*

Peco Foods Inc 662 738-5771
  559 W Main Brooksville (39739) *(G-557)*

Peco Foods Inc 601 855-0925
  200 Feather Ln Canton (39046) *(G-676)*

Peco Foods Inc 601 625-7819
  Hwy 21 Sebastopol (39359) *(G-4775)*

Peco Foods of Brooksville, Brooksville *Also called Peco Foods Inc (G-557)*

Peco Foods of Mississippi, Canton *Also called Peco Foods Inc (G-675)*

Peller Electric Motor Srvs 601 693-4621
  2125 Grand Ave Meridian (39301) *(G-3387)*

Peltz Medical LLC 601 831-3135
  3211 Wisconsin Ave Ste A Vicksburg (39180) *(G-5404)*

Pemco-Naval Engrg Works Inc 228 769-1080
  3614 Frederic St Pascagoula (39567) *(G-4062)*

Pen/Ron Company Inc 601 519-5096
  226 Woodlake Dr Brandon (39047) *(G-431)*

Pennington Wldg Sp Crane Rentl 662 838-2015
  1041 Highway 309 N Byhalia (38611) *(G-596)*

Peppers Machine & Wldg Co Inc 601 833-3038
  23 Auburn Rd Sw Brookhaven (39601) *(G-522)*

Pepsi America, Tupelo *Also called Pepsi Beverages Company (G-5202)*

Pepsi Beverages Company 662 841-8750
  620 E President Ave Tupelo (38801) *(G-5202)*

Pepsi Bottling Group 601 982-4160
  1651 Marquette Rd Brandon (39042) *(G-432)*

Pepsi Cola Btlg Co Gulfport, Gulfport *Also called Allen Beverages Incorporated (G-1721)*

Pepsi South Bottling 601 607-3011
  591 Highland Colony Pkwy Ridgeland (39157) *(G-4616)*

Pepsi-Cola Metro Btlg Co Inc 662 563-8622
  180 Corporate Dr Batesville (38606) *(G-118)*

Pepsico, Jackson *Also called Brown Bottling Group Inc (G-2344)*

Pepsico, Batesville *Also called Pepsi-Cola Metro Btlg Co Inc (G-118)*

Pepsico, Brandon *Also called Pepsi Bottling Group (G-432)*

Pepsico, Gulfport *Also called P-Americas LLC (G-1842)*

Pepsico, McComb *Also called P-Americas LLC (G-3263)*

Pepsico, Jackson *Also called Brown Bottling Group Inc (G-2345)*

Pepsico, Tupelo *Also called P-Americas LLC (G-5198)*

Pepsico, Natchez *Also called Brown Bottling Group Inc (G-3539)*

Perfect Promotions LLC 601 482-7710
  504b Highway 19 N Ste B Meridian (39307) *(G-3388)*

Performance Drilling Co LLC 601 969-6796
  115 E Business Park Brandon (39042) *(G-433)*

Performance Drilling Company 601 854-5661
  4326 Highway 80 Pelahatchie (39145) *(G-4171)*

Performance Logging LLC 601 656-3556
  10050 Eastmore Ln Philadelphia (39350) *(G-4232)*

Performance Paperboard Inc 601 856-3939
  218 N Wheatley St Ridgeland (39157) *(G-4617)*

Perma R Products Inc 662 226-8075
  2604 Sunset Dr Grenada (38901) *(G-1699)*

Pernells Repairs Inc 662 453-9702
  402 Highway 7 N Greenwood (38930) *(G-1645)*

Personal Touch Stone 228 219-3359
  6321 Gavin Hamilton Rd Moss Point (39562) *(G-3494)*

Perspecta Engineering Inc 571 313-6000
  1103 Balch Blvd Ste 218 Stennis Space Center (39529) *(G-4996)*

Petermans Cabinets 228 832-0353
  15362 Russell Rd Gulfport (39503) *(G-1848)*

Peters Brothers Logging 601 928-3591
  60 Lacy Evans Rd Wiggins (39577) *(G-5587)*

Petro-Hunt LLC 601 636-3448
  4940 Freetown Rd Vicksburg (39183) *(G-5405)*

Petroci Usa Inc 601 764-2222
  460 County Road 2339 Bay Springs (39422) *(G-171)*

Pettigrew Cabinets Inc 662 844-1368
  3449 Highway 6 Plantersville (38862) *(G-4313)*

Pevey Publishing LLC 601 503-7205
  405 Knights Cv W Brandon (39047) *(G-434)*

Pezant Logging LLC 601 303-3025
  169 New River Rd Tylertown (39667) *(G-5280)*

Pg Technologies LLC 317 240-2500
  135 Technology Blvd Ellisville (39437) *(G-1266)*

Phae I Bobs 662 332-3505
  512 Highway 1 N Greenville (38701) *(G-1590)*

Pharmaceutical Trade Svcs Inc 228 244-1530
  5820 Gulf Tech Dr Ocean Springs (39564) *(G-3775)*

Pharmedium Services LLC 662 846-5969
  913 N Davis Ave Cleveland (38732) *(G-803)*

Philips Day-Brite, Tupelo *Also called Signify North America Corp (G-5223)*

Philips Lighting Company, Tupelo *Also called Signify North America Corp (G-5222)*

Phillip Spring Logging In 601 567-2138
  319 Evans Rd Se Smithdale (39664) *(G-4842)*

Phillips Bark Proc Co Inc (PA) 601 605-1071
  428 County Farm Ln Ne Brookhaven (39601) *(G-523)*

Phillips Company Inc 662 844-3898
  372 Road 1438 Tupelo (38804) *(G-5203)*

Philumina LLC 228 363-4048
  122 Carroll Ave Long Beach (39560) *(G-2949)*

Phoenix Energy Inc Mississippi 601 445-3200
  118 Lower Woodville Rd Natchez (39120) *(G-3607)*

Phoenix Operating Inc 601 866-2223
  400 W Madison St Bolton (39041) *(G-313)*

Phone Booth Inc 662 286-6600
  809 Tate St Corinth (38834) *(G-1109)*

Phosphate Holdings Inc 601 898-9004
  100 Webster Cir Ste 4 Madison (39110) *(G-3138)*

Photowire Solar Producers 228 627-0088
  10530 Road 747 Philadelphia (39350) *(G-4233)*

Piave Broom & Mop Inc 601 584-7314
  106 Mc Aulay Dr Petal (39465) *(G-4195)*

Picayune Item, Picayune *Also called Newspaper Holding Inc (G-4281)*

Picayune Monument & Gran Works 601 798-7926
  411 Memorial Blvd Picayune (39466) *(G-4286)*

Pickens Hardwoods Inc 601 924-1199
  127 Richardson Dr Jackson (39209) *(G-2539)*

Pickett Equipment Co Inc 662 890-9095
  8464 Summit Cv Olive Branch (38654) *(G-3895)*

Pickett Productions 601 885-2720
  1923 Breeden Rd Utica (39175) *(G-5310)*

Pickle Larry 662 256-7239
  60018 Country Wood Rd Amory (38821) *(G-52)*

Pierce Body Works 601 939-1768
  203 Belaire Dr Jackson (39208) *(G-2663)*

Pierce Cabinets Inc 662 840-6795
  2259 Graham Dr Tupelo (38801) *(G-5204)*

Pierce Cnstr & Maint Co Inc 601 544-1321
  1505 Highway 11 Petal (39465) *(G-4196)*

Pierce Foam and Supply Inc 662 728-8070
  103 Superior Dr Booneville (38829) *(G-342)*

Pierce Well Service 601 947-4548
  5267 Highway 613 Agricola (39452) *(G-30)*

Pig Neon 662 638-3257
  711 N Lamar Blvd Oxford (38655) *(G-3993)*

Pigeon Roost News 662 838-4844
  157 S Center St Holly Springs (38635) *(G-2188)*

Pike County Ready-Mix Concrete, Magnolia *Also called Delta Industries Inc (G-3190)*

Pillows Plus 662 890-3699
  6645 Blue Bird Ln Olive Branch (38654) *(G-3896)*

Pine Belt Energy Services LLC 601 796-3299
  6466 Highway 13 Lumberton (39455) *(G-3037)*

Pine Belt Gas Inc 601 731-1144
  47 Pine Ln Columbia (39429) *(G-911)*

Pine Belt Industries 601 450-0431
  41 Bonhomie Rd Hattiesburg (39401) *(G-2042)*

Pine Belt Medical Equipment, Hattiesburg *Also called Advantage Medical and Phrm LLC (G-1916)*

Pine Belt Processing Inc 601 785-4476
  1122 Erwin Rd Stonewall (39363) *(G-4998)*

Pine Belt Ready Mix 601 544-7069
  2098 Glendale Ave Hattiesburg (39401) *(G-2043)*

Pine Belt Ready Mix Concrete 601 425-2559
  1104 W 1st St Ste 8 Laurel (39440) *(G-2819)*

Pine Belt Ready-Mix Con Inc (HQ) 601 425-2026
  1104 W 1st St Ste 8 Laurel (39440) *(G-2820)*

Pine Belt Ready-Mix Con Inc 601 765-4813
  38 Collins Indus Pk Dr Collins (39428) *(G-859)*

Pine Belt Truss Company Inc 601 729-4298
  246 Northridge Rd Soso (39480) *(G-4847)*

Pine Creek LLC 601 255-5036
  42 Pine Bark Cv Hattiesburg (39401) *(G-2044)*

Pinecrest Woodworks 601 677-3015
  414 Randy Coleman Rd Shuqualak (39361) *(G-4836)*

Pinion Prod 662 891-0930
  1746 County Road 278 Blue Springs (38828) *(G-298)*

Pink Apple 901 412-3926
  1686 Main St Southaven (38671) *(G-4892)*

Pink Peppermint Paper LLC 601 898-9232
  404 Saint Ives Dr Madison (39110) *(G-3139)*

Pink Star Industries 702 546-9883
  1386 Rader Creek Rd Sarah (38665) *(G-4735)*

Pinnacle Agriculture Dist Inc 662 453-7010
  62901 Highway 82 W Greenwood (38930) *(G-1646)*

Pinnacle Agriculture Dist Inc 662 265-5828
  1009 First St Inverness (38753) *(G-2276)*

Pinnacle Printing and Copying 601 944-1470
  2300 Lakeland Dr Flowood (39232) *(G-1387)*

Pinplanfix21 LLC 662 380-1961
  307 Park Dr Oxford (38655) *(G-3994)*

Pioneer, Meridian *Also called DEA Mississippi Inc (G-3327)*

Pioneer Aerospace Corporation 601 736-4511
  1 Pioneer Dr Columbia (39429) *(G-912)*

Pioneer Machinery and Sup Inc 662 286-5646
  901 S Tate St Corinth (38834) *(G-1110)*

(PA)=Parent Co (HQ)=Headquarters (DH)=Div Headquarters

2019 Harris Directory of
Mississippi Manufacturers

309

ALPHABETIC

ALPHABETIC SECTION

Pioneer Publishing Co 662 237-6010
20193 Highway 82 Carrollton (38917) *(G-702)*

Pioneer Well Service 601 399-1648
1475 Highway 84 E Laurel (39443) *(G-2821)*

Pipe Organ Specialties Inc 601 649-5581
3104 N 5th Ave Laurel (39440) *(G-2822)*

Piper Impact, New Albany *Also called Piper Metal Forming Corp (G-3691)*

Piper Metal Forming Corp 508 363-3937
795 Sam T Barkley Dr New Albany (38652) *(G-3691)*

Piranha Business Cards LLC 800 281-1916
106 Lone Wolf Dr Madison (39110) *(G-3140)*

Pistol Ridge Partners LLC 601 649-7639
2300 Hwy 11 N Laurel (39440) *(G-2823)*

Pitcocks Meat Processing Inc 662 563-9627
483 Liberty Hill Rd Pope (38658) *(G-4372)*

Pitney Bowes Inc 601 969-2900
175 E Capitol St Ste 300 Jackson (39201) *(G-2540)*

Pitney Bowes Inc 601 206-9039
119 Marketridge Dr Ste H Ridgeland (39157) *(G-4618)*

Pitsburgh Stone & Plaster 601 631-0006
715 China St Vicksburg (39183) *(G-5406)*

Pitts Companies Cabinets Mllwk (PA) 662 844-2772
1644 Cliff Gookin Blvd Tupelo (38801) *(G-5205)*

Pitts Swabbing Service Inc 601 422-0111
2777 Highway 84 E Laurel (39443) *(G-2824)*

Pk USA Inc 662 301-4800
150 Industrial Dr Senatobia (38668) *(G-4798)*

Plan House Printing (PA) 662 407-0193
607 W Main St Ste A Tupelo (38804) *(G-5206)*

Plan House Printing 601 336-6378
1 Churchill St Hattiesburg (39402) *(G-2045)*

Planhouse Publications Inc 601 825-1187
660 Katherine Dr Flowood (39232) *(G-1388)*

Plantronics Inc 662 893-7221
7769 Pleasant Hill Rd Olive Branch (38654) *(G-3897)*

Plaskolite South LLC 662 895-7007
10500 High Point Rd Olive Branch (38654) *(G-3898)*

Plaspros Inc 662 563-8635
175 Corporate Dr Batesville (38606) *(G-119)*

Plastics Plus Inc 228 832-4634
15132 Dedeaux Rd Gulfport (39503) *(G-1849)*

Platinum Publishing Inc 228 219-1020
630 Bay Cove Dr Unit 102 Biloxi (39532) *(G-273)*

Platte Chemical Co, Greenville *Also called Loveland Products Inc (G-1564)*

Play Coast 228 369-4582
1403 Churchill Dr Ocean Springs (39564) *(G-3776)*

Pleasant Grove Soaps 662 487-3050
9360 Highway 315 Sardis (38666) *(G-4743)*

Pledger Petroleum Inc 601 442-9871
606 Washington St Natchez (39120) *(G-3608)*

Plr Labs LLC 228 327-0939
996 N Halstead Rd Ocean Springs (39564) *(G-3777)*

Plum Trophy Sales 601 758-4834
4882 Highway 589 Sumrall (39482) *(G-5041)*

Plymouth Tube Company 662 258-2420
212 Industrial Park Rd Eupora (39744) *(G-1290)*

Pmq Inc 662 234-5481
612 Mclarty Rd Oxford (38655) *(G-3995)*

Pmq Inc 662 234-5481
605 Edison St Oxford (38655) *(G-3996)*

PO Boy Welding Inc 662 624-3696
1012 E 2nd St Clarksdale (38614) *(G-778)*

Pole Mill Optimizer LLC 601 928-8860
2175 Hwy 49 S Wiggins (39577) *(G-5588)*

Polks Meat Products Inc 601 849-9997
1801 Simpson Highway 49 Magee (39111) *(G-3180)*

Pollchaps LLC 601 706-4928
453 Holifield Cir Brandon (39042) *(G-435)*

Pollchaps Custom Screen Prtg 769 218-0824
100 Brooks Dr Brandon (39042) *(G-436)*

Polo Custom Products Inc 662 779-2009
15730 W Main St Louisville (39339) *(G-2976)*

Polychemie Inc (HQ) 228 533-5555
3080 Port And Harbor Dr Bay Saint Louis (39520) *(G-150)*

Polycon International LLC 601 898-1024
350 Industrial Dr S Madison (39110) *(G-3141)*

Polyvulc Usa Inc 601 638-8040
695 Industrial Dr Vicksburg (39183) *(G-5407)*

Pontotoc Die Cutting LLC 662 489-5874
363 Stafford Blvd Pontotoc (38863) *(G-4354)*

Pontotoc Machine Works Inc 662 489-8944
312 Highway 15 S Pontotoc (38863) *(G-4355)*

Pontotoc Progress Inc 662 489-3511
13 E Jefferson St Pontotoc (38863) *(G-4356)*

Pontotoc Spring, Pontotoc *Also called Matthew Warren Inc (G-4344)*

Pontotoc Springs, Pontotoc *Also called Union Spring & Mfg Corp (G-4366)*

Pooles Stone & Masonry Contrs 662 438-6643
671 County Road 993 Belmont (38827) *(G-201)*

Pop-A-Cart LLC 931 292-2150
405 Briarwood Dr Ste 103a Jackson (39206) *(G-2541)*

Poplarville Democrat, Poplarville *Also called Newspaper Holding Inc (G-4385)*

Port Gibson Reville News, Port Gibson *Also called Clairborne Publishing Co (G-4401)*

Portable Boring & Mch Works 601 922-9333
5556 Cahill Dr Jackson (39209) *(G-2542)*

Portable Boring Inc 601 922-9333
233 Saddlewood Dr Clinton (39056) *(G-833)*

Portabull Fuel Service LLC 601 549-5655
343 Highway 589 Purvis (39475) *(G-4447)*

Portland Chain, Meridian *Also called Webster - Portalloy Chains Inc (G-3419)*

Portstone Manufacturing Corp 601 922-0902
114 Riley Dr Jackson (39209) *(G-2543)*

Pottery By Helene 662 728-0988
797 County Rd 5051 Guntown (38849) *(G-1902)*

Powe Timber Company 601 788-6564
1356 Highway 15 Richton (39476) *(G-4542)*

Powe Timber Company (PA) 601 545-7600
114 S 10th Ave Hattiesburg (39401) *(G-2046)*

Power Dynamics Innovations LLC 601 229-0960
1301 Mlk Blvd Picayune (39466) *(G-4287)*

Power Plus Inc 601 264-1950
923 Highway 42 Sumrall (39482) *(G-5042)*

Power Torque Services LLC 601 835-2600
1344 Highway 84 E Brookhaven (39601) *(G-524)*

Power Transformer Div, Crystal Springs *Also called Kuhlman Electric Corporation (G-1144)*

Powerline Tags Inc 228 760-3072
23476 Ashleigh Dr Gulfport (39503) *(G-1850)*

Powertrain N Feuer Amer Inc 662 373-0050
2130 Csino Ctr Dr Extnded Robinsonville (38664) *(G-4676)*

PPG 4483, Hernando *Also called PPG Industries Inc (G-2148)*

PPG Industries Inc 601 932-0898
2106 Highway 80 E Pearl (39208) *(G-4138)*

PPG Industries Inc 662 449-4947
417 E Commerce St Hernando (38632) *(G-2148)*

Pps Plus Software, Biloxi *Also called Cks Productions Inc (G-229)*

Pqr Inc 662 289-7613
123 Pilsudski St Kosciusko (39090) *(G-2710)*

Prairie Adventure LLC 662 295-8807
126 Bus Blankenship Rd West Point (39773) *(G-5558)*

Prairie Farms Dairy Inc 601 969-1307
427 Dory St Jackson (39201) *(G-2544)*

Prairie Mills Feed & Farm Sup, Prairie *Also called Steve Schrock (G-4414)*

Prairie Welding & Supply, Macon *Also called Daniel Petre (G-3057)*

Prairie Wildlife 662 494-1235
3990 Old Vinton Rd West Point (39773) *(G-5559)*

Pratt (mississippi Box) Inc 601 366-3435
2031 Nw Progress Pkwy Jackson (39213) *(G-2545)*

Pratt Corrugated Holdings Inc 601 366-3435
2031 Nw Progress Pkwy Jackson (39213) *(G-2546)*

Pratt Industries, Jackson *Also called Pratt (mississippi Box) Inc (G-2545)*

Praxair Inc 662 343-8336
40433 Old Highway 45 S Hamilton (39746) *(G-1906)*

Praxair Inc 601 825-8214
214 Carbonic Dr Brandon (39042) *(G-437)*

Precast Concrete, Jackson *Also called Evans Refrigeration (G-2404)*

Precious Creative Caterpillars 228 424-3500
330 Kimberly Dr Gulfport (39503) *(G-1851)*

Precision Asp Sealcoating LLC 601 527-6381
12111 Maple Leaf Ln Collinsville (39325) *(G-874)*

Precision Automotive Machine, Moss Point *Also called Mitchell Buckhalter (G-3486)*

Precision Blades Inc 662 869-1034
120 Bauhaus Dr Saltillo (38866) *(G-4719)*

Precision Cultured Marble 662 838-5112
100 Lowry Dr Byhalia (38611) *(G-597)*

Precision Electric & Ltg Svc 662 893-3200
6229 Highway 305 N Ste G Olive Branch (38654) *(G-3899)*

Precision Fab Refurbishing 601 543-7752
3806 U S Highway 49 Hattiesburg (39401) *(G-2047)*

Precision Heat Treating Corp 601 355-4208
218 Yerger St Jackson (39203) *(G-2547)*

Precision Iron Works 228 341-0736
23213 Road 508 Saucier (39574) *(G-4761)*

Precision Mch Met Fbrction Inc 662 844-4606
502 Crossover Rd Tupelo (38801) *(G-5207)*

Precision Metalworks Inc 662 838-4605
64 Chase St Byhalia (38611) *(G-598)*

Precision Packaging Inc 601 352-2016
2805 Meter Rd Jackson (39204) *(G-2548)*

Precision Products Inc 228 475-7400
6500 Shortcut Rd Moss Point (39563) *(G-3495)*

Precision Rifle Ordnance LLC 601 825-0697
1024 Highway 471 Ste B Brandon (39042) *(G-438)*

Precision Spine, Pearl *Also called Spinal Usa Inc (G-4148)*

Precision Spine Inc 601 420-4244
5177 Old Brandon Rd Pearl (39208) *(G-4139)*

Precision Welding 601 730-0224
3069 Johnston Chapel Rd Summit (39666) *(G-5019)*

Precision/Delta Corporation 662 756-2810
205 W Floyce St Ruleville (38771) *(G-4698)*

ALPHABETIC SECTION

Purvis Jewelry Candles LLC

Precoat Metals Inc 601 372-0325
1095 Mendell Davis Dr Jackson (39272) *(G-2549)*

Premier Air Products LLC 662 890-9233
5230 Hacks Cross Rd Olive Branch (38654) *(G-3900)*

Premier Bride of Mississippi, Flowood *Also called Premier Publishing Inc (G-1389)*

Premier Building Salvage, Kosciusko *Also called Johnny Parks (G-2697)*

Premier Publishing Inc 601 957-1050
640 Lakeland East Dr A Flowood (39232) *(G-1389)*

Premier Shooting Solutions LLC 601 297-5778
557 Silverstone Dr Madison (39110) *(G-3142)*

Premiere Plastics Inc 662 489-2007
109 Ford St Pontotoc (38863) *(G-4357)*

Premiere Printing 662 488-9591
269 W Reynolds St Pontotoc (38863) *(G-4358)*

Premium Oilfield Services 601 425-5211
19 Service Blvd Laurel (39440) *(G-2825)*

Prentiss Headlight, Prentiss *Also called Prentiss Publishers Inc (G-4423)*

Prentiss Publishers Inc 601 792-4221
1020 Third St Prentiss (39474) *(G-4423)*

Press 4 U 901 361-0256
10340 Palmer Cv Olive Branch (38654) *(G-3901)*

Pressure Control 601 342-8051
1643 Highway 184 Laurel (39443) *(G-2826)*

Pressure Pro 601 331-7070
142 Ne Madison Dr Ridgeland (39157) *(G-4619)*

Prestage Farms Inc 662 494-0813
1550 W Church Hill Rd West Point (39773) *(G-5560)*

Prestige Cnstr & Land Svcs LLC 228 861-1292
18505 Robinson Rd Gulfport (39503) *(G-1852)*

Presto Manufacturing Company 601 366-3481
109 Presto Ln Jackson (39206) *(G-2550)*

Presto Printing Inc 228 678-9085
9471 Three Rivers Rd B Gulfport (39503) *(G-1853)*

Presto-Tap LLC 662 332-8559
3101 Little Theater Rd Greenville (38703) *(G-1591)*

Pretty Vixen Defense LLC 228 304-2173
6136 11th Ave Pearlington (39572) *(G-4161)*

Prevost Woodworking 615 836-9383
318 Fairview Dr Brandon (39047) *(G-439)*

Price Companies, The, Amory *Also called Chips Amory Inc (G-38)*

Pride of The Pond, Tunica *Also called Magnolia Processing Inc (G-5101)*

Primary Pharmaceuticals 228 872-1167
1019 Government St Ste E Ocean Springs (39564) *(G-3778)*

Prime Hospitality Group LLC 662 269-2892
95 Old Runway Rd Tupelo (38801) *(G-5208)*

Prime Manufacturing Svcs LLC 901 463-5844
622 Highway 305 N Senatobia (38668) *(G-4799)*

Primos Hunting Calls, Flora *Also called Primos Inc (G-1311)*

Primos Inc 601 879-9323
604 First St Flora (39071) *(G-1311)*

Print Brokers Inc 662 231-2556
219 Cedar Ridge Dr Booneville (38829) *(G-343)*

Print Press 601 342-2645
5229 Highway 84 W Laurel (39443) *(G-2827)*

Print Pros LLC 662 327-3222
1112 Main St Ste 3 Columbus (39701) *(G-1016)*

Print Shed 228 206-0077
12100 Highway 49 Ste 906 Gulfport (39503) *(G-1854)*

Print Shop 662 453-8497
1400 Sycamore Ave Greenwood (38930) *(G-1647)*

Print Shop 601 638-0962
3510 Manor Dr Vicksburg (39180) *(G-5408)*

Print Shop Inc 601 428-4602
1108 Trace Rd Laurel (39443) *(G-2828)*

Print Shop of Tupelo 662 841-0004
144 Hillview Dr Mooreville (38857) *(G-3443)*

Print Zone 601 799-3113
15 W Union Rd Carriere (39426) *(G-699)*

Printers Inc 601 792-8493
2233 Columbia Ave Prentiss (39474) *(G-4424)*

Printing Alley Ltd 601 371-1243
349 Springhill Dr Terry (39170) *(G-5075)*

Printing and Promotional Items, Tupelo *Also called P P I Inc (G-5197)*

Printing On Time Screen 601 707-7207
230 Christopher Cv Ridgeland (39157) *(G-4620)*

Printing Place 601 885-8327
4038 Old Port Gibson Rd Utica (39175) *(G-5311)*

Printshop Plus Inc 662 231-4790
461 Barry Spur Pontotoc (38863) *(G-4359)*

Prisock Brothers Logging Inc 662 773-8443
8270 Bluff Lake Rd Louisville (39339) *(G-2977)*

Pro Designs Inc 662 841-1867
1835 Nelle St Ste A Tupelo (38801) *(G-5209)*

Pro Logging Inc 662 720-9457
619 Highway 30 E Booneville (38829) *(G-344)*

Pro Shop The, Myrtle *Also called Proshop Inc (G-3513)*

Pro Signs 662 587-6036
550 County Road 538 Ripley (38663) *(G-4668)*

Pro Tool Inc 662 282-4419
3320 Highway 371 N Mantachie (38855) *(G-3203)*

Pro-Stone LLC 334 281-0048
8855 Cypress Woods Ln Olive Branch (38654) *(G-3902)*

Probuilt LLC 662 312-2159
47121 Ms Highway 14 E Macon (39341) *(G-3071)*

Process Engineering Co Inc 601 981-4931
4639 Medgar Evers Blvd Jackson (39213) *(G-2551)*

Process Mechanical Eqp Co 601 291-4082
110 Windrush Dr Ridgeland (39157) *(G-4621)*

Producers Rice Mill Inc 662 334-6266
105 Martin Luther King Dr Greenville (38703) *(G-1592)*

Product Services Company 866 886-3093
266 Upton Dr Jackson (39209) *(G-2552)*

Product Source Limited LLC 769 257-4620
144 Long Dr Florence (39073) *(G-1331)*

Production Machine & Tool Inc 662 287-4752
2500 Mason Saint Luke Rd Corinth (38834) *(G-1111)*

Professional Graphics Inc 601 924-9116
154 Wickstead Dr Clinton (39056) *(G-834)*

Profile Products LLC 662 685-4741
7250 Highway 15 Blue Mountain (38610) *(G-292)*

Proforma Southprint 901 734-2290
857 Amanda Cv Hernando (38632) *(G-2149)*

Prographics Inc (PA) 662 329-3341
1112 Main St Ste 2 Columbus (39701) *(G-1017)*

Progressive Atms 228 475-7234
10000 Saracennia Rd Moss Point (39562) *(G-3496)*

Prolon LLC 601 437-4211
305 Industrial Ave Port Gibson (39150) *(G-4405)*

Prop Straighteners Inc 662 423-9588
2080 Paul Edmondson Dr Iuka (38852) *(G-2305)*

Proshop Inc 662 333-7511
200 Dogwood Cir Myrtle (38650) *(G-3513)*

Prosigns Inc 601 791-5299
17252 Highway 26 W Lucedale (39452) *(G-3012)*

Prosperity7 Helping Hands LLC 800 597-6599
1046 Church Rd W # 106234 Southaven (38671) *(G-4893)*

Prosthetic Solutions Inc 228 220-4917
12311 Ashley Dr Ste B Gulfport (39503) *(G-1855)*

Protank LLC (PA) 662 895-4337
8971 Yahweh Rd Olive Branch (38654) *(G-3903)*

Protec Steel Industries LLC 228 364-4240
24101 Spyders Dr Pass Christian (39571) *(G-4094)*

Protees USA LLC 601 317-3649
2650 Livingston Rd Ste A Jackson (39213) *(G-2553)*

Protein Products Inc 662 569-3396
1042 Highway 3 Sunflower (38778) *(G-5047)*

Provine Machine Works 662 226-1512
719 Air Industrial Pk Rd Grenada (38901) *(G-1700)*

Prs 601 941-5104
113 Bridlewood Dr Brandon (39047) *(G-440)*

Pryor Packers Inc 601 649-4535
382 Trace Rd Laurel (39443) *(G-2829)*

PSL USA Inc (HQ) 228 533-7779
13092 Seaplane Rd Bay Saint Louis (39520) *(G-151)*

PSL-North America LLC 228 533-7779
13092 Sea Plane Road Bay Bay St Louis (39520) *(G-180)*

Psp Industries Inc 662 423-2033
27 County Road 342 Iuka (38852) *(G-2306)*

Pt, Columbus *Also called Mississippi Precision (G-1004)*

Ptc Inc 601 919-2688
185 Bridlewood Dr Brandon (39047) *(G-441)*

Public Art Project Ocean 228 872-0846
1924 Kensington St Ocean Springs (39564) *(G-3779)*

Pucci Petique Inc 662 429-3202
2400 Highway 51 S Ste 1 Hernando (38632) *(G-2150)*

Puckett Allen B Jr & Family 662 328-4931
114 Brickyard Rd Columbus (39701) *(G-1018)*

Pugh Tackle Co Inc 662 534-7393
1111 St Hwy 348 New Albany (38652) *(G-3692)*

Pura Vida, Ridgeland *Also called Tico Investments LLC (G-4641)*

Pure Air Filter, Greenwood *Also called Lott Enterprises Inc (G-1636)*

Pure Air Filter, Jackson *Also called Lott Enterprises Inc (G-2654)*

Pure Air Filter 228 867-0888
2518 Cypress Ave Gulfport (39501) *(G-1856)*

Purina Animal Nutrition LLC 662 726-4262
600 Pearl St Macon (39341) *(G-3072)*

Purple Bannana 228 466-2978
108 S Beach Blvd Bay Saint Louis (39520) *(G-152)*

Purple Label Candles 601 955-2217
1127 Gentry St Jackson (39213) *(G-2554)*

Purpose Designs LLC 601 480-2197
131 County Road 289 Pachuta (39347) *(G-4015)*

Purvis Forest Products Inc 601 794-8593
630 Highway 589 Purvis (39475) *(G-4448)*

Purvis Jewelry Candles 601 270-9687
505 S Main St Picayune (39466) *(G-4288)*

Purvis Jewelry Candles LLC 601 794-8977
176 Shelby Speights Dr # 9 Purvis (39475) *(G-4449)*

(PA)=Parent Co (HQ)=Headquarters (DH)=Div Headquarters

2019 Harris Directory of
Mississippi Manufacturers

311

Purvis Jewerly Rlc LLC

Purvis Jewerly Rlc LLC........................601 329-9002
176 Shelby Speights Dr # 9 Purvis (39475) *(G-4450)*

Purvis Machine........................601 947-6617
147 New Hope Church Rd Lucedale (39452) *(G-3013)*

Purvis Machine New Hope, Lucedale Also called Purvis Machine *(G-3013)*

Pvh Corp........................228 863-0017
10410 Factory Shop Blvd # 410 Gulfport (39503) *(G-1857)*

Q P P Inc........................662 356-4848
738 Main St Caledonia (39740) *(G-629)*

Q S C, Cleveland Also called Quality Steel Corporation *(G-804)*

Quad Inc........................601 656-2376
300 Choctaw Town Ctr Choctaw (39350) *(G-750)*

Quail Ridge Press Inc........................601 825-2063
101 Brooks Dr Brandon (39042) *(G-442)*

Qualified Fabrication Inc........................601 508-4389
174 Nancy Ln Lucedale (39452) *(G-3014)*

Quality Alum & HM Imprv Inc........................662 329-2525
1514 Gardner Blvd Columbus (39702) *(G-1019)*

Quality Beverage Packing Inc........................662 329-5976
82 Yorkville Park Sq Columbus (39702) *(G-1020)*

Quality Cabinet Company Inc........................662 429-1411
1662 Highway 51 S Hernando (38632) *(G-2151)*

Quality Cnstr & Engrg LLC........................601 786-8017
248 Medgar Evers Fayette (39069) *(G-1299)*

Quality Coatings Oxford........................662 234-2944
521 College Hill Rd Oxford (38655) *(G-3997)*

Quality Drilling Fluids Inc........................601 477-9085
2 Neil Gunn Dr Ellisville (39437) *(G-1267)*

Quality Engineering & Cnstr, Fayette Also called Quality Cnstr & Engrg LLC *(G-1299)*

Quality Engraving and Signs, Houston Also called Eddie Wiggs *(G-2239)*

Quality Fibers Inc........................662 620-7775
858 Mitchell Road Ext Tupelo (38801) *(G-5210)*

Quality Glass and Aluminum........................662 837-3615
1725 City Ave N Ripley (38663) *(G-4669)*

Quality Glass Inc-Ripley Miss, Ripley Also called Quality Glass and Aluminum *(G-4669)*

Quality Machine & Wldg of Miss........................601 798-8568
64 Mars Island Rd Picayune (39466) *(G-4289)*

Quality Manufacturing Group, Columbia Also called Quality Wldg & Fabrication Inc *(G-914)*

Quality Metal Roofing LLC........................601 669-4336
3810 Bouie Mill Rd Nw Brookhaven (39601) *(G-525)*

Quality Mud Products Co, Ellisville Also called Quality Drilling Fluids Inc *(G-1267)*

Quality Office Supply, Laurel Also called Chancellors Business Sup Inc *(G-2753)*

Quality Pipe & Fabrication LLC........................662 321-8542
1243 Highway 9 N Blue Springs (38828) *(G-299)*

Quality Plywood Company Inc (PA)........................601 735-3106
160 Marshall Durbin Dr Waynesboro (39367) *(G-5510)*

Quality Printing Inc........................601 353-9663
355 W Pearl St Jackson (39203) *(G-2555)*

Quality Production Products, Caledonia Also called Q P P Inc *(G-629)*

Quality Steel, Cleveland Also called L T Corporation *(G-798)*

Quality Steel & Supply LLC........................601 731-1222
2171 Highway 98 E Columbia (39429) *(G-913)*

Quality Steel Corporation (HQ)........................662 771-4243
2914 Hwy 61 Cleveland (38732) *(G-804)*

Quality Trim & Upholstery........................601 483-0077
3313 State Blvd Meridian (39307) *(G-3389)*

Quality Welding........................601 428-4724
3270 Ellisville Blvd Laurel (39440) *(G-2830)*

Quality Wldg & Fabrication Inc........................601 731-1222
2171 Highway 98 E Columbia (39429) *(G-914)*

Quantum Scientific Imaging Inc........................601 795-8824
12 Coteau Dr Poplarville (39470) *(G-4389)*

Quarter Inc........................228 701-0361
4300 Air Cargo Rd Gulfport (39501) *(G-1858)*

Quarter Rest Classics........................601 638-4207
2170 N Washington St Vicksburg (39183) *(G-5409)*

Quartermaster Security PR........................601 656-9882
10371 Road 391 Philadelphia (39350) *(G-4234)*

Queens Printing LLC........................228 234-5693
2009 Dartmouth Dr Gautier (39553) *(G-1502)*

Queens Reward Meadery LLC........................662 823-6323
1719 Mccullough Blvd Tupelo (38801) *(G-5211)*

Quick Printer, Ocean Springs Also called American Printing Copy Center *(G-3741)*

Quick Prints........................601 485-3278
2318 12th St Meridian (39301) *(G-3390)*

Quikrete Companies LLC........................601 798-6021
178 Huey Stockstill Rd Picayune (39466) *(G-4290)*

Quinton Hill Logging........................662 773-6864
4825 Bond Rd Louisville (39339) *(G-2978)*

Quitman County Democrat........................662 326-2181
330 Locust St Marks (38646) *(G-3222)*

Quitman Sporting Goods & Pawn........................601 776-3212
113 Sanders Ave Quitman (39355) *(G-4468)*

Quitman Tank Solutions LLC........................601 776-3800
502 S Archusa Ave Quitman (39355) *(G-4469)*

R & B Specialty Printing LLC........................662 260-2145
398 E Main St Ste 119 Tupelo (38804) *(G-5212)*

R & J Brown Logging & Trucking........................601 739-3338
639 County Road 13 Louin (39338) *(G-2963)*

R & M Paint Designs........................601 503-3631
5839 N Commerce Plz Ste A Jackson (39206) *(G-2556)*

R & R Crafts, Clarksdale Also called Renchers This & That *(G-779)*

R & R Lumber Inc........................662 568-7937
2466 Highway 15 N Houlka (38850) *(G-2227)*

R & S Sand & Gravel, Tremont Also called Martin Marietta Materials Inc *(G-5093)*

R & S Welding, Greenwood Also called Vera S Ray *(G-1655)*

R & W Hydraulics Inc........................601 649-0565
3039 Ellisville Blvd Laurel (39440) *(G-2831)*

R A Lesso Seafood Inc........................228 374-7200
598 Bayview Ave Biloxi (39530) *(G-274)*

R and B Welding LLC........................601 441-4398
197 Sanders Rd Columbia (39429) *(G-915)*

R and R Furniture Inc........................662 456-5888
112 County Road 66 Woodland (39776) *(G-5614)*

R D Graphix Sign Solutions........................601 736-0663
708 Main St Columbia (39429) *(G-916)*

R F Ederer Co Inc........................228 875-9345
4000 Bienville Blvd Ocean Springs (39564) *(G-3780)*

R Fournier & Sons Inc........................228 392-4293
9391 Fournier Ave Diberville (39540) *(G-1209)*

R K Metals LLC........................662 840-6060
703 Westmoreland Dr Tupelo (38801) *(G-5213)*

R R Donnelley, Senatobia Also called RR Donnelley & Sons Company *(G-4802)*

R W Delaney Construction Co (PA)........................601 442-0352
155 River Terminal Rd Natchez (39120) *(G-3609)*

R&M Harvesting, Quitman Also called Ronny P Moore *(G-4470)*

R&R Welding LLC........................601 335-2470
18 E L Loper Rd Laurel (39443) *(G-2832)*

R- Squared Aluminium LLC........................601 825-1171
2650 Hwy 18 Puckett (39151) *(G-4429)*

R-Squared Puckett Inc........................601 825-1171
2650 Hwy 18 Puckett (39151) *(G-4430)*

R2pg Inc........................601 747-0522
507 Market St Port Gibson (39150) *(G-4406)*

Ra Maxx LLC........................662 342-6212
3380 Goodman Rd E Southaven (38672) *(G-4894)*

RAC N Spurs Game Calls........................601 455-9484
578 Crooked Creek Rd Silver Creek (39663) *(G-4839)*

Raceway Express Shell........................662 335-5434
3195 Highway 82 E Greenville (38703) *(G-1593)*

Racor Div, Holly Springs Also called Parker-Hannifin Corporation *(G-2187)*

Radco Fishing & Rental Tls Inc........................601 736-8580
86 Pierce Ln Columbia (39429) *(G-917)*

Radzewicz Explration Drlg Corp........................601 445-8659
655 Highway 61 S Natchez (39120) *(G-3610)*

Rain Cii Carbon LLC........................601 794-2753
863 Old Richburg Rd Purvis (39475) *(G-4451)*

Rainbow Rentl Fishing Tls Inc........................601 425-3309
12 Donald Dr Laurel (39440) *(G-2833)*

Rainbow Signs........................228 354-8008
12487 Shortcut Rd Biloxi (39532) *(G-275)*

Rainbow Spring Water Inc........................228 769-6262
3310 Old Mobile Ave Pascagoula (39581) *(G-4063)*

Rainbow Stitchings........................662 378-5335
1047 Sisson Dr Greenville (38703) *(G-1594)*

Rainey Mill Works LLC........................601 583-1310
1909 Country Club Rd Hattiesburg (39401) *(G-2048)*

Rak-Master LLC........................601 906-1039
125 Vineyard Blvd Brandon (39047) *(G-443)*

Ralph Craven LLC........................601 425-0294
526 E 21st St Laurel (39440) *(G-2834)*

Ralph Morgan Logging Inc........................601 679-5291
3714 Lauderdale Rd Lauderdale (39335) *(G-2728)*

Ralph Rone........................662 674-5796
11670 Attala Road 5053 Ethel (39067) *(G-1283)*

Ram Petroleum LLC........................601 876-0807
84 A C Dillon Rd 1 Tylertown (39667) *(G-5281)*

Rand S Welding........................601 876-3736
44 Rand Rd Tylertown (39667) *(G-5282)*

Randell Mfg Inc........................601 372-3903
1055 Mendell Davis Dr Jackson (39272) *(G-2557)*

Randy A Elder........................504 301-7962
155 Burgetown Rd Carriere (39426) *(G-700)*

Randy Cummings........................662 547-2008
516 Erwin Rd Weir (39772) *(G-5521)*

Randy Judge Logging Inc........................601 775-3027
122 Little Warrior Rd Lake (39092) *(G-2724)*

Rankin County Industries, Brandon Also called Region 8 Mental Health Retrdat *(G-445)*

Rankin County News, Brandon Also called Rcn Corporation *(G-444)*

Rankin Ledger........................601 360-4600
201 S Congress St Jackson (39201) *(G-2558)*

Rankin Plastics LLC........................601 919-7883
307 Walker Cir Bldg L Richland (39218) *(G-4523)*

Rankin Printery........................662 287-4426
130 S Fillmore St Corinth (38834) *(G-1112)*

Rankin Publishing Company Inc........................601 992-4869
614 Grants Ferry Rd Flowood (39232) *(G-1390)*

Rankin Record, Flowood Also called Rankin Publishing Company Inc *(G-1390)*

ALPHABETIC SECTION

Rapad Drilling & Well Services (PA) 601 649-0760
217 W Capitol St Ste 201 Jackson (39201) *(G-2559)*

Rapad Drilling & Well Services 601 649-0760
1309 Hillcrest Dr Laurel (39440) *(G-2835)*

Rare Studios Publishing 770 316-0683
194 Davis Hill Rd Nw Roxie (39661) *(G-4693)*

Ratliff Fabricating Company 601 362-8942
100 Clay St Jackson (39213) *(G-2560)*

Rauschs Welding & Repair 662 841-0499
County Rd 736 Ste 136 Plantersville (38862) *(G-4314)*

Raven Happy Hour LLC 662 607-6604
1739 University Ave 132 Oxford (38655) *(G-3998)*

Ray Brooks Enterprises 662 342-0555
8068 Buckingham Dr Southaven (38671) *(G-4895)*

Ray Davis Logging Inc 601 687-1392
377 Matherville Poplar Waynesboro (39367) *(G-5511)*

Ray Smith Logging Inc 601 786-8428
979 Dennis Cross Rd Fayette (39069) *(G-1300)*

Ray's Trucking, Waynesboro *Also called Ray Davis Logging Inc (G-5511)*

Rayburn Publishing LLC 662 232-8900
1503 White Oak Ln Ste A Oxford (38655) *(G-3999)*

Raymond Granger 662 289-2502
2309 Attala Road 4237 Sallis (39160) *(G-4704)*

Raymond Mucillo Jr 662 429-8976
400 Getwell Rd Nesbit (38651) *(G-3656)*

Raymond Young Printing 601 947-8999
7188 Highway 198 E Lucedale (39452) *(G-3015)*

Rays Mobile Welding 601 966-0848
1320 Old Highway 49 S Jackson (39218) *(G-2664)*

Rays Welding 601 741-1114
101 Garrett Rd Terry (39170) *(G-5076)*

Raytheon Company 601 467-3730
19859 Highway 80 Forest (39074) *(G-1424)*

RC Cola Bottling Co, Jackson *Also called Frank Villines (G-2646)*

RC Cola Company 662 844-7947
2945 Mattox St Tupelo (38801) *(G-5214)*

RC Lonestar Inc 601 442-8651
60 Le Barry Rd Natchez (39120) *(G-3611)*

Rcl Components Inc 662 449-0401
3155 Industrail Dr Hernando (38632) *(G-2152)*

Rcn Corporation 601 825-8333
207 E Government St Brandon (39042) *(G-444)*

Ready Defense LLC 662 544-3478
481 Bonds Dr Holly Springs (38635) *(G-2189)*

Ready Mix Dispatch 662 842-6313
130 N Industrial Rd Tupelo (38801) *(G-5215)*

Real Meal Publishing LLC 601 697-7199
7657 Highway 13 N Lena (39094) *(G-2896)*

Real Yellow Pages 662 746-4958
7144 Tinsley Rd Tinsley (39173) *(G-5080)*

Real-Time Laboratories LLC 601 389-2212
375 Industrial Rd Ste 3 Choctaw (39350) *(G-751)*

Realpure Beverage Group LLC 601 849-9910
130 Coby Dr Magee (39111) *(G-3181)*

Realpure Bottling Inc 601 849-9910
130 Coby Dr Magee (39111) *(G-3182)*

Reaves Pure Water LLC 601 606-6789
2320 Eddy St Hattiesburg (39402) *(G-2049)*

Rebecca McCallum 662 501-0709
14265 Harrison Dr Byhalia (38611) *(G-599)*

Rebeccas Cstm EMB & Appliques 662 665-1846
48 County Road 258 Corinth (38834) *(G-1113)*

Rebel Boat Works & Shipyard, Biloxi *Also called Clyde E Burton (G-231)*

Rebel Butcher Supply Co Inc 601 939-2214
106 Flowood Dr Jackson (39232) *(G-2665)*

Rebel Quick Cash 662 326-9228
225 Martin Luther King Dr Marks (38646) *(G-3223)*

Reclamation Resources, Pachuta *Also called Diversified Petroleum Inc (G-4013)*

Recon Concealment Furn Eqp LLC 228 238-9149
7421 Joe Fountain Rd Ocean Springs (39564) *(G-3781)*

Record Imaging Systems 662 280-1286
963 Town And Country Dr Southaven (38671) *(G-4896)*

Red Creek Graphics LLC 228 864-3349
1829 25th Ave Gulfport (39501) *(G-1859)*

Red Lake Cedar Co LLC 877 469-5552
4209 Lakeland Dr Ste 279 Flowood (39232) *(G-1391)*

Red Penguin Jackson Ice Cream 601 519-9901
1524 Highway 80 W Jackson (39204) *(G-2561)*

Red Square Clothing Co 601 853-8960
1000 Highland Pkwy # 9004 Ridgeland (39157) *(G-4622)*

Red Star Digital Publishing 228 223-7638
14494 Williamsburg Dr Gulfport (39503) *(G-1860)*

Redco, Natchez *Also called Radzewicz Explration Drlg Corp (G-3610)*

Reddi Meals Inc 601 992-1503
679 Grants Ferry Rd Flowood (39232) *(G-1392)*

Reddy Ice Corporation 601 948-0900
607 S Jefferson St Jackson (39201) *(G-2562)*

Redi-Strip of Jackson Inc 601 355-3317
750 Boling St Ste C Jackson (39209) *(G-2563)*

Reebok International Ltd 228 822-9222
10360 Factory Shop Blvd # 360 Gulfport (39503) *(G-1861)*

Reed Food Technology Inc (PA) 601 939-4001
3151 Greenfield Rd Pearl (39208) *(G-4140)*

Reed Logging Inc 662 793-4951
231 Reed Rd Scooba (39358) *(G-4772)*

Reed Manufacturing Company Inc (PA) 662 842-4472
1321 S Veterans Mem Blvd Tupelo (38804) *(G-5216)*

Reed S Printing Inc 662 287-0311
258 State Line Rd Corinth (38834) *(G-1114)*

Reeds Reynolds 601 445-8206
33 Vaughn Dr Natchez (39120) *(G-3612)*

Reeves Cabinets 662 323-3633
112 Miley Dr Starkville (39759) *(G-4967)*

Refreshments Inc 662 286-6051
101 W Linden St Corinth (38834) *(G-1115)*

Rega Environmental Inc 228 447-1024
3586 Sangani Blvd Ste L Diberville (39540) *(G-1210)*

Reggie Waddle Logging Co 662 862-3106
812 W Main St Fulton (38843) *(G-1473)*

Region 8 Mental Health Retrdat 601 591-5553
600 Marquette Rd Brandon (39042) *(G-445)*

Regional Sites Inc 662 643-4595
6 County Road 251 Glen (38846) *(G-1508)*

Regional Stucco LLC 228 323-0290
7301 Mccann Rd Biloxi (39532) *(G-276)*

Rehabilitation Svcs Miss Dept 662 335-3359
385 W Reed Rd Greenville (38701) *(G-1595)*

Reid & Deese Llc 601 248-3143
263 Highway 27 S Tylertown (39667) *(G-5283)*

Reid Electric Motor Services 601 684-6040
1008 Office Park Ct Summit (39666) *(G-5020)*

Reid II Port Gibson, Port Gibson *Also called R2pg Inc (G-4406)*

Relevant Design Studios LLC 601 736-0663
907 Main St Columbia (39429) *(G-918)*

Reliable 2 Screen Printing 662 910-8272
1558 Woolfolk Rd Tunica (38676) *(G-5102)*

Reman Inc 601 635-4897
110 E 9th St Decatur (39327) *(G-1178)*

Reman Inc (PA) 601 537-3400
6586 Highway 13 Morton (39117) *(G-3454)*

Remy Reman LLC (HQ) 601 785-9504
214 Fellowship Rd Taylorsville (39168) *(G-5057)*

Renchers This & That 662 624-9825
1768 Sycamore St Clarksdale (38614) *(G-779)*

Renin US LLC 662 844-7191
1141 Ryder St Tupelo (38804) *(G-5217)*

Rentay's LLC, Jackson *Also called Taylor Rene (G-2604)*

Research and Development, Meridian *Also called Atlas Roofing Corporation (G-3301)*

Reservoir Signs LLC 601 898-1111
323 Trace Harbor Rd Madison (39110) *(G-3143)*

Reservoir Stationers, Madison *Also called Ksquared Inc (G-3116)*

Resinall Mississippi Inc 252 585-1445
102 Dixie Pine Rd Hattiesburg (39401) *(G-2050)*

Resolute FP US Inc 662 227-7900
1000 Paper Mill Rd Grenada (38901) *(G-1701)*

Resolute Ft US Inc 662 227-7948
1000 Paper Mill Rd Grenada (38901) *(G-1702)*

Resourcemfg 662 563-9617
101 Public Sq Batesville (38606) *(G-120)*

Resteel Express Inc 601 795-6110
9 Saw Rd Poplarville (39470) *(G-4390)*

Restora-Life Minerals Inc 601 789-5545
2140 Scr 97 Bay Springs (39422) *(G-172)*

Resurfacing Concepts Inc 662 489-6867
5024 New Hope Rd Pontotoc (38863) *(G-4360)*

Reuben Allred 601 734-2801
1730 Huckleberry Trl Sw Bogue Chitto (39629) *(G-304)*

Revolution Printing & Graphics 662 932-8176
8610 Highway 178 Olive Branch (38654) *(G-3904)*

Rex Lumber Brookhaven Llc 601 833-1990
810 Wl Behan Rd Brookhaven (39601) *(G-526)*

Rfc-Embroidery 601 463-0491
401 Highway 26 E Poplarville (39470) *(G-4391)*

Rfm Enterprises LLC 228 896-9498
1204 E Pass Rd Gulfport (39507) *(G-1862)*

Rheogistics LLC 601 749-8845
100 Polymer Dr Picayune (39466) *(G-4291)*

Rhino Graphics 601 445-8777
20 Fourth St Natchez (39120) *(G-3613)*

Rice Equipment Co LLC 662 323-5502
5893 Ms Highway 182 Starkville (39759) *(G-4968)*

Richard Armstrong 228 822-2238
7085 Turner Rd Long Beach (39560) *(G-2950)*

Richard B Brandon 601 238-2383
5945 N State St Jackson (39213) *(G-2564)*

Richard E Johnson (PA) 601 735-4737
148 Russell Dr Waynesboro (39367) *(G-5512)*

Richard Fick 601 848-7420
15438 Old Avera Rd State Line (39362) *(G-4988)*

(PA)=Parent Co (HQ)=Headquarters (DH)=Div Headquarters

2019 Harris Directory of
Mississippi Manufacturers

Richard H Bowers — ALPHABETIC SECTION

Richard H Bowers..601 264-0100
5243 Old Highway 11 Hattiesburg (39402) *(G-2051)*

Richard Melos..434 401-9496
11562 Old Highway 61 N Robinsonville (38664) *(G-4677)*

Richard Plastics Co...601 426-2810
1024 Hillcrest Dr Laurel (39440) *(G-2836)*

Richard Price Batton..601 892-5678
2133 Harmony Rd Crystal Springs (39059) *(G-1153)*

Richards Home Services......................................228 324-3482
9009 Seahorse Ave Ocean Springs (39564) *(G-3782)*

Richardson Marketing..662 234-3907
7 County Road 2064 Abbeville (38601) *(G-3)*

Richardson Molding LLC.......................................601 656-7921
931 Herman Alford Mem Hwy Philadelphia (39350) *(G-4235)*

Richton Dispatch Inc..601 788-6031
110 Walnut St Richton (39476) *(G-4543)*

Rickys Welding and Machine Sp............................601 638-8238
1721 Levee St Vicksburg (39180) *(G-5410)*

Ridgid Machining..228 383-3525
6307 W Benton St Bay St Louis (39520) *(G-181)*

Riedesigns Embroidery..601 262-5130
7869 County Road 350 Meridian (39301) *(G-3391)*

Rig Managers Inc...601 362-5121
1907 Dunbarton Dr Ste A Jackson (39216) *(G-2565)*

Ripley Industries Inc..662 423-6733
1409 Paul Edmondson Dr Iuka (38852) *(G-2307)*

Ripley Precision Tool & Die, Walnut *Also called Abby Manufacturing Co Inc (G-5453)*

Rising Son Welding LLC..601 344-0077
269 Will Young Rd Ovett (39464) *(G-3932)*

Rite-Kem Inc...662 840-6060
703 Westmoreland Dr Tupelo (38801) *(G-5218)*

River Bank Logging LLC.......................................601 639-4557
743 Otis Jackson Rd Crosby (39633) *(G-1135)*

River Bend Logging LLC.......................................601 466-1524
215 Carroll Loop Foxworth (39483) *(G-1435)*

River Cement Co...601 442-4881
60 L E Barry Rd Natchez (39121) *(G-3614)*

River City Pallet Co...601 415-0386
30 Sherard Dr Vicksburg (39180) *(G-5411)*

River Rads Drectional Drlg LLC.............................601 778-7179
3078 Highway 11 Moselle (39459) *(G-3459)*

River Rads Drectional Drlg LLC (PA)......................601 778-7179
3616 Industrial Blvd Laurel (39440) *(G-2837)*

River Road Jean Company....................................601 279-6571
2250 Eagle Lake Shore Rd Vicksburg (39183) *(G-5412)*

River Road Sand & Gravel LLC..............................601 582-9662
406 Hemphill St Hattiesburg (39401) *(G-2052)*

River Road Welding Inc..601 947-2511
1313 Vernal River Rd Lucedale (39452) *(G-3016)*

River Rock and Sand Co.......................................601 798-4292
79 Emmett Meitzler Rd Picayune (39466) *(G-4292)*

Rivers Gist Gainspoletti.......................................662 902-5415
38 Tiser Dr Cleveland (38732) *(G-805)*

Riverside AG Supply LLC......................................662 444-0600
109 Hwy 6 E Marks (38646) *(G-3224)*

Rives and Reynolds Lbr Co Inc (PA)......................662 773-5157
Hwy 15 N Louisville (39339) *(G-2979)*

Rives and Reynolds Lbr Co Inc..............................662 289-3823
Hwy 12 E Kosciusko (39090) *(G-2711)*

Rj Young..601 948-2222
2030 Nw Progress Pkwy Jackson (39213) *(G-2566)*

Rjb Enterprise Inc..202 830-3508
11520 Briarstone Pl Gulfport (39503) *(G-1863)*

Rjb Enterprises...601 639-4921
123 E Oak St Crosby (39633) *(G-1136)*

Rk Manufacturing Inc...601 956-7774
119 Marketridge Dr Ste D Ridgeland (39157) *(G-4623)*

Rkr Woodworking, Starkville *Also called Ronda K Gentry (G-4969)*

RLH Trucking Inc...662 462-5079
30 County Road 1461 Burnsville (38833) *(G-573)*

Rls Transport and Welding Svc, Moss Point *Also called Stringer Randal (G-3500)*

Rlt Publishing LLC...404 956-8344
3712 Thomas Jefferson Rd Jackson (39213) *(G-2567)*

Roadsafe Traffic Systems Inc................................601 922-5009
1416 Barnett Dr Jackson (39209) *(G-2568)*

Roadster Dream Publishing LLC.............................601 853-4443
809 Steels Pt Madison (39110) *(G-3144)*

Robbys Small Engine & Saw Repr..........................601 847-0323
3661 Simpson Hwy 493 Mendenhall (39114) *(G-3287)*

Robchem LLC...601 485-5502
981 Highway 19 S Meridian (39301) *(G-3392)*

Robchem Paints and Coatings, Meridian *Also called Robchem LLC (G-3392)*

Robco Inc...769 218-6457
113 E Second St Long Beach (39560) *(G-2951)*

Robert Bray Logging..601 269-3437
101 Scr 516 Raleigh (39153) *(G-4476)*

Robert E Monk..662 562-8729
30 Gwen Rd Senatobia (38668) *(G-4800)*

Robert L Leggett...601 833-7313
3525 Anderson Trl Brookhaven (39601) *(G-527)*

Robert R Stewart...601 408-0494
1701 James St Hattiesburg (39401) *(G-2053)*

Robert Smith Custom Cabinets..............................662 282-5007
869 Shiloh Rd Mantachie (38855) *(G-3204)*

Robert W Stubbs...601 849-9857
275 George Turner Rd Magee (39111) *(G-3183)*

Robert W Stubbs Logging, Magee *Also called Robert W Stubbs (G-3183)*

Roberts Welding LLC...228 697-4816
19451 28th St Long Beach (39560) *(G-2952)*

Robertson Fabrication Inc.....................................662 453-1551
5905 Highway 49 S Greenwood (38930) *(G-1648)*

Robertson-Ceco II Corporation..............................662 243-6400
2400 Highway 45 N Columbus (39705) *(G-1021)*

Robicheauxs Specialty Candy................................601 795-6833
2103 Fords Creek Rd Poplarville (39470) *(G-4392)*

Robin Jones Logging Co..601 687-5837
665 W Eucutta St Shubuta (39360) *(G-4833)*

Robine & Welch Machine & TI Co............................601 428-1545
3037 Ellisville Blvd Laurel (39440) *(G-2838)*

Robinson Woodworks...662 419-1864
2986 Topsy Rd Randolph (38864) *(G-4480)*

Robinsons Retail Inc...662 843-3950
110 N Sharpe Ave Cleveland (38732) *(G-806)*

Robison Adhesives Inc..662 997-8000
261 Murphey Ridge Rd Batesville (38606) *(G-121)*

Robot-Coupe Inc USA..601 898-8411
264 S Perkins St Ridgeland (39157) *(G-4624)*

Rock On Industries LLC..601 825-4857
116 Sunline Dr Brandon (39042) *(G-446)*

Rock or Not LLC..662 719-9120
702 Pecan Ct Brandon (39042) *(G-447)*

Rock Shop LLC..601 446-7625
241 John R Junkin Dr Natchez (39120) *(G-3615)*

Rockett Inc..601 939-9347
3640 Fourth St Flowood (39232) *(G-1393)*

Rockwool International, Byhalia *Also called Roxul USA Inc (G-600)*

Rocky BR Directional Drlg LLC...............................601 758-3340
196 Bob Graham Rd Sumrall (39482) *(G-5043)*

Rodger Holdeman S Signs.....................................662 436-0911
155 Northwood Forest Rd West Point (39773) *(G-5561)*

Rodgers Sales Company..662 902-1664
418 Jefferson Ave Clarksdale (38614) *(G-780)*

Roes Rims and Accessories...................................601 619-4489
2840 Clay St Vicksburg (39183) *(G-5413)*

Rog LLC..662 455-1364
110 Main St Greenwood (38930) *(G-1649)*

Roger Fillebaum...601 638-5473
7935 Warriors Trl Vicksburg (39180) *(G-5414)*

Roger Welch..601 649-3767
4457 Indian Springs Rd Laurel (39443) *(G-2839)*

Roger's Inspection Service, Laurel *Also called Roger Welch (G-2839)*

Rogers Automatic Screw Machine...........................601 849-2431
412 Raleigh Dr Ne Magee (39111) *(G-3184)*

Rogers Lumber 2, Columbia *Also called Rogers Lumber Corp (G-920)*

Rogers Lumber Corp (PA)......................................601 736-4472
8330 Old Hwy 90 Columbia (39429) *(G-919)*

Rogers Lumber Corp....601 736-4472
1120 Highway 13 S Columbia (39429) *(G-920)*

Rogers Machine...601 876-4476
298 Rushingtown Rd Tylertown (39667) *(G-5284)*

Rolison & Sons Logging Inc...................................662 837-9066
101 Walker Dr Ripley (38663) *(G-4670)*

Rolison Logging, Ripley *Also called Rolison & Sons Logging Inc (G-4670)*

Rolison Timber Logging..662 993-8115
1116 City Ave N Ripley (38663) *(G-4671)*

Rolls-Royce Marine North Amer.............................228 762-0728
3719 Industrial Rd Pascagoula (39581) *(G-4064)*

Rolls-Royce North America Inc..............................228 688-1003
5002 Test Site H1 Stennis Space Center (39529) *(G-4997)*

Romar Offshore Wldg Svcs LLC..............................228 475-4220
6524 Shortcut Rd Moss Point (39563) *(G-3497)*

Rome Chenille & Supply Co Inc...............................662 286-9947
1407a N Harper Rd Corinth (38834) *(G-1116)*

Ron Lor Window Fashions......................................662 329-1557
130 S Mccrary Rd Columbus (39702) *(G-1022)*

Ronald D Sterling...601 225-7772
3471 King Rd Liberty (39645) *(G-2916)*

Ronald E Christopher III..901 301-5922
7377 Grove Park Rd Olive Branch (38654) *(G-3905)*

Ronda K Gentry...662 418-9844
2225 Old Highway 12 Starkville (39759) *(G-4969)*

Rone Sawmill, Ethel *Also called Ralph Rone (G-1283)*

Ronnie Kolb..662 263-5252
Douglastown Rd Maben (39750) *(G-3049)*

Ronnies Auto Sales..662 773-9327
601 S Church Ave Louisville (39339) *(G-2980)*

Ronny P Moore..601 934-0113
543 Moorewood Ln Quitman (39355) *(G-4470)*

Rookie Boats...228 466-6377
10008 Highway 603 Bay Saint Louis (39520) *(G-153)*

ALPHABETIC SECTION

Roosevelt Wallace 662 627-7513
913 Desoto Ave Clarksdale (38614) *(G-781)*

Roseberry Welding LLC 601 408-1843
71 Walker Rd Hattiesburg (39401) *(G-2054)*

Roseburg Forest Products Co 601 785-4734
10599 Old Hwy 99 S Taylorsville (39168) *(G-5058)*

Roseburg Forest Products Co 662 236-8080
26 County Road 122 Oxford (38655) *(G-4000)*

Roseburg Forest Products Co 662 773-9868
122 Armstrong St Louisville (39339) *(G-2981)*

Rosson Exloopartion Company 601 969-2022
4021 N State St Jackson (39206) *(G-2569)*

Rosson Exploration Company 601 969-2022
814 N President St Jackson (39202) *(G-2570)*

Rossville Aluminum Castings 662 301-1147
211 Gwen Rd Senatobia (38668) *(G-4801)*

Roundtree & Associates Inc 601 355-4530
210 Trace Colony Park Dr Ridgeland (39157) *(G-4625)*

Roura Acquisition Inc 662 252-1421
100 S Industrial Park Rd Holly Springs (38635) *(G-2190)*

Roura Material Handling, Holly Springs Also called Roura Acquisition Inc *(G-2190)*

Rowell Publishing 601 981-0933
124 Peninsula Dr Brandon (39047) *(G-448)*

Roxul USA Inc (HQ) 662 851-4755
4594 Cayce Rd Byhalia (38611) *(G-600)*

Roy S Rides Inc 601 425-3700
94 Highway 28 W Laurel (39443) *(G-2840)*

Royal Canvas Studios 601 419-0809
110 Pine Knoll Dr Apt 261 Ridgeland (39157) *(G-4626)*

Royal Crown Bottling 662 843-3431
310 N Sharpe Ave Cleveland (38732) *(G-807)*

Royal Products, Plantersville Also called Superior Bedding Products of M *(G-4316)*

RPM Piping and Supply LLC 901 633-6083
1615 Epping Forest Dr Southaven (38671) *(G-4897)*

RR Donnelley & Sons Company 662 562-5252
121 Matthews Dr Senatobia (38668) *(G-4802)*

Rsileds LLC 228 697-5967
169 Balmoral Ave Biloxi (39531) *(G-277)*

RTC Logging Inc 601 517-6881
1731 Sunset Rd Collins (39428) *(G-860)*

Rubber & Specialties Inc 228 762-6103
2802 Andrew Ave Pascagoula (39567) *(G-4065)*

Ruby Press LLC 662 832-2255
207 Birch Tree Loop Oxford (38655) *(G-4001)*

Rufroggy Monograms 228 547-7060
18205 Prairie Dr Saucier (39574) *(G-4762)*

Rufus M Chancellor 601 776-5557
276 County Road 658 Quitman (39355) *(G-4471)*

Ruleville Manufacturing Co Inc 662 756-4363
902 N Oak Ave Ruleville (38771) *(G-4699)*

Run-N-Tri Company Llc 228 604-2227
9138 Carl Legett Rd D Gulfport (39503) *(G-1864)*

Runway Liquidation LLC 406 388-1988
2024 15th St Meridian (39301) *(G-3393)*

Runway Liquidation LLC 406 259-1280
109 State Highway 15 S New Albany (38652) *(G-3693)*

Runway Liquidation LLC 816 671-7922
11240 Highway 49 Gulfport (39503) *(G-1865)*

Rusken Packaging Inc 662 680-5060
1720 S Green St Tupelo (38801) *(G-5219)*

Russell Trucking 662 563-2616
106 Sherwood Cv Batesville (38606) *(G-122)*

Rustic Inn Publications Inc 856 983-4288
3233 N Polk St Corinth (38834) *(G-1117)*

Rutledge Publishing Co Inc 662 534-2116
100 Main St W New Albany (38652) *(G-3694)*

Rutn Cutn Deer Processing 601 892-5527
26029 Highway 27 Crystal Springs (39059) *(G-1154)*

Rykan Industries 601 900-2055
895 Greenwood Chapel Rd Carthage (39051) *(G-722)*

S & A Industries Corporation 330 733-6040
303 Futorian Way New Albany (38652) *(G-3695)*

S & A Industries Corporation 330 733-6040
2300 Munsford Dr New Albany (38652) *(G-3696)*

S & C Welding & Machine Works 601 845-5483
122 Lewis Rd S Florence (39073) *(G-1332)*

S & F Logging Inc 662 552-4701
597 Eddie Lee Rd Mantee (39751) *(G-3212)*

S & H Steel Corp 601 932-0250
2110 Highway 80 E Ste D Pearl (39208) *(G-4141)*

S & N Airoflo Inc 662 455-2804
1011 Sycamore Ave Greenwood (38930) *(G-1650)*

S & R Metals Inc 601 982-1171
2705 Lena St Jackson (39213) *(G-2571)*

S & S Custom Cabinets & Trims, Carrollton Also called Stanley D Stokes Jr *(G-703)*

S & S Frame Sales LLC 662 397-3725
155 Old Highway 45 Shannon (38868) *(G-4818)*

S & S Manufacturers Inc 662 489-2223
1998 Campground Rd Pontotoc (38863) *(G-4361)*

S & S Striping 662 449-4498
2340 Oak Woods Dr E Hernando (38632) *(G-2153)*

S & S Timber 601 833-8844
2411 Highway 550 Nw Wesson (39191) *(G-5529)*

S & S Welding & Repairs 662 834-1131
4275 Wash Bailey Rd Durant (39063) *(G-1228)*

S & W Welding & Machine Works 601 939-8516
131 Walker Cir Jackson (39218) *(G-2666)*

S and M Logging LLC 662 263-6711
200 Fulton St Mathiston (39752) *(G-3230)*

S and S Woodworking LLC 228 257-6846
10437 Lamey Bridge Rd I Diberville (39540) *(G-1211)*

S Circle Inc 601 792-4104
187 Rodeo Rd Newhebron (39140) *(G-3714)*

S H Wholesale Sign Co 228 865-4352
17500 Racetrack Rd Gulfport (39503) *(G-1866)*

S L Netterville Logging Inc 601 639-4915
2487 Netterville Rd Gloster (39638) *(G-1517)*

S Lavon Evans Jr Oper Co Inc 601 649-7639
2300 Hwy 11 N Laurel (39440) *(G-2841)*

S S S, Meridian Also called Structural Steel Services Inc *(G-3409)*

S W Krebs Woodworking Co LLC 228 762-1064
2009 Resca De La Palma St Pascagoula (39567) *(G-4066)*

S W M Company, Oxford Also called Blauer Manufacturing Co Inc *(G-3942)*

S&G Gutter & Sheet Metal Co 662 286-2924
206 Norman Rd Corinth (38834) *(G-1118)*

S&S Frames Inc 662 488-8996
240 Stepp Dr Ecru (38841) *(G-1232)*

S&S Signs 601 659-7783
117 Harper Ln Stonewall (39363) *(G-4999)*

S2s, Jackson Also called Spine Stability Surgical LLC *(G-2595)*

Sabbatini & Sons Incorporation 662 686-7713
410 N Broad St Leland (38756) *(G-2892)*

Sabic Innovative Plas US LLC 228 533-7855
13118 Webre Rd Bay Saint Louis (39520) *(G-154)*

Sabic Innovative Plas US LLC 228 466-3015
3531 Port And Harbor Dr Bay Saint Louis (39520) *(G-155)*

Saf T Cart Inc 662 624-6492
1322 Industrial Park Dr Clarksdale (38614) *(G-782)*

Saf-T Compliance Intl LLC 601 684-9495
1312c Harrison Ave McComb (39648) *(G-3264)*

Safilo 601 212-4136
2643 Highway 80 Brandon (39042) *(G-449)*

Safran Usa Inc 601 736-4511
1 Pioneer Dr Columbia (39429) *(G-921)*

Said Melinda 601 990-4022
129 W Cherokee St Brookhaven (39601) *(G-528)*

Sailmakers Supply 228 522-3232
3803 Old Spanish Trl Gautier (39553) *(G-1503)*

Saltillo Guntown Gazette 662 869-8380
2686 Highway 145 Saltillo (38866) *(G-4720)*

Sammy Evans Poultry 601 267-0521
110 Cliff Roten Rd Carthage (39051) *(G-723)*

Sample Lab 662 564-2498
3 Union Valley Rd Byhalia (38611) *(G-601)*

Samuel Son & Co (usa) Inc (HQ) 662 424-1460
26 County Road 351 Iuka (38852) *(G-2308)*

Samuel Moses Inc 601 669-0756
112 W Highland Dr Brookhaven (39601) *(G-529)*

Samuel Roll Form Group, Iuka Also called Samuel Son & Co (usa) Inc *(G-2308)*

Sanders, Greenwood Also called Pinnacle Agriculture Dist Inc *(G-1646)*

Sanders Home Health Inc 662 335-2326
1570 Highway 1 S Greenville (38701) *(G-1596)*

Sanders Industries Inc 662 895-1337
8158 Industrial Dr Olive Branch (38654) *(G-3906)*

Sanders Seed (PA) 800 844-5533
518 N Sharpe Ave Cleveland (38732) *(G-808)*

Sanders Sons Dvrsfd Wldg Entps 601 969-3119
1820 Valley St Jackson (39204) *(G-2572)*

Sanders Uniform, Greenville Also called Sanders Home Health Inc *(G-1596)*

Sanderson Farms Inc (PA) 601 649-4030
127 Flynt Rd Laurel (39443) *(G-2842)*

Sanderson Farms Inc 601 426-1316
195 County Line Rd Ellisville (39437) *(G-1268)*

Sanderson Farms Inc 601 894-3721
Hwy 28 E Hazlehurst (39083) *(G-2103)*

Sanderson Farms Inc Foods Div (HQ) 601 649-4030
127 Flynt Rd Laurel (39443) *(G-2843)*

Sanderson Farms Inc Foods Div 601 939-9790
4418 Mangum Dr Flowood (39232) *(G-1394)*

Sanderson Farms Inc Proc Div 601 765-8211
1111 N Fir Ave Collins (39428) *(G-861)*

Sanderson Farms Inc Proc Div (HQ) 601 649-4030
127 Flynt Rd Laurel (39443) *(G-2844)*

Sanderson Farms Inc Proc Div 601 428-5261
2535 Sanderson Dr Laurel (39440) *(G-2845)*

Sanderson Farms Inc Proc Div 601 684-9375
4039 River Rdg Rd Summit (39666) *(G-5021)*

Sanderson Farms Inc Prod Div 601 892-1145
19148 Highway 51 Hazlehurst (39083) *(G-2104)*

(PA)=Parent Co (HQ)=Headquarters (DH)=Div Headquarters

2019 Harris Directory of
Mississippi Manufacturers

315

Sanderson Farms Inc Prod Div

ALPHABETIC SECTION

Sanderson Farms Inc Prod Div 601 765-2221
3098 Highway 49 Collins (39428) *(G-862)*

Sanderson Redi-Mix Inc (PA) 662 256-9301
60068 Phlips Schlhuse Rd Amory (38821) *(G-53)*

Sandhill Group LLC (PA) 601 591-4030
3295 Highway 80 Brandon (39042) *(G-450)*

Sandstorm Entertainment 662 578-1357
208 Claude St Batesville (38606) *(G-123)*

Sandy Hook Machine Shop Inc 601 736-4041
283 Highway 48 E Sandy Hook (39478) *(G-4731)*

Sandy Ridge Sweet Potato Farm, Senatobia Also called Keith Murphree *(G-4793)*

Sandys Auto Parts & Machine Sp 662 342-1900
1759 Veterans Dr Southaven (38671) *(G-4898)*

Sani LLC 601 454-6047
102 Woodmoor Cv Clinton (39056) *(G-835)*

Santas & Such 662 773-2711
2090 Evergreen Rd Louisville (39339) *(G-2982)*

Sara Lee Coffee & Tea, Jackson Also called Hillshire Brands Company *(G-2441)*

Sarah Case-Price 601 818-4377
604 Adeline St Ste B Hattiesburg (39401) *(G-2055)*

Sardis Ready Mix LLC 662 512-2170
306 E Stonewall Rd Byhalia (38611) *(G-602)*

Sarub Inc 601 936-4490
5020 Highway 80 E Ste A Pearl (39208) *(G-4142)*

Sasser Logging Larry, Bogue Chitto Also called Larry Sasser Logging LP *(G-303)*

Sassones Timber LLC 601 542-5558
566 E Railroad Ave Osyka (39657) *(G-3929)*

Satchel LLC (PA) 901 515-8163
121 N State St Jackson (39201) *(G-2573)*

Satin Locs LLC 901 282-6823
6930 Black Oak Dr Walls (38680) *(G-5451)*

Satisfaction Welding 662 473-1518
49 County Road 484 Water Valley (38965) *(G-5474)*

Saul Jay Enterprises Inc 662 349-1660
3044 Goodman Rd E Southaven (38672) *(G-4899)*

Saunders Mfg Co Inc 601 693-3482
6604 Highway 80 W Meridian (39307) *(G-3394)*

Sc3 LLC 601 853-3690
112 Overlook Pointe Dr Ridgeland (39157) *(G-4627)*

Scanlon-Taylor Millwork Co 601 362-5333
2913 N West St Jackson (39216) *(G-2574)*

Scarborough Oilfield Supply Co, Natchez Also called Browning Oil Tools Inc *(G-3540)*

SCE, Bay St Louis Also called South Coast Electric LLC *(G-182)*

Scented Creations 601 362-5926
1441 Canton Mart Rd Ste 6 Jackson (39211) *(G-2575)*

Scentsational Scents, Olive Branch Also called D & G Enterprises *(G-3832)*

Schlumberger Technology Corp 601 649-3200
3750 Industrial Blvd Laurel (39440) *(G-2846)*

Schlumberger Technology Corp 601 442-7481
9 Covington Rd Natchez (39120) *(G-3616)*

Schlumberger Well Services, Natchez Also called Schlumberger Technology Corp *(G-3616)*

Schlumberger Wireline & Tstg, Laurel Also called Schlumberger Technology Corp *(G-2846)*

Scholastic Products and Awards 601 362-6990
1766 Lelia Dr Jackson (39216) *(G-2576)*

Schoolstatus LLC 601 620-0613
6222 U S Highway 98 Fl 2 Hattiesburg (39402) *(G-2056)*

Schudco Ltd 662 332-8678
335 Wilmont Rd Greenville (38701) *(G-1597)*

Schuyler C Jones 601 540-5841
115 Coventry Cv Madison (39110) *(G-3145)*

Scotch Plywood Company Miss 601 735-2881
110 Industrial Park Rd Waynesboro (39367) *(G-5513)*

Scott County Times, The, Forest Also called Scott Publishing Inc *(G-1425)*

Scott O Galbreath Jr 601 445-9924
65 S Concord Ave Natchez (39120) *(G-3617)*

Scott Publishing Inc 601 469-2561
311 Smith Ave Forest (39074) *(G-1425)*

Scott Strickland Sons Inc 601 928-2321
32 Lawson Oneal Rd Perkinston (39573) *(G-4180)*

Scotts Welding, Natchez Also called William Barnes *(G-3642)*

Scp, Booneville Also called South Central Polymers Inc *(G-345)*

Screen-Co, New Albany Also called Screenco Inc *(G-3697)*

Screenco Inc 662 534-8750
214 Carter Ave New Albany (38652) *(G-3697)*

Screenco Printing LLC 601 507-1986
280 Christopher Cv Ste C Ridgeland (39157) *(G-4628)*

Screening Room 601 626-0327
11611 Hitt Ln Collinsville (39325) *(G-875)*

Screw Conveyor Corporation 662 283-3142
781 Church St Winona (38967) *(G-5606)*

Scrubs Elite LLC (PA) 662 842-4011
917 S Gloster St Tupelo (38801) *(G-5220)*

Scs Signs and Service LLC 228 235-4839
15240 Camelot Dr Diberville (39540) *(G-1212)*

Sea Coast Echo, Bay Saint Louis Also called Bay St Louis Newspapers Inc *(G-135)*

Sea Robin Forge 601 798-0060
1423 Third Ave Picayune (39466) *(G-4293)*

Seago Enterprises Inc 601 684-3000
614 W Presley Blvd McComb (39648) *(G-3265)*

Seago Lumber, McComb Also called Seago Enterprises Inc *(G-3265)*

Seal Group At Hydradyne, Brookhaven Also called Hydradyne LLC *(G-501)*

Seal Master Mississippi 601 936-0080
1124 Weems St Pearl (39208) *(G-4143)*

Seamless One Seamles Gutters 228 832-0516
23044 N Carr Bridge Rd Saucier (39574) *(G-4763)*

Seb Mining 228 826-4466
8400 Jim Ramsay Rd Vancleave (39565) *(G-5320)*

Secorp Indus & Safety Sups Inc 601 422-0203
294 Victory Rd Laurel (39443) *(G-2847)*

Secure Shred LLC (PA) 662 563-5008
36124 Highway 315 Batesville (38606) *(G-124)*

Secure Shred LLC 662 563-5008
5850 Barnacre Rd Sardis (38666) *(G-4744)*

Seemann Composites LLC (PA) 228 314-8000
12481 Glascock Dr Gulfport (39503) *(G-1867)*

Seimens Industry Sector 662 245-4573
1961 Airport Rd Columbus (39701) *(G-1023)*

Seismic Drilling Contractor, Richton Also called J D Smith Drilling Company *(G-4536)*

Select Signs More 601 823-0717
664 Industrial Park Rd Ne Brookhaven (39601) *(G-530)*

Selex Inc 228 467-2000
7095 Roscoe Turner Rd Kiln (39556) *(G-2684)*

Self Serve Marine Inc 228 762-3628
4514 Flechas St Pascagoula (39567) *(G-4067)*

Seminole Furniture LLC 662 447-5222
269 S Carter St Okolona (38860) *(G-3797)*

Seminole Furniture Mfg, Okolona Also called Seminole Furniture LLC *(G-3797)*

Seminole Furniture Mfg Inc 662 447-5222
269 S Carter St Okolona (38860) *(G-3798)*

Seniors Bluebook 228 396-4602
15217 Shadow Creek Dr Biloxi (39532) *(G-278)*

Senter's Transit Mix, Verona Also called B & B Concrete Co Inc *(G-5327)*

Senter's Transit Mix, Tupelo Also called B & B Concrete Co Inc *(G-5111)*

Sentiments By Shele - Whmsical 662 812-3506
4257 Forest Hill Rd S Olive Branch (38654) *(G-3907)*

Seraphim Solar USA Mfg Inc 601 509-1265
3111 Lawson St Jackson (39213) *(G-2577)*

Serendipitee 228 872-4766
918 Washington Ave Ocean Springs (39564) *(G-3783)*

Seri 601 638-3355
1000 Rubber Way Vicksburg (39180) *(G-5415)*

Serigraphics 662 895-3553
7275 Lamb Rd Olive Branch (38654) *(G-3908)*

Service Connection, Horn Lake Also called Lawrence A Witherspoon *(G-2205)*

Service Lumber Company Inc 662 873-4334
20558 Highway 61 Rolling Fork (39159) *(G-4682)*

Service Lumber Holding Corp (PA) 662 873-4334
20558 Highway 61 Rolling Fork (39159) *(G-4683)*

Service Printers Inc 601 939-4910
1014 N Flowood Dr Flowood (39232) *(G-1395)*

Serviceknight 601 906-2810
201 N College St Ste 201 # 201 Brandon (39042) *(G-451)*

SERVPRO Oxfrd/Btsvll/Clrksdale, Oxford Also called Blue Note Management LLC *(G-3943)*

Severcorr LLC 662 245-4561
1409 Highway 45 S Columbus (39701) *(G-1024)*

Sevlo Solutions LLC 662 312-9507
39a Sadye Weir St Starkville (39759) *(G-4970)*

Sew Lucky Embroidery 662 550-5533
3022 N Wren St Hernando (38632) *(G-2154)*

Sew Southern Monograms 662 229-6564
1394 Highway 51 Winona (38967) *(G-5607)*

Sew Sweet 601 431-2304
4 Jason Ct Natchez (39120) *(G-3618)*

Shabazz Printing 601 786-9788
232 Medgar Evers Blvd Fayette (39069) *(G-1301)*

Shabby Chic S Etc 601 799-2800
505 S Main St Picayune (39466) *(G-4294)*

Shacks Welding Service Inc 601 939-5491
1260 Old Brandon Rd Flowood (39232) *(G-1396)*

Shale Energy Support LLC 601 798-7821
105 Street A Picayune (39466) *(G-4295)*

Shale Support, Picayune Also called Shale Energy Support LLC *(G-4295)*

Shamrock Drilling Inc 601 442-0785
118 Lwer Wdvlle Rd Unit 2 Natchez (39120) *(G-3619)*

Shamrock Farm 601 277-3053
10120 Old Port Gibson Rd Hazlehurst (39083) *(G-2105)*

Shamrock Plank Flooring, Horn Lake Also called JT Shannon Lumber Co Inc *(G-2203)*

Shamrock Plank Flooring, Horn Lake Also called Shamrock Wood Industries Inc *(G-2210)*

Shamrock Wood Industries Inc 662 393-2125
2200 Cole Rd Horn Lake (38637) *(G-2210)*

Shannon Fulgham Logging Inc 662 418-4449
1694 County Line Rd Maben (39750) *(G-3050)*

Sharones Innovative Prtg LLC 601 877-3727
5009 Alcorn Rd 552 W Lorman (39096) *(G-2962)*

Sharp Cypress Inc 601 249-2936
3194 Highway 98 E McComb (39648) *(G-3266)*

316

2019 Harris Directory of
Mississippi Manufacturers

(G-0000) Company's Geographic Section entry number

ALPHABETIC SECTION

Shaughnessy & Co Inc 228 436-4060
234 Caillavet St Biloxi (39530) *(G-279)*

Shaughnessy Clark D Prtg Co, Biloxi *Also called Shaughnessy & Co Inc* *(G-279)*

Shavers' Choice, Ridgeland *Also called Sc3 LLC* *(G-4627)*

Shaw Signs LLC 228 224-4971
21797 Ridgeview Dr Saucier (39574) *(G-4764)*

Shawn Kurtz 601 415-9540
344 Stenson Rd Vicksburg (39180) *(G-5416)*

Shcpi Greenwood Site 662 453-1445
616 Main St Greenwood (38930) *(G-1651)*

Shear View Mulching LLC 985 637-8402
35 Magnolia Ln Poplarville (39470) *(G-4393)*

Shears Fabrication & Wldg LLC 601 946-3268
1045 Chapel Hill Rd Utica (39175) *(G-5312)*

Shearwater Pottery Ltd 228 875-7320
102 Shearwater Dr Ocean Springs (39564) *(G-3784)*

Shed Bbq, The, Ocean Springs *Also called Shed Saucery LLC* *(G-3785)*

Shed Saucery LLC 228 875-7373
2 Choctaw Trl Ocean Springs (39564) *(G-3785)*

Shelby Dean Distributing 601 529-7936
800 Newitt Vick Dr Vicksburg (39183) *(G-5417)*

Shelby Group International Inc 901 795-5810
Hwy 32 E Charleston (38921) *(G-742)*

Shelby Logging LLC 601 609-7796
5521 Will O Run Cir Jackson (39212) *(G-2578)*

Shelby Manufactoring, Charleston *Also called Shelby Group International Inc* *(G-742)*

Sheldon Laboratory Systems, Crystal Springs *Also called Missco Corporation of Jackson* *(G-1149)*

Sheldon Laboratory Systems Inc 601 892-2731
102 Kirk St Crystal Springs (39059) *(G-1155)*

Shell Pipe Line Corporation 601 638-1921
20 Freetown Rd Vicksburg (39183) *(G-5418)*

Shelter From Rain 601 454-7602
2311 Breckinridge Rd Jackson (39204) *(G-2579)*

Shenise Productions Inc 601 437-3665
30 Pinehurst St Port Gibson (39150) *(G-4407)*

Sherwin-Williams Company 228 467-3938
214 Highway 90 Waveland (39576) *(G-5484)*

Shilpam Corp 601 933-9550
115 Metroplex Blvd Pearl (39208) *(G-4144)*

Shippers Carline, Bude *Also called American Railcar Inds Inc* *(G-567)*

Shirley McArthur Nobles 601 310-0890
956 Wpa Rd Sumrall (39482) *(G-5044)*

Shirtz Stuff 601 729-2472
180 Johnny Watkins Rd Laurel (39443) *(G-2848)*

Shocase of Homes, Flowood *Also called Blake Publishing Inc* *(G-1347)*

Shoffner Motor Co Inc 662 378-2909
105 Creekmore Rd Greenville (38701) *(G-1598)*

Shoreline Pool Mfr Inc 601 372-0577
3774 I 55 S Jackson (39212) *(G-2580)*

Short Line Manufacturing Co 662 754-6858
36 Choctaw Gin Rd Shaw (38773) *(G-4825)*

Shoulder Cords Unlimited 601 425-2195
1008 Strngthfrd Plsnt Grv Laurel (39443) *(G-2849)*

Shumpert Media 662 678-3742
30081 Seymore Rd Nettleton (38858) *(G-3667)*

Shuqualak Lumber Company Inc 662 425-5339
86 College St Shuqualak (39361) *(G-4837)*

Sideus Technologies, Biloxi *Also called TNT Investments LLC* *(G-284)*

Siemens Industry Inc 601 939-0550
44 Old Highway 49 S Richland (39218) *(G-4524)*

Sigma Plastics Group, Clinton *Also called McNeely Plastic Products Inc* *(G-830)*

Sign and Sing 601 954-9172
151 Taylor Way Brandon (39047) *(G-452)*

Sign Crafters 769 216-3936
316 Bay Park Dr Brandon (39047) *(G-453)*

Sign Design Plus, West Point *Also called Signs & More* *(G-5562)*

Sign Doctor LLC 601 286-3387
422 N Point Dr Meridian (39305) *(G-3395)*

Sign Graphics 601 445-0463
166 E Franklin St Natchez (39120) *(G-3620)*

Sign Gypsies Df North Ms 901 484-7357
4764 Thornbury Cv Southaven (38672) *(G-4900)*

Sign Gypsies Golden Triangle 662 368-3662
1742 Seed Tick Rd Caledonia (39740) *(G-630)*

Sign Here 601 847-3537
507 N West St Mendenhall (39114) *(G-3288)*

Sign Language 228 990-3609
17300 Popcorn Ave Vancleave (39565) *(G-5321)*

Sign Ministries 678 507-9912
2068b Appleway Ct Gulfport (39501) *(G-1868)*

Sign Plex 228 896-5999
560 Magnolia St Gulfport (39507) *(G-1869)*

Sign Pro Wholesale LLC 601 453-3082
345 Hawkins Crossing Dr Meridian (39301) *(G-3396)*

Sign Shop 662 328-7933
1835 Highway 45 N Columbus (39705) *(G-1025)*

Sign Shop 662 258-7186
559 Schaefer Rd Eupora (39744) *(G-1291)*

Sign Shop 601 735-1383
1204 Mississippi Dr Waynesboro (39367) *(G-5514)*

Sign Solutions of Saucier 228 265-4325
13056 Teague Rd Saucier (39574) *(G-4765)*

Signature Accents 601 853-9020
297 Ingleside Dr Madison (39110) *(G-3146)*

Signature Bedding LLC 663 523-8477
515 Crump Rd Tupelo (38801) *(G-5221)*

Signature Sound & Printing 601 272-5662
2116 1/2 Highway 45 N Columbus (39705) *(G-1026)*

Signature Sund Media Solutions, Columbus *Also called Signature Sound & Printing* *(G-1026)*

Signature Works 601 477-6187
1101 Highway 11 S Ellisville (39437) *(G-1269)*

Signature Works Division, Hazlehurst *Also called L C Industries Inc* *(G-2099)*

Signature Works Inc 601 894-1771
1 Signature Dr Hazlehurst (39083) *(G-2106)*

Signaturelink Inc 601 898-7359
605 Crescent Blvd Ste 200 Ridgeland (39157) *(G-4629)*

Signify North America Corp 662 842-7212
938 S Green St Tupelo (38804) *(G-5222)*

Signify North America Corp 662 842-7212
938 S Green St Tupelo (38804) *(G-5223)*

Signmark Inc 601 932-6699
228 N Pearson Rd Pearl (39208) *(G-4145)*

Signs & More 662 494-9451
1050 Northwood Forest Rd West Point (39773) *(G-5562)*

Signs & Stuff 662 393-9314
910 Goodman Rd E Apt C Southaven (38671) *(G-4901)*

Signs & Stuff Inc 662 895-4505
3674 Goodman Rd S Ste 1 Southaven (38672) *(G-4902)*

Signs By Schack 662 890-3683
9093 Deerfield Cv Olive Branch (38654) *(G-3909)*

Signs By Shaffier 601 833-8600
732 Zetus Rd Nw Brookhaven (39601) *(G-531)*

Signs First, Jackson *Also called Multimedia Graphics Inc* *(G-2514)*

Signs First, Hattiesburg *Also called Ets Signs Inc* *(G-1964)*

Signs First, Gulfport *Also called Red Creek Graphics LLC* *(G-1859)*

Signs First, Pearl *Also called Sarub Inc* *(G-4142)*

Signs First, Vicksburg *Also called Vicksburg Printing and Pubg Co* *(G-5440)*

Signs First, Southaven *Also called Ra Maxx LLC* *(G-4894)*

Signs First of North Miss, Tupelo *Also called Willcoxon Enterprises Inc* *(G-5259)*

Signs Plus 228 832-4634
15132 Dedeaux Rd Gulfport (39503) *(G-1870)*

Signs Plus 601 482-4217
9218 Whippoorwill Rd Meridian (39307) *(G-3397)*

Signs Plus Inc 228 832-4634
11325 Dye Rd Gulfport (39503) *(G-1871)*

Sille Biofuels LLC 601 400-2227
5513 Will O Run Dr Jackson (39212) *(G-2581)*

Simmons Farms, Yazoo City *Also called Simmons Frm Raised Catfish Inc* *(G-5646)*

Simmons Frm Raised Catfish Inc (PA) 662 746-5687
2628 Erickson Rd Yazoo City (39194) *(G-5646)*

Simple Solutions 228 588-9509
7004 Bentwood Dr Moss Point (39562) *(G-3498)*

Simple Stone Solutions 601 206-5566
5760 Gallant Dr Jackson (39206) *(G-2582)*

Simpson Brothers Inc 678 451-4259
4796 Attala Rd Mc Cool (39108) *(G-3237)*

Simpson County News, Magee *Also called Simpson Publishing Co Inc* *(G-3185)*

Simpson County News 601 847-2525
120 W Court Ave Mendenhall (39114) *(G-3289)*

Simpson County Ready Mix, Magee *Also called Delta Industries Inc* *(G-3176)*

Simpson Publishing Co Inc 601 849-3434
206 Main Ave N Magee (39111) *(G-3185)*

Sims Bark Co Inc 662 895-6501
5060 Hacks Xrd Olive Branch (38654) *(G-3910)*

Sims Metal Inc 601 649-2555
87 Crepe Myrtle Ln Laurel (39443) *(G-2850)*

Sincere Trading Inc 662 702-3822
1535 Sunridge Cv Greenville (38701) *(G-1599)*

Singin River Mental Health 228 497-0690
3407 Shamrock Ct Gautier (39553) *(G-1504)*

Sinhatech 662 234-6248
3607 Lyles Dr Oxford (38655) *(G-4002)*

Sipp Spinners and Lures LLC 601 620-6445
858 Willow Grande Cir Brandon (39047) *(G-454)*

Sir Speedy Printing Center 601 981-3045
2701 N State St Jackson (39216) *(G-2583)*

Sircle Laboratories LLC 601 897-4474
276 Nissan Pkwy Canton (39046) *(G-677)*

Sisters of Creations 662 615-3978
102 Green Hill Dr Starkville (39759) *(G-4971)*

Sisters Scents 901 283-9867
13191 Fairview Rd Byhalia (38611) *(G-603)*

Sistrunk Sheet Metal 601 825-5999
121 Pole Bridge Dr Brandon (39042) *(G-455)*

(PA)=Parent Co (HQ)=Headquarters (DH)=Div Headquarters

2019 Harris Directory of
Mississippi Manufacturers

SJ Ellington Inc

SJ Ellington Inc 228 369-0089
   5604 Belle Vale Dr Ocean Springs (39565) *(G-3786)*

Skillem Entrepises Inc 601 936-4461
   5020 Highway 80 E Ste D Pearl (39208) *(G-4146)*

Skin Sake LLC 870 853-5544
   2187 Highway 51 Madison (39110) *(G-3147)*

Skygolf, Ridgeland *Also called Skyhawke Technologies LLC (G-4630)*

Skyhawk LLC 601 619-6805
   1661 N Frontage Rd Vicksburg (39180) *(G-5419)*

Skyhawke Technologies LLC 601 605-6100
   274 Commerce Park Dr Ridgeland (39157) *(G-4630)*

Skylar Laboratories LLC 601 855-7678
   276 Nissan Pkwy Bldg A Canton (39046) *(G-678)*

Slate Springs Glove Company 662 637-2222
   148 Vance St Calhoun City (38916) *(G-644)*

Slaters Jigs Inc 662 887-3548
   185 Beaverdam Rd Indianola (38751) *(G-2270)*

Slaters Quality Outdoor Pdts, Indianola *Also called Slaters Jigs Inc (G-2270)*

Slay Steel Inc 601 483-3911
   6215 5th St Meridian (39307) *(G-3398)*

Sleep Innovations, Baldwyn *Also called Innocor East LLC (G-79)*

Sleeper Kraft LLC 662 620-9797
   131 Cedar St Plantersville (38862) *(G-4315)*

Sleepmadecom LLC (PA) 662 386-2222
   179 Tradewinds Dr Columbus (39705) *(G-1027)*

Slide Rule LLC 228 863-8583
   139 Bayou Cir Gulfport (39507) *(G-1872)*

Slip Protector, The, Gulfport *Also called Rjb Enterprise Inc (G-1863)*

Sly Inc 662 263-8234
   4526 Reed Rd Mathiston (39752) *(G-3231)*

Smallberry Mfg Co 601 847-3692
   125 Rosebud Trl Mendenhall (39114) *(G-3290)*

Smart Snacks LLC 228 239-6507
   8724 Live Oak Ave Ocean Springs (39564) *(G-3787)*

Smart Source 601 707-1150
   356 Highway 51 Ridgeland (39157) *(G-4631)*

Smart Synch 601 420-9959
   3010 Lakeland Cv Ste S Flowood (39232) *(G-1397)*

Smith & Associates Inc 228 864-2786
   207 Mcguire Dr Long Beach (39560) *(G-2953)*

Smith Boys Timber Inc 601 859-1628
   464 Covington Dr Canton (39046) *(G-679)*

Smith Brothers Forest Products 601 648-2892
   110 Carrson Rd Buckatunna (39322) *(G-565)*

Smith Brothers Logging Inc 601 322-7362
   5769 Highway 33 S Roxie (39661) *(G-4694)*

Smith Cabinet Shop Inc (PA) 662 287-2151
   1505 S Fulton Dr Corinth (38834) *(G-1119)*

Smith Chemical Company 901 849-4074
   9821 Bethel Rd Olive Branch (38654) *(G-3911)*

Smith Gravel and Trucking LLC 228 518-0766
   5564 Highway 53 Poplarville (39470) *(G-4394)*

Smith Machine & Iron Inc 662 375-8551
   2479 Hwy 49 E Sumner (38957) *(G-5032)*

Smith Mobile Home Company 662 566-7998
   2703 S Gloster St Tupelo (38801) *(G-5224)*

Smith Mobile Welding LLC 601 695-4640
   718 Watts Ln Nw Brookhaven (39601) *(G-532)*

Smith Printing & Off Sup Inc (PA) 601 442-2441
   294 1/2 Sgt Prentiss Dr Natchez (39120) *(G-3621)*

Smith S Bakery, Hattiesburg *Also called Bimbo Bakeries Usa Inc (G-1931)*

Smith Speed Shop, Purvis *Also called Smiths Speed Shop (G-4452)*

Smith Sr William Shayne 901 832-1998
   2807 Oliver Cv Southaven (38672) *(G-4903)*

Smith Tie and Timber LLC 662 258-7605
   14020 Ms Highway 9 Eupora (39744) *(G-1292)*

Smith Timber Inc 601 833-3968
   1511 Friendship Ln Nw Brookhaven (39601) *(G-533)*

Smith Tooling 662 234-1139
   941 Highway 7 N Abbeville (38601) *(G-4)*

Smith Transportation Eqp Inc 662 838-4486
   9045 Highway 178 Byhalia (38611) *(G-604)*

Smiths Machine & Wldg Co Inc 601 833-8787
   1423 Union Street Ext Ne Brookhaven (39601) *(G-534)*

Smiths Medical Asd Inc 662 895-8000
   9124 Polk Ln Ste 101 Olive Branch (38654) *(G-3912)*

Smiths Mobile Welding 901 626-1616
   828 Parham Cir Southaven (38671) *(G-4904)*

Smiths Speed Shop 601 794-2855
   1185 Rckhill To Brklyn Rd Purvis (39475) *(G-4452)*

Smithtrans, Byhalia *Also called Smith Transportation Eqp Inc (G-604)*

Smocking Bird Clothing LLC 662 453-6432
   1705 Highway 82 W Greenwood (38930) *(G-1652)*

Smokehouse Meats 662 489-5764
   426 Highway 41 Pontotoc (38863) *(G-4362)*

Smokers Express 601 483-5789
   804 Holland Ave Philadelphia (39350) *(G-4236)*

Smooth Transitions LLC 601 493-3787
   213 Mcginty St Ste 2247 Fayette (39069) *(G-1302)*

SMS Embroidery 601 635-2347
   891 Decatur Stratton Rd Decatur (39327) *(G-1179)*

Smw Manufacturing 517 596-3300
   36 County Road 166 Oxford (38655) *(G-4003)*

Smyda Woodworking Inc 601 591-0247
   154 Indian Mound Rdg Brandon (39042) *(G-456)*

Snap-It-Wreaths 228 596-0387
   12458 Crestwood Dr Gulfport (39503) *(G-1873)*

Snapshot Publishing LLC 601 624-8845
   3900 Lakeland Dr Ste 202 Flowood (39232) *(G-1398)*

Sneaker Addict Clothing 601 212-3205
   6468 Homewood Cir Jackson (39213) *(G-2584)*

Snells Concrete Tanks 601 845-1881
   180 Joe Dear Rd Harrisville (39082) *(G-1912)*

So Nuts and Confections LLC 901 398-9650
   6001 Highway 51 N Ste 3 Horn Lake (38637) *(G-2211)*

Soap & Stuff LLC 228 875-1721
   611 Pine Hills Rd Ocean Springs (39564) *(G-3788)*

Socrates Garrett Entps Inc 601 896-0084
   2659 Livingston Rd Jackson (39213) *(G-2585)*

Sojourner Timber Inc 601 892-4021
   2126 Sandy Yarn Rd Crystal Springs (39059) *(G-1156)*

Sokhom To 601 684-3300
   912 Delaware Ave McComb (39648) *(G-3267)*

Solaplast LLC 877 972-5449
   5168 Water Tower Rd Meridian (39301) *(G-3399)*

Solen Inc 601 833-0403
   1706 Highway 84 E Brookhaven (39601) *(G-535)*

Solomon Energy LLC 601 607-3070
   132 Adderley Blvd Madison (39110) *(G-3148)*

Solus Rx LLC 228 365-4501
   4063 Ginger Dr Ste E Diberville (39540) *(G-1213)*

Solvay Spclty Polymers USA LLC 228 533-0238
   13233 Webre Rd Bay Saint Louis (39520) *(G-156)*

Somefa LLC 601 506-1808
   2521 Harriotte Ave Jackson (39209) *(G-2586)*

Son Light Candles and More LLC 228 263-1661
   16037 Crestview Dr Gulfport (39503) *(G-1874)*

Sonic of Fulton 662 862-3000
   1620 S Adams St Fulton (38843) *(G-1474)*

Sonny Moore 662 585-4009
   13510 John Rankin Hwy Fulton (38843) *(G-1475)*

Sonnyboys Garment Printing LLC 601 415-2250
   3545 Rainey Rd Jackson (39212) *(G-2587)*

Sonoco Products Company 662 615-6204
   1025 Lynn Ln Starkville (39759) *(G-4972)*

Sonoco Prtective Solutions Inc 662 842-1043
   2612 President Ave Tupelo (38801) *(G-5225)*

Soperma USA Inc 228 701-1900
   12251 Seaway Rd Gulfport (39503) *(G-1875)*

Sophisticated Fabrications LLC 228 424-8346
   15553 Village Cir Biloxi (39532) *(G-280)*

Soprema, Gulfport *Also called Soperma USA Inc (G-1875)*

Sorg Printing LLC 228 392-3299
   10361 Auto Mall Pkwy Diberville (39540) *(G-1214)*

Soupbone Industries LLC 601 520-1317
   10 Melody Ln Purvis (39475) *(G-4453)*

Source 601 949-7878
   3645 Metro Dr Jackson (39209) *(G-2588)*

South Carlton Operating Co LLC 601 446-5992
   11179 St Natchez (39120) *(G-3622)*

South Center Printing 662 252-2793
   157 S Center St Holly Springs (38635) *(G-2191)*

South Central Group Inc 601 445-5101
   1124 Lower Woodville Rd Natchez (39120) *(G-3623)*

South Central Polymers Inc 662 728-9506
   535 Highway 145 N Booneville (38829) *(G-345)*

South Central Ready Mix, Jackson *Also called Delta Industries Inc (G-2380)*

South Central Ready Mix, Prentiss *Also called Delta Industries Inc (G-4416)*

South Coast Architectural, Moss Point *Also called Southern Cabinet & Woodwork (G-3499)*

South Coast Electric LLC 228 533-0002
   13061 Road D Bay St Louis (39520) *(G-182)*

South Coast Paddling Company (PA) 228 818-9442
   614 Magnolia Ave Ocean Springs (39564) *(G-3789)*

South Fork Logging LLC 601 218-4524
   6624 Warriors Trl Vicksburg (39180) *(G-5420)*

South Memphis Fence Co 662 526-5400
   307 Warren St Como (38619) *(G-1051)*

South Reporter Inc 662 252-4261
   157 S Center St Holly Springs (38635) *(G-2192)*

South Trucking, Fulton *Also called Clarence South Logging (G-1450)*

South Txas Lghthouse For Blind 601 679-3180
   224 Allen Rd Meridian (39309) *(G-3400)*

Southaven Raceway 662 393-9945
   580 Stateline Rd W Southaven (38671) *(G-4905)*

Southeast Miss Schl Pdts Co, Caledonia *Also called Southeast Miss Schl Pdts Inc (G-631)*

Southeast Miss Schl Pdts Inc 662 855-5048
   151 Gin Site Rd Ste B Caledonia (39740) *(G-631)*

Southeast Ready Mix Inc 601 735-4823
   3594 Highway 145 S Waynesboro (39367) *(G-5515)*

ALPHABETIC SECTION

Southern Tooling & Mch Works

Southeast Supply Header 601 947-9842
1154 Pete Miles Rd Lucedale (39452) **(G-3017)**

Southeastern Bulk Bag, Clarksdale *Also called Bag Connection LLC* **(G-758)**

Southeastern Concrete Co Inc (PA) 601 544-7000
105 Industrial Blvd Hattiesburg (39401) **(G-2057)**

Southeastern Concrete Co Inc 601 545-7811
2611 Lakeview Rd Hattiesburg (39401) **(G-2058)**

Southeastern Concrete Co Inc 601 544-7000
105 Industrial Blvd Hattiesburg (39401) **(G-2059)**

Southeastern Constructors Inc 601 825-9791
1148 Shiloh Rd Brandon (39042) **(G-457)**

Southeastern E & P Svcs Inc 601 849-9218
148 Clovis Jones Rd Magee (39111) **(G-3186)**

Southeastern Forest Produ 601 988-1131
502 Shalom Way Flowood (39232) **(G-1399)**

Southeastern Oilfield Pdts LLC 601 428-0603
1250 Ellisville Blvd Laurel (39440) **(G-2851)**

Southeastern Sample Company 662 282-4063
2710 Highway 371 N Mantachie (38855) **(G-3205)**

Southeastern Sign Company Inc 601 391-0023
120 Lone Wolf Dr Madison (39110) **(G-3149)**

Southeastern Timber Pdts LLC 662 285-3291
240 Pca Rd Ackerman (39735) **(G-29)**

Southern Advocate, Ashland *Also called Southern Sintinel Inc* **(G-65)**

Southern Application MGT 662 578-4684
21129 Highway 6 E Batesville (38606) **(G-125)**

Southern Band Saw Co Inc 662 332-4008
1309 Thornton St Greenville (38703) **(G-1600)**

Southern Bandsaw Company, Greenville *Also called Southern Band Saw Co Inc* **(G-1600)**

Southern Bell Clothing 662 258-2955
2860 E Roane Ave Eupora (39744) **(G-1293)**

Southern Belle 662 637-2264
2310 Sunset Dr Grenada (38901) **(G-1703)**

Southern Belle Tresses LLC 470 645-1777
426 Saddle Creek Dr Oxford (38655) **(G-4004)**

Southern Blle Sweet Dsigns LLC 901 598-7938
917 Cloverleaf Dr Southaven (38671) **(G-4906)**

Southern Cabinet & Woodwork 228 475-0912
6312 Shortcut Rd Moss Point (39563) **(G-3499)**

Southern Cabinets 901 461-6161
7879 Highway 178 Byhalia (38611) **(G-605)**

Southern Cabinets & Millwork 662 447-3885
106 N Gatlin St Okolona (38860) **(G-3799)**

Southern Canvas 601 951-6266
130 Belle Oak Dr Brandon (39042) **(G-458)**

Southern Carburetor 601 400-3716
5587 Robinson Road Ext Jackson (39204) **(G-2589)**

Southern Cast Products Inc 601 482-8518
1010 Wile Rd Meridian (39301) **(G-3401)**

Southern Charm Cstm Cbntry LLC 662 862-5058
261 Wilson Rd N Fulton (38843) **(G-1476)**

Southern Circuits & Components, De Kalb *Also called E M F Corp* **(G-1163)**

Southern Components Inc 662 844-7884
114 Old Runway Rd Tupelo (38801) **(G-5226)**

Southern Craftsmen Inc 601 484-5757
1193 Bonita Lakes Cir Meridian (39301) **(G-3402)**

Southern Design Finds 662 893-4303
631 Desoto Rd Byhalia (38611) **(G-606)**

Southern Discount Drugs of Cha (PA) 662 647-5172
1068 Factory Dr Charleston (38921) **(G-743)**

Southern Diversified Inds Inc 662 365-6720
1154 N 2nd St Baldwyn (38824) **(G-87)**

Southern Diversified Inds Inc 662 365-8800
1154 N 2nd St Baldwyn (38824) **(G-88)**

Southern Diversified Products 601 271-2588
2712 Hardy St Hattiesburg (39401) **(G-2060)**

Southern Division, Pearl *Also called Helmerich & Payne Intl Drlg Co* **(G-4126)**

Southern Door & Hardware, Madison *Also called Cox Hardware LLC* **(G-3090)**

Southern Electric Works Inc (PA) 601 833-8323
1557 Highway 51 Ne Brookhaven (39601) **(G-536)**

Southern Exteriors Fence Co 228 586-2110
31023 Crane Creek Rd Perkinston (39573) **(G-4181)**

Southern Fabricators, Collinsville *Also called Southern Gate Twr Fabricators* **(G-876)**

Southern Fabricators LLC 601 824-8855
980 Burnham Rd Brandon (39042) **(G-459)**

Southern Fastener Co Miss 662 335-2157
368 Air Field Rd At Arprt Greenville (38703) **(G-1601)**

Southern Fasteners, Greenville *Also called Southern Fastener Co Miss* **(G-1601)**

Southern Fiberglass Inc 601 876-2111
194 Cemetery Rd Tylertown (39667) **(G-5285)**

Southern Fibers Inc 662 568-3456
923 Highway 32 E Houlka (38850) **(G-2228)**

Southern Flow 601 591-1526
307a E Government St Brandon (39042) **(G-460)**

Southern Forestry Inc 662 416-3883
167 Main St Golden (38847) **(G-1530)**

Southern Fur Design 601 936-2005
3010 Lakeland Cv Ste V Flowood (39232) **(G-1400)**

Southern Gate Twr Fabricators 601 483-6710
3903 Highland Park Dr Collinsville (39325) **(G-876)**

Southern Graphics Inc 601 833-7448
400 Brookhaven St Brookhaven (39601) **(G-537)**

Southern Hens Inc 601 582-2262
327 Moselle Seminary Rd Moselle (39459) **(G-3460)**

Southern Hose & Hydraulics 601 922-9990
4958 Highway 80 W Jackson (39209) **(G-2590)**

Southern Images Printing Inc 601 649-3501
121 N 15th Ave Laurel (39440) **(G-2852)**

Southern Industrial Tech LLC 601 426-3866
25 County Road 17 Stringer (39481) **(G-5004)**

Southern Ionics Incorporated (PA) 662 494-3055
579 Commerce St West Point (39773) **(G-5563)**

Southern Ionics Incorporated 662 495-2583
506 W Broad St West Point (39773) **(G-5564)**

Southern Ionics Incorporated 662 328-0516
1825 Post Access Rd Columbus (39701) **(G-1028)**

Southern Kernels 601 336-9080
560 Weathersby Rd Hattiesburg (39402) **(G-2061)**

Southern Land Exploration Inc 662 369-7390
20671 Old Magnolia Hwy Prairie (39756) **(G-4413)**

Southern Land Solutions LLC 601 622-8581
1203 Crisler Rd Terry (39170) **(G-5077)**

Southern Logging Inc 601 657-4449
5411 Ms Highway 567 Liberty (39645) **(G-2917)**

Southern Lure Company Inc 662 327-4548
201a N Browder St Columbus (39702) **(G-1029)**

Southern Machining LLC 662 229-0026
23074 Highway 8 E Grenada (38901) **(G-1704)**

Southern Marketing Group 601 664-3880
199 Interstate Dr Ste F Jackson (39218) **(G-2667)**

Southern Metals Co Miss Inc 601 649-7475
144 Don Curt Rd Laurel (39440) **(G-2853)**

Southern Motion Inc 662 488-9301
298 Henry Southern Dr Pontotoc (38863) **(G-4363)**

Southern Oil Company 601 582-5455
501 N Main St Hattiesburg (39401) **(G-2062)**

Southern Petroleum Labs Inc 601 428-0842
1961 Bush Dairy Rd Laurel (39443) **(G-2854)**

Southern Pharmaceutical Corp 601 939-2525
5905 Old Brandon Rd # 10 Pearl (39208) **(G-4147)**

Southern Pharmaceutical Corp 662 844-5858
444 E President Ave Tupelo (38801) **(G-5227)**

Southern Print Company 601 898-8796
130 Langdon Dr Madison (39110) **(G-3150)**

Southern Prohibition Brewing 601 467-1057
2056 Oak Grove Rd Hattiesburg (39402) **(G-2063)**

Southern Prosthetic Care LLC 769 242-2555
4201 Highway 11 N Ste D Picayune (39466) **(G-4296)**

Southern Prtg & Silk Screening 228 452-7309
230 Davis Ave Pass Christian (39571) **(G-4095)**

Southern Roost Game Calls 601 441-0748
3007 Highway 13 N Columbia (39429) **(G-922)**

Southern Rubber Stamp Inc 601 373-6590
121 Eltonwoods East Dr Jackson (39212) **(G-2591)**

Southern Rustic Logwerks LLC 662 315-9677
313 Highway 278 W Amory (38821) **(G-54)**

Southern Sales and Service, Ellisville *Also called Watkins* **(G-1277)**

Southern Scents By Carla LLC 662 312-5610
41 Augusta Dr Starkville (39759) **(G-4973)**

Southern Scrap Meridian LLC 601 693-5323
75 Highway 19 N Meridian (39307) **(G-3403)**

Southern Sentinel, Ripley *Also called Southern Sintinel Inc* **(G-4672)**

Southern Sewage Systems 228 832-7400
23018 Highway 49 Saucier (39574) **(G-4766)**

Southern Signs, Gautier *Also called Ocean Springs Sign & Graphics* **(G-1500)**

Southern Signs 228 255-4122
13117 C Necaise Rd Pass Christian (39571) **(G-4096)**

Southern Signs Inc 601 445-5564
406 Liberty Rd Natchez (39120) **(G-3624)**

Southern Sintinel Inc (PA) 662 837-8111
1701 City Ave N Ripley (38663) **(G-4672)**

Southern Sintinel Inc 662 224-6681
114 Church Ave Ashland (38603) **(G-65)**

Southern Speed 662 842-3799
2028 Mccullough Blvd Tupelo (38801) **(G-5228)**

Southern States Bee Supply LLC 601 513-5151
109 Back St Taylorsville (39168) **(G-5059)**

Southern Sttch Canvas Uphl LLC 228 234-2515
14335 Creosote Rd Gulfport (39503) **(G-1876)**

Southern Systems & Service Co 601 264-4713
171 W Hills Dr Hattiesburg (39402) **(G-2064)**

Southern Technical Aquatic RES 601 590-6248
67 Hayes Rd Carriere (39426) **(G-701)**

Southern Tees Plus 601 896-7468
110 Aponaug Rd Kosciusko (39090) **(G-2712)**

Southern Timber Venture, Jackson *Also called Van Petroleum Inc* **(G-2620)**

Southern Tooling & Mch Works 662 256-7633
1421 Highway 25 S Amory (38821) **(G-55)**

A
L
P
H
A
B
E
T
I
C

(PA)=Parent Co (HQ)=Headquarters (DH)=Div Headquarters

2019 Harris Directory of
Mississippi Manufacturers

319

Southern Tooling and Mch Works, Amory *Also called Southern Tooling & Mch Works* **(G-55)**

Southern Touch Soap Works Inc 601 825-2676
115 Tiffany Dr Brandon (39042) **(G-461)**

Southern Traditions 662 534-0410
120 W Bankhead St New Albany (38652) **(G-3698)**

Southern WD Prsv Httesburg Inc 601 544-1140
627 Hood Rd Hattiesburg (39401) **(G-2065)**

Southern-Its Corporation 228 273-2585
624 Cypress Dr Diberville (39540) **(G-1215)**

Southland Container Inc 601 879-8816
493 Livingston Vernon Rd Flora (39071) **(G-1312)**

Southland Log Homes 601 605-4900
421 Business Park Dr Madison (39110) **(G-3151)**

Southland Oil Company 601 796-2331
7539 U S Highway 11 Lumberton (39455) **(G-3038)**

Southland Oil Company (HQ) 601 981-4151
5170 Galaxie Dr Jackson (39206) **(G-2592)**

Southland Oil Company 601 634-1361
2600 Dorsey St Vicksburg (39180) **(G-5421)**

Southland Supplies 662 647-2452
2167 Pressgrove Rd Cascilla (38920) **(G-729)**

Southstern Foam Fbrication LLC 601 540-8880
141 Township Ave Ste 305 Ridgeland (39157) **(G-4632)**

Southwark Metal Mfg Co 662 342-7805
8680 Stanton Rd Southaven (38671) **(G-4907)**

Southwest Mississippi Robotics 601 276-4276
1062 Golf Ln Summit (39666) **(G-5022)**

Southwest Publishers Inc 601 833-6961
128 N Railroad Ave Brookhaven (39601) **(G-538)**

Southwest Ready Mix Concrete, Summit *Also called Danny Berry* **(G-5010)**

Southwire Company LLC 662 324-6600
103 Airport Rd Starkville (39759) **(G-4974)**

Spain Incorporated 662 843-1301
470 Gaines Hwy Boyle (38730) **(G-352)**

Sparkles & Such 601 750-1270
510 Lee Ave Crystal Springs (39059) **(G-1157)**

Sparko Inc (PA) 662 690-5800
868 Mississippi Dr Tupelo (38804) **(G-5229)**

Sparks Printing & Graphics 662 842-4481
529 Road 1460 Tupelo (38804) **(G-5230)**

Sparks Welding Service 601 519-9573
5658 Highway 18 Brandon (39042) **(G-462)**

Spearman Ornamental Ironworks 901 301-7061
4234 Highgate Dr Horn Lake (38637) **(G-2212)**

Special TS 662 563-5138
1883 John Branch Rd Batesville (38606) **(G-126)**

Specialtees Etc 601 683-2552
108 Doolittle St Newton (39345) **(G-3728)**

Specialty Hose Fabrication Inc 228 831-1919
13309 Three Rivers Rd Gulfport (39503) **(G-1877)**

Specialty Lamps, Meridian *Also called Lighting Investment Group Inc* **(G-3360)**

Specialty Machine Works Inc 228 832-7123
11573 Three Rivers Rd Gulfport (39503) **(G-1878)**

Specialty Process Fabricators, Vicksburg *Also called Ergon Inc* **(G-5367)**

Specialty Roll Products Inc 601 693-1771
601 25th Ave Meridian (39301) **(G-3404)**

Specialty Services Group LLC 601 543-9474
71 Fillingane Rd Sumrall (39482) **(G-5045)**

Spectacles Inc 601 398-4662
120 District Blvd D109 Jackson (39211) **(G-2593)**

Spectech Service & Signs LLC 601 482-0816
202 Highway 19 N Meridian (39307) **(G-3405)**

Spectrum III Limited 662 234-2461
108 Sivley St Oxford (38655) **(G-4005)**

Speed Box LLC 910 964-7947
375 Whippoorwill Ln Ridgeland (39157) **(G-4633)**

Speediprint, Vicksburg *Also called Vicksburg Printing and Pubg Co* **(G-5439)**

Speeds Welding Works 601 917-2571
2653 Russell Mt Gilead Rd Meridian (39301) **(G-3406)**

Speedy Printing 228 466-5766
304 Highway 90 Ste D Waveland (39576) **(G-5485)**

Speedy Printing & Signs, Hattiesburg *Also called W T Leggett Inc* **(G-2081)**

Speights W Repair, Braxton *Also called Donald Speights Jr* **(G-477)**

Spencer Ready-Mix Jackson Inc 601 981-6080
9161 Highway 49 N Jackson (39209) **(G-2594)**

Spic-N-Span Crew LLC 601 248-2090
1019 Little Rock Ln McComb (39648) **(G-3268)**

Spider Blue Press LLC 601 770-0846
116 Milton Murrah Rd Lucedale (39452) **(G-3018)**

Spinal Usa Inc (PA) 601 420-4244
2050 Executive Dr Pearl (39208) **(G-4148)**

Spine Stability Surgical LLC 800 991-3723
2510 Lakeland Ter Ste 400 Jackson (39216) **(G-2595)**

Spiral Fab Inc 662 862-7999
606 S Spring St Fulton (38843) **(G-1477)**

Spiral Systems Inc (PA) 662 429-0373
860 Old Highway 51 N Nesbit (38651) **(G-3657)**

Spiral Systems Inc 901 521-8373
1700 Highway 51 S Hernando (38632) **(G-2155)**

Spirit Enterprises 662 236-2667
1296 N Lamar Blvd Oxford (38655) **(G-4006)**

Spirit Lifters Scented Candles 210 802-0149
248 Debuys Rd Apt 148 Biloxi (39531) **(G-281)**

Split Ends 601 619-0088
3412 Pemberton Square Blv Vicksburg (39180) **(G-5422)**

Spooner Petroleum Inc 601 969-1831
154 Meadowlark Ln Ridgeland (39157) **(G-4634)**

Spoonfudge Shoppe LLC (PA) 601 685-2000
113 S Main St Newton (39345) **(G-3729)**

Sport Trial 228 467-1885
5232 Highway 90 Bay Saint Louis (39520) **(G-157)**

Sportman Camo Covers Inc 662 489-7074
6564 Highway 15 N Ecru (38841) **(G-1233)**

Sports of All Sorts Inc 662 429-1162
345 E Commerce St Hernando (38632) **(G-2156)**

Sports Zone, Booneville *Also called Bo Enterprises Inc* **(G-320)**

Sports Zone 2, Meridian *Also called Bo Enterprises Inc* **(G-3311)**

Sportz Zone LLC 228 284-1654
100 Jeff Davis Ave Long Beach (39560) **(G-2954)**

Spot Cash Tire and Appliance (PA) 662 289-2611
140 Highway 12 W Kosciusko (39090) **(G-2713)**

Springer Dry Goods 662 263-8144
Hwy 15 N Maben (39750) **(G-3051)**

Springer Trckg & Car Crushing 601 649-4238
1500 Highway 84 E Laurel (39443) **(G-2855)**

Sprint Print, Tupelo *Also called Harden Enterprises Inc* **(G-5152)**

Sprint Print of Tupelo, Tupelo *Also called Harden Enterprises Inc* **(G-5151)**

Sqm North America Corporation 601 969-4710
1325 Boling St Jackson (39209) **(G-2596)**

Squelchfire Inc 601 434-2048
46 Shelby Thames Dr Hattiesburg (39402) **(G-2066)**

Sqwincher Activity Drink, Columbus *Also called Sqwincher Corporation* **(G-1030)**

Sqwincher Corporation 662 328-0400
1409 Highway 45 S Columbus (39701) **(G-1030)**

Ss Drilling LLC 740 207-5673
207 Pecan Blvd Brandon (39042) **(G-463)**

St Catherine Gravel Co Inc 601 442-1674
879 Hwy 61 N Washington (39190) **(G-5462)**

St Catherine Ready Mix Inc (PA) 601 445-8891
319 Lower Woodville Rd Natchez (39120) **(G-3625)**

St Engineer Halter Marine and 228 762-0010
601 Bayou Casotte Pkwy Pascagoula (39581) **(G-4068)**

St James Lighting LLC 601 444-4966
1491 Highway 13 N Columbia (39429) **(G-923)**

St Tammany Box Company 601 799-0775
205 Street A Picayune (39466) **(G-4297)**

Sta-Put-Hook LLC 601 622-7313
204 Belle Pointe Madison (39110) **(G-3152)**

Staco Decorative Iron 601 264-0064
5243 Old Highway 11 Hattiesburg (39402) **(G-2067)**

Staco Manufacturing Co, Hattiesburg *Also called Richard H Bowers* **(G-2051)**

Stacy Furniture, Pontotoc *Also called S & S Manufacturers Inc* **(G-4361)**

Stacy Robinson 662 289-4640
3077 Attala Road 1154 Kosciusko (39090) **(G-2714)**

Stained Glassworks Inc 662 329-2970
3067 Old West Point Rd Columbus (39701) **(G-1031)**

Stair Depot of Ms 334 467-5584
9465 Creosote Rd Bldg 30 Gulfport (39503) **(G-1879)**

Stakes Unlimited, Ripley *Also called Jeffrey Roberson* **(G-4662)**

Stamm Advertising Co Inc (PA) 601 636-7749
3400 Drummond St Vicksburg (39180) **(G-5423)**

Stamm Advertising Co Inc 601 922-3400
120 Upton Dr Jackson (39209) **(G-2597)**

Standard Dynamics LLC 228 383-2070
822 Taylor St Starkville (39760) **(G-4975)**

Standard Gravel Co Inc 601 584-6436
2094 Glendale Ave Hattiesburg (39401) **(G-2068)**

Standard Industrial Corp 662 624-2436
1410 Industrial Park Dr Clarksdale (38614) **(G-783)**

Standard Office Sup Prtg Inc 601 544-5361
400 W Pine St Hattiesburg (39401) **(G-2069)**

Standex Food Service Group, New Albany *Also called Standex International Corp* **(G-3699)**

Standex International Corp 662 534-9061
908 Highway 15 N New Albany (38652) **(G-3699)**

Standex International Corp 662 534-9061
908 State Highway 15 N New Albany (38652) **(G-3700)**

Standex International Corp 662 534-9061
Hwy 15 Bldg 2900 New Albany (38652) **(G-3701)**

Stanley Appraisal Company LLC 662 287-8543
504 N Cass St Apt 4 Corinth (38834) **(G-1120)**

Stanley Black & Decker Inc 662 844-7191
1141 Ryder St Tupelo (38804) **(G-5231)**

Stanley D Stokes Jr 662 237-6600
6796 County Road 100 Carrollton (38917) **(G-703)**

Stanley Home Decor, Tupelo *Also called Home Decor Company* **(G-5157)**

Stanley Logging, Shubuta *Also called Carey F Stanley* **(G-4828)**

Stanley McCaffrey Signs 228 832-0885
15254 Dedeaux Rd Gulfport (39503) **(G-1880)**

ALPHABETIC SECTION

Sunbelt Resources Inc

Stanley McCaffrey Signs (PA) 228 832-0885
231 Bradford Dr Richland (39218) *(G-4525)*

Star Herald 662 289-2251
207 N Madison St Kosciusko (39090) *(G-2715)*

Star Printing Co of Amory Inc 662 256-8424
1223 Highway 278 E Amory (38821) *(G-56)*

Stark Aerospace Inc (HQ) 662 798-4075
319 Charleigh Ford Jr Rd Columbus (39701) *(G-1032)*

Starkville Daily News, Starkville Also called Horizon Publications Inc *(G-4950)*

Starr, Carriere Also called Southern Technical Aquatic RES *(G-701)*

Status Leather, Corinth Also called Corinthian Inc *(G-1079)*

Staybrite Signs 901 490-0431
819 Autumn Woods Cv Southaven (38671) *(G-4908)*

Steel Dynamics Columbus LLC (HQ) 662 245-4200
1945 Airport Rd Columbus (39701) *(G-1033)*

Steel Service Corporation 601 939-9222
2260 Flowood Dr Jackson (39232) *(G-2668)*

Steel Specialties Miss Inc 601 939-2690
111 Midco Rd Pearl (39208) *(G-4149)*

Steel Technologies LLC 601 855-7242
576 Church Rd Madison (39110) *(G-3153)*

Steelpro LLC 662 456-3004
120 Wright Rd Houston (38851) *(G-2254)*

Steelsummit Holdings LLC 601 638-1819
901 Haining Rd Vicksburg (39183) *(G-5424)*

Steelsummit Mississippi, Vicksburg Also called Vicksmetal Corporation *(G-5442)*

Steiner Plastics Inc 662 895-7350
8805 Cypress Woods Ln Olive Branch (38654) *(G-3913)*

Stephens Printing LLC 601 845-7708
642 Highway 469 S Florence (39073) *(G-1333)*

Stephens-Adamson Division, Clarksdale Also called Metso Minerals Industries Inc *(G-774)*

Sterling Custom Cabinets LLC 601 996-1906
1131 Bennie Cassels Rd Gloster (39638) *(G-1518)*

Sterlng-Knght Phrmcuticals LLC 662 661-3232
106 E Mulberry St Ripley (38663) *(G-4673)*

Steve B White 601 939-8177
130 Shenandoah Dr Florence (39073) *(G-1334)*

Steve Hamblin Frames Inc 662 568-7299
780 County Road 408 Houlka (38850) *(G-2229)*

Steve Harris 228 769-8350
1902 Chicot St Pascagoula (39581) *(G-4069)*

Steve Schrock 662 369-6062
10111 Prairie Mills Rd Prairie (39756) *(G-4414)*

Stevens Machine & Tool Inc 662 728-6005
291 Highway 371 Marietta (38856) *(G-3218)*

Stevens Packing 601 795-6999
52 Foots Stevens Rd Poplarville (39470) *(G-4395)*

Stevens Sheet Metal & Ir Works 601 939-6943
420 Childre Rd Pearl (39208) *(G-4150)*

Stewart Sign & Screen Graphics 601 783-5377
2107 Highway 48 W McComb (39648) *(G-3269)*

Stewarts Screen Printing 601 932-8310
413 Roberts St Jackson (39208) *(G-2669)*

Stickman Logging LLC 601 782-4597
3367 Scr 540-2 Raleigh (39153) *(G-4477)*

Still Blessed Prints 601 810-8285
402 Eitel Pl Brookhaven (39601) *(G-539)*

Stinson & Son Logging 601 989-2311
Rr 1 Box 88 Richton (39476) *(G-4544)*

Stitched In Time 601 562-6715
12631 Road 759 Philadelphia (39350) *(G-4237)*

Stitches By Lee LLC 228 769-7460
903 Tucker Ave Pascagoula (39567) *(G-4070)*

Stitching and Stuff LLC 228 365-4735
4401 Beatline Rd Apt 3d Long Beach (39560) *(G-2955)*

Stockman Grass Farmer, Ridgeland Also called Mississippi Valley Publishing *(G-4607)*

Stockman Grass Farmer (PA) 601 853-1861
234 W School St Ridgeland (39157) *(G-4635)*

Stockman Grass Farmers, Ridgeland Also called Stockman Grass Farmer *(G-4635)*

Stockmans Supply LLC 601 750-2726
13545 Ms Highway 12 W Starkville (39759) *(G-4976)*

Stockstill Bros Invstments LLC 601 798-2981
130 Huey Stockstill Rd Picayune (39466) *(G-4298)*

Stockstill Land Dev LLC 601 273-2409
20 Joyce Dr Poplarville (39470) *(G-4396)*

Stone Associates Inc 662 838-4671
89 Edwards Rd Byhalia (38611) *(G-607)*

Stone County Enterprises Inc 601 928-4802
143 First St S Wiggins (39577) *(G-5589)*

Stone Perfection 662 895-4442
8822 Cypress Woods Ln Olive Branch (38654) *(G-3914)*

Stone Printing Inc 601 928-7050
2919 Highway 26 Wiggins (39577) *(G-5590)*

Stone Treated Materials 601 798-4422
403 Davis St Picayune (39466) *(G-4299)*

Storagetek, Jackson Also called Oracle America Inc *(G-2530)*

Stormcom LLC 601 918-5401
1230 Raymond Rd Jackson (39204) *(G-2598)*

Storsoft Technology Corp 954 436-9292
1910 31st Ave Gulfport (39501) *(G-1881)*

Stout Woodworks Inc 601 795-0727
59 Castleberry Dr Poplarville (39470) *(G-4397)*

Straughter Cabinets 662 247-2728
107 Van Buren St Belzoni (39038) *(G-206)*

Strayhorn Trucking & Cnstr LLC 662 560-6516
1250 Matthews Rd Sarah (38665) *(G-4736)*

Stribling Printing 601 656-4194
409 Center Ave N Philadelphia (39350) *(G-4238)*

Stringer Randal 228 623-0037
7402 Frank Griffin Rd Moss Point (39563) *(G-3500)*

Stringer Gun Works LLC 601 947-6796
18117 Highway 98 Lucedale (39452) *(G-3019)*

Stringer Industries Inc (PA) 601 876-3376
11 Highway 48 E Tylertown (39667) *(G-5286)*

Stringer Woodworks 601 372-5725
6795 Springridge Rd Raymond (39154) *(G-4493)*

Stringers Oilfield Service 601 736-4498
1320 Highway 13 N Columbia (39429) *(G-924)*

Strong Bros Logging Inc 601 764-9191
100 County Road 182a2 Bay Springs (39422) *(G-173)*

Structural Steel Holding Inc 601 485-1503
1601 60th Pl S Meridian (39307) *(G-3407)*

Structural Steel Holding Inc (PA) 601 483-5381
6210 Saint Louis St Meridian (39307) *(G-3408)*

Structural Steel Services Inc (HQ) 601 482-1668
6215 Saint Louis St Meridian (39307) *(G-3409)*

Structural Steel Services Inc 601 485-2619
533 65th Ave Meridian (39307) *(G-3410)*

Stryder & Associates LLC 662 579-8703
141b Walker Rd Cleveland (38732) *(G-809)*

Stryder Associates, Cleveland Also called Stryder & Associates LLC *(G-809)*

Stryke Ryte Lures 217 370-9461
1026 County Road 358 New Albany (38652) *(G-3702)*

Stuart Chaffin 601 807-1547
1086 Fender Trl Ne Brookhaven (39601) *(G-540)*

Stuart Timber Inc 601 943-8184
510 Martin Bass Rd Carson (39427) *(G-705)*

Studio Chane, Jackson Also called Swell O Phonic *(G-2601)*

Style-Line Furn Inc 662 566-1113
116 Godfrey Rd Verona (38879) *(G-5335)*

Stylecraft Home Collection Inc 662 429-5279
8474 Market Place Dr # 104 Southaven (38671) *(G-4909)*

Stylecraft Home Collections, Southaven Also called Stylecraft Home Collection Inc *(G-4909)*

Suburban Plastics Co 662 227-1911
1000 Enterprise Dr Grenada (38901) *(G-1705)*

Sudden Service Inc 601 650-9600
103 Industrial Park Rd Philadelphia (39350) *(G-4239)*

Suds N Squares 662 827-9991
516 East Ave N Hollandale (38748) *(G-2168)*

Sugar -N- Spice Confections 901 210-6181
3645 Pembrook Dr Horn Lake (38637) *(G-2213)*

Sugar -N- Spice Delights, Horn Lake Also called Sugar -N- Spice Confections *(G-2213)*

Sullivan Industrial/Farm Maint, Greenville Also called Merle E Sullivan *(G-1572)*

Sullivan Metals Inc 662 252-5050
260 S Industrial Park Rd Holly Springs (38635) *(G-2193)*

Sullivans Custom Processing 662 773-2839
610 Sullivan Rd Preston (39354) *(G-4428)*

Summerford Enterprises Inc 662 585-3584
4494 Tucker Rd Golden (38847) *(G-1531)*

Summit Cabinet Co LLC 601 684-1639
2060 Moak Rd Summit (39666) *(G-5023)*

Summit Plastics Inc 601 276-7500
107 S Laurel St Summit (39666) *(G-5024)*

Summit Truck Group Miss LLC 662 842-3401
1007 International Dr Tupelo (38804) *(G-5232)*

Sumrall Welding 601 876-4653
980 Highway 48 E Tylertown (39667) *(G-5287)*

Sumrall Welding Service LLC 601 498-1075
157 George Boutwell Rd Ovett (39464) *(G-3933)*

Sun Herald, Gulfport Also called Gulf Publishing Company Inc *(G-1801)*

Sun Sentinel, Charleston Also called Emmerich Newspapers Inc *(G-737)*

Sun-Air Products Incorporated 662 454-9577
18 Sun Air Dr Belmont (38827) *(G-202)*

Sun-Pine Corporation Ltd 601 825-2463
340 Barfield St Canton (39046) *(G-680)*

Sun-Pine Corporation Ltd (PA) 601 825-2463
331 W Jasper St Brandon (39042) *(G-464)*

Sunbeam Products Inc 601 671-2200
224 Russell Dr Waynesboro (39367) *(G-5516)*

Sunbeam Products Inc 601 296-5000
95 Wl Runnels Industrial Hattiesburg (39401) *(G-2070)*

Sunbeam Products Inc 601 296-5000
95 Wl Runnels Industrial Hattiesburg (39401) *(G-2071)*

Sunbelt Manufacturing Company 601 977-5292
5752 Gallant Dr Jackson (39206) *(G-2599)*

Sunbelt Resources Inc 601 853-8195
700 Northlake Ave V Ridgeland (39157) *(G-4636)*

(PA)=Parent Co (HQ)=Headquarters (DH)=Div Headquarters

2019 Harris Directory of
Mississippi Manufacturers

Sunday Best

Sunday Best..662 226-2214
  10 South St Grenada (38901) *(G-1706)*

Sunland Publishing Co Inc..................................601 957-1122
  246 Briarwood Dr Ste 101 Jackson (39206) *(G-2600)*

Sunset Screen Printing.......................................601 297-2754
  827 Snset Williamsburg Rd Collins (39428) *(G-863)*

Sunshine Mills Inc...662 842-6714
  2103 S Gloster St Tupelo (38801) *(G-5233)*

Sunshine Mills Inc...662 842-6175
  2103 S Gloster St Tupelo (38801) *(G-5234)*

Super Sagless, Tupelo *Also called Leggett & Platt Incorporated (G-5176)*

Superior Asphalt Inc..601 376-3000
  5990 I 55 S Byram (39272) *(G-624)*

Superior Bedding Products of M...........................662 841-1632
  224 Poplar St Plantersville (38862) *(G-4316)*

Superior Blinds and Shutters...............................901 270-8061
  3664 New Pointe Dr S Southaven (38672) *(G-4910)*

Superior Fish Products, Macon *Also called Noxubee County Producers Inc (G-3069)*

Superior Granite & Quartz....................................662 241-5664
  341 Island Rd Columbus (39701) *(G-1034)*

Superior Manufactured Fibers (PA)......................662 844-8255
  117 Cedar St Plantersville (38862) *(G-4317)*

Superior Mat Company Inc...................................601 765-8268
  1731 Sunset Rd Collins (39428) *(G-864)*

Superior Mfg Group Inc..601 544-8119
  133 Superior Dr Moselle (39459) *(G-3461)*

Superior Mfg Group Inc..601 544-8119
  133 Superior Dr Moselle (39459) *(G-3462)*

Superior Mulch Inc..772 878-5220
  1701 Sw Macedo Blvd Soso (39480) *(G-4848)*

Superior Optical Labs Inc (PA)............................228 875-3796
  6525 Sunplex Dr Ocean Springs (39564) *(G-3790)*

Superior Pallet Company......................................601 941-6254
  106 Creekwood Dr Brandon (39047) *(G-465)*

Superior Uniform Group Inc.................................662 834-4485
  Hwy 12 Bowling Green Rd Lexington (39095) *(G-2905)*

Superior Wldg Fabrication Inc..............................601 823-5999
  800 Magee Dr Apt 211 Brookhaven (39601) *(G-541)*

Supreme Electronics Corp....................................662 453-6212
  1714 Carrollton Ave Greenwood (38930) *(G-1653)*

Supreme International LLC...................................601 638-2403
  4000 S Frontage Rd # 101 Vicksburg (39180) *(G-5425)*

Surfacetechs...601 605-1900
  188 Woods Crossing Blvd Madison (39110) *(G-3154)*

Surgisure Inc...601 985-8125
  113 Trace Rdg Clinton (39056) *(G-836)*

Suzuki of Western Mass, Oxford *Also called Blauer Manufacturing Co Inc (G-3941)*

Swain Printing & Signs...662 773-7584
  15185 Highway 397 Louisville (39339) *(G-2983)*

Swamp Donkey LLC...228 369-4927
  14508 Low Point Rd Vancleave (39565) *(G-5322)*

Swap Shop Newspaper, Picayune *Also called Wrjw 1320 AM (G-4305)*

Swatprint Screen Printing....................................662 862-3004
  107 N Gaither St Fulton (38843) *(G-1478)*

Swd Acidizing Inc...601 442-7172
  429 Lower Woodville Rd Natchez (39120) *(G-3626)*

Sweet Scents..662 425-9305
  104 Sherard Cir Columbus (39705) *(G-1035)*

Sweet Sensations-Jackson...................................601 790-7553
  534 Brookstone Dr Madison (39110) *(G-3155)*

Sweet South Embroidery......................................601 277-3371
  3179 Smyrna Rd Hazlehurst (39083) *(G-2107)*

Sweet Tee Screen Printing...................................601 757-3435
  803 Robb St Summit (39666) *(G-5025)*

Sweet Thing Apparel, Grenada *Also called Hodge Podge Screen Prtg Inc (G-1685)*

Sweet Treats and Coffee Too................................662 286-5511
  501 Cardinal Dr Corinth (38834) *(G-1121)*

Sweetees..662 404-1966
  101 Sycamore St Sardis (38666) *(G-4745)*

Sweetwater Studios Inc.......................................601 584-8035
  318 Cook Rd Moselle (39459) *(G-3463)*

Swell O Phonic..601 981-3547
  2906 N St St Ste 103 Jackson (39216) *(G-2601)*

Swirlz..662 791-7822
  109 N Spring St Tupelo (38804) *(G-5235)*

Sxp Schulz Xtruded Products LP...........................662 429-0818
  2785 Mccracken Rd Hernando (38632) *(G-2157)*

Sxp Schulz Xtruded Products LP (PA)....................662 373-4114
  1001 Schulz Blvd Robinsonville (38664) *(G-4678)*

Sycpowersports...662 301-1563
  468 Christian College Rd Senatobia (38668) *(G-4803)*

Synergy Prosthetics Center..................................601 832-4975
  2 Old River Pl Ste D Jackson (39202) *(G-2602)*

Synergy Service and Supply LLC..........................601 597-9902
  1106 Highway 61 S Natchez (39120) *(G-3627)*

Synergy Service and Supply LLC (PA)....................601 492-4000
  294 Highland Blvd Natchez (39120) *(G-3628)*

Syntron Material Handling LLC (HQ).....................662 869-5711
  2730 Highway 145 Saltillo (38866) *(G-4721)*

Syntron Mtl Hdlg Group LLC.................................662 869-5711
  2730 Highway 145 Saltillo (38866) *(G-4722)*

Systems Auto Interiors LLC..................................662 862-1360
  1 Tb Way Mantachie (38855) *(G-3206)*

Systems Electro Coating LLC................................601 407-2340
  253 Old Jackson Rd Madison (39110) *(G-3156)*

T & G Pallet Inc...662 746-4499
  1138 Rialto Rd Yazoo City (39194) *(G-5647)*

T & J Machine..601 795-0853
  689 Progress Rd Poplarville (39470) *(G-4398)*

T & L Specialty Company Inc................................662 842-8143
  300 Air Park Rd Tupelo (38801) *(G-5236)*

T & S Machine Shop Inc.......................................601 825-8627
  1396 Highway 471 Brandon (39042) *(G-466)*

T & S Precision Mfg Inc..601 825-0878
  1396 Highway 471 Brandon (39042) *(G-467)*

T & T Communications, Ellisville *Also called T & T Welding Yard Inc (G-1271)*

T & T Inc...662 840-7500
  2348 S Green St Tupelo (38801) *(G-5237)*

T & T Logging Co...601 852-4281
  1377 Askew Ln Edwards (39066) *(G-1243)*

T & T Plating, Tupelo *Also called T & T Inc (G-5237)*

T & T Welding Inc..601 477-2884
  Ellisville Tuckr Crsng Rd Ellisville (39437) *(G-1270)*

T & T Welding Service, Ellisville *Also called T & T Welding Inc (G-1270)*

T & T Welding Yard Inc..601 477-2299
  1462 Tuckers Crossing Rd Ellisville (39437) *(G-1271)*

T A Netterville Logging Inc...................................601 888-0054
  2910 Shannon Dr Sw Bogue Chitto (39629) *(G-305)*

T and S Deer Processing......................................601 727-3725
  4419 County Road 31 Rose Hill (39356) *(G-4685)*

T and W Maintenance LLC...................................901 848-2511
  902 Acorn Cv Southaven (38671) *(G-4911)*

T Enterprises Inc...601 487-1100
  2125 Tv Rd Jackson (39204) *(G-2603)*

T G C, Lexington *Also called Transfrmer Gskets Cmpnents LLC (G-2906)*

T G Ferguson Company...662 563-0806
  117 Public Sq Batesville (38606) *(G-127)*

T JS Welding...601 498-1409
  244 Victory Rd Laurel (39443) *(G-2856)*

T K Stanley Inc (PA)..601 735-2855
  4025 Highway 35 N Columbia (39429) *(G-925)*

T K Stanley Inc...601 735-2855
  6739 Highway 184 Waynesboro (39367) *(G-5517)*

T L G Logging Inc..601 225-9743
  1881 Busy Corner Rd Gloster (39638) *(G-1519)*

T O Kimbrell LLC...601 446-6099
  118 Lower Woodville Rd Natchez (39120) *(G-3629)*

T R General Welding...901 481-0425
  5790 Landau Dr Southaven (38671) *(G-4912)*

T S Car Ports..601 797-9600
  5091 Highway 49 Mount Olive (39119) *(G-3511)*

T Shirt Shop & Design Firm LLC...........................662 329-9911
  5489 Ridge Rd Columbus (39705) *(G-1036)*

T Tommys...601 833-8620
  811 Highway 51 N Brookhaven (39601) *(G-542)*

T-N-T Printing...601 630-9553
  1211 Grammar St Vicksburg (39180) *(G-5426)*

T.J. Maxx, Oxford *Also called TJX Companies Inc (G-4007)*

T/S Car Ports, Mount Olive *Also called T S Car Ports (G-3511)*

Taber Extrusions LLC...228 863-2852
  1900 34th St Gulfport (39501) *(G-1882)*

Tabler Metals Gulfport, Gulfport *Also called Taber Extrusions LLC (G-1882)*

Tackle Technologies LLC.......................................228 206-1449
  5244 A Ave Long Beach (39560) *(G-2956)*

Tailored South, Madison *Also called Landing (G-3119)*

Tallahatchie Hardwoods Inc..................................662 647-5427
  336 N Market St Charleston (38921) *(G-744)*

Tally Student Service LLC.....................................601 782-9606
  214 Mimosa Dr Raleigh (39153) *(G-4478)*

Tally Trophies & Awards, Raleigh *Also called Tally Student Service LLC (G-4478)*

Tampa Sign Co...228 474-1945
  5625 Grierson St Moss Point (39563) *(G-3501)*

Tanners Enterprise LLC..601 894-5219
  4073 Tower Rd Hazlehurst (39083) *(G-2108)*

Tapco Inc..662 841-1635
  1813 Mccullough Blvd Tupelo (38801) *(G-5238)*

Tarantos Crawfish House......................................228 392-0806
  11085 Gorenflo Rd Ste A Diberville (39540) *(G-1216)*

Target Door and Supply Inc..................................601 790-9006
  208 Industrial Dr Ridgeland (39157) *(G-4637)*

Taste Maker Foods LLC..901 274-4407
  495 Vaiden Dr Hernando (38632) *(G-2158)*

Tato-Nut Donut Shop...228 872-2076
  1114 Government St Ocean Springs (39564) *(G-3791)*

Tatum Development Corp (PA)..............................601 544-6043
  3000 W 7th St Hattiesburg (39401) *(G-2072)*

Tavares Signs..662 289-5366
  12038 Highway 12 W Kosciusko (39090) *(G-2716)*

ALPHABETIC SECTION

Taw Power System Inc......................................601 939-3455
2702 Flowood Dr Flowood (39232) *(G-1401)*

Taylor & Sons Inc...601 483-0714
2622 N Frontage Rd Meridian (39301) *(G-3411)*

Taylor Brothers Cnstr Co.................................601 636-1749
213 Greenbriar Dr Vicksburg (39180) *(G-5427)*

Taylor Coml Foodservice Inc............................662 895-4455
11042 Wildwood Dr Olive Branch (38654) *(G-3915)*

Taylor Construction Co Inc..............................601 426-2987
28 Taylors Cir Laurel (39443) *(G-2857)*

Taylor Defense Products LLC...........................662 773-3421
3690 N Church Ave Louisville (39339) *(G-2984)*

Taylor Energy Company LLC............................601 736-9997
469 Circle Bar Rd Foxworth (39483) *(G-1436)*

Taylor Enterprises.......................................228 385-1245
2574 Hampton Ln Biloxi (39531) *(G-282)*

Taylor Environmental Products.........................662 773-8056
3690 N Church Ave Louisville (39339) *(G-2985)*

Taylor Industries LLC...................................601 856-8439
308 Distribution Dr Madison (39110) *(G-3157)*

Taylor Machine..601 650-9600
103 Industrial Park Rd Philadelphia (39350) *(G-4240)*

Taylor Machine Works Inc...............................303 289-2201
461 Highway 49 S Jackson (39218) *(G-2670)*

Taylor Made Labels Inc..................................601 936-0050
201 Industrial Dr Jackson (39218) *(G-2671)*

Taylor McKinley...601 792-2739
337 Park Fortenberry Rd Oak Vale (39656) *(G-3736)*

Taylor Power Systems Inc...............................601 932-6491
947 Indl Park Dr Clinton (39056) *(G-837)*

Taylor Redi-Mix Co, Laurel Also called Taylor Construction Co Inc *(G-2857)*

Taylor Rene..601 977-8928
521 N Canton Club Cir Jackson (39211) *(G-2604)*

Taylor S Flying Service Inc.............................601 885-9959
1460 Charlie Brown Rd Utica (39175) *(G-5313)*

Taylor Screen Printing...................................601 352-9779
700 S State St Jackson (39201) *(G-2605)*

Taylor, Mark Logging, Maben Also called Mark Taylor Logging *(G-3047)*

Tbei, Tishomingo Also called Truck Bodies & Eqp Intl Inc *(G-5089)*

Tc Engraving & Gifts.....................................601 684-6834
1722 Veterans Blvd McComb (39648) *(G-3270)*

Tdk Logging Inc...662 328-6625
6011 Highway 182 E Columbus (39702) *(G-1037)*

Team Safety Apparel Inc.................................601 892-3571
21155 Highway 51 Crystal Springs (39059) *(G-1158)*

Tech Assurance, Ridgeland Also called Cedotal Inc *(G-4561)*

Tech Smart LLC...662 417-8780
570 Sunset Dr Ste C Grenada (38901) *(G-1707)*

Tech Wire..773 669-7583
4588 Rock Hill Rd Starkville (39759) *(G-4977)*

Techform Manufacturing LLC...........................662 282-7771
100 Industrial Park Rd Mantachie (38855) *(G-3207)*

Techno-Catch LLC..662 289-1631
2087 Attala Road 5257 Kosciusko (39090) *(G-2717)*

Tecumseh Products Company...........................662 566-2231
5424 Hwy 145 S Verona (38879) *(G-5336)*

Tecumseh Products Company...........................662 407-0428
158 Plant Rd Tupelo (38804) *(G-5239)*

Teddy Doggett Logging Inc.............................601 687-5233
1631 Pleasant Grove Chapp Waynesboro (39367) *(G-5518)*

Tees By Taran...601 549-8384
300 Ash St Brookhaven (39601) *(G-543)*

Tees River Relics...662 501-9936
796 Barr Rd Coldwater (38618) *(G-851)*

Tees Snow White...662 420-2687
1403 W Woodward Ave Holly Springs (38635) *(G-2194)*

Teezers..662 560-5099
111 S Front St Senatobia (38668) *(G-4804)*

Tegra Medical (ms) LLC.................................662 429-5191
3414 Highway 51 S Hernando (38632) *(G-2159)*

Teikuro Corporation......................................601 482-0432
4847 Peavey Dr Meridian (39301) *(G-3412)*

Teleflex Medical Incorporated.........................662 892-9100
11245 N Distribution Cv Olive Branch (38654) *(G-3916)*

Telliers Sheetmetal Works..............................228 392-5319
4270d Popps Ferry Rd Diberville (39540) *(G-1217)*

Tellus Operating Group LLC...........................601 787-3014
3368 County Road 8 Heidelberg (39439) *(G-2119)*

Tellus Operating Group LLC (PA).....................601 898-7444
602 Crescent Pl Ste 100 Ridgeland (39157) *(G-4638)*

Telpico LLC..601 898-7444
602 Crescent Pl Ste 100 Ridgeland (39157) *(G-4639)*

Temputech Inc...662 838-3698
7869 Highway 178 Byhalia (38611) *(G-608)*

Ten Below LLC...601 453-2041
1814 N Frontage Rd Meridian (39301) *(G-3413)*

Tenax Tm LLC...601 352-1107
124 One Madison Plz # 2100 Madison (39110) *(G-3158)*

Tencarva Machinery Company LLC....................601 823-0510
984 Highway 84 E Brookhaven (39601) *(G-544)*

Tenn Tom Pallet Company Inc..........................662 369-9341
810 S Thayer Ave Aberdeen (39730) *(G-20)*

Tenrgys LLC (PA)...601 898-7444
602 Crescent Pl Ste 100 Ridgeland (39157) *(G-4640)*

Terex Corporation..662 393-1800
8800 Rostin Rd Southaven (38671) *(G-4913)*

Terminal..601 636-7781
639 Industrial Dr Vicksburg (39183) *(G-5428)*

Terra Houston Ammonia Inc.............................662 746-4131
Hwy 49 Yazoo City (39194) *(G-5648)*

Terra Industries Inc......................................662 456-3076
606 Franklin Dr Houston (38851) *(G-2255)*

Terra Mississippi Nitrogen Inc (HQ)..................662 746-4131
4612 Highway 49 E Yazoo City (39194) *(G-5649)*

Terrys Bits Machine Shop...............................601 736-6112
350 Pine Grove Church Rd Foxworth (39483) *(G-1437)*

Terumo Medical Corporation............................662 280-2643
8655 Commerce Dr Ste 105 Southaven (38671) *(G-4914)*

Texas Packaging..214 912-5833
711 Neal Rd Picayune (39466) *(G-4300)*

Texas Petroleum Investment Co........................601 796-4921
1497 Clear Creek Ch Rd Lumberton (39455) *(G-3039)*

Tg Missouri-Mississippi..................................662 563-1043
195 Corporate Dr Batesville (38606) *(G-128)*

The Clarion Ledger, Jackson Also called Gannett Co Inc *(G-2421)*

The Post..601 785-4333
124 Main St Taylorsville (39168) *(G-5060)*

The Touch..662 378-4188
143 Bayou Rd Greenville (38701) *(G-1602)*

Theleg5813 Photos & Prints............................601 927-1360
109 Quail Field Run Brandon (39042) *(G-468)*

Thermo-Kool, Laurel Also called Mid-South Industries Inc *(G-2803)*

Thermoprobe Inc..601 939-1831
112a Jetport Dr Pearl (39208) *(G-4151)*

Thermos LLC...800 831-9242
355 Thermos Dr Batesville (38606) *(G-129)*

Thibideau Enterprises LLC..............................662 471-3168
9461 Taylor Cv Olive Branch (38654) *(G-3917)*

Thine Mark, Jackson Also called Pearl Rubber Stamp & Sign Inc *(G-2662)*

Thomas Davis Gamblin...................................601 656-2759
12220 Marty Stuart Dr Philadelphia (39350) *(G-4241)*

Thomas E Windham Pumping...........................601 764-3965
22 Hendry Rd Bay Springs (39422) *(G-174)*

Thomas Gamblin Logging, Philadelphia Also called Thomas Davis Gamblin *(G-4241)*

Thomas Jewelry...601 264-8780
5057 Lincoln Road Ext Hattiesburg (39402) *(G-2073)*

Thomas Larry Hearn......................................601 922-2700
1631 Westhaven Blvd Jackson (39209) *(G-2606)*

Thomas Leslie Coleman..................................662 369-6000
40098 Pinebrook Cir Caledonia (39740) *(G-632)*

Thomas Logging Company Inc..........................662 862-7342
420 E Main St Fulton (38843) *(G-1479)*

Thomas LP Gas Inc.......................................662 252-5388
115 W Van Dorn Ave Holly Springs (38635) *(G-2195)*

Thomas Welding and Fabricating.......................601 408-1843
71 Walker Rd Hattiesburg (39401) *(G-2074)*

Thomas Wood Preserving Inc...........................662 226-2350
1964 Murff Dr Grenada (38901) *(G-1708)*

Thomasson Company (PA)...............................601 656-6000
1007 Saint Francis Dr Philadelphia (39350) *(G-4242)*

Thomasvlle Mtal Fbricators Inc.........................662 526-9900
305 S Main St Como (38619) *(G-1052)*

Thompson Backhoe Service, Wesson Also called Thompson Dozer & Gravel *(G-5530)*

Thompson Dozer & Gravel...............................601 835-2406
1633 Furrs Mill Dr Ne Wesson (39191) *(G-5530)*

Thompson Services Inc...................................662 369-9102
40284 Grubb Springs Rd Hamilton (39746) *(G-1907)*

Thompsons Welding Services Inc (PA)................662 343-8955
40005 Church Rd Hamilton (39746) *(G-1908)*

Thornhill Welding...601 248-6472
5228 Wilson Rd Summit (39666) *(G-5026)*

Thornton & Sons Cabinet Shop........................601 425-2172
2065 Highway 184 Laurel (39443) *(G-2858)*

Thornton Repair Shop....................................662 332-6853
248 Highway 1 S Greenville (38701) *(G-1603)*

Three Crafty Women......................................662 746-6844
519 Webster St Yazoo City (39194) *(G-5650)*

Throw Strikes Baseball Academy.......................662 931-4948
410 Solomon St Greenville (38703) *(G-1604)*

Thugrelatedpublishing....................................228 326-2476
2613 W Stevens Cir Gulfport (39503) *(G-1883)*

Thyssenkrupp Elevator Corp............................662 223-4025
50 Mitchell Ave Walnut (38683) *(G-5458)*

Tico Investments LLC....................................601 559-8161
131 Canterbury Pl Ridgeland (39157) *(G-4641)*

Tier-Rack Corporation....................................662 526-9900
305 S Main St Como (38619) *(G-1053)*

Tikal Prints LLC...601 954-0972
844 Lawrence Rd Jackson (39206) *(G-2607)*

(PA)=Parent Co (HQ)=Headquarters (DH)=Div Headquarters

2019 Harris Directory of
Mississippi Manufacturers

A
L
P
H
A
B
E
T
I
C

Tim Bennett 662 332-0020
3033 Highway 1 S Greenville (38701) *(G-1605)*

Tim Blake 662 256-8218
30225 Johnson Mill Rd Nettleton (38858) *(G-3668)*

Tim Breland Logging Inc 601 656-0382
10580 Road 537 Philadelphia (39350) *(G-4243)*

Tim Roark 662 746-8871
494 Eola Dr Yazoo City (39194) *(G-5651)*

Tim Rollins Logging 601 225-4972
5785 New Hope Rd Gloster (39638) *(G-1520)*

Tim Wilder Logging Inc 662 489-7632
830 Andrews Rd Ecru (38841) *(G-1234)*

Timber Creek Candles 601 818-6400
436 Longwood Trl Madison (39110) *(G-3159)*

Timber Creek Estates 228 392-0858
6271 Pocono Way Biloxi (39532) *(G-283)*

Timber Harvesters Inc 601 416-2078
27 Tommy Dr Philadelphia (39350) *(G-4244)*

Timber Products Co Ltd Partnr 662 287-3766
2701 S Harper Rd Corinth (38834) *(G-1122)*

Timber Products Mississippi, Corinth *Also called Timber Products Co Ltd Partnr (G-1122)*

Timber Resources Inc 601 681-6801
8998 Chapel Rd Meridian (39305) *(G-3414)*

Timberland Management Services (PA) 601 645-6440
2592 Hwy 24 Centreville (39631) *(G-733)*

Timberland Products Inc 601 442-8102
310 Auburn Ave Natchez (39120) *(G-3630)*

Timberline Logging Inc 662 423-3948
355 County Road 982 Iuka (38852) *(G-2309)*

Timberwood Logging LLC 662 633-7744
1238 Highway 51 Winona (38967) *(G-5608)*

Timothy D Jeter 662 266-0968
4740 Highway 15 Blue Mountain (38610) *(G-293)*

Timothy R Oglesby 601 835-0673
109 Doolittle Ln Sw Bogue Chitto (39629) *(G-306)*

Timothy Trigg 601 722-9581
1335 Highway 49 Seminary (39479) *(G-4784)*

Tin Roof Mercantile 901 596-6803
9808 Sequoia Ln Olive Branch (38654) *(G-3918)*

Tindall Corporation 228 246-0798
11450 Saracennia Rd Moss Point (39562) *(G-3502)*

Tinkerbelle Industries Inc 601 928-3520
230 Clear Creek Rd Wiggins (39577) *(G-5591)*

Tinks Bells 662 574-2685
94 South Pkwy Columbus (39705) *(G-1038)*

Tiny Prints 3d Imaging LLC 866 846-9733
118 E Canal St Picayune (39466) *(G-4301)*

Tippo Timber Company LLP 601 981-3303
2436 Massena Dr Jackson (39211) *(G-2608)*

Tishomingo Acquisition LLC 662 438-7800
1425 Highway 25 Tishomingo (38873) *(G-5087)*

Tishomingo County News Inc 662 423-2211
120 W Front St Iuka (38852) *(G-2310)*

Titan Specialties 601 477-3259
626 County Home Rd Ellisville (39437) *(G-1272)*

Tj Scarbrough Inc 601 648-9987
2265 Hghtway 45 S Bcktnna Buckatunna (39322) *(G-566)*

TJX Companies Inc 662 236-2856
500 Merchants Dr Oxford (38655) *(G-4007)*

Tlgllc/Magnolia Monogramming 662 838-2000
11560 Byhalia Rd Byhalia (38611) *(G-609)*

Tlh Consturction, Pass Christian *Also called Tommy L Henderson (G-4097)*

TMC Exploration Inc 601 807-1124
116 Lower Woodville Rd Natchez (39120) *(G-3631)*

TMI, Senatobia *Also called Mims Timber LLC (G-4796)*

Tms International LLC 601 932-8205
3630 Fourth St Flowood (39232) *(G-1402)*

Tnc Logging Llc 601 394-9760
1741 Mcdonald Rd Leakesville (39451) *(G-2879)*

TNT Investments LLC 228 860-8207
176 Wisteria Ln Biloxi (39530) *(G-284)*

Tokins Inc 601 939-1093
127 Tokins Dr Pearl (39208) *(G-4152)*

Toltec Company 662 427-9515
364 Highway 72 Burnsville (38833) *(G-574)*

Tom Lauderdale Paper Svcs Inc 662 767-9744
127 Bynum Ave Shannon (38868) *(G-4819)*

Tombigbee Lumber Co Ms LLC 662 862-7417
315 Vo Tech Rd Fulton (38843) *(G-1480)*

Tombigbee Lumber Company Inc 662 862-7417
315 Vo Tech Rd Fulton (38843) *(G-1481)*

Tombigbee Tooling Inc 662 282-4273
100 W E Hodges Indl Pk Rd Mantachie (38855) *(G-3208)*

Tombstone Game Calls 662 769-6364
3622 N County Line Rd Maben (39750) *(G-3052)*

Tomlinson Machine & Tool LLC 662 342-5043
2989 Stateline Rd W Southaven (38671) *(G-4915)*

Tommy L Henderson 228 452-4484
607 W North St Pass Christian (39571) *(G-4097)*

Tony Adams Logging 601 267-5174
7830 Ebenezer Rd Carthage (39051) *(G-724)*

Tony Nelson', Gulfport *Also called Tonys King of Steaks Inc (G-1884)*

Tony Pharr Logging 662 728-9426
591b Highway 4 E Booneville (38829) *(G-346)*

Tonys King of Steaks Inc 228 214-9668
11 Pass Rd Gulfport (39507) *(G-1884)*

Tool Tek LLC 937 399-4333
365 Highway 13 Wiggins (39577) *(G-5592)*

Tooneys Tire Center 601 479-2654
Hwy 16 W De Kalb (39328) *(G-1168)*

Top Brass Tackle, Starkville *Also called Cemco Inc (G-4933)*

Top of Line Woodwork 228 669-3363
17477 Robinwood Dr Saucier (39574) *(G-4767)*

Topre America Corporation 601 927-6723
151 Nissan Way Canton (39046) *(G-681)*

Torchd LLC 601 717-2044
3325 Northview Dr Jackson (39216) *(G-2609)*

Touba Hair Braiding Ms 769 524-4641
1910 E County Line Rd Ridgeland (39157) *(G-4642)*

Tower Automotive Operations 601 499-3300
440 Church Rd Madison (39110) *(G-3160)*

Tower Automotive Operations 601 678-4000
6305 Saint Louis St Meridian (39307) *(G-3415)*

Townes Construction Co Inc 662 226-4894
16398 Highway 8 W Grenada (38901) *(G-1709)*

Townes Ready Mix, Grenada *Also called Townes Construction Co Inc (G-1709)*

Townhouse Home Furnishings LLC (PA) 662 651-5442
60012 Industrial St D Smithville (38870) *(G-4845)*

Townsend Wrecker & Auto Repair, Kosciusko *Also called Townsnds Auto Repr Wricker Svc (G-2718)*

Townsnds Auto Repr Wricker Svc 662 289-6845
806 Highway 12 W Kosciusko (39090) *(G-2718)*

Toyota Boshoku Mississippi LLC 662 862-3322
1 Tb Way Mantachie (38855) *(G-3209)*

Toyota Motor Mfg Miss Inc 662 317-3000
1200 Magnolia Way Blue Springs (38828) *(G-300)*

Toyota Tsusho America Inc 662 620-8890
203 Service Dr Tupelo (38804) *(G-5240)*

Trace Industries Inc 662 456-4261
500 2nd Ave Houston (38851) *(G-2256)*

Trace Mountain LLC 662 862-2345
111 Martin Rd Fulton (38843) *(G-1482)*

Traceway Engineering and Mfg 662 489-1314
344 Presidents Dr Pontotoc (38863) *(G-4364)*

Traceway Tooling, Pontotoc *Also called Traceway Engineering and Mfg (G-4364)*

Trader Printing 662 767-9411
215 Broad St Shannon (38868) *(G-4820)*

Tradewinds Publications 601 992-3699
5719 Highway 25 Flowood (39232) *(G-1403)*

Trailboss Trailers Inc 800 345-2452
15722 Us Highway 45 Macon (39341) *(G-3073)*

Training Consultants Inc 662 226-6637
1820 Country Club Rd Grenada (38901) *(G-1710)*

Trainum Lumber Inc 662 224-8346
2411 Pleasant Hill Rd Ashland (38603) *(G-66)*

Trane US Inc 228 863-4445
14231 Seaway Rd Ste E9 Gulfport (39503) *(G-1885)*

Transforming Lives Pubg LLC 601 434-6583
403 Grant St Ellisville (39437) *(G-1273)*

Transfrac Logistics LLC 479 659-8186
1350 Fonsylvania Rd Vicksburg (39180) *(G-5429)*

Transfrmer Gskets Cmpnents LLC 601 854-6624
491 Bowling Green Rd Lexington (39095) *(G-2906)*

Transport Trailer Service Inc (PA) 662 844-4606
502 Crossover Rd Tupelo (38801) *(G-5241)*

Travis Construction Co LLC 228 539-4849
11258 Bayou Bernard Rd Gulfport (39503) *(G-1886)*

Travis Exploration Inc 601 879-8664
636 Mount Leopard Rd Flora (39071) *(G-1313)*

Travis Welding Services 601 684-9578
905 S Magnolia St McComb (39648) *(G-3271)*

Treated Materials Co Inc 228 896-5056
13334 Seaway Rd Gulfport (39503) *(G-1887)*

Tremac Resteel Inc 601 853-3123
2064 Main St Madison (39110) *(G-3161)*

Trens Screen Printing 662 578-9074
348 Highway 51 N Batesville (38606) *(G-130)*

Tri B Timber & Logging LLC 662 283-4824
646 Sawyer Rd Winona (38967) *(G-5609)*

Tri County Sheet Metal & Wldg 601 939-0803
1001 S Pearson Rd Pearl (39208) *(G-4153)*

Tri Resources Inc 601 583-8711
18 Chappell Hill Rd Petal (39465) *(G-4197)*

Tri Star Industrial 662 680-4331
3269 White Dr Belden (38826) *(G-192)*

Tri State Lumber Co Main, Fulton *Also called Tri-State Lumber Company Inc (G-1483)*

Tri State Ready Mix 662 893-3496
2734 Highway 309 N Byhalia (38611) *(G-610)*

ALPHABETIC SECTION

Tyson Foods Inc

Tri-C Wood Products Inc (PA)...........................601 774-8295
610 S Decatur St Union (39365) *(G-5303)*

Tri-Coast Industries Inc................................228 369-9924
1007 Del Norte Cir Pascagoula (39581) *(G-4071)*

Tri-County Industries..................................601 743-9931
14066 Highway 16 W De Kalb (39328) *(G-1169)*

Tri-State Athletic Group...............................901 395-6359
2893 Broadway Dr Southaven (38672) *(G-4916)*

Tri-State Ballers, Southaven *Also called Tri-State Athletic Group (G-4916)*

Tri-State Electric Corinth Inc.........................662 287-2451
1415 Sawyer Rd Corinth (38834) *(G-1123)*

Tri-State Environmental LLC...........................888 554-9792
4901 Highway 29 Petal (39465) *(G-4198)*

Tri-State Lumber Company Inc.........................662 862-2125
105 Homan Dr Off Hwy 25 S Fulton (38843) *(G-1483)*

Tri-State Pole & Piling Inc............................601 947-4285
103 Tri State Rd Lucedale (39452) *(G-3020)*

Tri-State Truck Center Inc.............................662 844-6000
3025 International Dr Tupelo (38801) *(G-5242)*

Triad of Mississippi LLC..............................601 373-7619
1685 Gregory Dr Jackson (39272) *(G-2610)*

Triangle Fastener Corporation.........................601 956-1824
854 Centre St Ridgeland (39157) *(G-4643)*

Triangle Recycling Services...........................601 352-5027
416 W Woodrow Wilson Ave Jackson (39213) *(G-2611)*

Trico Industries Inc...................................601 649-4467
1317 Hillcrest Dr Laurel (39440) *(G-2859)*

Tricounty Farm Services South.........................662 526-9100
206 Highway 51 Como (38619) *(G-1054)*

Tricounty Ready Mix Inc...............................601 649-2887
1241 Highway 15 Stringer (39481) *(G-5005)*

Trillium International, Pelahatchie *Also called Multicraft Intl Ltd Partnr (G-4169)*

Trillium Specialty Parts, Pelahatchie *Also called Multicraft Intl Ltd Partnr (G-4167)*

Trilloma Industries, Pelahatchie *Also called Multicraft Intl Ltd Partnr (G-4170)*

Trilogy Communications Inc...........................601 932-4461
4400 Mangum Dr Flowood (39232) *(G-1404)*

Trilogy Communications Inc (PA)......................601 932-4461
2910 Highway 80 E Pearl (39208) *(G-4154)*

Trimjoist Corporation.................................662 327-7950
5146 Highway 182 E Columbus (39702) *(G-1039)*

Triner Scale and Mfg Co Inc (PA).....................800 238-0152
8411 Hacks Cross Rd Olive Branch (38654) *(G-3919)*

Trinity Highway Products Llc..........................662 290-1500
2235 Attala Road 2202 Kosciusko (39090) *(G-2719)*

Trinity River Energy Oper LLC........................601 792-9686
8970 Highway 13 Newhebron (39140) *(G-3715)*

Trinity Steel Fabricators Inc..........................601 783-6625
5005 Highway 568 W Magnolia (39652) *(G-3195)*

Trinity Three LLC....................................601 249-8851
1009 Meadville St Summit (39666) *(G-5027)*

Triple E Door & Hardware Inc.........................601 940-7371
560 Turtle Ln Brandon (39047) *(G-469)*

Triple G Logging.....................................601 416-8733
11700 Road 397 Philadelphia (39350) *(G-4245)*

Triple J of Mississippi Inc............................662 624-4630
520 Sunbelt Dr Clarksdale (38614) *(G-784)*

Triple J Tie and Timber LLC..........................662 547-6600
609 Stewart Weir Rd Weir (39772) *(G-5522)*

Triple J Tie and Timber LLC..........................601 663-4275
12920 Road 832 Philadelphia (39350) *(G-4246)*

Triple L Logging.....................................601 656-9313
11761 Road 539 Philadelphia (39350) *(G-4247)*

Triple M Lures LLC...................................601 919-5515
13 Summit View Dr Perkinston (39573) *(G-4182)*

Triple R Trailers Inc.................................662 728-7975
194 County Road 547 Corinth (38834) *(G-1124)*

Triple S Logging, State Line *Also called Kenneth Smith (G-4987)*

Triple S Well Service Inc.............................601 736-8804
1798 Highway 98 E Columbia (39429) *(G-926)*

Triple Shots...228 872-2696
1415 Bienville Blvd Ocean Springs (39564) *(G-3792)*

Triton Automatic Teller Mchs.........................228 575-3292
522 E Railroad St Long Beach (39560) *(G-2957)*

Triton Stone Holdings LLC............................662 280-8041
2363 Stateline Rd W Southaven (38671) *(G-4917)*

Triton Systems Delaware LLC (PA).....................228 575-3100
21405 B St Long Beach (39560) *(G-2958)*

Trodat Marking Products Inc (HQ).....................601 500-5971
8339 Highway 18 W Jackson (39209) *(G-2612)*

Tronicsales..769 218-0432
1829 Meadowbrook Rd Jackson (39211) *(G-2613)*

Tronox Incorporated..................................662 343-8311
40034 Tronox Rd Hamilton (39746) *(G-1909)*

Trooper Publications.................................228 392-1442
10536 Auto Mall Pkwy C2 Diberville (39540) *(G-1218)*

Trophy Petroleum Corporation.........................601 298-0200
2042 Red Dog Rd Carthage (39051) *(G-725)*

Trophy Shop...662 236-3726
1533 University Ave Oxford (38655) *(G-4008)*

Tropical World Intl LLC...............................228 229-8413
309 Goose Pointe Blvd Biloxi (39531) *(G-285)*

Troy Custom Cabinets LLC............................662 902-5559
3246 Us Highway 49 E Tutwiler (38963) *(G-5260)*

Tru-Cut Inc...662 489-1879
89 Possum Trot Rd Pontotoc (38863) *(G-4365)*

Tru-Cut Frames, Pontotoc *Also called Tru-Cut Inc (G-4365)*

Truck Bodies & Eqp Intl Inc..........................662 438-7800
182 County Road 123 Tishomingo (38873) *(G-5088)*

Truck Bodies & Eqp Intl Inc..........................800 255-4345
1425 Highway 25 Tishomingo (38873) *(G-5089)*

Trucking Division, Como *Also called Cemex Cnstr Mtls Fla LLC (G-1046)*

Trucks Unlimited, Hattiesburg *Also called Fireplace Wholesale (G-1970)*

True Temper Sports Inc...............................662 256-5605
Hgwy 25 S Amory (38821) *(G-57)*

Trulite GL Alum Solutions LLC........................662 226-5551
501 E Govan St Grenada (38901) *(G-1711)*

TSA Embroidery LLC..................................662 538-1007
1186 State Highway 348 New Albany (38652) *(G-3703)*

Tucker Machine Services..............................601 582-4280
507 Peps Point Rd Hattiesburg (39401) *(G-2075)*

Tucker Manufacturing Co Inc..........................662 563-7220
120 Crown Dr Batesville (38606) *(G-131)*

Tuff-Wall Inc..601 264-8649
5266 Old Highway 11 Hattiesburg (39402) *(G-2076)*

Tullahoma Industries LLC............................601 222-2255
101 Ostrover Dr Tylertown (39667) *(G-5288)*

Tunica Publishing Co Inc.............................662 363-1511
986 Magnolia St Tunica (38676) *(G-5103)*

Tunica Times, Tunica *Also called Tunica Publishing Co Inc (G-5103)*

Tuohys J Sptg Gods of Columbus.......................662 328-1440
113 5th St S Columbus (39701) *(G-1040)*

Tupelo Advertiser Inc................................601 534-6635
713 Carter Ave New Albany (38652) *(G-3704)*

Tupelo Concrete Products Inc.........................662 842-7811
120 N Industrial Rd Tupelo (38801) *(G-5243)*

Tupelo Cupcakes Inc.................................205 269-4130
3978 N Gloster St Ste C Tupelo (38804) *(G-5244)*

Tupelo Daily Journal News Bur........................601 364-1000
200 N Congress St Ste 400 Jackson (39201) *(G-2614)*

Tupelo Elvis Presley Fan Club........................662 610-5301
114 Lake Crest Cir Tupelo (38801) *(G-5245)*

Tupelo Engraving & Rbr Stamp........................662 842-0574
605 W Main St Ste 15 Tupelo (38804) *(G-5246)*

Tupelo Fibers, Tupelo *Also called Fibrix LLC (G-5133)*

Tupelo Manufacturing, Pontotoc *Also called Wdtm Inc (G-4369)*

Tupelo Screen Printing LLC...........................662 523-0092
408 W Franklin St Tupelo (38804) *(G-5247)*

Tupelo Sleeper 0341, Tupelo *Also called Leggett & Platt Incorporated (G-5178)*

Turner Bamboo Fly Rods, Moss Point *Also called Turner Fly Rods LLC (G-3503)*

Turner Fly Rods LLC.................................228 623-6475
8005 Pecan Ridge Dr Moss Point (39562) *(G-3503)*

Turner Group LLC...................................601 394-5070
431 Main St Leakesville (39451) *(G-2880)*

Turner Jimmy Backhoe Dozer Svc......................662 988-2701
1875 County Road 478 Myrtle (38650) *(G-3514)*

Turners Tax Service..................................662 887-2066
124 Front Ave Baird (38751) *(G-69)*

Tvi Inc...662 343-5117
40537 Old Highway 45 S Hamilton (39746) *(G-1910)*

TW Logging LLC......................................601 657-8838
3333b Highway 48 Liberty (39645) *(G-2918)*

TWI Inc..601 736-1783
1256 Highway 98 E Columbia (39429) *(G-927)*

Twin Rivers Paper Company LLC.......................662 468-2183
196 Burrows Dr Pickens (39146) *(G-4307)*

Twisted Canvas......................................228 596-9332
6190 Beatline Rd Ste 2 Long Beach (39560) *(G-2959)*

Twister LLC..601 371-7276
36 Jennifer Ct Madison (39110) *(G-3162)*

Two-J Ranch Inc....................................601 445-8540
25 Hawthorne Pl Natchez (39120) *(G-3632)*

Tyler Printing and Cmpt Svc..........................601 279-6105
225 Sea Island Dr Vicksburg (39183) *(G-5430)*

Tylertown Times.....................................601 876-5111
727 Beulah Ave Tylertown (39667) *(G-5289)*

Tylertown Wear Parts Inc.............................601 876-4659
25 Industrial Park Rd Tylertown (39667) *(G-5290)*

Tyonek Svcs Overhaul-Facility.........................256 258-6200
7095 Roscoe Turner Rd Kiln (39556) *(G-2685)*

Tyson Foods Inc.....................................601 664-9102
110 Metroplex Blvd Ste F Pearl (39208) *(G-4155)*

Tyson Foods Inc.....................................601 298-5300
3865 Highway 35 N Carthage (39051) *(G-726)*

Tyson Foods Inc.....................................229 995-6800
305 Cleveland St Forest (39074) *(G-1426)*

Tyson Foods Inc.....................................601 469-1712
1225 Jack Lee Dr Forest (39074) *(G-1427)*

ALPHABETIC

(PA)=Parent Co (HQ)=Headquarters (DH)=Div Headquarters

2019 Harris Directory of
Mississippi Manufacturers

325

Tyson Foods Inc

Tyson Foods Inc 601 849-3351
  855 Industrial Park Dr Se Magee (39111) *(G-3187)*

Tyson Foods Inc 601 631-3600
  1785 Interplex Cir Vicksburg (39183) *(G-5431)*

Tyson Foods Inc 601 774-7551
  13001 Road 2219 Union (39365) *(G-5304)*

U S M I, Gulfport *Also called United States Marine Inc (G-1890)*

U S Metal Works Inc 601 657-4676
  438 Industrial Dr Liberty (39645) *(G-2919)*

U S Plastics Inc 662 456-5551
  242 Industrial Dr Houston (38851) *(G-2257)*

U S Safety Services Inc 601 833-3627
  1878 Pleasant Ridge Rd Nw Wesson (39191) *(G-5531)*

U S Weatherford L P 601 428-1551
  1315 Hillcrest Dr Laurel (39440) *(G-2860)*

Udt, West Point *Also called Ultra Drying Technology (G-5565)*

Ulmer Machine Company Inc 601 939-5812
  130 Aztec Dr Jackson (39218) *(G-2672)*

Ultra Comfort Foam Company 662 539-6004
  431 Garfield St New Albany (38652) *(G-3705)*

Ultra Drying Technology 662 494-5025
  2867 Oak Ridge Rd West Point (39773) *(G-5565)*

Ulysses Cooley 601 394-5485
  506 Steer Holw Leakesville (39451) *(G-2881)*

Uncle Ben's, Greenville *Also called Mars Food Us LLC (G-1569)*

Under Armour Inc 228 864-2791
  10110 Factory Shop Blvd Gulfport (39503) *(G-1888)*

Under Armour Inc 662 298-5269
  5205 Airways Blvd Ste 700 Southaven (38671) *(G-4918)*

Unified Brands Inc 888 994-7636
  1055 Mendell Davis Dr Jackson (39272) *(G-2615)*

Unified Brands Inc 601 372-3903
  1055 Mendell Davis Dr Byram (39272) *(G-625)*

Unified Buddist Church Inc 662 578-2077
  123 Towles Rd Batesville (38606) *(G-132)*

Uniforms Unlimited of Tupelo, Tupelo *Also called Scrubs Elite LLC (G-5220)*

Unik Ink Cstm Screen Prtg Inc 601 259-1004
  555 Hoy Rd Madison (39110) *(G-3163)*

Union Corrugating Company 601 661-0577
  1463 Interplex Cir Vicksburg (39183) *(G-5432)*

Union Directories 662 620-6366
  818 Shell St Tupelo (38801) *(G-5248)*

Union Spring & Mfg Corp 662 489-7846
  260 Industrial Dr Pontotoc (38863) *(G-4366)*

Unipres Southeast USA Inc 601 469-0234
  1001 Fountain Dr Forest (39074) *(G-1428)*

Unique Services LLC 601 326-9912
  4955 N State St Ste A Jackson (39206) *(G-2616)*

United Assoc Journeymen & 5 .... 228 863-1853
  1237 Pass Rd Gulfport (39501) *(G-1889)*

United Burial Vault Co & Cemtr 662 347-9319
  205 W Preston St Benoit (38725) *(G-207)*

United Comb & Novelty Corp 662 487-9248
  1052 Industrial Park Rd Sardis (38666) *(G-4746)*

United Fence Company 601 582-0406
  255 Mcleod St Hattiesburg (39401) *(G-2077)*

United Furniture Inds CA Inc 800 458-7212
  431 Highway 41 N Okolona (38860) *(G-3800)*

United Furniture Inds Inc 662 447-4000
  431 Highway 41 N Okolona (38860) *(G-3801)*

United Furniture Inds Inc 662 841-2321
  3301 Adams Farm Rd Belden (38826) *(G-193)*

United Furniture Inds NC LLC 662 447-5504
  431 Highway 41 N Okolona (38860) *(G-3802)*

United Gilsonite Laboratories 601 362-8619
  3908 Beasley Rd Jackson (39213) *(G-2617)*

United Pioneer, Corinth *Also called Corinth Acquisition Corp (G-1075)*

United Plastic Molders Inc 601 353-3193
  105 E Rankin St Jackson (39201) *(G-2618)*

United Plastics, Sardis *Also called United Comb & Novelty Corp (G-4746)*

United Print Services LLC 662 287-1090
  130 S Fillmore St Corinth (38834) *(G-1125)*

United Service Equipment Co 662 534-9061
  908 State Highway 15 N New Albany (38652) *(G-3706)*

United Solutions Inc 662 487-0068
  100 Rainwater St Sardis (38666) *(G-4747)*

United States Marine Inc 228 679-1005
  10011 Lorraine Rd Gulfport (39503) *(G-1890)*

United States Worldwide Inc 662 488-1840
  7118 Highway 41 Pontotoc (38863) *(G-4367)*

Universal Lighting Tech Inc 601 892-9828
  19120 Hwy 51 Gallman (39077) *(G-1486)*

Universal Scale & Conveyor, Nesbit *Also called Raymond Mucillo Jr (G-3656)*

University of Mississippi 662 915-5742
  301 Hill HI University (38677) *(G-5306)*

University of Southern Miss 601 266-5390
  118 College Dr Hattiesburg (39406) *(G-2078)*

University Press Mississippi (HQ) 601 432-6205
  3825 Ridgewood Rd Unit 5 Jackson (39211) *(G-2619)*

University Screen Print Inc 662 324-8277
  414 Highway 12 E Starkville (39759) *(G-4978)*

Upchurch Industrial LLC 662 453-6680
  6923 Pasadena Dr Horn Lake (38637) *(G-2214)*

Uphill Construction LLC 662 299-9654
  402 Ione St Greenwood (38930) *(G-1654)*

Upholstry, Meridian *Also called Watkins Trim Shop Inc (G-3417)*

Upper Kutz Barbr Style College, Greenville *Also called Upper Kutz LLC (G-1606)*

Upper Kutz LLC 662 807-8707
  813 S Martin Luther Greenville (38701) *(G-1606)*

UPS, Columbus *Also called Chism Rackard Enterprises LLC (G-947)*

UPS Store, The, Biloxi *Also called Jagg LLC (G-254)*

US Oil Recovery LLC 662 884-1050
  1136 Highway 49 S Indianola (38751) *(G-2271)*

USA Yeast Company LLC 601 545-2690
  457 J M Tatum Indus Dr Hattiesburg (39401) *(G-2079)*

Usaccess LLC 601 806-5034
  1005 W Broad St Monticello (39654) *(G-3440)*

Usedvending.com, Picayune *Also called Breaktime Vending Inc (G-4257)*

Usm Science & Technology, Hattiesburg *Also called University of Southern Miss (G-2078)*

Ustx Contract Services NC Inc 512 894-0008
  311a S Parkway St Corinth (38834) *(G-1126)*

Uswebworx LLC 601 813-8927
  455 Brookstone Dr Madison (39110) *(G-3164)*

Utility Poles & Piling, Wiggins *Also called Desoto Treated Materials Inc (G-5580)*

V & B International Inc 601 437-8279
  810 Market St Port Gibson (39150) *(G-4408)*

V A Sauls Inc 601 787-4321
  Highway 528 E Heidelberg (39439) *(G-2120)*

V E Brackett & Co Inc 662 840-5656
  1203 Maxwell St Tupelo (38804) *(G-5249)*

Vaiden Timber Co 662 464-7740
  300 Hwy 51 Vaiden (39176) *(G-5315)*

Valeo Front End Module, Canton *Also called Valeo North America Inc (G-682)*

Valeo North America Inc 931 446-9128
  300 Nissan Dr Canton (39046) *(G-682)*

Valioso Petroleum Company 601 936-3601
  504 Keywood Cir Flowood (39232) *(G-1405)*

Valley Farms 662 738-5861
  13462 Ms Highway 388 Brooksville (39739) *(G-558)*

Valley Gravel Co, Brooksville *Also called Valley Farms (G-558)*

Valley Publishing Inc 662 473-1473
  416 N Main St Water Valley (38965) *(G-5475)*

Valley Thing'y, Water Valley *Also called Gmn Group LLC (G-5468)*

Valley Tool Inc (PA) 662 473-3066
  101 Industrial Park Rd Water Valley (38965) *(G-5476)*

Valmet Inc 662 328-3841
  617 Yorkville Park Sq Columbus (39702) *(G-1041)*

Valvoline, Hernando *Also called Niteo Products LLC (G-2145)*

Vampco Inc 601 638-5133
  247 Armory Rd Vicksburg (39183) *(G-5433)*

Van Heusen, Gulfport *Also called Pvh Corp (G-1857)*

Van Petroleum Inc (PA) 601 982-8728
  1300 Meadowbrook Rd # 202 Jackson (39211) *(G-2620)*

Van S Leather Crafts 662 838-6269
  1909 Bubba Taylor Rd Byhalia (38611) *(G-611)*

Van's Deer Procesiing Sptg Gds, Brandon *Also called Vans Deer Processing Inc (G-470)*

Vance Nimrod 662 334-3713
  323 Central St Greenville (38701) *(G-1607)*

Vancleave Bait and Tackle, Vancleave *Also called Vancleave Portable Buildings (G-5323)*

Vancleave Portable Buildings 228 826-5151
  12214 Highway 57 Vancleave (39565) *(G-5323)*

Vanguard Solutions Inc 407 230-2887
  1616 Bayou Vista St Gautier (39553) *(G-1505)*

Vanleigh Rv Inc 662 612-4040
  26 Indl Access Rd Burnsville (38833) *(G-575)*

Vans Deer Processing Inc 601 825-9087
  777 Hwy 4689 Brandon (39042) *(G-470)*

Vape and Bake LLC 228 447-1566
  6716 Washington Ave Ste C Ocean Springs (39564) *(G-3793)*

Vapor Express LLC 601 559-8004
  3553 Dale Cir Pearl (39208) *(G-4156)*

Vapor Oilfield Services LLC 601 741-7171
  3340 Mills Rd Conehatta (39057) *(G-1055)*

Varco LP 601 428-1555
  721 E 22nd St Laurel (39440) *(G-2861)*

Vardaman Hardware, Vardaman *Also called P & R Aluminum (G-5325)*

Varsity Pro Inc 662 628-4172
  307 N Boland St Calhoun City (38916) *(G-645)*

Vbg Woodworks LLC 601 634-0313
  766 Rollingwood Dr Vicksburg (39183) *(G-5434)*

Vegasigns LLC 662 871-7337
  932 William St Tupelo (38801) *(G-5250)*

Velocity Inc 662 449-4026
  530 Vaiden Dr Hernando (38632) *(G-2160)*

Velocity Cnslting Spcalist LLC 229 726-6047
  46 Edgeware Petal (39465) *(G-4199)*

326

2019 Harris Directory of
Mississippi Manufacturers

(G-0000) Company's Geographic Section entry number

ALPHABETIC SECTION

Wade Services Inc

Venable Glass Services LLC (PA) 601 605-4443
660 Highway 51 Ridgeland (39157) *(G-4644)*

Vendworks LLC (HQ) 601 268-1906
201 Coca Cola Ave Hattiesburg (39402) *(G-2080)*

Vendworks LLC 601 684-2085
301 Oakdale Ave McComb (39648) *(G-3272)*

Veneer Division, Vicksburg Also called Anderson-Tully Company *(G-5339)*

Venevaa Jos LLC 850 501-4040
13230 Meadowland Ct Gulfport (39503) *(G-1891)*

Venture Oil & Gas Inc 601 428-3653
207 S 13th Ave Laurel (39440) *(G-2862)*

Venture Technologies, Ridgeland Also called VT Consolidated Inc *(G-4646)*

Vera S Ray 662 453-1615
4355 King Cir Greenwood (38930) *(G-1655)*

Verona Foam, Verona Also called Elite Comfort Solutions LLC *(G-5330)*

Vertechs Design Solutions LLC 228 671-1442
712 Spruce St Waveland (39576) *(G-5486)*

Vertex Aerospace 601 622-8940
133 Penn Rd Canton (39046) *(G-683)*

Vertex Aerospace LLC 601 856-2274
555 Industrial Dr S Madison (39110) *(G-3165)*

Vertex Manufacturing Corp 662 895-6263
8341 Industrial Dr Olive Branch (38654) *(G-3920)*

Vertiv Corporation 662 313-0813
710 Venture Dr Ste 200 Southaven (38672) *(G-4919)*

Veterans Monument Company LLC 662 549-1422
194 Quail Rdg Caledonia (39740) *(G-633)*

Veterans Service Officer, Bay St Louis Also called County of Hancock *(G-177)*

Vetguard Solutions, Madison Also called Schuyler C Jones *(G-3145)*

Vibra Shine Inc 601 785-9854
113 Fellowship Rd Taylorsville (39168) *(G-5061)*

Vibrant Screen Printing 601 291-1296
934 S Gallatin St Jackson (39204) *(G-2621)*

Vibrashine, Taylorsville Also called Vibra Shine Inc *(G-5061)*

Viceroy Pharmaceuticals Inc 732 762-6577
106 E Mulberry St Ripley (38663) *(G-4674)*

Vicksburg Alum & Met Pdts Co, Vicksburg Also called Vampco Inc *(G-5433)*

Vicksburg Engineering & Mfg, Vicksburg Also called Vicksburg Enterprise Mfg LLC *(G-5435)*

Vicksburg Engineering & Mfg, Vicksburg Also called Vicksburg Enterprise Mfg LLC *(G-5436)*

Vicksburg Enterprise Mfg LLC 601 631-0304
4 Chelsea Ln Vicksburg (39180) *(G-5435)*

Vicksburg Enterprise Mfg LLC (PA) 601 631-0304
1514 Walnut St Vicksburg (39180) *(G-5436)*

Vicksburg Metal Products, Vicksburg Also called Union Corrugating Company *(G-5432)*

Vicksburg Newsmedia LLC 601 636-4545
1601 N Frontage Rd Ste F Vicksburg (39180) *(G-5437)*

Vicksburg Post, Vicksburg Also called Vicksburg Printing and Pubg Co *(G-5438)*

Vicksburg Posts, The, Vicksburg Also called Vicksburg Newsmedia LLC *(G-5437)*

Vicksburg Printing and Pubg Co (PA) 601 636-4545
1601 N Frontage Rd Vicksburg (39180) *(G-5438)*

Vicksburg Printing and Pubg Co 601 638-2900
1601c N Frontage Rd Ste C Vicksburg (39180) *(G-5439)*

Vicksburg Printing and Pubg Co 601 631-0400
1601b N Frontage Rd Vicksburg (39180) *(G-5440)*

Vicksburg Ready Mix Concrete 601 634-6001
1730 Highway 80 Vicksburg (39180) *(G-5441)*

Vicksmetal Company, Vicksburg Also called Steelsummit Holdings Inc *(G-5424)*

Vicksmetal Corporation 601 636-1314
155 Industrial Dr Vicksburg (39183) *(G-5442)*

Victor Dale Harris, Exec Dir, Pearl Also called Signmark Inc *(G-4145)*

Victor P Smith Oil Producers 601 932-2223
2 Country Pl Jackson (39208) *(G-2673)*

Victor Umfress Gar Wldg Sp Inc 662 862-4213
404 S Spring St Fulton (38843) *(G-1484)*

Victory Logistics LLC 662 620-2829
4110 Westside Dr Ste C Tupelo (38801) *(G-5251)*

Victory Motor Company 601 573-1441
9373 Highway 18 Raymond (39154) *(G-4494)*

Vidette-Belmont News, Iuka Also called Tishomingo County News Inc *(G-2310)*

View Inc 662 892-3415
12380 Kirk Rd Olive Branch (38654) *(G-3921)*

Viking Capital Ventures Inc (PA) 662 455-1200
111 W Front St Greenwood (38930) *(G-1656)*

Viking Culinary Arts Center, Greenwood Also called Viking Capital Ventures Inc *(G-1656)*

Viking Manufacturing, Greenwood Also called Viking Range LLC *(G-1659)*

Viking Range LLC 770 932-7282
5601 Viking Rd Greenwood (38930) *(G-1657)*

Viking Range LLC 662 455-7522
5601 Viking Rd Greenwood (38930) *(G-1658)*

Viking Range LLC 662 455-1214
5601 County Rd 525 Greenwood (38930) *(G-1659)*

Viking Range LLC 662 455-7521
5601 Viking Rd Greenwood (38930) *(G-1660)*

Viking Range LLC 662 455-1200
5801 Viking Rd Greenwood (38930) *(G-1661)*

Viking Range LLC (HQ) 662 455-1200
111 W Front St Greenwood (38930) *(G-1662)*

Viking Range LLC 662 455-7522
5601 Viking Rd Greenwood (38930) *(G-1663)*

Viking Specialty Products, Greenwood Also called Viking Range LLC *(G-1657)*

Vines Operating Company Inc 601 442-8034
308 Greenfield Rd Church Hill (39120) *(G-755)*

Vineyard 769 251-1322
801 S Wheatley St Ste E Ridgeland (39157) *(G-4645)*

VIP Cinema LLC (PA) 662 841-5866
101 Industrial Dr New Albany (38652) *(G-3707)*

VIP Cinema Seating, New Albany Also called VIP Cinema LLC *(G-3707)*

VIP Vinyl and Embroidery LLC 601 624-7366
133 Mountain Creek Frm Rd Florence (39073) *(G-1335)*

Virgil Williams LLC 662 287-7734
46 County Road 405 Corinth (38834) *(G-1127)*

Vision Center PA 601 928-3914
1113 Central Ave E Wiggins (39577) *(G-5593)*

Vision Technologies Marine Inc 228 762-0010
601 Bayou Casotte Pkwy Pascagoula (39581) *(G-4072)*

Vital Care of Central Ms 601 859-8200
159 Fountains Blvd Madison (39110) *(G-3166)*

Vital Signs Unbound 662 363-6940
1286 Houston Ln Tunica (38676) *(G-5104)*

Vizaura LLC 228 363-4048
6514 Hanauma Ct Diamondhead (39525) *(G-1193)*

Vizionz Unlimited LLC 601 272-5040
5261 Greenway Drive Ext Jackson (39204) *(G-2622)*

Vmi Marine Inc 601 636-8700
4477 Highway 61 S Vicksburg (39180) *(G-5443)*

Vogue Home Furnishings, Tupelo Also called Paxton Sales Inc *(G-5201)*

Voith Fabrics Florence Inc 601 845-2202
220 Price St Florence (39073) *(G-1336)*

Voith Paper Fabrics & Roll Sys, Florence Also called Voith Fabrics Florence Inc *(G-1336)*

Voluptuous E-Juice LLC 662 297-8353
1085 Wise Bend Rd Pontotoc (38863) *(G-4368)*

Von Drehle Corporation 601 445-0100
30 Majorca Rd Natchez (39120) *(G-3633)*

Vonco of Mississippi Inc 601 446-7274
188 Highway 61 S Natchez (39120) *(G-3634)*

VT, Water Valley Also called Valley Tool Inc *(G-5476)*

VT Consolidated Inc (HQ) 601 956-5440
860 Centre St Ridgeland (39157) *(G-4646)*

VT Halter Marine Inc 228 475-1211
5801 Elder Ferry Rd Moss Point (39563) *(G-3504)*

VT Halter Marine Inc (HQ) 228 696-6888
900 Bayou Casotte Pkwy Pascagoula (39581) *(G-4073)*

VT Halter Marine Inc 228 712-2278
7801 Trinity Dr Moss Point (39562) *(G-3505)*

VT Marine, Pascagoula Also called Vision Technologies Marine Inc *(G-4072)*

Vulcan Materials Company, Calhoun City Also called MMC Materials Inc *(G-641)*

Vulcan Materials Company 601 425-3509
606 Avenue C Laurel (39440) *(G-2863)*

W & W Pallets LLC 662 706-0050
106 Woodgreen Rd Plantersville (38862) *(G-4318)*

W & W Special Components Inc 662 365-5648
10040 Highway 371 Marietta (38856) *(G-3219)*

W A Mathis Timber Co 601 684-7839
210 E Georgia Ave McComb (39648) *(G-3273)*

W E Birdsong Associates Inc 601 939-7448
1435 Monterey Rd Florence (39073) *(G-1337)*

W E Blain & Sons Inc 601 442-3032
693 Highway 61 N Natchez (39120) *(G-3635)*

W F Ferguson 601 453-1093
501 Montgomery St Greenwood (38930) *(G-1664)*

W F Ferguson Sand & Gravel, Greenwood Also called W F Ferguson *(G-1664)*

W G Yates & Sons Cnstr Co (HQ) 601 656-5411
1 Gully Ave Philadelphia (39350) *(G-4248)*

W L Byrd Lumber Co Inc (PA) 601 783-5711
2145 Highway 98 W Summit (39666) *(G-5028)*

W L Byrd Lumber Co Inc 601 567-2314
2145 Highway 98 W Summit (39666) *(G-5029)*

W L S Inc (PA) 601 687-1761
851 County Road 253 Shubuta (39360) *(G-4834)*

W L S Inc 601 687-1761
8207 County Road 630 Shubuta (39360) *(G-4835)*

W L Tisdale Cabinet Shop 601 763-3552
2741 Highway 588 Ellisville (39437) *(G-1274)*

W S Red Hancock Inc (PA) 662 755-0011
115 Pritchard Ave Bentonia (39040) *(G-213)*

W S Red Hancock Inc 601 399-0605
5349 Highway 11 N Ellisville (39437) *(G-1275)*

W T Drilling Co Inc 601 442-1607
231 Highway 61 S Natchez (39120) *(G-3636)*

W T Leggett Inc 601 544-2704
1002 Hardy St Hattiesburg (39401) *(G-2081)*

W W W Electric Company Inc 601 833-6666
523 Byrd St Brookhaven (39601) *(G-545)*

Wade Services Inc 601 399-1900
500 Eastview Dr Laurel (39443) *(G-2864)*

(PA)=Parent Co (HQ)=Headquarters (DH)=Div Headquarters

2019 Harris Directory of
Mississippi Manufacturers

327

Wade Services Inc (PA)

ALPHABETIC SECTION

Wade Services Inc (PA) 601 399-1900
30 Currie Rd Ellisville (39437) *(G-1276)*

Wag Corporation 662 844-8478
5522 W Main St Tupelo (38801) *(G-5252)*

Walker Parris 601 953-3023
1017 Riley Thomas Cir Port Gibson (39150) *(G-4409)*

Walker Auto Repair Service 601 969-5353
624 N Mill St Jackson (39202) *(G-2623)*

Walker Construction, Port Gibson Also called Walker Parris *(G-4409)*

Walker Enterprises 662 237-0240
1584 County Road 121 Carrollton (38917) *(G-704)*

Walker Machine 601 425-4635
1104 Susie B Ruffin Ave Laurel (39440) *(G-2865)*

Walker Memorial Co Inc 601 428-5337
1220 Ellisville Blvd Laurel (39440) *(G-2866)*

Walker Missionary Baptist Pars 662 585-3309
5 Antioch Church Rd Golden (38847) *(G-1532)*

Walker Printing Company, Hickory Also called J & S Enterprises LLC *(G-2162)*

Walker Welding and Fabrication 601 503-0340
1005 Prince Dr Brandon (39042) *(G-471)*

Wallace Art & Sign Service, Clarksdale Also called Roosevelt Wallace *(G-781)*

Wallace Express Freight Inc 662 890-3080
9305 Stateline Rd Apt 32a Olive Branch (38654) *(G-3922)*

Wallace Lumber Company 601 276-2834
6521 County Line Rd Summit (39666) *(G-5030)*

Wallace Welding LLC 601 734-6542
1033 Montgomery Rd Sw Bogue Chitto (39629) *(G-307)*

Waller Bros Inc 601 352-6556
524 E Pascagoula St Jackson (39201) *(G-2624)*

Walley Trucking 601 848-7576
19645 Mrtn Luther King Dr State Line (39362) *(G-4989)*

Walls Drapery & Bedspread Mfg 601 939-6014
422 Roberts St Pearl (39208) *(G-4157)*

Walls Drapery & Bedspreads, Pearl Also called Walls Drapery & Bedspread Mfg *(G-4157)*

Walsworth Logging 601 442-5406
530 Tate Rd Natchez (39120) *(G-3637)*

Walt Machine Inc 601 796-8269
891 Otho Davis Rd Lumberton (39455) *(G-3040)*

Walter Allen 601 924-1956
112 Country Cove Dr Clinton (39056) *(G-838)*

Walter L Perrigin 662 240-0056
1713 Ridge Rd Columbus (39705) *(G-1042)*

Walters Machine Works Inc 601 426-6092
1507 Highway 84 E Laurel (39443) *(G-2867)*

Waltman Pharmaceuticals Inc 601 939-0833
1 Lakeland Sq Ste B Flowood (39232) *(G-1406)*

Wamble Machine Shop, Kosciusko Also called Alan Dickerson Inc *(G-2687)*

Warco, Ripley Also called Biltrite Ripley Operations LLC *(G-4654)*

Wards Custom Screen Prin 601 384-4635
3055 Highway 84 W Meadville (39653) *(G-3278)*

Ware Milling Inc 662 456-9032
150 A F L Dr Houston (38851) *(G-2258)*

Wares Air Filter Service 228 832-8918
22061 E Bradis Rd Gulfport (39503) *(G-1892)*

Warhorse Industries LLC 601 856-2990
100 Darrowsby Pl Madison (39110) *(G-3167)*

Warmkraft Inc 601 659-3317
1122 Erwin Rd Stonewall (39363) *(G-5000)*

Warmkraft Inc (PA) 601 785-4476
113 Fellowship Rd Taylorsville (39168) *(G-5062)*

Warren Inc 601 765-8221
707 N Fir Ave Collins (39428) *(G-865)*

Warren Corporation UNI 888 913-7708
121 Southpointe Dr Ste E Byram (39272) *(G-626)*

Warrior Energy Services Corp 601 425-9684
339 Avenue A Laurel (39440) *(G-2868)*

Washington County Wide Shop 662 334-4322
3114 County Shop Rd Greenville (38703) *(G-1608)*

Washington Furniture Sales, Pontotoc Also called Behold Washington LLC *(G-4322)*

Waste Placement Inc 601 362-5343
4164 Crestview Pl Jackson (39211) *(G-2625)*

Wastewater Control Inc 601 845-5581
2056 Highway 49 S Florence (39073) *(G-1338)*

Watco Co Inc 601 553-1332
400 18th Ave S Meridian (39301) *(G-3416)*

Watco Mobile Services, Meridian Also called Watco Co Inc *(G-3416)*

Water Valley Poultry Inc 662 473-0016
507 Lafayette St Water Valley (38965) *(G-5477)*

Water Water LLC 662 721-7098
25 Gaston Dr Cleveland (38732) *(G-810)*

Water-Way Inc 662 423-0081
751 County Road 989 # 1010 Iuka (38852) *(G-2311)*

Waterfall Brand, Diberville Also called R Fournier & Sons Inc *(G-1209)*

Watermark Printers LLC 662 323-8750
1085 Stark Rd Starkville (39759) *(G-4979)*

Watersprings Media House 662 812-1568
10719 Oak Cir N Olive Branch (38654) *(G-3923)*

Watkins 601 752-2526
3165 Monroe Rd Ellisville (39437) *(G-1277)*

Watkins Mayola 601 826-8310
900 Scr120 # 120 Jackson (39212) *(G-2626)*

Watkins Jr H Vaughn 601 898-9347
125 S Congress St # 1820 Jackson (39201) *(G-2627)*

Watkins Trim Shop Inc 601 485-5512
2503 8th St Meridian (39301) *(G-3417)*

Watson Percy 662 931-6490
634 Hibiscus St Greenville (38701) *(G-1609)*

Watson Tj Property LLC 601 527-3587
2440 N Hlls St 105 Mrdian Meridian (39305) *(G-3418)*

Watthour Engineering Co Inc 601 933-0900
333 Cross Park Dr Pearl (39208) *(G-4158)*

Watts Timber Company Inc 601 754-0138
1124 Wroten Ln Nw Brookhaven (39601) *(G-546)*

Waveland Candle Company LLC 228 220-4716
1815 Nicholson Ave Waveland (39576) *(G-5487)*

Way Manufacture Inc 601 749-0362
204 Street A Picayune (39466) *(G-4302)*

Wayne A Potter 601 446-6090
417 Main St Natchez (39120) *(G-3638)*

Wayne Farms LLC 601 425-4721
525 N Mississippi Ave Laurel (39440) *(G-2869)*

Wayne Farms LLC 601 399-7000
525 Wayne Dr Laurel (39440) *(G-2870)*

Wayne Hmphrys/Plygraph Exminer 601 825-8640
101 Ferry Dr Brandon (39047) *(G-472)*

Wcs Oil & Gas Corporation 601 787-4565
141 Hale Rd Sandersville (39477) *(G-4726)*

Wdtm Inc 662 842-6161
3185 Highway 9 S Pontotoc (38863) *(G-4369)*

Weatherford Artificia 601 649-4467
2932 Industrial Blvd Laurel (39440) *(G-2871)*

Weaver Consolidated Group Inc (PA) 662 287-1433
601 Washington St Corinth (38834) *(G-1128)*

Weaver Consolidated Group Inc 662 842-1753
1 Hadley St Tupelo (38804) *(G-5253)*

Weavexx LLC 662 323-4064
401 Mississippi 12 W Starkville (39759) *(G-4980)*

Webb Machine and Supply Inc 662 375-8309
303 Hwy 49 E Webb (38966) *(G-5520)*

Webbs Cstm Wdwrk & Finshg LLC 601 824-2851
6621 Brock Cir Brandon (39042) *(G-473)*

Webbs Welding & Repair LLC 901 487-2400
14414 Hedge Row Cv Olive Branch (38654) *(G-3924)*

Webster - Portalloy Chains Inc (HQ) 419 447-8232
3800 2nd St Meridian (39301) *(G-3419)*

Webster Industry Inc 601 482-0183
3800 2nd St Meridian (39301) *(G-3420)*

Wedgeworth Welding and Fab 228 326-0937
558 W Mchenry Rd Mc Henry (39561) *(G-3239)*

Weekly Leader 601 825-5133
207 E Government St Brandon (39042) *(G-474)*

Weems Industries LLC 228 382-4423
20053 Yaupon Dr Saucier (39574) *(G-4768)*

Weise Communications, Biloxi Also called Glenn Weise *(G-244)*

Welborn Devices LLC 601 428-5912
1596 Sndrsville Sharon Rd Laurel (39443) *(G-2872)*

Welch Printing 662 283-3692
705 Fairground St Winona (38967) *(G-5610)*

Welco Inc 601 445-9851
114 Foster Mound Rd Natchez (39120) *(G-3639)*

Welding Research & Fabricatn 870 551-5650
201 Milford St Apt 59 Tupelo (38801) *(G-5254)*

Welding Services 662 321-2472
680a Road 1460 Tupelo (38804) *(G-5255)*

Welding Works LLC 662 323-8684
307 Industrial Park Rd Starkville (39759) *(G-4981)*

Well Lease Service, Shubuta Also called W L S Inc *(G-4835)*

Well Logging Solutions LLC 601 416-9241
1011 Hickory Ridge Dr Kosciusko (39090) *(G-2720)*

Well Made Goods LLC 917 853-3598
81 S Church St Grenada (38901) *(G-1712)*

Well-Dressed Man 601 213-8311
128 W Cherokee St Brookhaven (39601) *(G-547)*

Wellcheck Inc 228 872-3633
4013 Bienville Blvd Ocean Springs (39564) *(G-3794)*

Wells Lamont Div, Philadelphia Also called Lamont Wells LLC *(G-4222)*

Wells Wood Products, Noxapater Also called Larry Wells *(G-3732)*

Wendall Harrell (PA) 601 267-3094
589 Highway 488 Carthage (39051) *(G-727)*

Wendall Harrell 601 353-3539
607 S Jefferson St Jackson (39201) *(G-2628)*

Werth Servicing LLC 662 449-4410
1404 Big Ben N Hernando (38632) *(G-2161)*

Wesco Gas & Welding Supply Inc 228 475-1955
3830 Highway 63 Moss Point (39563) *(G-3506)*

Wesley Inc 601 731-9288
568 Pounds Rd Foxworth (39483) *(G-1438)*

West Backhoe Inc 662 566-7828
132 Gum Tree Run Tupelo (38801) *(G-5256)*

328

2019 Harris Directory of
Mississippi Manufacturers

(G-0000) Company's Geographic Section entry number

ALPHABETIC SECTION

Windmill Pallet Works Inc (PA)

West Body Shop & Salvage Inc 662 566-2161
1383 W Palmetto Rd Verona (38879) *(G-5337)*

West Express 601 321-8088
3727 N West St Jackson (39216) *(G-2629)*

West Farms Inc 601 277-3579
8012 Carter Hill Rd Hazlehurst (39083) *(G-2109)*

West Group Holding Company LLC 662 871-2344
251 County Road 631 Shannon (38868) *(G-4821)*

West Jones Press Box 601 729-2216
254 Springhill Rd Laurel (39443) *(G-2873)*

Westergard Boat Works Inc 228 214-4455
10220 Three Rivers Rd Gulfport (39503) *(G-1893)*

Westlake Chemical Corporation 601 892-5612
20043 Highway 51 Hazlehurst (39083) *(G-2110)*

Westlake Chemical Corporation 662 369-8111
715 Highway 25 S Aberdeen (39730) *(G-21)*

Westlake Compound, Madison Also called Axiall Corporation *(G-3081)*

Westlake Compounds LLC 601 206-3200
210 Industrial Dr N Madison (39110) *(G-3168)*

Westlake Compounds LLC 601 892-5612
20043 Us Hwy 51 S Gallman (39077) *(G-1487)*

Westlake Group, Booneville Also called North American Pipe Corp *(G-338)*

Westminster Software 601 214-5028
315 Westminster Ct Brandon (39047) *(G-475)*

Westpoint Home LLC 601 466-6738
1005 Oakleigh Dr Hattiesburg (39402) *(G-2082)*

Westrock Cp LLC 662 842-4940
1590 S Green St Tupelo (38802) *(G-5257)*

Westrock Cp LLC 662 895-1627
10333 High Point Rd Olive Branch (38654) *(G-3925)*

Westrock Cp LLC 662 869-5771
324 Turner Indus Pk Rd Saltillo (38866) *(G-4723)*

Westward Corporation 601 660-3857
1453 Main St Fayette (39069) *(G-1303)*

Wet Paint LLC 662 269-2412
4344 Mall Dr Tupelo (38804) *(G-5258)*

Wey Valve Inc 662 963-2020
175 Bryan Blvd Shannon (38868) *(G-4822)*

Weyerhaeuser 662 327-1961
297 Richardson Rd Columbus (39702) *(G-1043)*

Weyerhaeuser Company 601 650-7200
1016 Weyerhaeuser Rd Philadelphia (39350) *(G-4249)*

Weyerhaeuser Company 662 983-7311
106 Railroad St Bruce (38915) *(G-562)*

Weyerhaeuser Company 662 243-4000
4335 Carson Rd Columbus (39701) *(G-1044)*

Weyerhaeuser Company 662 243-6900
371 Manufacturers Rd Columbus (39701) *(G-1045)*

Wheat Construction Inc 601 772-9074
8124 Highway 43 N Poplarville (39470) *(G-4399)*

Wheel Polishing Pros Inc 601 259-9379
31234 Highway 12 Mc Cool (39108) *(G-3238)*

Wheeler Enterprises Inc 601 799-1440
1620 Highway 11 N Ste B Picayune (39466) *(G-4303)*

Where We Print Shirts LLC 601 348-5754
108 Kenbridge Ln Madison (39110) *(G-3169)*

White Jerleen 601 941-6886
5641 Highway 84 Prentiss (39474) *(G-4425)*

White Brothers Inc 601 948-0888
200 Commerce St Ofc Jackson (39201) *(G-2630)*

White Logging 601 783-2738
7759 Highway 568 W Magnolia (39652) *(G-3196)*

White Rhino Fabrication LLC 601 397-1118
494 Lincoln St Canton (39046) *(G-684)*

White Septic Backhoe LLC 662 251-8989
69 Mohave Ln Steens (39766) *(G-4992)*

White Shirt Networks LLC 601 292-7900
742 Magnolia St Madison (39110) *(G-3170)*

Whitehouse Industries 601 981-5866
728 Windward Rd Jackson (39206) *(G-2631)*

Whitestone Contracting LLC 601 800-8077
503 E Holly St Ellisville (39437) *(G-1278)*

Whiting Woodcraft LLC 662 895-1688
8823 Deerfield Dr Olive Branch (38654) *(G-3926)*

Whitney 662 268-8379
96 Lummus Dr Starkville (39759) *(G-4982)*

Whitney Engineering, Philadelphia Also called Mark A Whitney *(G-4224)*

Whitney Whitehead 662 380-0614
127 Ashley Way Sarah (38665) *(G-4737)*

Whittington Construction Co 601 442-8096
706 Orleans St Natchez (39120) *(G-3640)*

Who Is Sed Publishing LLC 601 634-8939
5015 Rllngwood Esttes Dr Vicksburg (39180) *(G-5444)*

Wholesale Electric Supply 601 501-6928
520 Depot St Vicksburg (39180) *(G-5445)*

Wicker Machine Co 662 827-5434
1400 East Ave N Hollandale (38748) *(G-2169)*

Wicks N Candle Company 662 891-4237
703 Pulltight Rd Saltillo (38866) *(G-4724)*

Wicks N More Inc 662 205-4025
558 Highway 371 Mooreville (38857) *(G-3444)*

Wicks N More Wholesale, Mooreville Also called Wicks N More Inc *(G-3444)*

Widups Woodworks LLC 601 966-0593
128 Rockwood Dr Madison (39110) *(G-3171)*

Wilbert Burial Vault Company 601 353-7084
820 Larson St Jackson (39202) *(G-2632)*

Wilbert Funeral Services Inc 800 323-7188
820 Larson St Jackson (39202) *(G-2633)*

Wilcox Energy Company 601 442-5191
304 Franklin St Natchez (39120) *(G-3641)*

Wilder Architecheral Designs, Pontotoc Also called Wilders Welding Shop *(G-4371)*

Wilder Bros Sawmill Inc 662 488-8692
830 Andrews Rd Ecru (38841) *(G-1235)*

Wilder Fitness Systems 662 489-8365
215 E Oxford St Pontotoc (38863) *(G-4370)*

Wilders Welding Shop 662 489-2772
321 W Oxford St Pontotoc (38863) *(G-4371)*

Wilderwood LLC 601 955-8539
129 Indian Creek Blvd Flowood (39232) *(G-1407)*

Wildlife Dominion MGT LLC 662 272-9550
1563 Penn Station Rd Crawford (39743) *(G-1131)*

Wilkinson County Museum 601 888-7151
203 Boston Row Woodville (39669) *(G-5619)*

Willcoxon Enterprises Inc 662 840-2300
510 S Gloster St Tupelo (38801) *(G-5259)*

William Barnes 601 446-6122
198 Devereaux Dr Natchez (39120) *(G-3642)*

William Carey University 601 318-6115
498 Tuscan Ave Hattiesburg (39401) *(G-2083)*

William Kilgore 601 582-3702
702 Sanford Rd Moselle (39459) *(G-3464)*

William M Stewart 662 393-7950
6815 Pinehurst Rd Horn Lake (38637) *(G-2215)*

William R Gatewood 601 636-0107
1431 Wisteria Dr Vicksburg (39180) *(G-5446)*

William Stephens 601 634-0498
3995 Highway 80 Vicksburg (39180) *(G-5447)*

William Zaremba 601 845-7238
2155 Cleary Rd Florence (39073) *(G-1339)*

Williams Companies Inc 662 895-7202
772 Wingo Rd Byhalia (38611) *(G-612)*

Williams J P Mch & Fabrication, Moss Point Also called Williams JP Mch & Fabrication *(G-3507)*

Williams JP Mch & Fabrication 228 474-1099
7206 Grierson St Moss Point (39563) *(G-3507)*

Williams Logging Company Inc 601 835-2771
835 Howard Rd Ne Brookhaven (39601) *(G-548)*

Williams Machine Works Inc 228 712-2667
5309 Industrial Rd Pascagoula (39581) *(G-4074)*

Williams Machine Works Inc (PA) 228 475-7651
5624 Main St Moss Point (39563) *(G-3508)*

Williams Prcsion Machining LLC (PA) 662 287-7734
46 County Road 405 Corinth (38834) *(G-1129)*

Williams Sonoma 901 795-2625
7755 Polk Ln Olive Branch (38654) *(G-3927)*

Williams Transportation Co LLC 601 428-2214
46 Don Curt Rd Laurel (39440) *(G-2874)*

Williamson & Son Logging LLC 601 736-7858
317 W Reservoir Rd Columbia (39429) *(G-928)*

Williamson Gin Repair 662 571-6084
1200 Rialto Rd Yazoo City (39194) *(G-5652)*

Williamson, James Co, Philadelphia Also called Clarence Sansing Jr *(G-4211)*

Willie B Sims Jr CPA Pllc 601 545-3930
908 Broadway Dr Hattiesburg (39401) *(G-2084)*

Willie Lynn Hunt 601 945-2237
161 Hunt Rd Lucedale (39452) *(G-3021)*

Willie Morgan 662 834-4366
159 Mallory Rd Lexington (39095) *(G-2907)*

Willies Woodworks 601 916-3574
12471 Old Kiln Rd Picayune (39466) *(G-4304)*

Willow Ansthesia Solutions LLC 662 550-4299
2704 West Oxford Loop Oxford (38655) *(G-4009)*

Willowood Dvelopmental Ctr Inc (PA) 601 366-0123
1635 Boling St Jackson (39213) *(G-2634)*

Wilson Branch Publishing LLC 601 656-2718
31 Terri Dr Philadelphia (39350) *(G-4250)*

Wilson Fabrication Inc 601 445-8119
252 Lower Woodville Rd Natchez (39120) *(G-3643)*

Wilson Solutions LLC 662 319-6063
10062a Homestead Rd Aberdeen (39730) *(G-22)*

Wilson Welding 601 483-3696
3211 Bolen Long Creek Rd Meridian (39301) *(G-3421)*

Wilsonart LLC 828 785-2796
98 County Road 122 Oxford (38655) *(G-4010)*

Wilsons Welding Service Inc (PA) 228 255-4825
5229 Jordan Rd Perkinston (39573) *(G-4183)*

Winchester Ammunition, Oxford Also called Olin Corporation *(G-3981)*

Windmill Pallet Works Inc (PA) 601 876-4498
70 Old Settlement Rd Tylertown (39667) *(G-5291)*

(PA)=Parent Co (HQ)=Headquarters (DH)=Div Headquarters

2019 Harris Directory of
Mississippi Manufacturers

329

ALPHABETIC

Windshield Repair Systems

Windshield Repair Systems 601 657-8303
3028 Highway 569 S Liberty (39645) *(G-2920)*

Winery At Williams Landing LLC 662 219-0596
500 Howard St Greenwood (38930) *(G-1665)*

Wings Aircraft Leasing, Holly Springs *Also called Jewell Aircrafting Inc* *(G-2178)*

Winona Hardwood Inc 662 283-3050
164 Sawyer Rd Winona (38967) *(G-5611)*

Winona Times, The, Winona *Also called Montgomery Publishing Co Inc* *(G-5604)*

Winston County Journal, Louisville *Also called Louisville Publishing Inc* *(G-2974)*

Wire Display Fabrication Inc 662 838-9650
33 Ms Sarah Byhalia (38611) *(G-613)*

Wiredless Network Inc 601 665-5307
127 W Peace St Fl 2 Canton (39046) *(G-685)*

Wis-Pak of Hattiesburg LLC 601 544-7200
2 WI Runnels Indus Dr Hattiesburg (39401) *(G-2085)*

Withers Oil & Gas LLC 601 982-3444
1837 Crane Ridge Dr Jackson (39216) *(G-2635)*

Wnc Satcom Group LLC (PA) 601 544-0311
208 W Pine St Ste 100 Hattiesburg (39401) *(G-2086)*

Wntz TV 601 442-4800
26 Col John Ptchford Pkwy Natchez (39120) *(G-3644)*

Wolf Industries Inc 228 864-9096
1418 31st Ave Gulfport (39501) *(G-1894)*

Wolf River Press 601 372-2679
815 Reaves St Jackson (39204) *(G-2636)*

Wolverton Enterprises Inc 601 355-9543
225 E Pearl St Jackson (39201) *(G-2637)*

Womack Willow 601 969-4120
418 N Farish St Jackson (39202) *(G-2638)*

Wonder Woods Inc 601 853-1956
376 Distribution Dr Madison (39110) *(G-3172)*

Wood Industries Inc 662 454-0005
21 Front St Belmont (38827) *(G-203)*

Wood Preserving Inc 601 833-8822
966 Sawmill Ln Ne Brookhaven (39601) *(G-549)*

Wood Work Solutions 662 890-8954
155 Downing St Olive Branch (38654) *(G-3928)*

Wood's Trailers, Golden *Also called Woods Trailers & Repair LLC* *(G-1533)*

Wooden Arts LLC 228 452-9943
22332 Freddie Frank Rd Long Beach (39560) *(G-2960)*

Wooden Arts Workshop, Long Beach *Also called Wooden Arts LLC* *(G-2960)*

Woodies Woodworks 478 973-8851
3840 York Rd Lauderdale (39335) *(G-2729)*

Woodrffs Prtble Wldg Fbrcation 662 728-3326
94 County Road 5131 Booneville (38829) *(G-347)*

Woods Farm Supply Inc 662 838-6754
3248 Highway 309 S Byhalia (38611) *(G-614)*

Woods Trading Co Inc 601 924-5015
100 Belmont St Clinton (39056) *(G-839)*

Woods Trailers & Repair LLC 662 585-3606
1 Industrial Park Golden (38847) *(G-1533)*

Woodson Flying Service Inc 662 983-4274
County Rd 219 Off Hwy 32 Bruce (38915) *(G-563)*

Woodville Civic Club, Woodville *Also called Wilkinson County Museum* *(G-5619)*

Woodworkings 662 255-3421
111 E Main St Baldwyn (38824) *(G-89)*

Wooly Booger Game Calls 662 587-3763
520 County Road 308 Walnut (38683) *(G-5459)*

Word Alive 601 307-3639
727 Central Ave W Wiggins (39577) *(G-5594)*

World Class Athltcsurfaces Inc 662 686-9997
817 N Broad St Leland (38756) *(G-2893)*

World Evangelism 662 283-1192
600 Devine St Winona (38967) *(G-5612)*

World Marine Mississippi LLC 228 762-0010
601 Bayou Casotte Pkwy Pascagoula (39581) *(G-4075)*

Worthen Bros Coastal Lawn 228 261-4785
11970 Summerhaven Cir Gulfport (39503) *(G-1895)*

Worthington Cylinder Corp 662 538-6500
795 Sam Barkley Dr New Albany (38652) *(G-3708)*

Worthington Cylinders Miss LLC 614 840-3802
795 Sam T Barkley Dr New Albany (38652) *(G-3709)*

Worthington Industries, New Albany *Also called Worthington Cylinders Miss LLC* *(G-3709)*

Wreath Haven 205 393-3015
102 Little John Dr Petal (39465) *(G-4200)*

Wreaths Charms and More, Biloxi *Also called Marilyn Turner* *(G-265)*

Wren Pest Control 601 276-6117
1160 Robb Street Ext E Summit (39666) *(G-5031)*

Wrestling USA Magazine Inc 406 360-9421
590 Royal Oak Dr Apt 18 Pass Christian (39571) *(G-4098)*

Wrestling USA Magazine Inc 406 549-4448
590 Royal Oak Dr Apt 18 Pass Christian (39571) *(G-4099)*

Wrjw 1320 AM 601 798-4835
2438 Highway 43 S Picayune (39466) *(G-4305)*

Wtf Lure Company, Brandon *Also called Jara L Miller* *(G-410)*

Wynnes Custom Coatings 601 664-3474
2560 Highway 80 E Pearl (39208) *(G-4159)*

X L Johnson & Sons Inc 601 776-3685
9110 County Road 511 Quitman (39355) *(G-4472)*

X Press Copy Centre, Picayune *Also called Wheeler Enterprises Inc* *(G-4303)*

X Treme Racing 601 947-9686
109 Mcmahan Dr Lucedale (39452) *(G-3022)*

Xerium Technologies Inc 662 323-4064
401 Highway 12 W Starkville (39759) *(G-4983)*

Xooma Worldwide 662 548-5361
2258 Linda Shore Dr Southaven (38672) *(G-4920)*

Xspire Pharma LLC 870 243-1687
121 Marketridge Dr Ste B Ridgeland (39157) *(G-4647)*

Xylem Water Solutions Usa 662 393-0275
1085 Sttline Rd E Ste 107 Southaven (38671) *(G-4921)*

Yak Mat, Columbia *Also called Dixie Mat and Hardwood Co* *(G-895)*

Yalls Products 601 391-3698
644 Church Rd Madison (39110) *(G-3173)*

Yank Threads LLC 601 201-3934
611 Patton Ave Jackson (39216) *(G-2639)*

Yates Industrial Services LLC 601 467-6232
131 Calvin Purvis Rd Purvis (39475) *(G-4454)*

Yazoo Herald, The, Yazoo City *Also called Yazoo Newspaper Co Inc* *(G-5653)*

Yazoo Newspaper Co Inc 662 746-4911
1035 Grand Ave Yazoo City (39194) *(G-5653)*

Yazoo Ready Mix Concrete, Yazoo City *Also called Delta Industries Inc* *(G-5631)*

Yellow Dog Printing Co LLC 601 776-6853
1065 County Road 430 Quitman (39355) *(G-4473)*

Yesco, Biloxi *Also called Young Electric Sign Company* *(G-287)*

Yna Pallets Sales 601 405-6545
250 Poplar St Florence (39073) *(G-1340)*

Yokohama Tire Manufactu 800 423-4544
1 Yokohama Blvd West Point (39773) *(G-5566)*

Yokohama Tire Mfg Miss LLC 800 423-4544
1 Yokohama Blvd West Point (39773) *(G-5567)*

Yonce & Comans Products LLC 601 270-7712
9128 Old River Rd Petal (39465) *(G-4201)*

York International Corporation 601 544-8911
77 Academy Dr Hattiesburg (39401) *(G-2087)*

Young E F Jr Manufacturing Co 601 483-8864
425 26th Ave Meridian (39301) *(G-3422)*

Young Dghters Prcsion Mch Wrks 662 286-6538
1500 Dcomsey Way Ext Extended Corinth (38834) *(G-1130)*

Young Electric Sign Co 228 354-8008
12487 Shortcut Rd Biloxi (39532) *(G-286)*

Young Electric Sign Company 228 354-8008
12487 Shortcut Rd Biloxi (39532) *(G-287)*

Young Welding Supply Inc 662 792-4061
723 Veterans Memorial Dr Kosciusko (39090) *(G-2721)*

Young's Trucking, Hattiesburg *Also called Malone Design & Contg LLC* *(G-2020)*

Youngs Leather & Custom Tees 662 424-3847
2499 County Road 961 Dennis (38838) *(G-1185)*

Your Dollar and More, McComb *Also called Bullocks Washteria* *(G-3244)*

Yum Yums Gourmet Popcorn LLC 662 470-6047
9049 Highway 51 N Southaven (38671) *(G-4922)*

Z A Construction LLC 601 259-5276
834 Cato Rd Mendenhall (39114) *(G-3291)*

Zaremba Machine, Florence *Also called William Zaremba* *(G-1339)*

Zavation LLC 601 919-1119
220 Lakeland Pkwy Flowood (39232) *(G-1408)*

Zeon Chemicals L P 601 583-5527
1301 W 7th St Hattiesburg (39401) *(G-2088)*

Zero Dead Miles LLC 769 208-8082
1245 Breckinridge Rd Jackson (39204) *(G-2640)*

Ziprint Inc 662 226-6864
1346 Sunset Dr Grenada (38901) *(G-1713)*

Zodiac Aerospace 601 657-8719
269 Main St Liberty (39645) *(G-2921)*

Zyaa Inc 601 321-9502
2729 Bailey Ave Jackson (39213) *(G-2641)*

PRODUCT INDEX

• Product categories are listed in alphabetical order.

A

ABRASIVES
ACCELERATION INDICATORS & SYSTEM COMPONENTS: Aerospace
ACCOUNTING SVCS, NEC
ACOUSTICAL BOARD & TILE
ACRYLIC RESINS
ACTUATORS: Indl, NEC
ADHESIVES
ADHESIVES & SEALANTS
ADHESIVES: Adhesives, paste
ADHESIVES: Epoxy
ADVERTISING AGENCIES
ADVERTISING AGENCIES: Consultants
ADVERTISING MATERIAL DISTRIBUTION
ADVERTISING REPRESENTATIVES: Magazine
ADVERTISING REPRESENTATIVES: Newspaper
ADVERTISING REPRESENTATIVES: Printed Media
ADVERTISING SPECIALTIES, WHOLESALE
ADVERTISING SVCS: Direct Mail
ADVERTISING SVCS: Display
AGENTS, BROKERS & BUREAUS: Personal Service
AGRICULTURAL CHEMICALS: Trace Elements
AGRICULTURAL EQPT: BARN, SILO, POULTRY, DAIRY/LIVESTOCK MACH
AGRICULTURAL EQPT: Fertilizing Machinery
AGRICULTURAL EQPT: Fertilizng, Sprayng, Dustng/Irrigatn Mach
AGRICULTURAL EQPT: Grounds Mowing Eqpt
AGRICULTURAL EQPT: Planting Machines
AGRICULTURAL EQPT: Soil Preparation Mach, Exc Turf & Grounds
AGRICULTURAL EQPT: Trailers & Wagons, Farm
AGRICULTURAL EQPT: Turf & Grounds Eqpt
AGRICULTURAL MACHINERY & EQPT: Wholesalers
AIR CLEANING SYSTEMS
AIR CONDITIONERS: Motor Vehicle
AIR CONDITIONING & VENTILATION EQPT & SPLYS: Wholesales
AIR CONDITIONING EQPT
AIR CONDITIONING REPAIR SVCS
AIRCRAFT & AEROSPACE FLIGHT INSTRUMENTS & GUIDANCE SYSTEMS
AIRCRAFT & HEAVY EQPT REPAIR SVCS
AIRCRAFT ASSEMBLY PLANTS
AIRCRAFT CONTROL SYSTEMS: Electronic Totalizing Counters
AIRCRAFT ELECTRICAL EQPT REPAIR SVCS
AIRCRAFT ENGINES & ENGINE PARTS: Air Scoops
AIRCRAFT ENGINES & ENGINE PARTS: Airfoils
AIRCRAFT ENGINES & PARTS
AIRCRAFT EQPT & SPLYS WHOLESALERS
AIRCRAFT MAINTENANCE & REPAIR SVCS
AIRCRAFT PARTS & AUXILIARY EQPT: Aircraft Training Eqpt
AIRCRAFT PARTS & AUXILIARY EQPT: Deicing Eqpt
AIRCRAFT PARTS & AUXILIARY EQPT: Military Eqpt & Armament
AIRCRAFT PARTS & AUXILIARY EQPT: Nacelles
AIRCRAFT PARTS & EQPT, NEC
AIRCRAFT PARTS WHOLESALERS
AIRCRAFT WHEELS
AIRCRAFT: Airplanes, Fixed Or Rotary Wing
AIRCRAFT: Motorized
AIRCRAFT: Research & Development, Manufacturer
AIRLOCKS
ALARMS: Burglar
ALKALIES & CHLORINE
ALTERNATORS & GENERATORS: Battery Charging
ALUMINUM
ALUMINUM & BERYLLIUM ORES MINING
ALUMINUM PRDTS
ALUMINUM: Coil & Sheet
ALUMINUM: Rolling & Drawing
AMMUNITION
AMMUNITION: Small Arms
AMPLIFIERS: RF & IF Power
AMUSEMENT & REC SVCS: Cake/Pastry Decorating Instruction

AMUSEMENT & RECREATION SVCS: Amusement Arcades
AMUSEMENT & RECREATION SVCS: Card Rooms
AMUSEMENT & RECREATION SVCS: Lottery Tickets, Sales
AMUSEMENT & RECREATION SVCS: Tour & Guide
AMUSEMENT MACHINES: Coin Operated
AMUSEMENT PARK DEVICES & RIDES
ANALGESICS
ANALYZERS: Network
ANESTHESIA EQPT
ANILINE OR NITROBENZENE
ANIMAL FEED & SUPPLEMENTS: Livestock & Poultry
ANIMAL FEED: Wholesalers
ANIMAL FOOD & SUPPLEMENTS: Dog
ANIMAL FOOD & SUPPLEMENTS: Dog & Cat
ANIMAL FOOD & SUPPLEMENTS: Feed Concentrates
ANIMAL FOOD & SUPPLEMENTS: Livestock
ANIMAL FOOD & SUPPLEMENTS: Meat Meal & Tankage
ANIMAL FOOD & SUPPLEMENTS: Slaughtering of nonfood animals
ANIMAL FOOD/SUPPLEMENTS: Feeds Fm Meat/Meat/Veg Combnd Meals
ANTENNAS: Satellite, Household Use
APPLIANCE PARTS: Porcelain Enameled
APPLIANCES, HOUSEHOLD: Kitchen, Major, Exc Refrigs & Stoves
APPLIANCES, HOUSEHOLD: Refrigs, Mechanical & Absorption
APPLIANCES: Household, NEC
APPLIANCES: Household, Refrigerators & Freezers
APPLIANCES: Major, Cooking
APPLIANCES: Small, Electric
ARCHITECTURAL SVCS
ARMATURE REPAIRING & REWINDING SVC
ART & ORNAMENTAL WARE: Pottery
ART GALLERIES
ART GOODS & SPLYS WHOLESALERS
ARTISTS' MATERIALS: Paints, China Painting
ARTISTS' MATERIALS: Paints, Exc Gold & Bronze
ARTS & CRAFTS SCHOOL
ASBESTOS REMOVAL EQPT
ASPHALT & ASPHALT PRDTS
ASPHALT COATINGS & SEALERS
ASPHALT PLANTS INCLUDING GRAVEL MIX TYPE
ASSOCIATIONS: Real Estate Management
ATOMIZERS
AUDIO COMPONENTS
AUDIO ELECTRONIC SYSTEMS
AUTHOR
AUTO & HOME SUPPLY STORES: Auto & Truck Eqpt & Parts
AUTO & HOME SUPPLY STORES: Automotive Access
AUTO & HOME SUPPLY STORES: Automotive parts
AUTO & HOME SUPPLY STORES: Batteries, Automotive & Truck
AUTO & HOME SUPPLY STORES: Speed Shops, Incl Race Car Splys
AUTO & HOME SUPPLY STORES: Truck Eqpt & Parts
AUTOMATIC REGULATING CONTROLS: AC & Refrigeration
AUTOMATIC REGULATING CONTROLS: Ice Maker
AUTOMATIC REGULATING CONTROLS: Refrig/Air-Cond Defrost
AUTOMATIC TELLER MACHINES
AUTOMOBILE RECOVERY SVCS
AUTOMOBILES & OTHER MOTOR VEHICLES WHOLESALERS
AUTOMOTIVE & TRUCK GENERAL REPAIR SVC
AUTOMOTIVE BODY SHOP
AUTOMOTIVE BRAKE REPAIR SHOPS
AUTOMOTIVE PAINT SHOP
AUTOMOTIVE PARTS, ACCESS & SPLYS
AUTOMOTIVE PARTS: Plastic
AUTOMOTIVE RADIATOR REPAIR SHOPS
AUTOMOTIVE REPAIR SHOPS: Diesel Engine Repair
AUTOMOTIVE REPAIR SHOPS: Electrical Svcs
AUTOMOTIVE REPAIR SHOPS: Engine Rebuilding
AUTOMOTIVE REPAIR SHOPS: Engine Repair
AUTOMOTIVE REPAIR SHOPS: Fuel System Repair
AUTOMOTIVE REPAIR SHOPS: Machine Shop
AUTOMOTIVE REPAIR SHOPS: Tire Repair Shop

AUTOMOTIVE REPAIR SHOPS: Trailer Repair
AUTOMOTIVE REPAIR SHOPS: Truck Engine Repair, Exc Indl
AUTOMOTIVE REPAIR SHOPS: Wheel Alignment
AUTOMOTIVE REPAIR SVCS, MISCELLANEOUS
AUTOMOTIVE SPLYS & PARTS, NEW, WHOL: Auto Servicing Eqpt
AUTOMOTIVE SPLYS & PARTS, NEW, WHOLESALE: Splys
AUTOMOTIVE SPLYS & PARTS, NEW, WHOLESALE: Trailer Parts
AUTOMOTIVE SPLYS & PARTS, WHOLESALE, NEC
AUTOMOTIVE SVCS, EXC REPAIR & CARWASHES: Lubrication
AUTOMOTIVE SVCS, EXC REPAIR & CARWASHES: Road Svc
AUTOMOTIVE SVCS, EXC REPAIR & CARWASHES: Trailer Maintenance
AUTOMOTIVE SVCS, EXC REPAIR: Washing & Polishing
AUTOMOTIVE TOPS INSTALLATION OR REPAIR: Canvas Or Plastic
AUTOMOTIVE TOWING SVCS
AUTOMOTIVE TRANSMISSION REPAIR SVC
AUTOMOTIVE UPHOLSTERY SHOPS
AUTOMOTIVE WELDING SVCS
AUTOMOTIVE: Seat Frames, Metal
AUTOMOTIVE: Seating
AWNINGS & CANOPIES: Fabric
AWNINGS: Metal

B

BABBITT (METAL)
BACKHOES
BADGES, WHOLESALE
BAGS & CONTAINERS: Textile, Exc Sleeping
BAGS: Canvas
BAGS: Duffle, Canvas, Made From Purchased Materials
BAGS: Food Storage & Trash, Plastic
BAGS: Garment, Plastic Film, Made From Purchased Materials
BAGS: Paper
BAGS: Paper, Made From Purchased Materials
BAGS: Plastic
BAGS: Plastic & Pliofilm
BAGS: Plastic, Made From Purchased Materials
BAGS: Shipping
BAGS: Textile
BAIT, FISHING, WHOLESALE
BAKERIES, COMMERCIAL: On Premises Baking Only
BAKERIES: On Premises Baking & Consumption
BAKERY FOR HOME SVC DELIVERY
BAKERY PRDTS: Bread, All Types, Fresh Or Frozen
BAKERY PRDTS: Cakes, Bakery, Exc Frozen
BAKERY PRDTS: Cakes, Bakery, Frozen
BAKERY PRDTS: Cookies
BAKERY PRDTS: Cookies & crackers
BAKERY PRDTS: Doughnuts, Exc Frozen
BAKERY PRDTS: Dry
BAKERY PRDTS: Frozen
BAKERY PRDTS: Pretzels
BAKERY PRDTS: Rolls, Bread Type, Fresh Or Frozen
BAKERY PRDTS: Yeast Goods, Sweet, Exc Frozen
BAKERY: Wholesale Or Wholesale & Retail Combined
BALCONIES: Metal
BALERS
BALLOONS: Novelty & Toy
BANNERS: Fabric
BAR
BARBECUE EQPT
BARRICADES: Metal
BARS, COLD FINISHED: Steel, From Purchased Hot-Rolled
BARS: Concrete Reinforcing, Fabricated Steel
BARS: Extruded, Aluminum
BATHMATS: Rubber
BATHTUBS: Concrete
BATTERIES, EXC AUTOMOTIVE: Wholesalers
BATTERIES: Alkaline, Cell Storage
BATTERIES: Lead Acid, Storage
BATTERIES: Storage

INDEX

PRODUCT INDEX

BATTERIES: Wet
BATTERY CHARGERS
BEADS: Unassembled
BEARINGS: Ball & Roller
BEAUTY & BARBER SHOP EQPT
BEAUTY & BARBER SHOP EQPT & SPLYS WHOLESALERS
BEAUTY SALONS
BEDDING, BEDSPREADS, BLANKETS & SHEETS: Comforters & Quilts
BEDS: Hospital
BEDSPREADS & BED SETS, FROM PURCHASED MATERIALS
BEDSPREADS, COTTON
BEEKEEPERS' SPLYS
BEER & ALE WHOLESALERS
BEER, WINE & LIQUOR STORES: Hard Liquor
BEER, WINE & LIQUOR STORES: Wine
BENTONITE MINING
BEVERAGE BASES & SYRUPS
BEVERAGE STORES
BEVERAGE, NONALCOHOLIC: Iced Tea/Fruit Drink, Bottled/Canned
BEVERAGES, ALCOHOLIC: Beer
BEVERAGES, ALCOHOLIC: Beer & Ale
BEVERAGES, ALCOHOLIC: Distilled Liquors
BEVERAGES, ALCOHOLIC: Vodka
BEVERAGES, ALCOHOLIC: Wines
BEVERAGES, NONALCOHOLIC: Bottled & canned soft drinks
BEVERAGES, NONALCOHOLIC: Carbonated
BEVERAGES, NONALCOHOLIC: Carbonated, Canned & Bottled, Etc
BEVERAGES, NONALCOHOLIC: Flavoring extracts & syrups, nec
BEVERAGES, NONALCOHOLIC: Soft Drinks, Canned & Bottled, Etc
BICYCLES WHOLESALERS
BILLIARD & POOL TABLES & SPLYS
BILLING & BOOKKEEPING SVCS
BINDING SVC: Books & Manuals
BIOLOGICAL PRDTS: Blood Derivatives
BIOLOGICAL PRDTS: Exc Diagnostic
BIOLOGICAL PRDTS: Vaccines & Immunizing
BLADES: Saw, Hand Or Power
BLANKBOOKS & LOOSELEAF BINDERS
BLANKBOOKS: Account
BLASTING SVC: Sand, Metal Parts
BLIMPS
BLINDS : Window
BLOCKS & BRICKS: Concrete
BLOCKS: Landscape Or Retaining Wall, Concrete
BLOCKS: Paving, Concrete
BLOCKS: Standard, Concrete Or Cinder
BLOOD RELATED HEALTH SVCS
BLOWERS & FANS
BLUEPRINTING SVCS
BOAT & BARGE COMPONENTS: Metal, Prefabricated
BOAT BUILDING & REPAIR
BOAT BUILDING & REPAIRING: Fiberglass
BOAT BUILDING & REPAIRING: Houseboats
BOAT BUILDING & REPAIRING: Hydrofoil
BOAT BUILDING & REPAIRING: Motorboats, Inboard Or Outboard
BOAT BUILDING & REPAIRING: Non-Motorized
BOAT BUILDING & REPAIRING: Tenders, Small Motor Craft
BOAT DEALERS
BOAT DEALERS: Marine Splys & Eqpt
BOAT LIFTS
BOAT REPAIR SVCS
BODIES: Truck & Bus
BODY PARTS: Automobile, Stamped Metal
BOLTS: Metal
BOLTS: Wooden, Hewn
BOTTLE CAPS & RESEALERS: Plastic
BOTTLED GAS DEALERS: Liquefied Petro, Dlvrd To Customers
BOTTLES: Plastic
BOXES & CRATES: Rectangular, Wood
BOXES & SHOOK: Nailed Wood
BOXES: Corrugated
BOXES: Filing, Paperboard Made From Purchased Materials
BOXES: Paperboard, Folding
BOXES: Wooden
BRAKES: Metal Forming
BRICK CLEANING SVCS

BRICK, STONE & RELATED PRDTS WHOLESALERS
BRICKS : Flooring, Clay
BRICKS: Clay
BRICKS: Concrete
BRIDAL SHOPS
BRIDGE COMPONENTS: Bridge sections, prefabricated, highway
BROADCASTING & COMMS EQPT: Antennas, Transmitting/Comms
BROKERS: Mortgage, Arranging For Loans
BROKERS: Printing
BROOMS
BROOMS & BRUSHES
BROOMS & BRUSHES: Household Or Indl
BUILDING & OFFICE CLEANING SVCS
BUILDING & STRUCTURAL WOOD MBRS: Timbers, Struct, Lam Lumber
BUILDING & STRUCTURAL WOOD MEMBERS
BUILDING BOARD: Gypsum
BUILDING COMPONENTS: Structural Steel
BUILDING EXTERIOR CLEANING SVCS
BUILDING MAINTENANCE SVCS, EXC REPAIRS
BUILDING PRDTS & MATERIALS DEALERS
BUILDING PRDTS: Concrete
BUILDINGS & COMPONENTS: Prefabricated Metal
BUILDINGS, PREFABRICATED: Wholesalers
BUILDINGS: Chicken Coops, Prefabricated, Wood
BUILDINGS: Mobile, For Commercial Use
BUILDINGS: Portable
BUILDINGS: Prefabricated, Metal
BUILDINGS: Prefabricated, Wood
BURIAL VAULTS: Concrete Or Precast Terrazzo
BURIAL VAULTS: Stone
BUSINESS ACTIVITIES: Non-Commercial Site
BUSINESS FORMS WHOLESALERS
BUSINESS FORMS: Printed, Continuous
BUSINESS FORMS: Printed, Manifold
BUYERS' CLUB

C

CABINETS & CASES: Show, Display & Storage, Exc Wood
CABINETS, HOUSING: For Radium, Metal Plate
CABINETS: Bathroom Vanities, Wood
CABINETS: Entertainment
CABINETS: Factory
CABINETS: Kitchen, Wood
CABINETS: Office, Wood
CABINETS: Show, Display, Etc, Wood, Exc Refrigerated
CABLE & OTHER PAY TELEVISION DISTRIBUTION
CABLE & PAY TELEVISION SVCS: Closed Circuit
CABLE & PAY TELEVISION SVCS: Direct Broadcast Satellite
CABLE: Coaxial
CAFES
CALCULATING & ACCOUNTING EQPT
CALIBRATING SVCS, NEC
CAMERA & PHOTOGRAPHIC SPLYS STORES
CAMERAS & RELATED EQPT: Photographic
CAMPERS: Truck, Slide-In
CAMSHAFTS
CANDLES
CANDLES: Wholesalers
CANDY & CONFECTIONS: Fruit, Chocolate Covered, Exc Dates
CANDY & CONFECTIONS: Nuts, Candy Covered
CANDY & CONFECTIONS: Popcorn Balls/Other Trtd Popcorn Prdts
CANDY, NUT & CONFECTIONERY STORE: Popcorn, Incl Caramel Corn
CANDY, NUT & CONFECTIONERY STORES: Candy
CANDY: Hard
CANNED SPECIALTIES
CANS: Metal
CANVAS PRDTS: Boat Seats
CARBIDES
CARBON BLACK
CARBURETORS
CARDS: Identification
CARPET & UPHOLSTERY CLEANING SVCS
CARPETS & RUGS: Tufted
CARPETS, RUGS & FLOOR COVERING
CARPETS: Hand & Machine Made
CARS: Electric
CASES: Carrying, Clothing & Apparel
CASTERS
CASTINGS GRINDING: For The Trade

CASTINGS: Bronze, NEC, Exc Die
CASTINGS: Die, Aluminum
CASTINGS: Steel
CAT BOX FILLER
CATALOG & MAIL-ORDER HOUSES
CATTLE WHOLESALERS
CEMENT: Hydraulic
CEMENT: Masonry
CEMENT: Portland
CEMETERY & FUNERAL DIRECTOR'S EQPT & SPLYS WHOLESALERS
CERAMIC FIBER
CHAIN: Welded, Made From Purchased Wire
CHANGE MAKING MACHINES
CHARCOAL
CHARCOAL: Activated
CHEMICAL ELEMENTS
CHEMICAL PROCESSING MACHINERY & EQPT
CHEMICAL SPLYS FOR FOUNDRIES
CHEMICALS & ALLIED PRDTS WHOLESALERS, NEC
CHEMICALS & ALLIED PRDTS, WHOLESALE: Alcohols
CHEMICALS & ALLIED PRDTS, WHOLESALE: Alkalines
CHEMICALS & ALLIED PRDTS, WHOLESALE: Carbon Dioxide
CHEMICALS & ALLIED PRDTS, WHOLESALE: Chemicals, Indl
CHEMICALS & ALLIED PRDTS, WHOLESALE: Chlorine
CHEMICALS & ALLIED PRDTS, WHOLESALE: Detergent/Soap
CHEMICALS & ALLIED PRDTS, WHOLESALE: Detergents
CHEMICALS & ALLIED PRDTS, WHOLESALE: Plastics Prdts, NEC
CHEMICALS & ALLIED PRDTS, WHOLESALE: Plastics Sheets & Rods
CHEMICALS & ALLIED PRDTS, WHOLESALE: Spec Clean/Sanitation
CHEMICALS & OTHER PRDTS DERIVED FROM COKING
CHEMICALS, AGRICULTURE: Wholesalers
CHEMICALS: Agricultural
CHEMICALS: Alcohols
CHEMICALS: Aluminum Sulfate
CHEMICALS: Alums
CHEMICALS: Ammonium Compounds, Exc Fertilizers, NEC
CHEMICALS: Anhydrous Ammonia
CHEMICALS: Caustic Soda
CHEMICALS: Formaldehyde
CHEMICALS: Fuel Tank Or Engine Cleaning
CHEMICALS: High Purity, Refined From Technical Grade
CHEMICALS: Hydrogen Peroxide
CHEMICALS: Inorganic, NEC
CHEMICALS: NEC
CHEMICALS: Organic, NEC
CHEMICALS: Reagent Grade, Refined From Technical Grade
CHEMICALS: Sodium/Potassium Cmpnds,Exc Bleach,Alkalies/Alum
CHEMICALS: Water Treatment
CHICKEN SLAUGHTERING & PROCESSING
CHILDREN'S WEAR STORES
CHIPPER MILL
CHLORINE
CHOCOLATE, EXC CANDY FROM BEANS: Chips, Powder, Block, Syrup
CIGARETTE & CIGAR PRDTS & ACCESS
CIRCUIT BOARDS, PRINTED: Television & Radio
CIRCUITS: Electronic
CLAY MINING, COMMON
CLAY: Ground Or Treated
CLEANERS: Boiler Tube
CLEANING EQPT: Commercial
CLEANING EQPT: High Pressure
CLEANING EQPT: Janitors' Carts
CLEANING OR POLISHING PREPARATIONS, NEC
CLEANING PRDTS: Ammonia, Household
CLEANING PRDTS: Automobile Polish
CLEANING PRDTS: Indl Plant Disinfectants Or Deodorants
CLEANING PRDTS: Polishing Preparations & Related Prdts
CLEANING PRDTS: Specialty
CLEANING SVCS
CLEANING SVCS: Industrial Or Commercial
CLIPBOARDS: Wood
CLIPS & FASTENERS, MADE FROM PURCHASED WIRE
CLOTHING & ACCESS STORES
CLOTHING & ACCESS, WOMEN, CHILD & INFANT, WHOL: Scarves

332

2019 Harris Directory of
Mississippi Manufacturers

PRODUCT INDEX

CLOTHING & ACCESS, WOMEN, CHILDREN & INFANT, WHOL: Uniforms
CLOTHING & ACCESS: Costumes, Theatrical
CLOTHING & ACCESS: Handicapped
CLOTHING & ACCESS: Hospital Gowns
CLOTHING & ACCESS: Men's Miscellaneous Access
CLOTHING & APPAREL STORES: Custom
CLOTHING & FURNISHINGS, MEN'S & BOYS', WHOLESALE: Shirts
CLOTHING & FURNISHINGS, MEN'S & BOYS', WHOLESALE: Uniforms
CLOTHING & FURNISHINGS, MEN/BOY, WHOL: Hats, Scarves/Gloves
CLOTHING STORES: Formal Wear
CLOTHING STORES: Shirts, Custom Made
CLOTHING STORES: T-Shirts, Printed, Custom
CLOTHING STORES: Teenage
CLOTHING STORES: Uniforms & Work
CLOTHING STORES: Unisex
CLOTHING STORES: Work
CLOTHING: Access
CLOTHING: Aprons, Harness
CLOTHING: Athletic & Sportswear, Men's & Boys'
CLOTHING: Athletic & Sportswear, Women's & Girls'
CLOTHING: Baker, Barber, Lab/Svc Ind Apparel, Washable, Men
CLOTHING: Bathing Suits & Swimwear, Girls, Children & Infant
CLOTHING: Belts
CLOTHING: Blouses, Women's & Girls'
CLOTHING: Bridal Gowns
CLOTHING: Burial
CLOTHING: Children & Infants'
CLOTHING: Children's, Girls'
CLOTHING: Coats & Suits, Men's & Boys'
CLOTHING: Coats, Hunting & Vests, Men's
CLOTHING: Coats, Overcoats & Vests
CLOTHING: Dresses
CLOTHING: Dresses & Skirts
CLOTHING: Furs
CLOTHING: Gloves & Mittens, Knit
CLOTHING: Gowns & Dresses, Wedding
CLOTHING: Gowns, Formal
CLOTHING: Hats & Caps, Leather
CLOTHING: Hats & Caps, NEC
CLOTHING: Hosiery, Pantyhose & Knee Length, Sheer
CLOTHING: Hospital, Men's
CLOTHING: Jackets & Vests, Exc Fur & Leather, Women's
CLOTHING: Jackets, Overall & Work
CLOTHING: Jeans, Men's & Boys'
CLOTHING: Maternity
CLOTHING: Men's & boy's clothing, nec
CLOTHING: Pants, Work, Men's, Youths' & Boys'
CLOTHING: Robes & Dressing Gowns
CLOTHING: Service Apparel, Women's
CLOTHING: Shirts
CLOTHING: Shirts & T-Shirts, Knit
CLOTHING: Shirts, Dress, Men's & Boys'
CLOTHING: Shirts, Knit
CLOTHING: Shirts, Sports & Polo, Men's & Boys'
CLOTHING: Shirts, Uniform, From Purchased Materials
CLOTHING: Slacks, Girls' & Children's
CLOTHING: Socks
CLOTHING: Suits, Men's & Boys', From Purchased Materials
CLOTHING: T-Shirts & Tops, Knit
CLOTHING: T-Shirts & Tops, Women's & Girls'
CLOTHING: Trousers & Slacks, Men's & Boys'
CLOTHING: Underwear, Women's & Children's
CLOTHING: Uniforms, Military, Men/Youth, Purchased Materials
CLOTHING: Uniforms, Policemen's, From Purchased Materials
CLOTHING: Uniforms, Team Athletic
CLOTHING: Uniforms, Work
CLOTHING: Work Apparel, Exc Uniforms
CLOTHING: Work, Men's
CLUTCHES, EXC VEHICULAR
COAL & OTHER MINERALS & ORES WHOLESALERS
COAL MINING SERVICES
COAL MINING: Bituminous Coal & Lignite-Surface Mining
COATING SVC
COATING SVC: Aluminum, Metal Prdts
COATING SVC: Hot Dip, Metals Or Formed Prdts
COATING SVC: Metals & Formed Prdts
COATING SVC: Metals, With Plastic Or Resins

COATINGS: Air Curing
COATINGS: Epoxy
COFFEE SVCS
COIL WINDING SVC
COILS & TRANSFORMERS
COILS: Electric Motors Or Generators
COKE: Calcined Petroleum, Made From Purchased Materials
COKE: Petroleum & Coal Derivative
COLLEGES, UNIVERSITIES & PROFESSIONAL SCHOOLS
COLORS: Pigments, Inorganic
COMB MOUNTINGS
COMBS, EXC HARD RUBBER
COMFORTERS & QUILTS, FROM MANMADE FIBER OR SILK
COMMERCIAL & OFFICE BUILDINGS RENOVATION & REPAIR
COMMERCIAL ART & GRAPHIC DESIGN SVCS
COMMERCIAL EQPT WHOLESALERS, NEC
COMMERCIAL EQPT, WHOL: Soda Fountain Fixtures, Exc Refrig
COMMERCIAL EQPT, WHOLESALE: Comm Cooking & Food Svc Eqpt
COMMERCIAL EQPT, WHOLESALE: Neon Signs
COMMERCIAL EQPT, WHOLESALE: Store Fixtures & Display Eqpt
COMMERCIAL PRINTING & NEWSPAPER PUBLISHING COMBINED
COMMODITY CONTRACTS BROKERS, DEALERS
COMMON SAND MINING
COMMUNICATIONS EQPT & SYSTEMS, NEC
COMMUNICATIONS EQPT: Microwave
COMMUNICATIONS SVCS: Data
COMMUNICATIONS SVCS: Internet Connectivity Svcs
COMMUNICATIONS SVCS: Internet Host Svcs
COMMUNICATIONS SVCS: Online Svc Providers
COMMUNICATIONS SVCS: Telephone, Data
COMMUNITY COLLEGE
COMMUTATORS: Electronic
COMPOSITION STONE: Plastic
COMPOST
COMPRESSORS: Air & Gas
COMPRESSORS: Refrigeration & Air Conditioning Eqpt
COMPRESSORS: Wholesalers
COMPUTER & COMPUTER SOFTWARE STORES
COMPUTER & COMPUTER SOFTWARE STORES: Peripheral Eqpt
COMPUTER & COMPUTER SOFTWARE STORES: Personal Computers
COMPUTER & COMPUTER SOFTWARE STORES: Software & Access
COMPUTER & COMPUTER SOFTWARE STORES: Software, Bus/Non-Game
COMPUTER & DATA PROCESSING EQPT REPAIR & MAINTENANCE
COMPUTER & OFFICE MACHINE MAINTENANCE & REPAIR
COMPUTER & SFTWR STORE: Modem, Monitor, Terminal/Disk Drive
COMPUTER PERIPHERAL EQPT REPAIR & MAINTENANCE
COMPUTER PERIPHERAL EQPT, NEC
COMPUTER PERIPHERAL EQPT: Input Or Output
COMPUTER PROGRAMMING SVCS
COMPUTER PROGRAMMING SVCS: Custom
COMPUTER RELATED SVCS, NEC
COMPUTER SOFTWARE DEVELOPMENT
COMPUTER SOFTWARE DEVELOPMENT & APPLICATIONS
COMPUTER SOFTWARE SYSTEMS ANALYSIS & DESIGN: Custom
COMPUTER STORAGE DEVICES, NEC
COMPUTER TERMINALS
COMPUTER-AIDED DESIGN SYSTEMS SVCS
COMPUTERS, NEC
COMPUTERS, PERIPHERALS & SOFTWARE, WHOLESALE: Software
COMPUTERS: Mainframe
COMPUTERS: Personal
CONCRETE CURING & HARDENING COMPOUNDS
CONCRETE PLANTS
CONCRETE PRDTS
CONCRETE PRDTS, PRECAST, NEC
CONCRETE: Asphaltic, Not From Refineries
CONCRETE: Dry Mixture
CONCRETE: Ready-Mixed

CONFECTIONERY PRDTS WHOLESALERS
CONFECTIONS & CANDY
CONNECTORS: Electronic
CONSTRUCTION & MINING MACHINERY WHOLESALERS
CONSTRUCTION & ROAD MAINTENANCE EQPT: Drags, Road
CONSTRUCTION EQPT: Backhoes, Tractors, Cranes & Similar Eqpt
CONSTRUCTION EQPT: Bulldozers
CONSTRUCTION EQPT: Dozers, Tractor Mounted, Material Moving
CONSTRUCTION EQPT: Finishers & Spreaders
CONSTRUCTION EQPT: Graders, Road
CONSTRUCTION EQPT: Hammer Mills, Port, Incl Rock/Ore Crush
CONSTRUCTION EQPT: Rakes, Land Clearing, Mechanical
CONSTRUCTION EQPT: Subgraders
CONSTRUCTION EQPT: Wrecker Hoists, Automobile
CONSTRUCTION MATERIALS, WHOL: Concrete/Cinder Bldg Prdts
CONSTRUCTION MATERIALS, WHOLESALE: Awnings
CONSTRUCTION MATERIALS, WHOLESALE: Block, Concrete & Cinder
CONSTRUCTION MATERIALS, WHOLESALE: Brick, Exc Refractory
CONSTRUCTION MATERIALS, WHOLESALE: Building Stone
CONSTRUCTION MATERIALS, WHOLESALE: Building Stone, Granite
CONSTRUCTION MATERIALS, WHOLESALE: Building Stone, Marble
CONSTRUCTION MATERIALS, WHOLESALE: Building, Exterior
CONSTRUCTION MATERIALS, WHOLESALE: Doors, Sliding
CONSTRUCTION MATERIALS, WHOLESALE: Fiberglass Building Mat
CONSTRUCTION MATERIALS, WHOLESALE: Millwork
CONSTRUCTION MATERIALS, WHOLESALE: Pallets, Wood
CONSTRUCTION MATERIALS, WHOLESALE: Paving Materials
CONSTRUCTION MATERIALS, WHOLESALE: Plywood
CONSTRUCTION MATERIALS, WHOLESALE: Sand
CONSTRUCTION MATERIALS, WHOLESALE: Septic Tanks
CONSTRUCTION MATERIALS, WHOLESALE: Sewer Pipe, Clay
CONSTRUCTION MATERIALS, WHOLESALE: Stucco
CONSTRUCTION MATERIALS, WHOLESALE: Tile & Clay Prdts
CONSTRUCTION MATERIALS, WHOLESALE: Veneer
CONSTRUCTION MATLS, WHOL: Lumber, Rough, Dressed/Finished
CONSTRUCTION MTRLS, WHOL: Exterior Flat Glass, Plate/Window
CONSTRUCTION SAND MINING
CONSTRUCTION SITE PREPARATION SVCS
CONSTRUCTION: Bank
CONSTRUCTION: Bridge
CONSTRUCTION: Commercial & Institutional Building
CONSTRUCTION: Commercial & Office Building, New
CONSTRUCTION: Heavy
CONSTRUCTION: Heavy Highway & Street
CONSTRUCTION: Indl Building & Warehouse
CONSTRUCTION: Indl Building, Prefabricated
CONSTRUCTION: Indl Buildings, New, NEC
CONSTRUCTION: Indl Plant
CONSTRUCTION: Land Preparation
CONSTRUCTION: Oil & Gas Pipeline Construction
CONSTRUCTION: Paper & Pulp Mill
CONSTRUCTION: Parking Lot
CONSTRUCTION: Pipeline, NEC
CONSTRUCTION: Railroad & Subway
CONSTRUCTION: Railway Roadbed
CONSTRUCTION: Residential, Nec
CONSTRUCTION: Retaining Wall
CONSTRUCTION: Roads, Gravel or Dirt
CONSTRUCTION: Sewer Line
CONSTRUCTION: Single-Family Housing
CONSTRUCTION: Single-family Housing, New
CONSTRUCTION: Single-family Housing, Prefabricated
CONSTRUCTION: Steel Buildings
CONSTRUCTION: Street Surfacing & Paving
CONSTRUCTION: Swimming Pools
CONSTRUCTION: Tennis Court
CONSTRUCTION: Transmitting Tower, Telecommunication
CONSTRUCTION: Utility Line

INDEX

PRODUCT INDEX

CONSTRUCTION: Water & Sewer Line
CONSULTING SVC: Business, NEC
CONSULTING SVC: Computer
CONSULTING SVC: Educational
CONSULTING SVC: Engineering
CONSULTING SVC: Financial Management
CONSULTING SVC: Management
CONSULTING SVC: Marketing Management
CONSULTING SVC: New Business Start Up
CONSULTING SVC: Online Technology
CONSULTING SVCS, BUSINESS: Environmental
CONSULTING SVCS, BUSINESS: Publishing
CONSULTING SVCS, BUSINESS: Safety Training Svcs
CONSULTING SVCS, BUSINESS: Sys Engnrg, Exc Computer/Prof
CONSULTING SVCS, BUSINESS: Systems Analysis & Engineering
CONSULTING SVCS, BUSINESS: Systems Analysis Or Design
CONSULTING SVCS: Geological
CONSULTING SVCS: Oil
CONSULTING SVCS: Scientific
CONTACT LENSES
CONTAINERS, GLASS: Water Bottles
CONTAINERS: Air Cargo, Metal
CONTAINERS: Corrugated
CONTAINERS: Glass
CONTAINERS: Metal
CONTAINERS: Plastic
CONTAINERS: Sanitary, Food
CONTAINERS: Shipping, Wood
CONTAINERS: Wood
CONTRACTOR: Dredging
CONTRACTOR: Rigging & Scaffolding
CONTRACTORS: Access Control System Eqpt
CONTRACTORS: Asphalt
CONTRACTORS: Awning Installation
CONTRACTORS: Building Eqpt & Machinery Installation
CONTRACTORS: Building Sign Installation & Mntnce
CONTRACTORS: Building Site Preparation
CONTRACTORS: Carpentry Work
CONTRACTORS: Carpentry, Cabinet & Finish Work
CONTRACTORS: Carpentry, Cabinet Building & Installation
CONTRACTORS: Carpentry, Finish & Trim Work
CONTRACTORS: Commercial & Office Building
CONTRACTORS: Computer Installation
CONTRACTORS: Concrete
CONTRACTORS: Construction Site Cleanup
CONTRACTORS: Countertop Installation
CONTRACTORS: Demolition, Building & Other Structures
CONTRACTORS: Directional Oil & Gas Well Drilling Svc
CONTRACTORS: Earthmoving
CONTRACTORS: Electrical
CONTRACTORS: Erection & Dismantling, Poured Concrete Forms
CONTRACTORS: Excavating
CONTRACTORS: Exterior Wall System Installation
CONTRACTORS: Fence Construction
CONTRACTORS: Fiber Optic Cable Installation
CONTRACTORS: Fire Sprinkler System Installation Svcs
CONTRACTORS: Floor Laying & Other Floor Work
CONTRACTORS: Flooring
CONTRACTORS: Foundation & Footing
CONTRACTORS: Gas Detection & Analysis Svcs
CONTRACTORS: Gas Field Svcs, NEC
CONTRACTORS: General Electric
CONTRACTORS: Glass, Glazing & Tinting
CONTRACTORS: Gutters & Downspouts
CONTRACTORS: Heating & Air Conditioning
CONTRACTORS: Highway & Street Construction, General
CONTRACTORS: Highway & Street Paving
CONTRACTORS: Highway & Street Resurfacing
CONTRACTORS: Highway Sign & Guardrail Construction & Install
CONTRACTORS: Hot Shot Svcs
CONTRACTORS: Hotel, Motel/Multi-Famly Home Renovtn/Remodel
CONTRACTORS: Hydraulic Eqpt Installation & Svcs
CONTRACTORS: Insulation Installation, Building
CONTRACTORS: Machinery Installation
CONTRACTORS: Mechanical
CONTRACTORS: Multi-Family Home Remodeling
CONTRACTORS: Oil & Gas Building, Repairing & Dismantling Svc

CONTRACTORS: Oil & Gas Field Geological Exploration Svcs
CONTRACTORS: Oil & Gas Field Geophysical Exploration Svcs
CONTRACTORS: Oil & Gas Field Tools Fishing Svcs
CONTRACTORS: Oil & Gas Well Casing Cement Svcs
CONTRACTORS: Oil & Gas Well Drilling Svc
CONTRACTORS: Oil & Gas Well Foundation Grading Svcs
CONTRACTORS: Oil & Gas Well On-Site Foundation Building Svcs
CONTRACTORS: Oil & Gas Well Redrilling
CONTRACTORS: Oil & Gas Well reworking
CONTRACTORS: Oil & Gas Wells Pumping Svcs
CONTRACTORS: Oil & Gas Wells Svcs
CONTRACTORS: Oil Field Haulage Svcs
CONTRACTORS: Oil Field Lease Tanks: Erectg, Clng/Rprg Svcs
CONTRACTORS: Oil Field Mud Drilling Svcs
CONTRACTORS: Oil Field Pipe Testing Svcs
CONTRACTORS: Oil/Gas Well Construction, Rpr/Dismantling Svcs
CONTRACTORS: On-Site Welding
CONTRACTORS: Ornamental Metal Work
CONTRACTORS: Paint & Wallpaper Stripping
CONTRACTORS: Painting & Wall Covering
CONTRACTORS: Painting, Commercial
CONTRACTORS: Painting, Residential
CONTRACTORS: Painting, Residential, Interior
CONTRACTORS: Patio & Deck Construction & Repair
CONTRACTORS: Pavement Marking
CONTRACTORS: Pipe Laying
CONTRACTORS: Plumbing
CONTRACTORS: Pole Cutting
CONTRACTORS: Prefabricated Window & Door Installation
CONTRACTORS: Pulpwood, Engaged In Cutting
CONTRACTORS: Rock Removal
CONTRACTORS: Roustabout Svcs
CONTRACTORS: Safety & Security Eqpt
CONTRACTORS: Sandblasting Svc, Building Exteriors
CONTRACTORS: Septic System
CONTRACTORS: Sheet Metal Work, NEC
CONTRACTORS: Ship Joinery
CONTRACTORS: Single-family Home General Remodeling
CONTRACTORS: Sound Eqpt Installation
CONTRACTORS: Special Trades, NEC
CONTRACTORS: Structural Iron Work, Structural
CONTRACTORS: Structural Steel Erection
CONTRACTORS: Svc Station Eqpt
CONTRACTORS: Svc Well Drilling Svcs
CONTRACTORS: Tile Installation, Ceramic
CONTRACTORS: Underground Utilities
CONTRACTORS: Unit Paver Installation
CONTRACTORS: Ventilation & Duct Work
CONTRACTORS: Vinyl Flooring Installation, Tile & Sheet
CONTRACTORS: Warm Air Heating & Air Conditioning
CONTRACTORS: Water Intake Well Drilling Svc
CONTRACTORS: Water Well Drilling
CONTRACTORS: Well Acidizing Svcs
CONTRACTORS: Well Bailing, Cleaning, Swabbing & Treating Svc
CONTRACTORS: Well Cleaning Svcs
CONTRACTORS: Well Logging Svcs
CONTRACTORS: Well Swabbing Svcs
CONTRACTORS: Wrecking & Demolition
CONTROL EQPT: Electric
CONTROLS & ACCESS: Indl, Electric
CONTROLS: Electric Motor
CONTROLS: Environmental
CONTROLS: Relay & Ind
CONVENIENCE STORES
CONVENTION & TRADE SHOW SVCS
CONVEYOR SYSTEMS: Bulk Handling
CONVEYORS & CONVEYING EQPT
COOKING EQPT, HOUSEHOLD: Ranges, Gas
COOKWARE, STONEWARE: Coarse Earthenware & Pottery
COSMETIC PREPARATIONS
COSMETICS & TOILETRIES
COSMETICS WHOLESALERS
COSMETOLOGIST
COSMETOLOGY & PERSONAL HYGIENE SALONS
COSTUME JEWELRY & NOVELTIES: Apparel, Exc Precious Metals
COSTUME JEWELRY STORES
COTTON COMPRESSES & WAREHOUSES
COUNTER & SINK TOPS

COUNTERS OR COUNTER DISPLAY CASES, WOOD
COUNTING DEVICES: Taximeters
COURIER SVCS: Package By Vehicle
COVERS & PADS Chair, Made From Purchased Materials
COVERS: Automotive, Exc Seat & Tire
CRANE & AERIAL LIFT SVCS
CRANKSHAFTS & CAMSHAFTS: Machining
CRANKSHAFTS: Motor Vehicle
CREDIT INSTITUTIONS: Personal
CRUDE PETROLEUM & NATURAL GAS PRODUCTION
CRUDE PETROLEUM & NATURAL GAS PRODUCTION
CRUDE PETROLEUM PRODUCTION
CULVERTS: Sheet Metal
CUPS & PLATES: Foamed Plastics
CURBING: Granite Or Stone
CURTAIN & DRAPERY FIXTURES: Poles, Rods & Rollers
CURTAINS: Window, From Purchased Materials
CUSHIONS & PILLOWS
CUSHIONS & PILLOWS: Bed, From Purchased Materials
CUSHIONS: Carpet & Rug, Foamed Plastics
CUSHIONS: Textile, Exc Spring & Carpet
CUT STONE & STONE PRODUCTS
CUTLERY
CYLINDER & ACTUATORS: Fluid Power
CYLINDERS: Pressure

D

DAIRY PRDTS STORE: Ice Cream, Packaged
DAIRY PRDTS WHOLESALERS: Fresh
DAIRY PRDTS: Cheese
DAIRY PRDTS: Dietary Supplements, Dairy & Non-Dairy Based
DAIRY PRDTS: Frozen Desserts & Novelties
DAIRY PRDTS: Ice Cream & Ice Milk
DAIRY PRDTS: Milk, Fluid
DAIRY PRDTS: Natural Cheese
DAIRY PRDTS: Yogurt, Exc Frozen
DAMAGED MERCHANDISE SALVAGING, SVCS ONLY
DATA PROCESSING SVCS
DEALERS: Tax Certificate
DECORATIVE WOOD & WOODWORK
DEFENSE SYSTEMS & EQPT
DELIVERY SVCS, BY VEHICLE
DENTAL EQPT & SPLYS: Enamels
DENTAL EQPT & SPLYS: Metal
DEPARTMENT STORES
DEPARTMENT STORES: Country General
DERMATOLOGICALS
DERRICKS: Oil & Gas Field
DESICCANTS, CLAY: Activated
DESIGN SVCS, NEC
DESIGN SVCS: Computer Integrated Systems
DIAGNOSTIC SUBSTANCES
DIAGNOSTIC SUBSTANCES OR AGENTS: Hematology
DIAGNOSTIC SUBSTANCES OR AGENTS: Radioactive
DIAGNOSTIC SUBSTANCES OR AGENTS: Veterinary
DIAMONDS, GEMS, WHOLESALE
DIAMONDS: Cutting & Polishing
DIAPERS: Disposable
DIE SETS: Presses, Metal Stamping
DIES & TOOLS: Special
DIODES: Light Emitting
DIRECT SELLING ESTABLISHMENTS: Food, Mobile, Exc Coffee-Cart
DIRECT SELLING ESTABLISHMENTS: Jewelry, House-To-House
DIRECT SELLING ESTABLISHMENTS: Telemarketing
DISASTER SVCS
DISHWASHING EQPT: Commercial
DISK & DRUM DRIVES & COMPONENTS: Computers
DISKS & DRUMS Magnetic
DISPENSERS: Soap
DISPLAY FIXTURES: Showcases, Wood, Exc Refrigerated
DISPLAY ITEMS: Corrugated, Made From Purchased Materials
DISPLAY LETTERING SVCS
DOOR PARTS: Sashes, Wood
DOORS & WINDOWS WHOLESALERS: All Materials
DOORS & WINDOWS: Screen & Storm
DOORS & WINDOWS: Storm, Metal
DOORS: Wooden
DRAFTING SVCS
DRAINAGE PRDTS: Concrete
DRAPERIES & CURTAINS
DRAPERIES & DRAPERY FABRICS, COTTON

2019 Harris Directory of
Mississippi Manufacturers

PRODUCT INDEX

DRAPERIES: Plastic & Textile, From Purchased Materials
DRAPERY & UPHOLSTERY STORES: Draperies
DRILLING MACHINERY & EQPT: Oil & Gas
DRINK MIXES, NONALCOHOLIC: Cocktail
DRINKING PLACES: Bars & Lounges
DRIVES: Hydrostatic
DRUG STORES
DRUG TESTING KITS: Blood & Urine
DRUGS & DRUG PROPRIETARIES, WHOLESALE: Pharmaceuticals
DRUGS AFFECTING NEOPLASMS & ENDOCRINE SYSTEMS
DRYCLEANING & LAUNDRY SVCS: Commercial & Family
DUCTS: Sheet Metal
DUMPSTERS: Garbage
DURABLE GOODS WHOLESALERS, NEC
DUST OR FUME COLLECTING EQPT: Indl

E

EATING PLACES
EDUCATIONAL PROGRAMS ADMINISTRATION SVCS
EDUCATIONAL SVCS
ELECTRIC MOTOR REPAIR SVCS
ELECTRICAL APPARATUS & EQPT WHOLESALERS
ELECTRICAL APPLIANCES, TELEVISIONS & RADIOS WHOLESALERS
ELECTRICAL CURRENT CARRYING WIRING DEVICES
ELECTRICAL EQPT & SPLYS
ELECTRICAL EQPT FOR ENGINES
ELECTRICAL EQPT REPAIR & MAINTENANCE
ELECTRICAL EQPT REPAIR SVCS: High Voltage
ELECTRICAL EQPT: Automotive, NEC
ELECTRICAL GOODS, WHOL: Antennas, Receiving/Satellite Dishes
ELECTRICAL GOODS, WHOLESALE: Burglar Alarm Systems
ELECTRICAL GOODS, WHOLESALE: Dishwashers
ELECTRICAL GOODS, WHOLESALE: Electrical Appliances, Major
ELECTRICAL GOODS, WHOLESALE: Fire Alarm Systems
ELECTRICAL GOODS, WHOLESALE: Generators
ELECTRICAL GOODS, WHOLESALE: Modems, Computer
ELECTRICAL GOODS, WHOLESALE: Motor Ctrls, Starters & Relays
ELECTRICAL GOODS, WHOLESALE: Motors
ELECTRICAL GOODS, WHOLESALE: Panelboards
ELECTRICAL GOODS, WHOLESALE: Radio & TV Or TV Eqpt & Parts
ELECTRICAL GOODS, WHOLESALE: Security Control Eqpt & Systems
ELECTRICAL GOODS, WHOLESALE: Telephone Eqpt
ELECTRICAL GOODS, WHOLESALE: Transformers
ELECTRICAL MEASURING INSTRUMENT REPAIR & CALIBRATION SVCS
ELECTRICAL SPLYS
ELECTROMEDICAL EQPT
ELECTRONIC EQPT REPAIR SVCS
ELECTRONIC PARTS & EQPT WHOLESALERS
ELECTRONIC SHOPPING
ELECTRONIC TRAINING DEVICES
ELEVATOR: Grain, Storage Only
ELEVATORS & EQPT
ELEVATORS WHOLESALERS
EMBLEMS: Embroidered
EMBROIDERING & ART NEEDLEWORK FOR THE TRADE
EMBROIDERING SVC
EMBROIDERING SVC: Schiffli Machine
EMBROIDERY ADVERTISING SVCS
EMERGENCY ALARMS
EMPLOYMENT AGENCY SVCS
EMPLOYMENT SVCS: Labor Contractors
ENCLOSURES: Screen
ENGINE PARTS & ACCESS: Internal Combustion
ENGINE REBUILDING: Diesel
ENGINEERING SVCS
ENGINEERING SVCS: Aviation Or Aeronautical
ENGINEERING SVCS: Civil
ENGINEERING SVCS: Industrial
ENGINEERING SVCS: Marine
ENGINEERING SVCS: Professional
ENGINES: Diesel & Semi-Diesel Or Duel Fuel
ENGINES: Gasoline, NEC
ENGINES: Internal Combustion, NEC
ENGRAVING SVC: Jewelry & Personal Goods
ENGRAVING SVCS
ENGRAVING: Steel line, For The Printing Trade

ENTERTAINMENT SVCS
ENVELOPES
EQUIPMENT: Rental & Leasing, NEC
ESTIMATING SVCS: Construction
ETCHING & ENGRAVING SVC
ETHYLENE-PROPYLENE RUBBERS: EPDM Polymers
EXPLORATION, METAL MINING
EXPLOSIVES
EXTRUDED SHAPES, NEC: Copper & Copper Alloy
EYEGLASSES
EYEGLASSES: Sunglasses
EYELASHES, ARTIFICIAL

F

FABRIC STORES
FABRICATED METAL PRODUCTS, NEC
FABRICS: Apparel & Outerwear, Cotton
FABRICS: Bonded-Fiber, Exc Felt
FABRICS: Broadwoven, Cotton
FABRICS: Broadwoven, Synthetic Manmade Fiber & Silk
FABRICS: Canvas
FABRICS: Canvas & Heavy Coarse, Cotton
FABRICS: Coated Or Treated
FABRICS: Cords
FABRICS: Denims
FABRICS: Glass & Fiberglass, Broadwoven
FABRICS: Hand Woven
FABRICS: Jean
FABRICS: Luggage, Cotton
FABRICS: Nonwoven
FABRICS: Papermakers Felt, Woven, Wool, Mohair/Similar Fiber
FABRICS: Print, Cotton
FABRICS: Satin
FABRICS: Scrub Cloths
FABRICS: Specialty Including Twisted Weaves, Broadwoven
FABRICS: Trimmings
FABRICS: Tubing, Textile, Varnished
FABRICS: Upholstery, Cotton
FABRICS: Upholstery, Wool
FACIAL SALONS
FACILITIES SUPPORT SVCS
FAMILY CLOTHING STORES
FARM & GARDEN MACHINERY WHOLESALERS
FARM MACHINERY REPAIR SVCS
FARM SPLY STORES
FARM SPLYS WHOLESALERS
FARM SPLYS, WHOLESALE: Feed
FARM SPLYS, WHOLESALE: Fertilizers & Agricultural Chemicals
FARM SPLYS, WHOLESALE: Greenhouse Eqpt & Splys
FARM SPLYS, WHOLESALE: Insecticides
FASTENERS: Notions, NEC
FELT PARTS
FELT, WHOLESALE
FELTS: Building
FENCE POSTS: Iron & Steel
FENCES & FENCING MATERIALS
FENCES OR POSTS: Ornamental Iron Or Steel
FENCING DEALERS
FENCING MATERIALS: Docks & Other Outdoor Prdts, Wood
FENCING MATERIALS: Plastic
FENCING: Chain Link
FERTILIZER MINERAL MINING
FERTILIZER, AGRICULTURAL: Wholesalers
FERTILIZERS: NEC
FERTILIZERS: Nitrogenous
FERTILIZERS: Phosphatic
FIBER & FIBER PRDTS: Elastomeric
FIBER & FIBER PRDTS: Organic, Noncellulose
FIBER & FIBER PRDTS: Polyester
FIBER & FIBER PRDTS: Synthetic Cellulosic
FIGURES, WAX
FILE FOLDERS
FILLERS & SEALERS: Wood
FILM & SHEET: Unsuppported Plastic
FILTER ELEMENTS: Fluid & Hydraulic Line
FILTERS
FILTERS & SOFTENERS: Water, Household
FILTERS: Air
FILTERS: General Line, Indl
FILTERS: Oil, Internal Combustion Engine, Exc Auto
FILTRATION DEVICES: Electronic
FINDINGS & TRIMMINGS: Apparel
FINDINGS & TRIMMINGS: Fabric

FINGERPRINT EQPT
FIRE ARMS, SMALL: Guns Or Gun Parts, 30 mm & Below
FIRE ARMS, SMALL: Rifles Or Rifle Parts, 30 mm & below
FIRE EXTINGUISHERS: Portable
FIRE OR BURGLARY RESISTIVE PRDTS
FIRE PROTECTION EQPT
FIRE PROTECTION SVCS: Contracted
FIRE PROTECTION, GOVERNMENT: Fire Department, Volunteer
FIREARMS: Large, Greater Than 30mm
FIREARMS: Small, 30mm or Less
FIREWORKS
FIREWORKS SHOPS
FISH & SEAFOOD PROCESSORS: Fresh Or Frozen
FISH FOOD
FISHING EQPT: Lures
FISHING EQPT: Nets & Seines
FITTINGS & ASSEMBLIES: Hose & Tube, Hydraulic Or Pneumatic
FITTINGS: Pipe
FITTINGS: Pipe, Fabricated
FIXTURES: Cut Stone
FLAGPOLES
FLAT GLASS: Window, Clear & Colored
FLEA MARKET
FLOOR COVERING STORES
FLOOR COVERING STORES: Carpets
FLOOR COVERING STORES: Floor Tile
FLOORING: Baseboards, Wood
FLOORING: Hard Surface
FLOORING: Hardwood
FLOORING: Rubber
FLOWER ARRANGEMENTS: Artificial
FLOWERS & FLORISTS' SPLYS WHOLESALERS
FLOWERS, ARTIFICIAL, WHOLESALE
FLOWERS: Artificial & Preserved
FLUID POWER PUMPS & MOTORS
FLUID POWER VALVES & HOSE FITTINGS
FLUXES
FOAM RUBBER
FOIL: Aluminum
FOOD COLORINGS: Bakers'
FOOD PRDTS, BREAKFAST: Cereal, Granola & Muesli
FOOD PRDTS, CANNED: Fruits
FOOD PRDTS, CANNED: Fruits & Fruit Prdts
FOOD PRDTS, CANNED: Jellies, Edible, Including Imitation
FOOD PRDTS, CANNED: Mexican, NEC
FOOD PRDTS, CONFECTIONERY, WHOLESALE: Snack Foods
FOOD PRDTS, DAIRY, WHOLESALE: Milk & Cream, Fluid
FOOD PRDTS, FISH & SEAFOOD, WHOLESALE: Seafood
FOOD PRDTS, FISH & SEAFOOD: Fish, Fresh, Prepared
FOOD PRDTS, FISH & SEAFOOD: Fish, Frozen, Prepared
FOOD PRDTS, FISH & SEAFOOD: Fresh, Prepared
FOOD PRDTS, FISH & SEAFOOD: Seafood, Frozen, Prepared
FOOD PRDTS, FISH & SEAFOOD: Shrimp, Fresh, Prepared
FOOD PRDTS, FROZEN: Dinners, Packaged
FOOD PRDTS, FROZEN: Fruits, Juices & Vegetables
FOOD PRDTS, FROZEN: NEC
FOOD PRDTS, FROZEN: Vegetables, Exc Potato Prdts
FOOD PRDTS, MEAT & MEAT PRDTS, WHOLESALE: Fresh
FOOD PRDTS, WHOLESALE: Beverages, Exc Coffee & Tea
FOOD PRDTS, WHOLESALE: Coffee & Tea
FOOD PRDTS, WHOLESALE: Natural & Organic
FOOD PRDTS, WHOLESALE: Specialty
FOOD PRDTS, WHOLESALE: Spices & Seasonings
FOOD PRDTS, WHOLESALE: Water, Mineral Or Spring, Bottled
FOOD PRDTS: Animal & marine fats & oils
FOOD PRDTS: Baking Powder, Soda, Yeast & Leavenings
FOOD PRDTS: Bologna, Poultry
FOOD PRDTS: Box Lunches, For Sale Off Premises
FOOD PRDTS: Bran, Rice
FOOD PRDTS: Cereals
FOOD PRDTS: Chicken, Processed, Cooked
FOOD PRDTS: Chicken, Processed, Fresh
FOOD PRDTS: Chicken, Slaughtered & Dressed
FOOD PRDTS: Coffee
FOOD PRDTS: Coffee Roasting, Exc Wholesale Grocers
FOOD PRDTS: Cottonseed Cooking & Salad Oil
FOOD PRDTS: Cottonseed Oil, Cake & Meal
FOOD PRDTS: Dressings, Salad, Raw & Cooked Exc Dry Mixes
FOOD PRDTS: Ducks, Slaughtered & Dressed

INDEX

2019 Harris Directory of
Mississippi Manufacturers

335

PRODUCT INDEX

FOOD PRDTS: Eggs, Processed
FOOD PRDTS: Eggs, Processed, Frozen
FOOD PRDTS: Emulsifiers
FOOD PRDTS: Fish Meal
FOOD PRDTS: Fish Oil
FOOD PRDTS: Fruit Juices
FOOD PRDTS: Fruits & Vegetables, Pickled
FOOD PRDTS: Honey
FOOD PRDTS: Ice, Cubes
FOOD PRDTS: Instant Coffee
FOOD PRDTS: Mixes, Bread & Bread-Type Roll
FOOD PRDTS: Mixes, Doughnut From Purchased Flour
FOOD PRDTS: Mixes, Seasonings, Dry
FOOD PRDTS: Nuts & Seeds
FOOD PRDTS: Oil, Partially Hydrogenated, Edible
FOOD PRDTS: Olive Oil
FOOD PRDTS: Popcorn, Popped
FOOD PRDTS: Pork Rinds
FOOD PRDTS: Potato & Corn Chips & Similar Prdts
FOOD PRDTS: Poultry Sausage, Lunch Meats/Other Poultry
  Prdts
FOOD PRDTS: Poultry, Processed, NEC
FOOD PRDTS: Poultry, Slaughtered & Dressed
FOOD PRDTS: Preparations
FOOD PRDTS: Rice, Milled
FOOD PRDTS: Seasonings & Spices
FOOD PRDTS: Soybean Lecithin
FOOD PRDTS: Spices, Including Ground
FOOD PRDTS: Syrups
FOOD PRDTS: Tea
FOOD PRDTS: Vegetable Oil Mills, NEC
FOOD PRODUCTS MACHINERY
FOOD STORES: Convenience, Independent
FOOTWEAR: Cut Stock
FORESTRY RELATED EQPT
FORGINGS
FORGINGS: Anchors
FORGINGS: Automotive & Internal Combustion Engine
FORGINGS: Nonferrous
FORGINGS: Plumbing Fixture, Nonferrous
FOUNDRIES: Aluminum
FOUNDRIES: Brass, Bronze & Copper
FOUNDRIES: Gray & Ductile Iron
FOUNDRIES: Nonferrous
FOUNDRIES: Steel
FOUNDRIES: Steel Investment
FREIGHT TRANSPORTATION ARRANGEMENTS
FRICTION MATERIAL, MADE FROM POWDERED METAL
FRUIT & VEGETABLE MARKETS
FUEL: Rocket Engine, Organic
FUELS: Diesel
FUELS: Ethanol
FUELS: Nuclear, Uranium Slug, Radioactive
FUELS: Oil
FUNERAL HOMES & SVCS
FUNGICIDES OR HERBICIDES
FURNACES & OVENS: Indl
FURNITURE & CABINET STORES: Cabinets, Custom Work
FURNITURE & CABINET STORES: Custom
FURNITURE COMPONENTS: Porcelain Enameled
FURNITURE PARTS: Metal
FURNITURE REFINISHING SVCS
FURNITURE STOCK & PARTS: Carvings, Wood
FURNITURE STOCK & PARTS: Dimension Stock, Hardwood
FURNITURE STOCK & PARTS: Frames, Upholstered Furni-
  ture, Wood
FURNITURE STOCK & PARTS: Hardwood
FURNITURE STOCK & PARTS: Turnings, Wood
FURNITURE STORES
FURNITURE STORES: Office
FURNITURE WHOLESALERS
FURNITURE, WHOLESALE: Beds
FURNITURE, WHOLESALE: Lockers
FURNITURE, WHOLESALE: Restaurant, NEC
FURNITURE, WHOLESALE: School Desks
FURNITURE: Assembly Hall
FURNITURE: Bed Frames & Headboards, Wood
FURNITURE: Benches, Office, Wood
FURNITURE: Box Springs, Assembled
FURNITURE: Breakfast Sets, Household, Metal
FURNITURE: Camp, Wood
FURNITURE: Chair & Couch Springs, Assembled
FURNITURE: Chairs, Cane
FURNITURE: Chairs, Folding
FURNITURE: Chairs, Household Upholstered

FURNITURE: Church
FURNITURE: Couches, Sofa/Davenport, Upholstered Wood
  Frames
FURNITURE: Frames, Box Springs Or Bedsprings, Metal
FURNITURE: Hospital
FURNITURE: Hotel
FURNITURE: Household, Metal
FURNITURE: Household, NEC
FURNITURE: Household, Upholstered, Exc Wood Or Metal
FURNITURE: Household, Wood
FURNITURE: Institutional, Exc Wood
FURNITURE: Juvenile, Upholstered On Wood Frames
FURNITURE: Juvenile, Wood
FURNITURE: Kitchen & Dining Room
FURNITURE: Kitchen & Dining Room, Metal
FURNITURE: Living Room, Upholstered On Wood Frames
FURNITURE: Mattresses & Foundations
FURNITURE: Mattresses, Box & Bedsprings
FURNITURE: Mattresses, Innerspring Or Box Spring
FURNITURE: NEC
FURNITURE: Office, Exc Wood
FURNITURE: Office, Wood
FURNITURE: Picnic Tables Or Benches, Park
FURNITURE: Recliners, Upholstered On Wood Frames
FURNITURE: Rockers, Wood, Exc Upholstered
FURNITURE: School
FURNITURE: Sleep
FURNITURE: Sofa Beds Or Convertible Sofas)
FURNITURE: Stools With Casters, Metal, Exc Home Or Office
FURNITURE: Upholstered
Furs

G

GAMES & TOYS: Automobiles & Trucks
GAMES & TOYS: Craft & Hobby Kits & Sets
GAMES & TOYS: Doll Clothing
GAMES & TOYS: Dolls, Exc Stuffed Toy Animals
GAMES & TOYS: Kits, Science, Incl Microscopes/Chemistry
  Sets
GAMES & TOYS: Puzzles
GARAGE DOOR REPAIR SVCS
GARMENT: Pressing & cleaners' agents
GAS & HYDROCARBON LIQUEFACTION FROM COAL
GAS & OIL FIELD EXPLORATION SVCS
GAS & OIL FIELD SVCS, NEC
GAS PROCESSING SVC
GAS PRODUCTION & DISTRIBUTION
GAS STATIONS
GAS: Refinery
GASES & LIQUIFIED PETROLEUM GASES
GASES: Acetylene
GASES: Carbon Dioxide
GASES: Hydrogen
GASES: Indl
GASES: Neon
GASES: Nitrogen
GASES: Nitrous Oxide
GASES: Oxygen
GASKETS
GASKETS & SEALING DEVICES
GASOLINE FILLING STATIONS
GASOLINE WHOLESALERS
GEARS: Power Transmission, Exc Auto
GENERATION EQPT: Electronic
GIFT SHOP
GIFT, NOVELTY & SOUVENIR STORES: Artcraft & carvings
GIFT, NOVELTY & SOUVENIR STORES: Gifts & Novelties
GIFTS & NOVELTIES: Wholesalers
GLASS & GLASS CERAMIC PRDTS, PRESSED OR
  BLOWN: Tableware
GLASS FABRICATORS
GLASS PRDTS, FROM PURCHASED GLASS: Glassware
GLASS PRDTS, FROM PURCHASED GLASS: Mirrored
GLASS PRDTS, FROM PURCHASED GLASS: Windshields
GLASS PRDTS, PRESSED OR BLOWN: Glassware, Art Or
  Decorative
GLASS PRDTS, PRESSED OR BLOWN: Glassware, Novelty
GLASS PRDTS, PRESSED/BLOWN: Glassware, Art,
  Decor/Novelty
GLASS PRDTS, PURCHSD GLASS: Ornamental, Cut, En-
  graved/Décor
GLASS STORE: Leaded Or Stained
GLASS STORES
GLASS: Fiber
GLASS: Indl Prdts

GLASS: Pressed & Blown, NEC
GLASS: Stained
GLOBAL POSITIONING SYSTEMS & EQPT
GLOVES: Fabric
GLOVES: Leather
GLOVES: Leather, Work
GLOVES: Safety
GLOVES: Work
GLOVES: Woven Or Knit, From Purchased Materials
GOLF CARTS: Powered
GOLF EQPT
GOLF GOODS & EQPT
GOURMET FOOD STORES
GOVERNMENT, EXECUTIVE OFFICES: County
  Supervisor/Exec Office
GRADING SVCS
GRANITE: Crushed & Broken
GRANITE: Cut & Shaped
GRAPHIC ARTS & RELATED DESIGN SVCS
GRASSES: Artificial & Preserved
GRAVE MARKERS: Concrete
GRAVEL MINING
GRINDING SVCS: Ophthalmic Lens, Exc Prescription
GROCERIES WHOLESALERS, NEC
GROCERIES, GENERAL LINE WHOLESALERS
GUARD SVCS
GUIDED MISSILES & SPACE VEHICLES
GUM & WOOD CHEMICALS
GUN SVCS
GUNSMITHS
GYPSUM PRDTS

H

HAIR & HAIR BASED PRDTS
HAIR ACCESS WHOLESALERS
HAIR CARE PRDTS
HAIR DRESSING, FOR THE TRADE
HAIR REPLACEMENT & WEAVING SVCS
HAIRDRESSERS
HANDYMAN SVCS
HARDWARE
HARDWARE STORES
HARDWARE STORES: Builders'
HARDWARE STORES: Chainsaws
HARDWARE STORES: Door Locks & Lock Sets
HARDWARE STORES: Tools, Power
HARDWARE WHOLESALERS
HARDWARE, WHOLESALE: Brads
HARDWARE, WHOLESALE: Nuts
HARDWARE, WHOLESALE: Padlocks
HARDWARE, WHOLESALE: Power Tools & Access
HARDWARE: Aircraft & Marine, Incl Pulleys & Similar Items
HARDWARE: Furniture, Builders' & Other Household
HARNESS ASSEMBLIES: Cable & Wire
HARNESS WIRING SETS: Internal Combustion Engines
HEALTH AIDS: Exercise Eqpt
HEALTH AIDS: Vaporizers
HEALTH SYSTEMS AGENCY
HEARING AID REPAIR SVCS
HEARING AIDS
HEARING TESTING SVCS
HEAT TREATING: Metal
HEATING & AIR CONDITIONING EQPT & SPLYS WHOLE-
  SALERS
HEATING & AIR CONDITIONING UNITS, COMBINATION
HEATING EQPT & SPLYS
HEELS, BOOT OR SHOE: Rubber, Composition Or Fiber
HELICOPTERS
HELP SUPPLY SERVICES
HOBBY, TOY & GAME STORES: Ceramics Splys
HOISTS: Aircraft Loading
HOLDING COMPANIES: Investment, Exc Banks
HOME CENTER STORES
HOME FOR THE MENTALLY RETARDED
HOME HEALTH CARE SVCS
HOME SHOPPING TELEVISION ORDER HOUSES
HOMEBUILDERS & OTHER OPERATIVE BUILDERS
HOMEFURNISHING STORE: Bedding, Sheet,
  Blanket,Spread/Pillow
HOMEFURNISHING STORES: Beddings & Linens
HOMEFURNISHING STORES: Fireplaces & Wood Burning
  Stoves
HOMEFURNISHING STORES: Pictures & Mirrors
HOMEFURNISHING STORES: Pottery
HOMEFURNISHINGS, WHOLESALE: Draperies

PRODUCT INDEX

HOMES, MODULAR: Wooden
HOMES: Log Cabins
HOPPERS: Sheet Metal
HORSE ACCESS: Harnesses & Riding Crops, Etc, Exc Leather
HOSE: Garden, Rubber
HOSPITAL BEDS WHOLESALERS
HOSPITAL EQPT REPAIR SVCS
HOSPITALS: Orthopedic
HOT TUBS
HOUSEHOLD APPLIANCE STORES
HOUSEHOLD ARTICLES, EXC KITCHEN: Pottery
HOUSEHOLD FURNISHINGS, NEC
HOUSEWARES, ELECTRIC: Appliances, Personal
HOUSEWARES, ELECTRIC: Blankets
HOUSEWARES, ELECTRIC: Dryers, Hair
HOUSEWARES, ELECTRIC: Heating, Bsbrd/Wall, Radiant Heat
HOUSEWARES, ELECTRIC: Irons, Household
HOUSEWARES: Dishes, Plastic
HOUSEWARES: Plates, Pressed/Molded Pulp, From Purchased Mtrl
HYDRAULIC EQPT REPAIR SVC
HYDRAULIC FLUIDS: Synthetic Based
Hard Rubber & Molded Rubber Prdts

I

ICE
ICE WHOLESALERS
IDENTIFICATION TAGS, EXC PAPER
INDL & PERSONAL SVC PAPER WHOLESALERS
INDL & PERSONAL SVC PAPER, WHOLESALE: Cardboard & Prdts
INDL & PERSONAL SVC PAPER, WHOLESALE: Paper Tubes & Cores
INDL CONTRACTORS: Exhibit Construction
INDL EQPT SVCS
INDL MACHINERY & EQPT WHOLESALERS
INDL MACHINERY REPAIR & MAINTENANCE
INDL PROCESS INSTRUMENTS: Data Loggers
INDL PROCESS INSTRUMENTS: On-Stream Gas Or Liquid Analysis
INDL SPLYS WHOLESALERS
INDL SPLYS, WHOLESALE: Bearings
INDL SPLYS, WHOLESALE: Filters, Indl
INDL SPLYS, WHOLESALE: Hydraulic & Pneumatic Pistons/Valves
INDL SPLYS, WHOLESALE: Mill Splys
INDL SPLYS, WHOLESALE: Rubber Goods, Mechanical
INNS
INSECTICIDES
INSECTICIDES & PESTICIDES
INSTRUMENTS, LABORATORY: Spectrometers
INSTRUMENTS, MEASURING & CNTRG: Plotting, Drafting/Map Rdg
INSTRUMENTS, MEASURING & CNTRL: Geophysical/Meteorological
INSTRUMENTS, MEASURING & CONTROLLING: Alidades, Surveying
INSTRUMENTS, MEASURING & CONTROLLING: Leak Detection, Liquid
INSTRUMENTS, OPTICAL: Light Sources, Standard
INSTRUMENTS, SURGICAL & MEDICAL: Blood & Bone Work
INSTRUMENTS, SURGICAL & MEDICAL: Lasers, Surgical
INSTRUMENTS: Analytical
INSTRUMENTS: Analyzers, Internal Combustion Eng, Electronic
INSTRUMENTS: Indl Process Control
INSTRUMENTS: Measurement, Indl Process
INSTRUMENTS: Measuring & Controlling
INSTRUMENTS: Measuring Electricity
INSTRUMENTS: Measuring, Electrical Energy
INSTRUMENTS: Medical & Surgical
INSTRUMENTS: Seismographs
INSTRUMENTS: Signal Generators & Averagers
INSTRUMENTS: Standards & Calibration, Electrical Measuring
INSULATION & CUSHIONING FOAM: Polystyrene
INSULATION MATERIALS WHOLESALERS
INSULATION: Fiberglass
INSURANCE AGENTS, NEC
INSURANCE CARRIERS: Direct Product Warranty
INSURANCE CARRIERS: Life
INTERIOR DESIGN SVCS, NEC

IRON OXIDES
IRRIGATION EQPT WHOLESALERS

J

JACKS: Hydraulic
JANITORIAL & CUSTODIAL SVCS
JANITORIAL EQPT & SPLYS WHOLESALERS
JEWELRY & PRECIOUS STONES WHOLESALERS
JEWELRY REPAIR SVCS
JEWELRY STORES
JEWELRY STORES: Precious Stones & Precious Metals
JEWELRY, PRECIOUS METAL: Cigar & Cigarette Access
JEWELRY, PRECIOUS METAL: Rings, Finger
JEWELRY, PRECIOUS METAL: Rosaries/Other Sm Religious Article
JEWELRY: Decorative, Fashion & Costume
JEWELRY: Precious Metal
JOB PRINTING & NEWSPAPER PUBLISHING COMBINED
JOB TRAINING & VOCATIONAL REHABILITATION SVCS
JOINTS: Expansion
JOISTS: Fabricated Bar

K

KAOLIN & BALL CLAY MINING
KITCHEN & COOKING ARTICLES: Pottery
KITCHEN UTENSILS: Food Handling & Processing Prdts, Wood
KITCHENWARE: Plastic

L

LABORATORIES: Biotechnology
LABORATORIES: Testing
LABORATORY APPARATUS & FURNITURE
LABORATORY APPARATUS: Laser Beam Alignment Device
LABORATORY APPARATUS: Physics, NEC
LABORATORY EQPT: Chemical
LABORATORY EQPT: Incubators
LAMINATED PLASTICS: Plate, Sheet, Rod & Tubes
LAMP & LIGHT BULBS & TUBES
LAND SUBDIVISION & DEVELOPMENT
LANTERNS
LASER SYSTEMS & EQPT
LAUNDRY SVCS: Indl
LAWN & GARDEN EQPT
LAWN & GARDEN EQPT STORES
LAWN & GARDEN EQPT: Plows
LAWN & GARDEN EQPT: Rototillers
LAWN MOWER REPAIR SHOP
LEASING & RENTAL SVCS: Cranes & Aerial Lift Eqpt
LEASING & RENTAL SVCS: Oil Field Eqpt
LEASING & RENTAL: Automobile With Driver
LEASING & RENTAL: Construction & Mining Eqpt
LEASING & RENTAL: Mobile Home Sites
LEASING & RENTAL: Other Real Estate Property
LEASING & RENTAL: Trucks, Indl
LEASING & RENTAL: Trucks, Without Drivers
LEASING & RENTAL: Utility Trailers & RV's
LEASING: Passenger Car
LEATHER GOODS: Aprons, Welders', Blacksmiths', Etc
LEATHER GOODS: NEC
LEATHER GOODS: Personal
LEATHER GOODS: Wallets
LEATHER: Upholstery
LECTURE BUREAU
LECTURING SVCS
LEGAL SVCS: General Practice Attorney or Lawyer
LETTERS: Cardboard, Die-Cut, Made From Purchased Materials
LIGHTING EQPT: Miners' Lamps
LIGHTING EQPT: Motor Vehicle, NEC
LIGHTING EQPT: Reflectors, Metal, For Lighting Eqpt
LIGHTING EQPT: Searchlights
LIGHTING FIXTURES WHOLESALERS
LIGHTING FIXTURES, NEC
LIGHTING FIXTURES: Airport
LIGHTING FIXTURES: Indl & Commercial
LIGHTING FIXTURES: Residential
LIGHTING FIXTURES: Residential, Electric
LIME
LIMESTONE: Crushed & Broken
LIMESTONE: Ground
LINERS & COVERS: Fabric
LININGS: Apparel, Made From Purchased Materials
LININGS: Vulcanizable Rubber

LIPSTICK
LOCKERS: Refrigerated
LOCKS & LOCK SETS, WHOLESALE
LOGGING
LOGGING CAMPS & CONTRACTORS
LOGGING: Fuel Wood Harvesting
LOGGING: Peeler Logs
LOGGING: Saw Logs
LOGGING: Timber, Cut At Logging Camp
LOGGING: Wooden Logs
LOOSELEAF BINDERS
LOTIONS OR CREAMS: Face
LOTIONS: SHAVING
LUGGAGE & LEATHER GOODS STORES
LUGGAGE REPAIR SHOP
LUMBER & BLDG MATRLS DEALERS, RET: Bath Fixtures, Eqpt/Sply
LUMBER & BLDG MTRLS DEALERS, RET: Insultn & Energy Consrvtn
LUMBER & BLDG MTRLS DEALERS, RET: Planing Mill Prdts/Lumber
LUMBER & BUILDING MATERIALS DEALER, RET: Door & Window Prdts
LUMBER & BUILDING MATERIALS DEALER, RET: Masonry Matls/Splys
LUMBER & BUILDING MATERIALS DEALERS, RETAIL: Brick
LUMBER & BUILDING MATERIALS DEALERS, RETAIL: Cement
LUMBER & BUILDING MATERIALS DEALERS, RETAIL: Countertops
LUMBER & BUILDING MATERIALS DEALERS, RETAIL: Flooring, Wood
LUMBER & BUILDING MATERIALS DEALERS, RETAIL: Modular Homes
LUMBER & BUILDING MATERIALS DEALERS, RETAIL: Sand & Gravel
LUMBER & BUILDING MATERIALS DEALERS, RETAIL: Siding
LUMBER & BUILDING MATERIALS RET DEALERS: Millwork & Lumber
LUMBER & BUILDING MATLS DEALERS, RET: Concrete/Cinder Block
LUMBER: Box
LUMBER: Dimension, Hardwood
LUMBER: Fiberboard
LUMBER: Furniture Dimension Stock, Softwood
LUMBER: Hardboard
LUMBER: Hardwood Dimension
LUMBER: Hardwood Dimension & Flooring Mills
LUMBER: Kiln Dried
LUMBER: Panels, Plywood, Softwood
LUMBER: Pilings, Treated
LUMBER: Plywood, Hardwood
LUMBER: Plywood, Hardwood or Hardwood Faced
LUMBER: Plywood, Prefinished, Hardwood
LUMBER: Plywood, Softwood
LUMBER: Plywood, Softwood
LUMBER: Poles & Pole Crossarms, Treated
LUMBER: Poles, Wood, Untreated
LUMBER: Posts, Treated
LUMBER: Resawn, Small Dimension
LUMBER: Silo Stock, Sawn
LUMBER: Stacking Or Sticking
LUMBER: Treated
LUMBER: Veneer, Softwood

M

MACHINE GUNS, WHOLESALE
MACHINE PARTS: Stamped Or Pressed Metal
MACHINE SHOPS
MACHINE TOOL ACCESS: Cutting
MACHINE TOOLS & ACCESS
MACHINE TOOLS, METAL CUTTING: Lathes
MACHINE TOOLS, METAL CUTTING: Vertical Turning & Boring
MACHINE TOOLS, METAL FORMING: Headers
MACHINE TOOLS: Metal Cutting
MACHINE TOOLS: Metal Forming
MACHINERY & EQPT, AGRICULTURAL, WHOL: Farm Eqpt Parts/Splys
MACHINERY & EQPT, AGRICULTURAL, WHOLESALE: Poultry Eqpt
MACHINERY & EQPT, INDL, WHOL: Meters, Consumption Registerng
MACHINERY & EQPT, INDL, WHOLESALE: Chainsaws

INDEX

2019 Harris Directory of
Mississippi Manufacturers

337

PRODUCT INDEX

MACHINERY & EQPT, INDL, WHOLESALE: Drilling Bits
MACHINERY & EQPT, INDL, WHOLESALE: Drilling, Exc Bits
MACHINERY & EQPT, INDL, WHOLESALE: Engines & Parts, Diesel
MACHINERY & EQPT, INDL, WHOLESALE: Engines, Gasoline
MACHINERY & EQPT, INDL, WHOLESALE: Engs/Transportation Eqpt
MACHINERY & EQPT, INDL, WHOLESALE: Food Manufacturing
MACHINERY & EQPT, INDL, WHOLESALE: Fuel Injection Systems
MACHINERY & EQPT, INDL, WHOLESALE: Hydraulic Systems
MACHINERY & EQPT, INDL, WHOLESALE: Lift Trucks & Parts
MACHINERY & EQPT, INDL, WHOLESALE: Safety Eqpt
MACHINERY & EQPT, INDL, WHOLESALE: Sawmill
MACHINERY & EQPT, INDL, WHOLESALE: Trailers, Indl
MACHINERY & EQPT, TEXTILE: Fabric Forming
MACHINERY & EQPT, WHOLESALE: Construction, General
MACHINERY & EQPT, WHOLESALE: Contractors Materials
MACHINERY & EQPT, WHOLESALE: Logging
MACHINERY & EQPT, WHOLESALE: Oil Field Eqpt
MACHINERY & EQPT: Farm
MACHINERY & EQPT: Gas Producers, Generators/Other Rltd Eqpt
MACHINERY & EQPT: Petroleum Refinery
MACHINERY & EQPT: Silver Recovery
MACHINERY, COMMERCIAL LAUNDRY: Washing, Incl Coin-Operated
MACHINERY, FOOD PRDTS: Choppers, Commercial
MACHINERY, FOOD PRDTS: Food Processing, Smokers
MACHINERY, FOOD PRDTS: Processing, Poultry
MACHINERY, MAILING: Postage Meters
MACHINERY, PRINTING TRADES: Type Cases
MACHINERY, SERVICING: Coin-Operated, Exc Dry Clean & Laundry
MACHINERY, TEXTILE: Embroidery
MACHINERY, TEXTILE: Rope & Cordage
MACHINERY, TEXTILE: Silk Screens
MACHINERY, WOODWORKING: Bandsaws
MACHINERY, WOODWORKING: Cabinet Makers'
MACHINERY/EQPT, INDL, WHOL: Cleaning, High Press, Sand/Steam
MACHINERY: Assembly, Exc Metalworking
MACHINERY: Automotive Maintenance
MACHINERY: Automotive Related
MACHINERY: Bottling & Canning
MACHINERY: Brick Making
MACHINERY: Construction
MACHINERY: Cotton Ginning
MACHINERY: Custom
MACHINERY: Dredging
MACHINERY: Electronic Component Making
MACHINERY: General, Industrial, NEC
MACHINERY: Industrial, NEC
MACHINERY: Kilns
MACHINERY: Kilns, Lumber
MACHINERY: Logging Eqpt
MACHINERY: Metalworking
MACHINERY: Milling
MACHINERY: Mining
MACHINERY: Packaging
MACHINERY: Recycling
MACHINERY: Road Construction & Maintenance
MACHINERY: Semiconductor Manufacturing
MACHINERY: Specialty
MACHINERY: Woodworking
MACHINES: Forming, Sheet Metal
MAIL-ORDER HOUSES: Computer Eqpt & Electronics
MAIL-ORDER HOUSES: Food
MAIL-ORDER HOUSES: General Merchandise
MAIL-ORDER HOUSES: Jewelry
MAILBOX RENTAL & RELATED SVCS
MANAGEMENT CONSULTING SVCS: Construction Project
MANAGEMENT CONSULTING SVCS: Hospital & Health
MANAGEMENT CONSULTING SVCS: Industrial & Labor
MANAGEMENT CONSULTING SVCS: Management Engineering
MANAGEMENT SERVICES
MANAGEMENT SVCS, FACILITIES SUPPORT: Environ Remediation
MANAGEMENT SVCS: Administrative
MANAGEMENT SVCS: Business

MANICURE PREPARATIONS
MANUFACTURING INDUSTRIES, NEC
MAPS
MARBLE BOARD
MARBLE, BUILDING: Cut & Shaped
MARBLE: Dimension
MARINE CARGO HANDLING SVCS
MARINE HARDWARE
MARINE RELATED EQPT
MARKING DEVICES
MARKING DEVICES: Date Stamps, Hand, Rubber Or Metal
MARKING DEVICES: Embossing Seals & Hand Stamps
MARKING DEVICES: Embossing Seals, Corporate & Official
MARKING DEVICES: Seal Presses, Notary & Hand
MARKING DEVICES: Textile Making Stamps, Hand, Rubber/Metal
MASTIC ROOFING COMPOSITION
MATERIALS HANDLING EQPT WHOLESALERS
MATS & MATTING, MADE FROM PURCHASED WIRE
MATS OR MATTING, NEC: Rubber
MATS, MATTING & PADS: Nonwoven
MATTRESS STORES
MEAT & FISH MARKETS: Seafood
MEAT CUTTING & PACKING
MEAT MARKETS
MEAT PRDTS: Dried Beef, From Purchased Meat
MEAT PRDTS: Ham, Boiled, From Purchased Meat
MEAT PRDTS: Sausages, From Purchased Meat
MEAT PRDTS: Spreads, Sandwich, From Purchased Meat
MEAT PROCESSED FROM PURCHASED CARCASSES
MEAT PROCESSING MACHINERY
MEDICAL & HOSPITAL EQPT WHOLESALERS
MEDICAL & SURGICAL SPLYS: Clothing, Fire Resistant & Protect
MEDICAL & SURGICAL SPLYS: Gynecological Splys & Appliances
MEDICAL & SURGICAL SPLYS: Limbs, Artificial
MEDICAL & SURGICAL SPLYS: Orthopedic Appliances
MEDICAL & SURGICAL SPLYS: Personal Safety Eqpt
MEDICAL & SURGICAL SPLYS: Prosthetic Appliances
MEDICAL & SURGICAL SPLYS: Sutures, Non & Absorbable
MEDICAL & SURGICAL SPLYS: Walkers
MEDICAL CENTERS
MEDICAL EQPT: Diagnostic
MEDICAL EQPT: Ultrasonic, Exc Cleaning
MEDICAL FIELD ASSOCIATION
MEDICAL HELP SVCS
MEDICAL RESCUE SQUAD
MEDICAL, DENTAL & HOSPITAL EQPT, WHOLESALE: Artificial Limbs
MEDICAL, DENTAL & HOSPITAL EQPT, WHOLESALE: Hearing Aids
MEDICAL, DENTAL & HOSPITAL EQPT, WHOLESALE: Med Eqpt & Splys
MEDICAL, DENTAL & HOSPITAL EQPT, WHOLESALE: Orthopedic
MEDICAL, DENTAL & HOSPITAL EQPT, WHOLESALE: Safety
MEMBERSHIP ORGANIZATIONS, BUSINESS: Contractors' Association
MEMBERSHIP ORGANIZATIONS, BUSINESS: Growers' Association
MEMBERSHIP ORGANIZATIONS, NEC: Charitable
MEMBERSHIP ORGS, BUSINESS: Shipping/Steamship Co Assoc
MEMORIALS, MONUMENTS & MARKERS
MEMORY DEVICES: Magnetic Bubble
MEN'S & BOYS' CLOTHING STORES
MEN'S & BOYS' CLOTHING WHOLESALERS, NEC
MEN'S & BOYS' WORK CLOTHING WHOLESALERS
MEN'S SUITS STORES
MESH, REINFORCING: Plastic
METAL & STEEL PRDTS: Abrasive
METAL FABRICATORS: Architechtural
METAL FABRICATORS: Plate
METAL FABRICATORS: Sheet
METAL FABRICATORS: Structural, Ship
METAL FINISHING SVCS
METAL ORES, NEC
METAL SERVICE CENTERS & OFFICES
METAL STAMPING, FOR THE TRADE
METALS SVC CENTERS & WHOL: Structural Shapes, Iron Or Steel
METALS SVC CENTERS & WHOLESALERS: Pipe & Tubing, Steel

METALS SVC CENTERS & WHOLESALERS: Rope, Wire, Exc Insulated
METALS SVC CENTERS & WHOLESALERS: Steel
METALS: Primary Nonferrous, NEC
METALWORK: Miscellaneous
METALWORK: Ornamental
MICROWAVE COMPONENTS
MILITARY INSIGNIA
MILLING: Corn Grits & Flakes, For Brewers' Use
MILLING: Rice
MILLWORK
MINE DEVELOPMENT, METAL
MINERAL MINING: Nonmetallic
MINERALS: Ground or Treated
MINING EXPLORATION & DEVELOPMENT SVCS
MISCELLANEOUS FIN INVEST ACTVTS: Mineral Royalty Dealer
MISCELLANEOUS FINANCIAL INVEST ACTIVITIES: Oil Royalties
MITTENS: Leather
MIXTURES & BLOCKS: Asphalt Paving
MOBILE HOMES
MODULES: Computer Logic
MOLDED RUBBER PRDTS
MOLDING SAND MINING
MOLDINGS & TRIM: Wood
MOLDINGS: Picture Frame
MOLDS: Indl
MOLDS: Plastic Working & Foundry
MONUMENTS & GRAVE MARKERS, EXC TERRAZZO
MONUMENTS: Cut Stone, Exc Finishing Or Lettering Only
MOPS: Floor & Dust
MOTION PICTURE PRODUCTION ALLIED SVCS
MOTOR HOMES
MOTOR REBUILDING SVCS, EXC AUTOMOTIVE
MOTOR REPAIR SVCS
MOTOR VEHICLE ASSEMBLY, COMPLETE: Autos, Incl Specialty
MOTOR VEHICLE ASSEMBLY, COMPLETE: Bus/Large Spclty Vehicles
MOTOR VEHICLE ASSEMBLY, COMPLETE: Cars, Armored
MOTOR VEHICLE ASSEMBLY, COMPLETE: Fire Department Vehicles
MOTOR VEHICLE ASSEMBLY, COMPLETE: Wreckers, Tow Truck
MOTOR VEHICLE DEALERS: Automobiles, New & Used
MOTOR VEHICLE DEALERS: Cars, Used Only
MOTOR VEHICLE DEALERS: Trucks, Tractors/Trailers, New & Used
MOTOR VEHICLE PARTS & ACCESS: Acceleration Eqpt
MOTOR VEHICLE PARTS & ACCESS: Body Components & Frames
MOTOR VEHICLE PARTS & ACCESS: Cylinder Heads
MOTOR VEHICLE PARTS & ACCESS: Electrical Eqpt
MOTOR VEHICLE PARTS & ACCESS: Engines & Parts
MOTOR VEHICLE PARTS & ACCESS: Engs & Trans,Factory, Rebuilt
MOTOR VEHICLE PARTS & ACCESS: Fuel Systems & Parts
MOTOR VEHICLE PARTS & ACCESS: Hoods
MOTOR VEHICLE PARTS & ACCESS: Manifolds
MOTOR VEHICLE PARTS & ACCESS: Pumps, Hydraulic Fluid Power
MOTOR VEHICLE PARTS & ACCESS: Sanders, Safety
MOTOR VEHICLE PARTS & ACCESS: Windshield Frames
MOTOR VEHICLE PARTS & ACCESS: Wiring Harness Sets
MOTOR VEHICLE SPLYS & PARTS WHOLESALERS: New
MOTOR VEHICLE: Radiators
MOTOR VEHICLE: Steering Mechanisms
MOTOR VEHICLES & CAR BODIES
MOTOR VEHICLES, WHOLESALE: Trailers, Truck, New & Used
MOTOR VEHICLES, WHOLESALE: Truck bodies
MOTOR VEHICLES, WHOLESALE: Truck tractors
MOTORCYCLE ACCESS
MOTORCYCLE DEALERS
MOTORCYCLE PARTS & ACCESS DEALERS
MOTORS: Electric
MOTORS: Generators
MOVING SVC: Local
MOWERS & ACCESSORIES
MUSEUMS
MUSICAL INSTRUMENTS & ACCESS: NEC
MUSICAL INSTRUMENTS: Bells
MUSICAL INSTRUMENTS: Guitars & Parts, Electric & Acoustic

338

2019 Harris Directory of
Mississippi Manufacturers

PRODUCT INDEX

MUSICAL INSTRUMENTS: Organ Parts & Materials

N

NAME PLATES: Engraved Or Etched
NAMEPLATES
NATIONAL SECURITY FORCES
NATURAL GAS COMPRESSING SVC, On-Site
NATURAL GAS DISTRIBUTION TO CONSUMERS
NATURAL GAS LIQUID FRACTIONATING SVC
NATURAL GAS LIQUIDS PRODUCTION
NATURAL GAS PRODUCTION
NATURAL LIQUEFIED PETROLEUM GAS PRODUCTION
NATURAL PROPANE PRODUCTION
NAUTICAL REPAIR SVCS
NAVIGATIONAL SYSTEMS & INSTRUMENTS
NETS: Camouflage
NEWS DEALERS & NEWSSTANDS
NEWSPAPERS & PERIODICALS NEWS REPORTING SVCS
NEWSPAPERS, WHOLESALE
NEWSSTAND
NONCURRENT CARRYING WIRING DEVICES
NONFERROUS: Rolling & Drawing, NEC
NOTEBOOKS, MADE FROM PURCHASED MATERIALS
NOVELTY SHOPS
NURSERIES & LAWN & GARDEN SPLY STORES, RETAIL:
   Top Soil
NURSERIES & LAWN/GARDEN SPLY STORE, RET: Lawn-
   mowers/Tractors
NURSERIES & LAWN/GARDEN SPLY STORES, RET: Gar-
   den Splys/Tools
NURSERY & GARDEN CENTERS
NURSERY STOCK, WHOLESALE

O

OFFICE EQPT WHOLESALERS
OFFICE MACHINES, NEC
OFFICE SPLY & STATIONERY STORES
OFFICE SPLY & STATIONERY STORES: Office Forms &
   Splys
OFFICE SPLY & STATIONERY STORES: Writing Splys
OFFICE SPLYS, NEC, WHOLESALE
OFFICES & CLINICS HLTH PRACTITIONERS: Christian Sci-
   ence
OFFICES & CLINICS OF DENTISTS: Specialist, Practitioners
OFFICES & CLINICS OF DOCTORS, MEDICINE: Gen & Fam
   Practice
OIL & GAS FIELD EQPT: Drill Rigs
OIL & GAS FIELD MACHINERY
OIL FIELD MACHINERY & EQPT
OIL FIELD SVCS, NEC
OILS: Lubricating
OPHTHALMIC GOODS
OPHTHALMIC GOODS: Frames, Lenses & Parts, Eyeglasses
OPHTHALMIC GOODS: Goggles, Sun, Safety, Indl, Etc
OPHTHALMIC GOODS: Spectacles
OPTICAL GOODS STORES: Contact Lenses, Prescription
OPTICAL GOODS STORES: Eyeglasses, Prescription
OPTICAL GOODS STORES: Opticians
OPTICAL INSTRUMENTS & APPARATUS
OPTICAL INSTRUMENTS & LENSES
OPTOMETRISTS' OFFICES
ORDNANCE: Flame Throwers
ORGAN TUNING & REPAIR SVCS
ORGANIZATIONS: Economic Research, Noncommercial
ORGANIZATIONS: Religious
ORGANIZATIONS: Research Institute
ORIENTED STRANDBOARD
OUTLETS: Electric, Convenience

P

PACKAGE DESIGN SVCS
PACKAGED FROZEN FOODS WHOLESALERS, NEC
PACKAGING MATERIALS, WHOLESALE
PACKAGING MATERIALS: Paper
PACKAGING MATERIALS: Paper, Coated Or Laminated
PACKAGING MATERIALS: Plastic Film, Coated Or Laminated
PACKAGING MATERIALS: Polystyrene Foam
PACKING & CRATING SVC
PACKING SVCS: Shipping
PADDING: Foamed Plastics
PADS: Mattress
PAINT & PAINTING SPLYS STORE
PAINT STORE
PAINTING SVC: Metal Prdts

PAINTS & ADDITIVES
PAINTS & ALLIED PRODUCTS
PAINTS, VARNISHES & SPLYS WHOLESALERS
PAINTS: Oil Or Alkyd Vehicle Or Water Thinned
PALLETS
PALLETS & SKIDS: Wood
PALLETS: Plastic
PALLETS: Wooden
PANEL & DISTRIBUTION BOARDS & OTHER RELATED AP-
   PARATUS
PANELS: Building, Metal
PANELS: Cardboard, Die-Cut, Made From Purchased Materi-
   als
PANELS: Wood
PAPER & BOARD: Die-cut
PAPER CONVERTING
PAPER MANUFACTURERS: Exc Newsprint
PAPER PRDTS: Facial Tissue
PAPER PRDTS: Infant & Baby Prdts
PAPER PRDTS: Pressed Pulp Prdts
PAPER PRDTS: Sanitary
PAPER PRDTS: Sanitary Tissue Paper
PAPER PRDTS: Towels, Napkins/Tissue Paper, From Purchd
   Mtrls
PAPER, WHOLESALE: Writing
PAPER: Adding Machine Rolls, Made From Purchased Materi-
   als
PAPER: Adhesive
PAPER: Bag
PAPER: Coated & Laminated, NEC
PAPER: Gift Wrap
PAPER: Newsprint
PAPER: Printer
PAPER: Soap Impregnated Papers & Paper Washcloths
PAPER: Specialty
PAPER: Tissue
PAPER: Wallpaper
PAPERBOARD
PAPERBOARD: Corrugated
PARACHUTES
PARALEGAL SVCS
PARTICLEBOARD
PARTICLEBOARD: Laminated, Plastic
PARTITIONS & FIXTURES: Except Wood
PARTITIONS: Wood & Fixtures
PATCHING PLASTER: Household
PATENT OWNERS & LESSORS
PATTERNS: Indl
PAVERS
PAWN SHOPS
PERFUMES
PERSONAL APPEARANCE SVCS
PERSONAL CREDIT INSTITUTIONS: Consumer Finance
   Companies
PERSONAL CREDIT INSTITUTIONS: Licensed Loan Compa-
   nies, Small
PERSONAL SVCS, NEC
PEST CONTROL SVCS
PESTICIDES
PET COLLARS, LEASHES, MUZZLES & HARNESSES:
   Leather
PET FOOD WHOLESALERS
PET SPLYS
PETROLEUM & PETROLEUM PRDTS, WHOLESALE Crude
   Oil
PETROLEUM & PETROLEUM PRDTS, WHOLESALE Diesel
   Fuel
PETROLEUM & PETROLEUM PRDTS, WHOLESALE Fuel
   Oil
PETROLEUM & PETROLEUM PRDTS, WHOLESALE Petro-
   leum Brokers
PETROLEUM & PETROLEUM PRDTS, WHOLESALE: Bulk
   Stations
PETROLEUM BULK STATIONS & TERMINALS
PETROLEUM PRDTS WHOLESALERS
PHARMACEUTICAL PREPARATIONS: Druggists' Prepara-
   tions
PHARMACEUTICAL PREPARATIONS: Medicines, Capsule
   Or Ample
PHARMACEUTICAL PREPARATIONS: Pills
PHARMACEUTICAL PREPARATIONS: Solutions
PHARMACEUTICAL PREPARATIONS: Tablets
PHARMACEUTICALS
PHARMACEUTICALS: Medicinal & Botanical Prdts
PHOSPHORIC ACID

PHOTOCOPY MACHINE REPAIR SVCS
PHOTOCOPYING & DUPLICATING SVCS
PHOTOFINISHING LABORATORIES
PHOTOGRAMMATIC MAPPING SVCS
PHOTOGRAPHIC EQPT & SPLY: Sound Recordg/Reprod
   Eqpt, Motion
PHOTOGRAPHIC EQPT & SPLYS
PHOTOGRAPHY SVCS: Commercial
PHOTOGRAPHY SVCS: Passport
PHOTOGRAPHY SVCS: Still Or Video
PHOTOGRAPHY: Aerial
PHYSICAL FITNESS CENTERS
PHYSICIANS' OFFICES & CLINICS: Medical
PICTURE FRAMES: Metal
PICTURE FRAMES: Wood
PIECE GOODS & NOTIONS WHOLESALERS
PIECE GOODS, NOTIONS & DRY GOODS, WHOLESALE:
   Fabrics
PIECE GOODS, NOTIONS & OTHER DRY GOODS,
   WHOLESALE: Bridal
PILOT SVCS: Aviation
PIPE & FITTING: Fabrication
PIPE & TUBES: Aluminum
PIPE & TUBES: Copper & Copper Alloy
PIPE & TUBES: Seamless
PIPE, CULVERT: Concrete
PIPE: Plastic
PIPE: Seamless Steel
PIPE: Sewer, Cast Iron
PIPE: Sheet Metal
PIPELINES, EXC NATURAL GAS: Coal
PIPELINES: Refined Petroleum
PIPES & FITTINGS: Fiber, Made From Purchased Materials
PIPES & TUBES
PIPES & TUBES: Steel
PIPES: Steel & Iron
PLANING MILL, NEC
PLASTER WORK: Ornamental & Architectural
PLASTIC PRDTS
PLASTICS FILM & SHEET
PLASTICS FILM & SHEET: Polyethylene
PLASTICS FILM & SHEET: Vinyl
PLASTICS FINISHED PRDTS: Laminated
PLASTICS MATERIAL & RESINS
PLASTICS MATERIALS, BASIC FORMS & SHAPES
   WHOLESALERS
PLASTICS PROCESSING
PLASTICS: Blow Molded
PLASTICS: Cast
PLASTICS: Finished Injection Molded
PLASTICS: Injection Molded
PLASTICS: Molded
PLASTICS: Polystyrene Foam
PLATES
PLATES: Plastic Exc Polystyrene Foam
PLATES: Sheet & Strip, Exc Coated Prdts
PLATING & POLISHING SVC
PLATING SVC: Electro
PLATING SVC: NEC
PLEATING & STITCHING FOR THE TRADE: Decorative &
   Novelty
PLEATING & STITCHING SVC
PLUMBING & HEATING EQPT & SPLY, WHOL: Htg
   Eqpt/Panels, Solar
PLUMBING & HEATING EQPT & SPLY, WHOL: Hy-
   dronic Htg Eqpt
PLUMBING & HEATING EQPT & SPLYS, WHOL: Fireplaces,
   Prefab
PLUMBING & HEATING EQPT & SPLYS, WHOL: Plumbing
   Fitting/Sply
PLUMBING FIXTURES
PLUMBING FIXTURES: Plastic
PLUMBING FIXTURES: Vitreous
POLICE PROTECTION: Local Government
POLISHING SVC: Metals Or Formed Prdts
POLYETHYLENE RESINS
POLYSTYRENE RESINS
POLYURETHANE RESINS
POLYVINYL CHLORIDE RESINS
POPCORN & SUPPLIES WHOLESALERS
PORTER SVC
PORTRAIT COPYING SVC
POSTAL EQPT: Locker Boxes, Exc Wood
POSTERS & DECALS, WHOLESALE
POTASH MINING

INDEX

PRODUCT INDEX

POTPOURRI
POTTERY
POTTING SOILS
POULTRY & SMALL GAME SLAUGHTERING & PROCESS-
ING
POULTRY SLAUGHTERING & PROCESSING
POWER SWITCHING EQPT
POWER TOOLS, HAND: Drills & Drilling Tools
POWER TRANSMISSION EQPT: Mechanical
PRECAST TERRAZZO OR CONCRETE PRDTS
PREFABRICATED BUILDING DEALERS
PRESSED FIBER & MOLDED PULP PRDTS, EXC FOOD
PRDTS
PRESTRESSED CONCRETE PRDTS
PRIMARY FINISHED OR SEMIFINISHED SHAPES
PRIMARY METAL PRODUCTS
PRINT CARTRIDGES: Laser & Other Computer Printers
PRINTED CIRCUIT BOARDS
PRINTERS: Computer
PRINTING & ENGRAVING: Invitation & Stationery
PRINTING & ENGRAVING: Poster & Decal
PRINTING & WRITING PAPER WHOLESALERS
PRINTING MACHINERY
PRINTING TRADES MACHINERY & EQPT REPAIR SVCS
PRINTING, COMMERCIAL Newspapers, NEC
PRINTING, COMMERCIAL: Business Forms, NEC
PRINTING, COMMERCIAL: Directories, Exc Telephone, NEC
PRINTING, COMMERCIAL: Envelopes, NEC
PRINTING, COMMERCIAL: Labels & Seals, NEC
PRINTING, COMMERCIAL: Letterpress & Screen
PRINTING, COMMERCIAL: Screen
PRINTING, COMMERCIAL: Stationery, NEC
PRINTING, LITHOGRAPHIC: Color
PRINTING, LITHOGRAPHIC: Decals
PRINTING, LITHOGRAPHIC: Forms, Business
PRINTING, LITHOGRAPHIC: Newspapers
PRINTING, LITHOGRAPHIC: Offset & photolithographic print-
ing
PRINTING, LITHOGRAPHIC: On Metal
PRINTING, LITHOGRAPHIC: Promotional
PRINTING: Books
PRINTING: Checkbooks
PRINTING: Commercial, NEC
PRINTING: Flexographic
PRINTING: Gravure, Invitations
PRINTING: Gravure, Job
PRINTING: Gravure, Rotogravure
PRINTING: Gravure, Stationery & Invitation
PRINTING: Letterpress
PRINTING: Lithographic
PRINTING: Offset
PRINTING: Pamphlets
PRINTING: Rotary Photogravure
PRINTING: Screen, Broadwoven Fabrics, Cotton
PRINTING: Screen, Fabric
PRINTING: Screen, Manmade Fiber & Silk, Broadwoven Fab-
ric
PRINTING: Thermography
PROFESSIONAL EQPT & SPLYS, WHOLESALE: Optical
Goods
PROFESSIONAL INSTRUMENT REPAIR SVCS
PROPELLERS: Boat & Ship, Cast
PROPELLERS: Boat & Ship, Machined
PROTECTION EQPT: Lightning
PUBLISHERS: Book
PUBLISHERS: Books, No Printing
PUBLISHERS: Comic Books, No Printing
PUBLISHERS: Guides
PUBLISHERS: Magazines, No Printing
PUBLISHERS: Miscellaneous
PUBLISHERS: Music Book
PUBLISHERS: Music Book & Sheet Music
PUBLISHERS: Newsletter
PUBLISHERS: Newspaper
PUBLISHERS: Newspapers, No Printing
PUBLISHERS: Periodicals, Magazines
PUBLISHERS: Periodicals, No Printing
PUBLISHERS: Telephone & Other Directory
PUBLISHERS: Trade journals, No Printing
PUBLISHING & BROADCASTING: Internet Only
PUBLISHING & PRINTING: Art Copy
PUBLISHING & PRINTING: Book Clubs
PUBLISHING & PRINTING: Books
PUBLISHING & PRINTING: Comic Books
PUBLISHING & PRINTING: Directories, NEC

PUBLISHING & PRINTING: Magazines: publishing & printing
PUBLISHING & PRINTING: Newsletters, Business Svc
PUBLISHING & PRINTING: Newspapers
PUBLISHING & PRINTING: Pamphlets
PUBLISHING & PRINTING: Posters
PUBLISHING & PRINTING: Technical Papers
PUBLISHING & PRINTING: Textbooks
PUBLISHING & PRINTING: Yearbooks
PULP MILLS
PULPWOOD, WHOLESALE
PUMP GOVERNORS: Gas Machines
PUMPS
PUMPS & PUMPING EQPT REPAIR SVCS
PUMPS & PUMPING EQPT WHOLESALERS
PUMPS: Oil Well & Field
PUPPETS & MARIONETTES
PURCHASING SVCS

Q

QUILTING SVC & SPLYS, FOR THE TRADE

R

RACEWAYS
RACKS: Pallet, Exc Wood
RADIO & TELEVISION COMMUNICATIONS EQUIPMENT
RADIO BROADCASTING STATIONS
RADIO COMMUNICATIONS: Airborne Eqpt
RADIO REPAIR & INSTALLATION SVCS
RAILROAD CARGO LOADING & UNLOADING SVCS
RAILROAD EQPT
RAILROAD EQPT: Cars & Eqpt, Dining
RAILROAD EQPT: Locomotives & Parts, Indl
RAILROAD TIES: Wood
REAL ESTATE AGENCIES & BROKERS
REAL ESTATE AGENCIES: Selling
REAL ESTATE AGENTS & MANAGERS
REAL ESTATE INVESTMENT TRUSTS
REAL ESTATE OPERATORS, EXC DEVELOPERS: Insurance
Building
RECLAIMED RUBBER: Reworked By Manufacturing Process
RECORDING TAPE: Video, Blank
RECORDS & TAPES: Prerecorded
RECREATIONAL SPORTING EQPT REPAIR SVCS
RECREATIONAL VEHICLE PARTS & ACCESS STORES
RECYCLABLE SCRAP & WASTE MATERIALS WHOLE-
SALERS
RECYCLING: Paper
REFINERS & SMELTERS: Nonferrous Metal
REFINERS & SMELTERS: Silver
REFINING: Petroleum
REFRACTORIES: Clay
REFRIGERATION & HEATING EQUIPMENT
REFRIGERATION EQPT & SPLYS WHOLESALERS
REFRIGERATION EQPT & SPLYS, WHOLESALE: Commer-
cial Eqpt
REFRIGERATION EQPT: Complete
REFRIGERATORS & FREEZERS WHOLESALERS
REFUSE SYSTEMS
REGISTERS: Air, Metal
REHABILITATION CTR, RESIDENTIAL WITH HEALTH CARE
INCIDENTAL
RELAYS & SWITCHES: Indl, Electric
RELAYS: Electronic Usage
RELIGIOUS SPLYS WHOLESALERS
REMOVERS & CLEANERS
RENTAL CENTERS: Tools
RENTAL SVCS: Aircraft
RENTAL SVCS: Business Machine & Electronic Eqpt
RENTAL SVCS: Costume
RENTAL SVCS: Garage Facility & Tool
RENTAL SVCS: Office Facilities & Secretarial Svcs
RENTAL SVCS: Oil Eqpt
RENTAL SVCS: Tent & Tarpaulin
REPRODUCTION SVCS: Video Tape Or Disk
RESEARCH, DEVELOPMENT & TEST SVCS, COMM: Cmptr
Hardware Dev
RESEARCH, DEVELOPMENT & TEST SVCS, COMM: Re-
search, Exc Lab
RESEARCH, DEVELOPMENT & TESTING SVCS, COMM:
Natural Resource
RESIDENTIAL REMODELERS
RESIDUES
RESISTORS
RESTAURANTS:Full Svc, Family, Independent
RESTAURANTS:Full Svc, Italian

RESTAURANTS:Limited Svc, Chicken
RESTAURANTS:Limited Svc, Ice Cream Stands Or Dairy
Bars
RETAIL BAKERY: Cakes
RETAIL BAKERY: Cookies
RETAIL BAKERY: Doughnuts
RETAIL BAKERY: Pretzels
RETAIL LUMBER YARDS
RETAIL STORES: Alarm Signal Systems
RETAIL STORES: Architectural Splys
RETAIL STORES: Art & Architectural Splys
RETAIL STORES: Artificial Limbs
RETAIL STORES: Awnings
RETAIL STORES: Banners
RETAIL STORES: Business Machines & Eqpt
RETAIL STORES: Cake Decorating Splys
RETAIL STORES: Cosmetics
RETAIL STORES: Decals
RETAIL STORES: Electronic Parts & Eqpt
RETAIL STORES: Engine & Motor Eqpt & Splys
RETAIL STORES: Engines & Parts, Air-Cooled
RETAIL STORES: Farm Eqpt & Splys
RETAIL STORES: Farm Tractors
RETAIL STORES: Hearing Aids
RETAIL STORES: Ice
RETAIL STORES: Insecticides
RETAIL STORES: Medical Apparatus & Splys
RETAIL STORES: Monuments, Finished To Custom Order
RETAIL STORES: Motors, Electric
RETAIL STORES: Orthopedic & Prosthesis Applications
RETAIL STORES: Picture Frames, Ready Made
RETAIL STORES: Plumbing & Heating Splys
RETAIL STORES: Rubber Stamps
RETAIL STORES: Telephone Eqpt & Systems
RETAIL STORES: Tombstones
RETAIL STORES: Training Materials, Electronic
RETAIL STORES: Typewriters & Business Machines
RETAIL STORES: Water Purification Eqpt
ROAD MATERIALS: Bituminous, Not From Refineries
ROLLING MILL EQPT: Galvanizing Lines
ROOF DECKS
ROOFING MATERIALS: Asphalt
RUBBER
RUBBER PRDTS: Reclaimed
RUBBER STAMP, WHOLESALE
RUBBER STRUCTURES: Air-Supported
RULES: Slide

S

SAFETY EQPT & SPLYS WHOLESALERS
SAILBOAT BUILDING & REPAIR
SAILS
SAND & GRAVEL
SAND MINING
SANDBLASTING SVC: Building Exterior
SANITARY SVC, NEC
SANITARY SVCS: Oil Spill Cleanup
SANITARY SVCS: Waste Materials, Recycling
SANITARY WARE: Metal
SANITATION CHEMICALS & CLEANING AGENTS
SATCHELS
SATELLITES: Communications
SAW BLADES
SAWING & PLANING MILLS
SAWING & PLANING MILLS: Custom
SAWMILL MACHINES
SAWS & SAWING EQPT
SAWS: Hand, Metalworking Or Woodworking
SCALES & BALANCES, EXC LABORATORY
SCALES: Indl
SCANNING DEVICES: Optical
SCHOOL FOR PHYSICALLY HANDICAPPED, NEC
SCHOOL SPLYS, EXC BOOKS: Wholesalers
SCHOOLS: Vocational, NEC
SCRAP & WASTE MATERIALS, WHOLESALE: Ferrous Metal
SCRAP & WASTE MATERIALS, WHOLESALE: Junk & Scrap
SCRAP & WASTE MATERIALS, WHOLESALE: Metal
SCREENS: Door, Metal Covered Wood
SCREENS: Window, Metal
SCREW MACHINE PRDTS
SCREW MACHINES
SCREWS: Metal
SEARCH & DETECTION SYSTEMS, EXC RADAR
SEARCH & NAVIGATION SYSTEMS
SEATING: Chairs, Table & Arm

2019 Harris Directory of
Mississippi Manufacturers

340

PRODUCT INDEX

SEATING: Stadium
SECURITY CONTROL EQPT & SYSTEMS
SECURITY DEVICES
SECURITY EQPT STORES
SECURITY PROTECTIVE DEVICES MAINTENANCE & MONITORING SVCS
SECURITY SYSTEMS SERVICES
SEEDS: Coated Or Treated, From Purchased Seeds
SEMICONDUCTORS & RELATED DEVICES
SEPTIC TANKS: Concrete
SEPTIC TANKS: Plastic
SEWAGE & WATER TREATMENT EQPT
SEWAGE TREATMENT SYSTEMS & EQPT
SEWING CONTRACTORS
SEWING MACHINE STORES
SEWING MACHINES & PARTS: Indl
SEWING, NEEDLEWORK & PIECE GOODS STORES: Sewing & Needlework
SEWING, NEEDLEWORK & PIECE GOODS: Weaving Goods & Splys
SHAPES: Extruded, Aluminum, NEC
SHEET METAL SPECIALTIES, EXC STAMPED
SHEETING: Laminated Plastic
SHELTERED WORKSHOPS
SHIP BLDG & RPRG: Drilling & Production Platforms, Oil/Gas
SHIP BUILDING & REPAIRING: Cargo, Commercial
SHIP BUILDING & REPAIRING: Combat Vessels
SHIP BUILDING & REPAIRING: Lighters, Marine
SHIP BUILDING & REPAIRING: Military
SHIP BUILDING & REPAIRING: Passenger, Commercial
SHIP BUILDING & REPAIRING: Towboats
SHIP COMPONENTS: Metal, Prefabricated
SHIPBUILDING & REPAIR
SHOE & BOOT ACCESS
SHOE MATERIALS: Quarters
SHOE MATERIALS: Rands
SHOE STORES
SHOE STORES: Custom & Orthopedic
SHOES: Athletic, Exc Rubber Or Plastic
SHOES: Plastic Or Rubber
SHOES: Rubber Or Rubber Soled Fabric Uppers
SHOT PEENING SVC
SHOWER STALLS: Plastic & Fiberglass
SHREDDERS: Indl & Commercial
SIDING MATERIALS
SIDING: Plastic
SIGN PAINTING & LETTERING SHOP
SIGNALS: Railroad, Electric
SIGNALS: Transportation
SIGNS & ADVERTISING SPECIALTIES
SIGNS & ADVERTISING SPECIALTIES: Artwork, Advertising
SIGNS & ADVERTISING SPECIALTIES: Novelties
SIGNS & ADVERTISING SPECIALTIES: Signs
SIGNS & ADVERTSG SPECIALTIES: Displays/Cutouts Window/Lobby
SIGNS, ELECTRICAL: Wholesalers
SIGNS, EXC ELECTRIC, WHOLESALE
SIGNS: Electrical
SIGNS: Neon
SILICON: Pure
SIRENS: Vehicle, Marine, Indl & Warning
SKIDS: Wood
SLAG: Crushed Or Ground
SOAPS & DETERGENTS
SOAPS & DETERGENTS: Dishwashing Compounds
SOFT DRINKS WHOLESALERS
SOFTWARE PUBLISHERS: Application
SOFTWARE PUBLISHERS: Business & Professional
SOFTWARE PUBLISHERS: Computer Utilities
SOFTWARE PUBLISHERS: Education
SOFTWARE PUBLISHERS: Home Entertainment
SOFTWARE PUBLISHERS: NEC
SOFTWARE PUBLISHERS: Operating Systems
SOFTWARE PUBLISHERS: Publisher's
SOFTWARE TRAINING, COMPUTER
SOIL CONDITIONERS
SOLAR CELLS
SOLDERING EQPT: Electrical, Handheld
SONAR SYSTEMS & EQPT
SOUND EFFECTS & MUSIC PRODUCTION: Motion Picture
SOUND EQPT: Electric
SOUND RECORDING STUDIOS
SOYBEAN PRDTS
SPACE RESEARCH & TECHNOLOGY PROGRAMS ADMINISTRATION

SPACE VEHICLE EQPT
SPEAKER SYSTEMS
SPECIALTY SAWMILL PRDTS
SPECULATIVE BUILDERS: Single-Family Housing
SPORTING & ATHLETIC GOODS: Arrows, Archery
SPORTING & ATHLETIC GOODS: Boomerangs
SPORTING & ATHLETIC GOODS: Bows, Archery
SPORTING & ATHLETIC GOODS: Camping Eqpt & Splys
SPORTING & ATHLETIC GOODS: Fishing Bait, Artificial
SPORTING & ATHLETIC GOODS: Fishing Tackle, General
SPORTING & ATHLETIC GOODS: Game Calls
SPORTING & ATHLETIC GOODS: Gymnasium Eqpt
SPORTING & ATHLETIC GOODS: Hunting Eqpt
SPORTING & ATHLETIC GOODS: Indian Clubs
SPORTING & ATHLETIC GOODS: Pools, Swimming, Exc Plastic
SPORTING & ATHLETIC GOODS: Rods & Rod Parts, Fishing
SPORTING & ATHLETIC GOODS: Shafts, Golf Club
SPORTING & ATHLETIC GOODS: Shooting Eqpt & Splys, General
SPORTING & ATHLETIC GOODS: Skateboards
SPORTING & ATHLETIC GOODS: Targets, Archery & Rifle Shooting
SPORTING & ATHLETIC GOODS: Team Sports Eqpt
SPORTING & ATHLETIC GOODS: Track & Field Athletic Eqpt
SPORTING & RECREATIONAL GOODS & SPLYS WHOLESALERS
SPORTING & RECREATIONAL GOODS, WHOLESALE: Boat Access & Part
SPORTING & RECREATIONAL GOODS, WHOLESALE: Fishing
SPORTING & RECREATIONAL GOODS, WHOLESALE: Golf
SPORTING & RECREATIONAL GOODS, WHOLESALE: Hot Tubs
SPORTING FIREARMS WHOLESALERS
SPORTING GOODS
SPORTING GOODS STORES, NEC
SPORTING GOODS STORES: Archery Splys
SPORTING GOODS STORES: Bait & Tackle
SPORTING GOODS STORES: Firearms
SPORTING GOODS STORES: Hunting Eqpt
SPORTING GOODS STORES: Playground Eqpt
SPORTING GOODS STORES: Specialty Sport Splys, NEC
SPORTING GOODS: Archery
SPORTING GOODS: Fishing Nets
SPORTING/ATHLETIC GOODS: Gloves, Boxing, Handball, Etc
SPORTS APPAREL STORES
SPRAYING EQPT: Agricultural
SPRINGS: Automobile
SPRINGS: Coiled Flat
SPRINGS: Steel
SPRINGS: Wire
STAINED GLASS ART SVCS
STAINLESS STEEL
STAIRCASES & STAIRS, WOOD
STAMPED ART GOODS FOR EMBROIDERING
STAMPINGS: Automotive
STAMPINGS: Metal
STATIONARY & OFFICE SPLYS, WHOLESALE: Looseleaf Binders
STATIONARY & OFFICE SPLYS, WHOLESALE: Manifold Business Form
STATIONARY & OFFICE SPLYS, WHOLESALE: Marking Devices
STATIONERY & OFFICE SPLYS WHOLESALERS
STATIONERY PRDTS
STEEL & ALLOYS: Tool & Die
STEEL FABRICATORS
STEEL MILLS
STEEL SHEET: Cold-Rolled
STEEL: Cold-Rolled
STITCHING SVCS
STOCK SHAPES: Plastic
STONE: Cast Concrete
STONEWARE PRDTS: Pottery
STORES: Auto & Home Supply
STOVES: Wood & Coal Burning
STRAW GOODS
STRUCTURAL SUPPORT & BUILDING MATERIAL: Concrete
STUCCO
STUDIOS: Artist
SUNDRIES & RELATED PRDTS: Medical & Laboratory, Rubber
SUPERMARKETS & OTHER GROCERY STORES

SURFACE ACTIVE AGENTS
SURFACE ACTIVE AGENTS: Oils & Greases
SURGICAL APPLIANCES & SPLYS
SURGICAL EQPT: See Also Instruments
SURGICAL IMPLANTS
SURVEYING & MAPPING: Land Parcels
SURVEYING SVCS: Aerial Digital Imaging
SVC ESTABLISH EQPT, WHOLESALE: Carpet/Rug Clean Eqpt & Sply
SVC ESTABLISHMENT EQPT & SPLYS WHOLESALERS
SVC ESTABLISHMENT EQPT, WHOL: Cleaning & Maint Eqpt & Splys
SVC ESTABLISHMENT EQPT, WHOLESALE: Beauty Parlor Eqpt & Sply
SVC ESTABLISHMENT EQPT, WHOLESALE: Sprinkler Systems
SWEEPING COMPOUNDS
SWIMMING POOL & HOT TUB CLEANING & MAINTENANCE SVCS
SWITCHES: Electronic
SWITCHES: Solenoid
SWITCHGEAR & SWITCHBOARD APPARATUS
SYNTHETIC RESIN FINISHED PRDTS, NEC
SYRUPS, DRINK

T

TABLE OR COUNTERTOPS, PLASTIC LAMINATED
TABLECLOTHS & SETTINGS
TABLEWARE OR KITCHEN ARTICLES: Commercial, Fine Earthenware
TABLEWARE: Household & Commercial, Semivitreous
TABLEWARE: Plastic
TAGS & LABELS: Paper
TALLOW: Animal
TANK REPAIR & CLEANING SVCS
TANK REPAIR SVCS
TANKS & OTHER TRACKED VEHICLE CMPNTS
TANKS: Concrete
TANKS: For Tank Trucks, Metal Plate
TANKS: Lined, Metal
TANKS: Plastic & Fiberglass
TANKS: Standard Or Custom Fabricated, Metal Plate
TARGET DRONES
TARPAULINS
TAX REFUND DISCOUNTING
TAX RETURN PREPARATION SVCS
TELECOMMUNICATION SYSTEMS & EQPT
TELECOMMUNICATIONS CARRIERS & SVCS: Wired
TELEMARKETING BUREAUS
TELEMETERING EQPT
TELEPHONE COUNSELING SVCS
TELEPHONE EQPT INSTALLATION
TELEPHONE EQPT: Modems
TELEPHONE EQPT: NEC
TELEPHONE SVCS
TELEPHONE: Fiber Optic Systems
TELEVISION: Closed Circuit Eqpt
TENTS: All Materials
TESTERS: Environmental
TEXTILE & APPAREL SVCS
TEXTILE FINISHING: Dyeing, Broadwoven, Cotton
TEXTILE PRDTS: Hand Woven & Crocheted
TEXTILE: Finishing, Cotton Broadwoven
TEXTILE: Goods, NEC
TEXTILES: Jute & Flax Prdts
TEXTILES: Linen Fabrics
THERMOSETTING MATERIALS
THREAD: Embroidery
THREAD: Thread, From Manmade Fiber
TILE: Asphalt, Floor
TILE: Brick & Structural, Clay
TILE: Clay, Drain & Structural
TIMBER DRIVING & BOOMING
TIMBER PRDTS WHOLESALERS
TIN
TIRE & INNER TUBE MATERIALS & RELATED PRDTS
TIRE CORD & FABRIC: Steel
TIRE DEALERS
TIRES & INNER TUBES
TIRES & TUBES WHOLESALERS
TOBACCO & PRDTS, WHOLESALE: Cigarettes
TOBACCO & TOBACCO PRDTS WHOLESALERS
TOBACCO REDRYING
TOBACCO STORES & STANDS
TOBACCO: Cigarettes

INDEX

2019 Harris Directory of
Mississippi Manufacturers

341

PRODUCT INDEX

TOBACCO: Smoking
TOILET PREPARATIONS
TOILET SEATS: Wood
TOILETRIES, COSMETICS & PERFUME STORES
TOILETRIES, WHOLESALE: Toiletries
TOOL & DIE STEEL
TOOLS: Carpenters', Including Levels & Chisels, Exc Saws
TOOLS: Hand
TOOLS: Hand, Ironworkers'
TOOLS: Hand, Mechanics
TOOLS: Hand, Power
TOWELS: Linen & Linen & Cotton Mixtures
TOWING SVCS: Mobile Homes
TOYS
TOYS & HOBBY GOODS & SPLYS, WHOLESALE: Arts/Crafts Eqpt/Sply
TOYS: Dolls, Stuffed Animals & Parts
TOYS: Kites
TRACTOR REPAIR SVCS
TRADE SHOW ARRANGEMENT SVCS
TRAILERS & PARTS: Boat
TRAILERS & PARTS: Truck & Semi's
TRAILERS & TRAILER EQPT
TRAILERS: Bodies
TRAILERS: Semitrailers, Truck Tractors
TRAILERS: Truck, Chassis
TRANSFORMERS: Electric
TRANSFORMERS: Power Related
TRANSPORTATION AGENTS & BROKERS
TRANSPORTATION EPQT & SPLYS, WHOL: Aircraft Engs/Eng Parts
TRANSPORTATION EPQT & SPLYS, WHOLESALE: Marine Crafts/Splys
TRANSPORTATION SVCS, AIR, NONSCHEDULED: Air Cargo Carriers
TRANSPORTATION SVCS, WATER: River, Exc St Lawrence Seaway
TRAPS: Animal & Fish, Wire
TRAVEL TRAILERS & CAMPERS
TROPHIES, PLATED, ALL METALS
TROPHY & PLAQUE STORES
TRUCK & BUS BODIES: Automobile Wrecker Truck
TRUCK & BUS BODIES: Beverage Truck
TRUCK & BUS BODIES: Dump Truck
TRUCK & BUS BODIES: Motor Vehicle, Specialty
TRUCK & BUS BODIES: Truck, Motor Vehicle
TRUCK BODIES: Body Parts
TRUCK DRIVER SVCS
TRUCK GENERAL REPAIR SVC
TRUCK PARTS & ACCESSORIES: Wholesalers
TRUCK STOPS
TRUCKING & HAULING SVCS: Contract Basis
TRUCKING & HAULING SVCS: Garbage, Collect/Transport Only
TRUCKING & HAULING SVCS: Heavy Machinery, Local
TRUCKING & HAULING SVCS: Heavy, NEC
TRUCKING & HAULING SVCS: Liquid Petroleum, Exc Local
TRUCKING & HAULING SVCS: Lumber & Timber
TRUCKING & HAULING SVCS: Machinery, Heavy
TRUCKING & HAULING SVCS: Timber, Local
TRUCKING, DUMP
TRUCKING: Except Local
TRUCKING: Local, Without Storage
TRUCKING: Long-Distance, Less Than Truckload
TRUCKS & TRACTORS: Industrial
TRUCKS: Forklift
TRUCKS: Indl
TRUSSES: Wood, Floor

TRUSSES: Wood, Roof
TUBE & TUBING FABRICATORS
TUBES: Paper
TUBES: Paper Or Fiber, Chemical Or Electrical Uses
TUBES: Steel & Iron
TUBING: Copper
TURBINE GENERATOR SET UNITS: Hydraulic, Complete
TURBINES & TURBINE GENERATOR SETS
TYPESETTING SVC
TYPESETTING SVC: Computer
TYPESETTING SVC: Hand Composition

U

UNIFORM SPLY SVCS: Indl
UNIFORM STORES
UNISEX HAIR SALONS
UNIVERSITY
UPHOLSTERY WORK SVCS
USED CAR DEALERS
UTENSILS: Household, Cooking & Kitchen, Metal
UTILITY TRAILER DEALERS

V

VACUUM CLEANERS: Household
VALVES
VALVES & PIPE FITTINGS
VALVES Solenoid
VALVES: Fire Hydrant
VALVES: Indl
VAN CONVERSIONS
VARNISHES, NEC
VARNISHING SVC: Metal Prdts
VEGETABLE OILS: Medicinal Grade, Refined Or Concentrated
VEHICLES: All Terrain
VEHICLES: Recreational
VENDING MACHINE OPERATORS: Candy & Snack Food
VENDING MACHINE OPERATORS: Food
VENDING MACHINES & PARTS
VETERINARY PHARMACEUTICAL PREPARATIONS
VIDEO CAMERA-AUDIO RECORDERS: Household Use
VIDEO EQPT
VIDEO PRODUCTION SVCS
VIDEO TAPE PRODUCTION SVCS
VINYL RESINS, NEC
VITAMINS: Natural Or Synthetic, Uncompounded, Bulk
VOCATIONAL REHABILITATION AGENCY
VOCATIONAL TRAINING AGENCY

W

WALL BASE: Terrazzo, Precast
WALLPAPER STORE
WAREHOUSE CLUBS STORES
WAREHOUSING & STORAGE FACILITIES, NEC
WAREHOUSING & STORAGE: Bulk St & Termnls, Hire, Petro/Chem
WAREHOUSING & STORAGE: Farm Prdts
WAREHOUSING & STORAGE: General
WAREHOUSING & STORAGE: General
WAREHOUSING & STORAGE: Lumber Terminal Or Storage For Hire
WARM AIR HEATING & AC EQPT & SPLYS, WHOL: Dust Collecting
WASHERS
WATER PURIFICATION EQPT: Household
WATER TREATMENT EQPT: Indl
WATER: Distilled

WATER: Pasteurized & Mineral, Bottled & Canned
WATER: Pasteurized, Canned & Bottled, Etc
WELDING EQPT
WELDING EQPT & SPLYS WHOLESALERS
WELDING EQPT REPAIR SVCS
WELDING EQPT: Electric
WELDING REPAIR SVC
WELDING SPLYS, EXC GASES: Wholesalers
WHEEL BALANCING EQPT: Automotive
WHEELCHAIR LIFTS
WHEELCHAIRS
WHEELS
WHEELS & PARTS
WINDMILLS: Electric Power Generation
WINDOW & DOOR FRAMES
WINDOW BLIND REPAIR SVCS
WINDOWS: Frames, Wood
WINDOWS: Storm, Wood
WINDOWS: Wood
WIRE
WIRE & CABLE: Aluminum
WIRE & WIRE PRDTS
WIRE FENCING & ACCESS WHOLESALERS
WIRE MATERIALS: Steel
WIRE ROPE CENTERS
WIRE WHOLESALERS
WIRE: Communication
WIRE: Nonferrous
WIRE: Nonferrous, Appliance Fixture
WOMEN'S & CHILDREN'S CLOTHING WHOLESALERS, NEC
WOMEN'S CLOTHING STORES
WOMEN'S CLOTHING STORES: Ready-To-Wear
WOOD & WOOD BY-PRDTS, WHOLESALE
WOOD CHIPS, PRODUCED AT THE MILL
WOOD PRDTS
WOOD PRDTS: Chicken Coops, Wood, Wirebound
WOOD PRDTS: Mulch, Wood & Bark
WOOD PRDTS: Oars & Paddles
WOOD PRDTS: Outdoor, Structural
WOOD PRDTS: Panel Work
WOOD PRDTS: Rulers & Rules
WOOD PRDTS: Rulers & Yardsticks
WOOD PRDTS: Survey Stakes
WOOD PRDTS: Trim
WOOD PRDTS: Trophy Bases
WOOD PRODUCTS: Reconstituted
WOOD TREATING: Bridges
WOOD TREATING: Millwork
WOOD TREATING: Railroad Cross-Ties
WOOD TREATING: Structural Lumber & Timber
WOOD TREATING: Vehicle Lumber
WOOD TREATING: Wood Prdts, Creosoted
WOODWORK & TRIM: Exterior & Ornamental
WOODWORK: Carved & Turned
WOODWORK: Interior & Ornamental, NEC
WOVEN WIRE PRDTS, NEC
WREATHS: Artificial
WRITING FOR PUBLICATION SVCS

X

X-RAY EQPT & TUBES

Y

YARN & YARN SPINNING
YARN: Needle & Handicraft, Spun
YARN: Specialty & Novelty

PRODUCT SECTION

Product category — **BOXES: Folding**
Edgar & Son Paperboard ....G....... 999 999-9999
  Yourtown **(G-11480)**
Ready Box Co.................................E....... 999 999-9999
  Anytown **(G-7097)**
City —

Indicates approximate employment figure
A = Over 500 employees, B = 251-500
C = 101-250, D = 51-100, E = 20-50
F = 10-19, G = 1-9
Business phone
Geographic Section entry number where full
company information appears.

See footnotes for symbols and codes identification.
- Refer to the Industrial Product Index preceding this section to locate product headings.

ABRASIVES
Covidien LP ....C....... 815 744-3766
  Olive Branch **(G-3830)**
Osborn ....F....... 601 366-9902
  Jackson **(G-2531)**

ACCELERATION INDICATORS & SYSTEM COMPONENTS: Aerospace
Eaton Aerospace LLC...................E....... 601 981-2811
  Jackson **(G-2396)**
T & S Machine Shop Inc ....E....... 601 825-8627
  Brandon **(G-466)**

ACCOUNTING SVCS, NEC
DLS Tax Consultants ....G....... 601 473-6623
  Jackson **(G-2387)**

ACOUSTICAL BOARD & TILE
Certainteed Gypsum Inc..............C....... 601 693-0254
  Meridian **(G-3318)**

ACRYLIC RESINS
Hybrid Plastics Incorporated.............E....... 601 544-3466
  Hattiesburg **(G-1997)**

ACTUATORS: Indl, NEC
Limoss Us LLC............................E....... 662 365-2200
  Baldwyn **(G-82)**

ADHESIVES
Accrabond Corporation.................F 662 895-4480
  Olive Branch **(G-3804)**
Robison Adhesives Inc ....G....... 662 997-8000
  Batesville **(G-121)**

ADHESIVES & SEALANTS
Label Express Inc ....F....... 662 566-7075
  Verona **(G-5334)**
United Gilsonite Laboratories.............E....... 601 362-8619
  Jackson **(G-2617)**

ADHESIVES: Adhesives, paste
Helmitin Inc................................F....... 662 895-4565
  Olive Branch **(G-3847)**

ADHESIVES: Epoxy
Hunt Process Corp-Southern ....G....... 601 856-8811
  Ridgeland **(G-4591)**

ADVERTISING AGENCIES
Ad Lines Inc................................G....... 662 893-6400
  Nesbit **(G-3646)**
Stamm Advertising Co Inc ....G....... 601 922-3400
  Jackson **(G-2597)**

ADVERTISING AGENCIES: Consultants
Gator Sign & Image Concepts ....G....... 601 684-8686
  McComb **(G-3251)**
Magnetic Arrow LLC ....G....... 601 653-2932
  Biloxi **(G-264)**

ADVERTISING MATERIAL DISTRIBUTION
Bear Creek Apparel Promotions...........G....... 601 259-8508
  Canton **(G-648)**

ADVERTISING REPRESENTATIVES: Magazine
Diamondhead Advertiser ....G....... 228 263-4377
  Waveland **(G-5480)**

ADVERTISING REPRESENTATIVES: Newspaper
Amory Advertiser........................G....... 662 256-5647
  Amory **(G-35)**
Lamar County News Inc ....G....... 601 268-2331
  Hattiesburg **(G-2014)**
Newspaper Holding Inc................G....... 601 795-2247
  Poplarville **(G-4385)**
Pigeon Roost News ....G....... 662 838-4844
  Holly Springs **(G-2188)**
Quitman County Democrat ....G....... 662 326-2181
  Marks **(G-3222)**
Valley Publishing Inc ....G....... 662 473-1473
  Water Valley **(G-5475)**
Yazoo Newspaper Co Inc ....F....... 662 746-4911
  Yazoo City **(G-5653)**

ADVERTISING REPRESENTATIVES: Printed Media
Madison County Herald................G....... 601 853-2899
  Madison **(G-3124)**

ADVERTISING SPECIALTIES, WHOLESALE
Barbara OMeallie........................G....... 228 255-7573
  Pass Christian **(G-4077)**
Brown Line Printing Inc................F....... 662 728-9881
  Booneville **(G-322)**
Swell O Phonic ....G....... 601 981-3547
  Jackson **(G-2601)**
Vicksburg Printing and Pubg Co...........G....... 601 631-0400
  Vicksburg **(G-5440)**

ADVERTISING SVCS: Direct Mail
Dallas Printing Inc......................E....... 601 968-9354
  Richland **(G-4511)**
First Amercn Prtg Direct Mail ....G....... 228 867-9808
  Gulfport **(G-1787)**
Willowood Dvelopmental Ctr Inc...........D....... 601 366-0123
  Jackson **(G-2634)**

ADVERTISING SVCS: Display
Major League Promotions..............G....... 601 672-4798
  Jackson **(G-2481)**
Major League Promotions LLC...........G....... 601 672-4798
  Jackson **(G-2482)**

AGENTS, BROKERS & BUREAUS: Personal Service
La Jolie Enterprises LLC...............G....... 601 909-8840
  Ridgeland **(G-4596)**
Livingston Log & Timber Co Inc...........G....... 601 425-2095
  Laurel **(G-2796)**

AGRICULTURAL CHEMICALS: Trace Elements
Trace Mountain LLC.....................G....... 662 862-2345
  Fulton **(G-1482)**

AGRICULTURAL EQPT: BARN, SILO, POULTRY, DAIRY/LIVESTOCK MACH
Techno-Catch LLC ....G....... 662 289-1631
  Kosciusko **(G-2717)**

AGRICULTURAL EQPT: Fertilizing Machinery
Kbh Corporation ....C....... 662 624-5471
  Clarksdale **(G-770)**

AGRICULTURAL EQPT: Fertilizng, Sprayng, Dustng/Irrigatn Mach
Ag Spray Equipment Inc ....G....... 662 453-4524
  Greenwood **(G-1610)**
H & H Chief Sales Inc...................E....... 601 267-9643
  Carthage **(G-716)**

AGRICULTURAL EQPT: Grounds Mowing Eqpt
Howse Implement Company Inc...........C....... 601 428-0841
  Laurel **(G-2782)**

AGRICULTURAL EQPT: Planting Machines
Harold Knight Sew Mchs & Appls ....G....... 601 425-2220
  Laurel **(G-2775)**

AGRICULTURAL EQPT: Soil Preparation Mach, Exc Turf & Grounds
Amco Manufacturing Company LLC....E....... 662 746-4464
  Yazoo City **(G-5621)**
Monroe-Tufline Mfg Co Inc............E....... 662 328-8347
  Columbus **(G-1008)**

AGRICULTURAL EQPT: Trailers & Wagons, Farm
Atlas Manufacturing Co Inc ....E....... 662 652-3900
  Tremont **(G-5091)**
Bell Inc......................................E....... 662 265-5841
  Inverness **(G-2274)**
Circle S Irrigation Inc..................F....... 662 627-7246
  Clarksdale **(G-761)**
Mc Comb Welding & Mch Works...........G....... 601 684-1921
  McComb **(G-3258)**

AGRICULTURAL EQPT: Turf & Grounds Eqpt
Air + Mak Industries Inc ....F....... 662 893-3444
  Olive Branch **(G-3809)**
Superior Mulch Inc......................G....... 772 878-5220
  Soso **(G-4848)**

AGRICULTURAL MACHINERY & EQPT: Wholesalers
Delta Farm & Auto LLC.................G....... 662 453-8340
  Greenwood **(G-1619)**

AIR CLEANING SYSTEMS
Natural Ozone Solutions LLC ....G....... 662 963-2157
  Nettleton **(G-3664)**

AIR CONDITIONERS: Motor Vehicle
Parker-Hannifin Corporation................C....... 662 563-4691
  Batesville **(G-117)**

Employee Codes: A=Over 500 employees, B=251-500
C=101-250, D=51-100, E=20-50, F=10-19, G=1-9

2019 Harris Directory of
Mississippi Manufacturers

343

AIR CONDITIONING & VENTILATION EQPT & SPLYS: Wholesales

PRODUCT SECTION

AIR CONDITIONING & VENTILATION EQPT & SPLYS: Wholesales

Watson Percy ....G..... 662 931-6490
Greenville (G-1609)

AIR CONDITIONING EQPT

Air Cond Htg & S/M Solutions ....G..... 601 720-5085
Terry (G-5063)
Carrier Corporation..............................C..... 662 890-3706
Byhalia (G-582)
Taylor Coml Foodservice Inc ....C..... 662 895-4455
Olive Branch (G-3915)

AIR CONDITIONING REPAIR SVCS

Air Tech of Waveland ....G..... 228 467-7547
Bay Saint Louis (G-133)
Browns Electrical Repair.......................G..... 662 226-8192
Grenada (G-1670)

AIRCRAFT & AEROSPACE FLIGHT INSTRUMENTS & GUIDANCE SYSTEMS

Bradford Enterprises LLC ....G..... 901 652-1491
Southaven (G-4856)
Selex Inc ....G..... 228 467-2000
Kiln (G-2684)
Tyonek Svcs Overhaul-Facility ....G..... 256 258-6200
Kiln (G-2685)

AIRCRAFT & HEAVY EQPT REPAIR SVCS

Gecas Asset MGT Svcs Inc ....G..... 662 455-1826
Greenwood (G-1626)

AIRCRAFT ASSEMBLY PLANTS

Air + Mak Industries Inc ....F..... 662 893-3444
Olive Branch (G-3809)
Airbus Helicopters Inc...........................E..... 662 327-6226
Columbus (G-933)
Carroll Aircraft LLC ....G..... 228 255-7460
Diamondhead (G-1186)
Diamondhead Aerolease LLC ....G..... 228 255-8491
Diamondhead (G-1190)
Lockheed Martin Corporation.................G..... 901 795-5943
Byhalia (G-589)
Lockheed Mrtin Space Oprations.........B..... 228 688-3675
Bay Saint Louis (G-148)
Mississippi Aerospace Corp ....F..... 601 749-5659
Picayune (G-4280)
Northrop Grumman Corp ....G..... 434 845-9181
Pascagoula (G-4057)
Northrop Grumman Systems Corp ....D..... 228 474-3700
Moss Point (G-3490)
Sinhatech ....G..... 662 234-6248
Oxford (G-4002)
Stark Aerospace Inc ....D..... 662 798-4075
Columbus (G-1032)
Vertex Aerospace ....G..... 601 622-8940
Canton (G-683)
Vertex Aerospace LLC ....A..... 601 856-2274
Madison (G-3165)

AIRCRAFT CONTROL SYSTEMS: Electronic Totalizing Counters

L3 Technologies Inc ....E..... 601 856-2274
Madison (G-3117)

AIRCRAFT ELECTRICAL EQPT REPAIR SVCS

Gecas Asset MGT Svcs Inc ....G..... 662 455-1826
Greenwood (G-1626)

AIRCRAFT ENGINES & ENGINE PARTS: Air Scoops

Aerojet Rocketdyne Inc ....C..... 228 813-1511
Stennis Space Center (G-4993)
Pg Technologies LLC ....C..... 317 240-2500
Ellisville (G-1266)

AIRCRAFT ENGINES & ENGINE PARTS: Airfoils

General Electric Company ....F..... 769 233-2828
Ellisville (G-1253)

AIRCRAFT ENGINES & PARTS

Abbott Industries Inc ....G..... 662 357-7360
Tunica (G-5095)
Eaton Aerospace LLC ....G..... 601 987-3273
Jackson (G-2397)
Eaton Aerospace LLC ....E..... 601 981-2811
Jackson (G-2396)
General Electric Company ....E..... 662 561-9800
Batesville (G-106)
Honeywell International Inc ....D..... 228 575-3706
Gulfport (G-1808)
Jewell Aircrafting Inc ....G..... 662 252-6377
Holly Springs (G-2178)
Lions Pride ....G..... 601 818-1308
Hattiesburg (G-2017)
Precoat Metals Inc ....G..... 601 372-0325
Jackson (G-2549)
Whitney ....G..... 662 268-8379
Starkville (G-4982)

AIRCRAFT EQPT & SPLYS WHOLESALERS

Pioneer Aerospace Corporation.............C..... 601 736-4511
Columbia (G-912)

AIRCRAFT MAINTENANCE & REPAIR SVCS

Mid Mississippi Maintenance..................F..... 601 953-1091
Edwards (G-1241)
Tenax Tm LLC ....F..... 601 352-1107
Madison (G-3158)

AIRCRAFT PARTS & AUXILIARY EQPT: Aircraft Training Eqpt

Raytheon Company ....B..... 601 467-3730
Forest (G-1424)

AIRCRAFT PARTS & AUXILIARY EQPT: Deicing Eqpt

Ground Support Specialist LLC ....E..... 662 342-1412
Horn Lake (G-2201)

AIRCRAFT PARTS & AUXILIARY EQPT: Military Eqpt & Armament

Air + Mak Industries Inc ....F..... 662 893-3444
Olive Branch (G-3809)

AIRCRAFT PARTS & AUXILIARY EQPT: Nacelles

General Electric Company ....F..... 769 233-2828
Ellisville (G-1253)

AIRCRAFT PARTS & EQPT, NEC

Aero-RAD Tech LLC ....G..... 662 328-0155
Columbus (G-932)
Atk Space Systems Inc ....E..... 662 423-7700
Iuka (G-2284)
Boeing Company ....A..... 601 936-8540
Jackson (G-2642)
Gecas Asset MGT Svcs Inc ....G..... 662 455-1826
Greenwood (G-1626)
Milpar Inc ....F..... 662 224-0426
Ashland (G-63)
Sinhatech ....G..... 662 234-6248
Oxford (G-4002)
Zodiac Aerospace ....G..... 601 657-8719
Liberty (G-2921)

AIRCRAFT PARTS WHOLESALERS

B & L International Inc ....G..... 601 261-5127
Purvis (G-4434)

AIRCRAFT WHEELS

Bearhawk Tailwheels LLC ....G..... 228 424-5096
Long Beach (G-2928)

AIRCRAFT: Airplanes, Fixed Or Rotary Wing

Boeing Company ....G..... 228 688-2281
Bay Saint Louis (G-138)

AIRCRAFT: Motorized

Dixon-Drone ....G..... 662 545-9303
Starkville (G-4942)

Drone Assist Incorporated ....G..... 228 265-0174
Gulfport (G-1775)
Emergent Technologies LLC ....G..... 601 497-8239
Madison (G-3097)

AIRCRAFT: Research & Development, Manufacturer

Aurora Flight Sciences Corp ....F..... 662 328-8227
Columbus (G-938)

AIRLOCKS

Airlock Insulation LLC ....F..... 601 526-4141
Ridgeland (G-4546)

ALARMS: Burglar

Alarm Company Inc ....F..... 601 898-3105
Madison (G-3077)
Amerione Security ....G..... 901 502-2295
Southaven (G-4853)

ALKALIES & CHLORINE

Axiall Corporation ....C..... 601 892-5612
Hazlehurst (G-2089)
Axiall Corporation ....D..... 601 206-3200
Madison (G-3081)
Axiall Corporation ....E..... 662 369-9586
Prairie (G-4411)

ALTERNATORS & GENERATORS: Battery Charging

Tri-County Industries.............................E..... 601 743-9931
De Kalb (G-1169)

ALUMINUM

Croft LLC ....E..... 601 684-6121
McComb (G-3247)
Onyx Xteriors LLC ....G..... 901 281-2887
Byhalia (G-594)
Parker-Hannifin Mobile Climate..............G..... 662 728-3141
Booneville (G-340)

ALUMINUM & BERYLLIUM ORES MINING

Hj Norris LLC ....G..... 228 217-6704
Moss Point (G-3479)

ALUMINUM PRDTS

Aei LLC ....D..... 662 562-6663
Senatobia (G-4786)
Afco Industries Inc ....C..... 662 895-8686
Olive Branch (G-3808)
Beaver Built Cherokee Mfg LLC ....F..... 901 258-2679
Byhalia (G-578)
Crown Cork & Seal Usa Inc ....B..... 662 563-7664
Batesville (G-102)
HMC Metal Forming Inc ....E..... 662 538-5447
New Albany (G-3682)
Metal Impact South LLC ....E..... 662 538-6500
New Albany (G-3685)
Saunders Mfg Co Inc ....F..... 601 693-3482
Meridian (G-3394)
Taber Extrusions LLC ....E..... 228 863-2852
Gulfport (G-1882)

ALUMINUM: Coil & Sheet

American Specialty Alloys ....E..... 662 368-1332
Columbus (G-934)
New Process Steel LP ....D..... 662 241-6582
Columbus (G-1010)

ALUMINUM: Rolling & Drawing

Magnolia Mtal Plastic Pdts Inc..............E..... 601 638-6912
Vicksburg (G-5393)
Nci Group Inc ....D..... 601 373-0374
Jackson (G-2516)

AMMUNITION

Fianna Systems LLC ....G..... 662 726-5200
Macon (G-3061)

AMMUNITION: Small Arms

2a Armaments LLC ....G..... 662 538-8118
New Albany (G-3669)

2019 Harris Directory of
Mississippi Manufacturers

(G-0000) Company's Geographic Section entry number

344

PRODUCT SECTION

ART GOODS & SPLYS WHOLESALERS

JMS Manufacturing Inc............................G...... 601 514-0660
Lucedale (G-3005)
Mac LLC...F...... 228 533-0157
Bay Saint Louis (G-149)
Olin Corporation.....................................G...... 662 513-2002
Oxford (G-3981)
Precision Rifle Ordnance LLC...............G...... 601 825-0697
Brandon (G-438)
Precision/Delta Corporation ....F...... 662 756-2810
Ruleville (G-4698)

AMPLIFIERS: RF & IF Power

Innovative Wireless LLC ....G...... 601 594-1201
Jackson (G-2447)

AMUSEMENT & REC SVCS: Cake/Pastry Decorating Instruction

Creative Cakes & Supplies Inc ....G...... 662 844-3080
Tupelo (G-5123)
Sugar -N- Spice Confections ....G...... 901 210-6181
Horn Lake (G-2213)

AMUSEMENT & RECREATION SVCS: Amusement Arcades

Laser Mania Inc ....G...... 601 543-0072
Hattiesburg (G-2016)

AMUSEMENT & RECREATION SVCS: Card Rooms

Bally Technologies Inc ....G...... 228 897-9059
Gulfport (G-1734)

AMUSEMENT & RECREATION SVCS: Lottery Tickets, Sales

Bg3 Delta LLC ....G...... 601 636-9828
Vicksburg (G-5344)

AMUSEMENT & RECREATION SVCS: Tour & Guide

Clay Necaise..G...... 228 233-7760
Bay Saint Louis (G-140)

AMUSEMENT MACHINES: Coin Operated

Bally Technologies Inc ....C...... 228 396-3480
Gulfport (G-1733)
Bally Technologies Inc ....G...... 228 897-9059
Gulfport (G-1734)

AMUSEMENT PARK DEVICES & RIDES

East Systems Inc ....G...... 662 244-7070
Columbus (G-965)

ANALGESICS

Fortus Pharma LLC.................................G...... 662 420-3094
Ocean Springs (G-3758)
Plr Labs LLC ....G...... 228 327-0939
Ocean Springs (G-3777)

ANALYZERS: Network

High Yield AG Solutions LLC.................G...... 662 546-4463
Starkville (G-4949)

ANESTHESIA EQPT

Precision Spine Inc.................................G...... 601 420-4244
Pearl (G-4139)
Willow Ansthesia Solutions LLC ....G...... 662 550-4299
Oxford (G-4009)

ANILINE OR NITROBENZENE

First Chemical Corporation....................D...... 228 762-0870
Pascagoula (G-4031)

ANIMAL FEED & SUPPLEMENTS: Livestock & Poultry

Central Industries Inc ....E...... 601 469-4421
Forest (G-1411)
Chickasaw Farm Services Inc................F...... 662 456-2008
Houston (G-2233)
J & J Bagging LLC ....E...... 662 746-5155
Yazoo City (G-5637)

Jasper Cooperative.................................G...... 601 428-4968
Stringer (G-5003)
Mar-Jac Poultry Ms LLC ....A...... 601 735-3132
Waynesboro (G-5505)
Moores II Inc ....E...... 662 488-0024
Pontotoc (G-4349)
Protein Products Inc...............................E...... 662 569-3396
Sunflower (G-5047)
Purina Animal Nutrition LLC ....E...... 662 726-4262
Macon (G-3072)
Sanderson Farms Inc Prod Div..............C...... 601 892-1145
Hazlehurst (G-2104)
Steve Schrock ....G...... 662 369-6062
Prairie (G-4414)
Sunshine Mills Inc ....D...... 662 842-6175
Tupelo (G-5234)
Tricounty Farm Services South ....G...... 662 526-9100
Como (G-1054)
Tyson Foods Inc......................................C...... 601 774-7551
Union (G-5304)

ANIMAL FEED: Wholesalers

Fishbelt Feeds Inc..................................E...... 662 246-5065
Moorhead (G-3445)
Steve Schrock ....G...... 662 369-6062
Prairie (G-4414)

ANIMAL FOOD & SUPPLEMENTS: Dog

Cottons Cafe LLC....................................G...... 662 380-1463
Oxford (G-3949)
Sunshine Mills Inc ....D...... 662 842-6714
Tupelo (G-5233)

ANIMAL FOOD & SUPPLEMENTS: Dog & Cat

Woods Trading Co Inc ....G...... 601 924-5015
Clinton (G-839)

ANIMAL FOOD & SUPPLEMENTS: Feed Concentrates

Lauderdale County Farm Sup Inc...........E...... 601 483-3363
Meridian (G-3356)

ANIMAL FOOD & SUPPLEMENTS: Livestock

Hawks Feed Mill ....G...... 662 564-2920
Hernando (G-2134)
Peco Foods Inc ....C...... 601 656-1865
Philadelphia (G-4231)
Peco Foods Inc ....A...... 601 764-4392
Bay Springs (G-170)
Ware Milling Inc ....F...... 662 456-9032
Houston (G-2258)
Woods Trading Co Inc ....G...... 601 924-5015
Clinton (G-839)

ANIMAL FOOD & SUPPLEMENTS: Meat Meal & Tankage

Central Industries Inc ....G...... 601 469-4421
Forest (G-1410)

ANIMAL FOOD & SUPPLEMENTS: Slaughtering of nonfood animals

Enslin and Son Packing Company.........E...... 601 582-9300
Hattiesburg (G-1963)

ANIMAL FOOD/SUPPLEMENTS: Feeds Fm Meat/Meat/Veg Combnd Meals

Moores Feed Store Inc ....G...... 662 488-0024
Pontotoc (G-4348)

ANTENNAS: Satellite, Household Use

High Edge Inc ....F...... 601 326-2025
Jackson (G-2440)
Wnc Satcom Group LLC..........................G...... 601 544-0311
Hattiesburg (G-2086)

APPLIANCE PARTS: Porcelain Enameled

Grenada Sales Management Inc.............C...... 662 226-1161
Grenada (G-1682)

APPLIANCES, HOUSEHOLD: Kitchen, Major, Exc Refrigs & Stoves

Kitchen Elegance LLC.............................G...... 228 248-0074
Gulfport (G-1818)
Knot Just Kitchens ....G...... 228 896-0584
Gulfport (G-1819)
Spot Cash Tire and Appliance ....G...... 662 289-2611
Kosciusko (G-2713)

APPLIANCES, HOUSEHOLD: Refrigs, Mechanical & Absorption

Watson Percy ....G...... 662 931-6490
Greenville (G-1609)

APPLIANCES: Household, NEC

Mr Appliance of Hattiesburg..................G...... 601 869-0434
Hattiesburg (G-2033)

APPLIANCES: Household, Refrigerators & Freezers

Kol Kraft Manufacturing Co ....G...... 662 429-7561
Hernando (G-2137)
Standex International Corp ....C...... 662 534-9061
New Albany (G-3701)
Viking Range LLC ....A...... 662 455-1214
Greenwood (G-1659)

APPLIANCES: Major, Cooking

Sunbeam Products Inc ....A...... 601 296-5000
Hattiesburg (G-2071)
Viking Range LLC ....D...... 770 932-7282
Greenwood (G-1657)
Viking Range LLC ....G...... 662 455-7521
Greenwood (G-1660)
Viking Range LLC ....G...... 662 455-1200
Greenwood (G-1661)
Viking Range LLC ....B...... 662 455-1200
Greenwood (G-1662)
Viking Range LLC ....B...... 662 455-7522
Greenwood (G-1663)

APPLIANCES: Small, Electric

Conair Corporation..................................E...... 662 280-6499
Southaven (G-4863)
Hamilton Beach Brands Inc ....F...... 662 890-9869
Olive Branch (G-3843)
Presto Manufacturing Company.............G...... 601 366-3481
Jackson (G-2550)
Sunbeam Products Inc ....E...... 601 296-5000
Hattiesburg (G-2070)
Warmkraft Inc ....E...... 601 659-3317
Stonewall (G-5000)

ARCHITECTURAL SVCS

Friede Goldman Delaware Inc................G...... 228 896-0029
Gulfport (G-1789)
Old House Depot LLC ....G...... 601 592-6200
Jackson (G-2529)

ARMATURE REPAIRING & REWINDING SVC

Indianola Electric Co Inc ....F...... 662 887-3292
Indianola (G-2266)
Sandys Auto Parts & Machine Sp ....G...... 662 342-1900
Southaven (G-4898)
TJX Companies Inc.................................G...... 662 236-2856
Oxford (G-4007)

ART & ORNAMENTAL WARE: Pottery

Beloved Pottery ....G...... 662 349-4430
Southaven (G-4854)
Wet Paint LLC..G...... 662 269-2412
Tupelo (G-5258)

ART GALLERIES

Giclee Fine Arts......................................G...... 228 586-2693
Kiln (G-2679)

ART GOODS & SPLYS WHOLESALERS

Advanced Dynamics Inc.........................G...... 601 677-3423
Preston (G-4426)

Employee Codes: A=Over 500 employees, B=251-500
C=101-250, D=51-100, E=20-50, F=10-19, G=1-9

2019 Harris Directory of
Mississippi Manufacturers

PRODUCT

345

ARTISTS' MATERIALS: Paints, China Painting

PRODUCT SECTION

ARTISTS' MATERIALS: Paints, China Painting

Wet Paint LLC..................................G.......662 269-2412
Tupelo (G-5258)

ARTISTS' MATERIALS: Paints, Exc Gold & Bronze

Rivers Gist Gainspoletti....................G.......662 902-5415
Cleveland (G-805)

ARTS & CRAFTS SCHOOL

Aberdeen School District...................G.......662 369-6886
Aberdeen (G-7)
Stained Glassworks Inc.....................G.......662 329-2970
Columbus (G-1031)

ASBESTOS REMOVAL EQPT

Saf-T Compliance Intl LLC.................G.......601 684-9495
McComb (G-3264)

ASPHALT & ASPHALT PRDTS

Adcamp Inc.....................................D.......601 939-4493
Flowood (G-1342)
Apac-Mississippi Inc.........................E.......662 378-8481
Greenville (G-1536)
Cold Mix Inc....................................G.......662 256-4529
Nettleton (G-3658)
J J Ferguson Sand & Grav Inc...........C.......662 453-5451
Greenwood (G-1630)
Klaas-Robbins Pavement Maint..........G.......601 362-4091
Ridgeland (G-4595)
Lehman-Roberts Company.................F.......662 563-2100
Batesville (G-113)
Mallette Brothers Cnstr Co ....E.......228 497-2523
Gautier (G-1499)
Pandle Inc......................................E.......228 762-3300
Pascagoula (G-4059)

ASPHALT COATINGS & SEALERS

Atlas Roofing Corporation..................E.......601 483-7111
Meridian (G-3302)
Lining & Coating Solutions LLC..........G.......662 453-6860
Greenwood (G-1635)
Majestic Metals Inc..........................E.......601 856-3600
Madison (G-3126)
Polycon International LLC..................F.......601 898-1024
Madison (G-3141)
Union Corrugating Company...............G.......601 661-0577
Vicksburg (G-5432)

ASPHALT PLANTS INCLUDING GRAVEL MIX TYPE

Apac-Mississippi Inc.........................D.......601 376-4000
Richland (G-4501)
Apac-Mississippi Inc.........................G.......601 376-4000
Richland (G-4502)
Bonds Company Inc..........................E.......601 376-4000
Richland (G-4507)

ASSOCIATIONS: Real Estate Management

5 K Corp...F.......601 736-5367
Columbia (G-877)
On The River LLC............................G.......601 442-7103
Natchez (G-3603)

ATOMIZERS

Bisco Industries Inc.........................G.......601 991-3308
Jackson (G-2338)
Gold Coast Manufacturing Inc............G.......228 261-6290
Pass Christian (G-4084)
King Mfg...G.......662 869-2069
Saltillo (G-4715)
Protec Steel Industries LLC...............G.......228 364-4240
Pass Christian (G-4094)
Saf-T Compliance Intl LLC.................G.......601 684-9495
McComb (G-3264)
Seminole Furniture Mfg Inc................D.......662 447-5222
Okolona (G-3798)
Truck Bodies & Eqp Intl Inc...............G.......800 255-4345
Tishomingo (G-5089)

AUDIO COMPONENTS

Mississppi Band Chctaw Indians.........G.......601 656-7350
Choctaw (G-746)

AUDIO ELECTRONIC SYSTEMS

Decibel Audio..................................G.......601 649-1144
Laurel (G-2760)
Innovative Wireless LLC....................G.......601 594-1201
Jackson (G-2447)
Peavey Electronics Corporation..........G.......601 483-5365
Meridian (G-3382)
Peavey Electronics Corporation..........G.......601 486-1760
Meridian (G-3383)
Peavey Electronics Corporation..........G.......601 486-1127
Meridian (G-3385)
Peavey Electronics Corporation..........F.......601 483-5365
Meridian (G-3386)

AUTHOR

Elizabeth Clayton.............................G.......601 371-1172
Terry (G-5066)

AUTO & HOME SUPPLY STORES: Auto & Truck Eqpt & Parts

Motor Parts Co of Yazoo City.............G.......662 746-1462
Yazoo City (G-5643)

AUTO & HOME SUPPLY STORES: Automotive Access

Dealership Services LLC...................G.......662 269-3897
Tupelo (G-5126)
Roes Rims and Accessories...............G.......601 619-4489
Vicksburg (G-5413)

AUTO & HOME SUPPLY STORES: Automotive parts

Calhoun Parts Inc............................G.......662 628-6621
Calhoun City (G-635)
Christians Automotive Machine...........G.......662 287-4500
Corinth (G-1070)
D & T Motors Inc.............................G.......662 773-5021
Louisville (G-2965)
Dahls Automotive Parts Inc...............G.......228 875-8154
Ocean Springs (G-3751)
Delta Auto Parts Inc........................F.......662 746-1143
Yazoo City (G-5630)
G & S Auto Parts Inc........................G.......662 837-9292
Ripley (G-4660)
Maximum Auto Parts & Supply............F.......228 863-1100
Gulfport (G-1825)
Sandys Auto Parts & Machine Sp........G.......662 342-1900
Southaven (G-4898)
Webb Machine and Supply Inc............F.......662 375-8309
Webb (G-5520)
Woodson Flying Service Inc...............G.......662 983-4274
Bruce (G-563)

AUTO & HOME SUPPLY STORES: Batteries, Automotive & Truck

Battco Inc.......................................G.......601 898-1200
Ridgeland (G-4552)
Dufour Battery One Source LLC..........G.......601 693-1500
Meridian (G-3333)
Johnson Wiley.................................G.......662 329-1495
Columbus (G-991)

AUTO & HOME SUPPLY STORES: Speed Shops, Incl Race Car Splys

Eagle Specialty Products Inc.............E.......662 796-7373
Southaven (G-4870)
Jims Auto Parts Inc..........................G.......662 494-4541
West Point (G-5547)
McMurtrys Automotive Mch Svc..........G.......228 832-8335
Saucier (G-4759)

AUTO & HOME SUPPLY STORES: Truck Eqpt & Parts

Aerial Truck Equipment Co Inc............G.......662 895-0993
Olive Branch (G-3807)
Fryfogle Manufacturing Inc................F.......601 947-8088
Lucedale (G-2996)

(continued)

M and S Sales Inc............................G.......662 453-6111
Greenwood (G-1637)

AUTOMATIC REGULATING CONTROLS: AC & Refrigeration

Siemens Industry Inc........................G.......601 939-0550
Richland (G-4524)

AUTOMATIC REGULATING CONTROLS: Ice Maker

Hoshizaki of Jackson........................G.......601 969-4200
Jackson (G-2442)

AUTOMATIC REGULATING CONTROLS: Refrig/Air-Cond Defrost

Bateman Airconditioning....................G.......601 225-4442
Gloster (G-1511)

AUTOMATIC TELLER MACHINES

At Xtree...G.......601 683-6494
Newton (G-3716)
Express Line....................................G.......662 328-3720
Columbus (G-971)
Kangaroo Express 1544.....................G.......662 563-4629
Batesville (G-111)
Payment Alliance Proc Corp...............G.......601 956-1222
Jackson (G-2537)
Pearl River Exxon............................F.......601 650-9393
Philadelphia (G-4230)
Progressive Atms.............................G.......228 475-7234
Moss Point (G-3496)
Triton Systems Delaware LLC............C.......228 575-3100
Long Beach (G-2958)

AUTOMOBILE RECOVERY SVCS

Region 8 Mental Health Retrdat..........D.......601 591-5553
Brandon (G-445)

AUTOMOBILES & OTHER MOTOR VEHICLES WHOLESALERS

Chuck Ryan Cars Inc........................G.......228 864-9706
Long Beach (G-2932)
Fowler Buick-Gmc Inc.......................E.......601 360-0200
Pearl (G-4120)

AUTOMOTIVE & TRUCK GENERAL REPAIR SVC

B & B Oil Well Service Co Inc.............F.......601 425-3836
Ellisville (G-1246)
Jerry Hailey....................................G.......662 349-2582
Southaven (G-4883)
Kogler Equipment Service Inc............E.......901 521-9742
Olive Branch (G-3861)
Sabbatini & Sons Incorporation..........G.......662 686-7713
Leland (G-2892)
Victor Umfress Gar Wldg Sp Inc.........G.......662 862-4213
Fulton (G-1484)

AUTOMOTIVE BODY SHOP

West Body Shop & Salvage Inc...........G.......662 566-2161
Verona (G-5337)

AUTOMOTIVE BRAKE REPAIR SHOPS

Victor Umfress Gar Wldg Sp Inc.........G.......662 862-4213
Fulton (G-1484)

AUTOMOTIVE PAINT SHOP

Sign Shop.......................................G.......601 735-1383
Waynesboro (G-5514)

AUTOMOTIVE PARTS, ACCESS & SPLYS

Aptiv Services Us LLC.......................B.......601 835-1983
Brookhaven (G-480)
Borgwarner Inc................................G.......601 785-9504
Taylorsville (G-5051)
Borgwarner Inc................................E.......662 473-3100
Water Valley (G-5463)
Cantrell Hot Rods LLC.......................G.......662 213-7184
Mooreville (G-3442)
Competition Cams Inc.......................G.......662 224-8972
Olive Branch (G-3825)

346

2019 Harris Directory of
Mississippi Manufacturers

(G-0000) Company's Geographic Section entry number

PRODUCT SECTION

AUTOMOTIVE WELDING SVCS

Competition Cams Inc ....G...... 662 890-9825
Olive Branch *(G-3826)*
Crane Cams Inc ....E...... 386 310-4875
Olive Branch *(G-3831)*
DEA Mississippi Inc ....C...... 800 821-2302
Meridian *(G-3327)*
Faurecia Interior Systems Inc ....C...... 601 855-2163
Canton *(G-658)*
Fowler Buick-Gmc Inc ....E...... 601 360-0200
Pearl *(G-4120)*
Habe-ISE USA Inc ....F...... 769 235-6650
Richland *(G-4519)*
Hunter Engineering Company ....C...... 662 653-3194
Durant *(G-1227)*
Hunterworks LLC ....G...... 601 771-0070
Collinsville *(G-871)*
Hyperco ....G...... 662 488-4567
Pontotoc *(G-4333)*
Martinrea Atmtv-Structures USA ....G...... 662 566-1023
Shannon *(G-4814)*
Multicraft Enterprises Inc ....G...... 601 854-5516
Pelahatchie *(G-4166)*
National Tank Inc ....F...... 662 429-5469
Hernando *(G-2143)*
Nexteer Automotive Corporation ....B...... 601 537-3099
Morton *(G-3452)*
Ottos Custom Trailers ....G...... 601 446-6469
Natchez *(G-3604)*
Parker-Hannifin Corporation ....C...... 662 895-1011
Olive Branch *(G-3894)*
Parker-Hannifin Corporation ....G...... 662 563-4691
Batesville *(G-117)*
Parts and Supply Inc ....G...... 228 832-6272
Gulfport *(G-1845)*
R-Squared Puckett Inc ....E...... 601 825-1171
Puckett *(G-4430)*
Reman Inc ....E...... 601 635-4897
Decatur *(G-1178)*
Sinhatech ....G...... 662 234-6248
Oxford *(G-4002)*
Tishomingo Acquisition LLC ....C...... 662 438-7800
Tishomingo *(G-5087)*
Topre America Corporation ....G...... 601 927-6723
Canton *(G-681)*
Valeo North America Inc ....G...... 931 446-9128
Canton *(G-682)*
Willowood Dvelopmental Ctr Inc ....D...... 601 366-0123
Jackson *(G-2634)*

AUTOMOTIVE PARTS: Plastic

Auto Parts Mfg Miss Inc ....B...... 662 365-3082
Guntown *(G-1898)*
Diversity-Vuteq LLC ....A...... 662 534-9250
New Albany *(G-3681)*
Euro American Plastics Inc ....F...... 601 879-0360
Flora *(G-1305)*
M-Tek Inc ....A...... 601 407-5000
Madison *(G-3123)*

AUTOMOTIVE RADIATOR REPAIR SHOPS

Johnnie Wright Radiator & Wldg ....G...... 601 428-5013
Laurel *(G-2788)*
Thornton Repair Shop ....G...... 662 332-6853
Greenville *(G-1603)*
Wilders Welding Shop ....G...... 662 489-2772
Pontotoc *(G-4371)*

AUTOMOTIVE REPAIR SHOPS: Diesel Engine Repair

Anderson Repair Shop ....G...... 601 783-2654
Magnolia *(G-3189)*
Thornton Repair Shop ....G...... 662 332-6853
Greenville *(G-1603)*

AUTOMOTIVE REPAIR SHOPS: Electrical Svcs

Quality Cnstr & Engrg LLC ....C...... 601 786-8017
Fayette *(G-1299)*

AUTOMOTIVE REPAIR SHOPS: Engine Rebuilding

Christians Automotive Machine ....G...... 662 287-4500
Corinth *(G-1070)*
Columbus Engine & Crank Shaft ....G...... 662 356-0068
Caledonia *(G-627)*

Kar Kleen ....G...... 601 638-8816
Vicksburg *(G-5384)*

AUTOMOTIVE REPAIR SHOPS: Engine Repair

Bakers Auto Machine & RAD Sp ....G...... 228 474-1222
Moss Point *(G-3468)*
TJX Companies Inc ....G...... 662 236-2856
Oxford *(G-4007)*
Walker Auto Repair Service ....G...... 601 969-5353
Jackson *(G-2623)*

AUTOMOTIVE REPAIR SHOPS: Fuel System Repair

K & D Fuel Injection Service ....G...... 601 849-9113
Magee *(G-3178)*

AUTOMOTIVE REPAIR SHOPS: Machine Shop

Christians Automotive Machine ....G...... 662 287-4500
Corinth *(G-1070)*
Deep S Mch Wrks Hydraulics LLC ....G...... 601 989-2977
Richton *(G-4529)*
Kar Kleen ....G...... 601 638-8816
Vicksburg *(G-5384)*
S & W Welding & Machine Works ....G...... 601 939-8516
Jackson *(G-2666)*

AUTOMOTIVE REPAIR SHOPS: Tire Repair Shop

Spot Cash Tire and Appliance ....G...... 662 289-2611
Kosciusko *(G-2713)*
Woods Trailers & Repair LLC ....G...... 662 585-3606
Golden *(G-1533)*

AUTOMOTIVE REPAIR SHOPS: Trailer Repair

Baldwyn Truck & Trailer Repair ....G...... 662 365-7888
Baldwyn *(G-73)*
Fryfogle Manufacturing Inc ....F...... 601 947-8088
Lucedale *(G-2996)*
Kogler Equipment Service Inc ....E...... 901 521-9742
Olive Branch *(G-3861)*
Magnolia Trailers Inc ....E...... 601 947-7990
Lucedale *(G-3010)*
Palmer Machine Works Inc ....E...... 662 256-2636
Amory *(G-50)*
Transport Trailer Service Inc ....D...... 662 844-4606
Tupelo *(G-5241)*
Woods Trailers & Repair LLC ....G...... 662 585-3606
Golden *(G-1533)*

AUTOMOTIVE REPAIR SHOPS: Truck Engine Repair, Exc Indl

Dean Weeks Repair & Welding ....G...... 601 833-2669
Wesson *(G-5526)*

AUTOMOTIVE REPAIR SHOPS: Wheel Alignment

Angels Truck Service LLC ....F...... 662 890-0417
Olive Branch *(G-3815)*

AUTOMOTIVE REPAIR SVCS, MISCELLANEOUS

Riverside AG Supply LLC ....G...... 662 444-0600
Marks *(G-3224)*

AUTOMOTIVE SPLYS & PARTS, NEW, WHOL: Auto Servicing Eqpt

Christians Automotive Machine ....G...... 662 287-4500
Corinth *(G-1070)*

AUTOMOTIVE SPLYS & PARTS, NEW, WHOLESALE: Splys

Delta Farm & Auto LLC ....G...... 662 453-8340
Greenwood *(G-1619)*

AUTOMOTIVE SPLYS & PARTS, NEW, WHOLESALE: Trailer Parts

Palmer Machine Works Inc ....E...... 662 256-2636
Amory *(G-50)*

AUTOMOTIVE SPLYS & PARTS, WHOLESALE, NEC

Calhoun Parts Inc ....G...... 662 628-6621
Calhoun City *(G-635)*
D & T Motors Inc ....G...... 662 773-5021
Louisville *(G-2965)*
Dahls Automotive Parts Inc ....G...... 228 875-8154
Ocean Springs *(G-3751)*
DEA Mississippi Inc ....C...... 800 821-2302
Meridian *(G-3327)*
Engine Rebuilders Co Inc ....F...... 662 332-2695
Greenville *(G-1554)*
G & S Auto Parts Inc ....G...... 662 837-9292
Ripley *(G-4660)*
Reman Inc ....E...... 601 635-4897
Decatur *(G-1178)*

AUTOMOTIVE SVCS, EXC REPAIR & CARWASHES: Lubrication

Christians Automotive Machine ....G...... 662 287-4500
Corinth *(G-1070)*
McMurtrys Automotive Mch Svc ....G...... 228 832-8335
Saucier *(G-4759)*
Mississippi Cylinder Head Svc ....G...... 662 328-0170
Columbus *(G-1002)*

AUTOMOTIVE SVCS, EXC REPAIR & CARWASHES: Road Svc

Angels Truck Service LLC ....F...... 662 890-0417
Olive Branch *(G-3815)*

AUTOMOTIVE SVCS, EXC REPAIR & CARWASHES: Trailer Maintenance

Equipment Maintenance Co ....G...... 662 393-9178
Horn Lake *(G-2198)*

AUTOMOTIVE SVCS, EXC REPAIR: Washing & Polishing

Kar Kleen ....G...... 601 638-8816
Vicksburg *(G-5384)*

AUTOMOTIVE TOPS INSTALLATION OR REPAIR: Canvas Or Plastic

Southern Sttch Canvas Uphl LLC ....G...... 228 234-2515
Gulfport *(G-1876)*

AUTOMOTIVE TOWING SVCS

Chops Wrecker & Welding Svc ....G...... 601 442-0092
Natchez *(G-3546)*
Townsnds Auto Repr Wricker Svc ....G...... 662 289-6845
Kosciusko *(G-2718)*

AUTOMOTIVE TRANSMISSION REPAIR SVC

Novelty Machine Works Inc ....F...... 601 948-2075
Jackson *(G-2524)*

AUTOMOTIVE UPHOLSTERY SHOPS

Quality Trim & Upholstery ....G...... 601 483-0077
Meridian *(G-3389)*

AUTOMOTIVE WELDING SVCS

Core Solutions LLC ....G...... 228 216-6848
Gulfport *(G-1765)*
Destinis Creations and Exquis ....G...... 601 317-3764
Pearl *(G-4114)*
Johnnie Wright Radiator & Wldg ....G...... 601 428-5013
Laurel *(G-2788)*
Kogler Equipment Service Inc ....E...... 901 521-9742
Olive Branch *(G-3861)*
M & M Chassis Shop LLC ....G...... 601 310-6078
Moselle *(G-3458)*
Riverside AG Supply LLC ....G...... 662 444-0600
Marks *(G-3224)*
Sabbatini & Sons Incorporation ....G...... 662 686-7713
Leland *(G-2892)*

Employee Codes: A=Over 500 employees, B=251-500
C=101-250, D=51-100, E=20-50, F=10-19, G=1-9

2019 Harris Directory of
Mississippi Manufacturers

347

PRODUCT

AUTOMOTIVE WELDING SVCS

PRODUCT SECTION

Southern Fabricators LLC....................F 601 824-8855
Brandon (G-459)
Thornton Repair Shop ....G 662 332-6853
Greenville (G-1603)
West Body Shop & Salvage Inc ....G 662 566-2161
Verona (G-5337)

AUTOMOTIVE: Seat Frames, Metal

Faurecia Mdson Auto Sating Inc ....C 601 407-2200
Madison (G-3098)
Sun-Air Products Incorporated ....E 662 454-9577
Belmont (G-202)

AUTOMOTIVE: Seating

Faurecia Auto Seating LLC ....B 248 288-1000
Cleveland (G-791)
Grammer Inc ....G 662 566-1660
Shannon (G-4807)
Johnson Controls Inc ....C 601 544-8911
Hattiesburg (G-2002)
Toyota Boshoku Mississippi LLC..........E 662 862-3322
Mantachie (G-3209)

AWNINGS & CANOPIES: Fabric

Duffell Metal Awning Co ....G 601 483-2181
Meridian (G-3332)
Quality Alum & HM Imprv Inc ....G 662 329-2525
Columbus (G-1019)

AWNINGS: Metal

Duffell Metal Awning Co ....G 601 483-2181
Meridian (G-3332)

BABBITT (METAL)

Clear Enterprise ....G 601 796-2429
Lumberton (G-3025)

BACKHOES

Eyesore Yrd Cleanup & Bushogng ....G 205 391-8232
Kosciusko (G-2693)
West Backhoe Inc ....G 662 566-7828
Tupelo (G-5256)
White Septic Backhoe LLC ....G 662 251-8989
Steens (G-4992)

BADGES, WHOLESALE

Major League Promotions ....G 601 672-4798
Jackson (G-2481)
Major League Promotions LLC..............G 601 672-4798
Jackson (G-2482)

BAGS & CONTAINERS: Textile, Exc Sleeping

Polo Custom Products Inc ....C 662 779-2009
Louisville (G-2976)

BAGS: Canvas

Brentwood Originals Inc ....C 662 781-5301
Walls (G-5448)

BAGS: Duffle, Canvas, Made From Purchased Materials

Southern Sttch Canvas Uphl LLC ....G 228 234-2515
Gulfport (G-1876)

BAGS: Food Storage & Trash, Plastic

United Solutions Inc ....F 662 487-0068
Sardis (G-4747)

BAGS: Garment, Plastic Film, Made From Purchased Materials

Bag Connection LLC ....F 662 624-6570
Clarksdale (G-758)

BAGS: Paper

Hood Packaging Corporation ....E 601 853-7260
Madison (G-3107)

BAGS: Paper, Made From Purchased Materials

Bemis Company Inc..............................B 402 734-6262
Madison (G-3084)

BAGS: Plastic

Hood Container Corporation ....C 601 582-1545
Hattiesburg (G-1992)
Hood Packaging Corporation ....D 770 981-5400
Madison (G-3106)
Innovex Inc ....E 662 328-9537
Columbus (G-988)
McNeely Plastic Products Inc ....F 601 926-1000
Hazlehurst (G-2100)
Mega Plastics Inc ....D 601 924-1712
Clinton (G-831)
Rankin Plastics LLC ....G 601 919-7883
Richland (G-4523)

BAGS: Plastic & Pliofilm

Novipax LLC ....D 662 226-8804
Grenada (G-1697)

BAGS: Plastic, Made From Purchased Materials

American Packaging Company Inc........F 601 856-0986
Madison (G-3078)
Bagit System Inc ....E 662 756-2600
Ruleville (G-4695)
Dixie Packaging Inc ....E 601 276-9317
Summit (G-5012)
Hood Flexible Packaging Corp ....D 903 593-1793
Hattiesburg (G-1993)

BAGS: Shipping

Hood Packaging Corporation ....D 770 981-5400
Madison (G-3106)

BAGS: Textile

Ao Liquidation Trust Inc ....E 662 675-8102
Coffeeville (G-841)
Superior Uniform Group Inc ....G 662 834-4485
Lexington (G-2905)

BAIT, FISHING, WHOLESALE

Global Seafood Tech Inc ....E 228 435-3632
Biloxi (G-245)

BAKERIES, COMMERCIAL: On Premises Baking Only

Adrienne Batla Cupcakes.....................G 260 348-5364
Clarksdale (G-756)
Bimbo Bakeries Usa Inc ....C 228 863-4302
Gulfport (G-1739)
Flowers Bkg Co Baton Rouge LLC ....G 601 932-7843
Pearl (G-4119)
Flowers Bkg Co Baton Rouge LLC ....G 601 583-2693
Hattiesburg (G-1971)
Flowers Bkg Co Lynchburg LLC ....G 601 502-1305
Raymond (G-4488)
Flowers Bkg Co Thomasville LLC ....G 662 245-1188
Columbus (G-976)
Flowers Bkg Co Thomasville LLC ....F 601 684-5481
McComb (G-3250)
Flowers Bkg Co Tuscaloosa LLC ....F 662 842-8613
Tupelo (G-5134)
La Ilucion ....G 662 536-0046
Horn Lake (G-2204)
Pauls Pastry Production LLC ....F 601 798-7457
Picayune (G-4284)
Pauls Pastry Shop ....E 601 798-7457
Picayune (G-4285)
Tupelo Cupcakes Inc ....G 205 269-4130
Tupelo (G-5244)

BAKERIES: On Premises Baking & Consumption

Bimbo Bakeries Usa Inc ....F 601 545-3782
Hattiesburg (G-1931)
La Ilucion ....G 662 536-0046
Horn Lake (G-2204)
Ole Country Bakery ....F 662 738-5795
Brooksville (G-556)

Pauls Pastry Production LLC ....F 601 798-7457
Picayune (G-4284)
So Nuts and Confections LLC ....G 901 398-9650
Horn Lake (G-2211)

BAKERY FOR HOME SVC DELIVERY

Johnson Wiley.....................................G 662 329-1495
Columbus (G-991)

BAKERY PRDTS: Bread, All Types, Fresh Or Frozen

Bimbo Bakeries Usa Inc ....C 601 693-4871
Meridian (G-3309)
Ole Country Bakery ....F 662 738-5795
Brooksville (G-556)
Samuel Moses Inc................................G 601 669-0756
Brookhaven (G-529)

BAKERY PRDTS: Cakes, Bakery, Exc Frozen

Creative Cakes & Supplies Inc ....G 662 844-3080
Tupelo (G-5123)
La Brioche LLC ....F 601 988-2299
Jackson (G-2466)
Lulus Sweet Shop LLC ....G 601 790-1951
Madison (G-3121)
Patycake Kids LLC...............................G 601 506-7117
Jackson (G-2536)
Sweet Sensations-Jackson ....G 601 790-7553
Madison (G-3155)

BAKERY PRDTS: Cakes, Bakery, Frozen

Heavenly Confections ....G 601 660-1986
Natchez (G-3568)
Jubilations Inc ....F 662 328-9210
West Point (G-5548)

BAKERY PRDTS: Cookies

Cookie Place Inc ....G 601 957-2891
Ridgeland (G-4565)
DBC Corporation..................................D 601 856-7454
Madison (G-3093)
Flathaus Fine Foods LLC ....F 601 582-9629
Petal (G-4185)

BAKERY PRDTS: Cookies & crackers

Patricia Betts ....G 601 863-9058
Ridgeland (G-4615)
Pauls Pastry Production LLC ....F 601 798-7457
Picayune (G-4284)
Pauls Pastry Shop ....E 601 798-7457
Picayune (G-4285)

BAKERY PRDTS: Doughnuts, Exc Frozen

Sokhom To...G 601 684-3300
McComb (G-3267)
Tato-Nut Donut Shop ....F 228 872-2076
Ocean Springs (G-3791)

BAKERY PRDTS: Dry

Connie S Kitchen ....F 662 686-2255
Leland (G-2886)

BAKERY PRDTS: Frozen

Dutch Ann Foods Inc ....E 601 445-4496
Natchez (G-3557)
So Nuts and Confections LLC ....G 901 398-9650
Horn Lake (G-2211)

BAKERY PRDTS: Pretzels

Cosentino Enterprises Inc ....G 228 392-6666
Diberville (G-1201)

BAKERY PRDTS: Rolls, Bread Type, Fresh Or Frozen

Mississippi Baking Co LLC....................D 601 854-5000
Pelahatchie (G-4165)

BAKERY PRDTS: Yeast Goods, Sweet, Exc Frozen

USA Yeast Company LLC......................E 601 545-2690
Hattiesburg (G-2079)

348

2019 Harris Directory of
Mississippi Manufacturers

(G-0000) Company's Geographic Section entry number

BAKERY: Wholesale Or Wholesale & Retail Combined

Bimbo Bakeries Usa Inc ....F 601 545-3782
Hattiesburg (G-1931)
Bimbo Bakeries Usa Inc ....E 601 479-8887
Meridian (G-3307)
Bimbo Bakeries Usa Inc ....E 601 693-4871
Meridian (G-3308)
Bunny Bread Inc ....G 228 868-0120
Gautier (G-1490)
Canada Bread ....G 662 494-1607
West Point (G-5539)
Flowers Bkg Co New Orleans LLC ....G 228 868-0120
Gulfport (G-1788)
Fresh Distributing Company LLC ....G 228 297-7655
Lumberton (G-3029)

BALCONIES: Metal

Independent Metal Craft LLC ....G 601 488-4789
Clinton (G-825)

BALERS

West Farms Inc ....G 601 277-3579
Hazlehurst (G-2109)

BALLOONS: Novelty & Toy

Vape and Bake LLC ....G 228 447-1566
Ocean Springs (G-3793)

BANNERS: Fabric

Multimedia Graphics Inc ....F 601 981-5001
Jackson (G-2514)

BAR

Kolinsky Corp ....G 601 544-5987
Hattiesburg (G-2011)
White Brothers Inc ....E 601 948-0888
Jackson (G-2630)

BARBECUE EQPT

Iron and Steel Design Works ....G 662 380-5662
Oxford (G-3962)
Sunbeam Products Inc ....E 601 296-5000
Hattiesburg (G-2070)

BARRICADES: Metal

Buy A Barricade LLC ....G 228 355-0146
Ocean Springs (G-3744)
Inline Barricades Met Pdts Inc ....G 800 229-4790
Pass Christian (G-4090)

BARS, COLD FINISHED: Steel, From Purchased Hot-Rolled

Ceca LLC ....E 662 993-8880
Ripley (G-4655)

BARS: Concrete Reinforcing, Fabricated Steel

Goff Steel Recting ....G 601 922-6014
Clinton (G-823)
Great River Industries LLC ....G 601 442-7568
Natchez (G-3564)
Holifield Engineering Inc ....G 601 276-3391
Summit (G-5015)
Miscellaneous Steel Supply LLC ....G 662 494-0090
West Point (G-5552)
Nichols Stl Sls & Fabrication ....G 662 378-2723
Greenville (G-1581)
Resteel Express Inc ....F 601 795-6110
Poplarville (G-4390)
Rockett Inc ....C 601 939-9347
Flowood (G-1393)

BARS: Extruded, Aluminum

Aluma-Form Inc ....D 662 677-6000
Walnut (G-5454)
Triple Shots ....G 228 872-2696
Ocean Springs (G-3792)

BATHMATS: Rubber

Innocor Foam Tech - Acp Inc ....G 662 365-5868
Baldwyn (G-80)

BATHTUBS: Concrete

Baymont Inc ....D 662 454-7993
Golden (G-1521)

BATTERIES, EXC AUTOMOTIVE: Wholesalers

Battco Inc ....G 601 898-1200
Ridgeland (G-4552)

BATTERIES: Alkaline, Cell Storage

Battco Inc ....G 601 898-1200
Ridgeland (G-4552)

BATTERIES: Lead Acid, Storage

Exide Technologies ....G 601 845-2236
Florence (G-1322)
Exide Technologies ....G 601 845-2281
Florence (G-1323)

BATTERIES: Storage

Exide Technologies ....F 601 936-7788
Pearl (G-4116)
Tri Star Industrial ....G 662 680-4331
Belden (G-192)

BATTERIES: Wet

Battco Inc ....G 601 898-1200
Ridgeland (G-4552)

BATTERY CHARGERS

Exide Technologies ....G 601 845-2236
Florence (G-1322)
Exide Technologies ....F 601 936-7788
Pearl (G-4116)
Exide Technologies ....G 601 845-2281
Florence (G-1323)

BEADS: Unassembled

Beaded Owls ....G 228 284-2712
Long Beach (G-2927)
Maurice Hinton ....G 601 857-5168
Terry (G-5072)

BEARINGS: Ball & Roller

Jpm of Mississippi Inc ....D 601 544-9950
Hattiesburg (G-2004)

BEAUTY & BARBER SHOP EQPT

Beauty Mart ....G 662 624-6738
Clarksdale (G-759)
Gatlin Corporation ....E 601 833-9475
Brookhaven (G-495)
Innovative Circuits Inc ....F 662 287-2007
Corinth (G-1092)
McNeely Plastic Products Inc ....E 601 926-1000
Clinton (G-830)
Nce Group Inc ....G 662 890-8778
Olive Branch (G-3888)
NY Beauty ....G 662 280-2573
Horn Lake (G-2209)
Oralia Mejia ....G 662 512-1906
Ripley (G-4667)
Prime Manufacturing Svcs LLC ....E 901 463-5844
Senatobia (G-4799)
Region 8 Mental Health Retrdat ....D 601 591-5553
Brandon (G-445)
Split Ends ....G 601 619-0088
Vicksburg (G-5422)
Stanley Appraisal Company LLC ....G 662 287-8543
Corinth (G-1120)

BEAUTY & BARBER SHOP EQPT & SPLYS WHOLESALERS

Antonio Tarrell LLC ....G 662 983-2486
Bruce (G-559)
Beauty Mart ....G 662 624-6738
Clarksdale (G-759)

BEAUTY SALONS

Antonio Tarrell LLC ....G 662 983-2486
Bruce (G-559)
Beauty Mart ....G 662 624-6738
Clarksdale (G-759)

BEDDING, BEDSPREADS, BLANKETS & SHEETS: Comforters & Quilts

Nitas Quilts ....G 601 825-2060
Brandon (G-429)

BEDS: Hospital

A B B Inc ....F 662 628-8196
Calhoun City (G-634)
Inhealth Medical ....G 662 283-5750
Winona (G-5602)

BEDSPREADS & BED SETS, FROM PURCHASED MATERIALS

Mid-South Drapery Inc ....E 662 454-3855
Belmont (G-200)

BEDSPREADS, COTTON

Commercial Drapery Svcs LLC ....E 662 893-1510
Olive Branch (G-3824)

BEEKEEPERS' SPLYS

Force Beekeeping LLC ....G 662 429-7586
Nesbit (G-3651)
Southern States Bee Supply LLC ....G 601 513-5151
Taylorsville (G-5059)

BEER & ALE WHOLESALERS

Clark Beverage Group Inc ....D 662 338-3400
Starkville (G-4934)

BEER, WINE & LIQUOR STORES: Hard Liquor

Liquor Locker Inc ....G 228 396-8557
Biloxi (G-263)

BEER, WINE & LIQUOR STORES: Wine

Bg3 Delta LLC ....G 601 636-9828
Vicksburg (G-5344)

BENTONITE MINING

Imerys Minerals Usa Inc ....F 662 369-6411
Aberdeen (G-14)

BEVERAGE BASES & SYRUPS

Sqwincher Corporation ....D 662 328-0400
Columbus (G-1030)

BEVERAGE STORES

Brown Bottling Group Inc ....G 601 442-5805
Natchez (G-3539)

BEVERAGE, NONALCOHOLIC: Iced Tea/Fruit Drink, Bottled/Canned

Grd Distributors LLC ....G 601 382-8802
Richland (G-4518)

BEVERAGES, ALCOHOLIC: Beer

Lucky Town Brewing Company LLC ....F 601 790-0142
Jackson (G-2473)
Mighty Miss Brewing Co LLC ....G 662 379-6477
Greenville (G-1574)
Southern Prohibition Brewing ....F 601 467-1057
Hattiesburg (G-2063)

BEVERAGES, ALCOHOLIC: Beer & Ale

White Brothers Inc ....E 601 948-0888
Jackson (G-2630)

BEVERAGES, ALCOHOLIC: Distilled Liquors

Cat Head Distillery LLC ....G 601 954-8207
Jackson (G-2355)
Czeiszperger Distiller LLC ....G 662 612-6160
Coldwater (G-844)

BEVERAGES, ALCOHOLIC: Vodka

BEVERAGES, ALCOHOLIC: Vodka

B Ficklin Investments LLC ....G...... 601 454-2724
Pearl *(G-4106)*

BEVERAGES, ALCOHOLIC: Wines

Hillbilly Wines LLC ....G...... 228 234-4411
Saucier *(G-4755)*
Queens Reward Meadery LLC ....G...... 662 823-6323
Tupelo *(G-5211)*
Scott O Galbreath Jr ....G...... 601 445-9924
Natchez *(G-3617)*
Vineyard ....G...... 769 251-1322
Ridgeland *(G-4645)*
Winery At Williams Landing LLC ....G...... 662 219-0596
Greenwood *(G-1665)*

BEVERAGES, NONALCOHOLIC: Bottled & canned soft drinks

Brown Bottling Group Inc ....G...... 601 442-5805
Natchez *(G-3539)*
Brown Bottling Group Inc ....E...... 601 824-3022
Brandon *(G-374)*
C C Clark Inc ....E...... 662 323-4317
Starkville *(G-4931)*
Ccbcc Operations LLC ....D...... 228 875-5426
Ocean Springs *(G-3748)*
Ccbcc Operations LLC ....E...... 601 428-0464
Hattiesburg *(G-1941)*
Clark Beverage Group Inc ....E...... 662 280-8540
Southaven *(G-4859)*
Clark Beverage Group Inc ....G...... 662 843-3241
Cleveland *(G-789)*
Clark Beverage Group Inc ....D...... 662 338-3400
Starkville *(G-4934)*
Coast Coca Cola Bottling Co ....D...... 228 864-1122
Gulfport *(G-1754)*
Coca-Cola Bottling Co Untd Inc ....G...... 228 864-1122
Gulfport *(G-1761)*
Coca-Cola Bottling Co Untd Inc ....D...... 601 684-8223
McComb *(G-3246)*
Coca-Cola Bottling Co Untd Inc ....G...... 601 264-8600
Hattiesburg *(G-1948)*
Coca-Cola Refreshments USA Inc ....G...... 601 442-1641
Natchez *(G-3548)*
Corinth Cc-Cola Btlg Works Inc ....D...... 662 287-1433
Corinth *(G-1077)*
Corinth Cc-Cola Btlg Works Inc ....E...... 662 286-2052
Corinth *(G-1078)*
Corinth Cc-Cola Btlg Works Inc ....D...... 662 842-1753
Tupelo *(G-5122)*
Dewmar International Bmc Inc ....G...... 877 747-5326
Clinton *(G-822)*
Hooper Sales Co Incorporated ....G...... 662 526-5668
Como *(G-1048)*
Meridian Coca-Cola Bottling Co ....C...... 601 483-5272
Meridian *(G-3367)*
Mississippi Coca Cola Btlg Co ....F...... 601 584-6644
Hattiesburg *(G-2025)*
Moak Bottling Co Inc ....G...... 662 844-0012
Tupelo *(G-5189)*
Niagara Bottling LLC ....G...... 215 703-0838
Byhalia *(G-592)*
Pepsi South Bottling ....E...... 601 607-3011
Ridgeland *(G-4616)*
Vendworks LLC ....E...... 601 268-1906
Hattiesburg *(G-2080)*
Vendworks LLC ....G...... 601 684-2085
McComb *(G-3272)*
Weaver Consolidated Group Inc ....G...... 662 287-1433
Corinth *(G-1128)*
Weaver Consolidated Group Inc ....E...... 662 842-1753
Tupelo *(G-5253)*

BEVERAGES, NONALCOHOLIC: Carbonated

Allen Beverages Incorporated ....D...... 228 831-4343
Gulfport *(G-1721)*
P-Americas LLC ....D...... 228 831-4343
Gulfport *(G-1842)*
P-Americas LLC ....E...... 601 684-2281
McComb *(G-3263)*
P-Americas LLC ....C...... 662 841-8750
Tupelo *(G-5198)*
Pepsi Beverages Company ....E...... 662 841-8750
Tupelo *(G-5202)*
Pepsi Bottling Group ....G...... 601 982-4160
Brandon *(G-432)*
Pepsi-Cola Metro Btlg Co Inc ....E...... 662 563-8622
Batesville *(G-118)*

Wis-Pak of Hattiesburg LLC ....F...... 601 544-7200
Hattiesburg *(G-2085)*

BEVERAGES, NONALCOHOLIC: Carbonated, Canned & Bottled, Etc

Calico Jacks Llc ....G...... 504 355-9639
Carriere *(G-689)*
Gulf States Canners Inc ....D...... 601 924-0511
Clinton *(G-824)*

BEVERAGES, NONALCOHOLIC: Flavoring extracts & syrups, nec

Anthony Syrup Company ....G...... 601 656-7052
Philadelphia *(G-4205)*

BEVERAGES, NONALCOHOLIC: Soft Drinks, Canned & Bottled, Etc

American Bottling Company ....D...... 601 939-5454
Richland *(G-4500)*
American Bottling Company ....D...... 662 844-7047
Tupelo *(G-5109)*
Brown Bottling Group Inc ....C...... 601 982-4160
Jackson *(G-2344)*
Dr Pepper/Seven Up Inc ....G...... 601 545-7511
Hattiesburg *(G-1958)*
Frank Villines ....G...... 601 939-5454
Jackson *(G-2646)*
Group Pepper Snapple Dr ....G...... 601 602-3695
Hattiesburg *(G-1977)*
Nehi Bottling Co of Cleveland ....F...... 662 843-3431
Cleveland *(G-802)*
RC Cola Company ....F...... 662 844-7947
Tupelo *(G-5214)*
Royal Crown Bottling ....E...... 662 843-3431
Cleveland *(G-807)*

BICYCLES WHOLESALERS

Main Street Cycle Inc ....G...... 662 438-6407
Tishomingo *(G-5086)*

BILLIARD & POOL TABLES & SPLYS

Espiritu Custom Cues ....G...... 601 825-7077
Brandon *(G-395)*

BILLING & BOOKKEEPING SVCS

Info Services Inc ....F...... 601 898-7858
Madison *(G-3109)*

BINDING SVC: Books & Manuals

Alpha Printing Inc ....G...... 601 371-2611
Jackson *(G-2324)*
Bourne Brothers Prtg Co Inc ....F...... 601 582-1808
Hattiesburg *(G-1938)*
Copy Cats Printing Inc ....F...... 601 582-3019
Hattiesburg *(G-1951)*
Dianne Gore ....G...... 510 697-2569
Jackson *(G-2383)*
Fedex Office & Print Svcs Inc ....E...... 601 957-3311
Jackson *(G-2407)*
Fedex Office & Print Svcs Inc ....F...... 601 264-6434
Hattiesburg *(G-1969)*
Hagen Corporation ....G...... 601 932-3138
Pearl *(G-4125)*
Harden Enterprises Inc ....F...... 662 841-9292
Tupelo *(G-5152)*
Jenkins Graphics Inc ....G...... 662 890-2851
Olive Branch *(G-3855)*
Lewis Yager Melbaleen J ....G...... 228 762-3152
Pascagoula *(G-4046)*
Mid South Publications Inc ....G...... 662 256-8209
Amory *(G-48)*
Natchez Printing Co ....G...... 601 442-3693
Natchez *(G-3596)*
Nick Strcklnds Quick Print Inc ....F...... 601 353-8672
Ridgeland *(G-4611)*
Nick Strcklnds Quick Print Inc ....E...... 601 898-1717
Jackson *(G-2521)*
Rankin Printery ....G...... 662 287-4426
Corinth *(G-1112)*
RR Donnelley & Sons Company ....B...... 662 562-5252
Senatobia *(G-4802)*
Smith Printing & Off Sup Inc ....G...... 601 442-2441
Natchez *(G-3621)*
Southern Systems & Service Co ....G...... 601 264-4713
Hattiesburg *(G-2064)*

Swain Printing & Signs ....G...... 662 773-7584
Louisville *(G-2983)*
Wolverton Enterprises Inc ....F...... 601 355-9543
Jackson *(G-2637)*
Womack Willow ....G...... 601 969-4120
Jackson *(G-2638)*

BIOLOGICAL PRDTS: Blood Derivatives

Immunotek Bio Centers LLC ....E...... 601 462-5145
Meridian *(G-3350)*

BIOLOGICAL PRDTS: Exc Diagnostic

Algix LLC ....G...... 877 972-5449
Meridian *(G-3296)*
Amite Bioenergy LLC ....G...... 770 743-4300
Gloster *(G-1509)*
Bio Plumber of Mississippi ....G...... 601 825-5190
Brandon *(G-371)*

BIOLOGICAL PRDTS: Vaccines & Immunizing

K & B Mississippi Corporation ....F...... 601 545-2056
Petal *(G-4189)*
K B Ms ....G...... 601 684-0510
McComb *(G-3255)*

BLADES: Saw, Hand Or Power

Milwaukee Electric Tool Corp ....B...... 662 451-5545
Greenwood *(G-1640)*
Milwaukee Electric Tool Corp ....C...... 662 895-4560
Olive Branch *(G-3879)*

BLANKBOOKS & LOOSELEAF BINDERS

Avery Products Corporation ....C...... 601 483-0611
Meridian *(G-3304)*
Southland Supplies ....G...... 662 647-2452
Cascilla *(G-729)*

BLANKBOOKS: Account

Norman Accounting Services ....G...... 662 347-4475
Greenville *(G-1582)*

BLASTING SVC: Sand, Metal Parts

Bdm Industrial Services LLC ....G...... 662 549-3055
Columbus *(G-939)*
Resurfacing Concepts Inc ....G...... 662 489-6867
Pontotoc *(G-4360)*

BLIMPS

Airworks Enterprises Inc ....G...... 601 372-8304
Raymond *(G-4482)*

BLINDS : Window

Hunter Douglas Inc ....C...... 662 690-8190
Shannon *(G-4810)*
Norman Vr Inc ....G...... 601 352-4819
Gulfport *(G-1838)*
Omni Blinds ....G...... 601 924-0326
Clinton *(G-832)*
Superior Blinds and Shutters ....G...... 901 270-8061
Southaven *(G-4910)*

BLOCKS & BRICKS: Concrete

Columbia Block & Brick Co Inc ....G...... 601 450-3791
Hattiesburg *(G-1949)*
Delta Industries Inc ....C...... 601 354-3801
Jackson *(G-2381)*
Lexington Concrete & Block Co ....G...... 662 834-3892
Lexington *(G-2904)*

BLOCKS: Landscape Or Retaining Wall, Concrete

Back Bay Lawnscapes LLC ....F...... 228 348-1299
Diberville *(G-1195)*
Daniels Lawn and Lanscape LLC ....G...... 601 965-6982
Clinton *(G-820)*
Lmg Diversified LLC ....G...... 601 635-5955
Newton *(G-3724)*
Magnolia Supply Group LLC ....G...... 601 454-1368
Jackson *(G-2480)*
Mid Mississippi Maintenance ....F...... 601 953-1091
Edwards *(G-1241)*

2019 Harris Directory of
Mississippi Manufacturers

(G-0000) Company's Geographic Section entry number

350

PRODUCT SECTION

BRICKS: Clay

Milieu Outdoor Image Solutions ....G....... 601 259-8570
Madison **(G-3129)**
Tropical World Intl LLC ....G....... 228 229-8413
Biloxi **(G-285)**

BLOCKS: Paving, Concrete

Pearson Enterprises ....G....... 662 289-7625
Kosciusko **(G-2709)**

BLOCKS: Standard, Concrete Or Cinder

American Concrete Products Inc ....E....... 601 583-2274
Hattiesburg **(G-1921)**
Tupelo Concrete Products Inc ....F....... 662 842-7811
Tupelo **(G-5243)**

BLOOD RELATED HEALTH SVCS

Willow Ansthesia Solutions LLC ....G....... 662 550-4299
Oxford **(G-4009)**

BLOWERS & FANS

Pure Air Filter ....G....... 228 867-0888
Gulfport **(G-1856)**
U S Metal Works Inc ....E....... 601 657-4676
Liberty **(G-2919)**
Ultra Drying Technology ....G....... 662 494-5025
West Point **(G-5565)**
Viking Range LLC ....D....... 770 932-7282
Greenwood **(G-1657)**

BLUEPRINTING SVCS

Lewis Yager Melbaleen J.....................G....... 228 762-3152
Pascagoula **(G-4046)**

BOAT & BARGE COMPONENTS: Metal, Prefabricated

Vertechs Design Solutions LLC.............G....... 228 671-1442
Waveland **(G-5486)**

BOAT BUILDING & REPAIR

A Step Above Marine Contrs LLC.........G....... 228 452-5122
Pass Christian **(G-4076)**
Betta Boats LLC ....G....... 228 363-2529
Bay St Louis **(G-176)**
Brian Smith ....G....... 601 259-9745
Gulfport **(G-1744)**
C Wells Trucking LLC ....G....... 601 273-0972
Picayune **(G-4258)**
Clyde E Burton ....G....... 228 432-0117
Biloxi **(G-231)**
Emerald Water LLC ....G....... 601 981-2430
Jackson **(G-2400)**
Knights Mar & Indus Svcs Inc ....C....... 228 769-5550
Pascagoula **(G-4045)**
Lynn Welding Shop LLC ....G....... 601 638-7235
Vicksburg **(G-5390)**
Mississippi Marine Corporation ....C....... 662 335-1175
Greenville **(G-1576)**
Nautic Star LLC ....C....... 662 256-5636
Amory **(G-49)**
Nichols Propeller Company ....E....... 662 378-2000
Greenville **(G-1580)**
Rookie Boats ....G....... 228 466-6377
Bay Saint Louis **(G-153)**
United States Marine Inc ....C....... 228 679-1005
Gulfport **(G-1890)**
VT Halter Marine Inc ....C....... 228 475-1211
Moss Point **(G-3504)**
VT Halter Marine Inc ....C....... 228 712-2278
Moss Point **(G-3505)**
Westergard Boat Works Inc ....G....... 228 214-4455
Gulfport **(G-1893)**

BOAT BUILDING & REPAIRING: Fiberglass

Kirkland Boats Inc ....E....... 662 647-0017
Charleston **(G-741)**

BOAT BUILDING & REPAIRING: Houseboats

Coastal Marine Sales LLC ....G....... 228 731-3955
Gulfport **(G-1760)**

BOAT BUILDING & REPAIRING: Hydrofoil

Prairie Adventure LLC ....G....... 662 295-8807
West Point **(G-5558)**

BOAT BUILDING & REPAIRING: Motorboats, Inboard Or Outboard

M M Flechas Shipyard Co Inc ....G....... 228 762-3628
Pascagoula **(G-4047)**
Prop Straighteners Inc ....G....... 662 423-9588
Iuka **(G-2305)**

BOAT BUILDING & REPAIRING: Non-Motorized

Boat Man..G....... 228 218-3080
Gautier **(G-1489)**
Jerry S Trolling Motor Repair................G....... 256 431-6564
Iuka **(G-2296)**

BOAT BUILDING & REPAIRING: Tenders, Small Motor Craft

Singin River Mental Health...................E....... 228 497-0690
Gautier **(G-1504)**

BOAT DEALERS

Rookie Boats ....G....... 228 466-6377
Bay Saint Louis **(G-153)**

BOAT DEALERS: Marine Splys & Eqpt

Brian Smith ....G....... 601 259-9745
Gulfport **(G-1744)**

BOAT LIFTS

Blue Bayou Boat Lifts Inc ....G....... 601 798-0659
Carriere **(G-688)**
Cannon Boat Lifts LLC ....G....... 601 540-8691
Madison **(G-3087)**

BOAT REPAIR SVCS

Brian Smith ....G....... 601 259-9745
Gulfport **(G-1744)**

BODIES: Truck & Bus

Parker-Hannifin Corporation.................C....... 662 895-1011
Olive Branch **(G-3894)**
Truck Bodies & Eqp Intl Inc ....G....... 662 438-7800
Tishomingo **(G-5088)**

BODY PARTS: Automobile, Stamped Metal

Unipres Southeast USA Inc ....C....... 601 469-0234
Forest **(G-1428)**

BOLTS: Metal

Southern Fastener Co Miss ....C....... 662 335-2157
Greenville **(G-1601)**

BOLTS: Wooden, Hewn

Hood Industries Inc ....G....... 601 264-2962
Hattiesburg **(G-1995)**

BOTTLE CAPS & RESEALERS: Plastic

Berry Global Inc ....C....... 601 584-4800
Hattiesburg **(G-1928)**
Berry Global Inc ....G....... 601 584-4778
Hattiesburg **(G-1929)**
Bprex Closures LLC ....D....... 601 584-4758
Hattiesburg **(G-1939)**

BOTTLED GAS DEALERS: Liquefied Petro, Dlvrd To Customers

Thomas LP Gas Inc...............................F....... 662 252-5388
Holly Springs **(G-2195)**

BOTTLES: Plastic

L C Industries Inc.................................B....... 601 894-1771
Hazlehurst **(G-2099)**
Signature Works Inc ....B....... 601 894-1771
Hazlehurst **(G-2106)**

BOXES & CRATES: Rectangular, Wood

Stanley D Stokes Jr ....G....... 662 237-6600
Carrollton **(G-703)**

BOXES & SHOOK: Nailed Wood

Bryan Industrial Co Inc.........................F....... 601 649-8786
Laurel **(G-2744)**
Hudspeth Wood Products Inc...............F....... 662 263-5902
Maben **(G-3046)**

BOXES: Corrugated

Airfloat Systems Inc ....G....... 662 566-0158
Verona **(G-5326)**
American Container Inc.........................E....... 662 890-0325
Olive Branch **(G-3810)**
Chickasaw Container Company ....D....... 662 447-3339
Okolona **(G-3795)**
Color-Box LLC ....C....... 601 854-6020
Pelahatchie **(G-4162)**
General Packaging Specialties ....F....... 662 844-7882
Tupelo **(G-5140)**
Gibson Corrugated LLC ....D....... 662 842-1862
Tupelo **(G-5143)**
Great Southern Industries Inc ....E....... 601 948-5700
Jackson **(G-2431)**
Hoerner Boxes Inc ....E....... 662 842-2491
Tupelo **(G-5156)**
Packaging Corporation America ....C....... 601 939-5111
Pearl **(G-4136)**
Packaging Corporation America ....E....... 662 895-4100
Olive Branch **(G-3893)**
Southland Container Inc ....E....... 601 879-8816
Flora **(G-1312)**
St Tammany Box Company....................E....... 601 799-0775
Picayune **(G-4297)**
Westrock Cp LLC ....E....... 662 842-4940
Tupelo **(G-5257)**
Westrock Cp LLC ....E....... 662 895-1627
Olive Branch **(G-3925)**
Westrock Cp LLC ....C....... 662 869-5771
Saltillo **(G-4723)**

BOXES: Filing, Paperboard Made From Purchased Materials

Rusken Packaging Inc...........................G....... 662 680-5060
Tupelo **(G-5219)**

BOXES: Paperboard, Folding

Fc Meyer Packaging LLC ....F....... 601 776-2117
Quitman **(G-4464)**
Region 8 Mental Health Retrdat............D....... 601 591-5553
Brandon **(G-445)**
Westrock Cp LLC ....E....... 662 842-4940
Tupelo **(G-5257)**

BOXES: Wooden

Chickasaw Wood Products Inc.............F....... 662 456-5357
Houston **(G-2234)**
Ronda K Gentry ....G....... 662 418-9844
Starkville **(G-4969)**

BRAKES: Metal Forming

Standard Industrial Corp......................D....... 662 624-2436
Clarksdale **(G-783)**

BRICK CLEANING SVCS

Dungans Outdoor Solutions Co ....G....... 228 382-7156
Ocean Springs **(G-3753)**

BRICK, STONE & RELATED PRDTS WHOLESALERS

Apac-Mississippi Inc ....G....... 662 746-7983
Yazoo City **(G-5623)**
Builders Marble Inc..............................E....... 601 922-5420
Clinton **(G-817)**
Fireplace Wholesale ....G....... 601 545-9876
Hattiesburg **(G-1970)**
Triton Stone Holdings LLC....................D....... 662 280-8041
Southaven **(G-4917)**

BRICKS : Flooring, Clay

Everett Industries Inc ....G....... 228 231-1556
Bay Saint Louis **(G-143)**

BRICKS: Clay

Louisville Brick Company ....E....... 800 530-7102
Louisville **(G-2973)**

Employee Codes: A=Over 500 employees, B=251-500
C=101-250, D=51-100, E=20-50, F=10-19, G=1-9

2019 Harris Directory of
Mississippi Manufacturers

351

PRODUCT

BRICKS: Concrete

PRODUCT SECTION

BRICKS: Concrete
General Shale Brick Inc..................F 662 840-8221
Tupelo (G-5141)

BRIDAL SHOPS
Formal Affair...........................G 228 497-7500
Gautier (G-1492)

BRIDGE COMPONENTS: Bridge sections, prefabricated, highway
Gipson Steel Inc.......................D 601 482-5131
Meridian (G-3340)

BROADCASTING & COMMS EQPT: Antennas, Transmitting/Comms
Mfj Enterprises Inc...................E 662 323-9538
Starkville (G-4959)
Omega-Tec LLC.........................G 601 750-8082
Vicksburg (G-5402)

BROKERS: Mortgage, Arranging For Loans
Delta Foundation Inc.................C 662 335-5291
Greenville (G-1547)

BROKERS: Printing
P P I Inc................................F 662 680-4332
Tupelo (G-5197)
Smart Source...........................G 601 707-1150
Ridgeland (G-4631)

BROOMS
L C Industries Inc....................B 601 894-1771
Hazlehurst (G-2099)
Piave Broom & Mop Inc.............F 601 584-7314
Petal (G-4195)
Signature Works Inc..................B 601 894-1771
Hazlehurst (G-2106)

BROOMS & BRUSHES
Easy Reach Supply LLC.............E 601 582-7866
Hattiesburg (G-1959)
Lighthouse For The Blind ....G 228 867-1565
Gulfport (G-1822)

BROOMS & BRUSHES: Household Or Indl
Hub City Brush Inc...................F 601 584-7314
Petal (G-4187)

BUILDING & OFFICE CLEANING SVCS
Aride Taxi Cab and Trnsp LLC.............G 601 620-4282
Byram (G-617)

BUILDING & STRUCTURAL WOOD MBRS: Timbers, Struct, Lam Lumber
CST Timber Company ....F 601 225-7887
Gloster (G-1513)
Mississippi Laminators Inc..........E 601 687-1621
Shubuta (G-4831)
Southeastern Forest Produ..................G 601 988-1131
Flowood (G-1399)

BUILDING & STRUCTURAL WOOD MEMBERS
Evergreen Lumber & Truss Inc............E 601 794-8404
Purvis (G-4437)
Frierson Building Supply Co ....C 601 922-1321
Jackson (G-2416)

BUILDING BOARD: Gypsum
Certainteed Gypsum Inc..................C 601 693-0254
Meridian (G-3318)

BUILDING COMPONENTS: Structural Steel
Accu-Fab and Construction Inc............E 228 475-0082
Moss Point (G-3465)
Industrial Fabricators Inc...........E 662 327-1776
Columbus (G-987)
Magnolia Steel Co Inc...............C 601 693-4301
Meridian (G-3363)

National Bank Builders & Eqp ....F 662 781-0702
Walls (G-5450)
Structural Steel Holding Inc ....F 601 485-1503
Meridian (G-3407)
Structural Steel Services Inc..............C 601 482-1668
Meridian (G-3409)
Structural Steel Services Inc..............E 601 485-2619
Meridian (G-3410)
Thomasvlle Mtal Fbricators Inc..............E 662 526-9900
Como (G-1052)

BUILDING EXTERIOR CLEANING SVCS
Dungans Outdoor Solutions Co ....G 228 382-7156
Ocean Springs (G-3753)
Emma Roberts ....G 601 638-3062
Vicksburg (G-5366)

BUILDING MAINTENANCE SVCS, EXC REPAIRS
Rjb Enterprise Inc ....G 202 830-3508
Gulfport (G-1863)

BUILDING PRDTS & MATERIALS DEALERS
Fortenberry Builders Supply ....G 601 825-3370
Brandon (G-397)
Jones Companies AVI MGT Inc ....G 844 500-2438
Hattiesburg (G-2003)
Service Lumber Holding Corp ....G 662 873-4334
Rolling Fork (G-4683)
Smith Cabinet Shop Inc..................E 662 287-2151
Corinth (G-1119)

BUILDING PRDTS: Concrete
Gilmore Bros Building Supply..................G 601 825-6292
Brandon (G-398)
Huey P Stockstill LLC.................C 601 798-2981
Picayune (G-4272)
Stair Depot of Ms ....G 334 467-5584
Gulfport (G-1879)

BUILDINGS & COMPONENTS: Prefabricated Metal
Better Built Portable Inc.................G 601 267-4607
Carthage (G-707)
Domes International Inc ....E 662 438-7186
Tishomingo (G-5085)
Glenn Weise ....G 228 435-4455
Biloxi (G-244)
Goldin Metals Incorporated ....F 228 575-7737
Gulfport (G-1794)
Johnny Parks ....G 662 289-5844
Kosciusko (G-2697)
Nci Group Inc ....G 601 373-3222
Jackson (G-2517)
Probuilt LLC ....G 662 312-2159
Macon (G-3071)

BUILDINGS, PREFABRICATED: Wholesalers
Majestic Metals Inc ....E 601 856-3600
Madison (G-3126)

BUILDINGS: Chicken Coops, Prefabricated, Wood
K & T Poultry Sales & Svc Inc..................F 601 764-3918
Bay Springs (G-167)

BUILDINGS: Mobile, For Commercial Use
Lifetime Portable Building LLC ....G 228 860-7715
Gulfport (G-1821)

BUILDINGS: Portable
AAA Portable Buildings LLC...............G 601 445-4034
Natchez (G-3516)
Custom-Bilt Portable Buildings.............G 601 932-2808
Florence (G-1319)
Derksen Portable Buildings...............G 601 528-5778
Wiggins (G-5579)
Fairview Portable Buildings..................G 662 837-8709
Ripley (G-4658)
First Monday Trade Day ....G 662 837-4051
Ripley (G-4659)
Gwendolyn Rucker ....G 919 337-6218
Diberville (G-1206)

Idom Enterprising Inc..................G 601 583-4852
Hattiesburg (G-1998)
Lakeview Metal Works ....G 601 947-8019
Lucedale (G-3007)
Majestic Metals Inc ....E 601 856-3600
Madison (G-3126)
Metal Builders Supply Inc..................G 601 932-0202
Pearl (G-4131)
Mini Systems Inc......................G 662 487-2240
Como (G-1050)
Nci Group Inc ....D 662 324-1845
Starkville (G-4963)
Payne Portable Building Inc..................G 601 426-9484
Laurel (G-2818)
Robertson-Ceco II Corporation ....D 662 243-6400
Columbus (G-1021)
Vancleave Portable Buildings..................G 228 826-5151
Vancleave (G-5323)

BUILDINGS: Prefabricated, Metal
Aci Building Systems LLC..................C 662 563-4574
Batesville (G-93)
Alexander Fabricating Co Inc ....G 601 485-5414
Meridian (G-3295)
Anderson Enterprises LLC..................G 601 928-0030
Wiggins (G-5570)
Chatham Enterprises Inc..................E 601 727-4951
Rose Hill (G-4684)
Kirby Bldg Systems Miss LLC..................C 662 323-8021
Starkville (G-4954)

BUILDINGS: Prefabricated, Wood
Cook Sales Inc ....E 662 229-9787
Grenada (G-1672)
Enercept Inc ....G 228 323-1666
Gulfport (G-1779)
Payne Portable Building Inc..................G 601 426-9484
Laurel (G-2818)

BURIAL VAULTS: Concrete Or Precast Terrazzo
Bates Vault & Services LLC...............G 601 303-0508
Tylertown (G-5263)
Bickes Inc ....E 601 353-7083
Jackson (G-2337)
United Burial Vault Co & Cemtr ....F 662 347-9319
Benoit (G-207)
Wilbert Burial Vault Company..................G 601 353-7084
Jackson (G-2632)
Wilbert Funeral Services Inc..................G 800 323-7188
Jackson (G-2633)

BURIAL VAULTS: Stone
Doric Burial Vault Co ....F 601 366-8390
Jackson (G-2388)

BUSINESS ACTIVITIES: Non-Commercial Site
A & D Timber Company Inc..................F 601 528-9357
Wiggins (G-5568)
Acme Fabrication LLC..................G 228 669-0004
Perkinston (G-4172)
Ada Newson ....G 601 810-6614
Richland (G-4498)
Advanced GnsInger Armament LLC........G 775 343-5633
Starkville (G-4923)
Automated Tech & Assembly LLC........G 662 213-9352
Rolling Fork (G-4679)
B&M Maintenance LLC ....G 228 273-5821
Vancleave (G-5318)
Bardo & Co ....G 601 397-1167
Kosciusko (G-2690)
Battlebells LLC ....G 662 312-5901
Starkville (G-4927)
BEC Fire and Safety LLC..................G 601 498-9108
Sumrall (G-5034)
Beloved Pottery........................G 662 349-4430
Southaven (G-4854)
Box Office 7 Studios....................G 662 633-2451
Brandon (G-372)
Calico Jacks Llc ....G 504 355-9639
Carriere (G-689)
Circle A LLC ....G 601 832-3698
Hazlehurst (G-2091)
Clifford A Crosby ....G 228 234-1649
Biloxi (G-230)

352

2019 Harris Directory of
Mississippi Manufacturers

(G-0000) Company's Geographic Section entry number

PRODUCT SECTION

CABINETS: Kitchen, Wood

Composite Fbrication Group LLC ....G...... 601 549-1789
Moselle *(G-3456)*

Cool Baby Water LLC ....G...... 850 748-0921
Lucedale *(G-2990)*

Creekside Envmtl Pdts LLC ....G...... 662 617-5553
Starkville *(G-4936)*

Crossroads Picks LLC ....G...... 662 902-1026
Clarksdale *(G-765)*

Custom Pallett LLC ....G...... 662 423-8127
Tishomingo *(G-5084)*

D D Rushing ....G...... 601 656-8842
Philadelphia *(G-4213)*

Delta Agricultural MGT Inc ....G...... 865 210-4605
Tunica *(G-5096)*

Destiny Apparel LLC ....G...... 228 383-2665
Biloxi *(G-236)*

Donald Speights Jr ....G...... 601 940-3847
Braxton *(G-477)*

Dwayne Timber Company ....G...... 601 695-6177
Wesson *(G-5527)*

Educate & Celebrate LLC ....G...... 228 547-0811
Gulfport *(G-1776)*

Elizabeth Clayton ....G...... 601 371-1172
Terry *(G-5066)*

Ell Holdings ....G...... 601 325-3317
Hattiesburg *(G-1961)*

Fast Track Planners LLC ....G...... 601 528-0558
Perkinston *(G-4175)*

Fiske International Group Corp ....G...... 601 622-5767
Madison *(G-3100)*

Fitmate Social Inc ....G...... 206 849-2447
Oxford *(G-3956)*

Flambeaux Cocktail Candle LLC ....G...... 601 826-1642
Ridgeland *(G-4583)*

Gmn Group LLC ....G...... 662 473-3094
Water Valley *(G-5468)*

Golden Source Inventors LLC ....G...... 601 325-4064
Hattiesburg *(G-1975)*

Guys Logging ....G...... 662 726-9301
Macon *(G-3063)*

Gw Ministries ....G...... 662 832-9756
Water Valley *(G-5469)*

Harlan Services LLC ....G...... 601 513-5318
Magee *(G-3177)*

Heavenly Confections ....G...... 601 660-1986
Natchez *(G-3568)*

Industrial Cleaning Svcs LLC ....F....... 662 397-6735
Saltillo *(G-4712)*

Ion Chemical Company ....G...... 601 781-0604
Carthage *(G-717)*

James L Brewer ....G...... 662 299-7247
Greenwood *(G-1631)*

Jason Fly Logging LLC ....F....... 662 316-3499
Batesville *(G-110)*

Jones Ldscp & Contrs Svc LLC ....G...... 601 780-2042
Jackson *(G-2460)*

Larry D Wallace ....G...... 601 384-4409
Roxie *(G-4691)*

Laurin Enterprises LLC ....G...... 228 207-5580
Biloxi *(G-259)*

Lawrence A Witherspoon ....G...... 662 404-5859
Horn Lake *(G-2205)*

M & M Chassis Shop LLC ....G...... 601 310-6078
Moselle *(G-3458)*

M & W Publishing Co LLC ....G...... 662 843-1358
Boyle *(G-350)*

Maelstrom Square LLC ....G...... 470 378-9064
Pascagoula *(G-4048)*

Magnetic Arrow LLC ....G...... 601 653-2932
Biloxi *(G-264)*

Mary Givens ....G...... 601 325-5599
Brandon *(G-419)*

Mc Consulting LLC ....G...... 601 735-2000
Waynesboro *(G-5506)*

Miller Timber LLC ....G...... 662 501-6150
Houlka *(G-2226)*

Natures Society Majestic Arts ....G...... 601 376-0447
Byram *(G-623)*

Newson Chenora ....G...... 601 596-3899
Hattiesburg *(G-2037)*

Pevey Publishing LLC ....G...... 601 503-7205
Brandon *(G-434)*

Pine Belt Gas Inc ....G...... 601 731-1144
Columbia *(G-911)*

Pop-A-Cart LLC ....G...... 931 292-2150
Jackson *(G-2541)*

Precision Asp Sealcoating LLC ....G...... 601 527-6381
Collinsville *(G-874)*

Richard B Brandon ....G...... 601 238-2383
Jackson *(G-2564)*

Richard Melos ....G...... 434 401-9496
Robinsonville *(G-4677)*

Ronald E Christopher III ....G...... 901 301-5922
Olive Branch *(G-3905)*

Ronda K Gentry ....G...... 662 418-9844
Starkville *(G-4969)*

Rsileds LLC ....G...... 228 697-5967
Biloxi *(G-277)*

Samuel Moses Inc ....G...... 601 669-0756
Brookhaven *(G-529)*

Schoolstatus LLC ....G...... 601 620-0613
Hattiesburg *(G-2056)*

Simpson Brothers Inc ....G...... 678 451-4259
Mc Cool *(G-3237)*

Sugar -N- Spice Confections ....G...... 901 210-6181
Horn Lake *(G-2213)*

Tinks Bells ....G...... 662 574-2685
Columbus *(G-1038)*

Travis Construction Co LLC ....F....... 228 539-4849
Gulfport *(G-1886)*

Tronicsales ....G...... 769 218-0432
Jackson *(G-2613)*

Twister LLC ....G...... 601 371-7276
Madison *(G-3162)*

Velocity Cnslting Spcalist LLC ....G...... 229 726-6047
Petal *(G-4199)*

Whitney Whitehead ....G...... 662 380-0614
Sarah *(G-4737)*

Williams Prcsion Machining LLC ....G...... 662 287-7734
Corinth *(G-1129)*

Wilson Solutions LLC ....G...... 662 319-6063
Aberdeen *(G-22)*

BUSINESS FORMS WHOLESALERS

Rutledge Publishing Co Inc ....G...... 662 534-2116
New Albany *(G-3694)*

BUSINESS FORMS: *Printed, Continuous*

Barber Printing Inc ....F....... 662 841-1584
Tupelo *(G-5112)*

BUSINESS FORMS: *Printed, Manifold*

Acco Brands USA LLC ....G...... 800 541-0094
Booneville *(G-314)*

Gpal LLC ....G...... 662 422-9351
Tupelo *(G-5146)*

Jackson Business Form Company ....E....... 601 932-5200
Flowood *(G-1370)*

BUYERS' CLUB

Great Southern Club Inc ....F....... 228 868-8619
Gulfport *(G-1796)*

CABINETS & CASES: *Show, Display & Storage, Exc Wood*

Stanley Black & Decker Inc ....E....... 662 844-7191
Tupelo *(G-5231)*

CABINETS, HOUSING: *For Radium, Metal Plate*

Richards Home Services ....G...... 228 324-3482
Ocean Springs *(G-3782)*

CABINETS: *Bathroom Vanities, Wood*

Smith Cabinet Shop Inc ....E....... 662 287-2151
Corinth *(G-1119)*

Viking Capital Ventures Inc ....F....... 662 455-1200
Greenwood *(G-1656)*

CABINETS: *Entertainment*

Bunyard Cabinetry ....G...... 601 757-8765
Brookhaven *(G-485)*

Pettigrew Cabinets Inc ....E....... 662 844-1368
Plantersville *(G-4313)*

CABINETS: *Factory*

Hartson-Kennedy Cabinet Top Co ....D...... 228 896-1548
Gulfport *(G-1805)*

CABINETS: *Kitchen, Wood*

Advantage Cabinet Doors ....G...... 662 494-9700
West Point *(G-5534)*

Andrews Cabinet Shop ....G...... 662 327-1070
Columbus *(G-935)*

Ash Millworks Inc ....E....... 601 544-3962
Petal *(G-4184)*

Associated Architectural Pdts ....F....... 662 245-0400
Columbus *(G-937)*

Bowman Cabinet Company ....G...... 662 564-2711
Holly Springs *(G-2172)*

Bridges Custom Cabinets & Trim ....G...... 601 954-5085
Canton *(G-650)*

Buchanan Custom Cabinets ....G...... 662 438-7435
Tishomingo *(G-5083)*

Bunyard Cabinetry ....G...... 601 757-8765
Brookhaven *(G-485)*

Burgess Kustom Cabinetry ....G...... 662 316-4294
New Albany *(G-3676)*

C & D Cabinets LLC ....F....... 228 466-4644
Waveland *(G-5478)*

Cabinet Specialists Inc ....G...... 601 992-3929
Jackson *(G-2352)*

Cabinetsource Inc ....G...... 228 385-8880
Gulfport *(G-1747)*

Carpenters Cabinets ....G...... 662 465-6453
Sturgis *(G-5006)*

CL Cabinets LLC ....G...... 228 860-9678
Long Beach *(G-2933)*

Clear Creek Cabinetry Inc ....G...... 601 684-7130
Summit *(G-5008)*

Coast Wood Products Inc ....G...... 228 466-4302
Bay Saint Louis *(G-141)*

Colon Cabinets and Trim ....G...... 662 347-8608
Greenville *(G-1539)*

D&H Construction Cabinetry Inc ....G...... 601 737-2010
Meridian *(G-3326)*

Darrells Custom Cabinets ....G...... 662 822-3936
Greenville *(G-1544)*

Davis & Cooke Custom Cabinetry ....G...... 601 580-0181
Laurel *(G-2759)*

Easley & Easley Millworks Inc ....F....... 601 372-8881
Jackson *(G-2395)*

Ellis Woodworks ....G...... 662 329-2605
Columbus *(G-970)*

Garner Millwork Inc ....F....... 662 844-7007
Tupelo *(G-5139)*

Graham Custom Cabinets & Trim ....G...... 803 381-6829
Crystal Springs *(G-1142)*

Heritage Custom Cabinets LLC ....G...... 228 323-8389
Gulfport *(G-1806)*

Hilderbrand Cabinet Doors LLC ....G...... 662 755-8626
Bentonia *(G-211)*

J M I Inc ....G...... 601 936-6800
Brandon *(G-409)*

Jakes Woodwork LLC ....G...... 601 651-6278
Laurel *(G-2786)*

Joes Custom Cabinets ....G...... 601 508-8284
Lucedale *(G-3006)*

Kitchen Elegance LLC ....G...... 228 248-0074
Gulfport *(G-1818)*

Kitchen Table ....F....... 601 261-3836
Hattiesburg *(G-2008)*

Lynn Hollis Rebel Cabinets ....G...... 228 588-2572
Moss Point *(G-3484)*

Magnolia Cabinet & Mllwk Inc ....G...... 662 282-7683
Mantachie *(G-3201)*

Magnolia Cabinet Works ....G...... 601 916-6538
Carriere *(G-697)*

McHan Cabinets ....G...... 601 636-8821
Vicksburg *(G-5394)*

Murphy Cabinet Company ....G...... 662 417-9717
Grenada *(G-1696)*

Nightengale Cabinets ....G...... 662 686-9004
Leland *(G-2891)*

Orman Cabinet Co LLC ....G...... 662 837-6352
Oxford *(G-3983)*

Petermans Cabinets ....G...... 228 832-0353
Gulfport *(G-1848)*

Pettigrew Cabinets Inc ....E....... 662 844-1368
Plantersville *(G-4313)*

Pierce Cabinets Inc ....E....... 662 840-6795
Tupelo *(G-5204)*

Pro-Stone LLC ....F....... 334 281-0048
Olive Branch *(G-3902)*

Rainey Mill Works LLC ....F....... 601 583-1310
Hattiesburg *(G-2048)*

Reeves Cabinets ....G...... 662 323-3633
Starkville *(G-4967)*

Robert Smith Custom Cabinets ....G...... 662 282-5007
Mantachie *(G-3204)*

Shawn Kurtz ....G...... 601 415-9540
Vicksburg *(G-5416)*

Southeastern Constructors Inc ....E....... 601 825-9791
Brandon *(G-457)*

Employee Codes: A=Over 500 employees, B=251-500
C=101-250, D=51-100, E=20-50, F=10-19, G=1-9

CABINETS: Kitchen, Wood
PRODUCT SECTION

Southern Cabinet & Woodwork ....E 228 475-0912
  Moss Point **(G-3499)**
Southern Cabinets ....G 901 461-6161
  Byhalia **(G-605)**
Southern Charm Cstm Cbntry LLC ......G 662 862-5058
  Fulton **(G-1476)**
Sterling Custom Cabinets LLC ....G 601 996-1906
  Gloster **(G-1518)**
Straughter Cabinets ....G 662 247-2728
  Belzoni **(G-206)**
Summit Cabinet Co LLC ....G 601 684-1639
  Summit **(G-5023)**
Superior Granite & Quartz ....G 662 241-5664
  Columbus **(G-1034)**
Thornton & Sons Cabinet Shop ....G 601 425-2172
  Laurel **(G-2858)**
Troy Custom Cabinets LLC ....G 662 902-5559
  Tutwiler **(G-5260)**
W L Tisdale Cabinet Shop ....G 601 763-3552
  Ellisville **(G-1274)**
Whittington Construction Co ....G 601 442-8096
  Natchez **(G-3640)**

CABINETS: Office, Wood

Ed Dangerfield Const Millwrks ....G 662 328-3877
  Columbus **(G-967)**
Quality Cabinet Company Inc ....E 662 429-1411
  Hernando **(G-2151)**
William Kilgore ....G 601 582-3702
  Moselle **(G-3464)**

CABINETS: Show, Display, Etc, Wood, Exc Refrigerated

Coleman Builders Inc ....G 662 234-0376
  Oxford **(G-3947)**
Shamrock Wood Industries Inc ....C 662 393-2125
  Horn Lake **(G-2210)**

CABLE & OTHER PAY TELEVISION DISTRIBUTION

Cable One Inc ....G 601 833-7991
  McComb **(G-3245)**

CABLE & PAY TELEVISION SVCS: Closed Circuit

Omega System Specialists LLC ....G 901 334-6742
  Nesbit **(G-3655)**

CABLE & PAY TELEVISION SVCS: Direct Broadcast Satellite

High Edge Inc ....F 601 326-2025
  Jackson **(G-2440)**

CABLE: Coaxial

Trilogy Communications Inc ....C 601 932-4461
  Flowood **(G-1404)**
Trilogy Communications Inc ....D 601 932-4461
  Pearl **(G-4154)**

CAFES

Cottons Cafe LLC ....G 662 380-1463
  Oxford **(G-3949)**

CALCULATING & ACCOUNTING EQPT

Triton Automatic Teller Mchs ....G 228 575-3292
  Long Beach **(G-2957)**

CALIBRATING SVCS, NEC

AA Calibration Services LLC ....F 662 716-0202
  Yazoo City **(G-5620)**
Gibson Electric Motor Svc Inc ....G 228 762-4923
  Pascagoula **(G-4033)**

CAMERA & PHOTOGRAPHIC SPLYS STORES

Alarm Company Inc ....F 601 898-3105
  Madison **(G-3077)**

CAMERAS & RELATED EQPT: Photographic

Quantum Scientific Imaging Inc ....F 601 795-8824
  Poplarville **(G-4389)**

CAMPERS: Truck, Slide-In

M and S Sales Inc ....G 662 453-6111
  Greenwood **(G-1637)**

CAMSHAFTS

Custom Cams Inc ....G 662 534-4881
  New Albany **(G-3678)**

CANDLES

Blue Deer Candles LLP ....G 662 275-2016
  West Point **(G-5538)**
Button Up Candles ....G 317 522-8060
  Vicksburg **(G-5349)**
Candle Creations By Melinda ....G 601 477-4942
  Ellisville **(G-1248)**
Candlelore Inc ....G 662 312-1060
  Starkville **(G-4932)**
Candles By Valorie ....G 601 394-3153
  Richton **(G-4528)**
Cozzytymzz Candles LLC ....G 662 471-1607
  New Albany **(G-3677)**
Desirepath Mississippi LLC ....E 662 324-2231
  Starkville **(G-4940)**
Eighty-Five 15 Candle Co LLC ....G 601 324-3064
  McComb **(G-3249)**
Flambeaux Candle Company ....G 769 251-0142
  Pearl **(G-4118)**
Flambeaux Cocktail Candle LLC ....G 601 826-1642
  Ridgeland **(G-4583)**
Fossil Creek Candle Co LLC ....G 601 730-3130
  Gloster **(G-1514)**
Fragrant Flames ....G 601 845-0759
  Florence **(G-1324)**
Grassroots A Natural Co LLC ....G 662 601-8808
  Columbus **(G-981)**
James H Kemp ....G 601 876-2331
  Tylertown **(G-5273)**
Laura Jane Company LLC ....G 662 629-0550
  Holly Springs **(G-2181)**
Lemon Tree Candles ....G 662 621-4312
  Clarksdale **(G-773)**
Lisas Candles ....G 601 384-7406
  Meadville **(G-3277)**
Love Your Light Candle Company ....G 769 572-1733
  Brandon **(G-415)**
Oxford Candle Company LLC ....G 662 816-7429
  Oxford **(G-3985)**
Pathway Candles ....G 601 297-0484
  Hattiesburg **(G-2040)**
Purple Label Candles ....G 601 955-2217
  Jackson **(G-2554)**
Purvis Jewelry Candles ....G 601 270-9687
  Picayune **(G-4288)**
Purvis Jewelry Candles LLC ....G 601 794-8977
  Purvis **(G-4449)**
Son Light Candles and More LLC ....G 228 263-1661
  Gulfport **(G-1874)**
Southern Design Finds ....G 662 893-4303
  Byhalia **(G-606)**
Spirit Lifters Scented Candles ....G 210 802-0149
  Biloxi **(G-281)**
Timber Creek Candles ....G 601 818-6400
  Madison **(G-3159)**
Timothy D Jeter ....G 662 266-0968
  Blue Mountain **(G-293)**
Torchd LLC ....G 601 717-2044
  Jackson **(G-2609)**
Waveland Candle Company LLC ....G 228 220-4716
  Waveland **(G-5487)**
Wicks N Candle Company ....G 662 891-4237
  Saltillo **(G-4724)**
Wicks N More Inc ....E 662 205-4025
  Mooreville **(G-3444)**

CANDLES: Wholesalers

Scented Creations ....G 601 362-5926
  Jackson **(G-2575)**

CANDY & CONFECTIONS: Fruit, Chocolate Covered, Exc Dates

Sugar -N- Spice Confections ....G 901 210-6181
  Horn Lake **(G-2213)**

CANDY & CONFECTIONS: Nuts, Candy Covered

Ada Newson ....G 601 810-6614
  Richland **(G-4498)**

CANDY & CONFECTIONS: Popcorn Balls/Other Trtd Popcorn Prdts

Southern Kernels ....G 601 336-9080
  Hattiesburg **(G-2061)**
Yum Yums Gourmet Popcorn LLC ....G 662 470-6047
  Southaven **(G-4922)**

CANDY, NUT & CONFECTIONERY STORE: Popcorn, Incl Caramel Corn

Yum Yums Gourmet Popcorn LLC ....G 662 470-6047
  Southaven **(G-4922)**

CANDY, NUT & CONFECTIONERY STORES: Candy

Nandys Candy & Ice Factory ....G 601 362-9553
  Jackson **(G-2515)**

CANDY: Hard

Miss Polka DOT Lollipop ....G 601 325-1779
  Hattiesburg **(G-2024)**

CANNED SPECIALTIES

Shelter From Rain ....G 601 454-7602
  Jackson **(G-2579)**

CANS: Metal

Crown Cork & Seal Usa Inc ....B 662 563-7664
  Batesville **(G-102)**
H&M Metal Express LLC ....G 601 798-4600
  Carriere **(G-693)**

CANVAS PRDTS: Boat Seats

Southern Sttch Canvas Uphl LLC ....G 228 234-2515
  Gulfport **(G-1876)**

CARBIDES

Aquavest ....G 662 287-0302
  Corinth **(G-1057)**

CARBON BLACK

Delta-Energy Group LLC ....G 601 348-4610
  Natchez **(G-3555)**

CARBURETORS

Borgwrner Emssions Systems LLC ....A 662 473-3100
  Water Valley **(G-5464)**
Southern Carburetor ....G 601 400-3716
  Jackson **(G-2589)**

CARDS: Identification

Sevlo Solutions LLC ....G 662 312-9507
  Starkville **(G-4970)**

CARPET & UPHOLSTERY CLEANING SVCS

Alfords Decorating Center ....G 662 455-3552
  Greenwood **(G-1612)**

CARPETS & RUGS: Tufted

Mohawk Steel Company ....G 601 467-6959
  Hattiesburg **(G-2030)**

CARPETS, RUGS & FLOOR COVERING

Belgique Inc ....G 601 368-1975
  Jackson **(G-2336)**
Biltrite Ripley Operations LLC ....G 662 837-9231
  Ripley **(G-4654)**
Boxcar Flooring Company LLC ....G 662 871-1417
  Saltillo **(G-4708)**
Dixie Mat LLC ....F 601 876-2427
  Sandy Hook **(G-4727)**
Fibrix LLC ....D 662 844-5595
  Tupelo **(G-5133)**
L and H Investment Inc ....G 601 636-4642
  Vicksburg **(G-5387)**

354

2019 Harris Directory of
Mississippi Manufacturers

(G-0000) Company's Geographic Section entry number

PRODUCT SECTION

CHEMICALS: Aluminum Sulfate

Serviceknight ....G....... 601 906-2810
Brandon (G-451)

Superior Mfg Group Inc ....D....... 601 544-8119
Moselle (G-3462)

Usaccess LLC ....E....... 601 806-5034
Monticello (G-3440)

CARPETS: Hand & Machine Made

D D Rushing ....G....... 601 656-8842
Philadelphia (G-4213)

CARS: Electric

Chuck Ryan Cars Inc ....G....... 228 864-9706
Long Beach (G-2932)

CASES: Carrying, Clothing & Apparel

Nicholes Cture Fashion Btq LLC..........G....... 601 493-6469
Natchez (G-3600)

Watkins Mayola ....G....... 601 826-8310
Jackson (G-2626)

CASTERS

Casters Den ....G....... 662 593-3214
Iuka (G-2286)

CASTINGS GRINDING: For The Trade

B B Stump Grinding.............................G....... 601 506-0997
Florence (G-1314)

B-Gone Stump Grinding Service ....G....... 228 762-2196
Pascagoula (G-4020)

C & M Tree Svc Stump Grinding...........G....... 662 675-8884
Coffeeville (G-842)

Capt Mikes Stump Grinding and ....G....... 985 892-9162
Picayune (G-4259)

Grind ....G....... 662 567-5211
Houston (G-2243)

CASTINGS: Bronze, NEC, Exc Die

Brimmer-Turan Fndry & Mch LLC ....G....... 228 896-9669
Gulfport (G-1745)

CASTINGS: Die, Aluminum

Leggett & Platt Incorporated................G....... 662 842-5704
Tupelo (G-5175)

Rossville Aluminum Castings ....F....... 662 301-1147
Senatobia (G-4801)

CASTINGS: Steel

Southern Cast Products Inc ....C....... 601 482-8518
Meridian (G-3401)

CAT BOX FILLER

Blue Mountain Refining Company ....D....... 662 685-4386
Blue Mountain (G-289)

CATALOG & MAIL-ORDER HOUSES

Ion Chemical Company ....G....... 601 781-0604
Carthage (G-717)

Proshop Inc ....G....... 662 333-7511
Myrtle (G-3513)

CATTLE WHOLESALERS

Russell Trucking ....G....... 662 563-2616
Batesville (G-122)

CEMENT: Hydraulic

Lafarge North America Inc ....E....... 601 859-4488
Canton (G-666)

CEMENT: Masonry

Pooles Stone & Masonry Contrs ....G....... 662 438-6643
Belmont (G-201)

CEMENT: Portland

RC Lonestar Inc ....G....... 601 442-8651
Natchez (G-3611)

River Cement Co ....G....... 601 442-4881
Natchez (G-3614)

CEMETERY & FUNERAL DIRECTOR'S EQPT & SPLYS WHOLESALERS

Rome Chenille & Supply Co Inc ....G....... 662 286-9947
Corinth (G-1116)

CERAMIC FIBER

Mackies Slip Inc ....G....... 601 722-4395
Seminary (G-4783)

Wesley Inc ....G....... 601 731-9288
Foxworth (G-1438)

CHAIN: Welded, Made From Purchased Wire

Webster - Portalloy Chains Inc ....C....... 419 447-8232
Meridian (G-3419)

CHANGE MAKING MACHINES

Hunter Engineering Company ....G....... 769 524-4949
Jackson (G-2445)

CHARCOAL

Kingsford Manufacturing Co ....G....... 510 271-6581
Glen (G-1507)

CHARCOAL: Activated

Calgon Carbon Corporation..................D....... 228 533-7171
Bay Saint Louis (G-139)

Hybrid Plastics Incorporated ....E....... 601 544-3466
Hattiesburg (G-1997)

CHEMICAL ELEMENTS

Elements Estate Sales ....G....... 601 482-4099
Meridian (G-3334)

CHEMICAL PROCESSING MACHINERY & EQPT

Champion Chemical Company LLC .....G....... 601 720-8908
Ruleville (G-4696)

CHEMICAL SPLYS FOR FOUNDRIES

Willie B Sims Jr CPA Pllc ....G....... 601 545-3930
Hattiesburg (G-2084)

CHEMICALS & ALLIED PRDTS WHOLESALERS, NEC

Baker Petrolite LLC..............................F....... 601 649-1955
Laurel (G-2739)

CTA Products Group LLC.....................G....... 662 536-1446
Southaven (G-4866)

Hancock Equipment & Oil Co LLC ....G....... 662 726-4556
Brooksville (G-555)

Helena Chemical Company ....G....... 662 563-9631
Batesville (G-108)

Socrates Garrett Entps Inc ....F....... 601 896-0084
Jackson (G-2585)

CHEMICALS & ALLIED PRDTS, WHOLESALE: Alcohols

Bottle Tree Beverage Co LLC ....F....... 601 667-3038
Jackson (G-2340)

CHEMICALS & ALLIED PRDTS, WHOLESALE: Alkalines

Xooma Worldwide.................................G....... 662 548-5361
Southaven (G-4920)

CHEMICALS & ALLIED PRDTS, WHOLESALE: Carbon Dioxide

Alig LLC ....F....... 601 829-9020
Brandon (G-361)

CHEMICALS & ALLIED PRDTS, WHOLESALE: Chemicals, Indl

Amerimac Chemical Co ....G....... 601 918-8321
Jackson (G-2328)

CHEMICALS & ALLIED PRDTS, WHOLESALE: Chlorine

Allied Universal Corp ....F....... 601 477-2550
Ellisville (G-1245)

CHEMICALS & ALLIED PRDTS, WHOLESALE: Detergent/Soap

Chemical Products & Systems ....G....... 601 354-1919
Jackson (G-2358)

CHEMICALS & ALLIED PRDTS, WHOLESALE: Detergents

Marietta American Inc..........................C....... 662 892-6959
Olive Branch (G-3870)

CHEMICALS & ALLIED PRDTS, WHOLESALE: Plastics Prdts, NEC

Curbell Plastics Inc.............................D....... 888 477-8173
Brandon (G-384)

CHEMICALS & ALLIED PRDTS, WHOLESALE: Plastics Sheets & Rods

M S Rubber Company...........................F....... 601 948-2575
Jackson (G-2474)

CHEMICALS & ALLIED PRDTS, WHOLESALE: Spec Clean/Sanitation

Taylor Industries LLC ....G....... 601 856-8439
Madison (G-3157)

CHEMICALS & OTHER PRDTS DERIVED FROM COKING

Smith Chemical Company.....................G....... 901 849-4074
Olive Branch (G-3911)

CHEMICALS, AGRICULTURE: Wholesalers

Helena Agri-Enterprises LLC ....G....... 662 283-3990
Winona (G-5600)

Woodson Flying Service Inc ....G....... 662 983-4274
Bruce (G-563)

CHEMICALS: Agricultural

Agriliance LLC ....F....... 662 738-4940
Brooksville (G-552)

Amerimac Synergy Veterans LLC ....G....... 601 326-3400
Jackson (G-2330)

Bayer Cropscience LP ....F....... 662 686-9235
Leland (G-2885)

Direct AG Source ....G....... 901 246-1487
Nesbit (G-3650)

Drexel Chemical Company ....E....... 662 363-1791
Tunica (G-5098)

E I Du Pont De Nemours & Co ....B....... 228 762-0870
Pascagoula (G-4030)

Ergon Biofuels LLC ....E....... 601 636-1976
Vicksburg (G-5368)

Gha Enterprises Incorporated ....G....... 601 812-7739
Jackson (G-2425)

Loveland Products Inc ....E....... 662 335-3394
Greenville (G-1565)

Magnolia Mobility LLC ....G....... 601 400-7292
Vicksburg (G-5392)

Monsanto Company..............................C....... 662 827-7212
Hollandale (G-2166)

Nufarm Americas Inc ....G....... 708 375-9010
Greenville (G-1584)

Odom Industries Inc ....C....... 601 735-0088
Waynesboro (G-5508)

Odom Industries Inc ....E....... 601 776-2035
Pachuta (G-4014)

Pinnacle Agriculture Dist Inc ....G....... 662 265-5828
Inverness (G-2276)

CHEMICALS: Alcohols

Bottle Tree Beverage Co LLC ....F....... 601 667-3038
Jackson (G-2340)

CHEMICALS: Aluminum Sulfate

Chemtrade Chemicals US LLC..............G....... 601 799-2380
Nicholson (G-3730)

Employee Codes: A=Over 500 employees, B=251-500
C=101-250, D=51-100, E=20-50, F=10-19, G=1-9

2019 Harris Directory of
Mississippi Manufacturers

355

CHEMICALS: Aluminum Sulfate

PRODUCT SECTION

Geo Specialty Chemical Inc .... G 601 587-7481
Monticello *(G-3431)*

CHEMICALS: Alums

Southern Ionics Incorporated .... E 662 494-3055
West Point *(G-5563)*
Southern Ionics Incorporated .... E 662 495-2583
West Point *(G-5564)*
Southern Ionics Incorporated .... G 662 328-0516
Columbus *(G-1028)*

CHEMICALS: Ammonium Compounds, Exc Fertilizers, NEC

Restora-Life Minerals Inc .... G 601 789-5545
Bay Springs *(G-172)*

CHEMICALS: Anhydrous Ammonia

CF Industries Inc .... C 662 746-4131
Yazoo City *(G-5625)*

CHEMICALS: Caustic Soda

Olin Corporation .... C 662 281-7900
Oxford *(G-3979)*

CHEMICALS: Formaldehyde

Koch Industries Inc .... F 601 785-6523
Taylorsville *(G-5055)*

CHEMICALS: Fuel Tank Or Engine Cleaning

Diversified Petroleum Inc .... G 601 727-4926
Pachuta *(G-4013)*

CHEMICALS: High Purity, Refined From Technical Grade

Bluff City Service Company .... G 662 534-2500
New Albany *(G-3675)*
Helena Agri-Enterprises LLC .... G 662 283-3990
Winona *(G-5600)*

CHEMICALS: Hydrogen Peroxide

Eko Peroxide LLC .... G 662 240-8571
Columbus *(G-968)*

CHEMICALS: Inorganic, NEC

3 F Chimica Americas Inc .... G 662 369-2843
Aberdeen *(G-5)*
Baker Petrolite .... G 601 442-2401
Natchez *(G-3522)*
Benny Evans .... G 601 264-8903
Hattiesburg *(G-1927)*
Channel Chemical Corporation .... E 228 864-6199
Gulfport *(G-1750)*
Chemours Company Fc LLC .... E 228 255-2100
Pass Christian *(G-4078)*
Desiccare Inc .... E 601 932-0405
Richland *(G-4513)*
Engelhard .... G 601 948-3966
Jackson *(G-2401)*
Exide Technologies .... F 601 936-7788
Pearl *(G-4116)*
Exide Technologies .... G 601 845-2281
Florence *(G-1323)*
Helena Chemical Company .... G 662 383-0004
Friars Point *(G-1442)*
Odom Industries Inc .... C 601 735-0088
Waynesboro *(G-5508)*
Odom Industries Inc .... E 601 776-2035
Pachuta *(G-4014)*

CHEMICALS: NEC

Agri-Afc LLC .... E 601 783-6080
Magnolia *(G-3188)*
Alvix Laboratories LLC .... E 601 714-1677
Ocean Springs *(G-3740)*
Basf-Chemical Co .... G 478 951-9985
Brandon *(G-369)*
BEC Fire and Safety LLC .... G 601 498-9108
Sumrall *(G-5034)*
CTA Products Group LLC .... G 662 536-1446
Southaven *(G-4866)*
Delta Protein Intl Inc .... F 662 279-8728
Sunflower *(G-5046)*
Helena Chemical Company .... G 662 563-9631
Batesville *(G-108)*

Highside Chemicals Inc .... G 228 896-9220
Gulfport *(G-1807)*
Ion Chemical Company .... G 601 781-0604
Carthage *(G-717)*
Kdl Solutions LLC .... G 601 434-0508
Hattiesburg *(G-2005)*
Niteo Products LLC .... D 662 429-0405
Hernando *(G-2144)*
Niteo Products LLC .... D 662 429-8292
Hernando *(G-2145)*
Odom Industries Inc .... E 601 776-2035
Pachuta *(G-4014)*
Rainbow Spring Water Inc .... F 228 769-6262
Pascagoula *(G-4063)*
Sille Biofuels LLC .... G 601 400-2227
Jackson *(G-2581)*
Squelchfire Inc .... G 601 434-2048
Hattiesburg *(G-2066)*
T & L Specialty Company Inc .... E 662 842-8143
Tupelo *(G-5236)*
Taylor Industries LLC .... G 601 856-8439
Madison *(G-3157)*
Way Manufacture Inc .... E 601 749-0362
Picayune *(G-4302)*

CHEMICALS: Organic, NEC

BASF Corporation .... C 601 948-3966
Jackson *(G-2335)*
CTA Products Group LLC .... G 662 536-1446
Southaven *(G-4866)*
Elevance Natchez Inc .... F 601 442-5330
Natchez *(G-3559)*
Ergon Biofuels LLC .... E 601 636-1976
Vicksburg *(G-5368)*
Ergon Ethanol Inc .... G 601 933-3000
Flowood *(G-1359)*
Hybrid Plastics Incorporated .... E 601 544-3466
Hattiesburg *(G-1997)*
Ion Chemical Company .... G 601 781-0604
Carthage *(G-717)*
Nouryon Pulp & Prfmce Chem LLC ... F 662 327-0400
Columbus *(G-1011)*
Nufarm Americas Inc .... G 708 375-9010
Greenville *(G-1584)*

CHEMICALS: Reagent Grade, Refined From Technical Grade

Polychemie Inc .... E 228 533-5555
Bay Saint Louis *(G-150)*

CHEMICALS: Sodium/Potassium Cmpnds,Exc Bleach,Alkalies/Alum

Allied Universal Corp .... F 601 477-2550
Ellisville *(G-1245)*

CHEMICALS: Water Treatment

Solen Inc .... E 601 833-0403
Brookhaven *(G-535)*

CHICKEN SLAUGHTERING & PROCESSING

Peco Foods Inc .... A 601 764-4964
Bay Springs *(G-169)*
Sanderson Farms Inc Proc Div .... A 601 428-5261
Laurel *(G-2845)*
Sanderson Farms Inc Proc Div .... A 601 684-9375
Summit *(G-5021)*
Shamrock Farm .... G 601 277-3053
Hazlehurst *(G-2105)*
William R Gatewood .... G 601 636-0107
Vicksburg *(G-5446)*

CHILDREN'S WEAR STORES

Carters Inc .... G 662 844-2667
Tupelo *(G-5119)*

CHIPPER MILL

Chip Jones Mill Inc .... F 601 876-6943
Columbia *(G-886)*
Chips Gloster Inc .... F 601 225-4405
Gloster *(G-1512)*

CHLORINE

Amerimac Chemical Co .... G 601 918-8321
Jackson *(G-2328)*

Olin Corporation .... C 662 234-4056
Oxford *(G-3980)*

CHOCOLATE, EXC CANDY FROM BEANS: Chips, Powder, Block, Syrup

Nandys Candy & Ice Factory .... G 601 362-9553
Jackson *(G-2515)*
Robicheauxs Specialty Candy .... F 601 795-6833
Poplarville *(G-4392)*

CIGARETTE & CIGAR PRDTS & ACCESS

Suds N Squares .... G 662 827-9991
Hollandale *(G-2168)*

CIRCUIT BOARDS, PRINTED: Television & Radio

Peavey Electronics Corporation .... B 601 483-5365
Decatur *(G-1177)*

CIRCUITS: Electronic

Connection Laboratories Inc .... G 662 429-1097
Hernando *(G-2126)*
E M F Corp .... E 601 743-2794
De Kalb *(G-1163)*
Temputech Inc .... F 662 838-3698
Byhalia *(G-608)*

CLAY MINING, COMMON

Clay Kentucky-Tennessee Co .... E 662 382-5262
Crenshaw *(G-1132)*
Wheat Construction Inc .... G 601 772-9074
Poplarville *(G-4399)*

CLAY: Ground Or Treated

Oil-Dri Production Company .... D 662 837-9263
Ripley *(G-4666)*

CLEANERS: Boiler Tube

Mini Mtrs Unlimited Sls & Svc .... G 662 356-4900
Steens *(G-4991)*

CLEANING EQPT: Commercial

Garrett Rowland G .... G 601 954-9841
Jackson *(G-2422)*
Hancock Equipment & Oil Co LLC ..... G 662 726-4556
Brooksville *(G-555)*

CLEANING EQPT: High Pressure

Bardo & Co .... G 601 397-1167
Kosciusko *(G-2690)*
Pressure Pro .... G 601 331-7070
Ridgeland *(G-4619)*

CLEANING EQPT: Janitors' Carts

Saf T Cart Inc .... E 662 624-6492
Clarksdale *(G-782)*

CLEANING OR POLISHING PREPARATIONS, NEC

Charlie Chemical and Supply .... G 662 332-9262
Greenville *(G-1537)*
Spic-N-Span Crew LLC .... G 601 248-2090
McComb *(G-3268)*
Sun-Pine Corporation Ltd .... E 601 825-2463
Canton *(G-680)*
Sun-Pine Corporation Ltd .... D 601 825-2463
Brandon *(G-464)*

CLEANING PRDTS: Ammonia, Household

Rjb Enterprise Inc .... E 202 830-3508
Gulfport *(G-1863)*

CLEANING PRDTS: Automobile Polish

Daves Mobile Car Wash .... G 601 940-6855
Ridgeland *(G-4570)*
R & M Paint Designs .... G 601 503-3631
Jackson *(G-2556)*

2019 Harris Directory of
Mississippi Manufacturers

(G-0000) Company's Geographic Section entry number

PRODUCT SECTION

CLOTHING: Coats & Suits, Men's & Boys'

CLEANING PRDTS: Indl Plant Disinfectants Or Deodorants

Davis Specialty Chemicals Inc ....G....... 601 856-5774
Ridgeland (G-4571)

CLEANING PRDTS: Polishing Preparations & Related Prdts

Frank Bradford Womack ....G....... 601 955-1841
Hazlehurst (G-2096)

CLEANING PRDTS: Specialty

Baxters Prssure Wshg..........................G....... 601 825-2990
Brandon (G-370)
Bell Environmental Svcs LLC ....G....... 662 873-4551
Delta City (G-1180)
Garrett Rowland G ....G....... 601 954-9841
Jackson (G-2422)
Industrial Cleaning Svcs LLC ....F 662 397-6735
Saltillo (G-4712)
Way Manufacture Inc ....G....... 601 749-0362
Picayune (G-4302)

CLEANING SVCS

Blue Note Management LLC ....F 601 281-1881
Oxford (G-3943)

CLEANING SVCS: Industrial Or Commercial

Dungans Outdoor Solutions Co ....G....... 228 382-7156
Ocean Springs (G-3753)

CLIPBOARDS: Wood

Cortez Byrd Chips Inc ....E 601 835-0333
Bogue Chitto (G-301)

CLIPS & FASTENERS, MADE FROM PURCHASED WIRE

Acco Brands USA LLC ....G....... 800 541-0094
Booneville (G-314)

CLOTHING & ACCESS STORES

Stewarts Screen Printing ....G....... 601 932-8310
Jackson (G-2669)

CLOTHING & ACCESS, WOMEN, CHILD & INFANT, WHOL: Scarves

Heritage Yarns ....G....... 601 956-1478
Jackson (G-2439)

CLOTHING & ACCESS, WOMEN, CHILDREN & INFANT, WHOL: Uniforms

Landau Uniforms Incorporated ....E 662 895-7200
Olive Branch (G-3864)

CLOTHING & ACCESS: Costumes, Theatrical

C & D Jarnagin Company Inc...............E 662 287-4977
Corinth (G-1062)
C & D Jarnagin Company Inc...............F 662 287-4977
Corinth (G-1063)
Gail McInnis......................................G....... 601 261-5077
Hattiesburg (G-1973)

CLOTHING & ACCESS: Handicapped

Swell O Phonic.....................................G....... 601 981-3547
Jackson (G-2601)

CLOTHING & ACCESS: Hospital Gowns

Dignity Garments LLC ....G....... 601 941-4636
Madison (G-3096)

CLOTHING & ACCESS: Men's Miscellaneous Access

Bo Enterprises Inc ....F 662 720-1211
Booneville (G-320)
Bo Enterprises Inc ....G....... 601 483-5571
Meridian (G-3311)
Golden Manufacturing Co Inc...............F 662 728-1300
Marietta (G-3215)
Yank Threads LLC ....G....... 601 201-3934
Jackson (G-2639)

CLOTHING & APPAREL STORES: Custom

J S Iupes ....G....... 601 856-7776
Madison (G-3112)
Monogram Express ....G....... 601 825-1248
Brandon (G-425)
T Shirt Shop & Design Firm LLC ....G....... 662 329-9911
Columbus (G-1036)

CLOTHING & FURNISHINGS, MEN'S & BOYS', WHOLESALE: Shirts

Harper Industries Inc ....G....... 601 947-2746
Lucedale (G-2999)
Southern Prtg & Silk Screening.............F 228 452-7309
Pass Christian (G-4095)

CLOTHING & FURNISHINGS, MEN'S & BOYS', WHOLESALE: Uniforms

Landau Uniforms Incorporated ....E 662 895-7200
Olive Branch (G-3864)

CLOTHING & FURNISHINGS, MEN/BOY, WHOL: Hats, Scarves/Gloves

Stryder & Associates LLC.....................G....... 662 579-8703
Cleveland (G-809)

CLOTHING STORES: Formal Wear

Formal Affair..G....... 228 497-7500
Gautier (G-1492)

CLOTHING STORES: Shirts, Custom Made

Park Avenue Printing.............................G....... 601 876-9095
Tylertown (G-5279)

CLOTHING STORES: T-Shirts, Printed, Custom

Airbrush & Signs By Debby ....G....... 601 656-6953
Philadelphia (G-4202)
Cap Co ....G....... 601 384-3939
Bude (G-568)
Gator Grafix Inc ....G....... 601 376-9004
Jackson (G-2423)
Ink Spot Inc...F 662 236-1985
Oxford (G-3960)
Tylertown Times ....F 601 876-5111
Tylertown (G-5289)

CLOTHING STORES: Teenage

Maelstrom Square LLC.........................G....... 470 378-9064
Pascagoula (G-4048)

CLOTHING STORES: Uniforms & Work

Lott Enterprises Inc ....G....... 601 932-4698
Jackson (G-2654)

CLOTHING STORES: Unisex

Dub Street Fashion Center LLC............G....... 601 483-0036
Meridian (G-3330)
Venevaa Jos LLC ....G....... 850 501-4040
Gulfport (G-1891)

CLOTHING STORES: Work

Choctaw Glove & Safety Co Inc............G....... 601 774-5555
Union (G-5296)
Golden Manufacturing Co Inc...............E 662 728-8200
Marietta (G-3214)
McNeely Plastic Products Inc ....E 601 926-1000
Clinton (G-830)
Springer Dry Goods..............................F 662 263-8144
Maben (G-3051)

CLOTHING: Access

Big River Classics Inc ....G....... 601 856-6607
Pearl (G-4107)
Coastal Waters LLC ....G....... 662 769-2944
Starkville (G-4935)
Cole Tempra Helmet & Vest LLC ....G....... 601 317-3842
Jackson (G-2361)
Ears Jewlery Box Sp Fashions ....G....... 769 234-1771
Foxworth (G-1429)
Smooth Transitions LLC ....G....... 601 493-3787
Fayette (G-1302)

CLOTHING: Aprons, Harness

Datco International Inc ....F 248 593-9142
Columbus (G-959)
Datco International Inc ....F 662 327-3995
Columbus (G-960)

CLOTHING: Athletic & Sportswear, Men's & Boys'

Asics America Corporation....................F 662 895-6800
Byhalia (G-577)
Reebok International Ltd ....G....... 228 822-9222
Gulfport (G-1861)
Ruleville Manufacturing Co Inc ....D....... 662 756-4363
Ruleville (G-4699)
Tuohys J Sptg Gods of Columbus ....E 662 328-1440
Columbus (G-1040)
Under Armour Inc ....G....... 228 864-2791
Gulfport (G-1888)
Under Armour Inc ....G....... 662 298-5269
Southaven (G-4918)
Varsity Pro Inc ....G....... 662 628-4172
Calhoun City (G-645)

CLOTHING: Athletic & Sportswear, Women's & Girls'

Reebok International Ltd ....F 228 822-9222
Gulfport (G-1861)

CLOTHING: Baker, Barber, Lab/Svc Ind Apparel, Washable, Men

Landau Uniforms Incorporated ....E 662 895-7200
Olive Branch (G-3864)

CLOTHING: Bathing Suits & Swimwear, Girls, Children & Infant

Backyard Escapes ....G....... 228 868-3938
Long Beach (G-2923)

CLOTHING: Belts

Thomas Larry Hearn............................G....... 601 922-2700
Jackson (G-2606)

CLOTHING: Blouses, Women's & Girls'

Alex Carol Limited ....G....... 601 956-0536
Ridgeland (G-4547)
Crystal Springs Apparel LLC ....E 601 856-8831
Ridgeland (G-4568)
Pvh Corp ....G....... 228 863-0017
Gulfport (G-1857)
Varsity Pro Inc ....G....... 662 628-4172
Calhoun City (G-645)

CLOTHING: Bridal Gowns

Belles & Beaus....................................G....... 228 396-1771
Diberville (G-1197)

CLOTHING: Burial

Destiny Apparel LLC............................G....... 228 383-2665
Biloxi (G-236)

CLOTHING: Children & Infants'

Carters Inc ....G....... 662 844-2667
Tupelo (G-5119)
Tuohys J Sptg Gods of Columbus ....E 662 328-1440
Columbus (G-1040)

CLOTHING: Children's, Girls'

Tuohys J Sptg Gods of Columbus ....E 662 328-1440
Columbus (G-1040)

CLOTHING: Coats & Suits, Men's & Boys'

Brigade Manufacturing Inc...................D....... 601 827-5062
Tylertown (G-5265)
Ek Embroidery LLC...............................G....... 228 868-8469
Gulfport (G-1777)
Golden Manufacturing Co Inc...............E 662 728-8200
Marietta (G-3214)
M & M Industries Inc ....E 601 799-2615
Mc Neill (G-3241)

Employee Codes: A=Over 500 employees, B=251-500
C=101-250, D=51-100, E=20-50, F=10-19, G=1-9

2019 Harris Directory of
Mississippi Manufacturers

357

PRODUCT

CLOTHING: Coats, Hunting & Vests, Men's

PRODUCT SECTION

CLOTHING: Coats, Hunting & Vests, Men's

Hunter Trading Company LLC ....G....... 866 521-5012
Olive Branch *(G-3849)*
Icon Outdoors LLC ....G....... 662 895-3651
Olive Branch *(G-3850)*

CLOTHING: Coats, Overcoats & Vests

Tullahoma Industries LLC ....G...... 601 222-2255
Tylertown *(G-5288)*

CLOTHING: Dresses

Runway Liquidation LLC ....G....... 406 388-1988
Meridian *(G-3393)*
Runway Liquidation LLC ....G....... 406 259-1280
New Albany *(G-3693)*
Runway Liquidation LLC ....G....... 816 671-7922
Gulfport *(G-1865)*

CLOTHING: Dresses & Skirts

Hemline ....G....... 601 898-3456
Ridgeland *(G-4589)*

CLOTHING: Furs

Southern Fur Design ....G....... 601 936-2005
Flowood *(G-1400)*

CLOTHING: Gloves & Mittens, Knit

Choctaw Glove & Safety Co Inc ....D....... 662 724-4178
Noxapater *(G-3731)*

CLOTHING: Gowns & Dresses, Wedding

Jasper & Assoc ....G....... 601 321-0811
Jackson *(G-2459)*
Le Fleur De Luis ....G....... 228 875-6628
Ocean Springs *(G-3769)*
Magnolia Mariee LLC ....G....... 601 446-6400
Natchez *(G-3583)*

CLOTHING: Gowns, Formal

A Stitch In Time ....G....... 662 257-0661
Amory *(G-33)*

CLOTHING: Hats & Caps, Leather

Consumer Products America LLC ......G....... 601 613-8583
Jackson *(G-2366)*

CLOTHING: Hats & Caps, NEC

Hat Shack Inc ....G....... 601 264-1017
Hattiesburg *(G-1983)*

CLOTHING: Hosiery, Pantyhose & Knee Length, Sheer

Magnolia Hosiery Mill Inc ....G....... 662 286-2221
Corinth *(G-1099)*

CLOTHING: Hospital, Men's

Sanders Home Health Inc ....G....... 662 335-2326
Greenville *(G-1596)*
Superior Uniform Group Inc ....G....... 662 834-4485
Lexington *(G-2905)*

CLOTHING: Jackets & Vests, Exc Fur & Leather, Women's

Landing ....G....... 601 707-7505
Madison *(G-3119)*

CLOTHING: Jackets, Overall & Work

Golden Manufacturing Co Inc ....B....... 662 454-3428
Golden *(G-1525)*

CLOTHING: Jeans, Men's & Boys'

West Group Holding Company LLC ......G....... 662 871-2344
Shannon *(G-4821)*

CLOTHING: Maternity

Henns Nest Inc ....G....... 601 268-3577
Hattiesburg *(G-1989)*

CLOTHING: Men's & boy's clothing, nec

Red Square Clothing Co ....G....... 601 853-8960
Ridgeland *(G-4622)*

CLOTHING: Pants, Work, Men's, Youths' & Boys'

Team Safety Apparel Inc ....E....... 601 892-3571
Crystal Springs *(G-1158)*

CLOTHING: Robes & Dressing Gowns

Foh Group Inc ....C....... 601 795-6470
Poplarville *(G-4382)*

CLOTHING: Service Apparel, Women's

Landau Uniforms Incorporated ....E....... 662 895-7200
Olive Branch *(G-3864)*

CLOTHING: Shirts

Blauer Manufacturing Co Inc ....D....... 662 281-0097
Oxford *(G-3942)*
County of Hancock ....G....... 228 467-2100
Bay St Louis *(G-177)*
Garan Incorporated ....E....... 601 656-1501
Philadelphia *(G-4215)*
Garan Manufacturing Corp ....C....... 662 323-4731
Starkville *(G-4945)*
Mossyoak Wildlife Conservatory ....G....... 662 495-9292
West Point *(G-5554)*

CLOTHING: Shirts & T-Shirts, Knit

Mojo Uprisin Inc ....G....... 662 983-8892
Bruce *(G-561)*

CLOTHING: Shirts, Dress, Men's & Boys'

Pvh Corp ....G....... 228 863-0017
Gulfport *(G-1857)*

CLOTHING: Shirts, Knit

American Apparel Inc ....G....... 601 654-9211
Lena *(G-2894)*

CLOTHING: Shirts, Sports & Polo, Men's & Boys'

Crystal Springs Apparel LLC ....E....... 601 856-8831
Ridgeland *(G-4568)*

CLOTHING: Shirts, Uniform, From Purchased Materials

Golden Manufacturing Co Inc ....B....... 662 454-3428
Golden *(G-1525)*

CLOTHING: Slacks, Girls' & Children's

Garan Manufacturing Corp ....C....... 662 323-4731
Starkville *(G-4945)*

CLOTHING: Socks

Lost Sock LLC ....G....... 601 946-1155
Madison *(G-3120)*

CLOTHING: Suits, Men's & Boys', From Purchased Materials

Kepler Boys Wear LLC ....G....... 601 738-1664
Vicksburg *(G-5386)*

CLOTHING: T-Shirts & Tops, Knit

Harper Industries Inc ....G....... 601 947-2746
Lucedale *(G-2999)*
Southern Prtg & Silk Screening ....F....... 228 452-7309
Pass Christian *(G-4095)*

CLOTHING: T-Shirts & Tops, Women's & Girls'

Boo Enterprises LLC ....G....... 228 475-8929
Moss Point *(G-3470)*
Garan Incorporated ....E....... 601 656-1501
Philadelphia *(G-4215)*
Garan Manufacturing Corp ....C....... 662 323-4731
Starkville *(G-4945)*

(continued)

Landing ....G....... 601 707-7505
Madison *(G-3119)*

CLOTHING: Trousers & Slacks, Men's & Boys'

Golden Manufacturing Co Inc ....E....... 662 728-8200
Marietta *(G-3214)*
Supreme International LLC ....E....... 601 638-2403
Vicksburg *(G-5425)*

CLOTHING: Underwear, Women's & Children's

Alex Carol Limited ....G....... 601 956-0536
Ridgeland *(G-4547)*

CLOTHING: Uniforms, Military, Men/Youth, Purchased Materials

Golden Manufacturing Co Inc ....B....... 662 454-3428
Golden *(G-1525)*
Pine Belt Processing Inc ....E....... 601 785-4476
Stonewall *(G-4998)*

CLOTHING: Uniforms, Policemen's, From Purchased Materials

Blauer Manufacturing Co Inc ....D....... 662 281-0097
Oxford *(G-3941)*
Blauer Manufacturing Co Inc ....D....... 662 281-0097
Oxford *(G-3942)*

CLOTHING: Uniforms, Team Athletic

Pak Uniform & EMB Shoppe LLC ....G....... 228 365-6695
Pascagoula *(G-4058)*

CLOTHING: Uniforms, Work

A and Y Uniform Shop ....G....... 601 553-1377
Meridian *(G-3293)*
Blauer Manufacturing Co Inc ....D....... 662 281-0097
Oxford *(G-3941)*
Blauer Manufacturing Co Inc ....D....... 662 281-0097
Oxford *(G-3942)*
Destiny Apparel LLC ....G....... 228 383-2665
Biloxi *(G-236)*
Mississippi Prison Inds Corp ....F....... 601 969-5760
Jackson *(G-2503)*
Reed Manufacturing Company Inc ....E....... 662 842-4472
Tupelo *(G-5216)*

CLOTHING: Work Apparel, Exc Uniforms

Pak Uniform & EMB Shoppe LLC ....G....... 228 365-6695
Pascagoula *(G-4058)*

CLOTHING: Work, Men's

G&K Services LLC ....E....... 601 788-6375
Richton *(G-4531)*
Malt Industries Inc ....E....... 601 794-4200
Purvis *(G-4446)*
National Textile and AP Inc ....E....... 601 892-4356
Hazlehurst *(G-2102)*
Ruleville Manufacturing Co Inc ....D....... 662 756-4363
Ruleville *(G-4699)*

CLUTCHES, EXC VEHICULAR

Marine Gears Inc ....E....... 662 332-8716
Greenville *(G-1568)*

COAL & OTHER MINERALS & ORES WHOLESALERS

Advanced Dynamics Inc ....G....... 601 677-3423
Preston *(G-4426)*

COAL MINING SERVICES

Waste Placement Inc ....G....... 601 362-5343
Jackson *(G-2625)*

COAL MINING: Bituminous Coal & Lignite-Surface Mining

Liberty Fuels Company LLC ....G....... 601 737-7000
Ackerman *(G-25)*
Liberty Fuels Company LLC ....D....... 601 737-7000
De Kalb *(G-1166)*

2019 Harris Directory of
Mississippi Manufacturers

(G-0000) Company's Geographic Section entry number

358

PRODUCT SECTION

COMMUTATORS: Electronic

Mississippi Lignite Mining Co ....C 662 387-5200
Ackerman (G-28)

COATING SVC

Booneville Industrial Coatings ....G 662 720-1147
Booneville (G-321)
Caston Creat & Coatings LLC...............G 228 588-0055
Lucedale (G-2987)
Coastal Prtective Coatings LLC ....G 214 882-8036
Lucedale (G-2988)
Gulf Coast Protective Coating ....G 601 261-9862
Hattiesburg (G-1978)
Quality Coatings Oxford......................G 662 234-2944
Oxford (G-3997)
Wynnes Custom Coatings ....G 601 664-3474
Pearl (G-4159)

COATING SVC: Aluminum, Metal Prdts

Double G Coatings Company LP...........D 601 371-3460
Jackson (G-2389)
Field Coatings LLC ....G 228 896-3535
Gulfport (G-1786)
Okin America Inc................................D 662 566-1000
Shannon (G-4817)

COATING SVC: Hot Dip, Metals Or Formed Prdts

Aztec Industries Inc ....F 601 939-8522
Richland (G-4504)

COATING SVC: Metals & Formed Prdts

Applied Safety Coatings Inc ....G 601 940-3004
Raymond (G-4483)
Precoat Metals Inc ....G 601 372-0325
Jackson (G-2549)
Systems Electro Coating LLC...............D 601 407-2340
Madison (G-3156)
W E Birdsong Associates Inc ....G 601 939-7448
Florence (G-1337)

COATING SVC: Metals, With Plastic Or Resins

K D M Custom Coatings LLC................F 662 842-9725
Tupelo (G-5166)

COATINGS: Air Curing

World Class Athltcsurfaces Inc ....F 662 686-9997
Leland (G-2893)

COATINGS: Epoxy

Belzona Mississippi Inc.......................G 228 475-1110
Moss Point (G-3469)
Lining & Coating Solutions LLC............F 662 893-0984
Olive Branch (G-3865)

COFFEE SVCS

1529 Coffee Company ....G 662 315-6951
Amory (G-32)

COIL WINDING SVC

Dubose Electric..................................G 601 425-5116
Laurel (G-2764)

COILS & TRANSFORMERS

Fortson Industrial Supply Co................G 601 948-2053
Jackson (G-2411)
Kuhlman Electric Corporation ....B 601 892-4661
Crystal Springs (G-1144)

COILS: Electric Motors Or Generators

Modine Grenada LLC...........................A 662 229-2000
Grenada (G-1692)
Modine Grenada LLC...........................A 662 226-3421
Grenada (G-1693)

COKE: Calcined Petroleum, Made From Purchased Materials

Rain Cii Carbon LLC ....G 601 794-2753
Purvis (G-4451)

COKE: Petroleum & Coal Derivative

Loresco Inc ....G 601 544-7490
Purvis (G-4445)

COLLEGES, UNIVERSITIES & PROFESSIONAL SCHOOLS

Johnson Education Firm LLC................G 662 347-9150
Greenville (G-1560)

COLORS: Pigments, Inorganic

Chemours Company Fc LLC.................E 228 255-2100
Pass Christian (G-4078)

COMB MOUNTINGS

Antonio Tarrell LLC............................G 662 983-2486
Bruce (G-559)

COMBS, EXC HARD RUBBER

Yalls Products ....G 601 391-3698
Madison (G-3173)

COMFORTERS & QUILTS, FROM MANMADE FIBER OR SILK

David Buford ....G 662 714-3031
Water Valley (G-5466)

COMMERCIAL & OFFICE BUILDINGS RENOVATION & REPAIR

Ustx Contract Services NC Inc ....E 512 894-0008
Corinth (G-1126)

COMMERCIAL ART & GRAPHIC DESIGN SVCS

Bear Creek Apparel Promotions............G 601 259-8508
Canton (G-648)
Ben Sessums ....G 601 856-3401
Madison (G-3085)
Global Screen Printing LLC ....G 601 919-2345
Brandon (G-399)
Magnetic Arrow LLC ....G 601 653-2932
Biloxi (G-264)
Mid South Publications Inc ....G 662 256-8209
Amory (G-48)
Park Avenue Printing..........................G 601 876-9095
Tylertown (G-5279)
Vizionz Unlimited LLC ....G 601 272-5040
Jackson (G-2622)

COMMERCIAL EQPT WHOLESALERS, NEC

Ag Spray Equipment Inc ....G 662 453-4524
Greenwood (G-1610)
City of Biloxi......................................C 228 435-6217
Biloxi (G-228)

COMMERCIAL EQPT, WHOL: Soda Fountain Fixtures, Exc Refrig

Brown Bottling Group Inc ....G 601 442-5805
Natchez (G-3539)

COMMERCIAL EQPT, WHOLESALE: Comm Cooking & Food Svc Eqpt

Mississippi Poultry ....G 601 732-8670
Morton (G-3450)

COMMERCIAL EQPT, WHOLESALE: Neon Signs

Stanley McCaffrey Signs......................G 228 832-0885
Richland (G-4525)

COMMERCIAL EQPT, WHOLESALE: Store Fixtures & Display Eqpt

H & L Millworks Inc ....G 228 392-9913
Biloxi (G-250)

COMMERCIAL PRINTING & NEWSPAPER PUBLISHING COMBINED

Bay St Louis Newspapers Inc...............E 228 467-5474
Bay Saint Louis (G-135)

Carpenter Newsmedia LLC ....G 601 445-3618
Natchez (G-3544)
Commercial Dispatch Pubg Inc ....D 662 328-2424
Columbus (G-955)
Deer Creek Publishing Company ....G 662 873-4354
Rolling Fork (G-4680)
George County Times ....G 601 947-2967
Lucedale (G-2997)
Grenada Newspaper Inc ....E 662 226-4321
Grenada (G-1681)
Gulf Publishing Company Inc ....C 228 896-2100
Gulfport (G-1801)
Houston Newspapers Inc ....F 662 456-3771
Houston (G-2245)
J O Emmerich & Assoc Inc ....E 601 684-2421
McComb (G-3254)
Jackson Advocate Inc ....G 601 948-4122
Jackson (G-2451)
Lawrence County Press Inc ....G 601 587-2781
Monticello (G-3435)
Montgomery Publishing Co Inc ....F 662 283-1131
Winona (G-5604)
New Albany Publishing Company ....F 662 534-6321
New Albany (G-3688)
Scott Publishing Inc ....G 601 469-2561
Forest (G-1425)
Tunica Publishing Co Inc ....G 662 363-1511
Tunica (G-5103)
Vicksburg Printing and Pubg Co ....D 601 636-4545
Vicksburg (G-5438)
Yazoo Newspaper Co Inc ....F 662 746-4911
Yazoo City (G-5653)

COMMODITY CONTRACTS BROKERS, DEALERS

Michael A Dent ....G 601 543-0157
Hattiesburg (G-2023)

COMMON SAND MINING

J J Ferguson Sand & Grav Inc ....C 662 453-5451
Greenwood (G-1630)

COMMUNICATIONS EQPT & SYSTEMS, NEC

Dvani Innovation Inc...........................G 601 992-5069
Brandon (G-392)

COMMUNICATIONS EQPT: Microwave

Microwave Service Co ....G 662 842-7620
Tupelo (G-5187)

COMMUNICATIONS SVCS: Data

Innovative Circuits Inc........................F 662 287-2007
Corinth (G-1092)

COMMUNICATIONS SVCS: Internet Connectivity Svcs

Awesome Sight and Sound...................G 601 215-8846
Picayune (G-4255)

COMMUNICATIONS SVCS: Internet Host Svcs

Localnet ....G 601 774-9338
Union (G-5300)

COMMUNICATIONS SVCS: Online Svc Providers

T G Ferguson Company ....G 662 563-0806
Batesville (G-127)

COMMUNICATIONS SVCS: Telephone, Data

Glenn Weise ....G 228 435-4455
Biloxi (G-244)

COMMUNITY COLLEGE

Johnson Education Firm LLC................G 662 347-9150
Greenville (G-1560)

COMMUTATORS: Electronic

Dufour Battery One Source LLC...........G 601 693-1500
Meridian (G-3333)

Employee Codes: A=Over 500 employees, B=251-500
C=101-250, D=51-100, E=20-50, F=10-19, G=1-9

2019 Harris Directory of
Mississippi Manufacturers

PRODUCT

359

COMPOSITION STONE: Plastic

COMPOSITION STONE: Plastic

Seemann Composites LLC ....D....... 228 314-8000
Gulfport *(G-1867)*

COMPOST

Creekside Envmtl Pdts LLC ....G....... 662 617-5553
Starkville *(G-4936)*

COMPRESSORS: Air & Gas

Compressed Air Tech Inc ....G....... 662 890-9782
Olive Branch *(G-3827)*
Tecumseh Products Company ....G....... 662 566-2231
Verona *(G-5336)*
Wood Industries Inc...............................E....... 662 454-0005
Belmont *(G-203)*

COMPRESSORS: Refrigeration & Air Conditioning Eqpt

Tecumseh Products Company ....G....... 662 566-2231
Verona *(G-5336)*

COMPRESSORS: Wholesalers

Archrock Inc..G....... 601 444-0055
Columbia *(G-880)*
Norton Equipment Company ....F....... 662 838-7900
Byhalia *(G-593)*

COMPUTER & COMPUTER SOFTWARE STORES

Chuck Jennings ....G....... 601 668-5704
Raymond *(G-4486)*
Harlan Services LLC ....G....... 601 513-5318
Magee *(G-3177)*
Landmark Spatial Solutions LLC...........G....... 662 769-5344
Starkville *(G-4955)*
Office Depot Inc ....E....... 662 378-2995
Greenville *(G-1585)*
Stanley McCaffrey Signs ....G....... 228 832-0885
Richland *(G-4525)*
T G Ferguson Company ....G....... 662 563-0806
Batesville *(G-127)*

COMPUTER & COMPUTER SOFTWARE STORES: Peripheral Eqpt

Business Systems Inc............................G....... 601 957-1500
Jackson *(G-2351)*

COMPUTER & COMPUTER SOFTWARE STORES: Personal Computers

Claude W Carnathan..............................G....... 662 834-3855
Lexington *(G-2899)*

COMPUTER & COMPUTER SOFTWARE STORES: Software & Access

Data Systems Management Inc ....F....... 601 925-6270
Clinton *(G-821)*

COMPUTER & COMPUTER SOFTWARE STORES: Software, Bus/Non-Game

Mac Financial Mgmt LLC.......................G....... 844 622-6468
Magnolia *(G-3193)*

COMPUTER & DATA PROCESSING EQPT REPAIR & MAINTENANCE

Cytec Software Systems Inc ....F....... 601 362-1612
Jackson *(G-2373)*
Incapitalmgcom LLC..............................G....... 601 268-0103
Hattiesburg *(G-1999)*

COMPUTER & OFFICE MACHINE MAINTENANCE & REPAIR

Business Communications Inc............E....... 601 898-1890
Ridgeland *(G-4559)*
Computer Works LLC.............................G....... 228 696-8889
Moss Point *(G-3475)*
Simple Solutions ....G....... 228 588-9509
Moss Point *(G-3498)*
T G Ferguson Company ....G....... 662 563-0806
Batesville *(G-127)*

Tech Smart LLC......................................G....... 662 417-8780
Grenada *(G-1707)*
Tronicsales ....G....... 769 218-0432
Jackson *(G-2613)*

COMPUTER & SFTWR STORE: Modem, Monitor, Terminal/Disk Drive

Incapitalmgcom LLC..............................G....... 601 268-0103
Hattiesburg *(G-1999)*
Rhino Graphics ....G....... 601 445-8777
Natchez *(G-3613)*

COMPUTER PERIPHERAL EQPT REPAIR & MAINTENANCE

Business Systems Inc............................G....... 601 957-1500
Jackson *(G-2351)*

COMPUTER PERIPHERAL EQPT, NEC

Adventure Leadership Cons LLC..........G....... 662 915-6736
Southaven *(G-4852)*
Bay Technical Associates Inc...............D....... 228 563-7334
Long Beach *(G-2925)*
Black Box Corporation ....G....... 601 939-9051
Flowood *(G-1346)*
Central Delta Cmnty Dev Corp...............G....... 601 215-0367
Jackson *(G-2357)*
Claude W Carnathan..............................G....... 662 834-3855
Lexington *(G-2899)*
Cosco Authorized Xerox Dealer ....G....... 601 568-5006
Philadelphia *(G-4212)*
Emma Roberts ....G....... 601 638-3062
Vicksburg *(G-5366)*
Howard Industries Inc ....F....... 601 399-5053
Ellisville *(G-1258)*
International Laser Sups LLC.................G....... 601 788-6475
Richton *(G-4535)*
Key Tronic Corporation ....G....... 662 665-3410
Corinth *(G-1094)*
Logitech Inc ....G....... 510 713-5429
Olive Branch *(G-3866)*
Tech Smart LLC......................................G....... 662 417-8780
Grenada *(G-1707)*
Thyssenkrupp Elevator Corp.................C....... 662 223-4025
Walnut *(G-5458)*
Tronicsales ....G....... 769 218-0432
Jackson *(G-2613)*
Wiredless Network Inc............................F....... 601 665-5307
Canton *(G-685)*

COMPUTER PERIPHERAL EQPT: Input Or Output

Storsoft Technology Corp ....G....... 954 436-9292
Gulfport *(G-1881)*

COMPUTER PROGRAMMING SVCS

Magnetic Arrow LLC ....G....... 601 653-2932
Biloxi *(G-264)*
Omni Technologies LLC..........................G....... 601 427-5898
Ridgeland *(G-4614)*
Storsoft Technology Corp ....G....... 954 436-9292
Gulfport *(G-1881)*
T G Ferguson Company ....G....... 662 563-0806
Batesville *(G-127)*

COMPUTER PROGRAMMING SVCS: Custom

Data Systems Management Inc ....F....... 601 925-6270
Clinton *(G-821)*

COMPUTER RELATED SVCS, NEC

Omni Technologies LLC..........................G....... 601 427-5898
Ridgeland *(G-4614)*

COMPUTER SOFTWARE DEVELOPMENT

Connect Technology LLC........................G....... 601 914-1713
Jackson *(G-2365)*
Nvision Solutions Inc ....D....... 228 242-0010
Diamondhead *(G-1192)*
Stormcom LLC ....G....... 601 918-5401
Jackson *(G-2598)*

COMPUTER SOFTWARE DEVELOPMENT & APPLICATIONS

Bdm It Services (us) Inc ....G....... 601 274-0347
Quitman *(G-4458)*
Kopis Mobile LLC....................................G....... 601 345-1753
Flowood *(G-1375)*
Relevant Design Studios LLC.................G....... 601 736-0663
Columbia *(G-918)*
Watthour Engineering Co Inc ....E....... 601 933-0900
Pearl *(G-4158)*
Wilson Solutions LLC.............................G....... 662 319-6063
Aberdeen *(G-22)*

COMPUTER SOFTWARE SYSTEMS ANALYSIS & DESIGN: Custom

Grayco Systems & Consulting ....G....... 601 583-0430
Hattiesburg *(G-1976)*
Jabr LLC...G....... 601 502-5587
Flowood *(G-1369)*
JMS Manufacturing Inc...........................G....... 601 514-0660
Lucedale *(G-3005)*
Vizaura LLC ....G....... 228 363-4048
Diamondhead *(G-1193)*

COMPUTER STORAGE DEVICES, NEC

Glassbridge Enterprises Inc ....G....... 662 280-6268
Southaven *(G-4875)*
Martin Caderwood ....G....... 714 456-0800
Oxford *(G-3970)*

COMPUTER TERMINALS

Incapitalmgcom LLC..............................G....... 601 268-0103
Hattiesburg *(G-1999)*

COMPUTER-AIDED DESIGN SYSTEMS SVCS

JMS Manufacturing Inc...........................G....... 601 514-0660
Lucedale *(G-3005)*

COMPUTERS, NEC

Columbia Computers Inc ....G....... 601 736-2204
Columbia *(G-888)*
Computer Consultant ....G....... 228 818-4486
Ocean Springs *(G-3750)*
Howard Technology Solutions ....G....... 601 428-2200
Laurel *(G-2781)*
Incapitalmgcom LLC..............................G....... 601 268-0103
Hattiesburg *(G-1999)*
Mississippi State University ....G....... 662 325-3149
Mississippi State *(G-3425)*
Omni Technologies LLC..........................G....... 601 427-5898
Ridgeland *(G-4614)*
PC Ace Computer Service.......................G....... 662 494-1925
West Point *(G-5557)*
Somefa LLC ....G....... 601 506-1808
Jackson *(G-2586)*
Storsoft Technology Corp ....G....... 954 436-9292
Gulfport *(G-1881)*
William M Stewart ....G....... 662 393-7950
Horn Lake *(G-2215)*

COMPUTERS, PERIPHERALS & SOFTWARE, WHOLESALE: Software

T G Ferguson Company ....G....... 662 563-0806
Batesville *(G-127)*

COMPUTERS: Mainframe

Cytec Software Systems Inc ....F....... 601 362-1612
Jackson *(G-2373)*

COMPUTERS: Personal

Apple Dapple ....G....... 228 539-3100
Gulfport *(G-1729)*
Harlan Services LLC ....G....... 601 513-5318
Magee *(G-3177)*
Olives & Apples LLC...............................G....... 662 419-0224
Pontotoc *(G-4352)*
Pink Apple ....G....... 901 412-3926
Southaven *(G-4892)*
TNT Investments LLC.............................G....... 228 860-8207
Biloxi *(G-284)*
Wilson Solutions LLC.............................G....... 662 319-6063
Aberdeen *(G-22)*

2019 Harris Directory of Mississippi Manufacturers

(G-0000) Company's Geographic Section entry number

PRODUCT SECTION

CONCRETE: Ready-Mixed

CONCRETE CURING & HARDENING COMPOUNDS

Hunt Process Corp-Southern ....G 601 856-8811
Ridgeland (G-4591)

CONCRETE PLANTS

Southeastern Concrete Co Inc ....E 601 545-7811
Hattiesburg (G-2058)

Southeastern Concrete Co Inc ....E 601 544-7000
Hattiesburg (G-2059)

CONCRETE PRDTS

Blaylocks Cement Manufacturing ....G 225 627-1006
Liberty (G-2910)

Castle Enclosures LLC ....G 228 238-6216
Biloxi (G-225)

Famco Company Inc ....F 228 831-4649
Gulfport (G-1782)

Foley Products Company ....E 601 792-3202
Prentiss (G-4417)

Forterra Pipe & Precast LLC ....E 662 526-0368
Como (G-1047)

H&R Consultants LLC ....G 601 613-2288
Edwards (G-1238)

Hills Brothers Cnstr & Engrg ....G 662 837-7415
Falkner (G-1294)

Legacy Vulcan LLC ....G 601 544-3523
Petal (G-4191)

Macon Ready-Mix Concrete Co ....F 662 726-4733
Macon (G-3065)

Mahans Concrete Septic Tanks ....G 662 234-3767
Water Valley (G-5471)

Mid South Cast Stone ....G 662 890-7669
Olive Branch (G-3874)

MMC Materials Inc ....G 662 327-1927
Columbus (G-1006)

MMC Materials Inc ....D 601 973-2093
Jackson (G-2508)

Pine Belt Ready Mix Concrete ....F 601 425-2559
Laurel (G-2819)

Quikrete Companies LLC ....E 601 798-6021
Picayune (G-4290)

CONCRETE PRDTS, PRECAST, NEC

Custom Precast Products Inc ....E 601 796-8531
Lumberton (G-3027)

Evans Refrigeration ....G 601 372-3482
Jackson (G-2404)

J J Ferguson Prestress- ....E 662 453-5451
Greenwood (G-1629)

Mid-South Ornamental Concrete ....F 662 224-3170
Michigan City (G-3423)

S & S Striping ....G 662 449-4498
Hernando (G-2153)

Tindall Corporation ....C 228 246-0798
Moss Point (G-3502)

CONCRETE: Asphaltic, Not From Refineries

Polycon International LLC ....F 601 898-1024
Madison (G-3141)

CONCRETE: Dry Mixture

Precision Packaging Inc ....E 601 352-2016
Jackson (G-2548)

CONCRETE: Ready-Mixed

Americrete Inc ....F 601 485-6507
Meridian (G-3297)

Americrete Ready Mix Inc ....G 601 656-5590
Philadelphia (G-4204)

Apac-Mississippi Inc ....G 662 494-5772
West Point (G-5535)

Apac-Mississippi Inc ....G 662 343-9300
Aberdeen (G-9)

B & B Concrete Co Inc ....F 662 286-6407
Corinth (G-1060)

B & B Concrete Co Inc ....G 662 489-2233
Pontotoc (G-4321)

B & B Concrete Co Inc ....F 662 234-7088
Oxford (G-3937)

B & B Concrete Co Inc ....G 662 837-3221
Ripley (G-4653)

B & B Concrete Co Inc ....F 662 534-2626
New Albany (G-3673)

B & B Concrete Co Inc ....E 662 869-1927
Saltillo (G-4706)

B & B Concrete Co Inc ....E 662 842-6312
Verona (G-5327)

B & B Concrete Co Inc ....E 662 842-7305
Tupelo (G-5111)

Baker Ready Mix & Cnstr LLC ....E 662 773-8054
Louisville (G-2964)

Bayou Concrete LLC ....D 228 868-1264
Gulfport (G-1736)

Bayou Concrete LLC ....G 601 898-4000
Ridgeland (G-4553)

Bayou Concrete LLC ....F 228 762-8911
Pascagoula (G-4022)

Canton Concrete ....E 601 859-4547
Canton (G-652)

Cemex Cnstr Mtls Fla LLC ....E 888 263-7093
Como (G-1046)

CMC Readymix Inc ....F 662 252-6479
Holly Springs (G-2174)

Coast Concrete Company Inc ....E 228 863-1364
Gulfport (G-1755)

Danny Berry ....G 601 276-6200
Summit (G-5010)

Delta Industries Inc ....F 601 634-6001
Vicksburg (G-5361)

Delta Industries Inc ....E 228 896-7400
Gulfport (G-1770)

Delta Industries Inc ....G 601 783-6030
Magnolia (G-3190)

Delta Industries Inc ....G 228 539-9333
Saucier (G-4752)

Delta Industries Inc ....G 601 849-2661
Magee (G-3176)

Delta Industries Inc ....D 601 354-3801
Jackson (G-2380)

Delta Industries Inc ....G 601 833-1166
Brookhaven (G-489)

Delta Industries Inc ....G 662 746-6646
Yazoo City (G-5631)

Delta Industries Inc ....F 601 825-7531
Brandon (G-387)

Delta Industries Inc ....G 228 475-2419
Moss Point (G-3476)

Delta Industries Inc ....G 662 323-7224
Starkville (G-4939)

Delta Industries Inc ....E 601 948-4245
Crystal Springs (G-1141)

Delta Industries Inc ....G 601 354-3801
Jackson (G-2381)

Delta Industries Inc ....G 601 792-4286
Prentiss (G-4416)

Dooley Brothers Ready Mix Inc ....G 601 888-3530
Woodville (G-5617)

Franklin Ready Mix Inc ....G 601 384-5445
Bude (G-569)

George B Ready ....G 662 429-7088
Hernando (G-2132)

Golden Triange Ready Mix Inc ....F 662 328-0153
Columbus (G-979)

Gulf Concrete Co Inc ....F 601 798-3181
Picayune (G-4269)

H S I Ready Mix ....G 601 798-1665
Picayune (G-4270)

Hernando Redi Mix Inc ....F 662 429-7571
Nesbit (G-3653)

HI Tech Concrete Inc ....G 228 452-2125
Pass Christian (G-4087)

Hills Brothers Cnstr & Engrg ....G 662 837-7415
Falkner (G-1294)

Huey P Stockstill LLC ....C 601 798-2981
Picayune (G-4273)

Iuka Concrete Products LLC ....G 662 423-6238
Iuka (G-2294)

J J Ferguson Sand & Grav Inc ....C 662 453-5451
Greenwood (G-1630)

John Ready Damond ....G 601 587-4381
Monticello (G-3434)

Jones Ready Mix LLC ....G 601 222-1919
Sandy Hook (G-4730)

Lamar Concrete Inc ....F 601 794-0049
Purvis (G-4444)

Legacy Vulcan LLC ....E 228 452-3000
Long Beach (G-2943)

Legacy Vulcan LLC ....G 228 474-1414
Moss Point (G-3483)

Lexington Concrete & Block Co ....F 601 859-4547
Canton (G-668)

Lexington Concrete & Block Co ....G 662 834-3892
Lexington (G-2904)

Lucedale Ready Mix Concrete Co ....G 601 947-4741
Lucedale (G-3009)

Macon Ready-Mix Concrete Co ....F 662 726-4733
Macon (G-3065)

Metro Concrete ....G 228 284-1660
Gulfport (G-1830)

Milligan Ready Mix Inc ....F 662 423-6238
Iuka (G-2300)

MMC Materials Inc ....G 601 898-4000
Ridgeland (G-4608)

MMC Materials Inc ....G 601 928-4941
Wiggins (G-5586)

MMC Materials Inc ....G 601 774-0443
Union (G-5302)

MMC Materials Inc ....G 601 833-4900
Brookhaven (G-519)

MMC Materials Inc ....E 601 684-7373
McComb (G-3260)

MMC Materials Inc ....F 601 469-2741
Forest (G-1423)

MMC Materials Inc ....G 601 582-8493
Petal (G-4193)

MMC Materials Inc ....G 662 624-9000
Clarksdale (G-776)

MMC Materials Inc ....G 662 332-5407
Greenville (G-1577)

MMC Materials Inc ....E 601 482-7007
Meridian (G-3375)

MMC Materials Inc ....G 662 628-6667
Calhoun City (G-641)

MMC Materials Inc ....D 662 393-7676
Horn Lake (G-2208)

MMC Materials Inc ....D 601 634-8787
Vicksburg (G-5399)

MMC Materials Inc ....G 662 453-9722
Greenwood (G-1642)

MMC Materials Inc ....F 601 268-9599
Hattiesburg (G-2028)

MMC Materials Inc ....D 251 408-0740
Gulfport (G-1833)

MMC Materials Inc ....G 662 887-4031
Greenville (G-1578)

MMC Materials Inc ....G 601 268-3005
Hattiesburg (G-2029)

MMC Materials Inc ....G 601 267-8278
Carthage (G-720)

MMC Materials Inc ....G 601 437-4321
Port Gibson (G-4403)

MMC Materials Inc ....F 601 445-5641
Natchez (G-3590)

MMC Materials Inc ....G 662 327-1927
Columbus (G-1006)

MMC Materials Inc ....D 601 973-2093
Jackson (G-2508)

MMC Materials Inc ....G 662 773-5656
Louisville (G-2975)

MMC Materials Inc ....F 662 323-0644
Starkville (G-4961)

MMC Materials Inc ....G 662 258-6096
Eupora (G-1289)

Morris Ready Mix Inc ....G 662 473-2505
Water Valley (G-5473)

Oxford Sand-Concrete Plant ....G 662 281-0355
Oxford (G-3990)

Pine Belt Ready Mix ....G 601 544-7069
Hattiesburg (G-2043)

Pine Belt Ready Mix Concrete ....F 601 425-2559
Laurel (G-2819)

Pine Belt Ready-Mix Con Inc ....G 601 425-2026
Laurel (G-2820)

Pine Belt Ready-Mix Con Inc ....G 601 765-4813
Collins (G-859)

Ready Mix Dispatch ....G 662 842-6313
Tupelo (G-5215)

Sanderson Redi-Mix Inc ....E 662 256-9301
Amory (G-53)

Sardis Ready Mix LLC ....G 662 512-2170
Byhalia (G-602)

Service Lumber Company Inc ....F 662 873-4334
Rolling Fork (G-4682)

Service Lumber Holding Corp ....G 662 873-4334
Rolling Fork (G-4683)

Southeast Ready Mix Inc ....F 601 735-4823
Waynesboro (G-5515)

Southeastern Concrete Co Inc ....E 601 544-7000
Hattiesburg (G-2057)

Southeastern Concrete Co Inc ....E 601 545-7811
Hattiesburg (G-2058)

Spencer Ready-Mix Jackson Inc ....E 601 981-6080
Jackson (G-2594)

St Catherine Ready Mix Inc ....F 601 445-8891
Natchez (G-3625)

Employee Codes: A=Over 500 employees, B=251-500
C=101-250, D=51-100, E=20-50, F=10-19, G=1-9

2019 Harris Directory of
Mississippi Manufacturers

361

PRODUCT

CONCRETE: Ready-Mixed

PRODUCT SECTION

Stockstill Bros Invstments LLC ....E 601 798-2981
Picayune **(G-4298)**

Terminal ....G 601 636-7781
Vicksburg **(G-5428)**

Townes Construction Co Inc ....F 662 226-4894
Grenada **(G-1709)**

Tri State Ready Mix ....G 662 893-3496
Byhalia **(G-610)**

Tricounty Ready Mix Inc ....F 601 649-2887
Stringer **(G-5005)**

Vicksburg Ready Mix Concrete ....G 601 634-6001
Vicksburg **(G-5441)**

CONFECTIONERY PRDTS WHOLESALERS

So Nuts and Confections LLC ....G 901 398-9650
Horn Lake **(G-2211)**

CONFECTIONS & CANDY

Alicia Vaughn ....G 601 888-7830
Woodville **(G-5615)**

Caramel Factory ....G 662 563-9900
Batesville **(G-101)**

Nandys Candy & Ice Factory ....G 601 362-9553
Jackson **(G-2515)**

Robicheauxs Specialty Candy ....F 601 795-6833
Poplarville **(G-4392)**

Southern Blle Sweet Dsigns LLC ....G 901 598-7938
Southaven **(G-4906)**

CONNECTORS: Electronic

Frank J Miller ....G 601 792-8795
Oak Vale **(G-3734)**

Rehabilitation Svcs Miss Dept ....E 662 335-3359
Greenville **(G-1595)**

CONSTRUCTION & MINING MACHINERY WHOLESALERS

Architectural Concepts ....G 850 471-7081
Brandon **(G-365)**

Caterpillar ....G 662 286-1274
Corinth **(G-1065)**

Larrys Equipment Inc ....G 662 423-0077
Iuka **(G-2298)**

Lyle Machinery Co ....G 601 276-3528
Summit **(G-5017)**

CONSTRUCTION & ROAD MAINTENANCE EQPT: Drags, Road

Duraco Inc ....E 601 932-2100
Pearl **(G-4115)**

CONSTRUCTION EQPT: Backhoes, Tractors, Cranes & Similar Eqpt

Crabtree Manufacturing Inc ....F 662 746-3041
Yazoo City **(G-5629)**

Reuben Allred ....G 601 734-2801
Bogue Chitto **(G-304)**

Richard Fick ....G 601 848-7420
State Line **(G-4988)**

CONSTRUCTION EQPT: Bulldozers

James Rachal ....G 601 442-1460
Church Hill **(G-754)**

CONSTRUCTION EQPT: Dozers, Tractor Mounted, Material Moving

Thompson Dozer & Gravel ....G 601 835-2406
Wesson **(G-5530)**

CONSTRUCTION EQPT: Finishers & Spreaders

Prestige Cnstr & Land Svcs LLC ....G 228 861-1292
Gulfport **(G-1852)**

CONSTRUCTION EQPT: Graders, Road

Holland Grading Service ....G 601 825-2364
Brandon **(G-406)**

CONSTRUCTION EQPT: Hammer Mills, Port, Incl Rock/Ore Crush

Grady Morrow ....G 769 230-6226
Jackson **(G-2428)**

CONSTRUCTION EQPT: Rakes, Land Clearing, Mechanical

Cooperation Jackson LLC ....F 601 355-7224
Jackson **(G-2368)**

Southern Land Solutions LLC ....G 601 622-8581
Terry **(G-5077)**

CONSTRUCTION EQPT: Subgraders

Jj Merchant ....G 601 596-4430
Purvis **(G-4442)**

CONSTRUCTION EQPT: Wrecker Hoists, Automobile

Around Clock Recovery ....G 662 455-1008
Greenwood **(G-1613)**

CONSTRUCTION MATERIALS, WHOL: Concrete/Cinder Bldg Prdts

Metro Concrete ....G 228 284-1660
Gulfport **(G-1830)**

CONSTRUCTION MATERIALS, WHOLESALE: Awnings

Better Signs Inc ....G 662 227-1235
Grenada **(G-1669)**

CONSTRUCTION MATERIALS, WHOLESALE: Block, Concrete & Cinder

Corinth Brick Company Inc ....G 662 287-2442
Corinth **(G-1076)**

CONSTRUCTION MATERIALS, WHOLESALE: Brick, Exc Refractory

Gulf Concrete Co Inc ....F 601 798-3181
Picayune **(G-4269)**

Tupelo Concrete Products Inc ....F 662 842-7811
Tupelo **(G-5243)**

CONSTRUCTION MATERIALS, WHOLESALE: Building Stone

Stone Associates Inc ....G 662 838-4671
Byhalia **(G-607)**

CONSTRUCTION MATERIALS, WHOLESALE: Building Stone, Granite

Jonathan Bigbie ....G 601 498-9890
Petal **(G-4188)**

Simple Stone Solutions ....G 601 206-5566
Jackson **(G-2582)**

CONSTRUCTION MATERIALS, WHOLESALE: Building Stone, Marble

A & W Marble Inc ....G 228 832-5037
Saucier **(G-4748)**

CONSTRUCTION MATERIALS, WHOLESALE: Building, Exterior

Georgia-Pacific LLC ....C 601 785-4721
Columbia **(G-900)**

Gilmore Bros Building Supply ....G 601 825-6292
Brandon **(G-398)**

Hood Industries Inc ....G 601 264-2962
Hattiesburg **(G-1995)**

Smith Cabinet Shop Inc ....E 662 287-2151
Corinth **(G-1119)**

CONSTRUCTION MATERIALS, WHOLESALE: Doors, Sliding

First Coastal Exteriors LLC ....G 769 251-1894
Pearl **(G-4117)**

CONSTRUCTION MATERIALS, WHOLESALE: Fiberglass Building Mat

Baymont Inc ....D 662 454-7993
Golden **(G-1521)**

CONSTRUCTION MATERIALS, WHOLESALE: Millwork

Ash Millworks Inc ....E 601 544-3962
Petal **(G-4184)**

CONSTRUCTION MATERIALS, WHOLESALE: Pallets, Wood

Inca Presswood-Pallets Ltd ....E 662 487-1016
Sardis **(G-4742)**

Windmill Pallet Works Inc ....F 601 876-4498
Tylertown **(G-5291)**

CONSTRUCTION MATERIALS, WHOLESALE: Paving Materials

Blacklidge Emulsions Inc ....E 228 863-3878
Gulfport **(G-1740)**

Cold Mix Inc ....G 662 256-4529
Nettleton **(G-3658)**

CONSTRUCTION MATERIALS, WHOLESALE: Plywood

Roseburg Forest Products Co ....B 662 236-8080
Oxford **(G-4000)**

CONSTRUCTION MATERIALS, WHOLESALE: Sand

Apac-Mississippi Inc ....G 601 376-4000
Richland **(G-4502)**

CONSTRUCTION MATERIALS, WHOLESALE: Septic Tanks

Lees Septic Inc ....F 662 369-9799
Aberdeen **(G-17)**

CONSTRUCTION MATERIALS, WHOLESALE: Sewer Pipe, Clay

Apm LLC ....G 907 279-0204
Gulfport **(G-1728)**

CONSTRUCTION MATERIALS, WHOLESALE: Stucco

Architectural Concepts ....G 850 471-7081
Brandon **(G-365)**

CONSTRUCTION MATERIALS, WHOLESALE: Tile & Clay Prdts

Baymont Inc ....D 662 454-7993
Golden **(G-1521)**

CONSTRUCTION MATERIALS, WHOLESALE: Veneer

Anderson-Tully Company ....B 601 629-3283
Vicksburg **(G-5339)**

CONSTRUCTION MATLS, WHOL: Lumber, Rough, Dressed/Finished

Barge Forest Products Co ....G 662 726-4426
Macon **(G-3055)**

Hankins Lumber Company Inc ....F 662 226-2961
Elliott **(G-1244)**

JC Jourdan Lumber Co Inc ....F 662 423-5238
Iuka **(G-2295)**

JT Shannon Lumber Co Inc ....E 662 393-3765
Horn Lake **(G-2203)**

Lincoln Lumber Co Inc ....D 601 833-4484
Brookhaven **(G-512)**

Magnolia Furniture LLC ....G 662 489-9337
Pontotoc **(G-4342)**

Nslc Southern Inc ....D 601 535-2205
Hermanville **(G-2122)**

Purvis Forest Products Inc ....E 601 794-8593
Purvis **(G-4448)**

2019 Harris Directory of
Mississippi Manufacturers

(G-0000) Company's Geographic Section entry number

PRODUCT SECTION

CONSULTING SVC: Educational

R & J Brown Logging & Trucking ....G...... 601 739-3338
Louin (G-2963)
Rives and Reynolds Lbr Co Inc ....E...... 662 289-3823
Kosciusko (G-2711)
Rogers Lumber Corp ....E...... 601 736-4472
Columbia (G-920)
Thomasson Company ....E...... 601 656-6000
Philadelphia (G-4242)
V & B International Inc ....E...... 601 437-8279
Port Gibson (G-4408)

CONSTRUCTION MTRLS, WHOL: Exterior Flat Glass, Plate/Window

La Rosa Glass Inc ....G...... 228 864-0751
Long Beach (G-2942)

CONSTRUCTION SAND MINING

Lehman-Roberts Company ....F...... 662 429-5237
Hernando (G-2138)

CONSTRUCTION SITE PREPARATION SVCS

Jwb Construction LLC ....F...... 601 439-7190
Mize (G-3427)
Southern Land Solutions LLC ....G...... 601 622-8581
Terry (G-5077)

CONSTRUCTION: Bank

National Bank Builders & Eqp ....F...... 662 781-0702
Walls (G-5450)

CONSTRUCTION: Bridge

J J Ferguson Sand & Grav Inc ....C...... 662 453-5451
Greenwood (G-1630)

CONSTRUCTION: Commercial & Institutional Building

Donald W Mason ....G...... 601 269-3782
Raleigh (G-4475)
Mathis Trucking & Cnstr LLC ....G...... 601 917-0237
Collinsville (G-873)
R W Delaney Construction Co ....D...... 601 442-0352
Natchez (G-3609)

CONSTRUCTION: Commercial & Office Building, New

Castle Hill Design ....G...... 601 918-8234
Canton (G-654)
Domes International Inc ....E...... 662 438-7186
Tishomingo (G-5085)
Tommy L Henderson ....G...... 228 452-4484
Pass Christian (G-4097)
Tropical World Intl LLC ....G...... 228 229-8413
Biloxi (G-285)
W G Yates & Sons Cnstr Co ....A...... 601 656-5411
Philadelphia (G-4248)
Whittington Construction Co ....G...... 601 442-8096
Natchez (G-3640)

CONSTRUCTION: Heavy

Merle E Sullivan ....G...... 662 347-4494
Greenville (G-1572)
Stockstill Land Dev LLC ....G...... 601 273-2409
Poplarville (G-4396)

CONSTRUCTION: Heavy Highway & Street

Apac-Mississippi Inc ....E...... 662 378-8481
Greenville (G-1536)
Apac-Mississippi Inc ....E...... 601 693-5025
Meridian (G-3299)
Huey P Stockstill LLC ....C...... 601 798-2981
Picayune (G-4273)
Lehman-Roberts Company ....F...... 662 563-2100
Batesville (G-113)

CONSTRUCTION: Indl Building & Warehouse

Smiths Machine & Wldg Co Inc ....E...... 601 833-8787
Brookhaven (G-534)

CONSTRUCTION: Indl Building, Prefabricated

Mini Systems Inc ....G...... 662 487-2240
Como (G-1050)

CONSTRUCTION: Indl Buildings, New, NEC

Castle Hill Design ....G...... 601 918-8234
Canton (G-654)
W G Yates & Sons Cnstr Co ....A...... 601 656-5411
Philadelphia (G-4248)

CONSTRUCTION: Indl Plant

Accu-Fab and Construction Inc ....E...... 228 475-0082
Moss Point (G-3465)
Yates Industrial Services LLC ....G...... 601 467-6232
Purvis (G-4454)

CONSTRUCTION: Land Preparation

Shear View Mulching LLC ....G...... 985 637-8402
Poplarville (G-4393)

CONSTRUCTION: Oil & Gas Pipeline Construction

Complete Welding Solutions ....G...... 601 791-5370
Lucedale (G-2989)
Hj Norris LLC ....G...... 228 217-6704
Moss Point (G-3479)
Southeastern E & P Svcs Inc ....G...... 601 849-9218
Magee (G-3186)

CONSTRUCTION: Paper & Pulp Mill

Complete Welding Solutions ....G...... 601 791-5370
Lucedale (G-2989)

CONSTRUCTION: Parking Lot

Apac-Mississippi Inc ....D...... 601 376-4000
Richland (G-4501)
Apac-Mississippi Inc ....G...... 601 376-4000
Richland (G-4502)
McDevitt Enterprises LLC ....G...... 601 453-2290
Meridian (G-3365)

CONSTRUCTION: Pipeline, NEC

Brocato Construction Inc ....G...... 662 563-4473
Batesville (G-100)
Williams Transportation Co LLC ....D...... 601 428-2214
Laurel (G-2874)

CONSTRUCTION: Railroad & Subway

AMS Services LLC ....G...... 662 449-2672
Nesbit (G-3648)

CONSTRUCTION: Railway Roadbed

Precision Asp Sealcoating LLC ....G...... 601 527-6381
Collinsville (G-874)

CONSTRUCTION: Residential, Nec

Donald W Mason ....G...... 601 269-3782
Raleigh (G-4475)
Mathis Trucking & Cnstr LLC ....G...... 601 917-0237
Collinsville (G-873)
McDevitt Enterprises LLC ....G...... 601 453-2290
Meridian (G-3365)
Taylor Brothers Cnstr Co ....G...... 601 636-1749
Vicksburg (G-5427)
Watkins ....G...... 601 752-2526
Ellisville (G-1277)

CONSTRUCTION: Retaining Wall

Hastys Mulch & Stone LLC ....G...... 601 485-2120
Meridian (G-3346)

CONSTRUCTION: Roads, Gravel or Dirt

Pen/Ron Company Inc ....G...... 601 519-5096
Brandon (G-431)
Socrates Garrett Entps Inc ....F...... 601 896-0084
Jackson (G-2585)

CONSTRUCTION: Sewer Line

Taylor Brothers Cnstr Co ....G...... 601 636-1749
Vicksburg (G-5427)
Turner Jimmy Backhoe Dozer Svc ....G...... 662 988-2701
Myrtle (G-3514)

CONSTRUCTION: Single-Family Housing

Cooperation Jackson LLC ....F...... 601 355-7224
Jackson (G-2368)
Jwb Construction LLC ....F...... 601 439-7190
Mize (G-3427)
Prestige Cnstr & Land Svcs LLC ....G...... 228 861-1292
Gulfport (G-1852)
Tommy L Henderson ....G...... 228 452-4484
Pass Christian (G-4097)
Watkins ....G...... 601 752-2526
Ellisville (G-1277)

CONSTRUCTION: Single-family Housing, New

Coleman Builders Inc ....G...... 662 234-0376
Oxford (G-3947)
D&H Construction Cabinetry Inc ....G...... 601 737-2010
Meridian (G-3326)
Whittington Construction Co ....G...... 601 442-8096
Natchez (G-3640)

CONSTRUCTION: Single-family Housing, Prefabricated

Domes International Inc ....E...... 662 438-7186
Tishomingo (G-5085)

CONSTRUCTION: Steel Buildings

Elite Const and Design ....G...... 662 307-2494
Grenada (G-1675)

CONSTRUCTION: Street Surfacing & Paving

Bonds Company Inc ....E...... 601 376-4000
Richland (G-4507)
Superior Asphalt Inc ....C...... 601 376-3000
Byram (G-624)

CONSTRUCTION: Swimming Pools

United Fence Company ....G...... 601 582-0406
Hattiesburg (G-2077)

CONSTRUCTION: Tennis Court

Castle Hill Design ....G...... 601 918-8234
Canton (G-654)

CONSTRUCTION: Transmitting Tower, Telecommunication

Innovative Wireless LLC ....G...... 601 594-1201
Jackson (G-2447)

CONSTRUCTION: Utility Line

Blue Note Management LLC ....F...... 662 281-1881
Oxford (G-3943)

CONSTRUCTION: Water & Sewer Line

Southern Sewage Systems ....G...... 228 832-7400
Saucier (G-4766)

CONSULTING SVC: Business, NEC

Imaging Informatics LLC ....G...... 228 332-0674
Pass Christian (G-4089)
Intellabuy Inc ....G...... 601 249-0508
McComb (G-3253)
Magnolia Accounting Services ....G...... 662 429-5852
Hernando (G-2141)
Rebecca McCallum ....G...... 662 501-0709
Byhalia (G-599)
Relevant Design Studios LLC ....G...... 601 736-0663
Columbia (G-918)
Z A Construction LLC ....F...... 601 259-5276
Mendenhall (G-3291)

CONSULTING SVC: Computer

Intelatool Solutions LLC ....G...... 601 594-8451
Richland (G-4520)

CONSULTING SVC: Educational

Excel By Four LLC ....G...... 228 355-8203
Gulfport (G-1780)

Employee Codes: A=Over 500 employees, B=251-500
C=101-250, D=51-100, E=20-50, F=10-19, G=1-9

2019 Harris Directory of
Mississippi Manufacturers

363

CONSULTING SVC: Engineering

PRODUCT SECTION

CONSULTING SVC: Engineering

Pace Brothers Inc ....G....... 601 736-9225
Columbia *(G-910)*

Patrick Enterprises Inc ....G....... 601 268-1115
Hattiesburg *(G-2041)*

CONSULTING SVC: Financial Management

Mac Financial Mgmt LLC ....G....... 844 622-6468
Magnolia *(G-3193)*

Seago Enterprises Inc ....D....... 601 684-3000
McComb *(G-3265)*

CONSULTING SVC: Management

Relevant Design Studios LLC ....G....... 601 736-0663
Columbia *(G-918)*

Wilcox Energy Company ....G....... 601 442-5191
Natchez *(G-3641)*

CONSULTING SVC: Marketing Management

Pmq Inc ....F....... 662 234-5481
Oxford *(G-3996)*

Uswebworx LLC ....G....... 601 813-8927
Madison *(G-3164)*

Vizionz Unlimited LLC ....G....... 601 272-5040
Jackson *(G-2622)*

Watersprings Media House ....G....... 662 812-1568
Olive Branch *(G-3923)*

CONSULTING SVC: New Business Start Up

Unique Services LLC ....G....... 601 326-9912
Jackson *(G-2616)*

CONSULTING SVC: Online Technology

Stormcom LLC ....G....... 601 918-5401
Jackson *(G-2598)*

CONSULTING SVCS, BUSINESS: Environmental

Greer Environmental Services ....G....... 601 734-2883
Ruth *(G-4701)*

CONSULTING SVCS, BUSINESS: Publishing

Wolf River Press ....G....... 601 372-2679
Jackson *(G-2636)*

CONSULTING SVCS, BUSINESS: Safety Training Svcs

Secorp Indus & Safety Sups Inc ....F....... 601 422-0203
Laurel *(G-2847)*

CONSULTING SVCS, BUSINESS: Sys Engnrg, Exc Computer/Prof

Nvision Solutions Inc ....D....... 228 242-0010
Diamondhead *(G-1192)*

Storsoft Technology Corp ....G....... 954 436-9292
Gulfport *(G-1881)*

CONSULTING SVCS, BUSINESS: Systems Analysis & Engineering

Kelsey Bailey Consulting LLC ....G....... 601 622-8319
Madison *(G-3115)*

CONSULTING SVCS, BUSINESS: Systems Analysis Or Design

Omega-Tec LLC ....G....... 601 750-8082
Vicksburg *(G-5402)*

CONSULTING SVCS: Geological

Patrick Enterprises Inc ....G....... 601 268-1115
Hattiesburg *(G-2041)*

CONSULTING SVCS: Oil

DAvion LLC ....G....... 601 724-5013
Brandon *(G-385)*

Donald L McKinnon ....G....... 601 319-3311
Laurel *(G-2763)*

Harbour Energy Inc ....G....... 601 992-2277
Brandon *(G-403)*

Inland Energy Company Inc ....G....... 601 969-1160
Jackson *(G-2446)*

James R Padgett ....G....... 601 763-3369
Ellisville *(G-1260)*

Rig Managers Inc ....G....... 601 362-5121
Jackson *(G-2565)*

SJ Ellington Inc ....E....... 228 369-0089
Ocean Springs *(G-3786)*

Southeastern Oilfield Pdts LLC ....G....... 601 428-0603
Laurel *(G-2851)*

Sunbelt Resources Inc ....G....... 601 853-8195
Ridgeland *(G-4636)*

Timothy R Oglesby ....G....... 601 835-0673
Bogue Chitto *(G-306)*

Welco Inc ....G....... 601 445-9851
Natchez *(G-3639)*

CONSULTING SVCS: Scientific

Sinhatech ....G....... 662 234-6248
Oxford *(G-4002)*

CONTACT LENSES

J & R Optical Co Inc ....G....... 601 977-0272
Jackson *(G-2450)*

Vision Center PA ....G....... 601 928-3914
Wiggins *(G-5593)*

CONTAINERS, GLASS: Water Bottles

Mississippi Beverage Co Inc ....E....... 601 693-3853
Meridian *(G-3372)*

CONTAINERS: Air Cargo, Metal

Zero Dead Miles LLC ....G....... 769 208-8082
Jackson *(G-2640)*

CONTAINERS: Corrugated

Ability Works Inc ....E....... 662 842-2144
Tupelo *(G-5107)*

Ability Works Inc ....G....... 662 328-0275
Columbus *(G-931)*

Corrugated Services America ....G....... 601 209-6297
Pearl *(G-4112)*

International Paper Company ....C....... 601 932-1422
Jackson *(G-2650)*

Midland Color Corp ....G....... 662 895-4100
Olive Branch *(G-3876)*

Pratt (mississippi Box) Inc ....E....... 601 366-3435
Jackson *(G-2545)*

Pratt Corrugated Holdings Inc ....D....... 601 366-3435
Jackson *(G-2546)*

Texas Packaging ....G....... 214 912-5833
Picayune *(G-4300)*

CONTAINERS: Glass

Owens-Brockway Glass Cont Inc ....F....... 601 584-4800
Hattiesburg *(G-2038)*

CONTAINERS: Metal

Dkh Distributing Inc ....G....... 901 734-4528
Hernando *(G-2129)*

CONTAINERS: Plastic

Jackson Fishing Sptg Accessory ....G....... 662 837-9089
Falkner *(G-1295)*

Southern Diversified Inds Inc ....G....... 662 365-8800
Baldwyn *(G-88)*

Speed Box LLC ....G....... 910 964-7947
Ridgeland *(G-4633)*

CONTAINERS: Sanitary, Food

Pactiv LLC ....E....... 662 585-3151
Fulton *(G-1472)*

CONTAINERS: Shipping, Wood

Ed Dangerfield Const Millwrks ....G....... 662 328-3877
Columbus *(G-967)*

CONTAINERS: Wood

Martin and Sons LLC ....E....... 601 825-4012
Brandon *(G-418)*

CONTRACTOR: Dredging

Townes Construction Co Inc ....F....... 662 226-4894
Grenada *(G-1709)*

CONTRACTOR: Rigging & Scaffolding

Danny Byrd LLC ....E....... 601 649-2524
Laurel *(G-2758)*

Tremac Resteel Inc ....E....... 601 853-3123
Madison *(G-3161)*

CONTRACTORS: Access Control System Eqpt

Chuck Jennings ....G....... 601 668-5704
Raymond *(G-4486)*

CONTRACTORS: Asphalt

Back Bay Lawnscapes LLC ....F....... 228 348-1299
Diberville *(G-1195)*

Precision Asp Sealcoating LLC ....G....... 601 527-6381
Collinsville *(G-874)*

CONTRACTORS: Awning Installation

Quality Alum & HM Imprv Inc ....G....... 662 329-2525
Columbus *(G-1019)*

CONTRACTORS: Building Eqpt & Machinery Installation

D & R Industrial Services LLC ....F....... 601 716-3140
Wiggins *(G-5578)*

Omega System Specialists LLC ....G....... 901 334-6742
Nesbit *(G-3655)*

CONTRACTORS: Building Sign Installation & Mntnce

Better Signs Inc ....G....... 662 227-1235
Grenada *(G-1669)*

J L McCool Contractors Inc ....F....... 228 769-9771
Moss Point *(G-3482)*

Munn Enterprises Inc ....D....... 601 264-7446
Hattiesburg *(G-2035)*

Southern Signs ....G....... 228 255-4122
Pass Christian *(G-4096)*

Southern Signs Inc ....G....... 601 445-5564
Natchez *(G-3624)*

CONTRACTORS: Building Site Preparation

Jwb Construction LLC ....F....... 601 439-7190
Mize *(G-3427)*

Shear View Mulching LLC ....G....... 985 637-8402
Poplarville *(G-4393)*

Southern Land Solutions LLC ....G....... 601 622-8581
Terry *(G-5077)*

CONTRACTORS: Carpentry Work

Omega System Specialists LLC ....G....... 901 334-6742
Nesbit *(G-3655)*

Pickens Hardwoods Inc ....G....... 601 924-1199
Jackson *(G-2539)*

Richard Fick ....G....... 601 848-7420
State Line *(G-4988)*

Taylor Brothers Cnstr Co ....G....... 601 636-1749
Vicksburg *(G-5427)*

CONTRACTORS: Carpentry, Cabinet & Finish Work

Andrews Cabinet Shop ....G....... 662 327-1070
Columbus *(G-935)*

Ash Millworks Inc ....E....... 601 544-3962
Petal *(G-4184)*

H & L Millworks Inc ....G....... 228 392-9913
Biloxi *(G-250)*

Southern Cabinet & Woodwork ....E....... 228 475-0912
Moss Point *(G-3499)*

Stanley D Stokes Jr ....G....... 662 237-6600
Carrollton *(G-703)*

CONTRACTORS: Carpentry, Cabinet Building & Installation

Bill Briscoe ....G....... 662 234-5669
Oxford *(G-3940)*

PRODUCT SECTION

CONTRACTORS: Hot Shot Svcs

Pierce Cabinets Inc............................E 662 840-6795
Tupelo *(G-5204)*

Richards Home Services.....................G...... 228 324-3482
Ocean Springs *(G-3782)*

CONTRACTORS: Carpentry, Finish & Trim Work

Efma Contracting LLC ....F 901 292-7221
Ridgeland *(G-4576)*

CONTRACTORS: Commercial & Office Building

Springer Trckg & Car Crushing ....F 601 649-4238
Laurel *(G-2855)*

Watkins ....G...... 601 752-2526
Ellisville *(G-1277)*

CONTRACTORS: Computer Installation

Tech Smart LLC ....G...... 662 417-8780
Grenada *(G-1707)*

CONTRACTORS: Concrete

Apac-Mississippi Inc ....E 662 378-8481
Greenville *(G-1536)*

Apac-Mississippi Inc ....E 601 693-5025
Meridian *(G-3299)*

Delta Industries Inc ....C 601 354-3801
Jackson *(G-2381)*

Lexington Concrete & Block Co ....F 601 859-4547
Canton *(G-668)*

Taylor Brothers Cnstr Co ....G...... 601 636-1749
Vicksburg *(G-5427)*

CONTRACTORS: Construction Site Cleanup

Prestige Cnstr & Land Svcs LLC ......G...... 228 861-1292
Gulfport *(G-1852)*

Walker Parris.....................................G...... 601 953-3023
Port Gibson *(G-4409)*

CONTRACTORS: Countertop Installation

Avalon Marble LLC ....F 601 798-3378
Picayune *(G-4253)*

Hartson-Kennedy Cabinet Top Co .....D....... 228 896-1548
Gulfport *(G-1805)*

Superior Granite & Quartz ....G...... 662 241-5664
Columbus *(G-1034)*

CONTRACTORS: Demolition, Building & Other Structures

5m Enterprises LLC ....G...... 601 416-0210
Sebastopol *(G-4773)*

Bell Environmental Svcs LLC ....G...... 662 873-4551
Delta City *(G-1180)*

CONTRACTORS: Directional Oil & Gas Well Drilling Svc

Energy Drilling Company ....C 601 446-5259
Natchez *(G-3560)*

Griffin Grffin Exploration LLC.............G...... 601 713-1146
Jackson *(G-2432)*

Helmerich & Payne Intl Drlg Co ....F 601 939-1589
Pearl *(G-4126)*

Performance Drilling Co LLC ....D....... 601 969-6796
Brandon *(G-433)*

River Rads Drectional Drlg LLC ....E 601 778-7179
Moselle *(G-3459)*

River Rads Drectional Drlg LLC ....G...... 601 778-7179
Laurel *(G-2837)*

Rocky BR Directional Drlg LLC ....G...... 601 758-3340
Sumrall *(G-5043)*

W T Drilling Co Inc ....D....... 601 442-1607
Natchez *(G-3636)*

CONTRACTORS: Earthmoving

U S Safety Services Inc ....G...... 601 833-3627
Wesson *(G-5531)*

W S Red Hancock Inc ....F 662 755-0011
Bentonia *(G-213)*

W S Red Hancock Inc ....C 601 399-0605
Ellisville *(G-1275)*

CONTRACTORS: Electrical

Brady Electric Inc...............................F 601 649-7862
Laurel *(G-2742)*

Dubose Electric ....G...... 601 425-5116
Laurel *(G-2764)*

Indianola Electric Co Inc ....F 662 887-3292
Indianola *(G-2266)*

K & T Poultry Sales & Svc Inc ....F 601 764-3918
Bay Springs *(G-167)*

CONTRACTORS: Erection & Dismantling, Poured Concrete Forms

Precision Asp Sealcoating LLC ....G...... 601 527-6381
Collinsville *(G-874)*

CONTRACTORS: Excavating

Ellis Dozer LLC..................................G...... 601 752-2207
Seminary *(G-4778)*

Magnolia Furniture LLC ....G...... 662 489-9337
Pontotoc *(G-4342)*

Stockstill Land Dev LLC ....G...... 601 273-2409
Poplarville *(G-4396)*

Townes Construction Co Inc ....F 662 226-4894
Grenada *(G-1709)*

CONTRACTORS: Exterior Wall System Installation

Applicated Images Inc ....G...... 601 992-1556
Brandon *(G-364)*

CONTRACTORS: Fence Construction

Frontier Contracting LLC ....G...... 662 809-1949
Grenada *(G-1678)*

Southern Exteriors Fence Co ....G...... 228 586-2110
Perkinston *(G-4181)*

CONTRACTORS: Fiber Optic Cable Installation

Business Communications Inc.............E 601 898-1890
Ridgeland *(G-4559)*

Harlan Services LLC ....G...... 601 513-5318
Magee *(G-3177)*

CONTRACTORS: Fire Sprinkler System Installation Svcs

First Class Fire Prtection LLC ....G...... 901 350-0499
Horn Lake *(G-2199)*

Huey P Stockstill LLC ....F 228 868-8678
Gulfport *(G-1810)*

CONTRACTORS: Floor Laying & Other Floor Work

Triton Stone Holdings LLC..................D....... 662 280-8041
Southaven *(G-4917)*

CONTRACTORS: Flooring

Boxcar Flooring Company LLC ....G...... 662 871-1417
Saltillo *(G-4708)*

Everett Industries Inc ....G...... 228 231-1556
Bay Saint Louis *(G-143)*

CONTRACTORS: Foundation & Footing

S Circle Inc ....D....... 601 792-4104
Newhebron *(G-3714)*

CONTRACTORS: Gas Detection & Analysis Svcs

Oil Well Logging Company Inc ....G...... 601 477-8315
Brandon *(G-430)*

CONTRACTORS: Gas Field Svcs, NEC

Cam2 International LLC.......................E 601 661-5382
Vicksburg *(G-5350)*

Cam2 International LLC.......................G...... 800 338-2262
Vicksburg *(G-5351)*

Masco Wireline Service Inc ....E 601 428-7966
Laurel *(G-2797)*

Williams Transportation Co LLC ....D....... 601 428-2214
Laurel *(G-2874)*

CONTRACTORS: General Electric

Ecs- Elec Cnstr Spcialists Inc............G...... 662 453-0588
Greenwood *(G-1621)*

W G Yates & Sons Cnstr Co ....A 601 656-5411
Philadelphia *(G-4248)*

CONTRACTORS: Glass, Glazing & Tinting

La Rosa Glass Inc ....G...... 228 864-0751
Long Beach *(G-2942)*

CONTRACTORS: Gutters & Downspouts

S&G Gutter & Sheet Metal Co ....G...... 662 286-2924
Corinth *(G-1118)*

Seamless One Seamles Gutters ....G...... 228 832-0516
Saucier *(G-4763)*

CONTRACTORS: Heating & Air Conditioning

Granger Mp AC & Htg ....G...... 601 894-3774
Hazlehurst *(G-2097)*

King Heating & AC ....G...... 662 227-1159
Grenada *(G-1689)*

Spiral Systems Inc ....F 662 429-0373
Nesbit *(G-3657)*

Telliers Sheetmetal Works ....G...... 228 392-5319
Diberville *(G-1217)*

CONTRACTORS: Highway & Street Construction, General

Apac-Mississippi Inc ....D....... 662 328-6555
Columbus *(G-936)*

Hammett Gravel Co Inc ....G...... 662 834-1867
Lexington *(G-2903)*

J J Ferguson Sand & Grav Inc ....C 662 453-5451
Greenwood *(G-1630)*

Mallette Brothers Cnstr Co ....E 228 497-2523
Gautier *(G-1499)*

W E Blain & Sons Inc ....E 601 442-3032
Natchez *(G-3635)*

CONTRACTORS: Highway & Street Paving

Adcamp Inc...D....... 601 939-4493
Flowood *(G-1342)*

Apac-Mississippi Inc ....D....... 601 376-4000
Richland *(G-4501)*

Apac-Mississippi Inc ....G...... 601 376-4000
Richland *(G-4502)*

Apac-Mississippi Inc ....E 662 348-2214
Guntown *(G-1897)*

Apac-Mississippi Inc ....E 601 634-6600
Vicksburg *(G-5341)*

Cold Mix Inc ....G...... 662 256-4529
Nettleton *(G-3658)*

Huey P Stockstill LLC ....C 601 798-2981
Picayune *(G-4272)*

Lehman-Roberts Company ....F 662 429-5237
Hernando *(G-2138)*

CONTRACTORS: Highway & Street Resurfacing

W G Yates & Sons Cnstr Co ....A 601 656-5411
Philadelphia *(G-4248)*

CONTRACTORS: Highway Sign & Guardrail Construction & Install

Gpp Charleston Industries LLC............E 800 647-2384
Charleston *(G-738)*

K & K Systems Inc ....D....... 662 566-2025
Tupelo *(G-5165)*

CONTRACTORS: Hot Shot Svcs

Hicks Hot Shot Services LLC...............G...... 601 498-7482
Stringer *(G-5001)*

Integrity Hot Shot Svcs LLC ....G...... 601 850-8881
Ridgeland *(G-4593)*

Kdh Trucking LLC ....G...... 601 730-2052
Liberty *(G-2913)*

Lees Hot Shot Service LLC ....G...... 601 383-1018
Florence *(G-1326)*

Employee Codes: A=Over 500 employees, B=251-500
C=101-250, D=51-100, E=20-50, F=10-19, G=1-9

2019 Harris Directory of
Mississippi Manufacturers

365

PRODUCT

CONTRACTORS: Hotel, Motel/Multi-Family Home Renovtn/Remodel

Everett Industries Inc ....G....... 228 231-1556
Bay Saint Louis *(G-143)*

CONTRACTORS: Hydraulic Eqpt Installation & Svcs

Peppers Machine & Wldg Co Inc ....E...... 601 833-3038
Brookhaven *(G-522)*

CONTRACTORS: Insulation Installation, Building

Masterbilt ....G....... 662 728-3227
Booneville *(G-335)*

CONTRACTORS: Machinery Installation

Industrial & Crane Svcs Inc ....E....... 601 914-4491
Pascagoula *(G-4039)*

CONTRACTORS: Mechanical

Greenville Metal Works Inc ....E....... 662 335-8510
Greenville *(G-1555)*
J & A Mechanical Inc ....G....... 662 890-4565
Olive Branch *(G-3853)*
Morrison Welding LLC ....G....... 601 845-5187
Florence *(G-1329)*

CONTRACTORS: Multi-Family Home Remodeling

Walker Parris ....G....... 601 953-3023
Port Gibson *(G-4409)*

CONTRACTORS: Oil & Gas Building, Repairing & Dismantling Svc

B & B Oil Well Service Co Inc ....F....... 601 425-3836
Ellisville *(G-1246)*
Crisco Swabbing Service Inc ....E....... 601 731-9008
Columbia *(G-892)*
Delta Royalty Company Inc ....G....... 601 982-0970
Jackson *(G-2382)*
Dixie Services and Supply LLC ....G....... 662 369-0907
Aberdeen *(G-11)*
Jack Black Oil Company Inc ....G....... 601 442-2620
Natchez *(G-3570)*
Pine Belt Energy Services LLC ....C....... 601 796-3299
Lumberton *(G-3037)*
Roundtree & Associates Inc ....F....... 601 355-4530
Ridgeland *(G-4625)*
T K Stanley Inc ....C....... 601 735-2855
Columbia *(G-925)*

CONTRACTORS: Oil & Gas Field Geological Exploration Svcs

Paradise & Associates Inc ....G....... 601 445-9710
Natchez *(G-3606)*
Pledger Petroleum Inc ....G....... 601 442-9871
Natchez *(G-3608)*
Solomon Energy LLC ....G....... 601 607-3070
Madison *(G-3148)*

CONTRACTORS: Oil & Gas Field Geophysical Exploration Svcs

Louisiana Well Service Co Inc ....G....... 601 442-6648
Natchez *(G-3580)*

CONTRACTORS: Oil & Gas Field Tools Fishing Svcs

Radco Fishing & Rental Tls Inc ....G....... 601 736-8580
Columbia *(G-917)*
Rainbow Rentl Fishing Tls Inc ....F....... 601 425-3309
Laurel *(G-2833)*

CONTRACTORS: Oil & Gas Well Casing Cement Svcs

Cyrus Resources LLC ....G....... 228 669-6955
Gulfport *(G-1767)*

CONTRACTORS: Oil & Gas Well Drilling Svc

5 K Corp ....F....... 601 736-5367
Columbia *(G-877)*
Akers Minerals LLC ....G....... 207 615-7591
Houston *(G-2230)*
Armadillo Service Inc Alabama ....F....... 601 857-0440
Raymond *(G-4484)*
Ccore Energy Holding Co LLC ....G....... 601 824-7900
Brandon *(G-376)*
Deepwell Energy Services LLC ....D....... 800 477-2855
Columbia *(G-894)*
Deepwell Energy Services LLC ....E....... 601 735-1393
Richland *(G-4512)*
Delta Petroleum Service Inc ....G....... 662 487-1701
Sardis *(G-4738)*
E & D Services Inc ....E....... 601 649-9044
Laurel *(G-2765)*
Expro Americas LLC ....E....... 281 576-5500
Ellisville *(G-1251)*
Jack Black Oil Company Inc ....G....... 601 442-2620
Natchez *(G-3570)*
Kelley Brothers Contrs Inc ....D....... 601 735-2541
Waynesboro *(G-5501)*
Mike Lowery LLC ....G....... 601 736-1096
Foxworth *(G-1434)*
Navidad Petroleum LLC ....G....... 601 442-9812
Natchez *(G-3598)*
Vonco of Mississippi Inc ....G....... 601 446-7274
Natchez *(G-3634)*

CONTRACTORS: Oil & Gas Well Foundation Grading Svcs

Jwb Construction LLC ....F....... 601 439-7190
Mize *(G-3427)*

CONTRACTORS: Oil & Gas Well On-Site Foundation Building Svcs

Southeastern E & P Svcs Inc ....G....... 601 849-9218
Magee *(G-3186)*

CONTRACTORS: Oil & Gas Well Redrilling

Mc Consulting LLC ....G....... 601 735-2000
Waynesboro *(G-5506)*

CONTRACTORS: Oil & Gas Well reworking

Coastal Petroleum Services Inc ....E....... 601 446-5888
Natchez *(G-3547)*

CONTRACTORS: Oil & Gas Wells Pumping Svcs

Air Tech of Waveland ....G....... 228 467-7547
Bay Saint Louis *(G-133)*
Thomas E Windham Pumping ....G....... 601 764-3965
Bay Springs *(G-174)*
Williams Companies Inc ....G....... 662 895-7202
Byhalia *(G-612)*

CONTRACTORS: Oil & Gas Wells Svcs

Radzewicz Explration Drlg Corp ....F....... 601 445-8659
Natchez *(G-3610)*
Tri Resources Inc ....G....... 601 583-8711
Petal *(G-4197)*
Triple S Well Service Inc ....F....... 601 736-8804
Columbia *(G-926)*
V A Sauls Inc ....D....... 601 787-4321
Heidelberg *(G-2120)*
Vines Operating Company Inc ....G....... 601 442-8034
Church Hill *(G-755)*

CONTRACTORS: Oil Field Haulage Svcs

T K Stanley Inc ....E....... 601 735-2855
Waynesboro *(G-5517)*
Transfrac Logistics LLC ....G....... 479 659-8186
Vicksburg *(G-5429)*

CONTRACTORS: Oil Field Lease Tanks: Erectg, Clng/Rprg Svcs

J & K Services LLC ....G....... 601 310-7728
Lumberton *(G-3032)*

CONTRACTORS: Oil Field Mud Drilling Svcs

Delta Directional Drilling LLC ....C....... 601 683-0879
Newton *(G-3719)*

CONTRACTORS: Oil Field Pipe Testing Svcs

Roger Welch ....G....... 601 649-3767
Laurel *(G-2839)*

CONTRACTORS: Oil/Gas Well Construction, Rpr/Dismantling Svcs

Agmyns ....G....... 228 831-0342
Gulfport *(G-1716)*
Archh LLC ....G....... 601 590-3519
Carriere *(G-687)*
Baker Hughes A GE Company LLC ......E....... 601 731-5004
Columbia *(G-882)*
Community Construction Co LLC ....E....... 601 894-5239
Hazlehurst *(G-2092)*
Consolidated Gulf Services LLC ....G....... 601 446-5992
Natchez *(G-3549)*
Danny Byrd LLC ....G....... 601 649-2524
Laurel *(G-2758)*
Dozer Inc ....F....... 601 442-1671
Natchez *(G-3556)*
Duckwrth Drlg Completion L L C ....G....... 601 848-6486
State Line *(G-4986)*
Elite Const and Design ....G....... 662 307-2494
Grenada *(G-1675)*
Fisher Construction Company ....E....... 769 257-9969
Jackson *(G-2408)*
Giexco LLC ....G....... 662 352-1128
Brooksville *(G-553)*
Jones Ldscp & Contrs Svc LLC ....G....... 601 780-2042
Jackson *(G-2460)*
Lee Small Engines Inc ....G....... 601 833-5431
Brookhaven *(G-510)*
Mid-South Contractors Inc ....G....... 601 544-2803
Ellisville *(G-1264)*
Rega Environmental Inc ....F....... 228 447-1024
Diberville *(G-1210)*
Springer Trckg & Car Crushing ....F....... 601 649-4238
Laurel *(G-2855)*
St Engineer Halter Marine and ....D....... 228 762-0010
Pascagoula *(G-4068)*
Synergy Service and Supply LLC ....G....... 601 597-9902
Natchez *(G-3627)*
Synergy Service and Supply LLC ....F....... 601 492-4000
Natchez *(G-3628)*
T & T Welding Inc ....E....... 601 477-2884
Ellisville *(G-1270)*
Vmi Marine Inc ....D....... 601 636-8700
Vicksburg *(G-5443)*
W S Red Hancock Inc ....F....... 662 755-0011
Bentonia *(G-213)*
W S Red Hancock Inc ....C....... 601 399-0605
Ellisville *(G-1275)*
Walker Parris ....G....... 601 953-3023
Port Gibson *(G-4409)*

CONTRACTORS: On-Site Welding

Advanced Fabrication Inc ....G....... 601 796-7977
Lumberton *(G-3023)*
Amerimac Machining Corporation ....G....... 601 940-7919
Jackson *(G-2329)*
B & O Machine & Wldg Co Inc ....F....... 601 833-3000
Brookhaven *(G-481)*
Block & Chip Iron Works Inc ....G....... 601 394-2964
Leakesville *(G-2876)*
Carrolls Welding Service ....G....... 228 875-3800
Ocean Springs *(G-3747)*
Daniel Petre ....G....... 662 726-2462
Macon *(G-3057)*
Dillard Machining Service ....F....... 662 329-4682
Columbus *(G-962)*
Edco Welding ....G....... 228 392-5600
Biloxi *(G-241)*
Electro Mech Solutions Ems Inc ....G....... 601 631-0138
Vicksburg *(G-5365)*
Hago Automotive Corp ....F....... 662 593-0491
Iuka *(G-2293)*
Havards Construction LLC ....G....... 601 766-9841
Lucedale *(G-3001)*
Kens Welding Shop Inc ....G....... 601 736-4136
Columbia *(G-902)*
Kustom Machine and Sheet Metal ....F....... 601 469-1062
Philadelphia *(G-4221)*
Mashburns Welding ....G....... 601 648-2886
Buckatunna *(G-564)*

PRODUCT SECTION

CONTRACTORS: Well Acidizing Svcs

McGregor Indstl Steel Fabrcatn............E 662 236-7006
Oxford (G-3973)
McKinnion Welding & Metal Fabr..........G....... 601 635-3983
Decatur (G-1175)
Mercer Welding Service ....G....... 601 649-4269
Laurel (G-2799)
Mitchells Welding LLC...........................G....... 601 554-6402
Kosciusko (G-2703)
Morrison Welding LLC...........................G....... 601 845-5187
Florence (G-1329)
Nations Welding Service Inc..................G....... 601 833-4949
Brookhaven (G-520)
Ormans Welding & Fab Inc....................F....... 662 494-9471
West Point (G-5556)
Plastics Plus Inc...................................G....... 228 832-4634
Gulfport (G-1849)
Resurfacing Concepts Inc.....................G....... 662 489-6867
Pontotoc (G-4360)
Sandy Hook Machine Shop Inc.............F....... 601 736-4041
Sandy Hook (G-4731)
T & T Welding Inc ....E....... 601 477-2884
Ellisville (G-1270)
T & T Welding Yard Inc ....G....... 601 477-2299
Ellisville (G-1271)
Tucker Machine Services ....G....... 601 582-4280
Hattiesburg (G-2075)

CONTRACTORS: Ornamental Metal Work

Olivers Iron Works ....G....... 662 252-3858
Holly Springs (G-2186)
Partridge Ornamental Iron Inc ....E....... 601 693-4021
Meridian (G-3380)

CONTRACTORS: Paint & Wallpaper Stripping

T & L Specialty Company Inc................E....... 662 842-8143
Tupelo (G-5236)

CONTRACTORS: Painting & Wall Covering

Picayune Monument & Gran Works ......G....... 601 798-7926
Picayune (G-4286)

CONTRACTORS: Painting, Commercial

S Circle Inc ....D....... 601 792-4104
Newhebron (G-3714)

CONTRACTORS: Painting, Residential

David Morehead ....G....... 601 469-2272
Forest (G-1413)

CONTRACTORS: Painting, Residential, Interior

Efma Contracting LLC ....F....... 901 292-7221
Ridgeland (G-4576)

CONTRACTORS: Patio & Deck Construction & Repair

Elite Const and Design ....G....... 662 307-2494
Grenada (G-1675)

CONTRACTORS: Pavement Marking

J L McCool Contractors Inc ....F....... 228 769-9771
Moss Point (G-3482)
Pearson Enterprises ....G....... 662 289-7625
Kosciusko (G-2709)
S & S Striping ....G....... 662 449-4498
Hernando (G-2153)

CONTRACTORS: Pipe Laying

Circle S Irrigation Inc...........................F....... 662 627-7246
Clarksdale (G-761)

CONTRACTORS: Plumbing

Hj Norris LLC.......................................G....... 228 217-6704
Moss Point (G-3479)

CONTRACTORS: Pole Cutting

Pole Mill Optimizer LLC........................G....... 601 928-8860
Wiggins (G-5588)

CONTRACTORS: Prefabricated Window & Door Installation

P & R Aluminum ....G....... 662 682-7939
Vardaman (G-5325)

CONTRACTORS: Pulpwood, Engaged In Cutting

Charles Donald Pulpwood Inc ....E....... 601 437-4012
Port Gibson (G-4400)
Cutshall D L & Sons Logging Co...........G....... 662 423-6965
Iuka (G-2288)
J & P Smith Logging Inc........................F....... 601 833-4286
Brookhaven (G-502)
Vaiden Timber Co.................................G....... 662 464-7740
Vaiden (G-5315)

CONTRACTORS: Rock Removal

McDevitt Enterprises LLC ....G....... 601 453-2290
Meridian (G-3365)

CONTRACTORS: Roustabout Svcs

Werth Servicing LLC.............................G....... 662 449-4410
Hernando (G-2161)

CONTRACTORS: Safety & Security Eqpt

Duffell Metal Awning Co ....G....... 601 483-2181
Meridian (G-3332)
Genesis Telecommunications ....G....... 601 626-7353
Collinsville (G-868)
Omega-Tec LLC...................................G....... 601 750-8082
Vicksburg (G-5402)

CONTRACTORS: Sandblasting Svc, Building Exteriors

Halls Welding Service...........................G....... 601 477-3925
Ellisville (G-1256)

CONTRACTORS: Septic System

Harold A Sparks Septic Tanks ....G....... 662 454-7244
Golden (G-1526)
Snells Concrete Tanks..........................G....... 601 845-1881
Harrisville (G-1912)
Southern Sewage Systems ....G....... 228 832-7400
Saucier (G-4766)

CONTRACTORS: Sheet Metal Work, NEC

Advanced Fabrication Inc ....G....... 601 796-7977
Lumberton (G-3023)
Telliers Sheetmetal Works ....G....... 228 392-5319
Diberville (G-1217)
Tri County Sheet Metal & Wldg ....G....... 601 939-0803
Pearl (G-4153)

CONTRACTORS: Ship Joinery

Jamestown Metal Marine Sls Inc ....D....... 228 762-3156
Pascagoula (G-4041)

CONTRACTORS: Single-family Home General Remodeling

Ed Dangerfield Const Millwrks ....G....... 662 328-3877
Columbus (G-967)
Whitestone Contracting LLC ....G....... 601 800-8077
Ellisville (G-1278)

CONTRACTORS: Sound Eqpt Installation

Awesome Sight and Sound....................G....... 601 215-8846
Picayune (G-4255)

CONTRACTORS: Special Trades, NEC

Trinity Three LLC ....G....... 601 249-8851
Summit (G-5027)

CONTRACTORS: Structural Iron Work, Structural

Partridge Ornamental Iron Inc ....E....... 601 693-4021
Meridian (G-3380)
Rickys Welding and Machine Sp ....G....... 601 638-8238
Vicksburg (G-5410)

CONTRACTORS: Structural Steel Erection

Careys Construction Co Inc...................E....... 601 922-7388
Jackson (G-2354)
Classic Window Design..........................G....... 662 893-5892
Olive Branch (G-3823)
Cws Grain Systems Inc ....E....... 662 332-5822
Greenville (G-1543)
Hesters Certified Welding ....G....... 662 566-7305
Tupelo (G-5155)
Steel Service Corporation ....C....... 601 939-9222
Jackson (G-2668)
Woodrffs Prtble Wldg Fbrcation ....G....... 662 728-3326
Booneville (G-347)

CONTRACTORS: Svc Station Eqpt

Custom Sign Co of Batesville................E....... 662 563-7371
Batesville (G-104)

CONTRACTORS: Svc Well Drilling Svcs

Performance Drilling Company ....G....... 601 854-5661
Pelahatchie (G-4171)
Saf-T Compliance Intl LLC ....G....... 601 684-9495
McComb (G-3264)

CONTRACTORS: Tile Installation, Ceramic

Foley Tile & Marble ....G....... 601 271-8415
Hattiesburg (G-1972)
Moulton Tile & Marble Inc ....G....... 228 863-7587
Long Beach (G-2945)
Pitsburgh Stone & Plaster.....................G....... 601 631-0006
Vicksburg (G-5406)

CONTRACTORS: Underground Utilities

Greater Gulf Development LLC ....G....... 228 392-6680
Diberville (G-1204)
Socrates Garrett Entps Inc....................F....... 601 896-0084
Jackson (G-2585)

CONTRACTORS: Unit Paver Installation

Pearson Enterprises ....G....... 662 289-7625
Kosciusko (G-2709)

CONTRACTORS: Ventilation & Duct Work

Capital City Metal Works Inc.................G....... 601 939-7467
Pearl (G-4108)
Clarence Sansing Jr ....G....... 601 656-4771
Philadelphia (G-4211)

CONTRACTORS: Vinyl Flooring Installation, Tile & Sheet

Efma Contracting LLC ....F....... 901 292-7221
Ridgeland (G-4576)

CONTRACTORS: Warm Air Heating & Air Conditioning

Air Tech of Waveland............................G....... 228 467-7547
Bay Saint Louis (G-133)
Browns Electrical Repair........................G....... 662 226-8192
Grenada (G-1670)
Chambers Air and Heat ....G....... 662 967-2002
West (G-5532)
Collins Filter Co Inc..............................F....... 228 896-0582
Gulfport (G-1762)
Larkowski Inc ....G....... 601 928-9501
Saucier (G-4757)
Metro Mechanical Inc............................D....... 601 866-9050
Bolton (G-312)

CONTRACTORS: Water Intake Well Drilling Svc

Schudco Ltd ....G....... 662 332-8678
Greenville (G-1597)

CONTRACTORS: Water Well Drilling

Luckett Pump & Well Svc Inc.................G....... 662 624-2398
Dublin (G-1219)

CONTRACTORS: Well Acidizing Svcs

Swd Acidizing Inc ....G....... 601 442-7172
Natchez (G-3626)

Employee Codes: A=Over 500 employees, B=251-500
C=101-250, D=51-100, E=20-50, F=10-19, G=1-9

2019 Harris Directory of
Mississippi Manufacturers

CONTRACTORS: Well Bailing, Cleaning, Swabbing & Treating Svc

PRODUCT SECTION

CONTRACTORS: Well Bailing, Cleaning, Swabbing & Treating Svc

C & F Swabbing Inc ....G...... 601 687-1171
Shubuta *(G-4827)*

CONTRACTORS: Well Cleaning Svcs

Oil Tools & Supplies Inc ....G...... 601 446-7229
Natchez *(G-3602)*

CONTRACTORS: Well Logging Svcs

Well Logging Solutions LLC ....G...... 601 416-9241
Kosciusko *(G-2720)*

CONTRACTORS: Well Swabbing Svcs

B & P Swab Service Inc ....E...... 601 731-6309
Columbia *(G-881)*
Thompson Services Inc ....F...... 662 369-9102
Hamilton *(G-1907)*

CONTRACTORS: Wrecking & Demolition

Magnolia Supply Group LLC ....G...... 601 454-1368
Jackson *(G-2480)*
Socrates Garrett Entps Inc ....F...... 601 896-0084
Jackson *(G-2585)*

CONTROL EQPT: Electric

Advanced Marine Inc ....G...... 228 374-6747
Biloxi *(G-217)*
Control Systems Inc ....E...... 601 355-8594
Jackson *(G-2367)*
ITT LLC...E...... 662 393-0275
Southaven *(G-4879)*
ITT LLC...C...... 662 256-7185
Amory *(G-45)*

CONTROLS & ACCESS: Indl, Electric

Lec Inc...E...... 601 939-8535
Pearl *(G-4128)*

CONTROLS: Electric Motor

Control Products Inc ....G...... 662 890-7920
Olive Branch *(G-3828)*

CONTROLS: Environmental

Ademco Inc..G...... 601 936-4842
Richland *(G-4499)*
Bio-Solutions Franchise Corp ....G...... 601 582-4000
Hattiesburg *(G-1933)*
Clyde Woodward Jr ....G...... 601 736-6115
Columbia *(G-887)*
Kuhlman Electric Corporation ....B...... 601 892-4661
Crystal Springs *(G-1144)*

CONTROLS: Relay & Ind

Ncv Testing Service ....G...... 662 728-3965
Booneville *(G-337)*
South Coast Electric LLC....................F...... 228 533-0002
Bay St Louis *(G-182)*
Thyssenkrupp Elevator Corp ....C...... 662 223-4025
Walnut *(G-5458)*

CONVENIENCE STORES

Jiffy Mart...G...... 601 947-6589
Lucedale *(G-3004)*

CONVENTION & TRADE SHOW SVCS

Premier Publishing Inc ....G...... 601 957-1050
Flowood *(G-1389)*

CONVEYOR SYSTEMS: Bulk Handling

Essmueller Company ....D...... 601 649-2400
Laurel *(G-2767)*

CONVEYORS & CONVEYING EQPT

BSK Resources LLC ....G...... 662 842-4716
Belden *(G-187)*
Chads LLC...G...... 601 919-3113
Brandon *(G-378)*
Chuck Jennings ....G...... 601 668-5704
Raymond *(G-4486)*

Conveyor Tech ....F...... 901 831-4760
Lyon *(G-3042)*
Esco Group LLC...................................C...... 601 683-3192
Newton *(G-3720)*
Havard Mfg Inc ....G...... 601 766-9170
Lucedale *(G-3000)*
Metal-Tech Fabricators Inc ....F...... 662 622-0400
Coldwater *(G-849)*
Metso Minerals Industries Inc...............D...... 662 627-5292
Clarksdale *(G-774)*
North Miss Conveyor Co Inc ....E...... 662 236-1000
Oxford *(G-3977)*
Raymond Mucillo Jr ....G...... 662 429-8976
Nesbit *(G-3656)*
Screw Conveyor Corporation ....C...... 662 283-3142
Winona *(G-5606)*
Tri County Sheet Metal & Wldg ....G...... 601 939-0803
Pearl *(G-4153)*
Webster Industry Inc ....G...... 601 482-0183
Meridian *(G-3420)*

COOKING EQPT, HOUSEHOLD: Ranges, Gas

Viking Range LLC ....D...... 662 455-7522
Greenwood *(G-1658)*
Viking Range LLC ....A...... 662 455-1214
Greenwood *(G-1659)*

COOKWARE, STONEWARE: Coarse Earthenware & Pottery

Williams Sonoma ....F...... 901 795-2625
Olive Branch *(G-3927)*

COSMETIC PREPARATIONS

Joyce Tillman ....G...... 228 896-4927
Gulfport *(G-1814)*
Million Dollar Makeup LLC ....G...... 318 331-5363
Picayune *(G-4279)*
Sample Lab ....G...... 662 564-2498
Byhalia *(G-601)*
Young E F Jr Manufacturing Co ....E...... 601 483-8864
Meridian *(G-3422)*

COSMETICS & TOILETRIES

Christian Pass Soap ....G...... 228 222-4303
Pass Christian *(G-4079)*
Elements Cosmetics LLC ....G...... 601 383-6352
Brandon *(G-393)*
Galexie Glister ....G...... 601 667-0004
Jackson *(G-2420)*
Kik Custom Products Inc ....B...... 901 947-5400
Olive Branch *(G-3860)*
Merle Norman Cosmetics Inc...............G...... 662 287-7233
Corinth *(G-1100)*
Newson Chenora..................................G...... 601 596-3899
Hattiesburg *(G-2037)*
Oxford Laboratories ....G...... 662 801-9764
Oxford *(G-3987)*
Sisters Scents ....G...... 901 283-9867
Byhalia *(G-603)*
Southern Scents By Carla LLC ....G...... 662 312-5610
Starkville *(G-4973)*
Sweet Scents ....G...... 662 425-9305
Columbus *(G-1035)*

COSMETICS WHOLESALERS

La Jolie Enterprises LLC......................G...... 601 909-8840
Ridgeland *(G-4596)*

COSMETOLOGIST

Million Dollar Makeup LLC ....G...... 318 331-5363
Picayune *(G-4279)*

COSMETOLOGY & PERSONAL HYGIENE SALONS

La Jolie Enterprises LLC......................G...... 601 909-8840
Ridgeland *(G-4596)*

COSTUME JEWELRY & NOVELTIES: Apparel, Exc Precious Metals

Maurice Hinton ....G...... 601 857-5168
Terry *(G-5072)*

COSTUME JEWELRY STORES

Southern Traditions ....G...... 662 534-0410
New Albany *(G-3698)*

COTTON COMPRESSES & WAREHOUSES

Cottonseed Co-Op Corporation............E...... 662 358-4481
Jonestown *(G-2675)*

COUNTER & SINK TOPS

Conceptual Designs Inc ....F...... 601 923-9922
Jackson *(G-2363)*
Galley Kitchen Bath ....G...... 662 455-6535
Greenwood *(G-1623)*
J N S Marble & Granite LLC ....F...... 662 280-2272
Southaven *(G-4880)*
Stone Perfection ....G...... 662 895-4442
Olive Branch *(G-3914)*

COUNTERS OR COUNTER DISPLAY CASES, WOOD

Superior Granite & Quartz.....................G...... 662 241-5664
Columbus *(G-1034)*

COUNTING DEVICES: Taximeters

Ben Mears Taxidermists & Sups ....G...... 662 282-4594
Mantachie *(G-3198)*

COURIER SVCS: Package By Vehicle

Johnson Wiley.....................................G...... 662 329-1495
Columbus *(G-991)*

COVERS & PADS Chair, Made From Purchased Materials

Rome Chenille & Supply Co Inc ....G...... 662 286-9947
Corinth *(G-1116)*

COVERS: Automotive, Exc Seat & Tire

Sportman Camo Covers Inc..................F...... 662 489-7074
Ecru *(G-1233)*

CRANE & AERIAL LIFT SVCS

B & O Machine & Wldg Co Inc ....F...... 601 833-3000
Brookhaven *(G-481)*
Glenn Machine Works Inc ....E...... 228 875-1877
Vancleave *(G-5319)*
Industrial & Crane Svcs Inc ....E...... 601 914-4491
Pascagoula *(G-4039)*

CRANKSHAFTS & CAMSHAFTS: Machining

Powertrain N Feuer Amer Inc................D...... 662 373-0050
Robinsonville *(G-4676)*

CRANKSHAFTS: Motor Vehicle

Jackson Powertrain Inc........................G...... 601 932-3159
Jackson *(G-2651)*
Powertrain N Feuer Amer Inc................D...... 662 373-0050
Robinsonville *(G-4676)*

CREDIT INSTITUTIONS: Personal

First Heritage Credit Corp ....G...... 662 283-4696
Winona *(G-5598)*
Unique Services LLC ....G...... 601 326-9912
Jackson *(G-2616)*

CRUDE PETROLEUM & NATURAL GAS PRODUCTION

Enbridge Processing LLC......................G...... 601 671-8800
Waynesboro *(G-5497)*
Gas Processors Inc ....F...... 601 736-1600
Columbia *(G-899)*
J R Pounds Inc ....G...... 601 649-1743
Laurel *(G-2785)*
Joe Fortunato Oil Prodcr RES ....G...... 601 442-6397
Natchez *(G-3572)*
S Lavon Evans Jr Oper Co Inc...............F...... 601 649-7639
Laurel *(G-2841)*
Tellus Operating Group LLC ....E...... 601 787-3014
Heidelberg *(G-2119)*

(G-0000) Company's Geographic Section entry number

PRODUCT SECTION

DATA PROCESSING SVCS

CRUDE PETROLEUM & NATURAL GAS PRODUCTION

American Midstream.................................G...... 601 671-8800
Waynesboro (G-5490)
American Midstream LLC.........................G...... 601 776-6721
Quitman (G-4456)
American Midstream LLC.........................G...... 601 798-9145
Picayune (G-4251)
Centerpint Enrgy Rsources Corp..............E...... 601 425-1461
Laurel (G-2750)
Central Resources Inc.............................G...... 601 776-3281
Quitman (G-4459)
Cline Ltd...G...... 601 649-6274
Laurel (G-2755)
Crosbys Creek Oil & Gas LLC..................G...... 601 898-0051
Ridgeland (G-4567)
D & D Oilfield Consultants Inc.................G...... 601 648-2282
State Line (G-4985)
David K Brooks......................................G...... 601 981-5722
Jackson (G-2377)
Denbury Resources Inc...........................G...... 601 829-0398
Brandon (G-388)
H O Hughes...G...... 601 261-3302
Hattiesburg (G-1979)
Howard E Stover....................................G...... 601 984-3702
Jackson (G-2443)
James W Elliot Jr....................................G...... 601 833-6201
Brookhaven (G-504)
Lion Oil Co..G...... 601 933-3000
Flowood (G-1378)
MRC Global (us) Inc................................F...... 601 965-5275
Jackson (G-2512)
Neal Clement Oil & Gas..........................G...... 601 982-5667
Jackson (G-2518)
Rosson Exploration Company...................G...... 601 969-2022
Jackson (G-2570)
US Oil Recovery LLC...............................G...... 662 884-1050
Indianola (G-2271)
Victor P Smith Oil Producers...................G...... 601 932-2223
Jackson (G-2673)
Wayne A Potter......................................G...... 601 446-6090
Natchez (G-3638)

CRUDE PETROLEUM PRODUCTION

A & B Pump & Supply Inc........................G...... 601 787-3741
Heidelberg (G-2111)
Anderson Oil Company Inc.......................G...... 601 442-2960
Natchez (G-3520)
Belle Oil Inc..G...... 601 442-6648
Natchez (G-3528)
Big Joe Oil Co Inc..................................G...... 601 442-5481
Natchez (G-3530)
Big Joe Operating Co Inc.........................G...... 601 442-5481
Natchez (G-3531)
Biglane Operating Co..............................G...... 601 442-2783
Natchez (G-3532)
Blue Lightning Enterprise LLC..................G...... 901 626-8587
Olive Branch (G-3820)
BP America Production Company.............E...... 228 762-3996
Moss Point (G-3471)
Bruxoil Inc..G...... 601 981-5722
Jackson (G-2346)
Callon Offshore Production......................D...... 601 442-1601
Natchez (G-3542)
Craft Exploration Company LLC...............G...... 601 859-0077
Canton (G-655)
El Toro Production Co Inc........................G...... 601 442-4159
Natchez (G-3558)
Gusoil Inc...G...... 601 735-2731
Waynesboro (G-5499)
Hughes Eastern Corporation....................G...... 601 957-1778
Ridgeland (G-4590)
Inland Energy Company Inc......................G...... 601 969-1160
Jackson (G-2446)
James Biglane..G...... 601 442-2783
Natchez (G-3571)
McGowan Working Partners Inc...............E...... 601 982-3444
Jackson (G-2484)
Meason Operating Co..............................F...... 601 442-3668
Natchez (G-3586)
Moco Inc...G...... 601 957-3550
Ridgeland (G-4609)
New David Oil Company Inc......................F...... 601 442-1607
Natchez (G-3599)
Partridge Production LLC.........................G...... 601 987-4911
Jackson (G-2535)
Petro-Hunt LLC.......................................F...... 601 636-3448
Vicksburg (G-5405)

Petroci Usa Inc......................................G...... 601 764-2222
Bay Springs (G-171)
Phoenix Operating Inc............................G...... 601 866-2223
Bolton (G-313)
Roundtree & Associates Inc.....................F...... 601 355-4530
Ridgeland (G-4625)
South Central Group Inc..........................G...... 601 445-5101
Natchez (G-3623)
Taylor Energy Company LLC.....................G...... 601 736-9997
Foxworth (G-1436)
Tellus Operating Group LLC.....................G...... 601 898-7444
Ridgeland (G-4638)
Texas Petroleum Investment Co...............G...... 601 796-4921
Lumberton (G-3039)
Waller Bros Inc......................................G...... 601 352-6556
Jackson (G-2624)
Wcs Oil & Gas Corporation......................G...... 601 787-4565
Sandersville (G-4726)
Wilcox Energy Company..........................G...... 601 442-5191
Natchez (G-3641)

CULVERTS: Sheet Metal

Contech Engnered Solutions LLC.............G...... 601 894-2041
Greenville (G-1540)

CUPS & PLATES: Foamed Plastics

Dart Cont Co Miss Ltd Lblty Co................C...... 601 776-3555
Quitman (G-4461)

CURBING: Granite Or Stone

G & G Granite..G...... 601 319-0905
Ellisville (G-1252)
Simple Stone Solutions............................G...... 601 206-5566
Jackson (G-2582)

CURTAIN & DRAPERY FIXTURES: Poles, Rods & Rollers

Amerson Cleophus Jr..............................G...... 601 362-3629
Jackson (G-2331)

CURTAINS: Window, From Purchased Materials

F S C Inc...G...... 662 434-0025
Columbus (G-972)

CUSHIONS & PILLOWS

Advanced Innovative Pdts LLC..................G...... 662 365-1640
Baldwyn (G-70)
Innocor East LLC....................................F...... 662 365-1640
Baldwyn (G-78)
Innocor East LLC....................................D...... 732 263-0800
Baldwyn (G-79)
Pillows Plus...G...... 662 890-3699
Olive Branch (G-3896)

CUSHIONS & PILLOWS: Bed, From Purchased Materials

Foamcraft Inc...E...... 662 844-6399
Tupelo (G-5135)

CUSHIONS: Carpet & Rug, Foamed Plastics

Fxi Inc..C...... 662 566-2382
Verona (G-5331)

CUSHIONS: Textile, Exc Spring & Carpet

Fibrix LLC...D...... 662 844-5595
Tupelo (G-5133)

CUT STONE & STONE PRODUCTS

AIA Countertops....................................G...... 574 457-2003
Guntown (G-1896)
Davidson Marble & Gran Works................G...... 662 289-1337
Kosciusko (G-2692)
Jonathan Bigbie.....................................G...... 601 498-9890
Petal (G-4188)
Precision Cultured Marble.......................G...... 662 838-5112
Byhalia (G-597)
Stone Associates Inc..............................G...... 662 838-4671
Byhalia (G-607)
Veterans Monument Company LLC............G...... 662 549-1422
Caledonia (G-633)

CUTLERY

Kut Tools Inc...G...... 601 876-4467
Tylertown (G-5276)

CYLINDER & ACTUATORS: Fluid Power

Gulf Hydraulics & Pneumatics...................F...... 228 392-1275
Diberville (G-1205)

CYLINDERS: Pressure

Worthington Cylinder Corp.......................C...... 662 538-6500
New Albany (G-3708)

DAIRY PRDTS STORE: Ice Cream, Packaged

Dairy Kream..G...... 662 256-7562
Amory (G-40)

DAIRY PRDTS WHOLESALERS: Fresh

Borden Dairy Company Ala LLC.................F...... 662 328-8755
Columbus (G-941)

DAIRY PRDTS: Cheese

Marathon Cheese Corporation..................D...... 662 728-6242
Booneville (G-333)

DAIRY PRDTS: Dietary Supplements, Dairy & Non-Dairy Based

Xooma Worldwide...................................G...... 662 548-5361
Southaven (G-4920)

DAIRY PRDTS: Frozen Desserts & Novelties

Caboose Cones.......................................G...... 228 860-4030
Ocean Springs (G-3745)
Dairy Kream..G...... 662 256-7562
Amory (G-40)
Red Penguin Jackson Ice Cream..............G...... 601 519-9901
Jackson (G-2561)

DAIRY PRDTS: Ice Cream & Ice Milk

Luvel Dairy Products Inc.........................C...... 662 289-2511
Kosciusko (G-2698)
Luvel Dairy Products Inc.........................G...... 601 693-0038
Meridian (G-3362)
Luvel Dairy Products Inc.........................G...... 662 334-6372
Greenville (G-1566)
Prairie Farms Dairy Inc...........................F...... 601 969-1307
Jackson (G-2544)

DAIRY PRDTS: Milk, Fluid

Borden Dairy Company Ala LLC.................E...... 251 456-3381
Hattiesburg (G-1936)
Borden Dairy Company Ala LLC.................F...... 662 328-8755
Columbus (G-941)
Borden Dairy Company Ala LLC.................D...... 601 268-2583
Hattiesburg (G-1937)
Foremost Dairies.....................................G...... 601 936-9606
Richland (G-4516)
Luvel Dairy Products Inc.........................C...... 662 289-2511
Kosciusko (G-2698)
Luvel Dairy Products Inc.........................G...... 601 693-0038
Meridian (G-3362)
Luvel Dairy Products Inc.........................G...... 662 334-6372
Greenville (G-1566)
Prairie Farms Dairy Inc...........................F...... 601 969-1307
Jackson (G-2544)

DAIRY PRDTS: Natural Cheese

Mississippi Cheese Straw Fctry................F...... 662 746-7171
Yazoo City (G-5640)

DAIRY PRDTS: Yogurt, Exc Frozen

Purple Bannana......................................G...... 228 466-2978
Bay Saint Louis (G-152)

DAMAGED MERCHANDISE SALVAGING, SVCS ONLY

Springer Trckg & Car Crushing.................F...... 601 649-4238
Laurel (G-2855)

DATA PROCESSING SVCS

Incapitalmgcom LLC...............................G...... 601 268-0103
Hattiesburg (G-1999)

Employee Codes: A=Over 500 employees, B=251-500
C=101-250, D=51-100, E=20-50, F=10-19, G=1-9

2019 Harris Directory of
Mississippi Manufacturers

PRODUCT

DATA PROCESSING SVCS

T Enterprises Inc ....F 601 487-1100
Jackson (G-2603)

DEALERS: Tax Certificate

Norman Accounting Services ....G 662 347-4475
Greenville (G-1582)

DECORATIVE WOOD & WOODWORK

Longleaf Forest Products LLC ....G 662 456-4444
Houston (G-2250)
Mary Tio ....G 228 392-0706
Biloxi (G-266)
Palmer Handrail & Custom Mllwk ....G 662 287-3090
Corinth (G-1107)
Pickens Hardwoods Inc ....G 601 924-1199
Jackson (G-2539)

DEFENSE SYSTEMS & EQPT

Eagle Eye Personal Defense ....G 662 816-2310
Oxford (G-3953)
Lone Star Defense ....G 662 701-5204
Amory (G-47)
Maritime Defense Strategy LLC ....G 352 302-1442
Pascagoula (G-4051)
Perspecta Engineering Inc ....G 571 313-6000
Stennis Space Center (G-4996)
Pretty Vixen Defense LLC ....G 228 304-2173
Pearlington (G-4161)
Ready Defense LLC ....G 662 544-3478
Holly Springs (G-2189)
Taylor Defense Products LLC ....G 662 773-3421
Louisville (G-2984)

DELIVERY SVCS, BY VEHICLE

Pepsi Beverages Company ....E 662 841-8750
Tupelo (G-5202)

DENTAL EQPT & SPLYS: Enamels

New Patients Number ....G 662 323-2803
Starkville (G-4964)
P Adam Middleton ....G 662 289-7076
Kosciusko (G-2708)

DENTAL EQPT & SPLYS: Metal

Gold Teeth Customs ....G 601 955-4653
Jackson (G-2427)

DEPARTMENT STORES

TJX Companies Inc ....G 662 236-2856
Oxford (G-4007)

DEPARTMENT STORES: Country General

Springer Dry Goods ....F 662 263-8144
Maben (G-3051)

DERMATOLOGICALS

Skin Sake LLC ....G 870 853-5544
Madison (G-3147)

DERRICKS: Oil & Gas Field

Pawn Investments Inc ....G 601 649-4059
Laurel (G-2817)

DESICCANTS, CLAY: Activated

Desiccare Inc ....E 601 932-0405
Richland (G-4513)

DESIGN SVCS, NEC

Castle Hill Design ....G 601 918-8234
Canton (G-654)
Elite Const and Design ....G 662 307-2494
Grenada (G-1675)

DESIGN SVCS: Computer Integrated Systems

Harlan Services LLC ....G 601 513-5318
Magee (G-3177)
Omega-Tec LLC ....G 601 750-8082
Vicksburg (G-5402)
Vizaura LLC ....G 228 363-4048
Diamondhead (G-1193)

DIAGNOSTIC SUBSTANCES

Cardinal Health 414 LLC ....G 662 680-8644
Tupelo (G-5118)
Mississippi Imaging ....G 601 656-6759
Philadelphia (G-4226)

DIAGNOSTIC SUBSTANCES OR AGENTS: Hematology

Accurate Drug Testing and Back ....G 601 500-7841
Flowood (G-1341)

DIAGNOSTIC SUBSTANCES OR AGENTS: Radioactive

Cardinal Health 414 LLC ....G 601 982-7345
Jackson (G-2353)

DIAGNOSTIC SUBSTANCES OR AGENTS: Veterinary

MSU Veterinary Diagnostics Lab ....E 601 420-4700
Pearl (G-4133)

DIAMONDS, GEMS, WHOLESALE

National Diamond Corp ....G 662 895-9633
Olive Branch (G-3883)

DIAMONDS: Cutting & Polishing

National Diamond Corp ....G 662 895-9633
Olive Branch (G-3883)

DIAPERS: Disposable

Leaf River Cellulose LLC ....B 601 964-8411
New Augusta (G-3711)

DIE SETS: Presses, Metal Stamping

Green Mold Die & Fixtures Inc ....F 601 879-8166
Flora (G-1308)
Magnolia Tool & Mfg Co ....G 601 856-4333
Ridgeland (G-4602)
Pro Tool Inc ....G 662 282-4419
Mantachie (G-3203)
Tool Tek LLC ....G 937 399-4333
Wiggins (G-5592)

DIES & TOOLS: Special

American Stamping Corporation ....G 662 895-5300
Olive Branch (G-3813)
Baldwyn Tool and Die Co ....G 662 365-8665
Baldwyn (G-72)
Boyle Tool & Die Inc ....G 662 846-0640
Boyle (G-348)
Davis Tool & Die Inc ....F 662 234-4007
Abbeville (G-2)
Dixie Dies Inc ....G 601 845-6029
Harrisville (G-1911)
Edge Tools and Designs Inc ....G 662 578-0363
Batesville (G-105)
Industrial Steel Rule Die Corp ....G 601 932-5555
Jackson (G-2649)
Jims Tool & Die Inc ....F 662 895-3287
Olive Branch (G-3856)
Metal Products of Corinth Inc ....G 662 287-3625
Corinth (G-1101)
Production Machine & Tool Inc ....G 662 287-4752
Corinth (G-1111)
Stevens Machine & Tool Inc ....G 662 728-6005
Marietta (G-3218)
Traceway Engineering and Mfg ....F 662 489-1314
Pontotoc (G-4364)

DIODES: Light Emitting

Rsileds LLC ....G 228 697-5967
Biloxi (G-277)

DIRECT SELLING ESTABLISHMENTS: Food, Mobile, Exc Coffee-Cart

From Our Cup To Yours ....G 601 214-7689
Pearl (G-4121)

DIRECT SELLING ESTABLISHMENTS: Jewelry, House-To-House

Scholastic Products and Awards ....F 601 362-6990
Jackson (G-2576)

DIRECT SELLING ESTABLISHMENTS: Telemarketing

High Edge Inc ....F 601 326-2025
Jackson (G-2440)

DISASTER SVCS

Excel By Four LLC ....G 228 355-8203
Gulfport (G-1780)

DISHWASHING EQPT: Commercial

Auto-Chlor System of Mid S LLC ....G 601 420-0331
Pearl (G-4105)

DISK & DRUM DRIVES & COMPONENTS: Computers

Grady Morrow ....G 769 823-1422
Jackson (G-2429)

DISKS & DRUMS Magnetic

Glassbridge Enterprises Inc ....G 662 280-6268
Southaven (G-4875)

DISPENSERS: Soap

AMaries Bath Happies & Body ....G 601 714-1887
Brandon (G-362)

DISPLAY FIXTURES: Showcases, Wood, Exc Refrigerated

H & L Millworks Inc ....G 228 392-9913
Biloxi (G-250)

DISPLAY ITEMS: Corrugated, Made From Purchased Materials

Wire Display Fabrication Inc ....G 662 838-9650
Byhalia (G-613)

DISPLAY LETTERING SVCS

Bloms Creative Signs Inc ....G 228 374-2566
Biloxi (G-221)

DOOR PARTS: Sashes, Wood

Target Door and Supply Inc ....G 601 790-9006
Ridgeland (G-4637)

DOORS & WINDOWS WHOLESALERS: All Materials

Tapco Inc ....E 662 841-1635
Tupelo (G-5238)

DOORS & WINDOWS: Screen & Storm

A Plus Tornado Shelters O ....G 601 879-0005
Jackson (G-2315)
French Awning & Screen Co Inc ....G 601 922-1132
Jackson (G-2414)
Tapco Inc ....E 662 841-1635
Tupelo (G-5238)

DOORS & WINDOWS: Storm, Metal

La Rosa Glass Inc ....G 228 864-0751
Long Beach (G-2942)
Masterbilt ....G 662 728-3227
Booneville (G-335)
National Custom Craft Inc ....G 662 963-7373
Nettleton (G-3663)
P & R Aluminum ....G 662 682-7939
Vardaman (G-5325)
Quality Glass and Aluminum ....G 662 837-3615
Ripley (G-4669)

DOORS: Wooden

Herrington Millworks ....G 601 845-8056
Florence (G-1325)

370

2019 Harris Directory of
Mississippi Manufacturers

(G-0000) Company's Geographic Section entry number

PRODUCT SECTION

ELECTRICAL EQPT & SPLYS

JC Manufacturing LLC..............................G....... 662 338-9004
Starkville (G-4952)

Masonite Corporation...............................D...... 601 422-2200
Laurel (G-2798)

Morgan Brothers Millwork Inc ....C...... 601 649-9188
Laurel (G-2807)

DRAFTING SVCS

Berry Enterprises of Miss ....G....... 601 928-4006
Perkinston (G-4174)

DRAINAGE PRDTS: Concrete

Design Precast & Pipe Inc.....................E...... 228 831-5833
Gulfport (G-1772)

DRAPERIES & CURTAINS

Beverly Robinson Decor ....G....... 601 201-1520
Madison (G-3086)

Blonzells Curtain Shop...........................G....... 601 635-3811
Decatur (G-1171)

Classic Window Design...........................G....... 662 893-5892
Olive Branch (G-3823)

Norman Vr Inc...G....... 601 352-4819
Gulfport (G-1838)

Ron Lor Window Fashions.....................G....... 662 329-1557
Columbus (G-1022)

DRAPERIES & DRAPERY FABRICS, COTTON

Rome Chenille & Supply Co Inc ....G....... 662 286-9947
Corinth (G-1116)

Said Melinda...G....... 601 990-4022
Brookhaven (G-528)

Walls Drapery & Bedspread Mfg ....G....... 601 939-6014
Pearl (G-4157)

DRAPERIES: Plastic & Textile, From Purchased Materials

Linas Interiors Inc..................................G....... 662 332-7226
Leland (G-2889)

Mid-South Drapery Inc............................E....... 662 454-3855
Belmont (G-200)

DRAPERY & UPHOLSTERY STORES: Draperies

Alfords Decorating Center ....G....... 662 455-3552
Greenwood (G-1612)

Linas Interiors Inc..................................G....... 662 332-7226
Leland (G-2889)

Rome Chenille & Supply Co Inc ....G....... 662 286-9947
Corinth (G-1116)

DRILLING MACHINERY & EQPT: Oil & Gas

Chevron Corporation...............................C...... 228 938-4600
Pascagoula (G-4025)

DRINK MIXES, NONALCOHOLIC: Cocktail

Liquor Locker Inc...................................G....... 228 396-8557
Biloxi (G-263)

DRINKING PLACES: Bars & Lounges

Lucky Town Brewing Company LLC.....F...... 601 790-0142
Jackson (G-2473)

DRIVES: Hydrostatic

Hydrostatic Transm Svc LLC ....G....... 662 680-8899
Tupelo (G-5160)

DRUG STORES

Doctors Specialty Pharmacy LLC ....G....... 228 806-1384
Biloxi (G-238)

Pharmedium Services LLC ....E....... 662 846-5969
Cleveland (G-803)

Southern Discount Drugs of Cha ....G....... 662 647-5172
Charleston (G-743)

DRUG TESTING KITS: Blood & Urine

Advanced Screening Solutiions ....G....... 662 205-4139
Tupelo (G-5108)

DRUGS & DRUG PROPRIETARIES, WHOLESALE: Pharmaceuticals

Oaklock LLC..G....... 601 855-7678
Canton (G-674)

Pharmaceutical Trade Svcs Inc ....F...... 228 244-1530
Ocean Springs (G-3775)

DRUGS AFFECTING NEOPLASMS & ENDOCRINE SYSTEMS

Follaine Pharmaceuticals LLC..............G....... 303 808-4104
Etta (G-1284)

DRYCLEANING & LAUNDRY SVCS: Commercial & Family

Mississppi Band Chctaw Indians ....G....... 601 656-7350
Choctaw (G-746)

DUCTS: Sheet Metal

Southwark Metal Mfg Co ....C...... 662 342-7805
Southaven (G-4907)

DUMPSTERS: Garbage

Construction Waste Management ....G....... 662 513-7999
Oxford (G-3948)

DURABLE GOODS WHOLESALERS, NEC

Wholesale Electric Supply ....G....... 601 501-6928
Vicksburg (G-5445)

DUST OR FUME COLLECTING EQPT: Indl

Greer Environmental Services..............G....... 601 734-2883
Ruth (G-4701)

Sly Inc ....G....... 662 263-8234
Mathiston (G-3231)

EATING PLACES

Midsouth Media Group ....F...... 662 890-3359
Olive Branch (G-3878)

Natchez Smokehouse & Cold Stor ....G....... 601 442-6116
Natchez (G-3597)

EDUCATIONAL PROGRAMS ADMINISTRATION SVCS

Rehabilitation Svcs Miss Dept ....E....... 662 335-3359
Greenville (G-1595)

EDUCATIONAL SVCS

Excel By Four LLC ....E....... 228 355-8203
Gulfport (G-1780)

Johnson Education Firm LLC.................G....... 662 347-9150
Greenville (G-1560)

Johnson Educational Sales Inc.............G....... 601 469-1924
Forest (G-1418)

ELECTRIC MOTOR REPAIR SVCS

Bay Motor Winding Inc ....F...... 228 863-0666
Long Beach (G-2924)

Betty Montgomery ....G....... 601 833-1461
Brookhaven (G-482)

Brady Electric Inc....................................F...... 601 649-7862
Laurel (G-2742)

Browns Electrical Repair........................G....... 662 226-8192
Grenada (G-1670)

Burford Electric Service Inc...................E....... 662 328-5679
Columbus (G-943)

Eaton Electric Motor Repair..................G....... 662 728-6187
Booneville (G-328)

Electric Motor & Equipment...................G....... 601 845-5561
Florence (G-1321)

Electric Motor Sales & Svc Inc ....E....... 662 327-1606
Columbus (G-969)

Electric Works ....G....... 662 342-5505
Horn Lake (G-2196)

Flannigan Electric Company..................E....... 601 354-2756
Jackson (G-2409)

Gibson Electric Motor Svc Inc ....G....... 228 762-4923
Pascagoula (G-4033)

Grenada Electric Company Inc..............G....... 662 226-5801
Grenada (G-1679)

Industrial Elc Mtr Works Inc..................E....... 601 679-5500
Meridian (G-3352)

McIlwains Electrical Supply ....G....... 601 735-1145
Waynesboro (G-5507)

Mid South Electric Motor Svc ....G....... 662 332-3512
Greenville (G-1573)

Mobley Auto Service...............................G....... 662 423-3516
Iuka (G-2301)

Patterson & Company Inc ....E....... 662 842-2807
Tupelo (G-5200)

Peller Electric Motor Srvs ....G....... 601 693-4621
Meridian (G-3387)

Reid Electric Motor Services ....G....... 601 684-6040
Summit (G-5020)

Southern Electric Works Inc ....F...... 601 833-8323
Brookhaven (G-536)

Taw Power System Inc ....G....... 601 939-3455
Flowood (G-1401)

Tri-State Electric Corinth Inc..................F...... 662 287-2451
Corinth (G-1123)

W W W Electric Company Inc ....F...... 601 833-6666
Brookhaven (G-545)

Walker Enterprises ....G....... 662 237-0240
Carrollton (G-704)

ELECTRICAL APPARATUS & EQPT WHOLESALERS

Ademco Inc...G....... 601 936-4842
Richland (G-4499)

Howard Industries Inc ....B....... 601 422-0033
Laurel (G-2779)

Legendary Lighting LLC..........................E....... 601 932-0707
Jackson (G-2653)

Wholesale Electric Supply ....G....... 601 501-6928
Vicksburg (G-5445)

ELECTRICAL APPLIANCES, TELEVISIONS & RADIOS WHOLESALERS

Hamilton Beach Brands Inc ....F...... 662 890-9869
Olive Branch (G-3843)

ELECTRICAL CURRENT CARRYING WIRING DEVICES

ABB Installation Products Inc ....B....... 662 342-1545
Southaven (G-4851)

Safran Usa Inc ....G....... 601 736-4511
Columbia (G-921)

Vicksburg Enterprise Mfg LLC ....G....... 601 631-0304
Vicksburg (G-5435)

Vicksburg Enterprise Mfg LLC ....G....... 601 631-0304
Vicksburg (G-5436)

ELECTRICAL EQPT & SPLYS

ABB Installation Products Inc ....B....... 662 342-1545
Southaven (G-4851)

Azz Inc...G....... 662 290-1500
Kosciusko (G-2689)

Azz Inc...E....... 601 939-9191
Richland (G-4505)

Azz Incorporated ....F...... 228 475-0342
Moss Point (G-3466)

Dave Strong Circuit Judge ....G....... 601 684-3400
McComb (G-3248)

Electric Contractors...............................G....... 662 470-3102
Southaven (G-4871)

High Tech Inc...E....... 228 868-6632
Long Beach (G-2940)

Innovative Circuits Inc...........................F...... 662 287-2007
Corinth (G-1092)

J & L Sales ....G....... 601 992-2495
Brandon (G-407)

Kopis Mobile LLC....................................G....... 601 345-1753
Flowood (G-1375)

McLan Electronics Inc ....G....... 601 373-2392
Raymond (G-4491)

Multicraft Intl Ltd Partnr ....G....... 601 854-1200
Pelahatchie (G-4168)

Multicraft Intl Ltd Partnr ....E....... 601 854-1200
Pelahatchie (G-4170)

Precision Electric & Ltg Svc ....G....... 662 893-3200
Olive Branch (G-3899)

Steelsummit Holdings Inc ....F...... 601 638-1819
Vicksburg (G-5424)

Tenax Tm LLC..F...... 601 352-1107
Madison (G-3158)

Vanguard Solutions Inc ....G....... 407 230-2887
Gautier (G-1505)

Wholesale Electric Supply ....G....... 601 501-6928
Vicksburg (G-5445)

Employee Codes: A=Over 500 employees, B=251-500
C=101-250, D=51-100, E=20-50, F=10-19, G=1-9

2019 Harris Directory of
Mississippi Manufacturers

371

PRODUCT

ELECTRICAL EQPT FOR ENGINES

ELECTRICAL EQPT FOR ENGINES

Delco Remy America ....G...... 601 785-6690
Taylorsville **(G-5053)**
Richard Melos ....G...... 434 401-9496
Robinsonville **(G-4677)**

ELECTRICAL EQPT REPAIR & MAINTENANCE

B & O Machine & Wldg Co Inc ....F 601 833-3000
Brookhaven **(G-481)**
Mason Overstreet Wldg Mch Work ....E 601 932-1794
Pearl **(G-4130)**
Triton Systems Delaware LLC ....G..... 228 575-3100
Long Beach **(G-2958)**

ELECTRICAL EQPT REPAIR SVCS: High Voltage

Garrett & Son Inc ....E 601 853-7865
Madison **(G-3102)**

ELECTRICAL EQPT: Automotive, NEC

Hattiesburg Motors LLC ....G...... 601 818-2255
Hattiesburg **(G-1987)**
Multicraft Intl Ltd Partnr ....G...... 601 854-5516
Pelahatchie **(G-4167)**

ELECTRICAL GOODS, WHOL: Antennas, Receiving/Satellite Dishes

High Edge Inc ....F 601 326-2025
Jackson **(G-2440)**

ELECTRICAL GOODS, WHOLESALE: Burglar Alarm Systems

Glenn Weise ....G...... 228 435-4455
Biloxi **(G-244)**

ELECTRICAL GOODS, WHOLESALE: Dishwashers

Viking Range LLC ....B 662 455-1200
Greenwood **(G-1662)**

ELECTRICAL GOODS, WHOLESALE: Electrical Appliances, Major

Viking Capital Ventures Inc ....F 662 455-1200
Greenwood **(G-1656)**

ELECTRICAL GOODS, WHOLESALE: Fire Alarm Systems

Genesis Telecommunications ....G...... 601 626-7353
Collinsville **(G-868)**

ELECTRICAL GOODS, WHOLESALE: Generators

Kennedy Engine Company Inc ....F 228 392-2200
Biloxi **(G-256)**

ELECTRICAL GOODS, WHOLESALE: Modems, Computer

Fed Service Hub LLC ....G...... 228 547-3498
Gulfport **(G-1784)**

ELECTRICAL GOODS, WHOLESALE: Motor Ctrls, Starters & Relays

Flannigan Electric Company ....E 601 354-2756
Jackson **(G-2409)**
Luckett Pump & Well Svc Inc ....G...... 662 624-2398
Dublin **(G-1219)**

ELECTRICAL GOODS, WHOLESALE: Motors

ABB Motors and Mechanical Inc ....E 662 328-9116
Columbus **(G-930)**
Applied Indus Tech - Dixie Inc ....G...... 601 649-4312
Laurel **(G-2731)**
Burford Electric Service Inc ....E 662 328-5679
Columbus **(G-943)**
Electric Motor Sales & Svc Inc ....E 662 327-1606
Columbus **(G-969)**

Gibson Electric Motor Svc Inc ....G...... 228 762-4923
Pascagoula **(G-4033)**
Industrial Elc Mtr Works Inc ....E 601 679-5500
Meridian **(G-3352)**
Mid South Electric Motor Svc ....G...... 662 332-3512
Greenville **(G-1573)**
Patterson & Company Inc ....E 662 842-2807
Tupelo **(G-5200)**
Southern Electric Works Inc ....F 601 833-8323
Brookhaven **(G-536)**

ELECTRICAL GOODS, WHOLESALE: Panelboards

North American Electric Inc ....E 662 429-8049
Hernando **(G-2146)**

ELECTRICAL GOODS, WHOLESALE: Radio & TV Or TV Eqpt & Parts

Mfj Enterprises Inc ....E 662 323-9538
Starkville **(G-4959)**

ELECTRICAL GOODS, WHOLESALE: Security Control Eqpt & Systems

A Square Innovative SEC LLC ....G...... 601 937-0318
Jackson **(G-2316)**

ELECTRICAL GOODS, WHOLESALE: Telephone Eqpt

Phone Booth Inc ....F 662 286-6600
Corinth **(G-1109)**

ELECTRICAL GOODS, WHOLESALE: Transformers

Garrett & Son Inc ....E 601 853-7865
Madison **(G-3102)**

ELECTRICAL MEASURING INSTRUMENT REPAIR & CALIBRATION SVCS

AA Calibration Services LLC ....F 662 716-0202
Yazoo City **(G-5620)**

ELECTRICAL SPLYS

Betty Montgomery ....G...... 601 833-1461
Brookhaven **(G-482)**
McIlwains Electrical Supply ....G...... 601 735-1145
Waynesboro **(G-5507)**

ELECTROMEDICAL EQPT

Curahe LLC ....G...... 662 325-2176
Starkville **(G-4937)**
Min Sheng Healthcare LLC ....G...... 601 212-6189
Madison **(G-3130)**

ELECTRONIC EQPT REPAIR SVCS

Dale Fulton ....G...... 662 327-4800
Columbus **(G-958)**
Southern Signs Inc ....G...... 601 445-5564
Natchez **(G-3624)**

ELECTRONIC PARTS & EQPT WHOLESALERS

McLan Electronics Inc ....G...... 601 373-2392
Raymond **(G-4491)**

ELECTRONIC SHOPPING

Brenda Ruth Designs LLC ....G...... 601 708-4227
Clinton **(G-815)**

ELECTRONIC TRAINING DEVICES

Training Consultants Inc ....G...... 662 226-6637
Grenada **(G-1710)**

ELEVATOR: Grain, Storage Only

Cws Grain Systems Inc ....E 662 332-5822
Greenville **(G-1543)**

ELEVATORS & EQPT

Midsouth Elevator LLC ....G...... 601 353-8283
Jackson **(G-2491)**

Thyssenkrupp Elevator Corp ....C 662 223-4025
Walnut **(G-5458)**

ELEVATORS WHOLESALERS

BSK Resources LLC ....G...... 662 842-4716
Belden **(G-187)**

EMBLEMS: Embroidered

Patrick Enterprises Inc ....G...... 601 268-1115
Hattiesburg **(G-2041)**

EMBROIDERING & ART NEEDLEWORK FOR THE TRADE

Ae Enterprises ....G...... 601 573-5954
Brandon **(G-359)**
American Stitching LLC ....G...... 601 919-7882
Ridgeland **(G-4549)**
At Home Embroidery ....G...... 228 365-4034
Saucier **(G-4749)**
B S Monogramming ....G...... 662 750-0505
Walnut **(G-5455)**
Blank 2 Beautiful EMB More LLC ....G...... 662 902-6195
Alligator **(G-31)**
Cg Monogram & Gifts ....G...... 662 401-5344
Fulton **(G-1448)**
Clementine Frazier ....G...... 601 572-7698
Utica **(G-5307)**
Coast Ink Wholesale Club ....G...... 601 948-4849
Ridgeland **(G-4564)**
Creative Designs & Sports ....G...... 662 327-5000
Columbus **(G-956)**
D J S Embroidery LLC ....G...... 662 547-9000
Mc Cool **(G-3235)**
Embroidery Nu Sun ....G...... 228 731-3781
Gulfport **(G-1778)**
Embroidme ....G...... 228 284-1689
Ocean Springs **(G-3755)**
Fashions Incorporated Jackson ....G...... 601 948-1119
Jackson **(G-2406)**
Hoop-It-Up Embroidery ....G...... 662 244-7212
Columbus **(G-984)**
Hoopla Monogramming & Gifts ....G...... 228 860-4774
Gulfport **(G-1809)**
It Could Happen Embroidery ....G...... 228 374-7674
Biloxi **(G-253)**
J J Monogram Embroidery ....G...... 662 226-0304
Grenada **(G-1688)**
Josh Gus Garcia ....G...... 228 255-7157
Perkinston **(G-4177)**
Khloes Closet and Monograms ....G...... 662 315-9425
Smithville **(G-4844)**
Krazy Kat Monograms ....G...... 901 832-1339
Southaven **(G-4885)**
Lil Ms Sew & Sew Inc ....G...... 601 992-3279
Flowood **(G-1377)**
Lucky Dog Monograms LLC ....G...... 662 321-7903
Tupelo **(G-5181)**
Lucy Lus Monogramming LLC ....G...... 662 417-9552
Winona **(G-5603)**
M & M Monograms ....G...... 601 856-7459
Madison **(G-3122)**
Main Street Embroidery ....G...... 601 876-0003
Tylertown **(G-5277)**
Mockingbird Monograms ....G...... 662 315-6213
Nettleton **(G-3662)**
Mollygrams ....G...... 601 856-5598
Madison **(G-3131)**
Monkey Business Unlimit ....G...... 662 895-1912
Olive Branch **(G-3880)**
Monogram Expressions ....G...... 662 571-0582
Yazoo City **(G-5642)**
Monogram Magic ....G...... 601 624-6917
Madison **(G-3132)**
Monogram Magick ....G...... 662 544-1392
Holly Springs **(G-2185)**
Monogram Mills ....G...... 601 749-1064
Brandon **(G-426)**
Monogram Stitch LLC ....G...... 601 649-1582
Laurel **(G-2806)**
Monograms By Rahaim ....G...... 601 310-0152
Hattiesburg **(G-2032)**
Monograms Plus ....G...... 662 327-3332
Columbus **(G-1007)**
Mr Stitch It ....G...... 601 543-8681
Hattiesburg **(G-2034)**
Needle Works ....G...... 601 425-4692
Laurel **(G-2811)**
Paxton Embroidery ....G...... 662 335-2160
Greenville **(G-1589)**

2019 Harris Directory of Mississippi Manufacturers

(G-0000) Company's Geographic Section entry number

PRODUCT SECTION

EYEGLASSES

Perfect Promotions LLC ....F 601 482-7710
Meridian (G-3388)
Rainbow Stitchings ....G 662 378-5335
Greenville (G-1594)
Rebeccas Cstm EMB & Appliques ....G 662 665-1846
Corinth (G-1113)
Rfc-Embroidery ....G 601 463-0491
Poplarville (G-4391)
Riedesigns Embroidery ....G 601 262-5130
Meridian (G-3391)
Robinsons Retail Inc ....F 662 843-3950
Cleveland (G-806)
Rufroggy Monograms ....G 228 547-7060
Saucier (G-4762)
Serendipitee ....G 228 872-4766
Ocean Springs (G-3783)
Sew Lucky Embroidery ....G 662 550-5533
Hernando (G-2154)
Sew Southern Monograms ....G 662 229-6564
Winona (G-5607)
Signature Accents ....G 601 853-9020
Madison (G-3146)
SMS Embroidery ....G 601 635-2347
Decatur (G-1179)
Stitched In Time ....G 601 562-6715
Philadelphia (G-4237)
Stitches By Lee LLC ....G 228 769-7460
Pascagoula (G-4070)
Stitching and Stuff LLC ....G 228 365-4735
Long Beach (G-2955)
Sweet South Embroidery ....G 601 277-3371
Hazlehurst (G-2107)
Tlgllc/Magnolia Monogramming ....G 662 838-2000
Byhalia (G-609)
TSA Embroidery LLC ....G 662 538-1007
New Albany (G-3703)
VIP Vinyl and Embroidery LLC ....G 601 624-7366
Florence (G-1335)

EMBROIDERING SVC

Anns Embroidery ....G 601 444-0011
Columbia (G-879)
Buzini Group LLC ....E 601 398-1311
Flowood (G-1350)
C & W Embroidery Inc ....E 662 462-8526
Rienzi (G-4648)
Cater 2u Embroidery ....G 662 253-8713
Southaven (G-4857)
City Sports Center ....G 228 474-2033
Moss Point (G-3474)
Embroidery Design LLC ....G 601 878-2606
Terry (G-5067)
Embroidery Plus ....G 662 590-7102
Yazoo City (G-5633)
Golden Needle ....G 662 842-0515
Tupelo (G-5145)
Just For You Embroidery ....G 228 769-8388
Pascagoula (G-4043)
Logo Sportswear ....G 601 845-5038
Florence (G-1327)
Mississippi Embroidery Co ....G 601 264-3255
Hattiesburg (G-2026)
Monogram Creations ....G 601 415-4970
Vicksburg (G-5401)
Monogram Hut ....G 601 268-9028
Hattiesburg (G-2031)
P & L Embroidery ....G 662 365-9852
Baldwyn (G-86)
T Shirt Shop & Design Firm LLC ....G 662 329-9911
Columbus (G-1036)
Three Crafty Women ....G 662 746-6844
Yazoo City (G-5650)

EMBROIDERING SVC: Schiffli Machine

Custom Sportswear USA Inc ....G 228 255-4795
Diamondhead (G-1188)

EMBROIDERY ADVERTISING SVCS

Bear Creek Apparel Promotions ....G 601 259-8508
Canton (G-648)
Monogram Hut ....G 601 268-9028
Hattiesburg (G-2031)

EMERGENCY ALARMS

Ademco Inc ....G 601 936-4842
Richland (G-4499)

EMPLOYMENT AGENCY SVCS

Nsc Technologies LLC ....F 251 338-0725
Moss Point (G-3491)

EMPLOYMENT SVCS: Labor Contractors

Knights Mar & Indus Svcs Inc ....C 228 769-5550
Pascagoula (G-4045)

ENCLOSURES: Screen

Seamless One Seamles Gutters ....G 228 832-0516
Saucier (G-4763)

ENGINE PARTS & ACCESS: Internal Combustion

Kennedy Engine Company Inc ....F 228 392-2200
Biloxi (G-256)

ENGINE REBUILDING: Diesel

TWI Inc ....G 601 736-1783
Columbia (G-927)

ENGINEERING SVCS

Lec Inc ....E 601 939-8535
Pearl (G-4128)
National Bank Builders & Eqp ....F 662 781-0702
Walls (G-5450)
Northrop Grumman Systems Corp ....D 228 872-7300
Ocean Springs (G-3773)
Quality Cnstr & Engrg LLC ....C 601 786-8017
Fayette (G-1299)
Tenax Tm LLC ....F 601 352-1107
Madison (G-3158)

ENGINEERING SVCS: Aviation Or Aeronautical

Mississippi Aerospace Corp ....F 601 749-5659
Picayune (G-4280)

ENGINEERING SVCS: Civil

Mark A Whitney ....G 601 575-4952
Philadelphia (G-4224)

ENGINEERING SVCS: Industrial

Kelsey Bailey Consulting LLC ....G 601 622-8319
Madison (G-3115)
Power Dynamics Innovations LLC ....E 601 229-0960
Picayune (G-4287)

ENGINEERING SVCS: Marine

Friede Goldman Delaware Inc..............G 228 896-0029
Gulfport (G-1789)
Nvision Solutions Inc ....D 228 242-0010
Diamondhead (G-1192)

ENGINEERING SVCS: Professional

Perspecta Engineering Inc ....G 571 313-6000
Stennis Space Center (G-4996)

ENGINES: Diesel & Semi-Diesel Or Duel Fuel

Paccar Engine Company ....G 662 329-6700
Columbus (G-1014)
Paccar Engine Company ....G 425 468-7400
Columbus (G-1015)

ENGINES: Gasoline, NEC

Bg3 Delta LLC ....G 601 636-9828
Vicksburg (G-5344)

ENGINES: Internal Combustion, NEC

Christians Automotive Machine ....G 662 287-4500
Corinth (G-1070)
Kohler Co ....B 601 582-3555
Hattiesburg (G-2009)
Mdh Marine Art ....G 228 769-1692
Pascagoula (G-4053)
P & B Enterprises Inc ....G 662 323-8565
Starkville (G-4965)

ENGRAVING SVC: Jewelry & Personal Goods

Awards Unlimited ....G 228 863-1814
Gulfport (G-1730)
Boardtown Trading Post ....G 662 324-7296
Starkville (G-4929)
Hunters Hollow Inc ....F 662 234-5945
Oxford (G-3958)
Monograms Plus ....G 662 327-3332
Columbus (G-1007)
Trophy Shop ....G 662 236-3726
Oxford (G-4008)

ENGRAVING SVCS

Awards Unlimited ....G 228 863-1814
Gulfport (G-1730)
Eddie Wiggs ....G 662 456-7080
Houston (G-2239)
Plum Trophy Sales ....G 601 758-4834
Sumrall (G-5041)

ENGRAVING: Steel line, For The Printing Trade

Toyota Tsusho America Inc ....G 662 620-8890
Tupelo (G-5240)

ENTERTAINMENT SVCS

Mississippi Puppetry Guild ....G 601 977-9840
Jackson (G-2505)

ENVELOPES

Consoldted Converting Svcs Inc ....E 601 545-1699
Hattiesburg (G-1950)
Parthenon Envelope Company LLC ......E 601 758-4788
Sumrall (G-5040)

EQUIPMENT: Rental & Leasing, NEC

Glenn Machine Works Inc ....E 662 328-4611
Columbus (G-978)
Glenn Machine Works Inc ....E 228 875-1877
Vancleave (G-5319)

ESTIMATING SVCS: Construction

Daily & Sons Construction Inc ....G 601 737-5847
Bailey (G-67)

ETCHING & ENGRAVING SVC

Alley Kats Glass ....G 662 324-3002
Starkville (G-4924)
Eddie Wiggs ....G 662 456-7080
Houston (G-2239)
Tc Engraving & Gifts ....G 601 684-6834
McComb (G-3270)

ETHYLENE-PROPYLENE RUBBERS: EPDM Polymers

Rheogistics LLC ....E 601 749-8845
Picayune (G-4291)

EXPLORATION, METAL MINING

Randy A Elder ....G 504 301-7962
Carriere (G-700)
TMC Exploration Inc ....G 601 807-1124
Natchez (G-3631)

EXPLOSIVES

365 Explosive Athc Performllc ....G 601 365-2318
Hattiesburg (G-1914)
Titan Specialties ....G 601 477-3259
Ellisville (G-1272)

EXTRUDED SHAPES, NEC: Copper & Copper Alloy

Piper Metal Forming Corp ....C 508 363-3937
New Albany (G-3691)

EYEGLASSES

Cook Eye Center ....G 601 553-2100
Meridian (G-3323)
D Dodd John Od ....G 662 286-5671
Corinth (G-1082)

Employee Codes: A=Over 500 employees, B=251-500
C=101-250, D=51-100, E=20-50, F=10-19, G=1-9

2019 Harris Directory of
Mississippi Manufacturers

373

EYEGLASSES

I Care Optical Inc..................E....... 601 352-3576
Terry *(G-5070)*

EYEGLASSES: Sunglasses

Cv Sunglasses LLC..................G....... 662 212-0993
Walnut *(G-5456)*
Saul Jay Enterprises Inc ....F....... 662 349-1660
Southaven *(G-4899)*

EYELASHES, ARTIFICIAL

La Jolie Enterprises LLC..................G....... 601 909-8840
Ridgeland *(G-4596)*

FABRIC STORES

Rfm Enterprises LLC ....G....... 228 896-9498
Gulfport *(G-1862)*

FABRICATED METAL PRODUCTS, NEC

Anchor Works ....G....... 601 264-8700
Hattiesburg *(G-1923)*
Bad Moon Customs ....G....... 601 520-7248
Hattiesburg *(G-1925)*
H & H Metal Fabrication Inc ....G....... 662 489-4626
Belden *(G-189)*

FABRICS: Apparel & Outerwear, Cotton

Corinth Acquisition Corp ....G....... 662 287-1476
Corinth *(G-1075)*
Cotton Capitol LLC ....D....... 601 498-4770
Tylertown *(G-5269)*
Venevaa Jos LLC ....G....... 850 501-4040
Gulfport *(G-1891)*

FABRICS: Bonded-Fiber, Exc Felt

Jason Industries Inc ....D....... 662 327-0756
Columbus *(G-990)*

FABRICS: Broadwoven, Cotton

Rfm Enterprises LLC ....G....... 228 896-9498
Gulfport *(G-1862)*
Westpoint Home LLC ....G....... 601 466-6738
Hattiesburg *(G-2082)*

FABRICS: Broadwoven, Synthetic Manmade Fiber & Silk

Trace Industries Inc ....E....... 662 456-4261
Houston *(G-2256)*

FABRICS: Canvas

ADB Canvas Art ....G....... 662 934-9449
Batesville *(G-94)*
Canvas & Cocktails LLC ....G....... 228 861-8444
Gulfport *(G-1748)*
Canvas Creations & Eatery ....G....... 404 514-3399
Waynesboro *(G-5495)*
Canvasbeauty Beauty ....G....... 601 282-5430
Marion *(G-3221)*
Royal Canvas Studios ....G....... 601 419-0809
Ridgeland *(G-4626)*
Southern Canvas ....G....... 601 951-6266
Brandon *(G-458)*
Twisted Canvas ....G....... 228 596-9332
Long Beach *(G-2959)*

FABRICS: Canvas & Heavy Coarse, Cotton

French Awning & Screen Co Inc............G....... 601 922-1132
Jackson *(G-2414)*

FABRICS: Coated Or Treated

Bills Organic Grdnng & Leaf..................G....... 901 315-8888
Olive Branch *(G-3819)*
Omnova Solutions Inc ....A....... 662 327-1522
Columbus *(G-1012)*

FABRICS: Cords

Shoulder Cords Unlimited..................G....... 601 425-2195
Laurel *(G-2849)*

FABRICS: Denims

CIC International LLC ....G....... 662 473-4724
Water Valley *(G-5465)*

FABRICS: Glass & Fiberglass, Broadwoven

Crossroads Picks LLC..................G....... 662 902-1026
Clarksdale *(G-765)*

FABRICS: Hand Woven

R2pg Inc ....F....... 601 747-0522
Port Gibson *(G-4406)*

FABRICS: Jean

Jane Little Inc ....G....... 601 694-2767
Newhebron *(G-3713)*

FABRICS: Luggage, Cotton

Evh Properties LLC ....G....... 662 571-1980
Yazoo City *(G-5634)*
Mardis 300 LLC ....G....... 601 936-3911
Flowood *(G-1380)*

FABRICS: Nonwoven

Carpenter Co ....B....... 662 566-2392
Verona *(G-5329)*
Fibrix LLC ....E....... 662 844-3803
Tupelo *(G-5132)*
Fibrix LLC ....E....... 662 844-5595
Tupelo *(G-5133)*
Fibrix LLC ....E....... 662 489-7908
Pontotoc *(G-4331)*
Master Fibers Inc ....G....... 662 568-3455
Houlka *(G-2225)*
Mississippi Fabritek Inc ....D....... 662 327-0745
Columbus *(G-1003)*
Trace Industries Inc ....E....... 662 456-4261
Houston *(G-2256)*

FABRICS: Papermakers Felt, Woven, Wool, Mohair/Similar Fiber

Voith Fabrics Florence Inc ....C....... 601 845-2202
Florence *(G-1336)*

FABRICS: Print, Cotton

Harris Custom Ink LLC ....E....... 662 338-4242
Olive Branch *(G-3844)*

FABRICS: Satin

Satin Locs LLC ....G....... 901 282-6823
Walls *(G-5451)*

FABRICS: Scrub Cloths

Scrubs Elite LLC ....G....... 662 842-4011
Tupelo *(G-5220)*

FABRICS: Specialty Including Twisted Weaves, Broadwoven

Weavexx LLC ....C....... 662 323-4064
Starkville *(G-4980)*

FABRICS: Trimmings

Charlottes EMB & Screen Prtg ....G....... 601 824-1080
Brandon *(G-379)*
Haygoods Industrial Engravers..................G....... 228 769-7488
Pascagoula *(G-4036)*
Southern Speed ....G....... 662 842-3799
Tupelo *(G-5228)*
Systems Auto Interiors LLC ....D....... 662 862-1360
Mantachie *(G-3206)*
T Tommys ....G....... 601 833-8620
Brookhaven *(G-542)*

FABRICS: Tubing, Textile, Varnished

Insituform Technologies LLC ....D....... 662 561-1378
Batesville *(G-109)*

FABRICS: Upholstery, Cotton

Culp Inc..................F....... 662 844-7144
Tupelo *(G-5124)*

FABRICS: Upholstery, Wool

Kdh Kustoms LLC..................G....... 601 730-2052
McComb *(G-3256)*
Mitchell Group ....G....... 662 488-0025
Pontotoc *(G-4347)*

Townhouse Home Furnishings LLC
Townhouse Home Furnishings LLC......C....... 662 651-5442
Smithville *(G-4845)*

FACIAL SALONS

Joyce Tillman ....G....... 228 896-4927
Gulfport *(G-1814)*

FACILITIES SUPPORT SVCS

Fallen Leaf Services LLC ....G....... 228 731-0919
Gulfport *(G-1781)*
Frontier Contracting LLC ....G....... 662 809-1949
Grenada *(G-1678)*

FAMILY CLOTHING STORES

Lauderdale County Farm Sup Inc..................E....... 601 483-3363
Meridian *(G-3356)*
T Shirt Shop & Design Firm LLC ....G....... 662 329-9911
Columbus *(G-1036)*

FARM & GARDEN MACHINERY WHOLESALERS

Cook Lawn & Tractor LLC ....G....... 601 445-0718
Natchez *(G-3550)*

FARM MACHINERY REPAIR SVCS

Leas Repair..................G....... 662 658-4462
Minter City *(G-3424)*
Williamson Gin Repair ....G....... 662 571-6084
Yazoo City *(G-5652)*

FARM SPLY STORES

Hawks Feed Mill ....G....... 662 564-2920
Hernando *(G-2134)*
Moores John ....G....... 662 488-2980
Pontotoc *(G-4350)*
Neshoba County Gin Assn AAL ....F....... 601 656-3463
Philadelphia *(G-4227)*
Taylor & Sons Inc ....G....... 601 483-0714
Meridian *(G-3411)*

FARM SPLYS WHOLESALERS

Central Industries Inc ....G....... 601 469-4421
Forest *(G-1410)*
Helena Agri-Enterprises LLC ....F....... 662 746-7466
Yazoo City *(G-5635)*
Huddleston Farm Service Inc ....G....... 662 728-5288
Booneville *(G-331)*
Hurley Farm & Feed ....G....... 228 588-9156
Hurley *(G-2260)*
Jasper Cooperative ....G....... 601 428-4968
Stringer *(G-5003)*
Terra Industries Inc ....E....... 662 456-3076
Houston *(G-2255)*
Woods Farm Supply Inc ....E....... 662 838-6754
Byhalia *(G-614)*

FARM SPLYS, WHOLESALE: Feed

Lauderdale County Farm Sup Inc..........E....... 601 483-3363
Meridian *(G-3356)*

FARM SPLYS, WHOLESALE: Fertilizers & Agricultural Chemicals

Agri-Afc LLC ....E....... 601 783-6080
Magnolia *(G-3188)*
Helena Chemical Company ....G....... 662 383-0004
Friars Point *(G-1442)*
J & J Bagging LLC ....E....... 662 746-5155
Yazoo City *(G-5637)*
Sanders Seed ....G....... 800 844-5533
Cleveland *(G-808)*

FARM SPLYS, WHOLESALE: Greenhouse Eqpt & Splys

Eakes Nursery Materials Inc ....G....... 601 722-4797
Seminary *(G-4777)*

FARM SPLYS, WHOLESALE: Insecticides

Pinnacle Agriculture Dist Inc ....G....... 662 265-5828
Inverness *(G-2276)*

PRODUCT SECTION

FIRE ARMS, SMALL: Guns Or Gun Parts, 30 mm & Below

FASTENERS: Notions, NEC

Bolt Company LLC ....G....... 601 696-9191
Meridian (G-3312)
Grenada Fasteners Inc ....G....... 662 227-1000
Grenada (G-1680)
Mjj Inc ....G....... 662 455-0126
Greenwood (G-1641)
Triangle Fastener Corporation..............G....... 601 956-1824
Ridgeland (G-4643)

FELT PARTS

Trace Industries Inc ....E....... 662 456-4261
Houston (G-2256)
Weavexx LLC ....C....... 662 323-4064
Starkville (G-4980)

FELT, WHOLESALE

Weavexx LLC ....C....... 662 323-4064
Starkville (G-4980)

FELTS: Building

Insituform Technologies LLC ....D....... 662 561-1378
Batesville (G-109)

FENCE POSTS: Iron & Steel

Garrett Welding & Iron........................G....... 601 372-3889
Terry (G-5068)
Southern Exteriors Fence Co ....G....... 228 586-2110
Perkinston (G-4181)

FENCES & FENCING MATERIALS

Johnsons Fencing ....G....... 601 833-3263
Brookhaven (G-505)

FENCES OR POSTS: Ornamental Iron Or Steel

Iron Innovations Inc ....F....... 601 924-0640
Clinton (G-826)
South Memphis Fence Co ....G....... 662 526-5400
Como (G-1051)

FENCING DEALERS

McKinnion Welding & Metal Fabr ....G....... 601 635-3983
Decatur (G-1175)

FENCING MATERIALS: Docks & Other Outdoor Prdts, Wood

Dungans Outdoor Solutions Co ....G....... 228 382-7156
Ocean Springs (G-3753)

FENCING MATERIALS: Plastic

Southern Exteriors Fence Co ....G....... 228 586-2110
Perkinston (G-4181)

FENCING: Chain Link

Laclede Chain Mfg Co LLC ....G....... 601 802-0134
Vicksburg (G-5388)

FERTILIZER MINERAL MINING

N-R-G Chemical Company ....G....... 601 519-5363
Laurel (G-2810)

FERTILIZER, AGRICULTURAL: Wholesalers

Advanced Dynamics Inc......................G....... 601 677-3423
Preston (G-4426)

FERTILIZERS: NEC

Agri-Afc LLC......................................E....... 601 783-6080
Magnolia (G-3188)
Delta Agricultural MGT Inc ....G....... 865 210-4605
Tunica (G-5096)
Eakes Nursery Materials Inc ....G....... 601 722-4797
Seminary (G-4777)
Helena Agri-Enterprises LLC ....F....... 662 746-7466
Yazoo City (G-5635)
Huddleston Farm Service Inc ....G....... 662 728-5288
Booneville (G-331)
Mississippi Agri-Products Inc ....G....... 601 879-3343
Flora (G-1310)
Neshoba County Gin Assn AAL ....F....... 601 656-3463
Philadelphia (G-4227)

Pinnacle Agriculture Dist Inc

Pinnacle Agriculture Dist Inc ....G....... 662 265-5828
Inverness (G-2276)
Terra Industries Inc ....E....... 662 456-3076
Houston (G-2255)
Woods Farm Supply Inc ....E....... 662 838-6754
Byhalia (G-614)
Woodson Flying Service Inc ....G....... 662 983-4274
Bruce (G-563)

FERTILIZERS: Nitrogenous

CF Industries Nitrogen LLC ....E....... 662 751-2616
Yazoo City (G-5626)
Forest Penick Products Inc...................E....... 662 726-5224
Macon (G-3062)
Melamine Chemicals Inc ....G....... 662 746-4131
Yazoo City (G-5639)
Terra Houston Ammonia Inc ....E....... 662 746-4131
Yazoo City (G-5648)
Terra Mississippi Nitrogen Inc ....B....... 662 746-4131
Yazoo City (G-5649)

FERTILIZERS: Phosphatic

CF Industries Nitrogen LLC ....E....... 662 751-2616
Yazoo City (G-5626)
Phosphate Holdings Inc ....B....... 601 898-9004
Madison (G-3138)
Terra Mississippi Nitrogen Inc ....B....... 662 746-4131
Yazoo City (G-5649)

FIBER & FIBER PRDTS: Elastomeric

Elite Elastomers Inc ....E....... 662 512-1770
Ripley (G-4657)

FIBER & FIBER PRDTS: Organic, Noncellulose

Fibrix LLC ....E....... 662 489-7908
Pontotoc (G-4331)
Omnova Solutions Inc ....A....... 662 327-1522
Columbus (G-1012)
Weyerhaeuser Company ....D....... 662 243-6900
Columbus (G-1045)

FIBER & FIBER PRDTS: Polyester

Best Fiber Inc ....E....... 662 840-1118
Tupelo (G-5115)
Quality Fibers Inc ....G....... 662 620-7775
Tupelo (G-5210)
Superior Manufactured Fibers...............G....... 662 844-8255
Plantersville (G-4317)

FIBER & FIBER PRDTS: Synthetic Cellulosic

Custom Nonwoven Inc ....F....... 662 539-6103
New Albany (G-3679)
Fibrix LLC ....E....... 662 844-3803
Tupelo (G-5132)
Fibrix LLC ....E....... 662 489-7908
Pontotoc (G-4331)
Kengro Corporation ....F....... 662 647-2456
Charleston (G-740)
Leggett Platt Components Inc ....F....... 662 844-4224
Tupelo (G-5179)
Southern Components Inc ....D....... 662 844-7884
Tupelo (G-5226)
Weyerhaeuser Company ....D....... 662 243-6900
Columbus (G-1045)

FIGURES, WAX

London War Room ....G....... 601 584-8533
Petal (G-4192)

FILE FOLDERS

Pqr Inc...C....... 662 289-7613
Kosciusko (G-2710)

FILLERS & SEALERS: Wood

Je Painting and Renovations.................G....... 601 470-2047
Hattiesburg (G-2001)

FILM & SHEET: Unsuppported Plastic

Ability Works Inc ....G....... 662 328-0275
Columbus (G-931)
Afco Industries Inc.............................C....... 662 895-8686
Olive Branch (G-3808)

Bag Connection LLC

Bag Connection LLC ....F....... 662 624-6570
Clarksdale (G-758)
Berry Global Inc ....C....... 601 584-4800
Hattiesburg (G-1928)
Berry Global Inc ....G....... 601 584-4778
Hattiesburg (G-1929)
Central Miss RES & EXT Ctr ....G....... 601 857-2284
Raymond (G-4485)
Dixie Packaging Inc ....E....... 601 276-9317
Summit (G-5012)
Lucite International ....G....... 662 893-5450
Olive Branch (G-3867)
Mega Plastics Inc ....D....... 601 924-1712
Clinton (G-831)
Mississippi Polymers Inc ....B....... 662 287-1401
Corinth (G-1103)
Omnova Solutions Inc ....A....... 662 327-1522
Columbus (G-1012)
Orbis Rpm LLC ....F....... 662 890-7646
Olive Branch (G-3891)

FILTER ELEMENTS: Fluid & Hydraulic Line

Ripley Industries Inc ....E....... 662 423-6733
Iuka (G-2307)

FILTERS

Filter Service Inc ....G....... 601 644-9840
Meridian (G-3338)
Monotech of Mississippi ....C....... 662 423-2033
Iuka (G-2303)

FILTERS & SOFTENERS: Water, Household

Ecowater Systems LLC ....C....... 662 837-9349
Ripley (G-4656)

FILTERS: Air

Collins Filter Co Inc ....F....... 228 896-0582
Gulfport (G-1762)
Filter Service Mississippi LLC ....G....... 601 693-4614
Meridian (G-3339)
Lott Enterprises Inc ....C....... 662 453-0034
Greenwood (G-1636)
Lott Enterprises Inc ....G....... 601 932-4698
Jackson (G-2654)
Wares Air Filter Service ....G....... 228 832-8918
Gulfport (G-1892)

FILTERS: General Line, Indl

Gulf Coast Filters Inc..........................G....... 601 528-5762
Perkinston (G-4176)
Holmes Industries LLC ....G....... 601 635-4409
Decatur (G-1173)
National Filter Media Corp ....D....... 662 895-4660
Olive Branch (G-3884)
Parker-Hannifin Corporation.................C....... 662 252-2656
Holly Springs (G-2187)

FILTERS: Oil, Internal Combustion Engine, Exc Auto

Eco Recovery Machine LLC..................G....... 713 829-1083
Pinola (G-4308)

FILTRATION DEVICES: Electronic

Turners Tax Service ....F....... 662 887-2066
Baird (G-69)

FINDINGS & TRIMMINGS: Apparel

Mount Vernon Mills Inc ....D....... 662 328-5670
Columbus (G-1009)

FINDINGS & TRIMMINGS: Fabric

Grammer Inc ....D....... 864 672-0702
Shannon (G-4808)

FINGERPRINT EQPT

Automtion Dsigns Solutions Inc ....G....... 601 992-4121
Brandon (G-367)

FIRE ARMS, SMALL: Guns Or Gun Parts, 30 mm & Below

2a Armaments LLC ....G....... 662 538-8118
New Albany (G-3669)

Employee Codes: A=Over 500 employees, B=251-500
C=101-250, D=51-100, E=20-50, F=10-19, G=1-9

2019 Harris Directory of
Mississippi Manufacturers

375

PRODUCT

FIRE ARMS, SMALL: Guns Or Gun Parts, 30 mm & Below

GI Armory LLC ....G....... 662 372-3389
Fulton (G-1454)
JMS Manufacturing Inc ....G....... 601 514-0660
Lucedale (G-3005)
John J Ishee ....G....... 601 847-2723
Mendenhall (G-3282)
Precision Rifle Ordnance LLC ....G....... 601 825-0697
Brandon (G-438)
Smiths Speed Shop ....G....... 601 794-2855
Purvis (G-4452)
Stringer Gun Works LLC ....G....... 601 947-6796
Lucedale (G-3019)

FIRE ARMS, SMALL: Rifles Or Rifle Parts, 30 mm & below

Dixie Precision Rifles LLC ....G....... 601 706-9100
Brandon (G-389)

FIRE EXTINGUISHERS: Portable

Integrity Fire Extinguish ....G....... 601 953-1927
Madison (G-3111)

FIRE OR BURGLARY RESISTIVE PRDTS

Griffin Inc ....D....... 662 838-2128
Byhalia (G-586)
River Road Welding Inc ....G....... 601 947-2511
Lucedale (G-3016)

FIRE PROTECTION EQPT

Southern Technical Aquatic RES ....G....... 601 590-6248
Carriere (G-701)

FIRE PROTECTION SVCS: Contracted

Blue Note Management LLC ....F....... 662 281-1881
Oxford (G-3943)

FIRE PROTECTION, GOVERNMENT: Fire Department, Volunteer

City of Biloxi..................................C....... 228 435-6217
Biloxi (G-228)

FIREARMS: Large, Greater Than 30mm

Robert E Monk ....G....... 662 562-8729
Senatobia (G-4800)

FIREARMS: Small, 30mm or Less

Dsp Armory Inc ....G....... 662 862-4272
Fulton (G-1452)
Fianna Systems LLC.........................G....... 662 726-5200
Macon (G-3061)
Maa Global Supply Ltd ....F....... 662 816-4802
Oxford (G-3968)
Military Firearms Parts ....G....... 228 596-1271
Gulfport (G-1831)
Sycpowersports ....G....... 662 301-1563
Senatobia (G-4803)

FIREWORKS

All Seasons Events..........................G....... 601 405-1417
Jackson (G-2321)
Eagle Fire Works Co Inc...................G....... 601 798-9291
Picayune (G-4265)

FIREWORKS SHOPS

Eagle Fire Works Co Inc...................G....... 601 798-9291
Picayune (G-4265)

FISH & SEAFOOD PROCESSORS: Fresh Or Frozen

Alabama Catfish Inc.........................F....... 662 265-5377
Inverness (G-2272)
Consoldted Ctfish Prducers LLC ....B....... 662 962-3101
Isola (G-2278)
Gollott Icehouse & Oil Dock..............G....... 228 280-8033
Biloxi (G-246)
Heartland Catfish Company Inc...........B....... 662 254-7100
Itta Bena (G-2280)
Omega Protein Corporation ....C....... 228 475-1252
Moss Point (G-3492)
R Fournier & Sons Inc ....E....... 228 392-4293
Diberville (G-1209)

Tarantos Crawfish House ....G....... 228 392-0806
Diberville (G-1216)

FISH FOOD

Fishbelt Feeds Inc ....E....... 662 246-5065
Moorhead (G-3445)
Indi-Bel Inc ....D....... 662 887-1226
Indianola (G-2265)
Sunshine Mills Inc ....D....... 662 842-6714
Tupelo (G-5233)

FISHING EQPT: Lures

Bain Manufacturing Co Inc ....F....... 662 226-7921
Grenada (G-1668)
Itawamba Classic Lures ....G....... 601 720-8810
Fulton (G-1458)
Jara L Miller ....G....... 601 421-6876
Brandon (G-410)
Mediator Lures Inc ....G....... 601 992-1577
Brandon (G-423)
Old River Lure Company LLC ....G....... 601 259-4323
Terry (G-5074)
Southern Lure Company Inc ....F....... 662 327-4548
Columbus (G-1029)
Stryke Ryte Lures ....G....... 217 370-9461
New Albany (G-3702)
Triple M Lures LLC ....G....... 601 919-5515
Perkinston (G-4182)

FISHING EQPT: Nets & Seines

R F Ederer Co Inc............................E....... 228 875-9345
Ocean Springs (G-3780)

FITTINGS & ASSEMBLIES: Hose & Tube, Hydraulic Or Pneumatic

Applied Indus Tech - Dixie Inc ....G....... 601 649-4312
Laurel (G-2731)
Dahls Automotive Parts Inc ....G....... 228 875-8154
Ocean Springs (G-3751)
Hattiesburg Hydraulics Sls Svc ....G....... 601 264-6606
Hattiesburg (G-1986)
Maximum Auto Parts & Supply...........F....... 228 863-1100
Gulfport (G-1825)
Rubber & Specialties Inc ....G....... 228 762-6103
Pascagoula (G-4065)
Specialty Hose Fabrication Inc ....G....... 228 831-1919
Gulfport (G-1877)
Tucker Machine Services ....G....... 601 582-4280
Hattiesburg (G-2075)

FITTINGS: Pipe

Mississippi Forge (pvf) Inc ....E....... 662 285-2995
Ackerman (G-27)
RPM Piping and Supply LLC ....G....... 901 633-6083
Southaven (G-4897)
United Assoc Journeymen & 5 ....G....... 228 863-1853
Gulfport (G-1889)

FITTINGS: Pipe, Fabricated

Lokring Gulf Coast LLC.....................G....... 228 497-0091
Gautier (G-1497)

FIXTURES: Cut Stone

K & D Cultured Marble Inc.................E....... 662 675-2928
Coffeeville (G-843)
Lighthouse Marble Works Inc ....E....... 228 392-3038
Biloxi (G-262)
Moulton Tile & Marble Inc ....G....... 228 863-7587
Long Beach (G-2945)

FLAGPOLES

Southeast Miss Schl Pdts Inc ....G....... 662 855-5048
Caledonia (G-631)

FLAT GLASS: Window, Clear & Colored

View Inc ....D....... 662 892-3415
Olive Branch (G-3921)

FLEA MARKET

First Monday Trade Day ....G....... 662 837-4051
Ripley (G-4659)

FLOOR COVERING STORES

Armstrong Flooring Inc ....C....... 601 354-1515
Jackson (G-2333)

FLOOR COVERING STORES: Carpets

Alfords Decorating Center ....G....... 662 455-3552
Greenwood (G-1612)

FLOOR COVERING STORES: Floor Tile

L & G Marble Inc.............................G....... 601 268-0225
Hattiesburg (G-2012)

FLOORING: Baseboards, Wood

Tri-C Wood Products Inc ....E....... 601 774-8295
Union (G-5303)

FLOORING: Hard Surface

Armstrong Flooring Inc ....C....... 601 354-1515
Jackson (G-2333)
Portstone Manufacturing Corp ....G....... 601 922-0902
Jackson (G-2543)

FLOORING: Hardwood

Clearspan Components Inc ....C....... 601 483-3941
Meridian (G-3321)
Everett Industries Inc ....G....... 228 231-1556
Bay Saint Louis (G-143)

FLOORING: Rubber

Everett Industries Inc ....G....... 228 231-1556
Bay Saint Louis (G-143)

FLOWER ARRANGEMENTS: Artificial

Sew Sweet ....G....... 601 431-2304
Natchez (G-3618)

FLOWERS & FLORISTS' SPLYS WHOLESALERS

Rome Chenille & Supply Co Inc ....G....... 662 286-9947
Corinth (G-1116)

FLOWERS, ARTIFICIAL, WHOLESALE

Marilyn Turner ....G....... 228 271-2551
Biloxi (G-265)

FLOWERS: Artificial & Preserved

Debra Thigpen.................................G....... 601 856-0019
Madison (G-3095)

FLUID POWER PUMPS & MOTORS

ABB Motors and Mechanical Inc ....E....... 662 328-9116
Columbus (G-930)
Eaton Aerospace LLC........................E....... 601 981-2811
Jackson (G-2396)
Franklin Electrofluid Co Inc ....G....... 601 969-7022
Jackson (G-2412)
Geartek ....F....... 662 286-2252
Corinth (G-1087)
Metaris Corporation.........................E....... 601 469-1987
Forest (G-1422)
Pickett Equipment Co Inc..................G....... 662 890-9095
Olive Branch (G-3895)
Plymouth Tube Company ....D....... 662 258-2420
Eupora (G-1290)

FLUID POWER VALVES & HOSE FITTINGS

Parker-Hannifin Corporation..............C....... 601 856-4123
Madison (G-3137)

FLUXES

Inspection Plus LLC ....G....... 601 525-6744
Leakesville (G-2877)

FOAM RUBBER

Best Foam Inc ....E....... 662 840-6700
Sherman (G-4826)
Elite Comfort Solutions LLC ....E....... 662 566-2322
Verona (G-5330)
Johnson Foam Sales Inc ....E....... 662 767-9007
Shannon (G-4811)

2019 Harris Directory of
Mississippi Manufacturers

(G-0000) Company's Geographic Section entry number

376

PRODUCT SECTION

FOOD PRDTS: Cottonseed Cooking & Salad Oil

Magnolia Furniture LLC.....................G...... 662 489-9337
Pontotoc (G-4342)
Mount Vernon Foam Sales ....F 662 844-3107
Tupelo (G-5190)

FOIL: Aluminum

Packaging Dynamics Corporation ....E 662 424-4000
Iuka (G-2304)

FOOD COLORINGS: Bakers'

Ada Newson ....G...... 601 810-6614
Richland (G-4498)

FOOD PRDTS, BREAKFAST: Cereal, Granola & Muesli

Great American Granola Co LLC ....G...... 228 369-0902
Ocean Springs (G-3759)

FOOD PRDTS, CANNED: Fruits

Althees Jellies & Jams LLC ....G...... 601 795-4118
Poplarville (G-4373)

FOOD PRDTS, CANNED: Fruits & Fruit Prdts

Global Food Concepts Inc ....C 601 940-5425
Flowood (G-1364)

FOOD PRDTS, CANNED: Jellies, Edible, Including Imitation

Gautier Mayhaw Co..............................G...... 228 497-6896
Gautier (G-1493)

FOOD PRDTS, CANNED: Mexican, NEC

Los Portrillos.....................................G...... 662 844-7350
Tupelo (G-5180)

FOOD PRDTS, CONFECTIONERY, WHOLESALE: Snack Foods

Westward Corporation ....G...... 601 660-3857
Fayette (G-1303)

FOOD PRDTS, DAIRY, WHOLESALE: Milk & Cream, Fluid

Borden Dairy Company Ala LLC ....D 601 268-2583
Hattiesburg (G-1937)

FOOD PRDTS, FISH & SEAFOOD, WHOLESALE: Seafood

Custom Pack Inc ....F 228 435-3632
Biloxi (G-235)
Gulf Pride Enterprises Inc....................F 228 432-2488
Biloxi (G-249)
R Fournier & Sons Inc ....E 228 392-4293
Diberville (G-1209)

FOOD PRDTS, FISH & SEAFOOD: Fish, Fresh, Prepared

Consoldted Ctfish Cmpanies LLC.........B 662 962-3101
Isola (G-2277)
Freshwater Farms Products LLC ....C 662 247-4205
Belzoni (G-205)
Lakes Farm Raised Catfish Inc.............G...... 662 363-1847
Dundee (G-1224)
Magnolia Processing Inc.......................C 662 363-3600
Tunica (G-5101)
Noxubee County Producers Inc ....C 662 726-2502
Macon (G-3069)

FOOD PRDTS, FISH & SEAFOOD: Fish, Frozen, Prepared

Simmons Frm Raised Catfish Inc..........E 662 746-5687
Yazoo City (G-5646)

FOOD PRDTS, FISH & SEAFOOD: Fresh, Prepared

Ocean Springs Seafood Mkt Inc............G...... 228 875-0104
Biloxi (G-269)
R A Lesso Seafood Inc ....E 228 374-7200
Biloxi (G-274)

FOOD PRDTS, FISH & SEAFOOD: Seafood, Frozen, Prepared

Lesso Freezing Company Inc ....G...... 228 374-7200
Biloxi (G-261)
Sanderson Farms Inc Foods Div ....G...... 601 649-4030
Laurel (G-2843)

FOOD PRDTS, FISH & SEAFOOD: Shrimp, Fresh, Prepared

Custom Pack Inc ....F 228 435-3632
Biloxi (G-235)
Global Seafood Tech Inc ....E 228 435-3632
Biloxi (G-245)
Gulf Pride Enterprises Inc....................F 228 432-2488
Biloxi (G-249)

FOOD PRDTS, FROZEN: Dinners, Packaged

Brm LLC ....G...... 601 501-1444
Vicksburg (G-5348)
J & K Restaurants Inc ....G...... 601 501-1444
Vicksburg (G-5381)
Sanderson Farms Inc Foods Div ....G...... 601 649-4030
Laurel (G-2843)
Sanderson Farms Inc Foods Div ....B 601 939-9790
Flowood (G-1394)

FOOD PRDTS, FROZEN: Fruits, Juices & Vegetables

Anusaya Fresh USA LLC.....................G...... 601 795-2008
Poplarville (G-4374)
Borden Dairy Company Ala LLC ....D 601 268-2583
Hattiesburg (G-1937)
Ishee Produce ....G...... 601 651-6643
Laurel (G-2784)

FOOD PRDTS, FROZEN: NEC

Ajinomoto Foods North Amer Inc..........D 662 623-7400
Oakland (G-3737)
Ajinomoto Windsor Inc........................G...... 662 647-1594
Batesville (G-95)
Dutch Ann Foods Inc ....E 601 445-4496
Natchez (G-3557)
Kims Processing Plant Inc....................F 662 627-2389
Clarksdale (G-771)

FOOD PRDTS, FROZEN: Vegetables, Exc Potato Prdts

Keith Murphree...................................G...... 662 292-7644
Senatobia (G-4793)

FOOD PRDTS, MEAT & MEAT PRDTS, WHOLESALE: Fresh

Fortenberrys Slaughter House ....G...... 601 798-2156
Carriere (G-692)

FOOD PRDTS, WHOLESALE: Beverages, Exc Coffee & Tea

Hooper Sales Co Incorporated ....G...... 662 526-5668
Como (G-1048)
RC Cola Company...............................F 662 844-7947
Tupelo (G-5214)
Sqwincher Corporation ....D 662 328-0400
Columbus (G-1030)

FOOD PRDTS, WHOLESALE: Coffee & Tea

1529 Coffee Company ....G...... 662 315-6951
Amory (G-32)
From Our Cup To Yours........................G...... 601 214-7689
Pearl (G-4121)

FOOD PRDTS, WHOLESALE: Natural & Organic

Shed Saucery LLC..............................G...... 228 875-7373
Ocean Springs (G-3785)

FOOD PRDTS, WHOLESALE: Specialty

Chef Rays Famous LLC........................G...... 601 559-8096
Byram (G-619)

FOOD PRDTS, WHOLESALE: Spices & Seasonings

TNT Investments LLC ....G...... 228 860-8207
Biloxi (G-284)

FOOD PRDTS, WHOLESALE: Water, Mineral Or Spring, Bottled

Cool Baby Water LLC ....G...... 850 748-0921
Lucedale (G-2990)
Grd Distributors LLC ....G...... 601 382-8802
Richland (G-4518)

FOOD PRDTS: Animal & marine fats & oils

Blue Ridge Beef Plant Inc ....G...... 864 338-5544
Greenwood (G-1615)
Central Industries Inc ....E 601 469-4421
Forest (G-1411)
Darling Ingredients Inc ....G...... 601 372-5212
Jackson (G-2376)

FOOD PRDTS: Baking Powder, Soda, Yeast & Leavenings

Becks Confection................................G...... 601 927-3137
Ridgeland (G-4554)

FOOD PRDTS: Bologna, Poultry

Sammy Evans Poultry ....G...... 601 267-0521
Carthage (G-723)

FOOD PRDTS: Box Lunches, For Sale Off Premises

West Group Holding Company LLC ......G...... 662 871-2344
Shannon (G-4821)

FOOD PRDTS: Bran, Rice

A & J Planting Company ....G...... 662 363-0039
Tunica (G-5094)

FOOD PRDTS: Cereals

Big Star of Belmont Inc ....G...... 662 454-3300
Belmont (G-196)

FOOD PRDTS: Chicken, Processed, Cooked

Peco Foods Inc ....C 601 855-0925
Canton (G-676)

FOOD PRDTS: Chicken, Processed, Fresh

Koch Foods of Mississippi LLC ....E 601 732-8911
Flowood (G-1374)
Koch Foods of Mississippi LLC ....E 601 732-3026
Morton (G-3449)

FOOD PRDTS: Chicken, Slaughtered & Dressed

Sanderson Farms Inc ....C 601 649-4030
Laurel (G-2842)
Sanderson Farms Inc Proc Div ....C 601 649-4030
Laurel (G-2844)

FOOD PRDTS: Coffee

An AMC LLC ....G...... 662 292-6973
Olive Branch (G-3814)
Aromica Coffee LLC ....G...... 901 848-1687
Olive Branch (G-3816)
Chenoa Coffee Company ....G...... 662 834-3917
Lexington (G-2898)
Mississippi Cold Drip Coffee ....G...... 601 624-5708
Jackson (G-2498)

FOOD PRDTS: Coffee Roasting, Exc Wholesale Grocers

1529 Coffee Company ....G...... 662 315-6951
Amory (G-32)

FOOD PRDTS: Cottonseed Cooking & Salad Oil

Cottonseed Co-Op Corporation.............E 662 358-4481
Jonestown (G-2675)

Employee Codes: A=Over 500 employees, B=251-500
C=101-250, D=51-100, E=20-50, F=10-19, G=1-9

2019 Harris Directory of
Mississippi Manufacturers

377

PRODUCT

FOOD PRDTS: Cottonseed Oil, Cake & Meal

PRODUCT SECTION

FOOD PRDTS: Cottonseed Oil, Cake & Meal

Delta Oil Mill ....E 662 358-4809
Jonestown *(G-2676)*

Omega Protein Corporation ....C 228 475-1252
Moss Point *(G-3492)*

FOOD PRDTS: Dressings, Salad, Raw & Cooked Exc Dry Mixes

Reed Food Technology Inc ....E 601 939-4001
Pearl *(G-4140)*

FOOD PRDTS: Ducks, Slaughtered & Dressed

Delta Duck Hunts Inc ....G 662 357-5152
Dundee *(G-1223)*

FOOD PRDTS: Eggs, Processed

Cal-Maine Foods Inc ....D 601 852-4970
Edwards *(G-1236)*

FOOD PRDTS: Eggs, Processed, Frozen

Cal-Maine Foods Inc ....G 601 852-4413
Edwards *(G-1237)*

FOOD PRDTS: Emulsifiers

No Time 2 Cook LLC ....G 662 236-9456
Oxford *(G-3976)*

Shcpi Greenwood Site ....G 662 453-1445
Greenwood *(G-1651)*

FOOD PRDTS: Fish Meal

Omega Protein Corporation ....C 228 475-1252
Moss Point *(G-3492)*

Protein Products Inc ....E 662 569-3396
Sunflower *(G-5047)*

FOOD PRDTS: Fish Oil

M G K Seining LLC ....G 662 453-8370
Greenwood *(G-1638)*

FOOD PRDTS: Fruit Juices

Realpure Beverage Group LLC ....F 601 849-9910
Magee *(G-3181)*

FOOD PRDTS: Fruits & Vegetables, Pickled

Gibson and Pickle Inc ....G 662 289-2400
Kosciusko *(G-2694)*

Jean Pickle ....G 662 256-7020
Amory *(G-46)*

Pickle Larry ....G 662 256-7239
Amory *(G-52)*

FOOD PRDTS: Honey

Honeyland Inc ....G 870 635-1160
Pass Christian *(G-4088)*

Live and Laff LLC ....G 662 816-5144
Taylor *(G-5049)*

FOOD PRDTS: Ice, Cubes

Ice Plant Inc ....F 601 485-9111
Meridian *(G-3347)*

FOOD PRDTS: Instant Coffee

From Our Cup To Yours ....G 601 214-7689
Pearl *(G-4121)*

FOOD PRDTS: Mixes, Bread & Bread-Type Roll

Reed Food Technology Inc ....E 601 939-4001
Pearl *(G-4140)*

FOOD PRDTS: Mixes, Doughnut From Purchased Flour

Taste Maker Foods LLC ....E 901 274-4407
Hernando *(G-2158)*

FOOD PRDTS: Mixes, Seasonings, Dry

Rebel Butcher Supply Co Inc ....G 601 939-2214
Jackson *(G-2665)*

Taste Maker Foods LLC ....E 901 274-4407
Hernando *(G-2158)*

FOOD PRDTS: Nuts & Seeds

Indianola Pecan House Inc ....G 601 693-1998
Meridian *(G-3351)*

FOOD PRDTS: Oil, Partially Hydrogenated, Edible

Sani LLC ....G 601 454-6047
Clinton *(G-835)*

FOOD PRDTS: Olive Oil

Grecian Oil Importers LLC ....G 662 372-4933
Tupelo *(G-5147)*

FOOD PRDTS: Popcorn, Popped

Ada Newson ....G 601 810-6614
Richland *(G-4498)*

FOOD PRDTS: Pork Rinds

Central Snacks Inc ....F 601 267-3112
Carthage *(G-712)*

Kims Processing Plant Inc ....F 662 627-2389
Clarksdale *(G-771)*

FOOD PRDTS: Potato & Corn Chips & Similar Prdts

Billy Purvis Distributing LLC ....G 601 480-3147
Meridian *(G-3306)*

Dkh Distributing Inc ....G 901 734-4528
Hernando *(G-2129)*

FOOD PRDTS: Poultry Sausage, Lunch Meats/Other Poultry Prdts

Tyson Foods Inc ....A 601 631-3600
Vicksburg *(G-5431)*

FOOD PRDTS: Poultry, Processed, NEC

Koch Foods of Mississippi LLC ....B 601 469-2337
Forest *(G-1421)*

Marshall Durbin Food Corp ....A 601 544-3141
Hattiesburg *(G-2021)*

Peco Foods Inc ....C 601 656-1865
Philadelphia *(G-4231)*

Peco Foods Inc ....A 601 764-4392
Bay Springs *(G-170)*

FOOD PRDTS: Poultry, Slaughtered & Dressed

Sanderson Farms Inc ....B 601 894-3721
Hazlehurst *(G-2103)*

FOOD PRDTS: Preparations

B K Industries Inc ....F 864 963-3471
New Albany *(G-3674)*

Blendco Inc ....E 888 253-6326
Hattiesburg *(G-1935)*

Borden Dairy Company Ala LLC ....D 601 268-2583
Hattiesburg *(G-1937)*

Charged Up Grill LLC ....G 228 224-4461
Gulfport *(G-1751)*

Chef Rays Famous LLC ....G 601 559-8096
Byram *(G-619)*

Family Feeding Dev Program ....G 662 357-8917
Tunica *(G-5100)*

Gateway America LLC ....G 228 331-1473
Gulfport *(G-1790)*

Healthy Growth Ntrtn Program ....G 901 493-7991
Olive Branch *(G-3846)*

Lisa Hibley ....F 601 736-6781
Columbia *(G-903)*

Melvin L Brewer Inc ....G 662 328-9191
Columbus *(G-999)*

Oxford Falls ....G 662 323-9696
Sallis *(G-4703)*

Reddi Meals Inc ....F 601 992-1503
Flowood *(G-1392)*

Refreshments Inc ....D 662 286-6051
Corinth *(G-1115)*

Tico Investments LLC ....G 601 559-8161
Ridgeland *(G-4641)*

FOOD PRDTS: Rice, Milled

Mars Food Us LLC ....C 662 335-8000
Greenville *(G-1569)*

Masterfoods USA ....G 662 335-8000
Greenville *(G-1570)*

Modern Mill Inc ....G 601 869-5050
McComb *(G-3261)*

FOOD PRDTS: Seasonings & Spices

Dottleys Spice Mart Inc ....G 601 629-6100
Vicksburg *(G-5362)*

FOOD PRDTS: Soybean Lecithin

B & H Hill Farm LLC ....G 662 207-7197
Indianola *(G-2261)*

FOOD PRDTS: Spices, Including Ground

McCormick & Company Inc ....G 662 274-1732
Byhalia *(G-590)*

FOOD PRDTS: Syrups

Hall Manufacturing LLC ....G 601 445-6640
Natchez *(G-3565)*

Warren Corporation UNI ....G 888 913-7708
Byram *(G-626)*

FOOD PRDTS: Tea

Chenoa Coffee Company ....G 662 834-3917
Lexington *(G-2898)*

Mississippi Cold Drip Coffee ....G 601 624-5708
Jackson *(G-2498)*

FOOD PRDTS: Vegetable Oil Mills, NEC

Clint Williams Company ....G 662 627-3243
Clarksdale *(G-762)*

FOOD PRODUCTS MACHINERY

Electro Mech Solutions Ems Inc ....G 601 631-0138
Vicksburg *(G-5365)*

Lamonts Food Products Inc ....G 662 838-3431
Byhalia *(G-588)*

Leonard Metal Fabricators Inc ....E 601 936-4994
Pearl *(G-4129)*

Marel USA Inc ....G 662 686-2269
Leland *(G-2890)*

Standex International Corp ....B 662 534-9061
New Albany *(G-3700)*

Welborn Devices LLC ....G 601 428-5912
Laurel *(G-2872)*

FOOD STORES: Convenience, Independent

Fastway Fuels 3 LLC ....G 228 452-7009
Long Beach *(G-2937)*

FOOTWEAR: Cut Stock

Biltrite Ripley Operations LLC ....G 662 837-9231
Ripley *(G-4654)*

Run-N-Tri Company Llc ....G 228 604-2227
Gulfport *(G-1864)*

Upper Kutz LLC ....G 662 807-8707
Greenville *(G-1606)*

FORESTRY RELATED EQPT

Chambers Delimbinator Inc ....G 662 285-2777
Ackerman *(G-23)*

Mathis Plow Inc ....F 662 323-5600
Starkville *(G-4957)*

Wicker Machine Co ....F 662 827-5434
Hollandale *(G-2169)*

FORGINGS

Ceca LLC ....E 662 993-8880
Ripley *(G-4655)*

Creative Iron Works Ms LLC ....G 985 960-2386
Picayune *(G-4263)*

Spearman Ornamental Ironworks ....G 901 301-7061
Horn Lake *(G-2212)*

Tremac Resteel Inc ....E 601 853-3123
Madison *(G-3161)*

2019 Harris Directory of
Mississippi Manufacturers

(G-0000) Company's Geographic Section entry number

PRODUCT SECTION

FURNITURE: Assembly Hall

FORGINGS: Anchors

South Central Group Inc ....G....... 601 445-5101
Natchez (G-3623)

FORGINGS: Automotive & Internal Combustion Engine

Eagle Specialty Products Inc..............E 662 796-7373
Southaven (G-4870)

FORGINGS: Nonferrous

Jpm of Mississippi Inc..........................D... 601 544-9950
Hattiesburg (G-2004)

FORGINGS: Plumbing Fixture, Nonferrous

Mueller Copper Fittings Co ....E 662 862-2181
Fulton (G-1465)

FOUNDRIES: Aluminum

Brimmer-Turan Fndry & Mch LLC ....G...... 228 896-9669
Gulfport (G-1745)
Rossville Aluminum Castings ....F........ 662 301-1147
Senatobia (G-4801)

FOUNDRIES: Brass, Bronze & Copper

Mueller Copper Fittings Co ....E 662 862-2181
Fulton (G-1465)
Rolls-Royce Marine North Amer ....D....... 228 762-0728
Pascagoula (G-4064)

FOUNDRIES: Gray & Ductile Iron

Laurel Machine and Foundry Co ....C 601 428-0541
Laurel (G-2793)

FOUNDRIES: Nonferrous

CL Dews Sons Fndry McHy Inc ....D....... 601 582-4427
Hattiesburg (G-1945)
Main Street Pascagoula........................G 228 219-1114
Pascagoula (G-4049)
Rossville Aluminum Castings ....F........ 662 301-1147
Senatobia (G-4801)

FOUNDRIES: Steel

Nucor Corporation ....E 601 936-6292
Jackson (G-2659)
Steel Technologies LLC ....E 601 855-7242
Madison (G-3153)

FOUNDRIES: Steel Investment

Mississippi Precision ....E 662 245-1155
Columbus (G-1004)
Samuel Son & Co (usa) Inc ....E 662 424-1460
Iuka (G-2308)

FREIGHT TRANSPORTATION ARRANGEMENTS

Galvian Group LLC ....G....... 662 374-1027
Greenwood (G-1624)
Malone Design & Contg LLC.................G....... 601 807-1279
Hattiesburg (G-2020)
Watson Tj Property LLC ....G....... 601 527-3587
Meridian (G-3418)

FRICTION MATERIAL, MADE FROM POWDERED METAL

Robertson Fabrication Inc ....F 662 453-1551
Greenwood (G-1648)

FRUIT & VEGETABLE MARKETS

Anusaya Fresh USA LLC.......................G....... 601 795-2008
Poplarville (G-4374)

FUEL: Rocket Engine, Organic

Vizaura LLC ....G....... 228 363-4048
Diamondhead (G-1193)

FUELS: Diesel

Express Biodiesel LLC ....E 662 453-4312
Greenwood (G-1622)

FUELS: Ethanol

27-55 Fuel Plaza LLC ....G....... 601 892-1643
Crystal Springs (G-1138)
Delta Biofuels Inc ....F 601 442-5330
Natchez (G-3554)
Fastway Fuels 3 LLC ....G....... 228 452-7009
Long Beach (G-2937)
Fossil Fuel ....G....... 601 790-7955
Ridgeland (G-4585)
Fuel Center ....G....... 601 664-1861
Richland (G-4517)
Fuel Time 5 ....G....... 601 372-1115
Jackson (G-2417)
Gulfport Harbor Fuel ....G....... 228 248-3474
Long Beach (G-2939)
Jns Biofuel LLC ....F 662 538-1005
New Albany (G-3683)
Jones Companies AVI MGT Inc ....G....... 844 500-2438
Hattiesburg (G-2003)
K & D Fuel Injection Service ....G....... 601 849-9113
Magee (G-3178)
Orrin F Fuelling ....G....... 601 485-2598
Meridian (G-3379)
Portabull Fuel Service LLC ....G....... 601 549-5655
Purvis (G-4447)

FUELS: Nuclear, Uranium Slug, Radioactive

Entergy Nuclear Fuels Company...........F 601 368-5750
Jackson (G-2402)

FUELS: Oil

Specialty Services Group LLC..............G....... 601 543-9474
Sumrall (G-5045)

FUNERAL HOMES & SVCS

Louisville Publishing Inc......................E 662 773-6241
Louisville (G-2974)

FUNGICIDES OR HERBICIDES

Bayer Cropscience LP ....D..... 662 686-2334
Leland (G-2883)

FURNACES & OVENS: Indl

Sly Inc ....G....... 662 263-8234
Mathiston (G-3231)

FURNITURE & CABINET STORES: Cabinets, Custom Work

McNeil Cabinet and Millwork ....E 601 764-2100
Bay Springs (G-168)
Pettigrew Cabinets Inc ....E 662 844-1368
Plantersville (G-4313)
Pitts Companies Cabinets Mllwk ....G....... 662 844-2772
Tupelo (G-5205)

FURNITURE & CABINET STORES: Custom

Pickens Hardwoods Inc........................G....... 601 924-1199
Jackson (G-2539)

FURNITURE COMPONENTS: Porcelain Enameled

Hsm Solutions.....................................G....... 352 622-7583
Verona (G-5333)

FURNITURE PARTS: Metal

Filing and Storage Miss LLC.................G....... 601 397-6452
Ridgeland (G-4580)

FURNITURE REFINISHING SVCS

Baddour Memorial Center Inc...............B 662 562-0100
Senatobia (G-4787)

FURNITURE STOCK & PARTS: Carvings, Wood

Cynthia Bowen ....G....... 228 463-7131
Waveland (G-5479)

FURNITURE STOCK & PARTS: Dimension Stock, Hardwood

Tommy L Henderson ....G....... 228 452-4484
Pass Christian (G-4097)

FURNITURE STOCK & PARTS: Frames, Upholstered Furniture, Wood

C & W Frames Inc ....F 662 728-2120
Booneville (G-323)
Carnes Frames Inc ....E 662 489-1984
Pontotoc (G-4325)
Davis & Son LLC..................................G....... 662 728-8396
Booneville (G-326)
J & W Furniture Frames Inc ....E 662 489-1991
Pontotoc (G-4338)
M R Furniture LLC................................G....... 662 882-8483
Dumas (G-1222)
Magnolia Furniture LLC........................G....... 662 489-9337
Pontotoc (G-4342)
Oak Wood Mills Inc ....G....... 662 542-9158
Houston (G-2252)
S&S Frames Inc...................................F 662 488-8996
Ecru (G-1232)
Steve Hamblin Frames Inc ....G....... 662 568-7299
Houlka (G-2229)

FURNITURE STOCK & PARTS: Hardwood

Chickasaw Wood Products Inc.............F 662 456-5357
Houston (G-2234)
Consolidated Inc ....F 601 425-2196
Laurel (G-2757)
Hodges Wood Products Inc ....E 662 728-3716
Marietta (G-3216)
K & L Furniture Frames Inc ....E 662 489-5355
Pontotoc (G-4340)
Shamrock Wood Industries Inc ....C 662 393-2125
Horn Lake (G-2210)

FURNITURE STOCK & PARTS: Turnings, Wood

Moss Woodturning Inc ....G....... 662 456-5043
Houston (G-2251)

FURNITURE STORES

Ashley Furniture Inds Inc.....................G....... 608 323-3377
Tupelo (G-5110)
Ashley Furniture Inds Inc.....................C 662 489-5655
Ecru (G-1230)
Linas Interiors Inc...............................G....... 662 332-7226
Leland (G-2889)
Springer Dry Goods.............................F 662 263-8144
Maben (G-3051)
Standard Office Sup Prtg Inc ....E 601 544-5361
Hattiesburg (G-2069)

FURNITURE STORES: Office

Star Printing Co of Amory Inc...............E 662 256-8424
Amory (G-56)

FURNITURE WHOLESALERS

Fusion Furniture Inc ....E 662 489-1296
Ecru (G-1231)
National Mattress LLC..........................G....... 662 205-4891
Plantersville (G-4311)

FURNITURE, WHOLESALE: Beds

Ark-Ell Springs Inc..............................C 662 568-3393
Houlka (G-2217)

FURNITURE, WHOLESALE: Lockers

Southeast Miss Schl Pdts Inc ....G....... 662 855-5048
Caledonia (G-631)

FURNITURE, WHOLESALE: Restaurant, NEC

Prime Hospitality Group LLC ....E 662 269-2892
Tupelo (G-5208)

FURNITURE, WHOLESALE: School Desks

Missco Corporation of Jackson ....F 601 352-7272
Jackson (G-2497)

FURNITURE: Assembly Hall

Great Southern Club Inc.......................F 228 868-8619
Gulfport (G-1796)

Employee Codes: A=Over 500 employees, B=251-500
C=101-250, D=51-100, E=20-50, F=10-19, G=1-9

2019 Harris Directory of
Mississippi Manufacturers

PRODUCT

FURNITURE: Bed Frames & Headboards, Wood

PRODUCT SECTION

FURNITURE: Bed Frames & Headboards, Wood

S & S Frame Sales LLC ....G....... 662 397-3725
Shannon *(G-4818)*

FURNITURE: Benches, Office, Wood

Mississipi Furniture Component ....G....... 662 566-8855
Tupelo *(G-5188)*

FURNITURE: Box Springs, Assembled

Fibrix LLC ....G....... 662 568-3393
Houlka *(G-2222)*
Leggett & Platt Incorporated ....G....... 662 842-5704
Tupelo *(G-5175)*
Leggett & Platt Incorporated ....E....... 662 842-5704
Tupelo *(G-5176)*

FURNITURE: Breakfast Sets, Household, Metal

Nowell Steps Incorporated ....G....... 601 964-8455
Richton *(G-4541)*

FURNITURE: Camp, Wood

Old House Depot LLC ....G....... 601 592-6200
Jackson *(G-2529)*

FURNITURE: Chair & Couch Springs, Assembled

Ark-Ell Springs Inc ....C....... 662 568-3393
Houlka *(G-2217)*

FURNITURE: Chairs, Cane

Allens Cane Shop ....G....... 662 429-2016
Nesbit *(G-3647)*

FURNITURE: Chairs, Folding

Spain Incorporated ....G....... 662 843-1301
Boyle *(G-352)*

FURNITURE: Chairs, Household Upholstered

Aw Manufacturing Inc ....C....... 662 767-2800
Shannon *(G-4806)*
Behold Home Inc ....E....... 662 651-4510
Smithville *(G-4843)*
La-Z-Boy Inc ....G....... 601 683-3354
Newton *(G-3722)*
Miss Eaton Inc ....D....... 662 489-4242
Pontotoc *(G-4346)*
Seminole Furniture Mfg Inc ....D....... 662 447-5222
Okolona *(G-3798)*

FURNITURE: Church

Larry Wells ....F....... 662 724-4355
Noxapater *(G-3732)*

FURNITURE: Couches, Sofa/Davenport, Upholstered Wood Frames

Albany Industries LLC ....B....... 662 534-9800
New Albany *(G-3672)*

FURNITURE: Frames, Box Springs Or Bedsprings, Metal

Leggett & Platt Incorporated ....G....... 662 842-5704
Tupelo *(G-5175)*
Leggett & Platt Incorporated ....E....... 662 842-5237
Tupelo *(G-5178)*

FURNITURE: Hospital

Knu LLC ....D....... 812 367-1761
Leland *(G-2888)*
Missco Corporation of Jackson ....D....... 601 892-7105
Crystal Springs *(G-1149)*
Missco Corporation of Jackson ....F....... 601 352-7272
Jackson *(G-2497)*

FURNITURE: Hotel

Lounora Industries Inc ....E....... 662 328-1685
Columbus *(G-994)*

Prime Hospitality Group LLC ....E....... 662 269-2892
Tupelo *(G-5208)*

FURNITURE: Household, Metal

B & O Machine & Wldg Co Inc ....F....... 601 833-3000
Brookhaven *(G-481)*
Kennedy Hall ....G....... 601 366-7301
Jackson *(G-2462)*
Krueger International Inc ....A....... 662 842-3124
Tupelo *(G-5167)*
Krueger International Inc ....D....... 662 840-7368
Tupelo *(G-5168)*

FURNITURE: Household, NEC

Birds Nest ....G....... 662 369-5757
Aberdeen *(G-10)*
Madison House Inc ....G....... 601 898-8090
Madison *(G-3125)*

FURNITURE: Household, Upholstered, Exc Wood Or Metal

Paxton Sales Inc ....E....... 662 841-1929
Tupelo *(G-5201)*
Springer Dry Goods ....F....... 662 263-8144
Maben *(G-3051)*
Varsity Pro Inc ....G....... 662 628-4172
Calhoun City *(G-645)*

FURNITURE: Household, Wood

Affordable Furn Mfg Co Inc ....B....... 662 568-7981
Houlka *(G-2216)*
Andrews Furniture Company Inc ....G....... 662 489-1107
Ecru *(G-1229)*
Behold Washington LLC ....B....... 662 489-6117
Pontotoc *(G-4322)*
Bill Briscoe ....G....... 662 234-5669
Oxford *(G-3940)*
Classic Furniture Mfg ....E....... 662 456-5900
Houston *(G-2235)*
Consolidated Inc ....F....... 601 425-2196
Laurel *(G-2757)*
Crossroads Furniture Inc ....G....... 662 627-2114
Clarksdale *(G-764)*
Delta Furniture Mfg LLC ....D....... 662 489-2128
Pontotoc *(G-4329)*
Ffm Inc ....E....... 662 256-9665
Amory *(G-42)*
From Our House To Yours ....G....... 601 956-1818
Madison *(G-3101)*
Grassy Ridge Gazebos ....G....... 662 738-6556
Brooksville *(G-554)*
Jakes Woodwork LLC ....G....... 601 651-6278
Laurel *(G-2786)*
Johnston-Tombigbee Furn Mfg Co ....C....... 662 328-1685
Columbus *(G-992)*
Krueger International Inc ....A....... 662 842-3124
Tupelo *(G-5167)*
Lounora Industries Inc ....E....... 662 328-1685
Columbus *(G-994)*
Southern Craftsmen Inc ....G....... 601 484-5757
Meridian *(G-3402)*
Southern Rustic Logwerks LLC ....G....... 662 315-9677
Amory *(G-54)*
Sunbeam Products Inc ....A....... 601 296-5000
Hattiesburg *(G-2071)*
Tru-Cut Inc ....E....... 662 489-1879
Pontotoc *(G-4365)*
Viking Capital Ventures Inc ....F....... 662 455-1200
Greenwood *(G-1656)*

FURNITURE: Institutional, Exc Wood

Business & Off Konnextions LLC ....G....... 601 965-5101
Jackson *(G-2350)*
Facilities Outfitters ....G....... 662 328-1977
Columbus *(G-973)*
Fletcher Cox ....G....... 601 956-2610
Ridgeland *(G-4584)*
Flexsteel Industries Inc ....B....... 662 323-5481
Starkville *(G-4944)*
James E Mattison Jr ....G....... 601 543-7313
Purvis *(G-4441)*
Krueger International Inc ....A....... 662 842-3124
Tupelo *(G-5167)*
Wdtm Inc ....D....... 662 842-6161
Pontotoc *(G-4369)*

FURNITURE: Juvenile, Upholstered On Wood Frames

Chapter 3 Inc ....D....... 662 568-7830
Houlka *(G-2220)*

FURNITURE: Juvenile, Wood

DIAS LLC ....E....... 662 628-1580
Calhoun City *(G-638)*
United States Worldwide Inc ....G....... 662 488-1840
Pontotoc *(G-4367)*

FURNITURE: Kitchen & Dining Room

Quality Cabinet Company Inc ....E....... 662 429-1411
Hernando *(G-2151)*

FURNITURE: Kitchen & Dining Room, Metal

Chromcraft Corporation ....C....... 662 562-8203
Senatobia *(G-4790)*

FURNITURE: Living Room, Upholstered On Wood Frames

Blue Mountain Furniture LLC ....F....... 662 685-4871
Blue Mountain *(G-288)*
Collums Furniture Inc ....D....... 662 568-7912
Houlka *(G-2221)*
Fusion Furniture Inc ....E....... 662 489-1296
Ecru *(G-1231)*
HM Richards Inc ....A....... 662 365-9485
Guntown *(G-1899)*
Kedron Furniture Mfg Inc ....G....... 662 963-3366
Plantersville *(G-4310)*
Lake Road Furniture Mfg Co ....E....... 662 568-3329
Houlka *(G-2224)*
Lucky Star Industries Inc ....F....... 662 840-4465
Tupelo *(G-5182)*
S & S Manufacturers Inc ....E....... 662 489-2223
Pontotoc *(G-4361)*
Style-Line Furn Inc ....C....... 662 566-1113
Verona *(G-5335)*
United Furniture Inds CA Inc ....G....... 800 458-7212
Okolona *(G-3800)*
United Furniture Inds Inc ....D....... 662 447-4000
Okolona *(G-3801)*
United Furniture Inds NC LLC ....D....... 662 447-5504
Okolona *(G-3802)*

FURNITURE: Mattresses & Foundations

Englander Sleep Products LLC ....C....... 800 370-8700
Olive Branch *(G-3839)*
Magnolia Furniture LLC ....G....... 662 489-9337
Pontotoc *(G-4342)*

FURNITURE: Mattresses, Box & Bedsprings

Elite Comfort Solutions LLC ....E....... 662 566-2322
Verona *(G-5330)*
Leggett & Platt Incorporated ....B....... 662 869-1060
Saltillo *(G-4717)*
Leggett & Platt Incorporated ....E....... 662 842-5237
Tupelo *(G-5178)*
Meridian Mattress Factory Inc ....F....... 601 693-3875
Meridian *(G-3368)*
National Mattress LLC ....G....... 662 205-4891
Plantersville *(G-4311)*
Signature Bedding LLC ....G....... 663 523-8477
Tupelo *(G-5221)*
Superior Bedding Products of M ....E....... 662 841-1632
Plantersville *(G-4316)*

FURNITURE: Mattresses, Innerspring Or Box Spring

Leggett & Platt Incorporated ....D....... 662 456-3053
Houston *(G-2249)*
Leggett & Platt Incorporated ....D....... 662 842-5704
Tupelo *(G-5177)*
Sleeper Kraft LLC ....E....... 662 620-9797
Plantersville *(G-4315)*

FURNITURE: NEC

Collins Woodworks ....G....... 228 452-2627
Pass Christian *(G-4080)*
Max Home LLC ....G....... 662 424-0005
Iuka *(G-2299)*
Recon Concealment Furn Eqp LLC ......G....... 228 238-9149
Ocean Springs *(G-3781)*

2019 Harris Directory of
Mississippi Manufacturers

(G-0000) Company's Geographic Section entry number

PRODUCT SECTION

GAS & OIL FIELD EXPLORATION SVCS

FURNITURE: Office, Exc Wood

Flexsteel Industries Inc ....B 662 323-5481
Starkville (G-4944)

Krueger International Inc ....A 662 842-3124
Tupelo (G-5167)

Office Chairs Mississippi LLC .....G 601 842-1004
Pearl (G-4135)

FURNITURE: Office, Wood

Flexsteel Industries Inc ....B 662 323-5481
Starkville (G-4944)

Grace Company of Ms Inc ....F 662 393-2443
Horn Lake (G-2200)

Krueger International Inc ....A 662 842-3124
Tupelo (G-5167)

Office Chairs Mississippi LLC .....G 601 842-1004
Pearl (G-4135)

Southeastern Constructors Inc ....E 601 825-9791
Brandon (G-457)

FURNITURE: Picnic Tables Or Benches, Park

Gmn Group LLC ....G 662 473-3094
Water Valley (G-5468)

T S Car Ports ....G 601 797-9600
Mount Olive (G-3511)

FURNITURE: Recliners, Upholstered On Wood Frames

Brazil Furniture Inc ....E 662 489-2063
Pontotoc (G-4323)

Franklin Corporation ....A 662 456-5771
Houston (G-2240)

Lane Furniture Industries Inc ......A 662 489-3815
Pontotoc (G-4341)

LFI Wind Down Inc ....A 662 566-7211
Belden (G-190)

R and R Furniture Inc ....E 662 456-5888
Woodland (G-5614)

United Furniture Inds Inc ....C 662 841-2321
Belden (G-193)

FURNITURE: Rockers, Wood, Exc Upholstered

Oiseys International Inc ....G 662 255-1545
Belden (G-191)

FURNITURE: School

Missco Corporation of Jackson ....F 601 352-7272
Jackson (G-2497)

Southeast Miss Schl Pdts Inc ......G 662 855-5048
Caledonia (G-631)

FURNITURE: Sleep

Sleepmadecom LLC ....G 662 386-2222
Columbus (G-1027)

FURNITURE: Sofa Beds Or Convertible Sofas)

Ashley Furniture Inds Inc ....C 662 837-7146
Ripley (G-4652)

FURNITURE: Stools With Casters, Metal, Exc Home Or Office

Filing and Storage Miss LLC ....G 601 397-6452
Ridgeland (G-4580)

FURNITURE: Upholstered

A-1 Family Furniture Inc ....E 662 257-6002
Amory (G-34)

Albany Industries Inc ....G 662 488-8281
Pontotoc (G-4320)

Ashley Furniture Inds Inc ....C 662 837-7146
Ripley (G-4652)

Ashley Furniture Inds Inc ....G 608 323-3377
Tupelo (G-5110)

Ashley Furniture Inds Inc ....C 662 489-5655
Ecru (G-1230)

Bauhaus Furniture Group LLC .....B 662 869-2664
Saltillo (G-4707)

Choctaw Glove & Safety Co Inc ...G 601 774-5555
Union (G-5296)

Classic Furniture Mfg ....E 662 456-5900
Houston (G-2235)

Corinthian Inc ....A 662 287-7835
Corinth (G-1079)

Dixieland Furniture Mfg Co Inc ....E 662 456-5378
Houston (G-2236)

Flexsteel Industries Inc ....B 662 323-5481
Starkville (G-4944)

Franklin Corporation ....B 662 456-4286
Houston (G-2241)

Franklin Development Co LLC ......G 662 456-5771
Houston (G-2242)

Homestretch Inc ....F 662 963-2494
Nettleton (G-3660)

Homestretch Holdings LLC ....B 662 963-2494
Nettleton (G-3661)

La-Z-Boy Incorporated ....A 601 683-3354
Newton (G-3723)

Leggett & Platt Incorporated ....E 662 842-5237
Tupelo (G-5178)

Max Home LLC ....B 662 862-9966
Fulton (G-1462)

Newport Home Furnishings LLC ...D 662 534-3030
New Albany (G-3690)

Quality Trim & Upholstery ....G 601 483-0077
Meridian (G-3389)

Seminole Furniture LLC ....D 662 447-5222
Okolona (G-3797)

Southern Motion Inc ....C 662 488-9301
Pontotoc (G-4363)

Furs

Desoto Fur Trappers LLC ....G 662 874-5605
Olive Branch (G-3835)

Dixie Specialties & Furn Inc ....G 662 369-8557
Aberdeen (G-12)

Feathers Fins & Fur Taxidermy .....G 228 860-3106
Biloxi (G-242)

GAMES & TOYS: Automobiles & Trucks

Gray Daniels Auto Family ....G 601 948-0576
Brandon (G-401)

GAMES & TOYS: Craft & Hobby Kits & Sets

American Plastic Toys Inc ....C 662 895-4055
Olive Branch (G-3812)

Crafts By Fenton ....G 601 477-9164
Ellisville (G-1250)

Janlynn Crafts ....G 601 956-1832
Jackson (G-2458)

Mabrys ....G 601 956-7238
Jackson (G-2475)

Natures Society Majestic Arts .....G 601 376-0447
Byram (G-623)

GAMES & TOYS: Doll Clothing

Smocking Bird Clothing LLC ....G 662 453-6432
Greenwood (G-1652)

Sneaker Addict Clothing ....G 601 212-3205
Jackson (G-2584)

GAMES & TOYS: Dolls, Exc Stuffed Toy Animals

Carol Baird ....G 601 924-5409
Clinton (G-818)

GAMES & TOYS: Kits, Science, Incl Microscopes/Chemistry Sets

Ladonna R Williams ....G 601 405-2200
Clinton (G-828)

GAMES & TOYS: Puzzles

Amandas Puzzles ....G 228 314-3930
Gulfport (G-1724)

Hint Hunter LLC ....G 228 273-4064
Diberville (G-1207)

GARAGE DOOR REPAIR SVCS

Core Solutions LLC ....G 228 216-6848
Gulfport (G-1765)

GARMENT: Pressing & cleaners' agents

Klean N Press ....G 662 563-5515
Batesville (G-112)

GAS & HYDROCARBON LIQUEFACTION FROM COAL

Exterran ....G 601 444-0055
Columbia (G-898)

GAS & OIL FIELD EXPLORATION SVCS

Action Drilling Company Inc ....G 601 892-5105
Wesson (G-5523)

Aldridge Operating Co LLC ....G 601 446-5585
Natchez (G-3517)

Allen Petroleum Service Inc ....G 601 442-3562
Natchez (G-3518)

Bass Associates LLC ....G 601 943-5229
Bassfield (G-90)

Belle Exploration Inc ....G 601 442-6648
Natchez (G-3527)

Big Joe Oil Co Inc ....G 601 442-5481
Natchez (G-3530)

Blackstone Investments LLC ....G 601 978-1763
Ridgeland (G-4557)

Bob Bertolet ....G 601 442-0424
Natchez (G-3535)

Brandon Petroleum Properties ......G 601 649-2261
Laurel (G-2743)

Callon Offshore Production ....G 601 442-1601
Natchez (G-3542)

Ceco Corp ....G 601 362-4737
Jackson (G-2356)

Centerpoint Energy Inc ....F 228 588-2977
Moss Point (G-3473)

Craft Exploration Company LLC .....G 601 859-0077
Canton (G-655)

Craft Operating Company Ix LLC ...G 601 427-9009
Canton (G-656)

Crtney G Aldridge Ptro Glogist ....G 601 446-5585
Natchez (G-3552)

Denbury Onshore LLC ....E 601 787-3111
Heidelberg (G-2115)

Denbury Onshore LLC ....E 601 276-2147
Ruth (G-4700)

Denbury Resources Inc ....G 601 729-2266
Soso (G-4846)

Denbury Resources Inc ....G 601 687-0089
Shubuta (G-4830)

Denbury Resources Inc ....G 601 835-0185
Brookhaven (G-490)

Denbury Resources Inc ....F 601 276-2677
Summit (G-5011)

Denbury Resources Inc ....F 601 823-4000
Brookhaven (G-491)

Durango Operating LLC ....F 601 420-2525
Ridgeland (G-4575)

Eastern Group LLC ....G 662 332-1890
Greenville (G-1552)

Ergon - St James Inc ....G 601 933-3000
Flowood (G-1356)

Erickson Oil ....G 601 362-7401
Jackson (G-2403)

Foil J Branton ....G 601 876-9678
Tylertown (G-5270)

Geo Seis Processing Inc ....G 601 936-0334
Jackson (G-2424)

Griffin Grffin Exploration LLC ....G 601 713-1146
Jackson (G-2432)

Intrepid Drilling LLC ....G 601 731-1010
Columbia (G-901)

Jiffy Mart ....G 601 947-6589
Lucedale (G-3004)

Julius Whittington ....G 601 532-6519
Meadville (G-3276)

Jura-Search Inc ....G 601 932-0002
Jackson (G-2461)

K F G Petroleum Corporation ....G 601 446-5219
Natchez (G-3575)

Kelley Brothers Contrs Inc ....D 601 735-2541
Waynesboro (G-5501)

Kfg Resources Ltd ....G 601 446-5219
Natchez (G-3576)

Lamoco Inc ....G 601 919-3777
Brandon (G-411)

Liberty Southern Partners LP ....G 214 450-8838
Ridgeland (G-4598)

Longleaf Enterprises Ltd ....F 601 225-4481
Gloster (G-1516)

Magee Energy LLC ....G 601 709-2930
Flowood (G-1379)

Manning Drilling Company Inc ....G 601 989-2805
Richton (G-4539)

Employee Codes: A=Over 500 employees, B=251-500
C=101-250, D=51-100, E=20-50, F=10-19, G=1-9

2019 Harris Directory of
Mississippi Manufacturers

381

PRODUCT

GAS & OIL FIELD EXPLORATION SVCS

PRODUCT SECTION

Medical Clinic ....G 601 587-7795
Monticello *(G-3436)*
Miller Land Professionals LLC ....G 601 969-1160
Jackson *(G-2493)*
Moon-Hns-Tigrett Operating Inc...........G 601 572-8300
Ridgeland *(G-4610)*
Natchez Exploration LLC ....G 601 442-7400
Natchez *(G-3594)*
Neill Oil LLC...G 601 984-9000
Jackson *(G-2519)*
On The River LLC.................................G 601 442-7103
Natchez *(G-3603)*
Oolite Investments Inc..........................G 601 853-0408
Madison *(G-3135)*
Pangaea Exploration Inc ....G 228 452-7544
Pass Christian *(G-4092)*
Par-Co Drilling Inc................................G 601 442-6421
Natchez *(G-3605)*
Phoenix Energy Inc Mississippi ....F 601 445-3200
Natchez *(G-3607)*
Pistol Ridge Partners LLC....................G 601 649-7639
Laurel *(G-2823)*
Radzewicz Explration Drlg Corp...........F 601 445-8659
Natchez *(G-3610)*
Ram Petroleum LLC..............................G 601 876-0807
Tylertown *(G-5281)*
Shamrock Drilling Inc ....F 601 442-0785
Natchez *(G-3619)*
South Carlton Operating Co LLC ....G 601 446-5992
Natchez *(G-3622)*
Southern Flow ....G 601 591-1526
Brandon *(G-460)*
Southern Land Exploration Inc.............G 662 369-7390
Prairie *(G-4413)*
Spooner Petroleum Inc.........................G 601 969-1831
Ridgeland *(G-4634)*
Stringers Oilfield Service ....E 601 736-4498
Columbia *(G-924)*
T O Kimbrell LLC..................................G 601 446-6099
Natchez *(G-3629)*
Telpico LLC ....G 601 898-7444
Ridgeland *(G-4639)*
Tenrgys LLC ....G 601 898-7444
Ridgeland *(G-4640)*
Tim Blake ....G 662 256-8218
Nettleton *(G-3668)*
Travis Exploration Inc ....G 601 879-8664
Flora *(G-1313)*
Trinity River Energy Oper LLC..............G 601 792-9686
Newhebron *(G-3715)*
Triple S Well Service Inc ....F 601 736-8804
Columbia *(G-926)*
Trophy Petroleum Corporation..............G 601 298-0200
Carthage *(G-725)*
Valioso Petroleum Company ....G 601 936-3601
Flowood *(G-1405)*
Van Petroleum Inc ....G 601 982-8728
Jackson *(G-2620)*
Venture Oil & Gas Inc ....F 601 428-3653
Laurel *(G-2862)*
Waller Bros Inc ....G 601 352-6556
Jackson *(G-2624)*
Walter Allen ....G 601 924-1956
Clinton *(G-838)*
Watkins Jr H Vaughn ....G 601 898-9347
Jackson *(G-2627)*

GAS & OIL FIELD SVCS, NEC

Bap Services Inc ....G 662 343-5216
Hamilton *(G-1903)*
Brazos Bend Oil and Gas LLC ....G 601 982-3444
Jackson *(G-2342)*
Cases Body & Paint ....G 601 833-3153
Brookhaven *(G-486)*
Fowler Consulting LLC..........................G 601 761-3696
Flora *(G-1306)*
Henry Lyell...G 601 355-1080
Jackson *(G-2438)*
Odat Energy LLC..................................G 601 736-0227
Columbia *(G-908)*

GAS PROCESSING SVC

Gasmax Fltration Solutions LLC ....G 601 790-1225
Ridgeland *(G-4586)*

GAS PRODUCTION & DISTRIBUTION

Tellus Operating Group LLC ....E 601 787-3014
Heidelberg *(G-2119)*

GAS STATIONS

Murphy USA Inc ....F 601 992-2041
Flowood *(G-1383)*

GAS: Refinery

Ergon Inc ....F 601 932-8365
Jackson *(G-2645)*
Ergon Marine & Industrial Sup ....G 601 636-6552
Vicksburg *(G-5369)*
Shell Pipe Line Corporation..................G 601 638-1921
Vicksburg *(G-5418)*

GASES & LIQUIFIED PETROLEUM GASES

Ergon Inc ....C 601 933-3000
Flowood *(G-1361)*

GASES: Acetylene

Wesco Gas & Welding Supply Inc.........G 228 475-1955
Moss Point *(G-3506)*

GASES: Carbon Dioxide

Messer LLC ....E 601 825-1422
Brandon *(G-424)*
Praxair Inc ....F 601 825-8214
Brandon *(G-437)*
Sandhill Group LLC ....E 601 591-4030
Brandon *(G-450)*

GASES: Hydrogen

Hydrogen Peroxide ....G 662 329-9085
Columbus *(G-985)*

GASES: Indl

Air Products and Chemicals Inc...........G 601 823-9850
Brookhaven *(G-479)*
Alig LLC ....F 601 829-9020
Brandon *(G-361)*
Brandon Boc Ms ....G 601 825-1422
Brandon *(G-373)*
Fallen Leaf Services LLC ....G 228 731-0919
Gulfport *(G-1781)*
Linde North America Inc ....F 601 829-9020
Brandon *(G-414)*
Praxair Inc ....G 662 343-8336
Hamilton *(G-1906)*
Premier Air Products LLC ....G 662 890-9233
Olive Branch *(G-3900)*

GASES: Neon

Neon Marketing ....G 601 960-4555
Jackson *(G-2520)*
Pig Neon ....G 662 638-3257
Oxford *(G-3993)*

GASES: Nitrogen

Matheson Tri-Gas Inc............................F 601 856-3000
Madison *(G-3127)*

GASES: Nitrous Oxide

Nitrous Oxide Corp ....G 662 746-7607
Yazoo City *(G-5644)*

GASES: Oxygen

Matheson Tri-Gas Inc............................F 228 255-6661
Pass Christian *(G-4091)*

GASKETS

M S Rubber Company ....F 601 948-2575
Jackson *(G-2474)*

GASKETS & SEALING DEVICES

Hydradyne LLC ....A 601 833-9475
Brookhaven *(G-501)*

GASOLINE FILLING STATIONS

Chevron Corporation.............................C 228 938-4600
Pascagoula *(G-4025)*
Raceway Express Shell ....G 662 335-5434
Greenville *(G-1593)*

GASOLINE WHOLESALERS

Richard E Johnson ....G 601 735-4737
Waynesboro *(G-5512)*

GEARS: Power Transmission, Exc Auto

Haley Clutch & Coupling Co Inc............E 662 332-8716
Greenville *(G-1556)*
Marine Gears Inc ....E 662 332-8716
Greenville *(G-1568)*

GENERATION EQPT: Electronic

Aluma-Form Inc.....................................D 662 677-6000
Walnut *(G-5454)*
American Payment Systems...................G 601 368-7382
Jackson *(G-2326)*
American Payment Systems...................G 601 713-3761
Jackson *(G-2327)*
Jackson Excavating & Lsg Co ....C 601 371-7935
Jackson *(G-2454)*

GIFT SHOP

Holmes Stationary and Gifts ....G 601 276-2700
Summit *(G-5016)*
Kewl Kites ....G 228 206-0322
Long Beach *(G-2941)*
Mackay Enterprises LLC ....G 662 328-8469
Columbus *(G-996)*
Monograms Plus ....G 662 327-3332
Columbus *(G-1007)*
Southern Traditions ....G 662 534-0410
New Albany *(G-3698)*

GIFT, NOVELTY & SOUVENIR STORES: Artcraft & carvings

Gulf States Fabrication Inc ....F 601 426-9006
Laurel *(G-2773)*

GIFT, NOVELTY & SOUVENIR STORES: Gifts & Novelties

Brenda Ruth Designs LLC ....G 601 708-4227
Clinton *(G-815)*
Mackay Enterprises LLC ....G 662 328-8469
Columbus *(G-995)*
Party City ....F 228 539-4476
Gulfport *(G-1846)*
So Nuts and Confections LLC ....G 901 398-9650
Horn Lake *(G-2211)*

GIFTS & NOVELTIES: Wholesalers

Linas Interiors Inc ....G 662 332-7226
Leland *(G-2889)*
Oneway Inc ....G 601 664-0007
Jackson *(G-2660)*

GLASS & GLASS CERAMIC PRDTS, PRESSED OR BLOWN: Tableware

Memaws Ceramics ....G 601 319-8263
Ellisville *(G-1263)*

GLASS FABRICATORS

Central Mississippi Glass Co..................G 601 469-5050
Forest *(G-1412)*
Corinth Cc-Cola Btlg Works Inc ....E 662 286-2052
Corinth *(G-1078)*
Stained Glassworks Inc.........................G 662 329-2970
Columbus *(G-1031)*
Venable Glass Services LLC..................F 601 605-4443
Ridgeland *(G-4644)*

GLASS PRDTS, FROM PURCHASED GLASS: Glassware

Plum Trophy Sales................................G 601 758-4834
Sumrall *(G-5041)*

GLASS PRDTS, FROM PURCHASED GLASS: Mirrored

Home Decor Company ....C 662 844-7191
Tupelo *(G-5157)*
Renin US LLC ....E 662 844-7191
Tupelo *(G-5217)*

2019 Harris Directory of
Mississippi Manufacturers

(G-0000) Company's Geographic Section entry number

382

PRODUCT SECTION

HAIR & HAIR BASED PRDTS

GLASS PRDTS, FROM PURCHASED GLASS: Windshields

Clear Sight Windshield Repair..............G....... 601 638-2892
Vicksburg (G-5356)
Windshield Repair Systems..................G....... 601 657-8303
Liberty (G-2920)

GLASS PRDTS, PRESSED OR BLOWN: Glassware, Art Or Decorative

Dollys Stained Glass ....G....... 662 887-3624
Indianola (G-2263)

GLASS PRDTS, PRESSED OR BLOWN: Glassware, Novelty

Vape and Bake LLC.............................G....... 228 447-1566
Ocean Springs (G-3793)

GLASS PRDTS, PRESSED/BLOWN: Glassware, Art, Decor/Novelty

Customized Stained Glass ....G....... 601 583-4720
Hattiesburg (G-1956)

GLASS PRDTS, PURCHSD GLASS: Ornamental, Cut, Engraved/Décor

Laurin Enterprises LLC ....G....... 228 207-5580
Biloxi (G-259)

GLASS STORE: Leaded Or Stained

Alley Kats Glass..................................G....... 662 324-3002
Starkville (G-4924)
Dollys Stained Glass ....G....... 662 887-3624
Indianola (G-2263)
Stained Glassworks Inc ....G....... 662 329-2970
Columbus (G-1031)

GLASS STORES

Quality Glass and Aluminum ....G....... 662 837-3615
Ripley (G-4669)
Trulite GL Alum Solutions LLC ....E....... 662 226-5551
Grenada (G-1711)
Windshield Repair Systems..................G....... 601 657-8303
Liberty (G-2920)

GLASS: Fiber

Cbl Architectural Fiberglass ....F 662 429-2277
Hernando (G-2124)

GLASS: Indl Prdts

Bekeson Glass LLC ....F 601 932-3676
Flowood (G-1345)

GLASS: Pressed & Blown, NEC

Stained Glassworks Inc ....G....... 662 329-2970
Columbus (G-1031)

GLASS: Stained

Sweetwater Studios Inc ....G....... 601 584-8035
Moselle (G-3463)

GLOBAL POSITIONING SYSTEMS & EQPT

Skyhawk LLC.......................................G....... 601 619-6805
Vicksburg (G-5419)

GLOVES: Fabric

Ao Liquidation Trust Inc ....E 662 675-8102
Coffeeville (G-841)
Armstrong Remodeling ....F 601 720-2097
Clinton (G-812)
Hawkeye Glove Manufacturing..............D....... 662 681-6278
Eupora (G-1286)
Hrd Safety ....G....... 601 213-6358
Jackson (G-2444)
Stryder & Associates LLC ....G....... 662 579-8703
Cleveland (G-809)

GLOVES: Leather

Choctaw Glove & Safety Co Inc............D....... 662 724-4178
Noxapater (G-3731)

GLOVES: Leather, Work

Rog LLC ....G....... 662 455-1364
Greenwood (G-1649)

GLOVES: Safety

Choctaw Glove & Safety Co Inc............D....... 662 724-4178
Noxapater (G-3731)

GLOVES: Work

Slate Springs Glove Company...............G....... 662 637-2222
Calhoun City (G-644)

GLOVES: Woven Or Knit, From Purchased Materials

Lamont Wells LLC................................D....... 601 656-2772
Philadelphia (G-4222)

GOLF CARTS: Powered

Eddie Martin Golf Cars Inc ....G....... 662 620-7242
Tupelo (G-5129)

GOLF EQPT

Green Save Inc ....G....... 662 566-0717
Verona (G-5332)
Sparko Inc ....G....... 662 690-5800
Tupelo (G-5229)

GOLF GOODS & EQPT

Green Save Inc ....G....... 662 566-0717
Verona (G-5332)

GOURMET FOOD STORES

Mackay Enterprises LLC ....G....... 662 328-8469
Columbus (G-996)
Mackay Enterprises LLC ....G....... 662 328-8469
Columbus (G-995)

GOVERNMENT, EXECUTIVE OFFICES: County Supervisor/Exec Office

County of Hancock ....G....... 228 467-2100
Bay St Louis (G-177)

GRADING SVCS

Taylor Brothers Cnstr Co ....G....... 601 636-1749
Vicksburg (G-5427)

GRANITE: Crushed & Broken

Martin Marietta Materials Inc.................G....... 662 383-2070
Friars Point (G-1443)
Martin Marietta Materials Inc.................G....... 601 859-4488
Canton (G-669)
Martin Marietta Materials Inc.................G....... 662 652-3836
Tremont (G-5093)

GRANITE: Cut & Shaped

Bacallao Silva Gran & Tile LLC............G....... 769 798-8816
Madison (G-3082)
International Granite LLC ....G....... 601 213-8287
Jackson (G-2448)
Personal Touch Stone ....G....... 228 219-3359
Moss Point (G-3494)
Rock Shop LLC ....G....... 601 446-7625
Natchez (G-3615)
Triton Stone Holdings LLC....................D....... 662 280-8041
Southaven (G-4917)

GRAPHIC ARTS & RELATED DESIGN SVCS

Creative Designs & Sports ....G....... 662 327-5000
Columbus (G-956)
Creative Ventures LLC..........................G....... 601 798-7758
Picayune (G-4264)
Mississippi Photo & Bluprt Co ....G....... 601 948-1119
Jackson (G-2502)
Plan House Printing ....G....... 601 336-6378
Hattiesburg (G-2045)
Purpose Designs LLC...........................G....... 601 480-2197
Pachuta (G-4015)

Revolution Printing & Graphics............G....... 662 932-8176
Olive Branch (G-3904)
Signature Sound & Printing ....G....... 601 272-5662
Columbus (G-1026)

GRASSES: Artificial & Preserved

Rome Chenille & Supply Co Inc ....G....... 662 286-9947
Corinth (G-1116)

GRAVE MARKERS: Concrete

Harris Ja Inc ....G....... 662 205-4370
Tupelo (G-5153)

GRAVEL MINING

Green Brothers Gravel Co Inc ....E....... 601 362-3620
Crystal Springs (G-1143)
Johnstons Sand & Gravel Inc ....E....... 601 787-4326
Heidelberg (G-2118)
North Simpson Gravel Co ....G....... 601 847-9500
Mendenhall (G-3286)
St Catherine Gravel Co Inc...................G....... 601 442-1674
Washington (G-5462)
Valley Farms ....E....... 662 738-5861
Brooksville (G-558)

GRINDING SVCS: Ophthalmic Lens, Exc Prescription

Dearlens Inc..G....... 601 693-1841
Meridian (G-3328)

GROCERIES WHOLESALERS, NEC

Brown Bottling Group Inc ....C....... 601 982-4160
Jackson (G-2344)
C C Clark Inc.......................................E....... 662 323-4317
Starkville (G-4931)
Coca-Cola Bottling Co Untd Inc ....G....... 228 864-1122
Gulfport (G-1761)
Corinth Cc-Cola Btlg Works Inc ....D....... 662 842-1753
Tupelo (G-5122)
P-Americas LLC ....E....... 601 684-2281
McComb (G-3263)
Tico Investments LLC...........................G....... 601 559-8161
Ridgeland (G-4641)

GROCERIES, GENERAL LINE WHOLESALERS

So Nuts and Confections LLC ....G....... 901 398-9650
Horn Lake (G-2211)
Tatum Development Corp ....G....... 601 544-6043
Hattiesburg (G-2072)

GUARD SVCS

Brock Outdoors...................................G....... 662 255-1121
Saltillo (G-4709)

GUIDED MISSILES & SPACE VEHICLES

Northrop Grumman Systems Corp ....D....... 228 474-3700
Moss Point (G-3490)

GUM & WOOD CHEMICALS

United Gilsonite Laboratories...............E....... 601 362-8619
Jackson (G-2617)

GUN SVCS

Hunters Hollow Inc ....F 662 234-5945
Oxford (G-3958)
Smiths Speed Shop ....G....... 601 794-2855
Purvis (G-4452)

GUNSMITHS

Big Buck Sports...................................G....... 601 605-2661
Ridgeland (G-4556)
Dixie Precision Rifles LLC....................G....... 601 706-9100
Brandon (G-389)

GYPSUM PRDTS

Georgia-Pacific LLC.............................F 601 939-7797
Pearl (G-4122)

HAIR & HAIR BASED PRDTS

Bouldin Essentials LLC ....G....... 769 216-7146
Jackson (G-2341)

Employee Codes: A=Over 500 employees, B=251-500
C=101-250, D=51-100, E=20-50, F=10-19, G=1-9

2019 Harris Directory of
Mississippi Manufacturers

PRODUCT

383

HAIR & HAIR BASED PRDTS

LLC Glass House ....G....... 769 251-1299
Jackson *(G-2470)*
My Fantasy Hair Inc ....G....... 925 289-4247
Olive Branch *(G-3881)*
Southern Belle Tresses LLC ....G....... 470 645-1777
Oxford *(G-4004)*

HAIR ACCESS WHOLESALERS

My Fantasy Hair Inc ....G....... 925 289-4247
Olive Branch *(G-3881)*

HAIR CARE PRDTS

My Fantasy Hair Inc ....G....... 925 289-4247
Olive Branch *(G-3881)*

HAIR DRESSING, FOR THE TRADE

Touba Hair Braiding Ms ....G....... 769 524-4641
Ridgeland *(G-4642)*

HAIR REPLACEMENT & WEAVING SVCS

LLC Glass House ....G....... 769 251-1299
Jackson *(G-2470)*

HAIRDRESSERS

Courtyard Mfg Jewelers ....G....... 601 825-6162
Brandon *(G-382)*
My Fantasy Hair Inc ....G....... 925 289-4247
Olive Branch *(G-3881)*

HANDYMAN SVCS

Mr Fix It ....G....... 601 852-4705
Edwards *(G-1242)*

HARDWARE

Alexander Fabricating Co Inc ....G....... 601 485-5414
Meridian *(G-3295)*
Fibrix LLC ....G....... 662 568-3393
Houlka *(G-2222)*
Gerrer Industrial LLC ....G....... 601 506-2709
Madison *(G-3104)*
Military Defense Systems Inc ....G....... 850 449-1910
Picayune *(G-4278)*
Moores John ....G....... 662 488-2980
Pontotoc *(G-4350)*
N C Enterprises Inc ....G....... 601 953-6977
Hazlehurst *(G-2101)*
Region 8 Mental Health Retrdat ....D....... 601 591-5553
Brandon *(G-445)*
Rolls-Royce Marine North Amer ....D....... 228 762-0728
Pascagoula *(G-4064)*
Southern Metals Co Miss Inc ....E....... 601 649-7475
Laurel *(G-2853)*

HARDWARE STORES

Delta Auto Parts Inc ....F....... 662 746-1143
Yazoo City *(G-5630)*
La Rosa Glass Inc ....G....... 228 864-0751
Long Beach *(G-2942)*
Mjj Inc ....G....... 662 455-0126
Greenwood *(G-1641)*
P & R Aluminum ....G....... 662 682-7939
Vardaman *(G-5325)*

HARDWARE STORES: Builders'

American Concrete Products Inc ....E....... 601 583-2274
Hattiesburg *(G-1921)*
Fortenberry Builders Supply ....G....... 601 825-3370
Brandon *(G-397)*
Hancock Equipment & Oil Co LLC ....G....... 662 726-4556
Brooksville *(G-555)*

HARDWARE STORES: Chainsaws

Motor Parts Co of Yazoo City ....G....... 662 746-1462
Yazoo City *(G-5643)*

HARDWARE STORES: Door Locks & Lock Sets

Necaise Lock Supply Inc ....G....... 228 864-9799
Gulfport *(G-1836)*

HARDWARE STORES: Tools, Power

Robbys Small Engine & Saw Repr ....G....... 601 847-0323
Mendenhall *(G-3287)*

HARDWARE WHOLESALERS

Milwaukee Electric Tool Corp ....C....... 662 895-4560
Olive Branch *(G-3879)*
Triple E Door & Hardware Inc ....G....... 601 940-7371
Brandon *(G-469)*

HARDWARE, WHOLESALE: Brads

Mjj Inc ....G....... 662 455-0126
Greenwood *(G-1641)*

HARDWARE, WHOLESALE: Nuts

Circle S Irrigation Inc ....F....... 662 627-7246
Clarksdale *(G-761)*

HARDWARE, WHOLESALE: Padlocks

Necaise Lock Supply Inc ....G....... 228 864-9799
Gulfport *(G-1836)*

HARDWARE, WHOLESALE: Power Tools & Access

Flannigan Electric Company ....E....... 601 354-2756
Jackson *(G-2409)*

HARDWARE: Aircraft & Marine, Incl Pulleys & Similar Items

Delta Auto Parts Inc ....F....... 662 746-1143
Yazoo City *(G-5630)*

HARDWARE: Furniture, Builders' & Other Household

Albany Fiber Sales Inc ....G....... 662 401-2342
New Albany *(G-3671)*

HARNESS ASSEMBLIES: Cable & Wire

Applied Geo Technologies Inc ....D....... 601 267-5681
Carthage *(G-706)*
Dison Electrical Solutions LLC ....G....... 228 234-7767
Saucier *(G-4753)*
Hardwire Inc ....F....... 662 285-2312
Louisville *(G-2971)*
Mississppi Band Chctaw Indians ....E....... 601 656-6038
Choctaw *(G-747)*
Multicraft Intl Ltd Partnr ....D....... 601 854-1200
Pelahatchie *(G-4169)*

HARNESS WIRING SETS: Internal Combustion Engines

Interstate Industries Miss LLC ....C....... 662 289-3877
Kosciusko *(G-2695)*

HEALTH AIDS: Exercise Eqpt

Wilder Fitness Systems ....G....... 662 489-8365
Pontotoc *(G-4370)*

HEALTH AIDS: Vaporizers

1810 Vapors ....G....... 662 523-7924
Saltillo *(G-4705)*
Vapor Express LLC ....G....... 601 559-8004
Pearl *(G-4156)*

HEALTH SYSTEMS AGENCY

Region 8 Mental Health Retrdat ....D....... 601 591-5553
Brandon *(G-445)*

HEARING AID REPAIR SVCS

Advanced Hearing and Balance ....G....... 601 450-0280
Hattiesburg *(G-1915)*

HEARING AIDS

ADP Hearing Inc ....G....... 662 874-6279
Olive Branch *(G-3805)*
Advanced Hearing and Balance ....G....... 601 450-0280
Hattiesburg *(G-1915)*
Hear Again ....G....... 601 626-0050
Collinsville *(G-869)*
J & B Athletics ....G....... 601 776-7557
Quitman *(G-4466)*

HEARING TESTING SVCS

Advanced Hearing and Balance ....G....... 601 450-0280
Hattiesburg *(G-1915)*

HEAT TREATING: Metal

Lundtek Inc ....E....... 662 252-2340
Holly Springs *(G-2183)*
Precision Heat Treating Corp ....F....... 601 355-4208
Jackson *(G-2547)*

HEATING & AIR CONDITIONING EQPT & SPLYS WHOLESALERS

Fiske International Group Corp ....G....... 601 622-5767
Madison *(G-3100)*

HEATING & AIR CONDITIONING UNITS, COMBINATION

Advanced Distributor Pdts LLC ....A....... 662 229-3000
Grenada *(G-1666)*

HEATING EQPT & SPLYS

Babcock & Wilcox Company ....C....... 662 494-1323
West Point *(G-5537)*
Hardy Manufacturing Co Inc ....E....... 601 656-5866
Philadelphia *(G-4217)*
Modine Grenada LLC ....B....... 662 229-4000
Grenada *(G-1694)*

HEELS, BOOT OR SHOE: Rubber, Composition Or Fiber

Biltrite Ripley Operations LLC ....G....... 662 837-9231
Ripley *(G-4654)*

HELICOPTERS

Advanced Dynamics Inc ....G....... 601 677-3423
Preston *(G-4426)*
Ai Evac Ems Inc ....G....... 662 335-3034
Greenville *(G-1535)*

HELP SUPPLY SERVICES

Mississppi Inds For The Blind ....E....... 601 693-5525
Meridian *(G-3373)*

HOBBY, TOY & GAME STORES: Ceramics Splys

Dogwood Ceramic Supply Inc ....G....... 228 831-4848
Gulfport *(G-1773)*

HOISTS: Aircraft Loading

Ground Support Specialist LLC ....E....... 662 342-1412
Horn Lake *(G-2201)*
Leas Repair ....G....... 662 658-4462
Minter City *(G-3424)*
Smith Transportation Eqp Inc ....E....... 662 838-4486
Byhalia *(G-604)*

HOLDING COMPANIES: Investment, Exc Banks

Ccore Energy Holding Co LLC ....G....... 601 824-7900
Brandon *(G-376)*
Hood Companies Inc ....D....... 601 582-1545
Hattiesburg *(G-1991)*

HOME CENTER STORES

W G Yates & Sons Cnstr Co ....A....... 601 656-5411
Philadelphia *(G-4248)*

HOME FOR THE MENTALLY RETARDED

Baddour Memorial Center Inc ....B....... 662 562-0100
Senatobia *(G-4787)*

HOME HEALTH CARE SVCS

Southern Pharmaceutical Corp ....G....... 601 939-2525
Pearl *(G-4147)*
Southern Pharmaceutical Corp ....G....... 662 844-5858
Tupelo *(G-5227)*

PRODUCT SECTION

INDL MACHINERY & EQPT WHOLESALERS

HOME SHOPPING TELEVISION ORDER HOUSES

Human Technology Inc ....G...... 662 349-4909
Southaven (G-4878)

HOMEBUILDERS & OTHER OPERATIVE BUILDERS

Correy Elder ....G...... 769 257-3240
Madison (G-3089)

HOMEFURNISHING STORE: Bedding, Sheet, Blanket,Spread/Pillow

Harold Knight Sew Mchs & Appls ....G...... 601 425-2220
Laurel (G-2775)
Hsm Solutions ....G...... 352 622-7583
Verona (G-5333)

HOMEFURNISHING STORES: Beddings & Linens

Bed Bath & Beyond Inc ....G...... 601 939-4840
Flowood (G-1344)

HOMEFURNISHING STORES: Fireplaces & Wood Burning Stoves

Fireplace Wholesale ....G...... 601 545-9876
Hattiesburg (G-1970)
Lavastone Industries Mid South...........G...... 662 844-5178
Tupelo (G-5172)

HOMEFURNISHING STORES: Pictures & Mirrors

Final Touch Accessories LLC ....E 662 594-1348
Corinth (G-1085)

HOMEFURNISHING STORES: Pottery

Ka Pottery ....G...... 601 722-4948
Seminary (G-4782)
Mississippi Mud Works Pottery............G...... 228 875-8773
Ocean Springs (G-3772)

HOMEFURNISHINGS, WHOLESALE: Draperies

Mid-South Drapery Inc...........................E 662 454-3855
Belmont (G-200)

HOMES, MODULAR: Wooden

C3 Design Inc ....F 662 392-5021
Greenwood (G-1617)

HOMES: Log Cabins

Great Southern Log Homes Inc.............G...... 601 833-0700
Brookhaven (G-497)
Southland Log Homes.............................G...... 601 605-4900
Madison (G-3151)

HOPPERS: Sheet Metal

Roura Acquisition Inc ....E 662 252-1421
Holly Springs (G-2190)

HORSE ACCESS: Harnesses & Riding Crops, Etc, Exc Leather

Joanna Freely.......................................G...... 662 272-8679
Starkville (G-4953)

HOSE: Garden, Rubber

Hydro Hose Corp ....F 662 842-2761
Tupelo (G-5159)

HOSPITAL BEDS WHOLESALERS

Zyaa Inc ....G...... 601 321-9502
Jackson (G-2641)

HOSPITAL EQPT REPAIR SVCS

Central Delta Cmnty Dev Corp..............G...... 601 215-0367
Jackson (G-2357)

HOSPITALS: Orthopedic

Medworx Compounding LLC ....F 601 859-5008
Ridgeland (G-4605)

HOT TUBS

Leisure Home Products Inc ....G...... 228 860-7727
Long Beach (G-2944)
Richard Armstrong ....G...... 228 822-2238
Long Beach (G-2950)

HOUSEHOLD APPLIANCE STORES

Pierce Cabinets Inc...............................E 662 840-6795
Tupelo (G-5204)

HOUSEHOLD ARTICLES, EXC KITCHEN: Pottery

Shearwater Pottery Ltd..........................F 228 875-7320
Ocean Springs (G-3784)

HOUSEHOLD FURNISHINGS, NEC

Corporate Housing ....G...... 601 853-8982
Ridgeland (G-4566)
Divine Creations...................................G...... 601 500-2764
Jackson (G-2385)
Elite Comfort Solutions LLC ....E 662 566-2322
Verona (G-5330)
Glen Jones & Associates Inc ....G...... 601 634-0877
Vicksburg (G-5374)
Kedron Furniture Mfg Inc ....G...... 662 963-3366
Plantersville (G-4310)
L C Industries Inc ....E 662 841-1640
Tupelo (G-5170)
Southeastern Sample Company...........F 662 282-4063
Mantachie (G-3205)

HOUSEWARES, ELECTRIC: Appliances, Personal

Canopy Breezes LLC ....G...... 972 207-2045
Madison (G-3088)

HOUSEWARES, ELECTRIC: Blankets

Sunbeam Products Inc ....D...... 601 671-2200
Waynesboro (G-5516)

HOUSEWARES, ELECTRIC: Dryers, Hair

Con Air ....G...... 662 280-6499
Southaven (G-4862)

HOUSEWARES, ELECTRIC: Heating, Bsbrd/Wall, Radiant Heat

Thomas LP Gas Inc................................F 662 252-5388
Holly Springs (G-2195)
Warmkraft Inc ....C...... 601 785-4476
Taylorsville (G-5062)

HOUSEWARES, ELECTRIC: Irons, Household

Bells Iron Works....................................G...... 662 254-7413
Itta Bena (G-2279)

HOUSEWARES: Dishes, Plastic

Prolon LLC...D....... 601 437-4211
Port Gibson (G-4405)

HOUSEWARES: Plates, Pressed/Molded Pulp, From Purchased Mtrl

L C Industries Inc ....B 601 894-1771
Hazlehurst (G-2099)
Signature Works Inc ....B 601 894-1771
Hazlehurst (G-2106)

HYDRAULIC EQPT REPAIR SVC

Atwood Mch Wldg & Hydraulics............F 601 735-0398
Waynesboro (G-5491)
Deep S Mch Wrks Hydraulics LLC ....G...... 601 989-2977
Richton (G-4529)
Geartek..F 662 286-2252
Corinth (G-1087)
Gulf Hydraulics & Pneumatics..............F 228 392-1275
Diberville (G-1205)
Hattiesburg Hydraulics Sls Svc............G...... 601 264-6606
Hattiesburg (G-1986)

Quality Welding

Quality Welding......................................G....... 601 428-4724
Laurel (G-2830)
Rcl Components Inc ....E 662 449-0401
Hernando (G-2152)
Tucker Machine Services ....G...... 601 582-4280
Hattiesburg (G-2075)

HYDRAULIC FLUIDS: Synthetic Based

Chancellor Inc ....F 601 518-0412
Laurel (G-2752)

Hard Rubber & Molded Rubber Prdts

Cade Rubber Co Inc...............................G...... 601 743-5717
De Kalb (G-1162)

ICE

Bay Ice Company Inc ....F 228 863-0981
Gulfport (G-1735)
Browns Ice Company ....G...... 662 862-3706
Fulton (G-1447)
Cube Ice Co ....G...... 662 563-8411
Batesville (G-103)
Fiske International Group Corp.............G...... 601 622-5767
Madison (G-3100)
Kolinsky Corp..G...... 601 544-5987
Hattiesburg (G-2011)
Party Time Ice Inc ....F 662 746-8899
Yazoo City (G-5645)
Reddy Ice Corporation ....E 601 948-0900
Jackson (G-2562)
Wendall Harrell ....G...... 601 267-3094
Carthage (G-727)
Wendall Harrell ....G...... 601 353-3539
Jackson (G-2628)

ICE WHOLESALERS

Party Time Ice Inc ....F 662 746-8899
Yazoo City (G-5645)

IDENTIFICATION TAGS, EXC PAPER

B-N/Associates......................................G...... 601 482-3939
Meridian (G-3305)
ID Group Inc ....G...... 601 982-2651
Ridgeland (G-4592)

INDL & PERSONAL SVC PAPER WHOLESALERS

Jagg LLC..G...... 228 388-1794
Biloxi (G-254)

INDL & PERSONAL SVC PAPER, WHOLESALE: Cardboard & Prdts

Davis Enterprises Inc ....G...... 662 488-9972
Pontotoc (G-4328)

INDL & PERSONAL SVC PAPER, WHOLESALE: Paper Tubes & Cores

Caraustar Industrial and Con................E 662 287-2492
Corinth (G-1064)

INDL CONTRACTORS: Exhibit Construction

S Circle Inc ....D....... 601 792-4104
Newhebron (G-3714)

INDL EQPT SVCS

Dnow LP...G...... 601 649-8671
Laurel (G-2762)
Ecs- Elec Cnstr Spcialists Inc..............G...... 662 453-0588
Greenwood (G-1621)
Equipment Maintenance Co...................G...... 662 393-9178
Horn Lake (G-2198)
Jerry Hailey...G...... 662 349-2582
Southaven (G-4883)
Outback Industries LLC ....F 662 591-5100
Nettleton (G-3666)
Pernells Repairs Inc..............................G...... 662 453-9702
Greenwood (G-1645)

INDL MACHINERY & EQPT WHOLESALERS

Ameitech/South......................................G...... 601 853-0830
Ridgeland (G-4548)

Employee Codes: A=Over 500 employees, B=251-500
C=101-250, D=51-100, E=20-50, F=10-19, G=1-9

2019 Harris Directory of
Mississippi Manufacturers

385

PRODUCT

INDL MACHINERY & EQPT WHOLESALERS

Atlas-Ssi Inc .....D..... 601 587-4511
Monticello **(G-3428)**
Hancock Equipment & Oil Co LLC .....G..... 662 726-4556
Brooksville **(G-555)**
Hunter Douglas Inc .....C..... 662 690-8190
Shannon **(G-4810)**
Keith Huber Corporation .....D..... 228 832-0992
Gulfport **(G-1816)**
Lyle Machinery Co .....G..... 601 276-3528
Summit **(G-5017)**
Valmet Inc .....D..... 662 328-3841
Columbus **(G-1041)**

INDL MACHINERY REPAIR & MAINTENANCE

Industrial & Crane Svcs Inc .....E..... 601 914-4491
Pascagoula **(G-4039)**
Lumpkin Repair Service LLC .....G..... 601 798-2027
Carriere **(G-694)**
Michaels Machine Shop Inc .....G..... 662 624-2376
Clarksdale **(G-775)**
Rickys Welding and Machine Sp .....G..... 601 638-8238
Vicksburg **(G-5410)**
Walker Machine .....G..... 601 425-4635
Laurel **(G-2865)**

INDL PROCESS INSTRUMENTS: Data Loggers

Bradford Enterprises .....G..... 601 442-2339
Natchez **(G-3538)**
Luckett Pump & Well Svc Inc .....G..... 662 624-2398
Dublin **(G-1219)**
S & S Timber .....F..... 601 833-8844
Wesson **(G-5529)**

INDL PROCESS INSTRUMENTS: On-Stream Gas Or Liquid Analysis

Hydrasep Inc .....G..... 662 429-4088
Hernando **(G-2135)**

INDL SPLYS WHOLESALERS

Choctaw Glove & Safety Co Inc .....G..... 601 774-5555
Union **(G-5296)**
Csa Logistics LLC .....G..... 601 264-2455
Hattiesburg **(G-1953)**
Gulf Coast Filters Inc .....G..... 601 528-5762
Perkinston **(G-4176)**
Hancock Equipment & Oil Co LLC .....G..... 662 726-4556
Brooksville **(G-555)**
Haynes Enterprises Inc .....G..... 662 843-4411
Cleveland **(G-795)**
Southern Technical Aquatic RES .....G..... 601 590-6248
Carriere **(G-701)**

INDL SPLYS, WHOLESALE: Bearings

Applied Indus Tech - Dixie Inc .....G..... 601 649-4312
Laurel **(G-2731)**

INDL SPLYS, WHOLESALE: Filters, Indl

Circle S Irrigation Inc .....F..... 662 627-7246
Clarksdale **(G-761)**
Ripley Industries Inc .....E..... 662 423-6733
Iuka **(G-2307)**

INDL SPLYS, WHOLESALE: Hydraulic & Pneumatic Pistons/Valves

Gulf Hydraulics & Pneumatics .....F..... 228 392-1275
Diberville **(G-1205)**
Hydradyne LLC .....A..... 601 833-9475
Brookhaven **(G-501)**

INDL SPLYS, WHOLESALE: Mill Splys

Glenn Machine Works Inc .....E..... 662 328-4611
Columbus **(G-978)**
Glenn Machine Works Inc .....E..... 228 875-1877
Vancleave **(G-5319)**
Laurel Machine and Foundry Co .....C..... 601 428-0541
Laurel **(G-2793)**

INDL SPLYS, WHOLESALE: Rubber Goods, Mechanical

M S Rubber Company .....F..... 601 948-2575
Jackson **(G-2474)**

Rubber & Specialties Inc .....G..... 228 762-6103
Pascagoula **(G-4065)**

INNS

Baymont Inc .....D..... 662 454-7993
Golden **(G-1521)**

INSECTICIDES

Bayer Cropscience LP .....G..... 662 686-9323
Leland **(G-2884)**

INSECTICIDES & PESTICIDES

Vance Nimrod .....G..... 662 334-3713
Greenville **(G-1607)**

INSTRUMENTS, LABORATORY: Spectrometers

Philumina LLC .....G..... 228 363-4048
Long Beach **(G-2949)**

INSTRUMENTS, MEASURING & CNTRG: Plotting, Drafting/Map Rdg

Kelsey Bailey Consulting LLC .....G..... 601 622-8319
Madison **(G-3115)**

INSTRUMENTS, MEASURING & CNTRL: Geophysical/Meteorological

Nvision Solutions Inc .....D..... 228 242-0010
Diamondhead **(G-1192)**

INSTRUMENTS, MEASURING & CONTROLLING: Alidades, Surveying

3d Laser Scanning LLC .....G..... 228 860-5952
Biloxi **(G-214)**

INSTRUMENTS, MEASURING & CONTROLLING: Leak Detection, Liquid

Presto-Tap LLC .....G..... 662 332-8559
Greenville **(G-1591)**

INSTRUMENTS, OPTICAL: Light Sources, Standard

Source .....G..... 601 949-7878
Jackson **(G-2588)**

INSTRUMENTS, SURGICAL & MEDICAL: Blood & Bone Work

Norwood Medical Supply LLC .....G..... 601 792-2224
Prentiss **(G-4422)**

INSTRUMENTS, SURGICAL & MEDICAL: Lasers, Surgical

Dr Erica Aesthetic Center .....G..... 662 284-9600
Corinth **(G-1084)**

INSTRUMENTS: Analytical

Inciteful Analytics Corp .....G..... 601 870-4004
Meadville **(G-3275)**

INSTRUMENTS: Analyzers, Internal Combustion Eng, Electronic

Rolls-Royce North America Inc .....G..... 228 688-1003
Stennis Space Center **(G-4997)**

INSTRUMENTS: Indl Process Control

Hydrolevel .....G..... 228 875-1821
Ocean Springs **(G-3765)**
Kuhlman Electric Corporation .....B..... 601 892-4661
Crystal Springs **(G-1144)**
Lec Inc .....E..... 601 939-8535
Pearl **(G-4128)**
Omni Instruments .....G..... 228 388-9211
Biloxi **(G-270)**
Real-Time Laboratories LLC .....G..... 601 389-2212
Choctaw **(G-751)**

INSTRUMENTS: Measurement, Indl Process

One Source Systems LLC .....E..... 601 636-6888
Vicksburg **(G-5403)**

INSTRUMENTS: Measuring & Controlling

1 A Lifesafer Inc .....G..... 800 634-3077
McComb **(G-3242)**
1 A Lifesafer Inc .....G..... 800 634-3077
Southaven **(G-4849)**
1 A Lifesafer Inc .....G..... 800 634-3077
Tupelo **(G-5105)**
1 A Lifesafer Inc .....G..... 800 634-3077
Pascagoula **(G-4016)**
1 A Lifesafer Inc .....G..... 800 634-3077
Gulfport **(G-1714)**
1 A Lifesafer Inc .....G..... 800 634-3077
Mathiston **(G-3225)**
1 A Lifesafer Inc .....G..... 800 634-3077
Meridian **(G-3292)**
1 A Lifesafer Inc .....G..... 800 634-3077
Hattiesburg **(G-1913)**
1 A Lifesafer Inc .....G..... 800 634-3077
Natchez **(G-3515)**
1 A Lifesafer Inc .....G..... 800 634-3077
Greenville **(G-1534)**
1 A Lifesafer Inc .....G..... 800 634-3077
Jackson **(G-2312)**
Carnet Technology .....G..... 601 857-8641
Terry **(G-5064)**
Delta Enterprises .....G..... 662 335-5291
Greenville **(G-1545)**
Fairbanks Scales Inc .....E..... 601 482-2073
Meridian **(G-3337)**
Heath Aviation .....G..... 662 283-9833
Winona **(G-5599)**
Mississippi State University .....D..... 662 325-2510
Starkville **(G-4960)**
Standard Dynamics LLC .....G..... 228 383-2070
Starkville **(G-4975)**
Thermoprobe Inc .....F..... 601 939-1831
Pearl **(G-4151)**

INSTRUMENTS: Measuring Electricity

Supreme Electronics Corp .....F..... 662 453-6212
Greenwood **(G-1653)**

INSTRUMENTS: Measuring, Electrical Energy

Watthour Engineering Co Inc .....E..... 601 933-0900
Pearl **(G-4158)**

INSTRUMENTS: Medical & Surgical

Central Medical Equipment .....G..... 661 843-6161
Carthage **(G-710)**
Coles Tool Works Inc .....C..... 662 429-5191
Hernando **(G-2125)**
Emergent Prtctive Pdts USA Inc .....F..... 517 489-5172
Hattiesburg **(G-1962)**
EZ Medical Wraps LLC .....G..... 321 961-0201
Brandon **(G-396)**
Kerex LLC .....G..... 210 494-5596
Jackson **(G-2463)**
Medical Arts Surgical Group .....F..... 601 693-3834
Meridian **(G-3366)**
Medtronic Inc .....C..... 662 895-2016
Olive Branch **(G-3873)**
Microtek Medical Inc .....B..... 662 327-1863
Columbus **(G-1000)**
Needle Specialty Products Corp .....C..... 662 843-8913
Boyle **(G-351)**
Smiths Medical Asd Inc .....F..... 662 895-8000
Olive Branch **(G-3912)**
Spinal Usa Inc .....D..... 601 420-4244
Pearl **(G-4148)**
Spine Stability Surgical LLC .....G..... 800 991-3723
Jackson **(G-2595)**
Tegra Medical (ms) LLC .....E..... 662 429-5191
Hernando **(G-2159)**
Teleflex Medical Incorporated .....D..... 662 892-9100
Olive Branch **(G-3916)**
Terumo Medical Corporation .....F..... 662 280-2643
Southaven **(G-4914)**

INSTRUMENTS: Seismographs

J D Smith Drilling Company .....G..... 601 989-2475
Richton **(G-4536)**

PRODUCT SECTION

LABORATORIES: Testing

INSTRUMENTS: Signal Generators & Averagers

Quality Cnstr & Engrg LLC ....C 601 786-8017
Fayette *(G-1299)*

INSTRUMENTS: Standards & Calibration, Electrical Measuring

AA Calibration Services LLC ....F 662 716-0202
Yazoo City *(G-5620)*

INSULATION & CUSHIONING FOAM: Polystyrene

Alaco of Mississippi Inc ....E 662 837-4041
Ripley *(G-4651)*
Atlas Roofing Corporation ....E 601 484-8900
Meridian *(G-3300)*
Atlas Roofing Corporation ....F 601 481-1474
Meridian *(G-3301)*
Atlas Roofing Corporation ....E 601 483-7111
Meridian *(G-3302)*
Carpenter Co ....B 662 566-2392
Verona *(G-5329)*
Foamcraft Inc ....E 662 844-6399
Tupelo *(G-5136)*
Hickory Springs Mfg Co ....E 662 489-6684
Pontotoc *(G-4332)*
Hood Companies Inc ....D 601 582-1545
Hattiesburg *(G-1991)*
Le Clair Industries Inc ....E 662 226-8075
Grenada *(G-1691)*
Perma R Products Inc ....C 662 226-8075
Grenada *(G-1699)*
Pierce Foam and Supply Inc ....E 662 728-8070
Booneville *(G-342)*

INSULATION MATERIALS WHOLESALERS

Certainteed Gypsum Inc ....C 601 693-0254
Meridian *(G-3318)*

INSULATION: Fiberglass

Johns Manville Corporation ....D 601 936-9841
Jackson *(G-2652)*
Molded Acstcal Pdts Easton Inc ....E 662 627-7811
Clarksdale *(G-777)*

INSURANCE AGENTS, NEC

Wallace Express Freight Inc ....F 662 890-3080
Olive Branch *(G-3922)*

INSURANCE CARRIERS: Direct Product Warranty

Wallace Express Freight Inc ....F 662 890-3080
Olive Branch *(G-3922)*

INSURANCE CARRIERS: Life

L T Corporation ....E 662 843-4046
Cleveland *(G-798)*

INTERIOR DESIGN SVCS, NEC

Laura Jane Company LLC ....G 662 629-0550
Holly Springs *(G-2181)*

IRON OXIDES

Tronox Incorporated ....D 662 343-8311
Hamilton *(G-1909)*

IRRIGATION EQPT WHOLESALERS

Circle S Irrigation Inc ....F 662 627-7246
Clarksdale *(G-761)*

JACKS: Hydraulic

Metaris Corporation ....E 601 469-1987
Forest *(G-1422)*
Power Dynamics Innovations LLC ....E 601 229-0960
Picayune *(G-4287)*

JANITORIAL & CUSTODIAL SVCS

McDevitt Enterprises LLC ....G 601 453-2290
Meridian *(G-3365)*

JANITORIAL EQPT & SPLYS WHOLESALERS

Bluff City Service Company ....G 662 534-2500
New Albany *(G-3675)*
Chemical Products & Systems ....G 601 354-1919
Jackson *(G-2358)*
Davis Specialty Chemicals Inc ....G 601 856-5774
Ridgeland *(G-4571)*
Haynes Enterprises Inc ....G 662 843-4411
Cleveland *(G-795)*
McNeely Plastic Products Inc ....E 601 926-1000
Clinton *(G-830)*
Rite-Kem Inc ....F 662 840-6060
Tupelo *(G-5218)*

JEWELRY & PRECIOUS STONES WHOLESALERS

Maelstrom Square LLC ....G 470 378-9064
Pascagoula *(G-4048)*

JEWELRY REPAIR SVCS

Courtyard Mfg Jewelers ....G 601 825-6162
Brandon *(G-382)*
Dunns Jewelry ....G 662 363-1501
Tunica *(G-5099)*
Joe Tonos Jeweler Inc ....G 662 335-1160
Greenville *(G-1559)*
Pav & Brome Wtchmkers Jewelers ....G 228 863-3699
Gulfport *(G-1847)*

JEWELRY STORES

Courtyard Mfg Jewelers ....G 601 825-6162
Brandon *(G-382)*
Quitman Sporting Goods & Pawn ....G 601 776-3212
Quitman *(G-4468)*

JEWELRY STORES: Precious Stones & Precious Metals

Beaded Owls ....G 228 284-2712
Long Beach *(G-2927)*
Dunns Jewelry ....G 662 363-1501
Tunica *(G-5099)*
Joe Tonos Jeweler Inc ....G 662 335-1160
Greenville *(G-1559)*
Pav & Brome Wtchmkers Jewelers ....G 228 863-3699
Gulfport *(G-1847)*
Thomas Jewelry ....G 601 264-8780
Hattiesburg *(G-2073)*

JEWELRY, PRECIOUS METAL: Cigar & Cigarette Access

Smokers Express ....G 601 483-5789
Philadelphia *(G-4236)*

JEWELRY, PRECIOUS METAL: Rings, Finger

Dunns Jewelry ....G 662 363-1501
Tunica *(G-5099)*

JEWELRY, PRECIOUS METAL: Rosaries/Other Sm Religious Article

Maelstrom Square LLC ....G 470 378-9064
Pascagoula *(G-4048)*

JEWELRY: Decorative, Fashion & Costume

Allens Trophies Inc ....E 601 582-7702
Hattiesburg *(G-1920)*
Crystal Crown Inc ....G 601 947-8074
Lucedale *(G-2992)*
Sparkles & Such ....G 601 750-1270
Crystal Springs *(G-1157)*

JEWELRY: Precious Metal

Courtyard Mfg Jewelers ....G 601 825-6162
Brandon *(G-382)*
Joe Tonos Jeweler Inc ....G 662 335-1160
Greenville *(G-1559)*
Mary Givens ....G 601 325-5599
Brandon *(G-419)*
Mast Management LLC ....G 601 833-8073
Brookhaven *(G-516)*
Pav & Brome Wtchmkers Jewelers ....G 228 863-3699
Gulfport *(G-1847)*

LABORATORIES: Testing

Southern Traditions ....G 662 534-0410
New Albany *(G-3698)*
Thomas Jewelry ....G 601 264-8780
Hattiesburg *(G-2073)*

JOB PRINTING & NEWSPAPER PUBLISHING COMBINED

Appeal Publishing Co Inc ....G 601 774-9433
Union *(G-5292)*
Banner Printing Co Inc ....G 662 247-3373
Belzoni *(G-204)*
Bolivar Newspaper Inc ....E 662 843-4241
Cleveland *(G-788)*
Mrs GS Computer Services ....G 601 376-0810
Jackson *(G-2513)*
Okolona Messenger Inc ....G 662 447-5501
Okolona *(G-3796)*
Pontotoc Progress Inc ....G 662 489-3511
Pontotoc *(G-4356)*
Simpson County News ....G 601 847-2525
Mendenhall *(G-3289)*
Simpson Publishing Co Inc ....E 601 849-3434
Magee *(G-3185)*
Tylertown Times ....F 601 876-5111
Tylertown *(G-5289)*

JOB TRAINING & VOCATIONAL REHABILITATION SVCS

Ability Works Inc ....G 662 328-0275
Columbus *(G-931)*
Ability Works Inc ....E 662 842-2144
Tupelo *(G-5107)*
Baddour Memorial Center Inc ....B 662 562-0100
Senatobia *(G-4787)*
L C Industries Inc ....E 662 841-1640
Tupelo *(G-5170)*
Mississppi Inds For The Blind ....E 601 693-5525
Meridian *(G-3373)*
Rehabilitation Svcs Miss Dept ....E 662 335-3359
Greenville *(G-1595)*
Singin River Mental Health ....E 228 497-0690
Gautier *(G-1504)*
Southern Technical Aquatic RES ....G 601 590-6248
Carriere *(G-701)*

JOINTS: Expansion

Steel Specialties Miss Inc ....F 601 939-2690
Pearl *(G-4149)*

JOISTS: Fabricated Bar

Buzzard Rebar Fabricators Inc ....F 228 832-8024
Gulfport *(G-1746)*

KAOLIN & BALL CLAY MINING

Clay Kentucky-Tennessee Co ....E 662 382-5262
Crenshaw *(G-1132)*

KITCHEN & COOKING ARTICLES: Pottery

Clay Canvas ....G 662 236-9798
Oxford *(G-3946)*
William Stephens ....G 601 634-0498
Vicksburg *(G-5447)*

KITCHEN UTENSILS: Food Handling & Processing Prdts, Wood

Gulf Shores Sea Products Inc ....G 228 323-6370
Lakeshore *(G-2726)*
Stringer Woodworks ....G 601 372-5725
Raymond *(G-4493)*

KITCHENWARE: Plastic

Unified Brands Inc ....A 601 372-3903
Byram *(G-625)*

LABORATORIES: Biotechnology

Leflore Technologies LLC ....G 601 572-1491
Brandon *(G-412)*

LABORATORIES: Testing

Lockheed Mrtin Space Oprations ....B 228 688-3675
Bay Saint Louis *(G-148)*

Employee Codes: A=Over 500 employees, B=251-500
C=101-250, D=51-100, E=20-50, F=10-19, G=1-9

2019 Harris Directory of
Mississippi Manufacturers

387

PRODUCT

LABORATORY APPARATUS & FURNITURE

Krueger International Inc ....A 662 842-3124
Tupelo **(G-5167)**

LABORATORY APPARATUS: Laser Beam Alignment Device

Bengal Resources and Assoc Inc ....G 404 312-4642
Columbia **(G-884)**

LABORATORY APPARATUS: Physics, NEC

University of Southern Miss ....E 601 266-5390
Hattiesburg **(G-2078)**

LABORATORY EQPT: Chemical

Sheldon Laboratory Systems Inc ....D 601 892-2731
Crystal Springs **(G-1155)**

LABORATORY EQPT: Incubators

North Miss Entp Initiative Inc ....G 662 281-0720
Oxford **(G-3978)**

LAMINATED PLASTICS: Plate, Sheet, Rod & Tubes

B & D Plastics LLC ....F 228 875-5865
Vancleave **(G-5317)**
Carlisle Syntec ....G 662 301-4509
Senatobia **(G-4789)**
Sabic Innovative Plas US LLC ....E 228 533-7855
Bay Saint Louis **(G-154)**
Southern Diversified Inds Inc ....D 662 365-6720
Baldwyn **(G-87)**
U S Plastics Inc ....E 662 456-5551
Houston **(G-2257)**

LAMP & LIGHT BULBS & TUBES

Capri Lighting ....G 662 842-7212
Tupelo **(G-5117)**
Stylecraft Home Collection Inc ....C 662 429-5279
Southaven **(G-4909)**

LAND SUBDIVISION & DEVELOPMENT

Pavco Industries Inc ....D 228 762-3959
Pascagoula **(G-4061)**

LANTERNS

Copper Sculptures Inc ....F 601 992-9955
Flowood **(G-1352)**
Legendary Lighting LLC ....E 601 932-0707
Jackson **(G-2653)**

LASER SYSTEMS & EQPT

Delta Positions Inc ....G 662 719-1194
Boyle **(G-349)**
Landmark Spatial Solutions LLC ....G 662 769-5344
Starkville **(G-4955)**

LAUNDRY SVCS: Indl

Landau Uniforms Incorporated ....E 662 895-7200
Olive Branch **(G-3864)**
Mississppi Band Chctaw Indians ....G 601 656-7350
Choctaw **(G-746)**

LAWN & GARDEN EQPT

Cook Lawn & Tractor LLC ....G 601 445-0718
Natchez **(G-3550)**
Mtd Products Inc ....A 662 566-2332
Tupelo **(G-5191)**
Oligarch Inc ....G 844 321-0016
Houston **(G-2253)**
Paul Garner Motors LLC ....G 601 785-4924
Taylorsville **(G-5056)**
Worthen Bros Coastal Lawn ....G 228 261-4785
Gulfport **(G-1895)**

LAWN & GARDEN EQPT STORES

Delta Auto Parts Inc ....F 662 746-1143
Yazoo City **(G-5630)**

LAWN & GARDEN EQPT: Plows

Lund Coating Technologies Inc ....E 662 252-2340
Holly Springs **(G-2182)**

LAWN & GARDEN EQPT: Rototillers

Maxim Holding Company Inc ....E 601 625-7471
Sebastopol **(G-4774)**

LAWN MOWER REPAIR SHOP

H & H Small Engine Repair ....G 662 423-2741
Iuka **(G-2292)**
Lee Small Engines Inc ....G 601 833-5431
Brookhaven **(G-510)**
Michael Williamson ....G 601 736-9156
Columbia **(G-906)**
Mini Mtrs Unlimited Sls & Svc ....G 662 356-4900
Steens **(G-4991)**
Power Plus Inc ....F 601 264-1950
Sumrall **(G-5042)**
TJX Companies Inc ....G 662 236-2856
Oxford **(G-4007)**

LEASING & RENTAL SVCS: Cranes & Aerial Lift Eqpt

Pennington Wldg Sp Crane Rentl ....G 662 838-2015
Byhalia **(G-596)**

LEASING & RENTAL SVCS: Oil Field Eqpt

Danny Byrd LLC ....E 601 649-2524
Laurel **(G-2758)**
Rainbow Rentl Fishing Tls Inc ....F 601 425-3309
Laurel **(G-2833)**

LEASING & RENTAL: Automobile With Driver

Allied Crawford Jackson Inc ....E 769 230-2220
Byram **(G-616)**

LEASING & RENTAL: Construction & Mining Eqpt

Glenn Machine Works Inc ....E 228 875-1877
Vancleave **(G-5319)**

LEASING & RENTAL: Mobile Home Sites

Lott Enterprises Inc ....G 601 932-4698
Jackson **(G-2654)**

LEASING & RENTAL: Other Real Estate Property

B & B Concrete Co Inc ....E 662 842-6312
Verona **(G-5327)**
Coast Observer ....G 228 875-0090
Ocean Springs **(G-3749)**

LEASING & RENTAL: Trucks, Indl

Barbers Timber & Logging ....G 662 382-7649
Sarah **(G-4732)**

LEASING & RENTAL: Trucks, Without Drivers

Cap Co ....G 601 384-3939
Bude **(G-568)**
Fowler Buick-Gmc Inc ....E 601 360-0200
Pearl **(G-4120)**

LEASING & RENTAL: Utility Trailers & RV's

A & A Trailer Sales LLC ....G 228 234-3420
Biloxi **(G-215)**

LEASING: Passenger Car

Allied Crawford Jackson Inc ....E 769 230-2220
Byram **(G-616)**
Fowler Buick-Gmc Inc ....E 601 360-0200
Pearl **(G-4120)**

LEATHER GOODS: Aprons, Welders', Blacksmiths', Etc

Sea Robin Forge ....G 601 798-0060
Picayune **(G-4293)**

LEATHER GOODS: NEC

Leather Lanyards ....G 662 902-5294
Clarksdale **(G-772)**

LEATHER GOODS: Personal

Mississippi Tantec Leather Inc ....G 601 429-6081
Vicksburg **(G-5398)**
Van S Leather Crafts ....G 662 838-6269
Byhalia **(G-611)**

LEATHER GOODS: Wallets

McLendon Holdings LLC ....G 858 255-9038
Gulfport **(G-1827)**

LEATHER: Upholstery

Kdh Kustoms LLC ....G 601 730-2052
McComb **(G-3256)**
Leather Works Inc ....G 662 538-4455
New Albany **(G-3684)**

LECTURE BUREAU

My Songs of Life ....G 901 303-8687
Olive Branch **(G-3882)**

LECTURING SVCS

Southern Technical Aquatic RES ....G 601 590-6248
Carriere **(G-701)**

LEGAL SVCS: General Practice Attorney or Lawyer

George B Ready ....G 662 429-7088
Hernando **(G-2132)**

LETTERS: Cardboard, Die-Cut, Made From Purchased Materials

Acco Brands USA LLC ....G 800 541-0094
Booneville **(G-314)**

LIGHTING EQPT: Miners' Lamps

Seb Mining ....G 228 826-4466
Vancleave **(G-5320)**

LIGHTING EQPT: Motor Vehicle, NEC

Exciting Lighting ....F 228 864-2995
Long Beach **(G-2936)**

LIGHTING EQPT: Reflectors, Metal, For Lighting Eqpt

Mississippi Delta Energy Agcy ....G 662 746-3741
Yazoo City **(G-5641)**

LIGHTING EQPT: Searchlights

Eap LLC ....G 601 636-1621
Vicksburg **(G-5363)**

LIGHTING FIXTURES WHOLESALERS

Precision Electric & Ltg Svc ....G 662 893-3200
Olive Branch **(G-3899)**

LIGHTING FIXTURES, NEC

Cooper Lighting LLC ....F 662 342-3100
Southaven **(G-4864)**
Cooper Lighting LLC ....B 601 638-1522
Vicksburg **(G-5357)**
Guth Lighting ....G 800 234-1890
Tupelo **(G-5148)**
Jji Lighting Group Inc ....G 662 842-7212
Tupelo **(G-5163)**
Lighting Investment Group Inc ....G 601 482-3983
Meridian **(G-3360)**
Morgan Billingsley Lighting ....G 662 429-3685
Nesbit **(G-3654)**
Proshop Inc ....G 662 333-7511
Myrtle **(G-3513)**

LIGHTING FIXTURES: Airport

Ecs- Elec Cnstr Spcialists Inc ....G 662 453-0588
Greenwood **(G-1621)**

LIGHTING FIXTURES: Indl & Commercial

Cooper Lighting LLC ....B 601 638-1522
Vicksburg **(G-5357)**
Eaton Custom Seating LLC ....D 662 489-4242
Pontotoc **(G-4330)**

388

2019 Harris Directory of
Mississippi Manufacturers

(G-0000) Company's Geographic Section entry number

PRODUCT SECTION

LOGGING

Five Stars Lighting Co Ltd ....G...... 610 533-6522
Vicksburg (G-5373)

H Fleming Contractor ....G...... 601 824-0902
Brandon (G-402)

Howard Industries Inc ....B...... 601 422-0033
Laurel (G-2779)

Jji Lighting Group Inc ....G...... 662 842-7212
Tupelo (G-5163)

Signify North America Corp ....A...... 662 842-7212
Tupelo (G-5222)

Signify North America Corp ....C...... 662 842-7212
Tupelo (G-5223)

Toltec Company ....F...... 662 427-9515
Burnsville (G-574)

LIGHTING FIXTURES: Residential

Chuck Jennings ....G...... 601 668-5704
Raymond (G-4486)

Cooper Lighting LLC ....B...... 601 638-1522
Vicksburg (G-5357)

Five Stars Lighting Co Ltd ....G...... 610 533-6522
Vicksburg (G-5373)

H Fleming Contractor ....G...... 601 824-0902
Brandon (G-402)

Stylecraft Home Collection Inc ....C...... 662 429-5279
Southaven (G-4909)

Toltec Company ....F...... 662 427-9515
Burnsville (G-574)

LIGHTING FIXTURES: Residential, Electric

St James Lighting LLC ....G...... 601 444-4966
Columbia (G-923)

LIME

Limeco Inc ....G...... 662 456-4226
West Point (G-5551)

Mississippi Lime Company ....E...... 601 636-0932
Vicksburg (G-5396)

LIMESTONE: Crushed & Broken

McDevitt Enterprises LLC ....G...... 601 453-2290
Meridian (G-3365)

Tropical World Intl LLC ....G...... 228 229-8413
Biloxi (G-285)

LIMESTONE: Ground

Two-J Ranch Inc ....G...... 601 445-8540
Natchez (G-3632)

LINERS & COVERS: Fabric

F S C Inc ....G...... 662 434-0025
Columbus (G-972)

LININGS: Apparel, Made From Purchased Materials

Zyaa Inc ....G...... 601 321-9502
Jackson (G-2641)

LININGS: Vulcanizable Rubber

Packaging Research and Design ....G...... 800 833-9364
Madison (G-3136)

LIPSTICK

Lipstick and Labels LLC ....G...... 601 501-4029
Vicksburg (G-5389)

LOCKERS: Refrigerated

Mid-South Industries Inc ....C...... 601 649-4600
Laurel (G-2803)

LOCKS & LOCK SETS, WHOLESALE

Necaise Lock Supply Inc ....G...... 228 864-9799
Gulfport (G-1836)

LOGGING

Alamiss Inc ....G...... 601 671-0840
Waynesboro (G-5489)

American Log Handlers LLC ....F...... 601 927-6692
Booneville (G-317)

Ancerstor Logging LLC ....G...... 601 701-7020
De Kalb (G-1161)

Ancestor Logging ....G...... 925 895-2306
Meridian (G-3298)

Anderson & Son Logging LLC ....G...... 662 688-1211
Tillatoba (G-5079)

Andy Jackson ....G...... 662 416-2614
Booneville (G-318)

Benny McDaniel ....G...... 601 253-0564
Philadelphia (G-4207)

Boco Logging LLC ....G...... 256 810-4777
Golden (G-1522)

Bogue Homa Logging ....G...... 601 426-3662
Heidelberg (G-2112)

Bradley Reid Inc ....F...... 601 810-6655
Tylertown (G-5264)

Brittany H Davis ....G...... 251 348-8858
Wiggins (G-5574)

Bubba Bond Logging LLC ....G...... 662 417-5242
Winona (G-5595)

Buie Loggin ....G...... 601 532-7186
Union Church (G-5305)

Burge Timber Contractors Inc ....F...... 601 796-3471
Lumberton (G-3024)

Burnie Dykes Logging Co Inc ....G...... 601 788-6211
Richton (G-4527)

Cade & Cade Logging Inc ....G...... 601 833-2557
Wesson (G-5525)

Cade Enterprises 2 ....G...... 662 283-3678
Winona (G-5596)

Campbell Global ....G...... 601 932-2729
Flowood (G-1351)

Chambers Logging Inc ....G...... 662 285-2777
Ackerman (G-24)

Charles Lance Griffin ....G...... 601 734-2683
Mc Call Creek (G-3232)

Chris G Gatlin ....G...... 601 498-6281
Heidelberg (G-2113)

Circle A LLC ....G...... 601 832-3698
Hazlehurst (G-2091)

Circle G Hauling LLC ....G...... 662 436-7028
Little Rock (G-2922)

Circle Lane Contractors LLC ....F...... 601 776-0129
Shubuta (G-4829)

Clark Harvison ....G...... 601 928-7929
Wiggins (G-5577)

Claude Guy ....G...... 601 848-7859
State Line (G-4984)

Conaway Logging Inc ....F...... 662 287-8830
Corinth (G-1072)

Crimm Bros Log Ltd Lblty Co ....G...... 662 552-0122
Mathiston (G-3228)

Crimm Logging LLC ....G...... 662 552-8511
Mantee (G-3211)

Curtis Wilson Logging ....G...... 601 943-6808
Prentiss (G-4415)

Danny Pat Martin ....G...... 601 267-3342
Carthage (G-714)

David Drew Sullivan ....G...... 601 656-3556
Philadelphia (G-4214)

David Kirkman ....G...... 662 418-5048
Maben (G-3044)

David M Eaves ....G...... 662 773-7056
Macon (G-3058)

DC Logging LLC ....G...... 662 251-4653
Columbus (G-961)

Delbert T Dickerson ....G...... 662 773-4747
Louisville (G-2967)

E & S Logging LLC ....G...... 601 866-7270
Bolton (G-309)

E Fairley Unlimited Svc LLC ....G...... 601 795-6933
Poplarville (G-4381)

Eddie Franklin ....G...... 601 225-4183
Centreville (G-730)

Edward C Mathis Logging ....G...... 601 776-2379
Quitman (G-4463)

F & F Timber Inc ....F...... 601 528-0023
Wiggins (G-5582)

G&L Logging LLC ....G...... 601 722-9781
Seminary (G-4781)

Gary L Thornton Trk ....G...... 601 835-4192
Brookhaven (G-494)

Greg Winstead Logging Inc ....F...... 601 774-9565
Union (G-5297)

Harper Timber Inc ....E...... 601 833-2121
Brookhaven (G-499)

Hood Industries Inc ....B...... 601 928-3737
Wiggins (G-5584)

Hood Industries Inc ....C...... 601 784-3414
Beaumont (G-185)

Hoop Logging LLC ....G...... 662 230-7553
Cascilla (G-728)

Hutchinson Logging ....G...... 601 943-5486
Bassfield (G-92)

Iron Horse Logging LLC ....G...... 601 416-5966
Union (G-5299)

Ironhorse Environmental LLC ....G...... 504 952-2516
Poplarville (G-4383)

Isaiah Ard Timber Inc ....E...... 601 833-9359
Ruth (G-4702)

J & L Transport LLC ....G...... 601 292-7044
Collins (G-854)

J W B Logging Co LLC ....G...... 601 437-8743
Port Gibson (G-4402)

James David Measell ....G...... 601 635-4441
Decatur (G-1174)

Jason Fly Logging LLC ....F...... 662 316-3499
Batesville (G-110)

Jasons Custom Logging LLC ....G...... 601 270-6818
Lumberton (G-3033)

Jennifer L Johnson Lpn ....G...... 601 573-7582
Canton (G-664)

Jerold Henderson Logging Inc ....F...... 601 989-2399
Richton (G-4537)

Joe K Smith ....G...... 601 786-8632
Fayette (G-1298)

John Albert Ware ....G...... 662 489-7824
Pontotoc (G-4339)

Jones Logging Co Inc ....G...... 601 877-3814
Lorman (G-2961)

Justin Alan Rankin ....G...... 601 297-4365
Lumberton (G-3034)

Keith Conaway Logging LLC ....G...... 662 415-5646
Walnut (G-5457)

Kenneth Smith ....G...... 601 848-7956
State Line (G-4987)

Kristina Thorn ....G...... 256 460-9798
Dennis (G-1183)

Ladner Logging LLC ....G...... 601 422-7822
Laurel (G-2792)

Laird Timber Inc ....G...... 601 833-4293
Brookhaven (G-507)

Lance Smith Logging Inc ....G...... 601 833-4855
Brookhaven (G-508)

Langston Logging Inc ....G...... 662 542-8704
Calhoun City (G-639)

Larry D Brabham ....G...... 601 551-4777
Liberty (G-2914)

Larry Wheeless Logging ....G...... 662 547-6863
Mc Cool (G-3236)

Larry Winstead ....F...... 601 656-6438
Philadelphia (G-4223)

Leroy Dees ....G...... 662 674-5356
Ethel (G-1282)

Lincoln Lumber Co Inc ....D...... 601 833-4484
Brookhaven (G-512)

Livingston Log & Timber Co Inc ....G...... 601 425-2095
Laurel (G-2796)

Lloyd Cox Jr ....G...... 662 462-5226
Rienzi (G-4650)

M&M Logging ....G...... 601 754-2796
Brookhaven (G-514)

Max White Logging Inc ....G...... 662 560-3460
Oxford (G-3972)

Mayo Logging ....G...... 601 270-4426
Richton (G-4540)

Mc Logging LLC ....G...... 601 678-6681
Union (G-5301)

McCrory Logging LLC ....G...... 601 613-1702
Brandon (G-420)

McDaniel Trucking ....G...... 601 656-1028
Philadelphia (G-4225)

McFarland Cascade Holdings Inc ....E...... 662 476-8000
Scooba (G-4771)

Mike Smith Logging Inc ....G...... 601 833-2043
Brookhaven (G-517)

Miller Timber LLC ....G...... 662 501-6150
Houlka (G-2226)

Mills Logging ....G...... 662 665-2718
Tiplersville (G-5081)

Mmj Logging Inc ....G...... 662 755-1163
Bentonia (G-212)

Money Tree Logging LLC ....G...... 740 891-1713
Gulfport (G-1835)

Mp Logging ....G...... 662 808-5411
Corinth (G-1104)

Nail Logging ....G...... 601 953-0071
Kosciusko (G-2705)

Nail Logging LLC ....G...... 601 825-3375
Brandon (G-428)

Narkeeta Forest Services Inc ....F...... 601 692-4777
Porterville (G-4410)

New South Logging LLC ....G...... 601 517-8457
Collins (G-856)

Employee Codes: A=Over 500 employees, B=251-500
C=101-250, D=51-100, E=20-50, F=10-19, G=1-9

2019 Harris Directory of
Mississippi Manufacturers

LOGGING

No Hope Trucking Inc ....G....... 601 320-1919
Monticello *(G-3438)*

Norman K Hillman ....G....... 601 525-3735
Neely *(G-3645)*

North Mississippi Timber & Log ....G....... 662 603-7944
Corinth *(G-1106)*

ONeal Power Corporation ....G....... 228 323-1059
Perkinston *(G-4179)*

Otis Logging Inc ....G....... 601 249-0963
McComb *(G-3262)*

Parker Logging Inc ....G....... 662 412-2435
Calhoun City *(G-643)*

Parker Trucking and Hlg LLC ....G....... 601 537-3670
Morton *(G-3453)*

Pearl River Logging LLC ....G....... 601 587-2516
Monticello *(G-3439)*

Performance Logging LLC ....G....... 601 656-3556
Philadelphia *(G-4232)*

Pezant Logging LLC ....G....... 601 303-3025
Tylertown *(G-5280)*

Ralph Morgan Logging Inc ....E....... 601 679-5291
Lauderdale *(G-2728)*

Randy Cummings ....G....... 662 547-2008
Weir *(G-5521)*

Randy Judge Logging Inc ....F....... 601 775-3027
Lake *(G-2724)*

Ray Davis Logging Inc ....G....... 601 687-1392
Waynesboro *(G-5511)*

Raymond Granger ....G....... 662 289-2502
Sallis *(G-4704)*

Reed Logging Inc ....G....... 662 793-4951
Scooba *(G-4772)*

Reid & Deese Llc ....G....... 601 248-3143
Tylertown *(G-5283)*

River Bank Logging LLC ....G....... 601 639-4557
Crosby *(G-1135)*

River Bend Logging LLC ....G....... 601 466-1524
Foxworth *(G-1435)*

Robert L Leggett ....G....... 601 833-7313
Brookhaven *(G-527)*

Rolison & Sons Logging Inc ....F....... 662 837-9066
Ripley *(G-4670)*

Rolison Timber Logging ....G....... 662 993-8115
Ripley *(G-4671)*

Ronald D Sterling ....G....... 601 225-7772
Liberty *(G-2916)*

RTC Logging Inc ....G....... 601 517-6881
Collins *(G-860)*

S & F Logging Inc ....F....... 662 552-4701
Mantee *(G-3212)*

Sassones Timber LLC ....E....... 601 542-5558
Osyka *(G-3929)*

Simpson Brothers Inc ....G....... 678 451-4259
Mc Cool *(G-3237)*

Smith Boys Timber Inc ....G....... 601 859-1628
Canton *(G-679)*

Smith Tie and Timber LLC ....E....... 662 258-7605
Eupora *(G-1292)*

Sojourner Timber Inc ....F....... 601 892-4021
Crystal Springs *(G-1156)*

Sonny Moore ....G....... 662 585-4009
Fulton *(G-1475)*

South Fork Logging LLC ....G....... 601 218-4524
Vicksburg *(G-5420)*

Southern Forestry Inc ....F....... 662 416-3883
Golden *(G-1530)*

Strong Bros Logging Inc ....G....... 601 764-9191
Bay Springs *(G-173)*

Stuart Timber Inc ....G....... 601 943-8184
Carson *(G-705)*

Summerford Enterprises Inc ....G....... 662 585-3584
Golden *(G-1531)*

T & T Logging Co ....G....... 601 852-4281
Edwards *(G-1243)*

T A Netterville Logging Inc ....F....... 601 888-0054
Bogue Chitto *(G-305)*

T L G Logging Inc ....G....... 601 225-9743
Gloster *(G-1519)*

Taylor McKinley ....F....... 601 792-2739
Oak Vale *(G-3736)*

Thomas Davis Gamblin ....F....... 601 656-2759
Philadelphia *(G-4241)*

Timber Harvesters Inc ....G....... 601 416-2078
Philadelphia *(G-4244)*

Timber Resources Inc ....G....... 601 681-6801
Meridian *(G-3414)*

Timberland Management Services ....G....... 601 645-6440
Centreville *(G-733)*

Timberland Products Inc ....G....... 601 442-8102
Natchez *(G-3630)*

Timberwood Logging LLC ....G....... 662 633-7744
Winona *(G-5608)*

Tnc Logging Llc ....G....... 601 394-9760
Leakesville *(G-2879)*

Trinity Three LLC ....G....... 601 249-8851
Summit *(G-5027)*

Ulysses Cooley ....G....... 601 394-5485
Leakesville *(G-2881)*

W L Byrd Lumber Co Inc ....E....... 601 567-2314
Summit *(G-5029)*

Walley Trucking ....G....... 601 848-7576
State Line *(G-4989)*

Williamson & Son Logging LLC ....G....... 601 736-7858
Columbia *(G-928)*

Willie Lynn Hunt ....G....... 601 945-2237
Lucedale *(G-3021)*

X L Johnson & Sons Inc ....G....... 601 776-3685
Quitman *(G-4472)*

LOGGING CAMPS & CONTRACTORS

A & D Timber Company Inc ....F....... 601 528-9357
Wiggins *(G-5568)*

Acy Logging ....G....... 601 833-5426
Brookhaven *(G-478)*

Adam Sterling Logging LLC ....F....... 601 657-1091
Liberty *(G-2908)*

Adams Logging Inc ....G....... 601 567-2988
Smithdale *(G-4840)*

Andy Massey Logging ....G....... 662 675-2647
Coffeeville *(G-840)*

Anthony Logging Inc ....G....... 601 731-2975
Kokomo *(G-2686)*

Autman Logging ....G....... 601 986-2555
Collinsville *(G-866)*

B P Graves Logging Co ....G....... 601 765-8956
Collins *(G-852)*

Barbers Timber & Logging ....G....... 662 382-7649
Sarah *(G-4732)*

Bazor Pulpwood Company Inc ....F....... 601 735-4017
Waynesboro *(G-5492)*

Beach Harvey & Son Logging ....F....... 601 446-5771
Natchez *(G-3526)*

Beane Logging ....G....... 662 862-9053
Fulton *(G-1445)*

Bo Logging Inc ....G....... 662 983-4225
Houlka *(G-2219)*

Box Logging ....G....... 662 547-6692
French Camp *(G-1439)*

Brad Warren Log & Trckg LLC ....G....... 601 416-8113
Union *(G-5294)*

Brent Hickman Logging LLC ....G....... 601 928-8840
Wiggins *(G-5573)*

Btc Logging Co ....G....... 601 735-3259
Waynesboro *(G-5493)*

C & L Logging Inc ....G....... 601 683-6349
Newton *(G-3718)*

C E Welch Timber Co Inc ....G....... 601 657-4577
Liberty *(G-2911)*

Carey F Stanley ....F....... 601 687-5247
Shubuta *(G-4828)*

Cecil D Johnson ....F....... 662 456-5846
Mantee *(G-3210)*

Chains Logging ....G....... 662 327-8240
Columbus *(G-946)*

Charles Jordan ....G....... 601 727-4753
Pachuta *(G-4011)*

Charles R Smith Logging Co ....G....... 601 267-9800
Carthage *(G-713)*

Clarence South Logging ....G....... 662 585-3724
Fulton *(G-1450)*

Cook Timber Co Inc ....G....... 601 727-4782
Pachuta *(G-4012)*

D & C Logging Inc ....G....... 662 862-9316
Nettleton *(G-3659)*

David Breazeale Logging LLC ....F....... 662 323-9991
Starkville *(G-4938)*

David L Vance Logging Co ....G....... 601 635-2105
Decatur *(G-1172)*

Delta Logging & Company Inc ....E....... 662 746-2066
Yazoo City *(G-5632)*

Dier Logging Inc ....G....... 601 384-5963
Meadville *(G-3274)*

Dixie Logging Inc ....F....... 601 532-6583
Mc Call Creek *(G-3233)*

Donald Gatlin Logging LLC ....G....... 601 425-4320
Heidelberg *(G-2116)*

Dunaways Logging Inc ....F....... 601 695-1232
Brookhaven *(G-493)*

Dwayne Timber Company ....G....... 601 695-6177
Wesson *(G-5527)*

Ellis Williams Logging ....G....... 601 734-3918
Bogue Chitto *(G-302)*

Evans Logging ....G....... 662 369-7151
Aberdeen *(G-13)*

F W Graves & Son Inc ....G....... 601 657-8750
Liberty *(G-2912)*

Falvey Logging ....G....... 601 546-2922
Pelahatchie *(G-4164)*

Flora Logging LLC ....G....... 662 552-5408
Maben *(G-3045)*

Freeman Reason Logging ....G....... 601 446-5938
Natchez *(G-3561)*

G A Pearson Logging Inc ....G....... 601 928-2105
Wiggins *(G-5583)*

Glendon Henderson Log & Trckg ....F....... 601 989-2638
Richton *(G-4532)*

Goodman Logging LLC ....G....... 601 644-3443
Meridian *(G-3342)*

Guys Logging ....G....... 662 726-9301
Macon *(G-3063)*

H Delane Tucker Logging Inc ....G....... 601 788-6320
Richton *(G-4534)*

Harrison Brothers Incorporated ....G....... 601 536-2069
Pulaski *(G-4431)*

Harrison Logging Inc ....G....... 662 226-7908
Grenada *(G-1684)*

J & K Enterprise Inc ....F....... 601 794-6005
Purvis *(G-4440)*

J T Horn Logging Inc ....G....... 662 585-3417
Golden *(G-1527)*

J W Priest & Sons Logging ....G....... 601 532-6237
Mc Call Creek *(G-3234)*

J&M Logging Inc ....G....... 601 645-5813
Centreville *(G-731)*

Jeff Shepherd Logging Inc ....F....... 601 416-1832
Philadelphia *(G-4219)*

Jeff Winstead Logging ....F....... 601 656-1448
Philadelphia *(G-4220)*

Jerry Harris Logging Inc ....G....... 662 728-7331
Booneville *(G-332)*

Jimmy Jones & Sons Sawmill ....G....... 601 253-2533
Walnut Grove *(G-5460)*

Johnny McCool Logging ....E....... 601 636-3824
Vicksburg *(G-5383)*

Johnny W Mills Timber Company ....G....... 601 989-2398
Richton *(G-4538)*

Jones & Young Logging LLC ....G....... 601 681-6801
Meridian *(G-3354)*

K & J Logging Inc ....G....... 601 639-4607
Roxie *(G-4690)*

K&D Wright Logging ....G....... 601 729-5675
Laurel *(G-2789)*

Kinard Burge & Sons Inc ....F....... 601 794-6829
Purvis *(G-4443)*

L & W Logging Inc ....G....... 601 927-3588
Crystal Springs *(G-1145)*

Larry Sasser Logging LP ....F....... 601 734-6002
Bogue Chitto *(G-303)*

Lea Logging ....G....... 601 833-8983
Brookhaven *(G-509)*

Lovorn Logging Inc ....G....... 662 637-2617
Calhoun City *(G-640)*

M & B Logging Inc ....G....... 601 384-6611
Bude *(G-571)*

M & T Logging ....G....... 662 673-1621
Benton *(G-209)*

Mar-Cal Inc ....G....... 601 825-7520
Mendenhall *(G-3283)*

Mark Taylor Logging ....G....... 662 418-0812
Maben *(G-3047)*

Martin Logging Inc ....F....... 601 644-3374
Meridian *(G-3364)*

McCloud Logging Inc ....G....... 601 835-3217
Jayess *(G-2674)*

McDaniel Logging Co Inc ....G....... 601 322-7701
Roxie *(G-4692)*

Moores Logging & Trucking ....G....... 662 289-5872
Kosciusko *(G-2704)*

Nickerson Logging ....G....... 662 289-9779
Kosciusko *(G-2707)*

No Hope Logging Inc ....G....... 601 587-5515
Monticello *(G-3437)*

Nolan Brothers ....F....... 662 862-3055
Fulton *(G-1470)*

North Mississippi Timber Brk ....G....... 662 728-7328
Booneville *(G-339)*

Peters Brothers Logging ....G....... 601 928-3591
Wiggins *(G-5587)*

Phillip Spring Logging In ....G....... 601 567-2138
Smithdale *(G-4842)*

2019 Harris Directory of
Mississippi Manufacturers

(G-0000) Company's Geographic Section entry number

390

PRODUCT SECTION

LUMBER & BUILDING MATERIALS RET DEALERS: Millwork & Lumber

Prisock Brothers Logging Inc..............G..... 662 773-8443
Louisville (G-2977)

Pro Logging Inc ....E..... 662 720-9457
Booneville (G-344)

Quinton Hill Logging ....F..... 662 773-6864
Louisville (G-2978)

R & J Brown Logging & Trucking.........G..... 601 739-3338
Louin (G-2963)

Ray Smith Logging Inc ....G..... 601 786-8428
Fayette (G-1300)

Reggie Waddle Logging Co ....G..... 662 862-3106
Fulton (G-1473)

Robert Bray Logging ....G..... 601 269-3437
Raleigh (G-4476)

Robert W Stubbs ....G..... 601 849-9857
Magee (G-3183)

Robin Jones Logging Co ....G..... 601 687-5837
Shubuta (G-4833)

S L Netterville Logging Inc ....G..... 601 639-4915
Gloster (G-1517)

Shannon Fulgham Logging Inc ....G..... 662 418-4449
Maben (G-3050)

Shelby Logging LLC ....G..... 601 609-7796
Jackson (G-2578)

Smith Brothers Logging Inc..............F..... 601 322-7362
Roxie (G-4694)

Smith Timber Inc ....G..... 601 833-3968
Brookhaven (G-533)

Southern Logging Inc ....F..... 601 657-4449
Liberty (G-2917)

Stickman Logging LLC ....G..... 601 782-4597
Raleigh (G-4477)

Stinson & Son Logging ....G..... 601 989-2311
Richton (G-4544)

Taylor S Flying Service Inc ....G..... 601 885-9959
Utica (G-5313)

Tdk Logging Inc ....F..... 662 328-6625
Columbus (G-1037)

Teddy Doggett Logging Inc................G..... 601 687-5233
Waynesboro (G-5518)

Thomas Logging Company Inc ....G..... 662 862-7342
Fulton (G-1479)

Tim Breland Logging Inc ....F..... 601 656-0382
Philadelphia (G-4243)

Tim Rollins Logging ....G..... 601 225-4972
Gloster (G-1520)

Tim Wilder Logging Inc ....F..... 662 489-7632
Ecru (G-1234)

Tony Adams Logging ....G..... 601 267-5174
Carthage (G-724)

Tony Pharr Logging ....G..... 662 728-9426
Booneville (G-346)

Tri B Timber & Logging LLC ....G..... 662 283-4824
Winona (G-5609)

Triple G Logging ....G..... 601 416-8733
Philadelphia (G-4245)

Triple L Logging ....F..... 601 656-9313
Philadelphia (G-4247)

TW Logging LLC ....G..... 601 657-8838
Liberty (G-2918)

W A Mathis Timber Co ....G..... 601 684-7839
McComb (G-3273)

Walsworth Logging ....G..... 601 442-5406
Natchez (G-3637)

Watts Timber Company Inc.................F..... 601 754-0138
Brookhaven (G-546)

White Logging ....G..... 601 783-2738
Magnolia (G-3196)

Williams Logging Company Inc ....G..... 601 835-2771
Brookhaven (G-548)

LOGGING: Fuel Wood Harvesting

Ckc Logging Inc ....G..... 601 754-1344
Monticello (G-3430)

LOGGING: Peeler Logs

East Mississippi Pole Company ....E..... 662 726-2932
Macon (G-3059)

LOGGING: Saw Logs

Jamie Valentine Logging LLC...............G..... 601 764-7271
Bay Springs (G-166)

LOGGING: Timber, Cut At Logging Camp

Austin Logging LLC ....G..... 662 296-6566
Randolph (G-4479)

Black Rver Timber Wildlife LLC............G..... 601 906-4099
Clinton (G-814)

Charles Horn Logging & Trckg ....F..... 662 585-3111
Golden (G-1524)

Diamond Land & Timber LLC ....G..... 601 310-3395
Hattiesburg (G-1957)

First Heritage Credit Corp ....G..... 228 762-7000
Pascagoula (G-4032)

First Heritage Credit Corp ....G..... 228 396-2620
Diberville (G-1203)

First Heritage Credit Corp ....G..... 601 636-6060
Vicksburg (G-5372)

First Heritage Credit Corp ....G..... 601 735-4543
Waynesboro (G-5498)

First Heritage Credit Corp ....G..... 601 799-1972
Picayune (G-4266)

First Heritage Credit Corp ....G..... 662 283-4696
Winona (G-5598)

First Heritage Credit Corp ....G..... 601 939-9309
Richland (G-4515)

Kelwood Products ....G..... 662 862-9494
Fulton (G-1461)

Mims Timber LLC ....G..... 662 301-5022
Senatobia (G-4796)

Molpus Timberlands Management ....G..... 601 969-7093
Jackson (G-2509)

North Ms Timber Harvester ....G..... 662 927-0013
Calhoun City (G-642)

Ronny P Moore ....G..... 601 934-0113
Quitman (G-4470)

S and M Logging LLC ....G..... 662 263-6711
Mathiston (G-3230)

Scott Strickland Sons Inc ....G..... 601 928-2321
Perkinston (G-4180)

Timber Creek Estates ....G..... 228 392-0858
Biloxi (G-283)

Tippo Timber Company LLP ....G..... 601 981-3303
Jackson (G-2608)

Triple J Tie and Timber LLC ....G..... 662 547-6600
Weir (G-5522)

LOGGING: Wooden Logs

Eddie Inc ....F..... 601 663-5755
Forest (G-1416)

Henry E Davis Logging ....G..... 601 677-3669
De Kalb (G-1165)

LOOSELEAF BINDERS

Acco Brands USA LLC ....D..... 662 720-1300
Booneville (G-315)

LOTIONS OR CREAMS: Face

Sc3 LLC ....G..... 601 853-3690
Ridgeland (G-4627)

LOTIONS: SHAVING

Diomedia Industries LLC ....G..... 601 882-7724
Jackson (G-2384)

LUGGAGE & LEATHER GOODS STORES

Mary Givens.......................................G..... 601 325-5599
Brandon (G-419)

LUGGAGE REPAIR SHOP

Boat Man ....G..... 228 218-3080
Gautier (G-1489)

LUMBER & BLDG MATRLS DEALERS, RET: Bath Fixtures, Eqpt/Sply

Pettigrew Cabinets Inc ....E..... 662 844-1368
Plantersville (G-4313)

LUMBER & BLDG MTRLS DEALERS, RET: Insultn & Energy Consrvtn

Cooperation Jackson LLC ....F..... 601 355-7224
Jackson (G-2368)

LUMBER & BLDG MTRLS DEALERS, RET: Planing Mill Prdts/Lumber

Crosby Wood Preserving Co Inc...........G..... 601 264-5249
Hattiesburg (G-1952)

Service Lumber Company Inc ....F..... 662 873-4334
Rolling Fork (G-4682)

LUMBER & BUILDING MATERIALS DEALER, RET: Door & Window Prdts

Fayard Millworks ....G..... 228 265-7787
Gulfport (G-1783)

LUMBER & BUILDING MATERIALS DEALER, RET: Masonry Matls/Splys

Blaylocks Cement Manufacturing ....G..... 225 627-1006
Liberty (G-2910)

MMC Materials Inc.............................G..... 601 774-0443
Union (G-5302)

MMC Materials Inc.............................D..... 662 393-7676
Horn Lake (G-2208)

MMC Materials Inc.............................G..... 662 327-1927
Columbus (G-1006)

Pittsburgh Stone & Plaster ....G..... 601 631-0006
Vicksburg (G-5406)

Vulcan Materials Company ....G..... 601 425-3509
Laurel (G-2863)

LUMBER & BUILDING MATERIALS DEALERS, RETAIL: Brick

General Shale Brick Inc ....F..... 662 840-8221
Tupelo (G-5141)

Meridian Brick LLC ....G..... 228 863-5451
Gulfport (G-1828)

Meridian Brick LLC ....G..... 601 296-0445
Hattiesburg (G-2022)

Meridian Brick LLC ....F..... 601 428-4364
Laurel (G-2800)

Meridian Brick LLC ....G..... 662 840-8884
Tupelo (G-5186)

Tupelo Concrete Products Inc ....F..... 662 842-7811
Tupelo (G-5243)

LUMBER & BUILDING MATERIALS DEALERS, RETAIL: Cement

Delta Industries Inc...........................G..... 228 475-2419
Moss Point (G-3476)

Delta Industries Inc...........................G..... 662 323-7224
Starkville (G-4939)

Metro Concrete ....G..... 228 284-1660
Gulfport (G-1830)

MMC Materials Inc.............................E..... 662 332-5407
Greenville (G-1577)

LUMBER & BUILDING MATERIALS DEALERS, RETAIL: Countertops

C & S Marble Co ....G..... 662 844-6873
Saltillo (G-4710)

LUMBER & BUILDING MATERIALS DEALERS, RETAIL: Flooring, Wood

Alfords Decorating Center ....G..... 662 455-3552
Greenwood (G-1612)

LUMBER & BUILDING MATERIALS DEALERS, RETAIL: Modular Homes

C3 Design Inc ....F..... 662 392-5021
Greenwood (G-1617)

LUMBER & BUILDING MATERIALS DEALERS, RETAIL: Sand & Gravel

Martin Marietta Materials Inc...............G..... 662 652-3836
Tremont (G-5093)

Pen/Ron Company Inc.........................G..... 601 519-5096
Brandon (G-431)

LUMBER & BUILDING MATERIALS DEALERS, RETAIL: Siding

Quality Glass and Aluminum ....G..... 662 837-3615
Ripley (G-4669)

LUMBER & BUILDING MATERIALS RET DEALERS: Millwork & Lumber

Ash Millworks Inc...............................E..... 601 544-3962
Petal (G-4184)

Frierson Building Supply Co ....C..... 601 922-1321
Jackson (G-2416)

Employee Codes: A=Over 500 employees, B=251-500
C=101-250, D=51-100, E=20-50, F=10-19, G=1-9

2019 Harris Directory of
Mississippi Manufacturers

391

PRODUCT

LUMBER & BUILDING MATERIALS RET DEALERS: Millwork & Lumber

PRODUCT SECTION

H & L Millworks Inc ....G...... 228 392-9913
Biloxi *(G-250)*

Herrington Millworks ....G...... 601 845-8056
Florence *(G-1325)*

Smith Tie and Timber LLC ....E 662 258-7605
Eupora *(G-1292)*

LUMBER & BUILDING MATLS DEALERS, RET: Concrete/Cinder Block

Columbia Block & Brick Co Inc ....G...... 601 450-3791
Hattiesburg *(G-1949)*

Macon Ready-Mix Concrete Co ....F 662 726-4733
Macon *(G-3065)*

LUMBER: Box

Anderson-Tully Company ....B 601 636-3876
Vicksburg *(G-5340)*

LUMBER: Dimension, Hardwood

Homans Wood Products ....E 662 862-2145
Fulton *(G-1457)*

LUMBER: Fiberboard

Certainteed Gypsum Inc ....C 601 693-0254
Meridian *(G-3318)*

Tom Lauderdale Paper Svcs Inc............F 662 767-9744
Shannon *(G-4819)*

LUMBER: Furniture Dimension Stock, Softwood

Kitchens Brothers Mfg Co......................C 601 885-6001
Utica *(G-5309)*

LUMBER: Hardboard

Carlmac Industries Inc ....G...... 601 794-5000
Purvis *(G-4435)*

LUMBER: Hardwood Dimension

Al-Tom Forest Products Inc ....E 601 989-2631
Richton *(G-4526)*

Kelwood Products Inc ....E 601 659-7027
Enterprise *(G-1280)*

LUMBER: Hardwood Dimension & Flooring Mills

Anderson-Tully Company ....B 601 636-3876
Vicksburg *(G-5340)*

Anderson-Tully Company ....B 601 629-3283
Vicksburg *(G-5339)*

Dixie Mat and Hardwood Co ....E 601 876-2427
Columbia *(G-895)*

Georgia-Pacific LLC.............................D 601 764-4806
Bay Springs *(G-161)*

Georgia-Pacific LLC.............................C 601 785-4721
Columbia *(G-900)*

Hood Industries Inc ....D 601 735-5038
Waynesboro *(G-5500)*

Marietta Wood Supply Inc ....E 662 728-9874
Marietta *(G-3217)*

Martin and Sons LLC ....E 601 825-4012
Brandon *(G-418)*

R & R Lumber Inc ....E 662 568-7937
Houlka *(G-2227)*

Reeds Reynolds ....E 601 445-8206
Natchez *(G-3612)*

Rives and Reynolds Lbr Co Inc ....E 662 289-3823
Kosciusko *(G-2711)*

Rjb Enterprises ....E 601 639-4921
Crosby *(G-1136)*

Tallahatchie Hardwoods Inc.................E 662 647-5427
Charleston *(G-744)*

Thomas Leslie Coleman ....G...... 662 369-6000
Caledonia *(G-632)*

Tombigbee Lumber Company Inc ....E 662 862-7417
Fulton *(G-1481)*

V & B International Inc..........................E 601 437-8279
Port Gibson *(G-4408)*

Weyerhaeuser Company ....C 662 983-7311
Bruce *(G-562)*

LUMBER: Kiln Dried

Tri-State Lumber Company Inc............D 662 862-2125
Fulton *(G-1483)*

LUMBER: Panels, Plywood, Softwood

American Pacific Inc............................D 662 252-1862
Holly Springs *(G-2171)*

Hood Industries Inc ....D 601 264-2962
Hattiesburg *(G-1994)*

LUMBER: Pilings, Treated

Tri-State Pole & Piling Inc ....F 601 947-4285
Lucedale *(G-3020)*

LUMBER: Plywood, Hardwood

Anderson-Tully Company ....B 601 629-3283
Vicksburg *(G-5339)*

Davis Wood Products of Miss ....C 662 534-2211
New Albany *(G-3680)*

Frierson Building Supply Co ....E 601 922-1321
Jackson *(G-2416)*

Hood Industries Inc ....B 601 928-3737
Wiggins *(G-5584)*

Hood Industries Inc ....D 601 735-5038
Waynesboro *(G-5500)*

Hood Industries Inc ....C 601 784-3414
Beaumont *(G-185)*

Quality Plywood Company Inc ....D 601 735-3106
Waynesboro *(G-5510)*

Scotch Plywood Company Miss ....D 601 735-2881
Waynesboro *(G-5513)*

Timber Products Co Ltd Partnr ....D 662 287-3766
Corinth *(G-1122)*

LUMBER: Plywood, Hardwood or Hardwood Faced

Georgia-Pacific LLC.............................G...... 601 225-4211
Gloster *(G-1515)*

LUMBER: Plywood, Prefinished, Hardwood

Commercial Mllwk Spcialist Inc............E 228 868-3888
Gulfport *(G-1763)*

LUMBER: Plywood, Softwood

Hood Industries Inc ....C 601 784-3414
Beaumont *(G-185)*

LUMBER: Plywood, Softwood

Georgia-Pacific LLC.............................G...... 601 225-4211
Gloster *(G-1515)*

Hood Industries Inc ....B 601 928-3737
Wiggins *(G-5584)*

LUMBER: Poles & Pole Crossarms, Treated

Carpenters Pole & Piling Co ....E 601 928-7400
Wiggins *(G-5576)*

Macon Treating Company ....G...... 662 726-2767
Macon *(G-3066)*

Southern WD Prsv Httesburg Inc ....F 601 544-1140
Hattiesburg *(G-2065)*

LUMBER: Poles, Wood, Untreated

Conway Investments Inc.......................G...... 601 964-3215
New Augusta *(G-3710)*

LUMBER: Posts, Treated

Treated Materials Co Inc......................F 228 896-5056
Gulfport *(G-1887)*

LUMBER: Resawn, Small Dimension

Hood Industries Inc ....D 601 264-2962
Hattiesburg *(G-1994)*

LUMBER: Silo Stock, Sawn

Crosby Wood Preserving Co Inc ....G...... 601 264-5249
Hattiesburg *(G-1952)*

LUMBER: Stacking Or Sticking

Jeffrey Roberson ....G...... 662 587-1991
Ripley *(G-4662)*

Rex Lumber Brookhaven Llc ....G...... 601 833-1990
Brookhaven *(G-526)*

LUMBER: Treated

Biewer Sawmill-Newton LLC ....F 601 357-6001
Newton *(G-3717)*

Brown Wood Preserving Co Inc ....G...... 601 656-2607
Philadelphia *(G-4209)*

Brown Wood Preserving Co Inc ....G...... 662 263-8272
Mathiston *(G-3227)*

Cpp LLC ....G...... 601 749-7140
Picayune *(G-4262)*

Deforest Wood Preserving Co ....G...... 601 866-4655
Bolton *(G-308)*

Desoto Treated Materials Inc ....E 601 928-3921
Wiggins *(G-5580)*

Electric Mills Wood Prsv LLC ....G...... 662 476-8000
Scooba *(G-4770)*

Elite Wood Care ....G...... 601 622-2278
Brandon *(G-394)*

Forest Penick Products Inc...................E 662 726-5224
Macon *(G-3062)*

Gordon Redd Lumber Company ....E 601 833-2311
Brookhaven *(G-496)*

Great Southern Wood Prsv Inc..............G...... 601 823-4865
Brookhaven *(G-498)*

Stone Treated Materials ....G...... 601 798-4422
Picayune *(G-4299)*

Thomas Wood Preserving Inc ....E 662 226-2350
Grenada *(G-1708)*

Tri-State Lumber Company Inc ....D 662 862-2125
Fulton *(G-1483)*

Wood Preserving Inc ....G...... 601 833-8822
Brookhaven *(G-549)*

LUMBER: Veneer, Softwood

Palmer Veneer Inc ....F 601 735-9717
Waynesboro *(G-5509)*

Scotch Plywood Company Miss.............D 601 735-2881
Waynesboro *(G-5513)*

MACHINE GUNS, WHOLESALE

Maa Global Supply Ltd ....F 662 816-4802
Oxford *(G-3968)*

MACHINE PARTS: Stamped Or Pressed Metal

L & L Tool & Machine Co LLC ....G...... 662 335-1181
Greenville *(G-1563)*

Tylertown Wear Parts Inc ....E 601 876-4659
Tylertown *(G-5290)*

MACHINE SHOPS

A K Sanders Mfg Inc ....G...... 901 647-1830
Southaven *(G-4850)*

Benvenutti Elctrcl Apprts & Rp ....G...... 228 831-0445
Gulfport *(G-1738)*

Bigbee Industries...............................G...... 662 568-7740
Houlka *(G-2218)*

D & T Motors Inc ....G...... 662 773-9041
Louisville *(G-2966)*

Fretwell (not Incorporated) ....G...... 601 649-0003
Laurel *(G-2768)*

Gulf Coast Fabrication Inc ....G...... 601 347-8403
Picayune *(G-4268)*

Helanbak LLC ....G...... 601 736-6112
Foxworth *(G-1431)*

Innovex Inc ....E 662 328-9537
Columbus *(G-988)*

Lindsey Machine Shop Inc....................G...... 662 365-8189
Baldwyn *(G-83)*

McGregor Indstl Steel Fabrcatn.............E 662 236-7006
Oxford *(G-3973)*

Msi Inc ....G...... 662 401-9781
Saltillo *(G-4718)*

P & S Welding & Manufacturing ....G...... 662 334-9881
Greenville *(G-1587)*

Parish Pumps and Machine Inc ....G...... 662 256-2052
Amory *(G-51)*

Redi-Strip of Jackson Inc......................F 601 355-3317
Jackson *(G-2563)*

Ridgid Machining ....G...... 228 383-3525
Bay St Louis *(G-181)*

MACHINE TOOL ACCESS: Cutting

J A C Industrial Tl & Sup LLC ....G...... 601 591-1321
Brandon *(G-408)*

2019 Harris Directory of
Mississippi Manufacturers

(G-0000) Company's Geographic Section entry number

392

PRODUCT SECTION

MACHINERY, FOOD PRDTS: Food Processing, Smokers

MACHINE TOOLS & ACCESS

Lunati LLC ....E 662 892-1518
Olive Branch **(G-3868)**
Novelty Machine Works Inc ....F 601 948-2075
Jackson **(G-2524)**
William Zaremba ....G 601 845-7238
Florence **(G-1339)**

MACHINE TOOLS, METAL CUTTING: Lathes

Electro Mech Solutions Ems Inc ....G 601 631-0138
Vicksburg **(G-5365)**

MACHINE TOOLS, METAL CUTTING: Vertical Turning & Boring

Accurate Edge ....G 228 832-2920
Gulfport **(G-1715)**
Metalworx LLC ....G 228 806-9112
Biloxi **(G-268)**

MACHINE TOOLS, METAL FORMING: Headers

Southeast Supply Header ....G 601 947-9842
Lucedale **(G-3017)**

MACHINE TOOLS: Metal Cutting

Cerbide Inc ....F 228 871-7123
Gulfport **(G-1749)**
Precision Metalworks Inc ....G 662 838-4605
Byhalia **(G-598)**

MACHINE TOOLS: Metal Forming

Developmental Industries Inc ....E 662 287-6626
Corinth **(G-1083)**
Union Spring & Mfg Corp ....D 662 489-7846
Pontotoc **(G-4366)**

MACHINERY & EQPT, AGRICULTURAL, WHOL: Farm Eqpt Parts/Splys

Fireplace Wholesale ....G 601 545-9876
Hattiesburg **(G-1970)**
Merle E Sullivan ....G 662 347-4494
Greenville **(G-1572)**

MACHINERY & EQPT, AGRICULTURAL, WHOLESALE: Poultry Eqpt

K & T Poultry Sales & Svc Inc ....F 601 764-3918
Bay Springs **(G-167)**

MACHINERY & EQPT, INDL, WHOL: Meters, Consumption Registerng

Gibson Electric Motor Svc Inc ....G 228 762-4923
Pascagoula **(G-4033)**

MACHINERY & EQPT, INDL, WHOLESALE: Chainsaws

Nhc Distributors Inc ....E 601 656-7911
Philadelphia **(G-4229)**

MACHINERY & EQPT, INDL, WHOLESALE: Drilling Bits

Vmi Marine Inc ....D 601 636-8700
Vicksburg **(G-5443)**

MACHINERY & EQPT, INDL, WHOLESALE: Drilling, Exc Bits

Richard E Johnson ....G 601 735-4737
Waynesboro **(G-5512)**

MACHINERY & EQPT, INDL, WHOLESALE: Engines & Parts, Diesel

Kennedy Engine Company Inc ....F 228 392-2200
Biloxi **(G-256)**

MACHINERY & EQPT, INDL, WHOLESALE: Engines, Gasoline

Barnetts Small Engines ....G 662 323-8993
Starkville **(G-4926)**

J and E Enterprises ....G 662 369-7324
Aberdeen **(G-15)**
Mini Mtrs Unlimited Sls & Svc ....G 662 356-4900
Steens **(G-4991)**
Power Plus Inc ....F 601 264-1950
Sumrall **(G-5042)**
Robbys Small Engine & Saw Repr ....G 601 847-0323
Mendenhall **(G-3287)**

MACHINERY & EQPT, INDL, WHOLESALE: Engs/Transportation Eqpt

Kar Kleen ....G 601 638-8816
Vicksburg **(G-5384)**

MACHINERY & EQPT, INDL, WHOLESALE: Food Manufacturing

Rebel Butcher Supply Co Inc ....G 601 939-2214
Jackson **(G-2665)**

MACHINERY & EQPT, INDL, WHOLESALE: Fuel Injection Systems

Mississippi Diesel Products ....E 601 847-2500
Mendenhall **(G-3285)**

MACHINERY & EQPT, INDL, WHOLESALE: Hydraulic Systems

Franklin Electrofluid Co Inc ....G 601 969-7022
Jackson **(G-2412)**
Geartek ....F 662 286-2252
Corinth **(G-1087)**
Hattiesburg Hydraulics Sls Svc ....G 601 264-6606
Hattiesburg **(G-1986)**
Metaris Corporation ....E 601 469-1987
Forest **(G-1422)**
Rcl Components Inc ....E 662 449-0401
Hernando **(G-2152)**
Tucker Machine Services ....G 601 582-4280
Hattiesburg **(G-2075)**

MACHINERY & EQPT, INDL, WHOLESALE: Lift Trucks & Parts

Chrisman Manufacturing Inc ....E 228 864-6293
Long Beach **(G-2931)**

MACHINERY & EQPT, INDL, WHOLESALE: Safety Eqpt

Choctaw Glove & Safety Co Inc ....D 662 724-4178
Noxapater **(G-3731)**

MACHINERY & EQPT, INDL, WHOLESALE: Sawmill

Pioneer Machinery and Sup Inc ....F 662 286-5646
Corinth **(G-1110)**

MACHINERY & EQPT, INDL, WHOLESALE: Trailers, Indl

M and S Sales Inc ....G 662 453-6111
Greenwood **(G-1637)**

MACHINERY & EQPT, TEXTILE: Fabric Forming

JP Williams Machine & Fabricat ....G 228 474-1099
Pascagoula **(G-4042)**

MACHINERY & EQPT, WHOLESALE: Construction, General

Electric Contractors ....G 662 470-3102
Southaven **(G-4871)**

MACHINERY & EQPT, WHOLESALE: Contractors Materials

Aerial Truck Equipment Co Inc ....G 662 895-0993
Olive Branch **(G-3807)**

MACHINERY & EQPT, WHOLESALE: Logging

Alamiss Inc ....G 601 671-0840
Waynesboro **(G-5489)**

MACHINERY & EQPT, WHOLESALE: Oil Field Eqpt

A & B Pump & Supply Inc ....G 601 787-3741
Heidelberg **(G-2111)**
Cameron International Corp ....G 601 649-8900
Laurel **(G-2747)**
Dnow LP ....G 601 649-8671
Laurel **(G-2762)**
Fretwell (not Incorporated) ....G 601 649-0003
Laurel **(G-2768)**
Oilfield Service & Sup Co Inc ....E 601 649-4461
Laurel **(G-2813)**
Pryor Packers Inc ....F 601 649-4535
Laurel **(G-2829)**
T & T Welding Yard Inc ....E 601 477-2299
Ellisville **(G-1271)**

MACHINERY & EQPT: Farm

Aerway Manufacturing Co ....G 662 726-4246
Macon **(G-3054)**
Autoflow LLC ....G 601 853-1021
Madison **(G-3079)**
Bigbee Metal Manufacturing Co ....E 662 652-3372
Tremont **(G-5092)**
Cases Cntrpint Hnting CLB Inc ....G 601 734-2373
Smithdale **(G-4841)**
CG&p Manufacturing Inc ....E 662 746-4464
Yazoo City **(G-5627)**
Evergreen AG Envmtl & Turf LLC ....F 662 263-4419
Mathiston **(G-3229)**
Hol-Mac Corporation ....C 601 764-4121
Bay Springs **(G-162)**
Knr Farm Supplies Inc ....G 228 574-8397
Lumberton **(G-3035)**
Mississippi Center For Freedom ....G 601 638-0962
Vicksburg **(G-5395)**
Rodgers Sales Company ....G 662 902-1664
Clarksdale **(G-780)**
Sarah Case-Price ....G 601 818-4377
Hattiesburg **(G-2055)**
Southern Application MGT ....G 662 578-4684
Batesville **(G-125)**
Welborn Devices LLC ....G 601 428-5912
Laurel **(G-2872)**
Wicker Machine Co ....F 662 827-5434
Hollandale **(G-2169)**

MACHINERY & EQPT: Gas Producers, Generators/Other Rltd Eqpt

Gasmax Fltration Solutions LLC ....G 601 790-1225
Ridgeland **(G-4586)**
Miller Bryant G Oil Gas Prpts ....G 601 360-2850
Jackson **(G-2492)**

MACHINERY & EQPT: Petroleum Refinery

Comet Street Inc ....F 601 981-4151
Jackson **(G-2362)**
Pascagoula Refinery ....G 228 938-4563
Pascagoula **(G-4060)**

MACHINERY & EQPT: Silver Recovery

Gulf States Silver ....G 601 415-4365
Vicksburg **(G-5375)**

MACHINERY, COMMERCIAL LAUNDRY: Washing, Incl Coin-Operated

Bullocks Washteria ....G 601 684-2332
McComb **(G-3244)**
Laundry Depot LLC ....F 601 527-2774
Meridian **(G-3357)**

MACHINERY, FOOD PRDTS: Choppers, Commercial

Robot-Coupe Inc USA ....E 601 898-8411
Ridgeland **(G-4624)**

MACHINERY, FOOD PRDTS: Food Processing, Smokers

Baader North America Corp ....G 662 887-5841
Indianola **(G-2262)**
Standex International Corp ....F 662 534-9061
New Albany **(G-3699)**

Employee Codes: A=Over 500 employees, B=251-500
C=101-250, D=51-100, E=20-50, F=10-19, G=1-9

2019 Harris Directory of
Mississippi Manufacturers

PRODUCT

393

MACHINERY, FOOD PRDTS: Processing, Poultry

PRODUCT SECTION

MACHINERY, FOOD PRDTS: Processing, Poultry

Pearl River Foods LLC ....G....... 678 343-3265
Carthage *(G-721)*

MACHINERY, MAILING: Postage Meters

Pitney Bowes Inc ....G....... 601 969-2900
Jackson *(G-2540)*

Pitney Bowes Inc ....E....... 601 206-9039
Ridgeland *(G-4618)*

MACHINERY, PRINTING TRADES: Type Cases

Cedotal Inc ....G....... 601 605-2660
Ridgeland *(G-4561)*

MACHINERY, SERVICING: Coin-Operated, Exc Dry Clean & Laundry

Klean N Press ....G....... 662 563-5515
Batesville *(G-112)*

Sunday Best ....G....... 662 226-2214
Grenada *(G-1706)*

MACHINERY, TEXTILE: Embroidery

Brenda Ruth Designs LLC ....G....... 601 708-4227
Clinton *(G-815)*

Magnolia Sewing Center ....G....... 601 261-9006
Hattiesburg *(G-2019)*

MACHINERY, TEXTILE: Rope & Cordage

D&J Twine Co ....G....... 662 726-2594
Macon *(G-3056)*

MACHINERY, TEXTILE: Silk Screens

Mitchell Signs Inc ....D....... 601 553-1557
Meridian *(G-3374)*

Shirtz Stuff ....G....... 601 729-2472
Laurel *(G-2848)*

MACHINERY, WOODWORKING: Bandsaws

Helanbak LLC ....G....... 601 736-6112
Foxworth *(G-1431)*

MACHINERY, WOODWORKING: Cabinet Makers'

Delta Fabricators ....G....... 662 862-2998
Fulton *(G-1451)*

Goodings Fine Woodworking ....G....... 228 255-9037
Pass Christian *(G-4085)*

MACHINERY/EQPT, INDL, WHOL: Cleaning, High Press, Sand/Steam

Baker Petrolite LLC ....F....... 601 649-1955
Laurel *(G-2739)*

MACHINERY: Assembly, Exc Metalworking

Ronald E Christopher III ....G....... 901 301-5922
Olive Branch *(G-3905)*

Southern Hose & Hydraulics ....F....... 601 922-9990
Jackson *(G-2590)*

MACHINERY: Automotive Maintenance

Crane Cams Inc ....E....... 386 310-4875
Olive Branch *(G-3831)*

Peppers Machine & Wldg Co Inc ....E....... 601 833-3038
Brookhaven *(G-522)*

MACHINERY: Automotive Related

Accusteer LLC ....G....... 601 483-0225
Meridian *(G-3294)*

Curbell Plastics Inc ....D....... 888 477-8173
Brandon *(G-384)*

Hol-Mac Corporation ....C....... 601 764-4121
Bay Springs *(G-162)*

MACHINERY: Bottling & Canning

S & N Airoflo Inc ....F....... 662 455-2804
Greenwood *(G-1650)*

MACHINERY: Brick Making

Puckett Allen B Jr & Family ....G....... 662 328-4931
Columbus *(G-1018)*

MACHINERY: Construction

B&Z Sales Inc ....G....... 601 825-1900
Brandon *(G-368)*

Bell Inc ....E....... 662 265-5841
Inverness *(G-2274)*

Bowen Titus ....G....... 662 327-3084
Steens *(G-4990)*

Brandi Bonner ....G....... 601 906-7224
Mendenhall *(G-3279)*

Caterpillar ....G....... 662 286-1274
Corinth *(G-1065)*

Caterpillar Dev Ctr Inc ....G....... 228 385-3900
Biloxi *(G-226)*

Caterpillar Inc ....C....... 662 720-2400
Booneville *(G-324)*

Caterpillar Inc ....A....... 662 286-5511
Corinth *(G-1068)*

Hol-Mac Corporation ....C....... 601 764-4121
Bay Springs *(G-162)*

L M & R Service Inc ....G....... 601 892-3034
Crystal Springs *(G-1146)*

Precious Creative Caterpillars ....G....... 228 424-3500
Gulfport *(G-1851)*

Roadsafe Traffic Systems Inc ....G....... 601 922-5009
Jackson *(G-2568)*

Stockstill Land Dev LLC ....G....... 601 273-2409
Poplarville *(G-4396)*

Sweet Treats and Coffee Too ....G....... 662 286-5511
Corinth *(G-1121)*

Terex Corporation ....C....... 662 393-1800
Southaven *(G-4913)*

MACHINERY: Cotton Ginning

Big Creek Gin Company Inc ....E....... 662 624-5233
Lyon *(G-3041)*

Williamson Gin Repair ....G....... 662 571-6084
Yazoo City *(G-5652)*

MACHINERY: Custom

B & B Mfg & Specialty Co Inc ....G....... 662 456-4313
Houston *(G-2231)*

Holmes Industries LLC ....G....... 601 635-4409
Decatur *(G-1173)*

Jims Tool & Die Inc ....F....... 662 895-3287
Olive Branch *(G-3856)*

Lauderdale-Hamilton Inc ....F....... 662 767-3928
Shannon *(G-4813)*

Pontotoc Machine Works Inc ....G....... 662 489-8944
Pontotoc *(G-4355)*

Precision Mch Met Fbrction Inc ....E....... 662 844-4606
Tupelo *(G-5207)*

Traceway Engineering and Mfg ....F....... 662 489-1314
Pontotoc *(G-4364)*

Transport Trailer Service Inc ....D....... 662 844-4606
Tupelo *(G-5241)*

MACHINERY: Dredging

Best Equipment Tech Inc ....E....... 601 795-2208
Poplarville *(G-4376)*

MACHINERY: Electronic Component Making

Ustx Contract Services NC Inc ....E....... 512 894-0008
Corinth *(G-1126)*

MACHINERY: General, Industrial, NEC

KC&c General Contractor ....G....... 601 668-4615
Edwards *(G-1239)*

Merle E Sullivan ....G....... 662 347-4494
Greenville *(G-1572)*

MACHINERY: Industrial, NEC

Hughes Outdoors & Marin ....G....... 662 287-8607
Corinth *(G-1090)*

Mashburns Welding ....G....... 601 648-2886
Buckatunna *(G-564)*

Pallet Machinery Svc ....G....... 662 726-5101
Macon *(G-3070)*

Southwest Mississippi Robotics ....G....... 601 276-4276
Summit *(G-5022)*

Taylor Machine ....G....... 601 650-9600
Philadelphia *(G-4240)*

Taylor Machine Works Inc ....G....... 303 289-2201
Jackson *(G-2670)*

MACHINERY: Kilns

Dogwood Ceramic Supply Inc ....G....... 228 831-4848
Gulfport *(G-1773)*

MACHINERY: Kilns, Lumber

JT Shannon Lumber Co Inc ....E....... 662 393-3765
Horn Lake *(G-2203)*

MACHINERY: Logging Eqpt

D & T Motors Inc ....G....... 662 773-5021
Louisville *(G-2965)*

MACHINERY: Metalworking

Hunter Engineering Company ....C....... 662 653-3194
Durant *(G-1227)*

Met-Tech Corp ....G....... 601 693-0061
Meridian *(G-3370)*

Ormans Welding & Fab Inc ....F....... 662 494-9471
West Point *(G-5556)*

MACHINERY: Milling

Freeman Milling LLC ....F....... 601 733-5444
Mize *(G-3426)*

M & M Milling Inc ....G....... 601 823-4630
Brookhaven *(G-513)*

MACHINERY: Mining

Glenn Mch Works Crane Rigging ....G....... 601 544-1275
Petal *(G-4186)*

Screw Conveyor Corporation ....C....... 662 283-3142
Winona *(G-5606)*

Syntron Material Handling LLC ....C....... 662 869-5711
Saltillo *(G-4721)*

Syntron Mtl Hdlg Group LLC ....C....... 662 869-5711
Saltillo *(G-4722)*

MACHINERY: Packaging

Packaging Machinery Systems ....G....... 601 992-5011
Flowood *(G-1386)*

MACHINERY: Recycling

L & W Print Finishers LLC ....G....... 662 890-0505
Olive Branch *(G-3862)*

Norton Equipment Company ....F....... 662 838-7900
Byhalia *(G-593)*

MACHINERY: Road Construction & Maintenance

Pace Brothers Inc ....G....... 601 736-9225
Columbia *(G-910)*

Washington County Wide Shop ....D....... 662 334-4322
Greenville *(G-1608)*

MACHINERY: Semiconductor Manufacturing

Galvian Group LLC ....G....... 662 374-1027
Greenwood *(G-1624)*

MACHINERY: Specialty

Beavers Enterprises ....G....... 601 569-1557
Picayune *(G-4256)*

Southern Diversified Products ....G....... 601 271-2588
Hattiesburg *(G-2060)*

MACHINERY: Woodworking

King Manufacturing Company Inc ....E....... 662 286-5504
Corinth *(G-1096)*

Pierce Cnstr & Maint Co Inc ....D....... 601 544-1321
Petal *(G-4196)*

MACHINES: Forming, Sheet Metal

A K Sanders Mfg Inc ....G....... 901 647-1830
Southaven *(G-4850)*

Mattuby Creek Machine Works ....G....... 662 369-8262
Aberdeen *(G-18)*

394

2019 Harris Directory of
Mississippi Manufacturers

(G-0000) Company's Geographic Section entry number

PRODUCT SECTION

MANUFACTURING INDUSTRIES, NEC

MAIL-ORDER HOUSES: Computer Eqpt & Electronics

Landmark Spatial Solutions LLC..........G...... 662 769-5344
Starkville *(G-4955)*

MAIL-ORDER HOUSES: Food

Westward Corporation ....G...... 601 660-3857
Fayette *(G-1303)*

MAIL-ORDER HOUSES: General Merchandise

Gmn Group LLC ....G.....662 473-3094
Water Valley *(G-5468)*

MAIL-ORDER HOUSES: Jewelry

Sparkles & Such................................G.......601 750-1270
Crystal Springs *(G-1157)*

MAILBOX RENTAL & RELATED SVCS

Jagg LLC...G...... 228 388-1794
Biloxi *(G-254)*
Mailbox Ranch...................................G...... 601 758-4767
Sumrall *(G-5038)*

MANAGEMENT CONSULTING SVCS: Construction Project

National Bank Builders & Eqp ....F..... 662 781-0702
Walls *(G-5450)*

MANAGEMENT CONSULTING SVCS: Hospital & Health

Min Sheng Healthcare LLC ....G...... 601 212-6189
Madison *(G-3130)*

MANAGEMENT CONSULTING SVCS: Industrial & Labor

Kelsey Bailey Consulting LLC ....G....... 601 622-8319
Madison *(G-3115)*

MANAGEMENT CONSULTING SVCS: Management Engineering

Stormcom LLC ....G...... 601 918-5401
Jackson *(G-2598)*

MANAGEMENT SERVICES

Crystal Springs Apparel LLC ....E 601 856-8831
Ridgeland *(G-4568)*
Dewmar International Bmc Inc ....G....... 877 747-5326
Clinton *(G-822)*
Sparko Inc ....G...... 662 690-5800
Tupelo *(G-5229)*

MANAGEMENT SVCS, FACILITIES SUPPORT: Environ Remediation

Socrates Garrett Entps Inc..................F 601 896-0084
Jackson *(G-2585)*
Tackle Technologies LLC ....G...... 228 206-1449
Long Beach *(G-2956)*

MANAGEMENT SVCS: Administrative

Saunders Mfg Co Inc ....F 601 693-3482
Meridian *(G-3394)*

MANAGEMENT SVCS: Business

Lmg Diversified LLC ....G...... 601 635-5955
Newton *(G-3724)*
Molpus Timberlands Management ....G....... 601 969-7093
Jackson *(G-2509)*

MANICURE PREPARATIONS

Belles ....G...... 662 617-8171
Starkville *(G-4928)*
Nail First ....G...... 601 892-4433
Crystal Springs *(G-1151)*

MANUFACTURING INDUSTRIES, NEC

ABC Scrity Fbrction Sltion LLC...........G....... 601 828-9010
Roxie *(G-4688)*

Accu-Fab Manufacturing LLC...............G...... 228 769-2532
Pascagoula *(G-4017)*
Action Industries...............................G...... 662 566-3173
Pontotoc *(G-4319)*
Armorlock Industries LLC ....G...... 228 466-2990
Bay St Louis *(G-175)*
Atco Industries ....G...... 601 407-6329
Canton *(G-647)*
B and P Cstome Meta L Fbrction.........G...... 228 474-0097
Moss Point *(G-3467)*
B&B Trailers & Mfg Co ....G...... 662 456-4313
Houston *(G-2232)*
Beaver Industries Inc ....G...... 601 664-6610
Richland *(G-4506)*
Bent Wrench Industries LLC ....G...... 601 934-7851
Florence *(G-1315)*
Blue Line Industries LLC ....G...... 901 335-2987
Gulfport *(G-1742)*
Cajun Planters LLC ....G...... 770 363-5638
Long Beach *(G-2930)*
Carters Machine Works ....G...... 601 507-5480
Carthage *(G-708)*
Cdr Manufacturing Inc ....G...... 662 665-3100
Corinth *(G-1069)*
Circle J Meat Manufacturing ....G...... 662 790-3448
Tupelo *(G-5120)*
Clay Stewart Industries LLC ....G...... 601 946-2332
Mendenhall *(G-3280)*
Coastal Fire and Safety LLC ....G...... 228 327-0563
Pascagoula *(G-4027)*
Craig Wilkes Design ....G...... 917 664-7255
Meridian *(G-3324)*
Crux Industries.................................F 662 873-3317
Anguilla *(G-58)*
Dkc Industries LLC ....G...... 800 308-5187
Jackson *(G-2386)*
Dogman Industries LLC ....G...... 662 832-3644
Oxford *(G-3952)*
Doubletap Industries ....G...... 601 506-3218
Terry *(G-5065)*
Easters Custom Woodworks LLC ....G...... 740 502-2039
Vicksburg *(G-5364)*
Faith Industries LLC ....G...... 662 618-0839
Lauderdale *(G-2727)*
Finnesse Fabrications & Steel ....G...... 228 216-2102
Pass Christian *(G-4083)*
First Class Industries LLC ....G...... 601 597-4787
Fayette *(G-1297)*
Foster & Thomas Manufacturing ....G...... 662 682-9094
Vardaman *(G-5324)*
G M Horne Commercial & Indus ....G...... 601 981-1600
Jackson *(G-2418)*
Garys Industries Inc ....G...... 662 415-1777
Corinth *(G-1086)*
Genie Industries ....G...... 662 393-1800
Southaven *(G-4874)*
Glad Industries ....G...... 601 422-0261
Laurel *(G-2771)*
GLC Mfg Inc ....G...... 662 565-2600
Duck Hill *(G-1221)*
Good News Industries Inc ....G...... 662 327-1988
Columbus *(G-980)*
Hampton Industries LLC ....G...... 601 441-7604
Hattiesburg *(G-1981)*
Highlands Industries Inc ....G...... 601 454-3901
Brandon *(G-405)*
Interstate Industries Miss LL ....G...... 601 856-5941
Ridgeland *(G-4594)*
Itawamba Ind Work Activities C............E 662 862-3392
Fulton *(G-1459)*
J2 Manufacturing Inc ....G...... 601 573-3134
Flowood *(G-1368)*
Jtwo Manufacturing LLC ....G...... 769 243-8914
Flowood *(G-1372)*
K and A Industries LLC ....G...... 601 763-3503
Ellisville *(G-1261)*
K M Industries ....G...... 228 497-7040
Gautier *(G-1495)*
Ksj Industries ....G...... 601 493-3991
Laurel *(G-2790)*
L T Industries Inc ....G...... 228 392-1172
Biloxi *(G-258)*
Lacknothing Enterprises LLC ....G...... 601 498-1000
Laurel *(G-2791)*
Leopold Inds Intrglaetical LLC ....G...... 662 324-0536
Starkville *(G-4956)*
Levan Industries ....G...... 601 446-7390
Natchez *(G-3579)*
Lit Industries Inc ....G...... 662 993-8088
Ripley *(G-4663)*

Lombardo Industries LLC ....G...... 601 783-3643
Magnolia *(G-3192)*
M & M Machine LLC ....G...... 601 749-4325
Carriere *(G-695)*
Magnolia Bites LLC ....G...... 601 709-9577
Brandon *(G-417)*
Magnolia Green Industries Inc ....G...... 601 466-3853
Hattiesburg *(G-2018)*
Manufacturing - ....G...... 408 514-6512
Olive Branch *(G-3869)*
Matco Industries LLC ....G...... 228 218-9813
Moss Point *(G-3485)*
Maybelle Mfg Co Inc ....G...... 228 863-4398
Gulfport *(G-1826)*
Microtech Industries Inc ....G...... 601 373-0177
Byram *(G-622)*
Mississippi Prison Industries ....G...... 601 346-4966
Jackson *(G-2504)*
Moore Industries ....G...... 662 862-3993
Fulton *(G-1463)*
Morton Industry ....G...... 601 732-6486
Morton *(G-3451)*
Mtm Industries LLC ....G...... 662 402-9750
Flowood *(G-1382)*
Mw Industries ....G...... 662 488-4551
Pontotoc *(G-4351)*
Nightwind Industries ....G...... 662 690-9709
Tupelo *(G-5193)*
Novi Creations LLC ....G...... 601 335-1902
Laurel *(G-2812)*
Odom Industries ....G...... 601 687-6325
Shubuta *(G-4832)*
Owl City Industries LLC ....G...... 901 268-6871
Hernando *(G-2147)*
Paine Industries ....G...... 601 336-2069
Jackson *(G-2533)*
Parker Dre Industries ....G...... 228 383-5967
Gulfport *(G-1843)*
Pine Belt Industries ....G...... 601 450-0431
Hattiesburg *(G-2042)*
Pink Star Industries ....G...... 702 546-9883
Sarah *(G-4735)*
Qualified Fabrication Inc ....F 601 508-4389
Lucedale *(G-3014)*
Randell Mfg Inc ....G...... 601 372-3903
Jackson *(G-2557)*
Resourcemfg ....G...... 662 563-9617
Batesville *(G-120)*
Rock On Industries LLC ....G...... 601 825-4857
Brandon *(G-446)*
Rykan Industries ....G...... 601 900-2055
Carthage *(G-722)*
Sanders Industries Inc ....G...... 662 895-1337
Olive Branch *(G-3906)*
Scented Creations ....G...... 601 362-5926
Jackson *(G-2575)*
Singin River Mental Health...................E 228 497-0690
Gautier *(G-1504)*
Sisters of Creations ....G...... 662 615-3978
Starkville *(G-4971)*
Smallberry Mfg Co ....G...... 601 847-3692
Mendenhall *(G-3290)*
Smw Manufacturing ....G...... 517 596-3300
Oxford *(G-4003)*
Sophisticated Fabrications LLC ....G...... 228 424-8346
Biloxi *(G-280)*
Soupbone Industries LLC ....G...... 601 520-1317
Purvis *(G-4453)*
Stuart Chaffin ....G...... 601 807-1547
Brookhaven *(G-540)*
Surgisure Inc ....G...... 601 985-8125
Clinton *(G-836)*
T & S Precision Mfg Inc ....G...... 601 825-0878
Brandon *(G-467)*
Techform Manufacturing LLC ....G...... 662 282-7771
Mantachie *(G-3207)*
Tinkerbelle Industries Inc ....G...... 601 928-3520
Wiggins *(G-5591)*
Tri-Coast Industries Inc ....G...... 228 369-9924
Pascagoula *(G-4071)*
Warhorse Industries LLC ....G...... 601 856-2990
Madison *(G-3167)*
Weems Industries LLC ....G...... 228 382-4423
Saucier *(G-4768)*
Whitehouse Industries ....G...... 601 981-5866
Jackson *(G-2631)*
Wolf Industries Inc ....G...... 228 864-9096
Gulfport *(G-1894)*

Employee Codes: A=Over 500 employees, B=251-500
C=101-250, D=51-100, E=20-50, F=10-19, G=1-9

2019 Harris Directory of
Mississippi Manufacturers

PRODUCT

395

MAPS

MAPS

MI-Da Maps................................G....... 662 429-0022
Hernando *(G-2142)*

MARBLE BOARD

Owens Custom Marble.....................G....... 662 627-7256
Lyon *(G-3043)*

Smith Cabinet Shop Inc.....................E....... 662 287-2151
Corinth *(G-1119)*

MARBLE, BUILDING: Cut & Shaped

A & W Marble Inc............................G....... 228 832-5037
Saucier *(G-4748)*

Apex Products Inc..........................G....... 601 992-5900
Jackson *(G-2332)*

Avalon Marble LLC........................F....... 601 798-3378
Picayune *(G-4253)*

C & S Marble Co............................G....... 662 844-6873
Saltillo *(G-4710)*

Foley Tile & Marble........................G....... 601 271-8415
Hattiesburg *(G-1972)*

L & G Marble Inc...........................G....... 601 268-0225
Hattiesburg *(G-2012)*

Lavastone Industries Mid South...........G....... 662 844-5178
Tupelo *(G-5172)*

North Miss Stone & Mem Co...............G....... 662 365-2721
Baldwyn *(G-85)*

MARBLE: Dimension

Avalon Marble LLC........................F....... 601 798-3378
Picayune *(G-4253)*

MARINE CARGO HANDLING SVCS

Galvian Group LLC..........................G....... 662 374-1027
Greenwood *(G-1624)*

MARINE HARDWARE

Southern Technical Aquatic RES.........G....... 601 590-6248
Carriere *(G-701)*

MARINE RELATED EQPT

Big River Shipbuilders Inc................G....... 601 802-9994
Vicksburg *(G-5346)*

Big River Shipbuilders Inc................E....... 601 636-9161
Vicksburg *(G-5345)*

Maymar Marine Supply Inc................G....... 228 762-2241
Pascagoula *(G-4052)*

MARKING DEVICES

Correy Elder................................G....... 769 257-3240
Madison *(G-3089)*

Documart of Mid-South LLC...............G....... 662 281-1474
Oxford *(G-3951)*

McMillan Stamp & Sign Co Inc...........G....... 601 353-4688
Jackson *(G-2485)*

Noyes Printing & Rbr Stamp Co...........G....... 662 332-5256
Greenville *(G-1583)*

Trodat Marking Products Inc..............G....... 601 500-5971
Jackson *(G-2612)*

MARKING DEVICES: Date Stamps, Hand, Rubber Or Metal

Labels & Stamps of Ellisville.............G....... 601 763-3092
Ellisville *(G-1262)*

MARKING DEVICES: Embossing Seals & Hand Stamps

Southern Rubber Stamp Inc...............G....... 601 373-6590
Jackson *(G-2591)*

MARKING DEVICES: Embossing Seals, Corporate & Official

Midsouth Corporate Housing..............G....... 901 239-4514
Olive Branch *(G-3877)*

MARKING DEVICES: Seal Presses, Notary & Hand

DLS Tax Consultants.......................G....... 601 473-6623
Jackson *(G-2387)*

Prosperity7 Helping Hands LLC...........G....... 800 597-6599
Southaven *(G-4893)*

MARKING DEVICES: Textile Making Stamps, Hand, Rubber/Metal

J & S Enterprises LLC......................G....... 601 646-3636
Hickory *(G-2162)*

MASTIC ROOFING COMPOSITION

Efma Contracting LLC......................F....... 901 292-7221
Ridgeland *(G-4576)*

MATERIALS HANDLING EQPT WHOLESALERS

Haynes Enterprises Inc...................G....... 662 843-4411
Cleveland *(G-795)*

Mel Vold Sales Co..........................G....... 601 371-4911
Jackson *(G-2487)*

MATS & MATTING, MADE FROM PURCHASED WIRE

Kdeb Manufacturing LLC.................G....... 601 750-9659
Morton *(G-3448)*

MATS OR MATTING, NEC: Rubber

Superior Mfg Group Inc....................D....... 601 544-8119
Moselle *(G-3462)*

MATS, MATTING & PADS: Nonwoven

Mat Sturgis Co Inc.........................E....... 662 465-8879
Sturgis *(G-5007)*

MATTRESS STORES

Meridian Mattress Factory Inc.............F....... 601 693-3875
Meridian *(G-3368)*

MEAT & FISH MARKETS: Seafood

Ocean Springs Seafood Mkt Inc...........G....... 228 875-0104
Biloxi *(G-269)*

MEAT CUTTING & PACKING

B and L Meat Processing...................G....... 601 218-0918
Vicksburg *(G-5343)*

Boon Docks Deer Processing..............G....... 601 789-5843
Raleigh *(G-4474)*

Boswell Meat Processing...................G....... 601 656-6015
Philadelphia *(G-4208)*

Dwights Custom Deer Processing..........G....... 601 857-2324
Raymond *(G-4487)*

Enslin and Son Packing Company.........E....... 601 582-9300
Hattiesburg *(G-1963)*

Family Meat Processing....................G....... 601 264-2344
Sumrall *(G-5036)*

Forbes Meat Processors...................G....... 601 736-6992
Sandy Hook *(G-4728)*

Fortenberrys Meat Processing.............G....... 601 876-2291
Sandy Hook *(G-4729)*

Fortenberrys Slaughter House............G....... 601 798-2156
Carriere *(G-692)*

Kershenstines Beef Jerky Inc.............G....... 662 258-2049
Eupora *(G-1288)*

Mississippi Poultry.........................G....... 601 732-8670
Morton *(G-3450)*

Murrays Deer Processing..................G....... 601 720-2769
Macon *(G-3068)*

Natchez Smokehouse & Cold Stor.......G....... 601 442-6116
Natchez *(G-3597)*

Pitcocks Meat Processing Inc.............G....... 662 563-9627
Pope *(G-4372)*

Polks Meat Products Inc..................C....... 601 849-9997
Magee *(G-3180)*

Prestage Farms Inc.......................C....... 662 494-0813
West Point *(G-5560)*

Rutn Cutn Deer Processing................G....... 601 892-5527
Crystal Springs *(G-1154)*

Sanderson Farms Inc Proc Div...........A....... 601 684-9375
Summit *(G-5021)*

Smokehouse Meats........................G....... 662 489-5764
Pontotoc *(G-4362)*

Stevens Packing...........................G....... 601 795-6999
Poplarville *(G-4395)*

Sullivans Custom Processing..............G....... 662 773-2839
Preston *(G-4428)*

T and S Deer Processing..................G....... 601 727-3725
Rose Hill *(G-4685)*

Tyson Foods Inc...........................G....... 601 664-9102
Pearl *(G-4155)*

Tyson Foods Inc...........................E....... 601 469-1712
Forest *(G-1427)*

MEAT MARKETS

Family Meat Processing....................G....... 601 264-2344
Sumrall *(G-5036)*

Honey Baked...............................G....... 228 875-5828
Ocean Springs *(G-3764)*

Pitcocks Meat Processing Inc.............G....... 662 563-9627
Pope *(G-4372)*

MEAT PRDTS: Dried Beef, From Purchased Meat

Kershenstines Beef Jerky Inc.............G....... 662 258-2049
Eupora *(G-1288)*

MEAT PRDTS: Ham, Boiled, From Purchased Meat

Honey Baked...............................G....... 228 875-5828
Ocean Springs *(G-3764)*

MEAT PRDTS: Sausages, From Purchased Meat

Enslin and Son Packing Company.........E....... 601 582-9300
Hattiesburg *(G-1963)*

MEAT PRDTS: Spreads, Sandwich, From Purchased Meat

Tonys King of Steaks Inc..................G....... 228 214-9668
Gulfport *(G-1884)*

MEAT PROCESSED FROM PURCHASED CARCASSES

Bryant Meats Inc...........................E....... 601 785-6507
Taylorsville *(G-5052)*

Fortenberrys Slaughter House............G....... 601 798-2156
Carriere *(G-692)*

Hillshire Brands Company.................B....... 662 890-6069
Olive Branch *(G-3848)*

Hillshire Brands Company.................G....... 601 948-4632
Jackson *(G-2441)*

Sanderson Farms Inc Foods Div..........B....... 601 939-9790
Flowood *(G-1394)*

MEAT PROCESSING MACHINERY

Blaylocks Wild Game Processing.........G....... 601 894-0087
Hazlehurst *(G-2090)*

Southern Hens Inc.........................A....... 601 582-2262
Moselle *(G-3460)*

Vans Deer Processing Inc................E....... 601 825-9087
Brandon *(G-470)*

MEDICAL & HOSPITAL EQPT WHOLESALERS

Air Products and Chemicals Inc...........G....... 601 823-9850
Brookhaven *(G-479)*

Covidien LP.................................C....... 815 744-3766
Olive Branch *(G-3830)*

Magnolia Mobility LLC....................G....... 601 400-7292
Vicksburg *(G-5392)*

MEDICAL & SURGICAL SPLYS: Clothing, Fire Resistant & Protect

Oxford Scrubs.............................G....... 662 513-0341
Oxford *(G-3991)*

MEDICAL & SURGICAL SPLYS: Gynecological Splys & Appliances

Memphis Obstetrics & Gynecolog........G....... 662 349-5554
Southaven *(G-4889)*

Ovation Womens Wellness LLC............G....... 601 326-6401
Jackson *(G-2532)*

MEDICAL & SURGICAL SPLYS: Limbs, Artificial

Gulf Coast Limb & Brace Inc..............G....... 228 864-4512
Gulfport *(G-1798)*

Hanger Prsthetcs & Ortho Inc.............G....... 662 844-6734
Tupelo *(G-5150)*

PRODUCT SECTION

METAL FABRICATORS: Plate

Jackson Brace Co ....F ... 601 353-2477
Jackson **(G-2453)**

Mid State Artificial Limb Inc ....F ... 601 981-2229
Jackson **(G-2490)**

MEDICAL & SURGICAL SPLYS: Orthopedic Appliances

Ability Prosthetics LLC ....G ... 662 842-3220
Tupelo **(G-5106)**

Central Fabrication Inc ....G ... 662 349-7122
Southaven **(G-4858)**

Custom Prosthetic & Orthotic ....G ... 601 708-4196
Clinton **(G-819)**

Hanger Prsthetcs & Ortho Inc ....G ... 662 451-7495
Greenwood **(G-1627)**

In Motion Orthotics ....G ... 662 258-8201
Eupora **(G-1287)**

J J Hill Brace & Limb Co Inc ....G ... 228 863-0381
Gulfport **(G-1812)**

MEDICAL & SURGICAL SPLYS: Personal Safety Eqpt

901 Safety LLC ....G ... 901 493-3841
Olive Branch **(G-3803)**

Logistical Services Intl Inc ....G ... 662 676-2823
Golden **(G-1529)**

MEDICAL & SURGICAL SPLYS: Prosthetic Appliances

Adams Prsthtics Orthdntics LLC ....G ... 601 665-4000
Jackson **(G-2318)**

Alatheia Prosthetic Reha ....F ... 601 919-2113
Brandon **(G-360)**

BMW Prosthetics Orthotics LLC ....E ... 601 414-0032
Jackson **(G-2339)**

Hanger Inc ....E ... 228 604-0818
Gulfport **(G-1803)**

Hanger Prosthetic Orthopedics ....G ... 601 939-2100
Jackson **(G-2647)**

Hanger Prsthetcs & Ortho Inc ....G ... 601 693-1002
Meridian **(G-3345)**

Hanger Prsthetcs & Ortho Inc ....G ... 662 335-6828
Greenville **(G-1557)**

Hanger Prsthetcs & Ortho Inc ....G ... 601 442-7742
Natchez **(G-3566)**

Hanger Prsthetcs & Ortho Inc ....G ... 662 323-3349
Starkville **(G-4947)**

Methodist and Prosthetics ....G ... 662 846-6555
Cleveland **(G-799)**

Parr Prosthetics ....G ... 601 749-7254
Picayune **(G-4283)**

Prosthetic Solutions Inc ....F ... 228 220-4917
Gulfport **(G-1855)**

Southern Prosthetic Care LLC ....G ... 769 242-2555
Picayune **(G-4296)**

Synergy Prosthetics Center ....G ... 601 832-4975
Jackson **(G-2602)**

MEDICAL & SURGICAL SPLYS: Sutures, Non & Absorbable

Medi-Vation LLC ....G ... 800 643-2134
Madison **(G-3128)**

MEDICAL & SURGICAL SPLYS: Walkers

Walker Missionary Baptist Pars ....G ... 662 585-3309
Golden **(G-1532)**

MEDICAL CENTERS

Central Delta Cmnty Dev Corp ....G ... 601 215-0367
Jackson **(G-2357)**

MEDICAL EQPT: Diagnostic

Desoto Sleep Diagnostics ....G ... 662 349-9802
Southaven **(G-4867)**

Mobile Diagnostics Inc ....G ... 601 445-9895
Natchez **(G-3591)**

Open Air M R I of Laurel ....G ... 601 428-5026
Laurel **(G-2815)**

MEDICAL EQPT: Ultrasonic, Exc Cleaning

Vital Care of Central Ms ....G ... 601 859-8200
Madison **(G-3166)**

MEDICAL FIELD ASSOCIATION

Mississippi State Phrm Assn ....G ... 601 981-0416
Jackson **(G-2506)**

MEDICAL HELP SVCS

City of Magee ....E ... 601 849-2366
Magee **(G-3174)**

MEDICAL RESCUE SQUAD

Southern Technical Aquatic RES ....G ... 601 590-6248
Carriere **(G-701)**

MEDICAL, DENTAL & HOSPITAL EQPT, WHOLESALE: Artificial Limbs

Hanger Prsthetcs & Ortho Inc ....G ... 662 335-6828
Greenville **(G-1557)**

MEDICAL, DENTAL & HOSPITAL EQPT, WHOLESALE: Hearing Aids

Advanced Hearing and Balance ....G ... 601 450-0280
Hattiesburg **(G-1915)**

MEDICAL, DENTAL & HOSPITAL EQPT, WHOLESALE: Med Eqpt & Splys

Hanger Prsthetcs & Ortho Inc ....G ... 228 822-0109
Gulfport **(G-1804)**

Kerex LLC ....G ... 210 494-5596
Jackson **(G-2463)**

Magnolia Supply Group LLC ....G ... 601 454-1368
Jackson **(G-2480)**

Norwood Medical Supply LLC ....G ... 601 792-2224
Prentiss **(G-4422)**

MEDICAL, DENTAL & HOSPITAL EQPT, WHOLESALE: Orthopedic

Jackson Brace Co ....F ... 601 353-2477
Jackson **(G-2453)**

MEDICAL, DENTAL & HOSPITAL EQPT, WHOLESALE: Safety

901 Safety LLC ....G ... 901 493-3841
Olive Branch **(G-3803)**

MEMBERSHIP ORGANIZATIONS, BUSINESS: Contractors' Association

Associated Gen Contrs of Miss ....G ... 601 981-1144
Jackson **(G-2334)**

MEMBERSHIP ORGANIZATIONS, BUSINESS: Growers' Association

Delta Agricultural MGT Inc ....G ... 865 210-4605
Tunica **(G-5096)**

MEMBERSHIP ORGANIZATIONS, NEC: Charitable

Natures Society Majestic Arts ....G ... 601 376-0447
Byram **(G-623)**

Orchard Oxford ....G ... 662 259-0094
Oxford **(G-3982)**

MEMBERSHIP ORGS, BUSINESS: Shipping/Steamship Co Assoc

Chism Rackard Enterprises LLC ....G ... 662 327-5200
Columbus **(G-947)**

MEMORIALS, MONUMENTS & MARKERS

Columbus Marble Works Inc ....E ... 662 328-1477
Columbus **(G-950)**

Mississippi Marble & Granite ....G ... 662 289-4111
Kosciusko **(G-2702)**

MEMORY DEVICES: Magnetic Bubble

Comfort Revolution LLC ....F ... 662 454-7526
Belmont **(G-197)**

MEN'S & BOYS' CLOTHING STORES

McCullar Long & Mccullough Inc ....G ... 662 842-4165
Tupelo **(G-5184)**

MEN'S & BOYS' CLOTHING WHOLESALERS, NEC

Corinth Acquisition Corp ....G ... 662 287-1476
Corinth **(G-1075)**

Harris Custom Ink LLC ....E ... 662 338-4242
Olive Branch **(G-3844)**

MEN'S & BOYS' WORK CLOTHING WHOLESALERS

Fashions Incorporated Jackson ....G ... 601 948-1119
Jackson **(G-2406)**

MEN'S SUITS STORES

Formal Affair ....G ... 228 497-7500
Gautier **(G-1492)**

MESH, REINFORCING: Plastic

Naum Myatt & Sons ....G ... 662 256-8104
Becker **(G-186)**

METAL & STEEL PRDTS: Abrasive

Atlas-Ssi Inc ....D ... 601 587-4511
Monticello **(G-3428)**

Kr Steel & Industrial Supply ....G ... 662 294-8888
Grenada **(G-1690)**

METAL FABRICATORS: Architechtural

Bills Welding ....G ... 901 216-6762
Byhalia **(G-579)**

Davis Custom Fabrication LLC ....G ... 228 832-7456
Gulfport **(G-1768)**

Fisher Ludlow ....G ... 601 853-9996
Madison **(G-3099)**

Industrial Fabricators Inc ....E ... 662 327-1776
Columbus **(G-987)**

Ironcrafters Security Products ....E ... 662 224-6658
Ashland **(G-62)**

Ironworks Inc ....G ... 601 352-3722
Jackson **(G-2449)**

J M Architectural Iron Wo ....G ... 228 234-1747
Brooklyn **(G-550)**

Majestic Metals Inc ....E ... 601 856-3600
Madison **(G-3126)**

Olivers Iron Works ....G ... 662 252-3858
Holly Springs **(G-2186)**

Union Corrugating Company ....G ... 601 661-0577
Vicksburg **(G-5432)**

METAL FABRICATORS: Plate

Aberdeen Machine Works Inc ....E ... 662 369-9357
Aberdeen **(G-6)**

Babcock & Wilcox Company ....C ... 662 494-1323
West Point **(G-5537)**

Cbl Architectural Fiberglass ....F ... 662 429-2277
Hernando **(G-2124)**

Contech Engnered Solutions LLC ....F ... 662 332-2625
Greenville **(G-1541)**

Contech Engnered Solutions LLC ....G ... 601 894-2041
Greenville **(G-1540)**

Laurel Machine and Foundry Co ....C ... 601 428-0541
Laurel **(G-2793)**

Matheson Tri-Gas Inc ....F ... 228 255-6661
Pass Christian **(G-4091)**

Olivers Iron Works ....G ... 662 252-3858
Holly Springs **(G-2186)**

Ratliff Fabricating Company ....F ... 601 362-8942
Jackson **(G-2560)**

Rickys Welding and Machine Sp ....G ... 601 638-8238
Vicksburg **(G-5410)**

Southern Metals Co Miss Inc ....E ... 601 649-7475
Laurel **(G-2853)**

Steel Service Corporation ....C ... 601 939-9222
Jackson **(G-2668)**

Structural Steel Holding Inc ....C ... 601 483-5381
Meridian **(G-3408)**

Structural Steel Services Inc ....E ... 601 485-2619
Meridian **(G-3410)**

Taylor Environmental Products ....G ... 662 773-8056
Louisville **(G-2985)**

Tokins Inc ....G ... 601 939-1093
Pearl **(G-4152)**

Employee Codes: A=Over 500 employees, B=251-500
C=101-250, D=51-100, E=20-50, F=10-19, G=1-9

2019 Harris Directory of
Mississippi Manufacturers

PRODUCT

397

METAL FABRICATORS: Sheet

METAL FABRICATORS: Sheet

Aberdeen Machine Works Inc ....E 662 369-9357
Aberdeen **(G-6)**

Advanced Fabrication Inc ....G 601 796-7977
Lumberton **(G-3023)**

Air Vent ....G 601 790-9397
Madison **(G-3076)**

Allen Sheetmetal Inc ....G 228 875-5336
Biloxi **(G-218)**

American Metalcraft ....G 769 486-5007
De Kalb **(G-1160)**

Aplimages Inc ....G 601 992-1556
Brandon **(G-363)**

Babcock & Wilcox Company ....C 662 494-1323
West Point **(G-5537)**

Brocato Construction Inc ....G 662 563-4473
Batesville **(G-100)**

Cbr Performance ....G 601 337-2928
Carriere **(G-690)**

Clarence Sansing Jr ....G 601 656-4771
Philadelphia **(G-4211)**

Conklin Metal Industries Inc ....F 601 933-0402
Richland **(G-4510)**

Contech Engnered Solutions LLC ....F 662 332-2625
Greenville **(G-1541)**

Daniel Petre ....G 662 726-2462
Macon **(G-3057)**

Edco Welding ....G 228 392-5600
Biloxi **(G-241)**

Fielders Welding and Orna Ir ....G 662 234-4256
Oxford **(G-3955)**

Gansman Sheet Metal Contrs ....G 662 890-6215
Olive Branch **(G-3841)**

Goldin Metals Incorporated ....D 228 575-7737
Gulfport **(G-1793)**

Goldin Metals Incorporated ....F 228 575-7737
Gulfport **(G-1794)**

Granger Mp AC & Htg ....G 601 894-3774
Hazlehurst **(G-2097)**

Hawkeye Industries Inc ....E 662 842-3333
Tupelo **(G-5154)**

Hunter Douglas Inc ....C 662 690-8190
Shannon **(G-4810)**

Hunter Engineering Company ....C 662 653-3194
Durant **(G-1227)**

Industrial Fabricators Inc ....E 662 327-1776
Columbus **(G-987)**

J & A Mechanical Inc ....G 662 890-4565
Olive Branch **(G-3853)**

King Heating & AC ....G 662 227-1159
Grenada **(G-1689)**

Koenig-Stimens Inc ....E 228 467-3888
Kiln **(G-2682)**

L D Sheet Metal ....G 662 838-6267
Byhalia **(G-587)**

Larkowski Inc ....G 601 928-9501
Saucier **(G-4757)**

Leonard Metal Fabricators Inc ....E 601 936-4994
Pearl **(G-4129)**

Majestic Metals Inc ....E 601 856-3600
Madison **(G-3126)**

McKinnion Welding & Metal Fabr ....G 601 635-3983
Decatur **(G-1175)**

Metaline Products Inc ....F 601 892-5610
Crystal Springs **(G-1147)**

Observa-Dome Laboratories Inc ....G 601 982-3333
Jackson **(G-2527)**

Onyx Xterirors ....G 901 281-2887
Byhalia **(G-595)**

Palmer Tool LLC ....E 228 832-0805
Saucier **(G-4760)**

Peppers Machine & Wldg Co Inc ....E 601 833-3038
Brookhaven **(G-522)**

Precision Mch Met Fbrction Inc ....E 662 844-4606
Tupelo **(G-5207)**

Quality Metal Roofing LLC ....G 601 669-4336
Brookhaven **(G-525)**

Ratliff Fabricating Company ....F 601 362-8942
Jackson **(G-2560)**

Rickys Welding and Machine Sp ....G 601 638-8238
Vicksburg **(G-5410)**

S & H Steel Corp ....F 601 932-0250
Pearl **(G-4141)**

S&G Gutter & Sheet Metal Co ....G 662 286-2924
Corinth **(G-1118)**

Sims Metal Inc ....G 601 649-2555
Laurel **(G-2850)**

Sistrunk Sheet Metal ....G 601 825-5999
Brandon **(G-455)**

Southern Metals Co Miss Inc ....E 601 649-7475
Laurel **(G-2853)**

Spiral Systems Inc ....G 901 521-8373
Hernando **(G-2155)**

Steve Harris ....G 228 769-8350
Pascagoula **(G-4069)**

T & T Welding Inc ....E 601 477-2884
Ellisville **(G-1270)**

Taber Extrusions LLC ....E 228 863-2852
Gulfport **(G-1882)**

Telliers Sheetmetal Works ....G 228 392-5319
Diberville **(G-1217)**

Viking Range LLC ....D 770 932-7282
Greenwood **(G-1657)**

White Rhino Fabrication LLC ....G 601 397-1118
Canton **(G-684)**

Woodrffs Prtble Wldg Fbrcation ....G 662 728-3326
Booneville **(G-347)**

METAL FABRICATORS: Structural, Ship

Bath Iron Works Corporation ....G 228 935-3872
Pascagoula **(G-4021)**

METAL FINISHING SVCS

Automatic Plating Inc ....F 601 785-6923
Taylorsville **(G-5050)**

METAL ORES, NEC

Pat S Pins ....G 662 562-8986
Coldwater **(G-850)**

METAL SERVICE CENTERS & OFFICES

Dillard Machining Service ....F 662 329-4682
Columbus **(G-962)**

Laurel Machine and Foundry Co ....C 601 428-0541
Laurel **(G-2793)**

New Process Steel LP ....D 662 241-6582
Columbus **(G-1010)**

Triangle Recycling Services ....F 601 352-5027
Jackson **(G-2611)**

METAL STAMPING, FOR THE TRADE

Ice Industries Inc ....E 419 842-3612
Grenada **(G-1686)**

King Manufacturing Company Inc ....E 662 286-5504
Corinth **(G-1096)**

Magnolia Tool & Mfg Co ....G 601 856-4333
Ridgeland **(G-4602)**

Magnolia Tool & Mfg Co ....G 601 856-4333
Ridgeland **(G-4603)**

Mayville Engineering Co Inc ....C 662 335-2325
Greenville **(G-1571)**

Production Machine & Tool Inc ....G 662 287-4752
Corinth **(G-1111)**

METALS SVC CENTERS & WHOL: Structural Shapes, Iron Or Steel

Allied Crawford Jackson Inc ....E 769 230-2220
Byram **(G-616)**

METALS SVC CENTERS & WHOLESALERS: Pipe & Tubing, Steel

Consolidated Pipe & Sup Co Inc ....F 228 769-1920
Pascagoula **(G-4028)**

METALS SVC CENTERS & WHOLESALERS: Rope, Wire, Exc Insulated

Nhc Distributors Inc ....E 601 656-7911
Philadelphia **(G-4229)**

METALS SVC CENTERS & WHOLESALERS: Steel

Construction Metals Co Inc ....G 601 939-2566
Jackson **(G-2643)**

Halls Welding Service ....G 601 477-3925
Ellisville **(G-1256)**

Miss-Lou Steel Supply Inc ....G 601 442-0846
Natchez **(G-3589)**

Slay Steel Inc ....D 601 483-3911
Meridian **(G-3398)**

METALS: Primary Nonferrous, NEC

Green Metals Inc ....G 662 534-5447
Blue Springs **(G-296)**

Purvis Jewerly Rlc LLC ....G 601 329-9002
Purvis **(G-4450)**

METALWORK: Miscellaneous

Ellis Steel Company Inc ....G 662 893-5955
Olive Branch **(G-3838)**

Foster Machine & Repair Svc ....G 662 755-2656
Bentonia **(G-210)**

H & H Metal Fabrication Inc ....G 662 489-4626
Belden **(G-189)**

Innovative Fabrications LLC ....G 601 485-1400
Meridian **(G-3353)**

Mississippi Prison Inds Corp ....F 601 969-5760
Jackson **(G-2503)**

T & J Machine ....G 601 795-0853
Poplarville **(G-4398)**

METALWORK: Ornamental

Iron and Steel Design Works ....G 662 380-5662
Oxford **(G-3962)**

Iron Effects ....G 662 871-5565
Thaxton **(G-5078)**

MICROWAVE COMPONENTS

L3 Technologies Inc ....E 601 856-2274
Madison **(G-3117)**

MILITARY INSIGNIA

Military Warehouse ....G 662 287-8234
Corinth **(G-1102)**

MILLING: Corn Grits & Flakes, For Brewers' Use

Delta Grind Stone Ground Pdts ....G 662 816-1254
Water Valley **(G-5467)**

MILLING: Rice

Producers Rice Mill Inc ....D 662 334-6266
Greenville **(G-1592)**

MILLWORK

601 Custom Woodworks ....G 601 588-0117
Beaumont **(G-183)**

A B S Woodworks ....G 601 425-3306
Laurel **(G-2730)**

Acadian Custom Woodworks ....G 601 572-4774
Brandon **(G-354)**

Alvin Schilling Wdwkg LLC ....G 601 268-1070
Purvis **(G-4432)**

Ameitech/South ....G 601 853-0830
Ridgeland **(G-4548)**

Ash Millworks Inc ....E 601 544-3962
Petal **(G-4184)**

Axsom Woodworks ....G 334 422-9766
Gulfport **(G-1731)**

B&M Maintenance LLC ....G 228 273-5821
Vancleave **(G-5318)**

Barnes Sawmill Woodworks ....G 901 605-7104
Olive Branch **(G-3818)**

Barrys Fine Wdwkg & Crafts LLC ....G 662 808-2268
Tupelo **(G-5113)**

Bayou View Woodworks ....G 985 290-0860
Bay Saint Louis **(G-136)**

Bennetts Wood Works ....G 662 862-6124
Fulton **(G-1446)**

Buckrdge Spclty Wods Mill Wrks ....G 601 667-3791
Canton **(G-651)**

Burns Fence & Woodworks LLC ....G 601 506-5226
Jackson **(G-2349)**

Chippewa Enterprises LLC ....G 228 832-0032
Gulfport **(G-1752)**

Colquitt Woodworks LLC ....G 229 425-6087
Diamondhead **(G-1187)**

Correro Woodworks ....G 662 334-9837
Greenville **(G-1542)**

Cox Works ....G 228 236-8402
Saucier **(G-4750)**

Cr Custom Woodworks ....G 601 624-2310
Pearl **(G-4113)**

Crown Simple Renovations Wdwkg ....G 601 850-8272
Florence **(G-1317)**

398

2019 Harris Directory of
Mississippi Manufacturers

(G-0000) Company's Geographic Section entry number

PRODUCT SECTION

MOPS: Floor & Dust

Crown Simple Renovations Wdwkg......G...... 601 850-8272
Florence *(G-1318)*
Custom Architectural Millwork ....G...... 662 562-7011
Sarah *(G-4733)*
DH Woodworks ....G...... 662 299-5486
Greenwood *(G-1620)*
Dimensions Wood Works ....G...... 228 254-6623
Ocean Springs *(G-3752)*
Donald W Mason ....G...... 601 269-3782
Raleigh *(G-4475)*
Donovan P Cain ....G...... 662 279-2124
Glen *(G-1506)*
Dunns Woodworking LLC ....G...... 601 736-0633
Columbia *(G-897)*
Ellis Custom Woodwork LLC ....G...... 601 983-8464
Jackson *(G-2399)*
Fleming True Value Lbr ....G...... 662 843-2763
Cleveland *(G-793)*
Frierson Building Supply Co ....C...... 601 922-1321
Jackson *(G-2416)*
Garner Millwork Inc ....F...... 662 844-7007
Tupelo *(G-5139)*
Georgia-Pacific LLC ....F...... 601 939-7797
Pearl *(G-4122)*
Georgia-Pacific LLC ....G...... 601 587-7711
Monticello *(G-3433)*
Guice Woodworks ....G...... 323 384-1826
Ocean Springs *(G-3760)*
Gulf Coast Cabinets & Mill ....G...... 228 206-7792
Gulfport *(G-1797)*
H & L Millworks Inc ....G...... 228 392-9913
Biloxi *(G-250)*
Halls Woodworking ....G...... 601 792-5955
Prentiss *(G-4421)*
Harris Frm Hven Spcltymillwork........G...... 601 953-2964
Canton *(G-660)*
High Country Woodworking ....G...... 228 396-2921
Biloxi *(G-251)*
Hobby Const Co ....G...... 662 803-1599
Louisville *(G-2972)*
Holcomb Handiman Svcs Cstm Woo ...G...... 601 394-4284
Laurel *(G-2778)*
Interior and Exterior WD Work ....G...... 662 587-2417
Ashland *(G-61)*
James Newton ....G...... 662 647-8968
Charleston *(G-739)*
Jims Woodworks LLC ....G...... 601 862-1025
Bolton *(G-310)*
Jjs Woodshed ....G...... 662 380-5034
Oxford *(G-3964)*
Js Woodworking ....G...... 228 257-6846
Biloxi *(G-255)*
Kings Woodworks ....G...... 662 403-0871
Hernando *(G-2136)*
Lamb Woodworking ....G...... 601 545-3052
Brooklyn *(G-551)*
Macs Small Engine Service ....F...... 601 932-8076
Richland *(G-4521)*
McLellan Woodworks ....G...... 336 425-8425
Brandon *(G-422)*
McMaster Custom Woodworks LLC....G...... 601 408-2252
Canton *(G-670)*
McNeil Cabinet and Millwork ....E...... 601 764-2100
Bay Springs *(G-168)*
Meridian Woodworking ....G...... 601 604-6147
Meridian *(G-3369)*
Mikes Woodworking ....G...... 601 966-1868
Canton *(G-671)*
Pearl River Door Company ....G...... 601 573-2572
Pearl *(G-4137)*
Pitts Companies Cabinets Mllwk..........G...... 662 844-2772
Tupelo *(G-5205)*
Prevost Woodworking ....G...... 615 836-9383
Brandon *(G-439)*
Robinson Woodworks ....G...... 662 419-1864
Randolph *(G-4480)*
Roseburg Forest Products Co ....E...... 662 773-9868
Louisville *(G-2981)*
S and S Woodworking LLC ....G...... 228 257-6846
Diberville *(G-1211)*
Scanlon-Taylor Millwork Co ....D...... 601 362-5333
Jackson *(G-2574)*
Sentiments By Shele - Whmsical ....G...... 662 812-3506
Olive Branch *(G-3907)*
Shirley McArthur Nobles ....G...... 601 310-0890
Sumrall *(G-5044)*
Smyda Woodworking Inc ....G...... 601 591-0247
Brandon *(G-456)*
Southern Cabinet & Woodwork ....E...... 228 475-0912
Moss Point *(G-3499)*

Southern Cabinets & Millwork ....G...... 662 447-3885
Okolona *(G-3799)*
Stout Woodworks Inc ....G...... 601 795-0727
Poplarville *(G-4397)*
Top of Line Woodwork ....G...... 228 669-3363
Saucier *(G-4767)*
Vbg Woodworks LLC ....G...... 601 634-0313
Vicksburg *(G-5434)*
Webbs Cstm Wdwrk & Finshg LLC ....G...... 601 824-2851
Brandon *(G-473)*
Whiting Woodcraft LLC ....G...... 662 895-1688
Olive Branch *(G-3926)*
Widups Woodworks LLC ....G...... 601 966-0593
Madison *(G-3171)*
Willies Woodworks ....G...... 601 916-3574
Picayune *(G-4304)*
Wood Work Solutions ....G...... 662 890-8954
Olive Branch *(G-3928)*
Wooden Arts LLC ....G...... 228 452-9943
Long Beach *(G-2960)*
Woodies Woodworks ....G...... 478 973-8851
Lauderdale *(G-2729)*
Woodworkings ....G...... 662 255-3421
Baldwyn *(G-89)*

MINE DEVELOPMENT, METAL

Nelsons Metal Inc ....G...... 662 454-7500
Dennis *(G-1184)*

MINERAL MINING: Nonmetallic

Walter L Perrigin ....G...... 662 240-0056
Columbus *(G-1042)*

MINERALS: Ground or Treated

Kengro Corporation ....F...... 662 647-2456
Charleston *(G-740)*
Nanocor LLC ....G...... 847 851-1500
Aberdeen *(G-19)*
Profile Products LLC ....E...... 662 685-4741
Blue Mountain *(G-292)*

MINING EXPLORATION & DEVELOPMENT SVCS

Greater Gulf Development LLC ....G...... 228 392-6680
Diberville *(G-1204)*

MISCELLANEOUS FIN INVEST ACTVTS: Mineral Royalty Dealer

Delta Royalty Company Inc..................G...... 601 982-0970
Jackson *(G-2382)*
Inland Energy Company Inc.................G...... 601 969-1160
Jackson *(G-2446)*

MISCELLANEOUS FINANCIAL INVEST ACTIVITIES: Oil Royalties

Wayne A Potter ....G...... 601 446-6090
Natchez *(G-3638)*

MITTENS: Leather

Itta Bena Plantation III ....G...... 662 254-7274
Itta Bena *(G-2281)*

MIXTURES & BLOCKS: Asphalt Paving

Apac-Mississippi Inc ....D...... 662 328-6555
Columbus *(G-936)*
Apac-Mississippi Inc ....E...... 601 693-5025
Meridian *(G-3299)*
Apac-Mississippi Inc ....E...... 662 348-2214
Guntown *(G-1897)*
Apac-Mississippi Inc ....E...... 601 634-6600
Vicksburg *(G-5341)*
Apac-Mississippi Inc ....G...... 662 746-7983
Yazoo City *(G-5623)*
Apac-Mississippi Inc ....D...... 601 376-4000
Richland *(G-4501)*
Apac-Mississippi Inc ....G...... 601 376-4000
Richland *(G-4502)*
Blacklidge Emulsions Inc....................G...... 228 864-3719
Gulfport *(G-1741)*
Boling Construction Inc ....G...... 601 833-0122
Wesson *(G-5524)*
CMC Paving LLC ....G...... 601 764-2787
Bay Springs *(G-160)*

Corinth Brick Company Inc.................G...... 662 287-2442
Corinth *(G-1076)*
Huey P Stockstill LLC ....F...... 228 868-8678
Gulfport *(G-1810)*
Jackson Asphalt & Concrete ....G...... 601 371-8707
Jackson *(G-2452)*
Land Shapers Inc ....G...... 228 864-3624
Gulfport *(G-1820)*
Lehman-Roberts Company ....F...... 662 429-5237
Hernando *(G-2138)*
Morgan Greg Asphalt and Cnstr..........G...... 601 479-3095
Chunky *(G-752)*
Seal Master Mississippi ....G...... 601 936-0080
Pearl *(G-4143)*
Southland Oil Company ....E...... 601 796-2331
Lumberton *(G-3038)*
Superior Asphalt ....C...... 601 376-3000
Byram *(G-624)*
W E Blain & Sons Inc ....E...... 601 442-3032
Natchez *(G-3635)*

MOBILE HOMES

Central Miss Manufacturing Hsing ....G...... 601 267-8353
Carthage *(G-711)*
Clayton Homes Inc ....G...... 601 939-0461
Pearl *(G-4110)*
Smith Mobile Home Company ....G...... 662 566-7998
Tupelo *(G-5224)*

MODULES: Computer Logic

Future Tek Inc....................................G...... 662 328-0900
Columbus *(G-977)*

MOLDED RUBBER PRDTS

Pearl Rubber Stamp & Sign Inc ....F...... 601 932-6699
Jackson *(G-2662)*
Seri ....G...... 601 638-3355
Vicksburg *(G-5415)*

MOLDING SAND MINING

Blue Note Management LLC ....F...... 662 281-1881
Oxford *(G-3943)*

MOLDINGS & TRIM: Wood

Burchwood Inc....................................F...... 662 841-2609
Mooreville *(G-3441)*

MOLDINGS: Picture Frame

Cotton Patch Framery ....G...... 662 895-6605
Olive Branch *(G-3829)*

MOLDS: Indl

Charles On Call Mold Removal.............G...... 662 352-8009
Meridian *(G-3319)*
JMS Manufacturing Inc.......................G...... 601 514-0660
Lucedale *(G-3005)*
Nichols Mold Shop..............................G...... 662 282-7560
Mantachie *(G-3202)*

MOLDS: Plastic Working & Foundry

Trulite GL Alum Solutions LLC ....E...... 662 226-5551
Grenada *(G-1711)*

MONUMENTS & GRAVE MARKERS, EXC TERRAZZO

Picayune Monument & Gran Works ......G...... 601 798-7926
Picayune *(G-4286)*

MONUMENTS: Cut Stone, Exc Finishing Or Lettering Only

Miller Enterprises ....F...... 601 798-3004
Carriere *(G-698)*
Walker Memorial Co Inc ....G...... 601 428-5337
Laurel *(G-2866)*

MOPS: Floor & Dust

L C Industries Inc ....B...... 601 894-1771
Hazlehurst *(G-2099)*
Piave Broom & Mop Inc ....F...... 601 584-7314
Petal *(G-4195)*
Signature Works Inc ....B...... 601 894-1771
Hazlehurst *(G-2106)*

Employee Codes: A=Over 500 employees, B=251-500
C=101-250, D=51-100, E=20-50, F=10-19, G=1-9

2019 Harris Directory of
Mississippi Manufacturers

399

PRODUCT

MOTION PICTURE PRODUCTION ALLIED SVCS

PRODUCT SECTION

MOTION PICTURE PRODUCTION ALLIED SVCS

Dianne Gore......................................G........ 510 697-2569
Jackson (G-2383)

Sevlo Solutions LLC ....G........ 662 312-9507
Starkville (G-4970)

MOTOR HOMES

All American Check Cashing Inc ....G........ 601 373-6115
Byram (G-615)

Companion Vans Inc..............................F........ 662 289-7711
Kosciusko (G-2691)

MOTOR REBUILDING SVCS, EXC AUTOMOTIVE

Walker Auto Repair Service ....G........ 601 969-5353
Jackson (G-2623)

MOTOR REPAIR SVCS

Summit Truck Group Miss LLC ....G........ 662 842-3401
Tupelo (G-5232)

MOTOR VEHICLE ASSEMBLY, COMPLETE: Autos, Incl Specialty

Greentech Automotive Inc ....D........ 662 996-1118
Robinsonville (G-4675)

Multicraft Intl Ltd Partnr ....G........ 601 854-1200
Pelahatchie (G-4168)

Myles Smith ....F........ 228 323-5052
Lumberton (G-3036)

Toyota Motor Mfg Miss Inc ....D........ 662 317-3000
Blue Springs (G-300)

MOTOR VEHICLE ASSEMBLY, COMPLETE: Bus/Large Spclty Vehicles

Burroughs Bus Sales Inc ....G........ 601 649-3062
Laurel (G-2745)

MOTOR VEHICLE ASSEMBLY, COMPLETE: Cars, Armored

Cite Armored Inc ....E........ 662 551-1066
Holly Springs (G-2173)

Roy S Rides Inc ....G........ 601 425-3700
Laurel (G-2840)

MOTOR VEHICLE ASSEMBLY, COMPLETE: Fire Department Vehicles

City of Magee...E........ 601 849-2366
Magee (G-3174)

Deep South Fire Trucks Inc...................D........ 601 722-4166
Seminary (G-4776)

MOTOR VEHICLE ASSEMBLY, COMPLETE: Wreckers, Tow Truck

ORears Garage and Wreck.....................G........ 662 585-3244
Fulton (G-1471)

Ronnies Auto Sales ....G........ 662 773-9327
Louisville (G-2980)

MOTOR VEHICLE DEALERS: Automobiles, New & Used

Fowler Buick-Gmc Inc ....E........ 601 360-0200
Pearl (G-4120)

Nissan North America Inc ....A........ 601 855-6000
Canton (G-673)

Toyota Motor Mfg Miss Inc ....D........ 662 317-3000
Blue Springs (G-300)

MOTOR VEHICLE DEALERS: Cars, Used Only

Carroll Ray Auto & Truck Sales ....G........ 662 226-1200
Grenada (G-1671)

Eddie Martin Golf Cars Inc.....................G........ 662 620-7242
Tupelo (G-5129)

Paul Garner Motors LLC.........................G........ 601 785-4924
Taylorsville (G-5056)

MOTOR VEHICLE DEALERS: Trucks, Tractors/Trailers, New & Used

Paul Garner Motors LLC.........................G........ 601 785-4924
Taylorsville (G-5056)

MOTOR VEHICLE PARTS & ACCESS: Acceleration Eqpt

American Howa Kentucky Inc.................G........ 601 506-0591
Canton (G-646)

MOTOR VEHICLE PARTS & ACCESS: Body Components & Frames

Automated Tech & Assembly LLC.........G........ 662 213-9352
Rolling Fork (G-4679)

MOTOR VEHICLE PARTS & ACCESS: Cylinder Heads

Mississippi Cylinder Head Svc ....G........ 662 328-0170
Columbus (G-1002)

MOTOR VEHICLE PARTS & ACCESS: Electrical Eqpt

Remy Reman LLC ....E........ 601 785-9504
Taylorsville (G-5057)

MOTOR VEHICLE PARTS & ACCESS: Engines & Parts

Caterpillar Inc..F........ 662 286-5511
Corinth (G-1066)

MOTOR VEHICLE PARTS & ACCESS: Engs & Trans,Factory, Rebuilt

Bunyards Garage ....G........ 601 632-4892
Toomsuba (G-5090)

MOTOR VEHICLE PARTS & ACCESS: Fuel Systems & Parts

Borgwrner Emssions Systems LLC ......A........ 662 473-3100
Water Valley (G-5464)

Mississippi Diesel Products ....E........ 601 847-2500
Mendenhall (G-3285)

MOTOR VEHICLE PARTS & ACCESS: Hoods

Southern Fiberglass Inc ....F........ 601 876-2111
Tylertown (G-5285)

MOTOR VEHICLE PARTS & ACCESS: Manifolds

R- Squared Aluminium LLC ....C........ 601 825-1171
Puckett (G-4429)

MOTOR VEHICLE PARTS & ACCESS: Pumps, Hydraulic Fluid Power

Cam2 International LLC..........................F........ 601 661-5382
Vicksburg (G-5352)

MOTOR VEHICLE PARTS & ACCESS: Sanders, Safety

Autoliv Asp Inc.......................................G........ 801 620-8018
Olive Branch (G-3817)

MOTOR VEHICLE PARTS & ACCESS: Windshield Frames

Dr James..G........ 601 238-7821
Jackson (G-2391)

MOTOR VEHICLE PARTS & ACCESS: Wiring Harness Sets

Mississppi Band Chctaw Indians ....E........ 601 267-5279
Carthage (G-719)

MOTOR VEHICLE SPLYS & PARTS WHOLESALERS: New

Grammer Inc...D........ 864 672-0702
Shannon (G-4808)

Maximum Auto Parts & Supply..............F........ 228 863-1100
Gulfport (G-1825)

MOTOR VEHICLE: Radiators

Bles Car Care ....F........ 770 292-0021
Columbus (G-940)

MOTOR VEHICLE: Steering Mechanisms

Reman Inc...E........ 601 537-3400
Morton (G-3454)

MOTOR VEHICLES & CAR BODIES

Companion Vans Inc..............................F........ 662 289-7711
Kosciusko (G-2691)

Grammer Inc...G........ 662 566-1660
Shannon (G-4807)

Griffin Inc..D........ 662 838-2128
Byhalia (G-586)

Multicraft Intl Ltd Partnr ....E........ 601 854-1200
Pelahatchie (G-4170)

Navistar Inc...D........ 662 284-8984
Corinth (G-1105)

Nissan North America Inc ....A........ 601 855-6000
Canton (G-673)

Shoffner Motor Co Inc ....G........ 662 378-2909
Greenville (G-1598)

Victory Motor Company ....G........ 601 573-1441
Raymond (G-4494)

MOTOR VEHICLES, WHOLESALE: Trailers, Truck, New & Used

Transport Trailer Service Inc..................D........ 662 844-4606
Tupelo (G-5241)

MOTOR VEHICLES, WHOLESALE: Truck bodies

Aerial Truck Equipment Co Inc..............G........ 662 895-0993
Olive Branch (G-3807)

H & H Chief Sales Inc............................E........ 601 267-9643
Carthage (G-716)

MOTOR VEHICLES, WHOLESALE: Truck tractors

Tri-State Truck Center Inc ....E........ 662 844-6000
Tupelo (G-5242)

MOTORCYCLE ACCESS

New Horizon Inc.....................................G........ 228 474-9918
Moss Point (G-3489)

MOTORCYCLE DEALERS

Taylor & Sons Inc...................................G........ 601 483-0714
Meridian (G-3411)

MOTORCYCLE PARTS & ACCESS DEALERS

Main Street Cycle Inc.............................G........ 662 438-6407
Tishomingo (G-5086)

MOTORS: Electric

ABB Motors and Mechanical Inc ....E........ 662 328-9116
Columbus (G-930)

Nidec Motor Corporation........................B........ 662 393-6910
Southaven (G-4891)

MOTORS: Generators

Generator Power Systems LLC ....G........ 662 231-0092
Tupelo (G-5142)

Kemp Enterprises ....G........ 662 574-0253
Hattiesburg (G-2006)

North American Electric Inc....................E........ 662 429-8049
Hernando (G-2146)

Sandys Auto Parts & Machine Sp ....G........ 662 342-1900
Southaven (G-4898)

MOVING SVC: Local

Watson Tj Property LLC ....G........ 601 527-3587
Meridian (G-3418)

MOWERS & ACCESSORIES

Bob Ladd & Associates Inc....................G........ 601 859-7250
Canton (G-649)

2019 Harris Directory of
Mississippi Manufacturers

(G-0000) Company's Geographic Section entry number

400

PRODUCT SECTION

OFFICE SPLY & STATIONERY STORES: Writing Splys

Delta Farm & Auto LLC ....G...... 662 453-8340
Greenwood *(G-1619)*

MUSEUMS

Wilkinson County Museum ....G...... 601 888-7151
Woodville *(G-5619)*

MUSICAL INSTRUMENTS & ACCESS: NEC

EZ Chord LLC ....G...... 601 329-3827
Diberville *(G-1202)*
Peavey Electronics Corporation............B...... 601 483-5365
Meridian *(G-3381)*
Peavey Electronics Corporation............G...... 601 486-1878
Meridian *(G-3384)*

MUSICAL INSTRUMENTS: Bells

Tinks Bells ....G...... 662 574-2685
Columbus *(G-1038)*

MUSICAL INSTRUMENTS: Guitars & Parts, Electric & Acoustic

Crossroads Picks LLC ....G...... 662 902-1026
Clarksdale *(G-765)*

MUSICAL INSTRUMENTS: Organ Parts & Materials

Pipe Organ Specialties Inc ....G...... 601 649-5581
Laurel *(G-2822)*

NAME PLATES: Engraved Or Etched

Tupelo Engraving & Rbr Stamp ....G...... 662 842-0574
Tupelo *(G-5246)*

NAMEPLATES

Eddie Wiggs ....G...... 662 456-7080
Houston *(G-2239)*

NATIONAL SECURITY FORCES

Dla Document Services ....G...... 662 434-7303
Columbus *(G-963)*
Dla Document Services ....G...... 228 377-2612
Biloxi *(G-237)*

NATURAL GAS COMPRESSING SVC, On-Site

Archrock Inc ....G...... 601 444-0055
Columbia *(G-880)*

NATURAL GAS DISTRIBUTION TO CONSUMERS

Centerpint Enrgy Rsources Corp ....E...... 601 425-1461
Laurel *(G-2750)*
Centerpoint Energy Inc ....F...... 228 588-2977
Moss Point *(G-3473)*
Oakland Ylbsha Natural Gas Dst ....G...... 662 623-5005
Oakland *(G-3738)*
Phae I Bobs ....G...... 662 332-3505
Greenville *(G-1590)*
Tatum Development Corp ....G...... 601 544-6043
Hattiesburg *(G-2072)*

NATURAL GAS LIQUID FRACTIONATING SVC

Ss Drilling LLC ....G...... 740 207-5673
Brandon *(G-463)*

NATURAL GAS LIQUIDS PRODUCTION

Gasmax Fltration Solutions LLC ....G...... 601 790-1225
Ridgeland *(G-4586)*
Nicks One Stop Port Gbson LLC ....G...... 601 437-3380
Port Gibson *(G-4404)*
Oakland Ylbsha Natural Gas Dst ....G...... 662 623-5005
Oakland *(G-3738)*
Phae I Bobs ....G...... 662 332-3505
Greenville *(G-1590)*

NATURAL GAS PRODUCTION

BP Corporation North Amer Inc.............E...... 228 712-3500
Moss Point *(G-3472)*
Devon Energy Corporation ....G...... 601 796-4243
Lumberton *(G-3028)*

NATURAL LIQUEFIED PETROLEUM GAS PRODUCTION

Mgc Terminal LLC ....G...... 601 482-5012
Meridian *(G-3371)*

NATURAL PROPANE PRODUCTION

Pine Belt Gas Inc ....G...... 601 731-1144
Columbia *(G-911)*

NAUTICAL REPAIR SVCS

Marine Gears Inc ....E...... 662 332-8716
Greenville *(G-1568)*

NAVIGATIONAL SYSTEMS & INSTRUMENTS

Linton Systems ....G...... 228 872-7300
Ocean Springs *(G-3771)*
Northrop Grumman Systems Corp ....D...... 228 872-7300
Ocean Springs *(G-3773)*

NETS: Camouflage

Mossy Oak 3d Fluid Grphics LLC..........G...... 662 494-9092
West Point *(G-5553)*

NEWS DEALERS & NEWSSTANDS

Baldwyn News ....G...... 662 365-3232
Baldwyn *(G-71)*

NEWSPAPERS & PERIODICALS NEWS REPORTING SVCS

Macon Beacon ....G...... 662 726-4747
Macon *(G-3064)*

NEWSPAPERS, WHOLESALE

George Nosser Jr ....G...... 601 446-7998
Natchez *(G-3563)*

NEWSSTAND

Madison County Herald ....G...... 601 853-2899
Madison *(G-3124)*

NONCURRENT CARRYING WIRING DEVICES

Vicksburg Enterprise Mfg LLC ....G...... 601 631-0304
Vicksburg *(G-5435)*
Vicksburg Enterprise Mfg LLC ....G...... 601 631-0304
Vicksburg *(G-5436)*

NONFERROUS: Rolling & Drawing, NEC

Lunati LLC ....E...... 662 892-1518
Olive Branch *(G-3868)*

NOTEBOOKS, MADE FROM PURCHASED MATERIALS

Avery Products Corporation ....C...... 601 483-0611
Meridian *(G-3304)*

NOVELTY SHOPS

Hodge Podge Screen Prtg Inc ....F...... 662 226-1636
Grenada *(G-1685)*

NURSERIES & LAWN & GARDEN SPLY STORES, RETAIL: Top Soil

Pen/Ron Company Inc ....G...... 601 519-5096
Brandon *(G-431)*

NURSERIES & LAWN/GARDEN SPLY STORE, RET: Lawnmowers/Tractors

Barnetts Small Engines ....G...... 662 323-8993
Starkville *(G-4926)*
Garys Small Engine ....G...... 601 545-7355
Hattiesburg *(G-1974)*
J and E Enterprises ....G...... 662 369-7324
Aberdeen *(G-15)*
Motor Parts Co of Yazoo City................G...... 662 746-1462
Yazoo City *(G-5643)*
Power Plus Inc ....F...... 601 264-1950
Sumrall *(G-5042)*
Robbys Small Engine & Saw Repr ....G...... 601 847-0323
Mendenhall *(G-3287)*

NURSERIES & LAWN/GARDEN SPLY STORES, RET: Garden Splys/Tools

Pinnacle Agriculture Dist Inc ....G...... 662 265-5828
Inverness *(G-2276)*

NURSERY & GARDEN CENTERS

Agri-Afc LLC ....E...... 601 783-6080
Magnolia *(G-3188)*
Baddour Memorial Center Inc ....B...... 662 562-0100
Senatobia *(G-4787)*
Lee Small Engines Inc ....G...... 601 833-5431
Brookhaven *(G-510)*
Taylor & Sons Inc ....G...... 601 483-0714
Meridian *(G-3411)*

NURSERY STOCK, WHOLESALE

Eakes Nursery Materials Inc ....G...... 601 722-4797
Seminary *(G-4777)*

OFFICE EQPT WHOLESALERS

Atkins Office Supply Inc........................G...... 662 627-2476
Clarksdale *(G-757)*
Oligarch Inc ....G...... 844 321-0016
Houston *(G-2253)*
Star Printing Co of Amory Inc...............E...... 662 256-8424
Amory *(G-56)*

OFFICE MACHINES, NEC

Rj Young ....G...... 601 948-2222
Jackson *(G-2566)*

OFFICE SPLY & STATIONERY STORES

Formal Affair...G...... 228 497-7500
Gautier *(G-1492)*
Monogram Express.................................G...... 601 825-1248
Brandon *(G-425)*
Office Depot Inc ....E...... 662 378-2995
Greenville *(G-1585)*

OFFICE SPLY & STATIONERY STORES: Office Forms & Splys

Atkins Office Supply Inc........................G...... 662 627-2476
Clarksdale *(G-757)*
Carthaginian Inc...................................F...... 601 267-4501
Carthage *(G-709)*
Chancellors Business Sup Inc ....F...... 601 426-6396
Laurel *(G-2753)*
Copy Write Printing Inc ....G...... 601 736-2679
Columbia *(G-891)*
Dement Printing Company.....................G...... 601 693-2721
Meridian *(G-3329)*
Dixie Print ....G...... 601 469-3350
Forest *(G-1414)*
East Holmes Publishing Entps ....G...... 662 834-1151
Lexington *(G-2901)*
Fletcher Printing & Office Sup...............G...... 662 487-3200
Sardis *(G-4739)*
Jeff Busby ....G...... 601 924-7979
Clinton *(G-827)*
Ksquared Inc ....F...... 601 956-2951
Madison *(G-3116)*
Lawrence County Press Inc ....G...... 601 587-2781
Monticello *(G-3435)*
Lawrence Printing Company ....D...... 662 453-6301
Greenwood *(G-1633)*
Meteor Inc ....F...... 601 892-2581
Crystal Springs *(G-1148)*
Rankin Printery ....G...... 662 287-4426
Corinth *(G-1112)*
Simpson Publishing Co Inc ....E...... 601 849-3434
Magee *(G-3185)*
Smith Printing & Off Sup Inc.................G...... 601 442-2441
Natchez *(G-3621)*
Standard Office Sup Prtg Inc ....E...... 601 544-5361
Hattiesburg *(G-2069)*
Star Printing Co of Amory Inc...............E...... 662 256-8424
Amory *(G-56)*
W T Leggett Inc ....G...... 601 544-2704
Hattiesburg *(G-2081)*

OFFICE SPLY & STATIONERY STORES: Writing Splys

Coopers Intl Screen Supply LLC ....G...... 601 353-2488
Jackson *(G-2369)*

Employee Codes: A=Over 500 employees, B=251-500
C=101-250, D=51-100, E=20-50, F=10-19, G=1-9

OFFICE SPLY & STATIONERY STORES: Writing Splys

Tylertown Times ....F........ 601 876-5111
Tylertown *(G-5289)*

OFFICE SPLYS, NEC, WHOLESALE

Atkins Office Supply Inc ....G....... 662 627-2476
Clarksdale *(G-757)*
Star Printing Co of Amory Inc.............E....... 662 256-8424
Amory *(G-56)*

OFFICES & CLINICS HLTH PRACTITIONERS: *Christian Science*

Elizabeth Newcomb ....G....... 662 596-1536
Rienzi *(G-4649)*

OFFICES & CLINICS OF DENTISTS: *Specialist, Practitioners*

Timber Products Co Ltd Partnr ....D....... 662 287-3766
Corinth *(G-1122)*

OFFICES & CLINICS OF DOCTORS, MEDICINE: *Gen & Fam Practice*

Medical Clinic ....G....... 601 587-7795
Monticello *(G-3436)*

OIL & GAS FIELD EQPT: *Drill Rigs*

Friede Goldman Delaware Inc...............G....... 228 896-0029
Gulfport *(G-1789)*

OIL & GAS FIELD MACHINERY

Browning Oil Tools Inc ....E....... 601 442-1800
Natchez *(G-3540)*
Global Vessel Tank ....G....... 601 649-5300
Laurel *(G-2772)*
Psp Industries Inc ....G....... 662 423-2033
Iuka *(G-2306)*
Q P P Inc ....G....... 662 356-4848
Caledonia *(G-629)*
Robine & Welch Machine & TI Co ....E....... 601 428-1545
Laurel *(G-2838)*
Trico Industries Inc ....G....... 601 649-4467
Laurel *(G-2859)*

OIL FIELD MACHINERY & EQPT

Harbison-Fischer Inc ....G....... 601 428-7919
Ellisville *(G-1257)*
P Delta Inc ....E....... 601 403-8100
Poplarville *(G-4387)*
Pressure Control ....G....... 601 342-8051
Laurel *(G-2826)*
Unified Brands Inc ....F....... 888 994-7636
Jackson *(G-2615)*

OIL FIELD SVCS, NEC

A & B Pump & Supply Inc ....G....... 601 787-3741
Heidelberg *(G-2111)*
Alpine Well Service Inc ....G....... 601 442-0021
Natchez *(G-3519)*
Armadillo Service Inc Alabama ....F....... 601 857-0440
Raymond *(G-4484)*
Baker Hghes Olfld Oprtions LLC ....F....... 601 649-4400
Laurel *(G-2733)*
Baker Hghes Olfld Oprtions LLC ....G....... 601 649-2704
Laurel *(G-2734)*
Baker Hughes A GE Company LLC ......G....... 601 649-7400
Laurel *(G-2735)*
Baker Hughes A GE Company LLC ......G....... 601 649-1955
Laurel *(G-2736)*
Baker Hughes A GE Company LLC ......F....... 601 649-4400
Laurel *(G-2737)*
Baker Hughes A GE Company LLC......F....... 601 425-1599
Laurel *(G-2738)*
Baker Petrolite LLC ....F....... 601 649-1955
Laurel *(G-2739)*
Bayou Oil Fill Supply LLC ....G....... 601 446-6284
Natchez *(G-3524)*
Bobbys Indus & Oilfld Repr ....G....... 601 833-3050
Brookhaven *(G-483)*
Cameron International Corp ....G....... 601 649-8900
Laurel *(G-2747)*
Cameron International Corp ....G....... 601 425-2377
Laurel *(G-2748)*
Cavins Corporation.......................G....... 601 833-2268
Brookhaven *(G-487)*

Cavins Corporation.......................G....... 601 428-0670
Laurel *(G-2749)*
Ccore Energy/Mariner LLC.................G....... 601 824-7900
Brandon *(G-377)*
Challnger Dpwell Servicing Inc ....E....... 601 736-2511
Columbia *(G-885)*
Clarkco Services Inc ....D....... 601 787-3447
Heidelberg *(G-2114)*
Cornwell Well Service Inc ....E....... 601 684-4951
Summit *(G-5009)*
Denbury Resources Inc ....G....... 972 673-2787
Pelahatchie *(G-4163)*
Dipstix Lube ....G....... 662 349-2810
Southaven *(G-4869)*
Dixie Oilfield Services Inc ....G....... 601 731-5541
Columbia *(G-896)*
Dixie Oilfield Supply LLC ....G....... 601 408-6027
Laurel *(G-2761)*
Dnow LP ....G....... 601 649-8671
Laurel *(G-2762)*
Eastern Fishing & Rental TI Co ....D....... 601 649-1454
Laurel *(G-2766)*
GE Oil & Gas Pressure Ctrl LP ....G....... 601 425-1436
Laurel *(G-2769)*
Gulf Pine Energy LP ....E....... 587 287-5400
Newhebron *(G-3712)*
Halliburton Energy Services ....D....... 601 649-9290
Sandersville *(G-4725)*
Kelley Brothers Contrs Inc ....D....... 601 735-2541
Waynesboro *(G-5501)*
Kenan Transportation.....................G....... 662 332-4223
Greenville *(G-1561)*
Kkam Services LLC ....G....... 903 707-0110
Wiggins *(G-5585)*
Lee & Lee Services Inc ....F....... 601 425-1060
Laurel *(G-2794)*
Liberty Oilfield Services & RE ....G....... 601 398-8511
Liberty *(G-2915)*
Logan Oil Field Services ....G....... 601 787-4407
Waynesboro *(G-5504)*
Louisiana Well Service Co Inc ....G....... 601 442-6648
Natchez *(G-3580)*
Mapp Oilfield Services Inc ....E....... 601 835-2013
Brookhaven *(G-515)*
Mk Oilfield Service ....G....... 662 328-2510
Columbus *(G-1005)*
Moncla Companies ....E....... 601 428-4322
Laurel *(G-2805)*
Multi-Chem Group LLC....................G....... 601 425-1131
Laurel *(G-2809)*
Newpark Drilling Fluids LLC ....F....... 281 362-6800
Summit *(G-5018)*
Oil Well Logging Company Inc ....G....... 601 477-8315
Ellisville *(G-1265)*
Oilfield Partners Energy ....G....... 601 444-0220
Columbia *(G-909)*
Oilfield Service & Sup Co Inc.............E....... 601 649-4461
Laurel *(G-2813)*
Old Ges Inc ....G....... 601 649-4920
Laurel *(G-2814)*
Pecanier Oil & Gas LLC...................G....... 601 982-3444
Jackson *(G-2538)*
Pierce Well Service ....G....... 601 947-4548
Agricola *(G-30)*
Pioneer Well Service ....E....... 601 399-1648
Laurel *(G-2821)*
Pitts Swabbing Service Inc ....F....... 601 422-0111
Laurel *(G-2824)*
Power Torque Services LLC................G....... 601 835-2600
Brookhaven *(G-524)*
Premium Oilfield Services.................G....... 601 425-5211
Laurel *(G-2825)*
Pryor Packers Inc ....F....... 601 649-4535
Laurel *(G-2829)*
Q P P Inc ....G....... 662 356-4848
Caledonia *(G-629)*
Quality Drilling Fluids Inc ....F....... 601 477-9085
Ellisville *(G-1267)*
R W Delaney Construction Co ....D....... 601 442-0352
Natchez *(G-3609)*
Ralph Craven LLC ....G....... 601 425-0294
Laurel *(G-2834)*
Rapad Drilling & Well Services ....G....... 601 649-0760
Jackson *(G-2559)*
Rapad Drilling & Well Services ....G....... 601 649-0760
Laurel *(G-2835)*
Richard E Johnson ....G....... 601 735-4737
Waynesboro *(G-5512)*
Rosson Exlopartion Company...............G....... 601 969-2022
Jackson *(G-2569)*

Rufus M Chancellor ....G....... 601 776-5557
Quitman *(G-4471)*
Schlumberger Technology Corp ....F....... 601 649-3200
Laurel *(G-2846)*
Schlumberger Technology Corp ....F....... 601 442-7481
Natchez *(G-3616)*
Secorp Indus & Safety Sups Inc ....F....... 601 422-0203
Laurel *(G-2847)*
Southern Petroleum Labs Inc ....G....... 601 428-0842
Laurel *(G-2854)*
Stringers Oilfield Service ....E....... 601 736-4498
Columbia *(G-924)*
T & T Welding Yard Inc ....G....... 601 477-2299
Ellisville *(G-1271)*
Taylor Construction Co Inc ....D....... 601 426-2987
Laurel *(G-2857)*
Tj Scarbrough Inc ....F....... 601 648-9987
Buckatunna *(G-566)*
Tri-State Environmental LLC ....E....... 888 554-9792
Petal *(G-4198)*
U S Safety Services Inc ....G....... 601 833-3627
Wesson *(G-5531)*
U S Weatherford L P ....G....... 601 428-1551
Laurel *(G-2860)*
Vapor Oilfield Services LLC ....G....... 601 741-7171
Conehatta *(G-1055)*
W L S Inc ....G....... 601 687-1761
Shubuta *(G-4834)*
W L S Inc ....F....... 601 687-1761
Shubuta *(G-4835)*
Warrior Energy Services Corp ....F....... 601 425-9684
Laurel *(G-2868)*
Weatherford Artificia ....G....... 601 649-4467
Laurel *(G-2871)*

OILS: *Lubricating*

Ergon Refining Inc ....C....... 601 638-4960
Vicksburg *(G-5370)*

OPHTHALMIC GOODS

Hoffman Lenses Inc ....G....... 662 815-2803
Blue Mountain *(G-291)*
I Care Optical Inc ....F....... 601 372-3801
Terry *(G-5069)*
I Care Optical Inc ....G....... 228 864-4397
Gulfport *(G-1811)*

OPHTHALMIC GOODS: *Frames, Lenses & Parts, Eyeglasses*

Superior Optical Labs Inc ....E....... 228 875-3796
Ocean Springs *(G-3790)*

OPHTHALMIC GOODS: *Goggles, Sun, Safety, Indl, Etc*

901 Safety LLC ....G....... 901 493-3841
Olive Branch *(G-3803)*

OPHTHALMIC GOODS: *Spectacles*

Spectacles Inc ....F....... 601 398-4662
Jackson *(G-2593)*

OPTICAL GOODS STORES: *Contact Lenses, Prescription*

Saul Jay Enterprises Inc ....F....... 662 349-1660
Southaven *(G-4899)*

OPTICAL GOODS STORES: *Eyeglasses, Prescription*

D Dodd John Od...........................G....... 662 286-5671
Corinth *(G-1082)*

OPTICAL GOODS STORES: *Opticians*

J & R Optical Co Inc.....................G....... 601 977-0272
Jackson *(G-2450)*

OPTICAL INSTRUMENTS & APPARATUS

Ferson LLC ....F....... 228 875-8146
Ocean Springs *(G-3757)*

OPTICAL INSTRUMENTS & LENSES

Design Tech Inc...........................G....... 601 798-5844
Carriere *(G-691)*

402

2019 Harris Directory of
Mississippi Manufacturers

(G-0000) Company's Geographic Section entry number

PRODUCT SECTION

PALLETS: Wooden

Ii-VI Incorporated ....G...... 662 615-5040
  Starkville **(G-4951)**

Nucor Grating ....G...... 601 853-9996
  Madison **(G-3134)**

Safilo ....G...... 601 212-4136
  Brandon **(G-449)**

OPTOMETRISTS' OFFICES

D Dodd John Od.....................................G...... 662 286-5671
  Corinth **(G-1082)**

Saul Jay Enterprises Inc ....F 662 349-1660
  Southaven **(G-4899)**

Spectacles Inc ....F 601 398-4662
  Jackson **(G-2593)**

ORDNANCE: Flame Throwers

Panama Pump Company.........................G...... 601 544-4251
  Hattiesburg **(G-2039)**

ORGAN TUNING & REPAIR SVCS

Pipe Organ Specialties Inc ....G...... 601 649-5581
  Laurel **(G-2822)**

ORGANIZATIONS: Economic Research, Noncommercial

Perspecta Engineering Inc....................G...... 571 313-6000
  Stennis Space Center **(G-4996)**

ORGANIZATIONS: Religious

Inner Sanctuary Inc...............................G...... 662 489-6772
  Pontotoc **(G-4337)**

ORGANIZATIONS: Research Institute

C & D Jarnagin Company Inc................F 662 287-4977
  Corinth **(G-1063)**

ORIENTED STRANDBOARD

Norbord Mississippi Inc ....C...... 662 348-2800
  Guntown **(G-1900)**

Norbord Mississippi LLC ....G...... 662 348-2800
  Guntown **(G-1901)**

OUTLETS: Electric, Convenience

Hudson Salvage Inc................................G...... 601 947-0092
  Lucedale **(G-3003)**

Shabby Chic S Etc ....G...... 601 799-2800
  Picayune **(G-4294)**

PACKAGE DESIGN SVCS

Mid-South Foam & Assembly Inc ....F 662 895-3334
  Olive Branch **(G-3875)**

PACKAGED FROZEN FOODS WHOLESALERS, NEC

So Nuts and Confections LLC ....G...... 901 398-9650
  Horn Lake **(G-2211)**

PACKAGING MATERIALS, WHOLESALE

American Container Inc..........................E 662 890-0325
  Olive Branch **(G-3810)**

Rusken Packaging Inc............................G...... 662 680-5060
  Tupelo **(G-5219)**

PACKAGING MATERIALS: Paper

Dunn Paper Inc.......................................C...... 800 253-1889
  Wiggins **(G-5581)**

General Packaging Specialties.............F 662 844-7882
  Tupelo **(G-5140)**

Hood Flexible Packaging Corp ....D...... 903 593-1793
  Hattiesburg **(G-1993)**

PACKAGING MATERIALS: Paper, Coated Or Laminated

Bemis Company Inc................................B 402 734-6262
  Madison **(G-3084)**

PACKAGING MATERIALS: Plastic Film, Coated Or Laminated

Mega Plastics Inc...................................D....... 601 924-1712
  Clinton **(G-831)**

PACKAGING MATERIALS: Polystyrene Foam

Cryovac Inc...D..... 662 226-8804
  Grenada **(G-1673)**

Independent Furn Sup Co Inc...............B 662 844-8411
  Tupelo **(G-5161)**

Mid-South Foam & Assembly Inc ....F 662 895-3334
  Olive Branch **(G-3875)**

Sonoco Prtective Solutions Inc.............E 662 842-1043
  Tupelo **(G-5225)**

W & W Special Components Inc............G..... 662 365-5648
  Marietta **(G-3219)**

PACKING & CRATING SVC

Willowood Dvelopmental Ctr Inc...........D..... 601 366-0123
  Jackson **(G-2634)**

PACKING SVCS: Shipping

West Group Holding Company LLC......G..... 662 871-2344
  Shannon **(G-4821)**

PADDING: Foamed Plastics

Confortaire Inc ....D..... 662 842-2966
  Tupelo **(G-5121)**

Thermos LLC ....D..... 800 831-9242
  Batesville **(G-129)**

Ultra Comfort Foam Company...............F 662 539-6004
  New Albany **(G-3705)**

PADS: Mattress

Cushions To Go LLC ....G..... 662 488-0350
  Pontotoc **(G-4327)**

Leggett & Platt Incorporated ....G..... 662 842-5704
  Tupelo **(G-5175)**

PAINT & PAINTING SPLYS STORE

Sherwin-Williams Company ....G..... 228 467-3938
  Waveland **(G-5484)**

PAINT STORE

Alfords Decorating Center ....G..... 662 455-3552
  Greenwood **(G-1612)**

Canvas & Cocktails LLC........................G..... 228 861-8444
  Gulfport **(G-1748)**

La Rosa Glass Inc ....G..... 228 864-0751
  Long Beach **(G-2942)**

Maximum Auto Parts & Supply ....F..... 228 863-1100
  Gulfport **(G-1825)**

PAINTING SVC: Metal Prdts

Amory Powder Coating LLC ....G..... 662 749-7081
  Amory **(G-36)**

Pierce Body Works ....G..... 601 939-1768
  Jackson **(G-2663)**

Resurfacing Concepts Inc......................G..... 662 489-6867
  Pontotoc **(G-4360)**

PAINTS & ADDITIVES

Sherwin-Williams Company ....G..... 228 467-3938
  Waveland **(G-5484)**

PAINTS & ALLIED PRODUCTS

Fuhr International LLC ....F 662 862-4903
  Fulton **(G-1453)**

Omnova Solutions Inc............................A 662 327-1522
  Columbus **(G-1012)**

PPG Industries Inc.................................F 601 932-0898
  Pearl **(G-4138)**

PPG Industries Inc.................................G..... 662 449-4947
  Hernando **(G-2148)**

Robchem LLC...G..... 601 485-5502
  Meridian **(G-3392)**

Tuff-Wall Inc...G..... 601 264-8649
  Hattiesburg **(G-2076)**

PAINTS, VARNISHES & SPLYS WHOLESALERS

Je Painting and Renovations................G..... 601 470-2047
  Hattiesburg **(G-2001)**

PAINTS: Oil Or Alkyd Vehicle Or Water Thinned

Bayou Inovations ....G....... 601 928-4143
  Perkinston **(G-4173)**

PALLETS

Cccl Pallet LLC ....G....... 662 494-0141
  West Point **(G-5540)**

Delta Pallets and Crates I.....................G....... 662 781-1633
  Walls **(G-5449)**

McMillon Pallet ....G....... 601 932-2299
  Jackson **(G-2656)**

Memphis Pallet Services LLC................G....... 901 334-6306
  Byhalia **(G-591)**

Pallet Exchange Network ....G....... 251 709-7021
  Gautier **(G-1501)**

River City Pallet Co ....G....... 601 415-0386
  Vicksburg **(G-5411)**

Superior Pallet Company ....G....... 601 941-6254
  Brandon **(G-465)**

T & G Pallet Inc......................................F 662 746-4499
  Yazoo City **(G-5647)**

Tenn Tom Pallet Company Inc ....G....... 662 369-9341
  Aberdeen **(G-20)**

W & W Pallets LLC.................................G....... 662 706-0050
  Plantersville **(G-4318)**

Windmill Pallet Works Inc ....F 601 876-4498
  Tylertown **(G-5291)**

PALLETS & SKIDS: Wood

All Star Forest Products Inc..................G....... 228 896-4117
  Gulfport **(G-1720)**

All Star Forest Products Inc..................G....... 662 294-8898
  Grenada **(G-1667)**

All Star Forest Products Inc..................G....... 601 664-0700
  Jackson **(G-2322)**

Coastal Transportation LLC ....G....... 601 876-2688
  Tylertown **(G-5268)**

Dixie Mat and Hardwood Co ....E 601 876-2427
  Columbia **(G-895)**

Inca Presswood-Pallets Ltd ....G....... 662 487-1016
  Sardis **(G-4741)**

Inca Presswood-Pallets Ltd ....E 662 487-1016
  Sardis **(G-4742)**

Martin and Sons LLC ....E 601 825-4012
  Brandon **(G-418)**

Rehabilitation Svcs Miss Dept..............E 662 335-3359
  Greenville **(G-1595)**

Robert R Stewart ....G....... 601 408-0494
  Hattiesburg **(G-2053)**

Superior Mat Company Inc ....G....... 601 765-8268
  Collins **(G-864)**

PALLETS: Plastic

Hewlett Industries Inc............................D...... 662 773-4626
  Starkville **(G-4948)**

PALLETS: Wooden

Bryan Industrial Co Inc..........................F 601 649-8786
  Laurel **(G-2744)**

Chep (usa) Inc ....E 601 352-6500
  Jackson **(G-2359)**

Coastal Tie & Timber Co Inc ....E 601 876-2688
  Tylertown **(G-5267)**

Custom Pallett LLC ....G....... 662 423-8127
  Tishomingo **(G-5084)**

Debra A Jones ....F 601 845-8946
  Florence **(G-1320)**

Gann Brothers Inc..................................G....... 662 568-2980
  Houlka **(G-2223)**

Hudspeth Wood Products Inc ....F 662 263-5902
  Maben **(G-3046)**

JC Jourdan Lumber Co Inc ....F 662 423-5238
  Iuka **(G-2295)**

Koestler Pallet Sales Inc ....F 601 852-2926
  Edwards **(G-1240)**

Pallet Source Inc ....E 662 851-3118
  Mount Pleasant **(G-3512)**

Pallets Inc ....F 601 876-2688
  Tylertown **(G-5278)**

Yna Pallets Sales ....G....... 601 405-6545
  Florence **(G-1340)**

Employee Codes: A=Over 500 employees, B=251-500
C=101-250, D=51-100, E=20-50, F=10-19, G=1-9

2019 Harris Directory of
Mississippi Manufacturers

403

PRODUCT

PANEL & DISTRIBUTION BOARDS & OTHER RELATED APPARATUS

PANEL & DISTRIBUTION BOARDS & OTHER RELATED APPARATUS

Kresec Enterprises Corp........................G....... 601 292-7015
Vaiden **(G-5314)**

PANELS: Building, Metal

Alply Archtctural Bldg Systems ....E....... 601 743-2623
De Kalb **(G-1159)**
Castle Hill Design.................................G....... 601 918-8234
Canton **(G-654)**
Goldin Metals Incorporated ....D....... 228 575-7737
Gulfport **(G-1793)**

PANELS: Cardboard, Die-Cut, Made From Purchased Materials

Martin Cardboard Company Inc ....G....... 662 489-5416
Pontotoc **(G-4343)**

PANELS: Wood

Pavco Industries Inc..............................D....... 228 762-3959
Pascagoula **(G-4061)**

PAPER & BOARD: Die-cut

Davis Enterprises Inc ....G....... 662 488-9972
Pontotoc **(G-4328)**
L C Industries Inc...................................E....... 662 841-1640
Tupelo **(G-5170)**
Pontotoc Die Cutting LLC ....F....... 662 489-5874
Pontotoc **(G-4354)**
Tom Lauderdale Paper Svcs Inc ....F....... 662 767-9744
Shannon **(G-4819)**

PAPER CONVERTING

Hattiesburg Paper Company LLC.........C....... 601 545-3400
Hattiesburg **(G-1988)**
Hpc LLC..G....... 601 545-3400
Hattiesburg **(G-1996)**
Pqr Inc...C....... 662 289-7613
Kosciusko **(G-2710)**
Specialty Roll Products Inc....................E....... 601 693-1771
Meridian **(G-3404)**

PAPER MANUFACTURERS: Exc Newsprint

Cryovac Inc..D....... 662 226-8804
Grenada **(G-1673)**
Domtar Paper Company LLC...................C....... 662 256-3526
Columbus **(G-964)**
Georgia-Pacific LLC...............................G....... 662 773-9454
Louisville **(G-2969)**
Georgia-Pacific LLC...............................G....... 601 587-7570
Monticello **(G-3432)**
Georgia-Pacific LLC...............................F....... 601 939-7797
Pearl **(G-4122)**
International Paper Company ....B....... 601 638-3665
Redwood **(G-4495)**
International Paper Company ....G....... 601 932-1422
Jackson **(G-2650)**
International Paper Company.................F....... 601 783-5011
Magnolia **(G-3191)**
International Paper Company ....F....... 662 893-3100
Olive Branch **(G-3852)**
International Paper Company.................C....... 662 456-4251
Houston **(G-2246)**
International Paper Company ....G....... 800 207-4003
Yazoo City **(G-5636)**
Lc Ind Signature Works Div ....G....... 601 206-9564
Ridgeland **(G-4597)**
Resolute Ft US Inc ....E....... 662 227-7948
Grenada **(G-1702)**
Weyerhaeuser ....G....... 662 327-1961
Columbus **(G-1043)**

PAPER PRDTS: Facial Tissue

L C Industries Inc ....E....... 662 841-1640
Tupelo **(G-5170)**

PAPER PRDTS: Infant & Baby Prdts

Kimberly-Clark Corporation..................C....... 601 545-3400
Hattiesburg **(G-2007)**
Kimberly-Clark Corporation..................B....... 662 287-8011
Corinth **(G-1095)**
Kimberly-Clark Corporation..................F....... 662 454-9274
Dennis **(G-1182)**

Kimberly-Clark Corporation..................C....... 662 284-3827
Baldwyn **(G-81)**

PAPER PRDTS: Pressed Pulp Prdts

Cand M Pupwood..................................G....... 601 445-9200
Natchez **(G-3543)**

PAPER PRDTS: Sanitary

Twin Rivers Paper Company LLC............E....... 662 468-2183
Pickens **(G-4307)**

PAPER PRDTS: Sanitary Tissue Paper

Kimberly-Clark Corporation..................C....... 601 545-3400
Hattiesburg **(G-2007)**
Kimberly-Clark Corporation..................B....... 662 287-8011
Corinth **(G-1095)**
Kimberly-Clark Corporation..................F....... 662 454-9274
Dennis **(G-1182)**
Kimberly-Clark Corporation..................C....... 662 284-3827
Baldwyn **(G-81)**

PAPER PRDTS: Towels, Napkins/Tissue Paper, From Purchd Mtrls

Jones Limber...G....... 601 894-3839
Hazlehurst **(G-2098)**
Magnolia Supply Group LLC..................G....... 601 454-1368
Jackson **(G-2480)**

PAPER, WHOLESALE: Writing

Jessica Williams ....G....... 601 738-0090
Rolling Fork **(G-4681)**

PAPER: Adding Machine Rolls, Made From Purchased Materials

International Paper Company ....G....... 662 243-4000
Columbus **(G-989)**

PAPER: Adhesive

Darrell Crum LLC ....G....... 806 224-7337
Madison **(G-3092)**

PAPER: Bag

Drumheller Packaging Inc......................E....... 662 627-2207
Clarksdale **(G-767)**

PAPER: Coated & Laminated, NEC

Domtar Paper Company LLC ....C....... 662 256-3526
Columbus **(G-964)**
Packaging Dynamics Corporation ....G....... 662 424-4000
Iuka **(G-2304)**

PAPER: Gift Wrap

Hilton National Corporation..................G....... 228 385-9800
Biloxi **(G-252)**

PAPER: Newsprint

Resolute FP US Inc ....C....... 662 227-7900
Grenada **(G-1701)**

PAPER: Printer

Giclee Fine Arts.....................................G....... 228 586-2693
Kiln **(G-2679)**

PAPER: Soap Impregnated Papers & Paper Washcloths

Newson Chenora...................................G....... 601 596-3899
Hattiesburg **(G-2037)**

PAPER: Specialty

Packaging Dynamics Corporation ....G....... 662 424-4000
Iuka **(G-2304)**

PAPER: Tissue

Twin Rivers Paper Company LLC..........E....... 662 468-2183
Pickens **(G-4307)**

PAPER: Wallpaper

David Morehead ....G....... 601 469-2272
Forest **(G-1413)**

PAPERBOARD

Ability Works Inc...................................E....... 662 842-2144
Tupelo **(G-5107)**
Georgia-Pacific LLC...............................F....... 601 939-7797
Pearl **(G-4122)**
International Paper Company ....B....... 601 638-3665
Redwood **(G-4495)**
Pontotoc Die Cutting LLC ....F....... 662 489-5874
Pontotoc **(G-4354)**
Sonoco Products Company.....................D....... 662 615-6204
Starkville **(G-4972)**

PAPERBOARD: Corrugated

Performance Paperboard Inc.................E....... 601 856-3939
Ridgeland **(G-4617)**

PARACHUTES

Pioneer Aerospace Corporation ....C....... 601 736-4511
Columbia **(G-912)**

PARALEGAL SVCS

Prosperity7 Helping Hands LLC ....G....... 800 597-6599
Southaven **(G-4893)**

PARTICLEBOARD

Roseburg Forest Products Co...............B....... 601 785-4734
Taylorsville **(G-5058)**

PARTICLEBOARD: Laminated, Plastic

American Pacific Inc..............................D....... 662 252-1862
Holly Springs **(G-2171)**
Roseburg Forest Products Co...............B....... 662 236-8080
Oxford **(G-4000)**

PARTITIONS & FIXTURES: Except Wood

Southeastern Constructors Inc ....E....... 601 825-9791
Brandon **(G-457)**
Standex International Corp ....B....... 662 534-9061
New Albany **(G-3700)**
Thomasvlle Mtal Fbricators Inc ....E....... 662 526-9900
Como **(G-1052)**

PARTITIONS: Wood & Fixtures

Baymont Wholesale Inc.........................G....... 662 424-2134
Belmont **(G-194)**
Hartson-Kennedy Cabinet Top Co.........D....... 228 896-1548
Gulfport **(G-1805)**
Pierce Cabinets Inc................................E....... 662 840-6795
Tupelo **(G-5204)**
Southern Cabinets & Millwork ....G....... 662 447-3885
Okolona **(G-3799)**

PATCHING PLASTER: Household

Ingram Roman Inc..................................G....... 601 954-8367
Madison **(G-3110)**

PATENT OWNERS & LESSORS

Mississppi Band Chctaw Indians ....E....... 601 656-6038
Choctaw **(G-747)**

PATTERNS: Indl

Jl Browne Inc...G....... 228 216-1137
Kiln **(G-2681)**

PAVERS

Kdeb Manufacturing LLC ....G....... 601 750-9659
Morton **(G-3448)**

PAWN SHOPS

Boardtown Trading Post ....G....... 662 324-7296
Starkville **(G-4929)**
Quitman Sporting Goods & Pawn ....G....... 601 776-3212
Quitman **(G-4468)**

PERFUMES

Yonce & Comans Products LLC ....G....... 601 270-7712
Petal **(G-4201)**

PERSONAL APPEARANCE SVCS

Joyce Tillman ....G....... 228 896-4927
Gulfport **(G-1814)**

PRODUCT SECTION

PHOTOGRAPHY SVCS: Passport

PERSONAL CREDIT INSTITUTIONS: Consumer Finance Companies

First Heritage Credit Corp ....G....... 228 762-7000
Pascagoula *(G-4032)*
First Heritage Credit Corp ....G....... 228 396-2620
Diberville *(G-1203)*
First Heritage Credit Corp ....G....... 601 636-6060
Vicksburg *(G-5372)*
First Heritage Credit Corp ....G....... 601 735-4543
Waynesboro *(G-5498)*
First Heritage Credit Corp ....G....... 601 799-1972
Picayune *(G-4266)*
First Heritage Credit Corp ....G....... 601 939-9309
Richland *(G-4515)*
L T Corporation ....E 662 843-4046
Cleveland *(G-798)*

PERSONAL CREDIT INSTITUTIONS: Licensed Loan Companies, Small

Galaxie Corporation ....G....... 601 366-8413
Jackson *(G-2419)*

PERSONAL SVCS, NEC

Destinis Creations and Exquis ....G....... 601 317-3764
Pearl *(G-4114)*

PEST CONTROL SVCS

Wren Pest Control ....G 601 276-6117
Summit *(G-5031)*

PESTICIDES

Loveland Products Inc ....C 662 335-3394
Greenville *(G-1564)*

PET COLLARS, LEASHES, MUZZLES & HARNESSES: Leather

Proshop Inc ....G 662 333-7511
Myrtle *(G-3513)*

PET FOOD WHOLESALERS

Sunshine Mills Inc ....D 662 842-6175
Tupelo *(G-5234)*

PET SPLYS

Pucci Petique Inc ....G 662 429-3202
Hernando *(G-2150)*

PETROLEUM & PETROLEUM PRDTS, WHOLESALE Crude Oil

Diversified Petroleum Inc ....G 601 727-4926
Pachuta *(G-4013)*

PETROLEUM & PETROLEUM PRDTS, WHOLESALE Diesel Fuel

Faststop Petroleum LLC ....G....... 601 466-3273
Bassfield *(G-91)*
Southland Oil Company ....F 601 981-4151
Jackson *(G-2592)*

PETROLEUM & PETROLEUM PRDTS, WHOLESALE Fuel Oil

Hancock Equipment & Oil Co LLC ....G....... 662 726-4556
Brooksville *(G-555)*

PETROLEUM & PETROLEUM PRDTS, WHOLESALE Petroleum Brokers

Galvian Group LLC ....G....... 662 374-1027
Greenwood *(G-1624)*

PETROLEUM & PETROLEUM PRDTS, WHOLESALE: Bulk Stations

Ergon Inc ....C 601 933-3000
Flowood *(G-1361)*

PETROLEUM BULK STATIONS & TERMINALS

Faststop Petroleum LLC ....G 601 466-3273
Bassfield *(G-91)*

PETROLEUM PRDTS WHOLESALERS

Chevron Corporation ....C 228 938-4600
Pascagoula *(G-4025)*
Ergon Inc ....C 601 933-3000
Flowood *(G-1361)*
Fiske International Group Corp ....G 601 622-5767
Madison *(G-3100)*
Nhc Distributors Inc ....E 601 656-7911
Philadelphia *(G-4229)*
Seago Enterprises Inc ....D 601 684-3000
McComb *(G-3265)*

PHARMACEUTICAL PREPARATIONS: Druggists' Preparations

Key Therapeutics LLC ....G 888 981-8337
Flowood *(G-1373)*
Levins Labs LLC ....G 228 334-2411
Ocean Springs *(G-3770)*
Solus Rx LLC ....G 228 365-4501
Diberville *(G-1213)*

PHARMACEUTICAL PREPARATIONS: Medicines, Capsule Or Ampule

Helping Hand Family Pharmacy ....G 601 631-6837
Vicksburg *(G-5378)*

PHARMACEUTICAL PREPARATIONS: Pills

Gentex Pharma LLC ....G 601 990-9497
Ridgeland *(G-4587)*

PHARMACEUTICAL PREPARATIONS: Solutions

Leflore Technologies LLC ....G 601 572-1491
Brandon *(G-412)*

PHARMACEUTICAL PREPARATIONS: Tablets

Skylar Laboratories LLC ....G 601 855-7678
Canton *(G-678)*

PHARMACEUTICALS

Advanced Pharmaceuticals LLC ....G 228 215-1911
Ocean Springs *(G-3739)*
Alvix Laboratories LLC ....E 601 714-1677
Ocean Springs *(G-3740)*
Ani Pharmaceuticals Inc ....D 228 863-1702
Gulfport *(G-1726)*
Arbor Therapeutics LLC ....G 303 808-4104
Oxford *(G-3935)*
Baxter Healthcare Corporation ....E 662 843-9421
Cleveland *(G-786)*
Bayer Cotton Seed Intl ....G 662 686-9235
Leland *(G-2882)*
Burel Pharmaceuticals Inc ....G 601 720-0111
Richland *(G-4508)*
Cardinal Health 414 LLC ....G 601 982-7345
Jackson *(G-2353)*
Cardinal Health 414 LLC ....G 662 680-8644
Tupelo *(G-5118)*
Carliss Pharmaceuticals ....G 228 875-2748
Ocean Springs *(G-3746)*
Celgene Corp ....G 908 673-9000
Ridgeland *(G-4562)*
Copharma Inc ....G 662 594-1594
Corinth *(G-1074)*
Cypress Pharmaceutical Inc ....G 800 856-4393
Madison *(G-3091)*
Denovo Labs LLC ....G 615 587-3099
Ridgeland *(G-4573)*
Doctors Specialty Pharmacy LLC ....G 228 806-1384
Biloxi *(G-238)*
Emilia Resources LLC ....D 601 743-9355
De Kalb *(G-1164)*
Forest Pharmaceuticals Inc ....G 662 841-2321
Belden *(G-188)*
Gcp Laboratories Inc ....D 228 863-1702
Gulfport *(G-1791)*
Larken Laboratories Inc ....G 601 855-7678
Canton *(G-667)*
Magnolia Therapeutics LLC ....G 662 281-0502
Ridgeland *(G-4601)*
Misemer Pharmaceutical Inc ....G 732 762-6577
Ripley *(G-4664)*
Novartis Corporation ....G 601 373-6148
Raymond *(G-4492)*

Numedrx Pharmacy Solutions LLC ....G 601 973-5501
Jackson *(G-2526)*
Oaklock LLC ....G 601 855-7678
Canton *(G-674)*
Pharmaceutical Trade Svcs Inc ....F 228 244-1530
Ocean Springs *(G-3775)*
Pharmedium Services LLC ....E 662 846-5969
Cleveland *(G-803)*
Primary Pharmaceuticals ....G 228 872-1167
Ocean Springs *(G-3778)*
Sircle Laboratories LLC ....G 601 897-4474
Canton *(G-677)*
Southern Pharmaceutical Corp ....G 601 939-2525
Pearl *(G-4147)*
Southern Pharmaceutical Corp ....G 662 844-5858
Tupelo *(G-5227)*
Sterlng-Knght Phrmcuticals LLC ....G 662 661-3232
Ripley *(G-4673)*
Velocity Cnslting Spcalist LLC ....G 229 726-6047
Petal *(G-4199)*
Viceroy Pharmaceuticals Inc ....G 732 762-6577
Ripley *(G-4674)*
Waltman Pharmaceuticals Inc ....G 601 939-0833
Flowood *(G-1406)*
Xspire Pharma LLC ....G 870 243-1687
Ridgeland *(G-4647)*

PHARMACEUTICALS: Medicinal & Botanical Prdts

CTA Products Group LLC ....G 662 536-1446
Southaven *(G-4866)*
Elizabeth Newcomb ....G 662 596-1536
Rienzi *(G-4649)*

PHOSPHORIC ACID

CF Industries Inc ....C 662 746-4131
Yazoo City *(G-5625)*

PHOTOCOPY MACHINE REPAIR SVCS

Filing and Storage Miss LLC ....G 601 397-6452
Ridgeland *(G-4580)*

PHOTOCOPYING & DUPLICATING SVCS

Clays Print Shop Inc ....G 228 868-8244
Gulfport *(G-1753)*
Delta Signs and Designs LLC ....G 662 822-0830
Greenville *(G-1550)*
Fedex Office & Print Svcs Inc ....F 601 264-6434
Hattiesburg *(G-1969)*
Fedex Office & Print Svcs Inc ....E 601 957-3311
Jackson *(G-2407)*
Mississippi Photo & Bluprt Co ....G 601 948-1119
Jackson *(G-2502)*
Wolverton Enterprises Inc ....F 601 355-9543
Jackson *(G-2637)*

PHOTOFINISHING LABORATORIES

Boardtown Trading Post ....G 662 324-7296
Starkville *(G-4929)*

PHOTOGRAMMATIC MAPPING SVCS

Nvision Solutions Inc ....D 228 242-0010
Diamondhead *(G-1192)*

PHOTOGRAPHIC EQPT & SPLY: Sound Recordg/Reprod Eqpt, Motion

Sandstorm Entertainment ....G 662 578-1357
Batesville *(G-123)*

PHOTOGRAPHIC EQPT & SPLYS

Exel Logistics Xerox ....G 662 393-7122
Southaven *(G-4872)*
Record Imaging Systems ....G 662 280-1286
Southaven *(G-4896)*

PHOTOGRAPHY SVCS: Commercial

Magnetic Arrow LLC ....G 601 653-2932
Biloxi *(G-264)*

PHOTOGRAPHY SVCS: Passport

Jagg LLC ....G 228 388-1794
Biloxi *(G-254)*

Employee Codes: A=Over 500 employees, B=251-500
C=101-250, D=51-100, E=20-50, F=10-19, G=1-9

2019 Harris Directory of
Mississippi Manufacturers

PRODUCT

PHOTOGRAPHY SVCS: Still Or Video

PRODUCT SECTION

PHOTOGRAPHY SVCS: Still Or Video

Dzt Photography and Event Prtg..........G...... 228 334-5253
Ocean Springs *(G-3754)*
Formal Affair.................................G...... 228 497-7500
Gautier *(G-1492)*

PHOTOGRAPHY: Aerial

Sevlo Solutions LLC.....................G...... 662 312-9507
Starkville *(G-4970)*

PHYSICAL FITNESS CENTERS

Throw Strikes Baseball Academy.........G...... 662 931-4948
Greenville *(G-1604)*

PHYSICIANS' OFFICES & CLINICS: Medical

Elizabeth Newcomb.......................G...... 662 596-1536
Rienzi *(G-4649)*

PICTURE FRAMES: Metal

Elims Art Cncpts & Dcrtv Dsgn.............G...... 601 540-4810
Jackson *(G-2398)*

PICTURE FRAMES: Wood

Art Horizons Inc...........................C...... 662 561-9733
Batesville *(G-96)*
Burtoni Fine Art Inc.....................G...... 601 581-1557
Meridian *(G-3314)*
Final Touch Accessories LLC..........E...... 662 594-1348
Corinth *(G-1085)*
Gallery..G...... 662 224-6694
Ashland *(G-60)*
Kathys Frame Works Inc................G...... 228 769-7672
Pascagoula *(G-4044)*

PIECE GOODS & NOTIONS WHOLESALERS

Culp Inc.......................................F...... 662 844-7144
Tupelo *(G-5124)*

PIECE GOODS, NOTIONS & DRY GOODS, WHOLESALE: Fabrics

F S C Inc......................................G...... 662 434-0025
Columbus *(G-972)*
Mitchell Group............................G...... 662 488-0025
Pontotoc *(G-4347)*

PIECE GOODS, NOTIONS & OTHER DRY GOODS, WHOLESALE: Bridal

Southern Design Finds....................G...... 662 893-4303
Byhalia *(G-606)*

PILOT SVCS: Aviation

Heath Aviation.............................G...... 662 283-9833
Winona *(G-5599)*

PIPE & FITTING: Fabrication

Babcock & Wilcox Company.............C...... 662 494-1323
West Point *(G-5537)*
Dmi Pipe Fabrication LLC.............F...... 225 272-1420
Woodville *(G-5616)*
J & A Mechanical Inc.....................G...... 662 890-4565
Olive Branch *(G-3853)*
Modine Grenada LLC....................B...... 662 229-4000
Grenada *(G-1694)*
Process Mechanical Eqp Co.............G...... 601 291-4082
Ridgeland *(G-4621)*
Quality Pipe & Fabrication LLC.............G...... 662 321-8542
Blue Springs *(G-299)*
Thomasvlle Mtal Fbricators Inc..........E...... 662 526-9900
Como *(G-1052)*
True Temper Sports Inc..................B...... 662 256-5605
Amory *(G-57)*
Upchurch Industrial LLC.................D...... 662 453-6680
Horn Lake *(G-2214)*

PIPE & TUBES: Aluminum

North American Pipe Corp.................D...... 662 728-2111
Booneville *(G-338)*

PIPE & TUBES: Copper & Copper Alloy

Mueller Copper Tube Co Inc.................B...... 662 862-1700
Fulton *(G-1466)*

PIPE & TUBES: Seamless

Maruichi Leavitt Pipe Tube LLC..............G...... 800 532-8488
Jackson *(G-2655)*

PIPE, CULVERT: Concrete

Travis Construction Co LLC..................F...... 228 539-4849
Gulfport *(G-1886)*

PIPE: Plastic

Advanced Drainage Systems Inc.........G...... 601 629-9040
Vicksburg *(G-5338)*
Advanced Drainage Systems Inc.........D...... 601 371-0678
Jackson *(G-2320)*
Contech Engnered Solutions LLC........G...... 601 894-2041
Greenville *(G-1540)*
Hancor Inc....................................E...... 601 629-9040
Vicksburg *(G-5376)*
North American Pipe Corp.................D...... 662 728-2111
Booneville *(G-338)*

PIPE: Seamless Steel

Helanbak LLC................................G...... 601 736-6112
Foxworth *(G-1431)*

PIPE: Sewer, Cast Iron

Apm LLC.......................................G...... 907 279-0204
Gulfport *(G-1728)*

PIPE: Sheet Metal

Spiral Systems Inc.........................F...... 662 429-0373
Nesbit *(G-3657)*

PIPELINES, EXC NATURAL GAS: Coal

Lining & Coating Solutions LLC...........F...... 662 893-0984
Olive Branch *(G-3865)*

PIPELINES: Refined Petroleum

BP America Production Company.......E...... 228 762-3996
Moss Point *(G-3471)*
Ergon Inc......................................C...... 601 933-3000
Flowood *(G-1361)*

PIPES & FITTINGS: Fiber, Made From Purchased Materials

Spiral Fab Inc...............................G...... 662 862-7999
Fulton *(G-1477)*

PIPES & TUBES

Eagle Pipe and Supply LLC.................G...... 601 487-7473
Jackson *(G-2394)*
PSL-North America LLC....................B...... 228 533-7779
Bay St Louis *(G-180)*

PIPES & TUBES: Steel

Allied Crawford Jackson Inc..................E...... 769 230-2220
Byram *(G-616)*
Contech Engnered Solutions LLC........G...... 601 894-2041
Greenville *(G-1540)*
Empire Services Inc.........................C...... 601 276-2500
Summit *(G-5014)*
Jindal Tubular USA LLC....................D...... 228 533-7779
Bay Saint Louis *(G-144)*
Leggett & Platt Incorporated..........F...... 417 358-8131
West Point *(G-5549)*
Midco Supply Co Inc.......................G...... 601 932-7311
Jackson *(G-2657)*
Plymouth Tube Company................D...... 662 258-2420
Eupora *(G-1290)*
PSL USA Inc..................................G...... 228 533-7779
Bay Saint Louis *(G-151)*

PIPES: Steel & Iron

Resurfacing Concepts Inc..................G...... 662 489-6867
Pontotoc *(G-4360)*
Sxp Schulz Xtruded Products LP..........D...... 662 429-0818
Hernando *(G-2157)*
Sxp Schulz Xtruded Products LP..........C...... 662 373-4114
Robinsonville *(G-4678)*

PLANING MILL, NEC

Foxworth & Thompson Inc..................G...... 601 736-3602
Foxworth *(G-1430)*

JC Jourdan Lumber Co Inc..................F...... 662 423-5238
Iuka *(G-2295)*
Jones Lumber Co Inc.......................D...... 601 445-8206
Natchez *(G-3573)*
JT Shannon Lumber Co Inc................E...... 662 393-3765
Horn Lake *(G-2203)*
Rives and Reynolds Lbr Co Inc..........D...... 662 773-5157
Louisville *(G-2979)*

PLASTER WORK: Ornamental & Architectural

Architectural Concepts...................G...... 850 471-7081
Brandon *(G-365)*

PLASTIC PRDTS

Coastal Solar and SEC Films.............G...... 228 369-3933
Biloxi *(G-232)*
Coastal Tire Wholesalers LLC.............G...... 810 257-9977
Long Beach *(G-2934)*
Diversity Vuteq LLC........................G...... 662 587-9633
Blue Springs *(G-295)*

PLASTICS FILM & SHEET

Adlam Films LLC............................E...... 662 823-1345
Shannon *(G-4805)*

PLASTICS FILM & SHEET: Polyethylene

Summit Plastics Inc.........................E...... 601 276-7500
Summit *(G-5024)*

PLASTICS FILM & SHEET: Vinyl

Intex Properties Perris Vly LP.............G...... 662 287-1455
Corinth *(G-1093)*

PLASTICS FINISHED PRDTS: Laminated

Quad Inc.......................................G...... 601 656-2376
Choctaw *(G-750)*
Superior Mfg Group Inc...................G...... 601 544-8119
Moselle *(G-3461)*

PLASTICS MATERIAL & RESINS

4m Enterprises LLC.........................G...... 601 664-0030
Pearl *(G-4101)*
Axiall LLC......................................E...... 601 856-8993
Madison *(G-3080)*
Axiall Corporation.........................C...... 601 892-5612
Hazlehurst *(G-2089)*
B & D Plastics Mississippi Inc.............F...... 228 875-5865
Ocean Springs *(G-3742)*
Carpenter Co.................................B...... 662 566-2392
Verona *(G-5329)*
Dak Americas Mississippi Inc.............E...... 228 533-4000
Bay Saint Louis *(G-142)*
Dealership Services LLC...................G...... 662 269-3897
Tupelo *(G-5126)*
Elite Comfort Solutions LLC.............E...... 662 566-2322
Verona *(G-5330)*
Fxi Inc..C...... 662 566-2382
Verona *(G-5331)*
George Pacific...............................C...... 662 779-1300
Louisville *(G-2968)*
Heritage Plastics Inc.......................C...... 404 425-1905
Picayune *(G-4271)*
Nanocor LLC..................................G...... 847 851-1500
Aberdeen *(G-19)*
Perma R Products Inc.......................C...... 662 226-8075
Grenada *(G-1699)*
Plaskolite South LLC.......................G...... 662 895-7007
Olive Branch *(G-3898)*
Resinall Mississippi Inc....................C...... 252 585-1445
Hattiesburg *(G-2050)*
Sabic Innovative Plas US LLC............C...... 228 466-3015
Bay Saint Louis *(G-155)*
Sabic Innovative Plas US LLC............E...... 228 533-7855
Bay Saint Louis *(G-154)*
Solaplast LLC................................G...... 877 972-5449
Meridian *(G-3399)*
Sonoco Prtective Solutions Inc..........E...... 662 842-1043
Tupelo *(G-5225)*
Westlake Compounds LLC...............G...... 601 206-3200
Madison *(G-3168)*
Westlake Compounds LLC...............E...... 601 892-5612
Gallman *(G-1487)*

406

2019 Harris Directory of
Mississippi Manufacturers

(G-0000) Company's Geographic Section entry number

PRODUCT SECTION

POSTERS & DECALS, WHOLESALE

PLASTICS MATERIALS, BASIC FORMS & SHAPES WHOLESALERS

South Central Polymers Inc ....D 662 728-9506
Booneville **(G-345)**

PLASTICS PROCESSING

Intex Properties Perris Vly LP ....G 662 287-1455
Corinth **(G-1093)**

Longbranch ....G 662 284-8585
Corinth **(G-1098)**

Omnova Solutions Inc ....A 662 327-1522
Columbus **(G-1012)**

Polyvulc Usa Inc ....E 601 638-8040
Vicksburg **(G-5407)**

Sinhatech ....G 662 234-6248
Oxford **(G-4002)**

Solvay Spclty Polymers USA LLC ....F 228 533-0238
Bay Saint Louis **(G-156)**

Stanley McCaffrey Signs ....G 228 832-0885
Richland **(G-4525)**

PLASTICS: Blow Molded

Hood Flexible Packaging Corp ....D 903 593-1793
Hattiesburg **(G-1993)**

PLASTICS: Cast

Easy Reach Supply LLC ....E 601 582-7866
Hattiesburg **(G-1959)**

PLASTICS: Finished Injection Molded

Custom Engineered Wheels Inc ....D 574 267-4005
Baldwyn **(G-75)**

Multicraft Intl Ltd Partnr ....G 601 854-5516
Pelahatchie **(G-4167)**

Richard Plastics Co ....F 601 426-2810
Laurel **(G-2836)**

Steiner Plastics Inc ....G 662 895-7350
Olive Branch **(G-3913)**

PLASTICS: Injection Molded

Acco Brands USA LLC ....G 800 541-0094
Booneville **(G-314)**

American National Molding LLC ....D 601 936-2722
Flowood **(G-1343)**

Canopy Breezes LLC ....G 972 207-2045
Madison **(G-3088)**

Caviness Woodworking Company ....D 662 628-5195
Calhoun City **(G-636)**

Excel Injection Molding Inc ....E 601 544-6133
Hattiesburg **(G-1966)**

Harrison Manufacturing LLC ....E 601 519-0558
Jackson **(G-2437)**

Magnolia Mtal Plastic Pdts Inc ....E 601 638-6912
Vicksburg **(G-5393)**

Plaspros Inc ....E 662 563-8635
Batesville **(G-119)**

Plastics Plus Inc ....G 228 832-4634
Gulfport **(G-1849)**

Richardson Molding LLC ....G 601 656-7921
Philadelphia **(G-4235)**

Rk Manufacturing Inc ....F 601 956-7774
Ridgeland **(G-4623)**

South Central Polymers Inc ....D 662 728-9506
Booneville **(G-345)**

Suburban Plastics Co ....D 662 227-1911
Grenada **(G-1705)**

United Plastic Molders Inc ....E 601 353-3193
Jackson **(G-2618)**

PLASTICS: Molded

United Comb & Novelty Corp ....F 662 487-9248
Sardis **(G-4746)**

PLASTICS: Polystyrene Foam

Bassco Foam Inc ....E 662 842-4321
Tupelo **(G-5114)**

Carlisle Construction Mtls LLC ....D 662 560-6474
Senatobia **(G-4788)**

Ideal Foam LLC ....D 662 489-2264
Pontotoc **(G-4334)**

Innocor Foam Tech - Acp Inc ....G 662 842-0123
Tupelo **(G-5162)**

Innocor Foam Technologies LLC ....F 662 622-7221
Coldwater **(G-847)**

S & A Industries Corporation ....E 330 733-6040
New Albany **(G-3695)**

S & A Industries Corporation ....G 330 733-6040
New Albany **(G-3696)**

Stewart Sign & Screen Graphics ....G 601 783-5377
McComb **(G-3269)**

PLATES

Copy Cats Printing Inc ....F 601 582-3019
Hattiesburg **(G-1951)**

Fedex Office & Print Svcs Inc ....F 601 264-6434
Hattiesburg **(G-1969)**

MDN Laser Engraving Inc ....G 662 397-5799
Tupelo **(G-5185)**

RR Donnelley & Sons Company ....B 662 562-5252
Senatobia **(G-4802)**

PLATES: Plastic Exc Polystyrene Foam

Intellabuy Inc ....G 601 249-0508
McComb **(G-3253)**

PLATES: Sheet & Strip, Exc Coated Prdts

Metro Mechanical Inc ....D 601 866-9050
Bolton **(G-312)**

PLATING & POLISHING SVC

ABB Installation Products Inc ....B 662 342-1545
Southaven **(G-4851)**

All That Glitters Ep Inc ....G 601 981-1947
Jackson **(G-2323)**

Columbus Roll Shop ....E 662 798-4149
Columbus **(G-952)**

R K Metals LLC ....G 662 840-6060
Tupelo **(G-5213)**

S Circle Inc ....G 601 792-4104
Newhebron **(G-3714)**

PLATING SVC: Electro

Process Engineering Co Inc ....E 601 981-4931
Jackson **(G-2551)**

PLATING SVC: NEC

Griffin Armor ....G 662 494-3421
West Point **(G-5545)**

Jackson Plating Co ....E 601 362-4623
Jackson **(G-2456)**

T & T Inc ....G 662 840-7500
Tupelo **(G-5237)**

Teikuro Corporation ....G 601 482-0432
Meridian **(G-3412)**

PLEATING & STITCHING FOR THE TRADE: Decorative & Novelty

Sew Sweet ....G 601 431-2304
Natchez **(G-3618)**

PLEATING & STITCHING SVC

Ability Works Inc ....G 662 328-0275
Columbus **(G-931)**

C W Embroidery Inc ....G 662 231-9206
Prairie **(G-4412)**

Get Stitched ....G 228 231-1162
Waveland **(G-5481)**

Mid-South Drapery Inc ....E 662 454-3855
Belmont **(G-200)**

PLUMBING & HEATING EQPT & SPLY, WHOL: Htg Eqpt/Panels, Solar

Magnolia Supply Group LLC ....G 601 454-1368
Jackson **(G-2480)**

PLUMBING & HEATING EQPT & SPLY, WHOLESALE: Hydronic Htg Eqpt

Comfort Designs Inc ....F 601 932-7555
Pearl **(G-4111)**

PLUMBING & HEATING EQPT & SPLYS, WHOL: Fireplaces, Prefab

Fireplace Wholesale ....G 601 545-9876
Hattiesburg **(G-1970)**

PLUMBING & HEATING EQPT & SPLYS, WHOL: Plumbing Fitting/Sply

Carr Plumbing Supply Inc ....G 601 824-9711
Brandon **(G-375)**

Haygoods Industrial Engravers ....G 228 769-7488
Pascagoula **(G-4036)**

Lees Septic Inc ....F 662 369-9799
Aberdeen **(G-17)**

PLUMBING FIXTURES

Carr Plumbing Supply Inc ....G 601 824-9711
Brandon **(G-375)**

National Pump Company ....G 662 895-1110
Olive Branch **(G-3886)**

PLUMBING FIXTURES: Plastic

Ability Works Inc ....E 662 842-2144
Tupelo **(G-5107)**

Builders Marble Inc ....E 601 922-5420
Clinton **(G-817)**

Hancor Inc ....E 601 629-9040
Vicksburg **(G-5376)**

K & D Cultured Marble Inc ....E 662 675-2928
Coffeeville **(G-843)**

PLUMBING FIXTURES: Vitreous

Tg Missouri-Mississippi ....G 662 563-1043
Batesville **(G-128)**

POLICE PROTECTION: Local Government

City of Magee ....E 601 849-2366
Magee **(G-3174)**

POLISHING SVC: Metals Or Formed Prdts

Vibra Shine Inc ....G 601 785-9854
Taylorsville **(G-5061)**

Wheel Polishing Pros Inc ....G 601 259-9379
Mc Cool **(G-3238)**

POLYETHYLENE RESINS

Dak Americas LLC ....C 228 533-4480
Bay St Louis **(G-178)**

Westlake Chemical Corporation ....G 601 892-5612
Hazlehurst **(G-2110)**

POLYSTYRENE RESINS

Gulf Concrete Technology LLC ....G 228 575-3500
Long Beach **(G-2938)**

POLYURETHANE RESINS

L & J Products & Sales Inc ....E 662 841-0710
Tupelo **(G-5169)**

POLYVINYL CHLORIDE RESINS

Axiall Corporation ....E 662 369-9586
Prairie **(G-4411)**

Westlake Chemical Corporation ....C 662 369-8111
Aberdeen **(G-21)**

POPCORN & SUPPLIES WHOLESALERS

Yum Yums Gourmet Popcorn LLC ....G 662 470-6047
Southaven **(G-4922)**

PORTER SVC

T S Car Ports ....G 601 797-9600
Mount Olive **(G-3511)**

PORTRAIT COPYING SVC

Delta Signs and Designs LLC ....G 662 822-0830
Greenville **(G-1550)**

POSTAL EQPT: Locker Boxes, Exc Wood

Krh Transport LLC ....G 769 244-1392
Centreville **(G-732)**

POSTERS & DECALS, WHOLESALE

Modeltruckin ....G 228 365-4124
Gulfport **(G-1834)**

Employee Codes: A=Over 500 employees, B=251-500
C=101-250, D=51-100, E=20-50, F=10-19, G=1-9

2019 Harris Directory of
Mississippi Manufacturers

407

PRODUCT

POTASH MINING

Terra Mississippi Nitrogen Inc..............B 662 746-4131
Yazoo City *(G-5649)*

POTPOURRI

D & G Enterprises ....G 662 895-4471
Olive Branch *(G-3832)*

POTTERY

Alleykat Ceramics LLC ....G 228 224-7775
Gulfport *(G-1722)*
Mississippi Mud Works Pottery ....G 228 875-8773
Ocean Springs *(G-3772)*

POTTING SOILS

Baddour Memorial Center Inc..............B 662 562-0100
Senatobia *(G-4787)*

POULTRY & SMALL GAME SLAUGHTERING & PROCESSING

B & S Farms.......................................G 601 656-5157
Philadelphia *(G-4206)*
Country Farms Quail ....G 601 947-4263
Lucedale *(G-2991)*
Debbie F Shelton................................G 601 535-7162
Pattison *(G-4100)*
Dg Foods LLC ....B 601 892-0333
Hazlehurst *(G-2094)*
Marshall Durbin Food Corp...................F 601 969-1248
Jackson *(G-2483)*
Peco Foods Inc ....A 601 859-6161
Canton *(G-675)*
Peco Foods Inc ....B 601 625-7819
Sebastopol *(G-4775)*
Sanderson Farms Inc ....G 601 426-1316
Ellisville *(G-1268)*
Sanderson Farms Inc Foods Div ....B 601 939-9790
Flowood *(G-1394)*
Sanderson Farms Inc Proc Div ....A 601 765-8211
Collins *(G-861)*
Sanderson Farms Inc Prod Div ....B 601 765-2221
Collins *(G-862)*
Tyson Foods Inc ....E 601 298-5300
Carthage *(G-726)*
Tyson Foods Inc ....G 229 995-6800
Forest *(G-1426)*
Tyson Foods Inc ....C 601 849-3351
Magee *(G-3187)*
Water Valley Poultry Inc ....E 662 473-0016
Water Valley *(G-5477)*
Wayne Farms LLC ....C 601 425-4721
Laurel *(G-2869)*
Wayne Farms LLC ....C 601 399-7000
Laurel *(G-2870)*

POULTRY SLAUGHTERING & PROCESSING

Peco Foods Inc ....C 662 738-5771
Brooksville *(G-557)*

POWER SWITCHING EQPT

Kuhlman Electric Corporation ....B 601 892-4661
Crystal Springs *(G-1144)*

POWER TOOLS, HAND: Drills & Drilling Tools

Martin Incorporated ....G 662 720-2445
Booneville *(G-334)*

POWER TRANSMISSION EQPT: Mechanical

Maurey Manufacturing Corp ....E 662 252-6583
Holly Springs *(G-2184)*
V E Brackett & Co Inc ....G 662 840-5656
Tupelo *(G-5249)*
Whitestone Contracting LLC ....G 601 800-8077
Ellisville *(G-1278)*

PRECAST TERRAZZO OR CONCRETE PRDTS

Civil Precast Corporation.....................G 601 853-1870
Ridgeland *(G-4563)*
Forterra Pipe & Precast LLC ....E 601 268-2081
Prentiss *(G-4418)*

Forterra Pipe & Precast LLC ....E 601 982-1100
Jackson *(G-2410)*
Forterra Pipe & Precast LLC ....G 601 792-3202
Prentiss *(G-4419)*

PREFABRICATED BUILDING DEALERS

Johnny Parks ....G 662 289-5844
Kosciusko *(G-2697)*

PRESSED FIBER & MOLDED PULP PRDTS, EXC FOOD PRDTS

Tri-County Industries ....E 601 743-9931
De Kalb *(G-1169)*

PRESTRESSED CONCRETE PRDTS

F-S Prestress LLC ....D 601 268-2006
Hattiesburg *(G-1967)*
Gulf Coast Pre-Stress Inc....................C 228 452-7270
Pass Christian *(G-4086)*

PRIMARY FINISHED OR SEMIFINISHED SHAPES

Piper Metal Forming Corp ....C 508 363-3937
New Albany *(G-3691)*

PRIMARY METAL PRODUCTS

Aerotec Ltd ....G 713 598-9410
Hattiesburg *(G-1918)*

PRINT CARTRIDGES: Laser & Other Computer Printers

Kdeb Manufacturing LLC ....G 601 750-9659
Morton *(G-3448)*

PRINTED CIRCUIT BOARDS

Ayrshire Electronics Miss LLC ....C 662 287-3771
Corinth *(G-1059)*
CM Solutions Inc................................F 662 287-8810
Corinth *(G-1071)*
Electro National Corporation ....E 601 859-5511
Canton *(G-657)*
Hunter Engineering Company ....C 601 857-8883
Raymond *(G-4489)*
Mississppi Band Chctaw Indians ....G 601 656-7350
Choctaw *(G-746)*
Tri-County Industries...........................E 601 743-9931
De Kalb *(G-1169)*

PRINTERS: Computer

Richardson Marketing ....G 662 234-3907
Abbeville *(G-3)*

PRINTING & ENGRAVING: Invitation & Stationery

Formal Affair ....G 228 497-7500
Gautier *(G-1492)*
Mackay Enterprises LLC ....G 662 328-8469
Columbus *(G-996)*
Monograms Plus ....G 662 327-3332
Columbus *(G-1007)*
Party City ....F 228 539-4476
Gulfport *(G-1846)*
Stribling Printing ....G 601 656-4194
Philadelphia *(G-4238)*

PRINTING & ENGRAVING: Poster & Decal

Modeltruckin.......................................G 228 365-4124
Gulfport *(G-1834)*

PRINTING & WRITING PAPER WHOLESALERS

T Enterprises Inc................................F 601 487-1100
Jackson *(G-2603)*

PRINTING MACHINERY

Ray Brooks Enterprises ....G 662 342-0555
Southaven *(G-4895)*

PRINTING TRADES MACHINERY & EQPT REPAIR SVCS

Passons Specialized Services..............G 601 939-3722
Jackson *(G-2661)*

PRINTING, COMMERCIAL Newspapers, NEC

Baldwyn News.....................................G 662 365-3232
Baldwyn *(G-71)*

PRINTING, COMMERCIAL: Business Forms, NEC

Dallas Printing Inc..............................E 601 968-9354
Richland *(G-4511)*
Nebco Inc...G 662 349-1400
Southaven *(G-4890)*

PRINTING, COMMERCIAL: Directories, Exc Telephone, NEC

Mississippi Gulf Coast ....G 228 896-3055
Gulfport *(G-1832)*

PRINTING, COMMERCIAL: Envelopes, NEC

Smart Source ....G 601 707-1150
Ridgeland *(G-4631)*

PRINTING, COMMERCIAL: Labels & Seals, NEC

Label Express Inc ....F 662 566-7075
Verona *(G-5334)*
Phillips Company Inc ....G 662 844-3898
Tupelo *(G-5203)*
Taylor Made Labels Inc.........................G 601 936-0050
Jackson *(G-2671)*

PRINTING, COMMERCIAL: Letterpress & Screen

Destiny Apparel LLC............................G 228 383-2665
Biloxi *(G-236)*
Harris Custom Ink LLC ....E 662 338-4242
Olive Branch *(G-3844)*
Her Heart Shop ....G 662 523-9568
Shannon *(G-4809)*
Onswoll Grafix LLC ....G 228 596-8409
Long Beach *(G-2947)*

PRINTING, COMMERCIAL: Screen

3 Men Moving & Storage LLC ....G 662 238-7774
Oxford *(G-3934)*
Ad Visuals Inc ....G 601 932-3060
Richland *(G-4497)*
American T Shirt Printing Co ....G 662 590-3272
Yazoo City *(G-5622)*
Anna Grace Tees LLC ....G 228 861-2661
Gulfport *(G-1727)*
Artistic Tees..G 662 234-5051
Oxford *(G-3936)*
Bangers and Mash Tees LLC ....G 801 803-8970
Madison *(G-3083)*
Barn Life Tees ....G 601 740-0696
Columbia *(G-883)*
Bear Creek Apparel Promotions...........G 601 259-8508
Canton *(G-648)*
Big Buck Sports ....G 601 605-2661
Ridgeland *(G-4556)*
Blax Screen Printing & EMB ....G 228 392-5022
Diberville *(G-1199)*
Brewer Screen Printing ....G 662 453-2255
Greenwood *(G-1616)*
Buzini Group LLC ....E 601 398-1311
Flowood *(G-1350)*
C F E N ....G 662 327-0031
Columbus *(G-945)*
Charlottes EMB & Screen Prtg ....G 601 824-1080
Brandon *(G-379)*
Coast Tees LLC ....G 228 234-1636
Gulfport *(G-1758)*
Cotton Tops ....G 662 287-4737
Corinth *(G-1081)*
Creative Designs & Sports...................G 662 327-5000
Columbus *(G-956)*
Custom Creations ....G 601 450-7600
Hattiesburg *(G-1954)*

408

2019 Harris Directory of
Mississippi Manufacturers

(G-0000) Company's Geographic Section entry number

PRODUCT SECTION

PRINTING: Commercial, NEC

Custom Sportswear USA Inc ....G..... 228 255-4795
Diamondhead *(G-1188)*

D Graphics Advertising ....G..... 601 373-4667
Jackson *(G-2374)*

Digital Kanvas LLC ....G..... 901 896-9690
Olive Branch *(G-3836)*

Dub Street Fashion Center LLC ....G..... 601 483-0036
Meridian *(G-3330)*

Dynastics Screen Printing ....G..... 601 353-1956
Jackson *(G-2393)*

Encore Products ....G..... 662 423-3484
Iuka *(G-2290)*

Express Printing ....G..... 601 856-5458
Ridgeland *(G-4579)*

Flatlanders Screen Printing ....G..... 662 846-0725
Cleveland *(G-792)*

G5 Tees ....G..... 662 403-1339
Coldwater *(G-846)*

Gator Grafix Inc ....G..... 601 376-9004
Jackson *(G-2423)*

Global Screen Printing LLC ....G..... 601 919-2345
Brandon *(G-399)*

Graphic Arts Productions Inc ....G..... 662 494-2549
West Point *(G-5544)*

Hobies Sports and Outdoors ....G..... 601 833-9700
Brookhaven *(G-500)*

Hodge Podge Screen Prtg Inc ....F..... 662 226-1636
Grenada *(G-1685)*

Image Screen Printing Inc ....E..... 662 489-5668
Pontotoc *(G-4336)*

Independents Service Company ....G..... 662 287-2431
Corinth *(G-1091)*

Ink Spot Inc ....G..... 662 236-2639
Oxford *(G-3959)*

Ink Spot Inc ....F..... 662 236-1985
Oxford *(G-3960)*

Inky BS Custom Tees LLC ....G..... 601 988-8558
Raymond *(G-4490)*

J M H Graphics ....G..... 601 261-2500
Hattiesburg *(G-2000)*

J S lupes ....G..... 601 856-7776
Madison *(G-3112)*

J&J Screen Printing ....G..... 662 342-6131
Southaven *(G-4881)*

JC Graphics LLC ....E..... 662 832-9291
Oxford *(G-3963)*

Lazarus Arts ....G..... 601 445-4576
Natchez *(G-3578)*

Mississippi Photo & Bluprt Co ....G..... 601 948-1119
Jackson *(G-2502)*

Mombo Graphixs ....G..... 228 466-2551
Waveland *(G-5483)*

Monogram Express ....G..... 601 825-1248
Brandon *(G-425)*

National Scrubwear Inc ....F..... 601 483-0796
Meridian *(G-3376)*

One of A Kind Art Creations ....G..... 662 328-1283
Columbus *(G-1013)*

Oneway Inc ....G..... 601 664-0007
Jackson *(G-2660)*

Oneway Screen Prtg & Graphics ....G..... 601 845-7777
Florence *(G-1330)*

Oxford Printwear LLC ....F..... 662 234-5051
Oxford *(G-3989)*

Park Avenue Printing ....G..... 601 876-9095
Tylertown *(G-5279)*

Pearl River Graphics & Prtg ....G..... 601 656-3636
Choctaw *(G-749)*

Pollchaps LLC ....G..... 601 706-4928
Brandon *(G-435)*

Print Shop of Tupelo ....G..... 662 841-0004
Mooreville *(G-3443)*

Pro Designs Inc ....G..... 662 841-1867
Tupelo *(G-5209)*

Protees USA LLC ....G..... 601 317-3649
Jackson *(G-2553)*

Roosevelt Wallace ....G..... 662 627-7513
Clarksdale *(G-781)*

Screenco Inc ....G..... 662 534-8750
New Albany *(G-3697)*

Screening Room ....G..... 601 626-0327
Collinsville *(G-875)*

Serigraphics ....G..... 662 895-3553
Olive Branch *(G-3908)*

Service Printers Inc ....E..... 601 939-4910
Flowood *(G-1395)*

Southern Bell Clothing ....G..... 662 258-2955
Eupora *(G-1293)*

Southern Belle ....G..... 662 637-2264
Grenada *(G-1703)*

Southern Graphics Inc ....G..... 601 833-7448
Brookhaven *(G-537)*

Southern Tees Plus ....G..... 601 896-7468
Kosciusko *(G-2712)*

Special TS ....G..... 662 563-5138
Batesville *(G-126)*

Specialtees Etc ....G..... 601 683-2552
Newton *(G-3728)*

Stamm Advertising Co Inc ....G..... 601 636-7749
Vicksburg *(G-5423)*

Stamm Advertising Co Inc ....G..... 601 922-3400
Jackson *(G-2597)*

Stewarts Screen Printing ....G..... 601 932-8310
Jackson *(G-2669)*

Swain Printing & Signs ....G..... 662 773-7584
Louisville *(G-2983)*

Sweetees ....G..... 662 404-1966
Sardis *(G-4745)*

T Shirt Shop & Design Firm LLC ....G..... 662 329-9911
Columbus *(G-1036)*

T Tommys ....G..... 601 833-8620
Brookhaven *(G-542)*

Tanners Enterprise LLC ....G..... 601 894-5219
Hazlehurst *(G-2108)*

Taylor Screen Printing ....G..... 601 352-9779
Jackson *(G-2605)*

Tees By Taran ....G..... 601 549-8384
Brookhaven *(G-543)*

Tees River Relics ....G..... 662 501-9936
Coldwater *(G-851)*

Tees Snow White ....G..... 662 420-2687
Holly Springs *(G-2194)*

Teezers ....G..... 662 560-5099
Senatobia *(G-4804)*

Youngs Leather & Custom Tees ....G..... 662 424-3847
Dennis *(G-1185)*

PRINTING, COMMERCIAL: Stationery, NEC

Office Depot Inc ....E..... 662 378-2995
Greenville *(G-1585)*

PRINTING, LITHOGRAPHIC: Color

Quality Printing Inc ....E..... 601 353-9663
Jackson *(G-2555)*

PRINTING, LITHOGRAPHIC: Decals

Modeltruckin ....G..... 228 365-4124
Gulfport *(G-1834)*

PRINTING, LITHOGRAPHIC: Forms, Business

Jackson Business Form Company ....E..... 601 932-5200
Flowood *(G-1370)*

Lawrence Printing Company ....D..... 662 453-6301
Greenwood *(G-1633)*

PRINTING, LITHOGRAPHIC: Newspapers

Richton Dispatch Inc ....G..... 601 788-6031
Richton *(G-4543)*

PRINTING, LITHOGRAPHIC: Offset & photolithographic printing

Meteor Inc ....F..... 601 892-2581
Crystal Springs *(G-1148)*

Stribling Printing ....G..... 601 656-4194
Philadelphia *(G-4238)*

PRINTING, LITHOGRAPHIC: On Metal

Action Printing Center Inc ....F..... 228 769-2676
Pascagoula *(G-4018)*

Dement Printing Company ....G..... 601 693-2721
Meridian *(G-3329)*

Joseph L Brown Printing Co ....G..... 601 693-6184
Meridian *(G-3355)*

Macon Beacon ....G..... 662 726-4747
Macon *(G-3064)*

Raymond Young Printing ....G..... 601 947-8999
Lucedale *(G-3015)*

PRINTING, LITHOGRAPHIC: Promotional

P P I Inc ....F..... 662 680-4332
Tupelo *(G-5197)*

Smart Source ....G..... 601 707-1150
Ridgeland *(G-4631)*

Vizionz Unlimited LLC ....G..... 601 272-5040
Jackson *(G-2622)*

PRINTING: Books

David Hollingsworth ....G..... 769 233-7769
Flowood *(G-1354)*

Lsc Communications Us LLC ....G..... 601 562-5252
Senatobia *(G-4794)*

RR Donnelley & Sons Company ....B..... 662 562-5252
Senatobia *(G-4802)*

PRINTING: Checkbooks

Rebel Quick Cash ....G..... 662 326-9228
Marks *(G-3223)*

PRINTING: Commercial, NEC

Advantage Tax & Printing Svc ....G..... 601 544-0602
Hattiesburg *(G-1917)*

Advantage Tax and Print ....G..... 601 557-5055
Quitman *(G-4455)*

American Printing Copy Center ....G..... 228 875-1398
Ocean Springs *(G-3741)*

Ashley Printing Co ....G..... 601 729-8950
Laurel *(G-2732)*

Betty Wright ....G..... 662 224-3000
Ashland *(G-59)*

Brown Line Printing Inc ....F..... 662 728-9881
Booneville *(G-322)*

Cap Co ....G..... 601 384-3939
Bude *(G-568)*

City of Biloxi ....C..... 228 435-6217
Biloxi *(G-228)*

Clayful Impressions ....G..... 601 918-0221
Brandon *(G-381)*

Darrells Screen Printing ....G..... 601 653-6924
Natchez *(G-3553)*

Dement Printing Company ....G..... 601 693-2721
Meridian *(G-3329)*

Emersons ....G..... 228 588-3952
Lucedale *(G-2994)*

First Amercn Prtg Direct Mail ....G..... 228 867-9808
Gulfport *(G-1787)*

First Amercn Prtg Direct Mail ....E..... 601 656-3636
Choctaw *(G-745)*

Fudge Inc ....F..... 601 932-4748
Flowood *(G-1363)*

Gt Screen Prtg & Promotions ....G..... 601 759-9858
Pearl *(G-4124)*

Hagen Corporation ....G..... 601 932-3138
Pearl *(G-4125)*

Hilgerson Printing ....G..... 601 684-6978
McComb *(G-3252)*

Holmes Stationary and Gifts ....G..... 601 276-2700
Summit *(G-5016)*

Jagg LLC ....G..... 228 388-1794
Biloxi *(G-254)*

Jenkins Graphics Inc ....G..... 662 890-2851
Olive Branch *(G-3855)*

JM Digital Corporation ....G..... 601 659-0599
Bay St Louis *(G-179)*

Magnolia Label Co Inc ....E..... 601 878-0951
Jackson *(G-2477)*

Mainline Printing ....G..... 662 301-8298
Senatobia *(G-4795)*

Mantachie Printing & Mktg LLC ....G..... 662 282-7625
Tupelo *(G-5183)*

Mid South Publications Inc ....G..... 662 256-8209
Amory *(G-48)*

Monogram Magic ....G..... 601 956-7117
Jackson *(G-2510)*

Nick Clark Printing and Signs ....G..... 601 607-7722
Madison *(G-3133)*

Office Huddle Small Business ....F..... 601 255-8650
Crowder *(G-1137)*

Pat Screen Printing ....G..... 662 301-8176
Senatobia *(G-4797)*

Plan House Printing ....G..... 662 407-0193
Tupelo *(G-5206)*

Plan House Printing ....G..... 601 336-6378
Hattiesburg *(G-2045)*

Printshop Plus Inc ....G..... 662 231-4790
Pontotoc *(G-4359)*

Revolution Printing & Graphics ....G..... 662 932-8176
Olive Branch *(G-3904)*

Shaughnessy & Co Inc ....G..... 228 436-4060
Biloxi *(G-279)*

Shenise Productions Inc ....G..... 601 437-3665
Port Gibson *(G-4407)*

Employee Codes: A=Over 500 employees, B=251-500
C=101-250, D=51-100, E=20-50, F=10-19, G=1-9

2019 Harris Directory of
Mississippi Manufacturers

409

PRODUCT

PRINTING: Commercial, NEC

Smith Printing & Off Sup Inc..............G...... 601 442-2441
Natchez **(G-3621)**
Standard Office Sup Prtg Inc...........E...... 601 544-5361
Hattiesburg **(G-2069)**
Star Printing Co of Amory Inc..........E...... 662 256-8424
Amory **(G-56)**
Steve B White...........................G...... 601 939-8177
Florence **(G-1334)**
Sweet Tee Screen Printing.............G...... 601 757-3435
Summit **(G-5025)**
Vicksburg Printing and Pubg Co.........G...... 601 638-2900
Vicksburg **(G-5439)**
Vizionz Unlimited LLC..................G...... 601 272-5040
Jackson **(G-2622)**
Watermark Printers LLC.................G...... 662 323-8750
Starkville **(G-4979)**
Watkins Trim Shop Inc..................G...... 601 485-5512
Meridian **(G-3417)**
Wheeler Enterprises Inc................G...... 601 799-1440
Picayune **(G-4303)**
Womack Willow..........................G...... 601 969-4120
Jackson **(G-2638)**
Yank Threads LLC.......................G...... 601 201-3934
Jackson **(G-2639)**

PRINTING: Flexographic

Quality Printing Inc...................E...... 601 353-9663
Jackson **(G-2555)**

PRINTING: Gravure, Invitations

Pink Peppermint Paper LLC..............G...... 601 898-9232
Madison **(G-3139)**

PRINTING: Gravure, Job

Rankin Printery........................G...... 662 287-4426
Corinth **(G-1112)**

PRINTING: Gravure, Rotogravure

Pcw (print Copy Webdesign LLC ....G...... 601 259-1945
Crystal Springs **(G-1152)**
Smart Source...........................G...... 601 707-1150
Ridgeland **(G-4631)**

PRINTING: Gravure, Stationery & Invitation

Celebrations Etc.......................G...... 601 268-0390
Hattiesburg **(G-1942)**
Newton Appeal..........................G...... 601 683-7810
Newton **(G-3726)**
Swirlz.................................G...... 662 791-7822
Tupelo **(G-5235)**
The Touch..............................G...... 662 378-4188
Greenville **(G-1602)**

PRINTING: Letterpress

Banner Printing Co Inc.................G...... 662 247-3373
Belzoni **(G-204)**
Barber Printing Inc....................F...... 662 841-1584
Tupelo **(G-5112)**
Coopers Intl Screen Supply LLC.........G...... 601 353-2488
Jackson **(G-2369)**
Country Printer Inc....................G...... 601 849-3637
Magee **(G-3175)**
Downs Corporation......................G...... 662 728-3237
Booneville **(G-327)**
Goodgames Inc..........................F...... 228 769-1827
Pascagoula **(G-4034)**
Iprint Inc.............................G...... 601 932-4414
Flowood **(G-1366)**
Natchez Printing Co....................G...... 601 442-3693
Natchez **(G-3596)**
Rutledge Publishing Co Inc.............G...... 662 534-2116
New Albany **(G-3694)**

PRINTING: Lithographic

506 Printing...........................G...... 662 361-4411
Macon **(G-3053)**
9r Screen Printing.....................G...... 601 303-0520
Tylertown **(G-5261)**
A-Squared Printing LLC.................G...... 601 497-0280
Pearl **(G-4102)**
Advantage Tax & Printing...............G...... 601 735-2023
Waynesboro **(G-5488)**
Advantage Tax & Printing Inc...........G...... 601 394-2898
Leakesville **(G-2875)**
Adware................................G...... 601 898-9194
Ridgeland **(G-4545)**

Aloha Printing Co......................G...... 601 483-6677
Marion **(G-3220)**
American Printing Blue PR..............G...... 601 544-7714
Hattiesburg **(G-1922)**
Atkins Office Supply Inc...............G...... 662 627-2476
Clarksdale **(G-757)**
Barbara OMeallie.......................G...... 228 255-7573
Pass Christian **(G-4077)**
Bay Printing & Design Shop LLC.........G...... 228 467-5833
Bay Saint Louis **(G-134)**
Bbs Printing...........................G...... 601 606-6980
Wiggins **(G-5572)**
Ben Sessums...........................G...... 601 856-3401
Madison **(G-3085)**
Boone Newspapers.......................E...... 601 442-9101
Natchez **(G-3537)**
Burr Creek Screen Printing.............G...... 601 297-2853
Moselle **(G-3455)**
Columbus Marble Works Inc..............E...... 662 328-1477
Columbus **(G-950)**
Commonwealth Publishing Inc............C...... 662 453-5312
Greenwood **(G-1618)**
Competitive Printing...................G...... 228 863-4001
Gulfport **(G-1764)**
Copy Write Printing Inc................G...... 601 736-2679
Columbia **(G-891)**
Creative Hands Printing Svcs...........G...... 601 631-1262
Vicksburg **(G-5358)**
Custom Printing........................G...... 662 227-9511
Grenada **(G-1674)**
Dallas Printing Inc....................E...... 601 968-9354
Richland **(G-4511)**
Delta-Democrat Pubg Co Inc.............D...... 662 335-1155
Greenville **(G-1551)**
Design Print & Advertise By Pj.........G...... 662 299-1148
Lexington **(G-2900)**
Diaz Brothers Printing.................G...... 601 247-0240
Diamondhead **(G-1191)**
Dittos Print & Copy Shop...............D...... 662 324-3838
Starkville **(G-4941)**
Dla Document Services..................G...... 662 434-7303
Columbus **(G-963)**
Dla Document Services..................G...... 228 377-2612
Biloxi **(G-237)**
Dogpound Printing LLC..................G...... 662 323-7425
Starkville **(G-4943)**
Dzt Photography and Event Prtg.........G...... 228 334-5253
Ocean Springs **(G-3754)**
Eclipse Screen Prints..................G...... 901 626-9029
Byhalia **(G-584)**
Eighteen-Seventeen Prtg LLC............G...... 601 300-0506
Summit **(G-5013)**
Elite Screen Printing..................F...... 601 450-1261
Hattiesburg **(G-1960)**
Fast Dog Print Co......................G...... 662 549-4450
Columbus **(G-974)**
Final Touch Productions................G...... 601 750-3940
Ridgeland **(G-4581)**
Franklin Printers Inc..................F...... 601 982-9383
Jackson **(G-2413)**
Gannett Co Inc.........................B...... 601 961-7000
Jackson **(G-2421)**
Gulf Publishing Company Inc............C...... 228 896-2100
Gulfport **(G-1801)**
Hall S Customized Printing.............G...... 601 261-2440
Hattiesburg **(G-1980)**
Harden Enterprises Inc.................F...... 662 841-9292
Tupelo **(G-5152)**
Hatchett Perfection Prints LLC.........G...... 662 260-6244
Southaven **(G-4876)**
Havard Printing Co.....................G...... 662 781-2613
Horn Lake **(G-2202)**
Hilgerson Printing.....................G...... 601 684-6978
McComb **(G-3252)**
Holmes Stationary and Gifts............G...... 601 276-2700
Summit **(G-5016)**
Inky Printing LLC......................G...... 504 858-6461
Ocean Springs **(G-3768)**
J&H Printing Inc.......................G...... 662 456-3654
Houston **(G-2247)**
J&J Screen Printing....................G...... 662 342-6131
Southaven **(G-4881)**
Jeff Busby.............................G...... 601 924-7979
Clinton **(G-827)**
Jonathan Sanford DBA...................G...... 601 297-2754
Collins **(G-855)**
K&A Customize Printing LLC.............G...... 225 326-9054
Madison **(G-3114)**
Kennith Humphrey - Paintings &.........G...... 601 218-2786
Vicksburg **(G-5385)**

Kingdom Life Printing..................G...... 601 398-4606
Jackson **(G-2465)**
Ksquared Inc...........................F...... 601 956-2951
Madison **(G-3116)**
Linda F Wilson.........................G...... 662 299-9656
Greenwood **(G-1634)**
Local Native Creative + Print..........G...... 662 401-4767
Baldwyn **(G-84)**
M & M Printing Co......................G...... 601 798-4316
Picayune **(G-4277)**
MADE Printing & Designin...............G...... 601 572-6967
Jackson **(G-2476)**
Magnificent Prints LLC.................G...... 662 469-5689
Horn Lake **(G-2206)**
Magnolia Printing and Signs............G...... 601 922-5076
Jackson **(G-2478)**
Martini Monday Inc.....................G...... 228 229-4872
Diberville **(G-1208)**
Mason Printing.........................G...... 662 563-3709
Batesville **(G-114)**
Media Solutions........................G...... 601 351-9303
Jackson **(G-2486)**
Mid South Publications Inc.............G...... 662 256-8209
Amory **(G-48)**
Minuteman Press International...........G...... 662 349-6675
Horn Lake **(G-2207)**
Mississippi Muddy Prints LLC...........G...... 601 757-2990
Brookhaven **(G-518)**
Ms Band of Choctaw Indians Db..........F...... 601 656-3636
Choctaw **(G-748)**
Newspaper Holding Inc..................D...... 601 693-1551
Meridian **(G-3377)**
Oce Corporate Printing Div.............G...... 228 863-0458
Gulfport **(G-1840)**
Panther Printing LLC...................G...... 601 425-4414
Laurel **(G-2816)**
Pat The Cat Prints.....................G...... 662 397-1038
Tupelo **(G-5199)**
Paw Print Visuals LLC..................G...... 662 332-2359
Greenville **(G-1588)**
Pinnacle Printing and Copying..........G...... 601 944-1470
Flowood **(G-1387)**
Piranha Business Cards LLC.............F...... 800 281-1916
Madison **(G-3140)**
Pollchaps Custom Screen Prtg...........G...... 769 218-0824
Brandon **(G-436)**
Presto Printing Inc....................G...... 228 678-9085
Gulfport **(G-1853)**
Print Brokers Inc......................G...... 662 231-2556
Booneville **(G-343)**
Print Pros LLC.........................G...... 662 327-3222
Columbus **(G-1016)**
Print Shed.............................G...... 228 206-0077
Gulfport **(G-1854)**
Print Shop.............................G...... 662 453-8497
Greenwood **(G-1647)**
Print Shop.............................G...... 601 638-0962
Vicksburg **(G-5408)**
Print Zone.............................G...... 601 799-3113
Carriere **(G-699)**
Printing Alley Ltd.....................G...... 601 371-1243
Terry **(G-5075)**
Printing On Time Screen................G...... 601 707-7207
Ridgeland **(G-4620)**
Proforma Southprint....................G...... 901 734-2290
Hernando **(G-2149)**
Prographics Inc........................G...... 662 329-3341
Columbus **(G-1017)**
Queens Printing LLC....................G...... 228 234-5693
Gautier **(G-1502)**
Quitman County Democrat................G...... 662 326-2181
Marks **(G-3222)**
R & B Specialty Printing LLC...........G...... 662 260-2145
Tupelo **(G-5212)**
Rankin Printery........................G...... 662 287-4426
Corinth **(G-1112)**
Reed S Printing Inc....................G...... 662 287-0311
Corinth **(G-1114)**
Reliable 2 Screen Printing.............G...... 662 910-8272
Tunica **(G-5102)**
Screenco Printing LLC..................G...... 601 507-1986
Ridgeland **(G-4628)**
Sharones Innovative Prtg LLC...........G...... 601 877-3727
Lorman **(G-2962)**
Shaughnessy & Co Inc...................G...... 228 436-4060
Biloxi **(G-279)**
Shilpam Corp...........................F...... 601 933-9550
Pearl **(G-4144)**
Sign Shop..............................G...... 662 328-7933
Columbus **(G-1025)**

PRODUCT SECTION

PROFESSIONAL INSTRUMENT REPAIR SVCS

Sir Speedy Printing Center ....G..... 601 981-3045
Jackson (G-2583)

Smith Printing & Off Sup Inc.................G..... 601 442-2441
Natchez (G-3621)

Sonnyboys Garment Printing LLC ....G..... 601 415-2250
Jackson (G-2587)

Southern Print Company.....................G..... 601 898-8796
Madison (G-3150)

Southern Prtg & Silk Screening ....F..... 228 452-7309
Pass Christian (G-4095)

Southwest Publishers Inc ....E..... 601 833-6961
Brookhaven (G-538)

Standard Office Sup Prtg Inc ....E..... 601 544-5361
Hattiesburg (G-2069)

Still Blessed Prints ....G..... 601 810-8285
Brookhaven (G-539)

Sunset Screen Printing ....G..... 601 297-2754
Collins (G-863)

Swain Printing & Signs ....G..... 662 773-7584
Louisville (G-2983)

Swatprint Screen Printing ....G..... 662 862-3004
Fulton (G-1478)

T Enterprises Inc ....F..... 601 487-1100
Jackson (G-2603)

T-N-T Printing ....G..... 601 630-9553
Vicksburg (G-5426)

Theleg5813 Photos & Prints ....G..... 601 927-1360
Brandon (G-468)

Tikal Prints LLC ....G..... 601 954-0972
Jackson (G-2607)

Tiny Prints 3d Imaging LLC ....G..... 866 846-9733
Picayune (G-4301)

Trader Printing ....G..... 662 767-9411
Shannon (G-4820)

Trens Screen Printing ....G..... 662 578-9074
Batesville (G-130)

Tupelo Screen Printing LLC ....G..... 662 523-0092
Tupelo (G-5247)

Tyler Printing and Cmpt Svc ....G..... 601 279-6105
Vicksburg (G-5430)

Unik Ink Cstm Screen Prtg Inc ....G..... 601 259-1004
Madison (G-3163)

Vibrant Screen Printing ....G..... 601 291-1296
Jackson (G-2621)

Wards Custom Screen Prin ....G..... 601 384-4635
Meadville (G-3278)

Watkins Trim Shop Inc ....G..... 601 485-5512
Meridian (G-3417)

Where We Print Shirts LLC ....G..... 601 348-5754
Madison (G-3169)

Womack Willow ....G..... 601 969-4120
Jackson (G-2638)

Yellow Dog Printing Co LLC ....G..... 601 776-6853
Quitman (G-4473)

PRINTING: Offset

A2z Printing Inc ....F..... 601 487-1100
Jackson (G-2317)

Acme Printing Company Inc ....F..... 601 856-7766
Madison (G-3075)

Allmond Printing Company Inc ....G..... 662 369-4848
Aberdeen (G-8)

Alpha Printing Inc ....G..... 601 371-2611
Jackson (G-2324)

American Printing and Converti ....G..... 601 222-0555
Tylertown (G-5262)

American Printing Copy Center............G..... 228 875-1398
Ocean Springs (G-3741)

Arrow Printers Inc ....F..... 601 924-1192
Clinton (G-813)

Bankingformscom Inc ....G..... 601 445-2245
Natchez (G-3523)

Bourne Brothers Prtg Co Inc ....F..... 601 582-1808
Hattiesburg (G-1938)

Boyanton Printing Inc.........................G..... 601 939-6725
Flowood (G-1348)

Budget Printing Company....................G..... 601 693-6003
Meridian (G-3313)

Bynum Printing ....G..... 601 735-5269
Waynesboro (G-5494)

C and P Printing Company Inc ....G..... 662 327-9742
Columbus (G-944)

Callahans Quick Print Inc ....G..... 662 234-8060
Oxford (G-3944)

Charleston Printing.............................G..... 662 647-2291
Charleston (G-734)

Clays Print Shop Inc ....G..... 228 868-8244
Gulfport (G-1753)

Coast Printing Company ....G..... 228 863-1018
Gulfport (G-1757)

Coopers Intl Screen Supply LLC..........G..... 601 353-2488
Jackson (G-2369)

Copy Cats Printing Inc ....F..... 601 582-3019
Hattiesburg (G-1951)

Country Printer Inc ....G..... 601 849-3637
Magee (G-3175)

Dixie Print ....G..... 601 469-3350
Forest (G-1414)

First Amercn Prtg Direct Mail ....G..... 228 867-9808
Gulfport (G-1787)

Fletcher Printing & Office Sup ....G..... 662 487-3200
Sardis (G-4739)

Gem Publications Inc ....G..... 601 879-3666
Flora (G-1307)

Goodgames Inc ....F..... 228 769-1827
Pascagoula (G-4034)

Hagen Corporation ....G..... 601 932-3138
Pearl (G-4125)

Harden Enterprises Inc ....G..... 662 841-9292
Tupelo (G-5151)

Hederman Brothers LLC ....D..... 601 853-7300
Madison (G-3105)

Impact Printing & Design ....G..... 601 764-9461
Bay Springs (G-165)

Impressions Inc ....G..... 601 477-9608
Ellisville (G-1259)

Jenkins Graphics Inc ....G..... 662 890-2851
Olive Branch (G-3855)

Knight-Abbey Coml Prtrs Inc ....D..... 228 702-3231
Biloxi (G-257)

Leonard Printing Company ....G..... 601 833-3912
Brookhaven (G-511)

Lewis Yager Melbaleen J ....G..... 228 762-3152
Pascagoula (G-4046)

Luke Printing Co Inc ....G..... 601 693-1144
Meridian (G-3361)

M & M Printing LLC ....G..... 601 798-4316
Picayune (G-4276)

Mackay Enterprises LLC ....G..... 662 328-8469
Columbus (G-995)

Magnolia Printing Co ....G..... 228 864-4401
Gulfport (G-1824)

McComb Printing Inc ....F..... 601 684-9841
McComb (G-3259)

Mississippi Rainbow Printing ....G..... 601 853-9513
Ridgeland (G-4606)

Murray Printing ....G..... 601 446-6558
Natchez (G-3593)

Natchez Printing Co ....G..... 601 442-3693
Natchez (G-3596)

Nelsons Printing Inc ....G..... 601 683-6651
Newton (G-3725)

Nick Strcklnds Quick Print Inc.............F..... 601 353-8672
Ridgeland (G-4611)

Nick Strcklnds Quick Print Inc.............E..... 601 898-1717
Jackson (G-2521)

Nick Strcklnds Quick Print Inc.............G..... 601 939-2781
Pearl (G-4134)

Nick Strcklnds Quick Print Inc.............G..... 601 355-8195
Ridgeland (G-4612)

Northtowne Printers Inc ....G..... 601 713-3200
Jackson (G-2523)

Noyes Printing & Rbr Stamp Co ....G..... 662 332-5256
Greenville (G-1583)

Overnight Printing Service ....G..... 662 895-9262
Olive Branch (G-3892)

P D Q Printing Inc ....G..... 228 392-4888
Biloxi (G-271)

Park Avenue Printing ....G..... 601 876-9095
Tylertown (G-5279)

Pavco Industries Inc ....D..... 228 762-3959
Pascagoula (G-4061)

Premiere Printing ....G..... 662 488-9591
Pontotoc (G-4358)

Print Shop Inc ....G..... 601 428-4602
Laurel (G-2828)

Printers Inc ....G..... 601 792-8493
Prentiss (G-4424)

Printing Place ....G..... 601 885-8327
Utica (G-5311)

Professional Graphics Inc ....G..... 601 924-9116
Clinton (G-834)

Quick Prints ....G..... 601 485-3278
Meridian (G-3390)

Rhino Graphics ....G..... 601 445-8777
Natchez (G-3613)

Rutledge Publishing Co Inc ....G..... 662 534-2116
New Albany (G-3694)

Shabazz Printing ....G..... 601 786-9788
Fayette (G-1301)

Sorg Printing LLC ....G..... 228 392-3299
Diberville (G-1214)

South Center Printing ....G..... 662 252-2793
Holly Springs (G-2191)

Southern Systems & Service Co ....G..... 601 264-4713
Hattiesburg (G-2064)

Sparks Printing & Graphics ....G..... 662 842-4481
Tupelo (G-5230)

Speedy Printing..................................G..... 228 466-5766
Waveland (G-5485)

Stephens Printing LLC ....G..... 601 845-7708
Florence (G-1333)

Stone Printing Inc ....G..... 601 928-7050
Wiggins (G-5590)

Turner Group LLC ....G..... 601 394-5070
Leakesville (G-2880)

United Print Services LLC ....G..... 662 287-1090
Corinth (G-1125)

Vicksburg Newsmedia LLC ....G..... 601 636-4545
Vicksburg (G-5437)

W T Leggett Inc ....G..... 601 544-2704
Hattiesburg (G-2081)

Welch Printing ....G..... 662 283-3692
Winona (G-5610)

Wolverton Enterprises Inc ....F..... 601 355-9543
Jackson (G-2637)

Ziprint Inc ....G..... 662 226-6864
Grenada (G-1713)

PRINTING: Pamphlets

Barber Printing Inc.............................F..... 662 841-1584
Tupelo (G-5112)

PRINTING: Rotary Photogravure

Standard Office Sup Prtg Inc ....E..... 601 544-5361
Hattiesburg (G-2069)

PRINTING: Screen, Broadwoven Fabrics, Cotton

Global Screen Printing LLC ....G..... 601 919-2345
Brandon (G-399)

Harris Custom Ink LLC ....E..... 662 338-4242
Olive Branch (G-3844)

University Screen Print Inc ....F..... 662 324-8277
Starkville (G-4978)

PRINTING: Screen, Fabric

Allistons ....G..... 228 832-8683
Gulfport (G-1723)

Ch Custom Designs & Prints LLC.........G..... 601 408-5068
Hattiesburg (G-1943)

Fashions Incorporated Jackson ....G..... 601 948-1119
Jackson (G-2406)

Gator Grafix Inc ....G..... 601 376-9004
Jackson (G-2423)

Global Screen Printing LLC ....G..... 601 919-2345
Brandon (G-399)

Graphic Arts Productions Inc ....G..... 662 494-2549
West Point (G-5544)

PRINTING: Screen, Manmade Fiber & Silk, Broadwoven Fabric

Harris Custom Ink LLC ....E..... 662 338-4242
Olive Branch (G-3844)

PRINTING: Thermography

Franklin Printers Inc ....F..... 601 982-9383
Jackson (G-2413)

PROFESSIONAL EQPT & SPLYS, WHOLESALE: Optical Goods

Ferson LLC ....F..... 228 875-8146
Ocean Springs (G-3757)

I Care Optical Inc ....G..... 228 864-4397
Gulfport (G-1811)

Superior Optical Labs Inc ....E..... 228 875-3796
Ocean Springs (G-3790)

PROFESSIONAL INSTRUMENT REPAIR SVCS

Baldwyn Truck & Trailer Repair............G..... 662 365-7888
Baldwyn (G-73)

Employee Codes: A=Over 500 employees, B=251-500
C=101-250, D=51-100, E=20-50, F=10-19, G=1-9

2019 Harris Directory of
Mississippi Manufacturers

PRODUCT

PROPELLERS: Boat & Ship, Cast

Nichols Propeller Company.................E....... 662 378-2000
Greenville *(G-1580)*

PROPELLERS: Boat & Ship, Machined

N Rolls-Ryce Amer Holdings Inc...........G....... 228 762-0728
Pascagoula *(G-4054)*
Rolls-Royce Marine North Amer............D....... 228 762-0728
Pascagoula *(G-4064)*

PROTECTION EQPT: Lightning

A-Z Lightning Protection LLC...............G....... 662 890-7041
Byhalia *(G-576)*

PUBLISHERS: Book

Books Plus LLC.................................G....... 228 209-5021
Biloxi *(G-223)*
Elizabeth Clayton..............................G....... 601 371-1172
Terry *(G-5066)*
Inner Sanctuary Inc............................G....... 662 489-6772
Pontotoc *(G-4337)*
Liberations Publishing LLC...................G....... 662 605-0382
West Point *(G-5550)*
Nautilus Publishing Company...............G....... 662 513-0159
Oxford *(G-3975)*
Pcp P Coast.....................................G....... 228 202-7872
Biloxi *(G-272)*
Pioneer Publishing Co..........................G....... 662 237-6010
Carrollton *(G-702)*
Raven Happy Hour LLC.........................G....... 662 607-6604
Oxford *(G-3998)*
Twister LLC.......................................G....... 601 371-7276
Madison *(G-3162)*
University Press Mississippi................E....... 601 432-6205
Jackson *(G-2619)*
Watersprings Media House...................G....... 662 812-1568
Olive Branch *(G-3923)*

PUBLISHERS: Books, No Printing

Lagniappe Books LLC..........................G....... 769 242-8104
Picayune *(G-4275)*
M & W Publishing Co LLC....................G....... 662 843-1358
Boyle *(G-350)*
My Songs of Life.................................G....... 901 303-8687
Olive Branch *(G-3882)*
Quail Ridge Press Inc..........................G....... 601 825-2063
Brandon *(G-442)*
Wilkinson County Museum...................G....... 601 888-7151
Woodville *(G-5619)*
World Evangelism...............................G....... 662 283-1192
Winona *(G-5612)*

PUBLISHERS: Comic Books, No Printing

Novia Cmmnications/ Novia Pubg.........G....... 601 985-9502
Jackson *(G-2525)*

PUBLISHERS: Guides

Jessica Williams.................................G....... 601 738-0090
Rolling Fork *(G-4681)*

PUBLISHERS: Magazines, No Printing

Bbq World Magazine............................F....... 228 363-2716
Long Beach *(G-2926)*
Downhome Publications Inc.................F....... 601 982-8418
Jackson *(G-2390)*
Goat Rancher.....................................G....... 662 562-9529
Sarah *(G-4734)*
Legend Publishing...............................G....... 662 844-2602
Tupelo *(G-5174)*
Midsouth Media Group........................F....... 662 890-3359
Olive Branch *(G-3878)*
Mississippi Valley Publishing...............F....... 601 853-1861
Ridgeland *(G-4607)*
Nautilus Publishing Company..............G....... 662 513-0159
Oxford *(G-3975)*
Parents and Kids Magazine..................G....... 601 366-0901
Jackson *(G-2534)*
Premier Publishing Inc........................G....... 601 957-1050
Flowood *(G-1389)*
Socrates Garrett Entps Inc...................F....... 601 896-0084
Jackson *(G-2585)*
Stockman Grass Farmer......................F....... 601 853-1861
Ridgeland *(G-4635)*
Wolf River Press.................................G....... 601 372-2679
Jackson *(G-2636)*
Wrestling USA Magazine Inc................G....... 406 549-4448
Pass Christian *(G-4099)*

PUBLISHERS: Miscellaneous

500 Degreez Entrnt LLC Not LLC.........G....... 678 948-8710
Mantachie *(G-3197)*
Abacus Publishing Co..........................G....... 601 684-0001
McComb *(G-3243)*
Action Success Press..........................G....... 601 824-7775
Brandon *(G-357)*
Ainz Publishing Company.....................G....... 662 728-6131
Booneville *(G-316)*
Beaty Street Publishing........................G....... 954 513-9441
Hattiesburg *(G-1926)*
Bijoubel LLC......................................G....... 228 344-3393
Bay Saint Louis *(G-137)*
Bits & PCs Press Inc...........................G....... 662 563-8661
Batesville *(G-99)*
Blake Publishing Inc............................G....... 601 992-6220
Flowood *(G-1347)*
Book Mart Corporation........................E....... 662 323-2844
Starkville *(G-4930)*
Book Publisher LLC.............................G....... 662 838-2633
Byhalia *(G-581)*
Bookpro Publishing Company...............G....... 769 208-6806
Natchez *(G-3536)*
Botr Press LLC...................................G....... 708 431-9668
Poplarville *(G-4378)*
Brew Barr LLC...................................G....... 601 218-7708
Jackson *(G-2343)*
Campbell Creek Publishing LLC............G....... 601 824-5932
Braxton *(G-476)*
Canton High Press Box........................G....... 601 859-4315
Canton *(G-653)*
Carney Publications LLC......................G....... 601 427-5694
Monticello *(G-3429)*
Carol Vincent & Associates..................G....... 662 624-8406
Clarksdale *(G-760)*
Catawomper Press LLC........................G....... 662 832-3897
Oxford *(G-3945)*
Chesser Publishing LLC.......................G....... 228 588-1111
Hurley *(G-2259)*
Cloud 12 Publishing.............................G....... 228 990-0434
Gautier *(G-1491)*
Country Kids Publishing LLC................G....... 662 509-0427
Pontotoc *(G-4326)*
Crooked Letter Publishing LLC.............G....... 228 334-4575
Gulfport *(G-1766)*
Cruise Street Press LLC......................G....... 601 720-4848
Pickens *(G-4306)*
Deals Xpress Lube..............................G....... 662 281-4417
Oxford *(G-3950)*
Deep Blue Press LLC..........................G....... 228 604-4643
Gulfport *(G-1769)*
Della West Publishing LLC...................G....... 601 618-8429
Vicksburg *(G-5360)*
Developing Resources For Educa.........G....... 601 933-9199
Jackson *(G-2644)*
Dogwood Press..................................G....... 601 919-3656
Brandon *(G-390)*
Dragon Breath Press LLC....................G....... 601 607-7007
Ridgeland *(G-4574)*
Elizabeth Newcomb.............................G....... 662 596-1536
Rienzi *(G-4649)*
Every Word Press LLC........................G....... 601 209-1379
Jackson *(G-2405)*
Express Lane Inc................................G....... 601 483-8872
Meridian *(G-3335)*
Fast Track Planners LLC.....................G....... 601 528-0558
Perkinston *(G-4175)*
Fishbowl International Inc...................G....... 601 384-0219
Roxie *(G-4689)*
Fishyrhythms Publishing LLC...............G....... 601 573-6771
Ridgeland *(G-4582)*
Freed Peoples Press LLC....................G....... 313 717-7819
Holly Springs *(G-2176)*
Fresh Press Creative LLC....................G....... 601 376-9449
Jackson *(G-2415)*
G Mark Lafrancis................................G....... 601 442-0980
Natchez *(G-3562)*
Gemlight Publishing LLC.....................G....... 601 509-1002
Gulfport *(G-1792)*
Grasslawn Publishing LLC...................G....... 228 896-5532
Gulfport *(G-1795)*
Great American Publishers...................G....... 601 854-5956
Lena *(G-2895)*
Gtp Publishing Group..........................G....... 228 348-2646
Biloxi *(G-248)*
Halftone Press LLC............................G....... 662 251-5036
Columbus *(G-983)*
Halo Southern Publishing LLC..............G....... 662 299-2999
Cleveland *(G-794)*
Heritage Press Pblications LLC............G....... 601 737-2086
Collinsville *(G-870)*
Hoopsnake Press -.............................G....... 662 260-5133
Tupelo *(G-5158)*
Hubbard Publishing LLC......................G....... 662 638-3821
Oxford *(G-3957)*
Informa Media Inc..............................G....... 662 624-8503
Clarksdale *(G-769)*
Jackson Publishing.............................G....... 662 349-2866
Southaven *(G-4882)*
Kanes Publishing Company LLC............G....... 601 345-5153
Forest *(G-1419)*
Kids Express.....................................G....... 601 352-3882
Jackson *(G-2464)*
Kings Judah Publishing Co LLC............G....... 228 342-3648
Perkinston *(G-4178)*
Lifestory Publishing............................G....... 601 594-0018
Jackson *(G-2469)*
Lightning Bloom Press LLC..................G....... 662 638-3611
Oxford *(G-3965)*
Long-Delayed Publishing LLC...............G....... 662 202-6229
Oxford *(G-3967)*
Low Pro Publishing.............................G....... 601 372-1875
Jackson *(G-2472)*
M P Johnson Publishing LLC................G....... 662 270-5544
Southaven *(G-4886)*
M&M Book Publishing Co.....................G....... 601 442-0980
Natchez *(G-3581)*
Magnetic Arrow LLC...........................G....... 601 653-2932
Biloxi *(G-264)*
Malius Press LLC...............................G....... 662 281-0955
Oxford *(G-3969)*
Mary Margaret Andrews.......................G....... 901 233-5463
Oxford *(G-3971)*
McKenzie/Lee Publishing LLC...............G....... 769 216-8049
Florence *(G-1328)*
Milk & Honey Prtg Press LLC...............G....... 662 739-4949
Kosciusko *(G-2701)*
Miracleworks Press.............................G....... 601 878-6686
Terry *(G-5073)*
Mobile One Lube Express Plus.............G....... 601 631-8000
Vicksburg *(G-5400)*
Moss Point Express............................G....... 228 475-4370
Moss Point *(G-3488)*
Ms Publishing Group LLC....................G....... 662 323-8800
West Point *(G-5555)*
Mueller Press Company Inc..................G....... 901 753-3200
Jackson *(G-2658)*
Newks Express Cafe of H....................G....... 601 602-0189
Hattiesburg *(G-2036)*
Old Blue Publishing LLC......................G....... 601 957-2530
Jackson *(G-2528)*
One Grower Publishing........................G....... 901 767-4020
Olive Branch *(G-3889)*
Outback Express Mississippi................G....... 662 378-8000
Greenville *(G-1586)*
Oxford Eagle Inc................................E....... 662 234-2222
Oxford *(G-3986)*
P Press..G....... 662 638-3571
Oxford *(G-3992)*
Pinion Prod.......................................G....... 662 891-0930
Blue Springs *(G-298)*
Planhouse Publications Inc..................G....... 601 825-1187
Flowood *(G-1388)*
Platinum Publishing Inc.......................G....... 228 219-1020
Biloxi *(G-273)*
Pmq Inc...F....... 662 234-5481
Oxford *(G-3996)*
Press 4 U..G....... 901 361-0256
Olive Branch *(G-3901)*
Print Press.......................................G....... 601 342-2645
Laurel *(G-2827)*
Prs..G....... 601 941-5104
Brandon *(G-440)*
Rare Studios Publishing......................G....... 770 316-0683
Roxie *(G-4693)*
Rayburn Publishing LLC......................G....... 662 232-8900
Oxford *(G-3999)*
Real Meal Publishing LLC....................G....... 601 697-7199
Lena *(G-2896)*
Red Star Digital Publishing..................G....... 228 223-7638
Gulfport *(G-1860)*
Rlt Publishing LLC.............................G....... 404 956-8344
Jackson *(G-2567)*
Roadster Dream Publishing LLC............G....... 601 853-4443
Madison *(G-3144)*
Ruby Press LLC.................................G....... 662 832-2255
Oxford *(G-4001)*

412 2019 Harris Directory of Mississippi Manufacturers (G-0000) Company's Geographic Section entry number

PRODUCT SECTION

PUBLISHING & PRINTING: Newspapers

Rustic Inn Publications Inc ....G...... 856 983-4288
Corinth *(G-1117)*

Sharp Cypress Inc ....G...... 601 249-2936
McComb *(G-3266)*

Snapshot Publishing LLC ....G...... 601 624-8845
Flowood *(G-1398)*

Spider Blue Press LLC ....G...... 601 770-0846
Lucedale *(G-3018)*

Stacy Robinson ....G...... 662 289-4640
Kosciusko *(G-2714)*

Thibideau Enterprises LLC ....G...... 662 471-3168
Olive Branch *(G-3917)*

Thugrelatedpublishing ....G...... 228 326-2476
Gulfport *(G-1883)*

Transforming Lives Pubg LLC ....G...... 601 434-6583
Ellisville *(G-1273)*

Trooper Publications ....G...... 228 392-1442
Diberville *(G-1218)*

Unified Buddist Church Inc ....G...... 662 578-2077
Batesville *(G-132)*

West Express ....G...... 601 321-8088
Jackson *(G-2629)*

West Jones Press Box ....G...... 601 729-2216
Laurel *(G-2873)*

Westminster Software ....G...... 601 214-5028
Brandon *(G-475)*

Who Is Sed Publishing LLC ....G...... 601 634-8939
Vicksburg *(G-5444)*

Wilson Branch Publishing LLC ....G...... 601 656-2718
Philadelphia *(G-4250)*

Word Alive ....G...... 601 307-3639
Wiggins *(G-5594)*

PUBLISHERS: Music Book

Exquisite Enterprise Pubg LLC ....G...... 708 362-4583
Durant *(G-1225)*

Grady Shady Music Inc ....G...... 601 278-3087
Canton *(G-659)*

PUBLISHERS: Music Book & Sheet Music

Exquisite Reads Publications ....G...... 662 400-0743
Macon *(G-3060)*

Michael A Dent ....G...... 601 543-0157
Hattiesburg *(G-2023)*

PUBLISHERS: Newsletter

Informa Business Media Inc ....E...... 662 624-8503
Clarksdale *(G-768)*

PUBLISHERS: Newspaper

24 Hour News Line ....G...... 662 241-5000
Columbus *(G-929)*

Amory Advertiser ....G...... 662 256-5647
Amory *(G-35)*

Beach Blvd Mag ....G...... 228 896-2499
Gulfport *(G-1737)*

Belmont Tshmngo Jrnl Incjurnal ....G...... 662 454-7196
Belmont *(G-195)*

Black Panther Newspaper ....G...... 877 388-6247
Hattiesburg *(G-1934)*

Bluff City Post Newspaper ....G...... 601 446-5218
Natchez *(G-3533)*

Campbell Newspapers LLC ....G...... 423 754-0312
Biloxi *(G-224)*

Chancellors Business Sup Inc ....F...... 601 426-6396
Laurel *(G-2753)*

Chronicle ....G...... 601 651-2000
Laurel *(G-2754)*

Coopwood Communications Inc ....F...... 662 843-2700
Cleveland *(G-790)*

George Nosser Jr ....G...... 601 446-7998
Natchez *(G-3563)*

Gin Creek Publishing ....G...... 601 649-9388
Laurel *(G-2770)*

Horizon Publications Inc ....G...... 662 494-1422
West Point *(G-5546)*

Lamar County News Inc ....G...... 601 268-2331
Hattiesburg *(G-2014)*

Natchez Newspapers Inc ....G...... 601 442-9101
Natchez *(G-3595)*

Newspaper Holding Inc ....G...... 601 795-2247
Poplarville *(G-4385)*

Ocean Springs Gazette ....G...... 228 875-1241
Ocean Springs *(G-3774)*

Pigeon Roost News ....G...... 662 838-4844
Holly Springs *(G-2188)*

Play Coast ....G...... 228 369-4582
Ocean Springs *(G-3776)*

Quitman County Democrat ....G...... 662 326-2181
Marks *(G-3222)*

Spirit Enterprises ....G...... 662 236-2667
Oxford *(G-4006)*

The Post ....G...... 601 785-4333
Taylorsville *(G-5060)*

Valley Publishing Inc ....G...... 662 473-1473
Water Valley *(G-5475)*

Vicksburg Newsmedia LLC ....G...... 601 636-4545
Vicksburg *(G-5437)*

Weekly Leader ....G...... 601 825-5133
Brandon *(G-474)*

Wrjw 1320 AM ....F...... 601 798-4835
Picayune *(G-4305)*

PUBLISHERS: Newspapers, No Printing

Buckley Newspapers Inc ....D...... 601 764-3104
Bay Springs *(G-159)*

Calhoun County Journal ....G...... 662 983-2570
Bruce *(G-560)*

Carthaginian Inc ....F...... 601 267-4501
Carthage *(G-709)*

Copiah County Courier Inc ....F...... 601 894-3141
Hazlehurst *(G-2093)*

Delta Press Publishing Co Inc ....F...... 662 627-2201
Clarksdale *(G-766)*

Democrat ....F...... 662 562-4414
Senatobia *(G-4792)*

Gannett Co Inc ....B...... 601 961-7000
Jackson *(G-2421)*

Lake Messenger ....G...... 601 775-3857
Lake *(G-2723)*

Louisville Publishing Inc ....E...... 662 773-6241
Louisville *(G-2974)*

Marion Publishing Co Inc ....F...... 601 736-2611
Columbia *(G-905)*

Mississippi Catholic ....G...... 601 969-3581
Jackson *(G-2499)*

Nautilus Publishing Company ....G...... 662 513-0159
Oxford *(G-3975)*

Neshoba Democrat Publishing Co ....F...... 601 656-4000
Philadelphia *(G-4228)*

News Commercial ....F...... 601 765-8275
Collins *(G-857)*

Newspaper Holding Inc ....D...... 601 693-1551
Meridian *(G-3377)*

Oxford Eagle Inc ....E...... 662 234-2222
Oxford *(G-3986)*

Panolian ....G...... 662 563-4591
Batesville *(G-116)*

Prentiss Publishers Inc ....G...... 601 792-4221
Prentiss *(G-4423)*

Rcn Corporation ....F...... 601 825-8333
Brandon *(G-444)*

South Reporter Inc ....F...... 662 252-4261
Holly Springs *(G-2192)*

Southern Sintinel Inc ....F...... 662 837-8111
Ripley *(G-4672)*

Sunland Publishing Co Inc ....F...... 601 957-1122
Jackson *(G-2600)*

Tishomingo County News Inc ....F...... 662 423-2211
Iuka *(G-2310)*

Tupelo Daily Journal News Bur ....G...... 601 364-1000
Jackson *(G-2614)*

Turner Group LLC ....G...... 601 394-5070
Leakesville *(G-2880)*

PUBLISHERS: Periodicals, Magazines

Associated Gen Contrs of Miss ....G...... 601 981-1144
Jackson *(G-2334)*

Breaktime Vending Inc ....G...... 601 749-8424
Picayune *(G-4257)*

Homeland Inc ....G...... 662 728-7799
Booneville *(G-329)*

Invitation Oxford Magazine ....F...... 662 701-8365
Oxford *(G-3961)*

Mississippi Baptist Paper ....G...... 601 426-3293
Laurel *(G-2804)*

Mississippi State Phrm Assn ....G...... 601 981-0416
Jackson *(G-2506)*

Oxford Eagle Inc ....E...... 662 234-2222
Oxford *(G-3986)*

Pmq Inc ....F...... 662 234-5481
Oxford *(G-3995)*

Regional Sites Inc ....G...... 662 643-4595
Glen *(G-1508)*

Rowell Publishing ....G...... 601 981-0933
Brandon *(G-448)*

University of Mississippi ....G...... 662 915-5742
University *(G-5306)*

PUBLISHERS: Periodicals, No Printing

Metro Christian Living ....G...... 601 790-9076
Jackson *(G-2489)*

Union Directories ....F...... 662 620-6366
Tupelo *(G-5248)*

PUBLISHERS: Telephone & Other Directory

Diamondhead Advertiser ....G...... 228 263-4377
Waveland *(G-5480)*

Real Yellow Pages ....G...... 662 746-4958
Tinsley *(G-5080)*

PUBLISHERS: Trade journals, No Printing

RR Donnelley & Sons Company ....B...... 662 562-5252
Senatobia *(G-4802)*

Tupelo Daily Journal News Bur ....G...... 601 364-1000
Jackson *(G-2614)*

PUBLISHING & BROADCASTING: Internet Only

Mobile Communications LLC ....G...... 662 570-4858
Itta Bena *(G-2282)*

Purpose Designs LLC ....G...... 601 480-2197
Pachuta *(G-4015)*

Rock or Not LLC ....G...... 662 719-9120
Brandon *(G-447)*

Uswebworx LLC ....G...... 601 813-8927
Madison *(G-3164)*

PUBLISHING & PRINTING: Art Copy

Giclee Fine Arts ....G...... 228 586-2693
Kiln *(G-2679)*

PUBLISHING & PRINTING: Book Clubs

Pevey Publishing LLC ....G...... 601 503-7205
Brandon *(G-434)*

PUBLISHING & PRINTING: Books

Seniors Bluebook ....G...... 228 396-4602
Biloxi *(G-278)*

PUBLISHING & PRINTING: Comic Books

Omni Fusion LLC ....G...... 601 765-6941
Collins *(G-858)*

PUBLISHING & PRINTING: Directories, NEC

Guides Publishing Inc ....G...... 601 981-7368
Jackson *(G-2435)*

PUBLISHING & PRINTING: Magazines: publishing & printing

Blue South Publishing Corp ....G...... 601 604-2963
Meridian *(G-3310)*

Bluffs & Bayou Magazine ....G...... 601 442-6847
Natchez *(G-3534)*

Jackpot Magazine ....G...... 228 385-7707
Gulfport *(G-1813)*

Journal Inc ....E...... 601 364-1000
Flowood *(G-1371)*

Shumpert Media ....G...... 662 678-3742
Nettleton *(G-3667)*

Wrestling USA Magazine Inc ....G...... 406 360-9421
Pass Christian *(G-4098)*

PUBLISHING & PRINTING: Newsletters, Business Svc

White Jerleen ....G...... 601 941-6886
Prentiss *(G-4425)*

PUBLISHING & PRINTING: Newspapers

Bolivar Cnty Dept Humn Rsurces ....G...... 662 843-8311
Cleveland *(G-787)*

Boone Newspapers ....E...... 601 442-9101
Natchez *(G-3537)*

Brent Aubry ....G...... 662 746-7600
Yazoo City *(G-5624)*

Clairborne Publishing Co ....G...... 601 437-5103
Port Gibson *(G-4401)*

Clarke County Tribune Inc ....G...... 601 776-3726
Quitman *(G-4460)*

Cleveland John ....G...... 901 359-2737
Byhalia *(G-583)*

Employee Codes: A=Over 500 employees, B=251-500
C=101-250, D=51-100, E=20-50, F=10-19, G=1-9

2019 Harris Directory of
Mississippi Manufacturers

PUBLISHING & PRINTING: Newspapers

Coast Motor News..............................G..... 228 868-1772
Gulfport (G-1756)
Coast Observer....................................G..... 228 875-0090
Ocean Springs (G-3749)
Commonwealth Publishing Inc.............C..... 662 453-5312
Greenwood (G-1618)
Daily & Sons Construction Inc ....G..... 601 737-5847
Bailey (G-67)
Delta-Democrat Pubg Co Inc ....D..... 662 335-1155
Greenville (G-1551)
East Holmes Publishing Entps ....G..... 662 834-1151
Lexington (G-2901)
Emmerich Newspapers Inc ....G..... 662 647-8462
Charleston (G-737)
Enterprise-Tocsin...............................G..... 662 887-2222
Indianola (G-2264)
Fayette Chronicle...............................G..... 601 786-3661
Fayette (G-1296)
Goodnews Gulf Coast ....G..... 228 435-2456
Biloxi (G-247)
Hattiesburg American ....G..... 601 582-4321
Hattiesburg (G-1984)
Hattiesburg American Pubg Co ....C..... 601 582-4321
Hattiesburg (G-1985)
Hh Services ....G..... 662 283-1131
Winona (G-5601)
Horizon Publications Inc ....E..... 662 323-1642
Starkville (G-4950)
Imes Communications of El Paso ....D..... 662 328-2424
Columbus (G-986)
Jackson Free Press Inc ....F..... 601 362-6121
Jackson (G-2455)
Journal Inc..C..... 662 842-2611
Tupelo (G-5164)
Journal Inc..G..... 662 862-3141
Fulton (G-1460)
Journal Publishing Houston ....G..... 662 456-3771
Houston (G-2248)
Lee County Courier Inc ....G..... 662 840-8819
Tupelo (G-5173)
Local Voice LLC ....G..... 662 232-8900
Oxford (G-3966)
Macon Beacon....................................G..... 662 726-4747
Macon (G-3064)
Madison County Herald ....G..... 601 853-2899
Madison (G-3124)
Madison County Publishing Inc ....G..... 601 853-4222
Ridgeland (G-4600)
Manolia Gazette..................................G..... 601 783-2441
Magnolia (G-3194)
McM Communications LLC...................F..... 228 435-0720
Biloxi (G-267)
Meteor Inc ....F..... 601 892-2581
Crystal Springs (G-1148)
Miss Lou Guide ....G..... 601 442-9101
Natchez (G-3588)
Newspaper Holding Inc ....E..... 601 798-4766
Picayune (G-4281)
Northeast Miss Daily Jurnl ....G..... 662 842-2622
Tupelo (G-5194)
Omni Fusion LLC ....G..... 601 765-6941
Collins (G-858)
Paxton Media Group LLC ....E..... 662 287-6111
Corinth (G-1108)
Paxton Media Group LLC ....G..... 662 728-6214
Booneville (G-341)
Rankin Ledger....................................G..... 601 360-4600
Jackson (G-2558)
Rankin Publishing Company Inc ....G..... 601 992-4869
Flowood (G-1390)
Saltillo Guntown Gazette......................G..... 662 869-8380
Saltillo (G-4720)
Southern Sentinel Inc ....G..... 662 224-6681
Ashland (G-65)
Southwest Publishers Inc ....E..... 601 833-6961
Brookhaven (G-538)
Star Herald ....G..... 662 289-2251
Kosciusko (G-2715)
Stone County Enterprises Inc...............G..... 601 928-4802
Wiggins (G-5589)
Tradewinds Publications ....G..... 601 992-3699
Flowood (G-1403)
Tupelo Advertiser Inc..........................E..... 601 534-6635
New Albany (G-3704)
Wayne Hmphrys/Plygraph Exminer ......G..... 601 825-8640
Brandon (G-472)
William Carey University ....G..... 601 318-6115
Hattiesburg (G-2083)

PUBLISHING & PRINTING: Pamphlets

Gods Inspiration For The Soul ....G..... 662 374-7785
Tupelo (G-5144)
Triad of Mississippi LLC......................G..... 601 373-7619
Jackson (G-2610)
White Jerleen ....G..... 601 941-6886
Prentiss (G-4425)

PUBLISHING & PRINTING: Posters

Illustrative Ink LLC ....G..... 228 354-9559
Saucier (G-4756)
Signature Sound & Printing ....G..... 601 272-5662
Columbus (G-1026)

PUBLISHING & PRINTING: Technical Papers

Multiforms..G..... 601 545-2312
Petal (G-4194)

PUBLISHING & PRINTING: Textbooks

Braxton Foxx LLC ....G..... 800 719-6811
Flowood (G-1349)

PUBLISHING & PRINTING: Yearbooks

Ms Yearbooks LLC..............................G..... 601 540-6132
Brandon (G-427)
Scholastic Products and Awards ....F..... 601 362-6990
Jackson (G-2576)

PULP MILLS

Domtar Paper Company LLC ....C..... 662 256-3526
Columbus (G-964)
Georgia-Pacific LLC............................F..... 601 939-7797
Pearl (G-4122)
James K Smith Logging ....F..... 601 859-1628
Canton (G-663)
Kaycan Inc ....G..... 662 252-9991
Holly Springs (G-2179)
Mike Culbreth Woodyard......................G..... 601 776-2422
Quitman (G-4467)
Weyerhaeuser Company ....E..... 662 243-4000
Columbus (G-1044)

PULPWOOD, WHOLESALE

Sassones Timber LLC ....E..... 601 542-5558
Osyka (G-3929)

PUMP GOVERNORS: Gas Machines

Dixie Pump & Machine Works ....F..... 601 823-0510
Brookhaven (G-492)
Met-Tech Corp ....G..... 601 693-0061
Meridian (G-3370)
Tencarva Machinery Company LLC ......F..... 601 823-0510
Brookhaven (G-544)

PUMPS

BSC Sales LLC ....G..... 662 890-1079
Olive Branch (G-3821)
Eaton Aerospace LLC..........................E..... 601 981-2811
Jackson (G-2396)
Fast Flow Pumps ....G..... 228 475-2468
Moss Point (G-3477)
Gravel Equipment & Supply Inc ....G..... 662 256-2052
Amory (G-43)
Harbison-Fischer Inc ....G..... 601 442-7961
Natchez (G-3567)
Luckett Pump & Well Svc Inc ....G..... 662 624-2398
Dublin (G-1219)
National Pump Co LLC ....E..... 662 895-1110
Olive Branch (G-3885)
Panama Pump Company ....G..... 601 544-4251
Hattiesburg (G-2039)
Parish Pumps and Machine Inc ....G..... 662 256-2052
Amory (G-51)
Xylem Water Solutions Usa ....F..... 662 393-0275
Southaven (G-4921)

PUMPS & PUMPING EQPT REPAIR SVCS

Harbison-Fischer Inc ....G..... 601 442-7961
Natchez (G-3567)

PUMPS & PUMPING EQPT WHOLESALERS

Baker Hghes Olfld Oprtions LLC...........G..... 601 649-2704
Laurel (G-2734)

PRODUCT SECTION

Browning Oil Tools Inc ....E..... 601 442-1800
Natchez (G-3540)
Flannigan Electric Company ....E..... 601 354-2756
Jackson (G-2409)
Harbison-Fischer Inc ....G..... 601 442-7961
Natchez (G-3567)
Pickett Equipment Co Inc ....G..... 662 890-9095
Olive Branch (G-3895)

PUMPS: Oil Well & Field

Browning Oil Tools Inc ....E..... 601 442-1800
Natchez (G-3540)

PUPPETS & MARIONETTES

Mississippi Puppetry Guild ....G..... 601 977-9840
Jackson (G-2505)

PURCHASING SVCS

Gecas Asset MGT Svcs Inc ....G..... 662 455-1826
Greenwood (G-1626)
Sparko Inc...G..... 662 690-5800
Tupelo (G-5229)

QUILTING SVC & SPLYS, FOR THE TRADE

Marcellas Quilt Shop ....G..... 662 262-7870
French Camp (G-1440)

RACEWAYS

Batesville Raceway LLC ....G..... 662 561-0065
Batesville (G-97)
Columbus Speedway ....G..... 662 327-3047
Columbus (G-954)
Flowood Raceway ....G..... 601 939-5048
Flowood (G-1362)
Golden Pine Raceway LLC ....G..... 601 506-8669
Prentiss (G-4420)
H and R Raceway LLC ....G..... 601 373-2490
Jackson (G-2436)
J&l&r Raceway LLC ....G..... 601 622-8458
Madison (G-3113)
Raceway Express Shell ....G..... 662 335-5434
Greenville (G-1593)
Southaven Raceway ....G..... 662 393-9945
Southaven (G-4905)

RACKS: Pallet, Exc Wood

Tier-Rack Corporation ....E..... 662 526-9900
Como (G-1053)

RADIO & TELEVISION COMMUNICATIONS EQUIPMENT

Lad2 LLC...G..... 601 584-9026
Hattiesburg (G-2013)
Mid South Communications Inc ....G..... 662 832-0538
Water Valley (G-5472)
Robco Inc...G..... 769 218-6457
Long Beach (G-2951)

RADIO BROADCASTING STATIONS

Community Broadcasting ....G..... 731 441-6962
Booneville (G-325)
Wrjw 1320 AM ....F..... 601 798-4835
Picayune (G-4305)

RADIO COMMUNICATIONS: Airborne Eqpt

Mstate Technologies LLC.....................G..... 662 418-0110
Starkville (G-4962)

RADIO REPAIR & INSTALLATION SVCS

Innovative Wireless LLC ....G..... 601 594-1201
Jackson (G-2447)

RAILROAD CARGO LOADING & UNLOADING SVCS

Williams Transportation Co LLC ....D..... 601 428-2214
Laurel (G-2874)

RAILROAD EQPT

American Railcar Inds Inc ....D..... 601 384-5841
Bude (G-567)
Gilcorp ....D..... 601 932-2100
Pearl (G-4123)

PRODUCT SECTION

RENTAL SVCS: Garage Facility & Tool

RAILROAD EQPT: Cars & Eqpt, Dining

Kdh Trucking LLC ....G....... 601 730-2052
Liberty (G-2913)
Trinity Highway Products Llc...............G....... 662 290-1500
Kosciusko (G-2719)

RAILROAD EQPT: Locomotives & Parts, Indl

Watco Co Inc ....G....... 601 553-1332
Meridian (G-3416)

RAILROAD TIES: Wood

M2 Corp......................G....... 662 342-2173
Southaven (G-4887)

REAL ESTATE AGENCIES & BROKERS

Paradise & Associates Inc ....G....... 601 445-9710
Natchez (G-3606)

REAL ESTATE AGENCIES: Selling

Tropical World Intl LLC..........................G....... 228 229-8413
Biloxi (G-285)

REAL ESTATE AGENTS & MANAGERS

Coast Observer ....G....... 228 875-0090
Ocean Springs (G-3749)

REAL ESTATE INVESTMENT TRUSTS

Correy Elder ....G....... 769 257-3240
Madison (G-3089)

REAL ESTATE OPERATORS, EXC DEVELOPERS: Insurance Building

Journal Inc......................C....... 662 842-2611
Tupelo (G-5164)

RECLAIMED RUBBER: Reworked By Manufacturing Process

Polyvulc Usa Inc ....E....... 601 638-8040
Vicksburg (G-5407)

RECORDING TAPE: Video, Blank

Primos Inc......................D....... 601 879-9323
Flora (G-1311)

RECORDS & TAPES: Prerecorded

Johnson Educational Sales Inc.............G....... 601 469-1924
Forest (G-1418)
Northside Partners......................G....... 601 982-4522
Jackson (G-2522)

RECREATIONAL SPORTING EQPT REPAIR SVCS

Tucker Manufacturing Co Inc...............E....... 662 563-7220
Batesville (G-131)

RECREATIONAL VEHICLE PARTS & ACCESS STORES

Woods Trailers & Repair LLC ....G....... 662 585-3606
Golden (G-1533)

RECYCLABLE SCRAP & WASTE MATERIALS WHOLESALERS

Nelsons Metal Inc......................G....... 662 454-7500
Dennis (G-1184)

RECYCLING: Paper

Energyzmart LLC ....G....... 650 630-1232
Grenada (G-1676)
Nelsons Metal Inc......................G....... 662 454-7500
Dennis (G-1184)
Profile Products LLC ....E....... 662 685-4741
Blue Mountain (G-292)

REFINERS & SMELTERS: Nonferrous Metal

Aluminum Recycling of Miss ....E....... 601 355-5777
Jackson (G-2325)
Columbus Scrap Material Co ....E....... 662 328-8176
Columbus (G-953)

Corinth Cc-Cola Btlg Works Inc ....E....... 662 286-2052
Corinth (G-1078)
Metal Management Inc......................G....... 662 455-2540
Greenwood (G-1639)
Metal Management Inc......................F....... 662 844-6441
New Albany (G-3686)
Northeast Metal Processors ....E....... 662 844-2164
Plantersville (G-4312)
Nucor Corporation ....E....... 601 936-6292
Jackson (G-2659)
Southern Scrap Meridian LLC ....E....... 601 693-5323
Meridian (G-3403)
Triangle Recycling Services ....F....... 601 352-5027
Jackson (G-2611)

REFINERS & SMELTERS: Silver

Attala Steel Industries LLC ....G....... 662 289-1980
Kosciusko (G-2688)

REFINING: Petroleum

Chevron Phillips Chem Co LLC...........A....... 228 938-4600
Pascagoula (G-4026)
Ergon Inc ....E....... 601 636-6888
Vicksburg (G-5367)
Ergon - West Virginia Inc ....G....... 601 933-3000
Flowood (G-1357)
Ergon Construction Group Inc ....E....... 601 939-3909
Richland (G-4514)
Ergon Europe Mea Inc ....E....... 601 933-3000
Flowood (G-1360)
Faststop Petroleum LLC ....G....... 601 466-3273
Bassfield (G-91)
Hunt Refining Company ....G....... 843 236-5098
Vicksburg (G-5379)
Hunt Refining Company ....E....... 601 426-1821
Heidelberg (G-2117)
Hunt Refining Company ....E....... 601 796-2331
Lumberton (G-3030)
Murphy USA Inc ....F....... 601 992-2041
Flowood (G-1383)
Southern Oil Company ....G....... 601 582-5455
Hattiesburg (G-2062)
Southland Oil Company ....E....... 601 796-2331
Lumberton (G-3038)
Southland Oil Company ....G....... 601 634-1361
Vicksburg (G-5421)

REFRACTORIES: Clay

Meridian Brick LLC ....G....... 228 863-5451
Gulfport (G-1828)
Restora-Life Minerals Inc ....G....... 601 789-5545
Bay Springs (G-172)

REFRIGERATION & HEATING EQUIPMENT

Caruthers AC & Htg LLC ....G....... 601 636-9433
Vicksburg (G-5355)
Donald E McCain......................G....... 601 824-1275
Brandon (G-391)
Kaz USA......................G....... 800 477-0457
Olive Branch (G-3859)
Lobell Sales LLC......................G....... 662 724-2940
Noxapater (G-3733)
Modine Grenada LLC......................B....... 662 229-4000
Grenada (G-1694)
Polyvulc Usa Inc ....E....... 601 638-8040
Vicksburg (G-5407)
Trane US Inc ....G....... 228 863-4445
Gulfport (G-1885)
United Service Equipment Co..............G....... 662 534-9061
New Albany (G-3706)
Wag Corporation ....G....... 662 844-8478
Tupelo (G-5252)
Watson Percy ....G....... 662 931-6490
Greenville (G-1609)
York International Corporation ....D....... 601 544-8911
Hattiesburg (G-2087)

REFRIGERATION EQPT & SPLYS WHOLESALERS

Haygoods Industrial Engravers.............G....... 228 769-7488
Pascagoula (G-4036)

REFRIGERATION EQPT & SPLYS, WHOLESALE: Commercial Eqpt

Taylor Coml Foodservice Inc ....C....... 662 895-4455
Olive Branch (G-3915)

REFRIGERATION EQPT: Complete

Modine Grenada LLC......................A....... 662 229-2000
Grenada (G-1692)
Modine Grenada LLC......................A....... 662 226-3421
Grenada (G-1693)
Standex International Corp ....B....... 662 534-9061
New Albany (G-3700)

REFRIGERATORS & FREEZERS WHOLESALERS

Taylor Coml Foodservice Inc ....C....... 662 895-4455
Olive Branch (G-3915)

REFUSE SYSTEMS

Aluminum Recycling of Miss ....E....... 601 355-5777
Jackson (G-2325)
Columbus Scrap Material Co ....E....... 662 328-8176
Columbus (G-953)
Corinth Cc-Cola Btlg Works Inc ....E....... 662 286-2052
Corinth (G-1078)
Exide Technologies ....F....... 601 936-7788
Pearl (G-4116)
Triangle Recycling Services ....F....... 601 352-5027
Jackson (G-2611)

REGISTERS: Air, Metal

Hart & Cooley Inc......................C....... 662 890-8000
Olive Branch (G-3845)

REHABILITATION CTR, RESIDENTIAL WITH HEALTH CARE INCIDENTAL

Alatheia Prosthetic Reha...................F....... 601 919-2113
Brandon (G-360)

RELAYS & SWITCHES: Indl, Electric

Electro National Corporation ....E....... 601 859-5511
Canton (G-657)

RELAYS: Electronic Usage

Omega System Specialists LLC ....G....... 901 334-6742
Nesbit (G-3655)

RELIGIOUS SPLYS WHOLESALERS

Sign Shop......................G....... 601 735-1383
Waynesboro (G-5514)

REMOVERS & CLEANERS

Aride Taxi Cab and Trnsp LLC...............G....... 601 620-4282
Byram (G-617)
Danny R Jansen......................G....... 601 636-1070
Valley Park (G-5316)
Mississippi Prison Inds Corp ....F....... 601 969-5760
Jackson (G-2503)

RENTAL CENTERS: Tools

Radco Fishing & Rental Tls Inc ....G....... 601 736-8580
Columbia (G-917)

RENTAL SVCS: Aircraft

Tenax Tm LLC ....F....... 601 352-1107
Madison (G-3158)

RENTAL SVCS: Business Machine & Electronic Eqpt

Pitney Bowes Inc ....G....... 601 969-2900
Jackson (G-2540)
Pitney Bowes Inc ....E....... 601 206-9039
Ridgeland (G-4618)

RENTAL SVCS: Costume

Party City ....F....... 228 539-4476
Gulfport (G-1846)

RENTAL SVCS: Garage Facility & Tool

Hills Welding & Crane Rental..................G....... 662 846-6789
Cleveland (G-796)

Employee Codes: A=Over 500 employees, B=251-500
C=101-250, D=51-100, E=20-50, F=10-19, G=1-9

2019 Harris Directory of
Mississippi Manufacturers

415

PRODUCT

RENTAL SVCS: Office Facilities & Secretarial Svcs

PRODUCT SECTION

RENTAL SVCS: Office Facilities & Secretarial Svcs

North Miss Entp Initiative Inc..............G....... 662 281-0720
Oxford *(G-3978)*

RENTAL SVCS: Oil Eqpt

Q P P Inc ....G....... 662 356-4848
Caledonia *(G-629)*
T & T Welding Yard Inc ....E....... 601 477-2299
Ellisville *(G-1271)*

RENTAL SVCS: Tent & Tarpaulin

United Burial Vault Co & Cemtr ....F....... 662 347-9319
Benoit *(G-207)*

REPRODUCTION SVCS: Video Tape Or Disk

Johnson Educational Sales Inc ....G....... 601 469-1924
Forest *(G-1418)*

RESEARCH, DEVELOPMENT & TEST SVCS, COMM: Cmptr Hardware Dev

Vizaura LLC ....G....... 228 363-4048
Diamondhead *(G-1193)*

RESEARCH, DEVELOPMENT & TEST SVCS, COMM: Research, Exc Lab

Gha Enterprises Incorporated ....G....... 601 812-7739
Jackson *(G-2425)*

RESEARCH, DEVELOPMENT & TESTING SVCS, COMM: Natural Resource

Harbour Energy Inc..............G....... 601 992-2277
Brandon *(G-403)*

RESIDENTIAL REMODELERS

Pooles Stone & Masonry Contrs ....G....... 662 438-6643
Belmont *(G-201)*

RESIDUES

Income Online Residual ....G....... 662 420-7636
Olive Branch *(G-3851)*

RESISTORS

Multicraft Intl Ltd Partnr ....G....... 601 854-5516
Pelahatchie *(G-4167)*

RESTAURANTS:Full Svc, Family, Independent

White Brothers Inc ....E....... 601 948-0888
Jackson *(G-2630)*

RESTAURANTS:Full Svc, Italian

Brm LLC..............G....... 601 501-1444
Vicksburg *(G-5348)*

RESTAURANTS:Limited Svc, Chicken

Richard E Johnson ....G....... 601 735-4737
Waynesboro *(G-5512)*

RESTAURANTS:Limited Svc, Ice Cream Stands Or Dairy Bars

Dairy Kream..............G....... 662 256-7562
Amory *(G-40)*

RETAIL BAKERY: Cakes

Jubilations Inc ....F....... 662 328-9210
West Point *(G-5548)*
Pauls Pastry Shop ....E....... 601 798-7457
Picayune *(G-4285)*

RETAIL BAKERY: Cookies

Cookie Place Inc ....G....... 601 957-2891
Ridgeland *(G-4565)*

RETAIL BAKERY: Doughnuts

Tato-Nut Donut Shop ....F....... 228 872-2076
Ocean Springs *(G-3791)*

RETAIL BAKERY: Pretzels

Cosentino Enterprises Inc ....G....... 228 392-6666
Diberville *(G-1201)*

RETAIL LUMBER YARDS

James K Smith Logging ....F....... 601 859-1628
Canton *(G-663)*
Pickens Hardwoods Inc ....G....... 601 924-1199
Jackson *(G-2539)*
Thomas Leslie Coleman ....G....... 662 369-6000
Caledonia *(G-632)*

RETAIL STORES: Alarm Signal Systems

Chambers Air and Heat ....G....... 662 967-2002
West *(G-5532)*

RETAIL STORES: Architectural Splys

Prographics Inc..............G....... 662 329-3341
Columbus *(G-1017)*

RETAIL STORES: Art & Architectural Splys

Mississippi Photo & Bluprt Co ....G....... 601 948-1119
Jackson *(G-2502)*

RETAIL STORES: Artificial Limbs

Gulf Coast Limb & Brace Inc ....G....... 228 864-4512
Gulfport *(G-1798)*
Hanger Prosthetic Orthopedics ....G....... 601 939-2100
Jackson *(G-2647)*
Hanger Prsthetcs & Ortho Inc..............G....... 662 844-6734
Tupelo *(G-5150)*

RETAIL STORES: Awnings

Quality Glass and Aluminum ....G....... 662 837-3615
Ripley *(G-4669)*

RETAIL STORES: Banners

Berry Signs & Stripes..............G....... 601 544-5600
Hattiesburg *(G-1930)*
Dan W Butler Signs..............G....... 601 948-5059
Jackson *(G-2375)*
Ets Signs Inc ....G....... 601 268-7275
Hattiesburg *(G-1964)*
Mike Stringer Signs ....G....... 601 736-8600
Columbia *(G-907)*
Sign Plex ....G....... 228 896-5999
Gulfport *(G-1869)*

RETAIL STORES: Business Machines & Eqpt

Atkins Office Supply Inc..............G....... 662 627-2476
Clarksdale *(G-757)*
Star Printing Co of Amory Inc..............E....... 662 256-8424
Amory *(G-56)*

RETAIL STORES: Cake Decorating Splys

Creative Cakes & Supplies Inc ....G....... 662 844-3080
Tupelo *(G-5123)*
McIlwains Electrical Supply ....G....... 601 735-1145
Waynesboro *(G-5507)*

RETAIL STORES: Cosmetics

Merle Norman Cosmetics Inc..............G....... 662 287-7233
Corinth *(G-1100)*

RETAIL STORES: Decals

All Signs Inc ....G....... 228 897-9100
Gulfport *(G-1719)*
Lightning Quick Signs..............G....... 228 467-1718
Waveland *(G-5482)*

RETAIL STORES: Electronic Parts & Eqpt

Advanced Marine Inc ....G....... 228 374-6747
Biloxi *(G-217)*
D & T Motors Inc ....G....... 662 773-5021
Louisville *(G-2965)*

RETAIL STORES: Engine & Motor Eqpt & Splys

H & H Small Engine Repair ....G....... 662 423-2741
Iuka *(G-2292)*

RETAIL STORES: Engines & Parts, Air-Cooled

Barnetts Small Engines..............G....... 662 323-8993
Starkville *(G-4926)*
J and E Enterprises ....G....... 662 369-7324
Aberdeen *(G-15)*

RETAIL STORES: Farm Eqpt & Splys

Fireplace Wholesale ....G....... 601 545-9876
Hattiesburg *(G-1970)*
Steve Schrock ....G....... 662 369-6062
Prairie *(G-4414)*

RETAIL STORES: Farm Tractors

Harold Knight Sew Mchs & Appls ....G....... 601 425-2220
Laurel *(G-2775)*

RETAIL STORES: Hearing Aids

Advanced Hearing and Balance ....G....... 601 450-0280
Hattiesburg *(G-1915)*

RETAIL STORES: Ice

Bay Ice Company Inc..............F....... 228 863-0981
Gulfport *(G-1735)*
Party Time Ice Inc ....F....... 662 746-8899
Yazoo City *(G-5645)*

RETAIL STORES: Insecticides

Pinnacle Agriculture Dist Inc ....G....... 662 265-5828
Inverness *(G-2276)*

RETAIL STORES: Medical Apparatus & Splys

Kerex LLC ....G....... 210 494-5596
Jackson *(G-2463)*
Norwood Medical Supply LLC ....G....... 601 792-2224
Prentiss *(G-4422)*

RETAIL STORES: Monuments, Finished To Custom Order

Davidson Marble & Gran Works ....G....... 662 289-1337
Kosciusko *(G-2692)*
Picayune Monument & Gran Works......G....... 601 798-7926
Picayune *(G-4286)*

RETAIL STORES: Motors, Electric

Burford Electric Service Inc..............E....... 662 328-5679
Columbus *(G-943)*
Peller Electric Motor Srvs ....G....... 601 693-4621
Meridian *(G-3387)*
Walker Enterprises ....G....... 662 237-0240
Carrollton *(G-704)*

RETAIL STORES: Orthopedic & Prosthesis Applications

Hanger Prsthetcs & Ortho Inc..............G....... 601 442-7742
Natchez *(G-3566)*
Hanger Prsthetcs & Ortho Inc..............G....... 662 323-3349
Starkville *(G-4947)*
Hanger Prsthetcs & Ortho Inc..............G....... 228 822-0109
Gulfport *(G-1804)*
Hanger Prsthetcs & Ortho Inc..............G....... 662 335-6828
Greenville *(G-1557)*

RETAIL STORES: Picture Frames, Ready Made

Cotton Patch Framery ....G....... 662 895-6605
Olive Branch *(G-3829)*
Kathys Frame Works Inc ....G....... 228 769-7672
Pascagoula *(G-4044)*

RETAIL STORES: Plumbing & Heating Splys

Filter Service Mississippi LLC ....G....... 601 693-4614
Meridian *(G-3339)*
Southern Sewage Systems ....G....... 228 832-7400
Saucier *(G-4766)*

RETAIL STORES: Rubber Stamps

Noyes Printing & Rbr Stamp Co..........G....... 662 332-5256
Greenville *(G-1583)*
Tupelo Engraving & Rbr Stamp..............G....... 662 842-0574
Tupelo *(G-5246)*

2019 Harris Directory of
Mississippi Manufacturers

(G-0000) Company's Geographic Section entry number

416

PRODUCT SECTION

SAWING & PLANING MILLS

RETAIL STORES: Telephone Eqpt & Systems

Phone Booth Inc ....F 662 286-6600
Corinth (G-1109)

RETAIL STORES: Tombstones

Miller Enterprises ....F 601 798-3004
Carriere (G-698)

RETAIL STORES: Training Materials, Electronic

Training Consultants Inc ....G 662 226-6637
Grenada (G-1710)

RETAIL STORES: Typewriters & Business Machines

Office Depot Inc ....E 662 378-2995
Greenville (G-1585)

RETAIL STORES: Water Purification Eqpt

Diomedia Industries LLC ....G 601 882-7724
Jackson (G-2384)

ROAD MATERIALS: Bituminous, Not From Refineries

Blacklidge Emulsions Inc ....E 228 863-3878
Gulfport (G-1740)

ROLLING MILL EQPT: Galvanizing Lines

Azz Incorporated ....F 228 475-0342
Moss Point (G-3466)

ROOF DECKS

Union Corrugating Company ....G 601 661-0577
Vicksburg (G-5432)

ROOFING MATERIALS: Asphalt

Atlas Roofing Corporation ....E 601 484-8900
Meridian (G-3300)
Certainteed Gypsum Inc ....C 601 693-0254
Meridian (G-3318)
Duro-Last Inc ....D 601 371-1973
Byram (G-621)
Hood Companies Inc ....D 601 582-1545
Hattiesburg (G-1991)
Soperma USA Inc ....G 228 701-1900
Gulfport (G-1875)

RUBBER

Valmet Inc ....D 662 328-3841
Columbus (G-1041)
Zeon Chemicals L P ....D 601 583-5527
Hattiesburg (G-2088)

RUBBER PRDTS: Reclaimed

Evercompounds LLC ....G 309 256-1166
Olive Branch (G-3840)

RUBBER STAMP, WHOLESALE

Labels & Stamps of Ellisville ....G 601 763-3092
Ellisville (G-1262)

RUBBER STRUCTURES: Air-Supported

Air Cruisers Company LLC ....C 601 657-8043
Liberty (G-2909)
Avon Engnered Fabrications LLC ....D 601 889-9050
Picayune (G-4254)

RULES: Slide

Slide Rule LLC ....G 228 863-8583
Gulfport (G-1872)

SAFETY EQPT & SPLYS WHOLESALERS

I Care Optical Inc..........................G 228 864-4397
Gulfport (G-1811)

SAILBOAT BUILDING & REPAIR

Classail Models International ....G 601 373-4833
Byram (G-620)

SAILS

Mainland Sails Inc ....G 228 374-7245
Gautier (G-1498)
Sailmakers Supply ....G 228 522-3232
Gautier (G-1503)

SAND & GRAVEL

Apac-Mississippi Inc ....D 662 328-6555
Columbus (G-936)
Baldwin Sand & Gravel ....G 662 834-6167
Lexington (G-2897)
Bell Gravel Co Inc ....G 228 452-2872
Long Beach (G-2929)
Bill Phillips Sand & Grav LLC ....G 662 284-6061
Corinth (G-1061)
Bullocks Gravel Service Inc ....G 601 833-7034
Brookhaven (G-484)
D M Yount Gravel ....G 662 292-1040
Senatobia (G-4791)
Delta Industries Inc ....E 601 948-4245
Crystal Springs (G-1141)
Doug McCormick ....G 662 256-9506
Amory (G-41)
Ellis Dozer LLC ....G 601 752-2207
Seminary (G-4778)
Florence Parker ....G 662 434-8555
Columbus (G-975)
Hard Rock Sand & Gravel ....G 601 876-2929
Tylertown (G-5271)
Honnoll Sand & Gravel LLC ....G 662 487-3854
Sardis (G-4740)
Huey P Stockstill LLC ....C 601 798-2981
Picayune (G-4273)
Jh Dirt & Gravel Llc ....G 601 831-3990
Vicksburg (G-5382)
Jordon Construction LLC ....G 601 502-6019
Terry (G-5071)
Kelly Dirt & Gravel LLC ....G 662 231-0249
Shannon (G-4812)
Kenneths Excavation Demo ....G 662 379-6771
Greenville (G-1562)
Lag Constructors ....G 601 720-0404
Madison (G-3118)
Legacy Vulcan LLC ....G 662 357-7675
Lake Cormorant (G-2725)
Legacy Vulcan LLC ....G 601 947-9717
Lucedale (G-3008)
Legacy Vulcan LLC ....G 601 553-2902
Meridian (G-3358)
Legacy Vulcan LLC ....G 228 522-6011
Gautier (G-1496)
Legacy Vulcan LLC ....F 601 482-7007
Meridian (G-3359)
Legacy Vulcan LLC ....G 601 631-8833
Jackson (G-2467)
Magnolia Frac Sand ....G 601 446-6023
Natchez (G-3582)
Malone Design & Contg LLC ....G 601 807-1279
Hattiesburg (G-2020)
McCoy Farms & Gravel ....G 601 847-5962
Mendenhall (G-3284)
Mississippi Sand Solutions LL ....G 870 291-8802
Vicksburg (G-5397)
MMC Materials Inc ....D 601 634-8787
Vicksburg (G-5399)
Nelson Materials Inc ....D 662 563-4972
Batesville (G-115)
Newell Sand & Gravel ....G 228 832-1215
Gulfport (G-1837)
Paul Bolling ....F 601 466-3398
Leakesville (G-2878)
Pen/Ron Company Inc ....G 601 519-5096
Brandon (G-431)
Pine Creek LLC ....G 601 255-5036
Hattiesburg (G-2044)
Prestige Cnstr & Land Svcs LLC ....G 228 861-1292
Gulfport (G-1852)
Rebecca McCallum ....G 662 501-0709
Byhalia (G-599)
Richard Price Batton ....G 601 892-5678
Crystal Springs (G-1153)
River Road Sand & Gravel LLC ....G 601 582-9662
Hattiesburg (G-2052)
River Rock and Sand Co ....G 601 798-4292
Picayune (G-4292)
Shear View Mulching LLC ....G 985 637-8402
Poplarville (G-4393)
Smith Gravel and Trucking LLC ....G 228 518-0766
Poplarville (G-4394)

Spectrum III Limited......................G 662 234-2461
Oxford (G-4005)
Standard Gravel Co Inc ....G 601 584-6436
Hattiesburg (G-2068)
Strayhorn Trucking & Cnstr LLC ....G 662 560-6516
Sarah (G-4736)
Uphill Construction LLC ....G 662 299-9654
Greenwood (G-1654)
W E Blain & Sons Inc ....E 601 442-3032
Natchez (G-3635)
W F Ferguson ....G 601 453-1093
Greenwood (G-1664)

SAND MINING

Hammett Gravel Co Inc ....G 662 834-1867
Lexington (G-2903)
Hutchinson Island Mining Corp ....F 601 799-4070
Picayune (G-4274)
Shale Energy Support LLC ....D 601 798-7821
Picayune (G-4295)

SANDBLASTING SVC: Building Exterior

Lumpkin Repair Service LLC ....G 601 798-2027
Carriere (G-694)
S Circle Inc ....D 601 792-4104
Newhebron (G-3714)

SANITARY SVC, NEC

Bell Environmental Svcs LLC ....G 662 873-4551
Delta City (G-1180)

SANITARY SVCS: Oil Spill Cleanup

Tackle Technologies LLC ....G 228 206-1449
Long Beach (G-2956)

SANITARY SVCS: Waste Materials, Recycling

Exide Technologies ....G 601 845-2281
Florence (G-1323)
Metal Management Inc ....G 662 455-2540
Greenwood (G-1639)

SANITARY WARE: Metal

Nokomis LLC ....G 601 743-2100
De Kalb (G-1167)

SANITATION CHEMICALS & CLEANING AGENTS

Desiccare Inc ....E 601 932-0405
Richland (G-4513)
Huffco LLC ....G 662 284-6517
Corinth (G-1089)
Kengro Corporation ....F 662 647-2456
Charleston (G-740)
Oil-Dri Production Company ....D 662 837-9263
Ripley (G-4666)
Profile Products LLC ....E 662 685-4741
Blue Mountain (G-292)
United Gilsonite Laboratories ....E 601 362-8619
Jackson (G-2617)

SATCHELS

Satchel LLC ....G 901 515-8163
Jackson (G-2573)

SATELLITES: Communications

Davids Satellite ....G 662 416-4697
Marietta (G-3213)
Wntz TV ....G 601 442-4800
Natchez (G-3644)

SAW BLADES

Precision Blades Inc ....F 662 869-1034
Saltillo (G-4719)

SAWING & PLANING MILLS

Al-Tom Forest Products Inc ....E 601 989-2631
Richton (G-4526)
Anderson-Tully Company ....B 601 629-3283
Vicksburg (G-5339)
Backwoods Tie and Timber LLC ....F 662 258-3388
Eupora (G-1285)
Bazor Lumber Company LLC ....E 601 776-2181
Quitman (G-4457)

Employee Codes: A=Over 500 employees, B=251-500
C=101-250, D=51-100, E=20-50, F=10-19, G=1-9

2019 Harris Directory of
Mississippi Manufacturers

417

PRODUCT

SAWING & PLANING MILLS

Buckhaults Sawmill & Pallets ....E 601 477-8403
Ellisville *(G-1247)*
Buntyn Sawmill ....G 601 774-8128
Union *(G-5295)*
Byrne Furn Co & Sawmill Svcs ....G 601 442-7363
Natchez *(G-3541)*
Central Mississippi Wood Inc ....G 662 724-2447
Philadelphia *(G-4210)*
Columbus Lumber Company LLC ....C 601 833-1990
Brookhaven *(G-488)*
Cooper Mar & Timberlands Corp ....G 662 454-9274
Dennis *(G-1181)*
Custom Rough Cut Lumber ....G 601 270-9518
Hattiesburg *(G-1955)*
Domtar Paper Company LLC ....C 662 256-3526
Columbus *(G-964)*
Enlow & Son Inc ....G 662 423-9073
Iuka *(G-2291)*
Fishers Sawmill ....G 662 967-2502
West *(G-5533)*
Fly Timber Co Inc ....F 662 226-2276
Grenada *(G-1677)*
Georgia-Pacific LLC ....D 601 764-4806
Bay Springs *(G-161)*
Georgia-Pacific LLC ....C 601 785-4721
Columbia *(G-900)*
Georgia-Pacific LLC ....F 601 939-7797
Pearl *(G-4122)*
Gordon Redd Lumber Company ....E 601 833-2311
Brookhaven *(G-496)*
H & G Sawmill LLC ....G 601 885-2179
Utica *(G-5308)*
Homan Industries Inc ....D 662 862-2125
Fulton *(G-1456)*
Jack Batte and Sons Inc ....E 601 536-3976
Forest *(G-1417)*
Jimmy Jones & Sons Sawmill ....G 601 253-2533
Walnut Grove *(G-5460)*
Kelwood Products Inc ....E 601 659-7027
Enterprise *(G-1280)*
King Lumber Company Inc ....D 601 469-3271
Forest *(G-1420)*
Leon Schommer Sawmill ....G 601 753-2687
Mc Lain *(G-3240)*
Lincoln Lumber Co Inc ....D 601 833-4484
Brookhaven *(G-512)*
Marion County Timber Inc ....F 601 736-0654
Foxworth *(G-1433)*
Maxwell Sawmill LLC ....G 601 894-3194
Wesson *(G-5528)*
Nslc Southern Inc ....D 601 605-0575
Ridgeland *(G-4613)*
Parkerson Lumber Inc ....E 662 547-6019
French Camp *(G-1441)*
Phillips Bark Proc Co Inc ....G 601 605-1071
Brookhaven *(G-523)*
Ralph Rone ....G 662 674-5796
Ethel *(G-1283)*
Rives and Reynolds Lbr Co Inc ....E 662 289-3823
Kosciusko *(G-2711)*
Rjb Enterprises ....E 601 639-4921
Crosby *(G-1136)*
RLH Trucking Inc ....G 662 462-5079
Burnsville *(G-573)*
Rogers Lumber Corp ....E 601 736-4472
Columbia *(G-919)*
Rogers Lumber Corp ....E 601 736-4472
Columbia *(G-920)*
Ronnie Kolb ....G 662 263-5252
Maben *(G-3049)*
Roseburg Forest Products Co ....E 662 773-9868
Louisville *(G-2981)*
Sims Bark Co Inc ....F 662 895-6501
Olive Branch *(G-3910)*
Smith Brothers Forest Products ....E 601 648-2892
Buckatunna *(G-565)*
Southeastern Timber Pdts LLC ....F 662 285-3291
Ackerman *(G-29)*
Thomas Leslie Coleman ....G 662 369-6000
Caledonia *(G-632)*
Tombigbee Lumber Company Inc ....E 662 862-7417
Fulton *(G-1481)*
Triple J Tie and Timber LLC ....G 601 663-4275
Philadelphia *(G-4246)*
W L Byrd Lumber Co Inc ....E 601 567-2314
Summit *(G-5029)*
Wilder Bros Sawmill Inc ....F 662 488-8692
Ecru *(G-1235)*
Winona Hardwood Inc ....G 662 283-3050
Winona *(G-5611)*

SAWING & PLANING MILLS: Custom

Elizabeth Newcomb ....G 662 596-1536
Rienzi *(G-4649)*

SAWMILL MACHINES

Pioneer Machinery and Sup Inc ....F 662 286-5646
Corinth *(G-1110)*
Stringer Industries Inc ....E 601 876-3376
Tylertown *(G-5286)*

SAWS & SAWING EQPT

Barnetts Small Engines ....G 662 323-8993
Starkville *(G-4926)*
Garys Small Engine ....G 601 545-7355
Hattiesburg *(G-1974)*
H & H Small Engine Repair ....G 662 423-2741
Iuka *(G-2292)*
Hurley Farm & Feed ....G 228 588-9156
Hurley *(G-2260)*
J and E Enterprises ....G 662 369-7324
Aberdeen *(G-15)*
Michael Williamson ....G 601 736-9156
Columbia *(G-906)*
Power Plus Inc ....F 601 264-1950
Sumrall *(G-5042)*
Robbys Small Engine & Saw Repr ....G 601 847-0323
Mendenhall *(G-3287)*

SAWS: Hand, Metalworking Or Woodworking

Southern Band Saw Co Inc ....F 662 332-4008
Greenville *(G-1600)*

SCALES & BALANCES, EXC LABORATORY

Raymond Mucillo Jr ....G 662 429-8976
Nesbit *(G-3656)*

SCALES: Indl

Gulf Coast Marine Supply Co ....F 228 762-9282
Pascagoula *(G-4035)*
Triner Scale and Mfg Co Inc ....F 800 238-0152
Olive Branch *(G-3919)*

SCANNING DEVICES: Optical

3d Laser Scanning LLC ....G 228 860-5952
Biloxi *(G-214)*

SCHOOL FOR PHYSICALLY HANDICAPPED, NEC

Willowood Dvelopmental Ctr Inc ....D 601 366-0123
Jackson *(G-2634)*

SCHOOL SPLYS, EXC BOOKS: Wholesalers

Fiskars Brands Inc ....C 662 393-3236
Southaven *(G-4873)*

SCHOOLS: Vocational, NEC

Rehabilitation Svcs Miss Dept ....E 662 335-3359
Greenville *(G-1595)*

SCRAP & WASTE MATERIALS, WHOLESALE: Ferrous Metal

Metal Management Inc ....F 662 844-6441
New Albany *(G-3686)*
Northeast Metal Processors ....E 662 844-2164
Plantersville *(G-4312)*
Southern Scrap Meridian LLC ....E 601 693-5323
Meridian *(G-3403)*

SCRAP & WASTE MATERIALS, WHOLESALE: Junk & Scrap

Columbus Scrap Material Co ....E 662 328-8176
Columbus *(G-953)*

SCRAP & WASTE MATERIALS, WHOLESALE: Metal

Aluminum Recycling of Miss ....E 601 355-5777
Jackson *(G-2325)*
MD Metals Scrap & Salvage ....G 601 635-4160
Decatur *(G-1176)*
Triple J Tie and Timber LLC ....G 601 663-4275
Philadelphia *(G-4246)*

SCREENS: Door, Metal Covered Wood

Magnolia Screens LLC ....G 601 942-3049
Jackson *(G-2479)*

SCREENS: Window, Metal

Vampco Inc ....G 601 638-5133
Vicksburg *(G-5433)*

SCREW MACHINE PRDTS

Automatic Machine Products Inc ....E 662 287-2467
Corinth *(G-1058)*
Cemco Inc ....E 662 323-1559
Starkville *(G-4933)*
Rogers Automatic Screw Machine ....G 601 849-2431
Magee *(G-3184)*
Sudden Service Inc ....E 601 650-9600
Philadelphia *(G-4239)*

SCREW MACHINES

Production Machine & Tool Inc ....G 662 287-4752
Corinth *(G-1111)*

SCREWS: Metal

Grenada Fasteners Inc ....G 662 227-1000
Grenada *(G-1680)*

SEARCH & DETECTION SYSTEMS, EXC RADAR

Proshop Inc ....G 662 333-7511
Myrtle *(G-3513)*

SEARCH & NAVIGATION SYSTEMS

Bae Systems Tech Sol Srvc Inc ....E 703 847-5820
Gautier *(G-1488)*
Coastal Charting Consultants ....G 601 590-0540
Picayune *(G-4260)*
Lockheed Martin Corporation ....F 228 864-7910
Gulfport *(G-1823)*
Lockheed Martin Corporation ....A 228 688-7997
Bay Saint Louis *(G-146)*
Lockheed Martin Corporation ....F 228 813-2160
Bay Saint Louis *(G-147)*
Mississippi Aerospace Corp ....F 601 749-5659
Picayune *(G-4280)*
Northrop Grumman Systems Corp ....D 228 474-3700
Moss Point *(G-3490)*

SEATING: Chairs, Table & Arm

Durfold Corporation ....E 601 922-4144
Jackson *(G-2392)*

SEATING: Stadium

VIP Cinema LLC ....D 662 841-5866
New Albany *(G-3707)*

SECURITY CONTROL EQPT & SYSTEMS

A Square Innovative SEC LLC ....G 601 937-0318
Jackson *(G-2316)*
Advanced Digital Fire & SEC ....G 901 240-8030
Olive Branch *(G-3806)*
Genesis Telecommunications ....G 601 626-7353
Collinsville *(G-868)*
Southern-Its Corporation ....F 228 273-2585
Diberville *(G-1215)*

SECURITY DEVICES

Awesome Sight and Sound ....G 601 215-8846
Picayune *(G-4255)*
Dale Fulton ....G 662 327-4800
Columbus *(G-958)*
Emergncy Eqp Professionals Inc ....F 662 280-4729
Horn Lake *(G-2197)*
Oxford Alarm Cmmunications Inc ....G 662 234-0505
Oxford *(G-3984)*
Quartermaster Security PR ....G 601 656-9882
Philadelphia *(G-4234)*
United Fence Company ....G 601 582-0406
Hattiesburg *(G-2077)*

SECURITY EQPT STORES

Reebok International Ltd ....F 228 822-9222
Gulfport *(G-1861)*

PRODUCT SECTION

SHREDDERS: Indl & Commercial

SECURITY PROTECTIVE DEVICES MAINTENANCE & MONITORING SVCS

A Square Innovative SEC LLC ....G 601 937-0318
Jackson *(G-2316)*

Brown Bottling Group Inc ....E 601 824-3022
Brandon *(G-374)*

SECURITY SYSTEMS SERVICES

White Shirt Networks LLC ....G 601 292-7900
Madison *(G-3170)*

SEEDS: Coated Or Treated, From Purchased Seeds

Pinnacle Agriculture Dist Inc ....G 662 453-7010
Greenwood *(G-1646)*

SEMICONDUCTORS & RELATED DEVICES

CM Manufacturing Inc ....D 601 545-7515
Hattiesburg *(G-1947)*

Daviscomms (s) Pte Ltd ....G 601 416-5043
Ridgeland *(G-4572)*

Lenoir Technology LLC ....G 769 926-5300
Biloxi *(G-260)*

SEPTIC TANKS: Concrete

Harold A Sparks Septic Tanks ....G 662 454-7244
Golden *(G-1526)*

Lees Precast Concrete Inc ....G 662 369-8935
Aberdeen *(G-16)*

Lees Septic Inc ....F 662 369-9799
Aberdeen *(G-17)*

Snells Concrete Tanks ....G 601 845-1881
Harrisville *(G-1912)*

SEPTIC TANKS: Plastic

Hancor Inc ....E 601 629-9040
Vicksburg *(G-5376)*

SEWAGE & WATER TREATMENT EQPT

Advanced Treatment Tech LLC ....G 601 506-3798
Brandon *(G-358)*

Enviro-Flo Inc ....G 601 939-2948
Flowood *(G-1355)*

SEWAGE TREATMENT SYSTEMS & EQPT

Southern Sewage Systems ....G 228 832-7400
Saucier *(G-4766)*

Wastewater Control Inc ....G 601 845-5581
Florence *(G-1338)*

SEWING CONTRACTORS

West Group Holding Company LLC ......G 662 871-2344
Shannon *(G-4821)*

SEWING MACHINE STORES

Magnolia Sewing Center ....G 601 261-9006
Hattiesburg *(G-2019)*

SEWING MACHINES & PARTS: Indl

Fab Products ....G 228 324-4133
Ocean Springs *(G-3756)*

SEWING, NEEDLEWORK & PIECE GOODS STORES: Sewing & Needlework

Just For You Embroidery ....G 228 769-8388
Pascagoula *(G-4043)*

Monogram Express ....G 601 825-1248
Brandon *(G-425)*

SEWING, NEEDLEWORK & PIECE GOODS: Weaving Goods & Splys

Heritage Yarns ....G 601 956-1478
Jackson *(G-2439)*

SHAPES: Extruded, Aluminum, NEC

L C Industries Inc ....B 601 894-1771
Hazlehurst *(G-2099)*

Piper Metal Forming Corp ....C 508 363-3937
New Albany *(G-3691)*

Signature Works Inc ....B 601 894-1771
Hazlehurst *(G-2106)*

SHEET METAL SPECIALTIES, EXC STAMPED

Capital City Metal Works Inc ....G 601 939-7467
Pearl *(G-4108)*

Fennell Sam Sheet Metal Mfg C ....G 228 864-1488
Gulfport *(G-1785)*

Groves Sheet Metal Co Inc ....G 601 922-6464
Jackson *(G-2434)*

John W McDougall Co Inc ....G 601 298-0079
Carthage *(G-718)*

SHEETING: Laminated Plastic

Acco Brands USA LLC ....D 662 720-1300
Booneville *(G-315)*

SHELTERED WORKSHOPS

Region 8 Mental Health Retrdat ....D 601 591-5553
Brandon *(G-445)*

SHIP BLDG & RPRG: Drilling & Production Platforms, Oil/Gas

Denbury Onshore LLC ....E 601 276-2147
Ruth *(G-4700)*

Withers Oil & Gas LLC ....E 601 982-3444
Jackson *(G-2635)*

SHIP BUILDING & REPAIRING: Cargo, Commercial

Ngss Ingalls Operations ....G 228 935-5731
Pascagoula *(G-4056)*

Patco Sales Inc ....G 228 207-4171
Pass Christian *(G-4093)*

SHIP BUILDING & REPAIRING: Combat Vessels

Huntington Ingalls Inc ....A 228 935-1122
Pascagoula *(G-4037)*

Huntington Ingalls Industries ....F 228 935-1122
Pascagoula *(G-4038)*

SHIP BUILDING & REPAIRING: Lighters, Marine

Complete Welding Solutions ....G 601 791-5370
Lucedale *(G-2989)*

Lynns Welding Shop LLC ....G 601 415-0012
Vicksburg *(G-5391)*

SHIP BUILDING & REPAIRING: Military

Gulf Ship LLC ....B 228 897-9189
Gulfport *(G-1802)*

Oms Shop ....E 601 835-1239
Brookhaven *(G-521)*

SHIP BUILDING & REPAIRING: Passenger, Commercial

Mississippi Marine Corporation ....C 662 332-5457
Greenville *(G-1575)*

SHIP BUILDING & REPAIRING: Towboats

Brian Smith ....G 601 259-9745
Gulfport *(G-1744)*

SHIP COMPONENTS: Metal, Prefabricated

Havards Construction LLC ....G 601 766-9841
Lucedale *(G-3001)*

SHIPBUILDING & REPAIR

Big River Shipbuilders Inc ....E 601 636-9161
Vicksburg *(G-5345)*

Coastal Marine Equipment Inc ....D 228 832-7655
Gulfport *(G-1759)*

Gulf Coast Shipyard Group Inc ....D 228 276-1051
Gulfport *(G-1800)*

Gulf Ship LLC ....G 985 601-4444
Flowood *(G-1365)*

Horizon Shipbuilding Inc ....C 251 824-1660
Moss Point *(G-3480)*

Ingalls Shipbuilding Inc ....G 877 871-2058
Pascagoula *(G-4040)*

Ingalls Shipbuilding Inc ....G 228 935-2887
Gautier *(G-1494)*

Jamestown Metal Marine Sls Inc ....D 228 762-3156
Pascagoula *(G-4041)*

Marine Flooring LLC ....G 832 472-0661
Pascagoula *(G-4050)*

Marine Service Solutions ....G 601 658-0772
Saucier *(G-4758)*

Mississippi Marine Corporation ....C 662 335-1175
Greenville *(G-1576)*

Naval Engineering Works Inc ....G 228 769-1080
Pascagoula *(G-4055)*

Nsc Technologies LLC ....F 251 338-0725
Moss Point *(G-3491)*

Omega Shipyard Inc ....E 228 475-9052
Pascagoula *(G-3493)*

Vision Technologies Marine Inc ....E 228 762-0010
Pascagoula *(G-4072)*

VT Halter Marine Inc ....C 228 475-1211
Moss Point *(G-3504)*

VT Halter Marine Inc ....C 228 696-6888
Pascagoula *(G-4073)*

VT Halter Marine Inc ....C 228 712-2278
Moss Point *(G-3505)*

World Marine Mississippi LLC ....C 228 762-0010
Pascagoula *(G-4075)*

SHOE & BOOT ACCESS

McCullar Long & Mccullough Inc ....G 662 842-4165
Tupelo *(G-5184)*

SHOE MATERIALS: Quarters

A Quarter Can Inc ....G 601 936-9915
Richland *(G-4496)*

C5 Trucking LLC ....G 601 797-9335
Mount Olive *(G-3510)*

Close Quarter Combat LLC ....G 601 325-5610
Hattiesburg *(G-1946)*

Mississippi Quarterhorse Assn ....G 601 692-5128
Walnut Grove *(G-5461)*

Quarter Inc ....G 228 701-0361
Gulfport *(G-1858)*

Quarter Rest Classics ....G 601 638-4207
Vicksburg *(G-5409)*

SHOE MATERIALS: Rands

Brian Rand ....G 601 519-5062
Bay Springs *(G-158)*

Faye Neldra Rand Spears ....G 601 722-0104
Seminary *(G-4780)*

SHOE STORES

Big Buck Sports ....G 601 605-2661
Ridgeland *(G-4556)*

SHOE STORES: Custom & Orthopedic

Southern Discount Drugs of Cha ....G 662 647-5172
Charleston *(G-743)*

SHOES: Athletic, Exc Rubber Or Plastic

Asics America Corporation ....F 662 895-6800
Byhalia *(G-577)*

SHOES: Plastic Or Rubber

Southern Discount Drugs of Cha ....G 662 647-5172
Charleston *(G-743)*

SHOES: Rubber Or Rubber Soled Fabric Uppers

Run-N-Tri Company Llc ....G 228 604-2227
Gulfport *(G-1864)*

SHOT PEENING SVC

Surfacetechs ....G 601 605-1900
Madison *(G-3154)*

SHOWER STALLS: Plastic & Fiberglass

Water-Way Inc ....E 662 423-0081
Iuka *(G-2311)*

SHREDDERS: Indl & Commercial

Cintas Corporation No 2 ....D 601 923-8664
Jackson *(G-2360)*

Employee Codes: A=Over 500 employees, B=251-500
C=101-250, D=51-100, E=20-50, F=10-19, G=1-9

2019 Harris Directory of
Mississippi Manufacturers

419

PRODUCT

Secure Shred LLC...G... 662 563-5008
Batesville *(G-124)*
Secure Shred LLC...G... 662 563-5008
Sardis *(G-4744)*

SIDING MATERIALS

First Coastal Exteriors LLC...G... 769 251-1894
Pearl *(G-4117)*

SIDING: Plastic

Kp Building Products Inc...D... 662 252-9991
Holly Springs *(G-2180)*

SIGN PAINTING & LETTERING SHOP

Better Signs Inc...G... 662 227-1235
Grenada *(G-1669)*
Mid-South Signs Inc...F... 662 327-7807
Columbus *(G-1001)*
Pearl Rubber Stamp & Sign Inc...F... 601 932-6699
Jackson *(G-2662)*

SIGNALS: Railroad, Electric

5m Enterprises LLC...G... 601 416-0210
Sebastopol *(G-4773)*

SIGNALS: Transportation

Gw Ministries...G... 662 832-9756
Water Valley *(G-5469)*
J L McCool Contractors Inc...F... 228 769-9771
Moss Point *(G-3482)*

SIGNS & ADVERTISING SPECIALTIES

A Plus Signs Inc...G... 601 355-9595
Jackson *(G-2314)*
A To B Sign Company...G... 601 924-6323
Clinton *(G-811)*
Ad Art Sign...G... 601 939-8000
Pearl *(G-4103)*
Address America Inc...G... 888 991-3322
Jackson *(G-2319)*
Airdesigns...D... 601 584-1000
Hattiesburg *(G-1919)*
Alden R Stockert...G... 228 731-2747
Gulfport *(G-1717)*
All In One Signs & Printing...G... 662 216-0737
Holly Springs *(G-2170)*
Allens Trophies Inc...E... 601 582-7702
Hattiesburg *(G-1920)*
AMC Signs & Lighting LLC...G... 901 831-7393
Iuka *(G-2283)*
Auto Trim Design of Meridian...G... 601 482-8037
Meridian *(G-3303)*
Ball Sign Co...G... 662 236-2338
Oxford *(G-3938)*
Be Joyful Signs...G... 601 540-6602
Natchez *(G-3525)*
Better Signs Inc...G... 662 227-1235
Grenada *(G-1669)*
Big D Signs...G... 228 860-1075
Diberville *(G-1198)*
Bloms Creative Signs Inc...G... 228 374-2566
Biloxi *(G-221)*
Blue Chip Signs Inc...G... 228 918-9511
Biloxi *(G-222)*
Brian Scott Moore...G... 901 831-7393
Tishomingo *(G-5082)*
C&C Signs LLC...G... 228 235-4839
Diberville *(G-1200)*
Charleston Manufacturing LLC...G... 901 853-3070
Olive Branch *(G-3822)*
Chism Rackard Enterprises LLC...G... 662 327-5200
Columbus *(G-947)*
Creative Ventures LLC...G... 601 798-7758
Picayune *(G-4264)*
Cupitsignscom LLC...G... 228 712-2322
Pascagoula *(G-4029)*
Custom Sign Co of Batesville...G... 662 844-6333
Tupelo *(G-5125)*
Custom Sign Co of Batesville...E... 662 563-7371
Batesville *(G-104)*
D & D Signs and Labels...G... 662 449-4956
Nesbit *(G-3649)*
D D Berryhill Signs...G... 662 298-3325
Hernando *(G-2128)*
Davids Signs Inc...G... 601 626-8934
Collinsville *(G-867)*
Delta Sign Shop...G... 662 334-9878
Greenville *(G-1549)*
Designs of Times Inc...G... 601 791-5299
Lucedale *(G-2993)*
Desoto Digital Services Llc...G... 662 336-2233
Olive Branch *(G-3834)*
Dixie Signs LLC...G... 228 255-5548
Pass Christian *(G-4081)*
Dotted Signs & Screenprinting...G... 601 506-2175
Forest *(G-1415)*
Dwain Mc Nair Signs & Screen...G... 601 267-9967
Carthage *(G-715)*
Dynamic Signs and More...G... 228 235-5660
Biloxi *(G-240)*
E Vegely Signs...G... 228 255-7543
Pass Christian *(G-4082)*
Econo Signs...G... 662 844-1554
Tupelo *(G-5128)*
Eyecatcher Signs...G... 601 604-2595
Meridian *(G-3336)*
Fast Signs...G... 601 602-5413
Hattiesburg *(G-1968)*
Fastwrapzcom LLC...G... 662 213-8771
Tupelo *(G-5131)*
Fred Windham Signs...G... 601 794-1445
Purvis *(G-4438)*
Gator Sign & Image Concepts...G... 601 684-8686
McComb *(G-3251)*
Gentry Signs...G... 662 323-3652
Starkville *(G-4946)*
Hancock Advg Specialities...G... 662 842-1820
Tupelo *(G-5149)*
Harris Signs...G... 601 624-4658
Brandon *(G-404)*
Hearz Yer Sign...G... 601 683-3636
Newton *(G-3721)*
Hospitality Sign Company...G... 601 898-8393
Madison *(G-3108)*
Houston Sign Design...G... 662 728-2327
Booneville *(G-330)*
Hudson Outdoor Sign LLC...G... 601 947-4608
Lucedale *(G-3002)*
Identities Graphic Solutions...G... 601 917-9983
Meridian *(G-3349)*
Images Galore Signs LLC...G... 228 818-5449
Ocean Springs *(G-3766)*
Independents Service Company...G... 662 287-2431
Corinth *(G-1091)*
Its Vinyl YAll LLC...G... 601 533-8885
Canton *(G-662)*
Jan Signs Inc...G... 601 785-9800
Taylorsville *(G-5054)*
John Sign & Co Inc...G... 662 843-3548
Cleveland *(G-797)*
K & K Systems Inc...D... 662 566-2025
Tupelo *(G-5165)*
King B Signs and Wonders Inc...G... 815 263-1546
Columbus *(G-993)*
Linco Safety Signs...G... 662 469-9569
Hernando *(G-2140)*
Major League Promotions...G... 601 672-4798
Jackson *(G-2481)*
Major League Promotions LLC...G... 601 672-4798
Jackson *(G-2482)*
McMillan Stamp & Sign Co Inc...G... 601 353-4688
Jackson *(G-2485)*
Mickeys Trophy & Sign Shop...G... 601 649-1263
Laurel *(G-2802)*
Mid South Sign Council...G... 601 446-6688
Natchez *(G-3587)*
Mid-Mississippi Vinyl...G... 601 910-6553
Flowood *(G-1381)*
Mike Stringer Signs...G... 601 736-8600
Columbia *(G-907)*
Multimedia Graphics Inc...F... 601 981-5001
Jackson *(G-2514)*
National Scrubwear Inc...F... 601 483-0796
Meridian *(G-3376)*
National Sign Tennessee Corp...G... 901 210-8023
Olive Branch *(G-3887)*
New Albany Sign Co...G... 662 538-5599
New Albany *(G-3689)*
Ocean Springs Sign & Graphics...G... 228 213-7933
Gautier *(G-1500)*
Outdoor Dimensions Inc...G... 601 749-9981
Picayune *(G-4282)*
Pearl Rubber Stamp & Sign Inc...F... 601 932-6699
Jackson *(G-2662)*
Pickett Productions...G... 601 885-2720
Utica *(G-5310)*
Plastics Plus Inc...G... 228 832-4634
Gulfport *(G-1849)*
Pro Signs...G... 662 587-6036
Ripley *(G-4668)*
Prosigns Inc...G... 601 791-5299
Lucedale *(G-3012)*
R D Graphix Sign Solutions...G... 601 736-0663
Columbia *(G-916)*
Ra Maxx LLC...G... 662 342-6212
Southaven *(G-4894)*
Rainbow Signs...G... 228 354-8008
Biloxi *(G-275)*
Red Creek Graphics LLC...G... 228 864-3349
Gulfport *(G-1859)*
Reservoir Signs LLC...G... 601 898-1111
Madison *(G-3143)*
Rodger Holdeman S Signs...G... 662 436-0911
West Point *(G-5561)*
Roosevelt Wallace...G... 662 627-7513
Clarksdale *(G-781)*
S H Wholesale Sign Co...G... 228 865-4352
Gulfport *(G-1866)*
Scs Signs and Service LLC...G... 228 235-4839
Diberville *(G-1212)*
Shaw Signs LLC...G... 228 224-4971
Saucier *(G-4764)*
Sign and Sing...G... 601 954-9172
Brandon *(G-452)*
Sign Crafters...G... 769 216-3936
Brandon *(G-453)*
Sign Doctor LLC...G... 601 286-3387
Meridian *(G-3395)*
Sign Graphics...G... 601 445-0463
Natchez *(G-3620)*
Sign Gypsies Df North Ms...G... 901 484-7357
Southaven *(G-4900)*
Sign Gypsies Golden Triangle...G... 662 368-3662
Caledonia *(G-630)*
Sign Here...G... 601 847-3537
Mendenhall *(G-3288)*
Sign Language...G... 228 990-3609
Vancleave *(G-5321)*
Sign Ministries...G... 678 507-9912
Gulfport *(G-1868)*
Sign Plex...G... 228 896-5999
Gulfport *(G-1869)*
Sign Pro Wholesale LLC...F... 601 453-3082
Meridian *(G-3396)*
Sign Shop...G... 662 258-7186
Eupora *(G-1291)*
Sign Solutions of Saucier...G... 228 265-4325
Saucier *(G-4765)*
Signature Works...G... 601 477-6187
Ellisville *(G-1269)*
Signmark Inc...G... 601 932-6699
Pearl *(G-4145)*
Signs & More...G... 662 494-9451
West Point *(G-5562)*
Signs By Schack...G... 662 890-3683
Olive Branch *(G-3909)*
Signs By Shaffier...G... 601 833-8600
Brookhaven *(G-531)*
Signs Plus...G... 228 832-4634
Gulfport *(G-1870)*
Signs Plus Inc...G... 228 832-4634
Gulfport *(G-1871)*
Southeastern Sign Company Inc...G... 601 391-0023
Madison *(G-3149)*
Southern Signs...G... 228 255-4122
Pass Christian *(G-4096)*
Staco Decorative Iron...G... 601 264-0064
Hattiesburg *(G-2067)*
Standex International Corp...B... 662 534-9061
New Albany *(G-3700)*
Staybrite Signs...G... 901 490-0431
Southaven *(G-4908)*
Tampa Sign Co...G... 228 474-1945
Moss Point *(G-3501)*
Tim Bennett...G... 662 332-0020
Greenville *(G-1605)*
Tupelo Engraving & Rbr Stamp...G... 662 842-0574
Tupelo *(G-5246)*
University Screen Print Inc...F... 662 324-8277
Starkville *(G-4978)*
Vegasigns LLC...G... 662 871-7337
Tupelo *(G-5250)*
Velocity Inc...E... 662 449-4026
Hernando *(G-2160)*
Vicksburg Newsmedia LLC...G... 601 636-4545
Vicksburg *(G-5437)*

PRODUCT SECTION

SOFTWARE PUBLISHERS: Education

Vicksburg Printing and Pubg Co ....G 601 631-0400
Vicksburg *(G-5440)*

Vital Signs Unbound ....G 662 363-6940
Tunica *(G-5104)*

Vizionz Unlimited LLC ....G 601 272-5040
Jackson *(G-2622)*

Willcoxon Enterprises Inc ....G 662 840-2300
Tupelo *(G-5259)*

Wren Pest Control ....G 601 276-6117
Summit *(G-5031)*

Young Electric Sign Co ....G 228 354-8008
Biloxi *(G-286)*

Young Electric Sign Company ....E 228 354-8008
Biloxi *(G-287)*

SIGNS & ADVERTISING SPECIALTIES: Artwork, Advertising

Relevant Design Studios LLC ....G 601 736-0663
Columbia *(G-918)*

SIGNS & ADVERTISING SPECIALTIES: Novelties

Oneway Inc ....G 601 664-0007
Jackson *(G-2660)*

SIGNS & ADVERTISING SPECIALTIES: Signs

Ad Lines Inc ....G 662 893-6400
Nesbit *(G-3646)*

Ainsworth Signs ....G 662 453-1904
Greenwood *(G-1611)*

Airbrush & Signs By Debby ....G 601 656-6953
Philadelphia *(G-4202)*

All Signs Inc ....G 228 897-9100
Gulfport *(G-1719)*

Berry Signs & Stripes ....G 601 544-5600
Hattiesburg *(G-1930)*

Computer Graphics By Connie ....G 662 343-8399
Hamilton *(G-1904)*

Dan W Butler Signs ....G 601 948-5059
Jackson *(G-2375)*

Dunaway Signs Inc ....G 228 392-5421
Biloxi *(G-239)*

Garys Graphics ....G 662 429-2924
Nesbit *(G-3652)*

H&S Sign Company ....G 662 473-9300
Water Valley *(G-5470)*

Lightning Quick Signs ....G 228 467-1718
Waveland *(G-5482)*

Peacocks Signs & Designs ....G 662 226-9206
Grenada *(G-1698)*

Roger Fillebaum ....G 601 638-5473
Vicksburg *(G-5414)*

S&S Signs ....G 601 659-7783
Stonewall *(G-4999)*

Sarub Inc ....G 601 936-4490
Pearl *(G-4142)*

Select Signs More ....G 601 823-0717
Brookhaven *(G-530)*

Sign Shop ....G 601 735-1383
Waynesboro *(G-5514)*

Signs & Stuff ....G 662 393-9314
Southaven *(G-4901)*

Signs & Stuff Inc ....G 662 895-4505
Southaven *(G-4902)*

Skillem Entreprises Inc ....G 601 936-4461
Pearl *(G-4146)*

Spectech Service & Signs LLC ....F 601 482-0816
Meridian *(G-3405)*

SIGNS & ADVERTSG SPECIALTIES: Displays/Cutouts Window/Lobby

Pop-A-Cart LLC ....G 931 292-2150
Jackson *(G-2541)*

SIGNS, ELECTRICAL: Wholesalers

Better Signs Inc ....G 662 227-1235
Grenada *(G-1669)*

SIGNS, EXC ELECTRIC, WHOLESALE

Better Signs Inc ....G 662 227-1235
Grenada *(G-1669)*

SIGNS: Electrical

59 Signs LLC ....G 601 798-3682
Carriere *(G-686)*

Budget Signs Inc ....F 601 354-4977
Jackson *(G-2348)*

Delta Signs and Designs LLC ....G 662 822-0830
Greenville *(G-1550)*

Dims Group ....G 302 562-2697
Southaven *(G-4868)*

Duncan Signs Inc ....G 662 842-0226
Tupelo *(G-5127)*

Ets Signs Inc ....G 601 268-7275
Hattiesburg *(G-1964)*

Federal Heath Sign Company LLC ....G 662 233-2999
Coldwater *(G-845)*

Gpp Charleston Industries LLC ....E 800 647-2384
Charleston *(G-738)*

Headrick Signs & Graphics Inc ....D 601 649-1977
Laurel *(G-2776)*

Jones Signs LLC ....G 662 453-2432
Greenwood *(G-1632)*

Mid-South Signs Inc ....F 662 327-7807
Columbus *(G-1001)*

Mitchell Signs Inc ....D 601 553-1557
Meridian *(G-3374)*

Munn Enterprises Inc ....D 601 264-7446
Hattiesburg *(G-2035)*

Signs Plus ....G 601 482-4217
Meridian *(G-3397)*

Southern Signs Inc ....G 601 445-5564
Natchez *(G-3624)*

SIGNS: Neon

Illusions Neon & Accessories ....G 662 299-6366
Greenwood *(G-1628)*

Manning Signs Inc ....G 662 332-4496
Greenville *(G-1567)*

Stanley McCaffrey Signs ....G 228 832-0885
Gulfport *(G-1880)*

Tavares Signs ....G 662 289-5366
Kosciusko *(G-2716)*

SILICON: Pure

Mississippi Silicon LLC ....C 662 696-2600
Burnsville *(G-572)*

SIRENS: Vehicle, Marine, Indl & Warning

L3 Technologies Inc ....E 601 856-2274
Madison *(G-3117)*

SKIDS: Wood

Stanley D Stokes Jr ....G 662 237-6600
Carrollton *(G-703)*

SLAG: Crushed Or Ground

Vulcan Materials Company ....G 601 425-3509
Laurel *(G-2863)*

SOAPS & DETERGENTS

Charlie Chemical and Supply ....G 662 332-9262
Greenville *(G-1537)*

Cottage Garden Ms LLC ....G 662 665-1918
Corinth *(G-1080)*

Ecolab Inc ....G 662 327-1863
Columbus *(G-966)*

Golden Source Inventors LLC ....G 601 325-4064
Hattiesburg *(G-1975)*

Kik Custom Products Inc ....B 901 947-5400
Olive Branch *(G-3860)*

Rite-Kem Inc ....F 662 840-6060
Tupelo *(G-5218)*

Soap & Stuff LLC ....G 228 875-1721
Ocean Springs *(G-3788)*

T & L Specialty Company Inc ....E 662 842-8143
Tupelo *(G-5236)*

Way Manufacture Inc ....E 601 749-0362
Picayune *(G-4302)*

Yonce & Comans Products LLC ....G 601 270-7712
Petal *(G-4201)*

SOAPS & DETERGENTS: Dishwashing Compounds

Chemical Products & Systems ....G 601 354-1919
Jackson *(G-2358)*

SOFT DRINKS WHOLESALERS

Clark Beverage Group Inc ....D 662 338-3400
Starkville *(G-4934)*

Royal Crown Bottling ....E 662 843-3431
Cleveland *(G-807)*

Weaver Consolidated Group Inc ....G 662 287-1433
Corinth *(G-1128)*

Weaver Consolidated Group Inc ....E 662 842-1753
Tupelo *(G-5253)*

SOFTWARE PUBLISHERS: Application

Box Office 7 Studios ....G 662 633-2451
Brandon *(G-372)*

Community Broadcasting ....G 731 441-6962
Booneville *(G-325)*

Connect Technology LLC ....G 601 914-1713
Jackson *(G-2365)*

Fed Service Hub LLC ....G 228 547-3498
Gulfport *(G-1784)*

Fitmate Social Inc ....G 206 849-2447
Oxford *(G-3956)*

Hydesoft Computing LLC ....G 601 629-8607
Vicksburg *(G-5380)*

Info Services Inc ....F 601 898-7858
Madison *(G-3109)*

Jabr LLC ....G 601 502-5587
Flowood *(G-1369)*

Orchard Oxford ....G 662 259-0094
Oxford *(G-3982)*

Perspecta Engineering Inc ....G 571 313-6000
Stennis Space Center *(G-4996)*

Pinplanfix21 LLC ....G 662 380-1961
Oxford *(G-3994)*

Ptc Inc ....G 601 919-2688
Brandon *(G-441)*

White Shirt Networks LLC ....G 601 292-7900
Madison *(G-3170)*

SOFTWARE PUBLISHERS: Business & Professional

3v Solutions LLC ....G 601 720-4999
Madison *(G-3074)*

5th Avenue Software LLC ....G 662 843-1200
Cleveland *(G-785)*

Assured Revenue Corporation ....G 662 323-5350
Starkville *(G-4925)*

Bdm It Services (us) Inc ....G 601 274-0347
Quitman *(G-4458)*

Beyondtrust Corporation ....E 601 519-0213
Ridgeland *(G-4555)*

Btm Solutions ....F 662 328-2400
Columbus *(G-942)*

Cks Productions Inc ....G 888 897-9136
Biloxi *(G-229)*

Corcoran Legal Group ....G 601 906-8227
Jackson *(G-2370)*

Grayco Systems & Consulting ....G 601 583-0430
Hattiesburg *(G-1976)*

Hey There App LLC ....G 228 238-0344
Ocean Springs *(G-3763)*

It Synergistics LLC ....G 855 866-7648
Flowood *(G-1367)*

Mac Financial Mgmt LLC ....G 844 622-6468
Magnolia *(G-3193)*

Magnolia Accounting Services ....G 662 429-5852
Hernando *(G-2141)*

Mega Tech South LLC ....G 662 538-3366
Shannon *(G-4816)*

Signaturelink Inc ....G 601 898-7359
Ridgeland *(G-4629)*

VT Consolidated Inc ....G 601 956-5440
Ridgeland *(G-4646)*

SOFTWARE PUBLISHERS: Computer Utilities

Stormcom LLC ....G 601 918-5401
Jackson *(G-2598)*

SOFTWARE PUBLISHERS: Education

Boyd Eductl Solutions Tech LLC ....G 601 951-2305
Ridgeland *(G-4558)*

L and J Global Marketing LLC ....G 662 420-9480
Olive Branch *(G-3863)*

Schoolstatus LLC ....G 601 620-0613
Hattiesburg *(G-2056)*

Employee Codes: A=Over 500 employees, B=251-500
C=101-250, D=51-100, E=20-50, F=10-19, G=1-9

2019 Harris Directory of
Mississippi Manufacturers

421

PRODUCT

SOFTWARE PUBLISHERS: Home Entertainment

SOFTWARE PUBLISHERS: Home Entertainment

Dataware LLC ....G...... 662 356-4978
Caledonia *(G-628)*

SOFTWARE PUBLISHERS: NEC

Aggeos Inc ....G...... 512 751-2160
Fulton *(G-1444)*
Applied Software System LLC ....G...... 601 605-0877
Ridgeland *(G-4550)*
Bartag Corporation ....G...... 769 233-0925
Byram *(G-618)*
Business Systems Inc ....G...... 601 957-1500
Jackson *(G-2351)*
Cable One Inc ....G...... 601 833-7991
McComb *(G-3245)*
Chuck Patrick ....G...... 601 278-7193
Brandon *(G-380)*
Citizen Health Foundation ....G...... 601 463-2436
Hattiesburg *(G-1944)*
Confederate Express LLC ....G...... 662 315-6625
Hamilton *(G-1905)*
Conflux Software LLC ....G...... 601 940-0182
Jackson *(G-2364)*
Custodis MGT Systems LLC ....G...... 601 207-1047
Meridian *(G-3325)*
Custom Accounting Solutions ....G...... 601 957-7500
Jackson *(G-2372)*
Data Medical Inc ....G...... 662 283-0463
Duck Hill *(G-1220)*
Data Systems Management Inc ....F...... 601 925-6270
Clinton *(G-821)*
Dqsi LLC ....G...... 228 688-3796
Stennis Space Center *(G-4994)*
End2end Public Safety LLC ....G...... 662 513-0999
Oxford *(G-3954)*
Environmental Tech of Amer ....G...... 601 607-3151
Ridgeland *(G-4577)*
Esoftware Solutions Inc ....E...... 601 919-2275
Ridgeland *(G-4578)*
Honey Island Software Inc ....G...... 985 265-4192
Pearlington *(G-4160)*
Ideal Software Systems Inc ....D...... 601 693-1673
Meridian *(G-3348)*
Imaging Informatics LLC ....G...... 228 332-0674
Pass Christian *(G-4089)*
In The Black Software LLC ....G...... 228 697-2120
Ocean Springs *(G-3767)*
Intelatool Solutions LLC ....G...... 601 594-8451
Richland *(G-4520)*
Lenders Software Incorporated ....G...... 601 919-6362
Brandon *(G-413)*
Localnet ....G...... 601 774-9338
Union *(G-5300)*
Mel Vold Sales Co ....G...... 601 371-4911
Jackson *(G-2487)*
NA Food Dash LLC ....G...... 662 266-0738
New Albany *(G-3687)*
Oracle America Inc ....G...... 601 352-6113
Jackson *(G-2530)*
Simple Solutions ....G...... 228 588-9509
Moss Point *(G-3498)*
Skyhawke Technologies LLC ....B...... 601 605-6100
Ridgeland *(G-4630)*

SOFTWARE PUBLISHERS: Operating Systems

Business Communications Inc ....E...... 601 898-1890
Ridgeland *(G-4559)*
Computer Works LLC ....G...... 228 696-8889
Moss Point *(G-3475)*

SOFTWARE PUBLISHERS: Publisher's

Catontech MGT Systems LLC ....G...... 601 207-1047
Meridian *(G-3316)*
Creations By Stephanie ....G...... 228 697-2899
Biloxi *(G-234)*
T G Ferguson Company ....G...... 662 563-0806
Batesville *(G-127)*

SOFTWARE TRAINING, COMPUTER

Storsoft Technology Corp ....G...... 954 436-9292
Gulfport *(G-1881)*

SOIL CONDITIONERS

Bio Soil Enhancers Inc ....G...... 601 582-4000
Hattiesburg *(G-1932)*

SOLAR CELLS

Seraphim Solar USA Mfg Inc ....E...... 601 509-1265
Jackson *(G-2577)*

SOLDERING EQPT: Electrical, Handheld

Robert E Monk ....G...... 662 562-8729
Senatobia *(G-4800)*

SONAR SYSTEMS & EQPT

Raytheon Company ....B...... 601 467-3730
Forest *(G-1424)*

SOUND EFFECTS & MUSIC PRODUCTION: Motion Picture

Michael A Dent ....G...... 601 543-0157
Hattiesburg *(G-2023)*

SOUND EQPT: Electric

Elvis and Company LLC ....G...... 662 616-9248
Greenville *(G-1553)*

SOUND RECORDING STUDIOS

Chuck Ryan Cars Inc ....G...... 228 864-9706
Long Beach *(G-2932)*

SOYBEAN PRDTS

Gold Coast Commodities Inc ....E...... 601 825-2508
Brandon *(G-400)*

SPACE RESEARCH & TECHNOLOGY PROGRAMS ADMINISTRATION

Michael A Dent ....G...... 601 543-0157
Hattiesburg *(G-2023)*

SPACE VEHICLE EQPT

Atk Space Systems Inc ....E...... 662 423-7700
Iuka *(G-2284)*
L3 Technologies Inc ....E...... 601 856-2274
Madison *(G-3117)*

SPEAKER SYSTEMS

Mississppi Band Chctaw Indians ....E...... 601 656-6038
Choctaw *(G-747)*

SPECIALTY SAWMILL PRDTS

Copiah Lumber Company ....E...... 601 892-2241
Crystal Springs *(G-1140)*
Homans Wood Products ....E...... 662 862-2145
Fulton *(G-1457)*
Reeds Reynolds ....E...... 601 445-8206
Natchez *(G-3612)*

SPECULATIVE BUILDERS: Single-Family Housing

Coleman Builders Inc ....G...... 662 234-0376
Oxford *(G-3947)*
Watkins ....G...... 601 752-2526
Ellisville *(G-1277)*

SPORTING & ATHLETIC GOODS: Arrows, Archery

Arrowmaker ....G...... 601 264-4748
Purvis *(G-4433)*

SPORTING & ATHLETIC GOODS: Boomerangs

Boomerang Services LLC ....G...... 601 649-6474
Laurel *(G-2741)*

SPORTING & ATHLETIC GOODS: Bows, Archery

Gator Archery & Outdoors LLC ....G...... 601 940-3570
Madison *(G-3103)*

SPORTING & ATHLETIC GOODS: Camping Eqpt & Splys

Kinards Kountry ....G...... 601 737-8378
Bailey *(G-68)*

SPORTING & ATHLETIC GOODS: Fishing Bait, Artificial

Clay Necaise ....G...... 228 233-7760
Bay Saint Louis *(G-140)*

SPORTING & ATHLETIC GOODS: Fishing Tackle, General

Cemco Inc ....E...... 662 323-1559
Starkville *(G-4933)*
Jackson Fishing Sptg Accessory ....G...... 662 837-9089
Falkner *(G-1295)*
Pugh Tackle Co Inc ....G...... 662 534-7393
New Albany *(G-3692)*
Slaters Jigs Inc ....G...... 662 887-3548
Indianola *(G-2270)*

SPORTING & ATHLETIC GOODS: Game Calls

Brock Outdoors ....G...... 662 255-1121
Saltillo *(G-4709)*
Conviction Game Calls ....G...... 662 295-9972
West Point *(G-5541)*
Coon Creek Custom Game Calls ....G...... 662 284-6932
Corinth *(G-1073)*
RAC N Spurs Game Calls ....G...... 601 455-9484
Silver Creek *(G-4839)*
Southern Roost Game Calls ....G...... 601 441-0748
Columbia *(G-922)*
Tombstone Game Calls ....G...... 662 769-6364
Maben *(G-3052)*
Wooly Booger Game Calls ....G...... 662 587-3763
Walnut *(G-5459)*

SPORTING & ATHLETIC GOODS: Gymnasium Eqpt

Mississssppi Bsktball Athltics ....G...... 601 957-7373
Jackson *(G-2507)*

SPORTING & ATHLETIC GOODS: Hunting Eqpt

Cjw Hunting LLC ....G...... 662 746-1863
Yazoo City *(G-5628)*
Icon Outdoors LLC ....G...... 662 895-3651
Olive Branch *(G-3850)*
Mstate Technologies LLC ....G...... 662 418-0110
Starkville *(G-4962)*
Primos Inc ....D...... 601 879-9323
Flora *(G-1311)*

SPORTING & ATHLETIC GOODS: Indian Clubs

Excel By Four LLC ....G...... 228 355-8203
Gulfport *(G-1780)*
Krewe of Natchez Indn Yth Ldrs ....E...... 601 392-1709
Natchez *(G-3577)*

SPORTING & ATHLETIC GOODS: Pools, Swimming, Exc Plastic

Shoreline Pool Mfr Inc ....G...... 601 372-0577
Jackson *(G-2580)*

SPORTING & ATHLETIC GOODS: Rods & Rod Parts, Fishing

Turner Fly Rods LLC ....G...... 228 623-6475
Moss Point *(G-3503)*

SPORTING & ATHLETIC GOODS: Shafts, Golf Club

True Temper Sports Inc ....B...... 662 256-5605
Amory *(G-57)*

SPORTING & ATHLETIC GOODS: Shooting Eqpt & Splys, General

Wilson Fabrication Inc ....G...... 601 445-8119
Natchez *(G-3643)*

2019 Harris Directory of Mississippi Manufacturers

(G-0000) Company's Geographic Section entry number

PRODUCT SECTION

STAMPINGS: Metal

SPORTING & ATHLETIC GOODS: Skateboards

Swell O Phonic ....G....... 601 981-3547
Jackson *(G-2601)*

SPORTING & ATHLETIC GOODS: Targets, Archery & Rifle Shooting

Advanced GnsInger Armament LLC .....G.... 775 343-5633
Starkville *(G-4923)*

SPORTING & ATHLETIC GOODS: Team Sports Eqpt

Johnson Education Firm LLC ....G....... 662 347-9150
Greenville *(G-1560)*

SPORTING & ATHLETIC GOODS: Track & Field Athletic Eqpt

Southeast Miss Schl Pdts Inc ....G....... 662 855-5048
Caledonia *(G-631)*

SPORTING & RECREATIONAL GOODS & SPLYS WHOLESALERS

Buzini Group LLC ....E....... 601 398-1311
Flowood *(G-1350)*
Clay Necaise ....G....... 228 233-7760
Bay Saint Louis *(G-140)*

SPORTING & RECREATIONAL GOODS, WHOLESALE: Boat Access & Part

Brian Smith ....G....... 601 259-9745
Gulfport *(G-1744)*
Mainland Sails Inc ....G....... 228 374-7245
Gautier *(G-1498)*
Rolls-Royce Marine North Amer ....D....... 228 762-0728
Pascagoula *(G-4064)*

SPORTING & RECREATIONAL GOODS, WHOLESALE: Fishing

Millennium Outdoors LLC ....F....... 601 932-5832
Pearl *(G-4132)*
Southern Lure Company Inc ....F....... 662 327-4548
Columbus *(G-1029)*

SPORTING & RECREATIONAL GOODS, WHOLESALE: Golf

Green Save Inc ....G....... 662 566-0717
Verona *(G-5332)*

SPORTING & RECREATIONAL GOODS, WHOLESALE: Hot Tubs

Baymont Inc ....D....... 662 454-7993
Golden *(G-1521)*
Richard Armstrong ....G....... 228 822-2238
Long Beach *(G-2950)*

SPORTING FIREARMS WHOLESALERS

2a Armaments LLC ....G....... 662 538-8118
New Albany *(G-3669)*

SPORTING GOODS

Ability Works Inc ....G....... 662 328-0275
Columbus *(G-931)*
Ao Liquidation Trust Inc ....E....... 662 675-8102
Coffeeville *(G-841)*
College Station Spt Stores Inc ....G....... 662 349-8988
Southaven *(G-4860)*
Dixons Hunting Lodge ....G....... 662 571-1908
Benton *(G-208)*
Gulf States Golf Cars ....G....... 601 853-1510
Ridgeland *(G-4588)*
Hanson Athletic Inc ....G....... 601 389-0403
Philadelphia *(G-4216)*
Huntin Camp LLC ....G....... 601 649-6334
Laurel *(G-2783)*
Outdoors Advantage ....G....... 662 257-9601
Tupelo *(G-5196)*
Outlaw Sporting Goods LLC ....G....... 662 459-9054
Greenwood *(G-1644)*
Proshop Inc ....G....... 662 333-7511
Myrtle *(G-3513)*

Quitman Sporting Goods & Pawn ....G....... 601 776-3212
Quitman *(G-4468)*
Sipp Spinners and Lures LLC ....G....... 601 620-6445
Brandon *(G-454)*
Sports of All Sorts Inc ....G....... 662 429-1162
Hernando *(G-2156)*
Sportz Zone LLC ....G....... 228 284-1654
Long Beach *(G-2954)*
Taylor Enterprises ....G....... 228 385-1245
Biloxi *(G-282)*
Tri-State Athletic Group ....G....... 901 395-6359
Southaven *(G-4916)*
Tucker Manufacturing Co Inc ....E....... 662 563-7220
Batesville *(G-131)*
Wonder Woods Inc ....G....... 601 853-1956
Madison *(G-3172)*

SPORTING GOODS STORES, NEC

3 Men Moving & Storage LLC ....G....... 662 238-7774
Oxford *(G-3934)*
Creative Designs & Sports ....G....... 662 327-5000
Columbus *(G-956)*
Emersons ....G....... 228 588-3952
Lucedale *(G-2994)*

SPORTING GOODS STORES: Archery Splys

Big Buck Sports ....G....... 601 605-2661
Ridgeland *(G-4556)*
Hickory Creek Inc ....G....... 228 832-2649
Saucier *(G-4754)*
Hunters Hollow Inc ....F....... 662 234-5945
Oxford *(G-3958)*

SPORTING GOODS STORES: Bait & Tackle

Pugh Tackle Co Inc ....G....... 662 534-7393
New Albany *(G-3692)*
Vancleave Portable Buildings ....G....... 228 826-5151
Vancleave *(G-5323)*

SPORTING GOODS STORES: Firearms

2a Armaments LLC ....G....... 662 538-8118
New Albany *(G-3669)*
Dixie Precision Rifles LLC ....G....... 601 706-9100
Brandon *(G-389)*

SPORTING GOODS STORES: Hunting Eqpt

Slaters Jigs Inc ....G....... 662 887-3548
Indianola *(G-2270)*

SPORTING GOODS STORES: Playground Eqpt

Wonder Woods Inc ....G....... 601 853-1956
Madison *(G-3172)*

SPORTING GOODS STORES: Specialty Sport Splys, NEC

Laser Mania Inc ....G....... 601 543-0072
Hattiesburg *(G-2016)*

SPORTING GOODS: Archery

Champion Custom Bow Strings ....G....... 662 652-3499
Fulton *(G-1449)*
Hickory Creek Inc ....G....... 228 832-2649
Saucier *(G-4754)*

SPORTING GOODS: Fishing Nets

Delta Net & Twine Co Inc ....F....... 662 332-0841
Greenville *(G-1548)*

SPORTING/ATHLETIC GOODS: Gloves, Boxing, Handball, Etc

Rog LLC ....G....... 662 455-1364
Greenwood *(G-1649)*

SPORTS APPAREL STORES

Creative Designs & Sports ....G....... 662 327-5000
Columbus *(G-956)*
Crux Industries ....F....... 662 873-3317
Anguilla *(G-58)*
Logo Sportswear ....G....... 601 845-5038
Florence *(G-1327)*

SPRAYING EQPT: Agricultural

Sanders Seed ....G....... 800 844-5533
Cleveland *(G-808)*
Warren Inc ....C....... 601 765-8221
Collins *(G-865)*

SPRINGS: Automobile

Deep S Suspension & ACC Inc ....G....... 601 371-7373
Jackson *(G-2378)*
Union Spring & Mfg Corp ....D....... 662 489-7846
Pontotoc *(G-4366)*

SPRINGS: Coiled Flat

Matthew Warren Inc ....G....... 574 753-6622
Pontotoc *(G-4345)*

SPRINGS: Steel

Matthew Warren Inc ....D....... 662 489-7846
Pontotoc *(G-4344)*
Quality Steel & Supply LLC ....F....... 601 731-1222
Columbia *(G-913)*

SPRINGS: Wire

Fibrix LLC ....G....... 662 568-3393
Houlka *(G-2222)*
Leggett & Platt Incorporated ....G....... 662 842-5704
Tupelo *(G-5175)*
Matthew Warren Inc ....D....... 662 489-7846
Pontotoc *(G-4344)*

STAINED GLASS ART SVCS

Alley Kats Glass ....G....... 662 324-3002
Starkville *(G-4924)*

STAINLESS STEEL

Grayson Blu LLC ....E....... 662 779-1291
Louisville *(G-2970)*
Nucor Steel Jackson Inc ....B....... 601 939-1623
Flowood *(G-1385)*

STAIRCASES & STAIRS, WOOD

Delta Enterprises ....G....... 662 335-5291
Greenville *(G-1545)*

STAMPED ART GOODS FOR EMBROIDERING

Hanging By A Thread LLC ....G....... 662 449-5198
Hernando *(G-2133)*

STAMPINGS: Automotive

Auto Parts Mfg Miss Inc ....B....... 662 365-3082
Guntown *(G-1898)*
Hago Automotive Corp ....F....... 662 593-0491
Iuka *(G-2293)*
Multicraft Intl Ltd Partnr ....G....... 601 854-5516
Pelahatchie *(G-4167)*
Tower Automotive Operations ....C....... 601 499-3300
Madison *(G-3160)*
Tower Automotive Operations ....C....... 601 678-4000
Meridian *(G-3415)*

STAMPINGS: Metal

Advance Tool and Die Inc ....G....... 601 939-1291
Pearl *(G-4104)*
Columbus Marble Works Inc ....E....... 662 328-1477
Columbus *(G-950)*
Heavy Duty Industries Inc ....G....... 601 425-1011
Laurel *(G-2777)*
Hunter Douglas Inc ....C....... 662 690-8190
Shannon *(G-4810)*
Ice Industries Inc ....G....... 662 226-1161
Grenada *(G-1687)*
Mississppi Inds For The Blind ....E....... 601 693-5525
Meridian *(G-3373)*
Pk USA Inc ....E....... 662 301-4800
Senatobia *(G-4798)*
Southern Metals Co Miss Inc ....E....... 601 649-7475
Laurel *(G-2853)*

Employee Codes: A=Over 500 employees, B=251-500
C=101-250, D=51-100, E=20-50, F=10-19, G=1-9

2019 Harris Directory of
Mississippi Manufacturers

423

STATIONARY & OFFICE SPLYS, WHOLESALE: Looseleaf Binders

PRODUCT SECTION

STATIONARY & OFFICE SPLYS, WHOLESALE: Looseleaf Binders

South Txas Lghthouse For Blind ....G...... 601 679-3180
Meridian *(G-3400)*

STATIONARY & OFFICE SPLYS, WHOLESALE: Manifold Business Form

Zyaa Inc..G...... 601 321-9502
Jackson *(G-2641)*

STATIONARY & OFFICE SPLYS, WHOLESALE: Marking Devices

Trodat Marking Products Inc ....G...... 601 500-5971
Jackson *(G-2612)*

STATIONERY & OFFICE SPLYS WHOLESALERS

Lawrence Printing Company ....D...... 662 453-6301
Greenwood *(G-1633)*
Mr Forms Printing Company Inc ....G...... 601 371-2567
Jackson *(G-2511)*
Oligarch Inc ....G...... 844 321-0016
Houston *(G-2253)*

STATIONERY PRDTS

Custom Signs and Banners ....G...... 662 327-8916
Columbus *(G-957)*

STEEL & ALLOYS: Tool & Die

Kustom Machine and Sheet Metal........F...... 601 469-1062
Philadelphia *(G-4221)*
Virgil Williams LLC ....G...... 662 287-7734
Corinth *(G-1127)*

STEEL FABRICATORS

Abby Manufacturing LLC ....D...... 662 223-5339
Walnut *(G-5452)*
Abby Manufacturing Co Inc ....E...... 662 223-5339
New Albany *(G-3670)*
Acme Fabrication LLC..........................G...... 228 669-0004
Perkinston *(G-4172)*
Addy Metal Fabrication ....G...... 601 635-4064
Decatur *(G-1170)*
Advanced Fabrication Inc ....G...... 601 796-7977
Lumberton *(G-3023)*
Alan Dickerson Inc..............................G...... 662 289-1451
Kosciusko *(G-2687)*
Amerimac Machining Corporation ....G...... 601 940-7919
Jackson *(G-2329)*
B & O Machine & Wldg Co Inc ....F...... 601 833-3000
Brookhaven *(G-481)*
B-Line Fabrication Co Ltd ....E...... 228 832-3286
Gulfport *(G-1732)*
Berry Enterprises of Miss ....G...... 601 928-4006
Perkinston *(G-4174)*
Big River Shipbuilders Inc ....E...... 601 636-9161
Vicksburg *(G-5345)*
Bryan E Presson & Assoc Inc...............F...... 601 925-0053
Clinton *(G-816)*
Cameron Rig Solutions Inc ....G...... 601 629-3300
Vicksburg *(G-5353)*
Careys Construction Co Inc ....E...... 601 922-7388
Jackson *(G-2354)*
Ci Metal Fabrication LLC......................E...... 601 483-6281
Meridian *(G-3320)*
Cives Corporation ....C...... 662 759-6265
Rosedale *(G-4687)*
CL Dews Sons Fndry McHy Inc ....D...... 601 582-4427
Hattiesburg *(G-1945)*
Coastal Metal Works LLC......................F...... 601 749-2611
Picayune *(G-4261)*
Columbus Mch & Wldg Works Inc........E...... 662 328-8473
Columbus *(G-951)*
Composite Fbrication Group LLC ....G...... 601 549-1789
Moselle *(G-3456)*
Construction Metals Co Inc ....G...... 601 939-2566
Jackson *(G-2643)*
Contech Engnered Solutions LLC.........G...... 601 894-2041
Greenville *(G-1540)*
Custom Metal Fabrication Inc..............G...... 662 628-8657
Calhoun City *(G-637)*
D & R Industrial Services LLC ....F...... 601 716-3140
Wiggins *(G-5578)*

Delta Fabrication LLC..........................E...... 662 335-2500
Greenville *(G-1546)*
Delta Machinery Inc ....F...... 662 827-2572
Hollandale *(G-2165)*
Dublin Steel Corporation Inc ....G...... 601 482-2102
Meridian *(G-3331)*
Ellis Steel Company Inc ....D...... 662 494-5955
West Point *(G-5542)*
Ellis Steel Company Inc ....G...... 662 893-5955
Olive Branch *(G-3838)*
Fab- Tek Central Miss Inc ....E...... 601 892-5017
Hazlehurst *(G-2095)*
Global Fabrication II LLC ....E...... 601 749-2209
Picayune *(G-4267)*
Gulf States Fabrication Inc ....F...... 601 426-9006
Laurel *(G-2773)*
Gulley S Welding Service ....G...... 601 938-6336
Meridian *(G-3343)*
Harrells Metal Works Inc ....E...... 662 226-0982
Grenada *(G-1683)*
Hawkeye Industries Inc ....E...... 662 842-3333
Tupelo *(G-5154)*
Industrial & Crane Svcs Inc ....E...... 601 914-4491
Pascagoula *(G-4039)*
Interntnal Wldg Fbrication Inc ....E...... 228 474-9353
Moss Point *(G-3481)*
Knights Mar & Indus Svcs Inc ....C...... 228 769-5550
Pascagoula *(G-4045)*
Laurel Machine and Foundry Co ....C...... 601 428-0541
Laurel *(G-2793)*
Lofton Corporation ....G...... 769 243-8427
Jackson *(G-2471)*
Majestic Metals Inc ....E...... 601 856-3600
Madison *(G-3126)*
McKinnion Welding & Metal Fabr ....G...... 601 635-3983
Decatur *(G-1175)*
McMahan Bulldog Enterprises ....G...... 601 606-5711
Sumrall *(G-5039)*
Metal Building Systems LLC..................F...... 601 649-9949
Laurel *(G-2801)*
Metal Tech Inc ....E...... 228 604-4604
Gulfport *(G-1829)*
Metaline Products Inc.........................F...... 601 892-5610
Crystal Springs *(G-1147)*
Mississippi Aerospace Corp ....F...... 601 749-5659
Picayune *(G-4280)*
Moore Fabrication and McHy ....F...... 601 892-5017
Gallman *(G-1485)*
Olivers Iron Works ....G...... 662 252-3858
Holly Springs *(G-2186)*
Oxford Metal Works LLC ....G...... 662 801-7969
Oxford *(G-3988)*
Pemco-Naval Engrg Works Inc ....E...... 228 769-1080
Pascagoula *(G-4062)*
Peppers Machine & Wldg Co Inc ....E...... 601 833-3038
Brookhaven *(G-522)*
Precision Products Inc........................F...... 228 475-7400
Moss Point *(G-3495)*
Quality Pipe & Fabrication LLC ....E...... 662 321-8542
Blue Springs *(G-299)*
Quality Wldg & Fabrication Inc..............D...... 601 731-1222
Columbia *(G-914)*
Ratliff Fabricating Company ....F...... 601 362-8942
Jackson *(G-2560)*
Richard H Bowers ....G...... 601 264-0100
Hattiesburg *(G-2051)*
Rickys Welding and Machine Sp ....G...... 601 638-8238
Vicksburg *(G-5410)*
S & H Steel Corp ....F...... 601 932-0250
Pearl *(G-4141)*
S&G Gutter & Sheet Metal Co ....G...... 662 286-2924
Corinth *(G-1118)*
Saf T Cart Inc ....E...... 662 624-6492
Clarksdale *(G-782)*
Shears Fabrication & Wldg LLC ....G...... 601 946-3268
Utica *(G-5312)*
Slay Steel Inc ....D...... 601 483-3911
Meridian *(G-3398)*
Southern Industrial Tech LLC ....F...... 601 426-3866
Stringer *(G-5004)*
Steel Service Corporation ....C...... 601 939-9222
Jackson *(G-2668)*
Steelpro LLC......................................E...... 662 456-3004
Houston *(G-2254)*
Stevens Sheet Metal & Ir Works ....E...... 601 939-6943
Pearl *(G-4150)*
Structural Steel Holding Inc ....G...... 601 483-5381
Meridian *(G-3408)*
Trinity Steel Fabricators Inc ....G...... 601 783-6625
Magnolia *(G-3195)*

Union Corrugating Company ....G...... 601 661-0577
Vicksburg *(G-5432)*
Watkins ....G...... 601 752-2526
Ellisville *(G-1277)*
Williams Machine Works Inc ....F...... 228 475-7651
Moss Point *(G-3508)*
Yates Industrial Services LLC...............G...... 601 467-6232
Purvis *(G-4454)*

STEEL MILLS

American Plant Services Inc.................D...... 228 762-1397
Pascagoula *(G-4019)*
Chrome Deposit Corporation.................E...... 662 798-4149
Columbus *(G-948)*
Commercial Metals Company ....F...... 601 796-5474
Lumberton *(G-3026)*
Consolidated Pipe & Sup Co Inc ....F...... 228 769-1920
Pascagoula *(G-4028)*
Contract Fabricators Inc ....E...... 662 424-0061
Iuka *(G-2287)*
Eagle Specialty Products Inc ....E...... 662 796-7373
Southaven *(G-4870)*
Industrial Steel Corporation.................G...... 601 932-5555
Pearl *(G-4127)*
Rain Cii Carbon LLC ....G...... 601 794-2753
Purvis *(G-4451)*
S & H Steel Corp ....F...... 601 932-0250
Pearl *(G-4141)*
Severcorr LLC ....G...... 662 245-4561
Columbus *(G-1024)*
Southern Scrap Meridian LLC ....E...... 601 693-5323
Meridian *(G-3403)*
Steel Dynamics Columbus LLC............B...... 662 245-4200
Columbus *(G-1033)*
Tms International LLC ....G...... 601 932-8205
Flowood *(G-1402)*
Vicksmetal Corporation.......................E...... 601 636-1314
Vicksburg *(G-5442)*

STEEL SHEET: Cold-Rolled

New Process Steel LP ....D...... 662 241-6582
Columbus *(G-1010)*

STEEL: Cold-Rolled

Miss-Lou Steel Supply Inc ....G...... 601 442-0846
Natchez *(G-3589)*
Steel Technologies LLC ....E...... 601 855-7242
Madison *(G-3153)*
Worthington Cylinders Miss LLC ....E...... 614 840-3802
New Albany *(G-3709)*

STITCHING SVCS

Southern Prtg & Silk Screening............F...... 228 452-7309
Pass Christian *(G-4095)*

STOCK SHAPES: Plastic

M S Rubber Company............................F...... 601 948-2575
Jackson *(G-2474)*

STONE: Cast Concrete

National Stone Imports Inc ....G...... 228 323-7239
Long Beach *(G-2946)*

STONEWARE PRDTS: Pottery

Ka Pottery ....G...... 601 722-4948
Seminary *(G-4782)*
Pottery By Helene ....G...... 662 728-0988
Guntown *(G-1902)*

STORES: Auto & Home Supply

Walker Enterprises ....G...... 662 237-0240
Carrollton *(G-704)*

STOVES: Wood & Coal Burning

B R Smith Enterprises Inc ....F...... 601 656-0846
Union *(G-5293)*

STRAW GOODS

Jerry D Smith......................................G...... 601 795-8760
Poplarville *(G-4384)*

2019 Harris Directory of
Mississippi Manufacturers

(G-0000) Company's Geographic Section entry number

PRODUCT SECTION

STRUCTURAL SUPPORT & BUILDING MATERIAL: Concrete

Gulf States Forming Systems ....F 601 428-1582
Laurel (G-2774)

STUCCO

All American Stucco ....G....... 228 669-0915
Gulfport (G-1718)
Outback Stucco & Coatings LLC...........G....... 228 224-2824
Gulfport (G-1841)
Regional Stucco LLC ....G....... 228 323-0290
Biloxi (G-276)

STUDIOS: Artist

Cynthia Bowen ....G....... 228 463-7131
Waveland (G-5479)

SUNDRIES & RELATED PRDTS: Medical & Laboratory, Rubber

Polo Custom Products Inc ....C....... 662 779-2009
Louisville (G-2976)
Schuyler C Jones ....G....... 601 540-5841
Madison (G-3145)
Xerium Technologies Inc...................G....... 662 323-4064
Starkville (G-4983)

SUPERMARKETS & OTHER GROCERY STORES

Bg3 Delta LLC ....G....... 601 636-9828
Vicksburg (G-5344)

SURFACE ACTIVE AGENTS

Product Services Company ....E 866 886-3093
Jackson (G-2552)

SURFACE ACTIVE AGENTS: Oils & Greases

Driven Racing Oil LLC ....G....... 866 611-1820
Olive Branch (G-3837)

SURGICAL APPLIANCES & SPLYS

Hanger Prsthetcs & Ortho Inc..............G....... 601 268-5520
Hattiesburg (G-1982)
Hanger Prsthetcs & Ortho Inc..............G....... 601 883-3341
Vicksburg (G-5377)
Hanger Prsthetcs & Ortho Inc..............G....... 228 822-0109
Gulfport (G-1804)
Hanger Prsthetcs & Ortho Inc..............G....... 228 875-8354
Ocean Springs (G-3761)
Hanger Prsthetcs & Ortho Inc..............G....... 601 939-2100
Jackson (G-2648)
Human Technology Inc.....................G....... 662 349-4909
Southaven (G-4878)
Spine Stability Surgical LLC ....G....... 800 991-3723
Jackson (G-2595)

SURGICAL EQPT: See Also Instruments

Cuff Toughener ....G....... 601 209-1609
Ridgeland (G-4569)
Medworx Compounding LLC ....F 601 859-5008
Ridgeland (G-4605)
Oligarch Inc ....G....... 844 321-0016
Houston (G-2253)
Peltz Medical LLC ....G....... 601 831-3135
Vicksburg (G-5404)

SURGICAL IMPLANTS

Ascend Surgical Sales LLC ....G....... 601 351-9866
Ridgeland (G-4551)
T & S Machine Shop Inc ....E 601 825-8627
Brandon (G-466)
Zavation LLC ....G....... 601 919-1119
Flowood (G-1408)

SURVEYING & MAPPING: Land Parcels

3d Laser Scanning LLC ....G....... 228 860-5952
Biloxi (G-214)

SURVEYING SVCS: Aerial Digital Imaging

Emergent Technologies LLC ....G....... 601 497-8239
Madison (G-3097)

SVC ESTABLISH EQPT, WHOLESALE: Carpet/Rug Clean Eqpt & Sply

Garrett Rowland G ....G....... 601 954-9841
Jackson (G-2422)

SVC ESTABLISHMENT EQPT & SPLYS WHOLESALERS

Larrys Equipment Inc ....G....... 662 423-0077
Iuka (G-2298)

SVC ESTABLISHMENT EQPT, WHOL: Cleaning & Maint Eqpt & Splys

Magnolia Supply Group LLC................G....... 601 454-1368
Jackson (G-2480)
Willie B Sims Jr CPA Pllc ....G....... 601 545-3930
Hattiesburg (G-2084)

SVC ESTABLISHMENT EQPT, WHOLESALE: Beauty Parlor Eqpt & Sply

NY Beauty ....G....... 662 280-2573
Horn Lake (G-2209)

SVC ESTABLISHMENT EQPT, WHOLESALE: Sprinkler Systems

First Class Fire Prtection LLC ....G....... 901 350-0499
Horn Lake (G-2199)

SWEEPING COMPOUNDS

Delta Dry LLC ....G....... 203 515-1528
Hollandale (G-2164)
Natures Broom Inc...........................G....... 662 931-5844
Hollandale (G-2167)
Tackle Technologies LLC ....G....... 228 206-1449
Long Beach (G-2956)

SWIMMING POOL & HOT TUB CLEANING & MAINTENANCE SVCS

Dale Fulton ....G....... 662 327-4800
Columbus (G-958)

SWITCHES: Electronic

Delta Foundation Inc ....C....... 662 335-5291
Greenville (G-1547)
Electro National Corporation ....E 601 859-5511
Canton (G-657)

SWITCHES: Solenoid

Multicraft Intl Ltd Partnr ....G....... 601 854-5516
Pelahatchie (G-4167)

SWITCHGEAR & SWITCHBOARD APPARATUS

South Coast Electric LLC...................F 228 533-0002
Bay St Louis (G-182)
Vertiv Corporation...........................F 662 313-0813
Southaven (G-4919)

SYNTHETIC RESIN FINISHED PRDTS, NEC

Builders Marble Inc..........................E 601 922-5420
Clinton (G-817)

SYRUPS, DRINK

Quality Beverage Packing Inc..............F 662 329-5976
Columbus (G-1020)
Warren Corporation UNI.....................G....... 888 913-7708
Byram (G-626)

TABLE OR COUNTERTOPS, PLASTIC LAMINATED

Counter Connections Inc ....G....... 662 342-5111
Southaven (G-4865)

TABLECLOTHS & SETTINGS

R2pg Inc.......................................F 601 747-0522
Port Gibson (G-4406)

TABLEWARE OR KITCHEN ARTICLES: Commercial, Fine Earthenware

Chambers Air and Heat ....G....... 662 967-2002
West (G-5532)

TABLEWARE: Household & Commercial, Semivitreous

Misccellaneous Items LLC ....G....... 601 918-0255
Jackson (G-2496)

TABLEWARE: Plastic

L C Industries Inc............................B 601 894-1771
Hazlehurst (G-2099)
Signature Works Inc ....B 601 894-1771
Hazlehurst (G-2106)

TAGS & LABELS: Paper

Capitol City Label Inc ....G....... 601 420-2375
Pearl (G-4109)

TALLOW: Animal

Griffin Industries LLC ....C....... 601 372-5212
Jackson (G-2433)

TANK REPAIR & CLEANING SVCS

American Tank & Vessel Inc ....C....... 601 947-7210
Lucedale (G-2986)

TANK REPAIR SVCS

Hesters Certified Welding ....G....... 662 566-7305
Tupelo (G-5155)

TANKS & OTHER TRACKED VEHICLE CMPNTS

Quality Wldg & Fabrication Inc.............D....... 601 731-1222
Columbia (G-914)

TANKS: Concrete

Desoto Concrete Products Inc ....G....... 662 890-1688
Olive Branch (G-3833)
Southern Sewage Systems ....G....... 228 832-7400
Saucier (G-4766)

TANKS: For Tank Trucks, Metal Plate

Keith Huber Corporation ....D....... 228 832-0992
Gulfport (G-1816)
L T Corporation ....E 662 843-4046
Cleveland (G-798)
Quality Steel Corporation ....D....... 662 771-4243
Cleveland (G-804)

TANKS: Lined, Metal

American Tank & Vessel Inc ....C....... 601 947-7210
Lucedale (G-2986)
Harbison-Fischer Inc ....G....... 601 428-7919
Ellisville (G-1257)
National Tank Inc ....F 662 429-5469
Hernando (G-2143)

TANKS: Plastic & Fiberglass

JKS International LLC ....F 228 689-8999
Stennis Space Center (G-4995)
Protank LLC...................................G....... 662 895-4337
Olive Branch (G-3903)

TANKS: Standard Or Custom Fabricated, Metal Plate

Commercial Construction Co Inc ....D....... 601 649-5300
Laurel (G-2756)
Mississippi Tank and Mfg Co...............C....... 601 264-1800
Hattiesburg (G-2027)
Quitman Tank Solutions LLC ....E 601 776-3800
Quitman (G-4469)

TARGET DRONES

DAvion LLC ....G....... 601 724-5013
Brandon (G-385)
Hiro Telemedicine Systems LLC ....G....... 312 835-1859
Hattiesburg (G-1990)

Employee Codes: A=Over 500 employees, B=251-500
C=101-250, D=51-100, E=20-50, F=10-19, G=1-9

2019 Harris Directory of Mississippi Manufacturers

TARGET DRONES

PRODUCT SECTION

Landmark Spatial Solutions LLC...........G....... 662 769-5344
Starkville *(G-4955)*

TARPAULINS

American Tarp & Awning Co...............G....... 601 656-5177
Philadelphia *(G-4203)*

TAX REFUND DISCOUNTING

Mac Financial Mgmt LLC......................G....... 844 622-6468
Magnolia *(G-3193)*

TAX RETURN PREPARATION SVCS

Advantage Tax & Printing Svc ....G....... 601 544-0602
Hattiesburg *(G-1917)*
DLS Tax Consultants ....G....... 601 473-6623
Jackson *(G-2387)*
Willie B Sims Jr CPA Pllc ....G....... 601 545-3930
Hattiesburg *(G-2084)*

TELECOMMUNICATION SYSTEMS & EQPT

King Manufacturing Company Inc.........E....... 662 286-5504
Corinth *(G-1097)*
King Manufacturing Company Inc.........E....... 662 286-5504
Corinth *(G-1096)*
Plantronics Inc ....G....... 662 893-7221
Olive Branch *(G-3897)*

TELECOMMUNICATIONS CARRIERS & SVCS: Wired

Cable One Inc ....G....... 601 833-7991
McComb *(G-3245)*

TELEMARKETING BUREAUS

Dewmar International Bmc Inc ....G....... 877 747-5326
Clinton *(G-822)*

TELEMETERING EQPT

L3 Technologies Inc ....E....... 601 856-2274
Madison *(G-3117)*

TELEPHONE COUNSELING SVCS

Hiro Telemedicine Systems LLC ....G....... 312 835-1859
Hattiesburg *(G-1990)*

TELEPHONE EQPT INSTALLATION

Oxford Alarm Cmmunications Inc.........G....... 662 234-0505
Oxford *(G-3984)*
Phone Booth Inc ....F....... 662 286-6600
Corinth *(G-1109)*

TELEPHONE EQPT: Modems

Continue Care Hlth Modem Line ....G....... 662 827-7107
Hollandale *(G-2163)*
Modem Guest ....G....... 601 442-5202
Natchez *(G-3592)*

TELEPHONE EQPT: NEC

Seimens Industry Sector ....G....... 662 245-4573
Columbus *(G-1023)*

TELEPHONE SVCS

Cable One Inc ....G....... 601 833-7991
McComb *(G-3245)*

TELEPHONE: Fiber Optic Systems

Innovative Wireless LLC ....G....... 601 594-1201
Jackson *(G-2447)*

TELEVISION: Closed Circuit Eqpt

Lady Bugs and Lily Pads ....G....... 601 735-0071
Waynesboro *(G-5503)*

TENTS: All Materials

Biloxi Tent and Awning Co Inc..............G....... 228 436-6161
Biloxi *(G-220)*

TESTERS: Environmental

Taylor Environmental Products.............G....... 662 773-8056
Louisville *(G-2985)*

TEXTILE & APPAREL SVCS

Warmkraft Inc ....C....... 601 785-4476
Taylorsville *(G-5062)*

TEXTILE FINISHING: Dyeing, Broadwoven, Cotton

Dyehouse Inc ....G....... 601 776-2189
Quitman *(G-4462)*

TEXTILE PRDTS: Hand Woven & Crocheted

Angies Crocheting Corner ....G....... 228 617-9342
Hattiesburg *(G-1924)*
Mks Crochet ....G....... 662 769-4982
Maben *(G-3048)*

TEXTILE: Finishing, Cotton Broadwoven

Gary Beall Enterprises LLC ....E....... 662 453-6100
Greenwood *(G-1625)*

TEXTILE: Goods, NEC

Product Source Limited LLC ....G....... 769 257-4620
Florence *(G-1331)*

TEXTILES: Jute & Flax Prdts

10 Below LLC ....G....... 769 243-8705
Jackson *(G-2313)*
Ten Below LLC ....G....... 601 453-2041
Meridian *(G-3413)*

TEXTILES: Linen Fabrics

Bed Bath & Beyond Inc ....G....... 601 939-4840
Flowood *(G-1344)*
Said Melinda ....G....... 601 990-4022
Brookhaven *(G-528)*

THERMOSETTING MATERIALS

Ergon Chemicals LLC ....B....... 601 933-3000
Flowood *(G-1358)*
McNeely Plastic Products Inc ....E....... 601 926-1000
Clinton *(G-830)*

THREAD: Embroidery

Dub Street Fashion Center LLC............G....... 601 483-0036
Meridian *(G-3330)*

THREAD: Thread, From Manmade Fiber

Fibrix LLC ....E....... 662 489-7908
Pontotoc *(G-4331)*

TILE: Asphalt, Floor

Precision Asp Sealcoating LLC.............G....... 601 527-6381
Collinsville *(G-874)*

TILE: Brick & Structural, Clay

Acme Brick Company............................G....... 601 714-2966
Brandon *(G-355)*
Columbus Brick Company ....E....... 662 328-4931
Columbus *(G-949)*
Corinth Brick Company Inc..................G....... 662 287-2442
Corinth *(G-1076)*
Meridian Brick LLC ....G....... 228 863-5451
Gulfport *(G-1828)*
Meridian Brick LLC ....G....... 601 296-0445
Hattiesburg *(G-2022)*
Meridian Brick LLC ....F....... 601 428-4364
Laurel *(G-2800)*
Meridian Brick LLC ....G....... 662 840-8884
Tupelo *(G-5186)*

TILE: Clay, Drain & Structural

Profile Products LLC ....E....... 662 685-4741
Blue Mountain *(G-292)*

TIMBER DRIVING & BOOMING

Mossy Island Land & Forest LLC ....G....... 662 207-6245
Inverness *(G-2275)*
Timberline Logging Inc ....F....... 662 423-3948
Iuka *(G-2309)*

TIMBER PRDTS WHOLESALERS

North Mississippi Timber Brk ....G....... 662 728-7328
Booneville *(G-339)*

TIN

Tin Roof Mercantile..............................G....... 901 596-6803
Olive Branch *(G-3918)*

TIRE & INNER TUBE MATERIALS & RELATED PRDTS

Yokohama Tire Manufactu ....G....... 800 423-4544
West Point *(G-5566)*
Yokohama Tire Mfg Miss LLC ....G....... 800 423-4544
West Point *(G-5567)*

TIRE CORD & FABRIC: Steel

Greenville Metal Works Inc ....E....... 662 335-8510
Greenville *(G-1555)*

TIRE DEALERS

B & B Oil Well Service Co Inc ....F....... 601 425-3836
Ellisville *(G-1246)*
Spot Cash Tire and Appliance ....G....... 662 289-2611
Kosciusko *(G-2713)*

TIRES & INNER TUBES

BF Kaufman Inc....................................G....... 662 253-8093
Southaven *(G-4855)*
Cooper Tire & Rubber Company ....E....... 662 624-4366
Clarksdale *(G-763)*
Tooneys Tire Center ....G....... 601 479-2654
De Kalb *(G-1168)*

TIRES & TUBES WHOLESALERS

Roes Rims and Accessories ....G....... 601 619-4489
Vicksburg *(G-5413)*

TOBACCO & PRDTS, WHOLESALE: Cigarettes

Newton Discount Tobacco ....G....... 601 683-6555
Newton *(G-3727)*

TOBACCO & TOBACCO PRDTS WHOLESALERS

Voluptuous E-Juice LLC.........................G....... 662 297-8353
Pontotoc *(G-4368)*

TOBACCO REDRYING

Lucky Leaf Discount Tobacco ....G....... 601 924-8818
Clinton *(G-829)*

TOBACCO STORES & STANDS

Lucky Leaf Discount Tobacco ....G....... 601 924-8818
Clinton *(G-829)*
Voluptuous E-Juice LLC.........................G....... 662 297-8353
Pontotoc *(G-4368)*

TOBACCO: Cigarettes

KS Tobacco & Brew ....G....... 662 869-0086
Saltillo *(G-4716)*
Newton Discount Tobacco ....G....... 601 683-6555
Newton *(G-3727)*
Voluptuous E-Juice LLC.........................G....... 662 297-8353
Pontotoc *(G-4368)*

TOBACCO: Smoking

Country Squire ....G....... 601 362-2233
Jackson *(G-2371)*

TOILET PREPARATIONS

Musee LLC..G....... 769 300-0485
Canton *(G-672)*

TOILET SEATS: Wood

Magnolia Beneke Inc ....E....... 662 328-4000
Columbus *(G-997)*

2019 Harris Directory of
Mississippi Manufacturers

(G-0000) Company's Geographic Section entry number

PRODUCT SECTION

TROPHY & PLAQUE STORES

TOILETRIES, COSMETICS & PERFUME STORES

Beauty Mart ....G...... 662 624-6738
Clarksdale (G-759)
Christian Pass Soap ....G...... 228 222-4303
Pass Christian (G-4079)

TOILETRIES, WHOLESALE: Toiletries

Oligarch Inc ....G...... 844 321-0016
Houston (G-2253)

TOOL & DIE STEEL

Advance Tool and Die Inc ....G...... 601 939-1291
Pearl (G-4104)
Etd Inc ....G...... 662 454-9349
Belmont (G-198)
Holly Tool & Die Inc ....G...... 662 252-1144
Holly Springs (G-2177)

TOOLS: Carpenters', Including Levels & Chisels, Exc Saws

Carsons Construction LLC ....E...... 601 301-0841
Vicksburg (G-5354)
Continental Interiors Inc ....G...... 662 382-3061
Crenshaw (G-1133)

TOOLS: Hand

Paslode Corporation............................G...... 662 489-4151
Pontotoc (G-4353)
Shelby Dean Distributing ....G...... 601 529-7936
Vicksburg (G-5417)

TOOLS: Hand, Ironworkers'

North Wind Fabrication Inc ....G...... 228 896-0230
Gulfport (G-1839)

TOOLS: Hand, Mechanics

Dern Mechanix ....G...... 228 832-3933
Gulfport (G-1771)

TOOLS: Hand, Power

B & L International Inc ....G...... 601 261-5127
Purvis (G-4434)
Hartley Equipment Company Inc ....G...... 601 499-0944
Canton (G-661)
Milwaukee Electric Tool Corp ....B...... 601 969-3033
Jackson (G-2495)
Milwaukee Electric Tool Corp ....B...... 662 451-5545
Greenwood (G-1640)
Milwaukee Electric Tool Corp ....C...... 662 895-4560
Olive Branch (G-3879)
Nichols Saw Service ....F...... 662 842-2129
Tupelo (G-5192)
Robine & Welch Machine & TI Co ....E...... 601 428-1545
Laurel (G-2838)

TOWELS: Linen & Linen & Cotton Mixtures

Medical Grade Innovations LLC ....G...... 601 899-9207
Ridgeland (G-4604)

TOWING SVCS: Mobile Homes

Stringer Randal ....G...... 228 623-0037
Moss Point (G-3500)

TOYS

Action Prsuit Games of Brandon ....G...... 601 825-1052
Brandon (G-356)
Laser Mania Inc ....G...... 601 543-0072
Hattiesburg (G-2016)
Parker Brothers 2 Inc ....G...... 662 283-2224
Winona (G-5605)

TOYS & HOBBY GOODS & SPLYS, WHOLESALE: Arts/Crafts Eqpt/Sply

Dogwood Ceramic Supply Inc ....G...... 228 831-4848
Gulfport (G-1773)

TOYS: Dolls, Stuffed Animals & Parts

Beryl Jones...G...... 601 442-4597
Natchez (G-3529)

Best Dressed Bunnies ....G...... 228 826-4619
Ocean Springs (G-3743)
Well Made Goods LLC ....G...... 917 853-3598
Grenada (G-1712)

TOYS: Kites

Kewl Kites ....G...... 228 206-0322
Long Beach (G-2941)

TRACTOR REPAIR SVCS

Ground Support Specialist LLC ....E...... 662 342-1412
Horn Lake (G-2201)
Sabbatini & Sons Incorporation ....G...... 662 686-7713
Leland (G-2892)

TRADE SHOW ARRANGEMENT SVCS

Journal Inc ....E...... 601 364-1000
Flowood (G-1371)

TRAILERS & PARTS: Boat

Bosarge Boats Inc ....G...... 228 762-0888
Pascagoula (G-4023)
Gulf Coast Shipyard Group Inc ....C...... 228 276-1000
Gulfport (G-1799)
Self Serve Marine Inc ....G...... 228 762-3628
Pascagoula (G-4067)

TRAILERS & PARTS: Truck & Semi's

A & A Trailer Sales LLC ....G...... 228 234-3420
Biloxi (G-215)
C & W Custom Design Trailers ....E...... 662 585-3146
Golden (G-1523)
Carroll Ray Auto & Truck Sales ....G...... 662 226-1200
Grenada (G-1671)
Deep South Trailer Sales LLC ....G...... 228 255-2026
Diamondhead (G-1189)
Innovative Fabrications LLC ....G...... 601 485-1400
Meridian (G-3353)
Mathis Trucking & Cnstr LLC ....G...... 601 917-0237
Collinsville (G-873)
Palmer Machine Works Inc ....E...... 662 256-2636
Amory (G-50)
Russell Trucking ....G...... 662 563-2616
Batesville (G-122)
Screw Conveyor Corporation ....C...... 662 283-3142
Winona (G-5606)
Timothy Trigg ....G...... 601 722-9581
Seminary (G-4784)
Truck Bodies & Eqp Intl Inc ....G...... 800 255-4345
Tishomingo (G-5089)
Wade Services Inc ....E...... 601 399-1900
Ellisville (G-1276)
Wade Services Inc ....G...... 601 399-1900
Laurel (G-2864)
Warren Inc ....C...... 601 765-8221
Collins (G-865)

TRAILERS & TRAILER EQPT

B & B Mfg & Specialty Co Inc ....G...... 662 456-4313
Houston (G-2231)
Barrentine Trailer Mfg Co Inc ....G...... 662 237-9650
Greenwood (G-1614)
Innovative Fabrications LLC ....G...... 601 485-1400
Meridian (G-3353)
Sport Trial ....G...... 228 467-1885
Bay Saint Louis (G-157)
Trailboss Trailers Inc ....E...... 800 345-2452
Macon (G-3073)
Triple R Trailers Inc ....G...... 662 728-7975
Corinth (G-1124)

TRAILERS: Bodies

Magnolia Trailers Inc ....E...... 601 947-7990
Lucedale (G-3010)

TRAILERS: Semitrailers, Truck Tractors

Baldwyn Truck & Trailer Repair ....G...... 662 365-7888
Baldwyn (G-73)

TRAILERS: Truck, Chassis

Fryfogle Manufacturing Inc ....F...... 601 947-8088
Lucedale (G-2996)

TRANSFORMERS: Electric

Emerald Transformer ....G...... 800 346-6164
Lexington (G-2902)
Howard Industries Inc ....G...... 601 847-5278
Mendenhall (G-3281)
Howard Industries Inc ....G...... 601 425-3151
Laurel (G-2780)

TRANSFORMERS: Power Related

ABB Inc ....E...... 601 892-6431
Crystal Springs (G-1139)
ABB Inc ....F...... 662 562-0700
Senatobia (G-4785)
Delta Municipal Energy Inc ....E...... 800 217-1519
Mound Bayou (G-3509)
Garrett & Son Inc ....E...... 601 853-7865
Madison (G-3102)
Howard Industries Inc ....B...... 601 422-0033
Laurel (G-2779)
Kuhlman Electric Corporation ....B...... 601 892-4661
Crystal Springs (G-1144)
Malibu Lighting Corporation ....G...... 662 290-1200
Kosciusko (G-2699)
Photowire Solar Producers ....G...... 228 627-0088
Philadelphia (G-4233)

TRANSPORTATION AGENTS & BROKERS

Kdh Trucking LLC ....G...... 601 730-2052
Liberty (G-2913)

TRANSPORTATION EPQT & SPLYS, WHOL: Aircraft Engs/Eng Parts

Gecas Asset MGT Svcs Inc ....G...... 662 455-1826
Greenwood (G-1626)

TRANSPORTATION EPQT & SPLYS, WHOLESALE: Marine Crafts/Splys

Rolls-Royce Marine North Amer ....D...... 228 762-0728
Pascagoula (G-4064)

TRANSPORTATION SVCS, AIR, NONSCHEDULED: Air Cargo Carriers

Tenax Tm LLC ....F...... 601 352-1107
Madison (G-3158)

TRANSPORTATION SVCS, WATER: River, Exc St Lawrence Seaway

Ergon Inc ....C...... 601 933-3000
Flowood (G-1361)

TRAPS: Animal & Fish, Wire

Wildlife Dominion MGT LLC ....G...... 662 272-9550
Crawford (G-1131)

TRAVEL TRAILERS & CAMPERS

Passport America Corporation ....F...... 228 452-9972
Long Beach (G-2948)
Vanleigh Rv Inc ....F...... 662 612-4040
Burnsville (G-575)

TROPHIES, PLATED, ALL METALS

Renchers This & That ....G...... 662 624-9825
Clarksdale (G-779)

TROPHY & PLAQUE STORES

Allistons...G...... 228 832-8683
Gulfport (G-1723)
Awards Unlimited..................................G...... 228 863-1814
Gulfport (G-1730)
Boardtown Trading Post ....G...... 662 324-7296
Starkville (G-4929)
Hunters Hollow Inc ....F...... 662 234-5945
Oxford (G-3958)
Mickeys Trophy & Sign Shop................G...... 601 649-1263
Laurel (G-2802)
Plum Trophy Sales................................G...... 601 758-4834
Sumrall (G-5041)
Trophy Shop ....G...... 662 236-3726
Oxford (G-4008)

Employee Codes: A=Over 500 employees, B=251-500
C=101-250, D=51-100, E=20-50, F=10-19, G=1-9

2019 Harris Directory of
Mississippi Manufacturers

427

PRODUCT

TRUCK & BUS BODIES: Automobile Wrecker Truck

PRODUCT SECTION

TRUCK & BUS BODIES: Automobile Wrecker Truck

AMS Services LLC ....G...... 662 449-2672
Nesbit *(G-3648)*

TRUCK & BUS BODIES: Beverage Truck

Innovative Fabrications LLC ....G...... 601 485-1400
Meridian *(G-3353)*

TRUCK & BUS BODIES: Dump Truck

Warren Inc ....C...... 601 765-8221
Collins *(G-865)*

TRUCK & BUS BODIES: Motor Vehicle, Specialty

Fireplace Wholesale ....G...... 601 545-9876
Hattiesburg *(G-1970)*

TRUCK & BUS BODIES: Truck, Motor Vehicle

Griffin Inc ....D...... 662 838-2128
Byhalia *(G-586)*

TRUCK BODIES: Body Parts

Aerial Truck Equipment Co Inc ....G...... 662 895-0993
Olive Branch *(G-3807)*
Tri-State Truck Center Inc ....E...... 662 844-6000
Tupelo *(G-5242)*

TRUCK DRIVER SVCS

Watson Tj Property LLC ....G...... 601 527-3587
Meridian *(G-3418)*

TRUCK GENERAL REPAIR SVC

Angels Truck Service LLC ....F...... 662 890-0417
Olive Branch *(G-3815)*
Tri-State Truck Center Inc ....E...... 662 844-6000
Tupelo *(G-5242)*

TRUCK PARTS & ACCESSORIES: Wholesalers

Aerial Truck Equipment Co Inc ....G...... 662 895-0993
Olive Branch *(G-3807)*
Paccar Engine Company ....G...... 662 329-6700
Columbus *(G-1014)*
Paccar Engine Company ....G...... 425 468-7400
Columbus *(G-1015)*

TRUCK STOPS

Stinson & Son Logging ....G...... 601 989-2311
Richton *(G-4544)*

TRUCKING & HAULING SVCS: Contract Basis

Burge Timber Contractors Inc ....F...... 601 796-3471
Lumberton *(G-3024)*
Ell Holdings ....G...... 601 325-3317
Hattiesburg *(G-1961)*
Fallen Leaf Services LLC ....G...... 228 731-0919
Gulfport *(G-1781)*
Howard Industries Inc ....B...... 601 422-0033
Laurel *(G-2779)*
Howard Industries Inc ....G...... 601 425-3151
Laurel *(G-2780)*
Howard Industries Inc ....G...... 601 847-5278
Mendenhall *(G-3281)*
Moores Logging & Trucking ....G...... 662 289-5872
Kosciusko *(G-2704)*

TRUCKING & HAULING SVCS: Garbage, Collect/Transport Only

Fallen Leaf Services LLC ....G...... 228 731-0919
Gulfport *(G-1781)*

TRUCKING & HAULING SVCS: Heavy Machinery, Local

Ell Holdings ....G...... 601 325-3317
Hattiesburg *(G-1961)*

TRUCKING & HAULING SVCS: Heavy, NEC

Bradford Enterprises ....G...... 601 442-2339
Natchez *(G-3538)*
Cutshall D L & Sons Logging Co ....G...... 662 423-6965
Iuka *(G-2288)*
Springer Trckg & Car Crushing ....F...... 601 649-4238
Laurel *(G-2855)*
Wade Services Inc ....G...... 601 399-1900
Laurel *(G-2864)*
Wade Services Inc ....E...... 601 399-1900
Ellisville *(G-1276)*

TRUCKING & HAULING SVCS: Liquid Petroleum, Exc Local

Ergon Inc ....F...... 601 932-8365
Jackson *(G-2645)*
Ergon Inc ....C...... 601 933-3000
Flowood *(G-1361)*
Ergon Marine & Industrial Sup ....G...... 601 636-6552
Vicksburg *(G-5369)*

TRUCKING & HAULING SVCS: Lumber & Timber

A & D Timber Company Inc ....F...... 601 528-9357
Wiggins *(G-5568)*
Bazor Pulpwood Company Inc ....F...... 601 735-4017
Waynesboro *(G-5492)*

TRUCKING & HAULING SVCS: Machinery, Heavy

Galvian Group LLC ....G...... 662 374-1027
Greenwood *(G-1624)*

TRUCKING & HAULING SVCS: Timber, Local

Circle Lane Contractors LLC ....F...... 601 776-0129
Shubuta *(G-4829)*

TRUCKING, DUMP

Jordon Construction LLC ....G...... 601 502-6019
Terry *(G-5071)*
Townes Construction Co Inc ....F...... 662 226-4894
Grenada *(G-1709)*

TRUCKING: Except Local

Ergon Inc ....E...... 601 636-6888
Vicksburg *(G-5367)*
Harper Timber Inc ....E...... 601 833-2121
Brookhaven *(G-499)*
McDaniel Trucking ....G...... 601 656-1028
Philadelphia *(G-4225)*
Structural Steel Holding Inc ....C...... 601 483-5381
Meridian *(G-3408)*
Watkins ....G...... 601 752-2526
Ellisville *(G-1277)*

TRUCKING: Local, Without Storage

C5 Trucking LLC ....G...... 601 797-9335
Mount Olive *(G-3510)*
Calico Jacks Llc ....G...... 504 355-9639
Carriere *(G-689)*
Clarence South Logging ....G...... 662 585-3724
Fulton *(G-1450)*
Coastal Petroleum Services Inc ....E...... 601 446-5888
Natchez *(G-3547)*
F & F Timber Inc ....F...... 601 528-0023
Wiggins *(G-5582)*
Harper Timber Inc ....E...... 601 833-2121
Brookhaven *(G-499)*
Ironhorse Environmental LLC ....G...... 504 952-2516
Poplarville *(G-4383)*
John Albert Ware ....G...... 662 489-7824
Pontotoc *(G-4339)*
Kdh Trucking LLC ....G...... 601 730-2052
Liberty *(G-2913)*
Reed Logging Inc ....G...... 662 793-4951
Scooba *(G-4772)*
Springer Trckg & Car Crushing ....F...... 601 649-4238
Laurel *(G-2855)*
Stockstill Land Dev LLC ....G...... 601 273-2409
Poplarville *(G-4396)*
Trinity Three LLC ....G...... 601 249-8851
Summit *(G-5027)*
W S Red Hancock Inc ....F...... 662 755-0011
Bentonia *(G-213)*

TRUCKING & HAULING SVCS: Heavy, NEC

W S Red Hancock Inc ....C...... 601 399-0605
Ellisville *(G-1275)*

TRUCKING: Long-Distance, Less Than Truckload

Johnson Wiley ....G...... 662 329-1495
Columbus *(G-991)*

TRUCKS & TRACTORS: Industrial

Bumper To Bumper ....G...... 601 928-5603
Wiggins *(G-5575)*
Caterpillar Inc ....F...... 662 284-5143
Corinth *(G-1067)*
Hunter Engineering Company ....C...... 662 653-3194
Durant *(G-1227)*
Lawrence A Witherspoon ....G...... 662 404-5859
Horn Lake *(G-2205)*
Rcl Components Inc ....E...... 662 449-0401
Hernando *(G-2152)*
Saf T Cart Inc ....E...... 662 624-6492
Clarksdale *(G-782)*
Screw Conveyor Corporation ....C...... 662 283-3142
Winona *(G-5606)*
U S Metal Works Inc ....E...... 601 657-4676
Liberty *(G-2919)*
Z A Construction LLC ....G...... 601 259-5276
Mendenhall *(G-3291)*

TRUCKS: Forklift

Chrisman Manufacturing Inc ....E...... 228 864-6293
Long Beach *(G-2931)*
Forklift LLC ....G...... 813 527-4093
Tupelo *(G-5137)*
Forklift LLC ....G...... 662 255-2581
Tupelo *(G-5138)*
Nmhg Financial Services ....G...... 601 304-0112
Natchez *(G-3601)*

TRUCKS: Indl

Black Diamond Construction LLC ....G...... 228 342-2742
Kiln *(G-2678)*
Harper Timber Inc ....E...... 601 833-2121
Brookhaven *(G-499)*
MERR Express LLC ....G...... 601 327-1554
Lucedale *(G-3011)*
Wallace Express Freight Inc ....F...... 662 890-3080
Olive Branch *(G-3922)*
Watson Tj Property LLC ....G...... 601 527-3587
Meridian *(G-3418)*

TRUSSES: Wood, Floor

Oldtown Truss ....G...... 662 412-2500
Pittsboro *(G-4309)*
Trimjoist Corporation ....E...... 662 327-7950
Columbus *(G-1039)*

TRUSSES: Wood, Roof

Clearspan Components Inc ....C...... 601 483-3941
Meridian *(G-3321)*
Mid-South Truss Co Inc ....G...... 662 728-0016
Booneville *(G-336)*
Pine Belt Truss Company Inc ....G...... 601 729-4298
Soso *(G-4847)*

TUBE & TUBING FABRICATORS

Cemco Inc ....E...... 662 323-1559
Starkville *(G-4933)*
Electro National Corporation ....E...... 601 859-5511
Canton *(G-657)*
Fabricated Pipe Inc ....F...... 601 684-3007
Fernwood *(G-1304)*
Mueller Castings Co ....G...... 662 862-7200
Fulton *(G-1464)*

TUBES: Paper

Caraustar Industrial and Con ....E...... 662 287-2492
Corinth *(G-1064)*
Caraustar Industries Inc ....G...... 601 703-0550
Meridian *(G-3315)*

TUBES: Paper Or Fiber, Chemical Or Electrical Uses

Larry Joe Gibson ....G...... 662 844-9113
Tupelo *(G-5171)*

2019 Harris Directory of Mississippi Manufacturers

(G-0000) Company's Geographic Section entry number

PRODUCT SECTION
VOCATIONAL REHABILITATION AGENCY

TUBES: Steel & Iron

True Temper Sports Inc ....B 662 256-5605
Amory (G-57)

TUBING: Copper

Mueller Copper Tube Pdts Inc ....F 662 862-2181
Fulton (G-1467)

TURBINE GENERATOR SET UNITS: Hydraulic, Complete

Vertex Manufacturing Corp ....G 662 895-6263
Olive Branch (G-3920)

TURBINES & TURBINE GENERATOR SETS

GE Wind Energy LLC ....C 662 892-2900
Olive Branch (G-3842)

TYPESETTING SVC

Alpha Printing Inc ....G 601 371-2611
Jackson (G-2324)
Boone Newspapers ....E 601 442-9101
Natchez (G-3537)
Bourne Brothers Prtg Co Inc ....F 601 582-1808
Hattiesburg (G-1938)
Composing Room Inc ....G 662 393-6652
Southaven (G-4861)
Copy Cats Printing Inc ....F 601 582-3019
Hattiesburg (G-1951)
Dement Printing Company ....G 601 693-2721
Meridian (G-3329)
Fedex Office & Print Svcs Inc ....E 601 957-3311
Jackson (G-2407)
Fedex Office & Print Svcs Inc ....F 601 264-6434
Hattiesburg (G-1969)
Harden Enterprises Inc ....F 662 841-9292
Tupelo (G-5152)
Holmes Stationary and Gifts ....G 601 276-2700
Summit (G-5016)
Jenkins Graphics Inc ....G 662 890-2851
Olive Branch (G-3855)
Lewis Yager Melbaleen J ....G 228 762-3152
Pascagoula (G-4046)
M & M Printing Co ....G 601 798-4316
Picayune (G-4277)
Mid South Publications Inc ....G 662 256-8209
Amory (G-48)
Nick StrckInds Quick Print Inc ....F 601 353-8672
Ridgeland (G-4611)
Nick StrckInds Quick Print Inc ....E 601 898-1717
Jackson (G-2521)
Nick StrckInds Quick Print Inc ....G 601 355-8195
Ridgeland (G-4612)
Rankin Printery ....G 662 287-4426
Corinth (G-1112)
RR Donnelley & Sons Company ....B 662 562-5252
Senatobia (G-4802)
Rutledge Publishing Co Inc ....G 662 534-2116
New Albany (G-3694)
Shaughnessy & Co Inc ....G 228 436-4060
Biloxi (G-279)
Smith Printing & Off Sup Inc ....G 601 442-2441
Natchez (G-3621)
Swain Printing & Signs ....G 662 773-7584
Louisville (G-2983)
Womack Willow ....G 601 969-4120
Jackson (G-2638)

TYPESETTING SVC: Computer

Printers Inc ....G 601 792-8493
Prentiss (G-4424)

TYPESETTING SVC: Hand Composition

Southern Images Printing Inc ....G 601 649-3501
Laurel (G-2852)

UNIFORM SPLY SVCS: Indl

G&K Services LLC ....E 601 788-6375
Richton (G-4531)

UNIFORM STORES

Landau Uniforms Incorporated ....E 662 895-7200
Olive Branch (G-3864)
Stitches By Lee LLC ....G 228 769-7460
Pascagoula (G-4070)

UNISEX HAIR SALONS

LLC Glass House ....G 769 251-1299
Jackson (G-2470)

UNIVERSITY

Mississippi State University ....D 662 325-2510
Starkville (G-4960)
Mississippi State University ....G 662 325-3149
Mississippi State (G-3425)
University of Mississippi ....G 662 915-5742
University (G-5306)
University of Southern Miss ....E 601 266-5390
Hattiesburg (G-2078)
William Carey University ....G 601 318-6115
Hattiesburg (G-2083)

UPHOLSTERY WORK SVCS

Kdh Kustoms LLC ....G 601 730-2052
McComb (G-3256)

USED CAR DEALERS

Fowler Buick-Gmc Inc ....E 601 360-0200
Pearl (G-4120)

UTENSILS: Household, Cooking & Kitchen, Metal

Taylor Rene ....G 601 977-8928
Jackson (G-2604)

UTILITY TRAILER DEALERS

M and S Sales Inc ....G 662 453-6111
Greenwood (G-1637)
Ottos Custom Trailers ....G 601 446-6469
Natchez (G-3604)
Warren Inc ....C 601 765-8221
Collins (G-865)

VACUUM CLEANERS: Household

Tupelo Elvis Presley Fan Club ....G 662 610-5301
Tupelo (G-5245)

VALVES

Tvi Inc ....G 662 343-5117
Hamilton (G-1910)

VALVES & PIPE FITTINGS

Consolidated Pipe & Sup Co Inc ....F 228 769-1920
Pascagoula (G-4028)
Mueller Copper Fittings Co ....E 662 862-2181
Fulton (G-1465)
Parker-Hannifin Corporation ....C 601 856-4123
Madison (G-3137)

VALVES Solenoid

Parker-Hannifin Corporation ....C 601 856-4123
Madison (G-3137)

VALVES: Fire Hydrant

First Class Fire Prtection LLC ....G 901 350-0499
Horn Lake (G-2199)

VALVES: Indl

ITT Engineered Valves LLC ....F 662 256-7185
Amory (G-44)
Southern Marketing Group ....G 601 664-3880
Jackson (G-2667)
Wey Valve Inc ....F 662 963-2020
Shannon (G-4822)

VAN CONVERSIONS

Aerial Truck Equipment Co Inc ....G 662 895-0993
Olive Branch (G-3807)
Companion Vans Inc ....F 662 289-7711
Kosciusko (G-2691)

VARNISHES, NEC

United Gilsonite Laboratories ....E 601 362-8619
Jackson (G-2617)

VARNISHING SVC: Metal Prdts

Consolidated Pipe Supply ....G 228 396-8818
Biloxi (G-233)

VEGETABLE OILS: Medicinal Grade, Refined Or Concentrated

Kenan Transportation ....G 662 332-4223
Greenville (G-1561)

VEHICLES: All Terrain

Csa Logistics LLC ....G 601 264-2455
Hattiesburg (G-1953)
Main Street Cycle Inc ....G 662 438-6407
Tishomingo (G-5086)
Swamp Donkey LLC ....G 228 369-4927
Vancleave (G-5322)

VEHICLES: Recreational

Johnsond Rv ....G 662 676-8716
Golden (G-1528)

VENDING MACHINE OPERATORS: Candy & Snack Food

Refreshments Inc ....D 662 286-6051
Corinth (G-1115)

VENDING MACHINE OPERATORS: Food

Breaktime Vending Inc ....G 601 749-8424
Picayune (G-4257)

VENDING MACHINES & PARTS

Brown Bottling Group Inc ....E 601 352-0366
Jackson (G-2345)
Luckett Pump & Well Svc Inc ....G 662 624-2398
Dublin (G-1219)
Smart Snacks LLC ....G 228 239-6507
Ocean Springs (G-3787)

VETERINARY PHARMACEUTICAL PREPARATIONS

Novartis Corporation ....G 662 844-2271
Tupelo (G-5195)
Stockmans Supply LLC ....F 601 750-2726
Starkville (G-4976)

VIDEO CAMERA-AUDIO RECORDERS: Household Use

Phone Booth Inc ....F 662 286-6600
Corinth (G-1109)

VIDEO EQPT

Mfj Enterprises Inc ....D 662 323-5869
Starkville (G-4958)

VIDEO PRODUCTION SVCS

Omni Fusion LLC ....G 601 765-6941
Collins (G-858)

VIDEO TAPE PRODUCTION SVCS

Box Office 7 Studios ....G 662 633-2451
Brandon (G-372)

VINYL RESINS, NEC

Axiall Corporation ....D 601 206-3200
Madison (G-3081)
Integrity Vnyl Sding Decks LLC ....G 601 723-1257
Lumberton (G-3031)

VITAMINS: Natural Or Synthetic, Uncompounded, Bulk

Gha Enterprises Incorporated ....G 601 812-7739
Jackson (G-2425)

VOCATIONAL REHABILITATION AGENCY

Itawamba Ind Work Activities C ....E 662 862-3392
Fulton (G-1459)
Willowood Dvelopmental Ctr Inc ....D 601 366-0123
Jackson (G-2634)

Employee Codes: A=Over 500 employees, B=251-500
C=101-250, D=51-100, E=20-50, F=10-19, G=1-9

2019 Harris Directory of
Mississippi Manufacturers

VOCATIONAL TRAINING AGENCY

Mississippi Prison Inds Corp..............F 601 969-5760
Jackson *(G-2503)*

WALL BASE: Terrazzo, Precast

Carsons Construction LLC ....E 601 301-0841
Vicksburg *(G-5354)*

WALLPAPER STORE

Linas Interiors Inc ....G 662 332-7226
Leland *(G-2889)*

WAREHOUSE CLUBS STORES

Maelstrom Square LLC ....G 470 378-9064
Pascagoula *(G-4048)*

WAREHOUSING & STORAGE FACILITIES, NEC

Automated Tech & Assembly LLC........G 662 213-9352
Rolling Fork *(G-4679)*

WAREHOUSING & STORAGE: Bulk St & Termnls, Hire, Petro/Chem

Sille Biofuels LLC ....G 601 400-2227
Jackson *(G-2581)*

WAREHOUSING & STORAGE: Farm Prdts

Stryder & Associates LLC ....G 662 579-8703
Cleveland *(G-809)*

WAREHOUSING & STORAGE: General

Garan Incorporated..........................E 601 656-1501
Philadelphia *(G-4215)*

WAREHOUSING & STORAGE: General

Hamilton Beach Brands Inc ....F 662 890-9869
Olive Branch *(G-3843)*
Mississippi Agri-Products Inc ....G 601 879-3343
Flora *(G-1310)*
West Group Holding Company LLC......G 662 871-2344
Shannon *(G-4821)*

WAREHOUSING & STORAGE: Lumber Terminal Or Storage For Hire

Jones Wood Products Inc ....G 601 876-2688
Tylertown *(G-5275)*

WARM AIR HEATING & AC EQPT & SPLYS, WHOL: Dust Collecting

Sly Inc ....G 662 263-8234
Mathiston *(G-3231)*

WASHERS

B & B Pressure Wshg & Ldscpg.........G 662 910-9105
Hernando *(G-2123)*

WATER PURIFICATION EQPT: Household

Kx Technologies LLC ....E 662 601-4140
Iuka *(G-2297)*

WATER TREATMENT EQPT: Indl

Water Water LLC ....G 662 721-7098
Cleveland *(G-810)*

WATER: Distilled

Bilal 100 All Natural Spring ....G 601 323-2237
Sumrall *(G-5035)*

WATER: Pasteurized & Mineral, Bottled & Canned

Realpure Bottling Inc ....F 601 849-9910
Magee *(G-3182)*
Reaves Pure Water LLC ....G 601 606-6789
Hattiesburg *(G-2049)*

WATER: Pasteurized, Canned & Bottled, Etc

Cool Baby Water LLC ....G 850 748-0921
Lucedale *(G-2990)*

Magnolia Bottled Water Company........G 662 329-9000
Columbus *(G-998)*

WELDING EQPT

Greenville Metal Works Inc ....E 662 335-8510
Greenville *(G-1555)*
Outback Industries LLC ....F 662 591-5100
Nettleton *(G-3666)*
Saf T Cart Inc ....E 662 624-6492
Clarksdale *(G-782)*

WELDING EQPT & SPLYS WHOLESALERS

Columbia Welding & Cnstr ....F 601 736-4332
Columbia *(G-890)*
Electro Mech Solutions Ems Inc..........G 601 631-0138
Vicksburg *(G-5365)*
Matheson Tri-Gas Inc.......................F 601 856-3000
Madison *(G-3127)*
PO Boy Welding Inc ....G 662 624-3696
Clarksdale *(G-778)*
Tatum Development Corp ....G 601 544-6043
Hattiesburg *(G-2072)*
Wesco Gas & Welding Supply Inc........G 228 475-1955
Moss Point *(G-3506)*

WELDING EQPT REPAIR SVCS

GE Oil & Gas Pressure Ctrl LP ....G 601 425-1436
Laurel *(G-2769)*
Oms Shop ....E 601 835-1239
Brookhaven *(G-521)*

WELDING EQPT: Electric

Powerline Tags Inc..........................G 228 760-3072
Gulfport *(G-1850)*

WELDING REPAIR SVC

Aberdeen Machine Works Inc ....E 662 369-9357
Aberdeen *(G-6)*
ABS Welding Inc ....F 601 444-9889
Columbia *(G-878)*
Adams Welding & Fabrication ....G 601 319-1865
Ovett *(G-3930)*
Advanced Fabrication Inc ....G 228 392-0400
Diberville *(G-1194)*
Ajs Welding Repair ....G 601 264-2571
Sumrall *(G-5033)*
Alcorn Fabricating ....G 662 462-5669
Corinth *(G-1056)*
All-Tech Metal Works Inc..................G 228 396-3800
Wiggins *(G-5569)*
Amerimac Machining Corporation ....G 601 940-7919
Jackson *(G-2329)*
Anderson Repair Shop ....G 601 783-2654
Magnolia *(G-3189)*
Angels Truck Service LLC ....F 662 890-0417
Olive Branch *(G-3815)*
ARC-Up Welding Inc ....G 601 638-1202
Vicksburg *(G-5342)*
Arky Welding & Handy Man ....G 662 494-4233
West Point *(G-5536)*
Atwood Mch Wldg & Hydraulics ....F 601 735-0398
Waynesboro *(G-5491)*
B R Smith Enterprises Inc ....F 601 656-0846
Union *(G-5293)*
Bakers Auto Machine & RAD Sp ....G 228 474-1222
Moss Point *(G-3468)*
Balius Dann Welding ....G 228 354-9647
Diberville *(G-1196)*
Beason Repair Shop ....G 662 256-9937
Amory *(G-37)*
Beckham Welding LLC ....G 662 832-0071
Oxford *(G-3939)*
Bergeron Machine & Marine ....G 504 416-6461
Poplarville *(G-4375)*
Berry Inc ....G 662 423-1984
Iuka *(G-2285)*
Big Johns Welding LLC ....G 570 660-1972
Poplarville *(G-4377)*
Bills Welding ....G 901 216-6762
Byhalia *(G-580)*
Billys Welding Service Inc ....G 601 649-1432
Laurel *(G-2740)*
Bk Edwards Fabrication & Wldg...........G 662 263-4320
Mathiston *(G-3226)*
Block & Chip Iron Works Inc...............G 601 394-2964
Leakesville *(G-2876)*
Bobs Welding & Repair ....G 662 685-4217
Blue Mountain *(G-290)*

Brocato Construction Inc...................G 662 563-4473
Batesville *(G-100)*
C B R Machinist Inc ....G 601 426-2326
Laurel *(G-2746)*
Carrolls Welding Service ....G 228 875-3800
Ocean Springs *(G-3747)*
Cg Welding Services LLC ....G 601 426-3922
Laurel *(G-2751)*
Chancellors Welding ....G 601 477-3552
Ellisville *(G-1249)*
Chops Wrecker & Welding Svc ....G 601 442-0092
Natchez *(G-3546)*
Chucks Welding & Mech LLC ....G 662 347-9941
Greenville *(G-1538)*
Clear Enterprise ....G 601 796-2429
Lumberton *(G-3025)*
Columbia Welding & Cnstr ....F 601 736-4332
Columbia *(G-890)*
Columbus Mch & Wldg Works Inc.........E 662 328-8473
Columbus *(G-951)*
Cottens Welding Shop ....G 662 647-2503
Charleston *(G-735)*
Crager Welding ....G 601 687-0019
Waynesboro *(G-5496)*
Creative Iron ....G 601 845-6290
Florence *(G-1316)*
Cuevas Machine Co Inc ....D 228 255-1384
Poplarville *(G-4380)*
Cwg Welding ....G 228 539-4121
Saucier *(G-4751)*
Cws Grain Systems Inc ....E 662 332-5822
Greenville *(G-1543)*
Daniel Petre ....G 662 726-2462
Macon *(G-3057)*
Davis Welding ....G 228 257-5231
Long Beach *(G-2935)*
Davis Welding Fabrication LLC ....G 662 614-2531
Columbia *(G-893)*
Davis Welding LLC ....G 662 423-2911
Iuka *(G-2289)*
Davis Wldg & Fabrication LLC..............G 601 258-0334
Beaumont *(G-184)*
Dean Weeks Repair & Welding ....G 601 833-2669
Wesson *(G-5526)*
Dees Welding Service LLC ....G 601 372-9361
Jackson *(G-2379)*
Dixie Welding ....G 662 417-0938
Winona *(G-5597)*
Dixie Welding Service Inc ....G 601 268-6949
Moselle *(G-3457)*
Donald Speights Jr ....G 601 940-3847
Braxton *(G-477)*
Double C Custom Welding & Fabg.........G 228 383-1243
Gulfport *(G-1774)*
Doves Machine & Welding Svc ....G 601 794-8112
Purvis *(G-4436)*
Ds Welding Services ....G 601 639-4988
Crosby *(G-1134)*
E C Welding & Fabricating ....G 662 429-1624
Hernando *(G-2130)*
E E Baird Shop Inc ....G 662 456-3467
Houston *(G-2238)*
Edco Welding ....G 228 392-5600
Biloxi *(G-241)*
Ellis Certified Welding ....G 662 869-2295
Saltillo *(G-4711)*
Ellis Welding ....G 601 752-2207
Seminary *(G-4779)*
Equipment Maintenance Co.................G 662 393-9178
Horn Lake *(G-2198)*
Fab Pro Wldg & Fabrication Co ....G 662 365-5557
Baldwyn *(G-76)*
Fielder Mfg.....................................G 601 630-9295
Vicksburg *(G-5371)*
Fielders Welding and Orna Ir ....G 662 234-4256
Oxford *(G-3955)*
G Hennig Jr Welding Shop ....G 228 374-7836
Biloxi *(G-243)*
G&K Fabrication & Trailer Repr ....G 228 249-6336
Moss Point *(G-3478)*
George Smith Welding Svc LLC ....G 601 752-5288
Ellisville *(G-1254)*
Gibbs & Sons Inc ....G 601 775-3467
Lake *(G-2722)*
Grace Welding Fabrication LLC ....G 601 788-2478
Richton *(G-4533)*
Gulleys Wldg Stl Erectors Inc..............E 601 482-3767
Meridian *(G-3344)*
H & H Fabrication Inc........................F 662 286-9475
Corinth *(G-1088)*

2019 Harris Directory of
Mississippi Manufacturers

(G-0000) Company's Geographic Section entry number

430

PRODUCT SECTION

WELDING SPLYS, EXC GASES: Wholesalers

H & H Welding LLC ....F...... 601 428-4788
Ellisville (G-1255)

Halls Welding Service ....G...... 601 477-3925
Ellisville (G-1256)

Harrell Welding Service LLC ....G...... 662 456-2444
Houston (G-2244)

Harrells Metal Works Inc ....E...... 662 226-0982
Grenada (G-1683)

Harrison Mobile Welding ....G...... 662 706-4692
Baldwyn (G-77)

Hesters Certified Welding ....G...... 662 566-7305
Tupelo (G-5155)

Hills Welding & Crane Rental ....G...... 662 846-6789
Cleveland (G-796)

Holloways Welding Service LLC ....G...... 601 729-4403
Stringer (G-5002)

Howells Welding & Fabricating ....G...... 601 663-6098
Union (G-5298)

J & J Welding ....G...... 662 456-6065
Woodland (G-5613)

Jackson Welding LLC ....G...... 662 680-4325
Saltillo (G-4714)

JC Welding LLC ....G...... 601 575-1307
Philadelphia (G-4218)

Jcbc Cs LLC ....G...... 662 560-7235
Coldwater (G-848)

Jennings & Jennings Inc ....G...... 662 887-1870
Indianola (G-2268)

Jennings Welding & Mch Works ....G...... 662 887-1870
Indianola (G-2269)

Jeremy Ray Welding Service LLC ....G...... 601 433-4905
Laurel (G-2787)

Jerome Rushing Welding ....G...... 601 303-0139
Tylertown (G-5274)

Jerry Hailey ....G...... 662 349-2582
Southaven (G-4883)

Kc Fabrication and Welding LLC ....G...... 504 427-8711
Bolton (G-311)

Kd Welding Services LLC ....G...... 228 863-2773
Gulfport (G-1815)

Kellys Welding Service ....G...... 601 879-8636
Flora (G-1309)

Kens Welding Shop Inc ....G...... 601 736-4136
Columbia (G-902)

Kirk Welding Inspection SE ....G...... 228 467-6586
Bay Saint Louis (G-145)

Lancaster Machine & Welding ....G...... 601 582-1400
Hattiesburg (G-2015)

Larry D Wallace ....G...... 601 384-4409
Roxie (G-4691)

Larrys Equipment Inc ....G...... 662 423-0077
Iuka (G-2298)

Lars Jordan ....G...... 601 544-2424
Petal (G-4190)

Lavelle Crabtree Welding ....G...... 662 746-7177
Yazoo City (G-5638)

Leeco Welding Service ....G...... 601 428-7896
Laurel (G-2795)

Lumpkin Repair Service LLC ....G...... 601 798-2027
Carriere (G-694)

Lums Welding & Machine ....G...... 601 825-1116
Brandon (G-416)

Lynn Welding Shop LLC ....G...... 601 638-7235
Vicksburg (G-5390)

Malley Inc ....G...... 228 255-7467
Kiln (G-2683)

Mark Williams Welding LLC ....G...... 601 431-5324
Natchez (G-3584)

Mashburns Welding ....G...... 601 648-2886
Buckatunna (G-564)

Mason Overstreet Wldg Mch Work ....E...... 601 932-1794
Pearl (G-4130)

Mc Comb Welding & Mch Works ....G...... 601 684-1921
McComb (G-3258)

McGee Welding LLC ....G...... 769 355-2339
Natchez (G-3585)

MD Metals Scrap & Salvage ....G...... 601 635-4160
Decatur (G-1176)

Mercer Welding Service ....G...... 601 649-4269
Laurel (G-2799)

Merle E Sullivan ....G...... 662 347-4494
Greenville (G-1572)

Metal Products of Corinth Inc ....G...... 662 287-3625
Corinth (G-1101)

Metallic Welding ....G...... 769 798-6498
Jackson (G-2488)

Michaels Machine Shop Inc ....G...... 662 624-2376
Clarksdale (G-775)

Mississippi Welding and Mchs ....G...... 662 726-5593
Macon (G-3067)

Mitchells Welding LLC ....G...... 601 554-6402
Kosciusko (G-2703)

Monotech of Mississippi ....G...... 662 862-2978
Iuka (G-2302)

Moore Machine & Welding Shop ....G...... 601 892-5026
Crystal Springs (G-1150)

Moores Welding & Fabrication ....G...... 662 402-5503
Cleveland (G-800)

Morris Welding Service ....G...... 601 729-2737
Laurel (G-2808)

Morrison Welding LLC ....G...... 601 845-5187
Florence (G-1329)

Mr Fix It ....G...... 601 852-4705
Edwards (G-1242)

Murphys Machine & Welding LLC ....G...... 601 849-2771
Magee (G-3179)

Murphys Welding LLC ....G...... 662 719-3879
Cleveland (G-801)

Nations Welding Service Inc ....G...... 601 833-4949
Brookhaven (G-520)

Novelty Machine Works Inc ....F...... 601 948-2075
Jackson (G-2524)

Opel Corp ....G...... 601 693-0771
Meridian (G-3378)

Ormans Welding & Fab Inc ....F...... 662 494-9471
West Point (G-5556)

Overstreet Welding LLC ....G...... 662 719-1269
Ruleville (G-4697)

P & S Welding & Manufacturing ....G...... 662 334-9881
Greenville (G-1587)

Patterson & Company Inc ....E...... 662 842-2807
Tupelo (G-5200)

Paul Yeatman ....G...... 662 323-7140
Starkville (G-4966)

Pennington Wldg Sp Crane Rentl ....G...... 662 838-2015
Byhalia (G-596)

Peppers Machine & Wldg Co Inc ....E...... 601 833-3038
Brookhaven (G-522)

PO Boy Welding Inc ....G...... 662 624-3696
Clarksdale (G-778)

Precision Fab Refurbishing ....G...... 601 543-7752
Hattiesburg (G-2047)

Precision Iron Works ....G...... 228 341-0736
Saucier (G-4761)

Precision Welding ....G...... 601 730-0224
Summit (G-5019)

Purvis Machine ....G...... 601 947-6617
Lucedale (G-3013)

Quality Machine & Wldg of Miss ....E...... 601 798-8568
Picayune (G-4289)

Quality Welding ....G...... 601 428-4724
Laurel (G-2830)

Quality Wldg & Fabrication Inc ....D...... 601 731-1222
Columbia (G-914)

R & W Hydraulics Inc ....G...... 601 649-0565
Laurel (G-2831)

R and B Welding LLC ....G...... 601 441-4398
Columbia (G-915)

R&R Welding LLC ....G...... 601 335-2470
Laurel (G-2832)

Rand S Welding ....G...... 601 876-3736
Tylertown (G-5282)

Rauschs Welding & Repair ....G...... 662 841-0499
Plantersville (G-4314)

Rays Mobile Welding ....G...... 601 966-0848
Jackson (G-2664)

Rays Welding ....G...... 601 741-1114
Terry (G-5076)

Rice Equipment Co LLC ....G...... 662 323-5502
Starkville (G-4981)

Rising Son Welding LLC ....G...... 601 344-0077
Ovett (G-3932)

Roberts Welding LLC ....G...... 228 697-4816
Long Beach (G-2952)

Romar Offshore Wldg Svcs LLC ....G...... 228 475-4220
Moss Point (G-3497)

Roseberry Welding LLC ....G...... 601 408-1843
Hattiesburg (G-2054)

S & C Welding & Machine Works ....G...... 601 845-5483
Florence (G-1332)

S & S Welding & Repairs ....G...... 662 834-1131
Durant (G-1228)

S & W Welding & Machine Works ....G...... 601 939-8516
Jackson (G-2666)

Sanders Sons Dvrsfd Wldg Entps ....G...... 601 969-3119
Jackson (G-2572)

Satisfaction Welding ....G...... 662 473-1518
Water Valley (G-5474)

Shacks Welding Service Inc ....G...... 601 939-5491
Flowood (G-1396)

Shears Fabrication & Wldg LLC ....G...... 601 946-3268
Utica (G-5312)

Smith Mobile Welding LLC ....G...... 601 695-4640
Brookhaven (G-532)

Smiths Machine & Wldg Co Inc ....E...... 601 833-8787
Brookhaven (G-534)

Smiths Mobile Welding ....G...... 901 626-1616
Southaven (G-4904)

Sparks Welding Service ....G...... 601 519-9573
Brandon (G-462)

Speeds Welding Works ....G...... 601 917-2571
Meridian (G-3406)

Stringer Randal ....G...... 228 623-0037
Moss Point (G-3500)

Sumrall Welding ....G...... 601 876-4653
Tylertown (G-5287)

Sumrall Welding Service LLC ....G...... 601 498-1075
Ovett (G-3933)

Superior Wldg Fabrication Inc ....G...... 601 823-5999
Brookhaven (G-541)

T & T Welding Inc ....E...... 601 477-2884
Ellisville (G-1270)

T & T Welding Yard Inc ....E...... 601 477-2299
Ellisville (G-1271)

T and W Maintenance LLC ....G...... 901 848-2511
Southaven (G-4911)

T JS Welding ....G...... 601 498-1409
Laurel (G-2856)

T R General Welding ....G...... 901 481-0425
Southaven (G-4912)

Taylor Brothers Cnstr Co ....G...... 601 636-1749
Vicksburg (G-5427)

Thomas Welding and Fabricating ....G...... 601 408-1843
Hattiesburg (G-2074)

Thompsons Welding Services Inc ....D...... 662 343-8955
Hamilton (G-1908)

Thornhill Welding ....G...... 601 248-6472
Summit (G-5026)

Travis Welding Services ....G...... 601 684-9578
McComb (G-3271)

Tri County Sheet Metal & Wldg ....G...... 601 939-0803
Pearl (G-4153)

Tucker Machine Services ....G...... 601 582-4280
Hattiesburg (G-2075)

Vera S Ray ....G...... 662 453-1615
Greenwood (G-1655)

Vertechs Design Solutions LLC ....G...... 228 671-1442
Waveland (G-5486)

Victor Umfress Gar Wldg Sp Inc ....G...... 662 862-4213
Fulton (G-1484)

Walker Welding and Fabrication ....G...... 601 503-0340
Brandon (G-471)

Wallace Welding LLC ....G...... 601 734-6542
Bogue Chitto (G-307)

Walters Machine Works Inc ....G...... 601 426-6092
Laurel (G-2867)

Webb Machine and Supply Inc ....F...... 662 375-8309
Webb (G-5520)

Webbs Welding & Repair LLC ....G...... 901 487-2400
Olive Branch (G-3924)

Wedgeworth Welding and Fab ....G...... 228 326-0937
Mc Henry (G-3239)

Welding Research & Fabricatn ....G...... 870 551-5650
Tupelo (G-5254)

Welding Services ....G...... 662 321-2472
Tupelo (G-5255)

Welding Works LLC ....G...... 662 323-8684
Starkville (G-4981)

Wilders Welding Shop ....G...... 662 489-2772
Pontotoc (G-4371)

William Barnes ....G...... 601 446-6122
Natchez (G-3642)

Willie Morgan ....G...... 662 834-4366
Lexington (G-2907)

Wilson Welding ....G...... 601 483-3696
Meridian (G-3421)

Wilsons Welding Service Inc ....F...... 228 255-4825
Perkinston (G-4183)

Woodrffs Prtble Wldg Fbrcation ....G...... 662 728-3326
Booneville (G-347)

Woods Trailers & Repair LLC ....G...... 662 585-3606
Golden (G-1533)

Yates Industrial Services LLC ....G...... 601 467-6232
Purvis (G-4454)

Young Welding Supply Inc ....G...... 662 792-4061
Kosciusko (G-2721)

WELDING SPLYS, EXC GASES: Wholesalers

Wesco Gas & Welding Supply Inc ....G...... 228 475-1955
Moss Point (G-3506)

Employee Codes: A=Over 500 employees, B=251-500
C=101-250, D=51-100, E=20-50, F=10-19, G=1-9

2019 Harris Directory of
Mississippi Manufacturers

WHEEL BALANCING EQPT: Automotive

WHEEL BALANCING EQPT: Automotive

Hunter Engineering Company ....C....... 601 857-8883
Raymond **(G-4489)**

WHEELCHAIR LIFTS

A B B Inc ....F....... 662 628-8196
Calhoun City **(G-634)**
Lagwenbre Designer Corporation ....G....... 469 230-8534
Brookhaven **(G-506)**

WHEELCHAIRS

Advantage Medical and Phrm LLC ....G....... 601 268-1422
Hattiesburg **(G-1916)**
Chariot Wheelchair and RPR ....G....... 228 967-7991
Biloxi **(G-227)**
National Seating Mobility Inc ....G....... 601 664-1090
Flowood **(G-1384)**

WHEELS

Roes Rims and Accessories ....G....... 601 619-4489
Vicksburg **(G-5413)**

WHEELS & PARTS

Custom Engineered Wheels Inc ....E....... 662 841-0756
Baldwyn **(G-74)**
Custom Engineered Wheels Inc ....D....... 574 267-4005
Baldwyn **(G-75)**

WINDMILLS: Electric Power Generation

American Energy Solutions LLC ....G....... 757 846-3261
Olive Branch **(G-3811)**
Taylor Power Systems Inc ....G....... 601 932-6491
Clinton **(G-837)**

WINDOW & DOOR FRAMES

Cox Hardware LLC ....E....... 713 923-9458
Madison **(G-3090)**

WINDOW BLIND REPAIR SVCS

Ron Lor Window Fashions ....G....... 662 329-1557
Columbus **(G-1022)**

WINDOWS: Frames, Wood

C E Russell Framing Components ....G....... 228 762-9267
Pascagoula **(G-4024)**
Easley & Easley Millworks Inc ....F....... 601 372-8881
Jackson **(G-2395)**

WINDOWS: Storm, Wood

Mid South Storm Shelters LLC ....G....... 901 619-0064
Como **(G-1049)**

WINDOWS: Wood

Croft LLC ....E....... 601 684-6121
McComb **(G-3247)**
M S I/Pozzi ....G....... 601 957-0085
Ridgeland **(G-4599)**

WIRE

Universal Lighting Tech Inc ....B....... 601 892-9828
Gallman **(G-1486)**

WIRE & CABLE: Aluminum

Southwire Company LLC ....E....... 662 324-6600
Starkville **(G-4974)**
Trilogy Communications Inc ....D....... 601 932-4461
Pearl **(G-4154)**

WIRE & WIRE PRDTS

Frontier Contracting LLC ....G....... 662 809-1949
Grenada **(G-1678)**
Nhc Distributors Inc ....E....... 601 656-7911
Philadelphia **(G-4229)**
Partridge Ornamental Iron Inc ....E....... 601 693-4021
Meridian **(G-3380)**
Ripley Industries Inc ....E....... 662 423-6733
Iuka **(G-2307)**
Saf T Cart Inc ....E....... 662 624-6492
Clarksdale **(G-782)**
Southern Gate Twr Fabricators ....G....... 601 483-6710
Collinsville **(G-876)**

Steel Service Corporation ....C....... 601 939-9222
Jackson **(G-2668)**
Voith Fabrics Florence Inc ....C....... 601 845-2202
Florence **(G-1336)**

WIRE FENCING & ACCESS WHOLESALERS

Southern Exteriors Fence Co ....G....... 228 586-2110
Perkinston **(G-4181)**
Southern Gate Twr Fabricators ....G....... 601 483-6710
Collinsville **(G-876)**

WIRE MATERIALS: Steel

Blue Springs Metals LLC ....E....... 662 539-2700
Blue Springs **(G-294)**
Illinois Tool Works Inc ....C....... 662 489-4151
Pontotoc **(G-4335)**
Southwire Company LLC ....E....... 662 324-6600
Starkville **(G-4974)**

WIRE ROPE CENTERS

Nhc Distributors Inc ....E....... 601 656-7911
Philadelphia **(G-4229)**

WIRE WHOLESALERS

Great Southern Industries Inc ....D....... 601 948-5700
Jackson **(G-2431)**

WIRE: Communication

Grady Morrow ....G....... 769 823-1422
Jackson **(G-2429)**

WIRE: Nonferrous

Electro National Corporation ....E....... 601 859-5511
Canton **(G-657)**
Southwire Company LLC ....E....... 662 324-6600
Starkville **(G-4974)**
Universal Lighting Tech Inc ....B....... 601 892-9828
Gallman **(G-1486)**

WIRE: Nonferrous, Appliance Fixture

Appliance Tech Authorized Svc ....G....... 228 392-0789
Biloxi **(G-219)**

WOMEN'S & CHILDREN'S CLOTHING WHOLESALERS, NEC

Alex Carol Limited ....G....... 601 956-0536
Ridgeland **(G-4547)**
Sincere Trading Inc ....G....... 662 702-3822
Greenville **(G-1599)**

WOMEN'S CLOTHING STORES

Massey Clothing Company LLC ....G....... 662 792-4046
Kosciusko **(G-2700)**
The Touch ....G....... 662 378-4188
Greenville **(G-1602)**

WOMEN'S CLOTHING STORES: Ready-To-Wear

Southern Prtg & Silk Screening ....F....... 228 452-7309
Pass Christian **(G-4095)**

WOOD & WOOD BY-PRDTS, WHOLESALE

Thomasson Company ....E....... 601 656-6000
Philadelphia **(G-4242)**

WOOD CHIPS, PRODUCED AT THE MILL

Chips Amory Inc ....F....... 662 256-1400
Amory **(G-38)**
Kermit Broome Sons WD Chipping ....E....... 601 264-8470
Sumrall **(G-5037)**

WOOD PRDTS

Andrews Woodshop LLC ....G....... 228 216-5563
Gulfport **(G-1725)**
ASpauljoy ....G....... 662 397-3661
Booneville **(G-319)**
Atwood Auto & Marine ....G....... 601 624-7012
Brandon **(G-366)**
Bobs Woodworking LLC ....G....... 601 661-8093
Vicksburg **(G-5347)**
Careys Fencing ....G....... 601 434-6510
Hattiesburg **(G-1940)**

Cottonport Hardwoods LLC ....G....... 601 442-9888
Natchez **(G-3551)**
Glenda Brock Woods Music LLC ....G....... 662 588-8343
Shaw **(G-4823)**
Lemonwood LLC ....G....... 601 792-5748
Oak Vale **(G-3735)**
Wilderwood LLC ....G....... 601 955-8539
Flowood **(G-1407)**

WOOD PRDTS: Chicken Coops, Wood, Wirebound

Grady 1&2 ....G....... 601 677-3390
Preston **(G-4427)**

WOOD PRDTS: Mulch, Wood & Bark

Hastys Mulch & Stone LLC ....G....... 601 485-2120
Meridian **(G-3346)**

WOOD PRDTS: Oars & Paddles

Caviness Woodworking Company ....D....... 662 628-5195
Calhoun City **(G-636)**
South Coast Paddling Company ....G....... 228 818-9442
Ocean Springs **(G-3789)**

WOOD PRDTS: Outdoor, Structural

Millennium Outdoors LLC ....F....... 601 932-5832
Pearl **(G-4132)**
Power Plus Inc ....F....... 601 264-1950
Sumrall **(G-5042)**

WOOD PRDTS: Panel Work

Clearspan Components Inc ....C....... 601 483-3941
Meridian **(G-3321)**
Great Southern Log Homes Inc ....G....... 601 833-0700
Brookhaven **(G-497)**

WOOD PRDTS: Rulers & Rules

Southland Supplies ....G....... 662 647-2452
Cascilla **(G-729)**

WOOD PRDTS: Rulers & Yardsticks

Eugene Flanders ....G....... 601 544-0345
Hattiesburg **(G-1965)**
Pinecrest Woodworks ....G....... 601 677-3015
Shuqualak **(G-4836)**

WOOD PRDTS: Survey Stakes

Loggins Woodwork ....G....... 662 283-5882
Kilmichael **(G-2677)**
Mississippi Wood Stakes Inc ....G....... 662 224-0975
Ashland **(G-64)**

WOOD PRDTS: Trim

Alfords Decorating Center ....G....... 662 455-3552
Greenwood **(G-1612)**
Fortenberry Builders Supply ....G....... 601 825-3370
Brandon **(G-397)**

WOOD PRDTS: Trophy Bases

Holmes Hilton ....G....... 601 736-5757
Foxworth **(G-1432)**
Tally Student Service LLC ....G....... 601 782-9606
Raleigh **(G-4478)**

WOOD PRODUCTS: Reconstituted

Industrial Timber LLC ....E....... 662 346-4488
Saltillo **(G-4713)**
Industrial Timber LLC ....D....... 662 282-4000
Mantachie **(G-3199)**
Industrial Timber LLC ....D....... 662 837-3213
Ripley **(G-4661)**
Purvis Forest Products Inc ....E....... 601 794-8593
Purvis **(G-4448)**
Roseburg Forest Products Co ....E....... 662 773-9868
Louisville **(G-2981)**
Saunders Mfg Co Inc ....F....... 601 693-3482
Meridian **(G-3394)**

WOOD TREATING: Bridges

Natural Wood Solutions LLC ....G....... 662 871-1625
Nettleton **(G-3665)**

2019 Harris Directory of
Mississippi Manufacturers

(G-0000) Company's Geographic Section entry number

PRODUCT SECTION

YARN: Specialty & Novelty

WOOD TREATING: Millwork

Abbeville Mill LLC ....G....... 662 238-7879
Abbeville **(G-1)**

WOOD TREATING: Railroad Cross-Ties

Powe Timber Company ....G....... 601 788-6564
Richton **(G-4542)**

WOOD TREATING: Structural Lumber & Timber

Columbus Lumber Company LLC ....C....... 601 833-1990
Brookhaven **(G-488)**
J and S Keene LLC ....G....... 601 833-8874
Brookhaven **(G-503)**
Pearl River Timber Llc ....G....... 985 516-7951
Poplarville **(G-4388)**

WOOD TREATING: Vehicle Lumber

Martin and Sons LLC ....E....... 601 825-4012
Brandon **(G-418)**

WOOD TREATING: Wood Prdts, Creosoted

L L Wood...G....... 662 454-0506
Belmont **(G-199)**
McFarland Cascade Holdings Inc........E....... 662 476-8000
Scooba **(G-4771)**

Powe Timber Company ....G....... 601 545-7600
Hattiesburg **(G-2046)**

WOODWORK & TRIM: Exterior & Ornamental

Triple E Door & Hardware Inc ....G....... 601 940-7371
Brandon **(G-469)**

WOODWORK: Carved & Turned

Red Lake Cedar Co LLC ....G....... 877 469-5552
Flowood **(G-1391)**

WOODWORK: Interior & Ornamental, NEC

Longleaf Forest Products LLC ....G....... 662 456-4444
Houston **(G-2250)**
Palmer Handrail & Custom Mllwk.........G....... 662 287-3090
Corinth **(G-1107)**

WOVEN WIRE PRDTS, NEC

Passons Specialized Services...............G....... 601 939-3722
Jackson **(G-2661)**

WREATHS: Artificial

Marilyn Turner ....G....... 228 271-2551
Biloxi **(G-265)**
Snap-It-Wreaths ....G....... 228 596-0387
Gulfport **(G-1873)**

Wreath Haven...G....... 205 393-3015
Petal **(G-4200)**

WRITING FOR PUBLICATION SVCS

Twister LLC..G....... 601 371-7276
Madison **(G-3162)**

X-RAY EQPT & TUBES

Deep South Physics Pllc ....G....... 601 613-8076
Brandon **(G-386)**

YARN & YARN SPINNING

Fine Fibers...G....... 901 590-9481
Byhalia **(G-585)**
National Council of Negro Wome ....G....... 952 361-6037
Kosciusko **(G-2706)**

YARN: Needle & Handicraft, Spun

Heritage Yarns.......................................G....... 601 956-1478
Jackson **(G-2439)**

YARN: Specialty & Novelty

Heritage Yarns.......................................G....... 601 956-1478
Jackson **(G-2439)**

Employee Codes: A=Over 500 employees, B=251-500
C=101-250, D=51-100, E=20-50, F=10-19, G=1-9

2019 Harris Directory of
Mississippi Manufacturers